Introducing

the Penguin Literature Library

Share your passion for reading!

Choose from hundreds of classic and contemporary favorites — from *Beowulf* to *Black Hawk Down*.

Teaching Support Available for every title!

Visit us online to browse the entire list
PHSchool.com/language_arts

TEACHER'S EDITION

PRENTICE HALL
LITERATURE

Timeless Voices, Timeless Themes

PLATINUM LEVEL

PEARSON
Prentice
Hall

Upper Saddle River, New Jersey

Needham, Massachusetts

ISBN 0-13-180442-1

5 6 7 8 9 10   09 08 07 06

Get results with Prentice

The nation's leading language arts program

Prentice Hall Literature:

- Features a powerful combination of great literature and superior instruction.

- Ensures student success with a proven, research-based reading approach.

- Provides meaningful, logical, and systematic language skills instruction.

- Helps you monitor student progress with a rich array of assessment tools.

- Allows you to share the same great literature with all your students.

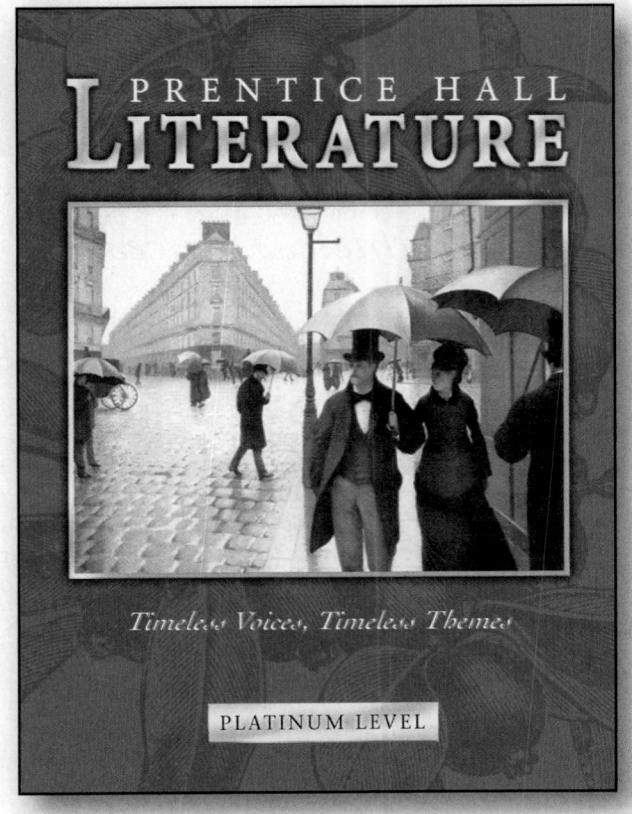

PRENTICE HALL
LITERATURE

Timeless Voices, Timeless Themes

PLATINUM LEVEL

Hall Literature.

What educators think about Prentice Hall Literature

Increases student achievement

"Our teachers are extremely pleased with the series and feel it has contributed to <u>improved student performance</u>."
—Dr. Karen Gibson, Program Leader, Appleton School District, Appleton, WI

"I stay in touch with quite a number of teachers in the district who report that <u>scores have increased</u> on high-stakes performance tests for students using the *Prentice Hall Literature* program."
—Audrey Hawkins, Language Arts Supervisor, Washington, D.C.

Connects to students' lives

"<u>The pre-reading activities are extremely helpful</u>. The importance of making connections with literature is immeasurable— it makes education 'real' for students."
—Matthew Scanlon, Language Arts Teacher, Chester, NJ

"The entire program is '<u>student-friendly</u>' and yet does not 'talk down' to them with simplistic comments. The layout is easy to read and the selections inviting!"
—Niki Locklear, Language Arts Teacher, Independence, KY

"All around the buildings, you see students reading the literature book on their own time. You hear about them discussing the literature with other kids or asking their teachers about it. There's just a lot of talk about the book."
—Patty Foster, Curriculum Consultant, Edmond Public School District, Edmond, OK

Delivers the most comprehensive support

"The best features of the program are the vocabulary instruction and supporting lessons, literary analysis and connecting elements, use of Bloom's taxonomy in the Review and Assess sections, and the quality of literary selections."
—Gail Hacker, Language Arts Teacher, North Charleston, SC

"I like having the <u>Literary Analysis</u> feature to help explain theme, plot, characterization, etc.—many textbooks do not have this."
—Sheila Colson, Language Arts Teacher, Philadelphia, PA

"My teachers have <u>enthusiastically praised the *Reader's Companions*</u>. These tools allow everyone in the class to participate in the discussion so that no one, especially the struggling reader, feels left out."
—Paulette Kirkwood, Communication Arts Supervisor, St. Louis, MO

"Overall, I give the *Prentice Hall Literature* program a grade of 'A'!"
—Kathy Litherland, Language Arts Teacher, Lincoln, IL

The Prentice Hall difference

The truth about the single-column format

It's about reading.

The ability to read and understand text is the most vital and crucial lifelong skill students will possess. Teachers recognize that, through a variety of systematic instructional features and nondistracting point-of-use reading tools in the Student Edition, *Prentice Hall Literature* offers students more reading support in the Student Edition than any other program—thanks to the single-column format.

How is the single-column format more reader-friendly than the dual-column format?

While there are many reasons why the single column can be regarded as more readable than the dual-column format, its greatest virtue is the way the single-column format allows for embedded, nondistracting reading support. This support appears in the form of point-of-use annotations with comprehension checks, vocabulary support, literary analysis, and critical thinking and reading strategies throughout each selection, acting as a kind of "personal reading tutor."

Why don't all publishers use the single-column format?

Actually, all educational publishers use the single-column format in one way or another, usually in texts in other reading-intensive content areas such as social studies or science. Some publishers even use the single-column format in the ancillary reading support of their literature programs, precisely for the unique benefits that the single-column format conveys. *Prentice Hall Literature*, however, is the only program that provides the benefits of the single-column format consistently for every selection throughout the student text, providing a greater degree of reading support than any other reading program.

For more information, ask your representative for the brochure, *It's About Reading: Why* Prentice Hall Literature *Is the Nation's Leading Literature Program.*

Our unique Comparing Literary Works feature helps students dig deeper!

Meaningful content, meaningful connections

Successful critical thinkers need ample practice comparing works of literature. This feature, unique to *Prentice Hall Literature*, traces common themes, elements, styles, and forms to help students gain a deeper insight into their reading.

Setting the stage

Beginning with the Prepare to Read page, *Prentice Hall Literature* presents an element or concept for comparative study. Through the use of examples and modeling, students know what to look for in their reading as they compare selections.

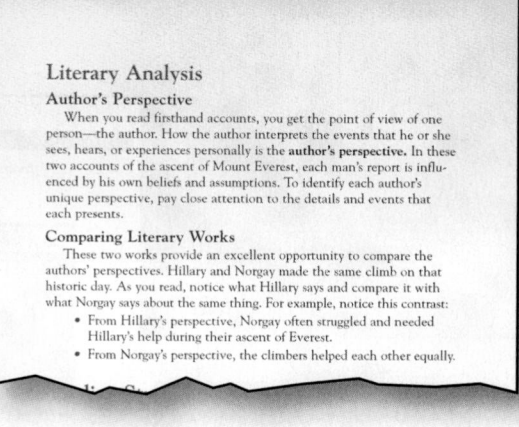

Putting it all together

Students demonstrate and apply critical thinking skills following the selection groups through scaffolded questioning strategies. A variety of instructional tools like graphic organizers assist students in collecting and analyzing their observations.

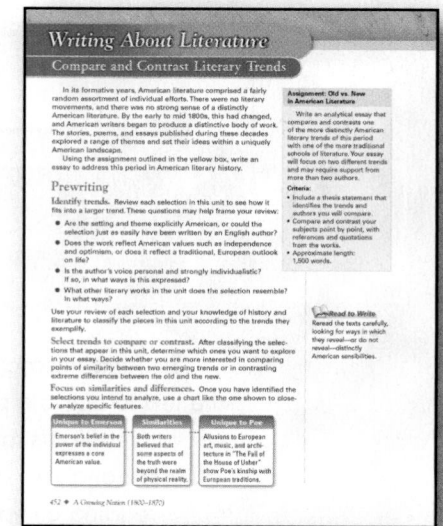

Especially for grades 11 and 12

The Writing About Literature feature, designed especially for grades 11 and 12, takes Comparing Literary Works to the next level as students employ the writing process to demonstrate their proficiency in literary analysis.

Share the same selection

Unique, appropriately leveled reading support that meets the needs of all your students.

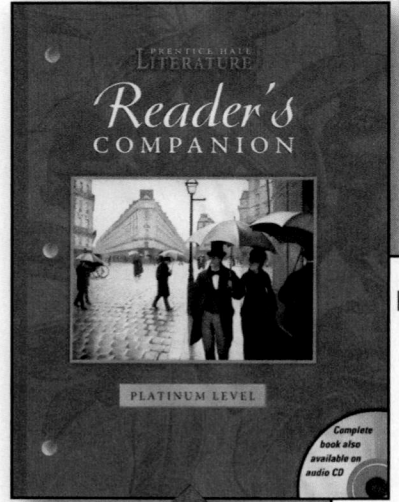

Note: Each of the skills presented here match those that are introduced in the Student Edition of *Prentice Hall Literature* for seamless lesson integration.

Each selection begins with a summary that lets students know what the selection is about before they read.

A visual summary shows students the important ideas or details graphically.

PREVIEW

from A Walk to the Jetty
from **Annie John**
Jamaica Kincaid

Summary
This story is part of a novel that is based on the life of the writer, Jamaica Kincaid. Like Kincaid, the main character has grown up on the Caribbean island of Antigua (an tē' gwə). Now a young woman, she is about to leave the island for the first time and travel by ship to England.

As she walks to the dock with her parents, she sees many things that bring back childhood memories. Some of the memories are pleasant, while others are not. She feels anxiety, gladness, and sorrow at the thought of leaving her home. Aboard the ship, she bids a hesitating and quiet goodbye to her father and a tearful, emotional farewell to her mother. Then, she begins her journey to adulthood.

Visual Summary

- singing in the choir
- being an apprentice
- buying dolls
- mother reading
- **Childhood Memories**
- opening a bank account
- porcelain dog
- wanting glasses

Reader's Companion   © Pearson Edu...

from A Walk to the Jetty
from **Annie John**
Jamaica Kincaid

How would you feel if you had to leave your family and your home to live without them in a new land? That is what the narrator of this story experiences

My mother had arranged with a stevedore[1] to take my trunk to the jetty ahead of me. At ten o'clock on the dot, I was dressed, and we set off for the jetty. An hour after that, I would board a launch that would take me out to sea, where I then would board the ship. Starting out, as if for old time's sake and without giving it a thought, we lined up in the old way: I walking between my mother and my father. I loomed way above my father and could see the top of his head. We must have made a strange sight: a grown girl all dressed up in the middle of a morning, in the middle of the week, walking in step in the middle between her two parents, for people we didn't know stared at us. It was all of half an hour's walk from our house to the jetty, but I was passing through most of the years of my life. We passed by the house where Miss Dulcie, the seamstress that I had been apprenticed to for a time, lived, and just as I was passing by, a wave of bad feeling for her came over me, because I suddenly remembered that the months I spent with her all she had me do was sweep the floor, which was always full of threads and pins and needles, and I never seemed to sweep it clean enough to please her. Then she would send me to the store to buy buttons or thread, though I was only allowed to do this if I was given a sample of the button or thread, and then she would find fault even though they were an exact match of the samples she had given me. And all the while she said to me, "A girl like you will never learn to sew properly, you know." At the time, I don't suppose I minded it, because it was customary to treat the first-year apprentice with such scorn, but now I placed on the dustheap of my life Miss Dulcie and everything that I had had to do with her.

Vocabulary Development: loomed (loomd) v. appeared in a large or threatening form
apprenticed (ə pren' tist) v. assigned to work a specified length of time in a craft or trade in return for instruction

1. **stevedore** (stē' və dôr) *n.* person whose job is loading and unloading ships.

© Pearson Education, Inc.   *from A Walk to the Jetty* 5

♦ Activate Prior Knowledge
Have you ever moved to a new home or to a new school where you knew no one and did not know what your future would hold? How did that make you feel?

♦ Literary Analysis
A writer uses a **flashback** to relate or describe an event from the past. Underline the flashback in the bracketed passage.

♦ Reading Strategy
When you **draw an inference**, you take a guess or reach a conclusion based on information that is provided. What inference can you make from the underlined passage about the way Annie John was treated by Miss Dulcie?

♦ Reading Check
Where is Annie going with her mother and father? Why?

Students interact directly with the text to activate prior knowledge, practice reading strategies, engage in literary analysis, and check their reading comprehension.

with all your students!

Choose the version that's right for your students

Reader's Companion

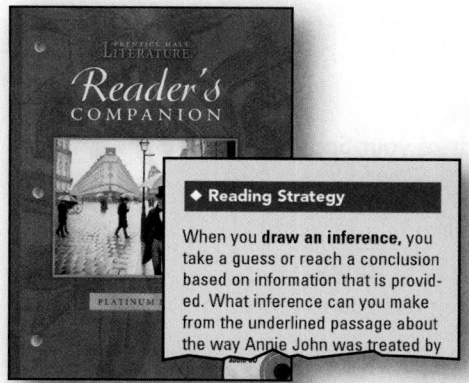

Basic reading support
- Full-length selections with interactive reading support
- Critical thinking questions
- Vocabulary and pronunciation guides

Adapted Version

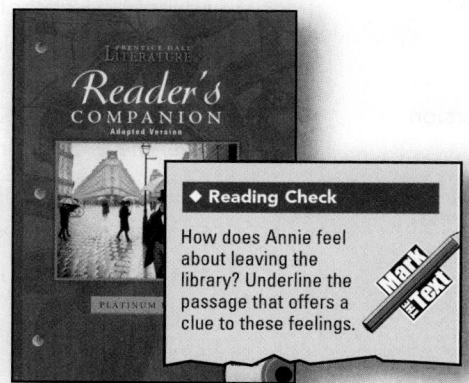

Enhanced reading support
- Selection adaptations and authentic text
- Enhanced design for easier readability
- Frequent Reading Checks and customized comprehension strategies

English Learner's Version

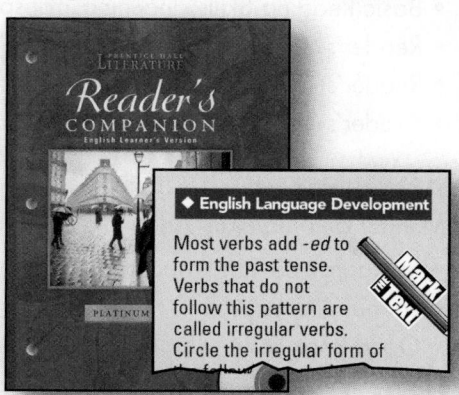

English learner's support
- Enhanced reading support
- Specialized vocabulary and pronunciation support
- Focus on idioms, colloquialisms, and cultural information

Need more reading support?

The Prentice Hall Reading Achievement System has the answer!

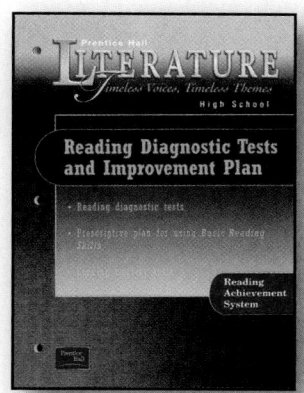

Reading Diagnostic Test and Improvement Plan
- Diagnostic tests determine what reading skills remediation is needed
- Individualized improvement plans guide teachers to specific skills lessons

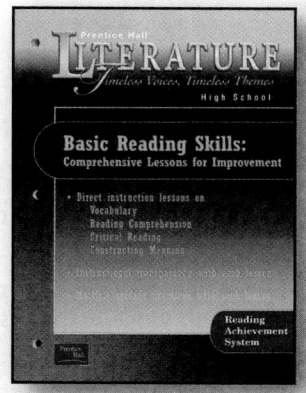

Basic Reading Skills: Comprehensive Lessons for Improvement
- Lesson plans for direct instruction
- Teaching transparencies for lesson modeling
- Blackline masters for student application and practice

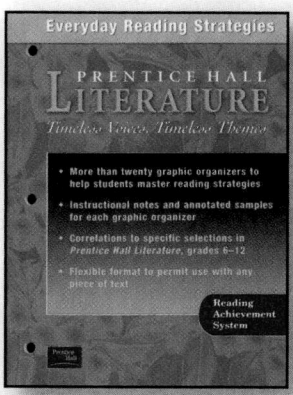

Everyday Reading Strategies
- More than 20 graphic organizers to help students master lifelong reading strategies
- Correlated to specific selections in *Prentice Hall Literature*

Prentice Hall Literature meets all your needs

Reading

Customize comprehensive reading instruction to ensure No Child Is Left Behind.

- Everyday Reading Strategies
- Teacher's Guidebook for Universal Access
- Reading Diagnostic and Improvement Plan
- Basic Reading Skills: Comprehensive Lessons for Improvement
- Basic Reading Skills: Teaching Transparencies
- Reader's Companion
- Reader's Companion, Adapted Version
- Reader's Companion, English Learner's Version

Assessment

Monitor and maintain Adequate Yearly Progress.

- Standardized Test Preparation: Diagnostic Tests
- Formal Assessment
- Open Book Tests
- Portfolio Assessment and Performance Management
- Review and Remediation Skillbook
- Skills Practice: Answers and Explanations Transparencies

Student Workbooks

Provide ample opportunities for skills practice and success on standardized tests.

- Selection Support: Skills Development Workbook
- Vocabulary and Spelling Practice Book
- Standardized Test Preparation Workbook
- Literary Analysis for Enrichment

Language Skills

Guarantee student success through consistent, systematic instruction in all language arts skills.

- Writing and Grammar Handbook Edition
- Integrated Lesson Planning Assistant
- Daily Language Practice Transparencies
- Vocabulary and Spelling Practice
- Writing Models and Graphic Organizers on Transparencies
- Fine Art Transparencies
- Extension Activities

Spanish Support

Meet the evolving needs of your Spanish speakers.

- *Literatura* Spanish Anthology (grades 6–8)
- *Literatura en español* Interactive Reader
- Spanish Readings Audio Program
- Spanish/English Summaries Audio Program

Technology

Plan, teach, and assess with a comprehensive, multimedia program for every grade level.

- Interactive Textbook Student Edition Online and on CD-ROM
- Standardized Test Preparation CD-ROM
- Reader's Companions Audio Program
- Listening to Literature Audio Program
- Listening to Music Audio Program
- Interest Grabber Video Program
- Got It! Assessment Video Program
- Literature in Performance Video Library

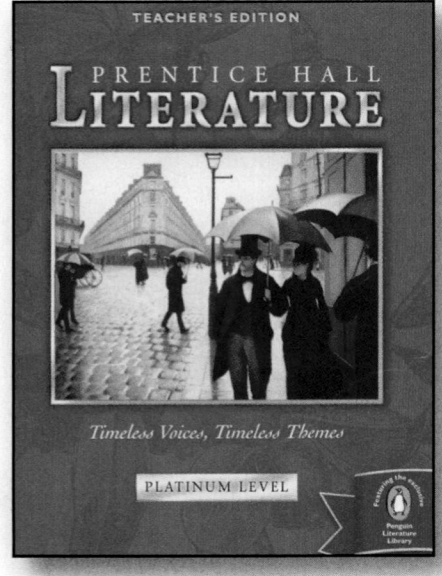

Prentice Hall Literature has the only Teacher's Edition that:

- provides a Time and Resource Manager for EVERY selection.
- encourages extensive planning support via direct instruction while helping set pace and priorities.
- gives all learners access to literature through ample customization notes.

ACADEMIC ACHIEVEMENT HANDBOOK

Research, Standards, and Planning Tools

Research Overview **T10**
An overview of the research used in the development of *Prentice Hall Literature*: what
types of research were consulted, how the research was gathered, and how it was utilized.

Research Bibliography **T20**
A comprehensive list of the articles, documents, essays, and other sources
cited in the Research Overview.

Professional Development **T21**
Summaries of recommended reference materials for ongoing professional development.

NCTE/IRA Standards Correlation **T22**
A chart showing where each NCTE and IRA standard is taught in the Student Edition.

Program Planner **T26**
An at-a-glance planning tool that shows the scope and sequence of skills instruction,
organized by unit and selection.

Strategies for Success **T47**
Suggestions from users of *Prentice Hall Literature* on how to teach the literature you
love and still prepare your students for high-stakes standardized tests.

PRENTICE HALL LITERATURE IS RESEARCH-BASED AND PROVEN TO WORK

The stakes for language arts educators are high. The plain fact is, you are expected to raise student achievement. Prentice Hall understands your dedicated efforts and gives you the confidence to meet this challenge. In developing Prentice Hall programs, the use of research studies is a central, guiding construct. Research on *Prentice Hall Literature* indicated key elements of a literature program that ensures student success: considerate text, consistent skills instruction, and an ongoing assessment strand. This research was conducted in three phases:

Phase 1: Exploratory Needs Assessment

Phase 2: Formative Research, Prototype Development, and Field Testing

Phase 3: Summative Research, Validation Research

1 EXPLORATORY NEEDS ASSESSMENT

In conjunction with Prentice Hall authors, research was done to explore educational research about reading. This research was incorporated into our instructional strategy and pedagogy to create a more effective literature program.

Along with periodic surveys concerning curriculum issues and challenges, we conducted specific product development research, which included discussions with teachers and advisory panels, focus groups, and quantitative surveys. We explored the specific needs of teachers, students, and other educators regarding each book we developed in *Prentice Hall Literature*.

2 FORMATIVE RESEARCH, PROTOTYPE DEVELOPMENT, AND FIELD TESTING

During this phase of research, we worked to develop prototype materials for each feature in *Prentice Hall Literature*. Then we tested the materials, including field testing with students and teachers and qualitative and quantitative evaluations of different kinds. We received solid feedback in our early prototype testing. Results were channeled back into the program development for improvement. For example, teachers commented positively on the easy navigation of instructional pages.

3 SUMMATIVE RESEARCH, VALIDATION RESEARCH

Finally, we conducted and continue to conduct longer-term research under actual classroom conditions. This research identifies what works and what can be improved in the next revision of *Prentice Hall Literature*. We also continue to monitor the program in the market. We talk to our users about what works, and then we begin the cycle over again. Highlights of this research follow in the next section.

PRENTICE HALL RESEARCH TIMELINE

Exploratory needs assessment
(Quantitative & qualitative)

- Reading research
- Teacher interviews
- Classroom observations
- Mail surveys
- Conference participation

Formative research
(Quantitative & qualitative)

- Field testing of prototypes
- Classroom observations
- Teacher reviews
- Supervisor reviews
- Educator advisory panels
- Prentice Hall sales force input

Summative research
(Experimental and quasi-experimental study designs & qualitative research)

- Prepublication learner verification research
- Postpublication validation studies
- Classroom observations
- Evaluation of in-market results on standardized tests

PRENTICE HALL LITERATURE

RESEARCH-BASED AND CLASSROOM-TESTED FOR PROVEN RESULTS

Average Mastery Levels in Instructional Objectives

† Scores between 0 and 49 are regarded as the nonmastery level. Scores between 50 and 74 are regarded as indications of partial mastery. Scores of 75 and above are regarded as the mastery level.

All tests were scored by CTB/McGraw Hill, the publisher of TerraNova™. Statistical analyses and conclusions were performed by an independent firm, Pulse Analytics, Inc., Ridgewood, New Jersey.

In a yearlong learner verification study, students using the *Prentice Hall Literature: Timeless Voices, Timeless Themes* program increased their mastery levels in several diagnostic skill areas for reading/language arts.

All students were tested at the start of the year with a nationally normed standardized test, the TerraNova™ Complete Battery Plus exam. At the end of the treatment period, students were retested with the same standardized test. Only students who completed both the pre- and post-tests were included in this analysis. All tests were scored by CTB/McGraw Hill, publisher of the TerraNova™.

In the study, students progressed from the partial mastery level to the mastery level (as defined by CTB/McGraw Hill)† in identifying reading strategies, analyzing text, writing strategies, and editing skills. In the other two reading objectives, Basic Understanding and Evaluate/Extend Meaning, the treatment group maintained mastery from the pre-test to the post-test.

PUTTING RESEARCH INTO PRACTICE

What Research Indicates

To aid comprehension, critical vocabulary words should be explained with meanings and background information before students read selections. To further improve reading fluency and comprehension, common prefixes and suffixes should be systematically introduced and explained (Carnine).

Studies indicate the efficacy of direct instruction of vocabulary, as well as programs that emphasize context. For a comprehensive approach, researchers advocate teaching decoding skills, introducing sight words, emphasizing context clues to determine if constructed meanings make sense, teaching vocabulary meanings explicitly, and extensively using comprehension strategies and modeling (Pressley, "What Should").

Integrate Language Skills

Vocabulary Development Lesson

Word Analysis: Latin Prefix *pre-*
The Latin prefix *pre-*, as found in *precluded*, means "before" or "in advance." Identify the word from the list below that best fits each definition.

preview   precaution   prejudice

1. To see in advance
2. Judgment without sufficient facts
3. Care taken in advance

Spelling Strategy
When you add an ending that begins with a vowel to a word that ends in a silent *e*, the *e* is usually dropped. For example, when adding *-ing* to the word *subside*, drop the silent *e* to form *subsiding*. Write the word formed by the

Concept Development: Antonyms
Identify the antonym, or opposite, of the first word.

1. precluded: (a) prevented, (b) aided, (c) started
2. retribution: (a) reward, (b) disaster, (c) assignment
3. accosted: (a) sought, (b) retreated, (c) discovered
4. subsided: (a) increased, (b) created, (c) challenged
5. afflicted: (a) weary, (b) skeptical, (c) blessed
6. explicit: (a) unnecessary, (b) vague, (c) impatient

Prentice Hall's Response

Vocabulary instruction in *Prentice Hall Literature* utilizes a combination of direct instruction and context-based approaches. Vocabulary words and their definitions are introduced before the selection, then again at point-of-use in the minor column of the selection. Reading strategies model the use of context-based approaches before the selection, then students are encouraged to use these approaches to answer questions after the selection. Also, students are given opportunities to assimilate new vocabulary words by applying them in exercises that follow the selection.

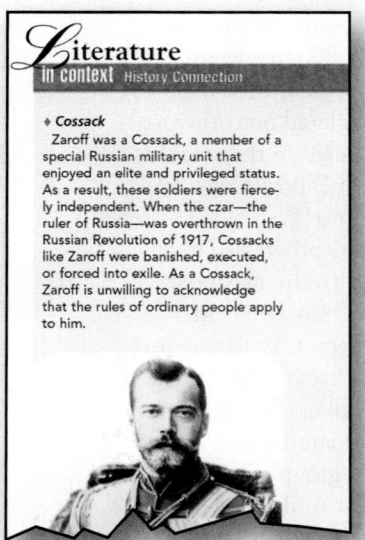

Literature in Context   History Connection

♦ Cossack
Zaroff was a Cossack, a member of a special Russian military unit that enjoyed an elite and privileged status. As a result, these soldiers were fiercely independent. When the czar—the ruler of Russia—was overthrown in the Russian Revolution of 1917, Cossacks like Zaroff were banished, executed, or forced into exile. As a Cossack, Zaroff is unwilling to acknowledge that the rules of ordinary people apply to him.

What Research Indicates

Schools that "beat the odds" in teaching middle- and high-school students to read and write well use materials that make overt connections among knowledge, skills, and ideas across lessons, classes, and grades, and across in-school and out-of-school applications (Langer).

Prentice Hall's Response

Prentice Hall Literature provides overt connections at the selection level with the Literature in Context features and at the unit level with the Connection to Literature features. The Teacher's Edition contains background information about each selection, author, and genre. Furthermore, students are encouraged to make connections between the literature selections and the fine art that illustrates the textbook. Extension Activities at the end of each selection and Reading Instructional Materials selections foster connections between students' reading and the world outside the classroom.

What Research Indicates

To enhance reading comprehension and retention, students must master reading strategies such as scanning, predicting, using background knowledge, summarizing main ideas, and asking questions (Every Child Reading).

Teaching a combination of reading comprehension techniques is the most effective way to increase students' understanding. When students use them appropriately, these techniques assist in recall, question answering, question generation, and summarization of texts. When used in combination, these techniques can improve results in standardized comprehension tests (National Reading Panel).

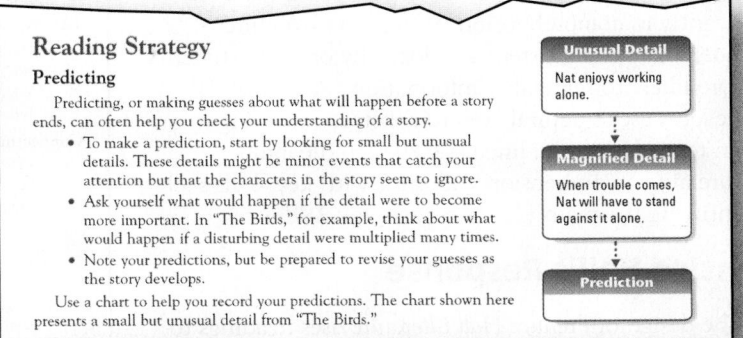

Prentice Hall's Response

Prentice Hall Literature provides extensive instruction in reading strategies with introduction, development, and conclusion of each reading skill. Reading strategies include predicting, questioning, rereading, scanning, drawing inferences, determining word meaning from context, using prior knowledge, identifying the main idea, and summarizing. Each reading skill is introduced in the Prepare to Read section of each selection. The skill is then practiced throughout the selection. Assessment of the skill occurs in the postselection material. Additionally, the Teacher's Edition provides direct instruction for the skills being taught at point-of-use in the selection.

What Research Indicates

In order to be effective, comprehension skills should be taught using a consistent format and sequence, with examples, practice, and review (Carnine).

Prentice Hall's Response

Comprehension skills are taught before the selection on the Prepare to Read page, along with appropriate examples. Students apply these skills by answering questions within the selection and directly afterward. In Reading Informational Material selections, reading skills are introduced before the selection, then tested immediately after.

STEP-BY-STEP TEACHING GUIDE	PACING GUIDE
PRETEACH	
Motivate Students and Provide Background	
Use the Motivation activity (ATE p. 4)	5 min.
Read and discuss the Preview material and Background information (SE/ATE p. 4) A	5 min.
Introduce the Concepts	
Introduce the Literary Analysis and Reading Strategy (SE/ATE p. 5) A	15 min.
Pronounce the vocabulary words and read their definitions (SE p. 5)	5 min.
TEACH	
Monitor Comprehension	
Informally monitor comprehension by circulating while students read independently or in groups A	30 min.
Monitor students' comprehension with the Reading Check notes (SE/ATE pp. 7, 9, 11)	as students read
Develop vocabulary with Vocabulary notes (SE pp. 7, 9, 11; ATE p. 7)	as students read
Develop Understanding	
Develop students' understanding of mood with the Literary Analysis annotations (SE p. 8; ATE pp. 7, 8, 9, 11) A	10 min.
Develop students' ability to break down confusing sentences with the Reading Strategy annotations (SE p. 10; ATE pp. 8,10)	10 min.
ASSESS	
Assess Mastery	
Assess students' mastery of the Reading Strategy and Literary Analysis by having them answer the Review and Assess questions (SE/ATE p. 13)	20 min.
Use one or more of the print and media Assessment Resources (ATE p. 15) A	up to 45 min.
EXTEND	
Apply Understanding	
Have students complete the Vocabulary Development Lesson and the Grammar Lesson (SE p. 14) A	20 min.
Apply students' ability to select precise details using the Writing Lesson (SE/ATE p. 15) A	45 min.
Apply students' understanding using one or more of the Extension Activities (SE p. 15)	20–90 min.

A ACCELERATED INSTRUCTION:
Use the strategies and activities identified with an A.

UNIVERSAL ACCESS
● = Below Level Students
▲ = On-Level Students
■ = Above Level Students

What Research Indicates

Text structure is vital to both comprehension and retention of information. "Signaling," through the use of headings, different typefaces, and pointer words, can aid significantly in comprehension. When text structure is "considerate," i.e. consistent and logically ordered, students are more likely to remember information (Armbruster).

Readers use structural cues to construct meaning from written texts. Headings, linguistic cues, and parallel structure aid comprehension and assist with key skills such as identifying the main idea in a passage (Goldman).

Prentice Hall's Response

The design of *Prentice Hall Literature* uses headings to identify particular skills or strategies, and uses graphic organizers to demonstrate skills such as identifying the main idea or making inferences. The structure and order of these various components is consistent throughout the program to maximize retention of information. Additionally, Reading Informational Materials selections explicitly identify the structure of informational materials such as brochures, contracts, and feature articles so that students will be familiar with the common features of these materials.

What Research Indicates

Because most real-world reading is nonfiction, students must gain fluency in reading informational texts. Necessary skills for reading nonfiction include activating prior knowledge, noting important headings and subheadings, skimming, determining a purpose for reading, finding main ideas and supporting details, using graphics and illustrations, and analyzing text structure (Harvey).

Prentice Hall's Response

In addition to the Nonfiction unit in each grade level of *Prentice Hall Literature*, every unit in each book includes at least one Reading Informational Materials selection. These selections consist of real-world nonfiction materials such as newspaper articles, product warranties, operating instructions, business letters, meeting agendas, and brochures. Skills taught with these informational materials include analyzing information, evaluating a text, using information to make a decision, questioning, recognizing different types of appeals, following steps in sequence, and following technical directions.

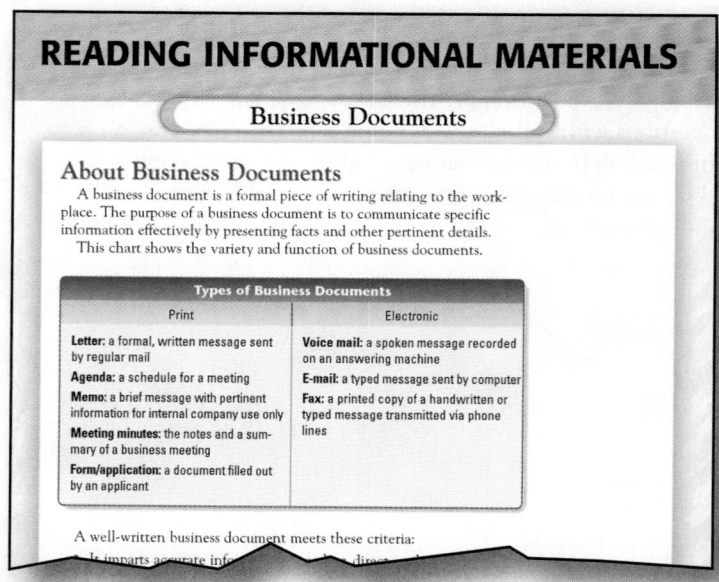

What Research Indicates

Research shows that engaged readers have higher achievement scores. Instructional techniques that can positively affect motivation include using reading strategies, linking to prior knowledge, introducing real-world interactions and related activities, promoting student choice in reading matter, having students ask their own questions, promoting collaboration between students, using scaffolding, assigning a variety of informational and literary texts, linking reading, writing, and knowledge through coherent instruction, and having students conduct self-evaluations of their work (Guthrie).

Prentice Hall's Response

Prentice Hall Literature incorporates multiple strategies to engage and motivate readers. Each selection is introduced with a section that connects to students' prior knowledge and demonstrates the reading strategy for the selection. These strategies motivate students to ask questions of the text and are specially designed to help foster reader autonomy. At each grade level, the literature selections include a diverse mixture of different genres, classic and contemporary works, and informational texts. The postselection section includes both response questions and scaffolded analytical questions that utilize the skills taught before the selection. Extension activities such as role plays and readers' panels promote collaboration among students. Writing Workshops and Listening and Speaking Workshops include rubrics and criteria charts that allow students to evaluate their work and that of their peers.

What Research Indicates

Schools that "beat the odds" in teaching middle- and high-school students to read and write well use test preparation that is integrated into ongoing goals, curriculum, and regular lessons (Langer).

Prentice Hall's Response

Prentice Hall Literature provides test preparation as a separate activity with Assessment Workshops at the end of each unit and with a Test Preparation workbook. The Test Preparation workbook is selection specific, allowing for integration of the assessment into regular lessons.

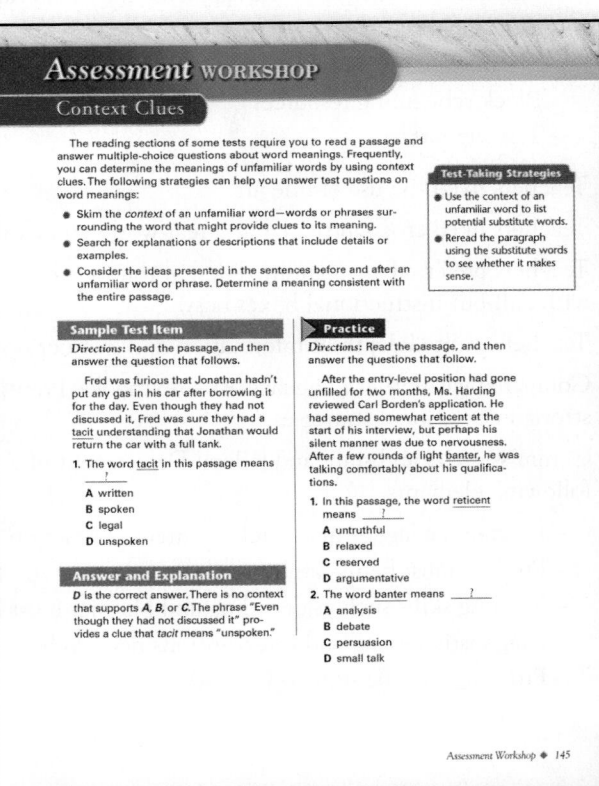

Incorporating Classroom Teacher Input

Market Needs Assessment

Prentice Hall conducted the following research to measure teacher responses to the literature textbooks in use in classrooms in 1999:

- **User Survey, September 9, 1999** Prentice Hall interviewed, by phone, 30 high-school teachers who used the previous edition of *Prentice Hall Literature*.

- **Focus Testing of Existing Programs, September 1999** Six focus groups of Grades 6–12 Language Arts teachers were conducted in three different cities. Participants reviewed then-current editions of *Prentice Hall Literature* and other literature programs.

- **Interviews with Department of Education Officials** Interviews were conducted in various key states in September and October 1999 and were ongoing through product development, December 2000.

Key Findings:

- The main reasons the program was adopted were:
  - Close fit with the curriculum
  - Selections offered
  - Amount and variety of the supplementary materials
  - Skill support
  - Thematic connections
  - Block scheduling resources
  - Test support

- Teachers liked the use of fine art.
- Teachers liked cross-curricular and real-world connections they perceived as solid and meaningful.
- Teachers preferred a streamlined design that was easy to work with; they considered the two-column design with call-out instructional boxes busy.
- Teachers wanted depth of information and instruction in Writing Workshops.
- Compared with other Language Arts textbooks, Prentice Hall was consistently cited by teachers as having strong instructional strategies.
- Commissioners and state and federal Department of Education officials asked that textbooks address the following elements:
  - Program pedagogy must include direct instruction in the Student Edition and Teacher's Edition.
  - Product must be research-based.
  - Reading skills such as decoding and phonics must be included.
  - Diagnostic testing and interventions need to be ongoing.
  - Program must be standards-based.

End Result:

In the new edition of *Prentice Hall Literature,* we've:

- retained the features that teachers love.

- developed a design that maintains a strong instructional focus through cleaner presentation. Selections appear in a single-column format, allowing instruction to be presented in a minor column.

- increased the length of Writing Workshops from two to four pages and included a full student model, a rubric, and more strategies for each stage of the writing process.

- developed the Student Edition and Teacher's Edition following the rules of direct instruction, defining terms at point-of-use and providing clear direction for students and teachers.

- consulted program authors and current research to confirm the direction and pedagogy of the series.

- developed Monitor Progress and Reteach notes in the Teacher's Edition for ongoing intervention opportunities.

- reviewed academic standards while instruction was developed.

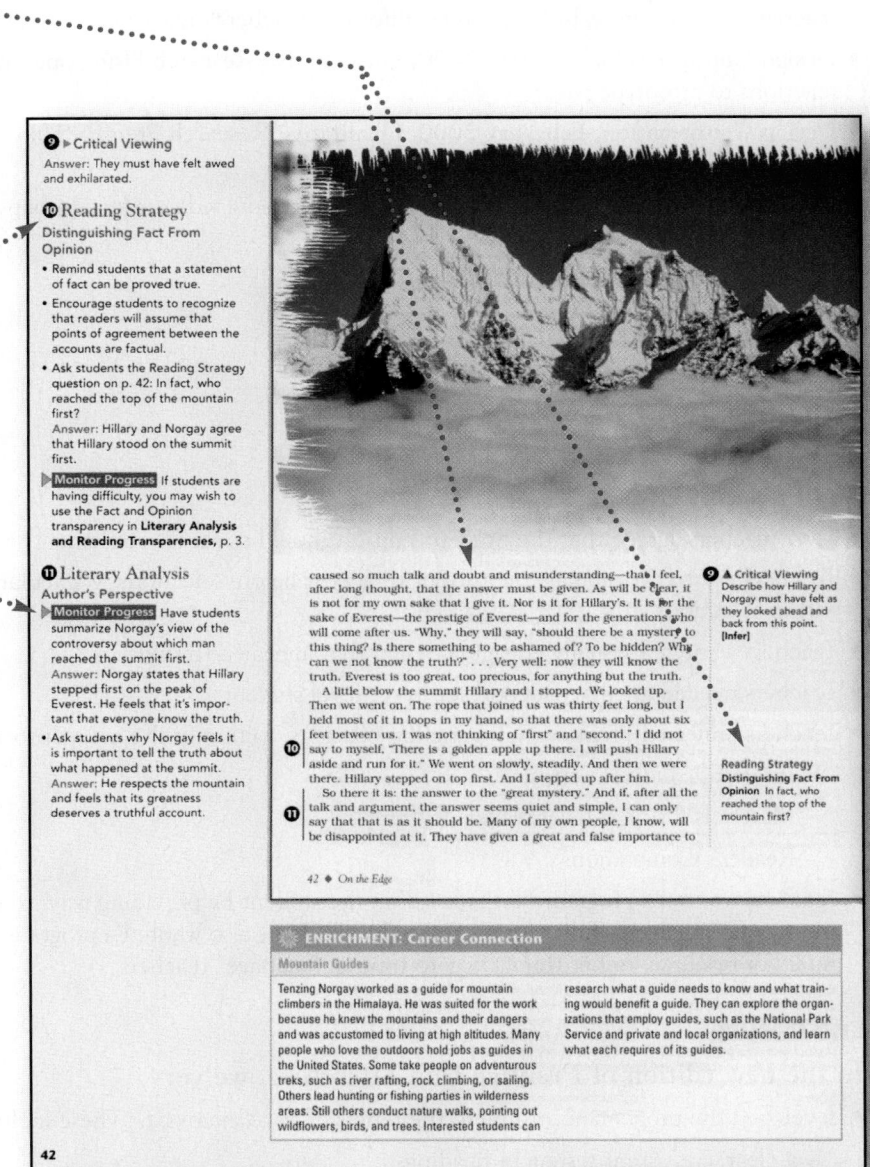

Formative Research

Prentice Hall conducted the following research to prototype and test new features, elements, and designs with teachers:

- **Prototype Testing: Focus Groups, December 1999** Focus groups were conducted among Grades 6–12 Language Arts teachers in New Jersey, Indiana, and California. Teachers reviewed several prototype versions of one literature selection.
- **Design Confirmation, February 2000, Quantitative Research** Using one-on-one interviews, Prentice Hall solicited reactions to prototype pages.
- **Design Confirmation, February 2000, Qualitative Research** Prentice Hall conducted two focus groups in New York for reactions to prototype pages.
- **Design Confirmation, April 2000** Prentice Hall conducted four focus groups in New Jersey and Oklahoma.

Ongoing Informal Research:

- In-school interviews
- Teacher advisory boards
- Adoption committee members

Key Findings:

- Most teachers agreed that the Student Edition should cover fewer elements in a more meaningful way.
- Teachers wanted vocabulary definitions to appear before selections; vocabulary words should be underlined at point-of-use within selections.
- Teachers wanted a visually engaging design that appealed to students.
- Teachers needed ancillary support for lower-level students.
- Teachers preferred Prentice Hall's ancillary package to that of the competitors, especially the following products:
    - Literature audiocassettes
    - Materials for high-level readers
    - Reader's Companions
- Teachers wanted a program that focused on the student by providing ways to engage and methods to teach important skills, and by offering accessibility for all ability levels. They also wanted a program that focused on the teacher by functioning as an aid or resource, rather than a way to train or "manage" teachers.

End Result:

In the new edition of *Prentice Hall Literature*, we've:

- developed the program according to the tenets of *considerate text*. These include:
    - a clear, consistent system of headings
    - chunked text to avoid paragraphs that are too dense
    - bulleted text when appropriate
    - boldfaced terms defined at point-of-use
- developed the Reading Achievement System to support lower-level students. Components include:
    - three levels of *Reader's Companions* to support struggling readers
    - *Basic Reading Skills: Comprehensive Lessons for Improvement*
    - *Teaching Guidebook for Universal Access*
- included panoramic images and large visuals to engage student interest.

Summary of Key Needs

Based on the collected research and classroom teacher input, Prentice Hall developed a literature program that meets these needs.

Strong skills instruction for successful test performance:

- Improved students' reading skills
- Strong instruction in communication skills
- Standardized test preparation

Strong teaching support and materials:

- Easy-to-follow materials for both students and teachers
- Instructional pathways to help all student populations— core, English-language learners, struggling readers, advanced students
- Companion Web site offering additional student activities, teacher resources, and professional development links

Standards-driven program with specific support/instruction for teachers:

- Strong skills activities and instruction with depth-based and standards-based outcomes
- Simple, direct lesson plans that clearly satisfy specific standards, including:
    - Daily lesson plans for special-education instruction
    - Daily lesson plans for English learners
    - Direct instruction in teaching reading and phonics

BIBLIOGRAPHY OF RESEARCH ARTICLES

Alexander, Patricia A., and Tamara Jetton. "Learning from Text: A Multidimensional and Developmental Perspective." In *Handbook of Reading Research*, vol. 3, ed. M. L. Kamil, P. B. Mosenthal, P. D. Pearson, and R. Barr, 285–310. Mahwah, N.J.: Lawrence Erlbaum Associates, 2000.

Armbruster, Bonnie, and Thomas H. Anderson. "On Selecting 'Considerate' Content Area Textbooks." *Remedial and Special Education* 9 (1): 47–52.

Blachowicz, Camille, and Peter Fisher. *Teaching Vocabulary in All Classrooms*. Upper Saddle River, N.J.: Prentice Hall, 1996.

Carnine, Douglas, Jerry Silbert, and Edward J. Kameenui. *Direct Instruction Reading. 3rd ed.* Upper Saddle River, N.J.: Prentice Hall, 1997.

Goldman, Susan R., and John A. Rakestraw, Jr. "Structural Aspects of Constructing Meaning From Text." In *Handbook of Reading Research*, vol. 3, ed. M. L. Kamil, P. B. Mosenthal, P. D. Pearson, and R. Barr, 311–335. Mahwah, N.J.: Lawrence Erlbaum Associates, 2000.

Guthrie, John T. and Allan Wigfield. "Engagement and Motivation in Reading." In *Handbook of Reading Research*, vol. 3, ed. M. L. Kamil, P. B. Mosenthal, P. D. Pearson, and R. Barr, 403–422. Mahwah, N.J.: Lawrence Erlbaum Associates, 2000.

Harvey, Stephanie, and Anne Goudvis. "Determining Importance in Text: The Nonfiction Connection." In *Strategies That Work: Teaching Comprehension to Enhance Understanding*. Portland, Me.: Stenhouse Publishers, 2000.

Langer, Judith. "Beating the Odds: Teaching Middle and High School Students to Read and Write Well," 1999. Center on English Learning and Achievement. May 2003. <http://cela.albany.edu/eie2/main.html>

Learning First Alliance. *Every Child Reading: An Action Plan*. Washington, D.C.: Learning First Alliance, 1998.

Morrow, Lesley Mandel. "Story Retelling: A Discussion Strategy to Develop and Assess Comprehension." In *Lively Discussions! Fostering Engaged Reading*, ed. Linda B. Gambrell and Janice F. Almasi, 265–285. Newark, Del.: International Reading Association, 1996.

National Reading Panel. *Teaching Children to Read: An Evidence-Based Assessment of the Scientific Research on Reading and Its Implications for Reading Instruction*. NIH Publication 00-4769. Bethesda, Md.: U.S. Department of Health and Human Services, 2000.

Pressley, Michael. "What Should Comprehension Instruction Be the Instruction Of?" In *Handbook of Reading Research*, vol. 3, ed. M. L. Kamil, P. B. Mosenthal, P. D. Pearson, and R. Barr, 545–562. Mahwah, N.J.: Lawrence Erlbaum Associates, 2000.

Pressley, Michael, Vera Woloshyn, et al. *Cognitive Strategy Instruction That REALLY Improves Children's Academic Performance*. Cambridge, Mass.: Brookline Books, 1995.

POWERFUL RESEARCH-BASED SOLUTIONS TO GUARANTEE TEACHER AND STUDENT SUCCESS!

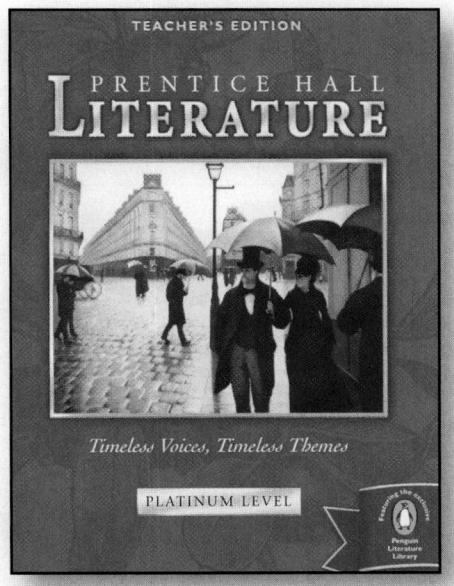

The Resource Teachers Use Most

The strategic instructional approach to teaching reading, grounded in reading research, is at the core of *Prentice Hall Literature*. This research is translated into direct program instruction to help teachers close the achievement gap in literacy.

Not only are teachers supported through research-based teaching techniques, but direct instruction within the Teacher's Edition offers customization ideas to reach students of all ability levels *before*, *during*, and *after* literary selections.

Anytime, Anywhere Professional Development

To enhance the powerful teacher support in *Prentice Hall Literature*, Prentice Hall offers the Online Literacy Series, powered by LessonLab. The *Prentice Hall Literature* authors lend their expertise to guide users of the Online Literacy Series toward exemplary practices and instructional methods. Five courses have been designed specifically to help teachers become even more proficient with their classroom materials, while mastering the skills they need to deliver the research-based strategy instruction.

Online Courses:

- Foundations of Coaching and Mentoring
- Active Learning: Structures to Engage All Students
- Vocabulary Development
- Comprehension of Literary and Informational Materials
- Literary Response and Analysis

The Online Literacy Series empowers administrators and teachers with the ability to:

- Observe a standards-based lesson
- Access resources, lesson plans, and student work
- Engage in ongoing dialogue with colleagues
- Apply best practices in your classroom
- Increase your content knowledge while building proficiency with your instructional materials

For more information, visit PHSchool.com/professional_development

NCTE/IRA STANDARDS CORRELATION

The National Council of Teachers of English (NCTE) and the International Reading Association (IRA), two professional organizations dedicated to improving the teaching and learning of English, have drafted a set of twelve comprehensive standards for the Language Arts. These standards are meant to provide a general framework for programs that encourage the development of language skills. The following pages show how *Prentice Hall Literature* meets these standards.

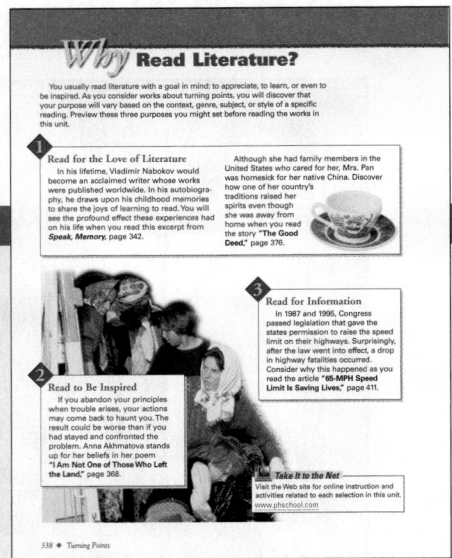

NCTE/IRA STANDARD	PRENTICE HALL LITERATURE
1. Students read a wide range of print and nonprint texts to build an understanding of texts, of themselves, and of the cultures of the United States and the world; to acquire new information; to respond to the needs and demands of society and the workplace; and for personal fulfillment. Among these texts are fiction and nonfiction, both classic and contemporary works.	• *Prentice Hall Literature* brings together the finest quality literature from around the world in a carefully balanced mix of classic and contemporary selections. • The Reading Informational Materials selections in each unit introduce students to real-world nonfiction texts and give them the tools to analyze informational materials, including editorials, warranties, business documents, critical reviews, and Web sites. • The Why Read Literature? page in each unit presents a variety of purposes for reading, each one connected to at least one selection in the unit.
2. Students read a wide range of literature from many periods in many genres to build an understanding of the many dimensions (e.g., philosophical, ethical, aesthetic) of human experience.	Following is a representative sampling of selections that support this standard: • **Short Stories** "The Monkey's Paw," W. W. Jacobs; "How Much Land Does a Man Need?" Leo Tolstoy; "The Cabuliwallah," Rabindranath Tagore; "There Will Come Soft Rains," Ray Bradbury; "The Censors," Luisa Valenzuela • **Poetry** "Thoughts of Hanoi," Nguyen Thi Vinh; "The Bean Eaters," Gwendolyn Brooks; "A Pace Like That," Yehuda Amichai; "Making a Fist," Naomi Shihab Nye; Haiku, Matsuo Bashō • **Nonfiction** from *The Way to Rainy Mountain*, N. Scott Momaday; "Keep Memory Alive," Elie Wiesel; "A Child's Christmas in Wales," Dylan Thomas; "Marian Anderson: Famous Concert Singer," Langston Hughes • **Drama** *The Tragedy of Julius Caesar*, William Shakespeare • **Epics and Legends** "Morte d'Arthur," Alfred, Lord Tennyson
3. Students apply a wide range of strategies to comprehend, interpret, evaluate, and appreciate texts. They draw on their prior experience, their interactions with other readers and writers, their knowledge of word meaning and of other texts, their word identification strategies, and their understanding of textual features (e.g., sound-letter correspondence, sentence structure, context, graphics).	• Reading skills and strategies are taught before, during, and after each selection. • The *Selection Support Skills Development Workbook* includes practice pages that reinforce the skills taught with every selection in the Student Edition, including vocabulary, grammar, reading strategies, and literary analysis.

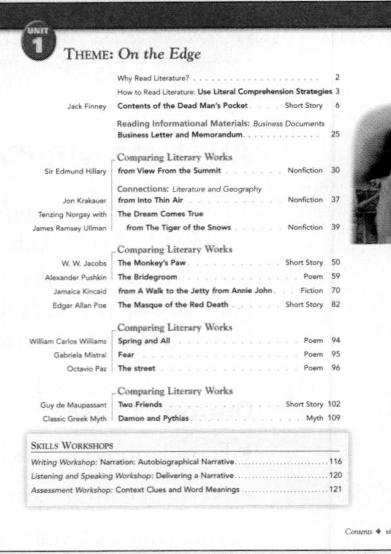

4. Students adjust their use of spoken, written, and visual language (e.g., conventions, style, vocabulary) to communicate effectively with a variety of audiences and for different purposes.

- Vocabulary skills and strategies are taught before, during, and after each selection.

- Writing lessons offered at both the selection level and the unit level provide instruction in the writing process. Each writing lesson contains links to *Prentice Hall Writing and Grammar* to further strengthen the program's support.

- Listening and Speaking activities are among the Extension Activities that follow each selection. In addition, each unit ends with a Listening and Speaking Workshop.

Extension Activities

Listening and Speaking With a partner, role-play a **television interview** with the narrator of "A Storm in the Mountains" to discuss his memorable mountain experience. In your dialogue, bring out the following:

- The narrator's knowledge of the mountains and what a storm would be like in that setting
- The narrator's emotions and reactions during and after the experience

Practice your interview, and then perform it for your class. **[Group Activity]**

Research and Technology The Black Mountain School, the artistic community in which Denise Levertov participated, had a major influence on the arts in America. Gather materials from a variety of sources—poems, photographs, audio- and videotapes—and then give a **multimedia presentation** about this school.

Take It to the Net www.phschool.com

Go online for an additional research activity using the Internet.

A Storm in the Mountains / In the Orchard / A Tree Telling of Orpheus ◆ 521

---

5. Students employ a wide range of strategies as they write and use different writing process elements appropriately to communicate with different audiences for a variety of purposes.

- In the selection-level Writing Lessons, students are given consistent instruction in prewriting, drafting, and revising, as well as in developing the appropriate voice and tone for a specific audience.

- Unit-level Writing Workshops provide in-depth instruction on prewriting strategies, such as note taking, outlining, and collecting source material; drafting strategies, such as point-by-point organization and pacing; and revising strategies, such as adding vivid language, adjusting tone, and varying sentence structure.

Writing WORKSHOP

Letter to the Editor

A letter to the editor is a type of business letter in which you present your opinion about a current event and support it with relevant facts, examples, or personal experiences. People write to the editors of magazines and newspapers to express their opinions on the content of the publication or on a public issue. In this workshop, you will write a letter to the editor of a publication.

Assignment Criteria Your letter to the editor should have the following characteristics:

- Standard business letter format, including heading, inside address, greeting, body, closing, and signature
- Formal language that states your opinion
- Relevant facts, examples, or personal experiences to support your opinion

To preview the criteria on which your letter to the editor may be assessed, see the Rubric on page 1083.

Prewriting

Choose a hot topic. Watch television, scan newspapers, or listen carefully to the issues your friends and family are discussing right now. In a chart like the one below, identify the two sides of several controversial topics, and then decide whether you feel strongly enough about any of the arguments to present it in a letter.

Narrow your topic. When you have chosen a topic, consider all the points you must make to convince your readers. Limiting your topic to one specific issue or problem enables you to cover your topic thoroughly. **Looping** is one strategy you can use.

Pro	Hot Topics	Con
Professional athletes have a responsibility to the public	Sports Heroes as Role Models	Excellent athletes are not necessarily models of non-sports skills.
Restrictions can protect our youngest citizens.	Laws restricting the Internet	Freedom of speech is denied by restrictions.

1. First, write freely on your topic for about five minutes.
2. Read what you have written, and circle the most important idea.
3. Then, write for five minutes on that idea.
4. Continue this process until you come to a topic that is narrow enough to address in your letter to the editor.
5. If you keep writing, you may even be able to identify a thesis statement, or main idea, that you want your letter to communicate.

1080 ◆ Epics and Legends

---

6. Students apply knowledge of language structure, language conventions (e.g., spelling and punctuation), media techniques, figurative language, and genre to create, critique, and discuss print and nonprint texts.

- Language arts skills development is thoroughly integrated in *Prentice Hall Literature.* Each selection includes applied grammar, usage, mechanics, writing, and word-study activities related to the reading.

- Grammar is presented sequentially so that students are able to cover and master the basic concepts before moving on to more complex structures. Grammar is taken from the context of the story so that authentic application comes naturally.

- Listening and speaking instruction ranges from Extension Activities, such as evaluating advertisements and analyzing media messages, to Listening and Speaking Workshops.

Integrate Language Skills

Vocabulary Development Lesson

Word Analysis: Anglo-Saxon Suffix -ly
Most words that end in the suffix -ly, such as *nonchalantly* and *audaciously,* are adverbs—words that modify a verb, an adjective, or another adverb.

Add -ly to the following words to make them adverbs. Then, write a sentence, using each adverb you formed.

1. confident   2. timid   3. hostile

Spelling Strategy
In *nonchalantly,* the *sh* sound is spelled with the letters *ch.* The *sh* sound can also be spelled with *sh* as in *shrill, ci* as in *audaciously, si* as in *mansion,* or *ti* as in *partial.* Spell these words correctly, using letters that spell an *sh* sound.

1. cons___ous   3. ten___on
2. poten___al

Fluency: Clarify Word Meaning
Review the vocabulary list on page 497. Then, in your notebook, write a response to each item.

1. Which character from the story behaves *audaciously?*
2. What animal has a *mottled coat?*
3. Describe a time when you acted *nonchalantly.*
4. What types of details give an advertisement *plausibility?*
5. Would you enjoy working for an *officious* person? Why or why not?
6. Which character in the story behaves *imperiously?*

Grammar Lesson

Prepositional Phrase or Infinitive?
The word *to* can be a preposition or part of an infinitive. In a **prepositional phrase,** *to* is followed by a noun or pronoun, as in *to the party* or *to her father.* In an **infinitive,** *to* is followed by a verb, as in *to dance* or *to talk.* Notice the prepositional phrase and the infinitive beginning with *to* in the following examples:

Preposition: He walked *to the laughter-filled*
NOUN
house.

Infinitive: He started *to lead* the way through
VERB
the maze of dancers.

Practice Copy the following sentences. Underline each prepositional phrase once and each infinitive twice.

1. The Cañon Road led across the mountains to the Sabinas Valley.
2. Welcome, stranger, welcome to our house.
3. Come and drink a toast to my daughter.
4. This young fool wants to meet you, my child.
5. A man clever enough to put the sheep has a right to play with the lamb.

Writing Application Write a single sentence that contains both a prepositional phrase beginning with *to* and an infinitive.

Prentice Hall Writing and Grammar Connection: Chapter 20, Section 1

508 ◆ Expanding Horizons

NCTE/IRA STANDARDS

NCTE/IRA STANDARD	PRENTICE HALL LITERATURE
7. Students conduct research on issues and interests by generating ideas and questions, as well as by posing problems. They gather, evaluate, and synthesize data from a variety of sources (e.g., print and nonprint texts, artifacts, people) to communicate their discoveries in ways that suit their purpose and audience.	• Extension Activities encourage students to explore additional dimensions of the selections through collaborative research, panel presentations, and discussions. • Each grade level includes unit-level workshops on writing and delivering a research paper. • Students practice research skills, such as asking questions and evaluating data, at the selection level and in the Reading Informational Materials features. 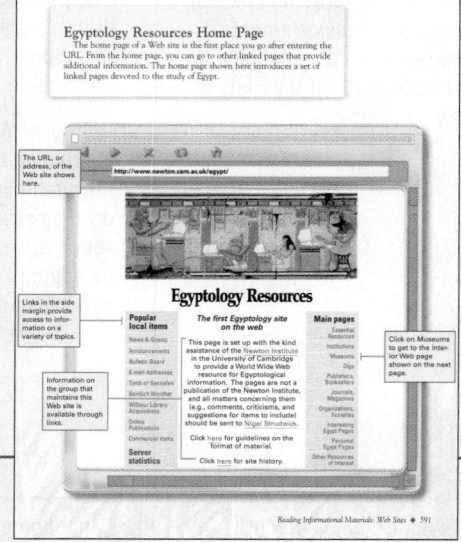
8. Students use a variety of technological and information resources (e.g., libraries, databases, computer networks, video) to gather and synthesize information and to create and communicate knowledge.	• Students practice research skills, such as searching the Internet and summarizing primary research articles, at the selection level in the Research and Technology Extension Activities and in the Reading Informational Materials features.
9. Students develop an understanding of and respect for diversity in language use, patterns, and dialects across cultures, ethnic groups, geographic regions, and social roles.	Following is a representative sampling of selections that support this standard: "A Visit to Grandmother," William Melvin Kelley; "Civil Peace," Chinua Achebe; "The Street of the Cañon," Josephina Niggli; from *Don Quixote,* Miguel de Cervantes; "Arthur Becomes King of Britain" from *The Once and Future King,* T. H. White; from *Sundiata: An Epic of Old Mali,* D. T. Niane; "Rama's Initiation" from the *Ramayana,* R. K. Narayan. • The Connections feature includes literary works from around the world, which are connected to individual selections in the Student Edition. 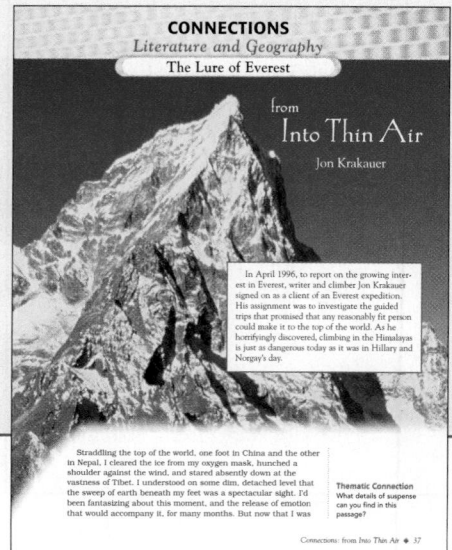

NCTE/IRA STANDARD	PRENTICE HALL LITERATURE
10. Students whose first language is not English make use of their first language to develop competency in the English language arts and to develop understanding of content across the curriculum.	• *Literatura en español* provides translations of one selection from each unit of the student textbook, along with summaries in English and Spanish of all textbook selections or groupings. • The *Spanish/English Summaries Audio CD*s include summaries of every selection in both English and Spanish. These summaries provide help for struggling readers, special-education students, and English learners prior to having them read. • *The Spanish Readings on Audio CD*s contain Spanish-language recordings of every selection in *Literatura en español*. • The *Teaching Guidebook for Universal Access* gives proven strategies for adapting instruction for English-language learners. In addition, the *Reader's Companion English Learner's Version* provides language support for students who are ready to work in English.

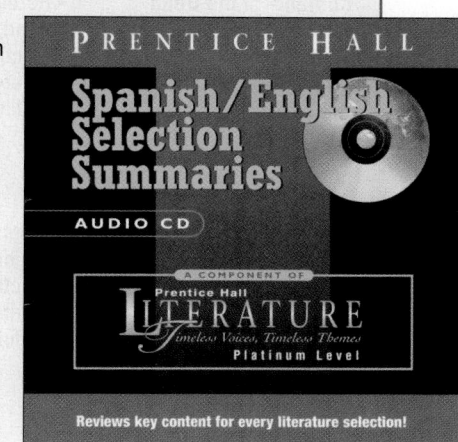

11. Students participate as knowledge-able, reflective, creative, and critical members of a variety of literacy communities.	• After each selection, the Extend Understanding question on the Review and Assess page and the Extension Activities invite students to go beyond the text to explore many connected areas. • The Writing Workshop in each unit includes several publishing and presenting opportunities that allow students to share their writing with classmates or with a larger audience. • Three levels of interactive readers—*Reader's Companion, Reader's Companion Adapted Version,* and *Reader's Companion English Learner's Version*—enable students at all ability levels to enjoy the same work of literature.

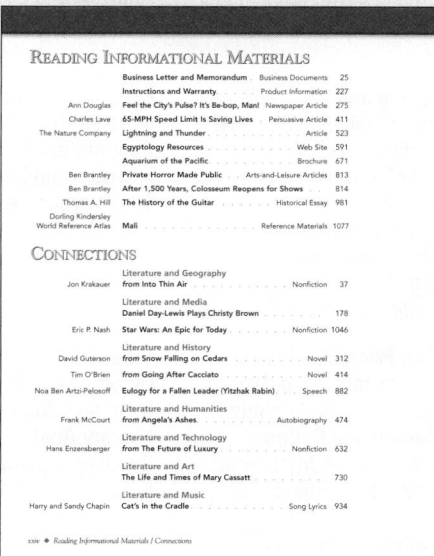

12. Students use spoken, written, and visual language to accomplish their own purposes (e.g., for learning, enjoyment, persuasion, and the exchange of information).	• Establishing a Purpose for Reading is one of the many Reading Strategies that are taught at each grade level. • Students learn to read for information in the Reading Informational Materials selections. The instruction that accompanies these selections teaches students to understand and utilize a vast array of real-world non-fiction texts. • Extension Activities at the selection level and Writing Lessons at the unit level often encourage students to choose their own topics for exploration.

Program Planner

Selection	Reading	Literary Analysis	Vocabulary	Grammar
"Contents of the Dead Man's Pocket," Jack Finney, SE p. 6 Reading Level: Average	• Rereading or Reading Ahead, SE p. 5; TR Selection Support, p. 3; TR Literary Analysis and Reading Transparencies, p. 1	• Suspense, SE p. 5; TR Selection Support, p. 4; TR Literary Analysis and Reading Transparencies, p. 2	• Vocabulary Development, SE p. 5: convoluted, grimace, deftness, imperceptibly, reveling, interminable • Latin Root -term-, SE p. 22; TR Selection Support, p.1	• Types of Nouns, SE p. 22; TR Selection Support, p. 2; WG Writing and Grammar, pp. 338–343
from *View From the Summit*, Edmund Hillary, SE p. 30 Reading Level: Average from *Into Thin Air*, Jon Krakauer, SE p. 37 Reading Level: Challenging "The Dream Comes True" from *The Tiger of the Snows*, Tenzing Norgay With James Ramsey Ullman, SE p. 39 Reading Level: Challenging	• Distinguishing Fact From Opinion, SE p. 29; TR Selection Support, p. 7; TR Literary Analysis and Reading Transparencies, p. 3	• Author's Perspective, SE p. 29; TR Selection Support, p. 8; TR Literary Analysis and Reading Transparencies, p. 4	• Vocabulary Development, SE p. 29: ample, aperture, belay, laboriously, feasible, formidable • Anglo-Saxon Prefix *be-*, SE p. 46; TR Selection Support, p. 5	• Noun Function, SE p. 46; TR Selection Support, p. 6; WG Writing and Grammar, p. 425
"The Monkey's Paw," W. W. Jacobs, SE p. 50 Reading Level: Average "The Bridegroom," Alexander Pushkin, SE p. 59 Reading Level: Average	• Predicting Outcomes, SE p. 49; TR Selection Support, p. 11; TR Literary Analysis and Reading Transparencies, p. 5	• Foreshadowing, SE p. 49; TR Selection Support, p. 12; TR Literary Analysis and Reading Transparencies, p. 6	• Vocabulary Development, SE p. 49: doughty, maligned, credulity, prosaic, avaricious, furtively, fusillade, foreboding, tumult • Latin Root -cred-, SE p. 66; TR Selection Support, p. 9	• Antecedents of Pronouns, SE p. 66; TR Selection Support, p. 10; WG Writing and Grammar, p. 344
from *A Walk to the Jetty* from *Annie John*, Jamaica Kincaid, SE p. 70 Reading Level: Average	• Drawing Inferences, SE p. 69; TR Selection Support, p. 15; TR Literary Analysis and Reading Transparencies, p. 7	• Flashback, SE p. 69; TR Selection Support, p. 16; TR Literary Analysis and Reading Transparencies, p. 8	• Vocabulary Development, SE p. 69: loomed, apprenticed, raked, stupor • Latin Root -stup-, SE p. 78; TR Sel. Support, p. 13	• Pronoun Case, SE p. 78; TR Selection Support, p. 14; WG Writing and Grammar, p. 544
"The Masque of the Red Death," Edgar Allan Poe, SE p. 82 Reading Level: Challenging	• Identifying Context Clues, SE p. 81; TR Selection Support, p. 19; TR Literary Analysis and Reading Transparencies, p. 9	• Symbols, SE p. 81; TR Selection Support, p. 20; TR Literary Analysis and Reading Transparencies, p. 10	• Vocabulary Development, SE p. 81: august, piquancy, arabesque, cessation, disapprobation, habiliments • Latin Suffix -tion, SE p. 90; TR Selection Support, p. 17	• Correct Use of Adjectives and Adverbs, SE p. 90; TR Selection Support, p. 18; WG Writing and Grammar, p. 368
"Spring and All," William Carlos Williams, SE p. 94 Reading Level: Average "Fear," Gabriela Mistral, SE p. 95 Reading Level: Easy "The Street," Octavio Paz, SE p. 96 Reading Level: Challenging	• Forming a Mental Image, SE p. 93; TR Selection Support, p. 23; TR Literary Analysis and Reading Transparencies, p. 11	• Imagery, SE p. 93; TR Selection Support, p. 24; TR Literary Analysis and Reading Transparencies, p. 12	• Vocabulary Development, SE p. 93: contagious, lifeless, clarity, stark, profound • Anglo-Saxon Suffix -less, SE p. 98; TR Selection Support, p. 21	• Coordinate Adjectives, SE p. 98; TR Selection Support, p. 22; WG Writing and Grammar, p. 657
"Two Friends," Guy de Maupassant, SE p. 102 Reading Level: Average "Damon and Pythias," Classic Greek Myth Retold by William F. Russell, SE p. 109 Reading Level: Easy	• Identifying Significant Details, SE p. 101; TR Selection Support, p. 27; TR Literary Analysis and Reading Transparencies, p. 13	• Climax, SE p.101; TR Selection Support, p. 28; TR Literary Analysis and Reading Transparencies, p. 14	• Vocabulary Development, SE p. 101: ardent, vernal, jauntiness, dire, detained, impediments, hindrances, annals • Latin Root -tain-, SE p.114; TR Selection Support, p. 25	• Degrees of Modifiers, SE p. 114; TR Selection Support, p. 26; WG Writing and Grammar, pp. 590–593

Key to Program References: SE: Student Edition **TR:** Teaching Resources **WG:** Writing and Grammar

Unit 1 *On the Edge*

Writing	Extension Activities	Assessment	Technology
• Writing Lesson: Cliffhanger Scene, SE p. 23; WG Writing and Grammar, p. 83	• Listening and Speaking: Dialogue, SE p. 23 • Research and Technology: Timeline, SE p. 23 • TR Extension Activities, p. 1	• Selection Test, TR Formal Assessment, pp. 1–3 • TR Open Book Test, pp. 1–3 • Writing Rubric and Listening and Speaking Rubric, TR Performance Assess. and Portfolio Mgmt., pp. 14, 31	• Interest Grabber Video, Tape 1 • Listening to Literature, Audiocassettes, Side 1; Audio CDs, CD 1 • Got It! Assessment Videotapes, Tape 1 • WG Writing and Grammar iText
• Writing Lesson: Comparison-and-Contrast Essay, SE p. 47; WG Writing and Grammar, p. 172	• Listening and Speaking: Advice for Future Climbers, SE p. 47 • Research and Technology: Video Game, SE p. 47 • TR Extension Activities, p. 2	• Selection Test, TR Formal Assessment, pp. 4–6 • TR Open Book Test, pp. 4–6 • Writing rubric and Listening and Speaking rubric, TR Performance Assess. and Portfolio Mgmt., p. 15	• Interest Grabber Video, Tape 1 • Listening to Literature, Audiocassettes, Sides 2, 3; Audio CDs, CDs 1, 2 • Got It! Assessment Videotapes, Tape 1 • WG Writing and Grammar iText
• Writing Lesson: Safety Instructions, SE p. 67; WG Writing and Grammar, p. 203	• Listening and Speaking: Dramatic Monologue, SE p. 67 • Research and Technology: Class Survey, SE p. 67 • TR Extension Activities, p. 3	• Selection Test, TR Formal Assessment, pp. 7–9 • TR Open Book Test, pp. 7–9 • Writing Rubric and Listening and Speaking Rubric, TR Performance Assess. and Portfolio Mgmt., p. 30	• Interest Grabber Video, Tape 1 • Listening to Literature, Audiocassettes, Sides 3, 4; Audio CDs, CD 2 • Got It! Assessment Videotapes, Tape 1 • WG Writing and Grammar iText
• Writing Lesson: Letter of Introduction, SE p. 79; WG Writing and Grammar, p. 56	• Listening and Speaking: Mock Telephone Interview, SE p. 79 • Research and Technology: Annotated Map, SE p. 79 • TR Extension Activities, p. 4	• Selection Test, TR Formal Assessment, pp. 10–12 • TR Open Book Test, pp. 10–12 • Writing Rubric and Listening and Speaking Rubric, TR Performance Assess. and Portfolio Mgmt., p. 27	• Interest Grabber Video, Tape 1 • Listening to Literature, Audiocassettes, Side 4; Audio CDs, CD 2 • Got It! Assessment Videotapes, Tape 1 • WG Writing and Grammar iText
• Writing Lesson: Journal of a Survivor, SE p. 91; WG Writing and Grammar, p. 57	• Listening and Speaking: Radio Script, SE p. 91 • Research and Technology: Multimedia Presentation, SE p. 91 • TR Extension Activities, p. 5	• Selection Test, TR Formal Assessment, pp. 13–15 • TR Open Book Test, pp. 13–15 • Writing Rubric and Listening and Speaking Rubric, TR Performance Assess. and Portfolio Mgmt., p. 28	• Interest Grabber Video, Tape 1 • Listening to Literature, Audiocassettes, Side 4; Audio CDs, CD 3 • Got It! Assessment Videotapes, Tape 1 • WG Writing and Grammar iText
• Writing Lesson: Description of a Natural Struggle, SE p. 99; WG Writing and Grammar, p. 107	• Listening and Speaking: Speech, SE p. 99 • Research and Technology: Comparison, SE p. 99 • TR Extension Activities, p. 6	• Selection Test, TR Formal Assessment, pp. 16–18 • TR Open Book Test, pp. 16–18 • Writing Rubric and Listening and Speaking Rubric, TR Performance Assess. and Portfolio Mgmt., pp. 19, 29	• Interest Grabber Video, Tape 1 • Listening to Literature, Audiocassettes, Side 5; Audio CDs, CD 3 • Got It! Assessment Videotapes, Tape 1 • WG Writing and Grammar iText
• Writing Lesson: Extended Definition of Friendship, SE p. 115; WG Writing and Grammar, p. 271	• Listening and Speaking: Debate, SE p.115 • Research and Technology: News Article, SE p.115 • TR Extension Activities, p.7	• Selection Test, TR Formal Assessment, pp. 19–21 • TR Open Book Test, pp. 19–21 • Writing Rubric and Listening and Speaking Rubric, TR Performance Assess. and Portfolio Mgmt., p. 19	• Interest Grabber Video, Tape 1 • Listening to Literature, Audiocassettes, Side 5, Audio CDs, CD 3 • Got It! Assessment Videotapes, Tape 1 • WG Writing and Grammar iText

Program Planner

Selection	Reading	Literary Analysis	Vocabulary	Grammar
from *In Commemoration: One Million Volumes,* Rudolfo A. Anaya, SE p. 128 Reading Level: Average	• Summarizing, SE p. 127; TR Selection Support, p. 31; TR Literary Analysis and Reading Transparencies, p. 15	• Author's Purpose, SE p. 127; TR Selection Support, p. 32; TR Literary Analysis and Reading Transparencies, p. 16	• Vocabulary Development, SE p. 127: induced, inherent, litany, dilapidated, satiated, enthralls, labyrinth, poignant, fomentation • Latin Prefix *in-*, SE p. 134; TR Selection Support, p. 29	• Action Verbs and Linking Verbs, SE p. 134; TR Selection Support, p. 30; WG Writing and Grammar, p. 352
"How Much Land Does a Man Need?," Leo Tolstoy, SE p. 138 Reading Level: Average	• Predicting Based on Character Traits, SE p.137; TR Selection Support, p. 35; TR Literary Analysis and Reading Transparencies, p. 17	• Parable, SE p. 137; TR Selection Support, p. 36; TR Literary Analysis and Reading Transparencies, p. 18	• Vocabulary Development, SE p. 137: piqued, disparaged, forbore, aggrieved, sheaf, arable, fallow • Context, SE p. 154; TR Selection Support, p. 33	• Regular and Irregular Verb Forms, SE p. 154; TR Selection Support, p. 34; WG Writing and Grammar, p. 520
"Success is counted sweetest," Emily Dickinson, SE p. 158 Reading Level: Easy "I dwell in Possibility—," Emily Dickinson, SE p. 159 Reading Level: Challenging "Uncoiling," Pat Mora, SE p. 160; Reading Level: Avg. "Columbus Dying," Vassar Miller, SE p. 162 Reading Level: Average	• Drawing Inferences, SE p. 157; TR Selection Support, p. 39; TR Literary Analysis and Reading Transparencies, p. 19	• Stated and Implied Themes in Poetry, SE p. 157; TR Selection Support, p. 40; TR Literary Analysis and Reading Transparencies, p. 20	• Vocabulary Development, SE p. 157: impregnable, thrall, vertigo • Latin Prefix *im-*, SE p.164; TR Selection Support, p. 37	• Subject and Verb Agreement, SE p. 164; TR Selection Support, p. 40; WG Writing and Grammar, p. 566
from *My Left Foot,* Christy Brown, SE p. 168 Reading Level: Average	• Identifying the Author's Purpose, SE p. 167; TR Selection Support, p. 43; TR Literary Analysis and Reading Transparencies, p. 21	• Epiphany, SE p. 167; TR Selection Support, p. 44; TR Literary Analysis and Reading Transparencies, p. 22	• Vocabulary Development, SE p. 167: impertinence, conviction, inert, contention, volition, taut • Latin Root *-vol-*, SE p. 176; TR Selection Support, p. 41	• Past and Past Perfect Tenses, SE p.176; TR Selection Support, p. 42; WG Writing and Grammar, p. 520
"A Visit to Grandmother," William Melvin Kelley, SE p. 182 Reading Level: Easy	• Clarifying, SE p. 181; TR Selection Support, p. 47; TR Literary Analysis and Reading Transparencies, p. 23	• Characterization, SE p.181; TR Selection Support, p. 48; TR Literary Analysis and Reading Transparencies, p. 24	• Vocabulary Development, SE p. 181: ventured, indulgence, grimacing, lacquered • Latin Word Origins: *ventured,* SE p.192; TR Selection Support, p. 45	• Progressive Verb Tenses, SE p. 192; TR Selection Support, p. 46; WG Writing and Grammar, p. 520
"After Apple Picking," Robert Frost, SE p. 196 Reading Level: Easy "Mowing," Robert Frost, SE p. 198; Reading Level: Avg.; "Style," Maya Angelou, SE p. 199; Reading Level: Easy "At Harvesttime," Maya Angelou, SE p. 200 Reading Level: Easy	• Interpreting, SE p. 195; TR Selection Support, p. 51; TR Literary Analysis and Reading Transparencies, p. 25	• Tone, SE p. 195; TR Selection Support, p. 52; TR Literary Analysis and Reading Transparencies, p. 26	• Vocabulary Development, SE p. 195: bough, trough, manifestation, disparaging, judicious, gibe, admonition, immutable, potency • Spelling vs. Pronunciation: *-ough,* SE p. 202; TR Selection Support, p. 49	• Adverb Function, SE p. 202; TR Selection Support, p. 50; WG Writing and Grammar, p. 380
"The Apple Tree," Katherine Mansfield, SE p. 206 Reading Level: Average	• Questioning, SE p. 205; TR Selection Support, p. 55; TR Literary Analysis and Reading Transparencies, p. 27	• Allusion, SE p. 205; TR Selection Support, p. 58; TR Literary Analysis and Reading Transparencies, p. 28	• Vocabulary Development, SE p. 205: paddocks, exquisite, bouquet, jovial • Words From Myths, SE p. 212; TR Selection Support, p. 53	• Confusing Verbs *lay* and *lie,* SE p. 212; TR Selection Support, p. 54; WG Writing and Grammar, p. 612

Key to Program References: SE: Student Edition **TR:** Teaching Resources **WG:** Writing and Grammar

Writing	Extension Activities	Assessment	Technology
• Writing Lesson: Reading Journal, SE p.135; WG Writing and Grammar, p. 284	• Listening and Speaking: Group Discussion, SE p. 135 • Research and Technology: Library Resources Chart, SE p. 135 • TR Extension Activities, p. 8	• Selection Test, TR Formal Assessment, pp. 26–28 • TR Open Book Test, pp. 22–24 • Writing rubric and Listening and Speaking rubric, TR Performance Assess. and Portfolio Mgmt., p. 30	• Interest Grabber Video, Tape 1 • Listening to Literature, Audiocassettes, Side 5; Audio CDs, CD 3 • Got It! Assessment Videotapes, Tape 1 • WG Writing and Grammar iText
• Writing Lesson: Video Script, SE p. 155; WG Writing and Grammar, p. 104	• Listening and Speaking: Eulogy, SE p. 155 • Research and Technology: Annotated Map, SE p. 155 • TR Extension Activities, p. 9	• Selection Test, TR Formal Assessment, pp. 29–31 • TR Open Book Test, pp. 25–27	• Interest Grabber Video, Tape 1 • Listening to Literature, Audiocassettes, Side 6; Audio CDs, CD 4 • Got It! Assessment Videotapes, Tape 1 • WG Writing and Grammar iText
• Writing Lesson: Submission Letter, SE p.165; WG Writing and Grammar, p. 287	• Listening and Speaking: Informal Debate, SE p. 165 • Research and Technology: Brochure, SE p. 165 • TR Extension Activities, p. 10	• Selection Test, TR Formal Assessment, pp. 32–34 • TR Open Book Test, pp. 28–30 • Writing rubric and Listening and Speaking rubric, TR Performance Assess. and Portfolio Mgmt., p. 18	• Interest Grabber Video, Tape 1 • Listening to Literature, Audiocassettes, Side 6; Audio CDs, CD 4 • Got It! Assessment Videotapes, Tape 1 • WG Writing and Grammar iText
• Writing Lesson: Personal Narrative, SE p.177; WG Writing and Grammar, p. 203	• Listening and Speaking: Speech, SE p. 177 • Research and Technology: Multimedia Presentation, SE p. 177 • TR Extension Activities, p. 11	• Selection Test, TR Formal Assessment, pp. 35–37 • TR Open Book Test, pp. 31–33 • Writing rubric and Listening and Speaking rubric, TR Performance Assess. and Portfolio Mgmt., pp. 9, 29	• Interest Grabber Video, Tape 1 • Listening to Literature, Audiocassettes, Side 6; Audio CDs, CD 4 • Got It! Assessment Videotapes, Tape 1 • WG Writing and Grammar iText
• Writing Lesson: Firsthand Biography of a Character, SE p. 193; WG Writing and Grammar, p. 71	• Listening and Speaking: Oral Anecdote, SE p. 193 • Research and Technology: Conflict-Resolution Workshop, SE p. 193 • TR Extension Activities, p.12	• Selection Test, TR Formal Assessment, pp. 38–40 • TR Open Book Test, pp. 34–36 • Writing rubric and Listening and Speaking rubric, TR Performance Assess. and Portfolio Mgmt., p. 28	• Interest Grabber Video, Tape 1 • Listening to Literature, Audiocassettes, Side 7; Audio CDs, CD 5 • Got It! Assessment Videotapes, Tape 1 • WG Writing and Grammar iText
• Writing Lesson: Advice Column, SE p. 203; WG Writing and Grammar, p. 239	• Listening and Speaking: Speech, SE p. 203 • Research and Technology: Timeline, SE p. 203 • TR Extension Activities, p. 13	• Selection Test, TR Formal Assessment, pp. 41–43 • TR Open Book Test, pp. 37–39 • Writing rubric and Listening and Speaking rubric, TR Performance Assess. and Portfolio Mgmt., p. 22	• Interest Grabber Video, Tape 1 • Listening to Literature, Audiocassettes, Side 7; Audio CDs, CD 5 • Got It! Assessment Videotapes, Tape 1 • WG Writing and Grammar iText
• Writing Lesson: Retelling a Story, SE p. 213; WG Writing and Grammar, p. 306	• Listening and Speaking: Monologue, SE p. 306 • Research and Technology: Annotated Map, SE p. 306 • TR Extension Activities, p. 14	• Selection Test, TR Formal Assessment, pp. 44–46 • TR Open Book Test, pp. 40–42 • Writing rubric and Listening and Speaking rubric, TR Performance Assess. and Portfolio Mgmt., p. 28	• Interest Grabber Video, Tape 1 • Listening to Literature, Audiocassettes, Side 8; Audio CDs, CD 5 • Got It! Assessment Videotapes, Tape 1 • WG Writing and Grammar iText

PROGRAM PLANNER

Program Planner

Selection	Reading	Literary Analysis	Vocabulary	Grammar
"Africa," David Diop, SE p. 216 ; Level: Challenging **"Old Song,"** Traditional, SE p. 217 Reading Level: Easy **"All,"** Bei Dao, SE p. 218 Reading Level: Challenging **"Also All,"** Shu Ting, SE p. 219 Reading Level: Average from **The Analects,** Confucius, SE p. 220 Reading Level: Average	• Relating to What You Know, SE p. 215; TR Selection Support, p. 59; TR Literary Analysis and Reading Transparencies, p. 29	• Aphorisms, SE p. 215; TR Selection Support, p. 60; TR Literary Analysis and Reading Transparencies, p. 30	• Vocabulary Development, SE p. 215: impetuous, lamentation, chastisements • Latin Suffix -ment, SE p. 224; TR Selection Support, p. 57	• Active and Passive Voice, SE p. 224; TR Selection Support, p. 58; WG Writing and Grammar, p. 534

Program Planner

Selection	Reading	Literary Analysis	Vocabulary	Grammar
"Through the Tunnel," Doris Lessing , SE p. 242 Reading Level: Average	• Questioning, SE p. 241; TR Selection Support, p. 63; TR Literary Analysis and Reading Transparencies, p. 31	• Internal Conflict, SE p. 241; TR Selection Support, p. 64; TR Literary Analysis and Reading Transparencies, p. 32	• Vocabulary Development, SE p. 241: contrition, promontories, luminous, supplication, frond, convulsive, gout • Latin Root -lum-, SE p. 252; TR Selection Support, p. 61	• Complete Subject, SE p. 252; TR Selection Support, p. 62; WG Writing and Grammar, p. 412
"The Dog That Bit People," James Thurber, SE p. 256 Reading Level: Average	• Forming Mental Images, SE p. 255; TR Selection Support, p. 67; TR Literary Analysis and Reading Transparencies, p. 33	• Humorous Essay, SE p. 255; TR Selection Support, p. 71; TR Literary Analysis and Reading Transparencies, p. 34	• Vocabulary Development, SE p. 255: incredulity, choleric, irascible, jangle, indignant, epitaph • Greek Prefix epi-, SE p. 262; TR Selection Support, p. 65	• Complete Predicates, SE p. 262; TR Selection Support, p. 66; WG Writing and Grammar, p. 412
"Conscientious Objector," Edna St. Vincent Millay, SE p. 266 Reading Level: Challenging **"A Man,"** Nina Cassian, SE p. 267 Reading Level: Easy **"The Weary Blues,"** Langston Hughes, SE p. 268 Reading Level: Challenging **"Jazz Fantasia,"** Carl Sandburg, SE p. 270 Reading Level: Average	• Responding to Images and Ideas, SE p. 265; TR Selection Support, p. 71; TR Literary Analysis and Reading Transparencies, p. 35	• Tone, SE p. 265; TR Selection Support, p. 75; TR Literary Analysis and Reading Transparencies, p. 36	• Vocabulary Development, SE p. 265: reap, pallor, melancholy • Greek Root -chol-, SE p. 272; TR Selection Support, p. 69	• Hard-to-Find Subjects, SE p. 272; TR Selection Support, p. 70; WG Writing and Grammar, p. 418
"Like the Sun," R. K. Narayan, SE p. 280 Reading Level: Average **"Tell all the Truth but tell it slant—,"** Emily Dickinson, SE p. 284 Reading Level: Average	• Analyzing Causes and Effects, SE p. 279; TR Selection Support, p. 75; TR Literary Analysis and Reading Transparencies, p. 37	• Irony, SE p. 279; TR Selection Support, p. 79; TR Literary Analysis and Reading Transparencies, p. 38	• Vocabulary Development, SE p. 279: essence, tempering, shirked, incessantly, ingratiating, stupefied, scrutinized • Latin Root -gratis-, SE p. 286; TR Selection Support, p. 73	• Direct and Indirect Objects, SE p. 286; TR Selection Support, p. 74; WG Writing and Grammar, p. 425
"Hearts and Hands," O. Henry, SE p. 290 Reading Level: Easy **"The Fish,"** Elizabeth Bishop, SE p. 293 Reading Level: Easy	• Predicting Outcomes, SE p. 289; TR Selection Support, p. 79; TR Literary Analysis and Reading Transparencies, p. 39	• Surprise Ending, SE p. 289; TR Selection Support, p. 83; TR Literary Analysis and Reading Transparencies, p. 40	• Vocabulary Development, SE p. 289: influx, forestalled, counterfeiting, sidled, venerable, infested, sullen • Latin Prefix counter-, SE p. 296; TR Selection Support, p. 77	• Compound Predicates, SE p. 296; TR Selection Support, p. 78; WG Writing and Grammar, p. 412

Key to Program References: SE: Student Edition **TR:** Teaching Resources **WG:** Writing and Grammar

Unit 2 *Striving for Success*

Writing	Extension Activities	Assessment	Technology
• Writing Lesson: Reading Journal, SE p.135; WG Writing and Grammar, p. 284	• Listening and Speaking: Group Discussion, SE p. 135 • Research and Technology: Library Resources Chart, SE p. 135 • TR Extension Activities, p. 8	• Selection Test, TR Formal Assessment, pp. 26–28 • TR Open Book Test, pp. 22–24 • Writing rubric and Listening and Speaking rubric, TR Performance Assess. and Portfolio Mgmt., p. 30	• Interest Grabber Video, Tape 1 • Listening to Literature, Audiocassettes, Side 5; Audio CDs, CD 3 • Got It! Assessment Videotapes, Tape 1 • WG Writing and Grammar iText
• Writing Lesson: Video Script, SE p. 155; WG Writing and Grammar, p. 104	• Listening and Speaking: Eulogy, SE p. 155 • Research and Technology: Annotated Map, SE p. 155 • TR Extension Activities, p. 9	• Selection Test, TR Formal Assessment, pp. 29–31 • TR Open Book Test, pp. 25–27	• Interest Grabber Video, Tape 1 • Listening to Literature, Audiocassettes, Side 6; Audio CDs, CD 4 • Got It! Assessment Videotapes, Tape 1 • WG Writing and Grammar iText
• Writing Lesson: Submission Letter, SE p.165; WG Writing and Grammar, p. 287	• Listening and Speaking: Informal Debate, SE p. 165 • Research and Technology: Brochure, SE p. 165 • TR Extension Activities, p. 10	• Selection Test, TR Formal Assessment, pp. 32–34 • TR Open Book Test, pp. 28–30 • Writing rubric and Listening and Speaking rubric, TR Performance Assess. and Portfolio Mgmt., p. 18	• Interest Grabber Video, Tape 1 • Listening to Literature, Audiocassettes, Side 6; Audio CDs, CD 4 • Got It! Assessment Videotapes, Tape 1 • WG Writing and Grammar iText
• Writing Lesson: Personal Narrative, SE p.177; WG Writing and Grammar, p. 203	• Listening and Speaking: Speech, SE p. 177 • Research and Technology: Multimedia Presentation, SE p. 177 • TR Extension Activities, p. 11	• Selection Test, TR Formal Assessment, pp. 35–37 • TR Open Book Test, pp. 31–33 • Writing rubric and Listening and Speaking rubric, TR Performance Assess. and Portfolio Mgmt., pp. 9, 29	• Interest Grabber Video, Tape 1 • Listening to Literature, Audiocassettes, Side 6; Audio CDs, CD 4 • Got It! Assessment Videotapes, Tape 1 • WG Writing and Grammar iText
• Writing Lesson: Firsthand Biography of a Character, SE p. 193; WG Writing and Grammar, p. 71	• Listening and Speaking: Oral Anecdote, SE p. 193 • Research and Technology: Conflict-Resolution Workshop, SE p. 193 • TR Extension Activities, p.12	• Selection Test, TR Formal Assessment, pp. 38–40 • TR Open Book Test, pp. 34–36 • Writing rubric and Listening and Speaking rubric, TR Performance Assess. and Portfolio Mgmt., p. 28	• Interest Grabber Video, Tape 1 • Listening to Literature, Audiocassettes, Side 7; Audio CDs, CD 5 • Got It! Assessment Videotapes, Tape 1 • WG Writing and Grammar iText
• Writing Lesson: Advice Column, SE p. 203; WG Writing and Grammar, p. 239	• Listening and Speaking: Speech, SE p. 203 • Research and Technology: Timeline, SE p. 203 • TR Extension Activities, p. 13	• Selection Test, TR Formal Assessment, pp. 41–43 • TR Open Book Test, pp. 37–39 • Writing rubric and Listening and Speaking rubric, TR Performance Assess. and Portfolio Mgmt., p. 22	• Interest Grabber Video, Tape 1 • Listening to Literature, Audiocassettes, Side 7; Audio CDs, CD 5 • Got It! Assessment Videotapes, Tape 1 • WG Writing and Grammar iText
• Writing Lesson: Retelling a Story, SE p. 213; WG Writing and Grammar, p. 306	• Listening and Speaking: Monologue, SE p. 306 • Research and Technology: Annotated Map, SE p. 306 • TR Extension Activities, p. 14	• Selection Test, TR Formal Assessment, pp. 44–46 • TR Open Book Test, pp. 40–42 • Writing rubric and Listening and Speaking rubric, TR Performance Assess. and Portfolio Mgmt., p. 28	• Interest Grabber Video, Tape 1 • Listening to Literature, Audiocassettes, Side 8; Audio CDs, CD 5 • Got It! Assessment Videotapes, Tape 1 • WG Writing and Grammar iText

Program Planner

Selection	Reading	Literary Analysis	Vocabulary	Grammar
"Africa," David Diop, SE p. 216 ; Level: Challenging **"Old Song,"** Traditional, SE p. 217 Reading Level: Easy **"All,"** Bei Dao, SE p. 218 Reading Level: Challenging **"Also All,"** Shu Ting, SE p. 219 Reading Level: Average from **The Analects,** Confucius, SE p. 220 Reading Level: Average	• Relating to What You Know, SE p. 215; TR Selection Support, p. 59; TR Literary Analysis and Reading Transparencies, p. 29	• Aphorisms, SE p. 215; TR Selection Support, p. 60; TR Literary Analysis and Reading Transparencies, p. 30	• Vocabulary Development, SE p. 215: impetuous, lamentation, chastisements • Latin Suffix -ment, SE p. 224; TR Selection Support, p. 57	• Active and Passive Voice, SE p. 224; TR Selection Support, p. 58; WG Writing and Grammar, p. 534

Program Planner

Selection	Reading	Literary Analysis	Vocabulary	Grammar
"Through the Tunnel," Doris Lessing , SE p. 242 Reading Level: Average	• Questioning, SE p. 241; TR Selection Support, p. 63; TR Literary Analysis and Reading Transparencies, p. 31	• Internal Conflict, SE p. 241; TR Selection Support, p. 64; TR Literary Analysis and Reading Transparencies, p. 32	• Vocabulary Development, SE p. 241: contrition, promontories, luminous, supplication, frond, convulsive, gout • Latin Root -lum-, SE p. 252; TR Selection Support, p. 61	• Complete Subject, SE p. 252; TR Selection Support, p. 62; WG Writing and Grammar, p. 412
"The Dog That Bit People," James Thurber, SE p. 256 Reading Level: Average	• Forming Mental Images, SE p. 255; TR Selection Support, p. 67; TR Literary Analysis and Reading Transparencies, p. 33	• Humorous Essay, SE p. 255; TR Selection Support, p. 71; TR Literary Analysis and Reading Transparencies, p. 34	• Vocabulary Development, SE p. 255: incredulity, choleric, irascible, jangle, indignant, epitaph • Greek Prefix epi-, SE p. 262; TR Selection Support, p. 65	• Complete Predicates, SE p. 262; TR Selection Support, p. 66; WG Writing and Grammar, p. 412
"Conscientious Objector," Edna St. Vincent Millay, SE p. 266 Reading Level: Challenging **"A Man,"** Nina Cassian, SE p. 267 Reading Level: Easy **"The Weary Blues,"** Langston Hughes, SE p. 268 Reading Level: Challenging **"Jazz Fantasia,"** Carl Sandburg, SE p. 270 Reading Level: Average	• Responding to Images and Ideas, SE p. 265; TR Selection Support, p. 71; TR Literary Analysis and Reading Transparencies, p. 35	• Tone, SE p. 265; TR Selection Support, p. 75; TR Literary Analysis and Reading Transparencies, p. 36	• Vocabulary Development, SE p. 265: reap, pallor, melancholy • Greek Root -chol-, SE p. 272; TR Selection Support, p. 69	• Hard-to-Find Subjects, SE p. 272; TR Selection Support, p. 70; WG Writing and Grammar, p. 418
"Like the Sun," R. K. Narayan, SE p. 280 Reading Level: Average **"Tell all the Truth but tell it slant—,"** Emily Dickinson, SE p. 284 Reading Level: Average	• Analyzing Causes and Effects, SE p. 279; TR Selection Support, p. 75; TR Literary Analysis and Reading Transparencies, p. 37	• Irony, SE p. 279; TR Selection Support, p. 79; TR Literary Analysis and Reading Transparencies, p. 38	• Vocabulary Development, SE p. 279: essence, tempering, shirked, incessantly, ingratiating, stupefied, scrutinized • Latin Root -gratis-, SE p. 286; TR Selection Support, p. 73	• Direct and Indirect Objects, SE p. 286; TR Selection Support, p. 74; WG Writing and Grammar, p. 425
"Hearts and Hands," O. Henry, SE p. 290 Reading Level: Easy **"The Fish,"** Elizabeth Bishop, SE p. 293 Reading Level: Easy	• Predicting Outcomes, SE p. 289; TR Selection Support, p. 79; TR Literary Analysis and Reading Transparencies, p. 39	• Surprise Ending, SE p. 289; TR Selection Support, p. 83; TR Literary Analysis and Reading Transparencies, p. 40	• Vocabulary Development, SE p. 289: influx, forestalled, counterfeiting, sidled, venerable, infested, sullen • Latin Prefix counter-, SE p. 296; TR Selection Support, p. 77	• Compound Predicates, SE p. 296; TR Selection Support, p. 78; WG Writing and Grammar, p. 412

Key to Program References: SE: Student Edition **TR:** Teaching Resources **WG:** Writing and Grammar

Unit 2 *Striving for Success*

Writing	Extension Activities	Assessment	Technology
• Writing Lesson: Evaluation, SE p. 225; WG Writing and Grammar, p. 181	• Listening and Speaking: Interview, SE p. 225 • Research and Technology: News Article, SE p. 225 • TR Extension Activities, p. 15	• Selection Test, TR Formal Assessment, pp. 47–49 • TR Open Book Test, pp. 43–45 • Writing rubric and Listening and Speaking rubric, TR Performance Assess. and Portfolio Mgmt., pp. 15, 27	• Interest Grabber Video, Tape 1 • Listening to Literature, Audiocassettes, Side 8; Audio CDs, CD 5 • Got It! Assessment Videotapes, Tape 1 • WG Writing and Grammar iText

Unit 3 *Clashing Forces*

Writing	Extension Activities	Assessment	Technology
• Writing Lesson: Travel Brochure, SE p. 253; WG Writing and Grammar, p. 162	• Listening and Speaking: Dialogue, SE p. 253 • Research and Technology: Safety Manual, SE p. 253 • TR Extension Activities, p. 16	• Selection Test, TR Formal Assessment, pp. 54–56 • TR Open Book Test, pp. 46–48 • Writing rubric and Listening and Speaking rubric, TR Performance Assess. and Portfolio Mgmt., pp. 20, 30	• Interest Grabber Video, Tape 2 • Got It! Assessment Videotapes, Tape 2 • WG Writing and Grammar iText
• Writing Lesson: News Article, SE p. 263; WG Writing and Grammar, p. 228	• Listening and Speaking: Radio Show, SE p. 263 • Research and Technology: Biographical Sketch, SE p. 263 • TR Extension Activities, p. 17	• Selection Test, TR Formal Assessment, pp. 57–59 • TR Open Book Test, pp. 49–51 • Writing rubric and Listening and Speaking rubric, TR Performance Assess. and Portfolio Mgmt., p. 22	• Interest Grabber Video, Tape 2 • Listening to Literature, Audiocassettes, Side 8; Audio CDs, CD 5 • Got It! Assessment Videotapes, Tape 2 • WG Writing and Grammar iText
• Writing Lesson: Interview With the Speaker, SE p. 273; WG Writing and Grammar, p. 835	• Listening and Speaking: Oral Reading, SE p. 273 • Research and Technology: Music Timeline, SE p. 273 • TR Extension Activities, p.18	• Selection Test, TR Formal Assessment, pp. 60–62 • TR Open Book Test, pp. 52–54 • Writing rubric and Listening and Speaking rubric, TR Performance Assess. and Portfolio Mgmt., p. 31	• Interest Grabber Video, Tape 2 • Listening to Literature, Audiocassettes, Side 9; Audio CDs, CD 5 • Got It! Assessment Videotapes, Tape 2 • WG Writing and Grammar iText
• Writing Lesson: Literary Comparison, SE p. 287; WG Writing and Grammar, p. 176	• Listening and Speaking: Oral Argument, SE p. 287 • Research and Technology: Multimedia Presentation, SE p. 287 • TR Extension Activities, p. 19	• Selection Test, TR Formal Assessment, pp. 63–65 • TR Open Book Test, pp. 55–57 • Writing rubric and Listening and Speaking rubric, TR Performance Assess. and Portfolio Mgmt., p. 15	• Interest Grabber Video, Tape 2 • Listening to Literature, Audiocassettes, Side 9; Audio CDs, CD 6 • Got It! Assessment Videotapes, Tape 2 • WG Writing and Grammar iText
• Writing Lesson: Letter to the Editor, SE p. 297; WG Writing and Grammar, p. 137	• Listening and Speaking: Sound-Effects Tape, SE p. 297 • Research and Technology: American Prisons Chart, SE p. 297 • TR Extension Activities, p. 20	• Selection Test, TR Formal Assessment, pp. 66–68 • TR Open Book Test, pp. 58–60 • Writing rubric and Listening and Speaking rubric, TR Performance Assess. and Portfolio Mgmt., p. 11	• Interest Grabber Video, Tape 2 • Listening to Literature, Audiocassettes, Sides 9, 10; Audio CDs, CD 6 • Got It! Assessment Videotapes, Tape 2 • WG Writing and Grammar iText

Program Planner

Selection	Reading	Literary Analysis	Vocabulary	Grammar
from **Desert Exile: The Uprooting of a Japanese-American Family**, Yoshiko Uchida, SE p. 300 Reading Level: Average **"Speech on Japanese American Internment,"** Gerald Ford, SE p. 308 Reading Level: Easy	• Using Background Knowledge, SE p. 299; TR Selection Support, p. 83; TR Literary Analysis and Reading Transparencies, p. 41	• Writer's Purpose, SE p. 299; TR Selection Support, p. 84; TR Literary Analysis and Reading Transparencies, p. 42	• Vocabulary Development, SE p. 299: cursory, euphemism, adept, destitute, unwieldy, communal, conspicuous, assuage • Latin Root -curs-, SE p. 310; TR Selection Support, p. 81	• Compound Subjects, SE p. 310; TR Selection Support, p. 82; WG Writing and Grammar, p. 414
"The Cabuliwallah," Rabindranath Tagore, SE p. 318 Reading Level: Average	• Engaging Your Senses, SE p. 317; TR Selection Support, p. 87; TR Literary Analysis and Reading Transparencies, p. 43	• Relationships Between Characters, SE p. 317; TR Selection Support, p. 88; TR Literary Analysis and Reading Transparencies, p. 44	• Vocabulary Development, SE p. 317: precarious, impending, judicious, euphemism, imploring, fettered, sordid, pervaded • Latin Root -jud-, SE p. 328; TR Selection Support, p. 85	• Predicate Nominatives and Predicate Adjectives, SE p. 328; TR Selection Support, p. 86; WG Writing and Grammar, pp. 432–434

Program Planner

Selection	Reading	Literary Analysis	Vocabulary	Grammar
from **Speak, Memory**, Vladimir Nabokov, SE p. 342 Reading Level: Average	• Recognizing Author's Purpose, SE p. 341; TR Selection Support, p. 91; TR Literary Analysis and Reading Transparencies, p. 45	• Personal Narrative, SE p. 341; TR Selection Support, p. 92; TR Literary Analysis and Reading Transparencies, p. 46	• Vocabulary Development, SE p. 341: procession, proficiency, laborious, portentously, limpid • Latin Prefix pro-, SE p. 348; TR Selection Support, p. 89	• Clauses, SE p. 348; TR Selection Support, p. 90; WG Writing and Grammar, p. 464
"Games at Twilight," Anita Desai, SE p. 352 Reading Level: Average	• Evaluating a Character's Decision, SE p. 351; TR Selection Support, p. 95; TR Literary Analysis and Reading Transparencies, p. 47	• Motivation, SE p. 351; TR Selection Support, p. 96; TR Literary Analysis and Reading Transparencies, p. 48	• Vocabulary Development, SE p. 351: superciliously, sidled, defunct, dogged • Latin Prefix super-, SE p. 362; TR Selection Support, p. 93	• Subordination, SE p. 362; TR Selection Support, p. 94; WG Writing and Grammar, p. 464
"The Bridge," Leopold Staff, SE p. 366 Reading Level: Average **"The Old Stoic,"** Emily Brontë, SE p. 367 Reading Level: Average **"I Am Not One of Those Who Left the Land,"** Anna Akhmatova, SE p. 368 Reading Level: Challenging **"Speech During the Invasion of Constantinople,"** Empress Theodora, SE p. 369 Reading Level: Average	• Identifying Author's Perspective, SE p. 365; TR Selection Support, p. 99; TR Literary Analysis and Reading Transparencies, p. 49	• Dramatic Situation, SE p. 365; TR Selection Support, p. 100; TR Literary Analysis and Reading Transparencies, p. 50	• Vocabulary Development, SE p. 365: implore, timorous, indomitable • Latin Root -dom-, SE p. 372; TR Selection Support, p. 97	• Adjective Clauses, SE p. 372; TR Selection Support, p. 98; WG Writing and Grammar, p. 465
"The Good Deed," Pearl S. Buck, SE p. 376 Reading Level: Average	• Drawing Inferences, SE p. 375; TR Selection Support, p. 103; TR Literary Analysis and Reading Transparencies, p. 51	• Static and Dynamic Characters, SE p. 375; TR Selection Support, p. 104; TR Literary Analysis and Reading Transparencies, p. 52	• Vocabulary Development, SE p. 375: contemplatively, revere, compelled, abashed, repressed, indignantly, assailed, expedition, conferred • Latin Root -pel-, SE p. 394; TR Selection Support, p. 101	• Adverb Clauses, SE p. 394; TR Selection Support, p. 102; WG Writing and Grammar, p. 470

Key to Program References: SE: Student Edition **TR:** Teaching Resources **WG:** Writing and Grammar

Unit 3 *Clashing Forces*

Writing	Extension Activities	Assessment	Technology
• Writing Lesson: Internment Camp Research Report, SE p. 311; WG Writing and Grammar, pp. 250–266	• Listening and Speaking: Persuasive Argument, SE p. 311 • Research and Technology: Oral History, SE p. 311 • TR Extension Activities, p. 21	• Selection Test, TR Formal Assessment, pp. 69–71 • TR Open Book Test, pp. 61–63 • Writing rubric and Listening and Speaking rubric, TR Performance Assess. and Portfolio Mgmt., pp. 13, 30	• Interest Grabber Video, Tape 2 • Listening to Literature, Audiocassettes, Sides 10, 11; Audio CDs, CD 6 • Got It! Assessment Videotapes, Tape 2 • WG Writing and Grammar iText
• Writing Lesson: Journal Entry, SE p. 329; WG Writing and Grammar, p. 63	• Listening and Speaking: Persuasive Speech, SE p. 329 • Research and Technology: Timeline, SE p. 329 • TR Extension Activities, p. 22	• Selection Test, TR Formal Assessment, pp. 72–74 • TR Open Book Test, pp. 64–66 • Writing rubric and Listening and Speaking rubric, TR Performance Assess. and Portfolio Mgmt., p. 30	• Interest Grabber Video, Tape 2 • Listening to Literature, Audiocassettes, Side 11; Audio CDs, CD 6 • Got It! Assessment Videotapes, Tape 2 • WG Writing and Grammar iText

Unit 4 *Turning Points*

Writing	Extension Activities	Assessment	Technology
• Writing Lesson: Personal Narrative, SE p. 349; WG Writing and Grammar, p. 57	• Listening and Speaking: Book Discussion, SE p. 349 • Research and Technology: Multimedia Presentation, SE p. 349 • TR Extension Activities, p. 23	• Selection Test, TR Formal Assessment, pp. 79–81 • TR Open Book Test, pp. 67–69 • Writing rubric and Listening and Speaking rubric, TR Performance Assess. and Portfolio Mgmt., p. 9	• Interest Grabber Video, Tape 2 • Listening to Literature, Audiocassettes, Side 11; Audio CDs, CD 7 • Got It! Assessment Videotapes, Tape 2 • WG Writing and Grammar iText
• Writing Lesson: Dialogue Between Children, SE p. 363; WG Writing and Grammar, p. 85	• Listening and Speaking: Playing Games, SE p. 363 • Research and Technology: Research Report, SE p. 363 • TR Extension Activities, p. 24	• Selection Test, TR Formal Assessment, pp. 82–84 • TR Open Book Test, pp. 70–72	• Interest Grabber Video, Tape 2 • Listening to Literature, Audiocassettes, Side 11; Audio CDs, CD 7 • Got It! Assessment Videotapes, Tape 2 • WG Writing and Grammar iText
• Writing Lesson: News Commentary, SE p. 373; WG Writing and Grammar, p. 21	• Listening and Speaking: Role-Play, SE p. 373 • Research and Technology: Collage, SE p. 373 • TR Extension Activities, p. 25	• Selection Test, TR Formal Assessment, pp. 85–87 • TR Open Book Test, pp. 73–75 • Writing rubric and Listening and Speaking rubric, TR Performance Assess. and Portfolio Mgmt., pp. 16, 30	• Interest Grabber Video, Tape 2 • Listening to Literature, Audiocassettes, Sides 11, 12; Audio CDs, CD 7 • Got It! Assessment Videotapes, Tape 2 • WG Writing and Grammar iText
• Writing Lesson: Award Speech for a Character, SE p. 395; WG Writing and Grammar, p. 286	• Listening and Speaking: Interview, SE p. 395 • Research and Technology: Multimedia Presentation, SE p. 395 • TR Extension Activities, p. 26	• Selection Test, TR Formal Assessment, pp. 88–90 • TR Open Book Test, pp. 76–78 • Writing rubric and Listening and Speaking rubric, TR Performance Assess. and Portfolio Mgmt., p. 27	• Interest Grabber Video, Tape 2 • Listening to Literature, Audiocassettes, Side 12; Audio CDs, CD 8 • Got It! Assessment Videotapes, Tape 2 • WG Writing and Grammar iText

Program Planner

Selection	Reading	Literary Analysis	Vocabulary	Grammar
"Thoughts of Hanoi," Nguyen Thi Vinh, SE p. 398 Reading Level: Average **"Auto Wreck,"** Karl Shapiro, SE p. 401 Reading Level: Easy **"Pride,"** Dahlia Ravikovitch, SE p. 402 Reading Level: Easy **"Before the Law,"** Franz Kafka, SE p. 404 Reading Level: Challenging	• Evaluating a Writer's Message, SE p. 397; TR Selection Support, p. 107; TR Literary Analysis and Reading Transparencies, p. 53	• Theme, SE p. 397; TR Selection Support, p. 108; TR Literary Analysis and Reading Transparencies, p. 54	• Vocabulary Development, SE p. 397: deranged, convalescents, banal, expedient, importunity, contemplation, insatiable • Latin Root -sat-, SE p. 408; TR Selection Support, p. 105	• Noun Clauses, SE p. 408; TR Selection Support, p. 106; WG Writing and Grammar, p. 474

Program Planner

Selection	Reading	Literary Analysis	Vocabulary	Grammar
"The Widow and the Parrot," Virginia Woolf, SE p. 430 Reading Level: Easy	• Drawing Inferences, SE p. 429; TR Selection Support, p. 111; TR Literary Analysis and Reading Transparencies, p. 55	• Motivation, SE p. 429; TR Selection Support, p. 112; TR Literary Analysis and Reading Transparencies, p. 56	• Vocabulary Development, SE p. 429: ford, dilapidated, sovereigns, sagacity • Forms of sagacity, SE p. 440; TR Selection Support, p. 109	• Appositives, SE p. 440; TR Selection Support, p. 110; WG Writing and Grammar, p. 445
"Civil Peace," Chinua Achebe, SE p. 444 Reading Level: Challenging	• Using Prior Knowledge, SE p. 443; TR Selection Support, p. 115; TR Literary Analysis and Reading Transparencies, p. 57	• Theme, SE p. 443; TR Selection Support, p. 116; TR Literary Analysis and Reading Transparencies, p. 58	• Vocabulary Development, SE p. 443: inestimable, disreputable, amenable, edifice, destitute, imperious, commiserate • Latin Root -reput-, SE p. 452; TR Selection Support, p. 113	• Present Participial Phrases, SE p. 452; TR Selection Support, p. 114; WG Writing and Grammar, p. 452
"How to React to Familiar Faces," Umberto Eco, SE p. 456 Reading Level: Easy **"The Bean Eaters,"** Gwendolyn Brooks, SE p. 458 Reading Level: Easy	• Responding to Connotations, SE p. 455; TR Selection Support, p. 119; TR Literary Analysis and Reading Transparencies, p. 59	• Tone, SE p. 455; TR Selection Support, p. 120; TR Literary Analysis and Reading Transparencies, p. 60	• Vocabulary Development, SE p. 455: expound, syndrome, amiably, protagonist • Latin Root -ami-, SE p. 460; TR Selection Support, p. 117	• Verb, Participle, or Gerund?, SE p. 460; TR Selection Support, p. 118; WG Writing and Grammar, p. 455
"A Picture From the Past: Emily Dickinson," Reynolds Price, SE p. 464 Reading Level: Average **"What Makes a Degas a Degas?,"** Richard Mühlberger, SE p. 466 Reading Level: Average	• Relating Text and Pictures, SE p. 463; TR Selection Support, p. 123; TR Literary Analysis and Reading Transparencies, p. 61	• Analytical Essay, SE p. 463; TR Selection Support, p. 124; TR Literary Analysis and Reading Transparencies, p. 62	• Vocabulary Development, SE p. 463: titanic, centenarian, austere, lacquered • Latin Root -cent-, SE p. 472; TR Selection Support, p. 121	• Infinitives and Infinitive Phrases, SE p. 472; TR Selection Support, p. 122; WG Writing and Grammar, p. 449
"The Orphan Boy and the Elk Dog," Native American (Blackfeet), SE p. 484 Reading Level: Average	• Interpreting, SE p. 483; TR Selection Support, p. 127; TR Literary Analysis and Reading Transparencies, p. 63	• Myth, SE p. 483; TR Selection Support, p. 128; TR Literary Analysis and Reading Transparencies, p. 64	• Vocabulary Development, SE p. 483: refuse, surpassed, emanating, relish, stifle • Homographs, SE p. 494; TR Selection Support, p. 125	• Commonly Confused Verbs: accept and except, SE p. 494; TR Selection Support, p. 126; WG Writing and Grammar, p. 612
"The Street of the Cañon" from **Mexican Village,** Josephina Niggli, SE p. 498 Reading Level: Easy	• Making Predictions, SE p. 497; TR Selection Support, p. 131; TR Literary Analysis and Reading Transparencies, p. 65	• Point of View, SE p. 497; TR Selection Support, p. 132; TR Literary Analysis and Reading Transparencies, p. 66	• Vocabulary Development, SE p. 497: officious, mottled, nonchalantly, audaciously, imperiously, plausibility • Anglo-Saxon Suffix -ly, SE p. 508; TR Selection Support, p. 129	• Prepositional Phrase or Infinitive?, SE p. 508; TR Selection Support, p. 130; WG Writing and Grammar, p. 460

Key to Program References: SE: Student Edition **TR:** Teaching Resources **WG:** Writing and Grammar

Unit 4 *Turning Points*

Writing	Extension Activities	Assessment	Technology
• Writing Lesson: Analysis of an Image, SE p. 409; WG Writing and Grammar, p. 285	• Listening and Speaking: Improvisational Skit, SE p. 409 • Research and Technology: Contrasting Maps, SE p. 409 • TR Extension Activities, p. 27	• Selection Test, TR Formal Assessment, pp. 91–93 • TR Open Book Test, pp. 79–81 • Writing rubric and Listening and Speaking rubric, TR Performance Assess. and Portfolio Mgmt., pp. 16, 28	• Interest Grabber Video, Tape 2 • Listening to Literature, Audiocassettes, Side 13; Audio CDs, CD 8 • Got It! Assessment Videotapes, Tape 2 • WG Writing and Grammar iText

Unit 5 *Expanding Horizons*

Writing	Extension Activities	Assessment	Technology
• Writing Lesson: Last Will and Testament, SE p. 441; WG Writing and Grammar, p. 204	• Listening and Speaking: Dialogue, SE p. 441 • Research and Technology: Internet Home Page, SE p. 441 • TR Extension Activities, p. 28	• Selection Test, TR Formal Assessment, pp. 98–100 • TR Open Book Test, pp. 82–84 • Writing rubric and Listening and Speaking rubric, TR Performance Assess. and Portfolio Mgmt., p. 16	• Interest Grabber Video, Tape 3 • Listening to Literature, Audiocassettes, Side 13; Audio CDs, CD 9 • Got It! Assessment Videotapes, Tape 3 • WG Writing and Grammar iText
• Writing Lesson: News Interview, SE p. 453; WG Writing and Grammar, p. 181	• Listening and Speaking: Dialogue, SE p. 453 • Research and Technology: Annotated Map, SE p. 453 • TR Extension Activities, p. 29	• Selection Test, TR Formal Assessment, pp. 101–103 • TR Open Book Test, pp. 85–87 • Writing rubric and Listening and Speaking rubric, TR Performance Assess. and Portfolio Mgmt., p. 28	• Interest Grabber Video, Tape 3 • Listening to Literature, Audiocassettes, Side 13; Audio CDs, CD 9 • Got It! Assessment Videotapes, Tape 3 • WG Writing and Grammar iText
• Writing Lesson: Persuasive Argument, SE p. 461; WG Writing and Grammar, p. 134	• Listening and Speaking: Introduction, SE p. 461 • Research and Technology: Research Report, SE p. 461 • TR Extension Activities, p. 30	• Selection Test, TR Formal Assessment, pp. 104–106 • TR Open Book Test, pp. 88–90 • Writing rubric and Listening and Speaking rubric, TR Performance Assess. and Portfolio Mgmt., pp. 11, 29	• Interest Grabber Video, Tape 3 • Listening to Literature, Audiocassettes, Side 14; Audio CDs, CD 9 • Got It! Assessment Videotapes, Tape 3 • WG Writing and Grammar iText
• Writing Lesson: Museum Placard, SE p. 473; WG Writing and Grammar, p. 256	• Listening and Speaking: Poetry Reading, SE p. 473 • Research and Technology: Art Exhibit, SE p. 473 • TR Extension Activities, p. 31	• Selection Test, TR Formal Assessment, pp. 107–109 • TR Open Book Test, pp. 91–93 • Writing rubric and Listening and Speaking rubric, TR Performance Assess. and Portfolio Mgmt., p. 19	• Interest Grabber Video, Tape 3 • Listening to Literature, Audiocassettes, Side 14; Audio CDs, CD 9 • Got It! Assessment Videotapes, Tape 3 • WG Writing and Grammar iText
• Writing Lesson: Retelling a Myth, SE p. 495; WG Writing and Grammar, p. 84	• Listening and Speaking: Debate, SE p. 495 • Research and Technology: Bar Graph, SE p. 495 • TR Extension Activities, p. 32	• Selection Test, TR Formal Assessment, pp. 110–112 • TR Open Book Test, pp. 94–96 • Writing rubric and Listening and Speaking rubric, TR Performance Assess. and Portfolio Mgmt., p. 14	• Interest Grabber Video, Tape 3 • Listening to Literature, Audiocassettes, Side 14; Audio CDs, CD 10 • Got It! Assessment Videotapes, Tape 3 • WG Writing and Grammar iText
• Writing Lesson: Comparison-and-Contrast Essay, SE p. 509; WG Writing and Grammar, p. 182	• Listening and Speaking: Debate, SE p. 509 • Research and Technology: Photo Essay, SE p. 509 • TR Extension Activities, p. 33	• Selection Test, TR Formal Assessment, pp. 113-115 • TR Open Book Test, pp. 97-99 • Writing rubric and Listening and Speaking rubric, TR Performance Assess. and Portfolio Mgmt., p. 15	• Interest Grabber Video, Tape 3 • Listening to Literature, Audiocassettes, Side 15; Audio CDs, CD 10 • Got It! Assessment Videotapes, Tape 3 • WG Writing and Grammar iText

PROGRAM PLANNER

Program Planner

Selection	Reading	Literary Analysis	Vocabulary	Grammar
"A Storm in the Mountains," Alexander Solzhenitsyn, SE p. 512 Reading Level: Average **"In the Orchard,"** Henrik Ibsen, SE p. 513 Reading Level: Average **"A Tree Telling of Orpheus,"** Denise Levertov, SE p. 514 Reading Level: Challenging	• Engaging the Senses, SE p. 511; TR Selection Support, p. 135; TR Literary Analysis and Reading Transparencies, p. 67	• Speaker, SE p. 511; TR Selection Support, p. 136; TR Literary Analysis and Reading Transparencies, p. 68	• Vocabulary Development, SE p. 511: terra firma, sultry, asunder • Latin Terms, SE p. 520; TR Selection Support, p. 133	• Gerunds and Gerund Phrases, SE p. 520; TR Selection Support, p. 134; WG Writing and Grammar, p. 454

Program Planner

Selection	Reading	Literary Analysis	Vocabulary	Grammar
"The Open Window," Saki (H. H. Munro), SE p. 540 Reading Level: Easy	• Identifying Relationships, SE p. 539; TR Selection Support, p. 139; TR Literary Analysis and Reading Transparencies, p. 69	• Plot, SE p. 539; TR Selection Support, p. 140; TR Literary Analysis and Reading Transparencies, p. 70	• Vocabulary Development, SE p. 539: delusion, imminent, mackintosh, pariah • Words From Names, SE p. 546; TR Selection Support, p. 137	• Placement of *only* and *just*, SE p. 546; TR Selection Support, p. 138; WG Writing and Grammar, p. 619
"Leiningen Versus the Ants," Carl Stephenson, SE p. 550 Reading Level: Average	• Making Predictions, SE p. 549; TR Selection Support, p. 143; TR Literary Analysis and Reading Transparencies, p. 71	• Conflict, SE p. 549; TR Selection Support, p. 144; TR Literary Analysis and Reading Transparencies, p. 72	• Vocabulary Development, SE p. 549: peons, flout, weir, provender, alluvium, fomentations • Latin Plural Forms, SE p. 572; TR Selection Support, p. 141	• Subject and Verb Agreement, SE p. 572; TR Selection Support, p. 142; WG Writing and Grammar, p. 566
"By the Waters of Babylon," Stephen Vincent Benét, SE p. 576 Reading Level: Challenging	• Drawing Conclusions, SE p. 575; TR Selection Support, p. 147; TR Literary Analysis and Reading Transparencies, p. 73	• Point of View, SE p. 575; TR Selection Support, p. 148; TR Literary Analysis and Reading Transparencies, p. 74	• Vocabulary Development, SE p. 575: purified, bowels, moreover, nevertheless • Conjunctive Adverbs, SE p. 588; TR Selection Support, p. 145	• Varying Sentence Beginnings, SE p. 588; TR Selection Support, p. 146; WG Writing and Grammar, p. 496
"A Problem," Anton Chekhov, SE p. 596 Reading Level: Average **"Luck,"** Mark Twain, SE p. 604 Reading Level: Average	• Drawing Inferences About Character, SE p. 595; TR Selection Support, p. 151; TR Literary Analysis and Reading Transparencies, p. 75	• Characters, SE p. 595; TR Selection Support, p. 152; TR Literary Analysis and Reading Transparencies, p. 76	• Vocabulary Development, SE p. 595: taciturn, rheumatic, vestibule, zenith, countenance, veracity, guileless, prodigious, sublimity • Latin Root -*ver*-, SE p. 610; TR Selection Support, p. 149	• Restrictive and Nonrestrictive Adjective Clauses, SE p. 610; TR Selection Support, p. 150; WG Writing and Grammar, p. 465
"There Will Come Soft Rains," Ray Bradbury, SE p. 614 Reading Level: Average **"The Garden of Stubborn Cats,"** Italo Calvino, SE p. 621 Reading Level: Average	• Clarifying, SE p. 613; TR Selection Support, p. 156; TR Literary Analysis and Reading Transparencies, p. 77	• Setting, SE p. 613; TR Selection Support, p. 156; TR Literary Analysis and Reading Transparencies, p. 78	• Vocabulary Development, SE p. 613: warrens, titanic, paranoia, tremulous, psychopathic, supernal, itinerary, indigence • Words From Myths, SE p. 630; TR Selection Support, p. 153	• Parallel Structure, SE p. 630; TR Selection Support, p. 154; WG Writing and Grammar, p. 138
"The Princess and All the Kingdom," Pär Lagerkvist, SE p. 638 Reading Level: Easy **"The Censors,"** Luisa Valenzuela, SE p. 641 Reading Level: Average	• Challenging the Writer's Message, SE p. 637; TR Selection Support, p. 159; TR Literary Analysis and Reading Transparencies, p. 79	• Theme, SE p. 637; TR Selection Support, p. 160; TR Literary Analysis and Reading Transparencies, p. 80	• Vocabulary Development, SE p. 637: ardent, venerable, sordid, ulterior, staidness • Latin Root -*ultra*-, SE p. 646; TR Selection Support, p. 157	• Consistency of Verb Tenses, SE p. 646; TR Selection Support, p. 159; WG Writing and Grammar, p. 232

Key to Program References: SE: Student Edition **TR:** Teaching Resources **WG:** Writing and Grammar

Unit 5 *Expanding Horizons*

Writing	Extension Activities	Assessment	Technology
• Writing Lesson: Monologue, SE p. 521; WG Writing and Grammar, p. 32	• Listening and Speaking: Television Interview, SE p. 521 • Research and Technology: Multimedia Presentation, SE p. 521 • TR Extension Activities, p. 34	• Selection Test, TR Formal Assessment, pp. 116-118 • TR Open Book Test, pp. 100-102 • Writing rubric and Listening and Speaking rubric, TR Performance Assess. and Portfolio Mgmt., p. 27	• Interest Grabber Video, Tape 3 • Listening to Literature, Audiocassettes, Side 15; Audio CDs, CD 10 • Got It! Assessment Videotapes, Tape 3 • WG Writing and Grammar iText

Unit 6 *Short Stories*

Writing	Extension Activities	Assessment	Technology
• Writing Lesson: Introduction for a Collection, SE p. 547; WG Writing and Grammar, p. 285	• Listening and Speaking: Storytelling, SE p. 547 • Research and Technology: Annotated Reading List, SE p. 547 • TR Extension Activities, p. 35	• Selection Test, TR Formal Assessment, pp. 123–125 • TR Open Book Test, pp. 103–105 • Writing rubric and Listening and Speaking rubric, TR Performance Assess. and Portfolio Mgmt., p. 31	• Interest Grabber Video, Tape 3 • Listening to Literature, Audiocassettes, Side 15; Audio CDs, CD 10 • Got It! Assessment Videotapes, Tape 3 • WG Writing and Grammar iText
• Writing Lesson: New Movie Scene, SE p. 573; WG Writing and Grammar, p. 84	• Listening and Speaking: Motivational Speech, SE p. 573 • Research and Technology: News Article, SE p. 573 • TR Extension Activities, p. 36	• Selection Test, TR Formal Assessment, pp. 126–128 • TR Open Book Test, pp. 106–108 • Writing rubric and Listening and Speaking rubric, TR Performance Assess. and Portfolio Mgmt., p. 30	• Interest Grabber Video, Tape 3 • Listening to Literature, Audiocassettes, Sides 16, 17; Audio CDs, CD 11 • Got It! Assessment Videotapes, Tape 3 • WG Writing and Grammar iText
• Writing Lesson: Character Sketch, SE p. 589; WG Writing and Grammar, p. 107	• Listening and Speaking: Radio Interview, SE p. 589 • Research and Technology: Annotated Map, SE p. 589 • TR Extension Activities, p. 37	• Selection Test, TR Formal Assessment, pp. 129–131 • TR Open Book Test, pp. 109–111 • Writing rubric and Listening and Speaking rubric, TR Performance Assess. and Portfolio Mgmt., pp. 19, 27	• Interest Grabber Video, Tape 3 • Listening to Literature, Audiocassettes, Side 18; Audio CDs, CD 12 • Got It! Assessment Videotapes, Tape 3 • WG Writing and Grammar iText
• Writing Lesson: Story Ending, SE p. 611; WG Writing and Grammar, p. 203	• Listening and Speaking: Monologue, SE p. 611 • Research and Technology: Multimedia Biography, SE p. 611 • TR Extension Activities, p. 38	• Selection Test, TR Formal Assessment, pp. 132–134 • TR Open Book Test, pp. 112–114 • Writing rubric and Listening and Speaking rubric, TR Performance Assess. and Portfolio Mgmt., p. 14	• Interest Grabber Video, Tape 3 • Listening to Literature, Audiocassettes, Side 19; Audio CDs, CD 12 • Got It! Assessment Videotapes, Tape 3 • WG Writing and Grammar iText
• Writing Lesson: Advertisement for a New Technology, SE p. 631; WG Writing and Grammar, p. 155	• Listening and Speaking: Persuasive Argument, SE p. 631 • Research and Technology: Floor Plan, SE p. 631 • TR Extension Activities, p. 39	• Selection Test, TR Formal Assessment, pp. 135–137 • TR Open Book Test, pp. 115–117 • Writing rubric and Listening and Speaking rubric, TR Performance Assess. and Portfolio Mgmt., pp. 20, 30	• Interest Grabber Video, Tape 3 • Listening to Literature, Audiocassettes, Sides 19, 20; Audio CDs, CD 13 • Got It! Assessment Videotapes, Tape 3 • WG Writing and Grammar iText
• Writing Lesson: Persuasive Essay, SE p. 647; WG Writing and Grammar, p. 137	• Listening and Speaking: Royal Speech, SE p. 647 • Research and Technology: Annotated List, SE p. 647 • TR Extension Activities, p. 40	• Selection Test, TR Formal Assessment, pp. 138–140 • TR Open Book Test, pp. 118–120 • Writing rubric and Listening and Speaking rubric, TR Performance Assess. and Portfolio Mgmt., p. 11	• Interest Grabber Video, Tape 3 • Listening to Literature, Audiocassettes, Side 20; Audio CDs, CD 13 • Got It! Assessment Videotapes, Tape 3 • WG Writing and Grammar iText

PROGRAM PLANNER

Program Planner

Selection	Reading	Literary Analysis	Vocabulary	Grammar
"The Marginal World," Rachel Carson, SE p. 660 Reading Level: Average	• Recognizing Patterns of Organization, SE p. 659; TR Selection Support, p. 163; TR Literary Analysis and Reading Transparencies, p. 81	• Expository Essay, SE p. 659; TR Selection Support, p. 164; TR Literary Analysis and Reading Transparencies, p. 82	• Vocabulary Development, SE p. 659: mutable, ephemeral, primeval, essence, marginal, subjectively, manifestations, cosmic • Latin Suffix -able, SE p. 668; TR Selection Support, p. 161	• Recognizing Degrees of Comparison, SE p. 668; TR Selection Support, p. 162; WG Writing and Grammar, p. 590
from **The Way to Rainy Mountain,** N. Scott Momaday, SE p. 676 Reading Level: Average from **Nobel Lecture,** Alexander Solzhenitsyn, SE p. 683 Reading Level: Challenging **"Keep Memory Alive,"** Elie Wiesel, SE p. 687 Reading Level: Average	• Analyzing Author's Purpose, SE p. 675; TR Selection Support, p. 167; TR Literary Analysis and Reading Transparencies, p. 83	• Reflective and Persuasive Essays, SE p. 675; TR Selection Support, p. 168; TR Literary Analysis and Reading Transparencies, p. 84	• Vocabulary Development, SE p. 675: engender, tenuous, reciprocity, assimilate, inexorably, oratory, transcends • Forms of reciprocity, SE p. 690; TR Selection Support, p. 165	• Irregular Comparative and Superlative Degrees, SE p. 690; TR Selection Support, p. 166; WG Writing and Grammar, p. 592
"A Child's Christmas in Wales," Dylan Thomas, SE p. 694 Reading Level: Average **"Marian Anderson: Famous Concert Singer,"** Langston Hughes, SE p. 702 Reading Level: Easy	• Recognizing Author's Attitude, SE p. 693; TR Selection Support, p. 171; TR Literary Analysis and Reading Transparencies, p. 85	• Biography and Autobiography, SE p. 693; TR Selection Support, p. 172; TR Literary Analysis and Reading Transparencies, p. 86	• Vocabulary Development, SE p. 693: sidle, prey, wallowed, crocheted, brittle, trod, forlorn, arias, staunch, repertoire • Musical Words, SE p. 708; TR Selection Support, p. 169	• Restrictive and Nonrestrictive Appositives, SE p. 708; TR Selection Support, p. 170; WG Writing and Grammar, p. 445
"Flood," Annie Dillard, SE p. 712 Reading Level: Easy	• Recognizing Facts and Impressions, SE p. 711; TR Selection Support, p. 175; TR Literary Analysis and Reading Transparencies, p. 87	• Descriptive Essay, SE p. 711; TR Selection Support, p. 176; TR Literary Analysis and Reading Transparencies, p. 88	• Vocabulary Development, SE p. 711: obliterates, opacity, usurped, mauled, malevolent, repressed • Latin Prefix mal-, SE p. 720; TR Selection Support, p. 173	• Commonly Confused Words: than and then, SE p. 720; TR Selection Support, p. 174; WG Writing and Grammar, p. 620
"Mothers & Daughters," Tillie Olsen and Estelle Jussim, SE p. 724 Reading Level: Average	• Interpreting Pictures, SE p. 723; TR Selection Support, p. 179; TR Literary Analysis and Reading Transparencies, p. 89	• Visual Essay, SE p. 723; TR Selection Support, p. 180; TR Literary Analysis and Reading Transparencies, p. 90	• Vocabulary Development, SE p. 723: hue, sullenness, implicit, fervor • Words About Color, SE p. 728; TR Selection Support, p. 177	• Use of Adjectives and Adverbs, SE p. 728; TR Selection Support, p. 178; WG Writing and Grammar, p. 368
"Star Wars—A Trip to a Far Galaxy That's Fun and Funny...," Vincent Canby, SE p. 734 Reading Level: Easy **"Star Wars: Breakthrough Film Still Has the Force,"** Roger Ebert, SE p. 737 Reading Level: Easy	• Identifying Evidence, SE p. 733; TR Selection Support, p. 183; TR Literary Analysis and Reading Transparencies, p. 91	• Critical Review, SE p. 733; TR Selection Support, p. 184; TR Literary Analysis and Reading Transparencies, p. 92	• Vocabulary Development, SE p. 733: apotheosis, eclectic, facetiousness, adroit, piously, condescension, watershed, synthesis, fastidious, effete, laconic • Connotations, SE p. 744; TR Selection Support, p. 181	• Commonly Confused Words: good and well, SE p. 744; TR Selection Support, p. 182; WG Writing and Grammar, p. 593
"Imitating Nature's Mineral Artistry," Paul O'Neil, SE p. 748 Reading Level: Challenging **"Work That Counts,"** Ernesto Ruelas Inzunza, SE p. 753 Reading Level: Easy	• Relating Diagrams to Text, SE p. 747; TR Selection Support, p. 187; TR Literary Analysis and Reading Transparencies, p. 93	• Technical Article, SE p. 747; TR Selection Support, p. 188; TR Literary Analysis and Reading Transparencies, p. 94	• Vocabulary Development, SE p. 747: synthetic, constituents, synthesized, metamorphosis, divulge, saturated, fortuitous, vigilance, myriad, topography • Greek Prefix syn-, SE p. 756; TR Selection Support, p. 185	• Placement of Modifiers, SE p. 756; TR Selection Support, p. 186; WG Writing and Grammar, p. 507

Key to Program References: SE: Student Edition **TR:** Teaching Resources **WG:** Writing and Grammar

Unit 7 *Nonfiction*

Writing	Extension Activities	Assessment	Technology
• Writing Lesson: Proposal for a Nature Documentary, SE p. 669; WG Writing and Grammar, p. 108	• Listening and Speaking: Multimedia Presentation, SE p. 669 • Research and Technology: Scientific Report, SE p. 669 • TR Extension Activities, p. 41	• Selection Test, TR Formal Assessment, pp. 145–147 • TR Open Book Test, pp. 121–123 • Writing rubric and Listening and Speaking rubric, TR Performance Assess. and Portfolio Mgmt., p. 19	• Interest Grabber Video, Tape 4 • Listening to Literature, Audiocassettes, Side 20; Audio CDs, CD 13 • Got It! Assessment Videotapes, Tape 4 • WG Writing and Grammar iText
• Writing Lesson: Letter to Solzhenitsyn, SE p. 691; WG Writing and Grammar, p. 132	• Listening and Speaking: Speech Analysis, SE p. 691 • Research and Technology: Report, SE p. 691 • TR Extension Activities, p. 42	• Selection Test, TR Formal Assessment, pp. 148–150 • TR Open Book Test, pp. 124–126 • Writing rubric and Listening and Speaking rubric, TR Performance Assess. and Portfolio Mgmt., p. 11	• Interest Grabber Video, Tape 4 • Listening to Literature, Audiocassettes, Side 21; Audio CDs, CD 14 • Got It! Assessment Videotapes, Tape 4 • WG Writing and Grammar iText
• Writing Lesson: Biographer's Account, SE p. 709; WG Writing and Grammar, p. 71	• Listening and Speaking: Musical Review, SE p. 709 • Research and Technology: Bibliography of Reference Materials, SE p. 709 • TR Extension Activities, p. 43	• Selection Test, TR Formal Assessment, pp. 151–153 • TR Open Book Test, pp. 127–129	• Interest Grabber Video, Tape 4 • Listening to Literature, Audiocassettes, Sides 21, 22; Audio CDs, CD 14 • Got It! Assessment Videotapes, Tape 4 • WG Writing and Grammar iText
• Writing Lesson: Radio Call-In Transcript, SE p. 721; WG Writing and Grammar, p. 107	• Listening and Speaking: Television Interview, SE p. 721 • Research and Technology: Flood Report, SE p. 721 • TR Extension Activities, p. 44	• Selection Test, TR Formal Assessment, pp. 154–156 • TR Open Book Test, pp. 130–132 • Writing rubric and Listening and Speaking rubric, TR Performance Assess. and Portfolio Mgmt., p. 19	• Interest Grabber Video, Tape 4 • Listening to Literature, Audiocassettes, Side 22; Audio CDs, CD 15 • Got It! Assessment Videotapes, Tape 4 • WG Writing and Grammar iText
• Writing Lesson: Introduction to an Art Exhibit, SE p. 729; WG Writing and Grammar, p. 35	• Listening and Speaking: Group Discussion, SE p. 729 • Research and Technology: Annotated Bibliography, SE p. 729 • TR Extension Activities, p. 45	• Selection Test, TR Formal Assessment, pp. 157–159 • TR Open Book Test, pp. 133–135 • Writing rubric and Listening and Speaking rubric, TR Performance Assess. and Portfolio Mgmt., p. 19	• Interest Grabber Video, Tape 4 • Listening to Literature, Audiocassettes, Side 23; Audio CDs, CD 15 • Got It! Assessment Videotapes, Tape 4 • WG Writing and Grammar iText
• Writing Lesson: Movie Review, SE p. 745; WG Writing and Grammar, p. 137	• Listening and Speaking: Music Analysis, SE p. 745 • Research and Technology: Comparison, SE p. 745 • TR Extension Activities, p. 46	• Selection Test, TR Formal Assessment, pp. 160–162 • TR Open Book Test, pp. 136–138 • Writing rubric and Listening and Speaking rubric, TR Performance Assess. and Portfolio Mgmt., pp. 11, 31	• Interest Grabber Video, Tape 4 • Listening to Literature, Audiocassettes, Side 23; Audio CDs, CD 15 • Got It! Assessment Videotapes, Tape 4 • WG Writing and Grammar iText
• Writing Lesson: Persuasive Letter, SE p. 757; WG Writing and Grammar, p. 135	• Listening and Speaking: Demonstration, SE p. 757 • Research and Technology: Conservation Update, SE p. 757 • TR Extension Activities, p. 47	• Selection Test, TR Formal Assessment, pp. 163–165 • TR Open Book Test, pp. 139–141 • Writing rubric and Listening and Speaking rubric, TR Performance Assess. and Portfolio Mgmt., pp. 11, 32	• Interest Grabber Video, Tape 4 • Listening to Literature, Audiocassettes, Side 24; Audio CDs, CD 15 • Got It! Assessment Videotapes, Tape 4 • WG Writing and Grammar iText

PROGRAM PLANNER

Program Planner

Selection	Reading	Literary Analysis	Vocabulary	Grammar
Antigone, Prologue Through Scene 2, Sophocles, SE p. 772 Reading Level: Average	• Questioning Characters' Motives, SE p. 771; TR Selection Support, p. 191; TR Literary Analysis and Reading Transparencies, p. 95	• Protagonist and Antagonist, SE p. 771; TR Selection Support, p. 192; TR Literary Analysis and Reading Transparencies, p. 96	• Vocabulary Development, SE p. 771: sated, anarchists, sententiously, sultry, transcends • Latin Prefix *trans-*, SE p. 789; TR Selection Support, p. 189	• Objective Pronouns, SE p. 789; TR Selection Support, p. 190; WG Writing and Grammar, p. 548
Antigone, Scenes 3 Through 5, Sophocles, SE p. 791 Reading Level: Average	• Identifying With a Character, SE p. 790; TR Selection Support, p. 195; TR Literary Analysis and Reading Transparencies, p. 97	• Tragic Character, SE p. 790; TR Selection Support, p. 196; TR Literary Analysis and Reading Transparencies, p. 98	• Vocabulary Development, SE p. 790: deference, vile, piety, blasphemy, lamentation, chorister • Greek Root *-chor-*, SE p. 810; TR Selection Support, p. 193	• Pronoun Case in Elliptical Clauses, SE p. 810; TR Selection Support, p. 194; WG Writing and Grammar, p. 556
The Tragedy of Julius Caesar, Act I, William Shakespeare, SE p. 822 Reading Level: Challenging	• Using Text Aids, SE p. 821; TR Selection Support, p. 199; TR Literary Analysis and Reading Transparencies, p. 99	• Exposition in Drama, SE p. 821; TR Selection Support, p. 200; TR Literary Analysis and Reading Transparencies, p. 100	• Vocabulary Development, SE p. 821: replication, spare, infirmity, surly, portentous, prodigious • Forms of *portent,* SE p. 839; TR Selection Support, p. 197	• Mood, SE p. 839; TR Selection Support, p. 198; WG Writing and Grammar, p. 518
The Tragedy of Julius Caesar, Act II, William Shakespeare, SE p. 841 Reading Level: Challenging	• Reading Blank Verse, SE p. 840; TR Selection Support, p. 203; TR Literary Analysis and Reading Transparencies, p. 101	• Blank Verse, SE p. 840; TR Selection Support, p. 204; TR Literary Analysis and Reading Transparencies, p. 102	• Vocabulary Development, SE p. 840: augmented, entreated, conspiracy, resolution, exploit, imminent • Latin Root *-spir-*, SE p. 859; TR Selection Support, p. 201	• Usage: *who, whom, who's,* and *whose,* SE p. 859; TR Selection Support, p. 202; WG Writing and Grammar, p. 552
The Tragedy of Julius Caesar, Act III, William Shakespeare, SE p. 861 Reading Level: Challenging	• Paraphrasing, SE p. 860; TR Selection Support, p. 207; TR Literary Analysis and Reading Transparencies, p. 103	• Dramatic Speeches, SE p. 860; TR Selection Support, p. 212; TR Literary Analysis and Reading Transparencies, p. 104	• Vocabulary Development, SE p. 860: suit, spurn, confounded, mutiny, vile, malice, oration, discourse • Latin Root *-ora-*, SE p. 881; TR Selection Support, p. 205	• Reflexive Pronouns, SE p. 881; TR Selection Support, p. 206; WG Writing and Grammar, p. 346
The Tragedy of Julius Caesar, Act IV, William Shakespeare, SE p. 884 Reading Level: Challenging	• Reading Between the Lines, SE p. 883; TR Selection Support, p. 211; TR Literary Analysis and Reading Transparencies, p. 105	• Conflict in Drama, SE p. 883; TR Selection Support, p. 212; TR Literary Analysis and Reading Transparencies, p. 106	• Vocabulary Development, SE p. 883: legacies, slanderous, covert, chastisement, philosophy • Greek Root *-phil-*, SE p. 899; TR Selection Support, p. 209	• Pronoun and Antecedent Agreement, SE p. 899; TR Selection Support, p. 210; WG Writing and Grammar, p. 577
The Tragedy of Julius Caesar, Act V, William Shakespeare, SE p. 901 Reading Level: Challenging	• Identifying Causes and Effects, SE p. 900; TR Selection Support, p. 215; TR Literary Analysis and Reading Transparencies, p. 107	• Tragedy, SE p. 900; TR Selection Support, p. 216; TR Literary Analysis and Reading Transparencies, p. 108	• Vocabulary Development, SE p. 900: presage, ensign, consorted, demeanor, disconsolate, misconstrued, envy • Anglo-Saxon Prefix *mis-*, SE p. 914; TR Selection Support, p. 213	• Words of Direct Address, SE p. 914; TR Selection Support, p. 214; WG Writing and Grammar, p. 659

Key to Program References: SE: Student Edition **TR:** Teaching Resources **WG:** Writing and Grammar

Unit 8 *Drama*

Writing	Extension Activities	Assessment	Technology
• Writing Lesson: Newspaper Article, SE p. 789; WG Writing and Grammar, p. 544	• Research and Technology: Presentation, SE p. 789 • TR Extension Activities, p. 48	• Selection Test, TR Formal Assessment, pp. 170–172 • TR Open Book Test, pp. 142–144 • Writing rubric and Listening and Speaking rubric, TR Performance Assess. and Portfolio Mgmt., p. 32	• Interest Grabber Video, Tape 4 • Listening to Literature, Audiocassettes, Side 25; Audio CDs, CD 16 • Got It! Assessment Videotapes, Tape 4 • WG Writing and Grammar iText
• Writing Lesson: Analytic Essay, SE p. 811; WG Writing and Grammar, p. 284	• Listening and Speaking: Mock Trial, SE p. 811 • Research and Technology: Multimedia Presentation, SE p. 811 • TR Extension Activities, p. 49	• Selection Test, TR Formal Assessment, pp. 173–175 • TR Open Book Test, pp. 145–147 • Writing rubric and Listening and Speaking rubric, TR Performance Assess. and Portfolio Mgmt., p. 16	• Interest Grabber Video, Tape 4 • Listening to Literature, Audiocassettes, Side 26; Audio CDs, CD 16 • Got It! Assessment Videotapes, Tape 4 • WG Writing and Grammar iText
• Writing Lesson: Interior Monologue, SE p. 839	• Listening and Speaking: Visual Symbol, SE p. 839 • TR Extension Activities, p. 50	• Selection Test, TR Formal Assessment, pp. 176–178 • TR Open Book Test, pp. 148–150	• Interest Grabber Video, Tape 4 • Listening to Literature, Audiocassettes, Side 27; Audio CDs, CD 17 • Got It! Assessment Videotapes, Tape 4 • WG Writing and Grammar iText
• Writing Lesson: Letter to the Editor, SE p. 859	• Listening and Speaking: Debate, SE p. 859 • TR Extension Activities, p. 51	• Selection Test, TR Formal Assessment, pp. 179–181 • TR Open Book Test, pp. 151–153 • Writing rubric and Listening and Speaking rubric, TR Performance Assess. and Portfolio Mgmt., pp. 18, 30	• Interest Grabber Video, Tape 4 • Listening to Literature, Audiocassettes, Side 28; Audio CDs, CD 17 • Got It! Assessment Videotapes, Tape 4 • WG Writing and Grammar iText
• Writing Lesson: Obituary, SE p. 881	• Listening and Speaking: Dramatic Reading, SE p. 881 • TR Extension Activities, p. 52	• Selection Test, TR Formal Assessment, pp. 182–184 • TR Open Book Test, pp. 154–156 • Writing rubric and Listening and Speaking rubric, TR Performance Assess. and Portfolio Mgmt., p. 19	• Interest Grabber Video, Tape 4 • Listening to Literature, Audiocassettes, Side 29; Audio CDs, CD 18 • Got It! Assessment Videotapes, Tape 4 • WG Writing and Grammar iText
• Writing Lesson: Profile, SE p. 899	• Research and Technology: Slide-Show Presentation, SE p. 899 • TR Extension Activities, p. 53	• Selection Test, TR Formal Assessment, pp. 185–187 • TR Open Book Test, pp. 157–159 • Writing rubric and Listening and Speaking rubric, TR Performance Assess. and Portfolio Mgmt., p. 19	• Interest Grabber Video, Tape 4 • Listening to Literature, Audiocassettes, Side 30; Audio CDs, CD 18 • Got It! Assessment Videotapes, Tape 4 • WG Writing and Grammar iText
• Writing Lesson: Persuasive Essay, SE p. 915; WG Writing and Grammar, p. 134	• Listening and Speaking: Perform a Scene, SE p. 915 • Research and Technology: Model, SE p. 915 • TR Extension Activities, p. 54	• Selection Test, TR Formal Assessment, pp. 188–190 • TR Open Book Test, pp. 160–162 • Writing rubric and Listening and Speaking rubric, TR Performance Assess. and Portfolio Mgmt., p. 11	• Interest Grabber Video, Tape 4 • Listening to Literature, Audiocassettes, Side 31; Audio CDs, CD 19 • Got It! Assessment Videotapes, Tape 4 • WG Writing and Grammar iText

PROGRAM PLANNER

Program Planner

Selection	Reading	Literary Analysis	Vocabulary	Grammar
"The Stolen Child," William Butler Yeats, SE p. 928 Reading Level: Average	• Responding, SE p. 927; TR Selection Support, p. 219; TR Literary Analysis and Reading Transparencies, p. 109	• Atmosphere, SE p. 927; TR Selection Support, p. 220; TR Literary Analysis and Reading Transparencies, p. 110	• Vocabulary Development, SE p. 927: herons, glosses, slumbering • Words With Multiple Meanings, SE p. 932; TR Selection Support, p. 217	• Common Usage Problems: *their, there,* and *they're,* SE p. 932; TR Selection Support, p. 218; WG Writing and Grammar, p. 620
"In Flanders Field," John McCrae, SE p. 938 **"The Kraken,"** Alfred, Lord Tennyson, SE p. 939 **"Meeting at Night,"** Robert Browning, SE p. 940 **"Reapers,"** Jean Toomer, SE p. 941 **"Prayer of First Dancers,"** Navajo, SE p. 942 Reading Level: Average, Challenging, Average, Easy, Easy	• Listening, SE p. 937; TR Selection Support, p. 223; TR Literary Analysis and Reading Transparencies, p. 111	• Musical Devices, SE p. 937; TR Selection Support, p. 224; TR Literary Analysis and Reading Transparencies, p. 112	• Vocabulary Development, SE p. 937: abysmal, millennial • Latin Prefix *mil-,* SE p. 946; TR Selection Support, p. 221	• Usage Problems: *among* and *between,* SE p. 946; TR Selection Support, p. 222; WG Writing and Grammar, p. 613
"The Wind—tapped like a tired Man," Emily Dickinson, SE p. 950 **"A Pace Like That,"** Yehuda Amichai, SE p. 951 **"Metaphor,"** Eve Merriam, SE p. 952 **"Right Hand,"** Philip Fried, SE p. 954 Reading Level: Average, Challenging, Easy, Average	• Paraphrasing, SE p. 949; TR Selection Support, p. 227; TR Literary Analysis and Reading Transparencies, p. 113	• Figurative Language, SE p. 949; TR Selection Support, p. 228; TR Literary Analysis and Reading Transparencies, p. 114	• Vocabulary Development, SE p. 949: countenance, tremulous, flurriedly, decipher, taciturn, eloquent, gutteral, diffused, garrulity • Latin Root *-tac-,* SE p. 956; TR Selection Support, p. 225	• Elliptical Clauses, SE p. 956; TR Selection Support, p. 226; WG Writing and Grammar, p. 472
"La Belle Dame sans Merci," John Keats , SE p. 960 Reading Level: Average **"Danny Deever,"** Rudyard Kipling, SE p. 963 Reading Level: Average	• Identifying the Speaker, SE p. 959; TR Selection Support, p. 231; TR Literary Analysis and Reading Transparencies, p. 115	• Narrative and Dramatic Poetry, SE p. 959; TR Selection Support, p. 232; TR Literary Analysis and Reading Transparencies, p. 116	• Vocabulary Development, SE p. 959: sedge, thrall, sojourn, whimpers, quickstep • Latin Root *-journ-,* SE p. 966; TR Selection Support, p. 229	• Hyphens, SE p. 966; TR Selection Support, p. 230; WG Writing and Grammar, p. 704
"Jade Flower Palace," Tu Fu, SE p. 970 **"The Moon at the Fortified Pass,"** Li Po, SE p. 971 **"The Guitar,"** Federico García Lorca, SE p. 972 **"What Are Friends For,"** Rosellen Brown, SE p. 974 **"Making a Fist,"** Naomi Shihab Nye, SE p. 975 **"Some Like Poetry,"** Wisława Szymborska, SE p. 976 Reading Level: Average, Average, Average, Easy, Easy, Easy	• Reading in Sentences, SE p. 969; TR Selection Support, p. 235; TR Literary Analysis and Reading Transparencies, p. 117	• Lyric Poetry, SE p. 969; TR Selection Support, p. 236; TR Literary Analysis and Reading Transparencies, p. 118	• Vocabulary Development, SE p. 969: pathos, wistful, monotonously • Greek Root *-path-,* SE p. 978; TR Selection Support, p. 233	• Usage Problems: Placement of *only,* SE p. 978; TR Selection Support, p. 234; WG Writing and Grammar, p. 612

Key to Program References: SE: Student Edition **TR:** Teaching Resources **WG:** Writing and Grammar

Unit 9 *Poetry*

Writing	Extension Activities	Assessment	Technology
• Writing Lesson: Crime Report, SE p. 933; WG Writing and Grammar, p. 109	• Listening and Speaking: Oral Presentation, SE p. 933 • Research and Technology: Timeline, SE p. 933 • TR Extension Activities, p. 55	• Selection Test, TR Formal Assessment, pp. 195–197 • TR Open Book Test, pp. 163–165 • Writing rubric and Listening and Speaking rubric, TR Performance Assess. and Portfolio Mgmt., p. 19	• Interest Grabber Video, Tape 5 • Listening to Literature, Audiocassettes, Side 32; Audio CDs, CD 19 • Got It! Assessment Videotapes, Tape 5 • WG Writing and Grammar iText
• Writing Lesson: Proposal for a Poetry Anthology, SE p. 947; WG Writing and Grammar, p. 181	• Listening and Speaking: Poetry Reading, SE p. 947 • Research and Technology: Visual Presentation, SE p. 947 • TR Extension Activities, p. 56	• Selection Test, TR Formal Assessment, pp. 198–200 • TR Open Book Test, pp. 166–168 • Writing rubric and Listening and Speaking rubric, TR Performance Assess. and Portfolio Mgmt., p. 11	• Interest Grabber Video, Tape 5 • Listening to Literature, Audiocassettes, Side 32; Audio CDs, CD 19 • Got It! Assessment Videotapes, Tape 5 • WG Writing and Grammar iText
• Writing Lesson: Analysis of a Poem, SE p. 957; WG Writing and Grammar, p. 285	• Listening and Speaking: Interview, SE p. 957 • Research and Technology: Biographical Report, SE p. 957 • TR Extension Activities, p. 57	• Selection Test, TR Formal Assessment, pp. 201–203 • TR Open Book Test, pp. 169–171 • Writing rubric and Listening and Speaking rubric, TR Performance Assess. and Portfolio Mgmt., p. 16	• Interest Grabber Video, Tape 5 • Listening to Literature, Audiocassettes, Side 33; Audio CDs, CD 19 • Got It! Assessment Videotapes, Tape 5 • WG Writing and Grammar iText
• Writing Lesson: News Bulletin, SE p. 967; WG Writing and Grammar, p. 84	• Listening and Speaking: Reading, SE p. 967 • Research and Technology: Dialect Chart, SE p. 967 • TR Extension Activities, p. 58	• Selection Test, TR Formal Assessment, pp. 204–206 • TR Open Book Test, pp. 172–174 • Writing rubric and Listening and Speaking rubric, TR Performance Assess. and Portfolio Mgmt., pp. 19, 28	• Interest Grabber Video, Tape 5 • Listening to Literature, Audiocassettes, Side 33; Audio CDs, CD 19 • Got It! Assessment Videotapes, Tape 5 • WG Writing and Grammar iText
• Writing Lesson: Lyric Poem, SE p. 979; WG Writing and Grammar, p. 118	• Listening and Speaking: Poetry Reading, SE p. 979 • Research and Technology: Research Report, SE p. 979 • TR Extension Activities, p. 59	• Selection Test, TR Formal Assessment, pp. 207–209 • TR Open Book Test, pp. 175–177 • Writing rubric and Listening and Speaking rubric, TR Performance Assess. and Portfolio Mgmt., p. 29	• Interest Grabber Video, Tape 5 • Listening to Literature, Audiocassettes, Sides 33, 34; Audio CDs, CD 19 • Got It! Assessment Videotapes, Tape 5 • WG Writing and Grammar iText

Program Planner

Selection	Reading	Literary Analysis	Vocabulary	Grammar
"The Waking," Theodore Roethke, SE p. 986; **Tanka,** Ki no Tsurayuki, SE p. 988; **Tanka,** Priest Jakuren, SE p. 988; **Haiku,** Matsuo Bashō, SE p. 989; **Haiku,** Kobayashi Issa, SE p. 989; **Sonnet 18,** William Shakespeare, SE p. 990 Reading Level: Average, Average, Challenging, Easy, Easy, Challenging	• Picturing the Imagery, SE p. 985; TR Selection Support, p. 239; TR Literary Analysis and Reading Transparencies, p. 119	• Poetic Forms, SE p. 985; TR Selection Support, p. 240; TR Literary Analysis and Reading Transparencies, p. 120	• Vocabulary Development, SE p. 985: camellia, lapping, temperate, eternal • Forms of *temperate,* SE p. 992; TR Selection Support, p. 237	• Commonly Confused Words: *to, too, two,* SE p. 992; TR Selection Support, p. 238; WG Writing and Grammar, p. 621

Program Planner

Selection	Reading	Literary Analysis	Vocabulary	Grammar
from **Don Quixote,** Miguel de Cervantes, SE p. 1006 Reading Level: Average	• Comparing and Contrasting, SE p. 1005; TR Selection Support, p. 243; TR Literary Analysis and Reading Transparencies, p. 121	• Parody, SE p. 1005; TR Selection Support, p. 244; TR Literary Analysis and Reading Transparencies, p. 122	• Vocabulary Development, SE p. 1005: lucidity, adulation, interminable, affable, sallying, requisite, sonorous, veracious, vanquish, extolled • Latin Root *-son-,* SE p. 1016; TR Selection Support, p. 241	• Capitalizing Proper Nouns and Adjectives, SE p. 1016; TR Selection Support, p. 242; WG Writing and Grammar, p. 635
"Morte d'Arthur," Alfred, Lord Tennyson, SE p. 1020 Reading Level: Challenging **"Arthur Becomes King of Britain"** from **The Once and Future King,** T. H. White , SE p. 1030 Reading Level: Average	• Recognizing Author's Attitude, SE p. 1019; TR Selection Support, p. 247; TR Literary Analysis and Reading Transparencies, p. 123	• Legend, SE p. 1019; TR Selection Support, p. 248; TR Literary Analysis and Reading Transparencies, p. 124	• Vocabulary Development, SE p. 1019: lamentation, swarthy, stickler, sumptuous, palfrey • Latin Suffix *-ous,* SE p. 1044; TR Selection Support, p. 245	• Quotation Marks With Other Punctuation, SE p. 1044; TR Selection Support, p. 246; WG Writing and Grammar, p. 686
"Rama's Initiation" from **The Ramayana,** R. K. Narayan, SE p. 1052 Reading Level: Challenging	• Drawing Inferences About Culture, SE p. 1051; TR Selection Support, p. 251; TR Literary Analysis and Reading Transparencies, p. 125	• The Epic Hero, SE p. 1051; TR Selection Support, p. 252; TR Literary Analysis and Reading Transparencies, p. 126	• Vocabulary Development, SE p. 1051: austerities, decrepitude, sublime, august, secular, obeisance, exuberance, diminuitive, esoteric • Latin Root *-min-,* SE p. 1060; TR Selection Support, p. 249	• Commas With Introductory Phrases, SE p. 1060; TR Selection Support, p. 250; WG Writing and Grammar, p. 659
from **Sundiata: An Epic of Old Mali,** D. T. Niane, SE p. 1064 Reading Level: Average	• Analyzing a Storyteller's Purpose, SE p. 1063; TR Selection Support, p. 255; TR Literary Analysis and Reading Transparencies, p. 127	• Epic Conflict, SE p. 1063; TR Selection Support, p. 256; TR Literary Analysis and Reading Transparencies, p. 128	• Vocabulary Development, SE p. 1063: fathom, taciturn, malicious, infirmity, innuendo, diabolical, estranged, affront • Latin Root *-firm-,* SE p. 1074; TR Selection Support, p. 253	• Semicolons, SE p. 1074; TR Selection Support, p. 254; WG Writing and Grammar, p. 671

Key to Program References: SE: Student Edition **TR:** Teaching Resources **WG:** Writing and Grammar

Unit 9 *Poetry*

Writing	Extension Activities	Assessment	Technology
• Writing Lesson: Consumer Report of Poetic Forms, SE p. 993; WG Writing and Grammar, p. 180	• Listening and Speaking: Oral Interpretation, SE p. 993 • Research and Technology: Poster, SE p. 993 • TR Extension Activities, p. 60	• Selection Test, TR Formal Assessment, pp. 210–212 • TR Open Book Test, pp. 178–180 • Writing rubric and Listening and Speaking rubric, TR Performance Assess. and Portfolio Mgmt., p. 15	• Interest Grabber Video, Tape 5 • Listening to Literature, Audiocassettes, Side 34; Audio CDs, CD 19 • Got It! Assessment Videotapes, Tape 5 • WG Writing and Grammar iText

Unit 10 *Epics and Legends*

Writing	Extension Activities	Assessment	Technology
• Writing Lesson: Profile of a Modern Superhero, SE p. 1017; WG Writing and Grammar, p. 57	• Listening and Speaking: Role-play, SE p. 1017 • Research and Technology: Biographical Brochure, SE p. 1017 • TR Extension Activities, p. 61	• Selection Test, TR Formal Assessment, pp. 217–219 • TR Open Book Test, pp. 181–183 • Writing rubric and Listening and Speaking rubric, TR Performance Assess. and Portfolio Mgmt., p. 28	• Interest Grabber Video, Tape 5 • Listening to Literature, Audiocassettes, Side 34; Audio CDs, CD 20 • Got It! Assessment Videotapes, Tape 5 • WG Writing and Grammar iText
• Writing Lesson: Letter of Recommendation, SE p. 1045; WG Writing and Grammar, p. 324	• Listening and Speaking: Panel Discussion, SE p. 1045 • Research and Technology: Chart, SE p. 1045 • TR Extension Activities, p. 62	• Selection Test, TR Formal Assessment, pp. 220–222 • TR Open Book Test, pp. 184–186 • Writing rubric and Listening and Speaking rubric, TR Performance Assess. and Portfolio Mgmt., p. 11	• Interest Grabber Video, Tape 5 • Listening to Literature, Audiocassettes, Side 35; Audio CDs, CD 20 • Got It! Assessment Videotapes, Tape 5 • WG Writing and Grammar iText
• Writing Lesson: Script Proposal, SE p. 1061; WG Writing and Grammar, p. 282	• Listening and Speaking: Write Dialogue, SE p. 1061 • Research and Technology: Annotated Poster, SE p. 1061 • TR Extension Activities, p. 63	• Selection Test, TR Formal Assessment, pp. 223–225 • TR Open Book Test, pp. 187–189 • Writing rubric and Listening and Speaking rubric, TR Performance Assess. and Portfolio Mgmt., p. 28	• Interest Grabber Video, Tape 5 • Listening to Literature, Audiocassettes, Side 36; Audio CDs, CD 20 • Got It! Assessment Videotapes, Tape 5 • WG Writing and Grammar iText
• Writing Lesson: Storytelling Notes, SE p. 1075; WG Writing and Grammar, p. 256	• Listening and Speaking: Family Story, SE p. 1075 • Research and Technology: Research Report, SE p. 1075 • TR Extension Activities, p. 64	• Selection Test, TR Formal Assessment, pp. 226–228 • TR Open Book Test, pp. 190–192 • Writing rubric and Listening and Speaking rubric, TR Performance Assess. and Portfolio Mgmt., pp. 14, 28	• Interest Grabber Video, Tape 5 • Listening to Literature, Audiocassettes, Side 36; Audio CDs, CD 20 • Got It! Assessment Videotapes, Tape 5 • WG Writing and Grammar iText

PROGRAM PLANNER

Unit Features

Unit	How to Read Literature	Reading Informational Materials	Writing Workshop	Listening and Speaking Workshop	Assessment Workshop
1 On the Edge	Literal Comprehension Strategies, p. 3	Business Documents: Analyze Structure and Format, p. 24	Autobiographical Narrative, p. 116	Delivering a Narrative, p. 120	Context Clues and Word Meanings, p. 121
2 Striving for Success	Interactive Reading Strategies, p. 125	Product Information: Technical Directions and Warranties, p. 226	Exposition: How-to Essay, p. 230	Descriptive Presentations, p. 234	Facts and Details, p. 235
3 Clashing Forces	Interactive Reading Strategies, p. 239	Newspaper Features: Evaluating Credibility of Information Sources, p. 274	Persuasion: Persuasive Essay, p. 330	Delivering Persuasive Arguments, p. 334	Stated and Implied Main Ideas, p. 335
4 Turning Points	Strategies for Reading Critically, p. 339	Persuasive Articles, p. 410	Reflective Essay, p. 418	Comparing Media Coverage, p. 422	Cause and Effect, p. 423
5 Expanding Horizons	Strategies for Reading Fiction, p. 427	Cause-and-Effect Articles, p. 522	Research Writing, p. 526	Analyzing Types of Arguments, p. 532	Graphic Aids, p. 533
6 Short Stories	Strategies for Constructing Meaning, p. 537	Web Sites: Evaluating Credibility of Sources, p. 590	Narration: Short Story, p. 648	Effective Listening, p. 652	Forms of Propaganda, p. 653
7 Nonfiction	Strategies for Reading Nonfiction, p. 657	Brochures: Skimming and Scanning, p. 670	Exposition: Comparison-and-Contrast Essay, p. 758	Analyze a Media Presentation, p. 762	Comparing and Contrasting, p. 763
8 Drama	Strategies for Reading Drama, p. 767	Arts-and-Leisure Articles: Comparing Information From Several Sources, p. 812	Response to Literature, p. 916	Oral Responses to Literature, p. 920	Characteristics of Text, p. 921
9 Poetry	Strategies for Reading Poetry, p. 925	Historical Essays: Analyzing Patterns of Organization, p. 980	Writing for Assessment, p. 994	Multimedia Presentation, p. 998	Analyzing an Author's Meaning, p. 999
10 Epics and Legends	Strategies for Reading Epics and Legends, p. 1003	Reference Materials: Skimming and Scanning, p. 1076	Letter to the Editor, p. 1080	Interviewing Techniques, p. 1084	Organization, p. 1085

Key to Program References: SE: Student Edition **TR:** Teaching Resources **WG:** Writing and Grammar

FROM THE CLASSROOM: STRATEGIES FOR SUCCESS

How do we teach the literature we love and still prepare students for high-stakes standardized tests?

The recent emphasis on state and national standards has increased the demands on teachers. Language arts instructors face a daunting balancing act in the classroom. We asked teachers who use *Prentice Hall Literature* for practical advice on confronting this challenge. Here are some of their responses.

Using the Student Edition

Make Cross-Curricular Connections Since I teach both world geography and world literature, my challenge is to open students' minds and hearts to diverse global viewpoints *while* preparing them to perform well on high-stakes standardized tests. In my classroom, I often pair Prentice Hall social studies texts with *Prentice Hall Literature*. The former points out how cultures are shaped by their geography; the latter provides thought-provoking excerpts from diverse classic works. What's more, Prentice Hall's well-rounded package of humanities enrichment materials adds depth and breadth to students' understanding of other cultures.

We must help students "read to understand" to succeed on standardized tests and to succeed in an integrated global society. Thanks to Prentice Hall, one does not have to be sacrificed for the other.

John Ludy
Fremont High School
Fremont, IN

Develop Themes I divide state standards into categories of concepts and themes. I then develop units around these themes. Prentice Hall textbooks provide me with ideas and literature selections to include in each unit. I simply choose the one main concept I want to focus on and center the unit on that particular work. This process connects literary works to specific state standards, while also making these works relevant to students' lives.

Agathaniki (Niki) Locklear
Simon Kenton High School
Independence, KY

Extend Learning I often use the Extension Activities in *Prentice Hall Literature* as resources for research and writing activities that connect with post-scholastic, "real world" problems. The challenge is to find an appropriate degree of difficulty for my students. I view the assignment in the Student Edition as a framework that I adjust to meet the identified objectives.

John Scott
Middlesex High School
Saluda, VA

Maximize Resources Prentice Hall has developed a cohesive program of reading selections, connections to extend meaning, skills lessons, vocabulary study, and grammatical and literary studies that provide the teacher with everything needed to promote learning and ensure students' success on standardized tests.

Martha L. Wildman
Lynn Middle School
Las Cruces, NM

Make Connections Prentice Hall's literary selections come complete with sidebars on reading strategies, literary analysis, critical viewing, vocabulary, and literature in context. I use these prompts as motivational hooks, mini-lessons, or assignment prompts. Such features help my students make meaningful connections in an effort to raise their test scores as well as their awareness of the world of ideas, language, and literature.

Charles E. Youngs
Bethel Park High School
Bethel Park, PA

Use Poetry for Practice Here's an idea to try with students who need help with handling poetry on a standardized test. Put a poem on the overhead for the students to see. As a class, read the poem twice, and then give students 7 to 10 minutes to write about the poem's structure and the ideas it conveys. When students have finished writing, comment quickly on structural and thematic issues, asking students to jot down any important points that they did not include in their own responses. As the year goes on, ask students to write longer responses. All *Prentice Hall Literature* textbooks have dozens of useful poems for this literature/high-stakes testing exercise.

Helen Mundy Hudson
Crawfordsville High School
Crawfordsville, IN

Using the Ancillaries

☑ **Monitor Progress** As a former language arts teacher, I have learned that familiarity doth breed . . . success! By using the Selection Tests in the *Formal Assessment* booklet, students become more comfortable with the accepted standardized test format—multiple choice. This workbook helps students not only learn to recognize the language of multiple-choice testing, but also to use the language to guide them in the process of elimination. Class time should be devoted to reviewing the test items and focusing on the specific language of the discriminators. This will increase students' comfort level and better prepare them for a variety of testing experiences.

In addition, the Literary Terms Handbook in the back of the Student Edition is a valuable resource that few make adequate use of.

Helen Spaith
Franklin Heights High School
Columbus, OH

☑ **Use Labels** An aspect of the Prentice Hall materials that I find very helpful is the labeling that accompanies the Thinking About the Selection questions in the Student Edition. These labels help students gain a better understanding of the language of standardized testing as it pertains to recalling, inferring, analyzing, evaluating, and extending information. Prentice Hall also provides materials for less proficient readers, allowing them to increase their level of understanding rather than struggling and becoming frustrated. Finally, Prentice Hall makes materials available on the Internet, allowing students to perform self-assessments and explore information without the time constraints of the classroom.

Holly Carr
Central Crossing High School
Grove City, OH

☑ **Review and Assess** Once students have read a selection in *Prentice Hall Literature* and we have reviewed the skills in focus, I assign the corresponding workbook pages in the *Selection Support: Skills Development Workbook.* Most of the time I allow students to work in pairs or groups. After students have completed the pages, we review and make any necessary corrections. Later these pages become study sheets for test preparation, as the pages can be easily removed from the workbook. Using the Resource Pro, I then design student tests. One of the best features of this portion of the CD-ROM is that the test questions include questions on the vocabulary, grammar, and literary analysis covered in the selection and practiced in the workbook.

Gail Hacker
North Charleston High School
North Charleston, SC

Using the Critical Viewing Questions

☑ **Practice Paragraph Development** One way that I help students prepare for standardized testing is to work on paragraph development. I use artwork in the Student Edition to give the students something to work from. The Critical Viewing question provides the writing prompt, and I show students on the overhead or the chalkboard how to turn the prompt into the topic sentence for a paragraph that answers the question. Then, I ask that students help me develop a paragraph that provides three pieces of evidence to support the topic sentence. This exercise can lead to stronger essays of the kind often asked for with free-responses or reading comprehension on state assessments.

Steve Thalheimer
Laurenceburg High School
Laurenceburg, IN

☑ **Use Picture Prompts** Although I have used *Prentice Hall Literature* consistently as a reading resource and teaching tool, I have found it useful in another invaluable way. The photographs and fine art in the Student Edition can be used as picture prompts, providing students with writing practice for standardized tests.

Linda Fund
Ezra L. Nolan Middle School
Jersey City, NJ

☑ **Analyze Art** Initially, one of the most challenging language arts standards for me to teach was viewing and representing. However, the fine art and Critical Viewing questions in *Prentice Hall Literature* have made this standard much more attainable. I select paintings from each unit in *Prentice Hall Literature* for my students to analyze critically. For example, my students view *Washington Crossing the Delaware* by Emanuel Gottlieb Leutze and answer questions about the setting, mood, and conflict. They then draw conclusions and make inferences about the action in the painting. This task covers an array of learning expectations and helps to prepare students for standardized tests. The questions for these assignments can be objective like most standardized tests or subjective to help students develop writing skills. Perhaps the best outcome is that my students now love "reading" art!

Cathy Robbs
Chattanooga Central High School
Harrison, TN

PRENTICE HALL
LITERATURE

Timeless Voices, Timeless Themes

PLATINUM LEVEL

PEARSON

Prentice
Hall

Upper Saddle River, New Jersey

Needham, Massachusetts

ISBN 0-13-180435-9

6 7 8 9 10   09 08 07 06 05

Cover: *Paris Street: Rainy Day,* oil on canvas, Gustave Caillebotte, Charles H. and Mary F. S. Worcester Collection, The Art Institute of Chicago

ACKNOWLEDGMENTS

Grateful acknowledgment is made to the following for permission to reprint copyrighted material:

Estate of Gwendolyn Brooks "The Bean Eaters" from *Blacks* by Gwendolyn Brooks. Copyright © 1991 by Gwendolyn Brooks. Used by permission.

Bancroft Library Excerpt from *Desert Exile: The Uprooting of a Japanese-American Family* by Yoshiko Uchida. Copyright © 1982 by Yoshiko Uchida. Reprinted courtesy of the Bancroft Library, University of California, Berkeley.

Elizabeth Barnett, Literary Executor of the Estate of Norma Vincent Millay Society "Conscientious Objector" by Edna St. Vincent Millay from *Collected Poems,* HarperCollins. Copyright © 1934, 1962 by Edna St. Vincent Millay and Norma Millay Ellis. Used by permission of Elizabeth Barnett, literary executor. All rights reserved.

Susan Bergholz Literary Services From THE ANAYA READER published as "The Magic of Words." Copyright © 1995 by Rudolfo Anaya. First published as "In Commemoration: One Million Volumes" from *A Million Stars: The Millionth Acquisition for University of New Mexico General Library,* University of New Mexico Press, 1982. Reprinted by permission of Susan Bergholz Literary Services, New York. All rights reserved.

Nguyen Ngoc Bich "Thoughts of Hanoi" by Nguyen Thi Vinh from *A Thousand Years of Vietnamese Poetry,* edited by Nguyen Ngoc Bich. Copyright © 1962, 1967, 1968, 1969, 1970, 1971, 1974 by The Asia Society and Nguyen Ngoc Bich. Reprinted by permission of Nguyen Ngoc Bich.

(Acknowledgments continue on page R53, which constitutes an extension of this copyright page.)

PRENTICE HALL

LITERATURE

Timeless Voices, Timeless Themes

COPPER

BRONZE

SILVER

GOLD

PLATINUM

THE AMERICAN EXPERIENCE

THE BRITISH TRADITION

CONTRIBUTING AUTHORS

The contributing authors guided the direction and philosophy of *Prentice Hall Literature: Timeless Voices, Timeless Themes*. Working with the development team, they helped to build the pedagogical integrity of the program and to ensure its relevance for today's teachers and students.

Kate Kinsella

Kate Kinsella, Ed.D., is a faculty member in the Department of Secondary Education at San Francisco State University. A specialist in second-language acquisition and adolescent reading and writing, she teaches coursework addressing language and literacy development across the secondary curricula. She has taught high-school ESL and directed SFSU's *Intensive English Program* for first-generation bilingual college students. She maintains secondary classroom involvement by teaching an academic literacy class for second-language learners through the University's *Step to College* partnership program. A former Fulbright lecturer and perennial institute leader for TESOL, the California Reading Association, and the California League of Middle Schools, Dr. Kinsella provides professional development nationally on topics ranging from learning-style enhancement to second-language reading. Her scholarship has been published in journals such as the *TESOL Journal,* the *CATESOL Journal,* and the *Social Studies Review.* Dr. Kinsella earned her M.A. in TESOL from San Francisco State University and her Ed.D. in Second Language Acquisition from the University of San Francisco.

Kevin Feldman

Kevin Feldman, Ed.D., is the Director of Reading and Early Intervention with the Sonoma County Office of Education (SCOE). His career in education spans thirty-one years. As the Director of Reading and Early Intervention for SCOE, he develops, organizes, and monitors programs related to K–12 literacy and prevention of reading difficulties. He also serves as a Leadership Team Consultant to the California Reading and Literature Project and assists in the development and implementation of K–12 programs throughout California. Dr. Feldman earned his undergraduate degree in Psychology from Washington State University and has a Master's degree in Special Education, Learning Disabilities, and Instructional Design from U.C. Riverside. He earned his Ed.D. in Curriculum and Instruction from the University of San Francisco.

Colleen Shea Stump

Colleen Shea Stump, Ph.D., is a Special Education supervisor in the area of Resource and Inclusion for Seattle Public Schools. She served as a professor and chairperson for the Department of Special Education at San Francisco State University. She continues as a lead consultant in the area of collaboration for the California State Improvement Grant and travels the state of California providing professional development training in the areas of collaboration, content literacy instruction, and inclusive instruction. Dr. Stump earned her doctorate at the University of Washington, her M.A. in Special Education from the University of New Mexico, and her B.S. in Elementary Education from the University of Wisconsin–Eau Claire.

Joyce Armstrong Carroll

In her forty-year career, Joyce Armstrong Carroll, Ed. D., has taught on every grade level from primary to graduate school. In the past twenty years, she has trained teachers in the teaching of writing. A nationally known consultant, she has served as president of TCTE and on NCTE's Commission on Composition. More than fifty of her articles have appeared in journals such as *Curriculum Review, English Journal, Media & Methods, Southwest Philosophical Studies, English in Texas,* and the *Florida English Journal.* With Edward E. Wilson, Dr. Carroll co-authored *Acts of Teaching: How to Teach Writing* and co-edited *Poetry After Lunch: Poetry to Read Aloud.* She co-directs the New Jersey Writing Project in Texas.

Edward E. Wilson

A former editor of *English in Texas,* Edward E. Wilson has served as a high-school English teacher and a writing consultant in school districts nationwide. Wilson has served on both the Texas Teacher Professional Practices Commission and NCTE's Commission on Composition. Wilson's poetry appears in Paul Janeczko's anthology *The Music of What Happens.* With Dr. Carroll, he co-wrote *Acts of Teaching: How to Teach Writing* and co-edited *Poetry After Lunch: Poetry to Read Aloud.* Wilson co-directs the New Jersey Writing Project in Texas.

PROGRAM ADVISORS

The program advisors provided ongoing input throughout the development of *Prentice Hall Literature: Timeless Voices, Timeless Themes*. Their valuable insights ensure that the perspectives of the teachers throughout the country are represented within this literature series.

Diane Cappillo
English Department Chair
Barbara Goleman Senior High School
Miami, Florida

Anita Clay
Language Arts Instructor
Gateway Institute of Technology
St. Louis, Missouri

Ellen Eberly
Language Arts Instructor
Catholic Memorial High School
West Roxbury, Massachusetts

Nancy Fahner
L.A.M.P. Lansing Area Manufacturing
   Partnership
Ingham Intermediate School District
Mason, Michigan

Terri Fields
Instructor of Language Arts,
   Communication Arts, and Author
Sunnyslope High School
Phoenix, Arizona

Susan Goldberg
Language Arts Instructor
Westlake Middle School
Thornwood, New York

Margo L. Graf
English Department Chair, Speech,
   Yearbook, Journalism
Lane Middle School
Fort Wayne, Indiana

Christopher E. Guarraia
Language Arts Instructor
Lakewood High School
Saint Petersburg, Florida

V. Pauline Hodges
Teacher, Educational Consultant
Forgan High School
Forgan, Oklahoma

Karen Hurley
Language Arts Instructor
Perry Meridian Middle School
Indianapolis, Indiana

Lenore D. Hynes
Language Arts Coordinator
Sunman-Dearborn Community
   Schools
Sunman, Indiana

Linda Kramer
Language Arts Instructor
Norman High School North
Norman, Oklahoma

Thomas S. Lindsay
Assistant Superintendent of Schools
Manheim District 83
Franklin Park, Illinois

Agathaniki (Niki) Locklear
English Department Chair
Simon Kenton High School
Independence, Kentucky

Mary Ellen Mastej
Language Arts Instructor
Scott Middle School
Hammond, Indiana

Ashley MacDonald
Language Arts Instructor
South Forsyth High School
Cumming, Georgia

Nancy L. Monroe
English, Speed Reading Teacher
Bolton High School
Alexandria, Louisiana

Jim Moody
Language Arts Instructor
Northside High School
Fort Smith, Arkansas

David Morris
Teacher of English, Writing,
   Publications, Yearbook
Washington High School
South Bend, Indiana

Rosemary A. Naab
English Department Chair
Ryan High School
Archdiocese of Philadelphia
Philadelphia, Pennsylvania

Ann Okamura
English Teacher
Laguna Creek High School
Elk Grove, California

Tucky Roger
Coordinator of Languages
Tulsa Public Schools
Tulsa, Oklahoma

Jonathan L. Schatz
English Teacher/Team Leader
Tappan Zee High School
Orangeburg, New York

John Scott
Assistant Principal
Middlesex High School
Saluda, Virginia

Ken Spurlock
Assistant Principal, Retired
Boone County High School
Florence, Kentucky

Dr. Jennifer Watson
Secondary Language Arts
   Coordinator
Putnam City Schools
Oklahoma City, Oklahoma

Joan West
Assistant Principal
Oliver Middle School
Broken Arrow, Oklahoma

Contents in Brief

Learn About Literature

Learn About Literature xxvi
Short Stories IN2
Nonfiction IN4
Drama IN6
Poetry IN8
Folk Literature IN10

Themes in Literature

Unit 1   On the Edge 1
Unit 2   Striving for Success 122
Unit 3   Clashing Forces 236
Unit 4   Turning Points 336
Unit 5   Expanding Horizons 424

Literary Genres

Unit 6   Short Stories 534
Unit 7   Nonfiction 654
Unit 8   Drama 764
Unit 9   Poetry 922
Unit 10   Epics and Legends 1000

Resources

Suggestions for Sustained Reading R1
Glossary R7

Handbooks

Tips for Improving Reading Fluency R10
Literary Terms Handbook R12
Rubric Handbook R20
Writing Handbook R24
Formatting Business Letters R29
Spelling Handbook R30
Grammar and Mechanics Handbook R34
Internet Research Handbook R39
Writing Criticism and Citing Sources R41

Indexes R44

Acknowledgments (continued) R53
Credits R56

Why Read Literature? 2

How to Read Literature: **Use Literal Comprehension Strategies** 3

Jack Finney   **Contents of the Dead Man's Pocket** . . . Short Story   6

Reading Informational Materials: *Business Documents*
Business Letter and Memorandum 25   **RC**

Comparing Literary Works

Sir Edmund Hillary   *from* **View From the Summit** . . . . . . Nonfiction   30

Connections: *Literature and Geography*

Jon Krakauer   *from* **Into Thin Air** . . . . Nonfiction   37

Tenzing Norgay *with*   **The Dream Comes True**

James Ramsey Ullman   *from* **The Tiger of the Snows** . . . . . . Nonfiction   39

Comparing Literary Works

W. W. Jacobs   **The Monkey's Paw** . . . . Short Story   50

Alexander Pushkin   **The Bridegroom** . . . . Poem   59

Jamaica Kincaid   *from* **A Walk to the Jetty** *from* **Annie John** . . . Fiction   70   **RC**

Edgar Allan Poe   **The Masque of the Red Death** . . . . . . Short Story   82   **RC**

Comparing Literary Works

William Carlos Williams   **Spring and All** . . . . Poem   94

Gabriela Mistral   **Fear** . . . . Poem   95

Octavio Paz   **The street** . . . . Poem   96

Comparing Literary Works

Guy de Maupassant   **Two Friends** . . . . Short Story   102

Classic Greek Myth   **Damon and Pythias** . . . . Myth   109   **RC**

SKILLS WORKSHOPS

Writing Workshop: Narration: Autobiographical Narrative 116

Listening and Speaking Workshop: Delivering a Narrative 120

Assessment Workshop: Context Clues and Word Meanings 121

RC   This selection is featured in
the *Reader's Companion* series.

UNIT 2

THEME: *Striving for Success*

	Why Read Literature?		124
	How to Read Literature: **Use Interactive Reading Strategies**		125
Rudolfo A. Anaya	*from* In Commemoration: One Million Volumes	Nonfiction	128
Leo Tolstoy	**How Much Land Does a Man Need?**	Short Story	138

Comparing Literary Works

Emily Dickinson	**Success is counted sweetest**	Poem	158
	I dwell in Possibility—	Poem	159
Pat Mora	**Uncoiling**	Poem	160
Vassar Miller	**Columbus Dying**	Poem	162
Christy Brown	*from* **My Left Foot**	Nonfiction	168

Connections: *Literature and Media*
| | **Daniel Day-Lewis Plays Christy Brown** | | 178 |
| William Melvin Kelley | **A Visit to Grandmother** | Short Story | 182 |

Comparing Literary Works

Robert Frost	**After Apple-Picking**	Poem	196
	Mowing	Poem	198
Maya Angelou	**Style**	Essay	199
	At Harvesttime	Essay	200
Katherine Mansfield	**The Apple Tree**	Short Story	206

Comparing Literary Works

David Diop	**Africa**	Poem	216
Traditional	**Old Song**	Poem	217
Bei Dao	**All**	Poem	218
Shu Ting	**Also All**	Poem	219
Confucius	*from* The Analects	Nonfiction	220

Reading Informational Materials: *Product Information*
| Instructions and Warranty | | 227 |

SKILLS WORKSHOPS

Writing Workshop: Exposition: How-to Essay 230

Listening and Speaking Workshop: Descriptive Presentation 234

Assessment Workshop: Facts and Details 235

UNIT 3

THEME: *Clashing Forces*

	Why Read Literature?		238
	How to Read Literature: **Use Interactive Reading Strategies**		239
Doris Lessing	**Through the Tunnel**	Short Story	242
James Thurber	**The Dog That Bit People**	Essay	256

Comparing Literary Works

Edna St. Vincent Millay	**Conscientious Objector**	Poem	266
Nina Cassian	**A Man**	Poem	267
Langston Hughes	**The Weary Blues**	Poem	268
Carl Sandburg	**Jazz Fantasia**	Poem	270

Reading Informational Materials: *Newspaper Features*

Ann Douglas	**Feel the City's Pulse? It's Be-bop, Man!**		275

Comparing Literary Works

R. K. Narayan	**Like the Sun**	Short Story	280
Emily Dickinson	**Tell all the Truth but tell it slant—**	Poem	284

Comparing Literary Works

O. Henry	**Hearts and Hands**	Short Story	290
Elizabeth Bishop	**The Fish**	Poem	293

Comparing Literary Works

Yoshiko Uchida	*from* **Desert Exile: The Uprooting of a Japanese-American Family**	Nonfiction	300
Gerald Ford	**Speech on Japanese American Internment**	Nonfiction	308

Connections: *Literature and History*

David Guterson	*from* **Snow Falling on Cedars**	Novel	312
Rabindranath Tagore	**The Cabuliwallah**	Short Story	318

SKILLS WORKSHOPS

Writing Workshop: Persuasion: Persuasive Essay 330

Listening and Speaking Workshop: Delivering Persuasive Arguments 334

Assessment Workshop: Stated and Implied Main Ideas 335

RC This selection is featured in the *Reader's Companion* series.

UNIT 4

THEME: *Turning Points*

	Why Read Literature?		338
	How to Read Literature: **Use Strategies for Reading Critically**		339
Vladimir Nabokov	*from* **Speak, Memory**	Nonfiction	342
Anita Desai	**Games at Twilight**	Short Story	352

Comparing Literary Works

Leopold Staff	**The Bridge**	Poem	366
Emily Brontë	**The Old Stoic**	Poem	367
Anna Akhmatova	**I Am Not One of Those Who Left the Land**	Poem	368 ✓
Empress Theodora	**Speech During the Invasion of Constantinople**	Speech	369
Pearl S. Buck	**The Good Deed**	Short Story	376 ✓

Comparing Literary Works

Nguyen Thi Vinh	**Thoughts of Hanoi**	Poem	398
Karl Shapiro	**Auto Wreck**	Poem	401
Dahlia Ravikovitch	**Pride**	Poem	402
Franz Kafka	**Before the Law**	Parable	404

	Reading Informational Materials: *Persuasive Articles*		
Charles Lave	**65-MPH Speed Limit Is Saving Lives**		411
	Connections: *Literature and History*		
Tim O'Brien	**Calling Home *from* Going After Cacciato**		414

SKILLS WORKSHOPS

Writing Workshop: Narration: Reflective Essay 418

Listening and Speaking Workshop: Comparing Media Coverage 422

Assessment Workshop: Cause and Effect 423

UNIT 5

THEME: *Expanding Horizons*

	Why Read Literature?		426	
	How to Read Literature: **Use Strategies for Reading Fiction**		427	
Virginia Woolf	**The Widow and the Parrot**	Short Story	430	RC
Chinua Achebe	**Civil Peace**	Short Story	444	RC

Comparing Literary Works
| Umberto Eco | **How to React to Familiar Faces** . . . . | Essay | 456 | |
| Gwendolyn Brooks | **The Bean Eaters** . . . . | Poem | 458 | ✓ |

Comparing Literary Works
| Reynolds Price | **A Picture From the Past: Emily Dickinson** . . . | Essay | 464 | |
| Richard Mühlberger | **What Makes a Degas a Degas?** . . . . | Essay | 466 | |

Connections: *Literature and Humanities*
Frank McCourt	*from* **Angela's Ashes.**	Autobiography	474	✓
Native American (Blackfeet)	**The Orphan Boy and the Elk Dog**	Myth	484	
Josephina Niggli	**The Street of the Cañon** *from* **Mexican Village**	Short Story	498	

Comparing Literary Works
Alexander Solzhenitsyn	**A Storm in the Mountains**	Prose	512	
Henrik Ibsen	**In the Orchard**	Poem	513	
Denise Levertov	**A Tree Telling of Orpheus**	Poem	514	

Reading Informational Materials: *Cause-and-Effect Articles*
| The Nature Company | **Lightning and Thunder** . . . . | | 523 | RC |

SKILLS WORKSHOPS

Writing Workshop: Research Writing. . . . . 526 ✓

Listening and Speaking Workshop: Analyzing Types of Arguments. . . . . 532 ✓

Assessment Workshop: Graphic Aids. . . . . 533 ✓

RC This selection is featured in the *Reader's Companion* series.

Contents xi

UNIT 6

GENRE: *Short Stories*

	Why Read Literature?		536
	How to Read Literature: **Use Strategies for Constructing Meaning**		537
RC	Saki (H. H. Munro)	**The Open Window**	Plot 540
	Carl Stephenson	**Leiningen Versus the Ants**	Conflict 550
	Stephen Vincent Benét	**By the Waters of Babylon**	Point of View 576
RC		**Reading Informational Materials:** *Web Sites* **Egyptology Resources**	Web Site 591

Comparing Literary Works

Anton Chekhov	**A Problem**	Character 596
Mark Twain	**Luck**	Character 604

Comparing Literary Works

Ray Bradbury	**There Will Come Soft Rains**	Setting 614
Italo Calvino	**The Garden of Stubborn Cats**	Setting 621

Connections: *Literature and Technology*

Hans Enzensberger   *from* **The Future of Luxury** 632

Comparing Literary Works

Pär Lagerkvist	**The Princess and All the Kingdom**	Theme 638
Luisa Valenzuela	**The Censors**	Theme 641

SKILLS WORKSHOPS

Writing Workshop: Narration: Short Story 648

Listening and Speaking Workshop: Effective Listening 652

Assessment: Forms of Propaganda 653

UNIT 7

GENRE: *Nonfiction*

	Why Read Literature?		656
	How to Read Literature: **Use Strategies for Reading Nonfiction**		657
Rachel Carson	**The Marginal World**	Expository Essay	660

Reading Informational Materials: *Brochures*
Aquarium of the Pacific . . . . Brochure 671 **RC**

Comparing Literary Works

N. Scott Momaday	*from* **The Way to Rainy Mountain**	Reflective Essay	676 **RC**
Alexander Solzhenitsyn	*from* **Nobel Lecture**	Persuasive Essay	683
Elie Wiesel	**Keep Memory Alive**	Persuasive Essay	687

Comparing Literary Works

Dylan Thomas	**A Child's Christmas in Wales**	Autobiography	694
Langston Hughes	**Marian Anderson: Famous Concert Singer**	Biography	702 **RC**
Annie Dillard	**Flood**	Descriptive Essay	712 **RC**
Tillie Olsen and Estelle Jussim	**Mothers & Daughters**	Visual Essay	724

Connections: *Literature and Art*
The Life and Times of Mary Cassatt 730

Comparing Literary Works

Vincent Canby	**Star Wars—A Trip to a Far Galaxy That's Fun and Funny** . . .	Critical Review	734
Roger Ebert	**Star Wars: Breakthrough Film Still Has the Force**	Critical Review	737

Comparing Literary Works

Paul O'Neil	**Imitating Nature's Mineral Artistry**	Technical Article	748
Ernesto Ruelas Inzunza	**Work That Counts**	Technical Article	753

SKILLS WORKSHOPS

Writing Workshop: Exposition: Comparison-and-Contrast Essay 758

Listening and Speaking Workshop: Analyze a Media Presentation 762

Assessment Workshop: Comparing and Contrasting 763

RC This selection is featured in the *Reader's Companion* series.

UNIT 8

GENRE: *Drama*

Why Read Literature? 766

How to Read Literature: **Use Strategies for Reading Drama** 767

Greek Theater 768

Sophocles **Antigone**

Prologue Through Scene 2 . Protagonist and Antagonist 772

Scenes 3 Through 5 . . . . Tragic Character 791

Reading Informational Materials: *Arts-and-Leisure Articles*

Ben Brantley **Private Horror Made Public** 813

Ben Brantley **After 1,500 Years, Colosseum Reopens for Shows** . . 814

Shakespeare on Stage 816

William Shakespeare 818

William Shakespeare **The Tragedy of Julius Caesar**

Act I . . . . Exposition in Drama 822

Act II . . . . Blank Verse 841

Act III . . . . Dramatic Speeches 861

Connections: *Literature and History*

Noa Ben Artzi-Pelossof **Eulogy for a Fallen Leader (Yitzhak Rabin)** 882

Act IV . . . . Conflict in Drama 884

Act V . . . . Tragedy 901

SKILLS WORKSHOPS

Writing Workshop: Response to Literature 916

Listening and Speaking Workshop: Oral Responses to Literature 920

Assessment Workshop: Characteristics of Text 921

UNIT 9

GENRE: *Poetry*

	Why Read Literature?	. . . .	924
	How to Read Literature: **Use Strategies for Reading Poetry**	925
William Butler Yeats	**The Stolen Child**	Atmosphere	928 ✓

Connections: *Literature and Music*

| Harry and Sandy Chapin | **Cat's in the Cradle** . . . . | Song | 934 |

Comparing Literary Works

John McCrae	**In Flanders Fields**	Musical Devices	938
Alfred, Lord Tennyson	**The Kraken**	Musical Devices	939
Robert Browning	**Meeting at Night**	Musical Devices	940
Jean Toomer	**Reapers**	Musical Devices	941
Native American (Navajo)	**Prayer of First Dancers**	Musical Devices	942

Comparing Literary Works

Emily Dickinson	**The Wind—tapped like a tired Man**	Figurative Language	950
Yehuda Amichai	**A Pace Like That**	Figurative Language	951
Eve Merriam	**Metaphor**	Figurative Language	952 ✓
Philip Fried	**Right Hand**	Figurative Language	954

Comparing Literary Works

| John Keats | **La Belle Dame sans Merci** . . . . . . | Narrative Poem | 960 ✓ **RC** |
| Rudyard Kipling | **Danny Deever** . . . . | Dramatic Poem | 963 **RC** |

(Continued on page xvi.)

RC This selection is featured in the *Reader's Companion* series.

UNIT 9

GENRE: *Poetry* (continued)

Comparing Literary Works

Tu Fu	**Jade Flower Palace**	Lyric Poem	970
Li Po	**The Moon at the Fortified Pass**	Lyric Poem	971
Federico García Lorca	**The Guitar**	Lyric Poem	972
Rosellen Brown	**What Are Friends For**	Free Verse	974
Naomi Shihab Nye	**Making a Fist**	Free Verse	975 ✓
Wisława Szymborska	**Some Like Poetry**	Free Verse	976

Reading Informational Materials: *Historical Essays*

Thomas A. Hill	**The History of the Guitar**	981

Comparing Literary Works

Theodore Roethke	**The Waking**	Poetic Forms	986
Ki Tsurayuki	**Tanka**	Poetic Forms	988
Priest Jakuren	**Tanka**	Poetic Forms	988
Matsuo Bashō	**Haiku**	Poetic Forms	989
Kobayashi Issa	**Haiku**	Poetic Forms	989
William Shakespeare	**Sonnet 18**	Poetic Forms	990 ✓

SKILLS WORKSHOPS

Writing Workshop: Writing for Assessment 994

Listening and Speaking Workshop: Multimedia Presentation 998

Assessment Workshop: Analyzing an Author's Meaning 999

UNIT 10

GENRE: *Epics and Legends*

Why Read Literature? 1002

How to Read Literature: **Use Strategies for Reading Epics and Legends** 1003

Miguel de Cervantes   *from* **Don Quixote** . . . . Parody 1006

Comparing Literary Works

Alfred, Lord Tennyson   **Morte d'Arthur** . . . . Legend 1020

T. H. White   **Arthur Becomes King of Britain** *from* **The Once and Future King** . . . . . Legend 1030

Connections: *Literature and Media*

Eric P. Nash   **Star Wars: An Epic for Today** . . . . Essay 1046 ✓

R. K. Narayan   **Rama's Initiation** *from* **the Ramayana** . . . Epic Hero 1052

D. T. Niane   *from* **Sundiata: An Epic of Old Mali** . . . Epic Conflict 1064

Reading Informational Materials: *Reference Materials*

Dorling Kindersley   **Mali** . . . . Atlas 1077

SKILLS WORKSHOPS

Writing Workshop: Letter to the Editor . . . . 1080 ✓

Listening and Speaking Workshop: Interviewing Techniques . . . . 1084 ✓

Assessment Workshop: Organization 1085

RC This selection is featured in the *Reader's Companion* series.

Complete Contents by Genre

Short Stories

Plot
Contents of the Dead Man's Pocket
Jack Finney. 6
The Monkey's Paw
W. W. Jacobs. 50
Two Friends
Guy de Maupassant 102
Through the Tunnel
Doris Lessing 242
Hearts and Hands
O. Henry. 290
The Open Window
Saki (H. H. Munro). 540
Leiningen Versus the Ants
Carl Stephenson 550

Point of View
from **A Walk to the Jetty** *from* **Annie John**
Jamaica Kincaid. 70
The Street of the Cañon *from* **Mexican Village**
Josephina Niggli. 498
By the Waters of Babylon
Stephen Vincent Benét 576

Theme
from **Snow Falling on Cedars**
David Guterson. 312
Like the Sun
R. K. Narayan. 280
Before the Law
Franz Kafka. 404
from **Going After Cacciato**
Tim O'Brien 414
Civil Peace
Chinua Achebe 444
The Princess and All the Kingdom
Pär Lagerkvist 638
The Censors
Luisa Valenzuela 641

Character
How Much Land Does a Man Need?
Leo Tolstoy. 137
A Visit to Grandmother
William Melvin Kelley. 182
The Cabuliwallah
Rabindranath Tagore 218
Games at Twilight
Anita Desai. 352

The Good Deed
Pearl S. Buck 376
The Widow and the Parrot
Virginia Woolf 430
A Problem
Anton Chekhov. 596
Luck
Mark Twain. 604

Setting
There Will Come Soft Rains
Ray Bradbury. 614
The Garden of Stubborn Cats
Italo Calvino. 621

Symbol
The Masque of the Red Death
Edgar Allan Poe 82
The Apple Tree
Katherine Mansfield 206

Poetry

Figurative Language
Africa
David Diop. 216
The Wind—tapped like a tired Man
Emily Dickinson. 950
A Pace Like That
Yehuda Amichai 951
Metaphor
Eve Merriam. 952
Right Hand
Philip Fried. 954

Theme
Success is counted sweetest
Emily Dickinson. 158
I dwell in Possibility—
Emily Dickinson. 159
Uncoiling
Pat Mora. 160
Columbus Dying
Vassar Miller. 162
Old Song
Traditional 217
The Bridge
Leopold Staff. 366
I Am Not One of Those Who Left the Land
Anna Akhmatova. 368

Auto Wreck
Karl Shapiro 401
Pride
Dahlia Ravikovitch 402

Speaker and Tone
After Apple-Picking
Robert Frost 196
Mowing
Robert Frost 198
All
Bei Dao 218
Also All
Shu Ting 219
Conscientious Objector
Edna St. Vincent Millay 266
A Man
Nina Cassian 267
The Weary Blues
Langston Hughes 268
Jazz Fantasia
Carl Sandburg 270
Thoughts of Hanoi
Nguyen Thi Vinh 398
The Bean Eaters
Gwendolyn Brooks 458
In the Orchard
Henrik Ibsen 513
A Tree Telling of Orpheus
Denise Levertov 514

Musical Devices
In Flanders Fields
John McCrae 938
The Kraken
Alfred, Lord Tennyson 939
Meeting at Night
Robert Browning 940
Reapers
Jean Toomer 941
Prayer of First Dancers
Native American (Navajo) 942

Word Choice and Imagery
Spring and All
William Carlos Williams 94
Fear
Gabriela Mistral 95
The street
Octavio Paz 96
Tell all the Truth but tell it slant—
Emily Dickinson 284
The Fish
Elizabeth Bishop 293

Poetic Forms
The Waking
Theodore Roethke 986
Tanka
Ki Tsurayuki; Priest Jakuren 988
Haiku
Matsuo Bashō; Kobayashi Issa 989
Sonnet 18
William Shakespeare 990

Narrative and Dramatic Poetry
The Bridegroom
Alexander Pushkin 59
The Stolen Child
William Butler Yeats 928
La Belle Dame sans Merci
John Keats 960
Danny Deever
Rudyard Kipling 963

Lyric Poetry
The Old Stoic
Emily Brontë 367
Cat's in the Cradle
Harry Chapin and Sandy Chapin 934
Jade Flower Palace
Tu Fu 970
The Moon at the Fortified Pass
Li Po 971
The Guitar
Federico García Lorca 972
What Are Friends For
Rosellen Brown 974
Making a Fist
Naomi Shihab Nye 975
Some Like Poetry
Wisława Szymborska 976

DRAMA

Antigone
Sophocles 772
The Tragedy of Julius Caesar
William Shakespeare 822

NONFICTION

Essays
from Into Thin Air
John Krakauer 37
Daniel Day-Lewis Plays Christy Brown 178

from **My Left Foot**
Christy Brown 168
Style
Maya Angelou 199
At Harvesttime
Maya Angelou 200
from **The Analects**
Confucius 220
The Dog That Bit People
James Thurber 256
How to React to Familiar Faces
Umberto Eco 457
A Picture From the Past: Emily Dickinson
Reynolds Price 464
What Makes a Degas a Degas?
Richard Mühlberger 466
The Marginal World
Rachel Carson 660
from **The Way to Rainy Mountain**
N. Scott Momaday 676
Flood
Annie Dillard 712
Star Wars: Breakthrough Film Still Has the Force
Roger Ebert 737
Star Wars—A Trip to a Far Galaxy That's Fun and Funny . . .
Vincent Canby 734
Imitating Nature's Mineral Artistry
Paul O'Neil 748
Work That Counts
Ernesto Ruelas Inzunza 753

Articles
Feel the City's Pulse? It's Be-bop, Man!
Ann Douglas 274
65-MPH Speed Limit Is Saving Lives
Charles Lave 410
Lightning and Thunder
The Nature Company 522
from **The Future of Luxury**
Hans Enzensberger 632
Mothers & Daughters
Tillie Olsen and Estelle Jussim 724
Greek National Theater Production of *Oedipus*
Ben Brantley 813
The History of the Guitar
Thomas A. Hill 980
Star Wars: An Epic for Today
Eric P. Nash 1046

Biographies and Autobiographies
The Dream Comes True
Tenzing Norgay 36

from **Desert Exile**
Yoshiko Uchida 300
from **Speak, Memory**
Vladimir Nabokov 342
from **Angela's Ashes**
Frank McCourt 474
A Child's Christmas in Wales
Dylan Thomas 694
Marian Anderson: Famous Concert Singer
Langston Hughes 702

Speeches
from **In Commemoration: One Million Volumes**
Rudolfo A. Anaya 128
Speech on Japanese American Internment
Gerald Ford 308
Speech During the Invasion of Constantinople
Empress Theodora 369
from **Nobel Lecture**
Alexander Solzhenitsyn 683
Keep Memory Alive
Elie Wiesel 687
Eulogy for a Fallen Leader (Yitzak Rabin)
Noa Ben Artzi-Pelossof 882

Workplace Writing
Business Letter and Memorandum 25
Instructions and Warranty 227
Aquarium of the Pacific 671

Other Media
from **View From the Summit**
Sir Edmund Hillary 30
Egyptology Resources 590
Mali (Atlas entry)
Dorling Kindersley 1076

EPICS, LEGENDS, AND MYTHS
Damon and Pythias
Retold by William F. Russell 109
The Orphan Boy and the Elk Dog
Native American (Blackfeet) 484
from **Don Quixote**
Miguel de Cervantes 1006
Morte d'Arthur
Alfred, Lord Tennyson 1020
Arthur Becomes King of Britain
from **The Once and Future King**
T. H. White 1030
Rama's Initiation *from* **the Ramayana**
R. K. Narayan 1052
from **Sundiata: An Epic of Old Mali**
D. T. Niane 1064

LITERATURE FROM AROUND THE WORLD

The Americas

from A Walk to the Jetty from Annie John
Jamaica Kincaid (Antigua) 70
Fear
Gabriela Mistral (Chile). 95
The street
Octavio Paz (Mexico) 96
The Censors
Luisa Valenzuela (Argentina) 641
Work That Counts
Ernesto Ruelas Inzunza (Mexico) 753
In Flanders Fields
John McCrae (Canada) 938

Eastern Europe

The Bridegroom
Alexander Pushkin (Russia) 59
How Much Land Does a Man Need?
Leo Tolstoy (Russia) 137
A Man
Nina Cassian (Romania). 267
from Speak, Memory
Vladimir Nabokov (Russia). 342
The Bridge
Leopold Staff (Poland) 366
I Am Not One of Those Who Left the Land
Anna Akhmatova (Russia) 368
Speech During the Invasion of Constantinople
Empress Theodora (Byzantine Empire). 369
Before the Law
Franz Kafka (Czechoslovakia) 404
A Storm in the Mountains • from Nobel Lecture
Alexander Solzhenitsyn (Russia) 512, 683
A Problem
Anton Chekhov (Russia). 596
Keep Memory Alive
Elie Wiesel (Romania). 687
Antigone
Sophocles (Ancient Greece) 772
Some Like Poetry
Wisława Szymborska (Poland) 976

Western Europe

Two Friends
Guy de Maupassant (France) 102
Damon and Pythias
Classic Greek Myth (Ancient Greece) 109
from My Left Foot
Christy Brown (Ireland). 168
How to React to Familiar Faces
Umberto Eco (Italy). 457
In the Orchard
Henrik Ibsen (Norway) 513

The Garden of Stubborn Cats
Italo Calvino (Italy) 621
The Princess and All the Kingdom
Pär Lagerkvist (Sweden). 638
The Stolen Child
William Butler Yeats (Ireland) 928
The Guitar
Federico García Lorca (Spain). 972
from Don Quixote
Miguel de Cervantes (Spain) 1006

Africa

Civil Peace
Chinua Achebe (Nigeria) 44
Africa
David Diop (Senegal). 216
Old Song
Traditional (West Africa). 217
Through the Tunnel
Doris Lessing (South Africa) 242
from Sundiata
D. T. Niane, Translator (Mali) 1064

Asia

from The Dream Comes True
Tenzing Norgay (Nepal) 39
from The Analects
Confucius (Ancient China). 220
All
Bei Dao (China). 218
Also All
Shu Ting (China) 219
Like the Sun • from the Ramayana
R. K. Narayan (India) 280, 1052
The Cabuliwallah
Rabindranath Tagore (India) 318
Thoughts of Hanoi
Nguyen Thi Vinh (Vietnam). 398
Jade Flower Palace
Tu Fu (China) 970
The Moon at the Fortified Pass
Li Po (China). 971
Tanka
Ki Tsurayuki; Priest Jakuren (Japan). 988
Haiku
Matsuo Bashō; Kobayashi Issa (Japan) 989

The South Pacific and the Middle East

The Apple Tree
Katherine Mansfield (New Zealand). 206
Pride
Dahlia Ravikovitch (Israel) 366
A Pace Like That
Yehuda Amichai (Israel) 951

COMPARING LITERARY WORKS

Comparing Author's Perspective
from View From the Summit
Sir Edmund Hillary 30
from Into Thin Air
Jon Krakauer. 37
The Dream Comes True *from* The Tiger of the Snows
Tenzing Norgay with James Ramsey Ullman 39

Comparing Theme
The Monkey's Paw
W. W. Jacobs 50
The Bridegroom
Alexander Pushkin 59

Comparing Sensory Language
Spring and All
William Carlos Williams 94
Fear
Gabriela Mistral. 95
The street
Octavio Paz 96

Comparing Universal Theme
Two Friends
Guy de Maupassant 102
Damon and Pythias
Classic Greek Myth. 109

Comparing Theme
Success is counted sweetest
Emily Dickinson. 158
I dwell in Possibility—
Emily Dickinson. 159
Uncoiling
Pat Mora. 160
Columbus Dying
Vassar Miller. 162

Comparing Imagery
After Apple-Picking
Robert Frost. 196
Mowing
Robert Frost. 198
Style
Maya Angelou. 199

Comparing Universal Theme
Africa
David Diop. 216
Old Song
Traditional 217
All
Bei Dao. 218
Also All
Shu Ting. 219

from The Analects
Confucius 220

Comparing Musical Devices
Conscientious Objector
Edna St. Vincent Millay 266
A Man
Nina Cassian 267
The Weary Blues
Langston Hughes 268
Jazz Fantasia
Carl Sandburg 270

Comparing Theme
Like the Sun
R. K. Narayan. 280
Tell all the Truth but tell it slant—
Emily Dickinson. 284

Comparing Surprise Endings
Hearts and Hands
O. Henry. 290
The Fish
Elizabeth Bishop 293

Comparing Writer's Purpose
from Desert Exile: The Uprooting of a Japanese-
American Family
Yoshiko Uchida 300
Speech on Japanese American Internment
Gerald Ford 308

Comparing Speaker
The Bridge
Leopold Staff. 366
The Old Stoic
Emily Brontë 367
I Am Not One of Those Who Left the Land
Anna Akhmatova. 368
Speech During the Invasion of Constantinople
Empress Theodora 369

Comparing Personification
Thoughts of Hanoi
Nguyen Thi Vinh. 398
Auto Wreck
Karl Shapiro 401
Pride
Dahlia Ravikovitch. 402
Before the Law
Franz Kafka. 404

Comparing Author's Attitude
How to React to Familiar Faces
Umberto Eco 456
The Bean Eaters
Gwendolyn Brooks 458

Comparing Writer's Purpose
A Picture From the Past: Emily Dickinson
Reynolds Price 464
What Makes a Degas a Degas?
Richard Mühlberger 466

Comparing Narrator/Speaker
A Storm in the Mountains
Alexander Solzhenitsyn 512
In the Orchard
Henrik Ibsen 513
A Tree Telling of Orpheus
Denise Levertov 514

Comparing Theme
A Problem
Anton Chekhov 596
Luck
Mark Twain 604

Comparing Irony
There Will Come Soft Rains
Ray Bradbury 614
The Garden of Stubborn Cats
Italo Calvino 621

Comparing Theme
The Princess and All the Kingdom
Pär Lagerkvist 638
The Censors
Luisa Valenzuela 641

Comparing Personal Experiences
from **The Way to Rainy Mountain**
N. Scott Momaday 676
from **Nobel Lecture**
Alexander Solzhenitsyn 683
Keep Memory Alive
Elie Wiesel 687

Comparing Autobiography/Biography
A Child's Christmas in Wales
Dylan Thomas 694
Marian Anderson: Famous Concert Singer
Langston Hughes 702

Comparing Writer's Perspective
Star Wars—A Trip to a Far Galaxy
That's Fun and Funny . . .
Vincent Canby 734
Star Wars: Breakthrough Film
Still Has the Force
Roger Ebert 737

Comparing Technical Articles
Imitating Nature's Mineral Artistry
Paul O'Neil 748
Work That Counts
Ernesto Ruelas Inzunza 753

Comparing Musical Devices
In Flanders Fields
John McCrae 938

The Kraken
Alfred, Lord Tennyson 939
Meeting at Night
Robert Browning 940
Reapers
Jean Toomer 941
Prayer of First Dancers
Native American (Navajo) 942

Comparing Figurative Language
The Wind—tapped like a tired Man
Emily Dickinson 950
A Pace Like That
Yehuda Amichai 951
Metaphor
Eve Merriam 952
Right Hand
Philip Fried 954

Comparing Plot
La Belle Dame sans Merci
John Keats 960
Danny Deever
Rudyard Kipling 963

Comparing Imagery
Jade Flower Palace
Tu Fu 970
The Moon at the Fortified Pass
Li Po 971
The Guitar
Federico García Lorca 972
What Are Friends For
Rosellen Brown 974
Making a Fist
Naomi Shihab Nye 975
Some Like Poetry
Wisława Szymborska 976

Comparing Poetic Forms
The Waking
Theodore Roethke 986
Tanka
Ki Tsurayuki 988
Tanka
Priest Jakuren 988
Haiku
Matsuo Bashō 989
Haiku
Kobayashi Issa 989
Sonnet 18
William Shakespeare 990

Comparing Dynamic Characters
Morte d'Arthur
Alfred, Lord Tennyson 1020
Arthur Becomes King of Britain
from **The Once and Future King**
T. H. White 1030

READING INFORMATIONAL MATERIALS

	Business Letter and Memorandum .	Business Documents	25
	Instructions and Warranty	Product Information	227
Ann Douglas	**Feel the City's Pulse? It's Be-bop, Man!**	Newspaper Article	275
Charles Lave	**65-MPH Speed Limit Is Saving Lives** .	Persuasive Article	411
The Nature Company	**Lightning and Thunder**	Article	523
	Egyptology Resources	Web Site	591
	Aquarium of the Pacific	Brochure	671
Ben Brantley	**Private Horror Made Public** . .	Arts-and-Leisure Articles	813
Ben Brantley	**After 1,500 Years, Colosseum Reopens for Shows** . .		814
Thomas A. Hill	**The History of the Guitar**	Historical Essay	981
Dorling Kindersley World Reference Atlas	**Mali**	Reference Materials	1077

CONNECTIONS

Literature and Geography

| Jon Krakauer | *from* **Into Thin Air** . . . . | Nonfiction | 37 |

Literature and Media

| | **Daniel Day-Lewis Plays Christy Brown** . . . . | | 178 |
| Eric P. Nash | **Star Wars: An Epic for Today** . . . . . . | Nonfiction | 1046 |

Literature and History

David Guterson	*from* **Snow Falling on Cedars**	Novel	312
Tim O'Brien	*from* **Going After Cacciato**	Novel	414
Noa Ben Artzi-Pelosoff	**Eulogy for a Fallen Leader (Yitzhak Rabin)** . . .	Speech	882

Literature and Humanities

| Frank McCourt | *from* **Angela's Ashes** . . . . | Autobiography | 474 |

Literature and Technology

| Hans Enzensberger | *from* **The Future of Luxury** . . . . | Nonfiction | 632 |

Literature and Art

| | **The Life and Times of Mary Cassatt** . . . . | | 730 |

Literature and Music

| Harry and Sandy Chapin | **Cat's in the Cradle** . . . . | Song Lyrics | 934 |

HOW TO READ LITERATURE

Use Literal Comprehension Strategies 3
Use Interactive Reading Strategies 125
Use Interactive Reading Strategies 239
Use Strategies for Reading Critically. 339
Use Strategies for Reading Fiction 427
Use Strategies for Constructing Meaning 537

Use Strategies for Reading Nonfiction 657
Use Strategies for Reading Drama 767
Use Strategies for Reading Poetry. 925
Use Strategies for Reading Epics
     and Legends. 1003

WRITING WORKSHOPS

Narration: Autobiographical Narrative 116

Exposition: How-to Essay 230

Persuasion: Persuasive Essay 330

Narration: Reflective Essay 418

Research Writing. 526

Narration: Short Story 648

Exposition: Comparison-and-Contrast Essay. . . 758

Response to Literature. 916

Writing for Assessment 994

Letter to the Editor 1080

LISTENING AND SPEAKING WORKSHOPS

Delivering a Narrative 120

Descriptive Presentations 234

Delivering Persuasive Arguments 334

Comparing Media Coverage 422

Analyzing Types of Arguments. 532

Effective Listening 652

Analyze a Media Presentation 762

Oral Responses to Literature 920

Multimedia Presentation 998

Interviewing Techniques 1084

ASSESSMENT WORKSHOPS

Context Clues and Word Meanings 121

Facts and Details 235

Stated and Implied Main Ideas 335

Cause and Effect. 423

Graphic Aids 533

Forms of Propaganda 653

Comparing and Contrasting. 763

Characteristics of Text 921

Analyzing an Author's Meaning 999

Organization 1085

Learn About Literature

Objectives

1. To identify the purposes and characteristics of the major literary genres
2. To apply an in-depth understanding of genre as an aid to reading comprehension

How to Use Learn About Literature

"Learn About Literature" pages help students become better readers by acquainting them with the conventions of the major literary genres. Each page contains definitions, sample passages, and comprehension questions about the major genres. These elements will help students build an in-depth understanding of genre that will improve their reading comprehension skills.

Literary Genres

Short Story and Nonfiction

- Have students read the definition of a short story and the accompanying excerpt. Then, ask them to respond to the question.
  Answer: Based on his envious references to Raghu and other "older, bigger, luckier children," Ravi seems to be a slight young boy, not yet as successful at games as he would like to be.

- Then, have students read the definition of nonfiction and respond to the question that follows.
  Answer: Students may say that the author's purpose is to demonstrate his teamwork with a fellow climber (Tenzing), in attacking the challenges of a mountain.

Forms of Literature

Short Story • Nonfiction • Poetry • Drama • Folk Literature

Just as there are different kinds of paintings, such as watercolors or oils, so too are there different types of literature. Each is called a genre, and each has its own distinct characteristics. On these pages, you will find explanations and examples of each genre. They will aid you in understanding and appreciating the literature in this anthology.

Short Story

A **short story** is a brief work of fiction. Usually in a short story, one main character faces a conflict that is resolved in the plot. Most short stories also convey a theme, or message about life. A short story is much shorter than a novel and, therefore, must convey its theme in far fewer words.

● **What do you learn about the character of Ravi in this passage from a short story?**

Ravi sat back on the harsh edge of the tub, deciding to hold out a bit longer. What fun if they were all found and caught—he alone left unconquered! He had never known that sensation. . . . To defeat Raghu—that hirsute, hoarse-voiced football champion—and to be the winner in a circle of older, bigger, luckier children—that would be thrilling beyond imagination.

FROM "GAMES AT TWILIGHT," ANITA DESAI, PAGE 352

Nonfiction

Nonfiction is writing that tells about real people, places, objects, events, and ideas. The nonfiction selections in this textbook include essays, biographies, autobiographies, and technical articles. All discuss the real world, as opposed to an imaginary one. The purpose of a nonfiction article may be to convey and explain information, to convince readers to accept a certain idea or an opinion, or simply to entertain and amuse readers.

● **What do you sense is the author's purpose in this nonfiction article?**

Above our camp was a great steep bulge of snow and, as my feet were still cold, I waved Tenzing on to take the lead. Surging on with impressive strength, he ploughed a knee-deep track upward and I was happy to follow behind. We reached the top of the bulge at 28,000 feet and, as my feet were now warmer, I took over the lead. Towering over our heads was the South Summit and running along from it to the right were the great menacing cornices overhanging the Kangshung Face.

FROM "VIEW FROM THE SUMMIT," SIR EDMUND HILLARY, PAGE 30

✳ ENRICHMENT: Literature Library

To extend students' understanding of different genres, use titles in the **Prentice Hall Literature Library**. This collection includes novels, plays, and special literature anthologies, each with its own study guide.

Novels
Animal Farm
Bless Me, Ultima
The Brothers Karamazov
Candide
The Hound of the Baskervilles
Lord of the Flies
The Red Badge of Courage
The Road to Memphis

Siddhartha
Silas Marner
Things Fall Apart
Waiting for the Rain

Play
Tartuffe

Special Anthologies
African American Literature
Appalachian Writers
Asian American Literature
Authors In Depth, Platinum Level
Latino Literature
Literature From Around the World

"The sole substitute for an experience which we have not our-selves lived through is art and literature."

—Alexander Solzhenitsyn

Poetry

Poetry is literature that appears in verse form. Many poems have a regular rhythm and, possibly, a rhyme scheme. Most poems use highly concise, musical, and powerful language to tell a story or to convey a single idea or an image.

● How do the poetry lines at right differ in form from the passages from "Games at Twilight" and "View From the Summit" on page xxvi?

I dwell in Possibility—
A fairer House than Prose—
More numerous of Windows—
Superior—for Doors—

FROM "I DWELL IN POSSIBILITY—," EMILY DICKINSON, PAGE 159

Drama

Drama is written to be performed by actors. The script consists of dialogue and monologue—the words the actors say—plus stage directions, which comment on how and where the action should occur.

● How does the appearance of this dramatic text differ from the appearance of a short story?

CREON. [*Slowly, dangerously*] And you, Antigone,
You with your head hanging,—do you confess this thing?
ANTIGONE. I do. I deny nothing.
CREON. [*To* SENTRY] You may go.
[*Exit* SENTRY.]

FROM ANTIGONE, SOPHOCLES, PAGE 772

Folk Literature

Folk literature is literature of a specific people or culture that is passed down orally from one generation to the next. Folk literature includes myths, folk tales, legends, and fables. Such stories express the hopes, fears, loves, dreams, and values of the people who tell them and pass them on.

● How does this passage from a myth suggest that the story may be a part of folk literature?

"I have come to find the mysterious Elk Dog."

"Ah, there I cannot help you," said the man, who was the spirit of the pond. "But if you travel further south, four-times-four days, you might chance upon a bigger lake and there meet one of my uncles. Possibly he might talk to you; then again, he might not. That's all I can tell you."

Long Arrow thanked the man, who went down to the bottom of the pond, where he lived.

FROM "THE ORPHAN BOY AND THE ELK DOG," NATIVE AMERICAN (BLACKFEET), PAGE 484.

Forms of Literature ◆ IN1

CUSTOMIZE INSTRUCTION FOR UNIVERSAL ACCESS

For Less Proficient Readers	For English Learners	For Advanced Readers
Ask students to find in this book an example of folk literature, a short story, a nonfiction article, and a poem. Then, have them point out the structural elements of each selection that reveal its genre.	Ask students to bring to class examples of each genre that they have encountered in their home language. Have them point out the key genre characteristics of each.	Have students read the first six pages of "Games at Twilight," pp. 352–357, to add more details to what they know about the story's characters, setting, and plot.

Discuss the Quotation

- Born in the Soviet Union, Alexander Solzhenitsyn found writing a hazardous undertaking. He was arrested while serving in front-line combat during World War II for having written disrespectfully of Joseph Stalin in letters to a friend. During his subsequent years of prison camp, exile, and illness, Solzhenitsyn began to write—but in secret, of course.

- Have students read Solzhenitsyn's quotation. Ask them whether they agree that art and literature are the "sole substitutes" for experiences not personally lived through.
  Possible response: Students may agree that art and literature allow viewers and readers a vicarious understanding of worlds and events beyond their own lives.

Literary Genres
Poetry, Drama, and Folk Literature

- Have students read the definition of poetry, and ask them to respond to the question.
  Answer: Students may note that the words are laid out in rhythmic lines that are punctuated with dashes, and that certain words are capitalized. Some students may sense that words themselves are used differently than in the passages on p. xxvi; the language is figurative rather than literal.

- Now, draw students' attention to the definition of drama, and have students respond to the accompanying question.
  Answer: Students may point out differences in format. Speakers' names appear in bold type; actions—stage directions—are printed in italic and bracketed.

- Finally, have students read the definition of folk literature and answer the question.
  Answer: The mixture of the mundane and the extraordinary, references to a mysterious Elk Dog, and a matter-of-fact conversation with a being that lives in the bottom of a pond all suggest elements of folk literature.

Short Stories

- Have a volunteer read aloud the introduction to short stories. Then, ask students to explain how short stories allow them to "travel" to different worlds
  Possible response: Short stories provide encounters with people and places readers might not otherwise get to know or visit.

- Have students work in pairs to write definitions of plot, characters, setting, point of view, and theme based on their prior knowledge. Then, as they read, have students compare their own definitions to those given in the book.

Elements of a Short Story
Plot

- Read the definition of plot. Then, have students copy the plot diagram into their notebooks. As a class, annotate the diagram by writing a short definition of each plot element.

- Have students answer the question about "The Masque of the Red Death," and then discuss their answers.
  Answer: The opening presents an immediate conflict with its description of a fatal contagion that is ravaging the country. The disease is characterized in some way by blood.

Elements of a Short Story
Characters

- After students read the definition of characters, have them explain in their own words the difference between flat and round, and static and dynamic characters. Ask them to name an example of each from a story they have read in the past, and to support their answers with evidence.

- Then, have students answer the question about Sasha from "A Problem."
  Answer: Sasha is a round character because he is "meek," "open," and "candid," yet capable of cashing a false promissory note.

Short Stories
Plot • Characters • Setting • Point of View • Theme

Short stories allow you to travel to fictional places, to meet interesting and unusual people, and to get involved with the problems the characters face. In this textbook, you will read a number of short stories. No two will be identical, although all the short stories will share certain characteristics and will conform to a common structure.

Plot

The **plot** of a short story is its sequence of events. It involves both characters and a conflict or problem. The plot begins with an exposition that introduces the characters, setting, and basic story. The action rises as the characters try to resolve the problem. Tension increases as events lead to a climax, or high point of interest or suspense. The climax is followed by falling action, leading to the resolution of the conflict.

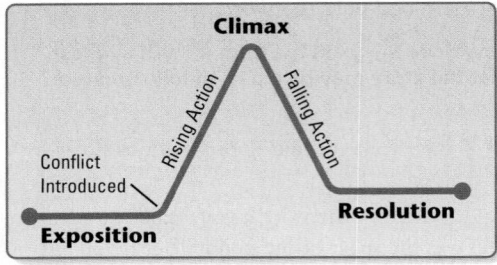

● **What plot details do you learn from the opening of this short story?**

The "Red Death" had long devastated the country. No pestilence had ever been so fatal, or so hideous. Blood was its Avatar and its seal—the redness and the horror of blood.

FROM "THE MASQUE OF THE RED DEATH," EDGAR ALLAN POE, PAGE 82

Characters

The **characters** in a short story are the people or animals that participate in the action. They may be round or flat, dynamic or static.
- A *round character* possesses many different personality traits.
- A *flat character* has only one basic trait.
- A *dynamic character* changes in a significant way by the end of the story.
- A *static character* remains the same, no matter what he or she experiences. The story's main character, or protagonist, is most often a round and dynamic character.

● **What details in the following passage indicate the type of character that Sasha is?**

Sasha Uskov, the young man of twenty-five who was the cause of all the commotion, had arrived some time before, and by the advice of kind-hearted Ivan Markovitch, his uncle, who was taking his part, he sat meekly in the hall by the door leading to the study, and prepared himself to make an open, candid explanation.

. . . The subject under discussion was an exceedingly disagreeable and delicate one. Sasha Uskov had cashed at one of the banks a false promissory note. . . .

FROM "A PROBLEM," ANTON CHEKHOV, PAGE 596

Setting

The **setting** of a story is the time and place of the action. Time can include not only the historical period—past, present, or future—but also a specific year, season, or time of day. Place may involve not only the geographical place—a region, country, state, town—but also the social, economic, or cultural environment.

◉ **What details in this passage help you identify the setting of the story?**

There were two orchards belonging to the old house. One, that we called the "wild" orchard, lay beyond the vegetable garden; it was planted with bitter cherries and damsons and transparent yellow plums. . . . But the other orchard, far away and hidden from the house, lay at the foot of a little hill and stretched right over to the edge of the paddocks—to the clumps of wattles bobbing yellow in the bright sun and the blue gums with their streaming sickle-shaped leaves. There, under the fruit trees, the grass grew so thick and coarse that it tangled and knotted in your shoes as you walked. . . .

FROM "THE APPLE TREE," KATHERINE MANSFIELD, PAGE 206

Point of View

The **point of view** in a story is the vantage point from which the story is told. In *first-person narration*, the storyteller is a character in the action. In *third-person narration*, the storyteller only reports events and does not participate in the action.

◉ **How does this passage indicate the point of view of the story from which it is taken?**

She picked herself up as best she could and trudged on again. It seemed to her that she had been walking for hours.

FROM "THE WIDOW AND THE PARROT," VIRGINIA WOOLF, PAGE 430

Theme

The **theme** of a short story is the key message or insight into life that it reveals. In some stories, theme is stated directly. In most stories, however, theme is only suggested or implied.

◉ **What might be a theme of this story, based on the following passage?**

"Do you not understand that one can fight, can conquer, without asking any reward other than one's happiness—not fame and gold, not land and power on earth? Well, then, I have conquered but ask for nothing, only to live happily with what, for me, is the only thing of value in life."

FROM "THE PRINCESS AND ALL THE KINGDOM," PÄR LAGERKVIST, PAGE 638

Short Stories ◆ IN3

Nonfiction

- Read the introduction to nonfiction to students, and then ask them which forms of nonfiction they read most frequently and why they do so.
- If possible, bring to class an assortment of articles, essays, journals, and biographical and autobiographical specimens. Have students work in small groups to categorize each item according to its form.

Forms of Nonfiction
Autobiography

- Have a volunteer read the definition of an autobiography, and then ask students to give examples of autobiographies they have read.
- Ask students to read the passage from "A Child's Christmas in Wales" and respond to the accompanying question.
  Answer: Students may agree that Thomas's description of his family's activities is intended to entertain and amuse readers.

Forms of Nonfiction
Biography

- Have students read the definition of biography. In distinguishing between biography and autobiography, students might find it helpful to invoke personal pronouns: An autobiography is an "I" account; a biography is a "he" or "she" account of a person's life.
- Ask students to read the passage from "Marian Anderson: Famous Concert Singer" and answer the accompanying question.
  Possible response: Students may perceive that the author chose to write about Marian Anderson to inspire readers.

Nonfiction

Autobiography • Biography • Essays • Informational Texts

Nonfiction is prose writing that presents and explains ideas or that tells about real people. Forms of nonfiction include essays, newspaper and magazine articles, journals, technical articles, biographies, and autobiographies. In this textbook, you will read a variety of nonfiction pieces, and you will have the chance to see similarities and differences among them.

Autobiography

An **autobiography** is nonfiction in which a person tells his or her own life story. An autobiography may tell about the person's whole life or only part of it. The author's purpose may be to explain his or her values, to teach lessons about life, to entertain or amuse readers, or any combination of these.

● What does this passage from Dylan Thomas's autobiography suggest about his purpose for writing?

> Always on Christmas night there was music. An uncle played the fiddle, a cousin sang "Cherry Ripe," and another uncle sang "Drake's Drum." It was very warm in the little house. Auntie Hannah, who had got on to the parsnip wine, sang a song about Bleeding Hearts and Death, and then another in which she said her heart was like a Bird's Nest; and then everybody laughed again; and then I went to bed.
> FROM "A CHILD'S CHRISTMAS IN WALES," DYLAN THOMAS, PAGE 694

Biography

A **biography** is a nonfiction work in which a writer tells the life story of another person. Biographies have been written about many famous historical and contemporary people, but they can be written about relatively unknown people, too. As with autobiography, biography is factual and may be written to express a person's values, to teach lessons about life, or to entertain or inspire readers. A biography often emphasizes the causes and effects of the subject's actions.

● Based on this passage, why do you think the author chose to write a biography of his subject?

> Sure enough, Marian Anderson did become a great success in the Scandinavian countries, where she learned to sing in both Finnish and Swedish, and her first concert tour of Europe became a critical triumph.
> FROM "MARIAN ANDERSON: FAMOUS CONCERT SINGER," LANGSTON HUGHES, PAGE 702

> *"'Tis strange—but true; for truth is always strange; Stranger than fiction."*
> —Lord Byron

Essays

An **essay** is a short nonfiction work about a particular subject. It contains a main idea that is supported with examples, facts, statistics, or anecdotes.

- A **descriptive essay** shows how something looks, feels, smells, sounds, or tastes.
- An **expository essay** gives information, discusses ideas, or explains a process.
- A **persuasive essay** tries to convince readers to do something or to accept the writer's point of view.
- A **reflective essay** presents the writer's reflections, or thoughts, on a topic of personal importance.
- A **visual essay** combines text with photographs, fine art, illustrations, charts, or diagrams to communicate an idea or a message.

● **What does this passage suggest about the type of essay from which it comes?**

It's summer. We had some deep spring sunshine about a month ago, in a drought; the nights were cold. It's been gray sporadically, but not oppressively, and rainy for a week, and I would think: When is the real hot stuff coming, the mind-melting weeding weather? It was rainy again this morning, the same spring rain, and then this afternoon a different rain came: a pounding, three-minute shower. And when it was over, the cloud dissolved to haze.

FROM "FLOOD," ANNIE DILLARD, PAGE 712

Informational Texts

In contrast to other forms of literature meant to entertain or inspire, **informational texts** are written to provide knowledge that guides and educates. Informational texts include magazine and newspaper articles on current topics, instructional manuals, technical articles, and workplace writing, such as business letters, memos, and agendas.

Most informational texts are written in objective language, using elaboration and support to clarify the writer's main ideas.

● **Based on this opening from a technical article, how might the text educate you about synthetic gems?**

In laboratories and factories, technicians can now create conditions of heat and chemical activity similar to those that give birth to gemstones deep within the earth. The result is synthetic gems, identical to their natural counterparts in chemistry and crystalline structure, and so similar in appearance that a microscope is often needed to tell them apart.

FROM "IMITATING NATURE'S MINERAL ARTISTRY," PAUL O'NEIL, PAGE 748

Nonfiction ◆ IN5

Drama

- Read the introduction to drama to students, emphasizing the importance of imagining a performance rather than simply reading a text.

- Ask students to share any experiences they have had in seeing a play performed or participating in a production.

Elements of Drama
Types of Plays

- Have a volunteer read the descriptions of the various types of plays, and then ask students to give examples of comedies, tragedies, and dramas they have read or seen.

- Ask students to read the passage from *The Tragedy of Julius Caesar* and respond to the accompanying question.
  Answer: The title is a giveaway, of course, but the lethal consequence of the scene also indicates that *Julius Caesar* is a tragedy.

Elements of Drama
Dialogue and Monologue

- Have students read the definitions of dialogue and monologue.

- Ask students to read the passage from *Antigone* and answer the accompanying question.
  Possible response: Students may infer that Antigone is fearless and determined and that Ismene is timid and cautious.

Drama

Types of Plays • Dialogue and Monologue •
Stage Directions • Plot and Conflict

Drama is writing that is meant to be performed by actors for an audience. The script consists of dialogue—the words the actors say—plus stage directions, which are comments on how and where the actors move and speak. As you read drama, you "set the stage" in your own mind, using your imagination to visualize the scenery, lighting, costumes, and actors.

Types of Plays

Not all plays are the same in their tone, mood, or theme. A **comedy** is a humorous play with a happy ending. A **tragedy** is a play in which a hero suffers a major downfall. A **drama** is also a serious play, although the consequences are not necessarily as dire as those in a tragedy.

◉ **From what type of play do you imagine this passage comes? Why?**

> **C**INNA. O Caesar—
> **CAESAR.**   Hence! Wilt thou lift up Olympus?
> **DECIUS.** Great Caesar—
> **CAESAR.**   Doth not Brutus bootless kneel?
> **CASCA.** Speak hands for me!
>   [*They stab* CAESAR.]
> **CAESAR.** *Et tu, Brutè?* Then fall, Caesar.   [*Dies*]
> FROM THE TRAGEDY OF JULIUS CAESAR, WILLIAM SHAKESPEARE, PAGE 822

Dialogue and Monologue

Dialogue in a play is conversation between two or more characters. A **monologue** is a lengthy speech that one character addresses to others on stage. The purposes of both dialogue and monologue are to reveal character traits and to advance the action of the story.

◉ **What do you learn about the speakers in this brief piece of dialogue?**

> **I**SMENE. Antigone, you are mad! What could I possibly do?
> **ANTIGONE.** You must decide whether you will help me or not.
> **ISMENE.** I do not understand you. Help you in what?
> **ANTIGONE.** Ismene, I am going to bury him. Will you come?
> **ISMENE.** Bury him! You have just said the new law forbids it.
> **ANTIGONE.** He is my brother. And he is your brother, too.
> **ISMENE.** But think of the danger! Think what Creon will do!
> FROM <u>ANTIGONE</u>, SOPHOCLES, PAGE 772

Stage Directions

Stage directions are the instructions for performing a play and the descriptions of settings, characters, and actions. When you read drama, the stage directions help you visualize the play. You can imagine where the scenery should be and how the actors are to move by following stage directions that indicate downstage, upstage, left, and right.

Wings (offstage)	Upstage Right	Upstage Center	Upstage Left	Wings (offstage)
	Right	Center	Left	
	Downstage Right	Downstage Center	Downstage Left	

Curtain Line

The Stage

Audience

● **How do these stage directions help you picture the setting of the play?**

> **S**cene. *Before the palace of* CREON, *King of Thebes. A central double door, and two lateral doors. A platform extends the length of the facade, and from this platform three steps lead down into the "orchestra," or chorus-ground.*
> FROM ANTIGONE, SOPHOCLES, PAGE 772

Plot and Conflict

A play, like a short story, contains a **plot,** or series of events, involving a **conflict** that one or more characters face. The conflict may be introduced early in the play, perhaps in the opening scene. Tension builds to the climax, and by the final scene of the play, the conflict has been resolved, either happily or unhappily. The resolution of the conflict reveals the play's theme, or general insight about life.

● **How does the following dialogue show the conflict between the characters?**

> **C**ASSIUS. Brutus, bait not me;
> I'll not endure it. You forget yourself
> To hedge me in. I am a soldier, I,
> Older in practice, abler than yourself
> To make conditions.
> **BRUTUS.**   Go to! You are not, Cassius.
> **CASSIUS.** I am.
> **BRUTUS.** I say you are not.
> **CASSIUS.** Urge me no more, I shall forget myself; Have mind upon your health; tempt me no farther.
> **BRUTUS.** Away, slight man!
> FROM THE TRAGEDY OF JULIUS CAESAR, WILLIAM SHAKESPEARE, PAGE 822

Discuss the Quotation

- Tell students that Shakespeare often included scenes from plays and discussions about the craft of acting within the context of his plays. For example, the amateur production of a play provides comic byplay in *A Midsummer Night's Dream.*

- Discuss the quotation with students. One possible meaning of the line is that one should follow through an action to its final consequences. Another meaning is that a play should be played, that is, performed. Point out that Shakespeare never meant his plays to be read from a book, but to be performed from a stage.

Elements of Drama
Stage Directions

- Read the explanation of stage directions. Demonstrate downstage and upstage by moving about the front of the classroom as if it were a stage.

- Have students read the passage from *Antigone.* Work as a class to answer the question by using the chalkboard to sketch the scene described in the stage directions.

Elements of Drama
Plot and Conflict

- After students read the definitions of plot and conflict, note that they should be familiar with these concepts from their experiences with short stories.

- Ask students to read the passage from *The Tragedy of Julius Caesar* and answer the question.
  Answer: Students should recognize that the exclamations, denials, and ultimatums in this passage demonstrate the conflict between Cassius and Brutus.

Poetry

- Read the introduction to poetry to students, emphasizing the importance of sound and structure.
- To give students a sense of the essential characteristics of poetry, read a lyric poem of your own choosing to the class or play a poem selected from the **Listening to Literature** Audiocassettes or Audio CDs in the Teaching Resources.

Elements of Poetry
Types of Poetry

- Have students read the definitions of the different types of poetry, and then ask them to give examples of narrative, lyric, and dramatic poems they have read.
- Ask students to read the passage from "Jade Flower Palace" and respond to the accompanying question.
  Answer: Students may cite the speaker's detailed description of the palace he or she observes.

Elements of Poetry
Poetic Form

- Have students read the definition of poetic form. If possible, bring to class examples of some of the various forms poems can take.
- Ask students to read the passage from "Also All" and answer the accompanying question.
  Possible response: Students may note that the poet achieves a strong dramatic emphasis by inserting single lines of text between the stanzas.

Poetry

Types of Poetry • Poetic Form • Rhythm and Rhyme • Figurative Language

Poetry is writing that combines language, images, and sounds to create a special emotional effect. A poem's sound and structure are different from that of prose, the writing you find in short stories and nonfiction. Poetry is arranged in lines and stanzas, and its language is more visual and musical than prose is. A story speaks to readers, but a poem sings to them.

Types of Poetry

There are many different types of poems:
- A **narrative poem**, like a short story, tells a story that includes a plot, characters, and a setting.
- A **lyric poem** expresses the observations and feelings of a speaker in a musical way.
- A **dramatic poem** employs the techniques of drama in the form of a monologue for one speaker or dramatic dialogue for two or more speakers.

● **What details in this passage suggest that it is from a lyric poem?**

The stream swirls. The wind moans in
The pines. Gray rats scurry over
Broken tiles. What prince, long ago,
Built this palace, standing in
Ruins beside the cliffs? There are
Green ghost fires in the black rooms.
FROM "JADE FLOWER PALACE," TU FU, PAGE 970

Poetic Form

Poetic form refers to the way the lines of a poem are shaped and arranged. Often, a poet groups lines into formal units called *stanzas*. A stanza may have any number of lines. Poetic form affects the way the poem is read aloud and, possibly, the message that the poem conveys.

● **Why do you think these stanzas are separated by single lines of text?**

Not all trees are felled by storms.
Not every seed finds barren soil.
Not all the wings of dream are broken,
nor is all affection doomed
to wither in a desolate heart.

No, not all is as you say.

Not all flames consume themselves,
shedding no light on other lives.
Not all stars announce the night
and never dawn. Not every song
will drift past every ear and heart.

No, not all is as you say.
FROM "ALSO ALL," SHU TING, PAGE 219

"It should be of the pleasure of a poem itself to tell how it can."

—Robert Frost

Rhythm and Rhyme

Rhythm in a poem is the pattern of stressed (´) and unstressed (˘) syllables in each line. For example:

˘   ´ ˘   ´   ˘   ´   ˘   ´   ˘   ´
In Flanders fields the poppies blow . . .

Rhyme in a poem is the repetition of sounds at the ends of words. For example:

In Flanders fields the poppies <u>blow</u>
Between the crosses, row on <u>row</u>, . . .

● **What rhythm and rhyme do you find in this poetry excerpt?**

> S hall I compare thee to a summer's day?
> Thou art more lovely and more temperate:
> Rough winds do shake the darling buds of
>   May,
> And summer's lease hath all too short a date: . . .
>
> FROM SONNET 18, WILLIAM SHAKESPEARE, PAGE 990

Figurative Language

Figurative language is writing or speech that is not meant to be taken literally. It is often used to create vivid impressions by establishing comparisons between dissimilar things. Three frequently used figures of speech are similes, metaphors, and personification.

- **Similes** use *like* or *as* to compare dissimilar things. (Boulders retreat *like* crabs.)
- **Metaphors** speak of one thing as though it were another. (Morning *is* a new sheet of paper.)
- **Personification** gives human characteristics to nonhuman things. (Now begins the cry of the guitar.)

● **What figurative language do you find in this poetry excerpt?**

> T he Wind—tapped like a tired
>   Man—
> And like a Host—"Come in"
> I boldly answered—entered then
> My Residence within
>
> FROM "THE WIND—TAPPED LIKE A TIRED MAN," EMILY DICKINSON, PAGE 950

Discuss the Quotation

- Tell students that Robert Frost used simple, almost conversational language to create some of the most powerful poems in modern American literature.
- Discuss the quotation with students, asking them to consider the possible ways a poem can express pleasure.

Elements of Poetry
Rhythm and Rhyme

- Read the definitions of rhythm and rhyme with the class. Have students read the example lines aloud several times; you may wish to augment these with other lines of your own choosing.
- Have students read the passage from Sonnet 18 and answer the accompanying question.
  Answer: Students should discover that words at the end of every other line rhyme (*abab*), and that the stress is on the second syllable of every pair of syllables. (You may wish to describe this rhythm as *iambic*.)

Elements of Poetry
Figurative Language

- After students read the definitions of similes, metaphors and personification, ask them to devise an example of each on their own. Have volunteers share their examples with the class.
- Ask students to read the passage from "The Wind—tapped like a tired Man" and answer the accompanying question.
  Answer: Students may recognize that "like a tired Man" and "like a Host" are similes. In identifying the wind as a man, the poet is using personification.

Folk Literature

- Read the introduction to folk literature to students, and then ask them to list examples of various types of folk literature they have read.

- Point out to students that one of the incidental characteristics of folk literature is the lack of identifiable authors. Usually, the author is unknown. When authors are attributed to works of folk literature, they may be simply the first to write down works that had long existed in oral tradition.

Forms of Folk Literature

Myth

- Have a volunteer read the definition of myth, and then ask students to give examples of myths with which they are familiar.

- Ask students to read the passage from "Damon and Pythias" and respond to the accompanying question.
  Answer: Students may cite the reference to "the Fates" as suggestive of myth.

Forms of Folk Literature

Legend

- Have students read the definition of legend and ask them to list any legends they recall reading. To help them distinguish between legend and myth, remind them that myths often include gods and goddesses and explanations of natural phenomena. Legends, by contrast, focus on the quests of humans.

- Ask students to read the passage from *The Once and Future King* and answer the accompanying question.
  Possible response: Students may cite the "days of yore" setting involving knights and magicians as characteristic of a legend. (Note, though, that White's retelling employs a modern conversational style.)

Folk Literature

Myth • Legend • Folk Tale • Epic

Not all stories were written down when they were first told. Folk literature comes from generations of peoples or cultures that passed down their favorite tales orally before ever recording them. Folk literature includes myths, legends, folk tales, and epics. Like a family heirloom, folk literature holds special enjoyment for those who benefit from it and then pass it on.

Myth

A **myth** is a fictional tale that explains the interactions of gods and humans. It may also explain causes of natural phenomena, such as tornados or the cycle of the seasons. Myths involve supernatural elements and have little historical truth to the events they describe. Among the most familiar myths today are those of the ancient Greeks and Romans.

● **What details in this passage indicate that it is from a myth?**

And, as the Fates would have it, by a strange turn of events, Pythias was detained far longer in his task than he had imagined. Though he never for a single minute intended to evade the sentence of death to which he had been so unjustly committed, Pythias met with several accidents and unavoidable delays. Now his time was running out and he had yet to overcome the many impediments that had been placed in his path.

FROM "DAMON AND PYTHIAS," WILLIAM F. RUSSELL, PAGE 109

Legend

A **legend** is a widely told story about the past that may or may not have a foundation in fact. Most legends have some basis in history, but the details may have become obscured or lost through centuries of retelling and embellishment. Often, a legend reflects a people's identity or cultural values. It generally emphasizes supernatural elements less than does a myth.

● **What details from this passage indicate that it is from a legend?**

Sir Ector said, "Come now, Merlyn, what's all this about? I don't understand all this a bit."

"I have come to say Goodbye, Sir Ector," said the old magician. "Tomorrow my pupil Kay will be knighted, and the next week my other pupil will go away as his squire. I have outlived my usefulness here, and it is time to go."

"Now, now, don't say that," said Sir Ector. "I think you're a jolly useful chap whatever happens. You just stay and teach me, or be the librarian or something. Don't you leave an old man alone, after the children have flown."

FROM THE ONCE AND FUTURE KING, T. H. WHITE, PAGE 1030

"There is a weird power in a spoken word." —Joseph Conrad

Folk Tale

A **folk tale** is a story composed orally and then passed from person to person by word of mouth. Folk tales originated among people who could neither read nor write. They entertained one another by telling stories aloud, often about heroes, adventure, magic, or romance.

○ **What elements in this passage from a Vietnamese folk tale make it an entertaining story?**

T'am's tears falling in the well
Made the water rise higher.
And from it rose Nâng Tien,
A lovely cloud-dressed fairy.
Her voice was a silver bell
Ringing clear in the moonlight.
"My child, why are you crying?"
"My dear little fish is gone!
He does not come when I call."

FROM "IN THE LAND OF THE SMALL DRAGON: A VIETNAMESE FOLK TALE" BY DANG MANH KHA, PAGE 80, LITERATURE FROM AROUND THE WORLD, PRENTICE HALL LITERATURE LIBRARY

Epic

An **epic** is a long narrative poem about the deeds of gods or heroes in war or in their travels. It has these characteristics:
• Poetic, elevated language
• The incorporation of myth, legend, and history
• The intervention of gods in the affairs of humans
• A serious mood

○ **What characteristics of an epic do you find in this excerpt from the *Ramayana*?**

Viswamithra looked steadily at the King and answered, "Yes. I am here to ask of you a favor. I wish to perform, before the next full moon, a yagna at Sidhasrama. Doubtless you know where it is?"

"I have passed that sacred ground beyond the Ganges many times."

The sage interrupted. "But there are creatures hovering about waiting to disturb every holy undertaking there, who must be overcome in the same manner as one has to conquer the five-fold evils within before one can realize holiness. . . ."

FROM "RAMA'S INITIATION," R. K. NARAYAN, PAGE 1052

Folk Literature ◆ IN11

Discuss the Quotation
• Tell students that Joseph Conrad was born in Poland and didn't begin to learn English until he was in his twenties. Despite his late start, he became one of the major novelists of the English language.
• Discuss the quotation with students, asking them to give examples of their own experience of the power of spoken—as opposed to written—language.

Forms of Folk Literature
Folk Tale
• Read the definition of folk tale with students. Ask them to mention some examples of folk tales they read or heard when they were children.
• Have students read the passage from "In the Land of the Small Dragon" and answer the accompanying question.
  Answer: Students may say that the Vietnamese names and the references to fairies and wishing suggest that it is an entertaining story.

Forms of Folk Literature
Epic
• After students read the definition of an epic, have them name an epic that they have read or know about.
• Ask students to read the passage from the *Ramayana* and answer the question.
  Answer: Students may identify the serious mood, the references to "sacred ground" and "holy undertaking," the legendary references to hovering "creatures," and the elevated language of discourse as being characteristic of an epic.

CUSTOMIZE INSTRUCTION FOR UNIVERSAL ACCESS

For English Learners	For Less Proficient Readers
Have students think of legends, myths, or folk tales from their home cultures. Ask them to describe the plot and characters to the class. Then, have the class seek parallels to legends, myths, or folk tales they know about. Discuss with students why folk stories from around the world share common elements.	To help students identify the setting of a legend, myth, or folk tale, have them keep a list of details related to time, place, and culture as they read. Pause frequently to allow students to share the details they have found. Then, discuss what these details reveal about the time and place in which the story occurs.

Unit Objectives

1. To read selections in different genres that develop the theme "On the Edge"

2. To apply a variety of reading strategies, particularly literal comprehension strategies, appropriate for reading these selections

3. To analyze literary elements

4. To use a variety of strategies to build vocabulary

5. To learn elements of grammar, usage, and style

6. To use recursive writing processes to write in a variety of forms

7. To develop listening and speaking skills

8. To express and support responses to various types of texts

9. To prepare, organize, and present literary interpretations

Meeting the Objectives

With each selection, you will find instructional materials through which students can meet these objectives. Further, you will find additional practice pages for reading strategies, literary analysis, vocabulary, and grammar in the **Selection Support: Skills Development Workbook** in your **Teaching Resources**.

Background

Art

Skateboard on the Edge, by Kazu Nitta

Kazu Nitta studied economics in Japan before coming to the United States to study media arts illustration. He has illustrated many children's books, including *My Many Colored Days* by Theodore Geisel (Dr. Seuss). He has also used his strong background in economics to develop assignments for *Newsweek*, IBM/Think, and many other companies.

Use the following question for discussion:

Why is this painting an appropriate illustration for the theme "On the Edge"?

Possible Answers: The painting evokes the senses of fear and possibility that often accompany this theme.

UNIT 1

On the Edge

Skateboard on the Edge, Kazu Nitta, The Stock Illustration Source Inc.

UNIT FEATURES

Connections	Reading Informational Materials
Every unit contains a feature that connects literature to a related topic, such as art, science, or history. In this unit, the excerpt from Jon Krakauer's *Into Thin Air* on pp. 37–38 offers an account of climbing the Himalayas.	These selections will help students learn to analyze and evaluate informational texts, such as workplace documents, technical directions, and consumer materials. They will expose students to the organization and features unique to nonnarrative texts.
Use the information and questions on the Connections pages to enrich students' understanding of the selections presented within the unit.	In this unit, students learn the structure and format of business documents.

....

Exploring the Theme

Your heart pounds, your brow perspires, your stomach twists in knots. Like riding a roller coaster, reading suspenseful literature can be nerve-racking, even frightening, but always exciting. Suspense—a literary technique that generates a sense of uneasiness, curiosity, and danger—can make you feel as if you have gone on the most delightful, daring ride of your life.

When you read "Contents of the Dead Man's Pocket," you will feel as though you are perched high above a city on a narrow ledge. As you read about one man's desperate struggle to safety, you will know the power of suspense—and the art of the writer who can bring you to the edge of your seat.

....

▲ **Critical Viewing** What details of this illustration suggest suspense and danger? **[Analyze]**

Exploring the Theme ◆ 1

ASSESSMENT RESOURCES

📖 **Selection Support: Skills Development Workbook**
📖 **Formal Assessment**
📖 **Open Book Tests**
📖 **Performance Assessment and Portfolio Management**
📖 **Extension Activities**

1

Why Read Literature?

The "Why Read Literature?" page in each unit presents a list of possible purposes for reading. Each purpose for reading is connected to one or more of the selections in the unit. Good readers set a purpose before reading to help them read actively and focus on meaningful details.

Unit 1 introduces three purposes for reading. "Read for the Love of Literature" encourages students to explore suspenseful situations. "Read to Appreciate the Author's Craft" focuses students' attention on the techniques that authors use to create engaging literature. "Read for Information" encourages students to learn more about an unfamiliar setting and challenge.

How to Use This Page

- Tell students that before reading each selection in this unit, they should set a purpose for reading. This will help them read in a more active and focused manner.

- Explain that they can increase their love of literature by reading about a woman's desire for revenge in "The Bridegroom."

- A reader will be more engaged with a story when he or she better understands the techniques that the author employs, such as the use of flashbacks in "A Walk to the Jetty."

- A third purpose for reading is to obtain information. Students should focus on the specific type of information they want to learn. In "View From the Summit," students might want to learn more about Sir Edmund Hillary's trek up Mt. Everest.

 Read Literature?

You read literature for a purpose: to learn, to appreciate, to be entertained, or to be inspired. Even as you read the literature of suspense, your purpose may vary depending on the context, genre, or style of a specific reading. Preview the three purposes that you might set before reading the works in this unit.

1

Read for the Love of Literature

Natasha kept silent for a reason: She had seen something she was not supposed to see. Ultimately, she could not let the evil deeds she had witnessed go unpunished. Follow her risky plan in **"The Bridegroom,"** by Alexander Pushkin, page 59.

Although he lived only a short time, Guy de Maupassant had a distinct writing style, a flair for detail, and a love of surprising endings. See for yourself as he describes the power of loyalty in **"Two Friends,"** page 102.

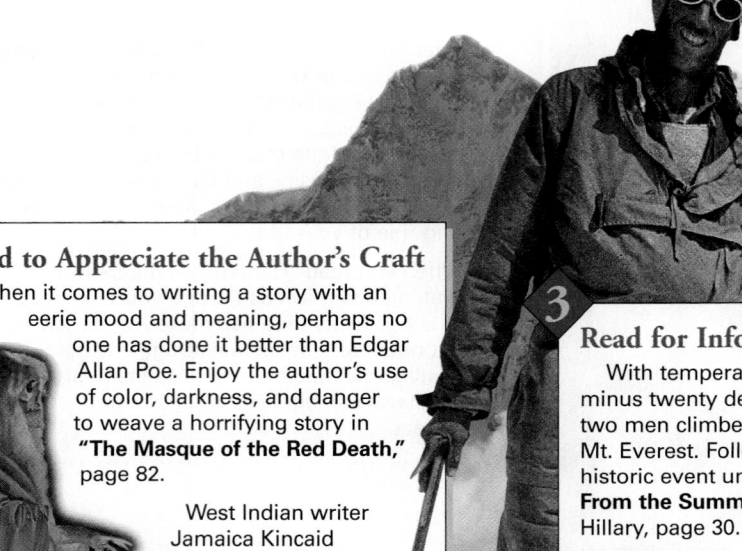

2

Read to Appreciate the Author's Craft

When it comes to writing a story with an eerie mood and meaning, perhaps no one has done it better than Edgar Allan Poe. Enjoy the author's use of color, darkness, and danger to weave a horrifying story in **"The Masque of the Red Death,"** page 82.

West Indian writer Jamaica Kincaid makes powerful use of flashbacks, a literary technique that involves interruptions of a narrative with memories of earlier events. See how flashbacks add depth to the narrative in **"A Walk to the Jetty,"** page 70.

3

Read for Information

With temperatures hovering at minus twenty degrees Celsius, two men climbed 29,028 feet up Mt. Everest. Follow along as this historic event unfolds in **"View From the Summit,"** by Sir Edmund Hillary, page 30.

Take It to the Net
Visit the Web site for online instruction and activities related to each selection in this unit.
www.phschool.com

2 ◆ On the Edge

✷ ENRICHMENT: Further Reading

Have students choose one or more of the works below to extend the unit theme "On the Edge" or to read more by the unit authors.

The Red Badge of Courage by Stephen Crane
In this novel, which can be found in the **Prentice Hall Literature Library,** a young man faces the horrors of the Civil War.

The Hound of the Baskervilles by Sir Arthur Conan Doyle
This suspenseful mystery involving Sherlock Holmes and his faithful sidekick Dr. Watson can be found in the **Prentice Hall Literature Library.**

The Strange Case of Dr. Jekyll and Mr. Hyde by Robert Louis Stevenson
The classic story of the double life of a respectable doctor who unlocks the door to his terrible alter ego can be found in the **Prentice Hall Literature Library.**

How to Read Literature

Use Literal Comprehension Strategies

With any piece of literature—from fiction to poetry—your first goal in reading is to understand what the writer is relating. Some writers have a clear, direct style that is easy to understand. Others may write in a way that is less clear. However, there are strategies you can apply to help you understand even the most complex writing.

1. Reread or read ahead.
- Reread passages that confuse you. You may have to review earlier passages to clarify a detail or an event that seems out of place later.
- If rereading does not clarify a passage, read ahead. You may find the answer in the next few sentences or paragraphs.

2. Distinguish facts from opinions.
- A *fact* is information that can be proved true or false.
- An *opinion* cannot be proved true or false.

When you read works of nonfiction, determine whether the author's statements are facts or opinions. For example, as you read the passage at right, ask yourself whether each statement can be proved true or false.

> **Fact vs. Opinion**
>
> We made our slow preparations for departure, eating well and consuming plenty of vital fluids. My boots were frozen solid and I cooked them over the primus stove until they were soft enough for me to pull on.
> —"View From the Summit"
>
> The words *slow*, *well*, and *plenty*, which are highlighted in yellow, suggest the writer's opinion. The statement about boots being frozen solid, highlighted in blue, is a fact because it can be tested and proved.

3. Predict outcomes.
As the events of a story unfold, ask yourself what will happen next. Watch for clues that hint at events to come. As you read further and find new information, you may need to revise your predictions, but this strategy keeps you actively involved in your reading.

4. Use context clues.
Context refers to the words, phrases, and sentences that surround a word. For example, you might be unfamiliar with the word *visage* in the following lines:

> The mask which concealed the *visage* was made so nearly to resemble the countenance of a stiffened corpse . . .
> —"The Masque of the Red Death"

The context clues *mask, concealed,* and *countenance* help you determine that *visage* means "face."

As you read the selections in this unit, apply these comprehension strategies to get the most out of what you read.

How to Read Literature ◆ 3

How to Read Literature
The "How to Read Literature" page in each unit presents a set of strategies to help readers understand authors' words and ideas. Each reading strategy is taught in conjunction with one or more of the selections within the unit. Good readers develop a bank of strategies from which they can draw as needed.

Unit 1 introduces four strategies for literal comprehension. To comprehend a selection fully, students must understand what the writer is saying. The strategies on this page help readers understand even the most complex writing.

How to Use This Page
Introduce the literal comprehension strategies, presenting each as a tool for developing understanding when reading the selections in this unit.

- As they read "Contents of the Dead Man's Pocket" (p. 6), students will learn how to clarify meaning by rereading or reading ahead.
- As they read "View From the Summit" (p. 30), students will learn how to distinguish between fact and opinion.
- As they read "The Monkey's Paw" (p. 50), students will learn how to predict outcomes to stay involved in what they are reading.
- As they read "The Masque of the Red Death" (p. 82), students will learn how to use context clues to determine the meanings of unfamiliar words.

MODEL A READING STRATEGY: Reread or Read Ahead

Explain to students that rereading or reading ahead in a selection can help them clarify details and events that seem confusing.

Model this strategy for students using "Contents of the Dead Man's Pocket." Tell students that they can read ahead to clarify that words such as *flimsy, carbon paper,* and *portable* in the first paragraph are related to typing.

3

Contents of the Dead Man's Pocket

Lesson Objectives

1. **To analyze and respond to literary elements**
   - Literary Analysis: Suspense
   - Connecting Literary Elements: Rising Action

2. **To read, comprehend, analyze, and critique a short story**
   - Reading Strategy: Rereading or Reading Ahead
   - Reading Check questions
   - Review and Assess questions
   - Assessment Practice (ATE)

3. **To develop word analysis skills, fluency, and systematic vocabulary**
   - Vocabulary Development Lesson: Latin Word Root: -*term*-

4. **To understand and apply written and oral language conventions**
   - Spelling Strategy
   - Grammar Lesson: Types of Nouns

5. **To understand and apply appropriate writing and research strategies**
   - Writing Lesson: Cliffhanger Scene
   - Extension Activity: Technology Timeline

6. **To understand and apply listening and speaking strategies**
   - Extension Activity: Dialogue

STEP-BY-STEP TEACHING GUIDE	PACING GUIDE
PRETEACH	
Motivate Students and Provide Background	
Use the Motivation activity (ATE p. 4)	5 min.
Read and discuss the Preview material and Background information (SE/ATE p. 4) **A**	5 min.
Introduce the Concepts	
Introduce the Literary Analysis and Reading Strategy (SE/ATE p. 5) **A**	15 min.
Pronounce the vocabulary words and read their definitions (SE p. 5)	5 min.
TEACH	
Monitor Comprehension	
Informally monitor comprehension by circulating while students read independently or in groups **A**	30 min.
Monitor students' comprehension with the Reading Check notes (SE/ATE pp. 7, 9, 11, 13, 15, 17, 19)	as students read
Develop vocabulary with Vocabulary notes (SE pp. 9, 12, 13, 16; ATE p. 16)	as students read
Develop Understanding	
Develop students' understanding of suspense with Literary Analysis annotations (SE pp. 8, 10, 12, 13, 14, 19, 20; ATE pp. 7, 8, 10, 11, 12, 13, 14, 19) **A**	10 min.
Develop students' understanding of rereading and reading ahead with the Reading Strategy annotations (SE pp. 7, 17; ATE pp. 7, 17, 18)	10 min.
ASSESS	
Assess Mastery	
Assess students' mastery of the Reading Strategy and Literary Analysis by having them answer the Review and Assess questions (SE/ATE p. 21)	20 min.
Use one or more of the print and media Assessment Resources (ATE p. 23) **A**	up to 50 min.
EXTEND	
Apply Understanding	
Have students complete the Vocabulary Development Lesson and the Grammar Lesson (SE p. 22) **A**	20 min.
Apply students' knowledge of sequence of events using the Writing Lesson (SE/ATE p. 23) **A**	45 min.
Apply students' understanding using one or more of the Extension Activities (SE p. 23)	20–90 min.

 ACCELERATED INSTRUCTION:
Use the strategies and activities identified with an **A**.

UNIVERSAL ACCESS
● = Below Level Students
▲ = On-Level Students
■ = Above Level Students

Time and Resource Manager

RESOURCES		
PRINT 📖	**TRANSPARENCIES**	**TECHNOLOGY**
• **Beyond Literature,** Workplace Skills: Making Decisions, p. 1 ▲ ■		• **Interest Grabber Video,** Tape 1 ● ▲ ■
• **Selection Support Workbook:** ● ▲ ■ Literary Analysis, p. 4 Reading Strategy, p. 3 Build Vocabulary, p. 1	• **Literary Analysis and Reading Transparencies,** pp. 1 and 2 ● ▲ ■	
		• **Listening to Literature** ● ▲ ■ Audiocassettes, Side 1 Audio CDs, CD 1
• **Literatura en español** ● ▲ • **Literary Analysis for Enrichment** ■	• **Fine Art Transparencies, Volume 1,** Art Transparency 19 ● ▲ ■	
• **Formal Assessment:** Selection Test, pp. 1–3 ● ▲ ■ • **Open Book Test,** pp. 1–3 ● ▲ ■ • **Performance Assessment and Portfolio Management,** pp. 14, 31 ● ▲ ■ • **ASSESSMENT SYSTEM** ● ▲ ■	• **ASSESSMENT SYSTEM** ● ▲ ■ Skills Practice Answers and Explanations on Transparencies	• **Test Bank Software** ● ▲ ■ • **Got It! Assessment Videotapes** ● ▲
• **Selection Support Workbook:** ● ▲ ■ Build Grammar Skills, p. 2 • **Writing and Grammar,** Platinum Level ● ▲ ■ • **Extension Activities,** p. 1 ● ▲ ■	• **Daily Language Practice Transparencies** ● ▲	• **Writing and Grammar iText CD-ROM** ● ▲ ■ 💻 *Take It to the Net* www.phschool.com

BLOCK SCHEDULING: Use one 90-minute class period to preteach the selection and have students read it. Use a second 90-minute class period to assess students' mastery of skills and have them complete one of the Extension Activities.

Motivation

Write the following sentences from the story on the chalkboard:

"For an instant he hung suspended between balance and falling, his fingertips pressed onto the quarter-inch wood strips."

"Quite realistically, he knew that he would fall; no one could stay out here on this ledge for four hours."

"All they'd find in his pockets would be the yellow sheet."

Have students try to piece together what the story is about based on these sentences. Then have them predict how the story might turn out.

Interest Grabber Video

As an alternative, you may wish to play "Forensic Science" on Tape 1 to engage student interest.

❶ Background

Culture

This story will take you back in time to the 1950s. In the mid-twentieth century, there were no photocopiers or personal computers, and most people still worked on typewriters or laboriously wrote things out in longhand. As a result, a single document was often unique.

Documents may have been one-of-a-kind in the 1950s, but time seemed to stretch out. For example, movies were often double features, combining two major films with previews and cartoons, lasting four or five hours. They also contained a newsreel, a short motion picture presenting current events, similar to today's TV news. It was not until 1957 that television sales soared and the TV news began to replace newsreels.

Prepare to Read

Contents of the Dead Man's Pocket

📷 Take It to the Net

Visit www.phschool.com for interactive activities and instruction related to to "Contents of the Dead Man's Pocket," including
* background
* graphic organizers
* literary elements
* reading strategies

Preview

Connecting to the Literature

Living means taking chances. You constantly take everyday risks, such as trying out for a team or asking someone you like for a date. "Contents of the Dead Man's Pocket" is about a man who takes a dramatic and foolish chance based on a moment's impulse.

❶ Background

Today's offices have laser printers, faxes, and high-tech hard drives that store information electronically for instant retrieval. In the 1950s, when this story takes place, there were no photocopiers or computers. Most people worked on typewriters or wrote things out in longhand. Losing a document, such as the one Tom Benecke wrote in this story, meant losing it forever.

4 ◆ On the Edge

TEACHING RESOURCES

The following resources can be used to enrich or extend the instruction for pp. 4–5.

Motivation

📺 **Interest Grabber Video**, Tape 1 ▪

Background

📖 **Beyond Literature**, p. 1

📷 **Take It to the Net**
Visit www.phschool.com for background and hotlinks for "Contents of the Dead Man's Pocket."

Literary Analysis

📖 **Literary Analysis and Reading Transparencies,** Suspense, p. 2 ▪

Reading

📖 **Selection Support:** Reading Strategy, p. 3; Build Vocabulary, p. 1

📖 **Literary Analysis and Reading Transparencies,** Rereading or Reading Ahead, p. 1 ▪

▪ **BLOCK SCHEDULING:** Resources marked with this symbol provide varied instruction during 90-minute blocks.

❷ Literary Analysis

Suspense

Another word for the tension and nervous uncertainty that some stories generate is **suspense.** This feeling keeps you guessing and turning pages, wondering about the outcome. Writers can create suspense by withholding key details or hinting at events to come. They can also create suspense by using vivid description to draw you into the tension of the moment. Look at this example from Finney's story:

> . . . he stood on the ledge outside in the slight, chill breeze, eleven stories above the street, . . .

Connecting Literary Elements

Rising action is part of a story's plot, or sequence of events. A story's rising action begins when the central problem is introduced, and it continues until the climax, or high point, is reached. To make a story's rising action suspenseful, writers often include descriptions of a character's efforts to solve a problem. They may also introduce twists and turns before the problem is solved. As you read "Contents of the Dead Man's Pocket," notice Tom Benecke's repeated attempts to save himself from a dangerous situation.

❸ Reading Strategy

Rereading or Reading Ahead

Reading can be a many-step process. On a first reading, you may miss details or have questions about what is happening. It makes sense, then, to go back and **reread** a passage to clarify details. Sometimes you may need to **read ahead** to find answers to questions or to understand why an author is presenting certain information.

A diagram like the one here can help you decide when to reread or read ahead to find an answer.

Reading
Take notes.
Ask questions.

Rereading
Clarify details.

Reading Ahead
Find answers.

Vocabulary Development

convoluted (kän′ və lōōt′ id) *adj.* intricate; twisted (p. 9)

grimace (grim′ is) *n.* twisted facial expression (p. 12)

deftness (deft′ nis) *n.* skillfulness (p. 12)

imperceptibly (im′ pər sep′ tə blē) *adv.* in such a slight way as to be almost unnoticeable (p. 13)

reveling (rev′ əl iŋ) *v.* taking great pleasure (p. 13)

interminable (in tʉr′ mi nə bəl) *adj.* seemingly endless (p. 16)

Contents of the Dead Man's Pocket ◆ 5

---

❷ Literary Analysis

Suspense

- Tell students that as they read "Contents of the Dead Man's Pocket," they will experience *suspense,* or the tension and nervous uncertainty that keep readers wondering what will happen next.

- Read the instruction about suspense together as a class. Draw students' attention to the example from the story.

- Use the instruction for Connecting Literary Elements to explain how writers use suspense to make a story's rising action intriguing.

- Use the Suspense transparency on page 2 of **Literary Analysis and Reading Transparencies** to show students how to recognize details that create suspense.

❸ Reading Strategy

Rereading or Reading Ahead

- Remind students that rereading means returning to a passage to clarify details, and reading ahead means moving on to find answers to questions.

- Then, tell students to use these strategies to make sure they understand what they read. Encourage them to use the chart on this page to help them decide when to use each strategy.

- Suggest that students record the questions they have while reading the story. Have them record the answers they find, as well.

Vocabulary Development

- Pronounce each vocabulary word for students, and read the definitions as a class. Have students identify any words with which they are already familiar.

CUSTOMIZE INSTRUCTION FOR UNIVERSAL ACCESS

For Less Proficient Readers	For English Learners	For Advanced Readers
Model for students how to create a chart for recording the questions they develop as they read the story. In the left column, have them write down questions. In the middle, have them decide which strategy to use to find the answer. In the right column, have them write down the answer.	Help English learners create a chart to record new words and their definitions. In the left column, have them write the word. In the middle, have them choose a strategy for finding the definition, such as rereading, reading ahead, or consulting the dictionary. In the right, have them record the definition.	Many advanced readers will naturally reread or read ahead when they encounter a difficult word or passage. Tell them that in addition to these strategies, they can visit www.phschool.com when they would like additional information, such as facts about the author's life and the influences on his writing.

 E-Teach

Visit E-Teach at www.phschool.com for teachers' essays on how to teach, with questions and answers.

Step-by-Step Teaching Guide for pp. 6–20

CUSTOMIZE INSTRUCTION
For Visual/Spatial Learners

Suggest that students write a screenplay based on one scene from Finney's story. Encourage them to study how Finney's visual effects created with words would be essential aspects of a screenplay. Students might benefit from locating and viewing film versions of Finney's writing.

❶ About the Selection

This suspenseful story captures what happens when Tom Benecke stays home to work on a business proposal while his wife goes to the movies alone. Clearly, Tom's ambition to get ahead is his top priority. However, when events lead Tom to a harrowing experience on the ledge of his apartment building, he is forced to reexamine his life and reshape his outlook. The suspenseful events in this story convey the message that sometimes people have to face a crisis in order to realize what is really important.

❷ ▶Critical Viewing

Answer: Students may suggest that the dark sky, the towering heights, and the feeling of isolation combine to create a feeling of suspense and danger.

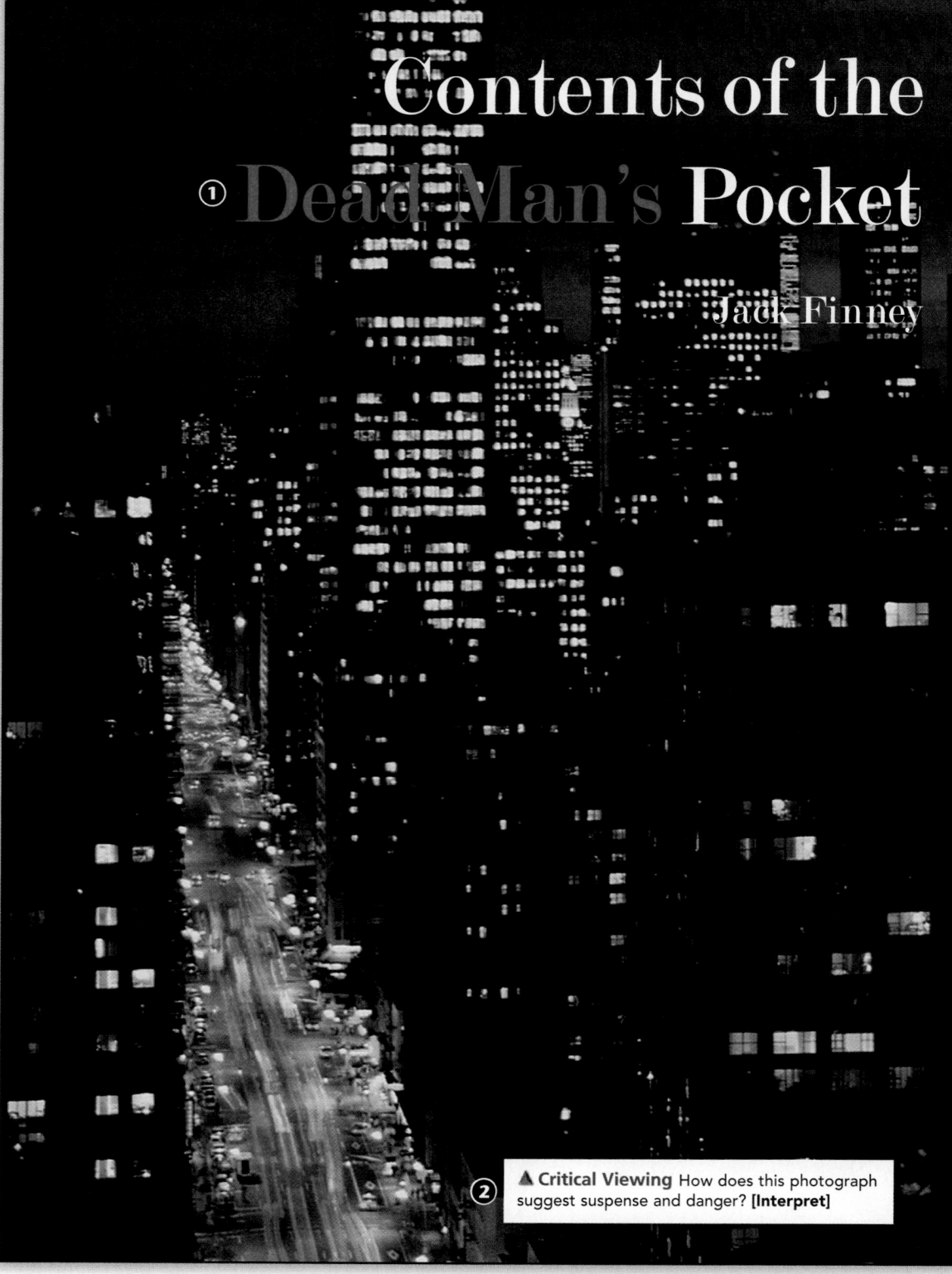

Contents of the
❶ Dead Man's Pocket

Jack Finney

▲ **Critical Viewing** How does this photograph suggest suspense and danger? **[Interpret]** ❷

TEACHING RESOURCES

The following resources can be used to enrich or extend the instruction for pp. 6–20.

Literary Analysis

📖 **Selection Support:** Literary Analysis, p. 4

▪ **Literary Analysis and Reading Transparencies,** Suspense, p. 2

Reading

🎧 **Listening to Literature Audiocassettes,** Side 1 ▪

💿 **Listening to Literature Audio CDs,** CD 1 ▪

Extension

▪ **Fine Art Transparencies, Volume 1,** Art Transparency 19 ▪

▪ **BLOCK SCHEDULING:** Resources marked with this symbol provide varied instruction during 90-minute blocks.

At the little living-room desk Tom Benecke rolled two sheets of flimsy[1] and a heavier top sheet, carbon paper sandwiched between them, into his portable. Interoffice Memo, the top sheet was headed, and he typed tomorrow's date just below this; then he glanced at a creased yellow sheet, covered with his own handwriting, beside the typewriter. "Hot in here," he muttered to himself. Then, from the short hallway at his back, he heard the muffled clang of wire coat hangers in the bedroom closet, and at this reminder of what his wife was doing he thought: Hot, no—guilty conscience.

He got up, shoving his hands into the back pockets of his gray wash slacks, stepped to the living-room window beside the desk and stood breathing on the glass, watching the expanding circle of mist, staring down through the autumn night at Lexington Avenue, eleven stories below. He was a tall, lean, dark-haired young man in a pullover sweater, who looked as though he had played not football, probably, but basketball in college. Now he placed the heels of his hands against the top edge of the lower window frame and shoved upward. But as usual the window didn't budge, and he had to lower his hands and then shoot them hard upward to jolt the window open a few inches. He dusted his hands, muttering.

But still he didn't begin his work. He crossed the room to the hallway entrance and, leaning against the doorjamb, hands shoved into his back pockets again, he called, "Clare?" When his wife answered, he said, "Sure you don't mind going alone?"

"No." Her voice was muffled, and he knew her head and shoulders were in the bedroom closet. Then the tap of her high heels sounded on the wood floor and she appeared at the end of the little hallway, wearing a slip, both hands raised to one ear, clipping on an earring. She smiled at him—a slender, very pretty girl with light brown, almost blonde, hair—her prettiness emphasized by the pleasant nature that showed in her face. "It's just that I hate you to miss this movie; you wanted to see it too."

"Yeah, I know." He ran his fingers through his hair. "Got to get this done though."

She nodded, accepting this. Then, glancing at the desk across the living room, she said, "You work too much, though, Tom—and too hard."

He smiled. "You won't mind though, will you, when the money comes rolling in and I'm known as the Boy Wizard of Wholesale Groceries?"

"I guess not." She smiled and turned back toward the bedroom.

At his desk again, Tom lighted a cigarette, then a few moments later as Clare appeared, dressed and ready to leave, he set it on the rim of the ash tray, "Just after seven," she said. "I can make the beginning of the first feature."

He walked to the front-door closet to help her on with her coat. He

---

1. **flimsy** (flim′ zē) n. thin typing paper for making carbon copies.

Contents of the Dead Man's Pocket ◆ 7

Reading Strategy

Reread or Read Ahead
Which words in this paragraph are unfamiliar to you? Read ahead to learn what they mean.

⑤ ✔Reading Check

Why does Tom decide not to go to the movies with his wife?

---

❸ Reading Strategy
Rereading or Reading Ahead

- As they read the first paragraph, have students record unfamiliar words in their notebooks.
- Ask students the Reading Strategy question on p. 7: Which words in this paragraph are unfamiliar to you?
- Have students read ahead to learn what the words mean.
  Answer: Explain that the word *portable* refers to a portable type-writer, one that is small and lightweight enough to be carried. Students should determine that the words *flimsy* and *carbon paper* are also connected to typing.

❹ Literary Analysis
Suspense

- Remind students that suspense is a feeling of tension and nervous uncertainty that keeps readers wondering what will happen next.
- Ask students why the writer might mention so early in the story that the window is stuck.
  Answer: Students may guess that the stuck window will play a crucial role in the story's suspense. Skilled readers may suggest that it is an example of foreshadowing.

❺ ✔Reading Check

Answer: Tom doesn't go to the movies because he wants to write an interoffice memo that will bolster his reputation at work.

CUSTOMIZE INSTRUCTION FOR UNIVERSAL ACCESS

For Less Proficient Readers	For English Learners	For Advanced Readers
Ask students to reread this page, making a list of details that might play an important role in the plot. Record their suggestions in a list on the chalkboard. Make sure they include the jammed window and the fact that Tom will be spending the evening alone. As they read ahead, encourage students to track how these details play out.	Before they read ahead, make sure students have a thorough understanding of the introduction. Ask them to reread this page, making a list of unfamiliar words. Help them obtain the definitions by rereading, reading ahead, or consulting the dictionary. Encourage students to keep a list of new words in their notebooks.	Before they read ahead, have students write a paragraph to predict what will happen next in the story. Make sure they consider significant details, such as the typewriter, the jammed window, and the fact that Tom will be home alone for the evening. Have volunteers share their predictions.

❻ Literary Analysis
Suspense

- Explain to students that small details, such as a threatening sound or object, often add to a story's suspense.

- Ask students the first Literary Analysis question on p. 8: How does the resisting door produce suspense?
  Answer: The narrow opening caused by the door creates a breeze close to the important papers on Tom's desk.

- Then, have students read the next paragraph and find at least two details that produce suspense.
  Possible responses: The white paper slowly drifting to the floor makes the reader wonder what will happen to the yellow paper. When the yellow paper hangs for an instant against the glass, the reader wonders whether it will eventually fall out the window.

❼ Literary Analysis
Suspense

- Ask students the second Literary Analysis question on p. 8: How does the description of Tom waiting for the yellow paper to move generate suspense?
  Answer: The description gives every detail of the paper's movement as it is carried by the wind. The reader can imagine Tom watching the paper in horror.

- Explain to students that drawing out a situation, rather than immediately telling the reader what will happen next, is one way that writers create suspense.

---

kissed her then and, for an instant, holding her close, smelling the perfume she had used, he was tempted to go with her; it was not actually true that he had to work tonight, though he very much wanted to. This was his own project, unannounced as yet in his office, and it could be postponed. But then they won't see it till Monday, he thought once again, and if I give it to the boss tomorrow he might read it over the weekend . . . "Have a good time," he said aloud. He gave his wife a little swat and opened the door for her, feeling the air from the building hallway, smelling faintly of floor wax, stream gently past his face.

❻ He watched her walk down the hall, flicked a hand in response as she waved, and then he started to close the door, but it resisted for a moment. As the door opening narrowed, the current of warm air from the hallway, channeled through this smaller opening now, suddenly rushed past him with accelerated force. Behind him he heard the slap of the window curtains against the wall and the sound of paper fluttering from his desk, and he had to push to close the door.

Turning, he saw a sheet of white paper drifting to the floor in a series of arcs, and another sheet, yellow, moving toward the window, caught in the dying current flowing through the narrow opening. As he watched, the paper struck the bottom edge of the window and hung there for an instant, plastered against the glass and wood. Then as the moving air stilled completely the curtains swinging back from the wall to hang free again, he saw the yellow sheet drop to the window ledge and slide over out of sight.

He ran across the room, grasped the bottom edge of the window and tugged, staring through the glass. He saw the yellow sheet, dimly now in the darkness outside, lying on the ornamental ledge a yard below the window. Even as he watched, it was moving, scraping slowly along the ledge, pushed by the breeze that pressed steadily against the building wall. He heaved on the window with all his strength and it shot open with a bang, the window weight rattling in the casing. But the paper was past his reach and, leaning out into the night, he watched it scud steadily along the ledge to the south, half plastered against the building wall. Above the muffled sound of the street traffic far below, he could hear the dry scrape of its movement, like a leaf on the pavement.

The living room of the next apartment to the south projected a yard or more farther out toward the street than this one; because of this the Beneckes paid seven and a half dollars less rent than their neighbors. And now the yellow sheet, sliding along the stone ledge, nearly invisible in the night, was stopped by the projecting blank wall of the next apartment. It lay motionless, then, in the corner formed by the two walls—a good five yards away, pressed firmly against the ornate corner ornament of the ledge, by the breeze that moved past Tom Benecke's face.

❼ He knelt at the window and stared at the yellow paper for a full minute or more, waiting for it to move, to slide off the ledge and fall,

Literary Analysis
Suspense How does the resisting door produce suspense?

Literary Analysis
Suspense How does the description of Tom waiting for the yellow paper to move generate suspense?

✷ ENRICHMENT: Cultural Connection

Architecture

Point out the architectural details that prove important to the plot—ornate corner ornaments and the narrow ledge. The height of the apartment buildings in New York City also contributes to the story's suspense. Ask students to note architectural details that distinguish the buildings in their area, such as tiled roofs or weathered siding. Students can speculate how events in this story might differ if the story were set in their community.

7 hoping he could follow its course to the street, and then hurry down in the elevator and retrieve it. But it didn't move, and then he saw that the paper was caught firmly between a projection of the <u>convoluted</u> corner ornament and the ledge. He thought about the poker from the fireplace, then the broom, then the mop—discarding each thought as it occurred to him. There was nothing in the apartment long enough to reach that paper.

It was hard for him to understand that he actually had to abandon it—it was ridiculous—and he began to curse. Of all the papers on his desk, why did it have to be this one in particular! On four long Saturday afternoons he had stood in supermarkets counting the people who passed certain displays, and the results were scribbled on that yellow sheet. From stacks of trade publications, gone over page by page in snatched half hours at work and during evenings at **8** home, he had copied facts, quotations, and figures onto that sheet. And he had carried it with him to the Public Library on Fifth Avenue, where he'd spent a dozen lunch hours and early evenings adding more. All were needed to support and lend authority to his idea for a new grocery-store display method; without them his idea was a mere opinion. And there they all lay, in his own improvised shorthand—countless hours of work—out there on the ledge.

For many seconds he believed he was going to abandon the yellow sheet, that there was nothing else to do. The work could be duplicated. But it would take two months, and the time to present this idea . . . was now, for use in the spring displays. He struck his fist on the window ledge. Then he shrugged. Even if his plan were adopted, he told himself, it wouldn't bring him a raise in pay—not immediately, anyway, or as a direct result. It won't bring me a promotion either, he argued—not of itself.

But just the same, and he couldn't escape the thought, this and other independent projects, some already done and others planned for the future, would gradually mark him out from the score of other young men in his company. They were the way to change from a name on the payroll to a name in the minds of the company officials. They were the beginning of the long, long climb to where he was determined to be, at the very top. And he knew he was going out there in the darkness, after the yellow sheet fifteen feet beyond his reach.

By a kind of instinct, he instantly began making his intention acceptable to himself by laughing at it. The mental picture of himself sidling along the ledge outside was absurd—it was actually comical—and he smiled. He imagined himself describing it; it would make a good story at the office and, it occurred to him, would add a special interest and

convoluted (kän′ və lōot′ id) *adj.* intricate; twisted

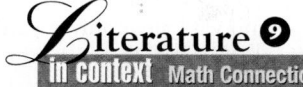
Literature **9**
in context Math Connection

Market Research

Tom Benecke spends countless hours collecting statistics to support his idea for a new grocery-store display method. Market research like this tests people's reactions and habits with the expectation that the information the research generates can predict consumer response. Most businesses take special care to test products, processes, or ideas before implementing them on a large scale. Tom's paper provides the detailed support for his ideas.

10 ✓ **Reading Check**

Why is the yellow paper so important to Tom?

Contents of the Dead Man's Pocket ◆ 9

---

8 **Critical Thinking**

Infer

- Ask students how Tom has been spending his free time. What does this imply about his attitude toward life?
  Answer: Tom has been compiling statistics and doing research during his free time. His attitude toward life seems to be that one should apply oneself relentlessly in order to get ahead.

- Explain to students that characters' attitudes and beliefs often influence their actions.

- Then, ask students whether they think Tom will attempt to retrieve the paper. Remind them to consider his attitude toward work.
  Possible response: Most students will say that Tom's desire to get ahead at work will lead him to try to retrieve the paper.

9 **Background**

Marketing

Retailers try to maximize sales through a variety of methods. For example, grocery retailers place "impulse purchase" items such as candy bars and magazines in checkout aisles where customers wait in line. Some companies have people hand out free samples of their products in grocery stores. Let students know that people who specialize in marketing plan and implement these selling strategies. Companies selling everything from books to cars use marketing strategies, though smaller companies may hire consulting firms rather than maintain their own marketing departments.

10 ✓ **Reading Check**

Answer: Tom spent months recording statistics on the yellow sheet while he was doing his supermarket research. It would take him months to duplicate the work he recorded on the paper.

CUSTOMIZE INSTRUCTION FOR UNIVERSAL ACCESS

For Special Needs Students	For Gifted/Talented Students
Have students reread the paragraph that begins, "He knelt at the window…." Then, make sure they understand exactly where the paper has landed by having them draw a picture of the scene. Guide students to include important details from the text, such as the ornate corner ornament on the stone ledge, and how far the paper is from Tom.	Have students reread the paragraph that begins, "He watched her walk…." Then, have interested students explain exactly how the force of the warm and cold air currents would draw the paper outside the room. Students may wish to use diagrams, charts, or other graphic organizers to demonstrate this effect.

❶ Critical Thinking

Draw Conclusions

- Ask students why getting the paper back is so important to Tom.
  Answer: The paper is crucial because it can help him distinguish himself from all the other young men in the company.

- Then, point out that when Tom decides to go after the paper, Finney writes that "he knew he'd better hurry and get this over with before he thought too much."

- Based on this detail, ask students how Tom feels about going out on the ledge.
  Answer: Tom is nervous about going out on the ledge. He seems to understand that it will be risky and dangerous.

❶ Literary Analysis

Suspense and Rising Action

- Remind students that a story's rising action starts when the central problem is introduced and continues until the climax, or high point, is reached.

  Monitor Progress Students who have difficulty following the story's events and how they lead to the central problem may benefit from completing a series-of-events chain like the one below.
  Reteach: Have students stop reading at the pause in this page. Then, ask them to restate what has happened so far, and have them record the important events in the chart. Encourage them to add to the chart as they continue reading.

- Ask students the Literary Analysis question on p. 10: What central problem is introduced in this paragraph?
  Answer: The central problem is that Tom Benecke is stuck on a twelve-inch-wide ledge high above the street.

10

---

importance to his memorandum, which would do it no harm at all.

To simply go out and get his paper was an easy task—he could be back here with it in less than two minutes—and he knew he wasn't deceiving himself. The ledge, he saw, measuring it with his eye, was about as wide as the length of his shoe, and perfectly flat. And every fifth row of brick in the face of the building, he remembered—leaning out, he verified this—was indented half an inch, enough for the tips of his fingers, enough to maintain balance easily. It occurred to him that if this ledge and wall were only a yard aboveground—as he knelt at the window staring out, this thought was the final confirmation of his intention—he could move along the ledge indefinitely.

On a sudden impulse, he got to his feet, walked to the front closet and took out an old tweed jacket; it would be cold outside. He put it on and buttoned it as he crossed the room rapidly toward the open window. In the back of his mind he knew he'd better hurry and get this over with before he thought too much, and at the window he didn't allow himself to hesitate.

He swung a leg over the sill, then felt for and found the ledge a yard below the window with his foot. Gripping the bottom of the window frame very tightly and carefully, he slowly ducked his head under it, feeling on his face the sudden change from the warm air of the room to the chill outside. With infinite care he brought out his other leg, his mind concentrating on what he was doing. Then he slowly stood erect. Most of the putty, dried out and brittle, had dropped off the bottom edging of the window frame, he found, and the flat wooden edging provided a good gripping surface, a half inch or more deep, for the tips of his fingers.

Now, balanced easily and firmly, he stood on the ledge outside in the slight, chill breeze, eleven stories above the street, staring into his own lighted apartment, odd and different-seeming now.

First his right hand, then his left, he carefully shifted his fingertip grip from the puttyless window edging to an indented row of bricks directly to his right. It was hard to take the first shuffling sideways step then—to make himself move—and the fear stirred in his stomach, but he did it, again by not allowing himself time to think. And now—with his chest, stomach, and the left side of his face pressed against the rough cold brick —his lighted apartment was suddenly gone, and it was much darker out here than he had thought.

Without pause he continued—right foot, left foot, right foot, left—his shoe soles shuffling and scraping along the rough stone, never lifting from it, fingers sliding along the exposed edging of brick. He moved on the balls of his feet, heels lifted slightly; the ledge was not quite as wide as he'd expected. But leaning slightly inward toward the face of the building and pressed against it, he could feel his balance firm and secure, and moving along the ledge was quite as easy as he had thought it would be. He could hear the buttons of his jacket scraping steadily along the rough bricks and feel them catch momentarily,

Literary Analysis
Suspense and Rising Action What central problem is introduced in this paragraph?

tugging a little, at each mortared crack. He simply did not permit himself to look down, though the compulsion to do so never left him; nor did he allow himself actually to think. Mechanically—right foot, left foot, over and again—he shuffled along crabwise, watching the projecting wall ahead loom steadily closer . . .

Then he reached it, and, at the corner—he'd decided how he was going to pick up the paper—he lifted his right foot and placed it carefully on the ledge that ran along the projecting wall at a right angle to the ledge on which his other foot rested. And now, facing the building, he stood in the corner formed by the two walls, one foot on the ledging of each, a hand on the shoulder-high indentation of each wall. His forehead was pressed directly into the corner against the cold bricks, and now he carefully lowered first one hand, then the other, perhaps a foot farther down, to the next indentation in the rows of bricks.

Very slowly, sliding his forehead down the trough of the brick corner and bending his knees, he lowered his body toward the paper lying between his outstretched feet. Again he lowered his fingerholds another foot and bent his knees still more, thigh muscles taut, his forehead sliding and bumping down the brick V. Half squatting now, he dropped his left hand to the next indentation and then slowly reached with his right hand toward the paper between his feet.

He couldn't quite touch it, and his knees now were pressed against the wall; he could bend them no farther. But by ducking his head another inch lower, the top of his head now pressed against the bricks, he lowered his right shoulder and his fingers had the paper by a corner, pulling it loose. At the same instant he saw, between his legs and far below, Lexington Avenue stretched out for miles ahead.

He saw, in that instant, the Loew's theater sign, blocks ahead past Fiftieth Street; the miles of traffic signals, all green now; the lights of

▲ Critical Viewing
Based on this picture, why do you think Tom should or should not look down? Explain. **[Draw Conclusions]**

✔ Reading Check
How was Tom able to reach the yellow paper on the ledge?

⑬ ▶ Critical Viewing
Answer: Students may suggest that looking down would make Tom feel scared and panicky. Responses should focus on the height of the buildings and the dizzying view of the streets far below.

⑭ Literary Analysis

Suspense

- Ask students to reread this paragraph and find a detail that suggests that Tom feels confident on the ledge.
  Possible answer: "…he could feel his balance firm and secure, and moving along the ledge was quite as easy as he thought it would be."

- Have students explain why the author includes scenes like this, showing Tom as confident and ignoring the danger of the situation.
  Answer: By minimizing the suspense now, the author increases his opportunity to build the suspense to greater peaks later in the story.

⑮ ✔ Reading Check
Answer: He got the paper between his feet, bent his knees, and then lowered his head and shoulder until he could grasp a corner of the paper.

CUSTOMIZE INSTRUCTION FOR UNIVERSAL ACCESS

For Less Proficient Readers	For English Learners	For Advanced Readers
Encourage students to use the photograph on this page to help them visualize the terror that Tom is experiencing. Ask students to make a list of emotions that Tom might feel as he looks down from the ledge high above the street.	To reinforce the terror of Tom's situation, you may wish to play the audiocassette recording of this portion of Finney's story as students read along in their books. Ask students to pay attention to the elements that convey terror, such as the reader's tone and specific words in the text.	Ask students to write a paragraph from Tom's point of view about his feelings as he walks along the ledge. Challenge them to include details that appeal to all five senses: touch, taste, smell, sight, and sound.

16 Literary Analysis

Suspense and Rising Action

- Remind students that all the events leading up to the climax in a story make up the rising action.

- Encourage students to keep a list of events in the story that make up the rising action.

- Ask students the Literary Analysis question on p. 12: How do Tom's efforts here add to the rising action of the story?
  Answer: Tom's fear causes him to move spasmodically and nearly fall. This accelerates the rising action and makes the scene more suspenseful.

17 Critical Thinking

Analyze

- Ask students to explain the cause of Tom's current bout of fear.
  Answer: Tom becomes terrified when he glimpses the street below him for the first time. He wishes he had looked down earlier and grown more accustomed to the sight.

- Then, have students analyze how Tom's emotions in this scene may affect his ability to get off the ledge safely.
  Answer: Students may say that Tom's panic might make him fall. When he was feeling more confident, he was able to move swiftly along the ledge.

---

cars and street lamps; countless neon signs; and the moving black dots of people. And a violent instantaneous explosion of absolute terror roared through him. For a motionless instant he saw himself externally— bent practically double, balanced on this narrow ledge, nearly half his body projecting out above the street far below—and he began to tremble violently, panic flaring through his mind and muscles, and he felt the blood rush from the surface of his skin.

In the fractional moment before horror paralyzed him, as he stared between his legs at that terrible length of street far beneath him, a fragment of his mind raised his body in a spasmodic jerk to an upright position again, but so violently that his head scraped hard against the wall, bouncing off it, and his body swayed outward to the **16** knife edge of balance, and he very nearly plunged backward and fell. Then he was leaning far into the corner again, squeezing and pushing into it, not only his face but his chest and stomach, his back arching; and his fingertips clung with all the pressure of his pulling arms to the shoulder-high half-inch indentation in the bricks.

He was more than trembling now; his whole body was racked with a violent shuddering beyond control, his eyes squeezed so tightly shut it was painful, though he was past awareness of that. His teeth were exposed in a frozen <u>grimace</u>, the strength draining like water from his knees and calves. It was extremely likely, he knew, that he would faint, to slump down along the wall, his face scraping, and then drop backward, a limp weight, out into nothing. And to save his life he concentrated on holding onto consciousness, drawing deliberate deep breaths of cold air into his lungs, fighting to keep his senses aware.

Then he knew that he would not faint, but he could neither stop shaking nor open his eyes. He stood where he was, breathing deeply, trying to hold back the terror of the glimpse he had had of what lay below him; and he knew he had made a mistake in not making himself stare down at the street, getting used to it and accepting it, when he had first stepped out onto the ledge.

It was impossible to walk back. He simply could not do it. He couldn't bring himself to make the slightest movement. The strength **17** was gone from his legs; his shivering hands—numb, cold and desperately rigid—had lost all <u>deftness</u>; his easy ability to move and balance was gone. Within a step or two, if he tried to move, he knew that he would stumble clumsily and fall.

Seconds passed, with the chill faint wind pressing the side of his face, and he could hear the toned-down volume of the street traffic far beneath him. Again and again it slowed and then stopped, almost to silence; then presently, even this high, he would hear the click of the traffic signals and the subdued roar of the cars starting up again. During a lull in the street sounds, he called out. Then he was shouting "*Help!*" so loudly it rasped his throat. But he felt the steady pressure of the wind, moving between his face and the blank wall, snatch up his cries as he uttered them, and he knew they must sound directionless and distant. And he remembered how habitually, here in New

Literary Analysis
Suspense and Rising Action How do Tom's efforts here add to the rising action of the story?

grimace (grim´ is) *n.* twisted facial expression

deftness (deft´ nis) *n.* skillfulness

✷ ENRICHMENT: Math Connection

Statistics in Business

Tom Benecke collects statistics to support his idea for a new grocery store display method. Statistics play an important role in many businesses. Collecting data through surveys and samples and then analyzing the data is essential to everything from test marketing a new soft drink to creating a safer automobile. Economists and meteorologists use statistical techniques to predict future economic and weather conditions. Ask students how statistics help to ensure the success of a product.

York, he himself heard and ignored shouts in the night. If anyone heard him, there was no sign of it, and presently Tom Benecke knew he had to try moving; there was nothing else he could do.

18 Eyes squeezed shut, he watched scenes in his mind like scraps of motion-picture film—he could not stop them. He saw himself stumbling suddenly sideways as he crept along the ledge and saw his upper body arc outward, arms flailing. He saw a dangling shoestring caught between the ledge and the sole of his other shoe, saw a foot start to move, to be stopped with a jerk, and felt his balance leaving him. He saw himself falling with a terrible speed as his body revolved in the air, knees clutched tight to his chest, eyes squeezed shut, moaning softly.

Out of utter necessity, knowing that any of these thoughts might be reality in the very next seconds, he was slowly able to shut his mind against every thought but what he now began to do. With fear-soaked slowness, he slid his left foot an inch or two toward his own impossibly distant window. Then he slid the fingers of his shivering left hand a cor-

19 responding distance. For a moment he could not bring himself to lift his right foot from one ledge to the other; then he did it, and became aware of the harsh exhalation of air from his throat and realized that he was panting. As his right hand, then, began to slide along the brick edging, he was astonished to feel the yellow paper pressed to the bricks underneath his stiff fingers, and he uttered a terrible, abrupt bark that might have been a laugh or a moan. He opened his mouth and took the paper in his teeth, pulling it out from under his fingers.

By a kind of trick—by concentrating his entire mind on first his left foot, then his left hand, then the other foot, then the other hand—he was able to move, almost <u>imperceptibly</u>, trembling steadily, very nearly without thought. But he could feel the terrible strength of the pent-up horror on just the other side of the flimsy barrier he had erected in his mind; and he knew that if it broke through he would lose this thin artificial control of his body.

During one slow step he tried keeping his eyes closed; it made him feel safer, shutting him off a little from the fearful reality of where he was. Then a sudden rush of giddiness swept over him and he had to open his eyes wide, staring sideways at the cold rough brick and angled lines of mortar, his cheek tight against the building. He kept his eyes open then, knowing that if he once let them flick outward, to stare for an instant at the lighted windows across the street, he would be past help.

He didn't know how many dozens of tiny sidling steps he had taken, his chest, belly, and face pressed to the wall; but he knew the slender hold he was keeping on his mind and body was going to break. He had a sudden mental picture of his apartment on just the other side of this wall—warm, cheerful, incredibly spacious. And he saw himself striding through it, lying down on the floor on his back, arms spread wide, <u>reveling</u> in its unbelievable security. The impossible remoteness of this utter safety, the contrast between it and where

---

Literary Analysis
Suspense and Rising Action How does the rising action in this paragraph increase the suspense of the story?

imperceptibly (im´ pər sep´ tə blē) *adv.* in such a slight way as to be almost unnoticeable

reveling (rev´ əl iŋ) *v.* taking great pleasure

20 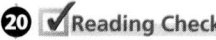 **Reading Check**
How does Tom feel about being on the ledge now?

Contents of the Dead Man's Pocket ◆ 13

---

18 Literary Analysis
Suspense and Rising Action
- Have students reread this paragraph. Make sure students understand that the action Tom describes here takes place in his mind.
- Then, ask students the Literary Analysis question on p. 13: How does the rising action in this paragraph increase the suspense of the story?
  Answer: As Tom sees himself falling, the reader becomes more and more worried that he will actually fall.

19 Critical Thinking
Analyze
- Have students analyze Tom's character in terms of his response to the pressure he feels here.
  Answer: Some students may realize that the pressure Tom is under has caused him to feel paralyzed; they may take his loss of control as a normal response to a dangerous situation. Other students may think that a stronger character would be able to master his body's response to terror.
- Ask students why they think Finney spends so much time describing Tom's thoughts and feelings, rather than focusing entirely on the action.
  Answer: The events in Tom's mind become as threatening as his actual movements. This intensifies the threat in the reader's mind.

20 Reading Check
Answer: Tom's nerves are starting to break, and he longs to be in the apartment where he can stretch out his body and relax.

CUSTOMIZE INSTRUCTION FOR UNIVERSAL ACCESS

For Less Proficient Readers	For Advanced Readers
In order to create suspense, Finney includes numerous details of both the actual scene and the scene in Tom's imagination. Help students separate the real events from those occurring in Tom's mind. In their notebooks, have them label one column on a sheet of paper "Reality" and the other "Tom's mind." Then, as they read, help them list each image in the proper column.	Finney's story is an excellent example of suspenseful writing. Help students appreciate his craft by asking them to make a list of words and images that create the tense, white-knuckled atmosphere. Have students keep this list in their notebooks for future reference in their own writing.

㉑ Literary Analysis

Suspense

- Ask students the Literary Analysis question on p. 14: What details build suspense here?
  Answer: All of Tom's movements—fingers scrabbling along the brick, his hand groping, and so on—build suspense by making it seem impossible that he can hang on.

- Then, tell students that Tom's stumbling here has a devastating result. Ask them to identify it.
  Answer: The window slams shut under the weight of Tom's sagging body. He is stuck outside on the ledge.

㉒ Literary Analysis

Suspense

- Explain to students that although Tom has solved the problem of retrieving the paper, he now faces another problem: He can't get into his apartment.

- Ask students to explain how this turn of events increases the story's tension and builds suspense.
  Answer: Just when Tom appears to be safe, his avenue of escape—the window—slams shut. As Tom looks at his apartment through the window, the reader understands his great desire to be inside.

he now stood, was more than he could bear. And the barrier broke then, and the fear of the awful height he stood on coursed through his nerves and muscles.

A fraction of his mind knew he was going to fall, and he began taking rapid blind steps with no feeling of what he was doing, sidling with a clumsy desperate swiftness, fingers scrabbling along the brick, almost hopelessly resigned to the sudden backward pull and swift motion outward and down. Then his moving left hand slid onto not brick but sheer emptiness, an impossible gap in the face of the wall, and he stumbled.

 His right foot smashed into his left anklebone; he staggered sideways, began falling, and the claw of his hand cracked against glass and wood, slid down it, and his fingertips were pressed hard on the puttyless edging of his window. His right hand smacked gropingly beside it as he fell to his knees; and, under the full weight and direct downward pull of his sagging body, the open window dropped shudderingly in its frame till it closed and his wrists struck the sill and were jarred off.

For a single moment he knelt, knee bones against stone on the very edge of the ledge, body swaying and touching nowhere else, fighting for balance. Then he lost it, his shoulders plunging backward, and he flung his arms forward, his hands smashing against the window casing on either side; and—his body moving backward—his fingers clutched the narrow wood stripping of the upper pane.

For an instant he hung suspended between balance and falling, his fingertips pressed onto the quarter-inch wood strips. Then, with utmost delicacy, with a focused concentration of all his senses, he increased even further the strain on his fingertips hooked to these slim edgings of wood. Elbows slowly bending, he began to draw the full weight of his upper body forward, knowing that the instant his fingers slipped off these quarter-inch strips he'd plunge backward and be falling. Elbows imperceptibly bending, body shaking with the strain, the sweat starting from his forehead in great sudden drops, he pulled, his entire being and thought concentrated in his fingertips. Then suddenly, the strain slackened and ended, his chest touching the window sill, and he was kneeling on the ledge, his forehead pressed to the glass of the closed window.

Dropping his palms to the sill, he stared into his living room—at the red-brown davenport[2] across the room, and a magazine he had left there; at the pictures on the walls and the gray rug; the entrance to the hallway; and at his papers, typewriter and desk, not two feet from his nose. A movement from his desk caught his eye and he saw that it was a thin curl of blue smoke; his cigarette, the ash long, was still burning in the ash tray where he'd left it—this was past all belief—only a few minutes before.

Literary Analysis
Suspense What details build suspense here?

---

2. **davenport** (dav´ ən pôrt´) n. couch.

His head moved, and in faint reflection from the glass before him he saw the yellow paper clenched in his front teeth. Lifting a hand from the sill he took it from his mouth; the moistened corner parted from the paper, and he spat it out.

For a moment, in the light from the living room, he stared wonderingly at the yellow sheet in his hand and then crushed it into the side pocket of his jacket.

He couldn't open the window. It had been pulled not completely closed, but its lower edge was below the level of the outside sill; there was no room to get his fingers underneath it. Between the upper sash and the lower was a gap not wide enough—reaching up, he tried—to get his fingers into; he couldn't push it open. The upper window panel, he knew from long experience, was impossible to move, frozen tight with dried paint.

Very carefully observing his balance, the fingertips of his left hand again hooked to the narrow stripping of the window casing, he drew back his right hand, palm facing the glass, and then struck the glass with the heel of his hand.

His arm rebounded from the pane, his body tottering, and he knew he didn't dare strike a harder blow.◆

But in the security and relief of his new position, he simply smiled; with only a sheet of glass between him and the room just before him, it was not possible that there wasn't a way past it. Eyes narrowing, he thought for a few moments about what to do. Then his eyes widened, for nothing occurred to him. But still he felt calm: the trembling, he realized, had stopped. At the back of his mind there still lay the thought that once he was again in his home, he could give release to his feelings. He actually would lie on the floor, rolling, clenching tufts of the rug in his hands. He would literally run across the room, free to move as he liked, jumping on the floor, testing and reveling in its absolute security, letting the relief flood through him, draining the fear from his mind and body. His yearning for this was astonishingly intense, and somehow he understood that he had better keep this feeling at bay.

He took a half dollar from his pocket and struck it against the pane, but without any hope that the glass would break and with very little disappointment when it did not. After a few moments of thought he drew his leg up onto the ledge and picked loose the knot of his shoelace. He slipped off the shoe and, holding it across the instep, drew back his arm as far as he dared and struck the leather heel against the glass. The pane rattled, but he knew he'd been a long way from breaking it. His foot was cold and he slipped the shoe back on.

Literature ㉓
in context Science Connection

Physics

Tom is on the ledge with only a pane of glass between him and safety. Why is he unable to break the glass? Newton's third law of motion explains this: For every action, there is an equal and opposite reaction.

If Tom hits the glass without enough force to break it, the opposite reaction of his hand bouncing off the glass will have enough force to throw him backward off the ledge.

㉔ ✔**Reading Check**
What prevents Tom from getting back into the apartment?

㉓ **Background**

Physics

Tom tries to break the window by hitting it with a half dollar and a shoe. He weighs his chances of successfully punching through the glass without having the rebound fling him backward and topple him off the ledge.

In his calculations, Tom deals with the science of physics, which concerns itself with the fundamental elements of the universe, the forces they exert on each other, and the results produced by these forces.

The Greek mathematician Archimedes designed devices to deal with force and motion, such as the lever. It was not until 1687, however, that the English mathematician Sir Isaac Newton stated the principles of mechanics. The subsequent development of physics owes much to Newton's laws of motion.

㉔ ✔**Reading Check**

Answer: The window is jammed shut, and Tom cannot break the glass.

CUSTOMIZE INSTRUCTION FOR UNIVERSAL ACCESS

For Special Needs Students	For Gifted/Talented Students
Students might get bogged down by the details in this passage. Suggest that they visualize each essential action the author describes: Tom takes the half dollar from his pocket; he strikes the pane with the half dollar; the pane doesn't break. Tom lifts his leg onto the ledge; he unties his shoelace; he takes off his shoe; he draws his arm back and hits the pane with his shoe. The glass doesn't break, so he puts the shoe back on.	Students might be interested in exploring in detail how the principles of physics affect Tom's attempts to break the window with the half dollar and the shoe. Have them research how Sir Isaac Newton's laws of motion, notably the second and third, affect Tom's chances of success. Have them write up their findings and make a recommendation to Tom about the safest and most effective way to break the window.

㉕ Critical Thinking

Synthesize

- Remind students that Jack Finney's stories are famous for their concern with time.

- Have students analyze how the author makes eight minutes seem like hours. Then have them analyze the effect of the time distortion here.
  Answer: Finney makes a short time seem endless by describing every detail of Tom's actions and every thought that goes through his mind. Students may say that Finney distorts time to create suspense. It seems that readers will never find out what happens to Tom in the end.

㉖ Vocabulary Development

The Latin Word Root -term-

- Call students' attention to the word *interminable* and its definition. Tell students that the Latin root *-term-* means "end."

- Have students suggest words that contain this root, and list them on the chalkboard. Possibilities include *terminal*, *termination*, and *terminate*.

- Next, have students look up the meanings of these words in a dictionary.

- Finally, ask students to write a sentence about the story that contains one of these words. Call on volunteers to read their sentences aloud.

㉗ ▶ Critical Viewing

Answer: Tom is very small in relation to the tall building. It would be difficult for someone to notice him, especially at night.

He shouted again experimentally, and then once more, but there was no answer.

The realization suddenly struck him that he might have to wait here till Clare came home, and for a moment the thought was funny. He could see Clare opening the front door, withdrawing her key from the lock, closing the door behind her, and then glancing up to see him crouched on the other side of the window. He could see her rush across the room, face astounded and frightened, and hear himself shouting instructions: "Never mind how I got here! Just open the wind—" She couldn't open it, he remembered, she'd never been able to; she'd always had to call him. She'd have to get the building superintendent or a neighbor, and he pictured himself smiling and answering their questions as he climbed in. "I just wanted to get a breath of fresh air, so—"

㉕ He couldn't possibly wait here till Clare came home. It was the second feature she'd wanted to see, and she'd left in time to see the first. She'd be another three hours or—He glanced at his watch; Clare had been gone eight minutes. It wasn't possible, but only eight minutes ago he had kissed his wife goodbye. She wasn't even at the theater yet!

It would be four hours before she could possibly be home, and he tried to picture himself kneeling out here, fingertips hooked to these narrow strippings, while first one movie, preceded by a slow listing of credits, began, developed, reached its climax and then finally ended. There'd be a newsreel next, maybe, and then an animated cartoon, and then <u>interminable</u> scenes from coming ㉖ pictures. And then, once more, the beginning of a full-length picture—while all the time he hung out here in the night.

He might possibly get to his feet, but he was afraid to try. Already his legs were cramped, his thigh muscles tired; his knees hurt, his feet felt numb and his hands were stiff. He couldn't possibly stay out here for four hours, or anywhere near it. Long before that his legs and arms would give out; he would be forced to try changing his position often—stiffly, clumsily, his coordination and strength gone—and he would fall. Quite realistically, he knew that he would fall; no one could stay out here on this ledge for four hours.

A dozen windows in the apartment building across the street were lighted. Looking over his shoulder, he could see the top of a man's head behind the newspaper he was reading; in another window he saw the blue-gray flicker of a television screen. No more than twenty-odd yards from his

interminable (in tur′ mi nə bəl) *adj.* seemingly endless

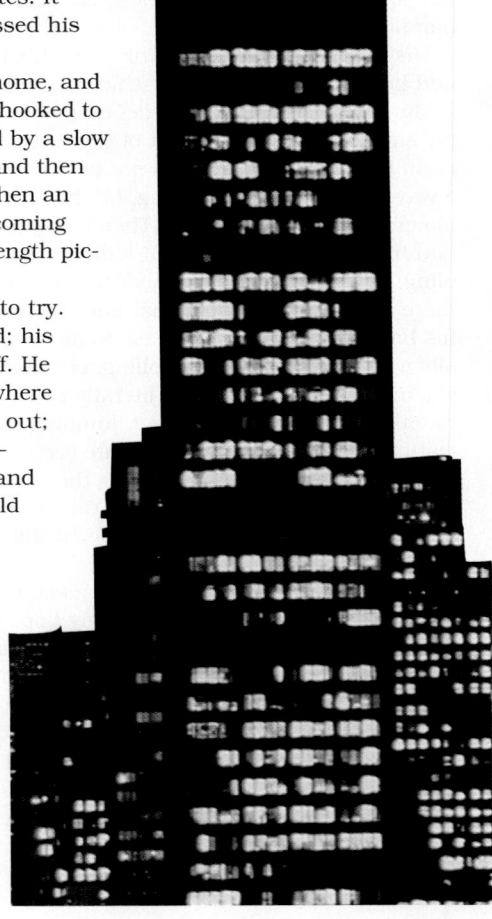

㉗ ▶**Critical Viewing** Based on this photograph, why do you think no one notices Tom on the ledge? **[Draw Conclusions]**

16 ◆ On the Edge

back were scores of people, and if just one of them would walk idly to his window and glance out. . . . For some moments he stared over his shoulder at the lighted rectangles, waiting. But no one appeared. The man reading his paper turned a page and then continued his reading. A figure passed another of the windows and was immediately gone.

In the inside pocket of his jacket he found a little sheaf of papers, and he pulled one out and looked at it in the light from the living room. It was an old letter, an advertisement of some sort; his name and address, in purple ink, were on a label pasted to the envelope. Gripping one end of the envelope in his teeth, he twisted it into a tight curl. From his shirt pocket he brought out a book of matches. He didn't dare let go the casing with both hands, but, with the twist of paper in his teeth, he opened the matchbook with his free hand; then he bent one of the matches in two without tearing it from the folder, its red-tipped end now touching the striking surface. With his thumb, he rubbed the red tip across the striking area.

He did it again, then again, and still again, pressing harder each time, and the match suddenly flared, burning his thumb. But he kept it alight, cupping the matchbook in his hand and shielding it with his body. He held the flame to the paper in his mouth till it caught. Then he snuffed out the match flame with his thumb and forefinger, careless of the burn, and replaced the book in his pocket. Taking the paper twist in his hand, he held it flame down, watching the flame crawl up the paper, till it flared bright. Then he held it behind him over the street, moving it from side to side, watching it over his shoulder, the flame flickering and guttering in the wind.

There were three letters in his pocket and he lighted each of them, holding each till the flame touched his hand and then dropping it to the street below. At one point, watching over his shoulder while the last of the letters burned, he saw the man across the street put down his paper and stand—even seeming, to Tom, to glance toward his window. But when he moved, it was only to walk across the room and disappear from sight.

There were a dozen coins in Tom Benecke's pocket and he dropped them, three or four at a time. But if they struck anyone, or if anyone noticed their falling, no one connected them with their source, and no one glanced upward.

His arms had begun to tremble from the steady strain of clinging to this narrow perch, and he did not know what to do now and was terribly frightened. Clinging to the window stripping with one hand, he again searched his pockets. But now—he had left his wallet on his dresser when he'd changed clothes—there was nothing left but the yellow sheet. It occurred to him irrelevantly that his death on the sidewalk below would be an eternal mystery; the window closed—why, how, and from where could he have fallen? No one would be able to identify his body for a time, either—the thought was somehow unbearable and increased his fear. All they'd find in his pockets would be the

Reading Stategy
Reread or Read Ahead
Read ahead to see what Tom will do with these papers.

**Reading Check**
Why does Tom light the papers from his pockets on fire?

㉘ Reading Strategy
Rereading or Reading Ahead

- Direct students to the Reading Strategy note on p. 17: Read ahead to see what Tom will do with these papers.
- Make sure students identify the paragraph that answers this question.
  Answer: He lights them on fire with matches from his pocket.

㉙ Critical Thinking
Connect

- Ask students why no one would be able to identify Tom's body if he fell.
  Answer: There is nothing on Tom to identify him—only the paper with the cryptic notes.
- Then, ask students to explain how this realization relates to the career goals he stated earlier.
  Answer: Tom begins to realize the emptiness of his driving ambition; he doesn't want to be defined only by his career.

㉚ ✔ Reading Check

Answer: He hopes that somebody in the street below will notice the fire and, therefore, notice him.

CUSTOMIZE INSTRUCTION FOR UNIVERSAL ACCESS

For Less Proficient Readers	For English Learners	For Advanced Readers
Make sure students understand why Tom decides to drop the coins and the burning letters to the street. Then, as a group, have them brainstorm for a list of other ways Tom might have drawn attention to himself. As students read ahead, have them compare these solutions to the one Tom actually finds.	In the scene in which Tom drops the burning letters to the street, Finney uses a variety of verbs relating to fire, such as *flare, snuff,* and *flicker.* Have students record and define these words in their notebooks. Then, have them use a dictionary or thesaurus to add at least two related verbs to the list. Examples include *blaze, ignite,* and *kindle.*	Ask students to imagine how the story might have ended if someone had discovered Tom after noticing the burning letters or the coins. Who might have noticed him? How would they have communicated? How would this person have rescued Tom? Have students write an outline for an alternative ending to the story.

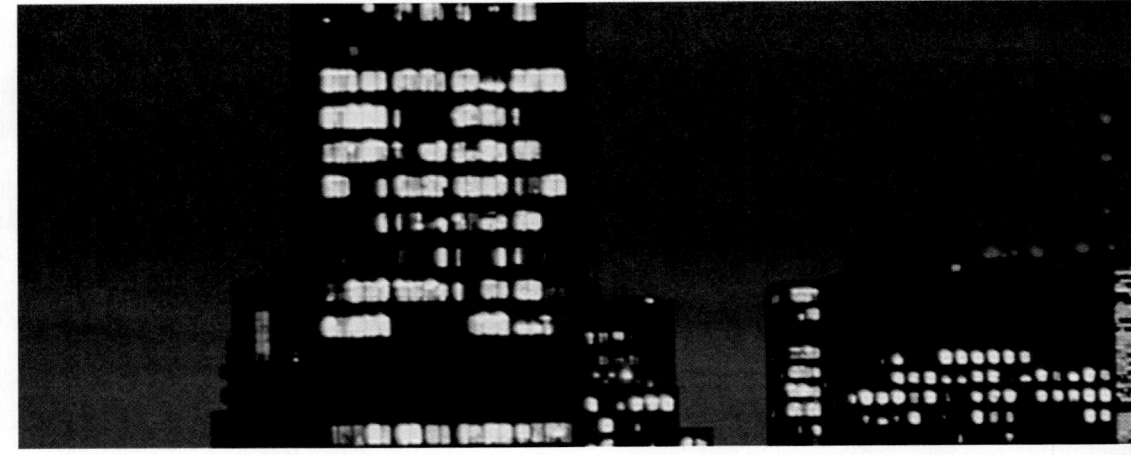

③① ▶Critical Viewing

Answer: Tom may look at the buildings with their lights on and wish he were one of the millions of people safely inside an apartment or office.

③② Reading Strategy

Rereading or Reading Ahead

- Direct students to return to the beginning of the story to remind themselves how important the yellow paper was to Tom.

- Then, have them explain Tom's current attitude toward work and the yellow paper.
  Answer: Tom regrets all the nights he spent alone working, rather than spending valuable time with his wife.

- Have students speculate about why Tom's attitude has changed.
  Possible answer: Tom believes that he doesn't have much time left to live, so he has begun to evaluate the way he spent his time in the past.

③③ Critical Thinking

Interpret

- Ask students what the phrase "contents of the dead man's pocket" signifies for Tom now.
  Answer: He puts the emphasis on dead man, and he realizes that if he did die, his life would have been wasted because he didn't take the time to enjoy what he had while he was alive.

- Ask students to write questions about how Tom will change his life if he returns safely to his apartment. For example, they might ask whether Tom will continue to work on this proposal.

- Encourage students to record their questions in a chart like the one below.

- Then, have students read ahead and look for answers to their questions.

Questions	Answers
Will Tom continue to work on his proposal?	

yellow sheet. *Contents of the dead man's pockets, he thought, one sheet of paper bearing penciled notations—incomprehensible.*

He understood fully that he might actually be going to die; his arms, maintaining his balance on the ledge, were trembling steadily now. And it occurred to him then with all the force of a revelation that, if he fell, all he was ever going to have out of life he would then, abruptly, have had. Nothing, then, could ever be changed; and nothing more—no least experience or pleasure—could ever be added to his life. He wished, then, that he had not allowed his wife to go off by herself tonight—and on similar nights. He thought of all the evenings he had spent away from her, working; and he regretted them. He thought wonderingly of his fierce ambition and of the direction his life had taken; he thought of the hours he'd spent by himself, filling the yellow sheet that had brought him out here. *Contents of the dead man's pockets,* he thought with sudden fierce anger, *a wasted life.*

He was simply not going to cling here till he slipped and fell; he told himself that now. There was one last thing he could try; he had been aware of it for some moments, refusing to think about it, but now he faced it. Kneeling here on the ledge, the fingertips of one hand pressed to the narrow strip of wood, he could, he knew, draw his other hand back a yard perhaps, fist clenched tight, doing it very slowly till he sensed the outer limit of balance, then, as hard as he was able from the distance, he could drive his fist forward against the glass. If it broke, his fist smashing through, he was safe; he might cut himself badly, and probably would, but with his arm inside the room, he would be secure. But if the glass did not break, the rebound, flinging his arm back, would topple him off the ledge. He was certain of that.

He tested his plan. The fingers of his left hand clawlike on the little stripping, he drew back his other fist until his body began teetering backward. But he had no leverage now—he could feel that there would be no force to his swing—and he moved his fist slowly forward till he

③① ▲ **Critical Viewing** In what ways does this picture help you appreciate Tom's feelings on the ledge? **[Connect]**

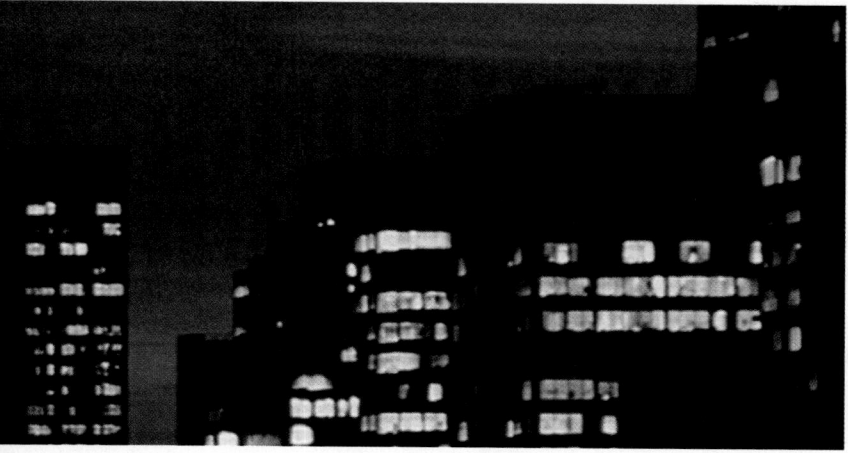

rocked forward on his knees again and could sense that his swing would carry its greatest force. Glancing down, however, measuring the distance from his fist to the glass, he saw that it was less than two feet.

It occurred to him that he could raise his arm over his head, to bring it down against the glass. But, experimenting in slow motion, he knew it would be an awkward . . . blow without the force of a driving punch, and not nearly enough to break the glass.

34 Facing the window, he had to drive a blow from the shoulder, he knew now, at a distance of less than two feet; and he did not know whether it would break through the heavy glass. It might; he could picture it happening, he could feel it in the nerves of his arm. And it might not; he could feel that too—feel his fist striking this glass and being instantaneously flung back by the unbreaking pane, feel the fingers of his other hand breaking loose, nails scraping along the casing as he fell.

He waited, arm drawn back, fist balled, but in no hurry to strike; this pause, he knew, might be an extension of his life. And to live even a few seconds longer, he felt, even out here on this ledge in the night, was infinitely better than to die a moment earlier than he had to. His arm grew tired, and he brought it down and rested it.

Then he knew that it was time to make the attempt. He could not kneel here hesitating indefinitely till he lost all courage to act, waiting till he slipped off the ledge. Again he drew back his arm, knowing this time that he would not bring it down till he struck. His elbow protruding over Lexington Avenue far below, the fingers of his other hand pressed down bloodlessly tight against the narrow stripping, he waited, feeling the sick tenseness and terrible excitement building. It grew and swelled toward the moment of action, his nerves tautening. He thought of Clare—just a wordless, yearning thought—and then drew his arm back just a bit more, fist so tight his fingers pained

Literary Analysis

Suspense Tom imagines actions that have not yet happened. How does this build suspense?

35 ☑ **Reading Check**

What makes Tom decide to break the window?

Contents of the Dead Man's Pocket ◆ 19

---

34 Literary Analysis

Suspense

- Ask students to reread this paragraph and identify the two scenarios that Tom imagines.
  Answer: Tom imagines first that he will succeed at breaking the glass, and then that he will fail, and be thrown backward off the ledge by the unyielding pane.

- Then, ask students the Literary Analysis question on p. 19: Tom imagines actions that have not yet happened. How does this build suspense?
  Answer: This increases the suspense because it makes the reader wonder which of the two scenarios will be the real outcome.

35 ☑ Reading Check

Answer: Tom believes that no one will save him, so he decides to act before he loses his courage. At the last minute, the thought of seeing Clare gives him motivation and strength.

CUSTOMIZE INSTRUCTION FOR UNIVERSAL ACCESS

For Special Needs Students	For Advanced Readers
To help students feel the tension of Tom's final moments on the ledge, play this scene on the Listening to Literature Audiotape. Have students listen to it once and then read it aloud on their own. Help students find the moments when Tom is the most fearful, and have them use their voice to convey that fear.	Have students reread the scene that depicts Tom's final moments on the ledge. Ask them to take note of the words and lines that most vividly express Tom's fear. Then, have students read the passage aloud to the class, using the tone, pitch, and volume of their voice to capture Tom's fear at the appropriate times.

36 Literary Analysis

Suspense

- Ask students the Literary Analysis question on p. 20: How and where does the suspense finally lift?

- Have students identify details in this paragraph that contribute to the lifting of the suspense. Make sure they pay attention to the author's choice of words.
Answer: The suspense lifts when Tom returns safely to his apartment. The author shows that the tension has eased by noting the grin on Tom's face and describing his calm, ordinary actions.

Answers for p. 20

Review and Assess

1. (a) Students may say they agreed with Tom's choice to break through the window. **(b)** Students may say they disagreed with his choice to go out the window in the first place.

2. (a) Tom goes out on the ledge to retrieve the yellow sheet containing the statistics he had gathered. **(b)** This shows that Tom cares deeply about his work, to the extent that he would risk his own safety.

3. (a) Tom feels terrified when he looks down at the street. **(b)** He becomes paralyzed and is convinced that he will faint.

4. (a) At the beginning of the story, he is interested only in his work; at the end of the story, he comes to realize that his relationship with his wife is more important than his work. **(b)** His close encounter with death makes him realize what is important to him. **(c)** He will probably spend less time on work and more time enjoying life with his wife.

5. Students may say they can learn to appreciate each moment in life, and spend time doing things that are truly meaningful.

6. Students may say that Finney's story would not make a good movie. It would be difficult to convey the suspense on a screen, since a lot of the tense "action" takes place in Tom's mind. In addition, the story contains only one main character and almost no dialogue.

---

him, and knowing he was going to do it. Then with full power, with every last scrap of strength he could bring to bear, he shot his arm forward toward the glass, and he said, "*Clare!*"

36 He heard the sound, felt the blow, felt himself falling forward, and his hand closed on the living-room curtains, the shards and fragments of glass showering onto the floor. And then, kneeling there on the ledge, an arm thrust into the room up to the shoulder, he began picking away the protruding slivers and great wedges of glass from the window frame, tossing them in onto the rug. And, as he grasped the edges of the empty window frame and climbed into his home, he was grinning in triumph.

He did not lie down on the floor or run through the apartment, as he had promised himself; even in the first few moments it seemed to him natural and normal that he should be where he was. He simply turned to his desk, pulled the crumpled yellow sheet from his pocket and laid it down where it had been, smoothing it out; then he absently laid a pencil across it to weight it down. He shook his head wonderingly, and turned to walk toward the closet.

There he got out his topcoat and hat and, without waiting to put them on, opened the front door and stepped out, to go find his wife. He turned to pull the door closed and the warm air from the hall rushed through the narrow opening again. As he saw the yellow paper, the pencil flying, scooped off the desk and, unimpeded by the glassless window, sail out into the night and out of his life, Tom Benecke burst into laughter and then closed the door behind him.

Literary Analysis

Suspense How and where does the suspense finally lift?

Jack Finney

(1911–1995)

Jack Finney combines fantastic events and realistic characters in his fascinating and sometimes frightening tales. In 1946, Finney worked for an advertising agency and dreamed of becoming a writer. He began to realize his dream when he entered his first short story in a contest sponsored by a magazine—and won!

He continued to combine real and imaginary details in his fiction, often writing about time travel. In many of his tales, the hero escapes from the present into a simpler and calmer time in the past. Finney's concern with time, and escaping from it, is reflected in the titles of some of his works: "About Time" (1986) and *From Time to Time*, the long-awaited sequel to *Time and Again*.

Review and Assess

Thinking About the Selection

1. **(a) Respond:** At what points in the story did you agree with Tom's choices? **(b)** When did you disagree with his choices?

2. **(a) Recall:** Why does Tom go out on the ledge? **(b) Draw Conclusions:** What does this reveal about his character?

3. **(a) Recall:** How does Tom feel when he looks between his legs down onto Lexington Avenue? **(b) Analyze:** How do Tom's feelings affect his ability to get off the ledge?

4. **(a) Compare and Contrast:** Contrast Tom's attitude toward life at the beginning of the story with his attitude at the end. **(b) Infer:** What causes his attitude to change? **(c) Extend:** What changes, if any, will Tom make in his life as a result of this experience?

5. **Apply:** What lesson can you learn from Tom's experiences?

6. **Evaluate:** Stories are often adapted into movies. Do you think that a movie based on Finney's story would be as effective as the story itself? Why or why not?

✎ ASSESSMENT PRACTICE: Reading Comprehension

Using Context Clues   (For more practice, see **Test Preparation Workbook, p. 1.**)

Some tests require that students be able to use context clues to determine the best meaning of selected words from a passage of reading. Answer the following sample question.

"As the door opening narrowed, the current of warm air from the hallway, <u>channeled</u> through this smaller opening now, suddenly rushed past him with accelerated force."

In this sentence, *channeled* means

A tumbled   **C** called
B widened   **D** sent

Have students read the sentence containing the underlined word and then carefully examine each answer choice. *A* can be eliminated because the sentence is about air; *B* can be eliminated because the opening is narrowed, not widened; and *C* does not relate to air. By process of elimination, *D* is the best answer.

Review and Assess

Literary Analysis

Suspense

1. **(a)** While you were reading the story, what was the main question that you had in mind? **(b)** How did this question produce a feeling of **suspense**?

2. Identify three details about Tom's situation that add to the suspense. Use a diagram like this one to record your ideas.

Tom looks down.

Suspense

3. How does the suspense in the story make you feel closer to Tom?

4. Why does the suspense make you more likely to think about what is really important in life?

Connecting Literary Elements

5. The **rising action** of this story begins when Tom steps out on the ledge. Identify three different events that increase the suspense during this part of the story.

6. Which event ends the rising action of the story? Why?

Reading Strategy

Rereading and Reading Ahead

7. Long before the reader knows why the document is so important, Tom Benecke agonizes about a piece of paper flying out of a window. Find the paragraph that describes this event. Then, **read ahead** to find information provided later that justifies his anxiety.

8. **Reread** to identify the significance of the title of this story.

9. In your own words, explain why rereading passages can help you more fully comprehend a work of literature.

Extend Understanding

10. **Career Connection: (a)** In what kinds of jobs is it routine to risk one's life? **(b)** Why are some people attracted to these jobs?

Quick Review

Suspense is the feeling of tension or curiosity about the outcome of events in a literary work.

All the events leading up to a narrative's climax, or high point, make up a story's **rising action.**

When you **reread,** you review a passage to find connections among the words.

When you **read ahead,** you gain information that helps you clarify your understanding.

 Take It to the Net

www.phschool.com

Take the interactive self-test online to check your understanding of the selection.

Contents of the Dead Man's Pocket ◆ *21*

ENRICHMENT: Further Reading

Other Works by Jack Finney

5 Against the House
The Body Snatchers
Time and Again

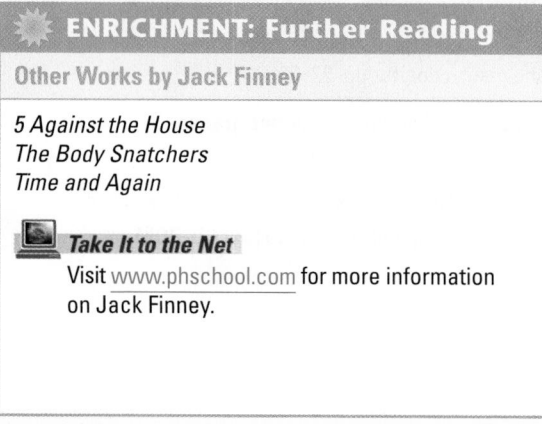 **Take It to the Net**
Visit www.phschool.com for more information on Jack Finney.

Answers for p. 22

❶ Vocabulary Development

Word Analysis

1. You hand in a term paper at the end of the term.
2. You would end the conversation.
3. A terminal disease causes the end of one's life.

Spelling Strategy

1. removing
2. grimacing
3. tiling

Concept Development: Synonyms

1. twisted
2. sneer
3. skill
4. unnoticeably
5. enjoying
6. unending

❷ Grammar

1. room (concrete); entrance (concrete)
2. window (concrete); strength (abstract); bang (abstract)
3. window (concrete); paper (concrete); minute (abstract); more (abstract)
4. hand (concrete); brick (concrete); emptiness (abstract); gap (concrete); face (concrete); wall (concrete)
5. power (abstract); scrap (concrete); strength (abstract); arm (concrete); glass (concrete)

Writing Application

Sample answer: The pitcher turned away from home plate to gather her confidence. She thought of the glory that would come with winning this game. Then, she took a deep breath, turned around, and prepared to throw one last strike.

Integrate Language Skills

❶ Vocabulary Development Lesson

Word Analysis: Latin Root -term-

The Latin root -term- means "end," and the prefix in- means "not" or "without." Combine these meanings to figure out that *interminable* means "without end" or "seemingly endless." Using this definition, answer the following questions.

1. When do you hand in a *term* paper?
2. How would you *terminate* a conversation?
3. What is a *terminal* disease?

Spelling Strategy

When adding a word ending that begins with a vowel to a word that ends in a silent *e*, you usually drop the *e* and add the suffix: *convolute + -ed = convoluted*. Combine the word parts below.

1. remove + -ing =
2. grimace + -ing =
3. tile + -ing =

Concept Development: Synonyms

Synonyms are words with similar meanings, such as *happy* and *cheerful*. On your paper, write the word whose meaning is closest to the meaning of the first word.

1. convoluted: (a) boisterous, (b) twisted, (c) greedy
2. grimace: (a) sneer, (b) buffoon, (c) sadness
3. deftness: (a) foolishness, (b) clumsiness, (c) skill
4. imperceptibly: (a) obviously, (b) visually, (c) unnoticeably
5. reveling: (a) mourning, (b) enjoying, (c) showing
6. interminable: (a) unending, (b) ageless, (c) noticeable

❷ Grammar Lesson

Types of Nouns

A **noun** is a word that names a person, place, thing, or idea. **Concrete nouns** name things that can be seen and touched, such as *beach* or *hand*. **Abstract nouns** name things that exist as concepts: ideas, qualities, and conditions, such as *freedom* or *courage*. In this example, the bold-faced nouns are abstract.

The impossible **remoteness** of this utter **safety**, the **contrast** between it and where he now stood, was more than he could bear.

Practice List the nouns in the sentences that follow. Label each noun as concrete or abstract.

1. He crossed the room to the entrance.
2. He heaved on the window with all his strength and it shot open with a bang.
3. He knelt at the window and stared at the yellow paper for a full minute or more.
4. Then his moving left hand slid onto not brick but sheer emptiness, an impossible gap in the face of the wall.
5. Then with full power, with every last scrap of strength he could bring to bear, he shot his arm forward toward the glass.

Writing Application Write a paragraph about a suspenseful situation. Use at least two abstract and two concrete nouns in your writing.

W̶G *Prentice Hall Writing and Grammar Connection: Chapter 16, Section 1*

TEACHING RESOURCES

The following resources can be used to enrich or extend the instruction for pp. 22–23.

Vocabulary

- **Selection Support:** Build Vocabulary, p.1
- **Vocabulary and Spelling Practice Book** (Use this booklet for skills enrichment.) ▪

Grammar

- **Selection Support:** Build Grammar Skills, p. 2
- W̶G **Writing and Grammar,** Platinum Level, pp. 338–343

Daily Language Practice Transparencies ▪

Writing

- W̶G **Writing and Grammar,** Platinum Level, p. 83
- **Writing and Grammar iText CD-ROM** ▪

BLOCK SCHEDULING: Resources marked with this symbol provide varied instruction during 90-minute blocks.

❸ Writing Lesson

Writing a Cliffhanger Scene

Tom's sidling dance on the ledge is as suspenseful as any movie's cliffhanger scene. Write your own "cliffhanger" with a dangerous setting that includes one or more characters, sound effects, and dialogue.

Prewriting Use your imagination to come up with a situation, such as a boy stuck in the railroad tracks with a train approaching or a jumbo jet that might crash. Then, use a flowchart like this one to map out the sequence of events that will occur.

Model: Planning a Sequence of Events

First	Next	Then	Finally
Foot caught in railroad tracks	Boy yells for help	Rumbling of approaching train heard	Foot comes free just before train passes

Drafting Describe the events using vivid details. Your details should be specific and create suspense. For example, if your scene is set on a railroad track, you might include the rumbling of the rails from the pressure of the approaching train.

Revising Review your writing to make sure you have included transitions that help indicate the sequence of events. Add transitions—such as *first, next, then,* and *finally*—that indicate time order.

W̧G *Prentice Hall Writing and Grammar Connection: Chapter 5, Section 2*

❹ Extension Activities

Listening and Speaking Suppose that Tom runs into Clare as he is walking out the door at the story's end. With a partner, write and perform a **dialogue** between Tom and Clare. Have Tom explain what has happened, and have Clare respond. Use these tips:

- Have the characters raise or lower their voices for effect.
- Use physical gestures to reinforce points each character makes.

Perform your dialogue. **[Group Activity]**

Research and Technology This story might not have taken place if the technology we use today had been available. Create a **timeline** that shows when photocopiers and personal computers were introduced to the market and how quickly they caught on.

 Take It to the Net www.phschool.com

Go online for an additional research activity using the Internet.

Contents of the Dead Man's Pocket ◆ 23

---

❸ Writing Lesson

- Make sure students understand that a "cliffhanger" scene is a scene or situation that is highly suspenseful.

- Tell students they will be writing their own cliffhanger scenes. Use the graphic organizer on p. 23 to model the sequence of events in a suspenseful scene.

- Point out the sensory details in the graphic organizer, such as the rumbling of the train. Encourage students to use sensory details to add drama to their scenes.

- Have students copy the graphic organizer in their notebooks and create their own sequence of events.

- Use the Short Story rubric in **Performance Assessment and Portfolio Management,** p. 14, to evaluate students' scenes.

❹ Listening and Speaking

- Have students pair up to do the role-play.

- Suggest that they try different reactions from Clare: confusion, amusement, anger, love, and relief.

- Explain to students that the characters can convey their emotions in many ways: word choice, tone of voice, expressions, and gestures.

- Have students use the rubric for Presenting an Oral Response to Literature, p. 31 in **Performance Assessment and Portfolio Management.**

CUSTOMIZE INSTRUCTION
For Universal Access

To address different learning styles, use the activities suggested in the **Extension Activities** booklet, p.1.

- For Intrapersonal Learners, use Activity 4.

- For Musical/Rhythmic and Verbal/Linguistic Learners, use Activity 5.

- For Visual/Spatial and Verbal/Linguistic Learners, use Activity 6.

Lesson Objectives

1. To analyze the structure and format of various business documents
2. To understand the purposes of various business documents
3. To distinguish between formal and informal business documents, such as letters and memos
4. To understand how the purpose of a business document is related to its form

About Business Documents

- Have students read "About Business Documents." Review the bulleted points to help focus students' attention on the function and format of different business documents.

- Ask students to discuss business documents that they have written or read in the past. Students may be familiar with these documents through their involvement in school organizations or after-school jobs.

- Ask students why they think it is important to learn about business letters and memos. Encourage them to discuss situations in the future in which they will have to write and read these types of documents.

Reading Strategy

Analyzing Structure and Format

- Review with students the elements of a successful business letter. Make sure students understand that these elements comprise the structure and format of effective business letters; the particular content of a letter will vary.

- Explain to students that understanding the structure and format of business documents will help them communicate in a business setting in a more efficient manner.

- Call students' attention to the chart of business document vocabulary and definitions on this page. Have students provide examples of each document with which they are familiar.

Business Documents

About Business Documents

Business documents include many different written products, all of which are fact-based and geared to communicate specific information in recognizable formats. Although you may encounter several forms of business documents, business letters and memorandums (memos) are among the most common.

A **business letter** or **memo** does the following:

- Conveys a message as clearly, directly, and briefly as possible within the chosen format
- Anticipates and answers any questions readers might have
- Addresses manageable topics and stays focused on those topics
- Follows a clear format and is organized effectively.

A business letter is written in formal, polite language, regardless of its content. In contrast, a memo is less formal and may be written with the assumption that the reader has a certain knowledge of the business.

Reading Strategy

Analyzing Structure and Format

Business letters serve a wide variety of purposes—from a letter of complaint to a letter congratulating a team of employees for a job well done. An effective business letter

- Includes six parts: the heading, the inside address, the salutation, the body, the closing, and the signature
- Contains formal, polite language, regardless of the content

A business memorandum usually contains

- Four headings—*Date*, *To*, *From*, and *Re*—each of which is followed by a colon (*Re* is short for *In re*, which means "in the matter of" or "as regards.")
- The body, which gives information or instruction about the topic referenced in the heading

---

Business Document Vocabulary and Definitions

Agenda: A schedule of items to be discussed in a meeting

Meeting Minutes: A written record of the issues discussed, the opinions expressed, and votes taken at a meeting

Phone Message: A written message that contains the name and phone number of the person who called and the time of the call, along with instructions for calling back

Job Application: A form filled out by a job applicant that provides pertinent information about that person's qualifications for the job

---

Business Letter to Confirm an Agreement

This business letter was sent from a building contractor to a potential client as a follow-up to a meeting about renovations to a house. It summarizes the decisions and puts these decisions in writing for future reference.

This letter is written in block format, a style in which each part of the letter begins at the left margin.

The **heading** includes the writer's address and the date on which the letter is sent. A designed letterhead, including a phone number or e-mail address, is optional.

The **inside address** includes the name and title of the addressee, as well as the company or organization name if there is one.

The **salutation** is a greeting. When the name of a specific person within the company is not known, the phrase "To whom it may concern" may apply.

In the **body** of the letter, the writer states the purpose of the letter and includes all the important details.

Options for a **closing** include "Sincerely," "Respectfully," "Regards," and "All the best."

R.A. BOSTWICK, INC.
RENOVATION / RESTORATION
37 HEMPSTEAD ROAD SPRING VALLEY, NEW YORK 10977
PHONE / FAX (914) 555-9920

November 29, 2000

Mary Van Houten
2 Bird Place
Spring Valley, NY 10977

Dear Mrs. Van Houten:

It was great to meet with you at your house last week. I think that your house has a lot of interesting 1940s detail, and I am glad to have the opportunity to work on it. I would like to outline the work that we agreed your house needed when we met.

1. The electrical service needs to be updated. The panel in the basement is too old. Your new air-conditioning system will require a 220-amp service.

2. The hot water in the bathtub does not work. That faucet will have to be replaced. If the problem goes further than the faucet, I will inform you of any additional cost.

3. The back hall will be repainted after the sheetrock is repaired.

I will be sending you a contract and a payment schedule early next week. Please let me know if I have forgotten anything. I am looking forward to working with you.

Sincerely,

R.A. Bostwick

R. A. Bostwick

Business Letter to Confirm an Agreement

- Tell students that they will encounter letters like this one after making agreements in person, on the telephone, or over the Internet. Explain that written confirmation letters clarify for both sides the terms of contract or an agreement.

- Have students read the letter and the notes that identify its main elements.

- Call students' attention to the note about the heading of the letter. Have students identify each element in the letter's heading. Explain that the actual style of the heading may vary, but that the type of information contained in it will not.

- Ask students why they think the information in the heading is important.
  Answer: The heading provides information that will allow the addressee to respond to the writer of the letter.

- Review with students the other notes on this page. Bring in an example of another business letter, and have students identify each of the parts.

CUSTOMIZE INSTRUCTION FOR UNIVERSAL ACCESS

For Special Needs Students	For Gifted/Talented Students
To help students distinguish among the different parts of the letter, work with them to code each part with a different colored highlighter. You can then assess their understanding by giving them another example of a business letter and having them highlight the different parts on their own.	Have students discuss the purpose of having a common style for business communication. What are the benefits of following this common style? What effect does this common style have on people's ability to communicate information in a wide variety of situations?

Memo to Start a Project

- Have students read the memo and the notes that accompany it.

- Ask students to identify the similarities between this memo and the letter of confirmation they read on p. 25.

- Then, have students discuss the differences between the two documents. Lead students to see that the purpose of the memo (to communicate information *within* a company) is related to its form. The memo has a more casual form, but the language is still clear and direct.

Memo to Start a Project

Based on the letter to his client, R. A. Bostwick drafted this memo to one of his employees. In it, he identifies parts of the job that should start right away.

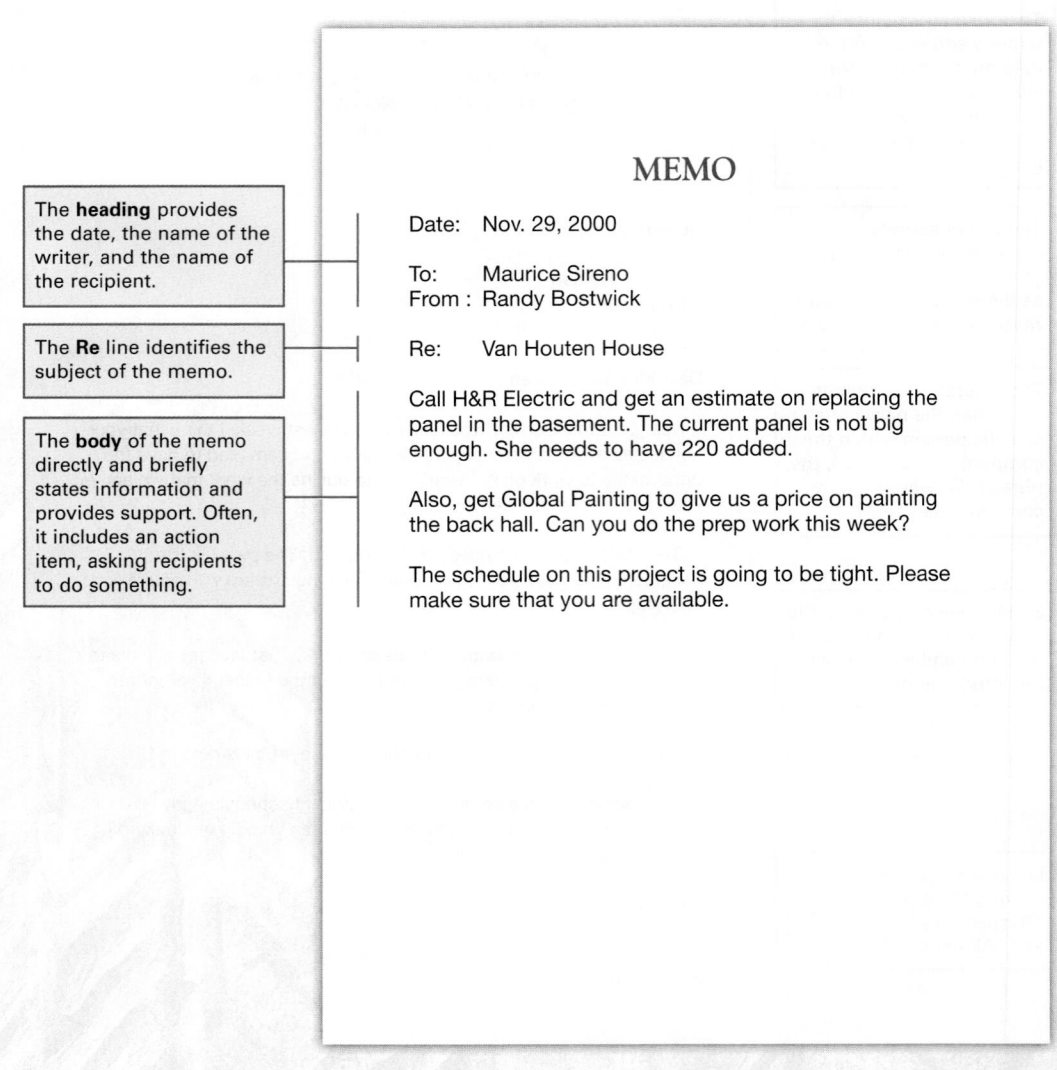

The **heading** provides the date, the name of the writer, and the name of the recipient.

The **Re** line identifies the subject of the memo.

The **body** of the memo directly and briefly states information and provides support. Often, it includes an action item, asking recipients to do something.

MEMO

Date: Nov. 29, 2000

To: Maurice Sireno
From : Randy Bostwick

Re: Van Houten House

Call H&R Electric and get an estimate on replacing the panel in the basement. The current panel is not big enough. She needs to have 220 added.

Also, get Global Painting to give us a price on painting the back hall. Can you do the prep work this week?

The schedule on this project is going to be tight. Please make sure that you are available.

Check Your Comprehension

1. What is the purpose of the business letter?
2. Why does R. A. Bostwick want to document in a letter a conversation that took place with the recipient?
3. What does R. A. Bostwick promise to do?
4. In the memo, why does Randy want an estimate on the electrical panel?
5. What does Randy want Maurice to do?

Applying the Reading Strategy

Analyzing Structure and Format

6. Why is it efficient to have two addresses on a business letter?
7. What purpose does the date line on a business document serve?
8. (a) Find an example of formal, polite language in the business letter. Why is it effective to use such a tone in the letter? (b) Find an example of less formal language in the memo. (c) In both cases, how does the language suit the format and the audience?

Activity

Write a Letter Requesting Information

Write a letter in proper business-letter format in which you request information about a product or service. State your purpose clearly, and be specific about what you want in response to your letter. Use a local phone book or the Internet to locate the appropriate address, and send your letter.

Comparing Informational Materials

Business Document Format

1. Find an example of a business letter and a memorandum. Using a chart like this one, specify the purpose, structure, and defining features of each document.
2. Decide which format would best suit each situation below. Then, explain your choice.

   - Applying for a job
   - Arranging an office party

3. Why is a business letter always formal and polite?
4. Why does a memo contain a *re* line?

Business Letter
Purpose:
Structure:
Defining Features:

Memorandum
Purpose:
Structure:
Defining Features:

Answers for p. 27

Check Your Comprehension

1. The purpose is to confirm an agreement between a company and a client.
2. Bostwick wants to make sure that the client agrees with the terms discussed in the conversation. Putting these terms in writing is the best way to ensure that both parties agree.
3. Bostwick promises to update the electrical service, replace a hot water faucet in the bathtub, and repair and repaint the back hall. He also promises to send a contract and payment schedule the following week.
4. Randy wants an estimate because the current panel is not big enough.
5. Randy wants Maurice to call H&R Electric to get an estimate and Global Painting for a price on painting the back hall.

Applying the Reading Strategy

6. It is efficient to have two addresses on a business letter so that both parties know how to contact one another.
7. The date line documents the date that the letter was written. This can be very important in business dealings.
8. (a) Students may cite "Please let me know if I have forgotten anything." It is effective to use such a tone because business dealings require a respectful tone. (b) Students may cite "Call H&R Electric . . . ." (c) In the business letter, the owner of the company is writing to confirm an agreement with a client, so formal, polite language is required. In the memo, the owner is communicating with an employee in the company, so less formal language is needed.

Activity

Suggest that students identify a product or service they are interested in before writing their letters. After they draft their letters, have students make sure they contain the necessary parts and use language suited to their purpose and audience. You may wish to have students read their letters to the class.

continued

Answers continued

Comparing Informational Materials

1. If students cannot find examples of letters and memos, they can use the examples on pp. 25–26.
2. A business letter would be appropriate for a job application, and a memo, for arranging an office party.
3. A business letter is a form of professional communication between two parties, so it always requires formal, polite language.
4. Memos contain a *re* line to indicate the topic of the memo.

View From the Summit ✦ The Dream Comes True

Lesson Objectives

1. **To analyze and respond to literary elements**
   - Literary Analysis: Author's Perspective
   - Comparing Literary Works
2. **To read, comprehend, analyze, and critique nonfiction**
   - Reading Strategy: Distinguishing Fact From Opinion
   - Reading Check questions
   - Review and Assess questions
   - Assessment Practice (ATE)
3. **To develop word analysis skills, fluency, and systematic vocabulary**
   - Vocabulary Development Lesson: Anglo-Saxon Prefix: *be-*
4. **To understand and apply written and oral language conventions**
   - Spelling Strategy
   - Grammar Lesson: Noun Function
5. **To understand and apply appropriate writing and research strategies**
   - Writing Lesson: Comparison-and-Contrast Essay
   - Extension Activity: Adventure Video Game
6. **To understand and apply listening and speaking strategies**
   - Extension Activity: Advice for Future Climbers

STEP-BY-STEP TEACHING GUIDE	PACING GUIDE
PRETEACH	
Motivate Students and Provide Background	
Use the Motivation activity (ATE p. 28)	5 min.
Read and discuss the Preview material and Background information (SE/ATE p. 28) **A**	5 min.
Introduce the Concepts	
Introduce the Literary Analysis and Reading Strategy (SE/ATE p. 29) **A**	15 min.
Pronounce the vocabulary words and read their definitions (SE p. 29)	5 min.
TEACH	
Monitor Comprehension	
Informally monitor comprehension by circulating while students read independently or in groups **A**	30 min.
Monitor students' comprehension with the Reading Check notes (SE/ATE pp. 31, 33, 35, 39, 41, 43)	as students read
Develop vocabulary with Vocabulary notes (SE pp. 31, 33, 34, 36; ATE p. 33)	as students read
Develop Understanding	
Develop students' understanding of author's perspective with Literary Analysis annotations (SE pp. 34, 43; ATE pp. 31, 32, 34, 40, 41, 42, 43) **A**	10 min.
Develop students' understanding of facts and opinions with Reading Strategy annotations (SE pp. 41, 42; ATE pp. 31, 33, 41, 42)	10 min.
ASSESS	
Assess Mastery	
Assess students' mastery of the Reading Strategy and Literary Analysis by having them answer the Review and Assess questions (SE/ATE p. 45)	20 min.
Use one or more of the print and media Assessment Resources (ATE p. 47) **A**	up to 50 min.
EXTEND	
Apply Understanding	
Have students complete the Vocabulary Development Lesson and the Grammar Lesson (SE p. 46) **A**	20 min.
Apply students' ability to compare and contrast using the Writing Lesson (SE/ATE p. 47) **A**	45 min.
Apply students' understanding using one or more of the Extension Activities (SE p. 47)	20–90 min.

 ACCELERATED INSTRUCTION:
Use the strategies and activities identified with an **A**.

UNIVERSAL ACCESS
● = Below Level Students
▲ = On-Level Students
■ = Above Level Students

Time and Resource Manager

Reading Level: Average, Challenging
Average Number of Instructional Days: 4

RESOURCES

PRINT	TRANSPARENCIES	TECHNOLOGY
• **Beyond Literature,** Cross-Curricular Connection: Physical Education, p. 2 ▲ ■		• **Interest Grabber Video,** Tape 1 ● ▲ ■
• **Selection Support Workbook:** ● ▲ ■ Literary Analysis, p. 8 Reading Strategy, p. 7 Build Vocabulary, p. 5	• **Literary Analysis and Reading Transparencies,** pp. 3 and 4 ● ▲ ■	
		• **Listening to Literature** ● ▲ ■ Audiocassettes, Sides 2, 3 Audio CDs, CDs 1, 2
• **Literatura en español** ● ▲ • **Literary Analysis for Enrichment** ■	• **Fine Art Transparencies, Volume 1,** Art Transparency 3 ● ▲ ■	
• **Formal Assessment:** Selection Test, pp. 4–6 ● ▲ ■ • **Open Book Test,** pp. 4–6 ● ▲ ■ • **Performance Assessment and Portfolio Management,** p. 15 ● ▲ ■ • **PRENTICE HALL ASSESSMENT SYSTEM** ● ▲ ■	• **PRENTICE HALL ASSESSMENT SYSTEM** ● ▲ ■ Skills Practice Answers and Explanations on Transparencies	• **Test Bank Software** ● ▲ ■ • **Got It! Assessment Videotapes** ● ▲
• **Selection Support Workbook:** ● ▲ ■ Build Grammar Skills, p. 6 • **Writing and Grammar,** Platinum Level ● ▲ ■ • **Extension Activities,** p. 2 ● ▲ ■	• **Daily Language Practice Transparencies** ● ▲ • **Writing Models and Graphic Organizers on Transparencies,** p. 95 ● ▲ ■	• **Writing and Grammar iText CD-ROM** ● ▲ ■ **Take It to the Net** www.phschool.com

BLOCK SCHEDULING: Use one 90-minute class period to preteach the selection and have students read it. Use a second 90-minute class period to assess students' mastery of skills and have them complete one of the Extension Activities.

PRETEACH

Step-by-Step Teaching Guide for pp. 28–29

Motivation

Engage students' interest by focusing their attention on the photo on this page. Explain to students that *summit* means not only "the top of the mountain peak," but "the highest degree." Point out to students that reaching the top of Everest can be seen as a summit in both senses—the highest elevation in the world, and the crown of the climber's greatest ambitions. Ask students to consider as they read whether Hillary and Norgay could reach another summit after climbing Everest.

▭ Interest Grabber Video

As an alternative, you may wish to play "Mount Everest" on Tape 1 to engage student interest.

❶ Background

Geography

29,028 feet is about $5\frac{1}{2}$ miles above sea level! The peoples who live on and around the mountain do not call it Mt. Everest. Those on the Tibetan side call it *Chomolungma,* while the Nepalese call it *Sagarmatha.*

Prepare to Read

View From the Summit ◆ The Dream Comes True

▭ Take It to the Net

Visit www.phschool.com for interactive activities and instruction related to these selections, including

- background
- graphic organizers
- literary elements
- reading strategies

Preview

Connecting to the Literature

Whether training to improve your running time or studying to get an A on your exam, you may have to convince yourself that your goal is worth the effort required to reach it. When Sir Edmund Hillary doubted his ability to reach the top of Mount Everest, he said to himself, "Ed, my boy, this is Everest—you've got to push it a bit harder!"

❶ Background

Sir Edmund Hillary and Tenzing Norgay, his climbing partner, were the first two people to reach the summit of Mount Everest in Nepal, 29,028 feet above sea level (the present official height)—the highest spot on Earth. The temperature on the day of their historic achievement was a frigid –27°C.

TEACHING RESOURCES

The following resources can be used to enrich or extend the instruction for pp. 28–29.

Motivation

▭ **Interest Grabber Video,** Tape 1 ▭

Background

▭ **Beyond Literature,** p. 2

▭ **Take It to the Net**
Visit www.phschool.com for background and hotlinks for the selections.

Literary Analysis

▭ **Literary Analysis and Reading Transparencies,** Author's Perspective, p. 4 ▭

Reading

▭ **Selection Support:** Reading Strategy, p. 7; Build Vocabulary, p. 5

▭ **Literary Analysis and Reading Transparencies,** Distinguishing Fact From Opinion, p. 3 ▭

▭ **BLOCK SCHEDULING:** Resources marked with this symbol provide varied instruction during 90-minute blocks.

Literary Analysis

Author's Perspective

When you read firsthand accounts, you get the point of view of one person—the author. How the author interprets the events that he or she sees, hears, or experiences personally is the **author's perspective.** In these two accounts of the ascent of Mount Everest, each man's report is influenced by his own beliefs and assumptions. To identify each author's unique perspective, pay close attention to the details and events that each presents.

Comparing Literary Works

These two works provide an excellent opportunity to compare the authors' perspectives. Hillary and Norgay made the same climb on that historic day. As you read, notice what Hillary says and compare it with what Norgay says about the same thing. For example, notice this contrast:

- From Hillary's perspective, Norgay often struggled and needed Hillary's help during their ascent of Everest.
- From Norgay's perspective, the climbers helped each other equally.

Reading Strategy

Distinguishing Fact From Opinion

Many people have died attempting to reach the summit of Everest. That is a fact—a statement that can be proved true using evidence. Mountain climbing is an exciting sport. That is an opinion—a statement that can be supported by facts but is not itself a fact.

When you **distinguish fact from opinion,** you can reach your own understanding of an event rather than simply accepting what the author says. Use a chart like the one shown to separate facts from opinions in these accounts.

Facts	Opinions
We reached the top at 11:30 A.M.	It was wonderful.
The temperature was –27°C	It was rather frightening.

Vocabulary Development

ample (am′ pəl) *adj.* more than enough; abundant (p. 31)

aperture (ap′ ər chər) *n.* opening in a camera through which light passes into the lens (p. 31)

belay (bi lā′) *n.* rope support (p. 33)

laboriously (lə bōr′ ē əs lē) *adv.* with difficulty (p. 34)

feasible (fē′ zə bəl) *adj.* capable of being done; possible (p. 36)

formidable (fôr′ mə də bəl) *adj.* causing fear or dread (p. 36)

---

❷ Literary Analysis
Author's Perspective

- Have students review the definition of author's perspective to make sure they understand it.
- Ask students to describe a time when they heard different versions of the same story from different people. For example, have family members disagreed about what happened at a family gathering?
- Finally, ask students how they can best determine just what happened when two accounts are presented. Do students try to understand the reasons behind the differences?

❸ Reading Strategy
Distinguishing Fact From Opinion

- Have students review the definitions of fact and opinion: A fact is provable; an opinion is not. To illustrate this point, review the fact-and-opinion chart on this page.
- Ask students to list examples of fact and opinion from their own experiences.
- Finally, instruct students to construct a fact-and-opinion chart to use as they read "View from the Summit" and "The Dream Comes True."

Vocabulary Development

- Pronounce each vocabulary word for students, and read the definitions as a class. Have students identify any words with which they are already familiar.

CUSTOMIZE INSTRUCTION FOR UNIVERSAL ACCESS

For Less Proficient Readers	For English Learners	For Advanced Readers
Model for students how to distinguish fact from opinion by using the Distinguishing Fact From Opinion transparency in **Literary Analysis and Reading Transparencies,** p. 3. Then, work with them to make a list of facts and opinions in the first paragraph on p. 31.	Model distinguishing between fact and opinion by prompting students to scan text for clue words such as "thought" or "seemed," which signal likely opinions.	Have students speculate as they read on how a court might evaluate Hillary's and Norgay's statements. Which might be treated as verifiable fact and admitted as testimony, and which as opinion and therefore unreliable?

 E-Teach

Visit E-Teach at www.phschool.com for teachers' essays on how to teach, with questions and answers.

Step-by-Step Teaching Guide for pp. 30–44

CUSTOMIZE INSTRUCTION
For Visual/Spatial Learners

Visual/spatial learners can best comprehend these narratives if they continue to look at the photographs provided with the selections. The photographs of the mountains provide a visual reinforcement of the details of the struggles and achievement that the writers describe.

❶ About the Selection

This nonfiction selection is about the last part of Edmund Hillary's climb to the highest peak of Mount Everest. He describes in detail the particular challenges of the climb and the views of the surrounding peaks.

❷ ▶ Critical Viewing

Answer: Edmund Hillary is brave and adventurous. He enjoys challenges.

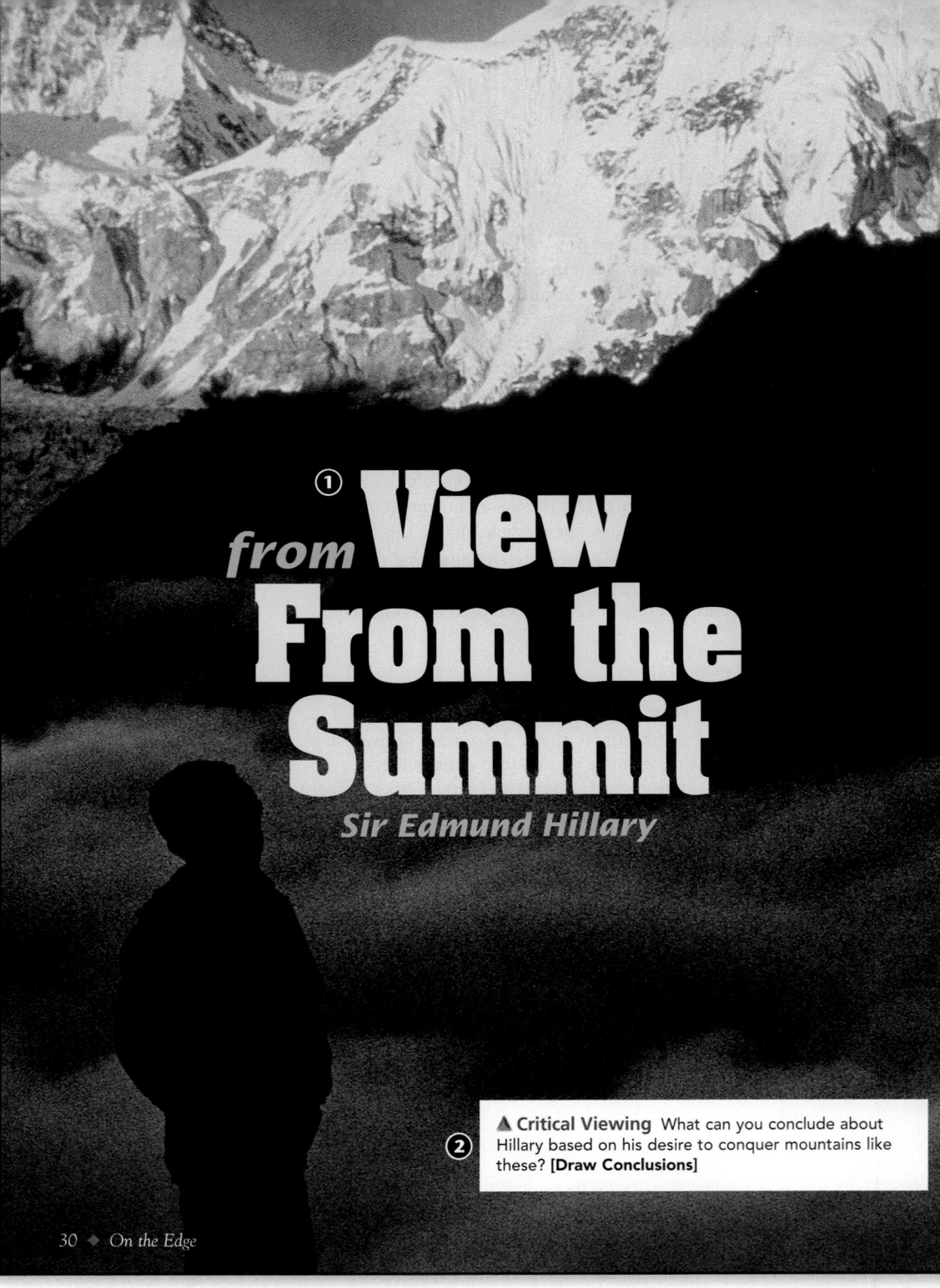

① *from* **View From the Summit**

Sir Edmund Hillary

▲ **Critical Viewing** What can you conclude about Hillary based on his desire to conquer mountains like these? **[Draw Conclusions]**

②

30 ◆ *On the Edge*

TEACHING RESOURCES

The following resources can be used to enrich or extend the instruction for pp. 30–44.

Literary Analysis

- 📖 **Selection Support:** Literary Analysis, p. 8 ■
- 📄 **Writing Models and Graphic Organizers on Transparencies,** p. 95

Reading

- 🎧 **Listening to Literature Audiocassettes,** Sides 2, 3 ■
- 💿 **Listening to Literature Audio CDs,** CDs 1, 2 ■

Extension

- 📄 **Fine Art Transparencies, Volume 1,** Art Transparency 3

■ **BLOCK SCHEDULING:** Resources marked with this symbol provide varied instruction during 90-minute blocks.

The setting sun bathed the giant peaks of Makalu and Lhotse[1] in warm red light. They seemed almost close enough to touch. Far below fleecy clouds floated above gloomy valleys. I joined Tenzing in the tent where he was cooking chicken noodle soup. Astonishingly for this height, we were really hungry. Out came all our delicacies, with the tinned apricots being a special treat. We also drank ample liquid. It was very cramped inside, particularly when we tried to crawl into our sleeping bags. I have such big feet that I decided to remove my boots for the night. Tenzing left his footwear on, while I used mine to prop the toe of my sleeping bag off the ice. Tenzing lay on the bottom ledge, almost overhanging the slope, while I stretched out on the top ledge with my legs across Tenzing in the bottom corner of the tent. We started getting the odd fierce gust of wind and I had some concern as to whether the tent would remain in place, but when I started our oxygen flowing we quickly warmed up and dropped off to sleep peacefully on and off for four hours and then wakened feeling cold and miserable.

At 4 a.m. I looked out the tent doors and could already see signs of the early morning light. Tenzing peered over my shoulder and then pointed and said, "Tengboche," and there, sure enough, was Tengboche Monastery,[2] 15,000 feet below us. The temperature was –27°C, chilly enough in our flimsy tent. We made our slow preparations for departure, eating well and consuming plenty of vital fluid. My boots were frozen solid and I cooked them over the primus stove until they were soft enough for me to pull on. We were wearing every piece of clothing we possessed and I checked my camera for the last time, setting it at a standard aperture and then placing it carefully inside my clothes and zipping up my windproofs. At 6:30 a.m. we crawled out of our tent and were ready to go.

---

1. **Makalu and Lhotse** mountains in the Himalayas in Nepal.
2. **Tengboche Monastery** Buddhist Monastery in Nepal that lies on the main route to the base camp of Mount Everest.

ample (amʹ pəl) *adj.* more than enough; abundant

aperture (apʹ ər chər) *n.* opening in a camera through which light passes into the lens

❺ ✓Reading Check

How did the climbers spend the night?

❸ Literary Analysis

Author's Perspective

- Review the definition of author's perspective with students—the author's attitude or point of view on the subject.
- Read the bracketed passage aloud. Point out details that indicate Hillary's perspective. (The description of his and Norgay's shared discomfort and delight in small luxuries; their seeming unity as they set out on the morning of the final approach.)
- Help students to identify words and phrases that provide clues to the author's perspective: *I joined Tenzing, cooking noodle soup, special treat,* as well as *fierce gust of wind, some concern,* and *cold and miserable.*

❹ Reading Strategy

Distinguishing Fact From Opinion

- Ask students to identify two examples of fact from this page. Possible responses: Tengboche was 15,000 feet below; the temperature was –27°C.
- Ask students to identify two examples of opinion from this page. Possible responses: The peaks of Makalu and Lhotse seemed almost close enough to touch; he describes the valleys as "gloomy."
- Point out to students how the facts were identifiable because of the statistics accompanying them, and how the opinions contained many adjectives and descriptive phrases.

❺ ✓Reading Check

Answer: After being warmed by food and oxygen, they were able to sleep for about four hours.

CUSTOMIZE INSTRUCTION FOR UNIVERSAL ACCESS

For Special Needs Students	For English Learners	For Gifted/Talented Students
Focus students' attention on the photograph on this spread. Ask them to characterize the scene using opinion words from the selection, such as *fleecy* or *gloomy.* Then ask for fact words such as *ledge, slope,* or *valleys.* Help students sound out the words and list them on a vocabulary sheet.	Fact and opinion evaluations may be difficult for English learners to articulate. You may wish to provide them with the option of making notes or constructing a graphic organizer containing adjectives and descriptive phrases that signal opinions in the text.	Suggest that students use the facts and opinions expressed in the selections to write a dialogue between Hillary and Norgay, discussing their achievement.

Author's Perspective

- Read the bracketed passage with students.

- Review the definition of author's perspective on p. 29, and let students know they can determine the author's perspective by scanning for clues about the author's feelings and point of view.

- Then, ask students which details in the paragraph reveal the author's perspective.
  Possible responses: Hillary's perspective is shown in his casual description of himself waving Norgay on to take the lead; his apparent admiration of Norgay's performance; and his description of himself as happy to trail behind Norgay.

7 ▶Critical Viewing

Answer: The mountain is much steeper closer to the summit and, therefore, more arduous for climbers. It takes as long to climb from Camp 8 to 9 as from Camp 3 to 4. Also, the air is much thinner toward the top, making it difficult for climbers to travel even short distances without a rest.

---

6 Above our camp was a great steep bulge of snow and, as my feet were still cold, I waved Tenzing on to take the lead. Surging on with impressive strength, he ploughed a knee-deep track upward and I was happy to follow behind. We reached the top of the bulge at 28,000 feet and, as my feet were now warmer, I took over the lead. Towering over our heads was the South Summit and running along from it to the right were the great menacing cornices overhanging the Kangshung Face. Ahead of me was a sharp narrow ridge, icy on the right and looking more manageable on the left. So it was to the left I went, at first making easy progress, but then experiencing one of the most unpleasant mountaineering conditions—breakable crust. The surface would hold my weight for a few seconds, shatter beneath me, then I lurched forward knee-deep in powder snow. For half an hour I persisted and was encouraged at how well I was moving in these difficult conditions. I crossed over a little bump and saw before me a small hollow on the ridge and in that hollow were the two oxygen bottles left by Evans and Bourdillon.[3] I wiped the snow off the dials and

7 ▼ Critical Viewing
Why do you think Camps 8 and 9 are so close together compared with Camps 3 and 4? **[Analyze]**

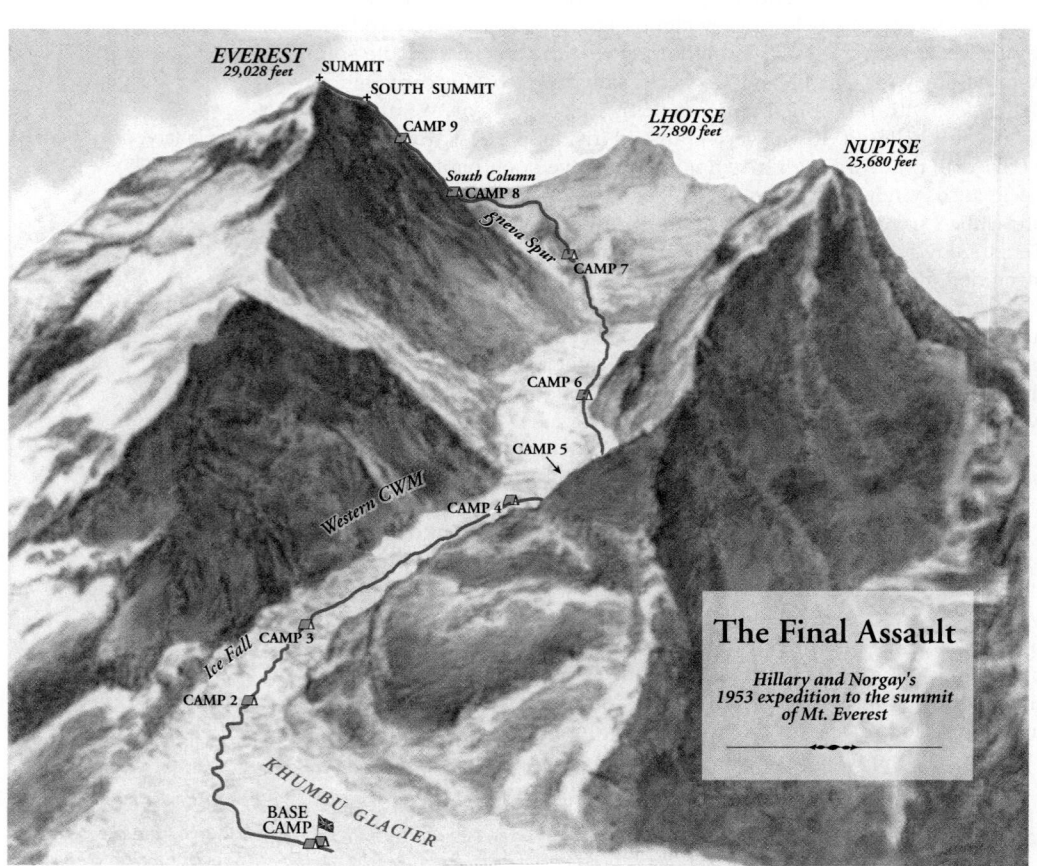

EVEREST 29,028 feet
SUMMIT
SOUTH SUMMIT
CAMP 9
LHOTSE 27,890 feet
NUPTSE 25,680 feet
South Column
CAMP 8
Geneva Spur
CAMP 7
CAMP 6
CAMP 5
Western CWM
CAMP 4
Ice Fall CAMP 3
CAMP 2
KHUMBU GLACIER
BASE CAMP

The Final Assault

Hillary and Norgay's 1953 expedition to the summit of Mt. Everest

---

✷ ENRICHMENT: Art Connection

Enhanced Photography

You may want to point out that the enhancement of this photo creates the visual effect of a map or diagram. Use these questions for discussion:

1. What can you learn from this map that you could not learn from an ordinary photograph?
Answer: This photograph shows the relative heights of the three mountains, the shape and terrain of the three mountains, and the route the climbers took.

2. Why did the climbers follow such a circuitous route to the summit?
Answer: They had to find a safe and accessible route to ascend the mountain.

3. What features does this map have that other maps you've seen do not share?
Answer: Students may note that the map has a three-dimensional quality and is very lifelike.

saw that the bottles were less than a third full of oxygen, but this could give us another hour of endurance on our return. That could be very useful later.

We had made considerable height, but there was much more ahead. A 400-foot-long snow slope rose steeply up toward the South Summit. Alternating the lead, we made our way forward, but it was an extremely uncomfortable experience. A thin skin of ice covered deep soft snow. On one occasion there was a dull breaking noise and a six-foot-wide piece of ice around me shattered and slid away down the mountainside. I slipped backward three or four steps and fortunately stopped, but the ice carried on with increasing speed far out of sight. It was rather frightening, but we had no alternative, we must keep going. With a considerable feeling of tension, we forced our way upward, the snow condition improved and we emerged with great relief onto the South Summit. We were now as high as anyone had ever been before. It was impossible not to dwell for a moment on the remarkable support we had received from our colleagues—John Hunt and Da Namgyal's lift to the depot on the South-East Ridge; George Lowe, Alf Gregory and Ang Nyima with their superb support to Camp IX; and the pioneer effort by Charles Evans and Toni Bourdillon to the South Summit. Their contribution had enabled us to make such good progress. But now the next move was up to us.

I looked carefully along the final summit ridge. It was impressive all right, but not impossible, despite what Charles Evans had said. We'd certainly give it a good try. We had a drink out of Tenzing's water bottle and I checked our oxygen supplies. Each of us had a bottle that was almost empty so, to save weight, we removed these and I attached our other full bottles firmly into place. It meant we had a total endurance of just under four hours. If we kept moving quickly it should be enough.

With a growing feeling of excitement, I moved down from the South Summit to the small saddle at the start of the summit ridge, cutting steps on the left-hand side below the great cornices and keeping just above the rock face sweeping into the Western Cwm. We moved cautiously, one at a time. I hacked a line of steps for forty feet, thrust my ice axe into the firm snow as a sound <u>belay</u>, and then brought Tenzing along to join me. After I had covered several rope-lengths, I noticed to my surprise that Tenzing was moving rather slowly and seemed in some distress. When he came up to me I examined his

---

3. **Evans and Bourdillon** Charles Evans and Tom Bourdillon were the first assault pair in the Everest expedition of 1953. They climbed to within 300 feet of the summit.

Literature ❽
in context Sports Connection

Climbing Essentials

Special equipment is used by climbers to help them get up snowy and icy slopes. Hillary mentions the following pieces of equipment:

ice axe: A tool designed to chop ice to give the climber a platform on which to stand.

crampons: Spiked platforms fastened on the climber's shoes to prevent slipping.

belay: A rope support that is attached to another person. As the climber climbs, the other person lets out the rope. If the climber were to fall, the person holding the belay rope would clamp down on the rope and prevent the climber from falling far.

Hillary and Norgay used ice axes to cut steps in the snow.

belay (bi lā′) *n.* rope support

❶❶ ✔**Reading Check**

What are some of the dangers that Hillary and Norgay encounter?

View From the Summit ◆ 33

---

❽ **Background**
Climbing Essentials

Climbing on snow and ice is much more dangerous than climbing on rock alone. The condition of the surface changes suddenly, often softening as the day progresses. As the ice warms, it may suddenly give way underfoot. Skillful use of the ice ax is therefore crucial to climbers. A multi-purpose tool, ice axes have a handle that tapers to a sharp spike, and a pick and adze (a chopping blade) at the head. It is used not only to cut steps in the ice and belay other climbers, but to measure the depth of snow and crevasses, and serve as a sturdy walking stick.

❾ **Reading Strategy**
Distinguishing Fact From Opinion

• Explain to students that an author's use of adjectives may signal the use of opinion.

• Ask students whether the words *impressive* and *impossible* represent fact or opinion. Make sure students support their responses. **Answer:** They represent opinion. Others might not be impressed with the ridge, and Evans might have found the climb impossible.

❿ **Vocabulary Development**
Anglo-Saxon Prefix *be-*

• Call students' attention to the word *belay* and its definition, "a rope support."

• Tell students that the noun form used here derives from the verb *belay,* combining *be-* (around) and *lay* (put or place).

• Guide students to see that a belay is a rope tied *around* an anchoring object.

❶❶ ✔**Reading Check**

Answer: Loose ice is breaking away from high cliffs. Their oxygen is almost gone, and their oxygen tubes are subject to clogging from ice.

oxygen equipment. The pressure seemed satisfactory but then I noticed that his face mask was choked up with ice. I squeezed the mask to dislodge the ice and was relieved to see Tenzing breathing freely again. I checked my own equipment—it, too, held some ice, but not enough to cause me concern, and I quickly cleared it away. I moved on again, cutting line after line of steps.

Ahead of me loomed the great rock step which we had observed from far below and which we knew might prove to be a major problem. I gazed up at the forty feet of rock with some concern. To climb it directly at nearly 29,000 feet would indeed be a considerable challenge. I looked to the right, there seemed a chance there. Clinging to the rock was a great ice cornice hanging over the mighty Kangshung Face. Under the effects of gravity, the ice had broken away from the rock and a narrow crack ran upward. Nervously, I wondered if the cornice might collapse under my pressure. There was only one way to find out!

Although it would be relatively useless, I got Tenzing to establish a belay; then I eased my way into the crack, facing the rock. I jammed my crampons into the ice behind me and then wriggled my way upward using every little handhold I could find. Puffing for breath, I made steady height—the ice was holding—and forty feet up I pulled myself out of the crack onto the top of the rock face. I had made it! For the first time on the whole expedition, I had a feeling of confidence that we were going to get to the top. I waved to Tenzing and brought in the rope as he, too, made his way <u>laboriously</u> up the crack and dragged himself out beside me, panting for breath.

Literary Analysis
Author's Perspective
How does Hillary feel about the belay that Norgay sets up?

laboriously (lə bôr′ ē əs lē) *adv.* with difficulty

⓭ ▼ Critical Viewing
What elements in this photograph suggest the dangers of climbing? **[Analyze]**

We didn't waste any time. I started cutting steps again, seeking now rather anxiously for signs of the summit. We seemed to go on forever, tired now and moving rather slowly. In the distance I could see the barren plateau of Tibet. I looked up to the right and there was a rounded snowy dome. It must be the summit! We drew closer together as Tenzing brought in the slack on the rope. I continued cutting a line of steps upward. Next moment I had moved onto a flattish exposed area of snow with nothing but space in every direction. Tenzing quickly joined me and we looked around in wonder. To our immense satisfaction, we realized we had reached the top of the world!

It was 11: 30 a.m. on 29th May 1953. In typical Anglo-Saxon fashion, I stretched out my arm for a handshake, but this was not enough for Tenzing who threw his arms around my shoulders in a mighty hug and I hugged him back in return. With a feeling of mild surprise I realized that Tenzing was perhaps more excited at our success than I was.

But time was short! I turned off my oxygen and removed my mask. Immediately my face was prickled sharply with ice splinters carried in the brisk wind. I removed my camera from the protection of my down jacket, stepped a little down the slope and photographed Tenzing on the summit with his ice axe upraised and the flags flapping in the breeze—the United Nations flag, the Indian flag, the Nepalese flag and the Union Jack. Tenzing didn't have a camera and, to tell the truth, the thought didn't enter my mind to try to organize a picture of

15 ✔**Reading Check**

What was the last obstacle to reaching the summit?

View From the Summit ◆ 35

14 **Background**

Geography

Explain to students that the Himalaya Mountains were formed 30 to 50 million years ago when two continental plates crashed together. The mountain system extends for about 1,500 miles through Pakistan, India, China, Nepal, Sikkim, Bhutan, and Tibet. The Himalaya are some of the highest mountains in the world. Many of the mountain passes are covered with snow most of the year and are completely impassable. In fact, in Sanskrit, the word *Himalaya* means "Snowy abode." Because of the difficult terrain, few roads for vehicles exist, and transportation is largely on foot. In places, the mountain range is as much as 250 miles wide. It is not difficult to understand why much of the area is uninhabited. The mountain system is still relatively young (in geological time) and experiences frequent earthquakes.

15 ✔**Reading Check**

Answer: The last obstacle they faced was a huge ice cornice with a split running through it vertically.

CUSTOMIZE INSTRUCTION FOR UNIVERSAL ACCESS

For Less Proficient Readers	For Special Needs Students
Ask students to reread the second paragraph on p. 35. Have them explain how Hillary's description of Norgay's reaction to reaching the summit reveals the differences between his own and Norgay's perspective.	Help students locate clues to Hillary's emotions in the text as a way to help them recognize the author's perspective. These include his use of exclamation points and phrases such as, "immense satisfaction" or "mild surprise."

Review and Assess

1. Students may have felt relieved, exultant, and perhaps envious.

2. **(a)** He believes that Norgay is having trouble breathing.
(b) Students' answers may vary.

3. **(a)** The last big obstacle was a huge ice cornice with a vertical fissure, up which Hillary and Norgay had to climb. **(b)** Hillary says very little about Norgay's helping him, and dismisses his belay at the ice cornice as "relatively useless," suggesting that Norgay was of little help.

4. **(a)** It took a tremendous amount of energy and effort to climb Mount Everest. **(b)** Possible response: The danger and difficulty of climbing peaks such as Everest requires that people work closely together, as when climbers monitor each other's condition or take turns belaying each other.

myself on top of the mountain. I felt a more urgent need to have photographic evidence that we had reached the summit, so quickly took shots down every major ridge. The view was most spectacular to the east, for here the giants Makalu and Kangchenjunga dominated the horizon and gave some idea of the vast scale of the Himalayas. Only a few miles away, Makalu, with its soaring rock ridges, was a remarkable sight. I could see all the northern slopes of the mountain and was immediately struck by the possibility of a feasible route to its summit. With a growing feeling of excitement, I took another photograph to study on returning to civilization—I was under no delusions that reaching the top of Everest would destroy my enthusiasm for further adventures.

The view to the north was a complete contrast—hundreds of miles of the arid Tibetan plateau. One scene was of particular interest. Almost under our feet it seemed, was the famous North Col and the East Rongbuk Glacier, where so many epic feats of courage and endurance were performed by the earlier British Everest expeditions. Part of the ridge up which they had established their high camps was visible, but the last thousand feet, which had proved such a formidable barrier, was concealed from our view as its rock slopes dropped away with frightening abruptness from the summit snow pyramid. It was a sobering thought to remember how often these men had reached 28,000 feet without the benefits of our modern equipment and reasonably efficient oxygen sets. Inevitably, my thoughts turned to Mallory and Irvine who had lost their lives on the mountain thirty years before. With little hope I looked around for some sign that they had reached the summit, but could see nothing.

feasible (fē´ zə bəl) *adj.* capable of being done; possible

formidable (fôr´ mə də bəl) *adj.* causing fear or dread

Review and Assess

Thinking About the Selection

1. **Respond:** How did you feel when Hillary and Norgay finally reached the summit of Everest? Explain your reaction.

2. **(a) Recall:** Why does Hillary examine Norgay's oxygen equipment? **(b) Make a Judgment:** Do you think Norgay's oxygen situation was as critical as Hillary made it seem? Explain.

3. **(a) Recall:** What was the last big obstacle to reaching the summit? **(b) Infer:** Does Hillary think that he needed Norgay's help to surmount the obstacle? Explain.

4. **(a) Generalize:** After reading "View From the Summit," how would you describe the amount of effort and energy required to conquer Everest? **(b) Apply:** How does the difficulty of climbing Mount Everest lead people of such different backgrounds as Hillary and Norgay to work together to succeed?

Sir Edmund Hillary

(b. 1919)
Few people can claim they have stood on top of the world—and only one person can claim to have been there first. That person is Sir Edmund Hillary.

Hillary has said of himself, "I've moved from being a child who dreamed a lot and read a lot of books about adventure, to actually getting involved in things like mountaineering, and then becoming a reasonably competent mountaineer. . . ." These are humble words for a man who has conquered eleven different peaks greater than 20,000 feet in the Himalayas of Tibet and Nepal.

CONNECTIONS
Literature and Geography
The Lure of Everest

from
Into Thin Air

Jon Krakauer

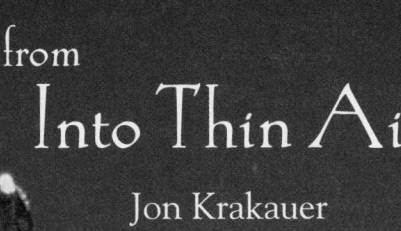

In April 1996, to report on the growing interest in Everest, writer and climber Jon Krakauer signed on as a client of an Everest expedition. His assignment was to investigate the guided trips that promised that any reasonably fit person could make it to the top of the world. As he horrifyingly discovered, climbing in the Himalayas is just as dangerous today as it was in Hillary and Norgay's day.

Straddling the top of the world, one foot in China and the other in Nepal, I cleared the ice from my oxygen mask, hunched a shoulder against the wind, and stared absently down at the vastness of Tibet. I understood on some dim, detached level that the sweep of earth beneath my feet was a spectacular sight. I'd been fantasizing about this moment, and the release of emotion that would accompany it, for many months. But now that I was

Thematic Connection
What details of suspense can you find in this passage?

Connections: from *Into Thin Air* ◆ 37

Lesson Objectives
1. To understand the connection between different accounts of scaling Mt. Everest
2. To explore the allure and dangers of mountain climbing

Connections
Both Hillary's and Krakauer's accounts convey important messages about people's desire to face challenging situations, and how they deal with the dangers inherent in these situations. Have students reread "View From the Summit" after they have read the excerpt from *Into Thin Air.* What similarities and differences can students identify between the ways in which the people in both accounts cope with danger and risk?

The Lure of Everest
- Explain to students that, like Hillary's account, this selection offers a firsthand view of the dangers inherent in climbing Mt. Everest.
- As students read the excerpt from Krakauer's account, have them pay attention to the ways in which technology has changed since Hillary and Norgay's time. Do students think that the changes in technology have made climbing the mountain easier?
- Focus students' attention on the role that nature plays in Krakauer's experience. Make sure that they understand the climbers were killed as a result of a violent and unforgiving storm that appeared virtually without warning.

Thematic Connection
Answer: Students may mention the dangerous cold, the high winds, and the vast emptiness that surrounds Krakauer.

finally here, actually standing on the summit of Mount Everest, I just couldn't summon the energy to care.

It was early in the afternoon of May 10, 1996. I hadn't slept in fifty-seven hours. The only food I'd been able to force down over the preceding three days was a bowl of ramen soup and a handful of peanut M&Ms. Weeks of violent coughing had left me with two separated ribs that made ordinary breathing an excruciating trial. At 29,028 feet up in the troposphere,[1] so little oxygen was reaching my brain that my mental capacity was that of a slow child. Under the circumstances, I was incapable of feeling much of anything except cold and tired.

. . . I snapped four quick photos of Harris and Boukreev[2] striking summit poses, then turned and headed down. My watch read 1:17 P.M. All told, I'd spent less than five minutes on the roof of the world.

A moment later, I paused to take another photo, this one looking down the Southeast Ridge, the route we had ascended. Training my lens on a pair of climbers approaching the summit, I noticed something that until that moment had escaped my attention. To the south, where the sky had been perfectly clear just an hour earlier, a blanket of clouds now hid Pumori, Ama Dablam, and the other lesser peaks surrounding Everest.

Later—after six bodies had been located, after a search for two others had been abandoned, after surgeons had amputated the <u>gangrenous</u> right hand of my teammate Beck Weathers—people would ask why, if the weather had begun to deteriorate, had climbers on the upper mountain not heeded the signs? Why did veteran Himalayan guides keep moving upward, ushering a <u>gaggle</u> of relatively inexperienced amateurs—each of whom had paid as much as $65,000 to be taken safely up Everest—into an apparent death trap?

Nobody can speak for the leaders of the two guided groups involved, because both men are dead. But I can attest that nothing I saw early on the afternoon of May 10 suggested that a murderous storm was bearing down.

---

1. **troposphere** (trō′ pō sfir′) *n.* atmospheric zone or shell below the tropopause, characterized by water vapor, vertical winds, weather, and decreasing temperatures with increasing altitude.
2. **Harris and Boukreev** Andrew Harris and Anatoli Boukreev were guides on the Everest expedition that Krakauer was on. Harris died in the storm.

Connecting Literature and Geography

1. Compare Krakauer's experiences with those of Hillary and Norgay. What role did natural elements play in both ascents?
2. How did the personality and goals of each man affect his experiences?

gangrenous (gaŋ′ grə nəs) *adj.* having gangrene, decay of tissue due to injury or disease

gaggle (gag′ əl) *n.* any group or cluster

Jon Krakauer

(b. 1954)
As a child, Jon Krakauer was already climbing rocks and developing an interest in volcanoes. As an adult, Krakauer, climber and writer, has never looked back.

Working primarily as a carpenter and fisherman in the backwoods of Oregon early in his life, Krakauer never really considered writing as a career until 1974, when a climbing magazine asked him to describe his first climb in Alaska. Krakauer, who lives with his wife in Seattle, Washington, has written a few books on climbing, most notably *Into Thin Air*, which is an account of his daunting experience climbing Mount Everest in 1996.

The Dream Comes True
from The Tiger of the Snows
Tenzing Norgay

Written in collaboration with James Ramsey Ullman

From the south summit we first had to go down a little. Then up, up, up. All the time the danger was that the snow would slip, or that we would get too far out on a cornice that would then break away; so we moved just one at a time, taking turns going ahead, while the second one wrapped the rope around his ax and fixed the ax in the snow as an anchor. The weather was still fine. We were not too tired. But every so often, as had happened all the way, we would have trouble breathing and have to stop and clear away the ice that kept forming in the tubes of our oxygen sets. In regard to this, I must say in all honesty that I do not think Hillary is quite fair in the story he later told, indicating that I had more trouble than he with breathing and that without his help I might have been in serious difficulty. In my opinion our difficulties were the same—and luckily never too great—and we each helped and were helped by the other in equal measure.

Anyhow, after each short stop we kept going, twisting always higher along the ridge between the cornices and the precipices. And at last we came to what might be the last big obstacle below the top. This was a cliff of rock rising straight up out of the ridge and blocking it off, and we had already known about it from aerial photographs and from seeing it through binoculars from Thyangboche.[1] Now it

❷ ▲ Critical Viewing Do you think this photograph of Hillary and Norgay was taken at the beginning or the end of the climb? Explain. **[Infer]**

❸ ☑Reading Check What kind of trouble did the climbers have?

---

1. **Thyangboche** (tän bō′ chā) village in Nepal.

- Draw students' attention to the last sentence of the second paragraph, "We were partners."

- Point out that this sentence sums up one of the key points of Norgay's account.

- Urge students to look carefully for other sentences that appear at the beginnings or ends of paragraphs and seem to express the author's perspective. Tell students that looking closely at opening and closing sentences is an effective reading strategy to help them determine an author's perspective.

▶ **Monitor Progress** Ask students to identify other sentences on pp. 40–41 that begin or end paragraphs and express the author's perspective.
Answers: The first sentence of the second paragraph on p. 40; the first sentence of the second paragraph on p. 41; the first sentence of the last paragraph on p. 41.

❺ ▶ Critical Viewing

Answer: Students should mention Norgay's love and respect for the mountain. He also needed and was helped by knowledge of the mountain, weather patterns, climbing techniques, and the ability to "read" the mountain.

was a question of how to get over or around it, and we could find only one possible way. This was along a steep, narrow gap between one side of the rock and the inner side of an adjoining cornice, and Hillary, now going first, worked his way up it, slowly and carefully, to a sort of platform above. While climbing, he had to press backwards with his feet against the cornice, and I belayed him from below as strongly as I could, for there was great danger of the ice giving way. Luckily, however, it did not. Hillary got up safely to the top of the rock and then held the rope while I came after.

Here again I must be honest and say that I do not feel his account, as told in *The Conquest of Everest*, is wholly accurate. For one thing, he has written that this gap up the rock wall was about forty feet high, but in my judgment it was little more than fifteen. Also, he gives the impression that it was only he who really climbed it on his own, and that he then practically pulled me, so that I "finally collapsed exhausted at the top, like a giant fish when it has just been hauled from the sea after a terrible struggle." Since then I have heard plenty about that "fish," and I admit I do not like it. For it is the plain truth that no one pulled or hauled me up the gap. I climbed it myself, just as Hillary had done; and if he was protecting me with the rope while I was doing it, this was no more than I had done for him. In speaking of this I must make one thing very plain. Hillary is my friend. He is a fine climber and a fine man, and I am proud to have gone with him to the top of Everest. But I do feel that in his story of our final climb he is not quite fair to me; that all the way through he indicates that when things went well it was his doing and when things went badly it was mine. For this is simply not true. Nowhere do I make the suggestion that I could have climbed Everest by myself; and I do not think Hillary should suggest that he could have, or that I could not have done it without his help. All the way up and down we helped, and were helped by, each other—and that was the way it should be. But we were not leader and
❹ led. We were partners.

On top of the rock cliff we rested again. Certainly, after the climb up the gap we were both a bit breathless, but after some slow pulls at the oxygen I am feeling fine. I look up; the top is very close now; and my heart thumps with excitement and joy. Then we are on our way again. Climbing again. There are still the cornices on our right and the precipice on our left, but the ridge is now less steep. It is only a row of snowy humps, one beyond the other, one higher than the other. But we are still afraid of the cornices and, instead of following

❺ ▲ **Critical Viewing**
What qualities do you think Norgay needed to guide climbers through mountains like these? **[Speculate]**

✹ **ENRICHMENT: Social Studies Connection**

Sherpas

Sherpas are a distinct ethnic group of Nepal. They live in the north in the high valleys and are accustomed to high altitudes, which make them effective as guides for Himalayan climbs. Many Sherpas make a living growing wheat and barley and herding goats, yaks, and sheep.

Although the Sherpa people served for many years as guides, cooks, and porters for European mountaineers, they are now claiming their own accomplishments. Sherpa climbers have now scaled Everest many times, setting records for speed and endurance. Sherpa Babu Chiri, father of six children, reached the summit repeatedly, often without oxygen. Once he did it in 16 hours, when most people take two weeks. He died on April 29, 2001, after falling into a crevasse.

the ridge all the way, cut over to the left, where there is now a long snow slope above the precipice. About a hundred feet below the top we come to the highest bare rocks. There is enough almost level space here for two tents, and I wonder if men will ever camp in this place, so near the summit of the earth. I pick up two small stones and put them in my pocket to bring back to the world below. Then the rocks, too, are beneath us. We are back among the snowy humps. They are curving off to the right, and each time we pass one I wonder, "Is the next the last one? Is the next the last?" Finally we reach a place where we can see past the humps, and beyond them is the great open sky and brown plains. We are looking down the far side of the mountain upon Tibet. Ahead of us now is only one more hump—the last hump. It is not a pinnacle. The way to it is an easy snow slope, wide enough for two men to go side by side. About thirty feet away we stop for a minute and look up. Then we go on. . . .

I have thought much about what I will say now: of how Hillary and I reached the summit of Everest. Later, when we came down from the mountain, there was much foolish talk about who got there first. Some said it was I, some Hillary. Some that only one of us got there—or neither. Still others that one of us had to drag the other up. All this was nonsense. And in Katmandu,[2] to put a stop to such talk Hillary and I signed a statement in which we said, "we reached the summit almost together." We hoped this would be the end of it. But it was not the end. People kept on asking questions and making up stories. They pointed to the "almost" and said, "What does that mean?" Mountaineers understand that there is no sense to such a question; that when two men are on the same rope they are *together*, and that is all there is to it. But other people did not understand. In India and Nepal, I am sorry to say, there has been great pressure on me to say that I reached the summit before Hillary. And all over the world I am asked, "Who got there first? Who got there first?"

Again I say: it is a foolish question. The answer means nothing. And yet it is a question that has been asked so often—that has

---

2. **Katmandu** (kät´män do͞o´) capital of Nepal.

⑥

Reading Strategy
Distinguishing Fact From Opinion Identify one fact and one opinion in this description of the climb.

⑦

⑧ ☑ **Reading Check**
Summarize the climb to the summit.

The Dream Comes True ◆ 41

⑥ Reading Strategy
Distinguishing Fact From Opinion

- Ask students the Reading Strategy question on p. 41: Identify one fact and one opinion in this description of the climb.
- Ask students to focus on Norgay's description of the terrain.
- Let students know that purely descriptive elements of Norgay's account are factual: the rocks, the bare space where a tent might be pitched, his picking up two stones.
- Help students to see that Norgay's characterization of the last snow slope as "easy" is his opinion, as others might find it difficult.

⑦ Literary Analysis
Author's Perspective

- Ask students how Norgay feels about the people who wanted to know who got to the summit first. Answer: He thinks that they are foolish. He thinks that when two people make such a climb together they are both first.
- Then, have students compare Hillary's perspective to Norgay's. Answer: Hillary is straightforward about having reached the summit first. He is less focused on the teamwork it took to get there.

⑧ ☑ Reading Check

Answer: They first had to go down a little, then up. They needed to climb one at a time because of the danger of snow slippage. They climbed along a ridge between the cornices and precipices. The last obstacle was a gap between rock and cornice that they had to climb. They continued climbing up the ridge next to the cornice and then along a snow slope above a precipice. Finally, there was an easy snow slope to the last hump, and they walked over it almost together.

CUSTOMIZE INSTRUCTION FOR UNIVERSAL ACCESS

For Less Proficient Readers	For English Learners	For Advanced Readers
To help students appreciate the contrasts between Hillary's and Norgay's views of the events, encourage them to record the points of view of the two men in a two-column table—one column for Norgay's views and one column for Hillary's.	To help students distinguish between fact and opinion in Norgay's account, have them focus on the pronouns in the text. Which "I" statements clearly signal that they are factual (I pick up two stones…)? Which indicate feelings, and therefore opinion (I am sorry to say…)?	Have students compare Hillary's and Norgay's points of view and focus on similarities and differences between the two. Are students inclined to think that similarities between the two accounts are likely to be factual? Have students discuss whether it is possible to discover all the facts from accounts such as these.

⑨ ▶ Critical Viewing

Answer: They must have felt awed and exhilarated.

⑩ Reading Strategy

Distinguishing Fact From Opinion

- Remind students that a statement of fact can be proved true.

- Encourage students to recognize that readers will assume that points of agreement between the accounts are factual.

- Ask students the Reading Strategy question on p. 42: In fact, who reached the top of the mountain first?
  Answer: Hillary and Norgay agree that Hillary stood on the summit first.

▶ **Monitor Progress** If students are having difficulty, you may wish to use the Fact and Opinion transparency in **Literary Analysis and Reading Transparencies,** p. 3.

⑪ Literary Analysis

Author's Perspective

▶ **Monitor Progress** Have students summarize Norgay's view of the controversy about which man reached the summit first.
Answer: Norgay states that Hillary stepped first on the peak of Everest. He feels that it's important that everyone know the truth.

- Ask students why Norgay feels it is important to tell the truth about what happened at the summit.
  Answer: He respects the mountain and feels that its greatness deserves a truthful account.

caused so much talk and doubt and misunderstanding—that I feel, after long thought, that the answer must be given. As will be clear, it is not for my own sake that I give it. Nor is it for Hillary's. It is for the sake of Everest—the prestige of Everest—and for the generations who will come after us. "Why," they will say, "should there be a mystery to this thing? Is there something to be ashamed of? To be hidden? Why can we not know the truth?" . . . Very well: now they will know the truth. Everest is too great, too precious, for anything but the truth.

⑩ A little below the summit Hillary and I stopped. We looked up. Then we went on. The rope that joined us was thirty feet long, but I held most of it in loops in my hand, so that there was only about six feet between us. I was not thinking of "first" and "second." I did not say to myself, "There is a golden apple up there. I will push Hillary aside and run for it." We went on slowly, steadily. And then we were there. Hillary stepped on top first. And I stepped up after him.

⑪ So there it is: the answer to the "great mystery." And if, after all the talk and argument, the answer seems quiet and simple, I can only say that that is as it should be. Many of my own people, I know, will be disappointed at it. They have given a great and false importance to

42 ◆ On the Edge

⑨ ▲ Critical Viewing
Describe how Hillary and Norgay must have felt as they looked ahead and back from this point.
[Infer]

Reading Strategy
Distinguishing Fact From Opinion In fact, who reached the top of the mountain first?

✳ **ENRICHMENT: Career Connection**

Mountain Guides

Tenzing Norgay worked as a guide for mountain climbers in the Himalaya. He was suited for the work because he knew the mountains and their dangers and was accustomed to living at high altitudes. Many people who love the outdoors hold jobs as guides in the United States. Some take people on adventurous treks, such as river rafting, rock climbing, or sailing. Others lead hunting or fishing parties in wilderness areas. Still others conduct nature walks, pointing out wildflowers, birds, and trees. Interested students can

research what a guide needs to know and what training would benefit a guide. They can explore the organizations that employ guides, such as the National Park Service and private and local organizations, and learn what each requires of its guides.

the idea that it must be I who was "first." These people have been good and wonderful to me, and I owe them much. But I owe more to Everest—and to the truth. If it is a discredit to me that I was a step behind Hillary, then I must live with that discredit. But I do not think it was that. Nor do I think that, in the end, it will bring discredit on me that I tell the story. Over and over again I have asked myself, "What will future generations think of us if we allow the facts of our achievement to stay shrouded in mystery? Will they not feel ashamed of us—two comrades in life and death—who have something to hide from the world?" And each time I asked it the answer was the same: "Only the truth is good enough for the future. Only the truth is good enough for Everest."

Now the truth is told. And I am ready to be judged by it.

We stepped up. We were there. The dream had come true. . . .

What we did first was what all climbers do when they reach the top of their mountain. We shook hands. But this was not enough for Everest. I waved my arms in the air and then threw them around Hillary, and we thumped each other on the back until, even with the oxygen, we were almost breathless. Then we looked around. It was eleven-thirty in the morning, the sun was shining, and the sky was the deepest blue I have ever seen. Only a gentle breeze was blowing, coming from the direction of Tibet, and the plume of snow that always blows from Everest's summit was very small. Looking down the far side of the mountain, I could see all the familiar landmarks from the earlier expeditions: the Rongbuk Monastery, the town of Shekar Dzong, the Kharta Valley, the Rongbuk and East Rongbuk Glaciers, the North Col, the place near the northeast ridge where we had made Camp Six in 1938. Then, turning, I looked down the long way we ourselves had come: past the south summit, the long ridge, the South Col; onto the Western Cwm, the icefall, the Khumbu Glacier; all the way down to Thyangboche and on to the valleys and hills of my homeland.

Beyond them, and around us on every side, were the great Himalayas, stretching away through Nepal and Tibet. For the closer peaks—giants like Lhotse, Nuptse and Makalu—you now had to look sharply downward to see their summits. And farther away, the whole sweep of the greatest range on earth—even Kangchenjunga[3] itself— seemed only like little bumps under the spreading sky. It was such a sight as I had never seen before and would never see again: wild, wonderful and terrible. But terror was not what I felt. I loved the mountains too well for that. I loved Everest too well. At that great moment for which I had waited all my life my mountain did not seem to me a lifeless thing of rock and ice, but warm and friendly and living. She was a mother hen, and the other mountains were chicks under her wings. I too, I felt, had only to spread my own wings to cover and shelter the brood that I loved.

---

3. **Kangchenjunga** (kän´ chən jŏŏn´ gə) third highest mountain in the world; lies near Mount Everest.

Literary Analysis
Author's Perspective How do Norgay's feelings about Everest, as described here, compare with Hillary's feelings?

 Reading Check
What did Hillary and Norgay do when they reached the summit?

The Dream Comes True ◆ 43

⓬ **Literary Analysis**
Author's Perspective

- Ask students the Literary Analysis question on p. 43: How do Norgay's feelings about Everest, as described here, compare with Hillary's feelings?
- Remind students to pay attention to the words that each author uses to describe his feelings.
  Answer: Norgay seems to feel a more personal connection to the mountain and the country, as he shows when he speaks of Everest as a warm, living thing. Because Everest is in his native land, Norgay perhaps feels more connected to it than Hillary does.

⓭ **Reading Check**
Answer: They shook hands, they hugged, and then Hillary began taking photographs of Norgay and the views from the summit.

CUSTOMIZE INSTRUCTION FOR UNIVERSAL ACCESS

For Less Proficient Readers	For Gifted/Talented Students	For Advanced Readers
To check understanding, have students pause at the end of the paragraph that begins, "We stepped up." Have them summarize what has happened up to this point. Then have them predict what will happen as the account progresses. Encourage them to jot down their predictions and then revise them as they continue reading.	Ask students to write a poem using Tenzing Norgay's author's perspective as expressed in the last paragraph. Make sure students incorporate the events of the climb as Norgay described them in this selection.	Have students rewrite the first three paragraphs of this page in their own words. Ask them to write a summary of what has happened up to this point. Then ask them to predict what might happen next, and to write a paragraph approximating what they think will happen next.

Answers for p. 44

Review and Assess

1. Possible responses: Hillary's account was more appealing because it was not argumentative. Norgay's account was more appealing because it reflected deeper emotions in the description of reaching the summit.

2. **(a)** Hillary says that Norgay is exhausted and needs a lot of help to reach the top of the crevice. **(b)** No, he does not. He feels that he and Hillary found the climb equally strenuous.

3. **(a)** He is familiar with the terrain, knowledgeable about mountain climbing, and respectful of the mountain. **(b)** It tells the reader that the author has self-respect and confidence.

4. **(a)** Everest is part of his homeland, and he feels a personal interest in it. **(b)** Norgay means that the truth about the ascent, including the truth about who first stood on the summit, should be told.

5. Possible responses: Norgay doesn't really feel Hillary is a friend, and he resents Hillary's account of his own climbing abilities as being inferior. Other students may feel that Norgay's respect for the truth argues that he is sincere, as does his candid account of the climb.

6. Norgay's purpose was to defend himself against Hillary's allegations of his weakness and finally to settle the question of who arrived first at the summit. Students' citations from the text should support this statement.

7. **(a)** Many people like to challenge themselves physically and mentally. They want to be the first to do something, especially something that is difficult and that requires courage. **(b)** Some climbers use sound judgment, and some do not. It is reasonable to try to climb Everest if you are in excellent physical condition and are an expert climber.

We turned off our oxygen. Even there on top of the world it was possible to live without it, so long as we were not exerting ourselves. We cleared away the ice that had formed on our masks, and I popped a bit of sweet into my mouth. Then we replaced the masks. But we did not turn on the oxygen again until we were ready to leave the top. Hillary took out his camera, which he had been carrying under his clothing to keep it from freezing, and I unwound the four flags from around my ax. They were tied together on a string, which was fastened to the blade of the ax, and now I held the ax up and Hillary took my picture. Actually he took three, and I think it was lucky, in those difficult conditions, that one came out so well. The order of the flags from top to bottom was United Nations, British, Nepalese, Indian; and the same sort of people who have made trouble in other ways have tried to find political meaning in this too. All I can say is that on Everest I was not thinking about politics. If I had been, I suppose I would have put the Indian or Nepalese flag highest—though that in itself would have been a bad problem for me. As it is, I am glad that the U.N. flag was on top. For I like to think that our victory was not only for ourselves—not only for our own nations—but for all men everywhere.

Review and Assess

Thinking About the Selection

1. **Respond:** Whose account of climbing Everest was more appealing to you—Hillary's or Norgay's? Why?

2. **(a) Recall:** How does Norgay say that Hillary describes him when he reaches the top of the crack? **(b) Connect:** Does Norgay feel that this description is accurate? Why or why not?

3. **(a) Evaluate:** What qualities does Norgay possess that helped contribute to his success? **(b) Infer:** What does Norgay's criticism of Hillary's account tell you about Norgay?

4. **(a) Analyze:** Why do you think Norgay is so concerned with the "prestige of Everest"? **(b) Analyze:** What does he mean by "Everest and the truth"?

5. **Evaluate:** Norgay calls Hillary his friend at the beginning of this excerpt. Do you think that was a sincere compliment? Why or why not?

6. **Infer:** What do you think Norgay's purpose was for writing this account? Cite examples to support your answer.

7. **(a) Extend:** What drives people like Hillary and Norgay to tackle the challenge of climbing Everest? **(b) Evaluate:** Do you think that climbers use sound judgment when they make the decision to climb Everest? Why or why not?

Tenzing Norgay

(1914–1986)

At 11:30 on the morning of May 29, 1953, Tenzing Norgay changed the course of his destiny—and began a journey toward international fame. At that moment, he and Edmund Hillary stood on the summit of Mount Everest in Nepal—a place where no man or woman had ever stood before and where few have stood since!

Norgay was born into a family of Sherpa farmers—Nepalese people of Tibetan descent. Norgay started guiding climbers at the age of fourteen. In 1953, he joined a Mount Everest expedition led by Sir John Hunt. Although all the other members of the expedition eventually turned back, Norgay and Hillary struggled on and fulfilled their dreams of being the first people ever to reach the summit.

ASSESSMENT PRACTICE: Reading and Vocabulary

Using Context Clues   (For more practice, see Test Preparation Workbook, p. 2.)

Students taking some assessment tests will encounter vocabulary questions based on sentences or reading passages that will require them to use context clues to select the best answer. To give students practice using context clues, use the following sample text item.

This sentence contains a blank which indicates that something has been omitted. Choose the word that, inserted in the sentence, best fits the meaning of the sentence as a whole.

"The pleasure of this safe belay after all the uncertainty below was like a _____ to a condemned man."

   A reproach   **C** reprimand

   B reprisal   **D** reprieve

Suggest that students apply an elimination strategy to make the corrrect selection. Have students read the sentence several times, inserting each word in turn until they decide that *D* is the best choice. Caution students not to be misled by the similar spelling of the answer choices.

Review and Assess

Literary Analysis

Author's Perspective

1. List three details in the account told from Hillary's **perspective** that are not included in Norgay's account.
2. List two details in the account told from Norgay's perspective that are not included in Hillary's account.
3. How do you think that each writer's background influenced his perspective?

Comparing Literary Works

4. Using the Venn diagram, compare the two **authors' perspectives** on the final moment of the climb: reaching the summit.

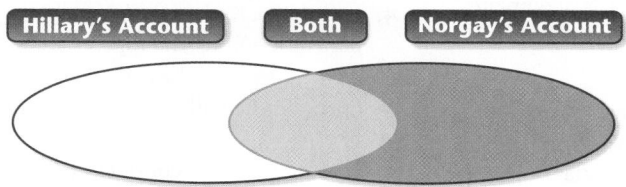

5. **(a)** What kinds of words does Norgay use in his descriptions of Mount Everest that are different from the words Hillary uses to describe the mountain? **(b)** How do you explain this difference?
6. Compare the similarities and differences in each writer's account of climbing the crack in the great rock step.

Reading Strategy

Distinguishing Fact From Opinion

7. Review each author's account, and identify one **fact** and one **opinion** that each states about the other.
8. Hillary describes Norgay "surging on with impressive strength." Explain whether this statement is a fact or an opinion.
9. List two examples of the writers' different opinions about the same events. What facts, if any, does each writer cite to support his opinions?

Extend Understanding

10. **Science Connection:** Hillary and Norgay describe a challenging climb. What health risks does such a climb present?

View From the Summit / The Dream Comes True ◆ 45

Quick Review

An **author's perspective** is the point of view from which he or she sees, hears, or experiences events personally.

A **fact** is a statement that can be proved.

An **opinion** is a statement that can be supported by facts but is not itself a fact.

 Take It to the Net

www.phschool.com

Take the interactive self-test online to check your understanding of these selections.

Answers continued

9. Hillary feels that Norgay was exhausted at the top of the crevice. Norgay says that he was not exhausted. The accounts disagree about the height of the crevice. The authors can only cite their own experience.

10. Risks include oxygen deprivation; trauma in a fall; altitude sickness and hypothermia.

Answers for p. 45

Review and Assess

1. Students might cite details about their last night in camp before the final assault, the condition of the snow crust, or the shearing off of a six foot slab of ice.

2. Students might mention the description of the two moving over the slopes and Norgay's spotting a level place on the rocks big enough for the tents.

3. Norgay's perspective is influenced by his being native to Tibet. Hillary's account is full of examples of his life as a mountain climber.

4. Hillary's Account: A handshake turned into a hug; he took off his mask; he photographed the surrounding views; he reminisced about other climbers. Both: It was May 29; they hugged; they described the surrounding mountains; they turned off their oxygen; the flags were raised; Hillary took Norgay's picture. Norgay's Account: They thumped each other on the back; the sun was shining; the sky was a deep blue; there was a gentle breeze blowing; he felt love for Everest.

5. **(a)** He uses the words *love, warm, friendly, living,* and *mother hen.* **(b)** Norgay thinks of Everest as a living thing.

6. Hillary says that the crevice was 40 feet high, and Norgay says it was only 15 feet. Hillary says that Norgay dragged himself up panting for breath, but Norgay says he found the climb no more difficult than did Hillary. Both say that Norgay belayed Hillary for the climb and that Hillary worked his way up slowly and carefully.

7. It is Norgay's opinion that Hillary exaggerates Norgay's difficulties. It is a fact stated by Norgay that the rope length between them as they neared the top was six feet. It is Hillary's opinion that Norgay climbs "laboriously" up the crevice. It is a fact stated by Hillary that Norgay hugged him.

8. Hillary's statement is an opinion because he uses the word *impressive,* which expresses a personal value. He can say that he is impressed with Norgay's strength but not whether anyone else would be.

continued

❶ Vocabulary Development

Word Analysis

1. befog—cover with fog
2. belie—tell lies about; give a false impression of
3. befriend—become a friend of

Spelling Strategy

1. discernible   3. eligible
2. fallible   4. feasible

Fluency

1. feasible   4. laboriously
2. ample   5. aperture
3. formidable   6. belay

❷ Grammar

1. subject; object
2. subject; object of preposition
3. subject; object
4. object; subject
5. predicate nominative; object of preposition

Writing Application

Students should use specific nouns and identify them properly.

Integrate Language Skills

❶ Vocabulary Development Lesson

Word Analysis: Anglo-Saxon Prefix *be-*

One meaning of the prefix *be-* is "about," changing the verb *moan*, which means "to complain," into the verb *bemoan*, which means "to complain about." In *belay*, the prefix means "around," creating a word that means "to tie a rope around." Give the meaning of the following words.

1. befog   2. belie   3. befriend

Spelling Strategy

Memorize words that end in *-ible*, such as *discernible*, *feasible*, *eligible*, and *fallible*. Complete each of the sentences with one of these words.

1. The birthmark was barely ___?___.
2. If you make mistakes, you are ___?___.
3. If you ski down this slope, you will be ___?___ for the intermediate class.
4. ___?___ means "possible."

Fluency: Sentence Completions

On a separate sheet of paper, complete each sentence below with the most appropriate word from the vocabulary list on page 29.

1. Although the path on the left looks ___?___, I think we should try the one on the right.
2. Even with ten people seated, there will be ___?___ room around the large table.
3. The mountain face appeared ___?___ as we stood at the bottom and looked up.
4. Inch by inch, the trembling child ___?___ pulled herself up the rope.
5. The ___?___ on the camera was completely open, but he still did not have enough light.
6. I would not even consider climbing up that rock unless I was on ___?___.

❷ Grammar Lesson

Noun Function

A **noun** is a word that names a person, place, thing, or idea. The following examples show the different functions—subject, object, object of a preposition, or predicate nominative—that the noun *mountain* can have in a sentence.

Subject:	The *mountain* rose before us.
Object:	Hillary and Norgay climbed the *mountain*.
Object of Preposition:	We went on our way up the *mountain*.
Predicate Nominative:	Our primary goal was the *mountain*.

Practice Identify the function of the italicized nouns in each sentence.

1. *Norgay* belays *Hillary* with a rope.
2. When the *snow* was crusted, the climbers' feet and legs plunged through the *ice*.
3. The *oxygen* would give Hillary and Norgay four more *hours*.
4. Hillary took *photographs* when the two *climbers* reached the summit.
5. Hillary and Norgay were the first *people* to stand on the summit of *Everest*.

Writing Application Write a paragraph about a challenge you have faced. Then, identify the function of five of the nouns you have used.

W̶G Prentice Hall Writing and Grammar Connection: Chapter 16, Section 1

TEACHING RESOURCES

The following resources can be used to enrich or extend the instruction for pp. 46–47.

Vocabulary

📖 **Selection Support:** Build Vocabulary, p. 5

📖 **Vocabulary and Spelling Practice Book** (Use this booklet for skills enrichment.)

Grammar

📖 **Selection Support:** Build Grammar Skills, p. 6 ▪

W̶G **Writing and Grammar,** Platinum Level, pp. 425–431

▪ **Daily Language Practice Transparencies**

Writing

W̶G **Writing and Grammar,** Platinum Level, pp. 172–191

🔵 **Writing and Grammar iText CD-ROM** ▪

▪ **Writing Models and Graphic Organizers on Transparencies,** p. 95

 BLOCK SCHEDULING: Resources marked with this symbol provide varied instruction during 90-minute blocks.

❸ Writing Lesson

Comparison-and-Contrast Essay

Hillary and Norgay achieved something that no other climbers had done before. Which of the two would you rather have as a climbing partner? Write a comparison-and-contrast essay in which you discuss the characteristics of both climbers.

Prewriting Use a Venn diagram to evaluate the characteristics of the men. Under the section labeled "Both," write things that they have in common. List their differences in their respective sections.

Drafting Write a paragraph about each climber, comparing him with the other climber. Write a final paragraph telling which one you would rather have as a climbing partner and why.

Revising Read your essay, making sure that you have organized your comparisons in a logical way. Your final conclusion should be well supported with facts. Proofread for spelling, grammar, and mechanics.

W/*G* *Prentice Hall Writing and Grammar Connection: Chapter 9, Section 3*

❹ Extension Activities

Listening and Speaking Using details from the accounts, prepare note cards and then deliver an **informal talk** in which you provide advice to aspiring climbers. Consider these strategies:

- Write key concepts and supporting evidence on your cards.
- Encourage questions. Address your classmates honestly, and review information if you feel there is any confusion.
- Stick to your key points, and stay focused on your topic.

Give your talk to the class.

Research and Technology With a partner, brainstorm for ideas for a **video game** based on this adventure. Design the graphics for the game, and present your ideas in a series of sketches. Show what the game screens will look like, how the players will move, and where the hazards will be. [**Group Activity**]

 Take It to the Net www.phschool.com
Go online for an additional research activity using the Internet.

View From the Summit / The Dream Comes True ◆ 47

47

The Monkey's Paw ✦ The Bridegroom

Lesson Objectives

1. **To analyze and respond to literary elements**
   - Literary Analysis: Foreshadowing
   - Comparing Literary Works
2. **To read, comprehend, analyze, and critique a short story and a poem**
   - Reading Strategy: Predicting Outcomes
   - Reading Check questions
   - Review and Assess questions
   - Assessment Practice (ATE)
3. **To develop word analysis skills, fluency, and systematic vocabulary**
   - Vocabulary Development Lesson: Latin Word Root: *-cred-*
4. **To understand and apply written and oral language conventions**
   - Spelling Strategy
   - Grammar Lesson: Antecedents of Pronouns
5. **To understand and apply appropriate writing and research strategies**
   - Writing Lesson: Safety Instructions
   - Extension Activity: Class Survey
6. **To understand and apply listening and speaking strategies**
   - Extension Activity: Dramatic Monologue

STEP-BY-STEP TEACHING GUIDE	PACING GUIDE
PRETEACH	
Motivate Students and Provide Background	
Use the Motivation activity (ATE p. 48)	5 min.
Read and discuss the Preview material and Background information (SE/ATE p. 48) **A**	5 min.
Introduce the Concepts	
Introduce the Literary Analysis and Reading Strategy (SE/ATE p. 49) **A**	15 min.
Pronounce the vocabulary words and read their definitions (SE p. 49)	5 min.
TEACH	
Monitor Comprehension	
Informally monitor comprehension by circulating while students read independently or in groups **A**	30 min.
Monitor students' comprehension with the Reading Check notes (SE/ATE pp. 51, 53, 55, 57, 59, 61, 63)	as students read
Develop vocabulary with Vocabulary notes (SE pp. 51, 53, 54, 59, 61; ATE pp. 51, 53)	as students read
Develop Understanding	
Develop students' understanding of foreshadowing with Literary Analysis annotations (SE pp. 52, 53, 56, 61, 63; ATE pp. 51, 52, 53, 56, 59, 61, 63) **A**	10 min.
Develop students' understanding of predicting outcomes with Reading Strategy annotations (SE pp. 50, 54, 59, 61; ATE pp. 50, 52, 54, 56, 59, 61)	10 min.
ASSESS	
Assess Mastery	
Assess students' mastery of the Reading Strategy and Literary Analysis by having them answer the Review and Assess questions (SE/ATE p. 65)	20 min.
Use one or more of the print and media Assessment Resources (ATE p. 67) **A**	up to 50 min.
EXTEND	
Apply Understanding	
Have students complete the Vocabulary Development Lesson and the Grammar Lesson (SE p. 66) **A**	20 min.
Apply students' knowledge of cause and effect using the Writing Lesson (SE p. 67) **A**	45 min.
Apply students' understanding of the selections using one or more of the Extension Activities (SE p. 67)	20–90 min.

 ACCELERATED INSTRUCTION:
Use the strategies and activities identified with an **A**.

UNIVERSAL ACCESS
- ● = Below Level Students
- ▲ = On-Level Students
- ■ = Above Level Students

Time and Resource Manager

RESOURCES

PRINT 📖	TRANSPARENCIES	TECHNOLOGY 💿 🎧 📼
• **Beyond Literature**, Cross-Curricular Connection: Community Action, p. 3 ▲ ■		• **Interest Grabber Video,** Tape 1 ● ▲ ■
• **Selection Support Workbook:** ● ▲ ■ Literary Analysis, p. 12 Reading Strategy, p. 11 Build Vocabulary, p. 9	• **Literary Analysis and Reading Transparencies,** pp. 5 and 6 ● ▲ ■	
		• **Listening to Literature** ● ▲ ■ Audiocassettes, Sides 3, 4 Audio CDs, CD 2
• **Literatura en español** ● ▲ • **Literary Analysis for Enrichment** ■		
• **Formal Assessment:** Selection Test, pp. 7–9 ● ▲ ■ • **Open Book Test,** pp. 7–9 ● ▲ ■ • **Performance Assessment and Portfolio Management,** pp. 21, 30 ● ▲ ■ • **ASSESSMENT SYSTEM** ● ▲ ■	• **ASSESSMENT SYSTEM** ● ▲ ■ Skills Practice Answers and Explanations on Transparencies	• **Test Bank Software** ● ▲ ■ • **Got It! Assessment Videotapes** ● ▲
• **Selection Support Workbook:** ● ▲ ■ Build Grammar Skills, p. 10 • **Writing and Grammar,** Platinum Level ● ▲ ■ • **Extension Activities,** p. 3 ● ▲ ■	• **Daily Language Practice Transparencies** ● ▲ • **Writing Models and Graphic Organizers on Transparencies,** p. 99 ● ▲ ■	• **Writing and Grammar iText CD-ROM** ● ▲ ■ 🖥️ **Take It to the Net** www.phschool.com

BLOCK SCHEDULING: Use one 90-minute class period to preteach the selection and have students read it. Use a second 90-minute class period to assess students' mastery of skills and have them complete one of the Extension Activities.

Step-by-Step Teaching Guide for pp. 48–49

Motivation

Engage students' attention by writing these story details on the chalkboard:

Who: An elderly man and wife and their son

Where: An isolated house near a factory

What: A guest carries a monkey's paw in his pocket

Invite volunteers to tell impromptu scary stories using these details and elaborating on them.

You could try the same with these details from "The Bridegroom":

Who: A young, unmarried woman

Where: A village in Russia years ago

What: A mysterious bridegroom comes to claim the young woman

Interest Grabber Video

As an alternative, you may wish to play "The Power of Imagination" on Tape 1 to engage student interest.

❶ Background

Social Studies

The English East India Company settled in India by 1611. They exported tea and textiles from India.

The English quickly became fascinated with Indian culture. Elephants, tigers, and monkeys were great novelties. Rajahs had outrageous wealth and many wives, fakirs did astonishing feats such as lying on beds of nails, and many people wore exotic clothing and jewelry. There were ornate temples and artwork, new foods, and unfamiliar beliefs, along with dreadful diseases, poisonous snakes, and mysterious cults. India became a symbol of the exotic.

Prepare to Read

The Monkey's Paw ◆ The Bridegroom

The Lights of Marriage, Marc Chagall, Kunsthaus, Zurich

🖥 *Take It to the Net*

Visit www.phschool.com for interactive activities and instruction related to these selections, including
- background
- graphic organizers
- literary elements
- reading strategies

Preview

Connecting to the Literature

Fate, chance, and *luck* are words that hint at mysterious forces beyond our immediate control. The characters in "The Monkey's Paw" and "The Bridegroom" believe that they can control their future. You will soon see whether or not they get the future they want.

❶ Background

India was a British colony from the late 1700s until 1947. India's culture was very different from British culture. Through letters and visits back home, soldiers—like Sergeant Major Morris in "The Monkey's Paw"—passed on information and misinformation about India. Before long, India became a symbol of the mysterious and exotic.

48 ◆ *On the Edge*

TEACHING RESOURCES

The following resources can be used to enrich or extend the instruction for pp. 48–49.

Motivation

 Interest Grabber Video, Tape 1 ▪

Background

📖 **Beyond Literature,** p. 3

🖥 *Take It to the Net*
Visit www.phschool.com for background and hotlinks for the selections.

Literary Analysis

📄 **Literary Analysis and Reading Transparencies,** Foreshadowing, p. 5 ▪

Reading

📖 **Selection Support:** Reading Strategy, p. 11; Build Vocabulary, p. 9

📄 **Literary Analysis and Reading Transparencies,** Predicting Outcomes, p. 6 ▪

▪ **BLOCK SCHEDULING:** Resources marked with this symbol provide varied instruction during 90-minute blocks.

Literary Analysis

Foreshadowing

Writers determine the outcome of *all* the events in the fictional worlds they construct. They keep you interested in what will happen next by giving you hints, called **foreshadowing,** of future events. To find the foreshadowing in "The Monkey's Paw," listen more carefully than the White family does to the sergeant major's tale early in the story.

> "The first man had his three wishes, yes," was the reply; "I don't know what the first two were, but the third was for death. That's how I got the paw."

This explanation, early in the story, hints at danger to follow.

Comparing Literary Works

Both "The Monkey's Paw" and "The Bridegroom" explore the role of fate in people's lives. However, the two pieces convey differing messages about the extent to which people are able to control their destinies. As you read, compare and contrast the degree to which fate shapes the events that occur.

Reading Strategy

Predicting Outcomes

You can use a writer's hints at future events to **predict outcomes,** or to make educated guesses, about what will happen in a literary work. For each selection, use these tips and jot down notes in a chart like this one.

- Find information that seems to hint at future events.
- Hypothesize about what the hints are predicting.

Predicting will keep you involved as you read.

Predictions	Actual Outcome
Something bad will happen to Herbert.	
The Whites will get the money.	
Everything will turn out fine.	

Vocabulary Development

doughty (dout´ ē) *adj.* brave; valiant (p. 51)

maligned (mə līnd´) *adj.* spoken ill of (p. 53)

credulity (krə dōō´ lə tē) *n.* tendency to believe too readily (p. 53)

prosaic (prō zā´ ik) *adj.* common-place; ordinary (p. 53)

avaricious (av´ ə rish´ əs) *adj.* greedy for riches (p. 54)

furtively (fur´ tiv lē) *adv.* secretly; stealthily (p. 54)

fusillade (fyōō´ sə lād´) *n.* something that is like the rapid firing of firearms (p. 58)

foreboding (fôr bōd´ iŋ) *n.* feeling that something bad will happen (p. 59)

tumult (tōō´ mult´) *n.* noisy commotion (p. 61)

The Monkey's Paw / The Bridegroom ◆ 49

---

❷ Literary Analysis
Foreshadowing

- Tell students that as they read "The Monkey's Paw," they should look for foreshadowing, or clues about what might happen later in the story.
- Suggest that students look for things that seem important, odd, or threatening.
- Tell students to note characters' statements and keep them in mind as they read. They may even want to jot notes about statements they think give clues about the story's outcome.
- Remind students that the author intends that they will remember the foreshadowing. Part of the impact of a story's ending is the anticipation created by the foreshadowing.
- Suggest that, when they finish reading, students review the clues they found. Do the clues match the ending?

❸ Reading Strategy
Predicting Outcomes

- Point out to students that foreshadowing can help them make predictions about what will happen in a story. Any time they notice something that seems like a clue, they should ask themselves what it suggests about the possible outcome.
- Have students create a chart like the one on p. 49. Then, tell them to enter a prediction about the story each time they encounter a clue.
- Tell students that they can change their predictions as they read, if they find a new clue or if an action proves a previous prediction wrong.
- Discuss in class which clues students found most helpful in predicting outcomes.

Vocabulary Development

- Pronounce each vocabulary word for students, and read the definitions as a class. Have students identify any words with which they are already familiar.

 E-Teach

Visit E-Teach at www.phschool.com for teachers' essays on how to teach, with questions and answers.

CUSTOMIZE INSTRUCTION FOR UNIVERSAL ACCESS

For Less Proficient Readers	For English Learners	For Advanced Readers
Organize groups of three to read aloud the long dialogue scene that opens the story. Include one less proficient reader in each group. Instruct students to follow the text carefully as others read aloud. Then, have the group discuss what they learn from the dialogue.	The dialogue scene that opens the story offers an opportunity for developing oral reading skills. Organize groups of three including at least one native speaker in each group. Have the native speaker read a line out loud, so that the English learner can hear the words pronounced.	Ask students to study the dialogue scene that opens the story, paying close attention to details that develop the characters. Then, have the students improvise additional lines of dialogue based on what they know of the characters. They may include what they learned in the Background note on page 48.

CUSTOMIZE INSTRUCTION
For Musical/Rhythmic Learners

Numerous sounds and noises echo through "The Monkey's Paw"—from the wind at the beginning of the story to Mrs. White's "long loud wail of disappointment" at the end. Invite students to notice these as they read, and identify how they help to create mood in the story.

❶ About the Selection

"The Monkey's Paw" is a chilling version of the "three wishes" tale told the world over. Like many renditions of the tale, it offers lessons in morality, but it distinguishes itself from other such tales through its aura of terror and suspense. Students will be taken on an emotional rollercoaster ride as the Whites are pushed to the brink of desperation, trying to reverse their wish and bring their son back from the dead.

❷ Reading Strategy

Predicting Outcomes

- Ask students to identify details in this section that create a gloomy and forbidding setting for the story. Possible answers: *beastly, slushy, torrent*

- Then, have students answer the Reading Strategy question on p. 50: What predictions can you make about the story based on the gloomy setting?
  Answer: The gloomy setting suggests that something unpleasant may happen. The eerie isolation of the Whites' house further hints that the family may become cut off from society or parted from one another.

❸ ▶Critical Viewing

Answer: Mr White is leaning toward the paw, and looks almost happy in his interest. Mrs. White looks nervous, playing with the cloth, her mouth slightly open in horror. The son is at a distance, and looks as if he doesn't believe in the charm.

---

❶The Monkey's Paw

W. W. Jacobs

I

Without, the night was cold and wet, but in the small parlor of Laburnam Villa the blinds were drawn and the fire burned brightly. Father and son were at chess, the former, who possessed ideas about the game involving radical changes, putting his king into such sharp and unnecessary perils that it even provoked comment from the white-haired old lady knitting placidly by the fire.

"Hark at the wind," said Mr. White, who, having seen a fatal mistake after it was too late, was amiably desirous of preventing his son from seeing it.

"I'm listening," said the latter, grimly surveying the board as he stretched out his hand. "Check."[1]

"I should hardly think that he'd come tonight," said his father, with his hand poised over the board.

"Mate,"[2] replied the son.

❷ "That's the worst of living so far out," bawled Mr. White, with sudden and unlooked-for violence; "of all the beastly, slushy, out-of-the-way places to live in, this is the worst. Pathway's a bog, and the road's a torrent. I don't know what people are thinking about. I suppose because only two houses on the road are let, they think it doesn't matter."

"Never mind, dear," said his wife, soothingly; "perhaps you'll win the next one."

Mr. White looked up sharply, just in time to intercept a knowing glance between mother and son. The words died away on his lips, and he hid a guilty grin in his thin gray beard.

"There he is," said Herbert White, as the gate banged to loudly and heavy footsteps came toward the door.

The old man rose with hospitable haste, and opening the door, was heard condoling with the new arrival. The new arrival also condoled with himself, so that Mrs. White said, "Tut, tut!" and coughed gently as her husband entered the room, followed by a tall, burly man, beady of eye and rubicund of visage.[3]

---

1. **check** *n.* chess move that threatens to capture the king.
2. **mate** *n.* checkmate, a chess move in which the king is captured and the game is over.
3. **rubicund** (rōō′ bə kund′) **of visage** (viz′ ij) *adj.* having a red complexion.

---

❸ ▲ Critical Viewing
How do you think each of the Whites is reacting to the object on the table? **[Infer]**

Reading Strategy
Predicting Outcomes
What predictions can you make about the story based on the gloomy setting?

TEACHING RESOURCES

The following resources can be used to enrich or extend the instruction for pp. 50–58.

Literary Analysis
- **Selection Support:** Literary Analysis, p. 12
- **Writing Models and Graphic Organizers on Transparencies,** p. 99

Reading
- **Listening to Literature Audiocassettes,** Sides 3, 4
- **Listening to Literature Audio CDs,** CD 2

BLOCK SCHEDULING: Resources marked with this symbol provide varied instruction during 90-minute blocks.

"Sergeant Major Morris," he said, introducing him.

The sergeant major shook hands, and taking the proffered seat by the fire, watched contentedly while his host got out tumblers and stood a small copper kettle on the fire.

At the third glass his eyes got brighter, and he began to talk, the little family circle regarding with eager interest this visitor from distant parts, as he squared his broad shoulders in the chair and spoke of wild scenes and doughty deeds; of wars and plagues and strange peoples.

"Twenty-one years of it," said Mr. White, nodding at his wife and son. "When he went away he was a slip of a youth in the warehouse. Now look at him."

"He don't look to have taken much harm," said Mrs. White, politely.

"I'd like to go to India myself," said the old man, "just to look round a bit, you know."

"Better where you are," said the sergeant major, shaking his head. He put down the empty glass, and sighing softly, shook it again.

"I should like to see those old temples and fakirs and jugglers," said the old man. "What was that you started telling me the other day about a monkey's paw or something, Morris?"

"Nothing," said the soldier, hastily. "Leastways nothing worth hearing."

"Monkey's paw?" said Mrs. White, curiously.

"Well, it's just a bit of what you might call magic, perhaps," said the sergeant major, offhandedly.

His three listeners leaned forward eagerly. The visitor absentmindedly put his empty glass to his lips and then set it down again. His host filled it for him.

"To look at," said the sergeant major, fumbling in his pocket, "it's just an ordinary little paw, dried to a mummy."

He took something out of his pocket and proffered it. Mrs. White drew back with a grimace, but her son, taking it, examined it curiously.

"And what is there special about it?" inquired Mr. White as he took it from his son, and having examined it, placed it upon the table.

"It had a spell put on it by an old fakir," said the sergeant major, "a very holy man."

"He wanted to show that fate ruled people's lives, and that those who interfered with it did so to their sorrow. He put a spell on it so that three separate men could each have three wishes from it."

His manner was so impressive that his hearers were conscious that their light laughter jarred somewhat.

"Well, why don't you have three, sir?" said Herbert White, cleverly.

The soldier regarded him in the way that middle age is wont to regard presumptuous youth. "I have," he said, quietly, and his blotchy face whitened.

"And did you really have the three wishes granted?" asked Mrs. White.

"I did," said the sergeant major, and his glass tapped against his strong teeth.

"And has anybody else wished?" persisted the old lady.

doughty (dout´ ē) *adj.*
brave; valiant

6 ✓ **Reading Check**
What is special about the monkey's paw?

The Monkey's Paw ◆ *51*

CUSTOMIZE INSTRUCTION FOR UNIVERSAL ACCESS

For Less Proficient Readers	For English Learners	For Advanced Readers
Tell students that Sergeant Major Morris gives many hints that the paw will cause danger. If students have trouble picking up on these hints, have them reread the page, paying close attention to the descriptions of the soldier's mood and appearance. Help them to see that he is hesitant to talk about the monkey's paw.	The description of Sergeant Major Morris is important because it reveals his feelings about the monkey's paw. Have students list the words used to describe him as he talks about the paw, such as *hastily, offhandedly,* and *absentmindedly.* Make sure students understand the meaning of each word.	Tell students that Sergeant Major Morris gives both verbal and nonverbal hints that he believes the paw will cause danger. Verbal hints include a speaker's word choice and tone of voice. Nonverbal hints include the speaker's appearance, gestures, and actions. Have students keep a list of both kinds of hints.

---

4 ● **Vocabulary Development**

- Have students locate the word *fakir* on this page. Suggest that they keep reading until they find a context clue that explains the term.
  Answer: The context clue is "a very holy man."

- Encourage students to use a dictionary to expand their understanding of the word meaning and to determine the correct pronunciation.

- Students should find that a *fakir* is someone who is believed to be able to cast spells and work wonders.

- Then, ask students to use the pronunciation guide to decide whether or not the word is pronounced the same as *faker*, someone who fakes.

5 ● Literary Analysis

Foreshadowing

- Explain to students that *fate* is the power that determines the outcome of events before they occur. One's fate is similar to one's destiny.

- Ask students how Sergeant Major Morris's warning about fate foreshadows a possible disaster.
  Answer: Sergeant Major Morris's words are a clear warning that interfering with fate by making wishes on the monkey's paw will bring unhappiness or misfortune.

▶ Monitor Progress Remind students that hints such as this one can help them make predictions about the story. Encourage students to think about who might be hurt by the paw, and how. Then, have them return to the chart on p. 49, and enter their predictions.

6 ✓ **Reading Check**

Answer: The monkey's paw can grant three wishes each to three different men.

51

Foreshadowing

- Ask students the Literary Analysis question on p. 52: Would it be a good idea to let the paw burn?

- Then, have students support their answers with details from the story. They might want to cite the sergeant major's earlier warnings about the paw.

  Answer: Students will probably say it would be a good idea to let the paw burn. They should support their answer with one of the sergeant's major's warnings, such as his reluctance to tell the Whites about the paw.

8 Reading Strategy

Predicting Outcomes

- Point out that the Whites have only "partly forgotten" about the paw while listening to the sergeant major's tales of India.

- Then, point out that the Whites listen to the tales of India "in an enthralled fashion."

- Explain that these words suggest that the Whites have a strong interest in India and exotic elements of its culture, such as the monkey's paw.

- Then, ask the students the Reading Strategy question on p. 52: Do you think the group will remain interested in the monkey's paw?

  Answer: Based on the hints mentioned above, the Whites are not likely to lose interest in the paw.

"The first man had his three wishes, yes," was the reply; "I don't know what the first two were, but the third was for death. That's how I got the paw."

His tones were so grave that a hush fell upon the group.

"If you've had your three wishes, it's no good to you now, then, Morris," said the old man at last. "What do you keep it for?"

The soldier shook his head. "Fancy, I suppose," he said, slowly. "I did have some idea of selling it, but I don't think I will. It has caused enough mischief already. Besides, people won't buy. They think it's a fairy tale, some of them, and those who do think anything of it want to try it first and pay me afterward."

"If you could have another three wishes," said the old man, eyeing him keenly, "would you have them?"

"I don't know," said the other. "I don't know."

He took the paw, and dangling it between his forefinger and thumb, suddenly threw it upon the fire. White, with a slight cry, stooped down and snatched it off.

"Better let it burn," said the soldier, solemnly.

"If you don't want it, Morris," said the other, "give it to me."

"I won't," said his friend doggedly. "I threw it on the fire. If you keep it, don't blame me for what happens. Pitch it on the fire again, like a sensible man."

The other shook his head and examined his new possession closely. "How do you do it?" he inquired.

"Hold it up in your right hand and wish aloud," said the sergeant major, "but I warn you of the consequences."

"Sounds like the *Arabian Nights*,"[4] said Mrs. White, as she rose and began to set the supper. "Don't you think you might wish for four pairs of hands for me?"

Her husband drew the talisman from his pocket, and then all three burst into laughter as the sergeant major, with a look of alarm on his face, caught him by the arm. "If you must wish," he said, gruffly, "wish for something sensible."

Mr. White dropped it back in his pocket, and placing chairs, motioned his friend to the table. In the business of supper the talisman was partly forgotten, and afterward the three sat listening in an enthralled fashion to a second installment of the soldier's adventures in India.

"If the tale about the monkey's paw is not more truthful than those he has been telling us," said Herbert, as the door closed behind their guest, just in time for him to catch the last train, "we shan't make much out of it."

"Did you give him anything for it, Father?" inquired Mrs. White, regarding her husband closely.

"A trifle," said he, coloring slightly. "He didn't want it, but I made him take it. And he pressed me again to throw it away."

"Likely," said Herbert, with pretended horror. "Why, we're going to

---

4. *Arabian Nights:* collection of stories from the ancient Near East.

Literary Analysis
Foreshadowing Would it be a good idea to let the paw burn? Explain your answer.

Reading Strategy
Predicting Outcomes Do you think the group will remain interested in the monkey's paw? Why?

ENRICHMENT: Cultural Connection

Folklore

The theme of wishing comes up again and again in the folklore of various cultures. One common variation features characters who have three wishes and who use them so foolishly that in the end, their lives do not change for the better. In a Jewish folk tale from Eastern Europe, a man is helped by a magical wishing ring, but he nearly dies when he reveals its existence to others. An ancient Chinese tale tells of the mother of heaven who tries to grant everyone's wishes, but who only causes more problems.

Many cultures also have proverbs about wishing. The French, for example, have the following saying: "After the act, wishing is in vain." The Italians say, "With wishing comes grieving." The Chinese warn, "Be careful what you wish for; you may get it."

Have interested students locate other folk tales and proverbs about wishing. Have them speculate about why wishing is a universal theme.

be rich, and famous and happy. Wish to be an emperor, Father, to begin with; then you can't be bossed around."

He darted round the table, pursued by the maligned Mrs. White armed with an antimacassar.[5]

Mr. White took the paw from his pocket and eyed it dubiously. "I don't know what to wish for, and that's a fact," he said, slowly. "It seems to me I've got all I want."

"If you only cleared the house, you'd be quite happy, wouldn't you?" said Herbert, with his hand on his shoulder. "Well, wish for two hundred pounds,[6] then; that'll just do it."

His father, smiling shamefacedly at his own credulity, held up the talisman, as his son, with a solemn face somewhat marred by a wink at his mother, sat down at the piano and struck a few impressive chords.

"I wish for two hundred pounds," said the old man distinctly.

A fine crash from the piano greeted the words, interrupted by a shuddering cry from the old man. His wife and son ran toward him.

"It moved," he cried, with a glance of disgust at the object as it lay on the floor. "As I wished it twisted in my hand like a snake."

"Well, I don't see the money," said his son as he picked it up and placed it on the table, "and I bet I never shall."

"It must have been your fancy, Father," said his wife, regarding him anxiously.

He shook his head. "Never mind, though; there's no harm done, but it gave me a shock all the same."

They sat down by the fire again while the two men finished their pipes. Outside, the wind was higher than ever, and the old man started nervously at the sound of a door banging upstairs. A silence unusual and depressing settled upon all three, which lasted until the old couple rose to retire for the night.

"I expect you'll find the cash tied up in a big bag in the middle of your bed," said Herbert, as he bade them good night, "and something horrible squatting up on top of the wardrobe watching you as you pocket your ill-gotten gains."

Herbert sat alone in the darkness, gazing at the dying fire, and seeing faces in it. The last face was so horrible and so simian[7] that he gazed at it in amazement. It got so vivid that, with a little uneasy laugh, he felt on the table for a glass containing a little water to throw over it. His hand grasped the monkey's paw, and with a little shiver he wiped his hand on his coat and went up to bed.

II

In the brightness of the wintry sun next morning as it streamed over the breakfast table Herbert laughed at his fears. There was an air of prosaic wholesomeness about the room which it had lacked on the previous night, and the dirty, shriveled little paw was pitched on the

---

5. **antimacassar** (an´ ti mə kas´ ər) n. small cover on the arms or back of a chair or sofa to prevent soiling.
6. **pounds** n. English money.
7. **simian** adj. monkeylike.

---

maligned (mə līnd´) adj. spoken ill of

credulity (krə do͞o´ lə tē) n. tendency to believe too readily

Literary Analysis
Foreshadowing How is the timing of the crash of the piano—immediately following Mr. White's wish—a foreshadowing of what might happen?

prosaic (prō zā´ ik) adj. commonplace; ordinary

⑪ ✓ **Reading Check**
What is the first wish?

The Monkey's Paw ◆ 53

---

⑨ **Vocabulary Development**
The Latin Word Root -cred-

- Call students' attention to the word *credulity* and its definition. Tell them that the Latin word root *-cred-* means "believe."

- Have students suggest other words that contain this root, and list them on the chalkboard. Possibilities include *credible*, *incredible*, *credentials*, and *credit*.

- Next, have students look up the meanings of these words in a dictionary.

- Finally, direct students to choose two of the words and use them in sentences about the characters in "The Monkey's Paw." Call on volunteers to read their sentences aloud.

⑩ **Literary Analysis**
Foreshadowing

- Ask the Literary Analysis question on p. 53: How is the timing of the crash of the piano—immediately following Mr. White's wish—a foreshadowing of what might happen? **Answer:** The crash is emotionally jarring, suggesting that something bad will happen. The crash is also surprising, hinting that the outcome of the wish may be a surprise even to the person making the wish.

- Remind students that so far, they have found examples of foreshadowing in the story's setting and in the characters' words.

- Explain that sensory details such as sound effects can also foreshadow a story's outcome. In this case, the crash of the piano adds to the threatening mood.

⑪ ✓ **Reading Check**
Answer: Mr. White uses the first wish to ask for two hundred pounds.

53

⑫ Critical Thinking

Analyze

• Have students reread this exchange among the family members. Then, ask students what the exchange reveals about each one.
Answer: Mrs. White shows common sense. Herbert appears to be carefree and a little silly. Mr. White is gullible and hopes, almost blindly, that the monkey's paw will work.

⑬ Reading Strategy

Predicting Outcomes

• Ask students the Reading Strategy question on p. 54: Predict why the stranger has come calling on the Whites.
Answer: The stranger has bad news of some sort, perhaps about Sergeant Major Morris, perhaps about Herbert, the monkey's paw, the Whites' house, or the two hundred pounds.

• Then, ask students to cite the details on which they based their predictions.
Answer: Some students may say they predicted the bad news would be about Herbert because Herbert was the only family member missing, and because his mother had already alluded to his return.

• Let students read ahead, comparing their predictions to the actual outcome.

---

sideboard with a carelessness which betokened no great belief in its virtues.

"I suppose all old soldiers are the same," said Mrs. White. "The idea of our listening to such nonsense! How could wishes be granted in these days? And if they could, how could two hundred pounds hurt you, Father?"

⑫ "Might drop on his head from the sky," said the frivolous Herbert.

"Morris said the things happened so naturally," said his father, "that you might if you so wished attribute it to coincidence."

"Well, don't break into the money before I come back," said Herbert, as he rose from the table. "I'm afraid it'll turn you into a mean, <u>avaricious</u> man, and we shall have to disown you."

His mother laughed, and following him to the door, watched him down the road, and, returning to the breakfast table, was very happy at the expense of her husband's credulity. All of which did not prevent her from scurrying to the door at the postman's knock, nor prevent her from referring somewhat shortly to retired sergeant majors of bibulous habits when she found that the post brought a tailor's bill.

"Herbert will have some more of his funny remarks, I expect, when he comes home," she said, as they sat at dinner.

"I dare say," said Mr. White, "but for all that, the thing moved in my hand; that I'll swear to."

"You thought it did," said the old lady soothingly.

"I say it did," replied the other. "There was no thought about it; I had just—What's the matter?"

His wife made no reply. She was watching the mysterious movements of a man outside, who, peering in an undecided fashion at the house, appeared to be trying to make up his mind to enter. In mental connection with the two hundred pounds, she noticed that the stranger was well dressed, and wore a silk hat of glossy newness. Three times he paused at the gate, and then walked on again. The fourth time he stood with his hand upon it, and then with sudden resolution flung it open and walked up the path. Mrs. White at the same moment placed her hands behind her, and hurriedly unfastening the strings of her apron, put that useful article of apparel beneath the cushion of her chair.

She brought the stranger, who seemed ill at ease, into the room. He gazed at her <u>furtively</u>, and listened in a preoccupied fashion as the old lady apologized for the appearance of the room, and her husband's coat, a garment which he usually reserved for the garden. She then waited patiently for him to broach his business, but he was at first strangely silent.

⑬ "I—was asked to call," he said at last, and stooped and picked a piece of cotton from his trousers. "I come from 'Maw and Meggins.'"

The old lady started. "Is anything the matter?" she asked, breathlessly. "Has anything happened to Herbert? What is it? What is it?"

Her husband interposed. "There, there, mother," he said, hastily. "Sit down, and don't jump to conclusions. You've not brought bad news, I'm sure, sir," and he eyed the other wistfully.

54 ◆ *On the Edge*

---

indirect char— what is revealed?

avaricious (av´ ə rish´ əs)
adj. greedy for riches

Reading Strategy
Predicting Outcomes
Predict why the stranger has come calling on the Whites.

furtively (fʉr´ tiv lē) *adv.*
secretly; stealthily

"I'm sorry—" began the visitor.

"Is he hurt?" demanded the mother, wildly.

The visitor bowed in assent. "Badly hurt," he said quietly, "but he is not in any pain."

"Oh, thank God!" said the old woman, clasping her hands. "Thank God for that! Thank—"

She broke off suddenly as the sinister meaning of the assurance dawned upon her and she saw the awful confirmation of her fears in the other's averted face. She caught her breath, and turning to her husband, laid her trembling old hand upon his. There was a long silence.

"He was caught in the machinery," said the visitor at length, in a low voice.

"Caught in the machinery," repeated Mr. White, in a dazed fashion, "yes."

He sat staring blankly out at the window, and taking his wife's hand between his own, pressed it as he had been wont to do in their old courting days nearly forty years before.

"He was the only one left to us," he said, turning gently to the visitor. "It is hard."

The other coughed, and, rising, walked slowly to the window. "The firm wished me to convey their sincere sympathy with you in your great loss," he said, without looking round. "I beg that you will understand I am only their servant and merely obeying orders."

There was no reply; the old woman's face was white, her eyes staring, and her breath inaudible; on the husband's face was a look such as his friend the sergeant might have carried into his first action.

"I was to say that Maw and Meggins disclaim all responsibility," continued the other. "They admit no liability at all, but in consideration of your son's services they wish to present you with a certain sum as compensation."

Mr. White dropped his wife's hand, and rising to his feet, gazed with a look of horror at his visitor. His dry lips shaped the words, "How much?"

"Two hundred pounds," was the answer.

Unconscious of his wife's shriek, the old man smiled faintly, put out his hands like a sightless man, and dropped, a senseless heap, to the floor.

III

In the huge new cemetery, some two miles distant, the old people buried their dead, and came back to a house steeped in shadow and silence. It was all over so quickly that at first they could hardly

[handwritten margin notes: rising action! Death of son! cost of fortune — suspense!]

14 ▲ Critical Viewing
How do the Whites appear to feel about the paw? **[Infer]**

16 ✔ Reading Check
How does the first wish come true?

The Monkey's Paw ◆ 55

14 ▶ Critical Viewing
Answer: Mr. White appears expectant, as though he hopes the paw can help them. Mrs. White looks frightened. She seems to sense that the monkey's paw can bring only heartache.

15 Critical Thinking
Interpret
• Have students reread the last three paragraphs in this section.
• Ask students why Mrs. White shrieks and Mr. White falls to the floor when they find out how much money they will receive.
Answer: They are devastated when they realize that their wish has come true, but with terrible consequences.
• Then, ask students to predict how they think the Whites will use their remaining wishes.

16 ✔ Reading Check
Answer: The Whites received two hundred pounds in compensation for the death of their son.

CUSTOMIZE INSTRUCTION FOR UNIVERSAL ACCESS

For Special Needs Students

Students may need additional practice using foreshadowing clues to predict outcomes in the plot. When they have finished reading "The Monkey's Paw," have students draw a sunburst diagram in their notebooks.

In the center of their diagrams, have the students list the final outcome of the story. Then, have them skim the story, looking for details that were hints or clues as to the final result. Have them write these hints on each arm.

Students should find it easier to locate these details as they reread because they know the final outcome, so they will know what to look for. For additional practice, suggest that students apply the same strategy to "The Bridegroom," which begins on p. 59. Discuss whether it was easier to make predictions about the short story or the ballad.

⓱ Reading Strategy

Predicting Outcomes

- Ask students to examine both Mrs. White's and Mr. White's attitude toward the paw.

- Point out that Mrs. White now desperately believes in the paw, but Mr. White no longer wants anything to do with it.

- Ask students the Reading Strategy question on p. 56: Do you think the Whites will make another wish? Why or why not?
  Answer: Students might predict that the Whites' desire to see their son will convince them to make another wish, despite Mr. White's reservations.

⓲ Literary Analysis

Foreshadowing

- Ask students the Literary Analysis question on p. 56: How might the outcome of the first wish foreshadow that of the other two wishes?
  Answer: Because the result of the first wish was so disastrous, it seems likely that the results of the other wishes might be just as bad or worse. Or, the other wishes might be more wisely and successfully made now that the Whites know the danger of the monkey's paw.

- Then, point out that Mr. White is afraid to wish for the return of his son. Ask students to explain the reason for his fear.
  Answer: Mr. White has realized that wishes can bring unintended consequences. He fears that if he wishes to have his son back, he will return as a decaying corpse.

realize it, and remained in a state of expectation as though of something else to happen—something else which was to lighten this load, too heavy for old hearts to bear.

⓱ But the days passed, and expectation gave place to resignation— the hopeless resignation of the old, sometimes miscalled apathy. Sometimes they hardly exchanged a word, for now they had nothing to talk about, and their days were long to weariness.

It was about a week after that the old man, waking suddenly in the night, stretched out his hand and found himself alone. The room was in darkness, and the sound of subdued weeping came from the window. He raised himself in bed and listened.

"Come back," he said, tenderly. "You will be cold."

"It is colder for my son," said the old woman, and wept afresh.

The sound of her sobs died away on his ears. The bed was warm, and his eyes heavy with sleep. He dozed fitfully, and then slept until a sudden wild cry from his wife awoke him with a start.

"The paw!" she cried wildly. "The monkey's paw!"

He started up in alarm. "Where? Where is it? What's the matter?"

She came stumbling across the room toward him. "I want it," she said quietly. "You've not destroyed it?"

"It's in the parlor, on the bracket," he replied, marveling. "Why?"

She cried and laughed together, and bending over, kissed his cheek.

"I only just thought of it," she said hysterically. "Why didn't I think of it before? Why didn't *you* think of it?"

"Think of what?" he questioned.

⓲ "The other two wishes," she replied rapidly. "We've only had one."

"Was not that enough?" he demanded, fiercely.

"No," she cried triumphantly; "we'll have one more. Go down and get it quickly, and wish our boy alive again."

The man sat up in bed and flung the bedclothes from his quaking limbs. "You are mad!" he cried, aghast.

"Get it," she panted; "get it quickly, and wish—Oh, my boy, my boy!"

Her husband struck a match and lit the candle. "Get back to bed," he said unsteadily. "You don't know what you are saying."

"We had the first wish granted," said the old woman feverishly; "why not the second?"

"A coincidence," stammered the old man.

"Go and get it and wish," cried his wife, quivering with excitement.

The old man turned and regarded her, and his voice shook. "He has been dead ten days, and besides he—I would not tell you else, but—I could only recognize him by his clothing. If he was too terrible for you to see then, how now?"

"Bring him back," cried the old woman, and dragged him toward the door. "Do you think I fear the child I have nursed?"

He went down in the darkness, and felt his way to the parlor, and then to the mantelpiece. The talisman was in its place, and a horrible fear that the unspoken wish might bring his mutilated son before him ere he could escape from the room seized upon him, and he caught

Reading Strategy
Predicting Outcomes Do you think the Whites will make another wish? Why or why not?

Literary Analysis
Foreshadowing How might the outcome of the first wish foreshadow that of the other two wishes?

CUSTOMIZE INSTRUCTION FOR UNIVERSAL ACCESS

For English Learners	For Gifted/Talented Students
Mr. White must be precise with his words when he makes his second wish. If he doesn't phrase his wish correctly, his son might come back as a corpse. Ask students to suggest how Mr. White should phrase his wish in order to get his son back alive and well. Tell them that if they have trouble coming up with the precise words they are looking for, they can consult a classmate, a dictionary, or a thesaurus.	Ask students to stop reading at the bottom of this page. Then, in small groups, have them determine what will happen next. Will Mr. White make a wish to get his son back? If so, how will he phrase his wish? Will Herbert return, and in what form? Have students write a script that answers these questions. Then, have them give a dramatic reading of it, using their words and expressions to convey the horror that the characters feel.

his breath as he found that he had lost the direction of the door. His brow cold with sweat, he felt his way round the table, and groped along the wall until he found himself in the small passage with the unwholesome thing in his hand.

Even his wife's face seemed changed as he entered the room. It was white and expectant, and to his fears seemed to have an unnatural look upon it. He was afraid of her.

"*Wish!*" she cried, in a strong voice.

"It is foolish and wicked," he faltered.

"*Wish!*" repeated his wife.

He raised his hand. "I wish my son alive again."

The talisman fell to the floor, and he regarded it fearfully. Then he sank trembling into a chair as the old woman, with burning eyes, walked to the window and raised the blind.

He sat until he was chilled with the cold, glancing occasionally at the figure of the old woman peering through the window. The candle-end, which had burned below the rim of the china candlestick, was throwing pulsating shadows on the ceiling and walls, until, with a flicker larger than the rest, it expired. The old man, with an unspeakable sense of relief at the failure of the talisman, crept back to his bed, and a minute or two afterward the old woman came silently and apathetically beside him.

Neither spoke, but lay silently listening to the ticking of the clock. A stair creaked, and a squeaky mouse scurried noisily through the wall. The darkness was oppressive, and after lying for some time screwing up his courage, he took the box of matches, and striking one, went downstairs for a candle.

At the foot of the stairs the match went out, and he paused to strike another; and at the same moment a knock so quiet and stealthy as to be scarcely audible, sounded on the front door.

The matches fell from his hand and spilled in the passage. He stood motionless, his breath suspended until the knock was repeated. Then he turned and fled swiftly back to his room, and closed the door behind him. A third knock sounded through the house.

"*What's that?*" cried the old woman, starting up.

"A rat," said the old man in shaking tones— "a rat. It passed me on the stairs."

His wife sat up in bed listening. A loud knock resounded through the house.

"It's Herbert!" she screamed. "It's Herbert!"

She ran to the door, but her husband was before her, and catching her by the arm, held her tightly.

"What are you going to do?" he whispered hoarsely.

"It's my boy; it's Herbert!" she cried, struggling mechanically. "I forgot it was two miles away. What are you holding me for? Let go. I must open the door."

> ### He raised his hand. "I wish my son alive again."

㉑ ✔Reading Check

Why does Mr. White hesitate to make the second wish?

The Monkey's Paw ◆ 57

⓳ Critical Thinking

Infer

- Ask students to explain why Mr. White would be afraid of his wife.
  Answer: He seems to fear her almost unnatural obsession with wishing on the monkey's paw as a way to bring their son back. He's afraid of what might really happen.

- Point out to students that the monkey's paw has caused yet another problem for Mr. and Mrs. White: It has created distance between them.

⓴ Critical Thinking

Analyze

- Read aloud the passage and ask students to identify details that create suspense in these paragraphs.
  Answer: The following details contribute to the suspense: their silent expectant waiting and the ticking of the clock and other sounds; Mr. White going downstairs in the dark; the knock on the door and its repetition.

- Ask students why they think the author decided to include suspenseful details in this paragraph.
  Answer: Students might say that the author wants the reader to feel the same tension that the Whites feel as they wonder whether their son will return.

㉑ ✔Reading Check

Answer: Mr. White fears that their son will return as a corpse.

57

Answers for p. 58

Review and Assess

1. Students might respond that the most frightening moment was when there was a knock at the door a second time. It could have been the mutilated Herbert.

2. **(a)** At the beginning of the story, it is a cold and blustery night outside, and the Whites are sitting inside by the fire when the sergeant major arrives. **(b)** The cold and blustery night suggests that danger is about to threaten the security of the White family.

3. **(a)** At first, Mr. White believes in the paw, Mrs. White is dubious, and Herbert is cynical and amused. **(b)** Herbert continues to joke, but the faces in the fire make him uneasy. Later, Mrs. White is desperate to believe in the paw's power to return her son, and Mr. White wants nothing to do with the paw.

4. **(a)** The first wish is fulfilled when the Whites receive two hundred pounds in compensation for the death of their son at work. **(b)** It seems unlikely that it was a coincidence because the amount was exactly what they wished for, and because it arrived promptly after the wish was made.

5. **(a)** Mr. White says, "I wish my son alive again." **(b)** If they had wished for Herbert to come back the way he was before the accident, the story might have turned out better.

6. Yes, the events prove the fakir's point of view. The Whites have brought tragedy into their lives by trying to change their fate.

"Don't let it in," cried the old man, trembling.

"You're afraid of your own son," she cried struggling. "Let me go. I'm coming Herbert; I'm coming."

There was another knock, and another. The old woman with a sudden wrench broke free and ran from the room. Her husband followed to the landing, and called after her appealingly as she hurried downstairs. He heard the chain rattle back and the bottom bolt drawn slowly and stiffly from the socket. Then the old woman's voice, strained and panting.

"The bolt," she cried, loudly. "Come down. I can't reach it."

But her husband was on his hands and knees groping wildly on the floor in search of the paw. If he could only find it before the thing outside got in. A perfect <u>fusillade</u> of knocks reverberated through the house, and he heard the scraping of a chair as his wife put it down in the passage against the door. He heard the creaking of the bolt as it came slowly back, and at the same moment he found the monkey's paw, and frantically breathed his third and last wish.

The knocking ceased suddenly, although the echoes of it were still in the house. He heard the chair drawn back and the door opened. A cold wind rushed up the staircase, and a long loud wail of disappointment and misery from his wife gave him courage to run down to her side, and then to the gate beyond. The street lamp flickering opposite shone on a quiet and deserted road.

fusillade (fyōō′ sə lād′) *n.* something that is like the rapid firing of firearms

Review and Assess

Thinking About the Selection

1. **Respond:** What was the most frightening moment in the story? Why?

2. **(a) Recall:** Describe the setting at the beginning of the story. **(b) Analyze:** How does that description set the mood for the story?

3. **(a) Recall:** How does each of the Whites react when the family first learns about the monkey's paw? **(b) Compare and Contrast:** Contrast the reactions of mother, father, and son to the paw as the story progresses.

4. **(a) Recall:** In what way is Mr. White's first wish fulfilled? **(b) Speculate:** Do you think the results of this first wish were coincidence? Explain why or why not.

5. **(a) Recall:** How did Mr. White phrase the second wish? **(b) Hypothesize:** Would things have turned out better if Mr. and Mrs. White had phrased the second wish more carefully?

6. **Draw Conclusions:** Explain whether you think the events of the story prove the fakir's point that "fate ruled people's lives, and that those who interfered with it did so to their sorrow."

W. W. Jacobs

(1863–1943)

As a boy, W. W. Jacobs often traveled vicariously through tales of adventure told by sailors he met at the dockside house where he lived. These tales shaped the stories he wrote as an adult—stories in which everyday life is disrupted by strange and fantastic events. "The Monkey's Paw" is his most famous tale of suspense and the supernatural. One reason for the story's popularity is that it hardly seems like a story that someone wrote. It is more like an age-old tale, made up by no one in particular, told around a campfire at night.

The Bridegroom

Alexander Pushkin   *Translated by D. M. Thomas*

For three days Natasha,
The merchant's daughter,
Was missing. The third night,
She ran in, distraught.
5 Her father and mother
Plied her with questions.
She did not hear them,
She could hardly breathe.

Stricken with <u>foreboding</u>
10 They pleaded, got angry,
But still she was silent;
At last they gave up.
Natasha's cheeks regained
Their rosy color.
15 And cheerfully again
She sat with her sisters.

Once at the shingle-gate
She sat with her friends
—And a swift troika[1]
20 Flashed by before them;
A handsome young man
Stood driving the horses;
Snow and mud went flying,
Splashing the girls.

25 He gazed as he flew past,
And Natasha gazed.
He flew on. Natasha froze.
Headlong she ran home.
"It was he! It was he!"
30 She cried. "I know it!
I recognized him! Papa,
Mama, save me from him!"

---

1. **troika** (troi′ kə) *n.* Russian carriage or sleigh drawn by a specially trained team of three horses harnessed side by side.

---

foreboding (fôr bōd′ iŋ) *n.* feeling that something bad will happen

Reading Strategy
Predicting Outcomes
What does Natasha's strange behavior followed by renewed cheerfulness lead you to predict about future events?

✔ Reading Check
What is Natasha's reaction to the young man in the troika?

The Bridegroom ◆ 59

---

22 About the Selection
"The Bridegroom" is a variation on the familiar folk motif of a worthy young person standing up to declare independence and becoming heroic by doing so. It raises questions about fate, wishes, and particularly about making choices for yourself.

23 Literary Analysis
Foreshadowing
• Draw students' attention to the word *foreboding* and its definition: the feeling that something bad will happen.
• Have students explain what the word *foreboding* suggests about the events that will follow.
   Answer: Students might say that the parents' fear of the future is a powerful clue that there will be trouble ahead.

24 Reading Strategy
Predicting Outcomes
• Ask students the Reading strategy question on p. 59: What does Natasha's strange behavior followed by renewed cheerfulness lead you to predict about future events?
   Answer: Students may say that her strange behavior, coupled with the fact that she's been gone for three days, points to a troubling future.
• Then, have students make predictions about what might happen next. Specifically, what do they think is the cause of Natasha's strange behavior?

25 ✔ Reading Check
Answer: Natasha is terrified of the young man in the troika.

TEACHING RESOURCES

The following resources can be used to enrich or extend the instruction for pp. 59–64.

Literary Analysis
📖 **Selection Support:** Literary Analysis, p. 12
📄 **Writing Models and Graphic Organizers on Transparencies,** p. 99

Reading
🎧 **Listening to Literature Audiocassettes,** Sides 3, 4 ▪
💿 **Listening to Literature Audio CDs,** CD 2 ▪

Full of grief and fear,
They shake their heads, sighing.
35 Her father says: "My child,
Tell me everything.
If someone has harmed you,
Tell us . . . even a hint."
㉖ She weeps again and
40 Her lips remain sealed.

The next morning, the old
Matchmaking woman
Unexpectedly calls and
Sings the girl's praises;
45 Says to the father: "You
Have the goods and I
A buyer for them:
A handsome young man.

"He bows low to no one,
50 He lives like a lord
With no debts nor worries;
He's rich and he's generous,
Says he will give his bride,
On their wedding-day,
55 A fox-fur coat, a pearl,
Gold rings, brocaded² dresses.

"Yesterday, out driving,
He saw your Natasha;
Shall we shake hands
60 And get her to church?"
The woman starts to eat
A pie, and talks in riddles,
While the poor girl
Does not know where to look.

65 "Agreed," says her father;
"Go in happiness
To the altar, Natasha;
It's dull for you here;
A swallow should not spend
70 All its time singing,
It's time for you to build
A nest for your children."

Natasha leaned against
The wall and tried

---

2. **brocaded** (brō kād′ əd) *adj.* woven, raised design in a cloth.

75 To speak—but found herself
Sobbing; she was shuddering
And laughing. The matchmaker
Poured out a cup of water,
Gave her some to drink,
80 Splashed some in her face.

Her parents are distressed.
Then Natasha recovered,
 And calmly she said:
"Your will be done. Call
85 My bridegroom to the feast,
Bake loaves for the whole world,
Brew sweet mead[3] and call
The law to the feast."

"Of course, Natasha, angel!
90 You know we'd give our lives
To make you happy!"
They bake and they brew;
The worthy guests come,
The bride is led to the feast,
95 Her maids sing and weep;
Then horses and a sledge[4]

With the groom—and all sit.
The glasses ring and clatter,
The toasting-cup is passed
100 From hand to hand in <u>tumult</u>,
The guests are drunk.

BRIDEGROOM
"Friends, why is my fair bride
Sad, why is she not
Feasting and serving?"

105 The bride answers the groom:
"I will tell you why
As best I can. My soul
Knows no rest, day and night
I weep; an evil dream
110 Oppresses me." Her father
Says: "My dear child, tell us
What your dream is."

---

3. **mead** (mēd) *n.* drink made of fermented honey and water.
4. **sledge** *n.* sleigh.

Literary Analysis
Foreshadowing What does Natasha's sobbing and shuddering foreshadow?

Reading Strategy
Predicting Outcomes Why do you think Natasha suddenly becomes calm?

tumult (too′ mult) *n.* noisy commotion

Reading Check
How is Natasha's marriage arranged?

The Bridegroom ◆ 61

28 Literary Analysis

Foreshadowing

• Ask students the Literary Analysis question on p. 61: What does Natasha's sobbing and shuddering foreshadow?
Answer: Natasha's sobbing and shuddering predict that she will not go happily into the wedding.

• Have students go back to the beginning of the poem and look for foreshadowing hints about what might happen at the wedding.
Answer: Students might guess that the young man on the troika will be involved somehow, since he elicited a strong reaction from Natasha.

▶ Monitor Progress If students are having difficulty picking up on foreshadowing hints, review the definition of *foreshadowing* and have students explain the concept in their own words.

29 Reading Strategy

Predicting Outcomes

• Ask students the Reading Strategy question on p. 61: Why do you think Natasha suddenly becomes calm?
Answer: Natasha becomes calm because she realizes she has no choice and will have to go through with the wedding.

• Then, ask students to predict what her calm state suggests about events to come.
Answer: Students might guess that Natasha has secretly hatched a plan to get out of the marriage.

• Have students read ahead to find out what Natasha has planned.

30 Reading Check

Answer: Natasha's marriage is arranged by a matchmaker who negotiates with her parents.

61

Answer: The strange, surrealistic quality of the painting suggests that Natasha's marriage will be less than perfect. Students may also note the distracted, disturbed look of the bride, who, like Natasha, seems to have more than a simple wedding on her mind.

32 Background

Art

The Lights of Marriage by Marc Chagall (1887–1985) depicts a wedding scene that is suggestive of the wedding scene described in "The Bridegroom."

Chagall was born in Russia. He studied painting under Leon Bakst in St. Petersburg. His paintings are distinguished by deeply colored landscapes in which people, objects, and animals fly and float in dreamlike fantasy. His work is associated with Surrealism and Cubism, two schools of painting that gave the world new, nonrealistic ways of looking at itself.

Use these questions for discussion:

- How is the mood of the painting similar to the mood of Natasha's wedding?
  Answer: Just as the painting creates a mysterious tension in the viewer with its unexplained human and animal figures flying about, so Natasha's wedding is unsettling to the guests and the reader with its vivid description of a mysterious, violent dream and its melodramatic revelation and conclusion.

- Natasha is the focus of the story. Who is the focus of the painting? Provide evidence to support your answer.
  Answer: The bride is the focus of the painting, too. The painter accomplishes this by placing the bride in the center of the painting and by using light and detail to draw our eyes to her.

"I dreamed," she says, "that I
Went into a forest,
115 It was late and dark;
The moon was faintly
Shining behind a cloud;
I strayed from the path;
Nothing stirred except
120 The tops of the pine-trees.

"And suddenly, as if
I was awake, I saw
A hut. I approach the hut
And knock at the door
125 —Silence. A prayer on my lips
I open the door and enter.
A candle burns. All
Is silver and gold."

31 ▼Critical Viewing
What might you infer about Natasha's marriage based on this painting? **[Infer]**

The Lights of Marriage, Marc Chagall, Kunsthaus, Zurich

BRIDEGROOM
"What is bad about that?
130 It promises wealth."

BRIDE
"Wait, sir, I've not finished.
Silently I gazed
On the silver and gold,
The cloths, the rugs, the silks,
135 From Novgorod,[5] and I
Was lost in wonder.

"Then I heard a shout
And a clatter of hoofs . . .
Someone has driven up
140 To the porch. Quickly
I slammed the door and hid
Behind the stove. Now
I hear many voices . . .
Twelve young men come in,

145 "And with them is a girl,
Pure and beautiful.
They've taken no notice
Of the ikons,[6] they sit
To the table without
150 Praying or taking off
Their hats. At the head,
The eldest brother,
At his right, the youngest;
At his left, the girl.
155 Shouts, laughs, drunken clamor . . . "

BRIDEGROOM
"That betokens merriment."

BRIDE
"Wait, sir, I've not finished.
The drunken din goes on
And grows louder still.
160 Only the girl is sad.

"She sits silent, neither
Eating nor drinking;
But sheds tears in plenty;
The eldest brother

---

5. **Novgorod:** city in the northwestern part of Russia.
6. **ikons** (ī´ känz´) *n.* images of Jesus, Mary, a saint, or another Christian religious figure.

Literary Analysis
Foreshadowing What does the repetition of line 131 in line 157 foreshadow about events to follow?

34 ☑ **Reading Check**
Summarize Natasha's dream.

The Bridegroom ◆ 63

---

33 Literary Analysis
Foreshadowing

- Ask students the Literary Analysis question on p. 63: What does the repetition of line 157 foreshadow about events to come?
  Answer: The repetition of the line, "Wait, sir, I've not finished," demonstrates Natasha's strength and determination and foreshadows her ultimate victory.

- Then, have students reread the description of the men's uncivilized behavior.

- Ask students how the men's behavior can help students predict what will happen next.
  Answer: The men's uncivilized behavior and dishonoring of religious symbols suggest that they do not live by any rules and may therefore perform some sort of evil deed.

34 ☑ **Reading Check**

Answer: In Natasha's dream, she hides behind the stove in a hut in the woods and watches twelve unruly men and a sad, quiet woman. One of the men kills the woman and cuts off her hand.

CUSTOMIZE INSTRUCTION FOR UNIVERSAL ACCESS

For Special Needs Students	For Gifted/Talented Students
Students will find the story more continuous and easy to follow if they are not slowed down by the frequent line and stanza breaks. Play the Listening to Literature Audiocassette and have students follow along in their books. Explain that they should think of stanzas as they think of paragraphs when reading prose. Like paragraphs, stanzas do not require the reader to pause for an extended amount of time. Rather, they signal a change in thought or scene.	Remind students that "The Bridegroom" is actually a ballad, and its stanzas can be thought of as verses in a song. Have interested students locate examples of ballads set to music. Then, have them find or create a piece of music to which they might set "The Bridegroom." Remind them to choose or create music that is appropriate for the events that take place in the poem. When they finish, have them share their finished piece with the class.

Answers for p. 64

Review and Assess

1. Students may admire Natasha's independence and resourcefulness in carrying through her plan to expose the bridegroom.

2. **(a)** After disappearing for three days, Natasha returns home distraught. She refuses to answer her parents' questions. **(b)** While she was missing, Natasha probably witnessed the murder that she later describes.

3. **(a)** At first Natasha is upset, but then she appears to resign herself to the marriage. **(b)** Possibly she felt that she would be safe in confronting the bridegroom as a murderer with her family and friends surrounding her.

4. **(a)** She tells him that she is sad because of a dream that has been haunting her. **(b)** Probably not; Natasha probably used the dream rather than making an outright accusation.

5. **(a)** At the beginning of the poem she seems fragile and timid. At the end, she is courageous and independent. **(b)** She has been able to bring the bridegroom to justice and avoid marrying him.

6. Students might say that the simplicity of the title hints at something much more complex and ominous.

7. **(a)** The poem could take place only in a culture that practices the custom of arranging marriages. **(b)** The poem might be realistic in some cultures today where marriages are still arranged.

---

165   Takes his knife and, whistling,
      Sharpens it; seizing her by
      The hair he kills her
      And cuts off her right hand."

      "Why," says the groom, "this
170   Is nonsense! Believe me,
      My love, your dream is not evil."
      She looks him in the eyes.
      "And from whose hand
      Does this ring come?"
175   The bride said. The whole throng
      Rose in the silence.

      With a clatter the ring
      Falls, and rolls along
      The floor. The groom blanches,
180   Trembles. Confusion . . .
      "Seize him!" the law commands.
      He's bound, judged, put to death.
      Natasha is famous!
      Our song at an end.

Review and Assess

Thinking About the Selection

1. **Respond:** Do you admire Natasha? Explain why or why not.

2. **(a) Recall:** Summarize the first eight lines of the poem. **(b) Infer:** Where was Natasha during the three days she was missing?

3. **(a) Recall:** Describe Natasha's changing reaction to the wedding. **(b) Infer:** What accounts for this switch in attitude?

4. **(a) Recall:** How does Natasha respond to her bridegroom's question about why his bride is sad? **(b) Interpret:** Do you think Natasha had the "evil" dream she describes? Explain.

5. **(a) Compare and Contrast:** How does Natasha's attitude at the beginning of the poem contrast with her behavior at the end? **(b) Draw Conclusions:** How can you account for this change in behavior?

6. **Evaluate:** Is the title of the poem effective in grabbing your attention and hinting at the events in the poem? Explain.

7. **(a) Evaluate:** Why is the setting important to this poem? **(b) Evaluate:** Would the events in the poem be realistic if it were set in today's world? Why or why not?

64 ◆ *On the Edge*

Alexander Pushkin

(1799–1837)

The father of modern Russian literature seems more like an adventurous teenager than a settled "father." Although born into the nobility, Pushkin had great sympathy for poor Russian peasants and criticized the absolute power and corruption of the government. In literature, too, he was a rebel. Pushkin drew on themes from folklore to express his democratic ideas. "The Bridegroom," for example, is like a literary version of a song passed on by word of mouth. In a manner perhaps foretold by his own dramatic nature, Pushkin died as the result of wounds suffered during a duel.

ASSESSMENT PRACTICE: Reading Comprehension

Using Context Clues   (For more practice, see Test Preparation Workbook, p. 3.)

Students preparing to take tests need practice using context clues to determine the meanings of words that appear in a reading passage. Have students read the description of the soldier's visit and storytelling on p. 52, and then give the following practice test item.

The word that best captures the meaning of enthralled is—

A bored   **C** envious

B captivated   **D** surprised

Suggest that students analyze each word as it applies to the context of the selection. The members of the family were not *bored, envious,* or *surprised* by their visitor's stories as much as they were charmed and entertained by him. Discuss with students that *captivated* captures the charm and entertainment that the visitor exudes, so the answer that provides the best meaning for *enthralled* is *B.*

Review and Assess

Literary Analysis

Foreshadowing

1. In "The Monkey's Paw," what event does the horrible thing that Herbert sees "squatting on top of the wardrobe" **foreshadow**?

2. Complete a chart like this one to identify three other clues from "The Monkey's Paw" that foreshadow events to come.

Clue	What Is Foreshadowed
Sergeant major's face whitens.	

3. In "The Bridegroom," why is Natasha's first reaction to the "handsome young man" an example of foreshadowing?

4. Natasha invites "the law" to her wedding. What specific later events does this invitation foreshadow?

Comparing Literary Works

5. Which of these selections suggests that people have little control over their own destinies? Support your answer.

6. Which of the pieces suggests that people do have a degree of control over their fates? Explain.

Reading Strategy

Predicting Outcomes

7. List three clues from "The Monkey's Paw" that might have helped you **predict** that the paw would bring sorrow to the Whites. Explain your choices.

8. At what point in "The Monkey's Paw" did you first predict that Mrs. White would ask her husband to wish her son alive again?

9. Explain how each of these other details helps you predict the outcome of "The Bridegroom": **(a)** Natasha's sudden decision to have the wedding, **(b)** her refusal to eat and drink at the wedding, **(c)** her tale of "an evil dream."

Extend Understanding

10. **Cultural Connection:** Many cultures have practiced the custom of arranged marriages. What are its potential benefits and drawbacks?

Quick Review

Foreshadowing is an author's use of clues to hint at or suggest events that have yet to occur.

When you **predict outcomes,** you identify details and hints to guess about what will happen in a work of literature.

 Take It to the Net
www.phschool.com

Take the interactive self-test online to check your understanding of these selections.

The Monkey's Paw / The Bridegroom ◆ 65

Answers for p. 65

Review and Assess

1. The horrible thing Herbert sees foreshadows his own death.

2. **Clues:**
   1. The paw moves in Mr. White's hand.
   2. The piano crashes after Mr. White makes a wish.
   3. Herbert sees the horrible face of the monkey in the fire.

   What Is Foreshadowed:
   1. The paw will grant Mr. White's wish.
   2. The wish will have jarring and unexpected consequences.
   3. Herbert will suffer at the hands of the monkey's paw.

3. Her reaction of terror indicates that she knew something about him, and that knowledge foreshadows the events to come.

4. It foreshadows the arrest of the bridegroom.

5. The characters in "The Monkey's Paw" suffer when they try to affect their destinies.

6. In "The Bridegroom," Natasha controls her own destiny when she publicly accuses the bridegroom of murder.

7. Clues include the sergeant major's warnings about the paw, his tossing the paw into the fire, and the simian face that appears in the flames.

8. Mrs. White reveals her intention when she says, "The other two wishes. . . . We've only had one."

9. **(a)** Natasha's sudden decision to have the wedding suggests that she has a plan. **(b)** Her refusal to eat or drink at the wedding suggests that she does not intend to celebrate. **(c)** When Natasha tells of her evil dream, the reader senses that the mystery of the bridegroom will be unraveled.

10. A potential benefit of arranged marriages is the fact that both families probably approve of both participants. A potential drawback is the possibility of a union based on finances or convenience rather than love.

Answers for p. 66

❶ Vocabulary Development

Word Analysis

1. not believable
2. believable
3. qualifications that make a person believable
4. a disposition to believe too readily
5. belief in the truth of someone or something

Spelling Strategy

1. creatively
2. shameful
3. malicious
4. believing
5. actively
6. gracious

Concept Development

1. criticized
2. ordinary
3. grasping
4. sneakily
5. commotion
6. brave
7. gullibility
8. barrage
9. forewarning

❷ Grammar

1. The Whites
2. paw
3. woman
4. Natasha
5. groom

Writing Application

1. At first, Natasha tells *her* parents nothing.
2. Natasha's parents do not hide *their* fear.
3. When Natasha sees the man in the troika, *she* is frightened.
4. During the wedding, Natasha tells of *her* dream.
5. Because of Natasha, the bridegroom is arrested for *his* crime.

Integrate Language Skills

❶ Vocabulary Development Lesson

Word Analysis: Latin Root -cred-

The Latin root *-cred-* means "believe." *Credulity* means "a tendency to believe something too quickly." Use a form of the word *believe* in defining each of these words:

1. incredible
2. credible
3. credentials
4. credulity
5. credit

Spelling Strategy

When adding a suffix that begins with a consonant to a word that ends in a silent *e*, keep the *e*: *furtive + -ly = furtively.* If the suffix begins with a vowel, drop the silent *e*: *avarice + -ious = avaricious.* Combine each of the pairs of word parts below.

1. creative + *-ly*
2. shame + *-ful*
3. malice + *-ious*
4. believe + *-ing*
5. active + *-ly*
6. grace + *-ious*

Concept Development: Synonyms

On your paper, write the word whose meaning is closest to that of the first word.

1. maligned: (a) praised, (b) criticized, (c) judged
2. prosaic: (a) ordinary, (b) unique, (c) odd
3. avaricious: (a) generous, (b) grasping, (c) mean
4. furtively: (a) obviously, (b) sneakily, (c) cleverly
5. tumult: (a) car, (b) peace, (c) commotion
6. doughty: (a) ill, (b) red, (c) brave
7. credulity: (a) gullibility, (b) disbelief, (c) futility
8. fusillade: (a) handful, (b) barrage, (c) shot
9. foreboding: (a) forewarning, (b) hindsight, (c) unawareness

❷ Grammar Lesson

Antecedents of Pronouns

Pronouns are words that act as stand-ins for nouns or for words that take the place of nouns. Pronouns—words such as *it, he,* or *they*—get their meanings from the words they stand for. These words are called **antecedents.** An antecedent may come before or after the pronoun, may be in another sentence, and might be more than one word.

>   ANTECEDENT   PRONOUN
> The **bridegroom** drove **his** troika past her house.
>
> The pronoun *his* agrees with its antecedent *bridegroom* in number, person, and gender.

Practice Identify the antecedent of each underlined pronoun in the following sentences.

1. The Whites opened <u>their</u> front door and let the sergeant major into the cozy room.
2. The monkey's paw had a spell put on <u>it</u>.
3. The matchmaking woman came in and gave <u>her</u> opinion to the girl's parents.
4. Natasha could not stop <u>her</u> sobbing at the thought of the handsome young man.
5. The groom tried to get the wedding guests to believe <u>him</u>.

Writing Application Write five sentences about a character in one of the selections. Include at least five pronouns and provide clear antecedents.

𝒲𝒢 Prentice Hall Writing and Grammar Connection: Chapter 16, Section 2

66 ◆ *On the Edge*

TEACHING RESOURCES

The following resources can be used to enrich or extend the instruction for pp. 66–67.

Vocabulary

📖 **Selection Support:** Build Vocabulary, p. 9

📖 **Vocabulary and Spelling Practice Book**
(Use this booklet for skills enrichment.)

Grammar

📖 **Selection Support:** Build Grammar Skills, p. 10

𝒲𝒢 **Writing and Grammar,** Platinum Level, p. 344

🖥 **Daily Language Practice Transparencies**

Writing

𝒲𝒢 **Writing and Grammar,** Platinum Level, p. 203

💿 **Writing and Grammar iText CD-ROM**

🖥 **Writing Models and Graphic Organizers on Transparencies,** p. 99 🖥

🖥 **BLOCK SCHEDULING:** Resources marked with this symbol provide varied instruction during 90-minute blocks.

Writing Lesson

Safety Instructions

Making wishes on the monkey's paw was a dangerous risk for the Whites to take. Perhaps if there had been a set of instructions on how to use the paw, the tragedy might not have occurred. Write instructions for the safe use of the monkey's paw.

Prewriting To figure out how to use the paw safely, work out some cause-and-effect scenarios. Brainstorm for a list of wishes. Then, think through all the things that could go wrong with each of your wishes.

Model: Identifying Causes and Effects

Wish	Possible Outcomes
Money	Could come from someone's life insurance
	Could fall out of the sky in a large bag onto your head
Fame	

> Brainstorming should have no limits. All ideas should be listed, and the list can be narrowed in drafting.

Drafting Once you have a set of guidelines, write them to show a logical, step-by-step process. Your instructions should cover how to wish and what to wish. Also, provide a list of precautions.

Revising Review your instructions with a partner. If your partner can suggest other dangers, revise your instructions to include them.

WG Prentice Hall Writing and Grammar Connection: Chapter 10, Section 2

Extension Activities

Listening and Speaking As the bridegroom, deliver a **dramatic monologue,** a speech given by one character to present that character's thoughts. The purpose of the monologue is to defend yourself after the bride has made her accusation in "The Bridegroom." Use these tips to make your performance effective:

- Use gestures and facial expressions that will attract sympathy from the audience.
- Use language that will persuade people that you are innocent.

Present your monologue to the class.

Research and Technology With a partner, take a **class survey** to identify ten wishes for your class. First, brainstorm for a list of ideas, which could range from such things as a field trip to a baseball game to a new school library. Using the list, survey your class and record your results on a bar graph or a pie chart. **[Group Activity]**

 Take It to the Net www.phschool.com

Go online for an additional research activity using the Internet.

The Monkey's Paw / The Bridegroom ◆ 67

ASSESSMENT RESOURCES

The following resources can be used to assess students' knowledge and skills.

Selection Assessment

- **Formal Assessment,** pp. 7–9
- **Open Book Test,** pp. 7–9
- **Got It! Assessment Videotapes,** Tape 1
- **Test Bank Software**
- **Take It to the Net**
  Visit www.phschool.com for self-tests and additional questions on the selections.

Writing Rubric

- **Performance Assess. and Portfolio Mgmt.,** p. 21

Listening and Speaking Rubric

- **Performance Assess. and Portfolio Mgmt.,** p. 30

 PRENTICE HALL ASSESSMENT SYSTEM

- **Workbook**
- **Skill Book**
- **Transparencies**
- **CD-ROM**

---

❸ Writing Lesson

- Explain to students that there is a cause-and-effect relationship between a wish and its fulfillment. For example, in "The Monkey's Paw," Mr. White's first wish ends up causing his son's death.
- Use the sample wishes on this page to model other cause-and-effect relationships.
- Explain to students that their safety instructions should tell users how to prevent their wishes from having negative effects.
- Use the Writing Lesson to guide students in developing safety instructions.
- Use the Cause-and-Effect rubric in **Performance Assessment and Portfolio Management,** p. 21, to evaluate students' work.

❹ Listening and Speaking

- Explain to students that the bridegroom's goal is to convince listeners of his innocence. In order to do this, he must convey sympathy.
- Have partners practice various expressions, gestures, and speaking tones that convey sympathy.
- Then, have the class brainstorm for phrases the bridegroom might use in his own defense. Have students vote on which phrases are the most powerful and convincing.
- Using these phrases, have students write their monologues. Volunteers can deliver their monologues to the class.
- Have students use the rubric for Delivering a Persuasive Argument, p. 30 in **Performance Assessment and Portfolio Management.**

CUSTOMIZE INSTRUCTION
For Universal Access

To address different learning styles, use the activities suggested in the **Extension Activities** booklet, p. 3.

- For Verbal/Linguistic Learners, use Activity 4.
- For Bodily/Kinesthetic and Interpersonal Learners, use Activity 5.
- For Visual/Spatial and Verbal/Linguistic Learners, use Activity 6.

from A Walk to the Jetty

Lesson Objectives

1. **To analyze and respond to literary elements**
   - Literary Analysis: Flashback
   - Connecting Literary Elements: First-person Point of View
2. **To read, comprehend, analyze, and critique a novel excerpt**
   - Reading Strategy: Drawing Inferences
   - Reading Check questions
   - Review and Assess questions
   - Assessment Practice (ATE)
3. **To develop word analysis skills, fluency, and systematic vocabulary**
   - Vocabulary Development Lesson: Latin Word Root: *-stup-*
4. **To understand and apply written and oral language conventions**
   - Spelling Strategy
   - Grammar Lesson: Pronoun Case
5. **To understand and apply appropriate writing and research strategies**
   - Writing Lesson: Letter of Introduction
   - Extension Activity: Annotated Map
6. **To understand and apply listening and speaking strategies**
   - Extension Activity: Telephone Interview

STEP-BY-STEP TEACHING GUIDE	PACING GUIDE
PRETEACH	
Motivate Students and Provide Background	
Use the Motivation activity (ATE p. 68)	5 min.
Read and discuss the Preview material and Background information (SE/ATE p. 68) **A**	5 min.
Introduce the Concepts	
Introduce the Literary Analysis and Reading Strategy (SE/ATE p. 69) **A**	15 min.
Pronounce the vocabulary words and read their definitions (SE p. 69)	5 min.
TEACH	
Monitor Comprehension	
Informally monitor comprehension by circulating while students read independently or in groups **A**	20 min.
Monitor students' comprehension with the Reading Check notes (SE/ATE pp. 71, 73, 75)	as students read
Develop vocabulary with Vocabulary notes (SE pp. 71, 76)	as students read
Develop Understanding	
Develop students' understanding of flashbacks with Literary Analysis annotations (SE p. 74; ATE pp. 72, 74) **A**	10 min.
Develop students' understanding of drawing inferences with Reading Strategy annotations (SE pp. 71, 73, 75; ATE pp. 71, 73, 74, 75)	10 min.
ASSESS	
Assess Mastery	
Assess students' mastery of the Reading Strategy and Literary Analysis by having them answer the Review and Assess questions (SE/ATE p. 77)	20 min.
Use one or more of the print and media Assessment Resources (ATE p. 79) **A**	up to 50 min.
EXTEND	
Apply Understanding	
Have students complete the Vocabulary Development Lesson and the Grammar Lesson (SE p. 78) **A**	20 min.
Apply students' ability to determine audience and purpose using the Writing Lesson (SE/ATE p. 79) **A**	45 min.
Apply students' understanding using one or more of the Extension Activities (SE p. 79)	20–90 min.

 ACCELERATED INSTRUCTION:
Use the strategies and activities identified with an **A**.

UNIVERSAL ACCESS
- ● = Below Level Students
- ▲ = On-Level Students
- ■ = Above Level Students

Time and Resource Manager

Reading Level: Average
Average Number of Instructional Days: 4

RESOURCES		
PRINT 📝	**TRANSPARENCIES**	**TECHNOLOGY** 💿 🎧 📼
• **Beyond Literature,** Cross-Curricular Connection: Social Studies, p. 4 ▲ ■		• **Interest Grabber Video,** Tape 1 ● ▲ ■
• **Selection Support Workbook:** ● ▲ ■ Literary Analysis, p. 16 Reading Strategy, p. 15 Build Vocabulary, p. 13	• **Literary Analysis and Reading Transparencies,** pp. 7 and 8 ● ▲ ■	
• **Adapted Reader's Companion** ● • **Reader's Companion** ●		• **Listening to Literature** ● ▲ ■ Audiocassettes, Side 4 Audio CDs, CD 2
• **English Learner's Companion** ● ▲ • **Literatura en español** ● ▲ • **Literary Analysis for Enrichment** ■		
• **Formal Assessment:** Selection Test, pp. 10–12 ● ▲ ■ • **Open Book Test,** pp. 10–12 ● ▲ ■ • **Performance Assessment and Portfolio Management,** pp. 19, 27 ● ▲ ■ • ⬤ PRENTICE HALL ASSESSMENT *SYSTEM* ● ▲ ■	• ⬤ PRENTICE HALL ASSESSMENT *SYSTEM* ● ▲ ■ Skills Practice Answers and Explanations on Transparencies	• **Test Bank Software** ● ▲ ■ • **Got It! Assessment Videotapes** ● ▲
• **Selection Support Workbook:** ● ▲ ■ Build Grammar Skills, p. 14 • **Writing and Grammar,** Platinum Level ● ▲ ■ • **Extension Activities,** p. 4 ● ▲ ■	• **Daily Language Practice Transparencies** ● ▲	• **Writing and Grammar iText CD-ROM** ● ▲ ■ 💻 **Take It to the Net** www.phschool.com

BLOCK SCHEDULING: Use one 90-minute class period to preteach the selection and have students read it. Use a second 90-minute class period to assess students' mastery of skills and have them complete one of the Extension Activities.

Step-by-Step Teaching Guide for pp. 68–69

Motivation

Invite students to picture themselves in the following situation: They are 16 years old, and they are leaving their family to begin life in another country. Help students generate a class list of the feelings that might surround these circumstances, such as fear of the unknown, excitement, and a sense of insecurity.

Discuss ways students could help themselves overcome fears and focus on the positive aspects of this situation. Tell the class that Annie John had this experience as a teenager, and she shares her thoughts and feelings in this selection.

▣ Interest Grabber Video

As an alternative, you may wish to play "Rites of Passage" on Tape 1 to engage student interest.

❶ Background
Geography

The island of Antigua is located in the Caribbean Sea, an arm of the Atlantic Ocean partially bounded on the west by Central America, the south by South America, and the north and east by the islands of the West Indies. The name of the sea derives from the Carib people, who inhabited the area when Spanish explorers arrived there in the fifteenth century. A popular resort area, the Caribbean is noted for its mild, tropical climate and cool ocean breezes.

Prepare to Read

from A Walk to the Jetty

Port de la Saline, Haiti, Lois Mailou Jones

▣ Take It to the Net

Visit www.phschool.com for interactive activities and instruction related to *A Walk to the Jetty,* including
• background
• graphic organizers
• literary elements
• reading strategies

Preview
Connecting to the Literature

Eventually, you may move away from home to go to college or to live on your own. Preparing to leave, you may be flooded with memories. The teenage girl in this story is leaving her island home, and her walk to the harbor is along a road of bittersweet memories.

❶ Background

Annie John, the main character in this story, is leaving Antigua. Most Antiguans are descendants of enslaved Africans captured to work on sugar cane plantations. Antigua became a British colony in the seventeenth century and won its independence in 1981. Because of the long-term British presence on the island, Antiguans speak English, use the British monetary system, and play the British game cricket.

68 ◆ *On the Edge*

TEACHING RESOURCES

The following resources can be used to enrich or extend the instruction for pp. 68–69.

Motivation
▣ **Interest Grabber Video,** Tape 1 ▣

Background
▣ **Beyond Literature,** p. 4

▣ **Take It to the Net**
Visit www.phschool.com for background and hotlinks for the excerpt from "A Walk to the Jetty."

Literary Analysis
▣ **Literary Analysis and Reading Transparencies,** Flashback, p. 8 ▣

Reading
▣ **Selection Support:** Reading Strategy, p. 15; Build Vocabulary, p. 13

▣ **Literary Analysis and Reading Transparencies,** Drawing Inferences, p. 7 ▣

▣ **BLOCK SCHEDULING:** Resources marked with this symbol provide varied instruction during 90-minute blocks.

Literary Analysis

Flashback

A **flashback** is a section of a literary work that interrupts the sequence of events to relate an event from an earlier time. Writers use flashbacks to show what motivates a character or to reveal something about a character's past. In this story, you learn about Annie John's childhood through a series of flashbacks triggered by sights as she walks through town. For example, as she walks past a seamstress's house, Annie says

> . . . I suddenly remembered that the months I spent with her all she had me do was sweep the floor, which was always full of threads and pins and needles, and I never seemed to sweep it clean enough to please her.

As you read, look for flashbacks that explain Annie's decision to leave.

Connecting Literary Elements

First-person point of view is characterized by the following:

- The narrator is the main character in the selection and tells the story from his or her point of view.
- The narrator uses the pronoun *I*.

In "A Walk to the Jetty," Annie John tells the story from her point of view, and her memories provide the flashbacks.

Reading Strategy

Drawing Inferences

You can **draw inferences**—reach conclusions—about characters in literature based on their speech, thoughts, and actions. Your inferences help you understand who the characters are and why they behave as they do. In "A Walk to the Jetty," a flashback shows you how proud Annie's mother was when her five-year-old daughter went on an errand alone. From this detail, you can infer that Annie and her mother had been very close.

Use a diagram like this one to draw inferences as you read.

Flashback	Inference
Sitting in mother's lap in the library	Reading was important to them.
Mother's eyes filled with tears when Annie came back from the chemist.	Mother was proud of her little daughter.

Vocabulary Development

loomed (lōōmd) *v.* appeared in a large or threatening form (p. 71)

apprenticed (ə prenʹ tist) *v.* assigned to work a specified length of time in a craft or trade in return for instruction (p. 71)

raked (rākt) *v.* scratched or scraped, as with a rake (p. 76)

stupor (stōōʹ pər) *n.* mental dullness, as if drugged (p. 76)

from A Walk to the Jetty ◆ 69

Flashback

- Have a volunteer read aloud the definition of a flashback.
- Remind students that writers use flashbacks to reveal information about a character by explaining events from his or her past.
- In this story, the flashbacks reveal Annie John's reasons for leaving Antigua.
- As they read, tell students to note places in the text where flashbacks begin and end. They should pay attention to phrases in the story that signal a shift in time, such as "I remembered," "I was five years old," and "I was a small child."

❸ **Reading Strategy**

Drawing Inferences

- Encourage students to draw inferences about the culture of Antigua as well as the characters in the story.
- For example, as she walks to the jetty, Annie John remembers Miss Dulcie, the seamstress to whom she was apprenticed. From this, students might infer that at the time, girls in Antigua were encouraged to learn a trade at an early age.
- Have students create charts like the one shown here. They can record flashbacks and the inferences they draw from each flashback as they read the selection.

Vocabulary Development

- Pronounce each vocabulary word for students, and read the definitions as a class. Have students identify any words with which they are already familiar.

CUSTOMIZE INSTRUCTION FOR UNIVERSAL ACCESS

For Special Needs Students	For Less Proficient Readers	For English Learners
Have students read the adapted version of "A Walk to the Jetty" in the **Adapted Reader's Companion.** This version provides basic-level instruction in an interactive format with questions and write-on lines. Completing the adapted version will prepare students to read the selection in the Student Edition.	Have students read the selection in the **Reader's Companion.** This version provides basic-level instruction in an interactive format with questions and write-on lines. After students finish the selection in the **Reader's Companion,** have them complete the questions and activities in the Student Edition.	Have students read the adapted version of the selection in the **English Learner's Companion.** This version provides basic-level instruction in an interactive format with questions and write-on lines. Completing the adapted version will prepare students to read the selection in the Student Edition.

 E-Teach

Visit E-Teach at www.phschool.com for teachers' essays on how to teach, with questions and answers.

69

**CUSTOMIZE INSTRUCTION
For Visual/Spatial Learners**

Encourage students to use the painting on this page to help them envision the story's setting. Have them note the colorfulness of the landscape, and draw their attention to the many flowers. Point out that the lush vegetation is typical of a tropical island.

❶ About the Selection

Fear, excitement, nostalgia, resentment, confusion, regret—this auto-biographical story captures all the complex emotions a young adult can feel when taking the first tentative steps toward independence. For Annie John, the emotions associated with leaving home are complicated by her conflicted relationship with her mother and her island home, as well as her need to rise above the low expectations for girls in her culture. Students will find much to identify with in this poignant leaving-home story.

❷ ▶ Critical Viewing

Answer: Annie John might want to move to a city to meet many different kinds of people or to have more educational or work opportunities.

from
❶ A Walk to the Jetty

from Annie John   Jamaica Kincaid

San Antonio de Oriente (detail), José Antonio Velásquez, Museum of Modern Art of Latin America, Washington, D.C.

❷ ▲ **Critical Viewing** Why might Annie John want to leave a home like this? **[Speculate]**

70 ◆ *On the Edge*

TEACHING RESOURCES

The following resources can be used to enrich or extend the instruction for pp. 70–76.

Literary Analysis

📖 **Selection Support:** Literary Analysis, p. 16

Reading

📖 **Reader's Companion**

📖 **English Learner's Companion**

🎧 **Listening to Literature Audiocassettes,** Side 4 ▪

💿 **Listening to Literature Audio CDs,** CD 2 ▪

▪ **BLOCK SCHEDULING:** Resources marked with this symbol provide varied instruction during 90-minute blocks.

My mother had arranged with a stevedore[1] to take my trunk to the jetty ahead of me. At ten o'clock on the dot, I was dressed, and we set off for the jetty. An hour after that, I would board a launch that would take me out to sea, where I then would board the ship. Starting out, as if for old time's sake and without giving it a thought, we lined up in the old way: I walking between my mother and my father. I loomed way above my father and could see the top of his head. We must have made a strange sight: a grown girl all dressed up in the middle of a morning, in the middle of the week, walking in step in the middle between her two parents, for people we didn't know stared at us. It was all of half an hour's walk from our house to the jetty, but I was passing through most of the years of my life. We passed by the house where Miss Dulcie, the seamstress that I had been apprenticed to for a time, lived, and just as I was passing by, a wave of bad feeling for her came over me, because I suddenly remembered that the months I spent with her all she had me do was sweep the floor, which was always full of threads and pins and needles, and I never seemed to sweep it clean enough to please her. Then she would send me to the store to buy buttons or thread, though I was only allowed to do this if I was given a sample of the button or thread, and then she would find fault even though they were an exact match of the samples she had given me. And all the while she said to me, "A girl like you will never learn to sew properly, you know." At the time, I don't suppose I minded it, because it was customary to treat the first-year apprentice with such scorn, but now I placed on the dustheap of my life Miss Dulcie and everything that I had had to do with her.

We were soon on the road that I had taken to school, to church, to Sunday school, to choir practice, to Brownie meetings, to Girl Guide meetings, to meet a friend. I was five years old when I first walked on this road unaccompanied by someone to hold my hand. My mother had placed three pennies in my little basket, which was a duplicate of her bigger basket, and sent me to the chemist's shop to buy a pennyworth of senna leaves, a pennyworth of eucalyptus leaves, and a pennyworth of camphor.[2] She then instructed me on what side of the road to walk, where to make a turn, where to cross, how to look carefully before I crossed, and if I met anyone that I knew to politely pass greetings and keep on my way. I was wearing a freshly ironed yellow dress that had printed on it scenes of acrobats flying through the air and swinging on a trapeze. I had just had a bath, and after it, instead of powdering me with my baby-smelling talcum powder, my mother had, as a special favor, let me use her own talcum powder, which smelled quite perfumy and came in a can that had painted on it people going out to dinner in nineteenth-century London and was called Mazie. How it pleased me to walk out the door and bend my head down to sniff at myself and see that I smelled just like my mother. I went to the chemist's shop, and he had to come

---

loomed (lo͞omd) *v.* appeared in a large or threatening form

apprenticed (ə pren' tist) *v.* assigned to work a specified length of time in a craft or trade in return for instruction

Reading Strategy
Drawing Inferences How does this first reminiscence of childhood help you infer why Annie might be leaving the island?

---

1. **stevedore** (stē' və dôr) *n.* person whose job is loading and unloading ships.
2. **chemist's shop . . . camphor** (kam' fər) the first phrase is a British term for a pharmacy. The items mentioned are small amounts of plant matter to be used in remedies.

5 ✔ **Reading Check**
Where is Annie going with her father and mother?

from A Walk to the Jetty ◆ 71

3 **Background**
Art

San Antonio de Oriente (detail) by José Antonio Velásquez

The primitivist painter José Antonio Velásquez has painted many pictures depicting San Antonio de Oriente, a small town in the Central American country of Honduras. In this painting, the rhythmic patterns of the roof tiles, flowers, and stone walls are offset by the smooth, solid planes of the white walls of the buildings and the colorful wash hung on a line in the foreground. Encourage students to study the painting and then use these questions for discussion.

1. What mood, or feeling, does the painting convey to you?
   Answer: Responses may range from peaceful, quiet, serene, unhurried, and relaxing to lazy and boring.

2. In what ways does this picture evoke a small-town feel?
   Answer: Students may note that the landscape has few buildings, people, or vehicles; the town is surrounded by nature; and the church seems to be the focus of the town.

4 **Reading Strategy**
Drawing Inferences

- Remind students that to draw inferences about a character's behavior, they should pay attention to his or her words, thoughts, and feelings.

- For example, students should note that the memory of Miss Dulcie the seamstress evokes a bad feeling in Annie John.

- Ask students the Reading Strategy question on p. 71: How does this first reminiscence of childhood help you to infer why Annie might be leaving the island?
   Answer: She might be leaving because there are few appealing work opportunities on the island.

5 ✔ **Reading Check**

Answer: They are on their way to the jetty.

Flashback

- Tell students that strong sensory experiences, such as a taste, a smell, or an image, often can result in a flashback.

- Ask students what details in this flashback help them to picture in their minds Annie's first walk. Possible responses: the three pennies, the little basket, the freshly ironed yellow dress printed with acrobats, the smell of Annie's mother's talcum powder, the scene on the can of talcum powder, the name of the talcum powder, her mother's tears of pride and joy at Annie's return, her being swooped up in her mother's arms, and her mother's proud words at Annie's accomplishments.

7 Background

Social Studies

Antigua is an island in the West Indies. The West Indies is an archipelago, or a group of islands, that extends in the Caribbean Sea from near Florida to the coast of Venezuela. When he arrived in 1492, Christopher Columbus named the islands the West Indies because he mistakenly believed that they were near the coast of India.

As time passed, other names came into use. Spain and France called the islands the Antilles, named after the mythological island of Antilla. The larger islands (Cuba, Jamaica, Hispaniola, and Puerto Rico) came to be known as the Greater Antilles, and the smaller islands were called the Lesser Antilles.

The islands of the West Indies comprise thirteen independent nations and a number of colonial territories. Sovereignty over these territories is distributed among the United States, France, the Netherlands, Venezuela, and Great Britain.

---

from behind the counter and bend down to hear what it was that I wanted to buy, my voice was so little and timid then. I went back just the way I had come, and when I walked into the yard and presented my basket with its three packages to my mother, her eyes filled with tears and she swooped me up and held me high in the air and said that I was wonderful and good and that there would never be anybody better. If I had just conquered Persia, she couldn't have been more proud of me.

We passed by our church—the church in which I had been christened and received[3] and had sung in the junior choir. We passed by a house in which a girl I used to like and was sure I couldn't live without had lived. Once, when she had mumps, I went to visit her against my mother's wishes, and we sat on her bed and ate the cure of roasted, buttered sweet potatoes that had been placed on her swollen jaws, held there by a piece of white cloth. I don't know how, but my mother found out about it, and I don't know how, but she put an end to our friendship. Shortly after, the girl moved with her family across the sea to somewhere else. We passed the doll store, where I would go with my mother when I was little and point out the doll I wanted that year for Christmas. We passed the store where I bought the much-fought-over shoes I wore to church to be received in. We passed the bank. On my sixth birthday, I was given, among other things, the present of a sixpence.[4] My mother and I then went to this bank, and with the sixpence I opened my own savings account. I was given a little gray book with my name in big letters on it, and in the balance column it said "6d." Every Saturday morning after that, I was given a sixpence—later a shilling, and later a two-and-sixpence piece—and I would take it to the bank for deposit. I had never been allowed to withdraw even a farthing from my bank account until just a few weeks before I was to leave; then the whole account was closed out, and I received from the bank the sum of six pounds ten shillings and two and a half pence.

We passed the office of the doctor who told my mother three times that I did not need glasses, that if my eyes were feeling weak a glass of carrot juice a day would make them strong again. This happened when I was eight. And so every day at recess I would run to my school gate and meet my mother, who was waiting for me with a glass of juice from carrots she had just grated and then squeezed, and I would drink it and then run back to meet my chums. I knew there was nothing at all wrong

---

3. **received** v. accepted into the congregation as a mature Christian.
4. **sixpence** n. monetary unit in the British commonwealth, worth six pennies (not of the same value as the pennies in United States currency). A shilling is worth two sixpence, a two-and-sixpence is two and one-half shillings, that is, two shillings and one sixpence. A pound is worth twenty shillings. A farthing is a "fourthing": one fourth of a penny.

Literature **7**
in context Geography Connection

The Landscape of Antigua

Annie John grew up on an island that is considered a vacation spot. White sand beaches, spectacular coral reefs, and an average temperature of 80 degrees make Antigua popular with tourists. There are 365 beaches on Antigua—one for each day of the year! Antigua is about 14 miles long and 11 miles wide, covering 108 square miles.

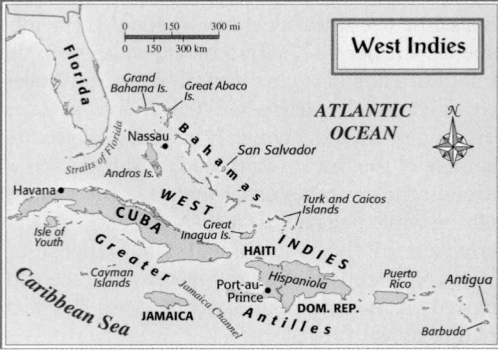

ENRICHMENT: Geography

Maps

Have students look at a variety of maps in an atlas or a social studies textbook and study the way the details are presented and how the map legend is constructed.

Suggest that students skim the selection and take notes of the details of Annie's walk that the author mentions. Some students may want to add further details to the list from their own imagination. Using their notes, have students create a map of Annie's neighborhood and the walk to the jetty. Some students may want to draw a stylized map that uses art materials and is colorful; others may prefer to create a detailed line drawing map, and they might use magazine photographs as illustrations.

Have students display their maps in the classroom. Assess students' projects based on completeness and accuracy of details, adherence to directions, and creativity.

with my eyes, but I had recently read a story in *The Schoolgirl's Own Annual* in which the heroine, a girl a few years older than I was then, cut such a figure to my mind with the way she was always adjusting her small, round, horn-rimmed glasses that I felt I must have a pair exactly like them. When it became clear that I didn't need glasses, I began to complain about the glare of the sun being too much for my eyes, and I walked around with my hands shielding them—especially in my mother's presence. My mother then bought for me a pair of sunglasses with the exact horn-rimmed frames I wanted, and how I enjoyed the gestures of blowing on the lenses, wiping them with the hem of my uniform, adjusting the glasses when they slipped down my nose, and just removing them from their case and putting them on. In three weeks, I grew tired of them and they found a nice resting place in a drawer, along with some other things that at one time or another I couldn't live without.

We passed the store that sold only grooming aids, all imported from England. This store had in it a large porcelain dog—white, with black spots all over and a red ribbon of satin tied around its neck. The dog sat in front of a white porcelain bowl that was always filled with fresh water, and it sat in such a way that it looked as if it had just taken a long drink. When I was a small child, I would ask my mother, if ever we were near this store, to please take me to see the dog, and I would stand in front of it, bent over slightly, my hands resting on my knees, and stare at it and stare at it. I thought this dog more beautiful and more real than any actual dog I had ever seen or any actual dog I would ever see. I must have outgrown my interest in the dog, for when it disappeared I never asked what became of it. We passed the library, and if there was anything on this walk that I might have wept over leaving, this most surely would have been the thing. My mother had been a member of the library long before I was born. And since she took me everywhere with her when I was quite little, when she went to the library she took me along there, too. I would sit in her lap very quietly as she read books that she did not want to take home with her. I could not read the words yet, but just the way they looked on the page was interesting to me. Once, a book she was reading had a large picture of a man in it, and when I asked her who he was she told me that he was Louis Pasteur[5] and that the book was about his life. It stuck in my mind, because she said it was because of him that she boiled my milk to purify it before I was allowed to drink it, that it was his idea, and that that was why the process was called pasteurization. One of the things I had put away in my mother's old trunk in which she kept all my childhood things was my library card. At that moment, I owed sevenpence in overdue fees.

As I passed by all these places, it was as if I were in a dream, for I didn't notice the people coming and going in and out of them, I didn't feel my feet touch ground, I didn't even feel my own body—I just saw these places as if they were hanging in the air, not having top or bottom,

---

5. **Louis Pasteur** (Pas tur′) (1822–1895) French chemist and bacteriologist who developed the process (pasteurization) for using heat to kill disease-causing bacteria in milk.

Reading Strategy
Drawing Inferences Infer why the library is such an important part of Annie's childhood.

❿ 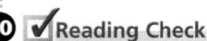**Reading Check**
What does Annie remember when she passes the doctor's office?

from A Walk to the Jetty ◆ 73

---

❽ Reading Strategy
Drawing Inferences
- Have students reread this episode about the carrot juice and Annie's demand for glasses.
- Ask students what this episode reveals about the personalities of Annie and her mother and their relationship.
  Answer: The episode shows that Annie is imaginative, impressionable, determined, and changeable. Her mother seems devoted to Annie's needs and desires and is eager to please her when possible.
- As they read, encourage students to continue recording inferences in a chart like this one.

Flashback	Inference
Annie's mother buys sunglasses for Annie.	Annie's mother is devoted to Annie's needs and desires.

❾ Reading Strategy
Drawing Inferences
- Ask students the Reading Strategy question on p. 73: Why is the library such an important part of Annie's childhood?
  Answer: Students may say that the library was important to Annie because it was important to her mother, and she wanted to be close to her mother.
- Then, ask students to speculate about how the library might have contributed to Annie's desire to leave Antigua.
  Answer: Students may say that the books in the library allowed the curious girl a view of the opportunities available in the world outside her island home.

❿ Reading Check
Answer: Annie remembers that when she was eight, she wanted a pair of glasses because she liked the way they looked and felt.

and as if I had gone in and out of them all in the same moment. The sun was bright; the sky was blue and just above my head. We then arrived at the jetty.

My heart now beat fast, and no matter how hard I tried, I couldn't keep my mouth from falling open and my nostrils from spreading to the ends of my face. My old fear of slipping between the boards of the jetty and falling into the dark-green water where the dark-green eels lived came over me. When my father's stomach started to go bad, the doctor had recommended a walk every evening right after he ate his dinner. Sometimes he would take me with him. When he took me with him, we usually went to the jetty, and there he would sit and talk to the night watchman about cricket[6] or some other thing that didn't interest me, because it was not personal; they didn't talk about their wives, or their children, or their parents, or about any of their likes and dislikes. They talked about things in such a strange way, and I didn't see what they found funny, but sometimes they made each other laugh so much that their guffaws would bound out to sea and send back an echo. I was always sorry when we got to the jetty and saw that the night watchman on duty was the one he enjoyed speaking to; it was like being locked up in a book filled with numbers and diagrams and what-ifs. For the thing about not being able to understand and enjoy what they were saying was I had nothing to take my mind off my fear of slipping in between the boards of the jetty.

Now, too, I had nothing to take my mind off what was happening to me. My mother and my father—I was leaving them forever. My home on an island—I was leaving it forever. What to make of everything? I felt a familiar hollow space inside. I felt I was being held down against my will. I felt I was burning up from head to toe. I felt that someone was tearing me up into little pieces and soon I would be able to see all the little pieces as they floated out into nothing in the deep blue sea. I didn't know whether to laugh or cry. I could see that it would be better not to think too clearly about any one thing. The launch was being made ready to take me, along with some other passengers, out to the ship that was anchored in the sea. My father paid our fares, and we joined a line of people waiting to board. My mother checked my bag to make sure that I had my passport, the money she had given me, and a sheet of paper placed between some pages in my Bible on which were written the names of the relatives—people I had not known existed—with whom I would live in England. Across from the jetty was a wharf, and some stevedores were loading and unloading barges. I don't know why seeing that struck me so, but suddenly a wave of strong feeling came over me, and my heart swelled with a great gladness as the words "I shall never see this again" spilled out inside me. But then, just as quickly, my heart shriveled up and the words "I shall never see this again" stabbed at me. I don't know what stopped me from falling in a heap at my parents' feet.

---

6. cricket *n.* British game, similar to baseball, but played with a flat bat by eleven players on each team.

When we were all on board, the launch headed out to sea. Away from the jetty, the water became the customary blue, and the launch left a wide path in it that looked like a road. I passed by sounds and smells that were so familiar that I had long ago stopped paying any attention to them. But now here they were, and the ever-present "I shall never see this again" bobbed up and down inside me. There was the sound of the sea-

Port de la Saline, Haiti, Lois Mailou Jones

gull diving down into the water and coming up with something silverish in its mouth. There was the smell of the sea and the sight of small pieces of rubbish floating around in it. There were boats filled with fishermen coming in early. There was the sound of their voices as they shouted greetings to each other. There was the hot sun, there was the blue sea, there was the blue sky. Not very far away, there was the white sand of the shore, with the run-down houses all crowded in next to each other, for in some places only poor people lived near the shore. I was seated in the launch between my parents, and when I realized that I was gripping their hands tightly I glanced quickly to see if they were looking at me with scorn, for I felt sure that they must have known of my never-see-this-again feelings. But instead my father kissed me on the forehead and my mother kissed me on the mouth, and they both gave over their hands to me, so that I could grip them as much as I wanted. I was on the verge of feeling that it had all been a mistake, but I remembered that I wasn't a child anymore, and that now when I made up my mind about something I had to see it through. At that moment, we came to the ship, and that was that.

The goodbyes had to be quick, the captain said. My mother introduced herself to him and then introduced me. She told him to keep an eye on me, for I had never gone this far away from home on my own. She gave him a letter to pass on to the captain of the next ship that I would board in Barbados.[7] They walked me to my cabin, a small space that I would share with someone else—a woman I did not know. I had never before slept in a room with someone I did not know. My father kissed me goodbye and told me to be good and to write home often. After he said this, he looked at me, then looked at the floor and swung his left foot, then looked at me again. I could see that he wanted to say something else, something that he had never said to me before, but then he just turned and walked away. My mother said, "Well," and then she threw her arms around me. Big tears streamed down her face, and it must have been that—for I could not bear to see my mother cry—

---

7. Barbados (bär bā´ dōs) easternmost island in the West Indies; southeast of Antigua.

14 ▲ **Critical Viewing** How does this jetty compare with the description of the jetty in the story? **[Compare]**

Reading Strategy
Drawing Inferences
What can you infer about Annie's relationship with her father based on their silent goodbye?

16 ☑ **Reading Check**
Where is Annie John going after leaving the island?

from A Walk to the Jetty ◆ 75

13 **Reading Strategy**
Drawing Inferences
• Point out to students the sentence "I shall never see this again."
• Ask students why these words first cause Annie's heart to swell with gladness and then shrivel up.
Answer: She has mixed emotions about leaving the people and places she knows. She longs for wider experience and opportunities, but she loves much of her past and fears her uncertain future.

14 ▶ **Critical Viewing**
Answer: Both jetties are crowded with people preparing to board boats and greet friends and relatives returning from sea. However, the jetty in the picture is surrounded by sailboats rather than fishing boats, and it does not appear to be near a wharf.

15 **Reading Strategy**
Drawing Inferences
• Ask students to summarize what they know so far about Annie's father.
• Then, ask the Reading Strategy question on p. 75: What can you infer about Annie's relationship with her father based on their silent goodbye?
Answer: Students may infer that their relationship is somewhat strained and that her father has a hard time expressing his emotions.

16 ☑ **Reading Check**
Answer: Annie John is going to Barbados to board another ship.

CUSTOMIZE INSTRUCTION FOR UNIVERSAL ACCESS

For Special Needs Students

Students may have difficulty following the story because the author's use of flashbacks disrupts its chronological flow. They might find it helpful to have a timeline to organize story events. Have students design a timeline on a piece of paper, using a straight edge to draw a line. Then, guide them as they reread the story and find details to place on the timeline as starting and ending points. They can then place other events in relation to these points.

If the author does not specify the date of a certain event, students must be prepared to make an educated guess as to where it should be placed. For example, at the beginning of the story, Annie says she is a "grown girl." Students may need to reread carefully to see whether the author mentions how old Annie is when she leaves home. Have students discuss in small groups the story details that indicate how they might create their timelines.

Answers for p. 76

Review and Assess

1. Students may admire Annie for leaving home because she was looking to better herself.

2. **(a)** Annie was five years old. **(b)** As she walks, she sees landmarks that remind her of other times in her life.

3. **(a)** On evening walks with her father, Annie usually went to the jetty. **(b)** This childhood fear returns as she is about to leave home because now—as then—she fears her uncertain, unknown future.

4. **(a)** Annie's mother clutches Annie tightly and sobs during the farewell. Annie's father looks as if he has something important to say, then walks away. **(b)** Her relationship with her father is loving but restrained. Her relationship with her mother is intimate and very expressive.

5. **(a)** Annie feels alone and afraid, imagining a vessel that has turned on its side and is emptying out. **(b)** Possible responses: Yes, she will be successful because she has courage and imagination. No, she won't be successful because she will miss her home too much to stay away.

---

which started me crying, too. She then tightened her arms around me and held me to her close, so that I felt that I couldn't breathe. With that, my tears dried up and I was suddenly on my guard. "What does she want now?" I said to myself. Still holding me close to her, she said, in a voice that <u>raked</u> across my skin, "It doesn't matter what you do or where you go, I'll always be your mother and this will always be your home."

I dragged myself away from her and backed off a little, and then I shook myself, as if to wake myself out of a <u>stupor</u>. We looked at each other for a long time with smiles on our faces, but I know the opposite of that was in my heart. As if responding to some invisible cue, we both said, at the very same moment, "Well." Then my mother turned around and walked out the cabin door. I stood there for I don't know how long, and then I remembered that it was customary to stand on deck and wave to your relatives who were returning to shore. From the deck, I could not see my father, but I could see my mother facing the ship, her eyes searching to pick me out. I removed from my bag a red cotton handkerchief that she had earlier given me for this purpose, and I waved it wildly in the air. Recognizing me immediately, she waved back just as wildly, and we continued to do this until she became just a dot in the matchbox-size launch swallowed up in the big blue sea.

I went back to my cabin and lay down on my berth. Everything trembled as if it had a spring at its very center. I could hear the small waves lap-lapping around the ship. They made an unexpected sound, as if a vessel filled with liquid had been placed on its side and now was slowly emptying out.

raked (rākt) *v.* scratched or scraped, as with a rake

stupor (stoo′ per) *n.* mental dullness, as if drugged

Jamaica Kincaid

(b. 1949)

Imagine leaving everyone and everything that is familiar to you and moving to a foreign country on your own. That is exactly what Jamaica Kincaid did. She left her home in Antigua to take a job caring for the children of a family in New York. Despite setbacks, she entered the New York publishing world and was soon writing articles for teen magazines.

Jamaica Kincaid has won acclaim for her autobiographical novels *Annie John* and *Lucy*. These works focus on the complex relationship between a mother and her daughter and how it changes, sometimes painfully. "A Walk to the Jetty" is the conclusion to *Annie John*. It describes the narrator's last walk through her childhood world, as she prepares to leave her native island.

Review and Assess

Thinking About the Selection

1. **Respond:** Do you admire Annie for leaving home? Why or why not?

2. **(a) Recall:** How old was Annie the first time she walked on the road alone? **(b) Analyze:** In what way is Annie walking through time as well as through space?

3. **(a) Recall:** Where did Annie go on evening walks with her father? **(b) Infer:** Why does Annie reexperience her old fear of falling through the boards of the jetty?

4. **(a) Recall:** Describe how Annie's mother and father say goodbye to her. **(b) Compare and Contrast:** How does the way they each say goodbye to Annie characterize the relationship Annie had with each of them?

5. **(a) Interpret:** Describe Annie's response to leaving the island. **(b) Extend:** Do you think she will be successful in her new life? Explain.

76 ◆ *On the Edge*

✐ ASSESSMENT PRACTICE: Reading Comprehension

Use Context Clues **(For more practice, see Test Preparation Workbook, p. 4.)**

Some tests may ask students to determine the best meaning of a vocabulary word from the context of a reading passage. Use the following sample question.

"She boiled my milk to <u>purify</u> it before I was allowed to drink it."

Which of the following represents the best meaning of the word <u>purify</u> as it is used in this sentence?

A free from guilt   C cleanse
B ceremoniously clean   D purge

Students should carefully read each answer choice to make the best selection, as more than one choice may answer the question. Milk would not be considered guilty, and boiling milk does not mean ceremoniously cleaning it, so *A* and *B* are incorrect. While *D* may seem to be a good choice, *C* is closer in meaning to the action of sterilizing milk by boiling. Therefore, *C* is the best choice.

Review and Assess

Literary Analysis

Flashback

1. In a chart like the one here, list three **flashbacks** from the story. Identify the place that sparked each flashback. Then, explain how the author uses precise details to make them vivid.

Location	Flashback	Precise Details

2. What do the flashbacks suggest about Annie's reasons for leaving home?

Connecting Literary Elements

3. What details about Annie's experiences do you learn because the story is told from her perspective?

4. Identify two ways that the **first-person point of view** adds to the emotion of this story.

5. Choose one experience from the story. Tell how Annie describes the experience. Then, tell how another character might describe it.

Reading Strategy

Drawing Inferences

6. What can you **infer** about Annie's relationship with her father based on her description of their evening walks to the jetty?

7. What can you infer about Annie's relationship with her mother when she drags herself out of her mother's embrace on the ship?

8. What can you infer about Annie's state of mind as her voyage finally begins? Support your inference with details.

Extend Understanding

9. **Social Studies Connection:** This story captures the emotions associated with leaving home to move to a new land. **(a)** What are some of the challenges that an immigrant like Annie John might face? Why? **(b)** What are some ways of meeting the challenges?

from *A Walk to the Jetty* ◆ 77

Quick Review

A **flashback** is a section of a literary work that interrupts the sequence of events to relate an event from an earlier time.

When a story is written in the **first-person point of view**, the narrator tells the story and is part of the action.

When you **draw inferences**, you reach conclusions about characters based on their speech, thoughts, and actions.

 Take It to the Net
www.phschool.com
Take the interactive self-test online to check your understanding of the selection.

Answers for p. 77

Review and Assess

1. Possible responses:
   Location: Miss Dulcie's house
   Flashback: Annie's apprenticeship
   Details: sweeping pins and needles off the floor; walking to the store to buy buttons and thread
   Location: the road to the chemist's
   Flashback: Annie's walk to the chemist's shop
   Details: the smell of her mother's powder; the dress with acrobats on it
   Location: Annie's friend's house
   Flashback: visiting her friend when she had the mumps
   Details: sitting on her friend's bed; eating roasted, buttered sweet potatoes

2. Some students will say the flashbacks suggest that Annie was overprotected and that her life in Antigua had its limitations; therefore, she wanted to leave home.

3. Readers learn about Annie's desire to be praised and her fear of leaving home. They also learn her perception of her parents.

4. The first-person point of view shows the depth of Annie John's love for her homeland and her parents. It also shows her fear of exploring a world beyond her island.

5. Annie thinks that her mother's goodbye was overwhelming and lasted too long. Her mother might say that the moment passed too quickly.

6. Students may infer that Annie does not understand her father and that she is not terribly interested in the things that interest him.

7. Annie sometimes finds her mother overbearing and overprotective.

8. Annie is lonely and scared when her voyage begins. She shows this by waving to her mother until she disappears from sight, and imagining a vessel slowly emptying out.

9. **(a)** Annie will face new people and customs, as well as a faster pace of life. **(b)** To meet people and learn about her new community, Annie might join local groups and organizations.

❶ Vocabulary Development

Word Analysis

1. b   3. c
2. a   4. a

Fluency

1. apprenticed   3. raked
2. loomed   4. stupor

Spelling Strategy

1. appear   3. accumulate
2. affirm

❷ Grammar

1. her; she   4. They
2. her; she   5. her; him; his
3. she; her

Writing Application

1. What is your purpose in leaving your homeland?
2. After you leave your parents, will they come to visit you?
3. Did your mother say that she would write to you?
4. Which of your memories will be most vivid?
5. Are you nervous about making new friends?

Integrate Language Skills

❶ Vocabulary Development Lesson

Word Analysis: Latin Root -stup-

In "A Walk to the Jetty," the main character shakes herself as if waking herself "out of a stupor." The word *stupor* contains the Latin root *-stup-*, which means "to be stunned or amazed." Choose the letter of the word or phrase whose meaning is closest to that of the first word.

1. stupefy: (a) entertain, (b) numb, (c) bring to life
2. stupendous: (a) astonishing, (b) excessive, (c) ridiculous
3. stupefaction: (a) alertness, (b) satisfaction, (c) bewilderment
4. stupid: (a) lacking normal intelligence, (b) wrong, (c) bent over

Fluency: Clarify Word Meaning

Complete each sentence with the most appropriate word from the vocabulary list on page 69.

1. Annie was ___?___ to a seamstress.
2. Annie ___?___ above her father and could see the top of his head.
3. Her mother's voice ___?___ across her skin.
4. For a moment, staring at her mother, Annie was in a ___?___.

Spelling Strategy

The prefix *ad-* means "to," "at," or "akin to." It changes spelling when it comes before certain consonants, as in *account*, *affront*, and *aggressor*. Make English words from the following:

1. *ad-* + *perere* (to come forth, be visible)
2. *ad-* + *firmare* (to make firm)
3. *ad-* + *cumulare* (to heap)

❷ Grammar Lesson

Pronoun Case

Pronoun case refers to the forms of a pronoun that indicate its function in a sentence.

> **Nominative case** The pronoun renames the subject: *I, we, you, she, it, he, they.*
> *Jane noticed the star when *she* looked up.*
>
> **Objective case** The pronoun functions as an object: *me, us, you, him, her, it, them.*
> *Aunt Susan bought *me* a dress.*
>
> **Possessive case** The pronoun indicates ownership: *my, mine, our, ours, your, yours, his, her, hers, its, their, theirs.*
> *My father gave me a hug.*

Practice Replace the noun or nouns in parentheses with the correct pronoun.

1. Annie withdrew (Annie's) money shortly before (Annie) left.
2. Annie's mother hugged (Annie) so hard, (Annie) could hardly breathe.
3. The woman (Annie) worked for would find fault with any choice made by (Annie).
4. (Annie and her mother) had been close.
5. Annie's father took (Annie) with (Annie's father) on (Annie's father) evening walks.

Writing Application Write five questions to ask Annie about why she is leaving the island. In your questions, use pronouns in all three cases.

W̶G Prentice Hall Writing and Grammar Connection: Chapter 23, Section 1

TEACHING RESOURCES

The following resources can be used to enrich or extend the instruction for pp. 78–79.

Vocabulary

📘 **Selection Support:** Build Vocabulary, p. 13

📖 **Vocabulary and Spelling Practice Book**
(Use this booklet for skills enrichment.)

Grammar

📘 **Selection Support:** Build Grammar Skills, p. 14

W̶G **Writing and Grammar,** Platinum Level, pp. 544–551

📄 **Daily Language Practice Transparencies** 📱

Writing

W̶G **Writing and Grammar,** Platinum Level, p. 56

💿 **Writing and Grammar iText CD-ROM** 📱

🔲 **BLOCK SCHEDULING:** Resources marked with this symbol provide varied instruction during 90-minute blocks.

Writing Lesson

Letter of Introduction

Annie John is leaving her home to begin a new life in England. As Annie John, write a letter of introduction to the family in England or to a place of business.

Prewriting Consider your audience and your purpose for writing this letter. You want to give pertinent information about yourself to someone who does not know you. If you are writing to the family in England, you will provide different details from those you would use in writing to a place of business.

Model: Determining Audience and Purpose

Who is my audience?

Why am I writing to this audience?

What details of my life does this audience need to know?

What will help me to get a job?

> Answers to these questions will help determine audience and purpose.

Drafting In the first paragraph, give some biographical information about yourself. In the next paragraph, describe your skills. Then, summarize the information about yourself in a final paragraph.

Revising Reread your letter. Make sure you included enough of the right kinds of details. If not, revise your letter to be more informative.

W̶G Prentice Hall Writing and Grammar Connection: Chapter 4, Section 2

Extension Activities

Listening and Speaking With a classmate, prepare a **mock telephone interview** with Annie John. Follow these suggestions:

- Review the story to identify the questions you will ask. This will show the interviewer's knowledge of Annie's experiences and will put her at ease. For the student playing Annie, it may help prompt the answers.
- Choose words that show respect for Annie.

When the interview is over, review the experience and evaluate its effectiveness. **[Group Activity]**

Research and Technology Using details from the story, make an **annotated map** showing Annie's walk to the jetty. Include all the landmarks mentioned in the story, and explain the significance of each. Using drawing software, make the map on your computer.

 Take It to the Net   www.phschool.com

Go online for an additional research activity using the Internet.

from A Walk to the Jetty ◆ 79

---

❸ Writing Lesson

- Remind students that depending on their audience, the content of their letter will change.
- For example, the family in England would probably be more interested in Annie's interests and hobbies than in her work experience.
- In addition, the language used in the letter will differ according to the audience. A letter to a place of business should have a more formal tone than a letter to the family in England.
- Use the Writing Lesson to guide students in drafting and revising their letters.
- Use the Description rubric in **Performance Assessment and Portfolio Management,** p. 19, to evaluate students' letters.

❹ Listening and Speaking

- In small groups, have students brainstorm for a list of questions they'd like to ask Annie John about her life.
- Then, have students draft their questions, making sure to include references to specific events in the story.
- Remind the students who play the role of Annie John that their answers should be consistent with details in the story about her life and personality.
- To assess their interviews, have students use the rubric for Interview Techniques, p. 27 in **Performance Assessment and Portfolio Management.**

CUSTOMIZE INSTRUCTION
For Universal Access

To address different learning styles, use the activities suggested in the **Extension Activities** booklet, p. 4.

- For Verbal/Linguistic and Interpersonal Learners, use Activity 4.
- For Logical/Mathematical and Verbal/Linguistic Learners, use Activity 5.
- For Visual/Spatial Learners, use Activity 6.

The Masque of the Red Death

Lesson Objectives

1. **To analyze and respond to literary elements**
   - Literary Analysis: Symbols
   - Connecting Literary Elements: Setting

2. **To read, comprehend, analyze, and critique a short story**
   - Reading Strategy: Identifying Context Clues
   - Reading Check questions
   - Review and Assess questions
   - Assessment Practice (ATE)

3. **To develop word analysis skills, fluency, and systematic vocabulary**
   - Vocabulary Development Lesson: Latin Suffix: -tion

4. **To understand and apply written and oral language conventions**
   - Spelling Strategy
   - Grammar Lesson: Correct Use of Adjectives and Adverbs

5. **To understand and apply appropriate writing and research strategies**
   - Writing Lesson: Journal of a Survivor
   - Extension Activity: Multimedia Presentation

6. **To understand and apply listening and speaking strategies**
   - Extension Activity: Radio Script

STEP-BY-STEP TEACHING GUIDE	PACING GUIDE
PRETEACH	
Motivate Students and Provide Background	
Use the Motivation activity (ATE p. 80)	5 min.
Read and discuss the Preview material and Background information (SE/ATE p. 80) **A**	5 min.
Introduce the Concepts	
Introduce the Literary Analysis and Reading Strategy (SE/ATE p. 81) **A**	15 min.
Pronounce the vocabulary words and read their definitions (SE p. 81)	5 min.
TEACH	
Monitor Comprehension	
Informally monitor comprehension by circulating while students read independently or in groups **A**	20 min.
Monitor students' comprehension with the Reading Check notes (SE/ATE pp. 83, 85, 87)	as students read
Develop vocabulary with Vocabulary notes (SE pp. 82, 85, 86, 87; ATE p. 85)	as students read
Develop Understanding	
Develop students' understanding of symbols with Literary Analysis annotations (SE pp. 85, 87; ATE pp. 83, 85, 87) **A**	10 min.
Develop students' understanding of context clues with Reading Strategy annotations (SE p. 84; ATE pp. 82, 84, 86, 88)	10 min.
ASSESS	
Assess Mastery	
Assess students' mastery of the Reading Strategy and Literary Analysis by having them answer the Review and Assess questions (SE/ATE p. 89)	20 min.
Use one or more of the print and media Assessment Resources (ATE p. 91) **A**	up to 50 min.
EXTEND	
Apply Understanding	
Have students complete the Vocabulary Development Lesson and the Grammar Lesson (SE p. 90) **A**	20 min.
Apply students' ability to describe a setting using the Writing Lesson (SE p. 91) **A**	45 min.
Apply students' understanding of the story using one or more of the Extension Activities (SE p. 91)	20–90 min.

 ACCELERATED INSTRUCTION:
Use the strategies and activities identified with an **A**.

UNIVERSAL ACCESS
● = Below Level Students
▲ = On-Level Students
■ = Above Level Students

Time and Resource Manager

Reading Level: Challenging
Average Number of Instructional Days: 4

RESOURCES		
PRINT 📝	**TRANSPARENCIES**	**TECHNOLOGY** 💿 🎧 📼
• **Beyond Literature,** Cross-Curricular Connection: Science, p. 5 ▲ ■		• **Interest Grabber Video,** Tape 1 ● ▲ ■
• **Selection Support Workbook:** ● ▲ ■ Literary Analysis, p. 20 Reading Strategy, p. 19 Build Vocabulary, p. 17	• **Literary Analysis and Reading Transparencies,** pp. 9 and 10 ● ▲ ■	
• **Adapted Reader's Companion** ● • **Reader's Companion** ● • **Authors In Depth,** Platinum Level ■		• **Listening to Literature** ● ▲ ■ Audiocassettes, Side 4 Audio CDs, CD 3
• **English Learner's Companion** ● ▲ • **Literatura en español** ● ▲ • **Literary Analysis for Enrichment** ■		
• **Formal Assessment:** Selection Test, pp. 13–15 ● ▲ ■ • **Open Book Test,** pp. 13–15 ● ▲ ■ • **Performance Assessment and Portfolio Management,** p. 28 ● ▲ ■ • PRENTICE HALL **ASSESSMENT** *SYSTEM* ● ▲ ■	PRENTICE HALL **ASSESSMENT** *SYSTEM* ● ▲ ■ Skills Practice Answers and Explanations on Transparencies	• **Test Bank Software** ● ▲ ■ • **Got It! Assessment Videotapes** ● ▲
• **Selection Support Workbook:** ● ▲ ■ Build Grammar Skills, p. 18 • **Writing and Grammar,** Platinum Level ● ▲ ■ • **Extension Activities,** p. 5 ● ▲ ■	• **Daily Language Practice Transparencies** ● ▲	• **Writing and Grammar iText CD-ROM** ● ▲ ■ 💻 *Take It to the Net* www.phschool.com

BLOCK SCHEDULING: Use one 90-minute class period to preteach the selection and have students read it. Use a second 90-minute class period to assess students' mastery of skills and have them complete one of the Extension Activities.

Step-by-Step Teaching Guide for pp. 80–81

Motivation

Ask students to discuss ways that people today protect themselves from diseases. They might mention inoculations, good hygiene, balanced diets, exercise, and donations to medical research. Then, explain that the main character in "The Masque of the Red Death" uses extreme measures to try to protect himself from a fatal disease.

▭ Interest Grabber Video

As an alternative, you may wish to play "Plagues" on Tape 1 to engage student interest.

❶ Background

The Black Death of the 1300s is not the only disease to have ravaged society. Bubonic plague appeared in 1664, scouring the city of London, England. For Poe and others living in the early nineteenth century, these outbreaks were a haunting memory. In addition, diseases such as influenza, cholera, typhoid, and smallpox were an ever-present threat. Today, AIDS (Acquired Immune Deficiency Syndrome) is spreading worldwide, infecting and killing millions, while diseases that were at one time under control, such as tuberculosis, are on the rise.

Prepare to Read

The Masque of the Red Death

Les Masques et la Mort 1897, © Estate of James Ensor/VAGA, New York, 1993

 Take It to the Net

Visit www.phschool.com for interactive activities and instruction related to "The Masque of the Red Death," including
- background
- graphic organizers
- literary elements
- reading strategies

Preview

Connecting to the Literature

To shield themselves from the public, some celebrities build elaborate homes protected by gates and guards. The prince in this story closes himself off in an abbey in order to escape from the sufferings of his subjects and the strange disease that ravages his country.

❶ Background

It seemed that no one was safe in medieval Europe. In the 1300s, a plague known as the Black Death swept across Europe, killing 25 million people. Most of the afflicted died within three to five days after their symptoms appeared. The "Red Death" is a plague Edgar Allan Poe invented for this story, but it is based on age-old fear.

80 ◆ *On the Edge*

TEACHING RESOURCES

The following resources can be used to enrich or extend the instruction for p. 80–81.

Motivation
▭ **Interest Grabber Video**, Tape 1 ▪

Background
📖 **Beyond Literature**, Cross-Curricular Connection: Science, p. 5 ▪

 Take It to the Net
Visit www.phschool.com for background and hotlinks for "The Masque of the Red Death."

Literary Analysis
▭ **Literary Analysis and Reading Transparencies**, Symbols, p. 9

Reading
▭ **Literary Analysis and Reading Transparencies**, Identifying Context Clues, p. 10 ▪

📖 **Selection Support:** Reading Strategy, p. 19; Build Vocabulary, p. 17 ▪

▪ **BLOCK SCHEDULING:** Resources marked with this symbol provide varied instruction during 90-minute blocks.

Literary Analysis

Symbols

If you wanted to create a **symbol** for the disease Poe calls the "Red Death"—a person, place, event, or thing that represented it—you might describe a skeleton in a red cape. Writers often use concrete symbols like this to help readers understand the meaning of a general idea like "disease" or "safety."

Poe's story is filled with symbols. As you read, jot down the symbols in the left column of a chart like this one. In the right column, write your ideas about what these items might represent.

Symbol	Possible Meaning
Prince	All people
Masquerade ball	
Plague	
Uninvited guest	

Connecting Literary Elements

A masquerade ball is an appropriate symbol for people who pretend that a disease does not exist. This **setting,** or the time and place in which events occur, is a key element in the story. As you read, notice how the luxurious setting provides a context for the main characters' actions and its description helps the writer convey an important message.

Reading Strategy

Identifying Context Clues

If you were to attend a masquerade, you would use **context clues**—hints from things in the surroundings, such as people's voices and actions—to figure out who the masked partygoers were. In a similar way, you can figure out the meanings of unfamiliar words by using context clues from the surrounding sentences. Look at the following example:

> All these and security were *within. Without* was the "Red Death."
> It was toward the close of the fifth or sixth month of his <u>seclusion</u>, and while the pestilence raged most furiously abroad, . . .

Using the words *within* and *without* from the surrounding text, you might determine that *seclusion* means "keeping inside" or "hiding."

Vocabulary Development

august (ô gust´) *adj.* imposing and magnificent (p. 82)

piquancy (pē´ kən sē) *n.* pleasantly sharp quality (p. 85)

arabesque (ar´ ə besk´) *adj.* elaborately designed (p. 85)

cessation (se sā´ shən) *n.* stopping, either forever or for some time (p. 86)

disapprobation (dis´ ap´ rə bā´ shən) *n.* disapproval (p. 86)

habiliments (hə bil´ ə mənts) *n.* clothing (p. 87)

The Masque of the Red Death ◆ 81

---

❷ Literary Analysis
Symbols

- Tell students that a symbol in a literary work is a person, animal, event, or idea that represents something in addition to itself.

- Have students suggest things they might use as a writer to symbolize the following: life, death, freedom, joy, despair.

- Read the instruction together as a class. Call students' attention to the example from the story.

- Use the instruction for Connecting Literary Elements to alert students to look for symbols in the setting of the story as they read.

- Use the Symbol transparency in **Literary Analysis and Reading Transparencies,** p. 9, to help students learn to identify symbols in reading.

❸ Reading Strategy
Identifying Context Clues

- Remind students that they can often figure out the meaning of an unfamiliar word by using *context clues*—hints from the words, phrases, and sentences surrounding the new word.

- You may want to have students create charts like the one below to keep track of unfamiliar words they encounter as they read the story.

New Word	Context Clues	Meaning
seclusion	within/ without	staying inside

Vocabulary Development

- Pronounce each vocabulary word for students, and read the definitions as a class. Have students identify any words with which they are already familiar.

E-Teach

Visit E-Teach at www.phschool.com for teachers' essays on how to teach, with questions and answers.

81

CUSTOMIZE INSTRUCTION
For Visual/Spatial Learners

To help students to understand the story, encourage them to render a blueprint or floorplan of the apartments or rooms in which Prince Prospero receives the guests. Have students label each room with its predominant color, as described in the text, and the manner in which no apartment is visible to the next. Share the drawings with the class, and ask students to discuss the effect of these rooms on someone in them.

❶ About the Selection

In addition to being a chilling horror story, this selection is a brilliant portrayal of the vanity of the rich and powerful and their illusions of invulnerability. Prince Prospero, the main character, believes he can save himself and a select few from the plague that menaces the country. In the story's climax, Prospero learns that wealth and privilege will not shield him from death.

❷ Reading Strategy

Identifying Context Clues

- Have a volunteer read aloud the bracketed sentence.
- Ask students to explain how the sequence "seizure, progress and termination" is a context clue that can help them figure out the meaning of *seizure*. Encourage them to define the word.
  Answer: The sequence refers to the stages of the disease. *Progress* refers to the movement of the disease from beginning to end, and *termination*, coming last in the sequence, means the end of the disease—literally "death." Therefore, *seizure*, used in this context, means the onset of disease, the moment when the sufferer is seized by sickness.

❶ The Masque¹ of the Red Death

Edgar Allan Poe

The "Red Death" had long devastated the country. No pestilence had ever been so fatal, or so hideous. Blood was its Avatar² and its seal—the redness and the horror of blood. There were sharp pains, and sudden dizziness, and then profuse bleeding at the pores, with dissolution. The scarlet stains upon the body and especially upon the face of the victim, were the pest ban which shut him out from the aid and from the sympathy of his fellow men. And the whole seizure, progress and termination of the disease, were the incidents of half an hour.

❷ But the Prince Prospero was happy and dauntless and sagacious. When his dominions were half depopulated, he summoned to his presence a thousand hale and lighthearted friends from among the knights and dames of his court, and with these retired to the deep seclusion of one of his castellated abbeys.³ This was an extensive and magnificent structure, the creation of the prince's own eccentric yet august taste. A strong and lofty wall

---

1. **Masque** (mask) *n.* ball at which costumes and masks are worn.
2. **Avatar** (av´ ə tär´) *n.* symbol or manifestation of an unseen force.
3. **castellated** (kas´ tə lāt´ id) **abbeys** (ab´ ēz) monasteries or convents with castlelike towers.

august (ô gust´) *adj.* imposing and magnificent

82   On the Edge

TEACHING RESOURCES

The following resources can be used to enrich or extend the instruction for pp. 82–88.

Literary Analysis
📖 **Selection Support:** Literary Analysis, p. 20

Reading
📖 **Reader's Companion**
📖 **English Learner's Companion**
🎧 **Listening to Literature Audiocassettes,** Side 4 ▣
💿 **Listening to Literature Audio CDs,** CD 3 ▣

Extension
📖 **Authors In Depth,** Platinum Level ▣
(The collection includes four additional selections by Poe for further reading.)

▣ **BLOCK SCHEDULING:** Resources marked with this symbol provide varied instruction during 90-minute blocks.

girdled it in. This wall had gates of iron. The courtiers, having entered, brought furnaces and massy[4] hammers and welded the bolts. They resolved to leave means neither of ingress or egress[5] to the sudden impulses of despair or frenzy from within. The abbey was amply provisioned. With such precautions the courtiers might bid defiance to contagion. The external world could take care of itself. In the meantime it was folly to grieve, or to think. The prince had provided all the appliances of pleasure. There were buffoons, there were improvisatori,[6] there were ballet dancers, there were musicians, there was Beauty, there was wine. All these and security were within. Without was the "Red Death."

It was toward the close of the fifth or sixth month of his seclusion, and while the pestilence raged most furiously abroad, that the Prince Prospero entertained his thousand friends at a masked ball of the most unusual magnificence.

It was a voluptuous scene, that masquerade. But first let me tell of the rooms in which it was held. There were seven—an imperial suite. In many palaces, however, such suites form a long and straight vista, while the folding doors slide back nearly to the walls on either hand, so that the view of the whole extent is scarcely impeded. Here the case was very different; as might have been expected from the duke's love of the bizarre. The apartments were so irregularly disposed that the vision embraced but little more than one at a time. There was a sharp turn at every twenty or thirty yards, and at each turn a novel effect. To the right and left, in the middle of each wall, a tall and narrow Gothic window looked out upon a

---

4. **massy** (mas´ ē) *adj.* massive or large.
5. **ingress** (in´ gres´) or **egress** (ē´ gres´) entering or leaving.
6. **improvisatori** (im präv´ i zə tôr´ ē) *n.* poets who improvise, or create verses without previous thought.

4 ☑ **Reading Check**

Why does Prince Prospero fortify his home?

5 ▶ **Critical Viewing**

Answer: Poe writes that the figures of the masqueraders contain "much of the wanton, much of the bizarre, something of the terrible, and not a little of that which might have excited disgust." The masks, rich fabrics, and bold colors reflect this description.

6 **Reading Strategy**

Identifying Context Clues

• Read aloud the bracketed passage to students. Ask them what Poe is describing here.
Answer: Poe describes the black chamber, which has the appearance of being full of blood because of the stained glass windows and the firelight that comes through them.

• Ask students the Reading Strategy question on this page: What clues in this paragraph hint at the meaning of *precincts*?
Possible response: The sentence describes a room that makes people in it look so dreadful that they are reluctant to enter it at all. This context suggests that the meaning of *precincts* is "surroundings," or "environment."

closed corridor which pursued the windings of the suite. These windows were of stained glass whose color varied in accordance with the prevailing hue of the decorations of the chamber into which it opened. That at the eastern extremity was hung, for example, in blue—and vividly blue were its windows. The second chamber was purple in its ornaments and tapestries, and here the panes were purple. The third was green throughout, and so were the casements. The fourth was furnished and lighted with orange—the fifth with white—the sixth with violet. The seventh apartment was closely shrouded in black velvet tapestries that hung all over the ceiling and down the walls, falling in heavy folds upon a carpet of the same material and hue. But in this chamber only, the color of the windows failed to correspond with the decorations. The panes here were scarlet—a deep blood color. Now in no one of the seven apartments was there any lamp or candelabrum amid the profusion of golden ornaments that lay scattered to and fro or depended from the roof. There was no light of any kind emanating from lamp or candle within the suite of chambers. But in the corridors that followed the suite, there stood, opposite to each window, a heavy tripod, bearing a brazier[7] of fire that projected its rays through the tinted glass and so glaringly illuminated the room. And thus were produced a multitude of gaudy and fantastic appearances. But in the western or black chamber the effect of the firelight that streamed upon the dark hangings through the blood-tinted panes, was ghastly in the extreme, and produced so wild a look upon the countenances of those who entered, that there were few of the company bold enough to set foot within its precincts at all.

It was in this apartment, also, that there stood against the western wall a gigantic clock of ebony. Its pendulum swung to and fro with a dull, heavy, monotonous clang; and when the minute-hand made the circuit of the face, and the hour was to be stricken, there came from the brazen lungs of the clock a sound which was clear and loud and deep and exceedingly musical, but of so peculiar a note and emphasis that, at each lapse of an hour, the musicians of the orchestra were constrained to pause, momentarily, in their performance, to hearken to the sound; and thus the waltzers perforce ceased their evolutions; and there was a brief disconcert of the whole gay company; and, while the chimes of the clock yet rang, it was observed that the giddiest grew pale, and the more aged and sedate passed their hands over their brows as if in

7. **brazier** (brā´ zhər) *n.* metal pan or bowl to hold burning coals or charcoal.

84 ◆ *On the Edge*

5 ▲ **Critical Viewing**
Compare this illustration with Poe's description of the costumes. [**Compare and Contrast**]

Reading Strategy
Identifying Context Clues
What clues in this paragraph hint at the meaning of *precincts*?

---

confused reverie or meditation. But when the echoes had fully ceased, a light laughter at once pervaded the assembly; the musicians looked at each other and smiled as if at their own nervousness and folly, and made whispering vows, each to the other, that the next chiming of the clock should produce in them no similar emotion; and then, after the lapse of sixty minutes, (which embrace three thousand and six hundred seconds of the Time that flies), there came yet another chiming of the clock, and then were the same disconcert and tremulousness and meditation as before.

But, in spite of these things, it was a gay and magnificent revel. The tastes of the duke were peculiar. He had a fine eye for colors and effects. He disregarded the decora[8] of mere fashion. His plans were bold and fiery, and his conceptions glowed with barbaric luster. There are some who would have thought him mad. His followers felt that he was not. It was necessary to hear and see and touch him to be sure that he was not.

He had directed, in great part, the movable embellishments of the seven chambers, upon occasion of this great fête; and it was his own guiding taste which had given character to the masqueraders. Be sure they were grotesque. There were much glare and glitter and piquancy and phantasm—much of what has been since seen in *Hernani*.[9] There were arabesque figures with unsuited limbs and appointments. There were delirious fancies such as the madman fashions. There was much of the beautiful, much of the wanton, much of the bizarre, something of the terrible, and not a little of that which might have excited disgust. To

---

8. **decora** (də kôr′ ə) *n.* requirements of good taste.
9. ***Hernani*** extravagant drama by the French author Victor Hugo.

The Masque of the Red Death ◆ 85

Literary Analysis
Symbols What does the clock symbolize?

piquancy (pē′ kən sē) *n.* pleasantly sharp quality

arabesque (ar′ ə besk′) *adj.* elaborately designed

⑨ ✓ **Reading Check**
What do the dancers do when the clock strikes?

⑦ **Vocabulary Development**
The Suffix *-tion*

- Call students' attention to the word *meditation* in the first paragraph on p. 85, and give the definition.
- Tell students that this word is constructed from the word *meditate,* which means to reflect or study. The suffix *-tion* means "the act or state of."
- Point out to students how the suffix makes a noun out of the verb *meditate.*
- Ask students to note other words in the story that end with *-tion.* Can students determine the root words from which they come?

⑧ **Literary Analysis**
Symbols

- Have a volunteer read aloud the bracketed passage (beginning on p. 84).
- Ask students to describe the clock, paying careful attention to Poe's description.
- Ask students what the clock may symbolize.
  Answer: The clock symbolizes time. It also symbolizes the nearing of death for the dancers, because each time it strikes, their end is closer.

▶ Monitor Progress Have students supply details that helped them reach the conclusion that the clock symbolizes the passage of time and impending death.
  Answer: Reasoning leading to this inference should include the color of the clock and the room (black), and its effect on the guests (pallor, fear).

⑨ ✓ **Reading Check**

Answer: The dancers stop dancing, grow pale, and some pass their hands over their brows as if they might be dreaming.

CUSTOMIZE INSTRUCTION FOR UNIVERSAL ACCESS

For Special Needs Students	For Gifted/Talented Students
Help students understand the story's symbolism by using a graphic organizer. Draw a T-chart on the chalkboard with the heading "Poe's Use of Symbols." In the left-hand column, list elements of the story, such as the abbey, the revellers, and the clock. In the right-hand column, help students record what the elements symbolize.	Students may wish to write a short radio script for this story. Remind them that listeners can only hear the action, not see it, so along with the dialogue, sound effects must be inserted into the script. Where would students insert sound effects? How might they create some of the sound effects needed in this story?

Les Masques et la Mort 1897
(Masks and Death), by James Ensor

James Ensor (1860–1949) was a
Belgian artist who found inspiration
in the stories of Edgar Allan Poe.
Although Ensor did not name his
work for a Poe story, it is not difficult
to surmise that "The Masque of the
Red Death" inspired it.

1. What details in the facial
   expressions of the masks make
   them especially horrifying?
   Answer: Students may mention
   the hollow eyes, the misshapen
   mouths, and the contorted
   expressions of the faces in the
   painting.

2. Why is Death smiling in the
   painting, whereas the masks all
   have contorted faces?
   Possible response: The grinning
   skull suggests that Death is
   laughing at the foolishness of
   the costumed figures.

⓫ ▶ Critical Viewing

Answer: As in the story, death is
present as a costumed reveller. The
masked figures appear to be as
grotesquely garbed as the people in
the story.

⓬ Reading Strategy

Identifying Context Clues

• Remind students that they can
  determine a word's meaning by
  looking for a synonym nearby. For
  example, in the bracketed
  passage, the phrase "taking *hue*
  from the *many-tinted* windows"
  contains two words that help to
  define each other.

• Read aloud the bracketed passage
  to students. Then, have them look
  for synonyms in this passage to
  determine the meaning of the
  words *ruddier, sable* and *ebony.*
  Answer: *Ruddier* is linked with the
  phrase "blood-colored," so it must
  mean "redder"; *sable* and *ebony*
  mean "black."

and fro in the seven chambers
there stalked, in fact, a multitude
of dreams. And these—the
dreams—writhed in and about,
taking hue from the rooms, and
causing the wild music of the
orchestra to seem as the echo of
their steps. And, anon, there
strikes the ebony clock which
stands in the hall of the velvet.
And then, for a moment, all is
still, and all is silent save the voice
of the clock. The dreams are stiff-
frozen as they stand. But the
echoes of the chime die away—
they have endured but an
instant—and a light, half-subdued
laughter floats after them as they
depart. And now again the music swells, and the dreams live, and
writhe to and fro more merrily than ever, taking hue from the many-
tinted windows through which stream the rays from the tripods. But to
the chamber which lies most westwardly of the seven, there are now
none of the maskers who venture; for the night is waning away; and
there flows a ruddier light through the blood-colored panes; and the
blackness of the sable drapery appalls; and to him whose foot falls upon
the sable carpet, there comes from the near clock of ebony a muffled
peal more solemnly emphatic than any which reaches their ears who
indulge in the more remote gaieties of the other apartments.

But these other apartments were densely crowded, and in them beat
feverishly the heart of life. And the revel went whirlingly on, until at
length there commenced the sounding of midnight upon the clock. And
then the music ceased, as I have told; and the evolutions of the waltzers
were quieted; and there was an uneasy cessation of all things as before.
But now there were twelve strokes to be sounded by the bell of the
clock; and thus it happened, perhaps, that more of thought crept, with
more of time, into the meditations of the thoughtful among those who
reveled. And thus, too, it happened, perhaps, that before the last echoes
of the last chime had utterly sunk into silence, there were many individuals in the crowd who had found leisure to become aware of the presence of a masked figure which had arrested the attention of no single
individual before. And the rumor of this new presence having spread
itself whisperingly around, there arose at length from the whole company a buzz, or murmur, expressive of disapprobation and surprise—
then, finally, of terror, of horror, and of disgust.

In an assembly of phantasms such as I have painted, it may well be
supposed that no ordinary appearance could have excited such sensation. In truth the masquerade license of the night was nearly unlimited;
but the figure in question had out-Heroded Herod,[10] and gone beyond

Les Masques et la Mort 1897, © Estate of James Ensor/VAGA, New York, 1993

⓫ ▲ Critical Viewing
How is the mood of "The
Masque of the Red
Death" reflected in the
details of this painting?
[Analyze]

cessation (se sā′ shən) *n.*
stopping, either forever
or for some time

disapprobation (dis′ ap′ rə
bā′ shən) *n.* disapproval

the bounds of even the prince's indefinite decorum. There are chords in the hearts of the most reckless which cannot be touched without emotion. Even with the utterly lost, to whom life and death are equally jests, there are matters of which no jest can be made. The whole company, indeed, seemed now deeply to feel that in the costume and bearing of the stranger neither wit nor propriety existed. The figure was tall and gaunt, and shrouded from head to foot in the <u>habiliments</u> of the grave. The mask which concealed the visage was made so nearly to resemble the countenance of a stiffened corpse that the closest scrutiny must have had difficulty in detecting the cheat. And yet all this might have been endured, if not approved, by the mad revelers around. But the mummer[11] had gone so far as to assume the type of the Red Death. His vesture was dabbled in *blood*—and his broad brow, with all the features of the face, was besprinkled with the scarlet horror.

When the eyes of Prince Prospero fell upon this spectral image (which with a slow and solemn movement, as if more fully to sustain its role, stalked to and fro among the waltzers) he was seen to be convulsed, in the first moment with a strong shudder either of terror or distaste; but, in the next, his brow reddened with rage.

"Who dares?" he demanded hoarsely of the courtiers who stood near him—"who dares insult us with this blasphemous mockery? Seize him and unmask him—that we may know whom we have to hang at sunrise, from the battlements!"

It was in the eastern or blue chamber in which stood the Prince Prospero as he uttered these words. They rang throughout the seven rooms loudly and clearly—for the prince was a bold and robust man, and the music had become hushed at the waving of his hand.

It was in the blue room where stood the prince, with a group of pale courtiers by his side. At first, as he spoke, there was a slight rushing movement of this group in the direction of the intruder, who at the moment was also near at hand, and now, with deliberate and stately step, made closer approach to the speaker. But from a certain nameless awe with which the mad assumptions of the mummer had inspired the whole party, there were found none who put forth hand to seize him; so that, unimpeded, he passed within a yard of the prince's person; and, while the vast assembly, as if with one impulse, shrank from the centers of the rooms to the walls, he made his way uninterruptedly, but with the same solemn and measured step which had distinguished him from the first, through the blue chamber to the purple—through the purple to the green—through the green to the orange—through this again to the

---

10. **out-Heroded Herod** behaved excessively, just as King Herod did. In the Bible, Herod slaughtered innocent babies, hoping to kill Jesus.
11. **mummer** *n.* masked and costumed person who acts out pantomimes.

The Masque of the Red Death ◆ 87

Literature in context — Science Connection

The Black Death

The "Red Death" is a fictitious disease made up by Poe for this eerie story. However, it is based on a real disease. The Black Death swept through Europe and Asia in the mid-1300s. The "Black Death" is another name for the bubonic plague, an epidemic carried by rats and other rodents. The plague is caused by a bacteria called *Yersinia pestis*, transmitted by fleas that live on the infected rodents. Poe took the fear associated with this kind of plague and based "The Masque of the Red Death" on it.

16 ✓ Reading Check

How does Prince Prospero react to the stranger?

---

⑰ Reading Strategy

Identifying Context Clues

- Ask students what happens in the last sentence of this paragraph. Answer: The revelers grab the guest and find there is nothing inside the clothing or under the mask.

- Have students use context clues to determine the meaning of the word *untenanted.*
Possible response: *Tangible* refers to something you can hold or touch. If there's nothing to grab hold of under the costume, then *untenanted* must mean "uninhabited" or "empty."

Answers for p. 88

Review and Assess

1. Some students might want Prospero as a friend because he likes to have fun, but others might suggest that his friendship is not worth the price they would have to pay.

2. **(a)** He hides to escape the Red Death. **(b)** Outside the abbey there is death and despair. Inside there is life and merriment.

3. **(a)** It is an abbey that has had the gates bolted shut so that no one may enter or leave. **(b)** He is a character who tries to escape misfortune, leaving his people to cope alone.

4. **(a)** The clock reminds them of time passing. **(b)** The clock is gigantic, heavy, and chimes loudly. All of these symbolize something lasting and important, something to which attention must be paid, such as the passing of life.

5. **(a)** The uninvited stranger is "tall and gaunt," wrapped in "habiliments of the grave," and wearing a mask that resembles a corpse. **(b)** When they notice him they begin expressing surprise and disapproval.

6. People engage in healthful activities to resist aging.

white—and even thence to the violet, ere a decided movement had been made to arrest him. It was then, however, that the Prince Prospero, maddening with rage and the shame of his own momentary cowardice, rushed hurriedly through the six chambers, while none followed him on account of a deadly terror that had seized upon all. He bore aloft a drawn dagger, and had approached, in rapid impetuosity, to within three or four feet of the retreating figure, when the latter, having attained the extremity of the velvet apartment, turned suddenly and confronted his pursuer. There was a sharp cry—and the dagger dropped gleaming upon the sable carpet, upon which, instantly afterwards, fell prostrate in death the Prince Prospero. Then, summoning the wild courage of despair, a throng of the revelers at once threw themselves into the black apartment, and, seizing the mummer, whose tall figure stood erect and motionless within the shadow of the ebony clock, gasped in unutterable horror at finding the grave cerements[12] and corpselike mask which they handled with so violent a rudeness, untenanted by any tangible form.

And now was acknowledged the presence of the Red Death. He had come like a thief in the night. And one by one dropped the revelers in the blood-bedewed halls of their revel, and died each in the despairing posture of his fall. And the life of the ebony clock went out with that of the last of the gay. And the flames of the tripods expired. And Darkness and Decay and the Red Death held illimitable dominion over all.

---

12. **cerements** (serʹ ə mənts) *n.* wrappings or shroud.

Review and Assess

Thinking About the Selection

1. **Respond:** Would you like to have the prince as a friend? Explain.

2. **(a) Recall:** Why does Prince Prospero hide in his palace? **(b) Compare and Contrast:** Contrast life outside the palace with life inside it.

3. **(a) Recall:** Describe the prince's fortification. **(b) Infer:** What does his desire to escape tell you about Prince Prospero?

4. **(a) Interpret:** Why does the ebony clock have such a dramatic effect on the dancers? **(b) Analyze:** What details of the description tell you what Poe meant for the clock to symbolize?

5. **(a) Recall:** Describe the uninvited guest. **(b) Connect:** What effect does his presence have on the other guests?

6. **Apply:** What methods do people use to try to avoid death?

Edgar Allan Poe

(1809–1849)

The American author Edgar Allan Poe died childless, but today he is credited with numerous literary grandchildren and great-grandchildren. Among these "descendants" are horror writer Stephen King and mystery writer Sir Arthur Conan Doyle.

Poe was born in Boston, Massachusetts, to a family of impoverished traveling actors. Within a year, his father had deserted the family and his mother had died. Poe was raised, but never formally adopted, by Mr. and Mrs. John Allan of Richmond, Virginia. In 1833, Poe entered a group of stories and a poem in a Baltimore literary contest. One of the stories, "MS. Found in a Bottle," won the fiction prize. His stories and poems continued to win him recognition, although Poe never did achieve financial success. He died a pauper in 1849.

ASSESSMENT PRACTICE: Reading Comprehension

Using Context Clues   (For more practice, see the Test Preparation Workbook, p. 5.)

Some tests require students to choose the appropriate meaning of multiple-meaning words by using context clues. Use the following sample:

In the passage on p. 82, *eccentric* means

  A not in the center
  B not concentric
  C deviating from a circular form
  D unusual or irregular

Discuss with students that *A*, *B*, and *C* describe objects, or mathematical figures, but not persons or a person's behavior. By process of elimination, students will be able to determine the best answer is *D*. Suggest that they then check the dictionary to confirm meanings of and synonyms for the word *eccentric*.

Review and Assess

Literary Analysis

Symbols

1. Describe the seventh apartment, and explain what it might represent.
2. What do you think the gigantic clock **symbolizes**?
3. Briefly explain what happens in this story. Then, look for another layer of meaning. What do you think Poe is trying to say?

Connecting Literary Elements

4. The boxes below are numbered 1 through 7 for the seven apartments that make up the **setting** of the story. Copy this diagram. In the boxes, put in details of each apartment.

blue east

5. Given the details you have gathered, what do you think the seven apartments symbolize?
6. How is the significance of the seventh apartment revealed at the end of the story?

Reading Strategy

Identifying Context Clues

7. Explain how **context clues** give hints to the meaning of *hue*.

   These windows were of stained glass whose color varied in accordance with the prevailing *hue* of the decorations. . . .

8. Which words are clues to the meaning of each italicized word?

   (a) This was an extensive and magnificent structure, the creation of the prince's own eccentric yet *august* taste.

   (b) And then the music ceased, as I have told; and the evolutions of the waltzers were quieted; and there was an uneasy *cessation* of all things as before.

Extend Understanding

9. **Science Connection:** What diseases do we fear today as much as the people in the story feared the Red Death?

The Masque of the Red Death ◆ 89

Answers for p. 89

Review and Assess

1. The seventh apartment is hung with black velvet curtains, and the floor is covered with a black velvet rug. The windowpanes are scarlet, the color of blood. The room represents death.

2. The clock symbolizes time passing, which in this context means approaching death.

3. A rich prince and his friends barricade themselves in a castle to dance, play, and avoid a plague that rages outside. The plague, in the form of an uninvited guest, enters the castle anyway and brings death to the inhabitants. Students may suggest that Poe is trying to say that no one is able to escape death, not even the rich and powerful.

4. **(1)** blue, facing east; **(2)** purple ornaments, tapestries, window panes; **(3)** green, including windows; **(4)** orange furnishings and light; **(5)** white; **(6)** violet; **(7)** hung with black velvet tapestries, black velvet rug, blood-red window panes

5. The rooms go from east to west, which might symbolize the movements of the sun and moon. This might represent the life cycle, ending in death in the black room. Discuss the symbols of different colors: blue represents water, or life; black means gloom, or death.

6. The uninvited guest reveals himself to be the Red Death. The seventh room symbolizes death.

7. The windows were of <u>stained</u> glass whose <u>color</u> varied in accordance with the prevailing <u>hue</u> of the decorations. The clue words suggest that <u>hue</u> is another word for color.

8. **(a)** <u>extensive</u>, <u>magnificent</u>; **(b)** <u>ceased</u>, <u>were</u> <u>quieted</u>

9. We fear AIDS, Ebola, and any new disease that appears suddenly, has little treatment and no cure, and is fatal.

---

❶ Vocabulary Development

1. the act of decorating
2. the act of creating
3. the state of being desperate

Spelling Strategy

1. unique   3. mystique
2. clique

Fluency: Clarify Word Meaning

1. They perceive him as august.
2. The costumes have arabesque patterns.
3. The uninvited guest wears habiliments of the grave and a mask that looks like that of a corpse.
4. The food has the quality of piquancy.
5. He views those who don't enjoy themselves with disapprobation.
6. When the clock strikes the hour there is a cessation of dancing.

❷ Grammar

1. closely; shrouded
2. loudly; struck
3. quickly; passed
4. slowly; walked
5. slow; progress

Writing Application

(a) The prince's friends were quick to take him up on his invitation. They dressed quickly to attend the ball.

(b) The guests felt safe inside the abbey. They lived there safely for several months.

Integrate Language Skills

❶ Vocabulary Development Lesson

Word Analysis: Latin Suffix -tion

The word *cessation* is built on the word *cease* with the Latin suffix *-tion*, which means "the act of" or "the quality of." Use the meaning of the suffix *-tion* to define each of these words:

    1. decoration 2. creation 3. desperation

Spelling Strategy

The word ending *-que* is pronounced like the letter *k* in a word. For example, the word *masque* has the same pronunciation as the word *mask*. Fill in the blank with the *-que* word below that fits the description.

    clique   mystique   unique

    1. one and only: ____?____
    2. an exclusive group of people: ____?____
    3. awe-inspiring aura: ____?____

Fluency: Clarify Word Meaning

On your paper, answer each question below with a sentence that contains a word from the vocabulary list on page 81.

1. How do the guests perceive Prince Prospero?
2. Describe the guests' costumes.
3. What is the uninvited guest wearing as he enters the costume ball?
4. What word could describe the food that may be served at the ball?
5. How does the prince view anyone who does not enjoy his ball?
6. What happens when the clock strikes the hour?

❷ Grammar Lesson

Correct Use of Adjectives and Adverbs

Do not confuse the use of adjectives and adverbs. **Adjectives** modify nouns, and **adverbs** modify verbs, adjectives, and other adverbs. A common mistake is the use of an adjective to modify a verb when an adverb is correct. In these examples, a form of the word *vivid* is used correctly as both an adjective and an adverb. Look at these examples:

> **Adjective:** The *vivid* color filled the room. (modifies noun *color*)

> **Adverb:** Its windows were *vividly* colored. (modifies verb *colored*)

Practice Choose the adjective or the adverb to correctly complete the sentence. Then, identify the word it modifies.

1. The seventh room was (close, closely) shrouded in black velvet tapestries.
2. The clock struck the hour (loud, loudly).
3. The time passed (quick, quickly).
4. The uninvited guest walked (slow, slowly) through the rooms.
5. The man saw his (slow, slowly) progress.

Writing Application Write sentence pairs demonstrating the correct use of the words below as adjectives and as adverbs.

(a) quick, quickly   (b) safe, safely

WG *Prentice Hall Writing and Grammar Connection: Chapter 17, Section 2*

TEACHING RESOURCES

The following resources can be used to enrich or extend the instruction for pp. 90–91.

Vocabulary

📖 **Selection Support:** Build Vocabulary, p. 17

📖 **Vocabulary and Spelling Practice Book** (Use this booklet for skills enrichment.)

Grammar

📖 **Selection Support:** Build Grammar Skills, p. 18

WG **Writing and Grammar,** Platinum Level, pp. 368–389

🖳 **Daily Language Practice Transparencies** 🖳

Writing

WG **Writing and Grammar,** Platinum Level, p. 57

💿 **Writing and Grammar iText CD-ROM** 🖳

🖳 **BLOCK SCHEDULING:** Resources marked with this symbol provide varied instruction during 90-minute blocks.

Writing Lesson

Journal of a Survivor

At the end of "The Masque of the Red Death," all the guests die. Imagine that one guest lives and is able to record his or her impressions of the setting and the events. Write a journal entry from the point of view of the surviving guest.

Prewriting   Gather details about the setting, the other guests, and the activities. Put your notes in a chart like the one below.

Brainstorming for Details

Setting	Guests	Activities
Seven different-colored chambers	Grotesque, masked figures	Waltzing
Wild music		Dining

Drafting   Begin your writing with a vivid description of the setting. Review your chart, keeping details that are relevant and discarding others. Your entry should tell the ways in which the setting affected you.

Revising   Although a journal entry is not written for a formal audience, you still want to preserve your memories with vivid descriptions. Enliven your descriptions by adding modifiers to dull sentences.

 Prentice Hall Writing and Grammar Connection: Chapter 6, Section 2

Extension Activities

Listening and Speaking   Write and perform a **radio script** for a scene from "The Masque of the Red Death." In a radio broadcast, what the audience hears must tell the whole story.

- Dialogue must be lively and descriptive.
- Actors must express emotions with voice only, so their performances must be "big."
- Sound effects must be realistic and obvious.

Record and share your script with classmates. [Group Activity]

Research and Technology   Give a **multimedia presentation** about an event that involves masks and costumes, such as the Venice carnival or the New Orleans Mardi Gras. If possible, include slides, music, and sound effects.

Take It to the Net   www.phschool.com

Go online for an additional research activity using the Internet.

The Masque of the Red Death ◆ 91

---

❸ Writing Lesson

- Have students use a journal entry of their own as a model for recording events as one of the guests. They may simply jot down the things that happened during the evening.

- Encourage students to note details of what the setting looked like, how they felt about the events, how other people were behaving, and so on. They might also explain how they survived.

- Use the Writing Lesson to guide students in developing their chart.

▶ **Monitor Progress**   Have students reread to confirm their details. Suggest that they note the page number and paragraph where each detail appears in their charts.

❹ Listening and Speaking

- Have students work in groups to make up dialogue for the Prince and his guests. Students may give each guest a name to make the activity more practical.

- Encourage the class to practice performing their dialogue showing different emotions—enjoyment, relief at being in a safe place, unease when the clock strikes, disapproval turning to terror when the uninvited guest appears, and so on.

- Have each group practice the dialogue and present it to the class.

- Have students use the rubric for Delivering a Narrative Presentation, p. 28 in **Performance Assessment and Portfolio Management.**

CUSTOMIZE INSTRUCTION
For Universal Access

To address different learning styles, use the activities suggested in the **Extension Activities** booklet, p. 5.

- For Musical/Rhythmic Learners, use Activity 4.
- For Visual/Spatial Learners, use Activity 5.
- For Logical/Mathematical Learners, use Activity 6.

Spring and All ✦ Fear ✦ The street

Lesson Objectives

1. **To analyze and respond to literary elements**
   - Literary Analysis: Imagery
   - Comparing Literary Works
2. **To read, comprehend, analyze, and critique poems**
   - Reading Strategy: Forming a Mental Image
   - Reading Check questions
   - Review and Assess questions
   - Assessment Practice (ATE)
3. **To develop word analysis skills, fluency, and systematic vocabulary**
   - Vocabulary Development Lesson: Anglo-Saxon Suffix: *-less*
4. **To understand and apply written and oral language conventions**
   - Spelling Strategy
   - Grammar Lesson: Coordinate Adjectives
5. **To understand and apply appropriate writing and research strategies**
   - Writing Lesson: Description of a Natural Struggle
   - Extension Activity: Comparison of Translations
6. **To understand and apply listening and speaking strategies**
   - Extension Activity: Speech About a Season

STEP-BY-STEP TEACHING GUIDE	PACING GUIDE
PRETEACH	
Motivate Students and Provide Background	
Use the Motivation activity (ATE p. 92)	5 min.
Read and discuss the Preview material and Background information (SE/ATE p. 92)	5 min.
Introduce the Concepts	
Introduce the Literary Analysis and Reading Strategy (SE/ATE p. 93) A	15 min.
Pronounce the vocabulary words and read their definitions (SE p. 93)	5 min.
TEACH	
Monitor Comprehension	
Informally monitor comprehension by circulating while students read independently or in groups A	15 min.
Develop vocabulary with Vocabulary notes (SE p. 94)	as students read
Develop Understanding	
Develop students' understanding of imagery with the Literary Analysis annotations (ATE pp. 94, 95) A	10 min.
Develop students' understanding of forming mental images with the Reading Strategy annotations (SE p. 96; ATE pp. 94, 96)	10 min.
ASSESS	
Assess Mastery	
Assess students' mastery of the Reading Strategy and Literary Analysis by having them answer the Review and Assess questions (SE/ ATE, p. 97)	20 min.
Use one or more of the print and media Assessment Resources (ATE p. 99) A	up to 50 min.
EXTEND	
Apply Understanding	
Have students complete the Vocabulary Development Lesson and the Grammar Lesson (SE p. 98) A	20 min.
Apply students' ability to use sensory details to the Writing Lesson (SE/ATE p. 99) A	45 min.
Apply students' understanding of the selections using one or more of the Extension Activities (SE p. 99)	20–90 min.

A **ACCELERATED INSTRUCTION:**
Use the strategies and activities identified with an A.

UNIVERSAL ACCESS
- ● = Below Level Students
- ▲ = On-Level Students
- ■ = Above Level Students

Time and Resource Manager

Reading Level: Average, Easy, Challenging
Average Number of Instructional Days: 4

PRINT	TRANSPARENCIES	TECHNOLOGY
• **Beyond Literature,** Humanities Connection: Fine Art, p. 6 ▲ ■		• **Interest Grabber Video,** Tape 1 ● ▲ ■
• **Selection Support Workbook:** ● ▲ ■ Literary Analysis, p. 24 Reading Strategy, p. 23 Build Vocabulary, p. 21	• **Literary Analysis and Reading Transparencies,** pp. 11 and 12 ● ▲ ■	
		• **Listening to Literature** ● ▲ ■ Audiocassettes, Side 5 Audio CDs, CD 3
• **Literatura en español** ● ▲ • **Literary Analysis for Enrichment** ■		
• **Formal Assessment:** Selection Test, pp. 16–18 ● ▲ ■ • **Open Book Test,** pp. 16–18 ● ▲ ■ • **Performance Assessment and Portfolio Management,** pp. 19, 29 ● ▲ ■ • **PRENTICE HALL ASSESSMENT SYSTEM** ● ▲ ■	• **PRENTICE HALL ASSESSMENT SYSTEM** ● ▲ ■ Skills Practice Answers and Explanations on Transparencies	• **Test Bank Software** ● ▲ ■ • **Got It! Assessment Videotapes** ● ▲
• **Selection Support Workbook:** ● ▲ ■ Build Grammar Skills, p. 22 • **Writing and Grammar,** Platinum Level ● ▲ ■ • **Extension Activities,** p. 6 ● ▲ ■	• **Daily Language Practice Transparencies** ● ▲	• **Writing and Grammar iText CD-ROM** ● ▲ ■ *Take It to the Net* www.phschool.com

BLOCK SCHEDULING: Use one 90-minute class period to preteach the selection and have students read it. Use a second 90-minute class period to assess students' mastery of skills and have them complete one of the Extension Activities.

Motivation

Present students with magazine pictures that reflect the feelings suggested by these poems: the burst of new life that is spring; the parting of mother and daughter, which might suggest abandonment; and a desolate street at night that would arouse fear. Have students share their impressions of these pictures. Then, explain that like pictures, the images created by the words in poems bring forth responses and make ideas concrete.

▣ Interest Grabber Video

As an alternative, you may wish to play "Reading and Student Response" on Tape 1 to engage student interest.

❶ Background

In addition to being good writers, translators must know both the original and the translation language well. Often, a word in one language can be translated into several possible words in another. For example, the word *niña* in the Spanish version of Mistral's poem "Fear" could be translated as "child" or "little girl." Those translating "Fear" must make many such choices, and each choice can alter the meaning of the poem. As a result, different translators can write different versions of the same poem or story.

Prepare to Read

Spring and All ◆ Fear ◆ The street

▣ Take It to the Net

Visit www.phschool.com for interactive activities and instruction related to these selections, including
- background
- graphic organizers
- literary elements
- reading strategies

Preview

Connecting to the Literature

As you grow older, you face new and sometimes difficult experiences. You may have to limit time with friends to work after school, or you may have to overcome your shyness to make a presentation. Like you, the subjects in these poems must face difficult and frightening challenges.

❶ Background

"Fear" and "The street" have been translated from their original Spanish. Translators face the difficult challenge of carrying the meaning of a poem from one language to another. In addition, a translator must maintain the literary quality of the poem. A word-for-word translation would not be inspiring to read. Therefore, a successful translator must be a good writer.

TEACHING RESOURCES

The following resources can be used to enrich or extend the instruction for pp. 92–93.

Motivation
▣ **Interest Grabber Video**, Tape 1 ▣

Background
📖 **Beyond Literature**, p. 6

▣ **Take It to the Net**
Visit www.phschool.com for background and hotlinks for the selections.

Literary Analysis
📄 **Literary Analysis and Reading Transparencies,** Imagery, p. 12 ▣

Reading
📖 **Selection Support:** Reading Strategy, p. 23; Build Vocabulary, p. 21

📄 **Literary Analysis and Reading Transparencies,** Forming a Mental Image, p. 11

▣ **BLOCK SCHEDULING:** Resources marked with this symbol provide varied instruction during 90-minute blocks.

Literary Analysis

Imagery

No matter what language they speak, people can understand the language of the senses. For that reason, the element of a poem that is often easiest to appreciate is its **imagery,** the descriptive language that re-creates sensory experiences. You can begin to enter the world each poem describes by identifying its imagery. In this excerpt from "Spring and All," notice the surprising picture that the poet paints of the season.

> Lifeless in appearance, sluggish
> dazed spring approaches—

Comparing Literary Works

In each of these poems, look at the **sensory language** the poets use to create images. In "Fear," Gabriela Mistral describes a swallow flying far away, choosing this image over that of another bird. In "The street," Octavio Paz's description creates a frightening scene. As you read each poem, make a diagram like the one here to analyze the ideas behind the poet's words. In the top box in the diagram, identify an image from the poem. Then, add the sensory language that the poet uses to build the image. Finally, note the effect that these details generate.

Reading Strategy

Forming a Mental Image

Reading a poem is like having a conversation with the poet. As you hear someone speak, you often **form a mental image,** a picture in your mind, of what that person is saying. In the same way, you can picture in your mind what these poets are saying. Enter the mysterious world of "The street," for example, by forming an image of the "dark and doorless" street that Paz describes. Glimpse the speaker in the "blackness" as he stumbles, falls, and rises.

Vocabulary Development

contagious (kən tā´ jəs) *adj.* spread by direct or indirect contact (p. 94)

lifeless (līf´ lis) *adj.* without life (p. 94)

clarity (klar´ ə tē) *n.* the quality or condition of being clear (p. 94)

stark (stark) *adj.* bare; plain (p. 94)

profound (prō found´) *adj.* deep (p. 94)

IMAGE
Street

⋮

Sensory Language
| long | silent | dark | doorless |

↓

Effect
frightening, eerie

Spring and All / Fear / The street ◆ 93

---

❷ Literary Analysis

Imagery

- Tell students that as they read these poems, they will focus on *imagery,* the descriptive language used by writers that appeals to readers' senses.

- Read the instruction about imagery with the class, and draw their attention to the example from "Spring and All."

- Use the instruction for Comparing Literary Works to help students create Image Charts on which they can enter specific images as they read, and identify the effect of each image.

- Use the Imagery transparency in **Literary Analysis and Reading Transparencies,** p. 12, to demonstrate how to identify sensory images.

❸ Reading Strategy

Forming a Mental Image

- Explain to students that as they watch a film, the images are presented to them. When they read, however, they must form their own mental images of what the writer is describing. Different readers will form different images.

- Have students read the instruction, and discuss what images they form based on the examples.

- Tell students that forming mental images will help them develop a more thorough understanding of the poems.

Vocabulary Development

- Pronounce each vocabulary word for students, and read the definitions as a class. Have students identify any words with which they are already familiar.

CUSTOMIZE INSTRUCTION FOR UNIVERSAL ACCESS

For Less Proficient Readers	For English Learners	For Advanced Readers
Give students practice in forming mental images by playing the first stanza of "Spring and All" on the **Listening to Literature Audio cassettes** or **Audio CDs**. After students hear the stanza, have them describe in writing the images that it brings to mind. Ask volunteers to compare their results.	Give students practice in forming mental images by having them read the first stanza of "Spring and All." First, define any words with which they are unfamiliar. Then, have them draw pictures of the mental images that the stanza brings to mind. Ask volunteers to compare their results.	Allow students to read the poems independently at their own pace. Tell them that if they have difficulty with a line or stanza, they should try to form a mental image based on the descriptions in it. Paying close attention to a poem's imagery can help to uncover its meaning.

 E-Teach

Visit E-Teach at www.phschool.com for teachers' essays on how to teach, with questions and answers.

93

CUSTOMIZE INSTRUCTION
For Musical/Rhythmic Learners

Have students select one of the poems and analyze whether it would make a good song. Encourage students to speculate as a group about the kind of music that would enhance the poem's imagery and rhythms.

❶ About the Selections

Although diverse in style and subject matter, these poems have one thing in common: Each explores a significant challenge or uncertainty that people face in life. In "Spring and All," the poet realizes that birth and renewal can be both joyous and difficult. In "Fear," a mother worries that her little girl might grow apart from her. In "The street," a man struggles with basic questions such as, "Who am I?" and "Where am I going?"

❷ Literary Analysis

Imagery

- Have students read the bracketed passage, and ask them which images they find particularly powerful.
  Answer: Students might find the image of the "contagious hospital" powerful because it is surprising in a poem about spring.

▶ Monitor Progress Some students may need extra help recognizing sensory images. If so, read the poems aloud, pausing to discuss the sensory details in each stanza.

❸ Reading Strategy

Forming a Mental Image

- Have a volunteer read aloud the bracketed passage.

- Then, have students discuss what image they form here and what ideas about spring the image suggests.
  Answer: Students may suggest that the "stiff curl of wildcarrot leaf" suggests a tightly coiled spring that is full of tension and potential energy, just like the season of spring.

---

❶ Spring and All
William Carlos Williams

By the road to the <u>contagious</u> hospital
under the surge of the blue
mottled clouds driven from the
northeast—a cold wind. Beyond, the
5   waste of broad, muddy fields
brown with dried weeds, standing and fallen

❷   patches of standing water
the scattering of tall trees

All along the road the reddish
10 purplish, forked, upstanding, twiggy
stuff of bushes and small trees
with dead, brown leaves under them
leafless vines—

<u>Lifeless</u> in appearance, sluggish
15 dazed spring approaches—

They enter the new world naked,
cold, uncertain of all
save that they enter. All about them
the cold, familiar wind—

❸   20 Now the grass, tomorrow
the stiff curl of wildcarrot leaf
One by one objects are defined—
It quickens: <u>clarity</u>, outline of leaf

But now the <u>stark</u> dignity of
25 entrance—Still, the <u>profound</u> change
has come upon them: rooted, they
grip down and begin to awaken

contagious (kən tā′ jəs) *adj.* spread by direct or indirect contact

lifeless (līf′ lis) *adj.* without life

clarity (klar′ ə tē) *n.* the quality or condition of being clear

stark (stark) *adj.* bare; plain

profound (prō found′) *adj.* deep

William Carlos Williams

(1883–1963)

Most people would agree that being a doctor is a full-time job. William Carlos Williams was both a doctor and a poet. When asked how he managed his double career, he replied that he treated his patients like poems and his poems like patients.

Williams believed that Americans should write about the details in the world around them. That is why the road in "Spring and All" describes a local route that he often took to see his patients.

TEACHING RESOURCES

The following resources can be used to enrich or extend the instruction for pp. 94–96.

Literary Analysis

📖 **Selection Support:** Literary Analysis, p. 24

Reading

🎧 **Listening to Literature Audiocassettes,** Side 5 ▪

💿 **Listening to Literature Audio CDs,** CD 3

▪ **BLOCK SCHEDULING:** Resources marked with this symbol provide varied instruction during 90-minute blocks.

Fear

Gabriela Mistral
Translated by **Doris Dana**

I don't want them to turn
my little girl into a swallow.
She would fly far away into the sky
and never fly again to my straw bed,
5 or she would nest in the eaves[1]
where I could not comb her hair.
I don't want them to turn
my little girl into a swallow.

I don't want them to make
10 my little girl a princess.
In tiny golden slippers
how could she play on the meadow?
And when night came, no longer
would she sleep at my side.
15 I don't want them to make
my little girl a princess.

And even less do I want them
one day to make her queen.
They would put her on a throne
20 where I could not go to see her.
And when nighttime came
I could never rock her . . .
I don't want them to make
my little girl a queen!

Woman With Child, Pablo Picasso, Museo Picasso, Barcelona, Spain

⑤ ▲ Critical Viewing What might the mother in this painting fear? Explain your answer. **[Draw Conclusions]**

---

1. **eaves** (ēvz) *n.* lower edge or edges of a roof, usually projecting beyond the sides of a building.

Gabriela Mistral

(1889–1957)

At fifteen, Gabriela Mistral (gä brē ā′ lä mē sträl′) was a full-time grade-school teacher in her native Chile. When Mistral (whose real name is Lucila Godoy Alcayaga) began publishing her poetry, she tried a variety of pen names, eventually settling on Gabriela Mistral. In 1945, Mistral became the first woman poet and the first Latin American to receive the Nobel Prize for Literature.

---

④ Literary Analysis

Imagery

• Read aloud the bracketed stanza to students. Point out that in this stanza, the poet compares the child to a swallow.

• Have students identify images that reinforce the image of the child as a bird.
   Answer: Images include "fly far away into the sky," "never fly again to my straw bed," and "nest in the eaves."

• Then, ask students how these images add to the poem's meaning.
   Answer: Students may say that the imagery emphasizes the idea that the speaker does not want the girl to "fly" away from her.

⑤ ▶ Critical Viewing

Answer: Students will probably connect the fear of the woman in the painting to that of the speaker in the poem. Based on the evidence that the mother in the painting appears worried and is clinging to her child, students might conclude she fears the dangers of the world and wants to protect her child.

⑥ Critical Thinking

Infer

• Have a volunteer read aloud the second stanza. Then, ask students to form mental images based on these lines.

• Ask volunteers to describe their mental images to the class.
   Possible Responses: Students might picture a young child playing in a meadow. They might also picture a mother and daughter sleeping peacefully in a warm home.

• Ask students what inferences they can make about the mother's hopes and fears, based on these images.
   Answer: The speaker fears that her little girl may not always be safe and close. She hopes that the girl will always be able to express her joy freely.

95

Forming a Mental Image

- Ask students the Reading Strategy question on p. 96: What words in the first two lines help you "see" the street?
  Answer: The words include *long*, *silent*, and *blackness*.

- Then, have students read the rest of the first stanza.

- Have them comment on the senses to which the images in the stanza appeal, as well as the overall impression they create.
  Answer: The images appeal to the senses of sight, sound, and touch. The overall impression is one of being lost and alone.

Answers for p. 96

Review and Assess

1. Students may say that it is difficult for a person without children to empathize with the speaker in "Fear." However, they may have feared losing someone close to them.

2. **(a)** The speaker notices new grass growing and says that new life will become clearer as spring approaches. **(b)** A plant faces danger trying to survive, just as patients may struggle to survive in a hospital.

3. **(a)** Spring is an awakening because it is a time of rebirth and renewal for plants, trees, and nature. **(b)** Students might suggest the words *enter*, *dignity*, and *begin*.

4. **(a)** She fears her daughter will turn into a swallow, a princess, or a queen. **(b)** The common element is that the daughter will become independent.

5. **(a)** The first stanza describes a man being pursued. The second stanza describes a man pursuing a phantom who is himself. **(b)** The two speakers are the man who is being pursued and the pursuer—actually the same person.

6. **(a)** Each poem describes a significant challenge or uncertainty that people face in life. **(b)** Students' choices will vary based on their life experiences.

The street

Octavio Paz

Translated by Muriel Rukeyser

❼

A long and silent street.
I walk in blackness and I stumble and fall
and rise, and I walk blind, my feet
stepping on silent stones and dry leaves.
5 Someone behind me also stepping on stones, leaves:
if I slow down, he slows;
if I run, he runs, I turn: nobody.

Everything dark and doorless.
Turning and turning among these corners
10 which lead forever to the street
where nobody waits for, nobody follows me,
where I pursue a man who stumbles
and rises and says when he sees me: nobody.

Reading Strategy
Forming a Mental Image
Which words in the first two lines help you "see" the street?

Review and Assess

Thinking About the Selections

1. **Respond:** Do you empathize with, or understand the feelings of, the speaker in "Fear"? Why or why not?

2. **(a) Recall:** Summarize the speaker's description of the approach of spring in "Spring and All." **(b) Infer:** Why do you think the poet sets the scene near a hospital?

3. **(a) Interpret:** Pointing to words such as *defined*, *clarity*, and *awaken* in "Spring and All," explain what the coming of spring means to Williams. **(b) Extend:** What other words could you add to strengthen your explanation?

4. **(a) Recall:** In "Fear," describe three fears that the speaker has. **(b) Draw Conclusions:** What is the common element in each of the fears that the speaker expresses?

5. **(a) Recall:** Describe the action in the first and the second stanzas of "The street." **(b) Interpret:** Show that there are two speakers in "The street," and explain who they are.

6. **(a) Compare and Contrast:** What common theme do you see in all three poems? **(b) Evaluate:** Which poem spoke the theme most clearly to you? Explain.

Octavio Paz

(1914–1998)

The wide-ranging travel of Mexican poet Octavio Paz (ok täv′ yō päs′) was matched by the freedom of his imagination. The universal appeal of his poetry earned Paz the Nobel Prize for Literature in 1990. Despite all the acclaim he won and the many places he visited, Paz remained deeply committed to his Mexican heritage.

✏ ASSESSMENT PRACTICE: Reading Comprehension

Using Context Clues   **(For more practice, see the Test Preparation Workbook, p. 6.)**

When students take assessment tests, they need to be prepared to use context clues to select the best word from a list of choices to complete a sentence. Ask students to read lines 1–10 of "Spring and All" on p. 94, and then use the following sample test item.

In line 5, <u>waste</u> most nearly means

   A spend uselessly   **C** uninhabited land

   B destroy   **D** gradually diminish

Although the meanings in answers *A, B,* and *D* are

definitions of the word *waste*, help students determine that answer *C* is best because context clues indicate (a) the word is used as a noun, and (b) "broad, muddy fields" are probably not inhabited.

To show students how to avoid confusion caused by "distractor" choices, do not give them the choices until they have used context clues and answered the item on their own. Then, they can see which answer most closely matches their own.

Review and Assess

Literary Analysis

Imagery

1. (a) Find a passage in "Spring and All" whose **imagery** describes experiences of both touch and sight. (b) Explain how this passage helps you appreciate the danger or uncertainty of spring.
2. How does the imagery of two sensory descriptions in "Fear" help you understand the speaker's anxiety about losing her daughter?
3. What images in "The street" create a mood of anxiety?

Comparing Literary Works

4. (a) Compare your image of "them" in "Fear" with your image of "nobody" in "The street." (b) Which **sensory language** helped build those images?
5. Which words in each of the poems generate images of a struggle?
6. Compare the language used to describe the road in "Spring and All" with that used to describe the street in "The street."

Reading Strategy

Forming a Mental Image

7. Using a diagram like the one below, briefly describe your **mental image** of "the road to the contagious hospital" in "Spring and All."

Taste	Sight	Sound

Sensory Details

Touch/Movement	Smell

8. Describe three ways that you can picture the girl in "Fear."
9. As you read "The street," what mental image did you form of the "Someone" who pursues the speaker?

Extend Understanding

10. **Cultural Connection:** What precautions do people you know take to protect themselves from the unknown? Do you think these are valid precautions or just reassuring rituals?

Spring and All / Fear / The street ◆ 97

Answers continued

9. Students may suggest that before they read the end of the poem, they pictured the "Someone" as a dangerous individual, perhaps a criminal wishing the narrator harm.
10. Students may discuss home, car, and business security systems. They might mention basic safety strategies, such as never walking alone at night.

Answers for p. 97

Review and Asess

1. **(a)** Students will probably cite lines 1–6 because "cold wind" evokes the sense of touch, and "the blue mottled clouds" and "muddy fields brown with dry weeds" call upon sight and touch. **(b)** The description in this passage seems to imply the danger that spring will never come to enliven the dead scene.
2. Both the images of the child as a bird flying away and as a princess in tiny golden slippers help readers understand that the mother fears her daughter will choose a life that excludes her.
3. Images that create anxiety include: "I walk in blackness and I stumble and fall and rise," "I walk blind," and "if I run, he runs."
4. **(a)** Students may suggest that "them" represents real people or society, while "nobody" is a phantom in a nightmare environment. **(b)** The images of the child becoming a bird, a princess, and a queen help form a mental image of "them" as all-powerful and uninterested in what the mother wants. The description of a silent pursuer makes "nobody" feel like a phantom.
5. Images of a struggle include "rooted, they grip down and begin to awaken," from "Spring and All"; the repetition of the phrase "I don't want them to turn my little girl into..." from "Fear"; and "if I slow down, he slows; if I run, he runs," from "The street."
6. The road in "Spring and All" is set in a landscape that will soon fill with flowers, plants, grass, and life. The road in "The street" is empty. It is black and silent, unrealistic and nightmarish.
7. Taste: wildcarrot leaf; Sight: blue mottled clouds, broad, muddy fields, brown with dried weeds; Sound: cold, familiar wind; Touch: movement of clouds, cold wind; Smell: the muddy fields, the grass, the leaves
8. The girl can be pictured as a swallow, a princess, or a queen.

continued

Answers for p. 98

❶ Vocabulary Development

Word Analysis

1. a   3. c
2. b

Spelling Strategy

1. tailless
2. wheelless
3. sailless

Concept Development: Analogies

1. contagious   4. profound
2. clarity   5. stark
3. lifeless

❷ Grammar

1. The small, dainty shoes were tied in bows.

2. A quiet, dark street wound through the neighborhood.

3. The sweet little girl was her mother's treasure.

4. The tall pine trees lined a peaceful lake.

5. The stone convalescent hospital overlooked a forest.

Writing Application

An owl flew above us, emitting an eerie, mournful call. Our shoes stuck constantly in the deep, muddy meadow. "That's it, I'm going home," whispered my brother.

Integrate Language Skills

❶ Vocabulary Development Lesson

Word Analysis: Anglo-Saxon Suffix -*less*

Knowing that the suffix -*less* means "without," you can figure out that *lifeless* means "without life." Choose the letter of the word that is the best antonym, or opposite, of the first word.

1. odorless: (a) fragrant, (b) flat, (c) pale
2. restless: (a) excited, (b) relaxed, (c) upset
3. speechless: (a) dull, (b) mute, (c) talkative

Spelling Strategy

When you add the suffix -*less* to a word ending in a single *l*, simply add the suffix. Thus, *soul* + *less* becomes *soulless*.

Add the suffix -*less* to each of these words:

    tail   wheel   sail

Concept Development: Analogies

Analogy exercises help you study vocabulary by analyzing the relationships among words. Common analogy relationships are **degree** (shout : speak), **part to whole** (leg : chair), **kind** (cauliflower : vegetable), **synonym** (problem : conflict), and **antonym** (conflict : peace). On your paper, write the word from the vocabulary list on page 93 that will make the relationship between the second pair of words similar to the relationship between the first pair.

1. *sickly : ill :: infectious :* ____?____
2. *darkness : gloom :: brightness :* ____?____
3. *alive : lively :: dead :* ____?____
4. *shallow : superficial :: deep :* ____?____
5. *costumed : naked :: adorned :* ____?____

❷ Grammar Lesson

Coordinate Adjectives

Use commas to separate **coordinate adjectives,** which are adjectives of equal rank. To determine whether adjectives are of equal rank, ask if the phrase retains its meaning when the adjectives are separated by *and* and if it retains its meaning when the adjectives are transposed.

> **Coordinate adjectives:** broad, muddy fields
> > broad and muddy fields
> > muddy, broad fields
>
> **Noncoordinate adjectives:** several dark doorways
> > several and dark doorways
> > dark several doorways
>
> *Several* and *dark* are not of equal rank.

Practice Copy the following sentences, adding commas if the adjectives are coordinate.

1. The small dainty shoes were tied in bows.
2. A quiet dark street wound through the neighborhood.
3. The sweet little girl was her mother's treasure.
4. The tall pine trees lined a peaceful lake.
5. The stone convalescent hospital overlooked a forest.

Writing Application Write a brief paragraph that describes an eerie scene. Use two sets of coordinate adjectives.

WG Prentice Hall Writing and Grammar Connection: Chapter 28, Section 2

TEACHING RESOURCES

The following resources can be used to enrich or extend the instruction for pp. 98–99.

Vocabulary

📖 **Selection Support:** Build Vocabulary, p. 21

📖 **Vocabulary and Spelling Practice Book** (Use this booklet for skills enrichment.) ▪

Grammar

📖 **Selection Support:** Build Grammar Skills, p. 22

WG **Writing and Grammar,** Platinum Level, p. 657

🗂 **Daily Language Practice Transparencies** ▪

Writing

WG **Writing and Grammar,** Platinum Level, p. 107

💿 **Writing and Grammar iText CD-ROM**

🗂 **BLOCK SCHEDULING:** Resources marked with this symbol provide varied instruction during 90-minute blocks.

❸ Writing Lesson

Description of a Natural Struggle

"Spring and All" describes some of the struggles that take place for life to begin anew in the spring. Using sensory language, write a description of a struggle that takes place in nature.

Prewriting   To find a topic, think about a struggle you have witnessed in your life or in nature films, such as a bean seed pushing through the ground or a newborn fawn struggling to stand. Using a chart like this one, jot down sensory images that describe the scene.

Sensory Details Chart

Sight	Sound	Taste	Touch/Movement	Smell
tiny green leaves	silence		cool spring breeze	fertilized soil
broken earth	soft whoosh of breeze		squatting by the garden	

Drafting   When you have gathered a wide range of sensory details, choose those that create a single mood. Paint a word picture so that readers can form a mental image from your writing.

Revising   Review your description to be sure that you have used vivid and precise words to describe your image. Delete details that detract from the overall mood of the image.

W͟G Prentice Hall Writing and Grammar Connection: Chapter 6, Section 4

❹ Extension Activities

Listening and Speaking The speaker in "Spring and All" vividly describes the drama of early spring. Write and deliver a **speech** to emphasize the drama and uncertainty of another season. Consider these tips:

- Tell what you see, hear, feel, taste, and smell.
- Use vivid adjectives and action verbs.
- Emphasize sensory words and descriptive phrases when you speak.

Present your speech to classmates.

Research and Technology In the library or online, find another translation of the poem "The street" by Octavio Paz. Then, write a **comparison** of the translations. Note similarities and differences, and back up your points with details from each translation.

 Take It to the Net   www.phschool.com

Go online for an additional research activity using the Internet.

ASSESSMENT RESOURCES

The following resources can be used to assess students' knowledge and skills.

Selection Assessment
- 📖 **Formal Assessment,** Selection Test, pp. 16–18
- 📖 **Open Book Test,** pp. 16–18
- 📼 **Got It! Assessment Videotapes,** Tape 1
- 💿 **Test Bank Software**
- 🖥 *Take It to the Net*
  Visit www.phschool.com for self-tests and additional questions on the selections.

Writing Rubric
- 📖 **Performance Assess. and Portfolio Mgmt.** p. 19

Listening and Speaking Rubric
- 📖 **Performance Assess. and Portfolio Mgmt.** p. 29

PRENTICE HALL
ASSESSMENT *SYSTEM*
- 📖 **Workbook**
- 📕 **Transparencies**
- 📖 **Skill Book**
- 💿 **CD-ROM**

---

❸ Writing Lesson

- Model a description of a struggle for students by reading the final stanza of "Spring and All."
- Invite students to recall struggles in the natural world they have witnessed: a bird pulling a worm from the ground, a flock of smaller birds chasing away a lone crow; or squirrels chasing each other from a source of food.
- Then, have students use the Sensory Details chart to record vivid details about the struggle they have chosen to write about.
- Use the Writing Lesson to guide students in writing their descriptions.
- Use the Description rubric in **Performance Assessment and Portfolio Management,** page 19, to evaluate students' descriptions.

❹ Listening and Speaking

- Divide the class into three groups, one for each season other than spring.
- Invite each group to make a list of sensory details that reflect its season. Have them work collectively to write a speech with the characteristics laid out in the lesson.
- Ask volunteers from each group to present the speech to the class.
- Have students use the rubric for Delivering a Descriptive Presentation, p. 29 in **Performance Assessment and Portfolio Management.**

CUSTOMIZE INSTRUCTION
For Universal Access

To address different learning styles, use the activities suggested in the **Extension Activities** booklet, p. 6.

- For Visual/Spatial and Verbal/Linguistic Learners, use Activity 4.
- For Intrapersonal and Bodily/Kinesthetic Learners, use Activity 5.
- For Verbal/Linguistic Learners, use Activity 6.

Two Friends ✦ Damon and Pythias

Lesson Objectives

1. **To analyze and respond to literary elements**
   - Literary Analysis: Climax
   - Comparing Literary Works
2. **To read, comprehend, analyze, and critique a short story and a myth**
   - Reading Strategy: Identifying Significant Details
   - Reading Check questions
   - Review and Assess questions
   - Assessment Practice (ATE)
3. **To develop word analysis skills, fluency, and systematic vocabulary**
   - Vocabulary Development Lesson: Latin Word Root: -tain-
4. **To understand and apply written and oral language conventions**
   - Spelling Strategy
   - Grammar Lesson: Degrees of Modifiers
5. **To understand and apply appropriate writing and research strategies**
   - Writing Lesson: Extended Definition of Friendship
   - Extension Activity: News Article
6. **To understand and apply listening and speaking**
   - Extension Activity: Debate

STEP-BY-STEP TEACHING GUIDE	PACING GUIDE
PRETEACH	
Motivate Students and Provide Background	
Use the Motivation activity (ATE p. 100)	5 min.
Read and discuss the Preview material and Background information (SE/ATE p. 100) ⒶA	5 min.
Introduce the Concepts	
Introduce the Literary Analysis and Reading Strategy (SE/ATE p. 101) ⒶA	15 min.
Pronounce the vocabulary words and read their definitions (SE p. 101)	5 min.
TEACH	
Monitor Comprehension	
Informally monitor comprehension by circulating while students read independently or in groups ⒶA	30 min.
Monitor students' comprehension with the Reading Check notes (SE/ATE pp. 103, 105, 107, 111)	as students read
Develop vocabulary with Vocabulary notes (SE pp. 103, 104, 110, 111, 112; ATE p. 111)	as students read
Develop Understanding	
Develop students' understanding of climax with Literary Analysis annotations (SE pp. 106, 107, 112; ATE pp. 106, 107, 111, 112) ⒶA	10 min.
Develop students' understanding of significant details with Reading Strategy annotations (SE pp. 103, 104, 105, 106, 107; ATE pp. 103, 104, 105, 106, 107, 108, 110)	10 min.
ASSESS	
Assess Mastery	
Assess students' mastery of the Reading Strategy and Literary Analysis by having them answer the Review and Assess questions (SE/ ATE, p. 113)	20 min.
Use one or more of the print and media Assessment Resources (ATE, p. 115) ⒶA	up to 50 min.
EXTEND	
Apply Understanding	
Have students complete the Vocabulary Development Lesson and the Grammar Lesson (SE p. 114) ⒶA	20 min.
Apply students' knowledge of concrete examples using the Writing Lesson (SE/ATE p. 115) ⒶA	45 min.
Apply students' understanding of the selections using one or more of the Extension Activities (SE p. 115)	20–90 min.

A **ACCELERATED INSTRUCTION:**
Use the strategies and activities identified with an Ⓐ.

UNIVERSAL ACCESS
- ● = Below Level Students
- ▲ = On-Level Students
- ■ = Above Level Students

Time and Resource Manager

Reading Level: Average, Easy
Average Number of Instructional Days: 4

RESOURCES		
PRINT 📖	**TRANSPARENCIES** 🗝	**TECHNOLOGY** 💿 🎧 📼
• **Beyond Literature,** Cross-Curricular Connection: Social Studies, p. 7 ▲ ■		• **Interest Grabber Video,** Tape 1 ● ▲ ■
• **Selection Support Workbook:** ● ▲ ■ Literary Analysis, p. 28 Reading Strategy, p. 27 Build Vocabulary, p. 25	• **Literary Analysis and Reading Transparencies,** pp. 13 and 14 ● ▲ ■	
• **Adapted Reader's Companion** ● • **Reader's Companion** ●		• **Listening to Literature** ● ▲ ■ Audiocassettes, Side 5 Audio CDs, CD 3
• **English Learner's Companion** ● ▲ • **Literatura en español** ● ▲ • **Literary Analysis for Enrichment** ■		
• **Formal Assessment:** Selection Test, pp. 19–21 ● ▲ ■ • **Open Book Test,** pp. 19–21 ● ▲ ■ • **Performance Assessment and Portfolio Management,** p. 19 ● ▲ ■ • **ASSESSMENT SYSTEM** ● ▲ ■	• **ASSESSMENT SYSTEM** ● ▲ ■ Skills Practice Answers and Explanations on Transparencies	• **Test Bank Software** ● ▲ ■ • **Got It! Assessment Videotapes** ● ▲
• **Selection Support Workbook:** ● ▲ ■ Build Grammar Skills, p. 26 • **Writing and Grammar,** Platinum Level ● ▲ ■ • **Extension Activities,** p. 7 ● ▲ ■	• **Daily Language Practice Transparencies** ● ▲ • **Writing Models and Graphic Organizers on Transparencies,** pp. 25–28 ● ▲ ■	• **Writing and Grammar iText CD-ROM** ● ▲ ■ 💻 *Take It to the Net* www.phschool.com

■ **BLOCK SCHEDULING:** Use one 90-minute class period to preteach the selection and have students read it. Use a second 90-minute class period to assess students' mastery of skills and have them complete one of the Extension Activities.

Step-by-Step Teaching Guide for pp. 100–101

Motivation

To capture students' interest, ask them to name and discuss a hall of fame with which they are familiar, such as a sports or rock-and-roll hall of fame. Elicit a list of the personal qualities of the people elected to these halls. Then, have students imagine a Friendship Hall of Fame that honors the world's closest and noblest friendships. What special qualities would a Friendship Hall of Fame honor? Let students know that both of the stories they are about to read pay tribute to unique friendships.

Interest Grabber Video

As an alternative, you may wish to play "On Friendship," Tape 1 to engage student interest.

❶ Background

Stories about friends have been set in many times and places. For example, the ancient Greeks placed such a high value on friendship that they saw it written in the sky. Castor and Pollux are characters in Greek mythology. When Castor was killed in a quarrel, Pollux begged his father, the god Zeus, to be allowed to die too so he would not be separated from his brother. The brothers were placed in the sky as the constellation Gemini ("the twins").

Prepare to Read

Two Friends ◆ Damon and Pythias

The Anglers, Georges Seurat, Musée National d'Art Moderne, Troyes, France

Take It to the Net

Visit www.phschool.com for interactive activities and instruction related to these selections, including

- background
- graphic organizers
- literary elements
- reading strategies

Preview

Connecting to the Literature

According to mathematics, if you share something with another person, you will each have less than the total amount. Friendship, however, proves this statement wrong. If you share a dream, a joke, or a story with a friend, it increases in value—and you both get to keep it.

"Two Friends" and "Damon and Pythias" show the value of friendship and the way life can test friendship.

❶ Background

"Two Friends" begins as the people of Paris are on the verge of surrender to the German army during the Franco-Prussian War. Paris had been under siege for months, and French forces were no match for the powerful German army. The war ended in May 1871, when the Treaty of Frankfurt was signed.

TEACHING RESOURCES

The following resources can be used to enrich or extend the instruction for pp. 100–101.

Motivation

Interest Grabber Video, Tape 1

Background

Beyond Literature, Cross-Curricular Connection: Social Studies, p. 7

Take It to the Net

Visit www.phschool.com for background and hotlinks for the selections.

Literary Analysis

Literary Analysis and Reading Transparencies, Climax, p. 14

Reading

Selection Support: Reading Strategy, p. 27; Build Vocabulary, p. 25

Literary Analysis and Reading Transparencies, Identifying Significant Details, p. 13

BLOCK SCHEDULING: Resources marked with this symbol provide varied instruction during 90-minute blocks.

❷ Literary Analysis

Climax

The **climax** of a story, novel, or play is the high point of interest or suspense at which the tension is greatest. It is also the point at which the outcome is about to be revealed. "Two Friends" and "Damon and Pythias" show two different ways of building toward a climax:

- *Expected:* The tension increases gradually, leading to a climax that you know is coming.
- *Unexpected:* The climax arrives suddenly and unexpectedly.

As you read each tale, decide whether the moment of greatest tension is expected or unexpected.

Comparing Literary Works

In both of these stories, a friendship is challenged by outside forces. Friendship, and the various issues relating to it, is a universal theme in literature. A **universal theme**—such as courage, love, and honor—is an idea or a statement that is relevant to people of almost any time or place. As you read, compare the messages each story conveys about friendship.

❸ Reading Strategy

Identifying Significant Details

Significant details in a story often hint at how events may turn out. Sometimes, these details describe character traits—human qualities that help determine the outcome of events. Other times, these details are events in the world that surround the characters.

As you read "Two Friends," notice significant details in the surroundings that hint at danger. Jot down the details in a cluster diagram like the one at right. For "Damon and Pythias," write the word *loyalty* in the center of the diagram and write in significant details relating to loyalty that give clues to the ending.

Vocabulary Development

ardent (är´ ənt) *adj.* intensely enthusiastic or devoted (p. 103)

vernal (vʉrn´ əl) *adj.* springlike (p. 103)

jauntiness (jônt´ ē nis) *n.* carefree attitude (p. 104)

dire (dīr) *adj.* calling for quick action; urgent (p. 110)

detained (dē tānd´) *v.* kept in custody (p. 111)

impediments (im ped´ ə mənts) *n.* something standing in the way (p. 111)

hindrances (hin´ drəns əz) *n.* people or things in the way; obstacles (p. 111)

annals (an´ əlz) *n.* historical records or chronicles; history (p. 112)

Two Friends / Damon and Pythias ◆ 101

---

❷ Literary Analysis
Climax

- Tell students that as they read these stories, they should take note of the *climax*—the point of highest interest in a story, at which the outcome is about to be revealed.
- Ask students to identify how they can tell that a climax is approaching as they watch a movie or read a story.
  Possible response: The suspense builds, and the action becomes more focused.
- Read the instruction for Climax and make sure students understand the two different kinds of climax. Encourage them to provide examples of each from stories they have read in the past.

❸ Reading Strategy
Identifying Significant Details

- Remind students that they can often make a good guess about the climax by paying attention to the significant details in a story.
- Tell students that significant details might include important details about characters, setting, or plot events.
- Encourage students to use cluster diagrams to record significant details about characters, setting, and plot as they read both stories.

Vocabulary Development

- Pronounce each vocabulary word for students, and read the definitions as a class. Have students identify any words with which they are already familiar.

 E-Teach

Visit E-Teach at www.phschool.com for teachers' essays on how to teach, with questions and answers.

CUSTOMIZE INSTRUCTION FOR UNIVERSAL ACCESS

For Special Needs Students	For Less Proficient Readers	For English Learners
Have students read the adapted version of "Damon and Pythias" in the **Adapted Reader's Companion.** This version provides basic-level instruction in an interactive format with questions and write-on lines. Completing the adapted version will prepare students to read the selection in the Student Edition.	Have students read the selection in the **Reader's Companion.** This version provides basic-level instruction in an interactive format with questions and write-on lines. After students finish the selection in the **Reader's Companion,** have them complete the questions and activities in the Student Edition.	Have students read the adapted version of the selection in the **English Learner's Companion.** This version provides basic-level instruction in an interactive format with questions and write-on lines. Completing the adapted version will prepare students to read the selection in the Student Edition.

Step-by-Step Teaching Guide for pp. 102–112

CUSTOMIZE INSTRUCTION
For Visual/Spatial Learners

Encourage students to use the painting on this page to help them visualize the story's foreign setting, which may seem to them incredibly remote. Have them note the ways in which the countryside in the painting differs from the area in which they live. Then, have them look for details in the painting that add to the details provided in the story. Encourage them to share their observations with classmates.

❶ About the Selection

In this story, Morissot (mô rē sō´) and Sauvage (sō väzh´) try to conduct their friendship in a business-as-usual manner against the backdrop of the Franco-Prussian War. War perplexes and disgusts them, and they wish only to recapture the simple pleasures they shared before it changed their lives. When they are captured by the enemy, they must choose between honor and survival. Students may recall times in which their own friendships have been challenged.

❷ ▶ Critical Viewing

Possible response: Students may describe the mood of the painting as peaceful, calm, or idyllic. The two men are sitting together companionably, as are Morissot and Sauvage in the story, exchanging few words.

The Anglers, Georges Seurat, Musée National d'Art Moderne, Troyes, France

❷ ▲ **Critical Viewing**
Compare this painting with the description in the story of an autumn afternoon. **[Compare and Contrast]**

❶ Two Friends

Guy de Maupassant
Translated by Gordon R. Silber

    The following story is set during the Franco-Prussian War. Beginning on July 19, 1870, the war was sparked by the Prussian prime minister Otto von Bismarck's belief that a war with France would strengthen the bond between the German states, along with French emperor Napoleon III's feeling that a successful conflict with Prussia would help him to gain support among the French people. As it turned out, the French army was no match for the German forces. After a series of victories, one of which ended in the capture of Napoleon III, the German army established a blockade around Paris on September 19, 1870. Led by a provisional government, Paris managed to hold out until January 28, 1871, though the city's inhabitants were plagued by famine and a sense of hopelessness. As Maupassant's story begins, the city is on the verge of surrender.

TEACHING RESOURCES

The following resources can be used to enrich or extend the instruction for pp. 102–112.

Literary Analysis

📖 **Writing Models and Graphic Organizers on Transparencies,** pp. 25–28

📖 **Selection Support:** Literary Analysis, p. 29

Reading

📖 **Reader's Companion**

📖 **English Learner's Companion**

📼 **Listening to Literature Audiocassettes,** Sides 5, 6 📼

💿 **Listening to Literature Audio CDs,** CD 3 💿

🖥 **BLOCK SCHEDULING:** Resources marked with this symbol provide varied instruction during 90-minute blocks.

Paris was blockaded, starved, in its death agony. Sparrows were becoming scarcer and scarcer on the rooftops and the sewers were being depopulated. One ate whatever one could get.

As he was strolling sadly along the outer boulevard one bright January morning, his hands in his trousers pockets and his stomach empty, M.[1] Morissot [mô rē sō´], watchmaker by trade but local militiaman for the time being, stopped short before a fellow militiaman whom he recognized as a friend. It was M. Sauvage [sō väzh´], a riverside acquaintance.

Every Sunday, before the war, Morissot left at dawn, a bamboo pole in his hand, a tin box on his back. He would take the Argenteuil railroad, get off at Colombes, and walk to Marante Island. As soon as he arrived at this ideal spot he would start to fish; he fished until nightfall.

Every Sunday he would meet a stout, jovial little man, M. Sauvage, a haberdasher[2] in Rue Notre-Dame-de-Lorette, another <u>ardent</u> fisherman. Often they spent half a day side by side, line in hand and feet dangling above the current. Inevitably they had struck up a friendship.

Some days they did not speak. Sometimes they did; but they understood one another admirably without saying anything because they had similar tastes and responded to their surroundings in exactly the same way.

On a spring morning, toward ten o'clock, when the young sun was drawing up from the tranquil stream wisps of haze which floated off in the direction of the current and was pouring down its <u>vernal</u> warmth on the backs of the two fanatical anglers,[3] Morissot would sometimes say to his neighbor, "Nice, isn't it?" and M. Sauvage would answer, "There's nothing like it." And that was enough for them to understand and appreciate each other.

On an autumn afternoon, when the sky, reddened by the setting sun, cast reflections of its scarlet clouds on the water, made the whole river crimson, lighted up the horizon, made the two friends look as ruddy as fire, and gilded the trees which were already brown and beginning to tremble with a wintery shiver, M. Sauvage would look at Morissot with a smile and say, "Fine sight!" And Morissot, awed, would answer, "It's better than the city, isn't it?" without taking his eyes from his float.

As soon as they recognized one another they shook hands energetically, touched at meeting under such changed circumstances. M. Sauvage, with a sigh, grumbled, "What goings-on!" Morissot groaned dismally, "And what weather! This is the first fine day of the year."

The sky was, in fact, blue and brilliant.

They started to walk side by side, absent-minded and sad. Morissot went on, "And fishing! Ah! Nothing but a pleasant memory."

"When'll we get back to it?" asked M. Sauvage.

---

1. **M.** abbreviation for *Monsieur* (mə syö´), or "Mister" or "Sir" (French).
2. **haberdasher** (hab´ ər dash´ ər) *n.* person who is in the business of selling men's clothing.
3. **anglers** (aŋ´ glərz) *n.* people who fish with hook and line.

Reading Strategy
Identifying Significant Details What important elements of the story are revealed in the first paragraph?

ardent (är´ ənt) *adj.* intensely enthusiastic or devoted

vernal (vɜrn´ əl) *adj.* springlike

 Reading Check
How do M. Morissot and M. Sauvage know each other?

---

❸ Reading Strategy
Identifying Significant Details

- Ask students the Reading Strategy question on p. 103: What important elements of the story are revealed in the first paragraph?
  Answer: Students should note that the story takes place in Paris, where the people are starving because of the blockade enacted by the Germans.

- Then, explain to students that readers can learn about characters' attitudes through the way they describe the world around them.

- Ask students what inferences they can make about the narrator's attitude toward the Franco-Prussian War based on this opening description.
  Answer: The narrator seems more concerned with the suffering that it caused—evidenced particularly by his mention of the sparrows—than with the issues over which it was being fought.

  ▶ Monitor Progress If students have difficulty with this concept, have them make a cluster diagram like the one on p. 101 for each character. As they read, they can jot down significant details about each character.

❹ Reading Check

Answer: Morissot and Sauvage used to fish together before the war.

CUSTOMIZE INSTRUCTION FOR UNIVERSAL ACCESS

For Special Needs Students	For English Learners	For Advanced Readers
Reread the background information on the Franco-Prussian War on p. 102 to make sure students understand why the people of Paris are suffering. Ask them why the war might prevent Morissot and Sauvage from engaging in activities such as fishing. Ask them what other everyday parts of life the war might affect.	Make sure students understand the background information on the Franco-Prussian War on p. 102. Help them make a list of words from the paragraph that relate to war, such as *blockade, provisional government,* and *surrender.* Define each one, and have students enter the words and definitions in their notebooks.	Students will learn the fate of Morissot and Sauvage, but they might be curious about the fate of the blockaded city of Paris, as well. Have interested students research what happened to Paris during the Franco-Prussian War, and share their findings with their classmates.

➎ Critical Thinking

Infer

- Ask students why it might have been easier for the men to avoid fishing as long as they did not see each other.

  Possible response: Their friendship was formed around fishing. As long as they did not see each other, they were not reminded of how much they missed fishing.

- Then, have students infer what leads the men to decide to go fishing again. Do students think it a wise decision?

  Answer: They have been discussing their pleasant memories of fishing. After several drinks, their desire to fish overcomes their concern about the circumstances. Students may suggest that it's not a wise decision, because of the blockade by the Prussian soldiers.

➏ Reading Strategy

Identifying Significant Details

- Explain to students that a blockade keeps people and important goods from getting in and out of a place. It can also involve attack by the blockading force.

- Have students reread the bracketed passage.

- Then, ask students to answer the Reading Strategy question on p. 104: What significant details suggest the possible danger of the setting?

  Answer: Students may note that the people in the area have fled; this suggests that an attack by the Prussians is a real possibility.

➐ ▶Critical Viewing

Answer: Students may say that the painting evokes the normal, peaceful times that the friends are trying to recapture. Others may suggest that the landscape is reminiscent of the "bare cherry trees" and "colorless fields" that the men see; in this respect, the painting evokes the eerie stillness of the wartime landscape.

They went into a little café and had an absinthe,[4] then resumed their stroll along the sidewalks.

Morissot stopped suddenly, "How about another, eh?" M. Sauvage agreed, "If you want." And they entered another wine shop.

On leaving they felt giddy, muddled, as one does after drinking on an empty stomach. It was mild. A caressing breeze touched their faces.

The warm air completed what the absinthe had begun. M. Sauvage **➎** stopped. "Suppose we went?"

"Went where?"

"Fishing, of course."

"But where?"

"Why, on our island. The French outposts are near Colombes. I know Colonel Dumoulin; they'll let us pass without any trouble."

Morissot trembled with eagerness: "Done! I'm with you." And they went off to get their tackle.

An hour later they were walking side by side on the highway. They reached the villa which the Colonel occupied. He smiled at their request and gave his consent to their whim. They started off again, armed with a pass.

Soon they passed the outposts, went through the abandoned village of Colombes, and reached the edge of the little vineyards which slope toward the Seine. It was about eleven.

➏ Opposite, the village of Argenteuil seemed dead. The heights of Orgemont and Sannois dominated the whole countryside. The broad plain which stretches as far as Nanterre was empty, absolutely empty, with its bare cherry trees and its colorless fields.

Pointing up to the heights, M. Sauvage murmured, "The Prussians are up there!" And a feeling of uneasiness paralyzed the two friends as they faced this deserted region.

"The Prussians!" They had never seen any, but for months they had felt their presence—around Paris, ruining France, pillaging, massacring, starving the country, invisible and all-powerful. And a kind of superstitious terror was superimposed on the hatred which they felt for this unknown and victorious people.

Morissot stammered, "Say, suppose we met some of them?"

His Parisian <u>jauntiness</u> coming to the surface in spite of everything, M. Sauvage answered, "We'll offer them some fish."

But they hesitated to venture into the country, frightened by the silence all about them.

Finally M. Sauvage pulled himself together: "Come on! On our way! But let's go carefully." And they climbed over into a vineyard, bent double, crawling, taking advantage of the vines to conceal themselves, watching, listening.

A stretch of bare ground had to be crossed to reach the edge of the river. They began to run, and when they reached the bank they plunged down among the dry reeds.

---

4. **absinthe** (ab´ sinth) n. type of liqueur.

Reading Strategy
Identifying Significant Details What significant details suggest the possible danger of the setting?

jauntiness (jônt´ ē nis) n. carefree attitude

➐ ▶Critical Viewing This painting does not suggest the horror or hardships of war. What aspects of this story does it illustrate? **[Draw Conclusions]**

Morissot glued his ear to the ground and listened for sounds of anyone walking in the vicinity. He heard nothing. They were indeed alone, all alone.

Reassured, they started to fish.

Opposite them Marante Island, deserted, hid them from the other bank. The little building which had housed a restaurant was shut up and looked as if it had been abandoned for years.

M. Sauvage caught the first gudgeon.[5] Morissot got the second, and from then on they pulled in their lines every minute or two with a silvery little fish squirming on the end, a truly miraculous draught.

Skillfully they slipped the fish into a sack made of fine net which they had hung in the water at their feet. And happiness pervaded their whole being, the happiness which seizes upon you when you regain a cherished pleasure of which you have long been deprived.

The good sun was pouring down its warmth on their backs. They heard nothing more; they no longer thought about anything at all; they forgot about the rest of the world—they were fishing!

But suddenly a dull sound which seemed to come from under ground made the earth tremble. The cannon were beginning.

Morissot turned and saw, over the bank to the left, the great silhouette of Mount Valérien wearing a white plume on its brow, powdersmoke which it had just spit out.

Reading Strategy
Identifying Significant Details What can you conclude based on Morissot's precautions?

9 ☑**Reading Check**
What causes the two friends to feel uneasy?

---

5. **gudgeon** (guj´ ən) *n.* small European freshwater fish.

Les Maisons Cabassud à la Ville D'Avray, Camille Corot

Two Friends ◆ 105

CUSTOMIZE INSTRUCTION FOR UNIVERSAL ACCESS

For Gifted/Talented Students	For Advanced Readers
Students may be interested in the territory that used to be called Prussia. Encourage students to prepare a list of relevant questions to find out more about this subject. For example, they may wish to locate a historic map of Prussia in an encyclopedia or other reference source to find out what city was the kingdom's capital (Berlin). They may choose to formulate questions to research the Franco-Prussian War or the formation of the country of Germany. When they finish, have students share their findings with the class.	Students may be interested in exploring literary criticism about Guy deMaupassant. Have them write a paragraph in response to this analysis of deMaupassant's work, written by literary critic Arthur Symons: "He attracts as certain men do, by a warm and blunt plausibility. He is so frank, and seems so broad; and is so skillful, and seems so living. All the exterior heat of life is in his work; and this exterior heat gives a more immediate illusion of what we call real life...."

---

8 ❽ **Reading Strategy**

Identifying Significant Details

- Have a volunteer read aloud the bracketed passage.

- Ask students the Reading Strategy question on p. 105: What can you conclude based on Morissot's precautions?

  Possible responses: Morissot wants to be sure no one else is around to observe the two men fishing in a forbidden area. He wants to make sure that there aren't any Prussians lying in wait.

9 ☑**Reading Check**

Answer: The friends feel uneasy because the Prussian soldiers are not far away.

10 ❿ **Background**

Art

Les Maisons Cabassud à la Ville d'Avray (The Cabassud Houses in the Town of Avray), by Camille Corot

During his long, distinguished career, French artist Camille Corot (1796–1875) became known primarily as a landscape painter. Classically trained, Corot traveled throughout Europe, painting pastures, villages, and mountainsides. His early landscapes were rendered in a highly detailed and realistic style. Later he adopted the softer, more romantic style represented by *Les Maisons Cabassud.* Use these questions for discussion:

1. What elements in the painting convey a sense of harmony and peacefulness?
   Answer: Students may point to the harmony between the color of the ground and the earthy colors of the buildings, and to the small, unhurried human figures.

2. Like Morissot and Sauvage, Corot—also a Parisian—was drawn to rural places. What do students think city-dwellers find most appealing about the country?
   Possible responses: Students might mention the opportunity to observe nature and experience life at a slower pace.

Identifying Significant Details

- Have students answer the Reading Strategy question on p. 106: Which details about the mountain may be significant? Why?
  Answer: Students may say that the cannon fire smoke coming from the mountain suggests that the war will intrude on the friends' peaceful day.
- Then, have students add this and other details that suggest danger to a graphic organizer like the one below

Significant Details

Paris blockaded

Danger

French outposts

⓬ Literary Analysis

Climax

- Point out to students that the soldiers appear just as the friends are laughing at a joke.
- Ask students why they think the author chose to introduce the soldiers at this moment.
  Answer: Students might say that the sudden change in the setting—from one of peace to one of danger—causes the tension to increase dramatically.
- Ask students the Literary Analysis question on p. 106: How does this change of setting build toward a climax?
  Answer: In earlier passages, the danger was at a distance. Now the danger is closer and it becomes very concrete. The fishermen have been captured, which creates more tension and moves the story closer to its climax.

And almost at once a second puff of smoke rolled from the summit, and a few seconds after the roar still another explosion was heard.

⓫ Then more followed, and time after time the mountain belched forth death-dealing breath, breathed out milky-white vapor which rose slowly in the calm sky and formed a cloud above the summit.

M. Sauvage shrugged his shoulders. "There they go again," he said.

As he sat anxiously watching his float bob up and down, Morissot was suddenly seized by the wrath which a peace-loving man will feel toward madmen who fight, and grumbled, "Folks sure are stupid to kill one another like that."

M. Sauvage answered, "They're worse than animals."

And Morissot, who had just pulled in a bleak, went on, "And to think that it will always be like this as long as there are governments."

M. Sauvage stopped him: "The Republic[6] wouldn't have declared war—"

Morissot interrupted: "Under kings you have war abroad; under the Republic you have war at home."

And they started a leisurely discussion, unraveling great political problems with the sane reasonableness of easygoing, limited individuals, and found themselves in agreement on the point that men would never be free. And Mount Valérien thundered unceasingly, demolishing French homes with its cannon, crushing out lives, putting an end to the dreams which many had dreamt, the joys which many had been waiting for, the happiness which many had hoped for, planting in wives' hearts, in maidens' hearts, in mothers' hearts, over there, in other lands, sufferings which would never end.

"That's life for you," opined M. Sauvage.

"You'd better say 'That's death for you,'" laughed Morissot.

⓬ But they shuddered in terror when they realized that someone had just come up behind them, and looking around they saw four men standing almost at their elbows, four tall men, armed and bearded, dressed like liveried[7] servants, with flat caps on their heads, pointing rifles at them.

The two fish lines dropped from their hands and floated off down stream.

In a few seconds they were seized, trussed up, carried off, thrown into a rowboat and taken over to the island.

And behind the building which they had thought deserted they saw a score of German soldiers.

A kind of hairy giant who was seated astride a chair smoking a porcelain pipe asked them in excellent French: "Well, gentlemen, have you had good fishing?"

Then a soldier put down at the officer's feet the sack full of fish

---

6. **The Republic** the provisional republican government that assumed control when Napoleon III was captured by the Prussians.
7. **liveried** (liv′ ər ēd) *adj.* uniformed.

Literary Analysis
Climax How does the change of setting build toward a climax?

CUSTOMIZE INSTRUCTION FOR UNIVERSAL ACCESS

For Gifted/Talented Students

Invite students to break up into pairs in order to role-play the two main characters in this story. Remind students that when they step into the shoes of characters, it is important that that they be true to those characters.

Before students begin, have them explore and discuss the characters' states of mind when the officer gives his ultimatum. Then, have students imagine that they have been given a short period of time to discuss what they will do. Lead students to consider these questions: Would the two men be completely certain of their choice, or would they feel some doubt? What reasons would they have for revealing the password? What reasons would they have for refusing?

Have pairs of students develop and practice their role-play conversations and then perform them for the class.

which he had carefully brought along. The Prussian smiled: "Aha! I see that it didn't go badly. But we have to talk about another little matter. Listen to me and don't get excited.

"As far as I am concerned, you are two spies sent to keep an eye on me. I catch you and I shoot you. You were pretending to fish in order to conceal your business. You have fallen into my hands, so much the worse for you. War is like that.

"But—since you came out past the outposts you have, of course, the password to return. Tell me that password and I will pardon you."

The two friends, side by side, pale, kept silent. A slight nervous trembling shook their hands.

The officer went on: "No one will ever know. You will go back placidly. The secret will disappear with you. If you refuse, it is immediate death. Choose."

They stood motionless, mouths shut.

The Prussian quietly went on, stretching out his hand toward the stream: "Remember that within five minutes you will be at the bottom of that river. Within five minutes! You have relatives, of course?"

Mount Valérien kept thundering.

The two fishermen stood silent. The German gave orders in his own language. Then he moved his chair so as not to be near the prisoners and twelve men took their places, twenty paces distant, rifles grounded.

The officer went on: "I give you one minute, not two seconds more."

Then he rose suddenly, approached the two Frenchmen, took Morissot by the arm, dragged him aside, whispered to him, "Quick, the password? Your friend won't know. I'll pretend to relent."

Morissot answered not a word.

The Prussian drew M. Sauvage aside and put the same question.

M. Sauvage did not answer.

They stood side by side again.

And the officer began to give commands. The soldiers raised their rifles.

Then Morissot's glance happened to fall on the sack full of gudgeons which was lying on the grass a few steps away.

A ray of sunshine made the little heap of still squirming fish gleam. And he almost weakened. In spite of his efforts his eyes filled with tears.

He stammered, "Farewell, Monsieur Sauvage."

M. Sauvage answered, "Farewell, Monsieur Morissot."

They shook hands, trembling from head to foot with a shudder which they could not control.

The officer shouted, "Fire!"

The twelve shots rang out together.

M. Sauvage fell straight forward, like a log. Morissot, who was taller, tottered, half turned, and fell crosswise on top of his comrade, face up, as the blood spurted from his torn shirt.

The German gave more orders.

Literary Analysis
Climax How does the officer's unemotional manner add to the tension?

Reading Strategy
Identifying Significant Details Why is it important that both men refuse to respond?

⓯ ✓ **Reading Check**
What does the Prussian officer want from the two friends?

⓭ **Literary Analysis**
Climax

- Read aloud the bracketed passage.
- Then, ask students to explain the officer's ultimatum in their own words.
  Answer: The officer says that the friends will die within five minutes if they do not reveal the password.
- Have students answer the Literary Analysis question on p. 107: How does the officer's unemotional manner add to the tension?
  Answer: The officer's cold manner lets both the men and readers know that he will not be swayed by feelings; the men have no way out.

⓮ **Reading Strategy**
Identifying Significant Details

- Have a volunteer read aloud the bracketed passage. Ask students what the officer hopes to gain by taking each man aside.
  Answer: He thinks that each is more likely to give up the password if his friend isn't present. In this way, he tries to break down the friends' sense of honor and loyalty.
- Ask students the Reading Strategy question on p. 107: Why is it important that both men refuse to respond?
  Answer: Both men refuse to respond, proving their loyalty to each other and to their country.

⓯ ✓ **Reading Check**
Answer: He wants the password so he and his troops can gain access to the town. He also wants to pit the friends against one another.

Identifying Significant Details

- Have a volunteer read aloud the bracketed passage.

- Then, ask students to note the significant details about the Prussian officer, based on his words and actions.
  Answer: Students should note the officer's callous and cold-blooded nature.

- Ask students whether the officer's behavior here is consistent with his behavior earlier in the story.
  Answer: The officer's behavior is consistent with the cold-blooded way in which he treated Morissot and Sauvage when they were captured.

- Explain to students that the officer represents the cold-blooded savagery of war.

Answers for p. 108

Review and Assess

1. Some students may say they did not expect the two friends to die for the honor of their country after discussing the folly of war.

2. **(a)** They have to forgo fishing because of the war. **(b)** Their decision to go fishing suggests that they value their friendship and will take risks in order to enjoy it.

3. **(a)** They believe war is pointless and destructive. **(b)** The setting adds to the tension because they have ventured into territory held by the Prussians.

4. **(a)** Their decision to keep the password to themselves leads to their execution. **(b)** One or both of the men could have decided to give the password. However, they still would likely have been executed.

5. **(a)** Simple, daily pleasures cannot be taken for granted; war destroys citizens' right to a peaceful life. **(b)** The story shows that even the simplest human activities become impossible in times of war.

6. The incident reinforces the shocking nature of the events and ironically refers to the friends' peaceful fishing.

His men scattered, then returned with rope and stones which they tied to the dead men's feet. Then they carried them to the bank.

Mount Valérien continued to roar, its summit hidden now in a mountainous cloud of smoke.

Two soldiers took Morissot by the head and the feet, two others seized M. Sauvage. They swung the bodies for a moment then let go. They described an arc and plunged into the river feet first, for the weights made them seem to be standing upright.

There was a splash, the water trembled, then grew calm, while tiny wavelets spread to both shores.

A little blood remained on the surface.

The officer, still calm, said in a low voice: "Now the fish will have their turn."

And he went back to the house.

⑯ And all at once he caught sight of the sack of gudgeons in the grass. He picked it up, looked at it, smiled, shouted, "Wilhelm!"

A soldier in a white apron ran out. And the Prussian threw him the catch of the two and said: "Fry these little animals right away while they are still alive. They will be delicious."

Then he lighted his pipe again.

Review and Assess

Thinking About the Selection

1. **Respond:** Were you shocked by the outcome of this story? Why or why not?

2. **(a) Recall:** How does the wartime situation in Paris affect the Sunday habits of Morissot and Sauvage? **(b) Analyze:** What does their decision to defy the war and fish again tell you about their friendship?

3. **(a) Recall:** What do the two men decide about the nature of war? **(b) Analyze:** How does the setting of their discussion add to the tension of the story?

4. **(a) Recall:** How does the men's final choice lead to the end of the story? **(b) Hypothesize:** How could the outcome of the story have been different?

5. **(a) Synthesize:** What message does Maupassant convey by showing how war breaks in on the peacefulness of fishing? **(b) Generalize:** What does this story suggest about the effects of modern warfare on everyday life?

6. **Evaluate:** Is it effective to end the story with the Prussian officer's order to cook the fish? Explain. In answering, consider what this detail does or does not add to the central idea of the story.

Guy de Maupassant

(1850–1893)

The short stories of Guy de Maupassant (gē də mō pä sän´) are filled with fascinating details of nineteenth-century life. In his writing, forces such as a person's family, surroundings, physical makeup, and personality determine the outcome of events.

Born into an aristocratic family, Maupassant was apparently destined for success. As a young man, he was a talented writer and won the attention of famous authors. Soon, he was famous in his own right. Unfortunately, his weaknesses caught up with him. Troubled by health problems, he died in his early forties. Yet he left a "fortune" to every future reader: 300 short stories.

Damon and Pythias

Retold by William F. Russell, Ed.D.

18

Damon and Pythias

◀ **Critical Viewing** **19**
What does this picture of Damon and Pythias reveal about their characters?
[Infer]

Damon and Pythias ◆ 109

17 **About the Selection**

In the myth "Damon and Pythias," two friends prove that they are willing to lay down their lives for each other. Students may be challenged to apply the standards of loyalty brought out in this story to their own friendships.

18 **Background**

Art

Damon and Pythias, artist unknown

An engraving is a picture printed from an image that has been cut into a metal plate. This engraving illustrates the climactic moment in which Pythias appears to save Damon, to the surprise of the tyrant Dionysius and the cheers of the crowd. Use these questions for discussion:

1. Call students' attention to the artist's use of diagonals. Have them identify various diagonal elements in the composition.
   Answer: Elements include the executioner's arm and sword; the upper half of Damon's body; and the outstretched arms of Pythias, Dionysius, and the spectator in the lower left corner.

2. What effect do all these diagonals create? In what way is this effect appropriate for the climax of the story?
   Answer: Students may say that the lines convey movement and action; the climax is the point at which the action is most intense.

19 ▶**Critical Viewing**

Answer: The picture shows Pythias trying to stop the killing of Damon. It suggests that the two characters are very loyal to each other.

CUSTOMIZE INSTRUCTION FOR UNIVERSAL ACCESS

For Special Needs Students	For Less Proficient Readers
Refer students to the reproduction of *Damon and Pythias.* Because this engraving directly illustrates a scene from the myth, it provides an excellent opportunity for students to absorb visual details to enhance their understanding of the story. Have the class carefully study the details of the engraving and consider how the depiction of the events and the characters is similar to or different from the way in which the characters and events are described in the selection. Encourage students to share their observations with classmates.	To help students understand the characters in this myth, refer them to the reproduction on this page. Ask students to describe the body language of Damon, Pythias, and Dionysius. Then, ask how each character's body language expresses what he is feeling. For example, students should note that Damon leans toward his friend, and that his eyes express relief, but not surprise, that he has returned.

20

Damon [dā′ mən] and Pythias [pith′ ē əs] were two noble young men who lived on the island of Sicily in a city called Syracuse. They were such close companions and were so devoted to each other that all the people of the city admired them as the highest examples of true friendship. Each trusted the other so completely that nobody could ever have persuaded one that the other had been unfaithful or dishonest, even if that had been the case.

Now it happened that Syracuse was, at that time, ruled by a famous tyrant named Dionysius [dī′ ə nish′ əs],* who had gained the throne for himself through treachery, and who from then on flaunted his power by behaving cruelly to his own subjects and to all strangers and enemies who were so unfortunate as to fall into his clutches. This tyrant, Dionysius, was so unjustly cruel that once, when he awoke from a restless sleep during which he dreamt that a certain man in the town had attempted to kill him, he immediately had that man put to death.

It happened that Pythias had, quite unjustly, been accused by Dionysius of trying to overthrow him, and for this supposed crime of treason Pythias was sentenced by the king to die. Try as he might, Pythias could not prove his innocence to the king's satisfaction, and so, all hope now lost, the noble youth asked only for a few days' freedom so that he could settle his business affairs and see to it that his relatives would be cared for after he was executed. Dionysius, the hardhearted tyrant, however, would not believe Pythias's promise to return and would not allow him to leave unless he left behind him a hostage, someone who would be put to death in his place if he should fail to return within the stated time.

Pythias immediately thought of his friend Damon, and he unhesitatingly sent for him in this hour of <u>dire</u> necessity, never thinking for a moment that his trusty companion would refuse his request. Nor did he, for Damon hastened straightaway to the palace—much to the amazement of King Dionysius—and gladly offered to be held hostage for his friend, in spite of the dangerous condition that had been attached to this favor. Therefore, Pythias was permitted to settle his earthly affairs before departing to the Land of the Shades,[1] while Damon remained behind in the dungeon, the captive of the tyrant Dionysius.

After Pythias had been released, Dionysius asked Damon if he did not feel afraid, for Pythias might very well take advantage of the

dire (dīr) *adj.* calling for quick action; urgent

---

1. **Land of the Shades** mythical place where people go when they die.

opportunity he had been given and simply not return at all, and then he, Damon, would be executed in his place. But Damon replied at once with a willing smile: "There is no need for me to feel afraid, O King, since I have perfect faith in the word of my true friend, and I know that he will certainly return before the appointed time—unless, of course, he dies or is held captive by some evil force. Even so, even should the noble Pythias be captured and held against his will, it would be an honor for me to die in his place."

Such devotion and perfect faith as this was unheard of to the friendless tyrant; still, though he could not help admiring the true nobility of his captive, he nevertheless determined that Damon should certainly be put to death should Pythias not return by the appointed time.

And, as the Fates would have it, by a strange turn of events, Pythias was <u>detained</u> far longer in his task than he had imagined. Though he never for a single minute intended to evade the sentence of death to which he had been so unjustly committed, Pythias met with several accidents and unavoidable delays. Now his time was running out and he had yet to overcome the many <u>impediments</u> that had been placed in his path. At last he succeeded in clearing away all the <u>hindrances</u>, and he sped back the many miles to the palace of the king, his heart almost bursting with grief and fear that he might arrive too late.

Meanwhile, when the last day of the allotted time arrived, Dionysius commanded that the place of execution should be readied at once, since he was still ruthlessly determined that if one of his victims escaped him, the other should not. And so, entering the chamber in which Damon was confined, he began to utter words of sarcastic pity for the "foolish faith," as he termed it, that the young man of Syracuse had in his friend.

In reply, however, Damon merely smiled, since, in spite of the fact that the eleventh hour had already arrived, he still believed that his lifelong companion would not fail him. Even when, a short time later, he was actually led out to the site of his execution, his serenity remained the same.

Great excitement stirred the crowd that had gathered to witness the execution, for all the people had heard of the bargain that had been struck between the two friends. There was much sobbing and cries of sympathy were heard all around as the captive was brought out, though he himself somehow retained complete composure even at this moment of darkest danger.

Presently the excitement grew more intense still as a swift runner could be seen approaching the palace courtyard at an astonishing speed, and wild shrieks of relief and joy went up as Pythias, breathless

detained (dē tānd') v. kept in custody

impediments (im ped' ə mentz) n. something standing in the way

hindrances (hin' drəns əz) n. people or things in the way; obstacles

㉔ ☑Reading Check
What compromise does Dionysius make with Pythias?

Damon and Pythias ◆ 111

㉒ Literary Analysis
Climax
- Before reading the bracketed passage, ask students what they expect the climax of the story to be, up to this point.
  Answer: Pythias will return in time to save Damon from execution.
- Then, have students read the bracketed passage. Ask them how the details add to the tension of the climax.
  Answer: The details add to the tension because although the reader trusts Pythias's loyalty to his friend, it begins to look as though he might not be able to fulfill his promise. In that case, Damon would be put to death, producing an unexpected and disappointing climax.

㉓ Vocabulary Development
The Latin Word Root -tain-
- Draw students' attention to the word *detained* and its definition, "kept in custody."
- Explain that the Latin word root -*tain*- means "to hold."
- Then, ask students to explain the relationship between the meaning of the word *detained* and the meaning of the root -*tain*-.
  Answer: To keep someone in custody is to *hold* him or her in custody.

㉔ ☑Reading Check
Answer: Dionysius agrees to let Pythias free to settle his affairs as long as Damon stays imprisoned in his place.

CUSTOMIZE INSTRUCTION FOR UNIVERSAL ACCESS

For English Learners

Write the story vocabulary and definitions on the chalkboard, and invite students to learn the words in a quiz show format. Ask students the following questions, and have them determine the answers as a group or by individual response. Students may also make up their own quiz questions, based on words from the story, to ask one another.

1. Which two words are synonyms? (*impediments* and *hindrances*)

2. For which vocabulary word are these words synonyms: *arrested, imprisoned?* (*detained*)

3. Which vocabulary word is a formal collection of events that you might note in a journal or diary? (*annals*)

4. Which word does not belong in this list: *hindrances, delays, captives, impediments?* (*captives*)

㉕ Literary Analysis

Climax

- Remind students that the climax of a story is the point at which the outcome is about to be revealed.
- Then, ask students the Literary Analysis question on p. 112: At what point does the story reach a climax?

  Answer: The climax of the story occurs when Pythias arrives at the execution site.

Answers for p. 112

Review and Assess

1. Students may cite the point at which "he had yet to overcome the many impediments that had been placed in his path."

2. **(a)** Damon and Pythias have the reputation of being noble and loyal, while Dionysius is considered treacherous and power hungry. **(b)** Because Dionysius is such a tyrant, he creates a situation that tests the friends' loyalty.

3. **(a)** Damon agrees to act as a hostage for Pythias. **(b)** Their friendship is such that either one would give his life for the other.

4. **(a)** Damon has faith that Pythias will return as he promised. **(b)** Students may say that the dramatic events that tested Pythias and Damon's friendship are not likely to occur in daily life today, but that in times of war similar circumstances could occur.

5. **(a)** Dionysius is so touched by the unselfishness of the two friends that he spares Pythias' life. **(b)** Dionysius' behavior at the beginning of the story is cold-blooded and cruel, while at the end he acts justly because he has been warmed by the friendship of Damon and Pythias.

6. Students may answer that it is not realistic; tyrants usually do not have sudden changes of heart.

㉕ and exhausted, rushed headlong through the crowd and flung himself into the arms of his beloved friend, sobbing with relief that he had, by the grace of the gods, arrived in time to save Damon's life.

This final exhibition of devoted love and faithfulness was more than even the stony heart of Dionysius, the tyrant, could resist. As the throng of spectators melted into tears at the companions' embrace, the king approached the pair and declared that Pythias was hereby pardoned and his death sentence canceled. In addition, he begged the pair to allow him to become their friend, to try to be as much a friend to them both as they had shown each other to be.

Thus did the two friends of Syracuse, by the faithful love they bore to each other, conquer the hard heart of a tyrant king, and in the annals of true friendship there are no more honored names than those of Damon and Pythias—for no person can do more than be willing to lay down his life for the sake of his friend.

Literary Analysis
Climax At what point does the story reach a climax?

annals (an′ əlz) *n.* historical records or chronicles; history

---

Review and Assess

Thinking About the Selection

1. **Respond:** At what point in the story were you most anxious about the return of Pythias? Explain.

2. **(a) Recall:** As the story begins, what are the reputations of Damon, Pythias, and Dionysius in Syracuse? **(b) Analyze:** How do these contrasting reputations set up the problem in the story?

3. **(a) Recall:** What does Damon agree to do for his friend? **(b) Interpret:** What does this decision tell you about the friendship of Damon and Pythias?

4. **(a) Infer:** Why is Damon patient and not fearful as he waits for Pythias? **(b) Extend:** Could a friendship like the one between Damon and Pythias exist in our own times? Why or why not?

5. **(a) Recall:** How does the outcome of the story affect Dionysius? **(b) Compare and Contrast:** Compare and contrast Dionysius' behavior at the beginning and at the end of the story.

6. **Evaluate:** Using your knowledge of tyrants, decide whether the king's change of heart is realistic.

About Myths

"Damon and Pythias" is a myth—a fictional story about gods and heroes. Myths may be ancient imaginary stories, but they attempt to explain real phenomena. They answer the most basic questions about the world and the human heart. We still need myths today because they offer timeless answers to timeless questions.

William F. Russell, the reteller of this myth, has retold many other myths so that modern readers can appreciate their universal messages. He is also the author of a widely read newspaper column on education.

✎ ASSESSMENT PRACTICE: Reading Comprehension

Analogies   **(For more practice, see the Test Preparation Workbook, p. 7.)**

When taking some tests, students may be asked to make analogy choices. To give them practice using the context of the words being compared in an analogy, use this sample item.

Read the related pair of words followed by the choices. Select the pair from the choices that best expresses a similar relationship.

RUDDY : CHEEKS

  A azure : sky   **C** crimson : lake
  B cinnamon : nutmeg   **D** snow : winter

Students must determine the meaning of *ruddy* from the context clues in the analogy: *Ruddy* is a color that a person's cheeks may be. Then, they can analyze the choices to see which is most similar in relationship. Students should determine that choice *A* has the closest meaning because it describes a color that the sky may be.

Review and Assess

Literary Analysis

Climax

1. For each story, list a few details that add to the tension. Then, identify the moment of **climax** in each.
2. In "Two Friends," Maupassant hints at the climax even though it arrives with shocking suddenness. (a) Find three of these hints. (b) Then, tell why a reader might overlook them.
3. (a) Which story's climax did you expect? Why? (b) Which climax surprised you? Why?

Comparing Literary Works

4. Using a Venn diagram, note details that show the friendships in each story. Place the common details in the overlapping area. Then, summarize the similarities and differences you see.

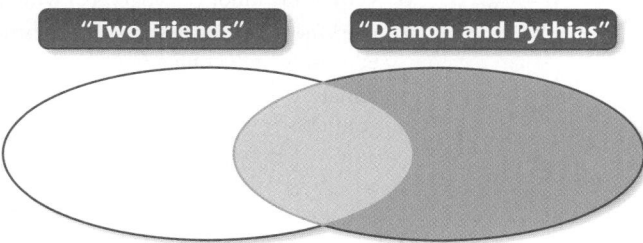

"Two Friends"   "Damon and Pythias"

5. What outside force challenges the friendship in each case?
6. (a) Combined, what theme about friendship do these stories convey? (b) What makes this a **universal theme**?

Reading Strategy

Identifying Significant Details

7. (a) In "Two Friends," identify two **significant details** of the trip to the island that create an uneasy feeling. (b) Explain your choices.
8. Find three significant details that suggest that Damon and Pythias' friendship is likely to survive a challenge.

Extend Understanding

9. **Social Studies Connection:** Was the officer in "Two Friends" or the tyrant in "Damon and Pythias" more realistic? Why?

Two Friends / Damon and Pythias ◆ 113

Quick Review

The **climax** is the point at which the tension is greatest. It is also the point at which the outcome is about to be revealed.

A **theme** is a central message or insight into life revealed through a literary work. A **universal theme** is relevant to people of almost any time and place.

Significant details are details that hint at the way events may turn out.

 Take It to the Net

www.phschool.com

Take the interactive self-test online to check your understanding of these selections.

Answers continued

7. **(a)** The empty landscape and the abandoned restaurant evoke an uneasy feeling. **(b)** Both details suggest a place that has become unsafe for human life.
8. Damon is willing to be held hostage for Pythias's return. Damon is unconcerned about Pythias taking advantage of the situation. Pythias fears that he will not return in time to save Damon's life.
9. The officer in "Two Friends" is more realistic because he behaves consistently throughout.

Answers for p. 113

Review and Assess

1. Details in "Two Friends" include the deserted town, the booming cannon, and the cool voice of the Prussian officer. The climax occurs when both men refuse to give the Prussian officer the password. Details in "Damon and Pythias" include the personality of Dionysius and the events that delay Pythias. The climax occurs when Pythias returns just as Damon is about to be executed.

2. **(a)** Hints include needing a pass to enter the war zone; the abandoned landscape and buildings on the way to the river; and smoke from cannon fire. **(b)** A reader might overlook these hints because they are woven into the story.

3. **(a)** Students might have expected the climax of "Damon and Pythias" because of the strength of the characters' friendship. **(b)** Students might say the climax of "Two Friends" was surprising because they didn't expect the men to die for a war they detested.

4.

Friendships in "Two Friends":

Common details:

Friendships in "Damon and Pythias":

Both men die rather than betray one another.

Both friendships demonstrate loyalty, trust, and the willingness to risk one's life.

The friends are willing to risk their lives for one another.

5. The Franco-Prussian war challenges the friendship in "Two Friends." The actions of a tyrant challenge the friendship in "Damon and Pythias."

6. **(a)** True friendship means loyalty even in the face of great challenges. **(b)** This is a universal theme because people form friendships in all societies.

continued

❶ **Vocabulary Development**

Word Analysis

1. to be able to hold
2. to hold in one's possession
3. to carry on

Spelling Strategy

1. silliness
2. steadying
3. dizzying
4. busily

Concept Development: Antonyms

1. b   5. a
2. c   6. c
3. c   7. a
4. b   8. c

❷ **Grammar**

1. most dismal   4. speedier
2. quieter   5. bravest
3. most enjoyable

Writing Application

My friend Ben is the funniest person I know. He can turn the dullest gathering into a circus. Whenever I feel down, I talk to Ben, and he makes me happier.

Integrate Language Skills

❶ Vocabulary Development Lesson

Word Analysis: Latin Root -tain-

Knowing that the Latin root -tain- means "to hold," you can guess that the vocabulary word *detained* means "held back." Write definitions for the following words:

1. contain   2. retain   3. maintain

Spelling Strategy

When adding a suffix to a word ending in y preceded by a consonant, change the y to i unless the suffix starts with an *i*. For example, *jaunty + -ness = jauntiness*. However, when the suffix *-ing* is added to a word ending in y, the y does not change to *i*. For example, *ready + -ing = readying*.

Add the suffix given to each word below. Make the appropriate spelling changes.

1. silly + -ness   3. dizzy + -ing
2. steady + -ing   4. busy + -ly

Concept Development: Antonyms

On your paper, write the letter of the word that is the antonym—opposite in meaning—of the first word.

1. dire: (a) urgent, (b) unimportant, (c) alive
2. detained: (a) restrained, (b) studied, (c) released
3. impediments: (a) footwear, (b) obstacles, (c) supports
4. hindrances: (a) fronts, (b) aids, (c) lances
5. ardent: (a) indifferent, (b) confident, (c) intent
6. vernal: (a) mild, (b) angry, (c) wintry
7. jauntiness: (a) seriousness, (b) lightheartedness, (c) reluctance
8. annals: (a) chronicles, (b) records, (c) fiction

❷ Grammar Lesson

Degrees of Modifiers

The **comparative degree** is usually formed with *-er* and compares two people, places, things, or ideas. If it would sound awkward with *-er*, a word forms the comparative with *more*.

> **Comparative:** Morissot was *taller*.
> Presently the excitement grew *more intense* still.

The **superlative degree** is usually formed with *-est* and compares three or more people, places, things, or ideas. If it would sound awkward with *-est*, a word forms the superlative with *most*.

> **Superlative:** the moment of *darkest* danger
> Damon and Pythias are perhaps the *most honored* names in friendship.

Practice Read these sentences. Change each adjective to its comparative or superlative form.

1. Paris was the (dismal) of all the cities.
2. Villages were (quiet) than they had been.
3. Fishing was Morissot's (enjoyable) hobby.
4. Pythias was (speedy) than he would have been if his friend were not waiting for him.
5. Damon was the (brave) of all Greeks.

Writing Application Write a brief paragraph about friendship. Use comparative and superlative forms of adjectives.

𝒲𝒢 *Prentice Hall Writing and Grammar Connection: Chapter 28, Section 2*

TEACHING RESOURCES

The following resources can be used to enrich or extend the instruction for pp. 114–115.

Vocabulary

📔 **Selection Support:** Build Vocabulary, p. 25

📖 **Vocabulary and Spelling Practice Book** (Use this booklet for skills enrichment.) ▪

Grammar

📔 **Selection Support:** Build Grammar Skills, p. 26

𝒲𝒢 **Writing and Grammar,** Platinum Level, pp. 590–592 ▪

📗 **Daily Language Practice Transparencies** ▪

Writing

𝒲𝒢 **Writing and Grammar** Platinum Level, p. 271

💿 **Writing and Grammar iText CD-ROM**

📄 **Writing Models and Graphic Organizers on Transparencies,** pp. 25–28

▪ **BLOCK SCHEDULING:** Resources marked with this symbol provide varied instruction during 90-minute blocks.

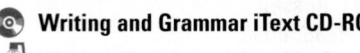

Writing Lesson

Extended Definition of Friendship

Use your own ideas and feelings as well as events in "Two Friends" and "Damon and Pythias" to write an extended definition of friendship. Unlike a dictionary definition, your extended definition should illustrate your ideas with concrete examples of friends and their behavior from literature, the movies, television, and your own experiences.

Prewriting Start with a two-column chart. In the left column, jot down general ideas about friendship. In the right column, note a concrete example that supports each idea.

Gathering Concrete Details

Friendship Ideas	Concrete Examples
Trust	Damon trusted Pythias to come back.

Drafting Use the ideas in the left column of your chart to write a general definition of friendship. Then, choose the best examples from the right column to make that definition more vivid.

Revising As you review your draft, be sure that you have illustrated each general point you have made about friendship with at least one concrete example.

W̶G Prentice Hall Writing and Grammar Connection: Chapter 12, Section 7

Extension Activities

Listening and Speaking With a small group, hold a **debate.** Take opposing sides to argue whether the friends in either or both of the stories behaved as you would behave and why. These tips will help you prepare for the debate:

- List your points to help clarify your opinions about your side of the issue.
- Make sure that you have convincing evidence to support each of your points.

As you argue, review your notes and stress your best evidence to persuade listeners.
[Group Activity]

Research and Technology In the library or online, research the setting of "Two Friends"—Prussia's blockade of Paris in 1870. Find examples of brutality that support the event that occurs in the story. Write a **news article** reporting on your findings.

 Take It to the Net   www.phschool.com
Go online for an additional research activity using the Internet.

Two Friends / Damon and Pythias ◆ 115

❸ **Writing Lesson**

- Have students brainstorm for a list of friendships they admire in books, movies, television shows, or their own lives.
- Make sure students can explain what they admire about each friendship on their list. Encourage them to use concrete examples.
- Then, based on their lists, have them compose basic definitions of friendship.
- Use the Writing Lesson to help students turn their basic definitions into extended definitions.
- Use the Description rubric in **Performance Assessment and Portfolio Management,** p. 19, to evaluate students' essays.

❹ **Research and Technology**

- Explain to students that a news article is an objective report on the facts of a situation or event.
- Before students begin their research, discuss the methods they should use. For example, if students are planning to perform an online search, what keywords might they use?
- When students have finished drafting their articles, you may want to encourage them to use word processing software to format their text like an actual news article.

CUSTOMIZE INSTRUCTION
For Universal Access

To address different learning styles, use the activities suggested in the **Extension Activities** booklet, p. 7.

- For Verbal/Linguistic and Logical/Mathematical Learners, use Activity 4.
- For Verbal/Linguistic and Visual/Spatial Learners, use Activity 5.
- For Musical/Rhythmic Learners, use Activity 6.
- For Verbal/Linguistic, Visual/Spatial, and Interpersonal Learners, use Activity 7.

Lesson Objectives

1. To write an autobiographical narrative
2. To use writing strategies to generate ideas, plan, organize, evaluate, and revise the narrative

Model From Literature

In the excerpt from "View From the Summit," Sir Edmund Hillary details his experience of climbing Mt. Everest.

Prewriting

- Students can use additional words to help them "consider the moment." Remind students of the importance of narrowing their topics so that they can describe the experience throughly in their narratives.

- Tell students that as they gather details about the setting, they should focus only on those details pertinent to establishing the time, place, and mood of the narrative.

- Remind students that conflict provides the basis of most narratives. Students should be able to identify the external conflicts without difficulty. Make sure they can also identify and detail any internal conflicts that occurred during the experience.

- Explain to students that the more details they can provide about the characters in their narratives, the more engaging and realistic the stories will be.

Writing WORKSHOP

Narration: Autobiographical Narrative

When you write an **autobiographical narrative,** you tell a story about an event or experience from your own life. In this workshop, you will write an autobiographical narrative about a memorable personal experience.

Assignment Criteria Your autobiographical narrative should have the following characteristics:

- The writer as the main character
- A sequence of events that is clearly significant
- Actions paced to include changes in time and mood
- Conflict or tension between characters or between a character and an outside force
- An interior monologue that reveals the writer's thoughts
- An insight gained by the writer

To preview the criteria on which your autobiographical narrative may be assessed, see the Rubric on page 119.

Prewriting

Choose a topic. Write your autobiographical narrative about an experience that is important to you. One strategy is to **consider the moment.** Write these words on a piece of paper: *Funny, Exciting, Interesting,* and *Puzzling.* Then, jot down moments in your life that fit each category. Choose one as the basis of your narrative.

Gather details about the setting. The setting is the specific time and place in which the events take place. You can use setting to establish mood and to orient your readers. Use a chart like the one shown here to gather details of setting.

Identify the conflict. To focus attention on the experience, clarify the conflicts. Write notes about whether the conflict is between you and someone or between you and something. Note whatever internal conflicts you had, such as specific worries or uncertainties. Your notes will help you develop the conflicts in your narrative.

Create a character profile. Gather the details needed to bring the character of each person to life by preparing a profile. Answer questions like these:

- What are the character's name and age?
- What are the character's personality, habits, and goals?
- Why is the character important to the narrative?

Gathering Details of Setting

Time/Year: August

Was eight

Just after grocery shopping

Place:

My backyard

Physical Details:

Blistering hot

TEACHING RESOURCES

The following resources can be used to enrich or extend the instruction for pp. 116–119.

📝 **Writing and Grammar,** Platinum Level, Chapter 4, pp. 48–67

📖 **Performance Assessment and Portfolio Management,** pp. 9, 37

📓 **Writing Models and Graphic Organizers on Transparencies,** pp. 17–23

💿 **Writing and Grammar iText CD-ROM**
Students can use the following tools as they complete their autobiographical narratives:

- Story Map
- Character Trait Word Bin
- Sentence Length

Student Model

Before you begin drafting, read this student model and review the characteristics of an interesting autobiographical narrative.

James C. Deavenport
Agoura Hills, California

Our Close Call

Sometimes things happen for a reason. I was never really sure what that meant until years after we adopted Benji. She was a shaggy brown dog who loved to run and play fetch.

> James is the main character in the narrative.

One blistering day in late August, my Mom, my sister, and I came home from the supermarket with a huge load of groceries. I was popping open a bag of chips when I heard a strange bark coming from the backyard. Quickly taking off my shoes, I went to see what the trouble was. First, I checked Benji's food and water bowls, thinking she was hungry or thirsty, but both were full. "What's the matter, Benji?" I asked. I began to return to the kitchen when she ran in front of me and let out a loud bark. It was unlike anything I had ever heard. I looked down, and there was a large brown-and-black rattlesnake curled up five inches from my bare feet. Benji had kept me from stepping on it. I walked backward slowly and called for Benji to follow. After a few moments she started toward me, when, suddenly, she let out a loud yelp.

> The order of events is significant. Benji's bark interrupts another activity, and the narrative moves logically from that point.

Benji had been bitten. I yelled for my mom. Dropping the last bag of groceries, she ran into the house to make two urgent phone calls: first, the vet for Benji and then, animal control to get rid of the snake. The vet was not in the office that Saturday. Instead, my mom located an emergency pet hospital about thirty minutes away. We knew time was frighteningly critical.

> Shorter sentences show that the pace of the action picks up after Benji has been bitten by the snake.

We all piled back into the family car and sped toward the hospital. The vet took Benji into the emergency room right away. He explained that she had been bitten on her cheek. Benji didn't need antivenom because we had gotten her to the vet quickly. However, she needed to be watched closely for a few days.

As I lay in bed that night, I thought about how close I had come to being bitten by the snake. I could not feel anything but a kind of pride: My dog would endanger her life to save mine. I thought about her often over the next few days, hoping and praying that she would get well so that I could return the love that she had shown me.

> The interior monologue reveals James's thoughts.

Benji recovered and lived many more years. We would go through a lot together. That day, however, will always remain in my mind. It was the day that I might have perished if it weren't for a shaggy brown dog named Benji.

> James concludes his narrative with an insight: He realizes how lucky he is to have a dog like Benji.

Student Model

- Explain that the Student Model is a sample, and that essays may be longer.
- Lead students to see that James varies the lengths of his sentences in order to create a rhythm that matches the pace of the action described.
- Point out that James uses details to describe how he thought and felt at the time, which allows readers to see the experience from his perspective.
- Remind students that an autobiographical narrative provides a personal insight gained from the particular experience. Lead students to see how James is careful to describe how the experience changed the way he looked at life.

Real-World Connection

Explain to students that autobiographical writing is not limited to nonfiction literary works. Students may be required to explain a significant event from their lives in college applications, for example.

CUSTOMIZE INSTRUCTION FOR UNIVERSAL ACCESS

For Less Proficient Writers	For English Learners	For Advanced Writers
If students have difficulty choosing a topic, model the process of considering the moment to help them select an experience about which to write.	Students might consider writing about an experience related to learning English. Has learning a new language presented them with any memorable encounters?	Once they have chosen a topic, encourage students to list as many sensory details as they can to help describe how they felt during the experience. Suggest that students use some of these details to make their narratives vivid.

Drafting

- Explain to students that their auto-biographical essays should have a plot with a clear beginning, middle, and end. Before they start writing, they should map out their plots on a plot diagram like the one shown here.

- Have students review the events listed on their plot diagrams. Encourage students to choose moments in each event that can be developed using sensory details. Tell students that using sensory details helps the reader picture what is being described in the narrative.

- Make sure students identify places in their narratives that will benefit from dialogue and interior monologues. Explain to students that these elements will help readers better understand their experiences from their perspective.

Revising

- Before students start to revise their work, have them write down the overall impression they wish to convey to the reader. As they read through their drafts, students should keep this impression in mind to help them determine whether each sentence works to develop and support this overall impression.

- Review the Revising Model with students. Have students describe how the changes James made improve the overall unity of his writing.

(continued on page 119)

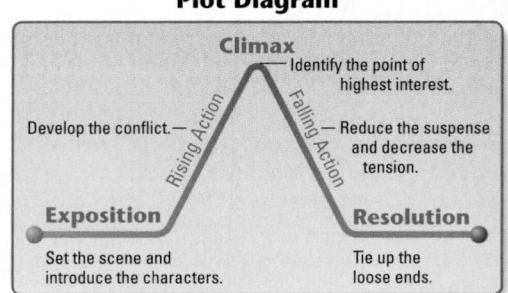

Writing WORKSHOP *continued*

Drafting

Write about a significant event. As you draft, include the significant events and order them in a logical sequence. Work to include the elements of a good story, just as you would if the narrative were fiction. Use your notes to identify the climax, or point of highest interest. Arrange the other events to fit the structure of the plot diagram shown here.

Include concrete sensory details. Think about what you saw, heard, smelled, tasted, and felt. As you write, choose precise words that evoke these sensory images and that can help your readers understand your experience.

Add dialogue and interior monologue. To add interest to your narrative, re-create conversations between people. Include interior monologues that reveal the thoughts that occurred to you while you were in the situation.

Revising

Revise to strengthen unity. Review your draft to make sure that all the elements are unified, or work together. Each paragraph should help develop the overall impression you want to leave with your readers. Each sentence should support the main idea of the paragraph.

Working at the paragraph level, review each sentence in every paragraph. Delete those sentences or details that do not move events forward or that do not create an image for the readers.

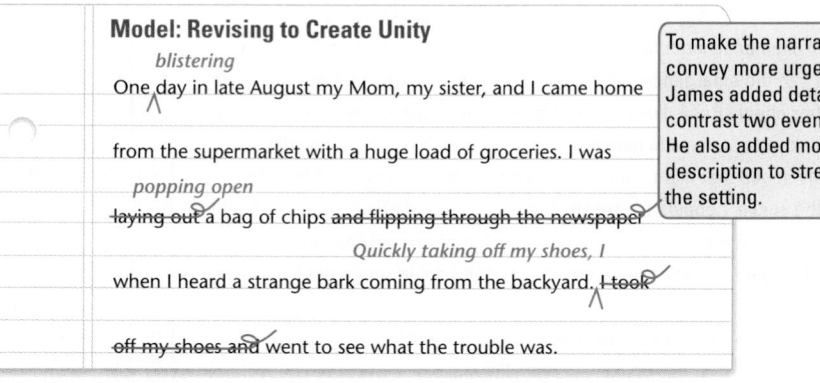

Model: Revising to Create Unity

blistering
One day in late August my Mom, my sister, and I came home

from the supermarket with a huge load of groceries. I was

popping open
~~laying out~~ a bag of chips ~~and flipping through the newspaper~~

Quickly taking off my shoes, I
when I heard a strange bark coming from the backyard. ~~I took~~

~~off my shoes and~~ went to see what the trouble was.

To make the narrative convey more urgency, James added details that contrast two events. He also added more description to strengthen the setting.

Plot Diagram

Climax — Identify the point of highest interest.

Develop the conflict. — *Rising Action* / *Falling Action* — Reduce the suspense and decrease the tension.

Exposition — Set the scene and introduce the characters.

Resolution — Tie up the loose ends.

USING TECHNOLOGY IN WRITING

If students are using word processors to draft and revise their autobiographical essays, suggest that they strike out lines they are unsure of, rather than immediately cutting them. This way, they can review this text later and decide whether they want to revise it or simply cut it.

Students can also use the organizing tools and revision checkers on the **Writing and Grammar iText CD-ROM.**

Revise to vary sentence length. Variety in sentence length can enliven your narrative. Break up passages that have consecutive short sentences or consecutive long sentences. Use different sentence types to help make your writing more interesting and mature.

Compare the model and nonmodel. Why is the model more interesting?

Nonmodel	Model
Notice the pattern of short sentences in this passage: Benji had been bitten. I yelled for my mom. She ran into the house to call the vet. She also called animal control to get rid of the snake.	Benji had been bitten. I yelled for my mom. Dropping the last bag of groceries, she ran into the house to make two urgent phone calls: first, the vet for Benji and then, animal control to get rid of the snake.

Publishing and Presenting

Choose one of the following ways to share your writing with classmates or a wider audience:

Publish in a print medium. Submit your narrative to a school newspaper or national magazine that publishes student writing. Consult your teacher or librarian for suggestions.

Tell your story. Rehearse reading your story aloud. Mark up a copy of the story, underlining words that you will emphasize and places where you will vary your reading rate. Then, read your story to your class.

WG Writing and Grammar Connection: Chapter 4

Speaking Connection
For instruction about narrative presentations, see the **Listening and Speaking Workshop** on page 120.

Rubric for Self-Assessment

Evaluate your autobiographical narrative using the following criteria and rating scale:

Criteria	Rating Scale				
	Not very				Very
Is the writer clearly established as the main character?	1	2	3	4	5
Are all events significant and is the sequence clear?	1	2	3	4	5
Are the actions paced to show changes in time and mood?	1	2	3	4	5
Does the narrative develop a conflict?	1	2	3	4	5
Does the narrative reveal an insight gained by the writer?	1	2	3	4	5
Does the narrative use interior monologues to reveal the writer's thoughts and feelings?	1	2	3	4	5

Revising (continued)

- Tell students that varying the lengths of their sentences will make their narratives more engaging for readers.
- Ask students to compare the model and nonmodel and respond to the question in their text: Why is the model more interesting than the nonmodel?
  Possible answer: The model is more interesting because the longer sentences allow the action to happen naturally, rather than breaking it up.

Publishing and Presenting

- Have students consider a publication for which their narrative would be well suited. Students should choose a publication whose audience is similar to the intended audience of their essay.
- Before students present their stories to the class, encourage them to practice reading them aloud. Remind them to speak clearly so their listeners can hear all of the details.

Assessment

- Review with students the assessment criteria.
- Have students choose three criteria from the rubric and score the Student Model. Make sure students support their scores with details from the model.
- The rubric on this page, and another rubric in an alternative format, can be found on pp. 9 and 37 in **Performance Assessment and Portfolio Management.**

TEST-TAKING TIP

When students are taking a test that requires them to respond to a narrative writing prompt, they should allot most of their time to the drafting stage. The key to effective writing is organizing one's thoughts while drafting. If students pay careful attention to the overall impression they want to make and ensure that the details they use contribute to this impression, they will have an easier time revising their responses.

Lesson Objectives

1. To deliver a narrative presentation in an effective manner
2. To choose a compelling story that engages the audience's interest
3. To modulate one's voice and use gestures and facial expressions to enhance the presentation of the narrative

Focus on Characteristics

- In addition to choosing a story that is appropriate for an oral retelling, students should also keep in mind the length of the work. You may want to establish a time limit so that students do not select works that are too long.
- Have students make a simple chart that lists the characteristics detailed on this page. As students search for an appropriate narrative to deliver, have them assess how well their choices demonstrate these characteristics.

Focus on the Speaker

- Explain to students that the speaker must convey the drama of the story through modulating the tone, volume, and speed of his or her voice.
- Encourage students to practice delivering their presentations with a variety of inflections and gestures. Students can then determine which inflections and gestures best suit the text.
- Tell students that to maintain eye contact with their audience, they should not read directly from their notes. They should be familiar enough with their story that they feel comfortable looking up often.

Listening and Speaking WORKSHOP

Delivering a Narrative

A **narrative presentation** provides a chronological, descriptive, and inspired retelling of a true-life or fictional story. Writers, poets, and filmmakers all use narratives to capture the imagination of their audience.

Focus on Characteristics

People use a wide range of techniques to deliver their narratives, depending on their purposes. As you plan, address these elements of narration:

Establish the chronology. Identify a beginning, a middle, and an end to help listeners keep the sequence of events clear. A consistent and logical organization is important to the chronology of your narrative.

Identify the setting. Make sure that the place where these events happen is clear so your audience has an understanding of the story's context. As you tell the story, include details of places and descriptions of each scene so that your audience can visualize the actions.

Set the pace. Keep the story moving by avoiding too much description. Focus more on the events that will interest your audience.

Focus on the Speaker

A good narrator can captivate an audience using strategies like these:

Adjust your voice. Experiment with different ways to tell the story. Change your volume and tone to indicate significant moments in your narrative. Consider using a different voice for each person in your story.

Speak clearly. Be careful to enunciate every word so that your audience can understand.

Take control of gestures and mannerisms. Nonverbal communication can be effective in establishing and rounding out a character. For example, if a character in your narrative uses his or her hands to embellish what he or she is saying, you may want to do the same. Similarly, avoid nervous motions that may detract from your presentation.

Maintain eye contact. Survey and engage your audience with your eyes. By doing so, you will be able to determine and adjust the moments of your narrative depending on your audience's reactions.

(Activity:)
Delivering a Narrative Presentation Choose a true-life or fictional story. Using the strategies outlined here, rehearse a presentation of the story. Then, deliver it to your class. Ask classmates to complete a feedback form like this one

Feedback Form for Narrative Presentation

Rating System
+ = Excellent   ✔ = average   – = wea

Content
Clear chronology _____
Description of setting _____
Interesting pace _____

Delivery
Voice modulation _____
Enunciation _____
Eye contact _____

Answer the following questions:
Was the narrative interesting or did the speaker lose your interest?

Could you hear everything that the speaker said?

CUSTOMIZE INSTRUCTION FOR UNIVERSAL ACCESS

For English Learners	For Less Proficient Readers
Before they deliver their narratives to the class, help students use a dictionary to determine the correct pronunciation of all unfamiliar words. Encourage them to use the dictionary for this purpose when they read texts or make oral presentations in the future.	Have students carefully practice their narratives, using self-sticking notes to identify any difficult or confusing passages. Students can then go back to these passages to improve both their comprehension of the text and their delivery.

Assessment WORKSHOP

Context Clues and Word Meanings

In the reading sections of some assessment tests, you may be required to use the context to understand words with multiple meanings or specialized and technical terms. Use these strategies to answer test questions with the help of context clues:

- Review the words surrounding the test word. They may help you figure out the meaning of the unfamiliar word.
- Look at the context to help determine which definition of a word with multiple meanings applies.
- Note the subject matter of a specialized or technical term to clarify the word's meaning.

Test-Taking Strategies

- To determine the subject of the writing, read an entire passage before studying the question.
- To find the best answer, substitute each answer choice for the underlined word. Eliminate those you know are wrong.

Sample Test Item

Directions: Read the passage, and then answer the question that follows.

Shayla always assumed she would go to Springfield State with Amy, one of her best friends, but her application was denied. Then, Shayla received a letter from a private college in a city 2,000 miles away. The letter informed her that she had been accepted for *matriculation*. Shayla knew she should jump at the opportunity—it was a noteworthy college in a beautiful location—but she would be far from home.

1. Use the context to determine which of the following is the meaning of *matriculation*:

   A refusal **C** humiliation

   B test **D** admission; registration

Answer and Explanation

Answer *D* is correct. Answer *C* can be eliminated because the context words "opportunity" and "noteworthy" are positive, and Shayla seems honored. The context does not support *B* because the passage implies that Shayla is being offered an opportunity, not a test. Shayla is considering attending the private college, so *A* can be eliminated.

▶ Practice

Directions: Read the passage, and then answer the questions that follow.

Before the Articles of Confederation could become law, each state had to *ratify* them. By 1779, only the state of Maryland had not voted in favor of the Articles. During colonial times, seven states had received *charters* granting them control of western lands. Maryland, one of six states that had not received western territory from Great Britain, wanted all western lands turned over to the federal government.

1. In the passage, the word *ratify* means

   A ignore

   B enjoy

   C approve

   D reject

2. Which word best defines *charters* as it is used in the passage?

   A legal documents granting privileges

   B letters from the government

   C contracts to build houses

   D documents creating institutions

Lesson Objective

To use context clues to understand words with multiple meanings or specialized and technical terms

Applying Reading Strategies

Tell students that they can use context clues to help them understand words that have more than one meaning. The surrounding words and phrases will help them pinpoint the precise meaning of the word as it is used in the passage. Students can also use this strategy to help them determine the meaning of technical terms.

Applying Test-Taking Strategies

- Have students read the Sample Test Item. Ask them to identify the word in the passage that they are being asked to define.
- Ask students to suggest the context clues they can use to determine the meaning of *matriculation*. Lead students to see that the words *application* and *accepted*, and the overall context of applying to college, can be used to determine that the meaning of the word is "admission."

Answers

1. The correct answer is *C*. Students should understand that in order for the Articles to become law, they first had to be considered and approved. For this reason, answers A and D are illogical, and answer B is irrelevant.

2. The correct answer is *A* because the states with charters were granted "control over western lands." Choice B is not specific enough; choices C and D are incorrect because they do not refer to land.

TEACHING RESOURCES

The following resources can be used to enrich or extend the instruction for p. 121.

PRENTICE HALL
ASSESSMENT SYSTEM

📖 **Workbook**   📄 **Transparencies**

📖 **Skill Book**   💿 **CD-ROM**

Unit Objectives

1. To read selections in different genres that develop the theme "Striving for Success"

2. To apply a variety of reading strategies, particularly interactive reading strategies, appropriate for reading these selections

3. To analyze literary elements

4. To use a variety of strategies to build vocabulary

5. To learn elements of grammar, usage, and style

6. To use recursive writing processes to write in a variety of forms

7. To develop listening and speaking skills

8. To express and support responses to various types of texts

9. To prepare, organize, and present literary interpretations

Meeting the Objectives

With each selection, you will find instructional materials through which students can meet these objectives. Further, you will find additional practice pages for reading strategies, literary analysis, vocabulary, and grammar in the **Selection Support: Skills Development Workbook** in your **Teaching Resources.**

Background

Art

Step to the Steps, by Brad Holland

In his early twenties, Brad Holland began writing and drawing for underground newspapers; he has since created covers for such mainstream publications as *The New Yorker, Newsweek,* and *U.S. News and World Report.* Use this question for discussion:

> Imagine that the man on the steps has already climbed a long way. How do you think he feels about seeing the next set of steps?

> Possible responses: He might feel discouraged that he is facing a much greater challenge; he might feel proud of having gotten so far.

UNIT 2 *Striving for Success*

Steps to the Steps, Brad Holland

UNIT FEATURES

Connections	Reading Informational Material
Every unit contains a feature that connects literature to a related topic, such as art, science, or history. This unit contains a discussion of the actor Daniel Day-Lewis's portrayal of Christy Brown in the film version of *My Left Foot.* Use the information and questions on the Connections pages to enrich students' understanding of the selections presented within the unit.	These selections will help students learn to analyze and evaluate informational texts, such as workplace documents, technical directions, and consumer materials. They will expose students to the organization and features unique to nonnarrative texts. In this unit, students will learn about the purpose of product information.

Exploring the Theme

You will strive to reach many goals in life—getting your driver's license, graduating from high school, establishing a career, starting a family—and along the way, you may have to overcome many obstacles. Let these poems, stories, and essays inspire you to strive for success and accomplish your goals. Share the determination and fear, the disappointments and hopes of people from a wide variety of times and places.

As you read the true and inspiring story from *My Left Foot*, you will feel as if you can accomplish anything you decide to do, no matter what stands in your way. In this autobiography, you will witness the critical moment when a boy's struggle to overcome severe physical limitations turns around, eventually leading to a productive life.

▲ **Critical Viewing** In what ways might these steps represent the challenge of meeting a goal? **[Analyze]**

Exploring the Theme ◆ 123

ASSESSMENT RESOURCES

📖 **Selection Support: Skills Development Workbook**
📖 **Formal Assessment**
📖 **Open Book Tests**
📖 **Performance Assessment and Portfolio Management**
📖 **Extension Activities**

Why Read Literature?

The "Why Read Literature?" page in each unit presents a list of possible purposes for reading. Each purpose for reading is connected to one or more of the selections in the unit. Good readers set a purpose before reading to help them read actively and focus on meaningful details.

Unit 2 introduces three purposes for reading. "Read for the Love of Literature" encourages students to appreciate the idea of measuring success in poetry and fiction. "Read to Be Inspired" provides students with an opportunity to celebrate great successes as they read. "Read for Information" encourages students to learn more about the teachings of Confucius.

How to Use This Page

- Tell students that by setting a purpose for reading, they will read in a more active and focused manner.

- Explain to students that they can increase their love of literature by exploring the theme of success in the poetry of Emily Dickinson.

- Students can draw inspiration from one man's courageous struggle against severe physical limitations, detailed in the excerpt from Christy Brown's *My Left Foot.*

- Students can read for information in order to learn about the teachings of Confucius.

 Read Literature?

You read literature about challenges with a specific purpose in mind—to appreciate, to learn, to be entertained, or even to be inspired. Your purpose will vary based on the context, genre, or style of each selection. Preview three purposes you might set before reading the works in this unit.

1

Read for the Love of Literature

Fame, wealth, and achievement are some common ways people measure success. Writers have challenged these ideas to show readers a deeper understanding of the best ways to measure success. Consider Emily Dickinson's ideas in her poems **"Success is counted sweetest,"** page 158, and **"I dwell in Possibility,"** page 159.

William Melvin Kelley weaves a complex story of the troubles that arise when communication among family members breaks down. Discover how their painful feelings lead to a resolution in **"A Visit to Grandmother,"** page 182.

2

Read to Be Inspired

When the library at the University of New Mexico acquired its one-millionth book, this became a cause for celebration. Rudolfo Anaya reflects on the value of libraries and the wider importance of sharing knowledge in **"In Commemoration: One Million Volumes,"** on page 128.

The rewards that success brings can often be more fulfilling when you have to overcome obstacles to attain them. See the barriers one man had to knock down just to communicate with his family in the excerpt from Christy Brown's *My Left Foot,* page 168.

3

Read for Information

Confucius is one of the world's best-known philosophers. His teachings, written more than two thousand years ago, are frequently quoted today. Find out why he is so well respected. Read his ideas in *The Analects,* page 220.

 Take It to the Net
Visit the Web site for online instruction and activities related to each selection in this unit.
www.phschool.com

 ENRICHMENT: Further Reading

Have students choose one or more of the works below to extend the unit theme "Striving for Success" or to read more by the unit authors.

Don Quixote by Miguel de Cervantes
The tale of knight-errant Don Quixote de La Mancha and his faithful squire, Sancho Panza, can be found in the **Prentice Hall Literature Library.**

My Lord, What a Morning: An Autobiography by Marian Anderson
In her autobiography, Anderson details her struggles to break through the color barrier in the world of opera.

Flowers for Algernon by Daniel Keyes
This award-winning novella chronicles the struggles of a mentally challenged young man.

Complete Poems of Emily Dickinson by Emily Dickinson
Students can further explore the poetry of Dickinson in this collection of her work.

How to Read Literature

Use Interactive Reading Strategies

You do not just watch a video game the way you watch a movie. Video games are interactive: Your choices affect the way the game turns out. Reading, too, is an interactive process—you become involved with the ideas, images, and events. The more involved you are, the richer your experience. Apply the following strategies to interact with what you read:

1. Identify the author's purpose.

Determine the author's reason for writing. It could be to entertain, to persuade, or to share an idea. Gather details from the text to make an informed decision about the author's purpose. As you read the passage at right, ask yourself, why did the author write this?

2. Question.

- Do not accept everything you read at face value.
- Ask yourself why certain details are included, and look for answers as you read.
- Consider how a fact or an idea fits in with what you have already read.

3. Clarify.

Clear up information or statements that you do not understand. Use these suggestions:

- Read ahead for more information, or reread to review what you have already learned.
- Represent information visually. Graphic organizers, such as cluster diagrams, can help you track key details and ideas.

4. Interpret.

Think about how authors convey their feelings or attitudes in their writing. In the following lines, notice how the author uses tomatoes and onions to make a larger point.

> . . . there are those who seem certain that if they plant tomato seeds, at harvesttime they can reap onions.
> —*from* **"At Harvesttime"**

When you interpret these lines, you may see that the writer uses this analogy to suggest that some people have unrealistic expectations about the effects of their behavior.

As you read the selections in this unit, apply interactive reading strategies to make your experience as rich as possible.

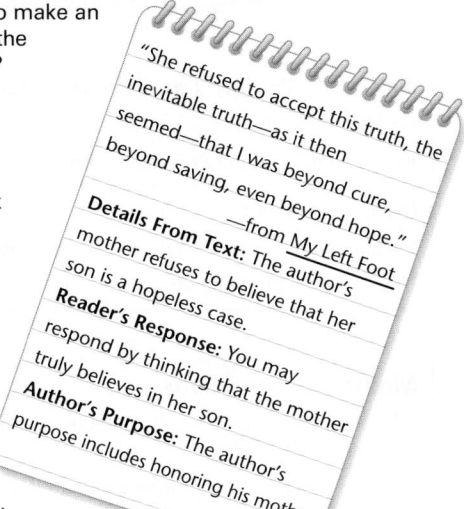

"She refused to accept this truth, the inevitable truth—as it then seemed—that I was beyond cure, beyond saving, even beyond hope."

—from *My Left Foot*

Details From Text: The author's mother refuses to believe that her son is a hopeless case.

Reader's Response: You may respond by thinking that the mother truly believes in her son.

Author's Purpose: The author's purpose includes honoring his mother.

How to Read Literature

The "How to Read Literature" page in each unit presents a set of strategies to help readers understand authors' words and ideas. Each reading strategy is taught in conjunction with one or more of the selections within the unit. Good readers develop a bank of strategies from which they can draw as needed.

Unit 2 introduces four strategies for comprehension. To understand a selection more fully, students should become actively involved in what they read.

How to Use This Page

Introduce the interactive reading strategies, presenting each as a tool for developing understanding when reading the selections in this unit.

- As they read the excerpt from *My Left Foot* (p. 168), students will learn how to identify the author's purpose for writing.
- As they read "The Apple Tree" (p. 206), students will learn how to ask questions about what they are reading and become more actively involved in the text as they look for answers to these questions.
- As they read "A Visit to Grandmother" (p. 182), students will learn how to avoid misunderstandings by checking their comprehension as they read.
- As they read poems such as "After Apple-Picking" (p. 196) and "Mowing" (p. 198), students will learn how to interpret the meanings of poetic images.

MODEL A READING STRATEGY: Clarify

Explain to students that rereading or reading ahead in a selection can help them clarify details and events that seem confusing.

Model this strategy for students using "In Commemoration: One Million Volumes." Explain to students that they can read ahead to help clarify the Spanish phrases that Anaya uses in the first paragraph of the selection.

from In Commemoration: One Million Volumes

Lesson Objectives

1. **To analyze and respond to literary elements**
   - Literary Analysis: Author's Purpose
   - Connecting Literary Elements: Tone
2. **To read, comprehend, analyze, and critique nonfiction**
   - Reading Strategy: Summarizing
   - Reading Check questions
   - Review and Assess questions
   - Assessment Practice (ATE)
3. **To develop word analysis skills, fluency, and systematic vocabulary**
   - Vocabulary Development Lesson: Latin Prefix: *in-*
4. **To understand and apply written and oral language conventions**
   - Spelling Strategy
   - Grammar Lesson: Action Verbs and Linking Verbs
5. **To understand and apply appropriate writing and research strategies**
   - Writing Lesson: Reading Journal
   - Extension Activity: Library Resources Chart
6. **To understand and apply listening and speaking strategies**
   - Extension Activity: Group Discussion

STEP-BY-STEP TEACHING GUIDE	PACING GUIDE
PRETEACH	
Motivate Students and Provide Background	
Use the Motivation activity (ATE p. 126)	5 min.
Read and discuss the Preview material and Background information (SE/ATE p. 126)	5 min.
Introduce the Concepts	
Introduce the Literary Analysis and Reading Strategy (SE/ATE p. 127) A	15 min.
Pronounce the vocabulary words and read their definitions (SE p. 127)	5 min.
TEACH	
Monitor Comprehension	
Informally monitor comprehension by circulating while students read independently or in groups A	20 min.
Monitor students' comprehension with the Reading Check notes (SE/ATE pp. 129, 131)	as students read
Develop vocabulary with Vocabulary notes (SE pp. 128, 129, 130, 131, 132; ATE p. 129)	as students read
Develop Understanding	
Develop students' understanding of author's purpose with the Literary Analysis annotations (SE p. 130; ATE pp. 129, 130, 131) A	10 min.
Develop students' understanding of summarizing with the Reading Strategy annotations (SE p. 128; ATE pp. 128, 130)	10 min.
ASSESS	
Assess Mastery	
Assess students' mastery of the Reading Strategy and Literary Analysis by having them answer the Review and Assess questions (SE/ATE p. 133)	20 min.
Use one or more of the print and media Assessment Resources (ATE p. 135) A	up to 50 min.
EXTEND	
Apply Understanding	
Have students complete the Vocabulary Development Lesson and the Grammar Lesson (SE p. 134) A	20 min.
Apply students' ability to keep a reading journal using the Writing Lesson (SE/ATE p. 135) A	45 min.
Apply students' understanding using one or more of the Extension Activities (SE p. 135)	20–90 min.

A ACCELERATED INSTRUCTION:
Use the strategies and activities identified with an A.

UNIVERSAL ACCESS
- ● = Below Level Students
- ▲ = On-Level Students
- ■ = Above Level Students

Time and Resource Manager

Reading Level: Average
Average Number of Instructional Days: 4

RESOURCES		
PRINT 📝	**TRANSPARENCIES**	**TECHNOLOGY** 💿 🎧 📼
• **Beyond Literature,** Community Connection: The Library, p. 8 ▲ ■		• **Interest Grabber Video,** Tape 1 ● ▲ ■
• **Selection Support Workbook:** ● ▲ ■ Literary Analysis, p. 32 Reading Strategy, p. 31 Build Vocabulary, p. 29	• **Literary Analysis and Reading Transparencies,** pp. 15 and 16 ● ▲ ■	
• **Adapted Reader's Companion** ● • **Reader's Companion** ●		• **Listening to Literature** ● ▲ ■ Audiocassettes, Side 5 Audio CDs, CD 3
• **English Learner's Companion** ● ▲ • **Literatura en español** ● ▲ • **Literary Analysis for Enrichment** ■		
• **Formal Assessment:** Selection Test, pp. 26–28 ● ▲ ■ • **Open Book Test,** pp. 22–24 ● ▲ ■ • **Performance Assessment and Portfolio Management,** pp. 30 ● ▲ ■ • **PRENTICE HALL** ASSESSMENT *SYSTEM* ● ▲ ■	• **PRENTICE HALL** ASSESSMENT *SYSTEM* ● ▲ ■ Skills Practice Answers and Explanations on Transparencies	• **Test Bank Software** ● ▲ ■ • **Got It! Assessment Videotapes,** Tape 1 ● ▲
• **Selection Support Workbook:** ● ▲ ■ Build Grammar Skills, p. 30 • **Writing and Grammar,** Platinum Level ● ▲ ■ • **Extension Activities,** p. 8 ● ▲ ■	• **Daily Language Practice Transparencies** ● ▲	• **Writing and Grammar iText CD-ROM** ● ▲ ■ 💻 *Take It to the Net* www.phschool.com

BLOCK SCHEDULING: Use one 90-minute class period to preteach the selection and have students read it. Use a second 90-minute class period to assess students' mastery of skills and have them complete one of the Extension Activities.

**Step-by-Step Teaching Guide
for pp. 126–127**

Motivation

Ask students to take out a piece of paper and write down the first things that come to mind when you say "library." Guide them to think about *everything* associated with a library, not just books and computers. What do the rooms of the library look like? With whom do students usually go to the library? What do they do there? What mood does a library evoke? Let volunteers share their writing, and then encourage students to compare their impressions of libraries with those of Rudolfo Anaya as they read this selection.

▣ Interest Grabber Video

As an alternative, you may wish to play "Rudolfo A. Anaya on His Love of Reading" on Tape 1 to engage student interest.

❶ Background

Social Studies

Libraries have existed since ancient times. The first public library in Greece was established in 330 B.C., and the first in Rome, in 40 B.C. In the United States, the first public library opened in Boston in 1848. In 1656, a subscription library was opened in Boston, but it was not available to everyone. Today, there are public libraries throughout the country and much of the world.

Prepare to Read

from In Commemoration: One Million Volumes

La Bibliothèque (The Library), 1949, Maria Elena Vieira da Silva, Musée National d'Art Moderne, Centre National d'Art et de Culture Georges Pompidou

▣ Take It to the Net

Visit www.phschool.com for interactive activities and instruction related to "In Commemoration: One Million Volumes," including
- background
- graphic organizers
- literary elements
- reading strategies

Preview

Connecting to the Literature

Throughout our lives, we remember specific dates, events, and numbers. They act as markers of our progress. In "One Million Volumes," author Rudolfo Anaya reflects on the importance of libraries, books, and words as he celebrates a milestone in the history of the University of New Mexico's library—reaching one million volumes.

❶ Background

When Anaya entered the University of New Mexico's library for the first time, he was astounded at the size of it compared with his neighborhood library. However, there are even larger libraries: The New York Public Library has more than ten million volumes, and the Library of Congress contains more than twenty-five million.

126 ◆ *Striving for Success*

TEACHING RESOURCES

The following resources can be used to enrich or extend the instruction for pp. 126–127.

Motivation

▣ **Interest Grabber Video**, Tape 1 ▣

Background

📖 **Beyond Literature**, Community Connection: The Library, p. 8

▣ *Take It to the Net*

Visit www.phschool.com for background and hotlinks for *from* "In Commemoration: One Million Volumes."

Literary Analysis

📄 **Literary Analysis and Reading Transparencies,** Author's Purpose, p. 16

Reading

📖 **Selection Support:** Reading Strategy, p. 31; Build Vocabulary, p. 29 ▣

📄 **Literary Analysis and Reading Transparencies,** Summarizing, p. 15

 BLOCK SCHEDULING: Resources marked with this symbol provide varied instruction during 90-minute blocks.

Literary Analysis

Author's Purpose

The **author's purpose** is his or her reason for writing. Anaya's general purpose in "One Million Volumes" is to share ideas. His specific purpose is to show the importance of libraries and books to people.

> . . . I visited the library of my childhood, the Santa Rosa Library . . . in that small room I found my shelter and retreat. If there were a hundred books there we were fortunate, but to me there were a million volumes.

As you read, notice the details Anaya includes and the direct statements he makes to clarify his purpose.

Connecting Literary Elements

In "One Million Volumes," the details, descriptive words, and images Anaya uses help achieve his purpose and also provide clues to the tone. The **tone** of a literary work is the writer's attitude toward his or her audience and subject. The tone of a work, like the tone of a person's voice, can often be described by a single adjective, such as humorous, angry, or serious.

Reading Strategy

Summarizing

When you **summarize,** you state the main idea of a piece of writing in your own words. Summarizing will help you keep track of the author's main points. To summarize, follow these steps:

- In one sentence, jot down the main point of the beginning.
- In one sentence, note the main ideas of the middle.
- In one sentence, write the main point of the end.
- Put sentences together concisely to summarize the piece.

Use a diagram like the one shown to summarize Anaya's essay.

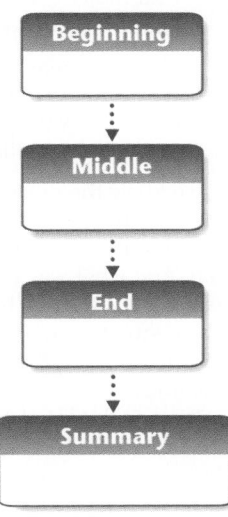

Vocabulary Development

induced (in do͞ost´) *v.* caused (p. 128)

inherent (in her´ ənt) *adj.* inborn (p. 129)

litany (lit´ ən ē) *n.* series of responsive religious readings (p. 129)

dilapidated (di lap´ ə dā´ tid) *adj.* broken down (p. 130)

satiated (sā´ shē ā tid) *adj.* having had enough; full (p. 130)

enthralls (en thrôlz´) *v.* captivates; fascinates (p. 131)

labyrinth (lab´ ə rinth) *n.* maze (p. 131)

poignant (poin´ yənt) *adj.* emotionally moving (p. 132)

fomentation (fō men tā´ shən) *n.* incitement; a stirring up (p. 132)

---

❷ Literary Analysis

Author's Purpose

- Explain to students that the author's purpose is his or her reason for writing. Tell them that an author's purpose can be to persuade, to entertain, to express an opinion, or to explain—or any combination of these.

- Draw students' attention to the excerpt from the selection. Point out that the details convey Anaya's purpose, which is to show what the Santa Rosa library meant to him.

- Read aloud the Connecting Literary Elements passage. Make sure that students see the connection between an author's purpose and his or her tone. Generally, the author's purpose for writing will influence the tone of the piece. For example, a persuasive essay might have a serious tone, while an entertaining piece might have a playful or comical tone.

❸ Reading Strategy

Summarizing

- Explain to students that a summary contains only the author's most important points.

- Remind students to write summaries in their own words. By using their own words, they will get a better understanding of the author's ideas.

- To help students better understand this strategy, ask them to summarize the ideas on this page.

Vocabulary Development

- Pronounce each vocabulary word for students, and read the definitions as a class. Have students identify any words with which they are already familiar.

CUSTOMIZE INSTRUCTION FOR UNIVERSAL ACCESS

For Special Needs Students	For Less Proficient Readers	For English Learners
Have students read the adapted version of *In Commemoration: One Million Volumes* in the **Adapted Reader's Companion**. This version provides basic-level instruction in an interactive format with questions and write-on lines. Completing the adapted version will prepare students to read the selection in the Student Edition.	Have students read the selection in the **Reader's Companion**. This version provides basic-level instruction in an interactive format with questions and write-on lines. After students finish the selection in **Reader's Companion**, have them complete the questions and activities in the Student Edition.	Have students read the adapted version of the selection in the **English Learner's Companion**. This version provides basic-level instruction in an interactive format with questions and write-on lines. Completing the adapted version will prepare students to read the selection in the Student Edition.

 E-Teach

Visit E-Teach at www.phschool.com for teachers' essays on how to teach, with questions and answers.

CUSTOMIZE INSTRUCTION
For Logical/Mathematical Learners

On the board, write the numerals for one million (1,000,000), one hundred million (100,000,000), and one billion (1,000,000,000). Invite students to think of logical items that might be indicated by these numbers, such as a million books, a hundred million people, and a billion stars. Encourage interested students to make bar graphs comparing other large collections.

❶ About the Selection

When the University of New Mexico library acquires its one millionth book, Rudolfo Anaya uses the occasion to reflect on the great importance of libraries as places that stimulate and nurture free thought. What makes this essay unique is that Anaya draws a connection between books and the many people and stories that opened his childhood mind to the natural and intellectual world.

❷ Reading Strategy

Summarizing

- Remind students that summarizing involves restating an author's main points in their own words.

- Have students reread the bracketed passage. Ask them to look for Anaya's main points as they read.

- Then, ask students the Reading Strategy question on p. 128: How would you summarize the beginning of Anaya's essay?
Answer: Anaya discusses the magic of the number one million. He remembers the awe that a million stars inspired in him and wonders whether a library with a million books can inspire the same feeling.

---

from In Commemoration:
❶ ONE MILLION VOLUMES

Rudolfo A. Anaya

A million volumes.

A magic number.

A million books to read, to look at, to hold in one's hand, to learn, to dream. . . .

I have always known there were at least a million stars. In the summer evenings when I was a child, we, all the children of the neighborhood, sat outside under the stars and listened to the stories of the old ones, los viejitos.[1] The stories of the old people taught us to wonder and imagine. Their adivinanzas[2] <u>induced</u> the stirring of our first questioning, our early learning.

I remember my grandfather raising his hand and pointing to the swirl of the Milky Way which swept over us. Then he would whisper his favorite riddle:

❷

> Hay un hombre con tanto dinero
> Que no lo puede contar
> Una mujer con una sábana tan grande
> Que no la puede doblar.

> There is a man with so much money
> He cannot count it
> A woman with a bedspread so large
> She cannot fold it

We knew the million stars were the coins of the Lord, and the heavens were the bedspread of his mother, and in our minds the sky was a million miles wide. A hundred million. Infinite. Stuff for the imagination. And what was more important, the teachings of the old ones made us see that we were bound to the infinity of that cosmic dance of life which swept around us. Their teachings created in us a thirst for knowledge. Can this library with its million volumes bestow that same inspiration?

❸ I was fortunate to have had those old and wise viejitos as guides into the world of nature and knowledge. They taught me with their stories; they taught me the magic of words. Now the words lie captured in ink,

---

1. **los viejitos** (lôs byä hē´ tôs) *n.* the old ones.
2. **adivinanzas** (a thē vē nan´ sas) *n.* riddles.

128 ◆ *Striving for Success*

induced (in do͞ost´) *v.* caused

Reading Strategy
Summarizing How would you summarize the beginning of Anaya's essay?

TEACHING RESOURCES

The following resources can be used to enrich or extend the instruction for pp. 128–132.

Literary Analysis

📖 **Selection Support:** Literary Analysis, p. 32

Reading

📖 **Reader's Companion**

📖 **English Learner's Companion**

🎧 **Listening to Literature Audiocassettes,** Side 5 ▪

💿 **Listening to Literature Audio CDs,** CD 3 ▪

▪ **BLOCK SCHEDULING:** Resources marked with this symbol provide varied instruction during 90-minute blocks.

but the magic is still there, the power <u>inherent</u> in each volume. Now with book in hand we can participate in the wisdom of mankind.

Each person moves from innocence through rites of passage into the knowledge of the world, and so I entered the world of school in search of the magic in the words. The sounds were no longer the soft sounds of Spanish which my grandfather spoke; the words were in English, and with each new awareness came my first steps toward a million volumes. I, who was used to reading my oraciones en español[3] while I sat in the kitchen and answered the <u>litany</u> to the slap of my mother's tortillas,[4] I now stumbled from sound to word to groups of words, head throbbing, painfully aware that each new sound took me deeper into the maze of the new language. Oh, how I clutched the hands of my new guides then!

Learn, my mother encouraged me, learn. Be as wise as your grandfather. He could speak many languages. He could speak to the birds and the animals of the field.

Yes, I remember the cuentos[5] of my grandfather, the stories of the people. Words are a way, he said, they hold joy, and they are a deadly power if misused. I clung to each syllable which lisped from his tobacco-stained lips. That was the winter the snow came, he would say, it piled high and we lost many sheep and cattle, and the trees groaned and broke with its weight. I looked across the llano[6] and saw the raging blizzard, the awful destruction of that winter which was imbedded in our people's mind.

And the following summer, he would say, the grass of the llano grew so high we couldn't see the top of the sheep. And I would look and see what was once clean and pure and green. I could see a million sheep and the pastores[7] caring for them, as I now care for the million words that pasture in my mind.

But a million books? How can we see a million books? I don't mean just the books lining the shelves here at the University of New Mexico

inherent (in her´ ənt) *adj.* inborn

litany (lit´ ən ē) *n.* series of responsive religious readings

---

3. **oraciones en español** (ô ra syôn´ ās en es pa nyōl´) prayers in Spanish.
4. **tortillas** (tôr tē´ yəs) *n.* thin, flat, round cakes of unleavened cornmeal.
5. **cuentos** (kwen´ tôs) *n.* stories.
6. **llano** (ya´ nō) *n.* plain.
7. **pastores** (pas tô´ rās) *n.* shepherds.

⑤ 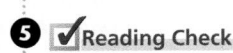Reading Check
What is Anaya's native language?

from *In Commemoration: One Million Volumes* ◆ 129

❸ Vocabulary Development
Latin Prefix: *in-*
- Have students reread the bracketed passage. Draw their attention to the vocabulary word *inherent* and its definition, "inborn."
- Then, ask students what Anaya means by "the power inherent in each volume."
  Answer: Anaya believes that books, like the stories of the *viejitos*, have a natural, inborn power to inspire and teach.

❹ Literary Analysis
Author's Purpose
- Remind students that one of Anaya's main purposes is to communicate how books can inspire readers.
- Have a volunteer read the bracketed passage aloud.
- Then, have students cite the phrase in this passage that encapsulates his purpose.
  Answer: The phrase that captures the purpose is "the worlds that lie waiting in each book." The phrase suggests that books have the power to introduce readers to new worlds.

❺ ✔Reading Check
Answer: Anaya's native language is Spanish.

CUSTOMIZE INSTRUCTION FOR UNIVERSAL ACCESS

For Special Needs Students	For Gifted/Talented Students
Give students a visual representation of the number of books in the University of New Mexico Library. Have them find out the number of volumes in your school and community libraries. Then, help them make a bar graph to compare and contrast the size of those libraries with the University of New Mexico Library (1,000,000 volumes) and the Library of Congress (more than 25,000,000 volumes).	Have students reread the Literature in Context note on p. 131, which explains that one million pieces of paper would make a row longer than a football field. Then, have them brainstorm for their own ways to design or construct a model representing the number one million, showing why it is used as a "magic" number. When they finish, have students share their ideas with their classmates.

Summarizing

- Have a volunteer read aloud the bracketed passage. Ask students to pay attention to the details about Anaya's reaction to reading.

- Remind students that a summary should not include every detail that an author brings up. Instead, students should make generalizations based on these details.

- Ask students to summarize the effects of books on the young Anaya.
  Answer: The young Anaya found the characters and stories in books to be fulfilling and exhilarating.

⑦ Literary Analysis

Author's Purpose and Tone

- Have students reread the bracketed passage. Then, ask them to describe its tone.
  Answer: Students might describe the tone as tender or loving.

- Then, ask students the Literary Analysis question on p. 130: What words and phrases in this paragraph help identify the author's tone?
  Answer: Words that convey Anaya's love of books are *exhilaration, love,* and *float on words to other worlds.*

- Then, explain to students that Anaya uses a loving tone to help accomplish his purpose, which is to convey his love and respect for books.

  ▶ Monitor Progress Students might want to keep lists of vivid details that Anaya includes. These details will help to reveal his tone.

Library, not just the fine worn covers, the intriguing titles; how can we see the worlds that lie waiting in each book? A million worlds. A million million worlds. And the beauty of it is that each world is related to the next, as was taught to us by the old ones. Perhaps it is easier for a child to see. Perhaps it is easier for a child to ask: How many stars are there in the sky? How many leaves in the trees of the river? How many blades of grass in the llano? How many dreams in a night of dreams?

So I worked my way into the world of books, but here is the paradox, a book at once quenches the thirst of the imagination and ignites new fires. I learned that as I visited the library of my childhood, the Santa Rosa Library. It was only a dusty room in those days, a room sitting atop the town's fire department, which was comprised of one <u>dilapidated</u> fire truck used by the town's volunteers only in the direst emergencies. But in that small room I found my shelter and retreat. If there were a hundred books there we were fortunate, but to me there were a million volumes. I trembled in awe when I first entered that library, because I realized that if the books held as much magic as the words of the old ones, then indeed this was a room full of power.

Miss Pansy, the librarian, became my new guide. She fed me books as any mother would nurture her child. She brought me book after book, and I consumed them all. Saturday afternoons disappeared as the time of day dissolved into the time of distant worlds. In a world that occupied most of my other schoolmates with games, I took the time to read. I was a librarian's dream. My tattered library card was my ticket into the same worlds my grandfather had known, worlds of magic that fed the imagination.

⑥ Late in the afternoon, when I was <u>satiated</u> with reading, when I could no longer hold in my soul the characters that crowded there, I heard the call of the llano, the real world of my father's ranchito, the solid, warm world of my mother's kitchen. Then to the surprise and bewilderment of Miss Pansy, I would rush out and race down the streets of our town, books tucked under my shirt, in my pockets, clutched tightly to my breast. Mad with the insanity of books, I would cross the river to get home, shouting my crazy challenge even at la Llorona,[8] and that poor spirit of so many frightening cuentos would wither and withdraw. She was no match for me.

⑦ Those of you who have felt the same exhilaration from reading—or from love—will know about what I'm speaking. Alas, the people of the town could only shake their heads and pity my mother. At least one of her sons was a bit touched. Perhaps they were right, for few will trade a snug reality to float on words to other worlds.

And now there are a million volumes for us to read here at the University of New Mexico Library. Books on every imaginable subject, in every field, a history of the thought of the world which we must keep free of censorship, because we treasure our freedoms. It is the word *freedom* which eventually must reflect what this collection, or the

---

8. la Llorona (la yô rô′ na) spirit of many stories, famous for shouting and crying for her lost love.

dilapidated (di lap′ ə dā′ tid) *adj.* broken down

satiated (sā′ shē ā tid) *adj.* having had enough; full

Literary Analysis
Author's Purpose and Tone What words and phrases in this paragraph help identify the author's tone?

✦ ENRICHMENT: Career Connection

Library Science

Anaya describes a number of different kinds of libraries: his one-room local library, his high-school library, and the huge university library that eventually acquires one million volumes. Each of these libraries has a system for ordering and cataloging books, so that patrons can find what they are looking for, or so the librarian can help them find a particular book or piece of information.

A trained, professional librarian learns different sys-

tems of cataloging books, such as the Dewey Decimal system and the Library of Congress system—both manually and in electronic database format. Most libraries contain materials besides books: audio- and video-tapes, CDs, electronic resources, and computers. Invite students to interview a school, community, or university librarian to learn about library ordering systems, the skills and duties of a librarian, and the education and training necessary to become a librarian.

collection of any library, is all about. We know that as we preserve and use the literature of all cultures, we preserve and regenerate our own. The old ones knew and taught me this. They eagerly read the few newspapers that were available. They kept their diaries, they wrote décimas[9] and cuentos, and they survived on their oral stories and traditions.

Another time, another library. I entered Albuquerque[10] High School Library prepared to study, because that's where we spent our study time. For better or for worse, I received my first contracts as a writer there. It was a place where budding lovers spent most of their time writing notes to each other, and when my friends who didn't have the gift of words found out I could turn a phrase I quickly had all the business I could do. I wrote poetic love notes for a dime apiece and thus worked my way through high school. And there were fringe benefits, because the young women knew very well who was writing the sweet words, and many a heart I was supposed to capture fell in love with me. And so, a library is also a place where love begins.

A library should be the heart of a city. With its storehouse of knowledge, it liberates, informs, teaches, and <u>enthralls</u>. A library indeed should be the cultural center of any city. Amidst the bustle of work and commerce, the great libraries of the world have provided a sanctuary where scholars and common man alike come to enlarge and clarify knowledge, to read and reflect in quiet solitude.

I knew a place like this, I spent many hours in the old library on Central Avenue and Edith Street. But my world was growing, and quite by accident I wandered up the hill to enroll in the University of New Mexico. And what a surprise lay in store for me. The libraries of my childhood paled in comparison to this new wealth of books housed in Zimmerman Library. Here there were stack after stack of books, and ample space and time to wander aimlessly in this <u>labyrinth</u> of new frontiers.

I had known the communal memory of my people through the newspapers and few books my grandfather read to me and through the rich oral tradition handed down by the old ones; now I discovered the collective memory of all mankind at my fingertips. I had only to reach for the books that laid all history bare. Here I could converse with the writers from every culture on earth, old and new, and at the same time I began my personal odyssey, which would add a few books to the collection which in 1981 would come to house a million volumes.

Those were exciting times. Around me swirled the busy world of the university, in many respects an alien world. Like many fellow undergraduates, I sought refuge in the library. My haven during those

---

9. **décimas** (dā′ sē mas) *n.* ten-line stanzas.
10. **Albuquerque** (al′ bə kur′ kē) city in central New Mexico.

from *In Commemoration: One Million Volumes* ◆ 131

Literature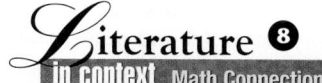
in context Math Connection ❽

How Much Is a Million?

Anaya celebrates a collection of one million books. How much is a million? There are more than one million stars in the sky. Counting aloud to one million would take you 23 days. What would a million look like? Imagine a row of sheets of paper standing on edge. One thousand sheets would make a row about four inches long. One million sheets would make a row more than 333 feet or 111 yards long—a row longer than a football field!

When Anaya applies the concept of a million to a library, he notes that the result is "A million million worlds . . . the collective memory of all mankind at my fingertips."

enthralls (en thrôlz′) *v.* captivates; fascinates

labyrinth (lab′ ə rinth) *n.* maze

 ☑**Reading Check** ❿

How did Anaya spend Saturdays as a child?

---

❽ **Background**
Million

The word *million* did not enter general usage until some time after the 13th century. Large numbers, such as a million, were mostly absent from mathematics at the time. The Egyptians, Greeks, and Romans, for example, had no need for this kind of a number. Up until the fourteenth century, people usually used the term *thousand thousand* to describe a very large amount. Maximus Planudes is believed to be the first mathematician to use the word *million*. However, it simply meant "great thousand" (*mille*, meaning "thousand" + *on*, meaning "great").

❾ **Literary Analysis**
Author's Purpose

• Have students read the bracketed passage to themselves. As they read, encourage them to pay attention to the details. Ask them what Anaya is describing in this paragraph.
Answer: In his high school library, Anaya made money writing love notes for friends because he had a way with words.

• Ask students to explain Anaya's purpose in including this information.
Answer: Anaya is trying to show the ways in which libraries are exciting places, and that reading and writing can be connected to real-world values, such as friendship, love, and even earning money.

❿ ☑**Reading Check**

Answer: Anaya read all day, lost track of time, and then, at the end of the day, raced home across the river that used to frighten him.

CUSTOMIZE INSTRUCTION FOR UNIVERSAL ACCESS

For Less Proficient Readers

Students who have trouble following the connection Anaya makes between stars, stories, and books may benefit by questioning ideas as they read. Encourage them to create two-column charts to track Anaya's ideas. As they read, students can fill in their charts. When they come to an idea that they find hard to understand, they can write a question about that passage in the left-hand column. As students continue to read, they can look for answers to their questions. When they have finished reading, discuss with them how the essay provided answers to their questions.

My Question	Answer found in selection
What do stars have to do with library books?	The infinite number of stars inspires the viewer's imagination, just as the million books in the library can inspire a person's thirst for knowledge.

⑪ Reading Strategy

Summarize

- Have students summarize the final paragraph in the essay.
  Answer: Anaya believes that a library should be a place for people to develop ideas through reading, thinking, and debating.

- Then, ask students to summarize Anaya's entire essay. Remind them to include only the main ideas.
  Answer: Anaya's love of words comes from a rich storytelling tradition; his love of stories, learning, and books grew in libraries; and he sees libraries as havens, gathering places, and storehouses of knowledge.

Answers for p. 132

Review and Assess

1. Students should think of nonfiction as well as fiction. Guide them toward a discussion of new ideas and insights gained through reading.

2. **(a)** *Los viejitos* were the old people in Anaya's community. **(b)** The old ones preserved and regenerated their culture through *cuentos*, the stories of the people.

3. **(a)** Anaya learned about the world his grandfather had known. **(b)** Anaya associates libraries with freedom because libraries represent ideas from many points of view in their uncensored collections.

4. **(a)** Anaya believes a library should contain "the collective memory of all mankind." **(b)** In books, we learn the answers to some questions, but those answers raise other questions. **(c)** Students should support their opinions.

5. Books are the written record of a culture. They transcend barriers of time and space and keep the thoughts and customs of a culture alive.

---

student university years was the reading room of the west wing of the old library. There I found peace. The carved vigas[11] decorating the ceiling, the solid wooden tables and chairs and the warm adobe color of the stucco were things with which I was familiar. There I felt comfortable. With books scattered around me, I could read and doze and dream. I took my breaks in the warm sun of the portal, where I ate my tortilla sandwiches, which I carried in my brown paper bag. There, with friends, I sipped coffee as we talked of changing the world and exchanged idealistic dreams.

That is a rich and pleasant time in my memory. No matter how far across the world I find myself in the future, how deep in the creation of worlds with words, I shall keep the simple and <u>poignant</u> memories of those days. The sun set golden on the ocher walls, and the green pine trees and the blue spruce, sacred trees to our people, whispered in the breeze. I remembered my grandfather meeting with the old men of the village in the resolana[12] of one of the men's homes, or against the wall of the church on Sundays, and I remembered the things they said. Later, alone, dreaming against the sun-warmed wall of the library, I continued that discourse in my mind.

Yes, the library is a place where people should gather. It is a place for research, reading, and for the quiet <u>fomentation</u> of ideas, but because it houses the collective memory of our race, it should also be a place where present issues are discussed and debated and researched in order for us to gain the knowledge and insight to create a better future. The library should be a warm place that reflects the needs and aspirations of the people.

---

11. **vigas** (bē´ gas) *n.* roof beams.
12. **resolana** (rā sô la´ na) *n.* place for enjoying the sun.

poignant (poin´ yənt) *adj.* emotionally moving

fomentation (fō men tā´ shən) *n.* incitement; a stirring up

Rudolfo Anaya

(b. 1937)
Rudolfo Anaya was born and raised in the rural village of Pastura in the desert southwest state of New Mexico. As a child, Anaya's imagination was fired by the *cuentos* of his people—stories that had been passed down from generation to generation. He realized then that he wanted to be a writer. His poems, short stories, novels, and articles reflect his Mexican American heritage.

In 1972, while a high-school English teacher, Anaya wrote *Bless Me, Ultima,* a highly praised novel about a young boy growing up in New Mexico.

Now a full-time writer, Anaya says, "Writing novels seems to be the medium which allows me to bring together all the questions I ask about life."

Review and Assess

Thinking About the Selection

1. **Respond:** Anaya talks about feeling "exhilaration from reading." What have you read that has exhilarated you? Why?

2. **(a) Recall:** Who were *los viejitos*? **(b) Interpret:** How did the "old ones" of Anaya's childhood preserve their culture?

3. **(a) Recall:** What did Anaya learn at the Santa Rosa Library during his childhood? **(b) Connect:** Why does Anaya associate libraries with freedom?

4. **(a) Deduce:** What kinds of books does Anaya think a library should have? **(b) Interpret:** What does he mean when he writes that "a book at once quenches the thirst of the imagination and ignites new fires"? **(c) Evaluate:** Do you agree with this statement? Explain.

5. **Extend:** How do books and reading help preserve a culture?

✐ ASSESSMENT PRACTICE: Reading Comprehension

Recognize Facts and Details   **(For more practice, see Test Preparation Workbook, p. 8.)**

Some tests ask students to recognize facts and details. Use this sample test item.

In the summer evenings when I was a child, we, all the children of the neighborhood, sat outside under the stars and listened to the stories of the old ones, *los viejitos*. The stories of the old people taught us to wonder and imagine. Their *adivinanzas* [riddles] induced the stirring of our first questioning, our early learning.

What did the children learn from the old ones?

A How to tell stories
B The answers to riddles
C To wonder, imagine, and question
D The number of stars in the sky

Help students notice that the word *taught* in the passage is a clue to what was learned, so the answer is *C*.

Review and Assess

Literary Analysis

Author's Purpose

1. This essay was written to be given as a speech at a celebration. How does that occasion influence the **author's purpose**?
2. Identify two details that support the author's purpose of acknowledging the importance of libraries in linking the wisdom of the past to the goals of the present.
3. If Anaya had a different purpose, he would have included different kinds of details in his writing. (a) What details or examples could he have used to persuade people to support their libraries through donations? (b) What details could he have used to honor the university?

Connecting Literary Elements

4. How do Anaya's personal experiences affect the **tone** of the writing?
5. Use a graphic organizer like this one to analyze the tone of the essay. Review the essay, noting at least five details or descriptive words. For each, identify the attitude the words convey.

Details or Descriptive Words		Attitude Toward Subject
to learn, to dream . . .	·····▶	
the magic of words	·····▶	
	·····▶	

6. What is the overall tone of the essay?

Reading Strategy

Summarizing

7. **Summarize** Anaya's essay by identifying the main points of these sections of the writing: (a) the beginning, (b) the middle, (c) the end.
8. For each main point you have identified, note two details that support the point.

Extend Understanding

9. **Literature Connection:** List a work of literature that inspired you or helped you reach a goal, and explain how it did so.

from *In Commemoration: One Million Volumes* ◆ 133

Quick Review

The **author's purpose** is his or her reason for writing.

The **tone** of a literary work is the writer's attitude toward his or her audience and subject.

To **summarize,** state the main ideas of a passage or literary work in your own words.

 Take It to the Net

www.phschool.com

Take the interactive self-test online to check your understanding of the selection.

Answers for p. 133

Review and Assess

1. Anaya's purpose is to acknowledge the importance of books and libraries. He celebrates not only the University of New Mexico Library, but libraries all over the world.

2. Anaya states that the Santa Rosa Library contains the worlds of his grandfather. He also says that the University of New Mexico Library contains "a history of the thought of the world."

3. **(a)** Anaya could have given examples of how donations can help libraries. **(b)** He could have given examples of great things that university graduates have accomplished.

4. Anaya has experienced joy and wonder with books, and this is reflected in his exuberant tone.

5. Possible responses:
Details: magic in the words; stumbled from sound to word to groups of words, head throbbing; I now care for the million words that pasture in my mind; ample space and time to wander aimlessly in this labyrinth; I shall keep the simple and poignant memories of those days tender. Attitudes: awe; wonder; tenderness; wonder; tenderness.

6. The overall tone is of wonder and tenderness.

7. **(a)** The main point of the beginning of the essay is that Anaya's love of words comes from a rich storytelling tradition. **(b)** The main point of the middle is that Anaya's love of stories, books, and learning grew in libraries. **(c)** The main point of the end is that Anaya sees libraries as havens, gathering places, and storehouses of knowledge.

8. Details from the beginning: "Their teachings created in us a thirst for knowledge"; "Learn, my mother encouraged me, learn." Details from the middle: "The libraries of my childhood paled in comparison to this new wealth of books housed in Zimmerman Library"; "I had only to reach for the books that laid all history bare." Details from the end: "I shall keep the simple and poignant memories of those days"; "it should be a place

continued

Answers continued

where present issues are discussed and debated"

9. Students should explain how the works inspired and motivated them.

❶ Vocabulary Development

Word Analysis

1. *Inhale* means "to breathe in."
2. *Include* means "to bring into."
3. *Internal* means "the state of being in or within."

Spelling Strategy

1. constancy
2. brilliance
3. absence

Fluency: Elaboration

1. A dilapidated car would be rusty, dented, and running poorly or not at all.
2. A meal that left you satiated, would leave you full and satisfied.
3. A book that enthralls fascinates the reader.
4. A poem like a litany would resemble a repetitive prayer.
5. A fomentation of ideas is an abundance and overflow of ideas.
6. A poignant movie scene is touching and emotionally moving.
7. Loyalty is an inherent quality of some cats.
8. A labyrinth of hallways is a maze.
9. A speech that induces sleep is monotonous and boring.

❷ Grammar

1. Anaya <u>feels</u> exhilarated by the power of words. LV
2. The people of his childhood village <u>told</u> him stories of his culture. AV
3. His love for stories <u>grew</u> in the library. AV
4. In college, he <u>grew</u> eager to learn even more. LV
5. He <u>delivered</u> this speech at the library of his alma mater. AV

Writing Application

Students should use action verbs and colorful adjectives in writing their descriptions. When they finish, have volunteers share their responses.

134

Integrate Language Skills

❶ Vocabulary Development Lesson

Word Analysis: Latin Prefix *in-*

The Latin prefix *in-* can mean "not" or "into." In the words *inherent* and *induced*, the prefix means "into." *Inherent* means "inborn," and *induced* means "led into" or "caused."

Define each word below in a sentence using the words *in* or *into*.

1. inhale
2. include
3. internal

Spelling Strategy

If a word ends in *-ent*, its parallel noun form ends in *-ence* or *-ency*, as in *persistent, persistence*. If a word ends in *-ant*, its noun form ends in *-ance* or *-ancy* as in *abundant, abundance*.

Spell the parallel noun form for each of these words.

1. constant
2. brilliant
3. absent

❷ Grammar Lesson

Action Verbs and Linking Verbs

There are two main categories of verbs. **Action verbs** express physical or mental action. **Linking verbs** express a state of being or tell what the subject is by linking it to one or more words that describe or identify it.

Action Verbs:	Then he would *whisper* his favorite riddle. They *taught* me with their stories.
Linking Verbs:	I *was* fortunate. I *am* satiated with reading. I *feel* proud to be here.

To determine whether a verb is an action verb or a linking verb, substitute *am*, *are*, or *is*. If the sentence makes sense, the original verb is a linking verb.

*W*_G *Prentice Hall Writing and Grammar Connection: Chapter 16, Section 3*

134 ◆ *Striving for Success*

Fluency: Elaboration

Review the list of vocabulary words on page 127. In complete sentences, describe each of the following:

1. *dilapidated* car
2. meal that left you *satiated*
3. book that *enthralls*
4. poem like a *litany*
5. *fomentation* of ideas
6. *poignant* movie scene
7. *inherent* quality of cats
8. *labyrinth* of hallways
9. speech that *induces* sleep

Practice Copy each of the following sentences. Underline the verb. Then, identify the verb as an action verb (*AV*) or a linking verb (*LV*).

1. Anaya feels exhilarated by the power of words.
2. The people of his childhood village told him stories of his culture.
3. His love for stories grew in the library.
4. In college, he grew eager to learn even more.
5. He delivered this speech at the library of his alma mater.

Writing Application Write a short description of your local or school library. Use action verbs to make your writing dynamic.

---

❸ Writing Lesson

Reading Journal

One way to explore the ideas you find in books is to respond to them in writing. For one week, keep a reading journal—a record of your thoughts and feelings about what you read and how the issues or topics apply to your life.

Prewriting While you are reading, keep your journal handy to jot down your reactions to specific passages and ideas. Sketch characters and settings, and record quotations you want to remember.

> ### Model: Keeping a Reading Journal
>
> 2/20 **Title:** from "In Commemoration: One Million Volumes"
>
> **Author:** Rudolfo Anaya
>
> I like the Spanish words scattered throughout. Books were valuable to Anaya. Library card is "ticket" to "world of magic." Library seen as a "room full of power."

> Memorable quotes or phrases help the reader remember the essay.

Drafting Review your notes, and write each entry as if you were speaking to a friend. Use complete sentences in the informal style of everyday language. Do not simply summarize. Explain your responses.

Revising In a personal journal, you do not need to revise extensively. Look over your entries, and add more detail if necessary.

𝒲𝒢 *Prentice Hall Writing and Grammar Connection: Chapter 3, Section 3*

❹ Extension Activities

Listening and Speaking As a class, hold a **group discussion** in which each group member presents a list of his or her favorite books and explains why the books should be included in the school library. Each group member should

- Give a brief summary of each book.
- Explain how the books inspired or exhilarated him or her.

At the end of the discussion, group members should narrow their lists to five books and share with the class their reasons for including these books in the library. **[Group Activity]**

Research and Technology When Anaya was a boy, libraries primarily contained books, magazines, and newspapers. Library catalogs consisted of file drawers with 3" × 5" cards. Interview your school librarian to find out what innovations have taken place in libraries in recent decades. Then, present your information in a **library resources chart,** showing how libraries have changed.

 Take It to the Net www.phschool.com

Go online for an additional research activity using the Internet.

from *In Commemoration: One Million Volumes* ◆ 135

Lesson Support for p. 135

❸ Writing Lesson

- Explain to students that they should record in their journals not only what they read, but their thoughts about what they have read and how it connects with their lives.

- Suggest that students return to their favorite books and freewrite about their responses to those books.

- Remind students that a journal does not require formal writing. However, they should make sure to support their main points with details from the books they have read.

❹ Listening and Speaking

- Suggest that students browse in the library to stir memories of their favorite authors and books.

- Remind students that their summaries should contain only the main ideas of each book.

- Encourage students to explain how the books have affected their lives, as Anaya does in his essay. Have students use the rubric for Delivering a Persuasive Argument, p. 30 in **Performance Assessment and Portfolio Management**.

CUSTOMIZE INSTRUCTION
For Universal Access

To address different learning styles, use the activities suggested in the **Extension Activities** booklet, p. 8.

- For Logical/Mathematical and Verbal/Linguistic Learners, use Activity 5.

- For Verbal/Linguistic and Interpersonal Learners, use Activity 6.

- For Visual/Spatial and Logical/Mathematical Learners, use Activity 7.

ASSESSMENT RESOURCES

The following resources can be used to assess students' knowledge and skills.

Selection Assessment

📖 **Formal Assessment**, pp. 26–28

📖 **Open Book Test**, pp. 22–24

📼 **Got It! Assessment Videotapes**, Tape 1

💿 **Test Bank Software**

Take It to the Net
Visit www.phschool.com for self-tests and additional questions on the selection.

Listening and Speaking Rubric

📖 **Performance Assess. and Portfolio Mgmt.**, p. 30

🅿️ PRENTICE HALL **ASSESSMENT** *SYSTEM*

📖 **Workbook** 📖 **Transparencies**

📖 **Skill Book** 💿 **CD-ROM**

How Much Land Does a Man Need?

Lesson Objectives

1. **To analyze and respond to literary elements**
   - Literary Analysis: Parable
   - Connecting Literary Elements: Flat and Round Characters

2. **To read, comprehend, analyze, and critique a short story**
   - Reading Strategy: Predicting Based on Character Traits
   - Reading Check questions
   - Review and Assess questions
   - Assessment Practice (ATE)

3. **To develop word analysis skills, fluency, and systematic vocabulary**
   - Vocabulary Development Lesson
   - Concept Development: Context

4. **To understand and apply written and oral language conventions**
   - Spelling Strategy
   - Grammar Lesson: Regular and Irregular Verb Forms

5. **To understand and apply appropriate writing and research strategies**
   - Writing Lesson: Video Script
   - Extension Activity: Annotated Map

6. **To understand and apply listening and speaking strategies**
   - Extension Activity: Eulogy

STEP-BY-STEP TEACHING GUIDE	PACING GUIDE
PRETEACH	
Motivate Students and Provide Background	
Use the Motivation activity (ATE p. 136)	5 min.
Read and discuss the Preview material and Background information (SE/ATE p. 136) **A**	5 min.
Introduce the Concepts	
Introduce the Literary Analysis and Reading Strategy (SE/ATE p. 137) **A**	15 min.
Pronounce the vocabulary words and read their definitions (SE p. 137)	5 min.
TEACH	
Monitor Comprehension	
Informally monitor comprehension by circulating while students read independently or in groups **A**	45 min.
Monitor students' comprehension with the Reading Check notes (SE/ATE pp. 139, 141, 143, 145, 147, 149, 151)	as students read
Develop vocabulary with Vocabulary notes (SE pp. 138, 141, 142, 143; ATE p. 142)	as students read
Develop Understanding	
Develop students' understanding of parables with the Literary Analysis annotations (SE pp. 139, 142, 145, 148, 151; ATE pp. 137, 139, 142, 145, 146, 148, 151) **A**	10 min.
Develop students' understanding of predictions with the Reading Strategy annotations (SE pp. 140, 144, 146, 149, 150; ATE pp. 137, 139, 140, 144, 146, 149, 150)	10 min.
ASSESS	
Assess Mastery	
Assess students' mastery of the Reading Strategy and Literary Analysis by having them answer the Review and Assess questions (SE/ATE p. 153)	20 min.
Use one or more of the print and media Assessment Resources (ATE p. 155) **A**	up to 50 min.
EXTEND	
Apply Understanding	
Have students complete the Vocabulary Development Lesson and the Grammar Lesson (SE p. 154) **A**	20 min.
Apply students' ability to incorporate clear directions using the Writing Lesson (SE/ATE p. 155) **A**	45 min.
Apply students' understanding using one or more of the Extension Activities (SE p. 155)	20–90 min.

 ACCELERATED INSTRUCTION:
Use the strategies and activities identified with an **A**.

UNIVERSAL ACCESS
● = Below Level Students
▲ = On-Level Students
■ = Above Level Students

Time and Resource Manager

RESOURCES		
PRINT 📝	**TRANSPARENCIES**	**TECHNOLOGY** 💿 🎧 📼
• **Beyond Literature**, Cross-Curricular Connection: Social Studies, p. 9 ▲ ■		• **Interest Grabber Video**, Tape 1 ● ▲ ■
• **Selection Support Workbook:** ● ▲ ■ Literary Analysis, p. 36 Reading Strategy, p. 35 Build Vocabulary, p. 33	• **Literary Analysis and Reading Transparencies,** pp. 17 and 18 ● ▲ ■	
		• **Listening to Literature** ● ▲ ■ Audiocassettes, Side 6 Audio CDs, CD 4
• **Literatura en español** ● ▲ • **Literary Analysis for Enrichment** ■		
• **Formal Assessment:** Selection Test, pp. 29–31 ● ▲ ■ • **Open Book Test**, pp. 25–27 ● ▲ ■ • PRENTICE HALL **ASSESSMENT** *SYSTEM* ● ▲ ■	• PRENTICE HALL **ASSESSMENT** *SYSTEM* ● ▲ ■ Skills Practice Answers and Explanations on Transparencies	• **Test Bank Software** ● ▲ ■ • **Got It! Assessment Videotapes**, Tape 1 ● ▲
• **Selection Support Workbook:** ● ▲ ■ Build Grammar Skills, p. 34 • **Writing and Grammar**, Platinum Level ● ▲ ■ • **Extension Activities**, p. 9 ● ▲ ■	• **Daily Language Practice Transparencies** ● ▲	• **Writing and Grammar iText CD-ROM** ● ▲ ■ 💻 *Take It to the Net* www.phschool.com

BLOCK SCHEDULING: Use one 90-minute class period to preteach the selection and have students read it. Use a second 90-minute class period to assess students' mastery of skills and have them complete one of the Extension Activities.

Step-by-Step Teaching Guide for pp. 136–137

Motivation

Capture students' attention by showing a range of consumer product ads from a magazine aimed at young people. Point to ads for clothes, jewelry, and sports or computer equipment. Generate a brief discussion with these questions: Do we buy more than we need? Let students know that Tolstoy asked these same questions in his time, as they will see when they read his parable about a peasant's quest for more and more land.

▣ Interest Grabber Video

As an alternative, you may wish to play "Czars and Peasants" on Tape 1 to engage student interest.

❶ Background

History

Serfdom was a legal practice in Russia beginning in the 1500s. At first, peasants had civil rights. But soon they became de facto slaves, and their condition was similar to that of slaves in the southern United States a century or two later. They could not own land, and they had to stay with their landowners. The Russian serfs were freed in 1861 (just as our Civil War to end slavery was beginning), and the peasants could now buy land from their landlords (at inflated prices). Of course, the peasants had no money, so they often borrowed it from the government; it could take twenty years or more to pay the money back. The resentment of these peasant "landowners" was one of the causes of the Russian Revolution of 1917.

Prepare to Read

How Much Land Does a Man Need?

▣ Take It to the Net

Visit www.phschool.com for interactive activities and instruction related to "How Much Land Does a Man Need?" including
- background
- graphic organizers
- literary elements
- reading strategies

Preview

Connecting to the Literature

"How Much Land Does a Man Need?" illustrates the widely held belief that a little more is never enough. Like the peasant in the story, most people have said, *Just a little more . . .* or *just a little longer . . .* from time to time and, like the peasant, they are still not satisfied.

❶ Background

From the sixteenth century to the mid-nineteenth century, Russian peasants were bound by law to work land they could rent but not own. They grew food they were not allowed to eat and cultivated crops they were not allowed to sell. This story is set after the laws had been changed to allow the peasants to own land, but the memory of those conditions affects the characters' actions.

TEACHING RESOURCES

The following resources can be used to enrich or extend the instruction for pp. 136–137.

Motivation

▣ **Interest Grabber Video,** Tape 1

Background

📖 **Beyond Literature,** Cross-Curricular Connection: Social Studies, p. 9 ▣

▣ **Take It to the Net**
Visit www.phschool.com for background and hotlinks for "How Much Land Does a Man Need?"

Literary Analysis

▣ **Literary Analysis and Reading Transparencies,** Parable, p. 18 ▣

Reading

📖 **Selection Support:** Literary Analysis, p. 36

▣ **Literary Analysis and Reading Transparencies,** Parable, p. 17

▣ **BLOCK SCHEDULING:** Resources marked with this symbol provide varied instruction during 90-minute blocks.

② Literary Analysis

Parable

"How Much Land Does a Man Need?" is a **parable,** a simple, brief story that teaches a lesson by using characters and events to stand for moral principles. When the Devil is introduced in this tale, readers know the story will test the character of the people involved:

> But the Devil had been sitting behind the stove and had heard all that had been said. He was pleased that the peasant's wife had led her husband into boasting. . . .

As you read, identify the moral principles the author addresses.

Connecting Literary Elements

Characters in literature can be classified as flat or round. **Round characters** are fully developed, displaying many different traits and faults as well as virtues. In contrast, **flat characters** demonstrate behaviors and attitudes that are limited to a few key characteristics. In parables, the characters are usually flat. Readers learn the parable's lesson because the characters succeed or fail for obvious reasons. As you read "How Much Land Does a Man Need?" notice that the main character exhibits the qualities of a flat character.

③ Reading Strategy

Predicting Based on Character Traits

In parables, you can usually predict the outcome before you actually read what happens. For clues to the ending, study the **character traits**—the actions, attitudes, and values each character displays.

- Casual remarks can help you guess how a character will act.
- Knowing how a character will act can help you predict what will happen.

For each character, use a chart like this one to record details to help you predict the outcome of the story.

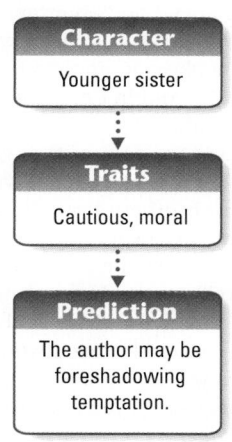

Vocabulary Development

piqued (pēkt) *adj.* offended (p. 138)

disparaged (di spar´ ijd) *v.* spoke slightly of; belittled (p. 138)

forbore (fôr bôr´) *v.* refrained from (p. 141)

aggrieved (ə grēvd´) *adj.* wronged (p. 142)

sheaf (shēf) *n.* bundle of grain (p. 142)

arable (ar´ ə bəl) *adj.* suitable for growing crops (p. 143)

fallow (fal´ ō) *adj.* plowed, but not planted (p. 143)

---

② Literary Analysis

Parable

- Explain that a *parable* is a story that uses characters and events to teach moral principles. Aesop's fables are examples of short parables.
- Review with students the information in Connecting Literary Elements. Highlight the difference between round and flat characters. Help students see this difference by explaining that *round* characters are three-dimensional, while *flat* characters are one-dimensional.
- As students read the selection, have them think about the ideas and principles represented by each character. In addition, urge them to watch for the lesson that this parable teaches.

③ Reading Strategy

Predicting Based on Character Traits

- Remind students that predicting is making educated guesses about future events based on present information.
- When students make predictions based on character traits, they use information about the characters to make educated guesses about events in a story.
- Help students see the connection between character types and the predictions that readers can make. For example, a flat character will tend to have only a few key character traits. This may make it easier to predict how he or she will behave in the future.
- Encourage students to use a chart like the one shown to help them record their ideas and make predictions as they read.

Vocabulary Development

- Pronounce each vocabulary word for students, and read the definitions as a class. Have students identify any words with which they are already familiar.

 E-Teach

Visit E-Teach at www.phschool.com for teachers' essays on how to teach, with questions and answers.

CUSTOMIZE INSTRUCTION FOR UNIVERSAL ACCESS

For Less Proficient Readers	For English Learners	For Advanced Readers
As students read the story, have them use sticky notes to mark passages where Pahom's character traits are revealed. Have them record the character trait on the sticky note and under it, a prediction based on the trait.	Students may benefit from first following the story while listening to the reading on the audiocassette. Encourage students to use sticky notes to mark passages where character traits are revealed. Then, have them volunteer predictions based on this information.	As students read the selection, have them look for clues in Pahom's actions that show how he is changing from his initial happiness at owning land to feeling possessive about his property. Ask students to consider whether Pahom's growing greed is inevitable, as the parable indicates, or if he might realize his mistake before it's too late.

**CUSTOMIZE INSTRUCTION
For Logical/Mathematical
Learners**

Pahom's land acquisition grows by
leaps and bounds. Have students
create a diagram or line graph showing how his holdings increase as the
story progresses.

❶ About the Selection

This parable illuminates Tolstoy's
sentiments about the perils of private ownership. A peasant named
Pahom seeks to acquire more and
more land. He rejects the advantages of cooperative ownership and
finds fault with each new land acquisition until, far from his home, he at
last dies in a final desperate grab for
even more land.

Tolstoy would have approved of the
peasants owning the land jointly.
Private property, this story tells us,
encourages individual greed.

❷ ▶ Critical Viewing

Answer: From the picture and the
story title, it appears that the story
will be about land.

❸ Background

Economics

Explain to students that the disparity
between town and country living was
far greater in Tolstoy's day than it is
today. A shopkeeper's wife, although
not rich, was in an entirely different
class from a peasant's wife and had
access to many more luxuries.

❹ Critical Thinking

Relate

• Read aloud the bracketed passage. Ask students to identify the
sentiment expressed here.

• Then, ask students to identify other
works or tales in which a character
expresses this sentiment.
Possible response: Students may
refer to the fable of "The Town
Mouse and the Country Mouse" or
works that have a similar theme.

How Much
❶ Land Does a

1

An elder sister came to visit her younger sister in the country. The
elder was married to a shopkeeper in town, the younger to a peasant in
the village. As the sisters sat over their tea talking, the elder began to
boast of the advantages of town life, saying how comfortably they lived
there, how well they dressed, what fine clothes her children wore, what
good things they ate and drank, and how she went to the theater, promenades,[1] and entertainments.

The younger sister was piqued, and in turn disparaged the life of a
shopkeeper, and stood up for that of a peasant.

"I wouldn't change my way of life for yours," said she. "We may live
roughly, but at least we're free from worry. You live in better style
than we do, but though you often earn more than you need, you're
very likely to lose all you have. You know the proverb, 'Loss and gain
are brothers twain.'[2] It often happens that people who're wealthy one
day are begging their bread the next. Our way is safer. Though a
peasant's life is not a rich one, it's long. We'll never grow rich, but
we'll always have enough to eat."

The elder sister said sneeringly:

"Enough? Yes, if you like to share with the pigs and the calves! What
do you know of elegance or manners! However much your good man
may slave, you'll die as you live—in a dung heap—and your children the
same."

"Well, what of that?" replied the younger sister. "Of course our work is

---

1. **promenades** (präm′ ə nādz′) *n.* balls or formal dances.
2. **twain** (twān) *n.* two.

138 ◆ *Striving for Success*

❷ ▲ Critical Viewing
Based on the title and
this photograph, what do
you think this story will
be about? **[Hypothesize]**

piqued (pēkt) *adj.*
offended

disparaged (di spar′ ijd) *v.*
spoke slightly of; belittled

TEACHING RESOURCES

The following resources can be used to enrich or extend the instruction for pp. 138–152.

Reading

📖 **Selection Support:** Reading Strategy, p. 35;
Build Vocabulary, p. 33 ▪

🎧 **Listening to Literature Audiocassettes,** Side 6 ▪

💿 **Listening to Literature Audio CDs,** CD 4 ▪

▪ **BLOCK SCHEDULING:** Resources marked with this symbol provide varied instruction during 90-minute blocks.

Man Need?

Leo Tolstoy

Translated by Louise and Aylmer Maude

rough and hard. But on the other hand, it's sure, and we need not bow to anyone. But you, in your towns, are surrounded by temptations; today all may be right, but tomorrow the Evil One may tempt your husband with cards, wine, or women, and all will go to ruin. Don't such things happen often enough?"

Pahom, the master of the house, was lying on the top of the stove and he listened to the women's chatter.

"It is perfectly true," thought he. "Busy as we are from childhood tilling mother earth, we peasants have no time to let any nonsense settle in our heads. Our only trouble is that we haven't land enough. If I had plenty of land, I shouldn't fear the Devil himself!"

The women finished their tea, chatted a while about dress, and then cleared away the tea things and lay down to sleep.

But the Devil had been sitting behind the stove and had heard all that had been said. He was pleased that the peasant's wife had led her husband into boasting and that he had said that if he had plenty of land he would not fear the Devil himself.

"All right," thought the Devil. "We'll have a tussle. I'll give you land enough; and by means of the land I'll get you into my power."

2

Close to the village there lived a lady, a small landowner who had an estate of about three hundred acres. She had always lived on good terms with the peasants until she engaged as her manager an old soldier, who took to burdening the people with fines. However careful Pahom tried to be, it happened again and again that now a horse of his got among the lady's oats, now a cow strayed into her garden, now his calves found

---

Literary Analysis
Parable Based on this discussion between the sisters, what subject do you think the parable will address?

Literary Analysis
Parable What effect does the introduction of the Devil have on your reading of the story?

❽ ✔Reading Check
What advantages does the country life have, according to the younger sister?

How Much Land Does a Man Need? ◆ 139

- Have a volunteer read aloud the bracketed passage. Then, have another volunteer summarize the information in this passage.

- Ask students to describe the traits of Pahom's character that they know thus far. Then, ask students the Reading Strategy question on p. 140: What do you predict that Pahom will do after hearing this news?

  Answer: Pahom has expressed a clear desire for land. He will definitely want to buy some of the available land.

▶ **Monitor Progress** Ask students whether they can predict, using what they know about Pahom, what will happen if he buys land.

❿ Reading Strategy

Predicting Based on Character Traits

- Ask students to list adjectives that describe Pahom based on the information they have learned about him.

- Then, ask students the Reading Strategy question on p. 140: Using what you know about Pahom's character, predict whether he will be happy now.

  Answer: Some students will observe that Pahom is ambitious and discontented, and they will predict Pahom will not be happy now. Other students may say that Pahom will be happy with the land.

their way into her meadows—and he always had to pay a fine.

Pahom paid up, but grumbled, and, going home in a temper, was rough with his family. All through that summer Pahom had much trouble because of this manager, and he was actually glad when winter came and the cattle had to be stabled. Though he grudged the fodder when they could no longer graze on the pasture land, at least he was free from anxiety about them.

In the winter the news got about that the lady was going to sell her land and that the keeper of the inn on the high road was bargaining for it. When the peasants heard this they were very much alarmed.

"Well," thought they, "if the innkeeper gets the land, he'll worry us with fines worse than the lady's manager. We all depend on that estate."

So the peasants went on behalf of their village council and asked the lady not to sell the land to the innkeeper, offering her a better price for it themselves. The lady agreed to let them have it. Then the peasants tried to arrange for the village council to buy the whole estate, so that it might be held by them all in common. They met twice to discuss it, but could not settle the matter; the Evil One sowed discord among them and they could not agree. So they decided to buy the land individually, each according to his means; and the lady agreed to this plan as she had to the other.

Presently Pahom heard that a neighbor of his was buying fifty acres, and that the lady had consented to accept one half in cash and to wait a year for the other half. Pahom felt envious.

"Look at that," thought he, "the land is all being sold, and I'll get none of it." So he spoke to his wife.

"Other people are buying," said he, "and we must also buy twenty acres or so. Life is becoming impossible. That manager is simply crushing us with his fines."

So they put their heads together and considered how they could manage to buy it. They had one hundred rubles[3] laid by. They sold a colt and one half of their bees, hired out one of their sons as a farmhand and took his wages in advance, borrowed the rest from a brother-in-law, and so scraped together half the purchase money.

Having done this, Pahom chose a farm of forty acres, some of it wooded, and went to the lady to bargain for it. They came to an agreement, and he shook hands with her upon it and paid her a deposit in advance. Then they went to town and signed the deeds, he paying half the price down, and undertaking to pay the remainder within two years.

So now Pahom had land of his own. He borrowed seed and sowed it on the land he had bought. The harvest was a good one, and within a year he had managed to pay off his debts both to the lady and to his brother-in-law. So he became a landowner, plowing and sowing his own land, making hay on his own land, cutting his own trees, and feeding his cattle on his own pasture. When he went out to plow his fields, or to look at his growing corn, or at his grass meadows, his heart would fill

---

3. **rubles** (rōō′ bəlz) *n.* Russian money.

Reading Strategy
Predicting Based on Character Traits What do you predict that Pahom will do after hearing this news? Explain.

Reading Strategy
Predicting Based on Character Traits Using what you know about Pahom's character, predict whether he will be happy now.

✳ ENRICHMENT: Cultural Connection

Councilpersons

The village council before which the peasants appear in this story is much like village, town, and city councils today. In the United States, councilpersons are elected officials. Although being a councilperson can be a full-time position in smaller municipalities, councilpersons usually hold other jobs as well.

Suggest that students learn who their city or town council members are. Encourage students to contact the office of one or more of the members, and if possible, interview someone there about how one becomes a member of the council, what the council does, and the council's recent decisions.

Cornfield at Ewell, c. 1846 (detail), William Holman Hunt, Tate Gallery, London

◀ **Critical Viewing**
Why would it be more satisfying for a farmer like the one in the painting to work on land that he owned? **[Speculate]**

with joy. The grass that grew and the flowers that bloomed there seemed to him unlike any that grew elsewhere. Formerly, when he had passed by that land, it had appeared the same as any other land, but now it seemed quite different.

3

So Pahom was well contented, and everything would have been right if the neighboring peasants would only not have trespassed on his wheatfields and meadows. He appealed to them most civilly, but they still went on: now the herdsmen would let the village cows stray into his meadows, then horses from the night pasture would get among his corn. Pahom turned them out again and again, and forgave their owners, and for a long time he <u>forbore</u> to prosecute anyone. But at last he lost patience and complained to the District Court. He knew it was the peasants' want of land, and no evil intent on their part, that caused the trouble, but he thought:

"I can't go on overlooking it, or they'll destroy all I have. They must be taught a lesson."

So he had them up, gave them one lesson, and then another, and two or three of the peasants were fined. After a time Pahom's neighbors began to bear him a grudge for this, and would now and then let their cattle onto his land on purpose. One peasant even got into Pahom's wood at night and cut down five young lime trees for their bark. Pahom, passing through the wood one day, noticed something white. He came nearer and saw the stripped trunks lying on the ground, and close by

forbore (fôr bôr´) *v.* refrained from

⓭ ☑**Reading Check**
How are Pahom and his wife able to buy the land?

How Much Land Does a Man Need? ◆ *141*

⓫ **Background**

Art

Cornfield at Ewell by William Holman Hunt

This landscape depicts a large field of grain similar to those Pahom would have cultivated in Russia. The artist was a member of the Pre-Raphaelite Brotherhood in England, a group of artists and poets who held to Renaissance ideals and standards in art. They strove to portray nature in a way that demonstrated both its detail and its simplicity. Use these questions for discussion:

1. What qualities does this field have that might appeal to Pahom?
   Answer: The field's vastness and potential productivity might appeal to Pahom.

2. Do you think this is an appropriate illustration for this story? Explain.
   Answer: The image of a lone man in a vast expanse of land suits the story well.

⓬ ▶**Critical Viewing**

Answer: Working his own land would be more satisfying to the farmer because ownership provides its own emotional reward and because any profits from the land would be the landowner's.

⓭ ☑**Reading Check**

Answer: They use their savings, sell some animals, put their son to work and take his wages, borrow some money, and arrange a payment plan with the owner.

CUSTOMIZE INSTRUCTION FOR UNIVERSAL ACCESS

For English Learners	For Special Needs Students
Students may have difficulty with some of the longer sentences in this selection. Choose some of these long sentences and model the process of breaking a sentence into its main subject and verb to determine its basic meaning. Ask "Whom or what is this sentence about? What is its subject? What is happening to that subject?"	Have students describe their favorite possession, their emotions about it, and how they feel about sharing it. Then, have them make a list of Pahom's feelings about his new land. Are any of these feelings similar?

⓮ Literary Analysis

Parable

• Have students stop reading at the bracketed passage. Have them summarize the information they have learned on this page and discuss how Pahom has changed now that he is a landowner.

Answer: Before Pahom became a landowner, his sympathies were with the peasants. When he was fined for trespassing, he was angry. Now he accuses and fines a peasant for trespassing.

• Ask students the Literary Analysis question on p. 142: How do Pahom's experiences begin to teach a lesson about greed?

Answer: Pahom's greed has alienated him from his community.

▶ Monitor Progress Ask students whether they know of other stories that teach lessons.

Answer: Students should mention fairy tales, television shows, or films that teach moral lessons.

⓯ Vocabulary Development

Context

• Read aloud the bracketed sentence to students. Point out the word *sheaf*, which means "a bundle of cut stalks of grain."

• Explain that the word *sheaf* may be used to refer more generally to a variety of items that are bundled together. Ask students to identify other bundled items that are referred to with the term *sheaf*.

Answer: Most students will mention paper.

---

stood the stumps where the trees had been. Pahom was furious.

"If he'd only cut one here and there it would have been bad enough," thought Pahom, "but the rascal has actually cut down a whole clump. If I could only find out who did this, I'd get even with him."

He racked his brains as to who it could be. Finally he decided: "It must be Simon—no one else could have done it." So he went to Simon's homestead to have a look around, but he found nothing and only had an angry scene. However, he now felt more certain than ever that Simon had done it, and he lodged a complaint. Simon was summoned. The case was tried, and retried, and at the end of it all Simon was acquitted, there being no evidence against him. Pahom felt still more aggrieved, and let his anger loose upon the Elders and the Judges.

"You let thieves grease your palms," said he. "If you were honest folk yourselves you wouldn't let a thief go free."

⓮ So Pahom quarreled with the judges and with his neighbors. Threats to burn his hut began to be uttered. So though Pahom had more land, his place in the community was much worse than before.

About this time a rumor got about that many people were moving to new parts.

"There's no need for me to leave my land," thought Pahom. "But some of the others may leave our village and then there'd be more room for us. I'd take over their land myself and make my estates somewhat bigger. I could then live more at ease. As it is, I'm still too cramped to be comfortable."

One day Pahom was sitting at home when a peasant, passing through the village, happened to drop in. He was allowed to stay the night, and supper was given him. Pahom had a talk with this peasant and asked him where he came from. The stranger answered that he came from beyond the Volga,[4] where he had been working. One word led to another, and the man went on to say that many people were settling in those parts. He told how some people from his village had settled there. They had joined the community there and had had twenty-five acres per man granted them. The land was so good, he said, that the rye sown on ⓯ it grew as high as a horse, and so thick that five cuts of a sickle made a sheaf. One peasant, he said, had brought nothing with him but his bare hands, and now he had six horses and two cows of his own.

Pahom's heart kindled with desire.

"Why should I suffer in this narrow hole, if one can live so well elsewhere?" he thought. "I'll sell my land and my homestead here, and with the money I'll start afresh over there and get everything new. In this crowded place one is always having trouble. But I must first go and find out all about it myself."

Toward summer he got ready and started out. He went down the Volga on a steamer to Samara,[5] then walked another three hundred miles on foot, and at last reached the place. It was just as the stranger

---

aggrieved (ə grēvd') *adj.* wronged

Literary Analysis
Parable How do Pahom's experiences begin to teach a lesson about greed?

sheaf (shēf) *n.* bundle of grain

---

4. **Volga** (väl' gə) the major river in western Russia.
5. **Samara** (sə mär' ə) city in eastern Russia.

✺ ENRICHMENT: Science Connection

Crop Rotation

The practice of rotating crops, that is, of sowing wheat for one or two years and then allowing a field to lie fallow until it is covered with grass, has a scientific justification. Certain crops, such as wheat and corn, leach nutrients from soil. Other crops, such as alfalfa and soybeans, can reconstitute the soil, making it ready for planting grain again. By rotating crops from year to year, farmers can increase the productivity of their land. Sometimes farmers let the land "rest" by not planting it and letting it lie fallow.

Students might like to speculate on how greed might make a farmer sacrifice productivity over time. If a farmer were shortsighted and planted grain year after year in hopes of making the best profit, eventually the grain crop would fail because the soil would be depleted of nutrients.

had said. The peasants had plenty of land: every man had twenty-five acres of communal land given him for his use, and anyone who had money could buy, besides, at a ruble and a half an acre, as much good freehold land[6] as he wanted.

Having found out all he wished to know, Pahom returned home as autumn came on, and began selling off his belongings. He sold his land at a profit, sold his homestead and all his cattle, and withdrew from membership in the village. He only waited till the spring, and then started with his family for the new settlement.

4

As soon as Pahom and his family reached their new abode, he applied for admission into the council of a large village. He stood treat to the Elders and obtained the necessary documents. Five shares of communal land were given him for his own and his sons' use: that is to say—125 acres (not all together, but in different fields) besides the use of the communal pasture. Pahom put up the buildings he needed and bought cattle. Of the communal land alone he had three times as much as at his former home, and the land was good wheat land. He was ten times better off than he had been. He had plenty of <u>arable</u> land and pasturage, and could keep as many head of cattle as he liked.

At first, in the bustle of building and settling down, Pahom was pleased with it all, but when he got used to it he began to think that even here he hadn't enough land. The first year he sowed wheat on his share of the communal land and had a good crop. He wanted to go on sowing wheat, but had not enough communal land for the purpose, and what he had already used was not available, for in those parts wheat is sown only on virgin soil or on <u>fallow</u> land. It is sown for one or two years, and then the land lies fallow till it is again overgrown with steppe grass. There were many who wanted such land, and there was not enough for all, so that people quarreled about it. Those who were better off wanted it for growing wheat, and those who were poor wanted it to let to dealers, so that they might raise money to pay their taxes. Pahom wanted to sow more wheat, so he rented land from a dealer for a year. He sowed much wheat and had a fine crop, but the land was too far from the village—the wheat had to be carted more than ten miles. After a time Pahom noticed that some peasant dealers were living on separate farms and were growing wealthy, and he thought:

"If I were to buy some freehold land and have a homestead on it, it would be a different thing altogether. Then it would all be fine and close together."

---

6. **freehold land** privately owned land that the owner can lease to others for a fee.

Literature
in context Geography Connection

Agricultural Vocabulary
The following terms used in agriculture will help you understand "How Much Land Does a Man Need?"

acre: a unit of land, equal to about 43,560 square feet

fodder: feed for farm animals, usually chopped stalks and leaves of grain plants mixed with hay

sow seed: to scatter seed over the ground, such as in a field, to grow crops

make hay: to cut and dry grass and other plants, such as clover or alfalfa, for fodder

harvest: the crop that is gathered

fallow land: land that is plowed and left unplanted during the growing season

flax: plant whose fibers are used to make textiles, especially linen

arable (ar′ ə bəl) *adj.* suitable for growing crops

fallow (fal′ ō) *adj.* plowed, but not planted

✔ Reading Check
What information does the stranger who comes to visit give Pahom?

How Much Land Does a Man Need? ◆ 143

---

⑯ Critical Thinking
Evaluate
- Read aloud the bracketed passage to students.
- Explain to students that the use of communal land is typical of many agrarian societies. Usually, a section of land is set aside on which everyone in a village can graze cattle or plant a garden. Ask students to briefly evaluate the pros and cons of such a system.
Possible responses: It is a good system because it is equitable, allows everyone to be productive, and fosters self-esteem. The system is rigid and does not allow people to get ahead on their own or to be independent.

⑰ Background
Agricultural Vocabulary
Students may be interested to know the etymology of these agricultural terms:
- *Acre* is derived from the Greek word *agros*, meaning "land."
- *Fodder* comes from the Old English term *fodor*, referring to food.
- *Sow* is derived from the Old English word *sawan*, meaning "to plant."
- *Harvest* comes from the Middle English word *hervest*, "autumn."
- *Fallow* is derived from the Middle English term *falow* or *falwe*, meaning "left unplanted after plowing."

⑱ ✔ Reading Check
Answer: The man says that many people are settling the land beyond the Volga River and are being granted twenty-five acres per man to use.

CUSTOMIZE INSTRUCTION FOR UNIVERSAL ACCESS

For Less Proficient Readers	**For English Learners**	**For Advanced Readers**
Students may have difficulty distinguishing between the land Pahom now holds and freehold land. Help them to identify the main idea of this passage. Point out that, once again, Pahom thinks others are doing better than he is and thinks he needs more land.	Use simpler language to explain the passage about communal land. Define the words *sowing* (planting), *fallow* (unplanted), and *arable* (fertile), and use a schematic map on the chalkboard to illustrate the uses of communal and freehold land.	Ask students to explain the principle behind freeholding land—how it benefits both the owner and the user. Suggest that they do research to discover whether any such system has ever been employed in the United States and, if so, how it worked.

144

The question of buying freehold land recurred to him again and again.

He went on in the same way for three years, renting land and sowing wheat. The seasons turned out well and the crops were good, so that he began to lay by money. He might have gone on living contentedly, but he grew tired of having to rent other people's land every year and having to scramble for it. Wherever there was good land to be had, the peasants would rush for it and it was taken up at once, so that unless you were sharp about it, you got none. It happened in the third year that he and a dealer together rented a piece of pasture land from some peasants, and they had already plowed it up, when there was some dispute and the peasants went to law about it, and things fell out so that the labor was all lost.

"If it were my own land," thought Pahom, "I should be independent, and there wouldn't be all this unpleasantness."

So Pahom began looking out for land which he could buy, and he came across a peasant who had bought thirteen hundred acres, but having got into difficulties was willing to sell again cheap. Pahom bargained and haggled with him, and at last they settled the price at fifteen hundred rubles, part in cash and part to be paid later. They had all but

Rest During the Harvest, Alexander Morosov, Tretyakov Gallery, Moscow, Russia

㉑ ▲Critical Viewing What are the benefits to these peasants of working communally? Contrast these benefits with the benefits of owning their own land. **[Contrast]**

144 ◆ *Striving for Success*

clinched the matter when a passing dealer happened to stop at Pahom's one day to get feed for his horses. He drank tea with Pahom, and they had a talk. The dealer said that he was just returning from the land of the Bashkirs,[7] far away, where he had bought thirteen thousand acres of land, all for a thousand rubles. Pahom questioned him further, and the dealer said:

"All one has to do is to make friends with the chiefs. I gave away about one hundred rubles' worth of silk robes and carpets, besides a case of tea, and I gave wine to those who would drink it; and I got the land for less than three kopecks[8] an acre." And he showed Pahom the title deed, saying:

"The land lies near a river, and the whole steppe[9] is virgin soil."

Pahom plied him with questions, and the dealer said:

"There's more land there than you could cover if you walked a year, and it all belongs to the Bashkirs. They're as simple as sheep, and land can be got almost for nothing."

"There, now," thought Pahom, "with my one thousand rubles, why should I get only thirteen hundred acres, and saddle myself with a debt besides? If I take it out there, I can get more than ten times as much for my money."

5

Pahom inquired how to get to the place, and as soon as the grain dealer had left him, he prepared to go there himself. He left his wife to look after the homestead, and started on his journey, taking his hired man with him. They stopped at a town on their way and bought a case of tea, some wine, and other presents, as the grain dealer had advised.

On and on they went until they had gone more than three hundred miles, and on the seventh day they came to a place where the Bashkirs had pitched their round tents. It was all just as the dealer had said. The people lived on the steppe, by a river, in felt-covered tents. They neither tilled the ground nor ate bread. Their cattle and horses grazed in herds on the steppe. The colts were tethered behind the tents, and the mares were driven to them twice a day. The mares were milked, and from the milk kumiss[10] was made. It was the women who prepared the kumiss, and they also made cheese. As far as the men were concerned, drinking kumiss and tea, eating mutton, and playing on their pipes was all they cared about. They were all stout and merry, and all the summer long they never thought of doing any work. They were quite ignorant, and knew no Russian, but were good-natured enough.

As soon as they saw Pahom, they came out of their tents and gathered around the visitor. An interpreter was found, and Pahom told them he had come about some land. The Bashkirs seemed very glad; they took Pahom and led him into one of the best tents, where they made

Literary Analysis
Round and Flat Characters What key characteristic does Pahom show here?

Literary Analysis
Parable What abstract idea do the Bashkirs represent?

24 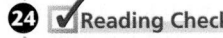 **Reading Check**
How does Pahom find out about the Bashkirs' land?

---

7. **Bashkirs** (bash kirz´) nomadic people who live in the plains of southwestern Russia.
8. **kopecks** (kō´ peks) *n.* Russian money, equal to one hundredth of a ruble.
9. **steppe** (step) *n.* high grassland of central Asia.
10. **kumiss** (kōō´ mis) *n.* mare's milk that has been fermented and is used as a drink.

㉒ Background
Geography
The Bashkirs live "far away" from Pahom's present home, but their land is still in Europe, not Asia. Pahom is moving eastward (somewhat like America's westward-moving pioneers) in search of cheaper and more abundant land.

㉓ Literary Analysis
Round and Flat Characters
• Have students review the traits Pahom has shown up to this point in the story. Then, have students decide whether Pahom is a round or flat character. Make sure that they support their responses with details from the story.
  Answer: Pahom has shown himself to be greedy and ambitious. He's a flat character because these are the only key traits he has shown.

• Then, ask students the Literary Analysis question on p. 145: What key characteristic does Pahom show here?
  Answer: The key trait he shows here is greed.

▶ **Monitor Progress** Ask students to name traits or behaviors that could be added to Pahom's character to make it more rounded.
  Possible Responses: Students may suggest doubt, compassion, caution, generosity, or humor.

㉔ ✓ Reading Check
Answer: He finds out from the grain dealer.

CUSTOMIZE INSTRUCTION FOR UNIVERSAL ACCESS

For Less Proficient Readers	For Gifted/Talented Students
Students may need help comparing Pahom's two opportunities for land. Direct them to compare the prices of the land and consider the debt involved with the first opportunity. Then, ask them to explain why the second opportunity is better.	Ask students to make calculations to demonstrate that Pahom's second opportunity for land on this page is better than his first. Have them discuss their calculations and the factors that Pahom has to consider. Then, have students write a paragraph describing Pahom's opportunities with regard to the two land opportunities. Ask them to explain Pahom's decision.

Parable

- Have a volunteer read aloud the bracketed passage. Ask students to review the description of the Bashkirs that begins on the bottom of p. 145.

- Ask students to think about the differences between the Bashkirs and Pahom and the peasants.
  Answer: The Bashkirs, unlike Pahom, don't care about work or investments. They're interested only in food and friendship. Unlike the peasants, they don't plow or plant the land, but they still live off it.

- Then, ask students the Literary Analysis question on p. 145: What abstract idea do the Bashkirs represent?
  Possible response: The abstract idea the Bashkirs represent is being contented with what they have, and being generous with others.

26 **Reading Strategy**

Predicting Based on Character Traits

- Have students summarize Pahom's meeting with the Bashkirs. Then, have students verbalize what Pahom wants out of this meeting.
  Answer: Pahom goes to meet with the Bashkirs, bringing gifts with him. To repay his kindness, the Bashkirs offer to give him something of theirs. Pahom wants their land.

- Finally, ask students the Reading Strategy question on p. 146: Predict how much land Pahom will try to get.
  Answer: Pahom will try to get as much land as he possibly can.

---

25 him sit on some down cushions placed on a carpet, while they sat around him. They gave him some tea and kumiss, and had a sheep killed, and gave him mutton to eat. Pahom took presents out of his cart and distributed them among the Bashkirs, and divided the tea amongst them. The Bashkirs were delighted. They talked a great deal among themselves and then told the interpreter what to say.

"They wish to tell you," said the interpreter, "that they like you and that it's our custom to do all we can to please a guest and to repay him for his gifts. You have given us presents, now tell us which of the things we possess please you best, that we may present them to you."

"What pleases me best here," answered Pahom, "is your land. Our land is crowded and the soil is worn out, but you have plenty of land, and it is good land. I never saw the likes of it."

The interpreter told the Bashkirs what Pahom had said. They talked among themselves for a while. Pahom could not understand what they were saying, but saw that they were much amused and heard them shout and laugh. Then they were silent and looked at Pahom while the interpreter said:

26 "They wish me to tell you that in return for your presents they will gladly give you as much land as you want. You have only to point it out with your hand and it is yours."

The Bashkirs talked again for a while and began to dispute. Pahom asked what they were disputing about, and the interpreter told him that some of them thought they ought to ask their chief about the land and not act in his absence, while others thought there was no need to wait for his return.

6

While the Bashkirs were disputing, a man in a large fox-fur cap appeared on the scene. They all became silent and rose to their feet. The interpreter said: "This is our chief himself."

Pahom immediately fetched the best dressing gown and five pounds of tea, and offered these to the chief. The chief accepted them and seated himself in the place of honor. The Bashkirs at once began telling him something. The chief listened for a while, then made a sign with his head for them to be silent, and addressing himself to Pahom, said in Russian:

"Well, so be it. Choose whatever piece of land you like; we have plenty of it."

"How can I take as much as I like?" thought Pahom. "I must get a deed to make it secure, or else they may say: 'It is yours,' and afterward may take it away again."

"Thank you for your kind words," he said aloud. "You have much land, and I only want a little. But I should like to be sure which portion is mine. Could it not be measured and made over to me? Life and death are in God's hands. You good people give it to me, but your children might wish to take it back again."

"You are quite right," said the chief. "We will make it over to you."

"I heard that a dealer had been here," continued Pahom, "and that

---

Reading Strategy
Predicting Based on Character Traits Predict how much land Pahom will try to get.

Interpreting

English learners should know that their language skills may be useful in the workplace. Point out the role of the interpreter in this story—he listens to both sides and translates what the people are saying and is equally fluent in Russian and the language of the Bashkirs.

Have students identify skills that a good interpreter should have, such as facility with languages, tact, good listening skills, and good speaking skills. Then, have students work in pairs to decide what kinds of businesses or services use interpreters and for what reasons. Are there any local businesses or individuals who might hire a student as an interpreter? What special kind of training or specific preparation might be required for interpreting? Ask them to formulate their ideas as lists to present to the class. Point out the variety of places where bilingual students might use their skills.

you gave him a little land, too, and signed title deeds to that effect. I should like to have it done in the same way."

The chief understood.

"Yes," replied he, "that can be done quite easily. We have a scribe, and we will go to town with you and have the deed properly sealed."

"And what will be the price?" asked Pahom.

"Our price is always the same: one thousand rubles a day."

Pahom did not understand.

"A day? What measure is that? How many acres would that be?"

"We do not know how to reckon it out," said the chief. "We sell it by the day. As much as you can go around on your feet in a day is yours, and the price is one thousand rubles a day."

Pahom was surprised.

"But in a day you can get around a large tract of land," he said.

The chief laughed.

"It will all be yours!" said he. "But there is one condition: If you don't return on the same day to the spot whence you started, your money is lost."

"But how am I to mark the way that I have gone?"

"Why, we shall go to any spot you like and stay there. You must start from that spot and make your round, taking a spade with you. Wherever you think necessary, make a mark. At every turning, dig a

27 ✓ **Reading Check**
What does Pahom ask of the Bashkirs in return for the gifts he gives them?

28 ▼ **Critical Viewing**
Based on this painting, what do you learn about the responsibility of owning a lot of land? **[Infer]**

The Hay Harvest, Boris Kustodiev, St. Petersburg, Russia

27 ✓ **Reading Check**
Answer: He asks for a written contract, or deed, for the land.

28 ▶ **Critical Viewing**
Answer: The people working the land indicate that the responsibility of the landowner will be to share the fruits of the land with the workers, either by paying them or by feeding them or both.

29 **Background**

Art

The Hay Harvest by Boris Kustodiev

In his day, Boris Kustodiev was famous for his brightly colored paintings of country and small-town life. Popular in the Soviet Union in the early twentieth century, his paintings celebrate Soviet ideals.

The Russian peasants harvesting hay in this painting are like the ones whom Tolstoy might have seen. Call students' attention to the color and tone of this painting, and then use these questions for discussion:

1. Does this painting have a joyous or a somber mood? Which part of the story would it best illustrate?
   Answer: The painting has a feeling of lively, joyous motion. The women seem happy working the land together. The painting depicts what life might have been like for Pahom and the other peasants if they had bought land together.

2. What does this painting tell you about the life of a peasant in Russia?
   Answer: It indicates that life involved hard work but perhaps that community feeling was strong.

147

Literary Analysis

Parable

- Read aloud the bracketed passage to students.

- Ask students to explain why Pahom is being laughed at in his dream.

  Possible responses: The figures in the dream laugh because they are all really the Devil.

- Ask students the first Literary Analysis question on p. 148: What should Pahom realize based on his dream?

  Answer: He should realize that something bad will happen as a result of this land deal and that perhaps his life is in danger.

Literary Analysis

Round and Flat Characters

- Remind students that round characters display many traits, whereas flat characters are limited to a few key characteristics.

- Ask students the second Literary Analysis question on p. 148: Pahom does not stop to analyze his dream. Is that action more typical of a round or flat character?

  Answer: It is more typical of a flat character, because it suggests that the character is content with a simple, surface-level understanding.

hole and pile up the turf; then afterward we will go around with a plow from hole to hole. You may make as large a circuit as you please, but before the sun sets you must return to the place you started from. All the land you cover will be yours."

Pahom was delighted. It was decided to start early next morning. They talked a while, and after drinking some more kumiss and eating some more mutton, they had tea again, and then the night came on. They gave Pahom a featherbed to sleep on, and the Bashkirs dispersed for the night, promising to assemble the next morning at daybreak and ride out before sunrise to the appointed spot.

7

Pahom lay on the featherbed, but could not sleep. He kept thinking about the land.

"What a large tract I'll mark off!" thought he, "I can easily do thirty-five miles in a day. The days are long now, and within a circuit of thirty-five miles what a lot of land there will be! I'll sell the poorer land or let it to peasants, but I'll pick out the best and farm it myself. I'll buy two ox teams and hire two more laborers. About a hundred and fifty acres shall be plowland, and I'll pasture cattle on the rest."

Pahom lay awake all night and dozed off only just before dawn. Hardly were his eyes closed when he had a dream. He thought he was lying in that same tent and heard somebody chuckling outside. He wondered who it could be, and rose and went out, and he saw the Bashkir chief sitting in front of the tent holding his sides and rolling about with laughter. Going nearer to the chief, Pahom asked: "What are you laughing at?" But he saw that it was no longer the chief but the grain dealer who had recently stopped at his house and had told him about the land. Just as Pahom was going to ask: "Have you been here long?" he saw that it was not the dealer, but the peasant who had come up from the Volga long ago, to Pahom's old home. Then he saw that it was not the peasant either, but the Devil himself with hoofs and horns, sitting there and chuckling, and before him lay a man, prostrate on the ground, barefooted, with only trousers and a shirt on. And Pahom dreamed that he looked more attentively to see what sort of man it was lying there, and he saw that the man was dead, and that it was himself. Horror-struck, he awoke.

"What things one dreams about!" thought he.

Looking around he saw through the open door that the dawn was breaking.

"It's time to wake them up," thought he. "We ought to be starting."

He got up, roused his man (who was sleeping in his cart), bade him harness, and went to call the Bashkirs.

"It's time to go to the steppe to measure the land," he said.

The Bashkirs rose and assembled, and the chief came, too. Then they began drinking kumiss again, and offered Pahom some tea, but he would not wait.

"If we are to go, let's go. It's high time," said he.

148 ◆ *Striving for Success*

Literary Analysis
Parable What should Pahom realize based on his dream?

Literary Analysis
Round and Flat Characters Pahom does not stop to analyze his dream. Is that action more typical of a round or flat character? Explain.

8

The Bashkirs got ready and they all started; some mounted on horses and some in carts. Pahom drove in his own small cart with his servant and took a spade with him. When they reached the steppe, the red dawn was beginning to kindle. They ascended a hillock (called by the Bashkirs a shikhan) and, dismounting from their carts and their horses, gathered in one spot. The chief came up to Pahom and, stretching out his arm toward the plain:

"See," said he, "all this, as far as your eye can reach, is ours. You may have any part of it you like."

Pahom's eyes glistened: it was all virgin soil, as flat as the palm of your hand, as black as the seed of a poppy, and in the hollows different kinds of grasses grew breast-high.

The chief took off his fox-fur cap, placed it on the ground, and said:

"This will be the mark. Start from here, and return here again. All the land you go around shall be yours."

Pahom took out his money and put it on the cap. Then he took off his outer coat, remaining in his sleeveless undercoat. He unfastened his girdle[11] and tied it tight below his stomach, put a little bag of bread into the breast of his coat, and, tying a flask of water to his girdle, he drew up the tops of his boots, took the spade from his man, and stood ready to start. He considered for some moments which way he had better go—it was tempting everywhere.

"No matter," he concluded, "I'll go toward the rising sun."

He turned his face to the east, stretched himself, and waited for the sun to appear above the rim.

"I must lose no time," he thought, "and it's easier walking while it's still cool."

The sun's rays had hardly flashed above the horizon when Pahom, carrying the spade over his shoulder, went down into the steppe.

Pahom started walking neither slowly nor quickly. After having gone a thousand yards he stopped, dug a hole, and placed pieces of turf one on another to make it more visible. Then he went on; and now that he had walked off his stiffness he quickened his pace. After a while he dug another hole.

Pahom looked back. The hillock could be distinctly seen in the sunlight, with the people on it, and the glittering iron rims of the cartwheels. At a rough guess Pahom concluded that he had walked three miles. It was growing warmer; he took off his undercoat, slung it across his shoulder, and went on again. It had grown quite warm now; he looked at the sun—it was time to think of breakfast.

"The first shift is done, but there are four in a day, and it's too soon yet to turn. But I'll just take off my boots," said he to himself.

He sat down, took off his boots, stuck them into his girdle, and went on. It was easy walking now.

"I'll go on for another three miles," thought he, "and then turn to the

---

11. **girdle** (gʉrd´ əl) *n.* belt or sash.

Reading Strategy

Predicting Based on Character Traits Based on Pahom's behavior so far, what do you think he feels and thinks as he looks at the land?

33 ✓ **Reading Check**
How is Pahom to mark the land he is claiming?

How Much Land Does a Man Need? ◆ 149

32 Reading Strategy
Predicting Based on Character Traits

• Ask students to discuss what land means to Pahom.

• Then, ask students the Reading Strategy question on p. 149: Based on Pahom's behavior so far, what do you think he feels and thinks as he looks at the land?
Answer: He feels very excited and thinks about how much land he can gain in one day.

33 ✓ **Reading Check**
Answer: He digs a hole and then piles mounds of turf next to it.

CUSTOMIZE INSTRUCTION FOR UNIVERSAL ACCESS

For Less Proficient Readers	For English Learners	For Advanced Readers
As students begin reading this new section, have them note when Pahom turns the three corners to form the sides of his new property. Breaking down the story this way will help them track the character's progress and make predictions about events in the story.	A few idioms on this page may need clarification. Have native English speakers assist their classmates by restating the following in their own words: *It's high time* and *Dawn was beginning to kindle.* The phrases mean "the time has come" and "the sun was beginning to rise."	Ask students to read the events of this page. Then, have them write a related subplot, something that might happen to Pahom on his walk that will change the direction of the story. Ask them to make notes about how the subplot will resolve.

Infer

• Have a volunteer read aloud the bracketed passage to students.

• Ask students to discuss how Pahom's observation might fore-shadow the outcome of the story.
Answer: The comment "a lifetime to live" is an ironic foreshadowing because Pahom may not live to enjoy the land.

35 Reading Strategy

Predicting Based on Character Traits

• Ask students how Pahom's greed is revealed by his actions in the bracketed paragraph.
Answer: Pahom rests very little because he sees it as a waste of time. Rather than taking what he can safely have, he keeps walking more and more so that he can have more land.

• Ask students the Reading Strategy question on p. 150: Predict whether Pahom will try to include any more land.
Answer: Yes, Pahom will try to include more land.

36 ▶ Critical Viewing

Answer: The land is rolling, so it's hard to judge the distance across it.

left. This spot is so fine that it would be a pity to lose it. The further one goes, the better the land seems."

He went straight on for a while, and when he looked around, the hillock was scarcely visible and the people on it looked like black ants, and he could just see something glistening there in the sun.

"Ah," thought Pahom, "I have gone far enough in this direction; it's time to turn. Besides, I'm in a regular sweat, and very thirsty."

He stopped, dug a large hole, and heaped up pieces of turf. Next he untied his flask, had a drink, and then turned sharply to the left. He went on and on; the grass was high, and it was very hot.

Pahom began to grow tired: he looked at the sun and saw that it was noon.

"Well," he thought, "I must have a rest."

34 He sat down, and ate some bread and drank some water; but he did not lie down, thinking that if he did he might fall asleep. After sitting a little while, he went on again. At first he walked easily; the food had strengthened him; but it had become terribly hot and he felt sleepy. Still he went on, thinking: "An hour to suffer, a lifetime to live."

He went a long way in this direction also, and was about to turn to the left again, when he perceived a damp hollow:

35 "It would be a pity to leave that out," he thought. "Flax would do well there." So he went on past the hollow and dug a hole on the other side of it before he made a sharp turn. Pahom looked toward the hillock. The heat made the air hazy: it seemed to be quivering, and through the haze the people on the hillock could scarcely be seen.

"Ah," thought Pahom, "I have made the sides too long; I must make this one shorter." And he went along the third side, stepping faster. He looked at the sun: it was nearly halfway to the horizon, and he had not yet done two miles of the third side of the square. He was still ten miles from the goal.

"No," he thought, "though it will make my land lopsided, I must hurry back in a straight line now. I might go too far, and as it is I have a great deal of land."

So Pahom hurriedly dug a hole and turned straight toward the hillock.

Reading Strategy
Predicting Based on Character Traits Predict whether Pahom will try to include any more land.

36 ▼ Critical Viewing
Why do you think it might be difficult to estimate distances in a landscape like this one? **[Speculate]**

150 ◆ *Striving for Success*

☀ ENRICHMENT: History

Russia

In 1922, Russia became part of the newly established Union of Soviet Socialist Republics (USSR), better known as the Soviet Union. The Soviet Union initially consisted of four republics, with the Russian Republic being the strongest and most influential. After World War II, the Soviet Union gained further territory. By 1991, disillusionment with communism and demands for greater freedoms led to the defeat of Communist party rule and to the dissolution of the Soviet Union. Throughout the Soviet era and the years that followed,

Russia has remained a highly agricultural society, like the one depicted in the story. However, Russia is adapting to a changing economic climate in an increasingly industrial and technological world.

9

Pahom went straight toward the hillock, but he now walked with difficulty. He was exhausted from the heat, his bare feet were cut and bruised, and his legs began to fail. He longed to rest, but it was impossible if he meant to get back before sunset. The sun waits for no man, and it was sinking lower and lower.

"Oh, Lord," he thought, "if only I have not blundered trying for too much! What if I am too late?"

He looked toward the hillock and at the sun. He was still far from his goal, and the sun was already near the rim of the sky.

Pahom walked on and on; it was very hard walking, but he went quicker and quicker. He pressed on, but was still far from the place. He began running, threw away his coat, his boots, his flask, and his cap, and kept only the spade which he used as a support.

"What am I to do?" he thought again. "I've grasped too much and ruined the whole affair. I can't get there before the sun sets."

And this fear made him still more breathless. Pahom kept on running; his trousers stuck to him, and his mouth was parched. His breast was working like a blacksmith's bellows, his heart was beating like a hammer, and his legs were giving way as if they did not belong to him. Pahom was seized with terror lest he should die of the strain.

Though afraid of death, he could not stop.

"After having run all that way they will call me a fool if I stop now," thought he.

And he ran on and on, and drew near and heard the Bashkirs yelling and shouting to him, and their cries inflamed his heart still more. He gathered his last strength and ran on.

The sun was close to the rim of the sky and, cloaked in mist, looked large, and red as blood. Now, yes, now, it was about to set! The sun was quite low, but he was also quite near his goal. Pahom could already see the people on the hillock waving their arms to make him hurry. He could see the fox-fur cap on the ground and the money in it, and the chief sitting on the ground holding his sides. And Pahom remembered his dream.

"There's plenty of land," thought he, "but will God let me live on it? I have lost my life, I have lost my life! Never will I reach that spot!"

Literary Analysis
Parable Do you think Pahom has learned a lesson about his greed?

38 ☑ **Reading Check**
How does Pahom's physical state change as the day goes on?

---

37 ◯ Literary Analysis
Parable

- Read aloud the bracketed passage to students. Ask them to describe Pahom's condition at this point.

- Have students decide what Pahom would do if he had learned his lesson. Then, ask students the Literary Analysis question on p. 151: Do you think Pahom has learned a lesson about his greed?
  Answer: Pahom has not learned his lesson; if he had, he would have stopped and rested instead of continuing to run.

38 ☑ **Reading Check**

Answer: He becomes weaker, hotter, and thirstier. His chest hurts because he is straining his heart.

CUSTOMIZE INSTRUCTION FOR UNIVERSAL ACCESS

For Special Needs Students	For English Learners	For Gifted/Talented Students
Ask students to identify with Pahom's emotional and physical states as the day draws to a close. Ask them to role-play Pahom and the Bashkirs to try to understand better Pahom's conflict and suffering.	Have students give words that describe Pahom's situation at this point in the story. Write their words on the chalkboard. Ask students to draw pictures of Pahom as he tries to make it back to the Bashkirs and close the border of his land. Have them caption their pictures with the words on the chalkboard.	Have students consider Pahom's history and what has happened to him on this day with the Bashkirs. Ask them to write a poem expressing Pahom's circumstance and emotional state of being.

Review and Assess

1. Some students may not sympathize with Pahom because his greed is a very unattractive trait. Other students may say Pahom doesn't deserve to die simply because he is foolish.

2. **(a)** At the beginning, he thinks the only problem peasants face is not having enough land. **(b)** He has no responsibility for land and thinks only of the positive aspects of having more of it.

3. **(a)** Pahom sells, borrows, and spends his savings to get his parcel of land. **(b)** He starts to fine the peasants himself after he becomes a landowner.

4. **(a)** First, a peasant tells him about land along the Volga; next, he decides he wants to freehold additional land so he can grow more wheat; then, he almost buys land from a peasant who had gotten into trouble; and finally, a grain dealer tells him about the Bashkirs and how easy it is to get their land for a few gifts. **(b)** He believes it will make him rich.

5. **(a)** The Bashkirs are not at all concerned about land ownership because they travel all the time; Pahom's primary concern in life is land. **(b)** The reader senses that Pahom will try to take advantage of the Bashkirs.

6. **(a)** On the last day of his life, Pahom tries to walk as far as he can in a day. He tries to walk too far in order to get more land and dies of exhaustion. **(b)** Many might try to get free land, but most would not want to risk death to get it.

7. Yes, Pahom deserves his end because he is so greedy. No, there is nothing wrong with ambition, and Pahom doesn't deserve to die for it.

Pahom looked at the sun, which had reached the earth: one side of it had already disappeared. With all his remaining strength he rushed on, bending his body forward so that his legs could hardly follow fast enough to keep him from falling. Just as he reached the hillock it suddenly grew dark. He looked up—the sun had already set!

He gave a cry: "All my labor has been in vain," thought he, and was about to stop, but he heard the Bashkirs still shouting and remembered that though to him, from below, the sun seemed to have set, they on the hillock could still see it. He took a long breath and ran up the hillock. It was still light there. He reached the top and saw the cap. Before it sat the chief, laughing and holding his sides. Again Pahom remembered his dream, and he uttered a cry: his legs gave way beneath him, he fell forward and reached the cap with his hands.

"Ah, that's a fine fellow!" exclaimed the chief. "He has gained much land!"

Pahom's servant came running up and tried to raise him, but he saw that blood was flowing from his mouth. Pahom was dead.

The Bashkirs clicked their tongues to show their pity.

His servant picked up the spade and dug a grave long enough for Pahom to lie in, and buried him in it.

Six feet from his head to his toes was all he needed.

Review and Assess

Thinking About the Selection

1. **Respond:** Do you sympathize with Pahom? Why or why not?

2. **(a) Recall:** At the start of this story, what does Pahom believe is the only trouble that peasants face? **(b) Analyze:** What details of his situation at the time lead him to think this way?

3. **(a) Recall:** How does Pahom come to buy his first parcel of land? **(b) Analyze Cause and Effect:** In what ways does Pahom's attitude toward the peasants begin to change with this first purchase? Why?

4. **(a) Recall:** How does Pahom learn about each new opportunity? **(b) Analyze:** Why is he eager to keep buying more land?

5. **(a) Compare and Contrast:** How do Pahom's and the Bashkirs' attitudes toward landownership differ? **(b) Infer:** How does this difference increase the tension of the story?

6. **(a) Summarize:** Briefly summarize what happens on the last day of Pahom's life. **(b) Evaluate:** Explain whether you think that most people would behave as Pahom does if they were put in his situation.

7. **Make a Judgment:** Do you think that Pahom deserves what he gets? Explain why or why not.

Leo Tolstoy

(1828–1910)

Tolstoy is remembered almost as much for his unusual life as for his work. Born into a rich family, he inherited his family estate at age nineteen and then tried to improve the lives of the peasants who lived on his land. At age thirty-four, he married an energetic woman who supported his work, copying his masterpiece *War and Peace* nine times by candlelight to send to publishers.

After the publication of *Anna Karenina*, his other masterpiece, Tolstoy suffered a spiritual crisis. He created his own religion, gave up drinking and smoking, and often wore peasants' clothes and worked in the fields. His strange behavior caused problems in his marriage and resulted in his leaving home. He died in an obscure railroad station in 1910.

ASSESSMENT PRACTICE: Reading Comprehension

Recognize Main Idea   (For more practice, see Test Preparation Workbook, p. 9.)

Many tests ask students to recognize the main idea in a passage. Use this sample test item.

> The grass that grew and the flowers that bloomed there seemed to him [Pahom] unlike any that grew elsewhere. Formerly, when he had passed by that land, it had appeared the same as any other land, but now it seemed quite different.

Which statement best sums up the main idea?

A Pahom had never noticed the land before.

B Pahom planted unusual flowers on his land.

C Pahom has worked to make the grass grow better than before.

D Owning the land changes Pahom's view of it.

Nothing indicates that Pahom had planted flowers or grass. The selection states that he has seen the land before. The words *Formerly* and *now* indicate that *D* is the correct choice.

Review and Assess

Literary Analysis

Parable

1. Use a flowchart like the one shown to outline the action in the **parable** "How Much Land Does a Man Need?"

Problem	Event	Event	Event	Conclusion

2. What is the lesson that Tolstoy's story teaches?
3. Parables are often used as a means of moral instruction. How might "How Much Land Does a Man Need?" be used for this purpose?

Connecting Literary Elements

4. What is the strongest personal characteristic of Pahom?
5. How does the author's decision to ignore any description of Pahom's wife after the start of the story contribute to the presentation of Pahom as a **flat character**?
6. How might Pahom's wife's inclusion, along with her thoughts and feelings about the events, hamper Tolstoy's ability to convey the parable's moral?

Reading Strategy

Predicting Based on Character Traits

7. Identify two things Pahom says or does that help you **predict** his behavior while interacting with the Bashkirs.
8. (a) Did you predict the ending of "How Much Land Does a Man Need?" (b) Do you find it satisfying? Surprising? Explain.

Extend Understanding

9. **Literature Connection:** Myths and fairy tales often have characters who have traits or flaws that lead to their downfall. (a) Name one other character who, like Pahom, is never satisfied with what he or she has. (b) What happens to this character? (c) What is the value of stories like these?

How Much Land Does a Man Need? ◆ 153

Quick Review

A **parable** is a simple, brief story that teaches a lesson.

Round characters exhibit a full range of emotions and actions.

Flat characters exhibit a limited number of behaviors and attitudes.

To **predict based on character traits,** study a character's actions, attitudes, and values to anticipate his or her behavior or the way the story will end.

 Take It to the Net
www.phschool.com

Take the interactive self-test online to check your understanding of the selection.

Answers continued

(b) The ending was satisfying because Pahom was punished. The ending was not satisfying because Pahom did not deserve to die.

9. **(a)** Students could name King Midas. **(b)** This character accidentally turns his child into gold. **(c)** They point out character flaws in stark relief, making it easy to see the harm they can cause.

Answers for p. 153

Review and Assess

1.

Problem
Pahom doesn't have enough land

⋮

Event
Pahom buys land with other peasants.

⋮

Event
Pahom buys land along the Volga.

⋮

Event
Pahom meets the Bashkirs and negotiates for more land.

⋮

Conclusion
Pahom dies overexerting himself while trying to fulfill the agreement with the Bashkirs.

2. It is better not to be greedy but rather to enjoy what you have, as the Bashkirs do.
3. It could be used to teach the lesson that greed is wrong.
4. His strongest personal characteristic is greed.
5. Because his wife is not there, Pahom doesn't have anyone to react to or any emotion to express except avarice.
6. If his wife were there, she might have challenged Pahom's greed, and he would have been influenced by her to think of other things besides land.
7. He says he wants more land, and he buys gifts for the Bashkirs to help him in his negotiations with them.
8. **(a)** Some students may have predicted that no good could come of Pahom's incessant greed. Others may have been hoping for a happier ending.

continued

Answers for p. 154

❶ Vocabulary Development

Words in Context

1. sheaf   2. fallow

Spelling Strategy

1. sleigh
2. chief
3. ceiling

Fluency: Sentence Completion

1. arable   5. forbore
2. disparaged   6. sheaf
3. aggrieved   7. fallow
4. piqued

❷ Grammar

1. became   4. become
2. seen   5. saw
3. known

Writing Application

A farmer named Pahom coveted more land. Every time he heard of an opportunity to buy land inexpensively, he took it, even if it meant moving far away. At last, he learned of an opportunity to buy a lot of land for very little money simply by befriending a nomadic tribe. They told him that he could buy at a low price whatever land he could walk around in a day. He tried to walk too far too fast, and his heart gave out.

Integrate Language Skills

❶ Vocabulary Development Lesson

Concept Development: Context

Words that have specific meanings in one context often have a broader meaning in other contexts. In agriculture, *sheaf* refers to a bundle of grain stalks. *Sheaf* is also used to describe a collection of things gathered together, such as a *sheaf* of paper. Use words from the vocabulary list on page 137 to complete each sentence.

1. The landowner stormed into the house, holding a ___?___ of bills in his hand.
2. His mind has gone ___?___ ; he has not read a book in a month.

Spelling Strategy

The word *aggrieved* follows this rule: Place *i* before *e* except after *c* or when sounded like *a* as in *neighbor* and *weigh*. Fill in the blanks to complete the spelling of each word.

1. sl__gh   2. ch__f   3. c__ling

❷ Grammar Lesson

Regular and Irregular Verb Forms

The past and past participles of **regular verbs** are formed by adding *-ed* or *-d* to the present form. The past and past participles of **irregular verbs** do not follow that pattern.

In this example, notice the difference between the ways in which the past tense of regular and irregular verbs are formed:

Regular: The women *finished* their tea, *chatted* a while about dress, and then *cleared* away the tea things. . . .

Irregular: As the sisters *sat* over their tea talking, the elder *began* to boast of the advantages of town life. . . .

𝒲G *Prentice Hall Writing and Grammar Connection: Chapter 22, Section 1*

154 ◆ *Striving for Success*

Fluency: Sentence Completion

Choose the word from the vocabulary list on page 137 that best completes each sentence.

1. Although the area used to be a desert, irrigation made the land ___?___.
2. Pahom's sister-in-law ___?___ the country ways.
3. The ___?___ peasants complained to the landowner.
4. Pahom was ___?___ by his neighbor's inconsiderate behavior.
5. When Pahom's neighbors let their animals in his fields, he ___?___ prosecuting them.
6. Pahom lovingly counted each ___?___ of wheat.
7. Pahom was unwilling to let any of his land lie ___?___.

Practice Choose a form of one of the irregular verbs below to complete each sentence.

Present	Past	Past Participle
know	knew	(have, had) known
see	saw	(have, had) seen
become	became	(have, had) become

1. Pahom _?_ upset. (become)
2. He had _?_ the animals in his fields. (see)
3. They had never _?_ how to do this. (know)
4. Pahom would have _?_ restless. (become)
5. He _?_ the vast land. (see)

Writing Application Summarize the story using the past tense.

TEACHING RESOURCES

The following resources can be used to enrich or extend the instruction for pp. 154–155.

Vocabulary

📖 **Vocabulary and Spelling Practice Book**
(Use this booklet for skills enrichment.)

Grammar

📖 **Selection Support:** Build Grammar Skills, p. 34

𝒲G **Writing and Grammar,** Platinum Level, p. 520 ▪

📄 **Daily Language Practice Transparencies**

Writing

𝒲G **Writing and Grammar,** Platinum Level, p. 104

💿 **Writing and Grammar iText CD-ROM** ▪

▪ **BLOCK SCHEDULING:** Resources marked with this symbol provide varied instruction during 90-minute blocks.

❸ Writing Lesson

Video Script

Some stories make great movies. Choose one part from "How Much Land Does a Man Need?" and write a video script for it. Your video script should give a clear explanation of the action, identifying camera angles and sound effects.

Prewriting   Draw a storyboard—a rough sketch of each scene in your video. Then, decide how you will make the visual transition from one image to another. Annotate your storyboard with directions for shooting the video. Describe the sounds as well as the sights.

Drafting   Write a draft showing what the characters say and do. Add camera directions to convey your storyboard ideas.

Model: Incorporating Clear Directions

[View field from a distance, bringing the camera in for a close-up on Pahom, who is sweaty and exhausted]

Pahom: [Stamps in frustration] What am I to do? I've ruined everything!

> [Clear explanations show everything that will be seen and heard but the dialogue.]

Revising   Compare your draft with your storyboards. If your script does not offer explicit directions for each shot you mapped out, add the necessary instructions.

𝒲G *Prentice Hall Writing and Grammar Connection: Chapter 6, Section 2*

❹ Extension Activities

Listening and Speaking   Prepare and deliver a **eulogy**—a speech about a person who has died—for Pahom. Look back over the story to recall facts of his life. Consider these tips:

- Say complimentary things about Pahom.
- Acknowledge his shortcomings in a kind or humorous way.
- Cast some of his behaviors in a positive light.

Deliver your eulogy to the class.

Research and Technology   Work with a partner to make an **annotated map** of Russia showing the location of the Bashkirs' lands. Download a map of Russia from the Internet or from a CD-ROM atlas and research the culture of the Bashkirs. On a map, label the location of the Bashkirs' lands. Beneath the map, write two or three paragraphs of your findings. **[Group Activity]**

 Take It to the Net   www.phschool.com

Go online for an additional research activity using the Internet.

How Much Land Does a Man Need? ◆ 155

---

❸ Writing Lesson

- If students are not familiar with a video script, you may wish to bring one in to class.
- Make sure students understand that their scripts should provide clear explanations of the action, camera angles, and sound effects. A person reading the script should be able to envision all of these elements.
- On the chalkboard, model creating a storyboard that contains several scenes. Annotate it with descriptions of sounds as well as sights.
- Tell students that scenes in a video need to be connected with visual transitions just as paragraphs in a story are connected with verbal transitions.

❹ Research and Technology

- Divide the class into groups. Have each group find information about the Bashkirs and their location in Russia.
- Review with students how they would find this information using a library or an online search engine.
- Have the students annotate maps with illustrations of the Bashkir dwellings and forms of livelihood.

CUSTOMIZE INSTRUCTION
For Universal Access

To address different learning styles, use the activities suggested in the **Extension Activities** booklet, p. 9.

- For Logical/Mathematical and Visual/Spatial learners, use Activity 5.
- For Verbal/Linguistic and Bodily/Kinesthetic learners, use Activity 6.
- For Visual/Spatial learners, use Activity 7.

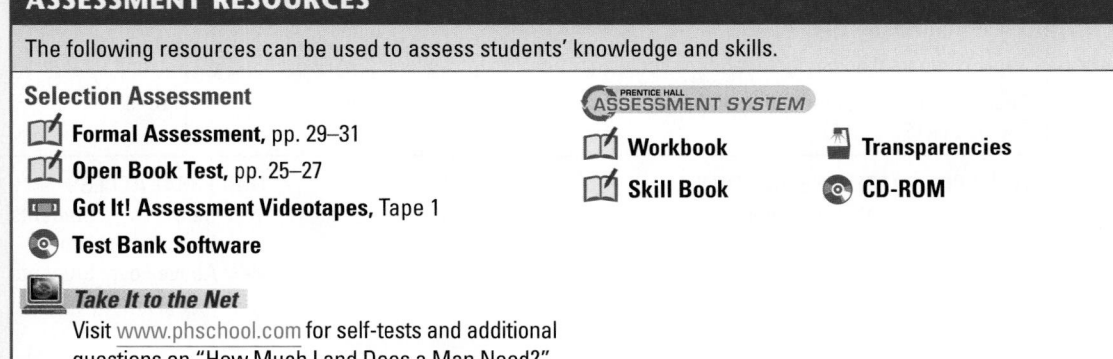

ASSESSMENT RESOURCES

The following resources can be used to assess students' knowledge and skills.

Selection Assessment

📖 **Formal Assessment,** pp. 29–31

📖 **Open Book Test,** pp. 25–27

📼 **Got It! Assessment Videotapes,** Tape 1

💿 **Test Bank Software**

💻 ***Take It to the Net***

Visit www.phschool.com for self-tests and additional questions on "How Much Land Does a Man Need?"

PRENTICE HALL ASSESSMENT SYSTEM

📖 **Workbook**   📄 **Transparencies**

📖 **Skill Book**   💿 **CD-ROM**

Success is counted sweetest ✦ I dwell in Possibility— ✦ Uncoiling ✦ Columbus Dying

Lesson Objectives

1. **To analyze and respond to literary elements**
   - Literary Analysis: Stated and Implied Themes in Poetry
   - Comparing Literary Works
2. **To read, comprehend, analyze, and critique poems**
   - Reading Strategy: Drawing Inferences
   - Review and Assess questions
   - Assessment Practice (ATE)
3. **To develop word analysis skills, fluency, and systematic vocabulary**
   - Vocabulary Development Lesson: Latin Prefix: *im-*
4. **To understand and apply written and oral language conventions**
   - Spelling Strategy
   - Grammar Lesson: Subject and Verb Agreement
5. **To understand and apply appropriate writing and research strategies**
   - Writing Lesson: Submission Letter
   - Extension Activity: Brochure
6. **To understand and apply listening and speaking strategies**
   - Extension Activity: Informal Debate

STEP-BY-STEP TEACHING GUIDE	PACING GUIDE
PRETEACH	
Motivate Students and Provide Background	
Use the Motivation activity (ATE p. 156)	5 min.
Read and discuss the Preview material and Background information (SE/ATE p. 156) **A**	5 min.
Introduce the Concepts	
Introduce the Literary Analysis and Reading Strategy (SE/ATE p. 157) **A**	15 min.
Pronounce the vocabulary words and read their definitions (SE p. 157)	5 min.
TEACH	
Monitor Comprehension	
Informally monitor comprehension by circulating while students read independently or in groups **A**	10 min.
Develop vocabulary with Vocabulary notes (SE pp. 159, 162)	as students read
Develop Understanding	
Develop students' understanding of stated and implied themes with the Literary Analysis annotations (ATE pp. 160, 161) **A**	10 min.
Develop students' understanding of drawing inferences with the Reading Strategy annotations (ATE pp. 160, 162)	10 min.
ASSESS	
Assess Mastery	
Assess students' mastery of the Reading Strategy and Literary Analysis by having them answer the Review and Assess questions (SE/ATE p. 163)	20 min.
Use one or more of the print and media Assessment Resources (ATE p. 165) **A**	up to 50 min.
EXTEND	
Apply Understanding	
Have students complete the Vocabulary Development Lesson and the Grammar Lesson (SE p. 164) **A**	20 min.
Apply students' knowledge of elaboration using the Writing Lesson (SE/ATE p. 165) **A**	45 min.
Apply students' understanding of the selections using one or more of the Extension Activities (SE p. 165)	20–90 min.

 ACCELERATED INSTRUCTION:
Use the strategies and activities identified with an **A**.

UNIVERSAL ACCESS
- ● = Below Level Students
- ▲ = On-Level Students
- ■ = Above Level Students

Time and Resource Manager

RESOURCES		
PRINT 📖	**TRANSPARENCIES**	**TECHNOLOGY** 💿 🎧 📼
• **Beyond Literature,** Humanities Connection: Impressionist Art, p. 10 ▲ ■		• **Interest Grabber Video,** Tape 1 ● ▲ ■
• **Selection Support Workbook:** ● ▲ ■ Literary Analysis, p. 40 Reading Strategy, p. 39 Build Vocabulary, p. 37	• **Literary Analysis and Reading Transparencies,** pp. 19 and 20 ● ▲ ■	
• **Authors In Depth,** Platinum Level, p. 29 ■		• **Listening to Literature** ● ▲ ■ Audiocassettes, Side 6 Audio CDs, CD 4
• **Literatura en español** ● ▲ • **Literary Analysis for Enrichment** ■	• **Fine Art Transparencies, Volume 1,** Art Transparency 10 ● ▲ ■	
• **Formal Assessment:** Selection Test, pp. 32–34 ● ▲ ■ • **Open Book Test,** pp. 28–30 ● ▲ ■ • **Performance Assessment and Portfolio Management,** p. 18 ● ▲ ■ • ⬭ PRENTICE HALL ⬭ ASSESSMENT SYSTEM ● ▲ ■	• ⬭ PRENTICE HALL ⬭ ASSESSMENT SYSTEM ● ▲ ■ Skills Practice Answers and Explanations on Transparencies	• **Test Bank Software** ● ▲ ■ • **Got It! Assessment Videotapes,** Tape 1 ● ▲
• **Selection Support Workbook:** ● ▲ ■ Build Grammar Skills, p. 38 • **Writing and Grammar,** Platinum Level ● ▲ ■ • **Extension Activities,** p. 10 ● ▲ ■	• **Daily Language Practice Transparencies** ● ▲	• **Writing and Grammar iText CD-ROM** ● ▲ ■ 💻 *Take It to the Net* www.phschool.com

BLOCK SCHEDULING: Use one 90-minute class period to preteach the selection and have students read it. Use a second 90-minute class period to assess students' mastery of skills and have them complete one of the Extension Activities.

Step-by-Step Teaching Guide
for pp. 156–157

Motivation

Read aloud or write on the chalkboard the first two lines of Dickinson's first poem: "Success is counted sweetest / By those who ne'er succeed." Ask students to imagine that this is a motto on a T-shirt or a bumper sticker. After discussing the meaning of these lines—that success is most glorified when it is most elusive—ask students whether they agree or disagree with the motto, and why. You might also ask them for their own definitions of success. Tell them that each of these poems focuses on an aspect of success students may not have considered before.

▦ Interest Grabber Video

As an alternative, play "Twisters" on Tape 1 to engage student interest.

❶ Background

Poetry

The poems by Emily Dickinson and Vassar Miller are examples of lyric poetry, or poetry that expresses the observations and feelings of a single speaker. A lyric poem does not tell a full story; rather, it zeros in on an experience or creates and explores a single effect.

Pat Mora's "Uncoiling" is a concrete poem, or a poem that uses the shape of the words on the page to symbolize an idea or image within the poem.

Prepare to Read

Success is counted sweetest ◆ I dwell in Possibility— ◆
Uncoiling ◆ Columbus Dying

The Terrace at Meríc, 1867, Frédéric Bazille, Cincinnati Museum of Art

▣ Take It to the Net

Visit www.phschool.com for interactive activities and instruction related to these selections, including
- background
- graphic organizers
- literary elements
- reading strategies

Preview

Connecting to the Literature

Every day, you make judgments about your experiences: Was it worth it? Was it a success or a failure? Like you, the poets in this group explore the positive and negative feelings that accompany the struggles in life.

❶ Background

Before you read a word, a poem can speak to you through its appearance on the page. In a traditional poem, lines are grouped into stanzas, and new lines always begin at the left margin. In other poems, the shape of the poem suggests an action, object, or idea. Three poems in this group have a traditional appearance. "Uncoiling," however, may surprise you—its appearance reflects the action named in the title.

156 ◆ Striving for Success

TEACHING RESOURCES

The following resources can be used to enrich or extend the instruction for pp. 156–157.

Motivation
▦ **Interest Grabber Video**, Tape 1

Background
📖 **Beyond Literature**, Humanities Connection: Impressionist Art, p. 10 ▦

▣ **Take It to the Net**
Visit www.phschool.com for background and hotlinks for the selections.

Literary Analysis
▤ **Literary Analysis and Reading Transparencies**, Stated and Implied Themes in Poetry, p. 20 ▦

Reading
📖 **Selection Support:** Reading Strategy, p. 39; Build Vocabulary, p. 37

▤ **Literary Analysis and Reading Transparencies**, Drawing Inferences, p. 19

156

 BLOCK SCHEDULING: Resources marked with this symbol provide varied instruction during 90-minute blocks.

❷ Literary Analysis

Stated and Implied Themes in Poetry

Poems, like most works of literature, convey a **theme**—a central idea, concern, or message about life.

- In some poems, the theme is directly **stated,** and readers can find it in the title or in the lines of poetry.
- In others, it is **implied**—suggested through events, actions of a character, a speaker's words and attitude, or other details.

One of these poems by Emily Dickinson has a stated theme: "Success is counted sweetest / By those who ne'er succeed." Look for the implied themes in the other poems in this group.

Comparing Literary Works

Even when three poets write about a single idea, their work will present very different views of the concept. The speakers in these poems describe facing and overcoming obstacles. Each poem may suggest to you a unique answer to these questions:

- What does it take to succeed?
- What are the costs?
- What are the benefits?

As you read, identify the theme in each poem. You will see that each poem has a different view of success.

❸ Reading Strategy

Drawing Inferences

To understand the message or theme of a poem, you may need to **draw inferences**—reach conclusions based on evidence. You can infer the theme of a poem when it is not stated from specific details and images. For example, when you begin reading "Columbus Dying," you will encounter images of sick, starving sailors. From these images, you can infer that this poem is not about the glory of Columbus's voyage. Use the details in these poems to draw inferences about their meanings.

Use a chart like the one shown to help you draw inferences and identify the themes of these poems.

Vocabulary Development

impregnable (im preg′ nə bəl) *adj.* unconquerable; not able to be captured (p. 159)

thrall (thrôl) *n.* servant; slave (p. 162)

vertigo (vʉr′ ti gō′) *n.* dizzy; confused state of mind (p. 162)

Image	Image
Fever, scabs	Buried in chains

Inference	Inference
Sickness	Regret

Theme

Columbus regretted the deaths of the sailors he commanded.

Success is counted sweetest / I dwell in Possibility— / Uncoiling / Columbus Dying ◆ 157

---

❷ Literary Analysis

Stated and Implied Themes in Poetry

- Tell students that as they read these poems, they will focus on their *themes,* or their central ideas about life.
- Read the instruction about theme together as a class. Call students' attention to the distinction between *stated* and *implied.*
- Next, use the transparency on p. 20 of **Literary Analysis and Reading Transparencies** to demonstrate for students how to identify a poem's theme.
- Then, use the instruction for Comparing Literary Works to compare the themes in the poems.

❸ Reading Strategy

Drawing Inferences

- Remind students that an *inference* is a conclusion drawn from evidence.
- Explain that drawing inferences based on a poem's details can help students understand its theme.
- Use the inference chart on this page to give students an example of how to infer a poem's theme.
- Then, instruct students to draw inference charts in their notebooks and fill them out as they read.

Vocabulary Development

- Pronounce each vocabulary word for students, and read the definitions as a class. Have students identify any words with which they are already familiar.

CUSTOMIZE INSTRUCTION FOR UNIVERSAL ACCESS

For Less Proficient Readers	For English Learners	For Advanced Readers
To ensure literal comprehension, review the "story" of each poem with students. Have them read each poem and then tell a partner, in their own words, what is happening in the poem.	Have students read the poems and make a list of unfamiliar words. Then, help students define the words, using context clues or a dictionary. Explain that when reading poetry, it is especially important to understand every word, because each one is so significant.	Invite students to compare the different styles and poetic devices that the three poets use. For example, they might compare Emily Dickinson's and Vassar Miller's use of rhyme, or Vassar Miller's and Pat Mora's use of imagery.

 E-Teach

Visit E-Teach at www.phschool.com for teachers' essays on how to teach, with questions and answers.

160

❹ About the Selections

These poems represent the dark side of success. Pat Mora's tornado "successfully" destroys all in its path. Vassar Miller shows that in succeeding, Columbus lost his faith in the meaning of life.

❺ Reading Strategy

Drawing Inferences

• Have a volunteer read aloud the bracketed stanza. Make sure the student uses a tone of voice that conveys the violence that takes place in the stanza.

• Then, ask students which details help them infer that the poem is about a tornado.

Answer: Students might say a tornado blows branches and is characterized by dark clouds and lightning.

▶ **Monitor Progress** Help students draw inferences by exploring specific images in the poems. Ask students to choose an image they like, such as "boulders retreat like crabs," and then describe the picture and feeling it brings to mind.

❻ Literary Analysis

Stated and Implied Themes

• Have students reread the poem and make a list of the violent images in it.

Answer: Students should mention both the tornado and people's reaction to it.

• Then, ask students to infer the poem's theme based on these images.

Answer: The poem's theme is destruction.

• Finally, ask students whether the theme is stated or implied. Make sure they explain their answers.

Answer: The theme is implied through images such as the frightened woman and the tornado blowing itself out into "sound."

❹ *Uncoiling*

Pat Mora

❺
      With thorns, she scratches
            on my window, tosses her hair dark with rain,
                  snares lightning, cholla,[1] hawks, butterfly
                        swarms in the tangles.

5   She sighs clouds,
            head thrown back, eyes closed, roars
                                    and rivers leap,

      boulders retreat like crabs
      into themselves.

❻
10   She spews gusts and thunder,
            spooks pale women who scurry to
                  lock doors, windows
                        when her tumbleweed skirt starts its spin.

❼
      They sing lace lullabies
15   so their children won't hear
                  her uncoiling
                        through her lips, howling
                              leaves off trees, flesh
                                    off bones, until she becomes

20   sound, spins herself
            to sleep, sand stinging her ankles,
                  whirring into her raw skin like stars.

---

1. **cholla** (chōl′ yä) *n.* spiny shrub found in the southwestern United States and Mexico.

❽ ▶ **Critical Viewing** Compare the shape of this picture with the shape of Mora's poem. **[Compare]**

Pat Mora

(b. 1942)

Pat Mora was born in El Paso, Texas, near the Mexican border. When she was young, she spoke Spanish at home, but she did not want her friends at school to know that she did. Now, she celebrates her Mexican American heritage. "I write," she says, "in part because Hispanic perspectives need to be part of our literary heritage," and also "because I am fascinated by the pleasure and power of words." Her work shows the beauty and surprise of the Southwest's landscape.

160 ◆ Striving for Success

CUSTOMIZE INSTRUCTION FOR UNIVERSAL ACCESS

For Advanced Readers

Suggest that students read additional works by Pat Mora. Provide students with the titles listed in the Enrichment box, ATE p. 163. You may also wish to use **Authors In Depth**, Platinum Level, which contains the following selections and more:

• Remembering Lobo (nonfiction, p. 31)

• Oral History (poem, p. 36)

• Secrets (poem, p. 37)

After students have read these or other works by Mora, have them form discussion groups in which they compare and contrast the selections they have read. Suggest criteria for comparison, such as setting, characters, and theme. To extend the activity, have volunteers present to the class brief oral reports on their favorite selections by Mora.

Uncoiling ◆ 161

Stated and Implied Themes

- Ask students to describe the shape of the poem.
  Answer: Students should note that the poem looks like a tornado.

- Then, ask how the poem's shape relates to its theme.
  Answer: The shape of the poem suggests a fast, spiraling motion. It extends the poem's theme of destruction.

- Remind students that poems that use the shape of the words on the page to symbolize an idea within the text are called concrete poems.

❽ ▶ **Critical Viewing**

Answer: The funnel shape in the picture is recreated in the poem, with lines that are progressively indented. The poem looks like a tornado.

✻ **ENRICHMENT: Science Connection**

Tornadoes

Most tornadoes form between a layer of cool, dry air from the north and warm, humid air from the south. Warm air naturally rises, while cool air sinks. When the warm air rises, more warm air rushes in to replace it, causing winds. The inrushing air also rises. If the warm air rises very rapidly, it may begin to rotate. The rotating air then forms the funnel shape of a tornado. In the United States, tornadoes are most common in the Midwest in the spring months.

Invite students to do research on tornadoes as well as on related storms: monsoons, cyclones, and hurricanes. Interested students might find out what causes the different storms, why they occur where they do, what types of damage they cause, and how people take precautions against them. Students can share their information with the class by presenting oral reports.

❾ Reading Strategy
Drawing Inferences

• Have students discuss the poet's meaning in these lines. What makes no difference?
Answer: Columbus no longer cares whether the world is flat (tumbling off the edge) or round (dropping from motion sickness).

• Then, ask students to infer the theme of this poem based on these images.
Answer: The theme is that success can sometimes be meaningless.

Answers for p. 162

Review and Assess

1. Students may feel sad because of the poems' destruction and human disappointment.

2. **(a)** Rivers leap; the boulders "retreat like crabs"; women lock doors and windows and sing lullabies to their children; and leaves blow off trees. **(b)** Words that suggest freedom and power are "tosses," "head thrown back," "leap," and "spins." **(c)** Words that suggest destruction are "howling leaves off trees" and "flesh off bones."

3. **(a)** It means the storm subsides. **(b)** Other human characteristics are tossing hair, sighing, throwing her head back, closing her eyes, howling through her lips, feeling sand sting her ankles, and having raw skin.

4. **(a)** Columbus found a world and quieted his scorners. **(b)** They seem trivial compared to its price: human life.

5. Students may not believe that Columbus despaired as much as the poem suggests.

6. Students might say that the price is too high when it exceeds the reward.

Columbus Dying
Vassar Miller

His men in fever, scabs, and hunger pains—
He found a world and put to scorn his scorners.
Yet having learned the living sea contains
No dragons gnawing on drowned sailors' brains,
5 He missed the angels guarding the four corners,
And begged that he be buried with his chains.
In token that he'd sworn to serve as <u>thrall</u>
His vision of men creeping to and fro,
Gum-footed flies glued to a spinning ball.
10 Whether they tumble off earth's edge or crawl
Till dropped dead in their tracks from <u>vertigo</u>,
He deemed would make no difference at all.

thrall (thrôl) *n.* servant; slave

vertigo (vʉr´ ti gō´) *n.* dizzy; confused state of mind

Review and Assess

Thinking About the Selections

1. **Respond:** What emotion do these poems spark in you? Explain.

2. **(a) Recall:** Identify three outcomes of the wind's actions in "Uncoiling." **(b)** Which words in the poem suggest freedom and power? **(c) Analyze:** Which words suggest destruction?

3. **(a) Interpret:** Explain what is meant by the phrase "spins herself to sleep" in lines 20–21 of "Uncoiling." **(b) Analyze:** What other human characteristics does Mora give her subject?

4. **(a) Recall:** According to Miller's poem, what were Columbus's achievements? **(b) Assess:** Does the poem make Columbus's achievements seem important or trivial? Explain.

5. **Evaluate:** How convincing do you find Miller's portrait of Columbus? Why?

6. **Apply:** As Columbus does in the poem, you may question whether a particular goal is as important as you originally thought. How do you decide when the price is too high?

Vassar Miller
(1924–1998)
Although she was born with cerebral palsy and could walk and speak only with great difficulty, Vassar Miller published ten volumes of poetry in her lifetime. Her work shows the faith and courage that helped her face her physical challenges. Her first poems were typed on a second-hand typewriter that her father brought home from his office. Miller was nominated for a Pulitzer Prize for Poetry and was twice named the poet laureate of Texas.

✎ ASSESSMENT PRACTICE: Reading Comprehension

Sequence (For more practice, see **Test Preparation Workbook, p. 10.**)

Some tests may ask students to recognize the logical flow of ideas. Some sequence words are *after, until, yet,* and *but.* Have students read "Uncoiling" by Pat Mora. Then, use this sample question.

The women comfort the children with lullabies while the wind is _____.

  A blowing
  B howling
  C whirring
  D spewing

Guide students to find the key word *until* in line 19, which indicates that the lullabies comfort the children while the wind is *howling,* choice *B.* Remind students to consider all of the answer choices before choosing one. In this case, all of the answers will complete the sentence; however, *howling* is accurate in the context of the entire sentence.

Review and Assess

Literary Analysis

Stated and Implied Themes in Poetry

1. (a) Restate the **theme** of "Success is . . ." in your own words.
   (b) Explain how the battle images clarify the theme.
2. (a) Give specific details, characters, or actions that support the **implied theme** of power in "Uncoiling." (b) How does this power relate to the general theme of success?
3. (a) What details in "Columbus Dying" support the implied theme of insignificance? (b) How does insignificance relate to success in this poem?

Comparing Literary Works

4. (a) Compare the theme of success in "Columbus Dying" and "Success is counted sweetest." Fill in a chart like this one with a statement about success that you infer from the images presented in each poem. (b) How do you think Columbus would feel about the message of Dickinson's poem? Explain.

"Success is counted sweetest" ◄ **Success** ► "Columbus Dying"

5. (a) Which of the four poems presents the most positive message?
   (b) Which presents the most negative? Explain.

Reading Strategy

Drawing Inferences

6. "I dwell in Possibility—" implies that the speaker lives in her imagination. What can you infer about the speaker based on this?
7. Based on her description of their powerlessness, what can you infer about the speaker's opinion of the "pale women" in "Uncoiling"?

Extend Understanding

8. **Media Connection:** In the final moments of a televised sports event, viewers are shown the winning team and the losing team. How do the images presented by the media compare with the ideas of Dickinson's poem "Success is counted sweetest"?

Quick Review

The **theme** of a poem is its message. Some themes are directly **stated**, and others are **implied** and must be inferred.

You **draw inferences** when you reach conclusions based on evidence.

 Take It to the Net
www.phschool.com

Take the interactive self-test online to check your understanding of these selections.

Success is counted sweetest / I dwell in Possibility— / Uncoiling / Columbus Dying ◆ 163

163

❶ Vocabulary Development

Word Analysis

1. impassable
2. impossible
3. immobile
4. impatient
5. immature
6. immodest

Fluency: True or False?

1. True
2. False
3. False

Spelling Strategy

1. illegal
2. irreversible
3. impartial
4. illiterate

❷ Grammar

1. plural; have
2. plural; are
3. singular; stings
4. plural; are
5. plural; scurry

Writing Application

Possible response: <u>Emily Dickinson</u> **may have experienced** the feeling of failure. <u>She</u> **had** little contact with the outside world and therefore little opportunity to achieve visible success. <u>She</u> **may have considered** herself to be one of the people for whom "<u>success</u> **is counted** sweetest."

Integrate Language Skills

❶ Vocabulary Development Lesson

Word Analysis: Latin Prefix *im-*

The Latin prefix *im-*, a variation of the prefix *in-*, usually means "not." In "I dwell in Possibility—" the poet uses the word *impregnable*, which means "not conquerable" or "not able to be captured." Supply an *im-* word for each definition.

1. cannot be passed, crossed, or traveled over
2. not capable of being, being done, or happening
3. not movable
4. feeling or showing a lack of patience
5. not mature or ripe
6. not shy or humble

Fluency: True or False?

Explain whether each of the following statements is true or false.

1. A king would most likely want his castle to be *impregnable*.
2. Most people would jump at the chance to become a *thrall*.
3. A person with *vertigo* would make an especially good tightrope walker.

Spelling Strategy

The prefix *in-* (meaning "not") becomes *il-* before *l* (illogical), *im-* before *m* (immaterial) and also usually before *b* (imbue) or *p* (imperfect), and *ir-* before *r* (irregular). Add the appropriate prefix to each of the words below.

1. legal
2. reversible
3. partial
4. literate

❷ Grammar Lesson

Subject and Verb Agreement

Although poetry is different from other forms of writing, some basic rules still apply. One of these rules is **subject-verb agreement**—using a verb form that agrees in number (singular or plural) with its subject.

Notice how the form of the verb is changed in these examples:

Singular:	A river *leaps*.
	She *sighs*.
	He *is* cold.
Plural:	Rivers *leap*.
	They *sigh*.
	They *are* cold.

Practice Copy each sentence. Label the subject as singular or plural, and choose the correct verb.

1. The rooms of "Possibility" (has, have) many windows.
2. Columbus's men (is, are) tired and hungry.
3. The wind (stings, sting) my face.
4. People who fail (is, are) the ones who know how sweet success is.
5. The women (scurries, scurry) back to their houses.

Writing Application Write a response to one of the poems in this group. Use a highlighter to identify each subject and verb pair in your writing. Then, make sure that your subjects and verbs agree.

WG Prentice Hall Writing and Grammar Connection: Chapter 24, Section 1

TEACHING RESOURCES

The following resources can be used to enrich or extend the instruction for pp. 164–165.

Vocabulary

📖 **Vocabulary and Spelling Practice Book** (Use this booklet for skills enrichment. ▪)

Grammar

📖 **Selection Support:** Build Grammar Skills, p. 38

WG **Writing and Grammar,** Platinum Level, pp. 566–575

▪ **Daily Language Practice Transparencies** ▪

Writing

WG **Writing and Grammar,** Platinum Level, p. 287

💿 **Writing and Grammar iText CD-ROM**

▪ **BLOCK SCHEDULING:** Resources marked with this symbol provide varied instruction during 90-minute blocks.

Writing Lesson

Submission Letter

When poets or other writers send their work to a magazine, they include a submission letter explaining why the work is appropriate for that publication. Write a submission letter to accompany one of the poems in this group.

Prewriting   Brainstorm for a list of reasons that you think the poem should be published. Avoid vague words like *nice* and *good*, which do not provide enough information to distinguish your poem from any other.

Drafting   Organize the letter around the main points you have identified. Elaborate on each point by quoting from the work or describing it.

Revising   Review your letter to identify the example or detail that elaborates on each point you wish to make. If you come across a point that does not have an example or a detail, underline it and then elaborate on the point by adding more information.

Model: Elaborating to Give Information

of the damage done by tornadoes,
"Uncoiling" not only contains dynamic images, but its shape
∧

on the page mirrors its meaning.

> The additional information supports the writer's claim.

 Prentice Hall Writing and Grammar Connection: Chapter 13, Section 3

Extension Activities

Listening and Speaking With a small group, have an **informal debate** on the following:

> Success is counted sweetest
> By those who ne'er succeed.

Divide the group in two, with one half taking one side of the argument and the other half taking the opposite side. Make sure that each side supports its argument with evidence to demonstrate the truth or falsehood of the poem's theme. Use situations from life, literature, or movies as support. **[Group Activity]**

Research and Technology Learn more about Columbus's successes and failures. Prepare a **brochure** about the conditions on Columbus's ships. Use the Internet to research the ships and their crews. Find pictures of the three ships on Columbus's original voyage, and use other graphics to illustrate your brochure.

Take It to the Net   www.phschool.com
Go online for an additional research activity using the Internet.

---

❸ Writing Lesson

- Have students form small groups with classmates who have chosen to work on the same poem.
- Ask each group to brainstorm for a list of its poem's strongest qualities. For example, they might mention its powerful imagery or provocative theme.
- Make sure students can support their main points with specific details from the poems.
- Using their notes, have students draft their submission letters individually.
- Use the Business Letter rubric in **Performance Assessment and Portfolio Management,** p. 18, to evaluate students' letters.

❹ Listening and Speaking

- First, make sure each side understands the position it will defend.
- Then, have both sides brainstorm for examples to support their positions. They might mention their own experiences or the experiences of characters in literature or movies.
- Encourage both sides to anticipate their opponents' arguments and design ways to discredit them.

CUSTOMIZE INSTRUCTION
For Universal Access

To address different learning styles, use the activities suggested in the **Extension Activities** booklet, p. 10.

- For Bodily/Kinesthetic and Musical/Rhythmic learners, use Activity 5.
- For Visual/Spatial learners, use Activity 6.
- For Verbal/Linguistic learners, use Activity 7.

ASSESSMENT RESOURCES

The following resources can be used to assess students' knowledge and skills.

Selection Assessment

- **Formal Assessment,** pp. 32–34
- **Open Book Test,** pp. 28–30
- **Got It! Assessment Videotape,** Tape 1
- **Test Bank Software**
- **Take It to the Net**
  Visit www.phschool.com for self-tests and additional questions on the selections.

Writing Rubric

- **Performance Assess. and Portfolio Mgmt.,** p. 18

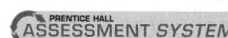 PRENTICE HALL
ASSESSMENT *SYSTEM*

- **Workbook**
- **Skill Book**
- **Transparencies**
- **CD-ROM**

from My Left Foot

Lesson Objectives

1. **To analyze and respond to literary elements**
   - Literary Analysis: Epiphany
   - Connecting Literary Elements: Autobiography

2. **To read, comprehend, analyze, and critique nonfiction**
   - Reading Strategy: Identifying Author's Purpose
   - Reading Check questions
   - Review and Assess questions
   - Assessment Practice (ATE)

3. **To develop word analysis skills, fluency, and systematic vocabulary**
   - Vocabulary Development Lesson: Latin Word Root: *-vol-*

4. **To understand and apply written and oral language conventions**
   - Spelling Strategy
   - Grammar Lesson: Past and Past Perfect Tenses

5. **To understand and apply appropriate writing and research strategies**
   - Writing Lesson: Personal Narrative
   - Extension Activity: Multimedia Presentation

6. **To understand and apply listening and speaking strategies**
   - Extension Activity: Speech

STEP-BY-STEP TEACHING GUIDE	PACING GUIDE
PRETEACH	
Motivate Students and Provide Background	
Use the Motivation activity (ATE p. 166)	5 min.
Read and discuss the Preview material and Background information (SE/ATE p. 166)	5 min.
Introduce the Concepts	
Introduce the Literary Analysis and Reading Strategy (SE/ATE p. 167)	15 min.
Pronounce the vocabulary words and read their definitions (SE p. 167)	5 min.
TEACH	
Monitor Comprehension	
Informally monitor comprehension by circulating while students read independently or in groups	20 min.
Monitor students' comprehension with the Reading Check notes (SE/ATE pp. 169, 171, 173)	as students read
Develop vocabulary with Vocabulary notes (SE pp. 170, 171, 173; ATE pp. 169, 173)	as students read
Develop Understanding	
Develop students' understanding of significant moments with the Literary Analysis annotations (SE pp. 170, 171, 172; ATE pp. 170, 171, 172, 173)	10 min.
Develop students' understanding of identifying the author's purpose with the Reading Strategy annotations (SE pp. 169, 170, 172; ATE pp. 169, 170, 171, 172)	10 min.
ASSESS	
Assess Mastery	
Assess students' mastery of the Reading Strategy and Literary Analysis by having them answer the Review and Assess questions (SE/ATE p. 175)	20 min.
Use one or more of the print and media Assessment Resources (ATE p. 177)	up to 50 min.
EXTEND	
Apply Understanding	
Have students complete the Vocabulary Development Lesson and the Grammar Lesson (SE p. 176)	20 min.
Apply students' knowledge of cause and effect using the Writing Lesson (SE/ATE p. 177)	45 min.
Apply students' understanding using one or more of the Extension Activities (SE p. 177)	20–90 min.

 ACCELERATED INSTRUCTION:
Use the strategies and activities identified with an .

UNIVERSAL ACCESS
● = Below Level Students
▲ = On-Level Students
■ = Above Level Students

Time and Resource Manager

PRINT 📖	TRANSPARENCIES 🗂	TECHNOLOGY 💿 🎧 📼
RESOURCES		
• **Beyond Literature,** Community Connection: Accommodating the Physically Challenged, p. 11 ▲ ■		• **Interest Grabber Video,** Tape 1 ● ▲ ■
• **Selection Support Workbook:** ● ▲ ■ Literary Analysis, p. 44 Reading Strategy, p. 43 Build Vocabulary, p. 41	• **Literary Analysis and Reading Transparencies,** pp. 21 and 22 ● ▲ ■	
• **Adapted Reader's Companion** ● • **Reader's Companion** ●		• **Listening to Literature** ● ▲ ■ Audiocassettes, Side 6 Audio CDs, CD 4
• **English Learner's Companion** ● ▲ • **Literatura en español** ● ▲ • **Literary Analysis for Enrichment** ■		
• **Formal Assessment:** Selection Test, pp. 35–37 ● ▲ ■ • **Open Book Test,** pp. 31–33 ● ▲ ■ • **Performance Assessment and Portfolio Management,** pp. 9, 29 ● ▲ ■ • **ASSESSMENT SYSTEM** ● ▲ ■	• **ASSESSMENT SYSTEM** ● ▲ ■ Skills Practice Answers and Explanations on Transparencies	• **Test Bank Software** ● ▲ ■ • **Got It! Assessment Videotapes,** Tape 1 ● ▲
• **Selection Support Workbook:** ● ▲ ■ Build Grammar Skills, p. 42 • **Writing and Grammar,** Platinum Level ● ▲ ■ • **Extension Activities,** p. 11 ● ▲ ■	• **Daily Language Practice Transparencies** ● ▲ • **Writing Models and Graphic Organizers on Transparencies,** pp. 17–23 ● ▲ ■	• **Writing and Grammar iText CD-ROM** ● ▲ ■ 🖥 **Take It to the Net** www.phschool.com

BLOCK SCHEDULING: Use one 90-minute class period to preteach the selection and have students read it. Use a second 90-minute class period to assess students' mastery of skills and have them complete one of the Extension Activities.

Motivation

Invite students to share what they know about Christopher Reeve and Stephen Hawking. Explain that the actor Reeve, known for his role as Superman before his spinal cord injury, and the physicist and author Hawking are both, in different ways, "locked" in their bodies. Yet, both have found unique and resourceful ways of accomplishing their goals. While being productive in their fields, they have also served as models of what physically challenged people can accomplish. Ask students what personal qualities and attitudes they think are necessary for a physically challenged person to find and use his or her hidden resources. Tell them that in the narrative they are about to read, Christy Brown discovers such resources in himself.

▣ Interest Grabber Video

As an alternative, you may wish to play "Living With a Disability" on Tape 1 to engage student interest.

❶ Background

Science

Born with cerebral palsy, Brown had no control over most of his limbs, could not talk, and had to be fed by hand. Many people assumed he was mentally retarded until one day he grabbed a piece of chalk with his left foot and scrawled the letter A. This action proved his intelligence and changed his life permanently.

Prepare to Read

from My Left Foot

 Take It to the Net

Visit www.phschool.com for interactive activities and instruction related to *My Left Foot*, including
- background
- graphic organizers
- literary elements
- reading strategies

Preview

Connecting to the Literature

Imagine having detention for five years. You could see your friends run off after school while you were trapped inside. If you can imagine this, then you might begin to understand how Christy Brown felt his whole life. Brown was able to think and feel emotions just like everyone else, but he was trapped inside a body he could not control.

❶ Background

Christy Brown, the author of *My Left Foot*, was born with cerebral palsy. People who suffer from this disorder have difficulty controlling their limbs, facial expressions, or both. Although some people with this condition are mentally challenged, others, such as Brown, have average or above-average intelligence.

TEACHING RESOURCES

The following resources can be used to enrich or extend the instruction for pp. 166–167.

Motivation

▣ **Interest Grabber Video**, Tape 1 ▣

Background

📖 **Beyond Literature**, p. 11

 Take It to the Net

Visit www.phschool.com for background and hotlinks for *My Left Foot*.

Literary Analysis

 Literary Analysis and Reading Transparencies, Epiphany, p. 22

Reading

📖 **Selection Support:** Reading Strategy, p. 43; Build Vocabulary, p. 41 ▣

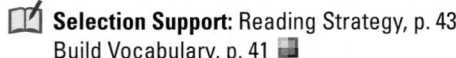 **Literary Analysis and Reading Transparencies**, Identify Author's Purpose, p. 21

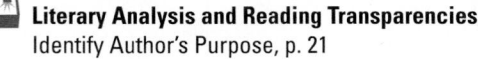 **BLOCK SCHEDULING:** Resources marked with this symbol provide varied instruction during 90-minute blocks.

Literary Analysis

Epiphany

In a nonfiction account, the writer often focuses on an **epiphany**—a moment when a character has a flash of insight about himself or herself, another character, or life in general. In this excerpt from his autobiography, Christy Brown describes the moment when he proved to his family that his physical disability had not affected his mental ability. In a single moment, Brown demonstrated his intelligence and changed the course of his life forever. As you read, notice the way the narrative builds to this critical point.

Connecting Literary Elements

Christy Brown's writing is an example of **autobiography,** a form of nonfiction in which a person tells his or her own life story. As you will see, these are characteristics of an autobiography:

- It may record personal thoughts as well as narrate events.
- It focuses mostly on the individual, not the times or public incidents.
- In contrast to a collection of letters or a diary, it is written and organized for a public audience.

Look for these characteristics as you read this excerpt.

Reading Strategy

Identifying Author's Purpose

When an author writes, he or she has a **purpose,** a reason for writing. This purpose might be to influence you to take a position, to inspire you to do something, or to make you laugh. The purpose shapes the writer's choice of language and use of details.

To help you determine Brown's purpose for writing, use a chart like the one shown here. In the first box, write all of the important details. In the next box, write your response to the details. Finally, review what you have written, and determine the author's purpose.

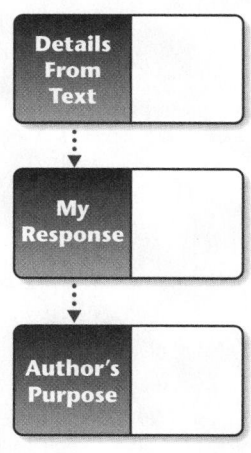

Vocabulary Development

impertinence (im pʉrt´ ən əns) n. inappropriate, rude action (p. 170)

conviction (kən vik´ shən) n. strong belief (p. 170)

inert (in ʉrt´) adj. lacking the power to move; inactive (p. 170)

contention (kən ten´ shən) n. statement that one argues for (p. 171)

volition (vō lish´ ən) n. the act of using the will (p. 173)

taut (tôt) adj. high-strung; tense (p. 173)

from My Left Foot ◆ 167

❷ Literary Analysis

Epiphany

- Ask students to share with the class epiphanies that they have experienced.
- Have students describe the prelude to the epiphanies. In other words, what events or circumstances led to their realizations?
- Tell students that as they read, they should look for both the moments that lead up to Brown's epiphany and the epiphany itself.
- Use the Epiphany transparency in **Literary Analysis and Reading Transparencies**, p. 22, to demonstrate for students how to identify the epiphany in a piece of writing.

❸ Reading Strategy

Identifying the Author's Purpose

- Explain to students that common purposes for writing are to persuade, entertain, describe, or inform. Sometimes a selection has only one purpose, and it is obvious—for example, a newspaper editorial's purpose is to persuade.
- More often, however, a selection has more than one purpose, and readers must figure them out.
- Tell students that Christy Brown has several purposes for writing. Encourage them to look for evidence of these purposes as they read the selection. Have them record their thoughts in a chart like the one here.

Vocabulary Development

- Pronounce each vocabulary word for students, and read the definitions as a class. Have students identify any words with which they are already familiar.

 E-Teach

Visit E-Teach at www.phschool.com for teachers' essays on how to teach, with questions and answers.

CUSTOMIZE INSTRUCTION
For Bodily/Kinesthetic Learners

Suggest that students pay particular attention to how Brown learns to write, as described on pp. 173–174. Students might demonstrate the technique.

❶ About the Selection

This personal narrative proves inspirational on two levels. It shows how the love and faith of Christy Brown's mother enhanced his development. Her faith was fully justified by Brown himself, a boy—and then a man—who determined he must be taken seriously. Through the nurturing atmosphere his mother created and his own drive to express himself truthfully, Brown overcame the limits of his cerebral palsy to become an artist and a writer of merit. Students may recognize aspects of his story in the lives of people they know.

❷ ▶ Critical Viewing

Answer: Brown's mother is showing pride and love. She "stands behind" him, showing that she supports him.

① from

My Left Foot

Christy Brown

② ▲ **Critical Viewing** Look at this still from the movie *My Left Foot*. Describe the feelings the actress playing Christy Brown's mother is showing in her expression. **[Interpret]**

TEACHING RESOURCES

The following resources can be used to enrich or extend the instruction for pp. 168–174.

Literary Analysis

- **Writing Models and Graphic Organizers on Transparencies,** pp. 17–23 ▪
- **Selection Support:** Literary Analysis, p. 44

Reading

- **Reader's Companion**
- **English Learner's Companion**
- **Listening to Literature Audiocassettes,** Side 6 ▪
- **Listening to Literature Audio CDs,** CD 4

▪ **BLOCK SCHEDULING:** Resources marked with this symbol provide varied instruction during 90-minute blocks.

I was born in the Rotunda Hospital on June 5th, 1932. There were nine children before me and twelve after me, so I myself belong to the middle group. Out of this total of twenty-two, seventeen lived, four died in infancy, leaving thirteen still to hold the family fort.

Mine was a difficult birth, I am told. Both mother and son almost died. A whole army of relations queued up[1] outside the hospital until the small hours of the morning, waiting for news and praying furiously that it would be good.

After my birth mother was sent to recuperate for some weeks and I was kept in the hospital while she was away. I remained there for some time, without name, for I wasn't baptized until my mother was well enough to bring me to church.

It was mother who first saw that there was something wrong with me. I was about four months old at the time. She noticed that my head had a habit of falling backwards whenever she tried to feed me. She attempted to correct this by placing her hand on the back of my neck to keep it steady. But when she took it away back it would drop again. That was the first warning sign. Then she became aware of other defects as I got older. She saw that my hands were clenched nearly all of the time and were inclined to twine behind my back; my mouth couldn't grasp the teat of the bottle because even at that early age my jaws would either lock together tightly, so that it was impossible for her to open them, or they would suddenly become limp and fall loose, dragging my whole mouth to one side.[2] At six months I could not sit up without having a mountain of pillows around me; at twelve months it was the same.

Very worried by this, mother told my father her fears, and they decided to seek medical advice without any further delay. I was a little over a year old when they began to take me to hospitals and clinics, convinced that there was something definitely wrong with me, something which they could not understand or name, but which was very real and disturbing.

Almost every doctor who saw and examined me, labelled me a very interesting but also a hopeless case. Many told mother very gently that I

---

1. **queued** (kyōōd) **up** joined a line of people.
2. **my hands . . . dragging my whole mouth to one side** characteristic behavior of a person with severe cerebral palsy, a condition sometimes caused by lack of oxygen to the brain during birth. It often occurs as a result of a difficult childbirth.

Literary Analysis
Epiphany and Autobiography How do you think Brown knows these things about his life?

5 **Reading Check**
What leads Christy's mother to notice that there is something wrong with him?

from *My Left Foot* ◆ 169

3 Background
As this excerpt begins, Christy Brown describes the number of children in his family. Out of 22 children, 17 lived. In the 1930s in Ireland, the infant mortality rate was between 6.3% and 15.6%. Brown tells readers that four of the Brown children died in infancy, a rate of 18%, higher than the national average.

As medical care has become more advanced, the infant mortality rate has declined. In 1950 in Ireland, 58 infants per thousand died. In 2001, the infant mortality rate was 5.53 infant deaths per 1,000 live births. This statistic compares favorably with those of other places in the world. The rate for 2001 in the United States, for example, was 6.76; in Kenya, 67.99; and in Pakistan, 80.5.

4 Literary Analysis
Epiphany and Autobiography
• Ask students whether they know any stories about their infancy. Then, ask them how they know about these events.
• Ask students the Literary Analysis question on p. 170: How do you think Brown knows these things about his life?
  Answer: His mother tells him about these events.
• Explain that even though autobiographies are about one's own life, writers still have to do research to tell their stories in a thorough manner.

5 Reading Check
Answer: When Brown's mother tried to feed him, she noticed that he couldn't hold his head up.

CUSTOMIZE INSTRUCTION FOR UNIVERSAL ACCESS

For Less Proficient Readers	For English Learners	For Advanced Readers
Tell students that Brown considered *My Left Foot* to be "too sentimental, too corny," compared with his other books. Have them isolate phrases or sentences that might support or contradict Brown's opinion of his own writing in this selection.	Brown often adds to his sentences many modifiers that make them difficult for English learners. Work with these students to isolate the modifiers so that they can grasp the basic meaning of the sentences.	Encourage students to examine the details of Brown's early life. What words and phrases does he use to describe how it felt to have cerebral palsy? Ask students to identify the phrases they find most powerful and to explain their choices.

❻ Reading Strategy

Identifying the Author's Purpose

- Remind students that they can determine an author's purpose by focusing on *what* the author is writing about and *how* he or she writes about it.
- Read aloud the bracketed passage, and then ask students to describe Brown's mother.
- Ask students the Reading Strategy question on p. 169: What do you think is Brown's purpose in focusing so strongly on his mother's belief that he was not hopeless? **Answer:** Brown wants readers to know the extent of his mother's faith in him. His purpose is both to emphasize her strong and loving nature and to begin to show how she would influence his development.

❼ Reading Strategy

Identifying the Author's Purpose

- Read aloud the bracketed passage to students. Have them focus on the parents' response to what friends and family tell them.
- Then, ask students the Reading Strategy question on p. 170: What do these details about Brown's parents reveal about them? **Possible response:** Brown's parents believe what they feel in their hearts rather than what other people tell them, and they are willing to act on these beliefs. They are loyal to their children and love them unconditionally.
- Tell students that one of Brown's purposes is to explain his parents' important role in his life.

▶ **Monitor Progress** As students discover Brown's purposes for writing, have them record them in a chart like the one on p. 167.

was mentally defective and would remain so. That was a hard blow to a young mother who had already reared five healthy children. The doctors were so very sure of themselves that mother's faith in me seemed almost an <u>impertinence</u>. They assured her that nothing could be done for me.

She refused to accept this truth, the inevitable truth—as it then seemed—that I was beyond cure, beyond saving, even beyond hope. She could not and would not believe that I was an imbecile, as the doctors told her. She had nothing in the world to go by, not a scrap of evidence to support her <u>conviction</u> that, though my body was crippled, my mind was not. In spite of all the doctors and specialists told her, she would not agree. I don't believe she knew why—she just knew without feeling the smallest shade of doubt.

❻ Finding that the doctors could not help in any way beyond telling her not to place her trust in me, or, in other words, to forget I was a human creature, rather to regard me as just something to be fed and washed and then put away again, mother decided there and then to take matters into her own hands. I was *her* child, and therefore part of the family. No matter how dull and incapable I might grow up to be, she was determined to treat me on the same plane as the others, and not as the 'queer one' in the back room who was never spoken of when there were visitors present.

That was a momentous decision as far as my future life was concerned. It meant that I would always have my mother on my side to help me fight all the battles that were to come, and to inspire me with new strength when I was almost beaten. But it wasn't easy for her because now the relatives and friends had decided otherwise. They contended that I should be taken kindly, sympathetically, but not seriously. That would be a mistake. "For your own sake," they told her, "don't look to this boy as you would to the others; it would only break your heart in the end." Luckily for me, mother and father held out against the lot of them. But mother wasn't content just to say that I was not an idiot, she set out to prove it, not because of any rigid sense ❼ of duty, but out of love. That is why she was so successful.

At this time she had the five other children to look after besides the 'difficult one', though as yet it was not by any means a full house. There were my brothers, Jim, Tony and Paddy, and my two sisters, Lily and Mona, all of them very young, just a year or so between each of them, so that they were almost exactly like steps of stairs.

Four years rolled by and I was now five, and still as helpless as a newly-born baby. While my father was out at bricklaying earning our bread and butter for us, mother was slowly, patiently pulling down the wall, brick by brick, that seemed to thrust itself between me and the other children, slowly, patiently penetrating beyond the thick curtain that hung over my mind, separating it from theirs. It was hard, heartbreaking work, for often all she got from me in return was a vague smile and perhaps a faint gurgle. I could not speak or even mumble, nor could I sit up without support on my own, let alone take steps. But I wasn't <u>inert</u> or motionless. I seemed indeed to be convulsed with

impertinence (im purt′ 'on əns) *n.* inappropriate, rude action

conviction (kən vik′ shən) *n.* strong belief

Reading Strategy
Identifying Author's Purpose What do you think is Brown's purpose in focusing so strongly on his mother's belief that he was not hopeless?

Reading Strategy
Identifying the Author's Purpose What do these details about Brown's parents reveal about them?

inert (in urt′) *adj.* lacking the power to move; inactive

✴ ENRICHMENT: Career Connection

Developmental Psychology

Brown's mother suspected that something was wrong with her son when he was four months old. Infants and children develop in predictable stages, conquering one developmental task before moving on to the next one.

Developmental psychologists study children's development in such areas as expressing needs appropriately, reasoning ability, and language acquisition. Have students gather information about child development stages and developmental psychologists, making a chart of their findings.

movement, wild, stiff, snake-like movement that never left me, except in sleep. My fingers twisted and twitched continually, my arms twined backwards and would often shoot out suddenly this way and that, and my head lolled and sagged sideways. I was a queer, crooked little fellow.

Mother tells me how one day she had been sitting with me for hours in an upstairs room, showing me pictures out of a great big storybook that I had got from Santa Claus last Christmas and telling me the names of different animals and flowers that were in them, trying without success to get me to repeat them. This had gone on for hours while she talked and laughed with me. Then at the end of it she leaned over me and said gently into my ear:

"Did you like it, Chris? Did you like the bears and the monkeys and all the lovely flowers? Nod your head for yes, like a good boy."

But I could make no sign that I had understood her. Her face was bent over mine, hopefully. Suddenly, involuntarily, my queer hand reached up and grasped one of the dark curls that fell in a thick cluster about her neck. Gently she loosened the clenched fingers, though some dark strands were still clutched between them.

Then she turned away from my curious stare and left the room, crying. The door closed behind her. It all seemed hopeless. It looked as though there was some justification for my relatives' contention that I was an idiot and beyond help.

They now spoke of an institution.

Literary Analysis
Epiphany What is the significance of this moment?

contention (kən ten′ shən) *n.* statement that one argues for

10 ✓ **Reading Check**

What momentous decision does Brown's mother make?

▲ **Critical Viewing** This still from the movie version of *My Left Foot* shows Brown as an adult with his mother. How does this photograph reinforce what you have learned about them in the narrative? **[Connect]**

from *My Left Foot* ◆ 171

8 **Reading Strategy**
Author's Purpose

• Have a volunteer read aloud the bracketed passage. Have students record the details that Brown uses to describe himself.

• Then, ask students what they think is the author's purpose in describing how unappealing he must have been as a young child.
Answer: Including these details underscores his mother's love, strength, and faith. She never let her son's disabilities shake her confidence in him.

9 **Literary Analysis**
Epiphany

• Read aloud the bracketed passage to students. Then, have a volunteer summarize Brown's recollection of this event.

• Ask students why they think Brown's mother cried.
Answer: She was upset because her son's condition had not improved in any way.

• Then, ask students the Literary Analysis question on p. 171: What is the significance of this moment?
Answer: Mrs. Brown is beginning to wonder whether her friends and family are right about Brown being hopeless.

10 ✓ **Reading Check**
Answer: Mrs. Brown decides to treat Christy on the same plane as her other children.

11 ▶ **Critical Viewing**
Answer: The mother's hand on her son's face and the proximity of their heads indicate closeness, caring, and trust.

CUSTOMIZE INSTRUCTION FOR UNIVERSAL ACCESS

For Special Needs Students	For Gifted/Talented Students
To help students identify the author's purpose, they can look for clues such as these in their reading:	Students will realize that one of Brown's purposes is to show how his mother influenced his life. Encourage them to study her character. Have them examine the conflict between the doctor's advice to Brown's mother and the action she decides to take. Invite them to write a journal entry or a poem that she might have written after seeing the doctors.

Clue	Purpose
silly situations	to entertain
advice	to persuade
facts	to inform
heroism	to inspire

⓬ Literary Analysis

Epiphany and Autobiography

- Ask students to describe some of the qualities of diary entries. Are diary entries usually informal or formal? What kinds of topics are they usually about?

- Have a volunteer read aloud the bracketed passage. Then, ask students the Literary Analysis question on p. 172: How is this passage similar to and different from a diary entry?
  Possible response: It is similar to a diary entry because it is in the first person and focuses on the writer's emotions. It is different because it goes on to analyze the event's significance. In addition, it is well written, organized, and grammatical—as though it were intended for an audience.

⓭ Reading Strategy

Identify Author's Purpose

- Read aloud the bracketed passage to students.

- Ask students to explain the significance of Brown's interest in the chalk.
  Answer: Chalk is for writing, which is a form of communicating. Brown wants to communicate.

- Then, ask students the Reading Strategy Question on p. 172: What effect do the details of Brown's response to the chalk have on you?
  Answer: Students are probably rooting powerfully for Brown at this point. They want him to take the chalk and communicate with his family.

"Never!" said my mother almost fiercely, when this was suggested to her. "I know my boy is not an idiot. It is his body that is shattered, not his mind. I'm sure of that."

Sure? Yet inwardly, she prayed God would give her some proof of her faith. She knew it was one thing to believe but quite another thing to prove.

I was now five, and still I showed no real sign of intelligence. I showed no apparent interest in things except with my toes—more especially those of my left foot. Although my natural habits were clean I could not aid myself, but in this respect my father took care of me. I used to lie on my back all the time in the kitchen or, on bright warm days, out in the garden, a little bundle of crooked muscles and twisted nerves, surrounded by a family that loved me and hoped for me and that made me part of their own warmth and humanity. I was lonely, imprisoned in a world of my own, unable to communicate with others, cut off, separated from them as though a glass wall stood between my existence and theirs, thrusting me beyond the sphere of their lives and activities. I longed to run about and play with the rest, but I was unable to break loose from my bondage.

Then, suddenly, it happened! In a moment everything was changed, my future life molded into a definite shape, my mother's faith in me rewarded and her secret fear changed into open triumph.

It happened so quickly, so simply after all the years of waiting and uncertainty that I can see and feel the whole scene as if it had happened last week. It was the afternoon of a cold, gray December day. The streets outside glistened with snow; the white sparkling flakes stuck and melted on the window-panes and hung on the boughs of the trees like molten silver. The wind howled dismally, whipping up little whirling columns of snow that rose and fell at every fresh gust. And over all, the dull, murky sky stretched like a dark canopy, a vast infinity of grayness.

Inside, all the family were gathered round the big kitchen fire that lit up the little room with a warm glow and made giant shadows dance on the walls and ceiling.

In a corner Mona and Paddy were sitting huddled together, a few torn school primers³ before them. They were writing down little sums on to an old chipped slate, using a bright piece of yellow chalk. I was close to them, propped up by a few pillows against the wall, watching.

It was the chalk that attracted me so much. It was a long, slender stick of vivid yellow. I had never seen anything like it before, and it showed up so well against the black surface of the slate that I was fascinated by it as much as if it had been a stick of gold.

Suddenly I wanted desperately to do what my sister was doing. Then—without thinking or knowing exactly what I was doing, I reached out and took the stick of chalk out of my sister's hand—*with my left foot.*

---

3. **primers** (prim′ ərz) *n.* small books for teaching young children reading, writing, and arithmetic.

172 ◆ *Striving for Success*

Literary Analysis
Epiphany and Autobiography How is this passage similar to and different from a diary entry?

Reading Strategy
Identifying Author's Purpose What effect do the details of Christy's response to the chalk have on you?

☀ ENRICHMENT: Cultural Connection

My Left Foot

The film version of *My Left Foot* was released in 1989 to general critical acclaim. The film, produced in Ireland, was directed by Jim Sheridan and starred Daniel Day-Lewis as Christy Brown and Brenda Fricker as his mother. Both actors won Academy Awards for their astonishing portrayals of these two inspiring people.

You may want to screen the film in class and have a discussion that compares and contrasts Brown's autobiography with the film adaptation.

I do not know why I used my left foot to do this. It is a puzzle to many people as well as to myself, for, although I had displayed a curious interest in my toes at an early age, I had never attempted before this to use either of my feet in any way. They could have been as useless to me as were my hands. That day, however, my left foot, apparently on its own <u>volition</u>, reached out and very impolitely took the chalk out of my sister's hand.

I held it tightly between my toes, and, acting on an impulse, made a wild sort of scribble with it on the slate. Next moment I stopped, a bit dazed, surprised, looking down at the stick of yellow chalk stuck between my toes, not knowing what to do with it next, hardly knowing how it got there. Then I looked up and became aware that everyone had stopped talking and were staring at me silently. Nobody stirred. Mona, her black curls framing her chubby little face, stared at me with great big eyes and open mouth. Across the open hearth,[4] his face lit by flames, sat my father, leaning forward, hands outspread on his knees, his shoulders tense. I felt the sweat break out on my forehead.

My mother came in from the pantry with a steaming pot in her hand. She stopped midway between the table and the fire, feeling the tension flowing through the room. She followed their stare and saw me, in the corner. Her eyes looked from my face down to my foot, with the chalk gripped between my toes. She put down the pot.

Then she crossed over to me and knelt down beside me, as she had done so many times before.

"I'll show you what to do with it, Chris," she said, very slowly and in a queer, jerky way, her face flushed as if with some inner excitement.

Taking another piece of chalk from Mona, she hesitated, then very deliberately drew, on the floor in front of me, *the single letter 'A'.*

"Copy that," she said, looking steadily at me. "Copy it, Christy."

I couldn't.

I looked about me, looked around at the faces that were turned towards me, tense, excited faces that were at that moment frozen, immobile, eager, waiting for a miracle in their midst.

The stillness was profound. The room was full of flame and shadow that danced before my eyes and lulled my <u>taut</u> nerves into a sort of waking sleep. I could hear the sound of the water-tap dripping in the pantry, the loud ticking of the clock on the mantel-shelf, and the soft hiss and crackle of the logs on the open hearth.

I tried again. I put out my foot and made a wild jerking stab with

---

4. **hearth** *n.* fireplace.

volition (vō lish´ ən) *n.* the act of using the will

In context Science Connection

Cerebral Palsy

Cerebral palsy is caused by an injury to the brain before, during, or shortly after birth. Christy Brown says that his was a "difficult birth," which may have been the cause of his cerebral palsy. If, during birth, the baby does not get enough oxygen or the baby's brain is injured during delivery, cerebral palsy may be the result. You cannot catch cerebral palsy from someone else and you cannot develop it later in life.

The condition may be barely noticeable or it may be extremely severe, as in Brown's case.

Scan of a normal brain

taut (tôt) *adj.* high-strung; tense

17 ✔ **Reading Check**

How does Christy pick up the chalk?

from *My Left Foot* ◆ 173

⓮ Background

Cerebral Palsy

Cerebral palsy is caused by brain damage before or during birth, resulting in a lack of muscular control and coordination. There are six different forms of the disability, depending on what part of the brain is damaged. Muscles may be flabby, or they may contract into unnatural positions. There is no cure for cerebral palsy, but physical and speech therapy can help. Brown's physical symptoms are severe, but he is one of the 75 percent of cerebral palsy sufferers without any mental impairment.

⓯ Vocabulary Development

The Latin Word Root -vol-

• Draw students' attention to the word *volition* and its definition, "the act of using the will."

• Explain that the root of *volition* is *vol,* which means "wish" or "will."

• Then, explain that when Brown's left foot takes the chalk "on its own volition," it acts on its own, without Brown's direction or command.

⓰ Literary Analysis

Epiphany

• Read aloud the bracketed passage to students.

• Ask students why Brown describes the scene in such precise detail. Answer: Brown wants the reader to know that he, as the silent child, was actually aware of all that was going on around him. Also, Brown as the adult writer wants to set the stage and draw out the suspense as the reader awaits the significant moment.

⓱ ✔ Reading Check

Answer: Brown picks up the chalk between the toes of his left foot.

CUSTOMIZE INSTRUCTION FOR UNIVERSAL ACCESS

For Less Proficient Readers	For English Learners	For Advanced Readers
Play the last scene of the story on the **Listening to Literature Audiocassette**, and have students read along. This will help them pick up on the significance of the scene. When the tape ends, ask students to explain the meaning of the story's title.	English learners might be confused by the use of the word *impolitely* in reference to Brown's taking the chalk from his sister's hand. Explain that Brown uses the word to inject humor into a tense situation. No one was concerned with manners in the midst of such a significant event.	Ask students to write a paragraph speculating about what Brown was feeling as he struggled with the piece of chalk. Make sure they trace the progression of his feelings from the moment he saw the chalk to the moment he wrote the letter A.

Review and Assess

1. Some readers may admire Brown because his determination and talent allowed him to overcome his physical limitations. Others may admire Brown's mother because her patience and faith were an inspiration.

2. **(a)** The doctors label him as interesting because his disability is so severe. They label him as hopeless because they cannot help him. **(b)** Brown's mother loves him too deeply to give up on him.

3. **(a)** He says that it is cold and gray and that the family has a fire going inside. **(b)** The description reveals that he can see, feel, and understand even though he has never been able to communicate.

4. **(a)** The incident with the chalk is the first time anyone knows that Brown can learn and that his cerebral palsy does not affect him mentally. **(b)** Brown was determined because he wanted to provide evidence of his intelligence. **(c)** Brown's determination and his desire to communicate with the world allowed him to succeed.

5. Her belief in Brown gave him confidence. Their loving relationship gave him enough affection for people to make him want to communicate.

---

the chalk which produced a very crooked line and nothing more. Mother held the slate steady for me.

"Try again, Chris," she whispered in my ear. "Again."

I did. I stiffened my body and put my left foot out again, for the third time. I drew one side of the letter. I drew half the other side. Then the stick of chalk broke and I was left with a stump. I wanted to fling it away and give up. Then I felt my mother's hand on my shoulder. I tried once more. Out went my foot. I shook, I sweated and strained every muscle. My hands were so tightly clenched that my fingernails bit into the flesh. I set my teeth so hard that I nearly pierced my lower lip. Everything in the room swam till the faces around me were mere patches of white. But—I drew it—*the letter 'A'*. There it was on the floor before me. Shaky, with awkward, wobbly sides and a very uneven centre line. But it *was* the letter 'A'. I looked up. I saw my mother's face for a moment, tears on her cheeks. Then my father stooped down and hoisted me on to his shoulder.

I had done it! It had started—the thing that was to give my mind its chance of expressing itself. True, I couldn't speak with my lips, but now I would speak through something more lasting than spoken words—written words.

That one letter, scrawled on the floor with a broken bit of yellow chalk gripped between my toes, was my road to a new world, my key to mental freedom. It was to provide a source of relaxation to the tense, taut thing that was me which panted for expression behind a twisted mouth.

Review and Assess

Thinking About the Selection

1. **Respond:** Whom do you admire most in this selection? Why?
2. **(a) Recall:** Why do the doctors label Brown as "interesting" but "hopeless"? **(b) Speculate:** Why does his mother refuse to believe this diagnosis?
3. **(a) Recall:** What descriptive details does Brown use to relate the December day at the end of this narrative? **(b) Interpret:** What does his description reveal about his condition?
4. **(a) Draw Conclusions:** Explain the significance of the incident with the chalk. **(b) Infer:** Why was Brown so determined to succeed in writing the letter A? **(c) Hypothesize:** Which of his character traits made it possible for him to overcome his physical disability to the extent that he did?
5. **Evaluate:** How did Mrs. Brown's belief in her son affect his life?

Christy Brown

(1932–1981)

Christy Brown was trapped in a body that he could not control. He was surrounded by people but unbearably alone. While his condition would crush most adults, he overcame great obstacles when he was just a child.

Brown was born in Dublin, Ireland, the tenth of twenty-two children. He wrote the manuscript for *My Left Foot* with a pencil that he held between the toes of his left foot. Later, after he taught himself to type, he wrote the novel *Down All the Days*, which became a bestseller in Ireland. In 1989, his life was portrayed in the popular and critically acclaimed film *My Left Foot*, which introduced the rest of the world to this remarkable man.

✎ ASSESSMENT PRACTICE: Reading Comprehension

Recognize Details   **(For more practice, see Test Preparation Workbook, p. 11.)**

Some tests require students to answer questions based on the details of reading passages. After students read the excerpt from *My Left Foot,* use this sample:

Which important event occurred first?

A Brown grasped his mother's hair after she read to him.

B Brown's mother decided to treat him on the same plane as the other children.

C Brown showed an interest in his toes.

D Brown wrote an *A* with a piece of chalk held in his left foot.

The best approach for answering this question is to go back to the passage and look for the details that support or contradict each choice. The event that occurred first is answer choice *B*.

Review and Assess

Literary Analysis

Epiphany

1. What event represents the **epiphany** in the selection?
2. Identify two details in the early part of the narrative that indicate the deep significance of this moment in the author's life.
3. (a) According to Brown, how was his life different after the epiphany? (b) What evidence can you find to support his claim?

Connecting Literary Elements

4. Using a chart like the one shown, list details that describe two events in the selection. For each, identify a passage in which Brown tells readers what he was feeling at the time.

Event	Narrator's Feelings or Thoughts

5. (a) Who is the intended audience of this **autobiography**? (b) What details helped you decide?
6. Do you think that Brown remembers most of the incidents he tells about in this excerpt from his autobiography? Why or why not?

Reading Strategy

Identifying the Author's Purpose

7. In addition to himself, Brown describes his mother in the most detail. List three obstacles that his mother overcomes.
8. (a) Identify a direct statement in which Brown expresses his mother's strength. (b) In your own words, describe the impact Brown's mother had on his life.
9. Using your answers to 7 and 8, as well as your own response to the excerpt, identify the **author's purpose**. Explain your answer.

Extend Understanding

10. **Cultural Connection:** Many famous and accomplished people have overcome severe physical or mental disabilities. What more could society do to support people with disabilities?

Quick Review

A **epiphany** is a moment when a character has a flash of insight about himself or herself, another character, or life in general.

An **autobiography** is a form of nonfiction in which a person tells his or her life story.

The **author's purpose** is his or her reason for writing.

 Take It to the Net

www.phschool.com

Take the interactive self-test online to check your understanding of the selection.

from *My Left Foot* ◆ 175

Answers for p. 175

Review and Assess

1. The epiphany occurs when Brown grasps the chalk and writes the letter *A* with his left foot.
2. Details leading up to the this moment include Mrs. Brown's blind conviction of her son's mental abilities and Brown's own frustration at not being able to signal that he understood his mother.
3. **(a)** After his epiphany, Brown begins to learn how to communicate with other people. **(b)** The fact that Brown wrote *My Left Foot* is evidence that he developed the ability to communicate.
4. Event: Brown picks up the chalk. Narrator's Feelings or Thoughts: He's excited but confused. He is not sure how his foot got the chalk. Event: The chalk breaks. Narrator's Feelings or Thoughts: He wants to throw the chalk down. He is discouraged and frustrated.
5. **(a)** Possible response: The autobiography is intended for families of physically challenged children. **(b)** The details about how Brown's family supported him suggest that family is the autobiography's focus.
6. Brown probably does not remember his infancy. However, he might remember the chalk incident because it was so significant.
7. Brown's mother overcomes the following obstacles: the hopelessness of Brown's doctors; the evidence that Brown might never communicate; and her own doubts about Brown.
8. **(a)** "But mother wasn't content just to say that I was not an idiot, she set out to prove it." **(b)** Brown's mother was his link to humanity. Because of her, he felt part of his family and was motivated to try to communicate with them.
9. The author's purpose is to show the importance of love and support to the development of a physically challenged child.

continued

Answers continued

10. People could take time to communicate with physically challenged children and adults. They could treat someone with a disability as they treat others.

❶ Vocabulary Development

Word Analysis

1. A volunteer works without being paid.
2. A benevolent passerby gave a dollar to the homeless person.
3. His help was voluntary; he wasn't required to give it.

Spelling Strategy

1. attention
2. decision
3. mathematician

Fluency: Word Meanings

1. c
2. a
3. b
4. c
5. b
6. c

❷ Grammar

1. Brown <u>had</u> always <u>known</u> he (was) different.
2. He (wanted) to be like the others.
3. His mother regularly (read) to him from the books that he <u>had received</u> for Christmas.
4. Even though doctors <u>had offered</u> no hope, his mother (continued) to believe in him.
5. Christy (copied) what they <u>had written</u>.

Writing Application

1. I had seen Arthur before I saw Susan.
2. Mark had already eaten, so we ate without him.
3. We walked the same path we had walked yesterday.

Integrate Language Skills

❶ Vocabulary Development Lesson

Word Analysis: Latin Root -vol-

The root of *volition* is *-vol-*, which means "wish" or "will." Brown's foot apparently grabs the chalk of its own *volition*, or free will. For each word that follows, write a sentence in which the word is defined.

1. volunteer
2. benevolent
3. voluntary

Spelling Strategy

A *shun* sound at the end of a word may be spelled in one of four ways: *contention*, *suspicion*, *dimension*, or *electrician*. Complete each word with the correct spelling of the *shun* sound.

1. atten ____
2. deci ____
3. mathemati ____

❷ Grammar Lesson

Past and Past Perfect Tenses

The **past tense** of a verb indicates that an action took place prior to the present. The **past perfect tense** indicates a past action that was completed before another action that took place in the past. It is formed with *had* and the past participle of a verb (the form ending in *-ed* or an irregular ending such as *-n* or *-t*). In the following sentences, note that the action of the underlined past perfect tense verbs was completed before the action of the italicized past tense verbs.

> Then I *looked* up and *became* aware that everyone <u>had stopped talking.</u>

> I <u>had</u> never <u>seen</u> anything like it before, and it *showed* up on the black slate so well.

W̶G̶ *Prentice Hall Writing and Grammar Connection: Chapter 22, Section 1*

Fluency: Word Meanings

On your paper, choose the letter of the word that best completes each sentence.

1. An *inert* ingredient is (a) important, (b) strong, (c) inactive.
2. A *taut* rope is (a) tight, (b) loose, (c) uncut.
3. A person with strong *convictions* (a) gives up easily, (b) stands by his or her beliefs, (c) is intelligent.
4. When interacting with other people, an *impertinent* person often generates (a) attraction, (b) boredom, (c) anger.
5. A *contention* is often raised by (a) a doctor, (b) a lawyer, (c) a gardener.
6. When people act on their own *volition*, they (a) do what they are told, (b) do nothing, (c) do what they want.

Practice Copy each of these sentences. Circle the verbs in the past tense, and underline the verbs in the past perfect tense.

1. Brown had always known he was different.
2. He wanted to be like the others.
3. His mother regularly read to him from the books that he had received for Christmas.
4. Even though doctors had offered no hope, his mother continued to believe in him.
5. Christy copied what they had written.

Writing Application Write three sentences using the verbs *see*, *eat*, and *walk*. In each sentence, use one verb in the past tense and another verb in the past perfect tense.

TEACHING RESOURCES

The following resources can be used to enrich or extend the instruction for pp. 176–177.

Vocabulary

📖 **Vocabulary and Spelling Practice Book**
(Use this booklet for skills enrichment.)

Grammar

📖 **Selection Support:** Build Grammar Skills, p. 42

W̶G̶ **Writing and Grammar,** Platinum Level, p. 520 ▦

📄 **Daily Language Practice Transparencies**

Writing

W̶G̶ **Writing and Grammar,** Platinum Level, p. 203

🔘 **Writing and Grammar iText CD-ROM** ▦

📄 **Writing Models and Graphic Organizers on Transparencies,** pp. 17–23

▦ **BLOCK SCHEDULING:** Resources marked with this symbol provide varied instruction during 90-minute blocks.

❸ Writing Lesson

Personal Narrative

The significant moment that Christy Brown describes shaped his whole life. Choose a significant moment from your life, and write a personal narrative about it. In your writing, explain how one event or condition leads to others.

Prewriting   Once you have identified the events to be included, map out the relationship between them visually. Use a chart like the one below to show the cause-and-effect relationship between events.

Model: Showing Cause and Effect

1	2	3	4	5
Failed in tryouts for basketball team	Dad took me to soccer game	Talked to some players after the game	Decided to try out for soccer	Made the team

Drafting   As you write, refer to your prewriting notes to make sure you connect related events. Use terms such as *because, consequently, as a result,* and *so* to show cause-and-effect relationships.

Revising   Read your draft, and mark places where you have not clearly established the cause-and-effect relationship between events. Add words or phrases that will clarify the relationship.

W𝒢 *Prentice Hall Writing and Grammar Connection: Chapter 10, Section 2*

❹ Extension Activities

Listening and Speaking   Suppose that Brown could clearly express his thoughts and feelings after writing the letter A. Improvise a **speech** that he might have spoken to his family.

- Keep in mind the years he suffered in silence, when people believed that he was mentally challenged and not aware of his surroundings.
- Show the emotion he must have felt when he was able to communicate for the first time.

Present your speech to the class.

Research and Technology   With a partner, create a **multimedia presentation** about cerebral palsy. Use computer software to prepare charts and graphs showing statistics about cerebral palsy. To build audience interest, obtain a video copy of the movie *My Left Foot*, and show the scenes described in this selection. **[Group Activity]**

 Take It to the Net   www.phschool.com

Go online for an additional research activity using the Internet.

---

❸ Writing Lesson

- Have students brainstorm for a list of significant moments in their lives. Tell them to think about important things they've learned or influential people they've met.
- Then, have students use a cause-and-effect chart like the one shown to determine the events that led up to the significant moment. Remind them that a *cause* is something that brings about a result, or an *effect*.
- Use the Writing Lesson to help students draft and revise their personal narratives.
- Use the rubric for Narration: Autobiographical Narrative, p. 9 in **Performance Assessment and Portfolio Management,** to assess students' work.

❹ Listening and Speaking

- Have students generate a list of emotions that Brown must have felt before he was able to communicate.
- Then, instruct them to organize their speeches around the two or three most powerful emotions on their list.
- Encourage them to end their speech by contrasting Brown's earlier emotions with those inspired by his breakthrough.
- Have students use the rubric for Speaking: Delivering a Descriptive Presentation, p. 29 in **Performance Assessment and Portfolio Management.**

CUSTOMIZE INSTRUCTION
For Universal Access

To address different learning styles, use the activities suggested in the **Extension Activities** booklet, p. 11.

- For Visual/Spatial learners, use Activity 5.
- For Interpersonal and Verbal/Linguistic learners, use Activity 6.
- For Visual/Spatial and Verbal/Linguistic learners, use Activity 7.

Connections

CONNECTIONS
Literature and Media
Daniel Day-Lewis Plays Christy Brown

It takes preparation, research, and talent to play a part in a movie. Just ask the actor Daniel Day-Lewis, who brilliantly transformed himself into Christy Brown in the 1989 film *My Left Foot,* based on Brown's autobiography. Day-Lewis worked tirelessly to perfect the difficult role and effectively portray Brown, the Irishman who overcame severe physical limitations and became an inspiration to everyone with whom he came into contact.

Careful Selection of Roles

Before they take a part and sign to do a movie, all actors set parameters about which roles they will choose. Some actors select roles because they mirror their own lives in some way, and others choose roles vastly different from their own experiences. In the role of Christy Brown, Day-Lewis saw the chance to detach himself from what was familiar to him.

". . . I'm attracted to people at some distance from my own life and other characters I've done," Day-Lewis said in a 1989 interview. "I most enjoy the loss of the self. That can only be achieved through detailed understanding of another life—not by limping and growing a mustache."

Wide Spectrum of Parts

Over his career, which has spanned nearly twenty years, Day-Lewis has appeared in seventeen motion pictures. From playing a boxer to a frontiersman to a quadriplegic, Day-Lewis has always been fascinated by parts that stretch the boundaries of his imagination.

"I suppose I have a highly developed capacity for self-delusion, so it's no problem for me to believe that I'm somebody else," Day-Lewis said in a 1985 interview.

A Role With Meaning

As he began reading the script for My *Left Foot*, Day-Lewis knew Brown was a good role for him. He was drawn to Brown because of the qualities the role demanded of the actor. However, he was also impressed by the message of the story: Brown forced nondisabled people to recognize that those who have physical disabilities possess their own strength and beauty. It was these attributes that Day-Lewis wanted to communicate in his portrayal of Brown.

"Christy gave me great license to say what I really thought," Day-Lewis said in a 1990 interview. "People have such firmly rooted fears of disability, of confronting something that offends our sense of order and aesthetic beauty. It's only the disabled people themselves that force us to confront that, and Christy was one of the pioneers."

Preparing for Christy Brown

Even though Daniel Day-Lewis had taken on many roles that pushed him to physical extremes, no part put more demands on his body than that of Christy Brown. To get into character, Day-Lewis spent two months in a clinic for the disabled, working with children afflicted with cerebral palsy. On the set of the movie, Day-Lewis spent six weeks twisted up in a wheelchair, eating only when others fed him. During this time, his only form of communication was grunts. Day-Lewis learned, just as Brown had had to, to write and paint with his left foot. In fact, many of the paintings shown in the film were painted by Day-Lewis.

When the film was released, it received positive reviews from audiences and critics. Day-Lewis's performance won him the Academy Award for Best Actor in 1989.

Connecting Literature and Media

1. What are the special challenges of playing the role of Christy Brown?
2. If you were trying out for a part in a movie, how would you prepare for and research the role?

Connections ◆ *179*

A Visit to Grandmother

Lesson Objectives

1. To analyze and respond to literary elements
- Literary Analysis: Characterization
- Connecting Literary Elements: Static and Dynamic Characters

2. To read, comprehend, analyze, and critique a short story
- Reading Strategy: Clarifying
- Reading Check questions
- Review and Assess questions
- Assessment Practice (ATE)

3. To develop word analysis skills, fluency, and systematic vocabulary
- Vocabulary Development Lesson: Latin Word Origins: *ventured*

4. To understand and apply written and oral language conventions
- Spelling Strategy
- Grammar Lesson: Progressive Verb Tenses

5. To understand and apply appropriate writing and research strategies
- Writing Lesson: Firsthand Biography
- Extension Activity: Conflict-Resolution Workshop

6. To understand and apply listening and speaking strategies
- Extension Activity: Oral Anecdote

STEP-BY-STEP TEACHING GUIDE	PACING GUIDE
PRETEACH	
Motivate Students and Provide Background	
Use the Motivation activity (ATE p. 180)	5 min.
Read and discuss the Preview material and Background information (SE/ATE p. 180) 🅰	5 min.
Introduce the Concepts	
Introduce the Literary Analysis and Reading Strategy (SE/ATE p. 181) 🅰	15 min.
Pronounce the vocabulary words and read their definitions (SE p. 181)	5 min.
TEACH	
Monitor Comprehension	
Informally monitor comprehension by circulating while students read independently or in groups 🅰	20 min.
Monitor students' comprehension with the Reading Check notes (SE/ATE pp. 183, 185, 187, 189)	as students read
Develop vocabulary with Vocabulary notes (SE pp. 183, 184, 190; ATE p. 183)	as students read
Develop Understanding	
Develop students' understanding of characterization with the Literary Analysis annotations (SE pp. 183, 186, 187, 188, 189; ATE pp. 181, 183, 184, 186, 187, 188, 189) 🅰	10 min.
Develop students' understanding of clarifying with the Reading Strategy annotations (SE pp. 185, 187; ATE pp. 185, 187, 189)	10 min.
ASSESS	
Assess Mastery	
Assess students' mastery of the Reading Strategy and Literary Analysis by having them answer the Review and Assess questions (SE/ATE p. 191)	20 min.
Use one or more of the print and media Assessment Resources (ATE p. 193) 🅰	up to 50 min.
EXTEND	
Apply Understanding	
Have students complete the Vocabulary Development Lesson and the Grammar Lesson (SE p. 192) 🅰	20 min.
Apply students' knowledge of providing examples using the Writing Lesson (SE/ATE p. 193) 🅰	45 min.
Apply students' understanding using one or more of the Extension Activities (SE p. 193)	20–90 min.

 ACCELERATED INSTRUCTION:
Use the strategies and activities identified with an 🅰.

UNIVERSAL ACCESS
- ● = Below Level Students
- ▲ = On-Level Students
- ■ = Above Level Students

Time and Resource Manager

RESOURCES		
PRINT 📖	**TRANSPARENCIES**	**TECHNOLOGY** 💿 🎧 📼
• **Beyond Literature**, Career Connection: Performing Arts, p. 12 ▲ ■		• **Interest Grabber Video**, Tape 1 ● ▲ ■
• **Selection Support Workbook:** ● ▲ ■ Literary Analysis, p. 48 Reading Strategy, p. 47 Build Vocabulary, p. 45	• **Literary Analysis and Reading Transparencies**, pp. 23 and 24 ● ▲ ■	
		• **Listening to Literature** ● ▲ ■ Audiocassettes, Side 7 Audio CDs, CD 5
• **Literatura en español** ● ▲ • **Literary Analysis for Enrichment** ■		
• **Formal Assessment:** Selection Test, pp. 38–40 ● ▲ ■ • **Open Book Test**, pp. 34–36 ● ▲ ■ • **Performance Assessment and Portfolio Management**, p. 28 ● ▲ ■ • **PRENTICE HALL ASSESSMENT SYSTEM** ● ▲ ■	• **PRENTICE HALL ASSESSMENT SYSTEM** ● ▲ ■ Skills Practice Answers and Explanations on Transparencies	• **Test Bank Software** ● ▲ ■ • **Got It! Assessment Videotapes**, Tape 1 ● ▲
• **Selection Support Workbook:** ● ▲ ■ Build Grammar Skills, p. 46 • **Writing and Grammar**, Platinum Level ● ▲ ■ • **Extension Activities**, p. 12 ● ▲ ■	• **Daily Language Practice Transparencies** ● ▲ • **Writing Models and Graphic Organizers on Transparencies**, p. 75 ● ▲ ■	• **Writing and Grammar iText CD-ROM** ● ▲ ■ 🖥️ *Take It to the Net* www.phschool.com

BLOCK SCHEDULING: Use one 90-minute class period to preteach the selection and have students read it. Use a second 90-minute class period to assess students' mastery of skills and have them complete one of the Extension Activities.

Step-by-Step Teaching Guide for pp. 180–181

Motivation

Ask students to name a book they've read or a TV show or movie they've seen that deals with a problem between a parent or adult family member and a teenager. Encourage students to share their thoughts about the book or show and to explain how the conflict did—or didn't—get resolved. Did students agree with the resolution? Point out that some parent-child conflicts continue into adulthood, when the child already has children of his or her own. Tell students that this kind of conflict is at the heart of "A Visit to Grandmother."

▣ Interest Grabber Video

As an alternative, you may wish to play "Reunions" on Tape 1 to engage student interest.

❶ Background

Technology

Let students know that part of this story takes place before many people had automobiles, and real horsepower was still common. The first "self-propelled vehicle" was built in France in 1789; its top speed was three miles per hour (an average person's walking speed). Advances in technology were slow to occur until the 1880s in Germany, when Gottlieb Daimler and Karl Benz produced gas-powered vehicles. In the 1890s, the first so-called horseless buggies began to appear in the United States. In 1913, Henry Ford began to mass-produce cars, and the average American soon took to the road. American auto sales were 4,000 in 1900; 896,000 in 1915; 1,135,000 in 1932; and 8.5 million in 1997.

Prepare to Read

A Visit to Grandmother

Spring Fever, 1978 From the Profile Part I: The Twenties series (Mecklenburg County), Collage on board, 7 x 9 3/8" Private Collection, ©Romare Bearden Foundation/Licensed by VAGA, New York, NY

▣ Take It to the Net

Visit www.phschool.com for interactive activities and instruction related to "A Visit to Grandmother," including

- background
- graphic organizers
- literary elements
- reading strategies

Preview

Connecting to the Literature

It makes no difference whether a family has two members or ten—there are always misunderstandings and disagreements. Through a confrontation, the family members in "A Visit to Grandmother" gain a better understanding of one another.

❶ Background

In "A Visit to Grandmother," one character sweet-talks his mother into taking a hair-raising ride with a wild horse and a borrowed buggy. Today, a character might suggest a spin in a new car, but in the late 1920s the automobile was still a novelty in the rural South, where this story takes place. The horse and buggy was not just transportation but was as much a status symbol as a sports car.

180 ◆ *Striving for Success*

TEACHING RESOURCES

The following resources can be used to enrich or extend the instruction for pp. 180–181.

Motivation
▣ **Interest Grabber Video,** Tape 1

Background
📖 **Beyond Literature,** p. 12 ▣

▣ Take It to the Net
Visit www.phschool.com for background and hotlinks for "A Visit to Grandmother."

Literary Analysis
📄 **Literary Analysis and Reading Transparencies,** Characterization, p. 24 ▣

Reading
📖 **Selection Support:** Reading Strategy, p. 47; Build Vocabulary, p. 45

📄 **Literary Analysis and Reading Transparencies,** Clarify, p. 23

▣ **BLOCK SCHEDULING:** Resources marked with this symbol provide varied instruction during 90-minute blocks.

Literary Analysis

Characterization

Characterization is the way a writer brings characters to life. Sometimes, writers use **direct characterization,** directly telling you about the character's personality. More frequently, writers use **indirect characterization,** revealing personality traits through the character's thoughts, words, and actions, as well as through other characters' comments. In this excerpt, the author uses indirect characterization to show one character's kindness:

> . . . when people ventured timidly into his office, it took only a
> few words from him to make them relax, and even laugh.

Notice details in this story—thoughts, actions, and reactions, as well as direct statements—that bring the characters to life.

Connecting Literary Elements

Part of a story's characterization is the growth each character demonstrates as a result of story events. Characters in a story can be either **static** or **dynamic.**

- A **static character** stays essentially the same throughout the story.
- A **dynamic character** is changed by story events.

As you read "A Visit to Grandmother," determine which characters are static and which are dynamic.

Reading Strategy

Clarifying

To avoid confusion when you read, **clarify**—check your understanding of—anything you do not understand. Use these techniques:

- Read ahead for more information.
- Read back to review what you have already learned.
- Define relationships among characters.

Use a family tree chart like the one shown to help you clarify the relationships among characters in this story.

Family Tree

Mama
Charles
Chig

Vocabulary Development

ventured (ven´ chərd) *v.* took a risk; went tentatively (p. 183)

indulgence (in dul´ jəns) *n.* leniency; forgiveness (p. 183)

grimacing (grim´ is iŋ) *v.* making a twisted or distorted facial expression (p. 184)

lacquered (lak´ ərd) *adj.* coated with varnish made from shellac or resin (p. 190)

A Visit to Grandmother ◆ 181

② Literary Analysis

Characterization

- Clarify for students that *direct characterization* involves making explicit statements about a character's personality and traits. Indirect characterization involves revealing a character's personality through his or her actions, thoughts, dialogue, and interaction with other characters, as well as other characters' thoughts and comments about that character.

- Have students discuss ways in which the example of indirect characterization could be rewritten as a form of direct characterization.

③ Reading Strategy

Clarifying

- Explain to students that *clarifying* involves refining their understanding of a story as they read.

- Students should reread relevant sections, read ahead, and define relationships between characters in order to help them fully understand what has happened in a story or why it has happened.

- Encourage students to create family trees for different characters in this selection and to fill them in as they read.

- Let students know that boxes for characters who are married to one of Mama's children should appear in a separate box joined with a horizontal line to the spouse's box.

Vocabulary Development

- Pronounce each vocabulary word for students, and read the definitions as a class. Have students identify any words with which they are already familiar.

CUSTOMIZE INSTRUCTION FOR UNIVERSAL ACCESS

For Less Proficient Readers	For English Learners	For Advanced Readers
Students might have difficulty with the dialect in which some of the dialogue in this selection is written. Having them listen to the recording of the story as they follow the text will aid in their comprehension.	Point out that the dialogue is written as informal speech and is often not standard English. Assist students in restating these ideas in standard English. Have students follow the text as they listen to a recording of the story to aid comprehension.	Suggest that students select a section of the story and rewrite it in dialect to reflect the grandmother's point of view. Advise them to use the characterizations presented in the story to write the story from the grandmother's first-person perspective.

 E-Teach

Visit E-Teach at www.phschool.com for teachers' essays on how to teach, with questions and answers.

Step-by-Step Teaching Guide for pp. 182–190

CUSTOMIZE INSTRUCTION
For Visual/Spatial Learners

Have students preview the illustrations on pages 182, 185, and 188. Ask them what expectations these pictures create about the characters and their way of life.

❶ About the Selection

This story shows how old grievances and tensions within a family can persist through the years, affecting even the most capable and accomplished people. Dr. Charles Dunford has achieved much in his life, and has applied his intelligence, determination, and empathy to serve others. Yet even as an adult, he is not exempt from the emotional burdens of sibling rivalry and feelings of rejection. When his bitter feelings finally emerge, the result is a shock to his family, including his admiring son.

❷ Background

Art

Strong Steady Hands by Alonzo Adams

Alonzo Adams was born in Harlem in New York City in 1961. As a painter, he specializes in capturing everyday scenes associated with contemporary African American life. Students might be interested to know that Bill Cosby, Jesse Jackson, Maya Angelou, and former Senator Bill Bradley all own works by Adams. Use these questions for discussion:

1. What personal quality might the woman in the picture share with the grandmother in the story?
   Answer: The woman shows strength and patience in finishing her task. The grandmother shows strength when she tells Chig she doesn't need help.

2. How would this painting be different without the quilt?
   Answer: The quilt is what makes the painting beautiful. Without it, the painting would be dull and dark.

❸ ▶ Critical Viewing

Answer: The woman seems patient, gentle, and wise.

Strong Steady Hands, Alonzo Adams

❸ ▲ **Critical Viewing** What "grandmotherly" qualities does this woman appear to have? As you read, compare and contrast Chig's grandmother with this woman. **[Compare and Contrast]**

182 ◆ Striving for Success

TEACHING RESOURCES

The following resources can be used to enrich or extend the instruction for pp. 182–190.

Literary Analysis

📖 **Writing Models and Graphic Organizers on Transparencies,** p. 75 ▪

📕 **Selection Support:** Literary Analysis, p. 48

Reading

🎧 **Listening to Literature Audiocassettes,** Side 7 ▪

💿 **Listening to Literature Audio CDs,** CD 5 ▪

▪ **BLOCK SCHEDULING:** Resources marked with this symbol provide varied instruction during 90-minute blocks.

A Visit to Grandmother

William Melvin Kelley

Chig knew something was wrong the instant his father kissed her. He had always known his father to be the warmest of men, a man so kind that when people <u>ventured</u> timidly into his office, it took only a few words from him to make them relax, and even laugh. Doctor Charles Dunford cared about people.

But when he had bent to kiss the old lady's black face, something new and almost ugly had come into his eyes: fear, uncertainty, sadness, and perhaps even hatred.

Ten days before in New York, Chig's father had decided suddenly he wanted to go to Nashville to attend his college class reunion, twenty years out. Both Chig's brother and sister, Peter and Connie, were packing for camp and besides were too young for such an affair. But Chig was seventeen, had nothing to do that summer, and his father asked if he would like to go along. His father had given him additional reasons: "All my running buddies got their diplomas and were snapped up by them crafty young gals, and had kids within a year—now all those kids, some of them gals, are your age."

The reunion had lasted a week. As they packed for home, his father, in a far too offhand way, had suggested they visit Chig's grandmother. "We this close. We might as well drop in on her and my brothers."

So, instead of going north, they had gone farther south, had just entered her house. And Chig had a suspicion now that the reunion had been only an excuse to drive south, that his father had been heading to this house all the time.

His father had never talked much about his family, with the exception of his brother, GL, who seemed part con man, part practical joker and part Don Juan;[1] he had spoken of GL with the kind of <u>indulgence</u> he would have shown a cute, but ill-behaved and potentially dangerous, five-year-old.

Chig's father had left home when he was fifteen. When asked why, he would answer: "I wanted to go to school. They didn't have a Negro high school at home, so I went up to Knoxville and lived with a cousin and went to school."

---

1. **Don Juan** (dän wän) an idle, immoral nobleman who enjoyed a great appeal for women.

ventured (ven´ chərd) *v.* took a risk; went tentatively

Literary Analysis
Characterization What does this detail indirectly reveal about the feelings Chig's father has?

indulgence (in dul´ jəns) *n.* leniency; forgiveness

6 ✓ **Reading Check**
What is Chig's father's excuse for driving south?

4 Vocabulary Development
Latin Word Origins: *ventured*
- Call students' attention to the word *ventured* and its definition. Tell students that the word comes from the Latin word *aventura*, meaning "a happening."
- Invite students to brainstorm for a list of English words that derive from the Latin word *aventura*. Such words include *adventure*, *venturesome*, and *venturous*.

5 Literary Analysis
Characterization
- Have a volunteer read aloud the bracketed passage.
- Ask students to characterize directly Chig's father's behavior in arranging the trip to Chig's grandmother's house.
- Then, ask students the Literary Analysis question on p. 183: What does this detail indirectly reveal about the feelings Chig's father has?
Answer: Chig's father is hiding his real reasons for the trip; he is making excuses for what he had planned all along.

6 ✓ **Reading Check**
Answer: Chig's father says he wants to go to his class reunion.

Infer

• Ask students what they can infer about Chig's grandmother from the fact that she asks Rose who's there.

Answer: Students can infer that Chig's grandmother's eyesight is extremely poor.

• What else can students infer about Chig's grandmother's life from this passage?

Answer: She is now dependent on others for many things.

❽ Literary Analysis

Characterization

• Read aloud the bracketed passage to students.

• Have students consider why Chig's father would never send him to see his grandmother. What does this suggest about his character?

• Then, ask students the Literary Analysis question on p. 184: What do you learn about Chig's father from what the old lady says?

Answer: Chig's father is not fond of his mother. Something may have happened in the past to cause an estrangement.

They had been met at the door by Aunt Rose, GL's wife, and ushered into the living room. The old lady had looked up from her seat by the window. Aunt Rose stood between the visitors.

❼ The old lady eyed his father. "Rose, who that? Rose?" She squinted. She looked like a doll, made of black straw, the wrinkles in her face running in one direction like the head of a broom. Her hair was white and coarse and grew out straight from her head. Her eyes were brown—the whites, too, seemed light brown—and were hidden behind thick glasses, which remained somehow on a tiny nose. "That Hiram?" That was another of his father's brothers. "No, it ain't Hiram; too big **❽** for Hiram." She turned then to Chig. "Now that man, he look like Eleanor, Charles's wife, but Charles wouldn't never send my grandson to see me. I never even hear from Charles." She stopped again.

"It Charles, Mama. That who it is." Aunt Rose, between them, led them closer. "It Charles come all the way from New York to see you, and brung little Charles with him."

The old lady stared up at them. "Charles? Rose, that really Charles?" She turned away, and reached for a handkerchief in the pocket of her clean, ironed, flowered housecoat, and wiped her eyes. "God have mercy, Charles." She spread her arms up to him, and he bent down and kissed her cheek. That was when Chig saw his face, <u>grimacing</u>. She hugged him; Chig watched the muscles in her arms as they tightened around his father's neck. She half rose out of her chair. "How are you, son?"

Chig could not hear his father's answer.

She let him go, and fell back into her chair, grabbing the arms. Her hands were as dark as the wood, and seemed to become part of it. "Now, who that standing there? Who that man?"

"That's one of your grandsons, Mama." His father's voice cracked. "Charles Dunford, junior. You saw him once, when he was a baby, in Chicago. He's grown now."

"I can see that, boy!" She looked at Chig squarely. "Come here, son, and kiss me once." He did. "What they call you? Charles too?"

"No, ma'am, they call me Chig."

She smiled. She had all her teeth, but they were too perfect to be her own. "That's good. Can't have two boys answering to Charles in the same house. Won't nobody at all come. So you that little boy. You don't remember me, do you. I used to take you to church in Chicago, and you'd get up and hop in time to the music. You studying to be a preacher?"

"No, ma'am. I don't think so. I might be a lawyer."

"You'll be an honest one, won't you?"

"I'll try."

"Trying ain't enough! You be honest, you hear? Promise me. You be honest like your daddy."

"All right. I promise."

"Good. Rose, where's GL at? Where's that thief? He gone again?"

"I don't know, Mama." Aunt Rose looked embarrassed. "He say he was going by the store. He'll be back."

Literary Analysis
Characterization
What do you learn about Chig's father from what the old lady says?

grimacing (grim′ is iŋ) v. making a twisted or distorted facial expression

---

✹ ENRICHMENT: Education Connection

African American Colleges

Because of the official segregation that existed during the early part of the twentieth century, Chig's father had to leave the South to get a high school education. He returned, however, for his college education, probably to attend one of the several noted colleges set up for the higher education of African American students.

Morehouse College is a small liberal arts college that has such renowned alumni as Dr. Martin Luther King, Jr., Olympic athlete Edwin Moses, filmmaker Spike Lee, and a number of congressmen and federal judges. Other African American colleges include Spelman College in Atlanta, Georgia; Howard University in Washington, D.C.; and Booker T. Washington's alma mater, Hampton University in Hampton, Virginia.

Springtime Rain, 1975, Ogden M. Pleissner

9

10 ◀ **Critical Viewing**
Compare this picture with the mental image you form of Chig's grandmother's house. **[Compare and Contrast]**

"Well, then where's Hiram? You call up those boys, and get them over here—now! You got enough to eat? Let me go see." She started to get up. Chig reached out his hand. She shook him off. "What they tell you about me, Chig? They tell you I'm all laid up? Don't believe it. They don't know nothing about old ladies. When I want help, I'll let you know. Only time I'll need help getting anywhere is when I dies and they lift me into the ground."

She was standing now, her back and shoulders straight. She came only to Chig's chest. She squinted up at him. "You eat much? Your daddy ate like two men."

"Yes, ma'am."

"That's good. That means you ain't nervous. Your mama, she ain't nervous. I remember that. In Chicago, she'd sit down by a window all afternoon and never say nothing, just knit." She smiled. "Let me see what we got to eat."

"I'll do that, Mama." Aunt Rose spoke softly. "You haven't seen Charles in a long time. You sit and talk."

The old lady squinted at her. "You can do the cooking if you promise it ain't because you think I can't."

Aunt Rose chuckled. "I know you can do it, Mama."

"All right. I'll just sit and talk a spell." She sat again and arranged her skirt around her short legs.

Chig did most of the talking, told all about himself before she asked. His father spoke only when he was spoken to, and then, only one word at a time, as if by coming back home, he had become a small boy

Reading Strategy
Clarifying What clues help you clarify whom Grandma is talking about?

12 ☑ **Reading Check**
When did Chig first meet his grandmother?

A Visit to Grandmother ◆ 185

CUSTOMIZE INSTRUCTION FOR UNIVERSAL ACCESS

For English Learners	For Gifted/Talented Students
Encourage students to express verbally their mental images of the grandmother. Have them list adjectives that describe her personality and appearance. Students should use a word web to record their ideas.	Encourage students to enlarge upon the description of the grandmother. Have them write a paragraph or two of colorful characterization that includes behavior as well as dialogue. Make sure students base their descriptions on information already in the story.

---

9 **Background**

Art

Springtime Rain by Ogden M. Pleissner

Odgen Pleissner was as comfortable in New York City as he was in rural settings such as the one shown here.

In addition to capturing the "essence" of a scene, Pleissner is known as a superb draftsman. The form and emotional expressiveness of his human figures is also admired by many critics.

Use the questions for discussion:

1. Why do you think Pleissner paints the scene from an angle?
   Answer: The angle gives a more immediate, realistic feel to the scene, as though the viewer is entering the scene.

2. How does Pleissner make the people seem realistic and capture their human qualities?
   Answer: The figures' poses make it seem as though they have been caught in a candid, unguarded moment.

10 ▶ **Critical Viewing**

Answer: Students may imagine a more urban scene, or they may say that this house is very much like what they imagine her house to be.

11 **Reading Strategy**

Clarifying

- Ask students to identify which strategies can help clarify parts of a story. Remind students that they can define relationships among characters, read ahead to find more information, or reread to review information they have already learned.

- Ask students the Reading Strategy question on page 185: What clues help you clarify whom Grandma is talking about?
  Answer: The phrase "those boys" implies that Hiram, together with GL, is another of Mama's sons.

- Ask students how they can verify their answers.
  Answer: Students can reread the passage on p. 184: "[Hiram] was another of father's brothers."

12 ☑ **Reading Check**

Answer: Chig met her once, when he was a baby.

185

Dialect

Dialect, as students have learned, is the particular variety of a language spoken in a distinct place by a distinct group of people. Dialects vary in pronunciation, vocabulary, sentence structure, grammatical construction, and use of expressions. Encourage students to name dialects with which they are familiar, as well as the specific variations attributed to these dialects.

Authors frequently use dialects in written dialogue to help establish the setting, define characters, and add color to their writing.

14 Literary Analysis

Characterization

- Read aloud the bracketed passage to students, emphasizing the grandmother's departures from standard English.
- Have students specify details of Grandma's dialect.
  Answer: Students will identify "no-good," "met up with," "brung," "I reckon" "don't rightly think," "wished I'd-a been there," "must-a been," and "mighty high-powered."
- Ask students the Literary Analysis question on p. 186: What is the effect of Mama's dialect in creating her character?
  Answer: Grandma's dialect brings her character to life, making her seem more realistic and alive. It makes her seem provincial in relation to Chig's family, especially his father, which adds to distance between mother and son.
- Encourage students to reread and identify other passages that exemplify Grandma's dialect.

---

again, sitting in the parlor while his mother spoke with her guests.

When Uncle Hiram and Mae, his wife, came they sat down to eat. Chig did not have to ask about Uncle GL's absence; Aunt Rose volunteered an explanation: "Can't never tell where the man is at. One Thursday morning he left here and next thing we knew, he was calling from Chicago, saying he went up to see Joe Louis[2] fight. He'll be here though; he ain't as young and footloose as he used to be." Chig's father had mentioned driving down that GL was about five years older than he was, nearly fifty.

Uncle Hiram was somewhat smaller than Chig's father; his short-cropped kinky hair was half gray, half black. One spot, just off his forehead, was totally white. Later, Chig found out it had been that way since he was twenty. Mae (Chig could not bring himself to call her Aunt) was a good deal younger than Hiram, pretty enough so that Chig would have looked at her twice on the street. She was a honey-colored woman, with long eyelashes. She was wearing a white sheath.

At dinner, Chig and his father sat on one side, opposite Uncle Hiram and Mae; his grandmother and Aunt Rose sat at the ends. The food was good; there was a lot and Chig ate a lot. All through the meal, they talked about the family as it had been thirty years before, and particularly about the young GL. Mae and Chig asked questions; the old lady answered; Aunt Rose directed the discussion, steering the old lady onto the best stories; Chig's father laughed from time to time; Uncle Hiram ate.

"Why don't you tell them about the horse, Mama?" Aunt Rose, over Chig's weak protest, was spooning mashed potatoes onto his plate. "There now, Chig."

"I'm trying to think." The old lady was holding her fork halfway to her mouth, looking at them over her glasses. "Oh, you talking about that crazy horse GL brung home that time."

"That's right, Mama." Aunt Rose nodded and slid another slice of white meat on Chig's plate.

Mae started to giggle. "Oh, I've heard this. This is funny, Chig."

 The old lady put down her fork and began: Well, GL went out of the house one day with an old, no-good chair I wanted him to take over to the church for a bazaar, and he met up with this man who'd just brung in some horses from out West. Now, I reckon you can expect one swindler to be in every town, but you don't rightly think there'll be two, and God forbid they should ever meet—but they did, GL and his chair, this man and his horses. Well, I wished I'd-a been there; there must-a been some mighty high-powered talking going on. That

---

2. **Joe Louis** U.S. boxer (1914–1981) and the world heavyweight champion from 1937 to 1949.

186 ◆ *Striving for Success*

Dialect

The people in this story speak in a southern dialect. Dialect is the variety of a spoken language peculiar to a region or community. Linguists, the people who study language, tell us that the southern highland dialect is directly related to the speech of North Britain in the seventeenth century. People from the Cumbria area in England emigrated to the United States and brought their speech patterns with them. In this dialect, *man* replaces "husband," *honey* is an endearment, *let on* replaces "tell," and *fixin'* to means "about to." The use of dialect in a story brings the reader right into the story and makes the characters' words seem realistic.

Literary Analysis
Characterization
What is the effect of Mama's dialect in creating her character?

---

man with his horses, he told GL them horses was half-Arab, half-Indian, and GL told that man the chair was an antique he'd stole from some rich white folks. So they swapped. Well, I was a-looking out the window and seen GL dragging this animal to the house. It looked pretty gentle and its eyes was most closed and its feet was shuffling.

"GL, where'd you get that thing?" I says.

"I swapped him for that old chair, Mama," he says. "And made myself a bargain. This is even better than Papa's horse."

Well, I'm a-looking at this horse and noticing how he be looking more and more wide awake every minute, sort of warming up like a teakettle until, I swears to you, that horse is blowing steam out its nose.

"Come on, Mama," GL says, "come on and I'll take you for a ride." Now George, my husband, God rest his tired soul, he'd brung home this white folks' buggy which had a busted wheel and fixed it and was to take it back that day and GL says: "Come on, Mama, we'll use this fine buggy and take us a ride."

"GL," I says, "no, we ain't. Them white folks'll burn us alive if we use their buggy. You just take that horse right on back." You see, I was sure that boy'd come by that animal ungainly.

"Mama, I can't take him back," GL says.

"Why not?" I says.

"Because I don't rightly know where that man is at," GL says.

"Oh," I says. "Well, then I reckon we stuck with it." And I turned around to go back into the house because it was getting late, near dinner time, and I was cooking for ten.

"Mama," GL says to my back. "Mama, ain't you coming for a ride with me?"

"Go on, boy. You ain't getting me inside kicking range of that animal." I was eying that beast and it was boiling hotter all the time. I reckon maybe that man had drugged it. "That horse is wild, GL," I says.

"No, he ain't. He ain't. That man say he is buggy and saddle broke and as sweet as the inside of a apple."

My oldest girl, Essie, had-a come out on the porch and she says: "Go on, Mama. I'll cook. You ain't been out the house in weeks."

"Sure, come on, Mama," GL says. "There ain't nothing to be fidgety about. This horse is gentle as a rose petal." And just then that animal snorts so hard it sets up a little dust storm around its feet.

"Yes, Mama," Essie says, "you can see he gentle." Well, I looked at Essie and then at that horse because I didn't think we could be looking at the same animal. I should-a figured how Essie's eyes ain't never been so good.

"Come on, Mama," GL says.

"All right," I says. So I stood on the porch and watched GL hitching that horse up to the white folks' buggy. For a while there, the animal was pretty quiet, pawing a little, but not much. And I was feeling a

---

Reading Strategy
Clarifying How does the first description of the horse compare with this one?

Literary Analysis
Characterization and Static and Dynamic Characters Up to this point, do you think GL is a static or a dynamic character? Explain.

17 ✓ **Reading Check**
How does GL get the horse?

A Visit to Grandmother ◆ 187

---

15 **Reading Strategy**
Clarifying

- Have students summarize the first description of the horse on this page.
  Answer: At the top of p. 187, Mama says that the horse looked gentle, its eyes were almost closed, and its feet were shuffling.

- Then, ask students the Reading Strategy question on p. 187: How does the first description of the horse compare with this one?
  Answer: In the first, the horse appears very gentle. In the second description, the animal is more alert and snorting like a teakettle.

16 **Literary Analysis**
Characterization and Static and Dynamic Characters

- Review the definition of static and dynamic characters with students.

- Ask students to review what they have learned about GL. Have them look carefully for any changes that occur as the story progresses.

- Then, ask students the Literary Analysis question on p. 187: Up to this point, do you think GL is a static or a dynamic character? Explain.
  Answer: GL seems unpredictable and immature, but also charming and funny. He has not changed through the course of the story up to this point, so he is a static character.

17 ✓ **Reading Check**
Answer: GL trades a chair for the horse.

CUSTOMIZE INSTRUCTION FOR UNIVERSAL ACCESS

For Special Needs Students	For Advanced Readers
Make sure students recognize that the incident with the horse occurred before Chig's visit to his grandmother. The grandmother is recounting the tale of the horse and chair to the family. Review with students what has occurred so far in the story. Suggest that they draw a time line showing what has occurred in the story up to this point.	Ask students to write a dialogue that might have taken place between GL and the man from the West. Have them use dialect to write dialogue that fits GL's character.

188

Spring Fever, 1978 From the Profile Part I: The Twenties series (Mecklenburg County). Collage on board, 7 x 9 3/8" Private Collection, © Romare Bearden Foundation/Licensed by VAGA, New York, NY

19 ▲ **Critical Viewing** What incident in the story does this picture suggest? **[Connect]**

20 little better about riding with GL behind that crazy-looking horse. I
could see how GL was happy I was going with him. He was scurrying
around that animal buckling buckles and strapping straps, all the
time smiling, and that made me feel good.

Then he was finished, and I must say, that horse looked mighty
fine hitched to that buggy and I knew anybody what climbed up there
would look pretty good too. GL came around and stood at the bottom
of the steps, and took off his hat and bowed and said: "Madam," and
reached out his hand to me and I was feeling real elegant like a fine
lady. He helped me up to the seat and then got up beside me and we
moved out down our alley. And I remember how black folks come out
on their porches and shook their heads, saying: "Lord now, will you
look at Eva Dunford, the fine lady! Don't she look good sitting up
there!" And I pretended not to hear and sat up straight and proud.

We rode on through the center of town, up Market Street, and all
the way out where Hiram is living now, which in them days was all
woods, there not being even a farm in sight and that's when that
horse must-a first realized he weren't at all broke or tame or maybe
thought he was back out West again, and started to gallop.

"GL," I says, "now you ain't joking with your mama, is you?
Because if you is, I'll strap you purple if I live through this."

Well, GL was pulling on the reins with all his meager strength, and
yelling, "Whoa, you. Say now, whoa!" He turned to me just long
enough to say, "I ain't fooling with you, Mama. Honest!"

188 ◆ *Striving for Success*

Literary Analysis
Characterization What
does Mama's willingness
to go for a ride despite
her better judgment imply
about her character?

I reckon that animal weren't too satisfied with the road, because it made a sharp right turn just then, down into a gulley and struck out across a hilly meadow. "Mama," GL yells. "Mama, do something!"

I didn't know what to do, but I figured I had to do something so I stood up, hopped down onto the horse's back and pulled it to a stop. Don't ask me how I did that; I reckon it was that I was a mother and my baby asked me to do something, is all.

"Well, we walked that animal all the way home; sometimes I had to club it over the nose with my fist to make it come, but we made it, GL and me. You remember how tired we was, Charles?"

"I wasn't here at the time." Chig turned to his father and found his face completely blank, without even a trace of a smile or a laugh.

"Well, of course you was, son. That happened in . . . in . . . it was a hot summer that year and—"

"I left here in June of that year. You wrote me about it."

The old lady stared past Chig at him. They all turned to him; Uncle Hiram looked up from his plate.

"Then you don't remember how we all laughed?"

"No, I don't, Mama. And I probably wouldn't have laughed. I don't think it was funny." They were staring into each other's eyes.

"Why not, Charles?"

"Because in the first place, the horse was gained by fraud. And in the second place, both of you might have been seriously injured or even killed." He broke off their stare and spoke to himself more than to any of them: "And if I'd done it, you would've beaten me good for it."

"Pardon?" The old lady had not heard him; only Chig had heard.

Chig's father sat up straight as if preparing to debate. "I said that if I had done it, if I had done just exactly what GL did, you would have beaten me good for it, Mama." He was looking at her again.

"Why you say that, son?" She was leaning toward him.

"Don't you know? Tell the truth. It can't hurt me now." His voice cracked, but only once. "If GL and I did something wrong, you'd beat me first and then be too tired to beat him. At dinner, he'd always get seconds and I wouldn't. You'd do things with him, like ride in that buggy, but if I wanted you to do something with me, you were always too busy." He paused and considered whether to say what he finally did say: "I cried when I left here. Nobody loved me, Mama. I cried all the way up to Knoxville. That was the last time I ever cried in my life."

"Oh, Charles." She started to get up, to come around the table to him. He stopped her. "It's too late."

"But you don't understand."

"What don't I understand? I understood then; I understand now."

Tears now traveled down the lines in her face, but when she spoke, her voice was clear. "I thought you knew. I had ten children. I had to give all of them what they needed most." She nodded. "I paid more mind to GL. I had to. GL could-a ended up swinging if I hadn't. But you was smarter. You was more growed up than GL when you was five and he was ten, and I tried to show you that by letting you do

Literary Analysis
Characterization What do Mama's comments reveal about the relationship between GL and her?

㉓ ✓Reading Check
How does Mama get the horse to stop?

A Visit to Grandmother ◆ 189

CUSTOMIZE INSTRUCTION FOR UNIVERSAL ACCESS

For Less Proficient Readers	For Gifted/Talented Students
Invite students to sit in groups, simulating the arrangement of the family members around the dinner table. Have group members read the parts, noting the facial expressions and gestures they might use as they act out this scene. Ask students why they use these gestures and what the gestures and dialogue reveal about the characters in the story.	Have students create a collage depicting the emotions of each of the characters in the story. To help them clarify the relationships among the characters, have them place images representing the grandmother in the center of the composition, with images relating to other characters radiating from hers.

㉑ Literary Analysis

Characterization

- Have a volunteer read aloud the bracketed passage.
- Call students' attention to the sentence "I reckon it was that I was a mother and my baby asked me to do something, is all." What do Mama's words imply about how she views GL?

  Answer: Mama refers to GL as her baby, which implies that she views him as a child.

- Then, ask students the Literary Analysis question on p. 189: What do Mama's comments reveal about the relationship between GL and her?

  Answer: By referring to her son as her baby, Mama reveals that she still sees him as an immature child in need of protection. She is willing to protect him even if it means risking her own life.

▶ **Monitor Progress** Ask students whether the passage is an example of direct or indirect characterization.

  Answer: The dialogue describes the grandmother's behavior, from which the reader learns something indirectly about the character.

㉒ Reading Strategy

Clarify

- Point out that the reader is about to find out what is really bothering Charles.
- Suggest that students reread in the story for passages where the author suggests that Charles has a troubled relationship with his mother.
- Then, have students read ahead to understand the source of the trouble. Ask students to identify the source of this trouble.

  Answer: Charles is jealous of GL because he thinks their mother favored him.

㉓ ✓Reading Check

Possible Answers: Mama jumps on the horse's back in order to force it to stop.

Answers for p. 190

Review and Assess

1. Some students may sympathize most with Chig, the narrator, because he is the person through whom we see the story. Others may sympathize with the grandmother because she is such a likable character. Some students may sympathize with Charles, because of his obvious pain.

2. **(a)** They are close to her home. **(b)** He wants to confront her about her apparent favoritism.

3. **(a)** Charles says he wanted to go to school, and there was no Negro high school at home. **(b)** He might have been unhappy at home because he felt unloved.

4. **(a)** He is angry. **(b)** She thinks it's funny. **(c)** Everyone except Charles thinks the story is funny.

5. **(a)** They each needed different things from her. **(b)** Students may say that Charles and his mother will reconcile their differences, and Charles may visit more often. Others may point out that Charles has been feeling resentful for thirty years, and hold out little hope for reconciliation.

6. Students may not agree with it because both sons needed her attention. Alternatively, students may agree with it because Charles didn't need as much guidance as GL did.

what you wanted to do."

"That's not true, Mama. You know it. GL was light-skinned and had good hair and looked almost white and you loved him for that."

"Charles, no. No, son. I didn't love any one of you more than any other."

"That can't be true." His father was standing now, his fists clenched tight. "Admit it, Mama . . . please!" Chig looked at him, shocked; the man was actually crying.

"It may not-a been right what I done, but I ain't no liar." Chig knew she did not really understand what had happened, what he wanted of her. "I'm not lying to you, Charles."

Chig's father had gone pale. He spoke very softly. "You're about thirty years too late, Mama." He bolted from the table. Silverware and dishes rang and jumped. Chig heard him hurrying up to their room.

They sat in silence for awhile and then heard a key in the front door. A man with a new, <u>lacquered</u> straw hat came in. He was wearing brown and white two-tone shoes with very pointed toes and a white summer suit. "Say now! Man! I heard my brother was in town. Where he at? Where that rascal?"

He stood in the doorway, smiling broadly, an engaging, open, friendly smile, the innocent smile of a five-year-old.

lacquered (lak´ ərd) *adj.* coated with varnish made from shellac or resin

Review and Assess

Thinking About the Selection

1. **Respond:** With which character in the story do you sympathize? Explain.

2. **(a) Recall:** What reason does Chig's father give for visiting his mother? **(b) Analyze:** What do you think is the real reason he wants to see her?

3. **(a) Recall:** What reason does Charles give for leaving home to go to Knoxville? **(b) Speculate:** What other reasons might he have had?

4. **(a) Recall:** What is Charles's reaction to the story that Mama tells about the horse? **(b) Analyze:** What is Mama's attitude about the story? **(c) Compare and Contrast:** How does Charles's reaction contrast with that of the others who hear the story?

5. **(a) Speculate:** Why did Mama treat her children differently? **(b) Hypothesize:** What do you think Charles's relationship with his mother will be like in the future?

6. **Evaluate:** Do you agree with the way Mama raised her children? Explain.

William Melvin Kelley

(b. 1937)

William Melvin Kelley is a man of questions. He says, "I am not a sociologist or a politician or a spokesman. Such people try to give answers. A writer, I think, should ask questions."

Kelley's questions about his own life have rarely found their answers in conformity. The title of his first book—*A Different Drummer*—reflects his belief in the importance of individuality. Kelley's stories focus on the problems of individual characters, some of whom are African Americans.

ASSESSMENT PRACTICE: Reading Comprehension

Recognize Details **(For more practice, see Test Preparation Workbook, p. 12.)**

Many tests ask students to identify details. Use this sample test item.

> Mae and Chig asked questions; the old lady answered; Aunt Rose directed the discussion, steering the old lady onto the best stories. Chig's father laughed from time to time; Uncle Hiram ate.
>
> Which family member is least interested in the discussion?

A Mae
B Chig's father
C Rose
D Hiram

Everyone is paying at least some attention to the discussion, except Uncle Hiram, who just eats. Therefore, the correct choice is *D*. Remind students to always read the questions first to get a sense of what to look for in their reading.

Review and Assess

Literary Analysis

Characterization

1. Identify one thing you learned about Charles through **direct characterization** and one thing you learned through **indirect characterization.**

2. Explain three things you learned about GL through indirect characterization.

3. Explain how the author reveals each of the details you listed.

Connecting Literary Elements

4. In a chart like the one below, list each character in either the **Static** or the **Dynamic** column. Then, explain your choice.

Static Character	Dynamic Character	Reason

5. Would you say that GL is a static or a dynamic character? Give indirect characterization from the story to explain your choice.

6. How does the presence of static characters help the author draw attention to Charles's troubles?

Reading Strategy

Clarifying

7. Explain how you **clarified** two ideas or relationships that were not at first clear to you.

8. Use a flowchart like the one here to list five of the events or actions in Charles's life that lead up to the moment of confrontation.

Charles and GL get in trouble, but only Charles is punished.

Extend Understanding

9. **Career Connection:** Describe the qualities you think are important in a person whose career involves guiding other people to communicate and resolve their differences.

Quick Review

Through **direct characterization,** writers tell you directly about a character's personality.
In **indirect characterization,** they reveal personality through the character's words and actions, as well as through other characters' comments.

A **static character** stays essentially the same throughout the story.

A **dynamic character** is changed by events or by interactions with other characters.

To **clarify,** you check your understanding of what you read.

 Take It to the Net

www.phschool.com

Take the interactive self-test online to check your understanding of the selection.

Answers for p. 191

Review and Assess

1. *Direct characterization:* Charles cares about people. *Indirect characterization:* He is somewhat secretive. He says they'll visit his mother because they're close by, but by his behavior later in the story, the reader realizes he wants to see his mother.

2. GL is funny; he's not very practical; he's childlike.

3. The family laughs when they talk about GL. He foolishly ends up with a wild horse. He panics and begs his mother to stop the runaway horse.

4. Static Characters: Hiram, Rose, Mae, and GL. Reason: Hiram, Rose, and Mae are bystanders to the action of the story. GL appears only at the very end, happy-go-lucky and childlike, as he was 30 years ago. Dynamic Characters: Charles, Grandmother, and Chig. Reason: Grandmother is grieved by Charles' pain, and tries to heal the rift. Charles is powerfully driven to see his family, and becomes a man who directly communicates long-held resentment. Chig is shocked to see his father's pain, and learns something new about him.

5. GL is a static character. All of his described behaviors are childlike and immature.

6. The static characters allow Charles's behavior and emotions to stand out in strong contrast.

7. Students may say they wondered why Charles was unhappy, but clarified that by the time they reached the end of the story. They may say they wondered why Charles really went to his mother's house, but this is clarified when he finally confronts his mother.

8. Students' flowcharts should contain events from Charles' life as he describes it to his mother, and end with his mother's anecdote about GL and Charles' outburst.

9. Such a career would require experience, wisdom, patience, objectivity, compassion, and fairness.

Answers for p. 192

❶ Vocabulary Development

Word Analysis

1. The words *navy* and *navigate* come from the Latin *navis*, which means "ship." The word *navigate* also contains a form of *agere*, meaning "to lead."

2. The words *pose* and *position* come from the Latin *positus*, a form of the verb "to place."

3. The words *matter* and *material* both come from the Latin *materia*, "matter."

Fluency: Context

1. lacquered   3. indulgence
2. grimacing   4. ventured

Spelling

1. achieving   3. including
2. storing   4. racing

❷ Grammar

1. was planning, past progressive

2. had been wanting, past perfect progressive

3. has been hoping, present perfect progressive

4. will be cooking, future progressive

5. will have been waiting, future perfect progressive

Writing Application
Possible Responses:

1. I am thinking about spring.

2. I will be thinking about soccer.

3. I was thinking about shoveling snow.

4. I have been thinking about daylight savings time.

5. I had been thinking about plowing driveways.

6. By fall, I will have been thinking about college for two years.

Integrate Language Skills

❶ Vocabulary Development Lesson

Latin Word Origins: *ventured*

It is no accident that *ventured* is similar to the word *adventure*. Both come from the Latin word *aventura*, which means "a happening." *Ventured* means "taking a risk," and an *adventure* usually involves some risk or excitement. Other related words are

event   advent   circumvent

Tracing the origins of words often reveals their relationships to words you already know. Use a good dictionary to look up the origins of the following pairs of related words. Then, explain the connection between each pair.

1. navigate, navy
2. pose, position
3. material, matter

Fluency: Context

Read each book title below. On your paper, write the word from the vocabulary list on page 181 that you would expect to find in that book.

1. *A History of Japanese Enamels*
2. *Smile Though Your Heart Is Breaking*
3. *Is Your Child Spoiled?*
4. *Business Risks in the Twenty-first Century*

Spelling Strategy

When the suffix *-ing* is added to a word ending in *e*, the *e* is dropped. For example, *grimace* becomes *grimacing*. (Exceptions to this rule are *eyeing* and *dyeing*.) On your paper, rewrite the following words, adding *-ing*.

1. achieve   3. include
2. store   4. race

❷ Grammar Lesson

Progressive Verb Tenses

Verb **tenses** show time—past, present, or future. The six tenses can be expressed in two different forms—basic and progressive. The progressive form is used for a continuing action. Here are the progressive forms of the verb *write*:

> **Present progressive:** He *is writing* a story.
> **Past progressive:** He *was writing* two stories.
> **Future progressive:** He *will be writing* it.
> **Present perfect progressive:** He *has been writing* stories for years.
> **Past perfect progressive:** He *had been writing* a novel when this story was published.
> **Future perfect progressive:** By then, he *will have been writing* stories for forty years.

Practice Copy the following sentences. Underline each progressive verb, and identify the tense.

1. Charles was planning to visit his mother.
2. He had been wanting to talk with her.
3. Chig has been hoping to go along.
4. Chig's grandmother will be cooking for days in preparation for the visit.
5. When Charles arrives, his mother will have been waiting for years to see him.

Writing Application Write six sentences, using a different form of the progressive tenses of the verb *think* in each.

W̶G̶ Prentice Hall Writing and Grammar Connection: Chapter 22, Section 1

192 ◆ Striving for Success

TEACHING RESOURCES

The following resources can be used to enrich or extend the instruction for pp. 192–193.

Vocabulary

📖 **Vocabulary and Spelling Practice Book** (Use this booklet for skills enrichment.) ▪

Grammar

📖 **Selection Support:** Build Grammar Skills, p. 46

W̶G̶ **Writing and Grammar,** Platinum Level, p. 520

📱 **Daily Language Practice Transparencies** ▪

Writing

W̶G̶ **Writing and Grammar Platinum Level,** p. 71

💿 **Writing and Grammar iText CD-ROM**

📱 **Writing Models and Graphic Organizers on Transparencies,** p. 75

 BLOCK SCHEDULING: Resources marked with this symbol provide varied instruction during 90-minute blocks.

Writing Lesson

Firsthand Biography of a Character

A firsthand biography is a narrative about a person with whom the writer has had direct experience. It can be about the life or an important episode in the life of that person. Choose one of the main characters from this story, and write a firsthand biography as if you knew the character personally.

Prewriting   Write your subject's name on a sheet of paper. Around the person's name, write words and phrases that capture his or her significant characteristics. Next to each of the characteristics, jot down examples.

Drafting   For each characteristic you want to stress in your biography, include at least one example that demonstrates that quality in your subject. Make sure you show the connection between the characteristic and the example.

Revising   Review your firsthand biography. Highlight the characteristics you have addressed, and underline examples that clarify your points. If needed, add more details to bring the subject to life.

Model: Revising to Provide Examples

Charles Dunford was a kind person. For example, when people ventured timidly into his office, it took only a few words from him to make them relax and even laugh. Even his most worried patients trusted him.

> Added support helps show Charles Dunford's kindness.

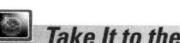 *Prentice Hall Writing and Grammar Connection Chapter 4, Section 2*

Extension Activities

Listening and Speaking In "A Visit to Grandmother," Mama tells a humorous story about a wild buggy ride. Choose a humorous or exciting incident from your own life, and tell it as an **oral anecdote**—a brief story told aloud.

- Choose the details and illustrations that show the humor or excitement of the event.
- Practice telling the story aloud for your family or friends.

Present the anecdote to the class.

Research and Technology Plan activities for a **conflict-resolution workshop** that could present strategies for working out differences. Use the library and the Internet to research strategies. Plan visual aids, such as charts and diagrams. Work with a small group of classmates to present an activity you have developed. **[Group Activity]**

Take It to the Net   www.phschool.com

Go online for an additional research activity using the Internet.

ASSESSMENT RESOURCES

The following resources can be used to assess students' knowledge and skills.

Selection Assessment

- 📖 **Formal Assessment,** pp. 38–40
- 📖 **Open Book Test,** pp. 34–36
- 📼 **Got It! Assessment Videotapes,** Tape 1
- 💿 **Test Bank Software**

 Take It to the Net

Visit www.phschool.com for self-tests and additional questions on the selections.

Listening and Speaking Rubric

- 📖 **Performance Assess. and Portfolio Mgmt.,** p. 28

PRENTICE HALL **ASSESSMENT SYSTEM**

- 📖 **Workbook**
- 📖 **Skill Book**
- 🗄 **Transparencies**
- 💿 **CD-ROM**

---

❸ Writing Lesson

- Make sure students understand the difference between a firsthand biography and a standard biography. A firsthand biography is written by someone who has had direct experience with the subject of the biography.
- Model the prewriting exercise by writing on the chalkboard the characteristics of an individual you know. For each characteristic, write an example that illustrates it.
- Remind students that they can rely on direct and indirect characterization to illustrate the characteristics they choose.

❹ Listening and Speaking

- Divide the class into groups to help students rehearse their anecdotes.
- Suggest to students that they use the Herringbone graphic organizer, p. 75 in **Writing Models and Graphic Organizers on Transparencies,** to help them organize their details.
- Ask students to present anecdotes in the group and get feedback and questions.
- Have students present their anecdotes to the class, using feedback from the small groups.
- Have students use the Speaking rubric for Delivering a Narrative Presentation, p. 28 in **Performance Assessment and Portfolio Management.**

CUSTOMIZE INSTRUCTION
For Universal Access

To address different learning styles, use the activities suggested in the **Extension Activities** booklet, p. 12.

- For Verbal/Linguistic and Bodily/Kinesthetic learners, use Activity 5.
- For Verbal/Linguistic and Logical/Mathematical learners, use Activity 6.
- For Visual/Spatial and Verbal/Linguistic learners, use Activity 7.

After Apple-Picking ✦ Mowing ✦ Style ✦ At Harvesttime

Lesson Objectives

1. **To analyze and respond to literary elements**
   - Literary Analysis: Tone
   - Comparing Literary Works

2. **To read, comprehend, analyze, and critique poems and essays**
   - Reading Strategy: Interpreting
   - Reading Check questions
   - Review and Assess questions
   - Assessment Practice (ATE)

3. **To develop word analysis skills, fluency, and systematic vocabulary**
   - Vocabulary Development Lesson: Spelling vs. Pronunciation: -ough

4. **To understand and apply written and oral language conventions**
   - Spelling Strategy
   - Grammar Lesson: Adverb Function

5. **To understand and apply appropriate writing and research strategies**
   - Writing Lesson: Advice Column
   - Extension Activity: Timeline

6. **To understand and apply listening and speaking strategies**
   - Extension Activity: Speech

STEP-BY-STEP TEACHING GUIDE	PACING GUIDE
PRETEACH	
Motivate Students and Provide Background	
Use the Motivation activity (ATE p. 194)	5 min.
Read and discuss the Preview material and Background information (SE/ATE p. 194) **A**	5 min.
Introduce the Concepts	
Introduce the Literary Analysis and Reading Strategy (SE/ATE p. 195) **A**	15 min.
Pronounce the vocabulary words and read their definitions (SE p. 195)	5 min.
TEACH	
Monitor Comprehension	
Informally monitor comprehension by circulating while students read independently or in groups **A**	10 min.
Monitor students' comprehension with the Reading Check notes (SE/ATE pp. 197, 199)	as students read
Develop vocabulary with Vocabulary notes (SE pp. 196, 199, 200; ATE p. 196)	as students read
Develop Understanding	
Develop students' understanding of tone with Literary Analysis annotations (ATE pp. 197, 199) **A**	10 min.
Develop students' understanding of interpreting with Reading Strategy annotations (ATE pp. 198, 200)	10 min.
ASSESS	
Assess Mastery	
Assess students' mastery of the Reading Strategy and Literary Analysis by having them answer the Review and Assess questions (SE/ATE p. 201)	20 min.
Use one or more of the print and media Assessment Resources (ATE p. 203) **A**	up to 50 min.
EXTEND	
Apply Understanding	
Have students complete the Vocabulary Development Lesson and the Grammar Lesson (SE p. 202) **A**	20 min.
Apply students' ability to brainstorm for topics using the Writing Lesson (SE p. 203) **A**	45 min.
Apply students' understanding using one or more of the Extension Activities (SE p. 203)	20–90 min.

 ACCELERATED INSTRUCTION:
Use the strategies and activities identified with an **A**.

UNIVERSAL ACCESS
● = Below Level Students
▲ = On-Level Students
■ = Above Level Students

Time and Resource Manager

Reading Level: Easy/Average/Easy/Easy
Average Number of Instructional Days: 4

RESOURCES

PRINT 📖	TRANSPARENCIES 🗂	TECHNOLOGY 💿 🎧 📼
• **Beyond Literature,** Career Connection: Farming, p. 13 ▲ ■		• **Interest Grabber Video,** Tape 1 ● ▲ ■
• **Selection Support Workbook:** ● ▲ ■ Literary Analysis, p. 52 Reading Strategy, p. 51 Build Vocabulary, p. 49	• **Literary Analysis and Reading Transparencies,** pp. 25 and 26 ● ▲ ■	
• **Adapted Reader's Companion** ● • **Reader's Companion** ●		• **Listening to Literature** ● ▲ ■ Audiocassettes, Side 7 Audio CDs, CD 5
• **English Learner's Companion** ● ▲ • **Literatura en español** ● ▲ • **Literary Analysis for Enrichment** ■		
• **Formal Assessment:** Selection Test, pp. 41–43 ● ▲ ■ • **Open Book Test,** pp. 37–39 ● ▲ ■ • **Performance Assessment and Portfolio Management,** p. 22 ● ▲ ■ • PRENTICE HALL **ASSESSMENT SYSTEM** ● ▲ ■	• PRENTICE HALL **ASSESSMENT SYSTEM** ● ▲ ■ Skills Practice Answers and Explanations on Transparencies	• **Test Bank Software** ● ▲ ■ • **Got It! Assessment Videotapes,** Tape 1 ● ▲
• **Selection Support Workbook:** ● ▲ ■ Build Grammar Skills, p. 50 • **Writing and Grammar,** Platinum Level ● ▲ ■ • **Extension Activities,** p. 13 ● ▲ ■	• **Daily Language Practice Transparencies** ● ▲ • **Writing Models and Graphic Organizers on Transparencies,** p. 91 ● ▲ ■	• **Writing and Grammar iText CD-ROM** ● ▲ ■ 📺 *Take It to the Net* www.phschool.com

BLOCK SCHEDULING: Use one 90-minute class period to preteach the selection and have students read it. Use a second 90-minute class period to assess students' mastery of skills and have them complete one of the Extension Activities.

Step-by-Step Teaching Guide for pp. 194–195

Motivation

To prepare students to read the poems and essays, write on the chalkboard, "You reap what you sow." If necessary, clarify for students that *reap* means "to harvest" or "to obtain a result," and *sow* means "to scatter seed for growing." Have them discuss both the literal and figurative meanings of this sentence. Then, apply it directly to students' lives, using a two-column chart on the chalkboard. Label the left column *Sow*, and write "works in a video store" and "misses three play rehearsals." Label the right column *Reap*, and write "earns money for a computer" and "forgets lines on stage." Lead students to see the relationship between reaping and sowing. After students have added examples to the list, tell them to keep this saying in mind as they read these selections.

▥ Interest Grabber Video

As an alternative, play "After the Harvest" on Tape 1 to engage student interest.

❶ Background

Apple Orchards

The United States is one of the world's leading apple-producing countries. Although Washington produces more apples than any other state, New England is home to many apple orchards as well. This area is well suited to growing apples because of its cold winters. While the fruit does not grow in the winter, the trees themselves grow best in areas where the average temperature approaches or reaches freezing for at least two months every year. The trees blossom in late spring, but apple growers do not begin harvesting the fruit until late summer or early fall.

Prepare to Read

After Apple-Picking ◆ Mowing ◆ Style ◆ At Harvesttime

 Take It to the Net

Visit www.phschool.com for interactive activities and instruction related to these selections, including
- background
- graphic organizers
- literary elements
- reading strategies

Preview

Connecting to the Literature

When you plant a bean seed, you cannot expect a daisy to sprout. In life as in gardening, what you put into an experience affects what you get out of it. As these selections remind you, success requires effort.

❶ Background

Most of Robert Frost's poems are set among the pastures, woods, and streams of rural New England. Life in New England is affected to a great extent by the four seasons. Winters are marked by long nights and snowy days. Spring is damp and cool, with misty mornings. Summer days are long and hot, but the nights are often cool. Autumn is harvest time, a time to go to work picking apples amid an array of brilliant leaves falling to the ground.

194 ◆ *Striving for Success*

TEACHING RESOURCES

The following resources can be used to enrich or extend the instruction for pp. 194–195.

Motivation

▥ **Interest Grabber Video,** Tape 1 ▤

Background

📖 **Beyond Literature,** Career Connection: Farming, p. 13

 Take It to the Net

Visit www.phschool.com for background and hotlinks for the selections.

Literary Analysis

📄 **Literary Analysis and Reading Transparencies,** Tone, p. 26

Reading

📖 **Selection Support:** Reading Strategy, p. 51; Build Vocabulary, p. 49 ▤

📄 **Literary Analysis and Reading Transparencies,** Interpreting, p. 25

▤ **BLOCK SCHEDULING:** Resources marked with this symbol provide varied instruction during 90-minute blocks.

❷ Literary Analysis

Tone

The attitude of the author toward his or her subject is known as the **tone** of a literary work. The tone may be, among other things, serious or casual, distant or personal, angry or humorous. In this example, the speaker in "Mowing" shows a respectful attitude toward his work:

> Anything more than the truth would have seemed too weak
> To the earnest love that laid the swale in rows,

Determine the tone of these works by looking carefully at each writer's choice of words and details.

Comparing Literary Works

Each of the writers presents ideas in the context of harvest **imagery**—language that paints word pictures and re-creates sensory experiences. For example, Maya Angelou's essay "At Harvesttime" expands on the saying "You reap what you sow" to address the concept of personal responsibility. Compare the imagery that each writer creates, and compare the message that each writer is expressing through the imagery in each work.

❸ Reading Strategy

Interpreting

Writers like Robert Frost and Maya Angelou use images to create a feeling and convey meaning. You can **interpret** these images by examining the feelings and attitudes associated with them. As you read, think about the associations and feelings the images create, as well as what the speakers' attitudes are toward those images. Use a chart like the one shown here to help you interpret the meanings of the images.

Image
Long whispering scythe

↓

Associations
Cutting tall grass

↓

Attitudes and Emotions
Solitude of outdoor work; tranquility; respect

↓

Interpretation
The scythe represents the speaker's pride in his work.

Vocabulary Development

bough (bou) *n.* tree branch (p. 196)

trough (trôf) *n.* shallow V-shaped container from which farm animals drink or eat (p. 196)

manifestation (man´ ə fes tā´ shən) *n.* something that is plainly revealed (p. 199)

disparaging (di spar´ ij iŋ) *adj.* belittling; showing contempt for (p. 199)

judicious (jōō dish´ əs) *adj.* showing good judgment; wise and careful (p. 199)

gibe (jīb) *v.* jeer; taunt (p. 199)

admonition (ad´ mə nish´ ən) *n.* warning; mild reprimand (p. 199)

immutable (im myōōt´ ə bəl) *adj.* unchangeable (p. 200)

potency (pōt´ ən sē) *n.* power (p. 200)

After Apple-Picking / Mowing / Style / At Harvesttime ◆ 195

---

❷ Literary Analysis

Tone

- Remind students that an author's tone is the attitude he or she takes toward his or her subject, and it can change within and between works.

- Suggest that students look carefully at an author's choice of words to understand his or her tone. For example, in the excerpt on this page, the words *truth* and *earnest love* convey the author's respectful tone.

- Have a volunteer read aloud the Comparing Literary Works section. Explain that an author's choice of images also affects a work's tone.

- To help students understand how word choice and imagery affect tone, ask them to write a sentence in a serious tone; then, have them change a few words or add an image so that the sentence takes on a comical tone.

❸ Reading Strategy

Interpreting

- Tell students to use the following questions to help them interpret the images they encounter: What associations do the images call to mind? What feelings or emotions do the images spark? What are the speakers' attitudes toward the images? What point or message do the images convey?

- As they read, have students use a chart like the one shown to record their interpretations of images.

Vocabulary Development

- Pronounce each vocabulary word for students, and read the definitions as a class. Have students identify any words with which they are already familiar.

E-Teach

Visit E-Teach at www.phschool.com for teachers' essays on how to teach, with questions and answers.

CUSTOMIZE INSTRUCTION FOR UNIVERSAL ACCESS

For Special Needs Students	For Less Proficient Readers	For English Learners
Have students read the adapted version of "Style" in the **Adapted Reader's Companion.** This version provides basic-level instruction in an interactive format with questions and write-on lines. Completing the adapted version will prepare students to read the selection in the Student Edition.	Have students read "Style" in the **Reader's Companion.** This version provides basic-level instruction in an interactive format with questions and write-on lines. After students finish the selection in the **Reader's Companion,** have them complete the questions and activities in the Student Edition.	Have students read the adapted version of "Style" in the **English Learner's Companion.** This version provides basic-level instruction in an interactive format with questions and write-on lines. Completing the adapted version will prepare students to read the selection in the Student Edition.

CUSTOMIZE INSTRUCTION
For Musical/Rhythmic Learners

Have students plan choral readings of the poems. As they prepare, they should work out the rhythms of the lines and determine which words and syllables should be stressed. When they finish, ask them how this exercise enhanced their understanding of the poems' meanings.

❶ About the Selections

Both of Frost's poems celebrate "the sweetest dream that labor knows" by focusing on the physicality of mowing and of harvesting. In "After Apple-Picking," the reader feels the exhaustion of the speaker who has just worked hard to harvest apples before the long winter sets in. In "Mowing," the scythe with which the speaker mows seems itself to be a sentient being, whispering and communicating with the land.

❷ ▶Critical Viewing

Answer: Students may appreciate the apples more, now that they know about the labor involved in harvesting them.

❸ Vocabulary Development

Spelling vs. Pronunciation: -ough

- Draw students' attention to the words *bough* and *trough*.

- Explain that although the words appear to rhyme with each other, *bough* actually rhymes with *now*, and *trough* rhymes with *off*.

- Have students list at least one other *-ough* word that rhymes with *now* and one that rhymes with *off*. Possible answers: *plough* rhymes with *now*, and *cough* rhymes with *off*.

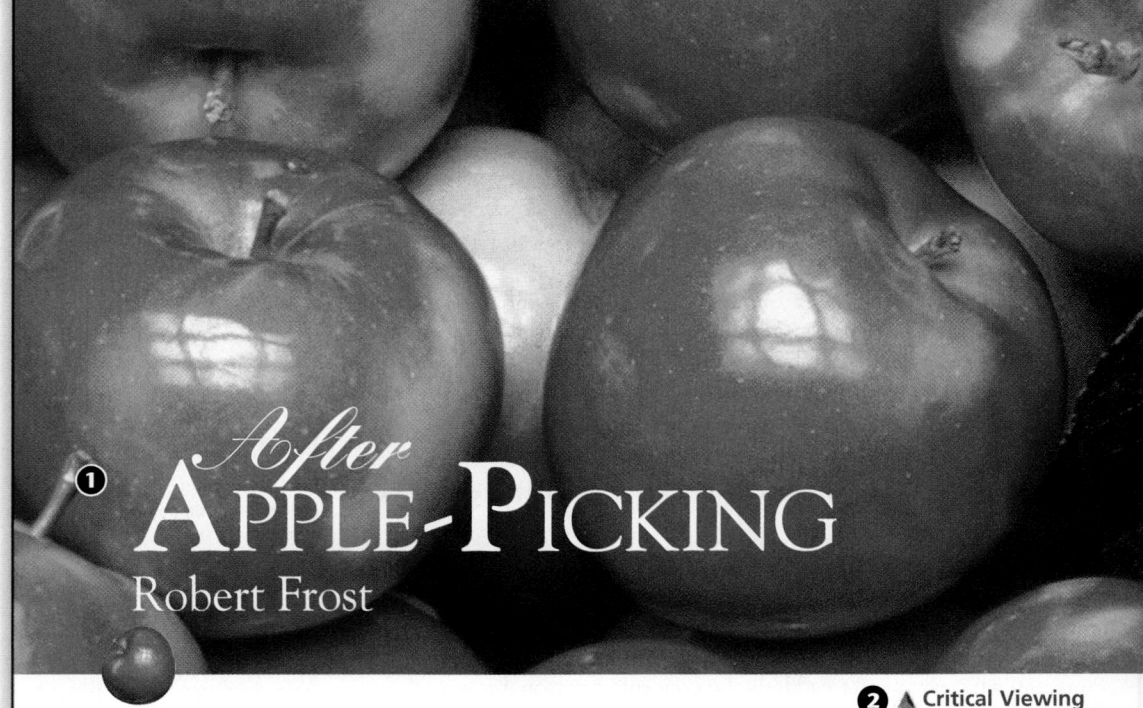

After
APPLE-PICKING
Robert Frost

My long two-pointed ladder's sticking through a tree
Toward heaven still,
And there's a barrel that I didn't fill
Beside it, and there may be two or three
5   Apples I didn't pick upon some <u>bough</u>.
But I am done with apple-picking now.
Essence of winter sleep is on the night,
The scent of apples: I am drowsing off.
I cannot rub the strangeness from my sight
10   I got from looking through a pane of glass
I skimmed this morning from the drinking <u>trough</u>
And held against the world of hoary[1] grass.
It melted, and I let it fall and break.
But I was well
15   Upon my way to sleep before it fell,
And I could tell
What form my dreaming was about to take.
Magnified apples appear and disappear,
Stem end and blossom end,
20   And every fleck of russet[2] showing clear.
My instep arch not only keeps the ache,

---

1. **hoary** (hō′ rē) *adj.* gray or white with age.
2. **russet** (rus′ it) *n.* strong reddish-brown color; type of winter apple having rough, reddish-brown skin.

196 ◆ *Striving for Success*

❷ ▲ Critical Viewing
How does the poem change your attitude about apples like these? **[Analyze]**

bough (bou) *n.* tree branch

trough (trôf) *n.* shallow V-shaped container from which farm animals drink or eat

---

TEACHING RESOURCES

The following resources can be used to enrich or extend the instruction for pp. 196–200.

Literary Analysis

📖 **Selection Support:** Literary Analysis, p. 52

🖥 **Writing Models and Graphic Organizers on Transparencies**, p. 91

Reading

📖 **Reader's Companion**

📖 **English Learner's Companion**

🎧 **Listening to Literature Audiocassettes,** Side 7 ▪

💿 **Listening to Literature Audio CDs**, CD 5 ▪

▪ **BLOCK SCHEDULING:** Resources marked with this symbol provide varied instruction during 90-minute blocks.

It keeps the pressure of a ladder-round.
I feel the ladder sway as the boughs bend.
And I keep hearing from the cellar bin
25 The rumbling sound
Of load on load of apples coming in.
For I have had too much
Of apple-picking: I am overtired
Of the great harvest I myself desired.
30 There were ten thousand thousand fruit to touch,
Cherish in hand, lift down, and not let fall.
For all
That struck the earth,
Not matter if not bruised or spiked with stubble,
35 Went surely to the cider-apple heap
As of no worth.
One can see what will trouble
This sleep of mine, whatever sleep it is.
Were he not gone,
40 The woodchuck could say whether it's like his
Long sleep, as I describe its coming on,
Or just some human sleep.

❺ ☑ Reading Check

What does the speaker want to do now that apple-picking is over?

After Apple-Picking ◆ 197

❹ Literary Analysis

Tone

- Have students read the bracketed passage. Ask them to pay attention to the repeated words.
- Then, ask students to describe the speaker's tone in these lines. Answer: The tone seems to reflect what the speaker is saying; it communicates a feeling of profound tiredness. The repetition of *sleep* adds to the weary tone.
- Have students note other lines in the poem that suggest the speaker's weariness. Possible responses: The detailed description of work yet to be done in lines 2–4 suggests exhaustion. Lines 27–29 suggest that the speaker has taken on more than he can accomplish.

❺ ☑ Reading Check

Answer: The speaker wants to sleep.

Mowing

Robert Frost

There was never a sound beside the wood but one,
And that was my long scythe[1] whispering to the ground.
What was it it whispered? I knew not well myself;
Perhaps it was something about the heat of the sun,
5 Something, perhaps, about the lack of sound—
And that was why it whispered and did not speak.
It was no dream of the gift of idle hours,
Or easy gold at the hand of fay[2] or elf:
Anything more than the truth would have seemed too weak
10 To the earnest love that laid the swale[3] in rows,
Not without feeble-pointed spikes of flowers
(Pale orchises),[4] and scared a bright green snake.
The fact is the sweetest dream that labor knows.
My long scythe whispered and left the hay to make.

---

1. **scythe** (sīth) *n.* slightly curved blade at the end of a long handle, used for cutting grass.
2. **fay** (fā) *n.* fairy.
3. **swale** (swāl) *n.* low-lying marshland.
4. **orchises** (ôr′ kis iz) *n.* orchids.

Review and Assess

Thinking About the Selections

1. **Respond:** What experiences do these poems call to mind?

2. **(a) Recall:** In "After Apple-Picking," what flashes through the speaker's mind as he drifts off to sleep? What does he feel? What does he hear? **(b) Deduce:** What is the cause of his condition?

3. **(a) Interpret:** In "After Apple-Picking," what is the speaker's attitude toward his day's work? **(b) Generalize:** Which do you think is more satisfying—physical or mental work? Why?

4. **(a) Recall:** In "Mowing," what is the one sound the speaker hears? **(b) Infer:** How does it add to the silence of the poem?

5. **(a) Recall:** What does the speaker of "Mowing" say is "the sweetest dream that labor knows"? **(b) Analyze:** Based on this line, what is the speaker's attitude toward his labor?

6. **Extend:** How do you think a person's attitude toward work affects his or her performance?

Robert Frost

(1874–1963)

Robert Frost spent most of his youth in New England, his family's original home. He worked as a farmer, an editor, and a schoolteacher, absorbing the ebb and flow of New England life that would form the themes of many of his poems.

In 1912, Frost moved to England, where he met the famous poets Ezra Pound and William Butler Yeats. Encouraged by their praise, he published his first volume of poetry, *A Boy's Will*, in 1913. Frost went on to become one of America's most successful poets, winning many awards, including four Pulitzer Prizes.

✺ ENRICHMENT: Career Connection

Landscape Architecture

Many high school students earn money from the land by mowing lawns, raking leaves, and shoveling snow. Students who are interested in working with the land may want to learn more about a career in landscape architecture. A landscape architect may design anything from a backyard garden to the grounds of a major corporate park. Have students investigate what a landscape architect does and the qualifications necessary to become one.

STYLE

MAYA ANGELOU ❼

Wind on the Water, Richard McDermott Miller

Content is of great importance, but we must not underrate the value of style. That is, attention must be paid to not only what is said but how it is said; to what we wear, as well as how we wear it. In fact, we should be aware of all we do and of how we do all that we do.

Manners and a respect for style can be developed if one is eager and has an accomplished teacher. On the other hand, any observant person can acquire the same results without a teacher simply by carefully watching the steady march of the human parade.

Never try to take the manners of another as your own, for the theft will be immediately evident and the thief will appear as ridiculous as a robin with peacock feathers hastily stuck on. Style is as unique and nontransferable and perfectly personal as a fingerprint. It is wise to take the time to develop one's own way of being, increasing those things one does well and eliminating the elements in one's character which can hinder and diminish the good personality.

Any person who has charm and some confidence can move in and through societies ranging from the most privileged to the most needy. Style allows the person to appear neither inferior in one location nor superior in the other. Good manners and tolerance, which are the highest <u>manifestation</u> of style, can often transform disaster into good fortune. Many people utter insults or <u>disparaging</u> remarks without thinking, but a wise or stylish person takes the time to consider the positive as well as negative possibilities in each situation. The <u>judicious</u> response to a <u>gibe</u> can disarm the rude person, removing the power to injure.

This is not another <u>admonition</u> to turn the other cheek, although I do think that that can be an effective ploy on certain occasions. Rather, this is an encouragement to meet adverse situations with the intent and style to control them. Falling into an entanglement with brutes will usually result in nothing more conclusive than a stimulated nervous system and an upset digestive tract.

manifestation (man´ ə fes tā´ shən) *n.* something that is plainly revealed

disparaging (di spar´ ij iŋ) *adj.* belittling; showing contempt for

judicious (jo͞o dish´ əs) *adj.* showing good judgment; wise and careful

gibe (jīb) *v.* jeer; taunt

admonition (ad´ mə nish´ ən) *n.* warning; mild reprimand

❾ ✔**Reading Check**

According to Angelou, what two items are necessary for acquiring style?

Style ◆ 199

---

❼ **About the Selections**

"Style" and "At Harvesttime" examine and expand upon the theme of "You reap what you sow." In these works, Angelou says that those who cultivate and remain true to their unique styles can successfully deal with most situations in life.

❽ **Literary Analysis**

Tone

- Have a volunteer read aloud the bracketed passage.
- Explain that Angelou is warning readers against using another's style as one's own.
- Have students identify the image that Angelou uses to illustrate her point.
  Answer: Angelou says that a person who steals another's style will look like "a robin with peacock feathers hastily stuck on."
- Then, ask students to identify the tone of this passage.
  Answer: Some students may say that Angelou's tone is serious because she is teaching something she considers important. Other students may say that the tone is humorous because the image of the robin with peacock feathers is funny.

▶ **Monitor Progress** To help students use images to determine tone, have them sketch the "robin with peacock feathers hastily stuck on" so they can see it clearly. Then, have them write a list of thoughts or emotions that the image calls up. Finally, have them examine the list and determine the overall feeling that the words convey.

❾ ✔**Reading Check**

Answer: To acquire style, one must either have an accomplished teacher or observe others.

CUSTOMIZE INSTRUCTION FOR UNIVERSAL ACCESS

For Special Needs Students	For Gifted/Talented Students
Remind students to read poetry in the same way they read prose—continue reading until you reach punctuation. Model for students the correct way to read poetry. Explain that they should come to a full stop at a period, colon, or dash; a shorter stop at a semicolon; and a brief pause at a comma.	Invite students to rewrite either "Style" or "At Harvesttime" as a poem. Encourage them to make the ideas vivid by incorporating the images that Angelou uses in her essays, and adding images of their own. For examples of how to use images in a poem, have students study Frost's "After Apple-Picking" and "Mowing." When they finish, have them discuss whether the new form affects the work's meaning.

ASSESS

⑩ Reading Strategy

Interpreting

- Have students read the bracketed passage and identify the image that Angelou uses.
  Answer: Angelou uses the image of planting tomato seeds and reaping onions.

- Then, have students interpret the image by filling in a graphic organizer like the one on p. 195.

- When students finish, ask them to share their interpretations.
  Answer: Angelou's image suggests that some people have unrealistic expectations about the effects that their present actions will have in the future.

Answers for p. 200

Review and Assess

1. Some students may say they find "Style" more meaningful because the advice it offers applies to almost any situation. Other students may say that "At Harvesttime" is more meaningful because it reminds them to think about the consequences of all of their actions.

2. **(a)** Good manners and tolerance are the proof of style. **(b)** They both involve treating others as we would like to be treated.

3. **(a)** Style is as important as content. **(b)** If you behave with style, as Angelou defines it, you will be successful in your interactions with people.

4. **(a)** Angelou proposes that people will reap what they sow. **(b)** Angelou believes that people's actions reproduce themselves. In other words, if you treat people well, they are likely to treat you well in return.

5. Planting and harvesting correlate to giving and getting things in life. You get back from others what you give to them, just as you harvest what you plant.

6. Students may say that our manner of presenting a message affects whether it will or will not be accepted.

200

AT HARVESTTIME

MAYA ANGELOU

⑩ There is an <u>immutable</u> life principle with which many people will quarrel.

Although nature has proven season in and season out that if the thing that is planted bears at all, it will yield more of itself, there are those who seem certain that if they plant tomato seeds, at harvesttime they can reap onions.

Too many times for comfort I have expected to reap good when I know I have sown evil. My lame excuse is that I have not always known that actions can only reproduce themselves, or rather, I have not always allowed myself to be aware of that knowledge. Now, after years of observation and enough courage to admit what I have observed, I try to plant peace if I do not want discord; to plant loyalty and honesty if I want to avoid betrayal and lies.

Of course, there is no absolute assurance that those things I plant will always fall upon arable land and will take root and grow, nor can I know if another cultivator did not leave contrary seeds before I arrived. I do know, however, that if I leave little to chance, if I am careful about the kinds of seeds I plant, about their <u>potency</u> and nature, I can, within reason, trust my expectations.

immutable (im myo͞ot´ ə bəl) *adj.* unchangeable

potency (pōt´ ən sē) *n.* power

Maya Angelou

(b. 1928)

Maya Angelou was born Marguerite Johnson in St. Louis, Missouri. She and her older brother were raised by their grandmother in Stamps, Arkansas. She records the experiences of her childhood in her autobiography, *I Know Why the Caged Bird Sings*.

In her adult life, Angelou has achieved success as a singer, an actress, a civil rights worker, and a writer of nonfiction, fiction, poetry, and plays.

Review and Assess

Thinking About the Selections

1. **Respond:** Which essay do you find more meaningful? Why?

2. **(a) Recall:** In the essay "Style," which two qualities are identified as the greatest proof of style? **(b) Analyze:** What do these qualities have in common?

3. **(a) Summarize:** Compared to content, how important is style to Angelou? **(b) Analyze:** In what ways can style help you achieve success?

4. **(a) Recall:** In "At Harvesttime," what does Angelou propose is a life principle that cannot be changed? **(b) Interpret:** How does she suggest that it applies to human behavior?

5. **Interpret:** How do the images of planting and harvesting help you understand the message in "At Harvesttime"?

6. **Evaluate:** Why is style sometimes more important than content?

ASSESSMENT PRACTICE: Reading Comprehension

Recognize Facts and Details   (For more practice, see Test Preparation Workbook, p. 13.)

Some test questions may ask students to identify facts and details that relate to the main idea of a text. Have students read "At Harvesttime" and then answer this sample question:

What does the author "plant" if she wants to avoid betrayal and lies?

  A courage
  B honesty
  C peace

  D contrary seeds

Students should skim the essay to review its details. They should recognize that all of the answer choices are details in the essay, but only choice *B*, honesty, helps the author avoid betrayal and lies.

Review and Assess

Literary Analysis

Tone

1. (a) How would you describe the **tone** of "After Apple-Picking"?
   (b) What words and phrases are most helpful in conveying this tone?
2. (a) Describe the tone of the essays "At Harvesttime" and "Style."
   (b) What words and phrases help convey this tone?

Comparing Literary Works

3. Compare the tone of Frost's poems and Angelou's essays.
4. The poems and essays are filled with **images** that appeal to different senses. (a) Use a chart like this one to classify the images.
   (b) Then, tell which images you find most vivid and why.

Selection	Sight	Sound	Taste	Feel	Smell
"Mowing"					
"Style"					

5. (a) Compare the image of harvesting in "After Apple-Picking" with the image of harvesting in "At Harvesttime." (b) How do these images contribute to each author's message?
6. (a) Compare the image you form of the farmer in "Mowing" with that of the farmer in "After Apple-Picking." (b) Which poem conveys a more positive tone? Explain.

Reading Strategy

Interpreting

7. (a) How does the speaker in "Mowing" feel about his work?
   (b) How do his feelings affect your interpretation of the poem?
8. (a) How does the speaker in "After Apple-Picking" feel at the end of the day? (b) How do his feelings affect your interpretation of the poem?
9. How do the images of planting and harvesting help you understand the message in "At Harvesttime"?

Extend Understanding

10. **Cultural Connection:** (a) How would you say we define success in our society? (b) Why do you agree or disagree with this definition?

Quick Review

Tone is the attitude of the author toward his or her subject.

Imagery is descriptive or figurative language that creates word pictures.

When you **interpret** images, you analyze what the images represent and decide how they contribute to the work's mood or meaning.

 Take It to the Net
www.phschool.com
Take the interactive self-test online to check your understanding of these selections.

After Apple-Picking / Mowing / Style / At Harvesttime ◆ 201

Answers for p. 201

Review and Assess

1. (a) The tone is tired and informal. (b) Words that convey exhaustion are "I am drowsing off," "My instep arch . . . keeps the ache," and "sleep."

2. (a) Students might find the tone either preachy or wise. (b) Words that convey these tones are "great importance," "attention must be paid," and "it is wise."

3. Students may say that Frost's tone is serious and personal, whereas Angelou's tone is serious but distant, like a lecture.

4. (a) Possible response for "Mowing": "bright green snake" (sight); "scythe whispering to the ground" (sound); "heat of the sun" (feel). Possible response for "Style": "plant tomato seeds . . . reap onions" (sight, smell, taste, feel); "arable land" (sight). (b) Students should explain why they found the details vivid.

5. (a) The harvest is of food in "After Apple-Picking" and of behavior in "At Harvesttime." (b) In both, the harvest is a time of great importance: It determines the well-being of the farmer during the winter, and it determines the success of the individual in "At Harvesttime."

6. (a) The farmer in "Mowing" is joyous, while the farmer in "After Apple-Picking" is numb with exhaustion. (b) The image in "Mowing" is more positive because the speaker loves his task.

7. (a) He respects his work. (b) His respect helps readers interpret mowing as a sacred act.

8. (a) He feels exhausted. (b) His exhaustion helps readers take a realistic look at the difficulty of labor.

9. The images reinforce Angelou's point about the relationship between actions and consequences.

10. (a) Some students may say that our society limits success to actual achievement. (b) Students may disagree, saying that success means finding work that is enjoyable and meaningful.

201

❶ Vocabulary Development

Spelling vs. Pronunciation

1. b   3. a
2. c

Spelling Strategy

1. labor   3. savor
2. rumor

Concept Development: Synonyms

1. c   6. a
2. g   7. e
3. i   8. d
4. f   9. b
5. h

❷ Grammar

1. *Quietly* answers *in what way* and modifies the verb *whispered.*
2. *Very* answers *to what extent* and modifies the adjective *tired.*
3. *Slowly* answers *in what way* and modifies the verb *moved; more* answers *to what extent* and modifies the adverb *slowly.*
4. *Down* answers *where* and modifies the verb *rolled.*
5. *Loudly* answers *in what way* and modifies the verb *speak; seldom* answers *when* and modifies the verb *speak.*

Writing Application

Possible answers:

1. Marcus dances fast to this music.
2. The doctor was not happy with the test results.
3. Vacation week passed quite quickly.

Integrate Language Skills

❶ Vocabulary Development Lesson

Spelling vs. Pronunciation: *-ough*

Although each is spelled with *-ough*, *bough* rhymes with *now* and *trough* rhymes with *off*. Match the word from the left column with the rhyming word in the right column.

1. bough   a. dough
2. trough   b. plough
3. though   c. cough

Spelling Strategy

The *ou* letter combination often indicates that a word originated in Middle English. Even today, the *ou* combination is used in words in British English that are spelled with an *o* in American English: *flavour, flavor*. Give the American English spelling of these words:

1. labour   2. rumour   3. savour

Concept Development: Synonyms

Synonyms are words that are similar in meaning. On your paper, match each word from the vocabulary list on page 195 with its synonym.

1. immutable   a. mild reprimand
2. bough   b. power
3. gibe   c. unchangeable
4. disparaging   d. wise
5. trough   e. evidence
6. admonition   f. critical
7. manifestation   g. branch
8. judicious   h. tub
9. potency   i. jeer

❷ Grammar Lesson

Adverb Function

An **adverb** modifies a verb, an adjective, or another adverb. Adverbs answer the questions *where, when, in what way,* or *to what extent.*

Modifying Verb:	ADV. *Now* I <u>have finished</u> with apple-picking. (*when*)
	ADV. Cherish in hand, <u>lift</u> *down*, and not let fall. (*where*)
Modifying Adjective:	ADV. Style is as *perfectly* <u>personal</u> as a fingerprint. (*to what extent*)
Modifying Adverb:	ADV You are *not* <u>exactly</u> correct. (*in what way*)

Practice Write each sentence, and circle the adverbs. Above each adverb, write the question it answers. Then, identify the words the adverbs modify, and write *verb, adjective,* or *adverb* over the words.

1. The scythe whispered quietly in the still air.
2. The man was very tired from his long day.
3. He moved more slowly at the end of the day.
4. The apples rolled down into the cellar.
5. People with style seldom speak loudly.

Writing Application Use each word in a sentence according to the function indicated.

1. *fast;* modifying a verb
2. *not;* modifying an adjective
3. *quite;* modifying an adverb

W̵G *Prentice Hall Writing and Grammar Connection: Chapter 17, Section 2*

TEACHING RESOURCES

The following resources can be used to enrich or extend the instruction for pp. 202–203.

Vocabulary

📖 **Selection Support:** Build Vocabulary, p. 49

📖 **Vocabulary and Spelling Practice Book**
(Use this booklet for skills enrichment.)

Grammar

📖 **Selection Support:** Build Grammar Skills, p. 50

W̵G **Writing and Grammar,** Platinum Level, p. 380

🖥 **Daily Language Practice Transparencies** 🖥

Writing

W̵G **Writing and Grammar,** Platinum Level, p. 239

💿 **Writing and Grammar iText CD-ROM** 🖥

🖨 **Writing Models and Graphic Organizers on Transparencies,** p. 91

 BLOCK SCHEDULING: Resources marked with this symbol provide varied instruction during 90-minute blocks.

Writing Lesson

Advice Column

"At Harvesttime" and "Style" offer good advice for people of any age. Write an **advice column,** including at least two letters from readers asking for advice. Use ideas from Angelou's essays as a basis for answering the letters.

> **Prewriting** Select a topic for each of your letters. The letters should state specific, real-life problems that can be answered with Angelou's ideas, such as how to deal with a person who insults or criticizes you.

Model: Brainstorming for Topics

Possible Problems:

— A girl in my class insults me by making fun of my name.

— I feel uncomfortable wearing the latest fashions.

— My friend is mean to me but gets mad when I am mean to him.

> Each idea presents a single problem to be addressed using ideas from the essays.

> **Drafting** Write your letters so that the problems are clearly identified. In your answers, suggest one or more possible solutions based on Angelou's ideas. Quote from her essays to make your points clear.

> **Revising** Read each letter, and make sure that you have defined the problem clearly. Then, make sure that your answer provides a solution.

W̶G Prentice Hall Writing and Grammar Connection: Chapter 11, Connected Assignment

Extension Activities

Listening and Speaking Practice reading one of the selections as a **speech.** Experiment with pauses, volume, and tone of voice. Use these tips to guide your presentation:

- Remember that you do not automatically pause at the end of each line.
- Pause according to the punctuation in the poem.

Present your speech to the class.

Research and Technology Although Frost's message about work is timeless, technology has dramatically changed the way farmers work. With a group, create a **timeline** that shows the impact of technology on a specific area of agriculture during the past century. Use library resources to find information. Include graphics that show the types of technology introduced. **[Group Activity]**

 Take It to the Net www.phschool.com
Go online for an additional research activity using the Internet.

After Apple-Picking / Mowing / Style / At Harvesttime ◆ 203

---

❸ Writing Lesson

- Have students brainstorm for a list of real-life problems to address. If they need suggestions, have them go to the library and read advice columns in newspapers.

- Then, have students reread the essays and find at least one quotation that will help to solve each problem.

- Students can use the Problem-Solution Organizer, p. 91 in **Writing Models and Graphic Organizers on Transparencies,** to organize their notes.

- Use the Writing Lesson to guide students in drafting and revising their advice columns.

- Use the rubric for Problem-Solution Essays, p. 22 in **Performance Assessment and Portfolio Management,** to assess students' work.

❹ Research and Technology

- Divide the class into groups, and have each group focus on a different aspect of agriculture. Help students use the library and online resources to find information on their topics.

- Have the students create timelines and present them to the class. Suggest that students illustrate their timelines with images that show how the technology has evolved over time. They might use drawings, photocopies of photographs, or downloaded images from the Internet.

CUSTOMIZE INSTRUCTION
For Universal Access

To address different learning styles, use the activities suggested in the **Extension Activities** booklet, p. 13.

- For Verbal/Linguistic and Interpersonal Learners, use Activity 5.

- For Visual/Spatial and Verbal/Linguistic learners, use Activity 6.

- For Bodily/Kinesthetic and Verbal/Linguistic learners, use Activity 7.

The Apple Tree

Lesson Objectives

1. To analyze and respond to literary elements
- Literary Analysis: Allusion
- Connecting Literary Elements: Connotation

2. To read, comprehend, analyze, and critique a short story
- Reading Strategy: Questioning
- Reading Check questions
- Review and Assess questions
- Assessment Practice (ATE)

3. To develop word analysis skills, fluency, and systematic vocabulary
- Vocabulary Development Lesson: Word Origins: Words From Myths

4. To understand and apply written and oral language conventions
- Spelling Strategy
- Grammar Lesson: Confusing Verbs: *lie* and *lay*

5. To understand and apply appropriate writing and research strategies
- Writing Lesson: Retelling a Story
- Extension Activity: Annotated Map

6. To understand and apply listening and speaking strategies
- Extension Activity: Monologue

STEP-BY-STEP TEACHING GUIDE	PACING GUIDE
PRETEACH	
Motivate Students and Provide Background	
Use the Motivation activity (ATE p. 204)	5 min.
Read and discuss the Preview material and Background information (SE/ATE p. 204) **A**	5 min.
Introduce the Concepts	
Introduce the Literary Analysis and Reading Strategy (SE/ATE p. 205) **A**	15 min.
Pronounce the vocabulary words and read their definitions (SE p. 205)	5 min.
TEACH	
Monitor Comprehension	
Informally monitor comprehension by circulating while students read independently or in groups **A**	10 min.
Monitor students' comprehension with the Reading Check notes (SE/ATE pp. 207, 209)	as students read
Develop vocabulary with Vocabulary notes (SE pp. 207, 209, 210)	as students read
Develop Understanding	
Develop students' understanding of allusion with Literary Analysis annotations (SE p. 207; ATE p. 207) **A**	10 min.
Develop students' understanding of questioning with Reading Strategy annotations (SE p. 209; ATE pp. 207, 209)	10 min.
ASSESS	
Assess Mastery	
Assess students' mastery of the Reading Strategy and Literary Analysis by having them answer the Review and Assess questions (SE/ATE p. 211)	20 min.
Use one or more of the print and media Assessment Resources (ATE p. 213) **A**	up to 50 min.
EXTEND	
Apply Understanding	
Have students complete the Vocabulary Development Lesson and the Grammar Lesson (SE p. 212) **A**	20 min.
Apply students' ability to show, not tell, using the Writing Lesson (SE/ATE p. 213) **A**	45 min.
Apply students' understanding of the selection using one or more of the Extension Activities (SE p. 213)	20–90 min.

 ACCELERATED INSTRUCTION:
Use the strategies and activities identified with an **A**.

UNIVERSAL ACCESS
- ● = Below Level Students
- ▲ = On-Level Students
- ■ = Above Level Students

Time and Resource Manager

Reading Level: Average
Average Number of Instructional Days: 4

RESOURCES		
PRINT 📖	**TRANSPARENCIES**	**TECHNOLOGY** 💿 🎧 📼
• **Beyond Literature**, Cross-Curricular Connection: Plant Science, p. 14 ▲ ■		• **Interest Grabber Video**, Tape 1 ● ▲ ■
• **Selection Support Workbook:** ● ▲ ■ Literary Analysis, p. 56 Reading Strategy, p. 55 Build Vocabulary, p. 53	• **Literary Analysis and Reading Transparencies**, pp. 27 and 28 ● ▲ ■	
		• **Listening to Literature** ● ▲ ■ Audiocassettes, Side 8 Audio CDs, CD 5
• **Literatura en español** ● ▲ • **Literary Analysis for Enrichment** ■		
• **Formal Assessment:** Selection Test, pp. 44–46 ● ▲ ■ • **Open Book Test**, pp. 40–42 ● ▲ ■ • **Performance Assessment and Portfolio Management**, p. 28 ● ▲ ■ • PRENTICE HALL ASSESSMENT *SYSTEM* ● ▲ ■	• PRENTICE HALL ASSESSMENT *SYSTEM* ● ▲ ■ Skills Practice Answers and Explanations on Transparencies	• **Test Bank Software** ● ▲ ■ • **Got It! Assessment Videotapes**, Tape 1 ● ▲
• **Selection Support Workbook:** ● ▲ ■ Build Grammar Skills, p. 54 • **Writing and Grammar**, Platinum Level ● ▲ ■ • **Extension Activities**, p. 14 ● ▲ ■	• **Daily Language Practice Transparencies** ● ▲ • **Writing Models and Graphic Organizers on Transparencies**, pp. 79–81, 103 ● ▲ ■	• **Writing and Grammar iText CD-ROM** ● ▲ ■ 💻 *Take It to the Net* www.phschool.com

BLOCK SCHEDULING: Use one 90-minute class period to preteach the selection and have students read it. Use a second 90-minute class period to assess students' mastery of skills and have them complete one of the Extension Activities.

Motivation

To capture students' interest, draw a simple sign on the chalkboard: "Private: Keep Out." Encourage students to exchange information about where and when they have encountered such a sign. Ask, What did you imagine was behind the sign? Did you ever find out? What is the effect of making something "off-limits" or forbidden? After discussing the effect of classifying something as forbidden, tell students that "The Apple Tree" centers on a forbidden fruit—the apple. Students will have a chance to compare their own responses to being forbidden to do something to those of the characters in this story.

▭ Interest Grabber Video

As an alternative, play "A Year at an Apple Orchard" on Tape 1 to engage student interest.

❶ Background

Literature

The biblical account of Adam and Eve eating from the Tree of Knowledge can be found in Chapter 3 of the Bible's first book, Genesis. According to the story, the fruit of this tree contained knowledge of good and evil. Although God had forbidden it, Adam and Eve ate fruit from this tree after being tempted by a serpent. The story gave rise to the literary and religious tradition that Adam and Eve's disobedience was mankind's first sin, and from it resulted all the unhappiness of human existence. More broadly, the image of the fall from grace is used to suggest, as Mansfield does in the story, that some knowledge may be painful but is part of adulthood. You may wish to provide students with a retelling of the Genesis story in order to help them recognize allusions to it in Mansfield's tale.

Prepare to Read

The Apple Tree

Apple Plenty, 1970, Herbert Shuptrine

 Take It to the Net

Visit www.phschool.com for interactive activities and instruction related to "The Apple Tree," including
- background
- graphic organizers
- literary elements
- reading strategies

Preview

Connecting to the Literature

If you have ever spent a long time waiting for something, you know how the characters in "The Apple Tree" feel. Based on your own experiences, predict whether or not the anticipated event will live up to the characters' expectations.

❶ Background

In "The Apple Tree," a man discovers a special apple tree in his orchard. He tells his children not to eat the fruit of the tree. The story is a variation of the biblical account of the tree in the Garden of Eden. The Bible relates that Adam and Eve are forbidden by God to eat the fruit of the Tree of Life in the center of the garden. However, Adam and Eve *do* eat the fruit, and they are banished from the Garden of Eden.

TEACHING RESOURCES

The following resources can be used to enrich or extend the instruction for pp. 204–205.

Motivation
▭ **Interest Grabber Video,** Tape 1

Background
📖 **Beyond Literature,** Cross-Curricular Connection: Plant Science, p. 14 ▪

 Take It to the Net
Visit www.phschool.com for background and hotlinks for "The Apple Tree."

Literary Analysis
📄 **Literary Analysis and Reading Transparencies,** Allusion, p. 28 ▪

Reading
📖 **Selection Support:** Reading Strategy, p. 55; Build Vocabulary, p. 53

📄 **Literary Analysis and Reading Transparencies,** Questioning, p. 27

▪ **BLOCK SCHEDULING:** Resources marked with this symbol provide varied instruction during 90-minute blocks.

Literary Analysis

Allusion

Author Katherine Mansfield's reference to the forbidden fruit is an **allusion,** a reference to a well-known person, place, event, literary work, or work of art. You may find literary allusions to current events, popular culture, or other fields, but the most common allusions are to

- The Bible
- Greek or Roman mythology
- Shakespeare's plays

Recognizing allusions will help you better understand and appreciate literature because these references often add layers of meaning to passages and events. As you read, look for biblical allusions that add depth to the author's story.

Connecting Literary Elements

Like allusions, connotations add layers of meaning to literary works. The **connotation** of a word is the set of ideas associated with it, in addition to its explicit meaning. In "The Apple Tree," for example, the father exclaims, "What a bouquet!" when he smells the apple. Imagine the difference if he had said, "What a smell!" or even "What an odor!" The word *bouquet* calls to mind something lovely and sweet, like flowers, setting up the expectation that the taste also will be sweet.

Reading Strategy

Questioning

When you **question** as you read, you ask yourself questions like these about the meaning of events, characters' actions, and key details:

- Why does a character act the way he or she does?
- Does a detail of the setting have an underlying meaning?

Try to piece together details that will enable you to answer such questions. Use a diagram like the one shown here to help you keep track of your questions and the clues to their answers.

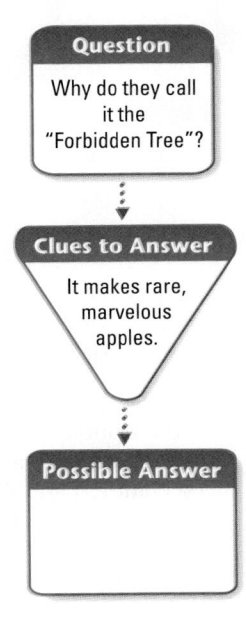

Vocabulary Development

paddocks (pad´ əks) *n.* small enclosed fields (p. 207)

exquisite (eks´ kwi zit) *adj.* delicately beautiful (p. 209)

bouquet (bo̅o̅ kā´) *n.* fragrance (p. 209)

jovial (jō´ vē əl) *adj.* full of good humor (p. 210)

The Apple Tree ◆ 205

---

❷ Literary Analysis

Allusion

- Remind students that most allusions are references to a historical or literary person, place, thing or event with which the reader is familiar.

- Encourage students to look for both subtle and explicit allusions to the Adam and Eve story as they read this selection. For example, in what ways are the orchards and grounds around the house like the Garden of Eden?

- Use the Allusion transparency in **Literary Analysis and Reading Transparencies**, p. 28, to demonstrate how to identify allusions.

❸ Reading Strategy

Questioning

- Explain to students that all readers ask questions as they read. Encourage students to become more aware of the questions they ask themselves when they are reading.

- Tell students that asking questions not only leads to a more active involvement in what they are reading, but can help them make predictions, interpret, analyze, and better comprehend what they read.

- Remind students that they should look for the answers to their questions as they read. Students may have to reread passages or read ahead in order to find answers to their questions.

- Encourage students to keep a chart of their questions and answers as they read.

Vocabulary Development

- Pronounce each vocabulary word for students, and read the definitions as a class. Have students identify any words with which they are already familiar.

 E-Teach

Visit E-Teach at www.phschool.com for teachers' essays on how to teach, with questions and answers.

Step-by-Step Teaching Guide
for pp. 206–210

CUSTOMIZE INSTRUCTION
For Linguistic Learners

You may wish to preview the footnotes to familiarize students with the terms that describe specific types of shrubs and apples. You may wish to review the use of context clues to help them to determine the general meaning of these references. After discussing the footnotes, tell students that as they encounter these terms in their reading, it is not necessary for them to interrupt their reading to consult the footnote, as long as they remember the general meaning of the reference. Encourage students to research the terms after they finish reading the selection.

❶ About the Selection

On its literal level, this is the story of how anticipation is rewarded—literally—with bitter disappointment. The children's disappointment at how terrible the magnificent apple tastes is matched only by their desire to shield their father from disappointment. Read as a story of a fall from grace, the story suggests that the fruit is not only bitter, but brings bitter knowledge. Though the children have permission to taste the fruit, they are driven from the innocence of their childhood Eden as they witness the foolishness of their adored father.

❷ ▶ Critical Viewing

Answer: Students might expect the story to be set in an apple orchard or a garden.

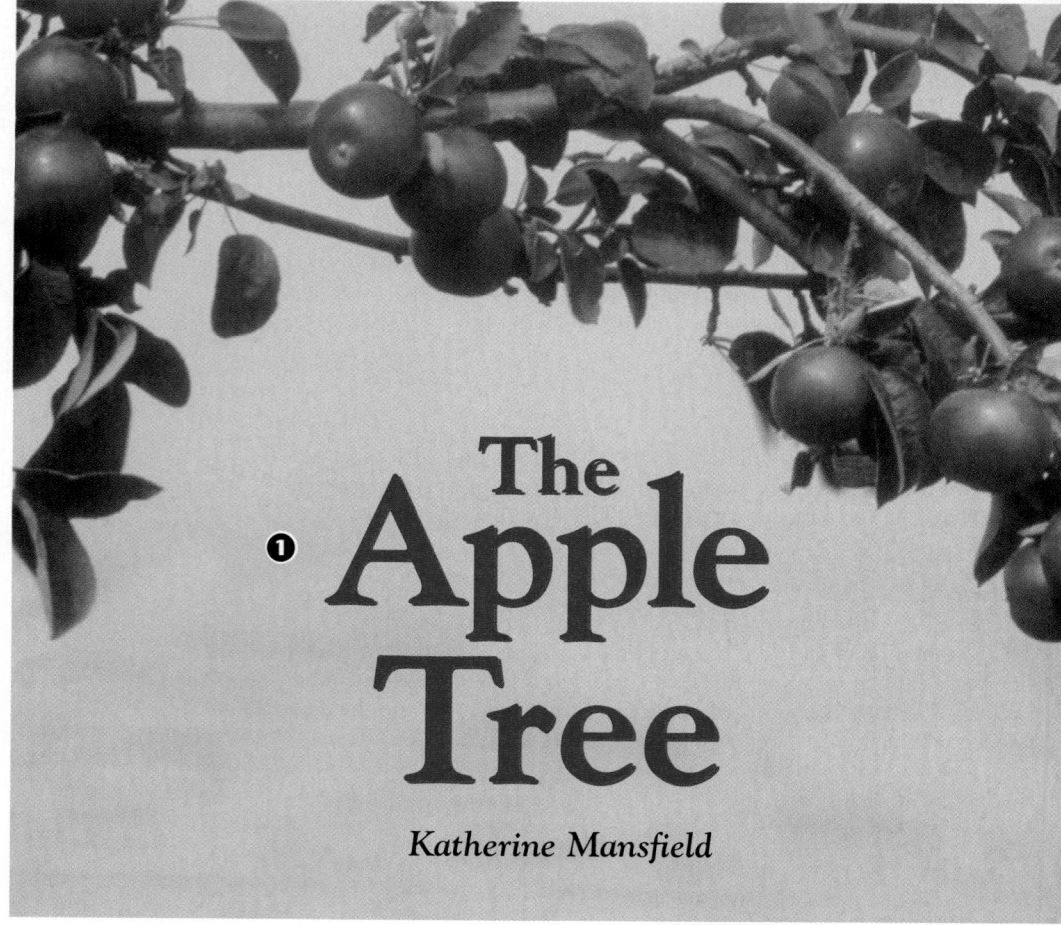

The
❶ Apple
Tree

Katherine Mansfield

❷ ▲ **Critical Viewing**
Based on this photograph, what type of setting do you expect this story to have? **[Speculate]**

There were two orchards belonging to the old house. One, that we called the "wild" orchard, lay beyond the vegetable garden; it was planted with bitter cherries and damsons[1] and transparent yellow plums. For some reason it lay under a cloud; we never played there, we did not even trouble to pick up the fallen fruit; and there, every Monday morning, to the round open space in the middle, the servant girl and the washerwoman carried the wet linen— Grandmother's nightdresses, Father's striped shirts, the hired man's cotton trousers and the servant girl's "dreadfully vulgar" salmon-pink flannelette drawers jigged and slapped in

---

1. **damsons** (dam′ zənz) *n.* small purple plums.

TEACHING RESOURCES

The following resources can be used to enrich or extend the instruction for pp. 206–210.

Literary Analysis

📖 **Selection Support:** Literary Analysis, p. 56

📑 **Writing Models and Graphic Organizers on Transparencies,** pp. 79–81 ▦

Reading

🎧 **Listening to Literature Audiocassettes,** Side 8 ▦

💿 **Listening to Literature Audio CDs,** CD 5 ▦

▦ **BLOCK SCHEDULING:** Resources marked with this symbol provide varied instruction during 90-minute blocks.

horrid familiarity. But the other orchard, far away and hidden from the house, lay at the foot of a little hill and stretched right over to the edge of the <u>paddocks</u>—to the clumps of wattles[2] bobbing yellow in the bright sun and the blue gums with their streaming sickle-shaped leaves. There, under the fruit trees, the grass grew so thick and coarse that it tangled and knotted in your shoes as you walked, and even on the hottest day it was damp to touch when you stopped and parted it this way and that, looking for windfalls—the apples marked with a bird's beak, the big bruised pears, the quinces,[3] so good to eat with a pinch of salt, but so delicious to smell that you could not bite for sniffing. . . .

One year the orchard had its Forbidden Tree. It was an apple tree discovered by Father and a friend during an after-dinner prowl one Sunday afternoon.

"Great Scott!" said the friend, lighting upon it with every appearance of admiring astonishment: "Isn't that a—?" And a rich, splendid name settled like an unknown bird on the tree.

"Yes, I believe it is," said Father lightly. He knew nothing whatever about the names of fruit trees.

"Great Scott!" said the friend again: "They're wonderful apples. Nothing like 'em—and you're going to have a tiptop crop. Marvelous apples! You can't beat 'em!"

"No, they're very fine—very fine," said Father carelessly, but looking upon the tree with new and lively interest.

"They're rare—they're very rare. Hardly ever see 'em in England nowadays," said the visitor and set a seal on Father's delight. For Father was a self-made man and the price he had to pay for everything was so huge and so painful that nothing rang so sweet to him as to hear his purchase praised. He was young and sensitive still. He still wondered whether in the deepest sense he got his money's worth. He still had hours when he walked up and down in the moonlight half deciding to "chuck this confounded rushing to the office every day—and clear out—clear out once and for all." And now to discover that he'd a valuable apple tree thrown in with the orchard—an apple tree that this Johnny from England positively envied!

"Don't touch that tree! Do you hear me, children!" said he, bland and firm; and when the guest had gone, with quite another voice and manner:

2. **wattles** (wät´ əlz) *n.* small flowering trees.
3. **quinces** (kwins´ iz) *n.* hard, greenish-yellow, apple-shaped fruit.

paddocks (pad´ əks) *n.* small enclosed fields

Literary Analysis
Allusion What allusion does the author make here?

☑ Reading Check
What did Father and his friend find in the orchard?

The Apple Tree ◆ 207

❸ Reading Strategy
Questioning

- Remind students that asking questions can help readers focus on important details as well as set a purpose for reading.
- Model the questioning strategy for students by asking them why the second orchard is so appealing to the narrator.
  Answer: It is hidden, grassy, cool, and more remote than the wild orchard.
- Explain that by asking and answering this question, readers begin to learn about the second orchard, which plays a key role in the story.

❹ Literary Analysis
Allusion

- Have a volunteer read aloud the bracketed passage.
- Direct students' attention to the phrase "Forbidden Tree." Ask students why they think these words are capitalized.
  Answer: The author wants to draw the reader's attention to them. It shows that the tree is an important element in the story.
- Then, ask students whether they have heard this term before. Ask students the Literary Analysis question on p. 207: What allusion does the author make here?
  Answer: The author is alluding to the Tree of Knowledge and the forbidden fruit on it in the Garden of Eden in the biblical story of Adam and Eve.

❺ ☑ Reading Check

Answer: Father and his friend found an apple tree that the friend says is very rare and bears wonderful apples.

CUSTOMIZE INSTRUCTION FOR UNIVERSAL ACCESS

For Less Proficient Readers	For Advanced Readers
Ask students to make a sensory detail chart to familiarize themselves with the information on this page. Students can use the Grid organizer in **Writing Models and Graphic Organizers on Transparencies,** pp. 79–81, and list *Sight, Sound, Taste, Touch,* and *Smell* in the left-hand column. Have them put sensory details from the story in the appropriate categories.	Ask students to make a sensory detail chart to categorize details on this page that appeal to the five senses. Then, have them add more sensory details that would fit into Mansfield's descriptive passage.

Art

Orchard With Flowering Fruit Trees, Springtime, Pontoise, 1877, by Camille Pissarro

This painting captures the delicate light and colors of springtime, which suggest the season of anticipation in which the characters in this story await the fruit of an apple tree.

Camille Pissarro (1830–1903) was a French Impressionist painter, the only painter to exhibit in all eight of the Impressionist group exhibitions of 1874 to 1886. Landscapes, often with peasant figures, were his main subjects. The blossoms on the fruit trees in this painting radiate light and seem to illuminate the orchard. As Mansfield's story focuses on a fleeting event in everyday life, this painting captures a spring day—one of nature's fleeting moments.

1. From the details in the painting and the title of the selection, what can you predict about this story?
   Answer: Students may say that the plot will revolve around an apple tree, and that there is something special or mysterious about a particular tree.

2. How is the orchard in the picture different from the second orchard described in the story?
   Answer: The orchard in the story is more remote and untended than the one in the picture—there would probably be no buildings in sight.

❼ ▶Critical Viewing

Answer: Both orchards are sunny and lie at the foot of a hill. The orchard in the story is hidden from the house, though the one in the painting is not.

❻

❼ ▲ **Critical Viewing** How does this orchard look like the one described in the story? How does it look different? **[Compare and Contrast]**

208 ◆ *Striving for Success*

✺ ENRICHMENT: Science Connection

Apple Orchards

Students may think that most work at an apple orchard occurs in the late summer and early fall, when the ripe apples are picked from the trees. However, growing apples involves year-round work.

From January to March, apple growers must prune the trees to remove small, nutrient-robbing branches and to allow more sunlight into the trees.

In April and May, growers spread fertilizer throughout the orchard and spray chemicals to kill pests and plant diseases. In late May, the apple trees begin to blossom. After the blossoms are pollinated by insects, the apple petals fall off, usually in early June. Growers then make sure that there aren't too many buds on a branch. This way, they'll end up with larger apples.

The remaining months of summer are spent thinning the apple trees and checking on the progress of the apples. By late August or early September, the apple harvesting finally begins.

"If I catch either of you touching those apples you shall not only go to bed—you shall each have a good sound whipping." Which merely added to its magnificence.

Every Sunday morning after church Father, with Bogey and me tailing after, walked through the flower garden, down the violet path, past the lace-bark tree, past the white rose and syringa[4] bushes, and down the hill to the orchard. The apple tree seemed to have been miraculously warned of its high honor, standing apart from its fellows, bending a little under its rich clusters, fluttering its polished leaves, important and exquisite before Father's awful eye. His heart swelled to the sight—we knew his heart swelled. He put his hands behind his back and screwed up his eyes in the way he had. There it stood—the accidental thing—the thing that no one had been aware of when the hard bargain was driven. It hadn't been counted in, hadn't in a way been paid for. If the house had been burned to the ground at that time it would have meant less to him than the destruction of his tree. And how we played up to him, Bogey and I,—Bogey with his scratched knees pressed together, his hands behind his back, too, and a round cap on his head with "H.M.S. Thunderbolt" printed across it.

The apples turned from pale green to yellow; then they had deep pink stripes painted on them, and then the pink melted all over the yellow, reddened, and spread into a fine clear crimson.

At last the day came when Father took out of his waistcoat pocket a little pearl penknife. He reached up. Very slowly and very carefully he picked two apples growing on a bough.

"Why, they're warm," cried Father in amazement. "They're wonderful apples! Tiptop! Marvelous!" he echoed. He rolled them over in his hands.

"Look at that!" he said. "Not a spot—not a blemish!" And he walked through the orchard with Bogey and me stumbling after, to a tree stump under the wattles. We sat, one on either side of Father. He laid one apple down, opened the penknife and neatly and beautifully cut the other in half.

"Look at that!" he exclaimed.

"Father!" we cried, dutiful but really enthusiastic, too. For the lovely red color had bitten right through the white flesh of the apple; it was pink to the shiny black pips lying so justly in their scaly pods. It looked as though the apple had been dipped in wine.

"Never seen *that* before," said Father. "You won't find an apple like that in a hurry!" He put it to his nose and pronounced an unfamiliar word. "Bouquet. What a bouquet!" And then he handed to Bogey one half, to me the other.

"Don't *bolt* it!"[5] said he. It was agony to give even so much away.

---

4. **syringa** (sə rin´ gə) *n.* genus of plants, which includes 30 species of fragrant, flowering shrubs such as lilac.
5. **Don't bolt it** Don't eat it all in one bite.

The Apple Tree ◆ 209

Reading Strategy
Questioning Why is Father so adamant that the children not touch the tree?

exquisite (eks´ kwi zit) *adj.* delicately beautiful

Reading Strategy
Questioning Why is Father so excited about the apple tree?

bouquet (bōō kā´) *n.* fragrance

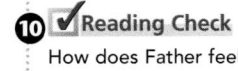 **Reading Check**
How does Father feel about the apple tree?

❽ Reading Strategy
Questioning
- Read aloud the bracketed passage to students.
- Ask students to paraphrase what Father says to the children about the apple tree. Make sure that they describe the father's tone.
  Answer: With a very angry and stern tone, Father tells the children not to touch the tree.
- Then, ask students the first Reading Strategy question on p. 209: Why is Father so adamant that the children not touch the tree?
  Answer: Students may say that Father issues the warning because he thinks the tree is very valuable.
- Lead students to see that by answering this question, they can predict how Father's new appreciation for the tree will affect events in the story.

❾ Reading Strategy
Questioning
- Have students read the bracketed passage.
- Have a volunteer summarize the events of the story up to this point.
- Then, ask students the second Reading Strategy question on p. 209: Why is Father so excited about the apple tree?
  Answer: Father believes the tree to be very rare, and the apples from it possibly very valuable.

❿ Reading Check
Answer: Father is very proud of the tree.

CUSTOMIZE INSTRUCTION FOR UNIVERSAL ACCESS

For Special Needs Students	For Gifted/Talented Students
These students may need practice questioning and making inferences from indirect characterization such as dialogue and descriptions of behavior. Have them make a chart with the following heads: *Behavior/Dialogue* and *Inference*. Show students how to list details from the story and then make inferences from them. For example, what do students infer about Father from his practice of inspecting the tree every Sunday morning? Encourage students to complete the chart as they read through the selection.	Have students choose a character in the story and make a list of his or her main traits. They can recognize these traits by making inferences based on the character's actions. Then, have students compose a journal entry for their character, expressing his or her feelings about the situation. The journal entry should be consistent with the story and reflect the character's main traits.

Answers for p. 210

Review and Assess

1. Some students may say they were surprised because of the characters' great expectation that the apples would be magnificent. Others may say that they knew the apples would be a disappointment because there was so much anticipation.

2. **(a)** The friend tells Father that the tree is very rare and wonderful. **(b)** He protects it and treasures it. **(c)** He is eager to listen because he really doesn't know very much about apples and hopes that he has acquired something extraordinary.

3. **(a)** The apples eventually became a "fine, clear crimson." **(b)** From their appearance, you would expect them to taste delicious.

4. **(a)** The children try to hide their disgust. **(b)** They pretend to enjoy the taste. In addition, their meaningful smiles at each other mask their new and ironic perception of their father. **(c)** They don't want their father to be disappointed or angry.

5. **(a)** The apples taste pulpy and bitter instead of sweet and juicy, as their appearance would indicate. **(b)** They learn that appearances can be deceiving.

6. These events disappoint because our imaginations are so powerful that nothing can live up to what we create in our minds.

7. Students may say that personally rewarding things, rather than possessions or money, are worth waiting for.

I knew it, while I took mine humbly and humbly Bogey took his.

Then he divided the second with the same neat beautiful little cut of the pearl knife.

I kept my eyes on Bogey. Together we took a bite. Our mouths were full of a floury stuff, a hard, faintly bitter skin—a horrible taste of something dry. . . .

"Well?" asked Father, very jovial. He had cut his two halves into quarters and was taking out the little pods. "Well?"

Bogey and I stared at each other, chewing desperately. In that second of chewing and swallowing a long silent conversation passed between us—and a strange meaning smile. We swallowed. We edged near Father, just touching him.

"Perfect," we lied. "Perfect—Father! Simply lovely!"

But it was no use. Father spat his out and never went near the apple tree again.

jovial (jō′ vē əl) *adj.* full of good humor

Review and Assess

Thinking About the Selection

1. **Respond:** Were you surprised by the story's ending? Explain why or why not.

2. **(a) Recall:** What does the friend from England tell Father about the apple tree? **(b) Recall:** How does Father treat the apple tree after hearing his friend's revelation? **(c) Infer:** Why is Father so eager to hear and believe what his friend has to say?

3. **(a) Recall:** Describe the apples' appearance. **(b) Speculate:** From their appearance, how would you expect the ripe apples to taste?

4. **(a) Recall:** When the children finally taste the apple, how do they react to its taste? **(b) Analyze:** Why does their outer reaction hide their true response? **(c) Infer:** Why do you think they react this way?

5. **(a) Compare and Contrast:** Explain how the taste of the apples compares with the characters' expectations. **(b) Draw Conclusions:** What lesson do Father and the children learn from this experience?

6. **Extend:** Why do you think that eagerly anticipated events so often fail to live up to people's expectations?

7. **Apply:** What things in life do you think are worth waiting for? Explain.

Katherine Mansfield

(1888–1923)
Katherine Mansfield was born in Wellington, the capital of New Zealand. While still in her teens, she moved to London to pursue a career in writing. However, she found London cold and impersonal, and this feeling is reflected in her early stories.

When her brother was killed in World War I, Mansfield began to write stories, including "The Apple Tree," based on her childhood in New Zealand. Although her life was cut short by tuberculosis, her work left a lasting mark. Katherine Mansfield is credited by critics with helping to refine and advance the art of the short story.

✐ ASSESSMENT PRACTICE: Reading Comprehension

Recognize Sequence   **(For more practice, see Test Preparation Workbook, p. 14.)**

Many tests require students to recognize sequential order in a reading passage. Give students practice by having them choose the item showing the correct order of events in "The Apple Tree."

A Father and a friend discover an apple tree; Father warns the children; the friend admires the tree.

B The friend admires the tree; Father and a friend discover an apple tree; Father warns the children.

C Father warns the children; Father and a friend discover the apple tree; the friend admires the tree.

D Father and a friend discover an apple tree; the friend admires the tree; Father warns the children.

By rereading the story, students should see that *D* is the right answer.

Review and Assess

Literary Analysis

Allusion

1. "The Apple Tree" contains **allusions** to the story of the tree in the Garden of Eden in the Bible. Use a Venn diagram like the one here to compare these stories. Consider the characters, the setting, the role of the tree, and the story's outcome.

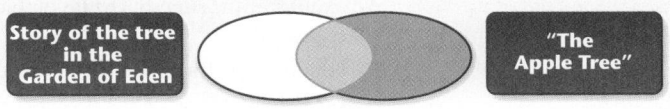

2. In the Bible, the tree stands for knowledge of worldly experience. What do you think the tree in "The Apple Tree" represents? Explain.
3. How does knowing the biblical story of the tree in the Garden of Eden increase your understanding and appreciation of "The Apple Tree"?

Connecting Literary Elements

4. (a) What words or phrases does the author use to describe the apple tree? (b) What are the **connotations** of those words and phrases?
5. For each of the following words or phrases, explain how connotation adds depth to the description: (a) a "pearl" penknife, (b) the "white flesh" of the apple, (c) the apple looked as though it had been "dipped in wine."
6. How do the connotations you have identified add to the story?

Reading Strategy

Questioning

7. What is the main **question** you have about Father's behavior?
8. After reading the story, how would you answer that question?

Extend Understanding

9. **Cultural Connection:** Father placed a high value on the apples based on the opinion of an acquaintance. Discuss how image and public approval play a role in determining the worth of some of the things we value.

Quick Review

An **allusion** is a reference to a well-known person, place, event, literary work, or work of art.

The **connotation** of a word is the set of ideas associated with it, in addition to its definition.

When you **question** as you read, you ask yourself about the meaning of events, characters' actions, and key details.

 Take It to the Net
www.phschool.com
Take the interactive self-test online to check your understanding of the selection.

The Apple Tree ◆ 211

Answers for p. 211
Review and Assess
Possible responses:

1.

God speaks to Adam and Eve. Serpent tempts Adam and Eve. — Garden of Eden

People are forbidden from eating the fruit. The fruit is eventually eaten.

Father speaks to children. Children obey Father. — The Apple Tree

2. The tree stands for worldly wealth and status because Father wants to make the most of his big investment.
3. Knowing the Bible story helps you appreciate the symbolism of forbidden fruit bringing painful knowledge.
4. (a) Possible answers: standing apart; bending a little under its rich clusters; fluttering its polished leaves. (b) The connotations are all positive and suggest wealth, rarity, and perfection.
5. (a) It suggests wealth. (b) It suggests perfection. (c) It suggests luxury.
6. They emphasize how much Father hoped for wealth and success.
7. Students may wonder why Father invested in the property at all, because it makes him so anxious.
8. Students may suggest that Father is foolish, or simply over-ambitious.
9. We may overvalue things because they make us appear better to others.

211

Answers for p. 212

❶ Vocabulary Development

Origins: Words From Myths

1. c   3. b
2. a

**Concept Development:
Synonyms**

1. c   3. a
2. b   4. a

Spelling Strategy

1. penknife   3. treehouse
2. applesauce

❷ Grammar

1. lay   4. lying
2. lay   5. lain
3. Lie

Writing Application

1. lay   2. lie

Integrate Language Skills

❶ Vocabulary Development Lesson

Origins: Words From Myths

Many English words come from Greek and Roman myths. For example, *jovial*, which means "full of good humor," comes from the name Jove, ruler of the Roman gods, who was supposedly playful and merry.

Use the clues below to match each word with the letter of its definition.

Pan: minor god who lived in wild places and sometimes frightened travelers

Chaos: formless confusion that existed before Earth or the gods appeared

Lethe: river of forgetfulness that separates the worlds of the living and the dead

1. lethal   a. completely confused
2. chaotic   b. sudden, hysterical fear
3. panic   c. deadly

Concept Development: Synonyms

On your paper, write the word or phrase whose meaning is closest to that of the first word.

1. jovial: (a) simple, (b) wealthy, (c) merry
2. paddock: (a) marsh, (b) pasture, (c) grove
3. exquisite: (a) superb, (b) favorable, (c) worldly
4. bouquet: (a) fragrance, (b) collection, (c) roses

Spelling Strategy

A compound word is a two-part word that functions as a single unit. The parts of a compound word may be written separately (fruit trees), hyphenated (half-moon), or closed up (windfall). Put the following words together in combinations that make three compound words.

knife   tree   pen   apple   sauce   house

❷ Grammar Lesson

Confusing Verbs: *lay* and *lie*

Because *lay* and *lie* seem similar and because the past tense of *lie* is *lay*, these verbs are often confused. **Lay** means "to put or set (something) down." Its principal parts—*lay*, *laying*, *laid*, and *laid*—are usually followed by a direct object. **Lie** means "to recline." Its principal parts—*lie*, *lying*, *lay*, and *lain*—are never followed by a direct object.

> D.O.
> He **laid** one apple down and picked up another. (past tense of *lay*)
>
> For some reason, the orchard **lay** under a cloud. (past tense of *lie*)

Practice For each item, identify the word that correctly completes the sentence.

1. The apple (lay, laid) there until it rotted.
2. Father (laid, lay) down under the tree.
3. (Lie, Lay) down, and I'll give you an ice pack.
4. What is that (laying, lying) in the grass?
5. We had (laid, lain) awake all night in anticipation.

Writing Application Replace the underlined words in these sentences with *lie* or *lay*.

1. I <u>put</u> the knives on the table.
2. The dog wants to <u>recline</u> on the sofa.

W/G *Prentice Hall Writing and Grammar Connection: Chapter 26, Section 2*

▪ **BLOCK SCHEDULING:** Resources marked with this symbol provide varied instruction during 90-minute blocks.

❸ Writing Lesson

Retelling a Story

On one level, "The Apple Tree" is a retelling of the biblical story of the tree in the Garden of Eden. Choose a story that you can retell from the Bible, classical mythology, or literature. Retell it, giving it a new setting or other twist.

Prewriting   Decide how to make your retelling unique. For example, you might recast *Romeo and Juliet* in modern times in your community. Then, list the key elements of the work or event you are adapting.

Drafting   Add interest by showing readers your setting and characters rather than simply telling about them. Use specific details and figurative language to show your readers what you want them to see.

> **Model: Drafting to Show, Not Tell**
>
>   When Rodney used his cellphone to call Jill, he excused himself from the table and ducked into a corner of the busy restaurant. As he dialed, he checked to see that no one was watching him. The sound of Jill's voice took him away from the crowd and back to the starry night they both remembered.
>
> > The writer does not say that Rodney is hiding his love for Jill. Instead, the writing shows it.

Revising   Compare your retelling with the original. Add descriptive details about the characters that show what you want readers to know.

W̶G   *Prentice Hall Writing and Grammar Connection: Chapter 13, Section 2*

❹ Extension Activities

Listening and Speaking Prepare a **monologue** in which you tell the story of "The Apple Tree" from Father's point of view. Imagine that you are Father, speaking your thoughts aloud.

- Describe your feelings about being told that the tree is valuable.
- Talk about your anticipation as you watch the apples ripen.
- Explain your disappointment when you finally taste the apple.

Share your monologue with classmates.

Research and Technology Use details from the story and your imagination to draw an **annotated map** of the family's property in "The Apple Tree." Show the locations of the two orchards and of "The Forbidden Tree." Include short descriptions from the story on your map. Generate the map with graphics software, using special fonts, shading, and design elements.

 Take It to the Net   www.phschool.com

Go online for an additional research activity using the Internet.

The Apple Tree ◆ 213

Lesson Support for p. 213

❸ Writing Lesson

- Model an outline of a biblical, classical, or contemporary story. Explain to students that an outline is a useful way of organizing one's thoughts before writing. You may wish to show students the Outline transparency on p.103 of **Writing Models and Graphic Organizers on Transparencies.**

- Have students make their own outlines of the stories they choose.

- Use the Writing Lesson to help students in developing a retelling of a story.

❹ Listening and Speaking

- Have students prepare index cards, each of which contains an idea they want Father to express.

- Have students annotate the cards with directions about gestures and tone of voice that would be appropriate for that idea.

- Have students deliver their monologues to the class.

- Have students use the rubric for Delivering a Narrative Presentation, p. 28 in **Performance Assessment and Portfolio Management.**

CUSTOMIZE INSTRUCTION
For Universal Access

To address different learning styles, use the activities suggested in the **Extension Activities** booklet, p. 14.

- For Verbal/Linguistic and Intrapersonal Learners, use Activity 5.
- For Interpersonal Learners, use Activity 6.

ASSESSMENT RESOURCES

The following resources can be used to assess students' knowledge and skills.

Selection Assessment

 Formal Assessment, pp. 44–46

 Open Book Test, pp. 40–42

▦ **Got It! Assessment Videotapes**, Tape 1

◉ **Test Bank Software**

💻 *Take It to the Net*
    Visit www.phschool.com for self-tests and additional questions on "The Apple Tree."

Listening and Speaking Rubric

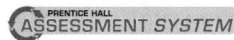 **Performance Assess. and Portfolio Mgmt.**, p. 28

PRENTICE HALL
ASSESSMENT *SYSTEM*

 Workbook   ▤ **Transparencies**

 Skill Book   ◉ **CD-ROM**

213

Africa ✦ Old Song ✦ All ✦ Also All ✦ *from* The Analects

Lesson Objectives

1. **To analyze and respond to literary elements**
   - Literary Analysis: Aphorisms
   - Comparing Literary Works: Universal themes

2. **To read, comprehend, analyze, and critique poetry and nonfiction**
   - Reading Strategy: Relating to What You Know
   - Reading Check questions
   - Review and Assess questions
   - Assessment Practice (ATE)

3. **To develop word analysis skills, fluency, and systematic vocabulary**
   - Vocabulary Development Lesson: Latin Suffix: *-ment*

4. **To understand and apply written and oral language conventions**
   - Spelling Strategy
   - Grammar Lesson: Active and Passive Voice

5. **To understand and apply appropriate writing and research strategies**
   - Writing Lesson: Evaluation
   - Extension Activity: News article

6. **To understand and apply listening and speaking strategies**
   - Extension Activity: Interview

STEP-BY-STEP TEACHING GUIDE	PACING GUIDE
PRETEACH	
Motivate Students and Provide Background	
Use the Motivation activity (ATE p. 214)	5 min.
Read and discuss the Preview material and Background information (SE/ATE p. 214)	5 min.
Introduce the Concepts	
Introduce the Literary Analysis and Reading Strategy (SE/ATE p. 215) 🅰	15 min.
Pronounce the vocabulary words and read their definitions (SE p. 215)	5 min.
TEACH	
Monitor Comprehension	
Informally monitor comprehension by circulating while students read independently or in groups 🅰	10 min.
Monitor students' comprehension with the Reading Check notes (SE/ATE p. 221)	as students read
Develop vocabulary with Vocabulary notes (SE pp. 216, 218, 221; ATE p. 221)	as students read
Develop Understanding	
Develop students' understanding of aphorisms with Literary Analysis annotations (SE p. 221; ATE pp. 215, 219, 220, 221) 🅰	10 min.
Develop students' understanding of relating to what you know with Reading Strategy annotations (ATE pp. 215, 216, 218, 221)	10 min.
ASSESS	
Assess Mastery	
Assess students' mastery of the Reading Strategy and Literary Analysis by having them answer the Review and Assess questions (SE/ATE p. 223)	20 min.
Use one or more of the print and media Assessment Resources (ATE p. 225) 🅰	up to 50 min.
EXTEND	
Apply Understanding	
Have students complete the Vocabulary Development Lesson and the Grammar Lesson (SE p. 224) 🅰	20 min.
Apply students' knowledge of revising to elaborate using the Writing Lesson (SE/ATE p. 225) 🅰	45 min.
Apply students' understanding using one or more of the Extension Activities (SE p. 225)	20–90 min.

A ACCELERATED INSTRUCTION:
Use the strategies and activities identified with an 🅰.

UNIVERSAL ACCESS
● = Below Level Students
▲ = On-Level Students
■ = Above Level Students

Time and Resource Manager

RESOURCES

PRINT 📖	TRANSPARENCIES	TECHNOLOGY 💿 🎧 📼
• **Beyond Literature,** Multicultural Connection: "Words to the Wise," p. 15 ▲ ■		• **Interest Grabber Video,** Tape 1 ● ▲ ■
• **Selection Support Workbook:** ● ▲ ■ Literary Analysis, p. 60 Reading Strategy, p. 59 Build Vocabulary, p. 57	• **Literary Analysis and Reading Transparencies,** pp. 29 and 30 ● ▲ ■	
		• **Listening to Literature** ● ▲ ■ Audiocassettes, Side 8 Audio CDs, CD 5
• **Literatura en español** ● ▲ • **Literary Analysis for Enrichment** ■	• **Fine Art Transparencies, Volume 1,** Art Transparencies 9, 17 ● ▲ ■	
• **Formal Assessment:** Selection Test, pp. 47–49 ● ▲ ■ • **Open Book Test,** pp. 43–45 ● ▲ ■ • **Performance Assessment and Portfolio Management,** pp. 15, 27 ● ▲ ■ **PRENTICE HALL** **ASSESSMENT** *SYSTEM* ● ▲ ■	**PRENTICE HALL** **ASSESSMENT** *SYSTEM* ● ▲ ■ Skills Practice Answers and Explanations on Transparencies	• **Test Bank Software** ● ▲ ■ • **Got It! Assessment Videotapes,** Tape 1 ● ▲
• **Selection Support Workbook:** ● ▲ ■ Build Grammar Skills, p. 58 • **Writing and Grammar,** Platinum Level ● ▲ ■ • **Extension Activities,** p. 15 ● ▲ ■	• **Daily Language Practice Transparencies** ● ▲ • **Writing Models and Graphic Organizers on Transparencies,** pp. 95–97 ● ▲ ■	• **Writing and Grammar iText CD-ROM** ● ▲ ■ 💻 *Take It to the Net* www.phschool.com

BLOCK SCHEDULING: Use one 90-minute class period to preteach the selection and have students read it. Use a second 90-minute class period to assess students' mastery of skills and have them complete one of the Extension Activities.

Step-by-Step Teaching guide for pp. 214–215

Motivation

Let students know that two poems in this grouping allude indirectly to the Tiananmen Square massacre in 1989. A large group of Chinese students gathered in Tiananmen Square in Beijing, China, to protest the actions of the Chinese government. The protesters wanted more freedom, including freedom of speech. In response to the protest, the Chinese government sent tanks and armed troops to stop the demonstration. Hundreds of people were killed.

Interest Grabber Video

As an alternative, play "Apartheid in South Africa" on Tape 1 to engage student interest.

❶ Background

Culture

Traditional African poetry was not written down. Instead, it was passed down orally from generation to generation, usually as chants and songs. This work included myths, epics, and religious chants, and covered almost every aspect of daily African life. These poetic works display a high degree of creativity and humor, while expressing the collective wisdom of many generations.

Prepare to Read

Africa ◆ Old Song ◆ All ◆ Also All ◆ *from* The Analects

Take It to the Net

Visit www.phschool.com for interactive activities and instruction related to these selections, including

- background
- graphic organizers
- literary elements
- reading strategies

Preview

Connecting to the Literature

You get advice from teachers, parents, and friends. Authors want to give you advice, too. The writers of these selections may not give you the same advice because they come from different backgrounds. As you read, think about what they suggest about a person's goals in life.

❶ Background

Many African societies passed on their wisdom in a rich oral tradition. In each village, elders handed down wisdom in the form of sayings, stories, and poems, like "Old Song." *The Analects,* or the collected sayings of the Chinese scholar Confucius, were also passed down orally. They were compiled in writing long after his death, more than two thousand years ago, and have survived for generations.

TEACHING RESOURCES

The following resources can be used to enrich or extend the instruction for pp. 214–215.

Motivation

📼 **Interest Grabber Video,** Tape 1

Background

📖 **Beyond Literature,** Multicultural Connection: "Words to the Wise," p. 15 ▪

Take It to the Net

Visit www.phschool.com for background and hotlinks for the selections.

Literary Analysis

📄 **Literary Analysis and Reading Transparencies,** Aphorisms, p. 30 ▪

Reading

📖 **Selection Support:** Reading Strategy, p. 59; Build Vocabulary, p. 57

📄 **Literary Analysis and Reading Transparencies,** Relating to What You Know, p. 29

▪ **BLOCK SCHEDULING:** Resources marked with this symbol provide varied instruction during 90-minute blocks.

❷ Literary Analysis

Aphorisms

The ideas of Confucius have endured partly because they were expressed as **aphorisms**—brief sayings that convey a basic truth. Many cultures pass on truths in the form of aphorisms, like gifts handed down from one generation to the next. Following is an example of an aphorism from "Old Song."

> Do not seek too much fame, / but do not seek obscurity.

As you read, look for other examples of aphorisms in the selections. Read them thoughtfully, contemplating what they say about life.

Comparing Literary Works

These selections come from distant parts of the globe—Africa and China—but if you look closely, you will discover that the themes expressed through their aphorisms are universal. **Universal themes** are messages that are relevant to people of almost any time and place. For example, people of all times and places have struggled with the expectations and behaviors associated with honor, one of the themes that Confucius addresses in *The Analects*. Compare the ways that the themes you identify in each work are supported by the cultural details and aphorisms the writer has used. Use a diagram like the one here to help you identify the themes.

❸ Reading Strategy

Relating to What You Know

The best way to judge advice is to think about how it applies to your own situation. Similarly, the best way to understand a writer's words is to **relate** them to **what you know**—find something in your own experience that helps you understand them. Consider their messages about survival, hope, dignity, and morality, and apply them to your own experiences.

Vocabulary Development

impetuous (im pech′ o͞o əs) *adj.* impulsive; sudden (p. 216)

lamentation (lam′ ən tā′ shən) *n.* act of crying out in grief; wailing (p. 218)

chastisements (chas′ tīz mənts) *n.* punishments (p. 221)

Aphorisms

Slow in word, but prompt in deed.

↓

Importance

Don't make promises rashly. Always honor your promises.

↓

Possible Theme

Honor; Integrity

❷ Literary Analysis
Aphorisms

- Emphasize the concise nature of the aphorism. Ask students to note how a very important truth is revealed in a very short statement.

- To help students grasp the concept, ask them to write aphorisms of their own or share aphorisms with which they are familiar.

- Read aloud the example from "Old Song," and ask students to discuss the truth contained in the lines.

- Have students look for aphorisms as they read these selections and identify the basic truths expressed in them.

❸ Reading Strategy
Relating to What You Know

- Explain to students that they should always try to make personal connections with what they read. Noting similarities between what they read and their own experiences will help them to more fully appreciate a text.

- Explain to students that they will better understand an aphorism if they identify its truth and then apply it to their own life.

- For example, have students explain how the aphorism on this page, "Do not seek too much fame, / but do not seek obscurity," relates to a situation they've experienced.

Vocabulary Development

- Pronounce each vocabulary word for students, and read the definitions as a class. Have students identify any words with which they are already familiar.

CUSTOMIZE INSTRUCTION FOR UNIVERSAL ACCESS

For Less Proficient Readers	For English Learners	For Advanced Readers
To help ensure their understanding of the poems, encourage students to work with partners to paraphrase the lines of poetry as they read.	Students may have difficulty pronouncing some of the longer words in these selections, such as *humbleness, impetuous, chastisements,* and *reverberates.* Encourage students to break down these words into smaller parts to help them sound out the pronunciations.	Have students list synonyms for words used in the poems. Encourage students to use the words on their lists to compose aphoristic poems on similar themes.

 E-Teach

Visit E-Teach at www.phschool.com for teachers' essays on how to teach, with questions and answers.

CUSTOMIZE INSTRUCTION
For Visual/Spatial Learners

Encourage students to analyze the imagery in David Diop's poem, "Africa." What associations do they make with the "young and sturdy tree," the "white and faded flowers," and the "fruits" that "grow to have/The bitter taste of liberty"? Why might the taste of liberty be bitter?

❶ About the Selections

These poems offer valuable insights intended to guide, caution, inspire, and ignite. The poem by David Diop searches for roots and renewal, while the traditional song offers quiet, steady strength.

❷ Reading Strategy

Relating to What You Know

• Have students read the poem to themselves. Then, focus their attention on the bracketed passage.

• Encourage students to think about their heritage. Ask them whether their ancestors had to overcome hardship and oppression and how this affected students' lives.
Answer: Students' responses should demonstrate how they have been influenced by previous generations in their families.

❸ ▶Critical Viewing

Answer: The painting shows Africans working together, though in a tiring, back-breaking task, as described in "Africa." "Old Song" describes values and traditions, such as working together, that are passed down from generation to generation.

---

❶ AFRICA

David Diop
Translated by Ulli Beier

Traditional Yam Harvest, John Mainga, LAMU, The Gallery of Contemporary African Art

To My Mother

❷

  Africa my Africa
  Africa of proud warriors in the ancestral savannahs[1]
  Africa my grandmother sings of
  Beside her distant river
5 I have never seen you
  But my gaze is full of your blood
  Your black blood spilt over the fields
  The blood of your sweat
  The sweat of your toil
10 The toil of slavery
  The slavery of your children
  Africa, tell me Africa,
  Are you the back that bends
  Lies down under the weight of humbleness?
15 The trembling back striped red
  That says yes to the sjambok[2] on the roads of noon?
  Solemnly a voice answers me
  "Impetuous child, that young and sturdy tree
  That tree that grows
20 There splendidly alone among white and faded flowers
  Is Africa, your Africa. It puts forth new shoots
  With patience and stubbornness puts forth new shoots
  Slowly its fruits grow to have
  The bitter taste of liberty."

---

1. **savannahs** (sə van´ əz) *n.* tropical grasslands containing scattered trees.
2. **sjambok** (sham´ bäk) *n.* whip.

216 ◆ *Striving for Success*

❸ ▲ **Critical Viewing**
Discuss how this painting reflects the thoughts conveyed in both poems. **[Synthesize]**

impetuous (im pech´ ‾oo əs) *adj.* impulsive; sudden

David Diop

(1927–1960)

David Diop published only one volume of poetry before his life was tragically cut short in a plane crash. That book, *Hammerblows*, reflects Diop's rejection of colonialism in Africa. His poem "Africa" captures the power and dignity of a continent struggling against oppression.

TEACHING RESOURCES

The following resources can be used to enrich or extend the instruction for pp. 216–222.

Literary Analysis

📖 **Selection Support:** Literary Analysis, p. 60

▦ **Writing Models and Graphic Organizers on Transparencies,** pp. 95–97 ▪

Reading

🎧 **Listening to Literature Audiocassettes,** Side 8 ▪

💿 **Listening to Literature Audio CDs,** CD 5 ▪

Extension

▦ **Fine Art Transparencies, Volume 1,** Art Transparencies 9, 17

▪ **BLOCK SCHEDULING:** Resources marked with this symbol provide varied instruction during 90-minute blocks.

OLD SONG

Do not seek too much fame,
but do not seek obscurity.
Be proud.
But do not remind the world of your deeds.
5   Excel when you must,
but do not excel the world.
Many heroes are not yet born,
many have already died.
To be alive to hear this song is a victory.

Review and Assess

Thinking About the Selections

1. **Respond:** Which poem did you find more powerful? Why?
2. **(a) Recall:** What question does the speaker of "Africa" ask?
   (b) Infer: What troubles the speaker of "Africa," causing him to ask his question?
3. **(a) Recall:** What answer does a voice provide? **(b) Analyze:** How do you think the speaker feels about the response? Explain.
4. **(a) Recall:** What advice about fame is found in "Old Song"? **(b) Interpret:** Is this poem written as a message of support or as a warning? Explain.
5. **Make a Judgment:** Which of these two poems has a more hopeful message? Explain.
6. **Extend:** These poems suggest that success can rise out of failure. Explain why you agree or disagree.

---

❹ Background

Art

Traditional Yam Harvest, by John Mainga

This colorful work echoes the style of a traditional wood cut. Use the following question for discussion:

How would you describe the mood of this painting? Use details from the painting to support your answer. Answer: Although the painting uses vivid colors, the mood is serious because the workers seem focused on their work.

Answers for p. 217

Review and Assess

1. Some students might cite "Africa" because of its strong tone; others might prefer the quiet power of "Old Song."
2. **(a)** The speaker asks whether Africa is meant to be treated as a slave. **(b)** He is troubled by Africa's legacy of slavery.
3. **(a)** The voice tells the speaker that the tree of liberty is slowly growing. **(b)** Students may say they think the speaker is deeply touched and comforted by the message.
4. **(a)** The advice is to seek neither fame nor obscurity. **(b)** Students may say that the poem is both a warning of behavior to avoid, and a message of support, telling the reader that his or her own life is a triumph.
5. Students may say that "Old Song" is more hopeful because it reveres life, whereas "Africa" calls the fruit of liberty "bitter."
6. Success can rise out of failure because when people have learned the lessons of failure, they can rise above it by acting on those lessons.

✸ ENRICHMENT: Social Studies

West Africa

David Diop's poem speaks of the oppression African people have suffered under colonial rule and apartheid governmental systems. The following historical background about West Africa, the location of Diop's homeland, Senegal, will enrich students' reading experience:

In the late 1800s, the French government looked to Africa as a potential source of much-needed land, resources, and human power. As French colonial rule spread, the African people were subjugated and exploited. Colonial rule has slowly been replaced by independence, but French dominance in many West African countries is still evident, and economic and educational opportunities are still far from equal. The people of post-colonial Africa remain faced with the challenge of overcoming the legacy of exploitation and re-establishing their cultural identities.

217

❺ All

Bei Dao

Translated by Donald Finkel
and Xueliang Chen

lamentation (lam´ ən tā´ shən) *n.* act of crying out in grief; wailing

All is fated,
all cloudy,

all an endless beginning,
all a search for what vanishes,

❻   5   all joys grave,
all griefs tearless,

❼   every speech a repetition,
every meeting a first encounter,

all love buried in the heart,
10   all history prisoned in a dream,

all hope hedged with doubt,
all faith drowned in <u>lamentation</u>.

Every explosion heralds an instant of stillness,
every death reverberates forever.

Bei Dao

(b. 1949)

Bei Dao seemed destined for a successful government career. However, he dropped out of school and joined the Red Guards, a movement of teenagers seeking to revitalize the Chinese Revolution. When he became disillusioned with the violent tactics of this movement, he turned to writing poetry. His poems became rallying cries for those who wanted China to become more democratic. He has lived outside China since 1989, when Chinese leaders ordered the massacre of protesting students in Tiananmen Square.

❺ Also All

In answer to Bei Dao's "All"

Shu Ting

Translated by Donald Finkel
and Jinsheng Yi

Not all trees are felled by storms.
Not every seed finds barren soil.
Not all the wings of dream are broken,
nor is all affection doomed
5 to wither in a desolate heart.

No, not all is as you say.

Not all flames consume themselves,
shedding no light on other lives.
Not all stars announce the night
10 and never dawn. Not every song
will drift past every ear and heart.

No, not all is as you say.

Not every cry for help is silenced,
nor every loss beyond recall.
15 Not every chasm spells disaster.
Not only the weak will be brought to their knees,
nor every soul be trodden under.

It won't all end in tears and blood.
Today is heavy with tomorrow—
20 the future was planted yesterday.
Hope is a burden all of us shoulder
though we might stumble under the load.

Old Trees by Cold Waterfall, 1470–1559, Wen Zhengming. The Los Angeles County Museum of Art

❾ ▲ Critical Viewing Which poem is better illustrated by this traditional artwork? **[Connect]**

Shu Ting

(b. 1952)

As a teenager, Shu Ting was forced by political events to leave Beijing and live in a small peasant village. She gained fame as a poet while she was still in her twenties, winning China's National Poetry Award in 1981 and 1983.

Also All ◆ 219

❽ Background

Art

Old Trees by Cold Waterfall, by Wen Zhengming

Chinese landscape painting follows an orderly set of rules, in keeping with the teachings of Confucius. Mountains, streams, rocks, and trees are delicately executed with only minimal brush strokes.

Wen Zhengming (1470–1559) was a Ming dynasty painter who was revered as the ideal scholar-artist. After a career as a government official and a historian, he decided to abandon his city position. He retired to the country, and for the last thirty years of his life devoted himself to painting, poetry, and calligraphy. Have students look at the painting and discuss the following question:

Why do you think the human figures in this painting are so small in relation to the landscape? What is the effect of this portrayal?
Answer: The small size of the human figures emphasizes the grandeur of the landscape.

❾ ▶ Critical Viewing

Answer: Students will say that the painting's peaceful portrayal of nature better illustrates the hopeful poem "Also All."

❿ Literary Analysis

Aphorisms

- Once students have read the poem, have a volunteer read aloud the last two lines.
- Remind students that an aphorism is a short statement that reveals a universal truth or lesson.
- Ask students whether they think these lines could be considered an aphorism. Why or why not?
Possible response: The lines are an aphorism because they teach a lesson in a succinct, spare manner.

CUSTOMIZE INSTRUCTION FOR UNIVERSAL ACCESS

For Less Proficient Readers	For English Learners	For Gifted/Talented Students
To help students grasp the literal meaning of the poems, have them read them aloud and in unison. Encourage students to identify how Shu Ting's poem answers Bei Dao's. Have them note that where Bei Dao sees "all love buried in the heart," Shu Ting replies with a more hopeful message about love.	Suggest that students paraphrase the poems in their own words to grasp their literal meaning. Point out, however, that the original language of the poem is much more effective in conveying the poem's mood.	Have students form debate teams. One team may take the position of the speaker in "All," and the other, of the speaker in "Also All." Have them debate the point under discussion, hope versus despair. Make sure students cite lines from the poems in support of their arguments.

from ***The Analects***

⓫ Confucius

Translated by Arthur Waley

孔夫子

⓬ ◀ Critical Viewing
How does this picture of Confucius relate to his teachings? **[Connect]**

220 ◆ *Striving for Success*

The Master[1] said, To learn and at due times to repeat what one has learnt, is that not after all[2] a pleasure? That friends should come to one from afar, is this not after all delightful? To remain unsoured even though one's merits are unrecognized by others, is that not after all what is expected of a gentleman?

The Master said, A young man's duty is to behave well to his parents at home and to his elders abroad, to be cautious in giving promises and punctual in keeping them, to have kindly feelings towards everyone, but seek the intimacy of the Good. If, when all that is done, he has any energy to spare, then let him study the polite arts.[3]

The Master said, (the good man) does not grieve that other people do not recognize his merits. His only anxiety is lest he should fail to recognize theirs.

The Master said, He who rules by moral force is like the pole-star,[4] which remains in its place while all the lesser stars do homage to it.

The Master said, If out of three hundred Songs[5] I had to take one phrase to cover all my teaching, I would say, "Let there be no evil in your thoughts."

The Master said, Govern the people by regulations, keep order among them by <u>chastisements</u>, and they will flee from you, and lose all self-respect. Govern them by moral force, keep order among them by ritual, and they will keep their self-respect and come to you of their own accord.

Meng Wu Po[6] asked about the treatment of parents. The Master said, Behave in such a way that your father and mother have no anxiety about you, except concerning your health.

The Master said, A gentleman can see a question from all sides without bias. The small man is biased and can see a question only from one side.

The Master said, Yu[7] shall I teach you what knowledge is? When you know a thing, to recognize that you know it, and when you do not know a thing, to recognize that you do not know it. That is knowledge.

The Master said, High office filled by men of narrow views, ritual performed without reverence, the forms of mourning observed without grief—these are things I cannot bear to see!

The Master said, In the presence of a good man, think all the time how you may learn to equal him. In the presence of a bad man, turn your gaze within!

The Master said, In old days a man kept a hold on his words,

---

1. **The Master** Confucius.
2. **after all** even though one does not hold public office.
3. **the polite arts** such activities as reciting from *The Book of Songs,* practicing archery, and learning proper behavior.
4. **pole-star** Polaris, the North Star.
5. **three hundred Songs** poems in *The Book of Songs.*
6. **Meng Wu Po** (muŋ wōō bō) the son of one of Confucius' disciples.
7. **Yu** (yōō) Tzu-lu, one of Confucius' disciples.

Literary Analysis
Aphorisms Express the aphorism "Let there be no evil in your thoughts" in modern English.

chastisements (chas′ tiz mənts) *n.* punishments

 ✓ **Reading Check**

What happens in a government run by regulation and chastisement?

from The Analects ◆ 221

⓯ **Literary Analysis**
Aphorisms

- Ask students the Literary Analysis question on p. 221: Express the aphorism "Let there be no evil in your thoughts" in modern English. **Possible response:** Think only good things.

- Then, ask students whether they have heard this sentiment expressed in another form. Encourage students to discuss situations when they have heard this advice, and whether it proved to be useful.

⓰ **Vocabulary Development**
The Latin Suffix *–ment*

- Draw students' attention to the word *chastisements* and its definition, "punishments."

- Explain that the Latin suffix *–ment* helps to create nouns. Therefore, *chastisements* is the noun form of *chastise,* which means "to punish."

- Have students turn other verbs into nouns by adding the suffix *–ment.* **Possible responses:** *government, statement, assignment, enrollment.*

⓱ **Reading Strategy**
Relating to What You Know

- Have students read the bracketed passage.

- Have students explain what Confucius is suggesting. **Answer:** Confucius suggests that children should behave in ways that do not make their parents worry about them.

- Then, ask students to relate this idea to their own lives. Do they agree with it? Do they consider it to be realistic?

⓲ ✓ **Reading Check**
Answer: The people will flee from you if you govern by regulation and chastisement.

CUSTOMIZE INSTRUCTION FOR UNIVERSAL ACCESS

For Special Needs Students	For Gifted/Talented Students
Discuss a few of the aphorisms, and have students rewrite them in their own words. Then, ask them to give examples of situations in which the aphorisms would prove helpful. Ask them to be as specific as possible.	Have these readers define *intelligence* and *wisdom.* Discuss with them the differences between the two and recognize the reason that someone who has one quality does not necessarily have the other. Ask them to discuss the kind of experiences that would lead a person to develop wisdom.

Review and Assess

1. Students may say that they would have been drawn to Confucius because they believe his advice to be wise.

2. **(a)** He says that everything comes to grief, including joy, love, hope, faith, and history. **(b)** The message is that there is no reason for hope.

3. **(a)** She believes that there is reason to have hope for the future. **(b)** She calls today "heavy"; she calls hope a "burden"; and she indicates that sometimes we will "stumble," or fail to keep up hope.

4. **(a)** She acknowledges that it is not easy to keep hope. **(b)** She says that all of us have it.

5. **(a)** He says that people should cause their parents no worry. **(b)** His belief suggests that every individual affects the lives of others.

6. **(a)** Knowledge is recognizing what you know and what you do not know. **(b)** Recognizing what you do not know is an aspect of humility.

7. **(a)** Governing by moral force means governing by strong moral principles, not by intimidation. **(b)** Yes, because seeing all sides of a question can help a ruler make compassionate and wise choices.

8. Possible response: "A gentleman is ashamed to let his words outrun his deeds." This might keep me from boasting or promising more than I can deliver.

9. Possible response: Students should mention events that cause people to lose hope.

---

fearing the disgrace that would ensue should he himself fail to keep pace with them.

The Master said, A gentleman covets the reputation of being slow in word but prompt in deed.

The Master said, In old days men studied for the sake of self-improvement; nowadays men study in order to impress other people.

The Master said, A gentleman is ashamed to let his words outrun his deeds.

The Master said, He who will not worry about what is far off will soon find something worse than worry close at hand.

The Master said, To demand much from oneself and little from others is the way (for a ruler) to banish discontent.

Review and Assess

Thinking About the Selections

1. **Respond:** If you had lived in China during the time of Confucius, do you think you would have been drawn to him and his ideas? Explain.

2. **(a) Recall:** Summarize what the poet says in "All."
   (b) Generalize: What is the theme or message of the poem?

3. **(a) Recall:** Summarize the speaker's view of life in "Also All."
   (b) Interpret: List three details in "Also All" that indicate that the speaker's optimism is difficult to maintain.

4. **(a) Interpret:** Explain the meaning of the last two lines of "Also All." **(b) Assess:** How do these two lines suggest the possibility of hope?

5. **(a) Recall:** How does Confucius believe people should behave toward parents? **(b) Generalize:** What does his belief suggest about the importance of the individual? Explain.

6. **(a) Recall:** What does Confucius believe knowledge is?
   (b) Connect: What does this definition reveal about the importance that Confucius attaches to humility?

7. **(a) Interpret:** What does Confucius mean when he says that a ruler should govern by "moral force"? **(b) Connect:** Do his attitudes about the importance of seeing all sides of a question support his ideas about "moral force"? Explain.

8. **Apply:** Which of Confucius' ideas do you think you could apply to your own life? Explain.

9. **Hypothesize:** Bei Dao's poem "All" is a response to political events in China. What events in the United States today might inspire someone to write a poem like this? Explain.

Confucius

(551?–479? B.C.)

Confucius was a scholar from Shandong province in northeast China. He became a teacher to the sons of noble families. In all his teachings, Confucius emphasizes the importance of moral conduct.

Confucius did not record his teachings, but his students often inscribed his answers to questions. In China, *K'ung* was a family name, and *Tze* meant "master." Thus, they wrote, "The Master K'ung says . . . ," or "K'ung Fu-Tze says . . ." When European visitors first heard of the great teacher K'ung Fu-Tze, they pronounced the name "Confucius."

The ideas of Confucius have influenced the pattern of Chinese life for more than two thousand years. His teachings have influenced the lives of many people in a number of other countries as well.

ASSESSMENT PRACTICE: Reading Comprehension

Recognize Details (For more practice, see **Test Preparation Workbook, p. 15.**)

Some test questions may require students to recognize and use details in order to select the best answer. Have students use the sample question below to practice this skill.

"The Master said, A young man's duty is to behave well to his parents at home and to his elders abroad, to be cautious in giving promises and punctual in keeping them, to have kindly feelings towards everyone. . . . "

The author's purpose in listing the details in this passage may be to teach young people to—

A stay at home
B respect other people
C always make promises
D always arrive on time

Each detail in the passage presents a way of respecting other people. Therefore, *B* is the best answer.

Review and Assess

Literary Analysis

Aphorisms

1. How do **aphorisms** illustrate the expression "Less is more"?
2. Find four aphorisms in the selections and paraphrase them, or express them in your own words, in a chart like the one here.

Aphorism	Paraphrase

3. Identify one basic truth conveyed both in the sayings of Confucius and in "Old Song."
4. Devise an aphorism that reflects a basic truth found in "Also All."

Comparing Literary Works

5. "Africa" and "Old Song" address the **universal themes** of work and status. Compare and contrast the messages of these poems.
6. Both "All" and "Also All" explore the universal themes of hope and despair. Which selection seems more hopeful? Why?
7. (a) How do Confucius' ideas support the message presented by Diop? (b) How do they compare or contrast with the ideas of "Old Song"?

Reading Strategy

Relating to What You Know

8. Compare the advice in "Old Song" with advice you have received from an older relative or friend.
9. Describe an experience in your life in which one of Confucius' principles was illustrated.
10. Explain how one person might be able to experience the feelings expressed in both "All" and "Also All."

Extend Understanding

11. **Social Studies Connection:** Which of Confucius' ideas do you think today's politicians should practice to gain more respect from voters?

Africa / Old Song / All / Also All / from The Analects ◆ 223

Quick Review

An **aphorism** is a brief saying that expresses a basic truth.

Universal themes are messages that are relevant to people of almost any time and place.

You **relate** an author's words **to what you know** by finding something in your own experience that helps you understand and evaluate the words.

 Take It to the Net
www.phschool.com
Take the interactive self-test online to check your understanding of these selections.

---

❶ Vocabulary Development

Word Analysis

1. statement
2. replacement
3. commandment
4. assignment
5. encouragement
6. employment
7. disappointment

Concept Development: Antonyms

1. b   3. a
2. c

Spelling

1. partial   3. conscience
2. tension

❷ Grammar

1. answers, active
2. reverberates, active
3. was planted, passive
4. Excel, active; must excel, active
5. will be brought, passive

Writing Application

1. The author has great hopes for Africa.
2. Africa experienced a difficult past.
3. For years, masters oppressed slaves. Passive: For years, slaves were oppressed by masters.
4. The author hopes for strength and renewal.
5. Patience and stubbornness will cause change. Passive: Change will be caused by patience and stubbornness.

Integrate Language Skills

❶ Vocabulary Development Lesson

Word Analysis: Latin Suffix -ment

In the excerpt from *The Analects*, you encounter the word *chastisements*. The Latin suffix *-ment* can help you figure out that this word is the noun form of the verb *chastise*, which means "punish." *Chastisements*, then, are "punishments."

Use the suffix *-ment* to form a noun for each of the following examples.

1. To state your opinion is to make a ___?___ .
2. You replace something with a ___?___ .
3. A ruler commands with a ___?___ .
4. A teacher assigns an ___?___ .
5. You encourage someone with ___?___ .
6. If you are not employed, you seek ___?___ .
7. A disappointed child expresses ___?___ .

❷ Grammar Lesson

Active and Passive Voice

A verb is in the **active voice** when the subject of the sentence performs the action. A verb is in the **passive voice** when the action is performed on the subject.

> **Active voice:** [subject performs action]
> Not all <u>stars</u> *announce* the night . . .
> Not all <u>flames</u> *consume* themselves, . . .
>
> **Passive voice:** [subject receives action]
> Not all <u>trees</u> *are felled* by storms.
> Not all the <u>wings</u> of dream *are broken*, . . .

When the performer of the action is not known or is not important, the writer uses the passive voice.

Concept Development: Antonyms

An **antonym** is a word that means the opposite of another word. Write the antonym for each word from the vocabulary list on page 215.

1. impetuous: (a) lively, (b) careful, (c) wise
2. lamentation: (a) despair, (b) interest, (c) rejoicing
3. chastisements: (a) rewards, (b) orders, (c) duties

Spelling Strategy

In the word *lamentation*, the letters *ti* produce the sound *sh*. Other letter combinations that may produce the *sh* sound include *ci* (social), *sci* (conscious), *si* (dimension), *ssi* (expression), *su* (sugar), and *xi* (anxious). Fill in the appropriate spelling for the *sh* sound in each of the following words.

1. par_al   2. ten_on   3. con_ence

Practice Copy the following sentences. Underline the verbs, and identify whether each is in the active or passive voice.

1. Solemnly a voice answers me.
2. Every death reverberates forever.
3. The future was planted yesterday.
4. Excel when you must excel.
5. Not only the weak will be brought to their knees.

Writing Application Write five sentences in the active voice about the poem "Africa." Then, change two sentences to the passive voice. Compare your sentences to evaluate the effect of the passive voice.

WG Prentice Hall *Writing and Grammar Connection: Chapter 22, Section 2*

TEACHING RESOURCES

The following resources can be used to enrich or extend the instruction for pp. 224–225.

Vocabulary

📖 **Selection Support:** Build Vocabulary, p. 57
📖 **Vocabulary and Spelling Practice Book** (Use this booklet for skills enrichment.) 📘

Grammar

📖 **Selection Support:** Build Grammar Skills, p. 58
WG **Writing and Grammar,** Platinum Level, p. 534
📙 **Daily Language Practice Transparencies** 📘

Writing

WG **Writing and Grammar,** Platinum Level, p. 181
💿 **Writing and Grammar iText CD-ROM**
 Writing Models and Graphic Organizers on Transparencies, pp. 95–97

❸ Writing Lesson

Evaluation

Shu Ting wrote "Also All" as a rebuttal to Bei Dao's "All." Write an evaluation in which you explain which poem makes a better case.

Prewriting	Review each poem to determine the poet's message. Then, find specific examples from the poems that illustrate each message.
Drafting	Using lines from each poem, describe the philosophy each poet suggests. Explain which philosophy best communicates your ideas.
Revising	To strengthen your evaluation, find places in your draft to elaborate. For example, highlight key ideas in your draft that need more explanation. Then, use self-sticking notes to jot down ideas to help you provide details from your own experiences.

Model: Revising to Elaborate

> **Add description about trying to inspire others who are down.**

In "Also All," Shu Ting says "Hope is a burden all of us shoulder." I think this is the main message of her poem. Hope is sometimes difficult to achieve when things are going wrong. Hope feels heavy at these times. However, there is hope, and so we should struggle on.

> **Concrete personal experiences will strengthen the evaluation.**

𝒲𝒢 *Prentice Hall Writing and Grammar Connection: Chapter 13, Section 4*

❹ Extension Activities

Listening and Speaking With a partner, role-play an **interview** with one of the writers. Follow these steps:

- Develop questions about the author's views and experiences.
- Base your answers on what you learned from your reading.
- Practice conducting the interview with your partner, with one of you role-playing the interviewer and the other, the author.

When you are ready, present your interview to the class. [**Group Activity**]

Research and Technology "All" and "Also All" are responses to political events in China during the 1980s. In April 1989, students took over Tiananmen Square in Beijing. Research this event, and write a **news article** on it for your class. Use the Internet as well as print and electronic sources in your research.

🖥 *Take It to the Net* www.phschool.com
Go online for an additional research activity using the Internet.

Africa / Old Song / All / Also All / from The Analects ◆ 225

---

❸ Writing Lesson

- Remind students that to *evaluate* means to form opinions about what they read. Explain to students that their evaluations should state their opinions and then support these opinions with details from the poems.
- To help students compare the messages and philosophies of each poem, encourage them to record their ideas in a Comparison-and-Contrast chart like the one on p. 97 of **Writing Models and Graphic Organizers on Transparencies.**
- Use the Comparison-and-Contrast Composition rubric in **Performance Assessment and Portfolio Management,** p. 15 to assess students' evaluations.

❹ Listening and Speaking

- Have students reread the selection by their chosen author, taking notes on lines or ideas they'd like to learn more about.
- Then, have students brainstorm for a list of interview questions. Remind them that these questions should focus on the author's views and experiences.
- Students can get answers from the selections or from doing research in the library or on the Internet.
- Use the rubric for Interview Techniques, p. 27 in **Performance Assessment and Portfolio Management**, to evaluate students' interviews.

CUSTOMIZE INSTRUCTION
For Universal Access

To address different learning styles, use the activities suggested in the **Extension Activities** booklet, p. 15.

- For Logical/Mathematical and Visual/Spatial Learners, use Activity 5.
- For Musical/Rhythmic and Interpersonal Learners, use Activity 6.
- For Intrapersonal and Verbal/Linguistic Learners, use Activity 7.

ASSESSMENT RESOURCES

The following resources can be used to assess students' knowledge and skills.

Selection Assessment
- 📓 **Formal Assessment,** pp. 47–49
- 📓 **Open Book Test,** pp. 43–45
- 📼 **Got It! Assessment Videotapes,** Tape 1
- 💿 **Test Bank Software**
- 🖥 *Take It to the Net*
  Visit www.phschool.com for self-tests and additional questions on the selections.

Writing Rubric
- 📓 **Performance Assess. and Portfolio Mgmt.,** p. 15

Listening and Speaking Rubric
- 📓 **Performance Assess. and Portfolio Mgmt.,** p. 27

PRENTICE HALL
ASSESSMENT *SYSTEM*
- 📓 **Workbook**
- 📓 **Skill Book**
- 📖 **Transparencies**
- 💿 **CD-ROM**

About Product Information

- Have students read "About Product Information." Then, discuss with students the kinds of products that usually come with technical directions and warranties.

- Ask students to discuss their personal experiences with technical directions and warranties.

- Have students consider why it is important to learn about these types of informational material.
Answer: Understanding technical directions and warranties can help a consumer use a product correctly and be protected from malfunctioning products.

Reading Strategy

Analyzing Purpose of Product Information

- Have students read the information about the Reading Strategy.

- Ask students to summarize the purposes of both technical directions and warranties. Have students explain the differences between the two.

- Review the table of contents from the owner's manual. Ask students to explain each type of information contained in this document.

Product Information: Technical Directions and Warranties

About Product Information

Product information—the material that accompanies consumer items from clock radios to new cars—helps you get the best performance from items you purchase. Product information also provides special instructions and guarantees to aid consumers in understanding how to use, protect, and maintain their products. These two documents are frequently included in product information:

- **Technical Directions** The directions, or instructions, tell you how to assemble and use the item safely and efficiently. Before you plug in a new popcorn maker or rice cooker, read the directions for using the product properly.

- **Warranties** A warranty is usually included with any new product. It is a guarantee of performance and a contract between you and the manufacturer. The warranty contains important information about what the manufacturer promises the customer and highlights the customers' responsibilities.

A warranty may be printed on a card that is included in the packaging, or it may be attached to other printed materials included with the product. Often, a warranty card must be signed and returned to the manufacturer.

Reading Strategy

Analyze Purpose of Product Information

To make the best use of product information, note the purpose and format of each type of document. This will save you time in locating the information you need.

- **Technical Directions** Often, step-by-step, detailed directions are provided in an owner's manual, written in simple language, accompanied by charts or graphics. The directions take you through the process of preparing, assembling, and maintaining your product.

- **Warranties** The purpose of a warranty is to outline the legal relationship between the consumer and the manufacturer. It is written in very formal language without excessive elaboration.

As you read, connect the purpose of the following documents with the level of language they include.

OWNER'S MANUAL
Table of Contents

Important Safeguards 2

Parts and Their Functions 4

Instructions for Use 5

Suggestions and Tips
for Optimum Use 12

Maintenance Instructions 15

Important Manufacturer
Information 18

Warranty 22

Instructions for Use

Before you use your rice cooker, become familiar with its operation. Here are detailed instructions for using the appliance:

Instructions for Use
- Tell students that they will encounter instructions for use with most of the electronic and household products they buy.
- Have students read the instructions and the accompanying notes.
- Call students' attention to the use of graphics in the instructions. Ask them how the absence of these graphics might affect their understanding of the instructions. Answer: The graphics help to clarify the written words in the instructions. Without the graphics, readers might misunderstand the instructions and use the cooker improperly.

The instructions offer detailed information on the use of the product.

Graphics help clarify instructions.

The instructions provide the consumer with examples of the proper use of the product.

The instructions include warnings to protect the user from injury.

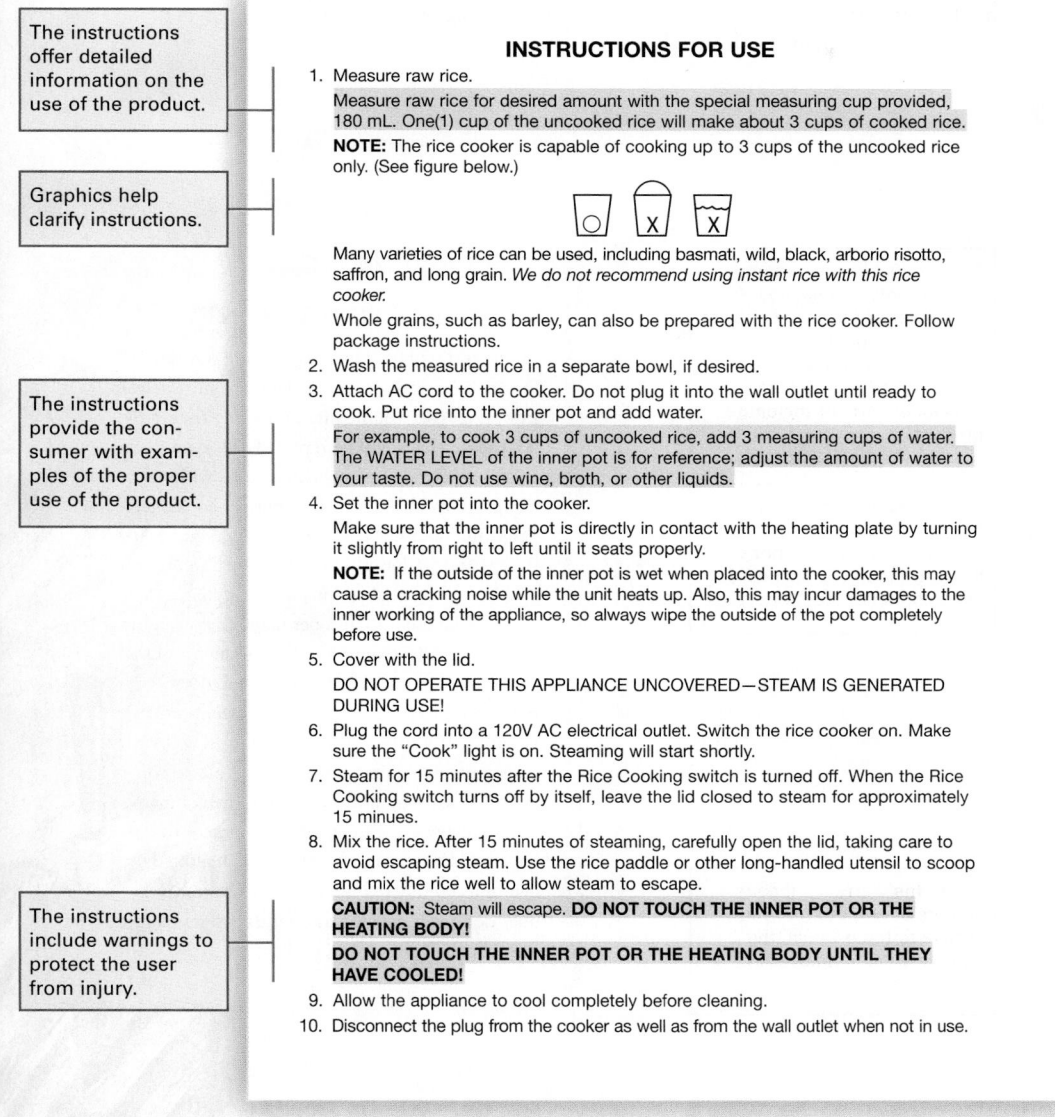

INSTRUCTIONS FOR USE

1. Measure raw rice.
   Measure raw rice for desired amount with the special measuring cup provided, 180 mL. One(1) cup of the uncooked rice will make about 3 cups of cooked rice.
   NOTE: The rice cooker is capable of cooking up to 3 cups of the uncooked rice only. (See figure below.)

   Many varieties of rice can be used, including basmati, wild, black, arborio risotto, saffron, and long grain. *We do not recommend using instant rice with this rice cooker.*
   Whole grains, such as barley, can also be prepared with the rice cooker. Follow package instructions.
2. Wash the measured rice in a separate bowl, if desired.
3. Attach AC cord to the cooker. Do not plug it into the wall outlet until ready to cook. Put rice into the inner pot and add water.
   For example, to cook 3 cups of uncooked rice, add 3 measuring cups of water. The WATER LEVEL of the inner pot is for reference; adjust the amount of water to your taste. Do not use wine, broth, or other liquids.
4. Set the inner pot into the cooker.
   Make sure that the inner pot is directly in contact with the heating plate by turning it slightly from right to left until it seats properly.
   NOTE: If the outside of the inner pot is wet when placed into the cooker, this may cause a cracking noise while the unit heats up. Also, this may incur damages to the inner working of the appliance, so always wipe the outside of the pot completely before use.
5. Cover with the lid.
   DO NOT OPERATE THIS APPLIANCE UNCOVERED—STEAM IS GENERATED DURING USE!
6. Plug the cord into a 120V AC electrical outlet. Switch the rice cooker on. Make sure the "Cook" light is on. Steaming will start shortly.
7. Steam for 15 minutes after the Rice Cooking switch is turned off. When the Rice Cooking switch turns off by itself, leave the lid closed to steam for approximately 15 minues.
8. Mix the rice. After 15 minutes of steaming, carefully open the lid, taking care to avoid escaping steam. Use the rice paddle or other long-handled utensil to scoop and mix the rice well to allow steam to escape.
   CAUTION: Steam will escape. **DO NOT TOUCH THE INNER POT OR THE HEATING BODY!**
   DO NOT TOUCH THE INNER POT OR THE HEATING BODY UNTIL THEY HAVE COOLED!
9. Allow the appliance to cool completely before cleaning.
10. Disconnect the plug from the cooker as well as from the wall outlet when not in use.

Reading Informational Materials: Product Information ◆ 227

CUSTOMIZE INSTRUCTION FOR UNIVERSAL ACCESS

For Special Needs Students	For Less Proficient Readers
Have students use the graphics provided to draw pictures that illustrate the steps in the instructions that they find confusing or difficult.	Have students work in pairs to read the instructions. Then, to check comprehension, have them quiz each other by asking questions about the steps.

Warranty for Rice Cooker

- Have students read the warranty and the notes that accompany it.
- Explain to students that the document provides information about the length of coverage of the warranty, as well as the conditions under which the warranty is valid.
- Remind students that a warranty is a legal agreement between the manufacturer and the consumer. Consumers must know what is meant by "normal consumer usage" in order to benefit from the coverage provided by the warranty.
- Have students identify situations under which the warranty is invalid.

Warranty for Rice Cooker

This particular warranty provides the consumer with a list of guarantees that the purchaser can expect from the manufacturer. For example, if a consumer discovers that a new rice cooker has a defect, the warranty states that the manufacturer will repair the product for up to one year from the purchase date.

The warranty also tells consumers what their responsibilities are. For example, this warranty states that it does not cover damage resulting from any unauthorized repairs to the product.

The product is covered under the warranty against any damage or defect for one year from the date of purchase. However, it is up to the company to decide whether to replace individual parts or the entire product.

This warranty does not protect against irresponsible handling or use of the product, nor does it cover damage sustained during shipping of the product.

Under the warranty, if consumers attempt to make any repairs to the product, the company will not cover any damage caused.

LIMITED WARRANTY

Products distributed by company are warranted for one year from date of purchase against defects in workmanship and material. During that period, these defects will be repaired or the product will be replaced at company's option, without charge. This warranty covers normal consumer usage and does not cover damage that occurs in shipment or failure that results from alteration, accident, misuse, abuse, neglect, installation, commercial use, or improper maintenance. This warranty is effective only if the product is purchased and operated in the USA and does not extend to any units that have been used in violation of written instructions furnished by the company or to units that have been altered or modified without authorization of the company, or to damage to products or parts thereof that have had the serial number removed, altered, defaced, or rendered illegible. This warranty does not cover damage that results from unauthorized repairs.

Check Your Comprehension

1. How many cups of rice can be cooked in the rice cooker?
2. What kind of rice does the company suggest you avoid using with this rice cooker?
3. Under the conditions of the warranty, what are some things you should not do to the rice cooker?
4. How long is the rice cooker's warranty in effect?

Apply the Reading Strategy

Analyzing Purpose of Product Information

5. Why does the rice cooker come with two pots?
6. Why do you think the directions for using the rice cooker are listed in the order shown?
7. What happens if you break the product by using it incorrectly?
8. Who gains more protection from this rice cooker's warranty, the consumer or the manufacturer? Explain your response with specific examples from the warranty.
9. Why do you think the warranty includes information about problems for which the company does not take responsibility?

Activity

Use Information
From Consumer Documents

Get copies of the product information for a product such as a new computer game or a disc player. Then, read the product's technical directions and warranty. Using a chart like the one shown here, generate a list of potential questions a consumer might have about the product. Complete the chart by finding the answers and indicating in which document you found the information.

Problem
or
Question:

Answer:

Source:

Contrasting Informational Materials

Technical directions that come with a product include instruction manuals, user's guides, and tips for caring for the product. These documents are different in purpose and structure from warranties. Compare and contrast the consumer documents below in terms of purpose and format.

Indicate the reasons you might consult the following sources of information.

1. advertisement
2. warranty
3. consumer report
4. technical directions

Lesson Objectives

1. To write a how-to essay
2. To use writing strategies to generate ideas, plan, organize, evaluate, and revise the manual

Model From Literature

In the excerpt from *The Analects* (p. 220), Confucius offers instruction on moral behavior.

Prewriting

- Encourage students to choose a topic with which they are familiar. This will enable them to describe the process in a clear and thorough manner.

- Once students have chosen a topic, explain that they must gather all the relevant details they will need to adequately describe the process. Remind students that they should omit any details that do not help to clarify the explanation.

- Students should identify their audience and keep it in mind as they begin to write. The age and background knowledge of their audience will help to determine the language that students use in their essays.

- Encourage students to use a problem-and-solution chart like the one shown to help them identify potential mistakes or problems that their readers may encounter with the instructions.

Writing WORKSHOP

Exposition: How-to Essay

A **how-to essay** is a document that explains how to do something—from fixing a lawn mower to speaking in public. In this workshop, you will write a how-to essay about a subject that you know well.

Assignment Criteria Your how-to essay should have the following characteristics:

- A process that is divided into clearly defined steps
- Transitions that signal the order in which steps should be taken
- A logical organization
- Simple, easy-to-understand language that uses definitions and examples
- Anticipation and resolution of potential mistakes and problems in understanding or following the directions

To preview the criteria on which your how-to essay may be assessed, refer to the Rubric on page 233.

Prewriting

Choose a topic. Write your how-to essay about how to behave in a specific situation. Try **putting yourself in a situation**. Imagine yourself in various roles, such as presiding over a committee meeting, programming a VCR, or packing for a vacation. Choose a situation, and analyze the stages of the activity.

Gather details. Observe the process or do research in the library, on the Internet, or by talking to experts. If possible, go through the process yourself, taking notes so you can give detailed and accurate specifications.

Identify your audience. To ensure that your work will be helpful to readers, ask and answer questions to learn about your audience, for example:

- Who are your readers?
- What do your readers already know about the subject and process?

Anticipate mistakes. Consider mistakes that readers might make or specific problems or misunderstandings that they might have. Then, provide solutions. You might analyze mistakes with a problem-and-solution chart like the one shown.

Situation: Traveling With Your Class	
Problem	**Solution**
Students act out	Remember they represent school
Students are bored on bus	Bring magazines or music along
Someone gets lost	Institute a buddy system

TEACHING RESOURCES

The following resources can be used to enrich or extend the instruction for pp. 230–233.

Writing and Grammar, Platinum Level, Chapter 11, pp. 220–236

Performance Assessment and Portfolio Management, p. 10

Writing Models and Graphic Organizers on Transparencies, pp. 65–68

Writing and Grammar iText CD-ROM
Students can use the following tools as they complete their how-to essays:

- Audience Profile
- Transition Word Bin
- Language Variety

Student Model

Before you begin drafting, read this student model and review the characteristics of an effective how-to essay.

Michael J. Hall
St. Petersburg, Florida

A Guide for Off-Campus Behavior

When you travel off school grounds for a school-related activity, you take on a double role. For yourself, you may be learning on a field trip or playing a sport. For others, though, you are representing your school. This manual will give simple guidelines for how to behave off campus.

I. Getting There: Stick to the Rules

While traveling to a school activity, students should obey the rules set by the teachers and by the operator of the vehicle used for transport.

In most cases, students will constitute the majority of passengers on board the vehicle. In cases where there are other passengers not associated with the student group, students should be extra careful about their behavior. To help fight the boredom of a long trip, students might bring magazines or music to help pass the time.

II. On Location: Keep Sticking to the Rules

While attending the event, students should obey their teachers and hosts. Students should be sensitive to other people at the site who are not traveling with the group. In addition, students should take extra care to avoid damage to property. If an item that belongs to the site is damaged or broken, it will give the students, the teacher, and the school a bad reputation.

III. The Age Game: Meet Expectations

As students get older, expectations for their good behavior increase. Elementary-school students need more supervision than do high-school students, who are expected to behave like young adults. No matter their age, all students should keep themselves under control without help from peers or teachers. When a student does lose control, a domino effect can occur—other students join in. At this point, the teacher has to take charge.

IV. Seize the Day: Surpass Expectations

While at the event, students should be active participants in the activities, making the most of the events. If students are involved, they will be less inclined to become distracted and act out. Instead, students should take the opportunity presented—listen to museum tour guides or really challenge themselves to compete well. If students witness most of their peers participating in the event, those with a tendency to bad behavior will be inclined to behave better.

These simple steps will guarantee a successful and memorable school outing.

> Michael has divided his process into clearly defined steps. The steps follow a logical chronological organization.

> Each step has a clear main idea that is supported with details and examples.

> Michael gives an example of what can happen when the rules are not followed.

> Michael uses simple, concise language to explain his instructions.

Student Model

- Explain that the Student Model is a sample, and that essays may be longer.
- Have students identify the topic of Michael's essay. Lead students to see that Michael has divided the process into steps, which he has ordered sequentially.
- For each of the steps, have students identify the main idea and the supporting details that Michael uses.
- Point out to students that Michael addresses potential problems by providing an example of what can happen when the rules are not followed.
- Finally, draw students' attention to Michael's choice of words. Lead students to see that Michael uses clear, direct language that other students will understand.

Real-World Connection

Explain that there are many times when students may have to write material of this nature. Many jobs require that people describe a particular process, such as a human resources employee who must explain company policies and procedures to new employees.

CUSTOMIZE INSTRUCTION FOR UNIVERSAL ACCESS

For Less Proficient Writers	For English Learners
Have students generate a list of questions and answers about their audience. Questions can include the audience's age, educational level, background knowledge, and skills. Have students refer to these lists as they begin to write their essays.	Have students work in small groups to role-play members of each student's audience. Explain to students that the goal of this exercise is to learn as much as possible about their intended audiences.

Drafting

- Tell students that a well-organized essay will communicate its ideas more clearly to the audience. Explain that, if possible, students should write their essays in chronological order; that is, the order in which the steps occur.

- Explain to students that transitional words and phrases make it easier for a reader to follow a set of steps or procedures. Review the transitional words and phrases with students. As students draft their essays, make sure they pay attention to places that will benefit from the use of these transitions.

- Remind students that visual aids can help clarify details in the process they are describing. Caution students against overusing visual aids; too many pictures will create clutter. Students should read through their drafts to determine the places that would benefit from visual explanations.

Revising

- Before students revise their work, have them refer to the notes they took about their intended audience.

- Have students reread their drafts, identifying points that require more clarification based on the traits of their audience. Students should try to anticipate and to address any questions their readers might have.

- Review the model with students. Have students describe how Michael's additional sentence anticipates possible concerns of the reader.

(continued on page 233)

232

Writing WORKSHOP *continued*

Drafting

Organize. Develop a draft that follows a logical organization. Usually, a how-to essay is written in chronological order. Provide specific and accurate details that explain what to do at every stage of the activity. Consider breaking the subject down into stages and addressing each one in turn—first, second, and so on. Use a timeline like the one shown to organize your draft.

Elaborate. Elaborate by explaining the purpose for each step. Give specific directions to clarify each stage.

Use transitions to show relationships. Signal any changes in time and place by using transitional words and phrases. Transitions showing order include the words *first, next, then, finally,* and *again.* Transitions signaling changes in place include the words and phrases *here, there, in front of, around,* and *on the other side.*

Include visual aids. Clarify your ideas by including diagrams and charts. Consider adding an illustrative chart or diagram to convey the basic information, along with options that readers might consider.

Revising

Revise to address reader's questions. Review your draft from the perspective of a reader who does not have your expertise. Consider the points that may need more clarification, and list a few questions that a reader might have about the process. Then, add information to address those concerns.

Beginning

Step 1: Getting there

Step 2: Rules for off-site actions

Step 3: Making the most of it

End

Model: Revising to Anticipate Readers' Concerns

Concern: Do you really want kids to sit still for an entire trip?

In cases in which there are other passengers not associated with the student group, students should be extra careful about their behavior. ∧*To help fight the boredom of a long trip, students might bring magazines or music to help pass the time.*

Michael added information to address a potential question.

USING TECHNOLOGY IN WRITING

If students are using word processors to draft and revise their essays, suggest that they use the thesaurus feature to help them vary their word choice. Remind students that their choice of words will depend on their intended audience.

Students can also use the organizing tools and revision checkers on the **Writing and Grammar iText CD-ROM.**

Revise to vary word choice. When writing about a process, it is easy to fall into the trap of repeating the same words over and over. This can make your writing dull and repetitive. Review your draft, highlighting words that appear more than three times. For each such word, break up repetition by substituting a synonym when appropriate.

> **Example:** Committee members should raise new business. Someone may ask the committee to consider a new proposal. Ask the committee member to explain the proposal.

> **Revision:** Committee members should raise new business. Someone may ask the group to consider a proposal.

Compare the model and nonmodel. Why is the model more interesting?

Nonmodel	Model
No matter the age of the students, students should keep themselves under control without help from fellow students or teachers.	No matter their age, all students should keep themselves under control without help from peers or teachers.

Publishing and Presenting

Choose one of the following ways to share your writing with classmates or a wider audience.

Publish your essay. Post your how-to essay on a classroom computer or on a Web site for others to read.

Give an oral report. Use your how-to essay as the basis for an oral presentation. You might enlarge graphic organizers or generate charts to use as props during your report.

Rubric for Self-Assessment

Evaluate your how-to essay using the following criteria and rating scale:

Criteria	Rating Scale Not very				Very
Have you divided the process into clearly defined steps?	1	2	3	4	5
Have you used transitions that clearly signal the order in which steps should be taken?	1	2	3	4	5
Have you organized the essay in a logical and effective way?	1	2	3	4	5
Is the essay written in simple language that uses definitions and examples?	1	2	3	4	5
Have you anticipated and solved potential mistakes and problems?	1	2	3	4	5

Revising (continued)

- Tell students that varying their word choice will make their essays more interesting for readers. Students also need to pay attention to their choice of words to make sure they are appropriate for their intended audience.

- Ask students to compare the model and nonmodel and respond to the question in their text: Why is the model more interesting? Answer: In the nonmodel, the repetition of the word *students* distracts readers from the main idea.

Publishing and Presenting

- Have students consider the intended audience for their essay. What Web sites might draw the attention of these readers?

- Before students give their oral reports, encourage them to make note cards that outline their main points. During their presentations, they can refer to these cards rather than reading directly from their essays.

Assessment

- Review with students the assessment criteria.

- Have students choose three criteria from the rubric and score the Student Model. Make sure students support their scores with details from the Model.

- The rubric on this page can be found on p. 10 in **Performance Assessment and Portfolio Management.**

TEST-TAKING TIP

When students are taking a test that requires them to explain the steps in a process, they should pay careful attention to the use of transitional words and phrases. Remind students that these words and phrases tell readers where they are in the process, and explain how one step relates to the next.

1. To deliver a descriptive presentation in an effective manner
2. To establish an audience and purpose for the presentation
3. To use descriptive language in order to make the topic come alive for the audience

Establish Audience and Purpose

- Students might create a brief audience profile to help them determine the language and level of detail they should use in their presentations.

- Review the purposes for sharing information listed on this page. Students should keep in mind what they hope to accomplish through their presentations. This will help them determine which details to include and what kind of language to use.

Make Your Topic Come Alive

- Students might want to circle all the verbs they used and then go back and replace weak verbs with precise and vivid ones.

- Students should identify points in their presentations that would benefit from visual aids. Explain that visual aids are helpful in clarifying complicated ideas and emphasizing main points.

Listening and Speaking WORKSHOP

Descriptive Presentations

Description can be useful in many kinds of presentations. Sportscasters use description to help viewers see the action of a sports event. Travel agents use description to tempt vacationers to exotic locations. Even scientists use description to help explain complicated findings. This workshop will help you prepare and deliver a descriptive presentation.

Establish Audience and Purpose

To prepare an effective presentation, follow these planning steps:

Identify your audience. An awareness of what your listeners already know about your topic can help you identify what to include and what to leave out. For example, if you plan to describe a baseball game to a group of fans, focus on the highlights of the action. In contrast, if your audience consists of people who do not know much about the game, you must explain some basic rules.

Clarify your purpose. Think about why you are sharing information. Consider these purposes:

- *To honor:* Include details that present your subject in a positive light.
- *To warn:* Use details that stress danger.
- *To entertain:* Focus on events or details that are funny.

Make Your Topic Come Alive

People who give descriptive presentations use techniques that demand attention. Below are a few ways to make your topic come to life.

Provide descriptive language. Use sensory language—words that apply and appeal to specific senses—to create vivid images.

Use vivid verbs. Use vivid verbs that paint a picture.
   Dull Verb: Ramirez *ran* to second base.
   Vivid Verb: Ramirez *zoomed* to second base.

Introduce visual aids. Use props, music, drawings, or slides to illustrate and enhance your presentation.

(Activity:) Descriptive Presentation — With your classmates, choose a recent school event as the topic of a descriptive presentation. Think about your audience, your purpose, and the most effective ways to present this event. After your presentation, have classmates use the Feedback Form to evaluate the presentation.

Feedback Form for Descriptive Presentation

Rating System
+ = Excellent   ✔ = Average   − = Weak

Content
Clear purpose _____
Use of vivid verbs, descriptive language _____
Use of visual aids _____

Delivery
Voice modulation _____
Enunciation _____
Eye contact _____

Answer the following questions:
Was the presentation interesting to you?

Were you able to see, hear, smell, taste, and feel what the speaker described?

---

234 ◆ *Striving for Success*

CUSTOMIZE INSTRUCTION FOR UNIVERSAL ACCESS

For Less Proficient Readers	For English Learners
Have students read through their drafts and circle any passages that seem dull or incomplete. Then, have them add descriptive details that answer the questions *Who? What? Where? When?* and *Why?* Students might find it helpful to make a five-column chart, with one of the five questions in each column. They can then fill in the chart with modifiers that answer each question.	Remind students that sensory details can be words, phrases, or clauses that engage the readers' senses. Encourage students to keep a list of vivid sensory details they encounter while reading, and to consider using some of these details in their writing when appropriate.

Assessment WORKSHOP

Facts and Details

In the reading sections of some tests, you may be required to understand the facts and details that support the main ideas in a variety of written texts. Use these strategies to help you answer questions about recognizing facts and details:

- Read the passage to determine the main idea.
- Search for facts and details that seem important to the main idea.
- If the passage is nonfiction, look for facts that elaborate on the main idea.
- If the passage is fiction, identify details that relate to the topic of the passage.

Test-Taking Strategies

- Look for clues about which details relate to the topic sentence.
- When you review answer choices, eliminate facts that are not stated in the passage.

Sample Test Item

Directions: Read the passage, and answer the question that follows.

Born in 1921 in Atlanta, Texas, Bessie Coleman became the first American woman to receive an international pilot's license from the Fédération Aéronautique Internationale in France. As an African American woman, Bessie Coleman had to overcome numerous obstacles to attain her goal.

1. Where did Coleman receive her pilot's license?
   A Atlanta
   B Texas
   C France
   D Africa

Answer and Explanation

The correct answer is *C* because it is a fact that is stated in the first sentence of the passage. Choice *A* is incorrect because it is the city of Coleman's birth. Choice *B* is incorrect because it is the state of Coleman's birth. Choice *D* is incorrect because it is the home of Coleman's ancestors.

Practice

Directions: Read the passage, and answer the question that follows.

Coleman attended college in Oklahoma after completing high school, but she could afford only one term. She moved to Chicago and earned a certificate as a manicurist. Her applications to flight schools in the United States were turned down because racial and gender barriers were formidable at the time. With the financial help of a benefactor, she was accepted to flight school in France. After receiving her license, she gave flying exhibitions in the United States. Coleman's pioneering role in aviation has been honored and cited in innumerable ways.

1. Which of the following was not an obstacle to Bessie Coleman's becoming a pilot?
   A She was an African American.
   B She was a woman.
   C She needed a college degree.
   D She did not have the money.

Lesson Objective

To understand the facts and details that are used to support the main ideas in a variety of written texts

Applying Reading Strategies

Review the bulleted points with students. Encourage them to clarify the main points they come across by rereading or reading ahead to locate examples of supporting facts and details.

Applying Test-Taking Strategies

- Have students read the Sample Test Item. Explain that they can read the question first to help focus their attention as they read the passage. Students will then know what supporting fact or detail they need to find.
- Students should see that they are being asked to identify the place where Coleman received her pilot's license. They can skim the text to find the phrase *pilot's license*. Then, they can read carefully to locate the correct answer to the question.

Answer

The correct answer to the Practice test item is *C*. Students should see that they are being asked to identify the detail that was *not* an obstacle to Coleman's becoming a pilot. The text clearly states that Coleman's applications to flight school in the U.S. were rejected because of her race and gender, making *A* and *B* incorrect. The text also states that Coleman did not have the necessary money and had to rely on a benefactor, so *D* is also incorrect.

TEACHING RESOURCES

The following resources can be used to enrich or extend the instruction for p. 235.

PRENTICE HALL ASSESSMENT SYSTEM

- Workbook
- Skill Book
- Transparencies
- CD-ROM

Unit Objectives

1. To read selections in different genres that develop the theme "Clashing Forces"

2. To apply a variety of reading strategies, particularly interactive reading strategies, appropriate for reading these selections

3. To analyze literary elements

4. To use a variety of strategies to build vocabulary

5. To learn elements of grammar, usage, and style

6. To use recursive writing processes to write in a variety of forms

7. To develop listening and speaking skills

8. To express and support responses to various texts

9. To prepare, organize, and present literary interpretations.

Meeting the Objectives

With each selection, you will find instructional materials through which students can meet these objectives. Further, you will find additional practice pages for reading strategies, literary analysis, vocabulary, and grammar in the **Selection Support: Skills Development Workbook** in your **Teaching Resources.**

Background

Art

Two Figures in a Windy Landscape
by Charles Goodenough

Ask students to identify details in the painting that suggest a windy day. Help students to see that the painting combines several different, conflicting ideas.

1. Describe the mood of the painting, supporting your answer.
   Possible response: The colors suggest hopelessness; the people's position suggests loneliness.

2. Why is the scene contradictory?
   Possible response: The people may be leaning into the wind, but there are two different winds. At the same time, they appear to be pushing at walls.

3. What do these idea suggest about conflict?
   Possible response: Conflict leads to struggle, communication failures, and confinement.

236

Two Figures in a Windy Landscape, 1991, Clifford Goodenough, Davidson Galleries

UNIT 3 *Clashing Forces*

236 ◆ *Clashing Forces*

UNIT FEATURES

Connections	Reading Informational Materials
Every unit contains a feature that connects literature to a related topic, such as art, science, or history. In this unit, the excerpt from David Guterson's *Snow Falling on Cedars* on pp. 312–315 captures what it was like for Japanese Americans to be sent to internment camps during World War II. Use the information and questions on the Connections pages to enrich students' understanding of the selections presented within the unit.	These selections will help students learn to analyze and evaluate informational texts, such as workplace documents, technical directions, and consumer materials. They will expose students to the organization and features unique to nonnarrative texts. In this unit, students will learn about newspaper feature articles.

Exploring the Theme

There are many clashing forces in life—good versus evil, right versus wrong, people versus nature. The stories, poems, and essays you are about to read share one theme: They all deal with the clashing forces that we encounter in life. Turn the page to see how real people and fictional characters respond to—and often overcome—obstacles and injustices.

When you read "Through the Tunnel," you will take a dark underwater journey, unsure when you will be able to come up for air. As you read about one boy's yearning for independence conflicting with his love for his mother, you will discover how powerful these colliding forces become in his life—and you will understand the skill of the writer who sheds light at the end of the journey.

▲ **Critical Viewing** How are the people in this painting working to overcome a conflict with nature? [**Analyze**]

ASSESSMENT RESOURCES

📖 **Selection Support: Skills Development Workbook**
📖 **Formal Assessment**
📖 **Open Book Tests**
📖 **Performance Assessment and Portfolio Management**
📖 **Extension Activities**

Assessing Student Progress

Listed below are the tools that are available to measure the degree to which students meet the unit objectives.

Informal Assessment

The questions in the Review and Assess sections are a first-level response to the concepts and skills presented with the selections. Students' responses provide a brief, informal measure of their grasp of the material. These responses can indicate where further instruction and practice are needed. Follow up with the practice pages in **Selection Support: Skills Development Workbook.**

Formal Assessment

The **Formal Assessment** booklet contains the Selection Tests and Unit Tests.

- Selection Tests measure comprehension and skills acquisition for each selection or group of selections.
- Each Unit Test provides students with thirty multiple-choice questions and five essay questions designed to assess students' knowledge of the literature and skills taught in the unit.

The **Open Book Tests** ask students to demonstrate their ability to synthesize and communicate information from selections or groups of selections.

To assess student writing, you will find rubrics and scoring models in the **Performance Assessment and Portfolio Management** booklet. In this booklet, you will also find scoring rubrics for listening and speaking activities.

Alternative Assessment

The **Extension Activities** booklet contains writing activities, listening and speaking activities, and research and technology activities that are appropriate for students with different ability levels. You may also use these activities as an alternative measure of students' growth.

▶**Critical Viewing**

Possible response: The people are resisting the wind, a natural force.

237

Why Read Literature?

The "Why Read Literature?" page in each unit presents a list of possible purposes for reading. Each purpose for reading is connected to one or more of the selections in the unit. Good readers set a purpose before reading to help them read actively and focus on meaningful details.

Unit 3 introduces three purposes for reading. "Read for the Love of Literature," encourages students to explore sounds in poetry and be surprised by the endings in short stories. "Read to Be Entertained" suggests that students enjoy what happens when telling the truth turns out not to be the best policy or when a certain little dog is not man's best friend. "Read for Information" encourages students to learn more about the aftermath of Japanese-American internment.

How to Use This Page

- Tell students that before reading each selection in this unit, they should set a purpose for reading. This will help them read in an active and focused manner.

- Explain that they can increase their love of literature by listening to the sounds of blues in the words of the poem "The Weary Blues."

- To be entertained, a reader must read actively, taking note of situations in which the unexpected happens. In "The Dog That Bit People," students will be surprised at the antics of dog and owner alike.

- A third purpose for reading is to obtain information. In the speech on "Japanese American Internment," students can read to learn more about the wrongdoings of our nation against people of Japanese descent. Students should focus on the specific type of information they want to learn.

Why Read Literature?

You read literature with a specific purpose in mind: to appreciate, to learn, or to be entertained. Even as you read about conflict or struggle, your purpose will vary, depending on the context, genre, or style of the reading. Preview these three purposes you might set before reading the works in this unit.

1

Read for the Love of Literature

O. Henry is a master of the surprise ending. Using elements of his life experiences, he creates Mr. Easton, a proud yet embarrassed young man. Read how this story unfolds in **"Hearts and Hands,"** page 290.

Poets are often inspired by the energetic and emotional sound of music called the blues. See how Langston Hughes puts the sounds of the blues into words in the poem **"The Weary Blues,"** page 268.

3

Read to Be Entertained

You have probably been told that honesty is the best policy. But you may be surprised by what happens when one man tells the whole truth for an entire day in **"Like the Sun,"** by R. K. Narayan, page 280.

A dog is sometimes called man's best friend, but this is not the case with Muggs, a mischievous and temperamental terrier. See what trouble he causes in the humorous essay **"The Dog That Bit People,"** by James Thurber, page 256.

 Take It to the Net

Visit the Web site for online instruction and activities related to each selection in this unit
www.phschool.com

2

Read for Information

During World War II, more than 100,000 Japanese Americans were detained in special camps in the United States. More than thirty years later, their internment became cause for a national apology. Read the carefully chosen words of Gerald Ford's **"Speech on Japanese American Internment,"** page 308.

238 ◆ Clashing Forces

 ENRICHMENT: Further Reading

Have students choose one or more of the works below to extend the unit theme "Clashing Forces" or to read more by the unit authors.

"The Gift of the Magi" by O. Henry
In this story, a husband and wife each sell a treasured possession in order to buy a gift for the other.

The Big Sea by Langston Hughes
This autobiography tells about Hughes' search for his place in this world, up until his first success as a writer.

The Hound of the Baskervilles by Sir Arthur Conan Doyle
This classic Sherlock Holmes mystery of the seemingly cursed Baskerville family—a mystery that has Dr. Watson at his wits' end—can be found in the **Prentice Hall Literature Library.**

How to Read Literature

Use Interactive Reading Strategies

Reading is interactive. When you interact with the words on a page, you can see the sights and hear the sounds of new worlds. If you just sit back and passively look at the words, it is like going on a field trip and never getting off the bus! When you read, apply the following strategies to help you get involved with the text:

1. Question.
- List questions that occur to you about the characters.
- Think about why the writer includes certain information.
- Look for answers to your questions.

2. Form mental images.
Use details from the selection to form pictures in your mind. These visualizations can clarify the writer's description of characters or events. For example, read the highlighted text in the passage at right, and imagine the action the writer describes.

3. Predict events.
- Look for hints or clues about a story's outcome.
- Make an educated guess about future events based on what you know about the characters, the situation, and the structure of a story or poem.
- Adjust your prediction as you gain more information.

4. Analyze causes and effects.
In life, you experience the effects of your actions—the results of what you do. When you analyze causes and effects in literature, you look for a relationship between events. In this quotation from "Like the Sun," you can see the immediate effect of one character's words.

. . . he said, "It isn't good. I'm unable to swallow it." He saw her wince and said to himself, Can't be helped. Truth is like the sun. — *from* "Like the Sun"

As you read the selections in this unit, review the reading strategies and look at the notes in the side columns. Use the suggestions to apply the strategies and interact with the text.

Forming a Mental Image

Muggs' first free leap carried him all the way across the table and into a brass fire screen in front of the gas grate but he was back on his feet in a moment and in the end he got Roy and gave him a pretty vicious bite in the leg.—*from* "The Dog That Bit People"

How to Read Literature ◆ 239

How to Read Literature

The "How to Read Literature" page in each unit presents a set of strategies to help readers understand authors' words and ideas. Each reading strategy is taught in conjunction with one or more of the selections within the unit. Good readers develop a bank of strategies from which they can draw as needed.

Unit 3 introduces four strategies for interactive reading. Students learn to question, to form mental images, to predict events, and to analyze causes and effects.

How to Use This Page

Introduce the strategies for interactive reading, presenting each as a tool for developing understanding when reading the selections in this unit.

- As they read "Through the Tunnel" (p. 242), students will learn to formulate and answer questions while reading in order to engage more deeply with the text.

- As they read "The Dog That Bit People" (p. 256), students will learn to form mental images using the details in the text.

- As they read "Hearts and Hands" (p. 290), students will learn to predict outcomes to help them better understand what they are reading.

- As they read, "Like the Sun" (p. 280), students will learn how to look for a relationship between events as they analyze causes and effects.

MODEL A READING STRATEGY: Predict Events

Explain to students that predicting events as they read keeps them involved with the story so they understand it better. Model this strategy for students using this passage from "Hearts and Hands":

> As they passed down the aisle of the coach the only vacant seat offered was a reversed one facing the attractive young woman. Here the linked couple seated themselves.

Tell students:

In this story, the author describes two handcuffed men boarding a train. He has already drawn attention to the young woman: She is the only passenger he describes besides the two handcuffed men. Now, he tells us that the three will be sitting together. Because of his focus, you can predict that the story will be about the interaction among these three characters. The very next sentence, in which the woman suddenly recognizes one of the men, helps confirm your prediction.

239

Through the Tunnel

Lesson Objectives

1. **To analyze and respond to literary elements**
   - Literary Analysis: Internal Conflict
   - Connecting Literary Elements: Climax

2. **To read, comprehend, analyze, and critique a short story**
   - Reading Strategy: Questioning
   - Reading Check questions
   - Review and Assess questions
   - Assessment Practice (ATE)

3. **To develop word analysis skills, fluency, and systematic vocabulary**
   - Vocabulary Development Lesson: Latin Word Root: -lum-

4. **To understand and apply written and oral language conventions**
   - Spelling Strategy
   - Grammar Lesson: Complete Subject

5. **To understand and apply appropriate writing and research strategies**
   - Writing Lesson: Travel Brochure
   - Extension Activity: Safety Manual

6. **To understand and apply listening and speaking strategies**
   - Extension Activity: Dialogue

STEP-BY-STEP TEACHING GUIDE	PACING GUIDE
PRETEACH	
Motivate Students and Provide Background	
Use the Motivation activity (ATE p. 240)	5 min.
Read and discuss the Preview material and Background information (SE/ATE p. 240)	5 min.
Introduce the Concepts	
Introduce the Literary Analysis and Reading Strategy (SE/ATE p. 241)	15 min.
Pronounce the vocabulary words and read their definitions (SE p. 241)	5 min.
TEACH	
Monitor Comprehension	
Informally monitor comprehension by circulating while students read independently or in groups	25 min.
Monitor students' comprehension with the Reading Check notes (SE/ATE pp. 243, 245, 247, 249)	as students read
Develop vocabulary with Vocabulary notes (SE pp. 242, 243, 244, 246, 249; ATE p. 243)	as students read
Develop Understanding	
Develop students' understanding of internal conflict with the Literary Analysis annotations (SE pp. 243, 246, 248; ATE pp. 243, 244, 246, 247, 248, 250)	10 min.
Develop students' understanding of questioning with Reading Strategy annotations (SE pp. 242, 244, 246, 249; ATE pp. 242, 244, 246, 249)	10 min.
ASSESS	
Assess Mastery	
Assess students' mastery of the Reading Strategy and Literary Analysis by having them answer the Review and Assess questions (SE/ATE p. 251)	20 min.
Use one or more of the print and media Assessment Resources (ATE p. 253)	up to 50 min.
EXTEND	
Apply Understanding	
Have students complete the Vocabulary Development Lesson and the Grammar Lesson (SE p. 252)	20 min.
Apply students' ability to use a persuasive tone using the Writing Lesson (SE p. 253)	45 min.
Apply students' understanding using one or more of the Extension Activities (SE p. 253)	20–90 min.

 ACCELERATED INSTRUCTION:
Use the strategies and activities identified with an .

UNIVERSAL ACCESS
- ● = Below Level Students
- ▲ = On-Level Students
- ■ = Above Level Students

Time and Resource Manager

RESOURCES		
PRINT 📖	**TRANSPARENCIES**	**TECHNOLOGY** 💿 🎧 📼
• **Beyond Literature**, Cross-Curricular Connection: Physical Education, p. 16 ▲ ■		• **Interest Grabber Video**, Tape 2 ● ▲ ■
• **Selection Support Workbook:** ● ▲ ■ Literary Analysis, p. 64 Reading Strategy, p. 63 Build Vocabulary, p. 61	• **Literary Analysis and Reading Transparencies,** pp. 31 and 32 ● ▲ ■	
• **Adapted Reader's Companion** ● • **Reader's Companion** ●		
• **English Learner's Companion** ● ▲ • **Literatura en español** ● ▲ • **Literary Analysis for Enrichment** ■		
• **Formal Assessment:** Selection Test, pp. 54–56 ● ▲ ■ • **Open Book Test,** pp. 46–48 ● ▲ ■ • **Performance Assessment and Portfolio Management,** pp. 20, 30 ● ▲ ■ • (PRENTICE HALL ASSESSMENT *SYSTEM*) ● ▲	• (PRENTICE HALL ASSESSMENT *SYSTEM*) ● ▲ ■ Skills Practice Answers and Explanations on Transparencies	• **Test Bank Software** ● ▲ ■ • **Got It! Assessment Videotapes,** Tape 2 ● ▲
• **Selection Support Workbook:** ● ▲ ■ Build Grammar Skills, p. 62 • **Writing and Grammar,** Platinum Level ● ▲ ■ • **Extension Activities,** p. 16 ● ▲ ■	• **Daily Language Practice Transparencies** ● ▲	• **Writing and Grammar iText CD-ROM** ● ▲ ■ 💻 *Take It to the Net* www.phschool.com

BLOCK SCHEDULING: Use one 90-minute class period to preteach the selection and have students read it. Use a second 90-minute class period to assess students' mastery of skills and have them complete one of the Extension Activities.

Motivation

Give students an opportunity to relate to the way time seems to expand during Jerry's physical ordeal. Have them close their eyes, and then tell them to keep their eyes closed and raise their hands when they think two minutes have passed. Most students will raise their hands before the time has elapsed. Point out that a boy in this story will spend that much time in a dark, frightening place, holding his breath and facing a great physical challenge, affecting his perception of time.

Interest Grabber Video

As an alternative, play "Athletes in Training," Tape 2 to engage student interest.

❶ Background

Art

Coast Scene, Isles of Shoals, by Childe Hassam

American-born Childe Hassam established himself as a key figure in the French Impressionist movement in the late nineteenth century. His goal as a painter was to capture sunlight and its effects on landscapes.

In this painting, the sunlit rocks look inviting and the sea appears calm, but the dark recesses of the churning water meeting the rocks in the foreground add an element of danger to the scene.

Have students study the painting and then answer the following question:
Based on the painting, what do you predict will be the main conflict of the story?
Answer: Students might predict that someone in the story will be in conflict with dangerous waters.

Prepare to Read

Through the Tunnel

Coast Scene, Isles of Shoals, 1901, Childe Hassam, The Metropolitan Museum of Art

 Take It to the Net

Visit www.phschool.com for interactive activities and instruction related to "Through the Tunnel," including
- background
- graphic organizers
- literary elements
- reading strategies

Preview

Connecting to the Literature

When you set personal goals, you challenge yourself to see just how far you can go. Whether or not you succeed, you learn something about yourself. The boy in "Through the Tunnel" sets himself a physical challenge that requires all his courage.

Background

Jerry, the young boy in "Through the Tunnel," keeps extending the amount of time he can hold his breath underwater. He deprives himself of oxygen, which is an important part of the air you breathe. Depriving the brain of oxygen can quickly cause dizziness and loss of consciousness. Upon losing consciousness, the body would automatically begin breathing. Then, Jerry would drown because people cannot obtain oxygen underwater.

240 ◆ *Clashing Forces*

TEACHING RESOURCES

The following resources can be used to enrich or extend the instruction for pp. 240–241.

Motivation

Interest Grabber Video, Tape 2

Background

Beyond Literature, Cross-Curricular Connection: Physical Education, p. 16

 Take It to the Net

Visit www.phschool.com for background and hotlinks for "Through the Tunnel."

Literary Analysis

Literary Analysis and Reading Transparencies, Internal Conflict, p. 32

Reading

Selection Support: Reading Strategy, p. 63; Build Vocabulary, p. 61

Literary Analysis and Reading Transparencies, Questioning, p. 31

BLOCK SCHEDULING: Resources marked with this symbol provide varied instruction during 90-minute blocks.

Literary Analysis

Internal Conflict

The personal challenge that Jerry sets for himself in "Through the Tunnel" involves an **internal conflict,** a struggle within a character between opposing feelings, beliefs, or needs. In this passage from the story, notice Jerry's mixed feelings and his inability to make a decision.

> He was frightened. Supposing he turned dizzy in the tunnel? Supposing he died there, trapped? Supposing—his head went around, in the hot sun, and he almost gave up.

As you read, use a chart like the one shown to identify Jerry's conflicting feelings.

Jerry's Feelings	
Wants to go to bay	Does not want to hurt mother's feelings

Connecting Literary Elements

The **climax** of a story is its high point of interest or suspense. It is the turning point at which readers learn how the conflict in the story will end. In "Through the Tunnel," Jerry's internal conflict causes increasing tension and gradually leads to the story's climax. Notice the steps that escalate Jerry's anxiety to the point at which he must act.

Reading Strategy

Questioning

You will understand stories better if you ask yourself **questions** and then look for the answers as you read.

- Ask yourself questions to make the story events, characters' actions, settings, and other details clear to you.
- Question why characters behave in a certain way and what their behavior reveals about them.

As you read "Through the Tunnel," question the events, characters, settings, and other details, and then look for the answers.

Vocabulary Development

contrition (kən trish´ ən) *n.* regret for having done something wrong (p. 242)

promontories (präm´ ən tôr´ ēz) *n.* high pieces of land extending out over a body of water (p. 243)

luminous (lōō´ mə nəs) *adj.* giving off light (p. 243)

supplication (sup´ lə kā´ shən) *n.* the act of asking humbly and earnestly (p. 244)

frond (fränd) *n.* leaflike shoot (p. 247)

convulsive (kən vul´ siv) *adj.* marked by an involuntary muscular contraction (p. 249)

gout (gout) *n.* spurt; splash; glob (p. 249)

Through the Tunnel ◆ 241

---

❷ Literary Analysis

Internal Conflict

- Remind students that an internal conflict is one that takes place within a character; for example, a character may experience a conflict between his conscience and his desires.
- Suggest that students give examples of internal conflicts experienced by characters in other stories they have read or movies they have seen.
- Review the graphic organizer with students. As they read the selection, have them complete the organizer by identifying details from the story that reveal Jerry's conflicting feelings.

❸ Reading Strategy

Questioning

- Explain to students that asking questions as they read will help them become more involved in and better comprehend what they are reading.
- Suggest that students jot down questions that occur to them as they read. Students can cross off questions as they answer them.
- Remind students that they may have to reread passages or read ahead in order to answer their questions.
- In addition, make sure students understand that not all of their questions will be answered when they finish reading. Readers often have to draw inferences based on information in the story.

Vocabulary Development

- Pronounce each vocabulary word for students, and read the definitions as a class. Have students identify any words with which they are already familiar.

CUSTOMIZE INSTRUCTION FOR UNIVERSAL ACCESS

For Special Needs Students	For Less Proficient Readers	For English Learners
Have students read the adapted version of "Through the Tunnel" in the **Adapted Reader's Companion.** This version provides basic-level instruction in an interactive format with questions and write-on lines. Completing the adapted version will prepare students to read the selection in the Student Edition.	Have students read the selection in the **Reader's Companion.** This version provides basic-level instruction in an interactive format with questions and write-on lines. After students finish the selection in **Reader's Companion,** have them complete the questions and activities in the Student Edition.	Have students read the adapted version of the selection in the **English Learner's Companion.** This version provides basic-level instruction in an interactive format with questions and write-on lines. Completing the adapted version will prepare students to read the selection in the Student Edition.

 E-Teach

Visit E-Teach at www.phschool.com for teachers' essays on how to teach, with questions and answers.

Step-by-Step Teaching Guide for pp. 242–250

CUSTOMIZE INSTRUCTION
For Verbal/Linguistic Learners

Suggest that interested students find out more about sea caves and how they are formed. They can expand their research to include cave study (speleology) and cave exploration (spelunking). Have students share their research information with the class in the form of written reports.

❶ About the Selection

In "Through the Tunnel," Doris Lessing establishes a level of tension that increases with every heart-pounding moment. The story reaches beyond suspense, however, to make profound points about a boy's conflict between love for his mother and desire for independence. For the boy, making the perilous journey through a dark underwater tunnel and breaking through to the light on the other end is an important rite of passage that helps him reconcile these two forces.

❷ Reading Strategy

Questioning

- Call students' attention to the bracketed passage. Ask students to describe the mental image they form when they read the phrase "young boy."

- Then, ask students the Reading Strategy question on p. 242: What might you ask about Jerry's age? Where would you find the answer?
  Answer: Students will most likely ask exactly how old Jerry is. They might find the answer by reading ahead.

❶ Through the Tunnel
Doris Lessing

❷   Going to the shore on the first morning of the vacation, the young English boy stopped at a turning of the path and looked down at a wild and rocky bay, and then over to the crowded beach he knew so well from other years. His mother walked on in front of him, carrying a bright striped bag in one hand. Her other arm, swinging loose, was very white in the sun. The boy watched that white, naked arm, and turned his eyes, which had a frown behind them, toward the bay and back again to his mother. When she felt he was not with her, she swung around. "Oh, there you are, Jerry!" she said. She looked impatient, then smiled. "Why, darling, would you rather not come with me? Would you rather—" She frowned, conscientiously worrying over what amusements he might secretly be longing for, which she had been too busy or too careless to imagine. He was very familiar with that anxious, apologetic smile. <u>Contrition</u> sent him running after her. And yet, as he ran, he looked back over his shoulder at the wild bay; and all morning, as he played on the safe beach, he was thinking of it.

   Next morning, when it was time for the routine of swimming and sun-bathing, his mother said, "Are you tired of the usual beach, Jerry? Would you like to go somewhere else?"

   "Oh, no!" he said quickly, smiling at her out of that unfailing impulse of contrition—a sort of chivalry. Yet, walking down the path with her, he blurted out, "I'd like to go and have a look at those rocks down there."

   She gave the idea her attention. It was a wild-looking place, and there was no one there; but she said, "Of course, Jerry. When you've had

Reading Strategy
Questioning Jerry is referred to as a "young English boy." What might you ask about his age? Where would you find the answer?

contrition (kən trish′ ən) *n.* regret for having done something wrong

242 ◆ *Clashing Forces*

TEACHING RESOURCES

The following resources can be used to enrich or extend the instruction for pp. 242–250.

Literary Analysis
📖 **Selection Support:** Literary Analysis, p. 65 ▪️

Reading
📖 **Reader's Companion**
📖 **English Learner's Companion**

▪️ **BLOCK SCHEDULING:** Resources marked with this symbol provide varied instruction during 90-minute blocks.

enough, come to the big beach. Or just go straight back to the villa, if you like." She walked away, that bare arm, now slightly reddened from yesterday's sun, swinging. And he almost ran after her again, feeling it unbearable that she should go by herself, but he did not.

She was thinking, Of course he's old enough to be safe without me. Have I been keeping him too close? He mustn't feel he ought to be with me. I must be careful.

He was an only child, eleven years old. She was a widow. She was determined to be neither possessive nor lacking in devotion. She went worrying off to her beach.

As for Jerry, once he saw that his mother had gained her beach, he began the steep descent to the bay. From where he was, high up among red-brown rocks, it was a scoop of moving bluish green fringed with white. As he went lower, he saw that it spread among small <u>promontories</u> and inlets of rough, sharp rock, and the crisping, lapping surface showed stains of purple and darker blue. Finally, as he ran sliding and scraping down the last few yards, he saw an edge of white surf and the shallow, <u>luminous</u> movement of water over white sand, and, beyond that, a solid, heavy blue.

He ran straight into the water and began swimming. He was a good swimmer. He went out fast over the gleaming sand, over a middle region where rocks lay like discolored monsters under the surface, and then he was in the real sea—a warm sea where irregular cold currents from the deep water shocked his limbs.

Literary Analysis
Internal Conflict
With what two opposing feelings does the mother struggle?

promontories (präm´ ən tôr´ ēz) *n.* high pieces of land extending out over a body of water

luminous (lōō´ mə nəs) *adj.* giving off light

⑤ ✓Reading Check
Where would Jerry rather go than with his mother?

Through the Tunnel ◆ 243

CUSTOMIZE INSTRUCTION FOR UNIVERSAL ACCESS

For Less Proficient Readers	For Gifted/Talented Students
Lessing's description of the wild bay on p. 243 is full of sensory images, such as "a scoop of moving bluish green" and "luminous movement of water over white sand." Have students identify the details that help them imagine this scene. Then, encourage them to describe the wild bay in their own words.	Suggest that students reread Lessing's description of the wild bay on p. 243. Then, have students write a poem about the wild bay, combining sensory images from the passage with sensory details and images of their own.

❻ Literary Analysis

Internal Conflict

- Point out to students that Jerry's interaction with the older boys highlights his desire to grow up and be independent of his mother.
- Ask students to notice how Jerry's actions in the next few paragraphs highlight his childlike side.

❼ Reading Strategy

Questioning

- Ask students what they already know about Jerry. Elicit that he is immature and wants to impress the older boys.
- Then, ask students the Reading Strategy question on p. 244: What might you ask at the end of this paragraph? What answer would you give to your question?
  Answer: Students might ask why Jerry wants to show off around the older boys. The answer is that he wants to impress the older boys.

When he was so far out that he could look back not only on the little bay but past the promontory that was between it and the big beach, he floated on the buoyant surface and looked for his mother. There she was, a speck of yellow under an umbrella that looked like a slice of orange peel. He swam back to shore, relieved at being sure she was there, but all at once very lonely.

On the edge of a small cape that marked the side of the bay away from the promontory was a loose scatter of rocks. Above them, some boys were stripping off their clothes. They came running, naked, down to the rocks. The English boy swam toward them, but kept his distance at a stone's throw. They were of that coast; all of them were burned smooth dark brown and speaking a language he did not understand. To be with them, of them, was a craving that filled his whole body. He swam a little closer; they turned and watched him with narrowed, alert dark eyes. Then one smiled and waved. It was enough. In a minute, he had swum in and was on the rocks beside them, smiling with a desperate, nervous supplication. They shouted cheerful greetings at him; and then, as he preserved his nervous, uncomprehending smile, they understood that he was a foreigner strayed from his own beach, and they proceeded to forget him. But he was happy. He was with them.

❻ They began diving again and again from a high point into a well of blue sea between rough, pointed rocks. After they had dived and come up, they swam around, hauled themselves up, and waited their turn to dive again. They were big boys—men, to Jerry. He dived, and they watched him; and when he swam around to take his place, they made way for him. He felt he was accepted and he dived again, carefully, proud of himself.

Soon the biggest of the boys poised himself, shot down into the water, and did not come up. The others stood about, watching. Jerry, after waiting for the sleek brown head to appear, let out a yell of warning; they looked at him idly and turned their eyes back toward the water. After a long time, the boy came up on the other side of a big dark rock, letting the air out of his lungs in a sputtering gasp and a shout of triumph. Immediately the rest of them dived in. One moment, the morning seemed full of chattering boys; the next, the air and the surface of the water were empty. But through the heavy blue, dark shapes could be seen moving and groping.

Jerry dived, shot past the school of underwater swimmers, saw a black wall of rock looming at him, touched it, and bobbed up at once to the surface, where the wall was a low barrier he could see across. There was no one visible; under him, in the water, the dim shapes of the swimmers had disappeared. Then one, and then another of the boys came up on the far side of the barrier of rock, and he understood that they had swum through some gap or hole in it. He plunged down again. He could see nothing through the stinging salt water but the blank rock. When he came up the boys were all on the diving rock, preparing to attempt the feat again. And now, in a panic of failure, he yelled up, in English, "Look at me! Look!" and he began splashing and

supplication (sup´ lə kā´ shən) *n.* the act of asking humbly and earnestly

Reading Strategy
Questioning What might you ask yourself at the end of this paragraph? What answer would that question generate?

244 ◆ *Clashing Forces*

✹ ENRICHMENT: Literature Connection

Symbolism

In literature, authors often use symbols to enhance the meaning of their stories. It's important for readers to look beyond the literal meaning of images that recur in a story. For example, a rose may be a symbol for beauty, and a bare tree may be a symbol for death.

In this story, the tunnel is a recurring image. Passing through the tunnel might be a symbol for birth, because a baby passes through the birth canal when he or she is born. Even though Jerry is a child, not a baby, he is,

in a sense, being born as a young man in this story.

Ask students to discuss why they think it can be more effective for an author to use a symbol than to state explicitly what he or she wants to say. Then, suggest that students note other recurring images in the story, and speculate about what they might symbolize.

The Beach Treat (detail), Suzanne Nagler

kicking in the water like a foolish dog.

They looked down gravely, frowning. He knew the frown. At moments of failure, when he clowned to claim his mother's attention, it was with just this grave, embarrassed inspection that she rewarded him. Through his hot shame, feeling the pleading grin on his face like a scar that he could never remove, he looked up at the group of big brown boys on the rock and shouted, *"Bonjour! Merci! Au revoir! Monsieur, monsieur!"*[1] while he hooked his fingers round his ears and waggled them.

Water surged into his mouth; he choked, sank, came up. The rock, lately weighted with boys, seemed to rear up out of the water as their weight was removed. They were flying down past him, now, into the water; the air was full of falling bodies. Then the rock was empty in the hot sunlight. He counted one, two, three. . . .

At fifty, he was terrified. They must all be drowning beneath him, in the watery caves of the rock! At a hundred, he stared around him at the empty hillside, wondering if he should yell for help. He counted faster, faster, to hurry them up, to bring them to the surface quickly, to drown them quickly—anything rather than the terror of counting on and on into the blue emptiness of the morning. And then, at a hundred and sixty, the water beyond the rock was full of boys blowing like brown whales. They swam back to the shore without a look at him.

He climbed back to the diving rock and sat down, feeling the hot roughness of it under his thighs. The boys were gathering up their bits of clothing and running off along the shore to another promontory.

---

1. **Bonjour! . . . monsieur!** (bōn zhoor´ . . . mə syŧr´) babbling of commonly known French words: "Hello! Thank you! Goodbye! Sir, sir!"

❾ ▲ **Critical Viewing**
Compare the details of this painting with the way you pictured the "big beach" in the story.
[Compare and Contrast]

❿ ☑ **Reading Check**
What do the other boys do that Jerry is not able to do?

Through the Tunnel ◆ 245

---

❽ Background

Art

The Beach Treat, by Suzanne Nagler
Suzanne Nagler's painting of a beach scene is, in some ways, similar to the description of the beach in the story. The artist's use of childlike primary colors emphasizes the safe, peaceful quality of this place.

Have students study the painting. Then, use the following questions for discussion:

1. What details in the painting give an impression of safety and tranquility?
   Possible responses: The building, which could be a home or a lifeguard station, gives a sense of permanence; phone lines link the remoteness of the beach to the rest of the world.

2. What important element of a beach scene is missing in this painting? Why do you think the artist omitted it?
   Answer: Encourage students to note that the ocean is missing. Suggest that the vastness and the motion of the sea would disturb the stability and calm of the beach scene.

❾ ▶ Critical Viewing

Answer: Students might say that the beach in the painting is less crowded than the one in the story. They may add more people and a woman sitting on a yellow towel or wearing a yellow bathing suit, sitting under an orange beach umbrella. They might also add the ocean and waves.

❿ ☑ Reading Check

Answer: The boys can swim through the tunnel, but Jerry cannot.

CUSTOMIZE INSTRUCTION FOR UNIVERSAL ACCESS

For English Learners	For Advanced Readers
Help students understand figurative expressions in the story, such as "anything rather than the terror of counting on and on into the blue emptiness of the morning." Help them to see that the counting seems as endless as the blue sky.	Have students write a paragraph that describes Jerry's thoughts and emotions as he waits for the boys to surface. Have them use sensory details to make the description as vivid as possible. Before they begin, students might make a list of Jerry's emotions. Then, they can think of sensory images that will convey these emotions.

- Have a volunteer read aloud the bracketed passage. Suggest that students list each of Jerry's actions as they follow the text.

- Then, ask students the Reading Strategy question on p. 246: What might you ask about Jerry's actions?

  Answer: Students might ask why Jerry is behaving this way toward his mother or why he wants the goggles so badly.

  ▶ **Monitor Progress** Make sure students find answers to their questions as they continue to read. If they have trouble, direct their attention to relevant passages and details.

- Have a volunteer paraphrase the action described in the bracketed passage. Ask students to identify Jerry's goal and then to describe how they think Jerry feels at this point. Make sure they support their responses with details from the passage.

  Answer: Students should note that Jerry's goal is to swim through the tunnel. He is frightened of the strange sights and sensations he encounters as he explores it.

- Then, ask students the Literary Analysis question on p. 247: Between what two needs is Jerry torn?

  Answer: Jerry is torn between his need to swim through the tunnel and his need to get out of the water due to his fear.

They were leaving to get away from him. He cried openly, fists in his eyes. There was no one to see him, and he cried himself out.

It seemed to him that a long time had passed, and he swam out to where he could see his mother. Yes, she was still there, a yellow spot under an orange umbrella. He swam back to the big rock, climbed up, and dived into the blue pool among the fanged and angry boulders. Down he went, until he touched the wall of rock again. But the salt was so painful in his eyes that he could not see.

He came to the surface, swam to shore and went back to the villa to wait for his mother. Soon she walked slowly up the path, swinging her striped bag, the flushed, naked arm dangling beside her. "I want some swimming goggles," he panted, defiant and beseeching.

She gave him a patient, inquisitive look as she said casually, "Well, of course, darling."

But now, now, now! He must have them this minute, and no other time. He nagged and pestered until she went with him to a shop. As soon as she had bought the goggles, he grabbed them from her hand as if she were going to claim them for herself, and was off, running down the steep path to the bay.

Jerry swam out to the big barrier rock, adjusted the goggles, and dived. The impact of the water broke the rubber-enclosed vacuum, and the goggles came loose. He understood that he must swim down to the base of the rock from the surface of the water. He fixed the goggles tight and firm, filled his lungs, and floated, face down, on the water. Now he could see. It was as if he had eyes of a different kind—fish eyes that showed everything clear and delicate and wavering in the bright water.

Under him, six or seven feet down, was a floor of perfectly clean, shining white sand, rippled firm and hard by the tides. Two grayish shapes steered there, like long, rounded pieces of wood or slate. They were fish. He saw them nose toward each other, poise motionless, make a dart forward, swerve off, and come around again. It was like a water dance. A few inches above them the water sparkled as if sequins were dropping through it. Fish again—myriads of minute fish, the length of his fingernail, were drifting through the water, and in a moment he could feel the innumerable tiny touches of them against his limbs. It was like swimming in flaked silver. The great rock the big boys had swum through rose sheer out of the white sand—black, tufted lightly with greenish weed. He could see no gap in it. He swam down to its base.

Again and again he rose, took a big chestful of air, and went down. Again and again he groped over the surface of the rock, feeling it, almost hugging it in the desperate need to find the entrance. And then, once, while he was clinging to the black wall, his knees came up and he shot his feet out forward and they met no obstacle. He had found the hole.

He gained the surface, clambered about the stones that littered the barrier rock until he found a big one, and, with this in his arms, let himself down over the side of the rock. He dropped, with the weight, straight to the sandy floor. Clinging tight to the anchor of stone, he lay on his side and looked in under the dark shelf at the place where his

246 ◆ *Clashing Forces*

feet had gone. He could see the hole. It was an irregular, dark gap; but he could not see deep into it. He let go of his anchor, clung with his hands to the edges of the hole, and tried to push himself in.

He got his head in, found his shoulders jammed, moved them in sidewise, and was inside as far as his waist. He could see nothing ahead. Something soft and clammy touched his mouth; he saw a dark <u>frond</u> moving against the grayish rock, and panic filled him. He thought of octopuses, of clinging weed. He pushed himself out backward and caught a glimpse, as he retreated, of a harmless tentacle of seaweed drifting in the mouth of the tunnel. But it was enough. He reached the sunlight, swam to shore, and lay on the diving rock. He looked down into the blue well of water. He knew he must find his way through that cave, or hole, or tunnel, and out the other side.

First, he thought, he must learn to control his breathing. He let himself down into the water with another big stone in his arms, so that he could lie effortlessly on the bottom of the sea. He counted. One, two, three. He counted steadily. He could hear the movement of blood in his chest. Fifty-one, fifty-two. . . . His chest was hurting. He let go of the rock and went up into the air. He saw that the sun was low. He rushed to the villa and found his mother at her supper. She said only, "Did you enjoy yourself?" and he said, "Yes."

All night the boy dreamed of the water-filled cave in the rock, and as soon as breakfast was over he went to the bay.

That night, his nose bled badly. For hours he had been underwater, learning to hold his breath, and now he felt weak and dizzy. His mother said, "I shouldn't overdo things, darling, if I were you."

That day and the next, Jerry exercised his lungs as if everything, the whole of his life, all that he would become, depended upon it. Again his nose bled at night, and his mother insisted on his coming with her the next day. It was a torment to him to waste a day of his careful self-training, but he stayed with her on that other beach, which now seemed a place for small children, a place where his mother might lie safe in the sun. It was not his beach.

He did not ask for permission, on the following day, to go to his beach. He went, before his mother could consider the complicated rights and wrongs of the matter. A day's rest, he discovered, had improved his count by ten. The big boys had made the passage while he counted a hundred and sixty. He had been counting fast, in his fright. Probably now, if he tried, he could get through that long tunnel, but he was not going to try yet. A curious, most unchildlike persistence, a controlled impatience, made him wait. In the meantime, he lay underwater on the white sand, littered now by stones he had brought down from the upper

Literature ⑬
in context   Health Connection

Water-Safety Rules
Jerry unwisely breaks most of the following common-sense rules regarding water safety.

1. He swims alone.
2. He swims into unknown areas.
3. He swims and dives in rocky areas and narrow passages.
4. He holds his breath too long underwater. He does not use underwater breathing equipment.
5. He swims even though he has a nosebleed.
6. He swims stained with blood. Blood attracts sharks.

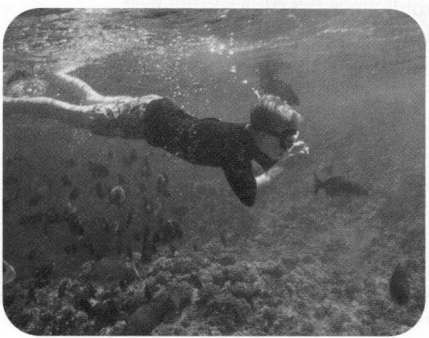

Literary Analysis
Internal Conflict
Between what two needs is Jerry torn?

frond (fränd) n. leaflike shoot

⑮ ✔**Reading Check**
What is Jerry's physical reaction to holding his breath for long periods?

Through the Tunnel ◆ 247

⑬ **Background**
Health Connection
The American Red Cross provides comprehensive information about water safety, from community swimming pools to lakes and oceans. Suggest that students visit the American Red Cross Web site, at www.redcross.org, for more information on being a safe swimmer.

⑭ **Literary Analysis**
Internal Conflict
• Ask students to explain why Jerry is waiting to swim through the tunnel. Why do they think Lessing calls his persistence "unchildlike"?
Answer: Jerry waits because he wants to be certain he will succeed. His persistence is unchildlike because most children do not exhibit this much self-control.

• Ask students whether Jerry's actions reveal any changes in his personality. Suggest that students compare Jerry's actions now with his behavior with his mother on p. 246.
Answer: Jerry is acting in a much more mature way now. His goal of swimming through the tunnel may be helping him to grow up.

⑮ ✔**Reading Check**
Answer: Jerry becomes dizzy and his nose bleeds profusely.

CUSTOMIZE INSTRUCTION FOR UNIVERSAL ACCESS

For Advanced Readers

Ask students to write a dialogue that takes place between Jerry and his mother in which he tries to explain to her why he needs to swim through the tunnel. Have him express himself excitedly and with great confidence.

Suggest that students elaborate on what they know about Jerry's mother so that she is a believable expanded version of the woman created by Doris Lessing.

Suggest that students use what they know about Jerry to create dialogue that reveals both his childishness and his growing determination to be independent.

When they finish writing, have students divide into pairs and perform their dialogues for the class.

air, and studied the entrance to the tunnel. He knew every jut and corner of it, as far as it was possible to see. It was as if he already felt its sharpness about his shoulders.

He sat by the clock in the villa, when his mother was not near, and checked his time. He was incredulous and then proud to find he could hold his breath without strain for two minutes. The words "two minutes," authorized by the clock, brought close the adventure that was so necessary to him.

In another four days, his mother said casually one morning, they must go home. On the day before they left, he would do it. He would do it if it killed him, he said defiantly to himself. But two days before they were to leave—a day of triumph when he increased his count by fifteen—his nose bled so badly that he turned dizzy and had to lie limply over the big rock like a bit of seaweed, watching the thick red blood flow onto the rock and trickle slowly down to the sea. He was frightened. Supposing he turned dizzy in the tunnel? Supposing he died there, trapped? Supposing—his head went around, in the hot sun, and he almost gave up. He thought he would return to the house and lie down, and next summer, perhaps, when he had another year's growth in him—*then* he would go through the hole.

But even after he had made the decision, or thought he had, he found himself sitting up on the rock and looking down into the water; and he knew that now, this moment, when his nose had only just stopped bleeding, when his head was still sore and throbbing—this was the moment when he would try. If he did not do it now, he never would. He was trembling with fear that he would not go; and he was trembling with horror at that long, long tunnel under the rock, under the sea. Even in the open sunlight, the barrier rock seemed very wide and very heavy; tons of rock pressed down on where he would go. If he died there, he would lie until one day—perhaps not before next year—those big boys would swim into it and find it blocked.

He put on his goggles, fitted them tight, tested the vacuum. His hands were shaking. Then he chose the biggest stone he could carry and slipped over the edge of the rock until half of him was in the cool, enclosing water and half in the hot sun. He looked up once at the empty sky, filled his lungs once, twice, and then sank fast to the bottom with the stone. He let it go and began to count. He took the edges of the hole in his hands and drew himself into it, wriggling his shoulders in sidewise as he remembered he must, kicking himself along with his feet.

The Diver, Dennis Angel

17 ▲ **Critical Viewing** How does the tranquillity of this painting compare with the emotion in the story? **[Compare and Contrast]**

Literary Analysis Climax and Internal Conflict What effect does Jerry's feeling of anxiety have on the tension of the story?

248

Soon he was clear inside. He was in a small rockbound hole filled with yellowish-gray water. The water was pushing him up against the roof. The roof was sharp and pained his back. He pulled himself along with his hands—fast, fast—and used his legs as levers. His head knocked against something; a sharp pain dizzied him. Fifty, fifty-one, fifty-two. . . . He was without light, and the water seemed to press upon him with the weight of rock. Seventy-one, seventy-two. . . . There was no strain on his lungs. He felt like an inflated balloon, his lungs were so light and easy, but his head was pulsing.

He was being continually pressed against the sharp roof, which felt slimy as well as sharp. Again he thought of octopuses, and wondered if the tunnel might be filled with weed that could tangle him. He gave himself a panicky, <u>convulsive</u> kick forward, ducked his head, and swam. His feet and hands moved freely, as if in open water. The hole must have widened out. He thought he must be swimming fast, and he was frightened of banging his head if the tunnel narrowed.

A hundred, a hundred and one. . . . The water paled. Victory filled him. His lungs were beginning to hurt. A few more strokes and he would be out. He was counting wildly; he said a hundred and fifteen, and then, a long time later, a hundred and fifteen again. The water was a clear jewel-green all around him. Then he saw, above his head, a crack running up through the rock. Sunlight was falling through it, showing the clean, dark rock of the tunnel, a single mussel shell, and darkness ahead.

He was at the end of what he could do. He looked up at the crack as if it were filled with air and not water, as if he could put his mouth to it to draw in air. A hundred and fifteen, he heard himself say inside his head—but he had said that long ago. He must go on into the blackness ahead, or he would drown. His head was swelling, his lungs cracking. A hundred and fifteen, a hundred and fifteen pounded through his head, and he feebly clutched at rocks in the dark, pulling himself forward, leaving the brief space of sunlit water behind. He felt he was dying. He was no longer quite conscious. He struggled on in the darkness between lapses into unconsciousness. An immense, swelling pain filled his head, and then the darkness cracked with an explosion of green light. His hands, groping forward, met nothing; and his feet, kicking back, propelled him out into the open sea.

He drifted to the surface, his face turned up to the air. He was gasping like a fish. He felt he would sink now and drown; he could not swim the few feet back to the rock. Then he was clutching it and pulling himself up on to it. He lay face down, gasping. He could see nothing but a red-veined, clotted dark. His eyes must have burst, he thought; they were full of blood. He tore off his goggles and a <u>gout</u> of blood went into the sea. His nose was bleeding, and the blood had filled the goggles.

He scooped up handfuls of water from the cool, salty sea, to splash on his face, and did not know whether it was blood or salt water he tasted. After a time, his heart quieted, his eyes cleared, and he sat up. He could see the local boys diving and playing half a mile away. He did

---

convulsive (kən vul′ siv) *adj.* marked by an involuntary muscular contraction

Reading Strategy
Questioning What might you ask about the outcome of the story at this point?

gout (gout) *n.* spurt; splash; glob

 20 ☑ **Reading Check**
Why was it difficult to swim through the tunnel?

Through the Tunnel ◆ *249*

---

19 Reading Strategy
Questioning

• Have students describe both Jerry's actions and his thoughts at this point in the story.

• Then, ask students the Reading Strategy question on p. 249: What might you ask about the outcome of the story at this point?
Answer: Students might ask whether or not Jerry will survive.

20 ☑ Reading Check
Answer: It was difficult because Jerry had to hold his breath for such a long time that he became dizzy, and his nose bled.

21 Literary Analysis
Internal Conflict

• Have students read the bracketed passage.

• Ask students how the passage is one indication of how Jerry's internal conflict has been resolved.
Answer: The fact that Jerry no longer wants or needs the approval of the older boys indicates a newfound independence and maturity.

CUSTOMIZE INSTRUCTION FOR UNIVERSAL ACCESS

For Special Needs Students	For Advanced Readers
Students may have difficulty following the action of the story as the suspense builds, especially due to the detailed descriptions of Jerry's deteriorating condition. Work with students to create storyboards for the action on pp. 248–249. Encourage them to read each paragraph carefully and then draw a simple image that visually captures the action.	Draw students' attention to the detailed description of Jerry's journey through the tunnel, and ask them to identify details that help to create suspense. For example, on p. 249, Lessing describes the "clear, jewel-green water" to make both Jerry and the reader think that Jerry is nearly out of the tunnel. When we realize that we are wrong and that Jerry is still in danger, the tension builds.

Answers for p. 250

Review and Assess

1. Some students may have welcomed the challenge; others may have decided that the situation was too dangerous.

2. **(a)** Jerry's relationship with his mother is close, but in some ways suffocating. **(b)** By the end of the story, Jerry doesn't feel it is necessary to challenge his mother to prove his independence.

3. **(a)** At first, the boys accept Jerry, but when he starts behaving immaturely, they ignore him. **(b)** Jerry's determination to prove himself by swimming through the tunnel is strengthened by the boys' rejection.

4. **(a)** Jerry knows he will have to hold his breath for a long time to get through the tunnel. **(b)** At first, Jerry wants to prove that he can do what the older boys do. By the end, however, his goal is to prove to himself that he can overcome his fear.

5. **(a)** Jerry has proven to himself that he has courage and strength. **(b)** He will probably be less afraid to meet other challenges.

6. While many students may feel that Jerry's experience has made him more mature and independent, others may point out that it was unwise to take a risk that might have cost him his life.

not want them. He wanted nothing but to get back home and lie down.

In a short while, Jerry swam to shore and climbed slowly up the path to the villa. He flung himself on his bed and slept, waking at the sound of feet on the path outside. His mother was coming back. He rushed to the bathroom, thinking she must not see his face with bloodstains, or tearstains, on it. He came out of the bathroom and met her as she walked into the villa, smiling, her eyes lighting up.

"Have a nice morning?" she asked, laying her hand on his warm brown shoulder a moment.

"Oh, yes, thank you," he said.

"You look a bit pale." And then, sharp and anxious, "How did you bang your head?"

"Oh, just banged it," he told her.

She looked at him closely. He was strained; his eyes were glazed-looking. She was worried. And then she said to herself, Oh, don't fuss! Nothing can happen. He can swim like a fish.

They sat down to lunch together.

"Mummy," he said, "I can stay under water for two minutes— three minutes, at least." It came bursting out of him.

"Can you, darling?" she said. "Well, I shouldn't overdo it. I don't think you ought to swim any more today."

She was ready for a battle of wills, but he gave in at once. It was no longer of the least importance to go to the bay.

Review and Assess

Thinking About the Selection

1. **Respond:** Would you have made the same decision that Jerry did? Explain.

2. **(a) Recall:** Describe Jerry's relationship with his mother at the beginning. **(b) Analyze:** How does their relationship change?

3. **(a) Recall:** What happens when Jerry encounters the local boys? **(b) Analyze Cause and Effect:** How does the encounter affect Jerry's subsequent actions?

4. **(a) Recall:** Why does Jerry practice holding his breath? **(b) Infer:** What does Jerry think he must prove to himself by swimming through the tunnel?

5. **(a) Draw Conclusions:** At the end of the story, why is going to the bay "no longer of the least importance" to Jerry? **(b) Extend:** How do you think his success in meeting this challenge will affect other aspects of his life?

6. **Make a Judgment:** Do you think Jerry's victory is worth the pain and risk it entails? Why or why not?

250 ◆ *Clashing Forces*

Doris Lessing

(b. 1919)

Doris May Taylor was born on October 22, 1919, in Persia (now Iran). In 1925, enticed by the prospect of getting rich by farming maize, her father moved the family to the colony of Rhodesia (now Zimbabwe) in southern Africa.

Lessing has never been one to shy away from controversy. When she was growing up, she saw firsthand the injustices suffered by black Africans under European colonialism. Lessing spotlighted those injustices in her first novel, *The Grass Is Singing* (1950). Her strong views provoked a strong reaction: In 1956, she was declared a "prohibited alien" by the government of Rhodesia. Settled in England, she sparked additional controversy with feminist novels like *The Golden Notebook* (1962). When apartheid ended in South Africa in 1996, Lessing was welcomed back as a hero.

ASSESSMENT PRACTICE: Reading Comprehension

Stated and Implied Main Ideas   (For more practice, see Test Preparation Workbook, p. 16.)

Many tests require that students recognize and understand main ideas of a reading passage. Ask students to read the paragraph that begins, "On the edge of a small cape..." near the top of p. 244. Then, have them answer the following sample question.

Which of the following best expresses the main idea of this paragraph?

A Jerry wants to befriend the boys.

B The boys are all good swimmers.

C Swimming on the small cape is dangerous.

D The beach is rocky.

Students should decide whether each answer states a supporting detail or expresses the paragraph's main idea. Answers *B, C,* and *D* represent details from the passage, but the best expression of the main idea is *A*—Jerry desperately wants to be friends with the boys.

Review and Assess

Literary Analysis

Internal Conflict

1. What are the two opposing forces of Jerry's **internal conflict**?
2. What is the resolution of the conflict suggested by the title?
3. How does the physical challenge make the internal conflict more exciting?
4. What internal conflict does Jerry's mother face?

Connecting Literary Elements

5. What is the **climax** of this story?
6. Identify three steps that escalate the story to its climax.
7. How does the climax resolve Jerry's inner conflict?

Reading Strategy

Questioning

8. (a) After reading the opening paragraphs, what **question** might you ask about the setting of the story? (b) What answer would further reading provide?
9. Use a chart like this one to list the questions you generated about the underwater tunnel and the details from the text that answer your questions.

My Questions About the Tunnel	Details From the Text That Answer My Questions

10. (a) As you read the story, what questions did you have about Jerry's behavior and motives? (b) What answers did you discover by the end of the story?

Extend Understanding

11. **Cultural Connection:** Why do many young people set up situations to test themselves, as Jerry does? Give examples.

Quick Review

An **internal conflict** is a struggle within a character between opposing feelings, beliefs, or needs.

In a story, the **climax** is the high point of interest or suspense.

To understand stories better, ask **questions** and then look for answers as you read.

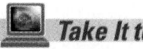 **Take It to the Net**

www.phschool.com

Take the interactive self-test online to check your understanding of the selection.

Through the Tunnel ◆ 251

Answers for p. 251

Review and Assess

1. Jerry wants to prove to himself that he can swim through the tunnel, but he is afraid of drowning in it. Dependence on and love for his mother versus independence from his mother are the forces.

2. Jerry swims through the tunnel despite his fear.

3. Jerry's internal conflict is intensified for readers by the knowledge that some of the dangers he feels are real possibilities.

4. Jerry's mother wants him to be safe, but she doesn't want to baby him or hold him back.

5. The climax of the story occurs when Jerry finally decides to make the dive.

6. Possible responses: Jerry realizes he can hold his breath for two minutes; he learns that they are leaving soon; he gets a bad nosebleed and considers delaying the dive for a year.

7. By making the dive, Jerry proves to himself that he has courage and strength.

8. (a) Students might wonder, like Jerry's mother does, what "amusements he might secretly be longing for." (b) Further reading would reveal that Jerry wants to be accepted by the older boys.

9. Possible responses: Question: How long does it take to swim through the tunnel? Details That Answer My Question: It takes about 160 seconds to swim through the tunnel.

10. (a) Possible questions: Why does Jerry prefer the wild bay to the safe beach? Why does Jerry persist in pursuing his goal, despite his dizziness and nosebleeds? (b) Possible answers: Jerry is looking for an adventure. Jerry needs to prove to himself that he can overcome his fears.

11. Students may suggest that young people feel the need to prove they are strong or mature. Encourage students to distinguish between healthy challenges, such as overcoming stage fright by auditioning for a play, or dangerous ones, such as Jerry's.

251

Answers for p. 252

❶ Vocabulary Development

Word Analysis

1. light up, fill with light
2. light, quality of light
3. shining person, a star

Spelling Strategy

1. entries
2. eddies
3. Jerrys
4. skies

Concept Development: Synonyms

1. gout
2. luminous
3. promontories
4. contrition
5. frond
6. supplication
7. convulsive

❷ Grammar

1. His mother
2. The biggest of the boys
3. Two grayish shapes
4. Something soft and clammy
5. Victory

Writing Application

Possible responses:

1. Both inexperienced and experienced swimmers should always swim with partners.
2. You should never swim into a cave.
3. A person who feels dizzy or tired should get out of the water.

Integrate Language Skills

❶ Vocabulary Development Lesson

Word Analysis: Latin Root -lum-

The Latin root -lum- means "light," and luminous means "giving off light." Use your knowledge of the root -lum- and the context clues in these sentences to help you determine the meanings of the words in italics.

1. The torches illuminate the dark cave.
2. The astronomer studied the star's luminosity.
3. The great scientist is considered a luminary of our time.

Spelling Strategy

To form the plurals of nouns that end in a consonant + y, change the y to i and add -es: promontory becomes promontories. Proper names are exceptions; for example, the plural of Duffy is Duffys. Write the plurals of each word.

1. entry
2. eddy
3. Jerry
4. sky

Concept Development: Synonyms

Synonyms are words with similar meanings. Rewrite the sentences, replacing each word in italics with a synonym from the vocabulary list on page 241.

1. A glob of blood fell to the floor.
2. The underwater world was mysterious and dimly glowing.
3. We walked on ridges that overlooked the sea.
4. After insulting her, he was filled with remorse.
5. She fanned herself with a palm leaf.
6. The dog's begging ended with a whimper when he got no bone.
7. With a shaking gesture, she dropped the vase.

❷ Grammar Lesson

Complete Subject

The **complete subject** of a sentence includes the noun or pronoun naming the actual person, place, or thing that the sentence is about. It also includes any words or phrases that modify or describe that noun or pronoun. The complete subject may be a single word or it may be many words. In the sentences below, the complete subject is italicized.

> The English boy swam toward them.
>
> The impact of the water broke the rubber-enclosed vacuum.
>
> They dove again and again.

Practice Copy the following sentences. Then, underline the complete subject in each.

1. His mother walked on in front of him.
2. The biggest of the boys poised himself and shot down into the water.
3. Two grayish shapes steered there, like long, rounded pieces of wood or slate.
4. Something soft and clammy touched his mouth.
5. Victory filled him.

Writing Application Write a list of water-safety rules that swimmers should follow. Underline the complete subject in each sentence.

*W*G Prentice Hall Writing and Grammar Connection: Chapter 19, Section 1

TEACHING RESOURCES

The following resources can be used to enrich or extend the instruction for pp. 252–253.

Vocabulary

📖 **Selection Support:** Build Vocabulary, p. 61

📖 **Vocabulary and Spelling Practice Book** (Use this booklet for skills enrichment.) ▪

Grammar

📖 **Selection Support:** Build Grammar Skills, p. 62

*W*G **Writing and Grammar,** Platinum Level, p. 412

📇 **Daily Language Practice Transparencies**

Writing

*W*G **Writing and Grammar,** Platinum Level, p. 162

💿 **Writing and Grammar iText CD-ROM** ▪

▪ **BLOCK SCHEDULING:** Resources marked with this symbol provide varied instruction during 90-minute blocks.

Writing Lesson

Travel Brochure

In "Through the Tunnel," Jerry and his mother visit a beach area for a vacation. Based on the descriptions in the story and your imagination, write a travel brochure about their vacation spot.

Prewriting List the specific sites and activities that you might mention in your brochure. Review your list, and circle the most popular and appealing sites and activities.

Drafting As you draft, state logical and compelling reasons for visiting the beach area, and use specific examples to support them. Make your description persuasive with words and phrases that present appealing images.

Model: Using Persuasive Tone in a Description

Santa Lucia is one of the loveliest islands in the Caribbean. After a fun-filled afternoon of local shopping, relax on our unspoiled beaches, where soft tropical breezes blow.

> The words *loveliest, fun-filled, unspoiled beaches,* and *soft tropical breezes* add to the persuasive tone.

Revising Review your draft, circling the verbs you have used. Then, evaluate each one, challenging yourself to replace vague verbs.

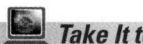 *Prentice Hall Writing and Grammar Connection: Chapter 8, Section 2*

Extension Activities

Listening and Speaking Imagine that one of Jerry's friends has discovered Jerry's plans to master the underwater tunnel and decides to talk him out of it. Role-play the **dialogue** that might take place between them. The friend should use the following tools to argue against Jerry's plans and to refute each claim or argument that Jerry offers.

• Emotional appeals
• Facts
• Personal experiences

Perform your dialogue. **[Group Activity]**

Research and Technology Find out more about underwater swimming and the breathing apparatus and other gear that could have made Jerry's swim safer. Use reliable, up-to-date print or Internet sources to obtain your information. Then, share your findings in the form of a **water safety manual.**

Take It to the Net www.phschool.com
Go online for an additional research activity using the Internet.

---

❸ Writing Lesson

• Bring in some examples of travel brochures for students to use as models. Remind students that travel brochures are designed to persuade travelers to visit a particular vacation spot.

• Suggest that students use specific sensory details and active verbs to describe the travel environment.

• Use the Advertisement rubric in **Performance Assessment and Portfolio Management,** p. 20, to assess students' brochures.

❹ Listening and Speaking

• Make sure students understand the difference between an emotional appeal and a fact. Facts can be used to present a logical argument, while emotional appeals bypass logic and focus on a person's emotional response.

• Suggest that students make a list of relevant facts, emotional appeals, and personal experiences. Then, have them circle the items they think will be most effective.

• Have students use the rubric for Delivering a Persuasive Argument, p. 30 in **Performance Assessment and Portfolio Management.**

CUSTOMIZE INSTRUCTION
For Universal Access

To address different learning styles, use the activities suggested in the **Extension Activities** booklet, p. 16.

• For Logical/Mathematical and Visual/Spatial Learners, use Activity 5.

• For Verbal/Linguistic and Logical/Mathematical Learners, use Activity 6.

• For Bodily/Kinesthetic and Intrapersonal Learners, use Activity 7.

ASSESSMENT RESOURCES

The following resources can be used to assess students' knowledge and skills.

Selection Assessment
📖 **Formal Assessment,** pp. 54–56
📖 **Open Book Test,** pp. 46–48
📹 **Got It! Assessment Videotapes,** Tape 2
💿 **Test Bank Software**

💻 *Take It to the Net*
Visit www.phschool.com for self-tests and additional questions on "Through the Tunnel."

Writing Rubric
📖 **Performance Assess. and Portfolio Mgmt.,** p. 20

Listening and Speaking Rubric
📖 **Performance Assess. and Portfolio Mgmt.,** p. 30

PRENTICE HALL
ASSESSMENT SYSTEM

📖 **Workbook**   🗐 **Transparencies**
📖 **Skill Book**   💿 **CD-ROM**

The Dog That Bit People

Lesson Objectives

1. **To analyze and respond to literary elements**
   - Literary Analysis: Humorous Essay
   - Connecting Literary Elements: External Conflict

2. **To read, comprehend, analyze, and critique an essay**
   - Reading Strategy: Forming Mental Images
   - Reading Check questions
   - Review and Assess questions
   - Assessment Practice (ATE)

3. **To develop word analysis skills, fluency, and systematic vocabulary**
   - Vocabulary Development Lesson: Greek Prefix: *epi-*

4. **To understand and apply written and oral language conventions**
   - Spelling Strategy
   - Grammar Lesson: Complete Predicates

5. **To understand and apply appropriate writing and research strategies**
   - Writing Lesson: News Article
   - Extension Activity: Biographical Sketch

6. **To understand and apply listening and speaking strategies**
   - Extension Activity: Radio Show

STEP-BY-STEP TEACHING GUIDE	PACING GUIDE
PRETEACH	
Motivate Students and Provide Background	
Use the Motivation activity (ATE p. 254)	5 min.
Read and discuss the Preview material and Background information (SE/ATE p. 254) [A]	5 min.
Introduce the Concepts	
Introduce the Literary Analysis and Reading Strategy (SE/ATE p. 255) [A]	15 min.
Pronounce the vocabulary words and read their definitions (SE p. 255)	5 min.
TEACH	
Monitor Comprehension	
Informally monitor comprehension by circulating while students read independently or in groups [A]	15 min.
Monitor students' comprehension with the Reading Check notes (SE/ATE pp. 257, 259)	as students read
Develop vocabulary with Vocabulary notes (SE pp. 257, 258, 259, 260; ATE p. 260)	as students read
Develop Understanding	
Develop students' understanding of humorous essays with Literary Analysis annotations (SE pp. 257, 258; ATE pp. 257, 258) [A]	10 min.
Develop students' understanding of forming mental images with Reading Strategy annotations (SE p. 258; ATE pp. 257, 258)	10 min.
ASSESS	
Assess Mastery	
Assess students' mastery of the Reading Strategy and Literary Analysis by having them answer the Review and Assess questions (SE/ATE p. 261)	20 min.
Use one or more of the print and media Assessment Resources (ATE p. 263) [A]	up to 50 min.
EXTEND	
Apply Understanding	
Have students complete the Vocabulary Development Lesson and the Grammar Lesson (SE p. 262) [A]	20 min.
Apply students' ability to write interview questions using the Writing Lesson (SE p. 263) [A]	45 min.
Apply students' understanding using one or more of the Extension Activities (SE p. 263)	20–90 min.

 ACCELERATED INSTRUCTION:
Use the strategies and activities identified with an [A].

UNIVERSAL ACCESS
- ● = Below Level Students
- ▲ = On-Level Students
- ■ = Above Level Students

Time and Resource Manager

PRINT 📖	TRANSPARENCIES	TECHNOLOGY 💿 🎧 📼
• **Beyond Literature,** Career Connection: Humor Columnist, p. 17 ▲ ■		• **Interest Grabber Video,** Tape 2 ● ▲ ■
• **Selection Support Workbook:** ● ▲ ■ Literary Analysis, p. 68 Reading Strategy, p. 67 Build Vocabulary, p. 65	• **Literary Analysis and Reading Transparencies,** pp. 33 and 34 ● ▲ ■	
• **Adapted Reader's Companion** ● • **Reader's Companion** ●		• **Listening to Literature** ● ▲ ■ Audiocassettes, Side 8 Audio CDs, CD 5
• **English Learner's Companion** ● ▲ • **Literatura en español** ● ▲ • **Literary Analysis for Enrichment** ■		
• **Formal Assessment:** Selection Test, pp. 57–59 ● ▲ ■ • **Open Book Test,** pp. 49–51 ● ▲ ■ • **Performance Assessment and Portfolio Management,** p. 22 ● ▲ ■ • PRENTICE HALL ASSESSMENT *SYSTEM* ● ▲	• PRENTICE HALL ASSESSMENT *SYSTEM* ● ▲ ■ Skills Practice Answers and Explanations on Transparencies	• **Test Bank Software** ● ▲ ■ • **Got It! Assessment Videotapes,** Tape 2 ● ▲
• **Selection Support Workbook:** ● ▲ ■ Build Grammar Skills, p. 66 • **Writing and Grammar,** Platinum Level ● ▲ ■ • **Extension Activities,** p. 17 ● ▲ ■	• **Daily Language Practice Transparencies** ● ▲	• **Writing and Grammar iText CD-ROM** ● ▲ ■ 💻 **Take It to the Net** www.phschool.com

BLOCK SCHEDULING: Use one 90-minute class period to preteach the selection and have students read it. Use a second 90-minute class period to assess students' mastery of skills and have them complete one of the Extension Activities.

Motivation

Have students brainstorm for a list of their favorite animated and live comedy shows. Ask them to describe the type of humor in each show and to identify some of the techniques used to create the humor. Students might suggest such elements as exaggeration, sight gags, and word play. Guide students to present specific examples from each show. Then, have students use the title and the introductory illustration to predict how Thurber will create humor in this essay.

 Interest Grabber Video

As an alternative, play "Dog Training," Tape 2 to engage student interest.

❶ Background

James Thurber enjoyed a dual career as a writer and a cartoonist. The lines of his drawings, as you can see, are as whimsical as the lines of his prose.

Thurber created nearly 500 cartoons—sketchy scribbles of men, women, children, and animals, especially dogs. The cartoon on this page is entitled "Lots of People Reported Our Dog to the Police." It adds humor to the essay about the vicious dog Muggs.

Prepare to Read

The Dog That Bit People

Lots of People Reported Our Dog to the Police, James Thurber

 Take It to the Net

Visit www.phschool.com for interactive activities and instruction related to "The Dog That Bit People," including

- background
- graphic organizers
- literary elements
- reading strategies

Preview

Connecting to the Literature

You may not think of yourself as a comedian—but you probably have made people laugh! If you give a little twist of the ridiculous to your stories, you are following in the footsteps of comic writers like James Thurber. In this essay, he turns an irritable family pet into an unforgettable character.

❶ Background

Thurber was a writer and a cartoonist. Despite failing eyesight, he illustrated his humorous tales with sketchy scribbles of his characters. In this selection, you will see the cartoon art that Thurber drew to illustrate "The Dog That Bit People." The cartoons combine with his prose to paint an amusing portrait of Muggs the dog and his long list of "victims."

TEACHING RESOURCES

The following resources can be used to enrich or extend the instruction for pp. 254–255.

Motivation

 Interest Grabber Video, Tape 2

Background

📖 **Beyond Literature**, Career Connection: Humor Columnist, p. 17 ▪

Take It to the Net
Visit www.phschool.com for background and hotlinks for "The Dog That Bit People."

Literary Analysis

Literary Analysis and Reading Transparencies, Humorous Essay, p. 34

Reading

📖 **Selection Support:** Reading Strategy, p. 67; Build Vocabulary, p. 65

Literary Analysis and Reading Transparencies, Forming Mental Images, p. 33 ▪

BLOCK SCHEDULING: Resources marked with this symbol provide varied instruction during 90-minute blocks.

Literary Analysis

Humorous Essay

A **humorous essay** is a nonfiction composition that presents the author's thoughts on a subject in an amusing, lighthearted way. In "The Dog That Bit People," James Thurber shares his thoughts about his family's experiences with a vicious pet dog named Muggs. As you can see in this passage, he achieves humor by exaggerating, by treating ridiculous situations seriously, and by treating serious situations lightly.

> One morning when Muggs bit me slightly, more or less in passing, I reached down and grabbed his short stumpy tail and hoisted him into the air.

Connecting Literary Elements

In "The Dog That Bit People," the humor stems from the struggle between Muggs the dog and several other characters in the story. Such a struggle—in which one character struggles with other characters or with an outside force—is called an **external conflict.** As you read the essay, look for other examples of external conflicts, identifying them on a chart like the one here.

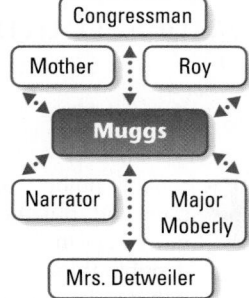

Reading Strategy

Forming Mental Images

Whether or not they draw actual cartoons like James Thurber, all comic writers create humorous images with words. By using the writers' words to **form mental images** of the situations they describe, you will better appreciate the humor of those situations.

As you read "The Dog That Bit People," try to picture the actions of all the characters, including Muggs the dog. Also, try to see the expressions on their faces.

Vocabulary Development

incredulity (in´ krə dōō´ lə tē) *n.* unwillingness or inability to believe (p. 256)

choleric (käl´ ər ik) *adj.* irritable (p. 257)

irascible (i ras´ ə bəl) *adj.* easily angered; quick-tempered (p. 258)

jangle (jaŋ´ gəl) *n.* discord; harsh sounds (p. 258)

indignant (in dig´ nənt) *adj.* feeling or expressing anger or scorn, especially at an injustice (p. 259)

epitaph (ep´ ə taf) *n.* inscription on a tomb or gravestone (p. 260)

The Dog That Bit People ◆ 255

---

❷ Literary Analysis

Humorous Essay

- Remind students that a humorous essay is an example of nonfiction writing. The author's purpose is to amuse the reader.

- Have students read the excerpt on this page and explain how the wording might differ if it were part of a serious essay.

- Call students' attention to the Connecting Literary Elements section. Explain that in this selection, they will focus on external conflicts—struggles that occur between characters or between a character and an outside force.

- Encourage students to identify the external conflicts as they read the selection. Have them record their responses in a chart like the one shown.

❸ Reading Strategy

Forming Mental Images

- Explain to students that they should use Thurber's descriptions of characters and events to help them form images in their minds. This will enrich their understanding and help them appreciate the humor of the selection.

- Ask students to read the excerpt in the Literary Analysis section and describe the mental images it evokes.

- Display the Forming Mental Images transparency in **Literary Analysis and Reading Transparencies,** p. 33, to model how to form mental images while reading.

Vocabulary Development

- Pronounce each vocabulary word for students, and read the definitions as a class. Have students identify any words with which they are already familiar.

 E-Teach

Visit E-Teach at www.phschool.com for teachers' essays on how to teach, with questions and answers.

CUSTOMIZE INSTRUCTION FOR UNIVERSAL ACCESS

For Special Needs Students	For Less Proficient Readers	For English Learners
Have students read the adapted version of "The Dog That Bit People" in the **Adapted Reader's Companion.** This version provides basic-level instruction in an interactive format with questions and write-on lines. Completing the adapted version will prepare students to read the selection in the Student Edition.	Have students read the selection in the **Reader's Companion.** This version provides basic-level instruction in an interactive format with questions and write-on lines. After students finish the selection in **Reader's Companion,** have them complete the questions and activities in the Student Edition.	Have students read the adapted version of the selection in the **English Learner's Companion.** This version provides basic-level instruction in an interactive format with questions and write-on lines. Completing the adapted version will prepare students to read the selection in the Student Edition.

**CUSTOMIZE INSTRUCTION
For Interpersonal Learners**

Suggest that students work in small groups to evaluate the problems with Muggs's behavior, and compile a list of possible solutions that Thurber might wish to try. They might solicit suggestions from friends and family members who have owned pets.

❶ About the Selection

Thurber uses exaggeration and contrast to achieve humor in this series of bad-dog anecdotes, but this master comic has other tricks up his sleeve as well. In addition, he uses understatement, irony, absurdity, and digression to keep his readers chuckling. Thurber's wry anecdotes will help students see that humor is a combination of keen observation of details and a unique style of reporting those details.

❷ Background

Art

Nobody Knew Exactly What Was the Matter With Him, by James Thurber

Thurber is well known for his sketches of sad-faced animals and frustrated humans trying to deal with zany situations. This cartoon of Muggs is typical of Thurber's cartoon style. It derives its humor from the dog's human facial expression and body position. Use these questions for discussion:

1. How does Thurber convey the human qualities that the dog seems to possess?
Answer: The furrowed brow and frowning mouth give the dog a human facial expression; the way the dog rests his head on his paw is a pose more likely to be seen in a human than a dog.

2. What can you infer about the dog's personality from this sketch?
Answer: The dog looks irritable and uncooperative.

❸ ▶ Critical Viewing

Answer: This dog looks ready to bite anyone who comes near him.

256

---

❶

The Dog That Bit People

❷

James Thurber

Nobody Knew Exactly What Was the Matter with Him

❹ Probably no one man should have as many dogs in his life as I have had, but there was more pleasure than distress in them for me except in the case of an Airedale[1] named Muggs. He gave me more trouble than all the other fifty-four or -five put together, although my moment of keenest embarrassment was the time a Scotch terrier named Jeannie, who had just had six puppies in the clothes closet of a fourth floor apartment in New York, had the unexpected seventh and last at the corner of Eleventh Street and Fifth Avenue during a walk she had insisted on taking. Then, too, there was the prize winning French poodle, a great big black poodle—none of your little, untroublesome white miniatures—who got sick riding in the rumble seat[2] of a car with me on her way to the Greenwich Dog Show. She had a red rubber bib tucked around her throat and, since a rain storm came up when we were halfway through the Bronx, I had to hold over her a small green umbrella, really more of a parasol. The rain beat down fearfully and suddenly the driver of the car drove into a big garage, filled with mechanics. It happened so quickly that I forgot to put the umbrella down and I will always remember, with sickening distress, the look of <u>incredulity</u> mixed with hatred that

---

1. **Airedale** (er′ dāl) *n.* any of a breed of large terrier having a hard, wiry tan coat with black markings.
2. **rumble seat** in some earlier automobiles, an open seat in the rear, behind the roofed seat, which could be folded shut when not in use.

256 ◆ *Clashing Forces*

❸ ▲ **Critical Viewing**
How do you think that a dog with this facial expression might behave? **[Predict]**

incredulity (in′ krə dʊ̄′ lə tē) *n.* unwillingness or inability to believe

---

came over the face of the particular hardened garage man that came over to see what we wanted, when he took a look at me and the poodle. All garage men, and people of that intolerant stripe, hate poodles with their curious hair cut, especially the pom-poms that you got to leave on their hips if you expect the dogs to win a prize.

But the Airedale, as I have said, was the worst of all my dogs. He really wasn't my dog, as a matter of fact: I came home from a vacation one summer to find that my brother Roy had bought him while I was away. A big, burly, <u>choleric</u> dog, he always acted as if he thought I wasn't one of the family. There was a slight advantage in being one of the family, for he didn't bite the family as often as he bit strangers. Still, in the years that we had him he bit everybody but mother, and he made a pass at her once but missed. That was during the month when we suddenly had mice, and Muggs refused to do anything about them. Nobody ever had mice exactly like the mice we had that month. They acted like pet mice, almost like mice somebody had trained. They were so friendly that one night when mother entertained at dinner the Friraliras, a club she and my father had belonged to for twenty years, she put down a lot of little dishes with food in them on the pantry floor so that the mice would be satisfied with that and wouldn't come into the dining room. Muggs stayed out in the pantry with the mice, lying on the floor, growling to himself—not at the mice, but about all the people in the next room that he would have liked to get at. Mother slipped out into the pantry once to see how everything was going. Everything was going fine. It made her so mad to see Muggs lying there, oblivious of the mice—they came running up to her—that she slapped him and he slashed at her, but didn't make it. He was sorry immediately, mother said. He was always sorry, she said, after he bit someone, but we could not understand how she figured this out. He didn't act sorry.

Mother used to send a box of candy every Christmas to the people the Airedale bit. The list finally contained forty or more names. Nobody could understand why we didn't get rid of the dog. I didn't understand it very well myself, but we didn't get rid of him. I think that one or two people tried to poison Muggs—he acted poisoned once in a while—and old Major Moberly fired at him once with his service revolver near the Seneca Hotel in East Broad Street—but Muggs lived to be almost eleven years old and even when he could hardly get around he bit a Congressman who had called to see my father on business. My mother had never liked the Congressman—she said the signs of his horoscope showed he couldn't be trusted (he was Saturn with the moon in Virgo)—but she sent him a box of candy that Christmas. He sent it right back, probably because he suspected it was trick candy. Mother persuaded herself it was all for the best that the dog had bitten him, even though father lost an important business association because of it. "I wouldn't be associated with such a man," mother said, "Muggs could read him like a book."

We used to take turns feeding Muggs to be on his good side, but that didn't always work. He was never in a very good humor, even

---

choleric (käl´ ər ik) *adj.* irritable

Literary Analysis
Humorous Essay Explain how the exaggeration of the mice's boldness adds humor to this scene.

6 ✔**Reading Check**
When did Muggs try to bite Mother?

---

4 **Reading Strategy**

Forming Mental Images

- As students read the bracketed passage, encourage them to picture it in their minds.
- Have students describe the image they form in their minds after reading this passage. Ask them which specific details elicited vivid images.

▶ Monitor Progress Have students verbalize what is funny about the mental images they form.
Answer: Lead students to grasp that the humor in this description comes from the absurdity of the mental image—the sight of a person holding a fancy green parasol over a poodle wearing a bib.

5 **Literary Analysis**

Humorous Essay

- Remind students that a humorous essay often relies on exaggeration to achieve its humor.
- Read aloud the bracketed passage, and have students focus on Thurber's description of the mice as you read.
- Ask students the Literary Analysis question on p. 257: Explain how the exaggeration of the mice's boldness adds humor to this scene.
Answer: The description of the "party" of mice eating from little dishes while the mother is hosting a dinner party adds a humorous image to the scene.

6 ✔**Reading Check**

Answer: Muggs tried to bite Mother when she slapped him for not attacking the mice.

CUSTOMIZE INSTRUCTION FOR UNIVERSAL ACCESS

For Special Needs Students	For Gifted/Talented Students
Encourage students to skim through the first two pages of the selection and list the descriptive, colorful words that Thurber uses. For example, they might list "white miniatures," "red rubber bib," and "parasol." Make sure students can define each word. Then, discuss how each word adds humor to the essay.	Have students choose a passage that contains a colorful and humorous description. Then, ask them to draw a cartoon that illustrates the passage. The cartoon should contain specific details from the passage and a humorous caption. When they finish, have volunteers share their cartoons.

after a meal. Nobody knew exactly what was the matter with him, but whatever it was it made him <u>irascible</u>, especially in the mornings. Roy never felt very well in the morning, either, especially before breakfast, and once when he came downstairs and found that Muggs had moodily chewed up the morning paper he hit him in the face with a grapefruit and then jumped up on the dining room table, scattering dishes and silverware and spilling the coffee. Muggs' first free leap carried him all the way across the table and into a brass fire screen in front of the gas grate but he was back on his feet in a moment and in the end he got Roy and gave him a pretty vicious bite in the leg. Then he was all over it; he never bit anyone more than once at a time. Mother always mentioned that as an argument in his favor; she said he had a quick temper but that he didn't hold a grudge. She was forever defending him. I think she liked him because he wasn't well. "He's not strong," she would say, pityingly, but that was inaccurate; he may not have been well but he was terribly strong.

One time my mother went to the Chittenden Hotel to call on a woman mental healer who was lecturing in Columbus on the subject of "Harmonious Vibrations." She wanted to find out if it was possible to get harmonious vibrations into a dog. "He's a large tan-colored Airedale," mother explained. The woman said that she had never treated a dog but she advised my mother to hold the thought that he did not bite and would not bite. Mother was holding the thought the very next morning when Muggs got the iceman but she blamed that slip-up on the iceman. "If you didn't think he would bite you, he wouldn't," mother told him. He stomped out of the house in a terrible <u>jangle</u> of vibrations.

One morning when Muggs bit me slightly, more or less in passing, I reached down and grabbed his short stumpy tail and hoisted him into the air. It was a foolhardy thing to do and the last time I saw my mother, about six months ago, she said she didn't know what possessed me. I don't either, except that I was pretty mad. As long as I held the dog off the floor by his tail he couldn't get at me, but he twisted and jerked so, snarling all the time, that I realized I couldn't hold him that way very long. I carried him to the kitchen and flung him onto the floor and shut the door on him just as he crashed against it. But I forgot about the backstairs. Muggs went up the backstairs and down the frontstairs and had me cornered in the living room. I managed to get up onto the mantelpiece above the fireplace, but it gave way and came down with a tremendous crash throwing a large marble clock, several vases, and myself heavily to the floor. Muggs was so alarmed by the racket that when I picked myself up he had disappeared. We couldn't find him anywhere, although we whistled and shouted, until old Mrs. Detweiler called after dinner that night. Muggs had bitten her once, in the leg, and she came into the living room only after we assured her that Muggs had run away. She had just seated herself when, with a great growling and scratching of claws, Muggs emerged from under a davenport[3] where he had been quietly hiding all the time, and bit her again.

---

3. **davenport** (dav´ ən pôrt´) *n.* large couch or sofa.

irascible (i ras´ ə bəl) *adj.* easily angered; quick-tempered

Literary Analysis
Humorous Essay and External Conflict What external conflict leads to the humor in this situation?

jangle (jaŋ´ gəl) *n.* discord; harsh sounds

Reading Strategy
Forming Mental Images What details help you form a mental picture of the incident between the narrator and Muggs?

Mother examined the bite and put arnica[4] on it and told Mrs. Detweiler that it was only a bruise. "He just bumped you," she said. But Mrs. Detweiler left the house in a nasty state of mind.

Lots of people reported our Airedale to the police but my father held a municipal office at the time and was on friendly terms with the police. Even so, the cops had been out a couple of times—once when Muggs bit Mrs. Rufus Sturtevant and again when he bit Lieutenant-Governor Malloy—but mother told them that it hadn't been Muggs' fault but the fault of the people who were bitten. "When he starts for them, they scream," she explained, "and that excites him." The cops suggested that it might be a good idea to tie the dog up, but mother said that it mortified him to be tied up and that he wouldn't eat when he was tied up.

Muggs at his meals was an unusual sight. Because of the fact that if you reached toward the floor he would bite you, we usually put his food plate on top of an old kitchen table with a bench alongside the table. Muggs would stand on the bench and eat. I remember that my mother's Uncle Horatio, who boasted that he was the third man up Missionary Ridge,[5] was splutteringly <u>indignant</u> when he found out that we fed the dog on a table because we were afraid to put his plate on the floor. He said he wasn't afraid of any dog that ever lived and that he would put the dog's plate on the floor if we would give it to him. Roy said that if Uncle Horatio had fed Muggs on the ground just before the battle he would have been the first man up Missionary Ridge. Uncle Horatio was furious. "Bring him in! Bring him in now!" he shouted. "I'll feed the—on the floor!" Roy was all for giving him a chance, but my father wouldn't hear of it. He said that Muggs had already been fed. "I'll feed him again!" bawled Uncle Horatio. We had quite a time quieting him.

In his last year Muggs used to spend practically all of his time outdoors. He didn't like to stay in the house for some reason or other—perhaps it held too many unpleasant memories for him. Anyway, it was hard to get him to come in and as a result the garbage man, the iceman, and the laundryman wouldn't come near the house. We had to haul the garbage down to the corner, take the laundry out and bring it back, and meet the iceman a block from home. After this had gone on for some time we hit on an ingenious arrangement for getting the dog in the house so that we could lock him up while the gas meter was read, and so on. Muggs was afraid of only one thing, an electrical storm. Thunder and lightning frightened him out of his senses (I think he thought a storm had broken the day the mantelpiece fell). He would

---

4. **arnica** (är´ ni kə) *n.* preparation made from certain plants, once used for treating sprains, bruises, and so forth.
5. **Missionary Ridge** hill south of Chattanooga, Tennessee, that was the site of a Civil War battle.

Muggs at His Meals Was an Unusual Sight, James Thurber

⑩ ▲ Critical Viewing
Compare this drawing of Muggs with the image you formed of him. **[Compare and Contrast]**

indignant (in dig´ nənt) *adj.* feeling or expressing anger or scorn, especially at an injustice

⑪ ☑ Reading Check
What advice about Muggs does a mental healer give Mother?

❾ Background
Art

Muggs at His Meals Was an Unusual Sight, by James Thurber

This cartoon shows Muggs eating his dinner at a table, as described in the essay. Through simple lines and basic forms, Thurber captures the essence of the humorous situation. The dog's turned head and annoyed expression hint that a confrontation is about to occur. Use these questions for discussion:

1. What does Muggs's posture suggest about his personality?
   Answer: Muggs is guarding his food. His posture conveys his combative personality.

2. How does this picture support what you've learned about Muggs from reading the essay?
   Answer: The essay indicates that the family made special accommodations for Muggs because of his irritable personality. The picture shows him eating at a table, probably another special accommodation the family has made.

⑩ ▶ Critical Viewing

Students might say they imagined the dog would have sharper features—an angular jaw, spiky fur, and more visible nails on his paws.

⑪ ☑ Reading Check

Answer: The mental healer advises Mother to hold the thought that Muggs does not and will not bite.

The Dog That Bit People ◆ 259

12 Vocabulary Development

12 Vocabulary Development

Greek Prefix: epi-

- Draw students' attention to the word *epitaph* and its definition, "inscription on a tomb or gravestone."

- Explain that the Greek prefix *epi-* can mean "upon," "over," "outside," or "among."

- Point out that in this case, *epi-* means "upon." An epitaph is written *upon* a tombstone.

Answers for p. 260

Review and Assess

1. Possible responses: Muggs's attack on Roy, Muggs's manner of eating, Muggs's attack on Thurber, and Muggs's reaction to the "storm machine."

2. **(a)** Muggs doesn't bite family members as much as he bites other people. **(b)** Mother loves him, Roy is annoyed by him, the narrator tolerates him, and Uncle Horatio finds him infuriating.

3. **(a)** Thurber foolishly grabbed Muggs by the tail in anger, and then realized that he couldn't let him go without being bitten. When released, Muggs chased Thurber onto a mantelpiece that came crashing down, frightening Muggs away. **(b)** He probably felt a mixture of fear and anger.

4. **(a)** They never get rid of Muggs because Mother loves him. **(b)** Students might say that they would take Muggs to a good trainer.

5. The essay would probably make a good television show because it is very visual and contains amusing dialogue and colorful characters.

---

rush into the house and hide under a bed or in a clothes closet. So we fixed up a thunder machine out of a long narrow piece of sheet iron with a wooden handle on one end. Mother would shake this vigorously when she wanted to get Muggs into the house. It made an excellent imitation of thunder, but I suppose it was the most roundabout system for running a household that was ever devised. It took a lot out of mother.

A few months before Muggs died, he got to "seeing things." He would rise slowly from the floor, growling low, and stalk stiff-legged and menacing toward nothing at all. Sometimes the Thing would be just a little to the right or left of a visitor. Once a Fuller Brush salesman got hysterics. Muggs came wandering into the room like Hamlet following his father's ghost. His eyes were fixed on a spot just to the left of the Fuller Brush man, who stood it until Muggs was about three slow, creeping paces from him. Then he shouted. Muggs wavered on past him into the hallway grumbling to himself but the Fuller man went on shouting. I think mother had to throw a pan of cold water on him before he stopped. That was the way she used to stop us boys when we got into fights.

Muggs died quite suddenly one night. Mother wanted to bury him in the family lot under a marble stone with some such inscription as "Flights of angels sing thee to thy rest" but we persuaded her it was against the law. In the end we just put up a smooth board above his grave along a lonely road. On the board I wrote with an indelible pencil "Cave Canem."[6] Mother was quite pleased with the simple **12** classic dignity of the old Latin <u>epitaph</u>.

epitaph (ep´ ə taf) *n.* inscription on a tomb or gravestone

---

6. **Cave Canem** (kä´ vā kä´ nem) Latin for "Beware the dog."

Review and Assess

Thinking About the Selection

1. **Respond:** Which of Muggs's escapades did you find the most amusing? Why?

2. **(a) Recall:** In Muggs's presence, what is the advantage of being one of the family? **(b) Compare and Contrast:** How do different family members react to the dog?

3. **(a) Recall:** Describe Thurber's "foolhardy" experience with Muggs. **(b) Analyze:** How do you think Thurber was feeling at the time the incident occurred?

4. **(a) Hypothesize:** Why do you think the family never does anything to get rid of Muggs? **(b) Apply:** What would you do if Muggs were your dog? Why?

5. **Evaluate:** Do you think that this story could be effectively adapted into an episode of a television situation comedy? Why or why not?

260 ◆ *Clashing Forces*

James Thurber

(1894–1961)

A native of Columbus, Ohio, James Thurber left college for a job with the U.S. State Department. He soon left that job to become a writer and cartoonist with the magazine *The New Yorker*. Winning fame for his whimsical depictions of human (and animal) foibles, Thurber published an autobiography in 1933, called *My Life and Hard Times*. By the 1940s, failing eyesight forced him to cut down on his cartoon illustrations. By 1952, Thurber was almost totally blind, but he was still contributing stories and articles to magazines.

ASSESSMENT PRACTICE: Reading Comprehension

Stated and Implied Main Ideas   (For more practice, see Test Preparation Workbook, p. 17.)

As students prepare for assessment tests, they should review strategies for determining main ideas. Ask students to read the first paragraph of "The Dog That Bit People."

What is the best title for this passage?

A Garage Men Hate Dogs
B Carefully Groomed Poodles
C Dogs Bring Pleasure and Pain
D Terrier Births Puppy on the Street

As students study the answer choices, remind them that main idea questions on some tests often have general answers. Students can probably arrive at the best answer by using the process of elimination to rule out answers that are too specific, or only partly true. By analyzing the choices, they should be able to determine that *A, B,* and *D* are specific details from the paragraph. Answer *C* is the most general and therefore the best choice for a passage title (or main idea).

Review and Assess

Literary Analysis

Humorous Essay

1. In this **humorous essay,** what is funny about the relationship between Mother and Muggs?
2. Find an example of the way Thurber creates humor by treating a silly situation as if it were serious.
3. On a chart like this one, list three incidents in which exaggeration helps Thurber achieve humor. For each, explain which details are exaggerated, and point out how the exaggeration creates humor.

Incident	Exaggerated Details	Effect

Connecting Literary Elements

4. (a) Identify three situations in which Muggs and another character are involved in an **external conflict.** (b) What is the outcome?
5. How does each example in the previous question add to the humor of the essay?
6. (a) Identify an external conflict between mother and another character. (b) How does this conflict add to the humor?

Reading Strategy

Forming Mental Images

7. In a chart like the one here, list details from the essay that help you **form a mental image** of Muggs the dog.

8. Which mental picture inspired by this essay is most vivid? Why?

Extend Understanding

9. **Humanities Connection:** Thurber describes an aspect of his home life in a humorous way. What other aspects of daily life do you think would make a good subject of a humorous essay? Why?

Quick Review

A **humorous essay** is a nonfiction composition that presents the author's thoughts on a subject in an amusing, lighthearted way.

An **external conflict** is a struggle between a character and an outside force, such as another character or an aspect of nature.

To **form a mental image,** use details to picture what is being described.

Take It to the Net
www.phschool.com
Take the interactive self-test online to check your understanding of the selection.

The Dog That Bit People ◆ 261

Answers for p. 261

Review and Assess

1. Mother attributes to Muggs qualities that do not match with his behavior, such as physical weakness and remorse for his actions.

2. Thurber describes the family's method for getting Muggs into the house as if he were explaining an ordinary household routine. Explaining this ridiculous activity in a serious, matter-of-fact way highlights just how silly the activity actually is.

3. Possible responses: In the incident with the garage men, their reaction to the poodle is exaggerated. In the incident with Roy, Roy's reaction to Mugg's behavior is exaggerated. In the incident with the mice, Mother's reaction to the mice is exaggerated.

4. (a) Possible responses: Roy throws a grapefruit at Muggs. Mother slaps Muggs for not chasing the mice. Muggs bites Thurber, and Thurber grabs him by the tail. (b) Muggs bites Roy in the leg. Muggs lunges at mother and misses. Muggs is scared away when the mantelpiece crashes to the floor.

5. Each example shows Muggs terrorizing the humans, which is amusing because we usually think of the dog as subservient to the human.

6. (a) Mother reasons that the congressman is a shady character, based on his astrological chart, and that Muggs had been able to see into his tainted soul. (b) Mother has rationalized Muggs' bad behavior and attributed to him human insight.

7. Details include *large, tan-colored, stumpy tail,* and *stiff-legged.*

8. Students should support their answers with specific details that make the image vivid.

9. Students should support their answers with an indication of humorous aspects of their choices.

❶ Vocabulary Development

Word Analysis

1. The epidermis covers the *outside* of the body.

2. The epicenter is the spot on the earth's surface directly *over* the origin of an earthquake.

3. An epidemic is a disease that spreads quickly *among* many individuals.

4. An epilogue is added *upon* the ending of a play or novel.

Spelling Strategy

1. dependably   3. terribly
2. probably

Fluency: Clarify Meaning

1. epitaph   4. choleric
2. indignant   5. irascible
3. incredulity   6. jangle

❷ Grammar

1. was never in a very good humor.

2. carried him all the way across the table.

3. contained forty or more names.

4. reported our Airedale to the police.

5. frightened him out of his senses.

Writing Application

1. Our family's German Shepherd <u>lunged furiously at bicycles.</u>

2. Our old tabby cat <u>had an ear-splitting yowl.</u>

3. Frodo, the black-and-white kitten, <u>knocked over the Christmas tree.</u>

Integrate Language Skills

❶ Vocabulary Development Lesson

Word Analysis: Greek Prefix *epi-*

An *epitaph* is an inscription on a tomb or gravestone. It contains the Greek prefix *epi-*, which can mean "upon," "over," "outside," or "among." Explain how one or another of these meanings contributes to the definition of each of these words:

1. epidermis   3. epidemic
2. epicenter   4. epilogue

Spelling Strategy

When adding -ly to a word ending in a consonant + le, drop the le; for example, *irascible* becomes *irascibly*. Add the suffix -ly to each of the following words, and then use each word in a sentence.

1. dependable 2. probable 3. terrible

Fluency: Clarify Meaning

On your paper, write the word from the vocabulary list on page 255 that best completes each sentence.

1. The ___?___ read "Rest in Peace."

2. The woman was ___?___ when I zoomed into the parking space ahead of her.

3. With his mouth hanging open, his ___?___ was obvious.

4. A ___?___ old man, he was always yelling at the children who stepped on his lawn.

5. My father is especially ___?___ in the morning before he has his coffee.

6. The fourth-grade band produced a ___?___ of music.

❷ Grammar Lesson

Complete Predicates

The **complete predicate** of a sentence tells what the subject does or is and includes a verb or verb phrase. For example, in the following sentence, the complete predicate is italicized. It includes an action verb and its adverbs, which describe *where* and *how* the action happened.

Action Verb: The rain *beat down fearfully.*

In the next sentence, the complete predicate contains a linking verb and its predicate nominative, which renames the subject.

Linking Verb: Muggs at his meals *was an unusual sight.*

Practice Copy the following sentences. Then, underline the complete predicate in each.

1. He was never in a very good humor.

2. Muggs' first free leap carried him all the way across the table.

3. The list contained forty or more names.

4. Lots of people reported our Airedale to the police.

5. Thunder and lightning frightened him out of his senses.

Writing Application Write three sentences about a pet you have known. Underline the complete predicate in each sentence.

𝒲𝒢 *Prentice Hall Writing and Grammar Connection: Chapter 19, Section 1*

262 ◆ *Clashing Forces*

TEACHING RESOURCES

The following resources can be used to enrich or extend the instruction for pp. 262–263.

Vocabulary

📖 **Selection Support:** Build Vocabulary, p. 65

📖 **Vocabulary and Spelling Practice Book**
(Use this booklet for skills enrichment.)

Grammar

📖 **Selection Support:** Build Grammar Skills, p. 66

𝒲𝒢 **Writing and Grammar,** Platinum Level, p. 412

📱 **Daily Language Practice Transparencies** ▪

Writing

𝒲𝒢 **Writing and Grammar,** Platinum Level, p. 228 ▪

💿 **Writing and Grammar iText CD-ROM**

▪ **BLOCK SCHEDULING:** Resources marked with this symbol provide varied instruction during 90-minute blocks.

❸ Writing Lesson

News Article

Write a news article about the neighborhood's quest to put a stop to Muggs's menacing ways. Answer the five standard W questions (*who, what, where, when,* and *why*) in your article.

Prewriting   To write an accurate news article, gather your facts carefully. Imagine interviewing people who were bitten by Muggs, and record the facts of each incident. Write a list of interview questions. When possible, gather details from the selection.

Model: Recording the Facts

Muggs Incident # _____

Who was bitten?

Where?

When?

Were there witnesses?

Was he provoked?

Drafting   Begin your article with a first line that will grab the reader's attention. Then, give the facts in an organized way.

Revising   Reread your article, and double-check it for accuracy. Correct any errors in facts or misleading statements.

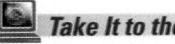 *Prentice Hall Writing and Grammar Connection: Chapter 11, Section 2*

❹ Extension Activities

Listening and Speaking With a group, produce a **radio show.** One person can play the part of Thurber, calling in with pet problems. Other group members should give advice. Use these tips:

- Choose specific incidents from the selection to write your questions.
- Research ways to modify animal behavior so that you can give advice.

When your show is ready, perform it for the class, using music and sound effects. **[Group Activity]**

Research and Technology Research the life of James Thurber, focusing on an aspect you think may have helped him see the world in such a humorous way. Write a **biographical sketch** of Thurber, emphasizing key points of his life.

 Take It to the Net   www.phschool.com

Go online for an additional research activity using the Internet.

The Dog That Bit People ◆ 263

Lesson Support for p. 263

❸ Writing Lesson

- Ask students to review newspaper articles for examples of good leads.
- Have students list the types of intriguing leads they encounter, such as quotations, questions, and surprising statements.
- Use the Writing Lesson to guide students in developing their news article.
- Use the rubric for Problem-Solution Essays, p. 22 of **Performance Assessment and Portfolio Management,** to evaluate students' work.

❹ Listening and Speaking

- You may want to begin by having students discuss what they know about radio call-in shows.
- Have students list behavior modification techniques for dogs after interviewing a trainer or skimming a dog-training manual.
- Tell students that when they write their scripts, they should use techniques from their lists to address Thurber's pet problems.

CUSTOMIZE INSTRUCTION
For Universal Access

To address different learning styles, use the activities suggested in the **Extension Activities** booklet, p. 17.

- For Logical/Mathematical and Visual/Spatial Learners, use Activity 5.
- For Verbal/Linguistic and Musical/Rhythmic Learners, use Activity 6.
- For Verbal/Linguistic and Logical/Mathematical Learners, use Activity 7.

ASSESSMENT RESOURCES

The following resources can be used to assess students' knowledge and skills.

Selection Assessment

📖 **Formal Assessment,** pp. 57–59

📖 **Open Book Test,** pp. 49–51

📼 **Got It! Assessment Videotapes,** Tape 2

💿 **Test Bank Software**

💻 *Take It to the Net*
Visit www.phschool.com for self-tests and additional questions on "The Dog That Bit People."

Writing Rubric

📖 **Performance Assess. and Portfolio Mgmt.,** p. 22

 PRENTICE HALL ASSESSMENT *SYSTEM*

📖 **Workbook**   🖥 **Transparencies**

📖 **Skill Book**   💿 **CD-ROM**

Conscientious Objector ✦ A Man ✦ The Weary Blues
Jazz Fantasia

Lesson Objectives

1. **To analyze and respond to literary elements**
   - Literary Analysis: Tone
   - Comparing Literary Works

2. **To read, comprehend, analyze, and critique poems**
   - Reading Strategy: Responding to Images and Ideas
   - Review and Assess questions
   - Assessment Practice (ATE)

3. **To develop word analysis skills, fluency, and systematic vocabulary**
   - Vocabulary Development Lesson: Greek Word Root: -chol-

4. **To understand and apply written and oral language conventions**
   - Spelling Strategy
   - Grammar Lesson: Hard-to-Find Subjects

5. **To understand and apply appropriate writing and research strategies**
   - Writing Lesson: Interview with the Speaker
   - Extension Activity: Music Timeline

6. **To understand and apply listening and speaking strategies**
   - Extension Activity: Oral Reading

STEP-BY-STEP TEACHING GUIDE	PACING GUIDE
PRETEACH	
Motivate Students and Provide Background	
Use the Motivation activity (ATE p. 264)	5 min.
Read and discuss the Preview material and Background information (SE/ATE p. 264) [A]	5 min.
Introduce the Concepts	
Introduce the Literary Analysis and Reading Strategy (SE/ATE p. 265) [A]	15 min.
Pronounce the vocabulary words and read their definitions (SE p. 265)	5 min.
TEACH	
Monitor Comprehension	
Informally monitor comprehension by circulating while students read independently or in groups [A]	10 min.
Develop vocabulary with Vocabulary notes (SE pp. 267, 268; ATE p. 268)	as students read
Develop Understanding	
Develop students' understanding of tone with Literary Analysis annotations (ATE pp. 266, 268, 270) [A]	10 min.
Develop students' understanding of responding to images and ideas with Reading Strategy annotations (ATE p. 267)	10 min.
ASSESS	
Assess Mastery	
Assess students' mastery of the Reading Strategy and Literary Analysis by having them answer the Review and Assess questions (SE/ATE p. 271)	20 min.
Use one or more of the print and media Assessment Resources (ATE p. 273) [A]	up to 50 min.
EXTEND	
Apply Understanding	
Have students complete the Vocabulary Development Lesson and the Grammar Lesson (SE p. 272) [A]	20 min.
Apply students' ability to use appropriate language for the audience using the Writing Lesson (SE p. 273) [A]	45 min.
Apply students' understanding using one or more of the Extension Activities (SE p. 273)	20–90 min.

 ACCELERATED INSTRUCTION:
Use the strategies and activities identified with an [A].

UNIVERSAL ACCESS
● = Below Level Students
▲ = On-Level Students
■ = Above Level Students

Time and Resource Manager

Reading Level: Challenging/Easy/Challenging/Average
Average Number of Instructional Days: 4

RESOURCES

PRINT 📖	TRANSPARENCIES	TECHNOLOGY
• **Beyond Literature**, Cross-Curricular Connection: Music, p. 18 ▲ ■		• **Interest Grabber Video**, Tape 2 ● ▲ ■
• **Selection Support Workbook:** ● ▲ ■ Literary Analysis, p. 72 Reading Strategy, p. 71 Build Vocabulary, p. 69	• **Literary Analysis and Reading Transparencies**, pp. 35 and 36 ● ▲ ■	
• **Authors In Depth**, Platinum Level ■		• **Listening to Literature** ● ▲ ■ Audiocassettes, Side 9 Audio CDs, CD 5
• **Literatura en español** ● ▲ • **Literary Analysis for Enrichment** ■	• **Fine Art Transparencies, Volume 1,** Art Transparency 8 ● ▲ ■	
• **Formal Assessment:** Selection Test, pp. 60–62 ● ▲ ■ • **Open Book Test**, pp. 52–54 ● ▲ ■ • **Performance Assessment and Portfolio Management**, p. 31 ● ▲ ■ • PRENTICE HALL ASSESSMENT *SYSTEM* ● ▲	• PRENTICE HALL ASSESSMENT *SYSTEM* ● ▲ ■ Skills Practice Answers and Explanations on Transparencies	• **Test Bank Software** ● ▲ ■ • **Got It! Assessment Videotapes**, Tape 2 ● ▲
• **Selection Support Workbook:** ● ▲ ■ Build Grammar Skills, p. 70 • **Writing and Grammar**, Platinum Level ● ▲ ■ • **Extension Activities**, p. 18 ● ▲ ■	• **Daily Language Practice Transparencies** ● ▲	• **Writing and Grammar iText CD-ROM** ● ▲ ■ 💻 *Take It to the Net* www.phschool.com

BLOCK SCHEDULING: Use one 90-minute class period to preteach the selection and have students read it. Use a second 90-minute class period to assess students' mastery of skills and have them complete one of the Extension Activities.

Step-by-Step Teaching Guide for pp. 264–265

Motivation

Tell students that a conscientious objector is a person who, for reasons of conscience, refuses to take part in warfare. Then, play the **Listening to Literature** audiocassette recording "Conscientious Objector." Tell students to listen for the examples of ways that some people collaborate with death. Then, ask students to suggest examples from recent history and current events. Point out that the poems in this group are affirmations of life and hope. Tell students to look for the way each poet celebrates life.

▦ Interest Grabber Video

As an alternative, play "Reading and Student Response" on Tape 2 to engage student interest.

❶ Background

Music

The earliest ancestors of the blues are African slave songs, which were musical forms of communication among slaves on plantations. The blues, which often deal with the hardships of life, became popular in the early 1900s, thanks to a bandleader named W. C. Handy. Since then, the blues have influenced musical styles as varied as jazz, rock-and-roll, rhythm-and-blues, and soul music.

Jazz, which developed out of the blues, is also rooted in the musical traditions of African Americans. Jazz is a form of improvisational music that combines many types of music, including African folk music, European classical music, gospel songs, and spirituals.

Prepare to Read

Conscientious Objector ◆ A Man ◆ The Weary Blues ◆ Jazz Fantasia

Solo Interval, 1987. Collage on board, 11 x 14"

▦ Take It to the Net

Visit www.phschool.com for interactive activities and instruction related to the selections, including
- background
- graphic organizers
- literary elements
- reading strategies

Preview

Connecting to the Literature

Chances are, whenever you hear your favorite song, it will influence how you feel. Music of any kind can evoke an emotional response. The poets of two of these poems focus specifically on types of music, but all poets express their ideas through the music of words.

❶ Background

In their poems, Langston Hughes and Carl Sandburg capture the spontaneity and originality of two distinctly American forms of music. The blues originated as African American folk music. Early blues was characterized by mournful vocals and repetitive lyrics that told a story. Jazz, which developed from blues, uses creative interpretation and improvisation to convey many moods and feelings.

264 ◆ Clashing Forces

TEACHING RESOURCES

The following resources can be used to enrich or extend the instruction for pp. 264–265.

Motivation

▦ **Interest Grabber Video**, Tape 2 ▦

Background

📖 **Beyond Literature**, Cross-Curricular Connection: Music, p. 18 ▦

 Take It to the Net
Visit www.phschool.com for background and hotlinks for the selections.

Literary Analysis

 Literary Analysis and Reading Transparencies, Tone, p. 36

Reading

📖 **Selection Support:** Reading Strategy, p. 71; Build Vocabulary, p. 69 ▦

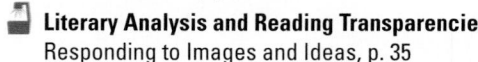 **Literary Analysis and Reading Transparencies**, Responding to Images and Ideas, p. 35

▦ **BLOCK SCHEDULING:** Resources marked with this symbol provide varied instruction during 90-minute blocks.

❷ Literary Analysis

Tone

A singer's attitude affects your response to a song. Similarly, your response to a poem is influenced by the **tone** of the poem, the attitude the poet takes toward the subject of the poem. In song or conversation, a person conveys a certain attitude mainly through the tone of voice. Usually, poets cannot speak their poems for you. They must convey attitudes by choosing precise words and specific images. Notice how the words *ebony* and *ivory* instead of *black* and *white* convey respect for the "poor" piano.

> With his ebony hands on each ivory key.
> He made the poor piano moan with melody.

As you read the poems, consider how word choice and images help convey tone. Note details of each poem on a chart like this one.

Comparing Literary Works

Both "Jazz Fantasia" and "The Weary Blues" address the subject of music, transforming words into the specific forms they describe. Even when poets turn their attention to other subjects, the poems they generate often have a musical quality.

Musical devices—including rhythm, rhyme, and other repeated sounds—can help a poet convey a specific tone. For example, lines with a quick, jingly rhythm and lots of rhymes can convey a childlike, happy tone, while lines with a slow rhythm and lots of long *o* sounds can seem sad and mournful. As you read "The Weary Blues" and "Jazz Fantasia," compare the effects of the musical devices.

Images
Piano moaning
Hands on keys

⬍

Tone

⬍

Word Choices
Ebony hands
Ivory key

---

❸ Reading Strategy

Responding to Images and Ideas

Your own experiences and knowledge influence the way you **respond to the images and ideas** in poetry. Even if you do not understand all the ideas in a poem, you can still have a strong emotional or sensory response to the images. As you read these poems, respond with your whole self—your mind, your heart, and your senses.

Vocabulary Development

reap (rēp) *v.* gather (p. 267)

pallor (pal′ ər) *n.* lack of color; unnatural paleness (p. 268)

melancholy (mel′ ən käl′ ē) *adj.* sad and depressed (p. 268)

Conscientious Objector / A Man / The Weary Blues / Jazz Fantasia ◆ 265

---

❷ Literary Analysis

Tone

- Explain to students that tone is the attitude of the writer toward his or her subject, and that tone can be conveyed through word choice and imagery.

- Tell students that the tone of a poem can be described using adjectives, such as *serious*, *playful*, or *respectful*.

- Use the Tone transparency in **Literary Analysis and Reading Transparencies,** p. 36, to demonstrate for students how to describe the tone of a poem.

❸ Reading Strategy

Responding to Images and Ideas

- Make sure students understand that responding to images and ideas means paying attention to how these elements make them *feel*.

- As students read the poems, encourage them to identify the details and imagery that they respond to. Suggest that they keep a list of the most vivid images and ideas.

Vocabulary Development

- Pronounce each vocabulary word for students, and read the definitions as a class. Have students identify any words with which they are already familiar.

CUSTOMIZE INSTRUCTION FOR UNIVERSAL ACCESS

For Less Proficient Readers	For English Learners	For Advanced Readers
As students read, have them create a chart like the one above for each poem. In the charts, have them list words and images that stand out. Then, have students share their choices, and discuss how they contribute to each poem's tone.	Help students understand the dialect and musical expressions in "The Weary Blues" and "Jazz Fantasia." For example, they may not be familiar with expressions such as *syncopated, mellow croon, raggy tune, tin pans,* and *can the rough stuff.* Encourage students to think about how these words help convey the tone of each poem.	Ask students to select one of the poems and describe what it might be like if it were set to music or transformed into a painting. Encourage students to discuss how the tone of the poem would be conveyed through music or line and color, rather than words.

 E-Teach

Visit E-Teach at www.phschool.com for teachers' essays on how to teach, with questions and answers.

Step-by-Step Teaching Guide for pp. 266–270

CUSTOMIZE INSTRUCTION
For Musical/Rhythmic Learners

After students read each poem, have them decide what instrument could best express its rhythm, content, and tone. Ask them to support their ideas with details from the text.

❶ About the Selections

In "Conscientious Objector," the proud, determined speaker refuses to cooperate in any way—passive or active—with the forces of death. Through allusions and figurative language, Millay communicates a timeless portrait of an individual who accepts that evil forces exist in the world but refuses to surrender to them.

In "A Man," Nina Cassian conveys the power of an individual's attitude through an image that students will easily connect with freedom and upward motion.

❷ ▶Critical Viewing

Answer: The upward flight of the bird reflects the freedom of the speaker in "Conscientious Objector."

❸ Literary Analysis

Tone

• Point out the emphasis that the poet creates in line 1 by using the word *shall*.

• Ask students to identify the ways that the poet immediately establishes a serious, determined tone.
Answer: The directness of the statement and the use of the word *shall* give the opening line a very serious tone, as if the speaker is making a proclamation.

❶ Conscientious Objector
Edna St. Vincent Millay

❸| I shall die, but that is all that I shall do for Death.

I hear him leading his horse out of the stall; I hear the
    clatter on the barn-floor.
He is in haste; he has business in Cuba, business in the
    Balkans, many calls to make this morning.
But I will not hold the bridle while he cinches the girth.[1]
5   And he may mount by himself: I will not give him a leg up.

Though he flick my shoulders with his whip, I will not tell
    him which way the fox ran.
With his hoof on my breast, I will not tell him where the
    black boy hides in the swamp.
I shall die, but that is all that I shall do for Death; I am not
    on his pay-roll.

I will not tell him the whereabouts of my friends nor of my
    enemies either.
10 Though he promise me much, I will not map him the route
    to any man's door.

Am I a spy in the land of the living, that I should deliver
    men to Death?
Brother, the password and the plans of our city are safe
    with me; never through me
Shall you be overcome.

---

1. **bridle . . . cinches . . . girth** *n., v., n.* terms that apply to horses. Harness; fastens on; band put around the belly of a horse for holding a saddle.

266 ◆ *Clashing Forces*

❷ ▲ Critical Viewing
Which details of this picture reflect the sentiments expressed in Millay's poem? **[Support]**

Edna St. Vincent Millay

(1892–1950)
Edna St. Vincent Millay was still in college when she first won fame as a poet. After graduation, she moved to New York City, where she acted in experimental plays and also pursued her writing career. Beautiful and outspoken, she won both praise and scorn for her controversial opinions on issues such as women's rights and political freedom. She retired from public life in 1925, moving to a farm in upstate New York, where she continued to write poetry.

TEACHING RESOURCES

The following resources can be used to enrich or extend the instruction for pp. 266–270.

Literary Analysis
📖 **Selection Support:** Literary Analysis, p. 72

Reading
🎧 **Listening to Literature Audiocassettes,** Side 9 ■
💿 **Listening to Literature Audio CDs,** CD 5 ■

Extension
■ **Fine Art Transparencies, Volume 1,** Art Transparency 8 (Have students compare and contrast the tone of the painting with that of "The Weary Blues" and "Jazz Fantasia.")
📖 **Authors In Depth,** Platinum Level ■ (The collection includes many additional selections by Langston Hughes for further reading.)

■ **BLOCK SCHEDULING:** Resources marked with this symbol provide varied instruction during 90-minute blocks.

A Man

Nina Cassian
Translated by Roy MacGregor-Hastie

While fighting for his country, he lost an arm
and was suddenly afraid:
'From now on, I shall only be able to do
   things by halves.

5 I shall <u>reap</u> half a harvest.
I shall be able to play either the tune
or the accompaniment on the piano,
but never both parts together.
I shall be able to bang with only one fist
10 on doors, and worst of all
I shall only be able to half hold
my love close to me.
There will be things I cannot do at all,
applaud for example,
at shows where everyone applauds.'

15 From that moment on, he set himself to do
everything with twice as much enthusiasm.
And where the arm had been torn away
a wing grew.

reap (rēp) v. gather

Review and Assess

Thinking About the Selections

1. **Respond:** How do you think the speakers of these two poems would feel about each other?

2. **(a) Recall:** In "Conscientious Objector," what are two things the speaker will not do? **(b) Speculate:** Why do you think the speaker will not tell the whereabouts of others?

3. **(a) Recall:** What was the man in "A Man" doing when he lost his arm? **(b) Infer:** What does this suggest about the kind of person he is?

4. **(a) Recall:** What does the man who lost his arm now "set himself to do"? **(b) Interpret:** What does the poet suggest about him in saying that his arm was replaced by a wing?

5. **(a) Synthesize:** What does the speaker in each poem say about the importance of living? **(b) Take a Position:** Do you agree or disagree with their philosophies? Explain.

Nina Cassian

(b. 1924)

Born in Galati, Romania, Nina Cassian is one of Romania's most notable poets. She studied at the Bucharest Conservatory of Music and was a Romanian State Prize Poet Laureate. Today, she lives and works in New York City.

A Man ◆ 267

---

4 Reading Strategy

Responding to Images and Ideas

- Ask students to identify the image described by the speaker.
  Answer: The speaker describes a man who cannot applaud because he has lost an arm.

- Have students discuss how the inability to applaud isolates the speaker more than the other adjustments he mentions.
  Answer: The speaker is able to participate to some degree in the other activities, but there is no way to applaud partially.

Answers for p. 267

Review and Assess

1. The speakers would probably admire each other's determination and optimism.

2. **(a)** The speaker will not help Death locate or conquer its victims. **(b)** The speaker won't tell where they are because he or she does not believe in cooperating with death.

3. **(a)** The man was fighting for his country. **(b)** It suggests that he is a brave and selfless man.

4. **(a)** He sets himself to do everything with twice as much enthusiasm. **(b)** The poet suggests that he has transcended his injury.

5. **(a)** Both suggest that living is a precious privilege. **(b)** Make sure students explain their responses.

❺ About the Selections

Hughes captures the languid repetition and syncopation of the blues by using long sentences punctuated with shorter ones. The repeated ō and ōō sounds echo the crooning of a blues singer. Like a story within a story, the poem conveys the "blues" of the life of a blues musician.

In "Jazz Fantasia," Sandburg combines slang and musical expressions to create a unique, jumpy rhythm that echoes the energetic rhythms of jazz.

❻ Literary Analysis

Tone

- Ask students to describe the tone of the poem. Then, ask them to identify the words in this passage that help to convey this tone.
Answer: The tone of the poem is relaxed but tired and sad. Words such as *poor piano*, *moan*, *rickety stool*, and *sad raggy tune* help to convey this tone.

▶ Monitor Progress Ask students why they think the poet chose this tone for this poem.
Answer: The melancholy tone echoes the sadness of the blues music that is the subject of the poem.

❼ Vocabulary Development

Greek Word Root: -chol-

- Draw students' attention to the word *melancholy* and its definition, "sad and depressed."

- Explain that the Greek root *–chol–* refers to bile, a digestive fluid that was once believed to be one of the four "humors," or bodily fluids governing health and disposition. *Melancholy*, which literally means "black bile," supposedly caused depression.

- Explain that the other "humors" are *choleric* (angry), *phlegmatic* (sluggish), and *sanguine* (cheerful).

❽ ▶ Critical Viewing

Answer: The musicians' relaxed poses and smiling faces, and the prominence of the instruments suggest that they enjoy playing the blues.

268

---

❺ The Weary Blues

Langston Hughes

Droning a drowsy syncopated[1] tune,
Rocking back and forth to a mellow croon,
    I heard a Negro play.
Down on Lenox Avenue the other night
5 By the pale dull <u>pallor</u> of an old gas light
    He did a lazy sway. . . .
    He did a lazy sway. . . .
To the tune o' those Weary Blues.
With his ebony hands on each ivory key
10 He made that poor piano moan with melody.
    O Blues!
Swaying to and fro on his rickety stool
He played that sad raggy tune like a musical fool.
    Sweet Blues!
15 Coming from a black man's soul.
    O Blues!
In a deep song voice with a <u>melancholy</u> tone
I heard that Negro sing, that old piano moan—
    "Ain't got nobody in all this world,

pallor (pal´ ər) *n.* lack of color; unnatural paleness

melancholy (mel´ ən käl´ ē) *adj.* sad and depressed

---

1. **syncopated** (siŋ´ kə pā´ tid) *adj.* with rhythm shifted, stressing beats that are ordinarily weak.

❽ ▼ **Critical Viewing**
How can you tell that these musicians enjoy playing the blues? **[Infer]**

268 ◆ *Clashing Forces*

CUSTOMIZE INSTRUCTION FOR UNIVERSAL ACCESS

For Special Needs Students

Poetry is often challenging for students to read, understand, and enjoy. Formulating a response to the images and ideas in the poem will enhance comprehension and reading pleasure. Students reading poetry will form a personal response to lines, phrases, and images. The work might please, frighten, anger, or bore them. Remind students that they may connect the poem with a personal experience or memory, and that they may agree or disagree with the poet's point of view. Let students know that their responses to poetry are all valid, as long as they can explain *why* they have a particular response.

For practice in responding to images and ideas, have students fold a piece of paper in half lengthwise. In the left column, have them record a line or phrase from a poem. In the right, have them respond to it by stating the thoughts, memories, or feelings it evokes.

20   Ain't got nobody but ma self.
        I's gwine to quit ma frownin'
        And put ma troubles on the shelf."
  Thump, thump, thump, went his foot on the floor.
  He played a few chords then he sang some more—
25   "I got the Weary Blues
        And I can't be satisfied.
        Got the Weary Blues
        And can't be satisfied—
        I ain't happy no mo'
30   And I wish that I had died."
  And far into the night he crooned that tune.
  The stars went out and so did the moon.
  The singer stopped playing and went to bed
  While the Weary Blues echoed through his head.
35 He slept like a rock or a man that's dead.

Review and Assess

Thinking About the Selection

1. **Respond:** Would you like to listen to the kind of music that is described in this poem? Why or why not?

2. **(a) Recall:** What words does Hughes use to describe the way the man plays the piano? **(b) Analyze:** Based on these descriptions, how would you describe the personality of the piano player?

3. **(a) Paraphrase:** Rewrite lines 19–22 in your own words. **(b) Analyze:** Based on lyrics such as these, how would you characterize the blues?

4. **(a) Evaluate:** How well does Hughes capture the music he describes? **(b) Support:** Cite details from the poem to support your answer.

5. **(a) Apply:** What emotions do you feel as you read this poem? **(b) Extend:** Why do you think people sing and play blues music?

Langston Hughes

(1902–1967)

Langston Hughes first won fame during the Harlem Renaissance, a flowering of African American arts in the 1920s. For decades, he remained at the forefront of African American literature, writing poems, plays, stories, and nonfiction in addition to encouraging younger writers. Hughes once defined poetry as "the human soul entire, squeezed like a lemon or lime, drop by drop, into atomic words." Often, he tried making music with words the way a blues musician plays notes on a saxophone.

The Weary Blues ◆ 269

CUSTOMIZE INSTRUCTION FOR UNIVERSAL ACCESS

For Advanced Readers

Suggest that students read additional works by Langston Hughes. Provide students with the titles listed in the Enrichment box, ATE p. 271. You may also wish to use **Authors In Depth,** Platinum Level, which contains the following selections and more:

- "Juke Box Love Song" (poem, p. 51)
- "Boogie: 1 A.M." (poem, p. 53)
- "Me and My Song" (poem, p. 54)

After students have read these or other works by Hughes, have them form discussion groups in which they compare and contrast the selections they have read. They might use the questions on pp. 60–61 of **Authors In Depth** to guide their discussions.

Tone

- Ask students to identify the words and expressions in the bracketed passage that express Sandburg's attitude toward his subject.
  Answer: Words such as *drum*, *batter*, *sob*, *sling*, and *ooze* indicate Sandburg's enjoyment of the music.
- Then, ask students to compare the tone of this poem with that of "The Weary Blues."
  Answer: Students should note that "Jazz Fantasia" is more upbeat and energetic than "The Weary Blues."

Answers for p. 270

Review and Assess

1. Some students might prefer the "rough stuff" of stanzas 2 and 3, but others might enjoy the soothing sounds of stanza 4.

2. **(a)** Sandburg uses words such as *drum*, *batter*, *sob*, *ooze*, *husha-husha-hush*, *moan*, *bang* and *hoo-hoo-hoo-oo*. **(b)** He uses it to echo the sounds and the moods of the instruments.

3. **(a)** Sandburg characterizes it very well with onomatopoeia and sound imagery.
   (b) Onomatopoeia includes *ooze*, *husha-husha-hush*, *moan*, *bang*, and *hoo-hoo-hoo-oo*. Sound imagery includes *drum*, *batter*, *sob*, *long cool winding*, and *cry*.

4. **(a)** Sandburg might say that jazz can be either rough or gentle.
   (b) Based on the varying moods in the poem, students will probably agree.

Jazz Fantasia — Carl Sandburg

❾

Drum on your drums, batter on your banjoes,
sob on the long cool winding saxophones.
Go to it, O jazzmen.

5 Sling your knuckles on the bottoms of the happy
tin pans, let your trombones ooze, and go husha-
husha-hush with the slippery sand-paper.

Moan like an autumn wind high in the lonesome treetops,
moan soft like you wanted somebody terrible, cry like a
racing car slipping away from a motorcycle cop,
10 bang-bang! you jazzmen, bang altogether drums, traps,
banjoes, horns, tin cans—make two people fight on the
top of a stairway and scratch each other's eyes in a
clinch[1] tumbling down the stairs.

Can[2] the rough stuff . . . now a Mississippi steamboat
15 pushes up the night river with a hoo-hoo-hoo-oo . . . and
the green lanterns calling to the high soft stars . . . a red
moon rides on the humps of the low river hills . . . go to it,
O jazzmen.

---

1. **clinch** (klinch) *n.* slang for *embrace*.
2. **Can** slang for *stop*.

Carl Sandburg

(1878–1960)

Carl Sandburg once observed that some poetry was perfect only in form, "all dressed up with nowhere to go." In contrast, his own poetry dresses in blue jeans, going everywhere and speaking in the voice of everyday people. Sandburg was one of a group of young poets who settled in Chicago in the early twentieth century. In addition to poetry, he is famous for his Pulitzer Prize-winning biography of Abraham Lincoln.

Review and Assess

Thinking About the Selection

1. **Respond:** Which kind of jazz would you rather listen to—the kind described in stanzas 2 and 3 or the kind described in stanza 4? Why?

2. **(a) Recall:** Which words does Sandburg use to describe the sound the different instruments make? **(b) Analyze:** Why do you think he uses language like that?

3. **(a) Evaluate:** How well does Sandburg capture the music he describes? **(b) Support:** Give examples from the poem.

4. **(a) Generalize:** Based on the shift in mood between the first three stanzas and the last one, how do you think Sandburg might define jazz? **(b) Make a Judgment:** Do you agree with his interpretation? Explain.

 ASSESSMENT PRACTICE: Reading Comprehension

Implied Main Ideas of Poetry   (For more practice, see Test Preparation Workbook, p. 18.)

On many tests, students will be asked to identify the main idea of a selection. To help prepare students to do this, have them read "A Man" on p. 267, and use the following sample question.

What is the author's main point in this poem?

  A The narrator of the poem is afraid to live.
  B The narrator cannot play the piano.
  C The narrator will not clap his hands.
  D The narrator wants to live life enthusiastically.

Students may wish to summarize the poem's central thought in their own words before they read the answer choices. Using this strategy will help students realize that *A*, *B*, and *C* are details of the narrator's loss, not the main idea of the poem. Answer *D* is the best choice because in lines 15–16, the narrator decides to make up for his loss by trying twice as hard.

Review and Assess

Literary Analysis

Tone

1. What words in "Conscientious Objector" give the poem a serious, purposeful **tone**?
2. What image helps convey the positive tone of "A Man"? Explain.
3. Describe the tone of "The Weary Blues." Support your answer with details from the poem.
4. Based on the tone of "Jazz Fantasia," what would you say is the poet's attitude toward jazz? Explain.

Comparing Literary Works

5. (a) Use a chart like the one here to list examples of the **musical devices** in "The Weary Blues" and "Jazz Fantasia." (b) Compare the ways the musical devices affect the tone of each poem.

Tone ◄··► "The Weary Blues" ◄··► Musical Devices (Rhythm, Rhyme, Repetition) ··► "Jazz Fantasia" ··► Tone

6. Which poem conveys the ideas or energies of music more effectively? Explain.

Reading Strategy

Responding to Images and Ideas

7. Which **image** in "Conscientious Objector" is most striking to you? Explain.
8. To which image in "A Man" do you respond most strongly? Why?
9. Do the descriptions in "Jazz Fantasia" and "The Weary Blues" inspire you to listen to these forms of music? Why or why not?

Extend Understanding

10. **Cultural Connection:** The speaker in "Conscientious Objector" describes many ways in which to refuse to "cooperate with Death." In what ways can ordinary people refuse to "cooperate with Death" in their day-to-day lives?

Conscientious Objector / A Man / The Weary Blues / Jazz Fantasia ◆ *271*

Quick Review

Tone is the attitude of a writer or speaker toward his or her subject or audience. It is often conveyed through word choice and images.

In poetry, **musical devices,** including rhythm, rhyme, and repetition, add to the tone of a work.

When you **respond to images and ideas** in poetry, you react to the sensory descriptions and thoughts in the poem.

 Take It to the Net
www.phschool.com

Take the interactive self-test online to check your understanding of these selections.

Answers for p. 271

Review and Assess

1. Students should note words such as *die, death, business,* and *pay-roll.*
2. The wing suggests that the man will "fly," that he will rise above his difficulties.
3. "The Weary Blues" has a relaxed, easygoing tone. Details include the swaying of the musician, the repetition of words and sounds, and words such as *droning* and *drowsy.*
4. Based on the happy, energetic tone, the poet seems to enjoy jazz.
5. **(a)** Musical Devices: Varied line lengths give "The Weary Blues" an easygoing rhythm, while long, interrupted sentences give "Jazz Fantasia" a fast, jumpy rhythm. "The Weary Blues" uses end rhymes and repeats both words and lines, while "Jazz Fantasia" uses some internal rhyme and repeats the line "Go to it, O jazzmen." **(b)** Tone: The tone of "Jazz Fantasia" is excited and driving. The tone of "The Weary Blues" is gentle and melancholy.
6. Students might choose "The Weary Blues" because it uses more rhyme and repetition.
7. Possible response: The most striking image is in line 6, "Though he flick my shoulders with his whip," because it contains vivid sensory details.
8. Some students might respond to the image of the wing. Others may respond to the individual examples of fear that the man expresses.
9. Students should include in their answers reasons based on the rhythms and instruments mentioned in the poems.
10. People can refuse to cooperate with death by avoiding unhealthy practices and substances, by not accepting injustice or cruelty, and by being aware of world events.

Other Works by the Authors

Works by Edna St. Vincent Millay
Selected Poems of Edna St. Vincent Millay
"Dirge Without Music"

Works by Nina Cassian
Call Yourself Alive?

Works by Langston Hughes
Selected Poems of Langston Hughes
"Dream Deferred"

Works by Carl Sandburg
The Complete Poems of Carl Sandburg
"Fog"

Take It to the Net
Visit www.phschool.com for more information on the authors.

Answers for p. 272

❶ Vocabulary Development

Word Analysis

1. b   3. a
2. c

Concept Development: Analogies

1. reap   3. pallor
2. melancholy

Spelling Strategy

1. attack   4. brusque
2. attic   5. mechanic
3. chlorine   6. khaki

❷ Grammar

1. Am, verb; I, subject
2. grew, verb; wing, subject
3. swayed, verb; musician, subject
4. he, subject; sang, verb
5. did play, verb; jazzmen, subject

Writing Application

1. Is there a trumpet in the band?
2. A trumpet is in the band.
3. On the stage, there is a trumpet in the band.

Integrate Language Skills

❶ Vocabulary Development Lesson

Word Analysis: Greek Root -chol-

Melancholy, which literally means "black bile," was one of the four "humors," the bodily fluids once thought to govern health and disposition. Having too much black bile was believed to cause depression and irritability. Today, *melancholy* has come to mean "sad" or "depressed."

Use your knowledge of the root *-chol-* to help you determine the meaning of the first word in each item.

1. choleric: (a) joyful, (b) quick-tempered, (c) simple
2. cholera: (a) crayon, (b) meeting, (c) disease
3. cholesterol: (a) substance formed in the liver, (b) earwax, (c) mouthwash

Concept Development: Analogies

In vocabulary study, analogies express a relationship between two pairs of words. On a separate paper, complete each of these analogies with one of the vocabulary words on page 265.

1. spring : plant :: autumn : ____?____
2. ecstasy : joyful :: depression : ____?____
3. embarrassment : blush :: sickness : ____?____

Spelling Strategy

In *melancholy,* the letters *ch* spell the sound of *k.* Other spellings of the *k* sound are *c* as in *cost,* *k* as in *king,* *ck* as in *back,* *qu* as in *physique,* and *kh* as in *khan.* Complete these words by using the correct spelling of the *k* sound.

1. atta__   4. brus__e
2. atti__   5. me__ani__
3. __lorine   6. __aki

❷ Grammar Lesson

Hard-to-Find Subjects

In some sentences, the usual subject-verb order is *inverted*—that is, reversed. Sentences that may be inverted in English include those that begin with *there* or *here* and questions. In addition, some sentences are inverted for emphasis.

>   V   S
> **Question:** Why was the singer on Lenox Road?
>
>   V   S
> **There:** There was a singer on Lenox Road.
>
>   V   S
> **Emphasis:** On Lenox Road stood the singer.

Practice Copy these sentences. Put an *S* over the subject and a *V* over the verb.

1. Am I a spy in the land of the living?
2. In place of an arm, there grew a wing.
3. Under the gas light swayed the musician.
4. In a melancholy tone, he sang the blues.
5. What did the jazzmen play?

Writing Application Using the instructions below, rewrite this sentence: *There is a trumpet in the band.*

1. Turn it into a yes-or-no question.
2. Start with the subject.
3. Add a prepositional phrase at the beginning.

𝒲𝒢 *Prentice Hall Writing and Grammar Connection: Chapter 19, Section 2*

272 ◆ Clashing Forces

TEACHING RESOURCES

The following resources can be used to enrich or extend the instruction for pp. 272–273.

Vocabulary

📖 **Selection Support:** Build Vocabulary, p. 69

📖 **Vocabulary and Spelling Practice Book** (Use this booklet for skills enrichment.) ▪

Grammar

📖 **Selection Support:** Build Grammar Skills, p. 70

𝒲𝒢 **Writing and Grammar,** Platinum Level, pp. 418–424

▪ **Daily Language Practice Transparencies**

Writing

𝒲𝒢 **Writing and Grammar,** Platinum Level, p. 835 ▪

💿 **Writing and Grammar iText CD-ROM**

▪ **BLOCK SCHEDULING:** Resources marked with this symbol provide varied instruction during 90-minute blocks.

Writing Lesson

Interview With the Speaker

Imagine that you were able to talk with one of the speakers from the poems in this grouping. You could ask the speaker any questions you liked about the poem. Plan and write an imaginary interview with the speaker of one of the poems.

Prewriting   Choose one of the poems and reread it. Then, write down questions that you would ask the speaker about the tone and the content of the poem. Keep in mind the audience for whom this interview is intended.

Model: Using Appropriate Language for the Audience

Audience	Language and Details
Journal	Informal language; details that vary
Critical Review	Formal language; details that illustrate the work's strengths and weaknesses; excerpts from the work
Literary Analysis	Very formal language; details that prove your ideas about the work; excerpts from the work

Drafting   Write out the interview, including the answers that the speaker of the poem would give. Choose details that will appeal to your audience and that will help you achieve your purpose.

Revising   Make sure that your questions and answers fit your specific purpose. If your language is too informal, change it.

W̶G   *Prentice Hall Writing and Grammar Connection: Chapter 13, Section 2*

Extension Activities

Listening and Speaking   With a small group, prepare and present an **oral reading** of one of the poems. To help you prepare, consider these ideas:

- Decide how you will use volume and tempo to express the tone of the poem.
- Experiment by having different voices read different lines.

When you are ready, read the poem to classmates as part of a poetry reading of all four poems. **[Group Activity]**

Research and Technology   Create a **music time-line** of the last ten decades. Researching online or in the library, find a major national or world event that represents each decade. Then, indicate what kind of music was popular during that time. Generate a timeline to represent the information you find.

 Take It to the Net   www.phschool.com

Go online for an additional research activity using the Internet.

Lesson Support for p. 273

❸ Writing Lesson

- Before students begin, have them determine the audience for whom this interview is intended. Make sure students keep this audience in mind as they complete the lesson.
- Model a list of possible interview questions on the chalkboard.
- Then, have students write their own questions. Remind students they will be interviewing the *speaker* of their chosen poem, not the *poet.*

❹ Listening and Speaking

- Suggest that students practice reciting the poem, paying attention to its rhythm, rhyme scheme, and punctuation.
- Encourage students to keep in mind the tone of the poem and to reflect this tone in the volume and pitch of their voice.
- Have students deliver their poems to the class.
- Have students use the rubric for Presenting an Oral Response to Literature, p. 31 in **Performance Assessment and Portfolio Management.**

CUSTOMIZE INSTRUCTION
For Universal Access

To address different learning styles, use the activities suggested in the **Extension Activities** booklet, p. 18.

- For Musical/Rhythmic and Interpersonal Learners, use Activity 5.
- For Visual/Spatial Learners, use Activity 6.
- For Verbal/Linguistic and Visual/Spatial Learners, use Activity 7.

ASSESSMENT RESOURCES

The following resources can be used to assess students' knowledge and skills.

Selection Assessment

- **Formal Assessment,** pp. 60–62
- **Open Book Test,** pp. 52–54
- **Got It! Assessment Videotapes,** Tape 2
- **Test Bank Software**
- **Take It to the Net**
  Visit www.phschool.com for self-tests and additional questions on the selections.

Listening and Speaking Rubric

- **Performance Assess. and Portfolio Mgmt.,** p. 31

PRENTICE HALL **ASSESSMENT** *SYSTEM*

- **Workbook**
- **Transparencies**
- **Skill Book**
- **CD-ROM**

Lesson Objectives

1. To learn how to evaluate the credibility of information sources

2. To understand the purposes of a newspaper feature article

3. To demonstrate the use and value of graphics in a newspaper article

About Newspaper Features

- Have students read "About Newspaper Features." Discuss with students what recent feature articles have caught their attention in the local newspaper.

- Engage students in a discussion about the value of feature articles. What purpose do they serve? Possible response: Students may say that feature articles give the reader a nice break from just straight news; they may offer more in-depth information on a general subject or reintroduce a subject to the public, perhaps generating renewed public interest.

Reading Strategy

Evaluating Credibility of Information Sources

- Have students read the information about the Reading Strategy.

- Encourage students to discuss why it is important to evaluate the credibility of sources. Ask them: Why should you not simply accept everything you read as true or accurate? Why is it important to question what you read? Possible response: Students may note that the information reported in various sources is not always accurate or unbiased. If they simply accept everything they read as true, they may be misled or, when accounts contradict each other, confused.

- Explain to students that by evaluating the credibility of their sources, they will be able to collect the most accurate information on a subject.

- Call students' attention to the chart on p. 274. Have students duplicate the chart in their notebooks and fill it in as they read "Feel the City's Pulse? It's Be-bop, Man!"

Newspaper Features

About Newspaper Features

In addition to up-to-the-minute news reporting, newspapers also include several other types of journalism, including sports reporting, editorials, and feature articles. A newspaper **feature article** is not necessarily about a current event. It can present information about a person, place, idea, or event that has been around for a long time. For example, this feature article by Ann Douglas is about a form of jazz that has been around since the early 1940s.

Unlike a news article, a feature article does not always give the *who*, *what*, *when*, *where*, and *why* of its subject. Instead, it may focus on just one or two of these questions.

Reading Strategy

Evaluating Credibility of Information Sources

When you read articles, you should be critical of the information presented. To avoid simply accepting everything you read, get in the habit of **evaluating the credibility of sources** to determine whether you should trust the validity, or truth, of the information.

"It's Be-bop, Man!" is from *The New York Times*, an established, trustworthy source. The writer is a cultural historian whose purpose is to give general historical background on be-bop. Therefore, you can trust her information on history, but you might want to be cautious about her remarks on music theory.

Using a chart like this one, rate the credibility of the article in each category listed.

	Example	Credibility	My Reasoning
Names, Places, Dates	1964: Monk defines jazz as "New York."	High credibility	The *Times* could easily check this date. The writer is a scholar accustomed to checking facts.
Accurate Quotations			
Historical Details			
Generalizations About the History of Jazz			

The New York Times

Feel the City's Pulse? It's Be-bop, Man!

ANN DOUGLAS

In 1964, Thelonious Monk, one of the pioneers of be-bop and perhaps jazz's greatest composer, was asked by an interviewer to define jazz. Though Monk disliked questions and usually ignored them, this time he didn't miss a beat: "New York, man. You can feel it. It's around in the air. . . ."

Be-bop (bop for short) was sometimes labeled "New York Jazz," and it is, in fact, the only major school of jazz to which the city can lay proprietary claim. Jazz of the 20's, dominated by Louis Armstrong, originated in New Orleans, migrating to New York only after a formative detour in Chicago. Armstrong inspired 30's swing, the music of the big bands led by Benny Goodman, Artie Shaw, Glenn Miller, Count Basie and Duke Ellington, the "mother bands," as Gillespie called them, whose music the be-boppers both emulated and revolutionized.

. . . Bop's wide-ranging allusiveness, its quick-silver expressivity, angular dissonance and shockingly extended palette of pitches and rhythms echoed the international mix, the fluidity and speed of New York life.

Jamming After Hours Bop began at roughly the same time as World War II, in 1940 when Monk, then 23, was hired to play with Kenny (Klook) Clarke, the man who transformed jazz drumming, at Minton's Playhouse in Harlem. Gillespie jammed with them after his regular engagement, and Parker joined them a year later. When Minton's closed for the night, they adjourned to Clark Monroe's Uptown House, an after-hours club where an extraordinary teen-age drummer named Max Roach played in the band.

The nation's entrance into the war in late 1941 imposed gas rationing, entertainment taxes and curfews, sharply restricting travel. The swing bands were touring bands, and some of them continued to tour, but now everyone was looking for a long-term base in a big city, easily accessible by public transit.

What hurt swing helped be-bop. The expense and risks of touring (especially down South) had been far greater for black musicians than for white. The cramped quarters of many city clubs suited the young bop musicians, eager to work with the small ensembles that maximized opportunities for experimentation. . . .

The word "be-bop," which both Monk and Gillespie claimed to have coined, described the music's unconventional stop-and-start form, especially Gillespie and Parker's witty eighth-note pair conclusions. The purpose of bop's irregular phrasings, side-sliding harmonies and whirlwind pace, was, in Kenny Clarke's words, to "raise the standards of musicianship," to tell people, "Whatever you go into, go into it intelligently." The be-boppers were the real New York intellectuals, the hippest, smartest men in town.

continued on page 276

A catchy title indicates the article is a feature and not straight news.

The writer provides some history of be-bop, describing how the war contributed to its expansion.

The writer describes be-bop and defines it as intellectual.

The article begins with a quotation, a good way to get the reader's attention.

Background information explains swing, a jazz form that preceded and influenced be-bop.

---

from *The New York Times:* Feel the City's Pulse? It's Be-bop, Man!

- Tell students that they will encounter feature articles like the one shown any time they read a newspaper—most newspapers include features on a regular basis.
- Remind students that, even though they may read such articles for enjoyment, they should critically evaluate the credibility of the information presented as they read.
- Have students read the article and the notes that identify elements of the feature.
- Ask students to discuss the title. Why did the writer choose this title?
  Answer: The writer chose the title in order to catch people's attention so they would read the article. It also prepares the reader for the hip, casual tone of the article. The title reflects the message that be-bop was born and bred in New York City, and echoes the life of the city.
- Ask students to discuss what they learned from the article. Which facts caught their interest? How would they rate the credibility of this information, and for what reasons?
  Possible response: Students may find the descriptions of be-bop style intriguing. They may rate these descriptions as moderately credible, since the writer is clearly knowledgeable about her subject but is not writing for an audience with technical expertise in music. Further, students should recognize that attempts to describe the "feel" of artworks are in part subjective and may not reflect everyone's experience.

CUSTOMIZE INSTRUCTION FOR UNIVERSAL ACCESS

For Less Proficient Readers	For Advanced Readers
To help students identify feature articles, bring in a few newspapers—either local, out of town, or national—and have students find the features in them. Tell students they may be able to locate them by title alone, or they may need to rely on other factors, such as the part of the paper in which they fall or the graphics they used.	To help students analyze the credibility of feature articles, bring in a few different newspapers. Have students create a list of criteria they would use to assess credibility. Then, have them determine which articles are the most credible sources. Allow time for students to present their opinions and reasonings to the class.

Graphics in Newspaper Features

- Have students read the information next to the map and the notes that accompany it.

- Ask students to discuss how this graphic complements the article they read on p. 275.
  Possible responses: The map encourages readers to imagine the bustling city life that the article says gave be-bop its spirit; the map fills in particular information about the events and personalities in the article; the map gives a sense of how a city can become a cultural center in which musicians congregate to live, work, and perform.

- Then, have students discuss the effectiveness of graphics in a newspaper. Encourage them to point out examples they have noticed in newspapers of other types of visuals that support articles (i.e. photographs, bulleted lists, maps) and graphics that stand on their own (i.e., weather maps, movie schedules). Ask what drawbacks there would be to a newspaper without graphics.
  Possible responses: Students may note that page upon page of text without the relief of graphics would not encourage casual readers to browse and would not catch their interest. Students may also note that a graphic format such as a map or timetable makes certain kinds of information easier to locate and digest, while photographs can add drama or human interest to an article.

Graphics in Newspaper Features

Visual representation is an important and effective way to communicate. The use of graphics, such as this annotated map, enables feature news writers to include more information in a small space. The map below helps readers make the connection between the places the article identifies and their location in Manhattan. In addition, the list provides further information.

Feel the City's Pulse? It's Be-bop, Man!

SITES OF BOP'S TRIUMPHS AND TRAGEDIES

Annotations to the map explain the importance of key sites.

1. **Savoy Ballroom,** Lenox Avenue and 140th Street, Harlem. Charlie Parker played in this legendary jazz and dance hall with the Jay McShann Orchestra in his early days in New York, . . .

2. **Minton's Playhouse,** 210 West 118th Street, Morningside Heights. Charlie Christian, Kenny Clarke, Thelonious Monk, Parker and Gillespie made musical history here in the early 1940s.

3. **St. Peter's Church,** 54th Street and Lexington Avenue, Manhattan (also its current site). Monk's funeral took place here on Feb. 22, 1982, with musicians playing for three hours.

Information is tightly connected to the article's content.

4. **52nd Street,** between Fifth and Sixth Avenues, known as "The Street." A magical block of jazz clubs . . . including the Onyx, Spotlite, Three Deuces and Kelly's Stable.

5. **Birdland,** 1678 Broadway, at 53rd Street, Manhattan. It opened on Dec. 15, 1949, with dozens of (caged) birds on view and Charlie (Bird) Parker presiding.

6. **216 West 19th Street.** Eager to become "a New York musician," Gillespie lived here with his brother, . . . when he first came to town from Philadelphia in 1937, eating for 25 cents a day.

Check Your Comprehension

1. How did Thelonius Monk define jazz?
2. When did be-bop begin?
3. Who inspired 1930s swing?
4. How did World War II affect two forms of jazz?
5. Who did the writer think were the real New York intellectuals?

Applying the Reading Strategy

Evaluating Credibility of Information Sources

6. How credible is the article as a source for explanations of be-bop's rise in popularity over swing? Explain.
7. How credible is the article as a source of theoretical explanations of music, such as the reference to the "extended palette of pitches"? Why?
8. Douglas's descriptions of be-bop are enthusiastic. Does this make them more credible or less credible? Explain.

Activity

Analyzing Feature Articles

Review a copy of a current city or regional daily newspaper. Locate two feature articles. Using the format shown at right, analyze the content of each one.

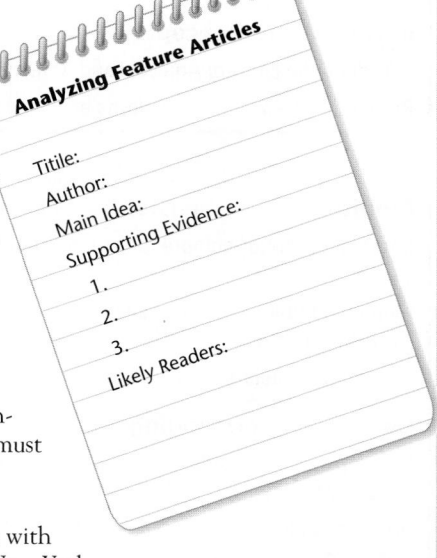

Analyzing Feature Articles

Title:
Author:
Main Idea:
Supporting Evidence:
1.
2.
3.
Likely Readers:

Contrasting Informational Materials

Feature Articles and News Articles

Feature articles suit a specific purpose—to provide readers with interesting and useful information. In contrast, news articles—even those focused on the arts—must be more tightly connected with newsworthy or time-sensitive events.

1. If Douglas's article had been written to coincide with the opening of a museum exhibit about jazz in New York City, what details would you expect to find in a news report about the opening?
2. If space limitations were suddenly tighter because of breaking news, feature articles might be cut and published at a later date. What is the value of feature articles like "Feel the City's Pulse?" Explain.

Like the Sun ✦ Tell all the Truth but tell it slant—

Lesson Objectives

1. **To analyze and respond to literary elements**
   - Literary Analysis: Irony
   - Comparing Literary Works

2. **To read, comprehend, analyze, and critique a short story and a poem**
   - Reading Strategy: Analyzing Causes and Effects
   - Reading Check questions
   - Review and Assess questions
   - Assessment Practice (ATE)

3. **To develop word analysis skills, fluency, and systematic vocabulary**
   - Vocabulary Development Lesson: Latin Word Root: *-gratis-*

4. **To understand and apply written and oral language conventions**
   - Spelling Strategy
   - Grammar Lesson: Direct and Indirect Objects

5. **To understand and apply appropriate writing and research strategies**
   - Writing Lesson: Literary Comparison
   - Extension Activity: Multimedia Presentation

6. **To understand and apply listening and speaking strategies**
   - Extension Activity: Oral Argument

STEP-BY-STEP TEACHING GUIDE	PACING GUIDE
PRETEACH	
Motivate Students and Provide Background	
Use the Motivation activity (ATE p. 278)	5 min.
Read and discuss the Preview material and Background information (SE/ATE p. 278) **A**	5 min.
Introduce the Concepts	
Introduce the Literary Analysis and Reading Strategy (SE/ATE p. 279) **A**	15 min.
Pronounce the vocabulary words and read their definitions (SE p. 279)	5 min.
TEACH	
Monitor Comprehension	
Informally monitor comprehension by circulating while students read independently or in groups **A**	15 min.
Monitor students' comprehension with the Reading Check notes (SE/ATE p. 281)	as students read
Develop vocabulary with Vocabulary notes (SE pp. 281, 282, 283; ATE p. 282)	as students read
Develop Understanding	
Develop students' understanding of irony with Literary Analysis annotations (SE p. 283; ATE p. 283) **A**	10 min.
Develop students' understanding of analyzing cause and effect with Reading Strategy annotations (SE p. 281; ATE pp. 281, 282, 283)	10 min.
ASSESS	
Assess Mastery	
Assess students' mastery of the Reading Strategy and Literary Analysis by having them answer the Review and Assess questions (SE/ATE p. 285)	20 min.
Use one or more of the print and media Assessment Resources (ATE p. 287) **A**	up to 50 min.
EXTEND	
Apply Understanding	
Have students complete the Vocabulary Development Lesson and the Grammar Lesson (SE p. 286) **A**	20 min.
Apply students' knowledge of supporting details using the Writing Lesson (SE p. 287) **A**	45 min.
Apply students' understanding of the selection using one or more of the Extension Activities (SE p. 287)	20–90 min.

 ACCELERATED INSTRUCTION:
Use the strategies and activities identified with an **A**.

UNIVERSAL ACCESS
● = Below Level Students
▲ = On-Level Students
■ = Above Level Students

Time and Resource Manager

RESOURCES

PRINT 📖	TRANSPARENCIES 🗂	TECHNOLOGY 💿 🎧 📼
• **Beyond Literature,** Cross-Curricular Connection: Science, p. 19 ▲ ■		• **Interest Grabber Video,** Tape 2 ● ▲ ■
• **Selection Support Workbook:** ● ▲ ■ Literary Analysis, p. 76 Reading Strategy, p. 75 Build Vocabulary, p. 73	• **Literary Analysis and Reading Transparencies,** pp. 37 and 38 ● ▲ ■	
		• **Listening to Literature** ● ▲ ■ Audiocassettes, Side 9 Audio CDs, CD 6
• **Literatura en español** ● ▲ • **Literary Analysis for Enrichment** ■		
• **Formal Assessment:** Selection Test, pp. 63–65 ● ▲ ■ • **Open Book Test,** pp. 55–57 ● ▲ ■ • **Performance Assessment and Portfolio Management,** p. 15 ● ▲ ■ • **PRENTICE HALL ASSESSMENT SYSTEM** ● ▲	• **PRENTICE HALL ASSESSMENT SYSTEM** ● ▲ ■ Skills Practice Answers and Explanations on Transparencies	• **Test Bank Software** ● ▲ ■ • **Got It! Assessment Videotapes,** Tape 2 ● ▲
• **Selection Support Workbook:** ● ▲ ■ Build Grammar Skills, p. 74 • **Writing and Grammar,** Platinum Level ● ▲ ■ • **Extension Activities,** p. 19 ● ▲ ■	• **Daily Language Practice Transparencies** ● ▲ • **Writing Models and Graphic Organizers on Transparencies,** p. 95 ● ▲ ■	• **Writing and Grammar iText CD-ROM** ● ▲ ■ 🖥 *Take It to the Net* www.phschool.com

BLOCK SCHEDULING: Use one 90-minute class period to preteach the selection and have students read it. Use a second 90-minute class period to assess students' mastery of skills and have them complete one of the Extension Activities.

Step-by-Step Teaching guide for pp. 278–279

Motivation

On the chalkboard, write the words "absolute truth." Ask students what they consider to be absolute truth. Then, lead the class in a discussion of whether it is possible or desirable to tell the absolute truth at all times. Then, read aloud the first paragraph of "Like the Sun." Tell students that this story will allow them to watch the adventures of a man who decides to tell what he considers the absolute truth for one full day.

▥ Interest Grabber Video

As an alternative, play "Music and Dance of India" on Tape 2 to engage student interest.

❶ Background

Music

The violin is widely used in southern Indian music. Percussion instruments featured in Indian music include the double-headed drum known as *mridangam* and the *ghatam*, a clay pot that the player may sometimes toss into the air.

Prepare to Read

Like the Sun ◆ Tell all the Truth but tell it slant—

Face in Sun, Hal Lose, Stock Illustration Source, Inc.

▥ Take It to the Net

Visit www.phschool.com for interactive activities and instruction related to the selections, including

- background
- graphic organizers
- literary elements
- reading strategies

Preview

Connecting to the Literature

Your closest friend has just given a less-than-impressive performance in the class play and asks for your honest response. You must decide whether to tell the truth or spare your friend's feelings. In different ways, Narayan's story and Dickinson's poem both pose this challenging dilemma.

❶ Background

Set in modern India, "Like the Sun" features a performance rooted in southern Indian musical traditions. In the story, the headmaster sings an *alapana*, or an improvisational piece, leading in to a song by Thyagaraja (1767–1847), one of southern India's most influential composers. Accompanying the headmaster's singing are a violinist and a drummer.

278 ◆ *Clashing Forces*

TEACHING RESOURCES

The following resources can be used to enrich or extend the instruction for pp. 278–279.

Motivation

▥ **Interest Grabber Video**, Tape 2 ▥

Background

▥ **Beyond Literature**, Cross-Curricular Connection: Science, p. 19

 Take It to the Net
Visit www.phschool.com for background and hotlinks for the selections.

Literary Analysis

▥ **Literary Analysis and Reading Transparencies**, Irony, p. 38

Reading

▥ **Selection Support:** Reading Strategy, p. 78; Build Vocabulary, p. 76 ▥

▥ **Literary Analysis and Reading Transparencies**, Analyzing Causes and Effects, p. 37

▥ **BLOCK SCHEDULING:** Resources marked with this symbol provide varied instruction during 90-minute blocks.

Literary Analysis

Irony

Irony is the literary technique that presents surprising, interesting, and sometimes amusing contradictions. The contradictions can result from these kinds of clashes:

- A contradiction between what a character believes and what is actually the case
- A contradiction between what a character expects to happen and what actually happens

By focusing on the clash between the main character's ideals and the real situation, you will understand the irony in "Like the Sun."

Comparing Literary Works

Emily Dickinson's poem "Tell all the Truth but tell it slant—" relates a surprising **theme,** or central message, related to truth. In fact, Dickinson would probably not agree with Sekhar's decision to tell the truth for a day, no matter what. Compare and contrast the lesson that Sekhar, the main character in "Like the Sun," learns with the ideas expressed in Dickinson's poem. Then, determine which philosophy you think is closest to your own.

Reading Strategy

Analyzing Causes and Effects

A **cause** is an event that makes something else happen, and an **effect** is the result that follows. "Like the Sun" is a perfect story with which to analyze the relationship between causes and effects. Sekhar makes an important decision at the beginning, a decision that seems to invite consequences. Fill out a graphic organizer like this one to help you connect Sekhar's actions with their results.

Vocabulary Development

essence (es′ əns) *n.* crucial element or basis (p. 281)

tempering (tem′ pər iŋ) *n.* modifying or adjusting (p. 281)

shirked (shʉrkt) *v.* neglected or avoided a responsibility (p. 281)

incessantly (in ses′ ənt lē) *adv.* constantly (p. 282)

ingratiating (in grā′ shē āt′ iŋ) *adj.* trying to please; accommodating (p. 282)

stupefied (stoo′ pə fīd′) *adj.* dazed; stunned (p. 282)

scrutinized (skroot′ ən īzd′) *v.* examined carefully (p. 283)

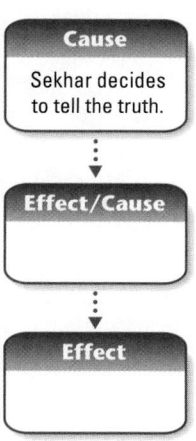

Cause

Sekhar decides to tell the truth.

Effect/Cause

Effect

❷ Literary Analysis

Irony

- Go over the definition of *irony* with students, emphasizing that it is a contradiction between what a character believes and what is true, or between what a character expects and what actually happens.

- Explain to students that irony can also result from a contradiction between what the reader expects and what actually happens. In addition, there can be a contradiction between what a character knows and what the reader knows.

- Encourage students to pay attention to these kinds of contradictions as they read the selections.

❸ Reading Strategy

Analyzing Causes and Effects

- Make sure students understand what causes and effects are and how they are related. Explain that an effect can also become the cause of yet another effect. This is known as a *cause-and-effect chain.*

- Explain to students that paying attention to how events are related through cause and effect will help them better understand plot events and characters' actions.

- Review the graphic organizer with students, and have them complete it as they read "Like the Sun."

Vocabulary Development

- Pronounce each vocabulary word for students, and read the definitions as a class. Have students identify any words with which they are already familiar.

CUSTOMIZE INSTRUCTION FOR UNIVERSAL ACCESS

For Less Proficient Readers	For English Learners	For Advanced Readers
To help students understand the story's irony, have them complete a chart like this one as they read:	Preview the Vocabulary Development list and footnotes with students, and substitute more familiar terms as needed. Make sure students can follow the events of the story so that they will be able to appreciate its irony.	Have groups of students work together to role-play one of the situations that Sekhar encounters. Suggest that they extend the dialogue to explore the character's expectations versus the reality of the situation in order to further explore the irony in the story.

Chart (For Less Proficient Readers):

What Sekhar expects	What happens

 E-Teach

Visit E-Teach at www.phschool.com for teachers' essays on how to teach, with questions and answers.

**CUSTOMIZE INSTRUCTION
For Visual/Spatial Learners**

Encourage students to create illustrations for a few scenes in this story. Have students use the details from their chosen scenes to incorporate in their illustrations. Students can share their work with the class when they are done.

❶ About the Selections

When Sekhar decides to tell the whole truth for one day, he hurts his wife's feelings, alienates a colleague, and insults his headmaster. Through the experiences of the main character, Narayan explores whether it is possible or wise to tell the unvarnished truth at all times. Emily Dickinson's poem suggests that it is not.

❷ Background

Art

Face in Sun, by Hal Lose

This artwork is an example of the paper cut-out technique, in which the image is composed of small pieces of cut paper. Have students study the image, and then use the following questions for discussion.

1. What personality has the artist given the sun?
   Answer: The arched eyebrows and big eyes suggest that this sun is observant and watchful. The smile suggests that the sun is amused by what it sees.

2. Based on its expression, what might the sun think of Sekhar?
   Answer: The sun might be a detached observer who chuckles at Sekhar's misadventures with the truth.

❶ *Like the Sun*

R. K. Narayan

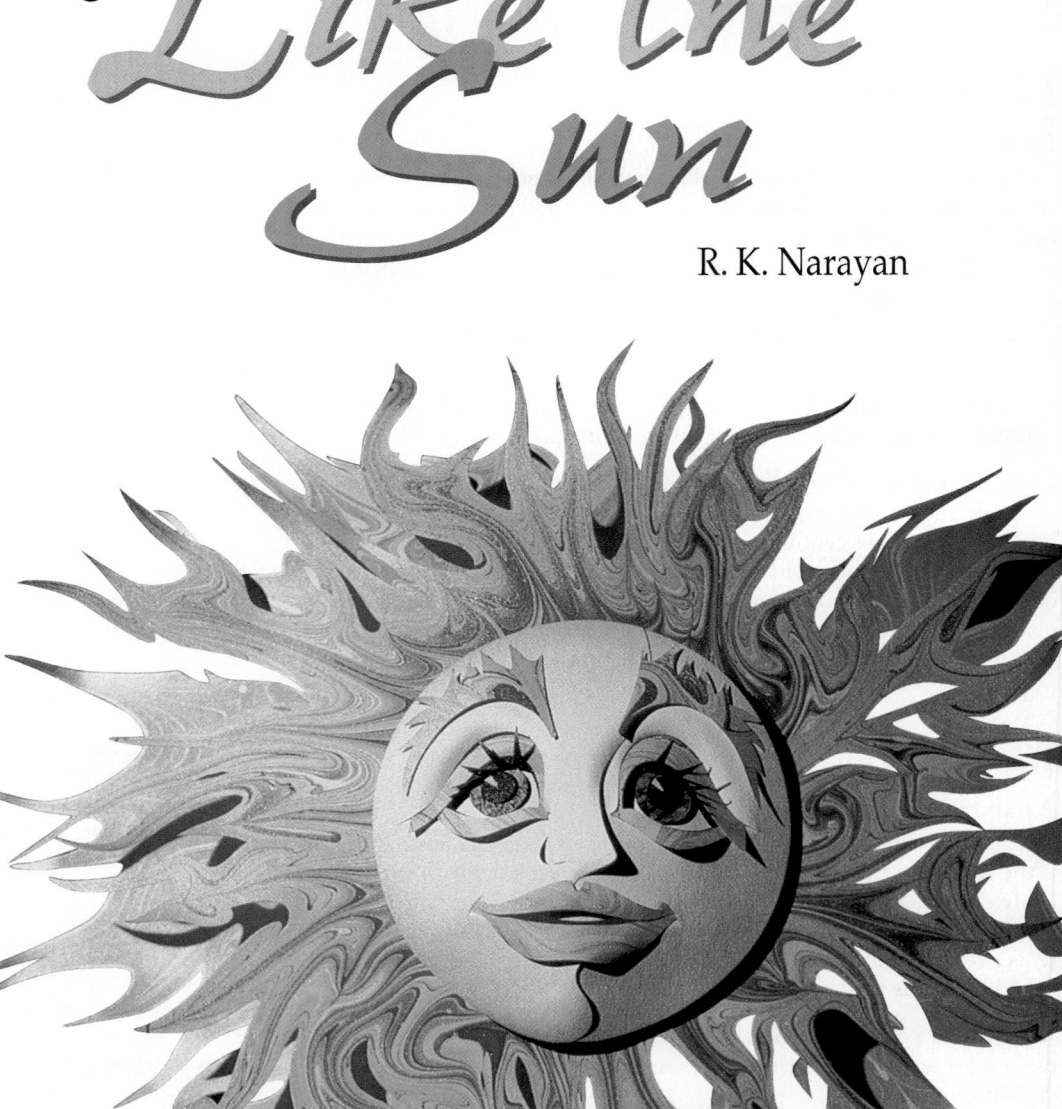

Face in Sun, Hal Lose,
Stock Illustration Source, Inc.

280 ◆ *Clashing Forces*

TEACHING RESOURCES

The following resources can be used to enrich or extend the instruction for pp. 280–284.

Literary Analysis

📖 **Selection Support:** Literary Analysis, p. 76

Reading

🎧 **Listening to Literature Audiocassettes,** Side 9 ▪

💿 **Listening to Literature Audio CDs,** CD 6 ▪

▪ **BLOCK SCHEDULING:** Resources marked with this symbol provide varied instruction during 90-minute blocks.

Truth, Sekhar reflected, is like the sun. I suppose no human being can ever look it straight in the face without blinking or being dazed. He realized that, morning till night, the essence of human relationships consisted in tempering truth so that it might not shock. This day he set apart as a unique day—at least one day in the year we must give and take absolute Truth whatever may happen. Otherwise life is not worth living. The day ahead seemed to him full of possibilities. He told no one of his experiment. It was a quiet resolve, a secret pact between him and eternity.

The very first test came while his wife served him his morning meal. He showed hesitation over a titbit, which she had thought was her culinary[1] masterpiece. She asked, "Why, isn't it good?" At other times he would have said, considering her feelings in the matter, "I feel full up, that's all." But today he said, "It isn't good. I'm unable to swallow it." He saw her wince and said to himself, Can't be helped. Truth is like the sun.

His next trial was in the common room when one of his colleagues came up and said, "Did you hear of the death of so-and-so? Don't you think it a pity?" "No," Sekhar answered. "He was such a fine man—" the other began. But Sekhar cut him short with: "Far from it. He always struck me as a mean and selfish brute."

During the last period when he was teaching geography for Third Form A, Sekhar received a note from the headmaster: "Please see me before you go home." Sekhar said to himself: It must be about these horrible test papers. A hundred papers in the boys' scrawls; he had shirked this work for weeks, feeling all the time as if a sword were hanging over his head.

The bell rang, and the boys burst out of the class.

Sekhar paused for a moment outside the headmaster's room to button up his coat; that was another subject the headmaster always sermonized about.

He stepped in with a very polite "Good evening, sir."

The headmaster looked up at him in a very friendly manner and asked, "Are you free this evening?"

Sekhar replied, "Just some outing which I have promised the children at home—"

"Well, you can take them out another day. Come home with me now."

"Oh . . . yes, sir, certainly. . . ." And then he added timidly, "anything special, sir?"

"Yes," replied the headmaster, smiling to himself. . . ."You didn't know my weakness for music?"

"Oh, yes, sir. . . ."

"I've been learning and practicing secretly, and now I want you to hear me this evening. I've engaged a drummer and a violinist to accompany me—this is the first time I'm doing it full-dress,[2] and I want your opinion. I know it will be valuable."

---

1. **culinary** (kyōō′ lə ner′ ē) *adj.* having to do with cooking or the kitchen.
2. **full-dress** complete in every respect.

---

essence (es′ əns) *n.* crucial element or basis

tempering (tem′ pər iŋ) *n.* modifying or adjusting

Reading Strategy
Analyzing Causes and Effects What is the first consequence of Sekhar's "pact" with "eternity"?

shirked (shʉrkt) *v.* neglected or avoided a responsibility

❺ **Reading Check**
What is unique about this day for Sekhar?

Like the Sun ◆ 281

❸ **Reading Strategy**
Analyzing Causes and Effects
- Point out that Sekhar's wife probably expected him to praise her cooking.
- Ask students the Reading Strategy question on p. 281: What is the first consequence of Sekhar's "pact" with "eternity"?
  Answer: Sekhar's decision to be candid has hurt his wife's feelings.

❹ **Critical Thinking**
Infer
- Ask students to describe what is happening in the bracketed paragraph. Elicit that Sekhar has a hundred test papers to grade, which he has been avoiding for weeks.
- Ask students what they can infer about Sekhar based on this information. How might this knowledge affect Sekhar's promise to tell the truth all day?
  Answer: Sekhar's procrastination indicates that he tries to avoid or put off unpleasant tasks. This would seem to indicate that if telling the absolute truth becomes unpleasant, he will be unable to do so for long.

❺ ✓ **Reading Check**
Answer: Sekhar has decided that he will tell nothing but the whole truth all day.

CUSTOMIZE INSTRUCTION FOR UNIVERSAL ACCESS

For Less Proficient Readers	For English Learners
Have students pause frequently while reading, perhaps at the end of each of Sekhar's encounters, to review what has happened thus far. Encourage students to describe the events in terms of causes and effects. For example, before students begin reading p. 282, ask them to predict what will happen when Sekhar goes to his headmaster's house to listen to him play. Elicit that Sekhar will probably disappoint his headmaster.	As they read, have students write unfamiliar words on index cards—one word per card. Have them look up the definitions and write them on the backs of the cards. Then, after they finish reading, have them review the flash cards occasionally to add the words to their permanent vocabulary.

Sekhar's taste in music was well known. He was one of the most dreaded music critics in the town. But he never anticipated his musical inclinations would lead him to this trial. . . . "Rather a surprise for you, isn't it?" asked the headmaster. "I've spent a fortune on it behind closed doors. . . ."

They started for the headmaster's house. "God hasn't given me a child, but at least let him not deny me the consolation of music," the headmaster said, pathetically, as they walked. He incessantly chattered about music: how he began one day out of sheer boredom; how his teacher at first laughed at him and then gave him hope; how his ambition in life was to forget himself in music.

At home the headmaster proved very ingratiating. He sat Sekhar on a red silk carpet, set before him several dishes of delicacies, and fussed over him as if he were a son-in-law of the house. He even said, "Well, you must listen with a free mind. Don't worry about these test papers." He added half humorously, "I will give you a week's time."

"Make it ten days, sir," Sekhar pleaded.

"All right, granted," the headmaster said generously. Sekhar felt really relieved now—he would attack them at the rate of ten a day and get rid of the nuisance.

The headmaster lighted incense sticks. "Just to create the right atmosphere," he explained. A drummer and a violinist, already seated on a Rangoon mat, were waiting for him. The headmaster sat down between them like a professional at a concert, cleared his throat and began an alapana,[3] and paused to ask, "Isn't it good Kalyani?"[4] Sekhar pretended not to have heard the question. The headmaster went on to sing a full song composed by Thyagaraja and followed it with two more. All the time the headmaster was singing, Sekhar went on commenting within himself, He croaks like a dozen frogs. He is bellowing like a buffalo. Now he sounds like loose window shutters in a storm.

The incense sticks burnt low. Sekhar's head throbbed with the medley of sounds that had assailed his eardrums for a couple of hours now. He felt half stupefied. The headmaster had gone nearly hoarse, when he paused to ask, "Shall I go on?" Sekhar replied, "Please don't, sir; I think this will do. . . ." The headmaster looked stunned. His face was beaded with perspiration. Sekhar felt the greatest pity for him. But he felt he could not help it. No judge delivering a sentence felt more pained and helpless. Sekhar noticed that the headmaster's wife peeped in from the kitchen, with eager curiosity. The drummer and the violinist put away their burdens with

---

3. **alapana** improvisational Indian music in the classical style.
4. **Kalyani** traditional Indian folk songs.

282 ◆ *Clashing Forces*

an air of relief. The headmaster removed his spectacles, mopped his brow, and asked, "Now, come out with your opinion."

"Can't I give it tomorrow, sir?" Sekhar asked tentatively.

"No. I want it immediately—your frank opinion. Was it good?"

"No, sir. . . ." Sekhar replied.

"Oh! . . . Is there any use continuing my lessons?"

"Absolutely none, sir. . . ." Sekhar said with his voice trembling. He felt very unhappy that he could not speak more soothingly. Truth, he reflected, required as much strength to give as to receive.

All the way home he felt worried. He felt that his official life was not going to be smooth sailing hereafter. There were questions of increment and confirmation[5] and so on, all depending upon the headmaster's goodwill. All kinds of worries seemed to be in store for him. . . . Did not Harishchandra[6] lose his throne, wife, child, because he would speak nothing less than the absolute Truth whatever happened?

At home his wife served him with a sullen face. He knew she was still angry with him for his remark of the morning. Two casualties for today, Sekhar said to himself. If I practice it for a week, I don't think I shall have a single friend left.

He received a call from the headmaster in his classroom next day. He went up apprehensively.

"Your suggestion was useful. I have paid off the music master. No one would tell me the truth about my music all these days. Why such antics at my age! Thank you. By the way, what about those test papers?"

"You gave me ten days, sir, for correcting them."

"Oh, I've reconsidered it. I must positively have them here tomorrow. . . ." A hundred papers in a day! That meant all night's sitting up! "Give me a couple of days, sir. . . ."

"No. I must have them tomorrow morning. And remember, every paper must be thoroughly <u>scrutinized</u>."

"Yes, sir," Sekhar said, feeling that sitting up all night with a hundred test papers was a small price to pay for the luxury of practicing Truth.

---

5. **increment and confirmation** salary increase and job security.
6. **Harishchandra** (hə rish chen´ drə) legendary Hindu king who was the subject of many Indian stories. His name has come to symbolize truth and integrity.

scrutinized (skrōōt´ ən īzd´) v. examined carefully

R. K. Narayan

(1906–2001)

R. K. Narayan's hometown of Mysore in southern India probably served as the basis for the fictional town of Malgudi, which is the setting for much of his fiction. A native Tamil speaker, Narayan wrote in English, a second language to many Indians. In addition to novels and short stories, he wrote a nonfiction memoir, *My Days*, and a noted English translation of the ancient Indian epic, the *Mahabharata*.

Like the Sun ◆ 283

❾ Literary Analysis

Irony

- Remind students that irony is based on a contradiction between a character's expectations and reality.
- Ask students to consider how the headmaster expects Sekhar to respond, and how they know Sekhar will really respond.
- Then, ask students to pinpoint the irony of the headmaster's invitation to Sekhar.
  Answer: If the invitation had come on any other day, the headmaster would have received the approval he desired.

❿ Reading Strategy

Analyzing Causes and Effects

- Have students go back and skim the selection up to this point.
- Ask them to identify the positive and negative effects of Sekhar's truth telling thus far.
  Answer: Sekhar's actions have hurt and angered his wife, upset a colleague, made Sekhar uncomfortable, and hurt the headmaster's feelings. Some students may point out that Sekhar won't have to keep eating food he doesn't like, or listening to the headmaster play. Also, the headmaster won't keep wasting money on music lessons.

CUSTOMIZE INSTRUCTION FOR UNIVERSAL ACCESS

For Special Needs Students	For Gifted/Talented Students
Ask students to share possible responses to the headmaster's question that Sekhar might have made if he didn't have to tell the absolute truth. Then, help them understand the difference in impact between those statements and the one Sekhar made.	Ask students to write a dialogue between Sekhar and the headmaster in which Sekhar does not tell the absolute truth about the headmaster's playing. Encourage students to explore the likely outcomes of that conversation.

⑪ Critical Thinking

Compare and Contrast

- Point out that in the bracketed passage, Dickinson compares the truth to a light that's too bright to be pleasing.
- Then, ask students to compare this message about the truth with the one in "Like the Sun." Answer: Sekhar believes that the truth, like the sun, cannot be looked in the face "without blinking or being dazed." Both suggest that the truth can be both illuminating and hurtful.

Answers for p. 284

Review and Assess

1. Students will probably reply that hearing the absolute truth all day would be difficult and uncomfortable.

2. (a) Sekhar plans to tell the absolute truth for one day. (b) Sekhar realizes that it is difficult for people to hear the absolute truth. He says, "If I practice for a week, I don't think I shall have a single friend left."

3. (a) The headmaster gives him dishes of delicacies, sits him on a red silk carpet, and burns incense for him. (b) He wants Sekhar to praise his music.

4. (a) Sekhar won't have to eat the food he doesn't like or listen to the music from his headmaster. (b) His wife realizes he doesn't like the food just as his headmaster realizes he doesn't like the music. Presumably, they won't subject him to these things any more.

5. It is a luxury because it is rare and because it demands a heavy price.

6. Students should base their answers on the full range of Sekhar's experiences.

7. (a) She compares it to lightning, which can blind. (b) Both Dickinson and Narayan compare the truth to a source of light, which can be illuminating but also painful.

8. A slanted "truth" might be dangerous for people to hear if it gives them a distorted picture of their abilities.

284

Tell all the Truth but tell it slant—

Emily Dickinson

> Tell all the Truth but tell it slant—
> Success in Circuit lies
> Too bright for our infirm Delight
> The Truth's superb surprise
> 5 As Lightning to the Children eased
> With explanation kind
> The Truth must dazzle gradually
> Or every man be blind—

⑪

Review and Assess

Thinking About the Selections

1. **Respond:** Explain how you might feel about hearing only the truth from other people.

2. (a) **Recall:** What experiment does Sekhar set for himself at the beginning of the story? (b) **Generalize:** What is the general result of the experiment?

3. (a) **Analyze:** What steps does the headmaster take to ensure Sekhar's comfort before the music begins? (b) **Hypothesize:** What is his likely motive for these actions?

4. (a) **Draw Conclusions:** Are there any benefits to Sekhar's truth telling? (b) **Support:** Cite story details and logical reasons to support your conclusion.

5. **Interpret:** Narayan uses the phrase "luxury of practicing Truth" at the end of the story. How can truth be a luxury?

6. **Make a Judgment:** Was Sekhar brave or foolish to tell the truth all day? Explain.

7. (a) **Recall:** What comparison does Dickinson use to describe truth in "Tell all the Truth but tell it slant—"? (b) **Compare and Contrast:** How do Dickinson's images in discussing truth relate to the opening of Narayan's story?

8. **Evaluate:** What are the dangers of Dickinson's suggestion?

Emily Dickinson

(1830–1886)

As a child, Dickinson was energetic and enjoyed the tasks of daily life. Her childhood seemed normal in many respects. However, as an adult she became increasingly isolated. Although she traveled as a young woman to Boston, Washington, D.C., and Philadelphia to visit friends, she rarely left her small valley town as she grew older. In fact, during the last ten years of her life, she would venture only into her garden.

For more on Emily Dickinson, see pages 159 and 950.

✎ ASSESSMENT PRACTICE: Reading Comprehension

Stated and Implied Main Ideas   (For more practice, see Test Preparation Workbook, p. 19.)

For practice in identifying main ideas and their supporting details, use the following sample question:

Read the first two paragraphs of "Like the Sun" on p. 281.

What is the main idea of these paragraphs?

A Telling the truth is easy.
B Telling lies is easy.
C Telling the truth is like looking at the sun.

D Human beings are dazed when they look at the sun.

In order to select the best answer, suggest that students paraphrase the paragraphs using their own words. This strategy will help them differentiate between the central idea and supporting details. Point out that the author does not imply answer *A* or *B* in the passage. *D* is a supporting detail from the paragraphs. By process of elimination, students will find that *C* is the best answer.

Review and Assess

Literary Analysis

Irony

1. Using a diagram like the one here, give three examples of contradictions in "Like the Sun" that show **irony.**

```
┌──────────────────┐   ╔═══════════════╗   ┌──────────────────┐
│ Sekhar wants     │   ║ Clashes with  ║   │                  │
│ to be truthful.  │   ╚═══════════════╝   │                  │
└──────────────────┘   ◄┄┄┄┄┄┄┄┄┄┄┄┄┄►    └──────────────────┘
```

2. What is ironic about the headmaster's demand for Sekhar's "frank opinion" of his performance?
3. (a) What do you think Sekhar believes might happen as a result of his poor review of the headmaster's performance? (b) What is the headmaster's actual reaction? (c) How is this ironic?

Comparing Literary Works

4. (a) What message does each writer suggest about telling the truth? (b) How are the messages similar? How are they different?
5. Why do you think that both writers use the image of bright light to describe truth?
6. Do you agree with the ideas expressed in Dickinson's poem or with Sekhar's ideals? Defend your answer.

Reading Strategy

Identifying Causes and Effects

7. Identify two **effects** of Sekhar's decision to tell the truth about the headmaster's performance.
8. In describing the effects of his vow, Sekhar calls them "casualties." Why?
9. Explain why Sekhar believes that if he keeps telling the truth, he will not have a single friend left.

Extend Understanding

10. **Social Studies Connection:** (a) Why do you think politicians do not consider it wise to tell the whole truth? (b) What is the potential effect of that attitude?

Like the Sun / Tell all the Truth but tell it slant— ◆ 285

Quick Review

Irony is the literary technique that portrays the contradictions between appearance and reality that sometimes occur in real life.

A **cause** is an event or circumstance that makes something else happen.

An **effect** is the result that follows.

 Take It to the Net
www.phschool.com
Take the interactive self-test online to check your understanding of these selections.

 ENRICHMENT: Further Reading

Other Works by the Authors

Works by R. K. Narayan
A Horse and Two Goats
An Astrologer's Day and Other Stories
Malgudi Days
Malgudi Landscapes: The Best of R. K. Narayan

Works by Emily Dickinson
"After Great Pain a Formal Feeling Comes"

 Take It to the Net
Visit www.phschool.com for more information on the authors.

❶ Vocabulary Development

Word Analysis

1. Gratitude is the feeling of thankfulness you have when someone does you a favor.

2. An ingrate is someone who does not appreciate a favor.

3. Something done gratis is done as a favor.

4. Something that is gratuitous is beyond what is required, or thrown in as a favor.

Spelling Strategy

1. essential   3. residential
2. confidential

Fluency: Sentence Completion

1. essence   5. scrutinized
2. tempering   6. stupefied
3. Incessantly   7. ingratiating
4. shirked

❷ Grammar

1. meal, direct object; him, indirect object

2. fear, direct object

3. none

4. truth, direct object; headmaster, indirect object

5. attention, direct object; tests, indirect object

Writing Application

Possible response: I'd like to be able to tell everyone the truth, but I agree with Emily Dickinson that this is not advisable. I will try, however, to tell myself the whole truth at all times.

Integrate Language Skills

❶ Vocabulary Development Lesson

Word Analysis: Latin Root -gratis-

Knowing that the root -gratis- comes from a Latin word meaning "pleasing" or "a favor," you can determine that *ingratiating* means "trying to please." Use your knowledge of the root -gratis- to define these words:

1. gratitude   3. gratis
2. ingrate   4. gratuitous

Spelling Strategy

When adding the suffix -ial to most words ending in the letters nce, change nce to ntial. For example, *sequence* becomes *sequential*. One exception to this rule is the word *finance*, which becomes *financial*. Write the adjective forms of these words:

1. essence   2. confidence   3. residence

❷ Grammar Lesson

Direct and Indirect Objects

A **direct object** is a noun or pronoun that receives the action of a verb. It answers the question *what* or *whom* after an action verb.

An **indirect object** is a noun or pronoun that names the person or thing that something is given to or done for. It answers the question *to* or *for whom* or *to* or *for what* after an action verb.

> DO
> Sekhar told the *truth*. (Sekhar told *what?*)
>
> IO   DO
> Sekhar told *everyone* the truth. (Sekhar told the truth *to whom?*)

Verbs such as *am, is, are, was,* and *were* are linking verbs. They do not take direct objects.

WG *Prentice Hall Writing and Grammar Connection: Chapter 19, Section 3*

286 ◆ *Clashing Forces*

Fluency: Sentence Completion

On your paper, write the word from the vocabulary list on page 279 that best fits each numbered blank in the paragraph below.

The ___1___ of Sekhar's vow was to tell the truth. This one day at least, he was not in favor of ___2___ the truth to protect people's feelings. ___3___ throughout the day, he ___4___ no opportunity to tell his wife and colleagues exactly what he thought. As they ___5___ his behavior, many of his colleagues were ___6___. They expected Sekhar to be more ___7___.

Practice Copy each sentence below. Then, put a single line under each direct object and a double line under each indirect object. Some sentences may not have direct or indirect objects.

1. Sekhar's wife served him his meal.
2. He showed fear.
3. Sekhar was a dreaded music critic in town.
4. No one would tell the headmaster the truth.
5. Sekhar gave the tests his attention.

Writing Application Write a response to Emily Dickinson's poem. Use at least two direct and two indirect objects in your writing.

TEACHING RESOURCES

The following resources can be used to enrich or extend the instruction for pp. 286–287.

Vocabulary

📖 **Selection Support:** Build Vocabulary, p. 73

📖 **Vocabulary and Spelling Practice Book**
(Use this booklet for skills enrichment.) ▪

Grammar

📖 **Selection Support:** Build Grammar Skills, p. 74

WG **Writing and Grammar,** Platinum Level, pp. 425–429 ▪

📖 **Daily Language Practice Transparencies**

Writing

WG **Writing and Grammar,** Platinum Level, p. 181

💿 **Writing and Grammar iText CD-ROM**

📖 **Writing Models and Graphic Organizers on Transparencies,** p. 95

■ **BLOCK SCHEDULING:** Resources marked with this symbol provide varied instruction during 90-minute blocks.

❸ Writing Lesson

Literary Comparison

Both writers have something to say about telling the truth. In a literary analysis, explain how Sekhar's experiences support or contradict the ideas in Dickinson's poem.

Prewriting   Review the poem to determine the poet's main idea. In a single sentence, summarize her attitude about truth. Then, gather details from the story that you can use to explain the connection between the story and the poem.

Drafting   First, introduce both selections and state the link between them. Then, in the body of your essay, elaborate on the main idea you have presented. Support your analysis with details from each selection.

Revising   Review your draft to evaluate the support you have included. Wherever appropriate, add direct quotations from the literature to back up your ideas.

Model: Adding a Direct Quotation

"He realized that . . . the essence of human relationships consisted in tempering truth so that it might not shock."

Sekhar comes to the same conclusion that Dickinson does in her poem: that telling the complete truth is not a good idea if you want to have positive relationships with other people.

The writer may need to provide a transition between analysis and the quotation from the story.

 Prentice Hall Writing and Grammar Connection: Chapter 9, Section 2

❹ Extension Activities

Listening and Speaking Suppose that Sekhar has been fired for telling the truth. As his attorney, prepare and deliver an **oral argument** summing up why he has been unfairly treated and why he should be rehired. Follow these tips:

- Use a pleasant but firm delivery style.
- Structure your ideas in a coherent, logical way.
- Support general statements with details.

Practice your argument before presenting it to classmates.

Research and Technology Learn more about the music at the center of the story. Working with a small group, research the traditional Indian folk songs known as *Kalyani*. Use resources at the library or on the Internet. Then, give a **multimedia presentation** of your findings, complete with charts, posters, photos or drawings of instruments, and musical recordings. [**Group Activity**]

Take It to the Net   www.phschool.com
Go online for an additional research activity using the Internet.

Lesson Support for p. 287

❸ Writing Lesson

- Make sure students can support their summary of the poem with details from it.
- Suggest that students use the Comparison-and-Contrast organizer, p. 95 in **Writing Models and Graphic Organizers on Transparencies,** to record the details they gather.
- Use the Writing Lesson to guide students in developing a literary comparison.
- Use the rubric for Comparison-and-Contrast Compositions in **Performance Assessment and Portfolio Management,** p. 15, to evaluate students' work.

❹ Research and Technology

- Encourage the groups to brainstorm for a list of terms to use in key-word searches, such as *Kalyani, Indian music,* and *India.*
- Suggest that students try to find recordings of Kalyani. They might download recordings from the Internet or check the music collection in the library.
- Ask students to present their research to the class, including illustrations of instruments and tapes of the music.

CUSTOMIZE INSTRUCTION
For Universal Access

To address different learning styles, use the activities suggested in the **Extension Activities** booklet, p. 19.

- For Verbal/Linguistic, Visual/Spatial, and Interpersonal Learners, use Activity 5.
- For Verbal/Linguistic and Logical/ Mathematical Learners, use Activity 6.
- For Verbal/Linguistic, Interpersonal, and Bodily/Kinesthetic Learners, use Activity 7.

ASSESSMENT RESOURCES

The following resources can be used to assess students' knowledge and skills.

Selection Assessment

- **Formal Assessment,** pp. 63–65
- **Open Book Test,** pp. 54–57
- **Got It! Assessment Videotapes,** Tape 2
- **Test Bank Software**

Take It to the Net
Visit www.phschool.com for self-tests and additional questions on the selections.

Writing Rubric

- **Performance Assess. and Portfolio Mgmt.,** p. 15

PRENTICE HALL **ASSESSMENT** *SYSTEM*

- **Workbook**
- **Skill Book**
- **Transparencies**
- **CD-ROM**

Hearts and Hands ✦ The Fish

Lesson Objectives

1. **To analyze and respond to literary elements**
   - Literary Analysis: Surprise Ending
   - Comparing Literary Works

2. **To read, comprehend, analyze, and critique a short story and a poem**
   - Reading Strategy: Predicting Outcomes
   - Reading Check questions
   - Review and Assess questions
   - Assessment Practice (ATE)

3. **To develop word analysis skills, fluency, and systematic vocabulary**
   - Vocabulary Development Lesson: Latin Prefix: *counter-*

4. **To understand and apply written and oral language conventions**
   - Spelling Strategy
   - Grammar Lesson: Compound Predicates

5. **To understand and apply appropriate writing and research strategies**
   - Writing Lesson: Letter to the Editor
   - Extension Activity: American Prisons Chart

6. **To understand and apply listening and speaking strategies**
   - Extension Activity: Sound-Effects Tape

STEP-BY-STEP TEACHING GUIDE	PACING GUIDE
PRETEACH	
Motivate Students and Provide Background	
Use the Motivation activity (ATE p. 288)	5 min.
Read and discuss the Preview material and Background information (SE/ATE p. 288) **A**	5 min.
Introduce the Concepts	
Introduce the Literary Analysis and Reading Strategy (SE/ATE p. 289) **A**	10 min.
Pronounce the vocabulary words and read their definitions (SE p. 289)	5 min.
TEACH	
Monitor Comprehension	
Informally monitor comprehension by circulating while students read independently or in groups **A**	10 min.
Monitor students' comprehension with the Reading Check notes (SE/ATE pp. 291, 293)	as students read
Develop vocabulary with Vocabulary notes (SE pp. 290, 291, 292, 293, 294; ATE p. 291)	as students read
Develop Understanding	
Develop students' understanding of surprise endings with Literary Analysis annotations (ATE pp. 289, 292) **A**	5 min.
Develop students' understanding of predicting events with Reading Strategy annotations (SE p. 291; ATE pp. 289, 291, 293)	5 min.
ASSESS	
Assess Mastery	
Assess students' mastery of the Reading Strategy and Literary Analysis by having them answer the Review and Assess questions (SE/ATE p. 295)	15 min.
Use one or more of the print and media Assessment Resources (ATE p. 297) **A**	up to 50 min.
EXTEND	
Apply Understanding	
Have students complete the Vocabulary Development Lesson and the Grammar Lesson (SE p. 296) **A**	20 min.
Apply students' knowledge of elaboration using the Writing Lesson (SE/ATE p. 297) **A**	45 min.
Apply students' understanding of the selection using one or more of the Extension Activities (SE p. 297)	20–90 min.

 ACCELERATED INSTRUCTION:
Use the strategies and activities identified with an **A**.

UNIVERSAL ACCESS
● = Below Level Students
▲ = On-Level Students
■ = Above Level Students

Time and Resource Manager

Reading Level: Easy/Easy
Average Number of Instructional Days: 3

RESOURCES

PRINT 📖	TRANSPARENCIES	TECHNOLOGY 💿 🎧 📼
• **Beyond Literature,** Community Connection: Random Acts of Kindness, p. 20 ▲ ■		• **Interest Grabber Video,** Tape 2 ● ▲ ■
• **Selection Support Workbook:** ● ▲ ■ Literary Analysis, p. 80 Reading Strategy, p. 79 Build Vocabulary, p. 77	• **Literary Analysis and Reading Transparencies,** pp. 39 and 40 ● ▲ ■	
		• **Listening to Literature** ● ▲ ■ Audiocassettes, Sides 9, 10 Audio CDs, CD 6
• **Literatura en español** ● ▲ • **Literary Analysis for Enrichment** ■		
• **Formal Assessment:** Selection Test, pp. 66–68 ● ▲ ■ • **Open Book Test,** pp. 58–60 ● ▲ ■ • **Performance Assessment and Portfolio Management,** p. 11 ● ▲ ■ • **PRENTICE HALL ASSESSMENT SYSTEM** ● ▲ ■	• **PRENTICE HALL ASSESSMENT SYSTEM** ● ▲ ■ Skills Practice Answers and Explanations on Transparencies	• **Test Bank Software** ● ▲ ■ • **Got It! Assessment Videotapes,** Tape 2 ● ▲
• **Selection Support Workbook:** ● ▲ ■ Build Grammar Skills, p. 78 • **Writing and Grammar,** Platinum Level ● ▲ ■ • **Extension Activities,** p. 20 ● ▲ ■	• **Daily Language Practice Transparencies** ● ▲ • **Writing Models and Graphic Organizers on Transparencies,** p. 75 ● ▲ ■	• **Writing and Grammar iText CD-ROM** ● ▲ ■ 💻 *Take It to the Net* www.phschool.com

BLOCK SCHEDULING: Use one 90-minute class period to preteach the selection and have students read it. Use a second 90-minute class period to assess students' mastery of skills and have them complete one of the Extension Activities.

Motivation

Show a video of magicians, such as Siegfried and Roy or David Copperfield, performing an illusion in which something or someone is exchanged for another. (If you have any amateur magicians in your class, invite them to perform an illusion.) Lead students to see that an illusion is like a surprise ending. When the curtain is whisked away, you see a person where a tiger used to be, or a quarter appears from behind your ear. Tell students that the selections they are about to read are like magic tricks. When the writers "whisk away the curtain" to reveal the ending, readers may not see what they had expected.

Interest Grabber Video

As an alternative, play "Through Different Eyes" on Tape 2 to engage student interest.

❶ Background

History

O. Henry was charged with embezzlement in 1896 from First National Bank, where he had been a teller two years earlier. The charges, which were for misappropriations of funds on three dates, were suspicious. The last date was almost a year after O. Henry had resigned from the bank. O. Henry denied the charges, but fled to Honduras rather than face the accusations in court. When he returned a year later to visit his sick wife, he was arrested, convicted of embezzlement, and sentenced to the Ohio State Penitentiary in Columbus.

Comparing Literary Works

Prepare to Read

Hearts and Hands ◆ The Fish

Take It to the Net

Visit www.phschool.com for interactive activities and instruction related to these selections, including
- background
- graphic organizers
- literary elements
- reading strategies

Preview

Connecting to the Literature

You may have helped someone out of an embarrassing or a difficult situation. You probably knew just how the other person felt, and you said or did something that made the other person feel better. As you read these selections, think about how showing compassion for others can give you a special feeling yourself.

❶ Background

In "Hearts and Hands," O. Henry, the author, makes us feel sympathy for a prisoner—perhaps because he had been one himself. Before he became a writer, O. Henry, whose real name was William Sydney Porter, was accused of embezzling funds from a bank in which he worked. He spent three years in jail. "Hearts and Hands" may have been inspired by his own journey to prison.

288 ◆ Clashing Forces

TEACHING RESOURCES

The following resources can be used to enrich or extend the instruction for pp. 288–289.

Interest Grabber Video, Tape 2

Background
📝 **Beyond Literature,** p. 20

 Take It to the Net
Visit www.phschool.com for background and hotlinks for the selections.

Literary Analysis
📝 **Selection Support:** Literary Analysis, p. 80

📄 **Literary Analysis and Reading Transparencies,** Surface Ending, p. 40

Reading
📄 **Literary Analysis and Reading Transparencies,** Predicting Outcomes, p. 39

BLOCK SCHEDULING: Resources marked with this symbol provide varied instruction during 90-minute blocks.

❷ Literary Analysis

Surprise Ending

Sometimes you can predict how a fictional piece will end. "Hearts and Hands" and "The Fish" make predicting a challenge because each has a **surprise ending**—a twist at the end that most readers do not expect. If you read carefully, however, you can pick up clues that the author has planted to help you predict the final outcome. This dialogue from "Hearts and Hands" holds a clue to the story's ending:

> "Will we see you again soon in Washington?" asked the girl.
> "Not soon, I think," said Easton. "My butterfly days are over, I fear."

Notice details that hint at unexpected but logical outcomes.

Comparing Literary Works

You are most likely to come across surprise endings in **fiction**—works of prose about imaginary characters and events. Surprise endings can also be found in **narrative poems**—stories told in verse. "The Fish," one of the selections you are about to read, is a narrative poem; "Hearts and Hands," the other piece, is a short story. As you read, compare and contrast the ways in which the two writers present clues about the outcome and reveal the surprise ending to readers. Consider how the differences relate to the form in which the two pieces are written.

❸ Reading Strategy

Predicting Outcomes

To get the most out of a work—especially one with a surprise ending—**predict**, or make educated guesses about, its outcome. Base your predictions on your own experiences, and consider details about the characters, the setting, and the situation. As you read each selection, list your predictions in a chart like the one here. When you come across details that change your expectations, revise your predictions.

Vocabulary Development

influx (in´ fluks´) *n.* a coming in (p. 290)

forestalled (fôr stôld´) *v.* prevented by acting ahead of time (p. 291)

counterfeiting (koun´ ər fit´ iŋ) *n.* making imitation money to pass off as real money (p. 291)

sidled (sīd´ əld) *v.* moved sideways (p. 292)

venerable (ven´ ər ə bəl) *adj.* worthy of respect or reverence because of age, character, or position (p. 293)

infested (in fest´ id) *v.* overrun (p. 293)

sullen (sul´ ən) *adj.* gloomy; sad (p. 294)

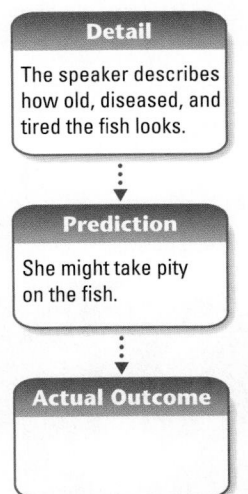

Detail

The speaker describes how old, diseased, and tired the fish looks.

Prediction

She might take pity on the fish.

Actual Outcome

---

❷ Literary Analysis

Surprise Ending

- Tell students that as they read the selections, they should look for clues that hint at a *surprise ending*, or an outcome that most readers do not expect.

- Discuss the example of a clue from "Hearts and Hands." Ask students what they think the clue is and what it might indicate. Record their ideas on the board.

- After students read the story, have them judge the accuracy of their interpretation of the clue.

- While reading the selections as a class, fill in the Surprise Ending transparency in **Literary Analysis and Reading Transparencies,** p. 40.

❸ Reading Strategy

Predicting Outcomes

- Encourage students to be active readers by making *predictions*—educated guesses based on story details and personal experience—about a story's outcome as they read.

- Remind students that their predictions may change as they read and learn new information. Revising predictions is part of the reading process.

- Read the selections as a class, pausing occasionally so that students can jot down or revise their predictions.

Vocabulary Development

- Pronounce each vocabulary word for students, and read the definitions as a class. Have students identify any words with which they are already familiar.

CUSTOMIZE INSTRUCTION FOR UNIVERSAL ACCESS

For Less Proficient Readers	For English Learners	For Advanced Readers
Have students pause frequently to review important details and visualize the action of the story. Ask students to make predictions based on their reviews and visualizations, and then guide them to identify details that support their predictions.	If students have trouble making predictions, it may be because they encounter unfamiliar words in the clues. Encourage students to make a list of new words and look up their definitions.	Allow students to read the selections independently while filling in their own prediction charts. Then, in groups, have them discuss the selections. Ask them to indicate the point at which they could accurately predict the outcome of the story and to identify the details that clued them into the ending.

 E-Teach

Visit E-Teach at www.phschool.com for teachers' essays on how to teach, with questions and answers.

CUSTOMIZE INSTRUCTION
For Interpersonal Learners

In small groups, have students put a different twist on O. Henry's story by retelling it with a new and different ending. Have each group act out its alternative ending, and then compare and contrast the groups' ideas.

❶ About the Selection

"Hearts and Hands" tells the story of a brief encounter among three characters on a train. Through dialogue, O. Henry hints at a past conflict between one young man and the young woman. At the end of the story, we realize that the real conflict, which is not between the young man and the young woman, is very much in the present, and that what characters say doesn't always reveal who they are.

❶ Hearts and Hands

O. Henry

At Denver there was an influx of passengers into the coaches on the eastbound B. & M. express. In one coach there sat a very pretty young woman dressed in elegant taste and surrounded by all the luxurious comforts of an experienced traveler. Among the newcomers were two young men, one of handsome presence with a bold, frank countenance and manner; the other a ruffled, glum-faced person, heavily built and roughly dressed. The two were handcuffed together.

As they passed down the aisle of the coach the only vacant seat offered was a reversed one facing the attractive young woman. Here the linked couple seated themselves. The young woman's glance fell upon them with a distant, swift disinterest; then with a lovely smile brightening her countenance and a

influx (in′ fluks′) *n.* a coming in

290 ◆ *Clashing Forces*

TEACHING RESOURCES

The following resources can be used to enrich or extend the instruction for pp. 290–294.

Literary Analysis

📖 **Writing Models and Graphic Organizers on Transparencies,** p. 75 ▪

Reading

📖 **Selection Support:** Reading Strategy, p. 79; Build Vocabulary, p. 77

🎧 **Listening to Literature Audiocassettes,** Sides 9, 10 ▪

💿 **Listening to Literature Audio CDs,** CD 6 ▪

▪ **BLOCK SCHEDULING:** Resources marked with this symbol provide varied instruction during 90-minute blocks.

tender pink tingeing her rounded cheeks, she held out a little gray-gloved hand. When she spoke her voice, full, sweet, and deliberate, proclaimed that its owner was accustomed to speak and be heard.

"Well, Mr. Easton, if you *will* make me speak first, I suppose I must. Don't you ever recognize old friends when you meet them in the West?"

The younger man roused himself sharply at the sound of her voice, seemed to struggle with a slight embarrassment which he threw off instantly, and then clasped her fingers with his left hand.

"It's Miss Fairchild," he said, with a smile. "I'll ask you to excuse the other hand; it's otherwise engaged just at present."

He slightly raised his right hand, bound at the wrist by the shining "bracelet" to the left one of his companion. The glad look in the girl's eyes slowly changed to a bewildered horror. The glow faded from her cheeks. Her lips parted in a vague, relaxing distress. Easton, with a little laugh, as if amused, was about to speak again when the other forestalled him. The glum-faced man had been watching the girl's countenance with veiled glances from his keen, shrewd eyes.

"You'll excuse me for speaking, miss, but I see you're acquainted with the marshal here. If you'll ask him to speak a word for me when we get to the pen he'll do it, and it'll make things easier for me there. He's taking me to Leavenworth prison. It's seven years for counterfeiting."

"Oh!" said the girl, with a deep breath and returning color. "So that is what you are doing out here? A marshal!"

"My dear Miss Fairchild," said Easton, calmly, "I had to do something. Money has a way of taking wings unto itself, and you know it takes money to keep step with our crowd in Washington. I saw this opening in the West, and—well, a marshalship isn't quite as high a position as that of ambassador, but—"

"The ambassador," said the girl, warmly, "doesn't call any more. He needn't ever have done so. You ought to know that. And so now you are one of these dashing Western heroes, and you ride and shoot and go into all kinds of dangers. That's different from the Washington life. You have been missed from the old crowd."

The girl's eyes, fascinated, went back, widening a little, to rest upon the glittering handcuffs.

"Don't you worry about them, miss," said the other man. "All marshals handcuff themselves to their prisoners to keep them from getting away. Mr. Easton knows his business."

"Will we see you again soon in Washington?" asked the girl.

"Not soon, I think," said Easton. "My butterfly days are over, I fear."

"I love the West," said the girl irrelevantly. Her eyes were shining softly. She looked away out the car window. She began to speak truly and simply, without the gloss of style and manner: "Mamma and I spent the summer in Denver. She went home a week ago because father was slightly ill. I could live and be happy in the West. I think the air here agrees with me. Money isn't everything. But people always misunderstand things and remain stupid—"

Reading Strategy
Predicting Outcomes
What do you predict is the reason that Mr. Easton feels embarrassed?

forestalled (fôr stôld´) *v.* prevented by acting ahead of time

counterfeiting (kount´ ər fit´ iŋ) *n.* making imitation money to pass off as real money

4 ✓ Reading Check
Why are the men handcuffed together?

Hearts and Hands ◆ 291

- Read aloud the bracketed passage. Have students pay attention to details that offer hints about the characters.

- Ask students the Reading Strategy question on p. 291: What do you predict is the reason that Mr. Easton feels embarrassed? Possible response: Easton's embarrassment is a clue that there is something he doesn't want the young woman to know. Students' predictions can springboard from this inference.

- Then, read aloud the last sentence of the bracketed passage. Ask students to predict what the "glum-faced man" will say. Possible Response: Some students may guess that the man is the prisoner since he's described as "glum-faced." If students pick up on the last few words—*keen, shrewd eyes*—they may guess that the man is not what he seems.

3 Vocabulary Development

The Latin Prefix *counter-*

- Draw students' attention to the vocabulary word *counterfeiting* and its definition, "making imitation money to pass off as real money."

- Explain that the prefix *counter-* means "in opposition."

- Ask students to explain how counterfeit money is "in opposition" to real money. Answer: Counterfeit money is in opposition to what it pretends to be.

4 ✓ Reading Check

Answer: The men are handcuffed together because one is a marshal taking a criminal to prison. The marshal does not want the prisoner to get away.

CUSTOMIZE INSTRUCTION FOR UNIVERSAL ACCESS

For Special Needs Students	For Gifted/Talented Students
Students may have trouble understanding the element of surprise in the ending. Discuss the last three paragraphs of the story with students. Ask students what the last sentence means, and encourage them to reenter the text to find out which man had his right hand in the handcuff.	Have students convert the short story into a play. Have them rewrite the text in script format, conveying all information through dialogue, rather than a narrator. Remind them that many of the details of the story are actions that can be performed rather than spoken. Have students perform their play for the class. Discuss afterwards whether the story was easier to understand when reading it or seeing it performed.

5 Literary Analysis

Surprise Ending

- Read aloud the bracketed passage. Ask students to identify the marshal and the prisoner.
  Answer: Easton is the prisoner; the other man is the marshal.

- Then, have students review the story and identify other clues that Easton is a prisoner and not a marshal.
  Possible responses: When Easton first meets Miss Fairchild he is embarrassed; his explanation of the handcuffs is interrupted by the other man; Easton indicates that he will not return to Washington by saying "My butterfly days are over, I fear"; Easton says, "I must go on to Leavenworth."

Answers for p. 292

Review and Assess

1. Encourage students to include in their reasons a response to Mr. Easton's character based on details in the story.

2. **(a)** The two men are handcuffed together. **(b)** Easton, who is well dressed and handsome, seems friendly, open, and happy. The marshal is described as "a ruffled, glum-faced person, heavily built and roughly dressed." He seems serious and unhappy.

3. **(a)** They knew each other socially in Washington. **(b)** The conversation suggests that at one time Easton was interested in Miss Fairchild romantically, but that he was without money and status and thought she preferred an ambassador (who probably had money).

4. **(a)** The glum-faced man tells Miss Fairchild that he is the prisoner. **(b)** The final exchange reveals that the glum-faced man is the marshal and that Mr. Easton is the prisoner.

5. **(a)** The marshal doesn't want to humiliate Easton in front of an old friend. **(b)** The marshal has a big heart that allows him to understand what might be in Easton's heart. This knowledge leads him to conceal the real reason that their hands are cuffed together. **(c)** Many students will say they admire the marshal because he respects

---

"Say, Mr. Marshal," growled the glum-faced man. "This isn't quite fair. Haven't had a smoke all day. Haven't you talked long enough? Take me in the smoker now, won't you? I'm half dead for a pipe."

The bound travelers rose to their feet, Easton with the same slow smile on his face.

"I can't deny a petition for tobacco," he said lightly. "It's the one friend of the unfortunate. Goodbye, Miss Fairchild. Duty calls, you know." He held out his hand for a farewell.

"It's too bad you are not going East," she said, reclothing herself with manner and style. "But you must go on to Leavenworth, I suppose?"

"Yes," said Easton. "I must go on to Leavenworth."

The two men **sidled** down the aisle into the smoker.

The two passengers in a seat nearby had heard most of the conversation. Said one of them: "That marshal's a good sort of chap. Some of these Western fellows are all right."

"Pretty young to hold an office like that, isn't he?" asked the other.

5 "Young!" exclaimed the first speaker, "why—Oh! didn't you catch on? Say—did you ever know an officer to handcuff a prisoner to his *right* hand?"

sidled (sĭd′ əld) v. moved sideways

Review and Assess

Thinking About the Selection

1. **Respond:** Would you have bailed Mr. Easton out of his uncomfortable situation? Why or why not?

2. **(a) Recall:** Why are the two men sitting together? **(b) Compare and Contrast:** In what ways do the two men look different and act differently from each other?

3. **(a) Recall:** Under what circumstances did Mr. Easton and Miss Fairchild know each other in the past? **(b) Draw Conclusions:** What do the details of their conversation suggest was the nature of their relationship?

4. **(a) Recall:** Why does Miss Fairchild think the glum-faced man is the prisoner? **(b) Connect:** What does the final exchange between the two other passengers reveal about the actual identities of the two men?

5. **(a) Speculate:** Why do you think the marshal deceives Miss Fairchild? **(b) Analyze:** How does the title of the story help explain his actions? **(c) Evaluate:** Based on his behavior, do you admire the marshal? Explain.

6. **Evaluate:** Should Mr. Easton have revealed the truth? Why or why not?

O. Henry

(1862–1910)

O. Henry, born William Sydney Porter in Greensboro, North Carolina, moved to Texas when he was twenty. While working as a bank teller, he was accused and convicted of embezzling funds. In prison, he took up writing, publishing short stories under his now-famous pen name. O. Henry's tales are noted for their surprise endings and their sympathetic look at human nature. His stories have remained so popular that the annual prizes for best American short stories are called the O. Henry Awards.

Easton's feelings and allows him to keep his dignity in front of Miss Fairchild.

6. Students might say that hiding the truth was a compassionate thing to do.

✹ ENRICHMENT: Writing Connection

A Very Prolific Writer

O. Henry moved to New York City after his release from prison and began his writing career. After living in New York for a while, he became fascinated by the street life there. The streets of New York City provide the setting for many of his later works.

O. Henry became one of America's most popular writers during the final ten years of his life. During that time he published over 500 short stories in dozens of periodicals. That's about one story a week!

The Fish

Elizabeth Bishop

I caught a tremendous fish
and held him beside the boat
half out of water, with my hook
fast in a corner of his mouth.
5   He didn't fight.
He hadn't fought at all.
He hung a grunting weight,
battered and <u>venerable</u>
and homely. Here and there
10   his brown skin hung in strips
like ancient wallpaper,
and its pattern of darker brown
was like wallpaper:
shapes like full-blown roses
15   stained and lost through age.
He was speckled with barnacles,
fine rosettes of lime,
and <u>infested</u>
with tiny white sea-lice,
20   and underneath two or three
rags of green weed hung down.
While his gills were breathing in
the terrible oxygen
—the frightening gills,
25   fresh and crisp with blood,
that can cut so badly—
I thought of the coarse white flesh
packed in like feathers,
the big bones and the little bones,
30   the dramatic reds and blacks
of his shiny entrails,
and the pink swim-bladder[1]
like a big peony.
I looked into his eyes
35   which were far larger than mine
but shallower, and yellowed,
the irises backed and packed
with tarnished tinfoil
seen through the lenses
40   of old scratched isinglass.[2]
They shifted a little, but not
to return my stare.
—It was more like the tipping
of an object toward the light.

1. **swim-bladder** gas-filled sac that keeps a fish from sinking.
2. **isinglass** (ī′zin glas′) *n.* semitransparent substance obtained from fish bladders and sometimes used for windows.

venerable (ven′ ər ə bəl) *adj.* worthy of respect or reverence because of age, character, or position

infested (in fest′ id) *v.* overrun

✔ Reading Check

What sort of fight does the fish put up?

The Fish ◆ 293

❻ About the Selection

At the opening of this poem, the conflict seems to be resolved—the fish is caught. As the poem continues, the speaker reveals an internal conflict that leads to an outcome most readers may not expect.

❼ Reading Strategy

Predicting Outcomes

• Read aloud the bracketed passage.

• Based on these lines, ask students to predict what the speaker will do with the fish. Encourage students to support their ideas with details from the text.
  Possible responses: The speaker is thinking about filleting the fish. Some students may interpret this passage as the speaker's reflection on the fish's living organs, which will lead to feeling compassion for the fish.

• Remind students to take the time to revise their predictions when necessary as they continue to read the poem.

▶ Monitor Progress If students are having trouble making predictions, suggest that they fold a piece of paper in half lengthwise to make two columns. Then, have them reread each line of the poem to see whether it contains a clue. If it does, have them write it in the first column. As they finish reading, have them analyze each clue again and put a check mark in the second column if it supported their prediction.

❽ ✔ Reading Check

Answer: The fish does not put up a fight at all.

CUSTOMIZE INSTRUCTION FOR UNIVERSAL ACCESS

For Special Needs Students	For Advanced Readers
Help students make connections between "Hearts and Hands" and "The Fish." On the chalkboard, draw one word web for the marshal and another for the speaker in "The Fish." Then, have students brainstorm for a list of the main qualities of each character, and record these in the webs. Finally, have students examine the completed webs, leading them to see that both characters demonstrate unexpected kindness and compassion.	Have students compare the marshal in "Hearts and Hands" with the speaker in "The Fish." They should discuss how the characters are similar and how they are different. Encourage them to speculate about what the characters would do if they switched places—what would the marshal do with the fish, and how would the speaker in "The Fish" treat Mr. Easton?

❾ ▶ Critical Viewing

Answer: Students may say that the thoughtful nature of the poem led them to picture the sense of quiet that the photograph portrays. Others may have imagined a more modern boat and a lake crowded with fishermen.

❿ Critical Thinking

Interpret

• Have students read the bracketed passage.

• Then, ask students what the speaker means by "victory filled up the little boat." Who has achieved victory—the speaker or the fish?

Answer: Students may say the fish has achieved victory because it has so many "medals" and battle scars. Others may say that the speaker feels victorious after catching such a venerable fish.

Answers for p. 294

Review and Assess

1. Some students may feel that, like the speaker, they would have felt admiration for the fish and released it. Others may say they would not release it, feeling that the fish is an even more valuable "prize" because it has eluded so many other anglers.

2. **(a)** The speaker finds four or five pieces of fish line and five hooks in the fish's jaw. **(b)** The discovery indicates that the fish had almost been caught four or five times, but had gotten away.

3. **(a)** In the end, the speaker lets the fish go. **(b)** The fact that the fish has successfully survived so many battles motivates the speaker to let him go. The speaker doesn't feel it would be fair to end the fish's life by keeping it.

4. A person who shows compassion is strong enough not to have to prove his or her strength.

---

45   I admired his <u>sullen</u> face,
the mechanism of his jaw,
and then I saw
that from his lower lip
—if you could call it a lip—
50   grim, wet, and weaponlike,
hung five old pieces of fish-line,
or four and a wire leader
with the swivel still attached,
with all their five big hooks
55   grown firmly in his mouth.
A green line, frayed at the end
where he broke it, two heavier lines
and a fine black thread
still crimped from the strain and snap
60   when it broke and he got away.
Like medals with their ribbons
frayed and wavering,
a five-haired beard of wisdom
trailing from his aching jaw.
❿ 65   I stared and stared
and victory filled up
the little rented boat,
from the pool of bilge[3]
where oil had spread a rainbow
70   around the rusted engine
to the bailer rusted orange,
the sun-cracked thwarts,[4]
the oarlocks on their strings,
the gunnels[5]—until everything
75   was rainbow, rainbow, rainbow!
And I let the fish go.

sullen (sul´ ən) *adj.* gloomy; sad

❾ ▲ Critical Viewing Compare this image with the mental image you formed while reading the poem. **[Compare and Contrast]**

---

3. **bilge** (bilj) *n.* dirty water in the bottom of a boat.
4. **thwarts** (thwôrts) *n.* rowers' seats lying across a boat.
5. **gunnels** (gun´ əlz) *n.* upper edges of the sides of a boat.

Review and Assess

Thinking About the Selection

1. **Respond:** Would you have let the fish go? Explain.

2. **(a) Recall:** What does the speaker find in the fish's lower lip?
   (b) Infer: What does this discovery indicate about the fish?

3. **(a) Recall:** What does the speaker do in the end?
   (b) Analyze: What seems to motivate the speaker's actions?

4. **Interpret:** Explain how compassion can be a sign of strength.

Elizabeth Bishop

(1911–1979)

Born and raised in Massachusetts, Elizabeth Bishop loved traveling and spent many years living in Brazil. In 1945, Bishop won a poetry contest, and this led to the publication of her first volume of poetry, *North and South*, which included "The Fish." Noted for her dramatic language and powerful images, Bishop won virtually every poetry prize in the United States at least once, including a Pulitzer Prize in 1956.

ASSESSMENT PRACTICE: Reading Comprehension

Stated and Implied Main Ideas   **(For more practice, see Test Preparation Workbook, p. 20.)**

Students will encounter questions on some tests that will test their ability to find the main idea of a selection and determine the details that best support the main idea. Give students the following sample test question for practice based on the first paragraph of "Hearts and Hands" on p. 290.

What is the main idea of this paragraph?

   A The woman is an experienced traveler.
   B The train is crowded.
   C The woman is wealthy.
   D The travelers have little in common.

Explain to students that answers *A, B,* and *C* are details from the paragraph, but *D* expresses the implied main idea—the handcuffed men have very little in common with a wealthy young woman.

Review and Assess

Literary Analysis

Surprise Ending

1. (a) What are you led to expect will happen between Mr. Easton and Miss Fairchild now that they have met again? (b) How does the ending change your thinking?

2. Write the **surprise ending** of "Hearts and Hands" in the diagram. Then, note three clues to the ending.

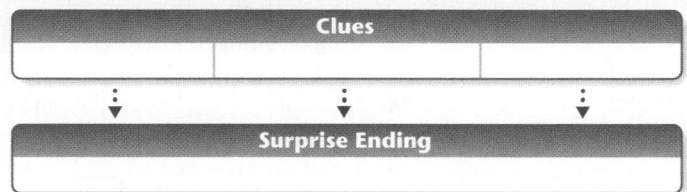

Clues

Surprise Ending

3. (a) At what point did you first suspect that the speaker in "The Fish" would release the catch? (b) What was your clue?

Comparing Literary Works

4. (a) Use the chart in question 2 to identify clues to the surprise ending in "The Fish." (b) Which selection has the most obvious clues? Explain.

5. How does an act of compassion contribute to the surprise ending in each selection?

Reading Strategy

Predicting Outcomes

6. In the opening of "Hearts and Hands," what do you **predict** the young woman will do after she smiles at the two men? Why?

7. In "Hearts and Hands," which details suggest that Mr. Easton and the other man are not who they say they are?

8. How do lines 34 and 45 help you predict the outcome of "The Fish"?

Extend Understanding

9. **Career Connection:** Is compassion needed by a person who works in law enforcement, as "Hearts and Hands" suggests? Explain.

Quick Review

A **surprise ending** is a final twist that is not expected by most readers.

When you **predict outcomes,** you make educated guesses about what will happen based on your own experience and the details provided.

Take It to the Net
www.phschool.com
Take the interactive self-test online to check your understanding of these selections.

Hearts and Hands / The Fish ◆ 295

Answers for p. 295

Review and Assess

1. **(a)** It seems as if Mr. Easton and Miss Fairchild may renew their relationship. **(b)** The ending reveals that Mr. Easton is going to prison and won't be able to have a relationship with Miss Fairchild.

2. Surprise Ending: Mr. Easton is the prisoner, and the other man is the marshal.
Clues: Mr. Easton's embarrassment, his comment that money takes wing, and his easy acceptance of the "prisoner's" request to leave the car.

3. **(a)** Students should explain how details from the poem led to their realization that the speaker would release the fish.
(b) Possible response: The clue was when the speaker looked into the fish's eyes.

4. **(a)** Clues: The speaker looks into the fish's eyes; the speaker admires the fish's face; the speaker stares at the hooks lodged in the fish's jaw.
(b) The poem has the more obvious clues because as soon as the speaker starts seeing the fish as a being, it becomes more and more clear that the speaker will let the fish go.

5. In "Hearts and Hands," the marshal's compassion leads him to conceal Easton's true identity. In "The Fish," the speaker's compassion motivates her to release the fish.

6. The woman's smile helps you predict that she knows one of the men.

7. Mr. Easton's embarrassment and his willingness to do what the other man wants him to do suggest that the men are not who they seem to be.

8. Lines 34 and 45 reveal that the speaker has begun to view the fish as a sentient being.

9. Many students will say that compassion is necessary for a balanced sense of justice; others may feel that it would prevent someone from punishing the guilty.

❶ Vocabulary Development

Word Analysis

1. Counterclockwise is the opposite direction from the way the hands on a clock move.

2. Counterproductive is the opposite of productive, or constructive, action.

3. A counterbalance is a weight or force placed in opposition so that it balances another weight.

4. Counterpoint is something (often a melody or an argument) set up to contrast or be opposite to another thing.

Spelling Strategy

1. coaches   4. addresses
2. taxes   5. waltzes
3. dashes   6. lenses

Fluency: Sentence Completions

1. infested   5. influx
2. venerable   6. sullen
3. forestalled   7. counterfeiting
4. sidled

❷ Grammar

1. I caught a fish (and) held him in the boat.

2. He did not fight at all (but) instead hung like a weight.

3. He either had barnacles on him (or) was infested with white lice.

4. His eyes seemed large (but) were shallow and yellow.

5. I stared at the fish, unhooked him, (and) released him back into the water.

Writing Application

Possible responses:

1. The fisherman baited his line and cast it into the water.

2. The fish grabbed at the bait and became caught on the hook.

Integrate Language Skills

❶ Vocabulary Development Lesson

Word Analysis: Latin Prefix *counter-*

Counterfeiting contains the Latin prefix *counter-*, which means "in opposition." *Counterfeiting* means "making something opposite of what it seems, or an imitation made to deceive."

With this knowledge, explain how *opposite* contributes to the meaning of each of the following words:

1. counterclockwise   3. counterbalance
2. counterproductive   4. counterpoint

Spelling Strategy

To form the plural of a noun ending in *ch, s, sh, x,* or *z,* you usually add *-es.* On your paper, write the plurals of these nouns.

1. coach   3. dash   5. waltz
2. tax   4. address   6. lens

Fluency: Sentence Completions

On your paper, complete each sentence with a word from the vocabulary list on page 289. Use each word only once.

1. The rotten apple was ___?___ with worms.
2. In his village, the old chief was known as a ___?___ man.
3. By apologizing, my brother ___?___ an argument with his friend.
4. The crab ___?___ across the sand toward the water.
5. The doctor has seen an ___?___ of patients who have the flu.
6. The glum-faced newcomer remained ___?___.
7. O. Henry's crime was embezzlement, not ___?___.

❷ Grammar Lesson

Compound Predicates

In a sentence, the predicate tells the action or condition of the subject. A **compound predicate** consists of two or more verbs or verb phrases that share the same subject and are joined by a conjunction, such as *and, but, or,* or *nor.* In the example, the two verbs in the compound predicate are printed in boldface and the conjunction is in italics.

The two linked men **rose** from their seats in the first coach *and* **continued** to the next car.

Practice Copy these sentences. Underline the two or three verbs in each compound predicate, and circle each conjunction that joins them.

1. I caught a fish and held him in the boat.

2. He did not fight at all but instead hung like a weight.

3. He either had barnacles on him or was infested with white lice.

4. His eyes seemed large but were shallow and yellow.

5. I stared at the fish, unhooked him, and released him back into the water.

Writing Application Add a second part to the predicate in each sentence to form a compound predicate.

1. The fisherman baited his line.
2. The fish grabbed at the bait.

WG *Prentice Hall Writing and Grammar Connection: Chapter 19, Section 1*

TEACHING RESOURCES

The following resources can be used to enrich or extend the instruction for pp. 296–297.

Vocabulary

📖 **Selection Support:** Build Vocabulary, p. 77

📖 **Vocabulary and Spelling Practice Book**
(Use this booklet for skills enrichment.) ▦

Grammar

📖 **Selection Support:** Build Grammar Skills, p. 78

WG **Writing and Grammar,** Platinum Level, p. 412

🖥 **Daily Language Practice Transparencies** ▦

Writing

WG **Writing and Grammar,** Platinum Level, p. 136

◉ **Writing and Grammar iText CD-ROM** ▦

🖼 **Writing Models and Graphic Organizers on Transparencies,** p. 75

▦ **BLOCK SCHEDULING:** Resources marked with this symbol provide varied instruction during 90-minute blocks.

❸ Writing Lesson

Letter to the Editor

Compassionate acts like those of O. Henry's marshal or the speaker in "The Fish" often go unacknowledged. Write a letter to the editor of a local newspaper about either the marshal or the fisher. Explain what the person has done and why it is praiseworthy.

Prewriting Make up an interview with the person you are acknowledging. Jot down notes to help you write your letter.

Drafting As you draft, elaborate with details, examples, and facts to support each main point in your letter.

Model: Elaborating on a Statement

Statement: The marshal is a kind man.

Elaboration: Even though his job requires him to be handcuffed to a prisoner, he still views the prisoner as a human being and shows him compassion by . . .

> Specific examples about the ways the marshal is compassionate give strong support to the original statement.

Revising Reread your draft, and highlight each main point. Then, use a colored pencil to underline the facts and examples that support each point. Evaluate your draft, and add details for more support.

W̶G Prentice Hall Writing and Grammar Connection: Chapter 7, Section 4

❹ Extension Activities

Listening and Speaking Working in a group, produce a **sound-effects tape** to accompany a dramatic reading of "The Fish." Experiment with ways to imitate the sounds of the actions. Here are some possible ways to generate sounds:

- Clap softly to imitate water striking a boat.
- Whistle lightly or fasten a zipper to imitate the sound of reeling.
- Drop a rock into a bucket of water to imitate freeing the fish.

Play your tape as you read the poem in class. [Group Activity]

Research and Technology Use books or Internet resources to find out more about what Leavenworth and other American prisons were like in the late nineteenth century, the setting of "Hearts and Hands." Then, present your findings in an American prisons **chart.** Include headings for prison location, number of prisoners, and prison conditions.

 Take It to the Net www.phschool.com

Go online for an additional research activity using the Internet.

Hearts and Hands / The Fish ◆ 297

---

❸ Writing Lesson

- After students have chosen a subject for their letters, help them brainstorm for a list of questions they might use in the "interview." Then, give them time to answer these questions.

- Have students trade papers with a partner, and place a check mark beside every answer that would benefit from more elaboration.

- You may want students to use the Herringbone Organizer in **Writing Models and Graphic Organizers on Transparencies,** p. 75, to help organize their main points and supporting details.

- When they finish collecting details, have students draft their letters.

- Use the rubric for Persuasive Compositions in **Performance Assessment and Portfolio Management,** p. 11, to evaluate students' letters.

❹ Listening and Speaking

- Once groups have decided on the sound effects they will use, encourage them to practice making those sounds while one group member reads the poem aloud.

- When groups have planned the timing of their sound effects, allow them to go to a quiet space to record their tape.

- When they finish, gather the class together to listen to each tape.

CUSTOMIZE INSTRUCTION for Universal Access

To address different learning styles, use the following activities suggested in the **Extension Activities** booklet, p. 20.

- For Visual/Spatial Learners, use Activity 5.
- For Verbal/Linguistic Learners, use Activity 6.
- For Logical/Mathematical Learners, use Activity 7.

ASSESSMENT RESOURCES

The following resources can be used to assess students' knowledge and skills.

Selection Assessment
- 📖 **Formal Assessment,** pp. 66–68
- 📖 **Open Book Test,** pp. 58–60
- 💿 **Test Bank Software**
- 📼 **Got It! Assessment Videotapes,** Tape 2

🖥 **Take It to the Net**
Visit www.phschool.com for self-tests and additional questions on the selections.

Writing Rubric
- 📖 **Performance Assess. and Portfolio Mgmt,** p. 11.

PRENTICE HALL
ASSESSMENT SYSTEM
- 📖 **Workbook**
- 🖥 **Transparencies**
- 📖 **Skill Book**
- 💿 **CD-ROM**

from Desert Exile: The Uprooting of a Japanese American Family ✦
Speech on Japanese American Internment

Lesson Objectives

1. **To analyze and respond to literary elements**
   - Literary Analysis: Writer's Purpose
   - Comparing Literary Works

2. **To read, comprehend, analyze, and critique nonfiction**
   - Reading Strategy: Using Background Knowledge
   - Reading Check questions
   - Review and Assess questions
   - Assessment Practice (ATE)

3. **To develop word analysis skills, fluency, and systematic vocabulary**
   - Vocabulary Development Lesson: Latin Word Root: *-curs-*

4. **To understand and apply written and oral language conventions**
   - Spelling Strategy
   - Grammar Lesson: Compound Subjects

5. **To understand and apply appropriate writing and research strategies**
   - Writing Lesson: Internment Camp Research Report
   - Extension Activity: Oral History

6. **To understand and apply listening and speaking strategies**
   - Extension Activity: Persuasive Argument

STEP-BY-STEP TEACHING GUIDE	PACING GUIDE
PRETEACH	
Motivate Students and Provide Background	
Use the Motivation activity (ATE p. 298)	5 min.
Read and discuss the Preview material and Background information (SE/ATE p. 298) **A**	5 min.
Introduce the Concepts	
Introduce the Literary Analysis and Reading Strategy (SE/ATE p. 299) **A**	15 min.
Pronounce the vocabulary words and read their definitions (SE p. 299)	5 min.
TEACH	
Monitor Comprehension	
Informally monitor comprehension by circulating while students read independently or in groups **A**	25 min.
Monitor students' comprehension with the Reading Check notes (SE/ATE pp. 301, 303, 305)	as students read
Develop vocabulary with Vocabulary notes (SE pp. 301, 302, 303, 304, 305, 307; ATE p. 301)	as students read
Develop Understanding	
Develop students' understanding of the writer's purpose with Literary Analysis annotations (SE pp. 302, 304; ATE pp. 302, 304, 306) **A**	10 min.
Develop students' understanding of background knowledge with Reading Strategy annotations (SE pp. 301, 307; ATE pp. 301, 304, 307)	10 min.
ASSESS	
Assess Mastery	
Assess students' mastery of the Reading Strategy and Literary Analysis by having them answer the Review and Assess questions (SE/ATE p. 309)	20 min.
Use one or more of the print and media Assessment Resources (ATE p. 311) **A**	up to 50 min.
EXTEND	
Apply Understanding	
Have students complete the Vocabulary Development Lesson and the Grammar Lesson (SE p. 310) **A**	20 min.
Apply students' knowledge of accuracy in writing using the Writing Lesson (SE/ATE p. 311) **A**	45 min.
Apply students' understanding using one or more of the Extension Activities (SE p. 311)	20–90 min.

 ACCELERATED INSTRUCTION:
Use the strategies and activities identified with an **A**.

UNIVERSAL ACCESS
- ● = Below Level Students
- ▲ = On-Level Students
- ■ = Above Level Students

Time and Resource Manager

Reading Level: Average/Easy
Average Number of Instructional Days: 4

RESOURCES		
PRINT 📖	**TRANSPARENCIES**	**TECHNOLOGY** 💿 🎧 📼
• **Beyond Literature,** Cross-Curricular Connection: Social Studies, p. 21 ▲ ■		• **Interest Grabber Video,** Tape 2 ● ▲ ■
• **Selection Support Workbook:** ● ▲ ■ Literary Analysis, p. 84 Reading Strategy, p. 83 Build Vocabulary, p. 81	• **Literary Analysis and Reading Transparencies,** pp. 41 and 42 ● ▲ ■	
• **Adapted Reader's Companion** ● • **Reader's Companion** ●		• **Listening to Literature** ● ▲ ■ Audiocassettes, Sides 10, 11 Audio CDs, CD 6
• **English Learner's Companion** ● ▲ • **Literatura en español** ● ▲ • **Literary Analysis for Enrichment** ■		
• **Formal Assessment:** Selection Test, pp. 69–71 ● ▲ ■ • **Open Book Test,** pp. 61–63 ● ▲ ■ • **Performance Assessment and Portfolio Management,** pp. 13, 30 ● ▲ ■ • PRENTICE HALL **ASSESSMENT** *SYSTEM* ● ▲ ■	• PRENTICE HALL **ASSESSMENT** *SYSTEM* ● ▲ ■ Skills Practice Answers and Explanations on Transparencies	• **Test Bank Software** ● ▲ ■ • **Got It! Assessment Videotapes,** Tape 2 ● ▲
• **Selection Support Workbook:** ● ▲ ■ Build Grammar Skills, p. 82 • **Writing and Grammar,** Platinum Level ● ▲ ■ • **Extension Activities,** p. 21 ● ▲ ■	• **Daily Language Practice Transparencies** ● ▲ • **Writing Models and Graphic Organizers on Transparencies,** pp. 75–78 ● ▲ ■	• **Writing and Grammar iText CD-ROM** ● ▲ ■ 🖥 *Take It to the Net* www.phschool.com

▨ **BLOCK SCHEDULING:** Use one 90-minute class period to preteach the selection and have students read it. Use a second 90-minute class period to assess students' mastery of skills and have them complete one of the Extension Activities.

Step-by-Step Teaching Guide for pp. 298–299

Motivation

Ask students to imagine the following situation: One day you are ordered to go live in a camp with other people whose families came originally from the same country as yours. Your parents have to leave their jobs, and you have to leave your home, school, and friends to live in a place that is crowded and uncomfortable. It's like being in prison. Have them discuss how they would respond to this situation. After discussion, make sure students know that the United States Government forced thousands of Japanese Americans into internment camps during World War II. Have students discuss whether or not a similar situation could ever arise in the United States today.

💻 Interest Grabber Video

As an alternative, play "Japanese American Internment" on Tape 2 to engage student interest.

❶ Background

Social Studies

Early on Sunday morning, December 7, 1941, Japanese airplanes zeroed in on the American naval base at Pearl Harbor, Hawaii. Although the planes were picked up on radar by American officers in Pearl Harbor, they ignored them, believing them to be American B-17s arriving from the West Coast. Since it was a Sunday, most of the antiaircraft guns—there were 780—were not manned, many military personnel were still on shore for the weekend, and hundreds were asleep on the ships targeted by the Japanese. The attack lasted two hours and killed 2,300 American military personnel.

Prepare to Read

from Desert Exile: The Uprooting of a Japanese-American Family ◆ Speech on Japanese American Internment

 Take It to the Net

Visit www.phschool.com for interactive activities and instruction related to these selections, including

- background
- graphic organizers
- literary elements
- reading strategies

Preview

Connecting to the Literature

Although it is unfair, people often judge by appearances rather than by actions. As this narrative and speech demonstrate, in 1942, thousands of Americans were judged by their appearance. They were wrongly imprisoned simply because they "looked like the enemy."

❶ Background

On December 7, 1941, Japan attacked the American naval base at Pearl Harbor. Two months later, under strong political pressure, President Franklin D. Roosevelt ordered many Japanese Americans from their homes and into government-run internment camps. More than thirty years after the war, President Gerald Ford apologized to Japanese Americans and signed a proclamation officially ending the old order.

298 ◆ *Clashing Forces*

TEACHING RESOURCES

The following resources can be used to enrich or extend the instruction for pp. 298–299.

💻 **Interest Grabber Video,** Tape 2 🔲

Background
📖 **Beyond Literature,** p. 21

 Take It to the Net
Visit www.phschool.com for background and hotlinks for the selections.

Literary Analysis
📑 **Selection Support:** Literary Analysis, p. 84
📑 **Literary Analysis and Reading Transparencies,** Writer's Purpose, p. 42

Reading
📑 **Literary Analysis and Reading Transparencies,** Using Background Knowledge, p. 41 🔲

🔲 **BLOCK SCHEDULING:** Resources marked with this symbol provide varied instruction during 90-minute blocks.

Literary Analysis

Writer's Purpose

A **writer's purpose**—reason for writing—often affects the writer's choice of details and writing style. For example, Gerald Ford's purpose in his speech is to acknowledge officially that an injustice had been done. He uses formal language appropriate to a historic speech:

> Executive Order 9066 ceased to be effective at the end of World War II. Because there was no formal statement of its termination, . . .

Yoshiko Uchida, author of *Desert Exile,* intends to present a picture of life in the camps through her memories. Use a diagram like the one shown here to record details that reflect each writer's purpose.

Comparing Literary Works

The excerpt from *Desert Exile* and the speech by President Ford have a common message: Japanese Americans were treated unfairly when they were interned in camps during World War II. Gerald Ford's speech is a public document. Uchida's narrative is a memoir of these years. Compare the details that each writer uses to achieve his or her purpose.

Reading Strategy

Using Background Knowledge

When you read nonfiction, you will understand it better if you apply **background knowledge**—what you already know about the subject. For instance, knowing that the United States was at war with Japan during World War II will help you focus on the two selections. As you read, keep your prior knowledge in mind, but look for new information at the same time. You will find details in the selections that add to your knowledge or even change your thinking about the subject.

Vocabulary Development

cursory (kur′ sə rē) *adj.* superficial; done without attention to detail (p. 301)

euphemism (yōō′ fə miz′ əm) *n.* word or phrase substituted for a more unpleasant word or phrase (p. 301)

adept (ə dept′) *adj.* expert; highly skilled (p. 302)

destitute (des′ tə tōōt′) *n.* those living in poverty (p. 302)

unwieldy (un wēl′ dē) *adj.* hard to manage because of shape or weight (p. 303)

communal (kə myōōn′ əl) *adj.* shared by the community; not private (p. 304)

conspicuous (kən spik′ yōō əs) *adj.* easy to see (p. 305)

assuage (ə swāj′) *v.* calm; satisfy (p. 307)

Writer's Purpose
Present a picture of life in camps

Details or Word Included
Smell of the stable

Description of "unprivate" bathrooms

from Desert Exile / Speech on Japanese American Internment ◆ 299

---

❷ **Literary Analysis**

Writer's Purpose

- Tell students that as they read the selections, they will focus on the writer's purpose, or the reasons for which the writer wrote the piece. Writers may write to entertain, to inform, to persuade, or to express an opinion.
- Read the instruction about writer's purpose together as a class. Discuss the example given from President Ford's apology speech.
- Use the instruction for Comparing Literary Works to compare each writer's purpose in writing the narrative and in giving the speech.
- Use the Writer's Purpose transparency in **Literary Analysis and Reading Transparencies,** p. 42, as a model for determining a writer's purpose.

❸ **Reading Strategy**

Using Background Knowledge

- Encourage students to use their background knowledge—what they already know about a topic—when reading these selections. Remind them that background knowledge includes their personal experiences and feelings about the topic.
- Explain that background knowledge helps readers better understand what they are reading.
- Employ the Using Background Knowledge transparency in **Literary Analysis and Reading Transparencies,** p. 41, to demonstrate how background knowledge creates richer understanding.

Vocabulary Development

- Pronounce each vocabulary word for students, and read the definitions as a class. Have students identify any words with which they are already familiar.

CUSTOMIZE INSTRUCTION FOR UNIVERSAL ACCESS

For Special Needs Students	For Less Proficient Readers	For English Learners
Have students read the adapted version of *Desert Exile* in the **Adapted Reader's Companion.** This version provides basic-level instruction in an interactive format with questions and write-on lines. Completing the adapted version will prepare students to read the selection in the Student Edition.	Have students read the selection in the **Reader's Companion.** This version provides basic-level instruction in an interactive format with questions and write-on lines. After students finish the selection in **Reader's Companion,** have them complete the questions and activities in the Student Edition.	Have students read the adapted version of the selection in the **English Learner's Companion.** This version provides basic-level instruction in an interactive format with questions and write-on lines. Completing the adapted version will prepare students to read the selection in the Student Edition.

 E-Teach

Visit E-Teach at www.phschool.com for teachers' essays on how to teach, with questions and answers.

**CUSTOMIZE INSTRUCTION
For Visual/Spatial Learners**

As students read, have them take notes on the details Uchida provides about the layout of Tanforan Internment camp. Have students draw maps of the camp to help them better understand its size and scale, and the difficulty of life there. Students might consult the photographs accompanying the selection to estimate how many barracks would have had to be constructed to house the 8,000 Japanese Americans at Tanforan.

❶ About the Selection

This narrative describes some details of one family's experiences in one of the Japanese American internment camps of the 1940s. The speech following the narrative is a belated apology for the treatment of Japanese Americans in these camps. Read together, they give a personal and a public perspective on a tragic episode in American history.

❷ ▶Critical Viewing

Answer: Call students' attention to the tags on each person in this picture. Elicit from students that the people's individual identity has been reduced to a name or number on a tag.

from Desert Exile:

❶The Uprooting of a Japanese-American Family

Yoshiko Uchida

❷ ▲ **Critical Viewing** What detail in this picture indicates that people in internment camps were not viewed as individuals? Explain. **[Analyze]**

300 ◆ Clashing Forces

TEACHING RESOURCES

The following resources can be used to enrich or extend the instruction for pp. 300–308.

Reading

📖 **Selection Support:** Reading Strategy, p. 83;
Build Vocabulary, p. 81

🎧 **Listening to Literature Audiocassettes,**
Sides 10, 11 ▪

💿 **Listening to Literature Audio CDs,** CD 6 ▪

▪ **BLOCK SCHEDULING:** Resources marked with this symbol provide varied instruction during 90-minute blocks.

A s the bus pulled up to the grandstand, I could see hundreds of Japanese Americans jammed along the fence that lined the track. These people had arrived a few days earlier and were now watching for the arrival of friends or had come to while away the empty hours that had suddenly been thrust upon them.

As soon as we got off the bus, we were directed to an area beneath the grandstand where we registered and filled out a series of forms. Our baggage was inspected for contraband,[1] a <u>cursory</u> medical check made, and our living quarters assigned. We were to be housed in Barrack 16, Apartment 40. Fortunately, some friends who had arrived earlier found us and offered to help us locate our quarters.

It had rained the day before and the hundreds of people who had trampled on the track had turned it into a miserable mass of slippery mud. We made our way on it carefully, helping my mother who was dressed just as she would have been to go to church. She wore a hat, gloves, her good coat, and her Sunday shoes, because she would not have thought of venturing outside our house dressed in any other way.

Everywhere there were black tar-papered barracks[2] that had been hastily erected to house the 8,000 Japanese Americans of the area who had been uprooted from their homes. Barrack 16, however, was not among them, and we couldn't find it until we had traveled half the length of the track and gone beyond it to the northern rim of the racetrack compound.

Finally one of our friends called out, "There it is, beyond that row of eucalyptus trees." Barrack 16 was not a barrack at all, but a long stable raised a few feet off the ground with a broad ramp the horses had used to reach their stalls. Each stall was now numbered, and ours was number 40. That the stalls should have been called "apartments" was a <u>euphemism</u> so ludicrous it was comical.

When we reached stall number 40, we pushed open the narrow door and looked uneasily into the vacant darkness. The stall was about ten by twenty feet and empty except for three folded Army cots lying on the floor. Dust, dirt, and wood shavings covered the linoleum that had been laid over manure-covered boards, the smell of horses hung in the air, and the whitened corpses of many insects still clung to the hastily white-washed walls.

High on either side of the entrance were two small windows which were our only source of daylight. The stall was divided into two sections by Dutch doors[3] worn down by teeth marks, and each stall in the stable was separated from the adjoining one only by rough partitions that

---

1. **contraband** (kän´ trə band´) *n.* smuggled goods.
2. **barracks** (bar´ əks) *n.* large, plain, often temporary housing.
3. **Dutch doors** doors split across the middle so the top and bottom halves can be opened separately.

Reading Strategy
Using Background Knowledge Why is an awareness of the historical setting important to understanding what is happening here?

cursory (kur´ sə rē) *adj.* superficial; done without attention to detail

euphemism (yōō´ fə miz´ əm) *n.* word or phrase substituted for a more unpleasant word or phrase

5 ✔**Reading Check**
Who are the people in this selection?

from Desert Exile ◆ *301*

---

3 Reading Strategy
Using Background Knowledge
- Read aloud the bracketed passage. Ask students whether they know where the narrator is.
  Answer: The narrator is entering a Japanese American internment camp.
- Ask students the Reading Strategy question on p. 301: Why is an awareness of the historical setting important in order to understand what is happening in the selection?
  Answer: It is important to know that during World War II the United States and Japan were at war, and that the United States government rounded up all Japanese Americans and detained them until the war—and the threat of spying for Japan—was over. Without some prior knowledge of these circumstances, a reader would not know what was going on.

4 Vocabulary Development
The Latin Word Root *-curs-*
- Draw students' attention to the word *cursory* and its definition. Tell students that the Latin root *-curs-* means, "to run."
- Ask students to identify how the root meaning, "to run," relates to the definition of the word *cursory*.
  Answer: It suggests haste, that something cursorily done has been done quickly and without attention.
- Have students look up the words *current, course,* and *recur* in a dictionary and record in their journals the meanings of the words and their relation to the Latin root.

5 ✔**Reading Check**
Answer: The people are Japanese Americans who are being forced to live in an internment camp.

CUSTOMIZE INSTRUCTION FOR UNIVERSAL ACCESS

For Special Needs Students	For English Learners
Some students may benefit from pausing two or three times on a page to discuss what is happening in the story. Have volunteers read a paragraph aloud, then stop. Then, ask students to summarize what they have just read and heard. Encourage students to reread to find details to include as they retell the action in their own words.	Students may be confused by the dual references to *apartment* and *stall.* Define and discuss *euphemism* with students. Ask them to comment on the government's use of the word *apartment* to denote a horse's stall. What background knowledge do students have about such use of language? What do they think it implies about the Uchidas' situation?

301

- Review with students the reasons for which a writer writes: to inform, to persuade, to entertain, or to express an opinion. Point out to students that a writer may have more than one purpose for writing a single piece.

- Ask the Literary Analysis question on p. 302: What is Uchida's purpose in revealing her feelings about standing in line?
  Answer: Guide students to see that Uchida includes these details to inform readers of the feelings of internees about the conditions they endured.

▶ **Monitor Progress** Encourage students to create a diagram like the one on p. 299 to record details that support Uchida's purpose in this passage.

7 ▶ Critical Viewing

Answer: This photo might illustrate how internees wait in line for dinner. Some students may say it also represents the many times they have to wait in line for something.

---

stopped a foot short of the sloping roof. The space, while perhaps a good source of ventilation for the horses, deprived us of all but visual privacy, and we couldn't even be sure of that because of the crevices and knotholes in the dividing walls.

Because our friends had already spent a day as residents of Tanforan, they had become <u>adept</u> at scrounging for necessities. One found a broom and swept the floor for us. Two of the boys went to the barracks where mattresses were being issued, stuffed the ticking with straw themselves, and came back with three for our cots.

Nothing in the camp was ready. Everything was only half-finished. I wondered how much the nation's security would have been threatened had the Army permitted us to remain in our homes a few more days until the camps were adequately prepared for occupancy by families.

By the time we had cleaned out the stall and set up the cots, it was time for supper. Somehow, in all the confusion, we had not had lunch, so I was eager to get to the main mess hall,[4] which was located beneath the grandstand.

The sun was going down as we started along the muddy track, and a cold, piercing wind swept in from the bay. When we arrived, there were six long weaving lines of people waiting to get into the mess hall. We took our place at the end of one of them, each of us clutching a plate and silverware borrowed from friends who had already received their baggage.

Shivering in the cold, we pressed close together trying to shield Mama from the wind. As we stood in what seemed a breadline for the <u>destitute</u>, I felt degraded, humiliated, and overwhelmed with a longing for home. And I saw the unutterable sadness on my mother's face.

This was only the first of many lines we were to endure, and we soon discovered that waiting in line was as inevitable a part of Tanforan as the north wind that swept in from the bay stirring up all the dust and litter of the camp.

Once we got inside the gloomy cavernous mess hall, I saw hundreds of people eating at wooden picnic tables, while those who had already eaten were shuffling aimlessly over the wet cement floor. When I reached the serving table and held out my plate, a cook reached into a dishpan full of canned sausages and dropped two onto my plate with his fingers. Another man gave me a boiled potato and a piece of butterless bread.

With 5,000 people to be fed, there were few unoccupied tables, so we separated from our friends and shared a table with an elderly man and a young family with two crying babies. No one at the table spoke to us, and even Mama could seem to find no friendly word to offer as she normally would have done. We tried to eat, but the food wouldn't go down.

"Let's get out of here," my sister suggested.

We decided it would be better to go back to our barrack than to linger in the depressing confusion of the mess hall. It had grown dark by now and since Tanforan had no lights for nighttime occupancy, we

---

4. **mess hall** room or building in which a group regularly meets for meals.

adept (ə dept´) *adj.* expert; highly skilled

destitute (des´ tə tōōt´) *n.* those living in poverty

Literary Analysis
Writer's Purpose What is Uchida's purpose in revealing her feelings about standing in line?

7 ▶ **Critical Viewing**
What part of the story could this photograph be illustrating? **[Connect]**

Japanese Houses

Explain to students that the arrangement of traditional Japanese homes stresses space, light, simplicity, and harmony of form. The rooms are divided by sliding screens made of wood and paper or glass. The floors are covered by *tatami,* woven grass mats. Bedding is hidden in closets during the day, and furniture is minimal. Often a home includes an alcove with a flower arrangement and a hanging scroll. Discuss with students why people used to this sort of home would find the internment camps especially difficult to bear. Call their attention to the contrast between the simple spacious elegance of a traditional Japanese home and the crowded squalor of the stalls.

Interested students may wish to research information and locate pictures of traditional Japanese architecture and home décor.

had to pick our way carefully down the slippery track.

Once back in our stall, we found it no less depressing, for there was only a single electric light bulb dangling from the ceiling, and a one-inch crevice at the top of the north wall admitted a steady draft of the cold night air. We sat huddled on our cots, bundled in our coats, too cold and miserable even to talk. My sister and I worried about Mama, for she wasn't strong and had recently been troubled with neuralgia,[5] which could easily be aggravated by the cold. She in turn was worrying about us, and of course we all worried and wondered about Papa.

Suddenly we heard the sound of a truck stopping outside.

"Hey, Uchida! Apartment 40!" a boy shouted.

I rushed to the door and found the baggage boys trying to heave our enormous "camp bundle" over the railing that fronted our stall.

"What ya got in here anyway?" they shouted good-naturedly as they struggled with the <u>unwieldy</u> bundle. "It's the biggest thing we got on our truck!"

I grinned, embarrassed, but I could hardly wait to get out our belongings. My sister and I fumbled to undo all the knots we had tied into the rope around our bundle that morning and eagerly pulled out the familiar objects from home.

We unpacked our blankets, pillows, sheets, tea kettle, and, most welcome of all, our electric hot plate. I ran to the nearest washroom to fill the kettle with water, while Mama and Kay made up the Army cots with our bedding. Once we hooked up the hot plate and put the

---

5. **neuralgia** (nōō ral′ jə) *n.* pain along the path of a nerve.

unwieldy (un wēl′ dē) *adj.* hard to manage because of shape or weight

⑩ ✔ **Reading Check**

How does the family feel about the food in the camp?

from *Desert Exile* ◆ 303

---

⑧ **Critical Thinking**

Draw Conclusions

- Call on a volunteer to read aloud the bracketed passage.
- Remind students that when they draw conclusions, they use information from the text to make judgments about what they have read.
- Ask students what conclusions they can draw about the mother's health based on the passage.
  Answer: The mother is not strong and suffers from neuralgia.
- Ask students to draw conclusions about the effect that imprisonment might have on the mother.
  Answer: Physically, she might suffer from cold, exhaustion, and hunger. Emotionally, the worry and crude conditions might depress her.

⑨ **Background**

Social Studies

Government instructions to Japanese Americans regarding what they would be allowed to bring with them included:

1. bedding and linens for each family member (no mattresses)
2. toiletries for each family member
3. extra clothing for each family member
4. enough knives, forks, spoons, cups, plates, and bowls for each family member
5. essential personal effects for each family member.

And they were limited by what they could carry themselves.

In many cases, the houses and personal belongings that Japanese Americans were forced to leave behind were lost.

⑩ ✔ **Reading Check**

Answer: The family does not like the food in the camp.

304

⓫ Reading Strategy

Using Background Knowledge

- Read aloud the bracketed passage. Ask students to think about the effects that hunger has on people.

- Ask students to use this knowledge about the effects of hunger to predict what lies in store for the Uchidas.
  Possible responses: The Uchidas face malnutrition, ill health, and emotional stress.

- Then, ask students why they think the writer compares the prunes they received to chocolate.
  Answer: The food that Tanforan offered was so bad, and the Uchidas were so hungry, that the prunes were a real treat to them.

⓬ Literary Analysis

Writer's Purpose

- Have a student volunteer read aloud the bracketed passage.

- Ask students to describe the passage's effect on the reader.
  Possible responses: Disgust, anger, compassion.

▶ Monitor Progress Ask students the Literary Analysis question on p. 304: What message or theme might the description of the bathroom support?
  Possible response: The description of the bathroom supports the message or theme that the conditions Japanese Americans had to endure were reprehensible.

---

kettle on to boil, we felt better. We sat close to its warmth, holding our hands toward it as though it were our fireplace at home.

⓫ Before long some friends came by to see us, bringing with them the only gift they had—a box of dried prunes. Even the day before, we wouldn't have given the prunes a second glance, but now they were as welcome as the boxes of Maskey's chocolate my father used to bring home from San Francisco.

Mama managed to make some tea for our friends, and we sat around our steaming kettle, munching gratefully on our prunes. We spent much of the evening talking about food and the lack of it, a concern that grew obsessive over the next few weeks, when we were constantly hungry.

Our stable consisted of twenty-five stalls facing north which were back to back with an equal number facing south, so we were surrounded on three sides. Living in our stable were an assortment of people—mostly small family units—that included an artist, my father's barber and his wife, a dentist and his wife, an elderly retired couple, a group of Kibei bachelors (Japanese born in the United States but educated in Japan), an insurance salesman and his wife, and a widow with two daughters. To say that we all became intimately acquainted would be an understatement. It was, in fact, <u>communal</u> living, with semi-private cubicles provided only for sleeping.

Our neighbors on one side spent much of their time playing cards, and at all hours of the day we could hear the sound of cards being shuffled and money changing hands. Our other neighbors had a teenage son who spent most of the day with his friends, coming home to his stall at night only after his parents were asleep. Family life began to show signs of strain almost immediately, not only in the next stall but throughout the entire camp.

One Sunday our neighbor's son fell asleep in the rear of his stall with the door bolted from inside. When his parents came home from church, no amount of shouting or banging on the door could awaken the boy.

"Our stupid son has locked us out," they explained, coming to us for help.

I climbed up on my cot and considered pouring water on him over the partition, for I knew he slept just on the other side of it. Instead I dangled a broom over the partition and poked and prodded with it, shouting, "Wake up! Wake up!" until the boy finally bestirred himself and let his parents in. We became good friends with our neighbors after that.

⓬ About one hundred feet from our stable were two latrines and two washrooms for our section of camp, one each for men and women. The latrines were crude wooden structures containing eight toilets, separated by partitions, but having no doors. The washrooms were divided into two sections. In the front section was a long tin trough spaced with spigots of hot and cold water where we washed our faces and brushed our teeth. To the rear were eight showers, also separated by partitions but lacking doors or curtains. The showers were difficult

communal (kə myōōn′ əl) *adj.* shared by the community; not private

Literary Analysis
Writer's Purpose What message or theme might the description of the bathroom support?

✸ ENRICHMENT: Social Studies Connection

Internment Camps

In the early 1940s, most Japanese Americans lived on the West Coast or in Hawaii. Many were successful farmers or business people.

After Pearl Harbor, many people said Japanese Americans might act as spies and help Japan invade the United States. No evidence of disloyalty existed. Nonetheless, President Roosevelt agreed to move Japanese Americans to inland camps set up by the Wartime Relocation Agency. Approximately 120,000

Japanese Americans were forced to sell their homes and businesses at great loss.

Years later, Americans began to recognize the injustice that had been done to Japanese Americans. Congress reviewed the government's wartime policy toward Japanese Americans. Lawmakers admitted that they could not right the wrong that had been done. They did, however, approve a payment of $20,000 to every survivor of the camps.

to adjust and we either got scalded by torrents of hot water or shocked by an icy blast of cold. Most of the Issei[6] were unaccustomed to showers, having known the luxury of soaking in deep pine-scented tubs during their years in Japan, and found the showers virtually impossible to use.

Our card-playing neighbor scoured the camp for a container that might serve as a tub, and eventually found a large wooden barrel. She rolled it to the showers, filled it with warm water, and then climbed in for a pleasant and leisurely soak. The greatest compliment she could offer anyone was the use of her private tub.

The lack of privacy in the latrines and showers was an embarrassing hardship especially for the older women, and many would take newspapers to hold over their faces or squares of cloth to tack up for their own private curtain. The Army, obviously ill-equipped to build living quarters for women and children, had made no attempt to introduce even the most common of life's civilities into these camps for us.

During the first few weeks of camp life everything was erratic and in short supply. Hot water appeared only sporadically, and the minute it was available, everyone ran for the showers or the laundry. We had to be clever and quick just to keep clean, and my sister and I often walked a mile to the other end of the camp where hot water was in better supply, in order to boost our morale with a hot shower.

Even toilet paper was at a premium, for new rolls would disappear as soon as they were placed in the latrines. The shock of the evacuation compounded by the short supply of every necessity brought out the baser instincts of the internees,[7] and there was little inclination for anyone to feel responsible for anyone else. In the early days, at least, it was everyone for himself or herself.

One morning I saw some women emptying bed pans into the troughs where we washed our faces. The sight was enough to turn my stomach, and my mother quickly made several large signs in Japanese cautioning people against such unsanitary practices. We posted them in <u>conspicuous</u> spots in the washroom and hoped for the best.

Across from the latrines was a double barrack, one containing laundry tubs and the other equipped with clotheslines and ironing boards. Because there were so many families with young children, the laundry

---

6. **Issei** Japanese who emigrated to the United States after 1907. They were not granted citizenship until 1952.
7. **internees** (in´ turn´ ēz´) *n.* prisoners, especially during wartime.

Literature in context 🔞 History Connection

Wartime Heroes

Uchida and her family were interned in camps like many other Japanese Americans. In 1943, the U.S. War Department came to the internment camps seeking volunteers for a new Japanese American combat unit to fight in Europe. Thousands of internees formed the 442nd Infantry Regiment, which became one of the most honored military groups in American history. The 442nd fought in seven major campaigns and earned more than 18,000 military decorations. Two veterans of the regiment later became U.S. senators. Japanese Americans in the camps were proud of the loyalty that their friends and family showed the United States.

conspicuous (kən spik´ yōō əs) *adj.* easy to see

🔞 ✔Reading Check

Describe one of the hardships of life in the camp.

from *Desert Exile* ◆ 305

🔞 Background

History Connection

President Roosevelt announced the formation of the 442nd Regiment with the famous words, "Americanism is not, and never was, a matter of race or ancestry." Those that answered the call astounded and probably shocked the Army. The original plan called for a quota of 3,000 volunteers from the mainland and 1,500 from Hawaii. Nearly 10,000 Hawaiian *nisei* (second generation Japanese Americans) volunteered and over 2,600 were accepted. Of the mainland Japanese from the internment camps, only 1,256 *nisei* volunteered, although there were some 23,606 *nisei* of draft age in the camps. From these camp volunteers, around 800 were inducted into the Army.

🔞 Critical Thinking

Make a Judgment

- Have a volunteer read aloud the bracketed passage.

- Ask students: What is Uchida's main point in this paragraph?
Answer: The situation in the camps brought out the worst in everyone.

- Ask students whether they agree that difficult conditions bring out the worst in people.
Answer: Some students may say that difficult conditions bring out the best in people, as evidenced by examples of cooperation and kindness Uchida offered earlier in the narrative. Other students may say that in general, difficult situations bring out the worst in people. Encourage students to offer examples from current events and literature as well as citing examples from the story.

🔞 ✔Reading Check

Answer: Students may describe living in a horse stall, the lack of privacy, the bathrooms, food, hot water shortage, unsanitary conditions, or shortage of necessities.

CUSTOMIZE INSTRUCTION FOR UNIVERSAL ACCESS

For Special Needs Students	For Advanced Readers
Have students read the story as they listen to the recorded version on the **Listening to Literature Audiocassettes,** Sides 12 and 13, or the **Listening to Literature Audio CDs,** CD 5. Take time to pause in the reading to check for comprehension by asking students to summarize what has happened.	Ask students to analyze and discuss why Uchida wanted to write about such a devastating experience. Have them consider to what degree people who live through historical events are obligated to record them. Can students make connections between Uchida's narrative and other first-person historical accounts?

Writer's Purpose

• Call on a volunteer to read aloud the bracketed passage.

• Ask students why Uchida uses the word *shamelessly*. What does that tell them about the author?
Possible response: The use of the word *shamelessly* indicates that although she would not normally ask for help so blatantly, the circumstances in which she found herself called for unusual actions.

• Then ask students for what purpose Uchida may have included this information about her non-Japanese friends.
Answer: She may have wanted readers to know that the government's distrust of Japanese Americans was not shared by all non-Japanese.

17 ▶ Critical Viewing

Answer: The small overnight cases that the people are carrying in the picture indicate that they did not have time to gather many belongings. The worried expressions on the faces of the people in line and the impatient expressions on the faces of the soldiers are another indication that Japanese Americans were forced out of their homes quickly.

tubs were in constant use. The hot water was often gone by 9:00 a.m., and many women got up at 3:00 and 4:00 in the morning to do their wash, all of which, including sheets, had to be done entirely by hand.

We found it difficult to get to the laundry by 9:00 a.m., and by then every tub was taken and there were long lines of people with bags of dirty laundry waiting behind each one. When we finally got to a tub, there was no more hot water. Then we would leave my mother to hold the tub while my sister and I rushed to the washroom where there was a better supply and carried back bucketfuls of hot water as everyone else learned to do. By the time we had finally hung our laundry on lines outside our stall, we were too exhausted to do much else for the rest of the day.

For four days after our arrival we continued to go to the main mess hall for all our meals. My sister and I usually missed breakfast because we were assigned to the early shift and we simply couldn't get there by 7:00 a.m. Dinner was at 4:45 p.m., which was a terrible hour, but not a major problem, as we were always hungry. Meals were uniformly bad and skimpy, with an abundance of starches such as beans and bread. I wrote to my non-Japanese friends in Berkeley **16** shamelessly asking them to send us food, and they obliged with large cartons of cookies, nuts, dried fruit, and jams.

17 ▲ Critical Viewing
What details indicate that these people were forced to leave their homes in a hurry? **[Draw Conclusions]**

We looked forward with much anticipation to the opening of a half dozen smaller mess halls located throughout the camp. But when ours finally opened, we discovered that the preparation of smaller quantities had absolutely no effect on the quality of the food. We went eagerly to our new mess hall only to be confronted at our first meal with chili con carne, corn, and butterless bread. To assuage our disappointment, a friend and I went to the main mess hall which was still in operation, to see if it had anything better. Much to our amazement and delight, we found small lettuce salads, the first fresh vegetables we had seen in many days. We ate ravenously and exercised enormous self-control not to go back for second and third helpings.

The food improved gradually, and by the time we left Tanforan five months later, we had fried chicken and ice cream for Sunday dinner. By July tubs of soapy water were installed at the mess hall exits so we could wash our plates and utensils on the way out. Being slow eaters, however, we usually found the dishwater tepid and dirty by the time we reached the tubs, and we often rewashed our dishes in the washroom.

Most internees got into the habit of rushing for everything. They ran to the mess halls to be first in line, they dashed inside for the best tables and then rushed through their meals to get to the wash-tubs before the suds ran out. The three of us, however, seemed to be at the end of every line that formed and somehow never managed to be first for anything.

One of the first things we all did at Tanforan was to make our living quarters as comfortable as possible. A pile of scrap lumber in one corner of camp melted away like snow on a hot day as residents salvaged whatever they could to make shelves and crude pieces of furniture to supplement the Army cots. They also made ingenious containers for carrying their dishes to the mess halls, with handles and lids that grew more and more elaborate in a sort of unspoken competition.

Because of my father's absence, our friends helped us in camp, just as they had in Berkeley, and we relied on them to put up shelves and build a crude table and two benches for us. We put our new camp furniture in the front half of our stall, which was our "living room," and put our three cots in the dark windowless rear section, which we promptly dubbed "the dungeon." We ordered some print fabric by mail and sewed curtains by hand to hang at our windows and to cover our shelves. Each new addition to our stall made it seem a little more like home.

One afternoon about a week after we had arrived at Tanforan, a messenger from the administration building appeared with a telegram for us. It was from my father, telling us he had been released on parole from Montana and would be able to join us soon in camp. Papa was coming home. The wonderful news had come like an unexpected gift, but even as we hugged each other in joy, we didn't quite dare believe it until we actually saw him. . . .

assuage (ə swāj′) v. calm; satisfy

Reading Strategy
Using Background Knowledge How does your prior knowledge of the conditions in the camp help you understand why many internees rush around?

Yoshiko Uchida

(1921–1992)

Yoshiko Uchida's life seemed normal until early in 1942. Then, under Executive Order 9066, she and her family were removed from their comfortable home in Berkeley, California, and sent first to Tanforan Racetrack near San Francisco—where they actually lived in a stable— and later to an internment camp in Utah. After the war, Uchida attended Smith College in Massachusetts. She became a teacher and an award-winning author who wrote more than thirty fiction and nonfiction books.

from *Desert Exile* ◆ 307

18 Reading Strategy
Using Background Knowledge

• Read aloud the bracketed passage. Then, ask a volunteer to summarize the passage.

• Ask students the Reading Strategy question on p. 307: How does your prior knowledge of the conditions in the camp help you understand why many internees rush around?
Answer: Students have already learned that if the internees don't rush they are likely to miss out on something.

19 Critical Thinking
Speculate

• Ask a volunteer to read aloud the bracketed passage.

• Have students consider why the Uchidas' friends helped them in the camp.

• Ask students why they think the Uchidas' friends could act so self-lessly under such difficult circumstances.
Answer: Students may suggest that difficult situations are complex—they bring out people's baser as well as their better instincts. The same person who ran to be first in line at the mess hall may give someone else part of her or his meal a few minutes later.

CUSTOMIZE INSTRUCTION FOR UNIVERSAL ACCESS

For Less Proficient Readers	For Gifted/Talented Students
Encourage students to imagine they were in the Uchidas' place. Have them list items they would want to take with them, as well as what they would do to make their new "homes" more comfortable and personalized. Ask them to consider whether they would help out others or if they would just try to make sure their families got what they needed—or if they might do both, depending on the situation.	Remind students that people in the camp community helped the Uchidas, making furniture and putting up shelves. Ask students to draft plans that people in the camp might have used to organize help for people in need, or to solve problems such as cold dishwater. Students may wish to read more of Uchida's writing about life at Tanforan in *Authors In Depth*, Silver Level.

Review and Assess

1. Students should choose one of the hardships of camp life and describe why they would dislike it most.

2. **(a)** Stall number 40 had a narrow door, it was ten by twenty feet, dark, cold, and empty except for three army cots. The floor was dirty, and it smelled liked horses. **(b)** It's ludicrous to call it an apartment because the word *apartment* indicates a home for human beings, not for horses.

3. **(a)** Brooms, mattresses, hot water, toilet paper, and food are scarce when the family first arrives. **(b)** Some people become more selfish, while others act more generously and help where they can.

4. **(a)** It publicly acknowledged the injustice of internment and formally terminated Executive Order 9066. **(b)** Students may suggest that it was never revoked because people assumed internment would never be enforced again.

5. **(a)** The conditions suggest that the government did not view Japanese Americans as citizens or individuals. **(b)** Although the United States was also at war with Germany and Italy, German Americans and Italian Americans were not placed in internment camps.

Speech on Japanese American Internment

Gerald Ford

Remarks Upon Signing a Proclamation Concerning Japanese American Internment During World War II, February 19, 1976

February 19, 1976, is the anniversary of a very, very sad day in American history. It was on that date in 1942 that Executive Order 9066 was issued resulting in the uprooting of many, many loyal Americans. Over 100,000 persons of Japanese ancestry were removed from their homes, detained in special camps, and eventually relocated.

We now know what we should have known then—not only was that evacuation wrong but Japanese Americans were and are loyal Americans. On the battlefield and at home the names of Japanese Americans have been and continue to be written in America's history for the sacrifices and the contributions they have made to the well-being and to the security of this, our common Nation.

Executive Order 9066 ceased to be effective at the end of World War II. Because there was no formal statement of its termination, there remains some concern among Japanese Americans that there yet may be some life in that obsolete document. The proclamation [4417] that I am signing here today should remove all doubt on that matter.

I call upon the American people to affirm with me the unhyphenated American promise that we have learned from the tragedy of that long ago experience—forever to treasure liberty and justice for each individual American and resolve that this kind of error shall never be made again.

Review and Assess

Thinking About the Selection

1. **Respond:** What part of life in the camps would you have disliked most? Why?

2. **(a) Recall:** Describe stall number 40. **(b) Analyze:** Why does Uchida feel that calling it an "apartment" was ludicrous?

3. **(a) Recall:** What necessities are scarce when the family first arrives at the camp? **(b) Analyze Causes and Effects:** How do the shortages affect the way people behave?

4. **(a) Recall:** What did Proclamation 4417 do? **(b) Speculate:** Why do you think Executive Order 9066 was not revoked before 1976?

5. **(a) Extend:** What do the conditions at the camp suggest about the government's attitude toward Japanese Americans? **(b) Make a Judgment:** Do you think other groups would have been treated the same way? Explain.

Gerald Ford

(b. 1913)

As a young man, Gerald Ford turned down the chance to play professional football, choosing instead to study law at Yale University. After graduation, he practiced law briefly and then was elected to the U.S. House of Representatives, where he served for nearly twenty-five years. In 1973, Ford was chosen by President Richard Nixon to replace Vice President Spiro Agnew, who had resigned. When Nixon resigned eight months later, Ford became the thirty-eighth president of the United States.

ASSESSMENT PRACTICE: Reading Comprehension

Stated and Implied Main Ideas   (For more practice, see Test Preparation Workbook, p. 21.)

As students prepare to take assessment tests they should review the process of finding the author's main idea. An author's purpose is to express a main idea and support it with details, secondary ideas, facts, and examples. For practice, have students read Gerald Ford's speech on p. 308, and answer the following sample question:

The primary purpose of the passage is to—

A Celebrate February 19 as an important date

B Remind all American citizens to value liberty

C Praise Japanese Americans

D Abolish an obsolete document

As a strategy, suggest that students reread to find the most important sentence of the speech: President Ford reminded all citizens of the value of liberty and freedom at the same time as he closed a tragic chapter in American history. Using this strategy, students will find that *B* is the best answer.

Review and Assess

Literary Analysis

Writer's Purpose

1. Using a chart like the one here, identify at least three details that help each writer achieve the stated **purpose.**

Purpose	Details
Uchida: to create a personal record	
Ford: to create a historic record acknowledging an injustice	

2. Identify one detail that Ford includes for the sake of history that would not be included in a personal account. Explain your choice.

Comparing Literary Works

3. What is the common message that the writers convey about the treatment of Japanese Americans during World War II?

4. (a) List two details that Uchida uses to imply her message. (b) Identify a sentence in Ford's remarks that states his message directly.

5. In your opinion, which selection achieves the writer's purpose more effectively? Explain.

Reading Strategy

Using Background Knowledge

6. Use a graphic organizer like this one to list ideas about internment camps that you knew before you read these selections and things that you learned from your reading.

Topic:	
What I Knew	What I Learned

7. Explain how your thinking about the camps did or did not change after reading these two works.

Extend Understanding

8. **Social Studies Connection:** How could requiring government leaders to read *Desert Exile* protect against such future injustices?

from *Desert Exile / Speech on Japanese American Internment* ◆ 309

Quick Review

The **writer's purpose** is his or her reason for writing.

To apply **background knowledge** as you read, use what you already know about a subject to help you understand new information about that subject.

  Take It to the Net

www.phschool.com

Take the interactive self-test online to check your understanding of these selections.

✷ ENRICHMENT: Further Reading

Other Works by Yoshiko Uchida

The Dancing Kettle
Picture Bride
The Sea of Gold and Other Tales from Japan
Journey to Topaz
Journey Home

Take It to the Net

Visit www.phschool.com for more information on Yoshiko Uchida.

Answers for p. 309

Review and Assess

1. Uchida: She writes about daily life in the camps. She tells about the selfish and generous acts of those around her. She tells how people felt in such an unjust situation. Ford: He mentions the historic significance of the date. He acknowledges the injustice of the internment of Japanese Americans. He revokes Executive Order 9066.

2. The number of the executive order, the number of the proclamation, and the formal appeal to the public would probably not be found in a personal account. Students may explain that these details would not help the writer of a personal account communicate the daily living experience in one of the camps.

3. Both messages convey that the internments were a tragic injustice done to innocent people.

4. Possible responses: **(a)** The details about the lack of privacy and living in a horse stall convey Uchida's message. **(b)** "We now know what we should have known then—not only was that evacuation wrong but Japanese Americans were and are loyal Americans."

5. Possible response: *Desert Exile* completes the writer's purpose more effectively because it is a personal account of what it was like to live in the camps.

6. What I Knew: Students may draw on the information presented in Background on p. 298, from a history class, friends or family, movies, plays, or novels on the subject. What I Learned: Students may say they learned about conditions within the camp and the daily life and treatment of the Japanese Americans.

7. Some students may say that the narrative gave them a deeper understanding of the conditions in the camps. Others may say the speech helped them realize some of the reasons people reacted as they did.

8. Students will say that requiring leaders to read *Desert Exile* would prevent such injustices from happening again.

309

❶ Vocabulary Development

Word Analysis

1. (b) connected and flowing
2. (b) movable
3. (a) to move

Spelling Strategy

1. traffic
2. graph
3. laughter

Fluency: Clarify Word Meaning

1. Both terms are euphemisms for "died."
2. Someone who is adept at sports could be described as highly skilled.
3. A destitute, or poor, person might assuage, or satisfy, his or her hunger by eating a meal.
4. A thief wouldn't want to be conspicuous, or highly noticeable, because he or she would be more easily caught.
5. A difficult adjustment to communal, or group, living might be learning to live with less privacy.
6. I would ask someone to help me move an unwieldy, or hard to handle, piece of furniture.
7. A cursory, or superficial, review of a contract could result in missing important information or conditions.

❷ Grammar

1. My family (and) I lived in stall 40.
2. Finding a broom (and) obtaining mattresses were important on that first day.
3. My sister (and) I worried about Mama.
4. Mama (or) Kay made up the army cots.
5. The lack of privacy (and) the rugged accommodations made our lives difficult.

Writing Application

1. My brother and sister served in the army.
2. The carpeting and furniture in the room were old.

310

Integrate Language Skills

❶ Vocabulary Development Lesson

Word Analysis: Latin Root -curs-

Cursory contains the Latin root -curs-, which means "to run." *Cursory* means "run through rapidly and without care." Use your knowledge of the Latin root -curs- to answer these questions:

1. Is *cursive* writing square and blocklike or connected and flowing?
2. Is a *cursor* on a computer screen fixed or movable?
3. Does a river *current* cause water to move or to stand still?

Spelling Strategy

In the word *euphemism*, the letters *ph* spell the sound of *f*. Other spellings of *f* are *f* as in *fast*, *ff* as in *stuff*, and *gh* as in *rough*. Spell these words correctly with letters that spell the sound of *f*:

1. tra__ic   2. gra__   3. lau__ter

❷ Grammar Lesson

Compound Subjects

The subject of a sentence names the person, place, or thing that the sentence is about. A **compound subject** is two or more subjects that have the same verb and are joined by a conjunction such as *and* or *or*. In the examples, the subjects are underlined and the conjunction is in italics.

> <u>Dust</u>, <u>dirt</u>, *and* <u>wood shavings</u> covered the linoleum that had been laid over manure-covered boards. . . .
>
> My <u>sister</u> *and* <u>I</u> fumbled to undo all the knots we had tied into the rope around our bundle.

Fluency: Clarify Word Meaning

Show that you understand the meanings of the words in italics by answering these questions:

1. Which of the following is a *euphemism* for "died": expired or passed away?
2. What adjective could you use to describe someone who is *adept* in sports?
3. What might the *destitute* do to *assuage* their hunger?
4. Why would a thief not want to be *conspicuous*?
5. What do you think would be the most difficult adjustment to *communal* living?
6. How would you move an *unwieldy* piece of furniture?
7. What problems could result from a *cursory* review of a contract?

Practice Copy these sentences. Underline the parts of each compound subject, and circle the conjunction that joins them.

1. My family and I lived in stall 40.
2. Finding a broom and obtaining mattresses were important on that first day.
3. My sister and I worried about Mama.
4. Mama or Kay made up the army cots.
5. The lack of privacy and the rugged accommodations made our lives difficult.

Writing Application Add a second subject to each sentence to form a compound subject.

1. My brother served in the army.
2. The carpeting in the room was old.

WG Prentice Hall Writing and Grammar Connection: Chapter 19, Section 1

310 ◆ Clashing Forces

TEACHING RESOURCES

The following resources can be used to enrich or extend the instruction for pp. 310–311.

Vocabulary

- **Selection Support:** Build Vocabulary, p. 81
- **Vocabulary and Spelling Practice Book** (Use this booklet for skills enrichment.)

Grammar

- **Selection Support:** Build Grammar Skills, p. 82
- *WG* **Writing and Grammar,** Platinum Level, p. 414
- **Daily Language Practice Transparencies** ▪

Writing

- *WG* **Writing and Grammar,** Platinum Level, pp. 244–266
- **Writing and Grammar iText CD-ROM** ▪
- **Writing Models and Graphic Organizers on Transparencies,** pp. 75–78

 BLOCK SCHEDULING: Resources marked with this symbol provide varied instruction during 90-minute blocks.

Writing Lesson

Internment Camp Research Report

Uchida describes one of the places that Japanese Americans were held during World War II. Write a research report that describes other internment camps.

Prewriting   Using books about World War II or other reliable print or online reference sources, compile data about the many internment centers set up during the war. Use several sources to ensure the accuracy of your information.

Drafting   As you write, include details that you learned from your research and explain how other camps compared or contrasted with the one in which Uchida lived.

Revising   Highlight all facts and figures in your draft. Place a check next to those you have confirmed. If necessary, qualify statements with terms like *approximately*, *nearly*, *more than*, or *about* to make your writing more accurate.

Model: Using Qualifiers for Accuracy

Two of the larger camps were established in Arizona. One

approximately

located near Poston housed 18,000 internees.

> A qualifier like *approximately* ensures the accuracy of this statement.

 Prentice Hall Writing and Grammar Connection: Chapter 12, Section 2

Extension Activities

Listening and Speaking   As a lawyer, prepare a **persuasive argument** to defend a Japanese American family against internment. Use details like these from the selections to impress the judge:

- Specific details about the family's life before the war
- Emotional appeals about mistreatment of internees in the camps
- Examples of this family's loyalty to the United States

Deliver your argument for classmates, and have them determine a verdict.

Research and Technology   With a partner, interview several people who lived during World War II. Take notes as they recount their memories of the war. Also, read eyewitness accounts of the war era, and note memorable quotations. Then, prepare an **oral history** in which you introduce each speaker and provide his or her remarks. If possible, include copies of period photographs of the speakers. **[Group Activity]**

 Take It to the Net   www.phschool.com

Go online for an additional research activity using the Internet.

---

❸ Writing Lesson

- Review the phases of the research writing process with students—research, prewriting, drafting, and final revision.

- Encourage students to use government sources as well as personal accounts of life in the camps. Many of these may be found on the Internet.

- On the chalkboard, model the use of index cards to collect and record supporting details.

❹ Research and Technology

- Allow students to choose their own partners.

- As a class, create a list of good interview questions. Go over interview etiquette with students and note-taking skills.

- If possible, arrange for a few people who remember World War II to visit your class on different days. Have students conduct a class-wide interview and take notes. Then encourage students to find at least one more outside person to interview themselves.

- Model how to create an oral history from the notes they've taken, as well as how you would like students to present their oral histories.

CUSTOMIZE INSTRUCTION
for Universal Access

To address different learning styles, use the following activities suggested in the **Extension Activities** booklet, p. 21.

- For Verbal/Linguistic Learners, use Activity 5.
- For Visual/Spatial and Verbal/Linguistic Learners, use Activity 6.
- For Logical/Mathematical Learners, use Activity 7.

ASSESSMENT RESOURCES

The following resources can be used to assess students' knowledge and skills.

Selection Assessment

- **Formal Assessment,** pp. 69–71
- **Open Book Test,** pp. 61–63
- **Test Bank Software**
- **Got It! Assessment Videotapes,** Tape 2

PRENTICE HALL ASSESSMENT SYSTEM

- **Workbook**
- **Skill Book**
- **Transparencies**
- **CD-ROM**

 Take It to the Net

Visit www.phschool.com for self-tests and additional questions on the selections.

Lesson Objectives

1. To understand the impact of Japanese internment on people
2. To explore the reactions of people to the bombing of Pearl Harbor

Connections

David Guterson accurately portrays through his fictional characters what it was like for people of Japanese descent to be sent to internment camps during the war. Have students reread the excerpt from *Desert Exile* once they have read the excerpt from *Snow Falling on Cedars*. Have students identify similarities and differences as they read between the ways in which the two authors portray this significant historical event.

Injustice for Japanese Americans

• Explain to students that this excerpt offers fictional characters in an historically accurate setting.

• As students read the excerpt from Guterson's novel, have them pay attention to the ways in which the different characters react to the news of the bombing of Pearl Harbor.

• Point out to students that a significant section of this selection is an excerpt from the fictional local newspaper. Discuss the way in which this device adds a feeling of authenticity and reality to the story.

CONNECTIONS
Literature and History
Japanese American Internment Camps

from

SNOW FALLING ON CEDARS

DAVID GUTERSON

In her personal narrative from *Desert Exile: The Uprooting of a Japanese-American Family*, Yoshiko Uchida describes how she and her family were taken from their home and imprisoned in a camp after the bombing of Pearl Harbor. Uchida's situation was not unusual, and it gave other writers the inspiration to show what she and thousands of others had to face during this period in history.

In his 1994 novel, *Snow Falling on Cedars*, David Guterson wrote about this significant event. Although the plot details a mystery, it is set against the historical facts of Japanese internment. The novel accurately and poignantly captures what it was like for Japanese Americans to be taken from their homes and held against their will after the bombing of Pearl Harbor.

In this excerpt from the novel, Guterson's fictional characters face the reaction to the bombing of Pearl Harbor.

✺ ENRICHMENT: Art Connection

War Memorial

Ruth Asawa created a panoramic bronze memorial dedicated to Japanese Americans who were forced to live in internment camps during World War II. The memorial, dedicated in March 1994, is located in San Jose, California, half a block away from the original site of the War Relocation Authority building for California, Arizona, and Washington. (The War Relocation Authority supervised the internment.)

Students can visit a Web site that tells about and has photographs of this memorial at http://www.scu.edu/SCU/Programs/Diversity/memorial.html. Encourage students to click on links to view close-up photographs of the panels described.

Arthur's war extra included an article entitled "Japanese Leaders Here Pledge Loyalty to America," in which Masato Nagaishi, Masao Uyeda, and Zenhichi Miyamoto, all strawberry men, made statements to the effect that they and all other island Japanese stood ready to protect the American flag. They spoke on behalf of the Japanese Chamber of Commerce, the Japanese-American Citizens' League, and the Japanese Community Center, and their pledges, said the *Review*, were "prompt and <u>unequivocal</u>," including Mr. Uyeda's promise that "if there is any sign of sabotage or spies, we will be the first ones to report it to the authorities." Arthur also ran his editor's column under the usual heading of "Plain Talk," which he'd composed wearily at two A.M. with a candle <u>propped</u> beside his typewriter.

If ever there was a community which faced a local emergency growing out of something over which it had no control, it is San Piedro Island[1] this Monday morning, December 8, 1941.

This is, indeed, a time for plain talk about things that matter to all of us.

There are on this island some 800 members of 150 families whose blood ties lie with a nation which yesterday committed an atrocity against all that is decent. That nation has committed itself to a war against us and has earned our swift and sure action. America will unite to respond courageously to the threat now facing us in the Pacific. And when the dust settles, America will have won.

In the meantime the task before us is grave and invites our strongest emotions. Yet these emotions, the *Review* must stress, should not include a blind, hysterical hatred of all persons who trace their ancestry to Japan. That some of these persons happen to be American citizens, happen to be loyal to this country, or happen to have no longer a binding tie with the land of their birth could all easily be swept aside by mob <u>hysteria</u>.

In light of this, the *Review* points out that those of Japanese descent on this island are not responsible for the tragedy at Pearl Harbor.[2] Make no mistake about it. They have pledged their loyalty to the United States and have been fine citizens of San Piedro for decades now. These people are our neighbors. They have sent six of their sons into the United States Army. They, in short, are not the enemy, any more than our fellow islanders of German or Italian descent. We should not allow ourselves to forget these things, and they should guide us in our behavior toward all our neighbors.

So of all islanders—of all ancestries—the *Review* would seek as calm an approach as possible in this emergency. Let us so live

unequivocal (un ē kwiv′ ə kəl) *adj.* certain; leaving no doubt

propped (präpt) *v.* supported by placing something under or against

hysteria (hi ster′ ē ə) *n.* nervous outburst; conduct exhibiting unmanageable fear or emotional excess

---

1. **San Piedro Island** *n.* island north of Puget Sound in Washington.
2. **Pearl Harbor** *n.* naval base and headquarters of the U.S. Pacific Fleet in Honolulu, Hawaii, where, in 1941, the Japanese made a surprise air attack that temporarily crippled the U.S. Fleet and resulted in the entry of the United States into World War II.

Connections: from *Snow Falling on Cedars* ◆ 313

Background

Internment Camps

The United States government imprisoned over 120,000 people of Japanese descent during the years 1942 to 1946. More than 70,000 of those people were U.S. citizens. The government officials mistakenly, and with very little evidence, believed that Japanese Americans posed a threat to national security. In all, there were 10 people convicted of spying for Japan—and all of them were Caucasian. For photographs, links, and more information about the camps, have interested students go to http://www.geocities.com/Athens/8420/main.html.

CUSTOMIZE INSTRUCTION FOR UNIVERSAL ACCESS

For Special Needs Students	For Less Proficient Readers
Make sure students understand that part of what they are reading is an editorial published in the fictional local newspaper the day after Japan bombed Pearl Harbor. Read the editorial only, then ask students to paraphrase what it says. Encourage students to think about how this editorial helps the story seem true, as if it were a work of nonfiction.	Engage students in a discussion about how the different characters react to the news of the bombing of Pearl Harbor. Ask them to think about what these reactions show us about each character. Why does Arthur feel the need to write the editorial? What is he afraid others on the island will do? How do the reactions of Arthur, Ishmael, and Hatsue differ? Who is most realistic in his or her reaction?

Thematic Connection

Answer: Hatsue's words echo the feeling that Japanese Americans have been treated unfairly simply because of their ethnic origins.

in this trying time that when it is all over we islanders can look one another in the eye with the knowledge that we have behaved honorably and fairly. Let us remember what is so easy to forget in the mad intensity of wartime: that prejudice and hatred are never right and never to be accepted by a just society.

Ishmael sat reading his father's words in the cedar tree; he was re-reading them when Hatsue, in her coat and scarf, ducked in and sat down on the moss beside him. "My father was up all night," said Ishmael. "He put this paper out."

"My father can't get our money from the bank," Hatsue replied to this. "We have a few dollars, and the rest we can't get. My parents aren't citizens."

"What will you do?"

"We don't know."

"I have twenty dollars from picking season," said Ishmael. "You can have all of it—you can just have it. I'll bring it to school in the morning."

"No," said Hatsue. "Don't bring it. My father will figure out something pretty soon. I could never accept your money."

Ishmael turned onto his side, toward her, and propped himself on his elbow. "It's hard to believe," he said.

"It's so unreal," answered Hatsue "It just isn't fair—it's not *fair*. How could they do this, just like that? How did we get ourselves into this?"

"*We* didn't get ourselves in it," said Ishmael. "The Japanese *forced* us

314

it. And on a Sunday morning, when no one was ready. It's cheap, if
ask me. They—"

Look at my face," interrupted Hatsue. "Look at my eyes, Ishmael. My
is the face of the people who did it—don't you see what I mean? My
—it's how the Japanese look. My parents came to San Piedro from
an. My mother and father, they hardly speak English. My family is
ad trouble now. Do you see what I mean? We're going to have trou-

Wait a minute," said Ishmael. "You're not Japanese. You're—"

You heard the news. They're arresting people. They're calling a lot of
le spies. Last night some men stopped at the Ichiyamas' and called
n names, Ishmael. They sat out front and honked their horn. How
this be happening?" she added. "How did things get like this?"

Connecting Literature and History

How does the mood of Uchida's story from *Desert Exile* compare
and contrast with the mood of Guterson's story?

Although one is nonfiction and the other is fiction, what similarities
and differences can you identify in each writer's story?

Why would a fiction writer like Guterson want to include such a
historically powerful event in a novel?

David Guterson

(b. 1956)
David
Guterson
drew praise
worthy of a
literary
giant for
his first
novel,
Snow Falling on Cedars. It
won the PEN/Faulkner
Award—the largest annual
literary prize in the United
States for fiction—in 1995.
Originally from Seattle,
Guterson moved to Puget
Sound in Washington,
where he taught high-
school English. He then
began writing for *Sports
Illustrated* and *Harper's* magazine. In 1999, Guterson
published his second book,
East of the Mountains.

Connections: from Snow Falling on Cedars ◆ 315

The Cabuliwallah

Lesson Objectives

1. **To analyze and respond to literary elements**
   - Literary Analysis: Relationships Between Characters
   - Connecting Literary Elements: Static and Dynamic Characters

2. **To read, comprehend, analyze, and critique a short story**
   - Reading Strategy: Engaging Your Senses
   - Reading Check questions
   - Review and Assess questions
   - Assessment Practice (ATE)

3. **To develop word analysis skills, fluency, and systematic vocabulary**
   - Vocabulary Development Lesson: Latin Word Root: *-jud-*

4. **To understand and apply written and oral language conventions**
   - Spelling Strategy
   - Grammar Lesson: Predicate Nominatives and Predicate Adjectives

5. **To understand and apply appropriate writing and research strategies**
   - Writing Lesson: Journal Entry
   - Extension Activity: Timeline

6. **To understand and apply listening and speaking strategies**
   - Extension Activity: Persuasive Speech

STEP-BY-STEP TEACHING GUIDE	PACING GUIDE
PRETEACH	
Motivate Students and Provide Background	
Use the Motivation activity (ATE p. 316)	5 min.
Read and discuss the Preview material and Background information (SE/ATE p. 316)	5 min.
Introduce the Concepts	
Introduce the Literary Analysis and Reading Strategy (SE/ATE p. 317) A	15 min.
Pronounce the vocabulary words and read their definitions (SE p. 317)	5 min.
TEACH	
Monitor Comprehension	
Informally monitor comprehension by circulating while students read independently or in groups A	20 min.
Monitor students' comprehension with the Reading Check notes (SE/ATE pp. 321, 323, 325)	as students read
Develop vocabulary with Vocabulary notes (SE pp. 320, 321, 322, 323, 324; ATE p. 321)	as students read
Develop Understanding	
Develop students' understanding of relationships between characters with Literary Analysis annotations (SE p. 324; ATE pp. 319, 321, 324, 325) A	10 min.
Develop students' understanding of engaging the senses with Reading Strategy annotations (SE pp. 320, 323; ATE pp. 320, 322, 323)	10 min.
ASSESS	
Assess Mastery	
Assess students' mastery of the Reading Strategy and Literary Analysis by having them answer the Review and Assess questions (SE/ATE p. 327)	20 min.
Use one or more of the print and media Assessment Resources (ATE p. 329) A	up to 50 min.
EXTEND	
Apply Understanding	
Have students complete the Vocabulary Development Lesson and the Grammar Lesson (SE p. 328) A	20 min.
Apply students' ability to use first-person pronouns using the Writing Lesson (SE/ATE p. 329) A	45 min.
Apply students' understanding using one or more of the Extension Activities (SE p. 329)	20–90 min.

A **ACCELERATED INSTRUCTION:**
Use the strategies and activities identified with an **A**.

UNIVERSAL ACCESS
● = Below Level Students
▲ = On-Level Students
■ = Above Level Students

Time and Resource Manager

Reading Level: Average
Average Number of Instructional Days: 4

RESOURCES

PRINT 📖	TRANSPARENCIES 🗂	TECHNOLOGY 💿 🎧 📼
• **Beyond Literature**, Cultural Connection: Wedding Customs and Traditions, p. 22 ▲ ■		• **Interest Grabber Video**, Tape 2 ● ▲ ■
• **Selection Support Workbook:** ● ▲ ■ Literary Analysis, p. 88 Reading Strategy, p. 87 Build Vocabulary, p. 85	• **Literary Analysis and Reading Transparencies**, pp. 43 and 44 ● ▲ ■	
		• **Listening to Literature** ● ▲ ■ Audiocassettes, Side 11 Audio CDs, CD 6
• **Literatura en español** ● ▲ • **Literary Analysis for Enrichment** ■		
• **Formal Assessment:** Selection Test, pp. 72–74 ● ▲ ■ • **Open Book Test**, pp. 64–66 ● ▲ ■ • **Performance Assessment and Portfolio Management**, p. 30 ● ▲ ■ • **ASSESSMENT SYSTEM** ● ▲ ■	• **ASSESSMENT SYSTEM** ● ▲ ■ Skills Practice Answers and Explanations on Transparencies	• **Test Bank Software** ● ▲ ■ • **Got It! Assessment Videotapes** ● ▲
• **Selection Support Workbook:** ● ▲ ■ Build Grammar Skills, p. 86 • **Writing and Grammar**, Platinum Level ● ▲ ■ • **Extension Activities**, p. 22 ● ▲ ■	• **Daily Language Practice Transparencies** ● ▲	• **Writing and Grammar iText CD-ROM** ● ▲ ■ 💻 *Take It to the Net* www.phschool.com

BLOCK SCHEDULING: Use one 90-minute class period to preteach the selection and have students read it. Use a second 90-minute class period to assess students' mastery of skills and have them complete one of the Extension Activities.

Motivation

Play a recording of the Beatles song "Yesterday." Encourage students to pay close attention to the lyrics. Ask them what they think the lyrics say about the nature of relationships. Lead a discussion in which students discuss ways people and relationships change. Tell students that "The Cabuliwallah" provides another perspective on the changing nature of relationships.

▣ Interest Grabber Video

As an alternative, play "Daily Life in India" on Tape 2 to engage student interest.

❶ Background

Social Studies

In the early 1970s, Afghanistan experienced great economic growth, aided in large part by the United States and the former Soviet Union. However, the 1979 Soviet invasion and the subsequent civil war severely hurt the country's economic development. Today, Afghanistan remains one of the world's poorest countries. Many of its people, such as the Cabuliwallah in this story, look for better economic opportunities abroad.

Prepare to Read

The Cabuliwallah

 Take It to the Net

Visit www.phschool.com for interactive activities and instruction related to "The Cabuliwallah," including
- background
- graphic organizers
- literary elements
- reading strategies

Preview

Connecting to the Literature

When you do not see someone for a long time, that person becomes "frozen" on the film in your memory. A childhood friend who moves away remains five years old in your mind, although he or she has obviously gotten older. The main character in this story experiences a conflict caused by such a "time freeze."

❶ Background

The Cabuliwallah in this story is a traveling salesman. The Indian word *wallah* means "salesman"; the *Cabuli*wallah is the "salesman from Cabul" (Kabul is the capital of Afghanistan). Like many poor people, he has left his homeland temporarily to find better economic opportunities in another place.

TEACHING RESOURCES

The following resources can be used to enrich or extend the instruction for pp. 316–317.

Motivation

▣ **Interest Grabber Video**, Tape 2 ▣

Background

📖 **Beyond Literature**, p. 22

 Take It to the Net

Visit www.phschool.com for background and hotlinks for "The Cabuliwallah."

Literary Analysis

📑 **Literary Analysis and Reading Transparencies**, Relationships Between Characters, p. 44

Reading

📖 **Selection Support:** Reading Strategy, p. 87; Build Vocabulary, p. 85 ▣

📑 **Literary Analysis and Reading Transparencies**, Engaging Your Senses, p. 43

▣ **BLOCK SCHEDULING:** Resources marked with this symbol provide varied instruction during 90-minute blocks.

Literary Analysis

Relationships Between Characters

The **relationships between characters**—the interactions and feelings that pass between people in a story—can reveal a lot about each character. In the following passage, the details in italics show a friendly relationship between Mini, the narrator's young daughter, and the Cabuliwallah.

> . . . I was startled to find Mini seated on a bench by the door, *laughing and talking with the great Cabuliwallah at her feet.* In all her life, it appeared, my small daughter had never found *so patient a listener,* except for her father.

As you read the story, focus on the relationships between characters and what they reveal.

Connecting Literary Elements

In some stories, characters seem to stay the same over time. In others, characters change or grow, and these changes can affect their relationships. A **static character** remains basically the same as a story unfolds. In contrast, a **dynamic character** changes and grows. Notice how the characters and their relationships in this story change over time.

Reading Strategy

Engaging Your Senses

When you read a story, **engage your senses**—use details of sight, sound, taste, smell, and touch—to experience the richness of the characters and setting. For example, when the narrator describes "tinkling chandeliers" or the warmth of the sun on his feet, engage your senses of sound and touch to experience these sensations yourself. To help you notice sensory details as you read, record the details on a chart like the one here.

Sight	Peddler's soiled clothing
Sound	Daughter's laughter
Touch	Warmth of sun on the father's feet
Taste	
Smell	

Vocabulary Development

precarious (prē ker′ ē əs) *adj.* dangerous; unstable (p. 320)

impending (im pen′ diŋ) *adj.* about to happen (p. 321)

judicious (jo͞o dish′ əs) *adj.* showing sound judgment or common sense (p. 321)

euphemism (yo͞o′ fə miz′ əm) *n.* word or phrase substituted for a more unpleasant word or phrase (p. 321)

imploring (im plôr′ iŋ) *v.* pleading with (p. 322)

fettered (fet′ ərd) *adj.* restrained, as with a chain (p. 323)

sordid (sôr′ did) *adj.* filthy or dirty (p. 324)

pervaded (pər vād′ id) *v.* spread throughout; filled (p. 324)

The Cabuliwallah ◆ 317

❷ Literary Analysis

Relationships Between Characters

- Tell students that they can learn a lot about a character by focusing on his or her relationships with others.

- As a class, read the excerpt from the story. Discuss with students what they can infer about Mini and the narrator from this short passage.

- As they read, have students use the Relationships Between Characters transparency in **Literary Analysis and Reading Transparencies,** p. 44, to learn about characters by examining their relationships.

❸ Reading Strategy

Engaging Your Senses

- As a class, read the instruction about engaging your senses.

- Encourage students to create a chart like the one shown to record sensory details as they read "The Cabuliwallah."

- Explain to students that they will appreciate the story more fully if they engage their senses while they read.

Vocabulary Development

- Pronounce each vocabulary word for students, and read the definitions as a class. Have students identify any words with which they are already familiar.

 E-Teach

Visit E-Teach at www.phschool.com for teachers' essays on how to teach, with questions and answers.

CUSTOMIZE INSTRUCTION
For Visual/Spatial Learners

Have students describe the sounds that might accompany the scene in this photograph. Encourage them to add details of sight, sound, touch, taste, and smell to their sensory details chart based on what they see in the photograph.

❶ About the Selection

This short story is set in India and describes a culture with customs very different from the culture in the United States. However, it treats themes that are universal: the love of fathers for their daughters, and the ways that relationships change as people change. In the beginning of the story, the narrator considers the Cabuliwallah very different from himself, but by the story's end, he realizes that the similarities between them are more important than the differences.

318 ◆ *Clashing Forces*

TEACHING RESOURCES

The following resources can be used to enrich or extend the instruction for pp. 318–326.

Literary Analysis

📖 **Selection Support:** Literary Analysis, p. 88

Reading

🎧 **Listening to Literature Audiocassettes,** Side 11 ▪

💿 **Listening to Literature Audio CDs,** CD 6 ▪

▪ **BLOCK SCHEDULING:** Resources marked with this symbol provide varied instruction during 90-minute blocks.

❶ The Cabuliwallah

Rabindranath Tagore

Translated From the Bengali Language

❷ Mini, my five-year-old daughter, cannot live without chattering. I really believe that in all her life she has not wasted one minute in silence. Her mother is often vexed at this and would stop her prattle, but I do not. To see Mini quiet is unnatural, and I cannot bear it for long. Because of this, our conversations are always lively.

One morning, for instance, when I was in the midst of the seventeenth chapter of my new novel, Mini stole into the room and, putting her hand into mine, said: "Father! Ramdayal the door-keeper calls a crow a krow! He doesn't know anything, does he?"

❸ ◀ **Critical Viewing** How does this market scene reflect the mood at the beginning of "The Cabuliwallah"? **[Connect]**

The Cabuliwallah ◆ *319*

❷ Literary Analysis
Relationships Between Characters

- Read aloud the bracketed passage.
- Ask students to describe the relationship between father and daughter at the beginning of the story.
  Answer: Students should describe the relationship as open, communicative, and comfortable.
- Make sure students find details in the text to support their answers.
  Possible responses: Mini's father enjoys her chattering. He describes their conversations as "lively."

❸ ▶ Critical Viewing
Answer: The busy, chaotic scene reflects the feeling of energy in the narrator's description of Mini. The scene suggests the lively variety that might draw a child of Mini's temperament to look out the window.

319

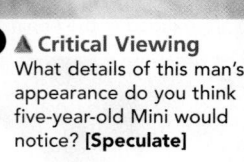

Before I could explain the language differences in this country, she was on the trace of another subject. "What do you
think, Father? Shola says there is an elephant in the clouds,
blowing water out of his trunk, and that is why it rains!"

The child had seated herself at my feet near the table
and was playing softly, drumming on her knees. I
was hard at work on my seventeenth chapter,
where Pratap Singh, the hero, had just caught
Kanchanlata, the heroine, in his arms and was
about to escape with her by the third-story window of the castle, when all of a sudden Mini left
her play and ran to the window, crying "A
Cabuliwallah! a Cabuliwallah!" Sure enough, in
the street below was a Cabuliwallah passing
slowly along. He wore the loose, soiled clothing
of his people, and a tall turban; there was a
bag on his back, and he carried boxes of
grapes in his hand.

I cannot tell what my daughter's feelings
were at the sight of this man, but she began to
call him loudly. Ah, I thought, he will come in,
and my seventeenth chapter will never be finished! At this exact moment the Cabuliwallah
turned and looked up at the child. When she
saw this, she was overcome by terror, fled to
her mother's protection, and disappeared. She
had a blind belief that inside the bag which the
big man carried were two or three children like
herself. Meanwhile, the peddler entered my
doorway and greeted me with a smiling face.

So <u>precarious</u> was the position of my hero and my heroine that my
first impulse was to stop and buy something, especially since Mini
had called to the man. I made some small purchases, and a conversation began about Abdurrahman, the Russians, the English, and the
frontier policy.[1]

As he was about to leave, he asked: "And where is the little girl, sir?"

I, thinking that Mini must get rid of her false fear, had her brought
out. She stood by my chair, watching the Cabuliwallah and his bag.
He offered her nuts and raisins, but she would not be tempted and
only clung closer to me, with all her doubts increased. This was their
first meeting.

 One morning, however, not many days later, as I was leaving the
house, I was startled to find Mini seated on a bench by the door,
laughing and talking with the great Cabuliwallah at her feet. In all
her life, it appeared, my small daughter had never found so patient a

---

1. **Abdurrahman . . . policy** political issues between Great Britain and Afghanistan at
the time of the story.

320 ◆ *Clashing Forces*

⑤ ▲ Critical Viewing
What details of this man's
appearance do you think
five-year-old Mini would
notice? **[Speculate]**

precarious (prē ker′ ē əs)
adj. dangerous; unstable

Reading Strategy
Engaging Your Senses
Which sensory details in
this paragraph help you
picture Mini and the
Cabuliwallah?

listener, except for her father. Already the corner of her little sari[2] was stuffed with almonds and raisins, gifts from her visitor. "Why did you give her those?" I said and, taking out an eight-anna piece,[3] handed it to him. The man accepted the money without delay, and slipped it into his pocket.

Alas, on my return an hour later, I found the unfortunate coin had made twice its own worth of trouble. The Cabuliwallah had given it to Mini, and her mother, seeing the bright round object, had pounced on the child with: "Where did you get that eight-anna piece?"

"The Cabuliwallah gave it to me," said Mini cheerfully.

"The Cabuliwallah gave it to you!" cried her mother much shocked. "O Mini! how could you take it from him?"

Entering at this moment, I saved her from <u>impending</u> disaster and proceeded to make my own inquiries. I found that it was not the first or the second time the two had met. The Cabuliwallah had overcome the child's first terror by a <u>judicious</u> bribery of nuts and almonds, and the two were now great friends.

They had many quaint jokes which afforded them a great deal of amusement. Seated in front of him, and looking with all her tiny dignity on his gigantic frame, Mini would ripple her face with laughter and begin "O Cabuliwallah! Cabuliwallah! what have you got in your bag?"

He would reply in the nasal accents of a mountaineer: "An elephant!" Not much cause for merriment, perhaps, but how they both enjoyed their joke! And for me, this child's talk with a grown-up man always had in it something strangely fascinating.

Then the Cabuliwallah, not to be caught behind, would take his turn with: "Well, little one, and when are you going to the father-in-law's house?"[4]

Now most small Bengali[5] maidens have heard long ago about the father-in-law's house, but we, being a little modern, had kept these things from our child, and at this question Mini must have been a trifle bewildered. But she would not show it and with instant composure replied: "Are you going there?"

Among men of the Cabuliwallah's class, however, it is well-known that the words "father-in-law's house" have a double meaning. It is a <u>euphemism</u> for jail, the place where we are well cared for at no expense. The sturdy peddler would take my daughter's question in this sense. "Ah," he would say, shaking his fist at an invisible policeman, "I will thrash my father-in-law!" Hearing this, and picturing the poor, uncomfortable relative, Mini would go into peals of laughter, joined by her formidable friend.

These were autumn mornings, the time of year when kings of old

---

2. **sari** (sä´ rē) *n.* garment worn by a Hindu woman, which consists of a long piece of cloth worn wrapped around the body, with one end forming an ankle-length skirt and the other end draped over one shoulder and, sometimes, around the head.
3. **eight-anna piece** coin formerly used in India.
4. **father-in-law's house** an expression meaning "getting married."
5. **Bengali** of or from Bengal, a region of eastern India and, now, Bangladesh.

impending (im pen´ diŋ) *adj.* about to happen

judicious (jо̄о̄ dish´ əs) *adj.* showing sound judgment or common sense

euphemism (yо̄о̄´ fə miz´ əm) *n.* word or phrase substituted for a more unpleasant word or phrase

❽ ✓ Reading Check

What did the Cabuliwallah do with the coin that was given to him by Mini's father?

The Cabuliwallah ◆ 321

❻ Vocabulary Development

Latin Word Root: -jud-

- Draw students' attention to the word *judicious* and its definition, "showing sound judgment or common sense."
- Explain that the root *-jud-* means "judge."
- Ask students to brainstorm for other words with this root, such as *judiciary*, *judgment*, and *adjudicate*. Then, have them define each word and explain its relation to the root *-jud-*.

❼ Literary Analysis

Relationships Between Characters

- Have students read the bracketed passage. Instruct them to look for details that offer clues about the relationship between the narrator and his daughter.
- Ask students the following question: How would you describe the relationship between the father and daughter?
  Answer: The father adores his daughter—he saves her from a conflict with her mother over the coin, and he is fascinated by her relationship with the Cabuliwallah. He is also protective of Mini. He does not tell her about the father-in-law's house at her young age, because he wants her to be happy and free for as long as possible.

▶ **Monitor Progress** Students may be confused about why Mini and the Cabuliwallah, who are so different from one another, develop a relationship. Have them brainstorm for reasons that they become friends.
  Answer: Students may say that, because the Cabuliwallah travels all the time, he has few friends and is lonely. Other students may suggest that the Cabuliwallah likes children, or that spending time with Mini allows him to relax and laugh.

❽ ✓ Reading Check

Answer: The Cabuliwallah gave the coin to Mini.

CUSTOMIZE INSTRUCTION FOR UNIVERSAL ACCESS

For Less Proficient Readers	For Gifted/Talented Students
Students who have trouble identifying the relationships between characters should examine the exchange about the elephant (p. 321) to understand the relationship between the Cabuliwallah and Mini. The private joke emphasizes that these two have found in each other a quality they do not find in other people.	Have students write a conversation between Mini and the Cabuliwallah. What subjects might these two people, whose ages and backgrounds are so different, talk about? What ideas or opinions might they share? What might each of them teach the other? When students finish writing, have them act out their conversations.

- Read aloud the bracketed passage.
- Encourage students to reread the passage to themselves, taking note of the sensory details the writer uses. Have them record examples of sensory details in a chart like the one on p. 317.
- Then, ask students to identify the sense or senses to which this passage appeals.
  Answer: The descriptions in this passage appeal mainly to the sense of sight.

❿ Background

Geography Connection

Calcutta, which is India's largest metropolitan area and a major port, is located on the eastern bank of the Hooghly River, an arm of the Ganges. It was founded in 1690 by British trader Job Charnock as a trading post of the British East India Company.

The city became famous in 1756, when it was captured by Siraj-Ud-Dawlah, a Bengal ruler. But the British regained their power in 1757 when the city was recaptured under Robert Clive. Warren Hastings, the first Governor-General of India, made it the seat of the supreme courts of justice and the supreme revenue administration, and Calcutta became the capital of British India in 1772. By 1800, Calcutta had become a busy and flourishing town, the center of the cultural, political, and economic life of the state of Bengal.

went forth to conquest; and I, never stirring from my corner in Calcutta,[6] would let my mind wander over the whole world. At the very name of another country, my heart would go out to it, and at the sight of a foreigner in the streets, I would fall to weaving a network of dreams: the mountains, the glens,[7] the forests of his distant homeland with a cottage in its setting, and the free and independent life of far-away wilds. Perhaps these scenes of travel pass in my imagination all the more vividly because I lead a vegetable existence such that a call to travel would fall upon me like a thunderbolt. In the presence of this Cabuliwallah I was immediately transported to the foot of mountains, with narrow defiles[8] twisting in and out amongst their towering, arid peaks. I could see the string of camels bearing merchandise, and the company of turbaned merchants carrying queer old firearms, and some of their spears down toward the plains. I could see—but at this point Mini's mother would intervene, <u>imploring</u> me to "beware of that man."

imploring (im plôr´ iŋ) *v.* pleading with

Unfortunately Mini's mother is a very timid lady. Whenever she hears a noise in the street or sees people coming toward the house, she always jumps to the conclusion that they are either thieves, drunkards, snakes, tigers, malaria, cockroaches, caterpillars, or an English sailor. Even after all these years of experience, she is not able to overcome her terror. Thus she was full of doubts about the Cabuliwallah and used to beg me to keep a watchful eye on him.

I tried to gently laugh her fear away, but then she would turn on me seriously and ask solemn questions.

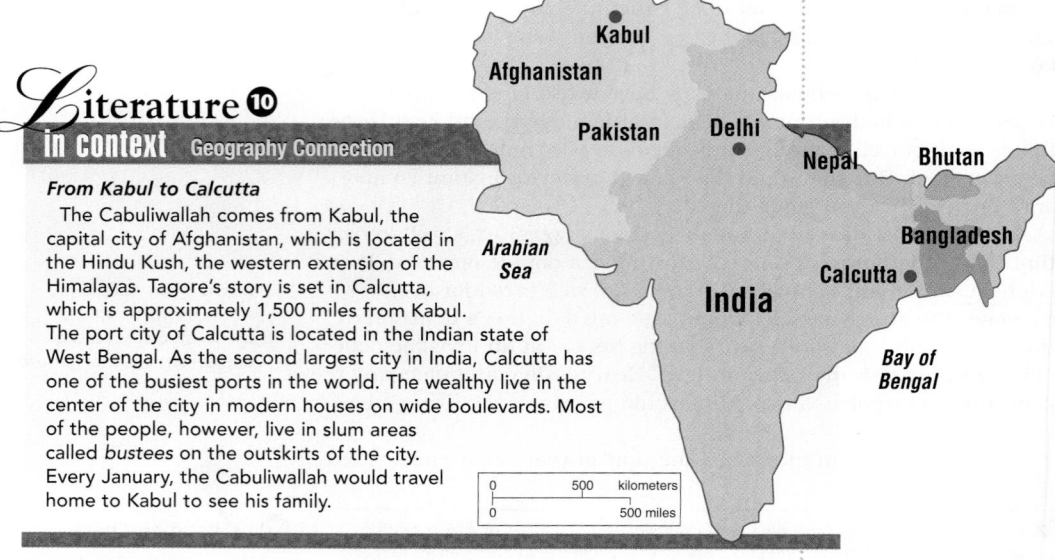

Literature ❿ in context   Geography Connection

From Kabul to Calcutta

The Cabuliwallah comes from Kabul, the capital city of Afghanistan, which is located in the Hindu Kush, the western extension of the Himalayas. Tagore's story is set in Calcutta, which is approximately 1,500 miles from Kabul. The port city of Calcutta is located in the Indian state of West Bengal. As the second largest city in India, Calcutta has one of the busiest ports in the world. The wealthy live in the center of the city in modern houses on wide boulevards. Most of the people, however, live in slum areas called *bustees* on the outskirts of the city. Every January, the Cabuliwallah would travel home to Kabul to see his family.

6. **Calcutta** large city in eastern India.
7. **glens** (glenz) *n.* valleys.
8. **defiles** (de fīls´) *n.* deep, narrow mountain passes.

322 ◆ *Clashing Forces*

✹ ENRICHMENT: Cultural Connection

The Caste System

Explain to students that the caste system is a class system in Hindu society. The top caste is the *Brahman,* or priest, caste. Below that are the *Kshatriyas,* or warriors; the *Vaisyas,* who are merchants and bankers; and the *Sudras,* artisans and laborers. Each of these broad divisions has many subdivisions—perhaps as many as 3,000 in all. There are also the untouchables, or outcasts, people in the lowest social group. The caste system was abolished in India in 1950, but discrimination against the untouchables is still a problem.

Tell students that Tagore's own caste was *pirali brahman*—one of the brahman castes. Suggest that interested students use research materials in the library or on the Internet to find out more about the caste system in Hindu society. Have them make a list of headings or topics that will help them locate information.

Writing Lesson

Journal Entry

In "The Cabuliwallah," Tagore describes the characters so vividly that they seem to be people he knows. Write a journal entry as if you were one of the characters in the story.

Prewriting Choose a character. Review the story, and pick a significant event in your subject's life. Write about that event as if you were the character.

Drafting As you draft, focus on bringing your subject to life. Along with factual details, include descriptions, feelings, and personal insights. Write in the first person to create an "I was there" feeling in your journal entry.

Model: Using First-Person Narration

I met a little girl today. She reminds me of my own Parbati. I miss her laugh. I wish I could hold her in my arms.

> First-person pronouns and personal insights make the entry seem real.

Revising Reread your draft carefully to see that you have used first-person pronouns and that your perspective is consistent.

 Prentice Hall Writing and Grammar Connection: Chapter 13, Section 2

Extension Activities

Listening and Speaking Imagine that you are the Cabuliwallah's lawyer at his trial. Deliver a **persuasive speech** to convince the court that your client should be given a light sentence. Drawing details from the story, try to gain sympathy by referring to these elements of the case:

- His positive character traits
- The circumstances of his life
- The validity of his claims

After you deliver your speech, ask your classmates to rate the quality of your defense.

Research and Technology To learn more about the author's homeland, research the history of India from the 1750s until its independence in 1947. Working in a group, use print and electronic sources for information, and list key dates and events on index cards. Organize your cards to develop a **timeline.** Illustrate and display your timeline. [Group Activity]

Take It to the Net   www.phschool.com

Go online for an additional research activity using the Internet.

The Cabuliwallah ◆ 329

Lesson Support for p. 329

❸ Writing Lesson

- Tell students to imagine themselves as the character they've chosen and write from that point of view.
- Use the Writing Lesson to guide students in writing their journal entries.
- During the revising stage, encourage students to pair up and read each other's entries. Have them ask each other questions in order to get more details into their writing.

❹ Listening and Speaking

- Have students reread the section on p. 323 that describes the Cabuliwallah's crime.
- Engage the class in a discussion about the Cabuliwallah's crime. Do students believe there are any mitigating factors?
- After students write their speeches, encourage them to rehearse them in small groups.
- Have students use the rubric for Delivering a Persuasive Argument in **Performance Assessment and Portfolio Management,** p. 30.

CUSTOMIZE INSTRUCTION for Universal Access

To address different learning styles, use the following activities suggested in the **Extension Activities** booklet, p. 22.

- For Visual/Spatial and Verbal/Linguistic Learners, use Activity 5.
- For Verbal/Linguistic and Interpersonal Learners, use Activity 6.
- For Musical/Rhythmic Learners, use Activity 7.

ASSESSMENT RESOURCES

The following resources can be used to assess students' knowledge and skills.

Selection Assessment

 Formal Assessment, pp. 72–74

Open Book Test, pp. 64–66

Test Bank Software

Got It! Assessment Videotapes, Tape 2

Take It to the Net
Visit www.phschool.com for self-tests and additional questions on "The Cabuliwallah."

Listening and Speaking Rubric

Performance Assess. and Portfolio Mgmt., p. 30

 PRENTICE HALL ASSESSMENT *SYSTEM*

Workbook   **Transparencies**

Skill Book   **CD-ROM**

Lesson Objectives

1. To write a persuasive essay
2. To learn the characteristics of a persuasive essay
3. To use writing strategies to generate ideas, plan, organize, evaluate, and revise the essay

Model From Literature

In "Style" (p. 199), Maya Angelou works to persuade the reader of the benefits of handling life with style.

Prewriting

- Have students suggest issues over which there is controversy, and list them on the board. Then select one of the topics and ask volunteers to tell why that issue is important to them.

- Discuss with students the pros and cons of the selected issue. Fill in a pro-and-con chart on the board as students offer their views.

- Have students select an issue to write on, either one of those discussed or an issue they have come up with on their own. Then, have them fill out a pro-and-con chart on the issue, just as you modeled for them.

- Tell students to review their charts and determine their own position on the issue.

- Have students begin compiling evidence to support their stand. Remind them that they don't have to use every fact they learn about their topic. Instead, students should compile evidence that solidly supports their main idea and that addresses opposing arguments.

- Explain to students that their audience will affect how they write their composition, what tone they use, and what information they include to support their opinion. For example, if they were to write a piece to be read by students on the benefits of school uniforms, it would be very different than one written for parents or school board members.

Writing WORKSHOP
Persuasion: Persuasive Essay

A **persuasive essay** is a work in which a writer tries to convince readers to accept a particular viewpoint or to take a certain action. In this workshop, you will write a persuasive essay on an issue of interest to you.

Assignment Criteria Your persuasive essay should have the following characteristics:

- A clearly stated opinion or argument on an issue that has more than one side
- A case study and other evidence that support the argument and address readers' concerns
- Memorable, convincing details and vivid, persuasive language
- A sustained and logical organization

To preview the criteria on which your persuasive essay may be assessed, see the Rubric on page 333.

Prewriting

Choose a topic. You should write your persuasive essay about an issue that is important to you. One strategy for finding a topic is to **scan a newspaper.** Find stories that make you angry, seem unfair, or demand change. Jot down some ideas about each of these stories, and choose a topic from among them.

Look at both sides. Build your argument by creating a pro-and-con chart to analyze your topic. In the left column, list your supporting arguments. In the right column, list the opposing arguments. Then, brainstorm for ways of countering the negative claims.

Gather evidence. While your own opinions form a good basis for your writing, gather evidence to support your ideas. Do research to gather precise and relevant evidence—facts, quotations, statistics, examples—from a variety of objective, bias-free sources. You might talk to an expert in the field, as well as review reports and interviews in news sources.

Consider your audience. Your audience may be friendly and supportive of your position, hostile to your views, or a mix of both. Identify the people who will read your essay, and plan your writing to address their concerns, biases, and expectations.

Pro-and-Con Chart	
Supporting	**Opposing**
– Honor roll students are responsible and dedicated.	– It is not fair to other students.
– They know the material.	– There would be inequality.

TEACHING RESOURCES

The following resources can be used to enrich or extend the instruction for pp. 330–333.

Writing and Grammar, Platinum Level, Chapter 7, pp. 124–145

Performance Assessment and Portfolio Management, p. 11

Writing Models and Graphic Organizers on Transparencies, pp. 45–52

Writing and Grammar iText CD-ROM Students can use the following tools as they complete their persuasive essays:

- Self-Interview
- Pros and Cons Chart
- Unity and Coherence Checker

Student Model

Before you begin drafting, read this student model and review the characteristics of powerful persuasion.

Esther Herrera
Hialeah, Florida

True Reward for Our Achievements

Straight-*A* students have been rewarded in different ways for their hard work. They have been given the chance to eat breakfast with the principal, they have received gifts and certificates, and they have been publicly acknowledged. Schools hope that these policies will not only serve as a reward to students but also as an inspiration to others to do well in their classes. However, these honor-roll students show little interest in the awards; they want something else. These students should be exempt from taking the final exam because they have demonstrated responsibility and dedication, they know the material, and most importantly they feel that other students will more likely be inspired to achieve the ultimate honor-roll goal.

> The writer clearly states her opinion on the issue.

Primarily, honor-roll students should be exempt from taking the final exam because they are responsible and dedicated. These students have stayed on task throughout the year, going out of their way to turn in a job well done. Sometimes, they sacrifice by staying up late to finish homework assignments. As one honor student recalled, "One time, I stayed up, literally, all night so that I could finish a project. The problem was not finishing it but making sure that it would come out perfect; it did."

> The writer states the argument and then supports it with valid reasons.

In addition, teachers should not have to give these students the final examination. Because they got *A*'s in the 1st, 2nd, 3rd, and 4th quarters, it is clear that the students know the material very well. Furthermore, the final exam is an added stress, because students worry and get nervous taking tests.

On the other hand, eleven out of twenty-five students whom I interviewed believe that such an exemption policy would not be fair to the other students. However, all students were given the same opportunity to get *A*'s. The striking thing about this survey is that many students who were in favor of an exemption policy were not honor students. Instead, they were students who might work harder to earn the privilege of not taking the final exam. What I say to the first eleven students is, Accept the challenge.

> By referring to a survey she conducted, the writer shows that she has consulted a range of her peers.

> Here, the writer addresses those who oppose her ideas.

In conclusion, honor-roll students should be exempt from taking the final exam because they have already proved themselves. These students deserve a true reward: the knowledge that their efforts have been recognized.

> The writer restates the opinion in her conclusion.

Student Model

- Explain that the Student Model is a sample and that persuasive essays may be longer.
- Ask students to state the issue and Esther's opinion.
  Answer: The issue is rewarding students who have performed well in school; Esther thinks that if students get A's for all 4 quarters, they should not have to take the final exam.
- Point out that Esther uses detailed arguments to support her opinion.
- Finally, ask students what Esther accomplishes in her final paragraph.
  Answer: She restates her opinion and concludes with a powerful image.

Real-World Connection

Explain to students that persuasive writing is not limited to nonfiction literary works and English class compositions. Many careers involve using your powers of persuasion: law, politics (local and national), activism, medicine, and teaching. Students may even be called on to persuade colleges to admit them (in an interview or essay) and employers to give them a job!

CUSTOMIZE INSTRUCTION FOR UNIVERSAL ACCESS

For Less Proficient Writers	For English Learners	For Advanced Writers
If students have difficulty choosing a topic, work through itemizing one of the issues suggested during the classroom discussion. If necessary, assign a topic.	Encourage students to focus on their experiences of different cultures to help them generate a topic for their persuasive composition. Students can also address an issue from their native cultures, but be sure to remind them to include enough details so their audience in the United States understands the issue well.	Encourage students to pick an issue about which they feel strongly but in which they are not experts. Challenge them to research both sides of the issue fully.

Drafting

- Explain to students that organization gives writing strength by making the point behind the words and arguments evident.

- Suggest that students write their main ideas with supporting evidence on slips of paper. They can then move these slips of paper around to see which order works best. The best arrangement can be used as a working outline for their essays. Encourage students to tape the slips in order onto another sheet of paper so they won't lose the organization.

- Ask students to make a note of which of their main ideas have too little supporting evidence. Tell them to find more support for or reconsider using each of these ideas.

- If students have chosen a topic of current general concern, encourage them to search the Internet and the periodical index of the library to uncover relevant statistics and expert opinions. If they have chosen an issue of local interest, encourage them to gather support by conducting their own interviews or surveys.

- To help students address readers' concerns, have students spend a few minutes with a partner, each helping the other think of possible objections.

Revising

- Supply students with red pens or pencils and have them follow the instructions in the text.

- Tell students that, in addition to evaluating the amount of support they have provided for each point, they should keep an eye on the type of support they used. For example, if they used only personal observations, they should consider adding other types of evidence, such as quotations or statistics.

- Also encourage students to make certain that each detail in a paragraph supports the key point of that paragraph.

(continued on page 333)

Writing WORKSHOP *continued*

Drafting

Organize to emphasize the strongest support. In your draft, introduce your topic and state your opinion in a clearly worded thesis statement. In the body of your essay, make the arguments that support and prove your thesis statement. Consider the organization shown at right.

Provide evidence. Build and support your argument with evidence, such as the following:

- **Case studies:** Give a detailed analysis of a case, or example, that illustrates and supports your position.

- **Statistics:** Provide numbers from research material or from surveys that you conducted to support your stand.

- **Expert opinion:** Include the advice of experts in the field. Use quotations when possible.

- **Personal anecdote:** Tell your readers about any of your own experiences or observations that support your view.

> ### Organizing a Persuasive Essay
>
> - Use your second-best argument for a good start.
> - Show and argue against an opposing view.
> - Organize the rest of your argument to lead up to your conclusion.
> * Save your best argument for a strong finish.

Revising

Revise to strengthen support. Review your draft to decide whether you have included enough supporting details.

1. Underline in red the topic sentence or the main idea of each paragraph.

2. Put a star next to each sentence that supports the topic sentence.

3. If a topic sentence has fewer than two supporting details, add more evidence or reconsider whether the point is worth including.

Model: Revising to Build Support

going out of their way to turn in a job well done. Sometimes, they sacrifice by staying up late to finish homework assignments.

Primarily, honor-roll students should be exempt from taking the final exam because they are responsible and dedicated. *These students have stayed on task throughout the year.

> Additional information helps to support Esther's claim.

USING TECHNOLOGY IN WRITING

If students are using word processors to draft and revise their persuasive compositions, suggest that they print out a copy of each draft before making any changes. Students will then have a record of the progress they have made throughout the writing process.

Students can also use the organizing tools and revision checkers available on the **Writing and Grammar iText CD-ROM.**

Revise to form parallel structures. Make the main points in your essay memorable by using *parallelism*—patterns or repetitions of grammatical structures. First, locate an important word, phrase, clause, or question. Then, build on that word or phrase to form parallel structures.

Example: We want *to learn, to shine,* and *to grow.*

Compare the model and nonmodel. Why is the model more interesting?

Nonmodel	Model
These students should be exempt from taking the final exam. They have responsibility and dedication. The material is mastered, and most importantly it will definitely stimulate other students. ...	These students should be exempt from taking the final exam because they have demonstrated responsibility and dedication, they know the material, and most importantly they feel that other students will more likely be inspired . . .

Publishing and Presenting

Choose one of the following ways to share your writing with classmates or a wider audience:

Publish in a print medium. If your topic relates to your school or community, submit your composition to your school newspaper. If it could appeal to a larger audience, consider submitting it as a letter to the editor of a local newspaper.

Deliver a speech. Use your persuasive essay as the basis for a speech. Present it to your class.

*W*G *Prentice Hall Writing and Grammar Connection: Chapter 7*

Speaking Connection
For instruction about persuasive presentations, see the **Listening and Speaking Workshop** on page 334.

Rubric for Self-Assessment

Evaluate your persuasive essay using the following criteria and rating scale:

Criteria	Rating Scale				
	Not very				Very
How clear and focused is the thesis statement?	1	2	3	4	5
How well is the thesis supported by evidence?	1	2	3	4	5
How well are readers' concerns anticipated and addressed?	1	2	3	4	5
How effectively are arguments organized?	1	2	3	4	5
How powerful is the persuasive language?	1	2	3	4	5

TEST-TAKING TIP

When students are taking a test that requires them to respond to a persuasive writing prompt, they should pace themselves as they work, allowing time for each stage of the writing process. For example, if they spend a few minutes organizing at the very beginning, it may save them time during the drafting stage. Suggest that students use a pro-and-con chart to jot down what they know about an assigned topic. If students are asked to choose between two topics, this exercise may also be used to help them identify the topic concerning which they have the most evidence.

Answers continued

- Have students choose three criteria from rubric and score the Student Model. Make sure students support their scores with details from the model. Then, have them score their own essays using the same criteria.
- The Rubric on this page, and another rubric in an alternative format, can be found on pp. 11 and 42 of **Performance Assessment and Portfolio Management.**

Revising (continued)

- To demonstrate the effective use of parallelism, write the following on the board:

  That the government of the people, by the people, for the people, shall not perish from the earth.

  Ask students to identify the use of parallelism in the sentence. Then have them rephrase the sentence without using parallelism. Ask: Which is more powerful? Why? Answer: Parallelism is found in the parallel prepositional phrases "of the people, by the people, for the people." Possible rephrasing: "The people's government shall not perish from the earth." The original is more powerful because it establishes a rhythm which lends it power.

- Ask students to compare the model and non-model and respond to the question in their text: Why is the model more interesting than the non-model? Possible response: The parallel clauses in the model make the sentence energetic, forceful, and convincing.

- Have students go through their compositions, looking for places where they could add parallelism to add power to their message.

Publishing and Presenting

- Ask students to think about the audience they had in mind when they wrote their compositions.
- Discuss ways in which students could reach their audiences. Encourage them to submit their composition to the school newspaper and to the local newspaper.
- If students are preparing to deliver their essays as speeches, have them practice in pairs. Each partner should offer the other suggestions about delivery.
- Have those preparing speeches identify the strongest statement of each main point in their essay. As they practice, they should use pacing and expression to emphasize each of these statements.

Assessment

- Review with students the assessment criteria.

continued

Lesson Objectives

1. To deliver a persuasive argument in an effective manner
2. To clearly state and argue for a position
3. To strengthen an argument by using rhetorical devices
4. To address opposing views
5. To vary one's pace and tone to enhance the presentation of the persuasive argument

Plan Your Content

- Remind students to organize their speeches the same way they would organize a persuasive essay. Their position should be clearly stated and well supported with valid evidence.
- Tell students to avoid broad generalizations (such as "Everyone agrees") and statements that are not completely logical (such as, "Since everyone else is doing it, why shouldn't we?").

Prepare Your Delivery

- Students should first practice to familiarize themselves with the text. Then, students can focus on their delivery.
- After students have familiarized themselves with their text, have them practice delivery in pairs. Partners should critique each others pace, tone, and eye contact. Each student should write out reminders to him- or herself based on his or her partner's comments.

Listening and Speaking WORKSHOP

Delivering Persuasive Arguments

Persuasive arguments have many of the same characteristics as persuasive essays. (To review the characteristics of effective persuasive essays, see the Writing Workshop, pages 330–333.) In a persuasive argument, you try to convince an audience to agree with your position or to take an action. The following strategies will help you deliver an effective persuasive argument.

Plan Your Content

Prepare your persuasive argument as you would a persuasive essay. Clearly define your position, and list all the reasons for your opinion. Gather supporting evidence, such as facts and statistics, expert opinions, and quotations from experts. Then, organize your argument logically.

Use rhetorical devices. Strengthen your argument by using rhetorical devices, such as questions or parallel structure, to support your reasoning. Consider personal anecdotes, case studies, or analogies. Explain the logic of your argument. Appeal to the emotions and beliefs of your audience.

Anticipate counterarguments. Members of your audience will undoubtedly have their own opinions. To be strong, your persuasive argument should analyze those beliefs, address them, and provide reasons that your ideas are better.

Prepare Your Delivery

Use these effective speaking techniques to make your argument lively, interesting, and engaging:

- **Vary your pace and tone.** Pace your speaking, slowing down to stress key statements and speeding up to emphasize emotion or to convey confidence in a long list of evidence.
- **Establish eye contact.** Keep your audience interested by making eye contact as often as possible, especially as you hit the crucial point of your argument.

Activity:
Presentation and Feedback

Choose a topic related to your school or community about which people disagree. Then, organize a presentation in which you take a stand. Practice your speech before a video recorder and a classmate. Ask your partner to use the Feedback Form to evaluate your content and delivery. Use the criticism to revise your delivery. Then, deliver your persuasive argument before your class.

> **Feedback Form for Persuasive Argument**
>
> **Rating System**
> + = Excellent   ✔ = Average   – = Weak
>
> **Content**
> Logically organized _____
> Effective appeal to reason and emotions using rhetorical devices _____
> Addresses listeners' concerns and counter-arguments _____
>
> **Delivery**
> Verbal techniques _____
> Nonverbal techniques _____
>
> ***Answer the following questions:***
> Have you clearly stated and explained your position?
>
> Do you have evidence to support each reason for your opinion?

CUSTOMIZE INSTRUCTION FOR UNIVERSAL ACCESS

For English Learners	For Less Proficient Readers
Students may feel overwhelmed with the task of delivering a persuasive argument while providing effective eye contact and variations in pace and tone. Suggest to students that they first become comfortable delivering the text and then focus on the speaking strategies one at a time. Once students feel comfortable with incorporating a strategy, they can move on to the next one.	Have students carefully practice their persuasive arguments, making notes in the margins where they want to remember to slow down, speed up, or change their tone. Students can work with partners to practice their delivery and improve their eye contact.

Assessment WORKSHOP

Stated and Implied Main Ideas

In the reading sections of some tests, you may be required to read a passage to identify a stated or implied main idea. The following strategies can help:

- Look for a topic sentence that states the subject of the passage.
- Recognize supporting details to help you identify the stated main idea.
- When a main idea is not stated directly, summarizing the author's points will help you identify the implied main idea.

Test-Taking Strategy

Read the entire passage, and consider what headline or title you might assign to it. Your label probably indicates the main idea.

Sample Test Item

Directions: Read the passage, and answer the question that follows.

Minerals are essential to good health. They control the body's water balance and constitute parts of hormones, enzymes, and vitamins. Eating a variety of foods will help ensure that the body receives enough minerals.

An overabundance of certain minerals, however, can lead to serious health problems. Most people get more sodium than they need. An adult's body requires only 500 milligrams of sodium a day.

1 What is the stated main idea of the second paragraph?
   A We need 500 milligrams of sodium a day.
   B Too much of certain minerals can be harmful.
   C Too much sodium can be harmful.
   D Minerals are essential to good health.

Answer and Explanation

The correct answer is **B** because it summarizes the main idea. Answer **A** is a supporting detail. Answer **C** is a detail not stated in the paragraph. Answer **D** is an idea from the first paragraph.

▶ Practice

Directions: Read the passage, and answer the questions that follow.

The critics of the proposed recycling initiative are concerned that recycling plastic and aluminum containers will create more work for citizens who already recycle glass and newspaper. While this notion is true, it misses a more important point.

By recycling plastic and aluminum, we will reduce the waste in our landfill. Most important, the initiative will better the planet. That is worth the extra time.

1 What is the implied main idea of the passage?
   A Citizens can extend the life of the landfill.
   B A compromise must be found.
   C Recycling plastic and aluminum containers is worth the time it takes.
   D The proposed recycling initiative should be accepted.

2 Which detail below could be added to strengthen the main idea of the passage?
   A Information about the history of recycling
   B Information about how plastic can be recycled
   C Facts about the elected officials
   D Statistics about how much glass is recycled.

Assessment Workshop ◆ 335

TEACHING RESOURCES

The following resources can be used to enrich or extend the instruction for p. 335.

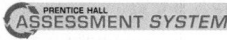

PRENTICE HALL
ASSESSMENT *SYSTEM*

- 📖 **Workbook**
- 📗 **Skill Book**
- 📄 **Transparencies**
- 💿 **CD-ROM**

Lesson Objective

To identify the stated and implied main ideas of a passage given on a test

Applying Reading Strategies

Explain to students that asking themselves questions about what they are reading can help them identify stated and implied main ideas. Encourage students to ask, for instance, why the writer includes certain information. Does that information offer support for another claim? That claim may be the main idea.

Applying Test-Taking Strategies

- Have students read the Sample Test Item. Ask them to identify what the passage is about.
  Answer: The passage is about minerals in one's diet.

- Next, ask students to find the main idea, or main message, of each paragraph, keeping in mind the general topic of minerals.
  Answer: First paragraph: Minerals are essential to good health. Second paragraph: The excessive consumption of certain minerals can be harmful.

- Have students use this strategy to answer the Practice questions on their own.

Answers

1. The correct answer is *D*. Students should see that the passage answers opponents of the initiative. Answers *A* and *C* are supporting arguments found in the passage. Answer *B* is clearly false.

2. The correct answer is *B*. *A* and *C* refer to irrelevant information. *D* would not help convince people to add plastic and aluminum to the list of recyclables. Information about plastic recycling, however, might help persuade readers to support such recycling.

Summer Breeze, 1995, Alice Dalton Brown, Courtesy Fischbach Gallery, NY

UNIT 4 Turning Points

336 ◆ *Turning Points*

UNIT FEATURES

Connections	Reading Informational Materials
Every unit contains a feature that connects literature to a related topic, such as art, science, or history. In this unit, the excerpt from Tim O'Brien's *Going After Cacciato* on pp. 414–417 tells about the changes war effects in a soldier's life.	These selections will help students learn to analyze and evaluate informational texts, such as workplace documents, technical directions, and consumer materials. They will expose students to the organization and features unique to nonnarrative texts.
Use the information and questions on the Connections pages to enrich students' understanding of the selections presented within the unit.	In this unit, students will learn how to analyze and evaluate the techniques of a persuasive article.

Exploring the Theme

Turning points can be exciting as well as frightening. Windows of opportunity open briefly, and life-changing decisions must be made. Stories, poems, and essays can show you how some people approach these fateful moments. Share the anticipation and anxiety of the writers and characters in this unit as they deal with chances and challenges that change their lives.

For example, when you read from the autobiography *Speak, Memory,* you will feel as though you have traveled back in time to the world where childhood memories are formed. One boy's pivotal and passionate experiences of learning to read on his own may remind you of the impression such experiences made on your life. They are a key turning point for every young person.

▲ **Critical Viewing** What details in the painting suggest to you a change or turning point ? **[Analyze]**

Exploring the Theme ◆ 337

ASSESSMENT RESOURCES

- Selection Support: Skills Development Workbook
- Formal Assessment
- Open Book Tests
- Performance Assessment and Portfolio Management
- Extension Activities

Assessing Student Progress

Listed below are the tools that are available to measure the degree to which students meet the unit objectives.

Informal Assessment

The questions in the Review and Assess sections are a first-level response to the concepts and skills presented with the selections. Students' responses provide a brief, informal measure of their grasp of the material. These responses can indicate where further instruction and practice are needed. Follow up with the practice pages in **Selection Support: Skills Development Workbook.**

Formal Assessment

The **Formal Assessment** booklet contains the Selection Tests and Unit Tests.

- Selection Tests measure comprehension and skills acquisition for each selection or group of selections.
- Each Unit Test provides students with thirty multiple-choice questions and five essay questions designed to assess students' knowledge of the literature and skills taught in the unit.

The **Open Book Tests** ask students to demonstrate their ability to synthesize and communicate information from selections or groups of selections.

To assess student writing, you will find rubrics and scoring models in the **Performance Assessment and Portfolio Management** booklet. In this booklet, you will also find scoring rubrics for listening and speaking activities.

Alternative Assessment

The **Extension Activities** booklet contains writing activities, listening and speaking activities, and research and technology activities that are appropriate for students with different ability levels. You may also use these activities as an alternative measure of students' growth.

▶ **Critical Viewing**

Answer: Students may suggest that the bareness of the room makes it look as if someone has just moved out or is about to move in. Others may say the breeze blowing the curtains suggests an imminent change in weather.

337

Why Read Literature?

The "Why Read Literature?" page in each unit presents a list of possible purposes for reading. Each purpose for reading is connected to one or more of the selections in the unit. Good readers set a purpose before reading to help them read actively and focus on meaningful details.

Unit 4 introduces three purposes for reading. "Read for the Love of Literature" encourages students to enjoy the windows that literature opens into memory and tradition. "Read to Be Inspired" encourages students to draw ethical examples from literature. In "Read for Information," students learn facts about a topic of national concern.

How to Use This Page

- Tell students that before reading each selection in this unit, they should set a purpose for reading. This will help them read in a more active and focused manner.

- Explain that students can increase their love of literature by reading a writer's childhood memories of learning to read in "Speak, Memory."

- A reader will feel inspired by the poem "I Am Not One of Those Who Left the Land," in which the speaker does not back down from her principles, even in the midst of war.

- Obtaining information is another valuable purpose for reading. Students should focus on the specific type of information they want to learn. In "65-MPH Speed Limit Is Saving Lives," students can read to learn how changes in the speed limit may have saved lives.

Why Read Literature?

You usually read literature with a goal in mind: to appreciate, to learn, or even to be inspired. As you consider works about turning points, you will discover that your purpose will vary based on the context, genre, subject, or style of a specific reading. Preview these three purposes you might set before reading the works in this unit.

1

Read for the Love of Literature

In his lifetime, Vladimir Nabokov would become an acclaimed writer whose works were published worldwide. In his autobiography, he draws upon his childhood memories to share the joys of learning to read. You will see the profound effect these experiences had on his life when you read this excerpt from *Speak, Memory,* page 342.

Although she had family members in the United States who cared for her, Mrs. Pan was homesick for her native China. Discover how one of her country's traditions raised her spirits even though she was away from home when you read the story **"The Good Deed,"** page 376.

2

Read to Be Inspired

If you abandon your principles when trouble arises, your actions may come back to haunt you. The result could be worse than if you had stayed and confronted the problem. Anna Akhmatova stands up for her beliefs in her poem **"I Am Not One of Those Who Left the Land,"** page 368.

3

Read for Information

In 1987 and 1995, Congress passed legislation that gave the states permission to raise the speed limit on their highways. Surprisingly, after the law went into effect, a drop in highway fatalities occurred. Consider why this happened as you read the article **"65-MPH Speed Limit Is Saving Lives,"** page 411.

 Take It to the Net
Visit the Web site for online instruction and activities related to each selection in this unit.
www.phschool.com

✹ ENRICHMENT: Further Reading

Have students choose one or more of the works below to extend the unit theme "Turning Points" or to read more by the unit authors.

Don Quixote by Miguel De Cervantes
This story about a man who actually lives out his dreams—despite reality—can be found in the **Prentice Hall Literature Library.**

The Lord of the Flies by William Golding
This chilling tale about a group of English schoolboys plane-wrecked on a deserted island can be found in the **Prentice Hall Literature Library.**

Siddhartha by Herman Hesse
The story of a young man seeking enlightenment and happiness can be found in the **Prentice Hall Literature Library.**

How to Read Literature

Use Strategies for Reading Critically

When you read a work that presents an individual's perspective or ideas on a subject, you should read the work critically. Examine and question the writer's ideas. Evaluate the information the writer includes as support. As a last step, form a judgment about the content and quality of the work. Here are specific strategies to help you read critically:

1. Recognize the author's purpose.

- Determine the author's reason for writing. It could be to inform, to entertain, or to share an important idea.
- Gather details, and use the information you have found in the text to make an informed decision about the author's purpose. In the passage below, for example, the author includes a detailed description of the overall experience of reading to show his enthusiasm for it.

> On later pages longer words appeared; and at the very end of the brown, inkstained volume, a real, sensible story unfolded its adult sentences, . . . the little reader's ultimate triumph and reward.
>
> —from *Speak, Memory*

2. Evaluate a character's decision.

- As you read fiction, examine the characters in the story and critically consider their actions.
- Notice relevant details that can give you insight into a character's motive or a character's effect on others.
- Assess the facts and actions in a character's life from various angles. Consider what would have happened had the character acted differently in the situation.

3. Recognize the author's perspective.

An author's perspective is his or her outlook on a subject. This perspective affects the choice of details and words that are included in the work, as well as the way an event or idea is presented.

4. Make inferences.

When you make inferences, you make logical assumptions about the characters based on what they say and how they act. For example, as you read the passage at right, ask yourself what inference can be made about the character.

As you read the selections in this unit, apply these critical reading strategies to help you get the most from what you read.

Making Inferences

"I cannot be responsible for what other persons do, but I must be responsible for my own kind," she declared.
—from "The Good Deed"

Inference: This character has a strong sense of morality.

How to Read Literature

The "How to Read Literature" page in each unit presents a set of strategies to help readers understand authors' words and ideas. Each reading strategy is taught in conjunction with one or more of the selections within the unit. Good readers develop a bank of strategies from which they can draw as needed.

Unit 4 introduces three strategies for reading critically. To understand a selection fully, students must examine and question the writer's ideas. The strategies on this page help readers evaluate the content and quality of a work.

How to Use This Page

Introduce the strategies for reading critically, presenting each as a tool for developing understanding when reading the selections in this unit.

- As they read the excerpt from "Speak, Memory" (p. 342), students will draw conclusions about the author's purpose by examining his decisions about which details to include.
- As they read "Games at Twilight" (p. 352), students will learn to engage with the text more deeply by making judgments about characters' motives and actions.
- As they read "I Am Not One of Those Who Left the Land" (p. 368), students will learn how to recognize an author's perspective to help them better understand what they are reading.
- As they read "The Good Deed" (p. 376), students will better understand the story when they draw inferences about the characters based on their actions and statements.

MODEL A READING STRATEGY: Evaluate a Character's Decision

Help students understand how to evaluate a character's decision, using this excerpt from "Games at Twilight":

> Ravi had never cared to enter such a dark and depressing mortuary of defunct household goods seething with such unspeakable and alarming animal life but, as Raghu's whistling grew angrier . . . Ravi suddenly slipped off the flower pot and through the crack and was gone.

Tell students:

Ravi decides to hide in an insect-infested shed during the game of hide-and-seek. To evaluate his decision, you should take a few factors into account. First, Ravi is showing courage, which is praiseworthy. However, he has not thought through his actions and the shed may be frightening or even dangerous inside. Since he is only hiding there to win a game, his decision is perhaps less than mature.

339

from Speak, Memory

Lesson Objectives

1. **To analyze and respond to literary elements**
   - Literary Analysis: Personal Narrative
   - Connecting Literary Elements: Allusion

2. **To read, comprehend, analyze, and critique nonfiction**
   - Reading Strategy: Recognizing Author's Purpose
   - Reading Check questions
   - Review and Assess questions
   - Assessment Practice (ATE)

3. **To develop word analysis skills, fluency, and systematic vocabulary**
   - Vocabulary Development Lesson: Latin Prefix: *pro-*

4. **To understand and apply written and oral language conventions**
   - Spelling Strategy
   - Grammar Lesson: Clauses

5. **To understand and apply appropriate writing and research strategies**
   - Writing Lesson: Personal Narrative
   - Extension Activity: Multimedia Presentation

6. **To understand and apply listening and speaking strategies**
   - Extension Activity: Book Discussion

STEP-BY-STEP TEACHING GUIDE	PACING GUIDE
PRETEACH	
Motivate Students and Provide Background	
Use the Motivation activity (ATE p. 340)	5 min.
Read and discuss the Preview material and Background information (SE/ATE p. 340) 🅰	5 min.
Introduce the Concepts	
Introduce the Literary Analysis and Reading Strategy (SE/ATE p. 341) 🅰	10 min.
Pronounce the vocabulary words and read their definitions (SE p. 341)	5 min.
TEACH	
Monitor Comprehension	
Informally monitor comprehension by circulating while students read independently or in groups 🅰	10 min.
Monitor students' comprehension with the Reading Check notes (SE/ATE pp. 343, 345)	as students read
Develop vocabulary with Vocabulary notes (SE pp. 343, 344, 345)	as students read
Develop Understanding	
Develop students' understanding of personal narratives with Literary Analysis annotations (SE p. 345; ATE p. 345) 🅰	5 min.
Develop students' understanding of determining the author's purpose with Reading Strategy annotations (ATE p. 343)	5 min.
ASSESS	
Assess Mastery	
Assess students' mastery of the Reading Strategy and Literary Analysis by having them answer the Review and Assess questions (SE/ATE p. 347)	15 min.
Use one or more of the print and media Assessment Resources (ATE p. 349) 🅰	up to 50 min.
EXTEND	
Apply Understanding	
Have students complete the Vocabulary Development Lesson and the Grammar Lesson (SE p. 348) 🅰	20 min.
Apply students' knowledge of sensory details using the Writing Lesson (SE p. 349) 🅰	45 min.
Apply students' understanding of the selection using one or more of the Extension Activities (SE p. 349)	20–90 min.

 ACCELERATED INSTRUCTION:
Use the strategies and activities identified with an 🅰.

UNIVERSAL ACCESS
● = Below Level Students
▲ = On-Level Students
■ = Above Level Students

Time and Resource Manager

Reading Level: Average
Average Number of Instructional Days: 3

RESOURCES		
PRINT 📖	**TRANSPARENCIES**	**TECHNOLOGY** 💿 🎧 📼
• **Beyond Literature,** Cross-Curricular Connection: Geography, p. 23 ▲ ■		• **Interest Grabber Video,** Tape 2 ● ▲ ■
• **Selection Support Workbook:** ● ▲ ■ Literary Analysis, p. 92 Reading Strategy, p. 91 Build Vocabulary, p. 89	• **Literary Analysis and Reading Transparencies,** pp. 45 and 46 ● ▲ ■	
• **Adapted Reader's Companion** ● • **Reader's Companion** ●		• **Listening to Literature** ● ▲ ■ Audiocassettes, Side 11 Audio CDs, CD 7
• **English Learner's Companion** ● ▲ • **Literatura en español** ● ▲ • **Literary Analysis for Enrichment** ■		
• **Formal Assessment:** Selection Test, pp. 79–81 ● ▲ ■ • **Open Book Test,** pp. 67–69 ● ▲ ■ • **Performance Assessment and Portfolio Management,** p. 9 ● ▲ ■ • **PRENTICE HALL ASSESSMENT SYSTEM** ● ▲	• **PRENTICE HALL ASSESSMENT SYSTEM** ● ▲ ■ Skills Practice Answers and Explanations on Transparencies	• **Test Bank Software** ● ▲ ■ • **Got It! Assessment Videotapes,** Tape 2 ● ▲
• **Selection Support Workbook:** ● ▲ ■ Build Grammar Skills, p. 90 • **Writing and Grammar,** Platinum Level ● ▲ ■ • **Extension Activities,** p. 23 ● ▲ ■	• **Daily Language Practice Transparencies** ● ▲	• **Writing and Grammar iText CD-ROM** ● ▲ ■ 🖥 *Take It to the Net* www.phschool.com

BLOCK SCHEDULING: Use one 90-minute class period to preteach the selection and have students read it. Use a second 90-minute class period to assess students' mastery of skills and have them complete one of the Extension Activities.

Motivation

Ask students why they think some memories are so vivid they stand out, while others just fade away. Invite students to share their ideas on what makes a particular memory last—its dramatic qualities, its emotional power, or some other quality. Let them know that in this excerpt from Nabokov's autobiography, *Speak, Memory*, the author "listened" as his memory "spoke," bringing forth unforgettable images and impressions from his childhood in Russia.

▨ Interest Grabber Video

As an alternative, play "The Russian Revolution," Tape 2 to engage student interest.

❶ Background

Vladimir Nabokov

Nabokov was only a teenager when his family was forced to leave Russia. While in exile, Nabokov completed his education at Cambridge University in England. There, in 1922, he learned that his father had been assassinated at a political gathering in Berlin. Students may wish to read all of *Speak, Memory*, in which Nabokov's great affection for his father and equally great feeling of loss are evident.

Prepare to Read

from *Speak, Memory*

 Take It to the Net

Visit www.phschool.com for interactive activities and instruction related to the selection, including

- background
- graphic organizers
- literary elements
- reading strategies

Preview

Connecting to the Literature

No two people have read exactly the same collection of books and stories. The special combination of books you have read contributes to your unique personality. In this section of his autobiography, the Russian writer Vladimir Nabokov fondly recalls his first reading experiences.

❶ Background

Nabokov's full autobiography records an upper-class life with loving parents. The Russian Revolution of 1917, however, snatched this lifestyle from the Nabokov family. Bad government and starvation led Russian citizens to overthrow the czar. Wealthy families like the Nabokovs were forced to flee from Russia.

340 ◆ *Turning Points*

TEACHING RESOURCES

The following resources can be used to enrich or extend the instruction for pp. 340–341.

Motivation

▨ **Interest Grabber Video,** Tape 2

Background

📖 **Beyond Literature,** Cross-Curricular Connection: Geography, p. 23

 Take It to the Net
Visit www.phschool.com for background and hotlinks for *Speak, Memory*.

Literary Analysis

▨ **Literary Analysis and Reading Transparencies,** Personal Narrative, p. 46 ▨

Reading

📖 **Selection Support:** Reading Strategy, p. 91; Build Vocabulary, p. 89

▨ **Literary Analysis and Reading Transparencies,** Recognizing Author's Purpose, p. 45

▨ **BLOCK SCHEDULING:** Resources marked with this symbol provide varied instruction during 90-minute blocks.

Literary Analysis

Personal Narrative

This episode from Vladimir Nabokov's autobiography is a **personal narrative**—a true story about a memorable person, event, or situation in the writer's life. As this passage from *Speak, Memory* demonstrates, writers tell such narratives from the first-person point of view, using the pronoun *I*.

> I learned to read English before I could read Russian. My first English friends were four simple souls in my grammar—Ben, Dan, Sam and Ned.

By indicating their thoughts and feelings about people and events, writers also hint at or state directly the meaning of their experiences. In his narrative, Nabokov captures memories of childhood reading.

Connecting Literary Elements

In *Speak, Memory*, Nabokov names many different books that he read as a child—some well known and some not so well known. An **allusion** is a reference to a well-known person, place, event, literary work, or work of art. Writers use allusions to add layers of information to a literary work. While reading, notice your own associations with the allusions that Nabokov includes.

Reading Strategy

Recognizing Author's Purpose

An **author's purpose** is his or her reason for writing, such as to inform or to persuade. In a personal narrative, for example, an author might want to reflect, inform, *and* entertain. To identify Nabokov's purpose, prepare a diagram like the one shown.

- List important details.
- Note your reactions to the details.
- Write the author's possible reasons for including the details.

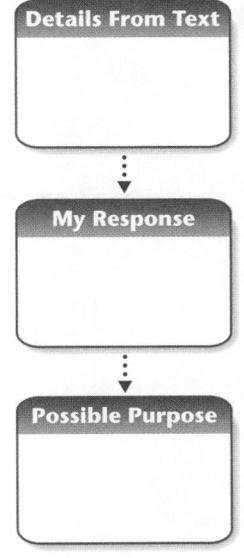

Vocabulary Development

procession (prō sesh′ ən) *n.* number of persons or things moving forward in an orderly or formal way (p. 343)

proficiency (prō fish′ ən sē) *n.* expertise (p. 344)

laborious (lə bôr′ ē əs) *adj.* involving much hard work; difficult (p. 344)

portentously (pôr ten′ təs lē) *adv.* ominously; scarily (p. 345)

limpid (lim′ pid) *adj.* perfectly clear; transparent (p. 345)

from *Speak, Memory* ◆ 341

---

❷ Literary Analysis

Personal Narrative

- Explain to students that a personal narrative is a true story told from the writer's personal point of view.

- Tell students that they can draw conclusions about the significance of a writer's experiences in much the same way that they can about characters in a fictional story.

- Let students know that sometimes information is stated directly by the writer, while at other times the reader must read between the lines to draw conclusions about the writer's experiences.

- Remind students that an allusion is a reference to a famous person, place, event, or work of art. Suggest that students keep a list of all the allusions they come across as they read the selection.

- Encourage students to note Nabokov's allusions as they read, and make a note of them for further discussion or research.

❸ Reading Strategy

Recognizing Author's Purpose

- Explain to students that an author may write to inform, persuade, entertain, or express an opinion. Often, an author will have more than one purpose for writing. Sometimes an author may state directly his or her purpose. At other times, readers must use details from the text to determine the author's purpose.

- Review the instruction for Recognizing Author's Purpose with students. Show students how they can use a diagram like the one shown to help them use the details in the selection to recognize Nabokov's purpose for writing.

Vocabulary Development

- Pronounce each vocabulary word for students, and read the definitions as a class. Have students identify any words with which they are already familiar.

 E-Teach

Visit E-Teach at www.phschool.com for teachers' essays on how to teach, with questions and answers.

**Step-by-Step Teaching Guide
for pp. 342–346**

CUSTOMIZE INSTRUCTION
For Verbal/Linguistic Learners

Have students examine Nabokov's
use of dashes. Ask them to suggest
how he uses this punctuation style
to evoke a mood. Then, encourage
them to compare his use of dashes
with that of other writers. You might
have them begin by looking at the
Emily Dickinson poems in this book.
What effect does the use of dashes
in this way have on the reader?

❶ About the Selection

In this excerpt from *Speak, Memory*,
Vladimir Nabokov blends memories
of events from his childhood, sensory
impressions, and historical facts to
create a unique autobiographical
reflection. The excerpt focuses primarily on Nabokov's early memories
of books—those his mother read to
him and those he first learned to
read by himself. These experiences
had a profound effect on Nabokov,
helping him to develop an enduring
love of language.

TEACHING RESOURCES

The following resources can be used to enrich or extend the instruction for pp. 342–346.

Literary Analysis

📖 **Selection Support:** Literary Analysis, p. 92

Reading

📖 **Reader's Companion**

📖 **English Learner's Companion**

🎧 **Listening to Literature Audiocassettes,** Side 11 ▪

💿 **Listening to Literature Audio CDs,** CD 7 ▪

▪ **BLOCK SCHEDULING:** Resources marked with this symbol provide varied instruction during 90-minute blocks.

from Speak, Memory

Vladimir Nabokov

1

The kind of Russian family to which I belonged—a kind now extinct—had, among other virtues, a traditional leaning toward the comfortable products of Anglo-Saxon civilization. Pears' Soap, tar-black when dry, topaz-like when held to the light between wet fingers, took care of one's morning bath. Pleasant was the decreasing weight of the English collapsible tub when it was made to protrude a rubber underlip and disgorge its frothy contents into the slop pail. "We could not improve the cream, so we improved the tube," said the English toothpaste. At breakfast, Golden Syrup imported from London would entwist with its glowing coils the revolving spoon from which enough of it had slithered onto a piece of Russian bread and butter. All sorts of snug, mellow things came in a steady <u>procession</u> from the English Shop on Nevski Avenue: fruit-cakes, smelling salts, playing cards, picture puzzles, striped blazers, talcum-white tennis balls.

I learned to read English before I could read Russian. My first

procession (prō sesh′ ən) *n.* number of persons or things moving forward in an orderly or formal way

❹ ✔Reading Check
Which English products did the Nabokov family enjoy?

❸ ◄ Critical Viewing Which details in this photograph make you think of remembering? **[Connect]**

---

❷ Reading Strategy
Recognizing Author's Purpose
- Have students read the bracketed passage, using the diagram from p. 341 to record the details they encounter.
- Then, ask students to discuss what these details reveal about the Nabokov family. Do students think the family was wealthy or poor? **Answer:** The family must have been wealthy to afford all of these imported English products.
- Then, ask students to identify Nabokov's purpose in detailing the English products that his family enjoyed and used. **Answer:** Nabokov's purpose for including these items is to inform the reader about his family.

❸ ►Critical Viewing
Answer: The boy's facial expression is thoughtful. Also, the blurred words look as if they are moving by him, which could be a visual representation of the act of reading.

❹ ✔Reading Check
Answer: The Nabokov family enjoyed English soap, a tub, tooth-paste, syrup, fruitcakes, smelling salts, playing cards, picture puzzles, striped blazers, and tennis balls.

CUSTOMIZE INSTRUCTION FOR UNIVERSAL ACCESS

For Special Needs Students	For Gifted/Talented Students
Write *Sight, Sound, Smell, Taste,* and *Touch* across the top of the chalkboard. Have students call out products from this page and say to which sense each appeals. Help students to understand how Nabokov's sensory details help him to accomplish his purpose for writing, to inform the reader about his childhood.	Encourage students to create a collage evoking the setting Nabokov describes. Make sure students include images of pre-Revolutionary Russia as well as images of the products Nabokov describes. Do the juxtaposed images help them deepen their understanding of the author's purpose in writing this personal narrative?

❺ Background

Soomerki

Just as it never gets dark in summer at this latitude, it never gets light in winter. Cold winter days are often as dark as night.

❻ Critical Thinking

Infer

• Have a volunteer read aloud the bracketed passage. Call students' attention to the sentence in parentheses.

• Ask students whether they think Nabokov is serious when he refers to the past in this way. What does this sentence reveal about Nabokov's feelings about the Russian Revolution?

Answer: Nabokov's use of the phrase "happy days" reveals the ironic humor with which he viewed the changes the Soviet Union brought to Russia.

English friends were four simple souls in my grammar—Ben, Dan, Sam and Ned. There used to be a great deal of fuss about their identities and whereabouts—"Who is Ben?" "He is Dan," "Sam is in bed," and so on. Although it all remained rather stiff and patchy (the compiler was handicapped by having to employ—for the initial lessons, at least—words of not more than three letters), my imagination somehow managed to obtain the necessary data. Wan-faced, big-limbed, silent nitwits, proud in the possession of certain tools ("Ben has an axe"), they now drift with a slow-motioned slouch across the remotest backdrop of memory; and, akin to the mad alphabet of an optician's chart, the grammar-book lettering looms again before me.

The schoolroom was drenched with sunlight. In a sweating glass jar, several spiny caterpillars were feeding on nettle[1] leaves (and ejecting interesting, barrel-shaped pellets of olive-green grass). The oilcloth that covered the round table smelled of glue. Miss Clayton smelled of Miss Clayton. Fantastically, gloriously, the blood-colored alcohol of the outside thermometer had risen to 24° Réaumur (86° Fahrenheit) in the shade. Through the window one could see kerchiefed peasant girls weeding a garden path on their hands and knees or gently raking the sun-mottled sand. ❻ (The happy days when they would be cleaning streets and digging canals for the State were still beyond the horizon.) Golden orioles in the greenery emitted their four brilliant notes: dee-del-dee-O!

Ned lumbered past the window in a fair impersonation of the gardener's mate Ivan (who was to become in 1918 a member of the local Soviet). On later pages longer words appeared; and at the very end of the brown, inkstained volume, a real, sensible story unfolded its adult sentences ("One day Ted said to Ann: Let us—"), the little reader's ultimate triumph and reward. I was thrilled by the thought that some day I might attain such <u>proficiency</u>. The magic has endured, and whenever a grammar book comes my way, I instantly turn to the last page to enjoy a forbidden glimpse of the <u>laborious</u> student's future, of that promised land where, at last, words are meant to mean what they mean.

2

❼ Summer *soomerki*✦—the lovely Russian word for dusk. Time: a dim point in the first decade of this unpopular century. Place: latitude[2]

---

1. **nettle** (net´ əl) *n.* any of various stinging or spiny plants.
2. **latitude** (lat´ ə tōōd) *n.* angular distance, measured in degrees, north or south from the equator.

♦ *Soomerki*

Nabokov remembers the summer *soomerki*—the long twilights of his childhood. He is referring to one of the effects of living in a northern latitude. His home was at 59° northern latitude, which is very far north. In the United States, it is as far north as southern Alaska. At that latitude, the summer sun never sinks far below the horizon, and *soomerki* (twilight or dusk) can last for hours. It virtually never gets dark in the summer.

proficiency (prō fish´ ən sē) *n.* expertise

laborious (lə bôr´ ē əs) *adj.* involving much hard work; difficult

---

59° north from your equator, longitude[3] 100° east from my writing hand. The day would take hours to fade, and everything—sky, tall flowers, still water—would be kept in a state of infinite vesperal[4] suspense, deepened rather than resolved by the doleful moo of a cow in a distant meadow or by the still more moving cry that came from some bird beyond the lower course of the river, where the vast expanse of a misty-blue sphagnum[5] bog, because of its mystery and remoteness, the Rukavishnikov children had baptized America.

In the drawing room of our country house, before going to bed, I would often be read to in English by my mother. As she came to a particularly dramatic passage, where the hero was about to encounter some strange, perhaps fatal danger, her voice would slow down, her words would be spaced <u>portentously</u>, and before turning the page she would place upon it her hand, with its familiar pigeon-blood ruby and diamond ring (within the <u>limpid</u> facets of which, had I been a better crystal-gazer, I might have seen a room, people, lights, trees in the rain—a whole period of émigré life for which that ring was to pay).

There were tales about knights whose terrific but wonderfully aseptic[6] wounds were bathed by damsels in grottoes.[7] From a windswept clifftop, a medieval maiden with flying hair and a youth in hose gazed at the round Isles of the Blessed. In "Misunderstood," the fate of Humphrey used to bring a more specialized lump to one's throat than anything in Dickens or Daudet[8] (great devisers of lumps), while a shamelessly allegorical story, "Beyond the Blue Mountains," dealing with two pairs of little travelers—good Clover and Cowslip, bad Buttercup and Daisy—contained enough exciting details to make one forget its "message."

There were also those large, flat, glossy picture books. I particularly liked the blue-coated, red-trousered, coal-black Golliwogg, with underclothes buttons for eyes, and his meager harem of five wooden dolls. By the illegal method of cutting themselves frocks out of the American flag (Peg taking the motherly stripes, Sarah Jane the pretty stars) two of the dolls acquired a certain soft femininity, once their neutral articulations had been clothed. The Twins (Meg and Weg) and the Midget remained stark naked and, consequently, sexless.

We see them in the dead of night stealing out of doors to sling snowballs at one another until the chimes of a remote clock ("But Hark!" comments the rhymed text) send them back to their toybox in the nursery. A rude jack-in-the-box shoots out, frightening my lovely

---

3. **longitude** (län´ jə tōōd) *n.* distance east or west on the Earth's surface, measured as an arc of the equator.
4. **vesperal** (ves´ pər əl) *adj.* eveninglike.
5. **sphagnum** (sfag´ nəm) *n.* highly absorbent, spongelike, grayish peat mosses found in bogs.
6. **aseptic** (ā sep´ tik) *adj.* free from or keeping away disease-producing microorganisms.
7. **grottoes** (grät´ ōz) *n.* caves.
8. **Dickens** (dik´ ənz) **or Daudet** (dō dā´) Charles Dickens and Alphonse Daudet, nineteenth-century novelists who sympathized with the common people.

Literary Analysis
Personal Narrative How do the details in this paragraph add power to the author's personal narrative?

portentously (pôr ten´ təs lē) *adv.* ominously; scarily

limpid (lim´ pid) *adj.* perfectly clear; transparent

Literary Analysis
Personal Narrative and Allusion What additional meaning does the allusion to Dickens and Daudet contribute to Nabokov's description of Humphrey?

9 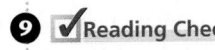 **Reading Check**
Why does Nabokov look forward to getting to the end of his grammar book?

from Speak, Memory ◆ 345

---

❼ Literary Analysis
Personal Narrative

- Help students' comprehension by having them break down the long last sentence of the bracketed passage into parts.
- Ask students the following question: In the bracketed passage, what effect does the author's use of time and place have on the reader? Possible response: Nabokov's specification of latitude and longitude and to the first decade of the twentieth century makes clear that the scene is set long ago, and far away. The reader may feel as though he or she is reading a scene from history or from a fairy tale.
- Ask students the Literary Analysis question on p. 345: How do the details in this paragraph add power to the author's personal narrative? Possible response: The images give the reader a full, powerful experience of *soomerki*.

▶ Monitor Progress Ask students how this passage might have been different if it were a biography written by someone who knew Nabokov.

❽ Literary Analysis
Personal Narrative

- Have students identify the example of allusion in the bracketed passage. Answer: Nabokov alludes to the writing of Dickens and Daudet.
- Then, ask students the Literary Analysis question on p. 345: What additional meaning does the allusion to Dickens and Daudet contribute to Nabokov's description of Humphrey? Answer: The allusion shows the reader how deeply Nabokov was affected by Humphrey's fate.

❾ ✓ Reading Check
Answer: Nabokov is looking forward to the day when he can become a more proficient reader.

Answers for p. 346

Review and Assess

1. Many students will have learned to read using grammar books and children's fiction.

2. **(a)** He has many luxuries, such as imported soaps, toothpaste, food, and clothes. **(b)** The Russian Revolution eradicated the aristocratic lifestyle the Nabokovs enjoyed.

3. **(a)** He mentions it when he describes his mother wearing it while she read to him. **(b)** He tells the reader that the sale of the ring paid for the Nabokovs' subsistence as émigrés.

4. **(a)** He read an English grammar book, "Misunderstood," "Beyond the Blue Mountains," and tales about knights and ladies. **(b)** They affected him powerfully because they were associated with the magic of learning to read.

5. **(a)** Nabokov has affectionate memories of his childhood experiences with reading because they played an important role in his life as a world-renowned writer. **(b)** The passage indicates that the author felt both sadness about and affection for his past.

6. He might like the story of King Arthur because it is about knights and ladies.

7. **(a)** In Nabokov's time, mainly middle- and upper-class families were literate. They had personal libraries of books. Today, many more people are literate, but there are other media that didn't exist during Nabokov's time, such as television, radio, and computers. **(b)** The power of reading is greater today because illiterate people cannot finish school or get jobs.

Sarah, and that picture I heartily disliked because it reminded me of children's parties at which this or that graceful little girl, who had bewitched me, happened to pinch her finger or hurt her knee, and would forthwith expand into a purple-faced goblin, all wrinkles and bawling mouth. Another time they went on a bicycle journey and were captured by cannibals; our unsuspecting travelers had been quenching their thirst at a palm-fringed pool when the tom-toms sounded. Over the shoulder of my past I admire again the crucial picture: the Golliwogg, still on his knees by the pool but no longer drinking; his hair stands on end and the normal black of his face has changed to a weird ashen hue. There was also the motorcar book (Sarah Jane, always my favorite, sporting a long green veil), with the usual sequel—crutches and bandaged heads.

And, yes—the airship. Yards and yards of yellow silk went to make it, and an additional tiny balloon was provided for the sole use of the fortunate Midget. At the immense altitude to which the ship reached, the aeronauts huddled together for warmth while the lost little soloist, still the object of my intense envy notwithstanding his plight, drifted into an abyss of frost and stars—alone.

Review and Assess

Thinking About the Selection

1. **Respond:** Compare the earliest books and stories you read with those that Nabokov read as a boy.

2. **(a) Recall:** What details in the beginning of the story show that Nabokov came from an aristocratic Russian family? **(b) Speculate:** Why does Nabokov say that the kind of family to which he belonged is "now extinct"?

3. **(a) Recall:** When does Nabokov refer to his mother's ruby and diamond ring? **(b) Draw Conclusions:** What does Nabokov intend for you to know about the ring?

4. **(a) Recall:** What books did Nabokov read or have read to him as a child? **(b) Analyze:** Why did these books affect Nabokov so strongly?

5. **(a) Infer:** Why do you think the author has such strong and affectionate memories of his childhood experiences with reading? **(b) Speculate:** How do you think these memories affected him as an adult?

6. **Apply:** Recommend a book or story that you think Nabokov would have liked. Give reasons for your recommendation.

7. **(a) Compare:** Compare the power of reading in Nabokov's time with the power of reading today. **(b) Evaluate:** During which time do you think reading was considered more important? Why?

Vladimir Nabokov

(1899–1977)

Besides being a novelist and poet, Russian-born Vladimir Nabokov was a passionate butterfly collector. Some critics have said that Nabokov, who wrote in both Russian and English, treated words like butterflies: each a rare, colorful specimen pinned to the page.

Nabokov was born into an upper-class but politically liberal Russian family. In 1919, following the Russian Revolution, his family went into exile. In 1940, Nabokov and his family immigrated to the United States to escape life in Nazi Germany.

Nabokov wrote carefully constructed novels, including *Bend Sinister* (1947), *Pnin* (1957), and *Ada* (1969). He also won acclaim for his autobiography, *Speak, Memory* (1967).

ASSESSMENT PRACTICE: Reading Comprehension

Recognizing Cause and Effect   **(For more practice, see Test Preparation Workbook, p. 23.)**

Use the following sample item to help students recognize implied cause-and-effect relationships.

Another time they went on a bicycle journey and were captured by cannibals; our unsuspecting travelers had been quenching their thirst at a palm-fringed pool when the tom-toms sounded. Over the shoulder of my past, I admire again the crucial picture: the Golliwogg, still on his knees by the pool but no longer drinking: his hair stands on end and the normal black of his face has changed to a weird ashen hue.

Why has the Golliwogg's face changed color?

  A The water in the pool is poisonous.

  B He has seen a cannibal.

  C The tom-toms are played by cannibals.

  D Golliwoggs always change colors.

The cause of the Golliwogg's pallor is fear of the unseen, so *C* is the correct answer.

Review and Assess

Literary Analysis

Personal Narrative

1. How does the first sentence of the selection indicate that this work is a **personal narrative**?
2. Identify two details that help you visualize the characters Ben, Dan, Sam, and Ned.
3. Using a diagram like this one, show how Nabokov appeals to every sense except taste in his description of the schoolroom.

Connecting Literary Elements

4. Identify two **allusions** that Nabokov uses in the selection.
5. Explain how one of these allusions adds layers of meaning to the story. Construct a cluster diagram like the one shown to explore ideas that you associate with the allusion.

Reading Strategy

Recognizing Author's Purpose

6. What was the **author's purpose** in writing these particular impressions of his childhood?
7. What details support this purpose?
8. How would the narrative have to be changed if Nabokov's purpose had been to criticize children's books?

Extend Understanding

9. **Cultural Connection:** In many cultures, children are taught English and other languages from an early age. How is this a benefit?

Quick Review

A **personal narrative** is a true story about a memorable person, event, or situation in the writer's life.

An **allusion** is a reference to a well-known person, place, event, literary work, or work of art.

The **author's purpose** is his or her reason for writing.

 Take It to the Net
www.phschool.com
Take the interactive self-test online to check your understanding of the selection.

from *Speak, Memory* ◆ 347

✳ ENRICHMENT: Further Reading

Other Works by Vladimir Nabokov

Speak, Memory
Nabokov's Dozen
Glory

Take It to the Net
Visit www.phschool.com for more information on Vladimir Nabokov.

Answers for p. 348

❶ Vocabulary Development

Word Analysis

1. d   4. a
2. f   5. b
3. c   6. e

Fluency: Clarify Word Meaning

1. procession   4. limpid
2. proficiency   5. portentously
3. laborious

Spelling Strategy

1. imagination   3. suspension
2. possessions

❷ Grammar

1. Independent: His mother read to him; Subordinate: when he was small

2. Independent: She placed her hand on the page; Subordinate: before she turned it

3. Independent: The stories of knights came alive.

4. Independent: he sat still; Subordinate: While his mother read

5. Independent: He loved literature as a child; he became a great writer

Writing Application

1. When I was a child, my mother read to me from *The Adventures of Tom Sawyer.*

2. When I was about seven, I could read to my sister from *Winnie the Pooh.*

3. When I was old enough, I got a library card.

Integrate Language Skills

❶ Vocabulary Development Lesson

Word Analysis: Latin Prefix *pro-*

Knowing that the Latin prefix *pro-* often means "before in place or time" or "moving forward," you can see the part it plays in the word *procession*, meaning "a number of persons or things moving forward." In your notebook, match each word below with the correct definition. Then, check your responses in a dictionary.

1. proceed   a. drive forward
2. prospect   b. something read before a drama
3. progress   c. to advance toward something better
4. propel   d. to push ahead
5. prologue   e. to jut out
6. protrude   f. something looked forward to

Fluency: Clarify Word Meaning

In your notebook, fill in the blanks with words from the vocabulary list on page 341.

Nabokov offers a ____?____ of sensory details, rendered with ____?____. The author is accurate without being ____?____. You can almost see the ____?____ facets of his mother's jewels and hear the way she ____?____ lowers her voice.

Spelling Strategy

The sound *shun* in a suffix is usually spelled *sion, tion,* or *ssion.* In your notebook, fill in the blanks to complete the spelling of the *shun* sound.

1. Stories kindle the imagina _____.
2. Are books your favorite posse _____s?
3. Some of the best stories are built upon the suspen _____ of reality.

❷ Grammar Lesson

Clauses

A **clause** is a group of words that has both a subject and a verb. An **independent clause** can stand by itself as a sentence. However, a **subordinate clause** cannot stand by itself. It must be linked to an independent clause to form a complete sentence. In these examples, each independent clause is underlined once. Each subordinate clause is underlined twice.

> I learned to read English before I could read Russian.

> Although it all remained rather stiff and patchy, my imagination somehow managed to obtain the necessary data.

Practice Copy the following sentences. Underline each independent clause once and each subordinate clause twice.

1. His mother read to him when he was small.
2. She placed her hand on the page before she turned it.
3. The stories of knights came alive.
4. While his mother read, he sat very still.
5. He loved literature as a child, and he became a great writer.

Writing Application Write three sentences about books that you remember reading as a child. At least one of your sentences should contain a subordinate clause.

W̶G *Prentice Hall Writing and Grammar Connection: Chapter 20, Section 2*

TEACHING RESOURCES

The following resources can be used to enrich or extend the instruction for pp. 348–349.

Vocabulary

📖 **Selection Support:** Build Vocabulary, p. 92

📖 **Vocabulary and Spelling Practice Book** (Use this booklet for skills enrichment.)

Grammar

📖 **Selection Support:** Build Grammar Skills, p. 93

W̶G **Writing and Grammar,** Platinum Level, p. 464

📰 **Daily Language Practice Transparencies** ▣

Writing

W̶G **Writing and Grammar,** Platinum Level, p. 57 ▣

💿 **Writing and Grammar iText CD-ROM**

📰 **BLOCK SCHEDULING:** Resources marked with this symbol provide varied instruction during 90-minute blocks.

Writing Lesson

Personal Narrative

Nabokov describes some of his favorite childhood books. Choose one or two of your favorite childhood books, and write a personal narrative about your memories of reading them.

Prewriting	Imagine yourself being read to as a child. From your memory, pick several key images, such as where you sat, what was read to you, and who read to you, and jot down details associated with these images. Gather sensory details to make your narrative come alive.
Drafting	Using the first-person point of view, describe your reading experience. Tell what you remember of your favorite books.
Revising	Reread your draft, highlighting words or phrases that are vague or dull and replacing them with details that appeal to the senses.

Model: Revising to Add Sensory Details

His lap was warm and cozy, and he would stroke my hair.

I remember sitting on my grandfather's lap. I had begged him to read my favorite book, Dr. Seuss's *Horton Hears a Who.* I liked the way he read to me.

The added information elaborates on an otherwise vague idea.

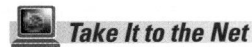 *Prentice Hall Writing and Grammar Connection: Chapter 4, Section 2*

Extension Activities

Research and Technology Working with a partner, research and report on the various ways the Russian Revolution of 1917 affected people like the Nabokovs. Look for information that you can use in a **multimedia presentation,** such as

- Film clips and photographs
- Quotations

Give your presentation to the class. [**Group Activity**]

Listening and Speaking Hold a **book discussion** to generate a list of books you might recommend to young children. As a group, discuss what was memorable about the books you enjoyed and prepare an annotated list that explains your choices. [**Group Activity**]

 Take It to the Net   www.phschool.com

Go online for an additional research activity using the Internet.

from *Speak, Memory* ◆ 349

Lesson Support for p. 349

❸ Writing Lesson

- Review with students the elements of a personal narrative. If necessary, have them reread the Literary Analysis instructional text on p. 341.
- When students have selected their books, have them list details on a sensory detail chart to help them with their narratives. Remind students that sensory details will help bring the events described in their narratives to life.
- Use the Autobiographical Narrative rubric in **Performance Assessment and Portfolio Management,** p. 9, to assess students' personal narratives.

❹ Listening and Speaking

- Students should choose one or two books as their favorites and be prepared to summarize the stories. They should also be prepared to discuss why they think the books are worthy of recommendation.
- You may also wish to have students go to a children's department at your local library and ask the librarian there to recommend children's authors, or have students interview their parents or younger siblings about favorite books for young children.

CUSTOMIZE INSTRUCTION
For Universal Access

To address different learning styles, use the activities suggested in the **Extension Activities** booklet, p. 23.

- For Verbal/Linguistic and Logical/Mathematical Learners, use Activity 5.
- For Bodily/Kinesthetic and Verbal/Linguistic Learners, use Activity 6.
- For Visual/Spatial Learners, use Activity 7.

ASSESSMENT RESOURCES

The following resources can be used to assess students' knowledge and skills.

Selection Assessment

- **Formal Assessment,** pp. 79–81
- **Open Book Test,** pp. 67–69
- **Got It! Assessment Videotapes,** Tape 2
- **Test Bank Software**
- **Take It to the Net**
  Visit www.phschool.com self-tests and additional questions on *Speak, Memory.*

Writing Rubric

- **Performance Assess. and Portfolio Mgmt.,** p. 9

PRENTICE HALL ASSESSMENT SYSTEM

- **Workbook**
- **Skill Book**
- **Transparencies**
- **CD-ROM**

Games at Twilight

Lesson Objectives

1. **To analyze and respond to literary elements**
   - Literary Analysis: Motivation
   - Connecting Literary Elements: Dialogue

2. **To read, comprehend, analyze, and critique a short story**
   - Reading Strategy: Evaluating a Character's Decision
   - Reading Check questions
   - Review and Assess questions
   - Assessment Practice (ATE)

3. **To develop word analysis skills, fluency, and systematic vocabulary**
   - Vocabulary Development Lesson: Latin Prefix: *super-*

4. **To understand and apply written and oral language conventions**
   - Spelling Strategy
   - Grammar Lesson: Subordination

5. **To understand and apply appropriate writing and research strategies**
   - Writing Lesson: Dialogue Between Children
   - Extension Activity: Research Report

6. **To understand and apply listening and speaking strategies**
   - Extension Activity: Explain and Play a Children's Game

STEP-BY-STEP TEACHING GUIDE	PACING GUIDE
PRETEACH	
Motivate Students and Provide Background	
Use the Motivation activity (ATE p. 350)	5 min.
Read and discuss the Preview material and Background information (SE/ATE p. 350)	5 min.
Introduce the Concepts	
Introduce the Literary Analysis and Reading Strategy (SE/ATE p. 351) A	15 min.
Pronounce the vocabulary words and read their definitions (SE p. 351)	5 min.
TEACH	
Monitor Comprehension	
Informally monitor comprehension by circulating while students read independently or in groups A	20 min.
Monitor students' comprehension with the Reading Check notes (SE/ATE pp. 353, 355, 357, 359)	as students read
Develop vocabulary with Vocabulary notes (SE pp. 355, 356, 357; ATE p. 355)	as students read
Develop Understanding	
Develop students' understanding of motivation with Literary Analysis annotations (SE pp. 353, 356, 358; ATE pp. 352, 353, 355, 356, 358) A	10 min.
Develop students' understanding of evaluating a character's decision with the Reading Strategy annotations (SE pp. 356, 358; ATE pp. 356, 358)	10 min.
ASSESS	
Assess Mastery	
Assess students' mastery of the Reading Strategy and Literary Analysis by having them answer the Review and Assess questions (SE/ATE p. 361)	20 min.
Use one or more of the print and media Assessment Resources (ATE p. 363) A	up to 50 min.
EXTEND	
Apply Understanding	
Have students complete the Vocabulary Development Lesson and the Grammar Lesson (SE p. 362) A	20 min.
Apply students' knowledge of of appropriate language using the Writing Lesson (SE p. 363) A	45 min.
Apply students' understanding using one or more of the Extension Activities (SE p. 363)	20–90 min.

A **ACCELERATED INSTRUCTION:**
Use the strategies and activities identified with an **A**.

UNIVERSAL ACCESS
- ● = Below Level Students
- ▲ = On-Level Students
- ■ = Above Level Students

Time and Resource Manager

Reading Level: Average
Average Number of Instructional Days: 4

RESOURCES

PRINT 📖	TRANSPARENCIES	TECHNOLOGY 💿 🎧 📼
• **Beyond Literature,** Cross-Curricular Connection: Science, p. 24 ▲ ■		
• **Selection Support Workbook:** ● ▲ ■ Literary Analysis, p. 96 Reading Strategy, p. 95 Build Vocabulary, p. 93	• **Literary Analysis and Reading Transparencies,** pp. 47 and 48 ● ▲ ■	
• **Adapted Reader's Companion** ● • **Reader's Companion** ●		• **Listening to Literature** ● ▲ ■ Audiocassettes, Side 11 Audio CDs, CD 7
• **English Learner's Companion** ● ▲ • **Literatura en español** ● ▲ • **Literary Analysis for Enrichment** ■		
• **Formal Assessment:** Selection Test, pp. 82–84 ● ▲ ■ • **Open Book Test,** pp. 70–72 ● ▲ ■ • **Performance Assessment and Portfolio Management,** p. 14 ● ▲ ■ • PRENTICE HALL ASSESSMENT *SYSTEM* ● ▲	• PRENTICE HALL ASSESSMENT *SYSTEM* ● ▲ ■ Skills Practice Answers and Explanations on Transparencies	• **Test Bank Software** ● ▲ ■ • **Got It! Assessment Videotapes,** Tape 2 ● ▲
• **Selection Support Workbook:** ● ▲ ■ Build Grammar Skills, p. 94 • **Writing and Grammar,** Platinum Level ● ▲ ■ • **Extension Activities,** p. 24 ● ▲ ■	• **Daily Language Practice Transparencies** ● ▲	• **Writing and Grammar iText CD-ROM** ● ▲ ■ 💻 **Take It to the Net** www.phschool.com

BLOCK SCHEDULING: Use one 90-minute class period to preteach the selection and have students read it. Use a second 90-minute class period to assess students' mastery of skills and have them complete one of the Extension Activities.

Motivation

Lead students in a discussion of the games they played when they were children. Did success depend on skill, physical superiority, persistence, or something else? What lessons about adult life can these games teach? Tell students that in this story, a child-hood game leads the main character to a difficult realization.

❶ Background

Cultural Connection

Popular sports in India include freestyle wrestling and a traditional Indian team sport called *kabaddi*, which requires quickness and strength. There are also a number of traditional games, played mainly by men. These include chess, which originated in India, and *pachisi*, a dice game.

Because of England's long colonial rule in India, Indians adopted many western games. For example, soccer is popular in Eastern India, and India's national cricket team competes at the highest interna-tional level. Children often play versions of English games, such as hide-and-seek.

Prepare to Read

Games at Twilight

 Take It to the Net

Visit www.phschool.com for interactive activities and instruction related to "Games at Twilight," including

- background
- graphic organizers
- literary elements
- reading strategies

Preview

Connecting to the Literature

Younger children often idolize older ones who run faster, know more, or just seem more self-confident. In this story, an Indian boy named Ravi tries to gain the respect of the older children by winning at a game of hide-and-seek.

❶ Background

Anita Desai, the author of "Games at Twilight," grew up in India in the final years of British rule. Great Britain had ruled India as a colony since 1858. In the early twentieth century, however, the Indians became increasingly dissatisfied with this situation. Demonstrations and violence occurred sporadically and led to Indian independence in 1947.

TEACHING RESOURCES

The following resources can be used to enrich or extend the instruction for pp. 350–351.

Background
 Beyond Literature, p. 24

Literary Analysis
 Literary Analysis and Reading Transparencies, Motivation, p. 48

 Take It to the Net
Visit www.phschool.com for background and hotlinks for "Games at Twilight."

Reading
 Selection Support: Reading Strategy, p. 95; Build Vocabulary, p. 93 ▪

 Literary Analysis and Reading Transparencies, Evaluating a Character's Decision, p. 47

BLOCK SCHEDULING: Resources marked with this symbol provide varied instruction during 90-minute blocks.

Literary Analysis

Motivation

A character's **motivation** is the reason behind his or her actions or words. Understanding why characters act in a certain way will help you understand story events. For example, in "Games at Twilight," the young Ravi sits alone in a dusty, dark, and scary shed for a long time. This peculiar behavior makes more sense if you understand that Ravi is motivated to show the older children that he can win at a game of hide-and-seek.

Connecting Literary Elements

Writers sometimes reveal motivation through dialogue. **Dialogue** is conversation between characters. Because it shows the characters' exact words, it is set off with quotation marks. Writers use dialogue for a variety of reasons:

- To move the plot forward
- To develop the characters
- To make the story more personal and real for the reader
- To reveal the characters' ideas

Reading Strategy

Evaluating a Character's Decision

In this story, Ravi makes a decision that he thinks will earn him the respect of the older children. As you read, evaluate his decision. Using the facts at hand, determine whether the decision he makes is the best one.

To **evaluate a character's decision** fairly, you have to look at it from many angles. Consider what would have happened had the character acted differently. Look to see what other options may have been available, and note the pros and cons of each option. Using a diagram like this one, evaluate Ravi's decision.

Problem		
	Option 1	Option 2
Pros		
Cons		
Decision		

⋮

Evaluation

Vocabulary Development

superciliously (soo′ pər sil′ ē əs lē) *adv*. contemptuously; acting as though one is above, or better than, others (p. 355)

sidled (sīd′ əld) *v*. moved slowly to the side to avoid attracting attention (p. 355)

defunct (dē funkt′) *adj*. no longer in use or existence; dead (p. 356)

dogged (dôg′ id) *adj*. stubborn (p. 357)

---

❷ Literary Analysis

Motivation

- Tell students that as they read "Games at Twilight," they will focus on character motivation, or the reasons that a character behaves a certain way.

- Use the instruction for Connecting Literary Elements to help students see how a character's words can help explain his or her motivation.

- Use the Motivation transparency in **Literary Analysis and Reading Transparencies,** p. 48, to demonstrate for students how to determine character motivation.

❸ Reading Strategy

Evaluating a Character's Decision

- Explain to students that when they evaluate a character's decisions, they make judgments about the actions that a character chooses to take. Often, understanding a character's motivation can help a reader make an informed evaluation.

- As a group, evaluate a decision made by a character in another story the class has read this year. Record students' responses in a chart like the one shown.

- Encourage students to create a chart to help them evaluate Ravi's decisions as they read the selection.

Vocabulary Development

- Pronounce each vocabulary word for students, and read the definitions as a class. Have students identify any words with which they are already familiar.

CUSTOMIZE INSTRUCTION FOR UNIVERSAL ACCESS

For Special Needs Students	For Less Proficient Readers	For English Learners
Have students read the adapted version of "Games at Twilight" in the **Adapted Reader's Companion**. This version provides basic-level instruction in an interactive format with questions and write-on lines. Completing the adapted version will prepare students to read the selection in the Student Edition.	Have students read the selection in the **Reader's Companion**. This version provides basic-level instruction in an interactive format with questions and write-on lines. After students finish the selection in **Reader's Companion,** have them complete the questions and activities in the Student Edition.	Have students read the adapted version of the selection in the **English Learner's Companion**. This version provides basic-level instruction in an interactive format with questions and write-on lines. Completing the adapted version will prepare students to read the selection in the Student Edition.

 E-Teach

Visit E-Teach at www.phschool.com for teachers' essays on how to teach, with questions and answers.

Step-by-Step Teaching Guide for pp. 352–360

Have these students notice the vivid imagery in the story's exposition. Ask them to create visual representations, such as drawings or paintings, of the way the children feel on this intensely hot afternoon. Their representations should include details from the text.

❶ About the Selection

On a hot afternoon, Ravi plays a game of hide-and-seek with his siblings and cousins. To prove that he can win, Ravi decides to hide in a dark and forbidding shed. He stays there all afternoon. Finally, when the hour has grown late, Ravi emerges from the shed to claim his victory, only to find that the game ended long ago and no one noticed his absence.

❷ Literary Analysis

Motivation

- Have students pay careful attention to the author's description of the setting in the bracketed passage.
- Ask students to describe the setting.
  Answer: The beginning of the story takes place inside a house on a very hot afternoon.
- Ask students to identify the children's motivation for wanting to go outside.
  Answer: The children want to get out of the stuffy house.

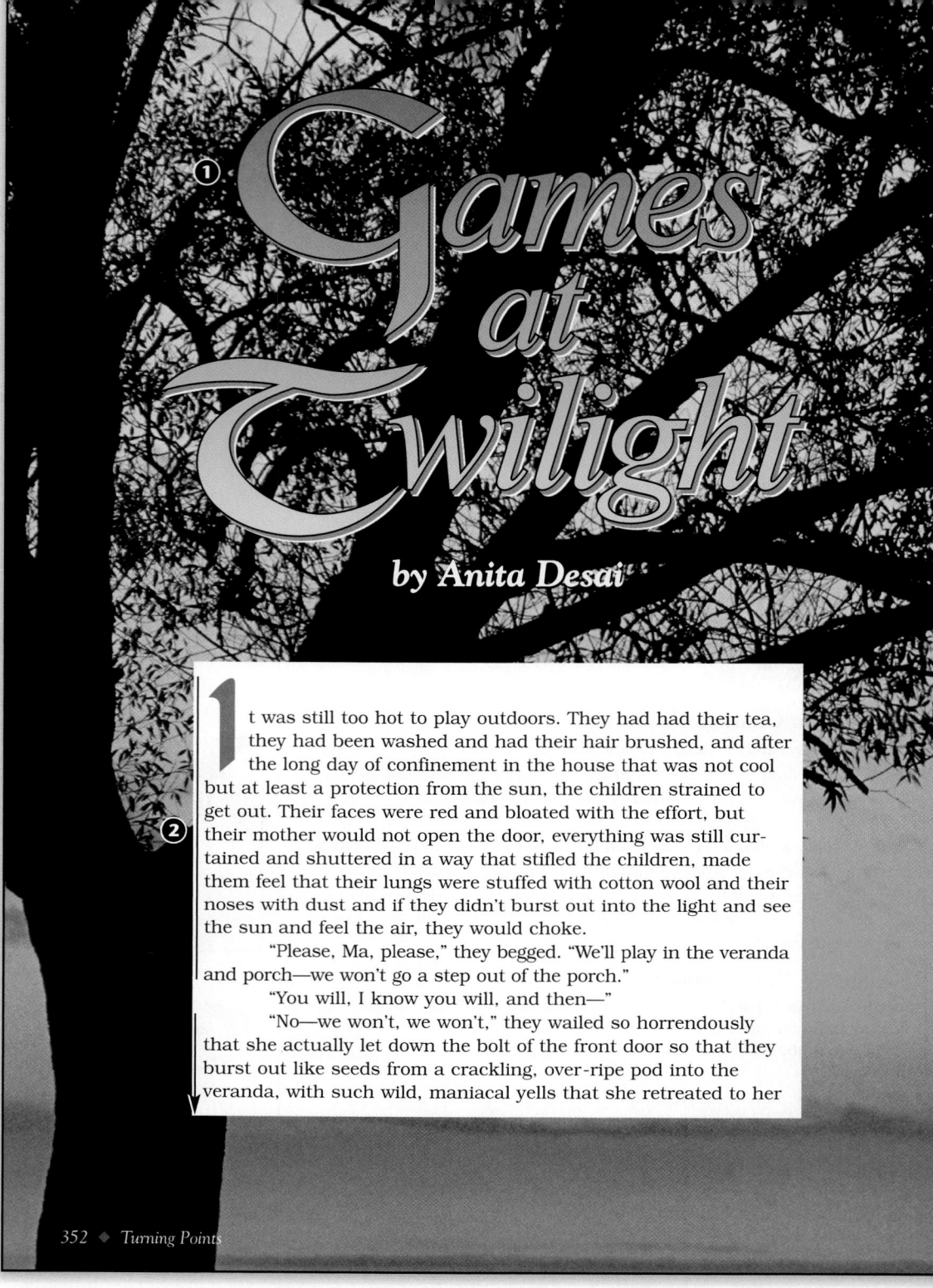

Games at Twilight

by Anita Desai

t was still too hot to play outdoors. They had had their tea, they had been washed and had their hair brushed, and after the long day of confinement in the house that was not cool but at least a protection from the sun, the children strained to get out. Their faces were red and bloated with the effort, but their mother would not open the door, everything was still curtained and shuttered in a way that stifled the children, made them feel that their lungs were stuffed with cotton wool and their noses with dust and if they didn't burst out into the light and see the sun and feel the air, they would choke.

"Please, Ma, please," they begged. "We'll play in the veranda and porch—we won't go a step out of the porch."

"You will, I know you will, and then—"

"No—we won't, we won't," they wailed so horrendously that she actually let down the bolt of the front door so that they burst out like seeds from a crackling, over-ripe pod into the veranda, with such wild, maniacal yells that she retreated to her

---

TEACHING RESOURCES

The following resources can be used to enrich or extend the instruction for pp. 352–360.

Literary Analysis

📖 **Selection Support:** Literary Analysis, p. 96

Reading

📖 **Reader's Companion**

📖 **English Learner's Companion**

🎧 **Listening to Literature Audiocassettes,** Side 11 ▪

💿 **Listening to Literature Audio CDs,** CD 7 ▪

▪ **BLOCK SCHEDULING:** Resources marked with this symbol provide varied instruction during 90-minute blocks.

bath and the shower of talcum powder and the fresh sari[1] that were to help her face the summer evening.

They faced the afternoon. It was too hot. Too bright. The white walls of the veranda glared stridently in the sun. The bougainvillea[2] hung about it, purple and magenta, in livid balloons. The garden outside was like a tray made of beaten brass, flattened out on the red gravel and the stony soil in all shades of metal—aluminum, tin, copper and brass. No life stirred at this arid time of day—the birds still drooped, like dead fruit, in the papery tents of the trees; some squirrels lay limp on the wet earth under the garden tap. The outdoor dog lay stretched as if dead on the veranda mat, his paws and ears and tail all reaching out like dying travelers in search of water. He rolled his eyes at the children—two white marbles rolling in the purple sockets, begging for sympathy—and attempted to lift his tail in a wag but could not. It only twitched and lay still.

Then, perhaps roused by the shrieks of the children, a band of parrots suddenly fell out of the eucalyptus tree, tumbled frantically in the still, sizzling air, then sorted themselves out into battle formation and streaked away across the white sky.

The children, too, felt released. They too began tumbling, shoving, pushing against each other, frantic to start. Start what? Start their business. The business of the children's day which is—play.

"Let's play hide-and-seek."

"Who'll be It?"

"You be It."

"Why should I? You be—"

"You're the eldest—"

"That doesn't mean—"

The shoves became harder. Some kicked out. The motherly Mira intervened. She pulled the boys roughly apart. There was a tearing sound of cloth but it was lost in the heavy panting and angry grumbling and no one paid attention to the small sleeve hanging loosely off a shoulder.

"Make a circle, make a circle!" she shouted, firmly pulling and pushing till a kind of vague circle was formed. "Now clap!" she roared and, clapping, they all chanted in melancholy unison: "Dip, dip, dip—my blue ship—" and every now and then one or the other saw he was safe by the way his hands fell at the crucial moment—palm on palm, or back of hand on palm—and dropped out of the circle with a yell and a jump of relief and jubilation.

Raghu was It. He started to protest, to cry "You cheated—Mira cheated—Amu cheated—" but it was too late, the others had all already streaked away. There was no one to hear when he called out, "Only in the veranda—the porch—Ma said—Ma *said* to stay in the porch!" No one had stopped to listen, all he saw were their brown legs

---

1. **sari** (sä′ rē) *n.* long piece of cloth wrapped around the body, forming a skirt, and draped over one shoulder; worn by Hindu women.
2. **bougainvillea** (bōō gən vil′ ē ə) *n.* woody, tropical vines with flowers.

Literary Analysis
Motivation What is the mother's motivation for allowing the children outside?

Literary Analysis
Motivation and Dialogue How realistic is this dialogue? Explain.

5 ✔Reading Check
Why are the children so anxious to get outside?

❸ Literary Analysis

Motivation

- Ask students to review the children's behavior and the situation inside the house.
- Then, ask students the first Literary Analysis question on p. 353: What is the mother's motivation for allowing the children outside?
  Answer: She lets them go outside because they are making a fuss, and because she wants to relax and cool off in the bath.

❹ Literary Analysis

Motivation and Dialogue

- Have a different student read each line of dialogue.
- Ask students why the author uses dashes at the end of some of the lines. What do the dashes signal?
  Answer: The dashes show that the children are interrupting each other.
- Ask students the second Literary Analysis question on p. 353: How realistic is this dialogue? Explain.
  Answer: The dialogue is very realistic because the children are excited and talk over each other.

❺ ✔Reading Check

Answer: The children feel stifled in the stuffy house.

CUSTOMIZE INSTRUCTION FOR UNIVERSAL ACCESS

For English Learners	For Gifted/Talented Students
Explain figurative expressions such as "They faced the afternoon," "the white walls . . . glared stridently," and "The garden . . . like a tray made of beaten brass." After you have explained the expressions, have students rewrite them in their own words. Encourage them to identify figurative expressions as they continue to read.	Draw students' attention to the vivid description of the heat. Ask them to write a few paragraphs describing an intensely hot or cold day they've experienced. Like Desai, have them use figurative language, such as similes and metaphors, to describe the extreme temperature. When they finish, have volunteers share their work with the class.

Racing Game, by Tony Wong

Tony Wong was born in China and later immigrated to the United States. His paintings were first shown in New York City in 1987.

Racing Game is executed in oil pastel, a type of chalk on paper. Here, Mr. Wong employs the same technique that makes his paintings so dramatic—he pulls brightly colored, expressive figures from a dark, heavily built-up background. The artist does not define the setting surrounding the figures. Instead, the viewer is left to decide where they are and what they are doing. In this case, they could be the children in the story running off to hide.

Use the following questions for discussion:

1. How does the artist convey the sense of urgency felt by the runners?
   Answer: Tension is conveyed in the runners' bodies. One looks back at the others, as if in fear.

2. How well does the painting portray the children at play from the story? Explain.
   Answer: The children resemble those in the story who are running off to hide.

❼ ▶Critical Viewing

Answer: It illustrates the universal similarity of children playing. These could be any children anywhere in the world. Students should recognize this universal behavior in the story.

❻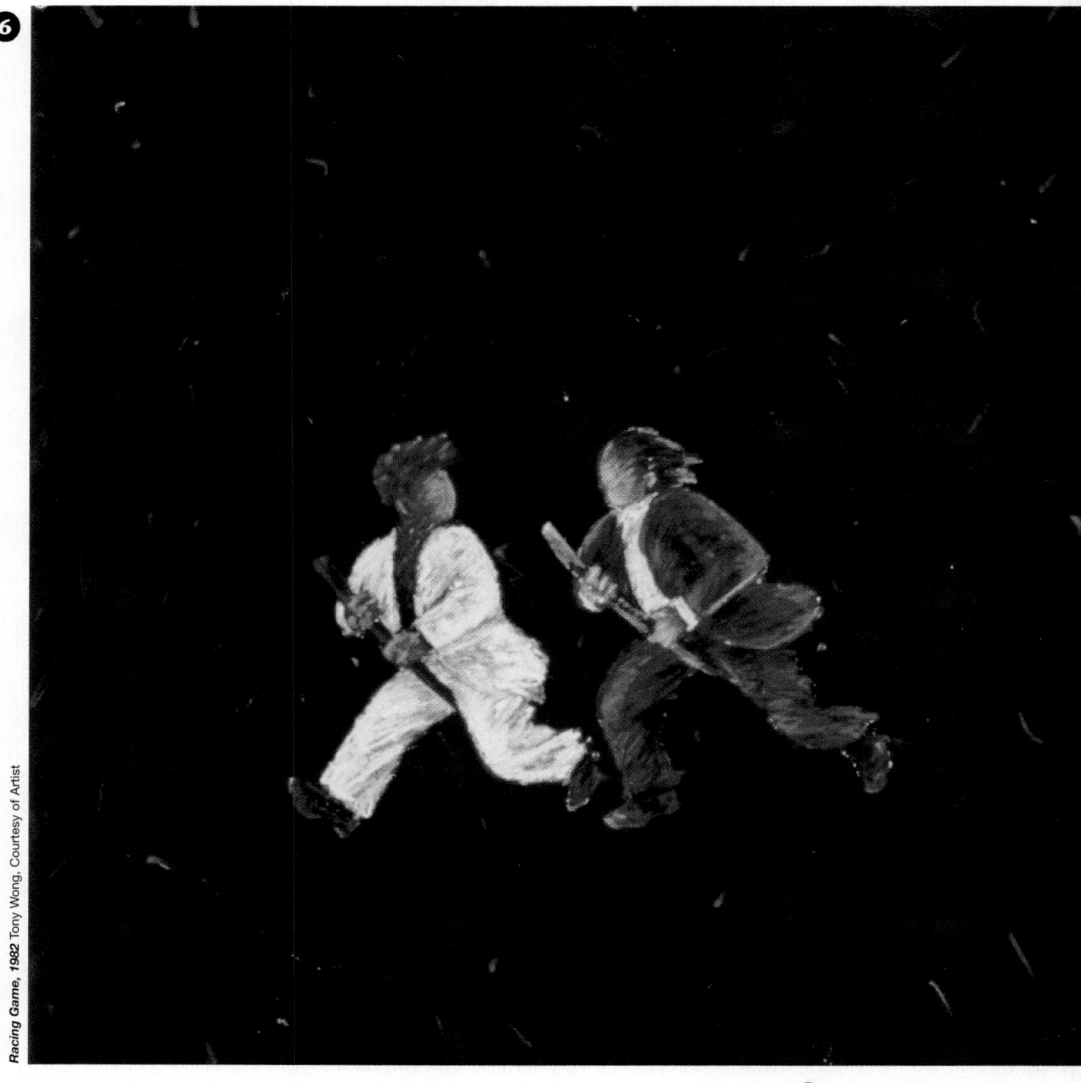

Racing Game, 1982 Tony Wong, Courtesy of Artist

flashing through the dusty shrubs, scrambling up brick walls, leaping over compost heaps and hedges, and then the porch stood empty in the purple shade of the bougainvillea and the garden was as empty as before; even the limp squirrels had whisked away, leaving everything gleaming, brassy and bare.

Only small Manu suddenly reappeared, as if he had dropped out of an invisible cloud or from a bird's claws, and stood for a moment in the center of the yellow lawn, chewing his finger and near to tears as he heard Raghu shouting, with his head pressed against the veranda

❼ ▲ Critical Viewing
How does the facelessness of the children in this image contribute to the mood of the story? **[Connect]**

✹ **ENRICHMENT: Cultural Connection**

Children's Games

The full text of the rhyme that the children in this story call out is as follows:

   Dip, dip, dip

   My blue ship

   Sailing on the water

   Like a cup and saucer

   Dip, dip, dip

   You are not it.

This counting-out rhyme (similar to our "eeny, meeny, miney, mo") was popular among British girls in the 1950s and 1960s.

wall, "Eighty-three, eighty-five, eighty-nine, ninety . . ." and then made off in a panic, half of him wanting to fly north, the other half counseling south. Raghu turned just in time to see the flash of his white shorts and the uncertain skittering of his red sandals, and charged after him with such a bloodcurdling yell that Manu stumbled over the hosepipe, fell into its rubber coils and lay there weeping, "I won't be It—you have to find them all—all—All!"

"I know I have to, idiot," Raghu said, <u>superciliously</u> kicking him with his toe. "You're dead," he said with satisfaction, licking the beads of perspiration off his upper lip, and then stalked off in search of worthier prey, whistling spiritedly so that the hiders should hear and tremble.

superciliously (soō′ pər sil′ ē əs lē) *adv.* contemptuously; acting as though one is above, or better than, others

R avi heard the whistling and picked his nose in a panic, trying to find comfort by burrowing the finger deep—deep into that soft tunnel. He felt himself too exposed, sitting on an upturned flower pot behind the garage. Where could he burrow? He could run around the garage if he heard Raghu come—around and around and around— but he hadn't much faith in his short legs when matched against Raghu's long, hefty, hairy footballer legs.[3] Ravi had a frightening glimpse of them as Raghu combed the hedge of crotons and hibiscus,[4] trampling delicate ferns underfoot as he did so. Ravi looked about him desperately, swallowing a small ball of snot in his fear.

The garage was locked with a great heavy lock to which the driver had the key in his room, hanging from a nail on the wall under his work-shirt. Ravi had peeped in and seen him still sprawling on his string-cot in his vest and striped underpants, the hair on his chest and the hair in his nose shaking with the vibrations of his phlegm-obstructed snores. Ravi had wished he were tall enough, big enough to reach the key on the nail, but it was impossible, beyond his reach for years to come. He had <u>sidled</u> away and sat dejectedly on the flower pot. That at least was cut to his own size.

sidled (sīd′ əld) *v.* moved slowly to the side to avoid attracting attention

But next to the garage was another shed with a big green door. Also locked. No one even knew who had the key to the lock. That shed wasn't opened more than once a year when Ma turned out all the old broken bits of furniture and rolls of matting and leaking buckets, and the white ant hills were broken and swept away and Flit sprayed into the spider webs and rat holes so that the whole operation was like the looting of a poor, ruined and conquered city. The green leaves of the door sagged. They were nearly off their rusty hinges. The hinges were large and made a small gap between the door and the walls—only just large enough for rats, dogs, and possibly, Ravi to slip through.

---

3. **footballer legs** the powerful legs of a soccer player.
4. **crotons** (krōt′ ənz) **and hibiscus** (hī bis′ kəs) types of tropical shrubs.

⓿ ☑ Reading Check

Why is Ravi in such a panic to find a hiding place?

---

❽ Vocabulary Development

Latin Prefix: *super-*

• Draw students' attention to the word *superciliously* and its definition, "acting as though one is above, or better than, others."

• Explain that the Latin prefix *super-* means "above" or "extra."

• Ask students to name and define other words that contain this root. **Possible responses:** *Superhuman* means "having powers above those of humans"; *superfluous* means "above what is necessary."

❾ Literary Analysis

Motivation

• Have students describe Ravi's behavior in the bracketed passage. Encourage students to cite details from the text to support their responses.
Answer: Ravi is trying frantically to find a good hiding spot. Students may cite words such as *panic*, *frightening*, and *desperately* to support their responses.

• Then, have students identify Ravi's motivation for trying so hard to find a good hiding spot.
Answer: Ravi wants to win the game to show that he can beat the older children.

▶ **Monitor Progress** Have students write a brief interior dialogue for Ravi that explains the motivation for his behavior.

❿ ☑ Reading Check

Answer: Ravi feels he must beat Raghu at the game to prove himself.

CUSTOMIZE INSTRUCTION FOR UNIVERSAL ACCESS

For Advanced Readers

Desai's story is filled with rich sensory details that make the setting and the action more vivid. Ask students to identify the sensory details in the story, explain which sense each detail appeals to, and describe how these details contribute to the story. They might use a sensory-details chart like the one shown here:

Sight	Smell	Sound	Taste	Touch

- Have students read the bracketed passage, paying close attention to the description of the shed.

- Have students explain what makes the shed both a good and a bad hiding place.

- Then, ask students the Reading Strategy question on p. 356: Explain whether or not you think Ravi has made a good decision to hide in the shed.

  Answer: Some students will say that Ravi made a good decision because it is unlikely that anyone will find him in the shed. Others will say he made a bad decision because the shed is scary and possibly dangerous.

⓬ Literary Analysis

Motivation

- As students read the bracketed passage, have them note the details that reveal how Ravi feels in the shed.

  Answer: Ravi is frightened. He "stood frozen" and he "shivered all over."

- Then, ask students the Literary Analysis question on p. 356: Why do you think that Ravi stays in the shed rather than finding a more pleasant hiding place?

  Answer: He probably stays in the shed because he knows it is unlikely that Raghu will go in there to find him.

Ravi had never cared to enter such a dark and depressing mortuary[5] of <u>defunct</u> household goods seething with such unspeakable and alarming animal life but, as Raghu's whistling grew angrier and sharper and his crashing and storming in the hedge wilder, Ravi suddenly slipped off the flower pot and through the crack and was gone. He chuckled aloud with astonishment at his own temerity so that Raghu came out of the hedge, stood silent with his hands on his hips, listening, and finally shouted "I heard you! I'm coming! *Got* you—" and came charging round the garage only to find the upturned flower pot, the yellow dust, the crawling of white ants in a mud-hill against the closed shed door—nothing. Snarling, he bent to pick up a stick and went off, whacking it against the garage and shed walls as if to beat out his prey.

R avi shook, then shivered with delight, with self-congratulation. Also with fear. It was dark, spooky in the shed. It had a muffled smell, as of graves. Ravi had once got locked into the linen cupboard and sat there weeping for half an hour before he was rescued. But at least that had been a familiar place, and even smelled pleasantly of starch, laundry and reassuringly, of his mother. But the shed smelled of rats, ant hills, dust and spider webs. Also of less definable, less recognizable horrors. And it was dark. Except for the white-hot cracks along the door, there was no light. The roof was very low. Although Ravi was small, he felt as if he could reach up and touch it with his finger tips. But he didn't stretch. He hunched himself into a ball so as not to bump into anything, touch or feel anything. What might there not be to touch him and feel him as he stood there, trying to see in the dark? Something cold, or slimy—like a snake. Snakes! He leapt up as Raghu whacked the wall with his stick—then quickly realizing what it was, felt almost relieved to hear Raghu, hear his stick. It made him feel protected.

But Raghu soon moved away. There wasn't a sound once his footsteps had gone around the garage and disappeared. Ravi stood frozen inside the shed. Then he shivered all over. Something had tickled the back of his neck. It took him a while to pick up the courage to lift his hand and explore. It was an insect—perhaps a spider—exploring *him.* He squashed it and wondered how many more creatures were watching him, waiting to reach out and touch him, the stranger.

There was nothing now. After standing in that position—his hand still on his neck, feeling the wet splodge of the squashed spider gradually dry—for minutes, hours, his legs began to tremble with the effort, the inaction. By now he could see enough in the dark to make out the large solid shapes of old wardrobes, broken buckets and bedsteads piled on top of each other around him. He recognized an old bathtub—patches of enamel glimmered at him and at last he lowered himself onto its edge.

---

5. **mortuary** (môr´ chōō er ē) *n.* place where dead bodies are kept before being buried or cremated.

---

defunct (dē funkt´) *adj.* no longer in use or existence; dead

Reading Strategy
Evaluating a Character's Decision Explain whether or not you think Ravi has made a good decision to hide in the shed.

Literary Analysis
Motivation Why do you think that Ravi stays in the shed rather than finding a more pleasant hiding place?

CUSTOMIZE INSTRUCTION FOR UNIVERSAL ACCESS

For Special Needs Students	For Gifted/Talented Students
Help students visualize the shed in which Ravi hides by having them draw a picture of it. To make sure they include details from the text, have them label in their drawings the items, such as the bathtub and the insect on Ravi's back, that Desai describes.	Have students write a journal entry about a challenging childhood experience. Have them answer the following questions: What was the challenge? By whom was it imposed? Did they meet it successfully, and why? What did they learn from it?

He contemplated slipping out of the shed and into the fray. He wondered if it would not be better to be captured by Raghu and be returned to the milling crowd as long as he could be in the sun, the light, the free spaces of the garden and the familiarity of his brothers, sisters and cousins. It would be evening soon. Their games would become legitimate. The parents would sit out on the lawn on cane basket chairs and watch them as they tore around the garden or gathered in knots to share a loot of mulberries or black, teeth-splitting *jamun*[6] from the garden trees. The gardener would fix the hosepipe to the water tap and water would fall lavishly through the air to the ground, soaking the dry yellow grass and the red gravel and arousing the sweet, the intoxicating scent of water on dry earth— that loveliest scent in the world. Ravi sniffed for a whiff of it. He half-rose from the bathtub, then heard the despairing scream of one of the girls as Raghu bore down upon her. There was the sound of a crash, and of rolling about in the bushes, the shrubs, then screams and accusing sobs of, "I touched the den—" "You did not—" "I did—" "You liar, you did *not*" and then a fading away and silence again.

Ravi sat back on the harsh edge of the tub, deciding to hold out a bit longer. What fun if they were all found and caught—he alone left unconquered! He had never known that sensation. Nothing more wonderful had ever happened to him than being taken out by an uncle and bought a whole slab of chocolate all to himself, or being flung into the soda-man's pony cart and driven up to the gate by the friendly driver with the red beard and pointed ears. To defeat Raghu—that hirsute,[7] hoarse-voiced football champion—and to be the winner in a circle of older, bigger, luckier children—that would be thrilling beyond imagination. He hugged his knees together and smiled to himself almost shyly at the thought of so much victory, such laurels.[8]

There he sat smiling, knocking his heels against the bathtub, now and then getting up and going to the door to put his ear to the broad crack and listening for sounds of the game, the pursuer and the pursued, and then returning to his seat with the <u>dogged</u> determination of the true winner, a breaker of records, a champion.

It grew darker in the shed as the light at the door grew softer, fuzzier, turned to a kind of crumbling yellow pollen that turned to yellow fur, blue fur, gray fur. Evening. Twilight. The sound of water gushing, falling. The scent of earth receiving water, slaking its thirst in great gulps and releasing that green scent of freshness, coolness.

---

6. *jamun* (jä´ mo͞on´) *n.* tart fruit with reddish-purple pulp and juice.
7. **hirsute** (hʉr´ so͞ot´) *adj.* hairy.
8. **laurels** (lôr´ əlz) *n.* foliage of the laurel tree, worn in a crown as a symbol of victory in a contest.

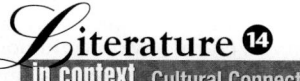

Literature in context Cultural Connection

Children's Games Around the World

In this story, the game hide-and-seek probably derives from English traditions. Hide-and-seek is a common game in Middle Eastern and most European countries.

In much of the world, many children's games involve a set of rules and few, if any, materials. Children make trees "home base," use a simple ball as the basis of their games, or even play at rhythm clapping.

At the end of the story, the children in "Games at Twilight" play another game that may seem familiar. Although the words are different, the game is similar to the English and American game of "London Bridge Is Falling Down."

dogged (dôg´ id) *adj.* stubborn

 Reading Check

What is unpleasant about Ravi's hiding place?

Games at Twilight ◆ 357

---

⑬ Critical Thinking

Infer

- Ask students to describe Ravi's feelings as he hears the other children being caught outside the shed.
  Answer: Ravi seems happy as the other children are caught.

- Then, ask students why Ravi feels this way.
  Answer: Ravi is thrilled by the thought of winning the game. He thinks that if he beats the bigger, older children, he will gain his family's respect.

⑭ Background

Children's Games

Students may not know that some children's games have a historical significance. For example, the game "Ring-Around-the-Rosy" refers to the Bubonic Plague, or the Black Death, that devastated Europe five hundred years ago. The lines of the song are as follows:

Ring around the rosy
A Pocket full of posy
Ashes, ashes
We all fall down.

"Rosy" is the wound caused by fleas infected with the disease; "posy" is an aromatic mixture thought to ward off the disease; and the last two lines refer to the hundreds of thousands of deaths it caused.

⑮ ✓Reading Check

Answer: The shed is dark, dusty, and filled with insects. Ravi can't see clearly, but he thinks there may be snakes inside.

16 ▶ Critical Viewing

Students will probably say that the painting captures the energy of the children because the girl who is "it" is tense with excitement, and the boy in the tree peeks down as if he can hardly contain himself.

17 Literary Analysis

Motivation

• As students read the bracketed passage, have them keep Ravi's goal in mind.

• Ask students the Literary Analysis question on p. 358: Why does Ravi feel angry and disgraced?
Answer: Ravi desperately wanted to win the game to gain respect from his siblings and cousins. The disappointment of not being recognized as the winner overwhelmed Ravi.

18 Reading Strategy

Evaluating a Character's Decision

• Ask students to explain why Ravi charged into the group.
Answer: Ravi was very upset that no one noticed that he won, so he took out his frustration on the group.

▶ Monitor Progress Ask students the Reading Strategy question on p. 358: Instead of charging into the group, how could Ravi have behaved differently?
Possible response: Ravi could have calmly told them that he actually won the game because Raghu never found him.

Through the crack Ravi saw the long purple shadows of the shed and the garage lying still across the yard. Beyond that, the white walls of the house. The bougainvillea had lost its lividity, hung in dark bundles that quaked and twittered and seethed with masses of homing sparrows. The lawn was shut off from his view. Could he hear the children's voices? It seemed to him that he could. It seemed to him that he could hear them chanting, singing, laughing. But what about the game? What had happened? Could it be over? How could it when he was still not found?

It then occurred to him that he could have slipped out long ago, dashed across the yard to the veranda and touched the "den." It was necessary to do that to win. He had forgotten. He had only remembered the part of hiding and trying to elude the seeker. He had done that so successfully, his success had occupied him so wholly that he had quite forgotten that success had to be clinched by that final dash to victory and the ringing cry of "Den!"

17 With a whimper he burst through the crack, fell on his knees, got up and stumbled on stiff, benumbed legs across the shadowy yard, crying heartily by the time he reached the veranda so that when he flung himself at the white pillar and bawled, "Den! Den! Den!" his voice broke with rage and pity at the disgrace of it all and he felt himself flooded with tears and misery.

Out on the lawn, the children stopped chanting. They all turned to stare at him in amazement. Their faces were pale and triangular in the dusk. The trees and bushes around them stood inky and sepulchral,[9] spilling long shadows across them. They stared, wondering at his reappearance, his passion, his wild animal howling. Their mother rose from her basket chair and came toward him, worried, annoyed, saying, "Stop it, stop it, Ravi. Don't be a baby. Have you hurt yourself?" Seeing him attended to, the children went back to clasping their hands and chanting "The grass is green, the rose is red. . . . "

18 But Ravi would not let them. He tore himself out of his mother's grasp and pounded across the lawn into their midst, charging at them with his head lowered so that they scattered in surprise. "I won, I won, I won," he bawled, shaking his head so that the big tears flew. "Raghu didn't find me. I won, I won—"

It took them a minute to grasp what he was saying, even who he was. They had quite forgotten him. Raghu had found all the others long ago. There had been a fight about who was to be It next. It had been so fierce that their mother had emerged from her bath and made them change to another game. Then they had played another and another. Broken mulberries from the tree and eaten them. Helped the driver wash the car when their father returned from work. Helped the gardener water the beds till he roared at them and swore he would complain to their parents. The parents had come out, taken up their

---

9. **sepulchral** (sə pul′ krəl) *adj.* dismal; gloomy.

---

16 ▶ **Critical Viewing**
Does this painting capture the energy of children playing as it is described in this story? Why or why not? **[Connect]**

Literary Analysis
Motivation Why does Ravi feel angry and disgraced?

Reading Strategy
Evaluating a Character's Decision Instead of charging into the group, how could Ravi have behaved differently?

 ENRICHMENT: Science Connection

Bougainvillea

Bougainvillea is a flowering vine that originally came from South America. It is commonly found in warm, tropical climates, including India and the southern United States. The flowers are very small, but they are surrounded by bright, showy modified leaves. These modified leaves are usually purple, orange, red, or white. The vine is named after Louis de Bougainville, a French explorer.

Hide and Seek Tony Wong, Courtesy of the Artist

positions on the cane chairs. They had begun to play again, sing and chant. All this time no one had remembered Ravi. Having disappeared from the scene, he had disappeared from their minds. Clean.

"Don't be a fool," Raghu said roughly, pushing him aside, and even Mira said, "Stop howling, Ravi. If you want to play, you can stand at the end of the line," and she put him there very firmly.

⓳ Background

Art

Hide and Seek, by Tony Wong

Although the paintings of contemporary Chinese American artist Tony Wong are executed in a modern, western style, they also show the eastern influence of his Chinese heritage.

"Hide and Seek," drawn in oil pastel on paper, is part of a series on the theme of childhood games. The blindfolded girl and the person hiding in the tree are the only figures that appear in this drawing. The artist manages to convey, through color and gesture, the impression that there are others players just out of sight, waiting with excitement to be discovered.

Use the following questions for discussion.

1. What details does the artist use to give the impression that this is a tropical setting?
Answer: The artist includes a tropical tree and a girl wearing a light dress.

2. What parallels can you draw between the way the artist and the writer describe the game of hide-and-seek?
Answer: Both the artist and the writer capture the children's excitement and tension.

⓴ ✔Reading Check

Answer: Ravi runs to the "den" only to discover that the game had ended and that the other children had forgotten about him.

⓴ ✔Reading Check

What happens when Ravi finally leaves the shed?

Review and Assess

1. Some students would have stayed in the shed because it would be unlikely that Raghu would find them there. Others would have left the frightening shed immediately.

2. **(a)** Ravi describes them as "long, hefty, hairy, footballer legs."
(b) He feels physically inferior to Raghu.

3. **(a)** The shed is dark and filled with insects. Ravi thinks it might contain snakes. **(b)** Ravi is willing to overcome his fear in order to achieve his goal.

4. **(a)** The children are too busy enjoying themselves at other games to be concerned with Ravi. **(b)** Possible response: They think that Ravi is foolish and immature.

5. **(a)** Ravi learns that he can be easily forgotten. **(b)** Ravi might continue to feel insignificant if the older children treat him that way. However, as he grows older, he will probably become less self-centered.

6. **(a)** Yes, she shows the conflicts that arise because some of the children take the game more seriously than others. **(b)** Older children may be anxious to prove their strength as they strive toward adulthood.

7. Students should support their answers with evidence from the story and from personal experiences.

The game proceeded. Two pairs of arms reached up and met in an arc. The children trooped under it again and again in a lugubrious[10] circle, ducking their heads and intoning

> "The grass is green,
> The rose is red;
> Remember me
> When I am dead, dead, dead, dead . . ."

And the arc of thin arms trembled in the twilight, and the heads were bowed so sadly, and their feet tramped to that melancholy refrain so mournfully, so helplessly, that Ravi could not bear it. He would not follow them, he would not be included in this funeral game. He had wanted victory and triumph—not a funeral. But he had been forgotten, left out and he would not join them now. The ignominy[11] of being forgotten—how could he face it? He felt his heart go heavy and ache inside him unbearably. He lay down full length on the damp grass, crushing his face into it, no longer crying, silenced by a terrible sense of his insignificance.

---

10. **lugubrious** (lə gōō′ brē əs) *adj.* sad and mournful, especially in an exaggerated way.
11. **ignominy** (ig′ nə min′ ē) *n.* shame; dishonor.

Review and Assess

Thinking About the Selection

1. **Respond:** Put yourself in Ravi's place. What would you have done after Raghu left the shed area? Explain your answer.

2. **(a) Recall:** How does Ravi describe Raghu's legs? **(b) Draw Conclusions:** How does Ravi feel about Raghu?

3. **(a) Recall:** What dangers does the shed present? **(b) Infer:** What do you know about Ravi's character based on the choices he makes in the story?

4. **(a) Recall:** Why have the other children stopped searching for Ravi? **(b) Draw Conclusions:** What do the other children think of Ravi?

5. **(a) Analyze:** What bitter lesson does Ravi learn at the end of the story? **(b) Apply:** Do you think that Ravi's sense of "insignificance" at the end of the story will remain strong? Explain.

6. **(a) Evaluate:** Do you think the author conveys the relationships among the children realistically? **(b) Generalize:** Why might older children treat younger children this way?

7. **Take a Position:** Do you think the treatment of the younger children was fair? Why or why not?

Anita Desai

(b. 1937)

Anita Desai was born in India to a German mother and an Indian father. As a child, she learned German, Hindi, and English. Today, Desai writes in English and is widely regarded as one of India's foremost novelists. She writes about contemporary Indian topics, producing works with strong characterization and powerful visual images. *Fire on the Mountain* (1977), *Clear Light of Day* (1980), *In Custody* (1984), and *Baumgartner's Bombay* (1988) are among her most successful books.

Of Desai's talent, the critic Victoria Glendinning has said, "She has the gift of opening up a closed world and making it clearly visible and, by the end, familiar." Desai lives in Cambridge, Massachusetts, with her husband and their four children.

✎ ASSESSMENT PRACTICE: Reading Comprehension

Recognizing Cause and Effect **(For more practice, see Test Preparation Workbook, p. 24.)**

Many tests require students to recognize cause-and-effect relationships. Have students read the paragraph on p. 357 that begins "Ravi sat back," and then answer the following question.

What causes Ravi to hide in the shed, even though he finds it scary?

A He wants a quiet place to rest.

B He wants to escape his siblings.

C He wants the best hiding spot.

D He thinks he can clean it up.

Students should notice that Ravi is thrilled by the thought of winning the game. He needs the best hiding spot to win, so *C* is the right answer.

Review and Assess

Literary Analysis

Motivation

1. What is Ravi's **motivation** for wanting to win the game?
2. What motives contribute to Ravi's desperate, hysterical race to the pillar? Record your answer on a diagram like the one shown here.

Motives	Action	Motives
Ravi is relieved to be out of the shed.	Ravi becomes hysterical.	

3. Compare the reasons that motivate Ravi and Raghu as they play hide-and-seek.
4. What motivates the children to play other games while Ravi is still hiding?

Connecting Literary Elements

5. What does **dialogue** reveal about the motivation of the children in the opening scene as they plan their games?
6. How does the dialogue that Ravi overhears while hiding in the shed motivate him to remain in hiding?

Reading Strategy

Evaluating a Character's Decision

7. While Ravi hides in the shed, Raghu pounds on it with his stick. How does this affect Ravi's decision to remain in the shed?
8. (a) Identify three reasons Ravi has for hiding in the shed.
   (b) **Evaluate** each reason, explaining your opinions.
9. At what point does Ravi's decision to hide in the shed become a bad choice? Explain.

Extend Understanding

10. **Cultural Connection:** What useful life lessons do children learn in the games they play? Explain your answer.

Quick Review

Motivation is the reason behind a character's action.

Dialogue is conversation between characters.

To **evaluate a character's decision**, assess whether the decision that the character makes is sound.

 Take It to the Net

www.phschool.com
Take the interactive self-test online to check your understanding of the selection.

Games at Twilight ◆ *361*

✳ **ENRICHMENT: Further Reading**

Other Works by Anita Desai

Fire on the Mountain
Clear Light of Day
In Custody
Baumgartner's Bombay

Take It to the Net
Visit www.phschool.com for more information on Anita Desai.

❶ Vocabulary Development

Word Analysis

1. superfluous
2. superhuman
3. superimpose

Fluency: Clarify Meaning

1. act with contempt.
2. throw it away.
3. determined.
4. approach them from the side.

Spelling Strategy

1. suspicious
2. ambitious
3. courageous

❷ Grammar

1. after he heard Raghu
2. When Ravi entered the shed
3. because he wanted to win
4. that he had to touch
5. Unless he touched the pillar

Writing Application

1. When I was a child, I played tag in the backyard.
2. Tag is similar to hide-and-seek because both games have an "it."
3. After we chose an "it," we ran as fast as we could.
4. While we were running, we tried to avoid "it."
5. We headed toward "home base," which we had to touch in order to win.

Integrate Language Skills

❶ Vocabulary Development Lesson

Word Analysis: Latin Prefix *super-*

The Latin prefix *super-* means "above" or "extra." As used in this story, *superciliously* means "acting in a manner that is above, or better than, others." Other words that contain the prefix *super-* include

superhuman   superimpose   superfluous

In your notebook, write the word from the list above that best completes each sentence. You may check your answers in a dictionary.

1. The family kept many ___?___ items they no longer used in the shed.
2. It took an almost ___?___ effort for Ravi to endure the unknown creatures that lurked in the shed.
3. Raghu was larger than the others and always tried to ___?___ his will on theirs.

Fluency: Clarify Word Meaning

Complete the following sentences:

1. When you treat someone *superciliously*, you . . .
2. If you had something that was *defunct*, you might . . .
3. Someone who is *dogged* is . . .
4. When you *sidle* up to someone, you . . .

Spelling Strategy

The word *supercilious* ends with the suffix *-ious*. In words whose root ends with *e*, this suffix becomes *-eous*, as in *advantageous*. In your notebook, fill in the blanks to complete the spelling of these words:

1. No one was suspic____ of Ravi.
2. Ravi's plan to win is ambit____.
3. Hiding in the shed was a courag____ act.

❷ Grammar Lesson

Subordination

Subordination is the process by which writers connect two unequal but related ideas in a complex sentence. The subordinate, or less important, idea limits, develops, describes, or adds meaning to the main idea of a sentence. To connect the ideas, the less important idea is introduced with subordinate conjunctions, such as *although*, *after*, *when*, *because*, *as if*, and *unless*, or by relative pronouns, such as *who*, *which*, and *that*.

> *Although Ravi was small*, he felt as if he could reach up and touch it with his fingertips.
>
> The garage was locked with a giant key, *which Ravi could not reach*.

Practice Copy the following sentences, and underline the subordinate clauses.

1. Ravi hid in the shed after he heard Raghu.
2. When Ravi entered the shed, he thought he was safe.
3. Ravi stayed in the shed because he wanted to win.
4. Ravi ran toward the pillar that he had to touch.
5. Unless he touched the pillar, he could not win.

Writing Application Write five sentences about games you played as a young child. Use subordinate clauses in your sentences.

𝒲𝒢 *Prentice Hall Writing and Grammar Connection: Chapter 20, Section 2*

TEACHING RESOURCES

The following resources can be used to enrich or extend the instruction for pp. 362–363.

Vocabulary

📖 **Selection Support:** Build Vocabulary, p. 93

📖 **Vocabulary and Spelling Practice Book** (Use this booklet for skills enrichment.) ▨

Grammar

📖 **Selection Support:** Build Grammar Skills, p. 94

𝒲𝒢 **Writing and Grammar,** Platinum Level, p. 464

▨ **Daily Language Practice Transparencies**

Writing

𝒲𝒢 **Writing and Grammar,** Platinum Level, p. 85

◎ **Writing and Grammar iText CD-ROM** ▨

▨ **BLOCK SCHEDULING:** Resources marked with this symbol provide varied instruction during 90-minute blocks.

❸ Writing Lesson

Dialogue Between Children

In "Games at Twilight," there are a number of dialogues among the children. Using these examples as inspiration, write your own dialogue between children. You can use characters from the story or make up two of your own.

Prewriting Focus on a decision or an event in your characters' lives. Then, brainstorm for a list of expressions that children might use. These phrases will make your dialogue sound realistic.

Drafting Bring your characters to life through your dialogue by using appropriate language. Make sure the words and phrases you use are consistent with the age, personality, and culture of the characters.

Revising Read your draft aloud. Decide whether the dialogue sounds realistic. Sometimes changing just a few words will fix it.

Model: Revising for Appropriate Language

Want
Sam: ~~Would you like~~ to play a game?

? Chess?
Charles: What ~~shall we play?~~

Nah. No way.
Sam: ~~I don't think so.~~

> Changes that make the language less formal help create dialogue that rings true.

W͞G *Prentice Hall Writing and Grammar Connection: Chapter 5, Section 3*

❹ Extension Activities

Listening and Speaking With three or four classmates, lead a **games discussion,** taking turns introducing and playing games you enjoy.

- Clearly state the objective of the game, and explain the rules.
- Describe how the game is organized and what the players do first, next, and so on.
- Have a practice game so that your classmates know what to expect.

After you play several different games, compare the experience of learning and playing each one. [Group Activity]

Research and Technology Desai's writing is often set in India. Using library and Internet resources, investigate the impact of British colonialism on the social and cultural traditions of that country. Begin by listing questions that you would like answered as a starting point for your research. Then, prepare a **report** that documents your information sources.

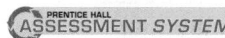 **Take It to the Net** www.phschool.com

Go online for an additional research activity using the Internet.

Lesson Support for p. 363

❸ Writing Lesson

- Suggest that students listen to how a group of children talk to each other. They might take notes on the words and expressions the children use.
- Use the Writing Lesson to guide students in developing their dialogue. Remind them to use words that are appropriate for the age level, personality, and culture of their characters.
- Encourage students to work with classmates to present their dialogues in dramatic performances.
- Use the rubric for Short Stories, p. 14 of **Performance Assessment and Portfolio Management,** to assess students' work.

❹ Research and Technology

- You may want to briefly review the history of British colonialism in India in order to help students focus on the topic.
- As a class, generate a list of questions that students can use as starting points for their research.
- Encourage students to use photographs and other images in their final reports.

CUSTOMIZE INSTRUCTION
For Universal Access

To address different learning styles, use the activities suggested in the **Extension Activities** booklet, p. 24.

- For Interpersonal and Bodily/Kinesthetic Learners, use Activity 5.
- For Visual/Spatial Learners, use Activity 6.
- For Verbal/Linguistic and Intrapersonal Learners, use Activity 7.

ASSESSMENT RESOURCES

The following resources can be used to assess students' knowledge and skills.

Selection Assessment

- **Formal Assessment,** pp. 82–84
- **Open Book Test,** pp. 70–72
- **Got It! Assessment Videotapes,** Tape 2
- **Test Bank Software**
- **Take It to the Net**
  Visit www.phschool.com for self-tests and additional questions on "Games at Twilight."

Writing Rubric

- **Performance Assess. and Portfolio Mgmt.,** p. 14
- PRENTICE HALL **ASSESSMENT** *SYSTEM*
- **Workbook**
- **Skill Book**
- **Transparencies**
- **CD-ROM**

The Bridge ✦ The Old Stoic ✦ I Am Not One of Those Who Left the Land ✦ Speech During the Invasion of Constantinople

Lesson Objectives

1. **To analyze and respond to literary elements**
   - Literary Analysis: Dramatic Situation
   - Comparing Literary Works

2. **To read, comprehend, analyze, and critique poems and a speech**
   - Reading Strategy: Identifying Author's Perspective
   - Reading Check questions
   - Review and Assess questions
   - Assessment Practice (ATE)

3. **To develop word analysis skills, fluency, and systematic vocabulary**
   - Vocabulary Development Lesson: Latin Word Root: *-dom-*

4. **To understand and apply written and oral language conventions**
   - Spelling Strategy
   - Grammar Lesson: Adjective Clauses

5. **To understand and apply appropriate writing and research strategies**
   - Writing Lesson: News Commentary
   - Extension Activity: Collage

6. **To understand and apply listening and speaking strategies**
   - Extension Activity: Role Play

STEP-BY-STEP TEACHING GUIDE	PACING GUIDE
PRETEACH	
Motivate Students and Provide Background	
Use the Motivation activity (ATE p. 364)	5 min.
Read and discuss the Preview material and Background information (SE/ATE p. 364)	5 min.
Introduce the Concepts	
Introduce the Literary Analysis and Reading Strategy (SE/ATE p. 365)	15 min.
Pronounce the vocabulary words and read their definitions (SE p. 365)	5 min.
TEACH	
Monitor Comprehension	
Informally monitor comprehension by circulating while students read independently or in groups	10 min.
Monitor students' comprehension with the Reading Check notes (SE/ATE p. 369)	as students read
Develop vocabulary with Vocabulary notes (SE pp. 367, 369; ATE p. 369)	as students read
Develop Understanding	
Develop students' understanding of dramatic situations with the Literary Analysis annotations (ATE pp. 368, 370)	10 min.
Develop students' understanding of author's perspective with the Reading Strategy annotations (SE p. 366; ATE pp. 366, 367, 368)	10 min.
ASSESS	
Assess Mastery	
Assess students' mastery of the Reading Strategy and the Literary Analysis by having them answer the Review and Assess questions (SE/ATE p. 371)	20 min.
Use one or more of the print and media Assessment Resources (ATE p. 373)	up to 50 min.
EXTEND	
Apply Understanding	
Have students complete the Vocabulary Development Lesson and the Grammar Lesson (SE p. 372)	20 min.
Apply students' knowledge of balancing fact and opinion using the Writing Lesson (SE p. 373)	45 min.
Apply students' understanding using one or more of the Extension Activities (SE p. 373)	20–90 min.

 ACCELERATED INSTRUCTION:
Use the strategies and activities identified with an .

UNIVERSAL ACCESS
● = Below Level Students
▲ = On-Level Students
■ = Above Level Students

Time and Resource Manager

RESOURCES

PRINT 📖	TRANSPARENCIES 🗂	TECHNOLOGY 💿 🎧 📼
• **Beyond Literature,** Humanities Connection: What Is Courage?, p. 25 ▲ ■		• **Interest Grabber Video,** Tape 2 ● ▲ ■
• **Selection Support Workbook:** ● ▲ ■ Literary Analysis, p. 100 Reading Strategy, p. 99 Build Vocabulary, p. 97	• **Literary Analysis and Reading Transparencies,** pp. 49 and 50 ● ▲ ■	
• **Authors In Depth,** Platinum Level ■		• **Listening to Literature** ● ▲ ■ Audiocassettes, Sides 11, 12 Audio CDs, CD 7
• **Literatura en español** ● ▲ • **Literary Analysis for Enrichment** ■		
• **Formal Assessment:** Selection Test, pp. 85–87 ● ▲ ■ • **Open Book Test,** pp. 73–75 ● ▲ ■ • **Performance Assessment and Portfolio Management,** pp. 16, 30 ● ▲ ■ ● **PRENTICE HALL** ASSESSMENT *SYSTEM* ● ▲	● **PRENTICE HALL** ASSESSMENT *SYSTEM* ● ▲ ■ Skills Practice Answers and Explanations on Transparencies	• **Test Bank Software** ● ▲ ■ • **Got It! Assessment Videotapes,** Tape 2 ● ▲
• **Selection Support Workbook:** ● ▲ ■ Build Grammar Skills, p. 98 • **Writing and Grammar,** Platinum Level ● ▲ ■ • **Extension Activities,** p. 25 ● ▲ ■	• **Daily Language Practice Transparencies** ● ▲	• **Writing and Grammar iText CD-ROM** ● ▲ ■ 🖥 *Take It to the Net* www.phschool.com

BLOCK SCHEDULING: Use one 90-minute class period to preteach the selection and have students read it. Use a second 90-minute class period to assess students' mastery of skills and have them complete one of the Extension Activities.

Motivation

Write on the chalkboard the following words: *money, love, fame, freedom, power*. Ask students why they think these are "big" themes—ones that have attracted writers from ancient to present times. Lead students to see that although each of these goals is desirable, each can lead to conflict or test people. Ask students to suggest some negative and positive results that might come from attaining each goal listed on the board. Tell students that the writers of these pieces highlight rewards and conflicts connected to these universal themes.

▥ Interest Grabber Video

As an alternative, play "Theodora's Speech" on Tape 2 to engage student interest.

❶ Background

At the height of its power in the fifth century A.D., the Byzantine empire (also known as the Eastern Roman Empire) included parts of southern and eastern Europe, as well as parts of northern Africa and the Middle East. Christianity, Greek culture, and Roman customs flourished in the empire, which served as a link between ancient and modern European civilization. Emperor Justinian ruled the empire from A.D. 527 to 565. Empress Theodora gave her speech in the year 532.

Prepare to Read

The Bridge ◆ The Old Stoic ◆ I Am Not One of Those Who Left the Land ◆ Speech During the Invasion of Constantinople

 Take It to the Net

Visit www.phschool.com for interactive activities and instruction related to these selections, including
- background
- graphic organizers
- literary elements
- reading strategies

Preview

Connecting to the Literature

In life, you may be forced to make tough decisions. It could be something as routine as deciding to try out for a play despite having terrible stage fright. In the following selections, however, you will encounter characters who show the courage to make decisions that could be a matter of life or death.

❶ Background

In 532, citizens of the Eastern Roman Empire rebelled against Emperor Justinian and Empress Theodora. When rebels stormed the castle, as you will read, Theodora encouraged her husband to face their attackers rather than flee. In the early 1900s, during the Russian Revolution, the poet Anna Akhmatova also refused to flee, even after her husband was killed and her son was imprisoned.

TEACHING RESOURCES

The following resources can be used to enrich or extend the instruction for pp. 364–365.

Motivation

▥ **Interest Grabber Video**, Tape 2 ▤

Background

📖 **Beyond Literature**, p. 25

 Take It to the Net

Visit www.phschool.com for background and hotlinks for the selections.

Literary Analysis

📄 **Literary Analysis and Reading Transparencies,** Dramatic Situation, p. 50

Reading

📖 **Selection Support:** Reading Strategy, p. 99; Build Vocabulary, p. 97 ▤

📄 **Literary Analysis and Reading Transparencies,** Identifying Author's Perspective, p. 49

 BLOCK SCHEDULING: Resources marked with this symbol provide varied instruction during 90-minute blocks.

Literary Analysis

Dramatic Situation

The **dramatic situation**—the circumstances that form the focal point of a literary work—gives you a framework in which you can appreciate a selection. For example, Anna Akhmatova's poem "I Am Not One of Those Who Left the Land" arises from the circumstances of the civil war in Russia. Because of food shortages, riots, and political oppression, many of Akhmatova's friends fled the country. Understanding this situation, you can appreciate the courage of her decision not to flee.

Look for the dramatic situation that forms the context in the selections that follow.

Comparing Literary Works

Each of the following literary works involves a speaker who is faced with a situation that requires courage. It is interesting to compare how each speaker shows courage in a difficult situation. The **speaker** is the imaginary voice assumed by the writer of a work of fiction. Determine how the perspective of the speaker enables him or her to behave courageously in each situation.

Reading Strategy

Identifying Author's Perspective

The details that are included in a work of literature depend on the **author's perspective**—the writer's outlook on the subject. Often, writers directly reveal their perspective. For example, Akhmatova indicates her outlook in the opening lines of her poem:

> I am not one of those who left the land
> to the mercy of its enemies.

In other cases, it is up to the reader to determine the author's perspective. To do this, you may need to go beyond the text and gather information about the historical or social context in which the work was written. Use a diagram like the one shown here to examine each author's perspective in the following works.

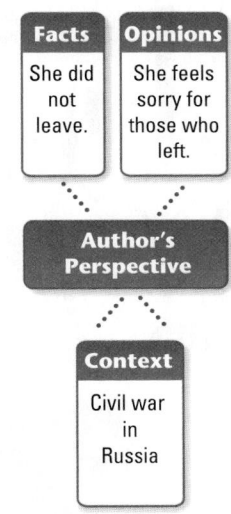

Vocabulary Development

implore (im plôr´) v. plead; ask for earnestly (p. 367)

timorous (tim´ ər es) adj. full of fear; timid (p. 369)

indomitable (in däm´ i tə bəl) adj. not easily defeated (p. 369)

---

❷ Literary Analysis

Dramatic Situation

- Explain to students that the dramatic situation is the context through which a selection can be understood. Many times, the dramatic situation involves larger social or cultural events and circumstances that motivate an author to write about something.

- Explain to students that they can determine the dramatic situation in a selection by looking for clues in the text and by doing additional research.

- Use the Dramatic Situation transparency in **Literary Analysis and Reading Transparencies,** p. 50, to help students use clues in the text to determine the dramatic situation.

❸ Reading Strategy

Identifying Author's Perspective

- Tell students that the author's perspective is a function of his or her experiences and historical environment. This is why readers must sometimes gather information about the larger historical and social context in which the author worked.

- Suggest that students look into the author's background to determine what his or her perspective might be.

- Students should also pay careful attention to an author's choice of words to see if they help to reveal the author's perspective.

- Encourage students to use a diagram like the one shown to record the information they find.

Vocabulary Development

- Pronounce each vocabulary word for students, and read the definitions as a class. Have students identify any words with which they are already familiar.

 E-Teach

Visit E-Teach at www.phschool.com for teachers' essays on how to teach, with questions and answers.

CUSTOMIZE INSTRUCTION FOR UNIVERSAL ACCESS

For Less Proficient Readers	For English Learners	For Advanced Readers
Help students with difficult vocabulary words before they read. Define words such as *fragile* and *wavered* in "The Bridge"; *esteem* and *endure* in "The Old Stoic"; *felon* and *wormwood* in "I Am Not One . . ."; and *convention* in "Speech During the Invasion of Constantinople."	English learners may be confused by the word order and sentence structure in the poems. For "The Bridge," help them rephrase the first sentence so "That I would cross that bridge" immediately follows "I didn't believe." For "The Old Stoic," help them rephrase the lines with inverted word order (e.g., "Riches I hold in light esteem").	Point out that poetry often reflects the poet's deep feelings. As they read the poems in this grouping, ask students to identify words and lines that strike them as especially emotional or powerful. Then, have them explain their choices.

CUSTOMIZE INSTRUCTION
For Visual/Spatial Learners

Have students close their eyes and visualize the speaker of "The Bridge" crossing the river. Then, have them make either an abstract or a realistic drawing of the scene.

❶ About the Selections

"The Bridge" metaphorically describes the anxiety and fear associated with life's risks and changes. Staff had to cross the bridge of the dangers and difficulties of wartime Poland, but people of any time can relate his theme to changes in their own lives.

In "The Old Stoic," Brontë celebrates the freedom of facing the future unafraid. Her wish is not for material wealth or for fame but for internal courage and a strong life spirit.

❷ Reading Strategy

Identifying Author's Perspective

- Ask students to identify details in the bracketed passage that show the speaker's perspective.
  Answer: Students should note that the speaker is standing on the edge of a "wide and swift" river.

- Then, ask students the Reading Strategy question on p. 366: What do the first four lines of the poem reveal about the author's perspective?
  Answer: At the beginning of the poem, the speaker tries to muster the courage to cross the bridge, or to take an important step in life.

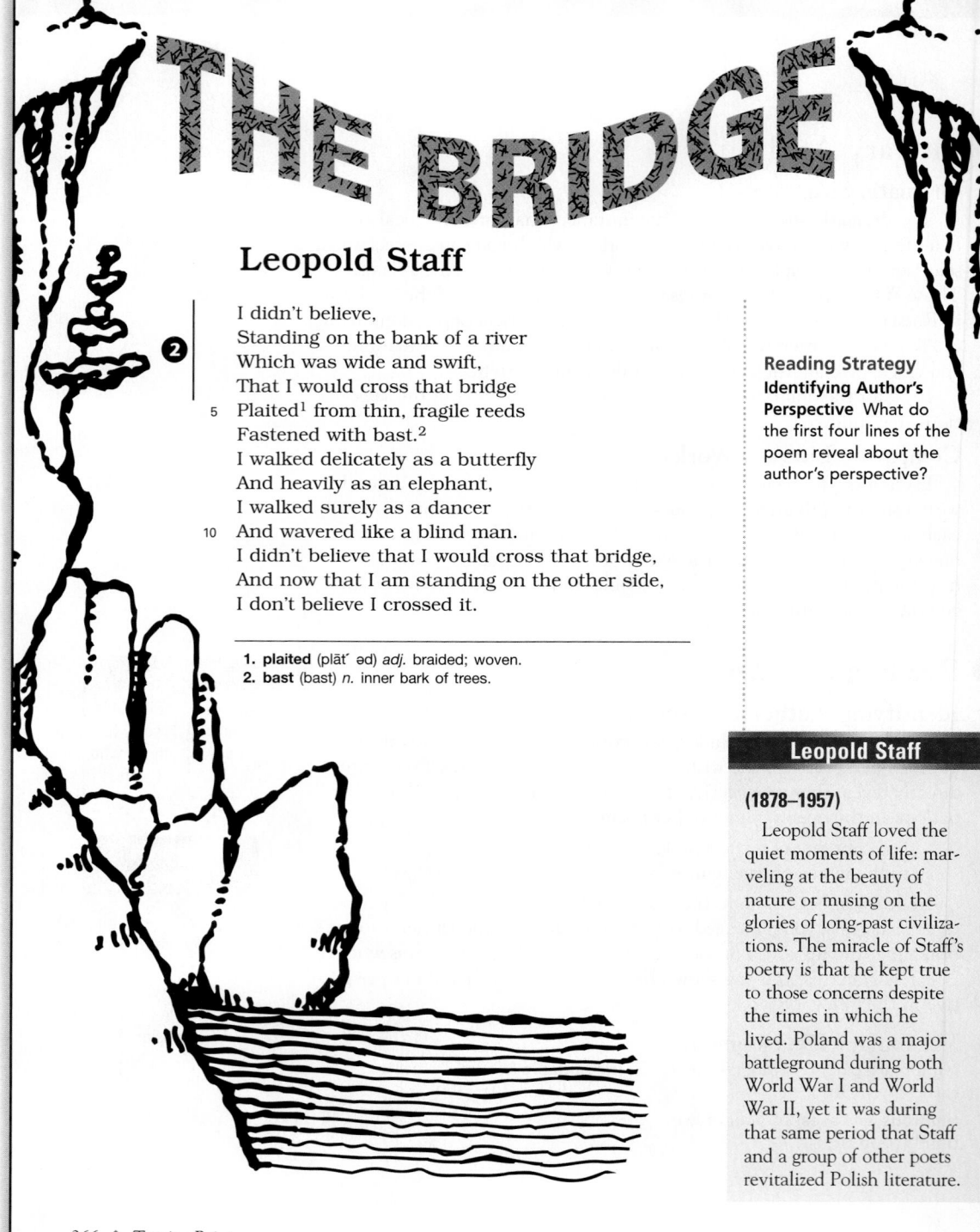

❶

THE BRIDGE

Leopold Staff

❷

I didn't believe,
Standing on the bank of a river
Which was wide and swift,
That I would cross that bridge
5 Plaited[1] from thin, fragile reeds
Fastened with bast.[2]
I walked delicately as a butterfly
And heavily as an elephant,
I walked surely as a dancer
10 And wavered like a blind man.
I didn't believe that I would cross that bridge,
And now that I am standing on the other side,
I don't believe I crossed it.

---

1. **plaited** (plāt′ əd) *adj.* braided; woven.
2. **bast** (bast) *n.* inner bark of trees.

Reading Strategy
Identifying Author's Perspective What do the first four lines of the poem reveal about the author's perspective?

Leopold Staff

(1878–1957)

Leopold Staff loved the quiet moments of life: marveling at the beauty of nature or musing on the glories of long-past civilizations. The miracle of Staff's poetry is that he kept true to those concerns despite the times in which he lived. Poland was a major battleground during both World War I and World War II, yet it was during that same period that Staff and a group of other poets revitalized Polish literature.

366 ◆ *Turning Point*

TEACHING RESOURCES

The following resources can be used to enrich or extend the instruction for pp. 366–370.

Literary Analysis

📖 **Selection Support:** Literary Analysis, p. 100

Reading

🎧 **Listening to Literature Audiocassettes,** Sides 11, 12

💿 **Listening to Literature Audio CDs,** CD 7 ▪

Extension

Authors In Depth, Platinum Level (The collection includes nine additional selections by Emily Brontë for extended reading.)

▪ **BLOCK SCHEDULING:** Resources marked with this symbol provide varied instruction during 90-minute blocks.

The Old Stoic

Emily Brontë

Riches I hold in light esteem,
And love I laugh to scorn;
And lust of fame was but a dream
That vanished with the morn:

5 And if I pray, the only prayer
That moves my lips for me
Is, "Leave the heart that now I bear,
And give me liberty!"

❸   Yes, as my swift days near their goal,
10   'Tis all that I implore—
Through life and death a chainless soul,
With courage to endure.

implore (im plôr´) v. plead;
ask for earnestly

Emily Brontë

(1818–1848)

To have one famous writer in a family is unusual, but to have three is extraordinary! The Brontë sisters—Emily, Charlotte, and Anne—were all successful novelists. They grew up in Yorkshire, England, in a landscape of bleak, windswept hills. When Emily was twenty-seven, Charlotte discovered some of her sister's poems. All three sisters then decided to publish their poems in a single volume. Just two years later, they each published a novel. Emily wrote *Wuthering Heights*, a classic story of love and revenge. Shortly after publication of her novel, Emily became ill and died of tuberculosis.

The Old Stoic ◆ 367

Review and Assess

Thinking About the Selections

1. **Respond:** What personal experiences do these works call to mind?

2. **(a) Recall:** How is the bridge made? **(b) Infer:** Why is the speaker in "The Bridge" afraid to cross it?

3. **(a) Recall:** What action surprises the speaker in "The Bridge"? **(b) Analyze:** Why do you think this action is surprising?

4. **Extend:** Do you think that you would cross the bridge described in the poem? Why or why not?

5. **(a) Recall:** What does the speaker in "The Old Stoic" value? **(b) Infer:** Why does the speaker in "The Old Stoic" scorn wealth and fame?

6. **(a) Recall:** What is the only thing the speaker in "The Old Stoic" wants? **(b) Interpret:** What does the speaker mean in saying that her "swift days near their goal"?

7. **Take a Position:** Do you agree with the speaker's opinion about what is important? Why or why not?

---

❸ **Reading Strategy**

Identifying Author's Perspective

- After reading the bracketed line, ask students to identify the author's perspective.
  Answer: The speaker is writing from the perspective of a person who is growing old, or who realizes that her life is nearing its end.

- Then, ask how the speaker's main points might have been different if she wrote from a different perspective.
  Answer: A younger speaker might have had different values.

Answers for p. 367

Review and Assess

1. Students will probably recall experiences that required courage.

2. **(a)** The bridge is woven from reeds and fastened with tree bark. **(b)** He is afraid because the river is swift and wide and the bridge does not look strong enough to hold him.

3. **(a)** He is surprised that he has crossed the bridge. **(b)** He is surprised because he still believes the act was difficult and dangerous.

4. Some students may say the bridge seems too flimsy to cross; others may say they would be willing to take the risk if it meant a better life on the other side.

5. **(a)** The speaker values independence and courage. **(b)** As the speaker has grown older, she has learned that wealth and fame are elusive.

6. **(a)** The speaker wants freedom and courage. **(b)** She is nearing her death.

7. Some students might say that fame, love, and riches are all passing things, but courage and freedom of spirit will endure. Others might argue that fame, love, and riches can bring people great happiness.

CUSTOMIZE INSTRUCTION FOR UNIVERSAL ACCESS

For Advanced Readers

Suggest that students read additional works by Emily Brontë. Provide students with the titles listed in the Enrichment box, ATE p. 371. You may also wish to use **Authors In Depth**, Platinum Level, which contains the following selections and more:

- "Song" (poem, p. 69)
- To Imagination (poem, p. 72)
- "A Diary Note—No. 5" (nonfiction, p. 74)

You might have students read pp. 62–64 in **Authors In Depth** to learn more about Brontë's life. Then, have students discuss how the author's perspective affects each poem.

❹ I Am Not One of Those Who Left the Land Anna Akhmatova
Translated by Stanley Kunitz

I am not one of those who left the land
to the mercy of its enemies.
Their flattery leaves me cold,
my songs are not for them to praise.

5   But I pity the exile's lot.
Like a felon, like a man half-dead,
dark is your path, wanderer;
wormwood infects your foreign bread.

❺   But here, in the murk of conflagration,[1]
10   where scarcely a friend is left to know,
we, the survivors, do not flinch
from anything, not from a single blow.

❻   Surely the reckoning will be made
after the passing of this cloud.
15   We are the people without tears,
straighter than you . . . more proud . . .

---

1. **conflagration** (kän' flə grā' shən) *n.* destructive fire.

❼ ▲ Critical Viewing Despite Akhmatova's opinion, what details in this photograph help explain why some people do leave war-torn lands? **[Speculate]**

368 ◆ *Turning Point*

Anna Akhmatova

(1889–1966)

Anna Akhmatova published her first poetry at the age of eighteen. She survived the most tumultuous events of modern times: two world wars, the Russian Revolution of 1917, and the "reign of terror" of the dictator Joseph Stalin. Through it all, Akhmatova's poetry celebrated the personal heroism she prized above everything else. At the time of her death, she was acknowledged as the foremost woman poet in Russian literature.

Speech During the Invasion of Constantinople

Empress Theodora

❽ **Background**

Art

Illustration for Speech During the Invasion of Constantinople

In this piece of art, the Emperor Justinian is receiving a supplicant. Behind him stands the Empress Theodora. Discuss these questions:

1. How is Theodora's speech different from the way she is portrayed in this picture?
   Answer: In the picture, she stands behind Justinian, but based on the speech, she seems to have a more prominent role.

2. Do you think the illustration represents Theodora truthfully?
   Possible answer: Although Theodora stands behind the throne, she is very possibly the "power behind the throne"— one whose influence was subtle but great.

❾ ▶**Critical Viewing**

Answer: Theodora assumes a confident, authoritative pose. While others respond to dramatic events, she seems to represent reasoned calm and wisdom.

❿ **Vocabulary Development**

The Latin Root -dom-

• Draw students' attention to the word *indomitable* and its definition, "not easily defeated."

• Then, explain that -dom- means "to rule" and in- means "not." Therefore, the word means "not able to be ruled," or "not easily defeated."

⓫ ✔**Reading Check**

Answer: The empress must convince her husband to stay in Constantinople and defend his government.

❾ ▲ **Critical Viewing** At the top of this picture, Theodora appears strong and triumphant. Which details in her speech reflect these qualities? **[Connect]**

I n his collection of historical speeches, Lend Me Your Ears, *William Safire wrote the following introduction to Empress Theodora's inspirational words.*

❖◆❖

Roman Emperor Justinian, on January 18 of the year 532, was certain he was about to be overthrown by rebel leader Hypatius and killed. A fast galley waited at the palace's private harbor to take him and Empress Theodora to safety in Thrace. His <u>timorous</u> *advisers persuaded him that the rebellion could not be stopped and that the way out for the imperial couple was flight. As the panicky leader made for the door, the* <u>indomitable</u> *empress rose from her throne and delivered a brief speech that kept her husband in Constantinople and led to the slaughter of the rebels.*

❖◆❖

timorous (tim´ ər es) *adj.* full of fear; timid

indomitable (in däm´ i tə bəl) *adj.* not easily defeated

⓫ **Reading Check**
What is the situation in which the empress finds herself?

CUSTOMIZE INSTRUCTION FOR UNIVERSAL ACCESS

For Special Needs Students	For Gifted/Talented Students
Help students rewrite the first paragraph of Empress Theodora's speech in simpler language. Define difficult words, such as *convention* and *council*, and explain that the "lords" are the members of her husband's court. Make sure students can identify what convention Theodora defies and why she decides to defy it.	Have students do research on the Internet and in the library to learn more about the Byzantine Empire, which was ruled by Justinian from A.D. 527 to 565. They might use an encyclopedia to determine the extent of the empire, and then indicate its boundaries on a contemporary map.

Identifying Author's Perspective

- Ask students what two options Theodora identifies.
  Answer: She says the options are to defend the empire or to seek personal safety.

- Ask students to explain how the author's perspective is reflected in the bracketed passage.
  Answer: The author implies that she believes it would be more noble to die than to give up the empire.

ASSESS

Answers for p. 370

Review and Assess

1. Students should support their answers with examples.

2. **(a)** The speaker is left cold by the flattery of those who left the land. **(b)** By not defending their land, they are in a sense participating in the crimes against it.

3. **(a)** She describes them as "half-dead" and wandering a "dark path." **(b)** The food they eat in their new countries is a symbol of the impurity of their actions.

4. **(a)** She calls it the "murk of conflagration where scarcely a friend is left to know." **(b)** She believes that she will be rewarded after the trouble has passed.

5. **(a)** She feels that it is better than leaving her country and her royal robes. **(b)** She says that after being an empress, it would be intolerable to be a fugitive.

6. **(a)** She means that she would rather die in her robes than give them up. **(b)** Her husband might have said that life, even as a fugitive, is precious.

7. The poem by Akhmatova appeals to pride, because she says that those who stay are "straighter" and "more proud." The speech by Empress Theodora appeals to courage, because she implores her listeners to be brave and avoid taking the easy way out.

8. Many students will recognize that staying to live in difficult circumstances is the more courageous choice because it involves standing up for one's principles.

My lords, the present occasion is too serious to allow me to follow the convention that a woman should not speak in a man's council. Those whose interests are threatened by extreme danger should think only of the wisest course of action, not of conventions.

⑫ In my opinion, flight is not the right course, even if it should bring us to safety. It is impossible for a person, having been born into this world, not to die; but for one who has reigned it is intolerable to be a fugitive. May I never be deprived of this purple robe, and may I never see the day when those who meet me do not call me empress.

If you wish to save yourself, my lord, there is no difficulty. We are rich; over there is the sea, and yonder are the ships. Yet reflect for a moment whether, when you have once escaped to a place of security, you would not gladly exchange such safety for death. As for me, I agree with the adage that the royal purple is the noblest shroud.

Review and Assess

Thinking About the Selections

1. **Respond:** Which of these speakers do you think demonstrates more courage? Explain your answer.

2. **(a) Recall:** In "I Am Not One of Those Who Left the Land," whose "flattery" leaves the speaker "cold"?
   (b) Speculate: Why does the speaker describe those who left as being like "felons"?

3. **(a) Recall:** How does the speaker describe the exile's lot?
   (b) Interpret: What does the speaker mean by the phrase "wormwood infects your foreign bread"?

4. **(a) Recall:** How does the speaker characterize her life?
   (b) Infer: What does she suggest about the eventual rewards of her decision to stay?

5. **(a) Recall:** How does the Empress Theodora in "Speech During the Invasion of Constantinople" feel about dying?
   (b) Infer: Why does she prefer dying to being a fugitive?

6. **(a) Interpret:** What does the speaker mean by the line "As for me, I agree with the adage that the royal purple is the noblest shroud"? **(b) Hypothesize:** What other view might her husband have presented?

7. **Compare and Contrast:** To what emotions does each work appeal? Explain.

8. **Evaluate:** Do you think it is more courageous to face the dangers of traveling across a continent and an ocean or to stay and live in difficult and dangerous circumstances? Explain.

Empress Theodora

(497?–548)

Theodora and her husband, the emperor Justinian, ruled the Eastern Roman Empire in the sixth century. Highly intelligent and politically astute, she was Justinian's most trusted advisor. In fact, some argue that she, rather than her husband, actually ruled the empire. She was one of the first rulers to advance the rights of women.

Theodora is best remembered for a single action: When a rebellion broke out against her and her husband, she persuaded Justinian to defend their palace in Constantinople rather than try to escape.

✎ ASSESSMENT PRACTICE: Reading Comprehension

Predicting Outcomes   **(For more practice, see Test Preparation Workbook, p. 25.)**

When taking some tests, students may be asked to use text evidence to make predictions. Have students read the first six lines of "The Bridge" on p. 366 and then answer the following sample question.

From this passage you may predict that the speaker

  A will drown
  B has crossed the bridge
  C will build another bridge
  D regrets not crossing the bridge

Guide students to understand that the speaker hasn't drowned (he's written the poem) and that there's no evidence to suggest he'll build another bridge. The line "I didn't believe . . ." suggests unexpected success, so the speaker doesn't have regrets. Therefore, *B* is the correct answer.

Review and Assess

Literary Analysis

Dramatic Situation

1. "The Bridge" was written in the aftermath of the devastation that Poland suffered during World War II. How does knowing this **dramatic situation** affect your understanding of the poem? Explain.

2. Akhmatova lived through terrible events in Russia while others fled. Why do the circumstances surrounding her decision make her situation more dramatic?

3. Theodora makes her speech just as she and Justinian are about to leave the palace to sail to Thrace. Why does this detail add to the drama of her remarks?

Comparing Literary Works

4. Who are the **speakers** in each of the selections?

5. Compare the way the speakers in "I Am Not . . ." and "Speech During the Invasion . . ." exhibit courage. Record similarities and differences in a Venn diagram like the one here.

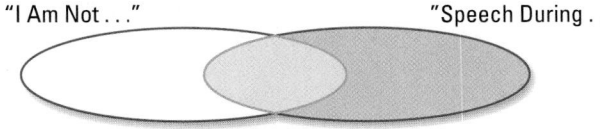

"I Am Not . . ."   "Speech During . . ."

6. Which of all the selections is most powerful to you? Explain.

Reading Strategy

Identifying Author's Perspective

7. What details in "The Bridge" indicate that the writer has lived through dangerous times?

8. (a) From what **perspective** does the speaker of "The Old Stoic" write? (b) What line in the poem tells you this?

9. What details of Theodora's speech are included that might not have been included in a speech by a common person during the insurrection?

Extend Understanding

10. **World Events Connection:** Akhmatova mentions a "cloud" that would one day pass from over Russia. Has the cloud completely passed? Explain.

The Bridge / The Old Stoic / I Am Not One of Those Who Left the Land / Speech During the Invasion of Constantinople ◆ *371*

Quick Review

A **dramatic situation** includes the circumstances and conflicts that form the focal point of a literary work.

The **speaker** is the imaginary voice assumed by the writer of a work of fiction.

The **author's perspective** is the writer's outlook on the subject.

 Take It to the Net
www.phschool.com
Take the interactive self-test online to check your understanding of these selections.

Answers for p. 372

❶ Vocabulary Development

Word Analysis: Latin Root -dom-

1. domain
2. dominant
3. domineer

Concept Development: Analogies

1. indomitable
2. implore
3. timorous

Spelling Strategy

1. wondrous
2. monotonous
3. vigorous

❷ Grammar

1. who stayed modifies *one*
2. who left modifies *those*
3. who remained behind modifies *People*
4. whose lives were disrupted modifies *Russians*
5. which has hung over Russia for years modifies *cloud*

Writing Application

1. He crossed the bridge that was made of reeds.
2. The stoic who sees death near hopes for courage.
3. The woman who decided to remain in the country was very brave.

Integrate Language Skills

❶ Vocabulary Development Lesson

Word Analysis: Latin Root -dom-

The word *indomitable* contains the Latin root *-dom-*, which means "to rule." With the prefix *in-*, meaning "not," you might guess that the meaning of *indomitable* is "not to be ruled," which is close to the actual meaning: "not easily defeated." Other words containing the root *-dom-* include the following:

domineer   domain   dominant

Write the following sentences on your paper, filling in the blanks with one of the words above.

1. The emperor refused to surrender his _____?_____.
2. After fighting off the invaders, the empress became more ___?___ in her husband's council.
3. Was it possible that she even began to ___?___ ?

Concept Development: Analogies

On your paper, complete the following word pairs with words from the vocabulary list on page 365.

1. courageous : hero :: ___?___ : conqueror
2. devour : eat :: ___?___ : ask
3. enraged : joyful :: ___?___ : brave

Spelling Strategy

Some words, like *timorous*, end with the suffix *-ous*, which is pronounced *us*. The suffix means "full of," "by the nature of," or "having the quality of." Words ending in *-ous* are always adjectives. Use the descriptions to spell adjectives ending in *-ous*.

1. full of wonder
2. having the quality of monotony
3. full of vigor

❷ Grammar Lesson

Adjective Clauses

An **adjective clause** is a group of words that contains a subject and verb and serves in a sentence to modify a noun or pronoun. Adjective clauses are subordinate clauses that tell *what kind* or *which one*. Usually, adjective clauses begin with *that, which, who, whom,* or *whose*. In the following examples, the adjective clause is italicized. The noun or pronoun that is modified is underlined.

I didn't believe, / Standing on the bank of a river / *Which was wide and swift,* . . .

I am not one of those *who left the land*. . . .

Practice Copy the following sentences. Underline the adjective clause in each. Draw an arrow from the clause to the word it modifies.

1. Akhmatova was one who stayed.
2. She condemns those who left.
3. People who remained behind suffered.
4. Russians whose lives were disrupted became stronger.
5. A cloud, which has hung over Russia for years, will one day blow away.

Writing Application Use adjective clauses to modify each of the following nouns in sentences: bridge, stoic, woman.

*W*G *Prentice Hall Writing and Grammar Connection: Chapter 20, Section 2*

372 ◆ Turning Points

TEACHING RESOURCES

The following resources can be used to enrich or extend the instruction for pp. 372–373.

Vocabulary

📖 **Selection Support:** Build Vocabulary, p. 97
📖 **Vocabulary and Spelling Practice Book** (Use this booklet for skills enrichment.)

Grammar

📖 **Selection Support:** Build Grammar Skills, p. 98
*W*G **Writing and Grammar,** Platinum Level, p. 465
📓 **Daily Language Practice Transparencies** ▥

Writing

*W*G **Writing and Grammar,** Platinum Level, p. 21
💿 **Writing and Grammar iText CD-ROM** ▥

▥ **BLOCK SCHEDULING:** Resources marked with this symbol provide varied instruction during 90-minute blocks.

Writing Lesson

News Commentary

Write a commentary that a newscaster might present following Empress Theodora's speech. Summarize what she said and why she said it. Then, discuss the impact that the speech may have had.

Prewriting	Review the speech and the explanatory text that comes before it to gather facts about the situation. Look for statements in the speech that could be used as quotations in your commentary.
Drafting	Begin your commentary with an attention-grabbing lead-in. Then, give background on the situation and tell the story. Express your opinion about what Theodora said and why she said it. Conclude with a description of the atmosphere following the speech.
Revising	Read over your report, and identify the exciting lead-in, the sequence of events leading to the speech, a summary of the speech, and a wrap-up. Highlight the facts in your commentary, and circle the opinions. Make sure that you have a good balance of both.

Model: Revising to Balance Fact and Opinion

Add more commentary: *turned convention on its ear and*

As the (fearful) emperor turned to flee from the palace, the (beautiful and brave) empress began to speak, "My lords, the present occasion is too serious to allow me to follow the convention that a woman should not speak in a man's council.

The words *fearful, beautiful,* and *brave* express the opinion of the writer and add commentary to the report.

 Prentice Hall Writing and Grammar Connection: Chapter 4, Section 2

Extension Activities

Listening and Speaking With a partner, **role-play** a conversation between Akhmatova and someone who chose to leave Russia.

- Use what you have learned in the poem and in the background information on page 364.
- Research to supplement your knowledge of the Russian Revolution and the era of communist rule.

Choose roles, and present your conversation to the class. [**Group Activity**]

Research and Technology Several of these works are written in response to specific historic events. Select one, and create a **collage** combining images with quotations that tell the story of the historic period. Build your collage from information you gather over the Internet or through library research. Try to represent all sides of the events.

Take It to the Net www.phschool.com

Go online for an additional research activity using the Internet.

The Bridge / The Old Stoic / I Am Not One of Those Who Left the Land / Speech During the Invasion of Constantinople ◆ 373

ASSESSMENT RESOURCES

The following resources can be used to assess students' knowledge and skills.

Selection Assessment
- **Formal Assessment,** pp. 85–87
- **Open Book Test,** pp. 73–75
- **Got It! Assessment Videotapes,** Tape 2
- **Test Bank Software**
- **Take It to the Net**
  Visit www.phschool.com self-tests and additional questions on the selections.

Writing Rubric
- **Performance Assess. and Portfolio Mgmt.,** p. 16

Listening and Speaking Rubric
- **Performance Assess. and Portfolio Mgmt.,** p. 30

PRENTICE HALL
ASSESSMENT *SYSTEM*

- **Workbook**
- **Skill Book**
- **Transparencies**
- **CD-ROM**

---

❸ Writing Lesson

- Remind students that a news commentary expresses an opinion about an important event.
- You may want to have students do additional research to find out more about the events that preceded and followed this speech. Students can use this information in their news commentaries.
- Encourage students to deliver their commentaries in the format of a television news show.
- Use the Response to Literature rubric, p. 16 in **Performance Assessment and Portfolio Management,** to assess students' work.

❹ Listening and Speaking

- Suggest that students do additional research about Akhmatova to help them better understand her perspective.
- Have students invent a person who has left Russia during the civil war, and brainstorm for a list of reasons that he or she chose to leave.
- Have students perform their dialogue with a partner.
- Use the rubric for Delivering a Persuasive Argument, p. 30 in **Performance Assessment and Portfolio Management,** to assess students' work.

CUSTOMIZE INSTRUCTION
For Universal Access

To address different learning styles, use the activities suggested in the **Extension Activities** booklet, p. 25.

- For Intrapersonal and Verbal/Linguistic Learners, use Activity 5.
- For Bodily/Kinesthetic and Interpersonal Learners, use Activity 6.
- For Verbal/Linguistic and Visual/Spatial Learners, use Activity 7.

The Good Deed

Lesson Objectives

1. **To analyze and respond to literary elements**
   - Literary Analysis: Static and Dynamic Characters
   - Connecting Literary Elements: Relationships Between Characters

2. **To read, comprehend, analyze, and critique a short story**
   - Reading Strategy: Drawing Inferences
   - Reading Check questions
   - Review and Assess questions
   - Assessment Practice (ATE)

3. **To develop word analysis skills, fluency, and systematic vocabulary**
   - Vocabulary Development Lesson: Latin Word Root: *-pel-*

4. **To understand and apply written and oral language conventions**
   - Spelling Strategy
   - Grammar Lesson: Adverb Clauses

5. **To understand and apply appropriate writing and research strategies**
   - Writing Lesson: Award Speech for a Character
   - Extension Activity: Multimedia Presentation

6. **To understand and apply listening and speaking strategies**
   - Extension Activity: Interview

STEP-BY-STEP TEACHING GUIDE	PACING GUIDE
PRETEACH	
Motivate Students and Provide Background	
Use the Motivation activity (ATE p. 374)	5 min.
Read and discuss the Preview material and Background information (SE/ATE p. 374) **A**	5 min.
Introduce the Concepts	
Introduce the Literary Analysis and Reading Strategy (SE/ATE p. 375) **A**	15 min.
Pronounce the vocabulary words and read their definitions (SE p. 375)	5 min.
TEACH	
Monitor Comprehension	
Informally monitor comprehension by circulating while students read independently or in groups **A**	35 min.
Monitor students' comprehension with the Reading Check notes (SE/ATE pp. 377, 379, 381, 383, 385, 387, 389, 391)	as students read
Develop vocabulary with Vocabulary notes (SE/ATE pp. 377, 378, 381, 383, 384, 387, 388, 389)	as students read
Develop Understanding	
Develop students' understanding of static and dynamic characters with Literary Analysis annotations (SE/ATE pp. 377, 378, 379, 382, 385, 386, 387, 388, 390, 391) **A**	10 min.
Develop students' understanding of drawing inferences with Reading Strategy annotations (SE pp. 377, 381, 384, 389, 391; ATE pp. 377, 380, 381, 384, 389, 391)	10 min.
ASSESS	
Assess Mastery	
Assess students' mastery of the Reading Strategy and Literary Analysis by having them answer the Review and Assess questions (SE/ATE p. 393)	20 min.
Use one or more of the print and media Assessment Resources (ATE p. 395) **A**	up to 50 min.
EXTEND	
Apply Understanding	
Have students complete the Vocabulary Development Lesson and the Grammar Lesson (SE p. 394) **A**	20 min.
Apply students' ability to write an introduction using the Writing Lesson (SE p. 395) **A**	45 min.
Apply students' understanding of the selection using one or more of the Extension Activities (SE p. 395)	20–90 min.

 ACCELERATED INSTRUCTION:
Use the strategies and activities identified with an **A**.

UNIVERSAL ACCESS
- ● = Below Level Students
- ▲ = On-Level Students
- ■ = Above Level Students

Time and Resource Manager

Reading Level: Average
Average Number of Instructional Days: 4

RESOURCES		
PRINT 📖	**TRANSPARENCIES**	**TECHNOLOGY** 💿 🎧 📼
• **Beyond Literature,** Cultural Connection: Dating Customs, p. 26 ▲ ■		• **Interest Grabber Video,** Tape 2 ● ▲ ■
• **Selection Support Workbook:** ● ▲ ■ Literary Analysis, p. 100 Reading Strategy, p. 99 Build Vocabulary, p. 97	• **Literary Analysis and Reading Transparencies,** pp. 51 and 52 ● ▲ ■	
		• **Listening to Literature** ● ▲ ■ Audiocassettes, Side 12 Audio CDs, CD 8
• **Literatura en español** ● ▲ • **Literary Analysis for Enrichment** ■		
• **Formal Assessment:** Selection Test, pp. 88–90 ● ▲ ■ • **Open Book Test,** pp. 76–78 ● ▲ ■ • **Performance Assessment and Portfolio Management,** p. 27 ● ▲ ■ • **PRENTICE HALL ASSESSMENT SYSTEM** ● ▲ ■	• **PRENTICE HALL ASSESSMENT SYSTEM** ● ▲ ■ Skills Practice Answers and Explanations on Transparencies	• **Test Bank Software** ● ▲ ■ • **Got It! Assessment Videotapes,** Tape 2 ● ▲
• **Selection Support Workbook:** ● ▲ ■ Build Grammar Skills, p. 98 • **Writing and Grammar,** Platinum Level ● ▲ ■ • **Extension Activities,** p. 26 ● ▲ ■	• **Daily Language Practice Transparencies** ● ▲ • **Writing Models and Graphic Organizers on Transparencies,** p. 71 ● ▲ ■	• **Writing and Grammar iText CD-ROM** ● ▲ ■ 💻 *Take It to the Net* www.phschool.com

BLOCK SCHEDULING: Use one 90-minute class period to preteach the selection and have students read it. Use a second 90-minute class period to assess students' mastery of skills and have them complete one of the Extension Activities.

Motivation

Discuss matchmaking with students. Do students believe that lasting relationships can be arranged between two people by a third party? Are matchmakers doing a good deed, or interfering in other people's lives? Encourage students to keep an open mind as they read about the custom of matchmaking—practiced in China and other cultures from ancient times—carried forward in this story by an older woman who finds herself settled in a new land.

Interest Grabber Video

As an alternative, play "Marriage Customs Around the World" on Tape 2 to engage student interest.

❶ Background

In the United States, Chinese immigrants have historically settled together to form strong communities. Most major U.S. cities have a Chinatown—an area in which Chinese immigrants settled to start a new life in a new country. These communities form a bridge between the old and new cultures, allowing the Chinese to live in a new place with the traditions and amenities of their home country.

Prepare to Read

The Good Deed

📷 Take It to the Net

Visit www.phschool.com for interactive activities and instruction related to "The Good Deed," including

- background
- graphic organizers
- literary elements
- reading strategies

Preview

Connecting to the Literature

Moving to someplace new can give you a feeling of uncertainty. Everything seems strange. Imagine how uncomfortable Mrs. Pan, the central character in this story, must feel after leaving China late in her life to live with her son in New York City.

❶ Background

In "The Good Deed," Mrs. Pan tries to arrange a marriage between two young Chinese Americans. Arranged marriages have long been a tradition in China. Parents choose their child's spouse and then negotiate with the parents of the prospective bride or groom. Although some arranged marriages still do take place in modern China and in Chinese American communities, most young people now choose their own marriage partners.

374 ◆ *Turning Points*

TEACHING RESOURCES

The following resources can be used to enrich or extend the instruction for pp. 374–375.

Motivation

📼 **Interest Grabber Video,** Tape 2

Background

📖 **Beyond Literature,** Cultural Connection: Dating Customs, p. 26 ▪

📷 **Take It to the Net**
Visit www.phschool.com for background and hotlinks for "The Good Deed."

Literary Analysis

📄 **Literary Analysis and Reading Transparencies,** Static and Dynamic Characters, p. 52

Reading

📖 **Selection Support Workbook:** Reading Strategy, p. 99; Build Vocabulary, p. 97

📄 **Literary Analysis and Reading Transparencies,** Drawing Inferences, p. 51

 BLOCK SCHEDULING: Resources marked with this symbol provide varied instruction during 90-minute blocks.

Literary Analysis

Static and Dynamic Characters

A character that changes or grows during the course of a literary work is a **dynamic character.** The changes that dynamic characters undergo affect their attitudes and beliefs. In contrast, a **static character** does not change. In this example, the words in italics show that Mrs. Pan is changing.

> She got up and tidied her hair . . . and opening the curtains a little she gazed into the street really *for the first time* since she came.

As you read, notice changes in the characters—especially in Mrs. Pan. Think about how the changes show growth.

Connecting Literary Elements

You can learn a lot about a story by examining the **relationships between characters**—the interactions and feelings that pass between the people in the story. If the characters are dynamic, their relationships will also change over time. For example, Mrs. Pan's relationship with her son changes during the story, and this change influences the story's outcome.

Reading Strategy

Drawing Inferences

Writers rarely announce that a character is changing, nor do they state directly what a character is feeling. Instead, you must **draw inferences,** or make logical assumptions, about the characters based on what they say and do. For example, the author never writes the words "Mr. Pan loves his mother," but, based on his actions, you can infer that he does.

Use a chart like the one shown to record your observations and draw inferences about the characters.

Vocabulary Development

contemplatively (kən tem´ plə tiv´ lē) *adv.* in a thoughtful way (p. 377)

revere (ri vir´) *v.* regard with deep respect and love (p. 378)

compelled (kəm peld´) *v.* forced to do something (p. 378)

abashed (ə basht´) *adj.* embarrassed (p. 381)

repressed (ri prest´) *v.* held back or restrained (p. 383)

indignantly (in dig´ nənt lē) *adv.* feeling anger as a reaction to unjust treatment (p. 384)

assailed (ə sāld´) *v.* attacked physically (p. 387)

expedition (eks´ pə dish´ ən) *n.* journey for a definite purpose (p. 388)

conferred (kən furd´) *v.* granted or bestowed (p. 389)

The Good Deed ◆ 375

---

❷ Literary Analysis
Static and Dynamic Characters

- Tell students that as they read "The Good Deed," they will meet a character who at first seems determined not to change or adapt to her new culture.

- Explain to students that they can remember how to distinguish between static and dynamic characters in this way: *static* things do not move (or change), while *dynamic* things do move (and change).

- Use the instruction for Connecting Literary Elements to illustrate for students how relationships between characters can show the difference between static and dynamic characters.

- Use the Static and Dynamic Characters transparency in **Literary Analysis and Reading Transparencies,** p. 52, to show students the process for determining whether a character in a particular selection is static or dynamic.

❸ Reading Strategy
Drawing Inferences

- Remind students that they must often infer, or make informed guesses about what a character is thinking or feeling or why he or she behaves in a certain way, because the information is not always stated directly. This process of making assumptions is called drawing inferences.

- Demonstrate for students how writers who show, rather than tell, about their characters prompt the reader to draw inferences about people and events in the story.

- Review the chart on this page with students. Encourage them to create a chart like this and use it to draw inferences about the characters in this selection.

Vocabulary Development

- Pronounce each vocabulary word for students, and read the definitions as a class. Have students identify any words with which they are already familiar.

 E-Teach

Visit E-Teach at www.phschool.com for teachers' essays on how to teach, with questions and answers.

CUSTOMIZE INSTRUCTION
For Visual/Spatial Learners

Suggest that students sketch quick storyboards for each scene in the narrative. Then, have them make notes under each scene describing what is happening in it, and use these notes to write a synopsis of the story.

❶ About the Selection

When her son brings her from China to New York, Mrs. Pan at first feels profoundly homesick. Her spirits lift, however, once she sets out to arrange a satisfactory marriage for Lili Yang, a young friend. The successful matchmaking effort rejuvenates Mrs. Pan, who discovers she can make a mark in her newly adopted country without abandoning her heritage.

❷ ▶Critical Viewing

Answer: Students might cite the clothing, hairstyle, and postures of the women, as well as the room furnishings.

❸ Background

Art

Mother and Daughter, Leaf from a Manchu family album

Manchu warriors frequently invaded China in the 1600s. They conquered northern China in 1644 and remained the ruling dynasty until 1912.

In the illustration, the Manchu mother and daughter are posed in a stiff and formal manner. Use the following question for discussion:

• What might the similarity between mother and daughter indicate about the old Manchu culture? Would Mrs. Pan approve or disapprove of this trait?
Answer: Children were expected to emulate their parents rather than develop their individuality. Mrs. Pan would approve.

---

❶ The Good Deed

Pearl S. Buck

Mother and Daughter: Leaf from a Manchu family album,
Unidentified artist, The Metropolitan Museum of Art

❷ ▲ **Critical Viewing** What details in this picture suggest traditional China? **[Analyze]**

376 ◆ *Turning Points*

TEACHING RESOURCES

The following resources can be used to enrich or extend the instruction for pp. 376–392.

Literary Analysis

📖 **Writing Models and Graphic Organizers on Transparencies,** p. 71

📓 **Selection Support:** Literary Analysis, p. 100

Reading

🎧 **Listening to Literature Audiocassettes,** Side 12 ▪

💿 **Listening to Literature Audio CDs,** CD 8 ▪

▪ **BLOCK SCHEDULING:** Resources marked with this symbol provide varied instruction during 90-minute blocks.

Mr. Pan was worried about his mother. He had been worried about her when she was in China, and now he was worried about her in New York, although he had thought that once he got her out of his ancestral village in the province of Szechuen and safely away from the local bullies, who took over when the distant government fell, his anxieties would be ended. To this end he had risked his own life and paid out large sums of sound American money, and he felt that day when he saw her on the wharf, a tiny, dazed little old woman, in a lavender silk coat and black skirt, that now they would live happily together, he and his wife, their four small children and his beloved mother, in the huge safety of the American city.

It soon became clear, however, that safety was not enough for old Mrs. Pan. She did not even appreciate the fact, which he repeated again and again, that had she remained in the village, she would now have been dead, because she was the widow of the large landowner who had been his father and therefore deserved death in the eyes of the rowdies in power.

Old Mrs. Pan listened to this without reply, but her eyes, looking very large in her small withered face, were haunted with homesickness.

"There are many things worse than death, especially at my age," she replied at last, when again her son reminded her of her good fortune in being where she was.

He became impassioned when she said this. He struck his breast with his clenched fists and he shouted, "Could I have forgiven myself if I had allowed you to die? Would the ghost of my father have given me rest?"

"I doubt his ghost would have traveled over such a wide sea," she replied. "That man was always afraid of the water."

Yet there was nothing that Mr. Pan and his wife did not try to do for his mother in order to make her happy. They prepared the food that she had once enjoyed, but she was now beyond the age of pleasure in food, and she had no appetite. She touched one dish and another with the ends of her ivory chopsticks,[1] which she had brought with her from her home, and she thanked them prettily. "It is all good," she said, "but the water is not the same as our village water; it tastes of metal and not of earth, and so the flavor is not the same. Please allow the children to eat it."

She was afraid of the children. They went to an American school and they spoke English very well and Chinese very badly, and since she could speak no English, it distressed her to hear her own language maltreated by their careless tongues. For a time she tried to coax them to a few lessons, or she told them stories, to which they were too busy to listen. Instead they preferred to look at the moving pictures in the box that stood on a table in the living room. She gave them up finally and merely watched them <u>contemplatively</u> when they were in the same room with her and was glad when they were gone. She liked her son's wife. She did not understand how there could be a Chinese woman who had never

---

1. **ivory chopsticks** thin pair of sticks used as eating utensils.

Reading Strategy
Drawing Inferences What can you infer about Mr. Pan's feelings concerning his mother?

contemplatively (kən tem′ plə tiv lē) *adv.* in a thoughtful way

6 ✓**Reading Check**
Why did Mr. Pan bring his mother to the United States?

The Good Deed ◆ 377

❹ Reading Strategy
Drawing Inferences

- Remind students that drawing inferences asks the reader to make judgments about characters and events when information is not directly stated.
- Ask students to cite examples of Mr. Pan's behavior toward his mother.
  Answer: He worried about her in the past, and he worries about her in the present; he risked his own life and paid much money to get her out of China and bring her to New York to live with him and his family.
- Have students respond to the Reading Strategy question on p. 377: What can you infer about Mr. Pan's feelings concerning his mother?
  Answer: Students will probably say that his actions on her behalf support the inference that he loves and respects his mother.

❺ Literary Analysis
Static and Dynamic Characters

- Remind students that static characters are those who do not change, and dynamic characters are those who do grow and change.
- Have students describe Mrs. Pan in this passage.
  Answer: She is haunted by homesickness, which she implies may be worse than death.
- Ask students whether Mrs. Pan is a static or dynamic character in this passage, and to explain their answers.
  Answer: She is a static character because she makes no effort to fit into her new home.

❻ ✓Reading Check
Answer: His mother would have been killed because she was the wife of a landowner who had already been killed by the people in power.

Static and Dynamic Characters

- Ask students to identify the things in this passage that make life miserable for Mrs. Pan.
  Answer: She does not approve of how her grandchildren have been raised; she feels useless; even the hot and cold water faucets are confusing to her.

- Ask students how Mrs. Pan spends her days.
  Answer: She sits all day, and will not even look out the window.

- Ask students to respond to the Literary Analysis question on p. 378: What changes do you see in old Mrs. Pan?
  Answer: She becomes more and more unhappy, and she grows thinner and thinner.

❽ Vocabulary Development

The Latin Root -pel-

- Call students' attention to the word *compelled* and its definition. Tell students that the word comes from the Latin word *pellere*, which means, "to drive."

- Invite students to brainstorm for a list of English words that derive from the Latin word *pellere*. Such words include *impel*, *repel*, and *dispel*.

---

been in China, but such her son's wife was. When her son was away, she could not say to her daughter-in-law, "Do you remember how the willows grew over the gate?" For her son's wife had no such memories. She had grown up here in the city and she did not even hear its noise. At the same time, though she was so foreign, she was very kind to the old lady, and she spoke to her always in a gentle voice, however she might shout at the children, who were often disobedient.

The disobedience of the children was another grief to old Mrs. Pan. She did not understand how it was that four children could all be disobedient, for this meant that they had never been taught to obey their parents and <u>revere</u> their elders, which are the first lessons a child should learn.

"How is it," she once asked her son, "that the children do not know how to obey?"

Mr. Pan had laughed, though uncomfortably. "Here in America the children are not taught as we were in China," he explained.

"But my grandchildren are Chinese nevertheless," old Mrs. Pan said in some astonishment.

"They are always with Americans," Mr. Pan explained. "It is very difficult to teach them."

Old Mrs. Pan did not understand, for Chinese and Americans are different beings, one on the west side of the sea and one on the east, and the sea is always between. Therefore, why should they not continue to live apart even in the same city? She felt in her heart that the children should be kept at home and taught those things which must be learned, but she said nothing. She felt lonely and there was no one who understood the things she felt and she was quite useless. That was the most difficult thing: She was of no use here. She could not even remember which spout the hot water came from and which brought the cold. Sometimes she turned on one and then the other, until her son's wife came in briskly and said, "Let me, Mother."

So she gave up and sat uselessly all day, not by the window, because the machines and the many people frightened her. She sat where she could not see out; she looked at a few books, and day by day she grew thinner and thinner until Mr. Pan was concerned beyond endurance.

One day he said to his wife, "Sophia, we must do something for my mother. There is no use in saving her from death in our village if she dies here in the city. Do you see how thin her hands are?"

"I have seen," his good young wife said. "But what can we do?"

"Is there no woman you know who can speak Chinese with her?" Mr. Pan asked. "She needs to have someone to whom she can talk about the village and all the things she knows. She cannot talk to you because you can only speak English, and I am too busy making our living to sit and listen to her."

Young Mrs. Pan considered. "I have a friend," she said at last, "a schoolmate whose family <u>compelled</u> her to speak Chinese. Now she is a social worker here in the city. She visits families in Chinatown and this is her work. I will call her up and ask her to spend some time here so

revere (ri vir´) *v.* regard with deep respect and love

Literary Analysis
Static and Dynamic Characters What changes do you see in old Mrs. Pan?

compelled (kəm peld´) *v.* forced to do something

✹ ENRICHMENT: Social Studies

China's Political Climate

"The Good Deed" is set against a backdrop of decades of political instability, civil war, and revolution in China.

In 1912, China's last emperor gave up his throne following a prolonged popular uprising. Over the years that followed, the new Nationalist party government was besieged by troubles as foreign powers, provincial war-lords, and a growing Communist movement all struggled to gain control of all or parts of the country. Finally, in 1949, Communist forces drove Nationalist forces from power.

It was during the years immediately after this Communist takeover—while the party was consolidating its control over China—that Mrs. Pan fled to join her son in the U.S. Other details indicate the time period in which the story is set, notably Lili Yang's description of a typical American courtship, which more closely resembles a 1950s-era ideal.

that our old mother can be happy enough to eat again."

"Do so," Mr. Pan said.

That very morning, when Mr. Pan was gone, young Mrs. Pan made the call and found her friend, Lili Yang, and she explained everything to her.

"We are really in very much trouble," she said finally. "His mother is thinner every day, and she is so afraid she will die here. She has made us promise that we will not bury her in foreign soil but will send her coffin back to the ancestral village. We have promised, but can we keep this promise, Lili? Yet I am so afraid, because I think she will die, and Billy will think he must keep his promise and he will try to take the coffin back and then he will be killed. Please help us, Lili."

Lili Yang promised and within a few days she came to the apartment and young Mrs. Pan led her into the inner room, which was old Mrs. Pan's room and where she always sat, wrapped in her satin coat and holding a magazine at whose pictures she did not care to look. She took up that magazine when her daughter-in-law came in, because she did not want to hurt her feelings, but the pictures frightened her. The women looked bold and evil, their bosoms bare, and sometimes they wore only a little silk stuff over their legs and this shocked her. She wondered that her son's wife would put such a magazine into her hands, but she did not ask questions. There would have been no end to them had she once begun, and the ways of foreigners did not interest her. Most of the time she sat silent and still, her head sunk on her breast, dreaming of the village, the big house there where she and her husband had lived together with his parents and where their children were born. She knew that the village had fallen into the hands of their enemies and that strangers lived in the house, but she hoped even so that the land was tilled.[2] All that she remembered was the way it had been when she was a young woman and before the evil had come to pass.

She heard now her daughter-in-law's voice, "Mother, this is a friend. She is Miss Lili Yang. She has come to see you."

Old Mrs. Pan remembered her manners. She tried to rise but Lili took her hands and begged her to keep seated.

"You must not rise to one so much younger," she exclaimed.

Old Mrs. Pan lifted her head. "You speak such good Chinese!"

"I was taught by my parents," Lili said. She sat down on a chair near the old lady.

Mrs. Pan leaned forward and put her hand on Lili's knee. "Have you been in our own country?" she asked eagerly.

Lili shook her head. "This is my sorrow. I have not and I want to know about it. I have come here to listen to you tell me."

"Excuse me," young Mrs. Pan said, "I must prepare the dinner for the family."

She slipped away so that the two could be alone and old Mrs. Pan looked after her sadly. "She never wishes to hear; she is always busy."

---

2. **tilled** (tild) *v.* plowed and fertilized to make ready for planting.

Literary Analysis
Static and Dynamic Characters What has Mrs. Pan done or said that leads you to think she is a static character? Explain.

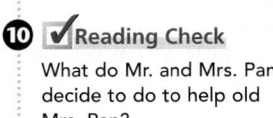

❿ ✓ **Reading Check**
What do Mr. and Mrs. Pan decide to do to help old Mrs. Pan?

The Good Deed ◆ 379

380

"You must remember in this country we have no servants," Lili reminded her gently.

"Yes," old Mrs. Pan said, "and why not? I have told my son it is not fitting to have my daughter-in-law cooking and washing in the kitchen. We should have at least three servants: one for me, one for the children and one to clean and cook. At home we had many more but here we have only a few rooms."

Lili did not try to explain. "Everything is different here and let us not talk about it," she said. "Let us talk about your home and the village. I want to know how it looks and what goes on there."

Old Mrs. Pan was delighted. She smoothed the gray satin of her coat as it lay on her knees and she began.

"You must know that our village lies in a wide valley from which the mountains rise as sharply as tiger's teeth."

"Is it so?" Lili said, making a voice of wonder.

"It is, and the village is not a small one. On the contrary, the walls encircle more than one thousand souls, all of whom are relatives of our family."

"A large family," Lili said.

"It is," old Mrs. Pan said, "and my son's father was the head of it. We lived in a house with seventy rooms. It was in the midst of the village. We had gardens in the courtyards. My own garden contained also a pool wherein are aged goldfish, very fat. I fed them millet[3] and they knew me."

"How amusing." Lili saw with pleasure that the old lady's cheeks were faintly pink and that her large beautiful eyes were beginning to shine and glow. "And how many years did you live there, Ancient One?"

"I went there as a bride. I was seventeen." She looked at Lili, questioning, "How old are you?"

Lili smiled, somewhat ashamed, "I am twenty-seven."

Mrs. Pan was shocked. "Twenty-seven? But my son's wife called you Miss."

⓬ "I am not married," Lili confessed.

Mrs. Pan was instantly concerned. "How is this?" she asked. "Are your parents dead?"

"They are dead," Lili said, "but it is not their fault that I am not married."

Old Mrs. Pan would not agree to this. She shook her head with decision. "It is the duty of the parents to arrange the marriage of the children. When death approached, they should have attended to this for you. Now who is left to perform the task? Have you brothers?"

"No," Lili said, "I am an only child. But please don't worry yourself, Madame Pan. I am earning my own living and there are many young women like me in this country."

Old Mrs. Pan was dignified about this. "I cannot be responsible for

---

3. **millet** (mil′ it) *n.* food grain.

380 ◆ *Turning Points*

---

what other persons do, but I must be responsible for my own kind," she declared. "Allow me to know the names of the suitable persons who can arrange your marriage. I will stand in the place of your mother. We are all in a foreign country now and we must keep together and the old must help the young in these important matters."

Lili was kind and she knew that Mrs. Pan meant kindness. "Dear Madame Pan," she said. "Marriage in America is very different from marriage in China. Here the young people choose their own mates."

"Why do you not choose, then?" Mrs. Pan said with some spirit.

Lili Yang looked <u>abashed</u>. "Perhaps it would be better for me to say that only the young men choose. It is they who must ask the young women."

"What do the young women do?" Mrs. Pan inquired.

"They wait," Lili confessed.

"And if they are not asked?"

"They continue to wait," Lili said gently.

"How long?" Mrs. Pan demanded.

"As long as they live."

Old Mrs. Pan was profoundly shocked. "Do you tell me that there is no person who arranges such matters when it is necessary?"

"Such an arrangement is not thought of here," Lili told her.

"And they allow their women to remain unmarried?" Mrs. Pan exclaimed. "Are there also sons who do not marry?"

"Here men do not marry unless they wish to do so."

Mrs. Pan was even more shocked. "How can this be?" she asked. "Of course, men will not marry unless they are compelled to do so to provide grandchildren for the family. It is necessary to make laws and create customs so that a man who will not marry is denounced as an unfilial[4] son and one who does not fulfill his duty to his ancestors."

"Here the ancestors are forgotten and parents are not important," Lili said unwillingly.

"What a country is this," Mrs. Pan exclaimed. "How can such a country endure?"

Lili did not reply. Old Mrs. Pan had unknowingly touched upon a wound in her heart. No man had ever asked her to marry him. Yet above all else she would like to be married and to have children. She was a good social worker, and the head of the Children's Bureau sometimes told her that he would not know what to do without her and she must never leave them, for then there would be no one to serve the people in Chinatown. She did not wish to leave except to be married, but how could she find a husband? She looked down at her hands, clasped in her lap, and thought that if she had been in her own country, if her father had not come here as a young man and married here, she would have been in China and by now the mother of many children. Instead what would become of her? She would grow older and older, and twenty-seven was already old, and at last hope must die. She knew

_____

4. **unfilial** (un fil′ ē əl) *adj.* unlike a loving, respectful son or daughter.

Reading Strategy
Drawing Inferences What do Mrs. Pan's words reveal about her character?

abashed (ə basht′) *adj.* embarrassed

⓮ ✔Reading Check
What shocks old Mrs. Pan about Lili Yang?

The Good Deed ◆ 381

⓭ Reading Strategy
Drawing Inferences

- Ask students what Mrs. Pan offers to do for Lili.
  Answer: She offers to stand in the place of Lili's mother in arranging Lili's marriage.

- Then, ask students how Mrs. Pan responds to Lili's statement that many women are in her position.
  Answer: Mrs. Pan says that she cannot be responsible for what others do, but must be responsible for her own kind, that is, other Chinese women.

- Have students respond to the Reading Strategy question on p. 381: What do Mrs. Pan's words reveal about her character?
  Answer: She feels responsible, and is prepared to act in accordance with her values.

⓮ ✔Reading Check
Answer: Mrs. Pan is shocked that no one has yet asked Lili to marry him, and is also shocked that she must wait to be asked.

CUSTOMIZE INSTRUCTION FOR UNIVERSAL ACCESS

For Special Needs Students	For Gifted/Talented Students
Students may benefit by watching "Marriage Customs Around the World" on Tape 2 of the **Interest Grabber Video**. Then, have students improvise a speech from Lili's point of view, expressing her feelings about Mrs. Pan's plan.	Have these students try retelling the story from Lili Yang's point of view. They can begin the story from the moment Sophia Pan asks Lili to help her mother-in-law. Encourage students to infer Lili's professional attitude toward helping an unhappy immigrant. Then, they can describe her meeting with Mrs. Pan from Lili's viewpoint.

- Ask students whether Mrs. Pan seems to become more dynamic in this passage. What evidence can they give that this is occurring?
  Answer: She focuses on Lili instead of on her own unhappiness.

- Have students answer the first Literary Analysis question on p. 382: How does old Mrs. Pan begin to change her relationship with Lili?
  Answer: Mrs. Pan begins to take an interest in Lili and her situation.

16 Literary Analysis

Static and Dynamic Characters

- Ask students to summarize Mrs. Pan's recollections in the bracketed passage.
  Answer: She was taken away from the village before she could see that the cabbage would be preserved correctly; she had left many other things undone, because she was compelled to leave by others; she now lives in idleness and she feels it is killing her.

- Ask students to respond to the second Literary Analysis question on p. 382: What is causing old Mrs. Pan to change?
  Possible answer: She sees an opportunity to accomplish something.

---

several American girls quite well; they liked her, and she knew that they faced the same fate. They, too, were waiting. They tried very hard; they went in summer to hotels and in winter to ski lodges, where men gathered and were at leisure enough to think about them, and in confidence they told one another of their efforts. They compared their experiences and they asked anxious questions. "Do you think men like talkative women or quiet ones?" "Do you think men like lipstick or none?" Such questions they asked of one another and who could answer them? If a girl succeeded in winning a proposal from a man, then all the other girls envied her and asked her special questions and immediately she became someone above them all, a successful woman. The job which had once been so valuable then became worthless and it was given away easily and gladly. But how could she explain this to old Mrs. Pan?

15 Meanwhile Mrs. Pan had been studying Lili's face carefully and with thought. This was not a pretty girl. Her face was too flat, and her mouth was large. She looked like a girl from Canton and not from Hangchow or Soochow. But she had nice skin, and her eyes, though small, were kind. She was the sort of girl, Mrs. Pan could see, who would make an excellent wife and a good mother, but certainly she was one for whom a marriage must be arranged. She was a decent, plain, good girl and, left to herself, Mrs. Pan could predict, nothing at all would happen. She would wither away like a dying flower.

16 Old Mrs. Pan forgot herself and for the first time since she had been hurried away from the village without even being allowed to stop and see that the salted cabbage, drying on ropes across the big courtyard, was brought in for the winter. She had been compelled to leave it there and she had often thought of it with regret. She could have brought some with her had she known it was not to be had here. But there it was, and it was only one thing among others that she had left undone. Many people depended upon her and she had left them, because her son compelled her, and she was not used to this idleness that was killing her day by day.

Now as she looked at Lili's kind, ugly face it occurred to her that here there was something she could do. She could find a husband for this good girl, and it would be counted for merit when she went to heaven. A good deed is a good deed, whether one is in China or in America, for the same heaven stretches above all.

She patted Lili's clasped hands. "Do not grieve anymore," she said tenderly. "I will arrange everything."

"I am not grieving," Lili said.

"Of course, you are," Mrs. Pan retorted. "I see you are a true woman, and women grieve when they are not wed so that they can have children. You are grieving for your children."

Lili could not deny it. She would have been ashamed to confess to any other person except this old Chinese lady who might have been her grandmother. She bent her head and bit her lip; she let a tear or two fall upon her hands. Then she nodded. Yes, she grieved in the secret places of her heart, in the darkness of the lonely nights, when she thought of

382 ◆ Turning Points

Literary Analysis
Relationships Between Characters How does old Mrs. Pan begin to change her relationship with Lili?

Literary Analysis
Static and Dynamic Characters What is causing old Mrs. Pan to change?

✳ ENRICHMENT: Social Studies

China's Geography and Population

Ask students the following "trick" question: "Is China the world's largest country? Vote yes or no." After students have voted, explain that either answer could be considered correct, depending on what is meant by "largest." With a population of over one billion, China is the largest country in terms of population. In terms of land area, it is the third largest, after Russia and Canada. Other references to places within China in the story include Szechuen, the province where Mrs. Pan's ancestral village is located; Shantung, the province that is the ancestral home of the Lim family; and the cities of Canton, Hangchow, and Soochow. Have students locate each of these places on a map of China.

the empty future of her life.

"Do not grieve," old Mrs. Pan was saying, "I will arrange it; I will do it."

It was so comforting a murmur that Lili could not bear it. She said, "I came to comfort you, but it is you who comfort me." Then she got up and went out of the room quickly because she did not want to sob aloud. She was unseen, for young Mrs. Pan had gone to market and the children were at school, and Lili went away telling herself that it was all absurd, that an old woman from the middle of China who could not speak a word of English would not be able to change this American world, even for her.

Old Mrs. Pan could scarcely wait for her son to come home at noon. She declined to join the family at the table, saying that she must speak to her son first.

When he came in, he saw at once that she was changed. She held up her head and she spoke to him sharply when he came into the room, as though it was her house and not his in which they now were.

"Let the children eat first," she commanded, "I shall need time to talk with you and I am not hungry."

He <u>repressed</u> his inclination to tell her that he was hungry and that he must get back to the office. Something in her look made it impossible for him to be disobedient to her. He went away and gave the children direction and then returned.

"Yes, my mother," he said, seating himself on a small and uncomfortable chair.

Then she related to him with much detail and repetition what had happened that morning; she declared with indignation that she had never before heard of a country where no marriages were arranged for the young, leaving to them the most important event of their lives and that at a time when their judgment was still unripe, and a mistake could bring disaster upon the whole family.

"Your own marriage," she reminded him, "was arranged by your father with great care, two families knowing each other well. Even though you and my daughter-in-law were distant in this country, yet we met her parents through a suitable go-between, and her uncle here stood in her father's place, and your father's friend in place of your father, and so it was all done according to custom though so far away."

Mr. Pan did not have the heart to tell his mother that he and his wife Sophia had fallen in love first, and then, out of kindness to their elders, had allowed the marriage to be arranged for them as though they were not in love, and as though, indeed, they did not know each other. They were both young people of heart, and although it would have been much easier to be married in the American fashion, they considered their elders.

"What has all this to do with us now, my mother?" he asked.

"This is what is to do," she replied with spirit. "A nice, ugly girl of our own people came here today to see me. She is twenty-seven years old and she is not married. What will become of her?"

"Do you mean Lili Yang?" her son asked.

repressed (ri prest') *v.* held back or restrained

Reading Strategy
Drawing Inferences What details from this scene might lead you to infer that Mr. Pan is a respectful son?

 Reading Check
What does old Mrs. Pan decide to do as a good deed?

The Good Deed ◆ 383

CUSTOMIZE INSTRUCTION FOR UNIVERSAL ACCESS

For Less Proficient Readers	For Advanced Readers
To help students make inferences about characters, have them list details about Lili and Mrs. Pan. Students should note Lili's grief and tears, Mrs. Pan's kindness and compassion, and Lili's statement that although she had come to comfort the older woman, Mrs. Pan had ended up comforting her. Draw their attention especially to Mrs. Pan's new sense of purpose. Ask students whether, using this information, they can make new guesses about the course the story will now take.	Challenge students to rewrite all or part of the narrative in dialogue form, to explore inferences they have made about characters and their motivations. Students should choose a scene from the story, such as a conversation between Mrs. Pan and her son, and have the characters talk more freely about their feelings and beliefs. Encourage students to form groups to perform their work. Students should discuss how the use of dialogue affects the narrative.

- Ask students what view of planning a marriage is implied by Mrs. Pan's comments in the bracketed passage.
Answer: Marriage is a matter that leads to embarrassment if the woman and man have to make the arrangements personally; it is more civilized to have a neutral party make the arrangements.

- Ask students to infer why Mrs. Pan believes that it is embarrassing to arrange one's own marriage.
Possible answer: Students should observe that Mrs. Pan knows that a woman such as Lili Yang would find it horribly embarrassing to tell a young man that she might not be pretty, but would still make a very good wife.

- Finally, have students respond to the Reading Strategy question on p. 384: What upsets Old Mrs. Pan? What can you infer about her values from this speech?
Answer: Mrs. Pan is upset because women who are not pretty are passed over for marriage. She has a strong feeling that this is unfair, and that matchmakers can help with this injustice.

"I do," she replied. "When I heard that she has no way of being married because, according to the custom of this country, she must wait for a man to ask her—"

Old Mrs. Pan broke off and gazed at her son with horrified eyes. "What now?" he asked.

"Suppose the only man who asks is one who is not at all suitable?"

"It is quite possible that it often happens thus," her son said, trying not to laugh.

"Then she has no choice," old Mrs. Pan said <u>indignantly</u>. "She can only remain unmarried or accept one who is unsuitable."

"Here she has no choice," Mr. Pan agreed, "unless she is very pretty, my mother, when several men may ask and then she has choice." It was on the tip of his tongue to tell how at least six young men had proposed to his Sophia, thereby distressing him continually until he was finally chosen, but he thought better of it. Would it not be very hard to explain so much to his old mother, and could she understand? He doubted it. Nevertheless, he felt it necessary at least to make one point.

"Something must be said for the man also, my mother. Sometimes he asks a girl who will not have him, because she chooses another, and then his sufferings are intense. Unless he wishes to remain unmarried he must ask a second girl, who is not the first one. Here also is some injustice."

Old Mrs. Pan listened to this attentively and then declared, "It is all barbarous.[5] Certainly it is very embarrassing to be compelled to speak of these matters, man and woman, face to face. They should be spared; others should speak for them."

She considered for a few seconds and then she said with fresh indignation, "And what woman can change the appearance her ancestors have given her? Because she is not pretty is she less a woman? Are not her feelings like any woman's; is it not her right to have husband and home and children? It is well-known that men have no wisdom in such matters; they believe that a woman's face is all she has, forgetting that everything else is the same. They gather about the pretty woman, who is surfeited with them,[6] and leave alone the good woman. And I do not know why heaven has created ugly women always good but so it is, whether here or in our own country, but what man is wise enough to know that? Therefore his wife should be chosen for him, so that the family is not burdened with his follies."

Mr. Pan allowed all this to be said and then he inquired, "What is on your mind, my mother?"

Old Mrs. Pan leaned toward him and lifted her forefinger. "This is what I command you to do for me, my son. I myself will find a husband for this good girl of our people. She is helpless and alone. But I know no one; I am a stranger, and I must depend upon you. In your business there must be young men. Inquire of them and see who stands for

---

5. **barbarous** (bär´ bə rəs) *adj.* uncivilized.
6. **is surfeited** (sʉr´ fit əd) **with them** has had enough of them.

✹ ENRICHMENT: Career Connection

Social Work

Lili Yang, a character in the story, is a social worker who works for the city's Children's Bureau; she serves the community by visiting families who need help.

In the United States, most social assistance and personal social service programs, such as the one for which Lili works, are organized and directed by local agencies. These receive substantial support from the federal government. The United States Department of Health and Human Services is the chief federal agency that oversees such social programs. Each state has a counterpart of this agency that administers and directs the delivery of services in the community.

The type of work that Lili does is called casework, and her field is known as family and child welfare. Caseworkers in this field may help families obtain financial assistance or medical care. They may also counsel people on family issues such as child care, education, and adoption.

them, so that we can arrange a meeting between them and me; I will stand for the girl's mother. I promised it."

Now Mr. Pan laughed heartily. "Oh, my mother!" he cried. "You are too kind, but it cannot be done. They would laugh at me, and do you believe that Lili Yang herself would like such an arrangement? I think she would not. She has been an American too long."

Old Mrs. Pan would not yield, however, and in the end he was compelled to promise that he would see what he could do. Upon this promise she consented to eat her meal, and he led her out, her right hand resting upon his left wrist. The children were gone and they had a quiet meal together, and after it she said she felt that she would sleep. This was good news, for she had not slept well since she came, and young Mrs. Pan led her into the bedroom and helped her to lie down and placed a thin quilt over her.

When young Mrs. Pan went back to the small dining room where her husband waited to tell her what his mother had said, she listened thoughtfully.

"It is absurd," her husband said, "but what shall we do to satisfy my mother? She sees it as a good deed if she can find a husband for Lili Yang."

Here his wife surprised him. "I can see some good in it myself," she declared. "I have often felt for Lili. It is a problem, and our mother is right to see it as such. It is not only Lili—it is a problem here for all young women, especially if they are not pretty." She looked quizzically at her husband for a moment and then said, "I too used to worry when I was very young, lest I should not find a husband for myself. It is a great burden for a young woman. It would be nice to have someone else arrange the matter."

"Remember," he told her, "how often in the old country the wrong men are arranged for and how often the young men leave home because they do not like the wives their parents choose for them."

"Well, so do they here," she said pertly. "Divorce, divorce, divorce!"

"Come, come," he told her. "It is not so bad."

"It is very bad for women," she insisted. "When there is divorce here, then she is thrown out of the family. The ties are broken. But in the old country, it is the man who leaves home and the woman stays on, for she is still the daughter-in-law and her children will belong to the family, and however far away the man wants to go, she has her place and she is safe."

Mr. Pan looked at his watch. "It is late and I must go to the office."

"Oh, your office," young Mrs. Pan said in an uppish[7] voice, "what would you do without it?"

They did not know it but their voices roused old Mrs. Pan in the bedroom, and she opened her eyes. She could not understand what they said for they spoke in English, but she understood that there was an argument. She sat up on the bed to listen, then she heard the door slam

---

7. **uppish** adj. haughty or arrogant.

Literary Analysis
Relationships Between Characters What does the discussion between Mr. and Mrs. Pan show about how they relate to each other?

21 ✔ Reading Check
What does old Mrs. Pan ask her son to do?

The Good Deed ◆ 385

---

20 Literary Analysis
Relationships Between Characters

- Ask students to explain why readers have, up to this point in the story, had little occasion to learn about Mr. and Mrs. Pan's relationship.
  Answer: The Pans' presence in the story so far has been largely to respond to the elder Mrs. Pan. Readers have not been shown the nature of their own relationship.

- Have students read the passage between Mr. and Mrs. Pan and focus on how they interact with one another.

- Ask students what Mr. Pan learns about his wife in this passage.
  Answer: He learns that she agrees that many young American women face the same problem that Lili does.

- Have students answer the Literary Analysis question on p. 385: What does the discussion between Mr. and Mrs. Pan show about how they relate to each other?
  Answer: Students may suggest that they relate to each other as equals, and that Mrs. Pan stands up for her point of view.

21 ✔ Reading Check

Answer: Mrs. Pan asks her son to inquire about possible husbands for Lili at his office.

CUSTOMIZE INSTRUCTION FOR UNIVERSAL ACCESS

For Less Proficient Readers	For English Learners
The elder Mrs. Pan uses a formal speech pattern and vocabulary that may challenge less proficient readers. Assist these students in previewing some of the words on this page that are not commonly used in conversation. Use the footnotes to clarify *barbarous* and *surfeited*. Discuss with students possible synonyms for words such as *compelled, inquire,* and *follies*. Point out related words such as *indignantly* and *indignation*. Students might wish to role-play or summarize the conversation in their own words.	Help students recognize relationships among characters by having them use a graphic organizer to track characters and their traits. Students can use the organizer to record the different points of view held by Mr. Pan, his mother, and his wife. You may wish to encourage students to use the Analysis Map transparency in **Writing Models and Graphic Organizers on Transparencies,** p. 71.

㉒ ▶Critical Viewing

Answer: Students may suggest that the shop might offer a place to find a possible husband for Lili Yang.

㉓ Literary Analysis

Static and Dynamic Characters

- Have students recall examples of Mrs. Pan's behavior that have shown her to be a static character.

- Lead students to see that Mrs. Pan has lived in the past, refused to see any good about her new home, and wished only to die and be buried in China.

- Have students read the passage and respond to the Literary Analysis question on p. 386: How do Mrs. Pan's actions indicate the beginning of a change in her character?

Answer: Mrs. Pan thinks that it would be interesting to look out the window. She gazes into the street for the first time since she came to the United States.

㉒ ▲ **Critical Viewing** How do you think that a china shop like this might fit into the story? [**Connect**]

and she knew her son was gone. She was about to lie down again when it occurred to her that it would be interesting to look out of the window to the street and see what young men there were coming to and from. One did not choose men from the street, of course, but still she could see what their looks were.

She got up and tidied her hair and tottered on her small feet over to the window and opening the curtains a little she gazed into the street really for the first time since she came. She was pleased to see many Chinese men, some of them young. It was still not late, and they loitered in the sunshine before going back to work, talking and laughing and looking happy. It was interesting to her to watch them, keeping in mind Lili Yang and thinking to herself that it might be this one or that one, although still one did not choose men from the street. She stood so long that at last she became tired and she pulled a small chair to the window and kept looking through the parted curtain.

Here her daughter-in-law saw her a little later, when she opened the door to see if her mother-in-law was awake, but she did not speak. She looked at the little satin-clad figure, and went away again, wondering why it was that the old lady found it pleasant today to look out of the window when every other day she had refused the same pleasure.

It became a pastime for old Mrs. Pan to look out of the window every day from then on. Gradually she came to know some of the

Literary Analysis
Static and Dynamic Characters How do Mrs. Pan's actions indicate the beginning of a change in her character?

✳ ENRICHMENT: Literary Criticism

Pearl Buck and Her Critics

Pearl Buck has always been considered a controversial author. Most critics think her reputation as a writer will always rest on *The Good Earth*, and that she never wrote anything else that equaled it. When she won the Nobel Prize in 1938, many critics were outraged that she defeated such writers as John Steinbeck and Ernest Hemingway, both of whom won in subsequent years.

Much of Buck's later fiction was written for women's magazines, and it has been described as "drippingly romantic." Buck said of her own writing, "The truth is I never write with a sense of mission or to accomplish any purpose whatever except the revelation of human character through a life situation."

young men, not by name but by their faces and by the way they walked by her window, never, of course looking up at her, until one day a certain young man did look up and smile. It was a warm day, and she had asked that the window be opened, which until now she had not allowed, for fear she might be <u>assailed</u> by the foreign winds and made ill. Today, however, was near to summer, she felt the room airless and she longed for freshness.

After this the young man habitually smiled when he passed or nodded his head. She was too old to have it mean anything but courtesy and so bit by bit she allowed herself to make a gesture of her hand in return. It was evident that he belonged in a china shop across the narrow street. She watched him go in and come out; she watched him stand at the door in his shirt sleeves on a fine day and talk and laugh, showing, as she observed, strong white teeth set off by two gold ones. Evidently he made money. She did not believe he was married, for she saw an old man who must be his father, who smoked a water pipe, and now and then an elderly woman, perhaps his mother, and a younger brother, but there was no young woman.

She began after some weeks of watching to fix upon this young man as a husband for Lili. But who could be the go-between except her own son?

She confided her plans one night to him, and, as always, he listened to her with courtesy and concealed amusement. "But the young man, my mother, is the son of Mr. Lim, who is the richest man on our street."

"That is nothing against him," she declared.

"No, but he will not submit to an arrangement, my mother. He is a college graduate. He is only spending the summer at home in the shop to help his father."

"Lili Yang has also been to school."

"I know, my mother, but, you see, the young man will want to choose his own wife, and it will not be someone who looks like Lili Yang. It will be someone who—"

He broke off and made a gesture which suggested curled hair, a fine figure and an air. Mrs. Pan watched him with disgust. "You are like all these other men, though you are my son," she said and dismissed him sternly.

Nevertheless, she thought over what he had said when she went back to the window. The young man was standing on the street picking his fine teeth and laughing at friends who passed, the sun shining on his glistening black hair. It was true he did not look at all obedient; it was perhaps true that he was no more wise than other men and so saw only what a girl's face was. She wished that she could speak to him, but that, of course, was impossible. Unless—

She drew in a long breath. Unless she went downstairs and out into that street and crossed it and entered the shop, pretending that she came to buy something! If she did this, she could speak to him. But what would she say, and who would help her cross the street? She did not want to tell her son or her son's wife, for they would suspect her

assailed (ə sāld') v. attacked physically

Literary Analysis
Relationships Between Characters What does the "concealed amusement" Mr. Pan often feels when listening to his mother indicate about how he relates to her?

Reading Check
Why does old Mrs. Pan look out the window every day?

The Good Deed ◆ 387

Literary Analysis
Relationships Between Characters

• Remind students that by observing the relationships between characters, readers can learn important facts about character motivation.

• Have students read the passage and identify how the author describes Mr. Pan's usual response to his mother.

• Elicit from students that Mr. Pan always listens with respect to his mother, as he does here, but he often is also secretly amused by her ideas about what should be done.

• Have students respond to the Literary Analysis question on p. 387: What does the "concealed amusement" Mr. Pan often feels when listening to his mother indicate about how he relates to her? Possible response: Students may suggest that Mr. Pan believes he owes his mother the respect due a parent and an elder, but he also reserves the right to have his own opinions about what she says.

Reading Check
Answer: Mrs. Pan looks out the window every day to keep track of the eligible men, and having found one, makes sure he learns to recognize her.

CUSTOMIZE INSTRUCTION FOR UNIVERSAL ACCESS

For English Learners

Remind students that throughout this selection, unless Mrs. Pan is speaking Chinese to her son or to Lily, she is surrounded by people who speak a language she cannot understand. Some students learning English will recognize the situation, and might share with the class some of the things they do to feel less isolated in this situation. For example, when they first began to learn English, did hearing a new language all day long help them to learn it, or only confuse them more? Read aloud the sentence near the top of p. 386: "[Mrs. Pan] could not understand what they said for they spoke in English, but she understood that there was an argument." You might invite students to share with the class whether they were aware of the emotional content of what is being said if they didn't understand the words.

- Ask students what they think is meant by the sentence, "Old Mrs. Pan reflected on the difficulty of her position as a lady in a barbarous and strange country."

- Elicit from students that the sentence means that Mrs. Pan's options are limited, because she is a woman without English language skills in a strange country.

- After students have read the passage, ask them whether they are surprised that Mrs. Pan is willing to venture outside the house as part of her plan. Why or why not? Possible response: Some students may say that they would have expected Mrs. Pan to be too frightened or depressed to leave the house; others may suggest that she is now determined to arrange a marriage for Lili and will do whatever she needs to in order to accomplish this.

- Have students answer the Literary Analysis question on p. 388: How does this plan show that Mrs. Pan's character is changing? Answer: She is willing to do several very challenging things in order to fulfill her promise to Lili.

and laugh. They teased her often even now about her purpose, and Lili was so embarrassed by their laughter that she did not want to come anymore.

Old Mrs. Pan reflected on the difficulty of her position as a lady in a barbarous and strange country. Then she thought of her eldest grandson, Johnnie. On Saturday, when her son was at his office and her son's wife was at the market, she could coax Johnnie to lead her across the street to the china shop; she would pay him some money, and in the shop she would say she was looking for two bowls to match some that had been broken. It would be an <u>expedition</u>, but she might speak to the young man and tell him—what should she tell him? That must first be planned.

This was only Thursday and she had only two days to prepare. She was very restless during those two days, and she could not eat. Mr. Pan spoke of a doctor whom she indignantly refused to see, because he was a man and also because she was not ill. But Saturday came at last and everything came about as she planned. Her son went away, and then her son's wife, and she crept downstairs with much effort to the sidewalk where her grandson was playing marbles and beckoned him to her. The child was terrified to see her there and came at once, and she pressed a coin into his palm and pointed across the street with her cane.

"Lead me there," she commanded and, shutting her eyes tightly, she put her hand on his shoulder and allowed him to lead her to the shop. Then to her dismay he left her and ran back to play and she stood wavering on the threshold, feeling dizzy, and the young man saw her and came hurrying toward her. To her joy he spoke good Chinese, and the words fell sweetly upon her old ears.

"Ancient One, Ancient One," he chided[8] her kindly. "Come in and sit down. It is too much for you."

He led her inside the cool, dark shop and she sat down on a bamboo chair.

"I came to look for two bowls," she said faintly.

"Tell me the pattern and I will get them for you," he said. "Are they blue willow pattern or the thousand flowers?"

"Thousand flowers," she said in the same faint voice, "but I do not wish to disturb you."

"I am here to be disturbed," he replied with the utmost courtesy.

He brought out some bowls and set them on a small table before her and she fell to talking with him. He was very pleasant; his rather large face was shining with kindness and he laughed easily. Now that she saw him close, she was glad to notice that he was not too handsome; his nose and mouth were big, and he had big hands and feet.

"You look like a countryman," she said. "Where is your ancestral home?"

Literary Analysis
Static and Dynamic Characters How does this plan show that Mrs. Pan's character is changing?

expedition (eks' pə dish' ən) *n.* journey for a definite purpose

---

8. chided (chīd' əd) *v.* gently scolded.

"It is in the province of Shantung," he replied, "and there are not many of us here."

"That explains why you are so tall," she said. "These people from Canton are small. We of Szechuen are also big and our language is yours. I cannot understand the people of Canton."

From this they fell to talking of their own country, which he had never seen, and she told him about the village and how her son's father had left it many years ago to do business here in this foreign country and how he had sent for their son and then how she had been compelled to flee because the country was in fragments and torn between many leaders. When she had told this much, she found herself telling him how difficult it was to live here and how strange the city was to her and how she would never have looked out of the window had it not been for the sake of Lili Yang.

"Who is Lili Yang?" he asked.

Old Mrs. Pan did not answer him directly. That would not have been suitable. One does not speak of a reputable young woman to any man, not even one as good as this one. Instead she began a long speech about the virtues of young women who were not pretty, and how beauty in a woman made virtue unlikely, and how a woman not beautiful was always grateful to her husband and did not consider that she had done him a favor by the marriage, but rather that it was he who <u>conferred</u> the favor, so that she served him far better than she could have done were she beautiful.

To all this the young man listened, his small eyes twinkling with laughter.

"I take it that this Lili Yang is not beautiful," he said.

Old Mrs. Pan looked astonished. "I did not say so," she replied with spirit. "I will not say she is beautiful and I will not say she is ugly. What is beautiful to one is not so to another. Suppose you see her sometime for yourself, and then we will discuss it."

"Discuss what?" he demanded.

"Whether she is beautiful."

Suddenly she felt that she had come to a point and that she had better go home. It was enough for the first visit. She chose two bowls and paid for them and while he wrapped them up she waited in silence, for to say too much is worse than to say too little.

When the bowls were wrapped, the young man said courteously, "Let me lead you across the street, Ancient One."

So, putting her right hand on his left wrist, she let him lead her across and this time she did not shut her eyes, and she came home again feeling that she had been a long way and had accomplished much. When her daughter-in-law came home she said quite easily, "I went across the street and bought these two bowls."

Young Mrs. Pan opened her eyes wide. "My mother, how could you go alone?"

"I did not go alone," old Mrs. Pan said tranquilly. "My grandson led me across and young Mr. Lim brought me back."

Reading Strategy
Drawing Inferences
What details of their conversation help you decide whether old Mrs. Pan approves of this man?

conferred (kən furd′) v. granted or bestowed

28 ✔**Reading Check**
What does old Mrs. Pan discuss with the young man in the china shop?

The Good Deed ◆ 389

27 **Reading Strategy**
Drawing Inferences

- Read aloud the bracketed passage to students.
- As you read, have students record important details from this passage about Old Mrs. Pan in a chart like the one on p. 375. Students' charts should look similar to the following:

Words	Actions
"come see her sometime for yourself"	talks with him about her past, avoids speaking directly about Lili

Inference
Old Mrs. Pan approves of this man

▶ **Monitor Progress** After students have completed the passage, have them use their charts to answer the Reading Strategy question on p. 389: What details of their conversation help you decide whether old Mrs. Pan approves of this man?
Answer: The fact that she tells him so much about her life in China suggests that she trusts him. The fact that he finds her description of Lili amusing suggests that he is a person of humor and kindness, which also makes her approve of him.

28 ✔**Reading Check**

Answer: Old Mrs. Pan talks about her life in China and then discusses the problems that virtuous but plain women have in finding husbands.

389

- Ask students to summarize Mr. Pan's responses to his mother's ideas up to this point in the story.

- Lead students to see that Mr. Pan has been willing to listen to his mother but largely discounts her ideas and does not do anything about them.

- After students have read the passage, ask them to respond to the Literary Analysis question on p. 390: How do Mr. Pan's actions indicate that he is beginning to change?

Answer: He begins to help old Mrs. Pan with her plan, though he does not tell her he is doing so.

Each had spoken in her own language with helpful gestures.

Young Mrs. Pan was astonished and she said no more until her husband came home, when she told him. He laughed a great deal and said, "Do not interfere with our old one. She is enjoying herself. It is good for her."

㉙ But all the time he knew what his mother was doing and he joined in it without her knowledge. That is to say, he telephoned the same afternoon from his office to Miss Lili Yang, and when she answered, he said, "Please come and see my old mother again. She asks after you every day. Your visit did her much good."

Lili Yang promised, not for today but for a week hence, and when Mr. Pan went home he told his mother carelessly, as though it were nothing, that Lili Yang had called him up to say she was coming again next week.

Old Mrs. Pan heard this with secret excitement. She had not gone out again, but every day young Mr. Lim nodded to her and smiled, and once he sent her a small gift of fresh ginger root. She made up her mind slowly but she made it up well. When Lili Yang came again, she would ask her to take her to the china shop, pretending that she wanted to buy something, and she would introduce the two to each other; that much she would do. It was too much, but, after all, these were modern times, and this was a barbarous country, where it did not matter greatly whether the old customs were kept or not. The important thing was to find a husband for Lili, who was already twenty-seven years old.

So it all came about, and when Lili walked into her room the next week, while the fine weather still held, old Mrs. Pan greeted her with smiles. She seized Lili's small hand and noticed that the hand was very soft and pretty, as the hands of most plain-faced girls are, the gods being kind to such women and giving them pretty bodies when they see that ancestors have not bestowed pretty faces.

"Do not take off your foreign hat," she told Lili. "I wish to go across the street to that shop and buy some dishes as a gift for my son's wife. She is very kind to me."

Lili Yang was pleased to see the old lady so changed and cheerful and in all innocence she agreed and they went across the street and into the shop. Today there were customers, and old Mr. Lim was there too, as well as his son. He was a tall, withered man, and he wore a small beard under his chin. When he saw old Mrs. Pan he stopped what he was doing and brought her a chair to sit upon while she waited. As soon as his customer was gone, he introduced himself, saying that he knew her son.

"My son has told me of your honored visit last week," he said. "Please come inside and have some tea. I will have my son bring the dishes, and you can look at them in quiet. It is too noisy here."

She accepted his courtesy, and in a few minutes young Mr. Lim came back to the inner room with the dishes while a servant brought tea.

Old Mrs. Pan did not introduce Lili Yang, for it was not well to embarrass a woman, but young Mr. Lim boldly introduced himself, in English.

"Are you Miss Lili Yang?" he asked. "I am James Lim."

☀ ENRICHMENT: Social Studies

The Chinese Language

Chinese is one of the world's oldest languages. It is spoken throughout China, Singapore, Hong Kong, and Taiwan, as well as in the Chinese American communities of many large North American cities.

The Chinese language has no alphabet. It has about 50,000 characters, many of which must be learned by scholars and others who wish to read ancient Chinese literature and documents. However, people who know about 5,000 characters can read Chinese newspapers and other books.

Written Chinese is the same everywhere, but spoken Chinese has many different dialects that vary so greatly that someone from one region may not be able to understand someone from another region. The major Chinese languages are Mandarin, Cantonese, Hsiang, Kan-Hakka, Min, and Wu.

"How did you know my name?" Lili asked, astonished.

"I have met you before, not face to face, but through Mrs. Pan," he said, his small eyes twinkling. "She has told me more about you than she knows."

Lili blushed. "Mrs. Pan is so old-fashioned," she murmured. "You must not believe her."

"I shall only believe what I see for myself," he said gallantly. He looked at her frankly and Lili kept blushing. Old Mrs. Pan had not done her justice, he thought. The young woman had a nice, round face, the sort of face he liked. She was shy, and he liked that also. It was something new.

Meanwhile old Mrs. Pan watched all this with amazement. So this was the way it was: The young man began speaking immediately, and the young woman blushed. She wished that she knew what they were saying but perhaps it was better that she did not know.

She turned to old Mr. Lim, who was sitting across the square table sipping tea. At least here she could do her duty. "I hear your son is not married," she said in a tentative way.

"Not yet," Mr. Lim said. "He wants first to finish learning how to be a Western doctor."

"How old is he?" Mrs. Pan inquired.

"He is twenty-eight. It is very old but he did not make up his mind for some years, and the learning is long."

"Miss Lili Yang is twenty-seven," Mrs. Pan said in the same tentative voice.

The young people were still talking in English and not listening to them. Lili was telling James Lim about her work and about old Mrs. Pan. She was not blushing anymore; she had forgotten, it seemed, that he was a young man and she a young woman. Suddenly she stopped and blushed again. A woman was supposed to let a man talk about himself, not about her.

"Tell me about your work," she said. "I wanted to be a doctor, too, but it cost too much."

"I can't tell you here," he said. "There are customers waiting in the shop and it will take a long time. Let me come to see you, may I? I could come on Sunday when the shop is closed. Or we could take a ride on one of the riverboats. Will you? The weather is so fine."

"I have never been on a riverboat," she said. "It would be delightful."

She forgot her work and remembered that he was a young man and that she was a young woman. She liked his big face and the way his black hair fell back from his forehead and she knew that a day on the river could be a day in heaven.

The customers were getting impatient. They began to call out and he got up. "Next Sunday," he said in a low voice. "Let's start early. I'll be at the wharf at nine o'clock."

"We do not know each other," she said, reluctant and yet eager. Would he think she was too eager?

He laughed. "You see my respectable father, and I know old Mrs. Pan very well. Let them guarantee us."

Reading Strategy
Drawing Inferences What can you infer about Lili Yang from her actions?

Literary Analysis
Relationships Between Characters How does the relationship between Lili Yang and James Lim change during their conversation?

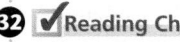 **Reading Check**

What happens when James Lim meets Lili Yang?

The Good Deed ◆ 391

Answers for p. 392

Review and Assess

1. Students might say that the successful matchmaking experience will open doors for Mrs. Pan, making her more outgoing and happy.

2. **(a)** She refuses to do anything and just sits in her room. **(b)** Homesickness and a sense of uselessness make her grow thinner and thinner.

3. **(a)** Mrs. Pan decides that she will arrange a marriage for Lili Yang. **(b)** The plan gets her out of the apartment and involved in the community.

4. **(a)** They are both American-born with Chinese parents; they both speak English; they both have an interest in medicine. **(b)** Mrs. Pan thinks they will be a good match because both are good people.

5. Choosing one's own mate clashes with the custom of arranged marriages. Both cultures respect family bonds.

6. **(a)** Children are not taught at home in the traditional way; they are not taught to revere their elders or learn Chinese. **(b)** Preserving diverse cultures allows us to learn from them.

He hurried away, and old Mrs. Pan said immediately to Lili, "I have chosen these four dishes. Please take them and have them wrapped. Then we will go home."

Lili obeyed, and when she was gone, old Mrs. Pan leaned toward old Mr. Lim.

"I wanted to get her out of the way," she said in a low and important voice. "Now, while she is gone, what do you say? Shall we arrange a match? We do not need a go-between. I stand as her mother, let us say, and you are his father. We must have their horoscopes read, of course, but just between us, it looks as though it is suitable, does it not?"

Mr. Lim wagged his head. "If you recommend her, Honorable Old Lady, why not?"

Why not, indeed? After all, things were not so different here, after all.

"What day is convenient for you?" she asked.

"Shall we say Sunday?" old Mr. Lim suggested.

"Why not?" she replied. "All days are good, when one performs a good deed, and what is better than to arrange a marriage?"

"Nothing is better," old Mr. Lim agreed. "Of all good deeds under heaven, it is the best."

They fell silent, both pleased with themselves, while they waited.

Review and Assess

Thinking About the Selection

1. **Respond:** How do you think Mrs. Pan's matchmaking experience will affect her life in the future?

2. **(a) Recall:** At the beginning of the story, how is Mrs. Pan behaving? **(b) Analyze Cause and Effect:** What are the causes of this behavior? How is her physical health affected?

3. **(a) Recall:** What does Mrs. Pan plan to do after she meets Lili Yang? **(b) Analyze Cause and Effect:** How does the plan change Mrs. Pan's life in New York?

4. **(a) Recall:** What do young Mr. Lim and Lili Yang have in common? **(b) Draw Conclusions:** Why does Mrs. Pan think they will be a good match?

5. **Interpret:** In what ways does the story reveal a clash of cultures? In what ways does it reveal similarities between cultures?

6. **(a) Evaluate:** According to the story, what valuable aspects of traditional Chinese life seem to be missing in Chinese American communities? **(b) Extend:** Why is it important to preserve diverse cultures?

Pearl S. Buck

(1892–1973)

Although Pearl Buck was born to American parents in West Virginia, she spent most of her first forty years in China. Her father was a missionary, and she grew up speaking both Chinese and English. It is not surprising, then, that most of Buck's literary works focus on China, its people, and its traditions.

Buck began publishing novels in the 1930s. Her second book, *The Good Earth* (1931), which earned a Pulitzer Prize, changed the way many Americans thought about the Chinese, erasing many false stereotypes. In 1938, Buck became the first American woman to win the Nobel Prize for Literature.

✎ ASSESSMENT PRACTICE: Reading Comprehension

Recognizing Cause and Effect   (For more practice, see Test Preparation Workbook, p. 26.)

Many tests ask students to recognize cause-and-effect relationships in a reading passage. Use this sample.

She was a decent, plain, good girl and, left to herself, Mrs. Pan could predict, nothing at all would happen. She would wither away like a dying flower. Old Mrs. Pan forgot herself for the first time since she had been hurried away from the village without even being allowed to stop and see that the salted cabbage, drying on ropes across the big courtyard, was brought in for the winter.

Mrs. Pan forgets herself because—

A she is unhappy about the girl's looks.

B she can think only of the salted cabbage.

C she regrets hasty departures.

D she is thinking about someone else.

Guide students to see that the passage focuses on Mrs. Pan's reaction to the girl (the cause), and that the effect of her interest is *D*, to forget herself.

Review and Assess

Literary Analysis

Static and Dynamic Characters

1. Is old Mrs. Pan a **dynamic** or a **static character**? Explain.
2. How does Mr. Pan change during "The Good Deed"? Using a diagram like the one here, cite examples of his attitude at the beginning, the end, and throughout the story.

3. Is Lili Yang a dynamic or a static character? Explain your answer.

Connecting Literary Elements

4. How does Mrs. Pan's **relationship** with her son change during the course of "The Good Deed"?
5. (a) Why does Mrs. Pan relate so well to both Lili Yang and James Lim? (b) How does connecting with them change her?
6. Why do you think Lili and James interact so well once they meet?

Reading Strategy

Drawing Inferences

7. What **inferences** can you draw about young Mrs. Pan based on the fact that old Mrs. Pan likes her?
8. What can you infer about Lili Yang based on her treatment of Mrs. Pan?
9. (a) What inferences can you draw about the feelings Lili Yang and James Lim have for each other? (b) List details from the story to support your inferences.

Extend Understanding

10. **Cultural Connection:** Do you think it is important for people to hold on to traditions as well as to accept changes of culture? Give examples to support your response.

Quick Review

A **dynamic character** changes during the course of a literary work.

A **static character** does not change during a literary work.

Relationships between characters are the interactions and feelings that pass between people in a story.

To **draw inferences,** make logical assumptions based on the evidence given.

 Take It to the Net
www.phschool.com
Take the interactive self-test online to check your understanding of the selection.

The Good Deed ◆ 393

---

❶ Vocabulary Development

1. push away   3. drive forward
2. drive out

Spelling Strategy

1. insisted   3. suspending
2. reluctantly

Fluency: Contrasting Definitions

1. thoughtfully; scornfully
2. a long trip; to speed up
3. these words are synonyms
4. restrained; strongly affected
5. these words are synonyms
6. angrily; persistently
7. attacked; helped
8. granted; guessed
9. forced; threw out

❷ Grammar

1. because Lili was not married.; Why?
2. when his mother revealed her plan.; When?
3. If the two young people meet,; Under what condition?
4. While Lili Yang and James Lim made plans to meet,; Under what condition? or When?
5. so that Mr. Lim could help a customer.; Why?

Writing Application

1. Mrs. Pan was unhappy when she first came to the United States.
2. Mrs. Pan went to the store so that she could meet the young man who had smiled at her.
3. Lili Yang met Mrs. Pan after Mr. and Mrs. Pan called her.

Integrate Language Skills

❶ Vocabulary Development Lesson

Word Analysis: Latin Root -pel-

Compelled, meaning "forced to act," contains the Latin root *-pel-*, which means "to drive" or "to push." On your paper, match each word that contains the root *-pel-* with its definition.

1. repel   a. drive forward
2. expel   b. drive out
3. propel   c. push away

Spelling Strategy

When a word ends in two consonants, keep both consonants when adding a suffix. For example, *repress + -ed = repressed*. Add the suffixes shown to these words:

1. insist (*-ed*)
2. reluctant (*-ly*)
3. suspend (*-ing*)

❷ Grammar Lesson

Adverb Clauses

A subordinate clause is a group of words that contains a subject and a verb but cannot stand alone. An **adverb clause** is a subordinate clause that modifies a verb, an adjective, or an adverb by telling *where*, *why*, *how*, *to what extent*, or *under what condition*. In the following example, the adverb clause is italicized.

> **Example:** Young Mrs. Pan was astonished, and she said no more *until her husband came home*, . . . (When?)

Practice Identify the adverb clause in each sentence below, and tell what question it answers.

1. She worried because Lili was not married.

𝒲𝒢 *Prentice Hall Writing and Grammar Connection: Chapter 20, Section 2*

394 ◆ *Turning Points*

Fluency: Contrasting Definitions

Review the words in the vocabulary list on page 375. Then, explain the differences between the following pairs of words. Use a dictionary to help define any words you do not know.

1. contemplatively, contemptuously
2. expedition, expedite
3. abashed, ashamed
4. repressed, impressed
5. revere, respect
6. indignantly, insistently
7. assailed, assisted
8. conferred, inferred
9. compelled, expelled

2. Mr. Pan listened when his mother revealed her plan.
3. If the two young people meet, they may marry some day.
4. While Lili Yang and James Lim made plans to meet, Mrs. Pan talked with old Mr. Lim.
5. Their talk was cut short so that Mr. Lim could help a customer.

Writing Application Expand each sentence below by adding an adverb clause.

1. Mrs. Pan was unhappy.
2. Mrs. Pan went to the store.
3. Lili Yang met Mrs. Pan.

Writing Lesson

Award Speech for a Character

Several characters in "The Good Deed" could win a community award for helping others. Write a brief speech introducing an award and explaining why the character deserves to win it.

Prewriting   Choose a character, and devise an award. Then, brainstorm for qualities that an award winner should possess. Select the strongest quality, and describe how the character demonstrates it.

Drafting   In an introduction, give the name of the award and identify a quality that a winner should possess. Then, name the winner, and provide examples or anecdotes to explain why he or she deserves the honor. In your draft, illustrate why the character deserves the award.

Model: Writing an Introduction

> The Chinese Star Award honors someone who shows respect for others in the Chinese community and for Chinese customs. Our winner has shown these qualities. For example, . . .

Starting with the award name and purpose emphasizes what is special about the award and its winner.

Revising   Read your draft, and circle the quality that the winner possesses. Highlight supporting examples, and add more if necessary.

WG *Prentice Hall Writing and Grammar Connection: Chapter 29, Section 1*

Extension Activities

Listening and Speaking Conduct an **interview** with old Mrs. Pan for a radio program about the experiences of recent immigrants. With a partner, research to learn about the experiences of immigrants and the challenges they face in fitting into American society. Follow these steps:

1. Combine your research with ideas from the story.
2. Develop interview questions and responses.
3. Assign roles: Mrs. Pan and the radio host.

Conduct the interview in front of your class. **[Group Activity]**

Research and Technology In the story, old Mrs. Pan notes that people from different parts of China speak differently. Prepare a **multimedia presentation** in which you focus on culture and traditions in different regions of China. Use quotations, articles, photographs, recipes, maps, or recordings to present information on languages, social conventions, art, music, and food in China.

 Take It to the Net   www.phschool.com

Go online for an additional research activity using the Internet.

The Good Deed ◆ 395

---

❸ Writing Lesson

- Have students list the characters from the selection whom they believe deserve a community award for helping others.
- Ask the class to vote on one award winner. Then, have them brainstorm for qualities they wish to highlight in their award speech to honor this person.
- Use the Writing Lesson to guide students in developing an introduction for such an award speech.
- Ask volunteers to present their speeches to the class.

❹ Listening and Speaking

- Have the class pair up.
- Based on information from the text and other research, have whichever partner is the interviewer conduct an interview with the partner playing Mrs. Pan about the character's life experiences.
- After pairs have practiced their presentation, ask volunteers to give their interview for the class.
- Use the rubric for Interview Techniques, p. 27 in **Performance Assessment and Portfolio Management,** to assess students' interviews.

**CUSTOMIZE INSTRUCTION
For Universal Access**

To address different learning styles, use the activities suggested in the **Extension Activities** booklet, p. 26.

- For Verbal/Linguistic and Visual/Spatial Learners, use Activity 5.
- For Verbal/Linguistic and Logical/Mathematical Learners, use Activity 6.
- For Verbal/Linguistic and Bodily/Kinesthetic Learners, use Activity 7.

ASSESSMENT RESOURCES

The following resources can be used to assess students' knowledge and skills.

Selection Assessment

- **Formal Assessment,** Selection Test, pp. 88–90
- **Open Book Test,** pp. 76–78
- **Got It! Assessment Videotapes,** Tape 2
- **Test Bank Software**
- ***Take It to the Net***
  Visit www.phschool.com for self-tests and additional questions on "A Good Deed."

Listening and Speaking Rubric

- **Performance Assess. and Portfolio Mgmt.,** p. 27

PRENTICE HALL *ASSESSMENT SYSTEM*

- **Workbook**
- **Skill Book**
- **Transparencies**
- **CD-ROM**

Thoughts of Hanoi ✦ Auto Wreck ✦ Pride ✦ Before the Law

Lesson Objectives

1. **To analyze and respond to literary elements**
   - Literary Analysis: Theme
   - Comparing Literary Works
2. **To read, comprehend, analyze, and critique poems and a parable**
   - Reading Strategy: Evaluating a Writer's Message
   - Reading Check questions
   - Review and Assess questions
   - Assessment Practice (ATE)
3. **To develop word analysis skills, fluency, and systematic vocabulary**
   - Vocabulary Development Lesson: Latin Word Root: *-sat-*
4. **To understand and apply written and oral language conventions**
   - Spelling Strategy
   - Grammar Lesson: Noun Clauses
5. **To understand and apply appropriate writing and research strategies**
   - Writing Lesson: Analysis of an Image
   - Extension Activity: Contrasting Maps
6. **To understand and apply listening and speaking strategies**
   - Extension Activity: Improvisational Skit

STEP-BY-STEP TEACHING GUIDE	PACING GUIDE
PRETEACH	
Motivate Students and Provide Background	
Use the Motivation activity (ATE p. 396)	5 min.
Read and discuss the Preview material and Background information (SE/ATE p. 396)	5 min.
Introduce the Concepts	
Introduce the Literary Analysis and Reading Strategy (SE/ATE p. 397)	15 min.
Pronounce the vocabulary words and read their definitions (SE p. 397)	5 min.
TEACH	
Monitor Comprehension	
Informally monitor comprehension by circulating while students read independently or in groups	15 min.
Monitor students' comprehension with the Reading Check notes (SE/ATE pp. 399, 405)	as students read
Develop vocabulary with Vocabulary notes (SE pp. 401, 405, 406)	as students read
Develop Understanding	
Develop students' understanding of theme with Literary Analysis annotations (SE pp. 399, 405; ATE pp. 399, 401, 402, 405)	10 min.
Develop students' understanding of evaluating a writer's message with Reading Strategy annotations (ATE pp. 399, 400, 405)	10 min.
ASSESS	
Assess Mastery	
Assess students' mastery of the Reading Strategy and Literary Analysis by having them answer the Review and Assess questions (SE/ATE p. 407)	20 min.
Use one or more of the print and media Assessment Resources (ATE p. 409)	up to 50 min.
EXTEND	
Apply Understanding	
Have students complete the Vocabulary Development Lesson and the Grammar Lesson (SE p. 408)	20 min.
Apply students' knowledge of the forms of the verb *to be* using the Writing Lesson (SE p. 409)	45 min.
Apply students' understanding using one or more of the Extension Activities (SE p. 409)	20–90 min.

A **ACCELERATED INSTRUCTION:**
Use the strategies and activities identified with an **A**.

UNIVERSAL ACCESS
- ● = Below Level Students
- ▲ = On-Level Students
- ■ = Above Level Students

Time and Resource Manager

RESOURCES		
PRINT 📖	**TRANSPARENCIES** 🗂	**TECHNOLOGY** 💿 🎧 📼
• **Beyond Literature,** Career Connection: Emergency Medical Technician, p. 27 ▲ ■		• **Interest Grabber Video,** Tape 2 ● ▲ ■
• **Selection Support Workbook:** ● ▲ ■ Literary Analysis, p. 108 Reading Strategy, p. 107 Build Vocabulary, p. 105	• **Literary Analysis and Reading Transparencies,** pp. 53 and 54 ● ▲ ■	
		• **Listening to Literature** ● ▲ ■ Audiocassettes, Side 13 Audio CDs, CD 8
• **Literatura en español** ● ▲ • **Literary Analysis for Enrichment** ■		
• **Formal Assessment:** Selection Test, pp. 91–93 ● ▲ ■ • **Open Book Test,** pp. 79–81 ● ▲ ■ • **Performance Assessment and Portfolio Management,** pp. 16, 28 ● ▲ ■ • PRENTICE HALL ASSESSMENT *SYSTEM* ● ▲ ■	• PRENTICE HALL ASSESSMENT *SYSTEM* ● ▲ ■ Skills Practice Answers and Explanations on Transparencies	• **Test Bank Software** ● ▲ ■ • **Got It! Assessment Videotapes,** Tape 2 ● ▲
• **Selection Support Workbook:** ● ▲ ■ Build Grammar Skills, p. 106 • **Writing and Grammar,** Platinum Level ● ▲ ■ • **Extension Activities,** p. 27 ● ▲ ■	• **Daily Language Practice Transparencies** ● ▲ • **Writing Models and Graphic Organizers on Transparencies,** p. 71 ● ▲ ■	• **Writing and Grammar iText CD-ROM** ● ▲ ■ 💻 *Take It to the Net* www.phschool.com

BLOCK SCHEDULING: Use one 90-minute class period to preteach the selection and have students read it. Use a second 90-minute class period to assess students' mastery of skills and have them complete one of the Extension Activities.

Step-by-Step Teaching Guide
for pp. 396–397

Motivation

Display pictures with bold headlines from newspapers and magazines, depicting the effects of natural disasters, wars, or accidents. Help students recognize that the media uses pictures like these because they grab attention and help sell publications. Lead a discussion about why people's attention is captured by tragic or frightening scenes. Then, guide students to recognize that traumatic events can be turning points for those involved and for those who witness them—either live or through the media. These events may have such a deep emotional effect that people who experience them are forever changed. Suggest that students keep this in mind as they read the selections.

▣ Interest Grabber Video

As an alternative, play "The Roots of the Vietnam War" on Tape 2 to engage student interest.

❶ Background

History

Just as Vietnam was divided during the war, the United States came to be divided on the legitimacy of the war. At first very few people protested, but when more and more Americans were killed, the country gradually questioned whether the military action should continue. Protesters also pointed out the terrible toll the war was taking on Vietnam, and made the point that the Vietnamese had a right to choose their own form of government without U.S. involvement. Eventually, based on discord at home and the victories of the Vietnamese forces overseas, the United States withdrew in April of 1975.

Prepare to Read

Thoughts of Hanoi ◆ Auto Wreck ◆ Pride ◆
Before the Law

 Take It to the Net

Visit www.phschool.com for interactive activities and instruction related to these selections, including

- background
- graphic organizers
- literary elements
- reading strategies

Preview

Connecting to the Literature

If you could control all the events that affect your life, you would win every game and pass every test. Sometimes, however, life throws you a curve ball. These selections show how people respond to circumstances that are (or seem to be) beyond their control.

❶ Background

Nguyen Thi Vinh wrote "Thoughts of Hanoi" about her home country, Vietnam, which was torn apart by a long civil war that lasted from just after World War II until 1975. A 1954 treaty divided the country into South Vietnam, which was supported by the United States, and North Vietnam, which was controlled by a communist government. Families became separated, and even former friends fought against each other.

396 ◆ *Turning Points*

TEACHING RESOURCES

The following resources can be used to enrich or extend the instruction for pp. 396–397.

Motivation

▣ **Interest Grabber Video,** Tape 2 ▣

Background

📖 **Beyond Literature,** p. 27

 Take It to the Net

Visit www.phschool.com for background and hotlinks for the selections.

Literary Analysis

▤ **Literary Analysis and Reading Transparencies,** Theme, p. 54

Reading

📖 **Selection Support:** Reading Strategy, p. 107; Build Vocabulary, p. 105

▤ **Literary Analysis and Reading Transparencies,** Evaluating a Writer's Message, p. 53

▣ **BLOCK SCHEDULING:** Resources marked with this symbol provide varied instruction during 90-minute blocks.

❶ Literary Analysis

Theme

The **theme** of a work is its central meaning—the comment the writer is making about human life and values. The theme is seldom stated directly but is usually revealed, instead, through the events and images that the writer presents. As these lines from "Pride" demonstrate, the poet not only describes how rocks act, but her description also offers a comment on how people live.

> They don't move, so the cracks stay hidden.
> A kind of pride.

As you read these selections, think about what each writer is saying about human life and values.

Comparing Literary Works

Giving rocks human traits, as in "Pride," is an example of a literary technique called personification. **Personification** is describing an object, animal, or idea as if it had human characteristics. Compare how the writers of these selections use this technique to imply truths about how people feel and act. Look for the following: what the writer personifies, which human characteristics the writer assigns, and why the writer chooses to personify them.

❷ Reading Strategy

Evaluating a Writer's Message

You **evaluate a writer's message** by identifying it and then judging whether it makes sense and is well supported. In "Pride," the poet conveys a message about how troubles affect people. To evaluate her message, think about how well she communicates and supports it. Identify the message in each of these selections, and then use a graphic organizer like the one here to evaluate it.

Strengths

Original images	Easy to understand

Message

Weaknesses

Vocabulary Development

deranged (dē rānjd´) *adj.* unsettled (p. 401)

convalescents (kän´ və les´ ənts) *n.* people who are recovering from illness (p. 401)

banal (bā´ nəl) *adj.* dull or stale because of overuse (p. 401)

expedient (ek spē´ dē ənt) *adj.* convenient (p. 401)

importunity (im´ pôr t‾o‾on´ i tē) *n.* persistence in requesting (p. 405)

contemplation (kän´ təm plā´ shən) *n.* thoughtful inspection (p. 405)

insatiable (in sā´ shə bəl) *adj.* unable to be satisfied (p. 406)

Thoughts of Hanoi / Pride / Auto Wreck / Before the Law ◆ 397

❷ Literary Analysis

Theme

- Tell students that the *theme* of a selection is its central meaning—the writer's main point about life, human nature, or values.

- Call students' attention to the example from the poem "Pride." Explain that the theme of a work can often be identified by exploring its central images.

- Use the Theme transparency in **Literary Analysis and Reading Transparencies,** p. 54, to demonstrate how the theme is expressed in one of the poems.

- Use the instruction for Comparing Literary Works to give students an example of personification. Invite them to look for more examples as they read the selections.

❸ Reading Strategy

Evaluating a Writer's Message

- Point out to students that after they have identified a theme, they should evaluate how well the writer has communicated it.

- Invite students to look for the ways in which the writers communicate their messages. For example, are their images clear and original? Are their ideas supported with sound evidence?

- Have students use the Evaluating a Writer's Message transparency in **Literary Analysis and Reading Transparencies,** p. 53, to record the evidence they will use to evaluate each message.

Vocabulary Development

- Pronounce each vocabulary word for students, and read the definitions as a class. Have students identify any words with which they are already familiar.

CUSTOMIZE INSTRUCTION FOR UNIVERSAL ACCESS

For Less Proficient Readers	For English Learners	For Advanced Readers
Students may have trouble identifying the theme when it is implied rather than stated. Remind them of the definition of *symbolism,* and help them determine which objects in the selections symbolize aspects of life or human nature.	Students may have trouble distinguishing between the subject and theme of each work. Explain that the word *subject* refers to what the piece is about, and the word *theme* refers to the central idea that the author wants to convey.	Once students have identified the theme of each selection, have them compare and contrast how each theme is conveyed. What symbols and images do the writers use? Which themes emerge at the end of the selection, and which are communicated from the beginning?

 E-Teach

Visit E-Teach at www.phschool.com for teachers' essays on how to teach, with questions and answers.

CUSTOMIZE INSTRUCTION
For Visual/Spatial Learners

These selections are rich with imagery. Invite pairs of students to choose and describe an image to a partner. The partners can add visual details, orally or in writing, to further enrich the image. Partners can then exchange roles, with one describing a scene and the other adding details.

❶ About the Selection

"Thoughts of Hanoi" looks at the deep and conflicted feelings associated with having a peacetime friend who has become a wartime enemy.

❷ ▶Critical Viewing

Answer: The figures in the boat are able to enjoy their friendship in peace, whereas the characters in the poem have been separated and turned into enemies by war.

❶ •Thoughts of Hanoi

Nguyen Thi Vinh
Translated by Nguyen Ngoc Bich
With Burton Raffel and W. S. Merwin

❷ ▲ **Critical Viewing** How do the figures in the boat compare and contrast with the characters in the poem? [**Connect**]

TEACHING RESOURCES

The following resources can be used to enrich or extend the instruction for pp. 398–406.

Literary Analysis

📄 **Writing Models and Graphic Organizers on Transparencies**, p. 71 ▪

📖 **Selection Support:** Literary Analysis, p. 108

Reading

🎧 **Listening to Literature Audiocassettes**, Side 13

💿 **Listening to Literature Audio CDs**, CD 8 ▪

▪ **BLOCK SCHEDULING:** Resources marked with this symbol provide varied instruction during 90-minute blocks.

The night is deep and chill
as in early autumn. Pitchblack,
it thickens after each lightning flash.
I dream of Hanoi:
5 Co-ngu[1] Road
ten years of separation
the way back sliced by a frontier of hatred.
I want to bury the past
to burn the future
10 still I yearn
still I fear
those endless nights
waiting for dawn.

Brother,
15 how is Hang Dao[2] now?
How is Ngoc Son[3] temple?
Do the trains still run
each day from Hanoi
to the neighboring towns?
20 To Bac-ninh, Cam-giang, Yen-bai,[4]
the small villages, islands
of brown thatch in a lush green sea?

The girls
    bright eyes
25   ruddy cheeks
    four-piece dresses
        raven-bill scarves
    sowing harvesting
        spinning weaving
30   all year round,
the boys
    ploughing
        transplanting
    in the fields
35   in their shops
    running across
        the meadow at evening
    to fly kites
        and sing alternating songs.

40 Stainless blue sky,
    jubilant voices of children
stumbling through the alphabet,
    village graybeards strolling to the temple,

---

1. **Co-ngu** (cô gōō)
2. **Hang Dao** (häṅ dou)
3. **Ngoc Son** (nōk sōn)
4. **Bac-ninh** (bäk nin), **Cam-giang** (cäm giäṅ), **Yen-bai** (ēṅ bī)

Literary Analysis
Theme How might the speaker's questions about Hanoi support the theme of the poem?

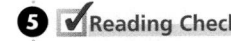 **Reading Check**
How many years have passed since the speaker was in Hanoi?

❸ **Literary Analysis**
Theme

• Ask students to identify at least two questions the speaker asks in the bracketed passage.
  Answer: She asks about the condition of Hang Dao and the Ngoc Sun temple. She also asks whether the trains still run.

• Point out that these questions show that the speaker still cares deeply about her homeland.

• Then, ask students the Literary Analysis question on p. 399: How might the speaker's questions about Hanoi support the theme of the poem?
  Answer: The questions ask how the war has influenced the country, which is one of the poem's themes.

❹ **Reading Strategy**
Evaluating a Writer's Message

• Have students point out the sensory details the speaker uses to describe Hanoi before the war.

• Then, ask how these details add to the writer's message that war changes the traditional way of life.
  Answer: The simple, peaceful images of Hanoi before the war contrast with the violent images brought about by the war.

❺ ✔**Reading Check**
Answer: Ten years have passed since the speaker was in Hanoi.

CUSTOMIZE INSTRUCTION FOR UNIVERSAL ACCESS

For Less Proficient Readers	For Advanced Students
The irregular layout of the poem's lines may be confusing to some students. Have them note the sections that depict the girls and boys. Point out that "The girls" has several indented lines beneath it, almost like an outline. All the lines through "all year round" refer to the girls. Ask students to identify the lines that describe the boys. Again, remind them to think of an outline.	Point out the metaphor in line 7, and explain that the "frontier of hatred" is the imaginary line dividing North Vietnam from South Vietnam, making enemies of countrymen. Ask students to identify other metaphors in the poem, such as "those roots go deep" in line 65, and determine what is being compared.

❻ Reading Strategy

Evaluating a Writer's Message

- Remind students that the writer's message is about the war's destructive focus on land and power.

- Have students explain how the bracketed passage relates to the writer's message.
  Answer: The writer suggests that friendship and family matter more than land and power.

Answers for p. 400

Review and Assess

1. Students might describe a time when a miscommunication was cleared up and an enemy became a friend.

2. **(a)** The speaker has been away from Hanoi for ten years. **(b)** The speaker fears experiencing the hatred and destruction caused by the war.

3. **(a)** The speaker is addressing a former friend who still lives in Vietnam. **(b)** The person is called Brother because the two are countrymen, though one has left.

4. **(a)** The speaker fears they will meet in battle. **(b)** The speaker does not want to shoot her friend.

5. Students might say that it is possible to shoot someone "not with hatred" because a soldier might feel he or she is fighting for a cause, not against a person.

---

grandmothers basking in twilight sun,
45   chewing betel leaves
while the children run—

Brother,
how is all that now?
Or is it obsolete?
50 Are you like me,
reliving the past,
imagining the future?
Do you count me as a friend
or am I the enemy in your eyes?
55 Brother, I am afraid
that one day I'll be with the March-North Army
meeting you on your way to the South.
I might be the one to shoot you then
or you me
60 but please
not with hatred.

For don't you remember how it was,
you and I in school together,
plotting our lives together?
65 Those roots go deep!

Brother, we are men,
conscious of more
than material needs.
How can this happen to us
70 my friend
my foe?

Review and Assess

Thinking About the Selection

1. **Respond:** Explain a situation in which someone you thought of as a "foe" became a friend.
2. **(a) Recall:** How long has the speaker been away from Hanoi? **(b) Speculate:** Why has the speaker not been back for a visit?
3. **(a) Recall:** Whom is the speaker addressing? **(b) Infer:** Why does the speaker call the person he is addressing "brother"?
4. **(a) Recall:** According to the speaker, how might the speaker and the other person meet some day? **(b) Infer:** Why is the speaker afraid of this meeting?
5. **Make a Judgment:** Do you think it is possible to shoot someone in war "not with hatred," as the poet describes? Explain your answer.

400 ◆ *Turning Points*

Nguyen Thi Vinh

(b. 1924)
Born in Hanoi, Nguyen Thi Vinh (noo´ yin tī vin) fled with her family to Saigon in the south when the communists took over the northern part of Vietnam in the late 1940s. She became a prominent editor, publishing executive, and writer of many novels, poems, and short stories. Among her works that are translated into English are *The Poetry of Nguyen Thi Vinh* and her story "Two Sisters," which appears in the anthology *Vietnamese Short Stories*.

She remained in Vietnam for eight years after the fall of Saigon to the communists in 1975, but then she joined her family in Norway as a refugee.

✹ ENRICHMENT: Social Studies

Hanoi

Located in the north on the Red River, Hanoi is the capital of Vietnam. In 1010, the first ruler of the Ly dynasty made Hanoi his capital city. It remained the capital until 1802, when the Nguyen dynasty moved the capital to the south. The name Hanoi was given to the city by the Nguyen. It means "city between two rivers." Under French rule, Hanoi again became the capital in 1902.

When Vietnam was divided in 1954, Hanoi became the capital of North Vietnam. From 1965 to 1972, Hanoi was the target of frequent bombings. Although most of Hanoi was destroyed, the Vietnamese rebuilt the city, and it again became the capital when the country was reunited in 1976.

Have students, knowing these facts, discuss why the poet Nguyen Thi Vinh selected Hanoi rather than another Vietnamese city as the subject of her poem.

Auto Wreck

Karl Shapiro

Its quick soft silver bell beating, beating,
And down the dark one ruby flare
Pulsing out red light like an artery,
The ambulance at top speed floating down
5 Past beacons and illuminated clocks
Wings in a heavy curve, dips down,
And brakes speed, entering the crowd.
The doors leap open, emptying light;
Stretchers are laid out, the mangled lifted
10 And stowed into the little hospital.
Then the bell, breaking the hush, tolls once,
And the ambulance with its terrible cargo
Rocking, slightly rocking, moves away,
As the doors, an afterthought, are closed.

15 We are <u>deranged</u>, walking among the cops
Who sweep glass and are large and composed.
One is still making notes under the light.
One with a bucket douches ponds of blood
Into the street and gutter.
20 One hangs lanterns on the wrecks that cling,
Empty husks of locusts, to iron poles.

Our throats were tight as tourniquets,[1]
Our feet were bound with splints, but now,
Like <u>convalescents</u> intimate and gauche,[2]
25 We speak through sickly smiles and warn
With the stubborn saw of common sense,
The grim joke and the <u>banal</u> resolution.
The traffic moves around with care,
But we remain, touching a wound
30 That opens to our richest horror.
Already old, the question Who shall die?
Becomes unspoken Who is innocent?

For death in war is done by hands;
Suicide has cause and stillbirth, logic;
35 And cancer, simple as a flower, blooms.
But this invites the occult mind,
Cancels our physics with a sneer,
And spatters all we knew of denouement[3]
Across the <u>expedient</u> and wicked stones.

---

1. **tourniquets** (tu̇r´ nə ketz) *n.* bandages to stop bleeding by compressing a blood vessel.
2. **gauche** (gōsh) *adj.* awkward.
3. **denouement** (dā´ no̅o̅ män´) *n.* outcome or the end.

deranged (dē rānjd´) *adj.* unsettled

convalescents (kän´ və les´ ənts) *n.* people who are recovering from illness

banal (bā´ nəl) *adj.* dull or stale because of overuse

expedient (ek spē´ dē´ ənt) *adj.* convenient

Karl Shapiro

(1913–2000)

American poet Karl Shapiro was a college professor, a critic, and an editor, as well as a Pulitzer Prize-winning poet. Shapiro said that he would like to see the elimination "of the line between poetry and prose." The harsh realism of "Auto Wreck" reflects Shapiro's preferred poetic style.

Auto Wreck ◆ 401

❼ About the Selections

The tone of these two poems shows that turning points can come upon one with a terrible and stunning suddenness ("Auto Wreck") or slowly over a period of time ("Pride").

❽ Literary Analysis

Personification

- As students read the bracketed passage, ask them to find the simile in the first few lines. What two things are being compared?
Answer: The red light of the ambulance is compared to an artery pulsing out blood.

- Point out that this is an example of personification. Ask students to identify other examples of personification as they read the poem.

❾ Literary Analysis

Theme

- Ask students to identify the kinds of death the speaker seems to think are understandable.
Possible response: Death in war, by suicide, at birth, and from cancer all seem understandable to the speaker.

- Then, have students identify the theme—the main message—of the poem.
Answer: Some forms of death, such as the sudden death caused by a car accident, seem to defy logic and order. If we see such a death, our outlook on life may be changed forever.

CUSTOMIZE INSTRUCTION FOR UNIVERSAL ACCESS

For Less Proficient Readers	For Gifted/Talented Students
Complex sentence structure makes the first seven lines of this poem particularly difficult. Help students find the subject (ambulance) and complete predicate with three verbs (<u>wings</u> in a heavy curve, <u>dips</u> down, <u>brakes</u> speed) in these opening lines.	Point out that in line 24, the speaker calls the spectators "convalescents." Explain that he is comparing them to people who feel that they are recovering from a life-threatening illness. Have students identify and explain other metaphors and similes in the poem, such as those in lines 22, 26, and 35.

10 ▶Critical Viewing

Answer: The rock stands strong despite being weathered by water and wind.

11 Literary Analysis

Theme

• Ask students to identify the subject of this poem.
Answer: The subject is a rock that has hidden cracks.

▶ Monitor Progress Invite students to identify the theme of this poem and to distinguish it from the subject.
Possible response: The theme is that with people, as with rocks, a crack that starts out small can turn into a complete break under pressure. The rock, which is the subject of the poem, represents a person.

12 Literary Analysis

Personification

• Explain to students that in this poem, the rock is being personified.

• Ask the class to identify the lines in which the rock is personified.
Answer: Examples of personification include: "they lie on their backs," "A kind of pride," and "And suddenly the rock has an open wound."

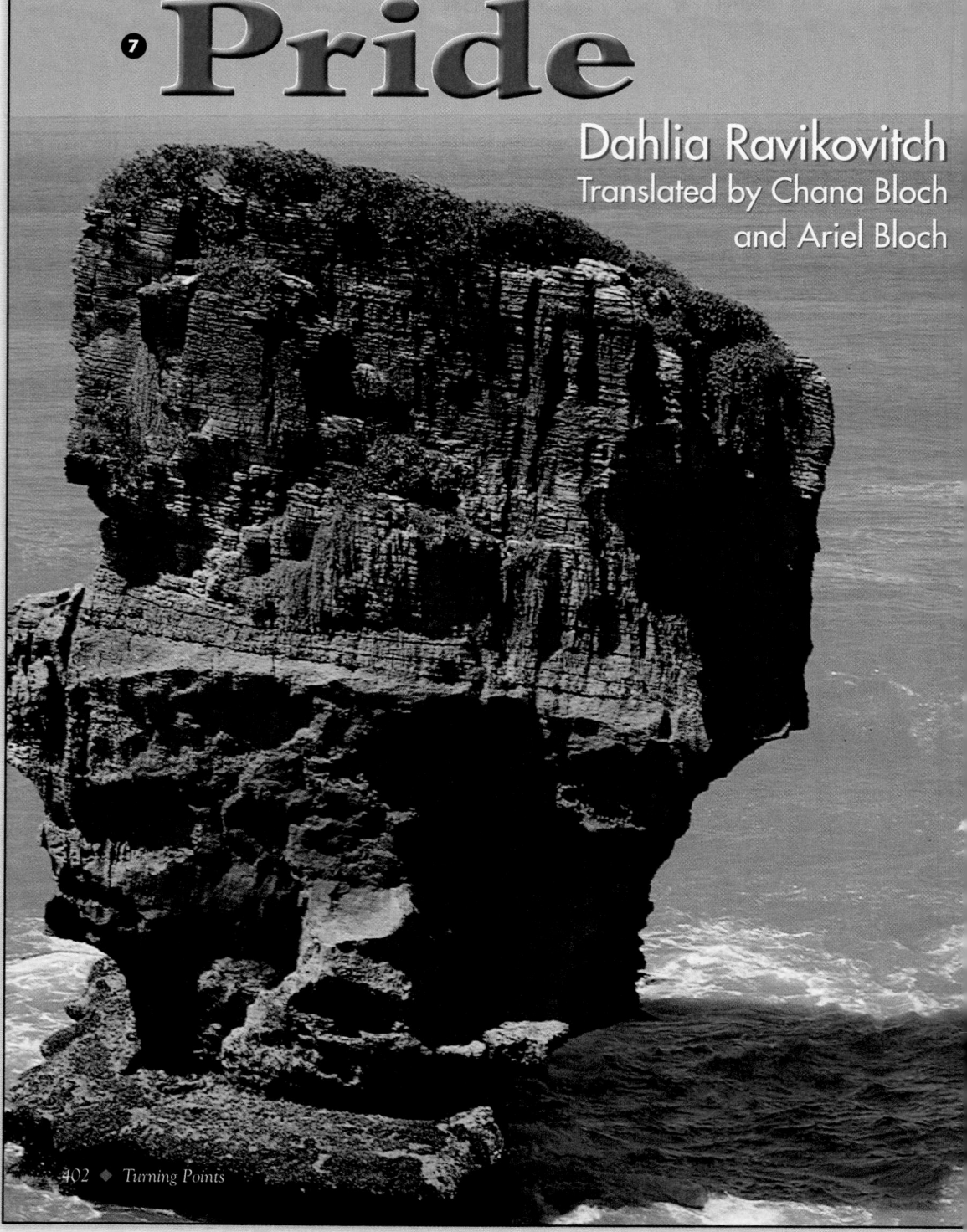

⁊ **Pride**

Dahlia Ravikovitch
Translated by Chana Bloch and Ariel Bloch

402 ◆ Turning Points

⚜ ENRICHMENT: Science Connection

Weathering

Weathering is visible all around us. The constant freezing and heating of rock surfaces gradually breaks down even the hardest composition. Weathering occurs faster in areas that have more water: In the arid southwest, weathering occurs slowly, while in humid regions, weathering speeds up. Weathering also occurs rapidly in areas that experience wide temperature changes—hot during the day, and freezing at night.

While a large rock, such as the one shown here, weathers, life colonizes it. As rock material eventually breaks down into pebbles and soil, this material fills the rock's cracks, and the seeds of mosses and other plants find a place to take root and grow. Plant life brings insects, which in turn bring birds. Ask students what will eventually become of the parts of the rock that loosen and fall into the sea.

I tell you, even rocks crack,
and not because of age.
For years they lie on their backs
in the heat and the cold,
5   so many years,
it almost seems peaceful.
They don't move, so the cracks stay hidden.
A kind of pride.
Years pass over them, waiting.
10 Whoever is going to shatter them
hasn't come yet.
And so the moss flourishes, the seaweed
whips around,
the sea pushes through and rolls back—
15 the rocks seem motionless.
Till a little seal comes to rub against them,
comes and goes away.
And suddenly the rock has an open wound.
I told you, when rocks break, it happens by surprise.
And people, too.

⑩ ◄ Critical Viewing
What details of this
photograph convey the
rock's sense of pride?

Review and Assess

Thinking About the Selections

1. **Respond:** Suggest another title that you think would fit one of these poems.
2. **(a) Recall:** What different groups of people are at the scene in "Auto Wreck"? **(b) Compare and Contrast:** How do the reactions of the police officers at the scene differ from those of the spectators?
3. **(a) Recall:** According to the poet, which kinds of death can be explained more easily than those by an auto wreck? **(b) Interpret:** Why does the poet think that death by an auto wreck disturbs people so much?
4. **(a) Recall:** According to the poet of "Pride," what do rocks hide from view? **(b) Interpret:** What might the hidden part represent?
5. **(a) Recall:** What happens when a seal rubs against the rocks? **(b) Deduce:** What might the seal represent?
6. **Make a Judgment:** Do you agree with the speaker in "Auto Wreck" that some forms of death seem to have a purpose? Why or why not?

Dahlia Ravikovitch

(b. 1936)

Israeli poet Dahlia Ravikovitch was born in a town near Tel Aviv and raised on a kibbutz, a collective settlement. Her father's death in an accident when she was six had a big impact on the poet, causing her to be deeply hurt at an early age. Her intensely personal poems focus on human emotion and also contain images from history, religion, and mythology.

Ravikovitch has translated the poetry of William Butler Yeats and T. S. Eliot into Hebrew. In turn, two of her books, *Dress of Fire* and *The Window*, have been translated into English.

Pride ◆ 403

Review and Assess

1. Sample alternative titles are "Shock" ("Auto Wreck") and "The Final Blow" ("Pride").
2. **(a)** Police officers, paramedics, and spectators are present at the wreck. **(b)** The police officers busy themselves with tasks, and the spectators wander around in a daze, trying to recover from their shock.
3. **(a)** The poet thinks that death in war, by suicide, at birth, and from cancer can be more easily explained. **(b)** Death in an auto accident comes suddenly and without warning.
4. **(a)** Rocks hide their cracks. **(b)** The hidden part represents the injuries that occur over time and do not fully heal.
5. **(a)** When a seal rubs the rock, it opens up a hidden crack. **(b)** The seal represents the last straw; not necessarily the worst thing that happens to a person, but the one that makes suddenly visible the crack that was there all along.
6. Students may say that yes, sometimes people die for a cause or to end suffering; or no, all death is random.

⓭ About the Selection

This parable describes the frustration and lost opportunity of a man waiting his turn to be allowed through a door. Students can read the selection on several levels, recognizing the message that sometimes a person must trigger a turning point through his or her own action rather than waiting for something to happen.

⓮ ▶ Critical Viewing

Answer: Students may cite the formal shapes and the largeness of the building compared with the smallness of the figure standing before it.

⓯ Background

Art

Enigma of the Hour, by Giorgio de Chirico

In this painting, a figure stands before a facade of arches with the face of a clock above. The identity of the figure, the place, and the historical period, as well as the significance of the clock, are all unclear.

Giorgio de Chirico was an Italian painter, born in Greece in 1888. Chirico's earlier paintings communicate a sense of reality very different from ordinary experience, and for that reason he is considered a forerunner of the Surrealist movement of the early 1920s. Use the following questions for discussion:

1. How does the mood of this painting reflect the mood of Kafka's story?
   Answer: Both are mysterious. The people and places in both are outside of ordinary reality. Both invite speculation and interpretation.

2. How can you connect the clock in the painting to the theme of the story?
   Answer: Students may say the clock reflects the idea that time runs out for the man in the story.

⓭ Before the Law

Franz Kafka
Translated by Willa and Edwin Muir

⓮ ▲ **Critical Viewing** What is it about this building that makes you think of "the Law"? **[Analyze]**

404 ◆ *Turning Points*

Enigma of the Hour, 1912, Giorgio de Chirico, Coll. Mattioli, Milan, Italy © Foundation Giorgio de Chirico/Licensed by VAGA

404

Before the Law stands a doorkeeper. To this doorkeeper there comes a man from the country and prays for admittance to the Law. But the doorkeeper says that he cannot grant admittance at the moment. The man thinks it over and then asks if he will be allowed in later. "It is possible," says the doorkeeper, "but not at the moment." Since the gate stands open, as usual, and the doorkeeper steps to one side, the man stoops to peer through the gateway into the interior. Observing that, the doorkeeper laughs and says: "If you are so drawn to it, just try to go in despite my veto.[1] But take note: I am powerful. And I am only the least of the doorkeepers. From hall to hall there is one doorkeeper after another, each more powerful than the last. The third doorkeeper is already so terrible that even I cannot bear to look at him." These are difficulties the man from the country has not expected; the Law, he thinks, should surely be accessible at all times and to everyone, but as he now takes a closer look at the doorkeeper in his fur coat, with his big sharp nose and long, thin, black Tartar[2] beard, he decides that it is better to wait until he gets permission to enter. The doorkeeper gives him a stool and lets him sit down at one side of the door. There he sits for days and years. He makes many attempts to be admitted, and wearies the doorkeeper by his importunity. The doorkeeper frequently has little interviews with him, asking him questions about his home and many other things, but the questions are put indifferently, as great lords put them, and always finish with the statement that he cannot be let in yet. The man, who has furnished himself with many things for his journey, sacrifices all he has, however valuable, to bribe the doorkeeper. The doorkeeper accepts everything, but always with the remark: "I am only taking it to keep you from thinking you have omitted anything." During these many years the man fixes his attention almost continuously on the doorkeeper. He forgets the other doorkeepers, and this one seems to him the sole obstacle preventing access to the Law. He curses his bad luck, in his early years boldly and loudly; later, as he grows old, he only grumbles to himself. He becomes childish, and since in his yearlong contemplation of the doorkeeper he has come to know even the fleas in his fur collar, he begs the fleas as well to help him and to change the doorkeeper's mind. At length his eyesight begins to fail, and he does not know whether the world is really darker or whether his eyes are only deceiving him. Yet in his darkness he is now aware of a radiance that streams inextinguishable from the gateway of the Law. Now he has not very long to live. Before he dies, all his experiences

---

1. **veto** (vē′ tō) *n.* order prohibiting some proposed or intended act.
2. **Tartar** (tär′ tər) member of a Turkic people living in a region of European Russia.

Literary Analysis
Theme Based on the doorkeeper's laugh and comments, what do you think might be the theme of this selection?

importunity (im′ pôr tōōn′ i tē) *n.* persistence in requesting

contemplation (kän′ təm plā′ shən) *n.* thoughtful inspection

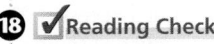 **Reading Check**
What or who prevents the man from gaining admittance to the Law?

---

16 Literary Analysis

Theme

- Ask students the Literary Analysis question on p. 405: Based on the doorkeeper's laugh and his comments, what do you think might be the theme of this selection?
  Answer: Students might recognize that the theme relates to the endless obstacles in life.

- As students continue to read, encourage them to take note of how the man deals with these obstacles. How does his action or inaction relate to the theme?
  Answer: Based on the man's inaction, students will say that the theme is that justice and success may never come to those who sit and wait for it.

17 Reading Strategy

Evaluating a Writer's Message

- Remind students that after they determine the theme of a selection, they should evaluate how well the writer has communicated this message.

- Ask students what the man does in this passage, and how his actions convey the writer's message.
  Answer: The man never takes any initiative to get beyond the doorkeeper, so he never gains admittance to "the Law."

- Ask students whether the man's fate clearly communicates the writer's message.
  Answer: Students will probably say that the message is communicated clearly because the result of the man's lack of action is made clear.

18 Reading Check

Answer: The doorkeeper and the man's unwillingness to stand up for himself prevent his admittance to the Law.

CUSTOMIZE INSTRUCTION FOR UNIVERSAL ACCESS

For Special Needs Students

Finding the theme of a work may challenge students who have trouble understanding the actual text of the literature. Students might benefit from a discussion about the works' events and their meanings. During the discussion, help students record each event and its meaning in a t-chart, with the columns labeled "Event" and "Meaning." Once students comprehend the texts thoroughly, they will probably understand the themes of the three poems. The message of "Before the Law" is ambiguous, though. Encourage students to determine the theme on their own.

Answers for p. 406

Review and Assess

1. Some students might say the frustration would lead them to take action; others might say it would be paralyzing.

2. **(a)** The doorkeeper wears a fur coat and has a big sharp nose and a long, thin, black Tartar beard. **(b)** The doorkeeper is sure of himself and his position; the man is not.

3. **(a)** The man has not been given permission to enter. **(b)** The doorkeeper says the man will find even more doorkeepers, each one more powerful than the last. **(c)** Some students may suggest that the man would have reached the Law if he tried; others may suggest that he would be continually thwarted.

4. **(a)** The doorkeeper explains that this gate has been made only for the man. **(b)** The man learns that his own character may have prevented him from gaining admittance to the Law.

5. **(a)** The man sits outside the door for days, then years. He sells all his possessions over time to bribe the doorkeeper, to no avail. He grows older and older. **(b)** At the end of the story, the doorkeeper shuts the gate.

6. **(a)** Students may suggest that the man never gained access to the Law because he was not courageous enough to confront the doorkeeper. **(b)** Students may suggest that the doorkeeper symbolizes life's injustices, and the man symbolizes people who do not stand up for their rights.

7. Students may suggest that the function of a government is to serve the people and that it should always be accessible.

---

in these long years gather themselves in his head to one point, a question he has not yet asked the doorkeeper. He waves him nearer, since he can no longer raise his stiffening body. The doorkeeper has to bend low toward him, for the difference in height between them has altered much to the man's disadvantage. "What do you want to know now?" asks the doorkeeper; "you are <u>insatiable</u>." "Everyone strives to reach the Law," says the man, "so how does it happen that for all these many years no one but myself has ever begged for admittance?" The doorkeeper recognizes that the man has reached his end, and, to let his failing senses catch the words, roars in his ear: "No one else could ever be admitted here, since this gate was made only for you. I am now going to shut it."

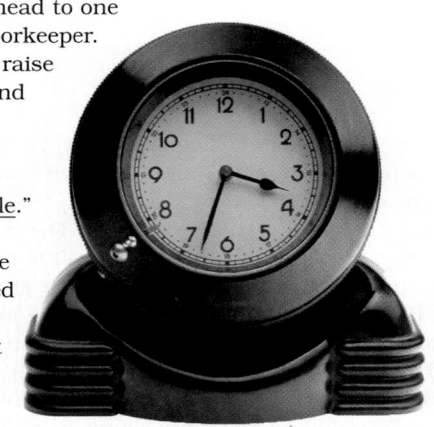

insatiable (in sā′ shə bəl)
adj. unable to be satisfied

Review and Assess

Thinking About the Selection

1. **Respond:** Describe the frustration you might feel if you were in this man's situation.

2. **(a) Recall:** Identify three details of the doorkeeper's appearance. **(b) Compare and Contrast:** How do the two men seem to differ?

3. **(a) Recall:** Why does the man not try to go past the doorkeeper to get to the Law? **(b) Connect:** What does the doorkeeper say that the man will find inside? **(c) Speculate:** Do you think the man might have succeeded in reaching the Law if he had tried to get past the doorkeeper? Why or why not?

4. **(a) Recall:** What does the doorkeeper say to explain why no one else has begged him for admittance to the Law? **(b) Interpret:** What does the man learn from the doorkeeper's explanation?

5. **(a) Analyze:** What details in the story suggest that time passes? **(b) Infer:** What happens to the man at the end of the story?

6. **(a) Draw Conclusions:** Why do you think the man never gained access to the Law? **(b) Interpret:** What do the main characters symbolize?

7. **Take a Position:** Are there some times or places in which limits to government access are appropriate? Explain.

Franz Kafka

(1883–1924)

In his will, the Czech writer Franz Kafka asked that all his unpublished literary works be burned and that all others be allowed to go out of print. Fortunately, his wishes were ignored, and much of Kafka's major work was published after his death.

In "Before the Law," as in most of his works, Kafka provides symbols that reflect his feelings of anxiety and alienation. Kafka's story "The Metamorphosis" is considered by many to be his best work.

✏ ASSESSMENT PRACTICE: Reading Comprehension

Predicting Outcomes (For more practice, see Test Preparation Workbook, p. 27.)

Use the following sample question to help students predict outcomes in reading passages on tests.

Since the gate stands open, as usual, and the doorkeeper steps to one side, the man stoops to peer through the gateway into the interior. Observing that, the doorkeeper laughs and says: "If you are so drawn to it, just try to go in despite my veto. But take note: I am powerful. And I am only the least of the doorkeepers. From hall to hall there is one doorkeeper after another, each more powerful than the last."

Information provided in the passage would lead you to predict that the man

A will try to get in.   C is not interested.
B will never get in.   D should give up.

Based on the unlimited number of doorkeepers, students can predict that *B*, the man will probably never get in.

Review and Assess

Literary Analysis

Theme

1. In your own words, state the **theme** of "Thoughts of Hanoi."
2. (a) What is the theme of "Pride"? (b) Explain how Ravikovitch communicates the theme without directly stating it.
3. What images does Karl Shapiro use to communicate his theme in "Auto Wreck"?
4. (a) Describe the feeling you get after reading "Before the Law." (b) How is this feeling a clue to Kafka's theme?

Comparing Literary Works

5. What objects or ideas do the writers **personify** in these selections? Use a chart like this one to present examples.

Object or Idea	How It Is Human	Effect

6. (a) Compare the effects of personification in "Pride" and "Auto Wreck." Which example is most effective? Explain. (b) Why do these poets use personification?

Reading Strategy

Evaluating a Writer's Message

7. How clearly does Nguyen Thi Vinh communicate her message in "Thoughts of Hanoi"? Give reasons to support your opinion.
8. (a) What is Ravikovitch's message in "Pride"? (b) Explain whether you think it is valid.
9. Do you think that Kafka has effectively conveyed his message in "Before the Law"? Why or why not?

Extend Understanding

10. **Social Studies Connection:** President Clinton's visit to Hanoi in November 2000 marked a clear indication that the Vietnam War was officially a part of the past. How do you think the speaker in "Thoughts of Hanoi" would feel about President Clinton's visit?

Thoughts of Hanoi / Pride / Auto Wreck / Before the Law ◆ 407

Quick Review

The **theme** of a work is its central meaning, a comment the writer is making about human life and values.

Personification describes an object, animal, or idea as if it had human characteristics.

To **evaluate a writer's message,** identify the message and then judge whether the message is clear and makes sense.

 Take It to the Net

www.phschool.com

Take the interactive self-test online to check your understanding of these selections.

Answers for p. 407

Review and Assess

1. Possible response: Individual friendships or family relationships can be destroyed by political divisions.
2. (a) People and objects can withstand pressure for only so long before they crack. (b) The message is communicated through images: the rock (pride) and the seal (final pressure).
3. He uses images such as "pulsing out red light like an artery" and "throats tight as tourniquets."
4. (a) Students may say they feel frustration. (b) This feeling suggests that Kafka's theme relates to futility.
5. Possible answers: "Pride": The rocks are personified because they lie on their backs and feel "a kind of pride." "Auto Wreck": The ambulance lights are personified because they are like arteries, pulsing blood.
6. (a) The personification in "Pride" is direct and lasts throughout the poem, but the personification in "Auto Wreck" is more sporadic and subtle. (b) Students should support their answers with evidence from the texts.
7. Students may suggest that the poet communicates her message clearly. They may cite the speaker's memories of Hanoi, which are vivid and full of sensory imagery.
8. (a) After years of withstanding pressure and assault, even the strongest object can crack. (b) Students should support their answers with reasons.
9. Students may say that Kafka has conveyed his message because his story evokes frustration in the reader.
10. Students may suggest that the poet "imagines" a better future, but does not believe that Hanoi will ever fully heal.

✳ ENRICHMENT: Further Reading

Other Works by the Authors

Works by Nguyen Thi Vinh
Two Sisters

Works by Dahlia Ravikovitch
The Window: New and Selected Poems

Works by Karl Shapiro
The Dome of Sunday

Works by Franz Kafka
The Metamorphosis

 Take It to the Net
Visit www.phschool.com for more information on the authors.

407

❶ Vocabulary Development

1. dissatisfied   3. satisfactory
2. satiate

Fluency: Words in Context

1. The salesperson called over and over, showing importunity.
2. He stood in front of the shelves in deep contemplation.
3. She has an insatiable appetite for books about whales.
4. After the earthquake, many survivors became deranged.
5. The convalescents stayed in the hospital while they healed.
6. The ideas in this new best seller are banal and without merit.
7. This product offers the most expedient method of cleaning your shower.

Spelling Strategy

1. improbable   3. irrepressible
2. illogical

❷ Grammar

1. whether it will rain; predicate nominative
2. What was necessary; subject
3. whatever he can to survive; direct object
4. what had caused the accident; direct object
5. Whoever joins the war; subject

Writing Application

1. The soldier asked when he could visit his buddy.
2. Whoever stands before the door would not let him pass.

Integrate Language Skills

❶ Vocabulary Development Lesson

Word Analysis: Latin Root -sat-

Insatiable contains the Latin root *-sat-*, which means "sufficient" or "enough." Because the prefix *in-* means "not," you can guess that *insatiable* means "unable to be satisfied." The root *-sat-* also appears in these words:

satiate   dissatisfied   satisfactory

Identify the word above that best fits each definition below.

1. Feeling as if you have not had enough:
   ____?____

2. Feed fully; provide more than enough:
   ____?____

3. Good enough to meet one's needs:
   ____?____

❷ Grammar Lesson

Noun Clauses

A subordinate clause is a group of words that contains a subject and a verb but cannot stand alone as a sentence. A **noun clause** is a subordinate clause used as a noun in a sentence. It can function as a subject, an object, or a predicate nominative.

> **As subject:** *Whoever is going to shatter them* has not come yet.
>
> **As direct object:** The man thinks it over and then asks *if he will be allowed in later.*
>
> **As predicate nominative:** To get into the building is *what I would like.*

📝 *Prentice Hall Writing and Grammar Connection: Chapter 20, Section 2*

Fluency: Words in Context

On your paper, write sentences as instructed.

1. Describe an action, using *importunity*.
2. Describe a library, using *contemplation*.
3. Describe a person, using *insatiable*.
4. Describe a character, using *deranged*.
5. Write about a hospital, using *convalescents*.
6. Write about a book, using *banal*.
7. Use *expedient* in an advertisement.

Spelling Strategy

The prefix *in-* becomes *il-* before *l* (illegible); *im-* before *b*, *m*, or *p* (imbalance, immature, impossible); and *ir-* before *r* (irregular). Fill in the blanks with the proper form of the prefix *in-*.

1. The accident seemed ____ probable to him.
2. The tragedy was ____ logical.
3. His grief was ____ repressible.

Practice Identify the noun clause in each sentence. Then, decide whether the noun clause functions as a subject, an object, or a predicate nominative.

1. The question is whether it will rain.
2. What was necessary was for him to fight.
3. He must do whatever he can to survive.
4. They knew what had caused the accident.
5. Whoever joins the war must be prepared.

Writing Application Replace the underlined words in each sentence with a noun clause.

1. The soldier asked <u>a question</u>.
2. <u>The doorkeeper</u> would not let him pass.

TEACHING RESOURCES

The following resources can be used to enrich or extend the instruction for pp. 408–409.

Vocabulary

📖 **Selection Support Workbook:** Build Vocabulary, p. 105

📖 **Vocabulary and Spelling Practice Book** (Use this booklet for skills enrichment.)

Grammar

📖 **Selection Support Workbook:** Build Grammar Skills, p. 106

📝 **Writing and Grammar,** Platinum Level, p. 474 ▪

▪ **Daily Language Practice Transparencies**

Writing

📝 **Writing and Grammar,** Platinum Level, p. 285 ▪

💿 **Writing and Grammar iText CD-ROM**

▪ **Writing Models and Graphic Organizers on Transparencies,** p. 71

 BLOCK SCHEDULING: Resources marked with this symbol provide varied instruction during 90-minute blocks.

Writing Lesson

Analysis of an Image

The words in each of these works of literature combine with your feelings and experiences to form images in your mind. Choose the image that is most striking to you from one of the works, and analyze it.

Prewriting Freewrite briefly to identify your response to the image you have chosen. Write down all the ideas that the image suggests.

Drafting After an introductory paragraph, explain your response to the image. Using your freewriting ideas, sensory details, and other language from the work, analyze how and why you formed that response.

Revising Review your draft to strengthen your verb choice. Highlight all forms of *to be*, including *be, am, is, are, was, were, being,* and *been,* and replace them with action verbs.

Model: Revising to Replace Forms of *to Be*

> writhes   Stoically, it waits
> A rock is in pain. It is stoic as salt water pours into the
> open wound and the waves break on the shore.

Changing the *to be* verbs to more descriptive verbs makes the analysis more interesting.

WG *Prentice Hall Writing and Grammar Connection: Chapter 13, Section 2*

Extension Activities

Listening and Speaking With a partner, perform an **improvisational skit**—a skit without preparation—based on "Before the Law." Make your presentation humorous. Keep these ideas in mind as you prepare for your role in the skit:

- Use dialogue that conveys your character's attitude and personality.
- Build a sense of frustration into the skit to match the mood of the selection.

After your presentation, ask classmates to rate your performance. **[Group Activity]**

Research and Technology On a computer or by hand, prepare **contrasting maps** of Vietnam. On the first map, show Vietnam when it was divided into two countries after 1954. On the second map, show Vietnam after the country was unified in 1976 following the communist takeover. Label the capital cities and other major cities on both maps. Then, write a caption to connect "Thoughts of Hanoi" to your maps.

Take It to the Net www.phschool.com
Go online for an additional research activity using the Internet.

---

❸ Writing Lesson

- Model an analysis for students by choosing an image from one of the selections and telling the class what feelings and ideas it brings to your mind.
- After students have chosen an image to analyze, have them gather ideas by freewriting or by using the Analysis Map on p. 71 of **Writing Models and Graphic Organizers on Transparencies.**
- Use the Writing Lesson to guide students in developing their analyses.
- Use the Response to Literature rubric in **Performance Assessment and Portfolio Management,** p. 16, to evaluate students' analyses.

❹ Listening and Speaking

- Divide the class into pairs. One member of each pair is to play the man, and the other is to play the doorkeeper.
- Encourage students to reread the selection to find places in which to insert humor.
- Ask volunteer pairs to present their skits to the class for review and evaluation.
- Use the rubric for Delivering a Narrative Presentation, p. 28, in **Performance Assessment and Portfolio Management** to assess students' skills.

CUSTOMIZE INSTRUCTION
For Universal Access

To address different learning styles, use the activities suggested in the **Extension Activities** booklet, p. 27.

- For Musical/Rhythmic and Bodily/Kinesthetic Learners, use Activity 5.
- For Visual/Spatial Learners, use Activity 6.
- For Interpersonal and Logical/Mathematical Learners, use Activity 7.

ASSESSMENT RESOURCES

The following resources can be used to assess students' knowledge and skills.

Selection Assessment

- **Formal Assessment,** Selection Test, pp. 91–93
- **Open Book Test,** pp. 79–81
- **Got It! Assessment Videotapes,** Tape 2
- **Test Bank Software**
- **Take It to the Net**
  Visit www.phschool.com for self-tests and additional questions on the selections.

Writing Rubric

- **Performance Assess. and Portfolio Mgmt.,** p. 16

Listening and Speaking Rubric

- **Performance Assess. and Portfolio Mgmt.,** p. 28

PRENTICE HALL
ASSESSMENT SYSTEM

- **Workbook**
- **Skill Book**
- **Transparencies**
- **CD-ROM**

Lesson Objectives

1. To learn to recognize inductive and deductive reasoning

2. To understand the elements of an effective persuasive article

3. To relate visuals to details in the text

About Persuasive Articles

- Have students read "About Persuasive Articles." Review the bulleted points to focus students' attention on the elements of an effective persuasive article.

- Point out to students that they use these same elements of a persuasive article when they are trying to persuade someone, like a friend or parent, to do something. Ask students for everyday, practical examples of these elements.

- Ask students why they think it is important to learn about persuasive articles. Encourage them to discuss situations in the future in which they will have to persuade someone to agree with them or to do something.

Reading Strategy

Recognizing Logical Modes of Persuasion: Induction and Deduction

- Have students read the information about the Reading Strategy.

- Explain to students that deductive reasoning involves starting with a general truth, applying it to a specific case, and then drawing a conclusion about that case. Inductive reasoning involves starting with specific cases or facts and drawing a general conclusion based on them.

- Explain to students that increasing their understanding of inductive and deductive reasoning will enhance their skills of persuasion and help them to build better arguments. Point out that it may also help them to identify faulty logic in other people's arguments.

- Call students' attention to the charts of deductive and inductive reasoning. Ask students to come up with their own examples of deduction and induction to share with the class.

About Persuasive Articles

A **persuasive article** is a piece of writing that tries to convince readers to accept a particular viewpoint or to take a certain action. Most effective persuasive articles contain the following:

- A clearly stated opinion or argument on an issue that has more than one side
- Evidence to support the opinion
- Memorable and convincing details and vivid, persuasive language
- Effective, logical organization

The article that follows gives the writer's reasoned opinion that higher speed limits can increase road safety. The writer first supports his opinion with statistics. Then, he describes the factors that contribute to increasing road safety with higher speed limits.

Reading Strategy

Recognizing Logical Modes of Persuasion: Induction and Deduction

The article "65-MPH Speed Limit Is Saving Lives" uses both deductive and inductive modes of persuasion. **Deductive reasoning** proves a conclusion by applying a principle to a specific case. In contrast, **inductive reasoning** leads from a number of examples to a generalization. Study the examples in the charts below. Then, as you read the article, analyze each argument, identifying it as induction or deduction.

Deduction	
Principle	If speed limits over 55 mph are unsafe, traffic deaths will go up when the speed limit is raised.
Specific Case	The speed limit was raised to 65 mph, but fatalities did not increase.
Conclusion	Speed limits over 55 mph are not inherently unsafe.

Induction	
Cases	In 1987 and 1996, the speed limit was raised.
Pattern	In each case, fatalities declined.
Generalization	Raising speed limits does not increase fatalities.

65-MPH SPEED LIMIT IS SAVING LIVES

Charles Lave

Consumers' Research Magazine

> **The writer begins his article with statistics, a good way to build credibility.**

Despite opposition from many national safety groups, in November 1995 Congress gave the states permission to raise speed limits. Opponents had testified that raising speed limits would cause an additional 4,400 to 6,000 deaths per year. Fortunately, it didn't work out that way.

Fatalities did not increase.

> **To build interest and support for his argument, the writer provides examples of a drop in fatalities following an increase in speed limits.**

They did not rise by the 10% to 14% expected by the opponents of the change, nor even by the 2% to 3% that would be expected from recent trends. Instead, fatalities fell by 0.7%. This surprising outcome was not the result of a decline in travel: Total vehicle miles rose 1.8% between 1995 and 1996.

Although Congress gave permission to raise speed limits in November 1995, it took the states a while to create and pass new legislation, and only half of those that did react had done so by May 1996.

A drop in fatalities following an increase in speed limits is not unprecedented. The 1987 change in speed limits produced similar results. In 1987 Congress gave the states permission to raise speed limits on portions of their Interstate highways. Some states raised speed limits, some did not. Comparing the subsequent fatality rates across these groups, holding constant a number of other factors, the states that raised speed limits experienced a 3.4% to 5.1% drop in fatality rates compared to the states that did not raise speed limits.

Why didn't fatalities increase in 1987 and 1996 as had been widely expected? My research cited three possible factors. Part of the answer is contained in testimony given to Congress by senior highway-patrol administrators. They said that pressure from the federal government to enforce compliance with a 55-mph limit had forced them to

> **The writer presents his theory, introducing the first of three factors that contribute to lower fatalities with higher speed limits.**

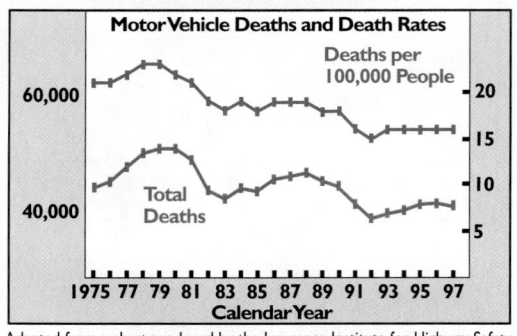

Adapted from a chart produced by the Insurance Institute for Highway Safety.

take patrol officers away from other safety activities and move them to the task of speed-limit enforcement on Interstate highways, even though they did not believe that action was the best use of their patrol resources. This opinion was widely shared among the state highway-patrol chiefs. In 1988 their national organization passed a resolution that stated: "[Federal demands to enforce the 55-mph limit] force the over-concentration of limited resources for the express purpose of attaining compliance rather than application of resources in a manner most effectively enhancing total highway safety."

Thus relaxing the speed laws eased the highway patrols' enforcement burden, allowing them to reallocate patrol resources to activities they considered more important for promoting safety.

There might also have been a reallocation of traffic when speed limits were raised. Previously, if a driver wanted to go faster than the limit on the heavily policed Interstate highways, he might have moved to one of the parallel two-lane roads. Though much more dangerous, these roads had very little speed enforcement. Raising speed limits would lure such drivers back to the Interstates, thus reallocating traffic from dangerous roads to safe ones.

Finally, speed variance among cars may have decreased when speed limits were raised. Speed variance is highly dangerous because it produces more overtaking and passing and hence more chances for collisions. Thus when setting speed limits, it is critical to choose a limit that drivers are willing to obey. Suppose most drivers wanted to go faster than 55 mph: Some obeyed the limit, some ignored it. Raising the limit would give the law-abiding drivers a chance to speed up, hence reducing speed variance and increasing safety.

These results do not imply that we should raise speed limits even further as a quick and easy way to increase highway safety. But it should be clear that the conventional wisdom — "speed kills" — is not a complete picture of the world. Highway safety is a much more complex matter, and should be analyzed as the outcome of a system of interdependent behaviors.

The writer presents statistics graphically as powerful support for his argument.

The writer provides quotations from experts to build his argument.

This paragraph addresses the second reason for his findings.

To finish a logical presentation of his ideas, the writer presents a third reason.

The writer presents his conclusion.

Check Your Comprehension

1. What was the occurrence of fatalities after the 1996 increase in speed limits?
2. What was the occurrence of fatalities after the 1987 increase in speed limits?
3. Identify the three factors contributing to the decrease in fatalities.

Applying the Reading Strategy

Recognizing Logical Modes of Persuasion: Induction and Deduction

4. The writer argues that a higher speed limit helps the police promote safety more effectively. Break this argument into steps to explain whether it represents deduction or induction.
5. What kind of argument—deductive or inductive—would the writer use to prove that there was a "reallocation" of traffic? Explain.
6. In arguing that lower "speed variance" leads to fewer fatalities, what assumption does the writer make?

Activity

Presenting an Opposing Point of View

Persuasive articles are written to support one position on a controversial topic. Using Lave's article as a basis, consider an opposing viewpoint. Complete a list like the one shown to provide reasons for setting lower speed limits—or keeping many roads to the federally regulated 55 miles per hour. Use the details you have gathered to write a short response to Lave's ideas.

Contrasting Informational Materials

Persuasive Articles and Other Forms of Persuasion

You can find persuasion at work in many types of informational materials. In addition, each writer brings unique experiences and purposes to a discussion of a controversial issue. Identify the purpose of each item below, and explain what opinion or slant you might expect the writer to present.

1. A pamphlet produced by a car manufacturer
2. A letter to the editor written by a school crossing guard
3. A commercial by the federal government aimed at student drivers

Considering the Opposition

1. Speed limits of 55 mph or less are safer in residential or business areas.

2.

3.

Reading Informational Materials: Persuasive Articles ◆ 413

Answers for p. 413

Check Your Comprehension

1. Fatalities fell by 0.7% after the 1996 increase in speed limits.
2. Fatality rates fell by 3.4% to 5.1% in states that increased speed limits.
3. The reallocation of patrol resources to safety-promoting activities, the incentive for fast drivers to use the safer inter-states rather than the less safe two-lane roads, and the decrease in speed variance among cars all contribute to the decrease in fatalities, according to the writer.

Apply the Reading Strategy

4. **Possible response:** 1. Other safety activities by the police are more effective than enforcing the speed limit. 2. When the speed limit is lower, more officers must be assigned to enforce speed limit compliance. 3. When the speed limit is higher, more can be assigned to more effective safety activities. Therefore, raising the speed limit helps the police promote safety. The argument is deductive because it applies a general principle to a specific case. (Students may note, though, that the author supports that principle inductively by pointing to facts about declining traffic deaths.)
5. The author would use inductive reasoning to prove that there was a reallocation of traffic. He would examine a large number of facts concerning the use of inter-states versus the use of local roads to show a pattern support-ing a general conclusion: Traffic moved onto the interstates.
6. By arguing the lower speed vari-ance leads to fewer fatalities, the author makes the assump-tion that many traffic deaths occur when one vehicle passes or overtakes another (cases of "speed variance").

Activity

Suggest that students consider not only safety but also fuel economy, wear and tear on cars and roads, and whether roads were designed to accommodate higher speeds. Students should clearly state their

continued

Answers continued

opposing viewpoint and offer strong support-ing evidence. They should research to find sta-tistics that support this viewpoint and find quotations from experts, if possible.

Contrasting Informational Materials

1. The purpose of the pamphlet would most likely be to persuade people to buy that manufacturer's cars. The writer would pres-ent these cars as powerful, exciting, sensi-ble, or affordable, depending on the targeted market.

2. The purpose of the letter to the editor would be to create community concern about an issue; a school crossing guard might caution drivers to show greater attention at school crossings for the safety of students.

3. The purpose of the commercial would most likely be to promote safety and responsibil-ity; it would most likely take a negative view of irresponsible driving.

Lesson Objectives

1. To make connections between different accounts of the Vietnam War
2. To explore the impact of war's traumatic events on life "back home"

Connections

Both Nguyen Thi Vinh's and O'Brien's accounts convey important messages about how war changes people's relation to normal life at home. Have students reread "Thoughts of Hanoi" after they have read the excerpt "Calling Home" from *Going After Cacciato*. What similarities and differences can students identify between the ways in which the people in both accounts cope with the changes effected by war?

The Vietnam War as a Literary Subject

- Explain to students that, like Vinh's account, this reading offers a first-hand view of the Vietnam War.
- As students read the excerpt from O'Brien's account, have them pay attention to the ways in which the soldiers react to their phone calls.
- Focus students' attention on how war changes all those involved—the soldiers and their families. Make sure that they understand the families in the United States lived in fear that their children serving in Vietnam would be killed, but at the same time had to continue living their own lives.

▶ **Critical Viewing**

Possible Response: Since the soldiers are young, it is probably hard for them to be away from home. Their experiences of overcoming challenges on their own may be more limited than those of older individuals, and so they may face greater self-doubt.

CONNECTIONS
Literature and History

The Vietnam War as a Literary Subject

Calling Home

from
Going After Cacciato

Tim O'Brien

In the poem "Thoughts of Hanoi," Nguyen Thi Vinh reflects upon the conflicted feelings associated with peacetime friends who become wartime enemies. Those feelings were triggered when the Vietnam War split Vietnam in half—and separated two people as countrymen and friends forever.

In the novel *Going After Cacciato*, Tim O'Brien tells the story of American soldiers who go to fight a war in Vietnam. In the chapter "Calling Home," soldiers who are on a week's leave call home and try to grasp what it is like there since they have been away. They realize that the home life they once knew has changed forever for them because of their experiences in Vietnam.

In August, after two months in the bush, the platoon returned to Chu Lai for a week's stand-down.

They swam, played mini-golf in the sand . . . wrote letters and slept late in the mornings. At night there were floor shows. There was singing . . . and dancing, and afterward there was homesickness. It was neither a good time nor a bad time. The war was all around them.

On the final day, Oscar and Eddie and Doc and Paul Berlin hiked down to the 82nd Commo Detachment. Recently the outfit had installed a radio-telephone hookup with the States.

"It's called MARS," said a young PFC[1] at the reception desk. "Stands for Military Affiliate Radio System." He was a friendly, deeply tanned redhead without freckles. On each wrist was a gold watch, and the boy kept glancing at them as if to correlate time. He seemed a little nervous.

While they waited to place their calls, the PFC explained how the system worked. A series of radio relays fed the signal across the Pacific to a telephone exchange in downtown Honolulu, where it was sent by regular undersea cable to San Francisco and from there to any telephone in

---

1. **PFC** *n.* Private First Class

414 ◆ *Turning Points*

▲ **Critical Viewing**
How might the youth of these soldiers—and the ones in the story—influence their feelings about home?

414

America. "Real <u>wizardry</u>," the boy said. "Depends a lot on the weather, but wow, sometimes it's like talkin' to the guy next door. You'd swear you was there in the same room."

They waited nearly an hour. Relay problems, the PFC explained. He grinned and gestured at Oscar's boots. "You guys are legs, I guess. Grunts."

"I guess so," Oscar said.

The boy nodded solemnly. He started to say something but then shook his head. "Legs," he murmured.

Eddie's call went through first.

The PFC led him into a small soundproof booth and had him sit behind a <u>console</u> equipped with speakers and a microphone and two pairs of headsets. Paul Berlin watched through a plastic window. For a time nothing happened. Then a red light blinked on and the PFC handed Eddie one of the headsets. Eddie began rocking in his chair. He held the microphone with one hand, squeezing it, leaning slightly forward. It was hard to see his eyes.

He was in the booth a long time. When he came out his face was bright red. He sat beside Oscar. He yawned, then immediately covered his eyes, rubbed them, then stretched and blinked. . . .

"Jeez," he said softly.

Then he laughed. It was a strange, scratchy laugh. He cleared his throat and smiled and kept blinking. . . .

"Jeez," he said.

"What—"

Eddie giggled, "It was. . . You shoulda heard her. 'Who?' she goes. Like that—'Who?' just like that."

He took out a handkerchief, blew his nose, shook his head. His eyes were shiny.

"Just like that—'Who?' 'Eddie,' I say, and Ma says, 'Eddie who?' and I say, 'Who do you think Eddie?' She almost passes out. Almost falls down or something. She gets this call from Nam and thinks maybe I been shot. 'Where you at?' she says, like maybe I'm callin' from Graves Registration or something, and—"

"That's great," Doc said. "That's really great, man."

"Yeah. It's—"

"Really great."

Eddie shook his head as though trying to clear stopped-up ears. He was quiet a time. Then he laughed.

"Honest, you had to hear it. 'Who?' she keeps saying. 'Who?' Real clear. Like in the next . . . And Petie! He's in . . . high school, you believe that? My brother. Can't even call him Petie no more. 'Pete,' he says. Real deep voice, just like that guy on Lawrence Welk—'Pete, not Petie,' he goes. You believe that?"

"It's terrific," Doc said. "It really is."

"And clear? Man! I could hear Ma's . . . cuckoo clock, *that* clear."

"Technology."

"Yeah," Eddie grinned. "Real technology. I say, 'Hey, Ma,' and what's she say? 'Who's this?' Real scared-soundin', you know? Man, I coulda just—"

"It's great, Eddie."

Doc was next, then Oscar. Both of them came out looking a little funny,

wizardry (wiz´ erd rē) *n.* seemingly magical transforming power or influence

console (kän´ sōl) *n.* panel or cabinet on which are mounted dials or switches used to control electrical or mechanical devices

☑️**Reading Check**
What do the soldiers do while on leave from their duties?

Background
The Vietnam War (1955–1975) began as a war between the French-created government of Vietnam and the communist opponents of French rule. The country was eventually divided by international agreement into Communist North Vietnam and Western-allied South Vietnam. The North Vietnamese and their allies in South Vietnam, the Viet Cong, fought against the South Vietnamese government, seeking to unify the country. In 1965, the United Sates began sending combat troops to fight for South Vietnam.

During the war, the United States relied on heavy aerial bombing of North Vietnam and search-and-destroy missions in the ground war in South Vietnam. Although the United States had superior fire power, the North Vietnamese army and the Viet Cong successfully used guerrilla tactics to beat off United States forces. The last American ground troops withdrew from Vietnam in 1975, and in 1976, the North Vietnamese succeeded in unifying the country. Over 58,000 American soldiers and as many as 2 million Vietnamese had died in the war.

☑️**Reading Check**
Answer: The soldiers sleep in, swim, play golf, sing, dance and miss their homes. Some of them try to call home through a special radio-telephone hookup.

CUSTOMIZE INSTRUCTION FOR UNIVERSAL ACCESS

For Less Proficient Readers	For Gifted/Talented Students
Students may need help understanding what transpires with the phone calls. Encourage groups to read aloud the dialogue, different students reading for each character. After having read and heard the dialogue aloud, engage students in a discussion about the phone calls. What did the soldiers learn? What did they talk about with their families? How did it make them feel? Why do you think they felt that way?	Challenge students to rewrite the excerpt as a play, without using a narrator. Encourage students to add actions or dialogue where necessary in order to present in their play all the same information they learned from reading the text. Allow time for them to write and practice their play. Remind students they may want to create or find props to use in their presentation. Have students present their play in front of the class.

not quite choked up but trying hard not to be. Very quiet at first, then laughing, then talking fast, then turning quiet again. It made Paul Berlin feel warm to watch them. Even Oscar seemed happy.

"Technology," Doc said. "You can't beat technology."

. . . "My old man, all he could say was 'Over.' Nothin' else—'Weather's fine,' he'd say 'Over.'" Oscar wagged his head. His father had been an RTO[2] in Italy. "You believe that? All he says is 'Over,' and 'Roger that.' Crazy."

They would turn pensive. Then one of them would chuckle or grin.

"Pirates are out of it this year. Not a prayer, Petie says."

"I bleed."

"Yeah, but Petie, he goes nuts over the Pirates. It's all he knows. Thinks we're over here fightin' the Russians. The Pirates, that's *all* he knows."

"Crazy," Oscar said. He kept wagging his head. "Over an' out."

It made Paul Berlin feel good. Like buddies. Genuine war buddies, he felt close to all of them. When they laughed, he laughed.

Then the PFC tapped him on the shoulder.

He felt giddy. Everything inside the booth was painted white. Sitting down, he grinned and squeezed his fingers together. He saw Doc wave at him through the plastic window.

Thematic Connection
How do you think the soldiers feel when they call home and things have changed?

"Ease up," the PFC said. "Pretend it's a local call."

The boy helped him with the headset. There was crisp clicking sound, then a long electric hum like a vacuum cleaner. He remembered how his mother always used the old Hoover on Saturdays. The smell of carpets, a fine powdery dust rising in the yellow window light. An uncluttered house. Things neatly in place.

He felt himself smiling. He pressed the headset tight. What day was it? Sunday, he hoped. His father liked to putz on Sundays. Putzing, he called it, which meant tinkering and dreaming and touching things with his hands, fixing them or building them or tearing them down, studying things. Putzing . . . He hoped it was Sunday. What would they be doing? What month was it? He pictured the telephone. It was there in the kitchen, to the left of the sink. It was black. Black, because his father hated pastels on his telephones. Then he imagined the ring. He remembered it clearly, both how it sounded in the kitchen and in the basement, where his father had rigged up an extra bell, much louder-sounding against the cement. He pictured the basement. He pictured the living room and den and kitchen. Pink Formica on the counters and speckled pink and white walls. His father always . . .

The PFC touched his arm. "Speak real clear," he said, "And after each time you talk you got to say 'Over,' it's in the regs, and the same for your loved ones. Got it?"

Paul Berlin nodded. Immediately the headphones buzzed with a different sort of sound.

He tried to think of something meaningful to say. Nothing forced: easy and natural, but still loving. Maybe start by saying he was getting along. Tell them things weren't really so bad. Then ask how his father's business was. Don't let on about being afraid. Don't make them worry—that was Doc

---

2. **RTO** *n.* Radio Telephone Operator

Peret's advice. Make it sound like a vacation, talk about the swell beaches, tell them how you're getting this spectacular tan. . . . That was Doc's advice. Tell them . . . The PFC swiveled the microphone so that it was facing him. The boy checked his two wristwatches, smiled, whispered something. The kitchen, Paul thought. He could see it now. The old walnut dining table that his mother had inherited from an aunt in Minnesota. And the big white stove, the refrigerator, stainless-steel cabinets over the sink, the black telephone, the windows looking out on Mrs. Stone's <u>immaculate</u> backyard. She was nuts, that Mrs. Stone. Something to ask his father about: Was the old lady still out there in winter, using her broom to sweep away the snow, even in blizzards, sweeping and sweeping, and in the autumn was she still sweeping leaves from her yard, and in summer was she sweeping away the dandelion fuzz? Sure! He'd get his father to talk about her. Something fun and cheerful. The time old Mrs. Stone was out there in the rain, sweeping the water off her lawn as fast as it fell, all day long, sweeping it out to the gutter and then sweeping it up the street, but how the street was at a slight angle so that the rainwater kept flowing back down on her, and, Lord, how Mrs. Stone was out there until midnight, ankle-deep, trying to beat gravity with her broom. Lord, his father always said, shaking his head. Neighbors. That was one thing to talk about. . . . They'd laugh. He wouldn't let on how afraid he was; he wouldn't mention Billy Boy or Frenchie or what happened to Bernie Lynn and the others. Yes, they'd laugh, and afterward, near the end of the conversation, maybe then he'd tell them he loved them. He couldn't remember ever telling them that, except at the bottom of letters, but this time maybe . . . The line buzzed again, then clicked, then there was the digital pause that always comes as a connection is completed, then he heard the first ring. He recognized it. Hollow, washed out by distance, but it was still the old ring. He'd heard it ten thousand times. He listened to the ring as he would listen to family voices, his father's voice and his mother's voice, older now and changed by what time does to voices, but still the same voice. He stopped thinking of things to say. He concentrated on the ringing. He saw the black phone, heard it ringing. The PFC held up a thumb but Paul Berlin barely noticed, he was smiling to the sound of the ringing.

"Tough luck," Doc said afterward.

Oscar and Eddie clapped him on the back, and the PFC shrugged and said it happened sometimes.

"What can you do?" Oscar said.

"Yeah."

"Maybe . . . Who knows? Maybe they was out takin' a drive or something. Buying groceries. The world don' stop."

Connecting Literature and History

1. What common things do the speaker of "Thoughts of Hanoi" and the American soldiers talk about while they are away from home?

2. (a) With what "side" of the war was each speaker connected?
   (b) How does this affiliation affect the details that each includes?

immaculate (im makʹ yōō lit) *adj.* spotless

Tim O'Brien

(b. 1946)
There is a good reason why the novels of Tim O'Brien focus on the Vietnam War: He lived it.

After graduating from college with a degree in political science, O'Brien was drafted and sent to Vietnam, where he was in the infantry from 1969 to 1970.

After his tour of duty in Vietnam, he enrolled as a graduate student at Harvard University. Eventually, he left Harvard to become a newspaper reporter for *The Washington Post*. O'Brien published his memoir *If I Die in a Combat Zone, Box Me Up and Ship Me Home* in 1973. His second novel, *Going After Cacciato*, won the National Book Award in 1979.

Connections: Calling Home ◆ 417

The Vietnam War as a Literary Subject

- Call students' attention to Paul's thoughts and feelings as the PFC sets up his phone call. Ask students: What inferences can you draw about Paul from these passages? Possible response: Paul is self-conscious about the call; he cares a great deal that it go well; he is concerned not to alarm his family by sharing his fears; he is not sure what to talk about; he carries a burden of fear; he has lost a few comrades in the war.

- No one picks up when Paul calls. Ask students what is suggested by the contrast between Paul's anticipation and his failure to connect. Possible response: The failure of the call to actually reach anyone confronts Paul with the fact that all of his thoughts and feelings about his family take place in isolation. He is isolated from his family by distance, uncertainty, fear, and his experiences of war. In a sense, the thoughts and feelings that connect him to them are deceptive; they affect him as if he were back home, when in fact he is cut off from home.

Answers
Connecting Literature and History

1. The poem's speaker and the soldiers both talk about the past, how things have changed, and that life goes on for others while they are stuck in a war.

2. **(a)** The poem's speaker is Vietnamese and is worried about the person he calls Brother who is in the midst of the war. The soldiers in "Calling Home" are United States soldiers. **(b)** The poem's speaker talks about life in Vietnam before the war; the American soldiers talk about their lives in the United States.

417

Lesson Objectives

1. To write a reflective essay
2. To learn the characteristics of a reflective essay
3. To use writing strategies to generate ideas, plan, organize, evaluate, and revise the essay

Model From Literature

In the excerpt from "Speak, Memory," Vladimir Nabokov reflects on the joys of learning to read that gave him an enduring love for language.

Prewriting

- Students will benefit from freewriting on their topic to discover the larger meaning of the specific event on which they are writing. Have them freewrite about the event for ten minutes, and then have them circle parts of their freewriting that suggest a general theme or lesson. If they cannot find one, they might review their freewriting for references to other events and look for the connection between those events and the one with which they started.

- Remind students that an effective reflective essay clearly connects a specific sequence of events with a general insight.

- Tell students that as they recall sensory details about the event, they should write down everything they can think of. They can later look at their lists of details and decide which they will use in their essays.

- Explain to students that the more details and concrete sensory images they can provide about the experience, the more engaging the essay will be for readers.

Writing WORKSHOP

Narration: Reflective Essay

A **reflective essay** is a piece of writing in which the writer describes a personal experience and then reflects on it by telling how it reveals some greater truth about life. In this workshop, you will write a reflective essay about an experience of special meaning to you.

Assignment Criteria Your reflective essay should have the following characteristics:

- The writer as the narrator
- An insight into a truth or an observation about life
- A sequence of events that forms the basis of the insight
- Scenes and incidents located in a clearly defined setting
- Effective use of concrete sensory images

To preview the criteria on which your reflective essay may be assessed, see the Rubric on page 421.

Prewriting

Choose a topic. To help find a topic, **brainstorm** for a list of events that you witnessed or experienced. Then, choose one event that is memorable and that holds special meaning for you.

Gather sensory details. Close your eyes, and recall the event as you experienced it. What did you see, feel, smell, taste, and hear? Complete a list like the one shown, to record words and phrases that describe your sensory experiences. Draw on these words when you begin to write.

Identify the setting. List details about the time and place in which the event occurred. Be specific, so that your readers can see the setting as if they were there.

Define your insight or main idea. Jot down some ideas to explain your experience. Then, write a statement that summarizes its significance for you or what it taught you about life. Keep the statement nearby as a reminder while you draft.

Example

I would much rather be a part of the world and feel and see everything possible.

Gathering Details

Sense	Descriptive Words
Sight	tiny chandelier flawless furniture
Hearing	
Touch	
Taste	chocolate chip ice cream
Smell	scent of pine

TEACHING RESOURCES

The following resources can be used to enrich or extend the instruction for pp. 418–421.

Writing and Grammar, Platinum Level, Chapter 4, pp. 48–70

Performance Assessment and Portfolio Management, p. 12

Writing Models and Graphic Organizers on Transparencies, pp. 5–16

Writing and Grammar iText CD-ROM Students can use the following tools as they complete their autobiographical narratives:

- Topic Web
- Sensory Details Word Bin
- Unity and Coherence Checker

Student Model

Before you begin drafting, read this student model and review the characteristics of a thought-provoking reflective essay.

Samantha Duffy
Santa Clarita, California

The Dollhouse

I was sitting on my couch eating chocolate chip ice cream when the front door was flung open. Suddenly, a huge colorfully wrapped box with a giant red bow appeared. The only other thing I could see was the strong hands of a man gripping the box tightly. He placed it carefully on the table in front of me.

> The essay focuses on the narrator's experience.

My father, glowing with pleasure at his gift to me, emerged from behind the box and said, "My daughter deserves the best present that money can buy for her birthday, and here it is. Go on, open it. What are you waiting for?"

I stood up and ripped the shiny paper from the box, but I could not help but stare when I saw what the paper had been hiding.

"Thank you, Daddy, it's truly beautiful," I said, hoping my eyes did not reveal the confusion I felt as I looked at the item.

In front of me was a delicately handcrafted dollhouse, and inside was a family of tiny porcelain dolls. The furniture in the dollhouse looked real, except that it had no flaws. There were pretty paintings on the wall and little glass chandeliers. It was amazing how peaceful and perfect the family inside appeared.

> Events are ordered sequentially.

It would have been a terrific birthday present except for one thing: The magical miniature world was enclosed in a glass case. My father brought it up to my bedroom and warned me never to touch the glass for fear I would destroy its perfection. The dollhouse was there for me to admire but never to touch or play with.

> Events are limited to a specific place and time.

The dollhouse sat in the same place for many years. I obeyed my father and never did touch it. At first, I was intrigued by this beautiful world and did as I was supposed to: I admired it. Time passed, though, and I started to find it boring and useless. I began to look at the dollhouse in a new light. Those pretty porcelain dolls had no expression. They would never experience life or feel the way real people do because in that perfect world there was no emotion.

> The writer shares an insight she gained through reflection.

On my eighth birthday, I received a gift that taught me a lot about what I want out of life: Many times I had imagined myself in that house, never being able to interact with the outside world. I do not think I could stand to be so closed off. I would much rather be a part of the world and feel and see everything possible. The dollhouse made me realize that as long as I opened myself up to the world, I would never be lonely. But if I shut the world out of my life, like one of those porcelain perfections, then I would be completely by myself.

> The writer includes a truth about life that she learned through events in this story.

Student Model

- Explain that the Student Model is a sample, and that reflective essays may be longer.
- Lead students to see that the first paragraph immediately puts the reader at the scene.
- Point out that Samantha uses rich sensory details to paint events. Discuss with students how this further draws in the reader.
- Point out that Samantha places events in the order in which they happened so the narrative is clear, and she limits the narrative to a specific sequence of events. She has chosen a narrow topic in order to be able to effectively describe it.
- Ask students what truth about life Samantha learned from this experience.
  Answer: She realized that she needed to open herself up to the world—that closing herself off would only leave her lonely and lifeless like her porcelain dolls.

Real-World Connection

Explain to students that reflective writing is not limited to nonfiction literary works. Students may be required to reflect on a significant event from their lives in a college application, for example. Reflective writing also helps develop the tools of thought and imagination that people use to evaluate their lives and make decisions about the right direction to take.

CUSTOMIZE INSTRUCTION FOR UNIVERSAL ACCESS

For Less Proficient Writers	For English Learners	For Advanced Writers
Have students gather sensory details in pairs. As one student describes an experience, the partner can take notes on it, paying special attention to the sensory details. Encourage the listener to ask questions, such as "What did it feel/look/smell/taste/sound like?" Then, have them switch roles.	As students gather more sensory details, encourage them to check a thesaurus and dictionary for vivid words to use to describe their experience.	Challenge students to present their reflective essays in creative ways, such as a mocked-up newspaper article or as information that a witness to a crime might give to a police officer. Tell them to choose words and write descriptions that suit their chosen format.

Drafting

- Explain to students that their reflective essays should order events sequentially. Students will have an easier time drafting their essays once they identify the order in which the events took place.

- As students begin elaborating on their topics, remind them that a reflective essay conveys personal experiences. To share the flavor of such experiences, good writers use effective figures of speech. An effective figure of speech brings a reader into an experience by connecting the experience to something the reader has experienced or can readily envision.

Revising

- Before students start to revise their work, have them write down the overall feeling they wish the essay to convey to a reader. As they read through their drafts, students should keep this feeling in mind to help them determine how each sentence in each paragraph develops or supports this overall feeling.

- Have students team up with peer editors as they revise. Have the peer editors use these guidelines: Does the essay convey a vivid and memorable mood or feeling? Is the writing personal and detailed? Is there a clear insight that the writer gained from the experience?

(continued on page 421)

Writing WORKSHOP *continued*

Drafting

Organize your writing. The incidents that form your experience or observation will be the basis for your reflective essay, so shape your narrative around them. You might devise a plot diagram like this one to organize and plan your draft.

Elaborate with figurative language. Use precise words and develop vivid images to first describe and then explain why the experience was significant. These types of figurative language may be helpful:

- A **simile** compares two unlike things using the words *like* or *as*. (My eyes were *as* wide *as* saucers.)
- A **metaphor** compares two unlike things by stating that one thing *is* the other. (Suddenly, the room *was* an emptied swimming pool.)
- **Personification** applies human qualities or behavior to something nonhuman. (Disappointment grabbed me, dragging me into deeper confusion.)

Plot Structure

Climax —identify the point of highest interest

Rising Action —develop the conflict

Falling Action —describe what happens after the climax

Exposition —establish setting and introduce characters

Resolution —tie up the loose ends

Revising

Revise for unity. Every paragraph, sentence, and detail should contribute to the main idea or feeling of your reflective essay. Jot down a few key words that summarize the feelings you want to convey in your writing. Then, review your draft, highlighting information that strays from these feelings.

Model: Revising for Unity

Key Feelings:
excitement
suspense
disappointment

My father, glowing with pleasure at his gift to me, emerged from behind the box. ~~He had been working all week and this was the first time I had seen him.~~ *and* He said, "My daughter deserves the best present that money can buy. . . ."

This information about Samantha's father pulls attention away from the suspense of the moment.

Revise to vary sentence length. In narrative writing, variety in sentence length can add interest to your narrative. Review your draft to find places in which your sentences fall into a pattern. Then, apply these revision strategies:

- Break up passages that have consecutive short sentences by combining sentences.
- Break up passages that have consecutive long sentences by splitting them into two or three simple sentences.

420 ◆ *Turning Points*

USING TECHNOLOGY IN WRITING

If students are using word processors to draft and revise their autobiographical essays, suggest that they strike out text rather than deleting it while elaborating and revising their drafts. This way, instead of cutting the chosen text, they can go back and review the text they marked to delete and decide if they want to revise it or simply cut it.

Students can also use the organizing tools and revision checkers available on the **Writing and Grammar iText CD-ROM.**

Revise to replace vague words. A vague word—whether it is a noun, a verb, or a modifier—cannot communicate your unique experience. Replace words that are vague, dull, or inaccurate with more precise words or phrases that better reflect what you are describing.

Vague: It was one of the best things I had ever seen.

Precise: It was one of the most colorful packages I had ever seen.

Compare the model and nonmodel. Why is the model more interesting?

Nonmodel	Model
It would have been a good birthday present except for one thing: the doll-house was in a glass case. My father put it in my bedroom. As he was leaving my room, he told me not to touch the glass. . . .	*It would have been a terrific birthday present except for one thing: The magical miniature world was enclosed in a glass case. My father brought it up to my bedroom and warned me never to touch the glass. . . .*

Publishing and Presenting

Choose one of the following ways to share your writing with classmates or a wider audience.

Publish electronically. Share your reflective essay by uploading it onto a classroom computer or posting it on a Web site.

Give a reading. Practice reading your reflective essay aloud. Mark it to show lines that you will emphasize and the places you will pause, slow down, or speed up. Read your essay to your class.

Read to Write

To read an example of a reflective essay, see the excerpt from **The Way to Rainy Mountain** on page 676.

Rubric for Self-Assessment

Evaluate your reflective essay using the following criteria and rating scale:

Criteria	Rating Scale				
	Not very				Very
How clearly does the essay convey an insight about life?	1	2	3	4	5
How clear is the sequence of events?	1	2	3	4	5
How effectively does each incident support the main idea of the essay?	1	2	3	4	5
How effectively is the essay developed with concrete sensory images?	1	2	3	4	5
How logically and effectively is the composition organized?	1	2	3	4	5

TEST-TAKING TIP

When students are taking a test that requires them to respond to a reflective writing prompt, they should focus on unity, the key to an effective reflective essay. If students pay careful attention during drafting and revising to the overall feeling they want to give the reader and ensure that the details they use contribute to this feeling, their essays will be successful.

Revising (continued)

- Write on the board:
    She went into the room.
    She stormed into the room.
    She floated into the room.
    She stomped into the room.
  Ask students to determine which are vague verbs in the sentences and which are vivid. Ask them what image or feeling the vivid verbs communicate.
  Answer: *Went* is a vague verb. *Stormed, floated,* and *stomped* are vivid, precise words. *Stormed* and *stomped* suggest anger; *floated* suggests happiness or dreaminess.

- Have student partners go over their essays together, looking for vague words. Encourage students to use a thesaurus to find more exact, vivid words to replace the vague words. Caution them to check the exact definition of synonyms in a dictionary before using them.

Publishing and Presenting

- Have students find two Web sites for which their essay would be well suited. Have students review their essays to make sure they are appropriate for the particular audience of the sites.

- Before students present their essays to the class, encourage them to practice reading them aloud. Have students make any notes about pacing and expression directly on a copy of their essay.

Assessment

- Review with students the assessment criteria.

- Have students choose three criteria from rubric and score the Student Model. Make sure students support their scores with details from the model. Then, have them score their own work using the same criteria.

- The rubric on this page can be found on p. 12 in **Performance Assessment and Portfolio Management.**

Evaluate Content

- Encourage students to think about where a news source finds its stories. Ask them if they would be more likely to believe a report based on one source or one based on multiple sources. Remind them to question everything—to not believe everything they read or hear. Tell them that the different media are businesses trying to make money, which they do by winning a large audience for programs and (often) by accepting advertising from other businesses.

- Have students complete the Activity on the student page. When they finish viewing two forms of coverage of an event and filling out a Feedback Form, have them present their findings to the class in an oral report.

Evaluate the Presentation

- Have students look at the presentation of the news events with a critical eye. Encourage them to ask themselves: Do I easily understand what is being presented or am I confused by it? What does this tell me about their use of clear and precise language?

- Ask students to name three types visual aids a media source might use to enhance their presentation or make complex issues more readily understandable.
  Possible response: Students may suggest the use of photographs, charts, diagrams, graphs, video footage, and computer simulations.

Listening and Speaking WORKSHOP

Comparing Media Coverage

Television, radio, and the Internet are readily available sources of detailed information on news events. However, different sources provide different levels and quality of coverage. The following listening strategies will help you compare the accuracy and validity of media coverage.

Evaluate Content

All news sources present information, but they may have different purposes, such as to inform, persuade, or, in some cases, entertain. They also have different resources for gathering and distributing news. The following will help you compare media coverage.

Identify the medium. You get news from television, newsmagazines, documentaries, and online sources. Each medium has its own strengths and weaknesses—timeliness, accessibility, and accuracy are among the most important.

Consider the purpose. News reports give information factually and objectively. Documentaries offer in-depth coverage but may reveal personal opinions. Television newsmagazines provide in-depth coverage that often includes subjective views. Editorials present a specific view or interpretation.

Question the source. Consider how a news source obtains its stories. Some news sources gather firsthand information, while others depend upon reports from news agencies. Some use multiple sources of information to corroborate, or support, their coverage, while others rely on fewer sources.

Evaluate the Presentation

To determine the value of a news source, compare and contrast the effectiveness with which it delivers and explains news events. Use these criteria:

- **Clarity and Coherence** The ideas should be presented in a logical order using language that is clear and precise.

- **Use of Visual Aids** Complex issues can be presented more effectively with photographs and video, diagrams, graphs, demonstrations, props, and other visual aids.

Activity:
Comparison and Feedback Choose a current event, and compare the way it is covered by two different media. Use the Feedback Form to evaluate the content and presentation. Share your findings in an oral report to your class.

Feedback Form for Comparing Media Coverage

Rating System
+ = Excellent   ✔ = Average   – = Weak

Content
Purpose clearly represented _____
Accuracy of information _____
Depth of coverage _____

Delivery
Logical presentation _____
Clear, precise language _____
Use of visual aids _____

Answer the following questions:
Is the media genre suited to cover the story effectively? Why?

Do you trust the media source to present information accurately and fairly?

CUSTOMIZE INSTRUCTION FOR UNIVERSAL ACCESS

For English Learners	For Less Proficient Readers
Students may have difficulty evaluating a news source in just one viewing. Have available for students videotaped news shows that they can either view during school hours or take home to watch. Encourage them to watch the coverage multiple times to ensure that they understand the stories. Have them compare and contrast different television news sources based on how easy they are to understand.	Encourage students to watch videotaped news shows. Have available for students videotaped news shows that they can view during class together as a group. As they watch the news coverage, pause the tape periodically to check for understanding and to discuss what they've seen so far. Ask them to point out the use of visual aids and in what way those visuals enhanced the presentation of the news.

Assessment WORKSHOP

Cause and Efffect

In the reading sections of some tests, you may be required to read a passage to identify cause-and-effect relationships. The following strategies can help:

- Identify the cause and effect. A *cause* is an event that makes something else happen, and an *effect* is the result that happens.
- Recognize cause-and-effect relationships by asking yourself: What happened? What was the result? What caused this occurrence?

Test-Taking Strategies

- Look for words and phrases such as *because* and *as a result*.
- Take the time to consider the answer you select, even if the first or second one seems correct at first glance.

Sample Test Item

Directions: Read the passage, and then answer the question that follows.

Last month's ski trip was a flop. Only eight of our thirty members came. Some had no transportation. Others had prior holiday commitments. In addition, the cost of the trip was more than most members could pay. We need to address these concerns before the next trip.

1 What effect did the holidays have on the trip?

  A Some members did not have any transportation.

  B Some members could not afford to go.

  C The organizers of the trip had not planned well.

  D Some members had other holiday plans.

Answer and Explanation

Answer **D** is correct because it explains how the holidays prevented some people from participating. Answers **A** and **B** refer to causes of low attendance on the trip, not to the effect of the holidays. Answer **C** does not provide details explaining why the holidays had an effect on the trip.

▶ Practice

Directions: Read the passage, and then answer the question that follows.

Gina and Phoebe had planned to study together for the next day's algebra exam, as they often did. They had agreed to meet at the library at six-thirty. But as Gina was leaving the house, her mother fell and hurt her arm. Gina had to rush her to the hospital. By the time she could call Phoebe, it was well past 11 P.M. Although it was not her fault that she missed their appointment, Gina was worried that Phoebe would be angry with her.

1 Why did Gina not meet Phoebe at the library?

  A Gina forgot that they had planned to meet.

  B Gina's mother hurt her arm.

  C Gina took her mother to the hospital.

  D It was past closing time at the library.

Applying Reading Strategies

Explain to students that to evaluate a character's decision, they may need to examine cause-and-effect relationships. Their judgment may depend on what caused a character to act or the effect of that action.

Applying Test-Taking Strategies

- Have students read the Sample Test Item. Ask them to identify the effect of all the causes listed.
- Next, ask students: What made people decide to not go on the ski trip? What were the causes of their decisions? What was the effect of their decisions?
  Answer: People decided to not go on the trip because they couldn't afford it, had no way to get there, or had made other plans for the holiday. The effect was that only eight people out of thirty went, and because of the low attendance, it was felt to be a "flop."
- Have students apply these cause-and-effect strategies to the Practice question.

Answer

The correct answer is *C*. Answers *A* and *D* are incorrect because they present information not found in the passage. Answer *B* is incorrect because the arm injury to Gina's mother did not by itself delay Gina; it was the trip to the hospital that did so.

TEACHING RESOURCES

The following resources can be used to enrich or extend the instruction for p. 423.

PRENTICE HALL
ASSESSMENT *SYSTEM*

- **Workbook**
- **Skill Book**
- **Transparencies**
- **CD-ROM**

Unit Objectives

1. To read selections in different genres that develop the theme "Expanding Horizons"
2. To apply a variety of reading strategies, particularly strategies for reading fiction, appropriate to these selections
3. To analyze literary elements
4. To use a variety of strategies to build vocabulary
5. To learn elements of grammar, usage, and style
6. To use recursive writing processes to write in a variety of forms
7. To develop listening and speaking skills
8. To express and support responses to various types of texts
9. To prepare, organize, and present literary interpretations

Meeting the Objectives

With each selection, you will find instructional materials through which students can meet these objectives. Further, you will find additional practice pages for reading strategies, literary analysis, vocabulary, and grammar in the **Selection Support: Skills Development Workbook** in your **Teaching Resources.**

Background

Art

Figure With Stars by Joy Gallowitz

Ask students to identify the three major elements represented in the picture: the person, the stars, and the forms suggesting galaxies or waves. Point out the artist's effort to integrate the person and the natural forms: The stars fall in a pattern set by the person's gaze, and the person's head rides or sends out the galaxies or waves. Ask students the following question:

What details suggest that a person's expectations or knowledge help shape their experiences? Possible responses: The stars emerge from, or brighten under, or collect inside the person's gaze, suggesting that *how* we see helps determine *what* we see. The person appears to ride the galaxies or waves, suggesting a collaboration between our lives and larger forces.

424

UNIT 5 Expanding Horizon

Figure with Stars, © Joy Gallowitz

424 ◆ *Expanding Horizons*

UNIT FEATURES

Connections

Every unit contains a feature that connects literature to a related topic, such as art, science, or history. In this unit, the excerpt from Frank McCourt's *Angela's Ashes* on pp. 474–481 tells of a young girl who opened the author's eyes to the world of poetry.

Use the information and questions on the Connections pages to enrich students' understanding of the selections presented within the unit.

Reading Informational Materials

These selections will help students learn to analyze and evaluate informational texts, such as workplace documents, technical directions, and consumer materials. They will expose students to the organization and features unique to nonnarrative texts.

In this unit, students will learn to analyze articles that explain cause-and-effect relationships.

Exploring the Theme

New places, new ideas, new friends—every new experience expands your horizons. Your world becomes larger when you consider new ways of seeing and doing. Through the stories, poems, and essays in this unit, you will travel from Nigeria to England, meeting a kindly old widow, celebrities, and a band of thieves. Your horizons will expand with a variety of new experiences and interesting people.

When you read the essay "What Makes a Degas a Degas?" you may see more in a painting than you have seen before. When you read "A Civil Peace," you may understand more about life in wartime. Every time you read, take the opportunity to learn more about the world around you.

▲ **Critical Viewing** What details in this picture convey the idea of expanding horizons? **[Analyze]**

ASSESSMENT RESOURCES

📖 **Selection Support: Skills Development Workbook**
📖 **Formal Assessment**
📖 **Open Book Tests**
📖 **Performance Assessment and Portfolio Management**
📖 **Extension Activities**

Assessing Student Progress

Listed below are the tools that are available to measure the degree to which students meet the unit objectives.

Informal Assessment

The questions in the Review and Assess sections are a first-level response to the concepts and skills presented with the selections. Students' responses provide a brief, informal measure of their grasp of the material. These responses can indicate where further instruction and practice are needed. Follow up with the practice pages in **Selection Support: Skills Development Workbook.**

Formal Assessment

The **Formal Assessment** booklet contains the Selection Tests and Unit Tests.

- Selection Tests measure comprehension and skills acquisition for each selection or group of selections.
- Each Unit Test provides students with thirty multiple-choice questions and five essay questions designed to assess students' knowledge of the literature and skills taught in the unit.

The **Open Book Tests** ask students to demonstrate their ability to synthesize and communicate information from selections or groups of selections.

To assess student writing, you will find rubrics and scoring models in the **Performance Assessment and Portfolio Management** booklet. In this booklet, you will also find scoring rubrics for listening and speaking activities.

Alternative Assessment

The **Extension Activities** booklet contains writing activities, listening and speaking activities, and research and technology activities that are appropriate for students with different ability levels. You may also use these activities as an alternative measure of students' growth.

▶**Critical Viewing**

Answer: The dual images of a rolling sea and a starry universe convey a sense of infinite possibilities, which the person seems open to or involved in discovering.

425

Why Read Literature?

The "Why Read Literature?" page in each unit presents a list of possible purposes for reading. Each purpose for reading is connected to one or more of the selections in the unit. Good readers set a purpose before reading to help them read actively and focus on meaningful details.

Unit 5 introduces three purposes for reading. "Read for the Love of Literature" encourages students to meet a famous poet and enjoy the renewal of spring. "Read to Be Entertained" suggests that students enjoy the surprises and mysteries good literature can create. "Read for Information" encourages students to learn more about a famous painter's techniques.

How to Use This Page

- Tell students that before reading each selection in this unit, they should set a purpose for reading. This will help them read in a more active and focused manner.

- Explain that they can increase their love of literature by reading about a blooming apple orchard in springtime in "In the Orchard."

- To be entertained, a reader must read actively, taking note of clues to mysterious and surprising happenings, as when a stranger who seems to know his way around crashes a party in "The Street of the Cañon."

- Reading to obtain information is another valuable purpose for reading. Students should focus on the specific type of information they want to learn. In "What Makes a Degas a Degas?" students can read to learn more about Edgar Degas' techniques with light, color, and brushstrokes in his paintings.

 Read Literature?

Especially when you read to expand your horizons, you have a reason or purpose in mind: to learn, to appreciate—or even to be entertained by something new. Preview three purposes you might set for yourself before reading the works in this unit.

1

Read for the Love of Literature

Reynolds Price uses an uncanny knack for description to bring his subjects to life. See how he uses this ability to reflect on a premier American poet in **"A Picture From the Past: Emily Dickinson,"** page 464.

The joys of being in a blooming apple orchard in spring may make the seasons that follow it seem bland in comparison. Henrik Ibsen blissfully captures this time of renewal in his poem **"In the Orchard,"** page 513.

2

Read to Be Entertained

Many people are charmed by the talents of parrots who acquire a small English vocabulary. What would they think of a parrot who could help solve a mystery? A parrot can be good for more than simply repeating the words humans say. Just ask Mrs. Gage, a poor elderly woman whose life takes on new meaning when she meets a mimicking yet intelligent bird, in Virginia Woolf's **"The Widow and the Parrot,"** page 430.

When a stranger from a rival village crashes a birthday party and leaves a mysterious package, no one is sure of his motives. Try to solve the mystery yourself as you read **"The Street of the Cañon"** by Josephina Niggli, page 498.

3

Read for Information

A nineteenth-century French painter named Edgar Degas was part of the artistic movement called Impressionism, a revolutionary new style of painting that focused on capturing the essence of objects through reproducing the shifting light and color. Learn more about his work in **"What Makes a Degas a Degas?"** by Richard Mühlberger, page 466.

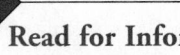 **Take It to the Net**

Visit the Web site for online instruction and activities related to each selection in this unit.
www.phschool.com

✸ ENRICHMENT: Further Reading

Have students choose one or more of the works below to extend the unit theme "Expanding Horizons" or to read more by the unit authors.

The Adventures of Huckleberry Finn by Mark Twain
In this classic novel, a young man finds adventure on the Mississippi.

The Road To Memphis by Mildred D. Taylor
This continuing saga of the Logan family can be found in the **Prentice Hall Literature Library.**

Silas Marner by George Eliot
This story of a recluse who befriends a child can be found in the **Prentice Hall Literature Library.**

How to Read Literature

Use Strategies for Reading Fiction

Imagine visiting a new and exciting place each week. If you read works of fiction, you can! Reading fiction allows you to explore unfamiliar places and unusual worlds without ever leaving your home. When you read fiction, use the following strategies to help you understand and enjoy what you are reading:

1. Draw inferences.

Fictional characters and situations do not come with clear labels like "villain" or "disaster"—you have to infer information from the clues you are given. Use a character's attitudes and actions to read "between the lines."

2. Predict.

- As you read, ask yourself what might happen next. Make educated guesses about the characters, the situation, and the text structure of a story or poem.

- Base your predictions on your own experiences in similar situations or on information that has been provided in the text. Adjust your predictions as you learn more information.

3. Use prior background knowledge.

- Your prior background knowledge is what you already know and can relate to a character's experiences and reactions. It can also guide you in understanding new experiences and ideas in literature.

- Look for details in the text that confirm opinions you already have, as well as details that change your opinions.

4. Engage your senses.

When you engage your senses, use the details of sight, sound, taste, smell, and touch to imagine a scene. Use the sensory details that a writer includes to fully experience the setting.

In the passage at right, the highlighted text shows the sensory language that makes the writing compelling.

As you read the selections in this unit, review the reading strategies and look at the notes in the side columns. Use the suggestions to apply the strategies and interact with the text.

Engaging Your Senses

The voice of the thunder filled the gorge, drowning the ceaseless roar of the rivers. Like the arrows of Sabaoth, the lightning flashes rained down on the peaks. . . .
— from "A Storm in the Mountains"

Sounds: voice of thunder
ceaseless roar
Sights: lightning flashes

How to Read Literature

The "How to Read Literature" page in each unit presents a set of strategies to help readers understand authors' words and ideas. Each reading strategy is taught in conjunction with one or more of the selections within the unit. Good readers develop a bank of strategies from which they can draw as needed.

Unit 5 introduces four strategies for reading fiction. Students learn to draw inferences about characters and situations, predict outcomes, apply their prior knowledge for enhanced understanding, and engage their senses for richer enjoyment.

How to Use This Page

Introduce the strategies for reading fiction, presenting each as a tool for developing understanding when reading the selections in this unit.

- As they read "The Widow and the Parrot" (p. 430), students will learn how to draw inferences about characters and situations, deepening their understanding of the work.

- As they read "The Street of the Cañon" (p. 498), students will learn how to predict outcomes to help them better understand what they are reading.

- As they read "Civil Peace" (p. 444), students will learn how to use their prior background knowledge to help them relate to the characters.

- As they read "In the Orchard" (p. 513), students will learn how to engage their senses to better imagine a scene.

MODEL A READING STRATEGY: Draw Inferences

Help students draw inferences by modeling the process, using this example from "The Widow and the Parrot":

> Mrs. Gage opened [the letter] and read:
>
> "Dear Madam: We have the honor to inform you of the death of your brother Mr. Joseph Brand.
>
> "Lawk a mussy," said Mrs. Gage. "Old brother Joseph gone at last."

Tell students:

Mrs. Gage learns of her brother's death by letter and is surprised. These facts suggest that she has not been in close contact with him. Otherwise, she might have been less surprised, or been by his side when he died. Her response, "gone at last," does not suggest great grief over the death but instead indicates quick acceptance of the inevitable. You can conclude that she was not close with her brother.

The Widow and the Parrot

Lesson Objectives

1. **To analyze and respond to literary elements**
   - Literary Analysis: Motivation
   - Connecting Literary Elements: Plot

2. **To read, comprehend, analyze, and critique a short story**
   - Reading Strategy: Drawing Inferences
   - Reading Check questions
   - Review and Assess questions
   - Assessment Practice (ATE)

3. **To develop word analysis skills, fluency, and systematic vocabulary**
   - Vocabulary Development Lesson: Forms of *sagacity*

4. **To understand and apply written and oral language conventions**
   - Spelling Strategy
   - Grammar Lesson: Appositives

5. **To understand and apply appropriate writing and research strategies**
   - Writing Lesson: Last Will and Testament
   - Extension Activity: Internet Home Page

6. **To understand and apply listening and speaking strategies**
   - Extension Activity: Dialogue

STEP-BY-STEP TEACHING GUIDE	PACING GUIDE
PRETEACH	
Motivate Students and Provide Background	
Use the Motivation activity (ATE p. 428)	5 min.
Read and discuss the Preview material and Background information (SE/ATE p. 428) [A]	5 min.
Introduce the Concepts	
Introduce the Literary Analysis and Reading Strategy (SE/ATE p. 429) [A]	15 min.
Pronounce the vocabulary words and read their definitions (SE p. 429)	5 min.
TEACH	
Monitor Comprehension	
Informally monitor comprehension by circulating while students read independently or in groups [A]	25 min.
Monitor students' comprehension with the Reading Check notes (SE/ATE pp. 431, 433, 435, 437)	as students read
Develop vocabulary with Vocabulary notes (SE pp. 431, 432, 437; ATE p. 437)	as students read
Develop Understanding	
Develop students' understanding of motivation with Literary Analysis annotations (SE pp. 431, 432; ATE pp. 431, 432, 436) [A]	10 min.
Develop students' understanding of drawing inferences with Reading Strategy annotations (SE pp. 433, 436, 437; ATE pp. 431, 433, 435, 436, 437)	10 min.
ASSESS	
Assess Mastery	
Assess students' mastery of the Reading Strategy and Literary Analysis by having them answer the Review and Assess questions (SE/ATE p. 439)	20 min.
Use one or more of the print and media Assessment Resources (ATE p. 441) [A]	up to 50 min.
EXTEND	
Apply Understanding	
Have students complete the Vocabulary Development Lesson and the Grammar Lesson (SE p. 440) [A]	20 min.
Apply students' knowledge of order of importance using the Writing Lesson (SE p. 441) [A]	45 min.
Apply students' understanding using one or more of the Extension Activities (SE p. 441)	20–90 min.

 ACCELERATED INSTRUCTION:
Use the strategies and activities identified with an [A].

UNIVERSAL ACCESS
● = Below Level Students
▲ = On-Level Students
■ = Above Level Students

Time and Resource Manager

RESOURCES

PRINT	TRANSPARENCIES	TECHNOLOGY
• **Beyond Literature**, Career Connection: Veterinary Science, p. 28 ▲ ■		• **Interest Grabber Video**, Tape 3 ● ▲ ■
• **Selection Support Workbook:** ● ▲ ■ Literary Analysis, p. 112 Reading Strategy, p. 111 Build Vocabulary, p. 109	• **Literary Analysis and Reading Transparencies,** pp. 55 and 56 ● ▲ ■	
• **Adapted Reader's Companion** ● • **Reader's Companion** ●		• **Listening to Literature** ● ▲ ■ Audiocassettes, Side 13 Audio CDs, CD 9
• **English Learner's Companion** ● ▲ • **Literatura en español** ● ▲ • **Literary Analysis for Enrichment** ■		
• **Formal Assessment:** Selection Test, pp. 98–100 ● ▲ ■ • **Open Book Test**, pp. 82–84 ● ▲ ■ • **Performance Assessment and Portfolio Management**, p. 16 ● ▲ ■ • PRENTICE HALL **ASSESSMENT** *SYSTEM* ● ▲ ■	• PRENTICE HALL **ASSESSMENT** *SYSTEM* ● ▲ ■ Skills Practice Answers and Explanations on Transparencies	• **Test Bank Software** ● ▲ ■ • **Got It! Assessment Videotapes**, Tape 3 ● ▲
• **Selection Support Workbook:** ● ▲ ■ Build Grammar Skills, p. 110 • **Writing and Grammar**, Platinum Level ● ▲ ■ • **Extension Activities**, p. 28 ● ▲ ■	• **Daily Language Practice Transparencies** ● ▲ • **Writing Models and Graphic Organizers on Transparencies**, pp. 53–55 ● ▲ ■	• **Writing and Grammar iText CD-ROM** ● ▲ ■ *Take It to the Net* www.phschool.com

BLOCK SCHEDULING: Use one 90-minute class period to preteach the selection and have students read it. Use a second 90-minute class period to assess students' mastery of skills and have them complete one of the Extension Activities.

Step-by-Step Teaching Guide for pp. 428–429

Motivation

Ask students what they would do if they suddenly learned that they had won or inherited a million dollars. Would they continue their lives much as they are living them now? Would they make any significant changes? What would they buy? Would they give any money away? After discussing what students would do if they received such an unexpected piece of good fortune, tell them they are about to read a story about a poor person who hears that she has inherited a large fortune.

▦ Interest Grabber Video

As an alternative, play "Canine Companions" on Tape 3 to engage student interest.

❶ Background

Math

The value of currency changes from day to day and from country to country, and the value of British and United States currency has tended to lessen with time because of inflation. This means that a person who, in the early twentieth century, inherited what seems to us to be a small sum might actually have been very well-off indeed. For example, the £3,000 inherited by the widow in this story was at that time worth about $15,000 in United States currency. Though that is certainly a lot of money even today, the reader should take into account that the purchasing power of that money was much greater than it is today. The widow inherited the modern-day equivalent of a fortune that would keep her in comfort for the rest of her life, and allow her to buy houses, land, and many other things that $15,000 could not buy today.

Prepare to Read

The Widow and the Parrot

▦ Take It to the Net

Visit www.phschool.com for interactive activities and instruction related to "The Widow and the Parrot," including
- background
- graphic organizers
- literary elements
- reading strategies

Preview

Connecting to the Literature

If you have ever had a pet, you know that the bond between people and animals can be a strong one. The woman in this story has a strong connection with animals. Her kindness to animals even changes her life for the better.

❶ Background

You might be surprised to find that someone who speaks American English might have difficulty understanding some words and expressions in British English. In "The Widow and the Parrot," Mrs. Gage mentions *pounds sterling* and *solicitors*. Although an American might think of *pounds* as weight and *solicitors* as salespeople, a resident of Great Britain thinks of *pounds* as British money and *solicitors* as lawyers.

TEACHING RESOURCES

The following resources can be used to enrich or extend the instruction for pp. 428–429.

Motivation
▦ **Interest Grabber Video,** Tape 3

Background
📖 **Beyond Literature,** p. 28 ▦

▦ **Take It to the Net**
Visit www.phschool.com com for background and hotlinks for "The Widow and the Parrot."

Literary Analysis
📖 **Selection Support:** Literary Analysis, p. 112 ▦

📄 **Literary Analysis and Reading Transparencies,** Motivation, p. 56

Reading
📄 **Literary Analysis and Reading Transparencies,** Drawing Inferences, p. 55

▦ **BLOCK SCHEDULING:** Resources marked with this symbol provide varied instruction during 90-minute blocks.

Literary Analysis

Motivation

When you understand a character's **motivation,** you know the reason for his or her actions or words. Knowing why characters act as they do will help you understand story events. For instance, in "The Widow and the Parrot," a rich old man leaves all his wealth to a sister whom he has not seen in years. His action makes sense if you look for the man's motive: He may have been sorry that he did not help her during his lifetime. Use a diagram like the one here to explore the motives behind the actions of the characters in this story.

Connecting Literary Elements

The motives of the characters are what moves a story through its **plot,** the sequence of events that make up a story.

- The **exposition** introduces characters and setting.
- The **conflict** or problem is introduced and developed, reaching its highest point of intensity at the **climax.**
- The **resolution** finishes the story by tying up loose ends.

As you read "The Widow and the Parrot," identify the climax. Then, look for events that come after the climax that tell you how the main character's life has changed as a result.

Motive

Sorrow that he has not been in touch

Action

Leaves money to his sister

Action

Action

Reading Strategy

Drawing Inferences

Writers do not always tell you everything directly. Instead, you have to **draw inferences**—reach conclusions—about characters based on their speech, thoughts, and actions. For example, in "The Widow and the Parrot," you can infer that Mrs. Ford does not like the parrot based on this speech:

> "Drat the bird!" said Mrs. Ford very peevishly, pointing to a large gray parrot. "He almost screams my head off."

As you read, draw inferences about characters based on the details of the story.

Vocabulary Development

ford (fôrd) *n.* shallow place in a river where people can cross (p. 431)

dilapidated (də lap′ ə dāt′ id) *adj.* shabby and neglected (p. 432)

sovereigns (säv′ rənz) *n.* British gold coins worth one pound each (p. 437)

sagacity (sə gas′ ə tē) *n.* wisdom (p. 437)

❷ Literary Analysis

Motivation

- Explain to students that, because they are modeled on human beings, characters in literature have motivations, or reasons, for their actions. Thinking about and understanding a character's motivation helps a reader better understand the story.

- Read the instruction about motivation together as a class. Ask students to theorize other reasons the rich old man may have left his sister the money.

- Encourage students to use a diagram like the one shown to determine characters' motives as they read the story.

❸ Reading Strategy

Drawing Inferences

- Tell students that when they draw an inference they are making a judgment about a character based on the character's actions, thoughts, and speech.

- As a class, read the instruction for drawing inferences. Focus students' attention on the example from the story. Discuss with students what else they might infer about Mrs. Ford.

- Remind students to think about what the characters say, do, and think, and what that tells the reader about them.

Vocabulary Development

- Pronounce each vocabulary word for students, and read the definitions as a class. Have students identify any words with which they are already familiar.

CUSTOMIZE INSTRUCTION FOR UNIVERSAL ACCESS

For Special Needs Students	For Less Proficient Readers	For English Learners
Have students read the adapted version of "The Widow and the Parrot" in the **Adapted Reader's Companion.** This version provides basic-level instruction in an interactive format with questions and write-on lines. Completing the adapted version will prepare students to read the selection in the Student Edition.	Have students read the selection in the **Reader's Companion.** This version provides basic-level instruction in an interactive format with questions and write-on lines. After students finish the selection in **Reader's Companion,** have them complete the questions and activities in the Student Edition.	Have students read the adapted version of the selection in the **English Learner's Companion.** This version provides basic-level instruction in an interactive format with questions and write-on lines. Completing the adapted version will prepare students to read the selection in the Student Edition.

 E-Teach

Visit E-Teach at www.phschool.com for teachers' essays on how to teach, with questions and answers.

**CUSTOMIZE INSTRUCTION
For Visual/Spatial Learners**

To help students to draw inferences about the story, point out that stories in movies and on television make a point of showing rather than telling about events. Suggest that students try to see their stories in the mind's eye as films. What is implied about motivation in the characters' actions as Woolf shows them? If students were filming the story, what scenes might they add to the story to further explore the characters' motivations?

❶ About the Selection

Kindly old Mrs. Gage gains an inheritance from her brother, but the miserly old man hides it where it cannot be found. After a series of apparent disasters, Mrs. Gage's kindness to her brother's pet parrot leads her to discover the missing fortune. The story ends happily, as the heroine's goodness to animals is rewarded by wealth.

❷ ▶Critical Viewing

Answer: Students may note that the title implies that a parrot will be a main character in the story.

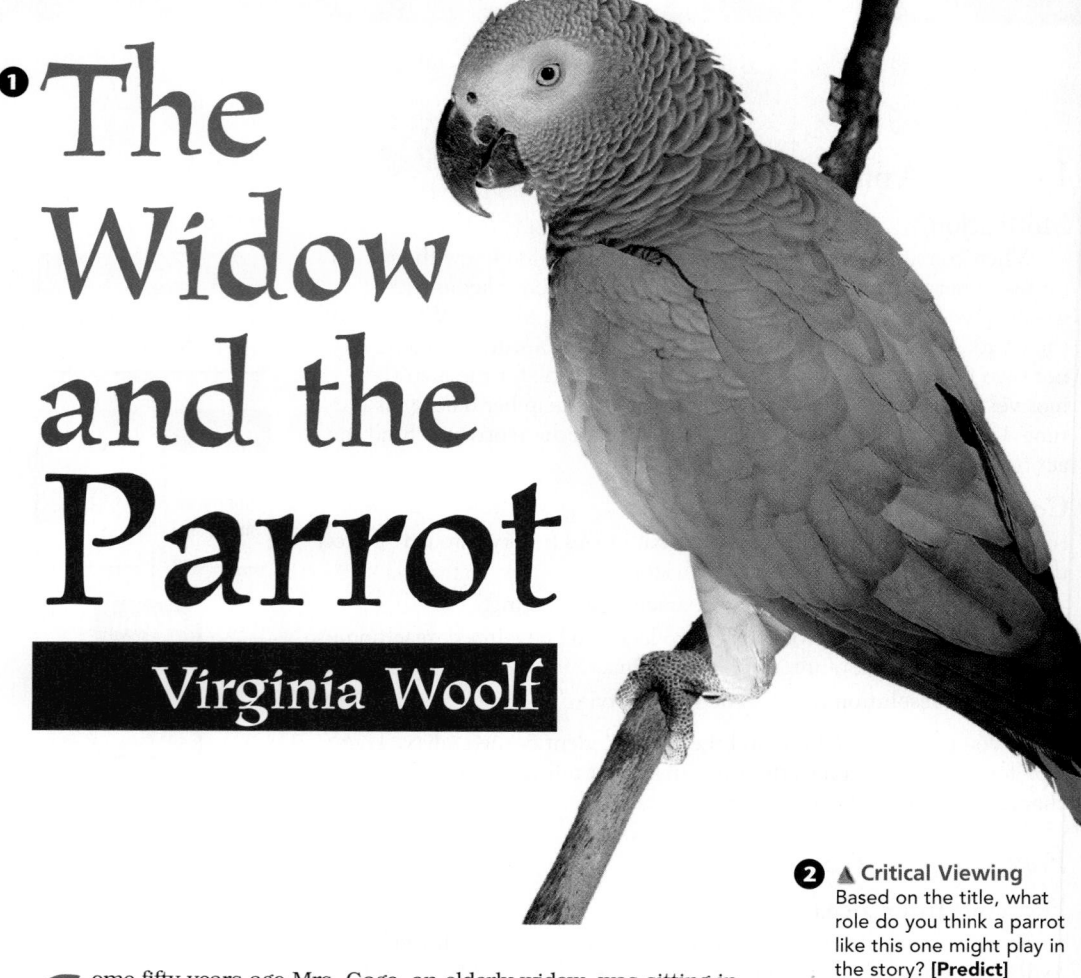

❶The Widow and the Parrot

Virginia Woolf

❷ ▲ Critical Viewing
Based on the title, what role do you think a parrot like this one might play in the story? **[Predict]**

Some fifty years ago Mrs. Gage, an elderly widow, was sitting in her cottage in a village called Spilsby in Yorkshire. Although lame and rather shortsighted she was doing her best to mend a pair of clogs, for she had only a few shillings a week to live on. As she hammered at the clog, the postman opened the door and threw a letter into her lap.

It bore the address "Messrs. Stagg and Beetle, 67 High Street, Lewes, Sussex."

Mrs. Gage opened it and read:

"Dear Madam: We have the honor to inform you of the death of your brother Mr. Joseph Brand."

"Lawk a mussy," said Mrs. Gage. "Old brother Joseph gone at last!"

"He has left you his entire property," the letter went on, "which consists of a dwelling house, stable, cucumber frames, mangles, wheelbarrows, etc., etc., in the village of Rodmell, near Lewes. He also bequeaths

430 ◆ Expanding Horizons

TEACHING RESOURCES

The following resources can be used to enrich or extend the instruction for pp. 430–438.

Literary Analysis

📖 **Writing Models and Graphic Organizers on Transparencies,** pp. 53–55 ■

Reading

📖 **Selection Support:** Reading Strategy, p. 111; Build Vocabulary, p. 109

📖 **Reader's Companion**

📖 **English Learner's Companion**

🎧 **Listening to Literature Audiocassettes,** Side 13 ■

💿 **Listening to Literature Audio CDs,** CD 9 ■

■ **BLOCK SCHEDULING:** Resources marked with this symbol provide varied instruction during 90-minute blocks.

to you his entire fortune; Viz: £3,000. (three thousand pounds[1]) sterling."

Mrs. Gage almost fell into the fire with joy. She had not seen her brother for many years, and, as he did not even acknowledge the Christmas card which she sent him every year, she thought that his miserly habits, well known to her from childhood, made him grudge even a penny stamp for a reply.

But now it had all turned out to her advantage. With three thousand pounds, to say nothing of house, etc., etc., she and her family could live in great luxury for ever.

She determined that she must visit Rodmell at once. The village clergyman, the Rev. Samuel Tallboys, lent her two pound ten, to pay her fare, and by next day all preparations for her journey were complete. The most important of these was the care of her dog Shag during her absence, for in spite of her poverty she was devoted to animals, and often went short herself rather than stint her dog of his bone.

She reached Lewes late on Tuesday night. In those days, I must tell you, there was no bridge over the river at Southease, nor had the road to Newhaven yet been made. To reach Rodmell it was necessary to cross the river Ouse by a <u>ford</u>, traces of which still exist, but this could only be attempted at low tide, when the stones on the riverbed appeared above the water. Mr. Stacey, the farmer, was going to Rodmell in his cart, and he kindly offered to take Mrs. Gage with him. They reached Rodmell about nine o'clock on a November night and Mr. Stacey obligingly pointed out to Mrs. Gage the house at the end of the village which had been left her by her brother. Mrs. Gage knocked at the door. There was no answer. She knocked again. A very strange high voice shrieked out "Not at home." She was so much taken aback that if she had not heard footsteps coming she would have run away. However, the door was opened by an old village woman, by name Mrs. Ford.

"Who was that shrieking out 'Not at home'?" said Mrs. Gage.

"Drat the bird!" said Mrs. Ford very peevishly, pointing to a large gray parrot. "He almost screams my head off. There he sits all day humped up on his perch like a monument screeching 'Not at home' if ever you go near his perch." He was a very handsome bird, as Mrs. Gage could see; but his feathers were sadly neglected. "Perhaps he is unhappy, or he may be hungry," she said. But Mrs. Ford said it was temper merely; he was a seaman's parrot and had learnt his language in the east. However, she added, Mr. Joseph was very fond of him, had called him James; and, it was said, talked to him as if he were a rational being. Mrs. Ford soon left. Mrs. Gage at once went to her box and fetched some sugar which she had with her and offered it to the parrot, saying in a very kind tone that she meant him no harm, but was his old master's sister, come to take possession of the house, and she would see to it that he was as happy as a bird could be. Taking a lantern she next

---

1. **three thousand pounds** British money worth about $15,000 at the time of the story.

Literary Analysis
Motivation Why is Mrs. Gage in such a hurry to visit Rodmell?

ford (fôrd) *n.* shallow place in a river where people can cross

5 ✓ **Reading Check**
What is Mrs. Gage's initial response to the inhospitable voice of the parrot?

---

❸ Literary Analysis
Motivation

- Call on a volunteer to read aloud the bracketed passage.
- Then, ask students the Literary Analysis question on p. 431: Why is Mrs. Gage in such a hurry to visit Rodmell?
  Answer: Mrs. Gage is in a hurry to visit Rodmell because she wants to collect the money her brother left to her, as well as see the condition of the house and other possessions he left her.

▶ Monitor Progress Have students create a motivation diagram for this passage like the one shown on p. 429.

Motive
visiting Rodmell immediately

Action	Action
borrowed money from Rev. Tallboys	arranged for the care of her dog

❹ Reading Strategy
Drawing Inferences

- Ask students the following question: What does the fact that Mrs. Gage is devoted to animals, even though she is poor, tell you about her character?
  Possible response: That she would sacrifice for her dog shows that she has a kind, unselfish nature.
- Encourage students to read ahead to find out whether their inferences about Mrs. Gage are correct.

❺ ✓ Reading Check
Answer: The inhospitable voice of the parrot surprised and somewhat frightened Mrs. Gage.

CUSTOMIZE INSTRUCTION FOR UNIVERSAL ACCESS

For English Learners	For Advanced Readers
As they read, ask students to list any words with which they are unfamiliar. Then, have students look up the meaning of those words. Encourage students to come up with a synonym for each word, directing them to use a thesaurus if necessary, and then to rewrite the original sentences with the synonyms in place of the unknown words.	Instruct students to use context clues to write their own definitions of the words *hobbled, uncanny,* and *prized* as Woolf uses them in the story. Then, have students find synonyms for each word by using a thesaurus. In each case have students compare and contrast the connotations of the words they've located. Finally, ask students to analyze Woolf's word choice, and compare her choices with the words that students found.

⑥ Critical Thinking

Identify Character Traits

- Instruct students to think about how Mrs. Gage handles her disappointment as you read aloud the bracketed passage.

- Then, ask students whether they would describe Mrs. Gage as an optimist or a pessimist. Why?
  Answer: She is an optimist; even though part of her inheritance has come to nothing, she is able to focus on the remainder. She looks for the positive.

⑦ Literary Analysis

Motivation

- Call students' attention to the bracketed sentence. Encourage them to think about Mrs. Gage's state of mind at this point.

- ▶ **Monitor Progress** Ask students the Literary Analysis question on p. 432: Why does Mrs. Gage decide to walk back to Rodmell in the rain?
  Possible Response: She walks back to Rodmell in the rain because she feels depressed after finding out that the lawyers don't know where the money is. It doesn't matter that it's raining because she's so unhappy.

- Ask students to identify with the character. Have students ever been so disappointed that they became indifferent to the weather?

⑧ Reading Strategy

Drawing Inferences

- Read aloud the bracketed passage. Ask students to note the details of Mrs. Gage's description of her brother as a child.

- Ask students whether they can infer from this description how the house Mrs. Gage inherited fell into such disrepair.
  Answer: Students will observe that even as a child, Joseph was stingy and cruel. He clearly was too miserly to keep the house in repair, and was unconcerned with his sister's well-being.

---

⑥ went round the house to see what sort of property her brother had left her. It was a bitter disappointment. There were holes in all the carpets. The bottoms of the chairs had fallen out. Rats ran along the mantelpiece. There were large toadstools growing through the kitchen floor. There was not a stick of furniture worth seven pence halfpenny; and Mrs. Gage only cheered herself by thinking of the three thousand pounds that lay safe and snug in Lewes Bank.

She determined to set off to Lewes next day in order to claim her money from Messrs. Stagg and Beetle the solicitors,[2] and then to return home as quick as she could. Mr. Stacey, who was going in to market with some fine Berkshire pigs, again offered to take her with him, and told her some terrible stories of young people who had been drowned through trying to cross the river at high tide, as they drove. A great disappointment was in store for the poor old woman directly she got in to Mr. Stagg's office.

"Pray take a seat, Madam," he said, looking very solemn and grunting slightly. "The fact is," he went on, "that you must prepare to face some very disagreeable news. Since I wrote to you I have gone carefully through Mr. Brand's papers. I regret to say that I can find no trace whatever of the three thousand pounds. Mr. Beetle, my partner, went himself to Rodmell and searched the premises with the utmost care. He found absolutely nothing—no gold, silver, or valuables of any kind—except a fine gray parrot which I advise you to sell for whatever he will fetch. His language, Benjamin Beetle said, is very extreme. But that is neither here nor there. I much fear you have had your journey for nothing. The premises are <u>dilapidated</u>; and of course our expenses are considerable." Here he stopped, and Mrs. Gage well knew that he wished her to go. She was almost crazy with disappointment. Not only had she borrowed two pound ten from the Rev. Samuel Tallboys, but she would return home absolutely empty handed, for the parrot James would have to be sold to pay her fare. It was raining hard, but Mr. Stagg did not press her to stay, ⑦ and she was too beside herself with sorrow to care what she did. In spite of the rain she started to walk back to Rodmell across the meadows.

Mrs. Gage, as I have already said, was lame in her right leg. At the best of times she walked slowly, and now, what with her disappointment and the mud on the bank, her progress was very slow indeed. As she plodded along, the day grew darker and darker, until it was as much as she could do to keep on the raised path by the river side. You might have heard her grumbling as she walked, and complaining of her ⑧ crafty brother Joseph, who had put her to all this trouble "Express," she said, "to plague me. He was always a cruel little boy when we were children," she went on. "He liked worrying the poor insects, and I've known him trim a hairy caterpillar with a pair of scissors before my

---

2. **solicitors** British legal representatives.

432 ◆ *Expanding Horizons*

dilapidated (də lap´ ə dāt´ id) *adj.* shabby and neglected

Literary Analysis
Motivation Why does Mrs. Gage decide to walk back to Rodmell in the rain?

✹ ENRICHMENT: Science Connection

Toadstools

Mrs. Gage found toadstools growing through the kitchen floor. Point out to students that toadstools are inedible forms of mushrooms. These are fungi consisting of two parts: a mycelium (stem) and a fruiting body (the umbrella-shaped top). Mushrooms vary greatly in size and color, rising from about 3/4 of an inch to about 15 inches in height, and ranging from whites and yellows to blue, violet, green, red, and black. Many species of mushroom live on decaying matter, although some live on living organisms such as trees and plants. In some instances the mushroom causes no harm to its host; however, many such growths are parasitic and can destroy the host plant.

There is no scientific difference between mushrooms and toadstools. Common edible mushrooms include the *Agaricus campestris,* often found in fields and meadows, or *Agaricus bisporus,* the mushroom grown commercially and seen in markets.

432

very eyes. He was such a miserly varmint too. He used to hide his pocket money in a tree, and if anyone gave him a piece of iced cake for tea, he cut the sugar off and kept it for his supper. I make no doubt he's all aflame at this very moment in fire, but what's the comfort of that to me?" she asked, and indeed it was very little comfort, for she ran slap into a great cow which was coming along the bank, and rolled over and over in the mud.

She picked herself up as best she could and trudged on again. It seemed to her that she had been walking for hours. It was now pitch dark and she could scarcely see her own hand before her nose. Suddenly she bethought her of Farmer Stacey's words about the ford. "Lawk a mussy," she said, "however shall I find my way across? If the tide's in, I shall step into deep water and be swept out to sea in a jiffy! Many's the couple that been drowned here; to say nothing of horses, carts, herds of cattle, and stacks of hay."

Indeed what with the dark and the mud she had got herself into a pretty pickle. She could hardly see the river itself, let alone tell whether she had reached the ford or not. No lights were visible anywhere, for, as you may be aware, there is no cottage or house on that side of the river nearer than Asheham House, lately the seat of Mr. Leonard Woolf. It seemed that there was nothing for it but to sit down and wait for the morning. But at her age, with the rheumatics in her system, she might well die of cold. On the other hand, if she tried to cross the river it was almost certain that she would be drowned. So miserable was her state that she would gladly have changed places with one of the cows in the field. No more wretched old woman could have been found in the whole county of Sussex; standing on the river bank, not knowing whether to sit or to swim, or merely to roll over in the grass, wet though it was, and sleep or freeze to death, as her fate decided.

At that moment a wonderful thing happened. An enormous light shot up into the sky, like a gigantic torch, lighting up every blade of grass, and showing her the ford not twenty yards away. It was low tide, and the crossing would be an easy matter if only the light did not go out before she had got over.

"It must be a comet or some such wonderful monstrosity," she said as she hobbled across. She could see the village of Rodmell brilliantly lit up in front of her.

"Bless and save us!" she cried out. "There's a house on fire—thanks be to the Lord"—for she reckoned that it would take some minutes at least to burn a house down, and in that time she would be well on her way to the village.

"It's an ill wind that blows nobody any good," she said as she hobbled along the Roman road. Sure enough, she could see every inch of the way, and was almost in the village street when for the first time it struck her: "Perhaps it's my own house that's blazing to cinders before my very eyes!"

Literature ❾
in context Science Connection

Animal Behavior: Talking Birds

African gray parrots, like James, are especially good at mimicking human speech. They can learn words and phrases with just a few hours of teaching. However, their ability to communicate using words is limited. Some can use words to express a few basic ideas, such as fear, hunger, or boredom. Most often, however, the words are meaningless sounds they have learned in order to please the human who feeds them.

In "The Widow and the Parrot," James appears to be an extraordinary parrot.

Reading Strategy
Drawing Inferences
What can you infer about Mrs. Gage based on the way she responds to these obstacles?

❶❶ ✔**Reading Check**
What results from Mrs. Gage's visit with the solicitors?

The Widow and the Parrot ◆ 433

❾**Background**
Science

Birds are very social animals. Pet birds often consider people to be part of their social group. That's why some will mimic human voices—they love communicating with their social group. Although tame birds are more likely to mimic human voices due to their interactions with humans, wild birds also have the ability to mimic and talk. Words spoken with excitement are usually what a bird picks up first. Common first words for such a bird might be laughing or calling the dog!

❶⓪**Reading Strategy**
Drawing Inferences

• Have students identify the obstacles that Mrs. Gage faces in this passage.

• Then, ask students the Reading Strategy question on p. 433: What can you infer about Mrs. Gage based on the way she responds to these obstacles?
  Possible Response: You can infer that, in her disappointment and in the face of these obstacles, Mrs. Gage has given up hope.

❶❶ ✔**Reading Check**

Answer: Mrs. Gage learns that the lawyers do not know where the money is, so she assumes that there is no money.

CUSTOMIZE INSTRUCTION FOR UNIVERSAL ACCESS

For Special Needs Students	For Advanced Readers
Since the use of dialect and British expressions pervade this story, students might benefit from reading along with a recorded version of this story. Use the **Listening to Literature Audiocassettes,** Side 15, or **Listening to Literature Audio CDs,** CD 7. Pause the recording occasionally to check for understanding and to answer students' questions.	Virginia Woolf was a sophisticated writer, acquainted with the works of many other writers. In this story, Woolf experiments with conventions of folk stories and oral tradition. Have students identify some of these conventions as they read. They might point out Woolf's use of dialect and the rustic setting. Students may also note the repetition of the line "Mrs. Gage, as I have already said, was lame in her right leg" to approximate an oral rendering.

433

She was perfectly right.

A small boy in his nightgown came capering up to her and cried out, "Come and see old Joseph Brand's house ablaze!"

All the villagers were standing in a ring round the house handing buckets of water which were filled from the well in Monk's house kitchen, and throwing them on the flames. But the fire had got a strong hold, and just as Mrs. Gage arrived, the roof fell in.

"Has anybody saved the parrot?" she cried.

"Be thankful you're not inside yourself, Madam," said the Rev. James Hawkesford, the clergyman. "Do not worry for the dumb creatures. I make no doubt the parrot was mercifully suffocated on his perch."

⑫ But Mrs. Gage was determined to see for herself. She had to be held back by the village people, who remarked that she must be crazy to hazard her life for a bird.

"Poor old woman," said Mrs. Ford, "she has lost all her property, save one old wooden box, with her night things in it. No doubt we should be crazed in her place too."

So saying, Mrs. Ford took Mrs. Gage by the hand and led her off to her own cottage, where she was to sleep the night. The fire was now

⑬ ▼ **Critical Viewing**
How do you think Mrs. Gage felt at seeing a sight like this and learning that it was her own house? **[Infer]**

434 ♦ Expanding Horizons

extinguished, and everybody went home to bed. But poor Mrs. Gage could not sleep. She tossed and tumbled thinking of her miserable state, and wondering how she could get back to Yorkshire and pay the Rev. Samuel Tallboys the money she owed him. At the same time she was even more grieved to think of the fate of the poor parrot James. She had taken a liking to the bird, and thought that he must have an affectionate heart to mourn so deeply for the death of old Joseph Brand, who had never done a kindness to any human creature. It was a terrible death for an innocent bird, she thought; and if only she had been in time, she would have risked her own life to save his.

She was lying in bed thinking these thoughts when a slight tap at the window made her start. The tap was repeated three times over. Mrs. Gage got out of bed as quickly as she could and went to the window. There, to her utmost surprise, sitting on the window ledge, was an enormous parrot. The rain had stopped and it was a fine moonlight night. She was greatly alarmed at first, but soon recognized the gray parrot, James, and was overcome with joy at his escape. She opened the window, stroked his head several times, and told him to come in. The parrot replied by gently shaking his head from side to side, then flew to

15 ✓ **Reading Check**

What concerns Mrs. Gage when she learns that it is her house that is burning?

The Widow and the Parrot 435

14 **Reading Strategy**

Drawing Inferences

• Call on a volunteer to read aloud the bracketed passage.

• Then, ask students what they can infer about Mrs. Gage by the way she reacts to having lost her entire inheritance.

Answer: Students will infer that she is a genuinely good-hearted and generous person since she is not the least bit concerned about her lost wealth, but rather the people and creatures in her life.

▶ **Monitor Progress** Discuss with students whether their inferences conflict with their impression of Mrs. Gage at the beginning of the story, when she reacts with joy to the news of her inheritance and her brother's death. Ask them these questions: Are her reactions inconsistent? How can you explain her reactions?

Possible response: Students may point out that Mrs. Gage is poor, and that she's happy to have come into some money. She probably isn't very sad over her brother's death since he wasn't a very nice person and never acknowledged the Christmas cards she sent him every year. In general, she puts others before herself. The reactions are therefore not inconsistent.

15 ✓ **Reading Check**

Answer: Mrs. Gage is concerned about the safety of the parrot.

CUSTOMIZE INSTRUCTION FOR UNIVERSAL ACCESS

For English Learners	For Gifted/Talented Students
An occasional Britishism or obsolete term such as *sovereign* or *half a crown* may pose problems to students. Explain these unfamiliar expressions as needed. Guide students to determine meanings of expressions such as "wealth of the Indies" from context.	Ask students to note the miraculous return of James the parrot. Challenge students to identify other narratives in which highly unlikely events determine the outcome of the plot. Have students pause here, and write speculative endings for the story. How do students think the parrot's return will resolve events?

16 Literary Analysis

Motivation

- Have students consider what they already know about Mrs. Gage's character.

- Ask students what motivates Mrs. Gage to follow the parrot. Answer: She likes the parrot and thinks he's intelligent; she treats him with as much respect as she would a human being. She may be motivated by her concern for him or by simple curiosity.

17 Reading Strategy

Drawing Inferences

- Discuss with students the possible reasons behind the parrot's behavior in the bracketed passage. Possible response: Students may suggest the parrot is trying to tell Mrs. Gage something. They may guess that the parrot wants Mrs. Gage to pick up the brick or start digging in the ground.

- Then, ask students the Reading Strategy question on p. 436: What can you infer about the parrot from its excited behavior? Possible Response: You can infer that the parrot knows something and is trying to communicate it to Mrs. Gage. It shows that the parrot is intelligent and likes Mrs. Gage as much as she likes him.

the ground, walked away a few steps, looked back as if to see whether Mrs. Gage were coming, and then returned to the window sill, where she stood in amazement.

"The creature has more meaning in its acts than we humans know," she said to herself. "Very well, James," she said aloud, talking to him as though he were a human being, "I'll take your word for it. Only wait a moment while I make myself decent."

16 So saying she pinned on a large apron, crept as lightly as possible downstairs, and let herself out without rousing Mrs. Ford.

The parrot James was evidently satisfied. He now hopped briskly a few yards ahead of her in the direction of the burnt house. Mrs. Gage followed as fast as she could. The parrot hopped, as if he knew his way perfectly, round to the back of the house, where the kitchen had originally been. Nothing now remained of it except the brick floor, which was still dripping with the water which had been thrown to put out the fire. Mrs. Gage stood still in amazement while James hopped about, pecking here and there, as if he were testing the bricks with his beak. It was a very uncanny sight, and had not Mrs. Gage been in the habit of living with animals, she would have lost her head, very likely, and hobbled back home. But stranger things yet were to happen. All this time the parrot had not said a word. He suddenly got into a state of the greatest excitement, fluttering his wings, tapping **17** the floor repeatedly with his beak, and crying so shrilly, "Not at home! Not at home!" that Mrs. Gage feared that the whole village would be roused.

"Don't take on so, James; you'll hurt yourself," she said soothingly. But he repeated his attack on the bricks more violently than ever.

"Whatever can be the meaning of it?" said Mrs. Gage, looking carefully at the kitchen floor. The moonlight was bright enough to show her a slight unevenness in the laying of the bricks, as if they had been taken up and then relaid not quite flat with the others. She had fastened her apron with a large safety pin, and she now prized this pin between the bricks and found that they were only loosely laid together. Very soon she had taken one up in her hands. No sooner had she done this than the parrot hopped onto the brick next to it, and, tapping it smartly with his beak, cried, "Not at home!" which Mrs. Gage understood to mean that she was to move it. So they went on taking up the bricks in the moonlight until they had laid bare a space some six feet by four and a half. This the parrot seemed to think was enough. But what was to be done next?

436 ❖ *Expanding Horizons*

Reading Strategy
Drawing Inferences
What can you infer about the parrot from its excited behavior?

✹ ENRICHMENT: Community Connection

Volunteer Fire Departments

In small villages at the time when this story is set, fires were generally put out by an army of neighbors working together with the tools they had at hand. Even today, many small communities that cannot afford a full-time fire department rely on volunteers to answer the call of "Fire!"

Have students find out whether their community has a paid fire department, a volunteer fire department, or a combination of the two. Interested students may want to find out the requirements for joining the volunteer squad. In most places, fire fighters must be at least 16 or 18 years old to join. Both men and women serve as fire fighters, and there is usually some training that one must go through to become an active volunteer.

Mrs. Gage now rested, and determined to be guided entirely by the behavior of the parrot James. She was not allowed to rest for long. After scratching about in the sandy foundations for a few minutes, as you may have seen a hen scratch in the sand with her claws, he unearthed what at first looked like a round lump of yellowish stone. His excitement became so intense that Mrs. Gage now went to his help. To her amazement she found that the whole space which they had uncovered was packed with long rolls of these round yellow stones, so neatly laid together that it was quite a job to move them. But what could they be? And for what purpose had they been hidden here? It was not until they had removed the entire layer on the top, and next a piece of oilcloth which lay beneath them, that a most miraculous sight was displayed before their eyes—there, in row after row, beautifully polished, and shining brightly in the moonlight, were thousands of brand new <u>sovereigns</u>!

This, then, was the miser's hiding place; and he had made sure that no one would detect it by taking two extraordinary precautions. In the first place, as was proved later, he had built a kitchen range over the spot where his treasure lay hid, so that unless the fire had destroyed it, no one could have guessed its existence; and secondly he had coated the top layer of sovereigns with some sticky substance, then rolled them in the earth, so that if by any chance one had been laid bare no one would have suspected that it was anything but a pebble such as you may see for yourself any day in the garden. Thus, it was only by the extraordinary coincidence of the fire and the parrot's <u>sagacity</u> that old Joseph's craft was defeated.

Mrs. Gage and the parrot now worked hard and removed the whole hoard—which numbered three thousand pieces, neither more nor less—placing them in her apron which was spread upon the ground. As the three thousandth coin was placed on the top of the pile, the parrot flew up into the air in triumph and alighted very gently on the top of Mrs. Gage's head. It was in this fashion that they returned to Mrs. Ford's cottage, at a very slow pace, for Mrs. Gage was lame, as I have said, and now she was almost weighted to the ground by the contents of her apron. But she reached her room without anyone knowing of her visit to the ruined house.

Next day she returned to Yorkshire. Mr. Stacey once more drove her into Lewes and was rather surprised to find how heavy Mrs. Gage's wooden box had become. But he was a quiet sort of man, and merely concluded that the kind people of Rodmell had given her a few odds and ends to console her for the dreadful loss of all her property in the fire. Out of sheer goodness of heart Mr. Stacey offered to buy the parrot off her for half a crown; but Mrs. Gage refused his offer with such indignation, saying that she would not sell the bird for all the wealth of the Indies, that he concluded that the old woman had been crazed by her troubles.

It now only remains to be said that Mrs. Gage got back to Spilsby

Reading Strategy
Drawing Inferences
What can you infer about the writer based on her description of James and the way he behaves?

sovereigns (säv´ rənz) *n.* British gold coins worth one pound each

sagacity (sə gas´ ə tē) *n.* wisdom

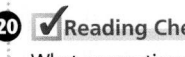 **Reading Check**
What precautions had Joseph taken in hiding the sovereigns?

The Widow and the Parrot ◆ 437

⓲ Reading Strategy
Drawing Inferences

- Encourage students to think about James's strange behavior. Have them consider why the author would choose the parrot to guide Mrs. Gage to her inheritance.
- Ask students the Reading Strategy question on p. 437: What can you infer about the writer based on her description of James and the way he behaves?
  Possible response: You can infer that the writer respects the intelligence of animals.

⓳ Vocabulary Development
Forms of *sagacity*

- Call students' attention to the word *sagacity* and its definition. Let students know that the word comes from the Latin word *sagax*, which means "keen" or "acute."
- Next, ask students whether they can suggest words that contain the same root. Words you might list on the chalkboard include *sage*, *sagacious*, and *sagaciousness*.
- Then, have students look up these words in a dictionary, and note their relationship to the Latin word root and to each other.
- Lastly, have students use the word to compose sentences about Mrs. Gage and her parrot.

⓴ ✔Reading Check

Answer: Joseph had made sure no one would find his hiding place for the sovereigns by taking two precautions: he had built a kitchen range directly over the spot where they were buried under the floor, and he had made the top layer of coins look like rocks by coating them with a sticky substance and then rolling them in dirt.

CUSTOMIZE INSTRUCTION FOR UNIVERSAL ACCESS

For Gifted/Talented Students	For Advanced Readers
Have students create the scene in which Mrs. Gage is on her deathbed, telling Mr. Talboys her fantastic tale. Instruct students to write the scene in the form of a play, with a dialogue between Mrs. Gage and the clergyman. Allow time for students to rehearse their scene and then perform it for the class. If there are enough interested students, have more than one group write the scene and then compare interpretations after the performances.	Virginia Woolf's fame is founded as much on her feminism as on her innovative writing style in books such as *To the Lighthouse* and *Mrs. Dalloway.* Ask students to read excerpts from *A Room of One's Own,* and evaluate "The Widow and the Parrot" in light of the ideas expressed there. What aspects of the story may be seen to illustrate Woolf's ideas about women's lives?

Review and Assess

1. Students should list responses in order of importance.

2. **(a)** Her dog and the parrot are important to Mrs. Gage. **(b)** She carefully arranges for her dog's care while she's away and immediately feeds the neglected parrot.

3. **(a)** Mrs. Gage is living in poverty, so the news of inherited wealth is good news. **(b)** She has been ill treated by her brother but has nevertheless extended her hand in friendship.

4. **(a)** Mrs. Gage cares for and befriends the neglected parrot; the parrot leads her to the buried treasure. **(b)** Her reaction to these events reveals that she is a thoughtful, kind, and generous person.

5. **(a)** Mrs. Gage's discovery of the gold is a surprise because she had been told that no one could find it. **(b)** Students may see the discovery of the gold as a reward for her kindness to James, the parrot. **(c)** Students should support their answers with details from their own observations and experiences.

in safety; took her black box to the Bank; and lived with James the parrot and her dog Shag in great comfort and happiness to a very great age.

It was not till she lay on her deathbed that she told the clergyman (the son of the Rev. Samuel Tallboys) the whole story, adding that she was quite sure that the house had been burnt on purpose by the parrot James, who, being aware of her danger on the river bank, flew into the scullery, and upset the oil stove which was keeping some scraps warm for her dinner. By this act, he not only saved her from drowning, but brought to light the three thousand pounds, which could have been found in no other manner. Such, she said, is the reward of kindness to animals.

The clergyman thought that she was wandering in her mind. But it is certain that the very moment the breath was out of her body, James the parrot shrieked out, "Not at home! Not at home!" and fell off his perch stone dead. The dog Shag had died some years previously.

Visitors to Rodmell may still see the ruins of the house, which was burnt down fifty years ago, and it is commonly said that if you visit it in the moonlight you may hear a parrot tapping with his beak upon the brick floor, while others have seen an old woman sitting there in a white apron.

Review and Assess

Thinking About the Selection

1. **Respond:** What would you do if you unexpectedly inherited a large sum of money?

2. **(a) Recall:** What animals are important to Mrs. Gage? **(b) Analyze:** How does she show her concern for them?

3. **(a) Recall:** Why is the news that Mrs. Gage receives at the beginning of the story so welcome to her? **(b) Infer:** What inferences can you draw about her relationship with her brother based on her reaction to this news and her comments about his will?

4. **(a) Summarize:** Describe the events that reverse Mrs. Gage's fortune. **(b) Analyze:** What does her reaction to these events reveal about her character?

5. **(a) Recall:** Why is Mrs. Gage's discovery of the gold a surprise? **(b) Make a Judgment:** Do you think Mrs. Gage's good fortune is a reward or merely a coincidence? Explain your answer. **(c) Generalize:** Do you think it is true that good things happen to good people? Why or why not?

Virginia Woolf

(1882–1941)

Virginia Woolf—whose father, Sir Leslie Stephen, was a critic, biographer, and an editor—grew up surrounded by books and met numerous writers. In 1912, she married Leonard Woolf, and together they founded the Hogarth Press. Their house became a meeting place for writers and thinkers, and her liberal beliefs flourished. She resented the sexism and corruption of English universities as well as other aspects of male-dominated Victorian England.

Woolf earned an international literary reputation with the publication of her novels, including *Mrs. Dalloway* (1925), *To the Lighthouse* (1927), and *The Waves* (1931).

ASSESSMENT PRACTICE: Reading Comprehension

Evaluate and Make Judgments	(For more practice, see Test Preparation Workbook, p. 28.)

Some tests require students to make judgments based on evidence from passages. Use the following sample test item to help students practice this skill:

Although lame and rather shortsighted Mrs. Gage was doing her best to mend a pair of clogs, for she had only a few shillings a week to live on. As she hammered at the clog, the postman opened the door and threw a letter into her lap.

The author provides evidence that Mrs. Gage is

A rude
B blind
C thrifty
D offhand

Help students to see that because Mrs. Gage is mending her shoes rather than buying new ones, *C* is the correct answer.

Review and Assess

Literary Analysis

Motivation

1. What **motivates** Mrs. Gage to be kind to the parrot?
2. Why do you think the parrot helps Mrs. Gage?
3. Using examples from the story, explain how a character's motivation may bring about unexpected results.

Connecting Literary Elements

4. The conflict of the story revolves around Mrs. Gage's attempts to get her money. Identify the climax of the story.
5. Complete a diagram like the one here by listing three details you learn in the story's resolution.

6. How do these details create a sense of closure in the story?

Reading Strategy

Drawing Inferences

7. Use a diagram like the one here to **draw inferences** about the actions of Mrs. Gage's brother, Joseph.

8. What can you infer about Mrs. Gage from her readiness to observe James's actions and to follow his directions?
9. What can you infer about the author based on the story?

Extend Understanding

10. **Health Connection:** Why might having a pet be beneficial?

Quick Review

A character's **motivation** is the reason for his or her actions or words.

Plot is the sequence of events that make up a story.
The **exposition** introduces characters and setting.
The **conflict** or problem is introduced and developed, reaching its highest point of intensity in the **climax.**
The **resolution** finishes a story by tying up its loose ends.

To **draw inferences,** consider the details, what the characters say and do, and what the narrator says.

 Take It to the Net
www.phschool.com
Take the interactive self-test online to check your understanding of the selection.

The Widow and the Parrot ◆ 439

Answers for p. 439

Review and Assess

1. Mrs. Gage feels compassion for the parrot.
2. The parrot recognizes Mrs. Gage's kindness and repays her in kind.
3. Students may cite Mrs. Gage's trust in the parrot as bringing the unexpected consequence of discovering the fortune.
4. The climax of the story occurs when Mrs. Gage follows the parrot to the house and discovers the hidden fortune.
5. Mrs. Gage got back home safely; she put her money in the bank; she lived happily with her dog and parrot.
6. These details create a sense of closure because we know what happens to Mrs. Gage and her animals—they live happily ever after.
7. Possible response:

Actions
He ignores his sister. He hides his money.

Inference
He is so miserly and mean that the only way his sister would find her inheritance is if the house were destroyed.

8. You can infer that she likes the parrot and thinks he's intelligent.
9. You can infer that the author has respect for the intelligence of animals.
10. Pets can enhance the lives of the elderly by providing companionship and help.

---

❶ Vocabulary Development

Word Analysis

1. wisdom
3. good
2. wise

Spelling Strategy

1. believe
3. their
2. foreign

Fluency: Clarify Word Meaning

1. No, because a ford is a shallow place in a river where one may cross without a bridge.
2. A dilapidated house is a shabby and neglected house.
3. The setting is most likely Britain because a sovereign is a British gold coin.
4. Judges are known for their sagacity because they act with wisdom.

❷ Grammar

1. They informed her of the death of her brother, Mr. Joseph Brand.
2. The village clergyman, the Rev. Samuel Tallboys, lent her two pound ten.
3. Mr. Stacey, the farmer, was going to town.
4. Mr. Beetle, my partner, went to Rodmell.
5. There is no house nearer than Asheham House, the seat of Mr. Leonard Woolf.

Writing Application

My dog, Brodie, is the cutest dog in the world. He's a small dog, a toy poodle, but he thinks he's much bigger. He loves to run around the yards—large groomed lawns—outside our apartment.

Integrate Language Skills

❶ Vocabulary Development Lesson

Word Analysis: Forms of *sagacity*

Sagacity and its related words come from the Latin word *sagax*, which means "keen" or "acute." *Sagacity* is a noun meaning "wisdom." Using this knowledge, provide a synonym for each word in italics:

1. Your decision shows *sagacity*.
2. Her grandmother was *sagacious*.
3. Offer a piece of *sage* advice.

Spelling Strategy

The rule of placing *i* before *e* except after *c* or when sounded like *a* as in *neighbor* or *weigh* has some exceptions. For instance, the *ei* in *sovereigns* is not pronounced like *a*. Complete the spelling of these words with *ie* or *ei* combinations:

1. bel___ve   2. for___gn   3. th___r

Fluency: Clarify Word Meaning

Review the words in the vocabulary list on page 429. Then, on your paper, answer the following questions. Define the italicized words in your answers.

1. If you *ford* a river, do you cross it on a bridge?
2. Why would most people choose not to move into a *dilapidated* house?
3. If a character reaches in his or her pocket and pulls out a *sovereign*, what is the likely setting of the story?
4. In what profession are people known for their *sagacity*?

❷ Grammar Lesson

Appositives

Virginia Woolf adds details about people and places using **appositives**—nouns or noun phrases placed near another noun or pronoun to explain it. An appositive is set off with commas or dashes when it is not essential to the meaning of the sentence.

Writers use appositives to add variety to sentence structure and to include more information concisely. In this example, the appositive is underlined and the word that is explained is in italics.

> Some fifty years ago *Mrs. Gage*, an elderly widow, was sitting in her cottage. . . .

𝒲𝒢 *Prentice Hall Writing and Grammar Connection: Chapter 20, Section 1*

Practice Copy the following sentences. Then, underline each appositive, and circle the word or phrase it renames or explains.

1. They informed her of the death of her brother, Mr. Joseph Brand.
2. The village clergyman, the Rev. Samuel Tallboys, lent her two pound ten.
3. Mr. Stacey, the farmer, was going to town.
4. Mr. Beetle, my partner, went to Rodmell.
5. There is no house nearer than Asheham House, the seat of Mr. Leonard Woolf.

Writing Application Write a brief description of a pet you know. Use appositives to add details to your writing.

TEACHING RESOURCES

The following resources can be used to enrich or extend the instruction for pp. 440–441.

Vocabulary

📖 **Selection Support:** Build Vocabulary, p. 109
📖 **Vocabulary and Spelling Practice Book** (Use this booklet for skills enrichment.) 🔲

Grammar

📖 **Selection Support:** Build Grammar Skills, p. 110
𝒲𝒢 **Writing and Grammar,** Platinum Level, p. 445
📺 **Daily Language Practice Transparencies** 🔲

Writing

𝒲𝒢 **Writing and Grammar,** Platinum Level, p. 204
💿 **Writing and Grammar iText CD-ROM** 🔲

🔲 **BLOCK SCHEDULING:** Resources marked with this symbol provide varied instruction during 90-minute blocks.

③ Writing Lesson

Last Will and Testament

Readers learn about Mrs. Gage's brother, in part, from his will and what he leaves behind. Write a last will and testament that tells others about Mrs. Gage.

Prewriting   List possessions that indicate what was important to Mrs. Gage. Jot down your ideas on note cards, writing a single thought on each one. Arrange the order of the cards to experiment with the organization.

Model: Organizing by Order of Importance

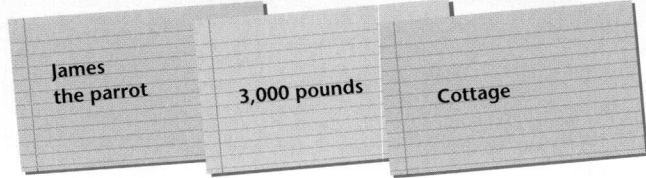

James the parrot   3,000 pounds   Cottage

Drafting   Use order-of-importance organization to show clear relationships among Mrs. Gage's possessions. Present the most important items first.

Revising   As you revise Mrs. Gage's last will and testament, be sure that you have conveyed the values and character of Mrs. Gage. Read your draft to be sure that each item is addressed in detail.

W̶G̶   *Prentice Hall Writing and Grammar Connection: Chapter 10, Section 3*

④ Extension Activities

Listening and Speaking   With a partner, discuss the relationship between Mrs. Gage and the parrot. Imagine what they would say to each other if the parrot really could talk. Then, conduct the **dialogue** between them.

- Choose roles, and have a conversation.
- Allow James to say everything that he has wanted to tell Mrs. Gage.
- Consider how language and delivery will create the proper mood and tone.

Present your dialogue before a group of classmates. **[Group Activity]**

Research and Technology   You have been assigned the creation of a "Best Short Stories" **home page** on the Internet. Write a brief review of "The Widow and the Parrot" that will make Web-surfers want to read the story. Sketch a home-page layout that is attractive and effective. Feature your review prominently.

 Take It to the Net   www.phschool.com

Go online for an additional research activity using the Internet.

The Widow and the Parrot ◆ 441

---

③ Writing Lesson

- Show students a simple model of a last will and testament.
- Encourage students to read it over, paying attention to the language and details. Elicit from students what they notice about the model in terms of format, formality and style of language, and details.
- Use the Writing Lesson to guide students through the process of writing a last will and testament for Mrs. Gage.

④ Research and Technology

- Provide students with some model reviews of books or short stories upon which to base their reviews.
- You may wish to have students consult Chapter 13 of **Writing and Grammar,** Platinum Level, p. 276, Response to Literature, for help in drafting their reviews.
- You may also use pp. 53–55 of **Writing Models and Graphic Organizers on Transparencies** to show students an example of a response to literature.

CUSTOMIZE INSTRUCTION for Universal Access

To address different learning styles, use the following activities suggested in the **Extension Activities** booklet, p. 30.

- For Logical/Mathematical Learners, use Activity 5.
- For Intrapersonal and Verbal/Linguistic Learners, use Activity 6.
- For Bodily/Kinesthetic and Interpersonal Learners, use Activity 7.

Civil Peace

Lesson Objectives

1. **To analyze and respond to literary elements**
   - Literary Analysis: Theme
   - Connecting Literary Elements: Characters' Attitudes

2. **To read, comprehend, analyze, and critique a short story**
   - Reading Strategy: Using Prior Knowledge
   - Reading Check questions
   - Review and Assess questions
   - Assessment Practice (ATE)

3. **To develop word analysis skills, fluency, and systematic vocabulary**
   - Vocabulary Development Lesson: Latin Word Root: *-reput-*

4. **To understand and apply written and oral language conventions**
   - Spelling Strategy
   - Grammar Lesson: Present Participial Phrases

5. **To understand and apply appropriate writing and research strategies**
   - Writing Lesson: News Interview
   - Extension Activity: Annotated Map

6. **To understand and apply listening and speaking strategies**
   - Extension Activity: Dialogue

STEP-BY-STEP TEACHING GUIDE	PACING GUIDE
PRETEACH	
Motivate Students and Provide Background	
Use the Motivation activity (ATE p. 442)	5 min.
Read and discuss the Preview material and Background information (SE/ATE p. 442) **A**	5 min.
Introduce the Concepts	
Introduce the Literary Analysis and Reading Strategy (SE/ATE p. 443) **A**	15 min.
Pronounce the vocabulary words and read their definitions (SE p. 443)	5 min.
TEACH	
Monitor Comprehension	
Informally monitor comprehension by circulating while students read independently or in groups **A**	15 min.
Monitor students' comprehension with the Reading Check notes (SE/ATE pp. 445, 447, 449)	as students read
Develop vocabulary with Vocabulary notes (SE pp. 445, 446, 448, 450; ATE p. 445)	as students read
Develop Understanding	
Develop students' understanding of theme with Literary Analysis annotations (SE p. 447; ATE pp. 445, 446, 447) **A**	10 min.
Develop students' understanding of using prior knowledge with the Reading Strategy annotations (SE p. 448; ATE p. 448)	10 min.
ASSESS	
Assess Mastery	
Assess students' mastery of the Reading Strategy and Literary Analysis by having them answer the Review and Assess questions (SE/ATE p. 451)	20 min.
Use one or more of the print and media Assessment Resources (ATE p. 453) **A**	up to 50 min.
EXTEND	
Apply Understanding	
Have students complete the Vocabulary Development Lesson and the Grammar Lesson (SE p. 452) **A**	20 min.
Apply students' knowledge of supporting details using the Writing Lesson (SE p. 453) **A**	45 min.
Apply students' understanding of the selection using one or more of the Extension Activities (SE p. 453)	20–90 min.

 ACCELERATED INSTRUCTION:
Use the strategies and activities identified with an **A**.

UNIVERSAL ACCESS
● = Below Level Students
▲ = On-Level Students
■ = Above Level Students

Time and Resource Manager

RESOURCES

PRINT 📖	TRANSPARENCIES 🖼	TECHNOLOGY 💿 🎧 📼
• **Beyond Literature,** Cross-Curricular Connection: Geography, p. 29 ▲ ■		• **Interest Grabber Video,** Tape 3 ● ▲ ■
• **Selection Support Workbook:** ● ▲ ■ Literary Analysis, p. 116 Reading Strategy, p. 115 Build Vocabulary, p. 113	• **Literary Analysis and Reading Transparencies,** pp. 57 and 58 ● ▲ ■	
• **Adapted Reader's Companion** ● • **Reader's Companion** ●		• **Listening to Literature** ● ▲ ■ Audiocassettes, Side 13 Audio CDs, CD 9
• **English Learner's Companion** ● ▲ • **Literatura en español** ● ▲ • **Literary Analysis for Enrichment** ■		
• **Formal Assessment:** Selection Test, pp. 101–103 ● ▲ ■ • **Open Book Test,** pp. 85–87 ● ▲ ■ • **Performance Assessment and Portfolio Management,** p. 28 ● ▲ ■ • **(PRENTICE HALL ASSESSMENT SYSTEM)** ● ▲ ■	• **(PRENTICE HALL ASSESSMENT SYSTEM)** ● ▲ ■ Skills Practice Answers and Explanations on Transparencies	• **Test Bank Software** ● ▲ ■ • **Got It! Assessment Videotapes,** Tape 3 ● ▲
• **Selection Support Workbook:** ● ▲ ■ Build Grammar Skills, p. 114 • **Writing and Grammar,** Platinum Level ● ▲ ■ • **Extension Activities,** p. 29 ● ▲ ■	• **Daily Language Practice Transparencies** ● ▲ • **Writing Models and Graphic Organizers on Transparencies,** pp. 13–16 ● ▲ ■	• **Writing and Grammar iText CD-ROM** ● ▲ ■ 🖥 ***Take It to the Net*** www.phschool.com

■ **BLOCK SCHEDULING:** Use one 90-minute class period to preteach the selection and have students read it. Use a second 90-minute class period to assess students' mastery of skills and have them complete one of the Extension Activities.

Motivation

Play a video segment from a documentary, or show pictures of a disaster area after such events as a flood, an earthquake, or a war. Ask students: What would be your first concerns if you found yourself in such a disaster area? Have students make a list of the first steps they would take. After students have compiled a list, tell them to read the story to find out how the characters in the story deal with a similar disaster.

▥ Interest Grabber Video

An an alternative, play "Chinua Achebe on Colonialism and Democracy" on Tape 3 to engage student interest.

❶ Background

Social Studies

Nigeria is the most populous country in Africa, with more than 126 million residents. Roughly the size of Texas and Kansas combined, Nigeria has more than five times as many people as those two states. Put another way, the population density of Nigeria is about 355 people per square mile. In contrast, the population density of the United States is about seventy-three people per square mile.

Prepare to Read

Civil Peace

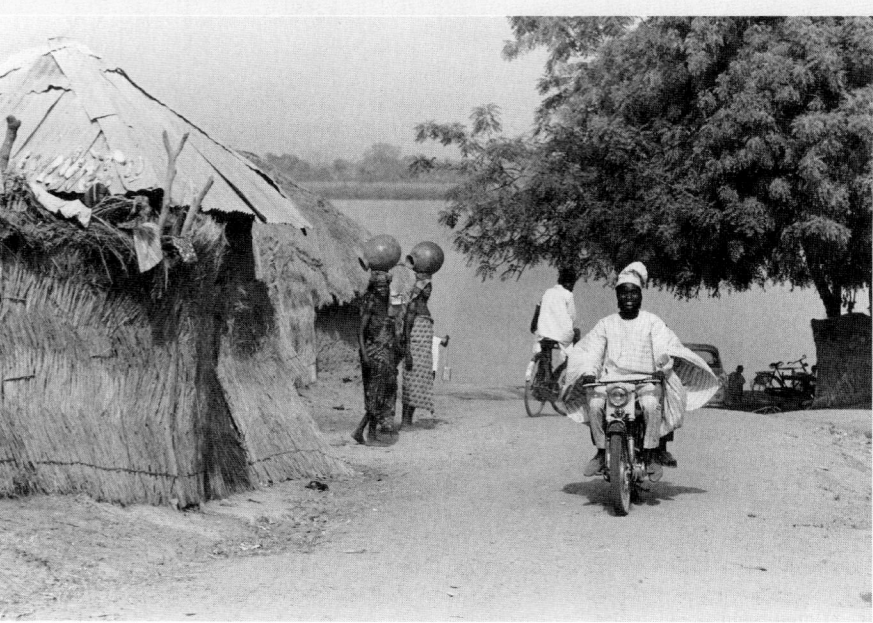

▤ Take It to the Net

Visit www.phschool.com for interactive activities and instruction related to "Civil Peace," including

- background
- graphic organizers
- literary elements
- reading strategies

Preview

Connecting to the Literature

Different factors, such as your outlook or your circumstances, influence the way you respond to a loss. The main character in this story by Chinua Achebe has survived a civil war. However, he considers himself lucky because he and his family are still alive.

❶ Background

In the late 1800s, the British annexed lands in West Africa and set up the colony of Nigeria. Local rulers resisted the British, and, in 1960, Nigeria won independence. The Ibo, one of the Nigerian peoples, seceded from Nigeria, setting up the independent Republic of Biafra. A civil war followed, and, in 1970, a defeated Biafra rejoined Nigeria. "Civil Peace" takes place in the aftermath of this civil war.

TEACHING RESOURCES

The following resources can be used to enrich or extend the instruction for pp. 442–443.

Motivation

▥ **Interest Grabber Video,** Tape 3 ▤

Background

📖 **Beyond Literature,** p. 29

▤ *Take It to the Net*

Visit www.phschool.com for background and hotlinks for "Civil Peace."

Literary Analysis

▧ **Literary Analysis and Reading Transparencies,** Theme, p. 58 ▤

Reading

📖 **Selection Support:** Reading Strategy, p. 111, Build Vocabulary, p. 113

▧ **Literary Analysis and Reading Transparencies,** Using Prior Knowledge, p. 57

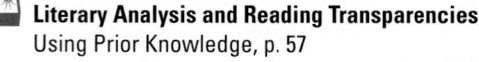 **BLOCK SCHEDULING:** Resources marked with this symbol provide varied instruction during 90-minute blocks.

Literary Analysis

Theme

Identifying the **theme** or central message of a story helps you understand it. An author can reveal a theme through key phrases that go beyond the events of the story and point to a general truth about life. Chinua Achebe uses repetition to emphasize one such phrase in "Civil Peace." Look for the repetition that marks this theme as you read the story. Using a chart like the one here, identify other key phrases that reflect the writer's message.

Key Phrase
Happy survival!

Theme

Connecting Literary Elements

In addition to key phrases that help to reveal the theme, authors also develop their ideas through the **characters' attitudes.** In this story, Jonathan Iwegbu has lived through a violent war, an experience that has changed his life. As you watch his reactions to the daily events of his life, you may notice that he thinks and behaves differently from the way other people might. If you ask why he behaves as he does, you may gain a better appreciation of the theme of the story.

Reading Strategy

Using Prior Knowledge

When a story takes you to another country or introduces you to unfamiliar people and places, you may feel the need for a guide. Your **prior knowledge**—what you already know and can relate to—can guide you in understanding the new experiences and ideas.

- Notice situations, circumstances, or events that seem familiar because of your reading or your experiences.
- Considering what you already know, apply this knowledge to fill in the gaps in the literature.

"Civil Peace" presents a man in a particular historical situation—returning home after the civil war in Nigeria. You can use your prior knowledge of coping with loss to try to understand the man's experiences.

Vocabulary Development

inestimable (in es´ tə mə bəl) *adj.* priceless; beyond measure (p. 445)

disreputable (dis rep´ yoo tə bəl) *adj.* not respectable (p. 445)

amenable (ə mē´ nə bəl) *adj.* responsive; open (p. 445)

edifice (ed´ i fis) *n.* building (p. 445)

destitute (des´ tə toot) *adj.* poverty-stricken; in great need (p. 446)

imperious (im pir´ ē əs) *adj.* commanding; powerful (p. 448)

commiserate (kə miz´ ər āt´) *v.* sympathize; share suffering (p. 450)

Civil Peace ◆ 443

**Step-by-Step Teaching Guide
for pp. 444–450**

CUSTOMIZE INSTRUCTION
For Intrapersonal Learners

Have students keep a reflective
journal as they read the story.
Encourage them to write their
thoughts and feelings each time
Jonathan Iwegbu states, "Nothing
puzzles God."

❶ About the Selection

"If life gives you lemons, make
lemonade." This expression sums up
the main character's ability to make
the best of the difficult situations
thrust upon him by a chaotic, lawless
post-civil war society. Having survived with most of his family intact,
Jonathan Iwegbu realizes that flexi-
bility is the key to success. If one
business doesn't work, another one
might. Even when thieves threaten
his family and steal his money,
Jonathan shows that a positive mental attitude helps one to adapt to
change and loss.

❷ ▶Critical Viewing

Answer: Students may observe that
the landscape appears vast and
rugged. As there are no automobiles visible, animals and bicycles
would be the most likely forms of
transportation.

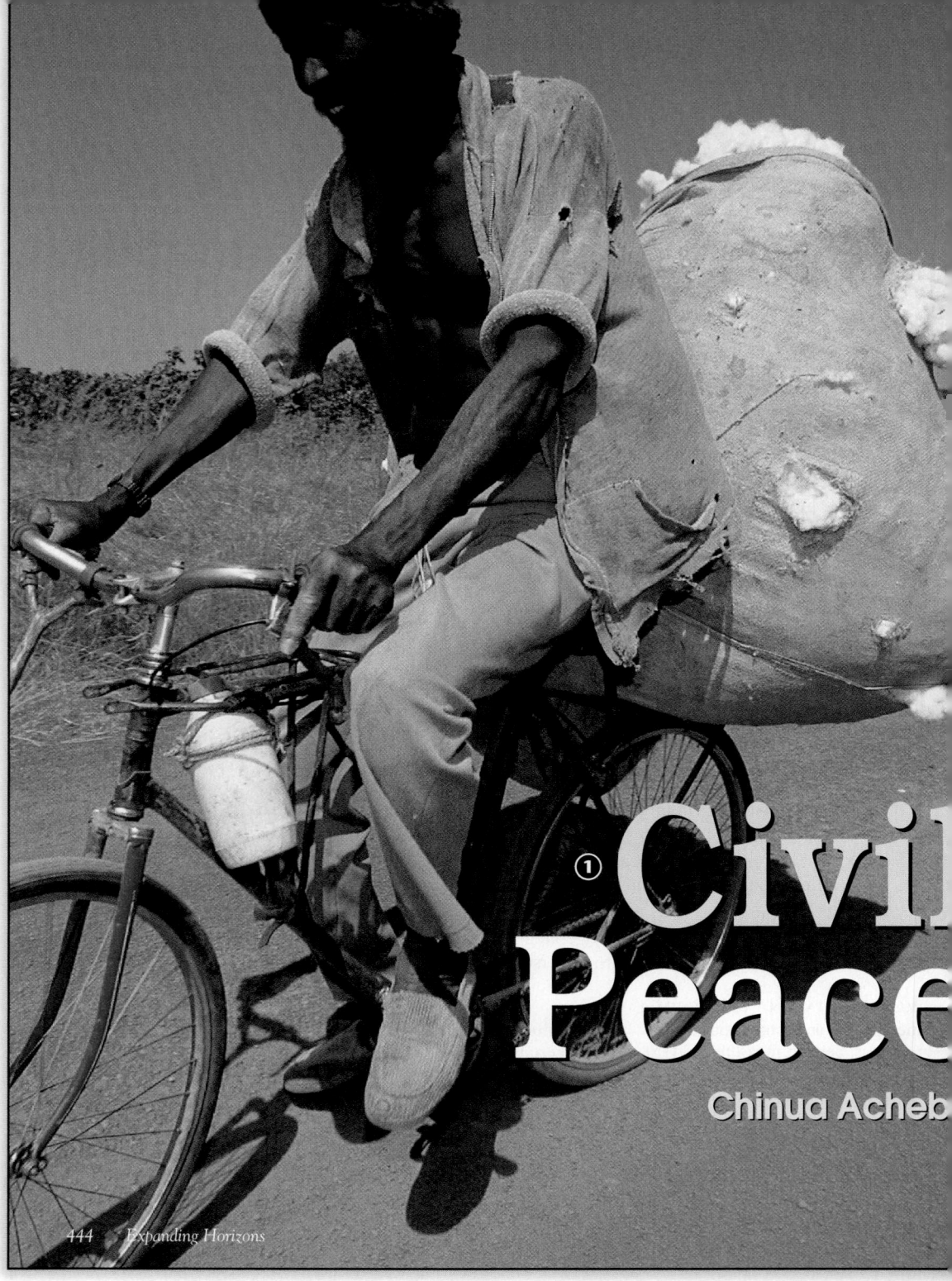

① **Civil
Peace**

Chinua Acheb[e]

444   *Expanding Horizons*

TEACHING RESOURCES

The following resources can be used to enrich or extend the instruction for pp. 444–450.

Literary Analysis

📖 **Selection Support:** Literary Analysis, p. 116

📓 **Writing Models and Graphic Organizers on
Transparencies**, p. 28 ▪

Reading

📖 **Reader's Companion**

📖 **English Learner's Companion**

🎧 **Listening to Literature Audiocassettes**, Side 13 ▪

💿 **Listening to Literature Audio CDs**, CD 9 ▪

▪ **BLOCK SCHEDULING:** Resources marked with this symbol provide varied instruction during 90-minute blocks.

J onathan Iwegbu counted himself extraordinarily lucky. "Happy survival!" meant so much more to him than just a current fashion of greeting old friends in the first hazy days of peace. It went deep to his heart. He had come out of the war with five <u>inestimable</u> blessings—his head, his wife Maria's head and the heads of three out of their four children. As a bonus he also had his old bicycle—a miracle too but naturally not to be compared to the safety of five human heads.

The bicycle had a little history of its own. One day at the height of the war it was commandeered "for urgent military action." Hard as its loss would have been to him he would still have let it go without a thought had he not had some doubts about the genuineness of the officer. It wasn't his <u>disreputable</u> rags, nor the toes peeping out of one blue and one brown canvas shoe, nor yet the two stars of his rank done obviously in a hurry in biro,[1] that troubled Jonathan; many good and heroic soldiers looked the same or worse. It was rather a certain lack of grip and firmness in his manner. So Jonathan, suspecting he might be <u>amenable</u> to influence, rummaged in his raffia bag and produced the two pounds with which he had been going to buy firewood which his wife, Maria, retailed to camp officials for extra stock-fish and corn meal, and got his bicycle back. That night he buried it in the little clearing in the bush where the dead of the camp, including his own youngest son, were buried. When he dug it up again a year later after the surrender all it needed was a little palm-oil greasing. "Nothing puzzles God," he said in wonder.

He put it to immediate use as a taxi and accumulated a small pile of Biafran[2] money ferrying camp officials and their families across the four-mile stretch to the nearest tarred road. His standard charge per trip was six pounds and those who had the money were only glad to be rid of some of it in this way. At the end of a fortnight[3] he had made a small fortune of one hundred and fifteen pounds.

Then he made the journey to Enugu and found another miracle waiting for him. It was unbelievable. He rubbed his eyes and looked again and it was still standing there before him. But, needless to say, even that monumental blessing must be accounted also totally inferior to the five heads in the family. This newest miracle was his little house in Ogui Overside. Indeed nothing puzzles God! Only two houses away a huge concrete <u>edifice</u> some wealthy contractor had put up just before the war was a mountain of rubble. And here was

---

1. **biro** (bir´ō) *n.* ballpoint pen.
2. **Biafran** (bē äf´ rən) *adj.* from the eastern part of the Gulf of Guinea on the west coast of Africa.
3. **fortnight** (fôrt´ nīt) *n.* two weeks.

◀ **Critical Viewing** Why would a bicycle be important to Jonathan, who lives in a landscape like the one shown? **[Infer]**

inestimable (in es´ tə mə bəl) *adj.* priceless; beyond measure

disreputable (dis rep´ yoo tə bəl) *adj.* not respectable

amenable (ə mē´ nə bəl) *adj.* responsive; open

edifice (ed´ i fis) *n.* building

❺ ✔ **Reading Check**
Why does Jonathan bury his bicycle rather than give it to the officer who wanted it?

Civil Peace ◆ 445

❸ **Literary Analysis**

Theme

- Ask students what they think the greeting "Happy survival" means and why it is used.
  Answer: "Happy survival" is the equivalent of our "hello" or "hi." It is used because people were so happy to have survived the war.

- Then, have students predict, on the basis of this opening paragraph, whether Jonathan will have a "happy survival."
  Answer: The optimistic key statement, "happy survival," sets the tone for the rest of the story, in which Jonathan looks at the positive side of all situations. Students may predict a happy survival for Jonathan.

▶ **Monitor Progress** Encourage students to predict what the theme of this story might be, based on what they have learned in this paragraph.
Possible Responses: Students may guess that the theme of the story is that there is always a positive side to every situation or that human life is more important than material belongings.

❹ **Vocabulary Development**

Latin Word Root: *-reput-*

- Draw students' attention to the word *disreputable* and its definition, "not respectable."

- Explain that the Latin root *–reput-* means "to think" or "to consider." Therefore, you "think badly of" someone who is *disreputable.*

- Encourage students to think of other words that contain this root, such as *reputation* or *reputed.*

❺ ✔ **Reading Check**

Answer: Jonathan buried his bicycle because he knew it would be very valuable after the war ended. He did not believe the disreputable officer would return it to him.

6 ▶ Critical Viewing

Answer: Students might say that the man in the photograph could be Jonathan Iwegbu because he looks as if he has suffered, but his eyes and mouth show the hint of a smile.

7 Literary Analysis

Characters' Attitudes

- Ask students to describe Jonathan's attitude toward the condition of his home.
  Answer: His attitude is positive; he is both grateful and happy that the house is salvageable.

- Then, ask students how someone else might react when faced with the same situation.
  Possible responses: Students might indicate that some people would be angry, upset, and discouraged about the missing doors and windows and the damaged roof.

- Discuss with students what this reveals about Jonathan's attitude toward life.
  Answer: This tells us that Jonathan is able to see the positive in the midst of many negatives.

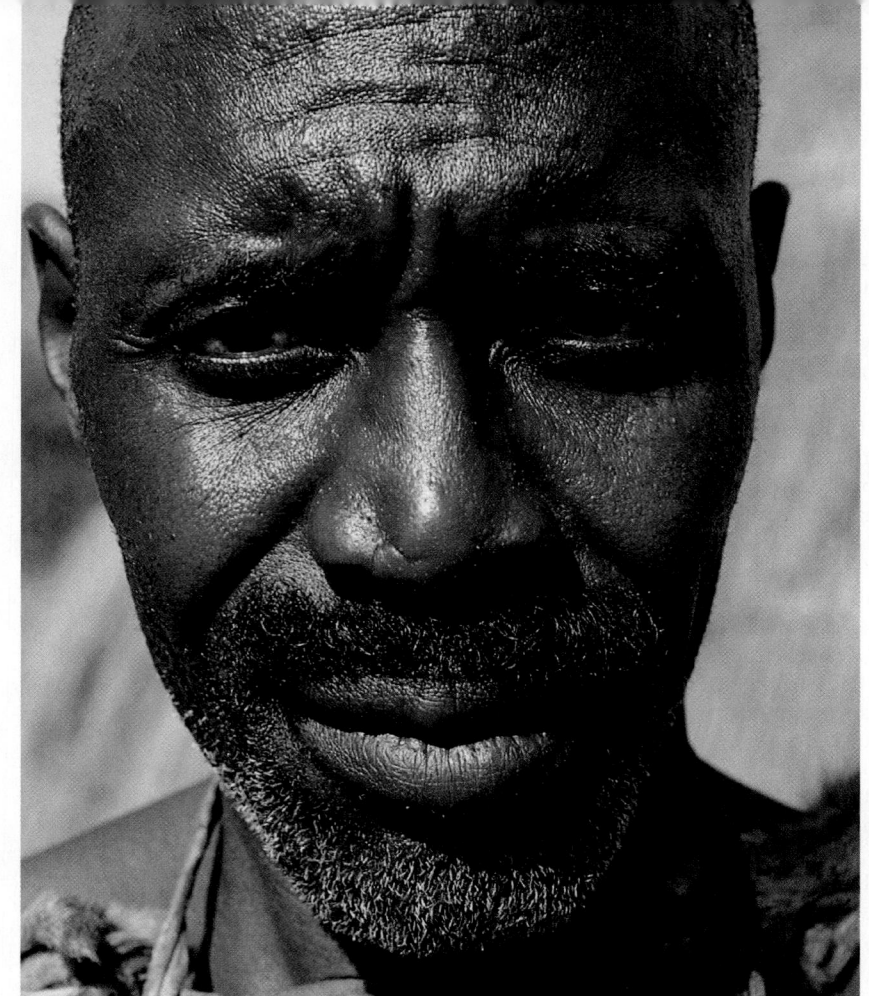

6 ▲ Critical Viewing Does this look like it could be the face of Jonathan Iwegbu? Why or why not? **[Analyze]**

7 Jonathan's little zinc house of no regrets built with mud blocks quite intact! Of course the doors and windows were missing and five sheets off the roof. But what was that? And anyhow he had returned to Enugu early enough to pick up bits of old zinc and wood and soggy sheets of cardboard lying around the neighborhood before thousands more came out of their forest holes looking for the same things. He got a <u>destitute</u> carpenter with one old hammer, a blunt plane and a few bent and rusty nails in his tool bag to turn this assortment of wood, paper and metal into door and window shutters for five Nigerian shillings or fifty Biafran pounds. He paid the pounds, and moved in with his overjoyed family carrying five heads on their shoulders.

destitute (des´ tə to͞ot´) *adj.* poverty-stricken; in great need

446 ◆ *Expanding Horizons*

✺ ENRICHMENT: Science Connection

Palm Trees

The story mentions palm oil, which Jonathan uses to grease his bicycle, and palm-wine, which he sells at his bar. Explain that palms are important in tropical regions, such as Nigeria, because they provide people with food, clothing, and building materials. There are more than 2,600 different kinds of palm trees throughout the world, varying greatly in size and the kind of flowers, leaves, and fruits they produce. Widely used food products made from palm trees include dried coconut, salad oils, margarine, dates, and sago, a

starch taken from palm trunks. Other palm products include baskets and chair bottoms woven from strips of palm leaves, furniture made from stems of the rattan palm, and soap.

Have interested students find out more about palm trees and their products. After students have collected their information, reserve some time for them to share with the class what they have discovered.

His children picked mangoes near the military cemetery and sold them to soldiers' wives for a few pennies—real pennies this time—and his wife started making breakfast akara balls[4] for neighbors in a hurry to start life again. With his family earnings he took his bicycle to the villages around and bought fresh palm-wine which he mixed generously in his rooms with the water which had recently started running again in the public tap down the road, and opened up a bar for soldiers and other lucky people with good money.

At first he went daily, then every other day and finally once a week, to the offices of the Coal Corporation where he used to be a miner, to find out what was what. The only thing he did find out in the end was that that little house of his was even a greater blessing than he had thought. Some of his fellow ex-miners who had nowhere to return at the end of the day's waiting just slept outside the doors of the offices and cooked what meal they could scrounge together in Bournvita tins. As the weeks lengthened and still nobody could say what was what Jonathan discontinued his weekly visits altogether and faced his palm-wine bar.

But nothing puzzles God. Came the day of the windfall when after five days of endless scuffles in queues[5] and counterqueues in the sun outside the Treasury he had twenty pounds counted into his palms as ex-gratia[6] award for the rebel money he had turned in. It was like Christmas for him and for many others like him when the payments began. They called it (since few could manage its proper official name) *egg-rasher*.

As soon as the pound notes were placed in his palm Jonathan simply closed it tight over them and buried fist and money inside his trouser pocket. He had to be extra careful because he had seen a man a couple of days earlier collapse into near-madness in an instant before that oceanic crowd because no sooner had he got his twenty pounds than some heartless ruffian picked it off him. Though it was not right that a man in such an extremity of agony should be blamed yet many in the queues that day were able to remark quietly at the victim's carelessness, especially after he pulled out the innards of his pocket and revealed a hole in it big enough to pass a thief's head. But of course he had insisted that the money had been in the other pocket, pulling it out too to show its comparative wholeness. So one had to be careful.

Jonathan soon transferred the money to his left hand and pocket so as to leave his right free for shaking hands should the need arise, though by fixing his gaze at such an elevation as to miss all approaching human faces he made sure that the need did not arise, until he got home.

---

4. **akara** (ə kär´ ə) **balls** balls made of ground beans that are deep fried.
5. **queues** (kyo͞oz) *n.* lines.
6. **ex-gratia** (eks grä´ shē ə) as a favor.

Literary Analysis
Theme What does the phrase "Nothing puzzles God" suggest about Jonathan Iwegbu's attitude toward good and bad events?

9 ☑**Reading Check**
Why does Jonathan receive twenty pounds?

Civil Peace ◆ 447

---

8 **Literary Analysis**

Theme

- Ask students the Literary Analysis question on p. 447: What does the phrase "Nothing puzzles God" suggest about Jonathan Iwegbu's attitude toward good and bad events?
  Answer: Jonathan is resilient and undaunted by setbacks; he accepts the good and the bad, and he believes that all is for the good, even if human beings cannot see the reasons.

 Monitor Progress Students can create a chart like the one on p. 443 to identify key phrases and their possible meanings. Students' charts should look similar to the one below.

Key Phrase
Nothing puzzles God.

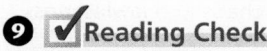

Theme
Everything happens for the best, even if it doesn't seem that way at first.

9 ☑**Reading Check**

Answer: Jonathan receives twenty pounds for turning in rebel money. His act is seen as a favor to the government and is called "ex-gratia."

CUSTOMIZE INSTRUCTION FOR UNIVERSAL ACCESS

For Less Proficient Readers	For Gifted/Talented Students
Encourage students to define the key phrase "Nothing puzzles God." Engage them in a discussion about the phrase's possible meanings as well as how it relates to Jonathan Iwegbu's attitude toward life. Have them consider the reason the writer repeated the phrase several times throughout the story.	Have these students compose their own proverbs that have the same meaning as "Nothing puzzles God," and then brainstorm for other proverbs and sayings that have a similar meaning. Encourage them to share their findings with the class.

- Have students put themselves in Jonathan's shoes and consider what they would do in the situation described in the bracketed paragraph.

▶ Monitor Progress Ask students the Reading Strategy question on p. 448: How does your experience with anxiety help you understand Jonathan's feelings here?

Answer: Students should recognize that anxiety can cause behavioral changes and sleeplessness. Jonathan does not look at people on the way home and even when he is safe at home, he has difficulty falling asleep.

⑪ Critical Thinking

Making Inferences

- Ask students whether they think it is normal for thieves to have so little fear of apprehension and punishment that they would make fun of a threat to call soldiers and police.

- Then, have students identify the cause of this strange situation.
Answer: Students should understand that chaos and lawlessness often follow war. In a peaceful society, an active police force is a deterrent to crime.

He was normally a heavy sleeper but that night he heard all the neighborhood noises die down one after another. Even the night watchman who knocked the hour on some metal somewhere in the distance had fallen silent after knocking one o'clock. That must have been the last thought in Jonathan's mind before he was finally carried away himself. He couldn't have been gone for long, though, when he was violently awakened again.

⑩ "Who is knocking?" whispered his wife lying beside him on the floor.

"I don't know," he whispered back breathlessly.

The second time the knocking came it was so loud and <u>imperious</u> that the rickety old door could have fallen down.

"Who is knocking?" he asked them, his voice parched and trembling.

"Na tief-man and him people," came the cool reply. "Make you hopen de door."[7] This was followed by the heaviest knocking of all.

Maria was the first to raise the alarm, then he followed and all their children.

"*Police-o! Thieves-o! Neighbors-o! Police-o! We are lost! We are dead! Neighbors, are you asleep? Wake up! Police-o!*"

This went on for a long time and then stopped suddenly. Perhaps they had scared the thief away. There was total silence. But only for a short while.

"You done finish?" asked the voice outside. "Make we help you small. Oya, everybody!"

"*Police-o! Tief-man-so! Neighbors-o! we done loss-o! Police-o! . . .*"

There were at least five other voices besides the leader's.

Jonathan and his family were now completely paralyzed by terror. Maria and the children sobbed inaudibly like lost souls. Jonathan groaned continuously.

⑪ The silence that followed the thieves' alarm vibrated horribly. Jonathan all but begged their leader to speak again and be done with it.

"My frien," said he at long last, "we don try our best for call dem but I tink say dem all done sleep-o . . . So wetin we go do now? Sometaim you wan call soja? Or you wan make we call dem for you? Soja better pass police. No be so?"

"Na so!" replied his men. Jonathan thought he heard even more voices now than before and groaned heavily. His legs were sagging under him and his throat felt like sandpaper.

"My frien, why you no de talk again. I de ask you say you wan make we call soja?"

"No."

"Awrighto. Now make we talk business. We no be bad tief. We no like for make trouble. Trouble done finish. War done finish and all

---

7. **"Na tief-man . . . hopen de door"** The man is speaking a dialect of English that includes some word forms and grammar of his own language. He is saying, "I am a thief with my accomplices. Open the door." As you read the rest of the story, read aloud when characters speak this way and try to figure out what they are saying.

imperious (im pir′ ē əs) *adj.* commanding; powerful

Reading Strategy
Using Prior Knowledge
How does your experience with anxiety help you understand Jonathan's feelings here?

☀ ENRICHMENT: Career Connection

Law Enforcement

Lawlessness and chaos often characterize a society in the aftermath of war. As they read on, students will see that restoration of order by ethical and well-trained law-enforcement officers helps life go on in a reasonable, orderly way.

Students interested in law enforcement can do research to find out what kind of background is necessary to become an officer of the law. Some questions students might consider include the following:

- How does one apply to become a police officer?

- What type of education is necessary?

- How does one become a detective or an FBI agent?

the katakata wey de for inside. No Civil War again. This time na Civil Peace. No be so?"

"Na so!" answered the horrible chorus.

"What do you want from me? I am a poor man. Everything I had went with this war. Why do you come to me? You know people who have money. We . . ."

"Awright! We know say you no get plenty money. But we sef no get even anini. So derefore make you open dis window and give us one hundred pound and we go commot. Orderwise we de come for inside now to show you guitar-boy like dis . . ."

A volley of automatic fire rang through the sky. Maria and the children began to weep aloud again.

"Ah, missisi de cry again. No need for dat. We done talk say we na good tief. We just take our small money and go nwayorly. No molest. Abi we de molest?"

"At all!" sang the chorus.

"My friends," began Jonathan hoarsely. "I hear what you say and I thank you. If I had one hundred pounds . . ."

"Lookia my frien, no be play we come play for your house. If we make mistake and step for inside you no go like am-o. So derefore . . ."

"To God who made me; if you come inside and find one hundred pounds, take it and shoot me and shoot my wife and children. I swear to God. The only money I have in this life is this twenty-pounds *egg-rasher* they gave me today . . ."

"Ok. Time de go. Make you open dis window and bring the twenty pound. We go manage am like dat."

There were now loud murmurs of dissent among the chorus: "Na lie de man de lie; e get plenty money . . . Make we go inside and search properly well . . . Wetin be twenty pound? . . ."

"Shurrup!" rang the leader's voice like a lone shot in the sky and silenced the murmuring at once. "Are you dere? Bring the money quick!"

"I am coming," said Jonathan fumbling in the darkness with the key of the small wooden box he kept by his side on the mat.

Literature in context ⓬
Geography Connection

Nigerian Civil War
Jonathan is delighted that his home in Enugu still stands—and for good reason. Enugu was at the center of the civil war that broke out in Nigeria. When the war began, Enugu became the capital of the new Republic of Biafra and, consequently, a target of the federal troops from Nigeria. The city was invaded just five months after Biafra had declared its independence. Jonathan and his family have to continue living in the wreckage of their former lives.

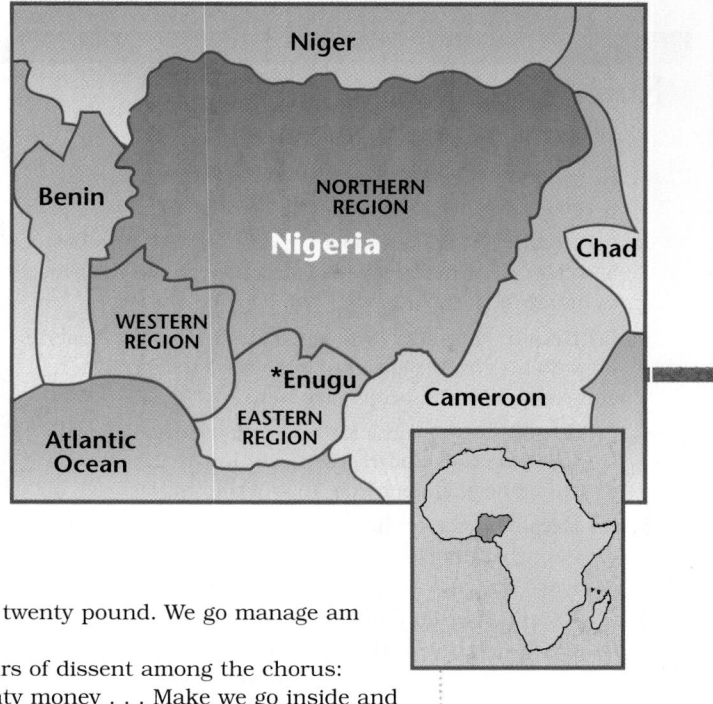

Niger · Benin · NORTHERN REGION · Nigeria · Chad · WESTERN REGION · *Enugu · Cameroon · Atlantic Ocean · EASTERN REGION

⓮ ✔ **Reading Check**
What deal does Jonathan work out with the thieves?

Civil Peace ◆ 449

⓬ **Background**
Nigeria
Civil war broke out in 1967 after the Eastern Region declared independence from Nigeria on May 30. It is estimated that over 1 million people became casualties of the war—many of whom were Biafrans (mostly Ibos) who had starved to death despite international relief efforts. On January 12, 1970, the Republic of Biafra capitulated, rejoining as part of the country of Nigeria.

⓭ **Critical Thinking**
Analyze
• Ask a volunteer to read aloud the bracketed passage and summarize what happens in it.
• Ask students why they think the thief decides to take the twenty pounds and leave Jonathan alone. Why doesn't he agree with his companions that they should go in and look for more money? **Answer:** Students may think the thief's attitude toward life is ironically similar to Jonathan's: He will take what he gets and be satisfied. Others may suggest that the thief doesn't want to get into a situation where he would hurt or kill anyone.

⓮ ✔ **Reading Check**
Answer: Jonathan gives the thieves twenty pounds, which is all the money he has. Even though this is eighty pounds less than what they wanted, they agree to leave Jonathan and his family alone.

CUSTOMIZE INSTRUCTION FOR UNIVERSAL ACCESS

For Gifted/Talented Students	For Advanced Readers
Encourage students to rewrite the scene between the thieves and Jonathan as a scene from a play. Have students think about what each line of dialogue means as they write their scenes—they can even provide literal "translations" of each line to help them better understand the language. They should practice speaking the dialect so it sounds natural when they perform. Allow time for students to perform their scenes for the class.	Have students reread the conversation between the thieves and Jonathan. Instruct them to rewrite the conversation in standard English. Encourage them to consider the characters' personalities, and to use language that the characters might actually use. Allow time for students to share their rewritten scenes with the class.

Review and Assess

1. Students may admire his positive attitude and his sense of priorities.

2. **(a)** Above all he is thankful that most of his family has survived the civil war. **(b)** The war has made him realize that the safety of his family is the most important thing in his life.

3. **(a)** Jonathan uses his bicycle as a taxi; then he uses it to supply a palm-wine business in his home. **(b)** The war has forced Jonathan and others to find work doing whatever will support their families.

4. **(a)** Thieves come to Jonathan's house and threaten to kill his family if he doesn't give them 100 pounds. He gives them all the money he has—twenty pounds—and they go away peacefully. **(b)** The thieves feel they can just take what they want; Jonathan knows how to create what he wants by working for it.

5. **(a)** The leader of the thieves wants Jonathan's money, but he does not want to make trouble. **(b)** The thieves are probably not hardened criminals. In the aftermath of the war they have become desperate for money, so they have resorted to stealing it.

6. **(a)** They return to their businesses as if nothing has happened. **(b)** Others may be angry, upset, or disappointed in the same situation.

7. Jonathan is optimistic, trusting, and peaceful.

8. The peace between Jonathan and the thieves is achieved with civility, without resorting to violence.

9. Students may say that to get through such difficult times, most people would have to develop courage similar to Jonathan's.

At the first sign of light as neighbors and others assembled to <u>commiserate</u> with him he was already strapping his five-gallon demijohn[8] to his bicycle carrier and his wife, sweating in the open fire, was turning over akara balls in a wide clay bowl of boiling oil. In the corner his eldest son was rinsing out dregs of yesterday's palm-wine from old beer bottles.

"I count it as nothing," he told his sympathizers, his eyes on the rope he was tying. "What is *egg-rasher*? Did I depend on it last week? Or is it greater than other things that went with the war? I say, let *egg-rasher* perish in the flames! Let it go where everything else has gone. Nothing puzzles God."

> **commiserate** (kə miz′ ər āt′) *v.* sympathize; share suffering

---

8. **demijohn** (dem′ i jän′) *n.* large bottle.

Review and Assess

Thinking About the Selection

1. **Respond:** In what ways do you identify with Jonathan Iwegbu? Explain.

2. **(a) Recall:** What does Jonathan count as his greatest blessings? **(b) Infer:** How do you think the war contributes to his attitude?

3. **(a) Recall:** How does Jonathan earn money? **(b) Analyze:** How do his postwar jobs reveal the ways that the war has affected the lives of people like him?

4. **(a) Recall:** Describe the robbery that Jonathan endures. **(b) Compare and Contrast:** How is Jonathan's attitude toward money different from that of the thieves?

5. **(a) Recall:** Describe the character of the leader of the thieves. **(b) Infer:** Do you think he and his followers are hardened criminals? Explain why or why not.

6. **(a) Recall:** How do Jonathan and his family behave after their money is stolen? **(b) Speculate:** How do you think people in other situations would have reacted?

7. **Interpret:** How would you sum up Jonathan's attitude toward life in general?

8. **Evaluate:** Why is "Civil Peace" an appropriate title for this story? Consider the meanings of the word *civil*.

9. **Make a Judgment:** Do you think that most people who face continual adversity share the courage that Jonathan displays? Explain.

Chinua Achebe

(b. 1930)

During the civil war in Nigeria, Chinua Achebe (chin wä′ ə cheb′ ā) survived the bombing of his house. He fled, leaving behind a book almost completed at the publishing company he had formed. That book was *How the Leopard Got His Claws*. When Achebe returned, only one copy of the book remained. This book and others, including *Things Fall Apart* (1958) and *Anthills of the Savannah* (1987), convey the history of tribal Africa's encounter with Europeans.

As a child, Achebe learned both the traditional values of the Ibo people and Western values. He believes that stories are a way to preserve important traditional values.

✎ ASSESSMENT PRACTICE: Reading Comprehension

Evaluate and Make Judgments   **(For more practice, see Test Preparation Workbook, p. 29.)**

Some tests require students to evaluate a text and make judgments. Use the following sample test item to teach this reading comprehension skill.

He was normally a heavy sleeper but that night he heard all the neighborhood noises die down one after another. Even the night watchman who knocked the hour on some metal somewhere in the distance had fallen silent after knocking one o'clock. That must have been the last thought in Jonathan's

mind before he was finally carried away himself.

Which of the following statements is supported by the evidence in the passage?

A The night watchman slept at midnight.

B Jonathan tried to keep himself awake.

C Jonathan had trouble sleeping that night.

D The neighborhood was very noisy.

The details in the passage prove *A, B,* and *D* wrong. *C* is the correct response.

Review and Assess

Literary Analysis

Theme

1. What does the phrase "Happy survival!" reveal about the **theme** of this story?
2. (a) Why do you think the proverb "Nothing puzzles God" is repeated in the story? (b) How does it help reveal the story's message about life?
3. (a) Jonathan brushes off the loss of his money by saying, "I count it as nothing." Why is his response a key phrase? (b) What might he count as "something"? Explain.

Connecting Literary Elements

4. Using a chart like the one here, show Jonathan's reaction to several negative events in the story. Then, describe how you might react to the same events.

Event	Jonathan's Reaction	My Reaction
3 out of 4 children survived war		

5. Based on the reactions in the chart above, summarize Jonathan's **attitude** in one sentence.

Reading Strategy

Using Prior Knowledge

6. Use your **prior knowledge** to explain why Jonathan's bicycle is so important to him.
7. Jonathan frequently quotes proverbs. What proverbs, or sayings, do you use to respond to events in your life? Compare one or two of them with the sayings that Jonathan uses.
8. Using your knowledge of people, do you think that Jonathan is an exceptionally optimistic person? Explain.

Extend Understanding

9. **Cultural Connection:** Do you think it is easier for a poor person or a rich person to accept the loss of material possessions? Explain.

Quick Review

The **theme** is the central message or idea about life that a story conveys.

Characters' attitudes are their values, ideas, and beliefs. Characters' attitudes may help reveal the author's theme.

To use **prior knowledge** as you read, connect your experiences and ideas with those of the characters.

 Take It to the Net

www.phschool.com
Take the interactive self-test online to check your understanding of the selection.

Civil Peace ◆ 451

Answers for p. 451

Review and Assess

1. The phrase reflects Jonathan's happiness in being alive.
2. (a) The proverb is repeated in the story to highlight Jonathan's attitude toward life. (b) It states the philosophy behind Jonathan's trust that all will work out for the best.
3. (a) It is a key phrase because Jonathan has learned that money is not very important. (b) He would count his family's safety as "something."
4. Possible response: Events: three out of four children survived the war; the house is missing doors and windows. Jonathan's reaction: relieved that most of the family survived; glad that most of the house has survived, and begins fixing it immediately. My reaction: sadness at the loss of a son; happy that I still had a home.
5. Jonathan is optimistic, trusting, and peaceful.
6. Jonathan knows his bike will help him support his family after the war.
7. Students may cite such sayings as "C'est la vie" (That's life) or "If at first you don't succeed, try, try again." *C'est la vie* is similar in meaning and use to "Nothing puzzles God."
8. Students may say that Jonathan is not exceptionally optimistic; rather, he simply focuses on the positive rather than the negative and makes do with what he has as he rebuilds his life.
9. Students may argue that rich people have more to lose and will mourn the loss of their possessions more. Others may say that although poor people are used to doing with less, they would mourn the loss of their possessions just as much.

451

Answers for p. 452

❶ Vocabulary Development

Word Analysis

1. reputed   3. disreputable
2. reputation   4. disrepute

Fluency: Clarify Word Meaning

1. edifice   5. destitute
2. imperious   6. inestimable
3. commiserate 7. disreputable
4. amenable

Spelling Strategy

1. inestimable   3. insensible
2. disreputable

❷ Grammar

1. Sleeping soundly, Jonathan's family was awakened by loud knocking.
2. The thieves, lurking outside, yelled.
3. The thief standing closest was the leader.
4. Listening intently, they heard nothing.
5. Jonathan, believing his family was in danger, gave them the money.

Writing Application

Sample response: My friend Peter, being an eternally cheerful person, always looks at the bright side of things. He never lets bad things get him down; he tries to find something positive in every event. Working on a project, he knows he is learning valuable skills even though it takes up lots of time. He knows that these types of situations help prepare him for college and his future, so he is able to smile his way through them.

Integrate Language Skills

❶ Vocabulary Development Lesson

Word Analysis: Latin Root -reput-

Disreputable contains the Latin root *-reput-*, which means "to think" or "to consider." Using other forms of *disreputable*, you might describe a *disreputable* person as someone whom others think badly of or someone who has fallen into *disrepute*.

Copy the sentences below, filling in the blanks with *disreputable*, *reputation*, *reputed*, or *disrepute*.

1. Jonathan is ___?___ to be a careful man.
2. He also has a ___?___ for honesty.
3. Unfortunately, he was robbed by some ___?___ men.
4. His good name has fallen into ___?___ .

❷ Grammar Lesson

Present Participial Phrases

A **present participial phrase** consists of a present participle—a verb form ending in *-ing*—modified by an adverb or adverb phrase or accompanied by a complement. The entire phrase acts as an adjective. In these examples from "Civil Peace," the participial phrase is in italics. The word modified is underlined.

> So <u>Jonathan</u>, *suspecting he might be amenable to influence*, rummaged in his raffia bag.

> Then he made the journey to Enugu and found another <u>miracle</u> *waiting for him*.

Fluency: Clarify Word Meaning

On a sheet of paper, write the word from the vocabulary list on page 443 that you would expect to find in each book listed here.

1. *The Architecture of Frank Lloyd Wright*
2. *Kings and Queens of the World*
3. *Sharing Your Pain*
4. *Getting Others to Agree*
5. *The Causes of Poverty*
6. *Jewels and Gemstones*
7. *Desperadoes of the Old West*

Spelling Strategy

Many English words end in *-ible* or *-able*. Complete each word below by adding *-ible* or *-able*. Use a dictionary if you need help.

1. inestim____   2. disreput____   3. insens____

Practice Copy the following sentences. Underline each participial phrase, and circle the word or phrase it modifies.

1. Sleeping soundly, Jonathan's family was awakened by loud knocking.
2. The thieves, lurking outside, yelled.
3. The thief standing closest was the leader.
4. Listening intently, they heard nothing.
5. Jonathan, believing his family was in danger, gave them the money.

Writing Application Write a paragraph describing an optimistic person. Use at least two present participial phrases to add variety to your writing.

WG *Prentice Hall Writing and Grammar Connection: Chapter 20, Section 1*

TEACHING RESOURCES

The following resources can be used to enrich or extend the instruction for pp. 452–453.

Vocabulary

📖 **Selection Support:** Build Vocabulary, p. 113

📖 **Vocabulary and Spelling Practice Book** (Use this booklet for skills enrichment.) ■

Grammar

📖 **Selection Support:** Build Grammar Skills, p. 114

WG **Writing and Grammar,** Platinum Level, p. 452

■ **Daily Language Practice Transparencies** ■

Writing

WG **Writing and Grammar,** Platinum Level, p. 181

💿 **Writing and Grammar iText CD-ROM** ■

📖 **Writing Models and Graphic Organizers on Transparencies,** pp. 13–16

 BLOCK SCHEDULING: Resources marked with this symbol provide varied instruction during 90-minute blocks.

❸ Writing Lesson

News Interview

As a reporter covering life after the civil war in Nigeria, prepare questions for an interview with Jonathan Iwegbu. Use details in the story to provide answers to your questions, and write your interview for the evening news.

Prewriting Reread the story as a journalist might, writing questions about Jonathan, his family, and his life after the war. Then, answer the questions with information from the text.

Drafting Begin your news story with a catchy introduction. Next, logically organize the information gathered from your questioning. Write topic sentences for each paragraph, and support each idea with details from the text. Wrap up your story with an insight about Jonathan and his attitude toward life.

Revising Underline each topic sentence, and highlight the details that support it. If you do not have enough details to support your idea, go back to the text and find support.

> My wife made akara balls to sell. I opened a bar. My children picked mangoes.

Model: Revising to Add Supporting Details

After the war, my wife and I had to find ways to support ourselves. We do not mind hard work.

> The details being added support the topic sentence.

✍ *Prentice Hall Writing and Grammar Connection: Chapter 9, Section 3*

❹ Extension Activities

Listening and Speaking Rewrite the **dialogue** between the thieves and Jonathan in language that is familiar to you. Use a combination of these techniques:

- Read the dialogue in the selection aloud.
- Sound out the sentences word by word.
- Guess at general ideas.

Then, with a partner, read your dialogue aloud before a group of classmates. **[Group Activity]**

Research and Technology Construct an **annotated map** of Nigeria showing places where Jonathan Iwegbu may have worked or lived. Research to show significant features of the country's ethnic diversity, industry, and culture. Include numbers on the map to correspond to your annotations. Then, share your map with the class.

 Take It to the Net www.phschool.com
Go online for an additional research activity using the Internet.

Civil Peace ◆ 453

Lesson Support for p. 453

❸ Writing Lesson

- Tell students that as they reread the story, they should look for answers to the questions *Who?*, *What?*, *When?*, *Where?*, and *Why?*.

- Use the Biographical Profile transparencies in **Writing Models and Graphic Organizers on Transparencies,** pp. 13–16, to show students how to take a similar assignment through the writing process.

- Use the Writing Lesson to guide students through writing their news interviews.

❹ Listening and Speaking

- Have students discuss why the dialect in the story might be difficult to understand.

- Divide the class into pairs. Consider placing English Learners, Special Needs Students, and Less Proficient Readers with a more advanced partner for this activity.

- Encourage the partners to work together to figure out the meaning of each line of dialogue. Remind them that reading the lines aloud and considering the context might help.

- Use the rubric for Delivering a Narrative Presentation in **Performance Assessment and Portfolio Management,** p. 28, to assess students' presentations.

CUSTOMIZE INSTRUCTION for Universal Access

To address different learning styles, use the following activities suggested in the **Extension Activities** booklet, p. 29.

- For Bodily/Kinesthetic and Intrapersonal Learners, use Activity 5.

- For Logical/Mathematical Learners, use Activity 6.

- For Logical/Mathematical and Verbal/Linguistic Learners, use Activity 7.

ASSESSMENT RESOURCES

The following resources can be used to assess students' knowledge and skills.

Selection Assessment

- 📖 **Formal Assessment**, pp. 101–103
- 📖 **Open Book Test**, pp. 85–87
- 📼 **Got It! Assessment Videotapes**, Tape 3
- 💿 **Test Bank Software**

 Take It to the Net
Visit www.phschool.com for self-tests and additional questions on "Civil Peace."

Listening and Speaking Rubric

- 📖 **Performance Assess. and Portfolio Mgmt.**, p. 28

 PRENTICE HALL **ASSESSMENT SYSTEM**

- 📖 **Workbook**
- 🖨 **Transparencies**
- 📖 **Skill Book**
- 💿 **CD-ROM**

How to React to Familiar Faces ✦ The Bean Eaters

Lesson Objectives

1. **To analyze and respond to literary elements**
   - Literary Analysis: Tone
   - Comparing Literary Works: Author's Attitude

2. **To read, comprehend, analyze, and critique a poem and an essay**
   - Reading Strategy: Responding to Connotations
   - Review and Assess questions
   - Assessment Practice (ATE)

3. **To develop word analysis skills, fluency, and systematic vocabulary**
   - Vocabulary Development Lesson: Latin Word Root: -ami-

4. **To understand and apply written and oral language conventions**
   - Spelling Strategy
   - Grammar Lesson: Verb, Participle, or Gerund?

5. **To understand and apply appropriate writing and research strategies**
   - Writing Lesson: Persuasive Argument
   - Extension Activity: Research Report

6. **To understand and apply listening and speaking strategies**
   - Extension Activity: Introduction

STEP-BY-STEP TEACHING GUIDE	PACING GUIDE
PRETEACH	
Motivate Students and Provide Background	
Use the Motivation activity (ATE p. 454)	5 min.
Read and discuss the Preview material and Background information (SE/ATE p. 454) **A**	5 min.
Introduce the Concepts	
Introduce the Literary Analysis and Reading Strategy (SE/ATE p. 455) **A**	10 min.
Pronounce the vocabulary words and read their definitions (SE p. 455)	5 min.
TEACH	
Monitor Comprehension	
Informally monitor comprehension by circulating while students read independently or in groups **A**	10 min.
Develop vocabulary with Vocabulary notes (SE pp. 456, 457; ATE p. 457)	as students read
Develop Understanding	
Develop students' understanding of tone with Literary Analysis annotations (ATE p. 456) **A**	5 min.
Develop students' understanding of connotation with Reading Strategy annotations (ATE p. 458)	5 min.
ASSESS	
Assess Mastery	
Assess students' mastery of the Reading Strategy and Literary Analysis by having them answer the Review and Assess questions (SE/ATE p. 459)	15 min.
Use one or more of the print and media Assessment Resources (ATE p. 461) **A**	up to 50 min.
EXTEND	
Apply Understanding	
Have students complete the Vocabulary Development Lesson and the Grammar Lesson (SE p. 460) **A**	20 min.
Apply students' knowledge of supporting and opposing evidence using the Writing Lesson (SE p. 461) **A**	45 min.
Apply students' understanding using one or more of the Extension Activities (SE p. 461)	20–90min.

 ACCELERATED INSTRUCTION:
Use the strategies and activities identified with an **A**.

UNIVERSAL ACCESS
- ● = Below Level Students
- ▲ = On-Level Students
- ■ = Above Level Students

Time and Resource Manager

RESOURCES

PRINT 📖	TRANSPARENCIES 📄	TECHNOLOGY 💿 🎧 📼
• **Beyond Literature,** Cross-Curricular Connection: Art, p. 30 ▲ ■		• **Interest Grabber Video,** Tape 3 ● ▲ ■
• **Selection Support Workbook:** ● ▲ ■ Literary Analysis, p. 120 Reading Strategy, p. 119 Build Vocabulary, p. 117	• **Literary Analysis and Reading Transparencies,** pp. 59 and 60 ● ▲ ■	
• **Authors In Depth,** Platinum Level ■		• **Listening to Literature** ● ▲ ■ Audiocassettes, Side 14 Audio CDs, CD 9
• **Literatura en español** ● ▲ • **Literary Analysis for Enrichment** ■	• **Fine Art Transparencies, Volume 1,** Art Transparency 1 ● ▲ ■	
• **Formal Assessment:** Selection Test, pp. 104–106 ● ▲ ■ • **Open Book Test,** pp. 88–90 ● ▲ ■ • **Performance Assessment and Portfolio Management,** pp. 11, 29 ● ▲ ■ • **PRENTICE HALL ASSESSMENT** *SYSTEM* ● ▲ ■	• **PRENTICE HALL ASSESSMENT** *SYSTEM* ● ▲ ■ Skills Practice Answers and Explanations on Transparencies	• **Test Bank Software** ● ▲ ■ • **Got It! Assessment Videotapes,** Tape 3 ● ▲
• **Selection Support Workbook:** ● ▲ ■ Build Grammar Skills, p. 118 • **Writing and Grammar,** Platinum Level ● ▲ ■ • **Extension Activities,** p. 30 ● ▲ ■	• **Daily Language Practice Transparencies** ● ▲ • **Writing Models and Graphic Organizers on Transparencies,** pp. 45–52 ● ▲ ■	• **Writing and Grammar iText CD-ROM** ● ▲ ■ *Take It to the Net* www.phschool.com

BLOCK SCHEDULING: Use one 90-minute class period to preteach the selection and have students read it. Use a second 90-minute class period to assess students' mastery of skills and have them complete one of the Extension Activities.

Step-by-Step Teaching Guide for pp. 454–455

Motivation

People Magazine . . . National Enquirer . . . Entertainment Tonight . . . Brainstorm with students to name some of the many magazines and television shows that focus on celebrities. Discuss with students the fascination people have for these subjects. Ask them why "ordinary people" are less likely to be subject to media attention. Tell them that the selections they will read offer some interesting insights on this topic.

▣ Interest Grabber Video

As an alternative, play "Growing Old Together" on Tape 3 to engage student interest.

❶ Background

Entertainers

The film actor Anthony Quinn was born in Chihuahua, Mexico, in 1916. Before he became an actor, Quinn won a scholarship to study architecture with the famous architect Frank Lloyd Wright. In fact, it was Wright who suggested that Quinn take acting lessons to re-train his speaking voice after having surgery.

After years of being stereotyped in such roles as a Mexican bandit and an Indian warrior, Quinn eventually achieved international fame, winning two Academy Awards. His film career spans six decades and includes 160 films.

Prepare to Read

How to React to Familiar Faces ◆ The Bean Eaters

Audience B, 1940, Diana Ong

▣ *Take It to the Net*

Visit www.phschool.com for interactive activities and instruction related to these selections, including
- background
- graphic organizers
- literary elements
- reading strategies

Preview

Connecting to the Literature

With television and film bringing the private details of celebrity life into our homes, it is easy to feel as if we know our favorite stars personally. These selections provide a contrast between the very private lives of ordinary people and the very public lives of celebrities.

❶ Background

In "How to React to Familiar Faces," Umberto Eco mentions several celebrities with whom you may not be familiar.
- Anthony Quinn was a film actor who won two Academy Awards.
- Charlton Heston won a Best-Actor Oscar for his role in *Ben Hur*.
- Johnny Carson was the host of *The Tonight Show* for thirty years.
- Oprah Winfrey is a successful talk-show host.

TEACHING RESOURCES

The following resources can be used to enrich or extend the instruction for pp. 454–455.

Motivation
 Interest Grabber Video, Tape 3

Background
▭ **Beyond Literature,** p. 30 ▪

▣ *Take It to the Net*
Visit www.phschool.com for background and hotlinks for the selections.

Literary Analysis
▭ **Selection Support:** Literary Analysis, p. 120 ▪

▣ **Literary Analysis and Reading Transparencies,** Tone, p. 60

Reading
▣ **Literary Analysis and Reading Transparencies,** Responding to Connotations, p. 59

 BLOCK SCHEDULING: Resources marked with this symbol provide varied instruction during 90-minute blocks.

Literary Analysis

Tone

Each of these selections has a distinct **tone**—that is, an attitude toward its readers and subject. A writer's tone may be formal or informal, friendly or distant, personal or impersonal. As you can see from this example, Eco's tone is lighthearted, amusing, and good-natured.

> I might as well have grabbed Anthony Quinn by the lapel, dragged him to a phone booth, and called a friend to say, "Talk about coincidence! I've run into Anthony Quinn. And you know something? He seems real!"

As you read, look for other passages that help you determine the author's tone.

Comparing Literary Works

In both of these selections, the authors describe people as they are seen by an outside observer—a situation in which the **author's attitude,** or the way he or she feels about the subject, is key to conveying a feeling to readers. In "How to React to Familiar Faces," the author describes people's reactions to seeing celebrities. Gwendolyn Brooks, author of "The Bean Eaters," describes an elderly couple living simply with their memories. As you read these selections, compare the ways the author's attitude colors your perception of the subjects of the works.

Reading Strategy

Responding to Connotations

When you see a familiar face, you respond based on associations you have with that person. Similarly, when you apply your own associations and feelings about a word, you are **responding to connotations,** or associations that go beyond a word's literal definition. For example, the title "The Bean Eaters" refers, literally, to people who eat beans, yet the phrase connotes simplicity and poverty. Using a chart like the one here, record other words and phrases in your reading that remind you of something else.

Vocabulary Development

expound (eks pound´) v. explain in detail (p. 456)

syndrome (sin´ drōm´) n. group of signs that occur together and may form a pattern (p. 456)

amiably (ā´ mē ə blē) adv. in a cheerful, friendly way (p. 457)

protagonist (prō tag´ ə nist) n. main character; person who plays a leading part (p. 457)

How to React to Familiar Faces / The Bean Eaters ◆ 455

---

❷ Literary Analysis

Tone

- Tell students that the tone of a selection is the writer's attitude toward his or her subject and readers.
- Read the instruction about tone together as a class. Explain that a writer's choice of words is a clue to his or her tone.
- Use the instruction for Comparing Literary Works to show how the writer's attitude affects the tone of a selection.
- Remind students to pay attention to the writer's tone as they read the selections.

❸ Reading Strategy

Responding to Connotations

- Remind students that the connotation of a word is the extra meaning they bring to the word from their own experiences. Explain that connotations can be either positive or negative.
- Have a volunteer look up the definition of *twinkling* and read it to the class (a quick sparkling or flashing, especially of the eyes; an instant).
- Have students compare the connotations of *twinkling* with the *denotation*, or dictionary definition.
- Encourage students to use a connotations chart like the one shown as they read the selections.

Vocabulary Development

- Pronounce each vocabulary word for students, and read the definitions as a class. Have students identify any words with which they are already familiar.

CUSTOMIZE INSTRUCTION FOR UNIVERSAL ACCESS

For Less Proficient Readers	For English Learners	For Advanced Readers
Students may need extra help in identifying the distinct tone of the selections. Help students by highlighting specific passages for them to consider. Ask such guiding questions as: Is the attitude expressed here light-hearted or serious? Joyous or sad? Formal or informal?	When determining a selection's tone, students should consider both the connotations and denotations of words. To help students determine connotations, allow them to translate words to their first language when thinking about their associations or experiences with it.	Encourage students to compare aspects of the two selections and distinguish between Umberto Eco's tone and that of Gwendolyn Brooks. Also, have them consider any common thread of theme or style that runs through each one.

 E-Teach

Visit E-Teach at www.phschool.com for teachers' essays on how to teach, with questions and answers.

**CUSTOMIZE INSTRUCTION
For Interpersonal Learners**

Have these students evaluate the attitude toward people that each of the authors expresses. Suggest that they work with partners to role-play an interview with Brooks and Eco to demonstrate these attitudes to classmates.

❶ About the Selection

Author and social critic Umberto Eco humorously analyzes the effects of the media on the way people react to celebrities. In a lighthearted tone, he raises questions on a serious theme.

❷ Literary Analysis

Tone

• Ask students to read the bracketed passage and think about its tone.

• Have students describe the tone of this passage.
  Answer: Students may describe the tone as humorous. They may note comic exaggerations when Eco writes, "It was too late to flee"; and "I might as well make the first move."

▶ Monitor Progress As students continue to read, encourage them to cite specific phrases that add to the selection's humorous tone.

❸ ▶ Critical Viewing

Answer: Students may cite his casual dress, his apparent lack of screen makeup, and the fact that he does not seem to be playing a role in a movie.

---

❶ # How to React to Familiar Faces

Umberto Eco

A few months ago, as I was strolling in New York, I saw, at a distance, a man I knew very well heading in my direction. The trouble was that I couldn't remember his name or where I had met him. This is one of those sensations you encounter especially when, in a foreign city, you run into someone you met back home, or vice versa. A face out of context creates confusion. Still, that face was so familiar that, I felt, I should certainly stop, greet him, converse; perhaps he would immediately respond, "My dear Umberto, how are you?" or "Were you able to do that thing you were telling me about?" And I ❷ would be at a total loss. It was too late to flee. He was still looking at the opposite side of the street, but now he was beginning to turn his eyes towards me. I might as well make the first move; I would wave and then, from his voice, his first remarks, I would try to guess his identity.

We were now only a few feet from each other, I was just about to break into a broad, radiant smile, when suddenly I recognized him. It was Anthony Quinn. Naturally, I had never met him in my life, nor he me. In a thousandth of a second I was able to check myself, and I walked past him, my eyes staring into space.

Afterwards, reflecting on this incident, I realized how totally normal it was. Once before, in a restaurant, I had glimpsed Charlton Heston and had felt an impulse to say hello. These faces inhabit our memory; watching the screen, we spend so many hours with them that they are as familiar to us as our relatives', even more so. You can be a student of mass communication, debate the effects of reality, or the confusion between the real and the imagined, and expound the way some people fall permanently into this confusion; but still you are not immune to the syndrome. And there is worse.

I have received confidences from people who, appearing fairly frequently on TV, have been subjected to the mass media over a certain period of time. I'm not talking about Johnny Carson or Oprah Winfrey, but public figures, experts who have participated in panel discussions often enough to become recognizable. All of them complain of the same disagreeable

❸ ▲ **Critical Viewing**
This photograph is of the movie star Anthony Quinn. What details of the photograph hide his celebrity? **[Analyze]**

expound (eks pound´) v. explain in detail

syndrome (sin´ drōm´) n. group of signs that occur together and may form a pattern

---

TEACHING RESOURCES

The following resources can be used to enrich or extend the instruction for pp. 456–458.

Literary Analysis

📖 **Writing Models and Graphic Organizers on Transparencies,** pp. 45–52

Reading

📖 **Selection Support:** Reading Strategy, p. 119; Build Vocabulary, p. 117

🎧 **Listening to Literature Audiocassettes,** Side 14 ■

💿 **Listening to Literature Audio CDs,** CD 9

Extension

📖 **Authors In Depth** Platinum Level (This collection includes eleven additional selections by Gwendolyn Brooks for extended reading.) ■

📖 **Fine Art Transparencies, Volume 1,** Art Transparency 1 (Have students compare and contrast the scene on the stairwell with the sidewalk scene in the essay.) ■

■ **BLOCK SCHEDULING:** Resources marked with this symbol provide varied instruction during 90-minute blocks.

experience. Now, as a rule, when we see someone we don't know person-ally, we don't stare into his or her face at length, we don't point out the person to the friend at our side, we don't speak of this person in a loud voice when he or she can overhear. Such behavior would be rude, even— if carried too far—aggressive. But the same people who would never point to a customer at a counter and remark to a friend that the man is wear-ing a smart tie behave quite differently with famous faces.

My guinea pigs insist that, at a newsstand, in the tobacconist's, as they are boarding a train or entering a restaurant toilet, they encounter others who, among themselves, say aloud, "Look there's X." "Are you sure?" "Of course I'm sure. It's X, I tell you." And they continue their conversation <u>amiably</u>, while X hears them, and they don't care if he hears them: it's as if he didn't exist.

Such people are confused by the fact that a <u>protagonist</u> of the mass media's imaginary world should abruptly enter real life, but at the same time they behave in the presence of the real person as if he still belonged to the world of images, as if he were on a screen, or in a weekly picture magazine. As if they were speaking in his absence.

I might as well have grabbed Anthony Quinn by the lapel, dragged him to a phone booth, and called a friend to say, "Talk about coinci-dence! I've run into Anthony Quinn. And you know something? He seems real!" (After which I would throw Quinn aside and go on about my business.)

The mass media first convinced us that the imaginary was real, and now they are convincing us that the real is imaginary; and the more reality the TV screen shows us, the more cinematic our everyday world becomes.

amiably (ā′ mē ə blē) *adv.* in a cheerful, friendly way

protagonist (prō tag′ ə nist) *n.* main character; person who plays a leading part

Review and Assess

Thinking About the Selection

1. **Respond:** Do you react to celebrities in the way Eco describes? Explain.
2. **(a) Recall:** Whom does the author see while strolling in New York? **(b) Infer:** How does Eco feel when he realizes who that person is?
3. **(a) Recall:** What reaction does Eco say most people have to celebrities? **(b) Infer:** How do you think Eco feels about the way people react to celebrities?
4. **(a) Recall:** Whose familiar faces does Eco mention? **(b) Connect:** How does the essay's title relate to its message?
5. **(a) Analyze:** Explain Eco's understanding of the role the media plays in our reaction to and attitude toward famous people. **(b) Make a Judgment:** Do you think that the media's treatment of famous people is fair? Explain.

Umberto Eco

(b. 1932)

Umberto Eco's personal library—holding more than 30,000 volumes—is larger than some school libraries! His extensive collec-tion is just one indication of the Italian author's strong interest in all forms of communication. At the University of Bologna in Italy, he teaches semiotics, the study of communica-tion through signs and symbols. He is also an avid follower of the information revolution taking place on the Internet.

Eco achieved an interna-tional audience with his 1983 novel *The Name of the Rose,* a suspenseful tale of murder in a Benedictine monastery.

How to React to Familiar Faces ◆ 457

457

❺ About the Selection

This selection explores the lives of ordinary people and how we view them. Poet Gwendolyn Brooks vividly evokes the texture of every-day lives and helps us glimpse the sensitive realities that lie beneath surface images.

❻ Reading Strategy

Responding to Connotations

• Encourage students to comment on the connotations of "this old yellow pair." Have them record their answers on a chart like the one on p. 455.
 Answer: Students may say that the description of their skin color as yellow evokes the qualities of wear and age.

• Tell students that one definition of *yellow* is "to change to a yellowish color through aging, as old paper."

Answers for p. 458

Review and Assess

1. Students might ask them about their work, friends and family, and their hobbies.

2. **(a)** The speaker uses the words *plain, chipware, creaking,* and *tin.* **(b)** The details indicate that the couple is poor.

3. **(a)** They reminisce as they eat. **(b)** The twinklings and twinges are happy and sad memories.

4. **(a)** Beads, receipts, dolls, cloths, tobacco crumbs, vases, and fringes fill the room. **(b)** The speaker believes that to the old couple, these objects are treasures because they help to spark their memories.

5. They are happy enough to care for themselves and share their memories with each other.

⑤ The Bean Eaters

Gwendolyn Brooks

❻ They eat beans mostly, this old yellow pair.
Dinner is a casual affair.
Plain chipware on a plain and creaking wood,
Tin flatware.

5 Two who are Mostly Good.
Two who have lived their day,
But keep on putting on their clothes
And putting things away.

And remembering . . .
10 Remembering, with twinklings and twinges,
As they lean over the beans in their rented back room
 that is full of beads and receipts and dolls
 and cloths, tobacco crumbs, vases and fringes.

Gwendolyn Brooks

(1917–2000)

Gwendolyn Brooks began writing in earnest at the age of seven and published her first poem, "Eventide," at the age of seventeen.

In many of her poems, Brooks explores the struggles and dreams of African Americans. She won a Pulitzer Prize (the first African American to do so) for her 1949 collection of poetry, *Annie Allen.* She received numerous other honors, including the title Poet Laureate of Illinois (1968) and an appointment as poetry consultant to the Library of Congress (1985–1986).

Review and Assess

Thinking About the Selection

1. **Respond:** If you could meet the people in "The Bean Eaters," what would you ask them?

2. **(a) Recall:** What words does the speaker use to describe the couple's dinnerware and table? **(b) Deduce:** What do these details indicate about the couple's standard of living?

3. **(a) Recall:** What do the people do as they eat their beans? **(b) Interpret:** What are the "twinklings and twinges" that the old couple feel?

4. **(a) Recall:** What kinds of things fill the couple's room? **(b) Draw Conclusions:** What might the poem's speaker want you to understand about their lives from these details?

5. **Hypothesize:** Do you think that the people in this poem are happy? Explain.

ASSESSMENT PRACTICE: Reading Comprehension

Evaluate and Make Judgments (For more practice, see **Test Preparation Workbook, p. 30.**)

Some tests require students to evaluate and make judgments about a text. Use the following sample test item to help students evaluate a poet's word choice.

 They eat beans mostly, this old yellow pair.

 Dinner is a casual affair.

 Plain chipware on a plain and creaking wood,

 Tin flatware.

The poet's choice of items used by the couple indicates that the use of the word *casual* may be ironic and the couple is probably

A vegetarian   **C** hungry
B tired   **D** poor

By noting the quality of the objects that the poet describes—chipped dinnerware and tin utensils—students should recognize that the couple is poor and that *D* is the correct answer.

Review and Assess

Literary Analysis

Tone

1. Find two statements in "How to React to Familiar Faces" that reflect a humorous **tone.**
2. (a) How does Eco's tone shift when he moves from talking about his encounter with Anthony Quinn to talking about the way the mass media affect our responses to famous people? (b) Why is this shift necessary?
3. (a) How do you think Gwendolyn Brooks feels about the people in her poem "The Bean Eaters"? (b) List two details that help you identify her feelings.

Comparing Literary Works

4. Using a chart like the one here, compare the **author's attitude** toward the people that are described. Give details from the text that illustrate each attitude.

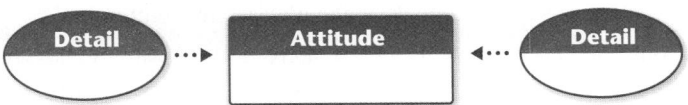

5. Based on the descriptions, which group of people—the bean eaters or the celebrity spotters—would you rather know? Why?

Reading Strategy

Responding to Connotations

6. (a) To which image in "How to React to Familiar Faces" do you respond strongly? (b) What **connotations** strengthen the image?
7. Keeping in mind the subject of "The Bean Eaters," what are some connotations of "Plain chipware" and "Tin flatware"?
8. How do you respond to the description of the old couple's home as a "rented back room"? Why?

Extend Understanding

9. **Cultural Connection:** (a) Do you think "The Bean Eaters" accurately describes the lives of the elderly? (b) What is one method that society could use to improve the lives of these people? Support your suggestion.

How to React to Familiar Faces / The Bean Eaters ◆ 459

Answers for p. 460

❶ Vocabulary Development

Word Analysis

1. An amiable approach would be accompanied by a smile.

2. You might have said, "Thanks for meeting with me" and "I appreciate your time."

3. Students may suggest good communication.

4. Some students may be willing to accept shorter vacations if they occur at more frequent intervals. Others may argue that they need a long vacation to rest from the pressures of school.

Fluency: Clarify Word Meaning

Possible responses:

1. A teacher might expound on the importance of reading.

2. You usually act amiably toward your parents and friends.

3. The protagonist is a small, white dog that saves the baby.

4. Students often suffer from sleepy brain waves on Monday mornings.

Spelling Strategy

1. symmetry; A checkerboard has perfect symmetry.

2. symposium; Our guest speaker leads a symposium on human rights.

3. symbolic; The flag is symbolic of patriotism and pride.

4. sympathy; Gwendolyn Brooks feels sympathy toward the bean eaters.

❷ Grammar

1. adjective   4. verb
2. verb   5. adjective
3. noun

Writing Application

Sample response: Steve Martin is my favorite movie star. He is a *living* genius, *displaying* talent at both *acting* and *writing*. When I am *watching* him, I always wind up *laughing*.

Integrate Language Skills

❶ Vocabulary Development Lesson

Word Analysis: Latin Root -ami-

The Latin root -ami- means "friend." It can be found in several English words, such as *amiable*, *amity*, and *amicable*. It is also the root in French and Spanish for the word *friend—ami* and *amigo*. Using this information, respond to the following questions.

1. Would a person have a smile or a frown if approaching you *amiably*? Explain.

2. Imagine that you have just finished meeting with your school's principal and you parted *amicably*. Write the last two things you might have said to each other.

3. Write one suggestion for developing *amity* between students and teachers.

4. Explain why you would or would not be *amenable* to shorter vacations.

Fluency: Clarify Word Meaning

On your paper, respond to the following items. Explain your answers.

1. Who might *expound* on the importance of reading?

2. To whom do you respond *amiably*?

3. Describe the *protagonist* in your favorite book.

4. Describe a humorous *syndrome* that might affect students on Monday morning.

Spelling Strategy

The *n* in the prefix *syn-* changes to *m* when the prefix is attached to a word that begins with *b*, *m*, or *p*. Write the words that result from the following, and use each in a sentence.

1. *syn-* + metry   3. *syn-* + bolic
2. *syn-* + posium   4. *syn-* + pathy

❷ Grammar Lesson

Verb, Participle, or Gerund?

Words ending in -ing may be parts of verb phrases, participles acting as adjectives, or gerunds (verb forms acting as nouns).

> **Verb:** A few months ago, I was *strolling* in New York.
>
> **Participle:** I saw a *strolling* man in front of me. (adjective)
>
> **Gerund:** *Strolling* can be a pleasurable pastime in New York. (noun)

Practice In each of the following sentences, tell whether the underlined word functions as a verb, an adjective, or a noun.

1. <u>Charming</u> people are nice to know.
2. Teenagers are <u>reading</u> more books.
3. <u>Eating</u> out at a restaurant is a treat.
4. I am <u>talking</u> about movie stars.
5. Acting is a <u>challenging</u> profession.

Writing Application Describe your favorite movie star. Use -ing words as adjectives, as verbs, and as nouns to add information to your description.

W̧G Prentice Hall Writing and Grammar Connection: Chapter 20, Section 1

TEACHING RESOURCES

The following resources can be used to enrich or extend the instruction for pp. 460–461.

Vocabulary

📖 **Selection Support:** Build Vocabulary, p. 117

📖 **Vocabulary and Spelling Practice Book** (Use this booklet for skills enrichment.) ▣

Grammar

📖 **Selection Support:** Build Grammar Skills, p. 118

W̧G **Writing and Grammar,** Platinum Level, p. 455

▣ **Daily Language Practice Transparencies** ▣

Writing

W̧G **Writing and Grammar,** Platinum Level, p. 134

💿 **Writing and Grammar iText CD-ROM** ▣

▣ **Writing Models and Graphic Organizers on Transparencies,** pp. 45–52

▣ **BLOCK SCHEDULING:** Resources marked with this symbol provide varied instruction during 90-minute blocks.

❸ Writing Lesson

Persuasive Argument

One response to Umberto Eco's essay "How to React to Familiar Faces" might be that "Publicity is part of the job of being a celebrity." Decide whether you agree or disagree with this statement. Then, prepare a persuasive argument with supporting evidence that you might present in a debate.

Prewriting   Using a T-chart, gather evidence for both sides of the argument. In the left column, list the "pros" or supporting evidence. In the right column, list the "cons" or opposing evidence. Your list will help you understand and defeat the opposition's argument.

Supporting	Opposing
Celebrities are paid to uphold an image.	Celebrities are people, too.

Drafting   Present the main points that you want to make. Then, write and elaborate statements that support your argument.

Revising   Have a peer read your argument and point out any holes in its logic or reasoning. Based on his or her feedback, work to fill those holes.

W︁G Prentice Hall Writing and Grammar Connection: Chapter 7, Section 2

❹ Extension Activities

Listening and Speaking With a partner, prepare and present an **introduction** for a talk-show guest. Imagine that you will be interviewing Anthony Quinn, Charlton Heston, Johnny Carson, or Oprah Winfrey. Use these tips to help you prepare your introduction:

- Research to find details that show your guest in a new light.
- Keep your introduction brief, giving just enough details to heighten the audience's interest.

When your material is ready, introduce your guest. [**Group Activity**]

Research and Technology Write a **research report** on the writer Gwendolyn Brooks. Using her biographical information on page 458, note a few questions on which to focus your research. Then, use suitable research methods to find information. Document any sources you use in a bibliography.

 Take It to the Net www.phschool.com

Go online for an additional research activity using the Internet.

How to React to Familiar Faces / The Bean Eaters ◆ 461

---

❸ Writing Lesson

- As students begin, encourage them to think about both sides of the question. They might use freewriting or have small-group discussions to explore their feelings on the topic of celebrity.

- Use **Writing Models and Graphic Organizers on Transparencies,** pp. 45–52, to show students how to use supporting and opposing evidence to strengthen their essays.

- Use the rubric for Persuasive Compositions in **Performance Assessment and Portfolio Management,** p. 11, to evaluate students' essays.

❹ Listening and Speaking

- Have students take notes on the information they find in the library or on the Internet.

- After students have completed their research, encourage them to use a colored pencil to circle any information that they believe their audience may not know. Students may then choose to focus on these details in the introduction.

- Use the rubric for Delivering a Descriptive Presentation in **Performance Assessment and Portfolio Management,** p. 29, to evaluate students' work.

CUSTOMIZE INSTRUCTION
for Universal Access

To address different learning styles, use the following activities suggested in the **Extension Activities** booklet, p. 30.

- For Intrapersonal and Verbal/Linguistic Learners, use Activity 5.

- For Verbal/Linguistic Learners, use Activity 6.

- For Interpersonal and Verbal/Linguistic Learners, use Activity 7.

A Picture From the Past: Emily Dickinson ✦
What Makes a Degas a Degas?

Lesson Objectives

1. **To analyze and respond to literary elements**
   - Literary Analysis: Analytical Essay
   - Comparing Literary Works: Purpose for Writing

2. **To read, comprehend, analyze, and critique essays**
   - Reading Strategy: Relating Text and Pictures
   - Reading Check questions
   - Review and Assess questions
   - Assessment Practice (ATE)

3. **To develop word analysis skills, fluency, and systematic vocabulary**
   - Vocabulary Development Lesson: Latin Word Root: -cent-

4. **To understand and apply written and oral language conventions**
   - Spelling Strategy
   - Grammar Lesson: Infinitives and Infinitive Phrases

5. **To understand and apply appropriate writing and research strategies**
   - Writing Lesson: Museum Placard
   - Extension Activity: Art Exhibit

6. **To understand and apply listening and speaking strategies**
   - Extension Activity: Poetry Reading

STEP-BY-STEP TEACHING GUIDE	PACING GUIDE
PRETEACH	
Motivate Students and Provide Background	
Use the Motivation activity (ATE p. 462)	5 min.
Read and discuss the Preview material and Background information (SE/ATE p. 462)	5 min.
Introduce the Concepts	
Introduce the Literary Analysis and Reading Strategy (SE/ATE p. 463)	15 min.
Pronounce the vocabulary words and read their definitions (SE p. 463)	5 min.
TEACH	
Monitor Comprehension	
Informally monitor comprehension by circulating while students read independently or in groups	10 min.
Monitor students' comprehension with the Reading Check notes (SE/ATE pp. 467, 469)	as students read
Develop vocabulary with Vocabulary notes (SE pp. 465, 469; ATE p. 465)	as students read
Develop Understanding	
Develop students' understanding of analytical essays with Literary Analysis annotations (SE p. 469; ATE pp. 467, 469)	10 min.
Develop students' understanding of relating text and pictures with Reading Strategy annotations (ATE pp. 465, 466, 468)	10 min.
ASSESS	
Assess Mastery	
Assess students' mastery of the Reading Strategy and Literary Analysis by having them answer the Review and Assess questions (SE/ATE p. 471)	20 min.
Use one or more of the print and media Assessment Resources (ATE p. 473)	up to 50 min.
EXTEND	
Apply Understanding	
Have students complete the Vocabulary Development Lesson and the Grammar Lesson (SE p. 472)	20 min.
Apply students' knowledge of anticipating questions using the Writing Lesson (SE p. 473)	45 min.
Apply students' understanding using one or more of the Extension Activities (SE p. 473)	20–90 min.

A **ACCELERATED INSTRUCTION:**
Use the strategies and activities identified with an **A**.

UNIVERSAL ACCESS
- ● = Below Level Students
- ▲ = On-Level Students
- ■ = Above Level Students

Time and Resource Manager

Reading Level: Average/Average
Average Number of Instructional Days: 4

RESOURCES

PRINT 📖	TRANSPARENCIES	TECHNOLOGY 💿 🎧 📼
• **Beyond Literature,** Humanities Connection: Art and Photography, p. 31 ▲ ■		• **Interest Grabber Video,** Tape 3 ● ▲ ■
• **Selection Support Workbook:** ● ▲ ■ Literary Analysis, p. 124 Reading Strategy, p. 123 Build Vocabulary, p. 121	• **Literary Analysis and Reading Transparencies,** pp. 61 and 62 ● ▲ ■	
		• **Listening to Literature** ● ▲ ■ Audiocassettes, Side 14 Audio CDs, CD 9
• **Literatura en español** ● ▲ • **Literary Analysis for Enrichment** ■	• **Fine Art Transparencies, Volume 1,** Art Transparency 4 ● ▲ ■	
• **Formal Assessment:** Selection Test, pp. 107–109 ● ▲ ■ • **Open Book Test,** pp. 91–93 ● ▲ ■ • **Performance Assessment and Portfolio Management,** p. 19 ● ▲ ■ • PRENTICE HALL ASSESSMENT *SYSTEM* ● ▲ ■	• PRENTICE HALL ASSESSMENT *SYSTEM* ● ▲ ■ Skills Practice Answers and Explanations on Transparencies	• **Test Bank Software** ● ▲ ■ • **Got It! Assessment Videotapes,** Tape 3 ● ▲
• **Selection Support Workbook:** ● ▲ ■ Build Grammar Skills, p. 122 • **Writing and Grammar,** Platinum Level ● ▲ ■ • **Extension Activities,** p. 31 ● ▲ ■	• **Daily Language Practice Transparencies** ● ▲ • **Writing Models and Graphic Organizers on Transparencies,** pp. 79, 88 ● ▲ ■	• **Writing and Grammar iText CD-ROM** ● ▲ ■ 💻 *Take It to the Net* www.phschool.com

BLOCK SCHEDULING: Use one 90-minute class period to preteach the selection and have students read it. Use a second 90-minute class period to assess students' mastery of skills and have them complete one of the Extension Activities.

Step-by-Step Teaching Guide
for pp. 462–463

Motivation

Engage students in a discussion about the difference between looking and seeing. Ask students to suggest reasons that people's eyes can be fooled. Explain that people's expectations affect their perceptions. Have students preview the pictures, jotting down details they notice. Tell students that the essays that analyze the pictures may help readers notice details they did not expect to see.

▭ Interest Grabber Video

As an alternative, play "Artistic Influences" on Tape 3 to engage student interest.

❶ Background

Art

Humans have a natural inclination to create art. Pieces of art date back as far as the Upper Paleolithic period (38,000 B.C.–10,000 B.C.), which marked the beginning of the human species. The art of each historical period gives us insight into the people who lived at that time—we learn about aspects of their culture, beliefs, and society.

Prepare to Read

A Picture From the Past: Emily Dickinson ◆
What Makes a Degas a Degas?

Two Dancers, Edgar Degas

 Take It to the Net

Visit www.phschool.com for interactive activities and instruction related to these selections, including

- background
- graphic organizers
- literary elements
- reading strategies

Preview

Connecting to the Literature

Looking at things in new ways can expand your horizons. When you look at a photograph or a painting, you may see the overall image, but when you focus on details, you may find something even more amazing. Reynolds Price and Richard Mühlberger, the authors of these essays, are able to look closely at pictures and see what most of us overlook. These essays will help you notice the subtle details.

❶ Background

Paintings have the power to transport viewers to distant places and to earlier periods in history. In fact, paintings and other works of art provide our only visual records of what life was like in the centuries before photography was invented in the 1830s.

462 ◆ *Expanding Horizons*

TEACHING RESOURCES

The following resources can be used to enrich or extend the instruction for pp. 462–463.

Motivation

▭ **Interest Grabber Video,** Tape 3

Background

▯ **Beyond Literature,** p. 31 ▭

 Take It to the Net

Visit www.phschool.com for background and hotlinks for the selections.

Literary Analysis

▯ **Selection Support:** Literary Analysis, p. 124 ▭

▯ **Literary Analysis and Reading Transparencies,** Analytical Essay, p. 62

Reading

▯ **Literary Analysis and Reading Transparencies,** Relating Text and Pictures, p. 61

 BLOCK SCHEDULING: Resources marked with this symbol provide varied instruction during 90-minute blocks.

❷ Literary Analysis

Analytical Essay

In an **analytical essay,** the author breaks down a large idea into parts, helping the reader understand how the pieces fit together and what they mean as a whole.

The authors of these two essays analyze pictures. Like mechanics working on a car engine, they take out the parts of the pictures, examine them, and determine how well they work together. By focusing on these details, your appreciation of the whole picture will increase. As you read, look for the details in the art that the authors bring to your attention.

Comparing Literary Works

While many writers choose artists as their subjects, their **purposes,** or reasons for writing, may differ. Although both these essays focus on analyzing pictures, the writers have different purposes for writing them. Compare the writers' purposes by considering the details that each writer includes in his essay and the conclusion that each reaches.

❸ Reading Strategy

Relating Text and Pictures

Sometimes, visual images and words are meant to complement each other. Together, they communicate a meaning that neither can convey alone. To **relate the text and pictures** in these essays,

- Pause as you read to look at the images.
- Note the details being described and interpreted.
- Compare the writers' interpretations of each image with your own impressions.

Use a diagram like the one here to help you. You may find that the authors' insights into the images will enhance your appreciation of what you see.

Vocabulary Development

titanic (tī tan´ ik) *adj.* huge and powerful (p. 465)

centenarian (sen´ tə ner´ ē ən) *n.* person who is at least one hundred years old (p. 465)

austere (ô stir´) *adj.* severe; stern (p. 465)

lacquered (lak´ ərd) *adj.* covered in tough, adherent varnish (p. 469)

A Picture From the Past: Emily Dickinson / What Makes a Degas a Degas? ◆ 463

---

❷ Literary Analysis
Analytical Essay

- Tell students that they will be reading two analytical essays—writings in which the subject is explored by taking a close look at small details.

- Discuss with students why someone might write analytical essays about pictures and paintings. Explain that art, like literature, often contains multiple layers of meaning.

- Encourage students to pause while reading to look at the art whenever the writer refers to details in it.

- Use the Analytical Essay transparency in **Literary Analysis and Reading Transparencies,** p. 62, to demonstrate for students how an analytical essay can enhance their own appreciation of art.

❸ Reading Strategy
Relating Text and Pictures

- Encourage students to flip back to a selection they've already read and look at the accompanying art.

- Ask students how the art complements the selection. Ask them to explain how the art helped to enrich their reading and understanding of the selection.

- Instruct students to create diagrams like the one shown here to explore some of the details in the art. Have them record both the authors' and their own interpretations as they read.

Vocabulary Development

- Pronounce each vocabulary word for students, and read the definitions as a class. Have students identify any words with which they are already familiar.

CUSTOMIZE INSTRUCTION FOR UNIVERSAL ACCESS

For Less Proficient Readers	For English Learners	For Advanced Readers
These essays require readers to move between pictures and text. Encourage students to use a placeholder—a finger, ruler, or the eraser tip of a pencil—to keep their place in the text.	Preview the pictures with students, having students describe in their own words what they see. As they read the essays, guide students to locate the portions of the picture being described.	After students have read the selections, challenge them to develop interpretations different from those presented by the writers. Have students share their own interpretations with their classmates in the form of a discussion or a debate.

 E-Teach

Visit E-Teach at www.phschool.com for teachers' essays on how to teach, with questions and answers.

**Step-by-Step Teaching Guide
for pp. 464–470**

CUSTOMIZE INSTRUCTION
For Logical/Mathematical
Learners

After they have read the selections, have students make a chart to compare and contrast the two paintings by Degas. Encourage them to use information they read in the essay, as well as their own observations and interpretations. You may want them to use the Grid Organizer in **Writing Models and Graphic Organizers on Transparencies,** p. 79.

❶ About the Selections

In this essay, Reynolds Price describes an image of Emily Dickinson and speculates on what the image reveals about the poet's personality and life. His analysis of the image raises questions about perceptions and appearances.

In "What Makes a Degas a Degas?," Richard Mühlberger analyzes Edgar Degas's painting style and points out the techniques he used to bring immediacy and the illusion of reality to his work.

❷ Background

Art

Emily Dickinson, daguerreotype, 1847 or 1848

The first popular method of photography was daguerreotype, a process named for Louis J.M. Daguerre, the Frenchman who perfected it in 1837. Daguerreotypes required subjects to remain still for a long period of time, resulting in the formal style seen in this image of Emily Dickinson. Use this question for discussion:

Why might Emily Dickinson have chosen to have a book in the picture? Answer: The book draws attention to the literary aspect of her life.

❸ ▶ Critical Viewing

Answer: Students may infer that she dressed in a conservative manner and that she enjoyed reading.

❶ *A Picture From the Past: Emily Dickinson* **Reynolds Price**

❸ ▲ **Critical Viewing** What can you infer about Emily Dickinson based on this photograph? **[Infer]**

464 ◆ *Expanding Horizons*

TEACHING RESOURCES

The following resources can be used to enrich or extend the instruction for pp. 464–470.

Literary Analysis

📖 **Writing Models and Graphic Organizers on Transparencies,** p. 79 ▪

Reading

📖 **Selection Support:** Reading Strategy, p. 123; Build Vocabulary, p. 121

🎧 **Listening to Literature Audiocassettes,** Side 14 ▪

💿 **Listening to Literature Audio CDs,** CD 9

Extend

📖 **Fine Art Transparencies, Volume 1,** Art Transparency 4 (Have students compare and contrast Gauguin's use of color with that of Degas in *Dancers, Pink and Green.*) ▪

▪ **BLOCK SCHEDULING:** Resources marked with this symbol provide varied instruction during 90-minute blocks.

Sorting the effects of an ancient aunt, in the wake of her death in the family homeplace or a merciless cell in an old-folks corral, you still might find such a picture and a face. The table drawers of middle-class America were once stuffed with them. No name, no date, no indication of why it's been saved to turn up now like a pebble from Mars in the glare of our world, where pictures of faces assail us at every glance and turn—assaulted children, the baffled old, the sleek in-betweeners.

A daguerreotype[1] the size of a calling card, hazed with the passage of more than a century; yet for all the immobility forced on the hapless sitter by a primitive process, it rides as lightly in your hand as a fragment of undoubted life, still pulsing. A homely girl with oddly dead eyes, set too far apart and flat as the eyes of a stunned fish in your stagnant bowl—or could she be warming to the verge of a blush and a big-toothed smile? A lopsided face, bigger on her right; a skewed part in the dark horsehair above the high forehead, unmatched eyebrows, a fleshy nose, unpainted bruised lips, an ample chin and a tall strong neck.

The hair, the ribbon around the neck, the sensible rough-knuckled hands and the complicated clinging dress date her to the midst of the 19th century. She's lasted somewhere between 16 and 20 years. Will she die shortly after this moment—consumption or childbirth—or will she endure through <u>titanic</u> throes and the ambush of pleasure to be your great-great-grandmother, say, or the maiden great-aunt your father remembers as a <u>centenarian</u> in his boyhood, a smuggler of priceless news to children—the secrets of solitude in the heart of the family but only on the rim, the watchful outrider?

None of those—no prior known option. Once this closely held girlhood ended, and the path ahead found no one waiting, she mastered solitude patiently as any rogue lioness, though she haunted her home's back room and kitchen (a sensible cook). Through the chilling or broiling hours in her upstairs room with the white door ajar on a chattering mother, an <u>austere</u> father, a loyal, silly sister, she wrote 1,800 lyrics—some clear as hill water, some dark as oak gall—that stand her yet, with no rival but Whitman,[2] at the head of our poetry: maiden aunt after all, our own Cassandra,[3] presiding mother of all this staggering nation still spooked as cubs by the mere glimpse of loneliness, that steady diet she ate by the hour all her lean years.

---

1. **daguerreotype** (də ger′ ō tip′) *n.* photographic image made by chemically treating a flat, thin piece of metal.
2. **Whitman** Walt Whitman (1819–1892), recognized as one of the most gifted American poets. Both he and Dickinson wrote poetry that was different from the standard poetry of their times.
3. **Cassandra** In Greek mythology, Cassandra was a prophetess whose predictions were always correct but never believed. Her name is used to refer to any prophet of doom.

titanic (tī tan′ ik) *adj.* huge and powerful

centenarian (sen′ tə ner′ ē ən) *n.* person who is at least one hundred years old

austere (ô stir′) *adj.* severe; stern

Reynolds Price

(b. 1933) American author Reynolds Price "photographs" his characters with words. He is known for creating characters that readers feel they have known all their lives. Most of his characters are drawn from the North Carolina cotton country where Price was raised. Although best known for his novels—including *A Long and Happy Life* and *A Generous Man*—Price has published essays, poetry, and a memoir in addition to his fiction works.

In this essay, Price uses his keen perception of characters to analyze the character of the very private American poet Emily Dickinson.

A Picture From the Past: Emily Dickinson ◆ 465

4 Reading Strategy

Relating Text and Pictures

- Have students look at the photograph on p. 464 as you read aloud the bracketed passage.
- Ask students whether they would have noticed the same details if they hadn't read the writer's interpretation.
  Possible Response: Students may say that they wouldn't have looked as closely at the small details of Dickinson's physical features had they not read the essay.
- Then, ask students how the writer describes Dickinson. Does he support his description well?
  Answer: Students should note that the author uses details to back up his point that Dickinson is "homely."

▶ **Monitor Progress** Ask students whether they agree with the writer's interpretation of the picture. If not, how would they describe Emily Dickinson?
Answer: If students see Dickinson differently, they should use the same details, interpreted differently, to back up their own views. Some students may also support their interpretations using details the writer did not mention.

5 Vocabulary Development

Latin Word Root: -cent-

- Draw students' attention to the word *centenarian* and its definition, "a person who is at least one hundred years old."
- Explain that the Latin root *–cent–* means "hundred," and ask students to list and define other words that contain this root.
  Answer: Students might mention *century* (period of one hundred years), and *centimeter* (one one-hundredth of a meter).

 E-Teach

Visit E-Teach at www.phschool.com for teachers' essays on how to teach, with questions and answers.

❻ Background

Art

Dancers, Pink and Green, by Edgar Degas

This piece of art is one of Degas's many paintings of ballet dancers. Most of Degas's ballet pictures were painted from the early 1870s to the early 1880s. Degas tried to capture the idea that ballet is work; sometimes dancers look tired or bored. In this painting, the body positions of the dancers reflect strength and energy as well as grace and delicacy. Use this question for discussion:

• If you had read the essay but never seen the painting, would you imagine it as it is or differently?
  Answer: Students should make specific references to details in the essay and the art.

❼ Reading Strategy

Relating Text and Pictures

• Have students match each detail in the passage with details in the painting.

• Then, ask students whether they would describe the painting in the same way or differently.
  Answer: Students' descriptions would probably be similar to the writer's.

• Instruct students to create diagrams like the one shown on p. 463. Have them fill in the diagrams with information from the text as well as their own interpretations.

466 ◆ *Expanding Horizons*

✳ ENRICHMENT: Art Connection

Photography

The word *photography* comes from the Greek roots *photo* and *graph*, meaning "light" and "drawing." Drawing with light is an accurate way to describe photography: A photograph is made when light (or some form of radiant energy) is shown on a light-sensitive surface in order to record a picture.

The daguerreotype made photography popular and accessible. The process was named for Louis J.M. Daguerre, the Frenchman who perfected it.

Daguerreotypes were capable of creating pictures of exquisitely fine detail, but the subjects of those photographs had to remain completely motionless for up to several minutes—even when taken in bright sunlight. That's why most people in daguerreotypes look so serious and formal; it's easier to sit still for several minutes when you're not smiling.

❶ What Makes a Degas a Degas?

Richard Mühlberger

DANCERS, PINK AND GREEN

Degas's famous ballet paintings witness his enthusiasm for dance and his intimacy with the private backstage areas of the Paris Opéra, the huge complex where the ballet made its home. He was equally familiar with the theater's more public boxes and stalls, where he watched many performances. During his lifetime, he produced about fifteen hundred drawings, prints, pastels, and oil paintings with ballet themes.

In *Dancers, Pink and Green*, each ballerina is caught in a characteristic pose as she waits to go on the stage. One stretches and flexes her foot. Another secures her hair, while a third is almost hidden. The fourth dancer, who looks at her shoulder strap as she adjusts it, holds a pose that was a favorite of the artist and one he used in many paintings. An upright beam separates her from the fifth ballerina, who also turns her head but in the opposite direction, full of anticipation. Above her in the distance are the box seats, which Degas simplified into a stack of six red and orange rectangles along the edge of the canvas. The vertical beam the ballerina is touching extends to the top and the bottom of the painting. The multicolored vertical shapes behind the dancers represent a large, painted landscape used as a backdrop for one of the dances. It will provide an immaterial, dreamworld quality to the performance, as it does to the painting.

Subscribers to the Opéra were allowed backstage in the theater, and some took advantage of this

Dancers, Pink and Green, Edgar Degas, Metropolitan Museum of Art

---

WHAT MAKES A DEGAS A DEGAS?

Notice the following techniques as you look at the paintings by Degas:

- As if viewing it from above, Degas tipped the stage upward to keep figures from blocking one another.

- Degas used patches of brilliant color to increase the feeling of movement.

- Degas cut figures off at the edge of the canvas, creating a candid effect.

- Degas used large, open spaces to move the eye deep into the picture.

---

❾ ✔**Reading Check**

How many dancers are pictured in *Dancers, Pink and Green*?

❿ ◀ **Critical Viewing** Which of Degas's techniques can you identify in this painting? **[Apply]**

What Makes a Degas a Degas? ◆ 467

467

access to pester dancers. On the far side of the tall wood column is the partial silhouette of a large man in a top hat. He seems to be trying to keep out of the way, but his protruding profile overlaps a ballerina. None of the dancers pay attention to him. They also ignore one another, for this scene represents the tense moments just before the curtain rises.

Degas discovered that with oil paints he could achieve the same fresh feeling conveyed with pastels. Although this painting took the same amount of time to finish as many of his others and was designed and executed in his studio, Degas wanted to make it look as though it had been executed quickly, backstage. To do this, he imitated the marks of a charcoal pencil with his brush, making narrow black lines that edge the dancers' bodies and costumes. Next, he

⓬ ▲ **Critical Viewing**
When you look at this picture, where is your eye first drawn? **[Analyze]**

Carriage at the Races, Edgar Degas, Museum of Fine Arts, Boston

used his own innovation of simulating the matte finish of pastels by taking the sheen out of oil paint, then filling in the sketchy "charcoal" outlines of his figures with a limited range of colors. The colors he used for the dancers extend to the floor and the background. The technique gives the impression that he applied the colors hastily while standing in the wings watching the dancers get ready.

The results of Degas's experiments could have been executed much more quickly had he used pastels instead of oils. What Degas wanted, however, was to make paint look spontaneous. This was part of his lifelong quest: to make viewers feel that they were right there, beside him.

CARRIAGE AT THE RACES

Paul Valpinçon was Degas's best friend in school and remained close to the artist all his life. Degas was a frequent visitor to his country house in Normandy, the northwest region of France, a long journey from Paris. Degas thought that the Normandy countryside was "exactly like England," and the beautiful horse farms there inspired him to paint equestrian subjects. During a visit in 1869, however, Degas found horses secondary to Paul Valpinçon's infant son, Henri. This becomes apparent by looking at the painting *Carriage at the Races.*

At first, Degas's composition seems lopsided. In one corner are the largest and darkest objects, a pair of horses and a carriage. Against the lacquered body of the carriage, the creamy white tones of the passengers stand out. They are framed by the dark colors rather than overwhelmed by them.

Degas placed a cream-colored umbrella in the middle of the painting above some of the figures in the carriage. Near it, balanced on the back of the driver's seat, is a black bulldog. Paul Valpinçon himself is the driver. Both Paul and the dog are gazing at the baby, who lies in the shade of the umbrella. With pink, dimpled knees, Henri, not yet a year old, sprawls on the lap of his nurse while his mother looks on.

IDEAS FROM THE EXOTIC, OLD, AND NEW

Degas always enjoyed looking at art. One of the thrills of his school years was being allowed to inspect the great paintings in the collection of Paul Valpinçon's father. Throughout his life, the artist drew inspiration from the masterpieces in the Louvre in Paris, one of the greatest museums in the world. He also found ideas in Japanese prints. They were considered cheap, disposable souvenirs in Japan,

Literary Analysis
Analytical Essay What details does the author use to support his point that Degas achieves the impression of quick execution?

lacquered (lak´ərd) *adj.* covered in tough, adherent varnish

Reading Check
How did Degas come to know Normandy, the setting of the painting *Carriage at the Races*?

What Makes a Degas a Degas? ◆ 469

⓭ Literary Analysis
Analytical Essay

- Read aloud the bracketed passage. Ask students to pay attention to the details the author uses to support his argument in this passage.

- Then, ask students the Literary Analysis question on p. 469: What details does the author use to support his point that Degas achieves the impression of quick execution? **Answer:** The author mentions Degas's technique of imitating the marks of a charcoal pencil, simulating the matte finish of pastels, and allowing the colors of the dancers to extend into the floor and the background.

⓮ Literary Analysis
Analytical Essay

- As students read the bracketed passage, have them identify each detail in the painting.

- Ask them which elements the essay helped them to notice. **Answer:** Students may mention the lopsided composition or the creamy white tones of the passengers standing out against the dark body of the carriage.

- Then, have students locate in the passage the larger idea that these details support. **Answer:** The larger idea is, "Degas found horses secondary to Paul Valpinçon's son, Henri." The details in this passage demonstrate how Degas made the baby the center of attention.

⓯ ✓ Reading Check
Answer: Degas traveled frequently to Normandy to visit his friend Paul Valpinçon.

CUSTOMIZE INSTRUCTION FOR UNIVERSAL ACCESS

For Gifted/Talented Students

Tell students that although Edgar Degas is considered one of the Impressionist painters, he did not share their enthusiasm for light and color. Instead, he focused on composition, drawing, and form. Have interested students research the Impressionists. Encourage them to find examples from many different Impressionist painters and compare them with Degas's work.

Degas also created many sculptures to study form and body movement. These "practice works" made Degas one of the most important sculptors in modern times. Have students find pictures of some of Degas's sculptures and compare them with his paintings. Then, have them give a presentation to the class about their findings. Encourage them to enhance their presentations by displaying the paintings and pictures of sculptures they found.

469

Answers for p. 470

Review and Assess

1. Students should support their opinions with specific reasons.

2. **(a)** He compares them to a pebble from Mars. **(b)** The comparison shows that the writer finds the photographer to be starkly out of place in today's world.

3. **(a)** He says she's one of our best poets. **(b)** Price believes that Dickinson's loneliness was both a consequence of her homeliness and a source of her sensitivity.

4. Students should support their opinions with specific details from the text and photograph.

5. **(a)** The setting is backstage before a ballet performance. **(b)** It illustrates the fact that subscribers went backstage to see the dancers.

6. **(a)** He creates a candid effect; it looks like he painted it quickly backstage. **(b)** The use of matte oil paints, sketchy outlines, and limited color range contribute to the effect.

7. **(a)** The dominant image is the family in the carriage. **(b)** It's surprising because it might have been expected that the horses would be prominent in that setting.

8. **(a)** Mühlberger says that Degas tried to make the viewer feel as if he or she were standing there beside him. **(b)** *Dancers, Pink and Green* illustrates the candid immediacy of Degas's art. *Carriage at the Races* appears more posed.

9. Degas imitated the effects of pastel artists and photographers; he was a leader in creating similar effects in oils.

10. Students might say that Degas and other artists draw our attention to small details we might not otherwise notice.

---

but were treasured by artists and others in the West as highly original, fascinating works of art. Photographs, then newly invented, also suggested to Degas ways of varying his paintings. He eventually became an enthusiastic photographer himself.

In *Carriage at the Races*, the way in which the horses and carriage are cut off recalls figures in photographs and Japanese prints. For Degas, showing only part of a subject made his paintings more intimate, immediate, and realistic. He wanted viewers to see the scene as if they were actually there.

Review and Assess

Thinking About the Selections

1. **Respond:** Would you like to see more of the work of Edgar Degas? Why or why not?

2. **(a) Recall:** To what does Price compare old pictures? **(b) Analyze:** How does this comparison effectively convey the writer's attitude toward the picture he finds?

3. **(a) Recall:** What does Price say about Dickinson's accomplishments as a poet? **(b) Infer:** How do you think Price feels about Dickinson? Explain.

4. **Evaluate:** Do you agree with Price's interpretation of the picture of Dickinson? Explain your answer.

5. **(a) Recall:** What is the setting for the painting *Dancers, Pink and Green*? **(b) Analyze:** How does the silhouette of the man in the top hat make the painting more realistic?

6. **(a) Recall:** What effect does Degas achieve by cutting off figures at the edges of his paintings and outlining his dancers in black lines? **(b) Connect:** What other elements of Degas's style contribute to this effect?

7. **(a) Recall:** What is the dominant image in the painting *Carriage at the Races*? **(b) Analyze:** What is surprising about the central image in the painting?

8. **(a) Recall:** What are the main points that Mühlberger tries to make about Degas's paintings? **(b) Apply:** Which of the two paintings better illustrates the points that Mühlberger makes? Why?

9. **Infer:** In his later years, Degas took up photography. What qualities in his paintings suggest that he might have been a good photographer?

10. **Extend:** How can the works of artists like Degas expand our view of the world?

Richard Mühlberger

(b. 1938)

You are most likely to find Richard Mühlberger's nonfiction in museum shops. In his book *What Makes a Degas a Degas?* he makes the work of a famous French artist understandable to the average viewer.

In this essay, he analyzes two works of the nineteenth-century French painter Edgar Degas. Degas studied art in both Paris and Italy. He intended to become a painter of historical scenes, but he soon turned to contemporary subjects. He became part of an artistic movement known as Impressionism, whose followers focused on capturing a momentary glimpse of a subject.

ASSESSMENT PRACTICE: Reading Comprehension

Evaluate and Make Judgments (For more practice, see Test Preparation Workbook, p. 31.)

Some tests require students to make judgments based on evidence from the text. Use the following sample test item to help students practice this skill:

The results of Degas's experiments could have been executed much more quickly had he used pastels instead of oils. What Degas wanted, however, was to make paint look spontaneous. This was part of his lifelong quest: to make viewers feel that they were right there, beside him.

The evidence in this passage suggests that the writer—

A approved of Degas's technique
B understood the qualities of oil paints
C did not study Degas's ideas
D conducted the same experiments as Degas

Help students see that, although the writer seems very knowledgeable about Degas, there is no evidence to support answers *A, C,* or *D*. The correct response is *B*.

Review and Assess

Literary Analysis

Analytical Essay

1. (a) On what details of Emily Dickinson's appearance does Price focus? (b) What personality traits does he relate to these details?
2. According to Mühlberger's analytical essay, why does Degas use a limited range of colors?
3. (a) What does Mühlberger say is Degas's lifelong quest? (b) Which of the techniques used by Degas to achieve his goal does Mühlberger identify?

Comparing Literary Works

4. Using a chart like the one here, identify the **author's purpose** in each of these essays.

Details From Text	My Response	Author's Purpose

5. Compare Mühlberger's purpose in writing "What Makes a Degas a Degas?" with Price's purpose in writing "A Picture From the Past."
6. (a) Which essay did you find more interesting? (b) How does the author's purpose help explain your answer?

Reading Strategy

Relating Text and Pictures

7. Explain whether you think Price's conclusions about Dickinson are supported by the details in the photograph.
8. Price asks, "could she be warming to the verge of a blush and a big-toothed smile?" What evidence in the photograph do you see to support this question?
9. Identify details from the paintings that illustrate three of the characteristics of Degas's work described by Mühlberger in his essay.

Extend Understanding

10. **Career Connection:** In what careers is it important to be able to see small details rather than just the big picture? Why?

A Picture From the Past: Emily Dickinson / What Makes a Degas a Degas? ◆ 471

Quick Review

In an **analytical essay,** the author breaks down a large idea into parts, examines them, and helps the reader understand how they fit together and what they mean.

The **author's purpose** is his or her reason for writing.

When you **relate text and pictures,** you compare what the author writes with what you find in the pictures.

 Take It to the Net

www.phschool.com

Take the interactive self-test online to check your understanding of these selections.

---

❶ Vocabulary Development

Word Analysis

1. e   4. c
2. d   5. a
3. b

Fluency: Clarify Word Meaning

1. Judges are often austere.
2. Critics might describe a powerful new movie as titanic.
3. You might buy a lacquered item in a gift shop.
4. The centenarian remembered historic events.

Spelling Strategy

1. severity   3. obscurity
2. actively   4. stately

❷ Grammar

1. To go on stage was her ultimate goal. (noun)
2. He wants to keep out of the way. (noun)
3. This painting took the same amount of time to finish. (adjective)
4. He was unable to dance. (adverb)
5. The dancers lived to perform. (adverb)

Writing Application

1. My mother likes to draw landscapes. (noun)
2. Portraits are my favorite things to draw. (adjective)
3. I always use pencils to draw. (adverb)

Integrate Language Skills

❶ Vocabulary Development Lesson

Word Analysis: Latin Root -cent-

The word *centenarian* refers to a person who has lived to be one hundred. A clue to the meaning of the word is the Latin root *-cent-*, which means "hundred." Use your knowledge of the root to match each word with its definition:

1. centigrade   a. one-hundredth of a dollar
2. century   b. one-hundredth anniversary
3. centennial   c. one one-hundredth of a meter
4. centimeter   d. period of one hundred years
5. cent   e. temperature scale in which one hundred degrees represents the boiling point of water

❷ Grammar Lesson

Infinitives and Infinitive Phrases

An **infinitive** is a form of the verb that generally appears with the word *to* and acts as a noun, an adjective, or an adverb. An **infinitive phrase** is an infinitive with modifiers or complements, all acting together as a single part of speech.

> **As Noun:** Degas wanted *to make it blue*.
>
> **As Adjective:** The dancers showed a willingness *to cooperate*.
>
> **As Adverb:** Subscribers used the access *to pester dancers*.

Fluency: Clarify Word Meaning

Copy each sentence. Fill in the blank with a word from the vocabulary list on page 463.

1. Judges are often ___?___.
2. Critics might describe a powerful new movie as ___?___.
3. You might buy a ___?___ item in a gift shop.
4. The ___?___ remembered historic events.

Spelling Strategy

When adding a suffix like *-ity*, which begins with a vowel, to a word ending in a silent *e*, drop the *e*: *austere* becomes *austerity*. When adding the suffix *-ly*, which begins with a consonant, keep the *e*. Form new words by attaching the suffix to the word given:

1. severe + *-ity*   3. obscure + *-ity*
2. active + *-ly*   4. state + *-ly*

Practice Copy the following sentences. Underline the infinitives. Then, identify the function each serves.

1. To go on stage was her ultimate goal.
2. He wants to keep out of the way.
3. This painting took the same amount of time to finish.
4. He was unable to dance.
5. The dancers lived to perform.

Writing Application Write sentences using the infinitive *to draw* as a noun, an adjective, and an adverb.

*W*G *Prentice Hall Writing and Grammar Connection: Chapter 20, Section 1*

472 ◆ *Expanding Horizons*

TEACHING RESOURCES

The following resources can be used to enrich or extend the instruction for pp. 472–473.

Vocabulary

📖 **Selection Support:** Build Vocabulary, p. 121

📖 **Vocabulary and Spelling Practice Book** (Use this booklet for skills enrichment.) ▪

Grammar

📖 **Selection Support:** Build Grammar Skills, p. 122

*W*G **Writing and Grammar,** Platinum Level, p. 458

📘 **Daily Language Practice Transparencies** ▪

Writing

*W*G **Writing and Grammar,** Platinum Level, p. 256

💿 **Writing and Grammar iText CD-ROM** ▪

📄 **Writing Models and Graphic Organizers on Transparencies,** p. 88

▪ **BLOCK SCHEDULING:** Resources marked with this symbol provide varied instruction during 90-minute blocks.

❸ Writing Lesson

Museum Placard

Write a **placard**—a small informational card—that might be displayed beside a Degas painting used in this selection. Do research to learn about the painting, such as when it was painted, the title, and the painter. Then, combining this with what you have learned from Mühlberger, write a few sentences that would help a reader appreciate the art.

Prewriting Choose a piece of art. Then, brainstorm for a list of questions that viewers might have. Choose one or two questions to answer that will give the most insight into the painting.

Model: Anticipating Questions

Where did Degas get his inspiration?

Who is the subject of the painting?

Did Degas know the people in the painting?

Why did he use those colors?

What are the subtle details?

> The answers to these questions might produce useful and interesting information for a placard.

Drafting Write basic information—such as title, date, and artist—clearly at the top of the placard. Then, write a short paragraph that includes other interesting facts you discovered through your research.

Revising Compare your question list against your draft. If you have not answered each question adequately, do more research or revise for clarity.

Prentice Hall Writing and Grammar Connection: Chapter 12, Section 3

❹ Extension Activities

Research and Technology With a small group, organize an **art exhibit** of famous paintings. Each group member should contribute one entry and research the painting and the artist.

- Display the paintings, with informational placards hung beneath.
- Invite your classmates to visit your art exhibit.

Hold a question-and-answer session in which your group explains its choices. **[Group Activity]**

Listening and Speaking To learn more about Emily Dickinson, have a **poetry reading** of some of her work. Find one or more Dickinson poems to read aloud to the class. Then, lead a discussion about what each poem reveals about the poet.

 Take It to the Net www.phschool.com

Go online for an additional research activity using the Internet.

A Picture From the Past: Emily Dickinson / What Makes a Degas a Degas? ◆ 473

Lesson Support for p. 473

❸ Writing Lesson

- Tell students that the information on a placard can influence the way people view a work of art just as the essay by Mühlberger did.
- Students may benefit from using the Cubing organizer in **Writing Models and Graphic Organizers on Transparencies,** p. 88, to brainstorm for the type of information they will include on their placards.
- When they finish, use the Description rubric, p. 19 in **Performance Assessment and Portfolio Management,** to assess students' placards.

❹ Research and Technology

- Before presenting this activity, arrange with your librarian to have art books collected for students.
- Have student groups go to the library to find paintings that interest them.
- Suggest that students follow the same procedure shown in the Writing Lesson to create the placards for their chosen art.
- Allow time for students to set up their exhibit and for the class to enjoy it. Encourage each group to explain its choices.

CUSTOMIZE INSTRUCTION for Universal Access

To address different learning styles, use the following activities suggested in the **Extension Activities** booklet, p. 31.

- For Verbal/Linguistic Learners, use Activity 5.
- For Visual/Spatial Learners, use Activity 6.
- For Logical/Mathematical and Verbal/Linguistic Learners, use Activity 7.

ASSESSMENT RESOURCES

The following resources can be used to assess students' knowledge and skills.

Selection Assessment

- **Formal Assessment,** pp. 107–109
- **Open Book Test,** pp. 91–93
- **Got It! Assessment Videotapes,** Tape 3
- **Test Bank Software**

Take It to the Net
Visit www.phschool.com for self-tests and additional questions on the selections.

Writing Rubric

- **Performance Assess. and Portfolio Mgmt.,** p. 19

PRENTICE HALL **ASSESSMENT SYSTEM**

- **Workbook**
- **Skill Book**
- **Transparencies**
- **CD-ROM**

Connections

In his paintings, Degas tried to create a feeling of immediacy, as if the viewer were a witness present at the moment captured on canvas. McCourt uses a literary style that accomplishes the same thing: readers feel as if they are a part of the scene and that they are experiencing it as they read. Ask students to note similarities and differences between the ways in which Degas and McCourt achieve this goal.

The Power of Art and Language

- Explain to students that this selection offers a firsthand account of recovering from typhoid fever as a child in a hospital in Ireland.

- As students read the excerpt from McCourt's book, have them pay attention to the way in which McCourt indicates dialogue. Do students find this style confusing or do they find it easier to understand? Does this style give the story more flow or slow them down?

▶ **Critical Viewing**

Answer: The water and the bridge suggest the story takes place in a town or city near a river. The boy's clothing—he is wearing a sweater and a jacket—suggest both that the story is set in a temperate part of the world and that it is set some years in the past, when clothing was more formal.

CONNECTIONS
Literature and Humanities
The Power of Art and Language

In the essay "What Makes a Degas a Degas?" Richard Mühlberger examines Edgar Degas's vibrant painting style, which lets viewers see his subjects as if they were actually there.

It is this type of eye-opening experience that Frank McCourt describes in his memoir *Angela's Ashes.* The 1997 Pulitzer Prize-winning book captures McCourt's boyhood, growing up in poverty and suffering from typhoid fever as a child in Ireland.

During an extended hospital stay, McCourt met a sick girl named Patricia, who introduced him to poetry. The language and sound of the poems made a strong impression on McCourt and introduced him to a world beyond his family's situation. Suddenly, through literature, he saw things in a new light.

▲ **Critical Viewing** What details in this picture give clues to the setting of this story? **[Infer]**

474 ◆ *Expanding Horizons*

⚙ **ENRICHMENT: Social Studies Connection**

Ireland

The selection is set in the Republic of Ireland, a country that takes up about five sixths of the island of Ireland; the other one sixth is Northern Ireland, which is part of the United Kingdom. English and Gaelic, the ancient language of Ireland, are the official languages of Ireland. The country is called Éire (AIR-uh) in Gaelic; it is also known by the poetic name Erin.

The beautiful green countryside of Ireland has given the country still another name: the Emerald Isle. It is well known for its rolling pasturelands, mountains, and coastal cliffs. Two thirds of Ireland is still farmland.

A largely Catholic country, Ireland fought for independence from Britain and became its own nation in 1921. The Protestant-dominated counties of Northern Ireland chose to remain part of Great Britain. Because of extensive emigration from Ireland to the United States, many in the United States have ties to the country.

from

Angela's Ashes

Frank McCourt

The other two beds in my room are empty. The nurse says I'm the only typhoid patient and I'm a miracle for getting over the crisis.

The room next to me is empty till one morning a girl's voice says, Yoo hoo, who's there?

I'm not sure if she's talking to me or someone in the room beyond.

Yoo hoo, boy with the typhoid, are you awake?

I am.

Are you better?

I am.

Well, why are you here?

I don't know. I'm still in the bed. They stick needles in me and give me medicine.

What do you look like?

I wonder, What kind of a question is that? I don't know what to tell her.

Yoo hoo, are you there, typhoid boy?

I am.

What's your name?

Frank.

That's a good name. My name is Patricia Madigan. How old are you?

Ten.

Oh. She sounds disappointed.

But I'll be eleven in August, next month.

Well, that's better than ten. I'll be fourteen in September. Do you want to know why I'm in the Fever Hospital?

I do.

Background
Typhoid Fever

Typhoid fever is caused by the bacterium *Salmonella typhi.* A serious disease that sometimes results in death, it is transferred indirectly from person to person through contaminated food or water. It was once fairly common in highly populated regions around the world, but improvements in sanitation and hygiene have decreased its occurrences. In fact, typhoid is quite rare in areas that have modern sanitation standards. However, this disease is still widespread in many underdeveloped countries.

CUSTOMIZE INSTRUCTION FOR UNIVERSAL ACCESS

For Less Proficient Readers	For Advanced Readers
Students may have difficulty distinguishing dialogue from the narrative due to the lack of dialogue punctuation. Encourage students to read the selection aloud in order to better understand where the dialogue begins and ends. You may want to guide students through the text, having them identify who is speaking each line of dialogue.	Encourage students to write about one of their own experiences, using the same style as McCourt. Challenge them to include dialogue without the usual punctuation, as McCourt does, but in a way that clearly indicates who's speaking. Have them analyze how McCourt achieves this, and then replicate it in their own writing.

Thematic Connection

Answer: The nurses do not allow patients, especially boys and girls to talk together. This restriction discourages patients from learning from one another's experiences and differing perspectives.

▶Critical Viewing

Answer: The hospital in the story has separate rooms for Frank and Patricia, while the photograph shows a ward with a number of beds. In the story, nurses pass in and out; the photograph suggests they are in constant attendance. The photograph does capture the austere, somber mood of the hospital in the story.

Thematic Connection

Answer: Based on this paragraph, Frank's experiences have most likely been very limited. The references to his father's periods of unemployment suggest that the family is poor. A chocolate bar is a luxury, suggesting that other pleasures such as books, trips, and elaborate toys may be absent from his childhood. His father's references to praying and to St. Jude show that religion is a prominent part of the family's life.

I have diphtheria and something else.

What's something else?

They don't know. They think I have a disease from foreign parts because my father used to be in Africa. I nearly died. Are you going to tell me what you look like?

I have black hair.

You and millions.

I have brown eyes with bits of green that's called hazel.

You and thousands.

I have stitches on the back of my right hand and my two feet where they put in the soldier's blood.

Oh, . . . did they?

They did.

You won't be able to stop marching and saluting.

There's a swish of habit and click of beads and then Sister Rita's voice. Now, now, what's this? There's to be no talking between two rooms especially when it's a boy and a girl. Do you hear me, Patricia?

I do, Sister.

Do you hear me, Francis?

I do, Sister.

You could be giving thanks for your two remarkable recoveries. You could be saying the rosary. You could be reading *The Little Messenger of the Sacred Heart* that's beside your beds. Don't let me come back and find you talking.

She comes into my room and wags her finger at me. Especially you, Francis, after thousands of boys prayed for you at the Confraternity. Give thanks, Francis, give thanks.

She leaves and there's silence for awhile. Then Patricia whispers, Give thanks, Francis, give thanks, and say your rosary, Francis, and I laugh so hard a nurse runs in to see if I'm all right. She's a very stern nurse from the County Kerry and she frightens me. What's this, Francis? Laughing? What is there to laugh about? Are you and that Madigan girl talking? I'll report you to Sister Rita. There's to be no laughing for you could be doing serious damage to your internal apparatus.

She plods out and Patricia whispers again in a heavy Kerry accent, No laughing, Francis, you could be doin' serious damage to your internal apparatus. Say your rosary, Francis, and pray for your internal apparatus.

Mam visits me on Thursdays. I'd like to see my father, too, but I'm out of danger, crisis time is over, and I'm allowed only one visitor. Besides, she says, he's back at work at Rank's Flour Mills and please God this job will last a while with the war on and the English desperate for flour. She brings me a chocolate bar and that proves Dad is working. She could never afford it on the dole.[1] He sends me notes. He tells me my brothers are all praying for me, that I should be a

---

1. **On the dole** the distribution by the government of relief payments to the unemployed.

Thematic Connection
What opportunities for growth do the nurses seem to restrict in the hospital?

▶ Critical Viewing
How does this image of a British hospital compare with the hospital that is described in the story? **[Compare and Contrast]**

Thematic Connection
How would you describe the range of McCourt's life experiences based on this paragraph?

good boy, obey the doctors, the nuns, the nurses, and don't forget to say my prayers. He's sure St. Jude pulled me through the crisis because he's the patron saint of desperate cases and I was indeed a desperate case.

Patricia says she has two books by her bed. One is a poetry book and that's the one she loves. The other is a short history of England and do I want it? She gives it to Seamus, the man who mops the floors every day, and he brings it to me. He says, I'm not supposed to be bringing anything from a diphtheria room to a typhoid room with all the germs flying around and hiding between the pages and if you ever catch diphtheria on top of the typhoid they'll know and I'll lose my good job and be out on the street singing patriotic songs with a tin cup in my hand, which I could easily do because there isn't a song ever written about Ireland's sufferings I don't know. . . .

Oh, yes, he knows Roddy McCorley. He'll sing it for me right enough but he's barely into the first verse when the Kerry nurse rushes in. What's this, Seamus? Singing? Of all the people in this hospital you should know the rules against singing. I have a good mind to report you to Sister Rita.

✔Reading Check

How do the nurses want children in the hospital to spend their time?

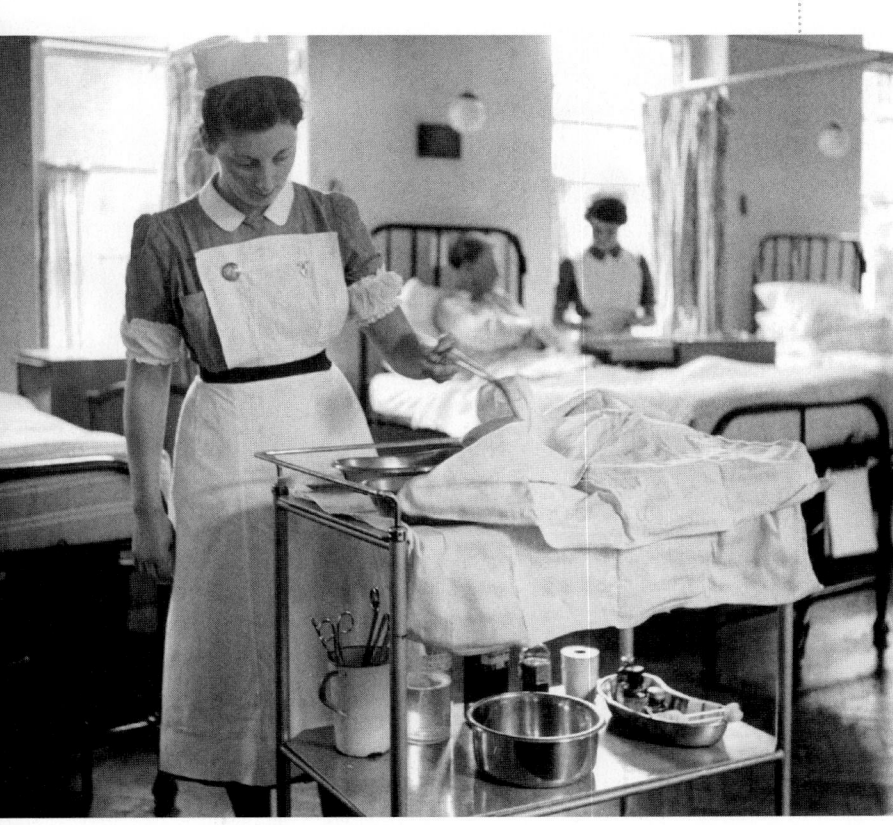

Connections: from *Angela's Ashes* ◆ 477

✔Reading Check

Answer: The nurses want the children in the hospital to pray, say the rosary, and read religious texts.

►Critical Viewing

Answer: Students may note that, like Sister Rita, the nurse in the photograph appears strict and disciplined. She is smiling, however, which might suggest she has the sense of humor Sister Rita lacks.

Ah, . . . don't do that, nurse.

Very well, Seamus. I'll let it go this one time. You know the singing could lead to a relapse in these patients.

When she leaves he whispers he'll teach me a few songs because singing is good for passing the time when you're by yourself in a typhoid room. He says Patricia is a lovely girl the way she often gives him sweets from the parcel her mother sends every fortnight. He stops mopping the floor and calls to Patricia in the next room, I was telling Frankie you're a lovely girl, Patricia, and she says, You're a lovely man, Seamus. He smiles because he's an old man of forty and he never had children but the ones he can talk to here in the Fever Hospital. He says, Here's the book, Frankie. Isn't is a great pity you have to be reading all about England after all they did to us, that there isn't a history of Ireland to be had in this hospital.

The book tells me all about King Alfred and William the Conqueror and all the kings and queens down to Edward, who had to wait forever for his mother, Victoria, to die before he could be king. The book has the first bit of Shakespeare I ever read.

▼ Critical Viewing
Compare the woman in the photograph with the image you formed of Sister Rita. **[Compare and Contrast]**

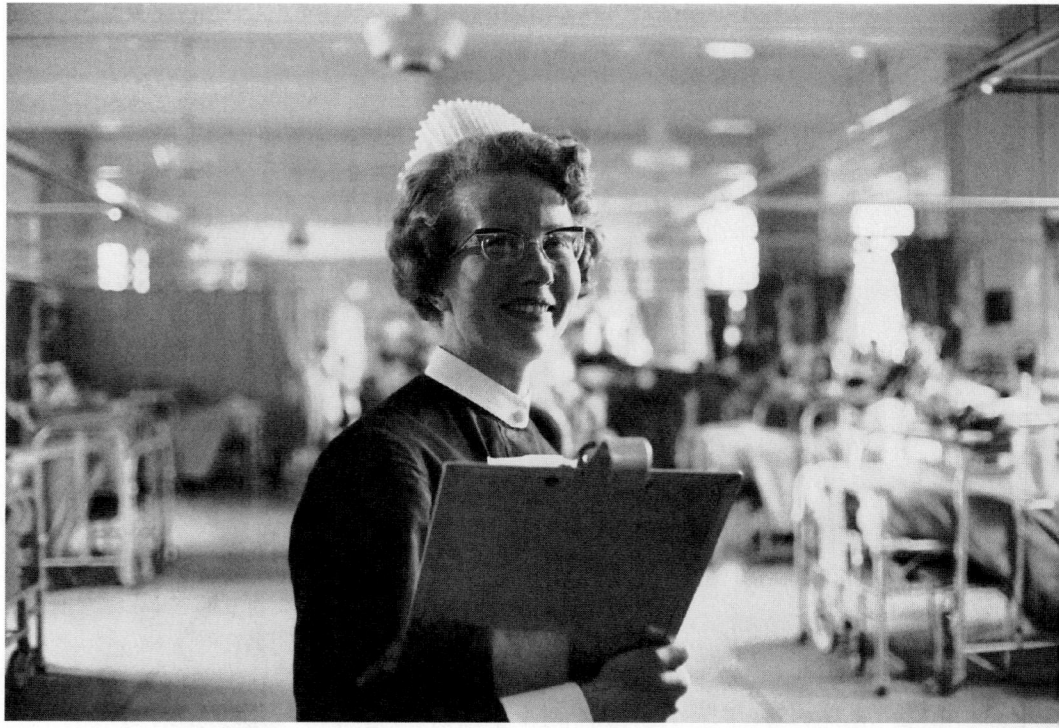

✳ ENRICHMENT: Literature Connection

"The Highwayman" by Alfred Noyes

The poem that enthralls Frank, "The Highwayman" (1906), is a beloved poem by Alfred Noyes (1880–1958). Modeled in form and subject after traditional English ballads, the poem tells the story of a young woman's sacrifice to save her lover, a highwayman, or bandit who robs travelers.

The woman, Bess, is the daughter of an innkeeper. Her love for the highwayman is discovered by a servant who informs on the two. British soldiers

("redcoats") gather at the inn and hold Bess prisoner while awaiting the highwayman's visit to her. As the highwayman approaches, Bess sacrifices her own life to give the signal that warns him away.

Popular in his own lifetime, Noyes wrote extensively on romantic subjects from history, such as the voyages of the English explorer Sir Francis Drake.

I do believe, induced by potent circumstances
That thou art mine enemy.

The history writer says this is what Catherine, who is a wife of Henry the Eighth, says to Cardinal Wolsey, who is trying to have her head cut off. I don't know what it means and I don't care because it's Shakespeare and it's like having jewels in my mouth when I say the words. If I had a whole book of Shakespeare they could keep me in the hospital for a year.

Patricia says she doesn't know what <u>induced</u> means or potent circumstances and she doesn't care about Shakespeare, she has her poetry book and she reads to me from beyond the wall a poem about an owl and a pussycat that went to sea in a green boat with honey and money and it makes no sense and when I say that Patricia gets huffy and says that's the last poem she'll ever read to me. She says I'm always reciting the lines from Shakespeare and they make no sense either. Seamus stops mopping again and tells us we shouldn't be fighting over poetry because we'll have enough to fight about when we grow up and get married. Patricia says she's sorry and I'm sorry too so she reads me part of another poem which I have to remember so I can say it back to her early in the morning or late at night when there are no nuns or nurses about,

> *The wind was a <u>torrent</u> of darkness among the gusty trees,*
> *The moon was a ghostly galleon tossed upon cloudy seas,*
> *The road was a ribbon of moonlight over the purple moor,*
> *And the highwayman came riding*
> > *Riding riding*
> *The highwayman came riding, up to the old inn-door.*
> *He'd a French cocked-hat on his forehead, a bunch of lace at his chin,*
> *A coat of the claret velvet, and breeches of brown doe-skin,*
> *They fitted with never a wrinkle, his boots were up to the thigh.*
> *And he rode with jeweled twinkle,*
> > *His pistol butts a-twinkle,*
> *His rapier hilt a-twinkle, under the jewelled sky.*

Every day I can't wait for the doctors and nurses to leave me alone so I can learn a new verse from Patricia and find out what's happening to the highwayman and the landlord's red-lipped daughter. I love the poem because it's exciting and almost as good as my two lines of Shakespeare. The redcoats are after the highwayman because they know he told her, I'll come to thee by moonlight. . . .

I'd love to do that myself, come by moonlight for Patricia in the next room. . . . She's ready to read the last few verses when in comes the nurse from Kerry shouting at her, shouting at me, I told ye there was to be no talking between rooms. Diphtheria is never allowed to talk to typhoid and visa versa. I warned ye. And she calls out,

---

Thematic Connection

How does discovering books while in the hospital expand Frankie's horizons?

induced (in doost') *adj.* convinced; led by a course of action

torrent (tôr´ ənt) *n.* heavy, uncontrolled outpouring

✔ Reading Check

How does the poem bring life to Frankie's days?

Connections: from *Angela's Ashes* ◆ 479

Thematic Connection

Answer: Discovering books expands Frank's horizons by introducing him to Shakespeare and poetic language. He is captivated by the sound and feel of the words, and he indicates that he will search out Shakespeare to read more in the future. Reading introduces him to feelings and ideas beyond his own limited experiences.

✔ Reading Check

Answer: Students will probably say that the poem brings life to Frank's days because each day he is anxious to learn more of the story. He now has something to look forward to, something that excites him and brings him joy, rather than just another quiet, lonely day of bed rest. He is enthralled with the story of the poem and thoroughly enjoys the poetic language.

CUSTOMIZE INSTRUCTION FOR UNIVERSAL ACCESS

For Special Needs Students	For Gifted/Talented Students
Students may need help understanding the excerpt from the poem "The Highwayman" that appears in the story. Use the information in the Enrichment note on page 478 to introduce them to the work. Then, guide students through the poem, pausing to have them paraphrase each line. Encourage students to help each other paraphrase, to work together as a group to decipher the poem.	Encourage interested students to research the song Seamus sings for McCourt, "Roddy McCorley." Ask them to try to find a recording of the song or sheet music for it. If they locate music, encourage them to learn to play or sing the song. Have them play or perform the song for the class.

Background

The Great Famine

Ireland's population grew rapidly during the 1800s. There was little industry in the country, and most people worked as farmers on rented land. Most of what they grew was given to the landlord as rent, and people struggled to subsist on what was left over.

When disease destroyed the potato crop of 1845–1850, the results were catastrophic. The struggling Irish farmers depended heavily on potatoes for food. With the failure of the crop, about one million Irish died. Another 1.5 million left the country, many emigrating to the United States. This period was known as the Great Famine.

The British, who ruled Ireland at the time, took a number of measures to help that actually worsened the situation. At first, they actually drove small farmers off the land in order to encourage large-scale farming. It was only later that they passed laws to protect poor farmers.

Seamus, take this one. Take the by. Sister Rita said one more word out of him and upstairs with him. We gave ye a warning to stop the blathering but ye wouldn't. Take the by, Seamus, take him.

Ah, now, nurse, sure isn't he harmless. 'Tis only a bit o'poetry.

Take that by, Seamus, take him at once.

He bends over me and whispers, Ah, . . . I'm sorry, Frankie. Here's your English history book. He slips the book under my shirt and lifts me from the bed. He whispers that I'm a feather. I try to see Patricia when we pass through her room but all I can make out is a blur of dark head on a pillow.

Sister Rita stops us in the hall to tell me I'm a great disappointment to her, that she expected me to be a good boy after what God had done for me, after all the prayers said by hundreds of boys at the Confraternity, after all the care from the nuns and nurses of the Fever Hospital, after the way they let my mother and father in to see me, a thing rarely allowed, and this is how I repaid them lying in the bed reciting silly poetry back and forth with Patricia Madigan knowing very well there was a ban on all talk between typhoid and diphtheria. She says I'll have plenty of time to reflect on my sins in the big ward upstairs and I should beg God's forgiveness for my disobedience reciting a pagan English poem about a thief on a horse and a maiden with red lips who commits a terrible sin when I could have been praying or reading the life of a saint. She made it her business to read that poem so she did and I'd be well advised to tell the priest in confession.

The Kerry nurse follows us upstairs gasping and holding on to the banister. She tells me I better not get the notion she'll be running up to this part of the world every time I have a little pain or a twinge.

There are twenty beds in the ward, all white, all empty. The nurse tells Seamus put me at the far end of the ward against the wall to make sure I don't talk to anyone who might be passing the door, which is very unlikely since there isn't another soul on this whole floor. She tells Seamus this was the fever ward during the Great Famine[2] long ago and only God knows how many died here brought in too late for anything but a wash before they were buried and there are stories of cries and moans in the far reaches of the night. She says 'twould break your heart to think of what the English did to us, that if they didn't put the blight on the

---

2. **Great Famine** a severe food shortage in Ireland from 1845–1849 caused by failed potato crops. Potato plants were infected by a disease that destroys the plants' leaves and roots. As a result, roughly one million Irish people died of starvation and nearly 1.5 million emigrated to Great Britain and the United States.

potato they didn't do much to take it off. No pity. No feeling at all for the people that died in this very ward, children suffering and dying here while the English feasted on roast beef and guzzled the best of wine in their big houses, little children with their mouths all green from trying to eat the grass in the fields beyond, God bless us and save us and guard us from future famines.

Seamus says 'twas a terrible thing indeed and he wouldn't want to be walking these halls in the dark with all the little green mouths gaping at him. The nurse takes my temperature, 'Tis up a bit, have a good sleep for yourself now that you're away from the chatter with Patricia Madigan below who will never know a gray hair.

She shakes her head at Seamus and he gives her a sad shake back.

Nurses and nuns never think you know what they're talking about. If you're ten going on eleven you're supposed to be simple like my uncle Pat Sheehan who was dropped on his head. You can't ask questions. You can't show you understand what the nurse said about Patricia Madigan, that's she's going to die, and you can't show you want to cry over this girl who taught you a lovely poem which the nun says is bad.

The nurse tells Seamus she has to go and he's to sweep the lint from under my bed and mop up a bit around the ward. Seamus tells me . . . that you can't catch a disease from a poem. . . . He never heard the likes of it, a little fella shifted upstairs for saying a poem and he has a good mind to go to the *Limerick Leader* and tell them print the whole thing except he has this job and he'd lose it if ever Sister Rita found out. Anyway, Frankie, you'll be outa here one of these fine days and you can read all the poetry you want though I don't know about Patricia below, I don't know about Patricia. . . .

He knows about Patricia in two days because she got out of the bed to go to the <u>lavatory</u> when she was supposed to use a bedpan and collapsed and died in the lavatory. Seamus is mopping the floor and there are tears on his cheeks and he's saying, 'Tis a dirty rotten thing to die in a lavatory when you're lovely in yourself. She told me she was sorry she had you reciting that poem and getting you shifted from the room, Frankie. She said 'twas all her fault.

It wasn't Seamus.

I know and didn't I tell her that.

lavatory (lav′ ə tôr′ ē) *n.* room equipped with a wash basin and a flush toilet

Frank McCourt

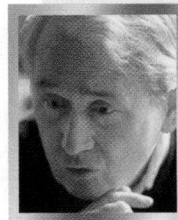

(b. 1930)
Born in Brooklyn, New York, to Irish immigrant parents, Frank McCourt traveled with his family to Ireland because his father had trouble keeping a job in New York.

In Ireland, McCourt lived out what he would later call a "miserable Irish childhood." At nineteen, McCourt managed to return to America, and he eventually enrolled in New York University. For thirty years afterward, he taught English in the New York City public schools. McCourt has published two memoirs—*Angela's Ashes* and *'Tis.* He currently lives in New York City and Connecticut with his wife, Ellen.

Connecting Literature and Humanities

1. How did literature improve Frankie's hospital experiences?
2. Basing your answer on McCourt's writing, what similarities can you find between the experiences of viewing paintings, such as those of Degas, and reading literature, such as "The Highwayman"?
3. What differences can you identify between these two art forms?

Answers

Connecting Literature and Humanities

1. Literature gave Frank something to look forward to, providing him a bit of joy and companionship during his long, lonely days in the hospital.

2. In his paintings, Degas strove to make viewers feel as if they were standing right next to him as he painted. The viewer would be absorbed in the immediacy of the moment. Similarly, the poem "The Highwayman" captivates Frank, bringing him directly into its drama and vivid word-pictures.

3. Some students may say that a story is more involved than a painting. A painting represents one moment, but a story takes the reader through many moments, so one might get more out of a story—a larger range of emotions and situations—than out of a painting.

The Orphan Boy and the Elk Dog

Lesson Objectives

1. **To analyze and respond to literary elements**
   - Literary Analysis: Myth
   - Connecting Literary Elements: Inciting Incident

2. **To read, comprehend, analyze, and critique a myth**
   - Reading Strategy: Interpreting
   - Reading Check questions
   - Review and Assess questions
   - Assessment Practice (ATE)

3. **To develop word analysis skills, fluency, and systematic vocabulary**
   - Vocabulary Development Lesson: Homographs

4. **To understand and apply written and oral language conventions**
   - Spelling Strategy
   - Grammar Lesson: Commonly Confused Verbs: *accept* and *except*

5. **To understand and apply appropriate writing and research strategies**
   - Writing Lesson: Retelling a Myth
   - Extension Activity: Bar Graph

6. **To understand and apply listening and speaking strategies**
   - Extension Activity: Debate

STEP-BY-STEP TEACHING GUIDE	PACING GUIDE
PRETEACH	
Motivate Students and Provide Background	
Use the Motivation activity (ATE p. 482)	5 min.
Read and discuss the Preview material and Background information (SE/ATE p. 482) [A]	5 min.
Introduce the Concepts	
Introduce the Literary Analysis and Reading Strategy (SE/ATE p. 483) [A]	15 min.
Pronounce the vocabulary words and read their definitions (SE p. 483)	5 min.
TEACH	
Monitor Comprehension	
Informally monitor comprehension by circulating while students read independently or in groups [A]	25 min.
Monitor students' comprehension with the Reading Check notes (SE/ATE pp. 485, 487, 489, 491)	as students read
Develop vocabulary with Vocabulary notes (SE pp. 485, 486, 489, 490; ATE p. 485)	as students read
Develop Understanding	
Develop students' understanding of myths with Literary Analysis annotations (SE pp. 488, 490; ATE pp. 488, 490) [A]	10 min.
Develop students' understanding of interpreting texts with Reading Strategy annotations (SE pp. 485, 486, 490; ATE pp. 485, 486, 490)	10 min.
ASSESS	
Assess Mastery	
Assess students' mastery of the Reading Strategy and Literary Analysis by having them answer the Review and Assess questions (SE/ATE p. 493)	20 min.
Use one or more of the print and media Assessment Resources (ATE p. 495) [A]	up to 50 min.
EXTEND	
Apply Understanding	
Have students complete the Vocabulary Development Lesson and the Grammar Lesson (SE p. 494) [A]	20 min.
Apply students' ability to use transitions using the Writing Lesson (SE/ATE p. 495) [A]	45 min.
Apply students' understanding using one or more of the Extension Activities (SE p. 495)	20–90 min.

 ACCELERATED INSTRUCTION:
Use the strategies and activities identified with an [A].

UNIVERSAL ACCESS
● = Below Level Students
▲ = On-Level Students
■ = Above Level Students

Time and Resource Manager

Reading Level: Average
Average Number of Instructional Days: 4

RESOURCES

PRINT 📖	TRANSPARENCIES	TECHNOLOGY 💿 🎧 📼
• **Beyond Literature,** Cultural Connection: The Role of the Horse in Different Cultures, p. 32 ▲ ■		• **Interest Grabber Video,** Tape 3 ● ▲ ■
• **Selection Support Workbook:** ● ▲ ■ Literary Analysis, p. 128 Reading Strategy, p. 127 Build Vocabulary, p. 125	• **Literary Analysis and Reading Transparencies,** pp. 63 and 64 ● ▲ ■	
		• **Listening to Literature** ● ▲ ■ Audiocassettes, Side 14 Audio CDs, CD 10
• **Literatura en español** ● ▲ • **Literary Analysis for Enrichment** ■		
• **Formal Assessment:** Selection Test, pp. 110–112 ● ▲ ■ • **Open Book Test,** pp. 94–96 ● ▲ ■ • **Performance Assessment and Portfolio Management,** p. 14 ● ▲ ■ • PRENTICE HALL **ASSESSMENT** *SYSTEM* ● ▲ ■	• PRENTICE HALL **ASSESSMENT** *SYSTEM* ● ▲ ■ Skills Practice Answers and Explanations on Transparencies	• **Test Bank Software** ● ▲ ■ • **Got It! Assessment Videotapes,** Tape 3 ● ▲
• **Selection Support Workbook:** ● ▲ ■ Build Grammar Skills, p. 126 • **Writing and Grammar,** Platinum Level ● ▲ ■ • **Extension Activities,** p. 32 ● ▲ ■	• **Daily Language Practice Transparencies** ● ▲ • **Writing Models and Graphic Organizers on Transparencies,** p. 83 ● ▲ ■	• **Writing and Grammar iText CD-ROM** ● ▲ ■ 🖥️ *Take It to the Net* www.phschool.com

BLOCK SCHEDULING: Use one 90-minute class period to preteach the selection and have students read it. Use a second 90-minute class period to assess students' mastery of skills and have them complete one of the Extension Activities.

Motivation

Read the following passage aloud to students:

"... he boldly jumped into the water. To his surprise, he found it did not make him wet, that it parted before him, that he could breathe and see."

Ask students what kind of story they think this excerpt comes from. On the chalkboard, list the qualities they might expect to find in such a story.

Answer: Students might say the story contains magic, adventure, and symbolic meanings.

▣ Interest Grabber Video

As an alternative, play "Great Plains Native Americans" on Tape 3 to engage student interest.

❶ Background

History

The Blackfeet had no horses before the 1700s. The Shoshone (another group of Plains Indians) had herds of horses as early as 1680. One daring Blackfoot, who may have been the inspiration for the "orphan boy" in this myth, slipped into a Shoshone camp with his companions, untied four horses, and led them away. To the amazed Blackfeet, these animals looked like elk-sized dogs. The easy mobility offered by horses eventually changed the Blackfeet way of life.

Prepare to Read

The Orphan Boy and the Elk Dog

Following the Buffalo Run, Charles M. Russell, Amon Carter Museum, Fort Worth, Texas

 Take It to the Net

Visit www.phschool.com for interactive activities and instruction related to the selection, including

- background
- graphic organizers
- literary elements
- reading strategies

Preview

Connecting to the Literature

When you need to go somewhere, you have many travel choices—car, airplane, train, bus, boat. Think how your life would be different without these ways to travel. In this selection, the Blackfeet discover horses, and the discovery will change their world.

❶ Background

This story comes from the Blackfeet, one of the many nations that have lived on the Great Plains of North America. At one time, most Plains Indians were farmers who lived in one place, grew their own food, and sometimes hunted buffalo on foot. Then, in the 1600s, many tribes captured and tamed wild horses. On horseback, the Indians could travel and hunt more efficiently. Hunting replaced farming, and the tribes became nomadic, following the buffalo herds.

482 ◆ *Expanding Horizons*

TEACHING RESOURCES

The following resources can be used to enrich or extend the instruction for pp. 482–483.

Motivation

▣ **Interest Grabber Video,** Tape 3

Background

📖 **Beyond Literature,** p. 32

 Take It to the Net

Visit www.phschool.com for background and hotlinks for "The Orphan Boy and the Elk Dog."

Literary Analysis

📖 **Literary Analysis and Reading Transparencies,** Myth, p. 64

Reading

📖 **Selection Support:** Reading Strategy, p. 127; Build Vocabulary, p. 125

📖 **Literary Analysis and Reading Transparencies,** Interpreting, p. 63

▣ **BLOCK SCHEDULING:** Resources marked with this symbol provide varied instruction during 90-minute blocks.

Literary Analysis

Myth

Myths are traditional stories, passed down from generation to generation, that usually involve "larger-than-life" characters, such as the man described below:

> There he came face to face with a tall man, fierce and scowling and twice the height of most humans.

As part of the oral tradition of cultures without a written language, myths attempt to explain facets of the world, including these specific elements:

- Natural phenomena
- The origin of humans or the universe
- The customs of a people

Indirectly, myths teach the values and ideals of a culture. This selection is a myth that explains how the Blackfeet came to have horses.

Connecting Literary Elements

In myths, as in other stories, a main character must deal with a central problem or conflict. The conflict is often introduced by an **inciting incident,** an event that propels the main character into the problem situation. The orphan boy's conflict in this myth involves a heroic quest. As you read, notice the details that show why he initiates his quest.

Reading Strategy

Interpreting

When you **interpret** literature, you try to determine what the author is saying. You might interpret a title, a figure of speech, an image, or the story as a whole. Interpreting will help you develop a deeper understanding of the meaning of a work. Use a diagram like the one here to help you interpret ideas as you read. In the center, write the idea to interpret. In the connecting boxes, write the ideas that it suggests.

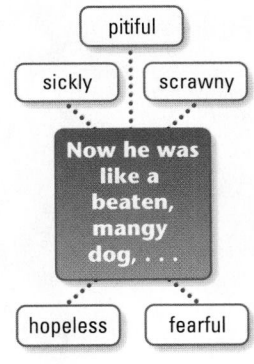

Vocabulary Development

refuse (ref´ yōōz) *n.* anything thrown away as useless (p. 485)

surpassed (sər past´) *v.* went beyond; excelled (p. 486)

emanating (em´ ə nāt´ iŋ) *v.* coming forth (p. 489)

relish (rel´ ish) *n.* pleasure and enjoyment (p. 489)

stifle (stī´ fəl) *v.* hold back (p. 490)

The Orphan Boy and the Elk Dog ◆ 483

---

❷ Literary Analysis

Myth

- Tell students that as they read "The Orphan Boy and the Elk Dog," they will focus on myths, traditional stories passed down through generations.

- Read the instruction about myths together as a class. Call students' attention to the myth's purpose, using the example from the story.

- Use the instruction for Connecting Literary Elements to help students identify the inciting incident in the myth.

- Display the Myth transparency in **Literary Analysis and Reading Transparencies,** p. 64, to help students explore the features of the myth as they read.

❸ Reading Strategy

Interpreting

- Explain to students that when they interpret, they are trying to determine what the author wants to say to the reader.

- Tell students that interpreting can reveal meanings within the text that are often different for each reader. Review the diagram on this page to show students how they can use details in the text to help them interpret key ideas.

- As they read, encourage students to create their own idea diagrams, interpreting for themselves what the author is trying to say.

Vocabulary Development

- Pronounce each vocabulary word for students, and read the definitions as a class. Have students identify any words with which they are already familiar.

CUSTOMIZE INSTRUCTION FOR UNIVERSAL ACCESS

For Less Proficient Readers	For English Learners	For Advanced Readers
Have students read the Review and Assess questions on p. 492 to help guide their reading. Then, ask students to read the story as a group, stopping periodically to record the main ideas.	Before they begin reading, have students preview the Review and Assess questions on p. 492. As they read, suggest that they look for key words in the text to find answers, and avoid getting stuck on unfamiliar words.	Have students read the selection independently at their own pace, keeping track of story elements and their own interpretations of the main ideas. When students finish reading, have them discuss their interpretations in small groups.

 E-Teach

Visit E-Teach at www.phschool.com for teachers' essays on how to teach, with questions and answers.

483

CUSTOMIZE INSTRUCTION
For Visual/Spatial Learners

Before students begin reading, have them view the painting on p. 484. From looking at this painting, what can the students infer about the story's setting and characters?

❶ About the Selection

So important were horses to the Plains Indians, that the explanation for how these animals came into their possession is an integral part of their cultural history. According to this myth, a young man who had been an outcast went on a danger-ous quest to prove himself to his people and to prove his own self-worth. By a feat of courage and dar-ing, and aided by magic, he returned with horses, or "Elk Dogs," which changed and improved the lives of his people. This myth, in addition to explaining an important aspect of life for the Blackfeet, con-veys important cultural values through the relationship of the young man to the old chief who adopted him: courage, respect for elders, generosity, and compassion.

❷ Background

Art

The Color of Sun by Howard Terpning

This painting shows a young Plains Indian brave riding a horse with bow and arrow strapped behind. The horse nuzzles the spring flowers as the brave scans the horizon. The horse's piebald coloring serves as effective camouflage against the dappled woodland background. Use this question for discussion:

> Based on the composition of the painting, how did the artist make the youth look brave and heroic?

> Possible responses: The young man and his horse take up most of the canvas; the horse and rider appear arrested in a moment of calm, awaiting action.

❶ The Orphan Boy and the Elk Dog
Native American (Blackfeet)

The Color of Sun, Howard Terpning, The Greenwich Workshop, Inc.

▲ **Critical Viewing** Use the selection title and this painting to predict what this story is about. **[Predict]**

TEACHING RESOURCES

The following resources can be used to enrich or extend the instruction for pp. 484–492.

Literary Analysis

📖 **Selection Support:** Literary Analysis, p. 128

🗂 **Writing Models and Graphic Organizers on Transparencies,** p. 83 ▪

Reading

🎧 **Listening to Literature Audiocassettes,** Side 14 ▪

💿 **Listening to Literature Audio CDs,** CD 10 ▪

▪ **BLOCK SCHEDULING:** Resources marked with this symbol provide varied instruction during 90-minute blocks.

In the days when people had only dogs to carry their bundles, two orphan children, a boy and his sister, were having a hard time. The boy was deaf, and because he could not understand what people said, they thought him foolish and dull-witted. Even his relatives wanted nothing to do with him. The name he had been given at birth, while his parents still lived, was Long Arrow. Now he was like a beaten, mangy dog, the kind who hungrily roams outside a camp, circling it from afar, smelling the good meat boiling in the kettles but never coming close for fear of being kicked. Only his sister, who was bright and beautiful, loved him.

Then the sister was adopted by a family from another camp, people who were attracted by her good looks and pleasing ways. Though they wanted her for a daughter, they certainly did not want the awkward, stupid boy. And so they took away the only person who cared about him, and the orphan boy was left to fend for himself. He lived on scraps thrown to the dogs and things he found on the <u>refuse</u> heaps. He dressed in remnants of skins and frayed robes discarded by the poorest people. At night he bedded down in a grass-lined dugout, like an animal in its den.

Eventually the game was hunted out near the camp that the boy regarded as his, and the people decided to move. The lodges were taken down, belongings were packed into rawhide bags and put on dog travois, and the village departed. "Stay here," they told the boy. "We don't want your kind coming with us."

For two or three days the boy fed on scraps the people had left behind, but he knew he would starve if he stayed. He had to join his people, whether they liked it or not. He followed their tracks, frantic that he would lose them, and crying at the same time. Soon the sweat was running down his skinny body. As he was stumbling, running, panting, something suddenly snapped in his left ear with a sound like a small crack, and a wormlike substance came out of that ear. All at once on his left side he could hear birdsongs for the first time. He took this wormlike thing in his left hand and hurried on. Then there was a snap in his right ear and a wormlike thing came out of it, and on his right side he could hear the rushing waters of a stream. His hearing was restored! And it was razor-sharp—he could make out the rustling of a tiny mouse in dry leaves a good distance away. The orphan boy laughed and was happy for the first time in his life. With renewed courage he followed the trail his people had made.

In the meantime the village had settled into its new place. Men were already out hunting. Thus the boy came upon Good Running, a kindly old chief, butchering a fat buffalo cow he had just killed. When the chief saw the boy, he said to himself, "Here comes that poor good-for-nothing boy. It was wrong to abandon him." To the boy Good Running said "Rest here, grandson, you're sweaty and covered with dust. Here, have some tripe."[1]

---

1. **tripe** (trīp) *n.* part of the stomach of an ox or cow when used as food.

refuse (ref′ yōōz) *n.* anything thrown away as useless

Reading Strategy
Interpreting What might the wormlike substance that comes out of Long Arrow's ears represent?

6 ☑**Reading Check**
Why did no one want to adopt the orphan boy?

The Orphan Boy and the Elk Dog ◆ 485

3 ▶**Critical Viewing**
Answer: Students may predict that the story will focus on a young Native American and a mysterious animal, perhaps a horse.

4 Vocabulary Development
Word Groups: Homographs
• Ask students to identify the part of speech for the word *close* in the bracketed sentence.
  Answer: *Close* is an adverb that modifies *coming*.
• Then, ask students to think of a homograph and its part of speech.
  Answer: *Close* can be a verb when pronounced differently, and when it serves a different function in a sentence.

5 Reading Strategy
Interpreting
• Remind students that when they interpret, they are trying to determine what the author is saying by reading "between the lines." Explain that interpreting a text gives a reader a deeper understanding of the meaning of the work.
• Ask students the Reading Strategy question on p. 485: What might the wormlike substance that comes out of Long Arrow's ears represent?
  Answer: The substance is a blockage falling out, enabling him to hear.

6 ☑**Reading Check**
Answer: Long Arrow was thought to be foolish and dull-witted because he was deaf.

CUSTOMIZE INSTRUCTION FOR UNIVERSAL ACCESS

For Less Proficient Readers	For English Learners	For Advanced Readers
Suggest that students imagine the myth as a movie and divide it into scenes, jotting down a brief summary of what happens in each.	Have students locate a mythical story in their native language to share with other students in English. Students should concentrate on the myth's purpose, its inciting incident, and the cultural values that it teaches.	Invite students to point out story elements that this myth shares with other myths or traditional tales they have read. For example, they might mention the magical objects in "Aladdin" or the difficult quests in the Grail legends.

485

- Ask students how Long Arrow's ambition to do something special is connected to his unusual early life.

  Answer: Because he was once ostracized, Long Arrow now feels he must prove his worth both to those who shunned him and to himself.

- Then, have students read the bracketed passage, paying careful attention to the details included about the Elk Dogs. Encourage students to record these details in a diagram like the one shown on p. 483.

- Ask students the Reading Strategy question on p. 486: What does the story of the Elk Dogs reveal about the culture of the Blackfeet?

  Possible response: The Blackfeet believe in "spirit people" and in mystery animals called "Elk Dogs."

The boy wolfed down the meat. He was not used to hearing and talking yet, but his eyes were alert and Good Running also noticed a change in his manner. "This boy," the chief said to himself, "is neither stupid nor crazy." He gave the orphan a piece of the hump meat, then a piece of liver, then a piece of raw kidney, and at last the very best kind of meat—a slice of tongue. The more the old man looked at the boy, the more he liked him. On the spur of the moment he said, "Grandson, I'm going to adopt you; there's a place for you in my tipi. And I'm going to make you into a good hunter and warrior." The boy wept, this time for joy. Good Running said, "They called you a stupid, crazy boy, but now that I think of it, the name you were given at birth is Long Arrow. I'll see that people call you by your right name. Now come along."

The chief's wife was not pleased. "Why do you put this burden on me," she said, "bringing into our lodge this good-for-nothing, this slow-witted crazy boy? Maybe you're a little slow-witted and crazy yourself!"

"Woman, keep talking like that and I'll beat you! This boy isn't slow or crazy; he's a good boy, and I have taken him for my grandson. Look—he's barefooted. Hurry up, and make a pair of moccasins for him, and if you don't do it well I'll take a stick to you."

Good Running's wife grumbled but did as she was told. Her husband was a kind man, but when aroused, his anger was great.

So a new life began for Long Arrow. He had to learn to speak and to understand well, and to catch up on all the things a boy should know. He was a fast learner and soon <u>surpassed</u> other boys his age in knowledge and skills. At last even Good Running's wife accepted him.

He grew up into a fine young hunter, tall and good-looking in the quilled buckskin outfit the chief's wife made for him. He helped his grandfather in everything and became a staff for Good Running to lean on. But he was lonely, for most people in the camp could not forget that Long Arrow had once been an outcast. "Grandfather," he said one day, "I want to do something to make you proud and show people that you were wise to adopt me. What can I do?"

Good Running answered, "Someday you will be a chief and do great things."

"But what's a great thing I could do now, Grandfather?"

The chief thought for a long time. "Maybe I shouldn't tell you this," he said. "I love you and don't want to lose you. But on winter nights, men talk of powerful spirit people living at the bottom of a faraway lake. Down in that lake the spirit people keep mystery animals who do their work for them. These animals are larger than a great elk, but they carry the burdens of the spirit people like dogs. So they're called Pono-Kamita—Elk Dogs. They are said to be swift, strong, gentle, and beautiful beyond imagination. Every fourth generation, one of our young warriors has gone to find these spirit folk and bring back an Elk Dog for us. But none of our brave young men has ever returned."

"Grandfather, I'm not afraid. I'll go and find the Elk Dog."

surpassed (sər past') *v.* went beyond; excelled

Reading Strategy
Interpreting What does the story of the Elk Dogs reveal about the culture of the Blackfeet?

✹ ENRICHMENT: Cultural Connection

Myths

"The Orphan Boy and the Elk Dog" is a myth that explains how the Blackfeet came to have horses. Stories like this one were regarded with great reverence, and there were strict observances in the telling of them. The season for telling myths was the winter, when people stayed inside for warmth and protection. It was considered inappropriate, and even sacrilegious, to tell these stories in the summer. The myths also served as entertainment for the long nights of winter, when dancing and powwows were impossible.

To fully enjoy the story, students should be encouraged to imagine they are hearing it told by someone they respect a great deal, surrounded by other listeners who feel the same way. The supernatural events are exciting to visualize, but they are secondary to the admirable bravery and good sense of the hero.

Crow Lodge of Twenty-five Buffalo Skins, George Catlin, National Museum of American Art, Washington, D.C.

▲ **Critical Viewing** Why do the Blackfeet live in houses like this one? **[Infer]**

"Grandson, first learn to be a man. Learn the right prayers and ceremonies. Be brave. Be generous and open-handed. Pity the old and the fatherless, and let the holy men of the tribe find a medicine for you which will protect you on your dangerous journey. We will begin by purifying you in the sweat bath."

So Long Arrow was purified with the white steam of the sweat lodge. He was taught how to use the pipe, and how to pray to the Great Mystery Power. The tribe's holy men gave him a medicine and made for him a shield with designs on it to ward off danger.

Then one morning, without telling anybody, Good Running loaded his best travois dog with all the things Long Arrow would need for traveling. The chief gave him his medicine, his shield, and his own fine bow and, just as the sun came up, went with his grandson to the edge of the camp to purify him with sweet-smelling cedar smoke. Long Arrow left unheard and unseen by anyone else. After a while

☑**Reading Check**

What does the chief tell Long Arrow that he can do to make him proud?

The Orphan Boy and the Elk Dog ◆ 487

❽ Background

Art

Crow Lodge of Twenty-five Buffalo Skins, by George Catlin

This painting documents a domestic scene centered on the tipi. The Crow are a Plains hunting people who lived along the Yellowstone River. They call themselves Absaroka, or "bird people." Use these questions for discussion:

1. What elements of the myth can you find in this painting?
   Answer: The tipi, the dog, the weapons, and the man and woman working are all mentioned in the myth.

2. How would life in a tipi differ from your life?
   Possible responses: Camping out in a tipi provides a closeness to nature that isn't possible in a house or an apartment building.

❾ ▶Critical Viewing

Possible answers: The Blackfeet probably live in tipis because they are made from buffalo skin, and buffaloes are plentiful on the Great Plains. Also, they have to travel frequently to find food, and tipis are easy to transport.

❿ ☑Reading Check

Answer: Long Arrow can look for the spirit people and bring back an Elk Dog.

Myth

- Remind students that an inciting incident introduces the conflict in a myth. This incident propels the action of the narrative.

▶ **Monitor Progress** Have students read the bracketed passage. Then, ask them the Literary Analysis question on p. 488: What effect does the meeting with the tall spirit man have on the action of the myth?

Answer: It is a critical turning point in the myth. Most humans would have been scared by the spirit man, but Long Arrow is unafraid. Because of his courage, Long Arrow is accepted by the powerful spirit and permitted to move forward to discover the Elk Dogs.

---

some people noticed that he was gone, but no one except his grandfather knew where and for what purpose.

Following Good Running's advice, Long Arrow wandered southward. On the fourth day of his journey he came to a small pond, where a strange man was standing as if waiting for him. "Why have you come here?" the stranger asked.

"I have come to find the mysterious Elk Dog."

"Ah, there I cannot help you," said the man, who was the spirit of the pond. "But if you travel further south, four-times-four days, you might chance upon a bigger lake and there meet one of my uncles. Possibly he might talk to you; then again, he might not. That's all I can tell you."

Long Arrow thanked the man, who went down to the bottom of the pond, where he lived.

Long Arrow wandered on, walking for long hours and taking little time for rest. Through deep canyons and over high mountains he went, wearing out his moccasins and enduring cold and heat, hunger and thirst.

Finally Long Arrow approached a big lake surrounded by steep pine-covered hills. There he came face to face with a tall man, fierce and scowling and twice the height of most humans. This stranger carried a long lance with a heavy spearpoint made of shining flint. "Young one," he growled, "why did you come here?"

"I came to find the mysterious Elk Dog."

The stranger, who was the spirit of the lake, stuck his face right into Long Arrow's and shook his mighty lance. "Little one, aren't you afraid of me?" he snarled.

"No, I am not," answered Long Arrow, smiling.

The tall spirit man gave a hideous grin, which was his way of being friendly. "I like small humans who aren't afraid," he said, "but I can't help you. Perhaps our grandfather will take the trouble to listen to you. More likely he won't. Walk south for four-times-four days, and maybe you'll find him. But probably you won't." With that the tall spirit turned his back on Long Arrow and went to the bottom of the lake, where he lived.

Long Arrow walked on for another four-times-four days, sleeping and resting little. By now he staggered and stumbled in his weakness, and his dog was not much better off. At last he came to the biggest lake he had ever seen, surrounded by towering snow-capped peaks and waterfalls of ice. This time there was nobody to receive him. As a matter of fact, there seemed to be no living thing around. "This must be the Great Mystery Lake," thought Long Arrow. Exhausted, he fell down upon the shortgrass meadow by the lake, fell down among the wild flowers, and went to sleep with his tired dog curled up at his feet.

When Long Arrow awoke, the sun was already high. He opened his eyes and saw a beautiful child standing before him, a boy in a dazzling white buckskin robe decorated with porcupine quills of many

Literary Analysis
Myth What effect does the meeting with the tall spirit man have on the action of the myth?

colors. The boy said, "We have been expecting you for a long time. My grandfather invites you to his lodge. Follow me."

Telling his dog to wait, Long Arrow took his medicine shield and his grandfather's bow and went with the wonderful child. They came to the edge of the lake. The spirit boy pointed to the water and said, "My grandfather's lodge is down there. Come." The child turned himself into a kingfisher and dove straight to the bottom.

Afraid, Long Arrow thought, "How can I follow him and not be drowned?" But then he said to himself, "I knew all the time that this would not be easy. In setting out to find the Elk Dog, I already threw my life away." And he boldly jumped into the water. To his surprise, he found it did not make him wet, that it parted before him, that he could breathe and see. He touched the lake's sandy bottom. It sloped down, down toward a center point.

Long Arrow descended this slope until he came to a small flat valley. In the middle of it stood a large tipi of tanned buffalo hide. The images of two strange animals were drawn on it in sacred vermilion[2] paint. A kingfisher perched high on the top of the tipi flew down and turned again into the beautiful boy, who said, "Welcome. Enter my grandfather's lodge."

Long Arrow followed the spirit boy inside. In the back at the seat of honor sat a black-robed old man with flowing white hair and such power <u>emanating</u> from him that Long Arrow felt himself in the presence of a truly Great One. The holy man welcomed Long Arrow and offered him food. The man's wife came in bringing dishes of buffalo hump, liver, tongues, delicious chunks of deer meat, the roasted flesh of strange, tasty water birds, and meat pounded together with berries, chokecherries, and kidney fat. Famished after his long journey, Long Arrow ate with <u>relish</u>. Yet he still looked around to admire the furnishings of the tipi, the painted inner curtain, the many medicine shields, wonderfully wrought weapons, shirts and robes decorated with porcupine quills in rainbow colors, beautifully painted rawhide containers filled with wonderful things, and much else that dazzled him.

---

2. **vermilion** (vər mil′ yən) n. bright red.

⑬ ▲ **Critical Viewing**
What mood or feeling does the artist invoke through his use of subtle color and shadow? What details or events in the myth also convey this feeling? **[Interpret]**

emanating (em′ ə nāt′ in) v. coming forth

relish (rel′ ish) n. pleasure and enjoyment

⑭ ☑ **Reading Check**
What does Long Arrow find in the Great Mystery Lake?

The Orphan Boy and the Elk Dog ◆ 489

---

⑫ **Background**

Art

***Wild Horses at Play,* by George Catlin**

This landscape painting shows a herd of horses gamboling on the prairie in the foreground, overseen by the mountain peak in the middle of the canvas. Large areas of uninterrupted land and sky give the painting a feeling of open space and freedom. Tell students that "wild" horses in North America, sometimes called mustangs, are actually the escaped descendants of domesticated horses brought by the Spanish in the 1500s. True wild horses had become extinct on this continent thousands of years earlier. Use these questions for discussion:

1. If, like Long Arrow's people, you had never seen horses before, what might you think of these animals?
   Possible answers: It would be reasonable to think of them as a kind of large dog or elk-like animal.

2. Which scene in the myth could this painting illustrate?
   Answer: The painting could illustrate the scene in which Long Arrow first sees the Elk Dogs.

⑬ ▶ **Critical Viewing**

Answer: The thin outlines and modulated tones of the horses and the landscape give the animals a mystical, shimmery quality like the "gamboling," "wonderful" animals of the myth.

⑭ ☑ **Reading Check**

Answer: Long Arrow finds the Great One's lodge, which is a large tipi in the middle of a valley.

CUSTOMIZE INSTRUCTION FOR UNIVERSAL ACCESS

For Less Proficient Readers	For Special Needs Students	For Gifted/Talented Students
Ask students how many days Long Arrow must travel farther south. Help students recognize the repeated pattern of Long Arrow's journey: four days to one lake, then four-times-four (four squared) days to another lake.	To help students follow the action of the myth, encourage them to make a list or a sketch of each leg of Long Arrow's journey. When they finish, have them compare their work with a partner and address any discrepancies they find by rereading the relevant part of the text.	Point out the repeated use of four in this myth: Long Arrow travels four days, then four-times-four days, then stays under the lake four days. Invite students to discuss and research the purpose of this motif. Does four have a mystical meaning in Blackfeet culture? Does the repetition have more to do with the unity in the myth than with the culture?

⓯ Reading Strategy

Interpreting

- Have students read the bracketed passage on this page, paying close attention to Long Arrow's description of the Elk Dogs.

- Based on the details he includes, what animals do students think Long Arrow sees?
  Answer: Long Arrow sees horses.

- Then, ask students the Reading Strategy question on p. 490: Why did the Blackfeet call horses Elk Dogs?
  Answer: Horses reminded the Blackfeet of elks because of their size, and of dogs because of their strength.

⓰ Literary Analysis

Myth

- Review with students the definition of myths: traditional stories passed down through generations.

- Read aloud the bracketed passage to students. Have them discuss and answer the Literary Analysis question on p. 490: What elements does this myth have in common with other myths you have read?
  Possible answers: Students should note the hero who undertakes a dangerous quest, the mentor figures, the magical powers granted to the hero, and the explanation of a cultural phenomenon.

After Long Arrow had stilled his hunger, the old spirit chief filled the pipe and passed it to his guest. They smoked, praying silently. After a while the old man said, "Some came before you from time to time, but they were always afraid of the deep water, and so they went away with empty hands. But you, grandson, were brave enough to plunge in, and therefore you are chosen to receive a wonderful gift to carry back to your people. Now, go outside with my grandson."

⓯ The beautiful boy took Long Arrow to a meadow on which some strange animals, unlike any the young man had ever seen, were galloping and gamboling, neighing and nickering. They were truly wonderful to look at, with their glossy coats fine as a maiden's hair, their long manes and tails streaming in the wind. Now rearing, now nuzzling, they looked at Long Arrow with gentle eyes which belied their fiery appearance.

"At last," thought Long Arrow, "here they are before my own eyes, the Pono-Kamita, the Elk Dogs!"

"Watch me," said the mystery boy, "so that you learn to do what I am doing." Gracefully and without effort, the boy swung himself onto the back of a jet-black Elk Dog with a high, arched neck. Larger than any elk Long Arrow had ever come across, the animal carried the boy all over the meadow swiftly as the wind. Then the boy returned, jumped off his mount, and said, "Now you try it." A little timidly Long Arrow climbed up on the beautiful Elk Dog's back. Seemingly regarding him as feather-light, it took off like a flying arrow. The young man felt himself soaring through the air as a bird does, and experienced a happiness greater even than the joy he had felt when Good Running had adopted him as a grandson.

When they had finished riding the Elk Dogs, the spirit boy said to Long Arrow, "Young hunter from the land above the waters, I want you to have what you have come for. Listen to me. You may have noticed that my grandfather wears a black medicine robe as long as a woman's dress, and that he is always trying to hide his feet. Try to get a glimpse of them, for if you do, he can refuse you nothing. He will then tell you to ask him for a gift, and you must ask for these three things: his rainbow-colored quilled belt, his black medicine robe, and a herd of these animals which you seem to like."

⓰ Long Arrow thanked him and vowed to follow his advice. For four days the young man stayed in the spirit chief's lodge, where he ate well and often went out riding on the Elk Dogs. But try as he would, he could never get a look at the old man's feet. The spirit chief always kept them carefully covered. Then on the morning of the fourth day, the old one was walking out of the tipi when his medicine robe caught in the entrance flap. As the robe opened, Long Arrow caught a glimpse of a leg and one foot. He was awed to see that it was not a human limb at all, but the glossy leg and firm hoof of an Elk Dog! He could not <u>stifle</u> a cry of surprise, and the old man looked over his shoulder and saw that his leg and hoof were exposed. The chief seemed a little embarrassed, but shrugged and said, "I tried to hide

Reading Strategy
Interpreting Why did the Blackfeet call horses Elk Dogs?

Literary Analysis
Myth What elements does this myth have in common with other myths you have read?

stifle (stī′ fəl) *v.* hold back

this, but you must have been fated to see it. Look, both of my feet are those of an Elk Dog. You may as well ask me for a gift. Don't be timid; tell me what you want."

Long Arrow spoke boldly: "I want three things: your belt of rainbow colors, your black medicine robe, and your herd of Elk Dogs."

"Well, so you're really not timid at all!" said the old man. "You ask for a lot, and I'll give it to you, except that you cannot have all my Elk Dogs; I'll give you half of them. Now I must tell you that my black medicine robe and my many-colored belt have Elk Dog magic in them. Always wear the robe when you try to catch Elk Dogs; then they can't get away from you. On quiet nights, if you listen closely to the belt, you will hear the Elk Dog dance song and Elk Dog prayers. You must learn them. And I will give you one more magic gift: this long rope woven from the hair of a white buffalo bull. With it you will never fail to catch whichever Elk Dog you want."

The spirit chief presented him with the gifts and said, "Now you must leave. At first the Elk Dogs will not follow you. Keep the medicine robe and the magic belt on at all times, and walk for four days toward the north. Never look back—always look to the north. On the fourth day the Elk Dogs will come up beside you on the left. Still don't look back. But after they have overtaken you, catch one with the rope of white buffalo hair and ride him home. Don't lose the black robe, or you will lose the Elk Dogs and never catch them again."

Long Arrow listened carefully so that he would remember. Then the old spirit chief had his wife make up a big pack of food, almost too heavy for Long Arrow to carry, and the young man took leave of his generous spirit host. The mysterious boy once again turned himself into a kingfisher and led Long Arrow to the surface of the lake, where his faithful dog greeted him joyfully. Long Arrow fed the dog, put his pack of food on the travois, and started walking north.

On the fourth day the Elk Dogs came up on his left side, as the spirit chief had foretold. Long Arrow snared the black one with the arched neck to ride, and he caught another to carry the pack of food. They galloped swiftly on, the dog barking at the big Elk Dogs' heels.

When Long Arrow arrived at last in his village, the people were afraid and hid. They did not recognize him astride his beautiful Elk Dog but took him for a monster, half man and half animal. Long Arrow kept calling, "Grandfather Good Running, it's your grandson. I've come back bringing Elk Dogs!"

Recognizing the voice, Good Running came out of hiding and wept for joy, because he had given Long Arrow up for lost. Then all the others

*L*iterature in context History Connection

When Horses Came to America

Long Arrow is amazed when he first sees the strange animals that he calls Elk Dogs. Horses were introduced to the North American mainland when Spanish explorer Hernando Cortés brought them to Mexico in 1519, and they quickly spread northward. A Spaniard who accompanied Cortés wrote that "the natives had never seen horses up to this time and thought the horse and rider were all one animal." The members of Long Arrow's tribe have the same reaction when he arrives on horseback at their village.

18 **Reading Check**
What three things does Long Arrow ask from the chief?

The Orphan Boy and the Elk Dog ◆ 491

Review and Assess

1. Possible response: Some students may respond to the journey favorably and liken it to an exciting wilderness trek. Others might consider it too dangerous.

2. **(a)** Long Arrow is disabled by his inability to hear, and people think he is stupid. **(b)** The villagers are not accepting of differences.

3. **(a)** He wants to make his grandfather proud and to gain the respect of the villagers. **(b)** He doesn't want to lose the boy to a dangerous quest. **(c)** He wants the villagers to accept Long Arrow and knows that this journey will expedite that acceptance. He also knows that Long Arrow is determined to do something to prove himself, and feels that he can properly guide him.

4. **(a)** It is a long journey, which requires walking for hours without rest in both cold and heat, and experiencing hunger and thirst. It is also a journey filled with fear: fear of the unknown, fear of the spirit people, and fear of the magical lake. **(b)** Courage and determination keep Long Arrow on his quest.

5. **(a)** The horses allow the Blackfeet to travel farther and faster when they hunt; the horses' great strength allows the Blackfeet to carry more possessions. **(b)** Long Arrow will probably be accepted by the tribe and highly regarded as a brave member.

6. Most students will say that the use of horses for the tribe is the greatest result. Others may say that the tribe's acceptance of Long Arrow is the greatest result.

---

emerged from their hiding places to admire the wonderful new animals.

Long Arrow said, "My grandfather and grandmother who adopted me, I can never repay you for your kindness. Accept these wonderful Elk Dogs as my gift. Now we no longer need to be humble footsloggers, because these animals will carry us swiftly everywhere we want to go. Now buffalo hunting will be easy. Now our tipis will be larger, our possessions will be greater, because an Elk Dog travois can carry a load ten times bigger than that of a dog. Take them, my grandparents. I shall keep for myself only this black male and this black female, which will grow into a fine herd."

"You have indeed done something great, grandson," said Good Running, and he spoke true. The people became the bold riders of the Plains and soon could hardly imagine how they had existed without these wonderful animals.

After some time Good Running, rich and honored by all, said to Long Arrow, "Grandson, lead us to the Great Mystery Lake so we can camp by its shores. Let's visit the spirit chief and the wondrous boy; maybe they will give us more of their power and magic gifts."

Long Arrow led the people southward and again found the Great Mystery Lake. But the waters would no longer part for him, nor would any of the kingfishers they saw turn into a boy. Nor, gazing down into the crystal-clear water, could they discover people, Elk Dogs, or a tipi. There was nothing in the lake but a few fish.

Review and Assess

Thinking About the Selection

1. **Respond:** Would you have wanted to travel with Long Arrow? Why or why not?

2. **(a) Recall:** Why do the villagers shun Long Arrow at the beginning of the story? **(b) Analyze:** What does this behavior tell you about the villagers?

3. **(a) Recall:** Why does Long Arrow ask Good Running for some great thing that he can do? **(b) Recall:** Why does Good Running hesitate to tell Long Arrow about the Elk Dogs? **(c) Infer:** Why does he finally decide to tell him?

4. **(a) Recall:** What obstacles does Long Arrow face on his journey? **(b) Interpret:** What qualities help him overcome these obstacles?

5. **(a) Analyze Cause and Effect:** What changes did Long Arrow's journey bring to his people? **(b) Speculate:** Predict what Long Arrow's position in the tribe will be in the future.

6. **Evaluate:** What do you think is the most important result of Long Arrow's journey? Why?

492 ◆ *Expanding Horizons*

Blackfeet

The Blackfeet are one of the many Native American nations that have lived on the Great Plains of North America. Like the other Plains Indians, the Blackfeet had no horses before the 1600s. Once they discovered these strange creatures, however, the people quickly recognized their value.

In time, the Blackfeet became skillful riders. Because the horse helped them travel farther and faster than before, the people raised fewer crops and hunted more. Eventually, horses transformed the Blackfeet way of life.

Today, the Blackfeet live on reservations in Montana and in Canada. Although they are no longer a nomadic people who follow the buffalo, traditional stories like "The Orphan Boy and the Elk Dog" reflect the importance of the horse to their culture.

ASSESSMENT PRACTICE: Reading Comprehension

Evaluate and Make Judgments   **(For more practice, see Test Preparation Workbook, p. 32.)**

Many tests require students to read passages and evaluate the evidence in order to make judgments. Use the following sample test item to review this strategy with students.

> He grew up into a fine young hunter, tall and good-looking in the quilled buckskin outfit the chief's wife made for him. He helped his grandfather in everything and became a staff for Good Running to lean on.

The passage provides evidence that—

A The boy described has disappointed his family.

B The culture described values hunting skills.

C The boy described is unhappy in his life.

D The culture described is technologically advanced.

Guide students to see that *A, C,* and *D* cannot be supported by the passage. *B* is the correct response.

Review and Assess

Literary Analysis

Myth

1. Use a chart like this one to analyze the story's **mythic** qualities.

Characteristics of Myths	How Shown in Story
Setting is distant past	
Characters may be supernatural beings	
Hero has special qualities	

2. What qualities make Long Arrow seem "larger than life"?
3. Identify three characteristics of Blackfeet culture that are revealed in this myth.

Connecting Literary Elements

4. (a) What is the central problem in this story? (b) Identify the **inciting incident** that leads Long Arrow to confront the problem.
5. What events in the early part of the myth inspire Long Arrow to make his journey?
6. Identify events that follow the inciting incident, including the highest point of interest and the resolution of the conflict.

Reading Strategy

Interpreting

7. What qualities does Good Running recognize in Long Arrow that lead to the boy's adoption?
8. Why does Long Arrow succeed on his mission when earlier seekers had failed to find the Elk Dogs?
9. Long Arrow's journey helps his tribe by bringing them horses. In what ways does the journey benefit him as an individual?

Extend Understanding

10. **Cultural Connection:** Long Arrow's gift of horses changes the lives of the Blackfeet. Describe someone in the last century who has given modern American society a gift that has changed some aspect of many people's lives.

Quick Review

A **myth** is a traditional story that involves "larger-than-life" characters and often reveals the values and customs of a culture.

An **inciting incident** is an event in the plot of a story that propels the main character into a problem situation or conflict.

When you **interpret,** you analyze the details of a work to determine what the author is conveying.

 Take It to the Net
www.phschool.com
Take the interactive self-test online to check your understanding of the selection.

The Orphan Boy and the Elk Dog ◆ 493

✳ ENRICHMENT: Further Reading

Other Native American Myths

American Indian Myths and Legends, edited by Richard Erdoes and Alfonso Ortiz
The Winged Serpent: American Indian Prose and Poetry, edited by Margot Astrov
They Dance in the Sky: Native American Star Myths, Jean Guard Monroe and Ray A. Williamson

 Take It to the Net
Visit www.phschool.com for more information on the authors.

Answers for p. 493

Review and Assess

1. **Setting is distant past:** Story begins with, "In the days when people had only dogs to carry their bundles . . . ." **Characters may be supernatural beings:** The Great One has legs resembling those of the Elk Dog. **Hero has special qualities:** Long Arrow's hearing suddenly returns.

2. Long Arrow endures extreme hardships on his journey and experiences magical powers in his descent to the underwater lodge of the Elk Dog.

3. The Blackfeet use steam sweat baths and cedar smoke for purification; they have a holy man who dispenses medicine; they revere the horse, or Elk Dog.

4. (a) Long Arrow wants to win the respect of his tribe and make his grandfather proud. (b) Long Arrow's grandfather suggests that Long Arrow set out on a journey to find the Elk Dogs.

5. Long Arrow's desire to prove himself to those who disparaged him inspire his journey.

6. Long Arrow overcomes hunger and exhaustion during his journey, and when he begins to meet the spirit people, he overcomes his fear. The highest point of interest occurs when Long Arrow decides to risk his life by following the kingfisher into the water. The resolution occurs when Long Arrow receives Elk Dogs, takes them back to his people, and wins their respect.

7. Good Running sees Long Arrow as a survivor and feels guilty for abandoning him. He notices Long Arrow's alert eyes and realizes he is not foolish or dull-witted.

8. Long Arrow's early life had prepared him to withstand the journey. In addition, he succeeds because he is brave and determined.

9. Long Arrow discovers his own strength and identity.

10. Students may identify an inventor, such as Thomas Edison, a political or social thinker, such as Dr. Martin Luther King, Jr., or an artist, writer, or musician.

❶ Vocabulary Development

Concept Development

1. After the parade, the streets were covered with refuse. I refuse to accept your criticism.

2. The content child played happily all morning. What is the content of that jar?

3. He stood in the entrance to the tipi, brooding. Puzzles and mysteries entrance my brother for hours on end.

4. The man on the horse has a bow and arrow. Bow to your elders to show your respect.

5. That brand of paint no longer contains lead. Lead the Elk Dog back to the village.

Fluency: Synonyms and Antonyms

1. S	**4.** A
2. S	**5.** S
3. A	

Spelling Strategy

1. starving	**3.** hiding
2. stifling	

❷ Grammar

1. accept	**4.** except
2. accepted	**5.** accepted
3. except	

Writing Application
The teacher accepted all essays except for those that were late.

494

Integrate Language Skills

❶ Vocabulary Development Lesson

Concept Development: Homographs

Refuse is a **homograph**—a word with at least two distinct meanings and pronunciations. In this myth, *refuse* (ref′ yōōz) is a noun meaning "garbage." Another word, *refuse* (ri fyōōz′), is a verb that means "to reject." The context in which a homograph appears will give you clues to its meaning. Use a dictionary to confirm the correct pronunciation.

Write two sentences for each homograph, showing its different meanings.

1. *refuse* as a noun and as a verb
2. *content* as an adjective and as a noun
3. *entrance* as a noun and as a verb
4. *bow* as a noun and as a verb
5. *lead* as a noun and as a verb

Fluency: Synonyms and Antonyms

Analyze the word pairs in each item. On your paper, write S for synonyms and A for antonyms.

1. refuse, garbage
2. surpassed, exceeded
3. emanating, suppressing
4. relish, loathe
5. stifle, smother

Spelling Strategy

When writing words ending in a silent *e*, drop the *e* before adding a suffix beginning with a vowel. For example, *emanate* becomes *emanating*. Add *-ing* to each of the following words.

1. starve   2. stifle   3. hide

❷ Grammar Lesson

Commonly Confused Verbs: *accept* and *except*

Accept is a verb meaning "to receive" or "to agree with." **Except** is usually a preposition meaning "not including," but it is sometimes a verb meaning "to leave out." These words are commonly confused because they have a similar look and sound, even though their meanings are different.

Notice the different meanings conveyed by *accept* and *except* in the following sentences.

> Good Running hoped his wife would *accept* the boy.

> No one *except* Good Running knew where the boy had gone and for what purpose.

Practice Write the following sentences, choosing the correct word in parentheses.

1. Good Running's wife asked if he would (accept, except) the moccasins.
2. Good Running (accepted, excepted) a ride.
3. None (accept, except) Long Arrow had ever returned from the lake.
4. The spirit chief looked normal (accept, except) for his leg and foot.
5. Long Arrow (accepted, excepted) the gifts.

Writing Application Write a single sentence in which you use *accept* and *except* correctly.

𝒲𝒢 *Prentice Hall Writing and Grammar Connection: Chapter 26, Section 2*

494 ◆ *Expanding Horizons*

TEACHING RESOURCES

The following resources can be used to enrich or extend the instruction for pp. 494–495.

Vocabulary

📖 **Selection Support:** Build Vocabulary, p. 125

📖 **Vocabulary and Spelling Practice Book**
(Use this booklet for skills enrichment.)

Grammar

📖 **Selection Support:** Build Grammar Skills, p. 126

𝒲𝒢 **Writing and Grammar,** Platinum Level, p. 612 ▦

📖 **Daily Language Practice Transparencies**

Writing

𝒲𝒢 **Writing and Grammar,** Platinum Level, p. 84

💿 **Writing and Grammar iText CD-ROM** ▦

Writing Lesson

Retelling a Myth

"The Orphan Boy and the Elk Dog" has been retold many times over many generations. Modernize the setting, and retell the myth in your own words.

Prewriting   Prepare a story map to organize your retelling. Include setting, characters, conflict, and events that develop and resolve the conflict. Make notes about the ways you can update the story.

Drafting   A myth needs a clear beginning, middle, and end. In the beginning, introduce the characters, setting, and conflict. In the middle, present events in logical order. Finally, tell how the conflict ends.

Revising   Reread your draft, making sure that you have kept the meaning of the original story. Review the connections between sentences. Place a check mark between sentences where the connection is clear. Add transitions where they would smooth your writing.

Model: Revising to Add Transitions

Before Leon started on his journey, he spent a full day resting.
☑ Then, he began his trip, driving southward on the

After four days,

freeway. ☑ He met a strange man. . . .

> Using transition words helps readers and listeners follow the order of events clearly.

Prentice Hall Writing and Grammar Connection: Chapter 5, Section 3

Extension Activities

Listening and Speaking   With a group, present a **debate** to decide whether Long Arrow will make a good chief. Use these strategies:

- Review the story, gathering details that support your opinion.
- Present your ideas, and listen to the ideas of the opposition.
- Allow time for each side to argue against the other.

At the conclusion of the debate, ask the audience to decide which team presented the stronger argument. **[Group Activity]**

Research and Technology   Buffalo were important to the Blackfeet, but their numbers plummeted after 1850. Research the decline in the buffalo population. First, develop a list of questions to guide your research, and then use library or Internet resources to find answers. Finally, construct a **bar graph** to show changes in the buffalo population over time.

 Take It to the Net   www.phschool.com

Go online for an additional research activity using the Internet.

The Orphan Boy and the Elk Dog ◆ 495

❸ Writing Lesson

- Encourage students to be creative when they retell the myth. Remind them that it can take place in any setting, and that the characters and the journey should reflect the setting they choose.
- Use the Writing Lesson to guide students in developing a story map to organize their retellings.
- Students may use the Story Map transparency in **Writing Models and Graphic Organizers on Transparencies,** p. 83, to record their notes.
- Use the Short Story rubric in **Performance Assessment and Portfolio Management,** p. 14, to evaluate students' myths.

❹ Extension Activity

Listening and Speaking

- Tell students that they should plan their arguments based on facts and details from the story, and form arguments that anticipate arguments from the other side.
- Form teams of two or three students. To prepare for the debate, have teams reread the myth and take notes on any points they feel might bear on Long Arrow's potential as a chief. They should then make an outline of their arguments and anticipated counterarguments.
- After rehearsing, have students debate Long Arrow's fitness as a chief.

CUSTOMIZE INSTRUCTION for Universal Access

To address different learning styles, use the following activities suggested in the **Extension Activities** booklet, p. 32.

- For Verbal Linguistic, Visual/Spatial, and Logical/Mathematical Learners, use Activity 5.
- For Verbal/Linguistic and Visual/Spatial Learners, use Activity 6.
- For Visual/Spatial Learners, use Activity 7.

ASSESSMENT RESOURCES

The following resources can be used to assess students' knowledge and skills.

Selection Assessment

📖 **Formal Assessment,** pp. 110–112

📖 **Open Book Test,** pp. 94–96

📼 **Got It! Assessment Videotapes,** Tape 3

💿 **Test Bank Software**

 Take It to the Net
Visit www.phschool.com for self-tests and additional questions on "The Orphan Boy and the Elk Dog."

Writing Rubric

📖 **Performance Assessment and Portfolio Management,** p. 14

 PRENTICE HALL **ASSESSMENT SYSTEM**

📖 **Workbook**   📖 **Transparencies**

📖 **Skill Book**   💿 **CD-ROM**

The Street of the Cañon

Lesson Objectives

1. **To analyze and respond to literary elements**
   - Literary Analysis: Point of View
   - Connecting Literary Elements: Conflict

2. **To read, comprehend, analyze, and critique a short story**
   - Reading Strategy: Making Predictions
   - Reading Check questions
   - Review and Assess questions
   - Assessment Practice (ATE)

3. **To develop word analysis skills, fluency, and systematic vocabulary**
   - Vocabulary Development Lesson: Anglo-Saxon Suffix: -ly

4. **To understand and apply written and oral language conventions**
   - Spelling Strategy
   - Grammar Lesson: Prepositional Phrase or Infinitive?

5. **To understand and apply appropriate writing and research strategies**
   - Writing Lesson: Comparison-and-Contrast Essay
   - Extension Activity: Photo Essay

6. **To understand and apply listening and speaking strategies**
   - Extension Activity: Debate

STEP-BY-STEP TEACHING GUIDE	PACING GUIDE
PRETEACH	
Motivate Students and Provide Background	
Use the Motivation activity (ATE p. 496)	5 min.
Read and discuss the Preview material and Background information (SE/ATE p. 496)	5 min.
Introduce the Concepts	
Introduce the Literary Analysis and Reading Strategy (SE/ATE p. 497) A	15 min.
Pronounce the vocabulary words and read their definitions (SE p. 497)	5 min.
TEACH	
Monitor Comprehension	
Informally monitor comprehension by circulating while students read independently or in groups A	20 min.
Monitor students' comprehension with the Reading Check notes (SE/ATE pp. 499, 501, 503, 505)	as students read
Develop vocabulary with Vocabulary notes (SE pp. 500, 501, 503; ATE p. 501)	as students read
Develop Understanding	
Develop students' understanding of point of view with Literary Analysis annotations (SE pp. 499, 503; ATE pp. 499, 503) A	10 min.
Develop students' understanding of making predictions with Reading Strategy annotations (SE pp. 499, 504, 505; ATE pp. 499, 500, 504, 505)	10 min.
ASSESS	
Assess Mastery	
Assess students' mastery of the Reading Strategy and Literary Analysis by having them answer the Review and Assess questions (SE/ATE p. 507)	20 min.
Use one or more of the print and media Assessment Resources (ATE p. 509) A	up to 50 min.
EXTEND	
Apply Understanding	
Have students complete the Vocabulary Development Lesson and the Grammar Lesson (SE p. 508) A	20 min.
Apply students' ability to evaluate structure using the Writing Lesson (SE/ATE p. 509) A	45 min.
Apply students' understanding of the selection using one or more of the Extension Activities (SE p. 509)	20–90 min.

A **ACCELERATED INSTRUCTION:**
Use the strategies and activities identified with an A.

UNIVERSAL ACCESS
- ● = Below Level Students
- ▲ = On-Level Students
- ■ = Above Level Students

Time and Resource Manager

Reading Level: Easy
Average Number of Instructional Days: 4

RESOURCES

PRINT 📝	TRANSPARENCIES	TECHNOLOGY 💿 🎧
• **Beyond Literature,** Community Connection: Social Dancing, p. 33 ▲ ■		• **Interest Grabber Video,** Tape 3 ● ▲ ■
• **Selection Support Workbook:** ● ▲ ■ Literary Analysis, p. 132 Reading Strategy, p. 131 Build Vocabulary, p. 129	• **Literary Analysis and Reading Transparencies,** pp. 65 and 66 ● ▲ ■	
		• **Listening to Literature** ● ▲ ■ Audiocassettes, Side 15 Audio CDs, CD 10
• **Literatura en español** ● ▲ • **Literary Analysis for Enrichment** ■		
• **Formal Assessment:** Selection Test, pp. 113–115 ● ▲ ■ • **Open Book Test,** pp. 97–99 ● ▲ ■ • **Performance Assessment and Portfolio Management,** p. 15 ● ▲ ■ • **PRENTICE HALL ASSESSMENT** *SYSTEM* ● ▲ ■	• **PRENTICE HALL ASSESSMENT** *SYSTEM* ● ▲ ■ Skills Practice Answers and Explanations on Transparencies	• **Test Bank Software** ● ▲ ■ • **Got It! Assessment Videotapes,** Tape 3 ● ▲
• **Selection Support Workbook:** ● ▲ ■ Build Grammar Skills, p. 130 • **Writing and Grammar,** Platinum Level ● ▲ ■ • **Extension Activities,** p. 33 ● ▲ ■	• **Daily Language Practice Transparencies** ● ▲ • **Writing Models and Graphic Organizers on Transparencies,** p. 95 ● ▲ ■	• **Writing and Grammar iText CD-ROM** ● ▲ ■ *Take It to the Net* www.phschool.com

BLOCK SCHEDULING: Use one 90-minute class period to preteach the selection and have students read it. Use a second 90-minute class period to assess students' mastery of skills and have them complete one of the Extension Activities.

Step-by-Step Teaching Guide for pp. 496-497

Motivation

Ask students to imagine themselves in the following situation: You are at a dance with all your friends from school. A mysterious stranger enters and proceeds to mix with group, even dancing with the most popular girl in the class. Ask students to think about how they would react to this stranger. How would he be treated by most of the students at the dance? Tell students that the story they will read includes a situation similar to this one. Have students look for clues that will enable them to identify the mysterious stranger and understand why he has come to the dance.

Interest Grabber Video

As an alternative, play "La Quinceañera" on Tape 3 to engage student interest.

❶ Background

Social Studies

Josephina Niggli and her family fled Mexico shortly after the Mexican Revolution of 1910; years later, as a writer, Niggli would be inspired by the colorful stories she had heard about two famous rebel leaders, Pancho Villa and Emiliano Zapata.

Villa and Zapata were leaders of two of the revolutionary bands that formed across Mexico to bring down the dictatorship of General Porfirio Diaz. In the years that followed, each led one of the many rival factions that opposed the presidents who assumed power in the wake of the Revolution. Zapata, an Indian, demanded more far-reaching land reforms. Villa became the notorious leader of a band of outlaws.

Prepare to Read

The Street of the Cañon

Fandango (detail), Gentilz, The Alamo Library

🖥 *Take It to the Net*

Visit www.phschool.com for interactive activities and instruction related to the selection, including
- background
- graphic organizers
- literary elements
- reading strategies

Preview

Connecting to the Literature

Some celebrations are held in public. Others, such as weddings or birthday parties, are usually limited to family and friends. In this story, a young woman celebrates her eighteenth birthday at a fiesta, to which her father has invited the whole town. The event becomes even more memorable when an uninvited guest appears.

❶ Background

Mexican courtship and marriage customs are important in this story. In some parts of Mexico, a man must ask the elders of a woman's family for permission to marry her. In others, parents arrange a match. In San Juan Iglesias, where this story is set, "to walk around the plaza with a girl" is a sign of engagement.

496 ◆ *Expanding Horizons*

TEACHING RESOURCES

The following resources can be used to enrich or extend the instruction for pp. 496–497.

Motivation

🖥 **Interest Grabber Video**, Tape 3

Background

📖 **Beyond Literature**, p. 33

🖥 *Take It to the Net*

Visit www.phschool.com for background and hotlinks for "The Street of the Cañon."

Literary Analysis

📖 **Literary Analysis and Reading Transparencies,** Point of View, p. 66

Reading

📖 **Selection Support:** Reading Strategy, p. 131; Build Vocabulary, p. 129

📖 **Literary Analysis and Reading Transparencies,** Making Predictions, p. 65

🖥 **BLOCK SCHEDULING:** Resources marked with this symbol provide varied instruction during 90-minute blocks.

❷ Literary Analysis

Point of View

Writers help you look into the minds of their characters through **point of view**—the vantage point from which the story is told. In a story told from the **third-person point of view,** a narrator outside the story reveals the thoughts and feelings of one main character. If the third-person point of view is all-knowing, or **omniscient,** the narrator reveals thoughts and feelings of more than one character and can even report events in separate locations, as in the example below:

> The long dark streets were empty because all of the people . . . were helping Don Roméo Calderón celebrate his daughter's eighteenth birthday.
>   On the other side of the town, . . . a tall slender man, . . . slipped from shadow to shadow.

As you read this selection, think about how the writer's omniscient point of view reveals some details that even the characters do not know.

Connecting Literary Elements

In a story written from a third-person omniscient point of view, readers are often able to view the action from several different angles. This is especially useful in building the **conflict**—the central problem that the main characters have to overcome. Consider the conflict in this story and how both the young woman and the young man handle it.

❸ Reading Strategy

Making Predictions

You can **predict** story events by making educated guesses about what will happen based on what the text reveals and what you know from experience. However, you may need to revise your predictions as you learn new information.

For each question you have as you read, use a chart like the one shown to keep track of your predictions and how they change.

Vocabulary Development

officious (ə fish′ əs) *adj.* overly ready to serve (p. 500)

mottled (mät′ əld) *adj.* marked with spots of different shades (p. 500)

nonchalantly (nän′ shə länt′ lē) *adv.* casually; indifferently (p. 501)

audaciously (ô dā′ shəs lē) *adv.* in a bold manner (p. 501)

imperiously (im pir′ ē əs lē) *adv.* arrogantly (p. 501)

plausibility (plô′ zə bil′ ə tē) *n.* believability (p. 503)

The Street of the Cañon ◆ 497

---

❷ Literary Analysis
Point of View

- Reinforce the idea that point of view is the vantage point from which a story is told. If a story is told in the third-person limited point of view, the reader can uncover the thoughts and feelings of one main character. If the point of view is all-knowing, or omniscient, the reader will be able to learn the thoughts and feelings of many characters.

- Read the story excerpt on this page, and call students' attention to the fact that the reader is able to "see" the same story from two different locations.

- Read the instruction for Connecting Literary Elements, and explain that in this story, students will be able to experience the conflict from two different points of view.

❸ Reading Strategy
Making Predictions

- Explain to students that predictions are informed guesses. Making predictions involves using what students know from experience and from what they already know about a story to guess what will happen next.

- Have students create a chart like the one on p. 497 to predict what will happen in "The Street of the Cañon." When they obtain new information as they read, students can change their predictions.

- When students finish reading, have them refer to the chart and determine how closely their predictions matched the actual outcome.

Vocabulary Development

- Pronounce each vocabulary word for students, and read the definitions as a class. Have students identify any words with which they are already familiar.

E-Teach

Visit E-Teach at www.phschool.com for teachers' essays on how to teach, with questions and answers.

CUSTOMIZE INSTRUCTION FOR UNIVERSAL ACCESS

For Less Proficient Readers	For English Learners	For Advanced Readers
In addition to having students predict story events, have them jot down key details that confirm or help them revise their predictions as they read. Doing so will help students keep track of important information that unfolds in bits and pieces throughout the story.	As students read, have them mark difficult or challenging passages with self-stick notes. They may want to stop after each page and discuss these passages with partners, or meet after finishing the story and share their strategies for working out the meaning of these passages.	Have students create their own endings to the story based on their original prediction charts. Have them note the ways in which their ending is similar to and different from Niggli's. Ask volunteers to share their work with the class.

CUSTOMIZE INSTRUCTION
For Visual/Spatial Learners

As students read, have them create a chart that relates key details to the manner in which they were revealed—that is, through the narrator, dialogue, or a character's thoughts. Students can then present their charts to the class.

❶ About the Selection

A stranger makes his way to Sarita Calderon's eighteenth-birthday celebration, carrying a mysterious package. Gradually, pieces of the puzzle—in the forms of conversations, glimpses into the stranger's and Sarita's thoughts, and further insights from the narrator—come together. It becomes clear that the stranger is Pepe Gonzalez—a notoriously daring young "devil" from a rival town. What remains intriguingly unclear, however, are Pepe's intentions toward Sarita—does he charm her because he genuinely wishes to marry her, or is winning her affection merely another one of his daring adventures?

❷ Background

Art

Fandango, by Theodore Gentilz

The paintings of the renowned Texas artist Theodore Gentilz (1819–1906) can be seen at the San Antonio Museum of Art in San Antonio, Texas.

Use the following question for discussion:

In addition to the partygoers' costumes, what details in the painting suggest that this celebration takes place in a past era?

Possible response: Students may cite the candlelight in the room and the old-fashioned dance being performed, in which a man holds a candle in one hand and his partner's hand in the other.

❸ ▶ Critical Viewing

Answers: The partygoers are dressed in elaborate costumes and performing traditional dances. A violinist plays music in the background.

❶ **The Street of the Cañon**
from Mexican Village Josephina Niggli

❷

Fandango (detail), Gentilz, The Alamo Library

❸ ▲ **Critical Viewing** What details in the painting suggest the celebration described in the story? **[Connect]**

498 ◆ *Expanding Horizons*

TEACHING RESOURCES

The following resources can be used to enrich or extend the instruction for pp. 498–506.

Literary Analysis

📖 **Selection Support:** Literary Analysis, p. 132

🖥 **Writing Models and Graphic Organizers on Transparencies,** p. 95 ▪

Reading

🎧 **Listening to Literature Audiocassettes,** Side 15 ▪

💿 **Listening to Literature Audio CDs,** CD 10 ▪

It was May, the flowering thorn was sweet in the air, and the village of San Juan Iglesias in the Valley of the Three Marys was celebrating. The long dark streets were empty because all of the people, from the lowest-paid cowboy to the mayor, were helping Don Roméo Calderón celebrate his daughter's eighteenth birthday.

On the other side of the town, where the Cañon Road led across the mountains to the Sabinas Valley, a tall slender man, a package clutched tightly against his side, slipped from shadow to shadow. Once a dog barked, and the man's black suit merged into the blackness of a wall. But no voice called out, and after a moment he slid into the narrow, dirt-packed street again.

The moonlight touched his shoulder and spilled across his narrow hips. He was young, no more than twenty-five, and his black curly head was bare. He walked swiftly along, heading always for the distant sound of guitar and flute. If he met anyone now, who could say from which direction he had come? He might be a trader from Monterrey, or a buyer of cow's milk from farther north in the Valley of the Three Marys. Who would guess that an Hidalgo[1] man dared to walk alone in the moonlit streets of San Juan Iglesias?

Carefully adjusting his flat package so that it was not too prominent, he squared his shoulders and walked jauntily across the street to the laughter-filled house. Little boys packed in the doorway made way for him, smiling and nodding to him. The long, narrow room with the orchestra at one end was filled with whirling dancers. Rigid-backed chaperones were gossiping together, seated in their straight chairs against the plaster walls. Over the scene was the yellow glow of kerosene lanterns, and the air was hot with the too-sweet perfume of gardenias, tuberoses, and the pungent scent of close-packed humanity.

The man in the doorway, while trying to appear at ease, was carefully examining every smiling face. If just one person recognized him, the room would turn on him like a den

___
1. Hidalgo (ē dal′ gō) *adj.* nearby village.

Literary Analysis
Point of View Whose thoughts are revealed in this passage?

Reading Strategy
Making Predictions What can you predict about the stranger based upon his actions so far?

6 ✓ **Reading Check**
What is the whole town celebrating?

The Street of the Cañon ◆ 499

---

❹ Literary Analysis
Point of View

- Have students read the bracketed passage, paying close attention to the thoughts and feelings of the man being described.
- Then, ask students the Literary Analysis question on p. 499: Whose thoughts are revealed in this passage?
  Answer: The "Hidalgo Man's" thoughts are revealed in this passage.

▶ **Monitor Progress** Based on the information revealed in this passage, have students describe the man in their own words.
  Answer: Students should describe the man as young and slender, and a stranger to the village of San Juan Iglesias.

❺ Reading Strategy
Making Predictions

- Have students review the story up to this point, taking careful note of the information provided about the stranger.
- Then, ask students the Reading Strategy question on p. 499: What can you predict about the stranger based upon his actions so far?
  Answer: Students should note that the man may have something to hide or that he has a secret purpose.
- Tell students as they read to note whether their original prediction about the young stranger holds true.

❻ ✓ Reading Check
Answer: The town is celebrating Don Calderón's daughter's eighteenth birthday.

---

❼ Background

Languages

Many words in English come directly from Spanish. Spanish words were introduced to American English through three primary sources: the Spanish Conquest and the subsequent settling of the American Southwest; Caribbean trade routes; and Spanish and Latin American cuisine. Words such as *patio* (Spanish), *fiesta* (Spanish), *corral* (Spanish), *barbecue* (Caribbean), *hammock* (Caribbean), *canoe* (Caribbean), *tamale* (Mexican Spanish), *tortilla* (Mexican Spanish), and *salsa* (Mexican Spanish) have greatly enriched American English.

❽ Reading Strategy

Making Predictions

- Remind students that their predictions will often change based on new information they gather as they read.

- Encourage students to make predictions about the guests' possible reasons for turning on the stranger.
  Answer: Students should note that there is some sort of hostility between the two towns.

▶ **Monitor Progress** Ask students whether the information in the bracketed passage affects the predictions they made about the reasons for the grudge between the two towns. In what way?
Answer: Students should note that they can now revise their predictions—an event in which Sarita was somehow involved has something to do with the hostilities.

---

of snarling mountain cats, but so far all the laughter-dancing eyes were friendly.

Suddenly a plump, <u>officious</u> little man, his round cheeks glistening with perspiration, pushed his way through the crowd. His voice, many times too large for his small body, boomed at the man in the doorway. "Welcome, stranger, welcome to our house." Thrusting his arm through the stranger's, and almost dislodging the package, he started to lead the way through the maze of dancers. "Come and drink a toast to my daughter—to my beautiful Sarita. She is eighteen this night."

In the square patio the gentle breeze ruffled the pink and white oleander bushes. A long table set up on sawhorses held loaves of flaky crusted French bread, stacks of thin, delicate tortillas, plates of barbecued beef, and long red rolls of spicy sausages. But most of all there were cheeses, for the Three Marys was a cheese-eating valley. There were yellow cheese and white cheese and curded cheese from cow's milk. There was even a flat white cake of goat cheese from distant Linares, a delicacy too expensive for any but feast days.

To set off this feast were bottles of beer floating in ice-filled tin tubs, and another table was covered with bottles of mescal, of tequila, of maguey wine.

Don Roméo Calderón thrust a glass of tequila into the stranger's hand. "Drink, friend, to the prettiest girl in San Juan. As pretty as my fine fighting cocks, she is. On her wedding day she takes to her man, and may she find him soon, the best fighter in my flock. Drink deep, friend. Even the rivers flow with wine."

The Hidalgo man laughed and raised his glass high. "May the earth be always fertile beneath her feet."

Someone called to Don Roméo that more guests were arriving, and with a final delighted pat on the stranger's shoulder, the little man scurried away. As the young fellow smiled after his retreating host, his eyes caught and held another pair of eyes—laughing black eyes set in a young girl's face. The last time he had seen that face it had been white and tense with rage, and the lips clenched tight to prevent an outgushing stream of angry words. That had been in February, and she had worn a white lace shawl over her hair. Now it was May, and a gardenia was a splash of white in the glossy dark braids. The moonlight had <u>mottled</u> his face that February night, and he knew that she did not recognize him. He grinned impudently back at her, and her eyes widened, then slid sideways to one of the chaperones. The fan in her small hand snapped shut. She tapped its parchment tip against her mouth and slipped away to join the dancing couples in the front room. The gestures of a fan translate into a coded language on the frontier. The stranger raised one eyebrow as he interpreted the signal.

500 ◆ *Expanding Horizons*

---

officious (ə fish′ əs) *adj.* overly ready to serve

𝓛iterature ❼
in context Language Connection

Spanish Vocabulary

Set in Mexico, the story contains several Spanish words and terms, including

cañon canyon

tío uncle

hola Spanish exclamation meaning "Hi"

don title of respect placed before a man's name, meaning "sir"

parada literally, "parade," but here it refers to a dance in which partners stride around together

mottled (mät′ əld) *adj.* marked with spots of different shades

---

⬟ ENRICHMENT: Social Studies Connection

Mexican Geography

The story's narrator and characters make several references to well-known places in Mexico. These references provide a good opportunity for students to learn more about the country's geography.

Read aloud each of the following passages. Challenge students to use the hints you provide to find each place on a map. (Be sure that the maps have indexes that provide coordinates that students can use to locate states, cities, and towns.)

- "…who could say from which direction he had come? He might be a trader from <u>Monterrey</u>…" (*Hint:* Monterrey is a large city in northern Mexico.)

- "Ask the people of Chihuahua, of Sonora. Ask the man on the bridge at Laredo, or the man in his boat at Tampico…" (*Hints:* Chihuahua and Tampico are cities; Sonora is a state; Laredo refers to Nuevo Laredo, a city with a famous bridge that crosses the Rio Bravo.)

But he did not move toward her at once. Instead, he inched slowly back against the table. No one was behind him, and his hands quickly unfastened the package he had been guarding so long. Then he <u>nonchalantly</u> walked into the front room.

The girl was sitting close to a chaperone. As he came up to her he swerved slightly toward the bushy-browed old lady.

"Your servant, señora. I kiss your hands and feet."

The chaperone stared at him in astonishment. Such fine manners were not common to the town of San Juan Iglesias.

"Eh, you're a stranger," she said. "I thought so."

"But a stranger no longer, señora, now that I have met you." He bent over her, so close she could smell the faint fragrance of talcum on his freshly shaven cheek.

"Will you dance the *parada* with me?"

This request startled her eyes into popping open beneath the heavy brows. "So, my young rooster, would you flirt with me, and I old enough to be your grandmother?"

"Can you show me a prettier woman to flirt with in the Valley of the Three Marys?" he asked <u>audaciously</u>.

She grinned at him and turned toward the girl at her side. "This young fool wants to meet you, my child."

The girl blushed to the roots of her hair and shyly lowered her white lids. The old woman laughed aloud.

"Go out and dance, the two of you. A man clever enough to pat the sheep has a right to play with the lamb."

The next moment they had joined the circle of dancers and Sarita was trying to control her laughter.

"She is the worst dragon in San Juan. And how easily you won her!"

"What is a dragon," he asked <u>imperiously</u>, "when I longed to dance with you?"

"Ay," she retorted, "you have a quick tongue. I think you are a dangerous man."

In answer he drew her closer to him, and turned her toward the orchestra. As he reached the chief violinist he called out, "Play the *Virgencita*, 'The Shy Young Maiden.'"

The violinist's mouth opened in soundless surprise. The girl in his arms said sharply, "You heard him, the *Borachita*, 'The Little Drunken Girl.'"

With a relieved grin, the violinist tapped his music stand with his bow, and the music swung into the sad farewell of a man to his sweetheart:

Farewell, my little drunken one,
I must go to the capital
To serve the master
Who makes me weep for my return.

nonchalantly (nän´ shə länt´ lē) *adv.* casually; indifferently

audaciously (ô dā´ shəs lē) *adv.* in a bold manner

imperiously (im pir´ ē əs lē) *adv.* arrogantly

❿ ✔**Reading Check**
What does the stranger do with the package he is carrying?

The Street of the Cañon ◆ 501

❾ Vocabulary Development
Anglo–Saxon Suffix: *-ly*

• Point out the suffix *-ly* in *audaciously.* Ask students what part of speech this word is, and what word it modifies.
  Answer: *Audaciously* is an adverb that modifies *asked.*

• Draw students' attention to the word's definition, "in a bold manner." Ask them to identify an instance in which the stranger acts *audaciously.*
  Answer: Students might say that his presence in San Juan Iglesias is audacious because he is from Hidalgo.

❿ ✔**Reading Check**
Answer: He places the package on the long table that holds the many cheeses and other foods.

CUSTOMIZE INSTRUCTION FOR UNIVERSAL ACCESS

For Advanced Readers

Stories about uninvited guests showing up at parties have always been popular. These scenes were a common device in romantic poems and novels of the early 1800s. Students may be familiar with "Lochinvar" by Sir Walter Scott and "The Masque of the Red Death" by Edgar Allan Poe. Ask students to take note of the ways that Niggli breathes life into this literary convention.

Answer: Students might notice Niggli's use of chang- ing perspectives, her colorful descriptions, and her careful attention to local customs and traditions. They might also point out the remarkably detailed description of the cheese, and the mystery of Pepe Gonzalez's motives.

⓫ ▶Critical Viewing
Answer: The dance might be especially open to danger because a stranger could easily blend into the swirling movements of the crowd. Also, the guests at the dance are probably full of joy, so they have let their guard down.

The stranger frowned down at her. "Is this a joke, señorita?" he asked coldly.

"No," she whispered, looking about her quickly to see if the incident had been observed. "But the *Virgencita* is the favorite song of Hidalgo, a village on the other side of the mountains in the next valley. The people of Hidalgo and San Juan Iglesias do not speak."

"That is a stupid thing," said the man from Hidalgo as he swung her around in a large turn. "Is not music free as air? Why should one town own the rights to a song?"

The girl shuddered slightly. "Those people from Hidalgo—they are wicked monsters. Can you guess what they did not six months since?"

⓫ ▲ Critical Viewing
What makes a festive dance like the one shown here and described in the story a setting that is especially open to strangers or danger? **[Analyze Cause and Effect]**

502 ◆ *Expanding Horizons*

✺ **ENRICHMENT: Cultural Connection**

Cultural Insight

Josephina Niggli and her family fled the country of Mexico shortly after the Mexican Revolution of 1910. Years later, Niggli would be inspired by the turbulence of these times as well as by her own cultural identity. The writer Pat Mora notes, "…Niggli is an interesting example of the complex issues of cultural identity. Her parents were Scandinavian Americans who moved to Mexico. We sometimes forget that the terms *bilingual* and *bicultural* can apply to people living in Mexico from the States or other countries since Mexico also has a diverse population not only of indigenous groups but of Blacks and Jews and Arabs and Chinese. Even members of the same family can define their nationality and culture differently."

The man started to point out that the space of time from February to May was three months, but he thought it better not to appear too wise. "Did these Hidalgo monsters frighten you, señorita? If they did, I personally will kill them all."

She moved closer against him and tilted her face until her mouth was close to his ear. "They attempted to steal the bones of Don Rómolo Balderas."

"Is it possible?" He made his eyes grow round and his lips purse up in disdain. "Surely not that! Why, all the world knows that Don Rómolo Balderas was the greatest historian in the entire Republic. Every school child reads his books. Wise men from Quintana Roo to the Río Bravo bow their heads in admiration to his name. What a wicked thing to do!" He hoped his virtuous tone was not too virtuous for plausibility, but she did not seem to notice.

"It is true! In the night they came. Three devils!"

"Young devils, I hope."

"Young or old, who cares? They were devils. The blacksmith surprised them even as they were opening the grave. He raised such a shout that all of San Juan rushed to his aid, for they were fighting, I can tell you. Especially one of them—their leader."

"And who was he?"

"You have heard of him doubtless. A proper wild one named Pepe Gonzalez."

"And what happened to them?"

"They had horses and got away, but one, I think, was hurt."

The Hidalgo man twisted his mouth remembering how Rubén the candymaker had ridden across the whitewashed line high on the cañon trail that marked the division between the Three Marys' and the Sabinas' sides of the mountains, and then had fallen in a faint from his saddle because his left arm was broken. There was no candy in Hidalgo for six weeks, and the entire Sabinas Valley resented that broken arm as fiercely as did Rubén.

The stranger tightened his arm in reflexed anger about Sarita's waist as she said, "All the world knows that the men of Hidalgo are sons of the mountain witches."

"But even devils are shy of disturbing the honored dead," he said gravely.

"'Don Rómolo was born in our village,' Hidalgo says. 'His bones belong to us.' Well, anyone in the valley can tell you he died in San Juan Iglesias, and here his bones will stay! Is that not proper? Is that not right?"

To keep from answering, he guided her through an intricate dance pattern that led them past the patio door. Over her head he could see two men and a woman staring with amazement at the open package on the table.

His eyes on the patio, he asked blandly, "You say the leader was one Pepe Gonzalez? The name seems to have a familiar sound."

plausibility (plô′ zə bil′ ə tē) *n.* believability

Literary Analysis
Point of View and Conflict What conflict must the young man and woman resolve, and how does each view the problem?

⑬ ✔Reading Check
Why do the people of Hidalgo and San Juan Iglesias refuse to speak to each other?

The Street of the Cañon ◆ 503

Making Predictions

- Remind students that they can make educated guesses about future events in a plot by reviewing the details and information they have already gleaned from the text.

- Draw students' attention to this sentence: "Realizing that this might be the last moment of peace he would have that evening, he bent toward her."

- Then, ask students the Reading Strategy question on p. 504: Do you think, as the stranger does, that there will be a fight? Why or why not?

  Possible responses: Students might say that when the contents of the package are discovered, there might be great unrest in the crowd of villagers.

15 Critical Thinking

Speculate

- Point out to students that both Sarita and the stranger know that to walk around the plaza with a girl means a wedding.

- Ask students to speculate on the stranger's motives for asking Sarita to walk with him.

  Possible responses: Some students may say that the stranger—Pepe Gonzales—fell in love with Sarita when he saw her three months ago, and has returned to court her in a characteristically bold way. Others may say that he is toying with her affections as part of a plan to get even with the people of San Juan Iglesias.

"But naturally. He has a talent." She tossed her head and stepped away from him as the music stopped. It was a dance of two *paradas*. He slipped his hand through her arm and guided her into place in the large oval of parading couples. Twice around the room and the orchestra would play again.

"A talent?" he prompted.

"For doing the impossible. When all the world says a thing cannot be done, he does it to prove the world wrong. Why, he climbed to the top of the Prow, and not even the long vanished Joaquín Castillo had ever climbed that mountain before. And this same Pepe caught a mountain lion with nothing to aid him but a rope and his two bare hands."

"He doesn't sound such a bad friend," protested the stranger, slipping his arm around her waist as the music began to play the merry song of the soap bubbles:

Pretty bubbles of a thousand colors
That ride on the wind
And break as swiftly
As a lover's heart.

The events in the patio were claiming his attention. Little by little he edged her closer to the door. The group at the table had considerably enlarged. There was a low murmur of excitement from the crowd.

"What has happened?" asked Sarita, attracted by the noise.

"There seems to be something wrong at the table," he answered, while trying to peer over the heads of the people in front of him. Realizing that this might be the **14** last moment of peace he would have that evening, he bent toward her.

"If I come back on Sunday, will you walk around the plaza with me?" She was startled into exclaiming, "Ay, no!"

"Please. Just once around."

"And you think I'd walk more than once with you, señor, even if you were no stranger? In San Juan Iglesias, to walk around the plaza **15** with a girl means a wedding."

"Ha, and you think that is common to San Juan alone? Even the devils of Hidalgo respect that law," he added hastily at her puzzled upward glance. "And so they do in all the villages." To cover his lapse he said softly, "I don't even know your name."

A mischievous grin crinkled the corners of her eyes. "Nor do I know yours, señor. Strangers do not often walk the streets of San Juan."

Reading Strategy
Making Predictions Do you think, as the stranger does, that there will be a fight? Why or why not?

Before he could answer, the chattering in the patio swelled to louder proportions. Don Roméo's voice lay on top, like thick cream on milk. "I tell you it is a jewel of a cheese. Such flavor, such texture, such whiteness. It is a jewel of a cheese."

"What has happened?" Sarita asked of a woman at her elbow.

"A fine goat's cheese appeared as if by magic on the table. No one knows where it came from."

"Probably an extra one from Linares," snorted a fat bald man on the right.

"Linares never made such a cheese as this," said the woman decisively.

"Silence!" roared Don Roméo. "Old Tío[2] Daniel would speak a word to us."

A great hand of silence closed down over the mouths of the people. The girl was standing on tiptoe trying vainly to see what was happening. She was hardly aware of the stranger's whispering voice although she remembered the words that he said. "Sunday night—once around the plaza."

She did not realize that he had moved away, leaving a gap that was quickly filled by the blacksmith.

Reading Strategy
Making Predictions Why does the stranger leave?

Old Tío Daniel's voice was a shrill squeak, and his thin, stringy neck jutted forth from his body like a turtle's from its shell. "This is no cheese from Linares," he said with authority, his mouth sucking in over his toothless gums between his sentences. "Years ago, when the great Don Rómolo Balderas was still alive, we had such cheese as this—ay, in those days we had it. But after he died and was buried in our own sainted ground, as was right and proper . . ."

"Yes, yes," muttered voices in the crowd. He glared at the interruption. As soon as there was silence again, he continued:

"After he died, we had it no more. Shall I tell you why?"

"Tell us, Tío Daniel," said the voices humbly.

"Because it is made in Hidalgo!"

The sound of a waterfall, the sound of a wind in a narrow cañon, and the sound of an angry crowd are much the same. There were no distinct words, but the sound was enough.

"Are you certain, Tío?" boomed Don Roméo.

"As certain as I am that a donkey has long ears. The people of Hidalgo have been famous for generations for making cheese like this—especially that wicked one, that owner of a cheese factory, Timotéo Gonzalez, father to Pepe, the wild one, whom we have good cause to remember."

"We do, we do," came the sigh of assurance.

"But on the whole northern frontier there are no vats like his to

---

2. Tío (tē′ ō) Spanish for uncle.

 Reading Check

What is in the package the stranger leaves on the table?

The Street of the Cañon ◆ 505

---

16 **Reading Strategy**
Making Predictions

• Have students use a graphic organizer to record the details related to the stranger's leaving. Students' organizers should look similar to the following:

• Then, ask students the Reading Strategy question on p. 505: Why does the stranger leave? Have students write their predictions in their organizers.
   Answer: Students should note that after the content of the package has been discovered, the stranger probably leaves because he does not want to be identified and caught.

▶ Monitor Progress Tell students to refer to their original predictions. Have students share them with the class and discuss how their predictions have changed during the course of the story.

17 ✔ **Reading Check**

Answer: The package is a fine goat's cheese from the village of Hidalgo.

CUSTOMIZE INSTRUCTION FOR UNIVERSAL ACCESS

For Less Proficient Readers	For Special Needs Students	For Advanced Readers
Students might be confused by the young man's gift. Have them form small groups and discuss why he might have decided to bring a gift of goat's cheese.	To make sure students understand the selection, show them the **Got It! Assessment Videotape.** Have them reread the passages that contain answers to the questions they answered incorrectly.	Suggest that students read additional works by Josephina Niggli. Provide students with the titles listed in the Enrichment box, ATE p. 507. After students have read these or other works by Niggli, have them form discussion groups in which they compare and contrast the works.

Answers for p. 506

Review and Assess

1. Students should give reasons for their opinions.
2. (a) Pepe Gonzalez behaves as if he has something to hide. (b) His secretive behavior suggests that he is bold, sneaky, and untrustworthy.
3. (a) Gonzalez arranges to dance with Sarita by charming her chaperone into making the arrangement for him. (b) Sarita calls him dangerous because he has a quick tongue and seems to be fearless.
4. (a) He brings cheese from Hidalgo. (b) Possible responses: Gonzalez wants to remind the people of San Juan Iglesias of the fine quality of the Hidalgo cheese, to upset the festivities by infiltrating as a spy, and to prove that he has again accomplished the impossible.
5. (a) They had attempted to dig up the grave of Don Rómolo Balderas and steal his bones. (b) The relationship has the potential to heal the rift between the two villages; it also has the potential to cause disaster. Students should support their speculations with specific reasons.
6. Gonzalez saw the festivities as an opportunity to prove himself as a threat to his enemies.

produce so fine a product. Ask the people of Chihuahua, of Sonora. Ask the man on the bridge at Laredo, or the man in his boat at Tampico, 'Hola, friend, who makes the finest goat cheese?' And the answer will always be the same, 'Don Timotéo of Hidalgo.'"

It was the blacksmith who asked the great question. "Then where did that cheese come from, and we haters of Hidalgo these ten long years?"

No voice said, "The stranger," but with one fluid movement every head in the patio turned toward the girl in the doorway. She also turned, her eyes wide with something that she realized to her own amazement was more apprehension than anger.

But the stranger was not in the room. When the angry, muttering men pushed through to the street, the stranger was not on the plaza. He was not anywhere in sight. A few of the more religious crossed themselves for fear that the Devil had walked in their midst. "Who was he?" one voice asked another. But Sarita, who was meekly listening to a lecture from Don Roméo on the propriety of dancing with strangers, did not have to ask. She had a strong suspicion that she had danced that night within the circling arm of Pepe Gonzalez.

Josephina Niggli

(1910–1983)

When Josephina Niggli was a child, she and her family fled Mexico to escape the turmoil of the Mexican Revolution. They settled in San Antonio, Texas, where Niggli grew up.

Niggli published her first book shortly after her high-school graduation. After college, she began writing and producing plays and later worked on movie scripts in Hollywood.

In 1945, she published *Mexican Village*, a collection of ten stories that capture the rich local color of her native Mexico. Because of her background in drama, Niggli's stories are noted for believable dialogue and vivid settings.

Review and Assess

Thinking About the Selection

1. **Respond:** Based on this story, would you like to read some of the other stories in Niggli's book *Mexican Village*? Why or why not?
2. (a) **Recall:** How does Pepe Gonzalez behave when he first arrives in the village the night of the party? (b) **Draw Conclusions:** What might Gonzalez's actions suggest about the kind of person he is?
3. (a) **Recall:** How does Gonzalez arrange to dance with Sarita? (b) **Infer:** When they begin dancing, Sarita says, "I think you are a dangerous man." What does she mean?
4. (a) **Recall:** What does Gonzalez bring to the party? (b) **Infer:** What are three possible reasons that Gonzalez brings this particular gift?
5. (a) **Recall:** What outrageous deed had men from Hidalgo attempted in San Juan Iglesias three months before? (b) **Speculate:** What do you think will happen now between Pepe and Sarita and between the two villages? Give reasons to support your answer.
6. **Make a Judgment:** Was Gonzalez wise to go to the party when doing so posed such a great danger? Explain.

ASSESSMENT PRACTICE: Reading Comprehension

Evaluate and Make Judgments   (For more practice, see Test Preparation Workbook, p. 33.)

Many tests require students to make judgments based on evidence in given passages. Use this sample test item to help students practice this skill.

The man in the doorway, while trying to appear at ease, was carefully examining every smiling face. If just one person recognized him, the room would turn on him like a den of snarling mountain cats, but so far all the laughter-dancing eyes were friendly.

The evidence in the passage indicates that the man in the doorway—

A is a coward
B is not expected
C is really a dog
D is looking for someone

The man is searching the faces not because he is looking for someone, *D*, but because he fears recognition. The correct response is *B*.

Review and Assess

Literary Analysis

Point of View

1. From what **point of view** does the author tell this story? Use a chart like this one to record clues that identify the point of view.

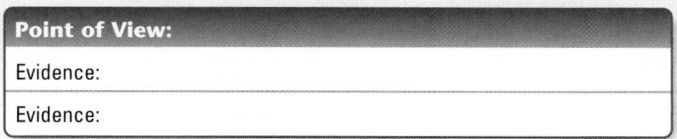

Point of View:
Evidence:
Evidence:

2. What is Sarita thinking at the end of the story?
3. Why do you think the author wants readers to know the thoughts and feelings of both Sarita and Pepe?

Connecting Literary Elements

4. What **conflict** does Pepe Gonzalez need to resolve in the story?
5. Using a diagram like the one here, analyze how Sarita and Pepe view the conflict differently.

Sarita's Feelings About the Conflict ···▶ **Conflict** ◀··· Pepe's Feelings About the Conflict

6. How do the differing viewpoints of these main characters help to move the plot of the story forward?

Reading Strategy

Making Predictions

7. When you first read about the stranger sneaking into the village, what **predictions** did you make about him? Why?
8. What details helped you predict the stranger's identity?
9. What details led you to revise, or at least reconsider, a prediction you made while reading? Explain.

Extend Understanding

10. **Social Studies Connection:** Think of two countries that have a conflict similar to that between the people of San Juan Iglesias and Hidalgo. Explain the cause of the problem, and predict whether it can be resolved.

Quick Review

Point of view is the vantage point from which an author tells a story.

The **conflict** in a story is the central problem that the main characters must resolve.

To **make a prediction,** make an educated guess based on your own experiences and what the text reveals about the characters and situation.

 Take It to the Net

www.phschool.com

Take the interactive self-test online to check your understanding of the selection.

The Street of the Cañon ◆ 507

Answers for p. 507

Review and Assess

1. **Point of view:** Third-person omniscient
   Evidence: Pepe Gonzalez reflects on his friend's broken arm.
   Evidence: Sarita's chaperone thinks that the stranger's good manners are astonishing.
   Evidence: Sarita does not realize that Gonzalez has left after the cheese has been discovered.

2. Sarita is thinking about her feelings for the stranger, who she has now learned is her enemy.

3. Niggli may want readers to see that the potential for healing the rift between two warring towns lies in personal relationships.

4. The conflict is the rift between the two villages concerning the location of Don Rómolo Balderas's grave.

5. Sarita believes that the bones should not be disturbed, and sees the men from Hidalgo as heartless thieves. Gonzalez believes he was right in trying to steal the bones because they should be buried in Hidalgo, where Don Rómolo Balderas was born.

6. The different viewpoints move the plot forward because they explain the tension between the villages and allow Gonzalez to drop hints as to his identity.

7. Students may have suspected that he meant to do harm to the festivities.

8. They could predict his identity from the direction he was taking on the Street of the Cañon and from his hiding in the shadows.

9. Possible response: Gonzalez's charm and pleasure at the festivities suggested that he was not there to harm anyone.

10. Possible response: Students may bring up the issue of Palestine and Israel fighting over holy lands. Have them predict whether a resolution will occur, and explain their predictions.

Answers for p. 508

❶ Vocabulary Development

Word Analysis

1. Feeling bold, Gonzalez dances confidently around the room with Sarita.
2. The nervous man entered the village timidly.
3. The villagers stared hostilely at the cheese brought by their enemy.

Spelling Strategy

1. con**sc**ious
2. poten**ti**al
3. ten**si**on

Fluency: Clarify Word Meaning

1. Gonzalez behaves audaciously by setting foot in the neighboring village.
2. A lynx has a mottled coat.
3. I would smile nonchalantly if I forgot someone's name.
4. Testimonials and statistics give an advertisement plausibility.
5. An officious person might be hard to work with because he'd be overly eager to give advice.
6. Gonzalez behaves imperiously when he dares to dance with Sarita.

❷ Grammar

1. across the mountains; to the Sabinas Valley
2. to our house
3. to my daughter
4. to meet
5. to pat; to play; with the lamb

Writing Application

Possible response: He wanted to go to the park.

Integrate Language Skills

❶ Vocabulary Development Lesson

Word Analysis: Anglo-Saxon Suffix -ly

Most words that end in the suffix -ly, such as *nonchalantly* and *audaciously*, are adverbs—words that modify a verb, an adjective, or another adverb.

Add -ly to the following words to make them adverbs. Then, write a sentence, using each adverb you formed.

    1. confident   2. timid   3. hostile

Spelling Strategy

In *nonchalantly*, the *sh* sound is spelled with the letters *ch*. The *sh* sound can also be spelled with *sh* as in *shrill*, *ci* as in *audaciously*, *si* as in *mansion*, or *ti* as in *partial*. Spell these words correctly, using letters that spell an *sh* sound.

    1. cons___ous   3. ten___on
    2. poten___al

Fluency: Clarify Word Meaning

Review the vocabulary list on page 497. Then, in your notebook, write a response to each item.

1. Which character from the story behaves *audaciously*?
2. What animal has a *mottled* coat?
3. Describe a time when you acted *nonchalantly*.
4. What types of details give an advertisement *plausibility*?
5. Would you enjoy working for an *officious* person? Why or why not?
6. Which character in the story behaves *imperiously*?

❷ Grammar Lesson

Prepositional Phrase or Infinitive?

The word *to* can be a preposition or part of an infinitive. In a **prepositional phrase,** *to* is followed by a noun or pronoun, as in *to the party* or *to her father*. In an **infinitive,** *to* is followed by a verb, as in *to dance* or *to talk*. Notice the prepositional phrase and the infinitive beginning with *to* in the following examples:

> **Preposition:** He walked *to the laughter-filled*
>   NOUN
>   house.
>
>   VERB
> **Infinitive:** He started *to lead* the way through the maze of dancers.

W/G **Prentice Hall Writing and Grammar Connection: Chapter 20, Section 1**

Practice Copy the following sentences. Underline each prepositional phrase once and each infinitive twice.

1. The Cañon Road led across the mountains to the Sabinas Valley.
2. Welcome, stranger, welcome to our house.
3. Come and drink a toast to my daughter.
4. This young fool wants to meet you, my child.
5. A man clever enough to pat the sheep has a right to play with the lamb.

Writing Application Write a single sentence that contains both a prepositional phrase beginning with *to* and an infinitive.

TEACHING RESOURCES

The following resources can be used to enrich or extend the instruction for pp. 508–509.

Vocabulary

📖 **Selection Support:** Build Vocabulary, p. 129
📖 **Vocabulary and Spelling Practice Book**
(Use this booklet for skills enrichment.)

Grammar

📖 **Selection Support:** Build Grammar Skills, p. 130
W/G **Writing and Grammar,** Platinum Level, p. 460 ▪
📑 **Daily Language Practice Transparencies**

Writing

W/G **Writing and Grammar,** Platinum Level, p. 182
💿 **Writing and Grammar iText CD-ROM** ▪
📚 **Writing Models and Graphic Organizers on Transparencies,** p. 95

 BLOCK SCHEDULING: Resources marked with this symbol provide varied instruction during 90-minute blocks.

❸ Writing Lesson

Comparison-and-Contrast Essay

In an essay, compare and contrast Pepe Gonzalez with another hero you know—real or fictional. Present readers with specific examples of the legends and feats surrounding each hero.

Prewriting	Review the story to gather details about Pepe as a hero. Then, jot down ideas and facts about another hero. Consider the risks and challenges each hero faces and the bravery each demonstrates. Identify the greatest similarities and differences between your subjects.
Drafting	Introduce both heroes before you start comparing. Using a point-by-point organization, discuss their similarities first and their differences next. For each main idea you present, include facts and examples.
Revising	Review your draft, underlining each point of comparison. Use separate colors to highlight references to each hero. If you have not addressed each hero equally, add information to balance your essay.

Model: Revising to Evaluate Structure

In this story, Pepe quietly goes undercover. In contrast, the Lone Ranger also lived undercover, but to a different end. In his mask, the Lone Ranger took on a new identity that people who needed him would recognize.

, sneaking into a party to which he would never have been invited

Highlighting reveals a need for more information about Pepe.

 Prentice Hall Writing and Grammar Connection: Chapter 9, Section 4

❹ Extension Activities

Listening and Speaking Break into two teams to present a **debate** on this question from the story: "Is not music free as air?" You might consider issues such as censorship and the rating of music.

- Do research, using the Internet, music magazines, and newspapers.
- Discuss your findings with your team.
- Outline your arguments logically.
- Divide up responsibility for presenting the arguments.

When the debate is complete, ask your audience to select the winning argument. **[Group Activity]**

Research and Technology To extend your understanding of the country Niggli describes, prepare a **photo essay** about Mexico. Begin by collecting photographs of Mexico from travel magazines, brochures, and the Internet. Select photographs that relate to a central theme or message. Then, using publishing software and graphics programs, arrange the photographs into a photo essay to display in your classroom.

 Take It to the Net   www.phschool.com

Go online for an additional research activity using the Internet.

The Street of the Cañon ◆ 509

---

❸ Writing Lesson

- Have students discuss real and fictional heroes they have read about to start gathering ideas.
- Ask the class for examples of what makes a person heroic. Students should be able to identify specific characteristics and feats.
- To prepare for the comparison-and-contrast essay, have students identify heroic details about Pepe Gonzalez and the other hero they have chosen. They might want to record their notes on the Comparison-and-Contrast organizer, p. 95 of **Writing Models and Graphic Organizers on Transparencies.**
- Use the Comparison-and-Contrast Composition rubric in **Performance Assessment and Portfolio Management,** p. 15, to evaluate students' essays.

❹ Extension Activity

Research and Technology

- Have students determine whether their photo essay will offer a historical perspective of Mexico or a picture of Mexico as it is today.
- Encourage students to write a caption and a brief explanation of each photograph they include. The explanations should clarify and enhance the information offered in the photos.
- When they finish, have students display their photo essays around the classroom.

CUSTOMIZE INSTRUCTION for Universal Access

To address different learning styles, use the following activities suggested in the **Extension Activities** booklet, p. 33.

- For Bodily/Kinesthetic and Musical/Rhythmic Learners, use Activity 5.
- For Verbal/Linguistic and Logical/Mathematical Learners, use Activity 6.
- For Verbal/Linguistic and Interpersonal Learners, use Activity 7.

ASSESSMENT RESOURCES

The following resources can be used to assess students' knowledge and skills.

Selection Assessment
- **Formal Assessment,** pp. 113–115
- **Open Book Test,** pp. 97–99
- **Got It! Assessment Videotapes,** Tape 3
- **Test Bank Software**
- **Take It to the Net**
  Visit www.phschool.com for self-tests and additional questions on "The Street of the Cañon."

Writing Rubric
- **Performance Assessment and Portfolio Management,** p. 15

PRENTICE HALL ASSESSMENT *SYSTEM*
- **Workbook**
- **Skill Book**
- **Transparencies**
- **CD-ROM**

A Storm in the Mountains ✦ In the Orchard ✦ A Tree Telling of Orpheus

Lesson Objectives

1. **To analyze and respond to literary elements**
   - Literary Analysis: Speaker
   - Comparing Literary Works

2. **To read, comprehend, analyze, and critique prose and poems**
   - Reading Strategy: Engaging the Senses
   - Reading Check questions
   - Review and Assess questions
   - Assessment Practice (ATE)

3. **To develop word analysis skills, fluency, and systematic vocabulary**
   - Vocabulary Development Lesson: Latin Terms

4. **To understand and apply written and oral language conventions**
   - Spelling Strategy
   - Grammar Lesson: Gerunds and Gerund Phrases

5. **To understand and apply appropriate writing and research strategies**
   - Writing Lesson: Monologue
   - Extension Activity: Multimedia Presentation

6. **To understand and apply listening and speaking strategies**
   - Extension Activity: Television Interview

STEP-BY-STEP TEACHING GUIDE	PACING GUIDE
PRETEACH	
Motivate Students and Provide Background	
Use the Motivation activity (ATE p. 510)	5 min.
Read and discuss the Preview material and Background information (SE/ATE p. 510) **A**	5 min.
Introduce the Concepts	
Introduce the Literary Analysis and Reading Strategy (SE/ATE p. 511) **A**	15 min.
Pronounce the vocabulary words and read their definitions (SE p. 511)	5 min.
TEACH	
Monitor Comprehension	
Informally monitor comprehension by circulating while students read independently or in groups **A**	15 min.
Monitor students' comprehension with the Reading Check notes (SE/ATE pp. 515, 517)	as students read
Develop vocabulary with Vocabulary notes (SE pp. 512, 513, 516)	as students read
Develop Understanding	
Develop students' understanding of identifying the speaker with Literary Analysis annotations (SE p. 515; ATE pp. 512, 513, 515) **A**	10 min.
Develop students' understanding of engaging the senses with Reading Strategy annotations (SE p. 517; ATE pp. 512, 514, 516, 517)	10 min.
ASSESS	
Assess Mastery	
Assess students' mastery of the Reading Strategy and Literary Analysis by having them answer the Review and Assess questions (SE/ATE p. 519)	20 min.
Use one or more of the print and media Assessment Resources (ATE p. 520) **A**	up to 50 min.
EXTEND	
Apply Understanding	
Have students complete the Vocabulary Development Lesson and the Grammar Lesson (SE p. 520) **A**	20 min.
Apply students' knowledge of sequence of events with the Writing Lesson (SE/ATE p. 521) **A**	45 min.
Apply students' understanding using one or more of the Extension Activities (SE p. 521)	20–90 min.

 ACCELERATED INSTRUCTION:
Use the strategies and activities identified with an **A**.

UNIVERSAL ACCESS
● = Below Level Students
▲ = On-Level Students
■ = Above Level Students

Time and Resource Manager

Reading Level: Average/Average/Challenging
Average Number of Instructional Days: 4

RESOURCES		
PRINT 📖	**TRANSPARENCIES**	**TECHNOLOGY** 💿 🎧
• **Beyond Literature,** Career Connection: Meteorology, p. 34 ▲ ■		• **Interest Grabber Video,** Tape 3 ● ▲ ■
• **Selection Support Workbook:** ● ▲ ■ Literary Analysis, p. 136 Reading Strategy, p. 135 Build Vocabulary, p. 133	• **Literary Analysis and Reading Transparencies,** pp. 67 and 68 ● ▲ ■	
		• **Listening to Literature** ● ▲ ■ Audiocassettes, Side 15 Audio CDs, CD 10
• **Literatura en español** ● ▲ • **Literary Analysis for Enrichment** ■		
• **Formal Assessment:** Selection Test, pp. 116–118 ● ▲ ■ • **Open Book Test,** pp. 100–102 ● ▲ ■ • **Performance Assessment and Portfolio Management,** p. 27 ● ▲ ■ • **PRENTICE HALL ASSESSMENT** *SYSTEM* ● ▲ ■	• **PRENTICE HALL ASSESSMENT** *SYSTEM* ● ▲ ■ Skills Practice Answers and Explanations on Transparencies	• **Test Bank Software** ● ▲ ■ • **Got It! Assessment Videotapes,** Tape 3 ● ▲
• **Selection Support Workbook:** ● ▲ ■ Build Grammar Skills, p. 134 • **Writing and Grammar,** Platinum Level ● ▲ ■ • **Extension Activities,** p. 34 ● ▲ ■	• **Daily Language Practice Transparencies** ● ▲	• **Writing and Grammar iText CD-ROM** ● ▲ ■ 💻 *Take It to the Net* www.phschool.com

BLOCK SCHEDULING: Use one 90-minute class period to preteach the selection and have students read it. Use a second 90-minute class period to assess students' mastery of skills and have them complete one of the Extension Activities.

Step-by-Step Teaching Guide
for pp. 510-511

Motivation

Read aloud the following passage from Alexander Solzhenitsyn's "A Storm in the Mountains":

"It caught us one pitch-black night at the foot of the pass. We crawled out of our tents and ran for shelter as it came towards us over the ridge."

Ask students to conjecture about what "it" might be. List students' responses on the chalkboard, and then tell them that the passage describes a storm in the mountains. Then, have students brainstorm for a list of comparisons they might use for different kinds of weather. Tell them that each of the selections they will read views nature as an entity with a life and voice of its own.

▣ Interest Grabber Video

As an alternative, play "Orpheus" on Tape 3 to engage student interest.

❶ Background
Poetry

Denise Levertov was part of a group of writers and poets affiliated with the experimental Black Mountain College in North Carolina. Levertov became associated with the group in 1948. These poets developed a poetic form known as projective verse that attempted to bring back the oral aspects of poetry to modern poetry writing. The leader of the group, Charles Olson, promoted a verse form that depended on the individual poet's breath rhythm to determine the poem's form. According to Olson, the emphasis should be placed on the syllable and not prescribed verse forms. This produced poems with varied spaces and unusual groupings of type on the page. "A Tree Telling of Orpheus" may have been written during Levertov's involvement with the Black Mountain poets.

Prepare to Read

A Storm in the Mountains ◆ In the Orchard ◆ A Tree Telling of Orpheus

▣ Take It to the Net

Visit www.phschool.com for interactive activities and instruction related to these selections, including
- background
- graphic organizers
- literary elements
- reading strategies

Preview

Connecting to the Literature

You dim the lights, put on headphones, and pop in a favorite CD. Suddenly, you are in a place free of daily pressures, a place that seems to be music itself. These selections help you reflect on the transforming powers of nature and music. As you read, connect with the sensations described and imagine what it feels like to be in the place each poet describes.

❶ Background

"A Tree Telling of Orpheus" is Denise Levertov's interpretation of a classic Greek myth. In that story, Orpheus' skill on the lyre (an ancient stringed instrument) was so great and his voice was so beautiful that trees were said to uproot themselves and follow him. Rivers also stopped flowing to listen to him, and wild beasts were made gentle by his music.

510 ◆ *Expanding Horizons*

TEACHING RESOURCES

The following resources can be used to enrich or extend the instruction for pp. 510–511.

Motivation
▣ **Interest Grabber Video**, Tape 3 ▣

Background
📖 **Beyond Literature**, p. 34 ▣

 Take It to the Net
Visit www.phschool.com for background and hotlinks for the selections.

Literary Analysis
▣ **Literary Analysis and Reading Transparencies**, Speaker, p. 68

Reading
📖 **Selection Support:** Reading Strategy, p. 135, Build Vocabulary, p. 133

▣ **Literary Analysis and Reading Transparencies**, Engaging the Senses, p. 67

▣ **BLOCK SCHEDULING:** Resources marked with this symbol provide varied instruction during 90-minute blocks.

Literary Analysis

Speaker

Each of the poems presented here has a **speaker,** the imaginary voice assumed by the writer. The speaker is the character—the poet, person, animal, or object—who narrates the work. As this passage from "A Tree Telling of Orpheus" reveals, the speaker is a tree.

> Fire he sang,
> that trees fear, and I, a tree, rejoiced in its flames.

As you read, focus on what you know about the speaker based on the speaker's words, actions, or feelings.

Comparing Literary Works

In poetry, the voice that tells the story is called the speaker. In narrative prose, the voice is known as the **narrator.** The speakers and the narrator in these selections each reflect a unique personality and perspective on nature. For example, one views nature with a grateful wonder and another expresses more bubbling enthusiasm. Compare and contrast the formality and level of the language as well as the attitude of each speaker or narrator.

Reading Strategy

Engaging the Senses

To fully appreciate poetry, **engage your senses**—allow the work to speak not just to your mind but to your senses of sight, hearing, touch, taste, and smell. For example, when the speaker of "A Storm in the Mountains" refers to the "ceaseless roar of the rivers," he expects you to use your sense of hearing to re-create the sound of a rushing river.

To help you engage your senses as you read, construct a chart like the one here for each selection. Fill in as many sensory details as you can.

"A Storm in the Mountains"	
Sight	Lightning flashes
Sound	Roaring rivers Voice of thunder
Smell	
Taste	
Touch	Belting rain

Vocabulary Development

terra firma (ter´ ə fur´ mə) Latin for "solid earth" (p. 512)

sultry (sul´ trē) *adj.* oppressively hot and moist; sweltering (p. 513)

asunder (ə sun´ dər) *adv.* into pieces or parts (p. 516)

A Storm in the Mountains / In the Orchard / A Tree Telling of Orpheus ◆ 511

---

❷ Literary Analysis

Speaker

- Explain to students that the speaker is the character who narrates a work of literature. The speaker may be the poet, a person, an animal, or an object.

- Have students read the excerpt from "A Tree Telling of Orpheus" on this page, and ask them to identify the speaker. Lead students to see that the appositive (*a tree*) indicates that the speaker is a tree.

- As students read the poems, have them use the Speaker transparency in **Literary Analysis and Reading Strategy Transparencies,** p. 68, to determine the speaker of each.

❸ Reading Strategy

Engaging the Senses

- Explain to students that when reading poetry, they should allow all of their senses to be engaged. This will help them develop a fuller understanding of each poem.

- Have the students review the sensory details chart on this page. As they read, encourage them to use a chart like this one to record examples of the many sensory details in the poems.

Vocabulary Development

- Pronounce each vocabulary word for students, and read the definitions as a class. Have students identify any words with which they are already familiar.

CUSTOMIZE INSTRUCTION FOR UNIVERSAL ACCESS

For Less Proficient Readers	For English Learners	For Advanced Readers
Demonstrate for students how to construct a sensory details chart by using the Engaging the Senses transparency in **Literary Analysis and Reading Transparencies,** p. 67. Have students read the poetry together, keeping track of the sensory details as a group.	Use context clues and pictures to help students determine the meaning of unfamiliar vocabulary words, such as *serpentine, primal, warblers, fruitage, sapling,* and *felled.*	Using the sensory details chart on this page, have students independently fill in sensory details while progressing through the readings. Have students compare their findings and determine whether some parts of the works engage different senses for different readers.

 E-Teach

Visit E-Teach at www.phschool.com for teachers' essays on how to teach, with questions and answers.

Step-by-Step Teaching Guide for pp. 512–518

CUSTOMIZE INSTRUCTION
For Visual/Spatial Learners

As students read, have them picture the landscapes suggested by the descriptive language in one of the works in this grouping and draw or collect photographs that illustrate them. They may use details they list in their sensory detail charts.

❶ About the Selection

The selections in this grouping explore different aspects of nature. In "A Storm in the Mountains," Solzhenitsyn describes a raging storm so overwhelming that individuals surrender to it, transcending their fear to feel at one with the powerful phenomenon—and with all of nature.

❷ Literary Analysis

Speaker

• Remind the students that the speaker is the character who narrates the work.

• Read aloud the bracketed passage. Ask students what information is revealed about the speaker in this first paragraph.
Answer: Readers can tell that the speaker is camping outdoors in a tent, and that he or she is not alone, since the plural pronouns *we, us* and *our* are used.

❸ Reading Strategy

Engaging the Senses

• Ask students to which senses the details in this passage appeal.
Possible responses: The thunder engages the sense of hearing; the lightning flashes engage the sense of sight.

• Remind students as they read to enter these sensory details into their charts.

---

❶ Alexander Solzhenitsyn
Translated by Michael Glenny

A Storm in the Mountains

❷ It caught us one pitch-black night at the foot of the pass. We crawled out of our tents and ran for shelter as it came towards us over the ridge.

Everything was black—no peaks, no valleys, no horizon to be seen, only the searing flashes of lightning separating darkness from light, and the gigantic peaks of Belaya-Kaya and Djuguturlyuchat[1] looming up out of the night. The huge black pine trees around us seemed as high as the mountains themselves. For a split second we felt ourselves on <u>terra firma</u>; then once more everything would be plunged into darkness and chaos.

The lightning moved on, brilliant light alternating with pitch blackness, flashing white, then pink, then violet, the mountains and pines always springing back in the same place, their hugeness filling us with awe; yet when they disappeared we could not believe that they had ever existed.

❸ The voice of the thunder filled the gorge, drowning the ceaseless roar of the rivers. Like the arrows of Sabaoth,[2] the lightning flashes rained down on the peaks, then split up into serpentine streams as though bursting into spray against the rock face, or striking and then shattering like a living thing.

As for us, we forgot to be afraid of the lightning, the thunder, and the downpour, just as a droplet in the ocean has no fear of a hurricane. Insignificant yet grateful, we became part of this world—a primal world in creation before our eyes.

terra firma (ter´ ə fur´ mə)
Latin for "solid earth"

Alexander Solzhenitsyn

(b. 1918)
Born in Russia, Alexander Solzhenitsyn (sōl´ zhə nēt´ sin) began writing after he was imprisoned in 1945 in a labor camp for criticizing communist leader Joseph Stalin.

Despite his 1970 Nobel Prize for Literature, Solzhenitsyn was exiled after the publication in Paris of parts of his work *The Gulag Archipelago*.

---

1. **Belaya-Kaya** (bye´ lĭ ə kĭ´ ə) and **Djuguturlyuchat** (djōō gōō tōor lyōō´ chət) Russian mountains.
2. **Sabaoth** (sab´ ā äth´) biblical word for "armies."

512 ◆ Expanding Horizons

TEACHING RESOURCES

The following resources can be used to enrich or extend the instruction for pp. 512–518.

Literary Analysis
📖 **Selection Support:** Literary Analysis, p. 136

Reading
🎧 **Listening to Literature Audiocassettes,** Side 15 ▪
💿 **Listening to Literature Audio CDs,** CD 10 ▪

▪ **BLOCK SCHEDULING:** Resources marked with this symbol provide varied instruction during 90-minute blocks.

In the Orchard

Henrik Ibsen
Translated by Sir Edmund Gosse

In the sunny orchard closes,[1]
    While the warblers sing and swing,
Care not whether blustering Autumn
    Break the promises of Spring!
5 Rose and white, the apple blossom
    Hides you from the <u>sultry</u> sky—
Let it flutter, blown and scatter'd,
    On the meadows by-and-by!

Will you ask about the fruitage
10   In the season of the flowers?
Will you murmur, will you question,
    Count the run of weary hours?
Will you let the scarecrow clapping
    Drown all happy sounds and words?
15 Brothers! there is better music
    In the singing of the birds.

From your heavy-laden garden
    Will you hunt the mellow thrush;
He will play you for protection
20   With his crown-song's liquid rush.
O but you will win the bargain,
    Though your fruit be spare and late,
For remember Time is flying
    And will shut the garden gate.

25 With my living, with my singing,
    I will tear the hedges down.
Sweep the grass and heap the blossom!
    Let it shrivel, pale and brown!
Swing the wicket![2] Sheep and cattle,
30   Let them graze among the best!
I broke off the flowers; what matter
    Who may revel with the rest?

---

1. **closes** enclosed place, as a farmyard.
2. **wicket** small door or gate.

In the Orchard ◆ 513

---

❹ About the Selection

Ibsen uses the seasons of spring and autumn as symbols of youth and old age—and ultimately, death. His poem urges readers to enjoy the budding blossoms of spring without thinking about the withered leaves of fall.

❺ Literary Analysis

Speaker

- Point out to students that the first stanza of the poem is an imperative sentence.
- Ask students: What is the speaker telling readers not to do? What does this reveal about the speaker?
  Possible responses: The speaker is telling readers not to let thoughts of autumn ruin their enjoyment of spring; in other words, not to let worrying about the future spoil their enjoyment of the present. The speaker is someone who feels qualified to give advice about life—perhaps an older person or a philosopher.

▶ **Monitor Progress** Have students paraphrase the passage.
Possible answer: When you are in your yard or garden and the birds are singing, don't ruin your experience of spring by thinking about the coming of fall.

❻ ▶ Critical Viewing

Answer: The lavish profusion of daffodils and apple blossoms suggests the speaker's message to celebrate life in its fullness.

❻ ▲ Critical Viewing

Explain how this photograph suggests the speaker's sense of celebration. **[Connect]**

sultry (sul´ trē) *adj.* oppressively hot and moist; sweltering

Henrik Ibsen

(1828–1906)

Henrik Ibsen's literary life began with poetry. Isolated on a small farm near the port town of Skien, Norway, the young Ibsen turned for solace to writing poetry. His first successful play, *Brand*, was, in fact, originally written as a narrative poem. It was his plays, however, that made him famous. His emphasis on character rather than the predictable plots popular at the time resulted in such realistic dramas as *A Doll's House* and *Hedda Gabler*.

CUSTOMIZE INSTRUCTION FOR UNIVERSAL ACCESS

For Special Needs Students	For Gifted/Talented Students	For Advanced Readers
Point out to students that Ibsen uses spring to symbolize youth, life, and happiness, and fall to symbolize old age. Ask them what qualities of spring and fall might lead a poet to choose them as symbols of youth and old age.	The writers in this section have all used literature to explore social issues: political oppression (Solzhenitsyn), equality for women (Ibsen), and world peace (Levertov). Have these students compile an anthology of poetry and other writings that explore social issues or current events that have particular meaning for them.	Tell students that it is common in literature to use the seasons to symbolize different stages in life. Ask them to name another story or poem they've read that uses these symbols, and to explain how they add to the work's meaning.

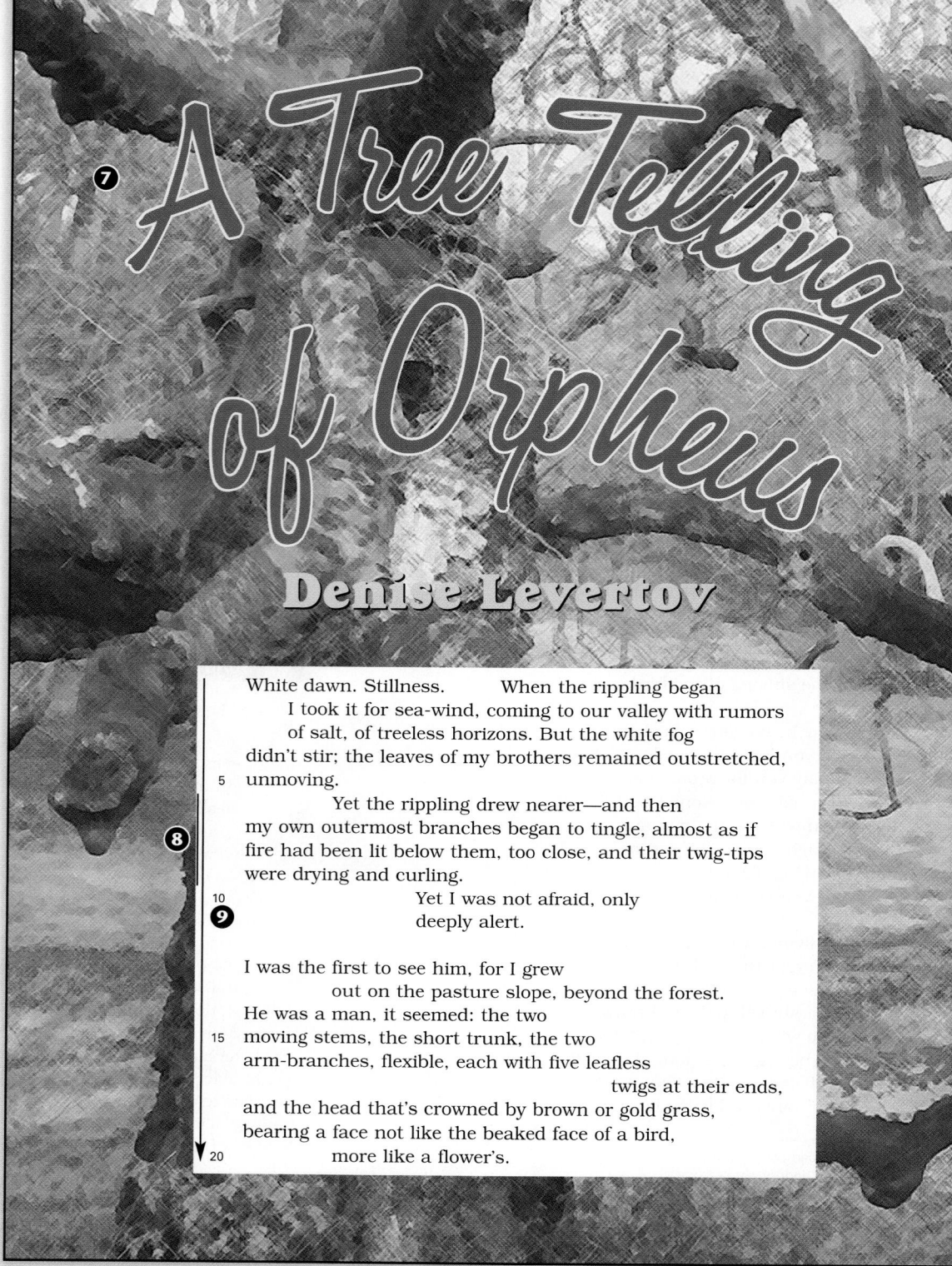

A Tree Telling of Orpheus

Denise Levertov

White dawn. Stillness.   When the rippling began
       I took it for sea-wind, coming to our valley with rumors
       of salt, of treeless horizons. But the white fog
didn't stir; the leaves of my brothers remained outstretched,
5   unmoving.
              Yet the rippling drew nearer—and then
my own outermost branches began to tingle, almost as if
fire had been lit below them, too close, and their twig-tips
were drying and curling.
10   Yet I was not afraid, only
              deeply alert.

I was the first to see him, for I grew
              out on the pasture slope, beyond the forest.
He was a man, it seemed: the two
15   moving stems, the short trunk, the two
arm-branches, flexible, each with five leafless
                            twigs at their ends,
and the head that's crowned by brown or gold grass,
bearing a face not like the beaked face of a bird,
20   more like a flower's.

He carried a burden made of
some cut branch bent while it was green,
strands of a vine tight-stretched across it. From this,
when he touched it, and from his voice
25 which unlike the wind's voice had no need of our
leaves and branches to complete its sound,
                              came the ripple,
But it was now no longer a ripple (he had come near and
stopped in my first shadow) it was a wave that bathed me
30   as if rain
                     rose from below and around me
            instead of falling.
And what I felt was no longer a dry tingling:

      I seemed to be singing as he sang, I seemed to know
35   what the lark knows; all my sap
            was mounting towards the sun that by now
                  had risen, the mist was rising, the grass
was drying, yet my roots felt music moisten them
deep under earth.

            He came still closer, leaned on my trunk:
40   the bark thrilled like a leaf still-folded.
Music! There was no twig of me not
                  trembling with joy and fear.

Then as he sang
45 it was no longer sounds only that made the music:
he spoke, and as no tree listens I listened, and language
            came into my roots
                        out of the earth,
            into my bark
50   out of the air,
            into the pores of my greenest shoots
                  gently as dew
and there was no word he sang but I knew its meaning.
He told of journeys,
55   of where sun and moon go while we stand in dark,
      of an earth-journey he dreamed he would take some day
deeper than roots . . .
He told of the dreams of man, wars, passions, griefs,
            and I, a tree, understood words—ah, it seemed
60 my thick bark would split like a sapling's that
                  grew too fast in the spring
when a late frost wounds it.

                  Fire he sang,
that trees fear, and I, a tree, rejoiced in its flames.

Literary Analysis
Speaker What do you know about this speaker after reading the first 25 lines?

Literary Analysis
Speaker Which descriptions in line 35 reveal the speaker's attitude about events?

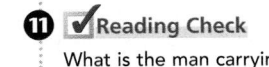 **Reading Check**
What is the man carrying?

A Tree Telling of Orpheus ◆ 515

---

❾ Literary Analysis
Speaker
- Have students read the first 25 lines of the poem. As they read, encourage them to record the details they learn about the speaker.
- Then, ask the first Literary Analysis question on p. 515: What do you know about this speaker after reading the first 25 lines?
  Answer: The speaker is a tree, as indicated by the words, "the leaves of my brothers remained outstretched…." The tree grows on a pasture and is the first tree to see Orpheus.

❿ Literary Analysis
Speaker
- Make sure students understand that the speaker in this poem is a tree.
- Read aloud line 35 to students. Ask them the second Literary Analysis question on p. 515: Which descriptions in line 35 reveal the speaker's attitude about events?
  Answer: The description of knowing "what the lark knows" indicates that the tree feels a deep, instinctual connection with the music from the lyre.

⓫ ✓Reading Check
Answer: The man, Orpheus, is carrying a lyre.

CUSTOMIZE INSTRUCTION FOR UNIVERSAL ACCESS

For Less Proficient Readers	For Gifted/Talented Students	For Advanced Readers
Have students make a list of words that describe the tree's feelings as they are revealed in the poem. They may then organize these words in a flow chart to indicate the changes as they evolve in the poem.	Levertov offers a detailed description of Orpheus. Have students prepare a list of details they would include if they were to create a painting of Orpheus. You might also ask students to add details Levertov omitted, basing their responses on the mood and tone of the poem.	Have students look at the picture of trees on this page. Ask them which of the trees' features give the appearance of movement and life. With which details in the poem do the trees pictured seem to correspond?

515

12 ▶ Critical Viewing

Possible response: Students may point out features of the tree that reflect movement, such as the graceful, arm-like lines of the branches, the interplay of light and shadow, and the contrasting textures.

13 Reading Strategy

Engaging the Senses

• Encourage students to focus on the sensory details throughout the bracketed passage.

• Ask students how these lines blend the senses of hearing and touch.

Answer: The phrase "Fire he sang" blends the heat of fire with the music of a song; "its chords flamed/up to the crown of me" blends the music of chords with the heat of a flame.

65　New buds broke forth from me though it was full summer.
　　　　As though his lyre[1] (now I knew its name)
　　　　　were both frost and fire, its chords flamed
up to the crown of me.
　　　　　　　　I was seed again.
70　　　　　　　　　I was fern in the swamp.
　　　　　　　　　　I was coal.

And at the heart of my wood
(so close I was to becoming man or a god)
　　　there was a kind of silence, a kind of sickness,
75　　　　something akin to what men call boredom,
　　　　　　　　　　something

(the poem descended a scale, a stream over stones)
　　　　that gives to a candle a coldness
　　　　　　in the midst of its burning, he said.

80　It was then,
　　　　when in the blaze of his power that
　　　　　　　　reached me and changed me
　　　　I thought I should fall my length,
that the singer began
85　　　　　　to leave me.　　　Slowly
　　　moved from my noon shadow
　　　　　　　　　to open light,
words leaping and dancing over his shoulders
back to me
90　　　rivery sweep of lyre-tones becoming
slowly again
　　　　ripple.
And I
　　　in terror
95　　　　but not in doubt of
　　　　　　　　what I must do
in anguish, in haste,
　　　　wrenched from the earth root after root,
the soil heaving and cracking, the moss tearing asunder—
100　and behind me the others: my brothers
forgotten since dawn. In the forest
they too had heard,
and were pulling their roots in pain
out of a thousand years' layers of dead leaves,
105　　　rolling the rocks away,
　　　　　　breaking themselves

14

12 ▼ Critical Viewing
Compare this tree to the speaker in this poem.
[Compare and Contrast]

asunder (ə sun′ dər) *adv.*
into pieces or parts

---

1. **lyre** (līr) *n.* small stringed instrument of the harp family that was used by the ancient Greeks to accompany singers.

516 ◆ *Expanding Horizons*

---

                                         out of
                                    their depths.
       You would have thought we would lose the sound of the lyre,
110   of the singing
       so dreadful the storm-sounds were, where there was no storm,
                       no wind but the rush of our
                    branches moving, our trunks breasting the air.
                       But the music!
                                    The music reached us.

       Clumsily,
                    stumbling over our own roots,
                                    rustling our leaves
                                             in answer,
120   we moved, we followed.

       All day we followed, up hill and down.
                                    We learned to dance,
       for he would stop, where the ground was flat,
                                             and words he said
125   taught us to leap and to wind in and out
       around one another   in figures   the lyre's measure designed.
       The singer
                    laughed till he wept to see us, he was so glad.
                                             At sunset
130   we came to this place I stand in, this knoll[2]
       with its ancient grove that was bare grass then.
                    In the last light of the day his song became
       farewell.
                    He stilled our longing.
135   He sang our sun-dried roots back into earth,
       watered them: all-night rain of music so quiet
                                    we could almost
                    not hear it in the
                                    moonless dark.
140   By dawn he was gone.
                    We have stood here since,
       in our new life.
                    We have waited.
                                    He does not return.
145   It is said he made his earth-journey, and lost
       what he sought.
                    It is said they felled him
       and cut up his limbs for firewood.
                                    And it is said
150   his head still sang and was swept out to sea singing.

---

2. **knoll** (nōl) *n.* mound.

Reading Strategy
Engaging the Senses
What images in these lines engage your senses of sight, touch, and hearing?

Reading Strategy
Engaging the Senses
What words in these lines appeal to several of your senses?

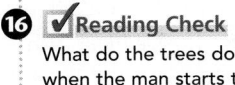

16 ☑ Reading Check
What do the trees do when the man starts to leave?

---

14 Reading Strategy
Engaging the Senses
- Call on a volunteer to read aloud the bracketed passage. Have students use a chart like the one on p. 511 to record the sensory details in the passage. Students' charts should look similar to the following:

Sight	"rush of our branches moving"
Touch	references to pain, wrenching, tearing, and pulling
Sound	"The music reached us"

- Then, ask students the first Reading Strategy question on p. 517: What images in these lines engage your senses of sight, touch, and hearing?
  Answer: References to pain, wrenching, tearing, and pulling engage the sense of touch. "But the music! The music reached us" engages the sense of hearing. "But the rush of our branches moving" engages the sense of sight.

15 Reading Strategy
Engaging the Senses
- Point out to students that some expressions can apply to more than one sense.
- Have students read the bracketed passage, and ask them the second Reading Strategy question on p. 517: What words in these lines appeal to several of your senses?
  Possible answers: "He sang our sun-dried roots back into the earth" appeals to sound, sight, and touch; "rain of music" appeals to sound, sight, and touch as well.

16 ☑ Reading Check
Answer: At first, the trees follow him, dancing. Then, he says farewell and the trees take root again in a new place.

517

Review and Assess

1. Possible response: Students may say that "A Tree Telling of Orpheus" is the most unusual because the poem's speaker is a tree telling a myth.

2. (a) Lightning illuminates the night. (b) Only when the lightning illuminates his surroundings does the speaker experience the earth beneath the him.

3. (a) While running for shelter, he watches the storm and the beauty that appears as lightning strikes. (b) He is saying they were overcome with the beauty of nature. (c) The speaker realizes his own insignificance and the power of such an event.

4. (a) The apple trees are in blossom and the warblers sing. (b) Spring represents youth and happiness.

5. (a) Signs of autumn include the scarecrow, the shriveling blossoms, and the closing gate. (b) Autumn is the end of the fruiting season, a sign of the coming winter, and of death. (c) The speaker wants the reader not to worry about the future but to celebrate life in its fullness.

6. (a) The speaker says the man has two moving stems, a short trunk, and two arm-branches with five leafless twigs at their ends. The man also has a face like a flower's. (b) The speaker is a tree, so the description parallels its experience and point of view.

7. (a) The trees come alive with the music. (b) The trees are inspired by the beauty of the music that overtakes them. (c) Students' answers will vary. Ask them to support their ideas with details.

8. (a) The trees are more alive than they were before they heard the music. (b) Ask students to support their answers with evidence from literature or from their own lives.

Perhaps he will not return.
                                  But what we have lived
comes back to us.
                  We see more.
155   We feel, as our rings increase,
something that lifts our branches, that stretches our furthest
                                                      leaf-tips
further.
                  The wind, the birds,
160   do not sound poorer but clearer,
recalling our agony, and the way we danced.
The music!

Review and Assess

Thinking About the Selections

1. **Respond:** Which selection gives you the most unexpected view of nature? Why?

2. (a) **Recall:** In "A Storm in the Mountains," why is there both darkness and light? (b) **Analyze:** What is the effect of the changing light on the narrator?

3. (a) **Recall:** What is the narrator in "A Storm in the Mountains" doing while the storm explodes around him? (b) **Interpret:** What does the narrator mean by saying his group "forgot to be afraid of the lightning"? (c) **Generalize:** What does the narrator learn from the experience?

4. (a) **Recall:** What signs of spring are mentioned at the beginning of "In the Orchard"? (b) **Interpret:** What does spring represent for the speaker?

5. (a) **Recall:** What signs of autumn are mentioned later in "In the Orchard"? (b) **Interpret:** What threat does autumn represent for the speaker? (c) **Analyze:** How does the speaker suggest that we deal with autumn's threat?

6. (a) **Recall:** In "A Tree Telling of Orpheus," what words does the speaker use to describe the man in the second stanza? (b) **Interpret:** Why might the speaker choose this language?

7. (a) **Recall:** What happens when Orpheus performs music for the trees? (b) **Analyze:** How does the speaker explain the reason for this action? (c) **Connect:** Does music have a similar or a different effect on you? Explain.

8. (a) **Deduce:** What lasting effect does Orpheus have on the trees? (b) **Take a Position:** Do you think a very positive or a very negative experience usually has a more lasting effect? Why?

Denise Levertov

(1923–1997)
When Denise Levertov moved to the United States from England in 1948, she became associated with the Black Mountain School, an experimental community of writers, painters, musicians, and dancers that thrived from 1933 to 1956. Levertov and the other Black Mountain poets began to change the rigid view of how a poem should read and look. She published many volumes of poetry, including *Relearning the Alphabet*, the 1970 collection in which "A Tree Telling of Orpheus" first appeared.

✎ ASSESSMENT PRACTICE: Reading Comprehension

Evaluate and Make Judgments   **(For more practice, see Test Preparation Workbook, p. 34.)**

Many tests require students to make judgments based on the evidence provided in a text. Use this sample test item to demonstrate this skill.

> As for us, we forgot to be afraid of the lightning, the thunder, and the downpour, just as a droplet in the ocean has no fear of a hurricane. Insignificant yet grateful, we became part of this world—a primal world in creation before our eyes.

Using the passage, fill in the blank in the sentence with the most appropriate word.

The evidence in this passage suggests that the speaker is—

A terrified
B exhausted
C awestruck
D careless

Help students to see that *C* is true and that *A, B,* and *D* cannot be supported by the passage.

Review and Assess

Literary Analysis

Speaker

1. What do you know about the **speaker** or **narrator** in each selection? Construct a chart like the one shown to record your answers.

Words	Actions	Feelings

2. Who is the most likely speaker of "In the Orchard": a tree, the wind, the poet, or a scarecrow? Explain your choice.

3. Why might Denise Levertov have chosen a tree to be the speaker of "A Tree Telling of Orpheus"?

Comparing Literary Works

4. (a) Which speaker or narrator uses the most formal language? (b) What does the word choice suggest about that character's personality?

5. Contrast the speakers' views about nature, citing details from each poem to support your answers. (a) Which speaker expresses the most wonder? (b) Which speaker expresses the most enthusiasm? (c) Which speaker is most thoughtful?

Reading Strategy

Engaging the Senses

6. What two senses do Solzhenitsyn's words "the searing flashes of lightning" call upon?

7. In which image in "In the Orchard" did you most sense the meaning of the poem? Explain your answer.

8. Choose a sensory detail from the poem "A Tree Telling of Orpheus." Then, explain why this detail is important to the poem.

Extend Understanding

9. **Environmental Connection:** How might an environmentalist use images or messages from these selections to illustrate the close connection between people and nature?

A Storm in the Mountains / In the Orchard / A Tree Telling of Orpheus ◆ 519

Quick Review

The **speaker** in a poem is the imaginary voice assumed by the poet to "tell" the poem.

In narrative prose, the imaginary voice is known as the **narrator.**

To **engage your senses,** be alert to the use of language and images that appeal to sight, hearing, taste, touch, and smell.

 Take It to the Net

www.phschool.com
Take the interactive self-test online to check your understanding of the selections.

☀ ENRICHMENT: Further Reading

Other Works by the Authors

Works by Alexander Solzhenitsyn
One Day in the Life of Ivan Denisovich
The First Circle

Works by Henrik Ibsen
A Doll's House
Peer Gynt

Works by Denise Levertov
Sands of the Wall
"The Springtime"

Take It to the Net
Visit www.phschool.com for more information on the authors.

Answers for p. 519

Review and Assess

1. **"A Storm in the Mountains"**
   Words: "we forgot to be afraid of the lightning"
   Actions: watches the storm in awe
   Feelings: feels that he or she "became part of this world"

   "In the Orchard"
   Words: "care not whether blustering Autumn/break the promises of Spring!"
   Actions: advises listeners to enjoy the present
   Feelings: feels it's important to avoid worrying about the future

   "A Tree Telling of Orpheus"
   Words: "as no tree listens I listened"
   Actions: uproots itself to follow Orpheus
   Feelings: feels deeply moved by the music

2. The speaker could be the poet or the wind, as in "With my living, with my singing" and "I broke off the flowers…"

3. The image of a tree so moved as to uproot itself and dance is a dramatic metaphor for the emotional power of music.

4. **(a)** The speaker in "In the Orchard" uses the most formal language. **(b)** The use of imperatives suggests the speaker considers himself or herself to be capable of giving advice about life.

5. **(a)** The speaker in "A Storm in the Mountains" expresses the most wonder. **(b)** The speaker in "In the Orchard" expresses the most enthusiasm. **(c)** The tree in "A Tree Telling of Orpheus" is the most thoughtful.

6. They call upon sight and touch.

7. Possible response: The image of time flying and shutting the gate underscores the "seize the day" theme.

8. Possible response: The image of the coldness in the candle (a combination of touch and sight) effectively suggests the lifelessness of the sickness of boredom, from which Orpheus' song has rescued the grove of trees.

9. Students may cite any of the poems to argue for preserving nature.

❶ Vocabulary Development

Word Analysis

1. ad hoc
2. de facto
3. status quo

Fluency

1. High humidity and temperatures in the region will produce <u>sultry</u> weather for the next few days.
2. The tremor split highways and buildings <u>asunder</u>.
3. View the magnificent volcano from <u>terra firma</u> in our earthquake-proof lodge.

Spelling Strategy

1. contrar<u>y</u>
2. coll<u>ie</u>
3. vall<u>ey</u>
4. fores<u>ee</u>

❷ Grammar

1. chirping of the birds, object of a preposition
2. a dry tingling, direct object
3. his playing, subject
4. singing, object of a preposition
5. our longing, direct object

Writing Application

Sample sentences:

1. Her speaking was inspirational to the crowd.
2. Many nights I wake up in the middle of dreaming about the next day.

Integrate Language Skills

❶ Vocabulary Development Lesson

Word Analysis: Latin Terms

The narrator in "A Storm in the Mountains" felt himself on *terra firma*. *Terra firma*—meaning "solid earth"—is one of many Latin phrases used in English. You may also encounter these Latin terms:

ad hoc: for a specific purpose

status quo: the existing state of things

de facto: in reality

Complete each sentence below with the correct Latin term from the list above.

1. The board assembled an ____?____ committee to handle budget issues.
2. Kim had the title of editor, but we knew that Ms. Lao was the ____?____ editor.
3. The group wanted to do something to change the ____?____.

Fluency: Clarify Word Meaning

Respond to the sentences using your knowledge of the words from the vocabulary list on page 511.

1. Write a weather forecast using *sultry*.
2. Use *asunder* to describe the effects of an earthquake.
3. Use *terra firma* in a passage about travel.

Spelling Strategy

The long *e* sound at the end of a word is often spelled with a *y*, as in *sultry*. It can also be spelled with *ie* as in *cookie*, *ey* as in *monkey*, or *ee* as in *agree*. Spell these words correctly, adding letters for the final long *e* sound:

1. contrar___
2. coll___
3. vall___
4. fores___

❷ Grammar Lesson

Gerunds and Gerund Phrases

A **gerund** is a verb form ending in *-ing* that acts as a noun. A **gerund phrase** includes a gerund with its modifiers and complements.

Gerunds and gerund phrases perform the same roles as nouns: subject, direct or indirect object, predicate nominative, object of a preposition, and appositive. Notice how gerunds are used in these examples:

Subject: *Singing* can be powerful.

Direct Object: We loved his *singing*.

Object of a Preposition: The tree responded to his *singing*.

Practice Copy the following sentences. Then, underline the gerunds or gerund phrases, and tell how each functions.

1. There is music in the chirping of the birds.
2. What I felt was no longer a dry tingling.
3. His playing of the lyre excited the trees.
4. You would have thought we would have lost the sound of the lyre, of the singing.
5. He stilled our longing.

Writing Application Use the following gerunds as indicated.

1. speaking (subject)
2. dreaming (object of a preposition)

*W*G *Prentice Hall Writing and Grammar Connection: Chapter 20, Section 1*

520 ◆ *Expanding Horizons*

TEACHING RESOURCES

The following resources can be used to enrich or extend the instruction for pp. 520–521.

Vocabulary

📖 **Selection Support:** Build Vocabulary, p. 133

📖 **Vocabulary and Spelling Practice Book**
(Use this booklet for skills enrichment.)

Grammar

📖 **Selection Support:** Build Grammar Skills, p. 134

*W*G **Writing and Grammar,** Platinum Level, p. 454 ■

📖 **Daily Language Practice Transparencies**

Writing

*W*G **Writing and Grammar,** Platinum Level, p. 32

💿 **Writing and Grammar iText CD-ROM** ■

■ **BLOCK SCHEDULING:** Resources marked with this symbol provide varied instruction during 90-minute blocks.

❸ Writing Lesson

Monologue

A monologue is a speech delivered by one character without interruption from others. "A Tree Telling of Orpheus" could be read as a monologue delivered by a tree. Paraphrase some of the tree's lines, and write a monologue delivered by the tree in the poem.

Prewriting Reread the poem, and make a timeline that puts the events in order. First, choose which event you want to write about. Then, decide what the speaker would say about the situation, and jot down ideas.

Tree senses   Tree rips roots out
the rippling.   of the ground.

Drafting Make sure your speaker responds to the situation with emotion. Bring out the speaker's personality and attitude with emotional words and comments.

Revising Review your monologue to determine whether you have effectively communicated the speaker's feelings and attitudes. If not, revise to strengthen these elements.

 Prentice Hall Writing and Grammar Connection: Chapter 3, Section 1

❹ Extension Activities

Listening and Speaking With a partner, role-play a **television interview** with the narrator of "A Storm in the Mountains" to discuss his memorable mountain experience. In your dialogue, bring out the following:

- The narrator's knowledge of the mountains and what a storm would be like in that setting
- The narrator's emotions and reactions during and after the experience

Practice your interview, and then perform it for your class. **[Group Activity]**

Research and Technology The Black Mountain School, the artistic community in which Denise Levertov participated, had a major influence on the arts in America. Gather materials from a variety of sources—poems, photographs, audio- and videotapes—and then give a **multimedia presentation** about this school.

 Take It to the Net   www.phschool.com

Go online for an additional research activity using the Internet.

---

❸ Writing Lesson

- Remind students that a monologue is a speech delivered by one person without interruption.
- Have students reread the poem and determine what they think the speaker would say in his or her monologue.
- Have students draft a monologue and revise with help from other students. Students can help determine whether the "voice" of the speaker is consistent throughout, and whether the speaker's emotion is communicated clearly.

❹ Extension Activities

Listening and Speaking

- Have students reread the poem to gather sensory details and infer emotions from the speaker's voice and word choice.
- Have students work in pairs to create a list of questions they would ask the speaker. Then, have them draft answers to each question.
- Tell students that they can use their imagination to supplement the information offered in the poem. However, this new information should be consistent with the speaker's attitude and experience.
- Use the rubric for Interview Techniques, p. 27 in **Performance Assessment and Portfolio Management,** to assess students' interviews.

CUSTOMIZE INSTRUCTION for Universal Access

To address different learning styles, use the following activities suggested in the **Extension Activities** booklet, p. 34.

- For Visual/Spatial Learners, use Activity 5.
- For Musical/Rhythmic and Interpersonal Learners, use Activity 6.
- For Bodily/Kinesthetic and Interpersonal Learners, use Activity 7.

ASSESSMENT RESOURCES

The following resources can be used to assess students' knowledge and skills.

Selection Assessment
- Formal Assessment, pp. 116–118
- Open Book Test, pp. 100–102
- Got It! Assessment Videotapes, Tape 3
- Test Bank Software

 Take It to the Net
Visit www.phschool.com for self-tests and additional questions on the selections.

Listening and Speaking Rubric
- Performance Assessment and Portfolio Management, p. 27

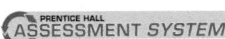 PRENTICE HALL ASSESSMENT *SYSTEM*
- Workbook
- Skill Book
- Transparencies
- CD-ROM

Lesson Objectives

1. To analyze cause-and-effect explanations
2. To understand the elements of cause-and-effect articles
3. To identify causes and effects in other texts and in real-life situations

About Cause-and-Effect Articles

- Have students read "About Cause-and-Effect Articles." Then, discuss cause-and-effect pieces students have read recently, including newspaper items, magazine articles, and textbook sections.

- Engage students in a discussion about the importance of cause-and-effect articles. Why are they written? Why do people read them?
  Possible response: Such articles are written to explain how something works. People read them in order to understand a subject better and to make informed decisions in matters such as diet, medical care, purchases of appliances, environmental issues, and in any other field where cause-and-effect relationships affect the quality of their lives.

Reading Strategy

Analyzing Cause and Effect

- Have students read the information about the Reading Strategy.

- Review with students the bulleted list of elements in a cause-and-effect article. Make sure students understand that each of these elements concerns effective communication with a reader—each makes it easier for a reader to understand a writer's cause-and-effect explanations.

- Explain to students that increasing their understanding of the structure of cause-and-effect articles will help them get more out of reading such articles.

- Call students' attention to the chart of causes and effects. Instruct them to create a similar chart in their notebooks and to fill it in as they read the article.

Cause-and-Effect Articles

About Cause-and-Effect Articles

Cause-and-effect relationships are explored in many types of writing as writers work to explain the reasons behind events or situations. Feature articles in your daily newspaper often describe causes and effects in politics, crime, or the environment. History textbooks are focused primarily on causes and effects, as well. Even something as common as a recipe may describe a cause-and-effect process.

In a cause-and-effect article, a writer explains how a process works. He or she relates the causes of a process with their corresponding effects. In "Lightning and Thunder," the writer explains the causes and effects of a natural phenomenon.

Reading Strategy

Analyzing Cause and Effect

Cause and effect is a structure that shows the connection between events. A **cause** is an event or a force that brings about another event (its **effect**). The effect of one event can also be the cause of another event.

In "Lightning and Thunder," the writer explains how the attraction between charges in a cloud and charges in the ground causes an effect—the flow of negative charges from the cloud to the ground below. This occurrence is one in the series that causes lightning.

Look for these elements as you read "Lightning and Thunder."

- A clearly stated topic that explains what cause-and-effect relationships will be explored
- An effective and logical method of organization
- Details and examples that elaborate upon the writer's statements
- Transitions that smoothly and clearly connect the writer's ideas

Use a chart like the one here to list three causes and their effects, as described in the article.

Negative charges collect at the bottom of a cloud.

Causes

Effect: Positive charges collect on the ground below.

Causes

Effect:

Lightning and Thunder

Science text from
The Nature Company Guides: Weather

Lightning is the result of a build-up of opposite electrical charges within a cumulonimbus cloud.[1] Exactly how this happens is not yet clear, but it seems that ice crystals, which form in the upper part of the cloud, are generally positively charged while water droplets, which tend to sink to the bottom of the cloud, are normally negatively charged. It may be that updrafts carry the positive charges up and downdrafts[2] drag the negative charges down.

As this build-up occurs, a positive charge also forms near the ground under the cloud and moves with the cloud.

Opposites Attract

The opposing electrical charges are strongly attracted to each other. Eventually, the insulating[3] layer of air between the charges cannot keep them apart any longer and a discharge takes place. Negative charges move toward positive charges in an invisible, jagged, zigzag pattern, called a stepped leader.

1. **cumulonimbus** (kyōō′ myōō lō nim′ bəs) **cloud** type of dense cloud developing vertically through all cloud levels; associated with thunder, lightning, and heavy showers.
2. **updrafts . . . downdrafts** air currents blowing up and down, respectively.
3. **insulating** (in′ sə lāt′ iŋ) *adj.* not allowing the passage of electric current.

> The writer provides a general description of what causes lightning.

> Transitional words and phrases help connect ideas logically.

Lightning and Thunder

- Tell students that they will encounter articles like the one shown in many situations in the future. Magazines of all subjects offer cause-and-effect articles, as do newspapers, political pamphlets, and brochures. Students will also see cause-and-effect explanations in television commercials and infomercials.
- Have students read the article and the notes that identify its main elements.
- Ask students why they think the writer begins the article with a general description of the cause of lightning.
  Answer: The general description gives readers an overview of the topic. They can then fit details in place as they continue reading, holding this general idea in mind.

CUSTOMIZE INSTRUCTION FOR UNIVERSAL ACCESS

For Special Needs Students	For Gifted/Talented Readers
To help students understand the technical descriptions, work with them to paraphrase each part of the article. You may want to draw concepts on the chalkboard or overhead projector so students have a visual to better understand.	Have students work with partners to draw diagrams of the technical concepts described in the article. Remind students to clearly label their diagrams. You may want to use these student diagrams when working through the article with Special Needs Students and Less Proficient Readers.

Diagrams in Cause-and-Effect Articles

- Have students examine the diagram and the note that accompanies it.
- Ask students to discuss how this diagram helps readers understand the complex ideas described in the article. Ask them: Which impresses on you most clearly the direction in which the visible lightning travels?

  Possible response: Students may note that the diagram, with its use of a clear, simple arrow, emphasizes more forcefully the idea that most lightning travels upward.

- Ask students: Which information do you need from the article to understand the diagram?

  Possible responses: Students may note that the discussion in the article of positive and negative charges helps them understand the plus and minus signs in the diagram; that the article explains the concept of a "leader"; that the article explains why lightning causes thunder, while the diagram merely shows at what point in the process thunder arises.

When the negative charge meets the positive charge, a massive electrical current—the lightning bolt—is created and then sustained[4] by a return positive charge back to the cloud. This positive charge travels extremely quickly—about 60,000 miles per second (96,000 kps).

> A diagram helps to clarify the process.

Stage I	Stage 2	Stage 3	Stage 4
Induction*	Stepped Leader	Lightning	Thunder

*Positive charges collect on the ground underneath the negatively charged cloud.

All of this can be repeated rapidly in the same lightning bolt, which gives the lightning its flickering appearance. The process continues until all the charges in the cloud have dissipated.[5]

> To explain causes and effects, the writer acknowledges what usually happens.

Most discharges take place within a cloud, between clouds, or between a cloud and the air if there is sufficient charge in the air. Only about one in four lightning bolts strikes the ground. When this happens, the descending leader attracts ground-level positive charges upward, usually from an elevated object such as a tree or building. A lightning bolt that travels all the way from the top of a cloud to negatively charged ground outside the area beneath the cloud is known as a positive flash.

All forms of lightning may appear as forked, sheet, or streaked lightning, depending on how far the observer is from the charge.

> The author also describes two rare forms of lightning: ball lightning and Saint Elmo's fire.

The Sound and the Fury

The temperature of a lightning bolt exceeds 40,000° F (22,000° C). When a bolt forms, the air around it is superheated, which causes the air to expand then contract rapidly. This creates sound waves that we hear as thunder.

---

4. **sustained** (sə stānd´) kept in existence.
5. **dissipated** (dis´ ə pāt´ id) disappeared; become scattered.

Because light waves travel much faster than sound waves, we see the lightning before hearing the thunder. It takes about 5 seconds for thunder to travel 1 mile (3 seconds/km), so it's possible to calculate how far away a storm is by counting the seconds between seeing the lightning flash and hearing the thunder, and dividing by five, for miles (or three, for km). Generally, thunder is inaudible farther than 20 miles (32 km) away.

Sparks May Fly

There are two other types of atmospheric electricity. A rare form, known as ball lightning, occurs when some of the charge from a cloud-to-ground strike forms a small, round ball. This ball of light may roll along the ground or climb objects until it either explodes or dissipates.

Sometimes, when the build-up of opposite charges is insufficient for a lightning bolt to form, a mass of sparks appears high above the ground in the vicinity of the thunderstorm. This phenomenon was first noted at the top of ships' masts and was subsequently named St. Elmo's fire, after the patron saint of sailors.

Check Your Comprehension

1. Where do the causes of lightning begin?
2. How fast do the positive charges travel?
3. What percentage of lightning bolts hit the ground?
4. Why do you see lightning before you hear thunder?
5. What causes St. Elmo's fire?

Applying the Reading Strategy

Analyzing Cause and Effect

6. Cite three cause-and-effect relationships described in the article.
7. Outline each step leading to the formation of a normal lightning flash between cloud and ground.
8. What prevents some lightning bolts from striking the ground?
9. What factor causes the difference between forked and sheet lightning?

Activity

Generating a Cause-and-Effect Flowchart

Consider the cause-and-effect connections related to one of the following aspects of modern life. Using a chart like the one shown, make a flowchart that shows at least two causes and two effects.

- Volunteerism
- Stress among students
- Rush-hour traffic
- War

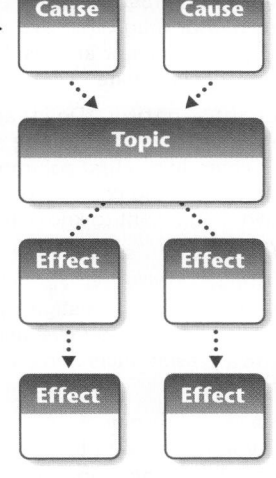

Contrasting Informational Materials

Cause-and-Effect Articles and Weather Reports

1. Contrast the information presented in this article with information you might gather while watching the weather report on television.
2. What accounts for the differences between the formats?
3. Would you recommend that television meteorologists adopt a more scientific approach to their broadcasts? Why or why not?

in the subject, and represent them clearly in their flow charts. You may want to display students' flow charts and have students discuss the different causes and effects they came up with for each subject.

Contrasting Informational Materials

1. The information in this article explains more about physical processes than a television weather report. A weather report, by contrast, describes particular existing weather patterns and uses them to make a prediction about future conditions. A weather report might tell you that lightning is expected, but not what takes place when it occurs.

2. A weather report's purpose is to alert people to what the weather will be like for the next few days—its purpose is not to explain how weather is created. The cause-and-effect article's purpose is to explain how lighting and thunder are created.

3. Possible response: Students might suggest that meteorologists give a weekly in-depth feature on the causes of the weather; they may note, though, that detailed explanations of these causes in every report would hinder viewers from quickly obtaining a clear idea of the forecast.

525

Lesson Objectives

1. To write a research report
2. To learn the elements of research writing
3. To use writing strategies to generate ideas, plan, organize, evaluate, and revise the report

Model From Literature

In the essay "What Makes a Degas a Degas?", Richard Mühlberger reports on Edgar Degas's painting style and techniques.

Prewriting

- To help students choose a topic for their reports, suggest they make a list of things that interest them. Tell them they can include people, careers, places, religions, groups, organizations, conflicts, and historical backgrounds on their lists.

- Remind students to find reliable sources as they research their topics. They must evaluate each source to ensure that the information it presents is credible. Also, instruct them to record every source they utilize and from which source quotations came. This will make double-checking facts, gathering additional details, and supplying citations and a bibliography much easier.

- Point out that, depending on their topics, some students may be able to conduct their own investigative research. Supply students with models of interview questions, polls, surveys, and experiments.

- Tell students that once they have compiled their research, they should take some time to think about what point they want to make with all this information. Encourage them to write a thesis statement to help them focus their writing as they begin the first draft.

Writing WORKSHOP

Research Writing

When you do **research writing,** you write about information gathered from outside sources. In this workshop, you will write a research report on a topic of interest to you.

Assignment Criteria Your research writing should have the following characteristics:

- A specific, narrow topic that is summarized in a thesis statement
- Relevant information from primary and secondary sources
- Logical, effective organization
- Identification of sources from which the information was drawn

To preview the criteria on which your research writing may be assessed, see the Rubric on page 531.

Prewriting

Choose a topic. Choose a topic for research writing by following your instincts and interests. If you seem to be stuck, try **scanning headlines** in a newspaper or magazine. Use a marker or self-sticking notes to indicate intriguing headlines or articles. Review your notes to find a topic you want to investigate.

Gather information. Do library research to build a foundation for your report. To organize and focus your search, make a K-W-L chart. In the first column, write what you already know. In the second column, generate research questions about what you want to know. In the final column, write what you learned.

Consider investigative research. Supplement your library research with investigative research. By conducting interviews, polls, surveys, and experiments, you can sometimes present facts and quotations that no one else has gathered.

Write a preliminary thesis statement. Even before your research begins, you might want to write a tentative thesis statement—a sentence that summarizes the point you will address in your research and in your paper. It will help you clarify your goals and focus your research. You can revise the thesis statement as you work and refine your ideas. When you are ready to begin a draft, include your thesis statement in your opening paragraph.

Sample
Thesis Statement: Dreams have always made a difference in people's lives.

Know | Want to Know | Learned

526 ◆ *Expanding Horizons*

TEACHING RESOURCES

The following resources can be used to enrich or extend the instruction for pp. 526–531.

WG **Writing and Grammar,** Platinum Level, Chapter 12, pp. 244–269

📖 **Performance Assessment and Portfolio Management,** p. 13

📄 **Writing Models and Graphic Organizers on Transparencies,** pp. 87–90

💿 **Writing and Grammar iText CD-ROM**
Students can use the following tools as they complete their research reports:

- Self-Interview
- Transition Word Bin
- Unity and Coherence Checker

Student Model

Before you begin drafting, read this student model and review the characteristics of effective research writing.

Lisa Maiden
Phoenix, Arizona

In Your Dreams

Ever since humans have existed, dreams have made a difference in people's lives. Julius Caesar's wife, Calpurnia, once dreamed that Caesar's statue spurted blood like a fountain while the Romans smiled and bathed in it. This nightmarish picture foreshadowed reality when Caesar was later assassinated. In 1793, Marie Antoinette had a dream of a red sun and pillar. After the sun rose, it suddenly set; this immediately preceded her beheading. Then, there is Robert Louis Stevenson, who believed his best stories came from dreams, including the infamous "Dr. Jekyll and Mr. Hyde." Neils Bohr dreamed of sitting on the sun with planets whizzing around him on small cords; he then developed the model of an atom. Even Genghis Khan claimed to receive his battle plans from his sleepy nights.

> The writer begins by introducing the topic in a concise sentence.

Who were the early interpreters of such dreams? Aristotle and Freud, of course, were among the scholars who labored over dream interpretation. Aristotle suggested that dreams were formed by disturbances in the body. Freud, however, believed that dreams were powerful tools for uncovering unconscious wishes. He said, "The purpose of dreams is to allow us to satisfy in fantasies the instinctual urges that society judges unacceptable" (Dreams: History, 2000).

Even today, creative people use their dreams in solving problems. A 1995 *Reader's Digest* article entitled "Why We Dream What We Dream" provides many examples. One such dreamer was the scientist Dmitri Ivanovich Mendeleev. He "saw" the periodic table of the elements in a dream and wrote it down the following day. Later, only one correction was needed. Screenwriter James Cameron dreamed of a robot with a red eye staring back at him. He woke up and wrote the script for *The Terminator*. Steve Allen's hit song "This Could Be the Start of Something Big" also began from a dream, as did the new way of swinging the club that allowed Jack Nicklaus to overcome his golfing problem (Kreisler, 28–38).

> In the body of her essay, the writer credits the source of her information.

> The writer incorporates a variety of sources in her research.

Besides being helpful in the creative aspect, dreams have, in many cases, foretold the future. In the weeks prior to his murder, Abraham Lincoln dreamed the White House was in mourning for an assassinated president. The video *The Secret World of Dreams* tells of a man whose dreams indicated a chronic illness even before it was diagnosed, as well as a man whose recurring nightmares of an explosion prepared him for the real thing and enabled him to save the life of a coworker. Unsolved mysteries.com shows

Writing Workshop ◆ 527

Student Model

- Explain that the Student Model is a sample, and that reports may be longer.
- Ask students to identify the topic and the thesis statement.
  Answer: The topic is dreams. The thesis statement is "Dreams have made a difference in people's lives."
- Point out that Lisa identifies the sources of her information throughout her report, and that she has used many different sources during her research.
- Point out that clear topic sentences and the use of details in a paragraph to support them also creates coherent organization.

Real-World Connection

Explain to students that research writing is not limited to nonfiction literary works. Students will most likely be required to produce research writing in college classes, as well as in business situations. For example, they may be asked to find out more information about a topic and report back to their company on their findings.

CUSTOMIZE INSTRUCTION FOR UNIVERSAL ACCESS

For Less Proficient Writers	For English Learners	For Advanced Writers
When students have decided on a topic, encourage them to us the Cubing organizer in **Writing Models and Graphic Organizers on Transparencies**, pp. 87–90, to better analyze their topic.	Once students have chosen a topic, have them analyze it in terms of *who?*, *what? when? where? why?* and *how?* Answers to these questions can form the outline for the report.	Challenge students to choose to report on an historical figure whom they do not admire, or a controversial event, or an event that had a negative impact on society.

Student Model

- Point out the organization of the report to students: After introducing the significance of dreams in creative work and as possible predictions of the future, the writer moves to aspects of the study of dreams, including dream symbols and the differences in dreams at various stages of life.

- Explain that this organization is made clear to the reader through the use of transitions. Ask students to identify the transitional sentences in paragraphs 5 and 6 and explain how they function as transitions.

  Answer: In paragraph 5, the transitional sentence is "However, to understand one's dreams, one must uncover the meaning of dream symbols." Using the word *however*, it signals a change of focus from the preceding paragraph, and it announces the new focus: dream symbols. In paragraph 6, the transitional sentence is "While dreams can be interpreted according to symbols, the most common types of dreams vary throughout the human life cycle." The word *while* signals the shift in focus; the sentence both refers to the subject of the preceding paragraph (the interpretation of dream symbols) and announces the new focus: the changes in type of dreams at various stages of life.

- Call students' attention to paragraph 6. Ask them to identify the topic sentence and supporting details.

  Answer: The topic sentence is "People at different places in their lives tend to dream differently." Supporting details include information about and examples of children's, men's, and women's dreams.

how dreams can bring luck with the report of a lottery winner from Maine whose dreams revealed a winning ticket (Unsolved Mysteries Home Page, screen 1). Given such cases as these, it is no mystery that modern psychology still believes in the prophetic power of dreams.

However, to understand one's dreams, one must uncover the meaning of dream symbols. Psychoanalyst Sigmund Freud said that the secret to the symbols in dreams lies within the dreamer (Bentley, p. 4). In other words, individuals can interpret dream symbols from their own lives and the imagery around them—not just by using a dream dictionary. Sleeps.com gives just a few examples of these symbols. For instance, to most dreamers, clothing symbolizes mood, attitude, or state of mind. One who wears a uniform in a dream may be influenced too much by society, while having clothes that are too short may suggest a longing for the pleasures of youth now gone. Death is also a recurring symbol. Whether the dreamer attends a funeral or is put in a coffin, these pictures signify a change in one's attitude toward life or one's emotional balance. Finally, other people occur in dreams as reflections of the person's own personality traits. For instance, if a dreamer is faced by the stares of others, that person may be worried about making a bad impression on other people (Dream Analysis and Interpretation, screens 6, 7).

While dreams can be interpreted according to symbols, the most common types of dreams vary throughout the human life cycle. People at different places in their lives tend to dream differently. Children's dreams reflect new impressions that they encounter each day. Bold geometric shapes are not just building blocks with which they play, but they represent a fixation with family relationships. For example, a triangle would signify the relationship among the father, mother, and child. Dreams of giants indicate a child's impression of his or her own size and sense of self-worth. Naturally, everything is bigger to a child, but a child with giant proportions compared to the world around him may have an increasing self-awareness (Bentley, p. 25). Much like a scene from *The Nutcracker,* toys come to life as the child lives out fantasies, showing developments of the young person's persona. As children become teens, they dream more about romance. Among adults, men and women dream differently. "It's biology and social conditioning," says Milton Kramer, director of the Bethesda Oak Hospital's Sleep Center in Cincinnati. Research has shown that men dream twice as often of other men as they do of women, while women tend to have an equal number of dreams of both sexes (*New Scientist,* p. 2). A study by Robert Van de Castle, author of

> Each paragraph includes a topic sentence, which is then supported in the paragraph with details.

528

Our Dreaming Mind, analyzed 1,000 dreams and found that men have more action-oriented dreams, while women imagine more emotional one-on-one struggles with loved ones (Van de Castle, p. 45).

Studies are also beginning to show that a person's attitude can influence his or her dreams. University of Pennsylvania professor Aaron Beck found that angry people are the ones throwing punches in their dreams, while depressed people often find themselves the victims of rejection. However, people who have a hard time standing up for themselves are the ones likely to suffer from restless nightmares. (Kreisler, 36)

Through the fascinating history of dreams, the interpretation of some dream symbols, and the secret dreams of different sleepers, it is evident that dreams are important. They provide valuable insights, help solve problems, spark new thoughts and creations, and even foretell the future. Maybe people should pay more attention to their dreams. The hours one spends sleeping could be the key to a better life.

Works Cited

Bentley, Peter. *Book of Dream Symbols.* Chronicle Books, 1995.

"Dream Analysis and Interpretation, Doing It!" 9 March 2000: 6,7.
　　<http://www.sleeps.com/analysis.html>

"Dreams: History." 22 Mar. 2000.
　　<http://library.thinkquest.org/11130/data/history/history.html>

"Get Real, Siggi." *New Scientist,* 26 April 1997: 2,5. 21 March 2000.
　　<http://www.newscientist.com/ns/970426/siggi.html>

Great Moments in Dream History Home Page. 7 March 2000: 1–3.
　　<http://www.dr-dream.com/hist.htm>

Kreisler, Kristin V. "Why We Dream What We Dream." *Reader's Digest,*
　　Feb. 1995: 28, 30, 34–36, 38.

Kramer, Milton. Personal Interview. 10 March 2000.

The Secret World of Dreams. Videotape. Questar Video, 1997. 80 min.

Van de Castle, Robert L. *Our Dreaming Mind.* Ballantine, 1995.

"Winning the Lottery in Your Dreams." Unsolved Mysteries Home Page.
　　11 March 2000: 1.
　　<http://unsolvedmysteries.com/usm397.html>

> Using a standard format, Lisa lists the sources from which her information was drawn.

Drafting

- Explain to students that their research reports should be organized logically and clearly. Students will have an easier time drafting their essays once they identify how they want to organize their research.

- Remind students that their goal should not be to fill up space on a page with everything they have learned, but rather to fill out a picture or prove a point using only information that directly and clearly applies.

Revising

- Before students start to revise their work, have them write down the overall point they wish to make in their report. As they read through their drafts, students should keep this point in mind to help them determine how each sentence in each paragraph works to develop and support this overall point.

- Review the model with students. Have students describe how Lisa ordered her information to create a strong, coherent report.

Drafting

Organize your information. To present the information you have gathered, develop a draft that follows a logical organization. Research writing may follow one of several organizational strategies, as this chart shows. Choose the order that matches the content and purpose of your writing.

Provide relevant support. As you draft, draw upon both your library research and your investigative research to provide relevant, substantive support for your thesis statement and related ideas. Avoid information that does not directly and clearly support your main ideas.

Organizational Strategy	Uses
Chronological Order	Use for historical topics and science experiments
Part-to-Whole Order	Use for examining how categories affect a larger subject
Order of Importance	Use when building a persuasive argument

Prepare to credit sources. When you include a direct quotation, present an original idea that is not your own, or report a fact that is available in only one source, you must include documentation. As you draft, circle ideas or words that are not your own. Use parentheses to note the author's last name and the page numbers of the material used. Later, you can use this record to make a formal citation list.

Revising

Revise to strengthen coherence. Because a research report is a big project, details can easily become lost or out of order. As a first step in revising, take a look at the big picture. What seems out of place? How can you strengthen the flow of information? Use this revision strategy:

1. On a separate sheet of paper, write the main idea of each paragraph.

2. Read your notes from beginning to end to see whether they flow together in a logical order.

3. Rearrange paragraphs or sections that sound awkward, or cut sections that stray from your thesis statement.

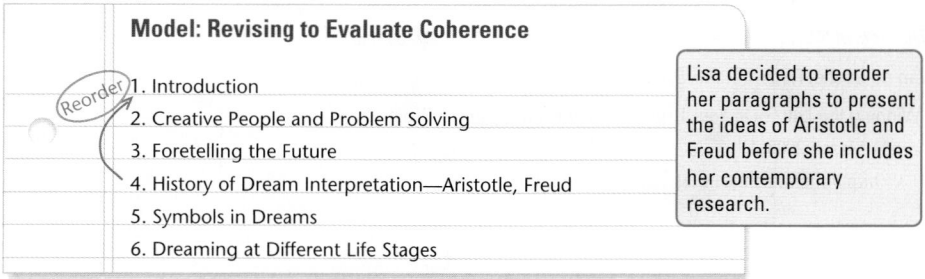

Model: Revising to Evaluate Coherence

Reorder 1. Introduction
2. Creative People and Problem Solving
3. Foretelling the Future
4. History of Dream Interpretation—Aristotle, Freud
5. Symbols in Dreams
6. Dreaming at Different Life Stages

Lisa decided to reorder her paragraphs to present the ideas of Aristotle and Freud before she includes her contemporary research.

USING TECHNOLOGY IN WRITING

If students are using word processors to draft and revise their research reports and decide they wish to order their information differently, suggest that they use the cut-and-paste function to quickly move their sentences and paragraphs to different places in the report.

Students can also use the organizing tools and revision checkers available on the **Writing and Grammar iText CD-ROM.**

Revise your sentences. When most of the sentences within a paper are similar in length, type, and structure, it can have a numbing effect on the reader. Review your draft to evaluate sentence length and the rhythm and flow of your writing. Add short sentences to break a pattern of long ones, or combine short sentences.

Revise your word choice. A research report often results in several pages of writing. Unnecessary words weigh it down and make it difficult to read.

> **Wordy:** Thus, in conclusion, one can see from careful observation that political conflict often leads to economic change.
>
> **Concise:** In conclusion, political conflict often leads to economic change.

Publishing and Presenting

Compile a reference list. As a final step in the preparation of your research report, your research writing should document your sources of information. A works-cited page provides readers with full bibliographic information on each source that you cite in your paper. Standards for documentation are set by several organizations.

Identify the format your teacher prefers. Follow that format, and check that each entry is complete and properly punctuated. (For more information, see Writing Criticism and Citing Sources, pages R26–R28.)

Choose one of the following ways to share your writing with classmates or a wider audience.

Publish on the Internet. Post your research writing on a Web site that publishes student writing, or send your report to a friend or relative by attaching it to an e-mail.

File your report with your librarian. Make a copy of your report, and ask your school librarian to place it in the library files. It can be a resource for other students researching the topic.

Rubric for Self-Assessment

Evaluate your research writing using the following criteria and rating scale:

Criteria	Rating Scale				
	Not very				Very
How clear and focused is the thesis statement?	1	2	3	4	5
How logically is the information organized?	1	2	3	4	5
How clear and well supported are the conclusions?	1	2	3	4	5
How well are the sources credited?	1	2	3	4	5
How fluent and error free is the language?	1	2	3	4	5

Revising (continued)

- Tell students that using fewer words to say something is always more desirable than using many words that add nothing to the meaning. Explain that it takes a kind of courage to eliminate unnecessary words, because it exposes exactly what one means to a reader. Encourage students to trust in the strength of their meaning as they revise.

Publishing and Presenting

- Make sure to provide students with your requirements for the bibliography page and a model for them to follow.
- Ask students to think about the audience they had in mind when they wrote their reports.
- Then, have them consider a publication or Web site for which their report would be well suited. Once students have decided on a publication or Web site, suggest that they review their reports to make sure they are appropriate for that particular audience.

Assessment

- Review with students the assessment criteria.
- Have students choose three criteria from the rubric and score the Student Model. Make sure students support their scores with details from the Model. Then, have them use the same criteria to score their own reports.
- The rubric on this page, and another rubric in an alternative format, can be found on pp. 13 and 47 of **Performance Assessment and Portfolio Management.**

TEST-TAKING TIP

When students are taking a test that requires them to respond to an expository writing prompt, they should spend some time organizing how they want to order the information in their responses. After students have brainstormed what they want to include in their responses, encourage them to use an outline to organize that information. A few minutes spent organizing will make the drafting and revising stages much easier.

Objectives

1. To learn to analyze and evaluate five common persuasive arguments and appeals
2. To learn to analyze and evaluate persuasive presentations

Evaluate the Content

- Have students read the "Evaluate the Content" section on p. 532.
- Tell students that when listening to a persuasive speech, they should analyze the types of strategies a speaker uses and how they are used.
- Ask students to name and define one type of argument or appeal. Encourage students to suggest an example of a person who characteristically uses this type of argument or appeal, such as the president or some other public speaker. Ask them where they can find this type of appeal in television commercials.

Evaluate the Presentation

- Have students read the "Evaluate the Presentation" section on p. 532.
- To prepare them to complete the Activity, explain to students that if a speaker's ideas are not clearly stated, the argument will be ineffective because listeners will either not understand the point or will not be persuaded.
- Remind students that they should think about the language a speaker uses. Is it appropriate to the occasion? Is it formal or informal? Does it seem apt or out of place?
- Encourage students to pay close attention to whether the speaker uses valid evidence to support his or her argument.
- Have students complete the Activity, and then hold a class discussion in which they share their results.

Listening and Speaking WORKSHOP

Analyzing Types of Arguments

Speakers use different strategies to convince listeners to accept their positions on issues. Before you agree with a speaker's point of view, consider the **types of arguments** used. The following listening strategies will help you analyze the effectiveness of the most common persuasive arguments. The Feedback Form will be a useful aid in your analysis.

Evaluate the Content

Persuasive strategies can be used fairly to build a reasonable argument, or they can be used inappropriately to influence listeners to respond emotionally without fully understanding the evidence.

Analyze types of arguments. Review these types of arguments:

- **Causation** The speaker explains how one event causes another and shows the specific advantages or disadvantages that result.
- **Analogy** The speaker provides a comparison to explain an argument.
- **Appeal to Authority** The speaker argues that evidence or a point of view is correct because an authority on the subject has said it is.
- **Appeal to Emotion** The speaker tries to win agreement by calling on the listener's sympathy, horror, anger, or other emotion.
- **Appeal to Logic** The speaker demonstrates the reasonableness of the position.

Evaluate the Presentation

Use the following techniques to analyze the presentation of the arguments.

Evaluate the organization and coherence. Any speaker's ideas should be clearly stated using a logical organization that demonstrates how the ideas are related.

Evaluate the diction and syntax. Diction is the speaker's choice of words. Syntax is the sentence structure. Together, they should make the arguments clear. Consider whether a speaker's language is appropriate to an occasion.

Analyze the effectiveness of the evidence. Persuasive appeals can enhance a speaker's power to convince. However, the speaker should use arguments to support evidence, not to replace it.

Activity:
Listening and Analysis Listen to an editorial or a commentary on a television news program, and analyze the types of arguments. Use the Feedback Form as a guide in your analysis. Share your findings in a class discussion.

Feedback Form for Analyzing Arguments

Rating System
+ = Excellent   ✔ = Average   – = Weak

Content
Causation _____
Analogies _____
Appeal to authority _____
Appeal to emotions _____
Appeal to logic _____

Presentation
Logical organization _____
Clear, precise diction and syntax _____
Evidence _____

Answer the following questions:
Did the speaker use the types of arguments fairly?

Were you convinced by the speaker's arguments?

CUSTOMIZE INSTRUCTION FOR UNIVERSAL ACCESS

For Less Proficient Readers	For English Learners
Students may have difficulty identifying the different types of argument. Work with students to break down a speech into an outline. Then, using the outline, have students compare the organization and information in the speech to the list of types of arguments or appeals. Engage them in a discussion about what category each argument or appeal falls under.	Students may need to listen to a speech a few times to be able to effectively analyze the argument. Provide such students with a videtaped speech, editorial, or commercial that they can view a few times in succession. Encourage students to analyze the presentation in groups, discussing its content and presentation and filling out a individual Feedback Form.

Assessment WORKSHOP

Graphic Aids

Lesson Objective
To interpret graphic aids in a test situation

In the reading sections of some tests, you may be required to interpret graphs, charts, diagrams, and tables. Use the following strategies:

● Graphs, charts, diagrams, and tables are devices for organizing and presenting information visually. To interpret graphic aids, read the titles, labels, captions, and keys.

● Look for a caption that summarizes or explains the information shown.

Test-Taking Strategies

● Be sure to read the numerical values in graphs in order to distinguish between the types of quantities represented.

● Locate and organize information according to the type of graphic aid that is being used.

Sample Test Item

Directions: Read the passage, and answer the question that follows.

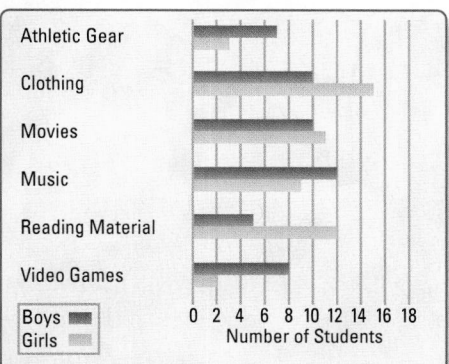

The bar graph above shows the results of a poll regarding student spending habits. Thirty-one students, 17 girls and 14 boys, were asked to list the categories in which they spent money in the last month. The poll shows that most spent money on clothing, movies, and music.

1 In which category do the spending habits of girls and boys differ most?

A clothing

B video games

C reading material

D athletic gear

Answer and Explanation

Answer *C* is correct because the difference between the number of boys and the number of girls spending money for reading material is 7, higher than for any other category. The difference for *A* is 5. The difference for *B* is 6, and the difference for *D* is 4.

▶ Practice

Directions: Refer again to the bar graph and the passage to answer the questions that follow:

1 In which category are the spending habits of girls and boys most alike?

A music

B athletic gear

C movies

D reading material

2 In which two categories do the fewest boys spend money?

A clothing and movies

B athletic gear and reading material

C movies and music

D reading material and video games

Applying Reading Strategies

Students can learn to predict what information will be presented upon first glance at a graphic aid. For example, looking at the bar graph on the student page, students can probably guess that the information is about student buying habits.

Applying Test-Taking Strategies

• Have students examine the bar graph in the Sample Test Item. Ask them to guess what information they think the graph presents.

• Then, have students read the paragraph below the bar graph. Ask students to write down the information contained in the bar graph. Answer: The bar graph shows the spending habits of thiry-one students.

Answers

1. The correct answer is C. The difference between the number of boys and the number of girls who spent money on movies is one. Answer A is incorrect, because the difference between the number of boys and the number of girls who spent money on music is three. Answer B is incorrect, because the difference here is four. Answer D is incorrect, because the difference is seven. Therefore, answer C shows the smallest difference between the two groups.

2. The correct answer is B. Only seven boys spent money on athletic gear and five on reading material. Answer A is incorrect, because ten boys spent money on clothing and ten spent money on movies. Answer C is incorrect, because ten boys spent money on movies and twelve spent money on music. Answer D is incorrect, because, although only five boys spent money on reading materials, eight boys spent money on video games. Answer B lists the categories in which the fewest boys spent money.

TEACHING RESOURCES

The following resources can be used to enrich or extend the instruction for p. 533.

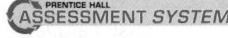

📖 **Workbook**   📖 **Transparencies**

📖 **Skill Book**   💿 **CD-ROM**

Unit Objectives

1. To read short stories which illustrate the different elements of the genre

2. To apply a variety of reading strategies, particularly strategies for constructing meaning, appropriate for reading these selections

3. To analyze literary elements

4. To use a variety of strategies to build vocabulary

5. To learn elements of grammar, usage, and style

6. To use recursive writing processes to write in a variety of forms

7. To develop listening and speaking skills

8. To express and support responses to short stories

9. To prepare, organize, and present literary interpretations

Meeting the Objectives

With each selection, you will find instructional materials through which students can meet these objectives. Further, you will find additional practice pages for reading strategies, literary analysis, vocabulary, and grammar in the **Selection Support: Skills Development Workbook** in your **Teaching Resources.**

Background

Art

Final Departure by Lisa Learner

Guide students through an analysis of the painting. It shows a platform for boarding trains or buses, covered by a barrel roof that lets in the sunlight. The artist draws attention to the contrast between the dark steps and the sunny platform, emphasized by the upward-tilted perspective. Ask students the following question:

If this were the opening of a short story, what might the story be about?

Possible response: Students may suggest the story would be about a character starting a new life.

Final Departure, Lisa Learner

UNIT 6 Short Stories

534 ◆ *Short Stories*

UNIT FEATURES

Connections	Reading Informational Materials
Every unit contains a feature that connects literature to a related topic, such as art, science, or history. In this unit, the excerpt from Hans Magnus Enzensberger's *The Future of Luxury,* pp. 633–635, offers a prediction about the luxuries of the future. Use the information and questions on the Connections pages to enrich students' understanding of the selections presented within the unit.	These selections will help students learn to analyze and evaluate informational texts, such as workplace documents, technical directions, and consumer materials. They will expose students to the organization and features unique to nonnarrative texts. In this unit, students will learn the elements of a Web site.

Exploring the Genre

There are no limits to the places short stories can take you. In a realistic short story, you might share the experiences of someone like yourself. In a science-fiction short story, you might travel to a future world. No matter where you go or whom you meet, however, you can be sure your brief encounter will enrich your life.

Despite their varied content, almost all short stories have the following elements in common:

- **Plot** is the sequence of events that take you through the story.
- **Characters** are the people, animals, or other beings that take part in the action of the story.
- **Setting** is the time and place in which the story takes place.
- **Theme** is the message about life that the story conveys.

▲ **Critical Viewing** What details of the scene in this painting make it a good place to set the beginning of a story? **[Analyze]**

Exploring the Genre ◆ 535

535

Why Read Literature?

The "Why Read Literature?" page in each unit presents a list of possible purposes for reading. Each purpose for reading is connected to one or more of the selections in the unit. Good readers set a purpose before reading to help them read actively and focus on meaningful details.

Unit 6 introduces three purposes for reading. "Read for the Love of Literature" encourages students to explore some surprising situations. "Read to Appreciate the Author's Craft" focuses students' attention on the techniques that authors use to create engaging literature. "Read for Information" encourages students to learn more about Web sites.

How to Use This Page

• Tell students that before reading each selection in this unit, they should set a purpose for reading. This will help them read in a more active and focused manner.

• Explain that they can increase their love of literature by reading about the luck of a bumbler in "Luck" or a little girl's powerful storytelling in "The Open Window."

• A reader will appreciate a story more when he or she better understands the techniques that authors employ, such as the use of suspense in "Leiningen Versus the Ants" or the use of narrative structure in "The Garden of Stubborn Cats."

• Reading to obtain information is another valuable purpose for reading. Students should focus on the specific type of information they want to learn. In "Egyptology Resources Web Site," students can read to learn more about scientists who study ancient cultures.

 # Why Read Literature?

When you read short stories, you have a goal in mind. Whether it is to appreciate, to learn, or even to be informed, you will find that your purpose will vary based on the subject or style of a particular reading. Preview these three purposes you might set before reading the works in this unit.

1 Read for the Love of Literature

As the saying goes, it is sometimes better to be lucky than it is to be good. Discover how one fortunate military officer succeeds despite his bumbling ways in **"Luck,"** by Mark Twain, page 604.

When it comes to mystery and surprise endings, Saki is one of the world's greatest masters. See his talent for yourself as you read **"The Open Window,"** page 540.

2 Read to Appreciate the Author's Craft

In a story about an army of carnivorous ants, Carl Stephenson artfully builds suspense. See how he keeps this tension mounting in **"Leiningen Versus the Ants,"** page 550.

Italo Calvino devised the "fable formula," explaining that all human stories follow a simple structure. See how he applies that idea in **"The Garden of Stubborn Cats,"** page 621.

3 Read for Information

When you go online, you can conduct research on almost any topic. Learn more about scientists who study ancient cultures by reviewing the **Egyptology Resources Web site,** page 591.

  Take It to the Net

Visit the Web site for online instruction and activities related to each selection in this unit.
www.phschool.com

536 ◆ *Short Stories*

⚙ ENRICHMENT: Further Reading

Have students choose one or more of the works below to extend their experience with the unit genre, the short story, or to read more by the unit authors.

"The Winner" by Barbara Kimenye
The story of a man who wins a lot of money

"The Dinner Party" by Mona Gardner
The suspenseful story of a cobra interrupting a dinner and disproving a chauvinistic character's opinion

"The Story of an Hour" by Kate Chopin
The surprising story of a woman who learns of her husband's death

How to Read Literature

Use Strategies for Constructing Meaning

In order to understand a piece of writing fully, you must do more than simply comprehend the writer's words. You have to go a step further and put the words and ideas together in your own mind. Why did the author write it? What idea does he or she want to convey? What does the work mean to you? In looking for answers to questions like these, you construct the meaning that the work has for you. Use these strategies to help you construct meaning:

1. Identify relationships.

- Look for the causes and effects of important actions in order to identify relationships.
- Clarify the sequence of events in the text, and identify which events are of greater and lesser importance.
- Evaluate the relationships among characters to determine motives or potential problems. Consider the relationship between characters in the following passage:

> "My aunt will be down presently, Mr. Nuttel," said a very self-possessed young lady of fifteen; "in the meantime you must try and put up with me." — *from* **"The Open Window"**

When you recognize that the young lady does not know Mr. Nuttel, you may see that she is obligated to entertain him while he waits for her aunt.

2. Draw conclusions.

A conclusion is a logical response that you can make and support with details from the text. Considering your own experience and knowledge may help you draw a conclusion.

3. Make predictions based on plot details.

- Note details that the writer shares. They may help you predict or guess future events.
- Adjust your prediction as you gather new hints from the text. The prediction at right is based on hints the author provides.

4. Clarify.

- Summarize the main idea to clarify things you do not understand.
- Read ahead for more information, or reread to review what you have already learned. You might want to review details of the setting or look back at the details of a key event.

As you read the selections in this unit, apply these strategies to get the most out of what you read.

> **Make Predictions**
>
> If by some miracle the ants managed to cross the water and reach the plantation, this "rampart of petrol" would be an absolutely impassable protection. . . . Such, at least, was Leiningen's opinion. . . .
> —from "Leiningen Versus the Ants"
>
> **Prediction:** The ants will reach the plantation, overcoming the rampart.
> **Reason:** The writer says that Leiningen's idea was only his "opinion."
> **Outcome:**

The "How to Read Literature" page in each unit presents a set of strategies to help readers understand authors' words and ideas. Each reading strategy is taught in conjunction with one or more of the selections within the unit. Good readers develop a bank of strategies from which they can draw as needed.

Unit 6 introduces four strategies for constructing meaning. Students learn to identify relationships among events and among characters, to move beyond the surface of the text by drawing conclusions, to engage more deeply with a story by making predictions, and to clarify difficult or confusing passages.

How to Use This Page

Introduce the strategies for constructing meaning, presenting each as a tool for developing understanding when reading the selections in this unit.

- As they read "The Open Window" (p. 540), students will learn to identify relationships among events and among characters.
- As they read "By the Waters of Babylon" (p. 576), students will learn how to draw conclusions based on details from the text.
- As they read "Leiningen Versus the Ants" (p. 550), students will learn how to predict outcomes to help them better understand what they are reading.
- As they read, "The Garden of Stubborn Cats" (p. 621), students will learn how to clarify parts of the story that seem confusing to them.

MODEL A READING STRATEGY: Clarify

Help students clarify as they read by modeling the process, using this example from "The Garden of Stubborn Cats":

> The city of cats and the city of men exist one inside the other, but they are not the same city. . . .

Say to students:

The first sentence of this story may confuse you: How can two cities "exist one inside the other"? When you read ahead with this question in mind, you will find a sentence suggesting that "the city of men" is those places that human activity makes unsafe or frightening for cats. When you read further, you will see that the "city of cats" is the neglected spaces in the city used by cats.

The Open Window

Lesson Objectives

1. **To analyze and respond to literary elements**
   - Literary Analysis: Plot
   - Connecting Literary Elements: Dialogue
2. **To read, comprehend, analyze, and critique a short story**
   - Reading Strategy: Identifying Relationships
   - Reading Check questions
   - Review and Assess questions
   - Assessment Practice (ATE)
3. **To develop word analysis skills, fluency, and systematic vocabulary**
   - Vocabulary Development Lesson: Words From Names
4. **To understand and apply written and oral language conventions**
   - Spelling Strategy
   - Grammar Lesson: Placement of *only* and *just*
5. **To understand and apply appropriate writing and research strategies**
   - Writing Lesson: Introduction for a Collection
   - Extension Activity: Annotated Reading List
6. **To understand and apply listening and speaking strategies**
   - Extension Activity: Storytelling

STEP-BY-STEP TEACHING GUIDE	PACING GUIDE
PRETEACH	
Motivate Students and Provide Background	
Use the Motivation activity (ATE p. 538)	5 min.
Read and discuss the Preview material and Background information (SE/ATE p. 538) **A**	5 min.
Introduce the Concepts	
Introduce the Literary Analysis and Reading Strategy (SE/ATE p. 539) **A**	10 min.
Pronounce the vocabulary words and read their definitions (SE p. 539)	5 min.
TEACH	
Monitor Comprehension	
Informally monitor comprehension by circulating while students read independently or in groups **A**	10 min.
Monitor students' comprehension with the Reading Check notes (SE/ATE pp. 541, 543)	as students read
Develop vocabulary with Vocabulary notes (SE pp. 542, 544; ATE p. 542)	as students read
Develop Understanding	
Develop students' understanding of plot with Literary Analysis annotations (SE p. 541; ATE p. 541) **A**	5 min.
Develop students' understanding of identifying relationships with Reading Strategy annotations (SE p. 542; ATE pp. 541, 542)	5 min.
ASSESS	
Assess Mastery	
Assess students' mastery of the Reading Strategy and Literary Analysis by having them answer the Review and Assess questions (SE/ATE p. 545)	15 min.
Use one or more of the print and media Assessment Resources (ATE p. 547) **A**	up to 50 min.
EXTEND	
Apply Understanding	
Have students complete the Vocabulary Development Lesson and the Grammar Lesson (SE p. 546) **A**	15 min.
Apply students' knowledge of identifying key points using the Writing Lesson (SE p. 547) **A**	45 min.
Apply students' understanding using one or more of the Extension Activities (SE p. 547)	20–90 min.

 ACCELERATED INSTRUCTION:
Use the strategies and activities identified with an **A**.

UNIVERSAL ACCESS
- ● = Below Level Students
- ▲ = On-Level Students
- ■ = Above Level Students

Time and Resource Manager

RESOURCES		
PRINT 📖	**TRANSPARENCIES** 🗂	**TECHNOLOGY** 💿 🎧 📼
• **Beyond Literature,** Workplace Skills: Letter of Recommendation, p. 35 ▲ ■		• **Interest Grabber Video,** Tape 3 ● ▲ ■
• **Selection Support Workbook:** ● ▲ ■ Literary Analysis, p. 140 Reading Strategy, p. 139 Build Vocabulary, p. 137	• **Literary Analysis and Reading Transparencies,** pp. 69 and 70 ● ▲ ■	
• **Adapted Reader's Companion** ● • **Reader's Companion** ●		• **Listening to Literature** ● ▲ ■ Audiocassettes, Side 15 Audio CDs, CD 10
• **English Learner's Companion** ● ▲ • **Literatura en español** ● ▲ • **Literary Analysis for Enrichment** ■		
• **Formal Assessment:** Selection Test, pp. 123–125 ● ▲ ■ • **Open Book Test,** pp. 103–105 ● ▲ ■ • **Performance Assessment and Portfolio Management,** p. 31 ● ▲ ■ • (ASSESSMENT *SYSTEM*) ● ▲ ■	• (ASSESSMENT *SYSTEM*) ● ▲ ■ Skills Practice Answers and Explanations on Transparencies	• **Test Bank Software** ● ▲ ■ • **Got It! Assessment Videotapes,** Tape 3 ● ▲
• **Selection Support Workbook:** ● ▲ ■ Build Grammar Skills, p. 138 • **Writing and Grammar,** Platinum Level ● ▲ ■ • **Extension Activities,** p. 35 ● ▲ ■	• **Daily Language Practice Transparencies** ● ▲ • **Writing Models and Graphic Organizers on Transparencies,** p. 99 ● ▲ ■	• **Writing and Grammar iText CD-ROM** ● ▲ ■ 💻 *Take It to the Net* www.phschool.com

BLOCK SCHEDULING: Use one 90-minute class period to preteach the selection and have students read it. Use a second 90-minute class period to assess students' mastery of skills and have them complete one of the Extension Activities.

Step-by-Step Teaching Guide for pp. 538-539

Motivation

Draw students into the selection by reading aloud the following passage from the story:

> The child was staring out through the open window with dazed horror in her eyes. In a chill shock of nameless fear Framton swung around in his seat and looked in the same direction.

Have students discuss what kind of story they would expect this quotation to come from. Students might suggest a horror story or a ghost story. Tell them to read "The Open Window" to find out.

▣ Interest Grabber Video

As an alternative, play "The Suspense of Saki" on Tape 3 to engage student interest.

❶ Background

Culture

Around the beginning of the twentieth century—when this story is set—people often presented themselves through letters of introduction—a kind of letter of recommendation that listed a person's accomplishments and personality traits. Mr. Nuttel, a character in this story, arrives at the country home of a "friend of a friend" with just such a letter. Ask students to discuss ways in which people present themselves and make friends today.

Prepare to Read

The Open Window

Summer Breeze, Alice Dalton Brown, Fischbach Gallery, New York

▣ Take It to the Net

Visit www.phschool.com for interactive activities and instruction related to "The Open Window," including
• background
• graphic organizers
• literary elements
• reading strategies

Preview

Connecting to the Literature

The popularity of horror movies shows that many people enjoy fictional stories that shock, frighten, or surprise. Sometimes the same movie that frightens one person may amuse another. In this story, two characters have very different feelings about the same tale.

❶ Background

In the early 1900s, when this story is set, social connections were very important in the leisure lives of people with money and land. A person was judged as much on whom he or she knew as on his or her personality and accomplishments. In this story, Framton Nuttel arrives at the home of a "friend of a friend" with a letter of introduction, hoping to make a new acquaintance.

538 ◆ *Short Stories*

▣ **BLOCK SCHEDULING:** Resources marked with this symbol provide varied instruction during 90-minute blocks.

Literary Analysis

Plot

Plot is the sequence of events that make up a story. In a short story, the plot usually contains five key elements.

- An **exposition** introduces the setting, characters, and situation.
- An **inciting incident** often leads to a central conflict or problem.
- The **conflict** intensifies during the rising action.
- The **climax** is the high point of interest or suspense.
- The **resolution** of the conflict leads to the end of the story.

As you read this story, note how the writer presents and develops each plot element.

Connecting Literary Elements

Dialogue is conversation between characters. Writers use dialogue to reveal character, to present events, to add variety to a narrative, and to interest readers. Dialogue helps move the plot forward by allowing the characters, rather than the narrator, to reveal what is happening and what is about to happen.

As you read, use a diagram like the one here to jot down parts of dialogue from the story. Then, explain how the information in the dialogue moves the story forward.

Reading Strategy

Identifying Relationships

To get the most out of this story, **identify relationships** in the text. For example, look for the causes and effects of important actions, follow the sequence of events, and identify which events are of greater or lesser importance. This will help you understand the plot and the significance of the dialogue.

Vocabulary Development

delusion (di lōō′ zhən) *n.* false belief held in spite of evidence to the contrary (p. 542)

imminent (im′ ə nənt) *adj.* likely to happen soon; threatening (p. 544)

mackintosh (mak′ in täsh′) *n.* waterproof raincoat (p. 544)

pariah (pə rī′ ə) *adj.* despised; outcast (p. 544)

Vera: "Then you know practically nothing about my aunt?"

Framton: "Only her name and address."

How Dialogue Advances the Plot

The two speakers do not know each other.

The Open Window ◆ 539

CUSTOMIZE INSTRUCTION FOR UNIVERSAL ACCESS

For Special Needs Students	For Less Proficient Readers	For English Learners
Have students read the adapted version of "The Open Window" in the **Adapted Reader's Companion.** This version provides basic-level instruction in an interactive format with questions and write-on lines. Completing the adapted version will prepare students to read the selection in the Student Edition.	Have students read "The Open Window" in the **Reader's Companion.** This version provides basic-level instruction in an interactive format with questions and write-on lines. After students finish the selection in **Reader's Companion,** have them complete the questions and activities in the Student Edition.	Have students read the adapted version of "The Open Window" in the **English Learner's Companion.** This version provides basic-level instruction in an interactive format with questions and write-on lines. Completing the adapted version will prepare students to read the selection in the Student Edition.

CUSTOMIZE INSTRUCTION
For Musical/Rhythmic Learners

Before they have finished reading
the story, have students find music
that would be appropriate for evok-
ing the mood of one of the scenes.
Have them read the scene to the
musical accompaniment, and then
explain why they chose that music.

❶ About the Selection

This story celebrates the power a
good storyteller can have over a
susceptible audience. Fifteen-year-
old Vera is bright, poised, and imaginative—with a wry sense of humor.
When she meets the nervous Mr.
Nuttel, she quickly determines that
he is the perfect victim and plays a
little joke on him, with spectacular
results. She tells Nuttel a story so
tragic and convincing that she has
him believing in ghosts—and seeing
them as well. When faced with
explaining the man's odd behavior
to her aunt, she invents an equally
bizarre story, making her aunt the
next unsuspecting victim.

❷ Background
Art

Nellie Kabel, by Gari Melchers

Gari Melchers was an American
painter who focused on human figures and faces. His best-known work
is a portrait of President Theodore
Roosevelt, painted in 1906. Once
students have learned more about
Vera, have them decide whether this
painting is a good illustration for the
story.
Answer: The character appears to
have traits similar to Vera's: self-
confidence and a mischievous streak.

❸ ▶ Critical Viewing

Possible response: The young
woman in the painting seems confident and self-possessed. Her
straightforward gaze and her
relaxed, open posture create this
impression, as do her comfortable
surroundings.

❶ The Open Window ❧ Saki

Nelli Kabel, Gari Melchers

❸ ▲ Critical Viewing Based on her posture, expression, and surroundings, what
is your impression of the girl in the painting? Would you call her "self-possessed,"
as Saki describes the young woman in the story? Explain. **[Compare]**

540 ◆ *Short Stories*

TEACHING RESOURCES

The following resources can be used to enrich or extend the instruction for pp. 540-544.

Literary Analysis

📖 **Writing Models and Graphic Organizers on
Transparencies,** p. 99

📖 **Selection Support:** Literary Analysis, p. 140

Reading

📖 **Reader's Companion**

📖 **English Learner's Companion**

🎧 **Listening to Literature Audiocassettes,** Side 15 ▪

💿 **Listening to Literature Audio CDs,** CD 10 ▪

▪ **BLOCK SCHEDULING:** Resources marked with this symbol provide varied instruction during 90-minute blocks.

"My aunt will be down presently, Mr. Nuttel," said a very self-possessed young lady of fifteen; "in the meantime you must try and put up with me."

Framton Nuttel endeavored to say the correct something that should duly flatter the niece of the moment without unduly discounting the aunt that was to come. Privately he doubted more than ever whether these formal visits on a succession of total strangers would do much towards helping the nerve cure which he was supposed to be undergoing.

"I know how it will be," his sister had said when he was preparing to migrate to this rural retreat; "you will bury yourself down there and not speak to a living soul, and your nerves will be worse than ever from moping. I shall just give you letters of introduction to all the people I know there. Some of them, as far as I can remember, were quite nice."

Framton wondered whether Mrs. Sappleton, the lady to whom he was presenting one of the letters of introduction, came into the nice division.

"Do you know many of the people round here?" asked the niece, when she judged that they had had sufficient silent communion.

"Hardly a soul," said Framton. "My sister was staying here, at the rectory, you know, some four years ago, and she gave me letters of introduction to some of the people here."

He made the last statement in a tone of distinct regret.

"Then you know practically nothing about my aunt?" pursued the self-possessed young lady.

"Only her name and address," admitted the caller. He was wondering whether Mrs. Sappleton was in the married or widowed state. An undefinable something about the room seemed to suggest masculine habitation.

"Her great tragedy happened just three years ago," said the child; "that would be since your sister's time."

"Her tragedy?" asked Framton; somehow in this restful country spot tragedies seemed out of place.

"You may wonder why we keep that window wide open on an October afternoon," said the niece, indicating a large French window that opened on to a lawn.

"It is quite warm for the time of the year," said Framton; "but has that window got anything to do with the tragedy?"

"Out through that window, three years ago to a day, her husband and her two young brothers went off for their day's shooting. They never came back. In crossing the moor to their favorite snipe-shooting ground[1]

---

1. **snipe-shooting ground** area for hunting snipe—wading birds who live chiefly in marshy places and have long, flexible bills.

clue

Literary Analysis
Plot Structure In the exposition, what do you learn about Framton Nuttel?

❻ ✔**Reading Check**
Why is Framton visiting Mrs. Sappleton?

The Open Window ◆ 541

---

❹ **Literary Analysis**
Plot

- Read the bracketed material aloud. Then, have students summarize what they know so far about the story's characters, setting, and basic situation.
  Possible responses: Characters: a "self-possessed" young lady; a delicate, sickly man; the young lady's aunt. Setting: a house in the country. Situation: the man has come to the country to undergo a "nerve cure." He knows no one in the neighborhood.

- Ask students the Literary Analysis question on p. 541: In the exposition, what do you learn about Framton Nuttel?
  Answer: Framton Nuttel is sickly, unsure of himself, and uncomfortable in social situations.

❺ **Reading Strategy**
Identifying Relationships

- Ask students to compare and contrast Vera and Mr. Nuttel.
  Answer: Students should notice that Vera is confident and talkative, while Mr. Nuttel seems shy and uncomfortable.

- Then, ask students how Mr. Nuttel's personality, especially in relation to Vera's, affects the plot.
  Answer: Mr. Nuttel's nervous personality convinces Vera that he is the perfect victim for her joke.

❻ ✔**Reading Check**
Answer: Framton is visiting Mrs. Sappleton because he is recovering from a nervous condition and needs to stay in a quiet, secluded place. His sister suggests that he try to befriend Mrs. Sappleton and others who live near his new home.

CUSTOMIZE INSTRUCTION FOR UNIVERSAL ACCESS

For Special Needs Students	For Less Proficient Readers	For English Learners
Tell students that Saki's stories are known for their surprise endings. As students read, have them take notes to help them predict the ending.	Because of the dialogue and short paragraphs, this selection is ideal for oral reading. Have students form a Read Around Circle in which students take turns reading a paragraph.	Help students paraphrase sections of dialogue that are peppered with unfamiliar "Britishisms," such as *rectory, moor,* and *bound*.

❼ Reading Strategy

Identifying Relationships

- Ask students the Reading Strategy question on p. 542: What effect does Vera's story have on Framton?

- To answer the Reading Strategy question, point out that the word *effect* in the question indicates a cause-and-effect relationship.

- Help students create charts to show the cause-and-effect relationship indicated by the question.

- Students' charts should look similar to the one below.

> Cause: Vera tells Framton a tragic and eerie story.

> Effect: Framton is horrified, and his imagination begins to run wild.

❽ Vocabulary Development

The Latin Suffix *-ion*

- Call students' attention to the word *delusion* and its definition. Tell students that the suffix *-ion* denotes an action, state, or result.

- Explain that in this case, *-ion* means "state," as in "the state of being misled, or deluded."

- Have students reread the story, looking for words with the Latin suffix *-ion*.

---

they were all three engulfed in a treacherous piece of bog. It had been that dreadful wet summer, you know, and places that were safe in other years gave way suddenly without warning. Their bodies were never recovered. That was the dreadful part of it." Here the child's voice lost its self-possessed note and became falteringly human. "Poor aunt always thinks that they will come back some day, they and the little brown spaniel that was lost with them, and walk in at that window just as they used to do. That is why the window is kept open every evening till it is quite dusk. Poor dear aunt, she has often told me how they went out, her husband with his white waterproof coat over his arm, and Ronnie, her youngest brother, singing, 'Bertie, why do you bound?' as he always did to tease her, because she said it got on her nerves. Do you know, sometimes on still, quiet evenings like this, I almost get a creepy feeling that they will walk in through that window—"

She broke off with a little shudder. It was a relief to Framton when the aunt bustled into the room with a whirl of apologies for being late in making her appearance.

"I hope Vera has been amusing you?" she said.

❼ "She has been very interesting," said Framton. *understatement*

"I hope you don't mind the open window," said Mrs. Sappleton briskly; "my husband and brothers will be home directly from shooting, and they always come in this way. They've been out for snipe in the marshes today, so they'll make a fine mess over my poor carpets. So like you menfolk, isn't it?"

She rattled on cheerfully about the shooting and the scarcity of birds, and the prospects for duck in the winter. To Framton, it was all purely horrible. He made a desperate but only partially successful effort to turn the talk on to a less ghastly topic; he was conscious that his hostess was giving him only a fragment of her attention, and her eyes were constantly straying past him to the open window and the lawn beyond. It was certainly an unfortunate coincidence that he should have paid his visit on this tragic anniversary.

"The doctors agree in ordering me complete rest, an absence of mental excitement, and avoidance of anything in the nature of violent physical exercise," announced Framton, who labored under the tolerably wide-spread delusion that total strangers and chance

❽ acquaintances are hungry for the least detail of one's ailments and infirmities, their cause and cure. "On the matter of diet they are not so much in agreement," he continued.

"No?" said Mrs. Sappleton, in a voice which only replaced a yawn at the last moment. Then she suddenly brightened into alert attention—but not to what Framton was saying.

"Here they are at last!" she cried. "Just in time for tea, and don't they look as if they were muddy up to the eyes!"

Framton shivered slightly and turned towards the niece with a look intended to convey sympathetic comprehension. The child was staring out through the open window with dazed horror in her eyes. In a

---

details

Reading Strategy
Identifying Relationships
What effect does Vera's story have on Framton?

He's a bore

delusion (di loo′ zhen) *n.* false belief held in spite of evidence to the contrary

The Hunters, Gari Melchers, Private Collection

▲ **Critical Viewing** How is this picture similar to and different from the scene Vera describes? **[Compare and Contrast]**

chill shock of nameless fear Framton swung round in his seat and looked in the same direction.

In the deepening twilight three figures were walking across the lawn towards the window; they all carried guns under their arms, and one of them was additionally burdened with a white coat hung over his shoulders. A tired brown spaniel kept close at their heels. Noiselessly they neared the house, and then a hoarse young voice chanted out of the dusk: "I said, Bertie, why do you bound?"

Framton grabbed wildly at his stick and hat; the hall door, the gravel drive, and the front gate were dimly noted stages in his headlong

☑ **Reading Check**

Why is Framton horrified by Mrs. Sappleton's discussion of her husband's hunting?

The Open Window ◆ 543

Review and Assess

1. Students might say that Framton would simply express horror at what he thought were ghosts.

2. **(a)** In the second paragraph, Framton refers to "these formal visits on a succession of total strangers." **(b)** If he knew the Sappletons, he would know that Vera's story was false.

3. **(a)** Framton is living in the country to calm a nervous condition. **(b)** Framton's nervous condition makes him a vulnerable target for Vera's joke.

4. **(a)** Vera says that her aunt expects her dead husband and brothers to return through the window. **(b)** The open window and the marshy area surrounding the house help to make Vera's story believable.

5. **(a)** Mrs. Sappleton cheerfully talks about the imminent return of her husband and brothers. **(b)** Her firm belief that the dead will return frightens Framton.

6. **(a)** She says that Nuttel told her that because of a horrifying experience in India, he is afraid of dogs. **(b)** Her new story suggests that her first story was made up.

7. Students may say that Vera was cruel to upset a sick man.

---

retreat. A cyclist coming along the road had to run into the hedge to avoid <u>imminent</u> collision.

"Here we are, my dear," said the bearer of the white <u>mackintosh</u>, coming in through the window; "fairly muddy, but most of it's dry. Who was that who bolted out as we came up?"

"A most extraordinary man, a Mr. Nuttel," said Mrs. Sappleton; "could only talk about his illnesses, and dashed off without a word of goodbye or apology when you arrived. One would think he had seen a ghost."

"I expect it was the spaniel," said the niece calmly; "he told me he had a horror of dogs. He was once hunted into a cemetery somewhere on the banks of the Ganges[2] by a pack of <u>pariah</u> dogs, and had to spend the night in a newly dug grave with the creatures snarling and grinning and foaming just above him. Enough to make anyone lose their nerve."

Romance at short notice was her specialty.

---

2. **Ganges** (gan′ jēz) river in northern India and Bangladesh.

imminent (im′ ə nənt) adj. likely to happen soon; threatening

mackintosh (mak′ in täsh′) n. waterproof raincoat

pariah (pə rī′ ə) adj. despised; outcast

Review and Assess

Thinking About the Selection

1. **Respond:** If you were Framton, what would you have said to Vera as the men approached the window?

2. **(a) Recall:** How do you know Framton has never met the Sappletons before his visit? **(b) Draw Conclusions:** Why is it important to the story that he know nothing about the Sappletons?

3. **(a) Recall:** Why is Framton living in the country? **(b) Connect:** Why is this detail critical to the outcome of the story?

4. **(a) Recall:** How does Vera explain the open window? **(b) Draw Conclusions:** What details in the house and the surrounding area make it believable?

5. **(a) Recall:** What does Mrs. Sappleton talk about when she meets Framton? **(b) Interpret:** Why do her words and actions seem "purely horrible" to him?

6. **(a) Recall:** How does Vera explain why Framton rushes from the house? **(b) Draw Conclusions:** What does her explanation tell you about the story involving her uncles?

7. **Take a Position:** What do you think about Vera's behavior toward a complete stranger?

Saki

(1870–1916)
Saki is the pen name of Hector Hugh Munro. Born to British parents in Akyab, Burma (now Myanmar), Saki lived in England most of his life. After contracting malaria during military service in Burma, Saki began writing political satires for newspapers in England and then turned to fiction.

He is most famous for his short stories, including "The Open Window," which are noted for their wit and humor as well as for their surprise endings.

Curiously, the story of Saki's own life ends with an ironic twist. After surviving childhood diseases and a bout with malaria, he was killed at the age of forty-five by a sniper's bullet during World War I.

ASSESSMENT PRACTICE: Reading Comprehension

Distinguish Between Fact and Nonfact   (For more practice, see Test Preparation Workbook, p. 35.)

Many tests require students to distinguish between facts and nonfacts in order to understand the writer's message. To help students prepare, introduce this sample test item.

Saki's award-winning tales are noted for their surprise endings. Curiously, the story of Saki's own life ends with an ironic twist. After surviving childhood diseases and a bout of malaria, he was killed at the age of forty-five by a sniper's bullet.

Which of the following is an OPINION expressed in the passage?

A Saki's tales have won awards.
B Saki died at age forty-five.
C Saki was killed by a bullet.
D Saki's death was ironic.

Point out that each statement can be found in the passage. However, only *D* states an opinion. Each other answer can be proven.

Review and Assess

Literary Analysis

Plot

1. Complete a **plot** diagram like the one shown. Use these questions to guide you: (a) What are two events that lead to the climax of the story? (b) What is the climax of the story? (c) What are two events that lead to the resolution of the story?

Climax

Inciting
Incident

Rising Action

Resolution

Exposition

Conclusion

2. At what point do you suspect that Vera's story might not be true?

Connecting Literary Elements

3. What does the **dialogue** at the beginning of the story tell you about the characters of Framton and Vera?
4. How does their dialogue help move the plot of the story forward?
5. How does the dialogue between Vera and Mrs. Sappleton at the end of the story help to resolve the plot?
6. Would the success of the story be different if it contained no dialogue? Explain.

Reading Strategy

Identifying Relationships

7. What is the effect of combining Framton's condition with Vera's mischievous nature?
8. What details help you determine whether Vera's story is true?
9. (a) In what way does the story have two endings? (b) How do the endings relate to each other?

Extend Understanding

10. **Psychology Connection:** Explain how a person's expectations can lead to misunderstanding obvious facts.

The Open Window ◆ 545

545

Answers for p. 546

❶ Vocabulary Development

Concept Development

1. c   3. b
2. a

Fluency: Clarify Meaning

1. You would need a mackintosh when it's raining. A *mackintosh* is a raincoat.
2. An event that is imminent will happen very soon. *Imminent* means "likely to happen soon."
3. Yes, because *pariah* means despised or outcast.
4. A *delusion* would be false, because it means "something that is falsely believed."

Spelling Strategy

1. confession   3. precision
2. expansion   4. relation

❷ Grammar

1. *Only* modifies *present*; I will present my letter and do nothing more.
2. *Only* modifies *you*; I will present my letter to you and no one else.
3. *Only* modifies *letter*; I will present my letter and nothing else.
4. *Just* modifies *learned*; I learned her name and address a short time ago.
5. *Just* modifies *name and address*; I learned her name and address and nothing more.

Writing Application
Possible responses:

1. I called only my brother two minutes ago. Meaning: My brother was the only one I called two minutes ago.
2. Just our English teacher is planning a test tomorrow. Meaning: No one but our English teacher is planning a test tomorrow.

Integrate Language Skills

❶ Vocabulary Development Lesson

Concept Development: Words From Names

A *mackintosh* is a type of raincoat named after the Scottish chemist who invented waterproof clothing. Other English words are also derived from the names of people. Match the following words with the definition and description of the person from whose name they derive.

1. draconian
2. maverick
3. vandal

     a. nonconformist; from a Texas rancher who refused to brand his cattle
     b. someone who willfully destroys property; from a Germanic tribe during the Dark Ages of Europe
     c. severe; from a harsh Athenian lawgiver

Fluency: Clarify Meaning

Answer each question, and explain your answer.

1. When would you need a *mackintosh*?
2. When would you expect an *imminent* event to occur?
3. Would you feel like a *pariah* if you had not been invited to a friend's party?
4. Would you expect a *delusion* to be true?

Spelling Strategy

The suffix that is pronounced *shun* is usually spelled *sion* as in *delusion*, *tion* as in *operation*, or *ssion* as in *possession*. Spell the *shun* sound in each word below.

1. confe___   3. preci___
2. expan___   4. rela___

❷ Grammar Lesson

Placement of *only* and *just*

The placement of modifying words can affect the meaning of a sentence. For example, when the placement of the word *just* or *only* is changed, the meaning of the sentence changes.

> She gave him *only* a fragment of her time. (Modifies *fragment*: She gave him a little time.)
> She gave *only* him a fragment of her time. (Modifies *him*: She gave him, and no one else, time.)
> She gave him a fragment of her *only* time. (Modifies *time*: She had very little time to give.)

Practice Explain how the placement of the word *just* or *only* influences the meaning of each sentence.

1. I shall *only* present my letter to you.
2. I shall present my letter *only* to you.
3. I shall present *only* my letter to you.
4. I *just* learned her name and address.
5. I learned *just* her name and address.

Writing Application Add *just* or *only* to each sentence below, and explain the meaning of the new sentence.

1. I called my brother two minutes ago.
2. Our English teacher is planning a test tomorrow.

𝒲𝒢 *Prentice Hall Writing and Grammar Connection: Chapter 26, Section 2*

546 ◆ *Short Stories*

Writing Lesson

Introduction for a Collection

You are compiling a short-story collection that includes Saki's "The Open Window." To introduce the collection, write an inviting essay that will draw readers into the collection. After the introduction, there will be an enticing summary of each story. Write the introduction and the summary for "The Open Window."

Prewriting   Consider the elements of successful short stories. Then, review "The Open Window" to locate and take notes on its key strengths.

> ### Model: Brainstorming to Identify Key Points
>
> A story should be . . . *exciting (There should be an interesting conflict.)*
>
> . . . *funny (It might have unusual characters or situations.)*

A sentence starter like the one shown can help writers generate ideas.

Drafting   To draft your introduction, present your opinions about the short-story format, describing the elements that readers can expect to find in your anthology. Devote a paragraph to your summary of "The Open Window."

Revising   Reread your essay as if you were considering reading the collection. If the introduction does not grab your interest, revise to make it more appealing.

Prentice Hall Writing and Grammar Connection: Chapter 13, Section 2

Extension Activities

Listening and Speaking   Retell one of Vera's tales using details she provides as well as some of your own that make the story seem more real. Use both verbal and nonverbal skills to make your **storytelling** believable.

- Add pauses for dramatic effect.
- Change your tone of voice to create mood and express emotions.
- Use facial expressions to enhance the meaning of your words.

Research and Technology   Saki, the author of "The Open Window," is well known for stories that feature practical jokes or surprise endings. Find out about some other Saki stories, and prepare an **annotated reading list.** Include short plot descriptions to entice potential readers.

 Take It to the Net   www.phschool.com

Go online for an additional research activity using the Internet.

The Open Window ◆ 547

Lesson Support for p. 547

③ Writing Lesson

- Before students write their introductions to "The Open Window," encourage them to think about what they enjoyed most about the story. Was it the humor? The suspense? The surprise ending? Have students list the story's most attractive features.

- Then, have students refer to their list as they write an introduction to the story. Remind them that the introduction's purpose will be to entice people to read the story, and that they shouldn't reveal information that will spoil the suspense or the surprise.

- Before they begin their summaries, remind students that a summary condenses a long passage into a few sentences or a paragraph. A summary should include the key events of a story in the order they occurred.

- Then, use the writing lesson to guide students in writing their summaries.

④ Listening and Speaking

- Divide the class into groups. Have each group discuss what Vera does to make her stories believable.

- Guide each group to the conclusion that successful stories have interesting details that are vivid enough to create "mind pictures" for the audience, and that a storyteller should use pauses, gestures, and facial expressions to help convey meaning.

- Let students work individually to enhance one of Vera's stories. Finally, have them present their stories to the class.

- Have students use the rubric for Presenting an Oral Response to Literature, p. 31 in **Performance Assessment and Portfolio Management.**

CUSTOMIZE INSTRUCTION
For Universal Access

To address different learning styles, use the activities suggested in the **Extension Activities** booklet, p. 35.

- For Verbal/Linguistic and Visual/Spatial Learners, use Activity 5.

- For Bodily/Kinesthetic Learners, use Activity 6.

547

Leiningen Versus the Ants

Lesson Objectives

1. **To analyze and respond to literary elements**
   - Literary Analysis: Conflict
   - Connecting Literary Elements: Climax

2. **To read, comprehend, analyze, and critique a short story**
   - Reading Strategy: Making Predictions
   - Reading Check questions
   - Review and Assess questions
   - Assessment Practice (ATE)

3. **To develop word analysis skills, fluency, and systematic vocabulary**
   - Vocabulary Development Lesson: Latin Plural Forms

4. **To understand and apply written and oral language conventions**
   - Spelling Strategy
   - Grammar Lesson: Subject and Verb Agreement

5. **To understand and apply appropriate writing and research strategies**
   - Writing Lesson: New Movie Scene
   - Extension Activity: News Article

6. **To understand and apply listening and speaking strategies**
   - Extension Activity: Motivational Speech

STEP-BY-STEP TEACHING GUIDE	PACING GUIDE
PRETEACH	
Motivate Students and Provide Background	
Use the Motivation activity (ATE p. 548)	5 min.
Read and discuss the Preview material and Background information (SE/ATE p. 548) Ⓐ	5 min.
Introduce the Concepts	
Introduce the Literary Analysis and Reading Strategy (SE/ATE p. 549) Ⓐ	15 min.
Pronounce the vocabulary words and read their definitions (SE p. 549)	5 min.
TEACH	
Monitor Comprehension	
Informally monitor comprehension by circulating while students read independently or in groups Ⓐ	45 min.
Monitor students' comprehension with the Reading Check notes (SE/ATE pp. 551, 553, 555, 557, 559, 561, 563, 565, 567, 569)	as students read
Develop vocabulary with Vocabulary notes (SE pp. 554, 555, 556, 560, 570)	as students read
Develop Understanding	
Develop students' understanding of conflict with Literary Analysis annotations (SE/ATE pp. 551, 557–559, 561–565, 568, 569) Ⓐ	10 min.
Develop students' understanding of making predictions with Reading Strategy annotations (SE/ATE pp. 551–554, 556, 558, 559, 561–564, 566, 567)	10 min.
ASSESS	
Assess Mastery	
Assess students' mastery of the Reading Strategy and Literary Analysis by having them answer the Review and Assess questions (SE/ATE p. 571)	20 min.
Use one or more of the print and media Assessment Resources (ATE p. 573) Ⓐ	up to 50 min.
EXTEND	
Apply Understanding	
Have students complete the Vocabulary Development Lesson and the Grammar Lesson (SE p. 572) Ⓐ	20 min.
Apply students' knowledge of setting the scene using the Writing Lesson (SE p. 573) Ⓐ	45 min.
Apply students' understanding using one or more of the Extension Activities (SE p. 573)	20–90 min.

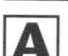 **ACCELERATED INSTRUCTION:**
Use the strategies and activities identified with an Ⓐ.

UNIVERSAL ACCESS
- ● = Below Level Students
- ▲ = On-Level Students
- ■ = Above Level Students

Time and Resource Manager

Reading Level: Average
Average Number of Instructional Days: 4

RESOURCES

PRINT 📖	TRANSPARENCIES	TECHNOLOGY
• **Beyond Literature,** Cross-Curricular Connection: Science, p. 36 ▲ ■		• **Interest Grabber Video,** Tape 3 ● ▲ ■
• **Selection Support Workbook:** ● ▲ ■ Literary Analysis, p. 144 Reading Strategy, p. 143 Build Vocabulary, p. 141	• **Literary Analysis and Reading Transparencies,** pp. 71 and 72 ● ▲ ■	
		• **Listening to Literature** ● ▲ ■ Audiocassettes, Sides 16, 17 Audio CDs, CD 11
• **Literatura en español** ● ▲ • **Literary Analysis for Enrichment** ■		
• **Formal Assessment:** Selection Test, pp. 126–128 ● ▲ ■ • **Open Book Test,** pp. 106–108 ● ▲ ■ • **Performance Assessment and Portfolio Management,** p. 30 ● ▲ ■ • **PRENTICE HALL ASSESSMENT SYSTEM** ● ▲ ■	• **PRENTICE HALL ASSESSMENT SYSTEM** ● ▲ ■ Skills Practice Answers and Explanations on Transparencies	• **Test Bank Software** ● ▲ ■ • **Got It! Assessment Videotapes,** Tape 3 ● ▲
• **Selection Support Workbook:** ● ▲ ■ Build Grammar Skills, p. 142 • **Writing and Grammar,** Platinum Level ● ▲ ■ • **Extension Activities,** p. 36 ● ▲ ■	• **Daily Language Practice Transparencies** ● ▲ • **Writing Models and Graphic Organizers on Transparencies,** p. 83 ● ▲ ■	• **Writing and Grammar iText CD-ROM** ● ▲ ■ 🖥 **Take It to the Net** www.phschool.com

BLOCK SCHEDULING: Use one 90-minute class period to preteach the selection and have students read it. Use a second 90-minute class period to assess students' mastery of skills and have them complete one of the Extension Activities.

**Step-by-Step Teaching Guide
for pp. 548–549**

Motivation

Ask students whether they have seen horror movies in which the "monster" was an insect. If they were making such a movie, which insect would they choose to be the monster? They might say spiders, locusts, or cockroaches.

Point out that the story they are about to read, "Leiningen Versus the Ants," was made into a horror movie titled *The Naked Jungle*, starring Charlton Heston. Have students speculate about the kind of ant that would be the more dramatic in a film—a monster ant or a giant mass of small, deadly ants?

Interest Grabber Video

As an alternative, play "Bees" on Tape 3 to engage student interest.

❶ Background

Science

Because of their large colony size, army ants must migrate in order to find food. They sometimes raid other ant colonies and capture slaves. During this migration phase, army ants march at night and stop to camp in daylight. Each of these rampages can last up to seventeen days. Once the need for food decreases, the ants begin a stationary phase. They form a nest that is actually made up of the ants themselves. They form walls and fasten onto each other by using their mandibles (jaws) and their legs. This way they can hang from a log or another surface, while the nest encloses the queen and her brood.

Prepare to Read

Leiningen Versus the Ants

Take It to the Net

Visit www.phschool.com for interactive activities and instruction related to "Leiningen Versus the Ants," including
- background
- graphic organizers
- literary elements
- reading strategies

Preview

Connecting to the Literature

Nature can be a terrifying enemy. Hurricanes and tornadoes are just two of the natural phenomena that can do serious damage. Compare these familiar catastrophes with the invasion of hungry ants that the main character in this story faces.

❶ Background

The ants in this story are army ants. Scientists divide army ants into two groups: *legionary ants* from South America and *driver ants* from the jungles of central Africa. These ant colonies, numbering from ten thousand to more than one million members, travel across the land in narrow columns, killing anything unlucky enough to get in their path—including other insects, lizards, and mammals.

548 ◆ *Short Stories*

TEACHING RESOURCES

The following resources can be used to enrich or extend the instruction for pp. 548–549.

Motivation

Interest Grabber Video, Tape 3

Background

Beyond Literature, p. 36

Take It to the Net
Visit www.phschool.com for background and hotlinks for "Leiningen Versus the Ants."

Literary Analysis

Literary Analysis and Reading Transparencies, Conflict, p. 72

Reading

Selection Support: Reading Strategy, p. 143; Build Vocabulary, p. 141

Literary Analysis and Reading Transparencies, Making Predictions, p. 71

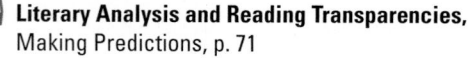 **BLOCK SCHEDULING:** Resources marked with this symbol provide varied instruction during 90-minute blocks.

Literary Analysis

Conflict

A story almost always contains a **conflict**—a struggle between opposing forces. An **internal conflict** takes place within a character, as he or she struggles with opposing feelings, beliefs, or needs. An **external conflict** occurs between two or more characters or between a character and a natural force. As the title suggests, the main character in this story faces an external conflict. This excerpt introduces the natural force:

> "Leiningen!" he shouted, "you're insane! They're not creatures you can fight—they're an elemental—an 'act of God'! Ten miles long, two miles wide— ants, nothing but ants!"

As you read, notice both the internal and external conflicts that the ants generate.

Connecting Literary Elements

The **climax** of a story is the point at which the tension is greatest. It is also the point at which the outcome is about to be revealed. In "Leiningen Versus the Ants," the climax of the story is caused by the escalation of the conflict between people and nature. Look for the event that marks the climax of this story.

Reading Strategy

Making Predictions

Stories follow a pattern that helps you predict or guess about story events. Your **predictions** may be based on details or evidence in the story and on what you know from your own experience.

- As this story opens, you learn that an army of flesh-eating ants is headed toward the main character's plantation.
- You can predict that the ants will get close enough to be a threat.

Details revealed in the story will enable you to make more specific predictions. Use a diagram like the one here to track your predictions.

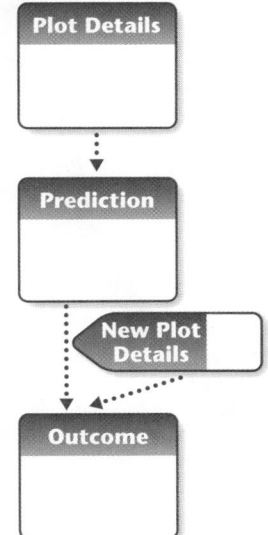

Vocabulary Development

peons (pē´ ənz) *n.* laborers (p. 554)

flout (flout) *v.* show open contempt (p. 555)

weir (wir) *n.* low dam (p. 556)

provender (präv´ ən dər) *n.* food; provisions (p. 560)

alluvium (ə lōō´ vē əm) *n.* material such as sand or clay deposited by moving water (p. 570)

fomentations (fō men tā´ shənz) *n.* applications of substances in the treatment of an injury (p. 570)

Leiningen Versus the Ants ◆ 549

CUSTOMIZE INSTRUCTION FOR UNIVERSAL ACCESS

For Less Proficient Readers	For English Learners	For Advanced Readers
Have students complete the prediction chart on this page as they read. Suggest that they pause at intervals during the story to check the predictions they have made and revise the predictions, if necessary.	You may wish to paraphrase idiomatic expressions, such as the following: *decent of you* (kind of you); *give me the tip* (warn me); and *do a bunk* (evacuate or leave). Discuss these expressions before students begin to read.	Challenge students to think about the internal conflict that Leiningen faces throughout the story, in addition to the external one. What forces are at war in him? Which force wins?

---

❷ Literary Analysis

Conflict

- Tell students that as they read "Leiningen Versus the Ants," they will focus on conflict, the struggle between opposing forces that forms the basis of most plots in literature.

- Make sure students understand the difference between internal conflict, in which the struggle takes place within a character, and external conflict, in which a character struggles against another character or an outside force.

- Use the instruction for Connecting Literary Elements to connect the climax of the story to its conflict. The climax of the story usually determines how the conflict will be resolved.

- Use the Conflict transparency in **Literary Analysis and Reading Transparencies,** p. 72, to demonstrate for students how to identify the conflicts in "Leiningen Versus the Ants."

❸ Reading Strategy

Making Predictions

- Explain to students that when they make predictions, they use details from a story to guess what will happen next.

- As they read the story, encourage students to think about what the characters may say or do next. Students should also try to make predictions about the story's climax and its resolution.

- Remind students that they may have to revise their predictions as they read to take into account new information and details.

- Have students use a diagram like the one shown to help them make predictions as they read.

Vocabulary Development

- Pronounce each vocabulary word for students, and read the definitions as a class. Have students identify any words with which they are already familiar.

 E-Teach

Visit E-Teach at www.phschool.com for teachers' essays on how to teach, with questions and answers.

549

**Step-by-Step Teaching Guide
for pp. 550–570**

CUSTOMIZE INSTRUCTION
For Visual/Spatial Learners

Direct students to infer from the
photograph on this page what the
story may be about.
Answer: Students may predict that
the story will feature giant ants.

❶ About the Selection

"Leiningen Versus the Ants" is in the
long tradition of "man against
nature" fiction. Leiningen is convinced that his superior intelligence
will enable him to win the war
against the voracious army of ants
that attacks his plantation. He has
planned long and carefully, but the
insects prove to be persistent and
resourceful. In the end, human intelligence and courage win out—but
not by much. Leiningen shows
bravado at the finale, but he has
also learned humility in the face of
nature's devastating threats.

❶ *Leiningen*
Versus
the
Ants

Carl Stephenson

TEACHING RESOURCES

The following resources can be used to enrich or extend the instruction for pp. 550–570.

Literary Analysis

📖 **Writing Models and Graphic Organizers on
Transparencies,** p. 83 ▪

📓 **Selection Support:** Literary Analysis, p. 144

Reading

🎧 **Listening to Literature Audiocassettes,** Sides 16, 17

💿 **Listening to Literature Audio CDs,** CD 11

▪ **BLOCK SCHEDULING:** Resources marked with this symbol provide varied instruction during 90-minute blocks.

"**U**nless they alter their course, and there's no reason why they should, they'll reach your plantation in two days at the latest."

Leiningen sucked placidly at a cigar about the size of a corn cob and for a few seconds gazed without answering at the agitated District Commissioner. Then he took the cigar from his lips and leaned slightly forward. With his bristling gray hair, bulky nose, and lucid eyes, he had the look of an aging and shabby eagle.

"Decent of you," he murmured, "paddling all this way just to give me the tip. But you're pulling my leg, of course, when you say I must do a bunk. Why, even a herd of saurians[1] couldn't drive me from this plantation of mine."

The Brazilian official threw up lean and lanky arms and clawed the air with wildly distended fingers. "Leiningen!" he shouted, "you're insane! They're not creatures you can fight—they're an elemental—an 'act of God'! Ten miles long, two miles wide—ants, nothing but ants! And every single one of them a fiend from hell; before you can spit three times they'll eat a full-grown buffalo to the bones. I tell you if you don't clear out at once there'll be nothing left of you but a skeleton picked as clean as your own plantation."

Leiningen grinned. "Act of God, my eye! Anyway, I'm not going to run for it just because an elemental's on the way. And don't think I'm the kind of fathead who tries to fend off lightning with his fists, either. I use my intelligence, old man. With me, the brain isn't a second blind gut;[2] I know what it's there for. When I began this model farm and plantation three years ago, I took into account all that could conceivably happen to it. And now I'm ready for anything and everything—including your ants."

The Brazilian rose heavily to his feet. "I've done my best," he gasped. "Your obstinacy endangers not only yourself, but the lives of your four hundred workers. *You don't know these ants!*"

Leiningen accompanied him down to the river, where the government launch was moored. The vessel cast off. As it moved downstream, the exclamation mark neared the rail and began waving arms frantically. Long after the launch had disappeared round the bend, Leiningen thought he could still hear that dimming, imploring voice. "You don't know them, I tell you! You don't know them!"

But the reported enemy was by no means unfamiliar to the planter. Before he started work on his settlement, he had lived long enough in the country to see for himself the fearful devastations sometimes wrought by these ravenous insects in their campaigns for food. But

---

1. **saurians** (sôr′ ē ənz) *n.* lizardlike animals.
2. **blind gut** reference to the appendix, which may have no function.

Leiningen Versus the Ants ◆ 551

Literary Analysis
Conflict What conflict with nature is the official describing?

Reading Check
What does the District Commissioner advise Leiningen to do?

❷ **Reading Strategy**
Making Predictions

• Ask students to use information from the title and the opening photograph to predict what the speaker is describing.
Answer: The speaker is describing the movement of vicious ants.

• Have students make a mental picture of the ants. As they read, have them adjust these pictures based on what they learn about the ants' size and speed.

❸ **Literary Analysis**
Conflict

• Ask students to consider the images described in the bracketed text.

• Then, ask students what they think the official means when he says the ants are an "act of God."
Answer: The official means that the ants are a force of nature that cannot be fought.

• Then, ask the Literary Analysis question on p. 551: What conflict with nature is the official describing?
Answer: The conflict is between the ants and anything that is in their path, including people.

❹ **Reading Check**
Answer: The District Commissioner advises Leiningen to leave the plantation.

CUSTOMIZE INSTRUCTION FOR UNIVERSAL ACCESS

For Special Needs Students	For Gifted/Talented Students
Based on his response to the official and on his decision to stay on the plantation, ask students to determine what they can tell about Leiningen's personality. Then, have them make predictions about how his personality traits will affect the plot.	Leiningen says that the human brain can conquer the elements. Have students discuss this idea and decide whether or not they agree with Leiningen. Answer: Some students will say that the human intellect is powerful when used wisely; others will say that the elements cannot always be predicted and can foil even the best-laid plans.

❺ **Reading Strategy**

Making Predictions

- As students read the bracketed passage, ask them to pay attention to both Leiningen's personality and his accomplishments.

- Then, ask the Reading Strategy question on p. 552: Which details in this passage about Leiningen help you predict his success against the ants? Explain.
  Answer: Leiningen's experience with other emergencies, including drought, flood, and plague, will help him now. His attitude that intelligence can conquer anything should also prove helpful.

❻ **Reading Strategy**

Making Predictions

- Ask students to describe how the animals are behaving.

- Then, ask the Reading Strategy question on p. 552: What can you predict about the ants based on the behavior of the animals?
  Answer: The ants must be very fierce in order to frighten the animals into a stampede.

since then he had planned measures of defense accordingly, and these, he was convinced, were in every way adequate to withstand the approaching peril.

Moreover, during his three years as planter, Leiningen had met and defeated drought, flood, plague, and all other "acts of God" which had come against him—unlike his fellow settlers in the district, who had made little or no resistance. This unbroken success he attributed solely to the observance of his lifelong motto: *The human brain needs only to become fully aware of its powers to conquer even the elements.* Dullards reeled senselessly and aimlessly into the abyss; cranks, however brilliant, lost their heads when circumstances suddenly altered or accelerated and ran into stone walls; sluggards drifted with the current until they were caught in whirlpools and dragged under. But such disasters, Leiningen contended, merely strengthened his argument that intelligence, directed aright, invariably makes man the master of his fate.

Yes, Leiningen had always known how to grapple with life. Even here, in this Brazilian wilderness, his brain had triumphed over every difficulty and danger it had so far encountered. First he had vanquished primal forces by cunning and organization, then he had enlisted the resources of modern science to increase miraculously the yield of his plantation. And now he was sure he would prove more than a match for the "irresistible" ants.

That same evening however, Leiningen assembled his workers. He had no intention of waiting till the news reached their ears from other sources. Most of them had been born in the district; the cry, "The ants are coming!" was to them an imperative signal for instant, panic-stricken flight, a spring for life itself. But so great was the Indians' trust in Leiningen, in Leiningen's word, and in Leiningen's wisdom, that they received his curt tidings, and his orders for the imminent struggle, with the calmness with which they were given. They waited, unafraid, alert, as if for the beginning of a new game or hunt which he had just described to them. The ants were indeed mighty, but not so mighty as the boss. Let them come!

They came at noon the second day. Their approach was announced by the wild unrest of the horses, scarcely controllable now either in stall or under rider, scenting from afar a vapor instinct with horror.

It was announced by a stampede of animals, timid and savage, hurtling past each other; jaguars and pumas flashing by nimble stags of the pampas;[3] bulky tapirs, no longer hunters, themselves hunted, outpacing fleet kinkajous; maddened herds of cattle, heads lowered, nostrils snorting, rushing through tribes of loping monkeys, chattering in a dementia[4] of terror; then followed the creeping and springing denizens of bush and steppe, big and little rodents, snakes, and lizards.

Pell-mell the rabble swarmed down the hill to the plantation, scattered right and left before the barrier of the water-filled ditch, then

---

3. **pampas** (päm´ pəz) *n.* South American grassland.
4. **dementia** (di men´ shə) *n.* insanity or madness.

Reading Strategy
Making Predictions
Which details in this passage about Leiningen help you predict his success against the ants? Explain.

Reading Strategy
Making Predictions
What can you predict about the ants based on the behavior of the animals?

✳ ENRICHMENT: Geography Connection

Brazil

The landscape of Brazil, where "Leiningen Versus the Ants" is set, is varied. The Northeast Region is made up of a coastal plain and high plateaus. The Central and Southern Plateau Region is fertile and includes large coffee plantations. The Amazon Region is located in the north and includes tropical rain forests and mountains. Most of the inhabitants of Brazil live in the plateaus, where the cities of São Paulo and Rio de Janeiro are located.

Display a physical map of Brazil, and have students decide in what region the story probably takes place (Southern Plateau) and what is probably grown on the plantation (coffee).

As students read the story, have them notice clues about the geographical features and animal and plant life of this region of Brazil.

sped onwards to the river, where, again hindered, they fled along its banks out of sight.

This water-filled ditch was one of the defense measures which Leiningen had long since prepared against the advent of the ants. It encompassed three sides of the plantation like a huge horseshoe. Twelve feet across, but not very deep, when dry it could hardly be described as an obstacle to either man or beast. But the ends of the "horseshoe" ran into the river which formed the northern boundary, and fourth side, of the plantation. And at the end nearer the house and outbuildings in the middle of the plantation, Leiningen had constructed a dam by means of which water from the river could be diverted into the ditch.

So now, by opening the dam, he was able to fling an imposing girdle of water, a huge quadrilateral with the river as its base, completely around the plantation, like the moat encircling a medieval city. Unless the ants were clever enough to build rafts, they had no hope of reaching the plantation, Leiningen concluded.

The twelve-foot water ditch seemed to afford in itself all the security

8 ☑ **Reading Check**
To what does Leiningen attribute his success in overcoming difficulties in the Brazilian wilderness?

▲ **Critical Viewing** What does this picture from a film based on the story suggest will happen to those who get too close to the ants? **[Draw Conclusions]**

Leiningen Versus the Ants ◆ 553

7 **Reading Strategy**
Making Predictions
- As students read the description of the ditch, have them sketch a picture of it so they see it clearly.
- Then, ask students what they think will happen to the ants when they reach the ditch.
  Answer: Leiningen will fill the ditch with water from the river, and the ants will have a hard time swimming across. Many of them will drown.

▶ Monitor Progress Have students return to their predictions after they have learned how the ditch affects the ants. Were their predictions correct? Why or why not?

8 ☑ **Reading Check**
Answer: Leiningen attributes his success to his intellect and to careful preparation for disasters.

9 ▶ **Critical Viewing**
Answer: The covered body of the dead man suggests that the ants will kill whatever they attack.

CUSTOMIZE INSTRUCTION FOR UNIVERSAL ACCESS

For Special Needs Students	For Gifted/Talented Students
Students may benefit from plotting out a map of the plantation. As they read, students can chart the advance of the ants to help them follow the action. Encourage them to use the Story Map Transparency on p. 83 of **Writing Models and Graphic Organizers on Transparencies**.	Have students discuss possible strategies for overcoming the ants. Have them produce at least two plans for eradicating the ants or altering their path before they reach the plantation. Have students share their plans with the class when they have finished.

needed. But while awaiting the arrival of the ants, Leiningen made a further improvement. The western section of the ditch ran along the edge of a tamarind wood,[5] and the branches of some great trees reached over the water. Leiningen now had them lopped so that ants could not descend from them within the "moat."

The women and children, then the herds of cattle, were escorted by <u>peons</u> on rafts over the river, to remain on the other side in absolute safety until the plunderers had departed. Leiningen gave this instruction, not because he believed the noncombatants were in any danger, but in order to avoid hampering the efficiency of the defenders.

Finally, he made a careful inspection of the "inner moat"—a smaller ditch lined with concrete, which extended around the hill on which stood the ranch house, barns, stables, and other buildings. Into this concrete ditch emptied the inflow pipes from three great petrol tanks.[6] If by some miracle the ants managed to cross the water and reach the plantation, this "rampart of petrol" would be an absolutely impassable protection for the besieged and their dwellings and stock. Such, at least, was Leiningen's opinion.

He stationed his men at irregular distances along the water ditch, the first line of defense. Then he lay down in his hammock and puffed drowsily away at his pipe until a peon came with the report that the ants had been observed far away in the south.

Leiningen mounted his horse, which at the feel of its master seemed to forget its uneasiness, and rode leisurely in the direction of the threatening offensive. The southern stretch of ditch—the upper side of the quadrilateral—was nearly three miles long; from its center one could survey the entire countryside. This was destined to be the scene of the outbreak of war between Leiningen's brain and twenty square miles of life-destroying ants.

It was a sight one could never forget. Over the range of hills, as far as eye could see, crept a darkening hem, ever longer and broader, until the shadow spread across the slope from east to west, then downward, downward, uncannily swift, and all the green herbage of that wide vista was being mown as by a giant sickle, leaving only the vast moving shadow, extending, deepening, and moving rapidly nearer.

When Leiningen's men, behind their barrier of water, perceived the approach of the long-expected foe, they gave vent to their suspense in screams and imprecations.

peons (pē´ ənz) *n.* laborers

Literature ⓫
in context Media Connection

The Naked Jungle

The vivid description and exciting action in "Leiningen Versus the Ants" inspired filmmakers to produce a screen version of Stephenson's short story. The film, starring Charlton Heston, was released in 1954 with the title *The Naked Jungle*. The photos you see in the story are stills from the film. Screenwriters Ranald MacDougall, Ben Maddow, and Philip Yordan expanded the cast of characters, adding a wife for Leiningen and increasing the roles of two plantation workers. Although the story presented here contains plenty of tension and excitement, the screenwriters also added several more "close calls" to the plot.

Charlton Heston as Leiningen (left)

---

5. **tamarind** (tam´ ə rind´) **wood** grove of leafy trees found in the tropics.
6. **petrol** (pe´ trəl) **tanks** gasoline tanks.

But as the distance began to lessen between the "sons of hell" and the water ditch, they relapsed into silence. Before the advance of that awe-inspiring throng, their belief in the powers of the boss began to steadily dwindle.

Even Leiningen himself, who had ridden up just in time to restore their loss of heart by a display of unshakable calm, even he could not free himself from a qualm of malaise. Yonder were thousands of millions of voracious jaws bearing down upon him and only a suddenly insignificant, narrow ditch lay between him and his men and being gnawed to the bones "before you can spit three times."

Hadn't his brain for once taken on more than it could manage? If the blighters decided to rush the ditch, fill it to the brim with their corpses, there'd still be more than enough to destroy every trace of that cranium of his. The planter's chin jutted; they hadn't got him yet, and he'd see to it they never would. While he could think at all, he'd <u>flout</u> both death and the devil.

The hostile army was approaching in perfect formation; no human battalions, however well drilled, could ever hope to rival the precision of that advance. Along a front that moved forward as uniformly as a straight line, the ants drew nearer and nearer to the water ditch. Then, when they learned through their scouts the nature of the obstacle, the two outlying wings of the army detached themselves from the main body and marched down the western and eastern sides of the ditch.

This surrounding maneuver took rather more than an hour to accomplish; no doubt the ants expected that at some point they would find a crossing.

During this outflanking movement by the wings, the army on the center and southern front remained still. The besieged were therefore able to contemplate at their leisure the thumb-long, reddish-black, long-legged insects; some of the Indians believed they could see, too, intent on them, the brilliant, cold eyes, and the razor-edged mandibles,[7] of this host of infinity.

It is not easy for the average person to imagine that an animal, not to mention an insect, can *think*. But now both the brain of Leiningen and the brains of the Indians began to stir with the unpleasant foreboding that inside every single one of that deluge of insects dwelled a thought. And that thought was: Ditch or no ditch, we'll get to your flesh!

Not until four o'clock did the wings reach the "horseshoe" ends of the ditch, only to find these ran into the great river. Through some kind of secret telegraphy, the report must then have flashed very swiftly indeed along the entire enemy line. And Leiningen, riding—no longer casually—along his side of the ditch, noticed by energetic and widespread movements of troops that for some unknown reason the news of the check had its greatest effect on the southern front, where the main army was massed. Perhaps the failure to find a way over

---

7. **mandibles** (man´ də bəlz) *n.* biting jaws.

Reading Strategy
Making Predictions What do you predict will happen when the ants reach the plantation?

flout (flout) *v.* show open contempt

15 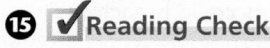**Reading Check**
What is the function of the "inner moat"?

Leiningen Versus the Ants ◆ 555

13 **Reading Strategy**
Making Predictions

- Point out to students that for the first time in the story, Leiningen's complete confidence has been shaken.
- Ask the Reading Strategy question on p. 555: What do you predict will happen when the ants reach the plantation?
  Answer: Based on Leiningen's reaction, students might predict that the ants will be able to cross the ditch.

14 **Critical Thinking**
Draw Conclusions

- Have students review the details about the ants' behavior as they move together.
- Ask them to think about what they know about insects from biology classes.
- Then, ask students whether they believe that the ants can actually think.
  Answer: They cannot think the way that humans do, but they do have an elaborate communication system that helps them to work together toward a goal.

15 **Reading Check**
Answer: The inner moat can be filled with gasoline in order to stop the ants.

⑯ Reading Strategy

Making Predictions

• Have students read the bracketed passage, and then consider what they know about the ants.

• Ask the Reading Strategy question on p. 556: Do you think the ants will survive the ditch? Why? Possible answer: Yes, some of the ants will survive the ditch because they have devised a way to use other ants as bridges.

⑰ Critical Thinking

Make a Judgment

• Ask students to explain in their own words how the ants plan to cross the ditch. If necessary, they can draw pictures of the ants' movements.

• Then, ask whether they think the ants are making an intelligent choice to cross the ditch or are simply operating instinctively. Answer: Some students may say the ants are acting intelligently by sacrificing the few so the many can reach the plantation.

⑱ ▶ Critical Viewing

Possible response: They may be looking at and discussing a place where the ants could breach their defenses.

the ditch was persuading the ants to withdraw from the plantation in search of spoils more easily attainable.

⑯ An immense flood of ants, about a hundred yards in width, was pouring in a glimmering black cataract down the far slope of the ditch. Many thousands were already drowning in the sluggish creeping flow, but they were followed by troop after troop, who clambered over their sinking comrades, and then themselves served as dying bridges to the reserves hurrying on in their rear.

Shoals of ants were being carried away by the current into the middle of the ditch, where gradually they broke asunder and then, exhausted by their struggles, vanished below the surface. Nevertheless, the wavering, floundering hundred-yard front was remorselessly if slowly advancing toward the besieged on the other bank. Leiningen had been wrong when he supposed the enemy would ⑰ first have to fill the ditch with their bodies before they could cross: instead, they merely needed to act as steppingstones, as they swam and sank, to the hordes ever pressing onwards from behind.

Near Leiningen a few mounted herdsmen awaited his orders. He sent one to the weir—the river must be dammed more strongly to

Reading Strategy Making Predictions Do you think the ants will survive the ditch? Why?

weir (wir) *n.* low dam

⑱ ▲ **Critical Viewing** What do you think Leiningen and his assistant are discussing here? **[Speculate]**

Insect Plagues

One of the most common themes of insect plagues in world folklore is that of the locust, a small type of grasshopper that swarms, eating all vegetation in its path. Plagues of locusts are mentioned in the Bible and by the ancient Greeks, who thought the little insects were mythological monsters. Special ceremonies to drive away the feared locusts exist in Dahomey (West Africa), India, and Syria, where the people simply make as much noise as possible to deter an oncoming swarm. The locust is also a symbol of death and destruction for many Native Americans, especially among the Yurok and Wiyot groups.

increase the speed and power of the water coursing through the ditch.

A second peon was dispatched to the outhouses to bring spades and petrol sprinklers. A third rode away to summon to the zone of the offensive all the men, except the observation posts, on the nearby sections of the ditch, which were not yet actively threatened.

The ants were getting across far more quickly than Leiningen would have deemed possible. Impelled by the mighty cascade behind them, they struggled nearer and nearer to the inner bank. The momentum of the attack was so great that neither the tardy flow of the stream nor its downward pull could exert its proper force; and into the gap left by every submerging insect, hastened forward a dozen more.

When reinforcements reached Leiningen, the invaders were halfway over. The planter had to admit to himself that it was only by a stroke of luck for him that the ants were attempting the crossing on a relatively short front: had they assaulted simultaneously along the entire length of the ditch, the outlook for the defenders would have been black indeed.

Even as it was, it could hardly be described as rosy, though the planter seemed quite unaware that death in a gruesome form was drawing closer and closer. As the war between his brain and the "act of God" reached its climax, the very shadow of annihilation began to pale to Leiningen, who now felt like a champion in a new Olympic game, a gigantic and thrilling contest, from which he was determined to emerge victor. Such, indeed, was his aura of confidence that the Indians forgot their fear of the peril only a yard or two away; under the planter's supervision, they began fervidly digging up to the edge of the bank and throwing clods of earth and spadefuls of sand into the midst of the hostile fleet.

The petrol sprinklers, hitherto used to destroy pests and blights on the plantation, were also brought into action. Streams of evil-reeking oil now soared and fell over an enemy already in disorder through the bombardment of earth and sand.

The ants responded to these vigorous and successful measures of defense by further developments of their offensive. Entire clumps of huddling insects began to roll down the opposite bank into the water. At the same time, Leiningen noticed that the ants were now attacking along an ever-widening front. As the numbers both of his men and his petrol sprinklers were severely limited, this rapid extension of the line of battle was becoming an overwhelming danger.

To add to his difficulties, the very clods of earth they flung into that black floating carpet often whirled fragments toward the defenders' side, and here and there dark ribbons were already mounting the inner bank. True, wherever a man saw these they could still be driven back into the water by spadefuls of earth or jets of petrol. But the file of defenders was too sparse and scattered to hold off at all points these landing parties, and though the peons toiled like mad men, their plight became momently more perilous.

Literary Analysis
Conflict How does Leiningen's response express the tension of the story?

 Reading Check
What do the peons do with the spades and the petrol sprinklers?

Leiningen Versus the Ants ◆ 557

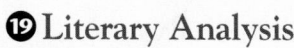 **Literary Analysis**
Conflict

- Ask students the Literary Analysis question on p. 557: How does Leiningen's response express the tension of the story?
  Answer: Leiningen is unwilling or unable to consider defeat, is highly competitive, and is blinded by his own determination. He sees life as a game.

- Then, have students discuss the advantages and disadvantages of Leiningen's total confidence. Do they think it will help him or harm him in the end?
  Answer: Students might say that Leiningen's total confidence will prevent him from seeing the true danger of the situation.

20 ✔ **Reading Check**
Answer: The peons use the spades to throw dirt at the ants, and they use the sprinklers to spray them with oil.

- Encourage students to speculate about how Leiningen's men are affected by watching their friend get devoured by the ants.
- Ask students the Literary Analysis question on p. 558: What kind of conflict concerns Leiningen here? Answer: He is worried about panic and failing morale among his men. He needs them to help him fight the ants.
- ▶ Monitor Progress Explain to students that the men are engaged in both an external conflict (against the ants) and an internal conflict (against fear and doubt).

22 Reading Strategy
Making Predictions

- Ask students what Leiningen means when he refers to "the unseen activity that can go on in a man's brain." Answer: Leiningen seems to be hatching another plan.
- Ask the Reading Strategy question on p. 558: What effect does this reference to Leiningen's thoughts have on your predictions for him? Explain. Possible response: Students may predict that Leiningen will use his reasoning to win the struggle.

One man struck with his spade at an enemy clump, did not draw it back quickly enough from the water; in a trice the wooden haft swarmed with upward scurrying insects. With a curse, he dropped the spade into the ditch; too late, they were already on his body. They lost no time; wherever they encountered bare flesh they bit deeply; a few, bigger than the rest, carried in their hindquarters a sting which injected a burning and paralyzing venom. Screaming, frantic with pain, the peon danced and twirled like a dervish.[8]

21 Realizing that another such casualty, yes, perhaps this alone, might plunge his men into confusion and destroy their morale, Leiningen roared in a bellow louder than the yells of the victim: "Into the petrol, idiot! Douse your paws in the petrol!" The dervish ceased his pirouette as if transfixed, then tore off his shirt and plunged his arm and the ants hanging to it up to the shoulder in one of the large open tins of petrol. But even then the fierce mandibles did not slacken; another peon had to help him squash and detach each separate insect.

Distracted by the episode, some defenders had turned away from the ditch. And now cries of fury, a thudding of spades, and a wild trampling to and fro, showed that the ants had made full use of the interval, though luckily only a few had managed to get across. The men set to work again desperately with the barrage of earth and sand. Meanwhile an old Indian, who acted as medicine man to the plantation workers, gave the bitten peon a drink he had prepared some hours before, which, he claimed, possessed the virtue of dissolving and weakening ants' venom.

Leiningen surveyed his position. A dispassionate observer would have estimated the odds against him at a thousand to one. But then such an onlooker would have reckoned only by what he saw—the advance of myriad battalions of ants against the futile efforts of a few defenders—and not by the unseen activity that can go on in a man's brain.

22 For Leiningen had not erred when he decided he would fight elemental with elemental. The water in the ditch was beginning to rise; the stronger damming of the river was making itself apparent.

Visibly the swiftness and power of the masses of water increased, swirling into quicker and quicker movement its living black surface, dispersing its pattern, carrying away more and more of it on the hastening current.

Victory had been snatched from the very jaws of defeat. With a hysterical shout of joy, the peons feverishly intensified their bombardment of earth clods and sand.

And now the wide cataract down the opposite bank was thinning and ceasing, as if the ants were becoming aware that they could not attain their aim. They were scurrying back up the slope to safety.

All the troops so far hurled into the ditch had been sacrificed in

---

8. **dervish** (dur′ vish) *n.* one who performs a ritual Muslim whirling dance.

Literary Analysis
Conflict What kind of conflict concerns Leiningen here?

Reading Strategy
Making Predictions What effect does this reference to Leiningen's thoughts have on your predictions for him? Explain.

vain. Drowned and floundering insects eddied in thousands along the flow, while Indians running on the bank destroyed every swimmer that reached the side.

Not until the ditch curved toward the east did the scattered ranks assemble again in a coherent mass. And now, exhausted and half-numbed, they were in no condition to ascend the bank. Fusillades of clods drove them round the bend toward the mouth of the ditch and then into the river, wherein they vanished without leaving a trace.

The news ran swiftly along the entire chain of outposts, and soon a long scattered line of laughing men could be seen hastening along the ditch toward the scene of victory.

For once they seemed to have lost all their native reserve, for it was in wild abandon now they celebrated the triumph—as if there were no longer thousands of millions of merciless, cold and hungry eyes watching them from the opposite bank, watching and waiting.

The sun sank behind the rim of the tamarind wood and twilight deepened into night. It was not only hoped but expected that the ants would remain quiet until dawn. But to defeat any forlorn attempt at a crossing, the flow of water through the ditch was powerfully increased by opening the dam still further.

In spite of this impregnable barrier, Leiningen was not yet altogether convinced that the ants would not venture another surprise attack. He ordered his men to camp along the bank overnight. He also detailed parties of them to patrol the ditch in two of his motor cars and ceaselessly to illuminate the surface of the water with headlights and electric torches.

After having taken all the precautions he deemed necessary, the farmer ate his supper with considerable appetite and went to bed. His slumbers were in no wise disturbed by the memory of the waiting, live, twenty square miles.

Dawn found a thoroughly refreshed and active Leiningen riding along the edge of the ditch. The planter saw before him a motionless and unaltered throng of besiegers. He studied the wide belt of water between them and the plantation, and for a moment almost regretted that the fight had ended so soon and so simply. In the comforting, matter-of-fact light of morning, it seemed to him now that the ants hadn't the ghost of a chance to cross the ditch. Even if they plunged headlong into it on all three fronts at once, the force of the now powerful current would inevitably sweep them away. He had got quite a thrill out of the fight—a pity it was already over.

He rode along the eastern and southern sections of the ditch and found everything in order. He reached the western section, opposite the tamarind wood, and here, contrary to the other battle fronts, he found the enemy very busy indeed. The trunks and branches of the trees and the creepers of the lianas,[9] on the far bank of the ditch, fairly swarmed with industrious insects. But instead of eating the

---

9. **lianas** (lē ä´ nəz) *n.* climbing vines found in the tropics.

Reading Strategy
Making Predictions
Predict whether this celebration is premature.

25 ✓**Reading Check**
Why does Leiningen think the fight is over?

Leiningen Versus the Ants ◆ 559

Background

Science

Army ants, like other ants, live in highly structured societies. Each colony has a queen, whose job is to reproduce, and legions of workers that perform the various tasks that are necessary to maintain the colony. Although real army ants are not quite as destructive as the author portrays, they are well-organized, carnivorous creatures that can cause great damage.

27 Critical Thinking

Connect

• Have students connect Macbeth's fate to the fate suggested for Leiningen.
Answer: Macbeth misinterpreted a prophecy and believed he was invulnerable; Leiningen's belief in the invulnerablitiy of his fortifications is about to be tested.

• Ask students to compare Macbeth's reaction to the leaf-covered soldiers with Leiningen's reaction to the leaf-covered ants.
Answer: Macbeth is surprised by the "moving trees" and he is very fearful because it seems that the witches' prophecy is being fulfilled. Leiningen is not surprised by the approach of the ants, and he still believes he can conquer them.

28 Background

Macbeth

Explain to students that in Greek mythology, a person's fate was determined by three women, sometimes called the "weird sisters." They were usually pictured spinning or weaving the fabric of a person's life, which was then arbitrarily cut. In fact, the Middle English word *werde* meant "fate."

In *Macbeth,* three witches (also known as the three weird sisters) appear throughout the play to foretell Macbeth's future and determine his fate.

---

leaves there and then, they were merely gnawing through the stalks, so that a thick green shower fell steadily to the ground.

No doubt they were victualing columns sent out to obtain <u>provender</u> for the rest of the army. The discovery did not surprise Leiningen. He did not need to be told that ants are intelligent, that certain species even use others as milch cows, watchdogs, and slaves. He was well aware of their power of adaptation, their sense of discipline, their marvelous talent for organization.

His belief that a foray to supply the army was in progress was strengthened when he saw the leaves that fell to the ground being dragged to the troops waiting outside the wood. Then all at once he realized the aim that rain of green was intended to serve.

Each single leaf, pulled or pushed by dozens of toiling insects, was borne straight to the edge of the ditch. Even as Macbeth watched the approach of Birnam Wood in the hands of his enemies,♦ Leiningen saw the tamarind wood move nearer and nearer in the mandibles of the ants. Unlike the fey Scot, however, he did not lose his nerve; no witches had prophesied his doom,[10] and if they had he would have slept just as soundly. All the same, he was forced to admit to himself that the situation was now far more ominous than that of the day before.

He had thought it impossible for the ants to build rafts for themselves—well, here they were, coming in thousands, more than enough to bridge the ditch. Leaves after leaves rustled down the slope to the water, where the current drew them away from the bank and carried them into midstream. And every single leaf carried several ants. This time the farmer did not trust to the alacrity of his messengers. He galloped away, leaning from his saddle and yelling orders as he rushed past outpost after outpost: "Bring petrol pumps to the southwest front! Issue spades to every man along the line facing the wood!" And arrived at the eastern and southern sections, he dispatched every man except the observation posts to the menaced west.

Then, as he rode past the stretch where the ants had failed to cross the day before, he witnessed a brief but impressive scene. Down the slope of the distant hill there came toward him a singular being, writhing rather than running, an animallike blackened statue with a shapeless head and four quivering feet that knuckled under almost ceaselessly. When the creature reached the far bank of the

provender (präv′ ən dər) *n.* food; provisions.

Literature 28
in context Humanities Connection

♦ *Macbeth*
"Even as Macbeth watched the approach of Birnam Wood in the hands of his enemies," Leiningen watches the ants. This is a reference to William Shakespeare's play *Macbeth*, set in eleventh-century Scotland. Macbeth murders King Duncan of Scotland. After he takes over the kingdom, Macbeth fears that he will be conquered by the dead king's supporters. He asks the witches for advice, and they predict that he will not be conquered "till Birnam forest come to Dunsinane." The prophecy is realized when soldiers carry boughs from Birnam Wood to use as shields as they come to attack Macbeth in the castle at Dunsinane.

Macbeth was surprised by the approach of Birnam Wood, but Leiningen was not surprised by the approach of the ants.

---

10. **fey** (fā) **Scot . . . doom** "fey Scot" refers to Macbeth, whose death was foretold by three witches.

ditch and collapsed opposite Leiningen, he recognized it as a pampas stag, covered over and over with ants.

It had strayed near the zone of the army. As usual, they had attacked its eyes first. Blinded, it had reeled in the madness of hideous torment straight into the ranks of its persecutors, and now the beast swayed to and fro in its death agony.

With a shot from his rifle Leiningen put it out of its misery. Then he pulled out his watch. He hadn't a second to lose, but for life itself he could not have denied his curiosity the satisfaction of knowing how long the ants would take—for personal reasons, so to speak. After six minutes the white polished bones alone remained. That's how he himself would look before you can—Leiningen spat once, and put spurs to his horse.

The sporting zest with which the excitement of the novel contest had inspired him the day before had now vanished; in its place was a cold and violent purpose. He would send these vermin back to the hell where they belonged, somehow, anyhow. Yes, but how was indeed the question; as things stood at present it looked as if the devils would raze him and his men from the earth instead. He had underestimated the might of the enemy; he really would have to bestir himself if he hoped to outwit them.

The biggest danger now, he decided, was the point where the western section of the ditch curved southward. And arrived there, he found his worst expectations justified. The very power of the current had huddled the leaves and their crews of ants so close together at the bend that the bridge was almost ready.

True, streams of petrol and clumps of earth still prevented a landing. But the number of floating leaves was increasing ever more swiftly. It could not be long now before a stretch of water a mile in length was decked by a green pontoon over which the ants could rush in millions.

Leiningen galloped to the weir. The damming of the river was controlled by a wheel on its bank. The planter ordered the man at the wheel first to lower the water in the ditch almost to vanishing point, next to wait a moment, then suddenly to let the river in again. This maneuver of lowering and raising the surface, of decreasing then increasing the flow of water through the ditch, was to be repeated over and over again until further notice.

This tactic was at first successful. The water in the ditch sank, and with it the film of leaves. The green fleet nearly reached the bed and the troops on the far bank swarmed down the slope to it. Then a violent flow of water at the original depth raced through the ditch, overwhelming leaves and ants, and sweeping them along.

This intermittent rapid flushing prevented just in time the almost completed fording of the ditch. But it also flung here and there squads of the enemy vanguard simultaneously up the inner bank. These seemed to know their duty only too well, and lost no time accomplishing it. The air rang with the curses of bitten Indians. They had removed their shirts and pants to detect the quicker the

Literary Analysis
Conflict How has the conflict changed in Leiningen's mind?

Reading Strategy
Making Predictions Which details help you predict whether this strategy will be successful?

③① ✓**Reading Check**
What new strategy are the ants employing?

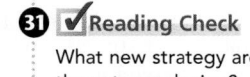

Leiningen Versus the Ants ◆ 561

㉙ Literary Analysis
Conflict

- As students read the passage, have them describe Leiningen's original attitude toward the ants. Then, have them review what the ants have thus far accomplished.
- Ask students the Literary Analysis question on p. 561: How has the conflict changed in Leiningen's mind?
  Answer: The conflict is now much more serious and challenging. It is no longer a game, but a struggle between good and evil, and the consequence of losing could be death.

㉚ Reading Strategy
Making Predictions

- Have students identify Leiningen's strategy, based on details in this passage.
  Answer: Leiningen has decided to lower and raise the surface of the water rapidly in order to destroy the ants' bridge.
- Ask the Reading Strategy question on p. 561: What details help you predict whether this strategy will be successful?
  Answer: The millions of ants and the "green pontoon" suggest that the ants are strong and sturdy enough to withstand this new strategy.

㉛ ✓**Reading Check**
Answer: The ants are using leaves to build a bridge across the ditch.

✺ **ENRICHMENT: Social Studies Connection**

Farming in Brazil

Explain to students that the interior of Brazil is a harsh region, with scarce grazing land and poor soil. Farmers there raise small crops of beans, corn, and cotton. On the coastal plains of the Northeast, there are cacao bean, sugar cane, and tobacco farms. In the Central and Southern Plateaus, where Leiningen's plantation is probably located, coffee is the largest crop. Farmers also grow potatoes, sugar cane, rice, and wheat.

Making Predictions

- After students read the bracketed passage, ask them to explain how the ants were able to cross the moat.
  Answer: The ants cross the moat by climbing over one another.
- Ask students the Reading Strategy question on p. 562: Now that the ants have crossed the moat, what do you think is going to happen?
  Answer: Leiningen and his men will rush to get behind the inner moat.

33 Literary Analysis

Conflict

- Ask students to summarize what Leiningen tells his men in this passage.
- Ask students the Literary Analysis question on p. 562: What internal conflict is expressed here?
  Answer: Leiningen realizes that he must give the men a chance to save their own lives. He hopes and expects that if he gives them a chance to leave, they will renew their loyalty to him and, therefore, fight harder than ever. Have students discuss what they might do in this situation, and why.

---

upward-hastening insects; when they saw one, they crushed it; and fortunately the onslaught as yet was only by skirmishers.

Again and again, the water sank and rose, carrying leaves and drowned ants away with it. It lowered once more nearly to its bed; but this time the exhausted defenders waited in vain for the flush of destruction. Leiningen sensed disaster; something must have gone wrong with the machinery of the dam. Then a sweating peon tore up to him:

"They're over!"

While the besieged were concentrating upon the defense of the stretch opposite the wood, the seemingly unaffected line beyond the wood had become the theater of decisive action. Here the defenders' front was sparse and scattered; everyone who could be spared had hurried away to the south.

Just as the man at the weir had lowered the water almost to the bed of the ditch, the ants on a wide front began another attempt at a direct crossing like that of the preceding day. Into the emptied bed poured an irresistible throng. Rushing across the ditch, they attained the inner bank before the Indians fully grasped the situation. Their frantic screams dumbfounded the man at the weir. Before he could direct the river anew into the safeguarding bed he saw himself surrounded by raging ants. He ran like the others, ran for his life.

When Leiningen heard this, he knew the plantation was doomed. He wasted no time bemoaning the inevitable. For as long as there was the slightest chance of success, he had stood his ground; and now any further resistance was both useless and dangerous. He fired three revolver shots into the air—the prearranged signal for his men to retreat instantly within the "inner moat." Then he rode toward the ranch house.

This was two miles from the point of invasion. There was therefore time enough to prepare the second line of defense against the advent of the ants. Of the three great petrol cisterns near the house, one had already been half emptied by the constant withdrawals needed for the pumps during the fight at the water ditch. The remaining petrol in it was now drawn off through underground pipes into the concrete trench which encircled the ranch house and its outbuildings.

And there, drifting in twos and threes, Leiningen's men reached him. Most of them were obviously trying to preserve an air of calm and indifference, belied, however, by their restless glances and knitted brows. One could see their belief in a favorable outcome of the struggle was already considerably shaken.

The planter called his peons around him.

"Well, lads," he began, "we've lost the first round. But we'll smash the beggars yet, don't you worry. Anyone who thinks otherwise can draw his pay here and now and push off. There are rafts enough and to spare on the river and plenty of time still to reach 'em."

Not a man stirred.

Leiningen acknowledged his silent vote of confidence with a laugh

Reading Strategy
Making Predictions Now that the ants have crossed the moat, what do you think is going to happen?

Literary Analysis
Conflict What internal conflict is expressed here?

CUSTOMIZE INSTRUCTION FOR UNIVERSAL ACCESS

For Special Needs Students	For Gifted/Talented Students
Students may benefit from having Leiningen's plan outlined for them. Explain that there are two lines of defense for the plantation, and that the men have had to retreat from the first line. The second line is much nearer to the house; retreating there means that the ants will destroy the crops grown on the plantation.	Encourage students to find words in the narrative that set the tone and place of the action. They should note that the writer uses words such as *quivering, toiling, ominous, rustled, galloped, blinded,* and *reeled.* Ask students to suggest music that might match the mood these words convey.

that was half a grunt. "That's the stuff, lads. Too bad if you'd missed the rest of the show, eh? Well, the fun won't start till morning. Once these blighters turn tail, there'll be plenty of work for everyone and higher wages all round. And now run along and get something to eat; you've earned it all right."

In the excitement of the fight the greater part of the day had passed without the men once pausing to snatch a bite. Now that the ants were for the time being out of sight, and the "wall of petrol" gave a stronger feeling of security, hungry stomachs began to assert their claims.

The bridges over the concrete ditch were removed. Here and there solitary ants had reached the ditch; they gazed at the petrol meditatively, then scurried back again. Apparently they had little interest at

Reading Strategy
Making Predictions What has Leiningen planned for the ants?

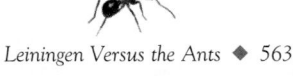 **Reading Check**

What does the signal of three revolver shots mean?

▲ **Critical Viewing** Imagine yourself in this situation. What would you need to do to survive? **[Connect]**

Leiningen Versus the Ants ◆ 563

34 **Reading Strategy**
Making Predictions
• Ask students whether they think the ants will swim in the petrol. Then, have students speculate about what Leiningen can do if the ants do indeed swim in the petrol.
• Ask students the Reading Strategy question on p. 563: What has Leiningen planned for the ants? **Answer:** Knowing that petrol is highly flammable may lead students to believe that Leiningen will set fire to the petrol and burn the ants.

35 ✓**Reading Check**
Answer: The signal means that Leiningen's men should retreat behind the inner moat.

36 ▶**Critical Viewing**
Possible responses: Students may say they would need to keep moving, cover their skin as completely as possible, and get to safety quickly.

③⑦ Literary Analysis

Conflict

- As students read the passage, have them pay careful attention to both the ants' and Leiningen's behavior.

- Ask students the Literary Analysis question on p. 564: What effect does nightfall have on the conflict? **Answer:** Nightfall seems to bring a truce in the conflict. The ants aren't moving, and Leiningen has retreated to do some paperwork. He seems confident and prepared to continue the battle in the morning.

③⑧ Reading Strategy

Making Predictions

- Read aloud the bracketed sentence to students. Call their attention to the words "At first it seemed," which suggest an unforeseen event.

- Ask students the Reading Strategy question on p. 564: How does the first sentence of this paragraph affect your predictions about the petrol trench? **Answer:** The sentence implies that what will actually happen will be different from what was expected. The petrol trench may not end up serving its purpose, and some of the ants will get to the inside of the moat.

▲ the moment for what lay beyond the evil-reeking barrier, the abundant spoils of the plantation were the main attraction. Soon the trees, shrubs and beds for miles around were hulled with ants zealously gobbling the yield of long weary months of strenuous toil.

As twilight began to fall, a cordon of ants marched around the petrol trench, but as yet made no move toward its brink. Leiningen posted sentries with headlights and electric torches, then withdrew to his office, and began to reckon up his losses. He estimated these as large, but, in comparison with his bank balance, by no means **③⑦** unbearable. He worked out in some detail a scheme of intensive cultivation which would enable him, before very long, to more than compensate himself for the damage now being wrought to his crops. It was with a contented mind that he finally betook himself to bed where he slept deeply until dawn, undisturbed by any thought that next day little more might be left of him than a glistening skeleton.

He rose with the sun and went out on the flat roof of his house. And a scene like one from Dante[11] lay around him; for miles in every direction there was nothing but a black, glittering multitude, a multitude of rested, sated, but nonetheless voracious ants; yes, look as far as one might, one could see nothing but that rustling black throng, except in the north, where the great river drew a boundary they could not hope to pass. But even the high stone breakwater, along the bank of the river, which Leiningen had built as a defense against inundations, was, like the paths, the shorn trees and shrubs, the ground itself, black with ants.

So their greed was not glutted in razing that vast plantation? Not by a long chalk; they were all the more eager now on a rich and certain booty—four hundred men, numerous horses, and bursting granaries.

③⑧ At first it seemed that the petrol trench would serve its purpose. The besiegers sensed the peril of swimming it, and made no move to plunge blindly over its brink. Instead they devised a better maneuver; they began to collect shreds of bark, twigs and dried leaves and dropped these into the petrol. Everything green, which could have been similarly used, had long since been eaten. After a time, though, a long procession could be seen bringing from the west the tamarind leaves used as rafts the day before.

Since the petrol, unlike the water in the outer ditch, was perfectly still, the refuse stayed where it was thrown. It was several hours before the ants succeeded in covering an appreciable part of the surface. At length, however, they were ready to proceed to a direct attack.

Their storm troops swarmed down the concrete side, scrambled over the supporting surface of twigs and leaves, and impelled these over the few remaining streaks of open petrol until they reached the

---

11. **Dante** (dän´ tā) Italian poet (1265–1321) who wrote *The Divine Comedy*, describing the horrors of hell.

Literary Analysis
Conflict What effect does nightfall have on the conflict?

Reading Strategy
Making Predictions How does the first sentence of this paragraph affect your predictions about the petrol trench?

✷ ENRICHMENT: Career Connection

Workplace Leadership

Point out to students that showing leadership in the workplace can help them achieve their goals. Invite students to describe a workplace situation in which they would be required to show leadership qualities. Have them consider these questions:

- What qualities does a leader need?

- How can a leader promote confidence in his or her workers?

- What aspects of a situation does a leader need to consider?

Have students discuss their answers. Then, have them note which of the qualities they have chosen are qualities Leiningen possesses, and whether they, as leaders, would have made the choices Leiningen made.

other side. Then they began to climb up this to make straight for the helpless garrison.

During the entire offensive, the planter sat peacefully, watching them with interest, but not stirring a muscle. Moreover, he had ordered his men not to disturb in any way whatever the advancing horde. So they squatted listlessly along the bank of the ditch and waited for a sign from the boss.

The petrol was now covered with ants. A few had climbed the inner concrete wall and were scurrying toward the defenders.

"Everyone back from the ditch!" roared Leiningen. The men rushed away, without the slightest idea of his plan. He stooped forward and cautiously dropped into the ditch a stone which split the floating carpet and its living freight, to reveal a gleaming patch of petrol. A match spurted, sank down to the oily surface—Leiningen sprang back; in a flash a towering rampart of fire encompassed the garrison.

This spectacular and instant repulse threw the Indians into ecstasy. They applauded, yelled and stamped. Had it not been for the awe in which they held their boss, they would infallibly have carried him shoulder high.

It was some time before the petrol burned down to the bed of the ditch, and the wall of smoke and flame began to lower. The ants had retreated in a wide circle from the devastation, and innumerable charred fragments along the outer bank showed that the flames had spread from the holocaust in the ditch well into the ranks beyond, where they had wrought havoc far and wide.

Yet the perseverance of the ants was by no means broken; indeed, each setback seemed only to whet it. The concrete cooled, the flicker of the dying flames wavered and vanished, petrol from the second tank poured into the trench—and the ants marched forward anew to the attack.

The foregoing scene repeated itself in every detail, except that on this occasion less time was needed to bridge the ditch, for the petrol was now already filmed by a layer of ash. Once again they withdrew; once again petrol flowed into the ditch. Would the creatures never learn that their self-sacrifice was utterly senseless? It really was senseless, wasn't it? Yes, of course it was senseless—provided the defenders had an *unlimited* supply of petrol.

When Leiningen reached this stage of reasoning, he felt for the first time since the arrival of the ants that his confidence was deserting him. His skin began to creep; he loosened his collar. Once the devils were over the trench there wasn't a chance for him and his men. What a prospect, to be eaten alive like that!

For the third time the flames immolated the attacking troops, and burned down to extinction. Yet the ants were coming on again as if nothing had happened. And meanwhile Leiningen had made a discovery that chilled him to the bone—petrol was no longer flowing into the ditch. Something must be blocking the outflow pipe of the third and last cistern—a snake or a dead rat? Whatever it was, the ants could

Literary Analysis
Conflict and Climax
What effect does the petrol fire have on your anticipation of the climax of the story?

Literary Analysis
Conflict What elements besides the ants influence the external conflict?

41 ✓**Reading Check**
What method are Leiningen and his men using to keep the ants from crossing the inner moat?

Leiningen Versus the Ants ◆ 565

Ants

Students may be interested to know that scientists sometimes view a colony of ants not as a group of individuals but rather as a single organism. Within the organism, different groups perform different tasks, just as organs of the body do.

43 Critical Thinking

Infer

• Have a volunteer read aloud the bracketed passage.

• Ask students to describe the mood of the group before the two men ran. Then, have students describe how the death of the men might affect the remaining men.

Answer: The men will probably be more resolved to continue fighting the ants now that they have seen that running will not help them.

44 Reading Strategy

Making Predictions

• Have students review the actions that Leiningen and his men have taken to combat the ants up to this point in this story.

• Have students identify the resources that Leiningen still has at his disposal to fight the ants.

• Then, ask students the Reading Strategy question on p. 566: What do you think Leiningen plans to do?

Answer: He will dam the river and drown the ants.

---

be held off no longer, unless petrol could by some method be led from the cistern into the ditch.

Then Leiningen remembered that in an outhouse nearby were two old disused fire engines. The peons dragged them out of the shed, connected their pumps to the cistern, uncoiled and laid the hose. They were just in time to aim a stream of petrol at a column of ants that had already crossed and drive them back down the incline into the ditch. Once more an oily girdle surrounded the garrison, once more it was possible to hold the position—for the moment.

It was obvious, however, that this last resource meant only the postponement of defeat and death. A few of the peons fell on their knees and began to pray; others, shrieking insanely, fired their revolvers at the black, advancing masses, as if they felt their despair was pitiful enough to sway fate itself to mercy.

At length, two of the men's nerves broke: Leiningen saw a naked Indian leap over the north side of the petrol trench, quickly followed by a second. They sprinted with incredible speed toward the river. But their fleetness did not save them; long before they could attain the rafts, the enemy covered their bodies from head to foot.

In the agony of their torment, both sprang blindly into the wide river, where enemies no less sinister awaited them. Wild screams of mortal anguish informed the breathless onlookers that crocodiles and sword-toothed piranhas were no less ravenous than ants, and even nimbler in reaching their prey.

In spite of this bloody warning, more and more men showed they were making up their minds to run the blockade. Anything, even a fight midstream against alligators, seemed better than powerlessly waiting for death to come and slowly consume their living bodies.

Leiningen flogged his brain till it reeled. Was there nothing on earth could sweep this devils' spawn back into the hell from which it came?

Then out of the inferno of his bewilderment rose a terrifying inspiration. Yes, one hope remained, and one alone. It might be possible to dam the great river completely, so that its waters would fill not only the water ditch but overflow into the entire gigantic "saucer" of land in which lay the plantation.

The far bank of the river was too high for the waters to escape that way. The stone break-water ran between the river and the plantation; its only gaps occurred where the "horseshoe" ends of the water ditch passed into the river. So its waters would not only be forced to inundate into the plantation, they would also be held there by the breakwater until they rose to its own high level. In half an hour,

---

Literature 42
in context Science Connection

Ants

All ants are social in habit, and they live in colonies. In fact, the social behavior of ants is more complex than that of any other insect. Ants communicate with one another in various ways. They may tap or buzz or give off chemicals called pheromones. The ants in the story seem to be able to tell each other what is happening.

Reading Strategy
Making Predictions What do you think Leiningen plans to do?

✳ ENRICHMENT: Science Connection

Poisonous Animal Bites

Point out that Leiningen's ants aren't the only animals with poisonous, or even fatal, bites. Spiders such as the black widow, tarantula, or brown spider can administer dangerous or even fatal bites. Mosquitoes can transmit diseases such as malaria and dengue fever that, if untreated, can kill. Some ticks transmit Lyme disease; bee stings, if the victim is allergic to them, can result in shock and death. Rattlesnakes and copperheads can kill with their venomous bites. Even mammals such as raccoons, skunks, and bats can transmit rabies, an infectious disease that is fatal if untreated.

perhaps even earlier, the plantation and its hostile army of occupation would be flooded.

The ranch house and outbuildings stood upon rising ground. Their foundations were higher than the breakwater, so the flood would not reach them. And any remaining ants trying to ascend the slope could be repulsed by petrol.

It was possible—yes, if one could only get to the dam! A distance of nearly two miles lay between the ranch house and the weir—two miles of ants. Those two peons had managed only a fifth of that distance at the cost of their lives. Was there an Indian daring enough after that to run the gauntlet five times as far? Hardly likely; and if there were, his prospect of getting back was almost nil.

No, there was only one thing for it, he'd have to make the attempt himself; he might just as well be running as sitting still, anyway, when the ants finally got him. Besides, there was a bit of a chance. Perhaps the ants weren't so almighty, after all; perhaps he had allowed the mass suggestion of that evil black throng to hypnotize him, just as a snake fascinates and overpowers.

The ants were building their bridges. Leiningen got up on a chair. "Hey, lads, listen to me!" he cried. Slowly and listlessly, from all sides of the trench, the men began to shuffle toward him, the apathy of death already stamped on their faces.

"Listen, lads!" he shouted. "You're frightened of those beggars, but I'm proud of you. There's still a chance to save our lives—by flooding the plantation from the river. Now one of you might manage to get as far as the weir—but he'd never come back. Well, I'm not going to let you try it; if I did, I'd be worse than one of those ants. No, I called the tune, and now I'm going to pay the piper.

"The moment I'm over the ditch, set fire to the petrol. That'll allow time for the flood to do the trick. Then all you have to do is to wait here all snug and quiet till I'm back. Yes, I'm coming back, trust me"—he grinned—"when I've finished my slimming cure."

He pulled on high leather boots, drew heavy gauntlets over his hands, and stuffed the spaces between breeches and boots, gauntlets and arms, shirt and neck, with rags soaked in petrol. With close-fitting mosquito goggles he shielded his eyes, knowing too well the ants' dodge of first robbing their victim of sight. Finally, he plugged his nostrils and ears with cottonwool, and let the peons drench his clothes with petrol.

He was about to set off when the old Indian medicine man came up to him; he had a wondrous salve, he said, prepared from a species of chafer[12] whose odor was intolerable to ants. Yes, this odor protected these chafers from the attacks of even the most murderous ants. The Indian smeared the boss's boots, his gauntlets, and his face over and over with the extract.

Leiningen then remembered the paralyzing effect of ants' venom,

---

12. chafer (chāf' ər) *n.* insect that feeds on plants.

Reading Strategy
Making Predictions Do you think Leiningen will succeed in his dash to the dam? Why?

 Reading Check
Why does Leiningen decide to go to the dam himself?

Leiningen Versus the Ants ◆ 567

---

45 Reading Strategy
Making Predictions

- Have students consider the power of the ants and the fate of the two men who tried to escape.

- Direct students to think about Leiningen's attitude and the way he has behaved thus far.

- Ask students the Reading Strategy question on p. 567: Do you think Leiningen will succeed in his dash to the dam? Why?
  Possible responses: Leiningen can't possibly make it because the other two men didn't. Leiningen's positive attitude and the fact that he will undoubtedly prepare himself for the run will enable him to succeed.

46 Critical Thinking
Draw Conclusions

- Draw students' attention to the description of Leiningen's men. Point out that they are on the verge of losing hope.

- Then, ask students to consider Leiningen's attitude and ask how it will affect the men's morale.
  Answer: Leiningen will probably revive their morale because he has a plan.

47 ☑ Reading Check

Answer: Leiningen realizes that he "called the tune," so he must "pay the piper." He has taken on this battle with the ants, so he must lead it.

㊽ Literary Analysis

Conflict

- Have students read the bracketed passage. Draw their attention to the ways in which Leiningen avoids the ants.

- Ask the first Literary Analysis question on p. 568: How does Leiningen avoid the ants at this point in the story?
  Answer: He keeps his feet off the ground as much as possible, and he avoids trees and shrubs where the ants would be able to jump on him.

㊾ Literary Analysis

Conflict and Climax

- Ask the second Literary Analysis question on p. 568: What details in this passage indicate that the tension of the story is reaching its highest point?
  Answer: Leiningen, the main character, is coated with ants, he is in great pain, and he begins the return journey seriously wounded.

- Ask students to predict whether Leiningen will survive his dangerous journey back to the plantation. Remind them to consider his personality and past actions when formulating their responses.

and the Indian gave him a gourd full of the medicine he had administered to the bitten peon at the water ditch.

The planter drank it down without noticing its bitter taste; his mind was already at the weir.

He started off toward the northwest corner of the trench. With a bound he was over—and among the ants.

The beleaguered garrison had no opportunity to watch Leiningen's race against death. The ants were climbing the inner bank again—the lurid ring of petrol blazed aloft. For the fourth time that day the reflection from the fire shone on the sweating faces of the imprisoned men, and on the reddish-black cuirasses[13] of their oppressors. The red and blue, dark-edged flames leaped vividly now, celebrating what? The funeral pyre of the four hundred, or of the hosts of destruction?

㊽ Leiningen ran. He ran in long, equal strides, with only one thought, one sensation, in his being—*he must* get through. He dodged all trees and shrubs; except for the split seconds his soles touched the ground, the ants should have no opportunity to alight on him. That they would get to him soon, despite the salve on his boots, the petrol on his clothes, he realized only too well, but he knew even more surely that he must, and that he would, get to the weir.

Apparently the salve was some use after all: not until he had reached halfway did he feel ants under his clothes, and a few on his face. Mechanically, in his stride, he struck at them, scarcely conscious of their bites. He saw he was drawing appreciably nearer the weir—the distance grew less and less—sank to five hundred—three—two—hundred yards.

Then he was at the weir and gripping the ant-hulled wheel. Hardly had he seized it when a horde of infuriated ants flowed over his hands, arms, and shoulders. He started the wheel—before it turned once on its axis the swarm covered his face. Leiningen strained like a madman, his lips pressed tight; if he opened them to draw breath . . .

He turned and turned; slowly the dam lowered until it reached the bed of the river. Already the water was overflowing the ditch. Another minute, and the river was pouring through the nearby gap in the breakwater. The flooding of the plantation had begun.

Leiningen let go the wheel. Now, for the first time, he realized he was coated from head to foot with a layer of ants. In spite of the petrol, his clothes were full of them, several had got to his body or were clinging to his face. Now that he had completed his task, he felt ㊾ the smart raging over his flesh from the bites of sawing and piercing insects.

Frantic with pain, he almost plunged into the river. To be ripped and slashed to shreds by piranhas? Already he was running the return journey, knocking ants from his gloves and jacket, brushing them from his bloodied face, squashing them to death under his clothes.

---

13. **cuirasses** (kwi ras´ ez) *n.* body armor; here, the ants' outer bodies.

Literary Analysis
Conflict How does Leiningen avoid the ants at this point in the story?

Literary Analysis
Conflict and Climax Which details in this passage indicate that the tension of the story is reaching its highest point?

✺ ENRICHMENT: Science Connection

Animals of Brazilian Rivers

Point out that the largest river in Brazil is the Amazon, which is home to a vast number of species of animals. Other rivers in the area would support the same wildlife, which includes the small but voracious piranha, which will attack any animal in the water; electric eels; giant anacondas; crocodiles; and freshwater stingrays. There are other less fearsome animals as well, such as the pirarucu, reputed to be the best-tasting and biggest freshwater fish in the world, and the giant catfish. Ask students why in "Leiningen Versus the Ants"

only the dangerous river inhabitants are mentioned.

Answer: Student should observe that only the dangerous animals contribute to the conflict in the story.

One of the creatures bit him just below the rim of his goggles; he managed to tear it away, but the agony of the bite and its etching acid drilled into the eye nerves; he saw now through circles of fire into a milky mist, then he ran for a time almost blinded, knowing that if he once tripped and fell. . . . The old Indian's brew didn't seem much good; it weakened the poison a bit, but didn't get rid of it. His heart pounded as if it would burst; blood roared in his ears; a giant's fist battered his lungs.

Then he could see again, but the burning girdle of petrol appeared infinitely far away; he could not last half that distance. Swift-changing pictures flashed through his head, episodes in his life, while in another part of his brain a cool and impartial onlooker informed this ant-blurred, gasping, exhausted bundle named Leiningen that such a rushing panorama of scenes from one's past is seen only in the moment before death.

A stone in the path . . . too weak to avoid it . . . the planter stumbled and collapsed. He tried to rise . . . he must be pinned under a rock . . . it was impossible . . . the slightest movement was impossible. . . .

Then all at once he saw, starkly clear and huge, and, right before his eyes, furred with ants, towering and swaying in its death agony, the pampas stag. In six minutes—gnawed to the bones. He *couldn't* die like that! And something outside him seemed to drag him to his feet. He tottered. He began to stagger forward again.

Through the blazing ring hurtled an apparition which, as soon as it reached the ground on the inner side, fell full length and did not move. Leiningen, at the moment he made that leap through the flames, lost consciousness for the first time in his life. As he lay there, with glazing eyes and lacerated face, he appeared a man returned from the grave. The peons rushed to him, stripped off his clothes, tore away the ants from a body that seemed almost one open wound; in some places the bones were showing. They carried him into the ranch house.

As the curtain of flames lowered, one could see in place of the illimitable host of ants an extensive vista of water. The thwarted river had swept over the plantation, carrying with it the entire army. The water had collected and mounted in the great "saucer," while the ants had in vain attempted to reach the hill on which stood the ranch house. The girdle of flames held them back.

And so, imprisoned between water and fire, they had been delivered into the annihilation that was their god. And near the farther mouth of the water ditch, where the stone mole had its second gap, the ocean swept the lost battalions into the river, to vanish forever.

The ring of fire dwindled as the water mounted to the petrol trench and quenched the dimming flames. The inundation rose higher and higher: because its outflow was impeded by the timber and underbrush it had carried along with it, its surface required some

Literary Analysis
Conflict What internal conflict is Leiningen facing?

51 ✔**Reading Check**
What does Leiningen accomplish at the dam?

Leiningen Versus the Ants ◆ 569

50 **Literary Analysis**
Conflict

• Ask students the Literary Analysis question on p. 569: What internal conflict is Leiningen facing?
Answer: His internal conflict is between his temptation to give up and the image of the stag's horrible death.

• Then, ask students why they think Leiningen was able to rise again and go on. Until now, he has relied on his intellect. What is he relying on now?
Answer: When Leiningen recalls the horrifying death of the stag, his instinct for survival forces him to get to his feet and continue.

51 ✔**Reading Check**
Answer: Leiningen lowers the dam and floods the plantation.

Review and Assess

1. Students may say that they would have left the plantation well before the ants arrived.

2. (a) The ants threaten to destroy his plantation and kill him and his workers. (b) Leiningen has a great deal of faith in the ability of his intellect to conquer nature.

3. (a) It first seems that Leiningen will be victorious when the ants cannot find a way to cross the moat. (b) The ants use the leaves as rafts to get across the river. (c) The ants' recovery shows that their instincts to survive can compete with Leiningen's intelligence.

4. (a) Leiningen opens the weir and lets the river overflow his plantation. (b) Possible response: Leiningen's nature is to fight back rather than surrender. He has tremendous self-confidence and seems incapable of giving up.

5. (a) Leiningen has a lot of experience with taming nature; he has determination and self-confidence; he has a powerful intellect. (b) Leiningen's self-confidence leads him to endanger the lives of others.

6. (a) The ants use each other as bridges and cut leaves to make rafts. (b) The ants' highly developed communication skills allow them to work together as a team.

7. Some students may say that Leiningen was justified because the plantation was the peons' home, too, and the peons needed a strong and experienced leader. Others may think that he was wrong to risk the lives of others to satisfy his own need for victory.

---

time to reach the top of the high stone breakwater and discharge over it the rest of the shattered army.

It swelled over ant-stippled shrubs and bushes, until it washed against the foot of the knoll whereon the besieged had taken refuge. For a while an <u>alluvium</u> of ants tried again and again to attain the dry land, only to be repulsed by streams of petrol back into the merciless flood.

Leiningen lay on his bed, his body swathed from head to foot in bandages. With <u>fomentations</u> and salves, they had managed to stop the bleeding, and had dressed his many wounds. Now they thronged around him, one question in every face. Would he recover? "He won't die," said the old man who had bandaged him, "if he doesn't want to."

The planter opened his eyes. "Everything in order?" he asked.

"They're gone," said his nurse. He held out to his master a gourd full of a powerful sleeping-draft. Leiningen gulped it down.

"I told you I'd come back," he murmured, "even if I am a bit streamlined."

alluvium (ə lōō´ vē əm) *n.* material such as sand or clay deposited by moving water

fomentations (fō mən tā´ shənz) *n.* applications of substances in the treatment of an injury

Review and Assess

Thinking About the Selection

1. **Respond:** Put yourself in Leiningen's place. What would you have done differently?

2. **(a) Recall:** What threat do the ants pose to Leiningen? **(b) Infer:** Why does Leiningen decide to stay and confront the ants?

3. **(a) Recall:** At what point in the story does it first seem that Leiningen has snatched victory "from the very jaws of defeat"? **(b) Recall:** How do the ants recover? **(c) Analyze:** What makes the ants' recovery so frightening?

4. **(a) Recall:** How does Leiningen finally defeat the ants? **(b) Analyze:** What do you think drives Leiningen beyond his physical limits in defeating the ants?

5. **(a) Analyze:** What qualities do you think make Leiningen well equipped to fight the ants? **(b) Connect:** What qualities might make him dangerous to others?

6. **(a) Interpret:** What behavior of the ants makes them appear to be intelligent beings? **(b) Generalize:** How does your knowledge of ants explain their behavior?

7. **Make a Judgment:** By staying to fight the ants, Leiningen risks others' lives as well as his own. Do you think he was justified? Why or why not?

Carl Stephenson

(1886–1954)

Although Carl Stephenson was born and lived his entire life in Germany, he vividly captures the torrid atmosphere and raw wilderness of the jungles of Brazil in "Leiningen Versus the Ants." This short story has been widely read and included in numerous anthologies since it was first published in *Esquire* magazine in 1938. It was also adapted for a radio program entitled *Suspense*, starring Vincent Price, and made into a film entitled *The Naked Jungle*, starring Charlton Heston.

Shying away from the spotlight, Stephenson insisted that "Leiningen Versus the Ants" be the only story published during his lifetime.

ASSESSMENT PRACTICE: Grammar and Language

Distinguish Between Fact and Nonfact   (For more practice, see Test Preparation Workbook, p. 36.)

Students preparing to take tests need to be able to distinguish fact from opinion. A fact can be verified or proved, and an opinion cannot. Use this sample test item to reinforce the concept.

The vivid descriptions and exciting action in the story inspired movie makers to create a film. The film version starring Charlton Heston was released in 1954 with the unusual title *The Naked Jungle*.

Which of the following is a FACT stated in the passage?

A The description in the story is vivid.

B The movie was released in 1954.

C The action in the story is exciting.

D The movie's title is unusual.

Remind students that adjectives such as *exciting*, *vivid*, or *unusual* state one person's opinion and cannot be proved. Only *B* is a fact that can be proved.

Review and Assess

Literary Analysis

Conflict

1. Using a diagram like this one, indicate what forces are in opposition in the **external conflict** of the story.

Force   vs.   Force

2. What is Leiningen's **internal conflict**?
3. (a) Which characters besides Leiningen experience an internal conflict? (b) For each, identify the conflict and explain how or whether it is revealed.

Connecting Literary Elements

4. (a) What event signals the **climax** of the story? (b) How do you know that this is the climax?
5. Using a diagram like the one here, describe three conflicts that escalate the tension in the story toward the climax.

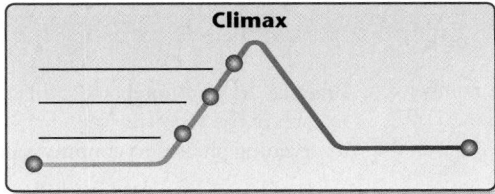

Climax

Reading Strategy

Making Predictions

6. (a) What did you **predict** would happen when the ants began crossing the ditch on leaves? Why? (b) What did you predict would happen when the men retreated to the ranch house? Why?
7. What hints suggest how the war against the ants will end?

Extend Understanding

8. **Literature Connection:** What other examples from literature can you recall in which a character makes a decision upon which others' lives depend? Compare the examples with those in this story.

Quick Review

Conflict is the struggle between opposing forces that is at the heart of a story's plot.

An **external conflict** occurs between two or more characters or between a character and a natural force.

An **internal conflict** takes place within a character, as he or she struggles with opposing feelings, beliefs, or needs.

The **climax** is the point at which the conflict reaches its highest intensity.

You can **make predictions,** or guesses about future events, based on the plot details that have already occurred in the story.

 Take It to the Net

www.phschool.com
Take the interactive self-test online to check your understanding of the selection.

Leiningen Versus the Ants ◆ 571

Answers for p. 572

❶ Vocabulary Development

Latin Plural Forms

1. data
2. curricula
3. antennae
4. octopi

Concept Development: Analogies

1. provender
2. flout
3. weir
4. alluvium
5. peons
6. fomentations

Spelling Strategy

1. veil
2. deceive
3. believe
4. correct

❷ Grammar

1. uses; delete "behind the hills"
2. float; delete "on their raft"
3. travels; delete "with great leaps"
4. was; delete "under the ants"
5. crawl; delete "on the spade"

Writing Application

Leiningen and his men battle a giant colony of killer ants. In the beginning, Leiningen prepares for the ants' arrival by lowering the dam on the river and filling kerosene sprayers with which to douse them. The ants use leaves as rafts to get across the outer ditch filled with water. Leiningen and his men escape to the safety of an inner moat that is filled with kerosene. There the ants are set on fire, but they still manage to advance over the ashes. Finally, Leiningen, protected by kerosene, salve, and goggles, runs to the weir to release the river in order to flood the plantation. The ants are swept away.

Integrate Language Skills

❶ Vocabulary Development Lesson

Concept Development: Latin Plural Forms

Some words in English that are borrowed from Latin, such as *alluvium*, retain their Latin plural forms. Change endings of words from Latin as follows to form plurals :

um becomes *a*
us becomes *i*
a becomes *ae*

In your notebook, write the plural forms of each of the following words:

1. datum
2. curriculum
3. antenna
4. octopus

❷ Grammar Lesson

Subject and Verb Agreement

A verb must agree with its subject in number and gender.

		S V
Singular:		The <u>ant builds</u> a dam.

		S V
Plural:		The <u>ants build</u> a dam.

Be careful not to confuse the subject with the object of a preposition that may follow it. In the following sentences, *Leiningen* is the subject:

No Prepositional Phrase:
<u>Leiningen</u> <u>races</u> against the ant army.

Intervening Prepositional Phrase:
<u>Leiningen</u> *with his employees* <u>races</u> against the ant army.

W͜G *Prentice Hall Writing and Grammar Connection: Chapter 24, Section 1*

572 ◆ *Short Stories*

Concept Development: Analogies

In your notebook, complete the analogies using the words from the vocabulary list on page 549.

1. water : plants :: ___ : animals
2. ignore : rule :: ___ : law
3. tourniquet : blood :: ___ : river
4. wall : bricks :: delta: ___
5. employee : manager :: ___ : master
6. patch : rip :: ___ : injury

Spelling Strategy

Place *i* before *e* except after *c* or when sounded like *a* as in *neighbor* and *weigh*. *Weir* and *weird* are exceptions. Rewrite misspelled words below.

1. viel
2. decieve
3. beleive
4. relief

Practice In your notebook, correct the verb form in each of the following sentences. Cross out any intervening phrases to confirm your decisions.

1. The peon behind the hills use kerosene on the leaves.
2. The ants on their raft floats across the river.
3. Leiningen with great leaps travel across the countryside.
4. The poor stag under the ants were doomed.
5. The ants on the spade crawls toward his hand.

Writing Application Write a brief summary of the story. After you draft your summary, confirm that subjects and verbs agree.

TEACHING RESOURCES

The following resources can be used to enrich or extend the instruction for pp. 572–573.

Vocabulary

📖 **Selection Support:** Build Vocabulary, p. 141

📖 **Vocabulary and Spelling Practice Book**
(Use this booklet for skills enrichment.) ▦

Grammar

📖 **Selection Support:** Build Grammar Skills, p. 142

W͜G **Writing and Grammar,** Platinum Level, p. 566

📄 **Daily Language Practice Transparencies**

Writing

W͜G **Writing and Grammar,** Platinum Level, p. 84

💿 **Writing and Grammar iText CD-ROM** ▦

📖 **Writing Models and Graphic Organizers on Transparencies,** p. 83

▦ **BLOCK SCHEDULING:** Resources marked with this symbol provide varied instruction during 90-minute blocks.

Writing Lesson

New Movie Scene

Stephenson's tale of terror has all the ingredients of a contemporary blockbuster movie—an exotic setting, a heroic main character, and a terrifying villain. Write a screenplay for the final scene. Include dialogue, description of characters' movements, camera angles, and other directions for the film crew.

Prewriting Reread the end of the story, jotting down crucial actions and words. Brainstorm for visual details that will add to the suspense.

Drafting Begin your scene with an image that will capture the mood you want to portray. Refer to your notes as you draft the scene to remind yourself of details that will translate into vivid on-screen images.

Model: Setting the Scene

[Camera zooms in over the ant-covered land surrounding the plantation to a close-up of Leiningen's face as he looks at the ants. Anxiety clouds his face only briefly, and then the look turns to resolve.]

Leiningen: Listen, lads! You're frightened of those beggars, but I'm proud of you.

> Camera direction and instructions to the actor set up the opening image for the scene.

Revising Reread your draft as if you were an actor who would use the screenplay. Fill in any gaps in the action, dialogue, and directions.

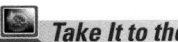 *Prentice Hall Writing and Grammar Connection: Chapter 5, Section 3*

Extension Activities

Listening and Speaking Review the tactics Leiningen uses on his workers. Then, develop your own **motivational speech** to raise morale and inspire courage in the frightened peons.

- Begin with an attention grabber—a quote or an anecdote.
- Keep your comments positive.
- Use short sentences that will hold your listeners' interest.
- Maintain eye contact with your audience.

Present the speech to the class. [**Group Activity**]

Research and Technology Using library or Internet resources, research actual invasions of army ants. Write a short **news article** detailing times, places, and casualties of such events. Also, report on any risk that you see of an ant invasion in the United States.

 Take It to the Net www.phschool.com

Go online for an additional research activity using the Internet.

Leiningen Versus the Ants ◆ 573

Lesson Support for p. 573

❸ Writing Lesson

- If possible, bring in a movie script for students to use as a model.
- Tell students that when they develop a movie scene, they should provide not only dialogue, but also details of the setting, special effects, and character movements.
- Encourage students to include imagery and music that will help to convey the scene's tension.
- When students have completed their scripts, encourage groups to perform staged readings for the class.

❹ Listening and Speaking

- Encourage students to brainstorm for a list of reasons that the peons should stay and fight the ants. Then, have them choose the most convincing reasons and use them in their speeches.
- Students should also consider the peons' fears, and present arguments that will allay these fears.
- Have students present their speeches in small groups.
- Have students use the rubric for Delivering a Persuasive Argument, p. 30 in **Performance Assessment and Portfolio Management.**

CUSTOMIZE INSTRUCTION
For Universal Access

To address different learning styles, use the activities suggested in the **Extension Activities** booklet, p. 36.

- For Verbal/Linguistic Learners, use Activity 5.
- For Visual/Spatial Learners, use Activity 6.
- For Logical/Mathematical Learners, use Activity 7.

ASSESSMENT RESOURCES

The following resources can be used to assess students' knowledge and skills.

Selection Assessment

- 📖 **Formal Assessment,** pp. 126–128
- 📖 **Open Book Test,** pp. 106–108
- 📼 **Got It! Assessment Videotapes,** Tape 3
- 💿 **Test Bank Software**
- 💻 **Take It to the Net**
  Visit www.phschool.com for self-tests and additional questions on "Leiningen Versus the Ants."

Listening and Speaking Rubric

- 📖 **Performance Assessment and Portfolio Management,** p. 30

 PRENTICE HALL ASSESSMENT SYSTEM

- 📖 **Workbook**
- 📖 **Skill Book**
- 📖 **Transparencies**
- 💿 **CD-ROM**

By the Waters of Babylon

Lesson Objectives

1. **To analyze and respond to literary elements**
   - Literary Analysis: Point of View
   - Connecting Literary Elements: Setting

2. **To read, comprehend, analyze, and critique a short story**
   - Reading Strategy: Drawing Conclusions
   - Reading Check questions
   - Review and Assess questions
   - Assessment Practice (ATE)

3. **To develop word analysis skills, fluency, and systematic vocabulary**
   - Vocabulary Development Lesson: Conjunctive Adverbs

4. **To understand and apply written and oral language conventions**
   - Spelling Strategy
   - Grammar Lesson: Varying Sentence Beginnings

5. **To understand and apply appropriate writing and research strategies**
   - Writing Lesson: Character Sketch
   - Extension Activity: Annotated Map

6. **To understand and apply listening and speaking strategies**
   - Extension Activity: Radio Interview

STEP-BY-STEP TEACHING GUIDE	PACING GUIDE
PRETEACH	
Motivate Students and Provide Background	
Use the Motivation activity (ATE p. 574)	5 min.
Read and discuss the Preview material and Background information (SE/ATE p. 574) [A]	5 min.
Introduce the Concepts	
Introduce the Literary Analysis and Reading Strategy (SE/ATE p. 575) [A]	15 min.
Pronounce the vocabulary words and read their definitions (SE p. 575)	5 min.
TEACH	
Monitor Comprehension	
Informally monitor comprehension by circulating while students read independently or in groups [A]	30 min.
Monitor students' comprehension with the Reading Check notes (SE/ATE pp. 577, 579, 581, 583, 585)	as students read
Develop vocabulary with Vocabulary notes (SE pp. 576, 579, 582, 583; ATE p. 583)	as students read
Develop Understanding	
Develop students' understanding of point of view with Literary Analysis annotations (SE pp. 577, 578, 581, 584; ATE pp. 577, 578, 580, 581, 582, 584) [A]	10 min.
Develop students' understanding of drawing conclusions with Reading Strategy annotations (SE pp. 578, 579, 580, 583; ATE pp. 578, 579, 580, 583)	10 min.
ASSESS	
Assess Mastery	
Assess students' mastery of the Reading Strategy and Literary Analysis by having them answer the Review and Assess questions (SE/ATE p. 587)	20 min.
Use one or more of the print and media Assessment Resources (ATE p. 589) [A]	up to 50 min.
EXTEND	
Apply Understanding	
Have students complete the Vocabulary Development Lesson and the Grammar Lesson (SE p. 588) [A]	20 min.
Apply students' ability to support generalizations using the Writing Lesson (SE p. 589) [A]	45 min.
Apply students' understanding using one or more of the Extension Activities (SE p. 589)	20–90 min.

 ACCELERATED INSTRUCTION:
Use the strategies and activities identified with an [A].

UNIVERSAL ACCESS
- ● = Below Level Students
- ▲ = On-Level Students
- ■ = Above Level Students

Time and Resource Manager

Reading Level: Challenging
Average Number of Instructional Days: 4

RESOURCES		
PRINT 📖	**TRANSPARENCIES**	**TECHNOLOGY** 💿 🎧
• **Beyond Literature,** Cross-Curricular Connection: Social Studies, p. 37 ▲ ■		• **Interest Grabber Video,** Tape 3 ● ▲ ■
• **Selection Support Workbook:** ● ▲ ■ Literary Analysis, p. 148 Reading Strategy, p. 147 Build Vocabulary, p. 145	• **Literary Analysis and Reading Transparencies,** pp. 73 and 74 ● ▲ ■	
		• **Listening to Literature** ● ▲ ■ Audiocassettes, Side 18 Audio CDs, CD 12
• **Literatura en español** ● ▲ • **Literary Analysis for Enrichment** ■		
• **Formal Assessment:** Selection Test, pp. 129–131 ● ▲ ■ • **Open Book Test,** pp. 109–111 ● ▲ ■ • **Performance Assessment and Portfolio Management,** p. 27 ● ▲ ■ • **ASSESSMENT** *SYSTEM* ● ▲ ■	• **ASSESSMENT** *SYSTEM* ● ▲ ■ Skills Practice Answers and Explanations on Transparencies	• **Test Bank Software** ● ▲ ■ • **Got It! Assessment Videotapes,** Tape 3 ● ▲
• **Selection Support Workbook:** ● ▲ ■ Build Grammar Skills, p. 146 • **Writing and Grammar,** Platinum Level ● ▲ ■ • **Extension Activities,** p. 37 ● ▲ ■	• **Daily Language Practice Transparencies** ● ▲ • **Writing Models and Graphic Organizers on Transparencies,** p. 13 ● ▲ ■	• **Writing and Grammar iText CD-ROM** ● ▲ ■ 💻 *Take It to the Net* www.phschool.com

BLOCK SCHEDULING: Use one 90-minute class period to preteach the selection and have students read it. Use a second 90-minute class period to assess students' mastery of skills and have them complete one of the Extension Activities.

Motivation

Ask students to imagine that they are exploring an empty building and come upon the following scene:

> He was sitting in his chair, by the window . . . and, for the first moment, I thought he was alive. Then I saw the skin on the back of his hand—it was like dry leather.

Discuss how students would react to this discovery. Then, tell students that the narrator of this story relates his adventures as he explores a place where danger and other frightening discoveries like this one lie in wait.

▭ Interest Grabber Video

As an alternative, play "New York City Landmarks" on Tape 3 to engage student interest.

❶ Background

History

This period in Jewish history is referred to as the Babylonian Captivity. It began in 586 B.C., when King Nebuchadnezzar II's army destroyed Jerusalem and deported the Israelites to Babylon. The period of captivity lasted until 538 B.C., when King Cyrus of Persia released them. Some of the Jews living in Babylon did not return to Palestine, but instead became part of the Jewish diaspora, or the body of Jews living outside Palestine.

Prepare to Read

By the Waters of Babylon

Red Hills and Bones, Georgia O'Keeffe, Philadelphia Museum of Art, The Alfred Stieglitz Collection

 Take It to the Net

Visit www.phschool.com for interactive activities and instruction related to "By the Waters of Babylon," including
- background
- graphic organizers
- literary elements
- reading strategies

Preview

Connecting to the Literature

The crumbling buildings you see when you look at pictures of ancient civilizations were once schools, businesses, and theaters. People of the past learned, worked, and socialized. In the future, people may look at ruins of the buildings of today and try to imagine the kinds of people who lived here.

❶ Background

The title "By the Waters of Babylon" is an allusion, or reference, to Psalm 137 in the Bible, in which the Israelites, who were being held captive in Babylon, wept over their lost homeland, Zion. Consider how these lines from the psalm relate to the story:

> By the rivers of Babylon, there we sat down, yea, we wept, when we remembered Zion.

TEACHING RESOURCES

The following resources can be used to enrich or extend the instruction for pp. 574–575.

Motivation
▭ **Interest Grabber Video,** Tape 3

Background
📖 **Beyond Literature,** Cross-Curricular Connection: Social Studies, p. 37 ▪

 Take It to the Net
Visit www.phschool.com for background and hotlinks for "By the Waters of Babylon."

Literary Analysis
▪ **Literary Analysis and Reading Transparencies,** Point of View, p. 74 ▪

Reading
📖 **Selection Support:** Reading Strategy, p. 147; Build Vocabulary, p. 145

▪ **Literary Analysis and Reading Transparencies,** Drawing Conclusions, p. 73

▪ **BLOCK SCHEDULING:** Resources marked with this symbol provide varied instruction during 90-minute blocks.

Literary Analysis

Point of View

Point of view is the perspective from which a story is told. Most stories are told from these common perspectives:

- **Third-person point of view,** in which the narrator does not participate in the action
- **First-person point of view,** in which the narrator is one of the characters and refers to himself or herself with the pronoun "I"

"By the Waters of Babylon" is told from the first-person point of view. The "I" is John, who introduces himself to the readers this way:

> I am the son of a priest. I have been in the Dead Places near us, with my father—at first, I was afraid.

Because John tells the story, you experience only what John sees, feels, and knows.

Connecting Literary Elements

A story's **setting** is the time and place in which the action of the story occurs. In "By the Waters of Babylon," the setting plays an important role as the reader tries to figure out where and when the story is set. The only evidence comes through a first-person narrator, who has a limited knowledge of the past. Look for clues to identify the setting as you read.

Reading Strategy

Drawing Conclusions

You **draw conclusions** based on facts and details given in a story. Sometimes an author creates a sense of mystery by presenting only a few details at a time. When each new detail is revealed, combine it with other details to draw conclusions. When you read, use charts like the one here to draw conclusions about the Dead Places and the Place of the Gods.

Dead Places

Details

We are forbidden to go there except to search for metal.

Conclusion

Vocabulary Development

purified (pyoo´ ə fīd´) *v.* cleansed; made pure (p. 576)

bowels (bou´ əlz) *n.* intestines (p. 579)

moreover (môr ō´ vər) *adv.* in addition to; further (p. 582)

nevertheless (nev´ ər thə les´) *adv.* in spite of that; however (p. 583)

By the Waters of Babylon ◆ 575

---

❷ Literary Analysis

Point of View

- Remind students that point of view is a narrative perspective. This perspective can come from a character in the story or from an outside observer.

- Encourage students to skim through some of the selections they have already read and identify the point of view from which the story is told.

- As they read, have students think about how John's point of view affects their understanding of the events in the story.

- Use the Point of View transparency in **Literary Analysis and Reading Transparencies,** p. 74, to demonstrate for students how to determine point of view.

❸ Reading Strategy

Drawing Conclusions

- Have students think of drawing conclusions as putting together a puzzle in which the details about characters and events are the different pieces.

- Write on the chalkboard three details that could lead to a conclusion. For example:
  Detail: A boat with rats on board has arrived in a port town.
  Detail: The rats have entered the sewer system of the port town.
  Detail: Residents of the port town are developing an illness that doctors have not seen before.

- Have students draw a conclusion from the details. (The rats are causing the mysterious illness.)

- Encourage students to use a chart like the one shown to help them record details from the story and then draw conclusions based on these details.

Vocabulary Development

- Pronounce each vocabulary word for students, and read the definitions as a class. Have students identify any words with which they are already familiar.

💻 E-Teach

Visit E-Teach at www.phschool.com for teachers' essays on how to teach, with questions and answers.

**CUSTOMIZE INSTRUCTION
For Visual/Spatial Learners**

Have students draw a picture of
how they envision the "Places of the
Gods." After John has traveled
there, have students compare their
pictures with John's findings.

❶ About the Selection

John's people are the survivors of
our own civilization after it is
destroyed in a war. They know little
of that civilization and call its ruins
"Places of the Gods." John's hunger
for knowledge drives him to enter
the forbidden ruins and learn the
secrets of the "gods." John, the son
of a priest, will reveal what he has
learned. Will his people embark on a
path toward their own destruction,
or will they avoid the mistakes of the
past? The story warns that unless we
use technology wisely, we may
destroy civilization.

❶ By the Waters of Babylon

Stephen Vincent Benét

The north and the west and the south are
good hunting ground, but it is forbidden to
go east. It is forbidden to go to any of the
Dead Places except to search for metal,
and then he who touches the metal must
be a priest or the son of a priest. Afterwards, both the
man and the metal must be <u>purified</u>! These are the rules
and the laws: they are well made. It is forbidden to cross
the great river and look upon the place that was the
Place of the Gods—this is most strictly forbidden. We do
not even say its name though we know its name. It is
there that spirits live, and demons—it is there that there
are the ashes of the Great Burning. These things are forbidden—they have been forbidden since the beginning of
time.

My father is a priest; I am the son of a priest. I have
been in the Dead Places near us, with my father—at first, I
was afraid. When my father went into the house to search
for the metal, I stood by the door and my heart felt small

purified (pyoor´ ə fid´) *v.*
cleansed; made pure

TEACHING RESOURCES

The following resources can be used to enrich or extend the instruction for pp. 576–586.

Literary Analysis

📄 **Writing Models and Graphic Organizers on
Transparencies,** p. 13

📖 **Selection Support:** Literary Analysis, p. 148

Reading

🎧 **Listening to Literature Audiocassettes,** Side 18 ▪

💿 **Listening to Literature Audio CDs,** CD 12

▪ **BLOCK SCHEDULING:** Resources marked with this symbol provide varied instruction during 90-minute blocks.

and weak. It was a dead man's house, a spirit house. It did not have the smell of man, though there were old bones in a corner. But it is not fitting that a priest's son should show fear. I looked at the bones in the shadow and kept my voice still.

Then my father came out with the metal—a good, strong piece. He looked at me with both eyes but I had not run away. He gave me the metal to hold—I took it and did not die. So he knew that I was truly his son and would be a priest in my time. That was when I was very young—nevertheless, my brothers would not have done it, though they are good hunters. After that, they gave me the good piece of meat and the warm corner by the fire. My father watched over me—he was glad that I should be a priest. But when I boasted or wept without a reason, he punished me more strictly than my brothers. That was right.

After a time, I myself was allowed to go into the dead houses and search for metal. So I learned the ways of those houses—and if I saw bones, I was no longer afraid. The bones are light and old—sometimes they will fall into dust if you touch them. But that is a great sin.

I was taught the chants and the spells—I was taught how to stop the running of blood from a wound and many secrets. A priest must know many secrets—that was what my father said. If the hunters think we do all things by chants and spells, they may believe so—it does not hurt them. I was taught how to read in the old books and how to make the old writings—that was hard and took a long time. My knowledge made me happy—it was like a fire in my heart. Most of all, I liked to hear of the Old Days and the stories of the gods. I asked myself many questions that I could not answer, but it was good to ask them. At night, I would lie awake and listen to the wind—it seemed to me that it was the voice of the gods as they flew through the air.

We are not ignorant like the Forest People—our women spin wool on the wheel, our priests wear a white robe. We do not eat grubs from the tree, we have not forgotten the old writings, although they are hard to understand. Nevertheless, my knowledge and my lack of knowledge burned in me—I wished to know more. When I was a man at last, I came to my father and said, "It is time for me to go on my journey. Give me your leave."

He looked at me for a long time, stroking his beard, then he said at last, "Yes. It is time." That night, in the house of the priesthood, I asked for and received purification. My body hurt but my spirit was a cool stone. It was my father himself who questioned me about my dreams.

He bade me look into the smoke of the fire and see—I saw and told what I saw. It was what I have always seen—a river, and, beyond it, a great Dead Place and in it the gods walking. I have always thought about that. His eyes were stern when I told him—he was no longer my father but a priest. He said, "This is a strong dream."

"It is mine," I said, while the smoke waved and my head felt light. They were singing the Star song in the outer chamber and it was like the buzzing of bees in my head.

He asked me how the gods were dressed and I told him how they

Literary Analysis
Point of View What words in this paragraph tell you that the story is written from the first-person point of view?

3 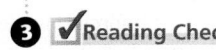Reading Check

What do the priests search for in the dead houses?

By the Waters of Babylon ◆ 577

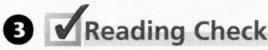Literary Analysis
Point of View

- Have students name some of the signal words they would expect to find in a story told from the first-person point of view.
- Read aloud the bracketed text. Ask students to listen for and jot down the words that signal the point of view from which this passage is told.
- Ask students the Literary Analysis question on p. 577: What words in this paragraph tell you that the story is written from the first-person point of view?
  Answer: Students should mention the words *my, me,* and *I.*

3 ✔Reading Check

Answer: The priests search for metal.

❹ Literary Analysis

Point of View

- Have students review the bracketed passage and look for words or phrases that signal the narrator's thoughts and emotions.
- Then, ask students the Literary Analysis question on p. 578: What details of the father's words help you understand the narrator's thoughts and feelings about his journey?

Answer: Students should note that while John agrees with his father, the words "it was my voice that spoke and not my spirit" suggest that he intends to explore the forbidden places.

▶ **Monitor Progress** Remind students that the point of view from which a story is told can greatly affect the information they learn about characters. Ask students how the information they learn about John in this passage would be affected if the story were told from the point of view of his father.

❺ Reading Strategy

Drawing Conclusions

- Ask students to read the bracketed passage and then explain why John is praying and waiting.
  Answer: John is awaiting guidance about where to go on his journey.
- Have students identify the signs that John receives and how he interprets them.
- Ask the Reading Strategy question on p. 578: What conclusion can you draw about John's plan based on these signs?
  Answer: John will go east because all the good signs point east.

---

were dressed. We know how they were dressed from the book, but I saw them as if they were before me. When I had finished, he threw the sticks three times and studied them as they fell.

"This is a very strong dream," he said. "It may eat you up."

"I am not afraid," I said and looked at him with both eyes. My voice sounded thin in my ears but that was because of the smoke.

He touched me on the breast and the forehead. He gave me the bow and the three arrows.

❹ "Take them," he said. "It is forbidden to travel east. It is forbidden to cross the river. It is forbidden to go to the Place of the Gods. All these things are forbidden."

"All these things are forbidden," I said, but it was my voice that spoke and not my spirit. He looked at me again.

"My son," he said. "Once I had young dreams. If your dreams do not eat you up, you may be a great priest. If they eat you, you are still my son. Now go on your journey."

I went fasting, as is the law. My body hurt but not my heart. When the dawn came, I was out of sight of the village. I prayed and purified myself, waiting for a sign. The sign was an eagle. It flew east.

❺ Sometimes signs are sent by bad spirits. I waited again on the flat rock, fasting, taking no food. I was very still—I could feel the sky above me and the earth beneath. I waited till the sun was beginning to sink. Then three deer passed in the valley, going east—they did not wind me or see me. There was a white fawn with them—a very great sign.

I followed them, at a distance, waiting for what would happen. My heart was troubled about going east, yet I knew that I must go. My head hummed with my fasting—I did not even see the panther spring upon the white fawn. But, before I knew it, the bow was in my hand. I shouted and the panther lifted his head from the fawn. It is not easy to kill a panther with one arrow but the arrow went through his eye and into his brain. He died as he tried to spring—he rolled over, tearing at the ground. Then I knew I was meant to go east—I knew that was my journey. When the night came, I made my fire and roasted meat.

It is eight suns' journey to the east and a man passes by many Dead Places. The Forest People are afraid of them but I am not. Once I made my fire on the edge of a Dead Place at night and, next morning, in the dead house, I found a good knife, little rusted. That was small to what came afterward, but it made my heart feel big. Always when I looked for game, it was in front of my arrow, and twice I passed hunting parties of the Forest People without their knowing. So I knew my magic was strong and my journey clean, in spite of the law.

Toward the setting of the eighth sun, I came to the banks of the great river. It was half-a-day's journey after I had left the god-road—we do not use the god-roads now for they are falling apart into great blocks of stone, and the forest is safer going. A long way off, I had seen the water through trees but the trees were thick. At last, I came out upon an open place at the top of a cliff. There was the great river below, like a giant in the sun. It is very long, very wide. It could eat all the streams we know

Literary Analysis
Point of View What details of the father's words help you understand the narrator's thoughts and feelings about his journey?

Reading Strategy
Drawing Conclusions All the good signs point east. What conclusion can you draw about the son's plan based on these signs?

❋ ENRICHMENT: Geography Connection

The Hudson River

The Hudson—which John calls "Ou-dis-sun"—originates in New York's Adirondack Mountains and flows 315 miles, emptying into New York Bay and the Atlantic Ocean at New York City. It is navigable by oceangoing vessels as far north as Albany. The New York State Barge Canal links the river to the Great Lakes. Among the points of interest on the Hudson are the United States Military Academy at West Point and the George Washington Bridge.

The beauty of the Hudson inspired the famous Hudson River school of nineteenth-century American painters. One of the river's most beautiful and imposing landmarks is the Palisades, a line of sheer cliffs on the west bank of the lower Hudson that rise as high as 550 feet. It is from these cliffs that John first sees the Place of the Dead.

Red Hills and Bones, Georgia O'Keeffe, Philadelphia Museum of Art, The Alfred Stieglitz Collection

▲ **Critical Viewing** Does this look like the land through which the narrator travels? Why or why not? **[Connect]**

and still be thirsty. Its name is Ou-dis-sun, the Sacred, the Long. No man of my tribe had seen it, not even my father, the priest. It was magic and I prayed.

Then I raised my eyes and looked south. It was there, the Place of the Gods.

How can I tell what it was like—you do not know. It was there, in the red light, and they were too big to be houses. It was there with the red light upon it, mighty and ruined. I knew that in another moment the gods would see me. I covered my eyes with my hands and crept back into the forest.

Surely, that was enough to do, and live. Surely it was enough to spend the night upon the cliff. The Forest People themselves do not come near. Yet, all through the night, I knew that I should have to cross the river and walk in the places of the gods, although the gods ate me up. My magic did not help me at all and yet there was a fire in my <u>bowels</u>, a fire in my mind. When the sun rose, I thought, "My journey has been clean. Now I will go home from my journey." But, even as I thought so, I knew I could not. If I went to the place of the gods, I would surely die, but, if I did not go, I could never be at peace with my spirit again. It is better to lose one's life than one's spirit, if one is a priest and the son of a priest.

Reading Strategy
Drawing Conclusions
What conclusion can you draw about the identity of the great river based on the name "Ou-dis-sun"?

bowels (bouʹ əlz) *n.* intestines

✓ Reading Check
What signs convince the narrator to go east?

By the Waters of Babylon ◆ 579

CUSTOMIZE INSTRUCTION FOR UNIVERSAL ACCESS

For Advanced Readers

Draw students' attention to the paragraph on p. 578 that begins, "My son,' he said." Have students discuss what the father means by dreams that "eat you up." Ask them to explain why the boy will become a great priest if he is not eaten up by his dreams.

Students should note that the father might be referring to dreams that are too big for the boy because they become obsessions and lead him into danger. If he is not eaten up by his dreams, the boy will become

a great priest because he will return from his journey with new and powerful knowledge that he will use for the good of his people.

❻ **Background**
Art

Red Hills and Bones, by Georgia O'Keeffe

In 1929, Georgia O'Keeffe (1887–1986) first visited New Mexico, and she lived there from 1946 on. From her first visit, she made increasing use of southwestern motifs in her work. Animal bones were frequent subjects, as in *Red Hills and Bones*.

Use these questions for discussion:

1. Do you think this is an appropriate illustration for the story? Why or why not?
   Possible response: Yes; the painting gives the impression of a "dead place," even though it portrays a desert rather than a city.

2. How would you describe the mood of the painting? How does the artist create that mood?
   Possible response: The mood is lonely, desolate, and eerie. The artist creates this mood by using only earth tones and including no living human or animal figures.

❼ ▶ **Critical Viewing**

Possible response: No, because this is a desert scene, and the narrator is traveling through the rolling hills of southeastern New York. However, both places seem lifeless.

❽ **Reading Strategy**
Drawing Conclusions

• Ask students to name rivers with which they are familiar. Do the names of any of these rivers sound similar to Ou-dis-sun when pronounced quickly?

• Then, ask students the Reading Strategy question on p. 579: What conclusion can you draw about the identity of the great river based on the name "Ou-dis-sun"?
   Answer: It is probably the Hudson, the great river that flows past Manhattan.

❾ **✓ Reading Check**

Answer: The narrator sees an eagle flying east and three deer going east with a white fawn.

Point of View

- On the chalkboard, write the following line: ". . . but the burning in my mind would not let me have peace."

- Ask students to rephrase these words as they would be spoken by a third-person narrator and contrast this version with the original. Answer: The passage might read, "John was troubled by the thoughts running through his mind." The statement seems more remote and less powerful in the third person.

⓫ Reading Strategy

Drawing Conclusions

- Have students read the bracketed passage, paying careful attention to the details about the god-roads.

- Ask students to identify an earlier passage in the story that describes the god-roads. Lead students to the description on p. 578.

- Then, ask students the Reading Strategy question on p. 580: Putting John's description together with the other things he has seen and found, draw a conclusion about the "god-roads." Answer: John has described the god-roads as made of stone and in disrepair. He sees god-roads that spanned the river, but now hang down like "broken vines" (cables). God-roads must be paved roads and bridges.

---

❿ Nevertheless, as I made the raft, the tears ran out of my eyes. The Forest People could have killed me without fight, if they had come upon me then, but they did not come. When the raft was made, I said the sayings for the dead and painted myself for death. My heart was cold as a frog and my knees like water, but the burning in my mind would not let me have peace. As I pushed the raft from the shore, I began my death song—I had the right. It was a fine song.

"I am John, son of John," I sang. "My people are the Hill People. They are the men.
I go into the Dead Places but I am not slain.
I take the metal from the Dead Places but I am not blasted.
I travel upon the god-roads and am not afraid. E-yah! I have killed the panther, I have killed the fawn!
E-yah! I have come to the great river. No man has come there before.
It is forbidden to go east, but I have gone, forbidden to go on the great river, but I am there.
Open your hearts, you spirits, and hear my song.
Now I go to the Place of the Gods, I shall not return.
My body is painted for death and my limbs weak, but my heart is big as I go to the Place of the Gods!"

All the same, when I came to the Place of the Gods, I was afraid, afraid. The current of the great river is very strong—it gripped my raft with its hands. That was magic, for the river itself is wide and calm. I could feel evil spirits about me, in the bright morning; I could feel their breath on my neck as I was swept down the stream. Never have I been so much alone—I tried to think of my knowledge, but it was a squirrel's heap of winter nuts. There was no strength in my knowledge any more, and I felt small and naked as a new-hatched bird—alone upon the great river, the servant of the gods.

⓫ Yet, after a while, my eyes were opened and I saw. I saw both banks of the river—I saw that once there had been god-roads across it, though now they were broken and fallen like broken vines. Very great they were, and wonderful and broken—broken in the time of the Great Burning when the fire fell out of the sky. And always the current took me nearer to the Place of the Gods, and the huge ruins rose before my eyes.

I do not know the customs of rivers—we are the People of the Hills. I tried to guide my raft with the pole but it spun around. I thought the river meant to take me past the Place of the Gods and out into the Bitter Water of the legends. I grew angry then—my heart felt strong. I said aloud, "I am a priest and the son of a priest!" The gods heard me—they showed me how to paddle with the pole on one side of the raft. The current changed itself—I drew near to the Place of the Gods.

When I was very near, my raft struck and turned over. I can swim in our lakes—I swam to the shore. There was a great spike of rusted metal sticking out into the river—I hauled myself up upon it and sat there, panting. I had saved my bow and two arrows and the knife I found in

Reading Strategy
Drawing Conclusions
Putting John's description together with the other things he has seen and found, draw a conclusion about the "god-roads."

 ENRICHMENT: Cultural Connection

Manhattan

The Dead Place that John explores is the ruins of Manhattan in New York City. Many people think that New York City and Manhattan are one and the same, but in fact the city has four other boroughs as well—the Bronx, Brooklyn, Queens, and Staten Island. However, Manhattan remains the cultural and commercial heart of the city. According to the 2000 census, Manhattan's population is more than 1,500,000.

Manhattan is a world capital for theater, music, and

other arts. The shops, such as those along Fifth Avenue, are equally renowned. Manhattan is a financial capital, as well; the New York Stock Exchange, on Wall Street, is among the most important of such institutions.

Discuss with students the effect of having Manhattan serve as the location of the Place of the Gods. Why is it significant that a great urban center is now in ruins?

the Dead Place but that was all. My raft went whirling downstream toward the Bitter Water. I looked after it, and thought if it had trod me under, at least I would be safely dead. Nevertheless, when I had dried my bow-string and restrung it, I walked forward to the Place of the Gods.

It felt like ground underfoot; it did not burn me. It is not true what some of the tales say, that the ground there burns forever, for I have been there. Here and there were the marks and stains of the Great Burning, on the ruins, that is true. But they were old marks and old stains. It is not true either, what some of our priests say, that it is an island covered with fogs and enchantments. It is not. It is a great Dead Place—greater than any Dead Place we know. Everywhere in it there are god-roads, though most are cracked and broken. Everywhere there are the ruins of the high towers of the gods.

How shall I tell what I saw? I went carefully, my strung bow in my hand, my skin ready for danger. There should have been the wailings of spirits and the shrieks of demons, but there were not. It was very silent and sunny where I had landed—the wind and the rain and the birds that drop seeds had done their work—the grass grew in the cracks of the broken stone. It is a fair island—no wonder the gods built there. If I had come there, a god, I also would have built.

How shall I tell what I saw? The towers are not all broken—here and there one still stands, like a great tree in a forest, and the birds nest high. But the towers themselves look blind, for the gods are gone. I saw a fish-hawk, catching fish in the river. I saw a little dance of white butterflies over a great heap of broken stones and columns. I went there and looked about me—there was a carved stone with cut-letters, broken in half. I can read letters but I could not understand these. They said UBTREAS. There was also the shattered image of a man or a god. It had been made of white stone and he wore his hair tied back like a woman's. His name was ASHING, as I read on the cracked half of a stone. I thought it wise to pray to ASHING, though I do not know that god.

How shall I tell what I saw? There was no smell of man left, on stone or metal. Nor were there many trees in that wilderness of stone. There are many pigeons, nesting and dropping in the towers—the gods must have loved them, or, perhaps, they used them for sacrifices. There are wild cats that roam the god-roads, green-eyed, unafraid of man. At night they wail like demons, but they are not demons. The wild dogs are more dangerous, for they hunt in a pack, but them I did not meet till later. Everywhere there are the carved stones carved with magical numbers or words.

I went North—I did not try to hide myself. When a god or a demon saw me, then I would die, but meanwhile I was no longer afraid. My hunger for knowledge burned in me—there was so much that I could not understand. After awhile, I knew that my belly was hungry. I could have hunted for my meat, but I did not hunt. It is known that the gods did not hunt as we do—they got their food from enchanted boxes and jars. Sometimes these are still found in the Dead Places—once, when I

Literary Analysis
Point of View and Setting What does John mean by the phrase "Bitter Water"?

Literary Analysis
Point of View What do you learn about the narrator based on the repetition of the line "How shall I tell what I saw?"

 Reading Check
What details in the Place of the Gods does John first notice?

By the Waters of Babylon ◆ 581

⓬ Literary Analysis

Setting

- Display a map of New York City or the northeast United States. Have students identify the Hudson River on the map.

- Ask students where the Hudson River ends. Lead them to see that the river empties into New York Harbor and then the Atlantic Ocean.

- Ask students the first Literary Analysis question on p. 581: What does John mean by the phrase "Bitter Water"?
  Answer: John means that the water is salty because of the sea into which the river empties.

⓭ Literary Analysis

Point of View

- Ask students to think about why the narrator would be wondering how to tell what he saw.

- Ask the second Literary Analysis question on p. 581: What do you learn about the narrator based on the repetition of the line "How shall I tell what I saw?"
  Possible response: The repetition of this phrase means that John intends to go back and admit that he went to the Place of the Gods.

⓮ ✔ Reading Check

Answer: John sees that the ground is not burning, that there are no fogs and enchantments, that the roads and bridges are broken, that there are no spirits or demons, and that it is silent and sunny.

⑮ Background

Geography

John has arrived in Lower Manhattan, one of the oldest parts of New York City. He could have found the remains of the Staten Island Ferry, a historic ferry that transports commuters between the boroughs of Manhattan and Staten Island.

⑯ Literary Analysis

Point of View

• Have students read the bracketed passage, and point out that John is becoming more comfortable in the Place of the Gods.

• Then, ask students to observe the effect of the first-person point of view on this passage.

Answer: Students may say that the author adds a dimension of humor when John observes that our food came not from hunting, but from "enchanted boxes and jars."

was a child and foolish, I opened such a jar and tasted it and found the food sweet. But my father found out and punished me for it strictly, for, often, that food is death. Now, though, I had long gone past what was forbidden, and I entered the likeliest towers, looking for the food of the gods.

I found it at last in the ruins of a great temple in the mid-city. A mighty temple it must have been, for the roof was painted like the sky at night with its stars—that much I could see, though the colors were faint and dim. It went down into great caves and tunnels—perhaps they kept their slaves there. But when I started to climb down, I heard the squeaking of rats, so I did not go—rats are unclean, and there must have been many tribes of them, from the squeaking. But near there, I found food, in the heart of a ruin, behind a door that still opened. I ate only the fruits from the jars—they had a very sweet taste. There was drink, too, in bottles of glass—the drink of the gods was strong and made my head swim. After I had eaten and drunk, I slept on the top of a stone, my bow at my side.

When I woke, the sun was low. Looking down from where I lay, I saw a dog sitting on his haunches. His tongue was hanging out of his mouth; he looked as if he were laughing. He was a big dog, with a gray-brown coat, as big as a wolf. I sprang up and shouted at him but he did not move—he just sat there as if he were laughing. I did not like that. When I reached for a stone to throw, he moved swiftly out of the way of the stone. He was not afraid of me; he looked at me as if I were meat. No doubt I could have killed him with an arrow, but I did not know if there were others. <u>Moreover</u>, night was falling.

I looked about me—not far away there was a great, broken god-road, leading North. The towers were high enough, but not so high, and while many of the dead-houses were wrecked, there were some that stood. I went toward this god-road, keeping to the heights of the ruins, while the dog followed. When I had reached the god-road, I saw that there were others behind him. If I had slept later, they would have come upon me asleep and torn out my throat. As it was, they were sure enough of me; they did not hurry. When I went into the dead-house, they kept watch at the entrance—doubtless they thought they would have a fine hunt. But a dog cannot open a door and I knew, from the books, that the gods did not like to live on the ground but on high.

I had just found a door I could open when the dogs decided to rush. Ha! They were surprised when I shut the door in their faces—it was a good door, of strong metal. I could hear their foolish baying beyond it, but I did not stop to answer them. I was in darkness—I found stairs and

Literature in context ⑮ Cultural Connection

Landmarks in New York City

John encounters the Subtreasury building and a statue of George Washington in the Place of the Gods. These are two New York City landmarks. The corner of Wall Street and Broad Street was the site of the City Hall of the eighteenth century. The Stamp Act Congress took place there in 1765. After the War for Independence, the Continental Congress met at City Hall. It was here that George Washington was sworn in as President of the United States. A statue of George Washington commemorates that event.

In 1862, the building on the site became the U.S. Subtreasury, where millions of dollars of gold and silver were kept in the basement vaults. Now, Federal Hall National Monument is located there.

Without full knowledge of these important events or even of the people or nation they involved, John does what an archaeologist would do—puts the pieces of the puzzles of the past together.

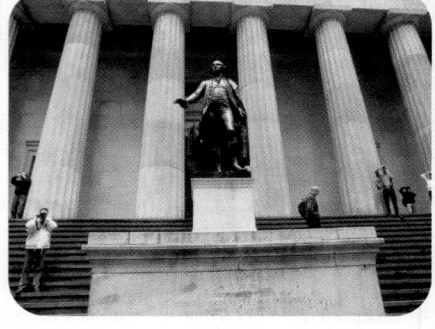

moreover (môr ōʹ vər) *adv.* in addition to; further

climbed. There were many stairs, turning around till my head was dizzy. At the top was another door—I found the knob and opened it. I was in a long small chamber—on one side of it was a bronze door that could not be opened, for it had no handle. Perhaps there was a magic word to open it, but I did not have the word. I turned to the door in the opposite side of the wall. The lock of it was broken and I opened it and went in.

Within, there was a place of great riches. The god who lived there must have been a powerful god. The first room was a small anteroom—I waited there for some time, telling the spirits of the place that I came in peace and not as a robber. When it seemed to me that they had had time to hear me, I went on. Ah, what riches! Few, even, of the windows had been broken—it was all as it had been. The great windows that looked over the city had not been broken at all though they were dusty and streaked with many years. There were coverings on the floors, the colors not greatly faded, and the chairs were soft and deep. There were pictures upon the walls, very strange, very wonderful—I remember one of a bunch of flowers in a jar—if you came close to it, you could see nothing but bits of color, but if you stood away from it, the flowers might have been picked yesterday. It made my heart feel strange to look at this picture—and to look at the figure of a bird, in some hard clay, on a table and see it so like our birds. Everywhere there were books and writings, many in tongues that I could not read. The god who lived there must have been a wise god and full of knowledge. I felt I had right there, as I sought knowledge also.

Nevertheless, it was strange. There was a washing-place but no water—perhaps the gods washed in air. There was a cooking-place but no wood, and though there was a machine to cook food, there was no place to put fire in it. Nor were there candles or lamps—there were things that looked like lamps but they had neither oil nor wick. All these things were magic, but I touched them and lived—the magic had gone out of them. Let me tell one thing to show. In the washing-place, a thing said "Hot" but it was not hot to the touch—another thing said "Cold" but it was not cold. This must have been a strong magic but the magic was gone. I do not understand—they had ways—I wish that I knew.

It was close and dry and dusty in their house of the gods. I have said the magic was gone but that is not true—it had gone from the magic things but it had not gone from the place. I felt the spirits about me, weighing upon me. Nor had I ever slept in a Dead Place before—and yet, tonight, I must sleep there. When I thought of it, my tongue felt dry in my throat, in spite of my wish for knowledge. Almost I would have gone down again and faced the dogs, but I did not.

I had not gone through all the rooms when the darkness fell. When it fell, I went back to the big room looking over the city and made fire. There was a place to make fire and a box with wood in it, though I do not think they cooked there. I wrapped myself in a floor-covering and slept in front of the fire—I was very tired.

Now I tell what is very strong magic. I woke in the midst of the night. When I woke, the fire had gone out and I was cold. It seemed to me that

Reading Strategy
Drawing Conclusions
What do you think this bronze door is?

nevertheless (nevʹ ər the lesʹ) *adv.* in spite of that; however

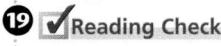**Reading Check**
Why does John decide to go into the tower?

By the Waters of Babylon ◆ 583

⑰ Reading Strategy
Drawing Conclusions

• Ask students to read the description in the bracketed passage. Then, have them consider what kind of doors do not have handles or knobs.

• Ask students the Reading Strategy question on p. 583: What do you think this bronze door is?
Answer: Students should say that this bronze door is most likely an elevator door.

⑱ Vocabulary Development
Conjunctive Adverbs

• Draw students' attention to the word *nevertheless* and its definition, "in spite of that; however."

• Explain that *nevertheless* is a conjunctive adverb. Conjunctive adverbs, such as *moreover, finally,* and *therefore,* show a relationship between ideas and often connect independent clauses.

• Ask students to write a sentence about the selection using the conjunctive adverb *nevertheless.*

⑲ ✓Reading Check
Answer: John goes into the tower to find food.

CUSTOMIZE INSTRUCTION FOR UNIVERSAL ACCESS

For Special Needs Students	For Gifted/Talented Students
Students may have difficulty understanding what John sees. Have them create illustrations based on John's description of the things he finds in the Place of the Gods. Have students share their illustrations with partners when they have finished.	Invite students to discuss how a third-person narrator would describe the room that John enters on this page. For example, a third-person narrator might say "carpets on the floors" instead of "coverings on the floors," and "the person who lived there" rather than "the god who lived there." Have students consider why the author has John describe it in this way.

20 Literary Analysis

Point of View

- As students read the bracketed passage, suggest that they look for ways that the author emphasizes John's point of view.

- Have students summarize what John experiences in this passage, noting any points that they think need clarification.

- Then, ask students the Literary Analysis question on p. 584: How does the first-person point of view affect the description? What questions do you have about John's situation?

Answer: The author uses the first-person point of view to describe what is real to him, but only imagined by the character. John imagines what the city once looked like when it was alive with light and sound. Students might wonder where the voices come from, and to whom they belong.

21 Literary Analysis

Point of View and Setting

- Have students read the bracketed passage and try to imagine themselves in John's place. Have them consider what aspects of the setting John would find unfamiliar.

- Ask students the Literary Analysis question on p. 584: How is John's perception of this setting different from what yours would be?

Answer: John comes from a less mechanized society, in which people travel only within a small area. He doesn't understand the restlessness of a society that has great bridges, planes, roads, and subway tunnels to carry people and goods from place to place.

all around me there were whisperings and voices. I closed my eyes to shut them out. Some will say that I slept again, but I do not think that I slept. I could feel the spirits drawing my spirit out of my body as a fish is drawn on a line.

20 Why should I lie about it? I am a priest and the son of a priest. If there are spirits, as they say, in the small Dead Places near us, what spirits must there not be in that great Place of the Gods? And would not they wish to speak? After such long years? I know that I felt myself drawn as a fish is drawn on a line. I had stepped out of my body—I could see my body asleep in front of the cold fire, but it was not I. I was drawn to look out upon the city of the gods.

It should have been dark, for it was night, but it was not dark. Everywhere there were lights—lines of light—circles and blurs of light—ten thousand torches would not have been the same. The sky itself was alight—you could barely see the stars for the glow in the sky. I thought to myself "This is strong magic" and trembled. There was a roaring in my ears like the rushing of rivers. Then my eyes grew used to the light and my ears to the sound. I knew that I was seeing the city as it had been when the gods were alive.

That was a sight indeed—yes, that was a sight: I could not have seen it in the body—my body would have died. Everywhere went the gods, on foot and in chariots—there were gods beyond number and counting and their chariots blocked the streets. They had turned night to day for their pleasure—they did not sleep with the sun. The noise of their coming and going was the noise of many waters. It was magic what they could do—it was magic what they did.

21 I looked out of another window—the great vines of their bridges were mended and the god-roads went East and West. Restless, restless, were the gods and always in motion! They burrowed tunnels under rivers—they flew in the air. With unbelievable tools they did giant works—no part of the earth was safe from them, for, if they wished for a thing, they summoned it from the other side of the world. And always, as they labored and rested, as they feasted and made love, there was a drum in their ears—the pulse of the giant city, beating and beating like a man's heart.

Were they happy? What is happiness to the gods? They were great, they were mighty, they were wonderful and terrible. As I looked upon them and their magic, I felt like a child—but a little more, it seemed to me, and they would pull down the moon from the sky. I saw them with wisdom beyond wisdom and knowledge beyond knowledge. And yet not all they did was well done—even I could see that—and yet their wisdom could not but grow until all was peace.

Then I saw their fate come upon them and that was terrible past speech. It came upon them as they walked the streets of their city. I have been in the fights with the Forest People—I have seen men die. But this was not like that. When gods war with gods, they use weapons we do not know. It was fire falling out of the sky and a mist that poisoned. It was the time of the Great Burning and the

Literary Analysis

Point of View How does the first-person point of view affect this description? What questions do you have about John's situation?

Literary Analysis

Point of View and Setting How is John's perception of this setting different from what yours would be?

Destruction. They ran about like ants in the streets of their city—poor gods, poor gods! Then the towers began to fall. A few escaped—yes, a few. The legends tell it. But, even after the city had become a Dead Place, for many years the poison was still in the ground. I saw it happen, I saw the last of them die. It was darkness over the broken city, and I wept.

All this, I saw. I saw it as I have told it, though not in the body. When I woke in the morning, I was hungry, but I did not think first of my hunger, for my heart was perplexed and confused. I knew the reason for the Dead Places but I did not see why it had happened. It seemed to me it should not have happened, with all the magic they had. I went through the house looking for an answer. There was so much in the house I could not understand—and yet I am a priest and the son of a priest. It was like being on one side of the great river, at night, with no light to show the way.

Then I saw the dead god. He was sitting in his chair, by the window, in a room I had not entered before and, for the first moment, I thought that he was alive. Then I saw the skin on the back of his hand—it was like dry leather. The room was shut, hot and dry—no doubt that had kept him as he was. At first I was afraid to approach him—then the fear left me. He was sitting looking out over the city—he was dressed in the clothes of the gods. His age was neither young nor old—I could not tell his age. But there was wisdom in his face and great sadness. You could see that he would have not run away. He had sat at his window, watching his city die—then he himself had died. But it is better to lose one's life than one's spirit—and you could see from the face that his spirit had not been lost. I knew, that, if I touched him, he would fall into dust—and yet, there was something unconquered in the face.

That is all of my story, for then I knew he was a man—I knew then that they had been men, neither gods nor demons. It is a great knowledge, hard to tell and believe. They were men—they went a dark road, but they were men. I had no fear after that—I had no fear going home, though twice I fought off the dogs and once I was hunted for two days by the Forest People. When I saw my father again, I prayed and was purified. He touched my lips and my breast, he said, "You went away a

City Night, Georgia O'Keeffe, Minneapolis Institute of Art

▲ **Critical Viewing** How does this picture of a city compare with John's descriptions of the Place of the Gods? **[Compare and Contrast]**

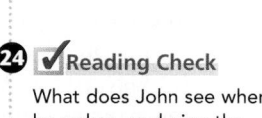

Reading Check
What does John see when he wakes up during the night?

By the Waters of Babylon ◆ 585

22 Background
Art

City Night, by Georgia O'Keeffe

Georgia O'Keeffe is considered one of the foremost twentieth-century American artists. The greater part of her life and work is associated with the American Southwest, particularly New Mexico. However, this painting of towering monolithic skyscrapers illuminated by the moon is typical of O'Keeffe's cityscapes, as it features a geometric design with no human figures. Use these questions for discussion:

1. What clue does this painting give you about the forbidden "Place of the Gods"?
   Answer: The painting could be a clue that the "Place of the Gods" is really a city.

2. How does the mood of the painting reflect the mood of the beginning of the story?
   Answer: The beginning of the story is mysterious because so much is left unexplained—Place of the Gods, Dead Places, the Great Burning. The painting reflects this mood because it, too, looks mysterious and eerie.

23 ▶ Critical Viewing

Answer: Both the painting and the description contain skyscrapers, and neither contains people.

24 ✓ Reading Check

Answer: John sees the Dead Place as it was when the gods lived there. He then sees their horrible fate—the Great Burning and Destruction.

CUSTOMIZE INSTRUCTION FOR UNIVERSAL ACCESS

For Special Needs Students

Some students may need extra help understanding point of view. When a story is told from first-person point of view, readers know only details that the narrator knows. To help students realize the difference a point of view makes, suggest that they think about the story as if it were a movie. Ask students to make a Venn diagram. Together, list details in one circle that only John, the narrator, knows. This includes how he feels and what he thinks. In the second circle, list details that only a viewer watching the action from outside might know. In the center, list details that would be known by both.

Answers for p. 586

Review and Assess

1. Students may say that our society is overwhelmed by information, and that people often don't have time to process it and to make good, informed decisions.

2. **(a)** John goes on his journey as a rite of passage to manhood. **(b)** His journey is unusual because he discovers secrets that will change his society.

3. **(a)** Possible response: John sees artwork, hot and cold water faucets, stoves, and great bridges and tunnels. **(b)** All of these things are unknown in his own society, so John believes them to be magic.

4 **(a)** John learns that the gods are really people, and that they died as the result of a great fire that fell from the sky.
(b) Possible response: John's father wants the truth to be revealed gradually. He does not want his people to acquire knowledge before they have the wisdom to use it properly, which is what happened to the "gods."

5. **(a)** The civilization ended as the result of bombs that fell on the city during a war. **(b)** Students may say that people can make sure that they do not "eat" knowledge too fast.

---

boy. You come back a man and a priest." I said, "Father, they were men! I have been in the Place of the Gods and seen it! Now slay me, if it is the law—but still I know they were men."

He looked at me out of both eyes. He said, "The law is not always the same shape—you have done what you have done. I could not have done it in my time but you come after me. Tell!"

I told and he listened. After that, I wished to tell all the people but he showed me otherwise. He said, "Truth is a hard deer to hunt. If you eat too much truth at once, you may die of the truth. It was not idly that our fathers forbade the Dead Places." He was right—it is better the truth should come little by little. I have learned that, being a priest. Perhaps, in the old days, they ate knowledge too fast.

Nevertheless, we make a beginning. It is not for the metal alone we go to the Dead Places now—there are the books and the writings. They are hard to learn. And the magic tools are broken—but we can look at them and wonder. At least, we make a beginning. And, when I am chief priest we shall go beyond the great river. We shall go to the Place of the Gods—the place newyork—not one man but a company. We shall look for the images of the gods and find the god ASHING and the others—the gods Lincoln and Biltmore[1] and Moses.[2] But they were men who built the city, not gods or demons. They were men. I remember the dead man's face. They were men who were here before us. We must build again.

---

1. **Biltmore** hotel in New York City.
2. **Moses** Robert Moses, former New York City municipal official who oversaw many large construction projects.

Review and Assess

Thinking About the Selection

1. **Respond:** After returning from the Dead Place, John thinks, "Perhaps, in the old days, they ate knowledge too fast." In your opinion, does our society "eat knowledge too fast"? Explain.

2. **(a) Recall:** Why does John set out on his journey?
   (b) Analyze: Why is John's journey unusual?

3. **(a) Recall:** Describe three things John sees in the Place of the Gods. **(b) Deduce:** Why does he think things are magic?

4. **(a) Recall:** What does John learn about the gods?
   (b) Speculate: Explain why John's father does not want others to know what John has learned about the gods.

5. **(a) Recall:** How did the civilization of the gods end?
   (b) Solve: How do you think John's people—or our society—can avoid repeating the mistakes that led to the destruction of civilization in the story?

Stephen Vincent Benét

(1898–1943)

When a clock strikes thirteen, you can expect strange things to happen. "By the Waters of Babylon" first appeared in a story collection by Stephen Vincent Benét with just that title—*Thirteen O'Clock* (1937).

Born in Bethlehem, Pennsylvania, Benét grew up listening to his father's evening poetry readings. As a young man, he took time off from his studies at Yale University to serve in the State Department during World War I. (His poor eyesight prevented him from serving in the army.) Much of Benét's work centers on American history and the establishment of American ideals.

Benét considered himself a poet first and foremost. His interest in American history and folklore, in addition to his interest in the ballad form, influenced his epic poem *John Brown's Body*, which won a Pulitzer Prize in 1929.

ASSESSMENT PRACTICE: Critical Reading

Distinguish Fact From Nonfact   (For more practice, see Test Preparation Workbook, p. 37.)

Many tests require students to distinguish fact from opinion. Use this sample test item.

Born in Bethlehem, Pennsylvania, Benét grew up listening to his father's evening poetry readings. As a young man, he took time off from his rigorous studies at Yale to serve in the State Department during World War I. (His poor eyesight prevented him from serving in the army.)

Which of the following is an opinion expressed in the passage?

A His poor eyesight prevented him from serving in the army.

B His father read poetry in the evenings.

C His studies at Yale were rigorous.

D Benét became a leading poet.

Choices *A* and *B* can be proved true or false, and choice *D* is not mentioned in the passage. *C* is the answer.

Review and Assess

Literary Analysis

Point of View

1. Your point of view is different from John's. Explain what you know about at least three of the mysterious objects that John has seen.
2. As the narrator, what does John reveal about his feelings toward the past?
3. Identify two ways that the **first-person point of view** adds to the mystery of this story.

Connecting Literary Elements

4. Using details from the story, identify both the time and place of the events of this story.
5. Using a diagram like the one here, find at least three facts, incidents, or details that reveal the time period.

6. Given your understanding of the **setting,** what do you think the term "Dead Places" means?

Reading Strategy

Drawing Conclusions

7. (a) What is the Great Burning? (b) Why and how did it happen? (c) Why did tales say that the ground would burn forever?
8. What three clues does the author give to the identity of the Place of the Gods?
9. Why are people forbidden to go to the Place of the Gods?

Extend Understanding

10. **Social Studies Connection:** (a) What warning do you think Benét is giving about the future? (b) What solutions might there be for potential disasters?

By the Waters of Babylon ◆ 587

Answers for p. 587

Review and Assess

1. **Possible responses:** The stove that doesn't require wood is an electric or gas stove. The bird and the flowers are art objects. The stone that says ASHING is a statue of George Washington.

2. The narrator reveals that the people of the past were great, but that they made mistakes that ended in their destruction.

3. The first-person point of view allows the reader to explore the mysterious ruins as John does. It also allows us to see over John's shoulder; the details allow us to solve the mystery before he does.

4. The place is New York City at a time in the future after bombs destroyed it during a war.

5. Details: the destroyed statue of George Washington; the ruins of tall skyscrapers; a river with a name similar to Hudson.

6. "Dead Places" refers to the ruins of cities.

7. **(a)** The Great Burning was the destruction of the city by bombs during a war. **(b)** Answers will vary, but students may say that civilization became too advanced and, during a war, managed to wipe itself out. **(c)** The tales are told to prevent people from exploring the Place of the Gods.

8. Possible clues are the references to the Hudson River, the buildings (including the Subtreasury Building), and "the place new-york."

9. People are forbidden to go to the Place of the Gods because their leaders do not believe they have the wisdom to handle the knowledge they would acquire.

10. **(a)** Benét's story warns that advanced technology can be used for destructive as well as constructive purposes. **(b) Possible response:** Humans must be aware of their destructive powers and work carefully to maintain peace.

587

❶ Vocabulary Development

Conjunctive Adverbs

1. therefore   3. moreover
2. nevertheless

Fluency: Context

1. We purified our water, ridding it of all toxins.
2. The subways are in the bowels, or guts, of the city.
3. The roast is cooked; moreover, the table is set, so let's have dinner.
4. Flowers won't make her forgive you; nevertheless, you might as well send them.

Spelling Strategy

1. clarified; clarifying
2. relied; relying
3. justified; justifying
4. terrified; terrifying

❷ Grammar

1. When my father went into the house, I stood by the door.
2. Later, my father questioned me.
3. Entering the building, John saw many stairs.
4. When I thought of it, my tongue felt dry in my throat.
5. All through the night, I knew that I would have to go.

Writing Application

1. I led my father to believe that I would not travel east, but I knew that I would.
2. Although I led my father to believe that I would not travel east, I knew that I would.
3. Knowing that I would travel east, I led my father to believe that I would not.
4. When I led my father to believe that I would not travel east, I knew that I would.
5. Earlier, I had led my father to believe that I would not travel east, but I knew that I would.

588

Integrate Language Skills

❶ Vocabulary Development Lesson

Concept Development: Conjunctive Adverbs

Conjunctive adverbs show a relationship between ideas and often connect independent clauses. *Moreover* indicates that the idea that follows is in addition to what has come before, such as "Moreover, night was falling." Other conjunctive adverbs include *nevertheless, finally, therefore,* and *however.* Copy the following sentences, completing each with a conjunctive adverb.

1. Our raft was sinking; __?__, we donned our life vests.
2. The elders had forbidden me to go; __?__, curiosity pushed me onward.
3. I needed to find shelter soon: Night was falling; __?__, the wolves would soon be out.

Fluency: Context

Review the words from the vocabulary list on page 575. Then, write sentences that suggest the definition of each one.

1. purified   3. moreover
2. bowels   4. nevertheless

Spelling Strategy

When adding a suffix to a word that ends in *y* preceded by a consonant, change the *y* to *i* and then add the suffix. *Purify* becomes *purified.* However, keep the *y* when adding *-ing: purifying.* Add the suffixes *-ed* and *-ing* to each of the following words:

1. clarify   3. justify
2. rely   4. terrify

❷ Grammar Lesson

Varying Sentence Beginnings

Writers use **sentence variety** to make their writing more interesting. Sentences can begin in some of these ways:

> **Subject:** The *current* is strong.
>
> **Adverb:** *Then*, my father came out.
>
> **Adverb Clause:** *When the raft was made*, I said the sayings for the dead.
>
> **Participle:** *Looking* down, I saw a dog sitting on his haunches.
>
> **Prepositional Phrase:** *After a time*, I was allowed to go into the dead houses.

Practice Write a new sentence beginning according to the information in parentheses for each sentence.

1. I stood by the door when my father went into the house. (adverb clause)
2. My father questioned me later. (adverb)
3. John, entering the building, saw many stairs. (participle)
4. My tongue felt dry in my throat when I thought of it. (adverb clause)
5. I knew all through the night that I would have to go. (prepositional phrase)

Writing Application Write a sentence about John. Then, write variations of your sentence by starting it four different ways.

WG *Prentice Hall Writing and Grammar Connection: Chapter 21, Section 3*

588 ◆ *Short Stories*

TEACHING RESOURCES

The following resources can be used to enrich or extend the instruction for pp. 588–589.

Vocabulary

📖 **Selection Support:** Build Vocabulary, p. 145

📖 **Vocabulary and Spelling Practice Book** (Use this booklet for skills enrichment.)

Grammar

📖 **Selection Support:** Build Grammar Skills, p. 146

WG **Writing and Grammar,** Platinum Level, p. 498

💻 **Daily Language Practice Transparencies** 📀

Writing

WG **Writing and Grammar,** Platinum Level, p. 107 📀

💿 **Writing and Grammar iText CD-ROM**

📖 **Writing Models and Graphic Organizers on Transparencies,** p. 13

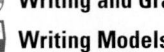 **BLOCK SCHEDULING:** Resources marked with this symbol provide varied instruction during 90-minute blocks.

Writing Lesson

Character Sketch

Because "By the Waters of Babylon" is written from the first-person point of view, the reader's knowledge of John is limited to John's words and actions. Write a character sketch of John from your own point of view.

Prewriting	Before you write your character sketch, gather details about John from the story that will help bring him to life. Describe his age, background, personality, habits, and likes or dislikes. Note his goals and achievements. You may have to infer many of the details.
Drafting	Begin with an introduction that makes a few generalizations about the character. Then, elaborate on each generalization in paragraphs that cite details and events from the story for support.
Revising	Look over your character sketch to make sure that you have provided enough support for your generalizations. If necessary, elaborate further on one of the character's traits.

"My knowledge and my lack of knowledge burned in me—I wished to know more."

Model: Supporting Generalizations

As a young man living with the Hill People, John is adventurous and very curious. In fact, he explains his feelings in the story.

The added quotation supports the writer's claim about John's curiosity.

 Prentice Hall Writing and Grammar Connection: Chapter 6, Section 2

Extension Activities

Listening and Speaking With a partner, improvise a one-minute **radio interview** in which one of you plays the role of a radio news reporter and the other plays the role of John, who has just arrived home from his journey. Use these tips to help you:

- Ask relevant questions.
- Demonstrate knowledge of the subject.
- Use language that conveys maturity, sensitivity, and respect.

When the interview is ready, perform it for the class. **[Group Activity]**

Research and Technology Work with a partner to produce an **annotated map** that traces the path of John's journey. To start, you will need a map of southern New York State. Make a poster-sized map, and near each place that you locate, show the text from the story that suggests this location. Determine where the Hill People live, and begin your map there. **[Group Activity]**

Take It to the Net www.phschool.com

Go online for an additional research activity using the Internet.

By the Waters of Babylon ◆ 589

❸ Writing Lesson

- As a model, show students the Biographical Profile transparency, p. 13 in **Writing Models and Graphic Organizers on Transparencies.**
- Help students begin the prewriting stage by jotting down a few details about John on the chalkboard.
- Remind students that they should support their generalizations with details from the story. Encourage students to trade their drafts with partners to determine whether they have provided enough support.
- Use the Writing Lesson to guide students in developing their character sketches.

❹ Listening and Speaking

- Suggest that the interviewer skim through the story, looking for questions to ask John.
- Suggest that the student playing John make a list of his personality traits, such as curious and daring. Then, have him or her prepare answers that seem natural for John.
- Use the rubric for Interview Techniques, p. 27 in **Performance Assessment and Portfolio Management,** to assess students' work.

CUSTOMIZE INSTRUCTION
For Universal Access

To address different learning styles, use the activities suggested in the **Extension Activities** booklet, p. 37.

- For Logical/Mathematical Learners, use Activity 5.
- For Bodily/Kinesthetic and Verbal/Linguistic Learners, use Activity 6.
- For Logical/Mathematical Learners, use Activity 7.

ASSESSMENT RESOURCES

The following resources can be used to assess students' knowledge and skills.

Selection Assessment

 Formal Assessment, pp. 129–131

Open Book Test, pp. 109–111

Got It! Assessment Videotapes, Tape 3

Test Bank Software

 Take It to the Net
Visit www.phschool.com for self-tests and additional questions on "By the Waters of Babylon."

Listening and Speaking Rubric

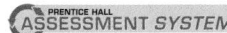 **Performance Assessment and Portfolio Management,** p. 27

 PRENTICE HALL **ASSESSMENT SYSTEM**

 Workbook   **Transparencies**

 Skill Book   **CD-ROM**

About Web Sites

- Have students read "About Web Sites."

- Ask students whether there are any sites they visit regularly. Have them discuss the reasons they use these sites.

- Ask students if anyone has created his or her own Web site, and have them talk about what information is on their Web sites and how they constructed them.

- Ask students why they think it is important to learn about Web sites. Encourage them to discuss situations in the future in which they will have to use the Internet.

Reading Strategy
Evaluating the Credibility of Sources

- Have students read the information about the Reading Strategy.

- Draw students' attention to the variety of agencies, businesses, and individuals who put up Web sites. Ask students why it is important to evaluate the credibility of Web sites. Possible response: Students may note that private individuals who put up sites may not check their information carefully; businesses that put up sites may allow their interest in profits and in maintaining appeal to customers influence their choices of information to include or not include on their sites.

- Explain to students that by evaluating the credibility of Web sites, they will be able to find the most accurate information available on the Internet.

- Call students' attention to the chart of common URL endings on p. 590. Explain that they might be inclined to trust a site the URL address for which ends in ".edu" or ".gov," since these endings indictate reliable sources—educational institutions and the government. Encourage them to use this information when researching on the Internet.

Web Sites

About Web Sites

A Web site is a collection of electronic documents containing graphics, text, or sound files that are linked together. Each Web site has its own URL (Uniform Resource Locator), or address, where it can be found on the Internet.

There are Web sites on nearly any topic. The Internet is a tremendous source of information and resources, but it also contains hundreds of advertisements and personal pages, which are not necessarily helpful to a researcher. As you become an Internet user, it will be important to be able to determine which material comes from a reliable source and is factual and accurate.

Reading Strategy

Evaluating the Credibility of Sources

Just as you would evaluate the quality, validity, and bias of any other research materials you locate, check the source of the information you find online. Use these tips for evaluating Internet sources:

- Consider who constructed and now maintains the Web page. Determine whether this author is a reputable source. Often, the URL endings indicate a source. The chart explains some common URL endings.

URL Ending	Description
.edu	Site is maintained by educational institution
.gov	Site is maintained by a government agency
.org	Site is probably maintained by a nonprofit organization
.com	Site is maintained commercially or personally

- Skim the official and trademarked Web pages first. It is safe to assume that the information you draw from Web pages of reputable institutions, online encyclopedias, and online versions of daily newspapers is as reliable as the material you could find in print.

- Check the credentials of writers of less "official" Web sites. You can obtain valuable information from these sites, but do not be fooled by official-looking graphics. Make sure that the page has been updated recently.

Egyptology Resources Home Page

The home page of a Web site is the first place you go after entering the URL. From the home page, you can go to other linked pages that provide additional information. The home page shown here introduces a set of linked pages devoted to the study of Egypt.

, or of the shows

http://www.newton.cam.ac.uk/egypt/

the side provide infor- n a f topics.

nformation on ne group that naintains this Web site is vailable through nks.

Egyptology Resources

Popular local items

News & Gossip

Announcements

Bulletin Board

E-mail Addresses

Tomb of Sennefen

Beinlich Wordlist

Wilbour Library Acquisitions

Online Publications

Commercial Items

Server statistics

The first Egyptology site on the web

This page is set up with the kind assistance of the Newton Institute in the University of Cambridge to provide a World Wide Web resource for Egyptological information. The pages are not a publication of the Newton Institute, and all matters concerning them (e.g., comments, criticisms, and suggestions for items to include) should be sent to Nigel Strudwick.

Click here for guidelines on the format of material.

Click here for site history.

Main pages

Essential Resources

Institutions

Museums

Digs

Publishers, Booksellers

Journals, Magazines

Organizations, Societies

Interesting Egypt Pages

Personal Egypt Pages

Other Resources of Interest

Click on Museums to get to the interior Web page shown on the next page.

Egyptology Resources Home Page

- Explain to students that the home page is usually the first page they will get to when they go to a Web site. Tell them that when they start exploring the site, they can usually get back to the home page through a link that appears on the other pages of the site.
- Have students examine the home page and the notes that identify its main elements.
- Ask students to identify the home page's address.
  Answer: http://www.newton.cam. ac.uk/egypt/
- Ask students what the paragraph in the middle of the page tells them about the credibility of information on the site.
  Answer: Students should say that the paragraph tells them who maintains the Web site. Because the Newton Institute is involved in funding the site, and because the Institute is associated with a world-renowned university, students may be inclined to rate the site as credible. They should note, however, that the paragraph gives direct responsibility for the information on the site to an individual, not to the Institute.
- Review with students the other notes on this page. Encourage individual students who have Internet experience to point out other elements of the home page they notice.

CUSTOMIZE INSTRUCTION FOR UNIVERSAL ACCESS

For Special Needs Students	For Advanced Readers
Students may benefit from examining the home page with teacher guidance and then visiting a specific Web site on the Internet. If available, allow students access to Internet-ready computers and provide them with a Web address to visit, such as www.pbs.org or an official Web site of a popular music group. Guide students through the home page and to links from that home page. Have students note at least three different categories of information they can uncover using links on the site.	Have students analyze the Egyptology home page. Then have students design the home page of a subject of their choosing. Remind students to include the same types of information and aids to navigation found on the sample home page. Have them create flowcharts showing the links among pages on the site and their layout, including the placement of graphics, pictures, music, and links to other sites.

Interior Web Page

- Have students examine the interior Web page and the notes that accompany it.

- Ask students to identify the similarities between this page and the home page on p. 591.

- Then, have students discuss the differences between the two pages. Lead students to see that the purpose of the home page is to give an overview of all the information that can be found on that site, and that the interior page gives more detailed information in a specific category. Ask them what information they can find on this interior page.
  Answer: This page lists museums with Egyptian collections that have Web sites.

- Ask students what two general navigation options the page offers.
  Answer: By clicking on the name of a museum, the user will be taken to the Web site of that museum. By clicking on "Back to Egyptology Resources home page," the user will be taken back to the home page of the site.

Interior Web Page

After clicking on the Museums link on the previous page, you arrive at this page. It has links to museums all over the world that have online Egyptian collections.

http://www.newton.cam.ac.uk/egypt/museum.html

Museums online with Egyptian collections

Many museums of course have WWW pages now. I have tried to select some of those which have more specific information on their Egyptian Collections, but I do also include the general Web presences of major museums with relevant material. Some of these links often go directly to the Egypt pages and bypass the home page. A more general set of links will be found in the ABZU indexes.

Egypt
- The Egyptian Museum, Cairo
- The Coptic Museum, Cairo

North America
- Museum of Fine Arts, Boston
- Metropolitan Museum, New York
- Michael C. Carlos Museum, Emory University, Atlanta
- Brooklyn Museum
- Oriental Institute, University of Chicago

Europe
- The British Museum, London COMPASS Project
- The Louvre, Paris
- Musées royaux d'art et d'art historie, Brussels
- Museo, Egizio, Torino
- Agyptisches Museum und Papyrussammlung Berlin-Charlottenburg
- Allard Pierson Museum
- Carsten Niebuhr Institute, University of Copenhagen, Papyrus Collection

Back to Egyptology Resources home page

All the museums listed have Web sites for the Egyptian artifacts in their collections.

This link takes you back to the home page of the Egyptology Resources Web site

Check Your Comprehension

1. What do you think would appear on the link entitled Institutions?
2. What link would you click on to learn about ongoing archaeological studies?
3. What is the link you would click on to find books about Egyptology?
4. What person, if any, should you contact for more information about this site?

Applying the Reading Strategy

Evaluating Credibility of Sources

Name two links on the Egyptology Resources home page that should lead you to reliable information, and name two links you should evaluate more cautiously. Provide reasons for your answers. Use a chart like this one to record your answers.

Evaluating Credibility

Web sites:
Accept: 1.
Why?

2.
Why?
Evaluate: 1.
Why?

2.
Why?

Activity

Researching a Web Site

Using the Internet, you can find information on almost any topic. Select a topic on which you might write a report. Then, find information on your topic by using one or more Web site addresses. As you find interesting facts, jot them down using a format like the one shown here.

Topic:

Web Addresses:

Interesting Facts:

Contrasting Informational Texts

Web Sites and Other Resources

Accessing the Egyptology Resources site would be one way to research Tutankhamen's tomb. Other resources, however, will have similar information. Suppose you wanted to find information without logging onto the Internet.

- How could you investigate your topic using the encyclopedia?
- How is using the encyclopedia different from using a Web site?
- Where would you look next if your topic was not in the encyclopedia?

A Problem ✦ Luck

Lesson Objectives

1. **To analyze and respond to literary elements**
   - Literary Analysis: Characters
   - Comparing Literary Works
2. **To read, comprehend, analyze, and critique short stories**
   - Reading Strategy: Drawing Inferences About Character
   - Reading Check questions
   - Review and Assess questions
   - Assessment Practice (ATE)
3. **To develop word analysis skills, fluency, and systematic vocabulary**
   - Vocabulary Development Lesson: Latin Word Root: -ver-
4. **To understand and apply written and oral language conventions**
   - Spelling Strategy
   - Grammar Lesson: Restrictive and Nonrestrictive Adjective Clauses
5. **To understand and apply appropriate writing and research strategies**
   - Writing Lesson: Story Ending
   - Extension Activity: Multimedia Biography
6. **To understand and apply listening and speaking strategies**
   - Extension Activity: Monologue

STEP-BY-STEP TEACHING GUIDE	PACING GUIDE
PRETEACH	
Motivate Students and Provide Background	
Use the Motivation activity (ATE p. 594)	5 min.
Read and discuss the Preview material and Background information (SE/ATE p. 594)	5 min.
Introduce the Concepts	
Introduce the Literary Analysis and Reading Strategy (SE/ATE p. 595) A	15 min.
Pronounce the vocabulary words and read their definitions (SE p. 595)	5 min.
TEACH	
Monitor Comprehension	
Informally monitor comprehension by circulating while students read independently or in groups A	25 min.
Monitor students' comprehension with the Reading Check notes (SE/ATE pp. 597, 599, 601, 605, 607)	as students read
Develop vocabulary with Vocabulary notes (SE pp. 598, 602, 605, 606; ATE p. 605)	as students read
Develop Understanding	
Develop students' understanding of characters with Literary Analysis annotations (SE pp. 600, 601, 606; ATE pp. 598, 599, 600, 601, 602, 606) A	10 min.
Develop students' understanding of drawing inferences about character with Reading Strategy annotations (SE pp. 597, 598, 601, 602; ATE pp. 597, 598, 601, 602, 606)	10 min.
ASSESS	
Assess Mastery	
Assess students' mastery of the Reading Strategy and Literary Analysis by having them answer the Review and Assess questions (SE/ATE p. 609)	20 min.
Use one or more of the print and media Assessment Resources (ATE p. 611) A	up to 50 min.
EXTEND	
Apply Understanding	
Have students complete the Vocabulary Development Lesson and the Grammar Lesson (SE p. 610) A	20 min.
Apply students' ability to analyze characters' decisions using the Writing Lesson (SE p. 611) A	45 min.
Apply students' understanding of the selection using one or more of the Extension Activities (SE p. 611)	20–90 min.

A **ACCELERATED INSTRUCTION:**
Use the strategies and activities identified with an A.

UNIVERSAL ACCESS
● = Below Level Students
▲ = On-Level Students
■ = Above Level Students

Time and Resource Manager

Reading Level: Average/Average
Average Number of Instructional Days: 4

RESOURCES

PRINT 📖	TRANSPARENCIES 📄	TECHNOLOGY 💿 🎧 📼
• **Beyond Literature,** Humanities Connection: Personal Honor, p. 38 ▲ ■		• **Interest Grabber Video,** Tape 3 ● ▲ ■
• **Selection Support Workbook:** ● ▲ ■ Literary Analysis, p. 152 Reading Strategy, p. 151 Build Vocabulary, p. 149	• **Literary Analysis and Reading Transparencies,** pp. 75 and 76 ● ▲ ■	
• **Authors In Depth,** Platinum Level ■		• **Listening to Literature** ● ▲ ■ Audiocassettes, Side 19 Audio CDs, CD 12
• **Literatura en español** ● ▲ • **Literary Analysis for Enrichment** ■		
• **Formal Assessment:** Selection Test, pp. 132–134 ● ▲ ■ • **Open Book Test,** pp. 112–114 ● ▲ ■ • **Performance Assessment and Portfolio Management,** p. 14 ● ▲ ■ • **PRENTICE HALL ASSESSMENT SYSTEM** ● ▲ ■	• **PRENTICE HALL ASSESSMENT SYSTEM** ● ▲ ■ Skills Practice Answers and Explanations on Transparencies	• **Test Bank Software** ● ▲ ■ • **Got It! Assessment Videotapes,** Tape 3 ● ▲
• **Selection Support Workbook:** ● ▲ ■ Build Grammar Skills, p. 150 • **Writing and Grammar,** Platinum Level ● ▲ ■ • **Extension Activities,** p. 38 ● ▲ ■	• **Daily Language Practice Transparencies** ● ▲ • **Writing Models and Graphic Organizers on Transparencies,** p. 83 ● ▲ ■	• **Writing and Grammar iText CD-ROM** ● ▲ ■ 💻 ***Take It to the Net*** www.phschool.com

BLOCK SCHEDULING: Use one 90-minute class period to preteach the selection and have students read it. Use a second 90-minute class period to assess students' mastery of skills and have them complete one of the Extension Activities.

PRETEACH

Step-by-Step Teaching Guide
for pp. 594–595

Motivation

Have two students role-play a situation in which a customer receives too much change for a purchase. The customer then has to decide whether to return the extra money. Ask the class to respond to the skit and discuss the questions about honesty that it raises. Then, tell them that these stories raise important questions about honesty, responsibility, and deception.

▣ Interest Grabber Video

As an alternative, play "The Art of Anton Chekhov" on Tape 3 to engage student interest.

❶ Background

Culture

The consequences of actions can vary according to the rules of a person's particular culture. Both stories in this selection feature characters who behave foolishly. The consequences that each character faces as a result of his foolishness, however, will surprise most students.

Prepare to Read

A Problem ◆ Luck

The Charge of the Light Brigade, Richard Caton Woodville, By permission of Cranston Fine Arts

▣ Take It to the Net

Visit www.phschool.com for interactive activities and instruction related to these selections, including
• background
• graphic organizers
• literary elements
• reading strategies

Preview

Connecting to the Literature

Have you ever heard the saying, "You can't tell a book by its cover"? In each of these selections, you may be surprised to find that what you see and hear does not always reflect what lies behind the actions and words of the main characters.

❶ Background

The aristocracy (people born to ruling families) of England, where the story "Luck" takes place, have more formal habits than English working people. This same situation existed in Russia before the communist revolution of 1917, where Anton Chekhov lived and wrote. For these privileged groups of people, appearance and honor often meant more than the truth of how each person thought and behaved.

594 ◆ *Short Stories*

TEACHING RESOURCES

The following resources can be used to enrich or extend the instruction for pp. 594–595.

Motivation

▣ **Interest Grabber Video,** Tape 3 ▣

Background

📖 **Beyond Literature,** p. 38

🖥 **Take It to the Net**
Visit www.phschool.com for background and hotlinks for the selections.

Literary Analysis

▥ **Literary Analysis and Reading Transparencies,** Characters, p. 76

Reading

📖 **Selection Support:** Reading Strategy, p. 151; Build Vocabulary, p. 149 ▣

▥ **Literary Analysis and Reading Transparencies,** Drawing Inferences About Character, p. 75

▣ **BLOCK SCHEDULING:** Resources marked with this symbol provide varied instruction during 90-minute blocks.

Literary Analysis

Characters

Characters are the people or animals who take part in the action of a work of fiction. Characters can be classified as either static or dynamic.

- **Static characters** do not change during the course of the story. They remain the same no matter what happens to them.
- **Dynamic characters** change and usually learn something. The changes they undergo affect their attitudes, beliefs, or behavior.

Notice whether each character in these selections either changes or does not change as the stories develop and reach resolution.

Comparing Literary Works

In each of these stories, characters are faced with choices and the consequences of those choices. In "A Problem," a family makes a decision regarding family honor and has to live with the consequences. In "Luck," a clergyman decides to help a struggling student. As you read, notice the consequences that result from the characters' decisions. Then, compare the points each story makes about choices and consequences.

Reading Strategy

Drawing Inferences About Character

When you meet new people, you probably notice their words and actions. When you put your impressions together to form an idea about a person, you **draw inferences** about his or her personality, beliefs, or qualities. You get to know fictional characters in a similar way. Their actions and words provide clues from which you draw inferences about them.

Use a chart like the one here to draw inferences about the characters in these selections.

Vocabulary Development

taciturn (tas´ ə turn´) *adj.* preferring not to talk (p. 598)

rheumatic (rōō mat´ ik) *adj.* suffering from a painful disease of the joints (p. 598)

vestibule (ves´ tə byōōl´) *n.* small entrance hall (p. 602)

zenith (zē´ nith) *n.* highest point (p. 605)

countenance (kɔun´ tə nəns) *n.* expression on a person's face (p. 605)

veracity (və ras´ ə tē) *n.* truthfulness; honesty (p. 605)

guileless (gīl´ lis) *adj.* without slyness or cunning (p. 605)

prodigious (prō dij´ əs) *adj.* enormous (p. 606)

sublimity (sə blim´ ə tē) *n.* noble or exalted state (p. 606)

> **Words**
> The Colonel says Sasha will not reform.
>
> ⋮
>
> **Inference**
> Sasha has disappointed his uncles before.
>
> ⋮
>
> **Actions**

A Problem / Luck ◆ 595

---

❷ Literary Analysis

Characters

- Tell students that as they read these stories, they will focus on characters.
- Reinforce for students the difference between static and dynamic characters. Explain that *static* means "not moving or progressing," so static characters do not change or develop. *Dynamic* means "relating to objects in motion," so dynamic characters undergo changes over the course of a story.
- Then, have students think of a few characters they have encountered in their readings. Have students identify whether each character is static or dynamic.
- Use the Characters transparency in **Literary Analysis and Reading Transparencies,** p. 76, to identify static and dynamic characters.

❸ Reading Strategy

Drawing Inferences About Character

- Explain to students that to draw an inference about a character is to form an idea about that character based on information in a story.
- Remind students that their inferences should be based on a character's actions and words.
- As students read the selections, encourage them to use a graphic organizer like the one shown to help them record the words and actions of the characters and then to draw inferences based on this information.

Vocabulary Development

- Pronounce each vocabulary word for students, and read the definitions as a class. Have students identify any words with which they are already familiar.

CUSTOMIZE INSTRUCTION FOR UNIVERSAL ACCESS

For Less Proficient Readers	For English Learners	For Advanced Readers
Suggest that students choose one main character in each story and list actions and words of that character as they read. Have them use a graphic organizer to keep track of details and the inferences they draw.	Define the word *inferences*. Explain to students that they will draw conclusions about characters just as they draw conclusions about each other by observing actions and words. As they read, have partners compare their inferences about characters.	Suggest that students draw inferences about characters as they read. Have them write predictions about each character, based on the inferences they have drawn.

 E-Teach

Visit E-Teach at www.phschool.com for teachers' essays on how to teach, with questions and answers.

595

Step-by-Step Teaching Guide for pp. 596–608

CUSTOMIZE INSTRUCTION
For Verbal/Linguistic Learners

Ask students to review the second paragraph of Chekhov's story. They should note that this is one compound sentence, garnished by many added phrases and clauses. Have students analyze the sentence and produce another that has the same structure.

❶ About the Selection

In "A Problem," three uncles grapple with the question of what to do about their errant nephew Sasha. Instead of welcoming their leniency as an opportunity to mend his ways, Sasha seizes it as an opportunity to continue in his irresponsible habits, with just one difference—he has gained self-knowledge. He now sees how he can manipulate his relatives and avoid facing up to the consequences he deserves. The story raises important questions about forgiveness and responsibility.

❷ Background
Art

Man on a Balcony, by Gustave Caillebotte

Caillebotte is best known as an art patron and collector. During the late 1800s, he helped organize the exhibits that introduced the works of such Impressionists as Monet, Manet, and Renoir.

Use these questions for discussion:

1. How does the setting in the painting reflect the setting of "A Problem"?
   Answer: The man's elegant clothing and surroundings suggest that he is in an expensive home or apartment; "A Problem" takes place in the home of an aristocratic family.

2. Which character in the story does the figure in the painting resemble? Why?
   Answer: The painting depicts an older man, apparently deep in thought. He could resemble either the uncle who is a former colonel or Ivan Markovitch, Sasha's maternal uncle.

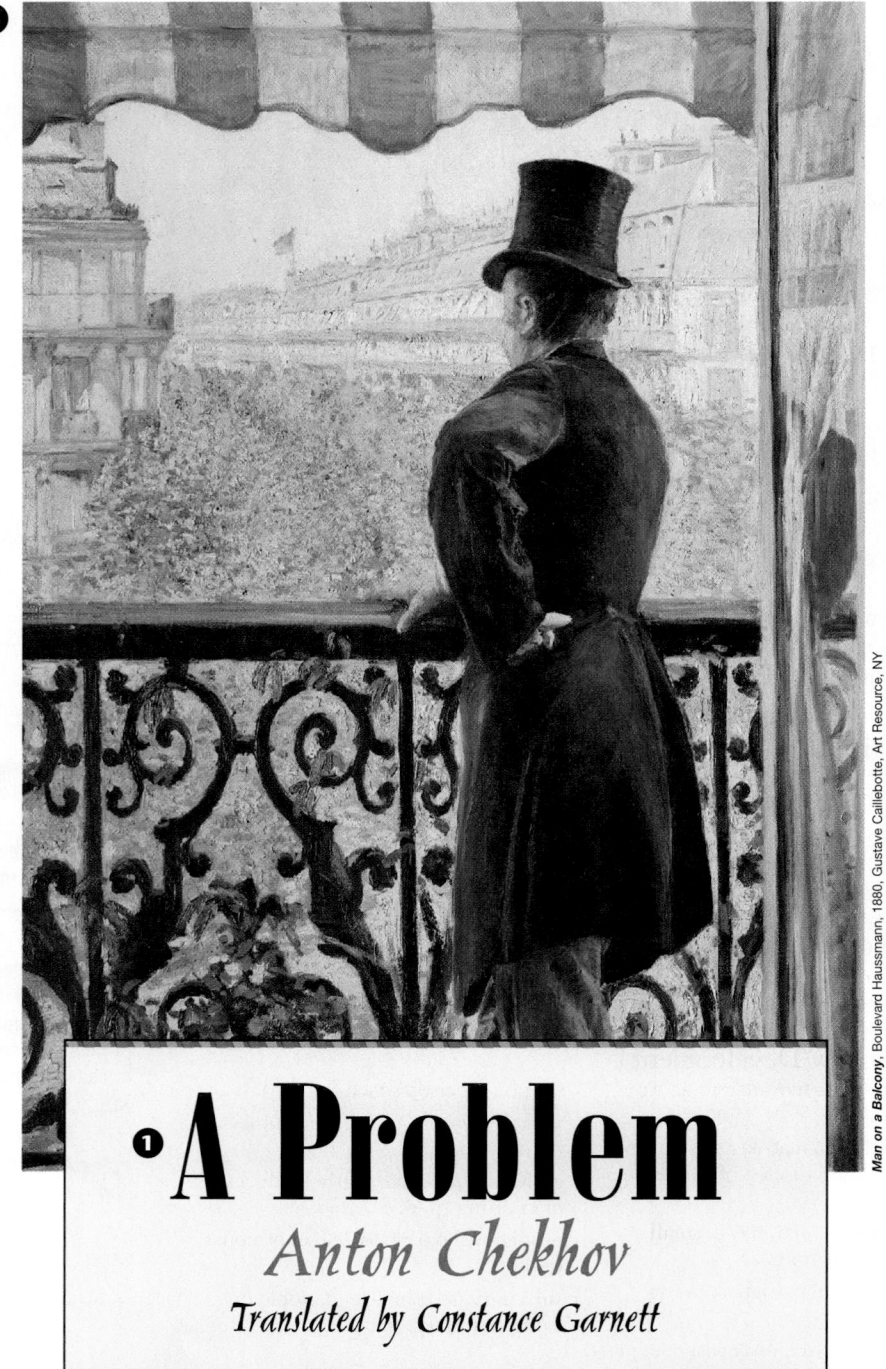

Man on a Balcony, Boulevard Haussmann, 1880, Gustave Caillebotte, Art Resource, NY

❷

❶ A Problem

Anton Chekhov
Translated by Constance Garnett

596 ◆ *Short Stories*

TEACHING RESOURCES

The following resources can be used to enrich or extend the instruction for pp. 596–608.

Literary Analysis

📖 **Writing Models and Graphic Organizers on Transparencies,** p. 83

📓 **Selection Support:** Literary Analysis, p. 152

Reading

🎧 **Listening to Literature Audiocassettes,** Side 19 ▪

💿 **Listening to Literature Audio CDs,** CD 12 ▪

Extension

📖 **Authors In Depth,** Platinum Level, p. 94 (The collection includes two additional selections by Anton Chekhov for extended reading.)

596

▪ **BLOCK SCHEDULING:** Resources marked with this symbol provide varied instruction during 90-minute blocks.

The strictest measures were taken that the Uskovs' family secret might not leak out and become generally known. Half of the servants were sent off to the theater or the circus; the other half were sitting in the kitchen and not allowed to leave it. Orders were given that no one was to be admitted. The wife of the Colonel, her sister, and the governess, though they had been initiated into the secret, kept up a pretense of knowing nothing; they sat in the dining room and did not show themselves in the drawing room or the hall.

Sasha Uskov, the young man of twenty-five who was the cause of all the commotion, had arrived some time before, and by the advice of kind-hearted Ivan Markovitch, his uncle, who was taking his part, he sat meekly in the hall by the door leading to the study, and prepared himself to make an open, candid explanation.

The other side of the door, in the study, a family council was being held. The subject under discussion was an exceedingly disagreeable and delicate one. Sasha Uskov had cashed at one of the banks a false promissory note,[1] and it had become due for payment three days before, and now his two paternal uncles and Ivan Markovitch, the brother of his dead mother, were deciding the question whether they should pay the money and save the family honor, or wash their hands of it and leave the case to go to trial.

To outsiders who have no personal interest in the matter such questions seem simple; for those who are so unfortunate as to have to decide them in earnest they are extremely difficult. The uncles had been talking for a long time, but the problem seemed no nearer decision.

"My friends!" said the uncle who was a colonel, and there was a note of exhaustion and bitterness in his voice. "Who says that family honor is a mere convention? I don't say that at all. I am only warning you against a false view; I am pointing out the possibility of an unpardonable mistake. How can you fail to see it? I am not speaking Chinese; I am speaking Russian!"

"My dear fellow, we do understand," Ivan Markovitch protested mildly.

"How can you understand if you say that I don't believe in family honor? I repeat once more; fa-mil-y ho-nor false-ly un-der-stood is a prejudice! Falsely understood! That's what I say: whatever may be the motives for screening a scoundrel, whoever he may be, and helping him to escape punishment, it is contrary to law and unworthy of a

---

1. **promissory note** written promise to pay a certain sum of money on demand; an IOU.

◀ **Critical Viewing** If you were in Sasha's situation, would you want to go to this man for help? Why or why not? **[Connect]**

Reading Strategy
Drawing Inferences About Character What do you infer about Sasha based on his behavior at this point in the story?

❺ ☑ **Reading Check**
What secret does the Uskov family have?

A Problem ◆ 597

❸ Reading Strategy
Drawing Inferences About Character

• Draw students' attention to the description of Sasha sitting meekly in the hall. Ask students to define the word *meekly*.
Answer: The word *meekly* means "patiently and mildly."

• Then, ask students the Reading Strategy question on p. 597: What do you infer about Sasha based on his behavior at this point in the story?
Answer: Sasha seems to be obedient because he obeyed his uncle's request. He also seems sorry about his wrongdoings, because he sits "meekly" and prepares to speak honestly about his actions.
▶ Monitor Progress As they continue to read, ask students to determine whether this first impression of Sasha is accurate.

❹ ▶ Critical Viewing
Answer: The man's posture makes him look stiff and stern. The fact that his head is turned away from the viewer creates a cold and impersonal impression. Therefore, students may say they would not want to ask him for help.

❺ ☑ Reading Check
Answer: Sasha Uskov has cashed a false promissory note at a bank.

CUSTOMIZE INSTRUCTION FOR UNIVERSAL ACCESS

For Less Proficient Readers	For Advanced Readers
This story contains long and complex sentences that may pose difficulty for students. Using examples from the story, model how to break down such sentences into smaller parts. Remind students to use punctuation marks, as well as signal words such as *if, that,* and *so,* as clues to the logic of the sentence.	As students read the works of well known and respected authors, encourage them to expand their own vocabulary by appreciating the author's selection of words. Have students make a list of interesting word choices in "A Problem," such as "purely anatomical peculiarities," and analyze how the words affect the story's tone.

➏ Literary Analysis

Character

- Have students read the bracketed passage, paying close attention to the differing views of the two paternal uncles.

- Then, ask students to contrast their views. How does one uncle's notion of family honor affect his opinion about how to treat Sasha?
  Answer: The uncle who is with the treasury is concerned with family honor in the sense of keeping up appearances. The uncle who was a colonel regards this approach to family honor as false and mistaken—he believes that covering up another person's wrongdoing is dishonorable, no matter the circumstances.

➐ Reading Strategy

Drawing Inferences About Character

- Remind students that inferences are conclusions they draw based on details in their reading.

- Have students summarize the main points of Ivan's speech.

- Then, ask students the Reading Strategy question on p. 598: What inferences can you make about Ivan Markovitch based on his speech?
  Answer: Ivan is a mild, forgiving man. His comments about Sasha show that he has an understanding, compassionate nature.

---

gentleman. It's not saving the family honor; it's civic cowardice! Take the army, for instance. . . . The honor of the army is more precious to us than any other honor, yet we don't screen our guilty members, but condemn them. And does the honor of the army suffer in consequence? Quite the opposite!"

➏ The other paternal uncle, an official in the Treasury, a <u>taciturn</u>, dull-witted, and <u>rheumatic</u> man, sat silent, or spoke only of the fact that the Uskovs' name would get into the newspapers if the case went for trial. His opinion was that the case ought to be hushed up from the first and not become public property; but, apart from publicity in the newspapers, he advanced no other argument in support of this opinion.

The maternal uncle, kind-hearted Ivan Markovitch, spoke smoothly, softly, and with a tremor in his voice. He began with saying that youth has its rights and its peculiar temptations. Which of us has not been young, and who has not been led astray? To say nothing of ordinary mortals, even great men have not escaped errors and mistakes in their youth. Take, for instance, the biography of great writers. Did not every one of them gamble, drink, and draw down upon himself the anger of right-thinking people in his young days? If Sasha's error bordered upon crime, they must remember that Sasha had received practically no education; he had been expelled from the high school in the fifth class; he had lost his parents in early childhood, and so had been left at the tenderest age without guidance and good, benevolent influences. He was nervous, excitable, had no firm ground under his feet, and, above all, he had been unlucky. Even if he were guilty, anyway he deserved indulgence and the sympathy of all compassionate souls. He ought, of course, to be punished, but he was punished as it was by his conscience and the agonies he was enduring now while awaiting the sentence of his relations. The comparison with the army made by the Colonel was delightful, and did credit to his lofty intelligence; his appeal to their feeling of public duty spoke for the chivalry of his soul, but they must not forget that in each individual the citizen is closely linked with the Christian. . . .

"Shall we be false to civic duty," Ivan Markovitch exclaimed passionately, "if instead of punishing an erring boy we hold out to him a helping hand?"

Ivan Markovitch talked further of family honor. He had not the honor to belong to the Uskov family himself, but he knew their distinguished family went back to the thirteenth century; he did not forget for a minute, either, that his precious, beloved sister had been the wife of one of the representatives of that name. In short, the family was dear to him for many reasons, and he refused to admit the idea that, for the sake of a paltry fifteen hundred rubles,[2] a blot should be cast on the escutcheon[3] that was beyond all price. If all the motives he had brought forward were not sufficiently convincing, he, Ivan

---

2. **rubles** (roo′ bəlz) *n.* Russian unit of currency.
3. **escutcheon** (e skuch′ ən) *n.* shield on which a coat of arms is displayed.

taciturn (tas′ ə turn′) *adj.* preferring not to talk

rheumatic (roo mat′ ik) *adj.* suffering from a painful disease of the joints

Reading Strategy
Drawing Inferences About Character What inferences can you make about Ivan Markovitch based on his speech?

Markovitch, in conclusion, begged his listeners to ask themselves what was meant by crime? Crime is an immoral act founded upon ill-will. But is the will of man free? Philosophy has not yet given a positive answer to that question. Different views were held by the learned. The latest school of Lombroso,[4] for instance, denies the freedom of the will, and considers every crime as the product of the purely anatomical peculiarities of the individual.

"Ivan Markovitch," said the Colonel, in a voice of entreaty, "we are talking seriously about an important matter, and you bring in Lombroso, you clever fellow. Think a little, what are you saying all this for? Can you imagine that all your thunderings and rhetoric will furnish an answer to the question?"

Sasha Uskov sat at the door and listened. He felt neither terror, shame, nor depression, but only weariness and inward emptiness. It seemed to him that it made absolutely no difference to him whether they forgave him or not; he had come here to hear his sentence and to explain himself simply because kind-hearted Ivan Markovitch had begged him to do so. He was not afraid of the future. It made no difference to him where he was: here in the hall, in prison, or in Siberia.

"If Siberia, then let it be Siberia, damn it all!"

He was sick of life and found it insufferably hard. He was inextricably involved in debt; he had not a farthing[5] in his pocket; his family had become detestable to him; he would have to part from his friends and his women sooner or later, as they had begun to be too contemptuous of his sponging on them. The future looked black.

Sasha was indifferent, and was only disturbed by one circumstance; the other side of the door they were calling him a scoundrel and a criminal. Every minute he was on the point of jumping up, bursting into the study and shouting in answer to the detestable metallic voice of the Colonel:

---

4. **Lombroso** Cesare Lombroso (1835–1909), an Italian physician and criminologist, believed that a criminal was a distinct human type, with specific physical and mental deviations, and that a criminal tendency was the result of hereditary factors.

5. **farthing** (fär´ thing) n. coin of little value.

Literature in context ❽ History Connection

Siberia

While he is awaiting the decision of his uncles, Sasha mentions ending up in Siberia.

Through the centuries, Russian and Soviet rulers have sent millions of prisoners to isolated parts of Siberia. There, they were forced to work building factories, mining minerals, and laying railroad tracks. Siberia is covered with ice and snow six months of the year. Ending up as a prisoner in Siberia would not be a pleasant prospect, but Sasha does not seem to care.

❿ ✔ Reading Check

What is one of Ivan Markovitch's arguments for helping Sasha?

A Problem ◆ 599

❽ Background

Siberia

The Siberian flag is white and green—white for the snow and green because Siberia has the largest forest in the world. Siberia is known for its harsh winters, and although people think of it as a desolate place, it has a rich and diverse ecosystem. Its mineral resources are vast, and its southern region produces such agricultural products as wheat, rye, oats, and sunflowers.

❾ Literary Analysis

Characters

- Ask students to describe Sasha's attitude toward his misdeed at this point.
  Answer: At this point, Sasha feels neither ashamed nor guilty about cashing the false promissory note.
- Remind students that a static character does not change during the course of a story.
- Suggest that students pay careful attention to any changes that Sasha may undergo as they continue to read the story.

❿ ✔ Reading Check

Answer: Ivan says that Sasha has already been punished for his misconduct by his own conscience.

CUSTOMIZE INSTRUCTION FOR UNIVERSAL ACCESS

For English Learners	For Gifted/Talented Students
Make sure students understand that a promissory note is an IOU, or a promise to pay an amount of money. In the story, Sasha forged an IOU and cashed it at a bank. If he cannot pay back the money he received, he will be charged with a crime.	Have students research the practice of sending criminals to Siberia. What types of crimes were punished by sending criminals to this region, and how did they live while they were there?

11 ▶ Critical Viewing

Answer: The picture is appropriate because the ruble relates to the main conflict in the story—how to deal with Sasha's fraudulent attempt to obtain money.

12 Literary Analysis

Characters and Theme

• Ask students to state in their own words Sasha's rationale for forging the Colonel's signature.
  Answer: Sasha claims that all the young people forge IOU's. Also, he feels that the problem was not his fault. He would have had the money if his friend Handrikov had followed through on his promise to lend him money.

• Ask students the Literary Analysis question on p. 600: How does Sasha feel about the family honor?
  Answer: Sasha does not care much about family honor; he says his family "had become detestable to him." On the other hand, he did not deliberately set out to ruin the family's honor. He said he "had no intention of causing anybody damage or loss."

11 ▲ **Critical Viewing** Why is a picture of rubles an appropriate illustration for this story? **[Connect]**

"You are lying!"

"Criminal" is a dreadful word—that is what murderers, thieves, robbers are; in fact, wicked and morally hopeless people. And Sasha was very far from being all that. . . . It was true he owed a great deal and did not pay his debts. But debt is not a crime, and it is unusual for a man not to be in debt. The Colonel and Ivan Markovitch were both in debt. . . .

"What have I done wrong besides?" Sasha wondered.

 He had discounted a forged note. But all the young men he knew did the same. Handrikov and Von Burst always forged IOU's from their parents or friends when their allowances were not paid at the regular time, and then when they got their money from home they redeemed them before they became due. Sasha had done the same, but had not redeemed the IOU because he had not got the money which Handrikov had promised to lend him. He was not to blame; it was the fault of circumstances. It was true that the use of another person's signature was considered reprehensible; but, still, it was

Literary Analysis
Characters How does Sasha feel about the family honor?

ENRICHMENT: Career Connection

Criminology

While arguing for leniency for Sasha, Ivan Markovitch brings up the latest theories of criminology—the scientific study of crime and criminal behavior. Although the particular ideas that this character cites have long been out of fashion, criminology remains an important field of social science.

Among the questions that criminologists study are the causes of crime, the nature of criminal organizations, how to prevent crime, and how to rehabilitate criminals.

Criminologists may work within the criminal justice system, or they may teach and conduct studies at a college or university.

Have students gather more information on criminology and report their findings to the class. For example, students may focus on why some background in criminology is important for lawyers, judges, and others who work in the criminal justice system.

not a crime but a generally accepted dodge, an ugly formality which injured no one and was quite harmless, for in forging the Colonel's signature Sasha had had no intention of causing anybody damage or loss.

"No, it doesn't mean that I am a criminal . . ." thought Sasha. "And it's not in my character to bring myself to commit a crime. I am soft, emotional. . . . When I have the money I help the poor. . . ."

Sasha was musing after this fashion while they went on talking the other side of the door.

"But, my friends, this is endless," the Colonel declared, getting excited. "Suppose we were to forgive him and pay the money. You know he would not give up leading a dissipated life, squandering money, making debts, going to our tailors and ordering suits in our names! Can you guarantee that this will be his last prank? As far as I am concerned, I have no faith whatever in his reforming!"

The official of the Treasury muttered something in reply; after him Ivan Markovitch began talking blandly and suavely again. The Colonel moved his chair impatiently and drowned the other's words with his detestable metallic voice. At last the door opened and Ivan Markovitch came out of the study; there were patches of red on his cleanshaven face.

"Come along," he said, taking Sasha by the hand. "Come and speak frankly from your heart. Without pride, my dear boy, humbly and from your heart."

Sasha went into the study. The official of the Treasury was sitting down; the Colonel was standing before the table with one hand in his pocket and one knee on a chair. It was smoky and stifling in the study. Sasha did not look at the official or the Colonel; he felt suddenly ashamed and uncomfortable. He looked uneasily at Ivan Markovitch and muttered:

"I'll pay it . . . I'll give it back. . . ."

"What did you expect when you discounted the IOU?" he heard a metallic voice.

"I . . . Handrikov promised to lend me the money before now."

Sasha could say no more. He went out of the study and sat down again on the chair near the door. He would have been glad to go away altogether at once, but he was choking with hatred and he awfully wanted to remain, to tear the Colonel to pieces, to say something rude to him. He sat trying to think of something violent and effective to say to his hated uncle, and at that moment a woman's figure, shrouded in the twilight, appeared at the drawing room door. It was the Colonel's wife. She beckoned Sasha to her, and, wringing her hands, said, weeping:

"*Alexandre*, I know you don't like me, but . . . listen to me; listen, I beg you. . . . But, my dear, how can this have happened? Why, it's awful, awful! For goodness' sake, beg them, defend yourself, entreat them."

Sasha looked at her quivering shoulders, at the big tears that were

---

Literary Analysis
Characters Ivan Markovitch talks "blandly and suavely again." Does this suggest he is a static or a dynamic character? Explain.

Reading Strategy
Drawing Inferences About Character What can you infer about Sasha based on this reaction?

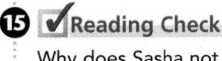 **Reading Check**
Why does Sasha not consider himself a criminal?

A Problem ◆ 601

⓭ **Literary Analysis**
Characters
• Ask students to explain how someone would sound if they spoke blandly and suavely. What might this manner of speaking indicate about the person?
• Then, draw students' attention to the word *again*. Point out that this indicates that Ivan is repeating an action that he already performed.
• Ask the Literary Analysis question on p. 601: Ivan Markovitch talks "blandly and suavely again." Does this suggest he is a static or dynamic character? Explain.
Answer: This suggests that Markovitch is a static character. He doesn't react to the Colonel's opinion or to Sasha's thin excuses. His viewpoint remains fixed.

⓮ **Reading Strategy**
Drawing Inferences About Character
• Ask students to read the bracketed passage and then describe Sasha's behavior.
• Ask the Reading Strategy question on p. 601: What can you infer about Sasha based on this reaction?
Answer: Sasha reacts strongly when people criticize his actions. Some students may say that Sasha's violent reaction indicates that he feels guilty about what he has done. However, he refuses to admit his guilt.

⓯ ✓**Reading Check**
Answer: Sasha doesn't consider himself a criminal because his friends write false promissory notes as well.

601

16 Reading Strategy

Drawing Inferences About Character

- Ask students to explain why the Colonel avoids walking in the hall.
  Answer: The Colonel wants to avoid Sasha. He is angry with his nephew and with the decision to conceal his misdeeds.

- Then, ask the Reading Strategy question on p. 602: What do you think the uncles expect will happen with Sasha?
  Answer: Except for Ivan Markovitch, they expect that he will repeat his bad behavior as soon as he has a chance.

17 Literary Analysis

Character

- Have students read the bracketed passage, and remind them that earlier in the story, Sasha refused to believe that he was a criminal.

- Then, ask students whether Sasha is a static or dynamic character, and why.
  Answer: Sasha is a dynamic character because he learns that he is a criminal. However, his actions will not change, so in this sense he could be considered a static character.

rolling down her cheeks, heard behind his back the hollow, nervous voices of worried and exhausted people, and shrugged his shoulders. He had not in the least expected that his aristocratic relations would raise such a tempest over a paltry fifteen hundred rubles! He could not understand her tears nor the quiver of their voices.

An hour later he heard that the Colonel was getting the best of it; the uncles were finally inclining to let the case go for trial.

"The matter's settled," said the Colonel, sighing. "Enough."

After this decision all the uncles, even the emphatic Colonel, became noticeably depressed. A silence followed.

"Merciful Heavens!" signed Ivan Markovitch. "My poor sister!"

And he began saying in a subdued voice that most likely his sister, Sasha's mother, was present unseen in the study at that moment. He felt in his soul how the unhappy, saintly woman was weeping, grieving, and begging for her boy. For the sake of her peace beyond the grave, they ought to spare Sasha.

The sound of a muffled sob was heard. Ivan Markovitch was weeping and muttering something which it was impossible to catch through the door. The Colonel got up and paced from corner to corner. The long conversation began over again.

But then the clock in the drawing room struck two. The family council was over. To avoid seeing the person who had moved him to such wrath, the Colonel went from the study, not into the hall, but into the <u>vestibule</u>. . . . Ivan Markovitch came out into the hall. . . . He was agitated and rubbing his hands joyfully. His tear-stained eyes looked good-humored and his mouth was twisted into a smile.

"Capital," he said to Sasha. "Thank God! You can go home, my dear, and sleep tranquilly. We have decided to pay the sum, but on condition that you repent and come with me tomorrow into the country and set to work."

A minute later Ivan Markovitch and Sasha in their greatcoats and caps were going down the stairs. The uncle was muttering something edifying. Sasha did not listen, but felt as though some uneasy weight were gradually slipping off his shoulders. They had forgiven him; he was free! A gust of joy sprang up within him and sent a sweet chill to his heart. He longed to breathe, to move swiftly, to live! Glancing at the street lamps and the black sky, he remembered that Von Burst was celebrating his name day[6] that evening at the "Bear," and again a rush of joy flooded his soul. . . .

"I am going!" he decided.

But then he remembered he had not a farthing, that the companions he was going to would despise him at once for his empty pockets. He must get hold of some money, come what may!

"Uncle, lend me a hundred rubles," he said to Ivan Markovitch.

His uncle, surprised, looked into his face and backed against a lamppost.

---

6. **name day** feast day of the saint after whom a person is named.

vestibule (ves′ tə byo͞ol) *n.* small entrance hall

**Reading Strategy
Drawing Inferences About Character** What do you think the uncles expect will happen with Sasha?

"Give it to me," said Sasha, shifting impatiently from one foot to the other and beginning to pant. "Uncle, I entreat you, give me a hundred rubles."

His face worked; he trembled, and seemed on the point of attacking his uncle. . . .

"Won't you?" he kept asking, seeing that his uncle was still amazed and did not understand. "Listen. If you don't, I'll give myself up tomorrow! I won't let you pay the IOU! I'll present another false note tomorrow!"

Petrified, muttering something incoherent in his horror, Ivan Markovitch took a hundred-ruble note out of his pocketbook and gave it to Sasha. The young man took it and walked rapidly away from him. . . .

Taking a sledge,[7] Sasha grew calmer, and felt a rush of joy within him again. The "rights of youth" of which kind-hearted Ivan Markovitch had spoken at the family council woke up and asserted themselves. Sasha pictured the drinking party before him, and, among the bottles, the women, and his friends, the thought flashed through his mind:

"Now I see that I am a criminal; yes, I am a criminal."

---

7. **sledge** (slej) *n.* strong, heavy sled.

Review and Assess

Thinking About the Selection

1. **Respond:** Of all the characters in this story, with whom do you sympathize? Why?

2. **(a) Recall:** Why does Sasha need help? **(b) Predict:** What will happen if Sasha's family helps him repay this debt?

3. **(a) Recall:** How does Uncle Ivan convince the other uncles to help Sasha? **(b) Speculate:** Why do you think the other two uncles do not want to help Sasha?

4. **(a) Infer:** Why do you think Sasha wrote a note he knew he could not pay? **(b) Support:** What details lead you to this conclusion?

5. **(a) Evaluate:** Do you think Uncle Ivan's attitude helps or harms Sasha? Explain. **(b) Relate:** What would you have done if you were one of Sasha's uncles?

6. **Evaluate:** Do you think what Sasha did was a crime? Why or why not?

7. **Take a Position:** What should Ivan Markovitch have done when Sasha accosted him on the street? Why?

Anton Chekhov

(1860–1904)
Anton Chekhov was born in the small coastal town of Taganrog in southern Russia. After the failure of his father's grocery business, his family moved to Moscow. Chekhov continued his schooling in Taganrog and then moved to Moscow to be with his family, enrolling in medical school. While a medical student, he wrote comic sketches and light short stories to earn money to help support his family. Although he suffered from tuberculosis, Chekhov continued to write until he died. *The Cherry Orchard,* one of his most famous plays, was written during the last year of his life.

A Problem ◆ 603

Answers for p. 603

Review and Assess

1. Students may say that they sympathize with Ivan Markovitch because his trust and kindness are betrayed by his nephew. Others may feel that Sasha is deeply troubled and needs help.

2. **(a)** Sasha needs help because he has cashed a false promissory note at the bank, and it has come due for payment. If his family does not cover the debt, Sasha will be tried in court, convicted, and probably sent to debtor's prison. **(b)** The appearance of family honor will be preserved, but Sasha might not learn his lesson.

3. **(a)** Ivan reminds the other relatives that Sasha is young, uneducated, and an orphan, and should therefore be treated with leniency. **(b)** The other two uncles believe that Sasha will never reform and that he will continue to disgrace the family.

4. **(a)** Sasha was playing financial roulette, believing he could cover one debt with another loan. **(b)** Sasha seems to care only about enjoying the moment; he is not concerned with responsibility or the future.

5. **(a)** Some students may say that, ultimately, Uncle Ivan's kindness will help Sasha to reform; others will say that Uncle Ivan is simply enabling Sasha to continue his irresponsible ways. **(b)** Encourage students to think carefully about the effect their actions would have on Sasha. What will help Sasha more—letting him off the hook or forcing him to face the consequences of his actions?

6. Most students will consider writing a false promissory note a crime.

7. Most students will say that Ivan should have walked away without giving Sasha any money because it is clear that Sasha needs to learn a lesson about responsibility.

603

18 About the Selection

In "Luck," a clergyman describes how he attempted to protect a military man from his own blundering ways—from the time the man was a cadet to his battlefield experience in the Crimean War. Due to luck, however, every situation in which the military man found himself seemed to work in his favor. Finally, the man became a renowned and highly decorated military leader. The reader has every reason to believe that the man will continue through life as the fortunate fool that he is.

19 Background

Art

Scotland Forever, by Elizabeth Butler

Elizabeth Butler's vividly realistic and patriotic depictions of battles and military life made her one of the most successful painters in Victorian England. Queen Victoria herself was a great admirer of Butler's works. Use these questions for discussion:

1. What elements in the painting convey a sense of movement and action?
   Answer: Elements include the soldiers with raised swords in the foreground; the turbulent, rolling clouds and gunsmoke; and the point of view, in which the horses appear to charge directly toward the viewer

2. Which side of Scoresby does the painting reflect—the "public" Scoresby or the "real" Scoresby, known only by the clergyman and the narrator? Explain.
   Answer: The painting reflects the public Scoresby—that is, the one who is regarded as a brilliant military hero.

20 ▶Critical Viewing

Answer: Some students may prefer to be a good soldier, because there is more satisfaction in being good at something than in being lucky. Others might point out that lucky soldiers will probably avoid getting wounded or killed.

18 LUCK *Mark Twain*

19

20 ▲ Critical Viewing Based on this painting, would you rather be a good soldier or a lucky one? Explain. **[Draw Conclusions]**

It was at a banquet in London in honor of one of the two or three conspicuously illustrious[1] English military names of this generation. For reasons which will presently appear, I will withhold his real name and titles, and call him Lieutenant-General Lord Arthur Scoresby, V.C., K.C.B., etc., etc., etc. What a fascination there is in a renowned name! There sat the man, in actual flesh, whom I had heard of so many thousands of times since that day, thirty years before, when his

---

1. **conspicuously** (kən spik′ yōō əs lē) **illustrious** (i lus′ trē əs) outstandingly famous.

604 ◆ *Short Stories*

name shot suddenly to the <u>zenith</u> from a Crimean battlefield,[2] to remain forever celebrated. It was food and drink to me to look, and look, and look at that demigod; scanning, searching, noting: the quietness, the reserve, the noble gravity of his <u>countenance</u>; the simple honesty that expressed itself all over him; the sweet unconsciousness of his greatness—unconsciousness of the hundreds of admiring eyes fastened upon him, unconsciousness of the deep, loving, sincere worship welling out of the breasts of those people and flowing toward him.

The clergyman at my left was an old acquaintance of mine—clergyman now, but had spent the first half of his life in the camp and field, and as an instructor in the military school at Woolwich. Just at the moment I have been talking about, a veiled and singular light glimmered in his eyes, and he leaned down and muttered confidentially to me—indicating the hero of the banquet with a gesture:

"Privately—he's an absolute fool."

This verdict was a great surprise to me. If its subject had been Napoleon,[3] or Socrates,[4] or Solomon,[5] my astonishment could not have been greater. Two things I was well aware of: that the Reverend was a man of strict <u>veracity</u>, and that his judgment of men was good. Therefore I knew, beyond doubt or question, that the world was mistaken about this hero: he was a fool. So I meant to find out, at a convenient moment, how the Reverend, all solitary and alone, had discovered the secret.

Some days later the opportunity came, and this is what the Reverend told me:

About forty years ago I was an instructor in the military academy at Woolwich. I was present in one of the sections when young Scoresby underwent his preliminary examination. I was touched to the quick with pity; for the rest of the class answered up brightly and handsomely, while he—why, dear me, he didn't know *anything*, so to speak. He was evidently good, and sweet, and lovable, and <u>guileless</u>; and so it was exceedingly painful to see him stand there, as serene as a graven image, and deliver himself of answers which were veritably miraculous for stupidity and ignorance. All the compassion in me was aroused in his behalf. I said to myself, when he comes to be examined again, he will be flung over, of course; so it will be simply a harmless act of charity to ease his fall as much as I can. I took him aside, and found that he knew a little of Caesar's history;[6] and as he

---

2. **Crimean** (krī mē′ ən) **battlefield** place of battle during the Crimean War (1853–1856), in which Russia was defeated in trying to dominate southeastern Europe.
3. **Napoleon** (nə pō′ lē ən) Napoleon Bonaparte (1769–1821), French military leader and emperor of France from 1804 to 1814.
4. **Socrates** (säk′ rə tēz′) Athenian philosopher and teacher (470?–399 B.C.).
5. **Solomon** (säl′ ə mən) in the Bible, the King of Israel who built the first temple and was noted for his wisdom.
6. **Caesar's** (sē′ zərz) **history** account of Julius Caesar (100?–44 B.C.), Roman emperor from 49 to 44 B.C.

---

zenith (zē′ nith) *n.* highest point

countenance (koun′ tə nəns) *n.* expression on a person's face

veracity (və ras′ ə tē) *n.* truthfulness; honesty

guileless (gīl′ lis) *adj.* without slyness or cunning

② Reading Check
What is the relationship between the clergyman and Scoresby?

Luck ◆ 605

㉑ Critical Thinking
Comparing and Contrasting

- Ask students to compare and contrast Scoresby's image in the eyes of the public and the clergyman.
  Answer: The public views him as a brilliant military hero; the clergyman views him as a lucky fool.

- Then, ask students to account for this difference of opinion. What do students think the clergyman knows about Scoresby that the public does not?

㉒ Vocabulary Development
Latin Root -ver-

- Call students' attention to the word *veritably*, and tell them that it means '"truly." Explain that the Latin root -ver- means "speaking truly."

- Have students suggest words and phrases that contain this root and list them on the chalkboard. Students might mention *verify*, *verisimilitude*, and *aver*.

- Next, have students look up the meanings of these words in the dictionary.

㉓ ✓ Reading Check
Answer: The clergyman is a former teacher who took pity on Scoresby and helped him pass his exams.

CUSTOMIZE INSTRUCTION FOR UNIVERSAL ACCESS

For Less Proficient Readers	For English Learners	For Advanced Readers
Make sure students understand the origin of the different viewpoints about Scoresby. Ask them to write one sentence explaining what the public thinks about Scoresby and another that explains what the clergyman thinks about Scoresby.	Make sure students understand the idiomatic expressions "shot . . . to the zenith," "it was food and drink for me to look," "honesty that expressed itself all over him," and "worship welling out of the breasts of those people."	As students read, have them compare the way Ivan Markovitch treats Sasha in "A Problem" with the way the clergyman treats Scoresby in "Luck." What do Markovitch and the clergyman intend to teach the young men? Do they succeed or fail? Why?

Making Inferences About Character

- Have students consider the image of mother and the crippled child in this passage to make inferences about the clergyman's character.

- Ask students what motives the clergyman might have for helping young Scoresby.
  Answer: He is caring and soft-hearted; he helps Scoresby out of kindness.

25 Critical Thinking

Make a Judgment

- Have students consider the clergy-man's character and why he behaved the way he did.

- Ask students why the clergyman goes off to war with Scoresby. Do they think it was wise or foolish?
  Answer: Scoresby has been pro-moted, and the clergyman fears that his participation in the war will result in disaster. Some students may say that the clergyman feels responsible because he got Scoresby into his position of responsibility. He feels he can pro-tect others from Scoresby's foolish mistakes. Other students may say that it is foolish—the clergyman should allow Scoresby to be exposed once and for all.

26 Literary Analysis

Characters

- Remind students that a static char-acter is one who does not change or develop over time.

- Ask the Literary Analysis question on p. 606: How does this observa-tion indicate that Scoresby is a static character?
  Answer: Scoresby did well in school by being lucky rather than intelligent. Now, he is doing well in the army for the same reason.

▶ Monitor Progress Based on the details he offers about his experi-ences with Scoresby, have stu-dents consider whether the clergyman is a static or dynamic character.

---

didn't know anything else, I went to work and drilled him like a galley slave on a certain line of stock questions concerning Caesar which I knew would be used. If you'll believe me, he went through with flying colors on examination day! He went through on that purely super-ficial "cram," and got compliments too, while others, who knew a thousand times more than he, got plucked. By some strangely lucky accident—an accident not likely to happen twice in a century—he was asked no question outside of the narrow limits of his drill.

24 It was stupefying. Well, all through his course I stood by him, with something of the sentiment which a mother feels for a crippled child; and he always saved himself—just by miracle, apparently.

Now of course the thing that would expose him and kill him at last was mathematics. I resolved to make his death as easy as I could; so I drilled him and crammed him, and crammed him and drilled him, just on the line of questions which the examiners would be most like-ly to use, and then launched him on his fate. Well, sir, try to conceive of the result: to my consternation he took the first prize! And with it he got a perfect ovation in the way of compliments.

Sleep? There was no more sleep for me for a week. My conscience tortured me day and night. What I had done I had done purely through charity, and only to ease the poor youth's fall—I never had dreamed of any such preposterous result as the thing that had hap-pened. I felt as guilty and miserable as the creator of Frankenstein. Here was a woodenhead whom I had put in the way of glittering pro-motions and prodigious responsibilities, and but one thing could hap-pen: he and his responsibilities would all go to ruin together at the first opportunity.

The Crimean War* had just broken out. Of course there had to be a war, I said to myself: we couldn't have peace and give this donkey a chance to die before he is found out. I waited for the earthquake. It came. And it made me reel when it did come. He was actually gazetted[7] to a captaincy in a marching regiment! Better men grow old and gray in the service before they climb to a sublimity like that. And who could ever have foreseen that they would go and put such a load of responsibility on such green and inadequate shoulders? I could just barely have stood it if they had made him a cornet;[8] but a cap-tain—think of it! I thought my hair would turn white.

25 Consider what I did—I who so loved repose and inaction. I said to myself, I am responsible to the country for this, and I must go along with him and protect the country against him as far as I can. So I took my poor little capital that I had saved up through years of work and grinding economy, and went with a sigh and bought a cornetcy in his regiment, and away we went to the field.

26 And there—oh dear, it was awful. Blunders?—why, he never did anything *but* blunder. But, you see, nobody was in the fellow's

---

7. **gazetted** (gə zet′ əd) v. officially promoted.
8. **cornet** (kôr net′) n. British cavalry officer who carried his troop's flag.

prodigious (prō dij′ əs) *adj.* enormous

sublimity (sə blim′ ə tē) *n.* noble or exalted state

Literary Analysis
Characters How does this observation indicate that Scoresby is a static character?

secret—everybody had him focused wrong, and necessarily misinterpreted his performance every time—consequently they took his idiotic blunders for inspirations of genius; they did, honestly! His mildest blunders were enough to make a man in his right mind cry; and they did make me cry—and rage and rave too, privately. And the thing that kept me always in a sweat of apprehension was the fact that every fresh blunder he made increased the luster of his reputation! I kept saying to myself, he'll get so high, that when discovery does finally come, it will be like the sun falling out of the sky.

He went right along up, from grade to grade, over the dead bodies of his superiors, until at last, in the hottest moment of the battle of * * * * down went our colonel, and my heart jumped into my mouth, for Scoresby was next in rank! Now for it, said I; we'll all land in Sheol[9] in ten minutes, sure.

The battle was awfully hot: the allies were steadily giving way all over the field. Our regiment occupied a position that was vital; a blunder now must be destruction. At this crucial moment, what does this immortal fool do but detach the regiment from its place and order a charge over a neighboring hill where there wasn't a suggestion of an enemy. "There you go!" I said to myself; "this *is* the end at last."

And away we did go, and were over the shoulder of the hill before the insane movement could be discovered and stopped. And what did we find? An entire and unsuspected Russian army in reserve! And what happened? We were eaten up? That is necessarily what would have happened in ninety-nine cases out of a hundred. But no, those Russians argued that no single regiment would come browsing around there at such a time. It must be the entire English army, and that the sly Russian game was detected and blocked; so they turned tail, and away they went, pell-mell, over the hill and down into the field, in wild confusion, and we after them; they themselves broke the solid Russian center in the field, and tore through, and in no time there was the most tremendous rout you ever saw, and the defeat of the allies was turned into a sweeping and splendid victory! Marshal Canrobert looked on, dizzy with astonishment, admiration, and delight; and sent right off for Scoresby, and

---

9. **Sheol** (shē´ ol) *n.* in the Bible, a place in the depths of the Earth where the dead are thought to dwell.

Literature in context History Connection

♦ **The Crimean War**

Scoresby achieved his greatest victory in the Crimean War, which lasted from October 1853 through February 1856. One factor causing the conflict was Russia's insistence on protecting Russian Orthodox subjects of the Ottoman sultan. The Russians fought against the British, French, and the Turks of the Ottoman Empire on the Crimean Peninsula along the north shore of the Black Sea. The Turks finally evacuated the Russians from their stronghold at Sebastopol on September 11, 1855, and Russia accepted preliminary peace terms on February 1, 1856.

RUSSIAN EMPIRE

Crimea

Sebastopol

BLACK SEA

OTTOMAN EMPIRE

Europe Black Sea

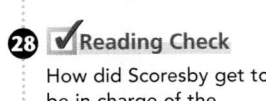

28 ✓ **Reading Check**

How did Scoresby get to be in charge of the regiment?

Luck ◆ 607

---

27 **Background**

The Crimean War

Students may be interested to know that Florence Nightingale was a hero of the Crimean war.

In 1854, while Nightingale was working as the superintendent of a women's hospital in London, the Secretary of War asked her to travel to the Crimea and take charge of nursing for the allied troops. The conditions she found there were wretched, but she and her staff did much to improve army hospitals and save lives. As a result of her work, Nightingale became a world-famous expert on field medicine—the care of sick and wounded soldiers. Several years later, during the American Civil War, she advised the United States on the operation and administration of military hospitals.

28 ✓ **Reading Check**

Answer: When the war broke out, Scoresby was promoted to captain based on his stellar performance on his examinations.

CUSTOMIZE INSTRUCTION FOR UNIVERSAL ACCESS

For Special Needs Students

Have students select one of the stories and analyze its static and dynamic characters. Have them list all the characters in the story down one side of a piece of paper, leaving space between each name. Then, have them fold the paper in an accordion fold so it has three additional columns. In the first column, students should note the traits of each character at the start of the story. Students can skim the story for details that indicate whether the character changed or remained the same during the story. If the character changed, have them mark an X in the second column, and if not, have them mark the third column.

Review and Assess

1. Some students may want to ask Scoresby to what he attributes his success.

2. **(a)** He describes Scoresby as a fool. **(b)** The narrator admires Scoresby; the clergyman thinks him a fool.

3. **(a)** He helps Scoresby with history and math; he joins Scoresby's regiment to help him in battle. **(b)** He finds Scoresby "lovable," but pities him for being such a fool.

4. **(a)** Scoresby is asked only questions to which he knows the answers on his examinations; he is made a captain in the army; his blunders in the war are taken for genius. **(b)** Possible response: Scoresby, if he is indeed a fool, probably thinks nothing of his successes.

5. **(a)** Scoresby wins a stunning military victory as a result of mistaking his right hand for his left. **(b)** Scoresby will probably continue to be successful because of his luck.

6. **(a)** Students should include evidence from the story as support. **(b)** The clergyman is a fool for enabling Scoresby to deceive those around him.

7. Possible response: It seems that luck is important, but the kindness of others is helpful, too.

---

hugged him, and decorated him on the field, in presence of all the armies!

And what was Scoresby's blunder that time? Merely the mistaking his right hand for his left—that was all. An order had come to him to fall back and support our right; and instead, he fell *forward* and went over the hill to the left. But the name he won that day as a marvelous military genius filled the world with his glory, and that glory will never fade while history books last.

He is just as good and sweet and lovable and unpretending as a man can be, but he doesn't know enough to come in when it rains. Now that is absolutely true. He is the supremest fool in the universe; and until half an hour ago nobody knew it but himself and me. He has been pursued, day by day and year by year, by a most phenomenal and astonishing luckiness. He has been a shining soldier in all our wars for a generation; he has littered his whole military life with blunders, and yet has never committed one that didn't make him a knight or a baronet or a lord or something. Look at his breast; why, he is just clothed in domestic and foreign decorations. Well, sir, every one of them is the record of some shouting stupidity or other; and taken together, they are proof that the very best thing in all this world that can befall a man is to be born lucky. I say again, as I said at the banquet, Scoresby's an absolute fool.

Review and Assess

Thinking About the Selection

1. **Respond:** If you could question Scoresby about his experiences, what would you ask him?

2. **(a) Recall:** How does the clergyman describe Scoresby? **(b) Distinguish:** How does the narrator's first impression of Scoresby contrast with the view the clergyman presents?

3. **(a) Recall:** What does the clergyman do to help Scoresby? **(b) Speculate:** Why does the clergyman help Scoresby?

4. **(a) Recall:** Summarize the series of lucky events that put Scoresby in a position of leadership. **(b) Speculate:** What do you think Scoresby thinks about his success?

5. **(a) Recall:** How does Scoresby achieve his "greatest victory"? **(b) Predict:** How do you think the rest of Scoresby's life will work out? Why?

6. **(a) Connect:** Do you agree with the clergyman that Scoresby is a fool? Explain. **(b) Support:** In what way is the clergyman also a fool?

7. **Take a Position:** What role do you think luck plays in a person's success? Support your response with examples.

Mark Twain

(1835–1910)

Mark Twain is the pen name of Samuel Langhorne Clemens, one of America's greatest writers. He was born in Florida, Missouri, and grew up in nearby Hannibal. Many of the characters and incidents that appear in his work were drawn from his boyhood experiences there.

Twain's formal education ended early. After he left school, he learned the printing trade. At various times, Twain worked as a printer, a riverboat pilot, and a prospector of gold. After his huge success as a writer, he lectured around the world. His two most widely read books are *The Adventures of Tom Sawyer* (1876) and *The Adventures of Huckleberry Finn* (1885).

✏ ASSESSMENT PRACTICE: Grammar and Language

Recognize Forms of Propaganda　　　　**(For more practice, see Test Preparation Workbook, p. 38.)**

Many tests require students to read critically and analyze passages that contain elements of propaganda. Use this sample test item to give students practice with these skills.

> Twain's formal education ended early. After he left school, he embarked on a colorful mix of jobs—at various times, he worked as a printer and a riverboat pilot, prospected for gold and gave rousing lectures around the world.

The author tries to convince the reader of Twain's eccentricity by—

　A describing Twain's personality.

　B questioning Twain's commitment.

　C showing why Twain disliked his formal education.

　D delineating Twain's varied career.

Guide students to see that *A, B,* and *C* are not supported by the passage. Only *D* accurately responds to the question.

Review and Assess

Literary Analysis

Characters

1. (a) Describe the behavior that led to Sasha Uskov's troubles in "A Problem." (b) Describe the way he behaves at the end of the story.
2. Compare Arthur Scoresby's character traits at the beginning of "Luck" and at the end of the selection.
3. Using a chart like the one here, explain which characters are **static** and which characters are **dynamic** in the two selections.

Character	Static or Dynamic?	Why?

Comparing Literary Works

4. (a) What are the consequences of the family's decision in "A Problem"? (b) In "Luck," what are the consequences of the clergyman's decision?
5. In which story are the consequences of the decision that was made more serious? Explain your answer.
6. What point do you think each author is making about choices and consequences? Support your ideas with examples.

Reading Strategy

Drawing Inferences About Character

7. What **inferences** can you **draw** about Sasha's character when he asks his uncle for money at the end of the story?
8. What do you infer about Scoresby based on the fact that all his advancements result from his blunders?
9. What can you infer about the clergyman's character and his motives for helping Scoresby the student?

Extend Understanding

10. **Cultural Connection:** How does Sasha's aristocratic background influence his bad behavior? What rules could his family enforce to teach him responsibility?

Quick Review

Static characters do not change during the course of a story.
Dynamic characters change as a result of what happens to them in a story.

You can **draw inferences about characters** by making guesses based on descriptions of them and on what they say and do.

 Take It to the Net
www.phschool.com
Take the interactive self-test online to check your understanding of these selections.

A Problem / Luck ◆ 609

Answers for p. 609

Review and Assess

1. **(a)** Sasha has forged his uncle's name on a promissory note in order to support his irresponsible lifestyle. **(b)** At the end of the story, he recklessly betrays his uncle's trust.
2. Scoresby is the same lucky blunderer throughout.
3. Sasha is dynamic, because he realizes he is a criminal at the end of the story. Ivan Markovitch is static, because he supports Sasha's criminality throughout the piece. Scoresby is static, because he remains a lucky blunderer throughout the selection.
4. **(a)** While they protect the family name, Sasha continues to be an irresponsible young man. **(b)** Scoresby continues to make foolish choices, and they continue to produce good results for him.
5. The consequences are potentially more serious in "Luck" because many soldiers' lives depend on Scoresby.
6. Possible responses: Chekhov is saying that honor based on deception is not actually honor. He believes that if the uncles support Sasha now, he will only bring dishonor on the family later. Twain is saying that those who create heroes, like the clergyman, should be held responsible for the false heroes' actions.
7. Sasha has no moral sense.
8. Scoresby is lucky.
9. The clergyman has a kind character, and his motives are good.
10. Because of his social standing, Sasha believes that he should have whatever he wants. His family could refuse to cover up Sasha's wrongdoings.

❶ Vocabulary Development

Word Analysis

1. c   3. a
2. b

Spelling Strategy

1. dining   3. gravity
2. daring

Fluency: Context

1. Someone who has reached the *zenith* of success has great happiness in his or her personal and professional life.

2. A clown usually displays a happy or comical *countenance*.

3. Politicians should have *veracity*; they should be honest.

4. A *guileless* burglar would fail because he would not be deceitful.

5. A grasshopper is not *prodigious* because it is small.

6. A person who is honored for her achievements is in a position of *sublimity*.

7. A *taciturn* person would be suited for a career that does not involve talking much with other people.

8. A *rheumatic* person would not be agile, so he or she probably would not be good at sports.

9. A *vestibule*, which is a small entrance hall or room, might hold a small table or some chairs.

❷ Grammar

1. who was a colonel; restrictive

2. which only I know; restrictive

3. who knew more than he; nonrestrictive

4. that you loaned me; restrictive

5. which resulted in a victory; nonrestrictive

Writing Application

The young man who is Ivan Markovitch's nephew causes all three of his uncles great anguish as a result of his selfishness. Sasha, who is selfish, short-sighted, and dishonest, uses his family as if their only purpose in life were to satisfy his whims.

Integrate Language Skills

❶ Vocabulary Development Lesson

Word Analysis: Latin Root *-ver-*

The root *-ver-* comes from the Latin *verox* and means "speaking truly." It forms the basis of a number of English words whose meanings relate to the idea of truth. In your notebook, match each numbered word with its corresponding definition.

1. veritable   a. a truth
2. verisimilitude   b. appearing true
3. verity   c. actual; in fact

Spelling Strategy

In words that end in a silent *e*, drop the *e* before adding a suffix beginning with a vowel. For example, *sublime* + *-ity* = *sublimity*. In your notebook, combine each word below with the suffix.

1. dine + *-ing* 2. dare + *-ing* 3. grave + *-ity*

❷ Grammar Lesson

Restrictive and Nonrestrictive Adjective Clauses

Adjective clauses contain both a subject and a verb and modify nouns or pronouns. An adjective clause is **restrictive** when it is necessary to complete the meaning of the noun or pronoun it modifies. It is not set off with a comma. A **nonrestrictive clause** adds details that are not necessary to the meaning of the sentence, so it is set off with commas.

> **Restrictive:** Orders were given *that no one was to be admitted.* (modifies *orders*)
>
> **Nonrestrictive:** . . . by the advice of . . . Ivan Markovitch, . . . *who was taking his part*, he sat meekly in the hall. . . . (modifies *Markovitch*)

W̶G̶ Prentice Hall Writing and Grammar Connection: Chapter 20, Section 2

Fluency: Context

In your notebook, answer the following questions. Explain your responses.

1. What are the signs that someone has reached the *zenith* of success?

2. What type of *countenance* does a clown typically display?

3. Why should politicians have *veracity*?

4. Why would a *guileless* burglar fail?

5. Is the grasshopper a *prodigious* creature? Explain.

6. Name a type of person who would be in a position of *sublimity*.

7. What careers are suitable for a *taciturn* person?

8. Would a *rheumatic* person be an athlete?

9. What furniture fits in a *vestibule*?

Practice Copy the following sentences. Underline the adjective clause in each, tell whether it is restrictive or nonrestrictive, and add appropriate punctuation.

1. "Help!" said the uncle who was a colonel.

2. For reasons that only I know, he left.

3. Others, who knew more than he, flunked.

4. I read the book that you loaned me.

5. Scoresby mistook his right hand for his left, which resulted in a victory.

Writing Application Write a paragraph giving your opinion of Sasha. Use at least one restrictive and one nonrestrictive adjective clause.

TEACHING RESOURCES

The following resources can be used to enrich or extend the instruction for pp. 610–611.

Vocabulary

📓 **Selection Support:** Build Vocabulary, p. 149

📖 **Vocabulary and Spelling Practice Book** (Use this booklet for skills enrichment.)

Grammar

📓 **Selection Support:** Build Grammar Skills, p. 150

W̶G̶ **Writing and Grammar,** Platinum Level, p. 465

📠 **Daily Language Practice Transparencies** ▪️

Writing

W̶G̶ **Writing and Grammar,** Platinum Level, p. 203

💿 **Writing and Grammar iText CD-ROM** ▪️

📠 **Writing Models and Graphic Organizers on Transparencies,** p. 83

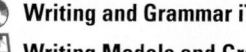 **BLOCK SCHEDULING:** Resources marked with this symbol provide varied instruction during 90-minute blocks.

Writing Lesson

Story Ending

Write a new story ending for either "Luck" or "A Problem" that shows one major character changing as a result of the events in the original story. To prepare, examine what motivated the characters' decisions.

Prewriting Choose a character from one of the stories. Using a chart like the one here, jot down the steps that led to your character's behavior. Then, consider what other decisions that character might have made.

Model: Analyzing Character's Behavior

Drafting After choosing the direction that the character will take, write a new ending for the story. Make sure that the character's new decisions are motivated by what has already happened in the story.

Revising Read your draft, and underline the details that motivate the character's decision. If the decision does not seem realistic or true, rewrite the ending so that it follows logically.

 Prentice Hall Writing and Grammar Connection: Chapter 10, Section 2

Extension Activities

Listening and Speaking Imagine yourself as the clergyman in "Luck," and prepare a **monologue** that describes the character of Scoresby. Base your description on details from the selection.

- Describe Scoresby's specific actions and movements.
- Give examples to support your inferences about his character.
- Tell how you feel about the decisions you made regarding him.

Rehearse your monologue until you are satisfied, and then present it to the class.

Research and Technology With a small group, produce a **multimedia biography** of either Mark Twain or Anton Chekhov. Use maps to show where the writer lived and the settings he described. To enhance your work, make a recording of a representative excerpt from the author's work. [Group Activity]

Take It to the Net www.phschool.com

Go online for an additional research activity using the Internet.

A Problem / Luck ◆ 611

Lesson Support for p. 611

❸ Writing Lesson

- Suggest that students lead up to the ending by writing what has already occurred to one of the major characters. They might write these notes on the Story Map transparency, p. 83 in **Writing Models and Graphic Organizers on Transparencies.**

- Encourage students to experiment with turning a static character, such as Scoresby, into a dynamic one, or vice versa.

- Use the Writing Lesson to help students write a story ending.

- Use the rubric for Narration: Short Story, p. 14 in **Performance Assessment and Portfolio Management,** to assess students' work.

❹ Research and Technology

- Divide the class into small groups.

- Have group members assign individuals to various tasks, such as gathering maps, gathering photos, and making a recording of the author's work.

- Have students present their multimedia biographies to their classmates when they finish.

CUSTOMIZE INSTRUCTION
For Universal Access

To address different learning styles, use the activities suggested in the **Extension Activities** booklet, p. 38.

- For Intrapersonal and Visual/Spatial Learners, use Activity 5.

- For Verbal/Linguistic and Logical/Mathematical Learners, use Activity 6.

- For Verbal/Linguistic, Musical/Rhythmic, and Interpersonal Learners, use Activity 7.

There Will Come Soft Rains ✦ The Garden of Stubborn Cats

Lesson Objectives

1. **To analyze and respond to literary elements**
   - Literary Analysis: Setting
   - Comparing Literary Works

2. **To read, comprehend, analyze, and critique short stories**
   - Reading Strategy: Clarifying
   - Reading Check questions
   - Review and Assess questions
   - Assessment Practice (ATE)

3. **To develop word analysis skills, fluency, and systematic vocabulary**
   - Vocabulary Development Lesson: Word Analysis: Words From Myths

4. **To understand and apply written and oral language conventions**
   - Spelling Strategy
   - Grammar Lesson: Parallel Structure

5. **To understand and apply appropriate writing and research strategies**
   - Writing Lesson: Advertisement for a New Technology
   - Extension Activity: Floor Plan

6. **To understand and apply listening and speaking strategies**
   - Extension Activity: Persuasive Argument

STEP-BY-STEP TEACHING GUIDE	PACING GUIDE
PRETEACH	
Motivate Students and Provide Background	
Use the Motivation activity (ATE p. 612)	5 min.
Read and discuss the Preview material and Background information (SE/ATE p. 612) **A**	5 min.
Introduce the Concepts	
Introduce the Literary Analysis and Reading Strategy (SE/ATE p.613) **A**	15 min.
Pronounce the vocabulary words and read their definitions (SE p. 613)	5 min.
TEACH	
Monitor Comprehension	
Informally monitor comprehension by circulating while students read independently or in groups **A**	35 min.
Monitor students' comprehension with the Reading Check notes (SE/ATE pp. 615, 617, 619, 621, 623, 625, 627)	as students read
Develop vocabulary with Vocabulary notes (SE pp. 615, 618, 620, 621, 626; ATE p. 620)	as students read
Develop Understanding	
Develop students' understanding of setting with Literary Analysis annotations (SE pp. 614, 617, 618, 622; ATE pp. 615, 617, 618, 622, 624) **A**	10 min.
Develop students' understanding of clarifying with Reading Strategy annotations (SE pp. 615, 616, 621, 624, 625, 626, 627; ATE pp. 615, 616, 621, 623, 624, 625, 626, 627)	10 min.
ASSESS	
Assess Mastery	
Assess students' mastery of the Reading Strategy and Literary Analysis by having them answer the Review and Assess questions (SE/ATE p. 629)	20 min.
Use one or more of the print and media Assessment Resources (ATE p. 631) **A**	up to 50 min.
EXTEND	
Apply Understanding	
Have students complete the Vocabulary Development Lesson and the Grammar Lesson (SE p. 630) **A**	20 min.
Apply students' ability to address a target audience by using the Writing Lesson (SE p. 631) **A**	45 min.
Apply students' understanding using one or more of the Extension Activities (SE p. 631)	20–90 min.

 ACCELERATED INSTRUCTION:
Use the strategies and activities identified with an **A**.

UNIVERSAL ACCESS
● = Below Level Students
▲ = On-Level Students
■ = Above Level Students

Time and Resource Manager

Reading Level: Average/Average
Average Number of Instructional Days: 4

RESOURCES

PRINT 📖	TRANSPARENCIES 🎞	TECHNOLOGY 💿 🎧 📼
• **Beyond Literature,** Community Connection: Automation in the Home, p. 39 ▲ ■		• **Interest Grabber Video,** Tape 3 ● ▲ ■
• **Selection Support Workbook:** ● ▲ ■ Literary Analysis, p. 156 Reading Strategy, p. 155 Build Vocabulary, p. 153	• **Literary Analysis and Reading Transparencies,** pp. 77 and 78 ● ▲ ■	
• **Adapted Reader's Companion** ● • **Reader's Companion** ●		• **Listening to Literature** ● ▲ ■ Audiocassettes, Sides 19, 20 Audio CDs, CD 13
• **English Learner's Companion** ● ▲ • **Literatura en español** ● ▲ • **Literary Analysis for Enrichment** ■	• **Fine Art Transparencies, Volume 1,** Art Transparency 5 ● ▲ ■	
• **Formal Assessment:** Selection Test, pp. 135–137 ● ▲ ■ • **Open Book Test,** pp. 115–117 ● ▲ ■ • **Performance Assessment and Portfolio Management,** pp. 20, 30 ● ▲ ■ • ⬡ PRENTICE HALL **ASSESSMENT SYSTEM** ● ▲ ■	• ⬡ PRENTICE HALL **ASSESSMENT SYSTEM** ● ▲ ■ Skills Practice Answers and Explanations on Transparencies	• **Test Bank Software** ● ▲ ■ • **Got It! Assessment Videotapes** ● ▲
• **Selection Support Workbook:** ● ▲ ■ Build Grammar Skills, p. 154 • **Writing and Grammar,** Platinum Level ● ▲ ■ • **Extension Activities,** p. 39 ● ▲ ■	• **Daily Language Practice Transparencies** ● ▲	• **Writing and Grammar iText CD-ROM** ● ▲ ■ 🖥 *Take It to the Net* www.phschool.com

BLOCK SCHEDULING: Use one 90-minute class period to preteach the selection and have students read it. Use a second 90-minute class period to assess students' mastery of skills and have them complete one of the Extension Activities.

PRETEACH

Step-by-Step Teaching Guide for pp. 612–613

Motivation

Have students anticipate technological developments by describing a typical day in the life of someone living fifty years from now. For example, what kind of gadgets would be available for preparing breakfast and what kinds of transportation would take the person to school or work? Ask students to brainstorm for technological developments as you go through a day from morning to evening. Then, tell them that these stories deal with the consequences of technology.

▦ Interest Grabber Video

As an alternative, play "There Will Come Soft Rains: The History of Nuclear Power" on Tape 3 to engage student interest.

❶ Background

Technology

Explain to students that the word *automation* contains the Greek root *autos*, which means "self." Automation refers to machines that are self-operating. These machines perform tasks that are too boring or dangerous for people to do. As more and more areas of business and personal life become automated, people continue to evaluate the effects of automation on society.

Prepare to Read

There Will Come Soft Rains ◆ The Garden of Stubborn Cats

 Take It to the Net

Visit www.phschool.com for interactive activities and instruction related to these selections, including

- background
- graphic organizers
- literary elements
- reading strategies

Preview

Connecting to the Literature

You have exchanged hundreds of e-mails with your best friend. You are starting to forget how he or she looks or sounds because all you have to do to communicate is type and press "send." Situations like this call your attention to the fact that new technology may have unexpected disadvantages. These stories highlight the need to examine the effects of progress.

❶ Background

Automation is the use of machines to perform tasks that require a decision. For example, thermostats "decide" when to turn up or down, and some traffic lights change based on the amount of traffic passing by. In "There Will Come Soft Rains," you will encounter a house of the future that has an impressive level of automation.

TEACHING RESOURCES

The following resources can be used to enrich or extend the instruction for pp. 612–613.

Motivation

▦ **Interest Grabber Video,** Tape 3 ▦

Background

📖 **Beyond Literature,** p. 39

💻 **Take It to the Net**
Visit www.phschool.com for background and hotlinks for the selections.

Literary Analysis

▥ **Literary Analysis and Reading Transparencies,** Setting, p. 78 ▦

Reading

📖 **Selection Support:** Reading Strategy, p. 155; Build Vocabulary, p. 153

▥ **Literary Analysis and Reading Transparencies,** Clarify, p. 77

▦ **BLOCK SCHEDULING:** Resources marked with this symbol provide varied instruction during 90-minute blocks.

❷ Literary Analysis

Setting

All stories have a **setting**—the time and place of the action. In some stories, the setting simply provides a backdrop for the events of the story. You will notice in these stories, however, that the setting plays a more important role. Place is emphasized in this passage from "The Garden of Stubborn Cats."

> . . . from the cat city there opened unsuspected peepholes onto the city of men: and one day the same tabby led him to discover the great Biarritz Restaurant.

For each selection, prepare a chart like the one shown, and record details that help you identify and understand each setting.

". . . Soft Rains"
Time Details
August 4, 2026 7:00 A.M.
Place Details
Allendale, California, house

Comparing Literary Works

The settings of these stories do not function as you would expect. Instead, they produce **irony**—a literary technique that presents a surprising or amusing contradiction. Irony often results from a clash between what the reader or character expects to happen and what actually happens. As you read, notice how the settings of the stories are ironic. Compare the effects of irony in each story to decide what the writer communicates about the future.

❸ Reading Strategy

Clarifying

As both of the stories develop, you may come to sections that are not clear to you. At these points, **clarify** information by identifying the word, phrase, detail, or event that confuses you. Then, stop, look back or ahead, and put details together to clarify what is confusing you.

Vocabulary Development

warrens (wôr′ ənz) *n.* mazelike passages (p. 615)

titanic (tī tan′ ik) *adj.* powerful (p. 615)

paranoia (par′ ə noi′ ə) *n.* mental disorder characterized by delusions of persecution (p. 615)

tremulous (trem′ yōō ləs) *adj.* trembling; quivering (p. 618)

psychopathic (sī′ kō path′ ik) *adj.* with a dangerous mental disorder (p. 620)

supernal (sə pʉrn′ əl) *adj.* celestial or divine (p. 621)

itinerary (ī tin′ ər er′ ē) *n.* route (p. 621)

indigence (in′ di jəns) *n.* poverty (p. 626)

There Will Come Soft Rains / The Garden of Stubborn Cats ◆ 613

---

❷ Literary Analysis

Setting

- Tell students that as they read "There Will Come Soft Rains" and "The Garden of Stubborn Cats," they will focus on setting, the time and place in which the action occurs.

- For each of the stories, have students prepare a setting chart like the one shown. Encourage them to think about which is more prominent in each story: time or place.

- Then, have students read the section on Comparing Literary Works. Explain that a setting can be ironic if it contributes to the clash between what is expected and what actually happens.

❸ Reading Strategy

Clarifying

- Lead students in a discussion of ways they can clarify meaning, such as by rereading a word, sentence, or passage; by checking a word's meaning in the dictionary; or by referring to earlier or later passages.

- Encourage students to use one of these strategies each time they encounter a difficult passage in the text.

Vocabulary Development

- Pronounce each vocabulary word for students, and read the definitions as a class. Have students identify any words with which they are already familiar.

CUSTOMIZE INSTRUCTION FOR UNIVERSAL ACCESS

For Special Needs Students	For Less Proficient Readers	For English Learners
Have students read the adapted version of "There Will Come Soft Rains" in the **Adapted Reader's Companion.** This version provides basic-level instruction in an interactive format with questions and write-on lines. Completing the adapted version will prepare students to read the selection in the Student Edition.	Have students read the selection in the **Reader's Companion.** This version provides basic-level instruction in an interactive format with questions and write-on lines. After students finish the selection in **Reader's Companion,** have them complete the questions and activities in the Student Edition.	Have students read the adapted version of the selection in the **English Learner's Companion.** This version provides basic-level instruction in an interactive format with questions and write-on lines. Completing the adapted version will prepare students to read the selection in the Student Edition.

 E-Teach

Visit E-Teach at www.phschool.com for teachers' essays on how to teach, with questions and answers.

CUSTOMIZE INSTRUCTION
For Verbal/Linguistic Learners

Certain cultures thriving today are strongly opposed to technology. For example, the Amish of Pennsylvania live in a society that bans the use of electricity and telephones. Ask students to write a few paragraphs about other cultures that have specific feelings about technology and the future. Have volunteers share their writings with the class.

❶ About the Selection

With no human characters, this story is an ironic reflection on the strengths and weaknesses of human nature. It is also a warning about the limits and dangers of technology. The same technical wizardry that enables people of the future to create a fully automated house is also responsible for the creation of the nuclear weapons that destroy the human race. What use is all our cleverness, Bradbury seems to ask, without the wisdom to accept our vulnerable position in the universe?

❷ Background
Art

Bikini, 1987, by Vernon Fisher

This image shows the aftermath of a nuclear explosion on the Pacific island of Bikini, where the United States once tested its nuclear weapons. Use these questions for discussion:

1. What do you know about the immediate and long-term effects of a nuclear explosion?
   Answer: Immediate effects include deadly firestorms; long-term effects include radioactive fallout, which consists of deadly particles that continue to fall days after the explosion.

2. How might the title of the story refer to these effects?
   Answer: The "soft rains" of the title might refer to radioactive fallout from a nuclear explosion.

❸ ▶ Critical Viewing

Answer: Students might say that the story will be about the aftermath of a nuclear explosion.

---

❶ There Will Come Soft Rains
Ray Bradbury

Bikini, 1987, Vernon Fisher, Kranner Art Museum

❸ ▲ **Critical Viewing** Based on the title of the story and this painting, make a prediction about the subject of the story. **[Predict]**

I n the living room the voice-clock sang, *Tick-tock, seven o'clock, time to get up, time to get up, seven o'clock!* as if it were afraid that nobody would. The morning house lay empty. The clock ticked on, repeating and repeating its sounds into the emptiness. *Seven-nine, breakfast time, seven-nine!*

❹   In the kitchen the breakfast stove gave a hissing sigh and ejected from its warm interior eight pieces of perfectly browned toast, eight eggs sunnyside up, sixteen slices of bacon, two coffees, and two cool glasses of milk.

"Today is August 4, 2026," said a second voice from the kitchen ceiling, "in the city of Allendale, California." It repeated the date three times for memory's sake. "Today is Mr. Featherstone's birthday.

Literary Analysis
Setting What details in the first three paragraphs show that the story is set in the future?

614 ◆ *Short Stories*

TEACHING RESOURCES

The following resources can be used to enrich or extend the instruction for pp. 614–628.

Literary Analysis
📖 **Selection Support:** Literary Analysis, p. 156

Reading
📖 **Reader's Companion**
📖 **English Learner's Companion**
🎧 **Listening to Literature Audiocassettes,** Sides 19, 20

💿 **Listening to Literature Audio CDs,** CD 13

Extension
📑 **Fine Art Transparencies, Volume 1,** Art Transparency 5 (Have students compare and contrast how the painting and "The Garden of Stubborn Cats" portray man's relationship with the natural environment.)

📕 **BLOCK SCHEDULING:** Resources marked with this symbol provide varied instruction during 90-minute blocks.

Today is the anniversary of Tilita's marriage. Insurance is payable, as are the water, gas, and light bills."

Somewhere in the walls, relays clicked, memory tapes glided under electric eyes.

Eight-one, tick-tock, eight-one o'clock, off to school, off to work, run, run, eight one! But no doors slammed, no carpets took the soft tread of rubber heels. It was raining outside. The weather box on the front door sang quietly: "Rain, rain, go away; rubbers, raincoats for today . . ." And the rain tapped on the empty house, echoing.

Outside, the garage chimed and lifted its door to reveal the waiting car. After a long wait the door swung down again.

At eight-thirty the eggs were shriveled and the toast was like stone. An aluminum wedge scraped them into the sink, where hot water whirled them down a metal throat which digested and flushed them away to the distant sea. The dirty dishes were dropped into a hot washer and emerged twinkling dry.

Nine-fifteen, sang the clock, *time to clean.*

Out of warrens in the wall, tiny robot mice darted. The rooms were acrawl with the small cleaning animals, all rubber and metal. They thudded against chairs, whirling their mustached runners, kneading the rug nap, sucking gently at hidden dust. Then, like mysterious invaders, they popped into their burrows. Their pink electric eyes faded. The house was clean.

Ten o'clock. The sun came out from behind the rain. The house stood alone in a city of rubble and ashes. This was the one house left standing. At night the ruined city gave off a radioactive glow which could be seen for miles.

Ten-fifteen. The garden sprinklers whirled up in golden founts, filling the soft morning air with scatterings of brightness. The water pelted windowpanes, running down the charred west side where the house had been burned evenly free of its white paint. The entire west face of the house was black, save for five places. Here the silhouette in paint of a man mowing a lawn. Here, as in a photograph, a woman bent to pick flowers. Still farther over, their images burned on wood in one titanic instant, a small boy, hands flung into the air; higher up, the image of a thrown ball, and opposite him a girl, hands raised to catch a ball which never came down.

The five spots of paint—the man, the woman, the children, the ball—remained. The rest was a thin charcoaled layer.

The gentle-sprinkler rain filled the garden with falling light.

Until this day, how well the house had kept its peace. How carefully it had inquired, "Who goes there? What's the password?" and, getting no answer from lonely foxes and whining cats, it had shut up its windows and drawn shades in an old-maidenly preoccupation with self-protection which bordered on a mechanical paranoia.

It quivered at each sound, the house did. If a sparrow brushed a window, the shade snapped up. The bird, startled, flew off! No, not even a bird must touch the house!

---

warrens (wôr′ ənz) *n.* mazelike passages

Reading Strategy
Clarifying How do you think the city has been destroyed?

---

titanic (tī tan′ ik) *adj.* powerful

---

paranoia (par′ ə noi′ ə) *n.* mental disorder characterized by delusions of persecution

---

❻ ☑Reading Check
Who are the people whose silhouettes are on the side of the house?

---

❹ Literary Analysis
Setting

- Read the bracketed passage aloud. Then, have students name details that relate to the setting. Students might mention these details: early in the morning, in an empty house full of automated devices.

- Then, ask students the Literary Analysis question on p. 614: What details in the first three paragraphs show that the story is set in the future?
  Answer: Students will probably mention futuristic and automated devices, such as the voice-clock and breakfast stove. They will also mention the voice from the ceiling and its announcement of the date—2026.

❺ Reading Strategy
Clarifying

- Read the bracketed passage aloud. Then, ask students the Reading Strategy question on p. 615: How was the city destroyed?
  Answer: It was probably destroyed by a nuclear explosion.

- Ask students to name some details that led them to this answer.
  Possible responses: Clues include "a city of rubble and ashes" and "radioactive glow."

❻ ☑Reading Check

Answer: The silhouettes are of the family members who lived in the house.

CUSTOMIZE INSTRUCTION FOR UNIVERSAL ACCESS

For Special Needs Students	For Less Proficient Readers	For Gifted/Talented Students
To help students understand the unfamiliar elements of the story's setting, have them draw a picture of the house and yard. Make sure they include details from the story, such as the breakfast stove and the silhouettes on the house's charred walls.	As they read, have students make a list of unfamiliar elements of the setting, such as the voice-clock and the breakfast stove. Discuss each element with students to make sure they understand its function.	Listening to the tones and rhythms of the house's automated voice and robots will help these students imagine the setting. Have students weigh the positive and negative aspects of audiovisual technology as it may someday be applied in the home environment.

- Ask students the Reading Strategy question on p. 616: Are these whirring mice real animals? What details from p. 615 clarify their description?

  Possible responses: The mice are mechanical. Details that show this are "robot mice made of rubber and metal," "whirling runners," "kneading," "sucking dust," and "electric eyes."

  ▷ Monitor Progress Remind students that irony is the clash between what is expected and what actually happens.

- Ask students to identify the irony in the description of the mice.

  Answer: Students will probably point out that since the mice are robotic, the description of them as angry is ironic.

The house was an altar with ten thousand attendants, big, small, servicing, attending, in choirs. But the gods had gone away, and the ritual of the religion continued senselessly, uselessly.

Twelve noon.

A dog whined, shivering, on the front porch.

The front door recognized the dog voice and opened. The dog, once huge and fleshy, but now gone to bone and covered with sores, moved in and through the house, tracking mud. Behind it whirred angry mice, angry at having to pick up mud, angry at inconvenience.

❼ For not a leaf fragment blew under the door but what the wall panels flipped open and the copper scrap rats flashed swiftly out. The offending dust, hair, or paper, seized in miniature steel jaws, was raced back to the burrows. There, down tubes which fed into the cellar, it was dropped into the sighing vent of an incinerator which sat like evil Baal[1] in a dark corner.

The dog ran upstairs, hysterically yelping to each door, at last realizing, as the house realized, that only silence was here.

It sniffed the air and scratched the kitchen door. Behind the door, the stove was making pancakes which filled the house with a rich baked odor and the scent of maple syrup.

The dog frothed at the mouth, lying at the door, sniffing, its eyes turned to fire. It ran wildly in circles, biting at its tail, spun in a frenzy, and died. It lay in the parlor for an hour.

Two o'clock, sang a voice.

Delicately sensing decay at last, the regiments of mice hummed out as softly as blown gray leaves in an electrical wind.

Two-fifteen.

The dog was gone.

In the cellar, the incinerator glowed suddenly and a whirl of sparks leaped up the chimney.

Two thirty-five.

Bridge tables sprouted from patio walls. Playing cards fluttered onto pads in a shower of pips. Glasses manifested on an oaken bench with egg-salad sandwiches. Music played.

But the tables were silent and the cards untouched.

At four o'clock the tables folded like great butterflies back through the paneled walls.

Four-thirty.

The nursery walls glowed.

Animals took shape: yellow giraffes, blue lions, pink antelopes, lilac panthers cavorting[2] in crystal substance. The walls were glass. They looked out upon color and fantasy. Hidden films clocked through well-oiled sprockets, and the walls lived. The nursery floor was woven to resemble a crisp, cereal meadow. Over this ran aluminum roaches and iron crickets, and in the hot still air butterflies of delicate red

---

1. **Baal** (bāʹ əl) ancient Phoenician and Canaanite deity.
2. **cavorting** (kə vôrtʹ iŋ) *v.* leaping or prancing about.

Literary Analysis
Setting What is unusual about the nursery?

✹ ENRICHMENT: Social Studies Connection

Nuclear Weapons

The world's first nuclear bomb was an atomic bomb developed by the United States. It was first tested by scientists in New Mexico in July of 1945. A few weeks later—near the end of World War II—it was used to bomb the Japanese cities of Hiroshima and Nagasaki. After the war, the United States and several other countries built thousands of nuclear weapons, many times more than enough to destroy each other. As these weapons proliferated, so did people's fears of a possible nuclear war. As tensions between the United States and the Soviet Union escalated during the Cold War, which lasted through the 1980s, American newspapers and magazines warned citizens of the dire consequences of a nuclear attack. In this story, Bradbury projects the fears of his own time onto a future setting.

Have students discuss whether fears of nuclear war still play an important part in American life. Ask what has happened since this story was written to increase or decrease such fears.

The Body of a House, #1 of 8, ©1993, Robert Beckman

▲ **Critical Viewing** How does the house in this picture compare with the house in the story? **[Compare and Contrast]**

tissue wavered among the sharp aroma of animal spoors![3] There was the sound like a great matted yellow hive of bees within a dark bellows, the lazy bumble of a purring lion. And there was the patter of okapi[4] feet and the murmur of a fresh jungle rain, like other hoofs, falling upon the summer-starched grass. Now the walls dissolved into distances of parched weed, mile on mile, and warm endless sky. The animals drew away into thorn brakes and water holes.

It was the children's hour.

Five o'clock. The bath filled with clear hot water.

Six, seven, eight o'clock. The dinner dishes manipulated like magic tricks, and in the study a *click.* In the hearth a fire now blazed up warmly.

---

3. **spoors** (spo͞orz) *n.* droppings of wild animals.
4. **okapi** (ō kä′ pē) *n.* African animal related to the giraffe but with a much shorter neck.

⑪ ✔**Reading Check**
What happens to the dog?

There Will Come Soft Rains ◆ 617

617

⑫ Literary Analysis

Setting and Irony

• Have students review the definition of irony on p. 613 and then read the bracketed material.

• Then, ask the Literary Analysis question on p. 618: What is ironic about the poem that the voice recites?
Possible responses: It is ironic that the computer would choose to read a poem about the soft, life-giving rains of spring at a time when the "soft rain" of deadly radioactivity is falling. It is also ironic that the poet should refer to the death of humankind, not knowing that it would actually happen.

⑬ Critical Thinking

Apply

• Ask students to summarize the topic of the poem.
Possible response: Life would go on even if humankind should perish.

• Then, ask how the words of the poem can be applied to the story.
Possible responses: The title of the story is taken from the first line of the poem; the poem describes the natural world continuing unawares, even after a war, much as the workings of the house continue after the family has perished.

Nine o'clock. The beds warmed their hidden circuits, for nights were cool here.

Nine-five. A voice spoke from the study ceiling:

"Mrs. McClellan, which poem would you like this evening?"

The house was silent.

The voice said at last, "Since you express no preference, I shall select a poem at random." Quiet music rose to back the voice. "Sara Teasdale. As I recall, your favorite. . . .

> *There will come soft rains and the smell of*
> *the ground,*
> *And swallows circling with their shimmering sound;*
>
> *And frogs in the pools singing at night,*
> *And wild plum trees in* <u>tremulous</u> *white;*
>
> **⑫** *Robins will wear their feathery fire,*
> *Whistling their whims on a low fence-wire;*
> **⑬**
>
> *And not one will know of the war, not one*
> *Will care at last when it is done.*
> *Not one would mind, neither bird nor tree,*
> *If mankind perished utterly;*
>
> *And Spring herself, when she woke at dawn*
> *Would scarcely know that we were gone."*

The fire burned on the stone hearth. The empty chairs faced each other between the silent walls, and the music played.

At ten o'clock the house began to die.

The wind blew. A falling tree bough crashed through the kitchen window. Cleaning solvent, bottled, shattered over the stove. The room was ablaze in an instant!

"Fire!" screamed a voice. The house lights flashed, water pumps shot water from the ceilings. But the solvent spread on the linoleum, licking, eating, under the kitchen door, while the voices took it up in chorus: "Fire, fire, fire!"

The house tried to save itself. Doors sprang tightly shut, but the windows were broken by the heat and the wind blew and sucked upon the fire.

The house gave ground as the fire in ten billion angry sparks moved with flaming ease from room to room and then up the stairs. While scurrying water rats squeaked from the walls, pistoled their water, and ran for more. And the wall sprays let down showers of mechanical rain.

But too late. Somewhere, sighing, a pump shrugged to a stop. The quenching rain ceased. The reserve water supply which had filled baths and washed dishes for many quiet days was gone.

tremulous (trem′ yoo ləs) *adj.* trembling; quivering

Literary Analysis
Setting and Irony What is ironic about the poem that the voice recites?

The fire crackled up the stairs. It fed upon Picassos and Matisses[5] in the upper halls, like delicacies, baking off the oily flesh, tenderly crisping the canvases into black shavings.

Now the fire lay in beds, stood in windows, changed the colors of drapes!

And then, reinforcements.

From attic trapdoors, blind robot faces peered down with faucet mouths gushing green chemical.

The fire backed off, as even an elephant must at the sight of a dead snake. Now there were twenty snakes whipping over the floor, killing the fire with a clear cold venom of green froth.

But the fire was clever. It had sent flame outside the house, up through the attic to the pumps there. An explosion! The attic brain which directed the pumps was shattered into bronze shrapnel on the beams.

The fire rushed back into every closet and felt of the clothes hung there.

The house shuddered, oak bone on bone, its bared skeleton cringing from the heat, its wire, its nerves revealed as if a surgeon had torn the skin off to let the red veins and capillaries quiver in the scalded air. Help, help! Fire! Run, run! Heat snapped mirrors like the first brittle winter ice. And the voices wailed Fire, fire, run, run, like a tragic nursery rhyme, a dozen voices, high, low, like children dying in a forest, alone, alone. And the voices fading as the wires popped their sheathings like hot chestnuts. One, two, three, four, five voices died.

In the nursery the jungle burned. Blue lions roared, purple giraffes bounded off. The panthers ran in circles, changing color, and ten million animals, running before the fire, vanished off toward a distant steaming river. . . .

Ten more voices died. In the last instant under the fire avalanche, other choruses, oblivious, could be heard announcing the time, playing music, cutting the lawn by remote-control mower, or setting an umbrella frantically out and in the slamming and opening front door, a thousand things happening, like a clock shop when each clock strikes the hour

The Body of a House, #6 of 8, ©1993, Robert Beckman

---

5. **Picassos** (pi kä´ sōz) **and Matisses** (mä tēs´ ez) works by the painters Pablo Picasso and Henri Matisse.

⓯ ▲ **Critical Viewing** Do the details in Bradbury's story seem as violent as the ones in this image? Explain. **[Compare and Contrast]**

⓰ ☑ **Reading Check**

What starts the fire in the house?

There Will Come Soft Rains ◆ 619

⓮ **Background**

Art

The Body of a House, #6 of 8,
by Robert Beckman

Remind students that this painting, like the one on p. 617, is based on actual film footage shot during the test of a nuclear weapon in Nevada in 1953. Use this question for discussion:

How is the painting different from what a person might actually see during a nuclear explosion?
Possible response: Such destruction would take place faster than the eye could see. The artist was able to stop the film footage to create his painting.

⓯ ▶ **Critical Viewing**

Possible response: The wild splotches of red and black convey more violence than the details in Bradbury's story, which despite the destruction it describes, maintains a stately and dignified mood.

⓰ ☑ **Reading Check**

Answer: The bough of a tree crashes through the kitchen window, knocking a bottle of flammable cleaning liquid onto the stove. The fire is fed by the wind coming through the windows broken by the heat.

CUSTOMIZE INSTRUCTION FOR UNIVERSAL ACCESS

For Advanced Readers

Ray Bradbury's writing is described by reviewer Christopher Jensen in the following statement:

"Depending on how you look at it, Ray Bradbury is either an expert creator of fiction and poetry, or a matchless stretcher of the truth. Either way, he is still a vital, respected, and well-loved literary giant. . . . He is thought of by many as the world's greatest living writer of science fiction and fantasy stories."

Read Jensen's evaluation of Bradbury's writing to the students and then use the following questions to stimulate discussion of his opinions:

1. Do you think Bradbury is a master of creating science fiction or a master of stretching the truth?
   Answer: Students may say that he creates a programmable house that could be created today, thereby arguing that he simply stretches the truth.
2. Find specific examples in "There Will Come Soft Rains" to support your answer.

Word Origins: Words From Myths

- Call students' attention to the word *psychopathic* and its definition. Explain that the word is derived from the Greek root *psyche*, meaning "breath," "life," or "soul." In Greek myth, Psyche was a beautiful maiden loved by the god Cupid. When Cupid abandoned her, Psyche searched the world for her lost love.

- Then, ask students to list other words derived from the word *psyche*.
  Possible responses: *psychology, psychic, psychiatrist, and psychosomatic.*

Answers for p. 620

Review and Assess

1. Some students may be more optimistic than Bradbury is. Whatever their ideas of the future, encourage them to give reasons for their opinions.

2. **(a)** The house announces each hour of the day; it opens and closes doors; it self-cleans with robot mice; it sets tables; it prepares food. **(b)** Possible answer: The house performs purely mechanical functions, such as cleaning and keeping track of the time, better than people do.

3. **(a)** All that's left of the house's inhabitants are silhouettes on the side of the house. **(b)** They were killed by the blast.

4. **(a)** The house reads a poem by Sara Teasdale. **(b)** Even if humankind should disappear, nature would go on. **(c)** Possible answer: The poem explains the title of the story and also implies Bradbury's theme—that perhaps someone "would mind . . . /If mankind perished utterly."

5. **(a)** The house, like a human, has a brain that controls its functions. It uses all its resources for self-preservation. **(b)** The house has no creativity, self-awareness, or empathy.

6. Students may find Bradbury's vision of the future exaggerated, now that the Cold War has ended.

---

insanely before or after the other, a scene of maniac confusion, yet unity; singing, screaming, a few last cleaning mice darting bravely out to carry the horrid ashes away! And one voice, with sublime disregard for the situation, read poetry aloud in the fiery study, until all the film spools burned, until all the wires withered and the circuits cracked.

The fire burst the house and let it slam flat down, puffing out skirts of spark and smoke.

⑰ In the kitchen, an instant before the rain of fire and timber, the stove could be seen making breakfasts at a psychopathic rate, ten dozen eggs, six loaves of toast, twenty dozen bacon strips, which, eaten by fire, started the stove working again, hysterically hissing!

The crash. The attic smashing into kitchen and parlor. The parlor into cellar, cellar into subcellar. Deep freeze, armchair, film tapes, circuits, beds, and all like skeletons thrown in a cluttered mound deep under.

Smoke and silence. A great quantity of smoke.

Dawn showed faintly in the east. Among the ruins, one wall stood alone. Within the wall, a last voice said, over and over again and again, even as the sun rose to shine upon the heaped rubble and steam: "Today is August 5, 2026, today is August 5, 2026, today is . . ."

psychopathic (sī´ kō path´ ik) *adj.* with a dangerous mental disorder

---

Review and Assess

Thinking About the Selection

1. **Respond:** Does the view presented in this story fit with your idea of a future world? Why or why not?

2. **(a) Recall:** List five automated functions the house performs. **(b) Make a Judgment:** What are some functions the house performs better than humans do?

3. **(a) Recall:** What evidence is left of the occupants of the house? **(b) Infer:** What do you think happened to them?

4. **(a) Recall:** What poem does the voice in the house read? **(b) Summarize:** How would you summarize the poem? **(c) Speculate:** Why do you think Bradbury chose to have the house broadcast this particular poem?

5. **(a) Compare and Contrast:** Compare the house—both in its normal operations and its final hours—to a human. **(b) Make a Judgment:** What important qualities of humans is the house missing? Explain.

6. **Evaluate:** How possible do you think the future described in the story is? Explain.

Ray Bradbury

(b. 1920)

Ray Bradbury, one of the world's most celebrated science-fiction writers, was born in Waukegan, Illinois, and grew up along the western shores of Lake Michigan. He began reading the stories of Edgar Allan Poe as a child and developed a fascination with horror movies and fantasy—especially futuristic fantasy. In many of his stories, including "There Will Come Soft Rains," Bradbury explores the consequences of future technological growth.

The Garden Of Stubborn Cats

Italo Calvino
Translated by William Weaver

The city of cats and the city of men exist one inside the other, but they are not the same city. Few cats recall the time when there was no distinction: the streets and squares of men were also streets and squares of cats, and the lawns, courtyards, balconies, and fountains: you lived in a broad and various space. But for several generations now domestic felines have been prisoners of an uninhabitable city: the streets are uninterruptedly overrun by the mortal traffic of cat-crushing automobiles; in every square foot of terrain where once a garden extended or a vacant lot or the ruins of an old demolition, now condominiums loom up, welfare housing, brand-new skyscrapers; every entrance is crammed with parked cars; the courtyards, one by one, have been roofed by reinforced concrete and transformed into garages or movie houses or storerooms or workshops. And where a rolling plateau of low roofs once extended, copings, terraces, water tanks, balconies, skylights, corrugated-iron sheds, now one general superstructure rises wherever structures can rise; the intermediate differences in height, between the low ground of the street and the <u>supernal</u> heaven of the penthouses, disappear; the cat of a recent litter seeks in vain the <u>itinerary</u> of its fathers, the point from which to make the soft leap from balustrade to cornice to drainpipe, or for the quick climb on the roof-tiles.

But in this vertical city, in this compressed city where all voids tend to fill up and every block of cement tends to mingle with other blocks of cement, a kind of counter-city opens, a negative city, that consists of empty slices between wall and wall, of the minimal distances ordained by the building regulations between two constructions, between the rear of one construction and the rear of the next; it is a city of cavities, wells, air conduits, driveways, inner yards, accesses to basements, like a network of dry canals on a planet of stucco and tar, and it is through this

Reading Strategy
Clarifying What does the author mean by his opening sentence?

supernal (sə pʉrn′ əl) *adj.* celestial or divine

itinerary (ī tin′ ər er′ ē) *n.* route

20 ✔**Reading Check**
Why is the city uninhabitable for cats?

The Garden of Stubborn Cats ◆ 621

18 **About the Selection**
In this story, an Italian worker named Marcovaldo becomes aware of cats and their pathways through a city. He discovers an old villa in a seedy garden where they congregate and resist the efforts of construction workers to build a new structure. For Calvino, the cats symbolize nature's mysterious, persistent presence even in a busy city. They also symbolize nature's resistance to human aims and designs.

19 **Reading Strategy**
Clarifying
• Have students read the opening sentence. Then, ask students to describe a "city of men" and a "city of cats."
Possible responses: The city of men includes traffic, apartment buildings, skyscrapers, and concrete. The city of cats would include gardens and grass and plenty of open spaces.

• Ask students the Reading Strategy question on p. 621: What does the author mean by his opening sentence? Have them look ahead to find information about the setting that clarifies the meaning of the sentence.
Answer: The first paragraph describes the city of men; the second paragraph describes the city of cats. The two exist within the same boundaries but are completely different; neither city is inhabitable by the population of the other.

20 ✔**Reading Check**
Answer: The city is uninhabitable for cats because the places they would normally live are occupied by extremely tall buildings. Moreover, the traffic is deadly.

CUSTOMIZE INSTRUCTION FOR UNIVERSAL ACCESS

For Less Proficient Readers	For English Learners	For Gifted/Talented Students
Based on the picture of the cat on p. 621, ask students to describe the type of environment that would be ideally suited for cats. Ask students to give reasons for their answers.	To make sure students understand the difference between the "city of men" and the "city of cats," have them create a quick sketch of each. The drawings should contain details from the selection, such as the skyscrapers and the "mortal" traffic.	Have students brainstorm for a description of a city that would be equally accommodating to men and cats. What passageways and green spaces would they include that would provide for cats' needs?

Setting

- Read aloud the bracketed passage on pp. 621–622. Ask students what the "negative city" consists of.
  Answer: The "negative city" consists of the in-between spaces that the cats inhabit.

- Then, ask students: What details help you envision the "negative city"?
  Possible responses: Details include cavities, wells, air conduits, inner yards, and accesses to basements.

22 Literary Analysis

Setting

- Read the bracketed passage aloud. Have students identify details relating to the setting.

- Then, ask the Literary Analysis question at the bottom of p. 622: What details help you picture the setting of the fancy restaurant?
  Possible responses: Students might cite gypsy violins; partridges and quails on silver platters; waiters wearing gloves, tailcoats, and patent-leather shoes; shining parquet floor; tablecloths and crystal; dwarf potted palms; champagne in ice buckets.

---

21 | network, grazing the walls, that the ancient cat population still scurries.

On occasion, to pass the time, Marcovaldo would follow a cat. It was during the work-break, between noon and three, when all the personnel except Marcovaldo went home to eat, and he—who brought his lunch in his bag—laid his place among the packing-cases in the warehouse, chewed his snack, smoked a half-cigar, and wandered around, alone and idle, waiting for work to resume. In those hours, a cat that peeped in at a window was always welcome company, and a guide for new explorations. He had made friends with a tabby, well fed, a blue ribbon around its neck, surely living with some well-to-do family. This tabby shared with Marcovaldo the habit of an afternoon stroll right after lunch; and naturally a friendship sprang up.

Following his tabby friend, Marcovaldo had started looking at places as if through the round eyes of a cat and even if these places were the usual environs of his firm he saw them in a different light, as settings for cattish stories, with connections practicable only by light, velvety paws. Though from the outside the neighborhood seemed poor in cats, every day on his rounds Marcovaldo made the acquaintance of some new face, and a miau, a hiss, a stiffening of fur on an arched back was enough for him to sense ties and intrigues and rivalries among them. At those moments he thought he had already penetrated the secrecy of the felines' society: and then he felt himself scrutinized by pupils that became slits, under the surveillance of the antennae of taut whiskers, and all the cats around him sat impassive as sphinxes, the pink triangles of their noses convergent on the black triangles of their lips, and the only things that moved were the tips of the ears, with a vibrant jerk like radar. They reached the end of a narrow passage, between squalid blank walls; and, looking around, Marcovaldo saw that the cats that had led him this far had vanished, all of them together, no telling in which direction, even his tabby friend, and they had left him alone. Their realm had territories, ceremonies, customs that it was not yet granted to him to discover.

On the other hand, from the cat city there opened unsuspected peepholes onto the city of men: and one day the same tabby led him to discover the great Biarritz Restaurant.

Anyone wishing to see the Biarritz Restaurant had only to assume the posture of a cat, that is, proceed on all fours. Cat and man, in this fashion, walked around a kind of dome, at whose foot some low, rectangular little windows opened. Following the tabby's example, Marcovaldo looked down. They were transoms through which the luxurious hall received air and light. To the sound of gypsy violins, partridges and quails swirled by on silver dishes balanced by the white-gloved fingers of waiters in tailcoats. Or, more precisely, above the partridges and quails the dishes whirled, and above the dishes the white gloves, and poised on the waiters' patent-leather shoes, the gleaming parquet floor, from which hung dwarf potted palms and tablecloths and crystal and buckets like bells with the champagne bottle for their clapper: everything was turned upside-down because

Literary Analysis
Setting Which details help you picture the setting of the fancy restaurant?

✹ ENRICHMENT: Art Connection

Representations of Cats

Because of their mysterious nature, their sensitivity to light and sound, and their skill as nighttime hunters, cats have been credited with supernatural powers in many cultures and have even been worshiped as gods. The ancient Egyptians, for example, produced many statues of cats in honor of their cat-goddess, Bastet. Later, cats were associated with witches in European cultures. Today, images of cats show our mixed feelings about these creatures. They are sometimes depicted as cute, cuddly balls of fluff and sometimes as mysterious, predatory hunters. Ask students how well the pictures of cats in this selection reflect their own feelings about these animals.

Marcovaldo, for fear of being seen, wouldn't stick his head inside the window and confined himself to looking at the reversed reflection of the room in the tilted pane.

But it was not so much the windows of the dining-room as those of the kitchens that interested the cat: looking through the former you saw, distant and somehow transfigured, what in the kitchens presented itself—quite concrete and within paw's reach—as a plucked bird or a fresh fish. And it was toward the kitchens, in fact, that the tabby wanted to lead Marcovaldo, either through a gesture of altruistic friendship or else because it counted on the man's help for one of its raids. Marcovaldo, however, was reluctant to leave his belvedere* over the main room: first as he was fascinated by the luxury of the place, and then because something down there had riveted his attention. To such an extent that, overcoming his fear of being seen, he kept peeking in, with his head in the transom.

In the midst of the room, directly under that pane, there was a little glass fish tank, a kind of aquarium, where some fat trout were swimming. A special customer approached, a man with a shiny bald pate, black suit, black beard. An old waiter in tailcoat followed him, carrying a little net as if he were going to catch butterflies. The gentleman in black looked at the trout with a grave, intent air; then he raised one hand and with a slow, solemn gesture singled out a fish. The waiter dipped the net into the tank, pursued the appointed trout, captured it, headed for the kitchens, holding out in front of him, like a lance, the net in which the fish wriggled. The gentleman in black, solemn as a magistrate who has handed down a capital sentence, went to take his seat and wait for the return of the trout, sauteed "à la meunière."[1]

If I found a way to drop a line from up here and make one of those trout bite, Marcovaldo thought, I couldn't be accused of theft; at worst, of fishing in an unauthorized place. And ignoring the miaus that called him toward the kitchens, he went to collect his fishing tackle.

Nobody in the crowded dining room of the Biarritz saw the long, fine line, armed with hook and bait, as it slowly dropped into the tank. The fish saw the bait, and flung themselves on it. In the fray one trout managed to bite the worm: and immediately it began to rise, rise, emerge from the water, a silvery flash, it darted up high, over the laid tables and the trolleys of hors d'oeuvres,[2] over the blue flames of the crêpes Suzette,[3] until it vanished into the heavens of the transom.

---

1. **sauteed "à la meunière"** (sô tād´ ä le me nyer´) fish prepared by being rolled in flour, fried in butter, and sprinkled with lemon juice and chopped parsley.
2. **hors d'oeuvres** (ôr durvz´) *n.* appetizers served at the beginning of a meal.
3. **crêpes Suzette** (krāp soō zet´) thin pancakes rolled or folded in a hot orange-flavored sauce and usually served in flaming brandy.

Literature in context 23 · Design Connection

♦ *Architectural Features*

Calvino describes these features of many of the buildings encountered by Marcovaldo and the tabby:

balustrade railing held up by posts

belvedere open, roofed gallery

capitals tops of columns

copings top layer of masonry, sloped to carry off water

cornice horizontal molding projecting above the top of a wall

transom small window

trestles frameworks of vertical or slanting beams

 Reading Check

What new places has Marcovaldo discovered while following cats?

The Garden of Stubborn Cats ◆ 623

Clarifying

- Remind students that the title of the story mentions "stubborn" cats.
- Ask the Reading Strategy question on p. 624: In what ways is the tabby stubborn?
  Answer: The tabby is stubborn in its refusal to give up the stolen trout.

27 Literary Analysis

Setting

- Have students read the bracketed passage and then record details about the "little rank garden" in a chart like the one on p. 613.
- Point out that this garden is the "Garden of Stubborn Cats," referred to in the story's title.
- Then, ask students why the windows of the skyscrapers might seem to look "disapprovingly" on the garden.
  Answer: The garden is one of the few areas of the city where a little bit of nature still remains, unconquered by urban development.

Marcovaldo had yanked the rod with the brisk snap of the expert fisherman, so the fish landed behind his back. The trout had barely touched the ground when the cat sprang. What little life the trout still had was lost between the tabby's teeth. Marcovaldo, who had abandoned his line at that moment to run and grab the fish, saw it snatched from under his nose, hook and all. He was quick to put one foot on the rod, but the snatch had been so strong that the rod was all the man had left, while the tabby ran off with the fish, pulling the line after it. Treacherous kitty! It had vanished.

26 But this time it wouldn't escape him: there was that long line trailing after him and showing the way he had taken. Though he had lost sight of the cat, Marcovaldo followed the end of the line: there it was, running along a wall; it climbed a parapet, wound through a doorway, was swallowed up by a basement . . . Marcovaldo, venturing into more and more cattish places, climbed roofs, straddled railings, always managed to catch a glimpse—perhaps only a second before it disappeared—of that moving trace that indicated a thief's path.

Now the line played out down a sidewalk, in the midst of the traffic, and Marcovaldo, running after it, almost managed to grab it. He flung himself down on his belly: there, he grabbed it! He managed to seize one end of the line before it slipped between the bars of a gate.

27 Beyond a half-rusted gate and two bits of wall buried under climbing plants, there was a little rank[4] garden, with a small, abandoned-looking building at the far end of it. A carpet of dry leaves covered the path, and dry leaves lay everywhere under the boughs of the two plane-trees, forming actually some little mounds in the yard. A layer of leaves was yellowing in the green water of a pool. Enormous buildings rose all around, skyscrapers with thousands of windows, like so many eyes trained disapprovingly on that little square patch with two trees, a few tiles, and all those yellow leaves, surviving right in the middle of an area of great traffic.

And in this garden, perched on the capitals and balustrades, lying on the dry leaves of the flowerbeds, climbing on the trunks of the trees or on the drainpipes, motionless on their four paws, their tails making a question-mark, seated to wash their faces, there were tiger cats, black cats, white cats, calico cats, tabbies, angoras, Persians, house cats and stray cats, perfumed cats and mangy cats. Marcovaldo realized he had finally reached the heart of the cats' realm, their secret island. And, in his emotion, he almost forgot his fish.

It had remained, that fish, hanging by the line from the branch of a tree, out of reach of the cats' leaps; it must have dropped from its kidnapper's mouth at some clumsy movement, perhaps as it was defended from the others, or perhaps displayed as an extraordinary prize. The line had got tangled, and Marcovaldo, tug as he would, couldn't manage to yank it loose. A furious battle had meanwhile been joined among the cats, to reach that unreachable fish, or rather,

4. **rank** (raŋk) *adj.* growing vigorously and coarsely.

Reading Strategy
Clarifying In what ways is the tabby "stubborn"?

 ENRICHMENT: Community Connection

Visiting Animal Shelters

In many cities and towns, the Society for the Prevention of Cruelty to Animals maintains animal shelters for abandoned pets, educates the public about pet ownership, and ensures the enforcement of laws protecting animals from cruel treatment. Have students visit a local animal shelter and report to the class on what is done in your community to ensure proper treatment of cats and other pets.

to win the right to try and reach it. Each wanted to prevent the others from leaping: they hurled themselves on one another, they tangled in midair, they rolled around clutching each other, and finally a general war broke out in a whirl of dry, crackling leaves.

After many futile yanks, Marcovaldo now felt the line was free, but he took care not to pull it: the trout would have fallen right in the midst of that infuriated scrimmage of felines.

It was at this moment that, from the top of the walls of the gardens, a strange rain began to fall: fish-bones, heads, tails, even bits of lung and lights. Immediately the cats' attention was distracted from the suspended trout and they flung themselves on the new delicacies. To Marcovaldo, this seemed the right moment to pull the line and regain his fish. But, before he had time to act, from a blind of the little villa, two yellow, skinny hands darted out: one was brandishing scissors; the other, a frying pan. The hand with the scissors was raised above the trout, the hand with the frying pan was thrust under it. The scissors cut the line, the trout fell into the pan; hands, scissors and pan withdrew, the blind closed: all in the space of a second. Marcovaldo was totally bewildered.

"Are you also a cat lover?" A voice at his back made him turn round. He was surrounded by little old women, some of them ancient, wearing old-fashioned hats on their heads; others, younger, but with the look of spinsters; and all were carrying in their hands or their bags packages of leftover meat or fish, and some even had little pans of milk. "Will you help me throw this package over the fence, for those poor creatures?"

All the ladies, cat lovers, gathered at this hour around the garden of dry leaves to take the food to their protégés.[5]

"Can you tell me why they are all here, these cats?" Marcovaldo inquired.

"Where else could they go? This garden is all they have left! Cats come here from other neighborhoods, too, from miles and miles around . . ."

"And birds, as well," another lady added. "They're forced to live by the hundreds and hundreds on these few trees . . ."

"And the frogs, they're all in that pool, and at night they never stop croaking . . . You can hear them even on the eighth floor of the buildings around here."

"Who does this villa belong to anyway?" Marcovaldo asked. Now, outside the gate, there weren't just the cat-loving ladies but also other people: the man from the gas pump opposite, the apprentices from a mechanic's shop, the postman, the grocer, some passers-by. And none of them, men and women, had to be asked twice: all wanted to have their say, as always when a mysterious and controversial subject comes up.

"It belongs to a Marchesa.[6] She lives there, but you never see her . . ."

"She's been offered millions and millions, by developers, for this little patch of land, but she won't sell . . ."

"What would she do with millions, an old woman all alone in the

---

5. **protégés** (prōt´ ə zhāz´) *n.* those guided and helped by another.
6. **Marchesa** (mär kā´ zä) title of an Italian noblewoman.

Reading Strategy
Clarifying To whom do you think the two yellow, skinny hands belong? Read ahead to find out.

29 ✓**Reading Check**
What has Marcovaldo found in the garden?

The Garden of Stubborn Cats ◆ 625

28 **Reading Strategy**
Clarifying

- Ask a volunteer to read the bracketed passage aloud.

- Then, ask the Reading Strategy question on p. 625: To whom do you think the two yellow, skinny hands belong? Give students time to read ahead to find out.
  Answer: The hands belong to the Marchesa.

- Ask a volunteer to point out details that enabled him or her to figure out that the hands belong to the Marchesa.
  Answer: Details include "From a blind in the little villa . . ." (p. 625) and "[The villa] belongs to a Marchesa . . ." (p. 626).

29 ✓**Reading Check**
Answer: Marcovaldo has found "the heart of the cats' realm."

CUSTOMIZE INSTRUCTION FOR UNIVERSAL ACCESS

For Less Proficient Readers	For Advanced Readers
Have students create an illustration of the Marchesa's garden in the middle of the city. Encourage them to use both original drawings and pictures cut from newspapers and magazines, as well as multimedia materials such as dried leaves and flower petals. They can include details from both the selection and their own imagination.	Remind students of the responsibilities of urban planners—that of balancing a community's need for progress and economic development with the need for a healthy environment that respects the natural world. Have students research this topic and find examples of cities that have successfully balanced these two opposing needs.

30 Reading Strategy

Clarifying

world? She wants to hold on to her house, even if it's falling to pieces, rather than be forced to move . . ."

"It's the only undeveloped bit of land in the downtown area . . . Its value goes up every year . . . They've made her offers—"

"Offers! That's not all. Threats, intimidation, persecution . . . You don't know the half of it! Those contractors!"

"But she holds out. She's held out for years . . ."

"She's a saint. Without her, where would those poor animals go?"

"A lot she cares about the animals, the old miser! Have you ever seen her give them anything to eat?"

"How can she feed the cats when she doesn't have food for herself? She's the last descendant of a ruined family!"

"She hates cats! I've seen her chasing them and hitting them with an umbrella!"

"Because they were tearing up her flowerbeds!"

"What flowerbeds? I've never seen anything in this garden but a great crop of weeds!"

30 Marcovaldo realized that with regard to the old Marchesa opinions were sharply divided: some saw her as an angelic being, others as an egoist and a miser.

"It's the same with the birds; she never gives them a crumb!"

"She gives them hospitality. Isn't that plenty?"

"Like she gives the mosquitoes, you mean. They all come from here, from that pool. In the summertime the mosquitoes eat us alive, and it's all the fault of that Marchesa!"

"And the mice? This villa is a mine of mice. Under the dead leaves they have their burrows, and at night they come out . . ."

"As far as the mice go, the cats take care of them . . ."

"Oh, you and your cats! If we had to rely on them . . ."

"Why? Have you got something to say against cats?"

Here the discussion degenerated into a general quarrel.

"The authorities should do something: confiscate the villa!" one man cried.

"What gives them the right?" another protested.

"In a modern neighborhood like ours, a mouse-nest like this . . . it should be forbidden . . ."

"Why, I picked my apartment precisely because it overlooked this little bit of green . . ."

"Green, hell! Think of the fine skyscraper they could build here!"

Marcovaldo would have liked to add something of his own, but he couldn't get a word in. Finally, all in one breath, he exclaimed: "The Marchesa stole a trout from me!"

The unexpected news supplied fresh ammunition to the old woman's enemies, but her defenders exploited it as proof of the <u>indigence</u> to which the unfortunate noblewoman was reduced. Both sides agreed that Marcovaldo should go and knock at her door to demand an explanation.

It wasn't clear whether the gate was locked or unlocked; in any case, it opened, after a push, with a mournful creak. Marcovaldo

Reading Strategy
Clarifying These lines present contrasting descriptions of the Marchesa. Read ahead to clarify the truth about this character.

indigence (in′ di jəns) *n.* poverty

picked his way among the leaves and cats, climbed the steps to the porch, knocked hard at the entrance.

At a window (the very one where the frying pan had appeared), the blind was raised slightly and in one corner a round, pale blue eye was seen, and a clump of hair dyed an undefinable color, and a dry skinny hand. A voice was heard, asking: "Who is it? Who's at the door?" the words accompanied by a cloud smelling of fried oil.

"It's me, Marchesa. The trout man," Marcovaldo explained. "I don't mean to trouble you. I only wanted to tell you, in case you didn't know, that the trout was stolen from me, by that cat, and I'm the one who caught it. In fact the line . . ."

"Those cats! It's always those cats . . . " the Marchesa said, from behind the shutter, with a shrill, somewhat nasal voice. "All my troubles come from the cats! Nobody knows what I go through! Prisoner night and day of those horrid beasts! And with all the refuse people throw over the walls, to spite me!"

"But my trout . . ."

"Your trout! What am I supposed to know about your trout!" The Marchesa's voice became almost a scream, as if she wanted to drown out the sizzle of oil in the pan, which came through the window along with the aroma of fried fish. "How can I make sense of anything, with all the stuff that rains into my house?"

"I understand, but did you take the trout or didn't you?"

"When I think of all the damage I suffer because of the cats! Ah, fine state of affairs! I'm not responsible for anything! I can't tell you what I've lost! Thanks to those cats, who've occupied house and garden for years! My life at the mercy of those animals! Go and find the owners! Make them pay damages! Damages? A whole life destroyed! A prisoner here, unable to move a step!"

"Excuse me for asking: but who's forcing you to stay?"

From the crack in the blind there appeared sometimes a round, pale blue eye, sometimes a mouth with two protruding teeth; for a moment the whole face was visible, and to Marcovaldo it seemed, bewilderingly, the face of a cat.

"They keep me prisoner, they do, those cats! Oh, I'd be glad to leave! What wouldn't I give for a little apartment all my own, in a nice clean modern building! But I can't go out . . . They follow me, they block my path, they trip me up!" The voice became a whisper, as if to confide a secret. "They're afraid I'll sell the lot . . . They won't leave me . . . won't allow me . . . When the builders come to offer me a contract, you should see them, those cats! They get in the way, pull out their claws; they even chased a lawyer off! Once I had the contract right here, I was about to sign it, and they dived in through the window, knocked over the inkwell, tore up all the pages . . ."

All of a sudden Marcovaldo remembered the time, the shipping department, the boss. He tiptoed off over the dried leaves, as the voice continued to come through the slats of the blind, enfolded in that cloud apparently from the oil of a frying pan. "They even scratched me . . . I

Reading Strategy
Clarifying What details of the Marchesa's words help you clarify her character?

32 ✓ **Reading Check**
What do some of the onlookers blame on the Marchesa?

The Garden of Stubborn Cats ◆ 627

31 **Reading Strategy**
Clarifying

- Have a volunteer read the bracketed passage. Then, ask students to paraphrase what the Marchesa says here.
  Answer: The Marchesa feels that her life is at the mercy of the cats; they keep her prisoner and have destroyed her life.
- Ask the Reading Strategy question on p. 627: What details of the Marchesa's words help you clarify her character?
  Answer: The Marchesa's lack of interest in the cats' fate suggests that her character represents self-interest.

32 ✓ **Reading Check**
Answer: They blame her for mistreating the cats and for attracting mice and mosquitoes.

CUSTOMIZE INSTRUCTION FOR UNIVERSAL ACCESS

For Less Proficient Readers	For Gifted/Talented Students
Play the **Listening to Literature** Audiocassette or CD as students follow along in the text. Allow them to listen to the neighbors' arguments about the fate of the Marchesa's land and decide for themselves which side of the argument sounds more convincing.	Students who prefer preserving the natural world over progress and development may cheer the cats, whereas students who believe progress and development are important may feel the cats should be removed. Have students write a continuation of the story that reflects their beliefs about the fate of the cats.

Review and Assess

1. According to the Marchesa, she is trapped because the cats thwart her attempts to sell or even to leave the villa.

2. **(a)** Because there are few gardens or vacant lots, the cats have few places to live and find food. They are also in great danger of being run over. **(b)** The "negative city" is the in-between spaces that the cats inhabit because there are no other places left for them.

3. **(a)** At first Marcovaldo follows the cat out of curiosity: later he chases it to retrieve the trout. **(b)** He discovers hidden peepholes onto the city of men; he discovers the Biarritz Restaurant.

4. **(a)** However unwillingly, the Marchesa provides a garden for the cats to live in. **(b)** Her supporters think she helps the cats by letting them live in her garden and by refusing to sell the villa; her critics think she abuses the cats.

5. **(a)** The opposing forces are technology and nature. **(b)** Possible response: Nature prevails at the end, with animals subverting the builders' efforts.

6. Students might say that the Marchesa had neither the financial means nor the energy to free herself from the cats.

---

still have the scar . . . All alone here at the mercy of these demons . . ."

Winter came. A blossoming of white flakes decked the branches and capitals and the cats' tails. Under the snow, the dry leaves dissolved into mush. The cats were rarely seen, the cat lovers even less; the packages of fish-bones were consigned only to cats who came to the door. Nobody, for quite a while, had seen anything of the Marchesa. No smoke came now from the chimneypot of the villa.

One snowy day, the garden was again full of cats, who had returned as if it were spring, and they were miauing as if on a moonlight night. The neighbors realized that something had happened: they went and knocked at the Marchesa's door. She didn't answer: she was dead.

In the spring, instead of the garden, there was a huge building site that a contractor had set up. The steam shovels dug down to great depths to make room for the foundations, cement poured into the iron armatures, a very high crane passed beams to the workmen who were making the scaffoldings. But how could they get on with their work? Cats walked along all the planks, they made bricks fall and upset buckets of mortar, they fought in the midst of the piles of sand. When you started to raise an armature, you found a cat perched on top of it, hissing fiercely. More treacherous pusses climbed onto the masons' backs as if to purr, and there was no getting rid of them. And the birds continued making their nests in all the trestles, the cab of the crane looked like an aviary . . . And you couldn't dip up a bucket of water that wasn't full of frogs, croaking and hopping . . .

Review and Assess

Thinking About the Selection

1. **Respond:** What is your impression of the Marchesa's circumstances in the story? Is she trapped? Explain.

2. **(a) Recall:** What are some threats that cats face in the "city of men"? **(b) Interpret:** What is the "negative city," and why do cats choose to live there?

3. **(a) Recall:** Why does Marcovaldo follow cats during his lunch break? **(b) Interpret:** What does Marcovaldo discover when he begins looking at the world as cats do?

4. **(a) Recall:** What does the Marchesa do for the cats? **(b) Compare and Contrast:** Why do her supporters believe she is helping the cats and her critics think she is not?

5. **(a) Interpret:** What are the opposing forces at work in this story? **(b) Draw Conclusions:** Which force do you think prevails? Why?

6. **Take a Position:** Should the Marchesa have tried harder to free herself, or do you think she wanted to live as she did? Explain.

Italo Calvino

(1923–1985)

Italo Calvino was born in Cuba, but as a young boy, he moved with his family to Italy. He settled in Turin after fighting in the Italian Resistance during World War II. Many of his works of fiction were inspired by his wartime experiences.

Calvino is best known for editing a large collection of fables. According to his theory, the "fable formula," which involves a child in the woods or a knight fighting beasts, is the scheme for all human stories. One fable element that can be found in almost all of Calvino's fiction, including this selection, is the tension between characters and the environment.

✐ ASSESSMENT PRACTICE: Reading Comprehension

Distinguish Between Fact and Nonfact   (For more practice, see Test Preparation Workbook, p. 39.)

To help students learn to distinguish between fact and opinion, use this sample test item.

> Automation is the use of machines to perform tasks that require a decision. Some familiar uses of automation are thermostats and traffic lights. Automation allows machines to perform tasks that are too boring or dangerous for people to do.

Which of the following lines is an OPINION?

A Automation is the use of machines to perform tasks that require a decision.

B Some tasks are too boring for people to do.

C Automation is at work in thermostats.

D People don't have to do work that machines do.

A, C, and *D* are supported by the passage, but only *B* is an opinion.

Review and Assess

Literary Analysis

Setting

1. (a) Identify three details that alert you that the **setting** of "There Will Come Soft Rains" is the future. (b) Why is this future setting essential to Bradbury's purpose?

2. (a) Describe the city in which Marcovaldo lives. (b) Is this a good or a bad setting for cats? Why?

3. Contrast the city with the garden Marcovaldo discovers. Compare them on the basis of physical appearance, inhabitants, sounds, kinds of activity, and mood.

Comparing Literary Works

4. (a) What is **ironic** about the setting of "There Will Come Soft Rains"? (b) What is ironic about the garden in "The Garden of Stubborn Cats"?

5. What other surprises do the authors present in these selections? Use a chart like the one shown to list ironic details.

Issue	What You Expect	Ironic Surprises
How is the house cleaned?		
What happens when the house burns?		
Where does Marcovaldo catch a fish?		
How does the Marchesa feel about cats?		

6. How is the irony different in the two stories?

Reading Strategy

Clarifying

7. How did the condition of the dog in "There Will Come Soft Rains" help you **clarify** the situation?

8. Identify three details that helped you clarify the opening statement of "The Garden of Stubborn Cats."

Extend Understanding

9. **Career Connection:** (a) What jobs might be eliminated or created in a future world in which houses provide the same services as in the Bradbury story? (b) What human touches would be lost?

Quick Review

Setting is the time and place in which the action of a story takes place.

Irony presents surprising or amusing contradictions between what readers or characters expect and what occurs.

To **clarify** the meaning of what you read, look ahead in the text or review what you have read.

 Take It to the Net
www.phschool.com
Take the interactive self-test online to check your understanding of these selections.

There Will Come Soft Rains / The Garden of Stubborn Cats ◆ 629

Answer continued

ceremonies, customs" that belong to the realm of cats; and the "unsuspected peepholes onto the city of men."

9. Students should be prepared to explain their responses.

Answers for p. 629

Review and Assess

1. **Possible responses: (a)** Details include the automated breakfast; the date, August 4, 2026; and the robot cleaning-mice. **(b)** The future setting is essential because Bradbury's purpose is to warn people of what could happen if nuclear weapons are allowed to proliferate.

2. **(a)** Marcovaldo's city is so overpopulated and built up that almost no traces of nature are left. **(b)** The setting is bad for cats and other animals because their lives are endangered by threats such as "cat-crushing automobiles."

3. In the city, building and technology seem to have obliterated nature, while in the garden nature grows wild. The garden looks untidy and rank, while the city is ordered and controlled. The garden is full of cats, birds, and frogs, while the city is overpopulated with people. The mood of the garden is one of life, while the mood of the city is one of sterility.

4. **(a)** The setting of "There Will Come Soft Rains" is ironic because the house is filled with technological advances aimed at making people's lives easier, but it is technology that destroyed the human race. **(b)** The garden in "The Garden of Stubborn Cats" is ironic because it teems with life in the middle of the sterile city and because its owner dislikes the cats.

5. **Possible responses:**
What You Expect: machines; the house will disappear; outside; she likes them. **Ironic Surprises:** machines made to resemble animals; the house fights for its life; in a restaurant; she hates them.

6. The irony is different in the two stories because "There Will Come Soft Rains" offers no hope of recovery from the destruction, while "The Garden of Stubborn Cats" hints that nature will yet survive.

7. The dog's sores indicate exposure to radioactivity.

8. Examples include the "network" through which the cat population moves; the "territories,

continued

629

❶ Vocabulary Development

Word Analysis

1. *Tantalize* means "tempt"; Tantalus was tempted by the food and drink he could not reach.
2. *Odyssey* means "long journey"; Odysseus went on a long journey.
3. *Mercurial* means "unpredictable, quickly changing"; Mercury traveled swiftly from one place to another.

Fluency: Words in Context

1. itinerary   5. supernal
2. warrens   6. tremulous
3. indigence   7. titanic
4. paranoia   8. psychopathic

Spelling Strategy

1. bouti*que*   3. roman*tic*
2. aci*dic*

❷ Grammar

1. The house was able to make beds, clean up messes, and fix breakfast.
2. The more I think about it, the more I am convinced that I do not like it.
3. Cats are known for their gracefulness, their ability to hunt, and their beauty.
4. The woman was unable to go to the store or to the bank.
5. During the day, cats are quiet, but during the night, they sing noisily.

Writing Application

Possible answer: After the explosion, people died, buildings collapsed into rubble, starving animals patrolled the neighborhood, and the ruined city glowed with radiation.

Integrate Language Skills

❶ Vocabulary Development Lesson

Word Analysis: Words From Myths

The word *titanic* comes from Greek mythology. The Titans were a race of giants who had great strength. *Titanic* describes something of great power or size. Use a dictionary to find the meaning of each word, and explain how it relates to the mythical character whose name is part of the word.

1. *tantalize:* from Tantalus, a Greek man for whom food and drink were always out of reach
2. *odyssey:* from Odysseus, a Greek hero who underwent a long and dangerous journey
3. *mercurial:* from Mercury, the speedy Roman messenger god

❷ Grammar Lesson

Parallel Structure

Parallelism involves using similar grammatical structures to express similar ideas. Sentences with **parallel structure** contain repeated grammatical patterns or repeated types of phrases or clauses within the sentence, as in the examples below.

> **Repeated Word:** . . . *how* well the house had kept its peace. *How* carefully it had inquired, "Who goes there?"

> **Repeated Pattern:** . . . *whirling* their mustached runners, *kneading* the rug nap, *sucking* gently at hidden dust.

Fluency: Words in Context

Identify the vocabulary word from the list on page 613 that is suggested by each sentence.

1. You use this word when planning a trip.
2. Rabbits live in these.
3. Ending this is a societal problem.
4. You think someone is watching you.
5. This word describes stars.
6. You might be this after meeting a bear.
7. This could describe a thunderstorm.
8. This kind of disorder may lead to violence.

Spelling Strategy

Many adjectives end in the suffix *-ic*, such as *titanic*, while several nouns end in *-ique*, such as *technique*. On your paper, spell each word correctly.

1. bout_____   2. acid_____   3. romant_____

Practice Rewrite the following sentences to achieve parallelism.

1. The house was able to make beds, to clean up messes, and also fixed breakfast.
2. The more I think about it, I am more convinced I do not like it.
3. Cats are known for their gracefulness, ability to hunt, and they are beautiful looking.
4. The woman had been unable to go to the store, nor could she go to the bank.
5. During the day, cats are quiet, but they sing noisily at night.

Writing Application Expand this sentence by adding parallel words or patterns.
After the explosion, people died. . . .

𝒲𝒢 *Prentice Hall Writing and Grammar Connection: Chapter 7, Section 4*

TEACHING RESOURCES

The following resources can be used to enrich or extend the instruction for pp. 630–631.

Vocabulary

📖 **Selection Support Workbook:** Build Vocabulary, p. 153

📖 **Vocabulary and Spelling Practice Book** (Use this booklet for skills enrichment.)

Grammar

📖 **Selection Support Workbook:** Build Grammar Skills, p. 154

𝒲𝒢 **Writing and Grammar,** Platinum Level, p. 138
▦ **Daily Language Practice Transparencies** ▦

Writing

𝒲𝒢 **Writing and Grammar,** Platinum Level, p. 133 ▦

💿 **Writing and Grammar iText CD-ROM**

▦ **BLOCK SCHEDULING:** Resources marked with this symbol provide varied instruction during 90-minute blocks.

Writing Lesson

Advertisement for a New Technology

The house in "There Will Come Soft Rains" is filled with automated devices. Choose one that you want to promote. Write an advertisement that describes the device, and persuade your audience that they need it.

Prewriting   Brainstorm to identify the characteristics of your audience. Provide information about their age range, education level, specialized training, technology awareness, and buying habits.

Drafting   Write directly to your target audience—the people to whom you are trying to sell your product. Address them in terms and language they can understand.

Model: Addressing a Target Audience

Are you tired of picking up after your family? Day after day, the children leave their toys all over, the dog tracks in mud. You need robot mice!

> Making a direct appeal to overworked parents targets a particular audience.

Revising   Ask for feedback on your ad from someone whose knowledge level is close to that of your target audience. Define any technical terms that are unclear. Add any missing details about the function or advantages of your product.

W̶G Prentice Hall Writing and Grammar Connection: Chapter 8, Section 2

Extension Activities

Listening and Speaking As Marcovaldo, prepare and present a **persuasive argument** to convince the Marchesa that she should stay in her villa and cultivate her garden. Follow these suggestions:

- Consider the ideas and approaches that would appeal to the Marchesa.
- Support your argument with reasons.

Present your argument to the class, and ask listeners to evaluate its effectiveness. [**Group Activity**]

Research and Technology Using Bradbury's story as a springboard, draw a **floor plan** to scale—one-half inch for one yard—of your ideal house of the future. Briefly describe its special features in annotations on your diagram.

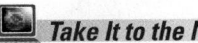 *Take It to the Net* www.phschool.com

Go online for an additional research activity using the Internet.

ASSESSMENT RESOURCES

The following resources can be used to assess students' knowledge and skills.

Selection Assessment

- 📖 **Formal Assessment**, pp. 135–137
- 📖 **Open Book Test**, pp. 115–117
- 📼 **Got It! Assessment Videotapes**, Tape 3
- 💿 **Test Bank Software**

- 🖥 *Take It to the Net*
  Visit www.phschool.com for self-tests and additional questions on the selections.

Writing Rubric

- 📖 **Performance Assess. and Portfolio Mgmt**, p. 20

Listening and Speaking Rubric

- 📖 **Performance Assess. and Portfolio Mgmt**, p. 30

PRENTICE HALL
ASSESSMENT *SYSTEM*

- 📖 **Workbook**
- 📖 **Skill Book**
- 🖨 **Transparencies**
- 💿 **CD-ROM**

CONNECTIONS
Literature and Technology
Thinking About the Future

In "There Will Come Soft Rains," Ray Bradbury imagines a world where technology makes the routines of daily life convenient, but he also raises the specter of mass destruction. In Bradbury's world, all the luxuries of home are easily accessible—from a breakfast prepared without effort to musical accompaniment chosen to reflect a listener's taste or mood.

Hans Magnus Enzensberger's writing is an essay, a brief nonfiction work that addresses not a fictional future but the probable outcome of today's trends. In this essay, Enzensberger discusses the changing definition of "luxury" and predicts that the luxuries of the future will be different from those of today.

L' Univers Demasque, René Magritte, Coll. Crik, Brussels, Belgium

▲ **Critical Viewing** What details in this picture suggest the future? **[Interpret]**

from The Future of Luxury

Hans Magnus Enzensberger
Translated by Linda Haverty Rugg

So one must ask if private luxury has any future at all. I hope and fear: yes. For if it is true that the struggle for difference is a part of the mechanism of evolution, and that the desire to squander has its roots in our natural drives, then luxury can never completely disappear, and the question is only which form it will take in its flight from its own shadow.

All we can offer is <u>conjecture</u>. And so I would guess that there will be completely different priorities in our future battles over distribution. Fast cars and gold watches, cases of champagne and perfume are available on every street corner; they are not scarce, rare, expensive or desirable in this age of raging consumerism. Instead, it is the elementary necessities of life that come at a great price: quiet, good water, and enough space.

It is a peculiar reversal of the logic of desire: the luxury of the future will turn away from excess and strive for the necessary; which, it is to be feared, will be available to only a select few. The things that matter will not be sold in any Duty Free Shop:[1]

1. *Time*. This is the most important of all luxury items. Strangely enough it is precisely the elite who have the least say over their own time. This is not primarily a question of quantity, though many members of this class work upward of eighty hours a week; it is much more a matter of the <u>multifarious</u> dependencies that enslave them. They are expected to be on call at all times. Besides that, they are bound to a day-planner that extends years into the future.

   But other professions, too, are bound to regulations that limit their temporal sovereignty to a minimum. Workers are tied to the pace of their machines, housewives (in Europe) to absurd shopping hours, parents to school functions, and almost all commuters have to travel at peak times. Under the circumstances, it is the person who always has time who lives in luxury; time for what he wants to do, and the power to decide what he does with his time, how much he does, when, and where he does it.

---

1. **Duty Free Shop** kind of variety store, usually found in airports, in which no taxes are imposed on items sold.

conjecture (kən jek´ chər) *n.* prediction based on guesswork

multifarious (mul´ tə far´ ē əs) *adj.* of great variety; diverse

✓**Reading Check**

What things does the author mention as being luxuries today?

---

from The Future of Luxury

- Call students' attention to the first two paragraphs.
- Ask them: What words or phrases suggest that this will be an essay of prediction?

  Answer: Students should point out that the essay starts with the author pondering a question and then uses the word *conjecture* in paragraph 2. These details indicate that the essay will be one of prediction.

✓**Reading Check**

Answer: The author says that today's luxuries include expensive cars, jewelry, champagne, and perfume, even though they seem to be readily available to everyone.

2. *Attention.* This, too, is a scarce commodity, with all the media competing bitterly for a piece. Watching the melee of money and politics, sports and art, technology, and advertising, leaves little attention leftover. Only the person who turns his back on these overbearing claims on his attention and turns off the roar of the channels can decide for himself what is worth his attention and what is not. In the barrage of <u>arbitrary</u> information our perceptive and <u>cognitive</u> capabilities decline, they grow when we limit our attention to those things and only those things that we ourselves want to see, hear, feel and know. In this we can see an occasion for luxury.

3. *Space.* As the day-planner[2] is to the economy of time, congestion is to space. In a sense, everywhere and everything is crowded. We have rising rents, housing shortages, and sardine-packed public transport. We feel the press of flesh on sidewalks, public swimming pools, discotheques, and tourist spots. All of this creates a density in living conditions that verges on a robbery of freedom. Anyone who can remove himself from this cagelike existence lives in luxury. But he must be prepared to shovel himself out from under a mountain of consumer items, as well. Usually our already-too-small living space is jammed with furniture, appliances, knick-knacks, and clothes. What is missing is the excess of space that is required for free movement. Today a room seems luxurious when it is empty.

4. *Quiet.* This, too, is a basic requirement that has become harder and harder to satisfy. Anyone who wants to escape the everyday din must be very extravagant. In general, apartments cost more the quieter they are; restaurants that do not pour musical pollution into the ears of their guests demand higher prices of their discerning clientele. The raging traffic, the howling sirens, the clatter of helicopters, the neighbor's droning stereo, the month-long roar of the street fair—the person who can elude all of that enjoys luxury.

5. *The Environment.* That one can breathe the air and drink the water, that it does not smoke and does not stink, is, as everyone knows, not a given but a privilege enjoyed by fewer and fewer. Anyone who does not produce his own food must pay a premium for nontoxic edibles. It is a problem for most to avoid the risk to life and limb in the workplace, in traffic, and in the dangerous bustle of leisure. In this arena, too, the possibility of withdrawal proves ever-more scarce.

6. *Security.* This is perhaps the most <u>precarious</u> of all luxury items. As the state has become less able to guarantee safety, the private demand for it has grown and driven the prices skyhigh. Bodyguards, security services, alarm systems—anything that promises security now belongs to the realm of privilege, and these businesses can count on further growth in the future. If one takes a look around the

---

2. **day-planner** a daily calendar-scheduling system for events or appointments that is usually listed in a portable datebook.

arbitrary (är´ bə trer´ ē) *adj.* random; not based on a system or rules

cognitive (käg´ nə tiv) *adj.* related to knowing, memory, and judgment

Thematic Connection

How does Enzensberger's view of the future compare with other views you have read or heard about?

precarious (prē ker´ ē əs) *adj.* uncertain; dependent on circumstances wealthier neighborhoods, one can already sense that luxury does not promise unmitigated pleasure. As in the past, it will bring with it not only freedom but obligations. For the person of privilege who wants to remain safe does not just lock others out, he locks himself in.

All in all, these speculations revolve on an about-face that is rich in ironies. If there is anything to them, the luxury of the future will depend not on increase, as it did in the past, but on decrease, not on accumulation but on avoidance. Excess will enter a new stage in which it negates itself. The answer to the paradox of mass exclusivity would then be a further paradox: minimalism and abstinence could prove to be just as rare, expensive, and desirable as <u>ostentatious</u> spending once was.

With that, in any case, luxury would <u>relinquish</u> its role as representation. Its privatization would be complete. It would no longer require viewers, but would exclude them. Its reason for being would be, precisely, to be invisible. But even with that kind of withdrawal from reality, luxury would still be true to its origins; it has always been at odds with the reality principle. Perhaps it has never been more than an attempt to flee life's monotony and misery.

New and bewildering, however, is another question that must be posed in light of future prospects: who will count among the beneficiaries of luxury in the future? The original <u>parameters</u> of social position, income, and fortune will no longer be the deciding factors. A top executive, star athlete, banker, or leading politician will quite simply not be able to afford the items discussed here. Such individuals can buy sufficient space and a certain degree of security. But they have no time and no peace.

On the other hand, the unemployed, the elderly, and refugees, who in the future will make up the majority of the world's population, usually dispose of their time as they like. But it would be sheer mockery to call that a privilege. Crammed into crowded living space, with no money or security, many of them can make little use of their empty time. It is difficult to say how the scarce commodities of the future will be distributed, but one thing is clear: anyone who has only one of them enjoys none of them. There can be as little hope of justice in the future as there was in the past. At least in this respect, luxury will remain what it always was—a stubborn opponent of equality.

Connecting Literature and Technology

1. What six items does Enzensberger identify as luxuries of the future?
2. How does the house in Ray Bradbury's story "There Will Come Soft Rains" address these luxuries, if at all?
3. Which scenario—Bradbury's world or Enzensberger's—do you think is more likely to happen? Explain.

---

ostentatious (äs´ tən tā´ shəs) *adj.* done as a showy display

relinquish (ri liŋ´ kwish) *v.* give up; abandon

parameters (pə ram´ ət ərz) *n.* factors; characteristics

Hans Magnus Enzensberger

(b. 1929)

Skilled in many writing forms, Hans Magnus Enzensberger offers cultural commentary in poetry, prose, drama, journalism, and essays. He has been called one of Germany's greatest living poets, and he is also respected for his ideas.

Enzensberger was born in Bavaria, a section of Germany, in 1929 and grew up in Nuremberg. At the age of seventeen, he began studying English translation. He quickly embraced a life and career revolving around literature and language.

Enzensberger has probably achieved his greatest fame as a cultural essayist and social critic on the subject of progress. "The Future of Luxury" is the final essay in his collection *Zig Zag: The Politics of Culture and Vice Versa* (1999).

Answers

Connecting Literature and Technology

1. Time, attention, space, quiet, the environment, and security are the luxuries of the future according to the author.

2. The house probably gave the people more time since they did not need to clean, cook or take care of the house. With more time, the people may have been able to focus their attention on things important to them. The house did not really address the luxuries of space and the environment. It was not quiet, since there were voices coming out of the walls relaying the time or reading poetry, but it did offer the people security in its state-of-the-art security system.

3. Students may say that aspects of both writers' scenarios will happen. People will probably have many automated features in their homes, but will probably value more the luxuries that Enzensberger covered.

The Princess and All the Kingdom ✦ The Censors

Lesson Objectives

1. **To analyze and respond to literary elements**
   - Literary Analysis: Theme
   - Comparing Literary Works

2. **To read, comprehend, analyze, and critique short stories**
   - Reading Strategy: Challenging the Writer's Message
   - Reading Check questions
   - Review and Assess questions
   - Assessment Practice (ATE)

3. **To develop word analysis skills, fluency, and systematic vocabulary**
   - Vocabulary Development Lesson: Latin Word Root: -ultra-

4. **To understand and apply written and oral language conventions**
   - Spelling Strategy
   - Grammar Lesson: Consistency of Verb Tenses

5. **To understand and apply appropriate writing and research strategies**
   - Writing Lesson: Persuasive Essay
   - Extension Activity: Annotated List

6. **To understand and apply listening and speaking strategies**
   - Extension Activity: Royal Speech

STEP-BY-STEP TEACHING GUIDE	PACING GUIDE
PRETEACH	
Motivate Students and Provide Background	
Use the Motivation activity (ATE p. 636)	5 min.
Read and discuss the Preview material and Background information (SE/ATE p. 636) **A**	5 min.
Introduce the Concepts	
Introduce the Literary Analysis and Reading Strategy (SE/ATE p. 637) **A**	15 min.
Pronounce the vocabulary words and read their definitions (SE p. 637)	5 min.
TEACH	
Monitor Comprehension	
Informally monitor comprehension by circulating while students read independently or in groups **A**	15 min.
Monitor students' comprehension with the Reading Check notes (SE/ATE pp. 639, 641, 643)	as students read
Develop vocabulary with Vocabulary notes (SE pp. 639, 643; ATE p. 642)	as students read
Develop Understanding	
Develop students' understanding of theme with Literary Analysis annotations (SE pp. 641, 643; ATE pp. 639, 641, 643) **A**	10 min.
Develop students' understanding of challenging the writer's message with Reading Strategy annotations (ATE p. 643)	10 min.
ASSESS	
Assess Mastery	
Assess students' mastery of the Reading Strategy and Literary Analysis by having them answer the Review and Assess questions (SE/ATE p. 645)	20 min.
Use one or more of the print and media Assessment Resources (ATE p. 647) **A**	up to 50 min.
EXTEND	
Apply Understanding	
Have students complete the Vocabulary Development Lesson and the Grammar Lesson (SE p. 646) **A**	20 min.
Apply students' ability to address the opposition using the Writing Lesson (SE p. 647) **A**	45 min.
Apply students' understanding of the selection using one or more of the Extension Activities (SE p. 647)	20–90 min.

 ACCELERATED INSTRUCTION:
Use the strategies and activities identified with an **A**.

UNIVERSAL ACCESS
● = Below Level Students
▲ = On-Level Students
■ = Above Level Students

Time and Resource Manager

RESOURCES		
PRINT 📖	**TRANSPARENCIES**	**TECHNOLOGY** 💿 🎧 📼
• **Beyond Literature,** Cross-Curricular Connection: Social Studies, p. 40 ▲ ■		• **Interest Grabber Video,** Tape 3 ● ▲ ■
• **Selection Support Workbook:** ● ▲ ■ Literary Analysis, p. 160 Reading Strategy, p. 159 Build Vocabulary, p. 157	• **Literary Analysis and Reading Transparencies,** pp. 79 and 80 ● ▲ ■	
• **Adapted Reader's Companion** ● • **Reader's Companion** ●		• **Listening to Literature** ● ▲ ■ Audiocassettes, Side 20 Audio CDs, CD 13
• **English Learner's Companion** ● ▲ • **Literatura en español** ● ▲ • **Literary Analysis for Enrichment** ■	• **Fine Art Transparencies, Volume 1,** Art Transparencies 7, 13 ● ▲ ■	
• **Formal Assessment:** Selection Test, pp. 138–140 ● ▲ ■ • **Open Book Test,** pp. 118–120 ● ▲ ■ • **Performance Assessment and Portfolio Management,** p. 11 ● ▲ ■ • **PRENTICE HALL ASSESSMENT SYSTEM** ● ▲ ■	• **PRENTICE HALL ASSESSMENT SYSTEM** ● ▲ ■ Skills Practice Answers and Explanations on Transparencies	• **Test Bank Software** ● ▲ ■ • **Got It! Assessment Videotapes** ● ▲
• **Selection Support Workbook:** ● ▲ ■ Build Grammar Skills, p. 158 • **Writing and Grammar,** Platinum Level ● ▲ ■ • **Extension Activities,** p. 40 ● ▲ ■	• **Daily Language Practice Transparencies** ● ▲ • **Writing Models and Graphic Organizers on Transparencies,** p. 83 ● ▲ ■	• **Writing and Grammar iText CD-ROM** ● ▲ ■ 🖥 *Take It to the Net* www.phschool.com

BLOCK SCHEDULING: Use one 90-minute class period to preteach the selection and have students read it. Use a second 90-minute class period to assess students' mastery of skills and have them complete one of the Extension Activities.

Motivation

Have students look at the dramatic piece of art on p. 642 and read the title, "Restricted Man." Ask them to speculate about the subject of the work. What might be the artist's message?
Possible response: The person appears to be trapped inside a cement box. The artist may be depicting political repression.

Ask students what kinds of traps people find themselves in. Then, have them predict what the theme might be in the stories they will read.

▶ Interest Grabber Video

As an alternative, play "Responsibilities" on Tape 3 to engage student interest.

❶ Background

Social Studies

Juan Domingo Perón was first elected president of Argentina in 1946. Once in power, he became increasingly authoritarian, jailing opponents, controlling education, and stifling the press. Support for Perón fell in the early 1950s as the economy weakened and his popular wife, Eva, passed away. The military seized power and Perón fled the country, but his ideas remained popular, and he regained power in 1973.

When Perón died in 1974, his third wife, Isabel Martinez de Perón, assumed the presidency but was unable to command much support. The armed forces intervened in 1976 and ruled until 1982, instituting one of the bloodiest regimes in South American history.

Prepare to Read

The Princess and All the Kingdom ◆ The Censors

▶ Take It to the Net

Visit www.phschool.com for interactive activities and instruction related to these selections, including
- background
- graphic organizers
- literary elements
- reading strategies

Preview

Connecting to the Literature

Have you ever fought for something and then found out that you got more than you had bargained for? In both these stories, people who believe they are pursuing noble goals find themselves in circumstances that are very different from those they had imagined.

❶ Background

Argentina, the setting of "The Censors," has not always been a democracy. During its history, Argentina has suffered under colonial rule and military dictatorships. In the 1970s, a military regime took power, brutally hunting down suspected political foes and censoring news and mail. Although democracy has now been restored, many Argentines remember sadly the "Dirty War" in which thousands were killed.

TEACHING RESOURCES

The following resources can be used to enrich or extend the instruction for pp. 636–637.

Motivation
▶ **Interest Grabber Video**, Tape 3 ▪

Background
📖 **Beyond Literature**, p. 40

▶ **Take It to the Net**
Visit www.phschool.com for background and hotlinks for the selections

Literary Analysis
📖 **Literary Analysis and Reading Transparencies**, Theme, p. 80 ▪

Reading
📖 **Selection Support:** Reading Strategy, p. 159; Build Vocabulary, p. 157

📖 **Literary Analysis and Reading Transparencies**, Challenge the Writer's Message, p. 79

▪ **BLOCK SCHEDULING:** Resources marked with this symbol provide varied instruction during 90-minute blocks.

Literary Analysis

Theme

At the heart of every short story is a **theme**—the message or general idea about life that the writer hopes to convey. Themes such as the importance of love, courage, and honor or the dangers of greed are illustrated by the events of a short story.

- "The Princess and All the Kingdom" presents a message about happiness and responsibility.
- "The Censors" addresses the themes of power and responsibility.

As you read these selections, complete a chart like the one shown to note the themes you find and to connect them to your life.

Comparing Literary Works

While both stories illustrate themes, their formats are strikingly different. "The Princess and All the Kingdom" uses a common fairy-tale format that makes the events of the story almost predictable and the theme practically transparent.

In contrast, "The Censors" uses a more standard story format, introducing and developing a unique character in an unusual situation. The theme is not so obvious in this story. Compare and contrast how the format and style of each story affect your ability to identify the theme.

Reading Strategy

Challenging the Writer's Message

When you see a television commercial that implies you will be able to jump as high as a sports star if you buy a specific brand of sneakers, you might want to buy the advertised shoes. If you are thinking critically, you will **challenge the message** behind the ad. Use the same critical strategy when you are reading. Look for the writer's message, which may be stated openly by a narrator or character or implied through the actions of characters. Then, ask yourself whether this message will prove true in real life.

Vocabulary Development

ardent (är´ dənt) *adj.* warm or intense in feeling (p. 639)

venerable (ven´ ər ə bəl) *adj.* worthy of respect by reason of age and dignity, character, or position (p. 639)

sordid (sôr´ did) *adj.* dirty; filthy (p. 639)

ulterior (ul tir´ ē ər) *adj.* undisclosed; beyond what is openly stated (p. 643)

staidness (stād´ nəs) *n.* state of being settled or resistant to change (p. 643)

Theme
With leadership comes responsibility.

⋮

How It Relates to My Life
Older children get privileges but more duties too.

The Princess and All the Kingdom / The Censors ◆ 637

---

❷ Literary Analysis

Theme

- Tell students that as they read "The Princess and All the Kingdom" and "The Censors," they will focus on theme—the message or general idea about life that the author hopes to convey.

- To determine a story's theme, students should focus on the important issues that the main character faces. For example, the prince in "The Princess and All the Kingdom" struggles to balance happiness and responsibility.

- Ask students to create charts like the one on p. 637 to connect the stories' themes with their own lives.

❸ Reading Strategy

Challenging the Writer's Message

- Ask students what is meant by a writer's message.
  Answer: The message is the idea that a writer hopes to convey.

- Point out that students should think critically about whether they agree with a writer's message or feel that it has any bearing on real life.

- Use the Challenge the Writer's Message transparency in **Literary Analysis and Reading Transparencies,** p. 79, to demonstrate this reading strategy.

- As they read, have students create similar charts to record their reactions to the messages in these selections.

Vocabulary Development

- Pronounce each vocabulary word for students, and read the definitions as a class. Have students identify any words with which they are already familiar.

CUSTOMIZE INSTRUCTION FOR UNIVERSAL ACCESS

For Special Needs Students	For Less Proficient Readers	For English Learners
Have students read the adapted version of "The Censors" in the **Adapted Reader's Companion.** This version provides basic-level instruction in an interactive format with questions and write-on lines. Completing the adapted version will prepare students to read the selection in the Student Edition.	Have students read the selection in the **Reader's Companion.** This version provides basic-level instruction in an interactive format with questions and write-on lines. After students finish the selection in **Reader's Companion,** have them complete the questions and activities in the Student Edition.	Have students read the adapted version of the selection in the **English Learner's Companion.** This version provides basic-level instruction in an interactive format with questions and write-on lines. Completing the adapted version will prepare students to read the selection in the Student Edition.

 E-Teach

Visit E-Teach at www.phschool.com for teachers' essays on how to teach, with questions and answers.

Step-by-Step Teaching Guide
for pp. 638–644

CUSTOMIZE INSTRUCTION
For Verbal/Linguistic Learners

Tell students to imagine that tomorrow they will be inaugurated as president of the United States. Have them write in a journal some of their concerns about the awesome responsibility they are about to undertake. Encourage them to consider both the rewards the position would offer and the toll it might it take on their personal lives.

❶ About the Selection

There is a saying, "Be careful what you wish for, because you just might get it." These words of wisdom could apply to the main character in "The Princess and All the Kingdom." In this story, a prince yearns for the lovely princess and fights bravely to win her. To his surprise and initial dismay, he also wins the entire kingdom—with all its problems and responsibilities. The story suggests that even in our victorious moments, we cannot evade responsibility.

❷ Background

Art

View of the Ile de la Cité, Paris,
by Jehan Fouquet

This piece of art illustrates a scene from a medieval kingdom. The stylized buildings with their turrets, towers, and banners evoke a fairy tale kingdom like the one in "The Princess and All the Kingdom." Use these questions for discussion:

1. What do you think is happening inside the castle?
Answer: It looks as though two kings are meeting; possibly, one is transferring power to another.

2. Looking at the painting, what do you think are some of the responsibilities of the ruler of this kingdom?
Answer: A ruler would have to make sure the kingdom is defended and that enough money is brought into the treasury to maintain courtly functions.

❷

View of the Ile de la Cité, Paris, Jehan Fouquet, Bibliothèque Nationale, Paris

❸ ▲ **Critical Viewing** What clues does this painting give you about the style and content of the story you are about to read? **[Deduce]**

638 ◆ *Short Stories*

TEACHING RESOURCES

The following resources can be used to enrich or extend the instruction for pp. 638–644.

Literary Analysis
📓 **Writing Models and Graphic Organizers,** p. 83
📖 **Selection Support:** Literary Analysis, p. 160

Reading
📖 **Reader's Companion**
📖 **English Learner's Companion**
🎧 **Listening to Literature Audiocassettes,** Side 20 ▪

🔘 **Listening to Literature Audio CDs,** CD 13 ▪

Extension
📓 **Fine Art Transparencies, Volume 1,** Art Transparencies 7, 13 (After students read "The Princess and All the Kingdom," display Transparency 13 to further their thinking about the topic of nobility. After they read "The Censors," have students compare and contrast the mood of the letter writer in the story and in the painting on Transparency 7.)

▪ **BLOCK SCHEDULING:** Resources marked with this symbol provide varied instruction during 90-minute blocks.

THE PRINCESS AND ALL THE KINGDOM

Pär Lagerkvist   Translated by Alan Blair

Once upon a time there was a prince, who went out to fight in order to win the princess whose beauty was greater than all others' and whom he loved above everything. He dared his life, he battled his way step by step through the country, ravaging it; nothing could stop him. He bled from his wounds but merely cast himself from one fight to the next, the most valiant nobleman to be seen and with a shield as pure as his own young features. At last he stood outside the city where the princess lived in her royal castle. It could not hold out against him and had to beg for mercy. The gates were thrown open; he rode in as conqueror.

When the princess saw how proud and handsome he was and thought of how he had dared his life for her sake, she could not withstand his power but gave him her hand. He knelt and covered it with ardent kisses. "Look, my bride, now I have won you!" he exclaimed, radiant with happiness. "Look, everything I have fought for, now I have won it!"

And he commanded that their wedding should take place this same day. The whole city decked itself out for the festival and the wedding was celebrated with rejoicing, pomp, and splendor.

When in the evening he went to enter the princess's bedchamber, he was met outside by the aged chancellor, a venerable man. Bowing his snow-white head, he tendered the keys of the kingdom and the crown of gold and precious stones to the young conqueror.

"Lord, here are the keys of the kingdom which open the treasuries where everything that now belongs to you is kept."

The prince frowned.

"What is that you say, old man? I do not want your keys. I have not fought for sordid gain. I have fought merely to win her whom I love, to win that which for me is the only costly thing on earth."

The old man replied, "This, too, you have won, lord. And you cannot set it aside. Now you must administer and look after it."

"Do you not understand what I say? Do you not understand that

ardent (är´ dənt) *adj.* warm or intense in feeling

venerable (ven´ ər ə bəl) *adj.* worthy of respect by reason of age and dignity, character, or position

sordid (sôr´ did) *adj.* dirty; filthy

 Reading Check

What motivates the prince's heroic actions?

The Princess and All the Kingdom ◆ 639

- Ask students to summarize the prince's reasons for not wanting the crown or the keys to the kingdom.
  Answer: The prince says he is not greedy. Even though he conquered the kingdom, he does not want fame, gold, land, or power.

- Ask students whether they think the prince is really being noble, or if there is another reason for his not wanting power.
  Possible answer: The prince is trying to avoid the responsibilities of running a kingdom. He wants happiness but does not want to pay a price for it.

Answers for p. 640

Review and Assess

1. Some students may say that power and responsibility are worth the price; others may say that the accompanying burdens may prevent happiness.

2. (a) He receives the crown of king and the keys to the treasury. (b) He rejects them because he is trying to evade his responsibilities. (c) The prince is carefree and irresponsible.

3. (a) The prince is carefree and irresponsible, while the chancellor is wise and responsible. (b) Wearing the crown and being addressed as "king" makes him realize the responsibilities he has incurred.

4. (a) Students may say that the change in the prince's attitude might help him become a wise and good ruler. (b) Some students may say they would like the rewards that would come with being in a high position; others may say that they would not like the burdens and lack of privacy that such a position entails.

---

6 one can fight, can conquer, without asking any reward other than one's happiness—not fame and gold, not land and power on earth? Well, then, I have conquered but ask for nothing, only to live happily with what, for me, is the only thing of value in life."

"Yes, lord, you have conquered. You have fought your way forward as the bravest of the brave, you have shrunk from nothing, the land lies ravaged where you have passed by. You have won your happiness. But, lord, others have been robbed of theirs. You have conquered, and therefore everything now belongs to you. It is a big land, fertile and impoverished, mighty and laid waste, full of riches and need, full of joy and sorrow, and all is now yours. For he who has won the princess and happiness, to him also belongs this land where she was born; he shall govern and cherish it."

The prince stood there glowering and fingering the hilt of his sword uneasily.

"I am the prince of happiness, nothing else!" he burst out. "Don't want to be anything else. If you get in my way, then I have my trusty sword."

But the old man put out his hand soothingly and the young man's arm sank. He looked at him searchingly, with a wise man's calm.

"Lord, you are no longer a prince," he said gently. "You are a king."

And lifting the crown with his aged hands, he put it on the other's head.

When the young ruler felt it on his brow he stood silent and moved, more erect than before. And gravely, with his head crowned for power on earth, he went in to his beloved to share her bed.

Review and Assess

Thinking About the Selection

1. **Respond:** Do you think the prince's prize is worth the price he has to pay? Why or why not?

2. (a) **Recall:** What does the prince receive in addition to the princess's hand in marriage? (b) **Infer:** Why does he reject these other "gifts" at first? (c) **Make a Judgment:** What does this rejection reveal about the prince's character?

3. (a) **Compare and Contrast:** How do the attitudes of the aged chancellor and the prince contrast with each other? (b) **Infer:** What causes the prince to change his attitude?

4. (a) **Speculate:** Do you think the prince will be able to live up to his new responsibilities? Explain. (b) **Take a Position:** Would you want the responsibilities that come with such a high-profile role? Why or why not?

Pär Lagerkvist

(1891–1974)
Swedish writer Pär Lagerkvist (pär la´gər kvist´) did not achieve much public recognition until late in his career. Finally, however, at age sixty, he won the attention of the world—he was awarded the Nobel Prize.

The son of a railway worker, Lagerkvist was one of the few people in his town to get a university education. His education led him to question many of his family's traditional beliefs. Because of his uncertainty, his early work is pessimistic. Although he continued to struggle with his beliefs, Lagerkvist's work gradually grew more optimistic. He reached a major turning point when he completed *The Triumph Over Life*, in which he expresses his growing faith in humanity.

The Censors

Luisa Valenzuela
Translated by David Unger

Poor Juan! One day they caught him with his guard down before he could even realize that what he had taken as a stroke of luck was really one of fate's dirty tricks. These things happen the minute you're careless, as one often is. Juancito let happiness—a feeling you can't trust—get the better of him when he received from a confidential source Mariana's new address in Paris and knew that she hadn't forgotten him. Without thinking twice, he sat down at his table and wrote her a letter. *The* letter that now keeps his mind off his job during the day and won't let him sleep at night (what had he scrawled, what had he put on that sheet of paper he sent to Mariana?).

Juan knows there won't be a problem with the letter's contents, that it's irreproachable, harmless. But what about the rest? He knows that they examine, sniff, feel, and read between the lines of each and every letter, and check its tiniest comma and most accidental stain. He knows that all letters pass from hand to hand and go through all sorts of tests in the huge censorship offices and that, in the end, very few continue on their way. Usually it takes months, even years, if there aren't any snags; all this time the freedom, maybe even the life, of both sender and receiver is in jeopardy. And that's why Juan's so troubled: thinking that something might happen to Mariana because of his letters. Of all people, Mariana, who must finally feel safe there where she always dreamt she'd live. But he knows that the *Censor's Secret Command* operates all over the world and cashes in on the discount in air fares; there's nothing to stop them from going as far as that hidden Paris neighborhood, kidnapping Mariana, and returning to their cozy homes, certain of having fulfilled their noble mission.

> **Literary Analysis**
> **Theme** What themes does the concept of strict censorship bring to mind?

> ❾ ✓ **Reading Check**
> What is troubling Juan?

The Censors ◆ 641

---

❼ **About the Selection**
In "The Censors," the main character, Juan, becomes a censor to reclaim a letter he has written, but in the process becomes obsessed with censorship. In his obsession, he seals his own fate in a way he never imagined. The story suggests that one's actions may have unintended consequences for which one has to take responsibility.

❽ **Literary Analysis**
Theme
• Ask students why a government might want to censor the correspondence of its citizens.
  Possible responses: It may want to conceal the truth about what is happening within its borders; it wants to control its public image.
  ▶ Monitor Progress Then, ask the Literary Analysis question on p. 641: What themes does the concept of strict censorship bring to mind?
  Possible responses: It brings to mind the themes of power, responsibility, and freedom.

❾ ✓ **Reading Check**
Answer: Juan is worried about what might happen to Mariana because he has sent her a letter.

CUSTOMIZE INSTRUCTION FOR UNIVERSAL ACCESS

For Less Proficient Readers	For Gifted/Talented Students	For Advanced Readers
To be sure that students understand the basic plot of the story, have them identify Juan and Mariana, and then invite them to summarize Juan's problem and his proposed solution.	Ask students to select one of the stories and write a newspaper review of it, explaining why they would or would not recommend the selection to a friend. Then, have students exchange their reviews and act as a censor of the other's writing.	Have students read the story with an eye to deciding which words and phrases they would cut if they were censoring the story for political reasons. Then, have them write out a censored page to show how it would look.

⑩

Restricted Man, 1961, © Jerry Uelsmann, Collection of the Center for Creative Photography, Tucson, Arizona

⑪ ▲ **Critical Viewing** In what ways does this art suggest the fear and repression of the story? **[Analyze]**

642 ◆ *Short Stories*

Well, you've got to beat them to the punch, do what everyone tries to do: sabotage the machinery, throw sand in its gears, get to the bottom of the problem so as to stop it.

This was Juan's sound plan when he, like many others, applied for a censor's job—not because he had a calling or needed a job: no, he applied simply to intercept his own letter, a consoling albeit unoriginal idea. He was hired immediately, for each day more and more censors were needed and no one would bother to check on his references.

Ulterior motives couldn't be overlooked by the _Censorship Division_, but they needn't be too strict with those who applied. They knew how hard it would be for the poor guys to find the letter they wanted and even if they did, what's a letter or two when the new censor would snap up so many others? That's how Juan managed to join the _Post Office's Censorship Division_, with a certain goal in mind.

The building had a festive air on the outside that contrasted with its inner <u>staidness</u>. Little by little, Juan was absorbed by his job, and he felt at peace since he was doing everything he could to get his letter for Mariana. He didn't even worry when, in his first month, he was sent to _Section K_ where envelopes are very carefully screened for explosives.

It's true that on the third day, a fellow worker had his right hand blown off by a letter, but the division chief claimed it was sheer negligence on the victim's part. Juan and the other employees were allowed to go back to their work, though feeling less secure. After work, one of them tried to organize a strike to demand higher wages for unhealthy work, but Juan didn't join in; after thinking it over, he reported the man to his superiors and thus got promoted.

You don't form a habit by doing something once, he told himself as he left his boss's office. And when he was transferred to _Section F_, where letters are carefully checked for poison dust, he felt he had climbed a rung in the ladder.

By working hard, he quickly reached _Section E_ where the job became more interesting, for he could now read and analyze the letters' contents. Here he could even hope to get hold of his letter, which, judging by the time that had elapsed, had gone through the other sections and was probably floating around in this one.

Soon his work became so absorbing that his noble mission blurred in his mind. Day after day he crossed out whole paragraphs in red ink, pitilessly chucking many letters into the censored basket. These were horrible days when he was shocked by the subtle and conniving ways employed by people to pass on subversive messages; his instincts were so sharp that he found behind a simple "the weather's unsettled" or "prices continue to soar" the wavering hand of someone secretly scheming to overthrow the Government.

His zeal brought him swift promotion. We don't know if this made

ulterior (ul tir′ ē ər) _adj._ undisclosed; beyond what is openly stated

staidness (stād′ nəs) _n._ state of being settled or resistant to change

Literary Analysis
Theme What theme do Juan's promotions illustrate?

⑮ 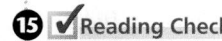**Reading Check**
What are Juan's responsibilities in _Section E_?

The Censors ◆ 643

CUSTOMIZE INSTRUCTION FOR UNIVERSAL ACCESS

For English Learners	For Gifted/Talented Students	For Advanced Readers
Encourage students to create a chart that follows Juan's progress within the organization. In the first column students can write his department and duties, and in the second they can record how his attitude changes with each promotion.	Ask students to imagine that they are Mariana, living in Paris, and have them write a letter to Juan explaining their reasons for leaving Argentina. Then, have students exchange their letters with a partner and act as a censor to the other's writing.	Have students use the Internet to locate information on groups whose purpose is to fight censorship. Have them create a chart showing their findings on at least two groups.

Review and Assess

1. Some students may think that it was a good idea, even if it went awry; others may think that a scheme based on deception was bound to fail.

2. **(a)** Juan worries that Mariana is endangered because of the letter he sent. **(b)** Juan seems prone to become obsessed with whatever is on his mind.

3. **(a)** Juan applies for the job so that he can protect himself and Mariana from persecution. **(b)** Juan's obsessiveness makes him a good censor.

4. **(a)** Because of his zealousness Juan receives many promotions. **(b)** Juan becomes so obsessed that he sees evil intent in the most innocent messages. He gets more and more absorbed in his job.

5. **(a)** Juan is executed as a traitor because in his zeal, he has censored his own letter. **(b)** Some students may feel that Juan deserves to die because of all the people he has turned in. Others may feel that Juan's overzealousness proves that he is insane and so does not deserve to die.

6. Most students will probably feel that Valenzuela's wry humor effectively sets off the gravity of the subject matter.

7. Some students may feel that Juan's tendency to be narrow-minded and obsessive makes his transformation believable.

---

him happy. Very few letters reached him in *Section B*—only a handful passed the other hurdles—so he read them over and over again, passed them under a magnifying glass, searched for microprint with an electronic microscope, and tuned his sense of smell so that he was beat by the time he made it home. He'd barely manage to warm up his soup, eat some fruit, and fall into bed, satisfied with having done his duty. Only his darling mother worried, but she couldn't get him back on the right track. She'd say, though it wasn't always true: Lola called, she's at the bar with the girls, they miss you, they're waiting for you. Or else she'd leave a bottle of red wine on the table. But Juan wouldn't overdo it: any distraction could make him lose his edge, and the perfect censor had to be alert, keen, attentive, and sharp to nab cheats. He had a truly patriotic task, both self-denying and uplifting.

His basket for censored letters became the best fed as well as the most cunning basket in the whole *Censorship Division*. He was about to congratulate himself for having finally discovered his true mission, when his letter to Mariana reached his hands. Naturally, he censored it without regret. And just as naturally, he couldn't stop them from executing him the following morning, another victim of his devotion to his work.

Review and Assess

Thinking About the Selection

1. **Respond:** Do you think it was a good idea for Juan to become a censor? Why or why not?

2. **(a) Recall:** What worries does Juan have after he mails the letter? **(b) Analyze:** What do you know about Juan's personality based on the nature of his worrying?

3. **(a) Recall:** Why does Juan apply for the job in the censor's office? **(b) Analyze:** What character traits make Juan a good censor?

4. **(a) Recall:** How does Juan's career as a censor progress? **(b) Draw Conclusions:** How and why does Juan's attitude about censorship change?

5. **(a) Recall:** What happens to Juan at the end of "The Censors"? **(b) Make a Judgment:** Do you think that Juan deserves what happens to him? Explain why or why not.

6. **Evaluate:** Is Valenzuela's use of humor an effective way to get across a serious message? Explain.

7. **Make a Judgment:** The writer implies that Juan's obsession with his job is so strong that it blocks his ability to reason enough to save his own life. Do you think such a turn of events is realistic? Why or why not?

Luisa Valenzuela

(b. 1938)

Born in Buenos Aires, the capital of Argentina, Luisa Valenzuela has lived around the world in places as diverse as New York City and Tepotzlán, Mexico, a little village with cobblestone streets where people still speak the ancient Aztec language.

Valenzuela travels to extremes in some of her work as well. She changes spellings, creates new words, and uses many puns.

Like many other Latin American writers, Valenzuela focuses on political issues. Having lived through a repressive regime herself, she is a strong defender of human rights. "The Censors" shows one aspect of the repression she has experienced.

✎ ASSESSMENT PRACTICE: Reading Comprehension

Distinguish Between Fact and Nonfact   **(For more practice, see Test Preparation Workbook, p. 40.)**

Many tests require students to distinguish between facts and nonfacts in a variety of texts. Use this sample test item.

Valenzuela has lived in New York City and Mexico. Because she was married to a French sailor she lived for a time in Normandy and Paris. Valenzuela travels to extremes in some of her work as well. She changes spellings, creates new words, and uses many puns.

Which of the following is an OPINION expressed in the passage?

A As a writer, Valenzuela travels to extremes.

B She changes spellings.

C She creates new words.

D She has lived in a number of cities.

All responses are supported by the passage. However, *B*, *C*, and *D* can be proven. *A* is the only opinion expressed in the passage; it is the correct answer.

Review and Assess

Literary Analysis

Theme

1. (a) What **theme** is illustrated by "The Princess and All the Kingdom"? (b) How might this message apply to the leadership of any country? (c) Explain how the message could apply to you and your friends.

2. State the theme of "The Censors" in your own words.

3. Juan sets out to beat a system that he feels is unjust. However, in the end, he becomes one of the most aggressive censors. Describe another situation in which someone might become part of the problem that he or she had hoped to solve.

Comparing Literary Works

4. What features of a fairy tale make it an effective form for communicating a theme?

5. How might "The Censors" change if it were written in a fairy-tale format?

6. Comparing your responses to each selection, in which story is the theme presented most successfully? Explain.

Reading Strategy

Challenging the Writer's Message

7. Using a chart like the one shown here, provide several details to **challenge the writer's message** in each selection.

Writer's Message	
Evidence in Support	Evidence Against

Your Opinion

8. Did you find the changes in Juan's attitude believable? Explain.

Extend Understanding

9. **History Connection:** If you could send "The Princess and All the Kingdom" to one ruler, to whom would you send it? Why?

Quick Review

A **theme** is the message or general idea about life that the writer hopes to convey.

To **challenge the writer's message,** determine the writer's message and decide for yourself whether it is valid.

 Take It to the Net

www.phschool.com

Take the interactive self-test online to check your understanding of these selections.

Answers for p. 645

Review and Assess

1. **(a)** The theme is that with happiness goes responsibility. **(b)** A military victory might force the conquering nation to protect and rule the vanquished. **(c)** For example, students who win elections must run their organizations; students with jobs must carry out their responsibilities.

2. The theme of "The Censors" is that power corrupts.

3. Sample response: In attempting to avenge a wrong, people might take the law into their own hands.

4. The simplicity of the plot and the uncomplicated nature of its characters make the fairy tale an effective vehicle for conveying a theme.

5. If it were written in a fairy tale format, "The Censors" would be less grave and sinister.

6. Some students may feel that the simple plot and uncomplicated characters in "The Princess and All the Kingdom" helped it express its theme more clearly. Others may feel that the sardonic humor and the realistic setting make "The Censors" a more effective story.

7. Possible responses:

Writer's Message: With happiness comes responsibility.	
Evidence in Support	**Evidence Against**
Most people have to balance happiness and responsibility.	Some people, such as lottery winners, are able to avoid responsibilities.
Your opinion: I agree with the writer.	

Writer's Message: Power corrupts.	
Evidence in Support	**Evidence Against**
Many powerful people become bullies.	Many people seek positions of power to help others.
Your opinion: I agree with the writer.	

8. Some students may feel that Juan is too exaggerated a character to be believable; others may feel that power can effect extreme changes in a person.

continued

Answers continued

9. Students should support their answers with historical facts. Encourage them to refer to their history textbooks, or to do research in the school library.

---

❶ Vocabulary Development

Word Analysis

1. e	**4.** c
2. d	**5.** a
3. b	

Concept Development: Synonyms

1. d	**4.** b
2. c	**5.** e
3. a	

Spelling Strategy

1. allotment   **2.** critically

❷ Grammar

Practice

1. When the prince saw how beautiful she was, he <u>fought</u> for her.
2. The prince was pleased when all the kingdom <u>bowed</u> down before him.
3. The princess saw that he was brave, and she <u>was</u> happy to marry him.
4. The chancellor confronted the prince and <u>told</u> him that the kingdom <u>was</u> now his.
5. Juan <u>opened</u> the letter and censored it without regret.

Writing Application

Possible response: Juan was so absorbed in his work that he did not eat proper meals.

Integrate Language Skills

❶ Vocabulary Development Lesson

Word Analysis: Latin Root *-ultra-*

Many English words contain the root *-ultra-*, which means "further" or "beyond." Variations of *-ultra-* are *-ulte-*, as in *ulterior*, meaning "beyond what is stated," and *-ulti-*, as in *ultimately*, meaning "at the furthest point," or "finally." On your paper, match each word with its correct definition.

1. ultrasensitive	a. extremely new
2. ultrasound	b. final offer or demand
3. ultimatum	c. finally
4. ultimately	d. high-speed waves used in medicine
5. ultramodern	e. having extreme feelings

Concept Development: Synonyms

On your paper, match each word with its closest synonym.

1. ardent	a. filthy
2. venerable	b. hidden
3. sordid	c. revered
4. ulterior	d. zealous
5. staidness	e. stuffiness

Spelling Strategy

When adding a suffix that begins with a consonant to a word that ends in a consonant, do not change either one. For example, *staid* + *-ness* = *staidness*. Add the suffixes to the base words below to spell the word correctly.

1. allot + *-ment*   2. critical + *-ly*

❷ Grammar Lesson

Consistency of Verb Tenses

In sentences containing more than one verb, the time sequence of **verb tenses** must be logical. In a story set in the past, for example, all verbs are in the past tense. Things that happened before are expressed in the past perfect.

> **Unnecessary Shift:** The prince *loved* the princess and *is fighting* to win her.
>
> **Correct Shift:** The princess *was impressed* that he *had dared* his life to win her. (he *had dared* before she *was impressed*)

Practice Rewrite the following sentences to keep tenses consistent.

1. When the prince saw how beautiful she was, he fights for her.
2. The prince was pleased when all the kingdom bows down before him.
3. The princess saw that he was brave, and she will be happy to marry him.
4. The chancellor confronted the prince and tells him that the kingdom is now his.
5. Juan opens the letter and censored it without regret.

Writing Application Rewrite the example below to include a second clause. Make sure the tense of the verb in the second clause is consistent with that in the first.

Juan was so absorbed in his work that

WG Prentice Hall Writing and Grammar Connection: Chapter 11, Section 4

646 ◆ *Short Stories*

646

Writing Lesson

Persuasive Essay on Censorship

Luisa Valenzuela's story addresses an issue so controversial that people in your own family, your school, and your community might disagree with one another over it. In a persuasive essay, identify and defend your own ideas about the topic.

Prewriting Talk with classmates, and take notes about opinions on both sides of the issue. Review your notes, and decide which side you most support.

Drafting In your introduction, explain the events of "The Censors." Then, state your own position. As you draft your body paragraphs, support your ideas with specific examples.

Revising To add strength to your persuasive essay, find a place in your writing to address the opposition. Return to your prewriting notes to find one argument for the opposing viewpoint. Address the idea briefly in your draft, and show how your ideas outweigh it.

> **Some would argue that information should be free in a free society, but**

Model: Addressing the Critics

 In a library where young children have access to computers and the Internet, the library acts appropriately as a parent, screening material that is not suitable for these patrons.

> By acknowledging the opposition, the writer strengthens the essay.

Prentice Hall Writing and Grammar Connection: Chapter 7, Section 4

Extension Activities

Listening and Speaking As the prince who has just become a king, give your first **royal speech** to your subjects.

- Plan your remarks, choosing a suitable topic for the occasion.
- Consider how your facial expressions and gestures will be viewed by your audience.

After a few rehearsals, present your speech to classmates.

Research and Technology The activity that goes on in "The Censors" violates the civil rights of people. Use the Internet to locate information on groups whose purpose is the advancement of human rights. Prepare an **annotated list** that shows your findings on at least four groups.

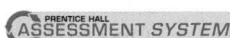 ***Take It to the Net*** www.phschool.com

Go online for an additional research activity using the Internet.

The Princess and All the Kingdom / The Censors ◆ 647

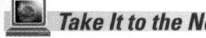
---

❸ Writing Lesson

- Lead students in a discussion about what censorship means. Encourage volunteers to explain any experiences they've had with censorship, and to express how they feel about the issue.
- Tell students that they are going to write a persuasive essay in which they will try to convince the reader to agree with their stand on the issue of censorship.
- Then, use the writing lesson to guide students in developing their persuasive essays.
- Use the rubric for Persuasive Composition, p. 11 in **Performance Assessment and Portfolio Management,** to assess students' essays.

❹ Listening and Speaking

- Have students consider the purpose of their speech as prince— for example, to make your subjects accept you as their new ruler, to persuade them to do something, or to explain something such as a war you are about to wage.
- Have students make a list of details and evidence that will support the purpose of their speech.
- After they have written and rehearsed their speeches, have students present them to the class.

CUSTOMIZE INSTRUCTION
For Universal Access

To address different learning styles, use the activities suggested in the **Extension Activities,** p. 40.

- For Verbal/Linguistic Learners, use Activity 5.
- For Visual/Spatial Learners, use Activity 6.
- For Intrapersonal and Verbal/Linguistic Learners, use Activity 7.

Lesson Objectives

1. To learn the elements of a short story

2. To use writing strategies to generate ideas, plan, organize, evaluate, and revise the narrative

3. To learn how to use dialogue to reveal character

Model From Literature

In the short story "The Open Window," Saki creates an engaging plot with a surprise ending.

Prewriting

- Remind students that the key to a good short story is conflict. As they are thinking of a topic to write about, students should consider the conflict their main characters will be involved in—what they must struggle against and overcome by the end of the story.

- Tell students that as they gather details about the characters, they should create a profile of each one that includes information about the following: the character's age, appearance, marked physical characteristics (such as a limp), distinctive phrases he or she uses, the kind of relationships he or she has with others, and the character's opinion of him- or herself. Encourage students to think of other aspects of characters they would want to know about, and write their ideas on the chalkboard.

- Explain to students that the more details they can provide about the setting of their short stories, the more real and engaging the stories will be for readers. Remind them that a character's conflict can be with an aspect of the setting.

Writing WORKSHOP

Narration: Short Story

A **short story** is a brief fictional narrative. Meant to be read in one sitting, it aims to create a powerful impression on the reader. In this workshop, you will write a short story that captures the imagination and interest of your readers.

Assignment Criteria Your short story should have the following characteristics:

- Main character who undergoes a change or learns something
- Setting—the time and location of the story
- Plot, or series of events, that leads to a climax
- Theme that is revealed by the story's end
- Effective descriptions using sensory details

To preview the criteria on which your short story may be assessed, see the Rubric on page 651.

Prewriting

Choose a topic. Sometimes topics for short stories come quickly to writers. When that does not happen, writers must use various strategies to find ideas. If you are struggling for an idea, try **sketching a character or a setting**. Use your imagination to make a drawing of a character or a setting. Then, review your sketch, and jot down story ideas that stem from it.

Gather details about characters. Characters are the people, animals, alien life-forms, or other creatures that take part in the action of a narrative. Before you begin drafting, get to know the characters you will develop. Examine each one to learn who he, she, or it is. Decide your characters' likes and dislikes, dreams and fears, and what others think of them.

Explore the setting. Plan your setting. Close your eyes, and imagine the place and time as if you were walking through it. Then, jot down notes describing it. Use sensory details to bring this setting to life for your readers.

Gathering Details About a Character

Character	Scarlett
Appearance	Pretty young woma
Actions	Goes to rallies
What the Character Says	
Thoughts	Wants suffrage
What Others Think of the Character	Some call her "Little Lady"

Example

There was a dull rumble in the distance, and a flicker of light illuminated the city around her. The cool breeze rustled her long skirt. . . .

648 ◆ *Short Stories*

TEACHING RESOURCES

The following resources can be used to enrich or extend the instruction for pp. 648–651.

𝒲𝒢 **Writing and Grammar,** Platinum Level, Chapter 5, pp. 76–93

Performance Assessment and Portfolio Management, p. 14

Writing Models and Graphic Organizers on Transparencies, pp. 83–86

Writing and Grammar iText CD-ROM
Students can use the following tools as they complete their short stories:

- Story Map
- Character Trait Word Bin
- Sentence Length Checker

Student Model

Before you begin drafting, read this student model and review the characteristics of an intriguing short story.

Aubrey Weatherford
Broken Arrow, Oklahoma

And Then the Rain Came

"Is it wrong for us to have a voice in our lives? We have to fight!" said the woman speaking to the crowd. Scarlett flashed instantly to the night of the fire. She could feel the young man holding her back; she could hear the child screaming in the burning building. She struggled to free herself, tears running down her face. Shaking herself back into reality, Scarlett walked slowly away from the park, the speaker's words fading as she went. There was a dull rumble in the distance, and a flicker of light illuminated the city around her. The cool breeze rustled her long skirt, and she began to quicken her pace for fear of being caught in the storm. Scarlett's mind was spinning, the speaker's words stirring her thoughts. The thought of speaking her opinion and of being able to choose whomever she wanted for public office, though she had never learned exactly what their jobs were. Just the thought of having the choice was enough to excite her.

> Aubrey introduces the main character in the first paragraph.

> Sensory details describe the setting.

"Little Lady, you had better hurry on home now. There's a gonna be quite a storm a comin'." An old, wrinkled man had approached Scarlett from the shadows, seemingly trying to help. She was looking at him patiently.

"Hey you, crazy man, leave the lady alone. You go on home now, you worthless old fool!" A middle-aged businessman had approached the two.

"Don't talk to him that way! He wasn't bothering me!" Scarlett said.

"You don't need to associate with street people like him. Go on home!"

"You have no right to speak to me in that fashion, good sir. I may associate with whomever I choose."

> The writer develops the conflict through dialogue.

The businessman turned on his heel and left.

"Thank yer for standing up for me little lady. Mighty appreciative."

"It was nothing. You remind me so much of, oh, never mind," Scarlett replied.

"I am sure I will walk by here again sometime. I will look for you. Good day, sir." Though Scarlett did not see it, the old man began to come out of the shadows as she made her way down the crowded street, though his appearance had greatly changed. He was no longer a wrinkled, old man but a tall, young man with sandy hair and piercing eyes. Carefully, he watched as Scarlett hurried along the sidewalk. Tiny drops of rain began to fall from the ashen sky as Scarlett disappeared into the crowd. . . .

> The writer reveals an interesting twist in the plot.

 Take It to the Net

www.phschool.com

Go online to read the rest of this story.

Student Model

- Explain that the Student Model is a sample, and that short stories may be longer.
- Ask students to identify the main character and where she is introduced in the story.
  Answer: The main character is Scarlett, and she is introduced in the first paragraph.
- Point out that Aubrey uses sensory details to describe the setting.
- Ask students: What is Scarlett's conflict? Is there more than one?
  Answer: Students should point out Scarlett's internal conflict—her struggle with the memory of the fire—and the external conflict with the businessman in the street.
- Point out that Aubrey adds a twist in the plot that further engages the reader in her story.

Real-World Connection

Explain to students that short stories can be found in many media. Many magazines and journals publish short stories, and most sitcoms and dramas on television are, in effect, dramatized short stories.

CUSTOMIZE INSTRUCTION FOR UNIVERSAL ACCESS

For Less Proficient Writers	For English Learners	For Advanced Writers
If students are having difficulty thinking of a plot, encourage them to write about an incident in their own lives. Make sure they write in the third person. Encourage them to enhance their story with fictional details and exaggeration.	Have these students form a clear picture of each character in their story, jotting down adjectives and comparisons to characters in movies and literature that help describe the character. Then, have them consult with peers and use dictionaries and thesauruses to generate a list of words they will use in their stories to describe each character.	Suggest that students plan out their short stories, beginning with a dramatic opening incident and building to a high point or climax. Encourage them to draft without too much concern for grammatical or other errors. Once students have completed a draft, they can make any revisions needed.

Drafting

- Explain to students that their short stories should have a clearly patterned plot. Students will have an easier time drafting their essays once they identify this pattern and the events that make it up.

- Encourage students to choose moments in each event that can be developed using sensory details. Tell students that using sensory details helps the reader picture what is being described in the narrative.

- Make sure students identify places in their short stories that will benefit from dialogue and interior monologues. Explain to students that using these elements will help readers better understand their characters' experiences and create a more engaging story.

Revising

- Before students start to revise their work, have them write down the overall mood they wish to communicate to the reader. As they read through their drafts, students should keep this mood in mind to help them determine how the words and images they have chosen work to develop and support this overall mood.

- Review the model with students. Have students describe the mood of Aubrey's story.

(continued on page 651)

Writing WORKSHOP *continued*

Drafting

Make a plot diagram. As you draft your story, keep your central conflict in mind and shape your story around it. An effective plot has the following components:

- **Exposition** Characters, setting, and the central conflict—the struggle between characters or between a character and another force—are introduced.
- **Rising Action** Tension builds as the conflict develops.
- **Climax** The story reaches the point of highest interest.
- **Falling Action** Immediately following the climax, these events lead to the resolution.
- **Resolution** The central conflict ends and an insight or a change is revealed.

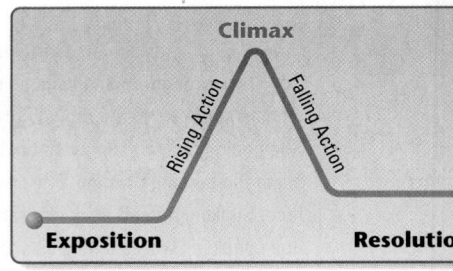

Elaborate, but keep pacing in mind. To keep your story moving, introduce the problem as soon as you can. Then, add events and details that intensify the problem. Once you know how your story will play out, elaborate in the rising action to intensify the conflict that leads to the climax.

Revising

Add dialogue to reveal the characters. Look for places that you can develop characters through dialogue and action. This revision will bring your story to life for readers. Reread your paragraphs, highlighting events, attitudes, or emotions that you have simply described. In these instances, consider letting the characters speak for themselves.

> **Model: Adding Dialogue**
>
> An old, wrinkled man had approached Scarlett from the shadows, seemingly trying to help. She was looking at him patiently ~~when she heard another voice call out.~~
>
> "Hey you, crazy man, leave the lady alone! You go on home now, you worthless old fool!" A middle-aged man had approached the two.
>
> "Don't talk to him that way! He wasn't bothering me!" Scarlett said.

Dialogue brings the scene and the characters to life.

USING TECHNOLOGY IN WRITING

If students are using word processors to draft and revise their short stories, suggest that they free write about each character and event in a separate document. They can then cut and paste effective descriptions or dialogue from these documents into their final drafts.

Students can also use the organizing tools and revision checkers available on the **Writing and Grammar iText CD-ROM**.

Revise your sentences. One way to engage your audience is to write in the active voice, which is livelier and more direct than the passive voice. In the active voice, the subject of the sentence performs the action. In the passive voice, the action is done to the subject.

> **Passive Voice:** He had been deserted by his friends during the night.
> **Active Voice:** His friends deserted him during the night.

Compare the model and nonmodel. Why is the model livelier and more direct?

Nonmodel	Model
She was being held back by the young man; she could hear the child screaming in the burning building.	She could feel the young man holding her back; she could hear the child screaming in the burning building.

Publishing and Presenting

Choose one of the following ways to share your writing with class-mates or a wider audience.

Give a dramatic reading. Practice reading your story aloud, experimenting with pace, emphasis, and tone. Then, read your story to a group of classmates.

Compile an anthology. Join with your classmates in collecting all your stories into an anthology. Organize them by theme, and place the collection in your school or class library.

W̶G *Prentice Hall Writing and Grammar Connection: Chapter 5*

Rubric for Self-Assessment

Evaluate your short story using the following criteria and rating scale:

Criteria	Rating Scale				
	Not very				Very
Does the main character undergo a change or learning experience?	1	2	3	4	5
How well is the setting described?	1	2	3	4	5
Are there clear plot events that lead to a climax?	1	2	3	4	5
How clearly is the theme revealed?	1	2	3	4	5
How effective is the descriptive language?	1	2	3	4	5

• The rubric on this page, and another rubric in an alternative format, can be found on pp. 14 and 54 of **Performance Assessment and Portfolio Management.**

Revising (continued)

• Tell students that using an active voice in the narrative of their short stories will be more engaging for readers.

• Write on the chalkboard:
She was grabbed by the shoulders and pulled out of sight by the man. He told her to be quiet.

The man grabbed her by the shoulders, pulling her out of sight. "Be quiet!" he urgently whispered.

Ask students to describe the difference between the two sentences.
Answer: Students should see that the second sentence is more engaging and tells the reader more about the situation and the characters. They should see that adding dialogue and using active voice makes writing more lively and interesting.

• Ask students to compare the Model and Nonmodel and respond to the question in their text: Why is the Model more interesting than the Nonmodel?
Answer: In the Model, events are described as the woman experiences them; the reader can identify with her feelings more easily than in the Nonmodel.

Publishing and Presenting

• Have students consider whether they would rather read their stories aloud or see them published in a class anthology. Have them think about whether one needs to read a story to really understand it or whether hearing it read aloud with expression would better convey its message.

• Before students present their stories to the class, encourage them to practice reading them aloud. Have students make any notes that might help them orally present their stories.

Assessment

• Review with students the assessment criteria.

• Have students choose three criteria from rubric and score the Student Model. Make sure students support their scores with details from the model. Then, have them score their own stories using the same criteria.

Lesson Objectives

1. To learn to listen effectively
2. To learn how to focus one's attention on the speaker and what he or she is saying
3. To learn methods for interpreting and analyzing what the speaker says

Focus Your Attention

- Have students make a list of things they find distracting when they are trying to listen. Encourage them to try to ignore the distractions as much as possible and to concentrate on the speaker.
- Tell them that when they notice they have become distracted, to consciously bring their attention back to the speaker. As they become more aware of distractions, they will become better at refocusing and listening.

Interpret the Information

- Review with students the bulleted elements. Discuss which students feel are more important and which they feel they can accomplish during the Activity.
- Have students complete the Activity. After they have chosen presentations to attend or listen to, discuss the subjects of the presentations with them. Have them identify a suitable purpose for listening. Encourage them to list questions to which they hope to learn the answer.

Listening and Speaking WORKSHOP

Effective Listening

There is more to listening than hearing what is said. **Effective listening** means preparing to listen and taking an active part in understanding what you hear. This workshop will help you hone your listening skills.

Focus Your Attention

You are probably aware that listening means more than hearing sounds. Like all communication, listening is interactive. It requires participation on the part of the listener. The most important step in listening is to focus your attention on the speaker and his or her words.

Recognize and counteract barriers. Work to ignore all people, objects, noises, and thoughts that can distract you from listening.

Set a purpose for listening. Decide what you want to gain from the listening experience. You can increase your interest in the subject by acquiring information about it and by finding a connection between the subject and your life.

Interpret the Information

When you listen to a speaker and interpret his or her message successfully, you identify and understand the key information that the speaker presents. Consider these suggestions to guide you:

- Listen for words and phrases that are emphasized and repeated.
- Visualize important statements, and test your understanding by rephrasing them in your own words.
- Take notes to summarize main ideas and support.
- Watch for nonverbal signals—tone of voice, gestures, and facial expressions—that may alert you to important ideas.
- Link the information to your prior knowledge, comparing what you hear with your own experiences.

When a presentation has concluded, respond to the information. Identify which elements of the presentation you found most useful, and decide whether you agree or disagree with the message. If possible, ask questions to clarify your understanding.

Activity: Analyzing a Speech

Choose a presentation given in school, on television, or elsewhere. Make appropriate plans for listening and taking notes. Use the Feedback Form to focus your listening. Share your conclusions in a class discussion.

Feedback Form for Effective Listening

Preparation
Set a purpose: _____
Identify three barriers that may prevent effective listening: _____

Interpretation
Main idea: _____
Identify three supports for the main idea: _____
_____
Link to your experience: _____

Response
Answer these questions:
1. Do you agree or disagree with the speaker's ideas? Why?
2. What was the most useful or interesting part of the presentation?

652 ◆ Short Stories

CUSTOMIZE INSTRUCTION FOR UNIVERSAL ACCESS

For English Learners	For Less Proficient Readers
Students may feel overwhelmed with the task of listening to a presentation and understanding it completely. Supply them with a videotaped television broadcast. Allow students to watch the presentation a few times to make sure they comprehend the message. Then, analyze the presentation in a group.	Suggest that students focus on accomplishing one of the bulleted items. If students are able to focus their attention closely during the Activity, they may surprise themselves by being able to accomplish more than they thought they could. Then, have them focus on another one of the bulleted strategies while viewing another presentation.

Assessment WORKSHOP

Forms of Propaganda

In the reading sections of some tests, you may be required to read a passage to recognize forms of propaganda. Use the following to help you answer test questions on this skill:

- Propaganda is information that may or may not be factual but is written to persuade the public that it is. Propaganda writers often use scare tactics or emotional appeals to communicate a specific position.
- As you read, determine what the writer's motives may be and whether or not the information is factual or misleading.

Test-Taking Strategies

- Use your prior knowledge to conclude whether the information in the text is accurate.
- Scan the answer choices to see which ones do not relate to the information in the passage.

Sample Test Item

Directions: Read the passage, and answer the question that follows.

The mayor blames our factory for polluting the river. His new program will force us to report our strategies for preventing industrial emissions from contaminating the air and water. If we do not comply, our company will face steep fines. The result? Workers will be laid off. The city cannot afford to take this risk! We should all protest the mayor's plan.

1 The writer tries to persuade readers by

  A working to reduce pollution.

  B presenting the mayor's plan in a positive way.

  C drawing the conclusion that jobs will be cut.

  D exposing other businesses that are polluters.

Answer and Explanation

The correct answer is **C** because the writer suggests that jobs will be lost. The writer does not speak of personal plans, so **A** is incorrect. **B** is incorrect because the writer does not praise the mayor's plan. **D** is incorrect because the writer mentions no other businesses.

▶ Practice

Directions: Read the passage, and answer the questions that follow.

We are all aware of our schools' budget deficits. Yet the majority of taxpayers do not support a tax increase to help fund the schools. Many school programs have been eliminated or cut back over the last two years. I ask you to think about what our students' future will be if we do not help them today. A tax increase is the only answer. Please give our students hope for the future.

1 You can tell from the passage that the speaker

  A is not telling the whole truth.

  B is trying only to discredit an opponent.

  C hopes to persuade the audience to take action.

  D wants to convince the audience to vote.

2 Which statement reflects the writer's opinion?

  A There is a budget deficit.

  B School programs have been cut.

  C A tax increase is the only answer.

  D The school board vote is essential.

Lesson Objective

To recognize forms of propaganda in passages on a test

Applying Reading Strategies

Tell students that they should draw conclusions about a writer's message and motives in order to identify propaganda. Students can use details in the text and the writer's tone to help them identify the writer's purpose. They can then draw conclusions from these details: Does the writer want to scare me or get me angry about something? Is the writer being misleading?

Applying Test-Taking Strategies

- Have students read the Sample Test Item. Ask them to describe the writer's tone.
  Answer: The writer's tone is urgent.
- Ask students to identify what the writer is trying to persuade them to do.
  Answer: The writer is trying to persuade readers to oppose the mayor's plan.
- Next, have them examine the writer's argument. Is it logical?
  Answer: The argument is not logical. The writer does not show that reporting strategies will cost jobs—the reader must wonder why the company does not simply report its strategies. The writer also fails to explain why the fines will force layoffs.

Answer

1. The correct answer is **C.** The writer hopes to persuade readers to support a tax increase to support the school budget. Answer A is incorrect because there is no evidence that the writer is concealing part of the truth. Answer B is incorrect because the writer makes a strong argument in favor of the position expressed, and does not discredit the only opponent mentioned—the majority of taxpayers. Answer D is incorrect because the writer makes no statements about voting.

continued

TEACHING RESOURCES

The following resources can be used to enrich or extend the instruction for p. 653.

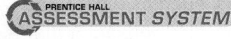
PRENTICE HALL
ASSESSMENT *SYSTEM*

📖 **Workbook**   📄 **Transparencies**

📖 **Skill Book**   💿 **CD-ROM**

Answers continued

2. The correct answer is **C.** The writer argues that a tax increase is the only solution to school budget problems. Answers A and B are incorrect because they identify facts set out in the passage, not opinions. Answer D is incorrect because the passage does not mention the vote.

Unit Objectives

1. To read a variety of types of nonfiction

2. To apply a variety of reading strategies appropriate for reading nonfiction

3. To analyze literary elements

4. To use a variety of strategies to build vocabulary

5. To learn elements of grammar and usage

6. To use recursive writing processes to write in a variety of forms

7. To develop listening and speaking skills

8. To express and support responses to various works of nonfiction

9. To prepare, organize, and present literary presentations

Meeting the Objectives

With each selection, you will find instructional materials through which students can meet these objectives. Further, you will find additional practice pages for reading strategies, literary analysis, vocabulary, and grammar in the **Selection Support: Skills Development Workbook** in your Teaching Resources.

Background

Art

The Last Painter on Earth, 1983, by James Doolin

Point out to students that if the painter is the "last painter on earth," as the title suggests, then there is no one else to paint his portrait. He can only paint what he sees of himself in the world—in this case, his shadow (lower left). Have students discuss other ways in which we "see" ourselves in the world around us—in the effects that we have on other people or in the clothing that reflects our tastes. Help them link these themes to the genre featured in the unit, nonfiction, by asking this question:

> In what ways can a person learn more about him- or herself by observing the world?
> Possible responses: By writing on nature, a person can learn more about how we fit into the world. By writing about events, a person can contrast his or her life with the lives of others.

654

UNIT 7 Nonfiction

The Last Painter on Earth, 1983, James Doolin, Koplin Gallery, Los Angeles, California

654 ◆ Nonfiction

UNIT FEATURES

Connections	Reading Informational Materials

Every unit contains a feature that connects literature to a related topic, such as art, science, or history. In this unit, the article on Mary Cassatt on pp. 730–731 discusses the artist's life, style, and the media in which she worked.
 	
   Use the information and questions on the Connections page to enrich students' understanding of the selections presented within the unit.
	These selections will help students learn to analyze and evaluate informational texts, such as workplace documents, technical directions, and consumer materials. They will expose students to the organization and features unique to nonnarrative texts.
	
	   In this unit, students will learn how to read and interpret an advertising brochure.

Exploring the Genre

Nonfiction introduces you to a wide variety of real people and places—some that are familiar to you and some that are far from your experiences. Through the essays, biographies, and articles in this unit, you can enjoy new experiences, consider new ideas, and learn new concepts.

Nonfiction encompasses many categories of writing, including the following, which you will encounter in this unit:

- A **biography** is the story of someone's life written by another person.

- An **autobiography** is the writer's own life story.

- An **essay** is a short work about a particular subject. Essays can be further categorized as *reflective, persuasive,* and *descriptive.* Another type is a *visual essay,* which combines text with images to convey its point.

- A **critical review** is a type of persuasive essay in which a writer shares his or her opinion on a book, a play, or a movie and attempts to persuade the reader.

- A **technical article** is writing that explains procedures, provides instructions, or presents specialized information.

▲ **Critical Viewing** What nonfiction topics does this painting suggest? **[Connect]**

Exploring the Genre ◆ 655

ASSESSMENT RESOURCES

- 📖 **Selection Support: Skills Development Workbook**
- 📖 **Formal Assessment**
- 📖 **Open Book Tests**
- 📖 **Performance Assessment and Portfolio Management**
- 📖 **Extension Activities**

Why Read Literature?

The "Why Read Literature?" page in each unit presents a list of possible purposes for reading. Each purpose for reading is connected to one or more of the selections in the unit. Good readers set a purpose before reading in order to help them read actively and focus on meaningful details.

Unit 7 introduces three purposes for reading. "Read for the Love of Literature" encourages students to appreciate the ways in which literature preserves and expresses values, such as holiday spirit or the right to speak the truth.

"Read for Information" suggests that reading can provide valuable information. "Read to Be Inspired" suggests that students can learn important life lessons from reading.

How to Use This Page

- Tell students that before reading each selection in this unit, they should set a purpose for reading. This will help them read in an active and focused manner.

- Explain that seeing writers celebrate what they cherish most—whether it is Dylan Thomas celebrating childhood memories or Alexander Solzhenitsyn affirming the right to speak the truth—will help increase their love for literature.

- A second purpose for reading is to obtain information. Explain that when setting a purpose, students should specify the type of information they want to learn. For example, when reading "Imitating Nature's Mineral Artistry," they might want to learn how people make artificial gems.

- To be inspired, students must see what elements of another person's life have meaning for their own life. In "Marian Anderson: Famous Concert Singer," for example, they will learn how an African American woman overcame racial prejudice to become an internationally known singer. In "Keep Memory Alive," they will learn the importance of acknowledging past suffering.

656

Why Read Literature?

You read nonfiction for a variety of purposes—from the practical to the academic to the inspirational. Your purpose varies depending on the context or style of the selection. Preview these three purposes you might set before reading the works in this unit.

1 Read for the Love of Literature

The holiday season is filled with falling snow, countless presents, and the promise of lasting memories. See how they all combine to make this time of year a magical one for children in Dylan Thomas's **"A Child's Christmas in Wales,"** page 694.

Although he was exiled from the country that had tried to silence his opinion, Russian writer Alexander Solzhenitsyn won the Nobel Prize for Literature—and the right to speak the truth. Read his thoughts on literature's role on the world stage in the excerpt from **"Nobel Lecture,"** page 683.

The Aunts, (detail and tint), Fritz Eichenberg etching,
© Fritz Eichenberg Trust/Licensed by VAGA, New York, NY

3 Read to Be Inspired

Despite the injustices she experienced throughout her life, the gifted Marian Anderson used her exceptional singing voice to bring people together. Discover how this African American artist became an international success in **"Marian Anderson: Famous Concert Singer,"** by Langston Hughes, page 702.

Silence can be deadly, especially when it represses those who have been through trauma. Discover why Holocaust survivor Elie Wiesel reminds people that victims of suffering and humiliation need to be heard, in **"Keep Memory Alive,"** page 687.

2 Read for Information

Diamonds, rubies, and sapphires are considered valuable because they are so rare. However, scientists are learning to make artificial gemstones. To investigate the process of making gems in a lab, read Paul O'Neil's **"Imitating Nature's Mineral Artistry,"** page 748.

 Take It to the Net

Visit the Web site for online instruction and activities related to each selection in this unit.
www.phschool.com

656 ◆ *Nonfiction*

✺ ENRICHMENT: Further Reading

Have students choose one or more of the works below to extend their experience with the unit genre, nonfiction, or to read more by the unit authors.

The Sea Around Us by Rachel Carson
Apart from *Silent Spring,* no other work of Carson's so fully displays the wonder of nature, and the connection between nature and writing that was so crucial to her life.

The Names: A Memoir by N. Scott Momaday
The author explores his personal and tribal past in this account of a Kiowa boyhood.

The Big Sea and I Wonder As I Wander by Langston Hughes

In two volumes of autobiography, Langston Hughes shows the reader how one of the most distinctive African American writers of the twentieth century developed his style and found his roots during the Harlem Renaissance.

How to Read Literature

Use Strategies for Reading Nonfiction

Most of what you read is probably nonfiction—textbooks, newspaper and magazine articles, information on the Internet. Reading nonfiction can open doors to new worlds, introduce you to interesting people, and help you look at ideas in new ways. Because nonfiction deals with information and ideas, you will benefit from these strategies that help you analyze it:

1. Analyze the author's purpose.

An author's purpose is the reason that he or she is writing. It may be to inform, to appreciate, or to entertain. Knowing this purpose will help you understand why the writer includes the information that he or she does.

2. Recognize facts and impressions.

- A fact is information that can be tested and proved. Facts can be supported by statistics, explanations, or evidence.

- In contrast, an impression is a feeling or an image retained from an experience. Impressions convey opinions and may be written in language that reflects this subjective quality.

As you read the passage at right, notice that details highlighted in blue are facts and that details in yellow are impressions.

> **Facts vs. Impressions**
>
> Some little children have discovered a snapping turtle as *big as a tray*. It's hard to believe that this creek could support a predator that size: its shell is a foot and a half across, and its head extends a good seven inches beyond the shell. —"Flood"

3. Identify evidence.

- Take note of the way the writer supports the points he or she makes. The author's reasoning should be believable and lead you to understand these points.

- Evidence that supports the writer's opinion comes in many forms. It may be in the form of facts, statistics, observations, examples, and quotations from experts. If you find the support unsatisfactory, you may not accept the writer's ideas.

4. Interpret pictures.

- Images frequently accompany nonfiction text. Interpret these pictures by "reading" their elements.

- Connect images, charts, and maps to the text to determine how they help you understand the meaning.

As you read the nonfiction in this unit, apply these skills to best appreciate the literature.

How to Read Literature

The "How to Read Literature" page in each unit presents a set of strategies to help readers understand authors' words and ideas. Each reading strategy is taught in conjunction with one or more of the selections within the unit. Good readers develop a bank of strategies from which they can draw as needed.

Unit 7 introduces four strategies for constructing meaning. Students will learn to analyze an author's purpose, to recognize and distinguish facts and impressions, to identify evidence for a point, and to interpret pictures.

How to Use This Page

Introduce the strategies for constructing meaning, presenting each as a tool for developing understanding when reading the selections in this unit.

- As they read "from *The Way to Rainy Mountain*" (p. 676), "from *Nobel Lecture*" (p. 683), and "Keep Memory Alive" (p. 687), students will determine the author's purpose, the reason the writer has for writing.

- As they read "Flood" (p. 712), students will learn to distinguish facts from impressions and to see how both can enrich a writer's work.

- As they read "Star Wars—A Trip to a Far Galaxy That's Fun and Funny . . ." (p. 734) and "Star Wars: Breakthrough Film Still Has the Force" (p. 737), students will see how writers present evidence to support a persuasive point.

- As they read *Mothers & Daughters* (p. 724), they will learn to interpret the important visual information that pictures can add to a written work.

MODEL A READING STRATEGY: Analyze the Author's Purpose

Tell students that when they read nonfiction they can determine the author's purpose by seeing what information is important to the author. Model the process by reading aloud the following phrases from the first page of *"from The Way to Rainy Mountain"*: "I returned to Rainy Mountain in July, My grandmother had died in the spring, and I wanted to be at her grave." "I like to think of her as a child. When she was born, the Kiowas were living the last great moment of their history." "Her name was Aho, and she belonged to the last culture to evolve in North America."

Tell students:

From these phrases and the other material at the beginning of Momaday's selection, you can determine that the author's purpose is to tell readers about his grandmother and also about his Native American culture. In these sentences, he emphasizes that his grandmother was important to him and that she is strongly linked for him with the proud tradition of the Kiowas. These concerns indicate his purpose.

The Marginal World

Lesson Objectives

1. **To analyze and respond to literary elements**
   - Literary Analysis: Expository Essay
   - Connecting Literary Elements: Descriptive Writing

2. **To read, comprehend, analyze, and critique an essay**
   - Reading Strategy: Recognizing Patterns of Organization
   - Reading Check questions
   - Review and Assess questions
   - Assessment Practice (ATE)

3. **To develop word analysis skills, fluency, and systematic vocabulary**
   - Vocabulary Development Lesson: Latin Suffix: -able

4. **To understand and apply written and oral language conventions**
   - Spelling Strategy
   - Grammar Lesson: Recognizing Degrees of Comparison

5. **To understand and apply appropriate writing and research strategies**
   - Writing Lesson: Proposal for a Nature Documentary
   - Extension Activity: Scientific Report

6. **To understand and apply listening and speaking strategies**
   - Extension Activity: Multimedia Presentation

STEP-BY-STEP TEACHING GUIDE	PACING GUIDE
PRETEACH	
Motivate Students and Provide Background	
Use the Motivation activity (ATE p. 658)	5 min.
Read and discuss the Preview material and Background information (SE/ATE p. 658) A	5 min.
Introduce the Concepts	
Introduce the Literary Analysis and Reading Strategy (SE/ATE p. 659) A	15 min.
Pronounce the vocabulary words and read their definitions (SE p. 659)	5 min.
TEACH	
Monitor Comprehension	
Informally monitor comprehension by circulating while students read independently or in groups A	15 min.
Monitor students' comprehension with the Reading Check notes (SE/ATE pp. 661, 663, 665)	as students read
Develop vocabulary with Vocabulary notes (SE pp. 661, 662, 664, 665, 666; ATE p. 661)	as students read
Develop Understanding	
Develop students' understanding of expository essays with Literary Analysis annotations (SE pp. 662, 663; ATE pp. 662, 663) A	10 min.
Develop students' understanding of patterns of organization with Reading Strategy annotations (SE p. 661; ATE pp. 661, 664, 665)	10 min.
ASSESS	
Assess Mastery	
Assess students' mastery of the Reading Strategy and Literary Analysis by having them answer the Review and Assess questions (SE/ATE p. 667)	20 min.
Use one or more of the print and media Assessment Resources (ATE p. 669) A	up to 50 min.
EXTEND	
Apply Understanding	
Have students complete the Vocabulary Development Lesson and the Grammar Lesson (SE p. 668) A	20 min.
Apply students' knowledge of using transitions to show comparison with the Writing Lesson (SE/ATE p. 669) A	45 min.
Apply students' understanding using one or more of the Extension Activities (SE p. 669)	20–90 min.

 ACCELERATED INSTRUCTION:
Use the strategies and activities identified with an A.

UNIVERSAL ACCESS
● = Below Level Students
▲ = On-Level Students
■ = Above Level Students

Time and Resource Manager

RESOURCES		
PRINT 📖	**TRANSPARENCIES**	**TECHNOLOGY** 💿 🎧 📼
• **Beyond Literature**, Cross-Curricular Connection: Science, p. 41 ▲ ■		• **Interest Grabber Video**, Tape 4 ● ▲ ■
• **Selection Support Workbook:** ● ▲ ■ Literary Analysis, p. 164 Reading Strategy, p. 163 Build Vocabulary, p. 161	• **Literary Analysis and Reading Transparencies**, pp. 81 and 82 ● ▲ ■	
		• **Listening to Literature** ● ▲ ■ Audiocassettes, Side 20 Audio CDs, CD 13
• **Literatura en español** ● ▲ • **Literary Analysis for Enrichment** ■	• **Fine Art Transparencies, Volume 1,** Art Transparency 2 ● ▲ ■	
• **Formal Assessment:** Selection Test, pp. 145–147 ● ▲ ■ • **Open Book Test**, pp. 121–123 ● ▲ ■ • **Performance Assessment and Portfolio Management**, p. 19 ● ▲ ■ • **PRENTICE HALL ASSESSMENT** *SYSTEM* ● ▲ ■	• **PRENTICE HALL ASSESSMENT** *SYSTEM* ● ▲ ■ Skills Practice Answers and Explanations on Transparencies	• **Test Bank Software** ● ▲ ■ • **Got It! Assessment Videotapes**, Tape 4 ● ▲
• **Selection Support Workbook:** ● ▲ ■ Build Grammar Skills, p. 162 • **Writing and Grammar**, Platinum Level ● ▲ ■ • **Extension Activities**, p. 41 ● ▲ ■	• **Daily Language Practice Transparencies** ● ▲	• **Writing and Grammar iText CD-ROM** ● ▲ ■ 🖥️ *Take It to the Net* www.phschool.com

BLOCK SCHEDULING: Use one 90-minute class period to preteach the selection and have students read it. Use a second 90-minute class period to assess students' mastery of skills and have them complete one of the Extension Activities.

Motivation

Have students look at the palms of their hands. To make the point that life exists on both visible and microscopic levels, show them a picture of skin cells from a science book or magazine. Suggest that looking at living things at a microscopic level can reveal whole new worlds. Rachel Carson uses this close focus to observe what happens in the place she calls "the marginal world"—that ever-changing sliver of space between land and sea. Where we might simply see a strip of sand, her close focus allows us to see that this limited space teems with animal and plant life.

▥ Interest Grabber Video

As an alternative, play "Tide Pools" on Tape 4 to engage student interest.

❶ Background

Science

Many organisms thrive in the "marginal world" because they have adapted to this unique environment. Some animals burrow in the sand, others live in tidal pools or crevices of rocks, and still others live within the protected world of a shell.

The survival of these organisms is crucial to the survival of other sea-dwelling creatures—and even to human survival. These tiny microorganisms are the beginning of a food chain that acts as a lifeline for countless species.

Prepare to Read

The Marginal World

 Take It to the Net

Visit www.phschool.com for interactive activities and instruction related to "The Marginal World," including

- background
- graphic organizers
- literary elements
- reading strategies

Preview

Connecting to the Literature

When you think of a place that has special meaning for you, you might remember a rocky shore that reminds you of vacations or the local park where you spend hours with your friends. For Rachel Carson, author of "The Marginal World," the edge of the sea is a special place of beauty and wonder.

❶ Background

In "The Marginal World," Carson describes the ocean's intertidal zone, or the zone between the high and low tide marks. Animals and organisms that live in this area must adapt to exposure to air and sun, changes in temperature, rain that dilutes salt water, evaporation that increases the salt level, and wave action. Despite these changing conditions, many organisms thrive there.

TEACHING RESOURCES

The following resources can be used to enrich or extend the instruction for pp. 658–659.

Motivation

▥ **Interest Grabber Video**, Tape 4 ▥

Background

📖 **Beyond Literature**, p. 41

 Take It to the Net
Visit www.phschool.com for background and hotlinks for "The Marginal World."

Literary Analysis

📕 **Literary Analysis and Reading Transparencies,** Expository Essay, p. 82 ▥

Reading

📖 **Selection Support Workbook:** Reading Strategy, p. 163; Build Vocabulary, p. 161

📕 **Literary Analysis and Reading Transparencies,** Recognizing Patterns of Organization, p. 81

▦ **BLOCK SCHEDULING:** Resources marked with this symbol provide varied instruction during 90-minute blocks.

Literary Analysis

Expository Essay

An **expository essay** is nonfiction writing that informs by explaining, defining, or interpreting an idea. In "The Marginal World," Carson uses several expository strategies for writing, including

- Presenting examples to illustrate her points
- Classifying the different types of life she discusses
- Explaining the cause-and-effect relationships affecting the survival of organisms

Connecting Literary Elements

Expository essays often include passages of **descriptive writing**—writing that presents a portrait in words of a person, place, or object. For example, Carson describes a hydroid as a plantlike creature "delicate as a wind flower." Notice how the descriptive writing in this essay helps you experience the ocean habitat through details that appeal to your senses.

Reading Strategy

Recognizing Patterns of Organization

One of the keys to understanding expository essays is recognizing how the material is organized. Writers can use a variety of patterns of organization, including

- **Chronological:** explaining events in the order that they occurred
- **Cause-and-effect:** showing the relationships between events
- **Comparison and contrast:** explaining similarities and differences

Carson organizes her observations by focusing on different places at different times of the day. Use a chart like the one here to jot down details about each time and place.

Time and Place
Observations

Vocabulary Development

mutable (myōōt´ ə bəl) *adj.* capable of change (p. 661)

ephemeral (e fem´ ər əl) *adj.* short-lived (p. 662)

primeval (prī mē´vəl) *adj.* ancient or primitive (p. 664)

essence (es´ əns) *n.* real nature of something (p. 664)

marginal (mär´ jə nəl) *adj.* at, on, or close to a border (p. 665)

subjectively (səb jek´ tiv lē) *adv.* personally (p. 666)

manifestations (man´ ə fes tā´ shənz) *n.* appearances or evidence (p. 666)

cosmic (käz´ mik) *adj.* relating to the universe (p. 666)

**Step-by-Step Teaching Guide
for pp. 660–666**

CUSTOMIZE INSTRUCTION
For Musical/ Rhythmic Learners

Carson's descriptions of the sea often call to mind aspects of music: *rush of water, surge of surf, pressure of incoming tides.* Suggest that students find descriptions in the selection that remind them of music. In a small group, they can compare and contrast the sounds of the sea to music. They might also want to create their own musical descriptions of the sea.

❶ About the Selection

Although Carson imparts a great deal of scientific knowledge about tidal zones in her essay, the main focus is philosophical. In language that is more often poetic than scientific, Carson describes the sights, sounds, and feelings that contribute to her appreciation of this delicate and changeable region.

By presenting three different sections of the "marginal world" at three different times of day, Carson leads readers to recognize the beauty and interdependence of all life forms.

❷ ▶ Critical Viewing

Possible responses: Students may speculate that the types of life that exist in the picture include sea plants, mussels, sea urchins, small fish, sea snails, and sea anemones.

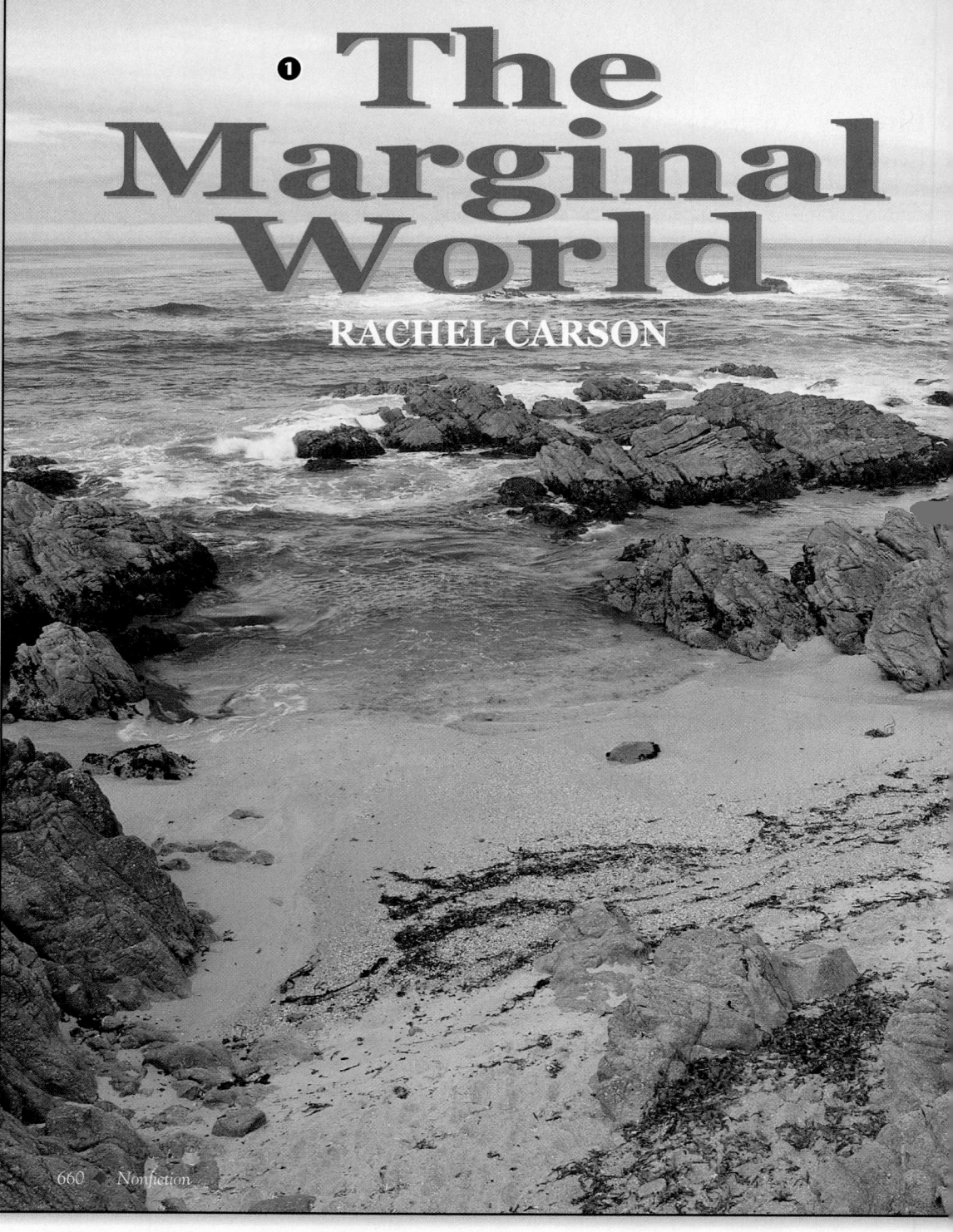

❶ The Marginal World
RACHEL CARSON

660 *Nonfiction*

TEACHING RESOURCES

The following resources can be used to enrich or extend the instruction for pp. 660–666.

Literary Analysis

📖 **Selection Support Workbook:** Literary Analysis, p. 164

Reading

🎧 **Listening to Literature Audiocassettes,** Side 20 ■

💿 **Listening to Literature Audio CDs,** CD 13 ■

Extension

📄 **Fine Art Transparencies, Volume 1,** Art Transparency 2 (Have students compare and contrast how the essay and the painting depict the relationship between man and the natural world.)

■ **BLOCK SCHEDULING:** Resources marked with this symbol provide varied instruction during 90-minute blocks.

The edge of the sea is a strange and beautiful place. All through the long history of Earth it has been an area of unrest where waves have broken heavily against the land, where the tides have pressed forward over the continents, receded, and then returned. For no two successive days is the shoreline precisely the same. Not only do the tides advance and retreat in their eternal rhythms, but the level of the sea itself is never at rest. It rises or falls as the glaciers melt or grow, as the floor of the deep ocean basins shifts under its increasing load of sediments, or as the earth's crust along the continental margins warps up or down in adjustment to strain and tension. Today a little more land may belong to the sea, tomorrow a little less. Always the edge of the sea remains an elusive and indefinable boundary.

The shore has a dual nature, changing with the swing of the tides, belonging now to the land, now to the sea. On the ebb tide it knows the harsh extremes of the land world, being exposed to heat and cold, to wind, to rain and drying sun. On the flood tide it is a water world, returning briefly to the relative stability of the open sea.

Only the most hardy and adaptable can survive in a region so mutable, yet the area between the tide lines is crowded with plants and animals. In this difficult world of the shore, life displays its enormous toughness and vitality by occupying almost every conceivable niche. Visibly, it carpets the intertidal rocks; or half hidden, it descends into fissures and crevices, or hides under boulders, or lurks in the wet gloom of sea caves. Invisibly, where the casual observer would say there is no life, it lies deep in the sand, in burrows and tubes and passageways. It tunnels into solid rock and bores into peat and clay. It encrusts weeds or drifting spars[1] or the hard, chitinous[2] shell of a lobster. It exists minutely, as the film of bacteria that spreads over a rock surface or a wharf piling; as spheres of protozoa, small as pinpricks, sparkling at the surface of the sea; and as Lilliputian[3] beings swimming through dark pools that lie between the grains of sand.

The shore is an ancient world, for as long as there has been an earth and sea there has been this place of the meeting of land and water. Yet it is a world that keeps alive the sense of continuing creation and of the relentless drive of life. Each time that I enter it, I gain some new awareness of its beauty and its deeper meanings,

---

1. **spars** (spärs) *n.* masts, booms, or other supports for sails.
2. **chitinous** (kī′ tin əs) *adj.* of a material that forms the tough outer covering of insects, crustaceans, and so on.
3. **Lilliputian** (lil′ ə pyōō′ shən) *adj.* tiny and thus like the tiny people who inhabit Lilliput in the book *Gulliver's Travels* by Jonathan Swift.

2 ◀ **Critical Viewing** What life do you think exists in the area pictured here? **[Speculate]**

Reading Strategy
Recognizing Patterns of Organization What does Carson compare in this paragraph about the tides?

mutable (myōōt′ ə bəl) *adj.* capable of change

5 ✓**Reading Check**
What is the marginal world?

The Marginal World ◆ 661

---

❸ Reading Strategy
Recognizing Patterns of Organization

- Read aloud the first sentence of this passage. Draw students' attention to the phrase *dual nature.*
- Explain that something with a dual nature has two different ways of being.
- Then, ask students the Reading Strategy question on p. 661: What does Carson compare in this paragraph about the tides?
  Possible responses: Carson compares the shore during the ebb tide and during the flood tide.

❹ Vocabulary Development
Latin Suffix: -able

- Read aloud the sentence that contains the word *mutable.* Have a student read the definition of *mutable* provided on p. 661.
- Point out that the Latin root -*mut*- means "change," and that the Latin suffix -*able* means "that can or will be." Explain that, therefore, a *mutable* region is one that "can or is able to change." Ask students why *mutable* is an appropriate word to describe the edge of the sea.
  Answer: At the edge of the sea, the crashing waves and changing tides ensure that nothing stays the same for very long.

❺ ✓Reading Check
Answer: The marginal world is the edge of the sea.

CUSTOMIZE INSTRUCTION FOR UNIVERSAL ACCESS

For Special Needs Students	For Gifted/ Talented Students
Have students view "Tide Pools" on Tape 4 of the **Interest Grabber Video** to get a visual introduction to the selection. Then, have them listen to Side 20 of **Listening to Literature** Audiocassettes as they read the essay. Pause the tape periodically to check comprehension and to discuss difficult passages.	Invite students to work together to create a classification chart of the animal and plant life in "The Marginal World." (For example, the phylum *Mollusca* includes the species lobster and ghost crab.) Invite students to display their chart for classmates.

Expository Essay

- Remind students of the strategies an author can use when developing an expository essay.

- Have students read the bracketed passage, and draw their attention to the phrase "exquisite beauty." Ask the students the Literary Analysis question on p. 662: What method does Carson use to develop the idea that this is a place of "exquisite beauty"?
Possible response: Carson uses examples to illustrate the idea that this is a place of great beauty.

▶ **Monitor Progress** Ask students to identify how this paragraph would be different if Carson had developed this idea by comparing and contrasting the pool with another place. What place might she have chosen, and why?

---

sensing that intricate fabric of life by which one creature is linked with another, and each with its surroundings.

In my thoughts of the shore, one place stands apart for its revelation of exquisite beauty. It is a pool hidden within a cave that one can visit only rarely and briefly when the lowest of the year's low tides fall below it, and perhaps from that very fact it acquires some of its special beauty. Choosing such a tide, I hoped for a glimpse of the pool. The ebb was to fall early in the morning. I knew that if the wind held from the northwest and no interfering swell ran in from a distant storm the level of the sea should drop below the entrance to the pool. **6** There had been sudden ominous showers in the night, with rain like handfuls of gravel flung on the roof. When I looked out into the early morning the sky was full of a gray dawn light but the sun had not yet risen. Water and air were pallid. Across the bay the moon was a luminous disc in the western sky, suspended above the dim line of distant shore—the full August moon, drawing the tide to the low, low levels of the threshold of the alien sea world. As I watched, a gull flew by, above the spruces. Its breast was rosy with the light of the unrisen sun. The day was, after all, to be fair.

Later, as I stood above the tide near the entrance to the pool, the promise of that rosy light was sustained. From the base of the steep wall of rock on which I stood, a moss-covered ledge jutted seaward into deep water. In the surge at the rim of the ledge the dark fronds of oarweeds swayed, smooth and gleaming as leather. The projecting ledge was the path to the small hidden cave and its pool. Occasionally a swell, stronger than the rest, rolled smoothly over the rim and broke in foam against the cliff. But the intervals between such swells were long enough to admit me to the ledge and long enough for a glimpse of that fairy pool, so seldom and so briefly exposed.

And so I knelt on the wet carpet of sea moss and looked back into the dark cavern that held the pool in a shallow basin. The floor of the cave was only a few inches below the roof, and a mirror had been created in which all that grew on the ceiling was reflected in the still water below.

Under water that was clear as glass the pool was carpeted with green sponge. Gray patches of sea squirts[4] glistened on the ceiling and colonies of soft coral[5] were a pale apricot color. In the moment when I looked into the cave a little elfin starfish hung down, suspended by the merest thread, perhaps by only a single tube foot. It reached down to touch its own reflection, so perfectly delineated that there might have been, not one starfish, but two. The beauty of the reflected images and of the limpid[6] pool itself was the poignant[7] beauty of things that are ephemeral, existing only until the sea should return to fill the little cave.

---

4. **sea squirts** *n.* sac-shaped water animals with tough outer coverings.
5. **coral** (kôr´ əl) *n.* animals with tentacles at the top of tubelike bodies.
6. **limpid** (lim´ pid) *adj.* clear.
7. **poignant** (poin´ yənt) *adj.* emotionally moving.

Literary Analysis
Expository Essay What method does Carson use to develop the idea that this is a place of "exquisite beauty"?

ephemeral (e fem´ ər əl) *adj.* short-lived

✳ ENRICHMENT: Career Connection

Oceanographer

The study of the sea, oceanography, is broken into four spheres of study:

- Geological oceanographers study the rocks and minerals of the sea floor.

- Biological oceanographers study marine life.

- Chemical oceanographers study sea water's chemical makeup and the effect of those chemicals on the ocean environment.

- Physical oceanographers study currents, tides, and the movement of water.

Have students suggest aspects of the marginal world described by Carson that might interest each type of oceanographer. For example, a physical oceanographer might be interested in measuring the difference between ebb and flood tides.

7 ◀ **Critical Viewing**
What details of this underwater photo might most interest Carson? Why? **[Connect]**

Whenever I go down into this magical zone of the low water of the spring tides, I look for the most delicately beautiful of all the shore's inhabitants—flowers that are not plant but animal, blooming on the threshold of the deeper sea. In that fairy cave I was not disappointed. Hanging from its roof were the pendent[8] flowers of the hydroid Tubularia, pale pink, fringed and delicate as the wind flower. Here were creatures so exquisitely fashioned that they seemed unreal, their beauty too fragile to exist in a world of crushing force. Yet every detail was functionally useful, every stalk and hydranth[9] and petallike tentacle fashioned for dealing with the realities of existence. I knew that they were merely waiting, in that moment of the tide's ebbing, for the return of the sea. Then in the rush of water, in the surge of surf and the pressure of the incoming tide, the delicate flower heads would stir with life. They would sway on their slender stalks, and their long tentacles would sweep the returning water, finding in it all that they needed for life.

And so in that enchanted place on the threshold of the sea the realities that possessed my mind were far from those of the land world I had left an hour before. In a different way the same sense of remoteness and of a world apart came to me in a twilight hour on a great beach on the coast of Georgia. I had come down after sunset and walked far out over sands that lay wet and gleaming, to the very edge of the retreating sea. Looking back across that immense flat, crossed by winding, waterfilled gullies and here and there holding shallow pools left by the tide, I was filled with awareness that this intertidal area, although abandoned briefly and rhythmically by the sea, is always reclaimed by the rising tide. There at the edge of low water the beach with its reminders of the land seemed far away. The only sounds were those of the wind and the sea and the birds. There was one sound of wind moving over water, and another of water sliding

Literary Analysis
Expository Essay and Descriptive Writing
What point does Carson make in comparing a hydroid to a wind flower?

9 ✓ **Reading Check**
When is the narrator able to get a look at the pool hidden within a cave?

---

8. **pendent** (pen′ dənt) *adj.* hanging.
9. **hydranth** (hī′ dranth′) *n.* feeding structure.

7 ▶ **Critical Viewing**
Possible response: Students' responses will vary. Make sure they support their answers with examples from Carson's essay.

8 **Literary Analysis**

Expository Essay and Descriptive Writing

• Have a volunteer read aloud the bracketed section. Ask students to list the details that Carson uses when describing the hydroid Tubularia.
  Answers: It hangs from the roof; it is pale pink, fringed, and delicate; all of its delicate parts are useful and necessary for staying alive.

• Then, ask students the Literary Analysis question on p. 663: What point does Carson make in comparing a hydroid to a wind flower?
  Possible response: Just as a wind flower is a delicate form of life that has adapted to survive in a windy environment, the delicate hydroid has adapted to survive in the tossing and turning tides.

9 ✓ **Reading Check**

Answer: The narrator can get a look into the pool when the lowest of the year's tides fall below the cave in which it is located.

Science

Sea birds are some of the more visible forms of life at the shoreline, in contrast to some of the smaller—even microscopic—forms of life found there. Yet all forms of life, both large and small, are part of a chain. The tiny links in the chain, such as the microorganisms, support the larger forms of life by providing sources of food. Each form of life at the shoreline is specially adapted yet dependent on others to maintain its place in the chain of life.

11 Reading Strategy

Recognizing Patterns of Organization

- Ask students to identify what time of day Carson describes, and how the time of day affects what she sees.
  Answer: Carson describes the shore at night. The darkness and silence makes the scene more elemental.

- Then, explain that this passage fits into Carson's strategy of organizing her essay chronologically—she describes different places at different times.

---

over the sand and tumbling down the faces of its own wave forms. The flats were astir with birds, and the voice of the willet* rang insistently. One of them stood at the edge of the water and gave its loud, urgent cry; an answer came from far up the beach and the two birds flew to join each other.

The flats took on a mysterious quality as dusk approached and the last evening light was reflected from the scattered pools and creeks. Then birds became only dark shadows, with no color discernible. Sanderlings* scurried across the beach like little ghosts, and here and there the darker forms of the willets stood out. Often I could come very close to them before they would start up in alarm—the sanderlings running, the willets flying up, crying. Black skimmers* flew along the ocean's edge silhouetted against the dull, metallic gleam, or they went flitting above the sand like large, dimly seen moths. Sometimes they "skimmed" the winding creeks of tidal water, where little spreading surface ripples marked the presence of small fish.

11 The shore at night is a different world, in which the very darkness that hides the distractions of daylight brings into sharper focus the elemental realities. Once, exploring the night beach, I surprised a small ghost crab in the searching beam of my torch. He was lying in a pit he had dug just above the surf, as though watching the sea and waiting. The blackness of the night possessed water, air, and beach. It was the darkness of an older world, before Man. There was no sound but the all-enveloping, <u>primeval</u> sounds of wind blowing over water and sand, and of waves crashing on the beach. There was no other visible life—just one small crab near the sea. I have seen hundreds of ghost crabs in other settings, but suddenly I was filled with the odd sensation that for the first time I knew the creature in its own world—that I understood, as never before, the <u>essence</u> of its being. In that moment time was suspended; the world to which I belonged did not exist and I might have been an onlooker from outer space. The little crab alone with the sea became a symbol that stood for life itself—for the delicate, destructible, yet incredibly vital force that somehow holds its place amid the harsh realities of the inorganic world.

The sense of creation comes with memories of a southern coast, where the sea and the mangroves,[10] working together, are building a wilderness of thousands of small islands off the southwestern coast of Florida, separated from each other by a

---

10. **mangroves** (maŋ´ grōvz) *n.* tropical trees that grow in swampy ground with spreading branches that send down roots and thus form more trunks.

◆ Sea Birds

Rachel Carson mentions three of the many sea birds that inhabit our shores.

- The *willet* is a shorebird, about 16 inches long, with a long bill. The bird's name comes from its loud call. Willets inhabit both coasts. They breed around ponds in places from southwestern Canada to Colorado, as far south as Mexico, and on the east coast from Nova Scotia to Florida, south to the West Indies.

- *Sanderlings*, a type of sandpiper, can be found worldwide. During the summer, they breed near the North Pole. In winter, they can be found on nearly every sandy beach.

- *Skimmers* live mainly in warm areas. They have an unusual bladelike bill that skims the surface of the water and scoops up small fish and crustaceans.

These birds play an important role in the intertidal zone.

A Sanderling

---

primeval (prī mē´ vəl) *adj.* ancient or primitive

essence (es´ əns) *n.* real nature of something

⊛ ENRICHMENT: Science Connection

Pesticides

Rachel Carson's book *Silent Spring* helped spark the environmental movement in this country. Through her work, the public learned about the way DDT and other pesticides can affect the broader environment. As a direct result, DDT was banned from general use in the United States by the early 1970s. DDT continues to be used in many nations, as are other pesticides that no longer are used in the United States.

tortuous[11] pattern of bays, lagoons, and narrow waterways, I remember a winter day when the sky was blue and drenched with sunlight; though there was no wind one was conscious of flowing air like cold clear crystal. I had landed on the surf-washed tip of one of those islands, and then worked my way around to the sheltered bay side. There I found the tide far out, exposing the broad mud flat of a cove bordered by the mangroves with their twisted branches, their glossy leaves, and their long prop roots reaching down, grasping and holding the mud, building the land out a little more, then again a little more.

The mud flats were strewn with the shells of that small, exquisitely colored mollusk,[12] the rose tellin, looking like scattered petals of pink roses. There must have been a colony nearby, living buried just under the surface of the mud. At first the only creature visible was a small heron in gray and rusty plumage—a reddish egret that waded across the flat with the stealthy, hesitant movements of its kind. But other land creatures had been there, for a line of fresh tracks wound in and out among the mangrove roots, marking the path of a raccoon feeding on the oysters that gripped the supporting roots with projections from their shells. Soon I found the tracks of a shore bird, probably a sanderling, and followed them a little; then they turned toward the water and were lost, for the tide had erased them and made them as though they had never been.

Looking out over the cove I felt a strong sense of the interchangeability of land and sea in this <u>marginal</u> world of the shore, and of the links between the life of the two. There was also an awareness of the past and of the continuing flow of time, obliterating much that had gone before, as the sea had that morning washed away the tracks of the bird.

The sequence and meaning of the drift of time were quietly summarized in the existence of hundreds of small snails—the mangrove periwinkles—browsing on the branches and roots of the trees. Once their ancestors had been sea dwellers, bound to the salt waters by every tie of their life processes. Little by little over the thousands and millions of years the ties had been broken, the snails had adjusted themselves to life out of water, and now today they were living many feet above the tide to which they only occasionally returned. And perhaps, who could say how many ages hence, there would be in their descendants not even this gesture of remembrance for the sea.

The spiral shells of other snails—these quite minute[13]—left winding tracks on the mud as they moved about in search of food. They were

---

11. **tortuous** (tôr´ choo əs) *adj.* full of twists and turns.
12. **mollusk** (mäl´ əsk) *n.* one of a large group of soft-bodied animals with shells, including clams and snails.
13. **minute** (mī noot´) *adj.* tiny.

⓬ ▲ **Critical Viewing**
What characteristics of the crab have helped it survive living in the intertidal zone? **[Analyze]**

marginal (mär´ jə nəl) *adj.* at, on, or close to a border

⓮ ✔ **Reading Check**
What do the sea and the mangroves build?

CUSTOMIZE INSTRUCTION FOR UNIVERSAL ACCESS

For English Learners

Students may have difficulty following the descriptions in this essay because they contain many specialized words that may be unfamiliar. They might find it helpful to look for the author's pattern of organization. On the chalkboard, draw a three-column chart. Use headings that indicate the three places she describes: the pool in the cave, the Georgia beach, and the Florida island. Have students suggest descriptive details to list under each heading.

Review and Assess

1. Students may name any aspect of nature—underwater life, stars and planets, woodland life. They should give reasons for their choices.

2. **(a)** Carson first visits a pool hidden in a cave in the early morning. **(b)** The pool can only be seen a few days each year, it is hard to reach, and it contains beautiful, tiny creatures both in the water and hanging from the roof of the cave.

3. **(a)** Carson visits the cave pool in early morning, a great beach in Georgia in the twilight, an island off the coast of Florida in the daytime. **(b)** They are all part of shore life, but the locales and life they support differ. The cave pool has sponges, sea squirts, coral, and starfish; the beach in Georgia has willets, sanderlings, and other birds; the island off the coast of Florida has various kinds of mollusk.

4. **(a)** The small snails represent the process of evolution. **(b)** Carson sees these snails continuing to change and adapt in the future, even as the rest of nature will change and adapt.

5. **(a)** Carson communicates the broader meaning that all in nature is related—to each other and to past and future times. **(b)** Possible responses: "Marine Life, Then and Now," "Changing Life on the Shore."

6. Students may say that the message still applies because plants and animals continue to adapt to both natural and manmade changes.

---

horn shells, and when I saw them I had a nostalgic moment when I wished I might see what Audubon[14] saw, a century and more ago. For such little horn shells were the food of the flamingo, once so numerous on this coast, and when I half closed my eyes I could almost imagine a flock of these magnificent flame birds feeding in that cove, filling it with their color. It was a mere yesterday in the life of the earth that they were there; in nature, time and space are relative matters, perhaps most truly perceived <u>subjectively</u> in occasional flashes of insight, sparked by such a magical hour and place.

There is a common thread that links these scenes and memories—the spectacle of life in all its varied <u>manifestations</u> as it has appeared, evolved, and sometimes died out. Underlying the beauty of the spectacle there is meaning and significance. It is the elusiveness of that meaning that haunts us, that sends us again and again into the natural world where the key to the riddle is hidden. It sends us back to the edge of the sea, where the drama of life played its first scene on earth and perhaps even its prelude; where the forces of evolution are at work today, as they have been since the appearance of what we know as life; and where the spectacle of living creatures faced by the <u>cosmic</u> realities of their world is crystal clear.

subjectively (səb jek´ tiv lē) *adv.* personally

manifestations (man´ ə fes tā´ shənz) *n.* appearances or evidence

cosmic (käz´ mik) *adj.* relating to the universe

17. **Audubon** (ôd´ ə bän´) John James Audubon (1785–1851), a famous ornithologist, naturalist, and painter famed for his paintings of North American birds.

Review and Assess

Thinking About the Selection

1. **Respond:** What aspects of nature intrigue you?

2. **(a) Recall:** What time and special place does Carson describe first? **(b) Infer:** Why does she seem to find this place especially mysterious and awe-inspiring?

3. **(a) Recall:** Summarize the three times, places, and experiences Carson describes. **(b) Compare and Contrast:** Compare the three different locations described. What are their similarities and differences?

4. **(a) Recall:** What do the small snails, the mangrove periwinkles, represent for Carson? **(b) Infer:** How does the future of these snails represent the future of all life on Earth?

5. **(a) Interpret:** What broader meaning about life does the "marginal world" that Carson describes help you to see? **(b) Connect:** Think of another title for this essay—one that states the meaning of the essay for you.

6. **Evaluate:** Rachel Carson wrote this essay more than thirty years ago. Does its message still apply? Why or why not?

Rachel Carson

(1907–1964)

Rachel Carson was successful in combining the two compelling interests of her life—nature and writing—into a career that spanned nearly a half century. Carson was a naturalist who specialized in marine biology, the study of sea life. In 1951, *The Sea Around Us* was published, winning a National Book Award.

Carson was also an environmental crusader. In *Silent Spring* (1962), she drew attention to the horrors and possible disasters resulting from the use of pesticides. Carson's work helped launch the modern environmental movement.

 ASSESSMENT PRACTICE: Reading Comprehension

Analyzing Literary Language (For more practice, see Test Preparation Workbook, p. 41.)

Some tests may require students to understand and analyze literary language. Provide students with the following sample question.

The shore has a dual nature, changing with the swing of the tides, belonging now to the land, now to the sea. On the ebb tide it knows the harsh extremes of the land world, being exposed to heat and cold, to wind, to rain and drying sun. On the flood tide it is a water world, returning

briefly to the relative stability of the open sea.

Which aspect of literary language best expresses the shore's dual nature?

A the repetition of phrases

B the descriptions of the harsh land

C the rhyming words within the sentences

D the descriptions of the water

Discuss repetition, description, and rhyme, and help students see that the correct answer is *A*.

Review and Assess

Literary Analysis

Expository Essay

1. Identify three reasons that Carson provides in her **expository essay** to explain why the level of the sea changes.
2. What differences does Carson identify between the shore at night and the shore in daylight?
3. Summarize the three main points that Carson makes about the "marginal world," and explain how she supports each point.

Connecting Literary Elements

4. List three **descriptive details** that Carson includes in the paragraph on page 663 that begins "And so in that enchanted place. . . ." Identify the sense to which each detail appeals.
5. List three "word portraits" from the essay that you find most vivid. Using a chart like the one here, cite the details that the author uses to create the portrait, and then identify the senses that are involved.

| Portrait | Detail: | Sense: |
| | Detail: | Sense: |

Reading Strategy

Recognizing Patterns of Organization

6. How does the pattern of comparison that Carson uses in the paragraph on page 661 that begins "The shore has a dual nature . . ." help you understand the point she is making?
7. What **pattern of organization** does Carson use on page 665 in the paragraph that begins "The mud flats were strewn . . ."?
8. Explain the overall organizational pattern of Carson's essay.

Extend Understanding

9. **Science Connection:** Rachel Carson wrote about the interconnectedness of life in the sea. What other places could help you experience the interconnectedness of life?

Quick Review

An **expository essay** is a short piece of nonfiction writing that informs by explaining, defining, or interpreting an idea, an event, or a process.

A **description** is a portrait in words of a person, a place, or an object.

A **pattern of organization** is the way in which writing is structured to best develop ideas.

 Take It to the Net
www.phschool.com

Take the interactive self-test online to check your understanding of the selection.

The Marginal World ◆ 667

ENRICHMENT: Further Reading

Other Works by Rachel Carson

The Edge of the Sea
Silent Spring

Take It to the Net
Visit www.phschool.com for more information on Rachel Carson.

Answers for p. 667

Review and Assess

1. The level of the sea changes as glaciers melt or grow, as the ocean floor shifts, and as the Earth's crust changes.

2. The daylight reveals different life forms and is filled with sounds of birds. The dark is quiet and so black that water, air, and beach seem to blend together.

3. Carson makes these points: (1) Life forms at the shore are enduring. Carson supports this with examples. (2) The shore is beautiful. Carson describes different locations at different times of day. (3) We can learn by studying the sea. Carson gives many examples of current and extinct species teaching us lessons about life.

4. Possible responses: "sands that lay wet and gleaming" appeals to the senses sight and touch; "The only sounds were those of the wind and the sea and the birds" appeals to the sense of sound; "one sound of wind moving over water, and another of water sliding over the sand" appeals to sense of sound.

5. Possible responses:
   Detail: "a little elfin starfish hung down . . . to touch its own reflection"
   Sense: Sight
   Detail: "the voice of the willet rang insistently"
   Sense: Sound
   Detail: "one was conscious of flowing air like cold clear crystal"
   Sense: Touch

6. Carson uses a back-and-forth pattern, like the ebb and flow of the tides.

7. Carson uses chronological organization.

8. Carson organizes her essay by describing different places at different times.

9. Students might suggest forests, canyons, fields, or mountains.

Answers for p. 668

❶ Vocabulary Development

Word Analysis

1. perishable—something that can die or be destroyed; c
2. comfortable—something that can provide a feeling of physical or mental well-being; b
3. believable—something that can be assumed to be true; a

Spelling Strategy

1. achievable   3. livable
2. achievement   4. lively

Concept Development: Synonym or Antonym?

1. S   5. A
2. S   6. A
3. S   7. S
4. A   8. A

❷ Grammar

1. darker   4. closer
2. stronger   5. smallest
3. cold

Writing Application

Possible answer: I saw two skunks scurry deep into the bushes. The second skunk was smaller than the first. The odor they left behind was the strongest I have ever encountered.

Integrate Language Skills

❶ Vocabulary Development Lesson

Word Analysis: Latin Suffix -able

Mutable combines the Latin root *-mut-*, meaning "change," with the Latin suffix *-able*, meaning "the ability to do, provide, or be something." Thus, a *mutable* region is one that has the ability to change. Define each of these words ending in *-able*. Then, match each word with the word most closely associated with it.

1. perishable   a. truth
2. comfortable   b. couch
3. believable   c. food

Spelling Strategy

To add a suffix beginning with a consonant to a word ending in a silent *e*, keep the *e*: *subjective + -ly = subjectively*. Add the suffix to each word:

1. achieve + *-able*   3. live + *-able*
2. achieve + *-ment*   4. live + *-ly*

❷ Grammar Lesson

Recognizing Degrees of Comparison

Most adjectives and adverbs have three different forms to modify and show **degrees of comparison**—the positive, the comparative, and the superlative.

> **Positive:** A ledge jutted seaward into *deep* water. (modifies one thing)
>
> **Comparative:** I gained some awareness of its *deeper* meanings. (compares two things)
>
> **Superlative:** Only the *most adaptable* can survive. (compares more than two things)

Concept Development: Synonym or Antonym?

A synonym is a word that is similar in meaning to another word. An antonym is a word opposite in meaning to another word. Study each of the following pairs of words. Write S on your paper if the words are synonyms and A if the words are antonyms.

1. essence, heart
2. manifestations, forms
3. marginal, borderline
4. mutable, solid
5. subjectively, disinterestedly
6. cosmic, earthly
7. ephemeral, short-lived
8. primeval, contemporary

Practice Complete the following sentences, inserting the correct word for the options presented.

1. The water is (dark, darker, darkest) than I had remembered it.
2. A swell (strong, stronger, strongest) than the last rolled smoothly over the rim.
3. I was conscious of flowing air like (cold, colder, coldest), clear crystal.
4. The birds allowed me to come (close, closer, closest) to them than I ever had.
5. The spiral shells of other snails were the (small, smaller, smallest) of all.

Writing Application Use modifiers in all three degrees of comparison to describe an animal you have seen.

W̶G Prentice Hall Writing and Grammar Connection: Chapter 25 Section 1

TEACHING RESOURCES

The following resources can be used to enrich or extend the instructions for pp. 660–666.

Vocabulary

📖 **Selection Support Workbook:** Build Vocabulary, p. 161

📖 **Vocabulary and Spelling Practice Book** (Use this booklet for skills enrichment.)

Grammar

📖 **Selection Support Workbook:** Build Grammar Skills, p. 162

W̶G **Writing and Grammar,** Platinum Level, p. 590

🖥 **Daily Language Practice Transparencies**

Writing

W̶G **Writing and Grammar,** Platinum Level, p. 108

💿 **Writing and Grammar iText CD-ROM** 🖥

🖥 **BLOCK SCHEDULING:** Resources marked with this symbol provide varied instruction during 90-minute blocks.

❸ Writing Lesson

Proposal for a Nature Documentary

The descriptive passages in "The Marginal World" lend themselves to spectacular documentary footage. Write a proposal for a documentary based on the essay in which you present a plan, summarize the content, and point out special features.

Prewriting   Review the selection to list all the elements you would capture on film, including scenery and sounds. Jot down comparisons that you would use to show the similarities or differences between two items.

Drafting   Use vivid descriptions to make your proposal appealing and to show how you would develop and support the main ideas. Include a summary of an exciting or beautiful scene you might include. Indicate similarities between scenes and ideas with transitional words, such as *like, likewise, in contrast, similarly,* and *in the same way.*

Model: Using Transitions to Show Comparisons

We could capture a small group of jellyfish moving slowly and gracefully through the water, their long tentacles trailing and swaying beneath, looking *like* a troop of ballerinas. Music could reinforce their grace.

> The word *like* compares the group of jellyfish to a troop of ballerinas.

Revising   Look over your proposal. Add transitions where necessary for clear comparisons.

W/G   *Prentice Hall Writing and Grammar Connection: Chapter 6, Section 3*

❹ Extension Activities

Listening and Speaking Use natural objects, photos, videos, and music to give a **multimedia presentation** about the beauty of the ocean to your class. Consider these suggestions:

- Identify the main idea you want to convey.
- Plan the timing and connections among items in your presention.
- Gather information and visual aids about your subject.

After your presentation, invite questions from classmates. [Group Activity]

Research and Technology Do research at the library, and then write a **scientific report** on an aspect of nature that you find interesting—a sunset, a blooming flower, a hawk's hunting habits. Be sure to include lively descriptions in your report. When you prepare your final draft, you may wish to include clip art from a computer program to illustrate your report.

🖥️ ***Take It to the Net***   www.phschool.com
Go online for an additional research activity using the Internet.

The Marginal World ◆ 669

Lesson Support for p. 669

❸ Writing Lesson

- Point out that students might want to envision a beautiful, wild, or exciting scene for their documentary proposals.

- If students have trouble getting started, have them try drawing the scene first to help them visualize the elements and action. Another strategy is to "storyboard" the scene by writing down and illustrating each element of the documentary and its accompanying action as the drama unfolds.

- Read aloud the model on p. 669 to help students see how comparisons, vivid descriptions, and transitional words help create a picture of the scene.

- Use the rubric for Description, p. 19 in **Performance Assessment and Portfolio Management,** to assess students' proposals.

❹ Listening and Speaking

- Show the students some natural objects and nature photos that could be examples of items to be used in a multimedia presentation. If possible, bring in some musical selections that would be appropriate as well.

- Divide students into small groups. Have them work as a team to brainstorm for their multimedia topic, gather visual and audio aids, and plan their presentation.

- Provide time for students not only to research and develop their project, but also to practice their presentation.

CUSTOMIZE INSTRUCTION for Universal Access

To address different learning styles, use the following activities suggested in the **Extension Activities** booklet, p. 41.

- For Verbal/ Linguistic and Interpersonal Learners, use Activity 5.

- For Musical/ Rhythmic Learners, use Activity 6.

- For Verbal/ Linguistic and Logical/ Mathematical Learners, use Activity 7.

About Brochures

Reading Strategy

Skimming and Scanning

670

About Brochures

A brochure combines elements of advertising with information on a place of interest or attraction. Whether it is highlighting a museum, zoo, or circus, a brochure usually includes a persuasive message financed by an individual or a company.

A brochure supplies an information preview, along with pictures, that tells what the place of interest or attraction offers. Brochures often give such information as facility hours, cost of admission, directions to the attraction, and the ages to which the exhibits appeal.

Reading Strategy

Skimming and Scanning

To get the most out of a brochure, set a specific purpose before reading it. One way to do so with this Aquarium of the Pacific brochure is to skim and scan it in order to identify and understand the contents.

- By *skimming*, you will be able to get an idea of the organization and scope of what is being presented. For example, if you are trying to find out if the aquarium has programs for children, skim the brochure until you spot that information.

- By *scanning*, you can locate specific information quickly. Let your eyes move rapidly but carefully over the page. Look for words related to the information you are seeking. As you read, note the bold-faced headings on the brochure. By doing this, you will gather important information that highlights the place of interest or attraction.

Use a chart like the one shown to list details from the brochure that fit your purpose for reading.

Scanning for Information
Programs for Children:
Programs for Families:
Programs for Groups:

Front Page of Brochure

The front of a brochure is designed to catch your attention with special type and bright images. This cover from a brochure produced by the Aquarium of the Pacific in California sets the tone for the information that the booklet presents.

Educational opportunities for every age at the *Aquarium of the Pacific*

PACIFIC Adventures

APRIL • MAY • JUNE 2001

The front page features the program title in an attractive typeface.

Ocean Exploration continues this spring at the *Aquarium of the Pacific.* All on-site classroom programs take place in the Sparkletts Learning Center. Call now to reserve a spot for you and your family. For questions or registration information, please call the Education Hotline at:

(562) 951-1630
or toll-free **(888) 826-7257**

AQUARIUM OF THE PACIFIC®
A non-profit institution

...umber in ...urges ...act on ...ation in ...ure.

This picture indicates that the aquarium is a family-oriented place.

Pacific Adventures

- Have students note that the information in the brochure is valid for the months of April, May, and June 2001.

- Have students read the brochure copy and the side notes. Based on the word *aquarium* and the title, how would they describe this facility?
  Answer: It is a facility on the Pacific coast that contains varieties of sea life and educates visitors about such life.

- Ask students which information is communicated through large print and what information is suggested by the two graphics.
  Answer: Large print gives the title of the program, the name of the facility, and the phone number. Graphics communicate that the facility focuses on marine life and is suitable for families.

CUSTOMIZE INSTRUCTION FOR UNIVERSAL ACCESS

For English Learners	For Gifted/Talented Students
Ask students to use a dictionary or their own knowledge to make a list of other words related to the word *aquarium.* From what Latin word do these words originate? Answer: Related words include *aqua, Aqua-Lung, Aquarius, aquatic, aqueduct, aquifer;* the words all come from the Latin *aqua,* which means "water."	Have students use color, bold graphics, and upbeat writing to create a brochure for an organization they like or support: for example, a humane society, a park conservation organization, a recycling center, or a bicycle shop. Have completed brochures displayed in the classroom.

Internal Brochure Page: Schedule

- Ask students to scan the schedule to see how the programs are categorized.

  Answer: The programs are created for specific age groups.

- Have students determine by skimming the method for identifying different age groups in the schedule.

  Answer: The different groups are color-coded, or marked in different colors, and assigned letters.

- Ask students to scan the material to learn if there is any way they can find out more about a specific program.

  Answer: There are program details inside the brochure.

Schedule of Events

Color-coded material on an internal page of the brochure provides information on special events and programs. Categorized according to age groups, these programs are specifically for the month of June.

Color-coded letters used below are explained here in the key.

Kids Only Aqua Club

Preschool
Ages 4-5; children only

Jr. Biologist
Ages 7-12; children only

K

Family Adventures

Sea Life Stroll
Infants with parent

Aqua Tots
Ages 2-3, with parent/adult

F

Saturday Family Fun
Ages 4-6, with parent/adult

Fintastic Fun Workshops
Ages 4-6, with parent/adult

Family Sleepovers
Ages 5 thru adult

Group Adventures & Tours

Pacific Explorers — 6-13 yrs;
1 chaperone/10 kids; min. 15

Youth Sleepovers — 9-14 yrs;
1 chaperone/10 children

G

Hide & Seek — Ages 4-5;
You set the date!

Behind the Scenes Tours —
Coming soon

Community Programs

18+ **Adult Programs**
18 years and over

N **Destination Nature** — Offsite
activities; Age restrictions
depending on activity

Events are listed chronologically for specific days in June.

More detailed information on programs can found inside the brochure

Times of events are listed.

JUNE 2001			*See listing on inside for program details*	
1 • Fri	F	**Family Sleepover**	5 yrs thru adult; 5:30 p.m. - 7:30 a.m.
2 • Sat	G	**Pacific Explorers**	6-13 yrs w/ chaperone; 1:00-3:00 p.m.
5 • Tue	K	**Preschool**	4-5 yrs; kids only; 2:30-4:30 p.m.
6 • Wed	F	**Sea Life Stroll**	Children up to 4 (in stroller) with an adult
8 • Fri	G	**Youth Sleepover**	9-14 yrs w/ chaperone; 5:30 p.m. - 7:30 a.m.
9 • Sat	K	**Jr. Biologist**	7-12 yrs; kids only; 2:00-3:30 p.m.
	G	**Pacific Explorers**	See June 2
13 • Wed	F	**Aqua Tots**	2-3 yrs w/ adult; 2:30-4:00 p.m.
15 • Fri	G	**Youth Sleepover**	9-14 yrs w/ chaperone; 5:30 p.m. - 7:30 a.m.
16 • Sat	18+	**Muffins to Morays**	18 yrs and up; 7:30-9:30 a.m.
	G	**Pacific Explorers**	See June 2
19 • Tue	F	**Aqua Tots**	2-3 yrs w/ adult; 2:30-4:00 p.m.
20 • Wed	K	**Preschool**	4-5 yrs; kids only; 2:30-4:30 p.m.
21 • Thu	G	**Pacific Explorers**	See June 2
23 • Sat	F	**Fintastic Workshop**	3 yrs & up; 10:00-11:00 a.m.
25-29	K	**Summer Day Camp**	1-week half- or full-day programs (kids only)
30 • Sat	F	**Saturday Family Fun**	Kids w/ adult; 1:00-2:30 p.m.
	G	**Pacific Explorers**	See June 2
	N	**Destination Nature**	11 yrs & up (11-16 yrs w/adult); 9 a.m.-Noon

Check Your Comprehension

1. What is the name of the aquarium?
2. What is the toll-free phone number?
3. Which programs are for preschool children?
4. How old must children be to participate in activities with the Pacific Explorers?
5. Which programs are available on Sundays?

Applying the Reading Strategy

Skimming and Scanning

6. What information on the front of the brochure stands out the most?
7. Why are the days in June color-coded?
8. Do you think that you would like to participate in an activity at this aquarium? Why or why not?
9. How do pictures add to the appeal of a brochure?

Activity

Analyzing a Brochure

- Find and read another brochure. Use a chart like the one shown to record the key features of the brochure.
- Based on the information you have recorded, what general impression does the brochure convey?
- Share your findings with a group.

Analyzing a Brochure

Topic:

Images:

Key Details:

Contact Information:

Contrasting Informational Materials

Brochures and Encyclopedia Articles

A brochure is a type of advertisement that you read to gather information about an attraction or an event. You could look up the site of the event in an encyclopedia, but you would discover different information. Compare and contrast these sources of information by answering these questions about purpose and structure:

1. (a) When is an encyclopedia a good resource? (b) When is a brochure a good resource?
2. How would the information you find in a brochure contrast with the materials you find in an encyclopedia?
3. Compare and contrast the structure and format of a brochure and an encyclopedia article.

from The Way to Rainy Mountain ✦ from Nobel Lecture ✦ Keep Memory Alive

Lesson Objectives

1. **To analyze and respond to literary elements**
   - Literary Analysis: Reflective and Persuasive Essays
   - Comparing Literary Works

2. **To read, comprehend, analyze, and critique essays**
   - Reading Strategy: Analyzing Author's Purpose
   - Reading Check questions
   - Review and Assess questions
   - Assessment Practice (ATE)

3. **To develop word analysis skills, fluency, and systematic vocabulary**
   - Vocabulary Development Lesson: Word Analysis: Forms of *reciprocity*

4. **To understand and apply written and oral language conventions**
   - Spelling Strategy
   - Grammar Lesson: Irregular Comparative and Superlative Degrees

5. **To understand and apply appropriate writing and research strategies**
   - Writing Lesson: Letter to Solzhenitsyn
   - Extension Activity: Report

6. **To understand and apply listening and speaking strategies**
   - Extension Activity: Speech Analysis

STEP-BY-STEP TEACHING GUIDE	PACING GUIDE
PRETEACH	
Motivate Students and Provide Background	
Use the Motivation activity (ATE p. 674)	5 min.
Read and discuss the Preview material and Background information (SE/ATE p. 674) **A**	5 min.
Introduce the Concepts	
Introduce the Literary Analysis and Reading Strategy (SE/ATE p. 675) **A**	15 min.
Pronounce the vocabulary words and read their definitions (SE p. 675)	5 min.
TEACH	
Monitor Comprehension	
Informally monitor comprehension by circulating while students read independently or in groups **A**	25 min.
Monitor students' comprehension with the Reading Check notes (SE/ATE pp. 677, 679, 681, 683, 685, 687)	as students read
Develop vocabulary with Vocabulary notes (SE pp. 679, 680, 683–687; ATE p. 683)	as students read
Develop Understanding	
Develop students' understanding of reflective and persuasive essays with Literary Analysis annotations (SE pp. 680, 682, 684; ATE pp. 680, 682, 684) **A**	10 min.
Develop students' understanding of analyzing the author's purpose with Reading Strategy annotations (SE pp. 677, 680, 683, 685; ATE pp. 677, 678, 679, 680, 683, 685)	10 min.
ASSESS	
Assess Mastery	
Assess students' mastery of the Reading Strategy and Literary Analysis by having them answer the Review and Assess questions (SE/ATE p. 689)	20 min.
Use one or more of the print and media Assessment Resources (ATE p. 691) **A**	up to 50 min.
EXTEND	
Apply Understanding	
Have students complete the Vocabulary Development Lesson and the Grammar Lesson (SE p. 690) **A**	20 min.
Apply students' ability to narrow their viewpoint using the Writing Lesson (SE/ATE p. 691) **A**	45 min.
Apply students' understanding using one or more of the Extension Activities (SE p. 691)	20–90 min.

 ACCELERATED INSTRUCTION:
Use the strategies and activities identified with an **A**.

UNIVERSAL ACCESS
● = Below Level Students
▲ = On-Level Students
■ = Above Level Students

Reading Level: Average/Challenging/Average
Average Number of Instructional Days: 4

RESOURCES		
PRINT 📖	**TRANSPARENCIES**	**TECHNOLOGY** 💿 🎧 📼
• **Beyond Literature,** Humanities Connection: Art, p. 42 ▲ ■		• **Interest Grabber Video,** Tape 4 ● ▲ ■
• **Selection Support Workbook:** ● ▲ ■ Literary Analysis, p. 168 Reading Strategy, p. 167 Build Vocabulary, p. 165	• **Literary Analysis and Reading Transparencies,** pp. 83 and 84 ● ▲ ■	
• **Adapted Reader's Companion** ● • **Reader's Companion** ●		• **Listening to Literature** ● ▲ ■ Audiocassettes, Side 21 Audio CDs, CD 14
• **English Learner's Companion** ● ▲ • **Literatura en español** ● ▲ • **Literary Analysis for Enrichment** ■		
• **Formal Assessment:** Selection Test, pp. 148–150 ● ▲ ■ • **Open Book Test,** pp. 124–126 ● ▲ ■ • **Performance Assessment and Portfolio Management,** p. 11 ● ▲ ■ • **PRENTICE HALL ASSESSMENT** *SYSTEM* ● ▲ ■	• **PRENTICE HALL ASSESSMENT** *SYSTEM* ● ▲ ■ Skills Practice Answers and Explanations on Transparencies	• **Test Bank Software** ● ▲ ■ • **Got It! Assessment Videotapes,** Tape 4 ● ▲
• **Selection Support Workbook:** ● ▲ ■ Build Grammar Skills, p. 166 • **Writing and Grammar,** Platinum Level ● ▲ ■ • **Extension Activities,** p. 42 ● ▲ ■	• **Daily Language Practice Transparencies** ● ▲ • **Writing Models and Graphic Organizers on Transparencies,** pp. 45–51 ● ▲ ■	• **Writing and Grammar iText CD-ROM** ● ▲ ■ 💻 *Take It to the Net* www.phschool.com

■ **BLOCK SCHEDULING:** Use one 90-minute class period to preteach the selection and have students read it. Use a second 90-minute class period to assess students' mastery of skills and have them complete one of the Extension Activities.

Step-by-Step Teaching Guide for pp. 674–675

Motivation

On the board, write the phrase "to bear witness." Then, ask students to imagine a scene: Strange-looking aliens come in and abduct their entire class. A week later, one student escapes and returns to school. Ask students why it would be important for this student to "bear witness," or explain what happened. Lead students to see that people who have experienced significant or harsh events need to inform others—both for their own sake and to try to prevent further atrocities. All the writers in this grouping have witnessed injustice: Momaday's Kiowa people have been oppressed, Wiesel fell victim to the Nazis, and Solzhenitsyn was a political prisoner. Writers who bear witness bring injustice to light.

Interest Grabber Video

As an alternative, play "N. Scott Momaday on the Importance of Research" on Tape 4 to engage student interest.

❶ Background

Literature

Alfred B. Nobel left $9 million in his will to establish the Nobel Prizes. Nobel was a chemist and engineer who was responsible for inventing dynamite. Nobel also contributed to the inventions of synthetic rubber, artificial silk, and synthetic leather. He held more than 350 patents. His interests were not limited to science; he was a lover of English literature and poetry and wrote several novels and poems. At his death, he left a library of more than 1,500 books, from fiction to philosophy.

Prepare to Read

from The Way to Rainy Mountain ◆ *from* Nobel Lecture ◆ Keep Memory Alive

Take It to the Net

Visit www.phschool.com for interactive activities and instruction related to these selections, including
- background
- graphic organizers
- literary elements
- reading strategies

Preview

Connecting to the Literature

We all have memories, and we cherish those that are most important to us. These three works of literature are the written records of three authors' recollections and reflections on important events in their lives.

❶ Background

One of the highest honors a person can receive is the Nobel Prize. Established by Alfred Nobel, a Swede, the Nobel Prizes include awards in physics, chemistry, medicine, literature, and peace. Nobel set up the fund to finance annual achievements and to present peace awards. The authors of two of these selections—Alexander Solzhenitsyn and Elie Wiesel— were awarded Nobel Prizes: Solzhenitsyn for literature and Wiesel for peace.

674 ◆ *Nonfiction*

TEACHING RESOURCES

The following resources can be used to enrich or extend the instruction for pp. 674–675.

Motivation

📼 **Interest Grabber Video**, Tape 4 ▪

Background

📖 **Beyond Literature**, p. 42

Take It to the Net
Visit www.phschool.com for background and hotlinks for the selections.

Literary Analysis

📄 **Literary Analysis and Reading Transparencies**, Reflective and Persuasive Essays, p. 84 ▪

Reading

📖 **Selection Support Workbook:** Reading Strategy, p. 167, Build Vocabulary, p. 165

📄 **Literary Analysis and Reading Transparencies**, Analyzing Author's Purpose, p. 83 ▪

▪ **BLOCK SCHEDULING:** Resources marked with this symbol provide varied instruction during 90-minute blocks.

Literary Analysis

Reflective and Persuasive Essays

In a **reflective essay,** an author shares his or her thoughts about an idea or a personal experience. In the excerpt from *The Way to Rainy Mountain*, author N. Scott Momaday, a Kiowa Indian, reflects on the death of his grandmother and the passing of the Kiowa culture.

A **persuasive essay** attempts to convince readers to adopt a particular opinion or course of action. Solzhenitsyn's and Wiesel's speeches use persuasive language and sound reasoning to convince you that their ideas are worth embracing.

Comparing Literary Works

In all of these selections, the authors introduce personal experiences in order to achieve a purpose beyond just telling a story. Each author reflects on events from the past and adds new meaning or draws new conclusions about them. As you read these essays, consider the experience each author shares and compare the ways each writer builds on these experiences to make another point.

Reading Strategy

Analyzing Author's Purpose

An **author's purpose** is the reason that he or she is writing—for example, to inform, to entertain, to persuade, or to reflect. This quotation from Wiesel's essay tells you he is writing to persuade people:

> We must always take sides. Neutrality helps the oppressor, never the victim. Silence encourages the tormentor, never the tormented.

As you read, complete a chart like the one shown by noting the kinds of details the writer includes. Then, use the details you find to help you determine the author's purpose.

Vocabulary Development

engender (en jen´ dər) *v.* bring about; cause; produce (p. 679)

tenuous (ten´ yōō əs) *adj.* slight; flimsy; not substantial or strong (p. 680)

reciprocity (res´ ə präs´ ə tē) *n.* mutual action; dependence (p. 683)

assimilate (ə sim´ ə lāt´) *v.* to absorb into a greater body (p. 684)

inexorably (in eks´ ə rə blē) *adv.* certainly (p. 685)

oratory (ôr´ ə tôr´ ē) *n.* skill in public speaking (p. 686)

transcends (tran sendz´) *v.* surpasses; exceeds (p. 687)

from *The Way to Rainy Mountain* / from *Nobel Lecture* / *Keep Memory Alive* ◆ 675

Step-by-Step Teaching Guide for pp. 676–688

CUSTOMIZE INSTRUCTION
For Interpersonal Learners

N. Scott Momaday explains how his grandmother could describe the Black Hills, where she had never been, because she had heard about them in stories. This is a common experience for many children. They may know details of their parents' or grandparents' past experiences. Invite students to share details of their own family's pasts that they may have learned from stories.

❶ About the Selection

Like all the essays in this grouping, "The Way to Rainy Mountain" focuses on the importance of memory in understanding the lessons of the past. In this essay, N. Scott Momaday weaves together his love for tradition, nature, and community to give his message a particular essence—the spiritual essence of the Kiowas.

❷ Background
Art

Old Ones Talking, by R. Brownell McGrew

R. Brownell McGrew is a Native American artist who often focuses on Native American life in his paintings.

Use this question for discussion: What elements of the painting emphasize the feelings of oneness with nature that comes forth in Momaday's essay?
Answer: The golden light of the sun through the trees illuminates the background and reflects off the colorful tones of the men's clothing, as it does off the ground and tree trunks, making the men seem a part of the natural surroundings.

❸ ▶ Critical Viewing

Possible responses: The men's expressions show that the essay will be about a serious subject; the men's clothing and necklaces indicate that the story will be about a Native American culture; and the title and the men's age suggest that it will be about times past.

676

---

from **The Way to**
❶ Rainy Mountain
N. Scott Momaday

❸ ▲ **Critical Viewing** Predict what the topic of this selection will be based on the title and this picture. **[Predict]**

676 ◆ *Nonfiction*

TEACHING RESOURCES

The following resources can be used to enrich or extend the instruction for pp. 676–688.

Literary Analysis
- 📖 **Selection Support:** Literary Analysis, p. 168
- 📱 **Writing Models and Graphic Organizers on Transparencies,** pp. 45–51

Reading
- 📖 **Reader's Companion**
- 📖 **English Learner's Companion**
- 🎧 **Listening to Literature Audiocassettes,** Side 21 ▪
- 💿 **Listening to Literature Audio CDs,** CD 14 ▪

Old Ones Talking, R. Brownell McGrew, Courtesy of the artist

A single knoll rises out of the plain in Oklahoma, north and west of the Wichita Range.[1] For my people, the Kiowas, it is an old landmark, and they gave it the name Rainy Mountain. The hardest weather in the world is there. Winter brings blizzards, hot tornadic winds arise in the spring, and in summer the prairie is an anvil's edge.[2] The grass turns brittle and brown, and it cracks beneath your feet. There are green belts along the rivers and creeks, linear groves of hickory and pecan, willow and witch hazel. At a distance in July or August the steaming foliage seems almost to writhe[3] in fire. Great green and yellow grasshoppers are everywhere in the tall grass, popping up like corn to sting the flesh, and tortoises crawl about on the red earth, going nowhere in the plenty of time. Loneliness is an aspect of the land. All things in the plain are isolate; there is no confusion of objects in the eye, but *one* hill or *one* tree or *one* man. To look upon that landscape in the early morning, with the sun at your back, is to lose the sense of proportion. Your imagination comes to life, and this, you think, is where Creation was begun.

I returned to Rainy Mountain in July. My grandmother had died in the spring, and I wanted to be at her grave. She had lived to be very old and at last infirm.[4] Her only living daughter was with her when she died, and I was told that in death her face was that of a child.

I like to think of her as a child. When she was born, the Kiowas were living the last great moment of their history. For more than a hundred years they had controlled the open range from the Smoky Hill River to the Red, from the headwaters of the Canadian to the fork of the Arkansas and Cimarron. In alliance with the Comanches, they had ruled the whole of the southern

---

1. **Wichita** (wĭch′ ə tô′) **Range** mountain range in southwestern Oklahoma.
2. **anvil's edge** edge of the iron or steel block on which metal objects are hammered into shape.
3. **writhe** (rīth) *v.* twist in pain and agony.
4. **infirm** (ĭn fʉrm′) *adj.* weak; feeble.

Reading Strategy
Analyzing Author's Purpose Why do you think Momaday included this detail about the Kiowas and their history?

 Reading Check
Why does the narrator return to Rainy Mountain?

from *The Way to Rainy Mountain* ◆ 677

Analyzing Author's Purpose

• Have a volunteer read aloud the bracketed passage. Ask other students to point out some of the details Momaday includes in this passage.

Possible responses: Momaday explains where his grandmother's people came from and offers details about their culture, beliefs, and language.

• Ask students why they think the author includes the information that the Kiowas' language has never been positively classified.

Answer: Momaday included the details to emphasize the group's uniqueness and to make it seem even more tragic that their traditions are fading away.

7 ▶ Critical Viewing

Analyze

Answer: The woman's skin is rough and wrinkled, which might indicate a difficult life. Her expression seems to be one of acceptance or resignation.

Plains. War was their sacred business, and they were among the finest horsemen the world has ever known. But warfare for the Kiowas was preeminently a matter of disposition rather than of survival, and they never understood the grim, unrelenting advance of the U.S. Cavalry. When at last, divided and ill-provisioned, they were driven onto the Staked Plains in the cold rains of autumn, they fell into panic. In Palo Duro Canyon they abandoned their crucial stores to pillage[5] and had nothing then but their lives. In order to save themselves, they surrendered to the soldiers at Fort Sill and were imprisoned in the old stone corral that now stands as a military museum. My grandmother was spared the humiliation of those high gray walls by eight or ten years, but she must have known from birth the affliction of defeat, the dark brooding of old warriors.

Her name was Aho, and she belonged to the last culture to evolve in North America. Her forebears came down from the high country in western Montana nearly three centuries ago. They were a mountain people, a mysterious tribe of hunters whose language has never been positively classified in any major group. In the late seventeenth century they began a long migration to the south and east.

6 It was a journey toward the dawn, and it led to a golden age. Along the way the Kiowas were befriended by the Crows, who gave them the culture and religion of the Plains. They acquired horses, and their ancient nomadic spirit was suddenly free of the ground. They acquired Tai-me, the sacred Sun Dance doll, from that moment the object and symbol of their worship, and so shared in the divinity of the sun. Not least, they acquired the sense of destiny, therefore courage and pride. When they entered upon the southern Plains they had been transformed. No longer were they slaves to the simple necessity of survival; they were a lordly and dangerous society of fighters and thieves, hunters and priests of the sun. According to their origin myth, they entered the world through a hollow log. From one point of view, their migration was the fruit of an old prophecy, for indeed they emerged from a sunless world.

Although my grandmother lived out her long life in the shadow of Rainy Mountain, the immense landscape of the continental interior lay like memory in her blood. She could tell of the Crows, whom she had never seen, and of the Black Hills, where she had never been. I

7 ▼ Critical Viewing
How are the struggles that the author's grandmother faced throughout her life reflected in the face of this Native American woman? [Analyze]

Annie Old Crow, James Bama, Courtesy of the Artist

---

5. **pillage** (pil´ ij) *n.* act of robbing and destroying, especially during wartime.

☀ ENRICHMENT: Cultural Connection

The Kiowa

Explain that the Kiowas lived in the southern plains of North America. Buffalo hunters, they lived in lodges made of skin that they could transport easily from place to place. Like many Native Americans, their lifestyle was compromised as settlers discovered the vast open spaces of the plains. The Kiowas vigorously protested white settlement in their territory and were hostile to settlers until 1868. After many Kiowa leaders were imprisoned and their horses taken, the Kiowas retreated to a reservation in southwestern Oklahoma.

wanted to see in reality what she had seen more perfectly in the mind's eye, and traveled fifteen hundred miles to begin my pilgrimage.

Yellowstone,[6] it seemed to me, was the top of the world, a region of deep lakes and dark timber, canyons and waterfalls. But, beautiful as it is, one might have the sense of confinement there. The skyline in all directions is close at hand, the high wall of the woods and deep cleavages of shade. There is a perfect freedom in the mountains, but it belongs to the eagle and the elk, the badger and the bear. The Kiowas reckoned their stature by the distance they could see, and they were bent and blind in the wilderness.

Descending eastward, the highland meadows are a stairway to the plain. In July the inland slope of the Rockies is luxuriant with flax and buckwheat, stonecrop and larkspur. The earth unfolds and the limit of the land recedes. Clusters of trees, and animals grazing far in the distance, cause the vision to reach away and wonder to build upon the mind. The sun follows a longer course in the day, and the sky is immense beyond all comparison. The great billowing clouds that sail upon it are shadows that move upon the brain like water, dividing light. Farther down, in the land of the Crows and Blackfeet, the plain is yellow. Sweet clover takes hold of the hills and bends upon itself to cover and seal the soil. There the Kiowas paused on their way; they had come to the place where they must change their lives. The sun is at home on the plains. Precisely there does it have the certain character of a god. When the Kiowas came to the land of the Crows, they could see the dark lees of the hills at dawn across the Bighorn River, the profusion of light on the grain shelves, the oldest deity ranging after the solstices. Not yet would they veer southward to the caldron[7] of the land that lay below; they must wean their blood from the northern winter and hold the mountains a while longer in their view. They bore Tai-me in procession to the east.

A dark mist lay over the Black Hills, and the land was like iron. At the top of a ridge I caught sight of Devil's Tower upthrust against the gray sky as if in the birth of time the core of the earth had broken through its crust and the motion of the world was begun. There are things in nature that engender an awful quiet in the heart of man; Devil's Tower is one of them. Two centuries ago, because they could not do otherwise, the Kiowas made a legend at the base of the rock. My grandmother said:

Eight children were there at play, seven sisters and their brother. Suddenly the boy was struck dumb; he trembled and began to run upon his hands and feet. His fingers became claws, and his body was covered with fur. Directly there was a bear where the boy had been. The sisters

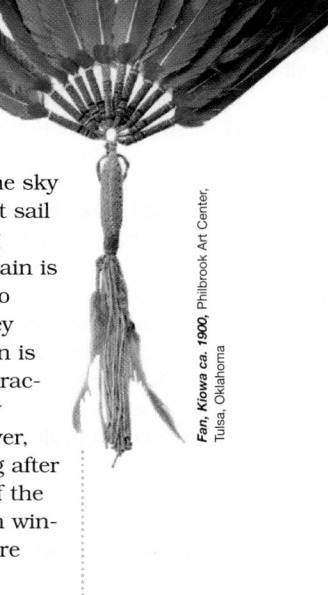

Fan, Kiowa ca. 1900, Philbrook Art Center, Tulsa, Oklahoma

engender (en jen′ dər) *v.* bring about; cause; produce

❾ **Reading Check**
Who gave the Kiowas the culture and religion of the Plains?

---

6. **Yellowstone** Yellowstone National Park, mostly in northwestern Wyoming but including narrow strips in southern Montana and eastern Idaho.
7. **caldron** (kôl′ drən) *n.* heat like that of a boiling kettle.

from *The Way to Rainy Mountain* ◆ 679

- Ask a student who enjoys reading aloud to read the legend to the class.

- Point out that Momaday knows the legend because he learned it from his grandmother, who learned it from her ancestors.

- Ask students the Reading Strategy question on p. 680: What is the author's purpose or purposes in retelling this legend?
  Possible answer: The author retells this legend to show that oral history and cultural stories were important ways that the Kiowa communicated their culture to future generations.

⑪ Literary Analysis

Reflective and Persuasive Essays

- Read aloud the bracketed passage, asking students to think about what the author might have been feeling as he wrote these words.

- Ask students the Literary Analysis question on p. 680: How do Momaday's recollections of his grandmother reflect his feelings for her?
  Answer: Momaday's recollections reflect his feelings of respect and affection for his grandmother by letting the reader "see" her through his eyes.

---

⑩ *were terrified; they ran, and the bear after them. They came to the stump of a great tree, and the tree spoke to them. It bade them climb upon it, and as they did so it began to rise in the air. The bear came to kill them, but they were just beyond its reach. It reared against the tree and scored the bark all around with its claws. The seven sisters were borne into the sky, and they became the stars of the Big Dipper.*

From that moment, and so long as the legend lives, the Kiowas have kinsmen in the night sky. Whatever they were in the mountains, they could be no more. However <u>tenuous</u> their well-being, however much they had suffered and would suffer again, they had found a way out of the wilderness.

My grandmother had a reverence for the sun, a holy regard that now is all but gone out of mankind. There was a wariness in her, and an ancient awe. She was a Christian in her later years, but she had come a long way about, and she never forgot her birthright. As a child she had been to the Sun Dances; she had taken part in those annual rites, and by them she had learned the restoration of her people in the presence of Tai-me. She was about seven when the last Kiowa Sun Dance was held in 1887 on the Washita River above Rainy Mountain Creek. The buffalo were gone. In order to consummate the ancient sacrifice—to impale the head of a buffalo bull upon the medicine tree—a delegation of old men journeyed into Texas, there to beg and barter for an animal from the Goodnight herd. She was ten when the Kiowas came together for the last time as a living Sun Dance culture. They could find no buffalo; they had to hang an old hide from the sacred tree. Before the dance could begin, a company of soldiers rode out from Fort Sill under orders to disperse the tribe. Forbidden without cause the essential act of their faith, having seen the wild herds slaughtered and left to rot upon the ground, the Kiowas backed away forever from the medicine tree. That was July 20, 1890, at the great bend of the Washita. My grandmother was there. Without bitterness, and for as long as she lived, she bore a vision of deicide.[8]

⑪ Now that I can have her only in memory, I see my grandmother in the several postures that were peculiar to her: standing at the wood stove on a winter morning and turning meat in a great iron skillet; sitting at the south window, bent above her beadwork, and afterwards, when her vision failed, looking down for a long time into the fold of her hands; going out upon a cane, very slowly as she did when the weight of age came upon her; praying. I remember her most often at prayer. She made long, rambling prayers out of suffering and hope, having seen many things. I was never sure that I had the right to hear, so exclusive were they of all mere custom and company. The last time I saw her she prayed standing by the side of her bed at night, naked to the waist, the light of a kerosene lamp moving upon her dark skin. Her long, black hair, always drawn and braided in the day, lay upon her shoulders and

---

8. **deicide** (dē′ ə sīd′) *n.* killing of a god.

tenuous (ten′ yoo əs) *adj.* slight; flimsy; not substantial or strong against her breasts like a shawl. I do not speak Kiowa, and I never understood her prayers, but there was something inherently sad in the sound, some merest hesitation upon the syllables of sorrow. She began in a high and descending pitch, exhausting her breath to silence; then again and again—and always the same intensity of effort, of something that is, and is not, like urgency in the human voice. Transported so in the dancing light among the shadows of her room, she seemed beyond the reach of time. But that was illusion; I think I knew then that I should not see her again.

Houses are like sentinels in the plain, old keepers of the weather watch. There, in a very little while, wood takes on the appearance of great age. All colors wear soon away in the wind and rain, and then the wood is burned gray and the grain appears and the nails turn red with rust. The windowpanes are black and opaque; you imagine there is nothing within, and indeed there are many ghosts, bones given up to the land. They stand here and there against the sky, and you approach them for a longer time than you expect. They belong in the distance; it is their domain.

Pouch Kiowa ca. 1890–1910, New York State Historical Association, Cooperstown

Once there was a lot of sound in my grandmother's house, a lot of coming and going, feasting and talk. The summers there were full of excitement and reunion. The Kiowas are a summer people; they abide the cold and keep to themselves, but when the season turns and the land becomes warm and vital they cannot hold still; an old love of going returns upon them. The aged visitors who came to my grandmother's house when I was a child were made of lean and leather, and they bore themselves upright. They wore great black hats and bright ample shirts that shook in the wind. They rubbed fat upon their hair and wound their braids with strips of colored cloth. Some of them painted their faces and carried the scars of old and cherished enmities. They were an old council of warlords, come to remind and be reminded of who they were. Their wives and daughters served them well. The women might indulge themselves; gossip was at once the mark and compensation of their servitude. They made loud and elaborate talk among themselves, full of jest and gesture, fright and false alarm. They went abroad in fringed and flowered shawls, bright beadwork and German silver. They were at home in the kitchen, and they prepared meals that were banquets.

There were frequent prayer meetings, and great nocturnal feasts. When I was a child I played with my cousins outside, where the lamplight fell upon the ground and the singing of the old people rose up around us and carried away into the darkness. There were a lot of good things to eat, a lot of laughter and surprise. And afterwards, when the quiet returned, I lay down with my grandmother and could hear the frogs away by the river and feel the motion of the air.

Now there is a funeral silence in the rooms, the endless wake of some final word. The walls have closed in upon my grandmother's

13 ✓ **Reading Check**

What ancient sacrifice was performed at the last Kiowa Sun Dance?

from The Way to Rainy Mountain ◆ 681

12 **Background**

Art

Explain that in the early 1800s, traders introduced glass beads to the Native Americans. Decorating in beads gradually replaced porcupine quill work. Women usually sewed beads onto buckskin clothing or bags, but some groups developed weaving techniques. The bead designs were mostly geometric, though around the turn of the century floral patterns became popular. The Cheyenne were known for creating sacred designs in beads; their decorations on cradle boards and moccasins symbolized protection and long life.

13 ✓ **Reading Check**

Answer: The ancient sacrifice of a buffalo was re-enacted at the last Kiowa Sun Dance.

- Ask the students to envision the view that Momaday sees. Some students may want to draw or paint this view.
- Ask the Literary Analysis question on p. 682: What does the cricket in this image represent in the author's imagination?
  Answer: The cricket represents his grandmother's life and the Kiowa culture, which he sees as so important even though they have passed away.

Answers for p. 682

Review and Assess

1. Students might be interested in exploring their cultural roots so that they can find out more about their personal identity.
2. **(a)** Momaday is paying homage to the lost way of life of the Kiowa and specifically to the life of his grandmother.
   (b) Momaday's grandmother was hardworking, strong, sensitive, religious, and dedicated to her culture and family.
3. **(a)** Students may offer details about feasting, talking, reminiscing, cooking, prayer meetings, or cousins playing. **(b)** Momaday's life has bridged two cultures—Kiowa and mainstream American culture—much more than did his grandmother's life.
4. **(a)** The legend explains the origins of the Big Dipper. **(b)** This legend helped the Kiowa people see a wide-open sky as the only way out of their earthly confinement.
5. **(a)** Momaday sees a cricket perched on a handrail with the moon behind it. **(b)** The image suggests that the spirit of the Kiowa culture lives on in eternity.
6. By reflecting on the past, students can put present-day events into perspective.

house. When I returned to it in mourning, I saw for the first time in my life how small it was. It was late at night, and there was a white moon, nearly full. I sat for a long time on the stone steps by the kitchen door. From there I could see out across the land; I could see the long row of trees by the creek, the low light upon the rolling plains, and the stars of the Big Dipper. Once I looked at the moon and caught sight of a strange thing. A cricket had perched upon the handrail, only a few inches away from me. My line of vision was such that the creature filled the moon like a fossil. It had gone there, I thought, to live and die, for there, of all places, was its small definition made whole and eternal. A warm wind rose up and purled[9] like the longing within me.

The next morning I awoke at dawn and went out on the dirt road to Rainy Mountain. It was already hot, and the grasshoppers began to fill the air. Still, it was early in the morning, and the birds sang out of the shadows. The long yellow grass on the mountain shone in the bright light, and a scissortail[10] hied above the land. There, where it ought to be, at the end of a long and legendary way, was my grandmother's grave. Here and there on the dark stones were ancestral names. Looking back once, I saw the mountain and came away.

---

9. **purled** (purld) *v.* moved in ripples or with a murmuring sound; swirled.
10. **scissortail** (siz′ ər tāl′) *n.* pale gray and pink variety of flycatcher.

Review and Assess

Thinking About the Selection

1. **Respond:** Would you be interested in searching out the roots of your culture in the way Momaday does? Explain.
2. **(a) Infer:** To whom and to what does Momaday pay homage in this essay? **(b) Draw Conclusions:** Describe the personality of Momaday's grandmother based on the details in this essay.
3. **(a) Recall:** Describe two activities at Momaday's grandmother's house in summer. **(b) Speculate:** How do you think his life differs from his grandmother's life?
4. **(a) Recall:** What natural phenomenon does the Kiowa legend explain? **(b) Interpret:** What transition in the culture of the Kiowa people does this legend mark?
5. **(a) Recall:** What image does Momaday describe seeing as he sits on the steps? **(b) Draw Conclusions:** What does the image signify about the Kiowa culture?
6. **Apply:** How can reflecting on the past help you understand yourself?

N. Scott Momaday

(b. 1934)
A Kiowa Indian, the writer N. Scott Momaday's interest in Native American culture and history began as a child, when he lived on several Indian reservations where his parents taught. Momaday earned a doctoral degree from Stanford University, where he also taught English. His first novel, *House Made of Dawn*, was awarded a Pulitzer Prize. *The Way to Rainy Mountain* includes his impressions of contemporary Kiowa culture and worldview, as well as their history and legends.

❂ ENRICHMENT: Cultural Connection

Community Feasts

Momaday describes great nighttime feasts that his grandmother's friends held. Discuss with students the community feasts, such as Fourth of July picnics, cultural fairs, or church suppers, that are held in their area. Have students compare their community feasts with the feasts the author describes. Have them reflect on why people hold and enjoy events like these.

Neille McClung 1873-1951

From
NOBEL LECTURE

Alexander Solzhenitsyn
Translated by F. D. Reeve

I am, however, encouraged by a keen sense of WORLD LITERATURE as the one great heart that beats for the cares and misfortunes of our world, even though each corner sees and experiences them in a different way.

In past times, also, besides age-old national literatures there existed a concept of world literature as the link between the summits of national literatures and as the aggregate[1] of reciprocal literary influences. But there was a time lag: readers and writers came to know foreign writers only belatedly, sometimes centuries later, so that mutual influences were delayed and the network of national literary high points was visible not to contemporaries but to later generations.

Today, between writers of one country and the readers and writers of another, there is an almost instantaneous reciprocity as I myself know. My books, unpublished, alas, in my own country, despite hasty and often bad translations have quickly found a responsive world readership. Critical analysis of them has been undertaken by such leading Western writers as Heinrich Böll.[2] During all these recent years, when both my work and my freedom did not collapse, when against the laws of gravity they held on seemingly in thin air, seemingly ON NOTHING, on the invisible, mute surface tension of sympathetic people,

---

1. **aggregate** (ag´ rə git) *n.* group of things gathered together and considered a whole.
2. **Heinrich Böll** (hin riH böl) German novelist (1917–1985) and winner of the Nobel Prize for Literature.

16 Reading Strategy
Analyzing Author's Purpose What is Solzhenitsyn's purpose in describing the role of world literature?

reciprocity (res´ ə präs´ ə tē) *n.* mutual action; dependence

18 ✔ Reading Check
What is the topic of this essay?

from Nobel Lecture ◆ 683

CUSTOMIZE INSTRUCTION FOR UNIVERSAL ACCESS

For Less Proficient Readers	For Gifted/ Talented Students
Have students read along as you play the recording of Solzhenitsyn's Nobel Lecture on the **Listening to Literature** Audiocassettes or CDs. Encourage students to summarize the main idea of each paragraph as they read through the selection.	Have students conduct research on Heinrich Böll. Students can begin by answering these questions: What did he write about? What was his connection to Solzhenitsyn?

with warm gratitude I learned, to my complete surprise, of the support of the world's writing fraternity. On my fiftieth birthday I was astounded to receive greetings from well-known European writers. No pressure put on me now passed unnoticed. During the dangerous weeks when I was being expelled from the Writers' Union,[3] THE PROTECTIVE WALL put forward by the prominent writers of the world saved me from worse persecution, and Norwegian writers and artists hospitably prepared shelter for me in the event that I was exiled from my country. Finally, my being nominated for a Nobel Prize was originated not in the land where I live and write but by François Mauriac[4] and his colleagues. Afterward, national writers' organizations expressed unanimous support for me.

 As I have understood it and experienced it myself, world literature is no longer an abstraction or a generalized concept invented by literary critics, but a common body and common spirit, a living, heartfelt unity reflecting the growing spiritual unity of mankind. State borders still turn crimson, heated red-hot by electric fences and machine-gun fire; some ministries of internal affairs still suppose that literature is "an internal affair" of the countries under their jurisdiction; and newspaper headlines still herald, "They have no right to interfere in our internal affairs!" Meanwhile, no such thing as INTERNAL AFFAIRS remains on our crowded Earth. Mankind's salvation lies exclusively in everyone's making everything his business, in the people of the East being anything but indifferent to what is thought in the West, and in the people of the West being anything but indifferent to what happens in the East. Literature, one of the most sensitive and responsive tools of human existence, has been the first to pick up, adopt, and <u>assimilate</u> this sense of the growing unity of mankind. I therefore confidently turn to the world literature of the present, to hundreds of friends whom I have not met face to face and perhaps never will see.

My friends! Let us try to be helpful, if we are worth anything. In our own countries, torn by differences among parties, movements, castes,

---

3. **the Writers' Union** official Soviet writers' organization.
4. **François Mauriac** (frän swä΄ mô΄ rē ak΄) French novelist and essayist (1885–1970).

684 ◆ *Nonfiction*

19 ▲ Critical Viewing
These stamps from various countries honor writers. What do they suggest about the importance of writers? **[Draw Conclusions]**

Literary Analysis
Reflective and Persuasive Essays What point does Solzhenitsyn want readers to support or accept?

assimilate (ə sim΄ ə lāt΄) *v.* to absorb into a greater body

---

and groups, who for ages past has been not the dividing but the uniting force? This, essentially, is the position of writers, spokesmen of a national language, of the chief tie binding the nation, the very soil which the people inhabit, and, in fortunate circumstances, the nation's spirit too.

I think that world literature has the power in these frightening times to help mankind see itself accurately despite what is advocated by partisans[5] and by parties. It has the power to transmit the condensed experience of one region to another, so that different scales of values are combined, and so that one people accurately and concisely knows the true history of another with a power of recognition and acute awareness as if it had lived through that history itself—and could thus be spared repeating old mistakes. At the same time, perhaps we ourselves may succeed in developing our own WORLDWIDE VIEW, like any man, with the center of the eye seeing what is nearby but the periphery[6] of vision taking in what is happening in the rest of the world. We will make correlations[7] and maintain worldwide standards.

Who, if not writers, are to condemn their own unsuccessful governments (in some states this is the easiest way to make a living; everyone who is not too lazy does it) as well as society itself, whether for its cowardly humiliation or for its self-satisfied weakness, or the lightheaded escapades of the young, or the youthful pirates brandishing knives?

We will be told: What can literature do against the pitiless onslaught of naked violence? Let us not forget that violence does not and cannot flourish by itself; it is inevitably intertwined with LYING. Between them there is the closest, the most profound and natural bond: nothing screens violence except lies, and the only way lies can hold out is by violence. Whoever has once announced violence as his METHOD must <u>inexorably</u> choose lying as his PRINCIPLE. At birth, violence behaves openly and even proudly. But as soon as it becomes stronger and firmly established, it senses the thinning of the air around it and cannot

---

5. **partisans** (pärt´ i zənz) *n.* unreasoning, emotional supporters of a party or viewpoint.
6. **periphery** (pə rif´ ər ē) *n.* boundary; perimeter.
7. **correlations** (kôr´ ə lā´ shənz) *n.* relationships; connections.

㉑ Reading Strategy
Analyzing Author's Purpose What details in this paragraph support Solzhenitsyn's purpose?

inexorably (in eks´ ə rə blē) *adv.* certainly

㉒ **Reading Check**

According to the author, what does world literature have the power to do?

from *Nobel Lecture* ◆ 685

 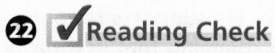
685

Review and Assess

1. Students might cite a work of literature from a culture different from their own and discuss how the author's background and reflections gave them special insight into that culture.

2. **(a)** "One great heart" refers to world literature. **(b)** The writers of the world were a great source of encouragement and support to Solzhenitsyn.

3. **(a)** Writers and artists can expose and dispel lies. **(b)** Lies screen, or hide, violence.

4. **(a)** "Internal affairs" are the goings-on within a country or group that affect only that group. **(b)** He supports his point well by explaining that in today's crowded world, something that happens in one country affects other countries, so these issues must all be brought out into the open. **(c)** Students should support their opinions with examples from current events.

5. **(a)** The proverb means that truth, even if it is told in a small voice, is more powerful than a world of lies or repression. **(b)** Students who agree may say that art has a universal power; those who disagree might think art is not strong enough or popular enough to expose lies.

---

go on without befogging itself in lies, coating itself with lying's sugary oratory. It does not always or necessarily go straight for the gullet; usually it demands of its victims only allegiance to the lie, only complicity in the lie.

The simple act of an ordinary courageous man is not to take part, not to support lies! Let *that* come into the world and even reign over it, but not through me. Writers and artists can do more: they can VANQUISH LIES! In the struggle against lies, art has always won and always will. Conspicuously, incontestably for everyone. Lies can stand up against much in the world, but not against art.

Once lies have been dispelled, the repulsive nakedness of violence will be exposed—and hollow violence will collapse.

That, my friends, is why I think we can help the world in its red-hot hour: not by the nay-saying of having no armaments, not by abandoning oneself to the carefree life, but by going into battle!

In Russian, proverbs about TRUTH are favorites. They persistently express the considerable, bitter, grim experience of the people, often astonishingly:

ONE WORD OF TRUTH OUTWEIGHS THE WORLD.

On such a seemingly fantastic violation of the law of the conservation of mass and energy[8] are based both my own activities and my appeal to the writers of the whole world.

> **oratory** (ôr′ ə tôr′ ē) *n.* skill in public speaking

---

8. **the law of conservation of mass and energy** This law states that in any physical or chemical change, neither mass nor energy can be lost.

Review and Assess

Thinking About the Selection

1. **Respond:** Tell how a work of literature has helped you to understand the values and traditions of different people.

2. **(a) Recall:** To what does the "one great heart" refer? **(b) Infer:** How did writers of the world influence Solzhenitsyn's career?

3. **(a) Recall:** What does Solzhenitsyn believe writers and artists can do? **(b) Analyze:** What connection does Solzhenitsyn see between lies and violence?

4. **(a) Analyze:** What does Solzhenitsyn mean by "internal affairs"? **(b) Make a Judgment:** How well do you think Solzhenitsyn supports his statement that "no such thing as INTERNAL AFFAIRS remains on our crowded Earth"? **(c) Take a Position:** Do you agree with him? Explain why or why not.

5. **(a) Interpret:** What is the meaning of the Russian proverb that Solzhenitsyn quotes? **(b) Assess:** Explain why you agree or disagree with the statement "Lies can stand up against much in the world, but not against art."

Alexander Solzhenitsyn

(b. 1918)

As an outspoken dissident, Russian writer Alexander Solzhenitsyn has departed from established opinion his whole literary life. His first book, *A Day in the Life of Ivan Denisovitch*—the story of an inmate in a Soviet labor camp—was banned in the Soviet Union.

Solzhenitsyn was tried for treason and exiled after the publication in Paris of parts of *The Gulag Archipelago*. Only since 1991 has his work been available to the people of his homeland. This excerpt from his Nobel lecture reflects on what it means to be part of a great world literature.

✹ ENRICHMENT: Career Connection

Publisher

Remind students that Solzhenitsyn's work is now published in many languages throughout the world. In a way, writers and publishers collaborate to bring individual ideas to the world at large. Discuss career roles in publishing, such as editors of newspapers, magazines, books, or Web sites. Invite students to consult career guides to find out more about these jobs and the education and training that prepare people for them.

KEEP MEMORY ALIVE

❷❸

Elie Wiesel

*I*t is with a profound sense of humility that I accept the honor you have chosen to bestow upon me. I know: your choice <u>transcends</u> me. This both frightens and pleases me.

It frightens me because I wonder: do I have the right to represent the multitudes who have perished? Do I have the right to accept this great honor on their behalf? I do not. That would be presumptuous. No one may speak for the dead, no one may interpret their mutilated dreams and visions.

transcends (tran sendz´) v. surpasses; exceeds

❷❺ ✔**Reading Check**
What feelings does Wiesel convey upon accepting his honor?

❷❹ ▲ **Critical Viewing** What emotion do you read on this boy's face? How does it relate to the title of this essay? **[Connect]**

Keep Memory Alive ◆ 687

Answers for p. 688

Review and Assess

1. A possible situation might involve ignoring a person who is sick or in trouble because of the stigma of being associated with him or her.

2. **(a)** He questions the right to represent multitudes who have perished. **(b)** He represents those who died by bearing witness to their sufferings through his writings.

3. **(a)** He can't believe this would happen in the twentieth century. **(b)** Students might guess that this device dramatizes the passing of time and illustrates the Jewish writer's accountability to his descendants.

4. **(a)** The term "fiery altar" refers to the Nazi death camps' crematoriums. **(b)** Not only was the future of the Jewish people sacrificed in the death camps, but also the innocence of children and others who believed that such an atrocity could never occur.

5. **(a)** He accuses the world of being a silent accomplice in the atrocities of the Holocaust. **(b)** This silence caused Wiesel to commit himself to speaking the truth about the events.

6. Students may answer that fear, ignorance, cruelty, or other reasons prevent people from speaking out against injustices.

It pleases me because I may say that this honor belongs to all the survivors and their children, and through us, to the Jewish people with whose destiny I have always identified.

I remember: it happened yesterday or eternities ago. A young Jewish boy discovered the kingdom of night. I remember his bewilderment, I remember his anguish. It all happened so fast. The ghetto. The deportation.[1] The sealed cattle car. The fiery altar upon which the history of our people and the future of mankind were meant to be sacrificed.

I remember: he asked his father: "Can this be true? This is the 20th century, not the Middle Ages. Who would allow such crimes to be committed? How could the world remain silent?"

And now the boy is turning to me: "Tell me," he asks. "What have you done with my future? What have you done with your life?"

And I tell him that I have tried. That I have tried to keep memory alive, that I have tried to fight those who would forget. Because if we forget, we are guilty, we are accomplices.

And then I explained to him how naive we were, that the world did know and remain silent. And that is why I swore never to be silent whenever and wherever human beings endure suffering and humiliation. We must always take sides. Neutrality helps the oppressor, never the victim. Silence encourages the tormentor, never the tormented.

---

1. **deportation** (dē´ pôr tā´ shen) *n.* expulsion from a country.

Review and Assess

Thinking About the Selection

1. **Respond:** Describe a situation today in which silently witnessing might do harm.

2. **(a) Recall:** What right, or claim, does Wiesel question? **(b) Infer:** How does Wiesel represent those who have died?

3. **(a) Recall:** Why is the boy incredulous as he is being deported? **(b) Deduce:** What is Wiesel's purpose in having his boy self talk to his man self?

4. **(a) Interpret:** Why does Wiesel use the term "the fiery altar"? **(b) Draw Conclusions:** How could the "future of mankind" be sacrificed on this altar?

5. **(a) Recall:** What does Wiesel call those who deliberately forget? **(b) Draw Conclusions:** At the end of the piece, of what crime does Wiesel accuse the world, and how has this crime affected the way Wiesel lives his life?

6. **Make a Judgment:** What do you think prevents people from speaking out against injustices.

688 ◆ *Nonfiction*

Elie Wiesel

(b. 1928)
The Romanian-born teacher, philosopher, and writer Elie Wiesel was deported to the Nazi death camp at Auschwitz at age sixteen. His parents and sister were killed, and he was forced into slave labor at Buchenwald, another Nazi death camp. After surviving the war, Wiesel studied in France and moved to the United States in 1956. In his first book, *Night*, Wiesel recounts the horrors of his experiences at the hands of the Nazis.

Elie Wiesel has been awarded the Congressional Gold Medal of Achievement and the Nobel Peace Prize. He delivered the speech here in 1986, in acceptance of that prize.

ASSESSMENT PRACTICE: Reading Comprehension

Comparing and Contrasting Texts   (For more practice, see Test Preparation Workbook, p. 42.)

Many tests require students to compare and contrast aspects of two texts. These aspects may include themes, conflicts, and allusions. After students have read the selections, write this sample test question on the board:

What common theme appears in both "The Way to Rainy Mountain" and "Keep Memory Alive"?

A the meaningfulness of landscape
B the importance of remembering
C the tragedy of the destruction of a culture
D the horror of the death camps

Suggest that students begin by ruling out choices that apply to only one selection, such as *A* and *D*. Then, help them recognize that *C* is not an accurate depiction of "Keep Memory Alive." *B* is the correct answer.

Review and Assess

Literary Analysis

Reflective and Persuasive Essays

1. How do Momaday's **reflections** on the death of his grandmother help him communicate a message about his Kiowa culture?

2. Analyze how well Solzhenitsyn argues his premise that world literature belongs to the world and not to a single country. What reasons does he give?

3. In your opinion, what is the most **persuasive** sentence in "Keep Memory Alive"? Explain your choice.

Comparing Literary Works

4. Using a chart like the one here, list one personal experience that each author shares with readers. In the second row of the chart, tell what you think each author's purpose is in sharing his personal experience.

	Momaday	Solzhenitsyn	Wiesel
Experience			
Purpose			

5. Which of these essays is most meaningful to you? Explain why.

Reading Strategy

Analyzing Author's Purpose

6. (a) What do you think was Momaday's **purpose** in writing? (b) Family ties among Kiowa Indians are very strong. How does this fact affect Momaday's purpose in writing?

7. (a) Identify Solzhenitsyn's purpose in writing. (b) Why would knowing some twentieth-century Russian history help you understand his work?

8. How does the title "Keep Memory Alive" reflect the author's purpose?

Extend Understanding

9. **Career Connection:** What are some careers that might be focused on keeping historical memories alive? Explain your answer.

from *The Way to Rainy Mountain* / from *Nobel Lecture* / Keep Memory Alive ◆ 689

Quick Review

In a **reflective essay,** an author shares his or her thoughts about an idea or a personal experience.

In a **persuasive essay,** an author attempts to convince readers to adopt a particular opinion or course of action.

The **author's purpose** is the reason that he or she is writing.

 Take It to the Net
www.phschool.com
Take the interactive self-test online to check your understanding of these selections.

✷ ENRICHMENT: Further Reading

Other Works by the Authors

Works by N. Scott Momaday
The Ancient Child
The Way to Rainy Mountain
House Made of Dawn

Works by Alexander Solzhenitsyn
One Day in the Life of Ivan Denisovich

Works by Elie Wiesel
Night

 Take It to the Net
Visit www.phschool.com for more information on the authors.

❶ Vocabulary Development

Word Analysis: Forms of *reciprocity*

1. reciprocal   3. reciprocate
2. reciprocity

Spelling Strategy

1. predictably   3. horribly
2. admirably

Students' sentences should use the words correctly.

Concept Development: Connotations

1. tenuous   5. transcends
2. assimilate   6. inexorably
3. reciprocity   7. engender
4. oratory

❷ Grammar

1. best   4. least
2. farther 5. worst
3. most

Writing Application

Possible response: I am the tallest child in our family and good at sports, but my brother gets better grades. It is hard to say who has the most achievements to be proud of or who will go farther in life.

Integrate Language Skills

❶ Vocabulary Development Lesson

Word Analysis: Forms of *reciprocity*

Reciprocity, which means "mutual action or dependence," has several forms—the adjective *reciprocal* and the verb *reciprocate*. Complete each sentence below with a form of *reciprocity*.

1. Pen pals have a ___?___ agreement.
2. The response to his writing demonstrates the ___?___ between readers and writers.
3. Although his situation did not allow him to ___?___, he appreciated the support.

Spelling Strategy

When adding *-ly* to a word that ends in the suffix *-ble*, drop the *le* and replace it with *-ly*. For example, *inexorable* becomes *inexorably*. Add the suffix *-ly* to each of the following words, and then use each word in a sentence.

1. predictable   2. admirable   3. horrible

Concept Development: Connotations

The connotation of a word is the set of ideas and emotions associated with it in addition to its denotation, or explicit meaning. In your notebook, write the word from the vocabulary list on p. 675 that is suggested by each of these song titles.

1. *Hanging by a Thread*
2. *(You Know) I Fit Right In*
3. *Give and Take*
4. *Speaking for Myself*
5. *My Love Is Higher Than the Sky*
6. *Without a Doubt (It Has to Be)*
7. *You've Created This Feeling*

❷ Grammar Lesson

Irregular Comparative and Superlative Degrees

While many modifiers follow a predictable pattern in forming the comparative and superlative degrees of adjectives and adverbs, other modifiers are irregular. The **irregular comparative** and **superlative forms** of certain adjectives and adverbs must be memorized. The forms of the adjectives and adverbs in the following chart are changed to show degrees of comparison:

Positive	Comparative	Superlative
bad	worse	worst
good	better	best
many	more	most
far	farther	farthest
little	less	least

𝒲𝒢 *Prentice Hall Writing and Grammar Connection: Chapter 25, Section 1*

690 ◆ *Nonfiction*

Practice Write each sentence using the correct comparative or superlative form of the adjective or adverb in parentheses.

1. The boy's ___?___ memories centered around summertime. (good)
2. Going a little ___?___ he found his grandmother's grave. (far)
3. He had taken the ___?___ risks. (many)
4. Of all the survivors, he was the ___?___ likely to represent the dead. (little)
5. He wrote about the ___?___ kind of memories. (bad)

Writing Application Write a paragraph describing your achievements. Use at least three irregular comparatives and superlatives in your writing.

TEACHING RESOURCES

The following resources can be used to enrich or extend the instruction for pp. 690–691.

Vocabulary

📖 **Selection Support:** Build Vocabulary, p. 165

📖 **Vocabulary and Spelling Practice Book** (Use this booklet for skills enrichment.)

Grammar

📖 **Selection Support:** Build Grammar Skills, p. 166

𝒲𝒢 **Writing and Grammar,** Platinum Level, p. 592 ▪

📄 **Daily Language Practice Transparencies**

Writing

𝒲𝒢 **Writing and Grammar,** Platinum Level, p. 132

📄 **Writing Models and Graphic Organizers on Transparencies,** pp. 45–51

💿 **Writing and Grammar iText CD-ROM** ▪

▪ **BLOCK SCHEDULING:** Resources marked with this symbol provide varied instruction during 90-minute blocks.

❸ Writing Lesson

Letter to Solzhenitsyn

As a student of world literature, you probably have opinions on its role in the world. Write a letter to Alexander Solzhenitsyn to tell him whether you agree or disagree with the main point of his Nobel Prize speech.

Prewriting   Identify the main point that Solzhenitsyn makes in his speech. Then, write freely about it for five minutes. Read what you have written, and circle the most important idea. Continue freewriting about the idea you circled. Repeat this process until you have narrowed down your viewpoint.

Model: Narrowing a Topic

I agree with Alexander Solzhenitsyn's ideas that there is (no such thing as "internal affairs.") We live in a world that has become too small to live behind walls. The key to future peace is communication.

"Internal" affairs describes . . .

> Picking one of the ideas expressed narrows the topic.

Drafting   Write your letter, and include details to elaborate and support your viewpoint.

Revising   Read your letter aloud to yourself, and determine whether your viewpoint is logical and well supported. If not, revise your letter.

 Prentice Hall Writing and Grammar Connection: Chapter 7, Section 2

❹ Extension Activities

Listening and Speaking   Analyze Wiesel's Nobel Prize speech, identifying the arguments he uses to persuade people to keep memory alive. Some types of arguments are

- *Analogy:* drawing a comparison
- *Authority:* citing the ideas of experts
- *Emotion:* appealing to people's feelings
- *Logic:* appealing to people's reason

Present your **speech analysis** to the class. Explain the arguments that Wiesel uses, and give examples from the speech to support your analysis.

Research and Technology   In a small group, prepare a report on the ritual dances of four Native American groups. Use books, library resources, and the Internet. If possible, locate a video recording of some of the dances. As a group, explain the dances to your class. **[Group Activity]**

Take It to the Net   www.phschool.com

Go online for an additional research activity using the Internet.

from *The Way to Rainy Mountain* / from *Nobel Lecture* / *Keep Memory Alive* ◆ 691

---

❸ Writing Lesson

- Have students freewrite about Solzhenitsyn's main point for five minutes. Then, have students circle the most important idea. Invite students to share these ideas with the class.

- Have students continue by following the directions for Prewriting, Drafting, and Revising in the Writing Lesson on p. 691.

- Use the transparencies for Persuasive Essay, pp. 45–51 in **Writing and Language Transparencies,** to show students a model of a persuasive essay. Remind them that their essays should be in the form of a letter.

- Use the Persuasion rubric in **Performance Assessment and Portfolio Management,** p. 11, to evaluate students' letters.

❹ Listening and Speaking

- Read aloud the types of persuasive arguments on this page, and make sure students understand each one.

- When students have completed their assignments, ask them to share some types of arguments they identified.

CUSTOMIZE INSTRUCTION for Universal Access

To address different learning styles, use the following activities suggested in the **Extension Activities** booklet, p. 42.

- For Verbal/Linguistic Learners, use Activity 5.
- For Visual/Spatial Learners, use Activity 6.
- For Verbal/Linguistic and Musical/Rhythmic Learners, use Activity 7.

ASSESSMENT RESOURCES

The following resources can be used to assess students' knowledge and skills.

Selection Assessment

- **Formal Assessment,** Selection Test, pp. 148–150
- **Open Book Test,** pp. 124–126
- **Got It! Assessment Videotapes,** Tape 4
- **Test Bank Software**

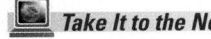 **Take It to the Net**
Visit www.phschool.com for self-tests and additional questions on the selections.

Writing Rubric

- **Performance Assess and Portfolio Mgmt.,** p. 11

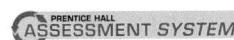 PRENTICE HALL ASSESSMENT SYSTEM

- **Workbook**
- **Transparencies**
- **Skill Book**
- **CD-ROM**

A Child's Christmas in Wales ✦
Marian Anderson: Famous Concert Singer

Lesson Objectives

1. To analyze and respond to literary elements
- Literary Analysis: Biography and Autobiography
- Comparing Literary Works

2. To read, comprehend, analyze, and critique a biography and an autobiography
- Reading Strategy: Recognizing Author's Attitude
- Reading Check questions
- Review and Assess questions
- Assessment Practice (ATE)

3. To develop word analysis skills, fluency, and systematic vocabulary
- Vocabulary Development Lesson: Musical Words

4. To understand and apply written and oral language conventions
- Spelling Strategy
- Grammar Lesson: Restrictive and Nonrestrictive Appositives

5. To understand and apply appropriate writing and research strategies
- Writing Lesson: Biographer's Account
- Extension Activity: Bibliography of Reference Materials

6. To understand and apply listening and speaking strategies
- Extension Activity: Musical Review

STEP-BY-STEP TEACHING GUIDE	PACING GUIDE
PRETEACH	
Motivate Students and Provide Background	
Use the Motivation activity (ATE p. 692)	5 min.
Read and discuss the Preview material and Background information (SE/ATE p. 692) **A**	5 min.
Introduce the Concepts	
Introduce the Literary Analysis and Reading Strategy (SE/ATE p. 693) **A**	15 min.
Pronounce the vocabulary words and read their definitions (SE p. 693)	5 min.
TEACH	
Monitor Comprehension	
Informally monitor comprehension by circulating while students read independently or in groups **A**	30 min.
Monitor students' comprehension with the Reading Check notes (SE/ATE pp. 695, 697, 699, 703, 705)	as students read
Develop vocabulary with Vocabulary notes (SE pp. 695–697, 699, 702, 703, 706; ATE p. 702)	as students read
Develop Understanding	
Develop students' understanding of biography and autobiography with Literary Analysis annotations (SE pp. 696, 700; ATE pp. 695, 696, 700) **A**	10 min.
Develop students' understanding of recognizing author's attitude with Reading Strategy annotations (SE pp. 695, 698, 703; ATE pp. 695, 698, 700, 703, 705)	10 min.
ASSESS	
Assess Mastery	
Assess students' mastery of the Reading Strategy and Literary Analysis by having them answer the Review and Assess questions (SE/ATE p. 707)	20 min.
Use one or more of the print and media Assessment Resources (ATE p. 709) **A**	up to 50 min.
EXTEND	
Apply Understanding	
Have students complete the Vocabulary Development Lesson and the Grammar Lesson (SE p. 708) **A**	20 min.
Apply students' knowledge of revising for objectivity using the Writing Lesson (SE/ATE p. 709) **A**	45 min.
Apply students' understanding using one or more of the Extension Activities (SE p. 709)	20–90 min.

 ACCELERATED INSTRUCTION:
Use the strategies and activities identified with an **A**.

UNIVERSAL ACCESS
- ● = Below Level Students
- ▲ = On-Level Students
- ■ = Above Level Students

Reading Level: Average/Easy
Average Number of Instructional Days: 4

RESOURCES		
PRINT 📖	**TRANSPARENCIES** 📑	**TECHNOLOGY** 💿 🎧 📼
• **Beyond Literature,** Career Connection: Music, p. 43 ▲ ■		• **Interest Grabber Video,** Tape 4 ● ▲ ■
• **Selection Support Workbook:** ● ▲ ■ Literary Analysis, p. 172 Reading Strategy, p. 171 Build Vocabulary, p. 169	• **Literary Analysis and Reading Transparencies,** pp. 85 and 86 ● ▲ ■	
• **Adapted Reader's Companion** ● • **Reader's Companion** ● • **Authors In Depth,** Platinum Level ■		• **Listening to Literature** ● ▲ ■ Audiocassettes, Sides 21, 22 Audio CDs, CD 14
• **English Learner's Companion** ● ▲ • **Literatura en español** ● ▲ • **Literary Analysis for Enrichment** ■	• **Fine Art Transparencies, Volume 1,** Art Transparency 20 ● ▲ ■	
• **Formal Assessment:** Selection Test, pp. 151–153 ● ▲ ■ • **Open Book Test,** pp. 127–129 ● ▲ ■ • **PRENTICE HALL ASSESSMENT SYSTEM** ● ▲ ■	• **PRENTICE HALL ASSESSMENT SYSTEM** ● ▲ ■ Skills Practice Answers and Explanations on Transparencies	• **Test Bank Software** ● ▲ ■ • **Got It! Assessment Videotapes,** Tape 4 ● ▲
• **Selection Support Workbook:** ● ▲ ■ Build Grammar Skills, p. 170 • **Writing and Grammar,** Platinum Level ● ▲ ■ • **Extension Activities,** p. 43 ● ▲ ■	• **Daily Language Practice Transparencies** ● ▲ • **Writing Models and Graphic Organizers on Transparencies,** p. 13 ● ▲ ■	• **Writing and Grammar iText CD-ROM** ● ▲ ■ 🖼 **Take It to the Net** www.phschool.com

BLOCK SCHEDULING: Use one 90-minute class period to preteach the selection and have students read it. Use a second 90-minute class period to assess students' mastery of skills and have them complete one of the Extension Activities.

Motivation

Prepare students to read the two selections of remembrances by taking five minutes to write two kinds of memories. First, ask students to remember sensations, such as being caught in a storm. Second, ask students to recall information about their favorite performer or sports star. Discuss how the type of memory students write about affects the style and language of their writing. Explain that they will see more clearly how subject matter can affect style in non-fiction when they read "A Child's Christmas in Wales" and "Marian Anderson: Famous Concert Singer."

▣ Interest Grabber Video

As an alternative, play "Christmas Traditions Around the World" on Tape 4 to engage student interest.

❶ Background

History

Philadelphia-born contralto Marian Anderson made musical history with her compelling interpretations of art songs, arias, and spirituals. She also made civil rights history with her April 1939 concert on the steps of the Lincoln Memorial and her January 1955 debut at the Metropolitan Opera Company.

Prepare to Read

A Child's Christmas in Wales ◆
Marian Anderson: Famous Concert Singer

Winter Scene, Philip Gale Fine Art, Chepstow, Gwent, Wales, UK

▣ *Take It to the Net*

Visit www.phschool.com for interactive activities and instruction related to these selections, including

- background
- graphic organizers
- literary elements
- reading strategies

Preview

Connecting to the Literature

Our remembrances take shape around people, places, and events from the past that have a special significance. In "A Child's Christmas in Wales," the author shares childhood memories of a holiday. Langston Hughes's account of Marian Anderson introduces new generations of readers to her.

❶ Background

It is remarkable that Marian Anderson achieved the level of success that she did. Because of racial prejudice in the United States, Anderson was unable to achieve the level of recognition of her white counterparts and traveled to Europe to find fame. Even after she achieved international recognition, Anderson was not permitted to sing in certain places in the United States because of her race.

692 ◆ *Nonfiction*

TEACHING RESOURCES

The following resources can be used to enrich or extend the instruction for pp. 692–693.

Motivation
▣ **Interest Grabber Video,** Tape 4 ▣

Background
▣ **Beyond Literature,** p. 43

▣ *Take It to the Net*
Visit www.phschool.com for background and hotlinks for the selections.

Literary Analysis
▣ **Selection Support Workbook:** Literary Analysis, p. 172 ▣

▣ **Literary Analysis and Reading Transparencies,** Biography and Autobiography, p. 84

Reading
▣ **Literary Analysis and Reading Transparencies,** Recognizing Author's Attitude, p. 85

▣ **BLOCK SCHEDULING:** Resources marked with this symbol provide varied instruction during 90-minute blocks.

❷ Literary Analysis

Biography and Autobiography

A **biography** is an account of a person's life written by another individual. The biographer gathers information from sources such as letters, diaries, and interviews. In his essay about Marian Anderson, Hughes focuses on the historical situation of prejudice in the United States and shows how Marian Anderson was able to overcome that prejudice.

An **autobiography** is a person's own account of his or her life. The writer of an autobiography can share personal thoughts and feelings, as Dylan Thomas does in "A Child's Christmas in Wales." As you read, notice the differences in the ways each author presents his material.

Comparing Literary Works

While a biography and an autobiography each relate true-life stories, the forms differ in a critical way—the writer's knowledge of the subject. Thomas shares his ideas through the filter of his own memory, choosing those details he wants to share with readers and revealing his personal connections to the events. In contrast, a biographer, like Hughes, has limited access to his subject, Marian Anderson. As you read, consider the ways in which the perspective of the writer colors the details included.

❸ Reading Strategy

Recognizing Author's Attitude

The **author's attitude** is the way he or she feels about the subject. The attitude that a biographer or an autobiographer brings to the subject is reflected in the way he or she presents information. To recognize an author's attitude, notice the details and events the author chooses to present. Use a diagram like the one here to help you identify the author's attitude.

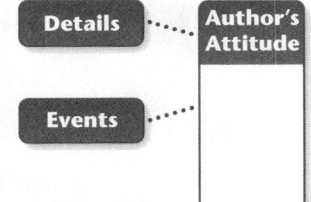

Vocabulary Development

sidle (sīd′ əl) v. move sideways in a sneaky way (p. 695)

prey (prā) n. animal hunted for food (p. 695)

wallowed (wäl′ ōd) v. enjoyed completely; took great pleasure (p. 696)

crocheted (krō shād′) adj. made with yarn woven with hooked needles (p. 697)

brittle (brit′ əl) adj. easily broken or shattered (p. 699)

trod (träd) v. walked (p. 699)

forlorn (fôr lôrn′) adj. abandoned; deserted (p. 699)

arias (är′ ē əz) n. melodies in an opera, especially for solo voice with instrumental accompaniment (p. 702)

staunch (stônch) adj. steadfast; loyal (p. 703)

repertoire (rep′ ər twär′) n. stock of songs that a singer is ready to perform (p. 706)

A Child's Christmas in Wales / Marian Anderson: Famous Concert Singer ◆ 693

---

❷ Literary Analysis
Biography and Autobiography

- Explain that a biography is an account of a person's life that is written by another person, called a *biographer*. The biographer gathers material from many sources, including letters, diaries, and interviews.

- Point out that an autobiography, by contrast, is a person's own account of his or her life. In an autobiography, the author can share thoughts, feelings, and comments about certain events and their effect on his or her life.

- Point out that an autobiography is a first-person account, so the pronoun "I" is frequently used. Ask students what pronoun(s) they would expect to see in a biography (he, she, they).

- Have students read and compare the first sentences of each selection as an illustration of this concept.

❸ Reading Strategy
Recognizing Author's Attitude

- Explain that both biographers and autobiographers express a particular attitude toward their subjects. Ask students to give examples of attitudes that can come across in writing (for example, angry, humorous, admiring, respectful, judgmental, matter-of-fact).

- Encourage students to take notes on events, words, and details that convey the authors' attitudes as they read the two selections.

Vocabulary Development

- Pronounce each vocabulary word for students, and read the definitions as a class. Have students identify any words with which they are already familiar.

CUSTOMIZE INSTRUCTION FOR UNIVERSAL ACCESS

For Special Needs Students	For Less Proficient Readers	For English Learners
Have students read the adapted version of "Marian Anderson: Famous Concert Singer" in the **Adapted Reader's Companion**. This version provides basic-level instruction in an interactive format with questions and write-on lines. Completing the adapted version will prepare students to read the selection in the Student Edition.	Have students read the selection in the **Reader's Companion**. This version provides basic-level instruction in an interactive format with questions and write-on lines. After students finish the selection in the **Reader's Companion**, have them complete the questions and activities in the Student Edition.	Have students read the adapted version of the selection in the **English Learner's Companion**. This version provides basic-level instruction in an interactive format with questions and write-on lines. Completing the adapted version will prepare students to read the selection in the Student Edition.

 E-Teach

Visit E-Teach at www.phschool.com for teachers' essays on how to teach, with questions and answers.

CUSTOMIZE INSTRUCTION
Visual/Spatial Learners

Encourage students to compare the details of the pictures that accompany the text to the text itself. Tell students that because the pictures were created specifically for this story, they should be able to identify significant details in the pictures that reflect Thomas's recollections.

❶ About the Selection

"A Child's Christmas in Wales" evokes the enchantment that holiday celebrations hold for children. In this famous work, the voice of the adult Dylan Thomas describes childhood Christmases, blended and transfigured by the magic of memory. With fondness and nostalgia, he recalls the activities, sensory details, and people he associates with this holiday.

❷ Background

Art

The Whistle, **by Fritz Eichenberg**

The German artist Fritz Eichenberg has illustrated many classic children's books, including Jonathan Swift's *Gulliver's Travels* and the modern classic *Black Beauty,* by Anna Sewell. Born in Cologne, Germany, Eichenberg traveled as a young man and eventually settled in Tuckahoe, New York. His highly rendered ink drawing "The Whistle," shown here, depicts a scene described in "A Child's Christmas in Wales." Use this question for discussion:

• Why did the artist depict the two boys as looking exactly alike?
  Answer: In the text, Thomas says that the other boy is the "spit image of myself," meaning he looks the same. The physical resemblance also suggests the cocky attitude the two boys share, as well as their similar Christmas experiences.

❸ ▶Critical Viewing

Answer: Students will expect the characters to be playful or mischievous boys who spend time outdoors in the winter.

694

---

❶
A Child's *Christmas* in Wales

Dylan Thomas

The Whistle (tinted), Fritz Eichenberg etching. © Fritz Eichenberg Trust/Licensed by VAGA, New York, NY

❷

❸ ▲ **Critical Viewing** Based on this picture, what kind of characters do you expect to find in Thomas's childhood memory? **[Draw Conclusions]**

694 ◆ *Nonfiction*

TEACHING RESOURCES

The following resources can be used to enrich or extend the instruction for pp. 694–706.

Reading

📖 **Selection Support:** Reading Strategy, p. 171; Build Vocabulary, p. 169

📖 **Reader's Companion**

📖 **English Learner's Companion**

🎧 **Listening to Literature Audiocassettes,** Sides 21 and 22 ▪

💿 **Listening to Literature Audio CDs,** CD 14 ▪

Extension

📖 **Authors In Depth,** Platinum Level (The collection includes eleven additional selections by Langston Hughes for extended reading.)

📖 **Fine Art Transparencies,** Volume 1, Art Transparency 20 (Use the art transparency to illustrate for students how an artist can use images and impressions to create a sense of "memory.")

▪ **BLOCK SCHEDULING:** Resources marked with this symbol provide varied instruction during 90-minute blocks.

One Christmas was so much like another, in those years around the sea-town corner now and out of all sound except the distant speaking of the voices I sometimes hear a moment before sleep, that I can never remember whether it snowed for six days and six nights when I was twelve or whether it snowed for twelve days and twelve nights when I was six. All the Christmases roll down toward the two-tongued sea, like a cold and headlong moon bundling down the sky that was our street; and they stop at the rim of the ice-edged, fish-freezing waves, and I plunge my hands in the snow and bring out whatever I can find. In goes my hand into that wool-white bell-tongued ball of holidays resting at the rim of the carol-singing seas, and out come Mrs. Prothero and the firemen.

It was on the afternoon of the day of Christmas Eve, and I was in Mrs. Prothero's garden, waiting for cats, with her son Jim. It was snowing. It was always snowing at Christmas. December, in my memory, is white as Lapland, though there were no reindeers. But there were cats. Patient, cold and callous, our hands wrapped in socks, we waited to snowball the cats. Sleek and long as jaguars and horrible-whiskered, spitting and snarling, they would slink and <u>sidle</u> over the white back-garden walls, and the lynx-eyed hunters, Jim and I, fur-capped and moccasined trappers from Hudson Bay,[1] off Mumbles Road, would hurl our deadly snowballs at the green of their eyes. The wise cats never appeared. We were so still, Eskimo-footed arctic marksmen in the muffling silence of the eternal snows—eternal, ever since Wednesday—that we never heard Mrs. Prothero's first cry from her igloo at the bottom of the garden. Or, if we heard it at all, it was, to us, like the far-off challenge of our enemy and <u>prey</u>, the neighbor's polar cat. But soon the voice grew louder. "Fire!" cried Mrs. Prothero, and she beat the dinner-gong.

And we ran down the garden, with the snowballs in our arms, toward the house; and smoke, indeed, was pouring out of the dining room, and the gong was bombilating,[2] and Mrs. Prothero was announcing ruin like a town crier in Pompeii.[3] This was better than all the cats in Wales standing on the wall in a row. We bounded into the house, laden with snowballs, and stopped at the open door of the smoke-filled room.

Something was burning all right; perhaps it was Mr. Prothero, who always slept there after midday dinner with a newspaper over his face. But he was standing in the middle of the room, saying "A fine Christmas!" and smacking at the smoke with a slipper.

"Call the fire brigade," cried Mrs. Prothero as she beat the gong.

---

1. **Hudson Bay** inland sea in northeastern Canada.
2. **bombilating** (bäm´ bə lāt iŋ) v. making a buzzing, droning sound as though a bomb were approaching.
3. **Pompeii** (päm pā´) city in Italy that was destroyed by the eruption of Mount Vesuvius in A.D. 79.

Reading Strategy
Recognizing Author's Attitude What details in this paragraph show the author's attitude about his Christmas memories?

sidle (sīd´ əl) v. move sideways in a sneaky way

prey (prā) n. animal hunted for food

6  **Reading Check**
In the Christmases of the writer's memory, what is the weather like?

A Child's Christmas in Wales ◆ 695

---

❼ Background

Wales

Wales is part of the United Kingdom and governed by England. However, the Welsh have fought many battles throughout history to resist English rule and maintain their unique identity.

❽ Literary Analysis

Biography and Autobiography

- Ask the students the Literary Analysis question on p. 696: Why does the author insist that the snows of his childhood were different?

  Possible response: People tend to exaggerate memories from their childhood because the world seems more intense and extreme from a child's point of view.

- Ask students to name other reasons that stories of the past tend to get exaggerated.

  Answer: Students might mention that memories blur and get mixed up with the passage of time. Or, storytellers might intentionally exaggerate to create a humorous or dramatic effect for readers.

"They won't be there," said Mr. Prothero, "it's Christmas."

There was no fire to be seen, only clouds of smoke and Mr. Prothero standing in the middle of them, waving his slipper as though he were conducting.

"Do something," he said.

And we threw all our snowballs into the smoke—I think we missed Mr. Prothero—and ran out of the house to the telephone box.

"Let's call the police as well," Jim said.

"And the ambulance."

"And Ernie Jenkins, he likes fires."

But we only called the fire brigade, and soon the fire engine came and three tall men in helmets brought a hose into the house and Mr. Prothero got out just in time before they turned it on. Nobody could have had a noisier Christmas Eve. And when the firemen turned off the hose and were standing in the wet, smoky room, Jim's aunt, Miss Prothero, came downstairs and peered in at them. Jim and I waited, very quietly, to hear what she would say to them. She said the right thing, always. She looked at the three tall firemen in their shining helmets, standing among the smoke and cinders and dissolving snowballs, and she said: "Would you like anything to read?"

Years and years and years ago, when I was a boy, when there were wolves in Wales, and birds the color of red-flannel petticoats whisked past the harp-shaped hills, when we sang and <u>wallowed</u> all night and day in caves that smelt like Sunday afternoons in damp front farmhouse parlors, and we chased, with the jawbones of deacons, the English and the bears, before the motor car, before the wheel, before the duchess-faced horse, when we rode the daft[4] and happy hills bareback, it snowed and it snowed. But here a small boy says: "It snowed last year, too. I made a snowman and my brother knocked it down and I knocked my brother down and then we had tea."

"But that was not the same snow," I say. "Our snow was not only shaken from whitewash buckets down the sky, it came shawling[5] out of the ground and swam and drifted out of the arms and hands and bodies of the trees; snow grew overnight on the roofs of the houses like a pure and grandfather moss, minutely white-ivied the walls and settled on the postman, opening the gate, like a dumb, numb thunderstorm of white, torn Christmas cards."

"Were there postmen then, too?"

"With sprinkling eyes and wind-cherried noses, on spread, frozen feet they crunched up to the doors and mittened on them manfully. But all that the children could hear was a ringing of bells."

---

4. **daft** *adj.* silly; foolish.
5. **shawling** *adv.* draping like a shawl.

Wales

Dylan Thomas was born in the southern seaport town of Swansea, a large industrial center in Wales, a principality located west of England. Wales along with England, Scotland, and Northern Ireland make up the United Kingdom, or Great Britain.

Wales has a maritime climate with a heavy annual precipitation of rain and snow. The Welsh have their own ancient language, but the Welsh citizens are bilingual and speak English as well. Winters in Wales held a special place in Thomas's memories, as you will discover in this selection.

wallowed (wäl´ ōd) *v.* enjoyed completely; took great pleasure

Literary Analysis

Biography and Autobiography Why does the author insist that the snows of his childhood were different?

"You mean that the postman went rat-a-tat-tat and the doors rang?"

"I mean that the bells that the children could hear were inside them."

"I only hear thunder sometimes, never bells."

"There were church bells, too."

"Inside them?"

"No, no, no, in the bat-black, snow-white belfries, tugged by bishops and storks. And they rang their tidings over the bandaged town, over the frozen foam of the powder and ice-cream hills, over the crackling sea. It seemed that all the churches boomed for joy under my window: and the weathercocks crew for Christmas, on our fence."

"Get back to the postmen."

"They were just ordinary postmen, fond of walking and dogs and Christmas and the snow. They knocked on the doors with blue knuckles. . . ."

"Ours has got a black knocker. . . ."

"And then they stood on the white Welcome mat in the little, drifted porches and huffed and puffed, making ghosts with their breath, and jogged from foot to foot like small boys wanting to go out."

"And then the presents?"

"And then the Presents, after the Christmas box. And the cold postman, with a rose on his button-nose, tingled down the tea-tray-slithered run of the chilly glinting hill. He went in his ice-bound boots like a man on fish-monger's slabs.[6] He wagged his bag like a frozen camel's hump, dizzily turned the corner on one foot, and was gone."

"Get back to the Presents."

"There were the Useful Presents: engulfing mufflers of the old coach days, and mittens made for giant sloths;[7] zebra scarfs of a substance like silky gum that could be tug-o'-warred down to the galoshes;[8] blinding tam-o'-shanters[9] like patchwork tea cozies[10] and bunny-suited busbies[11] and balaclavas[12] for victims of head-shrinking tribes; from aunts who always wore wool next to the skin there were mustached and rasping vests that made you wonder why the aunts had any skin left at all; and once I had a little <u>crocheted</u> nose bag from an aunt now, alas, no longer whinnying with us. And pictureless books in which small boys, though warned with quotations not to, *would* skate on Farmer Giles'

❿ ▲ Critical Viewing
How well does this picture capture the atmosphere of the holiday Thomas describes? **[Assess]**

crocheted (krō shād´) *adj.* made with yarn woven with hooked needles

---

6. **fish-monger's slabs** flat, slimy surface on which fish are displayed for sale.
7. **sloths** (slôths) *n.* two-toed mammals that hang from trees.
8. **galoshes** (gə läsh´ əz) *n.* rubber overshoes or boots.
9. **tam-o'-shanters** Scottish caps.
10. **tea cozies** knitted or padded covers placed over a teapot to keep the contents warm.
11. **busbies** (buz´ bēz) tall fur hats worn as part of the full-dress uniforms of guardsmen in the British army.
12. **balaclavas** (bäl´ ə klä´ vəz) knitted helmets with an opening for the nose and eyes.

⓫ ✔Reading Check
What are two of the Useful Presents?

A Child's Christmas in Wales ◆ 697

pond and did and drowned; and books that told me everything about the wasp, except why."

"Go on to the Useless Presents."

⓬ "Bags of moist and many-colored jelly babies[13] and a folded flag and a false nose and a tram-conductor's cap[14] and a machine that punched tickets and rang a bell; never a catapult;[15] once, by mistake that no one could explain, a little hatchet; and a celluloid duck that made, when you pressed it, a most unducklike sound, a mewing moo that an ambitious cat might make who wished to be a cow; and a painting book in which I could make the grass, the trees, the sea and the animals any color I pleased, and still the dazzling sky-blue sheep are grazing in the red field under the rainbow-billed and pea-green birds. Hard-boiled, toffee, fudge and allsorts, crunches, cracknels, humbugs, glaciers, marzipan, and butterwelsh[16] for the Welsh. And troops of bright tin soldiers who, if they could not fight, could always run. And Snakes-and-Families and Happy Ladders.[17] And Easy Hobbi-Games for Little Engineers, complete with instructions. Oh, easy for Leonardo![18] And a whistle to make the dogs bark to wake up the old man next door to make him beat on the wall with his stick to shake our picture off the wall. And a packet of cigarettes: you put one in your mouth and you stood at the corner of the street and you waited for hours, in vain, for an old lady to scold you for smoking a cigarette, and then with a smirk you ate it. And then it was breakfast under the balloons."

"Were there Uncles, like in our house?"

"There are always Uncles at Christmas. The same Uncles. And on Christmas mornings, with dog-disturbing whistle and sugar fags,[19] I would scour the swatched town for the news of the little world, and find always a dead bird by the white Post Office or by the deserted swings; perhaps a robin, all but one of his fires out. Men and women wading or scooping back from chapel, with taproom noses and wind-bussed cheeks, all albinos,[20] huddled their stiff black jarring feathers against the irreligious snow. Mistletoe hung from the gas brackets[21] in all the front parlors; there was sherry and walnuts and bottled beer and crackers by the dessert-spoons; and cats in their fur-abouts watched the

---

13. **jelly babies** candies in the shape of babies.
14. **tram-conductor's cap** streetcar or trolley car operator's cap.
15. **catapult** (kat´ ə pult´) ancient military machine for throwing or shooting stones or spears; slingshot.
16. **Hard-boiled . . . butterwelsh** various kinds of candy.
17. **Snakes-and-Families and Happy Ladders** games, the names of which Dylan Thomas mixes up on purpose. The games are actually Snakes-and-Ladders and Happy Families.
18. **Leonardo** Leonardo da Vinci (1452–1519), an Italian painter, sculptor, architect, engineer, and scientist.
19. **sugar fags** candy cigarettes.
20. **albinos** (al bī´ nōz) people who because of a genetic factor have unusually pale skin and white hair.
21. **gas brackets** wall fixtures for gaslights.

The Whistle (detail and tint), Fritz Eichenberg etching, © Fritz Eichenberg Trust/Licensed by VAGA, New York, NY

Reading Strategy
Recognizing Author's Attitude What do these sensory details indicate about the author's attitude?

---

fires; and the high-heaped fire spat, all ready for the chestnuts and the mulling pokers. Some few large men sat in the front parlors, without their collars, Uncles almost certainly, trying their new cigars, holding them out judiciously at arms' length, returning them to their mouths, coughing, then holding them out again as though waiting for the explosion; and some few small aunts, not wanted in the kitchen, nor anywhere else for that matter, sat on the very edges of their chairs, poised and <u>brittle</u>, afraid to break, like faded cups and saucers."

Not many those mornings <u>trod</u> the piling streets: an old man always, fawn-bowlered,[22] yellow-gloved and, at this time of year, with spats[23] of snow, would take his constitutional[24] to the white bowling green and back, as he would take it wet or fine on Christmas Day or Doomsday; sometimes two hale young men, with big pipes blazing, no overcoats and wind-blown scarfs, would trudge, unspeaking, down to the <u>forlorn</u> sea, to work up an appetite, to blow away the fumes, who knows, to walk into the waves until nothing of them was left but the two curling smoke clouds of their inextinguishable briars.[25] Then I would be slap-dashing home, the gravy smell of the dinners of others, the bird smell, the brandy, the pudding and mince, coiling up to my nostrils, when out of a snow-clogged side lane would come a boy the spit of myself, with a pink-tipped cigarette and the violet past of a black eye, cocky as a bullfinch, leering all to himself. I hated him on sight and sound, and would be about to put my dog whistle to my lips and blow him off the face of Christmas when suddenly he, with a violet wink, put *his* whistle to *his* lips and blew so stridently, so high, so exquisitely loud, that gobbling faces, their cheeks bulged with goose, would press against their tinseled windows, the whole length of the white echoing street. For dinner we had turkey and blazing pudding, and after dinner the Uncles sat in front of the fire, loosened all buttons, put their large moist hands over their watch chains, groaned a little and slept. Mothers, aunts and sisters scuttled to and fro, bearing tureens.[26] Auntie Bessie, who had already been frightened, twice, by a clock-work mouse, whimpered at the sideboard and had some elderberry wine. The dog was sick. Auntie Dosie had to have three aspirins, but Auntie Hannah, who liked port, stood in the middle of the snowbound back yard, singing like a big-bosomed thrush. I would blow up balloons to see how big they would blow up to; and, when they burst, which they all did, the Uncles jumped and rumbled. In the rich and heavy afternoon, the Uncles breathing like dolphins and the snow descending, I would sit among festoons[27] and Chinese lanterns and nibble dates and try to make a model man-o'-war[28] following the Instructions for Little Engineers, and produce what might be mistaken for a sea-going tramcar.

---

22. **fawn-bowlered** tan-hatted.
23. **spats** coverings for the instep and ankle.
24. **constitutional** walk taken for one's health.
25. **briars** pipes.
26. **tureens** (to͞o rēnz´) deep dishes with covers.
27. **festoons** wreaths and garlands.
28. **man-o'-war** warship.

brittle (brit´ əl) *adj.* easily broken or shattered

trod (träd) *v.* walked

forlorn (fôr lôrn´) *adj.* abandoned; deserted

The Whistle (detail and tint), Fritz Eichenberg etching. © Fritz Eichenberg Trust/Licensed by VAGA, New York, NY

14 ✓**Reading Check**

What does the narrator do after opening presents and before dinner?

A Child's Christmas in Wales ◆ 699

13 **Critical Thinking**
Compare and Contrast

• Ask students whether the adults described in this passage share the children's sense of wonder and excitement about Christmas. Have them support their answers with details from the passage.
Possible response: The adults do not seem to share the children's feelings. The uncles seem content but bored as they smoke their cigars. The aunts seem timid and uncomfortable.

• Ask students whether they can understand the sense of wonder expressed by the author. Invite them to share examples of similar experiences from their own childhood.

14 ✓**Reading Check**

Answer: The narrator walks the streets of his town, noticing who is out and about.

CUSTOMIZE INSTRUCTION FOR UNIVERSAL ACCESS

For English Learners	For Gifted/ Talented Students
Students might find some of the vocabulary in the narrative difficult to understand. To provide help with unfamiliar words, give students context sentences, such as this one: On his way to school, Sam *trod* on the sidewalks.	These students may enjoy performing an oral interpretation of "A Child's Christmas in Wales." Have them work together to analyze the feelings expressed in each section of the selection. Then, they can decide on specific paragraphs for each student to interpret and read aloud.

⓯ Reading Strategy

Recognizing Author's Attitude

- Ask students to point out two or three pretending games or pranks that the author describes in the story.
- Discuss with the students what attitude the author seems to take toward these games and pranks. Possible response: He is delighted by them and seems to miss this imaginative, uninhibited time of his life.

⓰ Literary Analysis

Biography and Autobiography

- Ask students the Literary Analysis question on p. 700: What does this brief story about caroling add to the selection? Possible response: The story about caroling gives the author a chance to recall ghost stories and other tall tales that are often told at holiday gatherings.
- Then, ask students whether families still tell ghost stories and tall tales at holiday gatherings. What other activities have replaced storytelling? Answer: Many students will say that television shows, movies, video games, and computer games have replaced storytelling at family gatherings.

Or I would go out, my bright new boots squeaking, into the white world, on to the seaward hill, to call on Jim and Dan and Jack and to pad through the still streets, leaving huge deep footprints on the hidden pavements.

"I bet people will think there's been hippos."

"What would you do if you saw a hippo coming down our street?"

"I'd go like this, bang! I'd throw him over the railings and roll him down the hill and then I'd tickle him under the ear and he'd wag his tail."

⓯ "What would you do if you saw *two* hippos?"

Iron-flanked and bellowing he-hippos clanked and battered through the scudding snow toward us as we passed Mr. Daniel's house.

"Let's post Mr. Daniel a snowball through his letter box."

"Let's write things in the snow."

"Let's write, 'Mr. Daniel looks like a spaniel' all over his lawn."

Or we walked on the white shore. "Can the fishes see it's snowing?"

The silent one-clouded heavens drifted on to the sea. Now we were snow-blind travelers lost on the north hills, and vast dewlapped[29] dogs, with flasks round their necks, ambled and shambled up to us, baying "Excelsior."[30] We returned home through the poor streets where only a few children fumbled with bare red fingers in the wheel-rutted snow and cat-called after us, their voices fading away, as we trudged uphill, into the cries of the dock birds and the hooting of ships out in the whirling bay. And then, at tea the recovered Uncles would be jolly; and the ice cake loomed in the center of the table like a marble grave. Auntie Hannah laced her tea with rum, because it was only once a year.

Bring out the tall tales now that we told by the fire as the gaslight bubbled like a diver. Ghosts whooed like owls in the long nights when I dared not look over my shoulder; animals lurked in the cubbyhole under the stairs where the gas meter ticked. And I remember that we went singing carols once, when there wasn't the shaving of a moon to light the flying streets. At the end of a long road was a drive that led to a large house, and we stumbled up the darkness of the drive that night, each one of us afraid, each one holding a stone in his hand in case, and all of us too brave to say a word. The wind through the trees made nois-

⓰ es as of old and unpleasant and maybe webfooted men wheezing in caves. We reached the black bulk of the house.

"What shall we give them? Hark the Herald?"

"No," Jack said, "Good King Wenceslas. I'll count three."

One, two, three, and we began to sing, our voices high and seemingly distant in the snow-felted darkness round the house that was occupied by nobody we knew. We stood close together, near the dark door.

> Good King Wenceslas
>   looked out
> On the Feast of Stephen . . .

---

29. **dewlapped** having loose folds of skin hanging from the throat.
30. **Excelsior** (eks sel′ sē ôr′) Latin phrase meaning "onward and upward."

700 ◆ *Nonfiction*

Literary Analysis
Biography and Autobiography What does this brief story about caroling add to the selection?

And then a small, dry voice, like the voice of someone who has not spoken for a long time, joined our singing: a small, dry, eggshell voice from the other side of the door: a small dry voice through the keyhole. And when we stopped running we were outside *our* house; the front room was lovely; balloons floated under the hot-water-bottle-gulping gas; everything was good again and shone over the town.

"Perhaps it was a ghost," Jim said.

"Perhaps it was trolls,"[31] Dan said, who was always reading.

"Let's go in and see if there's any jelly left," Jack said. And we did that.

Always on Christmas night there was music. An uncle played the fiddle, a cousin sang "Cherry Ripe," and another uncle sang "Drake's Drum." It was very warm in the little house. Auntie Hannah, who had got on to the parsnip wine, sang a song about Bleeding Hearts and Death, and then another in which she said her heart was like a Bird's Nest; and then everybody laughed again; and then I went to bed. Looking through my bedroom window, out into the moonlight and the unending smoke-colored snow, I could see the lights in the windows of all the other houses on our hill and hear the music rising from them up the long, steadily falling night. I turned the gas down, I got into bed. I said some words to the close and holy darkness, and then I slept.

---

31. **trolls** mythical Scandinavian beings.

Review and Assess

Thinking About the Selection

1. **Respond:** Do you find something familiar in Thomas's memories? Explain.
2. **(a) Recall:** How did Jim and Dylan respond to the fire at the Protheros' house? **(b) Analyze:** What details indicate that "A Child's Christmas in Wales" is a childhood memory narrated by an adult?
3. **(a) Recall:** Describe three events in Thomas's recollections of Christmas. **(b) Compare and Contrast:** In what ways was Christmas for the children different from Christmas for the adults?
4. **(a) Recall:** What is the difference between the Useful Presents and the Useless Presents? **(b) Interpret:** What does the classification of gifts tell you about the author's values?
5. **(a) Recall:** List several examples of exaggeration in the essay. **(b) Analyze:** What is the effect of these exaggerations?
6. **Evaluate:** How can something like Thomas's essay, which concentrates on the past, still be relevant in today's world?

Dylan Thomas

(1914–1953)

Dylan Thomas wanted to be a poet ever since he was a small child. In the poem "Fern Hill" (1946), he fondly evokes the memories of his early childhood. Thomas's first book of poetry was published when he moved to London at the age of twenty. His poetry readings in England and the United States brought him popular appeal but little income. Poverty and a stormy private life took their toll, and Thomas died in New York at the age of thirty-nine.

A Child's Christmas in Wales ◆ 701

CUSTOMIZE INSTRUCTION FOR UNIVERSAL ACCESS

For English Learners	For Advanced Readers
Have students who are familiar with the customs of Christmas caroling explain these customs to those who are not. If they know the carols mentioned here, have them sing or say their lyrics. In turn, English learners can describe or sing holiday songs in their native languages.	Students might want to try some of the author's techniques in their own autobiographical writing. One technique is having the small boy interrupt the narrator and request more details about certain parts. Another technique is listing objects or feelings to create atmosphere.

17 MARIAN ANDERSON
Famous Concert Singer
Langston Hughes

When Marian Anderson was born in a little red brick house in Philadelphia, a famous group of Negro singers, the Fisk Jubilee Singers, had already carried the spirituals all over Europe. And a colored woman billed as "Black Patti" had become famous on variety programs as a singer of both folk songs and the classics. Both Negro and white minstrels had popularized American songs. The all-Negro musical comedies of Bert Williams and George Walker had been successful on Broadway. But no well-trained colored singers performing the

18 ▲ Critical Viewing
Based on this photograph, what kind of music do you think Marian Anderson sang? **[Speculate]**

702 ◆ Nonfiction

great songs of Schubert, Handel, and the other masters, or the <u>arias</u> from famous operas, had become successful on the concert stage. And most people thought of Negro vocalists only in connection with spirituals. Roland Hayes[1] and Marian Anderson were the first to become famous enough to break this stereotype.

Marian Anderson's mother was a <u>staunch</u> church worker who loved to croon the hymns of her faith about the house, as did the aunt who came to live with them when Marian's father died. Both parents were from Virginia. Marian's mother had been a schoolteacher there, and her father a farm boy. Shortly after they moved to Philadelphia where three daughters were born, the father died, and the mother went to work at Wanamaker's department store. But she saw to it that her children attended school and church regularly. The father had been an usher in the Union Baptist Church, so the congregation took an interest in his three little girls. Marian was the oldest and, before she was eight, singing in the Sunday school choir, she had already learned a great many hymns and spirituals by heart.

One day Marian saw an old violin in a pawnshop window marked $3.45. She set her mind on that violin, and began to save the nickels and dimes neighbors would give her for scrubbing their white front steps—the kind of stone steps so characteristic of Philadelphia and Baltimore houses—until she had $3.00. The pawnshop man let her take the violin at a reduced price. Marian never became very good on the violin. A few years later her mother bought a piano, so the child forgot all about it in favor of their newer instrument. By that time, too, her unusual singing voice had attracted the attention of her choir master, and at the age of fourteen she was promoted to a place in the main church choir. There she learned all four parts of all the hymns and anthems and could easily fill in anywhere from bass to soprano.

Sensing that she had exceptional musical talent, some of the church members began to raise money so that she might have singing lessons. But her first teacher, a colored woman, refused to accept any pay for instructing so talented a child. So the church folks put their money into a trust fund called "Marian Anderson's Future," banking it until the time came for her to have advanced training. Meanwhile, Marian attended South Philadelphia High School for Girls and took part in various group concerts, usually doing the solo parts. When she was fifteen she sang a group of songs alone at a Sunday School Convention in Harrisburg and word of her talent began to spread about the state. When she was graduated from high school, the Philadelphia Choral Society, a Negro group, sponsored her further study and secured for her one of the best local teachers. Then in 1925 she journeyed to New York to take part, with three hundred other young singers, in the New York Philharmonic Competitions, where she won first place, and appeared with the orchestra at Lewisohn Stadium.

This appearance was given wide publicity, but very few lucrative

---

1. **Roland Hayes** (1887–1977) famous African American tenor in the United States.

Marian Anderson: Famous Concert Singer ◆ 703

---

arias (ärʹ ē əz) *n.* melodies in an opera, especially for solo voice with instrumental accompaniment

staunch (stônch) *adj.* steadfast; loyal

Reading Strategy
Recognizing Author's Attitude What words or phrases reveal the author's attitude toward Anderson in this passage?

22 **Reading Check**
For what reason does Marian Anderson journey to New York in 1925?

---

20 Vocabulary Development
Musical Words

- Draw students' attention to the word *arias* and its definition, "melodies in an opera, especially for solo voice with instrumental accompaniment."

- Ask students to list other words related to music that Hughes uses, such as *repertoire, soprano, croon,* and *hymns.* Define the words that are unfamiliar to students.

21 Reading Strategy
Recognizing Author's Attitude

- Point out that the author expresses his admiration for Marian Anderson even when she was a child, before she became famous.

- Ask students the Reading Strategy question on p. 703: What words or phrases reveal the author's attitude toward Anderson in this passage? Possible responses: Marian "set her mind" on a violin; before she was eight, she had already learned many songs by heart; she could sing all four parts in a hymn or anthem.

▶ Monitor Progress Have students list the details about Anderson that Hughes provides in this passage. For each detail, have students discuss how the detail reveals the author's attitude toward Anderson. Students should pay careful attention to Hughes's choice of words. They might record their findings in a chart like the one on p. 693.

22 Reading Check
Answer: Marian Anderson went to New York in 1925 to compete in the New York Philharmonic Competitions, in which she won first place.

CUSTOMIZE INSTRUCTION FOR UNIVERSAL ACCESS

For Advanced Readers

Suggest that students read additional works by Langston Hughes. Provide students with the titles listed in the Enrichment Box, ATE p. 707. You may also wish to use **Authors In Depth,** Platinum Level, which contains the following selections and more:

- "Me and My Song" (poem, p. 54)
- "Afro-American Fragment" (poem, p. 55)
- "Bouquet" (poem, p. 56)

After students have read these or other works by Hughes, ask them to identify the subject of each, and then identify the author's attitude toward it.

23 Critical Thinking

Infer

• Ask students to paraphrase the events that take place in the bracketed text.

• Then, ask students why Marian Anderson had to go to Europe to achieve her first major success. **Possible response:** Racial prejudice and stereotypes in the United States made it difficult for an American audience to accept an African American who sang classical music.

24 ▶ Critical Viewing

Possible response: The violin is a symbol of Marian Anderson's interest in music and her determination to pursue it as an important part of her life. Students should recall the old violin that she bought with "nickels and dimes" when she was a child.

engagements came in, so Marian continued to study. A Town Hall concert was arranged for her in New York, but it was unsuccessful. Meanwhile, she kept on singing with various choral groups, and herself gave concerts in churches and at some of the Negro colleges until, in 1930, a Rosenwald Fellowship made European study possible. During her first year abroad she made her debut in Berlin. A prominent Scandinavian concert manager read of this concert, but was attracted more by the name, Anderson, than by what the critics said about her voice. "Ah," he said, "a Negro singer with a Swedish name! She is bound to be a success in Scandinavia." He sent two of his friends to Germany to hear her, one of them being Kosti Vehanen who shortly became her accompanist and remained with her for many years.

23 Sure enough, Marian Anderson did become a great success in the Scandinavian countries, where she learned to sing in both Finnish and Swedish, and her first concert tour of Europe became a critical triumph. When she came back home to America, she gave several programs and appeared as soloist with the famous Hall Johnson Choir, but without financial success. However, the Scandinavian people, who had fallen in love with her, kept asking her to come back there. So, in 1933, she went again to Europe for 142 concerts in Norway, Sweden, Denmark, and Finland. She was decorated by the King of Denmark and the King of Sweden. Sibelius[2] dedicated a song to her. And the following spring she made her debut in Paris where she was so well received that she had to give three concerts that season at the Salle Gaveau.[3] Great successes followed in all the European capitals. In 1935 the famous conductor, Arturo Toscanini, listened to her sing at Salzburg.[4] He said, "What I heard today one is privileged to hear only once in a hundred years." It was in Europe that Marian Anderson began to be acclaimed by critics as "the greatest singer in the world."

When Marian Anderson again returned to America, she was a seasoned artist. News of her tremendous European successes had preceded her, so a big New York concert was planned. But a few days before she arrived at New York, in a storm on the liner crossing the Atlantic, Marian fell and broke her ankle. She refused to allow this to interfere with her concert, however, nor did she even want people to know about it. She wore a very long evening gown that night so that no one could see the plaster cast on her leg. She propped herself in a curve of the piano before the curtains parted, and gave her New York concert standing on one foot! The next day Howard Taubman wrote enthusiastically in *The New York Times*:

Marian Anderson has returned to her native land one of the great singers of our time. . . . There is no doubt of it, she was mistress of all she surveyed. . . . It was music making that proved too deep for words.

A coast-to-coast American tour followed. And, from that season on, Marian Anderson has been one of our country's favorite singers, rated,

24 ▲ **Critical Viewing**
Why is the violin significant in this essay? **[Connect]**

---

2. **Sibelius** (si bā´ lē ōōs) Jean Sibelius (1865–1957), a Finnish composer.
3. **Salle Gaveau** (sal ga vō´) concert hall in Paris, France.
4. **Salzburg** city in Austria noted for its music festivals.

704 ◆ *Nonfiction*

---

according to *Variety*,[5] among the top ten of the concert stage who earn over $100,000 a year. Miss Anderson has sung with the great symphony orchestras, and appeared on all the major radio and television networks many times, being a particular favorite with the millions of listeners to the Ford Hour. During the years she has returned often to Europe for concerts, and among the numerous honors accorded her abroad was a request for a command performance before the King and Queen of England, and a decoration from the government of Finland. Her concerts in South America and Asia have been as successful as those elsewhere. Since 1935 she has averaged over one hundred programs a year in cities as far apart as Vienna, Buenos Aires, Moscow, and Tokyo. Her recordings have sold millions of copies around the world. She has been invited more than once to sing at the White House. She has appeared in concert at the Paris Opera and at the Metropolitan Opera House in New York. Several colleges have granted her honorary degrees, and in 1944 Smith College made her a Doctor of Music.

In spite of all this, as a Negro, Marian Anderson has not been immune from those aspects of racial segregation which affect most traveling artists of color in the United States. In his book, *Marian Anderson*, her longtime accompanist, Vehanen, tells of hotel accommodations being denied her, and service in dining rooms often refused. Once after a concert in a Southern city, Vehanen writes that some white friends drove Marian to the railroad station and took her into the main waiting room. But a policeman ran them out, since Negroes were not allowed in that part of the station. Then they went into the smaller waiting room marked, Colored. But again they were ejected, because *white* people were not permitted in the cubby hole allotted to Negroes. So they all had to stand on the platform until the train arrived.

The most dramatic incident of prejudice in all Marian Anderson's career occurred in 1939 when the Daughters of the American Revolution, who own Constitution Hall in Washington, refused to allow her to sing there. The newspapers headlined this and many Americans were outraged. In protest a committee of prominent people, including a number of great artists and distinguished figures in the government, was formed. Through the efforts of this committee, Marian Anderson sang in Washington, anyway—before the statue of Abraham Lincoln—to one of the largest crowds ever to hear a singer at one time in the history of the world. Seventy-five thousand people stood in the open air on a cold clear Easter Sunday afternoon to hear her. And millions more listened to Marian Anderson that day over the radio or heard her in the newsreels that recorded the event. Harold Ickes, then Secretary of the Interior, presented Miss Anderson to that enormous audience standing

---

5. *Variety* show-business newspaper.

Musical Vocabulary

The following musical terms will help you understand this essay.

spiritual religious folk song, specifically originating with African Americans

minstrel performer in a variety show who sings, dances, tells jokes, and performs comic skits

aria vocal piece for a solo performer, with musical accompaniment, as in an opera

hymn song of thanksgiving or praise to God

anthem hymn of praise; music set to words from the Bible

bass tones in the lowest range of a voice or a musical instrument

soprano woman or young boy's highest singing voice, or a woman with such a voice

soloist person who performs solo, or alone

---

27 ☑**Reading Check**
Why did Marian Anderson wear a long evening gown for her New York concert?

---

25 **Reading Strategy**

Recognizing Author's Attitude

- Have students read the bracketed passage.
- Ask students why they think the author included these events in the story.
  Answer: The author included the events to point out Marian Anderson's musical success despite racial prejudice.

▶ **Monitor Progress** Ask students what inference they can make about Hughes's attitude toward the events he describes.
Answer: Hughes thought it was important for his readers to know that Anderson, despite her prominence, experienced racial prejudice. Students can infer that Hughes's attitude toward these injustices was one of anger or disgust.

26 **Background**

Musical Terms

Many musical terms come to us from Italian and Latin. For example, the word *soloist* is derived from the Latin *solo*, meaning "alone." The term *aria* comes directly from the Italian term for "air, tune, or melody." Have students find other musical terms and note their etymologies.

27 ☑**Reading Check**

Answer: Anderson wore a long evening gown so that no one could see the plaster cast on her leg.

Review and Assess

1. Possible responses: Anderson was a talented vocalist who pursued her goal in spite of racial prejudice. Even though she achieved worldwide acclaim, she maintained a sense of simplicity, humility, and generosity.

2. **(a)** The congregation took an interest in Marian and supported her musical talents by teaching her hymns and spirituals, giving her performing opportunities, and providing financial support. **(b)** People's reactions to Anderson confirm her upright character and extraordinary talent.

3. **(a)** Anderson first became a success in the Scandinavian countries. **(b)** Anderson's race was not a problem in these countries because they did not have the same racial prejudice against African Americans as did people in the United States.

4. **(a)** Anderson was often refused service in hotels, dining rooms, and on public transportation. **(b)** It was difficult for Anderson to find success in the United States because of the racial prejudice at that time.

5. **(a)** The Bok Award was presented in 1941 to Anderson in Philadelphia for outstanding public service. **(b)** The way Anderson chooses to spend her money shows her desire to support artistic talent without regard to race or creed.

6. Possible responses: Hughes, also an artist, appreciates Marian Anderson's accomplishments in a different artistic discipline. By including instances of racial prejudice that Anderson had to face, he allows the reader to contemplate this issue without directly stating his opinion, much as he would in writing a poem.

7. Possible responses: Marian Anderson showed exceptional courage because of the tremendous obstacles she had to face, including poverty and racial prejudice.

---

in the plaza to pay honor, as he said, not only to a great singer, but to the basic ideals of democracy and equality.

In 1943 Marian Anderson married Orpheus H. Fisher, an architect, and settled down—between tours—in a beautiful country house in Connecticut where she rehearses new songs to add to her already vast repertoire. Sometimes her neighbors across the fields can hear the rich warm voice that covers three octaves singing in English, French, Finnish, or German. And sometimes they hear in the New England air that old Negro spiritual, "Honor, honor unto the dying Lamb. . . ."

Friends say that Marian Anderson has invested her money in real estate and in government bonds. Certainly, throughout her career, she has lived very simply, traveled without a maid or secretary, and carried her own sewing machine along by train, ship, or plane to mend her gowns. When in 1941 in Philadelphia she was awarded the coveted Bok Award for outstanding public service, the $10,000 that came with the medallion she used to establish a trust fund for "talented American artists without regard to race or creed." Now, each year from this fund promising young musicians receive scholarships.

repertoire (rep´ ər twär) *n.* stock of songs that a singer is ready to perform

Review and Assess

Thinking About the Selection

1. **Respond:** After reading Hughes's essay, what are your impressions of Marian Anderson?

2. **(a) Recall:** How did Anderson's congregation help her? **(b) Infer:** What do people's reactions to Anderson say about her character and talent?

3. **(a) Recall:** Where did Anderson first become a success? **(b) Speculate:** Why do you think Anderson's race was not a problem there?

4. **(a) Recall:** What difficulties did Anderson face traveling in the United States? **(b) Interpret:** Why was it so difficult for Marian Anderson to gain success in the United States?

5. **(a) Recall:** What was the Bok Award received by Marian Anderson? **(b) Draw Conclusions:** What can you learn about Anderson from the way she chooses to spend the money from this award?

6. **Connect:** Langston Hughes is known as a poet. In what way does this selection reflect a poet's sensibility and use of language?

7. **Take a Position:** Do you think Marian Anderson showed exceptional courage? Why or why not?

706 ◆ *Nonfiction*

Langston Hughes

(1902–1967)

Langston Hughes traveled widely to such places as Africa, Europe, the Soviet Union (now Russia), China, and Japan, and he lived in Paris and Italy. However, his work is associated mostly with the Harlem Renaissance—a period when some of America's finest writers, artists, and musicians, who were based in Harlem, New York, brought the African American experience into the spotlight. Hughes, for instance, used the rhythm and mood of jazz and blues in his poetry. Although he has been called the poet laureate of the Harlem Renaissance, he also wrote nonfiction, novels, and plays, as well as scripts for opera, radio, and film.

✎ ASSESSMENT PRACTICE: Reading Comprehension

Analyzing Literary Language (For more practice, see Test Preparation Workbook, p. 43.)

Many tests require students to analyze literary language, such as evocative words, rhyme, repeated sounds, or rhythms. Have students read the first sentence of "A Child's Christmas in Wales," and then answer this sample question.

How does the repetition of the "o" sound and the numbers six and twelve reveal the author's attitude toward this subject?

A It shows that he is in a hurry to share his memories.

B It shows that he remembers best when falling asleep.

C It shows how much he loves the snow.

D It shows that his childhood memories blur together.

The correct answer is *D*. The repetitious sounds contribute to his vague but intense childhood memories.

Review and Assess

Literary Analysis

Biography and Autobiography
1. (a) Why do you think Thomas focuses on this particular part of his childhood? (b) What details support your opinion?
2. What incidents in "Marian Anderson: Famous Concert Singer" reveal Anderson's character?
3. (a) What aspects of Anderson's life has the author emphasized in the biography? (b) What has he left out?

Comparing Literary Works
4. (a) What elements do Thomas's autobiography and Hughes's biography have in common? (b) How are they different? Record your answer in a diagram like the one here.

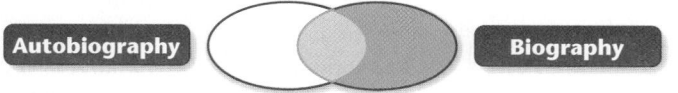

5. Which do you think is a more reliable record of someone's life—a biography or an autobiography? Explain.
6. Do you think Hughes's piece or Thomas's piece is more objective? Why?

Reading Strategy

Recognizing Author's Attitude
7. (a) What is Thomas's **attitude** about the snowstorms of his youth? (b) What are some words or phrases that convey this attitude?
8. What details does Thomas use to convey his attitude about the presents the children received for Christmas?
9. (a) What is Hughes's attitude toward Marian Anderson? (b) What are some words or phrases that convey this attitude?

Extend Understanding
10. **History Connection:** Why are biographies and autobiographies useful to people who study history or culture?

Quick Review

A **biography** is an account of a person's life written by another individual.

An **autobiography** is a person's own account of his or her life.

To **recognize an author's attitude,** note the details he or she uses and determine the way he or she feels about the subject.

 Take It to the Net
www.phschool.com

Take the interactive self-test online to check your understanding of these selections.

A Child's Christmas in Wales / Marian Anderson: Famous Concert Singer ◆ 707

Answers continued

9. (a) Hughes's attitude toward Marian Anderson is one of admiration and respect. (b) Words and phrases that convey this include "exceptional," "a critical triumph," "top ten of the concert stage," "numerous honors," and "she has lived very simply."

10. Biographies and autobiographies provide important details about many different aspects of life from a variety of perspectives.

Answers for p. 707
Review and Assess

1. (a) Thomas wants to share his experience of a particular and warm childhood. (b) He remembers details such as the kinds of presents exchanged with great clarity.

2. Incidents that reveal Anderson's character include her saving money to buy the second-hand violin and her performing with a broken ankle.

3. (a) He has emphasized aspects of her career and the obstacles she met in achieving success. (b) He has left out mention of her personal life—her life outside music.

4. (a) Both autobiographies and biographies tell a story about a person. (b) The autobiography is Thomas's own account of his life and includes details that only he would know. The biography is an account of Anderson's life that reveals factual information that emphasizes certain aspects of her character.

5. Possible response: A biography is probably a more reliable record because it contains facts that can be proven.

6. Possible response: Hughes's piece is more objective because it is based on facts gathered through research, not on personal recollections or personal opinions.

7. (a) Thomas's attitude is one of delight and ever-present mystery. (b) Possible responses: "Our snow ... came shawling out of the ground and swam and drifted out of the hands and bodies of the trees; snow grew overnight on the roofs and houses..."; "snowbound backyard"; "into the white world"

8. Thomas conveys his attitude about the Christmas gifts by categorizing the gifts into Useful Presents and Useless Presents, a tongue-in-cheek way of saying he liked the toys and games best.

Answers continued

❶ Vocabulary Development

Concept Development: Musical Words

1. *Soprano* is the highest vocal range for a woman or boy singer.
2. If you sing a song in a soft, sentimental way, you *croon* the song.
3. An *anthem* is a song of praise or devotion.

Spelling Strategy

1. ironed
2. considerable
3. remembering

Concept Development: Connotations

1. g
2. a
3. h
4. j
5. e
6. d
7. b
8. i
9. c
10. f

❷ Grammar

1. "a famous writer"; nonrestrictive
2. "Mabel"; nonrestrictive
3. "an African American woman"; nonrestrictive
4. "beloved singer"; nonrestrictive
5. "Orpheus H. Fisher"; restrictive

Writing Application

Possible response: I remember a Christmas when my sister Shannon and I were too sick to open our gifts. Our brother, Ben, opened our gifts as we watched. Not even our favorite gifts, new dolls and an art set, could cheer us up.

Integrate Language Skills

❶ Vocabulary Development Lesson

Concept Development: Musical Words

In Hughes's account of Anderson, he uses words such as *repertoire*, French for a group of songs that a musician knows well and is ready to perform.

Write sentences that define each of the following words:

1. soprano   2. croon   3. anthem

Spelling Strategy

If a word of more than one syllable ends in a single consonant following a single vowel and the accent is *not* on the last syllable, do *not* double the final consonant before adding a suffix beginning with a vowel. For example, *wallow* + *-ed* = *wallowed*. Combine the following words and suffixes to form the new word.

1. iron + *-ed*   3.   remember + *-ing*
2. consider + *-able*

Concept Development: Connotations

The connotation of a word is the set of ideas associated with it in addition to its explicit meaning. On your paper, match each word from the vocabulary list on page 693 with the word most closely associated with it.

1. staunch   a. burglar
2. sidle   b. shoes
3. prey   c. solos
4. wallowed   d. twigs
5. crocheted   e. sweater
6. brittle   f. music
7. trod   g. friend
8. forlorn   h. hunter
9. arias   i. lost child
10. repertoire   j. pig

❷ Grammar Lesson

Restrictive and Nonrestrictive Appositives

Appositives and **appositive phrases** provide more information about the noun they are placed near. A **restrictive appositive** is essential to the meaning of the sentence and is not set off by commas. A **nonrestrictive appositive** is not essential and is set off by commas.

> **Restrictive:** I was in Mrs. Prothero's garden . . . with her son *Jim*. (essential: which son?)
>
> **Nonrestrictive:** . . . a famous group of Negro singers, *the Fisk Jubilee Singers*, had already carried the spirituals all over Europe. (not essential: modifies *Singers*)

Practice Locate the appositive or appositive phrase in each sentence, and identify it as restrictive or nonrestrictive.

1. Dylan Thomas, a famous writer, shares his Christmas memories.
2. Jim's only aunt, Mabel, was staying with his family.
3. Her first teacher, an African American woman, refused to accept any pay.
4. Anderson, beloved singer, toured Europe.
5. Anderson married the architect Orpheus H. Fisher.

Writing Application Write a paragraph about a childhood memory. Use three appositives to add more information.

W̶G̶ *Prentice Hall Writing and Grammar Connection: Chapter 20, Section 1*

708 ◆ Nonfiction

---

③ Writing Lesson

Biographer's Account

Imagine that you are writing a biography of Dylan Thomas. Using his Christmas memories as a child in Wales, capture and report the ideas of this selection using a more objective viewpoint.

Prewriting   Reread the selection and choose a part of the Christmas celebration to describe. It might be the snow, the presents, or the relatives.

Drafting   As you draft, focus on bringing your subject to life for your audience. Include dialogue and vivid descriptions. Make sure that you attribute subjective information to Thomas with words like "according to Thomas," or "Thomas has said."

Revising   Read your draft, and circle anything that is not a fact. Edit to attribute the information to the person who provided it or delete the details.

Model: Revising for Objectivity

The family made music on Christmas night. An uncle played

Thomas said that

the fiddle and everyone sang. It was very warm in the house,

and there was a lot of laughter.

> To maintain the objective tone of biography, this subjective information is linked to its source.

W̶G̶ *Prentice Hall Writing and Grammar Connection: Chapter 4, Connected Assignment*

④ Extension Activities

Research and Technology   Prepare a **bibliography of reference materials** for a report on Marian Anderson. Your bibliography should include

- Print material, such as books, newspapers, magazines, and encyclopedia articles
- Material that can be found on the Internet
- Audio resources, such as Anderson's recordings

Use a style guide to present your bibliographic material in the proper format.

Listening and Speaking   Ask the librarian in your town's library or your school's library to help you locate one of Marian Anderson's recordings. Present the music to the class, and lead a **musical review** discussion. **[Group Activity]**

Take It to the Net   www.phschool.com

Go online for an additional research activity using the Internet.

A Child's Christmas in Wales / Marian Anderson: Famous Concert Singer ◆ 709

---

③ Writing Lesson

- Remind students that a biography is an account of a person's life written by another individual. In this case, the students will write a biography of Dylan Thomas.

- To show students a model of a biography, use the Biographical Profile transparency, p. 13 of **Writing Models and Graphic Organizers on Transparencies.**

- As students work on their drafts, point out the Writing Model. Explain that subjective information from the story can be made objective by attributing it to the author.

④ Extension Activities

Research and Technology

- Discuss reference sources that may be available in your school or local library, including books, recordings, and archived newspaper and magazine articles.

- Help students brainstorm for a list of key words they could use in an Internet search about Marian Anderson.

- Decide on a style students should use for their bibliographies. Encourage students to see **Writing and Grammar,** Platinum Level, pp. 851–854, for examples of the various styles.

CUSTOMIZE INSTRUCTION for Universal Access

To address different learning styles, use the following activities suggested in the **Extension Activities** booklet, p. 43.

- For Verbal/Linguistic, Bodily/Kinesthetic, and Visual/Spatial Learners, use Activity 5.
- For Musical/Rhythmic Learners, use Activity 6.
- For Verbal/Linguistic and Musical/Rhythmic Learners, use Activity 7.

ASSESSMENT RESOURCES

The following resources can be used to assess students' knowledge and skills.

Selection Assessment

- 📝 **Formal Assessment**, Selection Test, pp. 151–153
- 📝 **Open Book Test**, pp. 127–129
- 📼 **Got It! Assessment Videotapes**, Tape 4
- 💿 **Test Bank Software**

Take It to the Net
Visit www.phschool.com for self-tests and additional questions on the selections.

PRENTICE HALL ASSESSMENT SYSTEM

- 📝 **Workbook**
- 📝 **Skill Book**
- 📖 **Transparencies**
- 💿 **CD-ROM**

Flood

Lesson Objectives

1. **To analyze and respond to literary elements**
   - Literary Analysis: Descriptive Essay
   - Connecting Literary Elements: Simile

2. **To read, comprehend, analyze, and critique an essay**
   - Reading Strategy: Recognizing Facts and Impressions
   - Reading Check questions
   - Review and Assess questions
   - Assessment Practice (ATE)

3. **To develop word analysis skills, fluency, and systematic vocabulary**
   - Vocabulary Development Lesson: Latin Prefix: *mal-*

4. **To understand and apply written and oral language conventions**
   - Spelling Strategy
   - Grammar Lesson: Commonly Confused Words: *than* and *then*

5. **To understand and apply appropriate writing and research strategies**
   - Writing Lesson: Radio Call-In Transcript
   - Extension Activity: Flood Report

6. **To understand and apply listening and speaking strategies**
   - Extension Activity: Television Interview

STEP-BY-STEP TEACHING GUIDE	PACING GUIDE
PRETEACH	
Motivate Students and Provide Background	
Use the Motivation activity (ATE p. 710)	5 min.
Read and discuss the Preview material and Background information (SE/ATE p. 710) **A**	5 min.
Introduce the Concepts	
Introduce the Literary Analysis and Reading Strategy (SE/ATE p. 711) **A**	15 min.
Pronounce the vocabulary words and read their definitions (SE p. 711)	5 min.
TEACH	
Monitor Comprehension	
Informally monitor comprehension by circulating while students read independently or in groups **A**	20 min.
Monitor students' comprehension with the Reading Check notes (SE/ATE pp. 713, 715, 717)	as students read
Develop vocabulary with Vocabulary notes (SE pp. 714, 715, 717; ATE p. 716)	as students read
Develop Understanding	
Develop students' understanding of descriptive essays with Literary Analysis annotations (SE pp. 713, 714, 715; ATE pp. 713, 714, 715) **A**	10 min.
Develop students' understanding of recognizing facts and impressions with Reading Strategy annotations (SE pp. 712, 717; ATE pp. 713, 717)	10 min.
ASSESS	
Assess Mastery	
Assess students' mastery of the Reading Strategy and Literary Analysis by having them answer the Review and Assess questions (SE/ATE p. 719)	20 min.
Use one or more of the print and media Assessment Resources (ATE p. 721) **A**	up to 50 min.
EXTEND	
Apply Understanding	
Have students complete the Vocabulary Development Lesson and the Grammar Lesson (SE p. 720) **A**	20 min.
Apply students' knowledge of sensory language using the Writing Lesson (SE/ATE p. 721) **A**	45 min.
Apply students' understanding using one or more of the Extension Activities (SE p. 721)	20–90 min.

 ACCELERATED INSTRUCTION: Use the strategies and activities identified with an **A**.

UNIVERSAL ACCESS
- ● = Below Level Students
- ▲ = On-Level Students
- ■ = Above Level Students

Time and Resource Manager

Reading Level: Easy
Average Number of Instructional Days: 4

RESOURCES

PRINT 📖	TRANSPARENCIES 🗂	TECHNOLOGY 💿 🎧 📼
• **Beyond Literature,** Community Connection: Flood Control, p. 44 ▲ ■		• **Interest Grabber Video,** Tape 4 ● ▲ ■
• **Selection Support Workbook:** ● ▲ ■ Literary Analysis, p. 176 Reading Strategy, p. 175 Build Vocabulary, p. 173	• **Literary Analysis and Reading Transparencies,** pp. 87 and 88 ● ▲ ■	
• **Adapted Reader's Companion** ● • **Reader's Companion** ● • **Authors In Depth,** Platinum Level ■		• **Listening to Literature** ● ▲ ■ Audiocassettes, Side 22 Audio CDs, CD 15
• **English Learner's Companion** ● ▲ • **Literatura en español** ● ▲ • **Literary Analysis for Enrichment** ■		
• **Formal Assessment:** Selection Test, pp. 154–156 ● ▲ ■ • **Open Book Test,** pp. 130–132 ● ▲ ■ • **Performance Assessment and Portfolio Management,** p. 19 ● ▲ ■ • **PRENTICE HALL ASSESSMENT SYSTEM** ● ▲ ■	• **PRENTICE HALL ASSESSMENT SYSTEM** ● ▲ ■ Skills Practice Answers and Explanations on Transparencies	• **Test Bank Software** ● ▲ ■ • **Got It! Assessment Videotapes,** Tape 4 ● ▲
• **Selection Support Workbook:** ● ▲ ■ Build Grammar Skills, p. 174 • **Writing and Grammar,** Platinum Level ● ▲ ■ • **Extension Activities,** p. 44 ● ▲ ■	• **Daily Language Practice Transparencies** ● ▲	• **Writing and Grammar iText CD-ROM** ● ▲ ■ 💻 **Take It to the Net** www.phschool.com

BLOCK SCHEDULING: Use one 90-minute class period to preteach the selection and have students read it. Use a second 90-minute class period to assess students' mastery of skills and have them complete one of the Extension Activities.

Motivation

Ask students to name and briefly describe "disaster" movies—films that feature natural disasters such as earthquakes and tornadoes—they have seen. Why do they think these movies are so popular? (Students might respond that perhaps people like to feel shocked out of their everyday existence, that they "enjoy" being scared and then relieved when all comes to a happy conclusion.) Tell them that the selection they are about to read deals with a natural disaster. No special effects heighten this disaster; rather, Annie Dillard creates drama simply through telling the facts and giving her impressions.

▣ Interest Grabber Video

As an alternative, play "Flood Damage" on Tape 4 to engage student interest.

❶ Background

Science

Hurricane Agnes began as a tropical disturbance off the coast of the Yucatan Peninsula in Mexico on June 14, 1972. As the disturbance moved northward, it strengthened and became a tropical storm.

By the time Agnes made initial landfall along the Florida panhandle on June 19, she had become a hurricane. Agnes then proceeded through Georgia, South Carolina, and North Carolina before she moved back over the Atlantic off the North Carolina coast on June 21. After regaining strength over the Atlantic, she made landfall again over southeastern New York and moved westward in an arc over southern New York into north-central Pennsylvania. Dillard's home state of Pennsylvania was hit worst by flash floods from the hurricane.

Prepare to Read

Flood

▣ Take It to the Net

Visit www.phschool.com for interactive activities and instruction related to "Flood," including

- background
- graphic organizers
- literary elements
- reading strategies

Preview

Connecting to the Literature

You walk outside and find that a freezing rainstorm has left ice glittering everywhere you look. When nature transforms our everyday sights into something extraordinary, as it does in "Flood," we have a chance to see the world anew.

❶ Background

In 1972, Hurricane Agnes produced the worst floods in Virginia's history. The low-lying basins of rivers and creeks were all struck by flash flooding. Flash floods can erode riverbanks, destroy homes, carry cars and furniture downstream, and leave fish swimming in people's basements.

710 ◆ Nonfiction

TEACHING RESOURCES

The following resources can be used to enrich or extend the instruction for pp. 710–711.

Motivation
▣ **Interest Grabber Video,** Tape 4 ▣

Background
📖 **Beyond Literature,** p. 44

▣ **Take It to the Net**
Visit www.phschool.com for background and hotlinks for "Flood."

Literary Analysis
📋 **Literary Analysis and Reading Transparencies,** Descriptive Essay, p. 88 ▣

Reading
📖 **Selection Support Workbook:** Reading Strategy, p. 175, Build Vocabulary, p. 173

📋 **Literary Analysis and Reading Transparencies,** Recognizing Facts and Impressions, p. 87 ▣

▣ **BLOCK SCHEDULING:** Resources marked with this symbol provide varied instruction during 90-minute blocks.

❷ Literary Analysis

Descriptive Essay

Reading "Flood" might make you feel that you are hip-high in rising creek water. That is because "Flood" succeeds as a **descriptive essay,** a short nonfiction work that contains sensory details that show how something looks, feels, smells, sounds, or tastes. The descriptions in "Flood" have the effect of taking you off the page and into the flood. Notice the writer's use of sensory language:

> A knot of yellow, fleshy somethings, . . .

> . . . a high windy sound more like air than like water, . . .

Look for other examples of descriptive details as you read this selection.

Connecting Literary Elements

A **simile** is a figure of speech in which *like* or *as* is used to make a comparison between two basically unlike things. In the following example, a simile makes a description more vivid:

> It was a couple of garbage trucks, huge trash compacters humped *like* armadillos, . . .

By comparing the compacters to armadillos, the writer emphasizes the unusual shape of the trucks. When you notice the similes in this essay, consider their effect on strengthening the description.

❸ Reading Strategy

Recognizing Facts and Impressions

If you tell a friend that Dillard's essay describes the flooding of Tinker Creek in 1972, you are presenting a **fact**—information that can be proved. If you then say that the flood was really frightening, you are giving your **impression**—a feeling or image retained from an experience. Use a chart like the one here to separate the facts and impressions in "Flood."

Vocabulary Development

obliterates (ə blit′ ər āts′) *v.* destroys; erases without a trace (p. 714)

opacity (ō pas′ ə tē) *n.* quality of not letting light pass through (p. 714)

usurped (yōō surpt′) *v.* taken power over; held by force (p. 714)

mauled (môld) *adj.* roughly or clumsily handled (p. 715)

malevolent (mə lev′ ə lənt) *adj.* intended as evil or harmful (p. 717)

repressed (ri prest′) *adj.* held back; restrained (p. 717)

Flood ◆ 711

---

❷ Literary Analysis

Descriptive Essay

- Explain that a descriptive essay contains many sensory details to help the reader "experience" the topic of the essay.
- Read aloud the paragraph about descriptive essays and the excerpt from the selection. Ask students to pay attention to the sensory details, and have them identify the senses to which they appeal. Answer: They appeal to sight, touch, and sound.
- Use the Descriptive Essay transparency in **Literary Analysis and Reading Transparencies,** p. 88, to guide students in identifying sensory details in "Flood."

❸ Reading Strategy

Recognizing Facts and Impressions

- Explain to students that facts can be proven, while impressions— a person's feelings or images— cannot.
- Ask students to notice what is going on around them in the classroom. Then, ask them to offer facts about the classroom.
- Next, ask them to offer impressions about the classroom. Discuss how their facts differ from their impressions.
- Point out the chart on p. 711, and have students use it to record facts and impressions as they read "Flood."

Vocabulary Development

- Pronounce each vocabulary word for students, and read the definitions as a class. Have students identify any words with which they are already familiar.

CUSTOMIZE INSTRUCTION FOR UNIVERSAL ACCESS

For Special Needs Students	For Less Proficient Readers	For English Learners
Have students read the adapted version of "Flood" in the **Adapted Reader's Companion.** This version provides basic-level instruction in an interactive format with questions and write-on lines. Completing the adapted version will prepare students to read the selection in the Student Edition.	Have students read the selection in the **Reader's Companion.** This version provides basic-level instruction in an interactive format with question and write-on lines. After students finish the selection in the **Reader's Companion,** have them complete the questions and activities in the Student Edition.	Have students read the adapted version of the selection in the **English Learner's Companion.** This version provides basic-level instruction in an interactive format with questions and write-on lines. Completing the adapted version will prepare students to read the selection in the Student Edition.

 E-Teach

Visit E-Teach at www.phschool.com for teachers' essays on how to teach, with questions and answers.

Step-by-Step Teaching Guide for pp. 712–718

CUSTOMIZE INSTRUCTION
Musical/ Rhythmic Learners

Ask students to describe how sound effects and background music contribute to their appreciation of movie scenes. Then, encourage them to think of background music and sound effects that would enhance Dillard's vivid descriptions. Have students pause occasionally in their reading to explain the effects they would use and how these effects would enhance the scene.

❶ About the Selection

Annie Dillard's recollection of the Tinker Creek flood is sparked by a watchful, uneasy feeling brought on by a June rain. As the account of the flood unfolds, tension rises. The landscape undergoes a dramatic change as a small creek becomes a roiling river that snatches everything in its path and transforms the landscape into an other-worldly waterscape—complete with waves and waterfalls. For the people in the area, the flood is frightening, but it also holds a certain fascination. When it is over and the waters begin to recede, people take up their normal lives once again. Dillard's account of the flood gives readers a glimpse of nature's power and how people respond to it.

❷ ▶ Critical Viewing

Possible responses: Students may say that the physical damage is shocking and immediate; the emotional damage may linger long after the physical damage is repaired, as people try to rebuild their lives and come to terms with what they have lost.

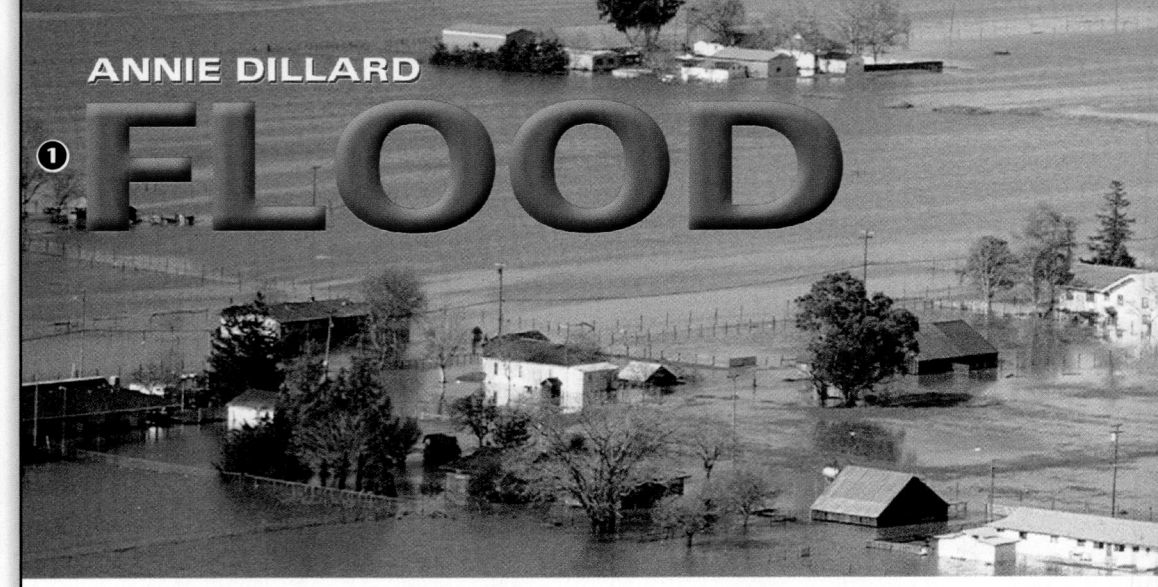

ANNIE DILLARD
❶ FLOOD

It's summer. We had some deep spring sunshine about a month ago, in a drought; the nights were cold. It's been gray sporadically, but not oppressively, and rainy for a week, and I would think: When is the real hot stuff coming, the mind-melting weeding weather? It was rainy again this morning, the same spring rain, and then this afternoon a different rain came: a pounding, three-minute shower. And when it was over, the cloud dissolved to haze. I can't see Tinker Mountain. It's summer now: the heat is on. It's summer now all summer long.

❸ The season changed two hours ago. Will my life change as well? This is a time for resolutions, revolutions. The animals are going wild. I must have seen ten rabbits in as many minutes. Baltimore orioles are here; brown thrashers seem to be nesting down by Tinker Creek across the road. The coot is still around, big as a Thanksgiving turkey, and as careless; it doesn't even glance at a barking dog.

The creek's up. When the rain stopped today I walked across the road to the downed log by the steer crossing. The steers were across the creek, a black clot on a distant hill. High water had touched my log, the log I sit on, and dumped a smooth slope of muck in its lee. The water itself was an opaque pale green, like pulverized jade, still high and very fast, lightless, like no earthly water. A dog I've never seen before, thin as death, was flushing rabbits.

A knot of yellow, fleshy somethings had grown up by the log. They didn't seem to have either proper stems or proper flowers, but instead only blind, featureless growth, like etiolated[1] potato sprouts in a root cellar. I tried to dig one up from the crumbly soil, but they all apparently grew from a single, well-rooted corm, so I let them go.

---

1. **etiolated** (ē′ tē ə lāt′ id) *adj.* made pale and unhealthy.

712 ◆ *Nonfiction*

❷ ▲ Critical Viewing
Do you think the physical damage or the emotional damage brought on by a natural disaster like this flood is harder to overcome? Why? **[Evaluate]**

Reading Strategy
Recognizing Facts and Impressions Is the author's claim that "The season changed two hours ago" a fact or an impression? Explain.

TEACHING RESOURCES

The following resources can be used to enrich or extend the instruction for pp. 712–718.

Literary Analysis

📓 **Selection Support Workbook:** Literary Analysis, p. 176

Reading

📓 **Reader's Companion**

📓 **English Learner's Companion**

🎧 **Listening to Literature Audiocassettes,** Side 22 ▪

💿 **Listening to Literature Audio CDs,** CD 15 ▪

Extension

📖 **Authors In Depth,** Platinum Level (The collection includes six additional selections by Annie Dillard for further reading.)

▪ **BLOCK SCHEDULING:** Resources marked with this symbol provide varied instruction during 90-minute blocks.

Still, the day had an air of menace. A broken whiskey bottle by the log, the brown tip of a snake's tail disappearing between two rocks on the hill at my back, the rabbit the dog nearly caught, the rabies I knew was in the county, the bees who kept unaccountably fumbling at my forehead with their furred feet . . .

I headed over to the new woods by the creek, the motorbike woods. They were strangely empty. The air was so steamy I could barely see. The ravine separating the woods from the field had filled during high water, and a dead tan mud clogged it now. The horny orange roots of one tree on the ravine's jagged bank had been stripped of soil; now the roots hung, an empty net in the air, clutching an incongruous light bulb stranded by receding waters. For the entire time that I walked in the woods, four jays flew around me very slowly, acting generally odd, and screaming on two held notes. There wasn't a breath of wind.

Coming out of the woods, I heard loud shots; they reverberated ominously in the damp air. But when I walked up the road, I saw what it was, and the dread quality of the whole afternoon vanished at once. It was a couple of garbage trucks, huge trash compacters humped like armadillos, and they were making their engines backfire to impress my neighbors' pretty daughters, high school girls who had just been let off the school bus. The long-haired girls strayed into giggling clumps at the corner of the road; the garbage trucks sped away gloriously, as if they had been the Tarleton twins on thoroughbreds cantering away from the gates of Tara.[2] In the distance a white vapor was rising from the waters of Carvin's Cove and catching in trailing tufts in the mountains' sides. I stood on my own porch, exhilarated, unwilling to go indoors.

Literary Analysis
Descriptive Essay How do the sensory details in this passage help create a mood?

---

2. **Tarleton twins . . . Tara** two suitors who try to win the love of Scarlett, the main character in *Gone With the Wind.*

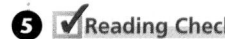**Reading Check**
Which season arrives in the opening paragraphs?

Flood ◆ 713

CUSTOMIZE INSTRUCTION FOR UNIVERSAL ACCESS

For English Learners	For Gifted/ Talented Students
Help students break down and interpret sentences that use figurative language, such as this one: "The water itself was an opaque pale green, like pulverized jade, still high and running fast, lightless, like no earthly water." Possible answer: The pale green water was the color of a piece of broken jade. The water was high, fast, and dark. It looked unlike any water the author had seen before.	Point out that although this is a prose selection, Dillard often uses poetic language, especially alliteration and simile. Have students examine and analyze her use of poetic language and imagery. They might rewrite several sentences without poetic language and compare them with the original.

❸ Reading Strategy
Recognizing Facts and Impressions

• Remind students that a fact can be proved. Then, read aloud the bracketed passage to students.

• Ask the Reading Strategy question on p. 712: Is the author's claim that "The season changed two hours ago" a fact or an impression?"
Possible answers: Students may argue that the claim is both a fact and an impression. It is a verifiable fact that the flood occurred on June 21, the first day of summer. But the author's statement that "the season changed two hours ago" seems to be more an impression that has arisen from the changing weather conditions.

❹ Literary Analysis
Descriptive Essay

• Remind students that sensory details are details that appeal to the senses of taste, touch, sound, sight, or smell.

• Read aloud the bracketed passage slowly, asking students to jot down some of the sensory details they notice. Ask volunteers to share their lists with the class.
Possible responses: empty woods; steamy air; dead tan mud; horny orange roots; stripped of soil; the roots hung, an empty net in the air; stranded by receding waters; four jays flew . . . screaming on two held notes; wasn't a breath of wind

▶ Monitor Progress After several students read their lists, ask them the Literary Analysis question on p. 713: How do the sensory details in this passage help create a mood?
Answer: Students might say that the details make the scene seem ominous, strange, frightening, and eerie.

❺ ✔Reading Check
Answer: Summer arrives in the opening paragraphs.

713

- Ask students the Literary Analysis question on p. 714: To what senses do each of the descriptive details in this paragraph about a helicopter appeal?
  Answer: The details refer to the senses of sound, smell, and touch.

- Then, ask students to point out at least one simile in this passage.
  Possible answers: Dillard compares the sound of the wind to "the run-together whaps of a helicopter's propeller." She also compares the smell of the air to fuel oil and insecticide.

It was just this time last year that we had the flood. It was Hurricane Agnes, really, but by the time it got here, the weather bureau had demoted it to a tropical storm. I see by a clipping I saved that the date was June twenty-first, the solstice, midsummer's night, the longest daylight of the year; but I didn't notice it at the time. Everything was so exciting, and so very dark. All it did was rain. It rained, and the creek started to rise. The creek, naturally, rises every time it rains; this didn't seem any different. But it kept raining, and, that morning of the twenty-first, the creek kept rising.

That morning I'm standing at my kitchen window. Tinker Creek is out of its four-foot banks, way out, and it's still coming. The high creek doesn't look like our creek. Our creek splashes transparently over a jumble of rocks; the high creek <u>obliterates</u> everything in flat <u>opacity</u>. It looks like somebody else's creek that has <u>usurped</u> or eaten our creek and is roving frantically to escape, big and ugly, like a blacksnake caught in a kitchen drawer. The color is foul, a rusty cream. Water that has picked up clay soils looks worse than other muddy waters, because the particles of clay are so fine; they spread out and cloud the water so that you can't see light through even an inch of it in a drinking glass.

Everything looks different. Where my eye is used to depth, I see the flat water, near, too near. I see trees I never noticed before, the black verticals of their rainsoaked trunks standing out of the pale water like pilings for a rotted dock. The stillness of grassy banks and stony ledges is gone; I see rushing, a wild sweep and hurry in one direction, as swift and compelling as a waterfall. The Atkins kids are out in their tiny rain gear, staring at the monster creek. It's risen up to their gates; the neighbors are gathering; I go out.

6 I hear a roar, a high windy sound more like air than like water, like the run-together whaps of a helicopter's propeller after the engine is off, a high million rushings. The air smells damp and acrid, like fuel oil, or insecticide. It's raining.

I'm in no danger; my house is high. I hurry down the road to the bridge. Neighbors who have barely seen each other all winter are there, shaking their heads. Few have ever seen it before: the water is *over* the bridge. Even when I see the bridge now, which I do every day, I still can't believe it: the water was *over* the bridge, a foot or two over the bridge, which at normal times is eleven feet above the surface of the creek.

Now the water is receding slightly; someone has produced empty metal drums, which we roll to the bridge and set up in a square to keep cars from trying to cross. It takes a bit of nerve even to stand on the bridge; the flood has ripped away a wedge of concrete that buttressed the bridge on the bank. Now one corner of the bridge hangs apparently unsupported while water hurls in an arch just inches below.

It's hard to take it all in, it's all so new. I look at the creek at my feet. It smashes under the bridge like a fist, but there is no end to its force; it hurtles down as far as I can see till it lurches round the

obliterates (ə blit′ ər āts′) *v.* destroys; erases without a trace

opacity (ō pas′ ə tē) *n.* quality of not letting light pass through

usurped (yo͞o surpt′) *v.* taken power over; held by force

Literary Analysis
Descriptive Essay
To what senses do each of the descriptive details in this paragraph about a helicopter appeal?

ENRICHMENT: Community Connection

Disaster Preparedness

The efforts and expertise of many different people, agencies, and organizations come into play when a disaster strikes. Cooperation, quick response, and up-to-the minute information is critical when coping with a disaster. Professionals and volunteers need to work together to implement safety measures, evacuate people in immediate danger, treat the injured, and orchestrate the clean-up. Smooth operation of these measures can mean the difference between life and death in the hours and days after a disaster occurs.

Have students find out about the people in your community who help ensure the safety of the population when a disaster hits: utility workers, fire fighters, police, volunteer ambulance drivers, and paramedics.

bend, filling the valley, flattening, mashing, pushed, wider and faster, till it fills my brain.

It's like a dragon. Maybe it's because the bridge we are on is chancy, but I notice that no one can help imagining himself washed overboard, and gauging his chances for survival. You couldn't live. Mark Spitz couldn't live. The water arches where the bridge's supports at the banks prevent its enormous volume from going wide, forcing it to go high; that arch drives down like a diving whale, and would butt you on the bottom. "You'd never know what hit you," one of the men says. But if you survived that part and managed to surface . . . ? How fast can you live? You'd need a windshield. You couldn't keep your head up; the water under the surface is fastest. You'd spin around like a sock in a clothes dryer. You couldn't grab onto a tree trunk without leaving that arm behind. No, you couldn't live. And if they ever found you, your gut would be solid red clay.

It's all I can do to stand. I feel dizzy, drawn, <u>mauled</u>. Below me the floodwater roils to a violent froth that looks like dirty lace, a lace that continuously explodes before my eyes. If I look away, the earth moves backwards, rises and swells, from the fixing of my eyes at one spot against the motion of the flood. All the familiar land looks as though it were not solid and real at all, but painted on a scroll like a backdrop, and that unrolled scroll has been shaken, so the earth sways and the air roars.

Everything imaginable is zipping by, almost too fast to see. If I stand on the bridge and look downstream, I get dizzy; but if I look upstream, I feel as though I am looking up the business end of an avalanche. There are dolls, split wood and kindling, dead fledgling songbirds, bottles, whole bushes and trees, rakes and garden gloves. Wooden, rough-hewn railroad ties charge by faster than any express. Lattice fencing bobs along, and a wooden picket gate. There are so many white plastic gallon milk jugs that when the flood ultimately recedes, they are left on the grassy banks looking from a distance like a flock of white geese.

I expect to see anything at all. In this one way, the creek is more like itself when it floods than at any other time: mediating, bringing things down. I wouldn't be at all surprised to see John Paul Jones coming round the bend, standing on the deck of the *Bon Homme Richard*, or Amelia Earhart waving gaily from the cockpit of her floating Lockheed. Why not a cello, a basket of breadfruit, a casket of antique coins? Here comes the Franklin expedition on snowshoes, and the three magi, plus camels, afloat on a canopied barge!

The whole world is in flood, the land as well as the water. Water streams down the trunks of trees, drips from hat-brims, courses across roads. The whole earth seems to slide like sand down a chute; water pouring over the least slope leaves the grass flattened, silver side up, pointing downstream. Everywhere windfall and flotsam twigs and leafy boughs, wood from woodpiles, bottles, and saturated straw spatter the ground or streak it in curving windrows. Tomatoes in flat

mauled (môld) *adj.* roughly or clumsily handled

Literary Analysis
Descriptive Essay In what specific ways is this passage typical of a descriptive essay?

8 ✓**Reading Check**
Why is the narrator in no imminent danger in the flood?

Flood ◆ 715

gardens are literally floating in mud; they look as though they have been dropped whole into a boiling, brown-gravy stew. The level of the water table is at the top of the toe of my shoes. Pale muddy water lies on the flat so that it all but drowns the grass; it looks like a hideous parody of a light snow on the field, with only the dark tips of the grass blades visible.

When I look across the street, I can't believe my eyes. Right behind the road's shoulder are waves, waves whipped in rhythmically peaking scallops, racing downstream. The hill where I watched the praying mantis lay her eggs is a waterfall that splashes into a brown ocean. I can't even remember where the creek usually runs—it is everywhere now. My log is gone for sure, I think—but in fact, I discover later, it holds, rammed between growing trees. Only the cable suspending the steers' fence is visible, and not the fence itself; the steers' pasture is entirely in flood, a brown river. The river leaps its banks and smashes into the woods where the motorbikes go, devastating all but the sturdiest trees. The water is so deep and wide it seems as though you could navigate the *Queen Mary* in it, clear to Tinker Mountain.

What do animals do in these floods? I see a drowned muskrat go by like he's flying, but they all couldn't die; the water rises after every hard rain, and the creek is still full of muskrats. This flood is higher than their raised sleeping platforms in the banks; they must just race for high ground and hold on. Where do the fish go, and what do they do? Presumably their gills can filter oxygen out of this muck, but I don't know how. They must hide from the current behind any barriers they can find, and fast for a few days. They must: otherwise we'd have no fish; they'd all be in the Atlantic Ocean. What about herons and kingfishers, say? They can't see to eat. It usually seems to me that when I see any animal, its business is urgent enough that it couldn't easily be suspended for forty-eight hours. Crayfish, frogs, snails, rotifers? Most things must simply die. They couldn't live. Then I suppose that when the water goes down and clears, the survivors have a field day with no competition. But you'd think the bottom would be knocked out of the food chain—the whole pyramid would have no base plankton, and it would crumble, or crash with a thud. Maybe enough spores and larvae and eggs are constantly being borne down from slower upstream waters to repopulate . . . I don't know.

Some little children have discovered a snapping turtle as big as a tray. It's hard to believe that this creek could support a predator that size: its shell is a foot and a half across, and its head extends a good seven inches beyond the shell. When the children—in the company of a shrunken terrier—approach it on the bank, the snapper rears up on its thick front legs and hisses very impressively. I had read earlier that since turtles' shells are rigid, they don't have bellows lungs; they have to gulp for air. And, also since their shells are rigid, there's only room for so much inside, so when they are frightened and planning a retreat, they have to expel air from their lungs to make room for head and feet—hence the malevolent hiss.

The next time I look, I see that the children have somehow maneuvered the snapper into a washtub. They're waving a broom handle at it in hopes that it will snap the wood like a matchstick, but the creature will not deign to oblige. The kids are crushed; all their lives they've heard that this is the one thing you do with a snapping turtle—you shove a broom handle near it, and it "snaps it like a matchstick." It's nature's way; it's sure-fire. But the turtle is having none of it. It avoids the broom handle with an air of patiently repressed rage. They let it go, and it beelines down the bank, dives unhesitatingly into the swirling floodwater, and that's the last we see of it.

A cheer comes up from the crowd on the bridge. The truck is here with a pump for the Bowerys' basement, hooray! We roll away the metal drums, the truck makes it over the bridge, to my amazement—the crowd cheers again. State police cruise by; everything's fine here; downstream people are in trouble. The bridge over by the Bings' on Tinker Creek looks like it's about to go. There's a tree trunk wedged against its railing, and a section of concrete is out. The Bings are away, and a young couple is living there, "taking care of the house." What can they do? The husband drove to work that morning as usual; a few hours later, his wife was evacuated from the front door in a *motorboat.*

I walk to the Bings'. Most of the people who are on our bridge eventually end up over there; it's just down the road. We straggle along in the rain, gathering a crowd. The men who work away from home are here, too; their wives have telephoned them at work this morning to say that the creek is rising fast, and they'd better get home while the gettin's good.

There's a big crowd already there; everybody knows that the Bings' is low. The creek is coming in the recreation-room windows; it's half-way up the garage door. Later that day people will haul out everything salvageable and try to dry it: books, rugs, furniture—the lower level was filled from floor to ceiling. Now on this bridge a road crew is trying to chop away the wedged tree trunk with a long-handled ax. The handle isn't so long that they don't have to stand on the bridge, in Tinker Creek. I walk along a low brick wall that was built to retain the creek away from the house at high water. The wall holds just fine, but now that the creek's receding, it's retaining water around the house. On the wall I can walk right out into the flood and stand in the middle of it. Now on the return trip I meet a young man who's going in the opposite direction. The wall is one brick wide; we can't pass. So we clasp hands and lean out backwards over the turbulent water; our feet

10

malevolent (mə lev´ ə lənt) *adj.* intended as evil or harmful

repressed (ri prest´) *adj.* held back; restrained

11 Reading Strategy
Recognizing Facts and Impressions Identify the facts and the impressions in this description of the truck's arrival.

12 ✔Reading Check
What does the narrator think happens to the animals during a flood?

Flood ◆ 717

Review and Assess

1. Some students might say their impression would be one of fear; others might say they would find the flood exhilarating.

2. **(a)** It's out of its four-foot banks; the color is rusty.
(b) Possible answer: The year gave Dillard time to reflect upon the flood and to develop her impressions of the events.

3. **(a)** The water's arches would knock people down; the water under the surface would move too fast for a person to keep his or her head up. **(b)** Students should infer that Dillard is a brave person. She is also curious and interested in observing the flood's effects.

4. **(a)** Items in the water include dolls, wood, dead birds, bottles, bushes, trees, rakes, garden gloves, railroad ties, lattice fencing, a gate, and white plastic milk jugs. **(b)** Dillard is probably trying to communicate the unusual power of the creek.

5. **(a)** Examples: Neighbors who don't usually see one another are now helping one another; women bring mugs of coffee to the road crew; Dillard and the stranger clasp hands to pass over the wall. **(b)** Students will likely agree that the statement is true in this situation; however, they may know of other disasters that resulted in looting and other behaviors that keep people apart.

---

interlace like teeth on a zipper, we pull together, stand, and continue on our ways. The kids have spotted a rattlesnake draping itself out of harm's way in a bush; now they all want to walk over the brick wall to the bush, to get bitten by the snake.

The little Atkins kids are here, and they are hopping up and down. I wonder if I hopped up and down, would the bridge go? I could stand at the railing as at the railing of a steamboat, shouting deliriously, "Mark three! Quarter-less-three! Half twain! Quarter twain! . . ." as the current bore the broken bridge out of sight around the bend before she sank. . . .

Everyone else is standing around. Some of the women are carrying curious plastic umbrellas that look like diving bells—umbrellas they don't put up, but on; they don't get under, but in. They can see out dimly, like goldfish in bowls. Their voices from within sound distant, but with an underlying cheerfulness that plainly acknowledges, "Isn't this ridiculous?" Some of the men are wearing their fishing hats. Others duck their heads under folded newspapers held not very high in an effort to compromise between keeping their heads dry and letting rain run up their sleeves. Following some form of courtesy, I guess, they lower these newspapers when they speak with you, and squint politely into the rain.

Women are bringing coffee in mugs to the road crew. They've barely made a dent in the tree trunk, and they're giving up. It's a job for power tools; the water's going down anyway, and the danger is past. Some kid starts doing tricks on a skateboard; I head home.

Review and Assess

Thinking About the Selection

1. **Respond:** What do you think would have been your immediate impression on first seeing this flood? Explain.

2. **(a) Recall:** What is different about Tinker Creek the morning before the flood? **(b) Infer:** Why do you think Dillard begins her description a year after the flood occurred?

3. **(a) Recall:** What are some reasons that someone would not survive in the flood waters? **(b) Infer:** What does the fact that Dillard is standing on the bridge tell you about her character? Explain.

4. **(a) Recall:** What are some items that rush by in the water? **(b) Speculate:** Why do you think Dillard lists the people and things she would not be surprised to see floating down the creek?

5. **(a) Defend:** Defend the following statement with examples from "Flood": Natural disasters bring people together. **(b) Take a Position:** Do you agree or disagree with this statement? Explain.

Annie Dillard

(b. 1945)
Annie Dillard grew up in Pittsburgh, Pennsylvania. As a child, she was encouraged to be creative and to explore her surroundings. From childhood on, her sense of awe set her apart from the doings of the proper society around her. She spent four seasons living near Tinker Creek, Virginia, an area of forests, creeks, and mountains that brim with wildlife of all kinds. She was twenty-nine when she wrote *Pilgrim at Tinker Creek*, a profound meditation on nature and religion that won the Pulitzer Prize in 1975.

✎ ASSESSMENT PRACTICE: Reading Comprehension

Analyzing Literary Language   **(For more practice, see Test Preparation Workbook, p. 44.)**

To help students prepare to analyze literary language, share this passage from "Flood."

> Tinker Creek is out of its four-foot banks, . . . The high creek doesn't look like our creek. . . . It looks like somebody else's creek that has usurped or eaten our creek and is roving frantically to escape, big and ugly, like a blacksnake caught in a kitchen drawer.

The words in this passage evoke the feeling—

  A that something is invading the author's home.

  B that the creek is cold and wet.

  C that everything is going to be all right.

  D of happiness and joy that rains have come.

Point out that the image of the "blacksnake in a kitchen drawer" suggests the feeling of a menacing invader; therefore, the answer is *A*.

Review and Assess

Literary Analysis

Descriptive Essay

1. What are some details that Dillard uses to **describe** things when the creek is in its normal state?
2. Which of Dillard's descriptions makes you feel that you are personally experiencing the flood? Why?
3. Using a chart like this one, find two examples of language that appeals to each of the five senses.

Sight	Sound	Touch/Texture	Smell	Taste

Connecting Literary Elements

4. List three **similes** from "Flood," and identify what is being compared. Complete a chart like the one here to analyze the similes you find.

Item		Item		Effect
	Compared to ·······▶		Suggests ·······▶	

5. What simile do you find most unusual or most striking? Why?

Reading Strategy

Recognizing Facts and Impressions

6. Analyze this sentence in terms of **fact and impression:** "The steers were across the creek, a black clot on a distant hill."
7. List two facts and two impressions that Dillard uses to describe the flood waters.
8. Find evidence that Dillard's knowledge of history and religion contributed to her impressions of the flood.

Extend Understanding

9. **Career Connection:** Describe the role of at least three kinds of professionals and volunteers who respond to natural disasters.

Quick Review

A **descriptive essay** is a short nonfiction work that contains details showing how something looks, feels, smells, sounds, or tastes.

A **simile** is a figure of speech in which *like* or *as* is used to make a comparison between two unlike things.

A **fact** is information that can be proved.

An **impression** is a feeling or an image retained from an experience.

 Take It to the Net

www.phschool.com

Take the interactive self-test online to check your understanding of the selection.

Flood ◆ 719

Answers for p. 719

Review and Assess

1. In its normal state, the creek "splashes transparently over a jumble of rocks"; stays within its banks and is deep; has grassy banks and stony ledges.

2. Students may respond to passages that contain descriptions with many sensory details.

3. Possible answers: Sight: "The creek's up." "It smashes under the bridge like a fist."
   Sound: "I heard loud shots." "I hear a roar."
   Touch/Texture: "A knot of yellow, fleshy somethings"; "The air was so steamy I could barely see."
   Smell: "The air smells damp like fuel oil or insecticide"; "a basket of breadfruit"
   Taste: "Tomatoes in flat gardens"; "a boiling, brown-gravy stew"

4. Possible responses: "Opaque pale green water . . . like pulverized jade . . ."suggests that the water looks greener and cloudier than normal; "White plastic milk jugs . . . like a flock of white geese . . ." suggests that they have sought refuge together on the shore; "The creek . . . it's like a dragon . . ." suggests a fluid, dangerous, living creature.

5. Possible answers: Students may choose similes such as "like a blacksnake caught in a kitchen drawer" that are both unusual and menacing.

6. Fact: The steers were across the creek.
   Impression: The steers looked like a black clot on a distant hill.

7. Possible response: Facts: The creek's up. You couldn't keep your head up. Impressions: The whole world is in flood. You'd spin around like a sock in a clothes dryer.

8. Evidence includes her mention of John Paul Jones, Amelia Earhart, the Franklin expedition, and the three magi.

9. Students may describe the work of paramedics, police or other rescue workers, helicopter pilots, road crews, or firefighters.

❶ Vocabulary Development

Word Analysis: Latin Prefix _mal-_

1. c
3. b
2. a

Spelling Strategy

1. searched
3. responded
2. slanting
4. appointing

Concept Development: Antonyms

1. d
4. b
2. d
5. c
3. a
6. c

❷ Grammar

1. then
4. than
2. than
5. than
3. then

Writing Application

Possible response: I've known Rex since third grade. Back then, I was taller than Rex. Now, Rex is five inches taller than I am.

Integrate Language Skills

❶ Vocabulary Development Lesson

Word Analysis: Latin Prefix _mal-_

Malevolent contains the Latin prefix _mal-_, which means "bad" or "evil." On your paper, match each word with its appropriate definition.

1. malice
2. malefactor
3. malfunction

a. criminal
b. fail to work properly
c. desire to do harm

Spelling Strategy

When adding a suffix to a word ending in more than one consonant, do not double the final consonant. For example, the word _usurp_ becomes _usurped_ when combined with the suffix _-ed_. In your notebook, write the following words combined with the suffix shown.

1. search (_-ed_)
3. respond (_-ed_)
2. slant (_-ing_)
4. appoint (_-ing_)

Concept Development: Antonyms

Review the list of vocabulary words on page 711. Choose the letter of the word that is the best antonym, or opposite, of the first word.

1. obliterates: (a) annihilates, (b) questions, (c) kills, (d) builds
2. usurped: (a) conquered, (b) swamped, (c) released, (d) shared
3. repressed: (a) freed, (b) oppressed, (c) bound, (d) analyzed
4. opacity: (a) depth, (b) translucence, (c) intelligence, (d) strength
5. mauled: (a) attacked, (b) smeared, (c) protected, (d) borrowed
6. malevolent: (a) corrupt, (b) injurious, (c) helpful, (d) spiteful

❷ Grammar Lesson

Commonly Confused Words: _than_ and _then_

The conjunction **_than_** is used to connect the two parts of a comparison. Do not confuse _than_ with the adverb **_then,_** which usually refers to time.

Than: The creek is more like itself when it floods _than_ at any other time. (shows a comparison)

Then: It was rainy again this morning, and _then_ this afternoon a different rain came. (shows time)

Practice Identify the word that correctly completes each sentence.

1. When the water level fell, (than, then) we could see the plastic jugs lining the bank.
2. Water that has picked up clay soils looks worse (than, then) other muddy waters.
3. The clouds dissolved in haze, and (than, then) the sun came out.
4. The flood caused more damage (than, then) any other in recent memory.
5. A dog I have never seen before, thinner (than, then) death, was flushing rabbits.

Writing Application Write several sentences comparing yourself with a friend of yours. In your writing, use the words _than_ and _then_ correctly at least once.

_W_G _Prentice Hall Writing and Grammar Connection: Chapter 26, Section 2_

TEACHING RESOURCES

The following resources can be used to enrich or extend the instructions for pp. 720–721.

Vocabulary

📖 **Selection Support:** Build Vocabulary, p. 173

📖 **Vocabulary and Spelling Practice Book** (Use this booklet for skills enrichment.)

Grammar

📖 **Selection Support:** Build Grammar Skills, p. 174

_W_G **Writing and Grammar,** Platinum Level, p. 620 ▪

📖 **Daily Language Practice Transparencies**

Writing

_W_G **Writing and Grammar,** Platinum Level, p. 107

💿 **Writing and Grammar iText CD-ROM** ▪

▪ **BLOCK SCHEDULING:** Resources marked with this symbol provide varied instruction during 90-minute blocks.

❸ Writing Lesson

Radio Call-In Transcript

The flood waters are rising. People are being evacuated from their homes. Write a transcript, or a written record of a conversation, of a radio call-in show addressing this situation. The transcript should include a conversation between the show's host and a caller from the flood area.

Prewriting Review the selection and then brainstorm for words and phrases that describe the sensory experiences of a flood. Appeal to as many of the senses as possible.

Drafting When writing, remember that the callers would be likely to mention verifiable facts along with their personal impressions of the flood.

Model: Using Sensory Language

Caller: The rain pelted me. I stepped outside and muddy water lapped around my knees in my own backyard! I felt like a paper cup being tossed in the current.

Action verbs—such as *pelted* and *lapped*—and figurative language, such as a comparison to a paper cup, stimulate the senses.

Rewriting Make sure that your transcript flows naturally, as dialogue should. Also, add sensory language to convey the chaos and destruction caused by the flood.

W͞G *Prentice Hall Writing and Grammar Connection: Chapter 6, Section 2*

❹ Extension Activities

Listening and Speaking Prepare and present a **television interview** between a talk-show host and Annie Dillard about the flood at Tinker Creek. Use the following interviewing techniques:

- Prepare and ask relevant questions.
- Make notes of responses to help you devise follow-up questions.
- Demonstrate knowledge of the subject.

Present your interview to the class. **[Group Activity]**

Research and Technology Gather information on the worst floods in history. Organize your findings into categories—such as locale, deaths, and property damage toll—in a **flood report.** Use a computer program to design the report. Include photographs where appropriate.

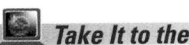 ***Take It to the Net*** www.phschool.com

Go online for an additional research activity using the Internet.

Flood ◆ 721

---

❸ Writing Lesson

- Lead students in brainstorming for words and phrases that describe the sensory experiences of a flood. List their ideas on the chalkboard.

- Have students work in pairs to draft their transcripts. Students can take turns acting as the show's host, asking questions about the flood to spark ideas in the caller's mind.

- In their answers, encourage the "callers" to use at least one simile to describe the water.

- Use the Description rubric in **Performance Assessment and Portfolio Management,** p. 19, to evaluate the students' transcripts.

❹ Research and Technology

- Have the class brainstorm for key words that will help them gather information during an Internet search.

- Have students work in small groups. Encourage each group to focus its research on three or four floods.

- Have students who are adept with computer programs design a report that will present the research findings in an organized manner.

- After groups have created their electronic reports, encourage them to share their work with the class.

CUSTOMIZE INSTRUCTION for Universal Access

To address different learning styles, use the following activities suggested in the **Extension Activities** booklet, p. 44.

- For Verbal/Linguistic Learners, use Activity 5.

- For Logical/Mathematical and Verbal/Linguistic Learners, use Activity 6.

- For Visual/Spatial Learners, use Activity 7.

ASSESSMENT RESOURCES

The following resources can be used to assess students' knowledge and skills.

Selection Assessment

📖 **Formal Assessment,** Selection Test, pp. 154–156

📖 **Open Book Test,** pp. 130–132

📺 **Got It! Assessment Videotapes,** Tape 4

💿 **Test Bank Software**

 Take It to the Net
Visit www.phschool.com for self-tests and questions on "Flood."

Writing Rubric

📖 **Performance Assess. and Portfolio Mgmt.,** p. 19

 ASSESSMENT *SYSTEM*

 📖 **Workbook**   📖 **Transparencies**

 📖 **Skill Book**   💿 **CD-ROM**

Mothers & Daughters

Lesson Objectives

1. To analyze and respond to literary elements
- Literary Analysis: Visual Essay
- Connecting Literary Elements: Tone

2. To read, comprehend, analyze, and critique a visual essay
- Reading Strategy: Interpreting Pictures
- Reading Check questions
- Review and Assess questions
- Assessment Practice (ATE)

3. To develop word analysis skills, fluency, and systematic vocabulary
- Vocabulary Development Lesson: Words About Color

4. To understand and apply written and oral language conventions
- Spelling Strategy
- Grammar Lesson: Use of Adjectives and Adverbs

5. To understand and apply appropriate writing and research strategies
- Writing Lesson: Introduction to an Art Exhibit
- Extension Activity: Annotated Bibliography

6. To understand and apply listening and speaking strategies
- Extension Activity: Group Discussion

STEP-BY-STEP TEACHING GUIDE	PACING GUIDE
PRETEACH	
Motivate Students and Provide Background	
Use the Motivation activity (ATE p. 722)	5 min.
Read and discuss the Preview material and Background information (SE/ATE p. 722) **A**	5 min.
Introduce the Concepts	
Introduce the Literary Analysis and Reading Strategy (SE/ATE p. 723) **A**	10 min.
Pronounce the vocabulary words and read their definitions (SE p. 723)	5 min.
TEACH	
Monitor Comprehension	
Informally monitor comprehension by circulating while students read independently or in groups **A**	5 min.
Monitor students' comprehension with the Reading Check notes (SE/ATE p. 725)	as students read
Develop vocabulary with Vocabulary notes (SE pp. 724, 725, 726)	as students read
Develop Understanding	
Develop students' understanding of visual essays with the Literary Analysis annotation (ATE p. 724) **A**	5 min.
Develop students' ability to interpret pictures with the Reading Strategy annotation (ATE p. 725)	5 min.
ASSESS	
Assess Mastery	
Assess students' mastery of the Reading Strategy and Literary Analysis by having them answer the Review and Assess questions (SE/ATE p. 727)	15 min.
Use one or more of the print and media Assessment Resources (ATE p. 729) **A**	up to 50 min.
EXTEND	
Apply Understanding	
Have students complete the Vocabulary Development Lesson and the Grammar Lesson (SE p. 728) **A**	15 min.
Apply students' knowledge of elaboration using the Writing Lesson (SE/ATE p. 729) **A**	45 min.
Apply students' understanding of the selection using one or more of the Extension Activities (SE p. 729)	20–90 min.

 ACCELERATED INSTRUCTION:
Use the strategies and activities identified with an **A**.

UNIVERSAL ACCESS
- ● = Below Level Students
- ▲ = On-Level Students
- ■ = Above Level Students

Time and Resource Manager

RESOURCES

PRINT 📖	TRANSPARENCIES 🗄	TECHNOLOGY 💿 🎧 📼
• **Beyond Literature,** Workplace Skills: Effective Listening, p. 46 ▲ ■		• **Interest Grabber Video,** Tape 4 ● ▲ ■
• **Selection Support Workbook:** ● ▲ ■ Literary Analysis, p. 184 Reading Strategy, p. 183 Build Vocabulary, p. 181	• **Literary Analysis and Reading Transparencies,** pp. 91 and 92 ● ▲ ■	
		• **Listening to Literature** ● ▲ ■ Audiocassettes, Side 23 Audio CDs, CD 15
• **Literatura en español** ● ▲ • **Literary Analysis for Enrichment** ■		
• **Formal Assessment:** Selection Test, pp. 160–162 ● ▲ ■ • **Open Book Test,** pp. 136–138 ● ▲ ■ • **Performance Assessment and Portfolio Management,** p. 19 ● ▲ ■ • PRENTICE HALL ASSESSMENT *SYSTEM* ● ▲ ■	• PRENTICE HALL ASSESSMENT *SYSTEM* ● ▲ ■ Skills Practice Answers and Explanations on Transparencies	• **Test Bank Software** ● ▲ ■ • **Got It! Assessment Videotapes,** Tape 4 ● ▲
• **Selection Support Workbook:** ● ▲ ■ Build Grammar Skills, p. 182 • **Writing and Grammar,** Platinum Level ● ▲ ■ • **Extension Activities,** p. 46 ● ▲ ■	• **Daily Language Practice Transparencies** ● ▲	• **Writing and Grammar iText CD-ROM** ● ▲ ■ 💻 *Take It to the Net* www.phschool.com

■ **BLOCK SCHEDULING:** Use one 90-minute class period to preteach the selection and have students read it. Use a second 90-minute class period to assess students' mastery of skills and have them complete one of the Extension Activities.

Motivation

Raise students' interest in this selection with a quick journal-writing activity. Have them visualize their favorite family photograph. Each student should then write a description of that photo along with some thoughts on what makes it meaningful. Follow up by letting students know that photographs can reveal unique aspects of interpersonal relationships. In this visual essay, text and photographs collaborate to create portraits of mothers and daughters together.

▦ Interest Grabber Video

As an alternative, play "Developing Photographs" on Tape 4 to engage student interest.

❶ Background

Art

Photographs are commonly taken to preserve moments and memories. Some, however, are taken to communicate or express the human condition or ideas. They are similar to paintings in that way—the photographer hopes you will feel something or understand something better after viewing the photographs. These photographs fall under the category of fine art and can be found on exhibit in most art museums today.

Prepare to Read

Mothers & Daughters

Untitled, Brookline, Massachusetts, 1986, Sage Sohier, Courtesy of the artist

🖥 *Take It to the Net*

Visit www.phschool.com for interactive activities and instruction related to "Mothers & Daughters," including

- background
- graphic organizers
- literary elements
- reading strategies

Preview

Connecting to the Literature

Many books and films have focused on the relationship between mothers and daughters. You probably have your own ideas about mother-daughter relationships from families you have known or from your own experiences. This selection offers insights through words and pictures.

❶ Background

Photography is one of the newest visual arts. Inventors produced the world's first photographs in the 1820s. Then, photographers such as Mathew Brady amazed the world by capturing the details of Civil War battle scenes. By 1888, George Eastman had produced a roll of paper film for ordinary Americans to use. The photographs in this essay owe their existence to these early pioneers.

722 ◆ *Nonfiction*

TEACHING RESOURCES

The following resources can be used to enrich or extend the instruction for pp. 722–723.

Motivation

▦ **Interest Grabber Video,** Tape 4 ▦

Background

📖 **Beyond Literature,** p. 46

🖥 *Take It to the Net*
Visit www.phschool.com for background and hotlinks for "Mothers & Daughters."

Literary Analysis

📖 **Selection Support:** Literary Analysis, p. 184 ▦

▦ **Literary Analysis and Reading Transparencies,** Visual Essay, p. 92

Reading

▦ **Literary Analysis and Reading Transparencies,** Interpreting Pictures, p. 91

 BLOCK SCHEDULING: Resources marked with this symbol provide varied instruction during 90-minute blocks.

❷ Literary Analysis

Visual Essay

Like a written essay, a **visual essay** presents information or makes a point about a subject. A visual essay has the following characteristics:

- It combines photographs or art with written text.
- The work addresses a single theme, but it may introduce several different angles or perspectives.

In this visual essay, a writer and a photographer have combined photographs with written passages from several authors to provide different perspectives on the relationships between mothers and daughters. Notice how the words and pictures convey feelings that many mothers and daughters have for each other.

Connecting Literary Elements

The **tone** of a literary work reflects the writer's attitude toward his or her subject. The tone may be serious, humorous, angry, sad, friendly, distant—to name just a few examples. In a visual essay, tone is revealed through both the writer's choice of words and the visual images used.

❸ Reading Strategy

Interpreting Pictures

To understand a story, you look carefully at the words to derive meaning. To **interpret pictures,** you "read" the elements of each picture. To interpret the photos in this selection, look at these elements:

- Facial expressions and other body language
- Closeness or distance between people
- Objects in the background
- Any other details that seem to convey meaning

Use a chart like the one shown to help you interpret the photos that accompany the text in this selection.

Element	Meaning Conveyed
Body language	Pride, independence
Position of people	Relationships may not be equal
Background	
Other details	

Vocabulary Development

hue (hyōō) *n.* color; tint (p. 724)

sullenness (sul´ ən nəs) *n.* gloom; sadness (p. 724)

implicit (im plis´ it) *adj.* essentially a part of; inherent (p. 725)

fervor (fur´ vər) *n.* passion; zeal (p. 726)

❷ Literary Analysis

Visual Essay

- Tell students that a visual essay conveys its point through photographs (or other visuals) as well as through written text.
- Read the instruction about visual essays together as a class.
- Use the instruction for Connecting Literary Elements to explain how tone is conveyed in a visual essay. Although students are familiar with identifying the tone of a work through an author's choice of words, they will learn how tone can be communicated through pictures as well.
- Use the Visual Essay transparency in **Literary Analysis and Reading Transparencies,** p. 92, to demonstrate the relationship between text and photographs in a visual essay.

❸ Reading Strategy

Interpreting Pictures

- Tell students that interpreting pictures means finding meaning in photographs—figuring out what the pictures tell them.
- Call students' attention to the photo on p. 722. Encourage them to discuss what the picture tells them about the people in it. Ask them to speculate about why the mother is hugging the cat instead of her daughter.
- Instruct students to create a chart like the one shown on p. 723 to interpret each photograph in the selection.

Vocabulary Development

- Pronounce each vocabulary word for students, and read the definitions as a class. Have students identify any words with which they are already familiar.

CUSTOMIZE INSTRUCTION FOR UNIVERSAL ACCESS

For Less Proficient Readers	For English Learners	For Advanced Readers
The stylistic variation among these texts may pose difficulties for some students. Guide students to see that the essays represent different voices, just as the photographs represent different visions. Also, encourage them to paraphrase the main points that each writer makes.	With essays by different writers, this selection presents an opportunity to review a variety of verb tenses with students. Point out the present tense "the eye seeks deeper vision" from Olsen's piece; the past tense "I learned" and the past perfect tense "I'd (I had) got in my own bed" from Welty's piece. Help students to see why each tense was used.	To take advantage of the different writing styles in the essays, encourage students to analyze the texts and photographs in terms of purpose and tone. For example, which essay(s) would they describe as intimate? Which are more formal? Which text is the most analytical? Students can discuss their choices in small groups.

 E-Teach

Visit E-Teach at www.phschool.com for teachers' essays on how to teach, with questions and answers.

**CUSTOMIZE INSTRUCTION
For Verbal/Linguistic Learners**

Suggest that students write captions
for each picture in this visual essay.
Encourage them to consider these
questions before writing: Who are
these people? What are they doing?
What do the details in each picture
reveal about the people's personalities and lives?

❶ About the Selection

The photographs and text in this
selection combine to evoke the rich
complexity of its theme. The photographers and writers explore the
relationship between mothers and
daughters from different perspectives. The overall multi-faceted
approach is fitting for a relationship
that cannot be summed up by a
single image or statement.

❷ ▶ Critical Viewing

Answer: Some students may say
that the photo shows "sullenness"
and "estrangement." They may cite
the expressions on the people's faces
and the distances between them.
Others may say that it shows "admiration" and "wordless closeness,"
arguing that the daughters and
mother feel secure enough within
themselves to stand on their own.

❸ Literary Analysis

Visual Essay

• Tillie Olsen's text refers to "a welter of images," and she calls these
photographic images "Multi,
multi-form."

• Ask students how Olsen's text is
itself a multiform welter of images
describing the mother-daughter
relationship.
Answer: Olsen captures the "multiform" nature of the images by
naming a wide variety of emotions,
conditions, and circumstances; she
conveys that every person and
every mother-daughter relationship
is unique.

---

❶ Mothers & Daughters

TILLIE OLSEN AND ESTELLE JUSSIM

August, New Mexico, 1979, Danny Lyon, Magnum Photos, Inc.

❷ ▲ **Critical Viewing** Which feelings described in the text do you think are shown in this photo? **[Interpret]**

Observations by Tillie Olsen and Julie Olsen Edwards

Here are daughters and mothers of every shape and human <u>hue</u>; in
every age and stage from mother and infant, to old daughter and old,
old mother; and here is the family resemblance in face, expression,
stance, body.

Here are mothers and daughters of lack and of privilege, in various
dress, settings, environments; posing for photographs or (unconcerned
with the camera) sharing tasks, ease, occasions, activities; holding,
embracing, touching; or in terrible isolation.

Here is <u>sullenness</u>, anger or controlled anger, resentment; admiration, distaste; playfulness, pride; joy, joy, joy in each other; estrangement; wordless closeness or intense communion.

❸ A welter[1] of images. Multi, multi-form.
The eye seeks deeper vision.

hue (hyōō) *n.* color; tint

sullenness (sul′ ən nes) *n.*
gloom; sadness

Tillie Olsen

(b. 1913)

Tillie Olsen and her
daughter, Julie Olsen Edwards, joined Estelle Jussim
to collect the materials included in *Mothers &
Daughters*. Olsen won the
O. Henry first prize for her
story "Tell Me a Riddle."

---

1. **welter** (wel′ tər) *n.* hodge-podge; number of things tossed and tumbled about.

724 ◆ *Nonfiction*

TEACHING RESOURCES

The following resources can be used to enrich or extend the instruction for pp. 724–726.

Reading

📖 **Selection Support:** Reading Strategy, p. 183;
Build Vocabulary, p. 181

🎧 **Listening to Literature Audiocassettes,** Side 23 ▪

💿 **Listening to Literature Audio CDs,** CD 15 ▪

▪ **BLOCK SCHEDULING:** Resources marked with this symbol provide varied instruction during 90-minute blocks.

Observations
by Estelle Jussim

from "The Heart of the Ineffable"

It has been widely recognized that even the greatest portrait can capture only so much of an individual's personality and character, not all of that person's physical attributes, and certainly not a permanently ascribable[2] mood. An attempt by a photographer to convey not only one, but two persons and their relationship, might seem to be exceedingly difficult, if not impossible. To portray two persons defined as mother and daughter is to define a relationship fraught[3] with cultural and emotional overtones. Such intensity of meaning would seem to demand skillful decoding. Perhaps, also, it requires a grasp of visual language that not all of us possess. Even if we did possess such a visual language, it might prove to be so ethnocentric and tempocentric[4] as to defy our desires for significant universal meanings. This collection makes no pretense of offering more than an intelligent sifting of contemporary imagery, which, upon examination, can reveal much about contemporary life and our <u>implicit</u> ideologies[5] concerning motherhood.

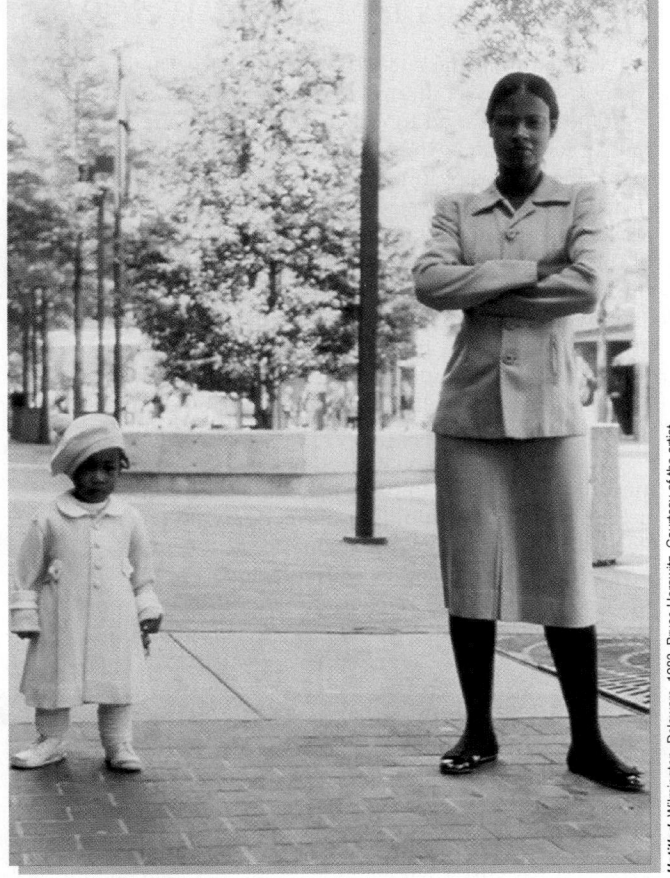

Untitled, Wilmington, Delaware, 1983, Bruce Horowitz, Courtesy of the artist

5 ▲ **Critical Viewing** What does this woman's body language and expression suggest about her? **[Draw Conclusions]**

implicit (im plis´ it) *adj.* essentially a part of; inherent

6 ✔ **Reading Check**
What does Jussim think is a weakness of portraits?

---

2. **ascribable** (ə skrīb´ ə bəl) *adj.* assignable; attributable.
3. **fraught** (frôt) *v.* filled; loaded.
4. **ethnocentric** (eth´ nō sen´ trik) **and tempocentric** (tem´ pō sen´ trik) *adj.* excessively concerned with race and time.
5. **ideologies** (ī´ dē äl´ ə jēz) *n.* ways of thinking; doctrines.

Mothers & Daughters ◆ 725

---

4 **Reading Strategy**
Interpreting Pictures
• Have students explain what Jussim means when she says that a portrait cannot capture a "permanently ascribable mood."
Answer: Jussim means that the moods and emotions captured in a photograph do not necessarily last longer than the moment in which the picture was snapped.

▶ **Monitor Progress** Ask students this question: What evidence in the picture on this page suggests that the two subjects are not caught in a "permanently ascribable mood," but rather in just one mood in a moment of time?
Answer: Although the mother seems proud of her daughter's independence, this is not a permanently ascribable mood. After the photograph is taken her mood might shift to one of protectiveness, anxiety, or something else. The daughter, who seems momentarily stunned in the photograph, might become joyous or fretful after the shutter has clicked.

5 ▶ **Critical Viewing**
Answer: Students may say that the woman shows strength, self-confidence, poise, and determination.

6 ✔ **Reading Check**
Answer: A weakness of portraits is that they cannot capture all of a person's personality, character, moods, and physical attributes.

CUSTOMIZE INSTRUCTION FOR UNIVERSAL ACCESS

For Special Needs Students	For Gifted/Talented Students
Students may have trouble understanding the connections between the written passages in this selection. Help them see that the theme of each passage is the relations between mothers and daughters. Encourage students to reread each passage and summarize it in their own words. Then, discuss the range of ideas about mothers and daughters presented in this selection.	Encourage students to take some time to study each photograph in depth. Then, have them choose one of the photographs and write a dialogue between the mother and daughter(s) in it. The dialogue should reflect the tone of the picture and shed light on the relationship between the mother and daughter(s). When they finish, have pairs of students read their dialogues to the class.

725

Answer: The mother's expression is proud, pleased, and forthright; she seems happy and comfortable about being photographed. The daughter's expression is more apprehensive and questioning. Students might note that the mother probably made their matching dresses and that the two might feel very differently about being photographed in them.

Answers for p. 726

Review and Assess

1. Students might choose photographs whose settings or subjects are particularly meaningful to them.

2. **(a)** They say these photographs convey sullenness, anger, resentment, admiration, distaste, playfulness, pride, joy, estrangement, closeness, or communion. **(b)** Students may say that they see estrangement, anger, sullenness, joy, and communion (the last two between mother and cat).

3. **(a)** It is hard to portray a mother-daughter relationship because it is too complicated to be seen in its entirety in a photograph. **(b)** Each mother-daughter relationship is different—a result of experiences, beliefs, emotions, and interactions unique to those two people.

4. **(a)** Welty shares the memory of being read to by her mother. **(b)** Welty's description of her relationship seems to fit well with the photo because the mother and daughter appear to share a close, loving bond.

5. Students may choose a picture that reflects how they feel about their parents or guardians.

Observations by Eudora Welty

I learned from the age of two or three that any room in our house, at any time of day, was there to read in, or to be read to. My mother read to me. She'd read to me in the big bedroom in the mornings, when we were in her rocker together, which ticked in rhythm as we rocked, as though we had a cricket accompanying the story. She'd read to me in the dining room on winter afternoons in front of the coal fire, with our cuckoo clock ending the story with "Cuckoo," and at night when I'd got in my own bed. I must have given her no peace. Sometimes she'd read to me in the kitchen while she sat churning, and the churning sobbed along with *any* story.

. . . She could still recite [the poems in McGuffey's Readers] in full when she was lying helpless and nearly blind, in her bed, an old lady. Reciting, her voice took on resonance and firmness, it rang with the old <u>fervor</u>, with ferocity even. She was teaching me one more, almost her last, lesson: emotions do not grow old. I knew that I would feel as she did, and I do.

Nellie G. Morgan and Tammie Pruitt Morgan, Bicentennial Celebration, Philadelphia.

⑦ ▲ **Critical Viewing**
What words would you use to describe each person's expression in this photograph? **[Analyze]**

fervor (fur´ vər) *n.* passion; zeal

Review and Assess

Thinking About the Selection

1. **Respond:** Which photograph do you like best? Why?

2. **(a) Recall:** What emotions do Tillie Olsen and Julie Olsen Edwards say these photographs convey? **(b) Interpret:** Which of these emotions do you see in the untitled photograph of the mother, daughter, and cat on page 722? Explain.

3. **(a) Recall:** According to Estelle Jussim, why is it so hard to portray in a photograph a relationship between a mother and daughter? **(b) Infer:** In what ways might a mother-daughter relationship be "fraught with cultural and emotional overtones"?

4. **(a) Recall:** What fond childhood memory does Eudora Welty share? **(b) Interpret:** How does Welty's relationship with her mother compare with that of the mother and daughter in the photograph "Bicentennial Celebration" above?

5. **Evaluate:** Which photograph do you feel is most successful in capturing how a mother and daughter may feel about each other? Explain.

726 ◆ *Nonfiction*

Estelle Jussim

(b. 1927)

Estelle Jussim is a professor at Simmons College, a writer, and an expert on photography, film, and popular imagery. She is the author of several award-winning books. In her essay for the book *Mothers & Daughters*, she explains how photographs can explore the unique relationships that mothers and daughters share.

✒️ ASSESSMENT PRACTICE: Reading Comprehension

Comparing and Contrasting Texts   **(For more practice, see Test Preparation Workbook, p. 46.)**

Students will encounter questions that require them to compare and contrast aspects of two texts on tests. Have them read the observations on pp. 724–725. Then, write this sample test question on the board:

What idea about taking photographs do both texts share?

    A Photographs capture emotions and moods.

    B Photographers use a visual language.

C A photograph cannot capture all aspects of a person.

D Daughters resemble their mothers in some ways.

Students should recognize that *B* and *C* refer only to the Jussim passage, while *D* refers only to the Olsen/Edwards passage. Therefore, to satisfy the qualifier *both* in the question, *A* is the correct answer.

Review and Assess

Literary Analysis

Visual Essay

1. Why do you need both the photography and the writing to understand the relationships between mothers and daughters presented in this **visual essay**?

2. What is the "visual language" that Estelle Jussim says is needed for a photograph to portray a complex relationship?

Connecting Literary Elements

3. Identify the **tone** in each of the three written passages and each of the four photographs.

4. Explain which photograph best matches the tone of the words that accompany it.

Reading Strategy

Interpreting Pictures

5. Describe the facial expressions and the body language of the mother and daughters in "August" on page 724.

6. What do you think is the relationship between the mother and daughter in "Bicentennial Celebration" on page 726? Use a diagram like the one shown to **interpret** details of the photo, and record your answer.

Detail	Detail	Detail

Relationship

7. What do you think is on the mother's mind in the photograph by Bruce Horowitz on page 725? Why?

Extend Understanding

8. **Social Studies Connection:** How has the development of the art of photography since the mid-1800s changed the way historical events are portrayed in print materials?

Quick Review

A **visual essay** is a presentation in which photographs or other visual forms are combined with written text.

The **tone** of a literary work or piece of art reflects the creator's attitude toward his or her audience and subject.

To **interpret pictures,** look for meaning in such elements as body language, people's positions, background, and other details.

Take It to the Net
www.phschool.com
Take the interactive self-test online to check your understanding of this selection.

Mothers & Daughters ◆ 727

Answers for p. 727

Review and Assess

1. The text and the photographs each contribute a different kind of language to make a whole picture. The text is analytical, reflective, and metaphoric, while the photos capture revealing details about people's lives.

2. Students might say that "visual language" means the poses and facial expressions that communicate the deep or hidden parts of a relationship.

3. Olsen/Edwards: intimate; Jussim: analytical; Welty: loving, warm; "Untitled" (Sohier): serious, tense; "August": open, but somewhat serious; "Untitled" (Horowitz): proud; "Bicentennial Celebration": proud, warm.

4. Students may say "Bicentennial Celebration" best matches the tone of the words because Welty wrote about the close bond she had with her mother, which is reflected beautifully in the people in the photograph.

5. The mother is squinting slightly from the sun, and she walks with pride and confidence. The daughters walk near their mother, but at a slight distance. They seem independent and comfortable with themselves.

6. Relationship: The mother and daughter feel differently about being photographed in matching dresses. Detail: The mother looks happy and comfortable. Detail: The daughter looks more apprehensive and questioning.

7. Students may say that the mother is thinking about how proud she is of her daughter.

8. Before photography was invented, historical events could only be captured in drawings and paintings, which took a long time and were not easily mass-produced in newspapers for public consumption. Now, events can be photographed in an instant, which means more visual information is available to more people in less time.

❶ Vocabulary Development

Word Analysis

1. tint
3. hue
2. shade

Fluency: Sentence Completion

1. fervor
3. hue
2. implicit
4. sullenness

Spelling Strategy

1. suddenness
3. meanness
2. thinness
4. openness

❷ Grammar

1. The photographer (worked) extremely quickly. (verb)
2. The (emotions) are implicit in this photograph. (noun)
3. The photographer always tried to (treat) her subjects respectfully. (verb)
4. She arranged the subjects for the photograph in a skillful (way.) (noun)
5. The woman seemed sadly (alone.) (adjective)

Writing Application

1. For a model, waiting to be photographed can be an arduous chore.
2. The photographer's subjects waited patiently for the picture to be taken.

Integrate Language Skills

❶ Vocabulary Development Lesson

Concept Development: Words About Color

The word *hue*, which Tillie Olsen uses, is just one of many English words that refer to differences in a color.

hue: particular shade of a color that distinguishes it from other shades

shade: degree of darkness of a color

tint: pale or delicate shade of a color

Choose the best word from those above to complete each sentence.

1. Many houses in Bermuda are painted in pastel ___?___s.
2. As night approached, the forest around them became a darker ___?___ of green.
3. Dust particles in the air sometimes give the sunset a pinkish ___?___.

❷ Grammar Lesson

Use of Adjectives and Adverbs

Adjectives modify nouns. **Adverbs** modify verbs, adjectives, and other adverbs. A common mistake is to use an adjective instead of an adverb to modify a verb.

Incorrect: The little girl *walked* too *slow*. (adjective modifying verb)

Correct: The little girl *walked* too *slowly*. (adverb modifying verb)

Practice Copy the following sentences, completing each with the correct adjective or adverb. Circle the word being modified, and label its part of speech.

1. The photographer worked extremely (quick, quickly).

Fluency: Sentence Completion

Write the vocabulary word from the list on page 723 that best completes each sentence.

1. Although the team's skill was limited, its ___?___ was enough to win the game.
2. The commercial's ___?___ message is that owning the car makes you popular.
3. The meat had a greenish ___?___, so I decided to throw it away.
4. The angry young boy could not hide his ___?___ during his sister's recital.

Spelling Strategy

When the suffix *-ness* is added to a word ending in *n*, keep all the letters intact. For example, *sullen + -ness = sullenness*. Add *-ness* to each of the following words.

1. sudden   2. thin   3. mean   4. open

2. The emotions are (implicit, implicitly) in this photograph.
3. The photographer always tried to treat her subjects (respectful, respectfully).
4. She arranged the subjects for the photograph in a (skillful, skillfully) way.
5. The woman seemed (sad, sadly) alone.

Writing Application Expand the sentences below, adding an adjective to the first sentence and an adverb to the second.

1. For a model, waiting to be photographed can be a chore.
2. The photographer's subjects waited for the picture to be taken.

𝒲𝒢 *Prentice Hall Writing and Grammar Connection: Chapter 17, Sections 1–2*

TEACHING RESOURCES

The following resources can be used to enrich or extend the instruction for pp. 728–729.

Vocabulary

📖 **Selection Support:** Build Vocabulary, p. 181

📖 **Vocabulary and Spelling Practice Book** (Use this booklet for skills enrichment.) ▪

Grammar

📖 **Selection Support:** Build Grammar Skills, p. 182

𝒲𝒢 **Writing and Grammar,** Platinum Level, p. 368

📖 **Daily Language Practice Transparencies** ▪

Writing

𝒲𝒢 **Writing and Grammar,** Platinum Level, p. 35

💿 **Writing and Grammar iText CD-ROM** ▪

▪ **BLOCK SCHEDULING:** Resources marked with this symbol provide varied instruction during 90-minute blocks.

❸ Writing Lesson

Introduction to an Art Exhibit

Write an introduction to an exhibit of the photographs in this selection, providing an overview of what visitors will see in the exhibit.

Prewriting	List the main points you want to make and the details to elaborate each idea. Your details might include the goals of the exhibit, information about the photographers, details about the style, and anything else that will help visitors understand and enjoy the show.
Drafting	Present each of your ideas in a topic sentence for a separate paragraph. Then, elaborate on each idea using the relevant details from your chart.

Model: Revising to Elaborate With Details

Need more details about styles.

There are formal and informal photographs in indoor and outdoor settings.
The exhibit includes photographs with the same subject—mothers and daughters—but in a variety of styles. The variety in the interpretation of the subject will ensure that there is something to interest every visitor.

The details tell readers more about the exhibit and engage their interests.

Revising	Ask a writing partner to read your draft. Your partner might make suggestions to indicate where ideas need to be further developed.

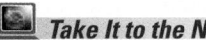 *Prentice Hall Writing and Grammar Connection: Chapter 3, Section 1*

❹ Extension Activities

Listening and Speaking In a **group discussion,** choose the photograph of the year. Use the following process:

- Each group member should bring in photos from recent newspapers or magazines.
- Study the photos, choosing your favorite. Prepare notes to support your choice.
- Hold a discussion to hear the arguments.
- Vote to identify the winning photograph.

Share your results with the rest of the class. [Group Activity]

Research and Technology With a group of classmates, prepare an **annotated bibliography** on the subject of mothers and daughters. Ask friends, relatives, teachers, and other students for their recommendations for books or articles on the subject. Compile a list that includes the title, the author, and a short description of each entry.

 Take It to the Net www.phschool.com
Go online for an additional research activity using the Internet.

Mothers & Daughters ◆ 729

ASSESSMENT RESOURCES

The following resources can be used to assess students' knowledge and skills.

Selection Assessment
- **Formal Assessment,** pp. 160–162
- **Open Book Test,** pp. 136–138
- **Got It! Assessment Videotapes,** Tape 4
- **Test Bank Software**

 Take It to the Net
Visit www.phschool.com for self-tests and additional questions on "Mothers & Daughters."

Writing Rubric
- **Performance Assess. and Portfolio Mgmt.,** p. 19

PRENTICE HALL **ASSESSMENT SYSTEM**
- **Workbook**
- **Skill Book**
- **Transparencies**
- **CD-ROM**

Lesson Support for p. 729

❸ Writing Lesson

- Explain to students that elaborating on an idea means using details that will help readers see it or understand it fully.
- Encourage students to decide on the main points they want to make in their introduction. Then, have them brainstorm for a list of details that will make their introductions both engaging and helpful to those who attend the exhibit.
- Use the Writing Lesson to guide students in writing their introductions.
- Use the Description rubric, p. 19 of **Performance Assessment and Portfolio Management,** to evaluate students' work.

❹ Research and Technology

- Divide the class into groups. Have each group come up with a list of people they will ask for book and article recommendations.
- Have groups compile their lists on a computer. Remind students to proofread and spell-check their work before they print out their final draft.
- Collect the groups' lists, photocopy them, and combine them in a booklet. Pass out the booklets to students.
- Then, have students discuss which books sound the most interesting to them.

CUSTOMIZE INSTRUCTION for Universal Access

To address different learning styles, use the following activities suggested in the **Extension Activities** booklet, p. 46.

- For Visual/Spatial and Intrapersonal Learners, use Activity 5.
- For Musical/Rhythmic Learners, use Activity 6.
- For Bodily/Kinesthetic and Musical/Rhythmic Learners, use Activity 7.

CONNECTIONS
Literature and Art
The Life and Times of Mary Cassatt

Just as the photographs in the essay from *Mothers & Daughters* tell very personal stories about the relationships of the subjects, American painter Mary Cassatt (1844–1926) captured moments of everyday life between mothers and daughters. Mary Cassatt's paintings and drawings communicate the special bond between mothers and daughters.

A Life in Art

At the age of sixteen, in 1860, Cassatt enrolled at the Pennsylvania Academy of the Fine Arts in Philadelphia. After honing her skills in drawing and painting for four years at the school, she traveled to Paris to study works of art by the Old Masters, such as Leonardo da Vinci and Rembrandt. By the age of thirty, Cassatt had established a permanent residence in France and set up her studio there.

Cassatt's clear talents gave her the chance to have her work exhibited in the Salon, France's annual art showcase. However, it was not until she met the Impressionist painter Edgar Degas that her work really began to develop and evolve into the style for which she is most noted.

Varied Mediums and Techniques

Along with Degas, Cassatt found inventive ways to exploit the medium of pastels—drawing crayons made from powdered pigments ground with chalk and mixed with gum water. The term also refers to drawings executed with these crayons.

In her printmaking, she drew inspiration from Japanese masters, such as Utamaro and Toyokuni. Their technique involves creating an inked impression from any of a variety of work surfaces, such as a wooden block, metal plate, or specially prepared stone.

Her Style

With her fondness for pastels becoming more apparent in her work, Cassatt moved away from social and urban themes, such as the figures of women drinking tea or enjoying outings with friends, which she had often explored. Instead, she began to focus on more domestic and intimate subjects. In *The Maternal Kiss,* Cassatt presents a daughter in her mother's embrace. The body language of the figures suggests complete trust and comfort.

Mother Combing Sara's Hair, Mary Cassatt, Christie's Images, London, UK

The pastel called *Mother Combing Sara's Hair* embodies the characteristics of Cassatt's pastel work in the 1890s. The work captures the emotional bond between the mother and daughter. Cassatt shows the connection through the child's gaze and the sensitive depiction of the mother's caress.

In all her paintings, pastels, and prints, Cassatt stresses the sensitive and caring relationship between mothers and daughters. Her work is displayed in museums worldwide, thus preserving for future viewers a glimpse into intimate moments captured more than a century ago.

Connecting Literature and Art

1. What comparisons can you draw between the work of Mary Cassatt and the visual essay from *Mothers & Daughters*?
2. Why are photographers and artists important to society?

Connections: The Life and Times of Mary Cassatt ◆ *731*

CUSTOMIZE INSTRUCTION FOR UNIVERSAL ACCESS

For Special Needs Students	For Advanced Students
Invite students to use pastels to depict a relationship of some kind. It may be a mother and daughter, but it may also be a child and animal, a son and father, or a group of teenagers. Then, ask them to write a paragraph on what the position of their figures shows about the relationship.	Students may benefit from comparing the style and subjects of Impressionist works. Have them view some of Degas's dancers and compare them with the children in Mary Cassatt's works. What are some similarities and differences between the two?

Star Wars—A Trip to a Far Galaxy That's Fun and Funny . . . ✦
Star Wars: Breakthrough Film Still Has the Force

Lesson Objectives

1. **To analyze and respond to literary elements**
   - Literary Analysis: Critical Review
   - Comparing Literary Works
2. **To read, comprehend, analyze, and critique critical reviews**
   - Reading Strategy: Identifying Evidence
   - Reading Check questions
   - Review and Assess questions
   - Assessment Practice (ATE)
3. **To develop word analysis skills, fluency, and systematic vocabulary**
   - Vocabulary Development Lesson: Connotations
4. **To understand and apply written and oral language conventions**
   - Spelling Strategy
   - Grammar Lesson: Commonly Confused Words: *good* and *well*
5. **To understand and apply appropriate writing and research strategies**
   - Writing Lesson: Movie Review
   - Extension Activity: Comparison
6. **To understand and apply listening and speaking strategies**
   - Extension Activity: Music Analysis

STEP-BY-STEP TEACHING GUIDE	PACING GUIDE
PRETEACH	
Motivate Students and Provide Background	
Use the Motivation activity (ATE p. 732)	5 min.
Read and discuss the Preview material and Background information (SE/ATE p. 732)	5 min.
Introduce the Concepts	
Introduce the Literary Analysis and Reading Strategy (SE/ATE p. 733)	15 min.
Pronounce the vocabulary words and read their definitions (SE p. 733)	5 min.
TEACH	
Monitor Comprehension	
Informally monitor comprehension by circulating while students read independently or in groups	20 min.
Monitor students' comprehension with the Reading Check notes (SE/ATE pp. 735, 737, 739, 741)	as students read
Develop vocabulary with Vocabulary notes (SE pp. 735, 736, 738, 741; ATE p. 741)	as students read
Develop Understanding	
Develop students' understanding of critical reviews with Literary Analysis annotations (SE pp. 740, 741; ATE pp. 736, 740, 741)	10 min.
Develop students' understanding of identifying evidence with Reading Strategy annotations (SE p. 740; ATE pp. 735, 739, 740)	10 min.
ASSESS	
Assess Mastery	
Assess students' mastery of the Reading Strategy and Literary Analysis by having them answer the Review and Assess questions (SE/ATE p. 743)	20 min.
Use one or more of the print and media Assessment Resources (ATE p. 745)	up to 50 min.
EXTEND	
Apply Understanding	
Have students complete the Vocabulary Development Lesson and the Grammar Lesson (SE p. 744)	20 min.
Apply students' ability to support opinions with evidence using the Writing Lesson (SE/ATE p. 745)	45 min.
Apply students' understanding using one or more of the Extension Activities (SE p. 745)	20–90 min.

A **ACCELERATED INSTRUCTION:**
Use the strategies and activities identified with an **A**.

UNIVERSAL ACCESS
● = Below Level Students
▲ = On-Level Students
■ = Above Level Students

Time and Resource Manager

Reading Level: Easy/Easy
Average Number of Instructional Days: 4

RESOURCES		
PRINT 📖	**TRANSPARENCIES** 🗂	**TECHNOLOGY** 💿 🎧 📼
• **Beyond Literature,** Media Connection: Classic Films, p. 45 ▲ ■		• **Interest Grabber Video,** Tape 4 ● ▲ ■
• **Selection Support Workbook:** ● ▲ ■ Literary Analysis, p. 180 Reading Strategy, p. 179 Build Vocabulary, p. 177	• **Literary Analysis and Reading Transparencies,** pp. 89 and 90 ● ▲ ■	
		• **Listening to Literature** ● ▲ ■ Audiocassettes, Side 23 Audio CDs, CD 15
• **Literatura en español** ● ▲ • **Literary Analysis for Enrichment** ■		
• **Formal Assessment:** Selection Test, pp. 157–159 ● ▲ ■ • **Open Book Test,** pp. 133–135 ● ▲ ■ • **Performance Assessment and Portfolio Management,** pp. 18, 31 ● ▲ ■ • ⬤ PRENTICE HALL ASSESSMENT *SYSTEM* ● ▲ ■	• ⬤ PRENTICE HALL ASSESSMENT *SYSTEM* ● ▲ ■ Skills Practice Answers and Explanations on Transparencies	• **Test Bank Software** ● ▲ ■ • **Got It! Assessment Videotapes,** Tape 4 ● ▲
• **Selection Support Workbook:** ● ▲ ■ Build Grammar Skills, p. 178 • **Writing and Grammar,** Platinum Level ● ▲ ■ • **Extension Activities,** p. 45 ● ▲ ■	• **Daily Language Practice Transparencies** ● ▲	• **Writing and Grammar iText CD-ROM** ● ▲ ■ 🖥 ***Take It to the Net*** www.phschool.com

BLOCK SCHEDULING: Use one 90-minute class period to preteach the selection and have students read it. Use a second 90-minute class period to assess students' mastery of skills and have them complete one of the Extension Activities.

Step-by-Step Teaching Guide for pp. 732–733

Motivation

If possible, show a brief clip from one of the *Star Wars* films. Point out that *Star Wars* has long been popular with movie fans of all ages, and that when it was re-released in theaters twenty years after its original opening, it was a smash hit all over again. Tell the class that the following selections are reviews of this film twenty years apart. Two outstanding movie critics write about why this amazing film became such a success originally, and why, two decades later, *Star Wars* is considered a classic.

▦ Interest Grabber Video

As an alternative, play "Movies and Outer Space" on Tape 4 to engage student interest.

❶ Background
Film

Together, the *Star Wars* films have made over $300 million. More impressive than that is the $4 billion merchandising gross from the movies. There are over two dozen novels, numerous action figures, computer games, trading cards, and Web sites devoted to the movie. In fact, some of the original plastic action figures from 1977, which sold for about $3 each at the time, are now worth about $1,400.

Prepare to Read

Star Wars—A Trip to a Far Galaxy That's Fun and Funny . . . ◆
Star Wars: Breakthrough Film Still Has the Force

 Take It to the Net

Visit www.phschool.com for interactive activities and instruction related to these selections, including
- background
- graphic organizers
- literary elements
- reading strategies

Preview

Connecting to the Literature

You are sitting in a crowded movie theater. The houselights dim. You are filled with anticipation. Excitement builds as you realize that the movie you are watching amazes you and changes the way you think about movies. For millions of people, *Star Wars* was just such a film.

❶ Background

As you travel, certain landmarks—a mountain, gorge, or building—may remain in your memory. They define a trip for you. In a similar way, movies and other art forms become cultural landmarks for entire generations. From the moment it opened in 1977, *Star Wars* made an impact on the lives of the people who saw it. These reviews may explain why it became such a cinematic landmark.

TEACHING RESOURCES

The following resources can be used to enrich or extend the instruction for pp. 732–733.

Motivation
▦ **Interest Grabber Video**, Tape 4

Background
📖 **Beyond Literature**, p. 45 ▦

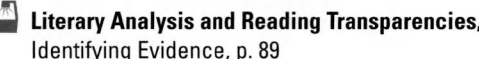 **Take It to the Net**
Visit www.phschool.com for background and hotlinks for the selections.

Literary Analysis
▱ **Literary Analysis and Reading Transparencies**, Critical Review, p. 90

Reading
📖 **Selection Support:** Reading Strategy, p. 179; Build Vocabulary, p. 177 ▦
▱ **Literary Analysis and Reading Transparencies**, Identifying Evidence, p. 89

▦ **BLOCK SCHEDULING:** Resources marked with this symbol provide varied instruction during 90-minute blocks.

Literary Analysis

Critical Review

Film critics write **critical reviews** in which they discuss the various elements of a film and try to persuade you to see it—or not to see it. In this example, the critic Vincent Canby builds interest in seeing the film:

> "Star Wars" . . . is the most elaborate, most expensive, most beautiful movie serial ever made.

As you read these selections, think about what the writers are trying to persuade you to do or think.

Comparing Literary Works

To assess a critical review, take into account the **writer's perspective**—the way a review reflects the critic's personal recollection of the experience of viewing the film. As you read these two reviews of *Star Wars*, compare how each one reflects the writer's interests and tastes.

Reading Strategy

Identifying Evidence

When you read a piece intended to persuade, you should **identify the evidence** the writer uses to support his or her claim. Evidence that supports the writer's opinion may be provided in several forms, including

- Facts and statistics
- Examples
- Observations
- Statements from authorities

Use a chart like the one shown to identify the evidence that supports the claims of each reviewer. Then, determine whether or not there is enough evidence to support the claim.

Claim
Star Wars has characteristics of a movie serial.

Evidence
• Series of adventures
• Characters get into and out of trouble
• Good vs. Evil

Vocabulary Development

apotheosis (ə păth´ ē ō´ sis) *n.* glorification of a person or thing (p. 735)

eclectic (ek lek´ tik) *adj.* composed of material from various sources (p. 735)

facetiousness (fə sē´ shəs nəs) *n.* act of making jokes (p. 735)

adroit (ə droit´) *adj.* skillful (p. 736)

piously (pī´ əs lē) *adv.* with religious devotion (p. 736)

condescension (kän´ di sen´ shən) *n.* snobbery; regarding as below one's dignity (p. 736)

watershed (wôt´ ər shed´) *n.* moment after which nothing is the same (p. 738)

synthesis (sin´ thə sis) *n.* combining parts to form a whole (p. 738)

fastidious (fas tid´ ē əs) *adj.* refined in an oversensitive way (p. 741)

effete (e fēt´) *adj.* overrefined (p. 741)

laconic (lə kän´ ik) *adj.* using few words (p. 741)

Star Wars—A Trip to a Far Galaxy That's Fun and Funny . . . / Star Wars: Breakthrough Film Still Has the Force ◆ 733

❷ Literary Analysis

Critical Review

- Engage students in a discussion about the purpose of critical reviews. Why do we read them? Why do reviewers write them?

- Guide students to understand that reviewers are trying to persuade readers to explore or avoid a work, such as a book or a movie, or to think in a certain way.

- Use the instruction for Comparing Literary Works to show how a review reflects the personal interests of the writer. Remind students that they should never accept a writer's opinions without first analyzing how the writer's own interests and tastes affect his or her point of view.

❸ Reading Strategy

Identifying Evidence

- Remind students that evidence is something that supports an opinion—it helps a writer show that his or her opinion is "right."

- Tell students that when they read, they should not only identify a writer's evidence, but also determine whether or not it is valid and convincing.

- Use the Identifying Evidence transparency in **Literary Analysis and Reading Transparencies,** p. 89, to demonstrate how to find evidence that supports the writers' opinions.

Vocabulary Development

- Pronounce each vocabulary word for students, and read the definitions as a class. Have students identify any words with which they are already familiar.

CUSTOMIZE INSTRUCTION FOR UNIVERSAL ACCESS

For Less Proficient Readers	For English Learners	For Advanced Readers
Suggest that students list the descriptive words and phrases that the reviewers use to evaluate *Star Wars*. When they've completed their lists, they can decide whether the words and phrases are positive or negative.	Before they read the selections, have students examine the photographs from the movie to get a sense of the plot and setting of *Star Wars*. This will help them follow Canby's and Ebert's reviews.	Vincent Canby compares *Star Wars* with elements of *Superman, Ivanhoe,* the Bible, and the legend of King Arthur and the Knights of the Round Table. Encourage students to do research to determine the specific ways in which *Star Wars* relates to one of these works.

 E-Teach

Visit E-Teach at www.phschool.com for teachers' essays on how to teach, with questions and answers.

Step-by-Step Teaching Guide for pp. 734–742

CUSTOMIZE INSTRUCTION
For Interpersonal Learners

In his review, Vincent Canby compares the move *Star Wars* to a comic-book adventure. Encourage students to work together to create their own comic-book adventure, complete with a hero or heroine, faithful sidekicks, a setting in a different time and place, and a simple plot of good against evil.

❶ About the Selection

In language that is exciting and enthusiastic, Vincent Canby reviews the first film in the *Star Wars* trilogy. He balances summary with evaluation, demonstrating for students the qualities of an effective review. In addition to offering an opinion on the movie itself, Canby analyzes the reasons the characters and situations may be appealing to audiences.

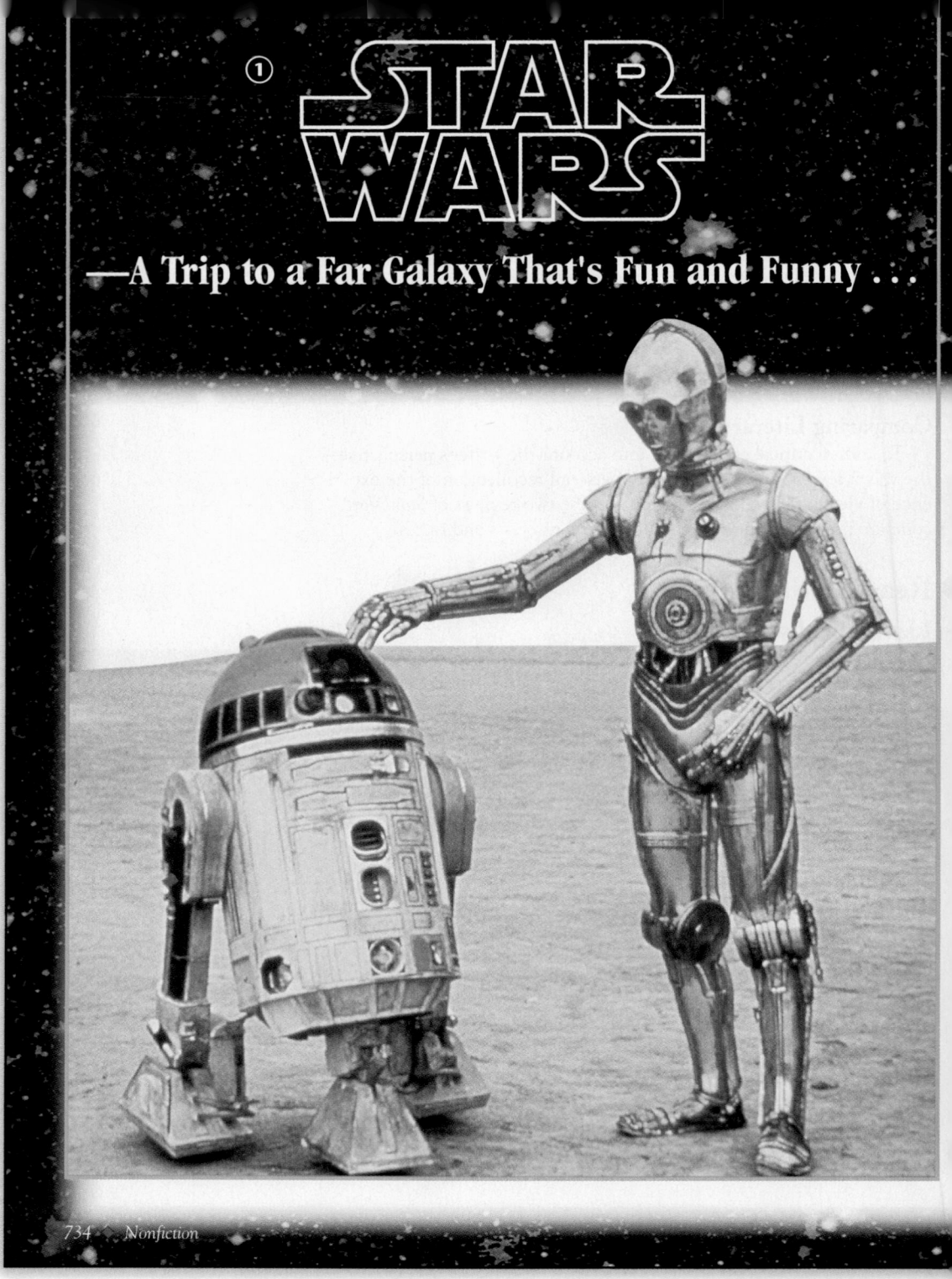

① **STAR WARS**

—A Trip to a Far Galaxy That's Fun and Funny . . .

734 • Nonfiction

TEACHING RESOURCES

The following resources can be used to enrich or extend the instruction for pp. 734–742.

Literary Analysis

📖 **Selection Support:** Literary Analysis, p. 180

Reading

🎧 **Listening to Literature Audiocassettes,** Side 23 ▪

💿 **Listening to Literature Audio CDs,** CD 15 ▪

▪ **BLOCK SCHEDULING:** Resources marked with this symbol provide varied instruction during 90-minute blocks.

VINCENT CANBY

from
The New York Times,
May 26, 1977

"Star Wars," George Lucas's first film since his terrifically successful "American Graffiti," is the movie that the teen-agers in "American Graffiti" would have broken their necks to see. It's also the movie that's going to entertain a lot of contemporary folk who have a soft spot for the virtually ritualized manners of comic-book adventure.

"Star Wars," which opened yesterday[1] at the Astor Plaza, Orpheum and other theaters, is the most elaborate, most expensive, most beautiful movie serial ever made. It's both an apotheosis of "Flash Gordon" serials and a witty critique that makes associations with a variety of literature that is nothing if not eclectic: "Quo Vadis?", "Buck Rogers," "Ivanhoe," "Superman," "The Wizard of Oz," "The Gospel According to St. Matthew," the legend of King Arthur and the knights of the Round Table.

All of these works, of course, had earlier left their marks on the kind of science-fiction comic strips that Mr. Lucas, the writer as well as director of "Star Wars," here remembers with affection of such cheerfulness that he avoids facetiousness. The way definitely not to approach "Star Wars," though, is to expect a film of cosmic implications or to footnote it with so many references that one anticipates it as if it were a literary duty. It's fun and funny.

The time, according to the opening credit card, is "a long time ago" and the setting "a galaxy far far away," which gives Mr. Lucas and his associates total freedom to come up with their own landscapes, housing, vehicles, weapons, religion, politics—all of which are variations on the familiar.

When the film opens, dark times have fallen upon the galactal empire once ruled, we are given to believe, from a kind of space-age Camelot. Against these evil tyrants there is, in progress, a rebellion led by a certain Princess Leia Organa, a pretty round-faced young woman of old-fashioned pluck who, before you can catch your breath, has been captured by the guardians of the empire. Their object is to retrieve

apotheosis (ə päth′ ē ō′ sis) *n.* glorification of a person or thing

eclectic (ek lek′ tik) *adj.* composed of material from various sources

facetiousness (fə sē′ shəs nəs) *n.* act of making jokes

---

1. **which opened yesterday:** Wednesday, May 25, 1977.

◀ **Critical Viewing** In what ways do these characters—R2D2 and C3PO— remind you of Laurel and Hardy? **[Compare]**

4 ✔ **Reading Check**
What is the setting of *Star Wars*?

Star Wars—A Trip to a Far Galaxy That's Fun and Funny . . . ◆ 735

---

⑤ Literary Analysis

Critical Review

- Remind students that film critics often use precise words to make their arguments more persuasive.
- Have students identify the persuasive language in this passage and point out Canby's supporting evidence.
  Answer: Persuasive language includes *stars, incredible,* and *fondness.* Canby supports his points with examples of the special effects and the elaborate settings.

▶ Monitor Progress After finishing the review, ask students: What is Canby trying to persuade the reader to do in this review? How can you tell?
Answer: Canby is trying to persuade the reader to see the movie. You can tell because he has written a glowing review of *Star Wars,* raving about its humor and its special effects.

some secret plans that can be the empire's undoing.

That's about all the plot that anyone of voting age should be required to keep track of. The story of "Star Wars" could be written on the head of a pin and still leave room for the Bible. It is, rather, a breathless succession of escapes, pursuits, dangerous missions, unexpected encounters, with each one ending in some kind of defeat until the final one.

These adventures involve, among others, an ever-optimistic young man named Luke Skywalker (Mark Hamill), who is innocent without being naive; Han Solo (Harrison Ford), a free-booting freelance, spaceship captain who goes where he can make the most money, and an old mystic named Ben Kenobi (Alec Guinness), one of the last of the Old Guard, a fellow in possession of what's called "the force," a mixture of what appears to be ESP and early Christian faith.

Accompanying these three as they set out to liberate the princess and restore justice to the empire are a pair of Laurel-and-Hardyish robots. The thin one, who looks like a sort of brass woodman, talks in the polished phrases of a valet ("I'm <u>adroit</u> but I'm not very knowledgeable"), while the squat one, shaped like a portable washing machine, who is the one with the knowledge, simply squeaks and blinks his lights. They are the year's best new comedy team.

In opposition to these good guys are the imperial forces led by someone called the Grand Moff Tarkin (Peter Cushing) and his executive assistant, Lord Darth Vader (David Prowse), a former student of Ben Kenobi who elected to leave heaven sometime before to join the evil ones.

⑤ The true stars of "Star Wars" are John Barry, who was responsible for the production design, and the people who were responsible for the incredible special effects—space ships, explosions of stars, space battles, hand-to-hand combat with what appear to be lethal neon swords. I have a particular fondness for the look of the interior of a gigantic satellite called the Death Star, a place full of the kind of waste space one finds today only in old Fifth Avenue mansions and public libraries.

There's also a very funny sequence in a low-life bar on a remote planet, a frontierlike establishment where they serve customers who look like turtles, apes, pythons and various amalgams of same, but draw the line at robots. Says the bartender <u>piously</u>: "We don't serve *their* kind here."

It's difficult to judge the performances in a film like this. I suspect that much of the time the actors had to perform with special effects that were later added in the laboratory. Yet everyone treats his material with the proper combination of solemnity and good humor that avoids <u>condescension</u>. One of Mr. Lucas's particular achievements is the manner in which he is able to recall the tackiness of the old comic strips and serials he loves without making a movie that is, itself, tacky. "Star Wars" is good enough to convince the most skeptical 8-year-old sci-fi buff, who is the toughest critic.

adroit (ə droit´) *adj.* skillful

piously (pī´ əs lē) *adv.* with religious devotion

condescension (kän´ di sen´ shən) *n.* snobbery; regarding as below one's dignity

Vincent Canby

(1924–2000)

If you had been looking for all the news fit to print about movies between 1969 and 1993, you would no doubt have read the film reviews of Vincent Canby, the leading film critic of *The New York Times* during those years. Canby served as chief theater critic from 1994 to 1996 and then returned to reviewing movies. In addition to theater and film reviews, Canby also wrote the play *After All* (1981) and the novel *Unnatural Scenery* (1979). A fellow critic wrote of Canby, "He was a wry and civilized man who took the job seriously but never took himself too seriously."

✳ ENRICHMENT: Art Connection

Film

At the end of the 19th century, the American inventor Thomas Edison devised the kinetoscope, the first successful machine for showing motion pictures. In 1903, *The Great Train Robbery* appeared; it was the first movie with a plot—and the first western. Shot in New Jersey, it was three minutes long.

Movies quickly grew longer, more ambitious, and more popular. Until 1927, they were silent; theater musicians provided the only accompaniment. Instead of spoken dialogue, films had printed titles between scenes.

In 1927, the first film with a sound track made its debut: *The Jazz Singer,* starring Al Jolson. Almost overnight, the movies switched to sound, and many actors whose voices recorded poorly saw their careers come to abrupt ends.

Today, motion pictures are a worldwide industry, whose stars are often better known than heads of government.

Star Wars

Breakthrough Film Still Has the Force

Roger Ebert
of the *Chicago Sun-Times*
from *The Oakland Press,* Friday, January 31, 1997

To see "Star Wars" again after 20 years is to revisit a place in the mind. George Lucas' space epic has colonized our imaginations, and it is hard to stand back and see it simply as a motion picture because it has so completely become part of our memories. It's as goofy as a children's tale, as shallow as an old Saturday afternoon serial, as corny as Kansas in August—and a masterpiece. Those who analyze its philosophy do so, I imagine, with a smile in their minds. May the Force be with them.

❼ ▲ **Critical Viewing**
Which traits of the characters of *Star Wars* do you think helped make them popular with viewers? **[Speculate]**

❽ ☑**Reading Check**
According to Ebert, why is it difficult to view *Star Wars* as just a motion picture?

Star Wars: Breakthrough Film Still Has the Force ◆ 737

CUSTOMIZE INSTRUCTION FOR UNIVERSAL ACCESS

For Gifted/Talented Students	For Advanced Readers
Ask students whether they have seen a television show in which two film reviewers discuss new films—a style of reviewing made popular by Roger Ebert and his late partner, Gene Siskel. Have students pair off and improvise this type of conversation about a film they have recently seen. They can discuss plot, dialogue, acting, music, costumes, and special effects.	Play the portions of *Star Wars* that Ebert describes. Have students evaluate his descriptions and opinions after viewing the scenes and settings themselves. If students find his descriptions lacking or inaccurate, encourage them to write a better description of their own. Then, allow time for students to share their descriptions with the class.

10 ⬤ **Background**

Film

Birth of a Nation (1915), by D.W. Griffith, is a technical milestone in film history—despite its content, which is considered quite dated. *Citizen Kane* (1941), made by Orson Welles at age 23, is considered to be one of the greatest screen achievements in the history of American film.

9 ▲ **Critical Viewing** This scene between Han Solo and Jabba the Hut was added to the reworked version of *Star Wars*. What can you learn about these characters from this picture? **[Analyze]**

10 ⬤   Like "Birth of a Nation" and "Citizen Kane," "Star Wars" was a technical <u>watershed</u> that influenced many of the movies that came after. These films have little in common, except for the way they came along at a crucial moment in cinema history, when new methods were ripe for <u>synthesis</u>. "Birth of a Nation" brought together the developing language and shots and editing. "Citizen Kane" married special effects, advanced sound, a new photographic style and a freedom from linear

watershed (wôt´ ər shed´) *n.* moment after which nothing is the same

synthesis (sin´ thə sis) *n.* combining parts to form a whole

738 ◆ *Nonfiction*

⬤ **ENRICHMENT: Science Connection**

Robots

The robots known as R2D2 and C3PO in *Star Wars* are historic and futuristic at the same time; they are yesterday's vision of what a robot looked like and what it could do.

The word *robot* originated in the Czech writer Karel Capek's 1921 play *R.U.R.* (Rossum's Universal Robots). In that play, mechanical beings that were manufactured to be slaves for humanity stage a rebellion and kill their creators. Robots of early science fiction

manifest people's fears that they will be overtaken by mechanization. The personalities of the *Star Wars* robots do not perpetuate that fear of the future. Today, it is difficult to distinguish robots from other forms of automation. However, robots are being used in some factories, and they are being developed to help people who have lost the use of their limbs.

- Ask students: What evidence has Ebert offered so far to support his assertion that *Star Wars* is a masterpiece?

  Answer: Ebert's evidence includes details about the incredible special effects, the fact that the movie began the high-action blockbuster trend that is still going on today, and the fact that so many movies since have tried to be the "next" *Star Wars*.

- As they read the rest of the review, encourage students to add to the list of the evidence Ebert offers to prove that *Star Wars* is a masterpiece.

⑫ ✔Reading Check

Answer: *Star Wars* focused the film-making industry on "big-budget special effects blockbusters."

storytelling. "Star Wars" combined a new generation of special effects with the high-energy action picture; it linked space opera and soap opera, fairy tales and legend, and packaged them as a wild visual ride.

"Star Wars" effectively brought to an end the golden era of early-1970s personal filmmaking and focused the industry on big-budget special effects blockbusters, blasting off a trend we are still living through. But you can't blame it for what it did; you can only observe how well it did it. In one way or another all the big studios have been trying to make another "Star Wars" ever since (pictures like "Raiders of the Lost Ark," "Jurassic Park" and "Independence Day" are its

⑫ ✔Reading Check

What did *Star Wars* do to the filmmaking industry?

Star Wars: Breakthrough Film Still Has the Force ◆ 739

CUSTOMIZE INSTRUCTION FOR UNIVERSAL ACCESS

For Advanced Readers

Point out to students that each film reviewer has an emotional response to *Star Wars* that is part of his critical response. Vincent Canby appreciates the humor in the movie, and warns against taking its message too seriously. Roger Ebert, viewing the film as a classic, marks its significance in the history of movie-making.

Offer students a choice of ways to examine these film reviews.

1. Have students write their own reviews of *Star Wars*, including comparisons of their responses with those of Canby and Ebert.

2. Have students search on the Internet to find other reviews of *Star Wars*, written either at its initial release or when it was re-released. They can compare these reviews with their own feelings or the reviews of Canby and Ebert.

Identifying Evidence

- Explain to students that in a film review, the details that a writer uses to support his or her main points may be facts, observations, examples, and statements from authorities.

- Ask a volunteer to read aloud the bracketed passage. Draw students' attention to Ebert's comment about people's tastes as they age.

▶ Monitor Progress Ask students the Reading Strategy question on p. 740: How does Ebert support his claim that people retain their tastes as they age?
Answer: Ebert supports his claim by saying that there is no other explanation for the allure of *Star Wars* to such a widespread audience.

14 Literary Analysis

Critical Review

- Ask students whether they are familiar with the film *2001: A Space Odyssey*. If any of the students have seen the film, ask them to describe the special effects.

- Then, ask the Literary Analysis question on p. 740: Why does Ebert compare *Star Wars* with *2001: A Space Odyssey*?
Answer: Ebert compares *Star Wars* with *2001: A Space Odyssey* because both films have masterful special effects that still hold up today.

15 Vocabulary Development

Connotations

- Point out the word *inspirations*, and explain that its denotation, or dictionary definition, is "ideas."

- Then, with students, consider the connotations of the word *inspirations*. Why did Ebert choose this word rather than *notions* or *ideas*?
Answer: The word *inspirations* connotes not simply ideas but brilliant or unique ideas. Ebert praises Lucas by using this word.

---

heirs). It located Hollywood's center of gravity at the intellectual and emotional level of a bright teenager.

13 It's possible, however, that as we grow older, we retain within the tastes of our earlier selves. How else to explain how much fun "Star Wars" is, even for those who think they don't care for science fiction? It's a good-hearted film in every single frame, and shining through is the gift of a man who knew how to link state-of-the-art technology with a deceptively simple, really very powerful, story. It was not by accident that George Lucas worked with Joseph Campbell, an expert on the world's basic myths, in fashioning a screenplay that owes much to man's oldest stories.

By now the ritual of classic film revival is well established: an older classic is brought out from the studio vaults, restored frame by frame, re-released in the best theaters, and then re-launched on home video. With this "special edition" of the "Star Wars" trilogy (which includes new versions of "Return of the Jedi" and "The Empire Strikes Back"), Lucas has gone one step beyond. His special effects were so advanced in 1977 that they spun off an industry, including his own Industrial Light & Magic Co., the computer wizards who do many of today's best special effects.

Now Lucas has put IL&M to work touching up the effects, including some that his limited 1977 budget left him unsatisfied with. Most of the changes are subtle: you'd need a side-by-side comparison to see that a new shot is a little better. There's about five minutes of new material, including a meeting between Han Solo and Jabba the Hut that was shot for the first version but not used. (We learn that Jabba is not immobile, but sloshes along in a kind of spongy undulation.) There's also an improved look to the city of Mos Eisley ("A wretched hive of scum and villainy," says Obi-Wan Kanobi). And the climactic battle scene against the Death Star has been rehabbed.[1]

14 The improvements are well done, but they point up how well the effects were done to begin with: If the changes are not obvious, that's because "Star Wars" got the look of the film so right in the first place. The obvious comparison is with Kubrick's "2001: A Space Odyssey," made 10 years earlier, in 1967, which also holds up perfectly well today. (One difference is that Kubrick went for realism, trying to imagine how his future world would really look, while Lucas cheerfully plundered the past; Han Solo's Millennium Falcon has a gun turret with a hand-operated weapon that would be at home on a World War II bomber, but too slow to hit anything at space velocities.)

15 Two Lucas inspirations started the story with a tease: He set the action not in the future but "long ago," and jumped into the middle of it with "Chapter 4: A New Hope." These seemingly innocent touches were actually rather powerful; they gave the saga the aura of an ancient tale, and an ongoing one.

---

1. **rehabbed** (rē´ habd´) *v.* rehabilitated.

Reading Strategy
Identifying Evidence
How does Ebert support his claim that people retain their tastes as they age?

Literary Analysis
Critical Review Why does Ebert compare *Star Wars* with *2001: A Space Odyssey*?

✸ ENRICHMENT: Career Connection

Motion Pictures and Television

Star Wars is the product of a gigantic industry. In addition to their original home in Hollywood, California, film studios are now found all over the map, and every major city has TV stations with studios and offices.

Let students know that actors comprise only a small fraction of the film and television work force. All studios have technical staffs: camera operators, electricians, carpenters, designers, and people skilled in lighting, sound, and editing. Major motion picture facilities employ specialists in areas such as wardrobe and properties, or props, such as futuristic weapons. In addition, special effects people are busy creating effects from exploding planets to Jabba the Hut. Designing special effects requires highly developed computer and electronic technology skills as well as design skills and a great imagination.

As if those two shocks were not enough for the movie's first moments, I learn from a review by Mark R. Leeper that this was the first film to pan the camera across a star field: "Space scenes had always been done with a fixed camera, and for a very good reason. It was more economical not to create a background of stars large enough to pan through." As the camera tilts up, a vast spaceship appears from the top of the screen and moves overhead, an effect reinforced by the surround sound. It is such a dramatic opening that it's no wonder Lucas paid a fine and resigned from the Directors' Guild rather than obey its demand that he begin with conventional opening credits.

The film has simple, well-defined characters, beginning with the robots R2D2 (childlike, easily hurt) and C3PO (fastidious, a little effete). The evil Empire has all but triumphed in the galaxy, but rebel forces are preparing an assault on the Death Star. Princess Leia (pert, sassy Carrie Fisher) has information pinpointing the star's vulnerable point, and feeds it into R2D2's computer; when her ship is captured, the robots escape from the Death Star and find themselves on Luke Skywalker's planet, where soon Luke (Mark Hamill as an idealistic youngster) meets the wise, old, mysterious Ben Kanobi (Alec Guinness) and they hire the freelance space jockey Han Solo (Harrison Ford, already laconic) to carry them to Leia's rescue.

The story is advanced with spectacularly effective art design, set decoration and effects. Although the scene in the intergalactic bar is famous for the menagerie of alien drunks, there is another scene, when the two robots are thrown into a hold with other used droids, which equally fills the scene with fascinating throwaway details. And a scene in the Death Star's garbage bin (inhabited by a snake with head curiously shaped like E.T.'s) is also well done.

Many of the planetscapes are startlingly beautiful, and owe something to Chesley Bonestell's imaginary drawings of other worlds. The final assault on the Death Star, when the fighter rockets speed between parallel walls, is a nod in the direction of "2001," with its light trip into another dimension: Kubrick showed, and Lucas learned, how to make the audience feel it is hurtling headlong through space.

Lucas fills his screen with loving touches. There are little alien rats hopping around the desert, and a chess game played with living creatures. Luke's weather-worn "Speeder" vehicle, which hovers over the sand, reminds me uncannily of a 1965 Mustang. And consider the details creating the presence, look and sound of Darth Vader, whose fanged face mask, black cape and hollow breathing are the setting for James Earl Jones's cold voice of doom.

Seeing the film the first time, I was swept away, and have remained swept ever since. Seeing this restored version, I tried to be more objective, and noted that the gun battles on board the space ships go on a bit too long; it is remarkable that the empire marksmen never hit anyone important; and the fighter rain on the enemy ship now

fastidious (fas tid′ ē əs) *adj.* refined in an oversensitive way

effete (e fēt′) *adj.* over-refined

laconic (lə kän′ ik) *adj.* using few words

Literary Analysis
Critical Review and Writer's Perspective
What personal feelings or tastes does the critic include in this passage?

✔ Reading Check
Before *Stars Wars*, why had space scenes always been shot with a fixed camera?

Star Wars: Breakthrough Film Still Has the Force ◆ 741

⓰ Literary Analysis
Critical Review

- Remind students that a reviewer's personal feelings or tastes will often enter into his or her review. Ask students how they can distinguish between the facts and the personal opinions in a review. Answer: Students should point out that facts can be proven.

- Then, ask students the Literary Analysis question on p. 741: What personal feelings or tastes does the critic include in this passage? Answer: Ebert feels the planet-scapes are beautiful; he refers to Lucas's "loving touches"; he mentions that the "Speeder" reminds him of an old car; he is very impressed with the look and sound of Darth Vader, specifically Jones's "cold voice of doom."

⓱ ✔ Reading Check

Answer: Before *Star Wars*, space scenes had always been shot with a fixed camera because it was cheaper and easier.

CUSTOMIZE INSTRUCTION FOR UNIVERSAL ACCESS	
For Less Proficient Readers	**For Advanced Readers**
Have students read the last paragraph on p. 740. Draw their attention to the words *saga* and *aura* in the last sentence. Encourage students to define the words based on the context of the sentence. Then, have them look up the words in the dictionary and find the meanings.	Encourage students to compare the writing styles of Vincent Canby and Roger Ebert. Have them describe the styles individually and discuss how they are different. Ask them whose style they prefer. Have students write opening paragraphs of their own movie reviews using one of the styles as a guide.

Answers for p. 742

Review and Assess

1. Some students may be most interested in reading about the special effects, while others will be interested in the plot or characterizations.

2. **(a)** *Star Wars* was inspired by old-fashioned comic books and serial movies. **(b)** It is like these sources in that it is a simple story about good versus evil and contains some fantastical characters and creatures. **(c)** It is different from these sources because it is not tacky.

3. **(a)** Yes, Canby enjoyed watching *Star Wars*. **(b)** He says it is "fun and funny" and describes the impressive special effects.

4. **(a)** There's a meeting between Han Solo and Jabba the Hut that was not in the original version; an improved look at the city of Mos Eisely; and a rehabilitated climactic battle scene. **(b)** He thinks the improvements are well done and also proves that the original special effects were excellent.

5. **(a)** He set the action in the past and then jumped into the middle of it. **(b)** Ebert thinks they are a powerful way to start the movie because they suggest it is part of an ancient, ongoing tale.

6. **(a)** Like these films, it was a technical watershed. **(b)** *Birth of a Nation* combined language, shots, and editing; *Citizen Kane* combined special effects with advanced sound and new photographic and nonlinear narrative styles; *Star Wars* combined improved special effects with high-energy action.

7. **(a)** *Star Wars* meets the criteria Ebert expresses because it has simple, well-defined characters and is a simple storyline based on mythic tales. **(b)** Students should give reasons for their choices.

---

plays like the computer games it predicted. I wonder, too, if Lucas could have come up with a more challenging philosophy behind the Force. As Kenobi explains it, it's basically just going with the flow. What if Lucas had pushed a little further to include elements of nonviolence or ideas about intergalactic conservation? (It's a great waste of resources to blow up star systems.)

The films that will live forever are the simplest-seeming ones. They have profound depths, but their surfaces are as clear to an audience as a beloved old story. The way I know this is because the stories that seem immortal—the "Odyssey," the "Tale of Genji," "Don Quixote," "David Copperfield," "Huckleberry Finn"—are all the same: a brave but flawed hero, a quest, colorful people and places, sidekicks, the discovery of life's underlying truths. If I were asked to say with certainty which movies will still be widely known a century or two from now, I would list "2001," and "The Wizard of Oz," and Keaton and Chaplin, and Astaire and Rogers, and probably "Casablanca" . . . and "Star Wars," for sure.

Review and Assess

Thinking About the Selections

1. **Respond:** Which aspect of *Star Wars* did you find most interesting or surprising in either review?

2. **(a) Recall:** According to Canby, what are two sources that inspired *Star Wars*? **(b) Compare:** In what ways is the film like these sources? **(c) Contrast:** What sets the film apart from them?

3. **(a) Infer:** Did Canby enjoy watching *Star Wars*? **(b) Support:** Give evidence to support your answer.

4. **(a) Recall:** Give two examples of aspects of the newer version of the film that, according to Roger Ebert's review, differ from the original. **(b) Infer:** What is Ebert's attitude toward these changes?

5. **(a) Recall:** What "shocks" does Lucas include at the beginning of *Star Wars*? **(b) Infer:** How does Ebert feel about these innovations? Explain.

6. **(a) Recall:** According to Ebert, what quality does *Star Wars* have in common with *Birth of a Nation* and *Citizen Kane*? **(b) Analyze:** How were all three breakthrough films?

7. **(a) Analyze:** In what ways does *Star Wars* fit Ebert's statement: "The films that will live forever are the simplest-seeming ones"? **(b) Make a Judgment:** Which movies do you think will be widely known a century or two from now? Why?

Roger Ebert

(b. 1942)

Along with fellow Chicagoan Gene Siskel (who died in 1999), Roger Ebert made famous the thumbs up and thumbs down symbols for movies worth seeing or avoiding. Siskel and Ebert were longtime cohosts of a weekly television program of movie reviews.

Ebert's reviews also appear in the *Chicago Sun-Times* and two hundred other newspapers around the country. He has won a Pulitzer Prize for his work. About viewing movies he has said, "The audience: In the dark, lined up facing the screen. The light comes from behind their heads—from back there where dreams come true."

✎ ASSESSMENT PRACTICE: Reading Comprehension

Comparing and Contrasting Texts   **(For more practice, see Test Preparation Workbook, p. 45.)**

Many tests require students to compare and contrast aspects of two texts. These aspects may include themes, conflicts, and allusions. After students have read both of the reviews in this selection grouping, write this sample test question on the board.

Both reviewers give their highest praise to—

A the quality of the acting

B the sophistication of the plot

C the fact that the movie is a classic

D the movie's special effects

By skimming over the reviews and noting main points, students will find that the best answer is *D*.

When taking tests, students may find it helpful to make notes about the main points of reading passages as they read them. They might underline or jot notes in the margin and refer to them when answering questions.

Review and Assess

Literary Analysis

Critical Review

1. What ideas in Canby's **critical review** persuade you the most—positively or negatively—about *Star Wars*?
2. (a) Where does Ebert use persuasive language in his review? (b) What message does he convey with this language?
3. (a) Which parts of the film does Ebert appreciate most? (b) What does he think could be improved?

Comparing Literary Works

4. In what ways do film critics approach movies from a different **perspective** from that of the average viewer?
5. How does Ebert have a different perspective on the film from Canby, based on seeing its remake twenty years later?
6. (a) On which elements in the film does each reviewer focus? (b) What do their choices tell you about their tastes?
7. Which reviewer seemed to like the film more? Support your answer.

Reading Strategy

Identifying Evidence

8. On a chart like the one shown here, list the **evidence** Canby uses to support his claim that "The way definitely not to approach *Star Wars* though, is to expect a film of cosmic implications. . . . It's fun and funny."

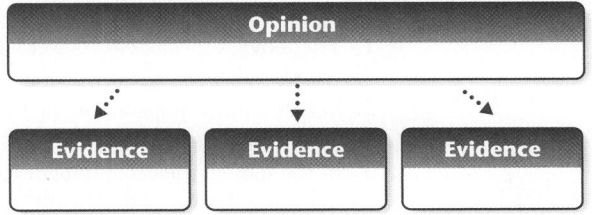

9. What evidence does Ebert give to support his claim that *Star Wars* presents a "deceptively simple, really very powerful, story"?

Extend Understanding

10. **Media Connection:** Using examples from films you know, explain how they reflect the best and worst of our culture.

Star Wars—A Trip to a Far Galaxy That's Fun and Funny . . . / Star Wars: Breakthrough Film Still Has the Force ◆ 743

Quick Review

Critical reviews discuss the various elements of a work and explain why readers should or should not read or see it.

A review often reflects the **writer's perspective**—the critic's personal outlook, interests, and recollection of the experience of viewing the film or performance or of reading the book.

Evidence includes facts and statistics, observations, examples, and statements from authorities that writers use to support their opinions.

 Take It to the Net
www.phschool.com
Take the interactive self-test online to check your understanding of these selections.

Answers for p. 743

Review and Assess

1. Students might be particularly persuaded by Canby's final statement that the movie is good enough to convince a skeptical eight-year-old sci-fi buff.
2. **(a)** Ebert begins the review with persuasive language. **(b)** His message is that *Star Wars* is a masterpiece.
3. **(a)** Ebert most appreciates the special effects. **(b)** He thinks perhaps the gun battles on board the space ships could be shorter and wonders whether the philosophy behind the Force could have been more challenging.
4. Film critics are more analytical and judgmental than many viewers. Also, they may have a greater knowledge of film and film history than the average viewer.
5. Ebert has seen the impact of *Star Wars* on the public and the film industry.
6. **(a)** Both reviewers focus on the movie's special effects and simple plot. **(b)** Their choices tell us that they enjoy being wowed by special effects and recognize the power of a simple, straightforward plot.
7. Students may say that Ebert enjoyed the movie more because his affection for it has withstood the test of time.
8. **Opinion:** *Star Wars* is fun and funny. **Evidence:** The Laurel and Hardy quality of R2D2 and C3PO; the funny scene in the alien bar; the stunning special effects.
9. He cites similar types of stories with simple plots and powerful themes.
10. Students' responses will vary. Make sure they support their answers with specific examples from the films.

❶ Vocabulary Development

Word Analysis

1. The slightly humorous connotation of the word *facetiousness* gives it an added dimension over *sarcasm*, which more straightforwardly means "harsh or bitter."

2. Both words imply a form of dexterity, but *cunning* carries with it a more negative connotation.

Spelling Strategy

1. instantaneous
2. ridiculous
3. contagious
4. courageous

Concept Development: Antonyms

1. d
2. f
3. b
4. g
5. i
6. a
7. k
8. j
9. e
10. h
11. c

❷ Grammar

1. well, modifies *done*
2. well, modifies *feel*
3. well, modifies *fought*
4. good, modifies *acting*
5. well, modifies *like*

Writing Application
At the state track meet, I ran well and had a good time.

Integrate Language Skills

❶ Vocabulary Development Lesson

Concept Development: Connotations

The connotation of a word is the thing, feeling, or idea that the word suggests. The following pairs of words have similar meanings. In your notebook, explain how the connotations of the words make them slightly different.

1. facetiousness, sarcasm
2. adroit, cunning

Spelling Strategy

Fastidious is one of many adjectives that end in *-ous*, pronounced *us*. Sometimes the *-ous* stands alone as in *jealous*, and sometimes it is preceded by *i* as in *facetious* or *e* as in *beauteous*. In your notebook, write each word below correctly, filling in the ending letters.

1. instantan_____
2. ridicul_____
3. contag_____
4. courag_____

Concept Development: Antonyms

In your notebook, write the letter of the word from the right column that is the best antonym, or opposite, of the word in the left column.

1. condescension   a. sloppy
2. eclectic   b. shame
3. apotheosis   c. solemnity
4. laconic   d. praise
5. effete   e. irreverently
6. fastidious   f. consistent
7. synthesis   g. talkative
8. watershed   h. clumsy
9. piously   i. vigorous
10. adroit   j. trifle
11. facetiousness   k. division

❷ Grammar Lesson

Commonly Confused Words:
good and well

Good is an adjective. *Well* is generally an adverb, but when it is used to mean "healthy," it is an adjective.

Incorrect:	The improvements show how *good* the effects were done.
Correct:	The improvements show how *well* the effects were done. (adverb modifies *done*)
Correct:	Han Solo did not feel *well* when he saw Jabba the Hut. (adjective meaning *healthy*)
Correct:	The movie was *good*. (adjective modifies *movie*)

Practice Choose the correct word to complete each sentence. Identify the word that *good* or *well* modifies.

1. The movie's special effects were done very (good, well).
2. I ate too much popcorn at the movie and did not feel (good, well).
3. In the movie, the rebels fought (good, well) and destroyed the Death Star.
4. The star's acting was very (good, well) throughout the film.
5. How (good, well) did you like the movie?

Writing Application Write one sentence in which you use both *good* and *well* correctly.

*W*G *Prentice Hall Writing and Grammar Connection: Chapter 25, Section 1*

744 ◆ Nonfiction

TEACHING RESOURCES

The following resources can be used to enrich or extend the instruction for pp. 744–745.

Vocabulary

📖 **Selection Support:** Build Vocabulary, p. 177

📖 **Vocabulary and Spelling Practice Book**
(Use this booklet for skills enrichment.) 📀

Grammar

📖 **Selection Support:** Build Grammar Skills, p. 178

*W*G **Writing and Grammar,** Platinum Level, p. 593

📕 **Daily Language Practice Transparencies** 📀

Writing

*W*G **Writing and Grammar,** Platinum Level, p. 137

💿 **Writing and Grammar iText CD-ROM** 📀

📕 **BLOCK SCHEDULING:** Resources marked with this symbol provide varied instruction during 90-minute blocks.

Writing Lesson

Movie Review

Prepare a **movie review** of a recent film that you liked or disliked. Your title and first paragraph should hook the reader and promote your point of view. In the rest of the review, provide specific evidence to support your opinions.

Prewriting Develop an idea web to organize ideas and list specific examples for your review. Write your overall opinion of the movie in the center of your paper. Then, add branches for aspects of the film you liked or disliked the most and specific examples for each.

Drafting State your opinion near the beginning of the review. Then, support your opinion with specific examples in the body paragraphs.

> **Model: Supporting Opinions With Evidence**
>
> The real strength of the movie is the way in which viewers feel the same fear that the characters are experiencing. The look in Helen's eyes when she hears the floorboards creak raises the anxiety level. . . .

Descriptions of the characters and the sounds in the scene provide the evidence the writer needs.

Revising Circle each main idea, and underline supporting evidence. If you find an unexplained opinion, include more examples or details.

 Prentice Hall Writing and Grammar Connection: Chapter 7, Section 4

Extension Activities

Listening and Speaking Play an excerpt from the *Star Wars* theme by composer John Williams. Then, present a **music analysis**, explaining how the music enhances the mood of specific scenes. Follow these steps to prepare your presentation:

1. Watch the movie to hear when the theme is used.
2. Determine the mood of the relevant scenes and the music to see whether they match well.

Follow up with an evaluation of the connection between the music and the action.

Research and Technology Work with a partner to find reviews of a movie that you have both seen. Search for movie reviews on the Internet. Do a **comparison** of the reviews in which you outline the main points each reviewer makes about the movie and state whether you agree or disagree with the points. **[Group Activity]**

 Take It to the Net www.phschool.com

Go online for an additional research activity using the Internet.

Star Wars—A Trip to a Far Galaxy That's Fun and Funny . . . / Star Wars: Breakthrough Film Still Has the Force ◆ 745

Imitating Nature's Mineral Artistry ✦ Work That Counts

Lesson Objectives

1. **To analyze and respond to literary elements**
   - Literary Analysis: Technical Article
   - Comparing Literary Works

2. **To read, comprehend, analyze, and critique technical articles**
   - Reading Strategy: Relating Diagrams to Text
   - Reading Check questions
   - Review and Assess questions
   - Assessment Practice (ATE)

3. **To develop word analysis skills, fluency, and systematic vocabulary**
   - Vocabulary Development Lesson: Greek Prefix: *syn-*

4. **To understand and apply written and oral language conventions**
   - Spelling Strategy
   - Grammar Lesson: Placement of Modifiers

5. **To understand and apply appropriate writing and research strategies**
   - Writing Lesson: Persuasive Letter
   - Extension Activity: Conservation Update

6. **To understand and apply listening and speaking strategies**
   - Extension Activity: Demonstration

STEP-BY-STEP TEACHING GUIDE	PACING GUIDE
PRETEACH	
Motivate Students and Provide Background	
Use the Motivation activity (ATE p. 746)	5 min.
Read and discuss the Preview material and Background information (SE/ATE p. 746)	5 min.
Introduce the Concepts	
Introduce the Literary Analysis and Reading Strategy (SE/ATE p. 747)	15 min.
Pronounce the vocabulary words and read their definitions (SE p. 747)	5 min.
TEACH	
Monitor Comprehension	
Informally monitor comprehension by circulating while students read independently or in groups	15 min.
Monitor students' comprehension with the Reading Check notes (SE/ATE pp. 749, 751, 753)	as students read
Develop vocabulary with Vocabulary notes (SE pp. 748, 749, 751, 752, 753; ATE p. 748)	as students read
Develop Understanding	
Develop students' understanding of technical articles with the Literary Analysis annotations (SE pp. 750, 754; ATE pp. 750, 753, 754)	10 min.
Develop students' ability to relate diagrams to text with the Reading Strategy annotations (ATE pp. 749, 751)	10 min.
ASSESS	
Assess Mastery	
Assess students' mastery of the Reading Strategy and Literary Analysis by having them answer the Review and Assess questions (SE/ATE p. 755)	20 min.
Use one or more of the print and media Assessment Resources (ATE p. 757)	up to 50 min.
EXTEND	
Apply Understanding	
Have students complete the Vocabulary Development Lesson and the Grammar Lesson (SE p. 756)	20 min.
Apply students' ability to support opinions with facts using the Writing Lesson (SE/ATE p. 757)	45 min.
Apply students' understanding using one or more of the Extension Activities (SE p. 757)	20–90 min.

 ACCELERATED INSTRUCTION:
Use the strategies and activities identified with an .

UNIVERSAL ACCESS
● = Below Level Students
▲ = On-Level Students
■ = Above Level Students

Time and Resource Manager

Reading Level: Challenging/Easy
Average Number of Instructional Days: 4

RESOURCES

PRINT 📖	TRANSPARENCIES	TECHNOLOGY 💿 🎧 📼
• **Beyond Literature,** Cross-Curricular Connection: Geography, p. 47 ▲ ■		• **Interest Grabber Video,** Tape 4 ● ▲ ■
• **Selection Support Workbook:** ● ▲ ■ Literary Analysis, p. 188 Reading Strategy, p. 187 Build Vocabulary, p. 185	• **Literary Analysis and Reading Transparencies,** pp. 93 and 94 ● ▲ ■	
		• **Listening to Literature** ● ▲ ■ Audiocassettes, Side 24 Audio CDs, CD 15
• **Literatura en español** ● ▲ • **Literary Analysis for Enrichment** ■		
• **Formal Assessment:** Selection Test, pp. 163–165 ● ▲ ■ • **Open Book Test,** pp. 139–141 ● ▲ ■ • **Performance Assessment and Portfolio Management,** pp. 11, 32 ● ▲ ■ • **PRENTICE HALL ASSESSMENT SYSTEM** ● ▲ ■	• **PRENTICE HALL ASSESSMENT SYSTEM** ● ▲ ■ Skills Practice Answers and Explanations on Transparencies	• **Test Bank Software** ● ▲ ■ • **Got It! Assessment Videotapes,** Tape 4 ● ▲
• **Selection Support Workbook:** ● ▲ ■ Build Grammar Skills, p. 186 • **Writing and Grammar,** Platinum Level ● ▲ ■ • **Extension Activities,** p. 47 ● ▲ ■	• **Daily Language Practice Transparencies** ● ▲ • **Writing Models and Graphic Organizers on Transparencies,** pp. 65–68 ● ▲ ■	• **Writing and Grammar iText CD-ROM** ● ▲ ■ 🖥️ ***Take It to the Net*** www.phschool.com

BLOCK SCHEDULING: Use one 90-minute class period to preteach the selection and have students read it. Use a second 90-minute class period to assess students' mastery of skills and have them complete one of the Extension Activities.

PRETEACH

Step-by-Step Teaching Guide for pp. 746–747

Motivation

Capture students' interest by asking this question: Should people strive to imitate nature or to appreciate nature? Encourage students to take a position and support it with information they have learned in science class or on their own. Help them to see that scientists have long tried to imitate nature (early aviators tried to imitate the flight of a bird; recently scientists have cloned sheep). Other scientists have made a career out of preserving and appreciating nature. These two technical articles show ways in which nature is imitated—and simply appreciated.

▭ Interest Grabber Video

As an alternative, play "Birds of Prey" on Tape 4 to engage student interest.

❶ Background

Science

The diamond is perhaps the most popular gem in the world. It's also the hardest natural substance on Earth. The word *diamond* comes from the Latin *adamas*, meaning "unconquerable." Industrial tools use diamond tips to cut through hard substances, like granite, as easily as a steel saw blade cuts through a piece of wood. In fact, diamond-tipped tools are needed to cut the facets on diamonds for jewelry!

Prepare to Read

Imitating Nature's Mineral Artistry ◆ Work That Counts

▭ *Take It to the Net*

Visit www.phschool.com for interactive activities and instruction related to these selections, including
- background
- graphic organizers
- literary elements
- reading strategies

Preview

Connecting to the Literature

Have you ever tasted a tomato that came from a scientist's lab? Chemists, biogeneticists, and other scientists are experimenting to create products that until recently were found only in nature. When you read "Imitating Nature's Mineral Artistry," think about why people try to imitate nature and consider the pros and cons of their ongoing efforts.

❶ Background

One indicator of a gemstone's value—whether it is natural or artificially made—is the number of carats (or karats). The word *carat* means "bean" in Arabic. Beans were once used to weigh gemstones. Today, a carat equals about 200 milligrams.

746 ◆ *Nonfiction*

TEACHING RESOURCES

The following resources can be used to enrich or extend the instruction for pp. 746–747.

Motivation
▭ **Interest Grabber Video**, Tape 4 ▭

Background
▭ **Beyond Literature**, p. 47

▭ *Take It to the Net*
Visit www.phschool.com for background and hotlinks for the selections.

Literary Analysis
▭ **Selection Support:** Literary Analysis, p. 188
▭ **Literary Analysis and Reading Transparencies,** Technical Article, p. 94

Reading
▭ **Literary Analysis and Reading Transparencies,** Relating Diagrams to Text, p. 93 ▭

▬ **BLOCK SCHEDULING:** Resources marked with this symbol provide varied instruction during 90-minute blocks.

Literary Analysis

Technical Article

These two selections are **technical articles**—writing that explains procedures, provides instructions, or presents specialized information. In this example from "Work That Counts," the writer explains why migrating birds use a certain route. Specialized language (italicized here) lets the writer be as specific as possible.

> The *topography* and *atmospheric conditions* . . . provide . . . conditions needed for migrating with the least expenditure of energy.

As you read, look for clues in the writing, notes, and visual aids to help you understand technical terms or ideas.

Comparing Literary Works

These articles differ in the complexity of their ideas and in the ways these ideas are demonstrated, but—like all technical articles—they both explain a process. Compare the ways each writer explains and illustrates his ideas.

Reading Strategy

Relating Diagrams to Text

Many technical writers use diagrams to illustrate their ideas and theories. Think of a diagram as a visual extension of the text. To **relate a diagram** to the text, take the following steps:

- Look for notations in the text that indicate where to find a related diagram.
- Study the pictures, captions, and labels for visual clues to details.

Use a chart like the one shown to record the connections you see between the diagrams and the text.

Subject	Flame-Fusion Growth of Ruby
Location of Related Text	First paragraph on page 749
How Diagram Helps	

Vocabulary Development

synthetic (sin thet´ ik) *adj.* artificially made (p. 748)

constituents (kən stich´ o͞o ənts) *n.* components; parts (p. 749)

synthesized (sin´ thə sīzd´) *v.* made by bringing together different elements (p. 749)

metamorphosis (met´ ə môr´ fə sis) *n.* change of form (p. 749)

divulge (də vulj´) *v.* reveal (p. 751)

saturated (sach´ ə rāt´ id) *adj.* completely filled (p. 751)

fortuitous (fôr to͞o´ ə təs) *adj.* accidental and beneficial at the same time (p. 751)

vigilance (vij´ ə ləns) *n.* watchfulness; alertness (p. 752)

myriad (mir´ ē əd) *adj.* seemingly countless (p. 753)

topography (tə päg´ rə fē) *n.* surface features of a place (p. 753)

---

❷ Literary Analysis

Technical Article

- Tell students that when reading technical articles—works that explain a process or provide specialized information—they will be learning new terminology and information.

- Read the instruction about technical articles together as a class.

- Call students' attention to the excerpt from the selection. Ask them what they think the italicized words mean. If there are terms they do not know, tell them to use context clues to help ascertain their meanings.

- Remind students that in addition to the text, the diagrams might also help to define unfamiliar terms.

❸ Reading Strategy

Relating Diagrams to Text

- Tell students that just as photographs add meaning to a text, diagrams help readers to better understand what is being described in the text.

- Ask students to provide examples of diagrams they encounter often, such as in instruction manuals or sports reports.

- Instruct students to create a chart like the one shown on p. 747 to record how the diagrams relate to the text as they read the first selection.

Vocabulary Development

- Pronounce each vocabulary word for students, and read the definitions as a class. Have students identify any words with which they are already familiar.

CUSTOMIZE INSTRUCTION FOR UNIVERSAL ACCESS

For Less Proficient Readers	For English Learners	For Advanced Readers
The selections contain several highly technical and detailed passages. Work with students to identify reading strategies that will help them deal with these passages, such as rereading, breaking down long sentences, paraphrasing, identifying main ideas, and taking notes.	Have students work in small groups made up of both English learners and native speakers. Students can work together to determine the meanings of both technical terms and challenging non-technical words, such as *hallmarks, fortuitous,* and *funnel*.	Encourage students to research and write explanatory notes for technical terms and references that appear in the articles but are not footnoted. For example, students might explain what a *plankton sample* is or what *crystal* and *crystalline* mean in the context of geology.

 E-Teach

Visit E-Teach at www.phschool.com for teachers' essays on how to teach, with questions and answers.

Step-by-Step Teaching Guide for pp. 748–754

CUSTOMIZE INSTRUCTION
For Visual/Spatial Learners

Have students create their own diagrams that illustrate concepts related to geology, chemistry, or ornithology. Encourage students to present their work to the class.

❶ About the Selection

In "Imitating Nature's Mineral Artistry," writer Paul O'Neil makes use of specialized terms, examples, comparisons, and numerical data as well as detailed diagrams to take readers on a guided tour of the high-tech world of gem synthesis.

❷ Vocabulary Development

Greek Prefix: *syn-*

- Draw students' attention to the word *synthetic* and its definition, "artificially made."

- Explain that the prefix *syn-* means "together with." A synthetic gem is one whose parts are brought together chemically instead of forming naturally.

- Ask students to name and define other words that contain this prefix.
  Answer: Students might mention *synonym, synchronize,* and *syntax.*

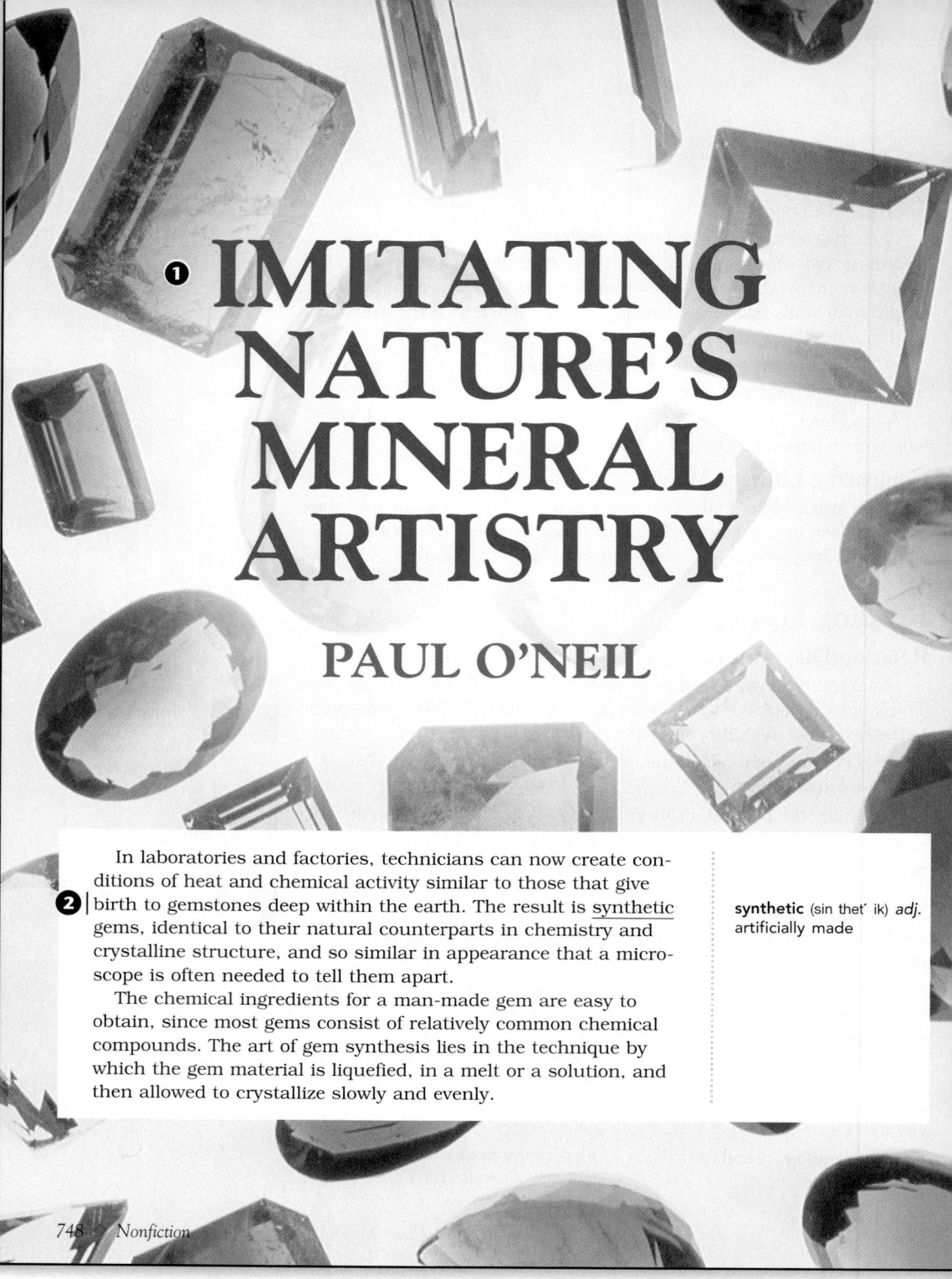

❶ IMITATING NATURE'S MINERAL ARTISTRY

PAUL O'NEIL

❷   In laboratories and factories, technicians can now create conditions of heat and chemical activity similar to those that give birth to gemstones deep within the earth. The result is <u>synthetic</u> gems, identical to their natural counterparts in chemistry and crystalline structure, and so similar in appearance that a microscope is often needed to tell them apart.

  The chemical ingredients for a man-made gem are easy to obtain, since most gems consist of relatively common chemical compounds. The art of gem synthesis lies in the technique by which the gem material is liquefied, in a melt or a solution, and then allowed to crystallize slowly and evenly.

synthetic (sin thet´ ik) *adj.* artificially made

748   Nonfiction

TEACHING RESOURCES

The following resources can be used to enrich or extend the instruction for pp. 748–754.

Literary Analysis

📖 **Writing Models and Graphic Organizers on Transparencies,** pp. 65–68 ▪

Reading

📖 **Selection Support:** Reading Strategy, p. 187; Build Vocabulary, p. 185

🎧 **Listening to Literature Audiocassettes,** Side 24 ▪

💿 **Listening to Literature Audio CDs,** CD 15 ▪

▪ **BLOCK SCHEDULING:** Resources marked with this symbol provide varied instruction during 90-minute blocks.

The so-called flame-fusion method, based on melting and gradual cooling, has been used to grow crystals of about 100 minerals and gems, including ruby, sapphire and spinel. But the ingredients of some gems decompose during the fierce heating needed to melt them, and others have extraordinarily high melting points. Such gems—among them emerald—are often manufactured by another process, called flux growth. In this process, the gem is crystallized from a solution of its <u>constituents</u> in a molten bath of a solvent, or flux—such as lead fluoride, boron oxide or lithium oxide.

Because of peculiarities in their internal structure, some gems cannot be <u>synthesized</u> by ordinary crystal growth. Opal, an orderly arrangement of minute, closely packed spheres of silica, is created in the laboratory by precipitating silica spheres through a chemical reaction, allowing them to settle to the bottom of the reaction vessel and then compressing and bonding them to form a compact and sturdy matrix.[1]

Artful as they are, synthetic gems nevertheless bear hallmarks of their laboratory origin: an array of microscopic inclusions and growth marks that contrast tellingly with the blemishes and inclusions of natural gems.

One of the gaudier uses of the Verneuil furnace is to make synthetic rutile[2] by sifting pure titanium dioxide through the flame. The boules thus produced—black in color because of oxygen deficiency—are then reheated in a jet of oxygen. As the rutile grows hotter, it oxidizes and changes in color to deep blue followed by light blue, green and, finally, a pale yellow. The color <u>metamorphosis</u> can be stopped at any stage by removing the heat source. Sold since 1948 under a profusion of names, including astryl and titania, the gems are soft, with a hardness of 6 to 6.5, but are even flashier than strontium titanate, with seven times the fire of diamond.

Since diamonds consist of only one element, synthesizing them

---

1. **matrix** (māˊ triksˊ) *n.* framework.
2. **rutile** (rooˊ tēlˊ) *n.* dark-red mineral.

Oxygen
Powdered Chemicals
Hydrogen
Combustion Chamber
Boule

Diagram A

Verneuil Furnace Flame-Fusion Growth of Ruby

The chemical ingredients of ruby—aluminum oxide with a chromium coloring agent—sift from a hopper at the top of the apparatus shown above into a jet of oxygen. In a combustion chamber, the oxygen combines with hydrogen in a 4,000° F flame—hot enough to melt the powdered ingredients, which shower onto a ceramic rod at the base of the furnace. There the material solidifies and accumulates in a rounder crystalline mass known as a boule.

constituents (kən stichˊ oo ənts) *n.* components; parts

synthesized (sinˊ thə sīzdˊ) *v.* made by bringing together different elements

metamorphosis (metˊ ə môrˊ fə sis) *n.* change of form

④ ✓Reading Check
Why are some gems unable to be synthesized by ordinary crystal growth?

❸ Reading Strategy
Relating Diagrams to Text
- Call on a volunteer to read aloud the bracketed passage.
- Then, have students look at the diagram on p. 749.
- Ask students: What key elements help readers connect the diagram to the concept that is introduced in this portion of the text? Answer: The caption, which refers to "flame-fusion growth of ruby" helps readers connect the diagram to the text.

▶ Monitor Progress   Instruct students to create a chart like the one shown on p. 747 to show how the diagram relates to the text. Answer: Charts should look similar to the one shown here.

Subject	Flame-Fusion Growth of Ruby
Location of Related Text	First paragraph on page 749
How Diagram Helps	The visual and the explanation that accompanies it explain the flame-fusion process in more detail. The reader gets to see what it looks like.

❹ ✓Reading Check
Answer: Some gems cannot be synthesized by ordinary crystal growth because of peculiarities in their internal structures.

Technical Article

- Once students have read the bracketed passage, ask them to identify the product that scientists were hoping to create.
  Answer: Scientists wanted to create diamonds.

- Then, have students identify how the scientists were hoping to achieve this.

- Ask students the Literary Analysis question on p. 750: What technical process is described in this paragraph?
  Answer: This paragraph describes the process of using a hydraulic press to create enough force to make synthetic diamonds.

⑥ Critical Thinking

Apply

- Have a volunteer read aloud the bracketed passage. Explain that an abrasive is a substance used for grinding or polishing.

- Then, encourage students to use their general knowledge about diamonds to explain why synthetic diamonds would make good industrial abrasives.
  Answer: Students may point out that diamonds are the hardest substance in nature and would therefore be the best choice for an industrial abrasive.

would seem to be relatively uncomplicated. The difficulty is one of technique, of creating—and containing—the enormous pressures and temperatures needed to pack carbon atoms tight enough to form diamond. Not surprisingly, many early attempts to synthesize diamond ended disastrously. Of the 80 experiments conducted in the late 19th Century by a Glasgow chemist named James Hannay, all but three were cut short by explosions, several of which wrecked the laboratory. Hannay was convinced that his pains had paid off: After several attempts, he discovered tiny flecks of diamond in his apparatus. But it is now thought that natural diamond dust from another of Hannay's projects had contaminated the experiment.

⑤ In the early 1950s, scientists at the General Electric Research Laboratories in Schenectady, New York, began experimenting with techniques for multiplying the force exerted by a hydraulic press. Using a pair of tapered pistons driven from opposite sides into the hole in a doughnut-shaped ring of tungsten carbide, they were able to subject the tiny intervening space to pressures of more than 1.5 million pounds per square inch. In a series of experiments directed by a chemist named H. Tracy Hall, the apparatus was loaded with a mixture of graphite powder and an iron compound, pressurized and heated with an electric current to more than 4,800° F.—hot enough to melt the iron and dissolve some of the graphite. The dissolved carbon, scientists hoped, would then crystallize out of the molten iron as diamond. Finally, on December 16, 1954, Hall removed a sample from the press and broke it open along a plate of tantalum, a rare element used to conduct electric current. Hall later recalled the moment: "My hands began to tremble; my heart beat rapidly; my knees weakened and no longer gave support. My eyes had caught the flashing light from dozens of tiny triangular faces of octahedral crystals that were stuck to the tantalum and I knew that diamonds had finally been made by man."

⑥ Today, the same basic method that yielded Hall's initial success annually produces some 44,000 pounds of industrial diamonds— small diamonds of no particular quality used as an industrial abrasive. Only a few minutes of high temperature and pressure are required to manufacture several

Literary Analysis
Technical Article What technical process is described in this paragraph?

Cover

Crucible

Solution

Crystals   **Furnace**

Diagram B

Flux Growth of Emerald

A saturated solution of emerald's chemical ingredients is produced by combining compounds of beryllium, aluminum, and silicone with a flux, or solvent, and heating the mixture to 1,500° F in an electric furnace. As the mixture cools, gem crystals begin to precipitate out at the bottom of the platinum crucible containing the solution, eventually forming clusters of emeralds.

✳ ENRICHMENT: Science Connection

Geology and Gemology

"Imitating Nature's Mineral Artistry" contains several terms used in the fields of geology and gemology. Groups of students can work together to research the meanings of these terms as well as explore and answer some basic questions related to these fields.

Suggest that students choose from among the following activities and questions.

- What is a rock? a mineral? a gem?
- What does *specific gravity* mean? What

does *refractive index* (sometimes called *index of refraction*) mean?

- What is an *inclusion?* What are *growth marks* and *growth lines?*
- Find out the name of the scale that is used to measure the hardness of gems and minerals. Name three minerals that are harder than synthetic rutile and three that are softer.

hundred carats of diamond grit from almost any carbon-containing material—paraffin, moth flakes, even sugar and peanuts. But the synthesis of gem-quality diamonds is another matter. In 1970, a painstaking variant of the General Electric method, using synthetic diamond grit as the feed material and maintaining the conditions of high temperature and pressure for stretches of a week, yielded a few gem-quality diamonds weighing up to a carat. But the cost of producing them was so high that it remains cheaper to mine gem diamonds.

Perhaps the finest products of humanity's age-old attempt to imitate nature in the creation of gemstones are synthetic emeralds. Beginning in the late 1930s, two pioneers, Carroll F. Chatham, a San Francisco chemist, and Pierre Gilson of France, succeeded in making emerald so close to the genuine article that it is worth several hundred dollars per carat—although that is still just 1/10 the price of natural emerald of similar quality. Chatham and Gilson did not divulge the details of their processes, but it is believed that both depend on a technique called flux growth, in which crystals are formed from raw materials dissolved in a flux—a substance that acts as a powerful solvent. In one type of flux growth, the chemical ingredients of emerald, in the form of natural beryl, are added to a 1,500° F. bath of flux to create a saturated solution, which circulates continuously through cooler parts of the container. There, the flux deposits crystals of emerald—so slowly that growth must continue for seven months to produce an emerald one quarter of an inch thick.

It is not easy to distinguish synthetic and natural emeralds, though the synthetic variety is often more transparent, richer in hue and in some ways more perfectly formed than natural emeralds. In addition, the synthetics have lower specific gravity and refractive indices. But the most telling test is usually a microscopic examination. Magnification of synthetic emeralds reveals fine, lacelike patterns formed by intersecting channels containing liquid flux. Natural emeralds, the fortuitous products of geologic turmoil, ordinarily display much coarser inclusions of pyrite, calcite, actinolite or other minerals. Another detection method is to expose the gems to ultraviolet light: The radiation has little effect on natural emeralds but causes Chatham emeralds to glow with a dull red fluorescence and Gilson synthetics to display an orange hue.

In synthetic rubies and sapphires, specific gravity and the refractive index are the same as in natural corundum. But visible under a microscope in natural gems are straight lines, called growth lines, set at definite angles. In Verneuil synthetics, the growth lines are curved, and spots, which are in fact gas-filled bubbles, may be seen. Synthetic spinel, which masquerades as any of several species, can be detected by its differing refractive index.

Still, distinguishing between synthetic and natural gemstones calls

8 ▲ **Critical Viewing** In what ways is the structure of this opal different from that of the emerald shown on page 752? **[Contrast]**

divulge (də vulj´) v. reveal

saturated (sach´ ə rāt´ id) adj. completely filled

fortuitous (fôr tōō´ ə təs) adj. accidental and beneficial at the same time

9 ✔ **Reading Check** How are industrial diamonds used?

Imitating Nature's Mineral Artistry ◆ 751

7 ❼ **Reading Strategy**
Relating Diagrams to Text
- Point out to students that the process of emerald synthesis through flux growth is further explained in Diagram B on p. 750.
- Ask students to study the diagram and its information carefully, and then identify the additional details that it provides.
  Answer: The diagram names the chemical raw materials (beryllium, aluminum, and silicone) that are dissolved in the flux; it shows the electric furnace in which emeralds are synthesized; it specifies how (precipitation while cooling) and where (the bottom of the platinum crucible) the clusters of emeralds form.

8 ▶ **Critical Viewing**
Answer: Students should note that the opal differs in color, in brilliance, and in texture—whereas the emerald has solid, smooth surfaces, the opal has a fragmented surface. Although it is solid, it resembles a sponge.

9 ✔ **Reading Check**
Answer: Industrial diamonds are used as an abrasive.

CUSTOMIZE INSTRUCTION FOR UNIVERSAL ACCESS

For Less Proficient Readers	For Gifted/Talented Students
Call students' attention to the specialized terms *specific gravity, refractive indices,* and *inclusions* in the third paragraph on p. 751. Have them use context clues to determine the approximate meanings of these terms. Also, have students explain where they might find the exact technical meanings of the terms—such as an encyclopedia, books on gems and minerals, or Web sites devoted to gemology or geology.	Have students write a detailed explanation of a process that they take for granted, such as making a sandwich, braiding hair, or tying shoes. Encourage them to use "Imitating Nature's Mineral Artistry" as a model. In addition, show them the Technical Writing transparencies, pp. 65–68 in **Writing Models and Graphic Organizers on Transparencies.** Encourage them to create diagrams that clarify their explanations.

10 ▶ **Critical Viewing**

Answer: According to the article, the imperfections of this emerald indicate that it is real.

Answers for p. 752

Review and Assess

1. Possible techniques include virtual reality and genetically altered foods.

2. **(a)** Two of the techniques are flux growth and flame-fusion growth. **(b)** Flame fusion is based on melting and gradual cooling. In the flux growth method, a gem is crystallized from a solution of its constituents in a molten bath of solvent, or flux.

3. **(a)** Flame fusion is used to make rubies; flux growth is used to make emeralds. **(b)** The chemicals of rubies can take the 4000°F heat, but the chemicals of emeralds decompose during the heating. The temperature for flux growth is only 1500°F.

4. **(a)** It took a long time to create an apparatus that would exert enough pressure on the compounds to create diamonds. **(b)** Industrial diamonds can be made from exposing any carbon-containing material to a few minutes of heat and pressure. For gem-quality diamonds, heat and pressure must be maintained for a week.

5. **(a)** Nassi wanted to make sure that they were real by inspecting them closely—probably under a microscope. **(b)** He would have lost a lot of money.

6. Students might say that creating synthetic diamonds for industrial use is beneficial and probably economical.

---

for vigilance, and sometimes even experts lower their guard. One Manhattan dealer who specializes in colored gemstones, Abraham Nassi, was offered three large red rubies while on an expedition to Burma. "They looked good," he remembered later, and he was prepared to pay the equivalent of $160,000 for the lot. But before any money changed hands, a fourth ruby was offered.

"I had an idea that the four might be worth a half a million dollars," he said, "but wanted to have them in New York and give them a real inspection before I paid." Nassi suggested a total price of $300,000—but only if the stones could first be examined in New York.

The Burmese refused his condition. "That seemed funnier yet. I found a Bangkok dealer who had a microscope and began looking at the stones under magnification. Their color was wonderful but their crystal structure was peculiar. I spent $200 to telephone the Gemological Institute of America in New York and described what I had seen. They told me what I'd been looking at: This gang had somehow gotten their hands on synthetic Kashan rubies, made in Texas for about $100 a carat, taken them into the jungle and had almost sold them to me as the real thing."

vigilance (vij′ ə ləns) *n.* watchfulness; alertness

10 ▲ **Critical Viewing** How can you tell from this picture and from clues in the text that the emerald is real and not synthetic? **[Analyze]**

Review and Assess

Thinking About the Selection

1. **Respond:** Besides those discussed in the selection, what are one or two other techniques you know in which people have tried to imitate nature? Explain.

2. **(a) Recall:** What are two techniques used to create synthetic gems? **(b) Compare and Contrast:** What are some differences between the two techniques?

3. **(a) Recall:** Which technique is used to make synthetic rubies? Which is used to make synthetic emeralds? **(b) Analyze:** What makes two techniques necessary?

4. **(a) Analyze:** Why did it take so long to synthesize diamonds successfully? **(b) Compare and Contrast:** Contrast the process for making industrial diamonds with that of producing gem-quality diamonds.

5. **(a) Draw Conclusions:** Why did Abraham Nassi want to take the rubies to New York before he paid for them? **(b) Speculate:** What might have happened if Nassi had bought the rubies from the Burmese?

6. **Take a Position:** Do you think making synthetic gems is ultimately helpful to society? Why or why not?

Paul O'Neil

(1909–1988)

After thirty years as a staff writer for the magazines *Time*, *Sports Illustrated*, and *Life*, Paul O'Neil became a freelance writer. He is the author of three volumes in the Time-Life series *The Old West*, and he also wrote *Barnstormers* and *Speed Kings* in the *Epic of Flight* series. "Imitating Nature's Mineral Artistry" comes from the Time-Life book *Gemstones*.

✹ ENRICHMENT: Community Connection

Community Bird Counts

In "Work That Counts," Ernesto Ruelas Inzunza quotes an 1897 account of the River of Raptors written by Frank M. Chapman. Chapman, who was curator of birds at the American Museum of Natural History, was also the founder of a bird count in which your students can participate—the annual Christmas Bird Count, now sponsored by the National Audubon Society.

Every year, more than 45,000 people take part in this nationwide event by spending one day between December 14 and January 5 identifying and counting birds within a designated area. The participants report their findings to the Audubon Society, which analyzes and publishes the data and uses it for long-term research on birds.

Interested students can learn more about the Christmas Bird Count by contacting their local chapter of the Audubon Society.

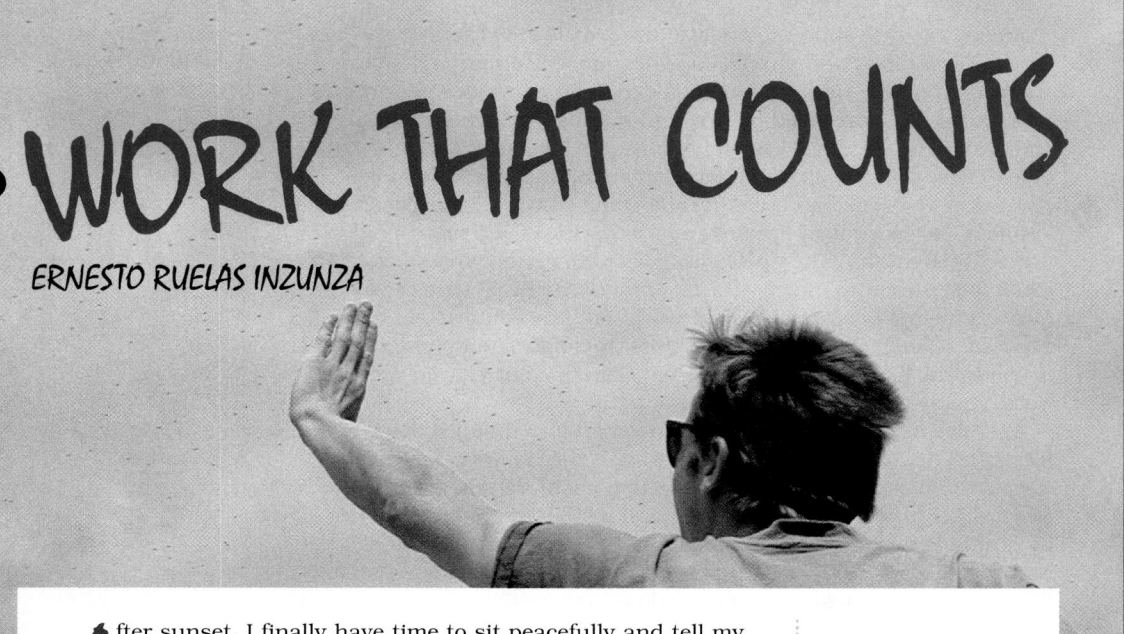

WORK THAT COUNTS

ERNESTO RUELAS INZUNZA

After sunset, I finally have time to sit peacefully and tell my friend Jeros, who is new to hawk watching, the story of the discovery of the River of Raptors.

It is the end of a long day of watching and counting birds of prey in the small town of Chichicaxtle in the state of Veracruz, Mexico. At eight this morning, as Jeros and I climbed the observation tower, about forty-five Swainson's hawks were just taking off from the nearby canyon where they had spent the night. Shortly afterward, we saw hundreds of them turning circles in the thermal columns of hot air, effortlessly gaining altitude. By eleven, the Swainson's had joined smaller numbers of broad-winged hawks and turkey vultures, forming long streams of migrants. Such large flocks, totaling more than 20,000 birds at times, can take up to thirty minutes to pass overhead. Resembling <u>myriad</u> moving organisms in a plankton sample, the raptors filled our binoculars' field of view. We watched the avian river continue north until it disappeared.

Each spring and fall, the spectacle of raptor migration fills the skies of Veracruz in eastern Mexico as the birds funnel through a narrow geographic corridor and above our monitoring stations at Chichicaxtle and Cardel. This bottleneck is formed where the Mexican central volcanic belt reaches the Gulf of Mexico and almost cuts the lowlands of the coastal plain in two. The <u>topography</u> and atmospheric conditions of the lowlands provide birds of prey and many other migrants with the conditions needed for migrating with the least expenditure of energy: tail winds and warm thermal updrafts.

myriad (mir´ ē əd) *adj.* seemingly countless

topography (tə päg´ rə fē) *n.* surface features of a place

☑ Reading Check
When do raptors migrate?

Work That Counts 753

⓫ About the Selection

In "Work That Counts," writer Ernesto Ruelas Inzunza combines the elements of a technical article with his sense of enthusiasm for his field to give readers an exciting account of an important project in the field of wildlife biology.

⓬ Literary Analysis

Technical Article

- Encourage students to explain what *tail winds* are.
  Answer: Tail winds are winds that blow in the same direction that one is flying—so the birds are going with the wind, rather than against it.
- Then, ask students why the birds choose the migratory path described in this passage.
  Answer: Birds choose this path because the environment and conditions are perfect for the birds and allow them to use less energy on their journey.

▶ **Monitor Progress** Point out the term *thermal updrafts*, which means "rising columns of warm air." Ask students what sources they could access to learn more about these phenomena.
Possible response: Possibilities include printed or online encyclopedias, meteorology books, or Web sites dealing with meteorology.

⓭ ☑ Reading Check

Answer: Raptors migrate each spring and fall.

CUSTOMIZE INSTRUCTION FOR UNIVERSAL ACCESS

For Gifted/Talented Students

Tell students that Ernest Ruelas Inzunza probably learned to identify so many different raptors by viewing charts with bird drawings or silhouettes. Have interested students research the raptors mentioned in the article using library or online sources. Allow sufficient time for students to find drawings or photographs of the birds and a few details of their habits. Then, have students create posters that would help a novice ornithologist identify the raptors. Students' posters should include drawings and information about the birds, such as the type of bird, its size and weight, and some of its habits.

Allow students time to share their posters with the class and, if applicable, encourage the class to identify which birds they have seen, either within the local area or on trips to other locations. Ask whether any students have gone bird-watching. Encourage interested students to find out more about local bird-watching groups and perhaps to arrange a class outing.

ASSESS

⑭ Literary Analysis

Technical Article

- As students read the bracketed passage, have them list or use a graphic organizer, such as a chart, to record the different technical information that Inzunza mentions.

- Then, ask students the Literary Analysis question on p. 754: What types of technical information does Inzunza include in this passage? **Answer:** Inzunza includes information about the specific types of migrating birds that have been seen in Veracruz, including the total counts of birds coming through Veracruz.

Answers for p. 754

Review and Assess

1. Students' responses will vary. Encourage them to be as specific as possible when describing the migrations they have seen.

2. **(a)** Tail winds and warm thermal updrafts allow birds to migrate with less energy. **(b)** Birds converge there because the topographic and atmospheric conditions are ideal for easy migrating.

3. **(a)** More than 220 species have been recorded at Veracruz. **(b)** Students will probably say that Veracruz has such a high number of migrating birds because birds from eastern, central, and western North America converge there.

4. **(a)** Inzunza watches and counts birds of prey for a conservation organization. **(b)** By counting and tracking the birds migrating each year, scientists know which species might be endangered.

5. **(a)** The title has both a literal and figurative meaning. Literally, it is about counting birds; figuratively, it describes a type of work that is meaningful and important. **(b)** The article includes information on how many species and birds have been recorded, and it describes why the work is important to the writer and the world.

754

Among the migrating raptors are turkey vultures; ospreys; swallow-tailed, Mississippi, and plumbeous kites; northern harriers; sharp-shinned, Cooper's, Harris's, red-shouldered, broad-winged, Swainson's, zone-tailed, and red-tailed hawks; and falcons, including kestrels, merlins, and peregrines. The migrations of a few other species—hook-billed kites, golden eagles and ferruginous hawks—are less well documented in Veracruz and are currently being studied. Five species of swallows, scissor-tailed flycatchers, white-winged and mourning doves, wood storks, white pelicans, cormorants, and white-faced and white ibises are also among the list of more than 220 species of migratory birds recorded at Veracruz. In fall, the count totals range between 2.5 million and 4 million birds, the highest count anywhere in the world, as birds journeying from eastern, central, and western North America converge here in Veracruz.

After five in the evening, when the temperature dropped down to 82° F and the thermals ceased to form, the pace slowed. Now I can respond in more detail to Jeros's question about the discovery of the River of Raptors. I read him a paragraph written in the spring of 1897 by ornithologist Frank M. Chapman, of the American Museum of Natural History: "On April 6 and 16, flights of hawks—I was unable to determine the species—were observed passing northward, exceeding in number any migration of these birds I have before seen." Almost a hundred years passed before bird counts were organized at Veracruz and Chapman's statements were borne out. Yet as long as these lowlands have been inhabited, the migration must have been seen and accepted by the local inhabitants as an autumn phenomenon. I conclude by telling my friend that perhaps the River of Raptors has always been known. And, he adds, admired.

Review and Assess

Thinking About the Selection

1. **Respond:** Describe any bird migrations that you have observed.

2. **(a) Recall:** What conditions allow birds to migrate with the least expenditure of energy? **(b) Draw Conclusions:** Why do so many birds converge where the Mexican central volcanic belt reaches the Gulf of Mexico?

3. **(a) Recall:** How many species of migratory birds have been recorded at Veracruz? **(b) Analyze:** Why does Veracruz have the highest count of migrating birds anywhere in the world?

4. **(a) Recall:** As it is described in this article, what is Inzunza's work? **(b) Synthesize:** Why is Inzunza's job important?

5. **(a) Analyze:** Explain the double meaning of the title of the article. **(b) Make a Judgment:** How does the article reflect both meanings?

754 ◆ *Nonfiction*

Literary Analysis
Technical Article What types of technical information does Inzunza include in this passage?

Ernesto Ruelas Inzunza

(b. 1968)

Ernesto Ruelas Inzunza is the executive director of Pronatura-Vera Cruz, a conservation organization in Veracruz, Mexico. Pronatura is raising money to meet a challenge grant from the National Fish and Wildlife Foundation and the Agency of International Development. The money will be used to build a nature center and bird observatory in Cardel, one of the monitoring stations mentioned in Inzunza's article. Contributors to this effort are dubbed "Friends of River of Raptors."

ASSESSMENT PRACTICE: Reading Comprehension

Comparing and Contrasting Texts   (For more practice, see Test Preparation Workbook, p. 47.)

In order to answer questions on tests that require them to compare and contrast aspects of two texts, students may need to determine which elements occur in just one selection, and which occur in both.

After students have read the technical articles in this selection grouping, write this sample test question on the board.

Which common element appears in both essays?

A a detailed explanation of how something is done

B a description of topography and atmospheric conditions

C the connection of history to the subject

D a description of bird migration

Through the process of elimination, help students determine that the correct answer is *C*.

Review and Assess

Literary Analysis

Technical Article

1. Explain one of the two technical processes for creating synthetic gems that O'Neil describes. Use a process diagram like the one shown for your explanation.

First	Then	Then	Then
Place chemicals in hopper.	Sift them into a jet of oxygen.		

2. Give two examples of specialized language in "Work That Counts." Then, explain what each term means.

3. What comparison does Inzunza use to help readers picture how many birds he observed from the observation tower?

Comparing Literary Works

4. (a) List three technical details that each article includes. (b) How do the writers handle technical details differently?

5. How does each writer's background, as described in their biographies on pages 752 and 754, have an impact on the purpose and tone of their articles?

6. Which article do you find easier to understand? Why?

Reading Strategy

Relating Diagrams to Text

7. Explain the purpose of Diagram A in "Imitating Nature's Mineral Artistry."

8. Use Diagram B to identify the states of flux growth.

9. (a) What kinds of **diagrams** could Inzunza have used to help illustrate his technical details? (b) Describe or sketch one such diagram.

Extend Understanding

10. **Science Connection:** What are the benefits of (a) creating synthetic gemstones and (b) understanding the migratory patterns of birds?

Quick Review

A **technical article** explains procedures, provides instructions, or presents specialized information.

To **relate a diagram** to the text, think of it as a visual extension of what you are reading.

 Take It to the Net
www.phschool.com
Take the interactive self-test online to check your understanding of these selections.

Answers continued

lowlands of the coastal plains highlighted. Arrows would be used to show tail winds and thermal updrafts.

10. **(a)** Synthetic gemstones are less expensive and more readily available than naturally formed gemstones. **(b)** Understanding the migratory patterns of birds shows scientists when a species becomes endangered.

Answers for p. 755

Review and Assess

1. **First:** Place chemicals in hopper. **Then:** Sift into a jet of oxygen. **Then:** Melt in combustion chamber with hydrogen in 4000°F heat. **Then:** Accumulate on ceramic rod at base. **Then:** Solidify into a boule.

2. A *raptor* is a bird of prey. *Tail winds* are winds going in the same direction as the bird is flying.

3. Inzunza compares the large migration of birds to moving organisms in a plankton sample.

4. **(a)** Possible answers: "Imitating Nature's Mineral Artistry" includes an explanation of flame-fusion growth, an explanation of flux growth, and a description of the internal structure of opals. "Work That Counts" includes the names, numbers, and homelands of migrating birds. **(b)** O'Neil uses diagrams to explain visually the complex processes and uses examples to demonstrate them. Inzunza uses comparisons and statistics.

5. O'Neil's purpose was to explain a process, and he has done a good deal of explanatory writing, which shows in his style. Inzunza's purpose was to tell of the importance of his work, which is also the focus of his biography.

6. Students may find Inzunza's article easier to understand because he does not describe a complex process.

7. The purpose of Diagram A is to help explain visually the process of creating gems using the flame-fusion technique.

8. A solution of emeralds' chemical ingredients is produced by combining a chemical compound with a flux; the solution is heated in an electric furnace; gem crystals precipitate out as they cool.

9. **(a)** Inzunza could use diagrams showing the geographic bottleneck of the area, as well as charts illustrating the statistical information. **(b)** The geographic bottleneck would show a map of Mexico with the central volcanic belt, the Gulf of Mexico, and the

continued

Answers for p. 756

❶ Vocabulary Development

Word Analysis

1. to move at the same time
2. number of symptoms occurring together
3. to put parts together into a whole

Spelling Strategy

1. tough   3. refinery
2. photograph

Concept Development: Analogies

1. divulge   6. topography
2. myriad   7. fortuitous
3. vigilance   8. saturated
4. constituents   9. metamorphosis
5. synthetic   10. synthesized

❷ Grammar

1. After the sun sets, I have time to sit peacefully and tell the story of the discovery.
2. With a smile, Hall removed the sample from the press.
3. Artful as they are, synthetic gems bear hallmarks of being made in laboratories.
4. Three red rubies were offered to Abraham Nassi while on an expedition to Burma.
5. We observed thousands of raptors flying in a distinctive pattern.

Writing Application

1. The scientists were able to produce synthetic diamonds that looked real.
2. Looking through binoculars, we observed several different species of raptors.

Integrate Language Skills

❶ Vocabulary Development Lesson

Word Analysis: Greek Prefix *syn-*

Synthetic contains the prefix *syn-*, which means "together with." A *synthetic* gem is one that is produced by bringing parts together chemically instead of being formed naturally.

Using your knowledge of the prefix *syn-*, define each of the words below. Consult a dictionary if needed.

1. synchronize   2. syndrome   3. synthesize

Spelling Strategy

The sound *f* can be spelled *ph* as in *phone*, *gh* as in *rough*, and *f* as in *fancy*. In your notebook, complete these words by adding the correct spelling of the *f* sound.

1. tou__   2. __otogra__   3. re__inery

❷ Grammar Lesson

Placement of Modifiers

To avoid confusion, a word, phrase, or clause that acts as a **modifier** should be placed close to the word it modifies.

> **Misplaced:** *Turning circles in the thermal columns of hot air,* we saw hundreds of birds. (phrase seems to modify *we*)
>
> **Correct:** We saw hundreds of birds *turning circles in the thermal columns of hot air.* (phrase correctly modifies *birds*)

Practice Rewrite the following sentences, moving the underlined modifier so that the sentence makes sense.

1. After the sun sets, <u>peacefully</u> I have time to sit and tell the story of the discovery.

W̶G̶ *Prentice Hall Writing and Grammar Connection: Chapter 21, Section 4*

756 ◆ *Nonfiction*

Concept Development: Analogies

An analogy draws a comparison by focusing on the relationship in word pairs. In your notebook, complete each analogy using the vocabulary words on page 747.

1. hide : conceal :: ___?___ : tell
2. few : three :: ___?___ : one million
3. concentration : relaxation :: ___?___ : sleep
4. ingredients : recipe :: ___?___ : whole
5. natural : earth :: ___?___ : laboratory
6. wave : ocean :: mountain : ___?___
7. unlucky : accident :: ___?___ : bonus
8. sold out : concert :: ___?___ : solution
9. oxidation : rust :: heat : ___?___
10. crops : grown :: compounds : ___?___

2. Hall removed the sample from the press <u>with a smile</u>.
3. Synthetic gems bear hallmarks of being made in laboratories, <u>artful as they are</u>.
4. <u>While on an expedition to Burma,</u> three red rubies were offered to Abraham Nassi.
5. <u>Flying in a distinctive pattern,</u> we observed thousands of raptors.

Writing Application Revise these sentences by adding the modifiers in the appropriate places.

1. The scientists were able to produce synthetic diamonds. (that looked real)
2. We observed several different species of raptors. (looking through binoculars)

TEACHING RESOURCES

The following resources can be used to enrich or extend the instruction for pp. 756–757.

Vocabulary

📖 **Selection Support:** Build Vocabulary, p. 185

📖 **Vocabulary and Spelling Practice Book** (Use this booklet for skills enrichment.) ▪

Grammar

📖 **Selection Support:** Build Grammar Skills, p. 186

W̶G̶ **Writing and Grammar,** Platinum Level, p. 507

▪ **Daily Language Practice Transparencies** ▪

Writing

W̶G̶ **Writing and Grammar,** Platinum Level, p. 135

💿 **Writing and Grammar iText CD-ROM** ▪

 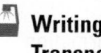 **Writing Models and Graphic Organizers on Transparencies,** pp. 65–68

▪ **BLOCK SCHEDULING:** Resources marked with this symbol provide varied instruction during 90-minute blocks.

Writing Lesson

Persuasive Letter

Suppose that you are Ernesto Ruelas Inzunza and you are raising money to continue your work. Write an introductory letter to a funding source, describing the importance of studying and protecting birds.

Prewriting   You will need facts and details from a variety of sources to support your position. To strengthen your letter, find unbiased research on the importance of raptors.

Drafting   As you draft, build and support your argument by providing evidence. Your first paragraph should introduce your project and explain why you think it is important. Discuss the importance of protecting birds in your body paragraphs, and conclude with your reasons for thinking that this funding source would benefit from investing in your work.

Model: Supporting Opinions With Facts

The protection of raptors is a worthwhile project because of the benefits their existence provides to the human race. Raptors eat rodents. Rodents spread disease and destroy crops.

> Facts about rodents support the opinion that protecting raptors is worthwhile.

Revision   Reread your letter to determine whether all of your arguments are supported. If needed, provide additional details to support them.

 Prentice Hall Writing and Grammar Connection: Chapter 7, Section 3

Extension Activities

Listening and Speaking With a partner, prepare a **demonstration** of a process you know—such as how to play your favorite computer game. Consider these tips:

- Make a detailed list of sequential steps in the process.
- Draw diagrams to clarify complicated steps.
- Anticipate questions from the audience, and prepare answers for them.

Present your demonstration to the class. **[Group Activity]**

Research and Technology Using pictures and research material from library resources or the Internet, prepare a **conservation update** on efforts to preserve the status of endangered birds worldwide. You might include graphs or charts developed on a computer graphics program to present statistics for your update.

Take It to the Net   www.phschool.com

Go online for an additional research activity using the Internet.

❸ Writing Lesson

- Help students brainstorm for a list of key words that they might use to find information in an Internet search.
- After students have written their first drafts, instruct them to read them, circle their arguments, and underline the supporting facts and details.
- If students find that some arguments are not well supported, remind them that they may need to return to their research to find more information.
- Use the Persuasive Composition rubric in **Performance Assessment and Portfolio Management,** p. 11, to evaluate students' letters.

❹ Listening and Speaking

- Tell students that they can use words and actions to show a process or skill in an oral demonstration.
- Remind students to present steps in a logical order and connect them with transition words such as *first, then, until,* and *after.*
- Use the rubric for Multimedia Presentations, p. 32 in **Performance Assessment and Portfolio Management,** to assess students' work.

CUSTOMIZE INSTRUCTION for Universal Access

To address different learning styles, use the following activities suggested in the **Extension Activities** booklet, p. 47.

- For Intrapersonal Learners, use Activity 5.
- For Logical/Mathematical and Verbal/Linguistic Learners, use Activity 6.
- For Visual/Spatial and Verbal/Linguistic Learners, use Activity 7.

ASSESSMENT RESOURCES

The following resources can be used to assess students' knowledge and skills.

Selection Assessment

- **Formal Assessment,** pp. 163–165
- **Open Book Test,** pp. 139–141
- **Got It! Assessment Videotapes,** Tape 4
- **Test Bank Software**
- **Take It to the Net**
  Visit www.phschool.com for self-tests and additional questions on the selections.

Writing Rubric

- **Performance Assess. and Portfolio Mgmt.,** p. 11

Listening and Speaking Rubric

- **Performance Assess. and Portfolio Mgmt.,** p. 32

PRENTICE HALL ASSESSMENT *SYSTEM*

- **Workbook**
- **Skill Book**
- **Transparencies**
- **CD-ROM**

Lesson Objectives

1. To write a compare-and-contrast essay
2. To use writing strategies to generate ideas, plan, organize, evaluate, and revise the composition

Model From Literature

In the excerpt from *The Marginal World* (p. 660), Rachel Carson compares and contrasts the world of the shore at high tide and low tide.

Prewriting

- Help students narrow down their topics. Remind them that topics such as Sports, Animals, or Music are all too broad. Help them see that within Sports, they might wish to compare the different skills needed to be a good soccer player or a good softball player, or they might compare and contrast the rules for each sport.

- Invite students to use a Venn Diagram to see if their topic has enough compare-and-contrast points to fill an essay.

- Have students begin to gather details to use in their essay. They may use their own knowledge as well as research to find points to use, and should continue to enter these points in the Venn Diagram they started earlier. Remind students that they need not use every point of difference or similarity they find in their research, but need focus only on major points of comparison and contrast.

- Work with students to write their theses statements. Emphasize clarity, brevity, and focus. A statement such as "Though they have many things in common, crocodiles and alligators are different in some ways, and you can learn to tell the difference," tells readers what they will learn and in what format.

- Before students draft their essays, have them review the Rubric for Self-Assessment, page 761, so they know what is expected.

Writing WORKSHOP

Exposition: Comparison-and-Contrast Essay

When you write a **comparison-and-contrast essay,** you show how two or more things are similar and how they are different. In this workshop, you will write a comparison-and-contrast essay about two subjects of your choice.

Assignment Criteria Your comparison-and-contrast essay should have the following characteristics:

- A purpose for comparison and contrast
- A clear thesis statement supported by evidence
- Factual details that reveal the similarities and differences between two or more subjects
- Transitions that show clear relationships between the subjects
- An effective organizational plan suited to its topic and purpose.

To preview the criteria on which your comparison-and-contrast essay may be assessed, see the Rubric on page 761.

Prewriting

Choose a topic. Write your comparison-and-contrast essay about a subject that interests you. To find a topic, try **listing**. First, choose a broad subject area, such as music, sports, or characters in a novel. Then, list items that come to mind, such as favorite examples. Finally, examine your list, and look for connections between two or more items that you can explore in an essay.

Evaluate your topic. To decide whether your subjects have enough points of comparison and contrast, use a Venn diagram like the one shown.

E-mail	Communication	Phone Call
-Typed -Not time-sensitive	-Communication -Can be informal	-Spontaneous -"Live" interaction

Gather details. Make notes to develop your ideas about the important similarities and differences between your subjects. Draw upon your personal knowledge and experience with the subjects. Then, conduct research using both primary and secondary sources.

Write a thesis statement. Write a thesis statement that identifies your subject and provides a clear focus for your essay. Include this statement in your introductory paragraph.

758 ◆ *Nonfiction*

TEACHING RESOURCES

The following resources can be used to enrich or extend the instruction for pp. 758–761.

*W*G **Writing and Grammar,** Platinum Level, Chapter 9, pp. 172–190

📖 **Performance Assessment and Portfolio Management,** Comparison-and-Contrast Composition, p. 15

📄 **Writing Models and Graphic Organizers on Transparencies,** pp. 95–98

 Writing and Grammar iText CD-ROM
Students can use the following tools as they complete their compare-and- contrast essays:

- Venn Diagram
- Transition Word Bin
- Language Variety Checker

Student Model

Before you begin drafting, read this student model and review the characteristics of an effective comparison-and-contrast essay.

Amanda Goodman
Glen Rock, New Jersey

You've Got Mail

Personal communications have gone through a major evolution in modern times. The letter gave way to the telephone call, and now they have both been overwhelmed in popularity by e-mail. While the three modes of communication have a lot in common, there are differences that let each stand out on its own.

Letters, phone calls, and e-mail are similar because they all involve personal communication. They allow people to share ideas and feelings with other people. Communicators do not have to be face to face; they can be across the world and get the same points across. Letter writers, phone callers, and e-mailers are generally not limited by time either. They can create and share their communications round the clock.

Despite their similarities, letters, phone calls, and e-mail communicate differently. Letters convey a personal touch and make recipients especially happy when received. They can be saved, to be reread (often over and over) at a later time. Unlike a letter, e-mail is usually more spontaneous and less likely to be reread. Phone call messages quickly fade. Of all three modes, letters take the longest time between the sender and the receiver. If time is important, letters are probably the worst format to use.

E-mail is seldom personal. It is more convenient than "snail mail," though. You never have to move away from your computer. Plus, you can edit without cross-outs. Once you send an e-mail, it is delivered instantly. This speed has its disadvantages. Because people create e-mails with such haste, they often do not stop to think carefully about what they want to say—or correct grammar or spelling mistakes—before they click an e-mail on its way.

A phone call is extremely personal, and it shows that you have set aside time for the other person. You are able to hear the tone of voice and expression of the other person. Phone calls may be expensive, temporary, and time-sensitive—unlike a letter or an e-mail, which a recipient can read when he or she has the time. Another problem with the phone is that once you say something, you cannot take it back, in contrast to the way you can edit writing.

There is a time and a place for all three types of communication. People are often so busy that they have time only for e-mail, but maybe people should set aside some time to write a letter or call a friend.

> In her introduction, Amanda identifies the subjects she will compare.

> This paragraph discusses the similarities three communication formats share.

> The third, fourth, and fifth paragraphs address the unique qualities of each form.

> Transitions help clarify the contrasts between subjects.

CUSTOMIZE INSTRUCTION FOR UNIVERSAL ACCESS

For Special Needs Students	For English Learners	For Advanced Writers
If students have listed too many points for their topic and are having difficulty deciding which to use, help them arrange the points on a continuum from most important to least important.	Write on the board: Music, Country/Western, and Rock, Different Singers, Instruments, and Specific Songs. Help students to see that comparing and contrasting country-western and rock music is too large a topic for a single essay, but that writing about two different singers is a reasonable task.	Suggest that students choose a topic that will help them, as they research and write about it, in their real life. For example, invite them to compare and contrast two possible after-school jobs or examine the similarities and differences between different junior year elective courses.

Student Model

- Explain that the Student Model is a sample, and that essays may be longer.
- Ask students to name the topic and the thesis statement.
  Possible response: The topic is a comparison of letters, telephone calls, and e-mail. The thesis statement is "While the three modes of communication have a lot in common, there are differences that let each stand out on its own."
- Discuss how Amanda supports her thesis by making a point-by-point comparison among the three forms of communication.
- Point out that Amanda uses the transitional word *Despite* at the beginning of her second paragraph to move the essay from similarities to differences.
- Have students note the way in which Amanda organizes her essay. The entire essay supports her original thesis statement. Within the essay, she begins each paragraph with a topic sentence, which she then supports with examples.
- Ask students what Amanda does in her final paragraph.
  Possible response: She draws a conclusion about the differences among the three types of communication.

Real-World Connection

Tell students that the ability to write effective compare-and-contrast material is important in many kinds of occupations. Scientists, natural history researchers, doctors, and many others must be able to communicate clearly about the work they do. How is the newly discovered dinosaur like or unlike those already unearthed? How is this new medical treatment different, though not necessarily better, than previous forms of treatment? What are the similarities and differences among several recycling programs?

Drafting

- Have students determine an audience for their essay. Do they want to address their classmates, adults such as teachers and parents, the wider community, or perhaps only one person? Remind students that an essay for a friend or groups of friends could be written in more informal language than an essay for adults and the wider community, which should be written in formal language.

- Explain to students that giving their essay a specific organization will help them write more clearly.

- Have students note that although the Student Model shows a point-by-point organization for a comparison-and-contrast essay, they may also use a subject-by-subject form of organization.

- As practice, ask the class to suggest different points for a comparison-and-contrast essay on the difference between country/western and rock music. What examples would they give for each under points such as Popularity, Representative Performers, Themes of the Music, and so forth?

- As students write their own essays, remind them to use not only facts but quotations from people who know about the subject. They may use quotations from classmates, teachers, and coaches as well. Remind them to be aware of their audience as they write.

Revising

- Supply students with colored pencils or highlighters and have them follow the instructions in the text.

- Provide a model by showing students how to highlight the writing example here.

- Have students note the kind of support they have provided for each of their compare-and-contrast subjects. For example, if they have provided only examples, have them insert some facts and direct quotations.

- Invite students to check their paragraph organization to be sure everything in a paragraph supports a main idea or key point.

- Where appropriate, encourage students to gather graphics for their essays.

(continued on p. 761)

760

Writing WORKSHOP *continued*

Drafting

Organize your essay. Usually, a comparison-and-contrast essay is organized in one of two ways. In a subject-by-subject organization, you discuss all the features of one subject and then discuss all the features of the second subject. If you follow a point-by-point organization, you discuss one point about both subjects and then move on to a second point, and so on. The diagram shown here demonstrates point-by-point organization.

Elaborate. Provide support for each of your statements. Support can take any of the following forms:

- **Examples:** Illustrate similarities and differences between your subjects.
- **Facts:** When possible, use hard evidence that will help readers gain a clear understanding of each subject.
- **Quotations:** Quotations from experts lend authority to the points you are making.

Point-by Point Organization

Point-by-Point
Point 1
- Subject A
- Subject B
Point 2
- Subject A
- Subject B

Subject by Subject
Subject A
- Point 1
- Point 2
Subject B
- Point 1
- Point 2

Revising

Revise to balance your organization. Because your essay has two or more subjects, clarity of organization is especially important. At every point of your essay, readers must know which subject you are talking about.

Read your draft, and identify the places where you address each subject. Use one color to highlight every instance in which you refer to one subject, use another color to underline every reference to the second subject, and use a third color for a third subject, if you include one. Review your highlighted draft to determine whether you have adequately addressed each subject.

Model: Revising to Balance Comparisons

Phone call messages quickly fade after the phone call is over.

Letters convey a personal touch and make recipients especially happy when received. They can be saved and stored, to be reread (often over and over) at a later time. Unlike a letter, an e-mail is usually more spontaneous and less likely to be reread. Of all three modes, letters take the longest time between the sender and the receiver.

Because she is comparing three formats, Amanda adds an example to address each one.

760 ◆ *Nonfiction*

USING TECHNOLOGY IN WRITING

If students are using word processors, they might want to use the Find feature of the software to locate conjunctions such as *and, but,* and *yet.* When they find each one, have them examine the sentence to see if it is a compound sentence. If it is, have students be sure that it has a comma before the conjunction, or, if the conjunction begins the sentence, to be sure it is capitalized.

Students may also use the **Writing and Grammar iText CD-ROM** for more assistance.

Revise your sentences. Review your draft, paying special attention to the way in which your ideas connect and flow together. If your sentences are choppy, consider combining them. When combining sentences, use appropriate conjunctions to indicate how the ideas are related.

Choppy: Brutus was a good man. He made bad decisions.
Connected: Brutus was a good man, but he made some bad decisions.

Compare the model and the nonmodel. Why is the model more interesting?

Nonmodel	Model
A phone call is extemely personal. It shows that you have made time for the other person. You get to actually hear someone's tone of voice. You get to hear his or her expression.	A phone call is extemely personal, and it shows that you have set aside time for the other person. You are able to hear the tone of voice and expression of the other person.

Publishing and Presenting

When you have completed your essay, choose one of the following ways to share your writing with classmates or a wider audience:

Give a presentation. Present your comparison-and-contrast essay to the class. Add charts or visuals to help listeners understand the points you make.

Publish your essay electronically. Post your essay on a Web site, or upload it onto a classroom computer.

> **Speaking Connection**
> For instruction about oral response to literature, see the Listening and Speaking Workshop on page 762.

Rubric for Self-Assessment

Evaluate your comparison-and-contrast essay using the following criteria and rating scale:

Criteria	Rating Scale Not very				Very
Are the subjects and purpose for comparison clearly identified?	1	2	3	4	5
Does the essay include a thesis statement?	1	2	3	4	5
Is the thesis supported by evidence?	1	2	3	4	5
Are there sufficient details to support each statement?	1	2	3	4	5
Are transitions between subjects smooth?	1	2	3	4	5
Is the organization logical and consistent?	1	2	3	4	5

Writing Workshop ◆ *761*

TEST-TAKING TIP

When taking a test that includes a compare-and-contrast writing prompt, students should be aware that the implied audience for such an essay on tests is well-educated adults unless otherwise specified. Students should choose points of comparison and supporting details that are appropriate for this audience. They should also use a formal tone and formal language, unless the test gives different instructions.

Revising (continued)

- Have students review the Model and Nonmodel. Explain that their job is not just to present details of comparison but to aid a reader's understanding with a smooth, flowing style.

- Ask students why the Model is preferable to the Nonmodel. **Answer:** The sentences in the Nonmodel are all the same length and style, creating repetition and a choppy effect. The sentences in the Model are varied and flow smoothly.

Publishing and Presenting

- Have students think of the audience they had in mind when they wrote their compare-and-contrast essay.

- Help students determine the best formats for publishing and presenting their essays.

- For students who have chosen to address their classmates, ask them to read their essays to the class.

- For students who have chosen to address the wider school community, have them e-mail their essays to a student publication Web site.

Assessment

- Review the assessment criteria in class.

- Before students proceed with self-assessment, have them score the Student Model in class, using one or more of the rubric categories, to help them see how to apply the criteria. For example, how would students score the essay in terms of Organization? Why would they give it this score?

- The rubric on this page, and another rubric in an alternative format, can be found on pp. 15 and 58 of **Performance Assessment and Portfolio Management.**

Evaluate the Content

- Remind students of the different types of media presentations. For example, an editorial is a legitimate place for strong opinion and bias, while a news report is not, or should not be, a place for such bias.

- Remind students to be alert to the difference between facts and statistics that are used to emotionally persuade and those used to support objective statements.

- After students complete the Activity on the student page, have them fill out the Feedback Form. When they finish, have them discuss their responses as a class or in small groups.

Evaluate the Presentation

- Have students evaluate photographs from newspapers in the classroom for persuasive bias. Have them find one photograph that they think tries to elicit a positive feeling and one that tries to elicit a negative feeling. How well does each photograph succeed?

- Invite students to use classroom newspapers to find examples of charged language in news stories. Ask them to compare this language with that in an editorial. In which form of presentation is such language acceptable?

- Have students judge news articles in terms of the "experts" quoted. Ask them to look for examples of articles in which many quotes on one side of an issue are "balanced" by one quote on the other side that is placed near the end of the article.

- Have students complete the Activity and present their conclusions in a class discussion.

Listening and Speaking WORKSHOP

Analyze a Media Presentation

The news you get about current events can be different in quality, thoroughness, and objectivity based on the sources you consult.

Evaluate the Content

There are many types of media presentations, such as news reports, documentaries, newsmagazines, and editorials. Each has its own main purpose—to inform, to persuade, or to entertain. Consider the following as you analyze media presentations:

Recognize the main idea. Like a headline, the first line of a broadcast report usually relates the main idea of a news story. Listen to identify the type of story being reported and the angle the reporter will present.

Identify supporting evidence. Facts, statistics, quotations, reasons, and other evidence should support statements. Be particularly alert for supporting evidence when one of the purposes is to persuade you.

Evaluate the Presentation

These are some of the techniques used to influence viewer response:

- **Images** A photograph captures a fleeting moment. The choice of image that is presented will influence your feelings about a topic.

- **Charged language** While journalists are trained to present facts objectively, those who present their views often use language intended to get a reaction. Compare these sentences:

  The budget was approved today. (*objective*)

  The budget was finally approved today. (*implies impatience*)

- **"Experts"** Be aware that the experts chosen to analyze the news also have their own opinions. For example, for a report on a trend in fashion, a reporter might choose the comments of an expert who finds fault with the new style and omit the commentary of the designer who created it.

- **Staging** Note the sets, the appearance and demeanor of the anchors, and the interaction among reporters. Also, notice the graphics and music that build your response to the programming.

Activity: Analysis and Discussion

Analyze a television newscast using the Feedback Form as a guide. Share your conclusions in a class discussion.

762 ◆ *Nonfiction*

Analyzing a Media Presentation

Rating System
+ = Excellent   ✔ = Average   – = Weak

Content
What is the topic of the story?_____
What is the main idea? _____

Supporting Evidence *Check off those that apply:*
___Interview (with whom? why?)
___Photographs/video (to what effect?)
___Charged language (which words? what effect?)

Presentation *Evaluate the impact of these items:*
___Set   ___Reporter's tone
___Graphics   ___Interaction among reporters
___Music

Answer the following questions:
Was the report objective?
What information may have been omitted?
Would you rely on this program as your source of news?

CUSTOMIZE INSTRUCTION FOR UNIVERSAL ACCESS

For Special Needs Students	For Less Proficient Students	For English Learners
Play a television documentary for students. Ask students to keep a list of ways in which the documentary tries to use images to present information in a favorable or unfavorable light. When the documentary has finished, ask students to write a brief critique of the use of images in the piece.	As students view the television documentary, have them take notes of important points they hear. When they have finished viewing, ask volunteers to state some of the main ideas from the documentary to the rest of the class. Then, ask them if they think the documentary was successful in communicating its information. Why or why not?	Have students keep track, as they watch and listen to the documentary, of charged words and phrases, and note them down on paper. After viewing, have them give examples to the class of such charged language, explaining in their own words what effect the charged language was intended to have on listeners.

Assessment WORKSHOP

Comparing and Contrasting

In the reading sections of some tests, you may be required to compare and contrast aspects—such as themes, conflicts, and allusions—of two texts. Use the following strategies to help you answer test questions on this skill:

- To compare and contrast, read each passage carefully and analyze the literary elements. For example, look for varying themes in each passage to determine similarities or differences in them.
- Consider the main point of each passage, and notice how each writer supports that point.

Test-Taking Strategies

- As you compare and contrast themes of two passages, think about the similarities or differences.
- If two passages have the same idea but varying details, jot down the details to compare them.

Sample Test Item

Directions: Read the passages, and answer the question that follows.

Passage A: The first settlers in the Western Hemisphere were faced with a world that was strange and unknown to them. They encountered unfamiliar lands, animals, and weather conditions. They had to learn to survive in a climate that could turn deadly in an instant.

Passage B: The crew of the space station had entered an uncharted universe. All their advanced equipment was useless to them. Unknown forces surrounded their ship. Intelligence experts on board raced to determine how to best counteract those forces.

1 What topic is addressed by both passages?

  A space travel
  B frontier life
  C entering unknown worlds
  D fighting off enemies

Answer and Explanation

The correct answer is *C*. Space travel appears only in the second passage, so *A* is incorrect. Only one passage deals with frontier life, so *B* is incorrect. Although there are dangers in both, *D* is not correct.

▶ Practice

Directions: Read the passages, and answer the question that follows.

Passage A: Television is a broadcast medium. Information is transmitted through airwaves and is delivered orally or spoken by professionals referred to as broadcast journalists.

Passage B: Newspapers and magazines are print media. Both provide information to the public through the printed word, which is read rather than heard. Newspapers and magazines are published by printing presses. People who write for newspapers and magazines are often referred to as print journalists.

1 Which is not a topic addressed by these passages?

  A journalists
  B information
  C media
  D printing press

Lesson Objective

To learn to compare two passages given on a test

Applying Reading Strategies

- Tell students that they should jot down a note about the topic of a passage after they read it. Then, they should read the passage again and revise their summary of its topic to reflect additional nuances or information they have overlooked. For instance, they might revise the topic summary "Space exploration" to the more accurate summary, "Funding space exploration."
- Tell students that for any question on a literary element in a passage, such as conflict, they should apply the same strategy.

Applying Test-Taking Strategies

- Have students read the Sample Test Item and jot down a note on the topic of each passage. Answer: The topic of the first passages is the unfamiliarity of the first settlers of the Western Hemisphere with the territory. The topic of the second is the entry of a space station crew into an unfamiliar universe.
- Have students answer the Sample Test Item and compare their answers with the explanation.
- Have students complete the Practice, applying the same strategy.

Answer

The correct answer is *D*. Only the second passage discusses the printing press. Both passages discuss journalists (answer A), information (answer B), and media (answer C).

TEACHING RESOURCES

The following resources can be used to enrich or extend the instruction for p. 763.

PRENTICE HALL ASSESSMENT *SYSTEM*

- 📖 **Workbook**
- 📖 **Skill Book**
- 📰 **Transparencies**
- 💿 **CD-ROM**

Unit Objectives

1. To read plays that exemplify classical Greek drama and Shakespearean drama
2. To apply a variety of strategies for reading drama
3. To analyze literary elements
4. To use a variety of strategies to build vocabulary
5. To learn elements of grammar, usage, and style
6. To use recursive writing processes to write in a variety of forms
7. To develop listening and speaking skills
8. To express and support responses to various dramas
9. To prepare, organize, and present literary interpretations

Meeting the Objectives

With each selection, you will find instructional materials through which students can meet these objectives. Further, you will find additional practice pages for reading strategies, literary analysis, vocabulary, and grammar in the **Selection Support: Skills Development Workbook** in your **Teaching Resources.**

Background

Art

Commedia dell' arte by André Rouillard

The title of this painting indicates a specific dramatic form, reflected in the gestures, expressions, and costumes. The masked figures have exaggerated comic costumes and features. The harlequin is a comic character well known in drama. The man in the hat wears a mask with a fake-nose caricature. The young man sitting center stage wears a mask, but with a subtle expression of sorrow.

> How might these characters be similar to those in a television situation comedy?
> Answer: The actors play fixed characters in situations that basically do not change.

Commedia dell'arte, Andre Rouillard

UNIT 8 Drama

UNIT FEATURES

Connections	Reading Informational Materials
Every unit contains a feature that connects literature to a related topic, such as art, science, or history. In this unit, "Eulogy for a Fallen Leader" (p. 882), communicates a granddaughter's sorrow at the assassination of her grandfather, Israel's Yitzhak Rabin. Use the information and questions on the Connections page to enrich students' understanding of the selections presented within the unit.	These selections will help students learn to analyze and evaluate informational texts, such as workplace documents, technical directions, and consumer materials. They will expose students to the organization and features unique to nonnarrative texts. In this unit, students will learn how to compare information from different sources.

Exploring the Genre

Drama is one of the earliest literary forms. People in ancient times acted out great triumphs, deep fears, or heartfelt wishes in religious rites. Since then, drama has evolved into its modern forms, which range from lively musicals to biting satires. It is the quality of action, or performance, that makes drama unique in literature.

As you read the dramas in this unit, notice the following elements, which can help bring the dramas to life.

- **Stage Directions:** These notes convey information about sound effects, movements and gestures, setting, and line readings to the cast, crew, and readers of the drama.

- **Dialogue:** In drama, much of what you learn about the characters, setting, and events is revealed through dialogue.

- **Characters:** Dramatic characters are brought to life by their dialogue and actions onstage.

- **Plot:** Most dramas contain a plot in which events unfold, rise to a climax, and are resolved.

- **Theme:** A theme is the central message that the playwright wishes to convey to the audience.

▲ **Critical Viewing** What elements of this painting suggest theater? **[Analyze]**

Exploring the Theme ◆ 765

ASSESSMENT RESOURCES

- Selection Support: Skills Development Workbook
- Formal Assessment
- Open Book Tests
- Performance Assessment and Portfolio Management
- Extension Activities

Assessing Student Progress

Listed below are the tools that are available to measure the degree to which students meet the unit objectives.

Informal Assessment

The questions in the Review and Assess sections are a first-level response to the concepts and skills presented within the selections. Students' responses provide a brief, informal measure of their grasp of the material. These responses can indicate where further instruction and practice are needed. Follow up with the practice pages in the **Selection Support: Skills Development Workbook.**

Formal Assessment

The **Formal Assessment** booklet contains the Selection Tests and Unit Tests.

- Selection Tests measure comprehension and skills acquisition for each selection or group of selections.

- Each Unit Test provides students with thirty multiple-choice questions and five essay questions designed to assess students' knowledge of the literature and skills taught in the unit.

The **Open Book Tests** ask students to demonstrate their ability to synthesize and communicate information from selections or groups of selections.

To assess student writing, you will find rubrics and scoring models in the **Performance Assessment and Portfolio Management** booklet. In this booklet, you will also find scoring rubrics for listening and speaking activities.

Alternative Assessment

The **Extension Activities** booklet contains writing activities, listening and speaking activities, and research and technology activities that are appropriate for students with different ability levels. You may also use these activities as an alternative measurement of students' growth.

▶**Critical Viewing**

Answer: Theater is suggested by the stage, as well as the players' costumes, masks, gestures and positions, and the watcher at the window.

765

Why Read Literature?

The "Why Read Literature" page in each unit presents a list of possible purposes for reading. Each purpose for reading is connected to one or more of the selections in the unit. Good readers set a purpose before reading in order to help them read actively and focus on meaningful details.

Unit 8 introduces three purposes for reading. "Read for the Love of Literature" encourages students to appreciate the portrayal of timeless events by one of the greatest writers in history. "Read to Appreciate the Author's Craft" encourages students to view the actions of strong characters created by a great Greek dramatist. When they "Read for Information," students will learn about the history of Greek and Shakespearean theater.

How to Use This Page

- Tell students that before reading each selection in this unit, they should set a purpose for reading. This will help them read in an active and focused manner.

- Explain that Shakespeare's drama of an emperor's betrayal by a friend will help increase their love for literature.

- To understand a character in a play, readers must attend to his or her actions, words, and thoughts. When they read to appreciate an author's craft, students will discover the techniques the writer uses to make his characters live.

- A third purpose for reading is to obtain information. Explain that when they set a purpose, students should specify the type of information they want to learn. For example, when reading "Greek Theater," they might wish to find out who the important figures were in the creation of the Greek theater.

Why Read Literature?

When you approach the classics of drama, you can bring several purposes to your reading. Whether it is to appreciate, to learn, or to be informed, you will find that the works of Shakespeare and Sophocles can support a wealth of reading purposes. Preview three purposes you might set before reading the works in this unit.

Read for the Love of Literature

Ever since they were written, William Shakespeare's plays have entertained audiences and students of literature. You can read Shakespeare for a number of reasons, including
- To learn about a theme
- To learn about Elizabethan theater
- To learn about iambic pentameter

Shakespeare wrote his plays with very strict attention to the rhythm his lines produced. Knowing this may help you enjoy or appreciate Shakespeare's skill even more.

Keep your friends close, but your enemies closer. This saying takes on new meaning for the Roman general Julius Caesar. Find out why when you read **The Tragedy of Julius Caesar,** Shakespeare's timeless drama based on historical events, page 822.

Read to Appreciate the Author's Craft

Etruscan Amphora, black-figured pontic fighting soldiers, white dove on shield, National Museum, Warsaw, Poland

Sophocles was one of the most respected Greek dramatists of his time, and the search for truth and self-awareness in his works is personified in the characters he created. Read the play **Antigone,** page 772.

Read for Information

Learn about the beginnings of modern theater in ancient Greece and how it changed by reading **Greek Theater,** page 768.

Most of Shakespeare's plays were staged in a theater that was open to the sky and held between 2,500 and 3,000 people. Read a description of the original theater and how it has been reconstructed in **Shakespeare on Stage,** page 816.

 Take It to the Net

Visit the Web site for online instruction and activities related to each selection in this unit.
www.phschool.com

766 ◆ *Drama*

 ENRICHMENT: Further Reading

Have students choose one or more of the works below to extend their experience of the genre featured in the unit or drama or to read more by the unit authors.

A Doll's House by Henrik Ibsen
This classic play portrays a woman's decision to reject her place in society, and therefore her protection within that society, and take the consequences.

Antigone by Jean Anouilh
The French playwright's version of the Greek classic serves as an allegory of life in France under the pro-German Vichy government during World War II.

Twelfth Night by William Shakespeare
Twins separated in their youth, a countess looking for a husband, a duke looking for a wife, a scheming steward—these are the main characters in a delightful comedy by the Master.

How to Read Literature

Use Strategies for Reading Drama

While plays share many elements with prose, fiction, and poetry, the greatest difference is that a drama is designed to be acted out on a stage before an audience. The story is told mostly through dialogue and action. Stage directions indicate when and how the actors move. When you read a play, you are reading a script, so keep in mind that it was written to be performed.

The following strategies will help you interact with the text of a drama and imagine the action and characters in performance.

1. Identify with a character.

- When you identify with a character, you put yourself in the character's place. This can give you greater insight into that character's motives and the events of the play.

- As you read the passage below, try to connect with the character's sense of justice. Then, imagine how you would feel if your beliefs or actions were challenged.

  > I have not sinned before God. Or if I have,
  > I shall know the truth in death. But if the guilt
  > Lies upon Creon who judged me, then, I pray,
  > May his punishment equal my own.— from *Antigone*

2. Use text aids.

- Text aids can enhance your reading of a play. Stage directions tell actors where and how to move. They can help you picture what is happening on the stage.

- Notes in the side margin define or clarify the language used in dialogue.

3. Paraphrase.

One way to approach dramatic language is to paraphrase, or restate passages in your own words. For example, the paraphrase of the passage at right may help you get to the heart of the meaning.

4. Read between the lines.

- By reading between the lines, you can discover a deeper or different meaning to a character's words or actions.

- Read dialogue carefully, considering each character's ideas and motives.

- Look for layers of meaning.

As you read the selections in this unit, use these suggestions to apply the strategies and interact with the text.

Paraphrasing

And men have lost their reason!
Bear with me; My heart is in the
coffin there with Caesar, And
I must pause till it come back
to me.
—from *The Tragedy of Julius Caesar*

Paraphrase: And people are not thinking clearly! Wait, I am so overcome with grief at Caesar's death that I cannot speak.

How to Read Literature

The "How to Read Literature" page in each unit presents a set of strategies to help readers understand the authors' words and ideas. Each reading strategy is taught in conjunction with one or more of the selections within the unit. Good readers develop a bank of strategies from which they can draw as needed.

Unit 8 introduces four strategies for reading drama. Students will learn to identify with characters, to use text aids such as footnotes, to paraphrase, and to read between the lines.

How to Use This Page

Introduce the strategies for constructing meaning, presenting each as a tool for developing understanding when reading the selections in this unit.

- As they read *Antigone* (p. 772), students will identify with the characters, particularly Antigone, to see why each one acts as he or she does.

- As they read *The Tragedy of Julius Caesar* (p. 822), students will learn to use text aids as a way to understand unfamiliar language, to paraphrase as a means for making difficult language understandable, and to read between the lines to find the hidden meaning in a characters' words.

MODEL A READING STRATEGY: Identifying With a Character

Tell students that when they identify with a character, they make that character's ideas and feelings their own or they determine which ideas of theirs are similar to those of the character, so as to understand him or her better.

Read to students Antigone's speech on p. 775, lines 84–88: "Go away, Ismeme: / I shall be hating you soon, and the dead will too, / For your words are hateful. Leave me my foolish plan: / I am not afraid of the danger: if it means death, / It will not be the worst of deaths—death without honor."

Tell students: From these lines, you can see that Antigone has made a plan that is dangerous and could lead to her death. But she believes that not following her plan means a worse kind of death—death without honor. To identify with Antigone, you might determine what actions and values are so important to you that you would be willing to die honorably in defense of such values.

Antigone, Prologue Through Scene 2

Lesson Objectives

1. **To analyze and respond to literary elements**
   - Literary Analysis: Protagonist and Antagonist
   - Connecting Literary Elements: Character's Decision

2. **To read, comprehend, analyze, and critique a play**
   - Reading Strategy: Questioning Characters' Motives
   - Reading Check questions
   - Review and Assess questions
   - Assessment Practice (ATE)

3. **To develop word analysis skills, fluency, and systematic vocabulary**
   - Vocabulary Development Lesson: Latin Prefix: *trans-*

4. **To understand and apply written and oral language conventions**
   - Spelling Strategy
   - Grammar Lesson: Objective Pronouns

5. **To understand and apply appropriate writing and research strategies**
   - Extension Activity: Newspaper Article
   - Extension Activity: Presentation

6. **To understand and apply listening and speaking strategies**
   - Extension Activity: Mock Trial (p. 811)

STEP-BY-STEP TEACHING GUIDE	PACING GUIDE
PRETEACH	
Motivate Students and Provide Background	
Use the Motivation activity (ATE p. 770)	5 min.
Read and discuss the Preview material and Background information (SE/ATE p. 768–770) **A**	5 min.
Introduce the Concepts	
Introduce the Literary Analysis and Reading Strategy (SE/ATE p. 771) **A**	15 min.
Pronounce the vocabulary words and read their definitions (SE p. 771)	5 min.
TEACH	
Monitor Comprehension	
Informally monitor comprehension by circulating while students read independently or in groups **A**	35 min.
Monitor students' comprehension with the Reading Check notes (SE/ATE pp. 773, 775, 777, 779, 781, 783, 785)	as students read
Develop vocabulary with Vocabulary notes (SE pp. 776, 780, 781, 787; ATE p. 786)	as students read
Develop Understanding	
Develop students' understanding of protagonists and antagonists with the Literary Analysis annotations (SE/ATE pp. 773, 774, 778, 780, 782, 783, 784) **A**	10 min.
Develop students' ability to question the characters' motives with the Reading Strategy annotations (SE/ATE pp. 774, 776, 779, 781, 782, 784, 785, 786)	10 min.
ASSESS	
Assess Mastery	
Assess students' mastery of the Reading Strategy and Literary Analysis by having them answer the Review and Assess questions (SE/ATE p. 788)	20 min.
Use one or more of the print and media Assessment Resources (ATE p. 789) **A**	up to 50 min.
EXTEND	
Apply Understanding	
Have students complete the Vocabulary Development Lesson and the Grammar Lesson (SE p. 789) **A**	20 min.
Apply students' understanding using one or more of the Extension Activities (SE p. 789)	20–90 min.

 ACCELERATED INSTRUCTION:
Use the strategies and activities identified with an **A**.

UNIVERSAL ACCESS
● = Below Level Students
▲ = On-Level Students
■ = Above Level Students

Time and Resource Manager

PRINT 📖	TRANSPARENCIES 📑	TECHNOLOGY 💿 🎧 📼
RESOURCES		
• **Beyond Literature,** Humanities Connection: The Greek Theater, p. 48 ▲ ■		• **Interest Grabber Video,** Tape 4 ● ▲ ■
• **Selection Support Workbook:** ● ▲ ■ Literary Analysis, p. 192 Reading Strategy, p. 191 Build Vocabulary, p. 189	• **Literary Analysis and Reading Transparencies,** pp. 95 and 96 ● ▲ ■	
• **Authors In Depth,** Platinum Level ■		• **Listening to Literature** ● ▲ ■ Audiocassettes, Side 25 Audio CDs, CD 16
• **Literatura en español** ● ▲ • **Literary Analysis for Enrichment** ■	• **Fine Art Transparencies, Volume 1,** Art Transparency 15 ● ▲ ■	
• **Formal Assessment:** Selection Test, pp. 170–172 ● ▲ ■ • **Open Book Test,** pp. 142–144 ● ▲ ■ • **Performance Assessment and Portfolio Management,** p. 32 ● ▲ ■ • **PRENTICE HALL ASSESSMENT SYSTEM** ● ▲ ■	**PRENTICE HALL ASSESSMENT SYSTEM** ● ▲ ■ Skills Practice Answers and Explanations on Transparencies	• **Test Bank Software** ● ▲ ■ • **Got It! Assessment Videotapes,** Tape 4 ● ▲
• **Selection Support Workbook:** ● ▲ ■ Build Grammar Skills, p. 190 • **Writing and Grammar,** Platinum Level ● ▲ ■ • **Extension Activities,** p. 48 ● ▲ ■	• **Daily Language Practice Transparencies** ● ▲	• **Writing and Grammar iText CD-ROM** ● ▲ ■ 🖥 **Take It to the Net** www.phschool.com

BLOCK SCHEDULING: Use one 90-minute class period to preteach the selection and have students read it. Use a second 90-minute class period to assess students' mastery of skills and have them complete one of the Extension Activities.

Background

Greek Tragedy

A Greek tragedy is usually centered on the suffering of a major character and ends in disaster. The origins of tragedy are obscure, but by the time Sophocles wrote, tragedy was a highly developed dramatic form, strongly linked with both religious ritual and artistic performance. It used poetic language as well as song and never completely abandoned its sacred origins.

Students living in secular societies will have some difficulty understanding the degree to which religion informed daily life in ancient Greece. The Greeks believed that the good will of the gods determined the city's welfare. Reverence, the fulfillment of religious duty, and patriotism were often synonymous.

Characters had human traits but were actually larger than life. Students accustomed to characters with personality and used to seeing cameras focus on revealing muscular twitches on the faces of tragic characters will miss these aspects in Greek drama. Although characters have their assigned traits, these characteristics are so universal that the personages represent examples or types rather than unique personalities.

Finally, tragedies were usually presented as part of a trilogy. Much of the content was based on myths familiar to the ancient Greeks. This inherited and familiar cultural background made it possible for the playwright to include pungent and subtle allusions whose importance could be understood by ancient Greek audiences without the benefit of explanation.

Greek Theater

Theater was a celebration in ancient Greece. The Athenians of the fifth century B.C. held festivals to honor Dionysos (dī´ ə nī´ səs), their god of wine. During these holidays, citizens gathered to watch competitions between playwrights, who presented plays derived from well-known myths. These plays depicted events that exposed arrogance and that emphasized reverence for the gods.

Thousands of Athenians saw the plays in outdoor theaters like the one shown in the photograph below, in which seats rose in a semicircle from a level orchestra area. The plays performed in these theaters had limited numbers of characters. There were no curtains to allow for changes of scenery between acts, so scenes were interspersed with songs. No violence or irreverence was depicted on stage, although both were central to the plots of many plays. Such events occurred offstage and were reported in dialogue.

The Presentation of the Plays

The playwrights of ancient Greece used a consistent format for most of their productions. Plays opened with a Prologue, or exposition, that presented the background to situate the conflict. The entering chorus then sang a parodos (par´ əd əs), or opening song. This was followed by the first scene. The chorus's song, called an ode, divided scenes, thus serving the same purpose as a curtain does in modern theater.

The Chorus The role of the chorus was central to the production and important in interpreting the meaning of the plays. During the odes, a leader, called the choragos (kō rā´ gəs), might exchange thoughts with the group in a dialogue. During that recital, the group would rotate from right to left, singing the strophe (strō´ fē). Then, the chorus would move in the opposite direction during the antistrophe. An epode, or stanza that follows the strophe and antistrophe, was included in some odes. At the conclusion, there was a paean (pē´ ən) of thanksgiving to Dionysos and an exodos (eks´ ə dəs), or final exiting scene. The chorus played an integral part in any play's success.

❶ ▼ Critical Viewing
What might be some advantages and disadvantages to watching a performance in a theater like this one? **[Assess]**

768 ● Drama

The Oedipus Myth

The Greek playwright Sophocles wrote three tragedies about the royal family of Thebes, a city in northeastern Greece. Called the Theban plays, these tragedies are *Oedipus the King, Oedipus at Colonus,* and *Antigone.* The stories of these plays were as familiar to the audience as the story of Noah's Ark is today.

Abandoned at Birth Oedipus was abandoned at birth by his parents, the Theban king Laios and his wife, Iocaste. A fortuneteller proclaimed that the infant would kill his father and marry his mother. Wishing to avoid that fate, the couple had a servant, who was to ensure the baby's death, take Oedipus to a mountaintop to be abandoned. The servant took pity on the newborn and gave him to a childless couple in a distant city, who raised the boy without ever mentioning his adoption. When Oedipus left to start his adult life, he still did not know that his real father was Laios and his mother was Iocaste. His travels took him toward Thebes, where he killed a man without knowing he was Laios. Through daring exploits, he eventually became a hero in the city of Thebes.

A Royal Marriage Iocaste, now a widow, agreed to marry the unknown champion. The couple lived happily and raised four children of their own. Then, a plague befell the city. During an investigation of this plague, Oedipus learned the facts of his birth. In horror, Iocaste committed suicide and Oedipus blinded himself. Iocaste's brother, Creon, took full control of the city and allowed one of Oedipus' children, Antigone, to lead Oedipus into exile, where he died.

A Daughter Mourns After her return to Thebes, Antigone was deeply troubled by her experience. Her sister, Ismene, and brothers, Eteocles and Polyneices, were also burdened by their background. They were haunted by the curse that caused their father to fulfill his own prophecy and to condemn his sons to kill each other for control of Thebes.

Order Restored By the time the play *Antigone* opens, Creon has restored some order to Thebes. The civil war between the brothers has just ended because Eteocles and Polyneices have killed each other in combat. Eteocles had supported Creon's established order and was buried with honors. Because Polyneices had rebelled against Thebes, Creon ordered that his corpse be left to rot. Antigone's decision to disobey that command is central to the play.

Greek Theater ◆ 769

✵ ENRICHMENT: Cultural Connection

The Development of Actors

Until the fifth century, tragic dramatists acted their own works—alone—with only the chorus to back them up. Early in his career, Aeschylus introduced a second actor. Dialogue could now occur between two characters. Playwrights continued to act in their own tragedies, however, until the early part of the fourth century B.C., when Sophocles introduced a third actor. He did not act in his own plays, and eventually other playwrights followed his example.

When awards for actors were introduced into the competitions (approximately 450 B.C.), the separation between actor and playwright was complete. The number of actors remained fixed at three, requiring a single actor to play many roles. The logistics of some plays even required that the same role be played by different actors in different scenes. Elaborate masks and costumes helped the audience identify each character, no matter which actor played the role.

❶ ▶Critical Viewing

Answer: Some students may enjoy watching a performance in the fresh air. Others may express concern over whether the actors could be seen or heard.

Background
The Big Three

The main contenders for the tragedy prize at the dramatic competitions were Aeschylus, Euripides, and Sophocles. Our knowledge of Greek tragedy is based mainly on the work of these three playwrights of the fifth century.

The oldest, Aeschylus, was born to an aristocratic family. As a young man, he earned fame as a soldier fighting against the Persians. He won his first prize for tragedy at approximately forty years of age. (He had been writing for sixteen years.) He won his last prize for tragedy when he was past sixty, with the *Oresteia,* a trilogy considered by many to be his masterpiece. Although Aeschylus wrote ninety plays, only seven of them have survived to the present day.

At the age of twenty-seven, Sophocles defeated Aeschylus in the playwrights' contest with his first tragedy. Like Aeschylus, Sophocles had served in the military. He held political positions as well and was a priest of Asclepius, the Greek god of healing. He was the most conservative of the three great tragedians, both socially and religiously.

Euripides, the youngest of the three, had surprisingly modern attitudes. His characters had greater psychological depth and were more human than the characters of the other two tragedians. In addition, his language was simpler and more colloquial. He disapproved of the prevailing Greek attitudes that subordinated women and glorified war. These beliefs, embedded in the social criticism in his plays, may account for the limited popularity of his plays in ancient Greece. (He won only four prizes in his lifetime.) Today he is acknowledged as one of the most powerful dramatists in history.

Step-by-Step Teaching Guide
for pp. 770–771

Motivation

Write the word *tragedy* in large capital letters on the chalkboard. Encourage students to jot down a list of current events they would describe as tragedies. Then, explain the definition of tragedy as it applies to drama: A person of importance, such as a king or princess, moves from happiness to disaster (and often to death) through some character flaw or error in judgment, or through the forces of fate. Lead a discussion in which students analyze their original suggestions of tragedies in light of this more specific definition. Then, tell them that this play, *Antigone,* is a famous Greek tragedy.

▣ Interest Grabber Video

As an alternative, play *Antigone* on Tape 4 to engage student interest.

❶ Background

Greek Tragedy

Greek tragedy is thought to have come out of dithyrambs—lyric hymns in praise of the Greek god of wine and fertility, Dionysus. Dithyrambs were sung by a chorus and their leader, and took the form of lyric exchanges. Originally spontaneous songs sung at Dionysian festivals, the dithyramb was shaped into a literary form by a seventh-century Greek poet, Arion.

Greek tragedy began as choral performances in which a group of 50 men danced and sang dithyrambs. The poet Thespis (6th-century B.C.) is said to have become the first true actor when he engaged in dialogue with the chorus. In the 5th century, Aeschylus reduced the chorus to twelve members. When Sophocles arrived on the scene, he added three more members to bring the total count to fifteen. Retaining the dithyrambic elements of lyric exchange, the chorus in Greek tragedy served as the collective voice of humanity.

Prepare to Read

Antigone

▣ Take It to the Net

Visit www.phschool.com for interactive activities and instruction related to *Antigone,* including

- background
- graphic organizers
- literary elements
- reading strategies

Preview

Connecting to the Literature

History is full of instances in which political situations cause family conflicts. The Greek playwright Sophocles (säf´ ə klēz´) dramatizes a complex dilemma faced by a young woman: Should she remain loyal to her family and obey the gods, or should she follow the laws of her government?

❶ Background

The chorus, which comments on and explains the action of the play, is an essential element of Greek drama. In an opening song—the *parodos* (par´ əd əs)—the chorus explains the central conflict of the play. Sometimes the chorus speaks in a single voice as a group, and sometimes there is dialogue between two sections of the group.

770 ◆ *Drama*

TEACHING RESOURCES

The following resources can be used to enrich or extend the instruction for pp. 770–771.

Motivation
▣ **Interest Grabber Video,** Tape 4 ▣

Background
▣ **Beyond Literature,** p. 48

▣ *Take It to the Net*
Visit www.phschool.com for background and hotlinks for *Antigone.*

Literary Analysis
▣ **Literary Analysis and Reading Transparencies,** Protagonist and Antagonist, p. 96 ▣

Reading
▣ **Selection Support:** Reading Strategy, p. 191; Build Vocabulary, p. 189

▣ **Literary Analysis and Reading Transparencies,** Questioning Characters' Motives, p. 95

 BLOCK SCHEDULING: Resources marked with this symbol provide varied instruction during 90-minute blocks.

❷ Literary Analysis

Protagonist and Antagonist

The main character in a literary work is called the **protagonist.** This character, who is at the center of the action, is the one with whom the audience most sympathizes. In contrast, the character who is in conflict with the protagonist is the **antagonist.**

In this play, Antigone is the protagonist. She is in conflict with Creon, the antagonist, who is her uncle and also the king.

Connecting Literary Elements

A **character's decision** is often the act that drives the plot of a literary work forward. Both Antigone and Creon make decisions and then refuse to change them. In time, this stubbornness leads to tragic consequences. As you read *Antigone*, keep track of each decision these characters make and observe how these decisions lead inevitably to ruin.

❸ Reading Strategy

Questioning Characters' Motives

To understand the conflict and resolution in any play, **question the characters' motives.** Look at each character's actions or words to determine the reasons that might be behind them. For example, at the beginning of the play, Antigone provokes her sister, Ismene, with this challange:

> And now you can prove what you are:
> A true sister, or a traitor to your family.

By questioning Antigone's motives for this challenge, as well as those of King Creon, you will better understand and appreciate the forces at work in this play. Use a chart like the one shown to record your ideas about characters' motives.

Significant Actions	Motives
Speaks harshly to her sister	

Vocabulary Development

sated (sāt′ əd) *adj.* satisfied or pleased (p. 776)

anarchists (an′ ər kists) *n.* those who disrespect laws or rules (p. 779)

sententiously (sen ten′ shəs lē) *adv.* pointed; expressing much in few words (p. 780)

sultry (sul′ trē) *adj.* oppressively hot or moist; inflamed (p. 781)

transcends (tran sendz′) *v.* goes above or beyond limits; exceeds (p. 787)

Antigone ◆ 771

❷ Literary Analysis

Protagonist and Antagonist

- Tell students that as they read *Antigone*, they will focus on the two main characters who are in conflict in the play—the protagonist and antagonist.

- Read the instruction about protagonist and antagonist together as a class. Remind students that the character in the play for which they will probably feel the most sympathy is the protagonist, Antigone.

- Use the instruction for Connecting Literary Elements to connect the fates of the protagonist and the antagonist to the decisions each makes.

❸ Reading Strategy

Questioning Characters' Motives

- Ask students what *motive* means. **Answer:** A motive is a person's reason for doing something.

- Point out that knowing a character's motives helps us understand the character and also gives us insight into the events taking place.

- As they read, have students keep track of characters' motives by creating charts like the one shown.

Vocabulary Development

- Pronounce each vocabulary word for students, and read the definitions as a class. Have students identify any words with which they are already familiar.

CUSTOMIZE INSTRUCTION FOR UNIVERSAL ACCESS

For Less Proficient Readers	For English Learners	For Advanced Readers
Unfamiliar Greek character names may be difficult for some students. Introduce the cast list, character identification information, and pronunciation guide on p. 772.	Tell students that the action in *Antigone* results when a character decides to act on loyalty to family rather than obeying the law. Ask students to consider the importance in their culture of loyalty to family. Are there situations in which loyalty to family might be less important than some other value?	Remind students that *Antigone* was written more than 2,000 years ago. Ask them to speculate about the qualities of a literary work that continues to be read and performed through the ages. Why would the problems of characters in an ancient play have any relevance to their own lives? Have students share their thoughts.

 E-Teach

Visit E-Teach at www.phschool.com for teachers' essays on how to teach, with questions and answers.

CUSTOMIZE INSTRUCTION
For Verbal/Linguistic Learners

As they would when reading poetry, students should pay attention to the punctuation cues in the play. Punctuation will help them know when a thought begins and ends. Demonstrate by reading one of Antigone's speeches, showing how it can be read aloud in sentence form.

❶ About the Selection

In the first part of the play, Sophocles establishes the main characters and the conflict. Proud and reckless, the fiery princess of Thebes, Antigone, breaks the law to bury her brother, who has been labeled a traitor by the king, her uncle. By so doing, she embarks on a course toward her own destruction and the destruction of those around her. As the play opens, the audience is invited to contrast Antigone with her sister, Ismene, who begs Antigone to be reasonable and accept the law. This contrast is a thread that runs throughout the play.

When Antigone argues her actions with Creon, her uncle and the king, the conflict between human law and divine law is firmly established.

❷ Background
Greek Tragedy

Explain that a prologue to a Greek tragedy is an introductory scene, which may be a monologue or a dialogue. In the prologue, the playwright sets up the situation. In this case, the prologue alerts readers that the sisters have lost two brothers who fought on opposite sides in a battle. One brother has been buried with honors; the other is left unburied by the king's orders.

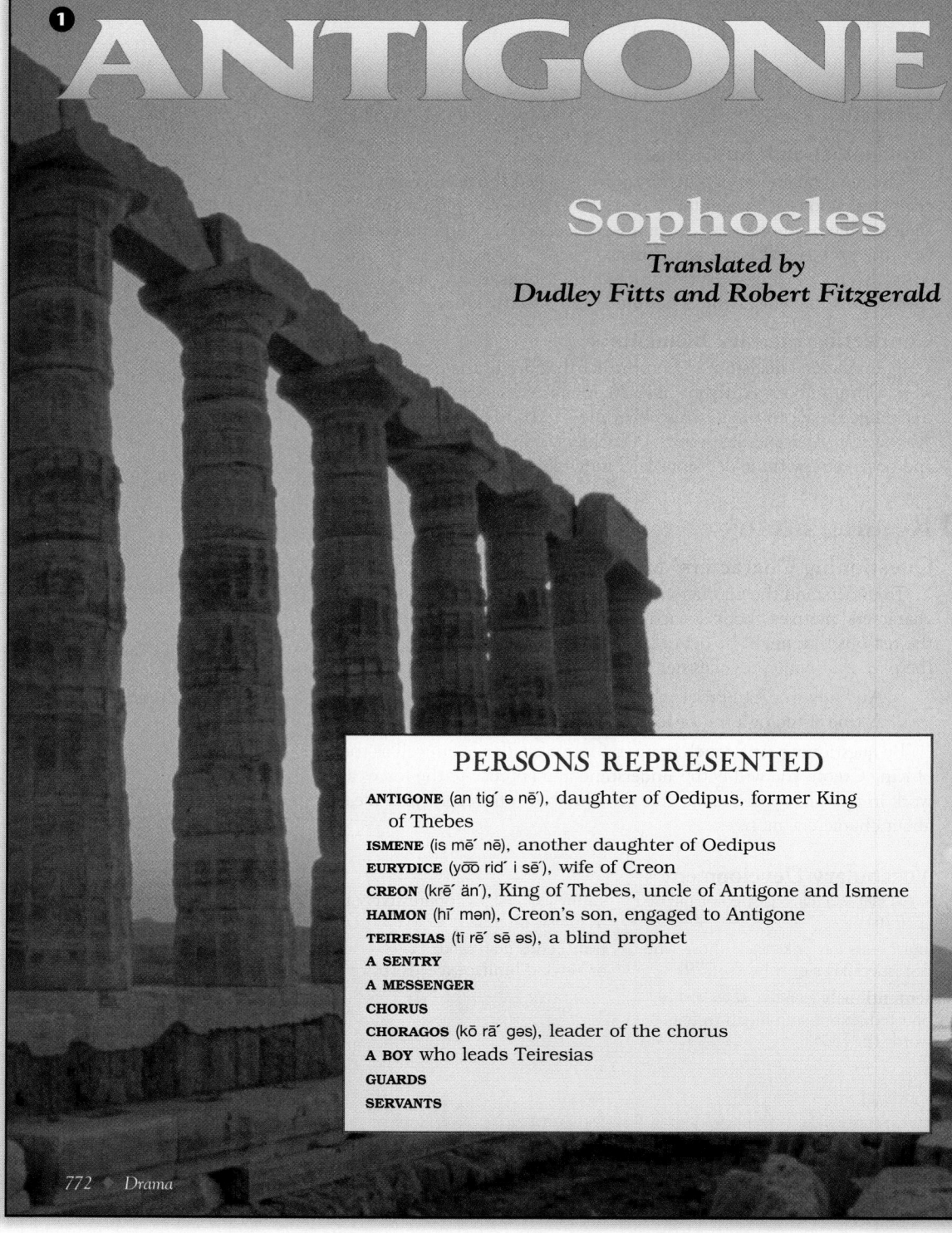

❶ ANTIGONE

Sophocles
Translated by
Dudley Fitts and Robert Fitzgerald

PERSONS REPRESENTED

ANTIGONE (an tig´ ə nē´), daughter of Oedipus, former King of Thebes
ISMENE (is mē´ nē), another daughter of Oedipus
EURYDICE (yōō rid´ i sē´), wife of Creon
CREON (krē´ än´), King of Thebes, uncle of Antigone and Ismene
HAIMON (hī´ mən), Creon's son, engaged to Antigone
TEIRESIAS (tī rē´ sē əs), a blind prophet
A SENTRY
A MESSENGER
CHORUS
CHORAGOS (kō rā´ gəs), leader of the chorus
A BOY who leads Teiresias
GUARDS
SERVANTS

772 *Drama*

TEACHING RESOURCES

The following resources can be used to enrich or extend the instruction for pp. 772–787.

Literary Analysis
📖 **Selection Support:** Literary Analysis, p. 192

Reading
🎧 **Listening to Literature Audiocassettes,** Side 25 ▪
💿 **Listening to Literature Audio CDs,** CD 16 ▪

Extension
Fine Art Transparencies, Volume 1
Art Transparency 15 (Display Art Transparency 15, and have students comment about details in the mosaic that suggest elements of Greek drama. Encourage them to refer to the information on Greek theater on pp. 768–769.)

▪ **BLOCK SCHEDULING:** Resources marked with this symbol provide varied instruction during 90-minute blocks.

Prologue–Scene 2

Scene. *Before the palace of* CREON, *King of Thebes. A central double door, and two lateral doors. A platform extends the length of the façade, and from this platform three steps lead down into the "orchestra," or chorus-ground.*

Time. *Dawn of the day after the repulse of the Argive[1] army from the assault on Thebes.*

Prologue

[ANTIGONE *and* ISMENE *enter from the central door of the Palace.*]

ANTIGONE. Ismene, dear sister,
You would think that we had already suffered enough
For the curse on Oedipus:[2]
I cannot imagine any grief
5   That you and I have not gone through. And now—
Have they told you of the new decree of our King Creon?

ISMENE. I have heard nothing: I know
That two sisters lost two brothers, a double death
In a single hour; and I know that the Argive army
10   Fled in the night; but beyond this, nothing.

ANTIGONE. I thought so. And that is why I wanted you
To come out here with me. There is something we must do.

ISMENE. Why do you speak so strangely?

ANTIGONE. Listen, Ismene:
15   Creon buried our brother Eteocles
With military honors, gave him a soldier's funeral,
And it was right that he should; but Polyneices,
Who fought as bravely and died as miserably,—
They say that Creon has sworn
20   No one shall bury him, no one mourn for him,
But his body must lie in the fields, a sweet treasure
For carrion birds[3] to find as they search for food.
That is what they say, and our good Creon is coming here
To announce it publicly; and the penalty—
25   Stoning to death in the public square!
                       There it is,
And now you can prove what you are:
A true sister, or a traitor to your family.

ISMENE. Antigone, you are mad! What could I possibly do?

◀ **Critical Viewing** What does this temple, dedicated to Poseidon, the god of the sea, suggest about the importance of the gods in ancient Greece? **[Draw Conclusions]**

1. Argive (är´ gīv´) from Argos, the capital of a section of ancient Greece.

2. curse on Oedipus this curse refers to the fate of Oedipus, who was doomed by a decree of the gods to kill his father and marry his mother while ignorant of their true identities.

Literary Analysis
Protagonist and Antagonist What qualities does Antigone show here that help you identify her as the protagonist?

3. carrion (kar´ ē ən) **birds** scavenger birds, such as vultures, that eat the decaying leftovers of another animal's kill.

5 ✓ **Reading Check**
Who are Eteocles and Polyneices?

Antigone, Prologue ◆ 773

---

❸ Literary Analysis
Protagonist and Antagonist

- Read the bracketed passage aloud. Then, ask students what conflict in the play is beginning to take shape.
  Answer: The conflict is between Antigone, who wants to honor her dead brother by burying him, and King Creon, who forbids it.

- Have students answer the Literary Analysis question on p. 773: What qualities does Antigone show here that help you identify her as the protagonist?
  Answer: Antigone sets the action in motion and shows love for her brothers by wanting them both to receive the honors of burial. Because she instigates the action and elicits readers' sympathy through her determination to "do the right thing," students can begin to identify her as the protagonist.

❹ ▶ Critical Viewing

Answer: The temple appears majestic and important. It indicates that the gods were important and honored at the time this temple was built.

❺ ✓ Reading Check

Answer: Eteocles and Polyneices are the dead brothers of Antigone and Ismene.

773

❻ Background

Culture

Antigone's determination to bury her dead brother may be clearer to students if they understand that the Greeks believed that the dead had to be buried before the soul could be at rest. This also explains Antigone's earlier statement that if Ismene doesn't help bury Polyneices, she is a traitor to her family.

❼ Literary Analysis

Protagonist and Antagonist

• Ask students the Literary Analysis question on p. 774: What conflict is outlined by Antigone's words here?
  Answer: Antigone challenges Ismene to defy the law and help her bury their dead brother, Polyneices.

• Then, invite students to identify personality traits that Ismene reveals in this speech that make her unlike Antigone.
  Answer: She is afraid of death; she believes women are weak and subordinate to men; she is afraid of authority.

❽ Reading Strategy

Questioning Characters' Motives

• Ask students to summarize Antigone's personality.
  Answer: She is determined, brave, and loyal to her family.

• Then, ask students the Reading Strategy question on p. 774: Why does Antigone want to bury her brother?
  Answer: Students may suggest that she wants to bury her brother out of family loyalty. She loves Polyneices and wants his body to have an honorable burial. Students should also note Antigone's words, "this crime is holy," and her reference to "the laws of the gods." Divine law is also one of her motives.

---

30   **ANTIGONE.** You must decide whether you will help me or not.

ISMENE. I do not understand you. Help you in what?

ANTIGONE. Ismene, I am going to bury him. Will you come?

❻   **ISMENE.** Bury him! You have just said the new law forbids it.

ANTIGONE. He is my brother. And he is your brother, too.

35   **ISMENE.** But think of the danger! Think what Creon will do!

❼   **ANTIGONE.** Creon is not strong enough to stand in my way.

ISMENE. Ah sister!
       Oedipus died, everyone hating him
       For what his own search brought to light, his eyes
40   Ripped out by his own hand; and Iocaste died,
       His mother and wife at once: she twisted the cords
       That strangled her life; and our two brothers died,
       Each killed by the other's sword. And we are left:
       But oh, Antigone,
45   Think how much more terrible than these
       Our own death would be if we should go against
          Creon
       And do what he has forbidden! We are only women,
       We cannot fight with men, Antigone!
       The law is strong, we must give in to the law
50   In this thing, and in worse. I beg the Dead
       To forgive me, but I am helpless: I must yield
       To those in authority. And I think it is dangerous
          business
       To be always meddling.

ANTIGONE.   If that is what you think,
55   I should not want you, even if you asked to come.
       You have made your choice, you can be what you want to be.
       But I will bury him; and if I must die,
       I say that this crime is holy: I shall lie down
       With him in death, and I shall be as dear
60   To him as he to me.
                           It is the dead,
       Not the living, who make the longest demands;
       We die for ever . . .
                           You may do as you like,
65   Since apparently the laws of the gods mean nothing to you.

ISMENE. They mean a great deal to me; but I have no strength
       To break laws that were made for the public good.

❽   **ANTIGONE.** That must be your excuse, I suppose. But as for me,
       I will bury the brother I love.

70   **ISMENE.**   Antigone,

774 ◆ *Drama*

Literary Analysis
Protagonist and Antagonist What conflict is outlined by Antigone's words here?

Reading Strategy
Questioning Characters' Motives Why does Antigone want to bury her brother?

✺ ENRICHMENT: Art Connection

Temple of Poseidon at Sounion

The photograph on p. 772 shows the Temple of Poseidon at Sounion. Built around 440 B.C., the temple sits on a promontory overlooking the sea, visible to the ships that pass beneath. It is a ruin now, but once it had six columns at each end and thirteen on each side. Archaeologists have found fragments of sculpture near the site that suggest that the front of the temple was decorated with a carved frieze depicting a battle against the Centaurs—wild mythical creatures that had the body of a horse and the arms, chest, and head of a man.

Explain to students that Greek temples fall into three categories based on how the capitals, or tops, of their columns were designed. This temple of Poseidon is *Doric;* that is, each column has a flat rectangular slab on top. Other temples are *Ionic,* with capitals carved in a ram's-horn design, while a third type, *Corinthian,* has capitals carved with a leaf or floral design.

Encourage interested students to do further research to find out more about Greek art and architecture.

I am so afraid for you!

ANTIGONE. You need not be:
You have yourself to consider, after all.

ISMENE. But no one must hear of this, you
must tell no one!

75 I will keep it a secret, I promise!

ANTIGONE. Oh tell it! Tell everyone!
Think how they'll hate you when it all
comes out
If they learn that you knew about it
all the time!

ISMENE. So fiery! You should be cold with
fear.

80 **ANTIGONE.** Perhaps. But I am doing only
what I must.

ISMENE. But can you do it? I say that
you cannot.

ANTIGONE. Very well: when my strength
gives out, I shall do no more.

ISMENE. Impossible things should
not be tried at all.

ANTIGONE. Go away, Ismene:

85 I shall be hating you soon, and the dead will too,
For your words are hateful. Leave me my foolish plan:
I am not afraid of the danger; if it means death,
It will not be the worst of deaths—death without honor.

ISMENE. Go then, if you feel that you must.

90 You are unwise,
But a loyal friend indeed to those who love you.

[*Exit into the Palace.* ANTIGONE *goes off, left. Enter the* CHORUS.]

 Parodos

CHORUS. [STROPHE 1]
Now the long blade of the sun, lying
Level east to west, touches with glory
Thebes of the Seven Gates.[4] Open, unlidded
Eye of golden day! O marching light
5 Across the eddy and rush of Dirce's stream,[5]
Striking the white shields of the enemy
Thrown headlong backward from the blaze of morning!

CHORAGOS. Polyneices their commander
Roused them with windy phrases,
10 He the wild eagle screaming

9 ▲ Critical Viewing
What emotions do you
see portrayed by
Antigone and Ismene in
this picture? [**Analyze**]

4. Seven Gates The city of
Thebes was defended by
walls containing seven
entrances.

5. Dirce's (dur´ sēz) **stream**
small river near Thebes into
which the body of Dirce, one
of the city's early queens,
was thrown after her murder.

11 ☑ Reading Check
What does Antigone want
her sister to help her do?

Antigone, Parodos ◆ 775

---

9 ▶ Critical Viewing
Possible response: Antigone looks
adamant and determined, while
Ismene looks beseeching.

10 Background
Literature
The chorus is an essential element of
Greek drama. This group comments
on and may explain the action of the
play. Sometimes the chorus speaks
with a single voice as a group, sometimes in dialogue between two sections of the group, and sometimes
with only one voice, that of the
choragos, the leader of the chorus.

In an opening song—the *parados*
(par´ əd əs)—the chorus explains the
central conflict of the play. Between
scenes, the chorus recites an *ode*.
During the ode, the group moves
from right to left, singing the
strophe. Then the chorus members
move in the opposite direction
during the *antistrophe*.

11 ☑ Reading Check
Answer: Antigone wants her sister
to help her bury their dead brother,
Polyneices.

CUSTOMIZE INSTRUCTION FOR UNIVERSAL ACCESS

For Gifted/Talented Students	For Advanced Readers
Remind students that the action in *Antigone* is caused by two characters who make decisions and take stands that will have profound consequences. Encourage students to create two versions of a skit about someone taking a stand on an issue. In one version the person should yield gracefully when shown to be wrong about the issue; in the other version, the person should not admit to making a mistake. The skits should include appropriate consequences.	Antigone believes so strongly in her brother's right to a burial that she is willing to put her life in danger—by her actions she makes the choice to face the consequences. Ask students to research and write about people from recent history who have chosen to face potentially dire consequences rather than back down from a stand they believed to be right. Suggest to students civil rights leaders, such as Martin Luther King Jr., Nelson Mandela, and Rosa Parks.

Questioning Characters' Motives

Insults above our land,
His wings their shields of snow,
His crest their marshalled helms.

    CHORUS.   [ANTISTROPHE 1]
15   Against our seven gates in a yawning ring
    The famished spears came onward in the night;
    But before his jaws were <u>sated</u> with our blood,
    Or pinefire took the garland of our towers,
    He was thrown back; and as he turned, great Thebes—
20   No tender victim for his noisy power—
    Rose like a dragon behind him, shouting war.

    CHORAGOS. For God hates utterly
    The bray of bragging tongues;
    And when he beheld their smiling,
    Their swagger of golden helms,
25   The frown of his thunder blasted
    Their first man from our walls.

    CHORUS.   [STROPHE 2]
    We heard his shout of triumph high in the air
    Turn to a scream; far out in a flaming arc
    He fell with his windy torch, and the earth struck him.
30   And others storming in fury no less than his
    Found shock of death in the dusty joy of battle.

    CHORAGOS. Seven captains at seven gates
    Yielded their clanging arms to the god
    That bends the battle-line and breaks it.
35   These two only, brothers in blood,
    Face to face in matchless rage,
    Mirroring each the other's death,
    Clashed in long combat.

    CHORUS.   [ANTISTROPHE 2]
    But now in the beautiful morning of victory
40   Let Thebes of the many chariots sing for joy!
    With hearts for dancing we'll take leave of war:
    Our temples shall be sweet with hymns of praise,
    And the long night shall echo with our chorus.

Scene 1

    CHORAGOS. But now at last our new King is coming:
    Creon of Thebes, Menoikeus'[6] son.
    In this auspicious dawn of his reign
    What are the new complexities
5   That shifting Fate has woven for him?
    What is his counsel? Why has he summoned
    The old men to hear him?

Side notes:

sated (sāt′ əd) *adj.* satisfied or pleased

**Reading Strategy
Questioning Characters' Motives** What motivates the brothers to fight to the death?

6. Menoikeus' (me noĭ′ kē əs)

✹ ENRICHMENT: History Connection

Seven Against Thebes

The battle known as "Seven Against Thebes" is renowned in legend and forms the basis for plays by Aeschylus and Euripides. According to legend, Oedipus' sons had agreed to occupy the throne on alternate years. To get around the agreement, during his year of reign, Eteocles banished his brother to Argos, where Polyneices married the daughter of the king. He gathered an army, which he led with six Argive heroes and returned to attack Thebes.

Each of the seven Argive leaders stationed himself at one of the seven gates that led to Thebes. In response, Eteocles sent six generals to man each of six gates, while he himself went to the gate where Polyneices waited. In the ensuing battle, six of the seven against Thebes were slain, including Polyneices, who killed his brother before succumbing himself.

[*Enter* CREON *from the Palace, center. He addresses the* CHORUS *from the top step.*]

CREON. Gentlemen: I have the honor to inform you that our Ship of
State, which recent storms have threatened to destroy, has
10 come safely to harbor at last, guided by the merciful wisdom of
Heaven. I have summoned you here this morning because I know
that I can depend upon you: your devotion to King Laïos was
absolute; you never hesitated in your duty to our late ruler
Oedipus; and when Oedipus died, your loyalty was transferred to
15 his children. Unfortunately, as you know, his two sons, the
princes Eteocles and Polyneices, have killed each other in battle;
and I, as the next in blood, have succeeded to the full power of
the throne.

I am aware, of course, that no Ruler can expect complete loyalty
20 from his subjects until he has been tested in office. Nevertheless,
I say to you at the very outset that I have nothing but contempt
for the kind of Governor who is afraid, for whatever reason, to
follow the course that he knows is best for the State; and as for
the man who sets private friendship above the public welfare,—I
25 have no use for him, either. I call God to witness that if
I saw my country headed for ruin, I should not be afraid to
speak out plainly; and I need hardly remind you that I would
never have any dealings with an enemy of the people. No one
values friendship more highly than I; but we must remember
30 that friends made at the risk of wrecking our Ship are
not real friends at all.

These are my principles, at any rate, and that is why I have
made the following decision concerning the sons of
Oedipus: Eteocles, who died as a man should die,
35 fighting for his country, is to be buried with full
military honors, with all the ceremony that is
usual when the greatest heroes die; but his
brother Polyneices, who broke his exile to
come back with fire and sword against his
40 native city and the shrines of his fathers' gods,
whose one idea was to spill the blood of his
blood and sell his own people into slavery—
Polyneices, I say, is to have no burial: no man
is to touch him or say the least prayer for him;
45 he shall lie on the plain, unburied; and the
birds and the scavenging dogs can do with him
whatever they like.

This is my command, and you can see the wisdom
behind it. As long as I am King, no traitor is
50 going to be honored with the loyal man. But whoever shows by word and deed that he is on the
side of the State,—he shall have my respect while
he is living, and my reverence when he is dead.

13 ☑ Reading Check
What event does the chorus describe?

15 ▼ Critical Viewing
How does Creon's body language reflect his status as King? **[Interpret]**

Antigone, Scene 1 ◆ 777

13 ☑ Reading Check
Answer: The chorus is describing the battle during which the brothers Polyneices and Eteocles killed each other.

14 Critical Thinking
Predict
• Ask students what Antigone planned to do to honor her dead brother Polyneices.
Answer: She planned to bury him.
• Based on his words, how do students predict Creon will react to Antigone's disobedience?
Answer: Most students will probably predict that Creon will treat Antigone as harshly as he would any other disobedient subject. His words "the man who sets private friendship above the public welfare" and "friends made at the risk of wrecking our Ship are not real friends at all" are indications that he does not allow his personal relationships to influence his official decisions.

15 ▶ Critical Viewing
Answer: Creon's body language shows that he takes his authority seriously and expects his commands to be obeyed.

CUSTOMIZE INSTRUCTION FOR UNIVERSAL ACCESS

For Less Proficient Readers	For Gifted/Talented Students	For Advanced Readers
Ask students to summarize what they have learned from the Prologue. Antigone and Ismene had two brothers who killed each other in battle. One was buried with honors, but their uncle, King Creon, will not allow the other to be buried. Antigone wants to bury him herself, but her sister, Ismene, is afraid to break the law.	Have students imagine that the dead brother Polyneices can speak to Antigone. What does he advise her to do? Does he want her to risk her life in order to bury him? Have students write down and then discuss what Polyneices might say to Antigone.	Ask students to point out the irony of Antistrophe 2. They should note that the Chorus is announcing the beginning of an era of peace and prosperity in Thebes. However, even more catastrophes are about to occur.

CHORAGOS. If that is your will, Creon son of Menoikeus,

You have the right to enforce it: we are yours.

55 CREON. That is my will. Take care that you do your part.

CHORAGOS. We are old men: let the younger ones carry it out.

CREON. I do not mean that: the sentries have been appointed.

CHORAGOS. Then what is it that you would have us do?

CREON. You will give no support to whoever breaks this law.

60 CHORAGOS. Only a crazy man is in love with death!

CREON. And death it is; yet money talks, and the wisest
    Have sometimes been known to count a few coins too many.

[Enter SENTRY from left.]

SENTRY. I'll not say that I'm out of breath from running, King,
    because every time I stopped to think about what I have to tell
65   you, I felt like going back. And all the time a voice kept saying,
    "You fool, don't you know you're walking straight into trou-
    ble?"; and then another voice: "Yes, but if you let somebody
    else get the news to Creon first, it will be even worse than that
    for you!" But good sense won out, at least I hope it was good
70   sense, and here I am with a story that makes no sense at all;
    but I'll tell it anyhow, because, as they say, what's going to
    happen's going to happen, and—

CREON. Come to the point. What have you to say?

SENTRY. I did not do it. I did not see who did it. You must not
    punish me for what someone else has done.

75 CREON. A comprehensive defense! More effective, perhaps,
    If I knew its purpose. Come: what is it?

SENTRY. A dreadful thing . . . I don't know how to put
    it—

CREON. Out with it!

SENTRY.   Well, then;
80   The dead man—
                Polyneices—

[*Pause. The* SENTRY *is overcome, fumbles for words.*
CREON *waits impassively.*]

                      out there—
                              someone,—
    New dust on the slimy flesh!

                 [*Pause. No sign from* CREON.]

Someone has given it burial that way, and

778 ◆ Drama

Gone . . .

[*Long pause.* CREON *finally speaks with deadly control.*]

85 **CREON.** And the man who dared do this?

SENTRY.   I swear I
Do not know! You must believe me!
                                                              Listen:
The ground was dry, not a sign of digging, no,
90 Not a wheeltrack in the dust, no trace of anyone.
It was when they relieved us this morning: and one of them,
The corporal, pointed to it.
                                There it was,
The strangest—
95   Look:
The body, just mounded over with light dust: you see?
Not buried really, but as if they'd covered it
Just enough for the ghost's peace. And no sign
Of dogs or any wild animal that had been there.

100 And then what a scene there was! Every man of us
Accusing the other: we all proved the other man did it,
We all had proof that we could not have done it.
We were ready to take hot iron in our hands,
Walk through fire, swear by all the gods,
105 *It was not I!*
I do not know who it was, but it was not I!

[CREON'S *rage has been mounting steadily, but the* SENTRY *is too intent
upon his story to notice it.*]

And then, when this came to nothing, someone said
A thing that silenced us and made us stare
Down at the ground: you had to be told the news,
110 And one of us had to do it! We threw the dice,
And the bad luck fell to me. So here I am,
No happier to be here than you are to have me:
Nobody likes the man who brings bad news.

CHORAGOS. I have been wondering, King: can it be that the gods
                        have done this?

CREON.
115 Stop! [*Furiously*]
Must you doddering wrecks
Go out of your heads entirely? "The gods!"
Intolerable!
The gods favor this corpse? Why? How had he served them?
120 Tried to loot their temples, burn their images,
Yes, and the whole State, and its laws with it!
Is it your senile opinion that the gods love to honor bad men?
A pious thought!—

Reading Strategy
**Questioning Characters'
Motives** What would the
sentry's motives have been
for proving that someone
else buried Polyneices?

Reading Strategy
**Questioning Characters'
Motives** Why does
Choragos suggest that
the gods might have
buried Polyneices?

㉑ ✓**Reading Check**

What does the sentry say
has happened to the body
of Polyneices?

Antigone, Scene 1 ◆ *779*

㉙ Reading Strategy

**Questioning Characters'
Motives**

• Ask students what punishment
Creon had promised to anyone
who buried Polyneices.
Answer: Creon had promised that
anyone who buried Polyneices
would be stoned to death.

• Ask students the Reading Strategy
question on p. 779: What would
the sentry's motives have been for
proving that someone else had
buried Polyneices?
Answer: All the sentries were motivated by the fear of death. They
believe that Creon's threat was not
idle.

㉚ Reading Strategy

**Questioning Characters'
Motives**

• Ask students whether Choragos is
in any danger of being suspected
of burying Polyneices.
Answer: No; Choragos was with
Creon when Polyneices was
buried.

• Then, ask students the Reading
Strategy question on p. 779: Why
does Choragos suggest that the
gods might have buried
Polyneices?
Answer: Choragos is hinting that
the gods are displeased with
Creon and are siding with
Antigone.

㉛ ✓**Reading Check**

Answer: The sentry tells Creon that
Polyneices' body had been covered
over with dust.

CUSTOMIZE INSTRUCTION FOR UNIVERSAL ACCESS

For Special Needs Students	For Less Proficient Readers	For Gifted/Talented Students
Have students listen to the section of the play covered so far on the **Listening to Literature** Audiocassettes or CDs. Pause periodically to clarify plot developments and characters' motives.	Ask students to write a paragraph describing Creon. What occupation do they think Creon would excel at in modern society? What would he do poorly?	Challenge students to write a news article about the story told in the drama. Remind students that they need to find details in the play that answer the questions *Who, What, When, Where,* and *Why.*

22 Literary Analysis

Character's Decision

- Ask students what Creon has accused the sentry of doing.
  Answer: The king accuses the sentry of burying Polyneices in exchange for money.

- Then, ask students what Creon's speech tells them about his character.
  Answer: Because Creon cannot yet punish the person who actually did the burying, he takes out his anger on the messenger. This suggests that Creon is allowing his fear and pride to lead him into rash actions.

- Have students answer the Literary Analysis question on p. 780: What decision does Creon make here that might have antagonistic consequences?
  Answer: Creon decides to punish the person who buried Polyneices.

23 Background

Religion

In ancient Greek mythology, a group of gods ruled heaven and earth, which is why the sentry swears by all the gods. When characters speak of a single "God," they mean Zeus, king of the gods.

No, from the very beginning
125   There have been those who have whispered together,
Stiff-necked <u>anarchists</u>, putting their heads together,
Scheming against me in alleys. These are the men,
And they have bribed my own guard to do this thing.

Money!   [*Sententiously*]
130   There's nothing in the world so demoralizing as money.
Down go your cities,
Homes gone, men gone, honest hearts corrupted,
Crookedness of all kinds, and all for money!

[*To* SENTRY]
But you—!
135   I swear by God and by the throne of God,
The man who has done this thing shall pay for it!
Find that man, bring him here to me, or your death
Will be the least of your problems: I'll string you up
Alive, and there will be certain ways to make you
140   Discover your employer before you die;
And the process may teach you a lesson you seem to have
     missed:
The dearest profit is sometimes all too dear:
That depends on the source. Do you understand me?
A fortune won is often misfortune.

145   SENTRY. King, may I speak?

CREON.   Your very voice distresses me.

SENTRY. Are you sure that it is my voice, and not your conscience?

CREON. By God, he wants to analyze me now!

SENTRY. It is not what I say, but what has been done, that hurts
        you.

150   CREON. You talk too much.

SENTRY.   Maybe; but I've done nothing.

CREON. Sold your soul for some silver: that's all you've done.

SENTRY. How dreadful it is when the right judge judges wrong!

CREON. Your figures of speech
155   May entertain you now; but unless you bring me the man,
You will get little profit from them in the end.

[*Exit* CREON *into the Palace.*]

SENTRY. "Bring me the man"—!
I'd like nothing better than bringing him the man!
But bring him or not, you have seen the last of me here.
160   At any rate, I am safe!

anarchists (an´ ər kists) *n.* those who disrespect laws or rules

sententiously (sen ten´ shəs lē) *adv.* pointed; expressing much in few words

Literary Analysis
Protagonist and Antagonist and Characters' Decision What decision does Creon make here that might have antagonistic consequences?

ENRICHMENT: Cultural Conncetion

The Golden Age of Greece

Sophocles lived during the "Golden Age of Greece" (461-431 B.C.). During this time, Athens was Greece's cultural center and its most powerful state. Many Athenians were wealthy and had leisure time to pursue interests such as philosophy and the arts. Many of the great art treasures created during this period may still be seen in museums throughout the world.

The Athenian political structure was based on the city-state, or *polis.* The governing body consisted of nine rulers called *archons,* ten generals, a citizen assembly, and ten executive committees. People's law courts administered justice.

In 431 B.C., surrounding city-states led by Sparta challenged Athenian power. The resulting conflict, the Peloponnesian Wars, led to the defeat of Athens. Sparta became Greece's most powerful city-state, but Athens remained Greece's intellectual center.

[Exit SENTRY.]

Ode 1

CHORUS.   [STROPHE 1]

    Numberless are the world's wonders, but none
    More wonderful than man; the stormgray sea
    Yields to his prows, the huge crests bear him high;
    Earth, holy and inexhaustible, is graven
5   With shining furrows where his plows have gone
    Year after year, the timeless labor of stallions.

                      [ANTISTROPHE 1]

    The lightboned birds and beasts that cling to cover,
    The lithe fish lighting their reaches of dim water,
    All are taken, tamed in the net of his mind;
10   The lion on the hill, the wild horse windy-maned,
    Resign to him; and his blunt yoke has broken
    The <u>sultry</u> shoulders of the mountain bull.

                    [STROPHE 2]

    Words also, and thought as rapid as air,
    He fashions to his good use; statecraft is his,
15   And his the skill that deflects the arrows of snow,
    The spears of winter rain: from every wind
    He has made himself secure—from all but one:
    In the late wind of death he cannot stand.

                  [ANTISTROPHE 2]

    O clear intelligence, force beyond all measure!
20   O fate of man, working both good and evil!
    When the laws are kept, how proudly his city stands!
    When the laws are broken, what of his city then?
    Never may the anarchic man find rest at my hearth,
    Never be it said that my thoughts are his thoughts.

Scene 2

        [Re-enter SENTRY leading ANTIGONE.]

CHORAGOS. What does this mean? Surely this
        captive woman
  Is the Princess, Antigone. Why should she
        be taken?

SENTRY. Here is the one who did it!
      We caught her
  In the very act of burying
      him.—Where is Creon?

5 **CHORAGOS.** Just coming from
      the house.

        [Enter CREON, center.]

sultry (sul′ trē) *adj.* oppressively hot or moist; inflamed

24 ✔**Reading Check**
What does the sentry want Creon to do?

25 ▼**Critical Viewing** How does Antigone appear to be feeling in this picture? **[Analyze]**

Antigone, Scene 2 ◆ 781

---

24 ✔**Reading Check**
Answer: The sentry wants Creon to believe him when he says he did not conspire to bury Polyneices.

25 ▶**Critical Viewing**
Possible response: Although grief-stricken, Antigone appears to be proud and defiant.

26 **Reading Strategy**
Questioning Characters' Motives

- Ask students why Antigone buried Polyneices the first time.
  Answer: She buried Polyneices out of love and loyalty—she wanted to honor him as her brother and to assure that his soul found rest.

- Then, ask students why Antigone buried her brother for the second time.
  Answer: Her work of burying him the first time was undone. She had the same motives for burying him the second time.

Questioning Characters' Motives

- Ask a volunteer to read the bracketed passage. Then, ask students to compare the sentry's present demeanor with his earlier one when he came to report that someone had buried Polyneices.
Answer: This time, the sentry seems confident and almost arrogant. This is in contrast to the fearful demeanor he presented the last time he came before the king.

- Then, ask the Reading Strategy question on p. 782: What motivates the sentry to return with Antigone despite Creon's threats?
Answer: The sentry is only too glad to prove the king wrong in suspecting that he had anything to do with burying Polyneices. He feels he no longer has anything to fear from the king.

㉘ Literary Analysis

Protagonist and Antagonist

- Read the bracketed passage aloud. Then, ask students: To what does the sentry compare Antigone?
Answer: He compares Antigone to a mother bird who is grieving because her babies have been taken from her.

- Ask students why the sentry compares Antigone to a mournful mother bird.
Answer: The sentry wants to show that Antigone acted out of love.

▶ Monitor Progress Ask the Literary Analysis question on p. 782: How does the sentry's description here of Antigone paint her in a positive light?
Answer: It reinforces that Antigone's motive is love for her brother rather than rebelliousness. Her repetition of the religious ritual indicates that she is also motivated by loyalty to divine law.

CREON.   What has happened?
Why have you come back so soon?

SENTRY.   [*Expansively*]
                    O King,
A man should never be too sure of anything:

10   I would have sworn
That you'd not see me here again: your anger
Frightened me so, and the things you threatened me with;
But how could I tell then
That I'd be able to solve the case so soon?

15   No dice-throwing this time: I was only too glad to come!

Here is this woman. She is the guilty one:
We found her trying to bury him.
Take her, then; question her; judge her as you will.
I am through with the whole thing now, and glad of it.

20   **CREON.** But this is Antigone! Why have you brought her here?

SENTRY. She was burying him, I tell you!

CREON. [*Severely*]   Is this the truth?

SENTRY. I saw her with my own eyes. Can I say more?

CREON. The details: come, tell me quickly!

25   **SENTRY.**   It was like this:
After those terrible threats of yours, King,
We went back and brushed the dust away from the body.
The flesh was soft by now, and stinking,
So we sat on a hill to windward and kept guard.

30   No napping this time! We kept each other awake.
But nothing happened until the white round sun
Whirled in the center of the round sky over us:
Then, suddenly,
A storm of dust roared up from the earth, and the sky

35   Went out, the plain vanished with all its trees
In the stinging dark. We closed our eyes and endured it.
The whirlwind lasted a long time, but it passed;
And then we looked, and there was Antigone!
I have seen

40   A mother bird come back to a stripped nest, heard
Her crying bitterly a broken note or two
For the young ones stolen. Just so, when this girl
Found the bare corpse, and all her love's work wasted,
She wept, and cried on heaven to damn the hands

45   That had done this thing.
                          And then she brought more dust
And sprinkled wine three times for her brother's ghost.

Reading Strategy
Questioning Characters' Motives What motivates the sentry to return with Antigone despite Creon's threats?

Literary Analysis
Protagonist and Antagonist How does the sentry's description here of Antigone paint her in a positive light?

☀ **ENRICHMENT: Performing Arts Connection**

The Greek Theater

Remind students that all the characters they have met so far would have been played by only three actors (all men) in the original ancient Greek performances. Have students review the play to this point and realize that, except for the chorus, there are usually only two characters on stage at a time. Encourage students to examine the play to see how the roles might have been broken up. For instance, point out that the actor who plays Antigone cannot also play Creon, since they are on stage at the same time. For more on Greek theater, see **Beyond Literature**, p. 48. Suggest that interested students find out more about the history of Greek drama and the types of costumes, masks, and stage settings that were often used.

We ran and took her at once. She was not afraid,
Not even when we charged her with what she had done.

50 She denied nothing.
                                 And this was a comfort to me,
And some uneasiness: for it is a good thing
To escape from death, but it is no great pleasure
To bring death to a friend.

55   Yet I always say
There is nothing so comfortable as your own safe skin!

CREON. [*Slowly, dangerously*] And you, Antigone,
You with your head hanging,—do you confess this thing?

ANTIGONE. I do. I deny nothing.

60 CREON. [*To* SENTRY]   You may go.

                                        [*Exit* SENTRY.]

[*To* ANTIGONE] Tell me, tell me briefly:
Had you heard my proclamation touching this matter?

ANTIGONE. It was public. Could I help hearing it?

CREON. And yet you dared defy the law.

65 ANTIGONE.   I dared.
It was not God's proclamation. That final Justice
That rules the world below makes no such laws.

Your edict, King, was strong,
But all your strength is weakness itself against

70 The immortal unrecorded laws of God.
They are not merely now: they were, and shall be,
Operative forever, beyond man utterly.

I knew I must die, even without your decree:
I am only mortal. And if I must die

75 Now, before it is my time to die,
Surely this is no hardship: can anyone
Living, as I live, with evil all about me,
Think Death less than a friend? This death of mine
Is of no importance; but if I had left my brother

80 Lying in death unburied, I should have suffered.
Now I do not.
                        You smile at me. Ah Creon,
Think me a fool, if you like; but it may well be
That a fool convicts me of folly.

85 CHORAGOS. Like father, like daughter: both headstrong, deaf to
                        reason!
She has never learned to yield.

CREON.   She has much to learn.
The inflexible heart breaks first, the toughest iron

Antigone, Scene 2 ◆ 783

Literary Analysis

Protagonist and Antagonist How does this scene reinforce the audience's sympathy for Antigone?

---

30 ✔ Reading Check

What is Antigone's response to the sentry when she is charged?

---

② Literary Analysis
Protagonist and Antagonist

- Ask four volunteers each to read a stanza of Antigone's speech. Then, ask what qualities Antigone shows in her speech.
  Answer: She shows bravery in her willingness to do what she feels is right, even though she will be put to death for it.

- Have students answer the Literary Analysis question on p. 783: How does this scene reinforce the audience's sympathy for Antigone?
  Answer: The audience is likely to feel sympathy and admiration for Antigone in her determination to do the right thing, especially because she acts out of loyalty to her family.

③ ✔ Reading Check

Answer: When the sentry charges Antigone with burying Polyneices, Antigone denies nothing.

CUSTOMIZE INSTRUCTION FOR UNIVERSAL ACCESS

For Gifted/Talented Students	For Advanced Readers
Have students role-play a scene between Creon and Ismene in which Ismene pleads for Creon to show mercy toward Antigone. How would Ismene justify Antigone's actions? How would she explain that Antigone meant no disrespect for Creon but was only showing her love for Polyneices and her respect for divine law? Encourage students to perform their skits for the class.	Imagine that you are Antigone. Write a letter to your sister Ismene telling her about your burial of Polyneices. What satisfaction did it give you? What would you say to Ismene about her refusal to help you? Can you forgive her, or will her refusal to participate become a continuing barrier between you and Ismene?

- Read the bracketed passage aloud. Ask students what transgressions Creon accuses Antigone of committing.

  Answer: He accuses Antigone of breaking the law and boasting about it.

- Then, ask the Reading Strategy question on p. 784: What additional motive beyond upholding the law does Creon reveal here?

  Answer: Creon feels that if he does not punish Antigone, he will be perceived as a weak leader.

32 Literary Analysis

Protagonist and Antagonist

- Ask students why Creon believes that Antigone's death will give him "everything."

  Answer: Creon feels that her death will show his strength and that it will eliminate the challenge to his authority.

- Then, ask the Literary Analysis question on p. 784: Which details in this scene solidify Antigone's role as protagonist and Creon's role as antagonist?

  Answer: Antigone says that the people agree with her, but they are too afraid to speak up because they fear Creon. This confirms that Antigone is sympathetic and that Creon is harsh and cruel.

Cracks first, and the wildest horses bend their necks
90   At the pull of the smallest curb.
                                         Pride? In a slave?
      This girl is guilty of a double insolence,
      Breaking the given laws and boasting of it.
      Who is the man here,
95   She or I, if this crime goes unpunished?
      Sister's child, or more than sister's child,
      Or closer yet in blood—she and her sister
      Win bitter death for this!

[*To* SERVANTS]   Go, some of you,
100   Arrest Ismene. I accuse her equally.
      Bring her: you will find her sniffling in the house there.

      Her mind's a traitor: crimes kept in the dark
      Cry for light, and the guardian brain shudders;
      But how much worse than this
105   Is brazen boasting of barefaced anarchy!

      ANTIGONE. Creon, what more do you want than my death?

      CREON.   Nothing.
      That gives me everything.

      ANTIGONE.   Then I beg you: kill me.
110   This talking is a great weariness: your words
      Are distasteful to me, and I am sure that mine
      Seem so to you. And yet they should not seem so:
      I should have praise and honor for what I have done.
      All these men here would praise me
115   Were their lips not frozen shut with fear of you.

                                                [*Bitterly*]
      Ah the good fortune of kings,
      Licensed to say and do whatever they please!

      CREON. You are alone here in that opinion.

      ANTIGONE. No, they are with me. But they keep their tongues in
                leash.

120   CREON. Maybe. But you are guilty, and they are not.

      ANTIGONE. There is no guilt in reverence for the dead.

      CREON. But Eteocles—was he not your brother too?

      ANTIGONE. My brother too.

      CREON.   And you insult his memory?

125   ANTIGONE. [*Softly*] The dead man would not say that I insult it.

      CREON. He would: for you honor a traitor as much as him.

      ANTIGONE. His own brother, traitor or not, and equal in blood.

784 ◆ Drama

Reading Strategy
Questioning Characters'
Motives What additional motive beyond upholding the law does Creon reveal here?

Literary Analysis
Protagonist and Antagonist Which details in this scene solidify Antigone's role as protagonist and Creon's role as antagonist?

✹ ENRICHMENT: Architecture Connection

Amphitheater

Sophocles' tragedies were formally performed in amphitheaters, open-air structures built expressly for public performances. (See the photograph on p. 772.) *Amphi-* means "on both sides," or "around," and an amphitheater is designed to place the audience on tiers of seats around the action of a play. The bowl-like structure of Greek amphitheaters resulted in remarkable acoustic properties; audiences could hear the actors' voices clearly, even when they spoke quietly.

A typical amphitheater might seat the audience in a semicircle facing the *proscenium,* or the front of the stage. At either side between audience and stage would be a corridor called a *parados,* through which the chorus might enter.

The most famous amphitheater in the world, the Coliseum, is Roman, not Greek. Roman amphitheaters were often built to house gladiatorial contests rather than dramas.

CREON. He made war on his country. Eteocles defended it.

ANTIGONE. Nevertheless, there are honors due all the dead.

130 **CREON.** But not the same for the wicked as for the just.

ANTIGONE. Ah Creon, Creon,
    Which of us can say what the gods hold wicked?

CREON. An enemy is an enemy, even dead.

ANTIGONE. It is my nature to join in love, not hate.

135 **CREON.** [*Finally losing patience*] Go join them, then; if you must
        have your love,
    Find it in hell!

CHORAGOS. But see, Ismene comes:

                [*Enter* ISMENE, *guarded.*]

    Those tears are sisterly, the cloud
    That shadows her eyes rains down gentle sorrow.

140 **CREON.** You too, Ismene,
    Snake in my ordered house, sucking my blood
    Stealthily—and all the time I never knew
    That these two sisters were aiming at my throne!
                           Ismene,
145   Do you confess your share in this crime, or deny it?
    Answer me.

ISMENE. Yes, if she will let me say so. I am guilty.

ANTIGONE. [*Coldly*] No, Ismene. You have no right to say so.
    You would not help me, and I will not have you help me.

150 **ISMENE.** But now I know what you meant; and I am here
    To join you, to take my share of punishment.

ANTIGONE. The dead man and the gods who rule the dead
    Know whose act this was. Words are not friends.

ISMENE. Do you refuse me, Antigone? I want to die with you:
    I too have a duty that I must discharge to the dead.

155 **ANTIGONE.** You shall not lessen my death by sharing it.

ISMENE. What do I care for life when you are dead?

ANTIGONE. Ask Creon. You're always hanging on his opinions.

ISMENE. You are laughing at me. Why, Antigone?

ANTIGONE. It's a joyless laughter, Ismene.

160 **ISMENE.**   But can I do nothing?

ANTIGONE. Yes. Save yourself. I shall not envy you.
    There are those who will praise you; I shall have honor, too.

Reading Strategy
Questioning Characters'
Motives Why does
Ismene now want to share
the guilt for burying
Polyneices?

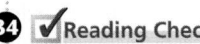 **Reading Check**

Who does Antigone say
agrees with her decision
to bury her brother?

Antigone, Scene 2 ◆ 785

㉝ Reading Strategy

Questioning Characters'
Motives

- Ask students to recall Ismene's
  response earlier in the play when
  Antigone asked for her help in
  burying their brother.
  Answer: Ismene refused to break
  the law by helping Antigone.

- Ask students what Ismene now
  wants to do.
  Answer: Ismene now wants to
  share the guilt for Antigone's
  crime.

- Then, ask the Reading Strategy
  question on p. 785: Why does
  Ismene now want to share the
  guilt for burying Polyneices?
  Answer: Ismene may feel guilty for
  not supporting her sister, or perhaps she feels guilty for not obeying the law of the gods.

㉞ ✔Reading Check

Answer: Antigone says that the men
of the chorus agree with her decision to bury her brother.

CUSTOMIZE INSTRUCTION FOR UNIVERSAL ACCESS

For English Learners	For Advanced Students
Have students put into a timeline the events leading up to Antigone's arrest and sentencing. Remind students that even events that occur offstage must be noted. Have students use their timeline to prompt them as they summarize the play.	Have students write character analyses of Antigone and Creon, highlighting the qualities of each that contribute to the conflict between them. Ask students to describe a quality that, if possessed by either Creon or Antigone, might have defused the conflict.

• Ask students to contrast the positions of Antigone and Ismene now and at the beginning of the play.
Answer: They are exactly opposite. At the beginning of the play, Antigone asked Ismene for her help in burying their brother, but Ismene refused. Now, Ismene asks Antigone to let her share in the guilt for burying Polyneices, but Antigone refuses.

• Then, ask students the Reading Strategy question on p. 786: Why does Antigone reject Ismene's wish to share in the blame?
Answer: Antigone may not want to give Ismene the satisfaction of making up for her earlier refusal, or Antigone may feel that since she alone committed the crime of burying her brother, she alone should pay the price.

36 ## Vocabulary Development

The Latin Prefix: *trans-*

• Call students' attention to the word *Transcends* in line 14 of the choral ode and to its definition. Tell students that the prefix *trans-* means "across, beyond, or through."

• Point out that the prefix can be followed by other Latin word parts, such as in *transmit, transpire, transient,* and *translate.* Another group of words combines the prefix *trans-* with English adjectives, such as in *transatlantic, transcontinental,* and *transoceanic.*

• Have students look up the meanings of these words in a dictionary, and add three new words of their own.

• Finally, have students share their new words with the rest of the class.

ISMENE. But we are equally guilty!

35

ANTIGONE. No more, Ismene.
165   You are alive, but I belong to Death.

CREON. [*To the* CHORUS] Gentlemen, I beg you to observe these girls:
     One has just now lost her mind; the other,
     It seems, has never had a mind at all.

ISMENE. Grief teaches the steadiest minds to waver, King.

170 **CREON.** Yours certainly did, when you assumed guilt with the guilty!

ISMENE. But how could I go on living without her?

CREON. You are.
     She is already dead.

ISMENE. But your own son's bride!

175 **CREON.** There are places enough for him to push his plow.
     I want no wicked women for my sons!

ISMENE. O dearest Haimon, how your father wrongs you!

CREON. I've had enough of your childish talk of marriage!

CHORAGOS. Do you really intend to steal this girl from your son?

180 **CREON.** No; Death will do that for me.

CHORAGOS. Then she must die?

CREON. [*Ironically*] You dazzle me.
     —But enough of this talk!

     [*To* GUARDS] You, there, take them away and guard them well:
     For they are but women, and even brave men run
185   When they see Death coming.

               [*Exit* ISMENE, ANTIGONE, *and* GUARDS.]

Ode II

CHORUS. [STROPHE 1]
     Fortunate is the man who has never tasted God's vengeance!
     Where once the anger of heaven has struck, that house is shaken
     For ever: damnation rises behind each child
     Like a wave cresting out of the black northeast,
5   When the long darkness under sea roars up
     And bursts drumming death upon the windwhipped sand.

               [ANTISTROPHE 1]
     I have seen this gathering sorrow from time long past
     Loom upon Oedipus' children: generation from generation
     Takes the compulsive rage of the enemy god.
10   So lately this last flower of Oedipus' line
     Drank the sunlight! but now a passionate word

✹ **ENRICHMENT: Literature Connection**

Tragedy Then and Now

While Sophocles fulfilled the requirements for tragedy set forth by Aristotle in his *Poetics,* drama evolved and changed over history so that modern dramatists do not now feel they must remain within the confines of Aristotle's famous definition. Willy Loman in Arthur Miller's *Death of a Salesman,* and Blanche Dubois in Tennessee Williams's *A Streetcar Named Desire,* for example, are noble of neither birth nor character. They are, on the other hand, very ordinary characters with whom the audience can more easily identify.

Two other requirements for tragedy, however, do survive in modern drama: that the audience be made to feel "pity and terror" and that at the end, a "catharsis," a cleansing, purification, or purging of the emotions, takes place. In other words, the audience sympathizes with and fears for the protagonist and then feels emotionally drained or exhausted at the end of the play.

And a handful of dust have closed up all its beauty.

[STROPHE 2]

What mortal arrogance
<u>Transcends</u> the wrath of Zeus?[7]
15 Sleep cannot lull him, nor the effortless long months
Of the timeless gods: but he is young for ever,
And his house is the shining day of high Olympos.[8]
All that is and shall be,
And all the past, is his.
20 No pride on earth is free of the curse of heaven.

[ANTISTROPHE 2]

The straying dreams of men
May bring them ghosts of joy:
But as they drowse, the waking embers burn them;
Or they walk with fixed eyes, as blind men walk.
25 But the ancient wisdom speaks for our own time:
Fate works most for woe
With Folly's fairest show.
Man's little pleasure is the spring of sorrow.

transcends (tran sendz´) *v.*
goes above or beyond
limits; exceeds

7. Zeus (zōōs) king of all
Greek gods, he was believed
to throw lightning bolts when
angry.

8. Olympos (ō lim´ pəs)
mountain in Greece, also
known as Olympus, where
the gods were believed to
live in ease and splendor.

Review and Assess

Thinking About the Selection

1. **Respond:** Antigone and Ismene disagree over the burial of Polyneices. With whom do you agree?

2. **(a) Recall:** Why do Ismene and Antigone quarrel as the play opens? **(b) Interpret:** Explain the stand that each takes.

3. **(a) Recall:** What reasons does Ismene give as she urges Antigone not to disobey Creon? **(b) Analyze:** How might Ismene's advice to her sister seem cowardly to some readers?

4. **(a) Recall:** What does Creon say to the chorus about the Ship of State? **(b) Analyze:** What does this remark reveal about his leadership style?

5. **(a) Recall:** How does Creon learn about Antigone's action? **(b) Interpret:** In his argument with Antigone, Creon declares, "An enemy is an enemy, even dead." What does he mean? Do you agree?

6. **(a) Recall:** What has Creon decided to do with Antigone? **(b) Speculate:** What do you predict will happen to Creon?

7. **Take a Position:** Strength of will and moral courage are usually thought of as virtues. Can they also seem foolish? Explain your answer.

Antigone, Scene 2 ◆ 787

ASSESSMENT PRACTICE: Reading Comprehension

Identify Patterns of Organization (For more practice, see Test Preparation Workbook, p. 48.)

As students prepare for tests, they need to refine their abilities to analyze the characteristics of clearly written texts. Use this sample test item to give students practice with this comprehension skill.

> Iocaste, now a widow, agreed to marry the unknown champion. The couple lived happily for years and raised four children of their own. Then a plague befell the city.

What pattern of organization is used in this passage?

A compare/contrast   **C** flashback
B chronological   **D** point-by-point

Words like *now, for years,* and *then* indicate that this narrative paragraph describes events in the order in which they happened. *B* is the correct response.

Answers for p. 788

Review and Assess

1. The conflict centers on which is more important, civil law or divine law and family loyalty.

2. Antigone's loyalty to her brother, her strong character, and her refusal to compromise her ideals contribute to her conflict with Creon, who is inflexible, proud, and fearful of any challenge to his authority.

3. Antigone is a sympathetic character, and readers want her to succeed because her actions seem admirable and noble. Creon's character is not sympathetic because his actions seem cruel and self-promoting.

4. **(a)** Antigone decides to bury her brother, and when she is caught, she decides not to repent.
(b) These actions cause Creon to react by sentencing her to death.

5. Effect: Antigone quarrels with Ismene.
Effect: Antigone buries Polyneices anyway.
Effect: Creon sentences Antigone to death.
Effect: Creon reveals himself as cold and inflexible.

6. Possible Answers: **(a)** Creon's behavior is cruel and inflexible. **(b)** Antigone's action is disobedient and brave.

7. Ismene's motive is fear for her life.

8. Antigone's motives are love for her brother, honor and loyalty to the gods, and belief in divine law.

9. As a new ruler, Creon must establish himself as all-powerful.

10. Some students may feel that Antigone is more believable because they sympathize and identify with her; others may give examples of authoritarian rulers in history to explain why they think that Creon is more believable.

11. Like Ismene, some students may think it just to punish individual acts of rebelliousness in order to maintain public order. Others may think that it's important to rebel against unjust laws or rules so as to hasten a change to such laws.

Review and Assess

Literary Analysis

Protagonist and Antagonist

1. What is the conflict between Antigone and Creon?
2. What qualities of each character contribute to the conflict?
3. Give examples of actions and language that show that Antigone is the **protagonist** and Creon is the **antagonist.**

Connecting Literary Elements

4. (a) What are two crucial **decisions** that Antigone makes?
   (b) How do these decisions contribute to furthering the plot?
5. Use a diagram like the one here to trace the effects of Creon's decision to forbid the burial of Polyneices.

Creon forbids the burial of Polyneices.

Effect   Effect   Effect   Effect

6. (a) Which adjectives can you use to describe the behavior of Creon?
   (b) Which adjectives would you use to describe Antigone's actions?

Reading Strategy

Questioning Characters' Motives

7. What was Ismene's **motive** for not going along with Antigone at first?
8. What is Antigone's motive for burying Polyneices?
9. What is Creon's motive for insisting on Antigone's death?
10. Which character is most believable? Explain.

Extend Understanding

11. **Civics Connection:** Ismene and Creon both argue that the law should be obeyed because it was made for the good of the country. Do you agree that obeying the law is always the right thing to do, or do you think Antigone is correct in following her conscience? Explain.

TEACHING RESOURCES

The following resources can be used to enrich or extend the instruction for pp. 788–789.

Vocabulary

 Selection Support: Build Vocabulary, p. 189

Vocabulary and Spelling Practice Book
(Use this booklet for skills enrichment.)

Grammar

Selection Support: Build Grammar Skills, p. 190

WG **Writing and Grammar,** Platinum Level, p. 548

Daily Language Practice Transparencies

Writing

Writing and Grammar iText CD-ROM

BLOCK SCHEDULING: Resources marked with this symbol provide varied instruction during 90-minute blocks.

Integrate Language Skills

❶ Vocabulary Development Lesson

Word Analysis: Latin Prefix *trans-*

The Latin prefix *trans-* means "through," "across," or "over." *Transcend* means "to go above or beyond limits." Use your knowledge of *trans-* to define each of the following words:

1. transparent   2. transmit   3. transplant

Spelling Strategy

When words end in a silent *e*, drop the *e* before a suffix that begins with a vowel. For example, when you add the suffix *-ed* to *sate*, you get *sated*. Add the suffix to each word below.

1. create + *-or*   3. care + *-ing*
2. fame + *-ous*   4. desire + *-able*

Fluency: Clarify Word Meaning

Review the words in the vocabulary list on page 771. Then, match each vocabulary word with its definition in the right column.

1. sated   a. pointedly
2. anarchists   b. oppressively hot or moist
3. sententiously   c. goes above or beyond the limit
4. sultry   d. satisfied or pleased
5. transcends   e. those who disrespect rules

❷ Grammar Lesson

Objective Pronouns

Objective pronouns are used when pronouns are the objects of verbs and prepositions. Objective pronouns include *me, you, him, her, it, us,* and *them.* In the following examples from *Antigone,* the objective pronoun is in italic type.

> **Direct Object:** No one shall bury *him,* . . .
>
> **Indirect Object:** Leave *me* my foolish plan: . . .
>
> **Object of Preposition:** . . . no one mourn for *him,* . . .

Practice Identify each objective pronoun in the sentences below, and tell how it is used in the sentence.

1. What new thing have you to tell us?
2. I admit my debt to you.
3. His parents are expecting him.
4. You see me now.
5. She was burying him.

Writing Application Write a summary of *Antigone* from the Prologue through Scene 2. Use five objective pronouns in your writing.

WG Prentice Hall Writing and Grammar Connection: Chapter 23, Section 1

❸ Extension Activities

Writing Write a **newspaper article** that would have appeared in a Thebes newspaper—if newspapers had existed at the time—the day after Polyneices was buried. Write a headline to announce the news, and answer the questions *who, what, when, where, why,* and *how* in your article.

❹ Research and Technology Work with a partner to plan a **presentation** on ancient Thebes. Write research questions, and use library and Internet resources to find the answers. Combine and organize your materials, and present your findings to your class. [Group Activity]

Antigone, Prologue–Scene 2 ◆ 789

Antigone, Scenes 3 Through 5

Lesson Objectives

1. **To analyze and respond to literary elements**
   - Literary Analysis: Tragic Character
   - Connecting Literary Elements: Resolution

2. **To read, comprehend, analyze, and critique a play**
   - Reading Strategy: Identifying With a Character
   - Reading Check questions
   - Review and Assess questions
   - Assessment Practice (ATE)

3. **To develop word analysis skills, fluency, and systematic vocabulary**
   - Vocabulary Development Lesson: Greek Root: -chor-

4. **To understand and apply written and oral language conventions**
   - Spelling Strategy
   - Grammar Lesson: Pronoun Case in Elliptical Clauses

5. **To understand and apply appropriate writing and research strategies**
   - Writing Lesson: Analytic Essay
   - Extension Activity: Multimedia Presentation

6. **To understand and apply listening and speaking strategies**
   - Extension Activity: Mock Trial

STEP-BY-STEP TEACHING GUIDE	PACING GUIDE
PRETEACH	
Motivate Students and Provide Background	
Use the Motivation activity (ATE p. 790)	5 min.
Read and discuss the Review and Anticipate information (SE p. 791)	5 min.
Introduce the Concepts	
Introduce the Literary Analysis and Reading Strategy (SE/ATE p. 790)	15 min.
Pronounce the vocabulary words and read their definitions (SE p. 790)	5 min.
TEACH	
Monitor Comprehension	
Informally monitor comprehension by circulating while students read independently or in groups	4 min.
Monitor students' comprehension with the Reading Check notes (SE/ATE pp. 793, 795, 797, 799, 801, 803, 805, 807)	as students read
Develop vocabulary with Vocabulary notes (SE pp. 791, 794, 795, 797, 803; ATE p. 796)	as students read
Develop Understanding	
Develop students' understanding of tragic characters with the Literary Analysis annotations (SE/ATE pp. 792, 793, 797, 800, 802, 806, 807)	10 min.
Develop students' ability to identify with a character with the Reading Strategy annotations (SE/ATE pp. 792, 794, 795, 798, 801, 802, 803, 805, 807)	10 min.
ASSESS	
Assess Mastery	
Assess students' mastery of the Reading Strategy and Literary Analysis by having them answer the Review and Assess questions (SE/ATE p. 809)	20 min.
Use one or more of the print and media Assessment Resources (ATE p. 811)	up to 50 min.
EXTEND	
Apply Understanding	
Have students complete the Vocabulary Development Lesson and the Grammar Lesson (SE p. 810)	20 min.
Apply students' ability to strengthen analysis using the Writing Lesson (SE/ATE p. 811)	45 min.
Apply students' understanding of the selection using one or more of the Extension Activities (SE p. 811)	20–90 min.

A ACCELERATED INSTRUCTION:
Use the strategies and activities identified with an .

UNIVERSAL ACCESS
- ● = Below Level Students
- ▲ = On-Level Students
- ■ = Above Level Students

Time and Resource Manager

Reading Level: Average
Average Number of Instructional Days: 5

RESOURCES		
PRINT 📖	**TRANSPARENCIES** 🗒	**TECHNOLOGY** 💿 🎧 📼
• **Beyond Literature,** Cross-Curricular Connection: History, p. 49 ▲ ■		• **Interest Grabber Video,** Tape 4 ● ▲ ■
• **Selection Support Workbook:** ● ▲ ■ Literary Analysis, p. 196 Reading Strategy, p. 195 Build Vocabulary, p. 193	• **Literary Analysis and Reading Transparencies,** pp. 97 and 98 ● ▲ ■	
• **Authors In Depth,** Platinum Level ■		• **Listening to Literature** ● ▲ ■ Audiocassettes, Side 26 Audio CDs, CD 16
• **Literatura en español** ● ▲ • **Literary Analysis for Enrichment** ■	• **Fine Art Transparencies, Volume 1,** Art Transparency 15 ● ▲ ■	
• **Formal Assessment:** Selection Test, pp. 173–175 ● ▲ ■ • **Open Book Test,** pp. 145–147 ● ▲ ■ • **Performance Assessment and Portfolio Management,** p. 16 ● ▲ ■ • **ASSESSMENT SYSTEM** ● ▲	• **ASSESSMENT SYSTEM** ● ▲ ■ Skills Practice Answers and Explanations on Transparencies	• **Test Bank Software** ● ▲ ■ • **Got It! Assessment Videotapes,** Tape 4 ● ▲
• **Selection Support Workbook:** ● ▲ ■ Build Grammar Skills, p. 194 • **Writing and Grammar,** Platinum Level ● ▲ ■ • **Extension Activities,** p. 49 ● ▲ ■	• **Daily Language Practice Transparencies** ● ▲ • **Writing Models and Graphic Organizers on Transparencies,** pp. 53–59 ● ▲ ■	• **Writing and Grammar iText CD-ROM** ● ▲ ■ 🖥 **Take It to the Net** www.phschool.com

BLOCK SCHEDULING: Use one 90-minute class period to preteach the selection and have students read it. Use a second 90-minute class period to assess students' mastery of skills and have them complete one of the Extension Activities.

Step-by-Step Teaching Guide for p. 790

Motivation

Tell students that Antigone's husband, Haimon, will play an important role in the rest of the play. Ask students to predict what he might do. After they share their ideas, tell them that Haimon is Creon's son, and ask them how that fact affects their predictions.

❶ Literary Analysis

Tragic Character

• Tell students that as they read Scenes 3 through 5 of *Antigone*, they will focus on the play's tragic characters, who experience reversals of fortune because of weaknesses called tragic flaws.

• Read the instruction about Tragic Character together as a class. Call students' attention to the example from the play.

• Use the instruction for Connecting Literary Elements to show how the tragic characters' actions lead to the play's resolution.

• Use the Tragic Character transparency in **Literary Analysis and Reading Transparencies,** p. 98, to show students how to analyze the tragic nature of the main characters in *Antigone*.

❷ Reading Strategy

Identifying With a Character

• Remind students that identifying with a character means putting oneself in the character's place and sympathizing with him or her.

• Point out that identifying with a character can give the reader greater insight into the character's motives and the events taking place.

• Have students complete a character diagram for Antigone like the one on p. 790. Then, have them fill out a diagram for Creon as well.

Prepare to Read

Antigone, Scenes 3 Through 5

❶ Literary Analysis

Tragic Character

A **tragic character** in a drama experiences a reversal of fortune as a result of fate or a flaw in his or her character. The tragic flaw is a fatal weakness in the character that causes this person to become enmeshed in events that lead to his or her downfall. This play has two tragic characters: Antigone and Creon. The chorus speaks to Antigone, proving that others see her tragic flaw.

> You have made your choice,
> Your death is the doing of your conscious hand.

As you read, observe how the Greek concept of fate combines with characters' flaws to lead to tragedy.

Connecting Literary Elements

The **resolution** is the final stage in plot development. It follows the climax, or turning point of the conflict, and tells how the struggle between characters or opposing forces is worked out. The resolution brings *Antigone* to a conclusion, following the path that is laid out by the decisions of the tragic characters.

❷ Reading Strategy

Identifying With a Character

When you **identify with a character,** you put yourself in that character's place, experiencing what he or she does and sympathizing with that character. For example, you may feel Antigone's anguish as she struggles to do what she thinks is right. Use a diagram like the one here to examine the feelings and issues confronting the characters in *Antigone*.

Vocabulary Development

deference (def´ ər əns) *n.* yielding in thought (p. 791)

vile (vīl) *adj.* extremely disgusting (p. 794)

piety (pī´ ə tē) *n.* holiness; respect for the divine (p. 795)

blasphemy (blas´ fə mē) *n.* disrespectful

action or speech against a deity (p. 797)

lamentation (lam´ ən tā´ shən) *n.* expression of grief; weeping (p. 797)

chorister (kôr´ is tər) *n.* member of a chorus (p. 803)

790 ◆ Drama

TEACHING RESOURCES

The following resources can be used to enrich or extend the instruction for p. 790.

Motivation

📺 **Interest Grabber Video,** Tape 4 ▪

Background

📖 **Beyond Literature,** p. 49

🖥 *Take It to the Net*
Visit www.phschool.com for background and hotlinks for *Antigone*.

Literary Analysis

📄 **Literary Analysis and Reading Transparencies,** Tragic Character, p. 98 ▪

Reading

📖 **Selection Support Workbook:** Reading Strategy, p. 195; Build Vocabulary, p. 193

📄 **Literary Analysis and Reading Transparencies,** Identifying With a Character, p. 97

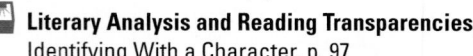 **BLOCK SCHEDULING:** Resources marked with this symbol provide varied instruction during 90-minute blocks.

❶ Scenes 3–5

Review and Anticipate

In Scenes 1 and 2, Antigone defies the order of her uncle, King Creon of Thebes, and buries her brother. When Creon finds out, he sentences her to death, refusing to pardon her just because she is his niece. As Scene 2 ends, the chorus sings, "*Fate works most for woe / With Folly's fairest show.*" In the final scenes of the play, you will see the truth of these words.

Scene 3

CHORAGOS. But here is Haimon, King, the last of all your sons.
Is it grief for Antigone that brings him here,
And bitterness at being robbed of his bride?

[*Enter* HAIMON.]

CREON. We shall soon see, and no need
of diviners.[1]

5 —Son,
You have heard my final judgment on
that girl:
Have you come here hating me, or
have you come
With <u>deference</u> and with love,
whatever I do?

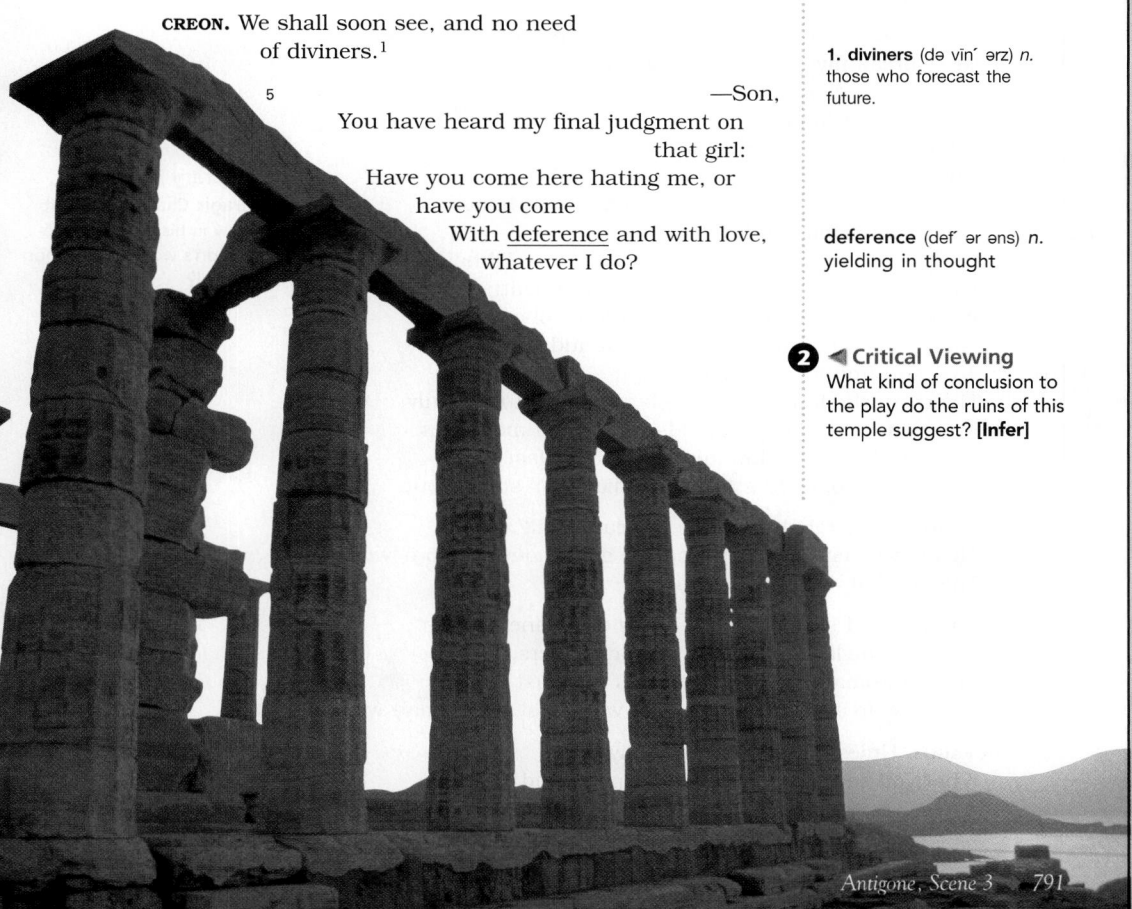

Antigone, Scene 3   791

1. diviners (də vīn′ ərz) *n.* those who forecast the future.

deference (def′ ər əns) *n.* yielding in thought

❷ ◀ Critical Viewing
What kind of conclusion to the play do the ruins of this temple suggest? **[Infer]**

CUSTOMIZE INSTRUCTION FOR UNIVERSAL ACCESS

For Less Proficient Readers	For English Learners	For Advanced Readers
To help students continue through the second part of the play, review with them the list of characters' names and the relationships between the characters.	Students will benefit from a review of the characters' names and relationships. In addition, have students write a few sentences about what they will find out in the second part of the play.	Have students write their predictions on the fates of Antigone and Creon. What do students think will happen to them? Is a happy ending in store for either Antigone or Creon? Why do students feel as they do?

TEACH

Step-by-Step Teaching Guide for pp. 791–808

❶ About the Selection

As the events in the second part of *Antigone* unfold, we watch Creon and Antigone move inexorably toward their respective fates. The events set in motion through their own strong-willed choices seem fated to lead each character to his or her downfall.

❷ ▶Critical Viewing

Answer: The ruins of the temple suggest that at the end of the play, the characters' lives will also be in ruins.

 E-Teach

Visit E-Teach at www.phschool.com for teachers' essays on how to teach, with questions and answers.

791

❸ Reading Strategy

Identifying With a Character

• Ask students to describe Haimon's words to his father.
 Answer: They are obsequious and almost fawning.

• Ask students why they think Haimon is talking to his father in this manner.
 Answer: Haimon may be trying hard not to antagonize his father. He may be hoping that he can persuade Creon to spare Antigone.

❹ Literary Analysis

Tragic Character

• Ask a volunteer to read Creon's speech aloud.

• Have students answer the Literary Analysis question on p. 792: What flaw in his character do Creon's words to Haimon reveal?
 Answer: Creon's words reveal his inflexible nature. He fears that he will appear weak if he softens his stance on Antigone's crime.

• Then, ask students how Creon's rigidity might drive him into a conflict that cannot be resolved.
 Answer: Creon has a tendency to see any deviation from submission to his will as "anarchy" and a threat to the state. This could lead to bitter conflict with anyone who challenges his will.

HAIMON. I am your son, father. You are my guide.
10   You make things clear for me, and I obey you.
  No marriage means more to me than your continuing wisdom.

CREON. Good. That is the way to behave: subordinate
  Everything else, my son, to your father's will.
  This is what a man prays for, that he may get
15   Sons attentive and dutiful in his house,
  Each one hating his father's enemies,
  Honoring his father's friends. But if his sons
  Fail him, if they turn out unprofitably,
  What has he fathered but trouble for himself
20   And amusement for the malicious?

                                    So you are right

  Not to lose your head over this woman.
  Your pleasure with her would soon grow cold, Haimon,
  And then you'd have a hellcat in bed and elsewhere.
25   Let her find her husband in Hell!
  Of all the people in this city, only she
  Has had contempt for my law and broken it.

  Do you want me to show myself weak before the people?
  Or to break my sworn word? No, and I will not.
30   The woman dies.
  I suppose she'll plead "family ties." Well, let her.
  If I permit my own family to rebel,
  How shall I earn the world's obedience?
  Show me the man who keeps his house in hand,
35   He's fit for public authority.

                            I'll have no dealings
  With law-breakers, critics of the government:
  Whoever is chosen to govern should be obeyed—
  Must be obeyed, in all things, great and small,
40   Just and unjust! O Haimon,
  The man who knows how to obey, and that man only,
  Knows how to give commands when the time comes.
  You can depend on him, no matter how fast
  The spears come: he's a good soldier, he'll stick it out.

45   Anarchy, anarchy! Show me a greater evil!
  This is why cities tumble and the great houses rain down,
  This is what scatters armies!

  No, no: good lives are made so by discipline.
  We keep the laws then, and the lawmakers,
50   And no woman shall seduce us. If we must lose,
  Let's lose to a man, at least! Is a woman stronger than we?

CHORAGOS. Unless time has rusted my wits,
  What you say, King, is said with point and dignity.

792 ◆ Drama

Literary Analysis
Tragic Character What flaw in his character do Creon's words to Haimon reveal?

TEACHING RESOURCES

The following resources can be used to enrich or extend the instruction for pp. 791–808.

Literary Analysis

📖 **Writing Models and Graphic Organizers,** pp. 53–59

📖 **Selection Support:** Literary Analysis, p. 196

Reading

🎧 **Listening to Literature Audiocassettes,** Side 26 ▪

💿 **Listening to Literature Audio CDs,** CD 16 ▪

Extension

📖 **Fine Art Transparencies, Volume 1,**
Art Transparency 15 (Have students bring the mosaic to life by taking the parts of the actors and discussing the play from their perspective.)

▪ **BLOCK SCHEDULING:** Resources marked with this symbol provide varied instruction during 90-minute blocks.

HAIMON. [*Boyishly earnest*] Father:

55　Reason is God's crowning gift to man, and you are right
　　To warn me against losing mine. I cannot say—
　　I hope that I shall never want to say!—that you
　　Have reasoned badly. Yet there are other men
　　Who can reason, too; and their opinions might be helpful.
60　You are not in a position to know everything
　　That people say or do, or what they feel:
　　Your temper terrifies them—everyone
　　Will tell you only what you like to hear.
　　But I, at any rate, can listen; and I have heard them
65　Muttering and whispering in the dark about this girl.
　　They say no woman has ever, so unreasonably,
　　Died so shameful a death for a generous act:
　　"She covered her brother's body. Is this indecent?
　　She kept him from dogs and vultures. Is this
　　　a crime?
　　Death?—She should have all the honor that
　　　we can give her!"

70　This is the way they talk out there in the city.

　　You must believe me:
　　Nothing is closer to me than your happiness.
　　What could be closer? Must not any son
　　Value his father's fortune as his father does his?
75　I beg you, do not be unchangeable:
　　Do not believe that you alone can be right.
　　The man who thinks that,
　　The man who maintains that only he has the
　　　power
　　To reason correctly, the gift to speak, the soul—
80　A man like that, when you know him, turns out
　　　empty.

　　It is not reason never to yield to reason!

　　In flood time you can see how some trees bend,
　　And because they bend, even their twigs are safe,
　　While stubborn trees are torn up, roots and all.
85　And the same thing happens in sailing:
　　Make your sheet fast, never slacken,—and over
　　　you go,

　　Head over heels and under: and there's your
　　　voyage.
　　Forget you are angry! Let yourself be moved!
　　I know I am young; but please let me say this:
90　The ideal condition

Antigone, Scene 3 793

6 ☑ **Reading Check**

What does Creon say is the most important thing a son can do?

7 ▼ **Critical Viewing**

Why might Creon hold his son this way as they talk? **[Infer]**

- Have volunteers take the parts of Creon and Haimon, and read aloud the argument between them.

- Then, ask students to summarize Creon's and Haimon's arguments in this passage.

  Answer: Creon implies that a man's judgment will always be better than a boy's. Then, he argues that Antigone breaks the law; she is a criminal, so Haimon should not stand up for her. Haimon argues that age is immaterial; what counts is who is right. He then implies that, if most people in the city deny that Antigone is a criminal, she must not be one.

- Ask the Reading Strategy question on p. 794: Do you identify more with Creon or with Haimon here? Why?

  Possible answer: Even students who are in favor of Creon's argument will probably identify more with Haimon because they sympathize with him as a young person and appreciate his statement that age is irrelevant in an argument.

Would be, I admit, that men should be right by instinct;
But since we are all too likely to go astray,
The reasonable thing is to learn from those who can teach.

CHORAGOS. You will do well to listen to him, King,
95   If what he says is sensible. And you, Haimon,
    Must listen to your father.—Both speak well.

CREON. You consider it right for a man of my years and experience
    To go to school to a boy?

HAIMON.   It is not right
100   If I am wrong. But if I am young, and right,
    What does my age matter?

CREON. You think it right to stand up for an anarchist?

HAIMON. Not at all. I pay no respect to criminals.

CREON. Then she is not a criminal?

❽ 105 **HAIMON.** The City would deny it, to a man.

CREON. And the City proposes to teach me how to rule?

HAIMON. Ah. Who is it that's talking like a boy now?

CREON. My voice is the one voice giving orders in this City!

HAIMON. It is no City if it takes orders from one voice.

110 **CREON.** The State is the King!

HAIMON.   Yes, if the State is a desert.

                                      [Pause]

CREON. This boy, it seems, has sold out to a woman.

HAIMON. If you are a woman: my concern is only for you.

CREON. So? Your "concern"! In a public brawl with your father!

115 **HAIMON.** How about you, in a public brawl with justice?

CREON. With justice, when all that I do is within my rights?

HAIMON. You have no right to trample on God's right.

CREON. *[Completely out of control]* Fool, adolescent fool! Taken in
    by a woman!

HAIMON. You'll never see me taken in by anything <u>vile</u>.

120 **CREON.** Every word you say is for her!

HAIMON. *[Quietly, darkly]*   And for you.
    And for me. And for the gods under the earth.

CREON. You'll never marry her while she lives.

HAIMON. Then she must die.—But her death will cause another.

Reading Strategy
Identifying With a Character Do you identify more with Creon or with Haimon here? Why?

vile (vīl) *adj.* extremely disgusting

✳ ENRICHMENT: Cultural Connection

The Library of Alexandria

Besides *Antigone*, six other tragedies by Sophocles survive today, as well as seven by Aeschylus and eighteen by Euripides. But historical records cite many other plays by these and other playwrights. Where are these plays? What happened to them?

In the early third century B.C., Ptolemy I, ruler of Egypt, built in the city of Alexandria a library to house all of Greek literature, or as much as could be found. He and Ptolemy II collected approximately 700,000

works over the years. The library at Alexandria was the first important library in the world and remained a center for scholars until 47 B.C.

In that year, the library burned, and most of its collection was lost. Some think that Roman soldiers under Octavius Caesar started the fire, but it may have been accidental. In addition some Greek literature was destroyed by officials of Roman libraries because it was deemed unfit to be saved for posterity.

125 CREON. Another?
　　　Have you lost your senses? Is this an open threat?

　　　HAIMON. There is no threat in speaking to emptiness.

　　　CREON. I swear you'll regret this superior tone of yours!
　　　You are the empty one!

130 HAIMON.　　　　　　　　　　　If you were not my father,
　　　I'd say you were perverse.

　　　CREON. You girlstruck fool, don't play at words with me!

　　　HAIMON. I am sorry. You prefer silence.

　　　CREON.　　　　　　　　　Now, by God—!
135 I swear, by all the gods in heaven above us,
　　　You'll watch it, I swear you shall!

[To the SERVANTS]　　　　　　　Bring her out!
　　　Bring the woman out! Let her die before his eyes!
　　　Here, this instant, with her bridegroom beside her!

140 HAIMON. Not here, no; she will not die here, King.
　　　And you will never see my face again.
　　　Go on raving as long as you've a friend to endure you.

　　　　　　　　　　　　　　[Exit HAIMON.]

　　　CHORAGOS. Gone, gone.
　　　Creon, a young man in a rage is dangerous!

145 CREON. Let him do, or dream to do, more than a man can.
　　　He shall not save these girls from death.

　　　CHORAGOS.　　　　　　　　These girls?
　　　You have sentenced them both?

　　　CREON.　　　　　　　　No, you are right.
150 I will not kill the one whose hands are clean.

　　　CHORAGOS. But Antigone?

　　　CREON. [Somberly] I will carry her far away
　　　Out there in the wilderness, and lock her
　　　Living in a vault of stone. She shall have food,
155 As the custom is, to absolve the State of her death.
　　　And there let her pray to the gods of hell:
　　　They are her only gods:
　　　Perhaps they will show her an escape from death,
　　　Or she may learn,
　　　　　　　　　though late,
160 That piety shown the dead is pity in vain.

　　　　　　　　　　[Exit CREON.]

Reading Strategy
Identifying With a Character In what ways can you identify with Haimon in this scene?

piety (pī' ə tē) n. holiness; respect for the divine

10 ✔**Reading Check**
Why are Haimon and Creon arguing?

Antigone, Scene 3 ◆ 795

---

❾ Reading Strategy
Identifying With a Character

• Have two volunteers read the bracketed exchange between Haimon and Creon.

• Ask students what Creon hopes to achieve if he carries out his threat. **Answer:** Creon wants to show the city of Thebes that no act against the state will go unpunished. He is making an example of Antigone.

• Then, ask the Reading Strategy question on p. 795: In what ways can you identify with Haimon in this scene? **Possible response:** Students may say that they can sympathize with Haimon's anger at his father for not listening reasonably to his point of view.

❿ ✔**Reading Check**
Answer: Haimon is trying to convince Creon to spare Antigone's life. Creon insists upon his right to do as he pleases.

CUSTOMIZE INSTRUCTION FOR UNIVERSAL ACCESS

For Less Proficient Readers	For Advanced Readers
Have students imagine that they write an advice column in a Theban newspaper. They receive a letter from a young man whose father does not pay attention to his point of view or heed any opinions except those that agree with his own. What advice would they offer the young man? Have them write their responses in the form of a letter.	Have students list in one column the reasons they think Creon should change his mind about punishing Antigone for burying her brother against his orders, and in a second column the reasons he should not change his mind. Which list has the stronger reasons? Have students write a few sentences giving advice to Creon on what they think he should do.

⓫ Vocabulary Development

Greek Root: -chor-

- Call students' attention to the word *chorus*. Tell them that *chorus* contains the Greek root *-chor-*, which comes from Terpsichore, the Greek Muse for song and dance.

- Explain to students that in Greek theater, the chorus was a company of actors whose singing, dancing, and narration provided explanation and interpretation of the play's main action. In contemporary theater, the chorus refers to an organized group of singers who sing in concert, or a group of singers or dancers who accompany a musical comedy or revue.

- Have students suggest other words that contain this word root, and list them on the chalkboard. **Possible responses:** Students might mention *chorale, choreography,* or *choir.*

- Have students look up any unfamiliar words in a dictionary, and write a sentence that reveals the definition of each.

Ode III

CHORUS.

Love, unconquerable   [STROPHE]
Waster of rich men, keeper

Of warm lights and all-night vigil
In the soft face of a girl:
5   Sea-wanderer, forest-visitor!
Even the pure Immortals cannot escape you,
And mortal man, in his one day's dusk,
Trembles before your glory.
Surely you swerve upon ruin   [ANTISTROPHE]
10   The just man's consenting heart,
As here you have made bright anger
Strike between father and son—
And none has conquered but Love!
A girl's glance working the will of heaven:
15   Pleasure to her alone who mocks us,
Merciless Aphrodite.[2]

Scene 4

CHORAGOS. [*As* ANTIGONE *enters guarded*] But I can no longer stand
      in awe of this,
   Nor, seeing what I see, keep back my tears.
   Here is Antigone, passing to that chamber
   Where all find sleep at last.

ANTIGONE.
5   Look upon me, friends, and pity me   [STROPHE 1]
   Turning back at the night's edge to say
   Good-by to the sun that shines for me no longer;
   Now sleepy Death
   Summons me down to Acheron,[3] that cold shore:
10   There is no bridesong there, nor any music.

CHORUS. Yet not unpraised, not without a kind of honor,
   You walk at last into the underworld;
   Untouched by sickness, broken by no sword.
   What woman has ever found your way to death?

ANTIGONE.
15   How often I have heard the story of Niobe,[4]   [ANTISTROPHE 1]
   Tantalos'[5] wretched daughter, how the stone
   Clung fast about her, ivy-close: and they say
   The rain falls endlessly
   And sifting soft snow; her tears are never done.
20   I feel the loneliness of her death in mine.

CHORUS. But she was born of heaven, and you
   Are woman, woman-born. If her death is yours,

796 ◆ *Drama*

---

2. Aphrodite (af´ rə dīt´ ē) goddess of beauty and love who is sometimes vengeful in her retaliation for offenses.

3. Acheron (ak´ ər än´) river in the underworld over which the dead are ferried.

4. Niobe (nī´ ō bē´) a queen of Thebes who was turned to stone while weeping for her slain children. Her seven sons and seven daughters were killed by Artemis and Apollo, the divine twins of Leto. These gods ruined Niobe after Leto complained that Niobe insulted her by bragging of maternal superiority. It was Zeus who turned the bereaved Niobe to stone, but her lament continued and her tears created a stream.

5. Tantalos' (tan´ tə ləs) Niobe's father, who was condemned to eternal frustration in the underworld because he revealed the secrets of the gods. Tantalos, also spelled Tantalus, was tormented by being kept just out of reach of the water and food that was near him but which he could never reach to enjoy.

✳ ENRICHMENT: Mythology Connection

Tantalus and Niobe

Antigone's reference to Niobe would have been very familiar to ancient Greek audiences. They would have known that Niobe was the daughter of Tantalus, who tried to humiliate the gods. As punishment, the gods placed Tantalus in a pool of water he could never drink from located in the midst of fruit trees he could never reach. Because he offended the gods so seriously, Tantalus' descendants were cursed as well. Niobe, Tantalus' daughter, ruled Thebes with her husband, Amphion. When she, like her father, challenged the gods, they struck down her seven children. In her grief, Niobe is said to have turned to stone—a stone forever wet with her tears.

Ask students to identify the connections between the stories of Tantalus and Niobe and Antigone. **Answer:** Students should notice that Niobe ruled Thebes, where Antigone lives. Like Niobe and her children, Antigone belongs to a cursed family. Excessive pride plays a role in both stories as well.

A mortal woman's, is this not for you
Glory in our world and in the world beyond?

ANTIGONE.   [STROPHE 2]
25 You laugh at me. Ah, friends, friends,
Can you not wait until I am dead? O Thebes,
O men many-charioted, in love with Fortune,
Dear springs of Dirce, sacred Theban grove,
Be witnesses for me, denied all pity,
30 Unjustly judged! and think a word of love
For her whose path turns
Under dark earth, where there are no more tears.

CHORUS. You have passed beyond human daring and come at last
Into a place of stone where Justice sits.
35 I cannot tell
What shape of your father's guilt appears in this.

ANTIGONE.   [ANTISTROPHE 2]
You have touched it at last: that bridal bed
Unspeakable, horror of son and mother mingling:
Their crime, infection of all our family!
40 O Oedipus, father and brother!
Your marriage strikes from the grave to murder mine.
I have been a stranger here in my own land:
All my life
The blasphemy of my birth has followed me.

45 CHORUS. Reverence is a virtue, but strength
Lives in established law: that must prevail.
You have made your choice,
Your death is the doing of your conscious hand.

ANTIGONE.   [EPODE]
Then let me go, since all your words are bitter,
50 And the very light of the sun is cold to me.
Lead me to my vigil, where I must have
Neither love nor lamentation; no song, but silence.

[CREON interrupts impatiently.]

CREON. If dirges and planned lamentations could put off death,
Men would be singing forever.

55 [To the SERVANTS]   Take her, go!
You know your orders: take her to the vault
And leave her alone there. And if she lives or dies,
That's her affair, not ours: our hands are clean.

ANTIGONE. O tomb, vaulted bride-bed in eternal rock,
60 Soon I shall be with my own again
Where Persephone[6] welcomes the thin ghosts underground:
And I shall see my father again, and you, mother,

blasphemy (blas′ fə mē) *n.*
disrespectful action or
speech against a deity

Literary Analysis
Tragic Character What
flaw in Antigone does the
chorus point out?

lamentation (lam′ ən tā′
shən) *n.* expression of
grief; weeping

6. **Persephone** (pər sef′ ə nē)
queen of the underworld.

13 ✓**Reading Check**
Whom does Antigone
blame for her fate?

Antigone, Scene 4 ◆ 797

---

12 **Literary Analysis**
Tragic Character
- Read the chorus's speech aloud.
Ask students what virtue in
Antigone the chorus points out.
  Answer: The chorus points out her
  reverence for the gods.
- Have students answer the Literary
Analysis question on p. 797: What
flaw in Antigone does the chorus
point out?
  Answer: The chorus points out her
  unwillingness to recognize human
  law.
- Then, ask students whom the cho-
rus blames for Antigone's fate.
  Answer: The chorus blames
  Antigone herself, saying that she
  chose to die when she opposed
  human law.

▶ Monitor Progress Ask students to
explain how having a passionate,
unyielding heart can be a fatal
flaw.
Answer: Antigone's passion and
her unwillingness to compromise
draw her into the conflict that
results in her death.

13 ✓**Reading Check**
Answer: Antigone blames her parents' marriage for her fate.

CUSTOMIZE INSTRUCTION FOR UNIVERSAL ACCESS

For Advanced Readers

Suggest that students read additional works by
Sophocles. Provide students with the titles listed in the
Enrichment box on p. 809. You may also wish to use
Authors In Depth, which contains an excerpt from
Oedipus the King.

    After students have read this or other works by
Sophocles, have them form discussion groups in
which they compare and contrast the tragic flaws of
the tragic characters in each work. They might also

discuss the role of fate in the plays.

❶❹ **Reading Strategy**

Identifying With a Character

• Ask students to read the bracketed passage and explain
Antigone's feelings at this point.
Answer: While she is certain that
she is right and feels justified as
she goes to her death, Antigone
can't help wishing that Creon will
be punished for his actions.

• Have students predict whether
Creon will be punished, and if so,
what form his punishment will take.

❶❺ ▶ **Critical Viewing**
Answer: Antigone is showing that
she has no respect or regard for the
king or his decrees.

❶❻ **Critical Thinking**

Making Inferences

• Ask a volunteer to read the
Chorus's speech. Then, ask why
the Chorus chooses to recount
Danae's story at this point.
Answer: Danae's story is similar to
Antigone's. Both were princesses
sealed away in a vault and left to
die.

• Then, ask students to explain why
the power of fate is shown to be
especially strong in the cases of
Danae and Antigone.
Answer: Danae's and Antigone's
high station did not shield them
from ruin.

And dearest Polyneices—
                                    dearest indeed
To me, since it was my hand
65 That washed him clean and poured the ritual wine:
And my reward is death before my time!

❶❹ And yet, as men's hearts know, I have done no wrong,
I have not sinned before God. Or if I have,
I shall know the truth in death. But if the guilt
70 Lies upon Creon who judged me, then, I pray,
May his punishment equal my own.

CHORAGOS.   O passionate heart,
Unyielding, tormented still by the same winds!

CREON. Her guards shall have good cause to regret their delaying.

75 ANTIGONE. Ah! That voice is like the voice of death!

CREON. I can give you no reason to think you are mistaken.

ANTIGONE. Thebes, and you my fathers' gods,
And rulers of Thebes, you see me now, the last
Unhappy daughter of a line of kings,
80 Your kings, led away to death. You will remember
What things I suffer, and at what men's hands,
Because I would not transgress the laws of heaven.

                                    [To the GUARDS, simply]

Come: let us wait no longer.

                                    [Exit ANTIGONE, left, guarded.]

Ode IV

CHORUS.
All Danae's beauty[7] was locked away   [STROPHE 1]
In a brazen cell where the sunlight
        could not come:
A small room, still as any grave,
        enclosed her.
Yet she was a princess too,
And Zeus in a rain of gold poured love
        upon her.
❶❻ O child, child,
No power in wealth or war
Or tough sea-blackened ships
Can prevail against untiring
        Destiny!

                                    [ANTISTROPHE 1]

10 And Dryas' son[8] also, that furious
        king,

7. Danae's (dan´ ā ēz´)
beauty Danae was imprisoned in a brazen, dark tower
when it was foretold that she
would mother a son who
would kill her father. Her
beauty attracted Zeus, who
visited her in the form of a
shower of gold. Perseus was
born of the union, and Danae
was exiled with the child
over stormy seas from which
Zeus saved them. Years later,
as prophesied, the boy did
kill the man he failed to
recognize as his grandfather.

8. Dryas' (drī´ əs) **son** Lycorgos (lī kʉr´ gəs), whose
opposition to the worship of
Dionysos was severely punished by the gods. He drove
the followers of the god from
Thrace and was driven insane
for having done so. Lycorgos
recovered from his madness
while imprisoned in a cave,
but he was later blinded by
Zeus as additional punishment
for his offense.

❶❺ ▼ **Critical Viewing**
What does Antigone's
body language say in this
photograph? **[Analyze]**

Greek Theater

Following is a glossary of terms from classical Greek
theater. Students might be interested in learning some
of them and identifying parts of *Antigone* to which they
could be applied.

Catharsis (ka thär´ sis): emotional relief or purification
that an audience was supposed to experience upon
watching a Greek tragedy

Exodus (eks´ ə dəs´): the departure of the chorus from
the stage at the end of a Greek tragedy

Hamartia (hə mär´ she): the tragic flaw that causes the
downfall of a tragic hero or heroine

Hubris (hyo͞o´ bris): excessive pride on the part of a
character; a common form of *hamartia*

Orchestra (ôr´ kis trə): the circular space in front of the
stage of a Greek theater in which the chorus performed

Parados (pa´ rə dəs): the initial entrance of the chorus
in a Greek tragedy; their entrance song

Bore the god's prisoning anger for his pride:
Sealed up by Dionysos[9] in deaf stone,
His madness died among echoes.
So at the last he learned what dreadful power
15 His tongue had mocked:
For he had profaned the revels,
And fired the wrath of the nine
Implacable Sisters[10] that love the sound of the flute.

[STROPHE 2]

And old men tell a half-remembered tale
20 Of horror done where a dark ledge splits the sea
And a double surf beats on the gray shores:
How a king's new woman, sick
With hatred for the queen he had imprisoned,
Ripped out his two sons' eyes with her bloody hands
25 While grinning Ares[11] watched the shuttle plunge
Four times: four blind wounds crying for revenge,

[ANTISTROPHE 2]

Crying, tears and blood mingled.—Piteously born,
Those sons whose mother was of heavenly birth!
Her father was the god of the North Wind
30 And she was cradled by gales,
She raced with young colts on the glittering hills
And walked untrammeled in the open light:
But in her marriage deathless Fate found means
To build a tomb like yours for all her joy.

Scene 5

[*Enter blind* TEIRESIAS, *led by a boy. The opening speeches of* TEIRESIAS *should be in singsong contrast to the realistic lines of* CREON.]

TEIRESIAS. This is the way the blind man comes, Princes, Princes,
   Lock-step, two heads lit by the eyes of one.
CREON. What new thing have you to tell us, old Teiresias?

TEIRESIAS. I have much to tell you: listen to the prophet, Creon.

5 CREON. I am not aware that I have ever failed to listen.

TEIRESIAS. Then you have done wisely, King, and ruled well.

CREON. I admit my debt to you.[12] But what have you to say?

TEIRESIAS. This, Creon: you stand once more on the edge of fate.

CREON. What do you mean? Your words are a kind of dread.

10 TEIRESIAS. Listen, Creon:
   I was sitting in my chair of augury,[13] at the place
   Where the birds gather about me. They were all a-chatter,
   As is their habit, when suddenly I heard
   A strange note in their jangling, a scream, a

9. Dionysos (dĭ ə nĭ´ səs) god of wine, in whose honor the Greek plays were performed.

10. nine / Implacable Sisters nine Muses, or goddesses, of science and literature. They are the daughters of Zeus and Mnemosyne (nē mäs´ i nē´)—Memory—who inspired invention and influenced the production of art. They are called implacable (im plak´ ə bəl) because they were unforgiving and denied inspiration to anyone who offended them.

11. Ares (er´ ēz´) god of war.

12. my debt to you Creon is here admitting that he would not have acquired the throne if Teiresias had not moved the former King, Oedipus, to an investigation of his own background that led eventually to his downfall. The news of his personal history, uncovered with help from Teiresias, forced Oedipus into exile.

13. chair of augury the seat near the temple from which Teiresias would deliver his predictions about the future. Augury was the skill of telling such fortunes from a consideration of omens, like the flight of birds or the positions of stars.

 Reading Check

How does Creon intend to get rid of Antigone?

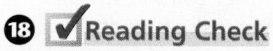 **Background**

Mythology

The Chorus refers to the story of King Phineas of Salmydessus in Thrace. Phineus imprisoned his first wife, Cleopatra (not the Egyptian queen) after marrying a second wife, Idaea. Out of jealousy, Idaea made false accusations of treachery against Cleopatra's sons, Plesippus and Pandion, and put out their eyes with a weaver's shuttle. Remind students that Oedipus put out his own eyes.

Reading Check

Answer: Creon plans to lock Antigone away in a vault.

CUSTOMIZE INSTRUCTION FOR UNIVERSAL ACCESS

For English Learners	For Advanced Readers	For Gifted/Talented Students
Have students skim through Ode IV looking for words whose meanings are unclear to them. Encourage students to look up the words in a dictionary or to work with a native English speaker to find out the meanings of the words.	Have students consider public figures in recent history. Can any of them be said to have tragic flaws that led or that appear to be leading them to their downfall? Have students discuss the question in a group and then present their conclusions to the class for further discussion.	Classical works such as Sophocles' *Antigone* provide students with an excellent opportunity to read with the purpose of appreciating an author's craft. Ask students to analyze the role of the chorus and decide whether Sophocles has created a likable "character" in this group of speakers.

799

Religion

Burnt offerings were traditional in many religions. Either whole animals or particular parts of animals were placed on an altar fire and burnt as a gift to please a god. If the offering did not burn, it was taken as a sign that the god in question was angry at some offense.

⓴ Literary Analysis

Tragic Character

• Ask a volunteer to read Creon's speech. Then, ask students to point out the part of his speech in which Creon seems to be placing himself above the gods.
Answer: In saying that he would not yield even if "the great eagles of God himself" were to carry Polyneices to heaven, Creon seems to be placing himself above the gods.

• Then, ask students the Literary Analysis question on p. 800: Which details in Creon's speech emphasize his role as a tragic character?
Answer: Creon's continuing refusal to yield and his pride in saying that he would defy even the gods emphasize his role as a tragic character.

---

15 Whirring fury; I knew that they were fighting,
Tearing each other, dying
In a whirlwind of wings clashing. And I was afraid.
I began the rites of burnt-offering at the altar,
But Hephaistos[14] failed me: instead of bright flame,
20 There was only the sputtering slime of the fat thigh-flesh
Melting: the entrails dissolved in gray smoke,
The bare bone burst from the welter. And no blaze!

This was a sign from heaven. My boy described it,
Seeing for me as I see for others.

25 I tell you, Creon, you yourself have brought
This new calamity upon us. Our hearths and altars
Are stained with the corruption of dogs and carrion birds
That glut themselves on the corpse of Oedipus' son.
The gods are deaf when we pray to them, their fire
30 Recoils from our offering, their birds of omen
Have no cry of comfort, for they are gorged
With the thick blood of the dead.
                                        O my son,
These are no trifles! Think: all men make mistakes,
35 But a good man yields when he knows his course is wrong,
And repairs the evil. The only crime is pride.

Give in to the dead man, then: do not fight with a corpse—
What glory is it to kill a man who is dead?
Think, I beg you:
40 It is for your own good that I speak as I do.
You should be able to yield for your own good.

CREON. It seems that prophets have made me their especial
    province.
All my life long
I have been a kind of butt for the dull arrows
45 Of doddering fortunetellers!
                                No, Teiresias:
If your birds—if the great eagles of God himself
Should carry him stinking bit by bit to heaven,
I would not yield. I am not afraid of pollution:
50 No man can defile the gods.
                                Do what you will,
Go into business, make money, speculate
In India gold or that synthetic gold from Sardis,[15]
Get rich otherwise than by my consent to bury him.
55 Teiresias, it is a sorry thing when a wise man
Sells his wisdom, lets out his words for hire!

TEIRESIAS. Ah Creon! Is there no man left in the world—

CREON. To do what?—Come, let's have the aphorism![16]

14. Hephaistos (hē fes′ təs) god of fire and the forge, who would be invoked, as he is here by Teiresias, for aid in the starting of ceremonial fires.

Literary Analysis
Tragic Character Which details in Creon's speech emphasize his role as a tragic character?

15. Sardis (sär′ dis) capital of ancient Lydia, which produced the first coins made from an alloy of gold and silver.
16. aphorism (af′ ə riz′ əm) *n.* brief, insightful saying. Creon is taunting the prophet and suggesting that the old man is capable of relying only on trite, meaningless expressions instead of any original thinking.

☀ ENRICHMENT: Humanities Connection

Greek Theater

Students may be interested in the ways Greek theater differs from modern theater. Point out these differences:

• The ancient Greeks used little scenery. Scenes were painted on the three sides of pyramid-shaped structures called *periaktoi* (pe re av′ toi). These structures could be swiveled around by "stage hands" to show changes of setting.

• Since no violence was supposed to appear on stage, if a character was killed, a "tableau," or wheeled platform with an actor playing the part of the dead character, would be pushed forward onto the stage.

• In some Greek dramas, gods appeared "flying" in baskets hung from cranes called *deus ex machina* (mä′ke nä), or "god on a machine."

• All actors were male, with boys playing female roles.

TEIRESIAS. No man who knows that wisdom outweighs any wealth?

60 **CREON.** As surely as bribes are baser than any baseness.

TEIRESIAS. You are sick, Creon! You are deathly sick!

CREON. As you say: it is not my place to challenge a prophet.

TEIRESIAS. Yet you have said my prophecy is for sale.

CREON. The generation of prophets has always loved gold.

65 **TEIRESIAS.** The generation of kings has always loved brass.

CREON. You forget yourself! You are speaking to your King.

TEIRESIAS. I know it. You are a king because of me.

CREON. You have a certain skill; but you have sold out.

TEIRESIAS. King, you will drive me to words that—

70 **CREON.**   Say them, say them!
    Only remember: I will not pay you for them.

TEIRESIAS. No, you will find them too costly.

CREON.   No doubt. Speak:
    Whatever you say, you will not change my will.

75 **TEIRESIAS.** Then take this, and take it to heart!
    The time is not far off when you shall pay back
    Corpse for corpse, flesh of your own flesh.
    You have thrust the child of this world into living night,
    You have kept from the gods below the child that is theirs:
80   The one in a grave before her death, the other,
    Dead, denied the grave. This is your crime:

22 ✔ **Reading Check**

What does Teiresias want Creon to do?

23 ▶ Critical Viewing What does Creon appear to be saying to Teiresias? **[Speculate]**

Antigone, Scene 5 ◆ 801

21 Critical Thinking

Analyze

• Ask students what Creon means by saying that Teiresias has "sold out."
Answer: He has been corrupted by money.

• Ask students whether they believe Creon's statement is true.
Answer: Most students probably do not believe that Creon is speaking the truth.

• Then, ask students what Creon's insistence that Teiresias has been corrupted suggests about Creon's thinking.
Answer: Students may say that Creon is unable to consider any viewpoint opposed to his and that he will entertain even a far-fetched rationale to discredit such a viewpoint. If necessary, point out that Creon has suspected both Antigone and the sentry of acting for money.

22 ✔ **Reading Check**

Answer: Teiresias wants Creon to give in and bury Polyneices.

23 ▶ Critical Viewing

Answer: Creon appears to be scolding or ridiculing Teiresias.

CUSTOMIZE INSTRUCTION FOR UNIVERSAL ACCESS

For Less Proficient Readers	For English Learners	For Advanced Readers
Help students understand the exchange between Creon and Teiresias by dividing it into two parts. First, have students identify what Teiresias did and saw before he encountered Creon. Then, have students describe the conflict between Creon and Teiresias.	Encourage students to discuss the photograph on p. 801. What emotions do the characters show? What emotions might they be holding back? Have students try to match one of Creon's speeches with the photograph.	Encourage students to discuss why it is ironic that Teiresias, a fortuneteller, is blind. Have them write a paragraph about why Teiresias was characterized in this manner. What effect might his blindness have on his ability to see the future?

㉔ Reading Strategy

Identifying With a Character

- Read Creon's lines aloud. Then, ask what human emotions Creon is showing for the first time.
  Answer: Creon is showing indecision and self-doubt.

- Then, ask the Reading Strategy question on p. 802: Which details help you identify with Creon's refusal to give in?
  Possible response: Creon has committed himself so totally to his course of action regarding Antigone that he cannot bring himself to change his mind, and must try to discredit the prophet instead.

㉕ Literary Analysis

Tragic Character

- Remind students that Creon's tragic flaw is his pride; until now, he believed that his own rules outweighed those of the gods.

- Then, ask students the Literary Analysis question on p. 802: How does Creon's statement reveal that he has begun to recognize his own tragic flaw?
  Answer: Creon admits the importance of serving the laws of the gods, rather than the laws of the state.

And the Furies[17] and the dark gods of Hell
Are swift with terrible punishment for you.

Do you want to buy me now, Creon?

85   Not many days,
And your house will be full of men and women weeping,
And curses will be hurled at you from far
Cities grieving for sons unburied, left to rot
Before the walls of Thebes.

90   These are my arrows, Creon: they are all for you.

But come, child: lead me home.   [*To* BOY]
Let him waste his fine anger upon younger men.
Maybe he will learn at last
To control a wiser tongue in a better head.

                           [*Exit* TEIRESIAS.]

95 **CHORAGOS.** The old man has gone, King, but his words
Remain to plague us. I am old, too,
But I cannot remember that he was ever false.

CREON. That is true. . . . It troubles me.
100   Oh it is hard to give in! but it is worse
To risk everything for stubborn pride.

CHORAGOS. Creon: take my advice.

CREON.   What shall I do?

CHORAGOS. Go quickly: free Antigone from her vault
And build a tomb for the body of Polyneices.

105 **CREON.** You would have me do this?

CHORAGOS.   Creon, yes!
And it must be done at once: God moves
Swiftly to cancel the folly of stubborn men.

CREON. It is hard to deny the heart! But I
110   Will do it: I will not fight with destiny.

CHORAGOS. You must go yourself, you
         cannot leave it to others.

CREON. I will go.
         —Bring axes, servants:
Come with me to the tomb. I buried her, I
115 Will set her free.
          Oh quickly!
My mind misgives—
The laws of the gods are mighty, and a man must serve them
To the last day of his life!

                     [*Exit* CREON.]

17. Furies (fyoor′ ēz) goddesses of vengence who made insane those whose crimes were unpunished, especially those who had sinned against their own families.

Reading Strategy
Identifying With a Character Which details help you identify with Creon's refusal to give in?

Literary Analysis
Tragic Character How does Creon's statement reveal that he has begun to recognize his own tragic flaw?

802 ◆ *Drama*

CUSTOMIZE INSTRUCTION FOR UNIVERSAL ACCESS

For English Learners	For Advanced Readers
Encourage students to focus on lines 77 through 81 on p. 801. Point out that there are three children mentioned in these lines. Have students figure out who they are. **Answer:** "Flesh of your own flesh" is Creon's son, who Teiresias says will die because of Creon; the child who is "in a grave before her death" is Antigone; the child who is "Dead, denied the grave" is Polyneices.	Taking Teiresias' admonitions and predictions into account, and keeping in mind that the play is a tragedy, have students write a prediction about what Creon's servants will find when they arrive at the vault in which Antigone is entombed.

802

Pæan

CHORAGOS.   [STROPHE 1]
    God of many names

CHORUS.   O Iacchos[18]

              son
    of Kadmeian Semele[19]
5   O born of the Thunder!
    Guardian of the West
              Regent
    of Eleusis' plain[20]
              O Prince of maenad Thebes[21]
10   and the Dragon Field by rippling Ismenos:[22]

CHORAGOS.   [ANTISTROPHE 1]
    God of many names

CHORUS.   the flame of torches
    flares on our hills
              the nymphs of Iacchos
15   dance at the spring of Castalia:[23]

    from the vine-close mountain
              come ah come in ivy:
    Evohe evohe![24] sings through the streets of Thebes

CHORAGOS.   [STROPHE 2]
    God of many names

20 CHORUS.   Iacchos of Thebes
    heavenly Child
              of Semele bride of the Thunderer!
    The shadow of plague is upon us:
25   come
    with clement feet[25]
             oh come from Parnasos[26]
    down the long slopes
             across the lamenting water

CHORAGOS.   [ANTISTROPHE 2]
30   Io[27] Fire! Chorister of the throbbing stars!
    O purest among the voices of the night!
    Thou son of God, blaze for us!

CHORUS. Come with choric rapture of circling Maenads
    Who cry *Io Iacche!*[28]
35   *God of many names!*

---

18. Iacchos (ē′ ə kəs) one of several alternate names for Dionysos.

19. Kadmeian Semele (sem′ ə lē′) Semele was a mortal and the mother of Dionysos. She was the daughter of Thebes' founder, Kadmos.

20. Eleusis' (e lōō′ sis) **plain** Located north of Athens, this plain was a site of worship for Dionysos and Demeter.

21. maenad (mē′ nad′) **Thebes** The city is here compared to a maenad, one of Dionysos' female worshipers. Such a follower would be thought of as uncontrolled or disturbed.

22. Dragon Field . . . Ismenos (is mē′ nas) The Dragon Field was located by the banks of Ismenos, a river near Thebes. Kadmos created warriors by sowing in the Dragon Field the teeth of the dragon he killed there.

23. Castalia (kas tā′ lē ə) location of a site sacred to Apollo.

24. Evohe (ē vō′ ē) triumphant shout of affirmation.

25. clement feet *Clement* means "kind" or "favorable."

26. Parnasos (pär nas′ es) mountain that was sacred to both Dionysos and Apollo, located in central Greece.

27. Io (ē′ ō′) Greek word for "behold" or "hail."

chorister (kôr′ is tər) *n.* member of a chorus

28. Io Iacche (ē′ ō′ ē′ ə ke) cry of celebration used by Dionysian worshipers.

27 ✔**Reading Check**

What does Teiresias say is Creon's crime?

---

26 **Reading Strategy**

Identifying With a Character

- Ask a volunteer to read Creon's speech aloud. Then, ask students what Creon plans to do.
  Answer: He plans to set Antigone free from the vault in which she is imprisoned.

- Point out that Creon's change of heart seems very sudden. Then, ask students to put themselves in Creon's place and to suggest reasons, based on events of the play and on what they know of him, for his change of heart.
  Possible response: Creon first began to waver when the Choragos pointed out that he had never known Teiresias to be wrong. Teiresias's warning combined with Creon's traditional fear of what the gods can do to those who offend them, may have been enough to sway him.

27 ✔**Reading Check**

Answer: Teiresias says that Creon's crime is pride.

28 Critical Thinking

Make Inferences

• Ask a volunteer to read the bracketed passage aloud. Then, ask students whether the messenger
brings bad news or good news.
Answer: He brings bad news.

• Then, ask students what has happened, based on the messenger's
words.
Answer: By saying that happiness
"has all gone from" Creon and
that "life's joy fails," the messenger implies that Antigone and
Haimon are dead.

29 ▶ Critical Viewing

Answer: Eurydice's face shows sto-
ical grief.

Exodus

[*Enter* MESSENGER, *left*.]

MESSENGER. Men of the line of Kadmos,[29] you who live
   Near Amphion's citadel:[30]
                I cannot say
   Of any condition of human life "This is fixed,
5   This is clearly good, or bad." Fate raises up,
   And Fate casts down the happy and unhappy alike:
   No man can foretell his Fate.
                    Take the case of Creon:
   Creon was happy once, as I count happiness:
10   Victorious in battle, sole governor of the land,
   Fortunate father of children nobly born.
   And now it has all gone from him! Who can say
   That a man is still alive when his life's joy fails?
   He is a walking dead man. Grant him rich,
15   Let him live like a king in his great house:
   If his pleasure is gone, I would not give
   So much as the shadow of smoke for all he owns.

CHORAGOS. Your words hint at sorrow: what is your news for us?

MESSENGER. They are dead. The living are guilty of their death.

20 CHORAGOS. Who is guilty? Who is dead? Speak!

MESSENGER.   Haimon.
   Haimon is dead; and the hand that killed him
   Is his own hand.

CHORAGOS.   His father's? or his own?

25 MESSENGER. His own, driven mad by the
        murder his father had done.

CHORAGOS. Teiresias, Teiresias, how clearly
        you saw it all!

29. Kadmos (kad´ məs)
founder of the city of Thebes,
whose daughter, Semele, gave
birth to Dionysos.

30. Amphion's (am fī´ ənz)
citadel Amphion was a king
of Thebes credited with
erecting the walls of the
fortress, or citadel, by using
a magic lyre.

29 ▼ Critical Viewing
Describe the emotions
you see in Eurydice's face.
[Connect]

804 ◆ Drama

✸ **ENRICHMENT: Social Studies Connection**

The Greek Legacy

The Greek legacy to the Western World comprises a
great deal more than drama. Every four years, athletes
from around the world meet to participate in the
Olympic games, which originated in Greece in 776 B.C.
Greek ideas abut law, freedom, justice, and government have influenced political thinking to the present
day. In the arts and sciences, Greek works became a
standard of excellence for the later people of Europe.
In fact, the word *museum* literally means "house of the
Muses." (The muses were nine Greek goddesses who
presided over the arts and sciences.) The achievements of the Greeks were especially remarkable
because they were produced by a scattering of tiny
city-states whose bitter rivalries eventually cost them
their freedom. Suggest that interested students do
research to find out more about the history of the
Olympic Games and how the current games compare
to those that were held originally. Have them prepare
an oral or written report to share the information they
find.

MESSENGER. This is my news: you must draw what
    conclusions you can from it.

CHORAGOS. But look: Eurydice, our Queen:
    Has she overheard us?

             [*Enter* EURYDICE *from the Palace, center.*]

30 **EURYDICE.** I have heard something, friends:
    As I was unlocking the gate of Pallas'[31] shrine,
    For I needed her help today, I heard a voice
    Telling of some new sorrow. And I fainted
    There at the temple with all my maidens about me.
35   But speak again: whatever it is, I can bear it:
    Grief and I are no strangers.

  MESSENGER.   Dearest Lady,
    I will tell you plainly all that I have seen.
    I shall not try to comfort you: what is the use,
40   Since comfort could lie only in what is not true?
    The truth is always best.
                   I went with Creon
    To the outer plain where Polyneices was lying,
    No friend to pity him, his body shredded by dogs.
45   We made our prayers in that place to Hecate[32]
    And Pluto,[33] that they would be merciful. And we bathed
    The corpse with holy water, and we brought
    Fresh-broken branches to burn what was left of it,
    And upon the urn we heaped up a towering barrow
50   Of the earth of his own land.
               When we were done, we ran
    To the vault where Antigone lay on her couch of stone.
    One of the servants had gone ahead,
    And while he was yet far off he heard a voice
55   Grieving within the chamber, and he came back
    And told Creon. And as the King went closer,
    The air was full of wailing, the words lost,
    And he begged us to make all haste. "Am I a prophet?"
    He said, weeping, "And must I walk this road,
60   The saddest of all that I have gone before?
    My son's voice calls me on. Oh quickly, quickly!
    Look through the crevice there, and tell me
    If it is Haimon, or some deception of the gods!"

    We obeyed; and in the cavern's farthest corner
65   We saw her lying:
    She had made a noose of her fine linen veil
    And hanged herself. Haimon lay beside her,
    His arms about her waist, lamenting her,
    His love lost underground, crying out

---

31. Pallas' (pal′ əs) Pallas
Athena, the goddess of
wisdom.

Reading Strategy
Identifying With a
Character Eurydice calmly
worries about "some new
sorrow." Why might she
say that she is accustomed
to grief?

32. Hecate (hek′ ə tē) goddess of the underworld.
33. Pluto (plo̅o̅t′ ō) god of
the underworld who man-
aged the souls of the
departed.

Reading Check
What news does the
messenger bring?

Antigone, Exodus ◆ 805

---

30 Reading Strategy
Identifying With a Character
• Ask students to review the relationship between Creon and
Oedipus, Antigone's father.
Answer: Creon's sister, Iocaste,
was Oedipus's mother and wife.
• Then, have students answer the
Reading Strategy question on
p. 805: Eurydice calmly worries
about "some new sorrow." Why
might she say that she is accustomed to grief?
Answer: Eurydice must have experienced a great deal of grief in the
aftermath of Iocaste's discovery
that she had married her own son.
If necessary, remind students that
Iocaste committed suicide and
that Oedipus put out his own
eyes.

31 Background
Religion
The ancient Greeks performed elaborate rituals over dead bodies. The
messenger here gives a brief
description of the rite that Creon
had earlier refused for Polyneices.

32 ✔ Reading Check
Answer: The messenger brings the
news that Antigone has killed herself and that Haimon is lamenting
her death.

CUSTOMIZE INSTRUCTION FOR UNIVERSAL ACCESS

For Less Proficient Readers	For Advanced Readers
Help students understand what has happened. They should understand that up to this point, Antigone has killed herself and that Haimon is beside himself with grief. Furthermore, the messenger bringing the bad news hints that more grief is yet to come, and that Creon is disconsolate.	Have students review the predictions they made about what Creon's servants would find when they arrived at the vault. How accurate were the predictions? Then, have students write predictions of what will happen between Creon and Haimon.

㉝ Literary Analysis

Tragic Character and Resolution

- To answer the Literary Analysis question on p. 806, review with students the definition of the resolution of a plot.

  Answer: The resolution is the final stage in plot development. It tells how the struggle between characters is worked out.

- Then, read the bracketed passage aloud. Ask students the Literary Analysis question on p. 806: What event here is one part of the resolution to the tragedy that Creon began with his decision to kill Antigone?

  Answer: Haimon's suicide is one part of the plot's resolution. It results from the decisions made by Antigone and Creon.

---

70 That his father had stolen her away from him.
    When Creon saw him the tears rushed to his eyes
    And he called to him: "What have you done, child? Speak to me.
    What are you thinking that makes your eyes so strange?
    O my son, my son, I come to you on my knees!"
75 But Haimon spat in his face. He said not a word,
    Staring—
              And suddenly drew his sword
    And lunged. Creon shrank back, the blade missed; and the boy,
    Desperate against himself, drove it half its length
80 Into his own side, and fell. And as he died
    He gathered Antigone close in his arms again,
    Choking, his blood bright red on her white cheek.
    And now he lies dead with the dead, and she is his
    At last, his bride in the houses of the dead.

                    [*Exit* EURYDICE *into the Palace.*]

85 **CHORAGOS.** She has left us without a word. What can this mean?

    MESSENGER. It troubles me, too; yet she knows what is best,
    Her grief is too great for public lamentation,
    And doubtless she has gone to her chamber to weep
    For her dead son, leading her maidens in his dirge.

90 **CHORAGOS.** It may be so: but I fear this deep silence.

                    [*Pause*]

    MESSENGER. I will see what she is doing. I will go in.

                    [*Exit* MESSENGER *into the Palace.*]

    [*Enter* CREON *with attendants, bearing* HAIMON'S *body.*]

    CHORAGOS. But here is the King himself: oh look at
         him,
    Bearing his own damnation in his arms.

    CREON. Nothing you say can touch me any more.
95   My own blind heart has brought me
    From darkness to final darkness. Here you see
    The father murdering, the murdered son—
    And all my civic wisdom!

    Haimon my son, so young, so young to die,
100   I was the fool, not you; and you died for me.

    CHORAGOS. That is the truth; but you were late in learning it.

    CREON. This truth is hard to bear. Surely a god
    Has crushed me beneath the hugest weight of heaven,
    And driven me headlong a barbaric way
105   To trample out the thing I held most dear.

806 ◆ *Drama*

Etruscan Amphora, black-figure, pontic fighting soldiers, white dove on shield, National Museum, Warsaw, Poland

Literary Analysis
Tragic Character and Resolution What event here is one part of the resolution to the tragedy that Creon began with his decision to kill Antigone?

✸ ENRICHMENT: Art Connection

Etruscan Amphora

Most of the ancient Greek painting that survives today is found on vases. Vase painters captured the myths, legends, wars, Olympic games, and domestic affairs of ancient Greece. One of the most popular vessels artists chose to paint on was the amphora—a two-handled jar such as the one seen here. Help students connect the art to the play with the following questions:

1. What events from *Antigone* might the scene on this vase portray?

Answer: The scene could be showing the battle in which Antigone's two brothers were killed.

2. Why might an artist choose to capture a scene such as this one?

Answer: Battles and heroic deeds were important to the ancient Greeks; capturing them in a painting was one way to tell the stories and preserve their history.

806

The pains that men will take to come to pain!

[*Enter* MESSENGER *from the Palace.*]

MESSENGER. The burden you carry in your hands is heavy,
But it is not all: you will find more in your house.

CREON. What burden worse than this shall I find there?

110 **MESSENGER.** The Queen is dead.

CREON. O port of death, deaf world,
Is there no pity for me? And you, Angel of evil,
I was dead, and your words are death again.
Is it true, boy? Can it be true?
115 Is my wife dead? Has death bred death?

MESSENGER. You can see for yourself.

[*The doors are opened, and the body of* EURYDICE *is disclosed within.*]

CREON. Oh pity!
All true, all true, and more than I can bear!
O my wife, my son!

120 **MESSENGER.** She stood before the altar, and her heart
Welcomed the knife her own hand guided,
And a great cry burst from her lips for Megareus³⁴ dead,
And for Haimon dead, her sons; and her last breath
Was a curse for their father, the murderer of her sons.
125 And she fell, and the dark flowed in through her closing eyes.

CREON. O God, I am sick with fear.
Are there no swords here? Has no one a blow for me?

MESSENGER. Her curse is upon you for the deaths of both.

CREON. It is right that it should be. I alone am guilty.
130 I know it, and I say it. Lead me in,
Quickly, friends.
I have neither life nor substance. Lead me in.

CHORAGOS. You are right, if there can be right in so much wrong.
The briefest way is best in a world of sorrow.

135 **CREON.** Let it come,
Let death come quickly, and be kind to me.
I would not ever see the sun again.

CHORAGOS. All that will come when it will; but we, meanwhile,
Have much to do. Leave the future to itself.

140 **CREON.** All my heart was in that prayer!

CHORAGOS. Then do not pray any more: the sky is deaf.

CREON. Lead me away. I have been rash and foolish.

Reading Strategy

Identifying With a Character In what way can you identify with Creon as he discovers his tragedy has suddenly been doubled?

34. **Megareus** (mə ga′ rē əs) oldest son of Creon and Eurydice, who was killed in the civil war by Argive forces invading Thebes.

35 ✓**Reading Check**

What are Eurydice's last words?

Antigone, Exodus ◆ 807

---

34 **Reading Strategy**

Identifying With a Character

- Ask a volunteer to read the bracketed passage aloud. Ask students what Creon means by saying, "I was dead, and your words are death again."
  Answer: Creon was already filled with grief over the death of Haimon, and now the death of his wife makes him despair even more.

- Then, ask the Reading Strategy question on p. 807: In what way can you identify with Creon as he discovers his tragedy has suddenly been doubled?
  Possible response: Given that Creon repented and tried to prevent Antigone's death, students can probably identify with his deep sorrow over the continuing tragedies in his life.

35 ✓**Reading Check**

Answer: Eurydice's last words are a curse on Creon for the deaths of their sons.

36 **Literary Analysis**

Tragic Character and Resolution

- Have students read the bracketed passage on p. 808. Then, ask to whom Creon refers when he says, "My comfort lies here dead."
  Answer: He is talking about his wife, Eurydice, whom he had expected to comfort him after the death of Haimon, their son.

▶ **Monitor Progress** Ask students: How does Creon sum up his own tragic end?
  Possible response: Creon says that his life has come to total ruin, and he places the blame on his fatal flaw—his pride.

CUSTOMIZE INSTRUCTION FOR UNIVERSAL ACCESS

For English Learners	For Gifted/Talented Students	For Advanced Readers
Help students organize the information on these pages by using a timeline. This visual representation will help them understand the relationships between the many events that are revealed in quick succession.	Have students evaluate the play and decide what Creon might have done that would have been fairer and brought about a happier ending. Suggest that they write their own "happy" ending in the form of a screenplay. Encourage them to work together to dramatize one of the screenplays for the class.	Suggest that students analyze the play and choose what they consider to be the best part and the worst part. Have them write short explanations citing the reasons they chose each part. Students can then exchange ideas with classmates in small-group discussions.

Review and Assess

1. Students may point out that if Creon had not changed his mind, events would have turned out the same way. Others may say that he was right to change his mind but should have done so earlier.

2. **(a)** Creon and Haimon argue over Creon's decision to have Antigone put to death. **(b)** Haimon believes that Antigone was right to obey divine law and bury Polyneices, rather than to obey the law of the state.

3. **(a)** Teiresias foretells that Haimon will die and that Creon's house will be filled with grief. **(b)** After Teiresias' prophecy, Creon sets out to bury Polyneices and free Antigone. **(c)** Events springing from Creon's decision to kill Antigone happen too quickly for him to stop them.

4. **(a)** The messenger tells Eurydice that Antigone and Haimon have killed themselves. **(b)** Creon has lost his beloved son and wife; his rigid pride has destroyed his power to rule.

5. **(a)** The play is based on the tension between individual, divine conscience (Antigone), and civil, human authority (Creon), with the potential for human reason (Haimon) to save the day. **(b)** Possible response: Although she lost her life in the process, Antigone won the battle. Polyneices was buried and Creon was ruined.

6. Creon's words are timeless. In every age, great effort often comes to naught. Have students offer examples from literature, movies, and current events.

7. Unwillingness to appear weak may make a person inflexible and unable to adjust to circumstances.

I have killed my son and my wife.
I look for comfort; my comfort lies here dead.
36 145 Whatever my hands have touched has come to nothing.
Fate has brought all my pride to a thought of dust.

[As CREON *is being led into the house, the* CHORAGOS *advances and speaks directly to the audience.*]

CHORAGOS. There is no happiness where there is no wisdom;
No wisdom but in submission to the gods.
Big words are always punished,
150 And proud men in old age learn to be wise.

Review and Assess

Thinking About the Selection

1. **Respond:** Do you think Creon should have changed his decision regarding Antigone? Why or why not?

2. **(a) Recall:** Why do Creon and Haimon argue? **(b) Analyze:** Is Haimon more concerned with divine law, to which Antigone turns for justification, or with human law? Support your answer.

3. **(a) Recall:** According to Teiresias, what terrible punishment awaits Creon? **(b) Recall:** What action does Creon take after the prophecy? **(c) Analyze:** Why is Creon unable to stop the tragedy?

4. **(a) Recall:** What news does the Messenger tell Eurydice before she leaves the stage during the Exodos? **(b) Interpret:** Why does Creon say "I have neither life nor substance" in the Exodos?

5. **(a) Analyze:** Explain how this play demonstrates the tension that sometimes exists between an individual's conscience and a designated authority. **(b) Evaluate:** In this play, who do you think wins that battle?

6. **Relate:** Near the end of the play, Creon says, "The pains that men will take to come to pain!" How do his words apply to contemporary society?

7. **Evaluate:** Both Antigone and Creon are unwilling to appear weak. How could this trait influence a person's actions and outlook on life?

Sophocles

(496?–406 B.C.)
The Greek dramatist Sophocles (săf′ ə klēz) wrote 123 plays, but only 7 remain in existence. His most famous are those chronicling the lives of Oedipus and his children: *Oedipus Rex* (Oedipus the King), *Oedipus at Colonus*, and *Antigone*. This trilogy was written over a span of forty years.

Born in Colonos, near Athens, Sophocles was one of the most respected Greek dramatists of his time. He was admired not only for his poetic and dramatic skills, but also for his good looks, athleticism, and musical ability.

ASSESSMENT PRACTICE: Reading Comprehension

Notice Word Choice   (For more practice, see Test Preparation Workbook, p. 49.)

To help students prepare for tests, offer them practice in analyzing the characteristics of texts. Use this sample test item to help students notice the effect of word choice.

Antigone is a stubborn young woman who will not give into the law of the land. Her sister, Ismene, begs desperately with her to change her mind, but Antigone will have none of her sister's pleading.

In this passage, the word *stubborn*—

A shows the writer's attitude toward Antigone

B provides a fact about Antigone

C shows how Antigone felt about herself

D shows how Ismene felt about Antigone

Since the word *stubborn* reveals bias, students should consider answers A, C, and D. There is not enough information in the passage to support C or D. Answer A is the best choice.

eview and Assess

erary Analysis

ic Character

. (a) In your opinion, is Antigone or Creon the more **tragic character**? (b) Which suffers the greater downfall? Give evidence from the play to support your answer.

. Using a chart like the one here, analyze the tragic flaws of Antigone and Creon.

	Character Flaw	How It Led to Tragedy
Antigone		
Creon		

. What role, if any, does fate—the Greek concept that lives are pre-determined—play in each downfall?

necting Literary Elements

. (a) How is the struggle between Antigone and Creon resolved? (b) Identify the climax, and list two events that take place in the **resolution** of the play.

. How does the resolution stress the tragic nature of the characters?

. How does the resolution reveal the play's theme, or central message?

ding Strategy

tifying With a Character

. (a) With which character do you most identify—Antigone, Creon, or one of the others? (b) Give reasons and evidence from the play to support your answer.

. Which actions, events, or lines in the play lead you to identify with the character you have chosen?

. How does your identification with that character draw you into the action of the play?

end Understanding

. **World Events Connection:** How do the checks and balances of a democracy protect against Creon's style of leadership?

Quick Review

A **tragic character** is a significant person in a drama who experiences a reversal of fortune as a result of fate or a flaw in his or her character.

The **resolution** is the final stage of the plot development that tells how the struggle between opposing characters or forces is worked out.

To **identify with a character,** put yourself in the character's place and try to understand his or her feelings and issues.

 Take It to the Net

www.phschool.com
Take the interactive self-test online to check your understanding of the selection.

Antigone, Scenes 3–5 ◆ 809

Answers for p. 809

Review and Assess

1. **(a)** Some students may choose Antigone because she lost her life; others may choose Creon because he lost his loved ones and his power. **(b) Possible response:** Creon suffers the greater downfall, because he lost everything that matters in life: his wife, his son, and the respect of his people.

2. Character Flaw: Antigone: passionate, unyielding heart; Creon: rigid and proud; How It Led to Tragedy: Antigone: unwillingness to compromise drew her into the conflict that resulted in her death; Creon: reliance on authority rather than on logic or common sense led him to disaster

3. The consequences of fate were brought before Creon by Teiresias to no avail, because he would not listen or use reason. Without reason, fate took its natural course.

4. **(a)** The struggle is resolved when Antigone kills herself. **(b)** The climax of the play occurs when Creon changes his mind and resolves to release Antigone from the vault. Two events that take place in the resolution are the deaths of Antigone and Haimon.

5. In the resolution, the tragic characters come to tragic ends.

6. The resolution shows that people who remain proud and rigid in their beliefs will come to tragic ends.

7. Possible response: **(a)** Students may identify most with Haimon. **(b)** For the love of his father and Antigone, he tried to guide his father with a wisdom that was beyond his years; he would have made a wise king.

8. Students should offer reasons that the lines or actions hold particular meaning for them.

9. Students may respond that they felt as though they could be the character, that this made the situation very real for them, instead of remote and distant.

10. The leader in a democracy cannot act unilaterally; she or he needs the support of the other branches of the government.

❶ Vocabulary Development

Word Analysis

1. c
2. a
3. d
4. b

Concept Development: Synonyms

1. d
2. a
3. f
4. b
5. c
6. e

Spelling Strategy

1. fierce
2. received
3. deceit

❷ Grammar

1. they (do).
2. he (was).
3. I (was).
4. she (is).
5. we (do).

Writing Application

Sample response: Antigone is a more passionate person than I. It would be hard to find anyone as idealistic as she. Would many of us be willing to do as she and lay down our lives for a principle?

Integrate Language Skills

❶ Vocabulary Development Lesson

Word Analysis: Greek Root -chor-

The root of *chorister* and *chorus* is *-chor-*, which comes from *Terpsichore* (tərp sik´ ə rē´), the Greek Muse of dance and song.

The words in the left column are based on the Greek root *-chor*. In your notebook, match each word in the left column with its definition in the right column.

1. choral   a. art of creating dances

2. choreography   b. group of singers

3. chorister   c. relating to a performance by a group of singers

4. choir   d. member or leader of a group of singers

Concept Development: Synonyms

Match each word in the left column with its synonym in the right column.

1. deference   a. corrupt
2. vile   b. disrepect
3. piety   c. mourning
4. blasphemy   d. respect
5. lamentation   e. singer
6. chorister   f. reverence

Spelling Strategy

Place *i* before *e* except after *c* or when sounded like *a* as in *neighbor* and *weigh*. Fill in the blanks with *ie* or *ei* to correctly spell each word below.

1. Two brothers fought a f___rce battle.
2. Both rec___ved mortal wounds.
3. Each accused the other of dec___t.

❷ Grammar Lesson

Pronoun Case in Elliptical Clauses

An **elliptical clause,** or an incomplete clause, is a type of construction in which some words are omitted because they are understood. When a pronoun occurs in an elliptical clause, its case is what it would be if the construction were complete. As the example shows, clauses beginning with *than* or *as* are often incomplete.

> **Example:** Is a woman stronger *than we?* [*are* is understood]

The understood word in the example is *are*. The completed clause would read, "Is a woman stronger *than we are?*" You can see that *we* is correct because you would not say, "Is a woman stronger than *us are?*"

Practice In your notebook, write the correct pronoun to complete each sentence. Then, identify the words that are needed to complete the elliptical clause.

1. The chorus sees all; no one sees more than (*they, them*).
2. No one was more enraged than (*he, him*).
3. My friend was as certain as (*I, me*).
4. Antigone is stronger than (*she, her*).
5. Antigone faces some of the same issues as (*we, us*).

Writing Application Write a brief comparison of Antigone and yourself. Use at least three elliptical clauses in your comparison.

*W*G *Prentice Hall Writing and Grammar Connection: Chapter 23, Section 2*

810 ◆ *Drama*

TEACHING RESOURCES

The following resources can be used to enrich or extend the instruction for pp. 810–811.

Vocabulary

📖 **Selection Support Workbook:** Build Vocabulary, p. 193

📖 **Vocabulary and Spelling Practice Book** (Use this booklet for skills enrichment.)

Grammar

📖 **Selection Support:** Build Grammar Skills, p. 194

*W*G **Writing and Grammar,** Platinum Level, p. 556

📄 **Daily Language Practice Transparencies** 📄

Writing

*W*G **Writing and Grammar,** Platinum Level, p. 284 📄

💿 **Writing and Grammar iText CD-ROM**

📄 **Writing Models and Graphic Organizers on Transparencies,** pp. 53–59

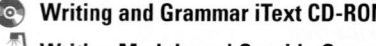 **BLOCK SCHEDULING:** Resources marked with this symbol provide varied instruction during 90-minute blocks.

Writing Lesson

Analytic Essay

After more than two thousand years, *Antigone* continues to touch audiences. In an essay, identify a theme from the play and analyze its relevance to today's readers.

Prewriting   Note conflicts, dialogue, or descriptions in the play that moved you. For each instance, consider what message made the writing effective. Choose one key moment on which to build your essay.

Drafting   State the message you think the play conveys. Use the body of your essay to summarize the key moment and to link that to the theme. Draw connections between the play's message and modern life.

Revising   Review your draft to evaluate whether you have effectively analyzed the theme of the play. If necessary, add more direct language that addresses the theme you have identified.

Model: Revising to Strengthen Analysis

When Antigone argues with Ismene, audiences see just how fiercely she holds her convictions—and how cowardly Ismene's own ideals really are. *Through this argument, Sophocles shows readers how difficult it can be to take an unpopular stand for your cause.*

> This additional sentence adds analysis to the summary.

WG *Prentice Hall Writing and Grammar Connection: Chapter 13, Section 2*

Extension Activities

Listening and Speaking Hold a **mock trial** in which both sides in the dispute between Antigone and Creon are argued before the class. Select students to play various roles:

- Judge
- Several defense attorneys
- Several prosecuting attorneys
- Witnesses

Have attorneys for both sides provide witnesses. The class should act as a jury to decide which argument is more convincing. **[Group Activity]**

Research and Technology Give a **multimedia presentation** on ancient Greek theater. Before you begin, prepare a list of research questions to guide your work, and use the Internet and library resources to gather information. Include illustrations or labeled diagrams, tape recordings of excerpts from *Antigone*, historical maps, timelines, and other items to enhance your presentation.

 Take It to the Net   www.phschool.com

Go online for an additional research activity using the Internet.

Lesson Support for p. 811

❸ Writing Lesson

- Lead students in a discussion about why *Antigone* is still relevant today. Encourage them to discuss figures from history who have, like Antigone, been willing to lay down their lives for a cause.

- Then, use the writing lesson to guide students in developing their analytic essays. As a model, show them the Interpreting a Work of Literature essay on pp. 53–59 of **Writing Models and Graphic Organizers on Transparencies.**

- Use the Response to Literature rubric in **Performance Assessment and Portfolio Management,** p. 16, to evaluate students' essays.

❹ Research and Technology

- Brainstorm with students for a list of topics they might focus on and questions they might ask.

- As small groups plan their presentations, suggest that they consider what technologies they will use. Encourage students to employ videos, maps, diagrams, recordings, and photographs.

- Have students conduct their research and prepare their presentations. When they finish, have them share their work with the class.

CUSTOMIZE INSTRUCTION
For Universal Access

To address different learning styles, use the activities suggested in the **Extension Activities** booklet, p. 49.

- For Logical/Mathematical Learners, use Activity 5.

- For Bodily/Kinesthetic Learners, use Activity 6.

- For Visual/Spatial and Logical/Mathematical Learners, use Activity 7.

Lesson Objectives

1. To learn how to compare information from several sources
2. To learn how to find specific information in one or more sources

About Arts-and-Leisure Articles

- Have students read "About Arts-and-Leisure Articles." Then have students discuss the different kinds of articles they have seen in their daily newspapers.
  Possible responses: Answers include a news story about the signing of a director and performers to make a new film.

- Ask students to discuss the similarities and differences among arts-and-leisure articles. How is the purpose of an article on a playwright, for example, different from the purpose of a review of the playwright's new play?
  Possible response: The purpose of an article about a playwright might be to give information about his or her life, while the purpose of a review of the new play would be to persuade readers of the critic's opinion.

- Ask students to think of situations in which they might read about the same person, event, or trend in more than one article.
  Possible responses: Answers include a news article about a local performer appearing in a new film and a review of the film; an article about the growing number of musicals being staged at local theaters and a news story on a director who specializes in directing musicals.

Reading Strategy

Comparing Information From Several Sources

- Have students read the information about the Reading Strategy.

- Ask students what a reader gains by reading more than one article about a topic.
  Possible response: Students may say that they will find different perspectives and information about different aspects of the topic.

- Have students fill out a Venn Diagram as they read the review and the article.

812

Arts-and-Leisure Articles

About Arts-and-Leisure Articles

Arts-and-leisure articles describe events that take place in the art world, addressing film, museums, music, theater, and style. There are three types: straight news, trends, and reviews. The article about the Colosseum is a straight news article, telling about a new theater that has been constructed within Rome's Colosseum. The other article is a review of a New York City production of the play *Oedipus Rex*, presented by the National Theater of Greece.

Reading Strategy

Comparing Information From Several Sources

When you read about an event in the news, you may find that several magazines, newspapers, or broadcast outlets cover the story. Instead of limiting yourself to only one source, you can compare the presentations to get a more complete and balanced understanding of the event.

The articles that follow were written by Ben Brantley of *The New York Times*. Each refers to the Greek National Theater. As you read, look for the information that is common to both. Then, look for the ways in which the writer addresses different angles of the story. Consider these questions:

- What is the main idea of each article?
- What details support the main idea?
- What information do both articles include?
- Is there contradictory information? If so, which article seems more reliable?

As you read, use a Venn diagram like the one shown to compare information from these articles.

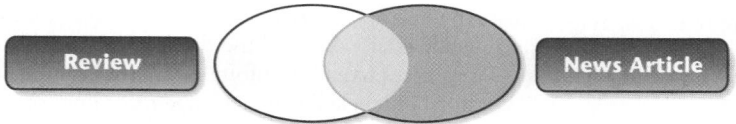

The New York Times

PRIVATE HORROR MADE PUBLIC
Theater Review

BEN BRANTLEY

The smothering sense of solitariness gets to you from the very beginning, that feeling of being helplessly on your own within a crowd. There he stands, the leader of a nation, so confident, so brisk, so firm of purpose as he speaks to his supplicating subjects. And also, clearly, so very very alone. The saddest part is that he doesn't even seem to know how alone he is. He will before the evening is over, of course. His name is Oedipus.

Few productions have so hauntingly conveyed the brutal isolation of those who would be king as the National Theater of Greece's exquisitely staged "Oedipus Rex," directed by Vassilis Papavassileiou, which runs at City Center through Sunday and which this summer famously reopened the Roman Colosseum as a theatrical space for the first time in 1,500 years.

This hypnotic re-creation of Sophocles's masterwork, a visually poetic staging that never sacrifices sense of feeling to style, examines the deepest wounds inflicted by the public exposure of private horrors. . . .

Mr. Papavassileiou's extraordinary achievement here is to convey the despair of a king whose destruction is particular to political circumstance, and at the same time to present a universal mirror as bleak and unsparing as Samuel Beckett's. Everything about the staging here emphasizes an impression of existence in a void. You feel those classic pangs of sorrow and pity before the production even begins.

Clearly, the proscenium stage at City Center is not the Colosseum of Rome. Yet Yorgos Ziakas's set, as underscored by Antonis Panayotopoulos's lighting, still suggests claustrophobic confinement and an empty vastness. Dimitris Kamarotos's instrumental music mixes percussive anxiety with the wandering, lonely melodies of reed instruments.

The audience entering the theater is greeted by a sight gag of sorts. Seven George Segal-style human statues in off-white monochromatic plaster and modern dress stand at the ready onstage. The dumb chorus prefigures the speaking one, which arrives in robes and half-masks that match the colors of the statues.

This combination of the classic and the contemporary ingeniously scrambles expectations. The obvious choice would have been to put the statues in ancient costume and the actors in street clothes. Mr. Papavassileiou and Mr. Ziakas will pluck images throughout the millennia here, but never randomly. There is always method in the mélange.

This is evident early in the visual confusion of the living and the unmoving choruses. And when Oedipus arrives on stage, in rich colors and garb associated with by-the-book Shakespeare productions, the contrast to the pale shrouded figures around him is shocking. . . .

The use of the chorus throughout is inventive and eloquent, incorporating ancient traditional devices (like the ceremonial beating of poles) into a flowing movement that embodies the fluctuations of sentiment among the citizens of Thebes. Individual speakers intone lines that are taken up by others, sometimes mutating into chants and song. You know these people, fretting over the state of their nation, shifting between certainty and frightened cluelessness. Today's pollsters would also find them familiar.

The supertitles are, inevitably, an encumbrance, especially early in the production, when one is still in a skeptical frame of mind. There are a few laughably awkward translations, as when Teiresias ominously tells Oedipus, "You sleep with your relatives."

News Article

- Have students state the subject of the article.

  Answer: The Roman Colosseum will stage a major event for the first time in 1,500 years.

- Ask students what has been done to the former underground areas for the gladiators and animals, in order for plays to take place at the Colosseum.

  Answer: A huge wooden structure has been built over this section.

AFTER 1,500 YEARS, COLOSSEUM REOPENS FOR SHOWS

BEN BRANTLEY

The opening paragraph provides the "lead," identifying the subject of the article.

Rome — The Colosseum, Rome's ancient arena of death and slaughter, will Wednesday stage its first major spectacle before a paying audience in 1,500 years.

This paragraph announces the plays to be produced in the theater.

The amphitheatre, completed under Roman Emperor Titus in 80 A.D., will not be hosting the gory combat brought vividly to life in the recent box office smash "Gladiator," but a more civilized festival of Greek tragedy.

"After 1,500 years, the Colosseum returns to its spectacular origins. This is an historical event for this monument and this country," Italian Culture Minister Giovanna Melandri told reporters after unveiling the 1.5 billion lire ($724,500) stage built over part of the floorless Colosseum.

The writer describes the restoration work.

The performances were made possible by building a wooden structure over a section of underground labyrinth that once housed gladiators and wild beasts, capping years of restoration work. The passages, clogged with earth over the centuries, were dug out on the order of French emperor Napoleon at the end of the 18th century.

"We are not going back to (the Colosseum's) gruesome and tragic origins but will instead give space to art and culture," Melandri said.

The festival will include three tragedies by ancient Greek playwright Sophocles performed between July 19 and Aug. 6.

"Oedipus Rex" by the Greek National Theater will be followed by "Antigone" by the Dramatic Arts Center of Tehran.

Rome's prestigious Santa Cecilia Academy will end the festival with the opera "Oedipus" by 19th-century German composer Felix Mendelssohn, adapted from Sophocles' "Oedipus in Colonus."

FIT FOR AN EMPEROR

Workers were preparing seats and standing room for 700 spectators at the eastern end of the Colosseum near the podium where the emperor, his court and senators used to give the thumbs-up or down to decide the gladiators' fate.

When ancient Rome ruled the western world, the then marble-clad building provided entertainment for up to 70,000 citizens, rich and poor.

Prices this time round are more than the couple of denarii the masses once paid. Standing room costs 40,000 lire and 100,000 will get you a seat.

The new wooden stage covers some 4,300 square feet of the 29,000 square foot arena. Actors will reach the stage via a wooden bridge linking the structure to the western end of the Colosseum and spanning the underground passages.

The decision to build the stage is part of a project to protect the remaining stone passages from further damage.

"The spirit behind this initiative is that of uniting preservation with cultural activities," Melandri said. "The stage is important because it also protects the monument."

Officials said it was not clear what will happen next as archaeologists will need to study the impact of the wooden structure on the ancient walls.

"This is an experiment. We'll see how it goes and then we will decide," Melandri said.

She said the Culture Ministry would be very rigorous in choosing future cultural initiatives for the Colosseum.

Check Your Comprehension

1. What is the mood of the play *Oedipus Rex*?
2. What does the audience see upon entering the City Center theater?
3. What is the purpose of the chorus in *Oedipus*?
4. Where within the Colosseum was the wooden structure of the theater built?
5. What were the first three productions presented in the newly opened Colosseum?

Applying the Reading Strategy

Comparing Information From Several Sources

6. What is the purpose of the review?
7. What is the purpose of the straight news article?
8. What information do the articles have in common?

Activity

Comparing Reviews

Find a review of a different production of the play *Oedipus Rex*, and compare it with the review of the Greek National Theater production on page 813. Answer the following questions, using a chart like the one at right.

1. How does the reviewer describe the mood of the play?
2. How does the reviewer describe the sets and costumes?
3. Which production would you rather see? Why?

Play Review

Sets

Costumes

Mood

Comparing Informational Materials

Reviews and Programs

Programs are given to the audience of a play before the play begins. They contain information that helps the audience understand and enjoy the play, such as background and historical notes, introductions of the actors, and an outline of the acts and scenes in the play. Compare the information you would find in a program with that in a review.

1. (a) Why would you read a review? (b) Why would you read a program?
2. Which might be more subjective? Why?
3. What information would be in a review that is not in a program?

Answers continued

information about the performers and other people connected with the production.

2. The review would be more subjective, because a review is based upon personal opinion.

3. Information about what is positive or negative about any aspect of the production would be in a review, but not in a program.

Check Your Comprehension

1. The mood is smothering, isolating, and solitary.

2. The audience sees several sculptures of human figures in modern dress, in the style of sculptor George Segal.

3. The chorus represents the citizens of Thebes, who respond emotionally to the events on stage.

4. The wooden structure was built over the section that used to house the underground areas for gladiators and animals.

5. The first three productions in the new Colosseum were Sophocles' *Oedipus Rex* and *Antigone* and Mendelssohn's *Oedipus*.

Applying the Reading Strategy

6. The purpose of the review is to give the writer's opinion of the production of the play.

7. The purpose of the straight news article is to give information about the restoration of the Roman Colosseum.

8. The articles both talk about the production of the National Theater of Greece's production of *Oedipus Rex*.

Activity

- Invite students to use the Internet to find a review of a different production of *Oedipus Rex*.

- Have students fill in the chart for both reviews, giving short versions of the reviewers' comments about the sets, costumes, and mood.

- Have students write their opinions of which production they would like to see, and explain why.

Comparing Informational Materials

Display one or more programs from dramatic productions at the school or in the community. Give students time to read them and compare them with the review on p. 813. Then, have them answer the questions.

Possible responses:

1. (a) You would read a review to get a specific opinion by a critic about the production. (b) You would read a program to get biographical and professional

continued

The Tragedy of Julius Caesar, Act I

Lesson Objectives

1. **To analyze and respond to literary elements**
   - Literary Analysis: Exposition in Drama
   - Connecting Literary Elements: Dialogue
2. **To read, comprehend, analyze, and critique a play**
   - Reading Strategy: Using Text Aids
   - Reading Check questions
   - Review and Assess questions
   - Assessment Practice (ATE)
3. **To develop word analysis skills, fluency, and systematic vocabulary**
   - Vocabulary Development Lesson: Related Words: Forms of *portent*
4. **To understand and apply written and oral language conventions**
   - Spelling Strategy
   - Grammar Lesson: Mood
5. **To understand and apply appropriate writing and research strategies**
   - Writing Lesson: Persuasive Essay (after Act V)
   - Extension Activity: Interior Monologue
6. **To understand and apply listening and speaking strategies**
   - Extension Activity: Visual Symbol

STEP-BY-STEP TEACHING GUIDE	PACING GUIDE
PRETEACH	
Motivate Students and Provide Background	
Use the Motivation activity (ATE p. 820)	5 min.
Read and discuss the Preview material and Background information (SE/ATE p. 820) **A**	5 min.
Introduce the Concepts	
Introduce the Literary Analysis and Reading Strategy (SE/ATE p. 821) **A**	15 min.
Pronounce the vocabulary words and read their definitions (SE p. 821)	5 min.
TEACH	
Monitor Comprehension	
Informally monitor comprehension by circulating while students read independently or in groups **A**	30 min.
Monitor students' comprehension with the Reading Check notes (SE/ATE pp. 823, 825, 827, 829, 831, 833, 835)	as students read
Develop vocabulary with Vocabulary notes (SE pp. 824, 832, 834, 835; ATE p. 834)	as students read
Develop Understanding	
Develop students' understanding of exposition in drama with the Literary Analysis annotations (SE/ATE pp. 824, 826, 827, 828, 831, 832, 836, 837) **A**	10 min.
Develop students' understanding of text aids with the Reading Strategy annotations (SE/ATE pp. 822, 823, 825, 833, 835)	10 min.
ASSESS	
Assess Mastery	
Assess students' mastery of the Reading Strategy and Literary Analysis by having them answer the Review and Assess questions (SE/ATE p. 838)	20 min.
Use one or more of the print and media Assessment Resources (ATE p. 839) **A**	up to 50 min.
EXTEND	
Apply Understanding	
Have students complete the Vocabulary Development Lesson and the Grammar Lesson (SE p. 839) **A**	20 min.
Apply students' knowledge of paraphrasing using the Writing Lesson (SE p. 915) **A**	45 min.
Apply students' understanding of the selection using one or more of the Extension Activities (SE p. 839)	20–90 min.

 ACCELERATED INSTRUCTION:
Use the strategies and activities identified with an **A**.

UNIVERSAL ACCESS
● = Below Level Students
▲ = On-Level Students
■ = Above Level Students

Time and Resource Manager

Reading Level: Challenging
Average Number of Instructional Days: 5

PRINT	TRANSPARENCIES	TECHNOLOGY
RESOURCES		
• **Beyond Literature,** Humanities Connection: The Globe Theater, p. 50 ▲ ■		• **Interest Grabber Video,** Tape 4 ● ▲ ■
• **Selection Support Workbook:** ● ▲ ■ Literary Analysis, p. 200 Reading Strategy, p. 199 Build Vocabulary, p. 197	• **Literary Analysis and Reading Transparencies,** pp. 99 and 100 ● ▲ ■	
		• **Listening to Literature** ● ▲ ■ Audiocassettes, Side 27 Audio CDs, CD 17
• **Literatura en español** ● ▲ • **Literary Analysis for Enrichment** ■		
• **Formal Assessment:** Selection Test, pp. 176–178 ● ▲ ■ • **Open Book Test,** pp. 148–150 ● ▲ ■ • PRENTICE HALL *ASSESSMENT SYSTEM* ● ▲ ■	• PRENTICE HALL *ASSESSMENT SYSTEM* ● ▲ ■ Skills Practice Answers and Explanations on Transparencies	• **Test Bank Software** ● ▲ ■ • **Got It! Assessment Videotapes,** Tape 4 ● ▲
• **Selection Support Workbook:** ● ▲ ■ Build Grammar Skills, p. 198 • **Writing and Grammar,** Platinum Level ● ▲ ■ • **Extension Activities,** p. 50 ● ▲ ■	• **Daily Language Practice Transparencies** ● ▲	• **Writing and Grammar iText CD-ROM** ● ▲ ■ *Take It to the Net* www.phschool.com

BLOCK SCHEDULING: Use one 90-minute class period to preteach the selection and have students read it. Use a second 90-minute class period to assess students' mastery of skills and have them complete one of the Extension Activities.

Background

Shakespeare's Globe Theater

Most of Shakespeare's plays were performed at the Globe Theater, built by Richard and Cuthbert Burbage. Their father James had built London's first theater (named simply The Theater).

Actors and playwrights occupied an odd position in London society. Although the elite looked down on actors, the common people clamored to see them perform in plays. They enjoyed reputations somewhat like those of modern rock stars: not quite respectable, but very much in demand.

The Globe was small enough for the actors' voices to reach the whole audience, but large enough to hold 2,500 to 3,000 people. Anyone who had a penny could buy admission to the Globe and stand in its central yard throughout the performance. The Globe's roof did not cover the pit, so the "groundlings," as they were called, got wet if it rained. On the other end of the scale, wealthy people sat in a gallery above and behind the stage. They came to the Globe hoping to be seen by the rest of the audience.

Renaissance technology allowed only a limited number of homemade sound effects. The Globe could be lit only by daylight, moonlight, or torches, which were dangerous in a wooden building with a thatched roof. Scenery was confined to the barest necessary pieces of furniture. Indications of light, sound, and setting were often written into the script. For example, at the beginning of a scene in *Macbeth*, a character looks around and remarks, "This castle hath a pleasant seat," thus informing the audience where the scene takes place.

The Globe burned to the ground in 1613, when a cannon fired during a performance of Shakespeare's *Henry VIII* set the theater's thatched roof on fire. The theater was rebuilt. The foundations of this second Globe were discovered in 1990.

Shakespeare on Stage

The Globe Theater

The Tragedy of Julius Caesar, like most of Shakespeare's plays, was produced in a public theater. Public theaters were built around roofless courtyards that had no artificial light. Performances, therefore, were given only during daylight hours. Surrounding the courtyard were three levels of galleries with benches where wealthier playgoers sat. Those who could not pay to sit, the "groundlings," stood and watched from the courtyard, which was called the pit.

Most of Shakespeare's plays were performed in the Globe theater. No one is certain exactly what the Globe looked like, though Shakespeare tells us it was round or octagonal. We know that it was open to the sky and that it held between 2,500 and 3,000 people. When the plans for a reconstruction of the Globe theater began in 1988, scholars and builders started with this information. As they worked, they learned more from the site of the original theater. The foundation was then discovered in 1990; its excavation has revealed clues about the plays, the actors, and the audience. The tiny part of the foundation initially uncovered yielded a great number of hazelnut shells. Hazelnuts were Elizabethan "popcorn"; people munched on them all during a performance.

The stage was a platform that extended into the pit. Actors entered and left the stage from doors located behind the platform. The portion of the galleries behind and above the stage was used primarily as dressing and storage rooms. The second-level gallery right above the stage, however, was used as an upper stage.

There was no scenery in the theaters of Shakespeare's day. Settings were indicated by references in the dialogue. As a result, one scene could follow another in rapid succession. The actors wore elaborate clothing—typical Elizabethan clothing, not costuming. Thus, the plays produced in Shakespeare's day were fast-paced, colorful productions that usually lasted two hours.

An important difference between Shakespeare's theater and theaters of today is that acting companies of the sixteenth century were made up only of men and boys. Women

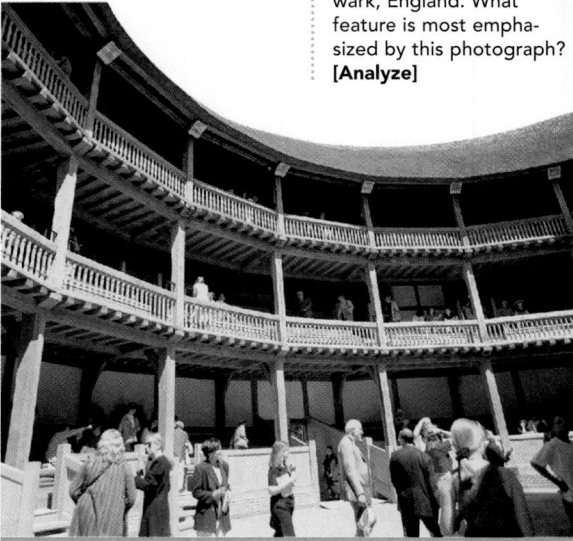

▼ **Critical Viewing**
Visitors enjoy the newly constructed Globe at the International Shakespeare Globe Centre in Southwark, England. What feature is most emphasized by this photograph? **[Analyze]**

✳ ENRICHMENT: History Connection

The Great Fire

A Londoner named Sir Henry Wotton wrote the following letter to his nephew, describing the burning of the Globe in 1613:

"The King's players had a new play . . . representing some principal pieces of the reign of Henry VIII, which was set forth with many extraordinary circumstances of pomp and majesty . . . sufficient in truth within a while to make greatness very familiar, if not ridiculous. Now, King Henry making a masque at the Cardinal Wolsey's house, and certain chambers being shot off at his entry, some of the paper . . . did light on the thatch . . . consuming within less than an hour the whole house to the very grounds. . . . [O]ne man had his breeches set on fire, that would perhaps have broiled him, if he had not by the benefit of a provident wit put it out with a bottle of ale."

did not perform on the stage, as it was not considered proper. Boys aged eleven, twelve, or thirteen—before their voices changed—performed the female roles.

Reconstructing the Globe

In 1988, on April 23 (believed to be Shakespeare's birthday), years of fund-raising and effort resulted in a remarkable birthday present for the playwright. Work began on a reconstruction of his Globe theater. The design is based on archaeological evidence and a drawing by Wendeslas Hollar. A contract drawn up in 1600 for the Fortune playhouse, a theater built by the same carpenter who built the Globe, provides additional details.

The new Globe, like the first two, is made of wood. Traditional sixteenth-century carpentry techniques were used for much of the construction. A thatched roof protects the stage and galleries, and lime plaster covers the walls. After long years of fund-raising and construction, the theater opened to its first full season on June 8, 1997, with a production of *Henry V.*

▲ **Critical Viewing**
This drawing shows the features of the Globe theater. Notice the stage, the doors through which actors enter and exit, the "upper stage," the galleries where wealthy people sit, and the pit where the groundlings stand. What modern-day structures does this theater suggest? **[Connect]**

Shakespeare on Stage ◆ 817

Background
The Globe Today

London's new Globe Theater is a remarkable replica of the Burbages' original. The new Globe is located near the site of the original on the south bank of the Thames River in a neighborhood called Southwark. It retains the circular shape, uncovered center, thatched roof, and bare bleacher-style seating of the original. The builders relied on surviving contracts for the Rose and Fortune theaters, which were built by the same carpenters who built the Globe, and on the existing foundations of the Rose, which were excavated in 1988. They used the same techniques and building materials as their predecessors 300 years earlier; the new Globe is held together by wooden pegs, not metal nails, and there are no bathrooms (these are in a museum building across the plaza from the theater). The only concession made to modern times is the signs for the fire exits.

The new Globe seats 1,000. The seats curve around the sides of the stage, giving everyone a view of the action. Some audience views are partly blocked by pillars, but no audience member is more than 50 feet from the stage. The pit has room for 450 groundlings; those in front rest their arms on the edge of the stage. As in Elizabethan times, the audience tends to join in the proceedings, booing the French army in *Henry V* and tossing coins to Autolycus, the clown in *A Winter's Tale*, when he sings them a song.

The atmosphere at the Globe is much like it was in Shakespeare's day. Audience members move around as they please, and vendors circulate selling sandwiches and chocolate bars. Sets and sound effects are minimal; no microphones are used. The experience is a contrast to performances in modern theater, which take place in darkened rooms with silent audiences who remain in their seats.

Shakespeare lived in the intellectual world of the Renaissance, the religious world of the Reformation, and the widening geographic world of the Age of Exploration. Although Shakespeare and his contemporaries did not apply these labels to their time, they were profoundly influenced by the climate of change and adventure.

Ironically, the more that boundaries and traditions were challenged, the more fiercely Elizabethans clung to them. For this reason, rank, social status, and rules of propriety were extremely important to the people of Shakespeare's day. So fanatic were the Elizabethans about social order that Clothing Acts—laws that specified the clothing to be worn by different classes of people—were passed. Not surprisingly, the Clothing Acts were largely ignored, but they reflect the sentiment of the times. Students will notice at the opening of Act I of *The Tragedy of Julius Caesar* that members of the working class are chided for going about in public without the proper attire that indicates their status and function.

Prepare to Read

The Tragedy of Julius Caesar

William Shakespeare (1564–1616)

William Shakespeare is regarded as the greatest writer in the English language. Nearly 400 years after his death, Shakespeare's plays continue to be read widely and produced throughout the world. They have the same powerful impact on today's audiences as they had when they were first staged in London.

What's Past Is Prologue Based on records showing that Shakespeare was baptized on April 26, 1564, scholars estimate the date of his birth as April 23 of the same year. He was born in Stratford-on-Avon, northwest of London. Shakespeare's father, John, was a successful glove maker and businessman. He was a respected man and a leader in the community.

Shakespeare's mother, whose maiden name was Mary Arden, was the daughter of his father's landlord. No written evidence of Shakespeare's boyhood exists, but given his father's status, it is probable that young Will attended the Stratford Grammar School, where he acquired a knowledge of Latin. In addition to Latin grammar, Shakespeare and his classmates would have read Latin dramas by Plautus and Terence; Latin poetry by Ovid, Horace, and Virgil; and studied logic, history, natural history, and some Greek. When Shakespeare left school, he had a solid foundation of classical literature and other subjects.

In late November or early December 1582, Shakespeare married Anne Hathaway. Records show that she was twenty-six and he was eighteen. The couple had a daughter, Susanna, in 1583, and twins, Judith and Hamnet, in 1585. Some scholars believe that for a brief time after his marriage, Shakespeare served as a country schoolmaster.

All the World's a Stage It is uncertain how Shakespeare came to be connected with the theater in the 1580s. Perhaps he was influenced by seeing

---

Familiar Expressions From Shakespeare

You have probably quoted Shakespeare without even realizing it! Look for familiar expressions and phrases in the following list. You may be surprised at how much Shakespeare you already know!

"Eaten out of house and home," *Henry IV*, Part 2, Act II, Scene i

"Cruel to be kind," *Hamlet*, Act III, Scene iv

"Knock,/knock! Who's there?" *Macbeth*, Act II, Scene iii

"Too much of a good thing," *As You Like It*, Act IV, Scene i

"Neither a borrower nor a lender be," *Hamlet*, Act I, Scene iii

"Something wicked this way comes," *Macbeth*, Act IV, Scene i

"To thine own self be true," *Hamlet*, Act I, Scene iii

"A tower of strength," *Richard III*, Act V, Scene iii

✹ ENRICHMENT: Literature Connection

Familiar Expressions From Shakespeare

Shakespeare's plays have not only had a powerful impact on audiences over the centuries, but they have also had a powerful impact on everyday contemporary English. Shakespeare invented dozens of familiar words and phrases—"catch cold," "laugh it off," and the slang word "lousy," to name just a few. As critic Christopher Morley has written, "Everyone is a Shakespeare scholar unconsciously. You yourself have probably quoted him today."

the traveling performers who stopped and performed in Stratford on their way to London. At the age of eighteen or nineteen, he is believed to have been acting in plays in London. Friends in London helped him financially and professionally. Soon, he was well established in social and theatrical circles. By 1594, he was part owner and principal playwright of the Lord Chamberlain's Men, one of the most successful theater companies in London.

In 1599, the company built the famous Globe theater, where most of Shakespeare's plays were performed. When James I became king in 1603, following the death of Elizabeth I, he took control of the Lord Chamberlain's Men and renamed the company the King's Men. A major stockholder in the company, Shakespeare continued to write for and act with this company.

Parting Is Such Sweet Sorrow
In about 1610, Shakespeare retired to Stratford, a prosperous middle-class man, having profited from his share in a successful theater company. He lived in the second-largest house in Stratford, invested in grain and farmland, and continued to write plays.

Shakespeare wrote his will on March 25, 1616. He left the bulk of his property to his oldest daughter, Susanna, and a smaller sum to his other daughter, Judith. (Hamnet had died in 1596.) According to the laws of the time, his widow automatically

received a lifetime income from one third of his estate. Although Susanna and Judith both had children, none lived to have children of their own. For this reason, Shakespeare has no living descendants. On April 23 (his birthday, if scholars are correct), 1616, Shakespeare died.

---

from *Shakespeare Alive!*
Joseph Papp and Elizabeth Kirkland

Joseph Papp, the founder and producer of the New York Shakespeare festival, devoted his life to making Shakespeare accessible to all. In Shakespeare Alive! he re-creates the England in which Shakespeare lived and worked.

Pounds of flesh in Venice; ambitious king-killers in Scotland; star-crossed lovers in Verona; daughterly ingratitude in ancient Britain; whimsical courtships in the Forest of Arden; sultry love and stern politics in ancient Egypt—Shakespeare's imagination appears to have cornered the market on exciting, inventive plot making. It seems there's no story he hasn't thought of. But how could all of these intriguing plots and stirring adventures possibly come from a single brain?

The answer is simple—they didn't. When it came to plots, Shakespeare was a borrower, not an inventor. It is astonishing to realize that not a single one of the stories in his plays was his own creation. Rather than growing his plots himself, he plucked them from the plentiful orchards of other authors.

Yet before we start suspecting Shakespeare of plagiarism, we'd better take a look at what everyone else was doing in the literary world. Although this business of outright lifting from other writers' work might seem dubious to us, it wasn't unusual in Shakespeare's time. Without copyright laws to protect an author's works, the business of writing and publishing was truly a "free trade" affair, and everyone's works were saleable commodities. Furthermore, the authors' originality just wasn't an issue; in fact, they were openly encouraged to imitate certain writing styles and literary models, especially, but not exclusively, the classical ones. The upshot of all this was that sixteenth-century authors and playwrights regularly raided both their predecessors and their colleagues, without giving it a second thought; one contemporary of Shakespeare's boasts proudly, "I have so written, as I have read."

In his far-flung borrowing, then, Shakespeare was a product of his times; and yet in this, as in so much else, he flew high above his contemporaries. Shakespeare's ultimate source was the broad spirit of the age, which he drew on in his own unique fashion.

William Shakespeare ◆ 819

Background
The Tragedy of Julius Caesar in Performance

In 1988, Joseph Papp's New York Shakespeare Festival produced *The Tragedy of Julius Caesar*. The performance starred Al Pacino as Mark Antony and Martin Sheen as Brutus. This was not the first time popular actors played these prestigious roles. Marlon Brando played Mark Antony in Metro-Goldwyn-Mayer's 1953 movie production of the play. Both Papp's and MGM's productions were traditional interpretations, with classic settings and period costumes. Others, however, have used the political themes in the play as a comment on contemporary social and political issues. In 1937, Orson Welles staged a production in which Antony's "Friends, Romans, countrymen" funeral oration was delivered amidst searchlights and symbols suggesting a Nazi rally. A 1993 production portrayed Cassius as an ambitious businessman and Mark Antony as a contemporary military leader. One of the first plays to be performed at the newly constructed Globe theater in 1599, *The Tragedy of Julius Caesar* has remained a vital and relevant production piece for more than four centuries.

☀ ENRICHMENT: Humanities Connection
Playwrights

Like Hollywood screenwriters, playwrights of the sixteenth century were subject in large part to the whims of the public. Plays were not judged successful based on their literary merit; they were assessed on the size of the audience they drew. And, like movie theaters, sixteenth-century theaters were constantly changing their offerings. This demand for fresh, new material in short order is part of what earned playwrights their reputations as hacks.

After a theater company bought a play from a playwright, they registered it with the office of the Master of Revels. Originally set up to organize court entertainment, the office of the Master of Revels became a powerful department through which government regulations, including censorship, were carried out.

In 1589, the Master of Revels was given power to "strike out such part and matters as they shall find unfit and undecent to be handled in plays."

819

Step-by-Step Teaching Guide
for pp. 820–821

Motivation

Ask students to name political assassinations they have studied or read about, such as the murder of President Lincoln by John Wilkes Booth. Ask students to discuss the motives for these murders. Do they believe that political assassinations are ever justified? Tell students that they are going to read a play about a political assassination and the reasons for it.

Interest Grabber Video

As an alternative, play "Caesar and the Roman Republic" on Tape 4 to engage student interest.

❶ Background
History

Plutarch was born about A.D. 45 in Boeotia. He studied philosophy in Athens and became a lecturer, teacher, and writer. Plutarch was much in demand as a lecturer on many topics. He wrote about philosophy, science, and literature. His *Lives*, biographies of famous people, is his best-known and most influential work. Plutarch wrote paired biographies of Greek and Roman historical figures. All the characters in Shakespeare's *Julius Caesar* except Brutus's servant Lucius appear in Plutarch's work.

Prepare to Read

The Tragedy of Julius Caesar

Take It to the Net

Visit www.phschool.com for interactive activities and instruction related to the play, including
- background
- graphic organizers
- literary elements
- reading strategies

Preview

Connecting to the Literature

Although political powers sometimes try to persuade each other with words, often they try to "persuade" each other with violence or war, too. Persuasion with both words and force plays an important role in this play.

❶ Background

Julius Caesar was a great general, a gifted speaker, and a popular ruler—so why would anyone want to kill him? Shakespeare did not make up this tragic tale of power and betrayal. He based his play on real people and real events. Shakespeare read about Caesar (and his friends and enemies) in the chronicles of Plutarch, a Greek biographer who delved into the psychological as well as factual details of his subjects' lives.

820 ◆ *Drama*

TEACHING RESOURCES

The following resources can be used to enrich or extend the instruction for pp. 820–821.

Motivation

Interest Grabber Video, Tape 4

Background

Beyond Literature, p. 50

Take It to the Net

Visit www.phschool.com for background and hotlinks for *Julius Caesar.*

Literary Analysis

Literary Analysis and Reading Transparencies, Exposition in Drama, p. 99

Reading

Selection Support: Reading Strategy, p. 199; Build Vocabulary, p. 197

Literary Analysis and Reading Transparencies, Using Text Aids, p. 100

BLOCK SCHEDULING: Resources marked with this symbol provide varied instruction during 90-minute blocks.

❷ Literary Analysis

Exposition in Drama

Like exposition in other forms of literature, the **exposition** in drama is the opening segment that introduces the characters, setting, situation, and other details crucial to understanding the work. For example, as *The Tragedy of Julius Caesar* opens, a man in the crowd declares, "We make holiday to see Caesar and to rejoice in his triumph." The tribunes respond angrily:

> And do you now cull out a holiday?
> And do you now strew flowers in his way
> That comes in triumph over Pompey's blood?
> Be gone!

This exchange reveals the play's situation: Caesar is returning victorious, the public loves him, and some leaders resent him.

Connecting Literary Elements

Dialogue is the conversation between characters in a work of literature. In a drama, it is the principal way in which the story is told. Shakespeare uses dialogue in the exposition to establish the situation, introduce the main characters, and bring the reader up to date with events.

❸ Reading Strategy

Using Text Aids

Text aids are directions provided for readers to help them understand a play. Stage directions that tell actors where and how to move and how to speak certain lines can help you, the reader, picture what is happening on stage. They are enclosed in brackets in the text.

Notes along the sides of the text explain the meanings of words and phrases that are no longer in use. Refer to these notes to clarify unfamiliar language. Use a chart like the one shown to help you rewrite some of the difficult passages in the play in your own words.

Vocabulary Development

replication (rep´ lə kā´ shən) *n.* echo or reverberation (p. 824)

spare (sper) *adj.* lean or thin (p. 830)

infirmity (in fur´ mə tē) *n.* illness; physical defect (p. 832)

surly (sur´ lē) *adv.* in a proud, commanding way (p. 834)

portentous (pôr ten´ təs) *adj.* foreboding; full of unspecified meaning (p. 834)

prodigious (prō dij´ əs) *adj.* impressively forceful (p. 835)

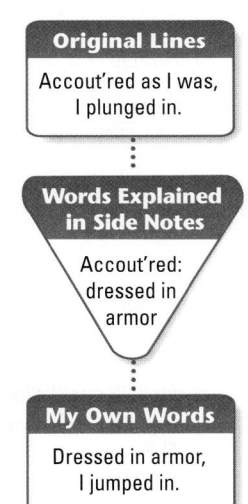

Original Lines

Accout'red as I was, I plunged in.

Words Explained in Side Notes

Accout'red: dressed in armor

My Own Words

Dressed in armor, I jumped in.

The Tragedy of Julius Caesar ◆ 821

CUSTOMIZE INSTRUCTION FOR UNIVERSAL ACCESS

For Less Proficient Readers	For English Learners	For Advanced Readers
The list of characters on p. 822 is an important text aid. Go over the list with students before they begin reading. Encourage them to refer to the list during their reading whenever new characters are introduced.	The margin notes throughout the play should be very helpful to students learning English. Summarize the acts for these students, and then encourage them to make frequent use of the margin notes as they read.	Have students write more detailed stage directions for each scene, using the stage directions already present and any clues in the dialogue. Students should describe each setting as fully as they can.

---

❷ Literary Analysis
Exposition in Drama

- Review plot structure from Saki's "The Open Window" (Unit 6). Remind students that all stories begin at some fixed point in time. The main purposes of the exposition are to inform readers of the setting and characters and to persuade them to continue reading.

- An exposition must identify the setting, the characters, and the situation. Playwrights often introduce two characters who convey this information to each other in dialogue, letting the audience listen in. Have students pay close attention to the opening dialogue among Marullus, Flavius, and the Cobbler as they begin reading *Julius Caesar*.

❸ Reading Strategy
Using Text Aids

- Explain that Shakespeare's plays contain few stage directions, and many of those were not written by him but were supplied by editors. By contrast, modern playwrights often provide detailed descriptions of settings and directions for the actors.

- Point out that Shakespeare gives only the barest indications of setting: "Rome. A street." Shakespeare's plays were performed on practically empty stages. This allowed the frequent changes of scene; actors simply entered and exited to indicate a new scene. No flats or furniture had to be moved. The various areas of the stage could represent indoors as well as outdoors. Shakespeare conveyed all visual information through the power of his language.

Vocabulary Development

- Pronounce each vocabulary word for students, and read the definitions as a class. Have students identify any words with which they are already familiar.

 E-Teach

Visit E-Teach at www.phschool.com for teachers' essays on how to teach, with questions and answers.

Step-by-Step Teaching Guide for pp. 822–837

CUSTOMIZE INSTRUCTION
For Interpersonal Learners

Suggest that students form a discussion group in which to analyze the conflicts introduced in this play. They can discuss external conflicts (between Caesar's supporters and detractors) and internal conflicts (Brutus's friendship with Caesar versus his patriotism). Have students continue their discussion as the conflicts develop throughout the play.

❶ About the Selection

Caesar returns to Rome triumphant after his defeat of Pompey, but many citizens worry that he will use his popularity to declare himself king. Cassius is especially bitter and envious of Caesar. Brutus is worried about the future of the empire. The two friends discuss their concerns.

A soothsayer warns Caesar to beware the ides of March. Caesar dismisses the warning. Mark Antony offers Caesar a crown three times; he reluctantly refuses it.

Cassius recruits Casca into the party of conspirators against Caesar. They go together to speak to Brutus about their plans against the Roman leader.

❷ Reading Strategy

Using Text Aids

• Go over the list of characters with students. Ask what they can learn from the list and how they might use it while reading the play.
  Answer: It gives the names of the characters and their relationships to one another. Refer to the list when new characters are introduced or if you need a reminder of who someone is.

• Point out the bracketed stage direction. Explain that stage directions in Shakespeare's plays are usually limited to indications of characters' exits and entrances.

---

❶ The Tragedy of JULIUS CAESAR
William Shakespeare

CHARACTERS

❷

JULIUS CAESAR	
OCTAVIUS CAESAR	Triumvirs* After
MARCUS ANTONIUS	the Death of
M. AEMILIUS LEPIDUS	Julius Caesar
CICERO	
PUBLIUS	Senators
POPILIUS LENA	
MARCUS BRUTUS	
CASSIUS	
CASCA	
TREBONIUS	Conspirators
LIGARIUS	Against Julius
DECIUS BRUTUS	Caesar
METELLUS CIMBER	
CINNA	
FLAVIUS	Tribunes
MARULLUS	
ARTEMIDORUS OF CNIDOS	Teacher of Rhetoric

CINNA	Poets
ANOTHER POET	
LUCILIUS	
TITINIUS	
MESSALA	Friends to Brutus
YOUNG CATO	and Cassius
VOLUMNIUS	
VARRO	
CLITUS	
CLAUDIUS	Servants to
STRATO	Brutus
LUCIUS	
DARDANIUS	
PINDARUS	Servant to Cassius
CALPURNIA	Wife to Caesar
PORTIA	Wife to Brutus
SOOTHSAYER	
SENATORS, CITIZENS, GUARDS, ATTENDANTS, AND SO ON	

Scene: During most of the play, at Rome; afterward near Sardis, and near Philippi.

*Triumvirs (trī um´ verz) n. in ancient Rome, a group of three rulers who share authority equally.

Act I

Scene i. Rome. A street.

[*Enter* FLAVIUS, MARULLUS, *and certain* COMMONERS[1] *over the stage.*]

  FLAVIUS. Hence! Home, you idle creatures, get you home!
    Is this a holiday? What, know you not,
    Being mechanical,[2] you ought not walk
    Upon a laboring day without the sign
5   Of your profession?[3] Speak, what trade art thou?

822 ◆ Drama

1. COMMONERS (käm´ ən erz) *n.* people not of the nobility or upper classes.

2. mechanical of the working class.

3. sign/Of your profession work clothes and tools.

TEACHING RESOURCES

The following resources can be used to enrich or extend the instruction for pp. 822–837.

Literary Analysis

📖 **Selection Support:** Literary Analysis, p. 200

Reading

🎧 **Listening to Literature Audiocassettes,** Side 27 ▪

💿 **Listening to Literature Audio CDs,** CD 17 ▪

▪ **BLOCK SCHEDULING:** Resources marked with this symbol provide varied instruction during 90-minute blocks.

CARPENTER. Why, sir, a carpenter.

MARULLUS. Where is thy leather apron and thy rule?
What dost thou with thy best apparel on?
You, sir, what trade are you?

10 **COBBLER.** Truly, sir, in respect of a fine workman,[4] I am but, as you
would say, a cobbler.[5]

MARULLUS. But what trade art thou? Answer me directly.

COBBLER. A trade, sir, that, I hope, I may use with a safe conscience,
15 which is indeed, sir, a mender of bad soles.

FLAVIUS. What trade, thou knave?[6] Thou naughty knave what trade?

COBBLER. Nay, I beseech you, sir, be not out with me: yet, if you be
out,[7] sir, I can mend you.[8]

MARULLUS. What mean'st thou by that? Mend me, thou saucy fellow?

20 **COBBLER.** Why, sir, cobble you.

FLAVIUS. Thou art a cobbler, art thou?

COBBLER. Truly, sir, all that I live by is with the awl:[9] I meddle with
no tradesman's matters, nor women's matters; but withal, I am
25 indeed, sir, a surgeon to old shoes: when they are in great danger, I recover them. As proper men as ever trod upon
neat's leather[10] have gone upon my handiwork.

FLAVIUS. But wherefore art not in thy shop today?
Why dost thou lead these men about
the streets?

30 **COBBLER.** Truly, sir, to wear out their
shoes, to get myself into more work. But
indeed, sir, we make holiday to see
Caesar and to rejoice in his triumph.[11]

---

4. **in respect of a fine workman** in relation to a skilled worker.

5. **cobbler** mender of shoes or a clumsy, bungling worker.

Reading Strategy
Using Text Aids What double meaning of *cobbler* applies here?

6. **knave** (nāv) *n.* tricky rascal; rogue.

7. **be not out . . . if you be out** be not angry . . . if you have worn-out shoes.

8. **mend you** mend your shoes or improve your disposition.

9. **awl** (ôl) *n.* small, pointed tool for making holes in leather.

10. **neat's leather** leather made from the hides of cattle.

11. **triumph** (trī′əmf) *n.* procession celebrating the return of a victorious general.

---

5 ▼ **Critical Viewing**
How can you tell that the man standing is a man of power? **[Infer]**

6 ✔ **Reading Check**
Why are the carpenter and the cobbler celebrating?

The Tragedy of Julius Caesar, Act I, Scene i ◆ 823

Exposition in Drama

- Ask students to identify the conflict indicated by Marullus's long speech.
  Answer: Marullus and Flavius support Pompey, and the working people of Rome support Caesar; this is an external conflict between the two groups of followers.

- What conflict do the scene's final four lines foreshadow?
  Answer: They foreshadow a conflict between Caesar's ambition to be king and the desire of many citizens to maintain the republic.

▶ **Monitor Progress** Ask students to describe the various ways Shakespeare has identified his characters and given the audience the necessary information for understanding the play's basic situation.
Answer: The Cobbler and Carpenter are asked to identify themselves. Marullus and Flavius are not named in the dialogue, but their actions show that they are responsible for keeping order in the streets and that they supported Pompey. The workmen support Caesar and "rejoice in his triumph." In their conversation, the characters give the audience the necessary information about Caesar's entry into Rome.

824

MARULLUS. Wherefore rejoice? What conquest brings he home?
   What tributaries[12] follow him to Rome,
35   To grace in captive bonds his chariot wheels?
   You blocks, you stones, you worse than senseless things!
   O you hard hearts, you cruel men of Rome,
   Knew you not Pompey?[13] Many a time and oft
   Have you climbed up to walls and battlements,
40   To tow'rs and windows, yea, to chimney tops,
   Your infants in your arms, and there have sat
   The livelong day, with patient expectation,
   To see great Pompey pass the streets of Rome.
   And when you saw his chariot but appear,
45   Have you not made an universal shout,
   That Tiber[14] trembled underneath her banks
   To hear the replication of your sounds
   Made in her concave shores?[15]
   And do you now put on your best attire?
50   And do you now cull out[16] a holiday?
   And do you now strew flowers in his way
   That comes in triumph over Pompey's blood?[17]
   Be gone!
   Run to your houses, fall upon your knees,
55   Pray to the gods to intermit the plague[18]
   That needs must light on this ingratitude.

FLAVIUS. Go, go, good countrymen, and, for this fault,
   Assemble all the poor men of your sort;
   Draw them to Tiber banks and weep your tears
60   Into the channel, till the lowest stream
   Do kiss the most exalted shores of all.[19]

   [All the commoners exit.]

   See, whe'r their basest mettle[20] be not moved,
   They vanish tongue-tied in their guiltiness.
   Go you down that way toward the Capitol;
65   This way will I. Disrobe the images,
   If you do find them decked with ceremonies.[21]

MARULLUS. May we do so?
   You know it is the feast of Lupercal.[22]

FLAVIUS. It is no matter; let no images
70   Be hung with Caesar's trophies. I'll about
   And drive away the vulgar[23] from the streets;
   So do you too, where you perceive them thick.
   These growing feathers plucked from Caesar's wing
   Will make him fly an ordinary pitch,[24]
75   Who else would soar above the view of men
   And keep us all in servile fearfulness.   *[Exit]*

12. tributaries (trib´ yoo ter´ ēz) *n.* captives.

13. Pompey (päm´ pē) A Roman general and triumvir defeated by Caesar in 48 B.C. and later murdered.

14. Tiber (tī´ bər) river that flows through Rome.

15. concave shores hollowed-out banks; overhanging banks.

replication (rep´ lə kā´ shən) *n.* echo or reverberation

16. cull out pick out; select.

17. Pompey's blood Pompey's sons, whom Caesar has just defeated.

18. intermit the plague (plāg) stop the calamity or trouble.

19. the most exalted shores of all the highest banks.

20. whe'r their basest mettle whether the most inferior material of which they are made.

21. Disrobe the images . . . decked with ceremonies strip the statues . . . covered with decorations.

22. feast of Lupercal (loo´ pər kal) ancient Roman festival celebrated on February 15.

23. vulgar (vul´ gər) *n.* common people.

24. pitch upward flight of a hawk.

✹ ENRICHMENT: History Connection

Pompey the Great

Pompey grew up in a wealthy Roman family during a time of war between the followers of Gaius Marius and those of Lucius Sulla. When Pompey was in his twenties, he raised his own army, allied himself with Sulla, and defeated Marius. Pompey became a popular hero. In 60 B.C., Pompey, Julius Caesar, and Marcus Crassus formed a triumvirate—a group of three rulers—and took control of Rome.

   Pompey grew more and more concerned with

Caesar's growing popularity and decided to crush him. Violent civil war broke out between their followers. Eventually, Caesar defeated Pompey, who escaped to Egypt only to be put to death by the Egyptian government.

Scene ii. A public place.

[Enter CAESAR, ANTONY *(for the course),*[1] CALPURNIA, PORTIA, DECIUS, CICERO, BRUTUS, CASSIUS, CASCA, *a* SOOTHSAYER; *after them,* MARULLUS *and* FLAVIUS.]

CAESAR. Calpurnia!

CASCA.   Peace, ho! Caesar speaks.

CAESAR.   Calpurnia!

CALPURNIA. Here, my lord.

CAESAR. Stand you directly in Antonius' way
     When he doth run his course. Antonius!

5 **ANTONY.** Caesar, my lord?

CAESAR. Forget not in your speed, Antonius,
     To touch Calpurnia; for our elders say
     The barren, touchèd in this holy chase,
     Shake off their sterile curse.[2]

ANTONY.   I shall remember:

10   When Caesar says "Do this," it is performed.

CAESAR. Set on, and leave no ceremony out.

SOOTHSAYER. Caesar!

CAESAR. Ha! Who calls?

CASCA. Bid every noise be still; peace yet again!

15 **CAESAR.** Who is it in the press[3] that calls on me?
     I hear a tongue, shriller than all the music,
     Cry "Caesar." Speak; Caesar is turned to hear.

SOOTHSAYER. Beware the ides of March.◆

iterature
in context Humanities Connection

◆ *The Ides of March*
   When the soothsayer mentions "the ides of March," he is referring to March 15. This term comes from the ancient Roman calendar, which did not number the days of each month. Instead, names were given to these three days:

   • Kalends (the first day of each month)
   • Nones (the seventh of March, May, July, and October and the fifth of other months)
   • the Ides (the fifteenth of March, May, July, and October and the thirteenth of other months)

   It was a complicated and awkward system. If Caesar were to ask Antony to meet on what we would call March 12, he would say, "Three days before the ides of March." In this play, the soothsayer's warning gives the ides a more ominous meaning.

The Tragedy of Julius Caesar, Act I, Scene ii ◆ 825

---

1. for the course ready for the foot race that was part of the Lupercal festivities.

Reading Strategy
Using Text Aids Which notes on this page did you use to clarify unfamiliar words or phrases?

2. barren . . . sterile curse It was believed that women who were unable to bear children (such as Calpurnia), if touched by a runner during this race, would then be able to bear children.

3. press *n.* crowd.

❾ ✓**Reading Check**

Why are Marullus and Flavius angry about the celebration of Caesar's victory?

---

❽ Reading Strategy
Using Text Aids

• Point out the stage direction "Exit" at the bottom of p. 824 and the beginning of Scene ii on p. 825. Explain that in Shakespeare's plays, the physical setting on the stage does not change from one scene to the next. When one group of characters leaves and another enters, usually by another entrance or onto a different area of the stage, the audience understands that a new scene is beginning. There is no pause in the action.

• Ask the Reading Strategy question on p. 825: Which notes on this page did you use to clarify unfamiliar words or phrases? **Answer:** Students probably used all of them, as the language is unfamiliar.

❾ ✓**Reading Check**

Answer: They support Pompey, whom Caesar has defeated.

❿ Background
History

According to the ancient Roman calendar, the year began in spring. A year was divided into 12 months: Martius, Aprilis, Maius, Junius, Quintilis, Sextilis, September, October, November, December, Januarius, and Februarius. The names *Quintilis–December* mean "fifth–tenth."

By Caesar's day, the Roman empire had swallowed up so many countries and provinces that Caesar decided to establish the first standard international calendar. The Julian calendar, adopted in 46 B.C., had a 365-day year with an extra day added every four years.

Augustus Caesar changed the name of Quintilis to July in honor of Julius Caesar, and renamed Sextilis August after himself. So that his month would not be shorter than July, he borrowed a day from Februarius. The Gregorian calendar, which we use today, established January 1 as the start of the year during the 1500s, but the months September–December were never renamed to reflect their new numbers.

CUSTOMIZE INSTRUCTION FOR UNIVERSAL ACCESS

For Special Needs Students	For Gifted/Talented Students
Assign peer tutors for these students. Have each pair work through the play scene by scene, reading the dialogue aloud. At the end of each scene, the tutor should make sure that his or her partner can identify the characters and summarize the action. For scenes with several characters, a few tutors and their partners may want to work together in a larger group.	Shakespeare's language was meant to be heard rather than read silently. Have students form a group in which to read the play aloud together. Readers can maintain the same roles or alternate so that everyone has a chance to read both major and minor characters. Have students discuss how hearing the language enriches their experience of the play.

CAESAR. What man is that?

BRUTUS. A soothsayer bids you beware the ides of March.

20 **CAESAR.** Set him before me; let me see his face.

CASSIUS. Fellow, come from the throng; look upon Caesar.

CAESAR. What say'st thou to me now? Speak once again.

SOOTHSAYER. Beware the ides of March.

CAESAR. He is a dreamer, let us leave him. Pass.

[*A trumpet sounds. Exit all but* BRUTUS *and* CASSIUS.]

25 **CASSIUS.** Will you go see the order of the course?[4]

BRUTUS. Not I.

CASSIUS. I pray you do.

BRUTUS. I am not gamesome:[5] I do lack some part
Of that quick spirit[6] that is in Antony.
30 Let me not hinder, Cassius, your desires;
I'll leave you.

CASSIUS. Brutus, I do observe you now of late;
I have not from your eyes that gentleness
And show of love as I was wont[7] to have;
35 You bear too stubborn and too strange a hand[8]
Over your friend that loves you.

BRUTUS. Cassius,
Be not deceived: if I have veiled my look,
I turn the trouble of my countenance
Merely upon myself.[9] Vexèd I am

4. **order of the course** the race.

5. **gamesome** (gām′ səm) *adj.* having a liking for sports.

6. **quick spirit** lively disposition.

7. **wont** (wōnt) accustomed.

8. **bear . . . hand** treat too harshly and too like a stranger.

9. **if I . . . upon myself** if I have been less open, my troubled face is due entirely to personal matters.

⓭ ▲ **Critical Viewing** At what or at whom do you think Caesar and Antony are looking? **[Infer]**

---

40   Of late with passions[10] of some difference,[11]
    Conceptions only proper to myself,[12]
    Which give some soil,[13] perhaps, to my behaviors;
    But let not therefore my good friends be grieved
    (Among which number, Cassius, be you one)
45   Nor construe any further my neglect
    Than that poor Brutus, with himself at war,
    Forgets the shows of love to other men.

    CASSIUS. Then, Brutus, I have much mistook your passion;
    By means whereof this breast of mine hath buried[14]
50   Thoughts of great value, worthy cogitations.[15]
    Tell me, good Brutus, can you see your face?

    BRUTUS. No, Cassius; for the eye sees not itself
    But by reflection, by some other things.

    CASSIUS. 'Tis just.[16]
55   And it is very much lamented,[17] Brutus,
    That you have no such mirrors as will turn
    Your hidden worthiness into your eye,
    That you might see your shadow.[18] I have heard
    Where many of the best respect[19] in Rome
60   (Except immortal Caesar), speaking of Brutus,
    And groaning underneath this age's yoke,[20]
    Have wished that noble Brutus had his eyes.

    BRUTUS. Into what dangers would you lead me, Cassius,
    That you would have me seek into myself
65   For that which is not in me?

    CASSIUS. Therefore, good Brutus, be prepared to hear;
    And since you know you cannot see yourself
    So well as by reflection, I, your glass
    Will modestly discover to yourself
70   That of yourself which you yet know not of.[21]
    And be not jealous on[22] me, gentle Brutus:
    Were I a common laughter,[23] or did use
    To stale with ordinary oaths my love
    To every new protester;[24] if you know
75   That I do fawn on men and hug them hard,
    And after scandal[25] them; or if you know
    That I profess myself in banqueting
    To all the rout,[26] then hold me dangerous.

                     [Flourish of trumpets and shout]

    BRUTUS. What means this shouting? I do fear the people
    Choose Caesar for their king.

80   **CASSIUS.**   Ay, do you fear it?
    Then must I think you would not have it so.

---

10. passions feelings; emotions.

11. of some difference in conflict.

12. Conceptions . . . myself thoughts that concern only me.

13. soil blemish.

14. By means . . . buried because of which I have kept to myself.

15. cogitations (kaj ə tā′ shənz) *n.* thoughts.

16. 'Tis just it is true.

17. lamented (lə men′ təd) *v.* regretted.

18. turn . . . shadow reflect your hidden noble qualities so you could see their image.

19. the best respect most respected people.

20. this age's yoke the tyranny of Caesar.

21. Will modestly . . . know not of will without exaggeration make known to you the qualities you have that you are unaware of.

22. be not jealous on do not be suspicious of.

23. common laughter object of ridicule.

24. To stale . . . new protester to make cheap my friendship to anyone who promises to be my friend.

25. scandal slander; gossip about.

26. profess myself . . . rout declare my friendship to the common crowd.

15 ✓ **Reading Check**

Why does Cassius think that Brutus is unhappy with him?

---

14 **Literary Analysis**

Exposition in Drama

• Ask students to describe the conflicts introduced in the conversation between Brutus and Cassius.
Answer: Brutus says he is "with himself at war": this introduces an internal conflict. The last few lines on the page suggest that neither Brutus nor Cassius supports Caesar; they are therefore in conflict with him and his supporters.

• Draw students' attention to the stage direction following line 78 and ask: what have you learned in the exposition to explain why the people are shouting?
Answer: Students have learned that a footrace is being run, that the people are celebrating the Lupercal holiday, and that they rejoice in Caesar's triumphant return to Rome.

15 ✓ **Reading Check**

Answer: Brutus seems distant and harsh, not friendly as usual.

The Tragedy of Julius Caesar, Act I, Scene ii ◆ 827

CUSTOMIZE INSTRUCTION FOR UNIVERSAL ACCESS

For Less Proficient Readers

One of Shakespeare's greatest strengths as a writer is his ability to create original, well-rounded, believable characters. Cassius and Brutus are two of the main characters of *Julius Caesar*, and in this scene they reveal a great deal about themselves in a long conversation. Challenge students to make word webs, one for each character. In the center of each web, they can write a character's name, and in the outer circles, his personality traits. They should note line numbers supporting their choices on the rays of the webs.

Students can use these graphic organizers for a group discussion about the two characters.

- Ask the Literary Analysis question on p. 828: How does Brutus's first statement illustrate his conflict? **Answer:** Brutus loves Caesar but does not want him to become king or dictator.

- Then, have students explain the conflict that troubles Cassius. **Answer:** Cassius thinks he is just as good a man as Caesar, so he is furious at having to bow down to him. He harps on Caesar's weaknesses, so he apparently doesn't love Caesar the way Brutus does.

▶ **Monitor Progress** As students continue reading, have them pay close attention to Brutus's internal conflict and Cassius's jealousy and bitterness. Have them pay attention to how these two characters try to resolve these conflicts.

BRUTUS. I would not, Cassius, yet I love him well.
But wherefore do you hold me here so long?
What is it that you would impart to me?
85   If it be aught toward the general good,[27]
Set honor in one eye and death i' th' other,
And I will look on both indifferently;[28]
For let the gods so speed[29] me, as I love
The name of honor more than I fear death.

90 **CASSIUS.** I know that virtue to be in you, Brutus,
As well as I do know your outward favor.[30]
Well, honor is the subject of my story.
I cannot tell what you and other men
Think of this life, but for my single self,
95   I had as lief not be,[31] as live to be
In awe of such a thing as I myself.[32]
I was born free as Caesar; so were you:
We both have fed as well, and we can both
Endure the winter's cold as well as he:
100   For once, upon a raw and gusty day,
The troubled Tiber chafing with[33] her shores,
Caesar said to me "Darest thou, Cassius, now
Leap in with me into this angry flood,
And swim to yonder point?" Upon the word,
105   Accout'red[34] as I was, I plungèd in
And bade him follow: so indeed he did.
The torrent roared, and we did buffet[35] it
With lusty sinews,[36] throwing it aside
And stemming it with hearts of controversy.[37]
110   But ere we could arrive the point proposed,
Caesar cried "Help me, Cassius, or I sink!"
I, as Aeneas,[38] our Great ancestor,
Did from the flames of Troy upon his shoulder
The old Anchises bear, so from the waves of Tiber
115   Did I the tired Caesar. And this man
Is now become a god, and Cassius is
A wretched creature, and must bend his body
If Caesar carelessly but nod on him.
He had a fever when he was in Spain,
120   And when the fit was on him, I did mark
How he did shake: 'tis true, this god did shake.
His coward lips did from their color fly,[39]
And that same eye whose bend[40] doth awe the world
did lose his[41] luster: I did hear him groan;
125   Ay, and that tongue of his, that bade the Romans
Mark him and write his speeches in their books,
Alas, it cried, "Give me some drink, Titinius,"
As a sick girl. Ye gods! It doth amaze me,
A man of such a feeble temper[42] should

27. aught . . . good anything to do with the public welfare.

28. indifferently without preference or concern.

29. speed give good fortune to.

30. favor face; appearance.

31. as lief not be just as soon not exist.

32. such a thing as I myself another human being (Caesar).

33. chafing with raging against.

34. Accout'red dressed in armor.

35. buffet (buf´ it) *v.* struggle against.

36. lusty sinews (sin´ yōoz) strong muscles.

37. stemming it . . . controversy making progress against it with our intense rivalry.

38. Aeneas (i nē´ əs) Trojan hero of the poet Virgil's epic poem *Aeneid*, who carried his old father, Anchises, from the burning city of Troy and later founded Rome.

39. His coward lips . . . fly color fled from his lips, which were like cowardly soldiers fleeing from a battle.

40. bend *n.* glance.

41. his its.

42. feeble temper weak physical constitution.

130 So get the start of[43] the majestic world,
   And bear the palm[44] alone.

                        [*Shout. Flourish of trumpets*]

BRUTUS. Another general shout?
   I do believe that these applauses are
   For some new honors that are heaped on Caesar.

135 CASSIUS. Why, man, he doth bestride the narrow world
   Like a Colossus,[45] and we petty men
   Walk under his huge legs and peep about
   To find ourselves dishonorable[46] graves.
   Men at some time are masters of their fates:
140 The fault, dear Brutus, is not in our stars,[47]
   But in ourselves, that we are underlings.[48]
   Brutus and Caesar: what should be in that "Caesar"?
   Why should that name be sounded[49] more than yours?
   Write them together, yours is as fair a name;
145 Sound them, it doth become the mouth as well;
   Weigh them, it is as heavy; conjure[50] with 'em,
   "Brutus" will start[51] a spirit as soon as "Caesar."
   Now, in the names of all the gods at once,
   Upon what meat doth this our Caesar feed,
150 That he is grown so great? Age, thou art shamed!
   Rome, thou hast lost the breed of noble bloods!
   When went there by an age, since the great flood,[52]
   But it was famed with[53] more than with one man?
   When could they say (till now) that talked of Rome,
155 That her wide walks encompassed but one man?
   Now is it Rome indeed, and room enough,
   When there is in it but one only man.
   O, you and I have heard our fathers say,
   There was a Brutus[54] once that would have brooked[55]
160 Th' eternal devil to keep his state in Rome
   As easily as a king.

BRUTUS. That you do love me, I am nothing jealous;[56]
   What you would work me to,[57] I have some aim;[58]
   How I have thought of this, and of these times,
165 I shall recount hereafter. For this present,
   I would not so (with love I might entreat you)
   Be any further moved. What you have said
   I will consider; what you have to say
   I will with patience hear, and find a time
170 Both meet to hear and answer such high things.
   Till then, my noble friend, chew upon[59] this:
   Brutus had rather be a villager
   Than to repute himself a son of Rome
   Under these hard conditions as this time

---

43. get the start of become the leader of.

44. palm symbol of victory; victor's prize.

45. Colossus (kə läs´ əs) *n.* gigantic statue of Apollo, a god of Greek and Roman mythology, which was set at the entrance to the harbor of Rhodes about 280 B.C. and was included among the seven wonders of the ancient world.

46. dishonorable (dis än´ ər ə bəl) *adj.* shameful (because they will not be of free men).

47. stars destinies. The stars were thought to control people's lives.

48. underlings inferior people.

49. sounded spoken or announced by trumpets.

50. conjure (kän´ jər) *v.* summon a spirit by a magic spell.

51. start raise.

52. great flood in Greek mythology, a flood that drowned everyone except Deucalion and his wife Pyrrha, who were saved by the god Zeus because of their virtue.

53. But it was famed with without the age being made famous by.

54. Brutus Lucius Junius Brutus had helped expel the last king of Rome and had helped found the Republic in 509 B.C.

55. brooked put up with.

56. nothing jealous not at all doubting.

57. work me to persuade me of.

58. aim idea.

59. chew upon think about.

 Reading Check

What happened when Caesar and Cassius held a swimming race in the river Tiber?

⓱ **Critical Thinking**
Making Judgments

• Ask students what kind of man they judge Cassius to be, based on his two long speeches on these two pages.
Answer: Cassius is a jealous and resentful man. He does not want the absolute power Caesar craves, but he resents the idea that Caesar should have power over him.

• What judgment does Brutus make about Cassius's comparison between him and Caesar (lines 142–147)? What judgment do students make about Cassius at this point?
Answer: Brutus appreciates the compliments Cassius pays him. Students may say that Cassius uses flattery to manipulate Brutus into joining in his plans.

⓲ **Critical Thinking**
Infer

• Have students read lines 158–161. What does Cassius imply?
Answer: He implies that Brutus has a duty to prevent Caesar from becoming king.

• Ask students to infer how Cassius thinks Brutus should do this. Have them explain their answers.
Answer: Students may suggest that Brutus should persuade Caesar that his ambitions would be bad for the empire. Others may say that Cassius's evident personal dislike of Caesar means that Cassius has violence in mind.

⓳ **Reading Check**

Answer: Cassius had to rescue Caesar from drowning.

CUSTOMIZE INSTRUCTION FOR UNIVERSAL ACCESS

For Advanced Readers

Have students identify and discuss the various conflicts described in Act I. Remind them that some conflicts, such as a war between two countries, are external. Others, such as a conflict between duty and inclination, are internal. Ask students to decide which seems to be the central conflict in *Julius Caesar* and to support their answers with specific details from the play. This activity can continue throughout the play; students can meet in discussion groups after reading each act and talk about new conflicts that have arisen, how conflicts introduced earlier have been resolved, and how various conflicts have developed.

Is like to lay upon us.

175   **CASSIUS.** I am glad
    That my weak words have struck but thus much show
    Of fire from Brutus.

[*Enter* CAESAR *and his* TRAIN.]

  BRUTUS. The games are done, and Caesar is returning.

  CASSIUS. As they pass by, pluck Casca by the sleeve,
180   And he will (after his sour fashion) tell you
    What hath proceeded worthy note today.

  BRUTUS. I will do so. But look you, Cassius,
    The angry spot doth glow on Caesar's brow,
    And all the rest look like a chidden train:[60]
185   Calpurnia's cheek is pale, and Cicero
    Looks with such ferret[61] and such fiery eyes
    As we have seen him in the Capitol,
    Being crossed in conference[62] by some senators.

  CASSIUS. Casca will tell us what the matter is.

190   **CAESAR.** Antonius.

  ANTONY. Caesar?

  CAESAR. Let me have men about me that are fat,
    Sleek-headed men, and such as sleep a-nights.
    Yond Cassius has a lean and hungry look;
195   He thinks too much: such men are dangerous.

  ANTONY. Fear him not, Caesar, he's not dangerous;
    He is a noble Roman, and well given.[63]

  CAESAR. Would he were fatter! But I fear him not.
    Yet if my name were liable to fear,
200   I do not know the man I should avoid
    So soon as that <u>spare</u> Cassius. He reads much,
    He is a great observer, and he looks
    quite through the deeds of men.[64] He loves no plays,
    As thou dost, Antony; he hears no music;
205   Seldom he smiles, and smiles in such a sort[65]
    As if he mocked himself, and scorned his spirit
    That could be moved to smile at anything.
    Such men as he be never at heart's ease
    Whiles they behold a greater than themselves,
210   And therefore are they very dangerous.
    I rather tell thee what is to be feared
    Than what I fear; for always I am Caesar.
    Come on my right hand, for this ear is deaf,
    And tell me truly what thou think'st of him.

[*A trumpet sounds.* CAESAR *and his* TRAIN *exit.*]

830 ◆ Drama

60. chidden train scolded attendants.

61. ferret (fer´ it) *n.* small animal, like a weasel, with reddish eyes.

62. crossed in conference opposed in debate.

63. well given well disposed.

64. looks . . . deeds of men sees through people's actions to their motives.

65. sort way.

spare (sper) *adj.* lean or thin

21 ▼ Critical Viewing
What details of Cassius' appearance can you see in this picture that might make Caesar distrust him? [Infer]

CASCA. You pulled me by the cloak; would you speak with me?

BRUTUS. Ay, Casca; tell us what hath chanced[66] today,
That Caesar looks so sad.

CASCA. Why, you were with him, were you not?

BRUTUS. I should not then ask Casca what had chanced.

220 **CASCA.** Why, there was a crown offered him; and being offered
him, he put it by[67] with the back of his hand, thus; and then
the people fell a-shouting.

BRUTUS. What was the second noise for?

CASCA. Why, for that too.

225 **CASSIUS.** They shouted thrice; what was the last cry for?

CASCA. Why, for that too.

BRUTUS. Was the crown offered him thrice?

CASCA. Ay, marry, was't, and he put it by thrice, every time gentler
than other; and at every putting-by mine honest neighbors
230 shouted.

CASSIUS. Who offered him the crown?

CASCA. Why, Antony.

BRUTUS. Tell us the manner of it, gentle Casca.

CASCA. I can as well be hanged as tell the manner of it: it was
235 mere foolery; I did not mark it. I saw Mark Antony offer him a
crown—yet 'twas not a crown neither, 'twas one of these coronets[68]—and, as I told you, he put it by once; but for all that, to
my thinking, he would fain[69] have had it. Then he offered it to
240 him again; then he put it by again; but to my thinking, he was
very loath to lay his fingers off it. And then he offered it the
third time. He put it the third time by; and still as he refused
it, the rabblement[70] hooted, and clapped their chopt[71] hands,
245 and threw up their sweaty nightcaps,[72] and uttered such a
deal of stinking breath because Caesar refused the crown, that
it had, almost, choked Caesar; for he swounded[73] and fell
down at it. And for mine own part, I durst not laugh, for fear of
250 opening my lips and receiving the bad air.

CASSIUS. But, soft,[74] I pray you; what, did Caesar swound?

CASCA. He fell down in the market place, and foamed at mouth,
and was speechless.

BRUTUS. 'Tis very like he hath the falling-sickness.[75]

255 **CASSIUS.** No, Caesar hath it not; but you, and I,
And honest Casca, we have the falling-sickness.[76]

CASCA. I know not what you mean by that, but I am sure Caesar

---

66. hath chanced has happened.

67. put it by pushed it away.

Literary Analysis
Exposition and Dialogue
How does this dialogue develop the situation set up in the exposition?

68. coronets (kôr′ ə nets′) *n.* ornamental bands used as crowns.

69. fain (fān) *adv.* gladly.

70. rabblement (rab′ əl mənt) *n.* mob.

71. chopt (chäpt) *adj.* chapped.

72. nightcaps workers' caps.

73. swounded swooned; fainted.

74. soft slowly.

75. falling-sickness epilepsy.

76. we have the falling-sickness We are becoming helpless under Caesar's rule.

23 ✓**Reading Check**
Why does Mark Antony offer Caesar a crown?

The Tragedy of Julius Caesar, Act I, Scene ii ◆ 831

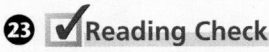

831

㉔ Literary Analysis
Exposition in Drama

- Ask the Literary Analysis question on p. 832: How did the exposition set the stage for this kind of action against Marullus and Flavius?
Answer: The exposition showed that there are two factions in Rome: supporters and detractors of Caesar. Brutus and Cassius hint at the idea of removing Caesar from power. Since Caesar has power, he will do anything to keep it.

- Ask students what this action in the exposition leads them to expect for the later scenes in the play.
Answer: Students may expect further violence and murder between the factions.

260 fell down. If the tag-rag people[77] did not clap him and hiss him, according as he pleased and displeased them, as they use[78] to do the players in the theater, I am no true man.

BRUTUS. What said he when he came unto himself?

CASCA. Marry, before he fell down, when he perceived the common herd was glad he refused the crown, he plucked me ope his 265 doublet[79] and offered them his throat to cut. An I had been a man of any occupation,[80] if I would not have taken him at a word, I would I might go to hell among the rogues. And so he fell. When he came to himself again, he said, if he had done or 270 said anything amiss, he desired their worships to think it was his infirmity.[81] Three or four wenches,[82] where I stood, cried "Alas, good soul!" and forgave him with all their hearts; but there's no heed to be taken of them; if Caesar had stabbed 275 their mothers, they would have done no less.

BRUTUS. And after that, he came thus sad away?

CASCA. Ay.

CASSIUS. Did Cicero say anything?

CASCA. Ay, he spoke Greek.

280 **CASSIUS.** To what effect?

CASCA. Nay, an I tell you that, I'll ne'er look you i' th' face again. But those that understood him smiled at one another and shook their heads; but for mine own part, it was Greek to me. I 285 could tell you more news too: Marullus and Flavius, for pulling scarfs off Caesar's images, are put to silence.[83] Fare you well. There was more foolery yet, if I could remember it.

CASSIUS. Will you sup with me tonight, Casca?

CASCA. No, I am promised forth.[84]

290 **CASSIUS.** Will you dine with me tomorrow?

CASCA. Ay, if I be alive, and your mind hold,[85] and your dinner worth the eating.

CASSIUS. Good; I will expect you.

CASCA. Do so. Farewell, both.   [*Exit*]

295 **BRUTUS.** What a blunt[86] fellow is this grown to be! He was quick mettle[87] when he went to school.

CASSIUS. So is he now in execution[88] Of any bold or noble enterprise, However he puts on this tardy form.[89] 300 This rudeness is a sauce to his good wit,[90] Which gives men stomach to disgest[91] his words With better appetite.

Side notes:

77. **tag-rag people** the rabble.

78. **use** are accustomed.

79. **doublet** (dub´ lit) *n.* close-fitting jacket.

80. **An I . . . occupation** if I had been a working-man (or a man of action).

infirmity (in fur´ mə tē) illness; physical defect

81. **infirmity** *n.* Caesar's illness is epilepsy.

82. **wenches** (wench´ əz) *n.* young women.

83. **for pulling . . . silence** for taking decorations off statues of Caesar, they have been silenced (by being forbidden to take part in public affairs, exiled, or perhaps even executed).

Literary Analysis
Exposition in Drama
How did the exposition set the stage for this kind of action against Marullus and Flavius?

84. **am promised forth** have a previous engagement.

85. **hold** does not change.

86. **blunt** dull; not sharp.

87. **quick mettle** of a lively disposition.

88. **execution** (ek´ sə kyo͞o´ shən) *n.* carrying out; doing.

89. **tardy form** sluggish appearance.

90. **wit** intelligence.

91. **disgest** digest.

✹ ENRICHMENT: Science Connection
"The Falling Sickness"

Casca tells Brutus and Cassius that Caesar "swounded [fainted] and fell down . . . and foamed at mouth, and was speechless." Brutus explains that Caesar "hath the falling-sickness." Historians believe that Caesar suffered from epilepsy, a general term used to cover a variety of chronic neurological disorders. Epileptics can suffer from seizures that involve muscle spasms and loss of consciousness. Some forms of epilepsy are known to be caused by injury or infection of the brain. Today, epileptic seizures like those Caesar suffered can be controlled by medications and diet.

BRUTUS. And so it is. For this time I will leave you.
   Tomorrow, if you please to speak with me,
305 I will come home to you; or if you will,
   Come home to me, and I will wait for you.

CASSIUS. I will do so. Till then, think of the world.[92]

                              [*Exit* BRUTUS.]

   Well, Brutus, thou art noble; yet I see
   Thy honorable mettle may be wrought
310 From that it is disposed;[93] therefore it is meet
   That noble minds keep ever with their likes;
   For who so firm that cannot be seduced?
   Caesar doth bear me hard,[94] but he loves Brutus.
   If I were Brutus now, and he were Cassius,
315 He should not humor me.[95] I will this night,
   In several hands,[96] in at his windows throw,
   As if they came from several citizens,
   Writings, all tending to the great opinion[97]
   That Rome holds of his name; wherein obscurely
320 Caesar's ambition shall be glancèd at.[98]
   And after this, let Caesar seat him sure;[99]
   For we will shake him, or worse days endure.   [*Exit*]

Scene iii. A street.

[*Thunder and lightning. Enter from opposite sides,* CASCA *and* CICERO.]

CICERO. Good even, Casca; brought you Caesar home?
   Why are you breathless? And why stare you so?

CASCA. Are not you moved, when all the sway of earth[1]
   Shakes like a thing unfirm? O Cicero,
5   I have seen tempests, when the scolding winds
   Have rived[2] the knotty oaks, and I have seen
   Th' ambitious ocean swell and rage and foam,
   To be exalted with[3] the threat'ning clouds;
   But never till tonight, never till now,
10 Did I go through a tempest dropping fire.
   Either there is a civil strife in heaven,
   Or else the world, too saucy[4] with the gods,
   Incenses[5] them to send destruction.

CICERO. Why, saw you anything more wonderful?

15 **CASCA.** A common slave—you know him well by sight—
   Held up his left hand, which did flame and burn
   Like twenty torches joined, and yet his hand,
   Not sensible of[6] fire, remained unscorched.
   Besides—I ha' not since put up my sword—
20 Against[7] the Capitol I met a lion,

---

92. the world present state of affairs.

93. wrought . . . is disposed shaped (like iron) in a way different from its usual form.

94. bear me hard dislikes me.

95. humor me win me over.

96. several hands different handwritings.

97. tending to the great opinion pointing out the great respect.

98. glancèd at hinted at.

99. seat him sure establish himself securely.

Reading Strategy

Using Text Aids How does the description of the weather add to the drama?

1. all the sway of earth the stable order of Earth.

2. Have rived have split.

3. exalted with lifted up to.

4. saucy rude; impudent.
5. Incenses enrages.

6. sensible of sensitive to.
7. Against opposite or near.

26 ✔ **Reading Check**

What has happened to Marullus and Flavius?

The Tragedy of Julius Caesar, Act I, Scene iii ◆ 833

---

25 **Reading Strategy**

Using Text Aids

- Point out the stage direction "Exit Brutus" just before line 308. Note that when Brutus leaves, Cassius is left alone on stage. This tells readers that the speech Cassius gives here is a soliloquy. A soliloquy is a special category of monologue in which a character speaks his thoughts aloud. The character's thoughts are understood to be audible only to the audience, not to any other character. In a soliloquy, a character is generally understood to be completely honest. Students will read more about soliloquies during Act III of *Julius Caesar.*

- Ask the Reading Strategy question on p. 833: How does the description of the weather add to the drama?
  Answer: The violence in the weather foreshadows the violence to come.

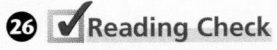 **Monitor Progress** Ask students why, given the printed stage direction, Casca describes the weather in his speech.
  Answer: The verbal description is needed for audience members who don't have any stage directions to read.

26 ✔ **Reading Check**

Answer: They have been "put to silence": probably either banished or executed.

Forms of *portent*

Draw students' attention to the word *portentous* and its definition, "foreboding; full of unspecified meaning."

- Write the word *portentous* on the chalkboard, and separate its parts: por|tent|ous. Explain that the Latin word *tendere* means "to stretch." Therefore, *portend* means "stretch forth," as a warning stretches forth a sign that there is trouble ahead.

- Give students the following words that contain this root, and have them define each and use it correctly in a sentence: *extend, intent, pretentious, attentive.*

Who glazed[8] upon me and went <u>surly</u> by
Without annoying me. And there were drawn
Upon a heap[9] a hundred ghastly[10] women,
Transformèd with their fear, who swore they saw
25   Men, all in fire, walk up and down the streets.
And yesterday the bird of night[11] did sit
Even at noonday upon the market place,
Hooting and shrieking. When these prodigies[12]
Do so conjointly meet,[13] let not men say,
30   "These are their reasons, they are natural,"
27   For I believe they are <u>portentous</u> things
Unto the climate that they point upon.[14]

CICERO. Indeed, it is a strange-disposèd[15] time:
But men may construe things after their fashion,[16]
35   Clean from the purpose[17] of the things themselves.
Comes Caesar to the Capitol tomorrow?

CASCA. He doth; for he did bid Antonius
Send word to you he would be there tomorrow.

CICERO. Good night then, Casca; this disturbèd sky
Is not to walk in.

40   CASCA.   Farewell, Cicero.   [*Exit* CICERO.]

[*Enter* CASSIUS.]

CASSIUS. Who's there?

CASCA.   A Roman.

CASSIUS.   Casca, by your voice.

CASCA. Your ear is good. Cassius, what night is this?

CASSIUS. A very pleasing night to honest men.

CASCA. Who ever knew the heavens menace so?

45   CASSIUS. Those that have known the earth so full of faults.
For my part, I have walked about the streets,
Submitting me unto the perilous night,
And thus unbracèd,[18] Casca, as you see,
Have bared my bosom to the thunder-stone;[19]
50   And when the cross[20] blue lightning seemed to open
The breast of heaven, I did present myself
Even in the aim and very flash of it.

CASCA. But wherefore did you so much tempt the heavens?
It is the part[21] of men to fear and tremble
55   When the most mighty gods by tokens send
Such dreadful heralds to astonish[22] us.

CASSIUS. You are dull, Casca, and those sparks of life
That should be in a Roman you do want,[23]

834 ◆ *Drama*

surly (sʉrʹ lē) *adv.* in a proud, commanding way

8. glazed stared.

9. were drawn . . . heap huddled together.

10. ghastly (gastʹ lē) *adj.* ghostlike; pale.

11. bird of night owl.

portentous (pôr tenʹ təs) *adj.* foreboding; full of unspecified meaning

12. prodigies (prädʹ ə jēz) *n.* extraordinary happenings.

13. conjointly meet occur at the same time and place.

14. portentous (pôr tenʹ təs) **. . . upon** bad omens for the country they point to.

15. strange-disposèd abnormal.

16. construe . . . fashion explain in their own way.

17. Clean from the purpose different from the real meaning.

18. unbracèd with jacket open.

19. thunder-stone thunderbolt.

20. cross zigzag.

21. part role.

22. by tokens . . . to astonish by portentous signs send such awful announcements to frighten and stun.

23. want lack.

Or else you use not. You look pale, and gaze,
60 And put on fear, and cast yourself in wonder,[24]
To see the strange impatience of the heavens;
But if you would consider the true cause
Why all these fires, why all these gliding ghosts,
Why birds and beasts from quality and kind,[25]
65 Why old men, fools, and children calculate,[26]
Why all these things change from their ordinance,[27]
Their natures and preformèd faculties,
To monstrous quality,[28] why, you shall find
That heaven hath infused them with these spirits[29]
70 To make them instruments of fear and warning
Unto some monstrous state.[30]
Now could I, Casca, name to thee a man
Most like this dreadful night,
That thunders, lightens, opens graves, and roars
75 As doth the lion in the Capitol;
A man no mightier than thyself, or me,
In personal action, yet <u>prodigious</u> grown
And fearful,[31] as these strange eruptions are.

CASCA. 'Tis Caesar that you mean, is it not, Cassius?

80 CASSIUS. Let it be who it is; for Romans now
Have thews[32] and limbs like to their ancestors;
But, woe the while![33] Our fathers' minds are dead,
And we are governed with our mothers' spirits;
Our yoke and sufferance[34] show us womanish.

85 CASCA. Indeed, they say the senators tomorrow
Mean to establish Caesar as a king;
And he shall wear his crown by sea and land,
In every place save here in Italy.

CASSIUS. I know where I will wear this dagger then;
90 Cassius from bondage will deliver[35] Cassius.
Therein,[36] ye gods, you make the weak most strong;
Therein, ye gods, you tyrants do defeat.
Nor stony tower, nor walls of beaten brass,
Nor airless dungeon, nor strong links of iron,
95 Can be retentive to[37] the strength of spirit;
But life, being weary of these worldly bars,
Never lacks power to dismiss itself.
If I know this, know all the world besides,
That part of tyranny that I do bear
I can shake off at pleasure.   [*Thunder still*]

100 CASCA.   So can I;
So every bondman in his own hand bears
The power to cancel his captivity.

24. put on . . . in wonder show fear and are amazed.

25. from quality and kind acting contrary to their nature.

26. calculate make predictions.

27. ordinance regular behavior.

Reading Strategy
Using Text Aids Using the side notes, explain what Cassius says in lines 57–71.

prodigious (prō dij´ əs) *adj.* impressively forceful

28. preformèd . . . quality established function to unnatural behavior.

29. infused . . . spirits filled them with supernatural powers.

30. monstrous state abnormal condition of government.

31. fearful causing fear.

32. thews (thyo͞oz) *n.* muscles or sinews; strength.

33. woe the while alas for the times.

34. yoke and sufferance slavery and meek acceptance of it.

35. will deliver will set free.

36. Therein in that way (by using his dagger on himself).

37. be retentive to confine.

29 ✔**Reading Check**
What bad omens have people noticed?

The Tragedy of Julius Caesar, Act I, Scene iii ◆ 835

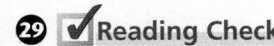

30 Literary Analysis

Exposition and Dialogue

- Ask the Literary Analysis question on p. 836: What is clarified between Cassius and Casca in lines 111–120?
  Answer: They agree that they both stand against Caesar.

- Ask why Cassius speaks so openly against Caesar before making sure that Casca agrees with him.
  Answer: Cassius despises Caesar so much that he can't control his spite.

- Ask what students think the conspirators have in mind for Caesar, given Cassius's speech (lines 120–130).
  Answer: It seems that they plan to kill him. Cassius speaks of "bloody, fiery, and most terrible" violence.

31 Literary Analysis

Exposition and Dialogue

- Ask students what they think may be on the papers that Cassius gives to Cinna. Ask why they think so.
  Answer: They are probably messages that will strengthen Brutus's resolve to be part of the conspiracy against Caesar.

- Ask the Literary Analysis question on p. 837: What is the connection between Cassius's speech and the sentiments expressed by the tribunes in the exposition in Scene i?
  Answer: The tribunes discussed Caesar's popularity and the statues that were decked with tributes to him. Cassius is planting more tributes to Caesar; this will make Brutus more certain that Caesar must be removed from power.

CASSIUS. And why should Caesar be a tyrant then?
Poor man, I know he would not be a wolf
105 But that he sees the Romans are but sheep;
He were no lion, were not Romans hinds.[38]
Those that with haste will make a mighty fire
Begin it with weak straws. What trash is Rome,
What rubbish and what offal,[39] when it serves
110 For the base matter[40] to illuminate
So vile a thing as Caesar! But, O grief,
Where hast thou led me? I, perhaps, speak this
Before a willing bondman; then I know
My answer must be made.[41] But I am armed,
115 And dangers are to me indifferent.

CASCA. You speak to Casca, and to such a man
That is no fleering tell-tale.[42] Hold, my hand.
Be factious[43] for redress of all these griefs,[44]
And I will set this foot of mine as far
As who goes farthest.   [*They clasp hands.*]

120 **CASSIUS.**   There's a bargain made.
Now know you, Casca, I have moved already
Some certain of the noblest-minded Romans
To undergo[45] with me an enterprise
Of honorable dangerous consequence;[46]
125 And I do know, by this[47] they stay for me
In Pompey's porch;[48] for now, this fearful night,
There is no stir or walking in the streets,
And the complexion of the element[49]
In favor's like[50] the work we have in hand,
130 Most bloody, fiery, and most terrible.

[*Enter* CINNA.]

CASCA. Stand close[51] awhile, for here comes one in haste.

CASSIUS. 'Tis Cinna; I do know him by his gait;[52]
He is a friend. Cinna, where haste you so?

CINNA. To find out you. Who's that? Metellus Cimber?

135 **CASSIUS.** No, it is Casca, one incorporate[53]
To our attempts. Am I not stayed[54] for, Cinna?

CINNA. I am glad on't.[55] What a fearful night is this!
There's two or three of us have seen strange sights.

CASSIUS. Am I not stayed for? Tell me.

CINNA.   Yes, you are.
140 O Cassius, if you could
But win the noble Brutus to our party—

CASSIUS. Be you content. Good Cinna, take this paper,

38. hinds (hīndz) *n.* female deer; peasants; servants.

39. offal (ôf´ əl) *n.* garbage.

40. base matter inferior or low material; foundation materials.

41. speak this . . . answer must be made say this before a willing servant of Caesar's; then I know I will have to answer for my words.

Literary Analysis
Exposition and Dialogue
What is clarified between Cassius and Casca in lines 111–120?

42. fleering tell-tale sneering tattletale.

43. factious (fak´ shəs) *adj.* active in forming a faction or a political party.

44. redress (ri dres´) **of all these griefs** setting right all these grievances.

45. undergo undertake.

46. consequence (kän´ sə kwens´) *n.* importance.

47. by this by this time.

48. Pompey's porch portico of Pompey's Theater.

49. complexion of the element condition of the sky; weather.

50. In favor's like in appearance is like.

51. close hidden.

52. gait (gāt) *n.* way of moving.

53. incorporate (in kôr´ pər it) *adj.* united.

54. stayed waited.

55. on't of it.

And look you lay it in the praetor's chair,[56]
Where Brutus may but find it;[57] and throw this
145   In at his window: set this up with wax
Upon old Brutus'[58] statue. All this done,
Repair to Pompey's porch, where you shall find us.
Is Decius Brutus and Trebonius there?

CINNA. All but Metellus Cimber, and he's gone
150   To seek you at your house. Well, I will hie,
And so bestow these papers as you bade me.

CASSIUS. That done, repair to Pompey's Theater.   [Exit CINNA.]

Come, Casca, you and I will yet ere day
See Brutus at his house; three parts of him
155   Is ours already, and the man entire
Upon the next encounter yields him ours.

CASCA. O, he sits high in all the people's hearts;
And that which would appear offense[59] in us,
His countenance,[60] like richest alchemy,[61]
160   Will change to virtue and to worthiness.

CASSIUS. Him, and his worth, and our great need of him,
You have right well conceited.[62] Let us go,
For it is after midnight, and ere day
We will awake him and be sure of him.   [Exit]

Literary Analysis
Exposition in Drama
What is the connection between Cassius' speech and the sentiments expressed by the tribunes in the exposition in Scene i?

56. praetor's (prē´ tərz) **chair** Roman magistrate's (or judge's) chair.

57. Where . . . find it where only Brutus (as the chief magistrate) will find it.

58. old Brutus' Lucius Junius Brutus, the founder of Rome.

59. offense (ə fens´) *n.* crime.

60. countenance (koun´ tə nəns) *n.* support.

61. alchemy (al´ kə mē) *n.* an early form of chemistry in which the goal was to change metals of little value into gold.

62. conceited (kən sēt´ id) understood.

Review and Assess

Thinking About Act I

1. **Respond:** Which character interests you most? Why?
2. **(a) Recall:** How do the workmen celebrate as the play begins? **(b) Analyze:** Why does their celebration annoy Flavius and Marullus?
3. **(a) Recall:** What warning does the soothsayer give to Caesar? **(b) Infer:** What does Caesar's reaction tell you about him?
4. **(a) Recall:** What does Brutus say when he hears the shouts of the people? **(b) Infer:** What mixed feelings does the shouting arouse in Brutus? **(c) Analyze:** How does Cassius take advantage of Brutus' conflicting feelings?
5. **Apply:** Explain how Brutus, Cassius, and Caesar represent qualities that can be found in people of any time period.
6. **Predict:** What do you suspect is going to happen in the next part of the play? Why?

The Tragedy of Julius Caesar, Act I, Scene iii ◆ 837

ASSESSMENT PRACTICE: Reading Comprehension

Identify Patterns of Organization   (For more practice, see Test Preparation Workbook, p. 50.)

Many tests require students to identify patterns of organization. Use this sample test item to help students practice this skill.

Although this business of outright lifting from other writers' works might seem dubious to us, it wasn't unusual in Shakespeare's time. Without copyright laws to protect an author's works, the business of writing and publishing was truly a free-trade affair.

The author makes a connection to the publishing world of today in order to ___.

A show a comparison
B show a contrast
C persuade
D entertain

The author shows a difference between the two time periods. The correct answer is *B*.

Review and Assess

1. Main characters: Brutus, Cassius, Caesar, Casca. Setting: Ancient Rome. Situation: Caesar has just defeated Pompey in a civil war and has returned to Rome in triumph.

2. He says that Pompey used to be as popular as Caesar is now.

3. Through statements made in conversations between characters, readers learn that Marullus, Flavius, Cassius, Brutus, and Casca resent Caesar's rise to power.

4. The commoners reveal the way the people feel about Caesar's power.

5. Possible answers: "Beware the ides of March"; "these hard conditions as this time/Is like to lay upon us"; "Indeed, it is a strange-disposed time."

6. Brutus likes to think things over before reaching a decision; he is reticent and quiet by nature. Cassius is bitterly jealous of Caesar's popularity and power. He is quick and active by nature. He is manipulative, exploiting Brutus's fears and concerns to make Brutus support his plot.

7. The technical resources of Shakespeare's theater were limited, but the descriptive and emotional power of language has no limits. It was easier to show more private scenes; battles, parades, and so on would have meant many actors on stage. In addition, he wanted to keep his plays within a certain length of time. He didn't want to slow down the action by showing unimportant scenes.

8. It helps readers understand the double meaning of *cobbler*.

9. The noises indicate that something official and significant is occurring offstage.

10. Possible response: They are similar. Supporters of rival officials still fight, some politicians are still ambitious, and many people are still concerned when they see someone trying to take absolute power.

Review and Assess

Literary Analysis

Exposition in Drama

1. Using a chart like the one shown, note what you learn about the characters, setting, and conflict in the **exposition** of the play.

Main Characters	Setting	Situation

2. What important information does Marullus reveal in Act I, Scene i, in his speech beginning at the top of page 824?

3. How do you learn that some in the government are resentful of Caesar?

4. What is the effect of Shakespeare's decision to open the play with a scene featuring a cobbler and other commoners? Explain.

Connecting Literary Elements

5. Identify three lines of **dialogue** in the exposition that show that there is unrest in Rome.

6. What does the dialogue between Cassius and Brutus reveal about their characters?

7. Why might Shakespeare use dialogue to tell about certain events—such as the offering of the crown—rather than showing them on stage?

Reading Strategy

Using Text Aids

8. How does the side note for Scene i, line 11, help readers understand the dialogue that follows?

9. The stage directions in Scene ii indicate a flourish of trumpets and shouts offstage during the conversation between Brutus and Cassius. Why do readers need to know about these offstage noises?

Extend Understanding

10. **Cultural Connections:** Compare and contrast the conflicts and rivalries that you see developing in this play with those that occur in modern American politics.

838 ◆ Drama

Quick Review

The **exposition in drama** is the opening part of the play that introduces the characters, setting, situation, and other details crucial to understanding the work.

Dialogue is the conversation that occurs between characters.

Text aids are the notes and stage directions that appear with the text of a play to help readers picture what is happening and understand difficult language.

 Take It to the Net

www.phschool.com
Take the interactive self-test on line to check your understanding of the selection.

TEACHING RESOURCES

The following resources can be used to enrich or extend the instruction for pp. 838–839

Vocabulary

📖 **Selection Support,** Build Vocabulary, p. 197

📖 **Vocabulary and Spelling Practice Book**
(Use this booklet for skills enrichment.) ▪

Grammar

📖 **Selection Support,** Build Grammar Skills, p. 198

📖 **Writing and Grammar,** Platinum Level, p. 518

📖 **Daily Language Practice Transparencies**

Writing

💿 **Writing and Grammar iText CD-ROM** ▪

▪ **BLOCK SCHEDULING:** Resources marked with this symbol provide varied instruction during 90-minute blocks.

Integrate Language Skills

➊ Vocabulary Development Lesson

Related Words: Forms of *portent*

The adjective *portentous* is related to the noun *portent*, meaning "omen" or "warning," and the verb *portend*, meaning "to be an omen or warning of." Use each word below in a sentence.

1. portentous   2. portend   3. portent

Spelling Strategy

In words such as *prodigious*, the *jus* sound is usually spelled *gious*. There are some exceptions, such as *courageous*, in which the *e* is retained from the base form. Complete these words with letters that correctly spell the *jus* sound.

1. relig____   2. contag____   3. gorg____

Concept Development: Synonyms

Choose the letter of the word that is the best synonym for the first word in each item.

1. replication: (a) original, (b) copy, (c) silence
2. spare: (a) fat, (b) muscular, (c) thin
3. infirmity: (a) strength, (b) weakness, (c) temper
4. surly: (a) bold, (b) timid, (c) polite
5. portentous: (a) optimistic, (b) unclear, (c) foreboding
6. prodigious: (a) passive, (b) forceful, (c) awkward

➋ Grammar Lesson

Mood

Modern English has three **moods**, or ways in which a verb can express an action or a condition: indicative, imperative, and subjunctive. The **indicative mood** is used to make statements of fact. The **subjunctive mood** is used to express ideas that are wishes or are contrary to fact. The **imperative mood** is used to give commands.

> **Indicative:** Because he *is* king, things *are* better. (fact)
>
> **Subjunctive:** If he *were* king, things *would be* better. (wish)
>
> **Imperative:** *Crown* him king! (command)

WG Prentice Hall Writing and Grammar Connection: Chapter 22, Section 1

Practice Identify the mood used in each of the following sentences:

1. If Brutus were less honorable, the plan would be easier.
2. Caesar refused the crown three times.
3. Seize the traitors!
4. If I had come sooner, he would be alive.
5. Antony is Caesar's biggest fan.

Writing Application Write two factual sentences about the plot that is forming in Act I. Recast your sentences in the subjunctive mood.

➌ Extension Activities

Writing Write an **interior monologue**—words that might go through a character's mind—for Cassius if Caesar had accepted the crown that Antony offered.

Listening and Speaking Julius Caesar's career brought Rome from the republican era to the imperial era. Research the art and visual symbols of both eras, and choose a **visual symbol** that captures the spirit of each.

The Tragedy of Julius Caesar, Act I ◆ 839

 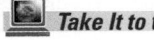

The Tragedy of Julius Caesar, Act II

Lesson Objectives

1. **To analyze and respond to literary elements**
   - Literary Analysis: Blank Verse
   - Connecting Literary Elements: Character Rank

2. **To read, comprehend, analyze, and critique a play**
   - Reading Strategy: Reading Blank Verse
   - Reading Check questions
   - Review and Assess questions
   - Assessment Practice (ATE)

3. **To develop word analysis skills, fluency, and systematic vocabulary**
   - Vocabulary Development Lesson: Latin Root: -spir-

4. **To understand and apply written and oral language conventions**
   - Spelling Strategy
   - Grammar Lesson: *who, whom, who's,* and *whose*

5. **To understand and apply appropriate writing and research strategies**
   - Writing Lesson: Persuasive Essay (After Act V)
   - Extension Activity: Letter to the Editor

6. **To understand and apply listening and speaking strategies**
   - Extension Activity: Debate

STEP-BY-STEP TEACHING GUIDE	PACING GUIDE
PRETEACH	
Motivate Students and Provide Background	
Read and discuss the Review and Anticipate information (SE/ATE p. 841)	5 min.
Introduce the Concepts	
Introduce the Literary Analysis and Reading Strategy (SE/ATE p. 840) A	15 min.
Pronounce the vocabulary words and read their definitions (SE p. 840)	5 min.
TEACH	
Monitor Comprehension	
Informally monitor comprehension by circulating while students read independently or in groups A	30 min.
Monitor students' comprehension with the Reading Check notes (SE/ATE pp. 841, 843, 845, 847, 849, 851, 853, 855)	as students read
Develop vocabulary with Vocabulary notes (SE pp. 842, 843, 844, 851, 853)	as students read
Develop Understanding	
Develop students' understanding of blank verse with the Literary Analysis annotations (SE/ATE pp. 841, 842, 843, 844, 846, 848, 851, 853, 854, 855, 856) A	10 min.
Develop students' understanding of reading blank verse with the Reading Strategy annotations (SE/ATE pp. 845, 847, 849, 850, 856)	10 min.
ASSESS	
Assess Mastery	
Assess students' mastery of the Reading Strategy and Literary Analysis by having them answer the Review and Assess questions (SE/ATE p. 858)	20 min.
Use one or more of the print and media Assessment Resources (ATE p. 859) A	up to 50 min.
EXTEND	
Apply Understanding	
Have students complete the Vocabulary Development Lesson and the Grammar Lesson (SE p. 859) A	20 min.
Apply students' knowledge of paraphrasing using the Writing Lesson (SE p. 915) A	45 min.
Apply students' understanding of the selection using one or more of the Extension Activities (SE p. 859)	20–90 min.

A **ACCELERATED INSTRUCTION:**
Use the strategies and activities identified with an **A**.

UNIVERSAL ACCESS
- ● = Below Level Students
- ▲ = On-Level Students
- ■ = Above Level Students

Time and Resource Manager

RESOURCES		
PRINT 📖	**TRANSPARENCIES** 🖼	**TECHNOLOGY** 💿 🎧 📼
• **Beyond Literature,** Multicultural Connection: Omens and Portents, p. 51 ▲ ■		• **Interest Grabber Video,** Tape 4 ● ▲ ■
• **Selection Support Workbook:** ● ▲ ■ Literary Analysis, p. 204 Reading Strategy, p. 203 Build Vocabulary, p. 201	• **Literary Analysis and Reading Transparencies,** pp. 101 and 102 ● ▲ ■	
		• **Listening to Literature** ● ▲ ■ Audiocassettes, Side 28 Audio CDs, CD 17
• **Literatura en español** ● ▲ • **Literary Analysis for Enrichment** ■		
• **Formal Assessment:** Selection Test, pp. 179–181 ● ▲ ■ • **Open Book Test,** pp. 151–153 ● ▲ ■ • **Performance Assessment and Portfolio Management,** p. 30 ● ▲ ■ • **ASSESSMENT SYSTEM** ● ▲ ■	• **ASSESSMENT SYSTEM** ● ▲ ■ Skills Practice Answers and Explanations on Transparencies	• **Test Bank Software** ● ▲ ■ • **Got It! Assessment Videotapes,** Tape 4 ● ▲
• **Selection Support Workbook:** ● ▲ ■ Build Grammar Skills, p. 202 • **Writing and Grammar,** Platinum Level ● ▲ ■ • **Extension Activities,** p. 51 ● ▲ ■	• **Daily Language Practice Transparencies** ● ▲	• **Writing and Grammar iText CD-ROM** ● ▲ ■ **Take It to the Net** www.phschool.com

BLOCK SCHEDULING: Use one 90-minute class period to preteach the selection and have students read it. Use a second 90-minute class period to assess students' mastery of skills and have them complete one of the Extension Activities.

Step-by-Step Teaching Guide for p. 840

❶ Literary Analysis
Blank Verse

- Ask students why a playwright might write in verse rather than prose. Suggest the following reasons: Verse is easier for both actors and audience to remember, because of its regular rhythm. In addition, verse gives dialogue a sound effect—a built-in rhythm and cadence—that prose doesn't have. Plays are meant to be heard, not read on paper.

- Have students turn back to Act I, Scene i, line 53: "Be gone!" Point out that this line is four iambic feet short of pentameter. This means a silence of about the length of time it would take to speak four more iambic feet. In this case, Marcellus may be waiting for the crowd to quiet down and pay attention.

- As students read, have them watch for lines that are short or long or that break from the iambic rhythm. Have them consider why Shakespeare breaks from the rhythm in each case.

❷ Reading Strategy
Reading Blank Verse

- Have a volunteer read aloud the two lines on this page, ignoring the stress marks and simply speaking the lines naturally, as though they were prose. Point out that the stresses remain the same. Iambic pentameter is the preferred meter for English verse plays because it echoes the natural rhythms of spoken English.

- Have students turn back to Act I, Scene i, and have a volunteer read lines 1–5 aloud to illustrate the proper way to read blank verse—as if it were prose.

 E-Teach

Visit E-Teach at www.phschool.com for teachers' essays on how to teach, with questions and answers.

840

Prepare to Read

The Tragedy of Julius Caesar, Act II

❶ Literary Analysis

Blank Verse

The Tragedy of Julius Caesar is written mainly in blank verse. **Blank verse** is unrhymed poetry written in iambic pentameter. **Iambic** means that an unaccented syllable is followed by an accented one. **Pentameter** means that there are five feet per line. (A foot is one beat set in the pattern of accented and unaccented syllables.) Notice how these lines follow the pattern of iambic pentameter. Straight lines separate the feet.

> Bў all | the gŏds | thăt Rŏ | măns bŏw | befŏre,
>
> Ĭ hĕre | discărd | mў sick | nĕss! Sŏul | ŏf Rŏme,

Shakespeare sometimes breaks with the rhythmic pattern of the lines to emphasize ideas and to keep the language fresh and interesting. (See Act II, Scene i, lines 14–15, for example.)

Connecting Literary Elements

In addition to generating rhythms, Shakespeare uses blank verse to establish **character rank** in the play. Blank verse is generally used for the dialogue of all aristocratic and important characters. In contrast, commoners and minor characters often speak in ordinary prose.

❷ Reading Strategy

Reading Blank Verse

In **reading blank verse,** do not confuse a line with a sentence. It is poetic convention that each line begins with a capital letter. However, to read for meaning, read in sentences. Pause over a comma at the end of a line, but do not stop until you come to a period. For troublesome passages, use a chart like the one shown. First, write the passage, marking pauses and stops. Once you find a complete sentence, rewrite it in your own words.

Vocabulary Development

augmented (ôg ment′ id) *v.* made greater (p. 842)

entreated (en trēt′ id) *v.* begged; pleaded with (p. 842)

conspiracy (kən spir′ ə sē) *n.* group plotting harm or the plot itself (p. 843)

resolution (rez′ ə lo͞o′ shən) *n.* strong determination (p. 844)

exploit (eks′ ploit′) *n.* act, especially a heroic achievement (p. 851)

imminent (im′ ə nənt) *adj.* about to happen (p. 853)

840 ◆ Drama

Passage
Between the acting of a dreadful thing/ And the first motion, all the interim is/ Like a phantasma, or a hideous dream.

Meaning
The time between acting and first planning something bad seems like a nightmare, or a bad dream.

TEACHING RESOURCES

The following resources can be used to enrich or extend the instruction for p. 840.

Motivation

📹 **Interest Grabber Video,** Tape 4

Background

📖 **Beyond Literature,** p. 51 ▪

💻 *Take It to the Net*
Visit www.phschool.com for background and hotlinks for *Julius Caesar.*

Literary Analysis

📄 **Literary Analysis and Reading Transparencies,** Blank Verse, p. 101 ▪

Reading

📖 **Selection Support:** Reading Strategy, p. 203; Build Vocabulary, p. 201

📄 **Literary Analysis and Reading Transparencies,** Reading Blank Verse, p. 102

▪ **BLOCK SCHEDULING:** Resources marked with this symbol provide varied instruction during 90-minute blocks.

❶ Review and Anticipate

In Act I, as Caesar returns victorious from war, he dismisses a warning to "beware the ides of March." The common people cry out for Caesar to be emperor. Although Caesar refuses three times, Cassius and others doubt his sincerity and form a conspiracy to stop him. Brutus is Caesar's friend, but he worries about Caesar's ambition, and the conspirators hope he will side with them. As Act II opens on the eve of the ides of March, Brutus is visited by Casca and Cassius. As you read this act, notice the warnings that Caesar ignores and the shift of power within the group of conspirators.

Act II

Scene i. Rome.

[*Enter* BRUTUS *in his orchard.*]

BRUTUS. What, Lucius, ho!
I cannot, by the progress of the stars,
Give guess how near to day. Lucius, I say!
I would it were my fault to sleep so soundly.
5   When, Lucius, when? Awake, I say! What, Lucius!

[*Enter* LUCIUS.]

LUCIUS. Called you, my lord?

BRUTUS. Get me a taper in my study, Lucius.
When it is lighted, come and call me here.

LUCIUS. I will, my lord.   [*Exit*]

10 **BRUTUS.** It must be by his death; and for my part,
I know no personal cause to spurn at[1] him,
But for the general.[2] He would be crowned.
How that might change his nature, there's the question.
It is the bright day that brings forth the adder,[3]
15   And that craves[4] wary walking. Crown him that,
And then I grant we put a sting in him
That at his will he may do danger with.
Th' abuse of greatness is when it disjoins
Remorse from power;[5] and, to speak truth of Caesar,
20   I have not known when his affections swayed[6]
More than his reason. But 'tis a common proof[7]
That lowliness[8] is young ambition's ladder,
Whereto the climber upward turns his face;

The Tragedy of Julius Caesar, Act II, Scene i ◆ 841

Literary Analysis
Blank Verse In the exchange between Lucius and Brutus, which character speaks in blank verse? Why?

1. **spurn at** kick against; rebel.

2. **the general** the public good.

3. **adder** (ad´ ər) *n.* poisonous snake.

4. **craves** requires.

5. **disjoins . . . power** separates mercy from power.

6. **affections swayed** emotions ruled.

7. **proof** experience.

8. **lowliness** humility.

❸ ✔**Reading Check**
Whom is Brutus addressing in this long speech?

TEACHING RESOURCES

The following resources can be used to enrich or extend the instruction for pp. 841–857.

Literary Analysis
📖 **Selection Support:** Literary Analysis, p. 204

Reading
🎧 **Listening to Literature Audiocassettes**, Side 28 ▪
💿 **Listening to Literature Audio CDs**, CD 17 ▪

TEACH

Step-by-Step Teaching Guide for pp. 841–857

CUSTOMIZE INSTRUCTION
For Musical/Rhythmic Learners
Have students lead groups in tapping out the iambic pentameter of the poetry in this act and finding the exceptions to the rule.

❶ Review and Anticipate

On the eve of the ides of March, Cassius and the other conspirators visit Brutus. All agree to kill Caesar the next day. Cassius proposes that they also kill Antony, who may be a danger to them, but Brutus objects.

As the conspirators leave, Brutus's wife Portia comes to him, pleading for his confidence. She reminds him that she is loyal and trustworthy and that as his wife she has the right to share in his troubles. Deeply moved, Brutus agrees to tell her everything.

The next morning, Calpurnia, fearing danger, begs Caesar to stay home. He agrees at first, but Decius Brutus persuades him to go to the Senate.

❷ Literary Analysis

Blank Verse

- Ask the Literary Analysis question on p. 841: In the exchange between Lucius and Brutus, which character speaks in blank verse? Why?
Answer: Brutus speaks in blank verse to show that he is a member of the upper classes. Lucius's lines are iambic (line 6 loosely so) but are three feet short of pentameter.

- Have students turn the page and read Lucius's speech (lines 35–38). Ask whether he is speaking in blank verse. Why might Shakespeare have made this decision? What is the effect?
Answer: He does speak in blank verse. He is a servant, so this is unusual. It may suggest that Brutus likes to maintain a very formal household or that Lucius is well-born even though he works as a servant. It may show Lucius' great respect for Brutus.

❸ ✔**Reading Check**

Answer: He is arguing with himself.

▪ **BLOCK SCHEDULING:** Resources marked with this symbol provide varied instruction during 90-minute blocks.

841

Making Judgments

• Ask students to share their reactions to Brutus's speech. Do they find his logic persuasive? Why or why not?

Possible answer: Brutus is overreacting. Caesar may or may not intend to take over Rome and end the republic. Brutus says himself that he has never known Caesar to make emotional rather than reasonable decisions.

• Ask students to give their opinions of Brutus based on what they have read so far.

Possible answers: Brutus likes to think things over carefully before taking any action. Brutus is conscientious; he cares for the welfare of the Roman people. He is not greedy for personal glory. He believes that duty is more important than friendship. He is perhaps too ready to assume the worst of Caesar.

❺ **Literary Analysis**

Blank Verse

• Have a volunteer read aloud lines 46–58. Ask students what they notice about the rhythm of this speech.

Answer: Lines 48 and 50 are two feet short of iambic pentameter.

• Ask students why they think Shakespeare departed from his regular cadence.

Possible answers: Both pauses separate Brutus's own words from the words in the letter. This helps the audience understand where the letter ends and Brutus's own words begin. The pauses also give Brutus a moment to think about the letter.

▶ Monitor Progress Point out that line 59 is a foot short of iambic pentameter. Ask students to suggest a reason.

Answer: The knock on the door fills the space of the last foot.

	But when he once attains the upmost round,
25	He then unto the ladder turns his back,
	Looks in the clouds, scorning the base degrees[9]
	By which he did ascend. So Caesar may;
	Then lest he may, prevent.[10] And, since the quarrel
❹		Will bear no color[11] for the thing he is,
30	Fashion it[12] thus: that what he is, <u>augmented</u>
	Would run to these and these extremities;[13]
	And therefore think him as a serpent's egg
	Which hatched, would as his kind grow mischievous,
	And kill him in the shell.

[*Enter* LUCIUS.]

35	LUCIUS. The taper burneth in your closet,[14] sir.
	Searching the window for a flint,[15] I found
	This paper thus sealed up, and I am sure
	It did not lie there when I went to bed. [*Gives him the letter*]

BRUTUS. Get you to bed again; it is not day.
| 40 | Is not tomorrow, boy, the ides of March? |

LUCIUS. I know not, sir.

BRUTUS. Look in the calendar and bring me word.

LUCIUS. I will, sir.   [*Exit*]

BRUTUS. The exhalations[16] whizzing in the air
| 45 | Give so much light that I may read by them. |

[*Opens the letter and reads*]

"Brutus, thou sleep'st; awake, and see thyself.
Shall Rome, &c.[17] Speak, strike, redress.
Brutus, thou sleep'st; awake."

Such instigations[18] have been often dropped
| 50 | Where I have took them up. |
"Shall Rome, &c." Thus must I piece it out:[19]
Shall Rome stand under one man's awe?[20] What, Rome?
My ancestors did from the streets of Rome
The Tarquin[21] drive, when he was called a king.
❺ | 55 | "Speak, strike, redress." Am I <u>entreated</u> |
To speak and strike? O Rome, I make thee promise,
If the redress will follow, thou receivest
Thy full petition at the hand of[22] Brutus!

[*Enter* LUCIUS.]

LUCIUS. Sir, March is wasted fifteen days. [*Knock within*]

| 60 | BRUTUS. 'Tis good. Go to the gate; somebody knocks.   [*Exit* LUCIUS.] |

---

9. base degrees low steps or people in lower positions.

10. lest . . . prevent in case he may, we must stop him.

11. the quarrel . . . no color our complaint cannot be justified in view of what he now is.
augmented (ôg ment´ id) *v.* made greater
12. Fashion it state the case.
13. extremities (ek strem´ ə tēz) *n.* extremes (of tyranny).

14. closet study.
15. flint stone used to start a fire.

16. exhalations (eks´ hə lā´ shənz) *n.* meteors.

17. & c. et cetera, Latin for "and so forth."

18. instigations (in´ stə gā´ shənz) *n.* urgings, incitements, or spurs to act.
19. piece it out figure out the meaning.

20. under one man's awe in fearful reverence of one man.

entreated (en trēt´ id) *v.* begged; pleaded with

21. Tarquin (tär´ kwin) king of Rome driven out by Lucius Junius Brutus, Brutus' ancestor.

22. Thy full . . . hand of all you ask from.

CUSTOMIZE INSTRUCTION FOR UNIVERSAL ACCESS

For Advanced Readers

Brutus is the central character in most of Act II. Have students write character analyses of Brutus based on what they know from Acts I and II. Students should pay attention to Brutus's thoughts (spoken in soliloquy), his actions, his words to others, and other characters' reactions to him. Students should analyze Brutus's character and discuss whether they think he is a hero. Have students revise their essays as needed after they have read the final three acts. Has their opinion of Brutus changed? Why or why not?

Since Cassius first did whet[23] me against Caesar,
I have not slept.
Between the acting of a dreadful thing
And the first motion,[24] all the interim is
65 Like a phantasma,[25] or a hideous dream.
The genius and the mortal instruments[26]
Are then in council, and the state of a man,
Like to a little kingdom, suffers then
The nature of an insurrection.[27]

[Enter LUCIUS.]

70 LUCIUS. Sir, 'tis your brother[28] Cassius at the door,
Who doth desire to see you.

BRUTUS.   Is he alone?

LUCIUS. No, sir, there are moe[29] with him.

BRUTUS.   Do you know them?

LUCIUS. No, sir; their hats are plucked about their ears,
And half their faces buried in their cloaks,
75 That by no means I may discover them
By any mark of favor.[30]

BRUTUS.   Let 'em enter.   [Exit LUCIUS.]

They are the faction. O conspiracy,
Sham'st thou to show thy dang'rous brow by night,
When evils are most free? O, then by day
80 Where wilt thou find a cavern dark enough
To mask thy monstrous visage? Seek none, conspiracy;
Hide it in smiles and affability:
For if thou path, thy native semblance on,[31]
Not Erebus◆ itself were dim enough
85 To hide thee from prevention.[32]

[Enter the conspirators, CASSIUS, CASCA, DECIUS, CINNA, METELLUS CIMBER, and TREBONIUS.]

Literature in Context ❽ Humanities Connection

◆ Erebus
When Brutus observes that the conspirators cannot hide their intentions even in Erebus, he is referring to a part of Hades, the underworld of Greek mythology. According to some myth versions, Erebus is a dim, dark place where people go as soon as they die. From Erebus, the dead who lived evil lives pass on to Tartarus, where they are imprisoned and punished, while the good go to the Elysian Fields to be rewarded.

The Tragedy of Julius Caesar, Act II, Scene i ◆ 843

23. whet (hwet) v. sharpen; incite.

24. motion idea; suggestion.

25. all the . . . a phantasma all the time between seems like a nightmare.

26. mortal instruments bodily powers.

27. insurrection (in′ sə rek′ shen) n. revolt.

28. brother brother-in-law (Cassius was married to Brutus' sister.)

29. moe more.

30. discover . . . favor identify them by their appearance.

31. path . . . semblance on walk looking as you normally do.

conspiracy (kən spir′ ə sē) n. group plotting harm or the plot itself

Literary Analysis

Blank Verse Which interjection does Shakespeare use to maintain the iambic pentameter of lines 77 and 79?

32. prevention being discovered and stopped.

❼ ✓**Reading Check**

What is troubling Brutus?

- Choose five volunteers to read lines 95–104 aloud. Ask students why they think line 95 is short.
  Answer: Having welcomed his guests, Brutus waits for someone to explain the reason for the visit. When no one says anything, he asks why they have come.

- Ask why line 100 is short. Point out the stage direction at the end of the line.
  Answer: The missing feet give the two actors a moment to walk a few steps away from the others, so that their conversation will be private.

▷ Monitor Progress Ask why Casca's line is so short and why Shakespeare chose not to incorporate it into a shared-meter line.
  Possible answers: Casca's "No" is so abrupt that the others may be startled and pause for a moment while they think of something else to say. It may be a comical moment; the others may have been expecting Casca to say more, so they wait until they realize he has nothing else to say.

CASSIUS. I think we are too bold upon[33] your rest.
  Good morrow, Brutus; do we trouble you?

BRUTUS. I have been up this hour, awake all night.
  Know I these men that come along with you?

90 **CASSIUS.** Yes, every man of them; and no man here
  But honors you; and every one doth wish
  You had but that opinion of yourself
  Which every noble Roman bears of you.
  This is Trebonius.

BRUTUS.   He is welcome hither.

CASSIUS. This, Decius Brutus.

95 **BRUTUS.**   He is welcome too.

CASSIUS. This, Casca; this, Cinna; and this, Metellus Cimber.

BRUTUS. They are all welcome.
  What watchful cares do interpose themselves
  Betwixt your eyes and night?[34]

100 **CASSIUS.** Shall I entreat[35] a word?   [*They whisper.*]

DECIUS. Here lies the east; doth not the day break here?

CASCA. No.

CINNA. O, pardon, sir, it doth; and yon gray lines
  That fret[36] the clouds are messengers of day.

105 **CASCA.** You shall confess that you are both deceived.
  Here, as I point my sword, the sun arises,
  Which is a great way growing on[37] the south,
  Weighing[38] the youthful season of the year.
  Some two months hence, up higher toward the north
110 He first presents his fire; and the high[39] east
  Stands as the Capitol, directly here.

BRUTUS. Give me your hands all over, one by one.

CASSIUS. And let us swear our resolution.

BRUTUS. No, not an oath. If not the face of men,
115 The sufferance of our souls, the time's abuse[40]—
  If these be motives weak, break off betimes,[41]
  And every man hence to his idle bed.
  So let high-sighted[42] tyranny range on
  Till each man drop by lottery.[43] But if these
120 (As I am sure they do) bear fire enough
  To kindle cowards and to steel with valor
  The melting spirits of women, then, countrymen,
  What need we any spur but our own cause

33. **upon** in interfering with.

34. **watchful . . . night** worries that keep you from sleep.

35. **entreat** (in trēt´) *v.* speak.

36. **fret** (fret) *v.* decorate with a pattern.

37. **growing on** tending toward.

38. **Weighing** considering.

39. **high** due.

resolution (rez´ ə lōō´ shən) *n.* strong determination

40. **the face . . . time's abuse** the sadness on men's faces, the suffering of our souls, the present abuses.

41. **betimes** quickly.

42. **high-sighted** arrogant (as a hawk about to swoop down on its prey).

43. **by lottery** by chance or in his turn.

✷ ENRICHMENT: History Connection

Cicero

In lines 141–153, the conspirators discuss inviting Cicero to join them. Marcus Tullius Cicero was one of the great speakers and writers of the age. His prose became the model for literary expression throughout Europe, and his orations are among the most commonly studied Latin works. Cicero studied philosophy and rhetoric in Greece. After returning to Rome in 66 B.C., he was elected praetor (administrator of civil justice). In 63 B.C., he was elected consul.

Cicero supported Pompey in his struggle with Caesar for control of Rome, and he approved of Caesar's assassination. In 43 B.C., when Octavius Caesar, Mark Antony, and Marcus Aemilius Lepidus assumed power as the Second Triumvirate (see Act IV, Scene i), Cicero was one of many whom they condemned to death. He was killed at his home in Tuscany.

To prick us to redress?[44] What other bond
125 Than secret Romans, that have spoke the word,
And will not palter?[45] And what other oath
Than honesty to honesty engaged[46]
That this shall be, or we will fall for it?
Swear priests and cowards and men cautelous,[47]
130 Old feeble carrions[48] and such suffering souls
That welcome wrongs; unto bad causes swear
Such creatures as men doubt; but do not stain
The even[49] virtue of our enterprise,
Nor th' insuppressive mettle[50] of our spirits,
135 To think that or our cause or[51] our performance
Did need an oath; when every drop of blood
That every Roman bears, and nobly bears,
Is guilty of a several bastardy[52]
If he do break the smallest particle
140 Of any promise that hath passed from him.

CASSIUS. But what of Cicero? Shall we sound him?[53]
I think he will stand very strong with us.

CASCA. Let us not leave him out.

CINNA.   No, by no means.

METELLUS. O, let us have him, for his silver hairs
145 Will purchase us a good opinion,
And buy men's voices to commend our deeds.
It shall be said his judgment ruled our hands;
Our youths and wildness shall no whit[54] appear,
But all be buried in his gravity.

150 **BRUTUS.** O, name him not! Let us not break with him;[55]
For he will never follow anything
That other men begin.

CASSIUS.   Then leave him out.

CASCA. Indeed, he is not fit.

DECIUS. Shall no man else be touched but only Caesar?

155 **CASSIUS.** Decius, well urged. I think it is not meet
Mark Antony, so well beloved of Caesar,
Should outlive Caesar; we shall find of[56] him
A shrewd contriver;[57] and you know, his means;
If he improve[58] them, may well stretch so far
160 As to annoy[59] us all; which to prevent,
Let Antony and Caesar fall together.

BRUTUS. Our course will seem too bloody, Caius Cassius,

The Tragedy of Julius Caesar, Act II, Scene i ◆ 845

---

44. prick us to redress goad or spur us on to correct these evils.

45. palter (pôl′ tər) talk insincerely.

46. honesty engaged personal honor pledged.

47. cautelous cautious.

48. carrions (kar′ ē ənz) *n.* decaying flesh.

49. even constant.

50. insuppressive mettle uncrushable courage.

51. or . . . or either our cause or.

52. guilty . . . bastardy is no true Roman.

53. sound him find out his opinion.

54. no whit (hwit) *n.* not the least bit.

55. break with him confide in him.

Reading Strategy
Reading Blank Verse
Where should you pause in reading the dialogue between Brutus and Cassius at lines 150–152?

56. of on.

57. contriver (kən trīv′ ər) *n.* schemer.

58. improve increase.

59. annoy harm.

⓬ ✔**Reading Check**

Why do the men want Cicero to join the conspiracy?

---

❿ Critical Thinking
Make Judgments

- Ask students to explain why Brutus doesn't want to swear an oath.
  Answer: He says that they are all virtuous, noble, and honest men, so no oath is necessary; they can all trust one another to be loyal.

- Ask whether students think Brutus is right. Have them support their answers.
  Possible answers: He is probably right because all the men want the same thing—to stop Caesar from becoming king. He may well be wrong because he is meeting some of these men for the first time and they may not be trustworthy. It is illogical to assume that men who intend murder are honest men.

⓫ Reading Strategy
Reading Blank Verse

- Ask the Reading Strategy question on p. 845: Where should you pause in reading the dialogue between Brutus and Cassius at lines 150–152?
  Answer: Stop after the exclamation point and pause after the semicolon in line 150.

- How quickly does Cassius's line "Then leave him out" follow Brutus's speech? How do you know?
  Answer: Cassius speaks immediately, barely waiting for Brutus to finish. There is no pause between their lines. "That other men begin./Then leave him out" is an example of shared meter.

⓬ ✔**Reading Check**

Answer: Cicero's age has given him a reputation for wisdom and gravity that will make the murder appear favorable to the people.

845

- Ask the Literary Analysis question on p. 846: In the last line of Brutus's speech what is Shakespeare trying to achieve with such a short line?

Answer: The abrupt ending of the speech echoes the image of the planned abrupt ending to Caesar's life.

▶ **Monitor Progress** Have students watch for other short lines as they read. Have them think about the effect Shakespeare achieves by breaking away from his usual rhythms.

⓮ ▶Critical Viewing

Answer: Their expressions are tense and urgent. They are probably trying to convince him to join their conspiracy.

To cut the head off and then hack the limbs,
Like wrath in death and envy afterwards;[60]
165   For Antony is but a limb of Caesar.
Let's be sacrificers, but not butchers, Caius.
We all stand up against the spirit of Caesar,
And in the spirit of men there is no blood.
O, that we then could come by Caesar's spirit,[61]
170   And not dismember Caesar! But, alas,
Caesar must bleed for it. And, gentle[62] friends,
Let's kill him boldly, but not wrathfully;
Let's carve him as a dish fit for the gods,
Not hew him as a carcass fit for hounds.
175   And let our hearts, as subtle masters do,
Stir up their servants[63] to an act of rage,
And after seem to chide 'em.[64] This shall make
Our purpose necessary, and not envious;
Which so appearing to the common eyes,
180   We shall be called purgers,[65] not murderers.
And for Mark Antony, think not of him;
For he can do no more than Caesar's arm
When Caesar's head is off.

⓭

CASSIUS.   Yet I fear him;
For in the ingrafted[66] love he bears to Caesar—

60. Like . . . envy afterwards as if we were killing in anger with hatred afterward.

61. come by Caesar's spirit get hold of the principles of tyranny for which Caesar stands.

62. gentle honorable; noble.

63. servants their hands.

64. chide 'em scold them.

65. purgers healers.

66. ingrafted deeply rooted.

Literary Analysis

Blank Verse In the last line of Brutus' speech, what is Shakespeare trying to achieve with such a short line?

⓮ ▼ **Critical Viewing**
What do you think the group is saying to Brutus here? **[Speculate]**

185 **BRUTUS.** Alas, good Cassius, do not think of him.
      If he love Caesar, all that he can do
      Is to himself—take thought[67] and die for Caesar.
      And that were much he should,[68] for he is given
      To sports, to wildness, and much company.

190 **TREBONIUS.** There is no fear in him; let him not die,
      For he will live and laugh at this hereafter.

                                    [*Clock strikes.*]

BRUTUS. Peace! Count the clock.

CASSIUS.   The clock hath stricken three.

TREBONIUS. 'Tis time to part.

CASSIUS.   But it is doubtful yet
      Whether Caesar will come forth today or no;
195 For he is superstitious grown of late,
      Quite from the main[69] opinion he held once
      Of fantasy, of dreams, and ceremonies.[70]
      It may be these apparent prodigies,
      The unaccustomed terror of this night,
200 And the persuasion of his augurers[71]
      May hold him from the Capitol today.

DECIUS.   Never fear that. If he be so resolved,
      I can o'ersway him;[72] for he loves to hear
                  That unicorns may be betrayed
                      with trees,[73]
205   And bears with glasses,[74] elephants
                      with holes,[75]
                  Lions with toils,[76] and men with
                      flatterers;
                  But when I tell him he hates
                      flatterers
                  He says he does, being then most
                      flatterèd.
                  Let me work;
210   For I can give his humor the true
                      bent,[77]
                  And I will bring him to the Capitol.

CASSIUS. Nay, we will all of us be there to
      fetch him.

BRUTUS. By the eighth hour; is that the
      uttermost?[78]

CINNA. Be that the uttermost, and fail
      not then.

The Tragedy of Julius Caesar, Act II, Scene i ◆ 847

---

67. take thought
become melancholy.

68. that were much he should It is unlikely he
would do that.

69. Quite from the main quite changed
from the strong.

70. ceremonies omens.

71. augurers (ô´ gər ərz) *n.*
officials who interpreted
omens to decide if they
were favorable or unfavor-
able for an undertaking.

72. I can o'ersway him
I can change his mind.

73. unicorns . . . trees story
that tells how standing in front
of a tree and stepping aside at
the last moment causes a
charging unicorn to bury his
horn in the tree and be caught.

74. glasses mirrors.

75. holes pitfalls.

76. toils nets; snares.

Reading Strategy
Reading Blank Verse
How does the accent on
"flatterèd" affect the way
you should read line 208?

**77. give his humor the
true bent** bend his feelings
in the right direction.

78. uttermost latest.

16 ✓**Reading Check**

Why does Brutus say that
Antony should not be
killed?

---

15 **Reading Strategy**
Reading Blank Verse

• Ask the Reading Strategy question
  on p. 847: How does the accent on
  "flatterèd" affect the way you
  should read line 208?
  Answer: Pronounce the word as if
  it had three syllables, so that the
  line will fit the rhythm of the
  iambic pentameter.

• Ask which line of the speech is not
  in iambic pentameter. Ask why the
  line is short.
  Answer: Line 209 is short. Decius
  may be looking around the circle
  of faces for agreement and
  approval or pausing to frame the
  summary of his argument.

16 ✓**Reading Check**

Answer: Brutus is willing to commit
murder only for noble reasons.
Murdering Antony would be a dishonorable and cowardly act.

CUSTOMIZE INSTRUCTION FOR UNIVERSAL ACCESS

For Gifted/Talented Students

Challenge students to stage Act II, Scene i from the
conspirators' entrance to their exit (lines 86–228). This
scene has roles for seven actors; other students may
want to take part in directing, staging, or costuming.
Meet with participants to discuss the scene's challenges and to hear students' ideas about staging.
Remind students that in Shakespeare's day, all female
roles were played by boys; this should encourage the
girls in your class to take on some of the male roles.
Give students sufficient time to rehearse and learn
their lines before they perform their scene for the
class.

847

⑰ Literary Analysis

Blank Verse

- Ask why Shakespeare contracts "upon us" to "upon 's" in line 221.
  Answer: The contraction maintains the rhythm of iambic pentameter. "Upon us" would have meant an extra syllable.

- Ask the Literary Analysis Question on p. 848: How many accented syllables are in line 223? Why might Shakespeare have broken away from pure iambic pentameter in this line?
  Answer: When spoken naturally, the line contains six stressed syllables: *what*, *said*, *show*, *-selves*, *true*, and *Ro-*. The line contains eleven syllables altogether, which is one too many for pure iambic pentameter.

⑱ Background

Language

Share the information on *thee* and *thou* on p. 823 of this teacher's edition. Remind students that these informal pronouns have passed out of use in modern times. Close friends and family members called one another *thou* instead of *you*. *You* was the pronoun used to show respect, formality, or politeness. Masters would call their servants *thou*, but servants would call masters *you*.

Thou has its own verb forms, which usually end in *-st*. Examples on this page include "thou hast" and "thou sleep'st." When the pronoun faded from use, the verb form also disappeared.

---

215   **METELLUS.** Caius Ligarius doth bear Caesar hard,[79]
      Who rated[80] him for speaking well of Pompey.
      I wonder none of you have thought of him.

   BRUTUS. Now, good Metellus, go along by him.
      He loves me well, and I have given him reasons;
220   Send him but hither, and I'll fashion[81] him.

   CASSIUS. The morning comes upon 's; we'll leave you, Brutus.
      And, friends, disperse yourselves; but all remember
      What you have said, and show yourselves true Romans.

   BRUTUS. Good gentlemen, look fresh and merrily.
225   Let not our looks put on[82] our purposes,
      But bear it[83] as our Roman actors do,
      With untired spirits and formal constancy.[84]
      And so good morrow to you every one.

                   [*Exit all but* BRUTUS.]

      Boy! Lucius! Fast asleep? It is no matter;
230   Enjoy the honey-heavy dew of slumber.
      Thou hast no figures nor no fantasies
      Which busy care draws in the brains of men;
      Therefore thou sleep'st so sound.

[*Enter* PORTIA.]

   PORTIA.   Brutus, my lord.

   BRUTUS. Portia, what mean you? Wherefore rise you now
235   It is not for your health thus to commit
      Your weak condition to the raw cold morning.

---

79. doth bear Caesar hard has a grudge against Caesar.

80. rated berated.

81. fashion mold.

Literary Analysis
Blank Verse How many accented syllables are in line 223? Why might Shakespeare have broken away from pure iambic pentameter in this line?

82. put on show.

83. bear it carry it off.

84. formal constancy consistent dignity.

Literature ⑱ in context   Vocabulary Connection

Archaic Word Forms

Shakespeare uses various word forms that are now archaic, or out of date. These words give the language a more formal—and also a more poetic—tone. Use the following glossary to interpret the word forms Shakespeare uses.

thou *pron.* nominative case meaning *you*
thee *pron.* objective case meaning *you*
thy *pron.* possessive case meaning *your*
dost *v.* third-person singular present tense of *do*
burneth *v.* third-person singular present tense of *burn*
sleep'st *v.* second-person singular present tense of *sleep*
receivest *v.* second-person singular present tense of *receive*
sham'st *v.* second-person singular present tense of *shame*

---

848 ◆ *Drama*

PORTIA. Nor for yours neither. Y'have ungently, Brutus,
 Stole from my bed; and yesternight at supper
 You suddenly arose and walked about,
240 Musing and sighing, with your arms across;
 And when I asked you what the matter was,
 You stared upon me with ungentle looks.
 I urged you further; then you scratched your head,
 And too impatiently stamped with your foot.
245 Yet I insisted, yet you answered not,
 But with an angry wafter[85] of your hand
 Gave sign for me to leave you. So I did,
 Fearing to strengthen that impatience
 Which seemed too much enkindled, and withal
250 Hoping it was but an effect of humor,
 Which sometime hath his[86] hour with every man.
 It will not let you eat, nor talk, nor sleep,
 And could it work so much upon your shape
 As it hath much prevailed on your condition,[87]
255 I should not know you[88] Brutus. Dear my lord,
 Make me acquainted with your cause of grief.

BRUTUS. I am not well in health, and that is all.

PORTIA. Brutus is wise and, were he not in health,
 He would embrace the means to come by it.

260 **BRUTUS.** Why, so I do. Good Portia, go to bed.

PORTIA. Is Brutus sick, and is it physical[89]
 To walk unbracèd and suck up the humors[90]
 Of the dank morning? What, is Brutus sick,
 And will he steal out of his wholesome bed,
265 To dare the vile contagion of the night,
 And tempt the rheumy and unpurgèd air[91]
 To add unto his sickness? No, my Brutus:
 You have some sick offense[92] within your mind.
 Which by the right and virtue of my place
270 I ought to know of; and upon my knees
 I charm[93] you, by my once commended[94] beauty,
 By all your vows of love, and that great vow[95]
 Which did incorporate and make us one,
 That you unfold to me, your self, your half,
275 Why you are heavy,[96] and what men tonight
 Have had resort to you; for here have been
 Some six or seven, who did hide their faces
 Even from darkness.

 BRUTUS.   Kneel not, gentle Portia.

PORTIA. I should not need, if you were gentle Brutus.

Reading Strategy
Reading Blank Verse
How many complete stops should the actor or reader make in Portia's speech (lines 237–256)?

85. wafter waving.

86. his its.

87. condition disposition.

88. I should not know you I would not recognize you as.

89. physical healthy.
90. humors dampness.

91. tempt . . . air risk exposing himself to the air that is likely to cause rheumatism and air that has not been purified by the sun.
92. sick offense harmful sickness.
93. charm beg.
94. commended praised.
95. great vow marriage vow.
96. heavy sorrowful.

20 ✔**Reading Check**
How does Portia know that Brutus is not physically sick?

---

19 **Reading Strategy**
Reading Blank Verse

- Ask the Reading Strategy question on p. 849: How many complete stops should the actor or reader make in Portia's speech (lines 237–256)?
 Answer: The speech contains seven sentences, so there should be seven full stops.
- Point out that Portia and Brutus use the formal pronoun *you* when speaking to each other. Given that they are husband and wife, ask students what effect this formality has.
 Answer: It echoes Lucius's formality in speaking to Brutus in blank verse. It suggests that Brutus is formal and somewhat distant with everyone, and that he doesn't show his emotions.

20 ✔**Reading Check**
Answer: He does not behave like a sick person; instead of resting, he paces the floor and wanders outdoors.

CUSTOMIZE INSTRUCTION FOR UNIVERSAL ACCESS

For Advanced Readers

Have students write brief essays on why Shakespeare included this scene with Portia in the play. Students may want to look ahead to Act IV, Scene iii, to see what happens to Portia and how Brutus reacts to it. Point out that Portia takes no active part in the story; her presence does not affect the plot. Why, therefore, is she included? Students may want to read this scene aloud with partners before they write their essays, to gain a better understanding of the relationship between Brutus and Portia.

㉑ Reading Strategy

Reading Blank Verse

- Ask students why they think Shakespeare chose to make line 290 two feet short of pentameter.
  Answer: The short line means a pause before the next speech. Portia may be too moved at Brutus's declaration to speak right away.

- Ask the Reading Strategy question on p. 850: Where should you pause in reading Brutus's speech (lines 302–304)?
  Answer: Pause at the exclamation points and period. An actor might also pause very slightly after the comma at the end of line 302.

280   Within the bond of marriage, tell me, Brutus,
       Is it excepted[97] I should know no secrets
       That appertain[98] to you? Am I your self
       But, as it were, in sort or limitation,[99]
       To keep with you at meals, comfort your bed,
285   And talk to you sometimes? Dwell I but in the suburbs[100]
       Of your good pleasure? If it be no more,
       Portia is Brutus' harlot, not his wife.

       BRUTUS. You are my true and honorable wife,
       As dear to me as are the ruddy drops[101]
290   That visit my sad heart.

       PORTIA. If this were true, then should I know this secret.
       I grant I am a woman; but withal
       A woman that Lord Brutus took to wife.
       I grant I am a woman; but withal
295   A woman well reputed, Cato's daughter.[102]
       Think you I am no stronger than my sex,
       Being so fathered and so husbanded?
       Tell me your counsels,[103] I will not disclose 'em.
       I have made strong proof of my constancy,
300   Giving myself a voluntary wound
       Here in the thigh; can I bear that with patience,
       And not my husband's secrets?

       BRUTUS.   O ye gods,
       Render[104] me worthy of this noble wife!   [*Knock*]
       Hark, hark! One knocks. Portia, go in a while,
305   And by and by thy bosom shall partake
       The secrets of my heart.
       All my engagements[105] I will construe to thee,
       All the charactery of my sad brows.[106]
       Leave me with haste.   [*Exit* PORTIA.]

       [*Enter* LUCIUS *and* CAIUS LIGARIUS.]

                                   Lucius, who's that knocks?

310   **LUCIUS.** Here is a sick man that would speak with you.

       BRUTUS. Caius Ligarius, that Metellus spake of.
       Boy, stand aside. Caius Ligarius! How?

       CAIUS. Vouchsafe good morrow from a feeble tongue.

       BRUTUS. O, what a time have you chose out,[107] brave Caius,
315   To wear a kerchief![108] Would you were not sick!

       CAIUS. I am not sick, if Brutus have in hand
       Any exploit worthy the name of honor.

97. excepted made an exception.

98. appertain (ap´ ər tān´) *v.* belong.

99. in sort or limitation within a limited way.

100. suburbs outskirts.

101. ruddy drops blood.

102. Cato's daughter Marcus Porcius Cato had been an ally of Pompey and enemy of Caesar. He killed himself rather than be captured by Caesar.

103. counsels secrets.

㉑

Reading Strategy
Reading Blank Verse
Where should you pause in reading Brutus' speech (lines 303–304)?

104. Render (ren´ dər) *v.* make.

105. engagements commitments.
106. All the charactery of my sad brows all that is written on my face.

107. chose out picked out.
108. To wear a kerchief Caius wears a scarf to protect himself from drafts because he is sick.

BRUTUS. Such an <u>exploit</u> have I in hand, Ligarius,
      Had you a healthful ear to hear of it.

320 **CAIUS.** By all the gods that Romans bow before,
      I here discard my sickness! Soul of Rome,
      Brave son, derived from honorable loins,[109]
      Thou, like an exorcist,[110] hast conjured up
      My mortifièd spirit.[111] Now bid me run,
325   And I will strive with things impossible.
      Yea, get the better of them. What's to do?

BRUTUS. A piece of work that will make sick men whole.

CAIUS. But are not some whole that we must make sick?

BRUTUS. That must we also. What it is, my Caius,
330   I shall unfold[112] to thee, as we are going
      To whom it must be done.

CAIUS. Set on[113] your foot,
      And with a heart new-fired I follow you,
      To do I know not what; but it sufficeth[114]
      That Brutus leads me on.   [*Thunder*]

BRUTUS.   Follow me, then.   [*Exit*]

Scene ii. Caesar's house.

[*Thunder and lightning. Enter* JULIUS CAESAR *in his nightgown.*]

CAESAR. Nor heaven nor earth have been at peace tonight:
      Thrice hath Calpurnia in her sleep cried out,
      "Help, ho! They murder Caesar!" Who's within?

[*Enter a* SERVANT.]

SERVANT. My lord?

5 **CAESAR.** Go bid the priests do present[1] sacrifice,
      And bring me their opinions of success.

SERVANT. I will, my lord.   [*Exit*]

[*Enter* CALPURNIA.]

CALPURNIA. What mean you, Caesar? Think you to walk forth?
      You shall not stir out of your house today.

10 **CAESAR.** Caesar shall forth. The things that threatened me
      Ne'er looked but on my back; when they shall see
      The face of Caesar, they are vanishèd.

CALPURNIA. Caesar, I never stood on ceremonies,[2]
      Yet now they fright me. There is one within,
15   Besides the things that we have heard and seen,

---

exploit (eks´ ploit´) *n.* act, especially a heroic achievement

109. derived from honorable loins descended from Lucius Junius Brutus, founder of Rome.

110. exorcist (ek´ sôr sist) *n.* one who calls up spirits.

111. mortifièd spirit paralyzed, as if dead, spirit.

112. unfold disclose.

113. Set on advance.

114. sufficeth (sə fis´ eth) *v.* is enough.

Literary Analysis
Blank Verse How can a speaker make the word *Calpurnia* work with the iambic rhythm?

1. present immediate.

2. stood on ceremonies paid attention to omens.

㉓ ✓**Reading Check**
Why does Portia think that Brutus should confide in her?

The Tragedy of Julius Caesar, Act II, Scene ii ◆ 851

㉒ Literary Analysis
Blank Verse

• Ask the Literary Analysis question on p. 851: How can a speaker make the word *Calpurnia* work with the rhythm?
  Answer: Pronounce it Cal-pur-nya, giving it three syllables.

• Have students turn the page and read the rest of Calpurnia's speech (to line 26). Ask them to point out a variation in the iambic pentameter.
  Answer: The word *horses* in line 23 reverses the iambic rhythm; it is strong-weak instead of weak-strong.

㉓ ✓**Reading Check**

Answer: She is his wife; she is trustworthy and intelligent; she is deeply concerned for him; their marriage gives her the right to share his troubles.

CUSTOMIZE INSTRUCTION FOR UNIVERSAL ACCESS

For Gifted/Talented Students	For Advanced Readers
Have students write an additional scene for Act II, in which Brutus keeps his promise to tell Portia what the conspirators are planning. Students may want to read the final scene of Act II, in which Portia appears. Have them consider what Brutus told her and how he expressed himself, given her mood in the act's final scene. Allow students to write their scenes in prose or blank verse. Have them try to maintain Shakespeare's style and diction. Students may want to choose partners with whom to read or perform their scenes.	Have students gather for a group discussion of the atmosphere of the play up to this point. Students should look at characters' descriptions of weather, their moods, their descriptions of various omens and strange sights, and their reactions to these things. Casca, for example, was badly frightened by the storm in Act I; Brutus's concerns for the future have made him gloomy. Have students try to define the play's atmosphere and mood and identify specific details with which Shakespeare creates this atmosphere.

Making Judgments

- Have students discuss their opinions of Caesar based on the three speeches he makes on this page.
Answer: Students may be impressed with Caesar's courage or irritated at his dismissal of the danger he may be in.

- Ask whether students think that Caesar is genuinely courageous or whether he simply wants to impress everyone with a show of courage. Have them give reasons for their answers.
Possible answer: He's genuinely brave, because he is ignoring powerful omens and warnings of danger. Since he is aware that Cassius may be plotting against him, he should know that his danger is real and that the omens are true.

Recounts most horrid sights seen by the watch.[3]
A lioness hath whelpèd[4] in the streets,
And graves have yawned, and yielded up their dead;
Fierce fiery warriors fought upon the clouds
20 In ranks and squadrons and right form of war,[5]
Which drizzled blood upon the Capitol;
The noise of battle hurtled[6] in the air,
Horses did neigh and dying men did groan,
And ghosts did shriek and squeal about the street.
25 O Caesar, these things are beyond all use,[7]
And I do fear them.

CAESAR.   What can be avoided
Whose end is purposed[8] by the mighty gods?
Yet Caesar shall go forth; for these predictions
Are to the world in general as to Caesar.[9]

30 CALPURNIA. When beggars die, there are no comets seen;
The heavens themselves blaze forth[10] the death of princes.

CAESAR. Cowards die many times before their deaths;
The valiant never taste of death but once.
Of all the wonders that I yet have heard,
35 It seems to me most strange that men should fear,
Seeing that death, a necessary end,
Will come when it will come.

24 [Enter a SERVANT.]

                                    What say the augurers?

SERVANT. They would not have you to stir forth today.
Plucking the entrails of an offering forth,[11]
40 They could not find a heart within the beast.

CAESAR. The gods do this in shame of[12] cowardice:
Caesar should be a beast without a heart
If he should stay at home today for fear.
No, Caesar shall not; Danger knows full well
45 That Caesar is more dangerous than he.
We are two lions littered[13] in one day,
And I the elder and more terrible,
And Caesar shall go forth.

CALPURNIA.   Alas, my lord,
Your wisdom is consumed in confidence.[14]
50 Do not go forth today. Call it my fear
That keeps you in the house and not your own.
We'll send Mark Antony to the Senate House,
And he shall say you are not well today.
Let me, upon my knee, prevail in this.

3. Recounts . . . watch tells about the awful sights seen by the watchman.

4. whelpèd given birth.

5. right form of war proper military formation of war.

6. hurtled (hʉrt´ əld) v. clashed together.

7. beyond all use contrary to all experience.

8. is purposed is intended.

9. for these . . . as to Caesar because these predictions apply to the rest of the world as much as they apply to Caesar.

10. blaze forth proclaim with meteors and comets.

11. Plucking . . . forth pulling out the insides of a sacrificed animal.

12. in shame of in order to shame.

13. littered born.

14. confidence overconfidence.

852 ◆ Drama

⚜ **ENRICHMENT: History Connection**

Caesar

Although he speaks few lines in the play of which he is the title character, Gaius Julius Caesar was one of the most powerful men in history. He began his political career as a director of public works and games in 65 B.C., about twenty years before the events of this play. In 62, he became praetor, the office ranking just below consul. In 60, he joined forces with Marcus Licinius Crassus and Gaeus Pompey. They ruled Rome as the First Triumvirate. In 59, Caesar married Calpurnia (his third wife), and Pompey married Caesar's daughter

Julia. In 58, Caesar began a campaign to conquer Gaul (modern France). A military genius, Caesar drove the Germans out of Gaul and marched all the way to Britain, which he and his troops invaded in 55 and again in 54.

(continued on page 853)

55 **CAESAR.** Mark Antony shall say I am not well,
And for thy humor,[15] I will stay at home.

[*Enter* DECIUS.]

Here's Decius Brutus, he shall tell them so.

DECIUS. Caesar, all hail! Good morrow, worthy Caesar;
I come to fetch you to the Senate House.

60 **CAESAR.** And you are come in very happy time[16]
To bear my greeting to the senators,
And tell them that I will not come today.
Cannot, is false; and that I dare not, falser:
I will not come today. Tell them so, Decius.

CALPURNIA. Say he is sick.

65 **CAESAR.** Shall Caesar send a lie?
Have I in conquest stretched mine arm so far
To be afeard to tell graybeards[17] the truth?
Decius, go tell them Caesar will not come.

DECIUS. Most mighty Caesar, let me know some cause,
70 Lest I be laughed at when I tell them so.

CAESAR. The cause is in my will: I will not come.
That is enough to satisfy the Senate.
But for your private satisfaction,
Because I love you, I will let you know.
75 Calpurnia here, my wife, stays me at home.
She dreamt tonight she saw my statue,
Which, like a fountain with an hundred spouts,
Did run pure blood, and many lusty Romans
Came smiling and did bathe their hands in it.
80 And these does she apply for[18] warnings and portents
And evils <u>imminent</u>, and on her knee
Hath begged that I will stay at home today.

DECIUS. This dream is all amiss interpreted;
It was a vision fair and fortunate:
85 Your statue spouting blood in many pipes,
In which so many smiling Romans bathed,
Signifies that from you great Rome shall suck
Reviving blood, and that great men shall press
For tinctures, stains, relics, and cognizance.[19]
90 This by Calpurnia's dream is signified.

CAESAR. And this way have you well expounded[20] it.

DECIUS. I have, when you have heard what I can say;
And know it now, the Senate have concluded

---

15. **humor** whim.

16. **in very happy time** at just the right moment.

Literary Analysis
Blank Verse and Character Rank How does Shakespeare demonstrate that Decius is a noble character and not a servant?

17. **afeard to tell graybeards** afraid to tell old men (the senators).

18. **apply for** consider to be. **imminent** (im′ ə nənt) *adj.* about to happen

19. **shall press . . . cognizance** Decius interprets Calpurnia's dream with a double meaning. To Caesar he suggests that people will beg for badges to show they are Caesar's servants. To the audience, that people will seek remembrances of his death.

20. **expounded** (eks pound′ id) *v.* interpreted; explained.

26 ✔**Reading Check**
Why does Calpurnia ask Caesar to stay home?

The Tragedy of Julius Caesar, Act II, Scene ii ◆ 853

---

25 **Literary Analysis**
Blank Verse and Character Rank
- Ask the Literary Analysis question on p. 853: How does Shakespeare demonstrate that Decius is a noble character and not a servant?
Answer: Decius speaks in blank verse.

- Point out Calpurnia's short line "Say he is sick." Ask why Shakespeare makes line 65 a shared-meter line.
Answer: There is no pause between Caesar's "Tell them so, Decius" and Calpurnia's line. Caesar speaks again immediately after she is finished. This gives the effect of an interruption and adds realism to the scene; a worried wife might well interrupt her husband.

26 ✔**Reading Check**
Answer: She is worried for his safety because of the omens.

Caesar *(continued from page 852)*

By 49, Pompey had become alarmed at Caesar's tremendous success and popularity. He and a group of allies ordered Caesar to give up his army. Caesar's response was to attack Pompey's troops, thus starting a civil war. Pompey's army retreated from Rome to Greece and then to Egypt, where Pompey was executed. In Egypt, Caesar fell in love with Queen Cleopatra; he helped her to take firm control over her country. Cleopatra bore Caesar a child. She followed Caesar when he returned to Rome, leaving the city shortly before his assassination. Later, she would begin a long love affair with Mark Antony. Shakespeare wrote about their relationship in the play *Antony and Cleopatra*.

On his return to Rome, Caesar was acknowledged supreme ruler of the Roman empire. He pardoned all Pompey's followers and was made dictator for a ten-year term and later for life.

27 Literary Analysis

Blank Verse

- Ask students why they think line 101 is short of pentameter.
  Answer: Decius pauses to let his suggestion that Caesar will look cowardly sink in and impress Caesar. He pauses for effect and emphasis.

- Line 107 is short. Ask students to describe the effect this has on them.
  Answer: The short line is as emphatic as the words "I will go." The line is very direct and strong.

28 ▶ Critical Viewing
Answer: If these men are the conspirators, they are not sincere.

To give this day a crown to mighty Caesar.
95 If you shall send them word you will not come,
Their minds may change. Besides, it were a mock
Apt to be rendered,[21] for someone to say
"Break up the Senate till another time,
When Caesar's wife shall meet with better dreams."
100 If Caesar hide himself, shall they not whisper
"Lo, Caesar is afraid"?
Pardon me, Caesar, for my dear dear love
To your proceeding[22] bids me tell you this,
And reason to my love is liable.[23]

27 105 **CAESAR.** How foolish do your fears seem now, Calpurnia!
I am ashamèd I did yield to them.
Give me my robe,[24] for I will go.

[*Enter* BRUTUS, LIGARIUS, METELLUS CIMBER, CASCA, TREBONIUS, CINNA, *and* PUBLIUS.]

And look where Publius is come to fetch me.

PUBLIUS. Good morrow, Caesar.

CAESAR.   Welcome, Publius.
110 What, Brutus, are you stirred so early too?
Good morrow, Casca. Caius Ligarius.
Caesar was ne'er so much your enemy[25]
As that same ague[26] which hath made
       you lean.

21. mock . . . rendered jeering comment likely to be made.

22. proceeding advancing in your career.
23. reason . . . liable my judgment is not as strong as my affection for you is.

24. robe toga.

25. Caius Ligarius . . . your enemy Caesar had recently pardoned Ligarius for supporting Pompey during the civil war.

26. ague (ā´ gyōō) *n.* fever.

What is't o'clock?

BRUTUS. Caesar, 'tis strucken eight.

115 **CAESAR.** I thank you for your pains and courtesy.

[*Enter* ANTONY.]

See! Antony, that revels[27] long a-nights,
Is notwithstanding up. Good morrow, Antony.

ANTONY. So to most noble Caesar.

CAESAR. Bid them prepare[28] within.
I am to blame to be thus waited for.
120 Now, Cinna; now, Metellus; what Trebonius,
I have an hour's talk in store for you;
Remember that you call on me today;
Be near me, that I may remember you.

TREBONIUS. Caesar, I will [*aside*] and so near will I be,
125 That your best friends shall wish I had been further.

CAESAR. Good friends, go in and taste some wine with me,
And we (like friends) will straightway go together.

BRUTUS. [*Aside*] That every like is not the same,[29] O Caesar,
The heart of Brutus earns[30] to think upon. [*Exit*]

Scene iii. A street near the Capitol, close to Brutus' house.

[*Enter* ARTEMIDORUS, *reading a paper.*]

ARTEMIDORUS. "Caesar, beware of Brutus; take heed of Cassius;
come not near Casca; have an eye to Cinna; trust not
Trebonius; mark well Metellus Cimber; Decius Brutus loves
thee not; thou hast wronged Caius Ligarius. There is but one
5 mind in all these men, and it is bent against Caesar. If thou
beest not immortal, look about you: security gives way to
conspiracy.[1] The mighty gods defend thee!
                                    Thy lover,[2] ARTEMIDORUS."

10 Here will I stand till Caesar pass along,
And as a suitor[3] will I give him this.
My heart laments that virtue cannot live
Out of the teeth of emulation.
If thou read this, O Caesar, thou mayest live;
15 If not, the Fates with traitors do contrive.[4] [*Exit*]

Scene iv. Another part of the street.

[*Enter* PORTIA *and* LUCIUS.]

PORTIA. I prithee, boy, run to the Senate House;
Stay not to answer me, but get thee gone.

27. revels (rev′ əlz) *v.*
makes merry.

28. prepare set out
refreshments.

**29. That every like . . .
the same** that everyone
who seems to be a friend
may actually be an enemy.
30. earns sorrows.

**1. security . . . conspir-
acy** overconfident care-
lessness allows the
conspiracy to proceed.

2. lover devoted friend.

3. suitor (so̅o̅t′ ər) *n.*
person who requests,
petitions, or entreats.

4. contrive conspire.

30 ✓**Reading Check**

How does Decius
convince Caesar to go to
the Senate House?

The Tragedy of Julius Caesar, Act II, Scene iv ◆ 855

---

29 **Literary Analysis**

Blank Verse

- Artemidorus's letter is in prose.
  Ask students why they think
  Shakespeare made this choice.
  Answer: The entire act up to this
  point has been in blank verse. The
  prose is a change of rhythm and
  cadence on the audience's ears. It
  draws their attention to the letter
  and gives the letter extra emphasis.

- Ask students what they can tell
  about Artemidorus from his
  speech (lines 10–15).
  Answer: He is probably not a commoner since he speaks in blank
  verse.

30 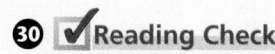**Reading Check**

Answer: He tells Caesar that the
senators are planning to present him
with a crown, and that they will scoff
at him if he stays home because of
Calpurnia's fears.

Reading Blank Verse

- Ask the Reading Strategy question on p. 856: Where should you pause when reading Portia's speech in lines 13–16? Why?
  Answer: Pause at the semicolon, and come to a full stop at the period.

- Have three volunteers read this scene aloud, up to line 24. Ask students what they notice about the lines of iambic pentameter in this scene and to describe the effect.
  Answer: The scene has many shared-meter lines; Portia keeps breaking off in the middle of a line, which Lucius finishes for her. The broken lines emphasize Portia's anxiety and give the scene a breathless quality that adds to the suspense.

32 Literary Analysis

Blank Verse and Character Rank

- Ask the Literary Analysis question on p. 857: How does Shakespeare reveal whether the soothsayer is an aristocrat or a common man?
  Answer: The soothsayer can't be a commoner, because he speaks in blank verse.

- Point out that although Lucius is a servant, he speaks in blank verse. Ask students to give reasons why a commoner might speak in blank verse.
  Possible answers: A commoner might speak in blank verse to show respect for an upper-class character; to put on airs; to pretend that he or she is upper class; to cover a disguise.

Why dost thou stay?

LUCIUS.   To know my errand, madam.

PORTIA. I would have had thee there and here again
5   Ere I can tell thee what thou shouldst do there.
    O constancy,[1] be strong upon my side;
    Set a huge mountain 'tween my heart and tongue!
    I have a man's mind, but a woman's might.[2]
    How hard it is for women to keep counsel![3]
    Art thou here yet?

10 LUCIUS.   Madam, what should I do?
    Run to the Capitol, and nothing else?
    And so return to you, and nothing else?

PORTIA. Yes, bring me word, boy, if thy lord look well,
    For he went sickly forth; and take good note
15 What Caesar doth, what suitors press to him.
    Hark, boy, what noise is that?

LUCIUS. I hear none, madam.

PORTIA.   Prithee, listen well.
    I heard a bustling rumor like a fray,[4]
    And the wind brings it from the Capitol.

20 LUCIUS. Sooth, madam, I hear nothing.

[Enter the SOOTHSAYER.]

PORTIA. Come hither, fellow. Which way hast thou been?

SOOTHSAYER. At mine own house, good lady.

PORTIA. What is't o'clock?

SOOTHSAYER.   About the ninth hour, lady.

PORTIA. Is Caesar yet gone to the Capitol?

25 SOOTHSAYER. Madam, not yet; I go to take my stand,
    To see him pass on the Capitol.

PORTIA. Thou hast some suit[5] to Caesar, hast thou not?

SOOTHSAYER. That I have, lady; if it will please Caesar
    To be so good to Caesar as to hear me,
30 I shall beseech him to befriend himself.

PORTIA. Why, know'st thou any harm's intended towards him?

SOOTHSAYER. None that I know will be, much that I fear may chance.
    Good morrow to you. Here the street is narrow;
    The throng that follows Caesar at the heels,
35 Of senators, of praetors, common suitors,

1. constancy (kän′ stən sē) *n.* firmness of mind or purpose; resoluteness.

2. might strength.

3. counsel secret.

Reading Strategy
Reading Blank Verse
Where should you pause when reading Portia's speech in lines 13–16? Why?

4. fray (frā) *n.* fight or brawl.

5. suit (so͞ot) *n.* petition.

32 **Literary Analysis**
Character Rank
How does Shakespeare reveal whether the soothsayer is an aristocrat or a common man?

ENRICHMENT: Social Studies Connection

Soothsayers

The characters of *Julius Caesar* vary in their reactions to the soothsayer's warning, to the omens, and to the augurers' predictions. In the fourth century B.C., the Romans conquered the Etruscans, who had ruled Rome along with most of what is now Italy. The Romans retained some features of the Etruscan religion, which placed a great deal of emphasis on prophecy and divination. Soothsayers predicted the future by studying such phenomena as the flight of birds and the intestines of animals.

Will crowd a feeble man almost to death.
I'll get me to a place more void,[6] and there
Speak to great Caesar as he comes along.

[*Exit*]

PORTIA. I must go in. Ay me, how weak a thing
40   The heart of woman is! O Brutus,
The heavens speed[7] thee in thine enterprise![8]
Sure, the boy heard me—Brutus hath a suit
That Caesar will not grant—O, I grow faint.
45   Run, Lucius, and commend me[9] to my lord;
Say I am merry; come to me again,
And bring me word what he doth say to thee.

[*Exit separately*]

6. **void** empty.

7. **speed** prosper.

8. **enterprise** (en′ tər priz′) *n.* undertaking; project.

9. **commend me** (kə mend′) *v.* give my kind regards.

Review and Assess

Thinking About Act II

1. **Respond:** If you had been a Roman citizen, would you have sided with the conspirators? Why or why not?

2. **(a) Recall:** What reasons does Brutus give for killing Caesar? **(b) Interpret:** How do Brutus' comments about the serpent's egg in Act II, Scene i, lines 32–35, help explain his thoughts about killing Caesar? **(c) Analyze:** In what ways is his analogy faulty or illogical?

3. **(a) Recall:** What does the writer of the letter that Lucius finds urge Brutus to do? **(b) Infer:** Why do you think the writer leaves gaps in the letter? **(c) Infer:** What inferences can you draw from the way Brutus fills in these gaps?

4. **(a) Recall:** What two changes does Brutus recommend in the assassination plan? **(b) Infer:** What can you tell about the relationship between Brutus and the others based on their response to his suggestions?

5. **(a) Analyze:** Why does Brutus decide to join the conspirators? **(b) Assess:** Which of Brutus' reasons do you find most convincing? Explain.

6. **(a) Compare and Contrast:** Compare the ways Calpurnia and Decius interpret dreams to try to influence Caesar's decision about going to the Capitol. **(b) Draw Conclusions:** What do you learn about Caesar's character based on his reactions to Calpurnia and Decius?

7. **Relate:** How might an unwillingness to seem weak lead some people to take unnecessary risks?

The Tragedy of Julius Caesar, Act II, Scene iv ◆ 857

ASSESSMENT PRACTICE: Reading Comprehension

Identify Patterns of Organization   **(For more practice, see Test Preparation Workbook, p. 51.)**

Many tests require students to identify patterns of organization. Use this sample test item to help students practice this skill.

Cowards die many times before their deaths;

The valiant never taste of death but once.

What pattern of organization is used in this passage?

  A flashback
  B chronological order
  C cause and effect
  D comparison and contrast

The speaker contrasts what death means to two groups, the cowards and the valiant. The correct answer is *D*.

Review and Assess

1. **(a)** These lines should be marked as standard iambic pentameter; lines 162 and 165 each end in an extra weak syllable. **(b)** These lines should be marked as standard iambic pentameter. The word *augurers* would be pronounced AU-grers.

2. It gives them added dignity and makes their speech seem more formal and educated.

3. Caesar: Yes, Aristocrat
   Calpurnia: Yes, Aristocrat
   Soothsayer: Yes, Aristocrat

4. There are six sentences.

5. Mark pauses or breaths at commas and other punctuation marks.

6. VA-nish-ED; the accent mark on the *e* tells you to pronounce *ed* as a separate syllable.

7. They suggest that omens and dreams are signs from their gods.

Review and Assess

Literary Analysis

Blank Verse

1. Copy the following passages from the play. Then, indicate the pattern of accented (´) and unaccented (˘) syllables in each line.
   (a) Act II, Scene i, lines 162–165
   (b) Act II, Scene ii, lines 33–37

Connecting Literary Elements

2. What might explain Shakespeare's decision to have the aristocratic characters speak in blank verse rather than in ordinary prose?

3. Identify the aristocratic and common people in Act II based on whether or not they speak in blank verse. Record your answers on a chart like the one shown.

Character	Speaks in Blank Verse?	Rank
Brutus	Yes	Aristocrat
Lucius	No	Commoner
Caesar		
Calpurnia		
Soothsayer		

Reading Strategy

Reading Blank Verse

4. Read lines 162–174 in Act II, Scene i. How many sentences are in this passage?

5. Copy lines 162–174 as a paragraph. Read your paragraph aloud, and mark it to indicate where it is natural to take a breath or a pause.

6. How should you pronounce "vanishèd" in Scene ii, line 12, in order to maintain iambic pentameter? How do you know?

Extend Understanding

7. **Cultural Connection:** How do the reactions to signs and dreams by characters such as Casca, Calpurnia, Brutus, and Caesar reflect the culture and religion of people in Rome during Caesar's time?

Quick Review

Blank verse is unrhymed poetry written in iambic pentameter. Iambic pentameter has five feet per line. Each foot consists of one unaccented syllable followed by one accented syllable.

In *The Tragedy of Julius Caesar,* you can identify **character rank**—social position—by noting whether or not characters speak in blank verse.

When you read **blank verse,** do not confuse a line with a sentence. Pause only for commas, and stop only for end punctuation.

 Take It to the Net
www.phschool.com
Take the interactive self-test online to check your understanding of the selection.

TEACHING RESOURCES

The following resources can be used to enrich or extend the instruction for p. 859.

Vocabulary
- **Selection Support**, Build Vocabulary, p. 204

- **Vocabulary and Spelling Practice Book**
  (Use this booklet for skills enrichment.)

Grammar
- **Selection Support**, Build Grammar Skills, p. 202
- **Writing and Grammar**, Platinum Level, p. 552

- **Daily Language Practice Transparencies**

Writing
- **Writing and Grammar iText CD-ROM**

BLOCK SCHEDULING: Resources marked with this symbol provide varied instruction during 90-minute blocks.

Integrate Language Skills

❶ Vocabulary Development Lesson

Word Analysis: Latin Root -spir-

Conspiracy contains the Latin root *-spir-*, meaning "to breathe." The root *-spir-* also appears in the following familiar words: *inspire*, *spirit*, *expire*, and *respiration*. Use each of these words in a sentence that includes the word *breathe*.

Spelling Strategy

When adding a suffix to a word ending in two consonants, do not change the consonants. Thus, *imminent* becomes *imminently*. Add the word ending to each word below.

1. health + -y
2. resort + -ed
3. augment + -ing
4. predict + -ion

Fluency: Clarify Word Meaning

Review the words in the vocabulary list on page 84. Then, in your notebook, match the word on the left with its definition on the right.

1. augmented   a. heroic deed
2. entreated   b. plot
3. conspiracy   c. about to happen
4. resolution   d. begged
5. exploit   e. made greater
6. imminent   f. determination

❷ Grammar Lesson

Usage: *who, whom, who's,* and *whose*

The pronouns *who, whom, who's,* and *whose* are easy to confuse. Like the pronoun *he, who* is a nominative case pronoun used as a subject. Like the pronoun *him, whom* is an objective case pronoun used as a direct object, an object of a verbal, or an object of a preposition. *Who's* is a contraction of *who is,* and *whose* is a possessive pronoun.

> *Who* desires to see you? (subject)
> . . . to *whom* it must be done. (object of a preposition)
> *Who's* within? (contraction)
> *Whose* end is served? (shows possession)

Practice Complete each sentence with *who, whom, who's,* or *whose.*

1. ___?___ is the leader of the conspirators?
2. To ___?___ does Cassius look for help?
3. It is Caesar ___?___ life is in danger.
4. It is Calpurnia ___?___ here.
5. I know to___?___ Brutus refers.

Writing Application Write one sentence containing both *who* and *whom* and another sentence containing both *who's* and *whose.*

W̄G *Prentice Hall Writing and Grammar Connection: Chapter 23, Section 2*

❸ Extension Activities

Writing As one of the tribunes, write a **letter to the editor** of the *Roman Times* expressing your feelings about the changing loyalties of the common people. Include evidence from the play to support your ideas.

Listening and Speaking Hold a **debate** on this question: Is Brutus an honorable man? Each side should organize arguments by introducing a position, providing evidence, and concluding with a summary. **[Group Activity]**

The Tragedy of Julius Caesar, Act II ◆ 859

The Tragedy of Julius Caesar, Act III

Lesson Objectives

1. **To analyze and respond to literary elements**
   - Literary Analysis: Dramatic Speeches
   - Connecting Literary Elements: Compare Dramatic Speeches

2. **To read, comprehend, analyze, and critique a play**
   - Reading Strategy: Paraphrasing
   - Reading Check questions
   - Review and Assess questions
   - Assessment Practice (ATE)

3. **To develop word analysis skills, fluency, and systematic vocabulary**
   - Vocabulary Development Lesson: Latin Word Root: *-ora-*

4. **To understand and apply written and oral language conventions**
   - Spelling Strategy
   - Grammar Lesson: Reflexive Pronouns

5. **To understand and apply appropriate writing and research strategies**
   - Writing Lesson: Persuasive Essay (after Act V)
   - Extension Activity: Obituary

6. **To understand and apply listening and speaking strategies**
   - Extension Activity: Dramatic Reading

STEP-BY-STEP TEACHING GUIDE	PACING GUIDE
PRETEACH	
Motivate Students and Provide Background	
Read and discuss the Review and Anticipate information (SE/ATE p. 861) 🅰	5 min.
Introduce the Concepts	
Introduce the Literary Analysis and Reading Strategy (SE/ATE p. 860) 🅰	15 min.
Pronounce the vocabulary words and read their definitions (SE p. 860)	5 min.
TEACH	
Monitor Comprehension	
Informally monitor comprehension by circulating while students read independently or in groups 🅰	35 min.
Monitor students' comprehension with the Reading Check notes (SE/ATE pp. 861, 863, 865, 867, 869, 871, 873, 875, 877, 879)	as students read
Develop vocabulary with Vocabulary notes (SE pp. 861, 862, 864, 867, 870, 871; ATE p. 870)	as students read
Develop Understanding	
Develop students' understanding of dramatic speeches with the Literary Analysis annotations (SE/ATE pp. 866, 867, 868, 869, 870, 873, 874, 877) 🅰	10 min.
Develop students' understanding of paraphrasing with the Reading Strategy annotations (SE/ATE pp. 862, 865, 872, 874, 875, 876)	10 min.
ASSESS	
Assess Mastery	
Assess students' mastery of the Reading Strategy and Literary Analysis by having them answer the Review and Assess questions (SE/ATE p. 880	20 min.
Use one or more of the print and media Assessment Resources (ATE p. 881) 🅰	up to 50 min.
EXTEND	
Apply Understanding	
Have students complete the Vocabulary Development Lesson and the Grammar Lesson (SE p. 881) 🅰	20 min.
Apply students' knowledge of paraphrasing using the Writing Lesson (SE p. 915) 🅰	45 min.
Apply students' understanding of the selection using one or more of the Extension Activities (SE p. 881)	20–90 min.

 ACCELERATED INSTRUCTION:
Use the strategies and activities identified with an 🅰.

UNIVERSAL ACCESS
- ● = Below Level Students
- ▲ = On-Level Students
- ■ = Above Level Students

Time and Resource Manager

Reading Level: Challenging
Average Number of Instructional Days: 5

RESOURCES		
PRINT 📖	**TRANSPARENCIES**	**TECHNOLOGY** 💿 🎧 📼
• **Beyond Literature,** Community Connection: Eulogies, p. 52 ▲ ■		• **Interest Grabber Video,** Tape 4 ● ▲ ■
• **Selection Support Workbook:** ● ▲ ■ Literary Analysis, p. 208 Reading Strategy, p. 207 Build Vocabulary, p. 205	• **Literary Analysis and Reading Transparencies,** pp. 103 and 104 ● ▲ ■	
• **Adapted Reader's Companion** ● • **Reader's Companion** ●		• **Listening to Literature** ● ▲ ■ Audiocassettes, Side 29 Audio CDs, CD 18
• **English Learner's Companion** ● ▲ • **Literatura en español** ● ▲ • **Literary Analysis for Enrichment** ■		
• **Formal Assessment:** Selection Test, pp. 182–184 ● ▲ ■ • **Open Book Test,** pp. 154–156 ● ▲ ■ • **Performance Assessment and Portfolio Management,** p. 19 ● ▲ ■ • **PRENTICE HALL** (ASSESSMENT *SYSTEM*) ● ▲ ■	• **PRENTICE HALL** (ASSESSMENT *SYSTEM*) ● ▲ ■ Skills Practice Answers and Explanations on Transparencies	• **Test Bank Software** ● ▲ ■ • **Got It! Assessment Videotapes,** Tape 4 ● ▲
• **Selection Support Workbook:** ● ▲ ■ Build Grammar Skills, p. 206 • **Writing and Grammar,** Platinum Level ● ▲ ■ • **Extension Activities,** p. 52 ● ▲ ■	• **Daily Language Practice Transparencies** ● ▲	• **Writing and Grammar iText CD-ROM** ● ▲ ■ 💻 *Take It to the Net* www.phschool.com

BLOCK SCHEDULING: Use one 90-minute class period to preteach the selection and have students read it. Use a second 90-minute class period to assess students' mastery of skills and have them complete one of the Extension Activities.

Step-by-Step Teaching Guide for p. 860

❶ Literary Analysis

Dramatic Speeches

- Go over the three types of speeches described. Challenge students to find at least one example of each in the previous two acts.

  Answers: Monologue: Cassius's speech, Act I, Scene ii, lines 90–131. Soliloquy: Brutus's speech, Act II, Scene i, lines 10–34. Aside: Act II, Scene ii, lines 124–125 and 128–129.

- Ask students why a playwright would write soliloquies for his characters. Explain that while a novelist can describe a character's thoughts to a reader, a playwright must accomplish everything in dialogue. Therefore, characters speak their thoughts aloud.

- Characters are understood to be entirely honest when speaking in soliloquy. Even a villainous liar like Iago in Shakespeare's tragedy *Othello* is assumed to be honest in his own thoughts.

- As students read, have them think about not only the purpose but the effect of the different types of speeches.

❷ Reading Strategy

Paraphrasing

- When students have difficulty with a speech and want to paraphrase it, they might find it helpful to write out the speech as if it were prose. This way line breaks will not distract them from finding the speech's meaning.

- Encourage students to use the margin notes to help themselves paraphrase speeches.

E-Teach

Visit E-Teach at www.phschool.com for teachers' essays on how to teach, with questions and answers.

860

Prepare to Read

The Tragedy of Julius Caesar, Act III

❶ Literary Analysis

Dramatic Speeches

Shakespeare's characters often make **dramatic speeches** that fall into the following categories:

- An **aside** is a brief comment a character makes to reveal his or her thoughts to the audience or to one other character.
- A **soliloquy** is a longer speech in which a character—usually alone on stage—speaks as if to himself or herself.
- Similar to a soliloquy is a **monologue**—a long, uninterrupted speech by one character that others can hear.

Connecting Literary Elements

Playwrights use dramatic speeches to achieve several purposes: to provide background, to reveal a character's thoughts, and to advance the plot. In Act III, two key monologues advance the plot by inspiring the citizens of Rome to act. As you read Act III, record the function of each dramatic speech on a chart like the one shown.

Type	Soliloquy
Speaker	Antony
Location	Act III, Scene ii, lines 254–275
Function	Reveals Antony's true thoughts

❷ Reading Strategy

Paraphrasing

Shakespeare's writing is difficult to understand. One way to approach complex passages is to **paraphrase,** or restate, them in your own words.

> **Shakespeare's version:** Trebonius doth desire you to o'er-read, At your best leisure, this his humble suit.

> **Paraphrase:** Trebonius would like you to read over his petition as soon as possible.

As you read, paraphrase difficult passages to help you understand them.

Vocabulary Development

suit (so͞ot) *n.* old word meaning "petition" (p. 861)

spurn (spʉrn) *v.* old word meaning "to kick disdainfully" (p. 862)

confounded (kən found´ id) *adj.* confused (p. 864)

mutiny (myo͞ot´ ən ē) *n.* open rebellion against authority (p. 864)

malice (mal´ is) *n.* desire to harm or see harm done to others (p. 867)

oration (ō rā´ shən) *n.* formal speech (p. 870)

discourse (dis´ kôrs´) *v.* speak formally and at length (p. 870)

vile (vīl) *adj.* depraved (p. 871)

860 ◆ Drama

The following resources can be used to enrich or extend the instruction for p. 860.

Motivation
- 📼 **Interest Grabber Video,** Tape 4

Background
- 📖 **Beyond Literature,** p. 52 ▪

- 💻 **Take It to the Net**
  Visit www.phschool.com for background and hotlinks for *Julius Caesar.*

Literary Analysis
- 📄 **Literary Analysis and Reading Transparencies,** Dramatic Speeches, p. 103 ▪

Reading
- 📖 **Selection Support:** Reading Strategy, p. 207; Build Vocabulary, p. 209

- 📄 **Literary Analysis and Reading Transparencies,** Paraphrasing, p. 104

▪ **BLOCK SCHEDULING:** Resources marked with this symbol provide varied instruction during 90-minute blocks.

❶ Review and Anticipate

Having ignored the warnings of the soothsayer in Act I and those of his wife, Calpurnia, in Act II, Caesar proceeds to the Capitol on the ides of March. Decius has told Caesar that the Senate will confer a crown upon him. The conspirators, led by Cassius and Brutus, accompany Caesar and his friend Mark Antony. As the events of Act III unfold, more warnings are ignored, and the common people again show how easily their loyalties can be swayed. This act is the turning point that sets irreversible wheels in motion.

Act III

Scene i. Rome. Before the Capitol.

[*Flourish of trumpets. Enter* CAESAR, BRUTUS, CASSIUS, CASCA, DECIUS, METELLUS CIMBER, TREBONIUS, CINNA, ANTONY, LEPIDUS, ARTEMIDORUS, PUBLIUS, POPILIUS, *and the* SOOTHSAYER.]

CAESAR. The ides of March are come.

SOOTHSAYER. Ay, Caesar, but not gone.

ARTEMIDORUS. Hail, Caesar! Read this schedule.[1]

DECIUS. Trebonius doth desire you to o'er-read,
5   At your best leisure, this his humble <u>suit</u>.

ARTEMIDORUS. O Caesar, read mine first; for mine's a suit
    That touches Caesar nearer. Read it, great Caesar.

CAESAR. What touches us ourself shall be last served.

ARTEMIDORUS. Delay not, Caesar; read it instantly.

CAESAR. What, is the fellow mad?

10 **PUBLIUS.**   Sirrah, give place.[2]

CASSIUS. What, urge you your petitions in the street?
    Come to the Capitol.

[CAESAR *goes to the Capitol, the rest following.*]

POPILIUS. I wish your enterprise today may thrive.

CASSIUS. What enterprise, Popilius?

POPILIUS.   Fare you well.

                    [*Advances to* CAESAR]

15 **BRUTUS.** What said Popilius Lena?

---

1. schedule (ske´ jool) *n.* paper.

suit (sōōt) *n.* old word meaning "petition"

2. give place get out of the way.

❷ ✔**Reading Check**
What does Artemidorus want Caesar to do?

The Tragedy of Julius Caesar, Act III, Scene i ◆ 861

CASSIUS. He wished today our enterprise might thrive.
   I fear our purpose is discoverèd.

BRUTUS. Look how he makes to³ Caesar; mark him.

CASSIUS. Casca, be sudden,⁴ for we fear prevention.
20   Brutus, what shall be done? If this be known,
   Cassius or Caesar never shall turn back,⁵
   For I will slay myself.

BRUTUS.   Cassius, be constant.⁶
   Popilius Lena speaks not of our purposes;
   For look, he smiles, and Caesar doth not change.⁷

25 **CASSIUS.** Trebonius knows his time; for look you, Brutus,
   He draws Mark Antony out of the way.

                    [*Exit* ANTONY *and* TREBONIUS.]

DECIUS. Where is Metellus Cimber? Let him go
   And presently prefer his suit⁸ to Caesar.

BRUTUS. He is addressed.⁹ Press near and second¹⁰ him.

30 **CINNA.** Casca, you are the first that rears your hand.

CAESAR. Are we all ready? What is now amiss
   That Caesar and his Senate must redress? ¹¹

METELLUS. Most high, most mighty, and most puissant¹² Caesar,
   Metellus Cimber throws before thy seat
   An humble heart.   [*Kneeling*]

35 **CAESAR.**   I must prevent thee, Cimber.
   These couchings and these lowly courtesies¹³
   Might fire the blood of ordinary men,
   And turn preordinance and first decree
   Into the law of children.¹⁴ Be not fond¹⁵
40   To think that Caesar bears such rebel blood
   That will be thawed from the true quality¹⁶
   With that which melteth fools—I mean sweet words,
   Low-crookèd curtsies, and base spaniel fawning.¹⁷
   Thy brother by decree is banishèd.
45   If thou dost bend and pray and fawn for him,
   I spurn thee like a cur out of my way.
   Know, Caesar doth not wrong, nor without cause
   Will he be satisfied.

METELLUS. Is there no voice more worthy than my own,
50   To sound more sweetly in great Caesar's ear
   For the repealing of my banished brother?

BRUTUS. I kiss thy hand, but not in flattery, Caesar,
   Desiring thee that Publius Cimber may
   Have an immediate freedom of repeal.

862 ◆ *Drama*

3. **makes to** approaches.

4. **be sudden** be quick.

5. **Cassius . . . back** either Cassius or Caesar will not return alive.

6. **constant** firm; calm.

7. **change** change the expression on his face.

8. **presently prefer his suit** immediately present his petition.

9. **addressed** ready.

10. **second** support.

11. **amiss . . . redress** wrong that Caesar and his Senate must correct.

12. **puissant** (pyo͞o′ i sənt) *adj.* powerful.

13. **couchings . . . courtesies** low bowings and humble gestures of reverence.

14. **And turn . . . law of children** and change what has already been decided as children might change their minds.

15. **fond** *adj.* foolish.

Reading Strategy

Paraphrasing Paraphrase Caesar's disdainful words to Metellus.

spurn (spʉrn) *v.* old word meaning "to kick disdainfully"

16. **rebel . . . quality** unstable disposition that will be changed from firmness.

17. **base spaniel fawning** low doglike cringing.

CAESAR. What, Brutus?

55 CASSIUS.   Pardon, Caesar; Caesar, pardon!
    As low as to thy foot doth Cassius fall
    To beg enfranchisement[18] for Publius Cimber.

    CAESAR. I could be well moved, if I were as you;
    If I could pray to move,[19] prayers would move me;
60 But I am constant as the Northern Star,
    Of whose true-fixed and resting[20] quality
    There is no fellow[21] in the firmament.[22]
    The skies are painted with unnumb'red sparks,
    They are all fire and every one doth shine;
65 But there's but one in all doth hold his[23] place.
    So in the world; 'tis furnished well with men,
    And men are flesh and blood, and apprehensive;[24]
    Yet in the number I do know but one
    That unassailable holds on his rank,[25]
70 Unshaked of motion;[26] and that I am he,
    Let me a little show it, even in this—
    That I was constant. Cimber should be banished,
    And constant do remain to keep him so.

    CINNA. O Caesar—

75 CAESAR.   Hence! Wilt thou lift up Olympus?◆

    DECIUS. Great Caesar—

    CAESAR.   Doth not Brutus bootless[27] kneel?

    CASCA. Speak hands for me!   [*They stab* CAESAR.]

    CAESAR. *Et tu, Brutè?*[28] Then fall, Caesar.   [*Dies*]

    CINNA. Liberty! Freedom! Tyranny is dead!
    Run hence, proclaim, cry it about the streets.

18. **enfranchisement** (en fran´ chīz mənt) *n.* freedom.

19. **pray to move** beg others to change their minds.

20. **resting** immovable.

21. **fellow** equal.

22. **firmament** (fur´ mə mənt) *n.* sky.

23. **his** its.

24. **apprehensive** (ap´ rə hen´ siv) *adj.* able to understand.

25. **unassailable . . . rank** unattackable, he maintains his position.

26. **Unshaked of motion** unmoved by his own or others' impulses.

27. **bootless** uselessly.

28. *Et tu, Brutè?* Latin for *And you, Brutus?*

❺ ✓Reading Check

Why does Metellus Cimber petition Caesar?

*L*iterature **❻**
in context Humanities Connection

◆ *Mount Olympus*
   Caesar makes a comparison between himself and Mount Olympus. Located in northeastern Greece, rising 9,570 feet, it is the highest mountain in the country. According to Greek mythology, Mount Olympus was also the home of the gods. In comparing himself to Olympus, then, Caesar is elevating himself to the status of a god.

The Tragedy of Julius Caesar, Act III, Scene i ◆ 863

Compare and Contrast

• Choose six students to read lines 78–95 (beginning on p. 863) aloud, each reading the lines of one of the conspirators. Have students compare and contrast the various reactions to the murder.
Answer: Cinna and Cassius seem excited and triumphant. Brutus is calm. Metellus is frightened.

• Ask what the reactions suggest about the various motivations for the crime.
Answer: Brutus is calm because he believes he did his duty. Cassius is triumphant because he envied Caesar and was bitter over his success. Metellus may be frightened because he feels guilty.

❽ ▶ Critical Viewing
Answer: While several conspirators distract his attention, one assassin stabs him in the back.

80　**CASSIUS.** Some to the common pulpits,[29] and cry out
　　　"Liberty, freedom, and enfranchisement!"

BRUTUS. People, and senators, be not affrighted.
　　Fly not; stand still; ambition's debt is paid.[30]

CASCA. Go to the pulpit, Brutus.

DECIUS.　　　　　　　　　　　　And Cassius too.

85　**BRUTUS.** Where's Publius?

CINNA. Here, quite <u>confounded</u> with this <u>mutiny</u>.

❼

METELLUS. Stand fast together, lest some friend of Caesar's
　　Should chance—

BRUTUS. Talk not of standing. Publius, good cheer;
90　　There is no harm intended to your person,
　　Nor to no Roman else. So tell them, Publius.

CASSIUS. And leave us, Publius, lest that the people
　　Rushing on us should do your age some mischief.

BRUTUS. Do so; and let no man abide[31] this deed
95　　But we the doers.

29. pulpits (pul´ pits) *n.* speakers' platforms.

30. ambition's . . . paid ambition received what it deserved.

31. let no man abide let no man take responsibility for.

confounded (kən found´ id) *adj.* confused
mutiny (myo͞ot´ ən ē) *n.* open rebellion against authority

❽ ▼ Critical Viewing
Explain how this picture captures the deception of the conspirators.
[Analyze]

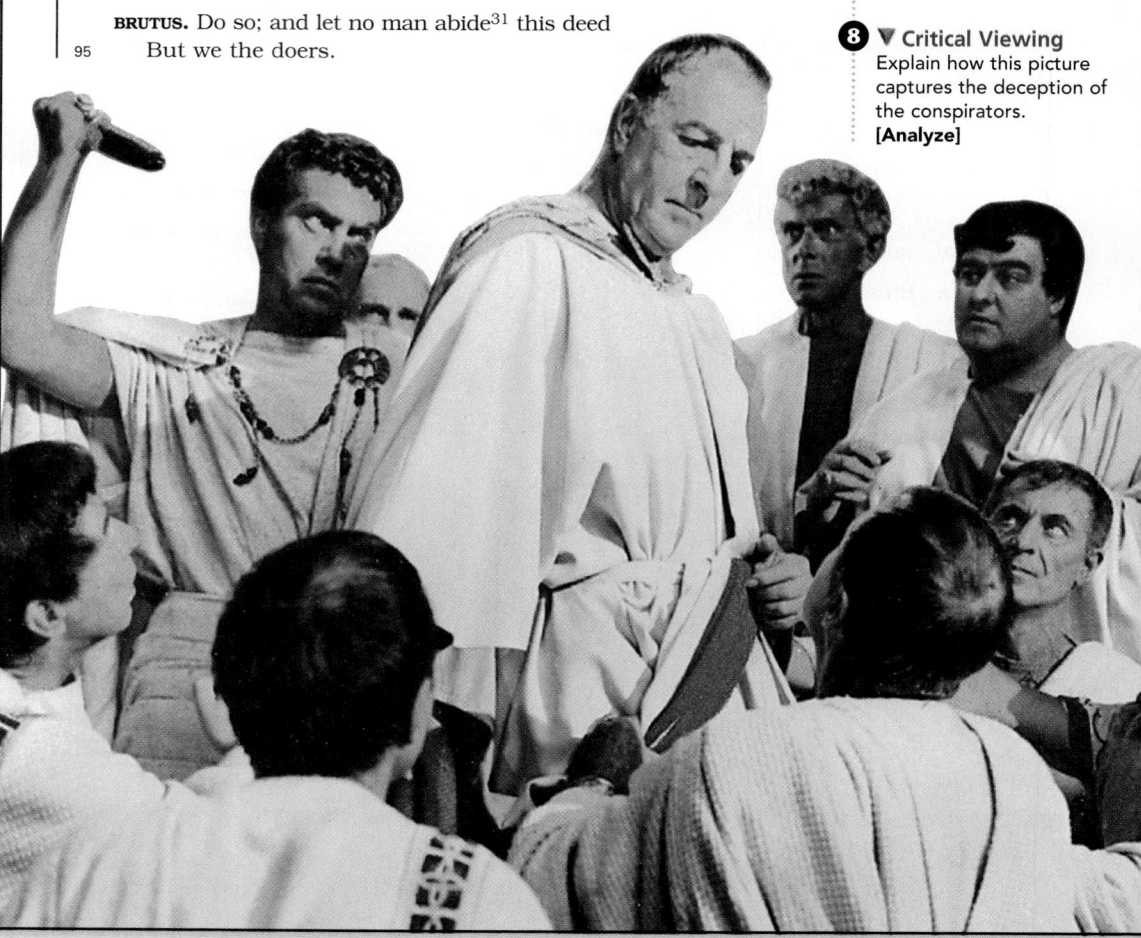

[Enter TREBONIUS.]

CASSIUS. Where is Antony?

TREBONIUS.   Fled to his house amazed.[32]
Men, wives, and children stare, cry out and run,
As[33] it were doomsday.

BRUTUS.   Fates, we will know your pleasures.
That we shall die, we know; 'tis but the time,
100 And drawing days out, that men stand upon.[34]

CASCA. Why, he that cuts off twenty years of life
Cuts off so many years of fearing death.

BRUTUS. Grant that, and then is death a benefit.
So are we Caesar's friends, that have abridged
105 His time of fearing death. Stoop, Romans, stoop,
And let us bathe our hands in Caesar's blood
Up to the elbows, and besmear our swords.
Then walk we forth, even to the market place,
And waving our red weapons o'er our heads,
110 Let's all cry "Peace, freedom, and liberty!"

CASSIUS. Stoop then, and wash. How many ages hence
Shall this our lofty scene be acted over
In states unborn and accents yet unknown!

BRUTUS. How many times shall Caesar bleed in sport,[35]
115 That now on Pompey's basis lies along[36]
No worthier than the dust!

CASSIUS.   So oft as that shall be,
So often shall the knot[37] of us be called
The men that gave their country liberty.

DECIUS. What, shall we forth?

CASSIUS.   Ay, every man away.
120 Brutus shall lead, and we will grace his heels[38]
With the most boldest and best hearts of Rome.

[Enter a SERVANT.]

BRUTUS. Soft, who comes here? A friend of Antony's.

SERVANT. Thus, Brutus, did my master bid me kneel;
Thus did Mark Antony bid me fall down;
125 And, being prostrate, thus he bade me say:
Brutus is noble, wise, valiant, and honest;
Caesar was mighty, bold, royal, and loving.
Say I love Brutus and I honor him;
Say I feared Caesar, honored him, and loved him.
130 If Brutus will vouchsafe that Antony
May safely come to him and be resolved[39]

The Tragedy of Julius Caesar, Act III, Scene i ◆ 865

---

32. amazed astounded.

33. As as if.

34. drawing . . . upon
prolonging life that
people care about.

Reading Strategy
Paraphrasing Paraphrase
Brutus' justifications for
killing Caesar.

35. in sport in plays.
**36. on Pompey's basis
lies along** by the
pedestal of Pompey's
statue lies stretched out.
37. knot group.

38. grace his heels honor
him by following him.

39. be resolved have it
explained.

Reading Strategy
Paraphrasing The servant
carries a message from
Mark Antony to Brutus.
Paraphrase the message
only.

11 ✔ **Reading Check**
What does Mark Antony
do after Caesar is stabbed?

---

9 Reading Strategy

Paraphrasing

- Ask the Reading Strategy question
  on p. 865: Paraphrase Brutus's
  justifications for killing Caesar.
  Answer: Lines 99–100: Everyone
  will die eventually. Lines 103–105:
  We have done Caesar a favor by
  shortening the years during which
  he would have feared death.

- Ask students whether they think
  Brutus is serious and whether they
  agree with him.
  Answer: Students should recall
  that in Act II, Scene ii, Caesar commented that death "will come
  when it will come," and he did not
  understand why anyone would
  fear it (lines 34–37). Therefore,
  Caesar did not need to be
  "saved" from a fear of death.

10 Reading Strategy

Paraphrasing

- Have students paraphrase lines
  111–116.
  Answer: Cassius wonders about
  the actors who, in future centuries,
  will play Caesar and the conspirators on stage. Brutus wonders how
  often an actor, as Caesar, will pretend to die.

- Ask students to discuss the effect
  of these lines on the audience.
  Answer: The lines remind the audience that it is watching a play, not
  real events. The lines are ironic
  and probably cause a laugh.

- Ask the Reading Strategy question
  on p. 865: The servant carries a
  message from Mark Antony to
  Brutus. Paraphrase the message
  only.
  Answer: I love and honor Brutus,
  and I loved and honored Caesar. I
  ask Brutus to explain why Caesar
  deserved to die, and Brutus's word
  will satisfy me. I will be loyal to
  him.

11 ✔ Reading Check

Answer: He leaves the Senate, sending a message requesting an explanation from Brutus.

CUSTOMIZE INSTRUCTION FOR UNIVERSAL ACCESS

For Advanced Readers

Remind students of Calpurnia's dream (Act II, Scene
ii), in which she saw Romans bathing in the blood
flowing from a statue of Caesar. Have students compare Calpurnia's dream with the conspirators' actions
in lines 105–111 above. Remind students of the definition of *foreshadowing*: "the use in a literary work of
clues that suggest events that have yet to occur."
Have students discuss this use of foreshadowing.
Would the effect of seeing the conspirators bathing
in Caesar's blood be less horrifying without the

foreshadowing? Why or why not? Have students write
brief analyses of Shakespeare's use of this literary
technique.

Dramatic Speeches

- Have two students read lines 143–146 aloud. Ask students whether they agree with Brutus or with Cassius and to explain why.
  Answer: Students will probably agree with Cassius because Antony offered Caesar a crown in Act I, and because Antony and Caesar were close.

- Ask the Literary Analysis question on p. 866: What is the purpose of the monologue that Antony delivers to the conspirators?
  Answer: Antony sincerely mourns Caesar and wants the conspirators to know this. His suggestion that they kill him may be a test of their motives and their intentions.

▶ Monitor Progress Have students watch for more of Antony's speeches in this act. Have them consider the purpose of each speech.

How Caesar hath deserved to lie in death,
Mark Antony shall not love Caesar dead
So well as Brutus living; but will follow
135   The fortunes and affairs of noble Brutus
Thorough the hazards of this untrod state[40]
With all true faith. So says my master Antony.

BRUTUS. Thy master is a wise and valiant Roman;
   I never thought him worse.
140   Tell him, so[41] please him come unto this place,
   He shall be satisfied and, by my honor,
   Depart untouched.

SERVANT.   I'll fetch him presently.

                     [*Exit* SERVANT]

BRUTUS. I know that we shall have him well to friend.[42]

CASSIUS. I wish we may. But yet have I a mind
145   That fears him much; and my misgiving still
   Falls shrewdly to the purpose.[43]

[*Enter* ANTONY.]

BRUTUS. But here comes Antony. Welcome, Mark Antony.

ANTONY. O mighty Caesar! Dost thou lie so low?
   Are all thy conquests, glories, triumphs, spoils,
150   Shrunk to this little measure? Fare thee well.
   I know not, gentlemen, what you intend,
   Who else must be let blood,[44] who else is rank.[45]
   If I myself, there is no hour so fit
   As Caesar's death's hour, nor no instrument
155   Of half that worth as those your swords, made rich
   With the most noble blood of all this world.
   I do beseech ye, if you bear me hard,[46]
   Now, whilst your purpled hands[47] do reek and smoke,
   Fulfill your pleasure. Live[48] a thousand years,
160   I shall not find myself so apt[49] to die;
   No place will please me so, no mean of death,[50]
   As here by Caesar, and by you cut off,
   The choice and master spirits of this age.

BRUTUS. O Antony, beg not your death of us!
165   Though now we must appear bloody and cruel,
   As by our hands and this our present act
   You see we do, yet see you but our hands
   And this the bleeding business they have done.
   Our hearts you see not; they are pitiful;[51]
170   And pity to the general wrong of Rome—
   As fire drives out fire, so pity pity[52]—
   Hath done this deed on Caesar. For your part,

40. Thorough . . . state through the dangers of this new state of affairs.

41. so if it should.

42. to friend as a friend.

43. my misgiving . . . to the purpose my doubts always turn out to be justified.

Literary Analysis
Dramatic Speeches What is the purpose of the monologue that Antony delivers to the conspirators?

44. be let blood be killed.

45. rank too powerful; in need of bloodletting.

46. bear me hard have a grudge against me.

47. purpled hands bloody hands.

48. Live if I live.

49. apt ready.

50. mean of death way of dying.

51. pitiful full of pity.

52. pity pity pity for Rome drove out pity for Caesar.

To you our swords have leaden[53] points, Mark Antony:
Our arms in strength of <u>malice</u>, and our hearts
175 Of brothers' temper,[54] do receive you in
With all kind love, good thoughts, and reverence.

CASSIUS. Your voice[55] shall be as strong as any man's
In the disposing of new dignities.[56]

BRUTUS. Only be patient till we have appeased
180 The multitude, beside themselves with fear,
And then we will deliver[57] you the cause
Why I, that did love Caesar when I struck him,
Have thus proceeded.

ANTONY. I doubt not of your wisdom.
Let each man render me his bloody hand.
185 First, Marcus Brutus, will I shake with you;
Next, Caius Cassius, do I take your hand;
Now, Decius Brutus, yours; now yours, Metellus;
Yours, Cinna; and, my valiant Casca, yours;
Though last, not least in love, yours, good Trebonius.
190 Gentlemen all—alas, what shall I say?
My credit[58] now stands on such slippery ground
That one of two bad ways you must conceit[59] me,
Either a coward or a flatterer.
That I did love thee, Caesar, O, 'tis true!
195 If then thy spirit look upon us now,
Shall it not grieve thee dearer[60] than thy death
To see thy Antony making his peace,
Shaking the bloody fingers of thy foes,
Most noble, in the presence of thy corse?[61]
200 Had I as many eyes as thou hast wounds,
Weeping as fast as they stream forth thy blood,
It would become me better than to close[62]
In terms of friendship with thine enemies.
Pardon me, Julius! Here wast thou bayed,[63] brave hart;[64]
205 Here didst thou fall, and here thy hunters stand,
Signed in thy spoil[65] and crimsoned in thy Lethe.[66]
O world, thou wast the forest to this hart;
And this indeed, O world, the heart of thee.
How like a deer, stroken[67] by many princes.
210 Dost thou here lie!

CASSIUS. Mark Antony—

ANTONY. Pardon me, Caius Cassius.
The enemies of Caesar shall say this;
Then, in a friend, it is cold modesty.[68]

CASSIUS. I blame you not for praising Caesar so;
215 But what compact[69] mean you to have with us?

---

53. **leaden** dull; blunt.

malice (mal′ is) *n.* desire to harm or see harm done to others

54. **Of brothers' temper** filled with brotherly feelings.
55. **voice** vote.
56. **dignities** offices.

57. **deliver** tell to.

58. **credit** reputation.
59. **conceit** (kən sēt′) *v.* think of.

60. **dearer** more deeply.

61. **corse** corpse.

62. **close** (clōz) *v.* reach an agreement.
63. **bayed** cornered.
64. **hart** (härt) *n.* deer.
65. **Signed in thy spoil** marked by signs of your decaying parts.
66. **Lethe** (lēth′ ē) river in Hades, but in this case, a river of blood.

67. **stroken** struck down.
68. **cold modesty** calm, moderate speech.
69. **compact** (käm′ pakt) *n.* agreement.

⓮ ✔**Reading Check**
When he arrives, what is Antony prepared to do?

---

❸ **Literary Analysis**
Dramatic Speeches

- Ask students to identify the type of dramatic speech Antony makes and to explain their answers.
 Answer: The speech is a monologue. It is a long speech addressed to everyone on stage.

- Ask students to analyze the second half of the speech, in which Antony addresses Caesar's corpse. How would they characterize the speech? What effect does it have on the listeners?
 Answers: Antony's language is emotional and exaggerated. He uses the pronoun *thou* to emphasize his emotional closeness and intimacy with Caesar and his personal grief at Caesar's murder. He stresses the horror and violence of the murder. The audience's sympathy may be shifting from the conspirators to the victim.

⓮ ✔**Reading Check**

Answer: Antony asks the conspirators to kill him, then asks for an explanation of their murder of Caesar.

Dramatic Speeches

- Ask students to determine where the aside beginning at line 232 ends. Have them explain their answers.

  Answer: It ends after line 243. In the next line, Brutus speaks directly to Antony, which shows that he and Cassius have rejoined the group.

- Ask the Literary Analysis Question on p. 868: Why does Cassius want to prevent other characters from hearing what he says to Brutus in this aside?

  Answer: Cassius's main concern is probably to prevent Antony from hearing him. Cassius doesn't want Antony to know that he suspects Antony's intentions.

- Ask students which character they think is right, Brutus or Cassius. Have them give reasons for their answers.

  Answer: Students will probably agree with Cassius. Antony is obviously deeply upset at Caesar's murder, and he probably wants revenge.

⑯ Critical Thinking

Speculate

- Ask students why Antony is pleased with Brutus's insistence that he has to speak last.

  Answer: Students should say that Brutus has given Antony an advantage. The last speaker is in the most powerful position because his or her words will be remembered best.

- Have students speculate about the use Antony may make of this advantage. Have them support their predictions with evidence from the text.

  Answer: Antony is so shaken by Caesar's death and loved Caesar so much that he probably intends to use his opportunity to stir up the people of Rome against the conspirators.

868

> Will you be pricked[70] in number of our friends,
> Or shall we on,[71] and not depend on you?
>
> ANTONY. Therefore I took your hands, but was indeed
>   Swayed from the point by looking down on Caesar.
> 220   Friends am I with you all, and love you all,
>   Upon this hope, that you shall give me reasons
>   Why, and wherein, Caesar was dangerous.
>
> BRUTUS. Or else were this a savage spectacle.
>   Our reasons are so full of good regard[72]
> 225   That were you, Antony, the son of Caesar,
>   You should be satisfied.
>
> ANTONY.   That's all I seek;
>   And am moreover suitor that I may
>   Produce[73] his body to the market place,
>   And in the pulpit, as becomes a friend,
> 230   Speak in the order[74] of his funeral.
>
> BRUTUS. You shall, Mark Antony.
>
> CASSIUS.   Brutus, a word with you.
>   [*Aside to* BRUTUS] You know not what you do; do not consent
>   That Antony speak in his funeral.
>   Know you how much the people may be moved
>   By that which he will utter?
>
> 235 BRUTUS.   By your pardon:
>   I will myself into the pulpit first,
>   And show the reason of our Caesar's death.
>   What Antony shall speak, I will protest[75]
>   He speaks by leave and by permission,
> 240   And that we are contented Caesar shall
>   Have all true rites and lawful ceremonies.
>   It shall advantage more than do us wrong.[76]
>
> CASSIUS. I know not what may fall;[77] I like it not.
>
> BRUTUS. Mark Antony, here, take you Caesar's body.
> 245   You shall not in your funeral speech blame us,
>   But speak all good you can devise of Caesar,
>   And say you do't by our permission;
>   Else shall you not have any hand at all
>   About his funeral. And you shall speak
> 250   In the same pulpit whereto I am going,
>   After my speech is ended.
>
> ANTONY.   Be it so;
>   I do desire no more.
>
> BRUTUS. Prepare the body then, and follow us.
>
>   [*Exit all but* ANTONY.]

70. pricked marked.

71. on proceed.

72. so full of good regard so carefully considered.

73. Produce bring forth.

74. order course of the ceremonies.

Literary Analysis
Dramatic Speeches Why does Cassius want to prevent other characters from hearing what he says to Brutus in this aside?

75. protest declare.

76. advantage . . . wrong benefit us more than hurt us.

77. what may fall what may happen.

868 ◆ *Drama*

✹ ENRICHMENT: History Connection

The Roman Forum

In line 228, Antony says, "Produce his body to the market place." Antony speaks of the Roman Forum, the true center of the city.

The Senate House, the Temples of Saturn and Concord, and the *Tabularium* (Hall of Records) were all located on the Roman Forum. It was a great open space that was ideal for large gatherings. Romans came to the Forum to conduct a great deal of everyday business and to meet their friends. The Forum is the setting for Caesar's funeral orations; later, it saw the crowning of Octavius Caesar as the first Roman emperor.

Archaeologists have excavated much of the Forum. Today, people can examine the ruins and remains of its buildings and understand something of the grandeur it displayed in ancient times.

ANTONY. O pardon me, thou bleeding piece of earth,
255 That I am meek and gentle with these butchers!
Thou art the ruins of the noblest man
That ever livèd in the tide of times.[78]
Woe to the hand that shed this costly blood!
Over thy wounds now do I prophesy
260 (Which like dumb mouths do ope their ruby lips
To beg the voice and utterance of my tongue),
A curse shall light upon the limbs of men;
Domestic fury and fierce civil strife
Shall cumber[79] all the parts of Italy;
265 Blood and destruction shall be so in use,[80]
And dreadful objects so familiar,
That mothers shall but smile when they behold
Their infants quartered with the hands of war,
All pity choked with custom of fell deeds;[81]
270 And Caesar's spirit, ranging[82] for revenge,
With Ate[83] by his side come hot from hell,
Shall in these confines[84] with a monarch's voice
Cry "Havoc,"[85] and let slip[86] the dogs of war,
That this foul deed shall smell above the earth
275 With carrion[87] men, groaning for burial.

[*Enter* OCTAVIUS' SERVANT.]

You serve Octavius Caesar, do you not?

SERVANT. I do, Mark Antony.

ANTONY. Caesar did write for him to come to Rome.

SERVANT. He did receive his letters and is coming,
280 And bid me say to you by word of mouth—
O Caesar! [*Seeing the body*]

ANTONY. Thy heart is big;[88] get thee apart and weep.
Passion, I see, is catching, for mine eyes,
Seeing those beads of sorrow stand in thine,
285 Began to water. Is thy master coming?

SERVANT. He lies tonight within seven leagues* of Rome.

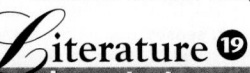iterature ⑲
in context Vocabulary Connection

♦ *Terms of Measurement: League*
  The servant reports that Octavius is camped 7 leagues from Rome. A *league* is an ancient unit of measure that has not always been the same distance. Today, a league is usually understood to equal 3 miles (4.8 km). In Roman times, however, the *league* equaled 1,500 paces, or steps. A pace was 5 feet (1.5 m), making a Roman league approximately 7,500 feet—not quite a mile and a half. So 7 leagues equaled about 10 miles.

78. tide of times course of all history.

79. cumber (kum´ bər) *v.* distress; burden.

80. in use customary.

81. fell deeds cruel acts.

82. ranging roaming like a wild beast in search of prey.

83. Ate (ā´ tē) Greek goddess personifying reckless ambition in man.

84. confines (kän´ finz) *n.* boundaries.

85. Havoc Latin for "no quarter," a signal for general slaughter.

86. slip loose.

87. carrion (kar´ ē ən) *adj.* dead and rotting.

88. big swollen with grief.

The Tragedy of Julius Caesar, Act III, Scene ii ◆ 869

ANTONY. Post[89] back with speed, and tell him what hath chanced.[90]
Here is a mourning Rome, a dangerous Rome,
No Rome of safety for Octavius yet.
290 Hie hence and tell him so. Yet stay awhile;
Thou shalt not back till I have borne this corse
Into the market place; there shall I try[91]
20 In my <u>oration</u> how the people take
The cruel issue[92] of these bloody men;
295 According to the which, thou shalt <u>discourse</u>
To young Octavius of the state of things.
Lend me your hand. [*Exit*]

Scene ii. The Forum

[*Enter* BRUTUS *and goes into the pulpit, and* CASSIUS, *with the* PLEBEIANS.[1]]

PLEBEIANS. We will be satisfied![2] Let us be satisfied!

BRUTUS. Then follow me, and give me audience, friends.
Cassius, go you into the other street
And part the numbers.[3]
5 Those that will hear me speak, let 'em stay here;
Those that will follow Cassius, go with him;
And public reasons shall be renderèd
Of Caesar's death.

FIRST PLEBEIAN. I will hear Brutus speak.

SECOND PLEBEIAN. I will hear Cassius, and compare their reasons,
10 When severally[4] we hear them renderèd.

[*Exit* CASSIUS, *with some of the* PLEBEIANS.]

THIRD PLEBEIAN. The noble Brutus is ascended. Silence!

BRUTUS. Be patient till the last.
Romans, countrymen, and lovers,[5] hear me for my cause, and be silent, that you may hear. Believe me
15 for mine honor, and have respect to mine honor, that you may believe. Censure[6] me in your wisdom, and awake your senses,[7] that you may the better judge. If there be any in this assembly, any dear friend of Caesar's, to him I say that Brutus' love to Caesar was
21 20 no less than his. If then that friend demand why Brutus rose against Caesar, this is my answer: Not that I loved Caesar less, but that I loved Rome more. Had you rather Caesar were living, and die all slaves, than that Caesar were dead, to live all free men? As
25 Caesar loved me, I weep for him; as he was fortunate, I rejoice at it; as he was valiant, I honor him; but, as he was ambitious, I slew him. There is tears, for his love; joy, for his fortune; honor, for his valor; and

89. Post hasten.

90. hath chanced has happened.

91. try test.

92. cruel issue outcome of the cruelty.

oration (ō rā′ shən) *n.* formal speech

discourse (dis′ kôrs′) *v.* speak formally and at length

1. Plebeians (ple bē′ ənz) *n.* commoners; members of the lower class.

2. be satisfied get an explanation.

3. part the numbers divide the crowd.

4. severally (sev′ ər əl ē) *adv.* separately.

5. lovers dear friends.

6. Censure (sen′ shər) *v.* condemn as wrong; criticize.

7. senses powers of reason.

death, for his ambition. Who is here so base,[8] that
would be a bondman?[9] If any, speak; for him have I
offended. Who is here so rude, [10] that would not be a
Roman? If any, speak; for him have I offended. Who is
here so vile, that will not love his country? If any,
speak; for him have I offended. I pause for a reply.

ALL. None, Brutus, none!

BRUTUS. Then none have I offended. I have done no
more to Caesar than you shall do to Brutus. The
question of his death is enrolled in the Capitol;[11] his
glory not extenuated,[12] wherein he was worthy, nor
his offenses enforced,[13] for which he suffered death.

[*Enter* MARK ANTONY, *with* CAESAR'S *body.*]

Here comes his body, mourned by Mark Antony,
who, though he had no hand in his death, shall receive
the benefit of his dying, a place in the commonwealth, as which of you shall not? With this I depart,
that, as I slew my best lover for the good of Rome,
I have the same dagger for myself, when it shall
please my country to need my death.

ALL. Live, Brutus! Live, live!

FIRST PLEBEIAN. Bring him with triumph home unto his house.

The Tragedy of Julius Caesar, Act III, Scene ii ◆ 871

22 ▲ Critical Viewing
Based on his stance and
his gestures, what do you
think Antony is trying to
convey? Explain. **[Connect]**

8. base low.

9. bondman slave.

10. rude ignorant.

vile (vīl) *adj.* depraved

**11. The question . . . in the
Capitol** the whole matter of
his death is on record in the
Capitol.

12. extenuated (ik sten´
yōō wāt id) *v.* underrated.

13. enforced (en fôrsd´) *v.*
given force to.

24 ✔ Reading Check
Why does Brutus say that
he killed Caesar?

22 ▶ Critical Viewing
Answer: Antony gestures as if to
hold back the crowd, or to protect
the body that lies at his feet.

23 Critical Thinking
Analyze
• Ask students how the crowd
reacts to Brutus's speech.
Answer: The plebeians seem to
accept his explanation and absolve
him from any blame.
• Ask students to analyze how
Brutus achieved this effect.
Answer: Brutus's speech is full of
parallel structure and repetition.
These techniques impress his
words on the plebeians and make
them remember what he says.
Brutus suggests that the murder
will benefit the plebeians, so they
support it.

24 ✔ Reading Check
Answer: He says that he loved
Rome more than he loved Caesar.

CUSTOMIZE INSTRUCTION FOR UNIVERSAL ACCESS

For Less Proficient Readers	For English Learners
Students may not understand many of the archaic and unfamiliar contractions Shakespeare uses. Examples from this act include *o'er, unnumb'red,* and *'tis.* Have students use context clues to figure out what these contractions mean. Point out that in some cases, Shakespeare uses them because the full word would have been too long for a line of iambic pentameter. Help students write out each contraction in full. Partners can help one another define the words.	Help students restate the formal, stylized language in this scene in simpler English. Mark Antony's entrance as announced by Brutus could be rephrased as "Here comes Antony carrying Caesar's body. He didn't help kill him, but he will benefit from his death. You all will."

• Ask students to paraphrase the Fourth Plebeian's speech (lines 51–52).
Answer: We will crown Brutus king, because he embodies Caesar's better qualities.

• Ask the Reading Strategy question on p. 872: What does Brutus ask of his countrymen in this speech?
Answer: He asks them to listen to Antony's speech rather than escort him (Brutus) home.

50   **SECOND PLEBEIAN.** Give him a statue with his ancestors.

THIRD PLEBEIAN. Let him be Caesar.

FOURTH PLEBEIAN. Caesar's better parts[14]
     Shall be crowned in Brutus.

FIRST PLEBEIAN. We'll bring him to his house with shouts and
     clamors.

BRUTUS.   My countrymen—

SECOND PLEBEIAN. Peace! Silence! Brutus speaks.

55   **FIRST PLEBEIAN.**   Peace, ho!

BRUTUS. Good countrymen, let me depart alone,
     And, for my sake, stay here with Antony.
     Do grace to Caesar's corpse, and grace his speech
     Tending to Caesar's glories,[15] which Mark Antony
60   By our permission, is allowed to make.
     I do entreat you, not a man depart,
     Save I alone, till Antony have spoke. [*Exit*]

FIRST PLEBEIAN. Stay, ho! And let us hear Mark Antony.

THIRD PLEBEIAN. Let him go up into the public chair;
65   We'll hear him. Noble Antony, go up.

ANTONY. For Brutus' sake, I am beholding[16] to you.

FOURTH PLEBEIAN. What does he say of Brutus?

THIRD PLEBEIAN.   He says, for Brutus' sake,
     He finds himself beholding to us all.

FOURTH PLEBEIAN. 'Twere best he speak no harm of
     Brutus here!

FIRST PLEBEIAN. This Caesar was a tyrant.

70   **THIRD PLEBEIAN.**   Nay, that's certain.
     We are blest that Rome is rid of him.

SECOND PLEBEIAN. Peace! Let us hear what Antony can say.

ANTONY. You gentle Romans—

ALL.   Peace, ho! Let us hear him.

ANTONY. Friends, Romans, countrymen, lend me your ears;
75   I come to bury Caesar, not to praise him.
     The evil that men do lives after them,
     The good is oft interrèd with their bones;
     So let it be with Caesar. The noble Brutus
     Hath told you Caesar was ambitious.
80   If it were so, it was a grievous fault,
     And grievously hath Caesar answered[17] it.

14. parts qualities.

Reading Strategy
Paraphrasing What does Brutus ask of his country-men in this speech?

15. Do grace . . . glories honor Caesar's body and the speech telling of Caesar's achievements.

16. beholding indebted.

Literary Analysis
Dramatic Speeches Notice how Antony's speech reflects the style and structure of Brutus' monologue. What is the effect of this similarity?

17. answered paid the penalty for.

✳ ENRICHMENT: Literature Connection

Rhetoric

Artemidorus, who tried to warn Caesar of danger at the beginning of Act III, is described in the cast list on p. 822 as a teacher of rhetoric. The speeches given by Brutus (pp. 870–871) and Antony (above) are examples of rhetoric—the art of public speaking.

The Latin *orare*, meaning "to speak," is derived from the Greek *rhetor*, meaning "speaker." Famous Greek orators and teachers of rhetoric included Pericles, Demosthenes, and Aristotle. Rhetoric was a necessary skill for Roman youths embarking on careers in law or politics.

An orator must speak loudly enough to be heard at some distance, and clearly enough that his words can be easily understood. The other important aspect of rhetoric is style. Rhetorical devices in Brutus and Antony's speeches include parallelism and repetition.

Here, under leave of Brutus and the rest
(For Brutus is an honorable man,
So are they all, all honorable men),
85   Come I to speak in Caesar's funeral.
He was my friend, faithful and just to me;
But Brutus says he was ambitious,
And Brutus is an honorable man.
He hath brought many captives home to Rome,
90   Whose ransoms did the general coffers fill;
Did this in Caesar seem ambitious?
When that the poor have cried, Caesar hath wept;
Ambition should be made of sterner stuff.
Yet Brutus says he was ambitious;
95   And Brutus is an honorable man.
You all did see that on the Lupercal
I thrice presented him a kingly crown,
Which he did thrice refuse. Was this ambition?
Yet Brutus says he was ambitious;
100   And sure he is an honorable man.
I speak not to disprove what Brutus spoke,
But here I am to speak what I do know.
You all did love him once, not without cause;
What cause withholds you then to mourn for him?
105   O judgment, thou art fled to brutish beasts,
And men have lost their reason! Bear with me;
My heart is in the coffin there with Caesar,
And I must pause till it come back to me.

FIRST PLEBEIAN. Methinks there is much reason in his sayings.

110   **SECOND PLEBEIAN.** If thou consider rightly of the matter,
Caesar has had great wrong.

THIRD PLEBEIAN.   Has he, masters?
I fear there will a worse come in his place.

FOURTH PLEBEIAN. Marked ye his words? He would not take the
crown,
Therefore 'tis certain he was not ambitious.

115   **FIRST PLEBEIAN.** If it be found so, some will dear abide it.[18]

SECOND PLEBEIAN. Poor soul, his eyes are red as fire
with weeping.

THIRD PLEBEIAN. There's not a nobler man in Rome
than Antony.

FOURTH PLEBEIAN. Now mark him, he begins again to
speak.

ANTONY. But yesterday the word of Caesar might
120   Have stood against the world; now lies he there,

18. dear abide it pay
dearly for it.

27 ✔**Reading Check**

What does Brutus ask the
Plebeians to do?

28 ▼ **Critical Viewing**
How does this actor
portray Antony's passion
in delivering Caesar's
eulogy? **[Connect]**

The Tragedy of Julius Caesar, Act III, Scene ii ◆ 873

26 **Literary Analysis**
Dramatic Speeches

• Ask the Literary Analysis question
on p. 872: Notice how Antony's
speech reflects the style and structure of Brutus's monologue. What
is the effect of this similarity?
Answer: Antony refutes Brutus's
speech point by point. Like Brutus,
he uses parallelism and repetition.
The effect is that the crowd
believes that Brutus was wrong.

• Ask students what effect Antony
achieves by speaking in verse
instead of prose.
Answer: Antony sounds more
impressive, and his speech is more
emotional.

27 ✔**Reading Check**

Answer: He asks them to stay and
listen to Antony's speech.

28 ▶**Critical Viewing**

Answer: His facial expression is
intense, and his pose is dramatic
and striking.

Paraphrasing

- Ask the Reading Strategy question on p. 874: Paraphrase Antony's words to the crowd.

  Answer: If I tried to stir up your anger against the conspirators, I would do them wrong, because they are honest men. I would rather harm you or myself than such good and honest men. I found Caesar's will in his room. If you heard what it says, you would honor his memory.

- Discuss the paraphrased version of the speech with the class until everyone understands exactly what it says.

▶ Monitor Progress As students continue reading, have them pay close attention to the crowd's reactions to Antony's words.

30 Literary Analysis

Dramatic Speeches

- Ask the Literary Analysis question on p. 874: What is Antony's purpose in making this speech about the will?

  Answer: His purpose is to make the crowd eager to hear the will.

- Why does Antony repeatedly refuse to read the will?

  Answer: He knows this will make the crowd more eager to hear it.

- What does the crowd's reaction suggest about Antony's decision temporarily to withhold the will?

  Answer: Their insistence on hearing the will suggests that he made the right decision; his refusals whetted their appetites to hear the will's contents.

And none so poor to[19] do him reverence.
O masters! If I were disposed to stir
Your hearts and minds to mutiny and rage,
I should do Brutus wrong and Cassius wrong,
125   Who, you all know, are honorable men.
I will not do them wrong; I rather choose
To wrong the dead, to wrong myself and you,
Than I will wrong such honorable men.
But here's a parchment with the seal of Caesar;
130   I found it in his closet; 'tis his will.
Let but the commons[20] hear this testament,
Which, pardon me, I do not mean to read,
And they would go and kiss dead Caesar's wounds,
And dip their napkins[21] in his sacred blood;
135   Yea, beg a hair of him for memory,
And dying, mention it within their wills,
Bequeathing it as a rich legacy
Unto their issue.[22]

FOURTH PLEBEIAN. We'll hear the will; read it, Mark Antony.

140   **ALL.** The will, the will! We will hear Caesar's will!

ANTONY. Have patience, gentle friends, I must not read it.
It is not meet you know how Caesar loved you.
You are not wood, you are not stones, but men;
And being men, hearing the will of Caesar,
145   It will inflame you, it will make you mad.
'Tis good you know not that you are his heirs;
For if you should, O, what would come of it?

FOURTH PLEBEIAN. Read the will! We'll hear it, Antony!
You shall read us the will, Caesar's will!

150   **ANTONY.** Will you be patient? Will you stay awhile?
I have o'ershot myself[23] to tell you of it.
I fear I wrong the honorable men
Whose daggers have stabbed Caesar; I do fear it.

FOURTH PLEBEIAN. They were traitors. Honorable men!

155   **ALL.** The will! The testament!

SECOND PLEBEIAN. They were villains, murderers! The will! Read the will!

ANTONY. You will compel me then to read the will?
Then make a ring about the corpse of Caesar,
160   And let me show you him that made the will.
Shall I descend? And will you give me leave?

ALL. Come down.

SECOND PLEBEIAN. Descend.   [ANTONY *comes down.*]

19. to as to.

Reading Strategy
Paraphrasing Paraphrase Antony's words to the crowd.

20. commons plebeians; commoners.

21. napkins handkerchiefs.

22. issue heirs.

Literary Analysis
Dramatic Speeches
What is Antony's purpose in making this speech about the will?

23. o'ershot myself gone too far.

✦ ENRICHMENT: History Connection

Roman Society

Roman society was divided into two main groups. About ten percent of the Roman population, including aristocrats, wealthy businessmen, and plebeians, were citizens. Citizens could live anywhere in the Roman empire. Citizens had a great stake in whether or not Caesar became king, because citizens were able to vote. They had the most to lose if the republic were to become a monarchy.

Ninety percent of the population were not citizens. They included commoners, foreigners, slaves, and condemned criminals. In ancient Rome, slavery carried no racial or class stigma: Most slaves were European, and many were well-educated. Slave status simply meant a lack of legal rights. Women throughout the empire had no legal rights either, but women of the upper classes had a great deal of power and influence.

THIRD PLEBEIAN. You shall have leave.

165 **FOURTH PLEBEIAN.** A ring! Stand round.

FIRST PLEBEIAN. Stand from the hearse,[24] stand from the body!

SECOND PLEBEIAN. Room for Antony, most noble Antony!

ANTONY. Nay, press not so upon me; stand far off.

ALL. Stand back! Room! Bear back.

170 **ANTONY.** If you have tears, prepare to shed them now.
You all do know this mantle;[25] I remember
The first time ever Caesar put it on:
'Twas on a summer's evening, in his tent,
That day he overcame the Nervii.
175 Look, in this place ran Cassius' dagger through;
See what a rent[26] the envious[27] Casca made;
Through this the well-belovèd Brutus stabbed,
And as he plucked his cursèd steel away,
Mark how the blood of Caesar followed it,
180 As[28] rushing out of doors, to be resolved[29]
If Brutus so unkindly knocked, or no;
For Brutus, as you know, was Caesar's angel.
Judge, O you gods, how dearly Caesar loved him!
This was the most unkindest cut of all;
185 For when the noble Caesar saw him stab,
Ingratitude, more strong than traitors' arms,
Quite vanquished him. Then burst his mighty heart;
And, in his mantle muffling up his face,
Even at the base of Pompey's statue
190 (Which all the while ran blood) great Caesar fell.
O, what a fall was there, my countrymen!
Then I, and you, and all of us fell down,
Whilst bloody treason flourished[30] over us.
O, now you weep, and I perceive you feel
195 The dint[31] of pity; these are gracious drops.
Kind souls, what[32] weep you when you but behold
Our Caesar's vesture[33] wounded? Look you here,
Here is himself, marred as you see with[34] traitors.

FIRST PLEBEIAN. O piteous spectacle!

200 **SECOND PLEBEIAN.** O noble Caesar!

THIRD PLEBEIAN. O woeful day!

FOURTH PLEBEIAN. O traitors, villains!

FIRST PLEBEIAN. O most bloody sight!

SECOND PLEBEIAN. We will be revenged.

205 **ALL.** Revenge! About![35] Seek! Burn! Fire! Kill! Slay!

24. hearse (hurs) *n.* coffin.

25. mantle (man´ təl) *n.* cloak; toga.

26. rent (rent) *n.* torn place.
27. envious (en´ vē əs) *adj.* spiteful.

28. As as if.
29. to be resolved to learn for certain.

Reading Strategy
Paraphrasing What does Antony say about Caesar's mantle?

30. flourished (flur´ isht) *v.* grew; triumphed.

31. dint *n.* force.
32. what why.
33. vesture (ves´ chər) *n.* clothing.
34. with by.

35. About let us go.

32 ✓**Reading Check**
What reason does Antony give for not reading the people Caesar's will?

The Tragedy of Julius Caesar, Act III, Scene ii ◆ 875

31 **Reading Strategy**
Paraphrasing

- Ask the Reading Strategy question on p. 875: What does Antony say about Caesar's mantle?
  Answer: He reminds the crowd of the first time Caesar put it on. He attributes each bloodstain and rip in the mantle to one of the conspirators.

- What effect does Antony's speech about the mantle have on the plebeians? How does Antony manipulate them into reacting this way?
  Answer: Antony appeals to their emotions by holding up the blood-stained mantle and describing the wounds that tore it. The plebeians are full of pity and indignation on behalf of the victim. They forget that if Caesar had become king, they would have been deprived of their voting rights.

32 ✓**Reading Check**

Answer: He says that they don't want to know how generous Caesar was to them.

CUSTOMIZE INSTRUCTION FOR UNIVERSAL ACCESS

For Less Proficient Readers

To help students distinguish among the different types of dramatic speeches, have them use a chart like the one shown here. Encourage students to look for examples of each type of speech in this act. Students can complete the chart by identifying act, scene, and line numbers, and by naming the speaker of each dramatic speech.

Aside	Soliloquy	Monologue

- Have students paraphrase lines 227–231 (beginning with, "But were I Brutus . . ."). What is Antony saying?

  Answer: If Brutus were in my place, his power of rhetoric would stir you up to mutiny. Antony says that Brutus is a much better and more charismatic speaker than he.

- What is ironic about Antony's statement?

  Answer: Antony has spoken to the plebeians in high-flown, emotional blank verse and has played on their feelings. Brutus spoke calmly, logically, reasonably, and in prose. Antony pretends that the opposite is true; that he is the "plain blunt man" and Brutus the orator.

- Ask the Reading Strategy question on p. 876: Restate lines 236–240 in your own words.

  Answer: Friends, you don't know what you're doing. You don't know what Caesar has done to deserve your love. I'll have to read you his will.

Let not a traitor live!

ANTONY. Stay, countrymen.

FIRST PEBEIAN. Peace there! Hear the noble Antony.

210 **SECOND PLEBEIAN.** We'll hear him, we'll follow him, we'll die with him!

ANTONY. Good friends, sweet friends, let me not stir you up
    To such a sudden flood of mutiny.
    They that have done this deed are honorable.
    What private griefs[36] they have, alas, I know not,
215 That made them do it. They are wise and honorable,
    And will, no doubt, with reasons answer you.
    I come not, friends, to steal away your hearts;
    I am no orator, as Brutus is;
    But (as you know me all) a plain blunt man
220 That love my friend, and that they know full well
    That gave me public leave[37] to speak of him.
    For I have neither writ, nor words, nor worth,
    Action, or utterance,[38] nor the power of speech
    To stir men's blood; I only speak right on.[39]
225 I tell you that which you yourselves do know,
    Show you sweet Caesar's wounds, poor poor dumb mouths,
    And bid them speak for me. But were I Brutus,
    And Brutus Antony, there were an Antony
    Would ruffle up your spirits, and put a tongue
230 In every wound of Caesar's that should move
    The stones of Rome to rise and mutiny.

ALL. We'll mutiny.

FIRST PLEBEIAN.   We'll burn the house of Brutus.

33 **THIRD PLEBEIAN.** Away, then! Come, seek the conspirators.

ANTONY. Yet hear me, countrymen. Yet hear me speak.

235 **ALL.** Peace, ho! Hear Antony, most noble Antony!

ANTONY. Why, friends, you go to do you know not what:
    Wherein hath Caesar thus deserved your loves?
    Alas, you know not; I must tell you then:
    You have forgot the will I told you of.

240 **ALL.** Most true, the will! Let's stay and hear the will.

ANTONY. Here is the will, and under Caesar's seal.
    To every Roman citizen he gives,
    To every several man, seventy-five drachmas.

SECOND PLEBEIAN. Most noble Caesar! We'll revenge his death!

245 **THIRD PLEBEIAN.** O royal Caesar!

ANTONY. Hear me with patience.

36. griefs (grēfs) *n.* grievances.

37. leave permission.

38. neither writ . . . utterance (ut′ ∂r ∂ns) neither written speech, nor fluency, nor reputation, nor gestures, nor style of speaking.

39. right on directly.

Reading Strategy
Paraphrasing Restate lines 236–240 in your own words.

ALL. Peace, ho!

ANTONY. Moreover, he hath left you all his walks,
His private arbors, and new-planted orchards,[40]
250 On this side Tiber; he hath left them you,
And to your heirs forever: common pleasures,[41]
To walk abroad and recreate yourselves.
Here was a Caesar! When comes such another?

FIRST PLEBEIAN. Never, never! Come, away, away!
255 We'll burn his body in the holy place,
And with the brands[42] fire the traitors' houses.
Take up the body.

SECOND PLEBEIAN. Go fetch fire.

THIRD PLEBEIAN. Pluck down benches.

260 **FOURTH PLEBEIAN.** Pluck down forms, windows, anything!

[*Exit* PLEBEIANS *with the body.*]

ANTONY. Now let it work: Mischief, thou art afoot,
Take thou what course thou wilt.

[*Enter* SERVANT.]

How now, fellow?

SERVANT. Sir, Octavius is already come to Rome.

ANTONY. Where is he?

265 **SERVANT.** He and Lepidus are at Caesar's
house.

40. walks . . . orchards
parks, his private trees, and
newly planted gardens.
41. common pleasures
public places of recreation.

42. brands torches.

Literary Analysis
Dramatic Speeches How
does this aside indicate
the true intentions behind
Antony's monologue?

35 ✔ **Reading Check**

What has Caesar left the
citizens of Rome in his will?

Extispicium relief (inspection of entrails) from the Forum of Trajan, Rome,
Louvre, Paris, France

36 ▲ **Critical Viewing** Why do you think sculptors of ancient Rome portrayed
political scenes such as this one? **[Speculate]**

The Tragedy of Julius Caesar, Act III, Scene ii ◆ 877

34 **Literary Analysis**
Dramatic Speeches

• Ask the Literary Analysis question
on p. 877: How does this aside
indicate the true intentions behind
Antony's monologue?
Answer: It reveals that Antony
intended all along to stir up the
plebeians' anger against the
conspirators.

• Ask students how this aside
affects their opinions of Antony.
Answer: Students may have sympathized with Antony's grief up to
this point, but they may now
doubt whether the grief was real.
Antony seems to be seizing his
chance to take power by stirring
up the crowd against the conspirators. The aside is cold and calculating, which would not be the case if
personal grief were Antony's only
motivation.

35 ✔ **Reading Check**

Answer: He left them 75 drachmas
each and declared that his orchards,
gardens, and walks would now be
public parks and common areas.

36 ▶ **Critical Viewing**

Possible answer: As events in this
play illustrate, Romans were very
involved in the workings of their
political system and followed the
activities of their leaders closely.

CUSTOMIZE INSTRUCTION FOR UNIVERSAL ACCESS

For Gifted/Talented Students

Have students analyze Shakespeare's use of the plebeians in this scene. Students should note that these
characters have no individual identity and no differences among their reactions. They form a collective
character. Have students discuss the effectiveness of
Shakespeare's use of the crowd. Do students find it
realistic? Are real crowds usually as easily swayed as
this crowd? Have students think about times when
they have been in crowds listening to speeches. Does
everyone always react alike? Why would Shakespeare
have wanted to handle his crowd of plebeians as he
does? What does the crowd contribute to the overall
effect of the play?

Analyze

- Have students summarize what happens in this scene.
  Answer: The plebeians, eager for revenge after hearing Antony's speech, attack and kill an innocent man because he has the same name as one of the conspirators.

- Have students analyze the effect of this scene on their opinions of Antony.
  Answer: The scene makes Antony seem even crueler and more calculating than before; Antony incited the plebeians to riot, so he is responsible for Cinna's death.

- Have students analyze the effect of the scene on the play as a whole. Why did Shakespeare include this scene?
  Answer: He included it to point out Antony's cruelty and, by contrast, to make the audience admire Brutus even more, since Brutus killed only for noble motives. One theme of the play is violence: Shakespeare is showing violence in one of its many forms.

ANTONY. And thither[43] will I straight to visit him;
  He comes upon a wish. Fortune is merry,
  And in this mood will give us anything.

SERVANT. I heard him say, Brutus and Cassius
270 Are rid[44] like madmen through the gates of Rome.

ANTONY. Belike[45] they had some notice of the people,[46]
  How I had moved them. Bring me to Octavius.   [*Exit*]

43. **thither** there.

44. **Are rid** have ridden.

45. **Belike** probably.

46. **notice of the people** word about the mood of the people.

Scene iii. A street.

[*Enter* CINNA THE POET, *and after him the* PLEBEIANS.]

CINNA. I dreamt tonight that I did feast with Caesar,
  And things unluckily charge my fantasy.[1]
  I have no will to wander forth of doors,[2]
  Yet something leads me forth?

5 **FIRST PLEBEIAN.** What is your name?

SECOND PLEBEIAN. Whither are you going?

THIRD PLEBEIAN. Where do you dwell?

FOURTH PLEBEIAN. Are you a married man or a bachelor?

SECOND PLEBEIAN. Answer every man directly.

10 **FIRST PLEBEIAN.** Ay, and briefly.

FOURTH PLEBEIAN. Ay, and wisely.

THIRD PLEBEIAN. Ay, and truly, you were best.

CINNA. What is my name? Whither am I going? Where do I dwell?
  Am I a married man or a bachelor? Then, to answer every man
15 directly and briefly, wisely and truly: wisely I say, I am a
  bachelor.

SECOND PLEBEIAN. That's as much as to say, they are fools that
  marry; you'll bear me a bang[3] for that, I fear. Proceed directly.

20 **CINNA.** Directly, I am going to Caesar's funeral.

FIRST PLEBEIAN. As a friend or an enemy?

CINNA. As a friend.

SECOND PLEBEIAN. That matter is answered directly.

FOURTH PLEBEIAN. For your dwelling, briefly.

25 **CINNA.** Briefly, I dwell by the Capitol.

THIRD PLEBEIAN. Your name, sir, truly.

CINNA. Truly, my name is Cinna.

FIRST PLEBEIAN. Tear him to pieces! He's a conspirator.

1. **things . . . fantasy** The events that have happened weigh heavily on my imagination.

2. **of doors** outdoors.

3. **bear me a bang** get a blow from me.

✹ ENRICHMENT: History Connection

Emperors of Rome

In 27 B.C., Octavius, with whom Antony hopes to join forces, took the name of Augustus and became the first emperor of Rome. Rome was then no longer a republic, but a monarchy, as Brutus, Cassius, and the other conspirators had feared. The reign of Augustus, however, marked the beginning of the *Pax Romana* (Roman peace), which lasted for 200 years, during which commerce flourished and the standard of living rose.

Among other emperors of this period were Tiberius (14–37 A.D.), Caligula (37–41), Claudius (41–54), Nero (54–68), Trajan (98–117), and Marcus Aurelius (161–180). Suggest that students choose one of these Roman emperors to research.

CINNA. I am Cinna the poet! I am Cinna the poet!

30 **FOURTH PLEBEIAN.** Tear him for his bad verses! Tear him for his
bad verses!

CINNA. I am not Cinna the conspirator.

FOURTH PLEBEIAN. It is no matter, his name's Cinna; pluck but his
35 name out of his heart, and turn him going.⁴

THIRD PLEBEIAN. Tear him, tear him! [*They attack him.*]
Come, brands, ho! Firebrands!⁵ To Brutus', to Cassius'!
Burn all! Some to Decius' house, and some to
Casca's; some to Ligarius'! Away, go!

[*Exit all the* PLEBEIANS *with* CINNA.]

4. **turn him going** send
him on his way.

5. **Firebrands** people
who stir up others to
revolt.

Review and Assess

Thinking About Act III

1. **Respond:** If you had been in the crowd at Caesar's funeral in
Scene ii, how would you have responded to Antony's speech?

2. **(a) Recall:** Artemidorus implores Caesar to read a paper he
has. How does Caesar react to this plea? **(b) Speculate:** Why
might Shakespeare include this brief scene with Artemidorus?

3. **(a) Recall:** How does Antony respond to the conspirators
after the assassination? **(b) Analyze:** What are the motives
behind his actions?

4. **(a) Recall:** How does Cassius feel about allowing Antony to
speak at the funeral? Why? **(b) Analyze:** Why does Brutus
allow Antony to speak?

5. **(a) Compare and Contrast:** How do the funeral monologues
delivered by Brutus and Antony compare in style and purpose?
(b) Analyze: How does each speaker attempt to sway the
people? **(c) Evaluate:** Which speaker more successfully
achieves his purpose? How do you know?

6. **(a) Interpret:** Why does Antony read Caesar's will to the
people? **(b) Interpret:** What effect does the reading of the
will have on the people?

7. **(a) Interpret:** How does Shakespeare build emotion into this
act of the play? **(b) Predict:** What effect do you think the
buildup of emotion will have on what happens next?

8. **Take a Position:** Do you think that Caesar has any
responsibility for his own death? Why or why not?

The Tragedy of Julius Caesar, Act III, Scene iii ◆ 879

ASSESSMENT PRACTICE: Reading Comprehension

Notice Word Choice (For more practice, see Test Preparation Workbook, p. 52.)

Many tests require students to analyze word choice.
Use this sample test item to help students practice this
skill.

Low-crooked curtsies, and base spaniel fawning.

Thy brother by decree is banished.

If thou dost bend and pray and fawn for him,

I spurn thee like a cur out of my way.

The words *base, cur,* and *spurn* reveal the speaker's

A anger toward his audience
B love for his audience
C bewilderment about his audience
D jealousy of his audience

The highlighted words are contemptuous. The correct answer is *A*.

879

Review and Assess

1. **Sample answers:** Aside: Scene i, lines 232–234: Cassius speaks to Brutus. Soliloquy: Scene i, lines 254–275: Antony speaks to himself. Monologue: Scene i, lines 148–163: Antony speaks to Caesar's corpse and to the conspirators.

2. He is speaking his true feelings. The speech is consistent with his soliloquies and speeches in Act II. He loved Caesar, but his duty to Rome was stronger. He appeals to the plebeians' reason.

3. Brutus is a straightforward man who trusts others; he feels that if he is truthful, others will understand and approve. Antony is less trusting; he believes that he needs to manipulate the people to get them to do what he wants.

4. It turns the listeners against the conspirators.

5. The aside shows that Antony is using the plebeians to help him avenge Caesar's death.

6. His speech to the other characters is calm and reasonable. His soliloquy shows his tremendous emotion.

7. Like the North Star, I cannot be moved. It is the only star that maintains its place in the heavens, and I am the only man who refuses to change his mind. I will not pardon Cimber.

8. Mark Antony asked me to tell Brutus that he loves and honors both Brutus and Caesar. If Brutus will guarantee Antony's safety, he will return to the Senate and ask why the conspirators killed Caesar. If the explanation is satisfactory, he will remain loyal to them.

9. Brutus says that Caesar was ambitious. If this is true, Caesar has paid for his fault. Caesar was my friend. Caesar has profited Rome financially, and Caesar sympathizes with the poor. Caesar refused three times to accept the crown I offered him. But Brutus says that Caesar was ambitious, and Brutus is honest, so it must be true. I don't challenge Brutus, but I speak the truth.

10. **Sample answer:** President Kennedy's assassination united the country in deep mourning.

880

Review and Assess

Literary Analysis

Dramatic Speeches

1. Find an example of an **aside**, a **soliloquy**, and a **monologue** in Act III. On a chart like the one shown, list where the speech is found, the speaker, and the listener(s), if any.

Type	Location	Speaker	Audience
Aside			
Soliloquy			
Monologue			

2. Examine Brutus' monologue in Act III, Scene ii, lines 12–34. Do you think Brutus is speaking his true feelings? Explain.

3. What do the monologues delivered by Brutus and Antony reveal about each man's character and intentions?

Connecting Literary Elements

4. How does Antony's monologue in Act III, Scene ii, lines 74–253, serve the purpose of advancing the plot?

5. What purpose does Shakespeare accomplish in Antony's brief aside in Act III, Scene ii, lines 262–263?

6. Compare and contrast what Antony says to the other characters in Act III, Scene i, lines 218–222, with what he says in his soliloquy in Scene i, lines 254–275.

Reading Strategy

Paraphrasing

7. **Paraphrase** Caesar's speech in Scene i, lines 58–73.

8. Paraphrase the servant's speech in Scene i, lines 123–137.

9. Paraphrase Antony's speech in Scene ii, lines 78–108.

Extend Understanding

10. **History Connection:** Recall a political assassination that you have heard about or studied. What impact did the death of the political leader have on the country's government or people?

880 ◆ *Drama*

Quick Review

There are three common types of **dramatic speeches:**

An **aside** is a brief comment a character makes that reveals his or her thoughts to the audience or to another character.

A **soliloquy** is a longer speech in which a character speaks as if to himself or herself.

A **monologue** is a long, uninterrupted speech by one character.

When you **paraphrase** a passage, you restate it in your own words.

 Take It to the Net

www.phschool.com

Take the interactive self-test online to check your understanding of the selection.

Integrate Language Skills

❶ Vocabulary Development Lesson

Word Analysis: Latin Root -ora-

The Latin root -ora-, from the Latin verb *orare*, which means "to speak," is found in *oration* and in many other words.

Define each of these words in a sentence using a form of "to speak": *oral, orator, oratory*

Spelling Strategy

When adding a suffix that begins with a vowel to a word that ends in a single consonant preceded by two vowels, do not double the final consonant. For example, *repeal* + *-ing* = *repealing*. Add the ending indicated to each word below.

1. speak + *-er*   2. fail + *-ure*   3. appeal + *-ing*

Concept Development: Analogies

In your notebook, complete each analogy with words from the vocabulary list on page 860.

1. riot : prison :: _____?_____ : ship
2. eulogy : funeral :: _____?_____ : graduation
3. helpful : nurse :: _____?_____ : criminal
4. goodwill : volunteer :: _____?_____ : murderer
5. application : job :: _____?_____ : favor
6. running : motion :: _____?_____ : communication
7. punch : fight :: _____?_____ : insult
8. wise : enlightened :: _____?_____ : ignorant

❷ Grammar Lesson

Reflexive Pronouns

A **reflexive pronoun** is a personal pronoun that ends with *-self* or *-selves* and adds information to a sentence by referring back to an antecedent earlier in the sentence. In these examples from the play, the reflexive pronoun is underlined and the antecedent is in italics.

> *I* have the same dagger for <u>myself</u> . . . (refers to *I*)
>
> . . . he hath left them to *you*, . . . / To walk abroad and recreate <u>yourselves</u>. (refers to *you*)

Practice Write the following sentences in your notebook, adding a reflexive pronoun to fill each blank. Underline each antecedent.

1. The senators decide to kill Caesar ____?____.
2. Brutus concerns ____?____ with the speech.
3. Read Antony's speech aloud to ____?____ .
4. Caesar considered ____?____ to be safe.
5. I answered all of the questions ____?____.

Writing Application Write two sentences about Act III using the reflexive pronouns *himself* and *themselves*.

W̶G̶ *Prentice Hall Writing and Grammar Connection: Chapter 16, Section 2*

❸ Extension Activities

Writing Write a newspaper obituary to announce Caesar's death. An **obituary** contains facts about a person's life and, in some cases, the circumstances of his or her death. In your writing, use details about Caesar from Acts I–III.

Listening and Speaking As either Brutus or Antony, give a **dramatic reading** of one of the soliloquies in this act. Rehearse to determine the most effective ways to deliver the lines.

The Tragedy of Julius Caesar, Act III ◆ 881

ASSESSMENT RESOURCES

The following resources can be used to assess students' knowledge and skills.

Selection Assessment

- **Formal Assessment,** pp. 182–184
- **Open Book Test,** pp. 154–156
- **Got It! Assessment Videotapes,** Tape 4
- **Test Bank Software**
- **Take It to the Net**
  Visit www.phschool.com for self-tests and additional questions on *Julius Caesar.*

Writing Rubric

- **Performance Assess. and Portfolio Mgmt.,** p. 19

 PRENTICE HALL **ASSESSMENT** *SYSTEM*

- **Workbook**
- **Skill Book**
- **Transparencies**
- **CD-ROM**

The Tragedy of Julius Caesar, Act IV

Lesson Objectives

1. **To analyze and respond to literary elements**
   - Literary Analysis: Conflict in Drama
   - Connecting Literary Elements: Suspense

2. **To read, comprehend, analyze, and critique a play**
   - Reading Strategy: Reading Between the Lines
   - Reading Check questions
   - Review and Assess questions
   - Assessment Practice (ATE)

3. **To develop word analysis skills, fluency, and systematic vocabulary**
   - Vocabulary Development Lesson: Greek Root: -phil-

4. **To understand and apply written and oral language conventions**
   - Spelling Strategy
   - Grammar Lesson: Pronoun and Antecedent Agreement

5. **To understand and apply appropriate writing and research strategies**
   - Writing Lesson: Persuasive Essay (after Act V)
   - Extension Activity: Slide-Show Presentation

6. **To understand and apply listening and speaking strategies**
   - Extension Activity: Perform a Scene (after Act V)

STEP-BY-STEP TEACHING GUIDE	PACING GUIDE
PRETEACH	
Motivate Students and Provide Background	
Read and discuss the Review and Anticipate information (SE/ATE p. 884)	5 min. 5 min.
Introduce the Concepts	
Introduce the Literary Analysis and Reading Strategy (SE/ATE p. 883) A	15 min.
Pronounce the vocabulary words and read their definitions (SE p. 883)	5 min.
TEACH	
Monitor Comprehension	
Informally monitor comprehension by circulating while students read independently or in groups A	25 min.
Monitor students' comprehension with the Reading Check notes (SE/ATE pp.885, 887, 889, 891, 893, 895)	as students read
Develop vocabulary with Vocabulary notes (SE p. 884, 885, 888, 892)	as students read
Develop Understanding	
Develop students' understanding of conflict in drama with the Literary Analysis annotations (SE pp. 885, 887, 889, 891, 892, 894, 896; ATE pp. 884, 886, 889, 891, 892, 894, 896) A	10 min.
Develop students' understanding of reading between the lines with the Reading Strategy annotations (SE pp. 887, 888, 890, 896; ATE pp. 887, 888, 890, 893, 895, 896)	10 min.
ASSESS	
Assess Mastery	
Assess students' mastery of the Reading Strategy and Literary Analysis by having them answer the Review and Assess questions (SE/ATE p. 898)	20 min.
Use one or more of the print and media Assessment Resources (ATE p. 899) A	up to 50 min.
EXTEND	
Apply Understanding	
Have students complete the Vocabulary Development Lesson and the Grammar Lesson (SE p. 899) A	20 min.
Apply students' knowledge of paraphrasing using the Writing Lesson (SE p. 915) A	45 min.
Apply students' understanding of the selection using one or more of the Extension Activities (SE p. 899)	20–90 min.

A ACCELERATED INSTRUCTION:
Use the strategies and activities identified with an A.

UNIVERSAL ACCESS
- ● = Below Level Students
- ▲ = On-Level Students
- ■ = Above Level Students

Time and Resource Manager

RESOURCES

PRINT 📖	TRANSPARENCIES	TECHNOLOGY
• **Beyond Literature,** Career Connection: Political Science, p. 53 ▲ ■		• **Interest Grabber Video,** Tape 4 ● ▲ ■
• **Selection Support Workbook:** ● ▲ ■ Literary Analysis, p. 212 Reading Strategy, p. 211 Build Vocabulary, p. 209	• **Literary Analysis and Reading Transparencies,** pp. 105 and 106 ● ▲ ■	
		• **Listening to Literature** ● ▲ ■ Audiocassettes, Side 30 Audio CDs, CD 18
• **Literatura en español** ● ▲ • **Literary Analysis for Enrichment** ■		
• **Formal Assessment:** Selection Test, pp. 185–187 ● ▲ ■ • **Open Book Test,** pp. 157–159 ● ▲ ■ • **Performance Assessment and Portfolio Management,** p. 19 ● ▲ ■ • **PRENTICE HALL ASSESSMENT** *SYSTEM* ● ▲ ■	• **PRENTICE HALL ASSESSMENT** *SYSTEM* ● ▲ ■ Skills Practice Answers and Explanations on Transparencies	• **Test Bank Software** ● ▲ ■ • **Got It! Assessment Videotapes,** Tape 4 ● ▲
• **Selection Support Workbook:** ● ▲ ■ Build Grammar Skills, p. 210 • **Writing and Grammar,** Platinum Level ● ▲ ■ • **Extension Activities,** p. 53 ● ▲ ■	• **Daily Language Practice Transparencies** ● ▲	• **Writing and Grammar iText CD-ROM** ● ▲ ■ 💻 **Take It to the Net** www.phschool.com

BLOCK SCHEDULING: Use one 90-minute class period to preteach the selection and have students read it. Use a second 90-minute class period to assess students' mastery of skills and have them complete one of the Extension Activities.

Connections

In Antony's eulogy for Caesar in *Julius Caesar,* Shakespeare writes in blank verse, mourning Caesar politically in formal words and phrases and at the same time suggesting with his praise of Brutus that Brutus was in fact responsible for Caesar's murder. In her eulogy for Yitzhak Rabin, Noa Ben Artzi-Pelossof speaks of memories of her grandfather.

Eulogy for a Fallen Leader

- Tell students that the word *eulogy* comes from the Greek prefix *eu-* and the Greek root *logos,* meaning "well" and "speak."
- If possible, bring in samples of other eulogies, such as Ossie Davis's for Malcolm X or eulogies from the funeral of Dr. Martin Luther King, Jr.
- Point out that both Julius Caesar and Yitzhak Rabin were assassinated not by their outside political enemies but by fellow citizens who disagreed with their policies.

Connecting Literature and History

1. Both speakers admire their subjects, but Antony uses irony to make his points about Caesar's death. Arzi-Pelossof speaks in a more straightforward manner about her feelings. Both speakers express sorrow at the loss of the subject. Antony uses his eulogy to place blame and stir up a conflict. Artzi-Pelossof does not express desire for revenge.
2. People who are unwilling to negotiate or who are denied peaceful and public means to express their disagreement with a leader may feel they need to use violence to make a point. In their answers, students may identify some of the peaceful means a person might use instead.

Eulogy for a Fallen Leader
NOA BEN ARTZI-PELOSSOF

All leaders live in some danger of violence against them. Like Julius Caesar, Yitzhak Rabin's life was cut short by an assassin.

Yitzhak Rabin was the prime minister of Israel from 1974 to 1977 and 1992 to 1995. In 1994, Rabin received the Nobel Prize for Peace for his work toward peace. He was assassinated on November 4, 1995.

Noa Ben Artzi-Pelossof is the granddaughter of Rabin. In her eulogy, Artzi-Pelossof expresses her personal feelings about this public man.

"Grandfather, you were the pillar of fire in front of the camp and now we are left in the camp alone, in the dark; and we are so cold and so sad.

"I know that people talk in terms of a national tragedy, and of comforting an entire nation, but we feel the huge void that remains in your absence when grandmother doesn't stop crying.

"Few people really knew you. Now they will talk about you for quite some time, but I feel that they really don't know just how great the pain is, how great the tragedy is; something has been destroyed.

"Grandfather, you were and still are our hero. I want you to know that every time I did anything, I saw you in front of me.

"Your appreciation and your love accompanied us every step down the road, and our lives were always shaped by your values. You, who never abandoned anything, are now abandoned. And here you are, my ever-present hero, cold, alone, and I cannot do anything to save you. You are missed so much.

"Others greater than I have already eulogized you, but none of them ever had the pleasure I had to feel the caresses of your arms, your soft hands, to merit your warm embrace that was reserved only for us, to see your half-smile that always told me so much, that same smile which is no longer, frozen in the grave with you.

"I have no feelings of revenge because my pain and feelings of loss are so large, too large. The ground has been swept out from below us, and we are groping now, trying to wander about in this empty void, without any success so far.

"I am not able to finish this; left with no alternative, I say goodbye to you, hero, and ask you to rest in peace, and think about us, and miss us, as down here we love you so very much. I imagine angels are accompanying you now, and I ask them to take care of you because you deserve their protection.

"We will love you, Saba, forever."

882 ◆ *Drama*

Connecting Literature and History

1. Compare and contrast the message of Noa Ben Artzi-Pelossof's eulogy for her grandfather and Antony's eulogy for Caesar.
2. Why do you think some people express their disagreement with a leader's policies with violence?

✲ ENRICHMENT: History Connection

Research

To avoid an oversimplified comparison between Caesar and Rabin, encourage students to conduct further research and discussion of the careers of these leaders. Both men gained prestige from military success and, upon reaching the highest political office, were assassinated by fellow citizens. However, students should consider the contrasting ways in which Caesar and Rabin prioritized their desires for power and peace. For example, Caesar conquered and exploited hostile territories with the goal of aggrandizing himself and enriching Rome. A small group of his constituents killed him out of fear that he would acquire too much power as sole ruler of Rome. By contrast, Rabin dedicated his career to improving diplomatic relations between Israel and other nations, working in particular toward an Israeli-Arab peace settlement. Ultimately, Rabin's willingness to concede land and water rights in disputed territories prompted his assassination by an extremist Israeli law student.

Prepare to Read

The Tragedy of Julius Caesar, Act IV

Literary Analysis

Conflict in Drama

Conflict, the struggle between two forces, is what creates drama. The conflict may be **external**—between two characters, groups, or forces—or it may be **internal,** involving a character's struggle to decide between two opposing ideas or values. The climax of the play is the point at which the internal and external conflicts are greatest. Usually, the action rises to the climax and then falls as the conflicts are resolved.

Connecting Literary Elementss

As the conflict in a play develops, suspense builds. **Suspense** is a feeling of tension about how things are going to turn out. Playwrights often build suspense by letting the audience see the outcome of events before the characters can. This technique builds a special tension:

- The characters wonder *whether* something is going to happen.
- The audience wonders *when* the inevitable will occur.

In Act IV, it becomes clear to the audience how the upcoming battle will end. There is a grisly fascination in watching the characters move inevitably toward their fates.

● Reading Strategy

Reading Between the Lines

People and situations in drama are not always what they appear to be on the surface. Although you must read line by line to follow the action, by **reading between the lines** you can discover a deeper or different meaning in a character's words or actions.

For example, at the opening of Act IV, Mark Antony describes Lepidus as "Meet to be sent on errands." Between the lines, he is saying that Lepidus is capable of little more. Make a diagram like the one shown to analyze passages and to read between the lines.

> **What Character Says**
>
> **BRUTUS.** Thou hast described A hot friend cooling.

> **What I Understand**
>
> Brutus is concerned that Cassius is no longer his ally.

Vocabulary Development

legacies (leg´ ə sēz) *n.* money, property, or position left in a will to someone (p. 884)

slanderous (slan´ dər əs) *adj.* damaging to a person's reputation (p. 884)

covert (kō´ vərt) *adj.* secret (p. 885)

chastisement (chas tīz´ mənt) *n.* punishment; severe criticism (p. 888)

philosophy (fə läs´ ə fē) *n.* system of principles or beliefs (p. 892)

The Tragedy of Julius Caesar, Act IV ◆ 883

TEACHING RESOURCES

The following resources can be used to enrich or extend the instruction for p. 883.

Motivation

📼 **Interest Grabber Video,** Tape 4

Background

📖 **Beyond Literature,** p. 53 ■

💻 *Take It to the Net*
Visit www.phschool.com for background and hotlinks for *Julius Caesar.*

Literary Analysis

📄 **Literary Analysis and Reading Transparencies,** Conflict in Drama, p. 105 ■

Reading

📖 **Selection Support:** Reading Strategy, p. 211; Build Vocabulary, p. 209

📄 **Literary Analysis and Reading Transparencies,** Reading Between the Lines, p. 106

■ **BLOCK SCHEDULING:** Resources marked with this symbol provide varied instruction during 90-minute blocks.

PRETEACH

Step-by-Step Teaching Guide for p. 883

❶ Literary Analysis

Conflict in Drama

- Review the various conflicts from Acts I–III. Write the headings *External Conflicts* and *Internal Conflicts* on the chalkboard, and have students list conflicts from the play's first three acts under the appropriate heading.

- Remind students that a long literary work like this contains many conflicts, major and minor. In Act II, Portia and Brutus are in conflict: She wants to know what is troubling him, and he prefers to keep his troubles to himself. This conflict drives the scene and is resolved at the end of it. *Julius Caesar* is full of such minor conflicts, which maintain the audience's interest in the story and characters.

- As students read Act IV, have them pay attention to the appearance of new conflicts and the resolution of old ones.

❷ Reading Strategy

Reading Between the Lines

- Explain that to read between the lines, students must pay attention to the words that are left unspoken.

- Have students apply this skill to Antony's speeches to the plebeians in Act III. Point out that the plebeians don't read between the lines. They take what Antony says at face value, and therefore he is easily able to manipulate them. To read between the lines, a plebeian would have had to ask, "Why is Antony speaking in this way? What does he want us to believe? Can we trust him?" Questions such as these help people read to find the meaning below the surface.

- As students read Act IV, have them think about what the characters truly feel and compare it with what they say.

 E-Teach

Visit E-Teach at www.phschool.com for teachers' essays on how to teach, with questions and answers.

Step-by-Step Teaching Guide
for pp. 884–897

CUSTOMIZE INSTRUCTION
For Bodily/Kinesthetic Learners

Have pairs and small groups of students stage the various scenes in Act IV. Make sure each pair or group is assigned a different scene. Give students time to learn their lines and work out how the characters will enter, exit, and move about during the scene. Students can perform their scenes in class.

❶ Review and Anticipate

Antony and Octavius Caesar prepare for battle against the conspirators and their troops.

Tension between Brutus and Cassius explodes into anger, but they make up their quarrel as Brutus tells Cassius that Portia has killed herself. The conspirators agree to march on Philippi. Later that night, when Brutus is alone, he is visited by Caesar's ghost, who tells him that they will meet again at Philippi.

❷ Literary Analysis
Conflict in Drama

- Ask the Literary Analysis question on p. 885: What conflict exists between Antony and Lepidus?
  Answer: Lepidus expects to have a share of power equal to that of Octavius and Antony. Antony intends to control and use Lepidus for his own purposes.

- How does Octavius react to this conflict?
  Answer: Octavius agrees to let Antony have his way, but he thinks more highly of Lepidus than Antony does.

▶ **Monitor Progress** Have students predict how the conflicts in this scene may develop.
Possible answers: Lepidus will soon discover what Antony thinks of him, and he will resent it. Octavius and Lepidus may side together against Antony. Antony may intend to rule alone; he may have as much concealed contempt for Octavius as he does for Lepidus.

Review and Anticipate

❶ After the conspirators assassinate Caesar, both Brutus and Antony give funeral orations. Brutus explains that Caesar's death was necessary to keep Romans free. Then, Antony convinces the crowd that Caesar was a great man and Brutus is a traitor. The crowd rushes off to find and destroy the conspirators.

As Act IV opens, Antony, Lepidus, and Octavius are deciding which of their political rivals must be killed. The remainder of the act reveals the growing conflict between Cassius and Brutus. As the act closes, a mysterious visitor foreshadows Brutus' fate.

➤➤➤➤➤➤➤➤ Act IV ⬅⬅⬅⬅⬅⬅⬅

Scene i. A house in Rome.

[*Enter* ANTONY, OCTAVIUS, *and* LEPIDUS.]

ANTONY. These many then shall die; their names are pricked.

OCTAVIUS. Your brother too must die; consent you, Lepidus?

LEPIDUS. I do consent—

OCTAVIUS.   Prick him down, Antony.

LEPIDUS. Upon condition Publius shall not live,
5   Who is your sister's son, Mark Antony.

ANTONY. He shall not live; look, with a spot I damn him.[1]
    But, Lepidus, go you to Caesar's house;
    Fetch the will hither, and we shall determine
    How to cut off some charge in <u>legacies</u>.

10 **LEPIDUS.** What, shall I find you here?

OCTAVIUS. Or[2] here or at the Capitol.   [*Exit* LEPIDUS.]

ANTONY. This is a slight unmeritable[3] man,
    Meet to be sent on errands; is it fit,
    The threefold world[4] divided, he should stand
    One of the three to share it?

15 **OCTAVIUS.**   So you thought him,
    And took his voice[5] who should be pricked to die
    In our black sentence and proscription.[6]

ANTONY. Octavius, I have seen more days[7] than you;
    And though we lay these honors on this man,
20   To ease ourselves of divers <u>sland'rous</u> loads,[8]

884 ◆ Drama

---

1. with a spot . . . him with a mark on the tablet, I condemn him.

2. Or either.

3. slight unmeritable insignificant and without merit.

4. threefold world three areas of the Roman Empire—Europe, Asia, and Africa.

legacies (leg´ ə sēz) *n.* money, property, or position left in a will to someone

5. voice vote; opinion.

6. proscription list of those sentenced to death or exile.

7. have seen more days am older.

8. divers sland'rous loads various burdens of blame.

slanderous (slan´ dər əs) *adj.* damaging to a person's reputation

---

TEACHING RESOURCES

The following resources can be used to enrich or extend the instruction for pp. 884–897.

Literary Analysis

📖 **Selection Support:**, Literary Analysis, p. 212

Reading

🎧 **Listening to Literature Audiocassettes,** Side 30 ■
💿 **Listening to Literature Audio CDs,** CD 18 ■

 BLOCK SCHEDULING: Resources marked with this symbol provide varied instruction during 90-minute blocks.

He shall but bear them as the ass bears gold,
To groan and sweat under the business,
Either led or driven, as we point the way;
And having brought our treasure where we will,
25 Then take we down his load, and turn him off,
(Like to the empty ass) to shake his ears
And graze in commons.⁹

OCTAVIUS.   You may do your will;
But he's a tried and valiant soldier.

ANTONY. So is my horse, Octavius, and for that
30 I do appoint him store of provender.¹⁰
It is a creature that I teach to fight,
To wind,¹¹ to stop, to run directly on,
His corporal motion governed by my spirit.¹²
And, in some taste,¹³ is Lepidus but so.
35 He must be taught, and trained, and bid go forth.
A barren-spirited¹⁴ fellow; one that feeds
On objects, arts, and imitations,¹⁵
Which, out of use and staled¹⁶ by other men,
Begin his fashion.¹⁷ Do not talk of him
40 But as a property. And now, Octavius,
Listen great things. Brutus and Cassius
Are levying powers;¹⁸ we must straight make head.¹⁹
Therefore let our alliance be combined,
Our best friends made, our means stretched;²⁰
45 And let us presently go sit in council
How covert matters may be best disclosed,
And open perils surest answerèd.²¹

OCTAVIUS. Let us do so; for we are at the stake,²²
And bayed about with many enemies;
50 And some that smile have in their hearts, I fear,
Millions of mischiefs.²³   [Exit]

Scene ii. Camp near Sardis.

[Drum. Enter BRUTUS, LUCILIUS, LUCIUS, and the ARMY. TITINIUS and
PINDARUS meet them.]

BRUTUS. Stand ho!

LUCILIUS. Give the word, ho! and stand.

BRUTUS. What now, Lucilius, is Cassius near?

LUCILIUS. He is at hand, and Pindarus is come
5   To do you salutation¹ from his master.

BRUTUS. He greets me well. Your master, Pindarus,
In his own change, or by ill officers,
Hath given me some worthy cause to wish

The Tragedy of Julius Caesar, Act IV, Scene ii ◆ 885

Literary Analysis
Conflict in Drama What conflict exists between Antony and Lepidus?

9. **in commons** on public pasture.

10. **appoint . . . provender** give him a supply of food.

11. **wind** (wind) v. turn.

12. **His . . . spirit** his body movements governed by my mind.

13. **taste** degree.

14. **barren-spirited** without ideas of his own.

15. **feeds/On objects, arts, and imitations** enjoys curiosities, arts, and styles.

16. **staled** cheapened.

17. **Begin his fashion** he begins to use. (He is hopelessly behind the times.)

18. **levying powers** enlisting troops.

covert (kō̆′ vərt) adj. secret

19. **straight make head** quickly gather soldiers.

20. **stretched** used to the fullest advantage.

21. **How . . . answerèd** how secrets may be discovered and dangers met.

22. **at the stake** like a bear tied to a stake and set upon by many dogs.

23. **mischiefs** plans to injure us.

1. **To do you salutation** to bring you greetings.

④ ✔Reading Check
What does Antony think of Lepidus?

---

❸ Critical Thinking
Making Judgments

• Ask students what they think of Antony's character at this point in the play. What kind of person is he? Do they admire him? Why or why not?
Answer: Antony is cool and calculating. Students should sympathize with his grief over Caesar but also notice his clever manipulation of the plebeians. They may admire some of his qualities and dislike others.

• Ask students how Antony's speech (lines 29–47) affects their judgment of him.
Answer: Antony is decisive. He thinks quickly and makes decisions swiftly. He takes charge of situations. He is not straightforward; he deceives Lepidus about how much power Lepidus will have in the triumvirate.

④ ✔Reading Check

Answer: Antony thinks Lepidus may be useful, but he doesn't respect or admire him.

CUSTOMIZE INSTRUCTION FOR UNIVERSAL ACCESS

For Less Proficient Readers	For English Learners	For Advanced Readers
Students may need assistance in recognizing that the discussion between Octavius and Antony concerns the man who just left the room. Point out the stage direction "Exit Lepidus" on p. 884, and remind students to take note of such text aids.	Help students understand that Antony compares Lepidus to a horse to highlight Lepidus's inability to think and act as one of the triumvirate. Have students point out words and phrases in which Antony names specific qualities that Lepidus shares with a horse.	Suggest that students rewrite a passage in "plain English" —words that explicitly express its meaning. Then, have students compare the two versions and discuss why Shakespeare chose language that required readers to apply more effort and read between the lines.

⑤ Literary Analysis

Conflict in Drama

- Have students identify the conflict being discussed in this conversation. Is it internal or external?
  Answer: Brutus and Lucilius discuss an external conflict between Brutus and Cassius.

- Have students read lines 6–10 and 19–27 carefully, then explain the source of the conflict.
  Answer: Brutus suggests that now that the murder has been committed, Cassius is not dedicated to the battle ahead.

- Ask the Literary Analysis question on p. 887: Which details of the meeting between Brutus and Lucilius indicate the increasing tension of the conflict?
  Answer: Lucilius says that Cassius seems less friendly than usual. Brutus fears that Cassius will let them all down in the coming battle with Antony's forces.

⑥ ▶ Critical Viewing

Answer: Details include their costumes, their confident postures and expressions, and the hearty meal they are eating.

Things done undone;[2] but if he be at hand,
I shall be satisfied.

10 **PINDARUS.**   I do not doubt
But that my noble master will appear
Such as he is, full of regard and honor.

BRUTUS. He is not doubted. A word, Lucilius,
How he received you; let me be resolved.[3]

⑤

15 **LUCILIUS.** With courtesy and with respect enough,
But not with such familiar instances,[4]
Nor with such free and friendly conference[5]
As he hath used of old.

BRUTUS.   Thou hast described
A hot friend cooling. Ever note, Lucilius,
20 When love begins to sicken and decay
It useth an enforcèd ceremony.[6]
There are no tricks in plain and simple faith;
But hollow[7] men, like horses hot at hand,[8]
Make gallant show and promise of their mettle;

[Low march within] ⑥

2. In his own . . . done undone has changed in his feelings toward me or has received bad advice from subordinates and has made me wish we had not done what we did.

3. resolved fully informed.

4. familiar instances marks of friendship.

5. conference conversation.

6. enforcèd ceremony forced formality.

7. hollow insincere.

8. hot at hand full of spirit when reined in.

▼ Critical Viewing
What details in this picture indicate that these are important, powerful men? **[Draw Conclusions]**

886 *Drama*

✱ ENRICHMENT: History Connection

After the Battle

At the opening of Act IV, Octavius, Antony, and Lepidus join forces. After defeating Brutus and his troops in battle, the three took over Rome as the Second Triumvirate. At the time, Octavius was only 19 years old.

As the disagreements between Octavius and Antony and Antony's contempt for Lepidus imply, the triumvirate would not last. Lepidus was forced into retirement. Antony, who had fallen passionately in love with Cleopatra, joined forces with her and fought Octavius's forces, but the Egyptian fleet was sunk in 31 B.C., leaving Octavius in control of Rome. He became Rome's first emperor in 27 B.C.

25 But when they should endure the bloody spur,
   They fall their crests, and like deceitful jades
   Sink in the trial.[9] Comes his army on?

  LUCILIUS. They mean this night in Sardis to be quartered;
   The greater part, the horse in general,[10]
   Are come with Cassius.

[*Enter* CASSIUS *and his Powers.*]

30 **BRUTUS.**   Hark! He is arrived.
   March gently[11] on to meet him.

  CASSIUS. Stand, ho!

  BRUTUS. Stand, ho! Speak the word along.

  FIRST SOLDIER. Stand!

35 **SECOND SOLDIER.** Stand!

  THIRD SOLDIER. Stand!

  CASSIUS. Most noble brother, you have done me wrong.

  BRUTUS. Judge me, you gods! Wrong I mine enemies?
   And if not so, how should I wrong a brother?

40 **CASSIUS.** Brutus, this sober form[12] of yours hides wrongs;
   And when you do them—

  BRUTUS.   Cassius, be content.[13]
   Speak your griefs softly; I do know you well.
   Before the eyes of both our armies here
   (Which should perceive nothing but love from us)
45 Let us not wrangle. Bid them move away;
   Then in my tent, Cassius, enlarge[14] your griefs,
   And I will give you audience.

  CASSIUS.   Pindarus,
   Bid our commanders lead their charges[15] off
   A little from this ground.

50 **BRUTUS.** Lucilius, do you the like, and let no man
   Come to our tent till we have done our conference.
   Let Lucius and Titinius guard our door.

          [*Exit all but* BRUTUS *and* CASSIUS]

Scene iii. Brutus' tent.

  CASSIUS. That you have wronged me doth appear in this:
   You have condemned and noted[1] Lucius Pella
   For taking bribes here of the Sardians;
   Wherein my letters, praying on his side,[2]
5 Because I knew the man, was slighted off.[3]

  BRUTUS. You wronged yourself to write in such a case.

Literary Analysis

Conflict in Drama Which details of the meeting between Brutus and Lucilius indicate the increasing tension of the conflict?

9. They fall . . . the trial They drop their necks, and like worn-out worthless horses, fail the test.

10. horse in general cavalry.

11. gently slowly.

12. sober form serious manner.

13. be content be patient.

Reading Strategy

Reading Between the Lines Read between the lines to explain why Brutus and Cassius want to meet away from their troops.

14. enlarge freely express.

15. charges troops.

1. noted publicly denounced.

2. praying on his side pleading on his behalf.

3. slighted off disregarded.

❽ ✔ Reading Check

What does Brutus say is happening with Cassius?

---

❼ Reading Strategy

Reading Between the Lines

- Choose students to read the entrance of Cassius aloud (lines 30–37). Ask students what effect they can read between the lines. Have them explain their answers.
  Answer: The short, sharp words and exclamations—"Hark!" "Stand, ho!" "Stand!"—create an atmosphere of hostility. It is almost as if Cassius were an enemy soldier coming to negotiate, rather than a commander on the same side as Brutus. Cassius's line, "you have done me wrong," suggests deep-seated resentment and unresolved conflict.

- Ask the Reading Strategy question on p. 887: Read between the lines to explain why Brutus and Cassius want to meet away from their troops.
  Answer: They want to present a united front to their troops. Their followers might easily lose courage if they think the leaders no longer agree.

❽ ✔ Reading Check

Answer: Brutus thinks Cassius is losing heart for the struggle ahead.

CUSTOMIZE INSTRUCTION FOR UNIVERSAL ACCESS

For Less Proficient Readers	For English Learners	For Advanced Readers
In Act I, Scene i, lines 32–36, Cassius accused Brutus of being less friendly than usual. Now Brutus notices the same thing about Cassius. Have students reread Act I, Scene i and this scene "between the lines" and discuss the change in the characters' relationship.	Explain that the idiom "reading between the lines" means "looking beyond the literal meaning of what people say." Reading between the lines means picking up hints and interpreting them.	Have students read between the lines to analyze Cassius's character. What do they think causes the change Lucilius describes in Scene ii, lines 15–18? Students should reread Cassius's speeches from the first three acts, as well as Act IV, Scene iii, to answer this question.

- Ask the Reading Strategy question on p. 888: What is Brutus suggesting when he asks what villain stabbed Caesar "not for justice"?
  Answer: He suggests that Cassius acted from personal, dishonorable motives.

- Have students reread some of the conversation between the two men and describe the mood Shakespeare creates.
  Answer: The mood is tense, hostile, and dark.

- What does the mood suggest Brutus and Cassius might be feeling but not saying directly?
  Answer: Brutus loved Caesar and may feel guilty about the murder. He may feel that Cassius has in some way manipulated him to commit murder not for honorable motives but from Cassius's personal jealousy and dislike of Caesar. Cassius may feel guilty because he knows his motives for the assassination were not pure. He may resent Brutus for causing the current situation by disregarding Cassius's suggestion to kill Antony or at least not to let him speak over Caesar's body.

CASSIUS. In such a time as this it is not meet
That every nice offense should bear his comment.[4]

BRUTUS. Let me tell you, Cassius, you yourself
10   Are much condemned to have an itching palm,[5]
To sell and mart[6] your offices for gold
To undeservers.

CASSIUS.   I an itching palm?
You know that you are Brutus that speaks this,
Or, by the gods, this speech were else your last.

15 **BRUTUS.** The name of Cassius honors[7] this corruption,
And <u>chastisement</u> doth therefore hide his head.

CASSIUS. Chastisement!

BRUTUS. Remember March, the ides of March remember.
Did not great Julius bleed for justice' sake?
20   What villain touched his body, that did stab,
And not[8] for justice? What, shall one of us,
That struck the foremost man of all this world
But for supporting robbers,[9] shall we now
Contaminate our fingers with base bribes,
25   And sell the mighty space of our large honors[10]
For so much trash[11] as may be grasped thus?
I had rather be a dog, and bay[12] the moon,
Than such a Roman.

CASSIUS.   Brutus, bait[13] not me;
I'll not endure it. You forget yourself
30   To hedge me in.[14] I am a soldier, I,
Older in practice, abler than yourself
To make conditions.[15]

BRUTUS.   Go to! You are not, Cassius.

CASSIUS. I am.

BRUTUS. I say you are not.

35 **CASSIUS.** Urge[16] me no more, I shall forget myself;
Have mind upon your health;[17] tempt me no farther.

BRUTUS. Away, slight[18] man!

CASSIUS. Is't possible?

BRUTUS.   Hear me, for I will speak.
Must I give way and room to your rash choler?[19]
40   Shall I be frighted when a madman stares?

CASSIUS. O ye gods, ye gods! Must I endure all this?

BRUTUS. All this? Ay, more: fret till your proud heart break.
Go show your slaves how choleric[20] you are,

4. every . . . comment every petty fault should receive its criticism.

5. condemned . . . palm accused of having a hand eager to accept bribes.

6. mart trade.

7. honors gives respectability to.

chastisement (chas tīz´ mənt) *n.* punishment; severe criticism

8. And not except.

Reading Strategy
Reading Between the Lines What is Brutus suggesting when he asks what villain stabbed Caesar "not for justice"?

9. But . . . robbers Here Brutus says, for the first time, that Caesar's officials were also involved in taking bribes and that this was a motive in his assassination.

10. honors offices.

11. trash dirty money.

12. bay howl at.

13. bait harass (as a bear tied to a stake is harassed by dogs).

14. hedge me in restrict my actions.

15. conditions decisions.

16. Urge drive.

17. health safety.

18. slight insignificant.

19. choler (käl´ ər) *n.* anger.

20. choleric (käl´ ər ik) *adj.* quick-tempered.

And make your bondmen tremble. Must I budge?[21]
Must I observe you?[22] Must I stand and crouch
Under your testy humor?[23] By the gods,
You shall digest the venom of your spleen,[24]
Though it do split you; for, from this day forth,
I'll use you for my mirth,[25] yea, for my laughter,
When you are waspish.[26]

50 CASSIUS.   Is it come to this?

BRUTUS. You say you are a better soldier:
Let it appear so; make your vaunting[27] true,
And it shall please me well. For mine own part,
I shall be glad to learn of[28] noble men.

55 CASSIUS. You wrong me every way; you wrong me, Brutus;
I said, an elder soldier, not a better.
Did I say, better?

BRUTUS.   If you did, I care not.

CASSIUS. When Caesar lived, he durst not thus have
moved[29] me.

BRUTUS. Peace, peace, you durst not so have tempted
him.

60 CASSIUS. I durst not?

BRUTUS. No.

CASSIUS. What? Durst not tempt him?

BRUTUS.   For your life you durst not.

CASSIUS. Do not presume too much upon my love;
I may do that I shall be sorry for.

65 BRUTUS. You have done that you should be sorry for.
There is no terror, Cassius, in your threats;
For I am armed so strong in honesty
That they pass by me as the idle wind,
Which I respect not. I did send to you
70 For certain sums of gold, which you denied me;
For I can raise no money by vile means.
By heaven, I had rather coin my heart
And drop my blood for drachmas than to wring
From the hard hands of peasants their vile trash
75 By any indirection.[30] I did send
To you for gold to pay my legions,
Which you denied me. Was that done like Cassius?
Should I have answered Caius Cassius so?
When Marcus Brutus grows so covetous[31]
80 To lock such rascal counters[32] from his friends,

---

21. **budge** flinch away
from you.

22. **observe you** show
reverence toward you.

23. **testy humor** irritability.

24. **digest . . . spleen** eat
the poison of your spleen.
(The spleen was thought to
be the source of anger.)

25. **mirth** amusement.
26. **waspish** bad-tempered.
27. **vaunting** (vônt´ iŋ) *n.*
boasting.

28. **learn of** hear about;
learn from.

29. **moved** irritated.

Literary Analysis
**Conflict in Drama and
Suspense** How does this
conflict between Cassius
and Brutus build
suspense?

30. **indirection** irregular
methods.

31. **covetous** (kuv´ ət əs)
adj. greedy.

32. **rascal counters**
worthless coins.

⓫ ✔Reading Check
Why are Brutus and
Cassius arguing?

The Tragedy of Julius Caesar, Act IV, Scene iii ◆ 889

⓵ Literary Analysis
Conflict in Drama and Suspense

- Ask students to identify the surface matters about which Brutus
and Cassius quarrel. What does
this suggest about both men's
present state of mind?
  Answer: They are quarreling about
  petty matters: who is a better soldier, whether Cassius was afraid of
  Caesar. This suggests that both
  are tense and edgy.

- Ask the Literary Analysis question
on p. 889: How does this conflict
between Cassius and Brutus build
suspense?
  Answer: The audience wonders
  whether they will come to blows,
  whether one will surrender to
  Antony, or whether one may kill
  the other.

▶ Monitor Progress Ask students to
identify what they think are the real
causes for this quarrel. They may
find some causes in this scene, or
they may want to review previous
encounters between Brutus and
Cassius.
  Answers: Cassius may blame
  Brutus for showing mercy to
  Antony and thus causing all the
  present trouble. Brutus may be
  angry because Cassius urged the
  conspiracy on him and now seems
  to lack the courage and heart to
  fight to the end. Brutus apparently
  doubts Cassius's motives for the
  murder.

⓫ ✔Reading Check
Answer: Cassius failed to provide
Brutus with necessary funds for his
army.

CUSTOMIZE INSTRUCTION FOR UNIVERSAL ACCESS

For Gifted/Talented Students

Have partners read aloud the play's crucial conversations between Brutus and Cassius: Act I, Scene ii,
lines 25–177, and Act IV, Scene iii, lines 1–122.
Students should also review the Act II and Act III
scenes in which these two characters exchange dialogue. Have partners analyze the causes and the
course of the conflict between the two friends. What
is their conflict in Act I? Is the conflict the same in Act
III? How might their relationship have changed its
course? What might have happened between them if

Brutus had accepted any of Cassius's advice in Acts II
and III? Is the conflict resolved in Act IV? If so, how? If
not, is it resolved in Act V? If so, at what point?

- Ask the Reading Strategy question
on p. 890: What can you read
between the lines to explain why
Cassius is so offended by Brutus's
words?
  Answer: Cassius's language
  throughout the scene and elsewhere shows that he has great
  respect for Brutus. He is especially
  hurt by Brutus's scolding because
  he cares for Brutus's good opinion.

- Ask students to infer why Brutus
drops the quarrel at line 106.
  Possible answers: Brutus has said
  as much as he needed to say. He
  sees that he has hurt Cassius's
  feelings, and he regrets that. The
  two men are too close to continue
  a quarrel for long.

- Ask how Brutus may feel when
Cassius suggests that Brutus kill
him. Why might Brutus feel this
way?
  Answer: This suggestion may
  remind him uncomfortably of the
  murder of Caesar. He may think
  Cassius is overdramatizing; Brutus
  is calm, quiet, and reasonable, and
  may not understand Cassius's passionate nature.

Be ready, gods, with all your thunderbolts,
Dash him to pieces!

CASSIUS.   I denied you not.

BRUTUS. You did.

CASSIUS.   I did not. He was but a fool
85 That brought my answer back. Brutus hath rived[33] my heart.
A friend should bear his friend's infirmities;
But Brutus makes mine greater than they are.

BRUTUS. I do not, till you practice them on me.

CASSIUS. You love me not.

BRUTUS.   I do not like your faults.

CASSIUS. A friendly eye could never see such faults.

90 **BRUTUS.** A flatterer's would not, though they do appear
As huge as high Olympus.

CASSIUS. Come, Antony, and young Octavius, come,
Revenge yourselves alone[34] on Cassius,
For Cassius is aweary of the world:
95 Hated by one he loves; braved[35] by his brother;
Checked like a bondman;[36] all his faults observed,
Set in a notebook, learned and conned by rote[37]
To cast into my teeth. O, I could weep
My spirit from mine eyes! There is my dagger,
100 And here my naked breast; within, a heart
Dearer than Pluto's mine,[38] richer than gold;
If that thou be'st a Roman, take it forth.
I, that denied thee gold, will give my heart.
Strike as thou didst at Caesar; for I know,
105 When thou didst hate him worst, thou lovedst him better
Than ever thou lovedst Cassius.

BRUTUS.   Sheathe your dagger.
Be angry when you will, it shall have scope.[39]
Do what you will, dishonor shall be humor.[40]
O Cassius, you are yokèd[41] with a lamb
110 That carries anger as the flint bears fire,
Who, much enforcèd,[42] shows a hasty spark,
And straight is cold again.

CASSIUS.   Hath Cassius lived
To be but mirth and laughter to his Brutus
When grief and blood ill-tempered vexeth him?

115 **BRUTUS.** When I spoke that, I was ill-tempered too.

CASSIUS. Do you confess so much? Give me your hand.

BRUTUS. And my heart too.

---

33. **rived** (rivd) v. broken.

Reading Strategy
Reading Between the Lines What can you read between the lines to explain why Cassius is so offended by Brutus' words?

34. **alone** only.
35. **braved** bullied.
36. **Checked like a bondman** scolded like a slave.
37. **conned by rote** memorized.
38. **Pluto's mine** mytho-logical Roman god of the underworld and of riches symbolized by his mine.

39. **scope** free play.
40. **dishonor . . . humor** any dishonorable acts will be considered just your irritable disposition.
41. **yokèd** in partnership.
42. **enforcèd** provoked.

CASSIUS.   O Brutus!

BRUTUS.   What's the matter?

CASSIUS. Have not you love enough to bear with me
       When that rash humor which my mother gave me
       Makes me forgetful?

120 BRUTUS.   Yes, Cassius, and from henceforth,
       When you are overearnest with your Brutus,
       He'll think your mother chides, and leave you so.[43]

[*Enter a* POET, *followed by* LUCILIUS, TITINIUS, *and* LUCIUS.]

    POET. Let me go in to see the generals;
        There is some grudge between 'em; 'tis not meet
125   They be alone.

    LUCILIUS. You shall not come to them.

    POET. Nothing but death shall stay me.

    CASSIUS. How now? What's the matter?

    POET. For shame, you generals! What do you mean?
130   Love, and be friends, as two such men should be;

Literary Analysis
Conflict in Drama How does the conflict between Brutus and Cassius reflect Brutus' internal conflict over his participation in the conspiracy?

43. **your mother . . . so**
it is just your inherited disposition and let it go at that.

⑭ ◄ **Critical Viewing** How do the expressions and body language of these actors playing Brutus and Cassius indicate conflict? **[Analyze]**

⑮ ☑**Reading Check**
What happens between Brutus and Cassius?

The Tragedy of Julius Caesar, Act IV, Scene iii ◆ 891

⑬ **Literary Analysis**
Conflict in Drama

• Ask the Literary Analysis question on p. 891: How does the conflict between Brutus and Cassius reflect Brutus's internal conflict over his participation in the conspiracy?
Answer: Brutus loved Caesar but felt it his duty to murder him. Brutus loves Cassius but feels it his duty to scold him.

• Ask students whether they detect an internal conflict in Cassius in this scene. If so, what is it?
Answer: Students may suggest that Cassius is torn between his duty to fight alongside Brutus and his desire to give up the entire enterprise. They may suggest he is torn between a desire to earn Brutus's respect and a desire to do things his own way.

⑭ ▶**Critical Viewing**

Tell students that Cassius is at the left of the photo and Brutus is at the right.
Answer: Brutus is scowling; Cassius is drawing his dagger. Brutus's pose, with hands on hips, indicates anger or impatience.

⑮ ☑**Reading Check**

Answer: Brutus and Cassius end their conflict by blaming it on their "ill tempers" and "rash humors."

CUSTOMIZE INSTRUCTION FOR UNIVERSAL ACCESS

For Gifted/Talented Students	For Advanced Readers
Remind students that Act IV, Scene iii marks the second time a poet wanders into a scene. The first occurs at the end of Act III, when Cinna the Poet is mistaken for a conspirator and attacked. The poet in Act IV, Scene iii tries to mend the quarrel between Brutus and Cassius, only to be insulted and told to leave. Ask students to brainstorm for reasons that poets appear as comic characters in this play.	Have students analyze the language of the quarrel between Cassius and Brutus. Have them look at such things as line length, length of individual speeches, and the language the characters use to each other. Do students notice repetition? Do people really speak like Brutus and Cassius when they are angry? Students may want to compare the scene with one in which two characters are talking as friends. Have students write brief essays analyzing the way Shakespeare's use of language makes (or fails to make) this quarrel realistic.

Conflict in Drama

- Ask the Literary Analysis question on p. 892: With what internal conflicts is Brutus struggling?
  Answer: Brutus struggles between wanting to mourn Portia and knowing that he must conceal his grief because the military situation is desperate.

- Ask students why they think Brutus delayed so long before telling Cassius of Portia's death.
  Answer: He was angry at Cassius. He thought he should settle his business with Cassius before discussing private matters.

- Ask students whether they think Cassius feels a new internal conflict once he is told of Portia's death. Have them explain their answers.
  Answer: Students should note that Cassius now feels terribly guilty for having quarreled with Brutus.

⑰ Background

History

According to Shakespeare's major source for this play, the Thomas North translation of Plutarch's *Lives*, Portia "took hot burning coals and cast them in her mouth, and kept her mouth so closed that she choked herself."

For I have seen more years, I'm sure, than ye.

CASSIUS. Ha, ha! How vilely doth this cynic[44] rhyme!

BRUTUS. Get you hence, sirrah! Saucy fellow, hence!

CASSIUS. Bear with him, Brutus, 'tis his fashion.

135 BRUTUS. I'll know his humor when he knows his time.[45]
What should the wars do with these jigging[46] fools?
Companion,[47] hence!

CASSIUS. 　　　　　　Away, away, be gone! 　　　[*Exit* POET.]

BRUTUS. Lucilius and Titinius, bid the commanders
Prepare to lodge their companies tonight.

140 CASSIUS. And come yourselves, and bring Messala with you
Immediately to us. 　　　　[*Exit* LUCILIUS *and* TITINIUS.]

BRUTUS. 　　　　　　Lucius, a bowl of wine. 　[*Exit* LUCIUS.]

CASSIUS. I did not think you could have been so angry.

BRUTUS. O Cassius, I am sick of many griefs.

CASSIUS. Of your philosophy you make no use,
145 If you give place to accidental evils.[48]

BRUTUS. No man bears sorrow better. Portia is dead.

CASSIUS. Ha? Portia?

BRUTUS. She is dead.

⑯ CASSIUS. How scaped I killing when I crossed you so?[49]
150 O insupportable and touching loss!
Upon[50] what sickness?

BRUTUS. 　　　　　　Impatient of my absence,
And grief that young Octavius with Mark Antony
Have made themselves so strong—for with her death
That tidings[51] came—with this she fell distract,[52]
⑰ 155 And (her attendants absent) swallowed fire.

CASSIUS. And died so?

BRUTUS. 　　　　　　Even so.

CASSIUS. 　　　　　　O ye immortal gods!

[*Enter* LUCIUS, *with wine and tapers.*]

BRUTUS. Speak no more of her. Give me a bowl of wine
In this I bury all unkindness, Cassius. 　　[*Drinks*]

CASSIUS. My heart is thirsty for that noble pledge.
160 Fill, Lucius, till the wine o'erswell the cup;
I cannot drink too much of Brutus' love.

44. cynic rude fellow.

45. I'll know . . . time
I'll accept his eccentricity when he chooses a proper time to exhibit it.

46. jigging rhyming.

47. Companion fellow (used to show contempt).

philosophy (fə läs′ ə fē) *n.* system of principles or beliefs

Literary Analysis
Conflict in Drama With what internal conflicts is Brutus struggling?

48. Of your philosophy . . . accidental evils Brutus' philosophy was Stoicism. As a Stoic, he believed that nothing evil would happen to a good man.

49. How scaped . . . you so? How did I escape being killed when I opposed you so?

50. Upon as a result of.

51. tidings news.

52. fell distract became distraught.

CUSTOMIZE INSTRUCTION FOR UNIVERSAL ACCESS

For Special Needs Students	For Less Proficient Readers
Have students read along in their textbooks while you play the **Listening to Literature** Audiocassettes or CDs. Pause the recording occasionally, and work with students to discuss developments in plot and characters in the scene they have just read.	Students may have an easier time understanding the play if they read its scenes aloud, either in small groups or with partners. If necessary, students can trade or alternate roles so that everyone gets plenty of chances to read and to listen. At the end of each scene, students can summarize what they have read, making sure they can all identify the characters and briefly explain what happened in the scene.

[*Drinks. Exit* LUCIUS.]

[*Enter* TITINIUS *and* MESSALA.]

BRUTUS. Come in, Titinius! Welcome, good Messala.
　　Now sit we close about this taper here,
　　And call in question[53] our necessities.

CASSIUS. Portia, art thou gone?

165　**BRUTUS.**　　　　　　　　No more, I pray you.
　　Messala, I have here receivèd letters
　　That young Octavius and Mark Antony
　　Come down upon us with a mighty power,[54]
　　Bending their expedition toward Philippi.[55]

170　**MESSALA.** Myself have letters of the selfsame tenure.[56]

BRUTUS. With what addition?

MESSALA. That by proscription and bills of outlawry
　　Octavius, Antony, and Lepidus
　　Have put to death an hundred senators.

175　**BRUTUS.** Therein our letters do not well agree.
　　Mine speak of seventy senators that died
　　By their proscriptions, Cicero being one.

CASSIUS. Cicero one?

MESSALA.　　　　　Cicero is dead,
　　And by that order of proscription.

180　　Had you your letters from your wife, my lord?

BRUTUS. No, Messala.

MESSALA. Nor nothing in your letters writ of her?

BRUTUS. Nothing, Messala.

MESSALA.　　　　　　　That methinks is strange.

BRUTUS. Why ask you? Hear you aught[57] of her in yours?

185　**MESSALA.** No, my lord.

BRUTUS. Now as you are a Roman, tell me true.

MESSALA. Then like a Roman bear the truth I tell,
　　For certain she is dead, and by strange manner.

BRUTUS. Why, farewell, Portia. We must die, Messala.
190　　With meditating that she must die once,
　　I have the patience to endure it now.

MESSALA. Even so great men great losses should endure.

CASSIUS. I have as much of this in art[58] as you,
　　But yet my nature could not bear it so.

---

53. **call in question**
examine.

54. **power** army.
55. **Bending . . . Philippi** (fi
lip′ ī) directing their rapid
march toward Philippi.

56. **selfsame tenure**
same message.

57. **aught** (ôt) *n.* anything
at all.

58. **have . . . art** have as
much Stoicism in theory.

⑲ ✓Reading Check
What has happened to
Portia?

The Tragedy of Julius Caesar, Act IV, Scene iii ◆ 893

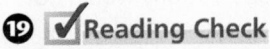

- Ask the Literary Analysis question on p. 894: How does the discussion over where to meet Antony and Octavius add to the suspense? Answer: It indicates that the final showdown between the two factions is nearing.

- Point out that once again, as in Acts II and III, Cassius and Brutus disagree over the best course of action. Once again, Cassius gives way to Brutus. Ask students how this adds to the suspense of the moment. Answer: Students should note that so far, Cassius has been right, and Brutus has been wrong. If the conspirators had killed Antony or refused to let him speak over Caesar's body, Antony would not now be in a position to destroy them. Students should expect that once again, Brutus's suggested course of action will turn out badly. This fear that things will go wrong adds to the suspense.

---

195 **BRUTUS.** Well, to our work alive.[59] What do you think
    Of marching to Philippi presently?

CASSIUS. I do not think it good.

BRUTUS.   Your reason?

CASSIUS.   This it is:
    'Tis better that the enemy seek us;
    So shall he waste his means, weary his soldiers,
200   Doing himself offense,[60] whilst we, lying still,
    Are full of rest, defense, and nimbleness.

BRUTUS. Good reasons must of force[61] give place to better.
    The people 'twixt Philippi and this ground
    Do stand but in a forced affection;[62]
205   For they have grudged us contribution.[63]
    The enemy, marching along by them,
    By them shall make a fuller number up,[64]
    Come on refreshed, new-added[65] and encouraged;
    From which advantage shall we cut him off
210   If at Philippi we do face him there,
    These people at our back.

CASSIUS.   Hear me, good brother.

BRUTUS. Under your pardon.[66] You must note beside
    That we have tried the utmost of our friends,
    Our legions are brimful, our cause is ripe.
215   The enemy increaseth every day;
    We, at the height, are ready to decline.
    There is a tide in the affairs of men
    Which, taken at the flood, leads on to fortune;
    Omitted,[67] all the voyage of their life
220   Is bound[68] in shallows and in miseries.
    On such a full sea are we now afloat,
    And we must take the current when it serves,
    Or lose our ventures.

CASSIUS.   Then, with your will,[69] go on;
    We'll along ourselves and meet them at Philippi.

225 **BRUTUS.** The deep of night is crept upon our talk,
    And nature must obey necessity,
    Which we will niggard with a little rest.[70]
    There is no more to say?

CASSIUS.   No more. Good night.
    Early tomorrow will we rise and hence.[71]

[*Enter* LUCIUS.]

BRUTUS. Lucius, my gown.[72]   [*Exit* LUCIUS.]
230   Farewell, good Messala.

---

59. to our work alive
Let us go about the work we have to do as living men.

60. offense harm.

Literary Analysis
Conflict in Drama and Suspense How does the discussion over where to meet Antony and Octavius add to the suspense?

61. of force of necessity.

62. Do stand . . . affection support us only by fear of force.

63. grudged us contribution given us aid and supplies grudgingly.

64. shall make . . . up will add more to their numbers.

65. new-added reinforced.

66. Under your pardon excuse me.

67. Omitted neglected.

68. bound confined.

69. with your will as you wish.

70. niggard . . . rest satisfy stingily with a short sleep.

71. hence leave.

72. gown nightgown.

Good night, Titinius. Noble, noble Cassius,
Good night, and good repose.

CASSIUS.   O my dear brother,
This was an ill beginning of the night.
Never come⁷³ such division 'tween our souls!
Let it not, Brutus.

[*Enter* LUCIUS, *with the gown.*]

235 BRUTUS.   Everything is well.

CASSIUS. Good night, my lord.

BRUTUS.   Good night, good brother.

TITINIUS, MESSALA. Good night, Lord Brutus.

BRUTUS.   Farewell, every one.

[*Exit*]

Give me the gown. Where is thy instrument?⁷⁴

LUCIUS. Here in the tent.

BRUTUS.   What, thou speak'st drowsily?
240 Poor knave,⁷⁵ I blame thee not; thou art o'erwatched.⁷⁶
Call Claudius and some other of my men;
I'll have them sleep on cushions in my tent.

LUCIUS. Varro and Claudius!

[*Enter* VARRO *and* CLAUDIUS.]

VARRO. Calls my lord?

245 BRUTUS. I pray you, sirs, lie in my tent and sleep.
It may be I shall raise⁷⁷ you by and by
On business to my brother Cassius.

VARRO. So please you, we will stand and watch your pleasure.

250 BRUTUS. I will not have it so; lie down, good sirs;
It may be I shall otherwise bethink me.⁷⁸

[VARRO *and* CLAUDIUS *lie down.*]

Look. Lucius, here's the book I sought for so;
I put it in the pocket of my gown.

LUCIUS. I was sure your lordship did not give it me.

BRUTUS. Bear with me, good boy, I am much forgetful.
255 Canst thou hold up thy heavy eyes awhile,
And touch⁷⁹ thy instrument a strain or two?

LUCIUS. Ay, my lord, an't⁸⁰ please you.

BRUTUS.   It does, my boy.
I trouble thee too much, but thou art willing.

73. **Never come** may
there never come.

74. **instrument** lute
(probably).

75. **knave** (nāv) *n.* servant.
76. **o'erwatched**
weary with too much
watchfulness.

77. **raise** wake.

78. **otherwise bethink
me** change my mind.

79. **touch** play.
80. **an't** if it.

22 ✔ Reading Check
Why does Brutus say they
must march to Philippi to
meet the enemy?

The Tragedy of Julius Caesar, Act IV, Scene iii ◆ 895

21 Reading Strategy
Reading Between the Lines

- Students should note that in this passage, Brutus is aware of the weariness of his servant and his men.

- Tell students that this passage reflects the complexity of Brutus's personality. Have them explain the complexity.
  Answer: Only a short time ago, Brutus was able to put his wife's death out of his mind to discuss a battle plan. In this passage, we see a gentle, compassionate side of Brutus's personality.

22 ✔ Reading Check

Answer: Brutus wants to prevent the enemy army from picking up reinforcements.

CUSTOMIZE INSTRUCTION FOR UNIVERSAL ACCESS

For Special Needs Students	For Advanced Readers
Have students meet to go over their answers to the Review and Assess questions on p. 897. If they disagree, have them go back through Act IV to find supporting evidence for their answers. Then, have them work together as a small group to answer the questions on p. 898.	Have students improvise a monologue or write a journal entry that captures Brutus's thoughts and feelings at this point in the play. Encourage students to refer to details from the play that affect his situation and his feelings about it.

Conflict in Drama

- Make sure students understand that the ghost is that of Caesar, although he does not identify himself in the dialogue. Ask the Literary Analysis question on p. 896: What is the effect of the appearance of the ghost?
  Answer: The audience is probably startled and intrigued.

- Ask students to describe the ghost's effect on Brutus. What does this suggest about the internal conflicts from which Brutus is suffering?
  Answer: Brutus loved Caesar and is honest and good by nature. Therefore, Brutus must feel some guilt and regret over the murder. His reaction to the ghost suggests that he is not entirely at ease with his own action.

- Ask what the appearance of Caesar's ghost suggests about conflicts within Caesar. Have students draw on their prior knowledge of ghosts in literature.
  Answer: If a ghost in a literary work walks, he or she often has some unresolved business among the living. Caesar's ghost apparently wants to get his own revenge on the men who killed him.

24 Reading Strategy

Reading Between the Lines

- Ask the Reading Strategy question on p. 896: What warning can you discover in the ghost's message by reading between the lines?
  Answer: The ghost suggests that Brutus will die at Philippi. Brutus will not see the ghost again until he is a ghost himself.

- Ask why Brutus might want "to hold more talk with" the ghost. What might he ask the ghost?
  Answer: Brutus might think the ghost can foretell the future. He may want the ghost to tell him what will happen at Philippi. He may hope that the ghost can give him news of Portia, who is dead.

896

LUCIUS. It is my duty, sir.

260 **BRUTUS.** I should not urge thy duty past thy might;
I know young bloods[81] look for a time of rest.

LUCIUS. I have slept, my lord, already.

BRUTUS. It was well done, and thou shalt sleep again;
I will not hold thee long. If I do live,
265 I will be good to thee.

[*Music, and a song*]

This is a sleepy tune. O murd'rous[82] slumber!
Layest thou thy leaden mace[83] upon my boy,
That plays thee music? Gentle knave, good night;
I will not do thee so much wrong to wake thee.
270 If thou dost nod, thou break'st thy instrument;
I'll take it from thee; and, good boy, good night.
Let me see, let me see; is not the leaf[84] turned down
Where I left reading? Here it is, I think.

[*Enter the ghost of* CAESAR.]

How ill this taper burns. Ha! Who comes here?
275 I think it is the weakness of mine eyes
That shapes this monstrous apparition.[85]
It comes upon[86] me. Art thou anything?
Art thou some god, some angel, or some devil,
That mak'st my blood cold, and my hair to stare?[87]
280 Speak to me what thou art.

GHOST. Thy evil spirit, Brutus.

BRUTUS.   Why com'st thou?

GHOST. To tell thee thou shalt see me at Philippi.

BRUTUS. Well; then I shall see thee again?

GHOST. Ay, at Philippi.

285 **BRUTUS.** Why, I will see thee at Philippi then.

[*Exit* GHOST.]

Now I have taken heart thou vanishest.
Ill spirit, I would hold more talk with thee.
Boy! Lucius! Varro! Claudius! Sirs, awake!
Claudius!

290 **LUCIUS.** The strings, my lord, are false.[88]

BRUTUS. He thinks he still is at his instrument. Lucius, awake!

LUCIUS. My lord?

BRUTUS. Didst thou dream, Lucius, that thou so criedst out?

896 ◆ *Drama*

---

81. young bloods young bodies.

82. murd'rous deathlike.

83. mace (mās) *n.* staff of office (an allusion to the practice of tapping a person on the shoulder with a mace when arresting him).

84. leaf page.

Literary Analysis
Conflict in Drama and Suspense What is the effect of the appearance of the ghost?

85. monstrous apparition ominous ghost.

86. upon toward.

87. stare stand on end.

Reading Strategy
Reading Between the Lines What warning can you discover in the ghost's message by reading between the lines?

88. false out of tune.

✸ **ENRICHMENT: Drama Connection**

Elizabethan Ghosts

Several of Shakespeare's plays feature ghosts. In *Hamlet*, the ghost of King Hamlet appears to his son, urging him to avenge his murder. In *Macbeth*, the ghost of Banquo appears to Macbeth at a banquet, terrifying the man who earlier that day ordered his murder.

On the Elizabethan stage, ghosts were assumed to be real, not figments of a character's imagination. The audience accepted the notion that a ghost had the power to make itself visible at will. Banquo's ghost appears in a crowded room but is visible only to Macbeth; the ghost of King Hamlet is seen by various guards and by Hamlet's friend Horatio, although he speaks only to Hamlet. Caesar's ghost may blame Brutus more than anyone else for Caesar's death, because Brutus is the only person the ghost visits.

295 **LUCIUS.** My lord, I do not know that I did cry.

BRUTUS. Yes, that thou didst. Didst thou see anything?

LUCIUS. Nothing, my lord.

BRUTUS. Sleep again, Lucius. Sirrah Claudius!

[*To* VARRO] Fellow thou, awake!

300 **VARRO.** My lord?

CLAUDIUS. My lord?

BRUTUS. Why did you so cry out, sirs, in your sleep?

BOTH. Did we, my lord?

BRUTUS.   Ay. Saw you anything?

VARRO. No, my lord, I saw nothing.

CLAUDIUS.   Nor I, my lord.

305 **BRUTUS.** Go and commend me[89] to my brother Cassius;
      Bid him set on his pow'rs betimes before,[90]
      And we will follow.

BOTH.   It shall be done, my lord.   [*Exit*]

89. commend me carry my greetings.

90. set on . . . before advance his troops.

Review and Assess

Thinking About Act IV

1. **Respond:** With whom do you sympathize in Act IV—Brutus, Cassius, or neither? Why?

2. (a) **Recall:** Why do Octavius and Antony argue in Scene i?
   (b) **Compare and Contrast:** How is their argument different from the one between Brutus and Cassius in Scene ii?

3. (a) **Recall:** How does Portia die? (b) **Infer:** Why do you think Brutus delays in telling Cassius of her death?
   (c) **Compare and Contrast:** Compare and contrast the reactions of Brutus and Cassius to Portia's death.

4. (a) **Recall:** Whose ghost appears to Brutus? (b) **Draw Conclusions:** What does the ghost mean when he says to Brutus, "thou shalt see me at Philippi"?

5. (a) **Recall:** Why have Brutus and Cassius decided to attack Antony and Octavius at Philippi rather than wait for them to attack? (b) **Speculate:** Who do you think will be the victor in the upcoming battle? Explain.

6. **Evaluate:** Which character in this act do you feel would make the best leader for Rome? Explain.

The Tragedy of Julius Caesar, Act IV, Scene iii ◆ 897

✏ ASSESSMENT PRACTICE: Reading Comprehension

Notice Word Choice   (For more practice, see Test Preparation Workbook, p. 53.)

Many tests require students to notice how word choice reveals character and attitude. Use this sample test item to help students practice this skill.

OCTAVIUS:

   Let us do so, for we are at the stake,
   And bayed about with many enemies;
   And some that smile have in their hearts, I fear,
   Millions of mischiefs.

What do the words *stake, bayed,* and *enemies* reveal about Octavius's mood?

   A He feels that he is at a crossroads.
   B He fears that he will be set on fire.
   C He plans an attack.
   D He feels he is in danger.

Octavius compares his situation with that of someone who is surrounded by enemies. The correct answer is *D*.

Review and Assess

1. Internal: Grief over Portia's death versus need to put it aside for more pressing matters. Guilt over Caesar's murder versus duty to continue with his battle against Antony's troops. External: Anger at Cassius versus love for him. Conflict between his faction and Antony's faction.

2. Antony faces a need to keep Lepidus from taking an equal share of power and a conflict with Brutus, Cassius, and their supporters.

3. Brutus still feels some guilt over Caesar's murder.

4. Cassius acted against Caesar from personal motives, not patriotic duty.

5. The conflict between Cassius and Brutus heightens the sense that the conspirators' plan is falling apart. Their quarrel weakens their side.

6. They don't know about the plans Antony and Octavius have made.

7. Antony is clearly the leader. He makes the decisions and does so for practical reasons. Octavius follows Antony's lead; when they disagree, Octavius gives in.

8. He implies that Cassius has a reputation for taking bribes.

9. Brutus might want to ask the ghost about Portia. He might want to ask the ghost what will happen at Philippi. He might want to know what the underworld is like.

10. Students' responses will vary. Make sure students support their answers with details from the text and their own experiences.

Review and Assess

Literary Analysis

Conflict in Drama

1. Use a chart like the one shown to analyze the **internal conflicts** and **external conflicts** that trouble Brutus.

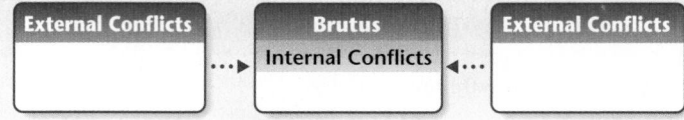

2. What external conflicts does Antony face?
3. What internal conflicts are revealed by the way Brutus responds to the ghost of Caesar?

Connecting Literary Elements

4. What have you known about Cassius that Brutus just begins to realize in this act?
5. How does the conflict between Cassius and Brutus heighten the **suspense** of the larger conflict to come?
6. Brutus and Cassius believe that they must fight now to succeed. What do they fail to see that builds the audience's suspense?

Reading Strategy

Reading Between the Lines

7. By **reading between the lines** of the argument between Antony and Octavius in Scene i, what do you learn about each man's character?
8. In Scene iii, Brutus says, "Cassius, you yourself / Are much condemned to have an itching palm, / To sell and mart your offices for gold / To undeservers." What is Brutus saying about Cassius?
9. Brutus tells the ghost, "I would hold more talk with thee." What can you infer that he would like to discuss with the ghost?

Extend Understanding

10. **Cultural Connection:** (a) What ideas about religion, medicine, and politics included in Act IV seem to belong more in ancient Rome than in our time? (b) What ideas still seem modern?

898 ◆ *Drama*

Quick Review

Conflict is a struggle between two forces. It may be **external**— between two characters or groups—or **internal,** involving a character's struggle to decide between opposing ideas or values.

Suspense is a feeling of tension about the way a conflict is going to turn out.

When you **read between the lines,** you discover deeper or different meanings to a character's words or actions.

 Take It to the Net

www.phschool.com

Take the interactive self-test online to check your understanding of the selection.

TEACHING RESOURCES

The following resources can be used to enrich or extend the instruction for p. 899.

Vocabulary

📖 **Selection Support,** Build Vocabulary, p. 209

📖 **Vocabulary and Spelling Practice Book** (Use this booklet for skills enrichment.) ▪

Grammar

📖 **Selection Support,** Build Grammar Skills, p. 210

✍ **Writing and Grammar,** Platinum Level, p. 577

📠 **Daily Language Practice Transparencies**

Writing

💿 **Writing and Grammar iText CD-ROM**

Integrate Language Skills

Vocabulary Development Lesson

Word Analysis: Greek Root *-phil-*

The Greek root *-phil-*, which means "love," appears in words such as *philosophy*, which can be defined as "a love of wisdom." Using this knowledge, define each *-phil-* word in a sentence using the word *love*.

1. philanthropist   3. Philadelphia
2. philharmonic   4. philology

Spelling Strategy

Form the plural of words ending in *y* preceded by a consonant by changing the *y* to an *i* and adding *-es*. For example, the plural form of *legacy* is *legacies*. Write the plural form of each word below.

1. philosophy   2. army   3. enemy

Fluency: Clarify Word Meaning

Copy the following sentences, completing each with a word from the vocabulary list on page 883.

1. In the atmosphere of suspicion following the assassination of Caesar, Antony and Octavius make ___?___ plans.
2. Cassius denies Brutus' ___?___ accusations.
3. What ___?___ did Caesar leave behind?
4. Brutus followed a ___?___ of Stoicism.
5. Brutus' ___?___ of Cassius for accepting bribery leads the men to engage in a bitter argument.

Grammar Lesson

Pronoun and Antecedent Agreement

Pronouns take the place of nouns or words that represent nouns. A pronoun must agree with its **antecedent** (the noun or pronoun it replaces) in **number** (singular or plural) and in **gender** (masculine, feminine, or neuter). In the example, the pronoun that is underlined agrees in number and gender with its antecedent in italics.

> *Cassius* is weary of the world;
> Hated by one <u>he</u> loves. (*singular, masculine*)

Practice Copy each sentence, completing it with a pronoun that agrees with its antecedent.

1. Cassius claims ___?___ has more experience.
2. The men prepared ___?___ army.
3. Portia has taken ___?___ own life.
4. Lucius went to get ___?___ lute.
5. The horse saw them and ___?___ neighed.

Writing Application Write two sentences about Act IV. Use a singular and a plural antecedent.

W_G Prentice Hall Writing and Grammar Connection: Chapter 24, Section 2

Extension Activities

Research and Technology Using computer software, produce a **slide-show presentation** on the philosophical movement called Stoicism. Determine which character in the play best embodies Stoicism, and include slides explaining your choice.

Writing Write a **profile** of Brutus for a magazine-style television news program. To describe him for audiences, include interviews with friends, "co-workers," and family members.

The Tragedy of Julius Caesar, Act IV ◆ 899

ASSESSMENT RESOURCES

The following resources can be used to assess students' knowledge and skills.

Selection Assessment
- 📖 **Formal Assessment**, pp. 185–187
- 📖 **Open Book Test**, pp. 157–159
- 📼 **Got It! Assessment Videotapes**, Tape 4
- 💿 **Test Bank Software**
- 💻 **Take It to the Net**
  Visit www.phschool.com for self-tests and additional questions on *Julius Caesar.*

Writing Rubric
- 📖 **Performance Assess. and Portfolio Mgmt.**, p. 19

PRENTICE HALL
ASSESSMENT *SYSTEM*
- 📖 **Workbook**   📕 **Transparencies**
- 📖 **Skill Book**   💿 **CD-ROM**

The Tragedy of Julius Caesar, Act V

Lesson Objectives

1. **To analyze and respond to literary elements**
   - Literary Analysis: Tragedy
   - Connecting Literary Elements: Tragic Flaw
2. **To read, comprehend, analyze, and critique a play**
   - Reading Strategy: Identifying Causes and Effects
   - Reading Check questions
   - Review and Assess questions
   - Assessment Practice (ATE)
3. **To develop word analysis skills, fluency, and systematic vocabulary**
   - Vocabulary Development Lesson: Anglo-Saxon Prefix: *mis-*
4. **To understand and apply written and oral language conventions**
   - Spelling Strategy
   - Grammar Lesson: Words of Direct Address
5. **To understand and apply appropriate writing and research strategies**
   - Writing Lesson: Persuasive Essay
   - Extension Activity: Model
6. **To understand and apply listening and speaking strategies**
   - Extension Activity: Perform a Scene

STEP-BY-STEP TEACHING GUIDE	PACING GUIDE
PRETEACH	
Motivate Students and Provide Background	
Read and discuss the Review and Anticipate information (SE/ATE p. 901)	5 min. 5 min.
Introduce the Concepts	
Introduce the Literary Analysis and Reading Strategy (SE/ATE p. 900) A	15 min.
Pronounce the vocabulary words and read their definitions (SE p. 900)	5 min.
TEACH	
Monitor Comprehension	
Informally monitor comprehension by circulating while students read independently or in groups A	25 min.
Monitor students' comprehension with the Reading Check notes (SE/ATE pp. 901, 903, 905, 907, 909, 911)	as students read
Develop vocabulary with Vocabulary notes (SE pp. 903, 904, 905, 907, 908, 912)	as students read
Develop Understanding	
Develop students' understanding of tragedy with the Literary Analysis annotations (SE pp. 902, 910, 911; ATE pp. 902, 910, 911) A	10 min.
Develop students' ability to identify cause and effect with the Reading Strategy annotations (SE pp. 901, 903, 905, 906, 908, 909, 910; ATE pp. 901, 903, 905, 906, 908, 909, 910)	10 min.
ASSESS	
Assess Mastery	
Assess students' mastery of the Reading Strategy and Literary Analysis by having them answer the Review and Assess questions (SE/ATE p. 913)	20 min.
Use one or more of the print and media Assessment Resources (ATE p. 915) A	up to 50 min.
EXTEND	
Apply Understanding	
Have students complete the Vocabulary Development Lesson and the Grammar Lesson (SE p. 914) A	20 min.
Apply students' knowledge of paraphrasing using the Writing Lesson (SE p. 915) A	45 min.
Apply students' understanding of the selection using one or more of the Extension Activities (SE p. 915)	20–90 min.

A **ACCELERATED INSTRUCTION:**
Use the strategies and activities identified with an **A**.

UNIVERSAL ACCESS
- ● = Below Level Students
- ▲ = On-Level Students
- ■ = Above Level Students

Time and Resource Manager

Reading Level: Challenging
Average Number of Instructional Days: 5

RESOURCES		
PRINT 📖	**TRANSPARENCIES**	**TECHNOLOGY** 💿 🎧
• **Beyond Literature,** Workplace Connection: Leadership Skills, p. 54 ▲ ■		• **Interest Grabber Video,** Tape 4 ● ▲ ■
• **Selection Support Workbook:** ● ▲ ■ Literary Analysis, p. 216 Reading Strategy, p. 215 Build Vocabulary, p. 213	• **Literary Analysis and Reading Transparencies,** pp. 107 and 108 ● ▲ ■	
		• **Listening to Literature** ● ▲ ■ Audiocassettes, Side 31 Audio CDs, CD 19
• **Literatura en español** ● ▲ • **Literary Analysis for Enrichment** ■		
• **Formal Assessment:** Selection Test, pp. 188–190 ● ▲ ■ • **Open Book Test,** pp. 160–162 ● ▲ ■ • **Performance Assessment and Portfolio Management,** p. 11 ● ▲ ■ • PRENTICE HALL ASSESSMENT *SYSTEM* ● ▲ ■	• PRENTICE HALL ASSESSMENT *SYSTEM* ● ▲ ■ Skills Practice Answers and Explanations on Transparencies	• **Test Bank Software** ● ▲ ■ • **Got It! Assessment Videotapes,** Tape 4 ● ▲
• **Selection Support Workbook:** ● ▲ ■ Build Grammar Skills, p. 214 • **Writing and Grammar,** Platinum Level ● ▲ ■ • **Extension Activities,** p. 54 ● ▲ ■	• **Daily Language Practice Transparencies** ● ▲	• **Writing and Grammar iText CD-ROM** ● ▲ ■ 🖥 *Take It to the Net* www.phschool.com

■ **BLOCK SCHEDULING:** Use one 90-minute class period to preteach the selection and have students read it. Use a second 90-minute class period to assess students' mastery of skills and have them complete one of the Extension Activities.

Step-by-Step Teaching Guide for p. 900

❶ Literary Analysis
Tragedy

- Go over the definition of *tragedy* with students. Help them to see that in literature, tragedy is not a generic term for "anything sad or horrible," but a genre with specific characteristics.

- Explain that the main character in a tragedy is often called the tragic hero. Discuss the characteristics of the tragic hero listed in the textbook. Ask students to list tragic heroes from real life or other works of literature.

- Have students think about which characters in this play qualify as tragic heroes—Brutus? Antony? Caesar? Cassius? Portia? Have students explain their answers. Remind them to use the definitions and explanations on this page.

❷ Reading Strategy
Identifying Causes and Effects

- Write a simple story in three sentences on the chalkboard, such as: *The dog smells the roast. The dog wants the roast. The dog steals the roast.* Help students see that these three sentences are linked by cause and effect. The first sentence causes the second; the second causes the third.

- Point out that a chain of causes and effects like this continues in both directions. Challenge students to suggest a cause for the dog's interest in the roast and an effect of its having stolen the roast. (Possible cause: forgetting to feed the dog. Possible effect: scolding.)

- List a few events from the first four acts of the play, and challenge students to name one cause and one effect of each.

 E-Teach

Visit E-Teach at www.phschool.com for teachers' essays on how to teach, with questions and answers.

Prepare to Read

The Tragedy of Julius Caesar, Act V

❶ Literary Analysis
Tragedy

Tragedy is a dramatic form that was first defined around 330 B.C. by the Greek philosopher Aristotle. It has these key characteristics:
- The main character is involved in a struggle that ends in disaster.
- This character is always a person of high rank who inevitably comes to ruin.

Tragedy arouses fear and pity in the audience and also may convey a sense of the nobility of the human spirit, even in the midst of suffering.

Connecting Literary Elements

The main character in a tragedy falls because of a **tragic flaw,** or weakness, in his or her character. The tragic flaw may be excessive ambition, pride, jealousy, or some other human frailty. As the play unfolds, Brutus' blindness to the true motives of the other conspirators leads him into disastrous alliances and actions. His downfall is tragic because he is a noble man who did the wrong thing for the right reason.

❷ Reading Strategy
Identifying Causes and Effects

A **cause** is what makes something occur; an **effect** is the result. Tragedies are carefully constructed with a chain of causes and effects that leads to the final tragic outcome.

To track interlocking causes and effects in *The Tragedy of Julius Caesar,* use a chart like the one shown.

Vocabulary Development

presage (prē sāj´) *v.* warn of a future event (p. 903)

ensign (en´ sīn) *n.* old word for a standard bearer; one who carries a flag (p. 903)

consorted (kən sôrt´ id) *v.* joined; accompanied (p. 904)

demeanor (di mēn´ ər) *n.* behavior (p. 905)

disconsolate (dis kän´ sə lit) *adj.* so unhappy that nothing will comfort (p. 907)

misconstrued (mis´ kən strōōd´) *v.* misunderstood; misinterpreted (p. 908)

envy (en´ vē) *n.* feeling of desire for another's possessions or qualities and jealousy at not having them (p. 912)

Cause
Caesar's interest in a crown

⋮
▼

Effect 1
Brutus thinks Caesar is too ambitious.

⋮
▼

Effect 2
Brutus helps plan and carry out Caesar's assassination.

TEACHING RESOURCES

The following resources can be used to enrich or extend the instruction for p. 900.

Motivation
 Interest Grabber Videotapes, Tape 4

Background
📖 **Beyond Literature,** p. 54

🖥 *Take It to the Net*
Visit www.phschool.com for background and hotlinks for *Julius Caesar.*

Literary Analysis
📄 **Literary Analysis and Reading Transparencies,** Tragedy, p. 107

Reading
📖 **Selection Support:** Reading Strategy, p. 215; Build Vocabulary, p. 213

📄 **Literary Analysis and Reading Transparencies,** Identifying Causes and Effects, p. 108

■ **BLOCK SCHEDULING:** Resources marked with this symbol provide varied instruction during 90-minute blocks.

Review and Anticipate

In Act IV, the alliance between Brutus and Cassius begins to fall apart. Brutus accuses Cassius of accepting bribes, and Cassius questions Brutus' abilities as a leader in war. After they resolve their differences, Brutus is visited by Caesar's ghost, who promises he will see him at Philippi.

❶ Act V opens on the plains of Philippi, with the armies ready for battle. Nothing less than the future of Rome is at stake.

Act V

Scene i. The plains of Philippi.

[*Enter* OCTAVIUS, ANTONY, *and their Army.*]

OCTAVIUS. Now, Antony, our hopes are answerèd;
You said the enemy would not come down,
But keep the hills and upper regions.
It proves not so; their battles¹ are at hand;
5 They mean to warn² us at Philippi here,
Answering before we do demand of them.³

❷ ANTONY. Tut, I am in their bosoms,⁴ and I know
Wherefore⁵ they do it. They could be content
To visit other places, and come down
10 With fearful bravery,⁶ thinking by this face⁷
To fasten in our thoughts⁸ that they have courage;
But 'tis not so.

[*Enter a* MESSENGER.]

MESSENGER.   Prepare you, generals,
The enemy comes on in gallant show;
Their bloody sign⁹ of battle is hung out,
15 And something to be done immediately.

ANTONY. Octavius, lead your battle softly¹⁰ on
Upon the left hand of the even¹¹ field.

OCTAVIUS. Upon the right hand I; keep thou the left.

ANTONY. Why do you cross me in this exigent?¹²

20 OCTAVIUS. I do not cross you; but I will do so.   [*March*]

[*Drum. Enter* BRUTUS, CASSIUS, *and their Army;* LUCILIUS, TITINIUS, MESSALA, *and others.*]

BRUTUS. They stand, and would have parley.¹³

---

1. **battles** armies.

2. **warn** challenge.

3. **Answering . . . of them** appearing in opposition to us before we challenge them.

4. **am in their bosoms** know what they are thinking.

Reading Strategy
Identifying Causes and Effects According to Antony, what has caused Brutus and Cassius to leave the hills and bring their armies to Philippi?

5. **Wherefore** why.

6. **fearful bravery** awesome show of bravery covering up their fear.

7. **face** appearance.

8. **fasten in our thoughts** convince us.

9. **bloody sign** red flag.

10. **softly** slowly.

11. **even** level.

12. **exigent** critical situation.

13. **parley** conference between enemies.

❸ ✓**Reading Check**
What news does the messenger bring?

The Tragedy of Julius Caesar, Act V, Scene i ◆ 901

TEACH

Step-by-Step Teaching Guide for pp. 901–912

CUSTOMIZE INSTRUCTION
For Musical/Rhythmic Learners
Invite students to share a piece of music that captures the mood of the battle scene. Have the rest of the class analyze the music and explain its suitability.

❶ Review and Anticipate
Antony and Octavius exchange insults with Brutus and Cassius at Philippi. Cassius realizes that today is his birthday. He and Brutus bid each other an affectionate farewell in case either or both are killed or captured.

Believing that his best friend Titinius has been captured, Cassius kills himself. Realizing that the battle is ending and Antony's side will win, Brutus kills himself. Antony and Octavius agree to give him an honorable state funeral.

❷ Reading Strategy
Identifying Causes and Effects
• Ask the Reading Strategy question on p. 901: According to Antony, what has caused Brutus and Cassius to leave the hills and bring their armies to Philippi?
Answer: Antony thinks they want to prove their courage.

• Ask why Octavius thinks they have attacked at Philippi.
Answer: Octavius thinks that the enemy prefers to attack first, instead of defending itself against an attack.

❸ ✓Reading Check
Answer: The messenger brings word that the enemy is ready to attack.

TEACHING RESOURCES

The following resources can be used to enrich or extend the instruction for pp. 901–912.

Literary Analysis
📖 **Selection Support:** Literary Analysis, p. 216

Reading
🎧 **Listening to Literature Audiocassettes,** Side 31 ▪
💿 **Listening to Literature Audio CDs,** CD 19 ▪

▪ **BLOCK SCHEDULING:** Resources marked with this symbol provide varied instruction during 90-minute blocks.

Tragedy

- Ask the Literary Analysis question on p. 902: How do Brutus' words in line 29—and Antony's response—highlight the tragedy?
  Answer: The words are a reminder of the assassination that has been Brutus' downfall.

- Ask students how Cassius' words (lines 45–47) help them define Brutus' tragic flaw.
  Possible answers: Brutus acted against his own noble nature when he took part in killing Caesar. His tragic flaw is his erroneous judgment, which led him to conspire with Cassius and to accept Antony's speeches in Act III at face value.

❺ ▶ Critical Viewing

Answer: The men hold weapons and shields and are wearing helmets and armor.

CASSIUS. Stand fast, Titinius, we must out and talk.

OCTAVIUS. Mark Antony, shall we give sign of battle?

ANTONY. No, Caesar, we will answer on their charge.[14]
25   Make forth;[15] the generals would have some words.

OCTAVIUS. Stir not until the signal.

BRUTUS. Words before blows; is it so, countrymen?

OCTAVIUS. Not that we love words better, as you do.

BRUTUS. Good words are better than bad strokes, Octavius.

30 ANTONY. In your bad strokes, Brutus, you give good words;
    Witness the hole you made in Caesar's heart,
    Crying "Long live! Hail, Caesar!"

CASSIUS.   Antony,
    The posture[16] of your blows are yet unknown;
    But for your words, they rob the Hybla bees,[17]
    And leave them honeyless.

35 ANTONY.   Not stingless too.

❹ BRUTUS. O, yes, and soundless too;
    For you have stol'n their buzzing, Antony,
    And very wisely threat before you sting.

ANTONY. Villains! You did not so, when your vile daggers
40   Hacked one another in the sides of Caesar.
    You showed your teeth[18] like apes, and fawned like hounds,
    And bowed like bondmen, kissing Caesar's feet;
    Whilst damnèd Casca, like a cur, behind
    Struck Caesar on the neck. O you flatterers!

45 CASSIUS. Flatterers! Now, Brutus, thank yourself;
    This tongue had not offended so today,
    If Cassius might have ruled.[19]

14. **answer on their charge** meet their advance.

15. **Make forth** go forward.

Literary Analysis
Tragedy How do Brutus' words in line 29—and Antony's response—highlight the tragedy?

16. **posture** quality.

17. **Hybla bees** bees from the town of Hybla in Sicily, noted for their sweet honey.

18. **showed your teeth** grinned.

19. **If Cassius might have ruled** if Cassius had had his way when he urged that Antony be killed.

❺ ▼ **Critical Viewing**
What details in this sculpture indicate that the subjects are preparing for battle? **[Analyze]**

Relief of Domitius Ahenobarbus, Louvre, Paris, France

Antony and Cleopatra

Mark Antony, one of the main characters of *Julius Caesar*, appears as one of the title characters of another, later Shakespearean tragedy—*Antony and Cleopatra*.

After Antony, Octavius, and Lepidus take power in Rome, Antony travels to Egypt, where he and Cleopatra fall passionately in love. Antony delays his return to Rome, too charmed to carry out his business of ensuring Egypt's alliance in Rome's war against

Sextus Pompey (son of the Pompey mentioned in *Julius Caesar*). When Antony marries Octavia (Octavius' sister) for political reasons, Cleopatra declares herself his enemy. Loyalties shift again: Antony and Cleopatra reunite and side with Pompey. Believing that Cleopatra is dead, Antony kills himself. Cleopatra, unwilling to live without him, also commits suicide. As in *Julius Caesar*, Octavius is left alive to order honorable funerals for his defeated enemies.

OCTAVIUS. Come, come, the cause.[20] If arguing make us sweat,
The proof[21] of it will turn to redder drops.

50　Look,
I draw a sword against conspirators.
When think you that the sword goes up[22] again?
Never, till Caesar's three and thirty wounds
Be well avenged; or till another Caesar

55　Have added slaughter to the sword of traitors.[23]

BRUTUS. Caesar, thou canst not die by traitors' hands,
Unless thou bring'st them with thee.

OCTAVIUS.　　　　　　　　　　　So I hope.
I was not born to die on Brutus' sword.

BRUTUS. O, if thou wert the noblest of thy strain,[24]

60　Young man, thou couldst not die more honorable.

CASSIUS. A peevish[25] schoolboy, worthless of such honor,
Joined with a masker and a reveler.[26]

ANTONY. Old Cassius still!

OCTAVIUS.　　　　　　　　Come, Antony; away!
Defiance, traitors, hurl we in your teeth.

65　If you dare fight today, come to the field;
If not, when you have stomachs.[27]

[Exit OCTAVIUS, ANTONY, *and Army.]*

CASSIUS. Why, now blow wind, swell billow, and swim bark![28]
The storm is up, and all is on the hazard.[29]

BRUTUS. Ho, Lucilius, hark, a word with you.

*[*LUCILIUS *and* MESSALA *stand forth.]*

LUCILIUS.　　　　　　　　　My lord?

*[*BRUTUS *and* LUCILIUS *converse apart.]*

CASSIUS. Messala.

MESSALA.　　　　　What says my general?

70　**CASSIUS.**　　　　　　　　　　　Messala,
This is my birthday; as this very day
Was Cassius born. Give me thy hand, Messala:
Be thou my witness that against my will
(As Pompey was)[30] am I compelled to set[31]

75　Upon one battle all our liberties.
You know that I held Epicurus strong,[32]
And his opinion; now I change my mind.
And partly credit things that do presage.
Coming from Sardis, on our former[33] ensign

80　Two mighty eagles fell,[34] and there they perched,

---

20. **cause** business at hand.

21. **proof** test.

22. **goes up** goes into its scabbard.

23. **till another Caesar . . . traitors** until I, another Caesar, have also been killed by you.

24. **noblest of thy strain** best of your family.

25. **peevish** silly.

26. **a masker and a reveler** one who takes part in masquerades and festivities.

27. **stomachs** appetites for battle.

28. **bark** ship.

29. **on the hazard** at stake.

Reading Strategy
Identifying Causes and Effects According to Cassius, what past action of Brutus has permitted Antony to insult them now?

30. **As Pompey was** Against his own judgment, Pompey was urged to do battle against Caesar. The battle resulted in Pompey's defeat and murder.

31. **set** stake.

32. **held Epicurus strong** believed in Epicurus' philosophy that the gods do not interest themselves in human affairs and that omens are merely superstitions.

presage (prē sāj´) v. warn of a future event

ensign (en´ sin´) n. old word for a standard bearer; one who carries a flag

33. **former** foremost.

34. **fell** swooped down.

❼ ✓Reading Check
What inspires Octavius and the others to battle?

The Tragedy of Julius Caesar, Act V, Scene i ◆ 903

---

❽ Critical Thinking

Compare and Contrast

- Have students compare and contrast Brutus' and Cassius' attitudes toward the coming battle.
  Answer: Cassius wants to bid a final farewell in case the worst happens; Brutus would rather not look ahead to what might happen.

- Ask students which attitude they agree with and why.
  Answer: Most students will probably agree with Cassius; it is better to be prepared for the worst.

❾ Background

Omens

Romans were extremely superstitious. It was an omen of disaster for a black cat to enter the house, a snake to fall from the roof into the yard, or a beam of the house to split. To spill wine, oil, or even water could also be a sign that bad things were about to happen. Another prophecy of bad luck was to encounter a mule carrying an herb called hipposelinum, which was used to decorate tombs. To stumble over the doorstep when leaving one's house was considered a bad omen. Many would choose to read this as a sign and hence spend the day at home.

> Gorging and feeding from our soldiers' hands,
> Who to Philippi here <u>consorted</u> us.
> This morning are they fled away and gone,
> And in their steads do ravens, crows, and kites◆
> 85 Fly o'er our heads and downward look on us
> As we were sickly prey; their shadows seem
> A canopy most fatal,[35] under which
> Our army lies, ready to give up the ghost.
>
> **MESSALA.** Believe not so.
>
> **CASSIUS.**   I but believe it partly,
> 90 For I am fresh of spirit and resolved
> To meet all perils very constantly.[36]
>
> **BRUTUS.** Even so, Lucilius.
>
> **CASSIUS.**   Now, most noble Brutus,
> The gods today stand friendly, that we may,
> Lovers in peace, lead on our days to age!
> 95 But since the affairs of men rest still incertain,[37]
> Let's reason with the worst that may befall.[38]
> If we do lose this battle, then is this
> The very last time we shall speak together.
> What are you then determinèd to do?
>
> ❽ 100 **BRUTUS.** Even by the rule of that philosophy
> By which I did blame Cato for the death
> Which he did give himself; I know not how,
> But I do find it cowardly and vile,
> For fear of what might fall, so to prevent
> 105 The time of life,[39] arming myself with patience
> To stay the providence[40] of some high powers
> That govern us below.
>
> **CASSIUS.**   Then, if we lose this battle,

consorted (kən sôrt′ id) v. joined; accompanied

35. A canopy most fatal a rooflike covering foretelling death.

36. very constantly most resolutely.

37. rest still incertain always remain uncertain.

38. befall happen.

39. so to prevent . . . life thus to anticipate the natural end of life.

40. stay the providence await the ordained fate.

---

❾ 𝓛iterature
in context Humanities Connection

◆ **Omens**

In observing the flight of eagles, ravens, crows, and kites, Cassius is looking for omens—signs of good or bad luck. The actions of animals as well as natural events, such as the storm in Act I, were regarded as omens in ancient times. It was believed that the gods sent these signs to warn humans of the consequences of their actions.

A Raven

You are contented to be led in triumph[41]
Thorough[42] the streets of Rome?

110 **BRUTUS.** No, Cassius, no; think not, thou noble Roman,
That ever Brutus will go bound to Rome;
He bears too great a mind. But this same day
Must end that work the ides of March begun;
And whether we shall meet again I know not.
115 Therefore our everlasting farewell take.
Forever, and forever, farewell, Cassius!
If we do meet again, why, we shall smile;
If not, why then this parting was well made.

CASSIUS. Forever, and forever, farewell, Brutus!
120 If we do meet again, we'll smile indeed;
If not, 'tis true this parting was well made.

BRUTUS. Why then, lead on. O, that a man might know
The end of this day's business ere it come!
But it sufficeth that the day will end,
125 And then the end is known. Come, ho! Away! [*Exit*]

Scene ii. *The field of battle.*

[*Call to arms sounds. Enter* BRUTUS *and* MESSALA.]

BRUTUS. Ride, ride, Messala, ride, and give these bills[1]
Unto the legions on the other side. [2]

[*Loud call to arms*]

Let them set on at once; for I perceive
But cold <u>demeanor</u>[3] in Octavius' wing,
5 And sudden push gives them the overthrow,[4]
Ride, ride, Messala! Let them all come down. [5]   [*Exit*]

Scene iii. *The field of battle.*

[*Calls to arms sound. Enter* CASSIUS *and* TITINIUS.]

CASSIUS. O, look, Titinius, look, the villains[1] fly!
Myself have to mine own turned enemy.[2]
This ensign here of mine was turning back;
I slew the coward, and did take it[3] from him.

5 **TITINIUS.** O Cassius, Brutus gave the word too early,
Who, having some advantage on Octavius,
Took it too eagerly; his soldiers fell to spoil,[4]
Whilst we by Antony are all enclosed.

[*Enter* PINDARUS.]

PINDARUS. Fly further off, my lord, fly further off!
10 Mark Antony is in your tents, my lord.
Fly, therefore, noble Cassius, fly far off!

---

41. in triumph as a captive in the victor's procession.

42. Thorough through.

**Reading Strategy
Identifying Causes and Effects** What causes Brutus to bid Cassius a final farewell?

1. bills written orders.

2. other side wing of the army commanded by Cassius.

3. cold demeanor (di mēn´ ər) lack of spirit in their conduct.

demeanor (di mēn´ ər) *n.* behavior

4. sudden push . . . overthrow sudden attack will defeat them.

5. Let . . . down attack all at once.

1. villains his own men.

2. Myself . . . enemy I have become an enemy to my own soldiers.

3. it banner or standard.

4. fell to spoil began to loot.

⑪ ✓Reading Check
What does Cassius believe the ravens, crows, and kites foretell?

---

⑩ Reading Strategy

Identifying Causes and Effects

- Ask the Reading Strategy question on p. 905: What causes Brutus to bid Cassius a final farewell?
  Answer: Brutus knows that they may not meet again.

- Why does Brutus refuse to "go bound to Rome"?
  Answer: Brutus would find it humiliating to be dragged through the streets in chains by his enemies.

⑪ ✓Reading Check

Answer: Cassius believes they foretell defeat and death.

The Tragedy of Julius Caesar, Act V, Scene iii ◆ 905

⓬ Reading Strategy

Identifying Causes and Effects

- Ask the Reading Strategy questions on p. 906: What causes Cassius to ask Pindarus to kill him? What might be some effects of Cassius' death?

  Answer: Cassius believes that his best friend Titinius has been captured. His death may mean the beginning of defeat for the conspirators; his soldiers are left without a commander.

- Ask why Cassius reacts so strongly to Titinius' capture.

  Answer: They are the closest of friends; Cassius feels responsible for Titinius because Cassius is the one who insisted on killing Caesar.

CASSIUS. This hill is far enough. Look, look, Titinius!
Are those my tents where I perceive the fire?

TITINIUS. They are, my lord.

CASSIUS. Titinius, if thou lovest me,
15 Mount thou my horse and hide[5] thy spurs in him
Till he have brought thee up to yonder troops
And here again, that I may rest assured
Whether yond troops are friend or enemy.

TITINIUS. I will be here again even with a thought.[6] [*Exit*]

CASSIUS. Go, Pindarus, get higher on that hill;
20 My sight was ever thick.[7] Regard[8] Titinius,
And tell me what thou not'st about the field.

[*Exit* PINDARUS.]

This day I breathèd first. Time is come round,
And where I did begin, there shall I end.
My life is run his compass.[9] Sirrah, what news?

25 **PINDARUS.** [*Above*] O my lord!

CASSIUS. What news?

PINDARUS. [*Above*] Titinius is enclosèd round about
With horsemen that make to him on the spur;[10]
Yet he spurs on. Now they are almost on him.
30 Now, Titinius! Now some light.[11] O, he lights too!
He's ta'en![12][*Shout*] And, hark! They shout for joy.

CASSIUS. Come down; behold no more.
O, coward that I am, to live so long,
To see my best friend ta'en before my face!

35 [*Enter* PINDARUS.]

⓬ Come hither, sirrah.
In Parthia did I take thee prisoner;
And then I swore thee, saving of thy life,
That whatsoever I did bid thee do,
40 Thou shouldst attempt it. Come now, keep thine oath.
Now be a freeman, and with this good sword,
That ran through Caesar's bowels, search[13] this bosom.
Stand not[14] to answer. Here, take thou the hilts,
And when my face is covered, as 'tis now,
45 Guide thou the sword—Caesar, thou art revenged,
Even with the sword that killed thee. [*Dies*]

PINDARUS. So, I am free; yet would not so have been,
Durst I have done my will. O Cassius!
Far from this country Pindarus shall run,
50 Where never Roman shall take note of him. [*Exit*]

5. **hide** sink.

6. **even with a thought** as quick as a thought.

7. **thick** dim.

8. **Regard** observe.

9. **his compass** its full course.

10. **make . . . spur** ride toward him at top speed.

11. **light** dismount from their horses.

12. **ta'en** taken; captured.

Reading Strategy

Identifying Causes and Effects What causes Cassius to ask Pindarus to kill him? What might be some effects of Cassius' death?

13. **search** penetrate.

14. **Stand not** do not wait.

▲ **Critical Viewing** This battle is the outcome of events that were set in motion earlier in the play. What is the original cause that leads to this battle? **[Analyze]**

[*Enter* TITINIUS *and* MESSALA.]

    MESSALA. It is but change,[15] Titinius; for Octavius
        Is overthrown by noble Brutus' power,
        As Cassius' legions are by Antony.

    TITINIUS. These tidings will well comfort Cassius.

    MESSALA. Where did you leave him?

55   **TITINIUS.**   All <u>disconsolate</u>,
        With Pindarus his bondman, on this hill.

    MESSALA. Is not that he that lies upon the ground?

    TITINIUS. He lies not like the living. O my heart!

    MESSALA. Is not that he?

    TITINIUS.   No, this was he, Messala,
60   But Cassius is no more. O setting sun,
        As in thy red rays thou dost sink to night,
        So in his red blood Cassius' day is set.
        The sun of Rome is set. Our day is gone;
        Clouds, dews, and dangers come; our deeds are done!
65   Mistrust of my success[16] hath done this deed.

    MESSALA. Mistrust of good success hath done this deed.
        O hateful Error, Melancholy's child,[17]
        Why dost thou show to the apt thoughts of men
        The things that are not?[18] O Error, soon conceived,[19]
70   Thou never com'st unto a happy birth,
        But kill'st the mother that engend'red thee![20]

    TITINIUS. What, Pindarus! Where art thou, Pindarus?

15. change an exchange.

disconsolate (dis kän´ sə lit) *adj.* so unhappy that nothing will comfort

16. Mistrust . . . success fear that I would not succeed.

17. Melancholy's child one of despondent temperament.

18. Why dost . . . are not? Why do you fill these easily impressed men with thoughts of imagined fears?

19. conceived created.

20. mother . . . thee Cassius (in this case), who conceived the error.

⓮ ✔Reading Check
What does Cassius think has happened to Titinius?

The Tragedy of Julius Caesar, Act V, Scene iii ◆ 907

⓭ ▶Critical Viewing

Point out to students that no battle scene like this takes place in the play as it is written. Shakespeare's stage was not large enough to accommodate many actors at once, and most of the fighting took place offstage. In a film, of course, there are no limitations of space, and it is dramatically appropriate to stage this scene. Answer: Students may say that Caesar's ambition leads to the battle, or they may say that his murder, or Antony's reaction to the murder, are the original causes of the battle.

⓮ ✔Reading Check

Answer: Cassius thinks Titinius has been captured by the enemy.

CUSTOMIZE INSTRUCTION FOR UNIVERSAL ACCESS

For Special Needs Students	For Gifted/Talented Students
Students may find the battle scenes confusing, because the characters on stage are describing fighting that occurs offstage. Have students work together in a group to read the battle scenes aloud and write out a brief summary of the battle as a whole.	Have students discuss the effectiveness of the battle scenes in the play. Note that the fighting takes place offstage. Ask how well students think Shakespeare solved the problem of having to keep the battles offstage. Students may want to watch the 1953 movie on video to compare and contrast the film's approach to staging the battles with the play's approach.

- Ask the Reading Strategy question on p. 908: What series of effects results from Pindarus' false report? **Answer:** Cassius kills himself. When Titinius discovers the body and the reason for Cassius' death, he also kills himself.

- Ask what effect Cassius' death is likely to have on Brutus. **Answer:** Brutus will probably feel sincere personal grief for his friend and doubts about the army's ability to win the battle without him.

MESSALA. Seek him, Titinius, whilst I go to meet
The noble Brutus, thrusting this report

75   Into his ears. I may say "thrusting" it;
For piercing steel and darts envenomèd[21]
Shall be as welcome to the ears of Brutus
As tidings of this sight.

TITINIUS.   Hie you, Messala,
And I will seek for Pindarus the while.   [*Exit* MESSALA.]

80   Why didst thou send me forth, brave[22] Cassius?
Did I not meet thy friends, and did not they
Put on my brows this wreath of victory,
And bid me give it thee? Didst thou not hear their shouts?
Alas, thou hast misconstrued everything!

85   But hold thee,[23] take this garland on thy brow;
Thy Brutus bid me give it thee, and I
Will do his bidding. Brutus, come apace,[24]
And see how I regarded[25] Caius Cassius.
By your leave,[26] gods. This is a Roman's part:[27]

⓯ 90   Come, Cassius' sword, and find Titinius' heart.   [*Dies*]

[*Call to arms sounds. Enter* BRUTUS, MESSALA, YOUNG CATO, STRATO,
VOLUMNIUS, *and* LUCILIUS.]

BRUTUS. Where, where, Messala, doth his body lie?

MESSALA. Lo, yonder, and Titinius mourning it.

BRUTUS. Titinius' face is upward.

CATO.   He is slain.

BRUTUS. O Julius Caesar, thou art mighty yet!

95   Thy spirit walks abroad, and turns our swords
In our own proper entrails.[28]   [*Low calls to arms*]

CATO.   Brave Titinius!
Look, whe'r[29] he have not crowned dead Cassius.

BRUTUS. Are yet two Romans living such as these?
The last of all the Romans, fare thee well!

100   It is impossible that ever Rome
Should breed thy fellow.[30] Friends, I owe moe tears
To this dead man than you shall see me pay.
I shall find time, Cassius; I shall find time.
Come, therefore, and to Thasos[31] send his body;

105   His funerals shall not be in our camp,
Lest it discomfort us.[32] Lucilius, come,
And come, young Cato; let us to the field.
Labeo and Flavius set our battles[33] on.
'Tis three o'clock; and, Romans, yet ere night

110   We shall try fortune in a second fight.   [*Exit*]

21. **envenomèd** poisoned.

22. **brave** noble.

misconstrued (mis´ kən
strood´) *v.* misunderstood;
misinterpreted

23. **hold thee** wait a moment.

24. **apace** quickly.

25. **regarded** honored.

26. **By your leave** with your permission.

27. **part** role; duty.

Reading Strategy
**Identifying Causes and
Effects** What series of
effects result from
Pindarus' false report?

28. **own proper entrails** very own inner organs.

29. **whe'r** whether.

30. **fellow** equal.

31. **Thasos** an island not far from Philippi.

32. **discomfort us** discourage our soldiers.

33. **battles** armies.

❉ ENRICHMENT: Career Connection

Military Careers

Military battles play important roles in many of Shakespeare's tragedies. While the United States has not been involved in a major war for decades, more than 500,000 U. S. Army personnel are on active duty today. Women as well as men pursue careers in the Army, Navy, Air Force, and Marines. Have students find out about career opportunities in the military, including training, education, pay, benefits, and years of service required.

Scene iv. *The field of battle.*

[*Call to arms sounds. Enter* BRUTUS, MESSALA, YOUNG CATO, LUCILIUS, *and* FLAVIUS.]

BRUTUS. Yet, countrymen, O, yet hold up your heads!

[*Exit, with followers*]

CATO. What bastard[1] doth not? Who will go with me?
I will proclaim my name about the field.
I am the son of Marcus Cato,[2] ho!
5   A foe to tyrants, and my country's friend.
I am the son of Marcus Cato, ho!

[*Enter* SOLDIERS *and fight.*]

LUCILIUS. And I am Brutus, Marcus Brutus, I;
Brutus, my country's friend; know me for Brutus![3]

[YOUNG CATO *falls.*]

O young and noble Cato, art thou down?
10   Why, now thou diest as bravely as Titinius,
And mayst be honored, being Cato's son.

FIRST SOLDIER. Yield, or thou diest.

LUCILIUS.   Only I yield to die.[4]
There is so much that thou wilt kill me straight;[5]
Kill Brutus, and be honored in his death.

15 **FIRST SOLDIER.** We must not. A noble prisoner!

[*Enter* ANTONY.]

SECOND SOLDIER. Room, ho! Tell Antony, Brutus is ta'en.

FIRST SOLDIER. I'll tell thee news. Here comes the general.
Brutus is ta'en, Brutus is ta'en, my lord.

ANTONY. Where is he?

20 **LUCILIUS.** Safe, Antony; Brutus is safe enough.
I dare assure thee that no enemy
Shall ever take alive the noble Brutus.
The gods defend him from so great a shame!
When you do find him, or alive or dead,
25   He will be found like Brutus, like himself.[6]

ANTONY. This is not Brutus, friend, but, I assure you,
A prize no less in worth. Keep this man safe;
Give him all kindness. I had rather have
Such men my friends than enemies. Go on,
30   And see whe'r Brutus be alive or dead,
And bring us word unto[7] Octavius' tent
How everything is chanced.[8]

                                           [*Exit*]

Reading Strategy
Identifying Causes and Effects What does Brutus hope will be the effect of this command to his troops?

1. bastard person who is not a true Roman.

2. Marcus Cato Brutus' wife's father

3. And I am . . . Brutus Lucilius impersonates Brutus in order to protect him and confuse the enemy.

4. Only . . . die I will surrender only to die.

5. much . . . straight much honor in it that you will kill me immediately.

6. like himself behaving in a noble way.

7. unto in.

8. is chanced has happened.

17 ✔**Reading Check**
Why does Lucilius say that he is Brutus?

The Tragedy of Julius Caesar, Act V, Scene iv ◆ 909

16 **Reading Strategy**
Identifying Causes and Effects
- Ask the Reading Strategy question on p. 909: What does Brutus hope will be the effect of this command to his troops?
  Answer: He hopes that they will not lose courage.
- Why does Brutus think his command will have this effect?
  Answer: He knows that his men will obey him because he is their leader and because they respect him.

17 ✔**Reading Check**
Answer: Lucilius is ready to die in Brutus' place.

CUSTOMIZE INSTRUCTION FOR UNIVERSAL ACCESS

For Advanced Readers

Students interested in learning more about Julius Caesar, Octavius, and the other Roman emperors will enjoy dipping into *The Twelve Caesars*, a lively, gossipy account of Rome's first dozen absolute rulers by Roman historian Gaius Suetonius Tranquillus (c. A.D. 69–140). Suetonius briefly practiced law but spent most of his career as a palace official, including a secretaryship under the emperor Hadrian. Suetonius lived through nearly 30 years of the events he described. His sources included official imperial and senatorial records, memoirs, and various public documents. Encourage students to read Suetonius' accounts of one or more of the Caesars and to share their findings with the class.

Identifying Causes and Effects

- Ask the Reading Strategy questions on p. 910: What is the cause of Brutus' despair? What is the effect?

  Answer: Brutus knows that the battle is lost. He has decided to kill himself.

- Ask why the ghost of Caesar comes to visit Brutus again.

  Answer: The ghost wants to be sure of his revenge.

⓳ Literary Analysis

Tragedy

- Ask the Literary Analysis question on p. 910: What characteristics of tragedy are evoked by Brutus' words?

  Answer: Brutus' words reveal that his downfall is complete.

- Have students try to define the aspects of Brutus' character that cause his fall.

  Answer: Brutus' tragic flaw is his error in judgment. He was wrong in trusting Cassius' motives for killing Caesar and for trusting Antony to speak over Caesar's body.

Scene v. *The field of battle.*

[*Enter* BRUTUS, DARDANIUS, CLITUS, STRATO, *and* VOLUMNIUS.]

BRUTUS. Come, poor remains[1] of friends, rest on this rock.

CLITUS. Statilius showed the torchlight,[2] but, my lord,
  He came not back; he is or ta'en or slain.

BRUTUS. Sit thee down, Clitus. Slaying is the word;
5 It is a deed in fashion. Hark thee, Clitus. [*Whispers*]

CLITUS. What, I, my lord? No, not for all the world!

BRUTUS. Peace then, no words.

CLITUS.   I'll rather kill myself.

BRUTUS. Hark thee, Dardanius.   [*Whispers*]

DARDANIUS.   Shall I do such a deed?

CLITUS. O Dardanius!

10 DARDANIUS. O Clitus!

⓲ CLITUS. What ill request did Brutus make to thee?

DARDANIUS. To kill him, Clitus. Look, he meditates.

CLITUS. Now is that noble vessel[3] full of grief,
  That it runs over even at his eyes.

15 BRUTUS. Come hither, good Volumnius; list[4] a word.

⓳ VOLUMNIUS. What says my lord?

BRUTUS.   Why, this, Volumnius:
  The ghost of Caesar hath appeared to me
  Two several[5] times by night; at Sardis once,
  And this last night here in Philippi fields.
  I know my hour is come.

20 VOLUMNIUS.   Not so, my lord.

BRUTUS. Nay, I am sure it is, Volumnius.
  Thou seest the world, Volumnius, how it goes;
  Our enemies have beat us to the pit.[6]

                         [*Low calls to arms*]

  It is more worthy to leap in ourselves
25 Than tarry till they push us.[7] Good Volumnius,
  Thou know'st that we two went to school together;
  Even for that our love of old, I prithee
  Hold thou my sword-hilts whilst I run on it.

VOLUMNIUS. That's not an office[8] for a friend, my lord.

                         [*Call to arms still*]

Reading Strategy
Identifying Causes and Effects What is the cause of Brutus' despair? What is the effect?

1. poor remains pitiful survivors.

2. showed the torchlight signaled with a torch.

3. vessel human being.

4. list hear.

5. several separate.

Literary Analysis
Tragedy What characteristics of tragedy are evoked by Brutus' words?

6. pit trap or grave.

7. tarry . . . us wait until they kill us.

8. office task.

☀ ENRICHMENT: History Connection

The Roman Empire

The year 27 B.C. marked the end of the Roman republic. In that year, Octavius became Rome's first emperor. He held supreme authority over Rome, with the aid and advice of the Senate. The emperor or the army appointed each successive emperor.

As time went on, the Senate lost its power. Rome became an absolute monarchy that controlled many provinces. It reached from northern Britain to the shores of the Red Sea and the Persian Gulf.

Provinces of the empire included Hibernia, Britannia, Gallia or Gaul, Hispania, Achaia, and Aegyptus (Scotland, England, France, Spain, Greece, and Egypt). The provinces were ruled by Roman governors and staffs of military assistants. Local officials were allowed to manage some local affairs.

CLITUS. Fly, fly, my lord, there is no tarrying here.

BRUTUS. Farewell to you; and you; and you,
    Volumnius.
    Strato, thou hast been all this while asleep;
    Farewell to thee too, Strato. Countrymen,
35 My heart doth joy that yet in all my life
    I found no man but he was true to me.
    I shall have glory by this losing day
    More than Octavius and Mark Antony
    By this vile conquest shall attain unto.[9]
    So fare you well at once, for Brutus' tongue
40 Hath almost ended his life's history.
    Night hangs upon mine eyes; my bones
        would rest,
    That have but labored to attain this hour.[10]

[*Call to arms sounds. Cry within, "Fly, fly, fly!"*]

CLITUS. Fly, my lord, fly!

BRUTUS.   Hence! I will follow.

[*Exit* CLITUS, DARDANIUS, *and* VOLUMNIUS.]

    I prithee, Strato, stay thou by thy lord,
45 Thou art a fellow of a good respect.[11]
    Thy life hath had some smatch[12] of honor in it;
    Hold then my sword, and turn away thy face,
    While I do run upon it. Wilt thou, Strato?

STRATO. Give me your hand first. Fare you well, my lord.

50 **BRUTUS.** Farewell, good Strato—Caesar, now be still;
    I killed not thee with half so good a will.   [*Dies*]

[*Call to arms sounds. Retreat sounds. Enter* ANTONY, OCTAVIUS, MESSALA, LUCILIUS, *and the Army.*]

OCTAVIUS. What man is that?

MESSALA. My master's man.[13] Strato, where is thy master?

STRATO. Free from the bondage you are in, Messala;
55 The conquerors can but make a fire of him
    For Brutus only overcame himself,
    And no man else hath honor[14] by his death.

LUCILIUS. So Brutus should be found. I thank thee, Brutus,
    That thou hast proved Lucilius' saying[15] true.

60 **OCTAVIUS.** All that served Brutus, I will entertain them.[16]
    Fellow, wilt thou bestow[17] thy time with me?

STRATO. Ay, if Messala will prefer[18] me to you.

OCTAVIUS. Do so, good Messala.

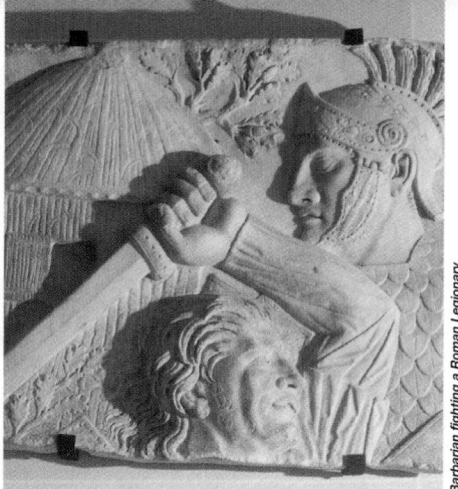

Barbarian fighting a Roman Legionary,
Roman stone relief 2nd cent, Louvre, Paris, France

▲ **Critical Viewing** What details in this sculpture indicate conflict, triumph, and defeat? **[Analyze]** ⓴

9. By this . . . unto by this evil victory shall gain. (Brutus sees the victory of Octavius and Antony as causing the downfall of Roman freedom.)

10. this hour time of death.

11. respect reputation.

12. smatch smack or taste.

Literary Analysis
Tragedy How do Brutus' final words reflect his nobility?

13. man servant.

14. no man else hath honor no other man gains honor.

15. Lucilius' saying see Act V, Scene iv, lines 21, 22.

16. entertain them take them into my service.

17. bestow spend.

18. prefer recommend.

⓶⓶ ✓**Reading Check**
What does Brutus whisper to Dardanius?

The Tragedy of Julius Caesar, Act V, Scene v ◆ 911

⓴ ▶**Critical Viewing**
Answer: The sword and war helmet indicate conflict. The facial expressions indicate triumph and defeat.

㉑ **Literary Analysis**
Tragedy

• Have a volunteer read lines 31–42 aloud. Ask how these lines support the notion of Brutus as a tragic hero.
  Answer: Brutus says "I found no man but he was true to me"; this states Brutus' tragic flaw. In different ways, Cassius, Caesar, and Antony were all untrue to him. Cassius used Brutus for his own purposes when he manipulated him into joining the conspiracy; Caesar betrayed Brutus' trust with his plans to become emperor; Antony lied to Brutus and deliberately stirred up the people of Rome against him.

• Ask the Literary Analysis question on p. 911: How do Brutus' final words reflect his nobility?
  Answer: Brutus shows concern and kindness toward his soldiers, urging them to save themselves (line 43), and courageously determines to take responsibility for his own fate.

▶ Monitor Progress Ask students what they think of Brutus' decision. Does he deserve to die? Why or why not?
  Answer: Students will probably admire him and feel sorry for his death; some may say that since he is an assassin he deserves to die; some may point out that he would have been executed by his enemies, and it is better for him to die with honor.

㉒ ✓**Reading Check**
Answer: Brutus asks Dardanius to hold his sword while he impales himself on it.

CUSTOMIZE INSTRUCTION FOR UNIVERSAL ACCESS

For Advanced Readers

Challenge students who enjoyed this play to form a small reading group in which to read and discuss *Macbeth*, a later tragedy by Shakespeare. *Macbeth* and *Julius Caesar* share many of the same themes and issues. A man of high rank assassinates the king; a ghost appears to warn him of his fate; political intrigue and conflict abound. In their discussion of the play, students should compare and contrast it to *Julius Caesar*. How are the heroes of the plays alike? How are they different? What role does the supernatural

play in each story? Students may want to perform a scene or two from *Macbeth* for the class so that everyone can participate in a discussion.

Answers for p. 912

Review and Assess

1. Possible answers: If a good person does something wrong for the right reasons, it can still turn out badly. Beware of whose company you keep. Watch out for flatterers. Never underestimate your enemy.

2. **(a)** He sees ravens, kites, and crows. **(b)** He thinks they are signs of defeat and death.

3. **(a)** Neither wants to be dragged through the streets of Rome as a defeated prisoner. They are too proud. **(b)** Cassius asks Pindarus to kill him. Brutus asks several men, who all refuse. Strato finally agrees to hold the sword so that Brutus can kill himself. **(c)** Cassius' death will put an end to his own grief, but Brutus' death will put an end to the fighting, and therefore save many lives.

4. **(a)** Brutus orders his men to get to a place of safety, leaving him behind. He speaks kindly to Strato and claims that he kills himself with a good will. **(b)** He does what he sees as his duty without complaining and after having taken care of his responsibility to his followers.

5. **(a)** Antony has hated Brutus and described him as a butcher and a traitor. **(b)** He acknowledges that Brutus acted from a sense of duty to Rome and that he was a good man.

6. **(a)** Students can assume that Antony and Octavius will rule Rome; some may know the history and say that Octavius eventually becomes emperor. **(b)** Students who don't know the history might say it will be bad for Rome because Octavius and Antony are not sympathetic characters, and because the people might lose the rights they had when Rome was a republic. Those who know that Octavius became emperor will say that he brought peace to the empire, so it was good for Rome.

MESSALA. How died my master, Strato?

65 STRATO. I held the sword, and he did run on it.

MESSALA. Octavius, then take him to follow thee,
That did the latest service to my master.

ANTONY. This was the noblest Roman of them all.
All the conspirators save[19] only he
70 Did that[20] they did in <u>envy</u> of great Caesar;
He, only in a general honest thought
And common good to all, made one of them.[21]
His life was gentle,[22] and the elements
So mixed[23] in him that Nature might stand up
75 And say to all the world, "This was a man!"

OCTAVIUS. According to his virtue,[24] let us use[25] him
With all respect and rites of burial.
Within my tent his bones tonight shall lie,
Most like a soldier ordered honorably.[26]
80 So call the field[27] to rest, and let's away
To part[28] the glories of this happy day.   [*Exit all.*]

19. **save** except.

20. **that** what.

21. **made one of them** became one of the conspirators.

envy (en′ vē) *n.* feeling of desire for another's possessions or qualities and jealousy at not having them

22. **gentle** noble.

23. **So mixed** well balanced.

24. **virtue** excellence.

25. **use** treat.

26. **ordered honorably** treated with honor.

27. **field** army.

28. **part** share.

Review and Assess

Thinking About Act V

1. **Respond:** What lessons did you learn from the play?

2. **(a) Recall:** What omens does Cassius see before the battle? **(b) Analyze Cause and Effect:** What effect do the omens have on him?

3. **(a) Recall:** Why do Cassius and Brutus both plan to kill themselves should they lose the battle? **(b) Compare and Contrast:** What are some key differences in their deaths? **(c) Interpret:** How do these differences reflect the contrast in each man's character?

4. **(a) Recall:** What are Brutus' final words? **(b) Interpret:** How do these words reveal his essential nobility?

5. **(a) Recall:** How has Antony felt toward Brutus throughout most of the play? **(b) Infer:** How and why does Antony's attitude toward Brutus change at the end?

6. **(a) Speculate:** Now that Octavius and Antony have triumphed, what do you think will become of the Roman republic? **(b) Evaluate:** Do you think this will be a good or a bad thing?

912 ◆ Drama

ASSESSMENT PRACTICE: Reading Comprehension

Identify Patterns of Organization   **(For more practice, see Test Preparation Workbook, p. 54.)**

Many tests require students to identify patterns of organization. Use this sample test item.

The main character of a tragedy is always a person of high rank whose ruin is caused by a tragic flaw such as ambition, pride, or jealousy. As this play unfolds, Brutus' blindness leads him into disastrous alliances.

Which pattern of organization does the passage demonstrate?

A cause and effect
B order of importance
C chronological
D specific to general

The phrase "is caused by" shows that the correct answer is *A*.

Review and Assess

Literary Analysis

Tragedy

1. Using a chart like the one shown, list examples from the play that illustrate its qualities as a **tragedy**.

Qualities of Tragedy	Examples from *Julius Caesar*
Main character is person of rank	Brutus is a Roman nobleman and military leader.
Main character comes to ruin	

2. In Act V, Scene i, both Brutus and Antony refer to "bad strokes" and "good words." How do these words summarize the tragedy?
3. Find two passages in the play that show that Brutus is a noble man.

Connecting Literary Elements

4. What is Brutus' **tragic flaw**?
5. Once Brutus joined the conspirators, could he turn back? Explain.
6. (a) In what ways is Caesar also a tragic hero? (b) What was his tragic flaw?

Reading Strategy

Identifying Causes and Effects

7. Using a chart like the one shown, identify three **effects** that are **caused** by Caesar's death.

8. (a) What is the immediate cause of Cassius' death? (b) What are two effects of his death?
9. (a) What is the immediate cause of Brutus' suicide? (b) What do you think its effect will be?

Extend Understanding

10. **History Connection:** Compare another defeated leader from history to Brutus. Explain how the circumstances, possible motives, and outcomes are similar or different.

The Tragedy of Julius Caesar, Act V ◆ 913

Quick Review

A **tragedy** is a dramatic form in which a character of high rank is involved in a struggle that ends in disaster.

A **tragic flaw** is a weakness in the main character of a tragedy that causes his or her downfall.

A **cause** is the reason something occurs.

An **effect** is the result of another event or circumstance.

 Take It to the Net

www.phschool.com

Take the interactive self-test online to check your understanding of the selection.

✸ **ENRICHMENT: Further Reading**

Other Works by William Shakespeare

Antony and Cleopatra
Titus Andronicus
Macbeth

Take It to the Net

Visit www.phschool.com for more information on William Shakespeare.

Answers for p. 914

❶ Vocabulary Development

Word Analysis

1. A misnomer is a wrong name.
2. A misanthrope thinks humankind is bad.
3. Misconduct is bad behavior.

Spelling Strategy

1. believing
2. arguably
3. fortunate

Concept Development: Synonyms

1. a
2. c
3. c
4. b
5. b
6. a
7. b

❷ Grammar

1. Prepare, <u>you generals</u>! The enemy comes on.
2. <u>Octavius</u>, lead your battle softly on.
3. No, <u>Caesar</u>, we will answer on their charge.
4. Flatterers! Now, <u>Brutus</u>, thank yourself.
5. <u>Mark Antony</u>, shall we give sign of battle?

Writing Application

1. Tell me, Lucius, how the battle is going.
2. Look, Casca, and you will see a great man.

914

Integrate Language Skills

❶ Vocabulary Development Lesson

Word Analysis: Anglo-Saxon Prefix *mis-*

The word *misconstrued* contains the Anglo-Saxon prefix *mis-*, meaning "wrong" or "bad." *Misconstrue* means "make the wrong interpretation." In your notebook, define each word in a sentence using *wrong* or *bad*.

1. misnomer
2. misanthrope
3. misconduct

Spelling Strategy

When a word ends in a silent *e*, drop the *e* before adding a suffix that begins with a vowel. For example, *disconsolate* + *-ation* = *disconsolation*. In your notebook, write each word, adding the suffix in parentheses.

1. believe (*-ing*)
2. argue (*-ably*)
3. fortune (*-ate*)

Concept Development: Synonyms

Choose the letter of the word that is a synonym for the first word.

1. misconstrued: (a) confused, (b) insulted, (c) understood
2. presage: (a) help, (b) review, (c) predict
3. disconsolate: (a) joyful, (b) angry, (c) cheerless
4. consorted: (a) abandoned, (b) accompanied, (c) served
5. demeanor: (a) feelings, (b) behavior, (c) respect
6. ensign: (a) flag-bearer, (b) signature, (c) jailer
7. envy: (a) love, (b) jealousy, (c) sadness

❷ Grammar Lesson

Words of Direct Address

Dialogue is the backbone of any drama: With the exceptions of asides and soliloquies, the characters are always speaking to one another. To emphasize the person or thing to whom a character is speaking, the playwright sets off these **words of direct address** with commas and, to show intense emotion, an exclamation point. Look at these examples from Act V:

> Now, *Antony*, our hopes are answerèd.
>
> Fly further off, *my lord*, fly further off!
>
> O *Cassius!*/ Far from this country Pindarus shall run, . . .

Practice Write these sentences in your notebook, underlining words of direct address and inserting the proper punctuation.

1. Prepare you generals the enemy comes on.
2. Octavius lead your battle softly on.
3. No Caesar we will answer on their charge.
4. Flatterers now Brutus thank yourself.
5. Mark Antony shall we give sign of battle?

Writing Application Revise the sentences below, adding words of direct address and punctuating them correctly.

1. Tell me how the battle is going.
2. Look and you will see a great man.

𝒲𝒢 *Prentice Hall Writing and Grammar Connection: Chapter 28, Section 2*

914 ◆ *Drama*

Writing Lesson

Persuasive Essay

Throughout the play, Brutus defends his reasons for killing Caesar. Antony just as eloquently states why Caesar should not have been killed. Write a position paper taking either Brutus' or Antony's part.

Prewriting Decide which part you want to take, and gather details from the play that support that position. Paraphrase the reasons given by either Brutus or Antony, depending on which part you choose.

> **Model: Paraphrasing**
>
> **Brutus:** "Had you rather Caesar were living, and die all slaves, than that Caesar were dead, to live all free men?" (III, ii, 23–24)
>
> **Paraphrase:** Would it be better if Caesar were alive and you were all slaves or if Caesar were dead and you were all free? (III, ii, 23–24)

A paraphrase of key lines from the play clarify each man's position.

Drafting Begin your paper with a statement of the position you have chosen. Elaborate on your statement by providing details and quotations to explain and illustrate your ideas.

Revising Once you have completed your first draft, make sure that it contains the details needed to be effective. Check to be sure that you have developed and supported your argument in the body of the paper.

 Prentice Hall Writing and Grammar Connection: Chapter 7, Section 2

Extension Activities

Listening and Speaking If you can, view a Shakespeare play by attending a local live production or by renting a video of one to watch in a small group. After viewing, **perform a scene** from the play.

- Choose a scene that the group found especially moving or dramatic.
- Assign roles for the scene.
- Have group members read their parts in a dramatic way.

Compare your group's treatment with that in the production you saw. **[Group Activity]**

Research and Technology Many of Shakespeare's plays were first performed at the Globe theater. Do research on the structure and design of the Globe, using library and Internet resources. Then, make a **model** of the Globe to help your classmates understand how Shakespeare's plays were originally performed.

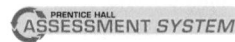 *Take It to the Net* www.phschool.com

Go online for an additional research activity using the Internet.

The Tragedy of Julius Caesar ◆ 915

Lesson Support for p. 915

❸ Writing Lesson

- Have students begin by rereading the speeches in Act III.
- Remind students that both Brutus' and Antony's speeches are persuasive speeches. Have students note the different styles and consider which is more effective.
- Use the Writing Lesson to guide students in writing their persuasive essays.
- Use the Persuasive Composition rubric in **Performance Assessment and Portfolio Management,** p. 11, to evaluate students' essays.

❹ Listening and Speaking

- Tell students that the 1953 film of *Julius Caesar* that was used to illustrate this textbook is available on video.
- Help students to choose a scene that won't present too many difficulties in production. You may need to discourage them from the battle scene, for example.

CUSTOMIZE INSTRUCTION
For Universal Access

To address different learning styles, use the following activities suggested in the **Extension Activities** booklet, p. 54.

- For Logical/Mathematical Learners, use Activity 5.
- For Verbal/Linguistic Learners, use Activities 5 and 6.
- For Visual/Spatial Learners, use Activity 7.

ASSESSMENT RESOURCES

The following resources can be used to assess students' knowledge and skills.

Selection Assessment

- **Formal Assessment,** pp. 188–190
- **Open Book Test,** pp. 160–162
- **Got It! Assessment Videotapes,** Tape 4
- **Test Bank Software**

 Take It to the Net
Visit www.phschool.com for self-tests and additional questions on *Julius Caesar.*

Writing Rubric

- **Performance Assess. and Portfolio Mgmt.,** p. 11

 PRENTICE HALL ASSESSMENT *SYSTEM*

- **Workbook**
- **Skill Book**
- **Transparencies**
- **CD-ROM**

Lesson Objectives

1. To write a response to literature

2. To learn the characteristics of a response to literature

3. To open and end their essays with power

Model From Literature

Vincent Canby's and Roger Ebert's reviews of *Star Wars* are examples of a response to a special kind of literature—a movie.

Prewriting

• Remind students that their strong feelings about a character or work can be negative as well as positive.

• Invite students to use a hexagonal writing graphic organizer to gather details for their response to literature.

• Urge students to give some thought to their intended audience. Will they write an informal critique of a work for their classmates and family, or will they write a formal criticism for a school report?

• Work with students to write their thesis statements, emphasizing clarity, brevity, and focus. For example, the thesis statement "Julius Caesar really should have seen what was coming, and in my view this blindness on his part is what makes him such an interesting and modern character" draws in a reader by stating that the writer, who admires the character of Caesar, is going to write about one of Caesar's major character flaws.

• Before students draft their essays, have them review the Rubric for Self-Assessment, p. 919, so they know what is expected of their work.

Writing WORKSHOP

Response to Literature

A **response to literature** is a reader's reaction to any aspect of a literary work. Some responses are formal and academic, and others are informal and personal. In this workshop, you will write a response to a favorite piece of literature.

Assignment Criteria Your response to literature should have the following characteristics:

● A response to the significant ideas in a poem, story, essay, or other piece of literature

● Accurate, detailed references to the text or other works

● References to personal and literary allusions, quotations, and other examples

● An effective and logical organization plan

● A conclusion or an evaluation that sums up your response

To preview the criteria on which your response to literature may be assessed, see the Rubric on page 919.

Prewriting

Choose a topic. The best topic for a response to literature is a work about which you have strong ideas. Use **listing** to generate ideas. Write down the names of characters in stories and poems about whom you have the most to say. Review your list, and choose as your topic a character or a work that you find most intriguing.

Gather details. Make sure you have enough details to fuel your writing. You might use the technique of **hexagonal writing**. A hexagon is a six-sided figure that can be used to explore six aspects of a work of literature. Follow the directions in the chart shown here to complete a hexagonal based on your topic.

Consider your audience. Identify your audience, and assess their interests and knowledge about your topic. Choose details that will appeal to your readers.

Example:
Topic: Similarity Between Antony and Cassius
Audience: Classmates
What they know: They are familiar with the work. I will not have to spend much time on a review of plot or characters.
What they do not know: Most have not read other works by this author.

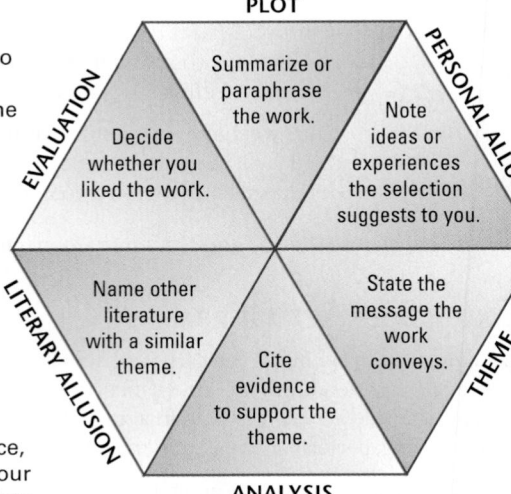

PLOT — Summarize or paraphrase the work.

PERSONAL ALLUSION — Note ideas or experiences the selection suggests to you.

THEME — State the message the work conveys.

ANALYSIS — Cite evidence to support the theme.

LITERARY ALLUSION — Name other literature with a similar theme.

EVALUATION — Decide whether you liked the work.

916 ◆ *Drama*

TEACHING RESOURCES

The following resources can be used to enrich or extend the instruction for pp. 916–919.

𝒲𝒢 **Writing and Grammar,** Platinum Level, Chapter 13, pp. 276–297

📖 **Performance Assessment and Portfolio Management,** p. 16

📄 **Writing Models and Graphic Organizers on Transparencies,** pp. 53–60

💿 **Writing and Grammar iText CD-ROM**
Students can use the following tools as they complete their response to literature essays:

• Hexagonal Graphic Organizer

• Topic Bin

• Character Trait Word Bin

• Unity and Coherence Revising Tool

Student Model

Before you begin drafting, read this student model and review the characteristics of an insightful response to literature.

Christopher Rich
Omaha, Nebraska

Response to *The Tragedy of Julius Caesar*

In all tales, modern or ancient, characters at odds often share some personality traits. However, significant character traits often put them at odds. No exception to this rule, Shakespeare's Antony and Cassius of *The Tragedy of Julius Caesar* share many characteristics but come to very different ends.

> Christopher begins his response with a thesis statement.

Marcus Antonius and Caius Cassius, both patricians and warriors, are presented as two of Rome's most noble citizens. Both are seen by plebeians as noble and honest men (not without their flaws, however), but they are among the most manipulative Romans in the play. Cassius is the first to exploit his talent, using it to coerce Brutus onto the side of the conspirators. Flattering Brutus, "*I know that virtue to be in you, Brutus, / As well as I do know your outward favor.*" (I, ii, 90–91) and challenging his honor as a Roman, Cassius wins the support of his brother-in-law. Antony, however, shows his ability in a far less conspicuous way. After the assassination of Caesar in Act III, Antony cleverly manipulates the commoners. His subtle and smooth way of controlling the crowd with a pause in his voice reflects his manipulative ability.

> The writer accurately quotes significant passages from the text.

Despite their powers of persuasion, these two show great allegiance to their loved ones. Over Caesar's body, in Act III, Scene i, Antony says he is willing to throw his country into civil war. Later, Cassius kills himself when he thinks that his best friend has been killed, taking loyalty to the extreme.

Though people may have many similarities, it is the differences that separate warriors and politicians. Always at the beck and call of the dictator who would be king, Antony is known by the common folk to be a possible successor to the "coronet." Cassius, however, is opposed to Caesar, not only politically but also personally, and is one of Caesar's least favorite people, "*Yond Cassius has a lean and hungry look*" (I, ii, 194). Cassius himself admits to his own dislike of Caesar by telling a story from their youth, in Act 1, Scene ii, lines 97–131. It is the differences that determine the eventual fate of each character.

> A point-by-point plan of organization is used to discuss similarities first and then differences.

In the end, the obvious similarities of these characters are not as important as their differences. The fate that each meets—Cassius commits suicide and Antony becomes part of the triumvirate that rules Rome—is determined by how each uses his personality traits.

> The conclusion restates the thesis statement and provides an insight that takes the analysis further.

Writing Workshop ◆ 917

Student Model

- Explain that the Student Model is a sample, and that responses to literature may be longer.
- Ask students to identify the thesis statement.
  Answer: The thesis statement is "No exception to this rule, Shakespeare's Antony and Cassius of *The Tragedy of Julius Caesar* share many characteristics, but come to very different ends."
- Point out that Christopher quotes a significant passage from the play to make his point that Brutus is subject to flattery. Ask students to find other examples of quotations from the play.
- Have students note that Christopher follows a consistent point-by-point organization.
- Remind students that a good conclusion to a response to literature restates the thesis, and may also go beyond the original analysis. Ask students what new insight Christopher offers in his conclusion.
  Answer: The differences between the characters determine their respective fate.

Real-World Connection

People learn from others. Our obvious teachers are our parents or other relatives, teachers, and friends. Some not-so-obvious teachers are the real people we meet in biography or nonfiction and the imaginary characters we meet in fiction and drama. Responding to these people, and the events through which they live, helps us learn and grow, as well as to discard ideas or plans that we might have once considered.

CUSTOMIZE INSTRUCTION FOR UNIVERSAL ACCESS

For Special Needs Students	For English Learners	For Advanced Writers
If students are having difficulty formulating a response to literature, have them choose a favorite piece and skim thorough it looking for a favorite passage or idea. When they have written down the passage, have them determine why they like it and use that as a basis for developing a wider response.	To help students formulate a response to literature, have them look for the ways in which characters use the language. What do they like about a character's language, or what do they dislike about it?	Perhaps students will wish to respond to a piece of literature or a character by comparing it with another. Some students might wish to compare one or more poems in terms of language, meter, or theme, while others might wish to choose similar characters from different works.

Drafting

- Remind students to organize their response in three parts—introduction, body, and conclusion.

- Suggest that students write down their main ideas and supporting details and then mark each with the numeral 1, 2, or 3 to identify which part of their response each idea fits.

- Remind students to elaborate on elements such as tone and mood, and to insert relevant quotations.

Revising

- Have students reread their introductory thesis statement to be sure it frames everything they want to say in their essay.

- Ask students to read the body of their response to be sure each supporting detail is connected with the thesis statement. This is the time to add more supporting details if necessary.

- Finally, have students be sure their introductory thesis statement and conclusion reinforce the same point.

(continued on p. 919)

Writing WORKSHOP *continued*

Drafting

Draft a thesis statement. Review your notes, and consider the main point you want to make about the piece of literature. Then, write a thesis statement to summarize your idea. Include the thesis in your introduction.

Organize your response. Follow a logical organization plan as you draft. A compelling response to literature is typically organized in three parts, as shown at right.

Elaborate. Support your response with specific references to the work or to other sources. You might refer to significant ideas, such as theme or character, or to specific details, such as stylistic devices, tone, or mood. If you use quotations, enclose them in quotation marks and indicate the source.

Example:
"I know that virtue to be in you, Brutus, / As well as I do know your outward favor." (I, ii, 90–91)

Revising

Revise your introduction and conclusion. Your opening and closing paragraphs should frame your analysis and present the main message of your response. Make sure your introduction and conclusion match.

Read through your introduction and your conclusion, and underline the important points that you make in them. If they do not make the same points, revise to clarify your draft.

> **Organizing a Response to Literature**
>
> **Introduction**
> **State Your Thesis**
> - Summarize your main points.
> - Give an overview of the literary piece.
>
> **Body**
> - Elaborate on your thesis.
> - Give details—quotations, anecdotes, and examples—to support your thesis.
>
> **Conclusion**
> - Restate your reaction to the literary piece.

Model: Matching Introduction to Conclusion

Introduction

In all tales, . . . characters at odds share some personality traits. However, significant character traits often put them at odds.

In the end, the obvious similarities of these characters are not as important as their differences.

Conclusion

~~In the end, the similarities of two people do not amount to a hill of beans in this world because all we see are the differences—the discrepancies, the conflicts, the two noble, warrior Romans on opposite sides of the battlefield.~~

Christopher revised his conclusion to match his introduction.

918 ◆ *Drama*

USING TECHNOLOGY IN WRITING

Students with access to the Internet might wish to create a Web literary page to share their responses to literature with others. Most Web pages use a computer language called HTML. Students can learn the basic HTML codes fairly quickly, or use a Web design software that writes the necessary codes for them. Elements students might include on home pages include: images, reviews, lists of favorites, and lists of recommendations.

Revise for clarity. When writing about literature, avoid generating confusion about who or what is being discussed. Read your draft, and make sure that each sentence has a clear subject. You may choose to replace pronouns with nouns to make the subjects of sentences more obvious.

Compare the model and nonmodel. Why is the meaning of the model clearer?

Nonmodel	Model
Cassius, however, is opposed to him, not only politically but also personally, and is one of Julius' least favorite people....	Cassius, however, is opposed to Caesar, not only politically but also personally, and is one of Caesar's least favorite people....

Publishing and Presenting

Choose one of the following ways to share your writing with classmates or a wider audience.

Present your response to a book club. Share your response to literature with members of a book club. Invite a group of students, friends, or family to read the work of literature you will address. Set a meeting time, and give a brief introduction to the book or work before sharing your ideas. Prepare notes to use as you speak. Then, compare your ideas with those of others in a free-form discussion.

Publish an online review. Post a literary review on a student or bookstore Web site. Remember to check with each site for specific submission requirements.

 Prentice Hall Writing and Grammar Connection: Chapter 13

Speaking Connection
For instruction on an oral response to literature, see the **Listening and Speaking Workshop** on page 920.

Rubric for Self-Assessment

Evaluate your response to literature using the following criteria and rating scale:

Criteria	Rating Scale				
	Not very				Very
How well have I covered the significant ideas of the piece?	1	2	3	4	5
Is my reaction well supported with accurate and detailed references to the text and other works?	1	2	3	4	5
Have I used personal and literary allusions, quotations, and other examples effectively?	1	2	3	4	5
How logical is the organization?	1	2	3	4	5
How effectively does the conclusion sum up my response?	1	2	3	4	5

TEST-TAKING TIP

Tell students that when they respond to a test prompt on literary elements such as character and theme, they should read the questions first to determine what elements they are being asked about. They should then read the passage, paying special attention to these elements.

- Tell students that revising, rather than indicating poor work, is a way to enhance one's work. Ask students what effect Christopher's change (p. 918), has on his response to literature.
  Answer: The change makes his conclusion stronger because it is shorter and more to the point.
- Have students compare the Nonmodel and Model, identifying which words are changed. Discuss how the changes affect the clarity of the Model.
  Answer: The word *him* is changed to Caesar, and the word *Julius'* is changed to the word Caesar's. The changes make it clear who in the sentence is being discussed as the object of Cassius' opposition.
- Have students read through their essays, replacing unclear pronoun referents with nouns, or rewriting sentences for clarity.

Publishing and Presenting

- Ask students to think of the audience they had in mind when they wrote their response.
- Based on their audience, have students choose one of the two methods of presenting their responses to a group. If they present it to a book club, have them report back to the class on the club's response to their review. If they publish it on a Web site, ask them to report back to the class on opinions they received from others using the site.

Assessment

- Review the assessment criteria in class.
- Before students proceed with self-assessment, have them score the Student Model in class, using one or more of the rubric categories to help them see how to apply the criteria. For example, ask students how they would score the essay in terms of literary allusions and quotations and why they would give it this score.
- The rubric on this page, and another rubric in an alternative format, can be found on pp. 16 and 62 of **Performance Assessment and Portfolio Management.**

Lesson Objectives

1. To make a formal or informal oral response to literature
2. To focus on main ideas about the literature and advance a judgment about them
3. To support main ideas with significant details from life and from the text

Prepare Content

- Remind students that they may need to give some background to listeners for the literature to which they are responding. Is the text fiction or nonfiction? Is it a novel or a short story?
- Tell students to focus on the main ideas of the literature and give their judgment about why these main ideas are important.
- If students feel strongly that the literature does not succeed in presenting a clear story, characterization, or logical progression of ideas, have them explain why they feel this way.
- After students complete the Activity on the student page, have them fill out the Feedback Form. When they finish, have them discuss their answers as a class or in small groups.

Prepare Your Delivery

- Help students determine the best pattern of organization for their response. If they are going to respond to two or more characters in literature, they might use a compare-and-contrast pattern. If they plan to talk about the plot events, they would likely use a chronological pattern.
- Have students rehearse their presentation at home in front of a mirror or for family members. Ask them to solicit listeners for feedback and incorporate any that is helpful.

Listening and Speaking WORKSHOP

Oral Responses to Literature

Whenever you react verbally to something you have read, you make an **oral response to literature**. Some responses are formal and academic, and others are informal and personal. The following strategies will help you prepare and present an effective response to a literary piece.

Prepare Content

In preparing an oral response, stay focused on your main idea so that everything will hang together. Review the Writing Workshop on page 916. Then, consider these suggestions to develop the content:

Advance a judgment about significant ideas. Clearly state the main ideas in the literature. Discuss ways in which the ideas are developed and why they are important.

Support important ideas and viewpoints. Your views will carry more weight if you support them with references to the text or to other works.

Assess ambiguities, nuances, and complexities within the text. Authors do not state all of their ideas directly. Help your audience understand the questions that the literature raises. Explore these subtle aspects of literature in your presentation.

Prepare Your Delivery

Use the following techniques to prepare the presentation of your response:

Choose a logical pattern of organization. You might present your ideas chronologically, in order of importance, or parts to whole.

Develop the introduction and conclusion. Plan an introduction that will capture your audience's attention as well as a conclusion that will make it memorable.

Rehearse you presentation. Although your ideas may be serious, work to make your presentation conversational and comfortable. Try not to read an essay word for word. Instead, use your notes as a guide.

Activity:
Presentation and Feedback
Select a short story or a short piece of nonfiction, and prepare a three-minute oral response to it. Use the Feedback Form to guide your preparation. Present your response to your class.

920 ◆ Drama

Feedback Form for an Oral Response to Literature

Rating System
+ = Excellent   ✔ = Average   – = Weak

Content
Judgment expressed _____
Ideas supported _____
Subtleties of text explored _____

Delivery
Logical organization _____
Strong introduction _____
Memorable conclusion _____
Conversational tone _____

Answer the following questions:
Is my presentation unified, with every statement supporting my main idea?

Is my opinion of this literary work clearly stated?

Assessment WORKSHOP

Characteristics of Text

In the reading sections of some tests, you may be required to analyze the characteristics of clear texts, including patterns of organization. Use the following strategies to help you answer test questions on these skills:

- Writers may organize information to compare and contrast, to establish chronological order, or to show a cause-and-effect relationship.
- A compare-and-contrast organization shows the similarities and differences between subjects.
- Chronological order shows events in time order.
- A cause-and-effect organizational pattern within a text helps to reinforce the relationship between actions and events.

Test-Taking Strategies

- Look for words or phrases that identify patterns of organization.
- Support your answer for patterns of organization by citing evidence from the text.

Sample Test Item

Directions: Read the passage, and write a short answer to the question that follows.

The use of automobiles has increased around the world. Twenty years ago, you could travel to many places without encountering a noisy, exhaust-spewing car. As global trade and world economies have expanded, more people have purchased cars. Environmentalists contend that this increase is not a healthy trend. For instance, in parts of China today, it is nearly impossible to breathe because of the glut of cars on the roads. Twenty years ago, those same roads were filled with nonpolluting bicycles.

1 What patterns of organization are used in this passage? Support your answer.

Answer and Explanation

Chronology is used in speaking of the number of cars twenty years ago and today. Comparison is used in comparing these two times. Cause and effect is used in mentioning the effects of expanded trade and the polluting effects of cars.

▶ Practice

Directions: Read the passage, and write a short answer to the questions that follow.

At the end of World War II, the United States and the Soviet Union distrusted each other. The two superpowers competed to influence other nations. The Soviet Union supported a system called communism. The United States embraced democracy for its freedom-loving people. Tensions mounted as each country built nuclear weapons. As a result, each side stockpiled enough weapons to destroy each other—and the world. Then, the two countries began to reduce their arms. By the 1980s, the reduction of nuclear weapons had resulted in decreased world tensions.

1 Explain how the writer has used patterns of organization. Support your answer.

2 Which other organizational patterns could the writer have used? Explain your answer.

Lesson Objective

To comprehend texts using a variety of strategies, including analyzing text structures such as compare and contrast, cause and effect, and chronological order for how they influence understanding

Applying Reading Strategies

- Explain to students that when they seek to identify a pattern of organization, they should look for clue words and phrases.
- Tell students that in a chronological pattern of organization, for example, they might find words and phrases such as *first, next, last year,* or *several years ago.* In a compare-and-contrast pattern, they would look for facts and details that show how two or more subjects are similar or different. In a cause-and-effect format, they would look for information that ties one event as a cause to another event as an effect.

Applying Test-Taking Strategies

- Have students read the Sample Test Item. Ask them to identify the clue words and phrases indicating its organization.
  Answer: Clues include *Twenty years ago, As* (chronological order); *those same roads* (comparison).
- Then, ask students to complete the Practice using the same strategies.

Answers

1. The writer uses a chronological pattern to view the Soviet Union and the United States at the end of World War II and in the 1980s. A compare-and-contrast pattern is used to show the different political systems of the two countries. Finally, a cause-and-effect pattern is used to explain what led to a stockpiling of dangerous nuclear weapons.

2. The main organization of the passage is chronological. The writer could have used cause and effect to focus on the reasons for the arms race. The writer could also have used comparison to emphasize the different political systems in the countries.

TEACHING RESOURCES

The following resources can be used to enrich or extend the instruction for p. 920–921.

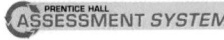

PRENTICE HALL
ASSESSMENT *SYSTEM*

- 📖 **Workbook**
- 📖 **Skill Book**
- 💻 **Transparencies**
- 💿 **CD-ROM**

Unit Objectives

1. To read a variety of poems
2. To apply a variety of reading strategies appropriate for reading poetry
3. To analyze literary elements in poetry
4. To use a variety of strategies to build vocabulary
5. To learn elements of grammar, usage, and style
6. To use recursive writing processes to write in a variety of forms
7. To develop listening and speaking skills
8. To express and support responses to various poems
9. To prepare, organize, and present literary interpretations

Meeting the Objectives

With each selection, you will find instructional materials through which students can meet these objectives. Further, you will find additional practice pages for reading strategies, literary analysis, vocabulary, and grammar in the **Selection Support: Skills Development Workbook** in your **Teaching Resources.**

Background

Art

Awaiting Spring by Scott Burdick

Call attention to the balance of elements in this painting. Students might note the two figures at either end of the staircase. Help them see the balance between the heavily carved staircase and the delicate tree and cloudy sky. There is also the balance between what is fixed—the carved figure and staircase—and what can change—the living woman, the tree about to bud, and the clouds. Have students link this painting with the focus of Unit 9, poetry, through the following question:

> Poems are memorable for their images and figures of speech. What figure of speech (imaginative comparison) does this painting suggest?
> Possible responses: Students might suggest a metaphor like "Spring cracks the stones of winter" or a simile like "Spring comes like a statue springing to life."

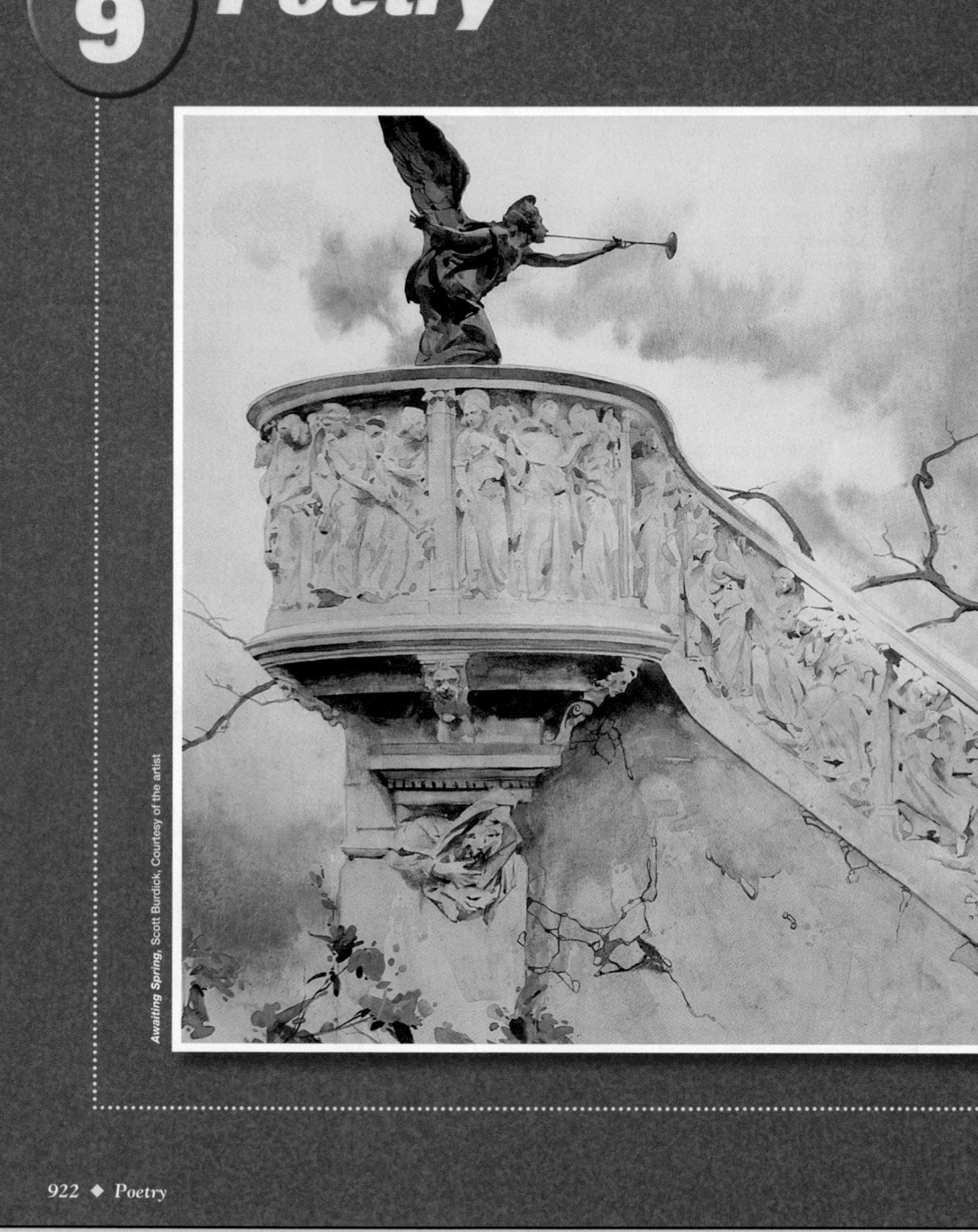

Awaiting Spring, Scott Burdick, Courtesy of the artist.

UNIT 9 Poetry

922 ◆ Poetry

UNIT FEATURES

Connections	Reading Informational Materials
Every unit contains a feature that connects literature to a related topic, such as art, science, or history. In this unit, the lyrics to "Cat's in the Cradle" on p. 934 inspire a study of the music of Harry Chapin. Use the information and questions on the Connections page to enrich students' understanding of the selections presented within the unit.	These selections will help students learn to analyze and evaluate informational texts, such as workplace documents, technical directions, and consumer materials. They will expose students to the organization and features unique to nonnarrative texts. In this unit, students will learn to read and interpret a historical essay.

Exploring the Genre

There are almost as many definitions of poetry as there are poets. Poetry can appear in neat stanzas, or it can look almost like prose on a page. Sometimes, it even forms a picture with the words. It can tell a story, express an idea, define a character, convey an emotion, describe a setting, or examine a situation. The poems in this unit will give you a sense of the wide range of literature that we call poetry.

As you explore the poetry in this unit, you will encounter the following terms:

- **Lyric poetry** is poetry that expresses vivid thoughts and feelings.

- **Narrative poetry** tells a story.

- **Dramatic poetry** creates the illusion that the reader is actually witnessing a dramatic event.

- **Musical devices**—such as alliteration, onomatopoeia, assonance, consonance, meter, and repetition and rhyme—give poems a musical quality.

- **Figurative language** refers to the use of figures of speech, such as simile, metaphor, and personification, which present a fresh and unusual way of looking at things.

▲ **Critical Viewing** In what ways is a poet similar to the winged sculpture? **[Connect]**

Exploring the Genre ◆ 923

Assessing Student Progress

Listed below are the tools that are available to measure the degree to which students meet the unit objectives.

Informal Assessment

The questions in the Review and Assess sections are a first-level response to the concepts and skills presented within the selections. Students' responses provide a brief, informal measure of their grasp of the material. These responses can indicate where further instruction and practice are needed. Follow up with the practice pages in the **Selection Support: Skills Development Workbook.**

Formal Assessment

The **Formal Assessment** booklet contains the Selection Tests and Unit Tests.

- Selection Tests measure comprehension and skills acquisition for each selection or group of selections.

- Each Unit Test provides students with thirty multiple-choice questions and five essay questions designed to assess students' knowledge of the literature and skills taught in the unit.

The **Open Book Tests** ask students to demonstrate their ability to synthesize and communicate information from selections or groups of selections.

To assess student writing, you will find rubrics and scoring models in the **Performance Assessment and Portfolio Management** booklet. In this booklet you will also find scoring rubrics for listening and speaking activities.

Alternative Assessment

The **Extension Activities** booklet contains writing activities, listening and speaking activities, and research and technology activities that are appropriate for students with different ability levels. You may also use these activities as an alternative measurement of students' growth.

▶Critical Viewing

Possible responses: A poet soars above ordinary existence to find extraordinary images, ideas, or truths about life. When the poet commits his or her vision to paper, readers read and hear his or her ideas, just as listeners hear the angel's horn.

Why Read Literature?

The "Why Read Literature?" page in each unit presents a list of possible purposes for reading. Each purpose for reading is connected to one or more of the selections in the unit. Good readers set a purpose before reading in order to help them read actively and focus on meaningful details.

Unit 9 introduces three purposes for reading. "Read for the Love of Literature" introduces students to the sorrowful sound of a guitar and the joys of waking to each new day, both announced in poetry. "Read to Appreciate the Author's Craft" suggests that students read to understand how the spiritual elements of a Navajo chant are communicated through rhythm. When they "Read for Information," students learn about the musical history of the guitar.

How to Use This Page

- Tell students that before reading each selection in this unit, they should set a purpose for reading. This will help them read in an active and focused manner.

- Explain that reading poems by two masters of this genre—García Lorca and Roethke—will help increase their love of literature.

- To appreciate an author's craft, a reader must see how the writer uses literary elements. As they read "Prayer of First Dancers," students will note the use of rhythm as a means of storytelling.

- A third purpose for reading is to obtain information. Explain that when setting a purpose, students should specify the type of information they want to learn. For example, in "The History of the Guitar," they will learn how the guitar evolved.

 Read Literature?

When you read, you have a purpose in mind. It might be for entertainment or for information. As you approach the genre of poetry, you can find several different purposes that apply to reading these selections. Preview the three purposes you might set before reading the works in this unit.

1 Read for the Love of Literature

When played in a certain way, the guitar can evoke powerful emotions and images. Federico García Lorca hears sorrow in its music. Discover how he transcribes the sound into words in **"The Guitar,"** page 972.

As you shake off the sleepy feeling after a restful night, you find that a new day with endless possibilities awaits you. Read Theodore Roethke's take on this idea in **"The Waking,"** page 986.

2 Read to Appreciate the Author's Craft

Rhythm is one device poets use to create a mood and tell a story. See how the repetitive and spiritual elements of a chant establish a sense of rhythm in the Navajo poem **"Prayer of First Dancers,"** page 942.

3 Read for Information

The *cithara* and *citharis* are musical instruments called *fides*—from the ancient Greek word for "strings." To learn why these instruments were vital to the evolution of the guitar, read **"The History of the Guitar,"** by Thomas A. Hill, page 981.

 Take It to the Net

Visit the Web site for online instruction and activities related to each selection in this unit.
www.phschool.com

❋ ENRICHMENT: Further Reading

Have students choose one or more of the works below to extend their experience of the unit genre, poetry, or to read more by the unit authors.

The Poetry of Robert Frost
In this anthology are collected some of the most famous poems of one of the best loved poets of the United States.

"The Lady of Shalott" by Alfred, Lord Tennyson
In this poem, Tennyson draws from the Camelot of Arthurian lore, telling the story of the cursed Lady of Shalott.

"The Man Who Dreamed of Fairyland" by William Butler Yeats
In this poem, Yeats effectively uses Irish folk traditions to reawaken the magic of nature.

How to Read a Poem by Burton Raffel
The author skillfully guides the reader through the various facets of poetry, unlocking its riches for even those whom it intimidates.

How to Read Literature

Use Strategies for Reading Poetry

Poetry is a distinct kind of writing. It differs from other forms of writing in its appearance, its use of language, and its sound. A poet's imaginative use of language can sometimes make a poem seem complex or hard to understand. These strategies will help you read poetry successfully and enjoy it as well:

1. Listen.

One of the things that distinguishes poetry from prose is its sound. Poetry is usually meant to be read aloud; only by doing so will you hear the music of the poet's words.

2. Identify the speaker.

When you read a poem, you are hearing the voice of the speaker of the poem. The speaker is not necessarily the poet, although it can be or it can be a part of the poet's personality.

The speaker may be a character created by the poet. Determine who you think is "telling" the poem, and try to determine his or her perspective on the situation in the poem. Recognizing the speaker and his or her perspective will give you insight into the meaning of the poem.

3. Read in sentences.

- Keep in mind that even if a poem is shaped to fit a particular rhythm and rhyme, the words are usually put together and punctuated as sentences.
- Do not stop at the end of each line unless a punctuation mark—period, comma, colon, semicolon, or dash—stops you.

4. Picture the imagery.

- Use your senses to experience the pleasures of a poem. To appreciate the images that the poet uses, form mental pictures based on the words in the poem.
- When you form mental pictures, you use your memory and imagination to see, feel, hear, smell, and taste what the poet describes.

For example, as you read the lines from Shakespeare's Sonnet 18 at right, try to picture the images that the poet describes.

As you read the selections in this unit, review the reading strategies and look at the notes in the side columns. Use the suggestions to apply the strategies and to interact with the text.

Picturing the Imagery

Rough winds do shake the darling buds of May, and summer's lease hath all too short a date: . . .

—from Sonnet 18

Image	Association
"darling buds of May"	Warm sun Bright colors

MODEL A READING STRATEGY: Identify the Speaker

Explain to students that, in many poems, the speaker is a fictional personality, not the poet him- or herself. Model the process of identifying the speaker using "In Flander Fields" (p. 938).

Read the first stanza aloud as students follow along. Tell students:

The word *our* in line 3 makes it clear that the poem has a group of speakers.

Read the second stanza aloud. Tell students:

In this stanza, the speakers identify themselves: They are the Dead. Knowing that the poem is set in wartime, you can figure out that they are soldiers killed in battle.

How to Read Literature

The "How to Read Literature" page in each unit presents a set of strategies to help readers understand authors' words and ideas. Each reading strategy is taught in conjunction with one or more of the selections within the unit. Good readers develop a bank of strategies from which they can draw as needed.

Unit 9 introduces four strategies for reading poetry. To understand a selection fully, students must understand how poetry communicates in ways different from other writing. The strategies on this page help readers decode poetry's sometimes complex structure in order to enjoy its ideas and imagery.

How to Use This Page

Introduce the strategies for understanding poetry, presenting each as a tool for developing understanding when reading the selections in this unit.

- As they read "In Flanders Field" (p. 938), "The Kraken" (p. 939), "Meeting at Night" (p. 940), "Reapers" (p. 941), and "Prayer of First Dancers" (p. 942), students will learn to listen to the music a poet creates with words.

- As they read "La Belle Dame sans Merci" (p. 960) and "Danny Deever" (p. 963), students will learn to identify the speaker, who is not necessarily the poet, and determine his or her perspective.

- As they read "Jade Flower Palace" (p. 970), "The Moon at the Fortified Pass" (p. 971), "The Guitar" (p. 972), "What Are Friends For" (p. 974), "Making a Fist" (p. 975), and "Some Like Poetry" (p. 976), students will learn that reading poetry as sentences rather than as lines will give them a greater grasp of its meaning.

- As they read "The Waking" (p. 986), selected tanka (p. 988) and haiku (p. 989), and Sonnet 18 (p. 990), students will learn to picture the sensory experiences that the poet conveys.

The Stolen Child

Lesson Objectives

1. **To analyze and respond to literary elements**
   - Literary Analysis: Atmosphere
   - Connecting Literary Elements: Alliteration

2. **To read, comprehend, analyze, and critique a poem**
   - Reading Strategy: Responding
   - Reading Check questions
   - Review and Assess questions
   - Assessment Practice (ATE)

3. **To develop word analysis skills, fluency, and systematic vocabulary**
   - Vocabulary Development Lesson: Words With Multiple Meanings

4. **To understand and apply written and oral language conventions**
   - Spelling Strategy
   - Grammar Lesson: *their, there,* and *they're*

5. **To understand and apply appropriate writing and research strategies**
   - Writing Lesson: Crime Report
   - Extension Activity: Timeline

6. **To understand and apply listening and speaking strategies**
   - Extension Activity: Oral Presentation

STEP-BY-STEP TEACHING GUIDE	PACING GUIDE
PRETEACH	
Motivate Students and Provide Background	
Use the Motivation activity (ATE p. 926)	5 min.
Read and discuss the Preview material and Background information (SE/ATE p. 926)	5 min.
Introduce the Concepts	
Introduce the Literary Analysis and Reading Strategy (SE/ATE p. 927) 🅰	10 min.
Pronounce the vocabulary words and read their definitions (SE p. 927)	5 min.
TEACH	
Monitor Comprehension	
Informally monitor comprehension by circulating while students read independently or in groups 🅰	xx min.
Monitor students' comprehension with the Reading Check notes (SE/ATE p. 929)	as students read
Develop vocabulary with the Vocabulary note (SE p. 929)	as students read
Develop Understanding	
Develop students' understanding of atmosphere with the Literary Analysis annotations (SE p. 929; ATE p. 929) 🅰	5 min.
Develop students' ability to respond to a poem with the Reading Strategy annotation (ATE p. 929)	5 min.
ASSESS	
Assess Mastery	
Assess students' mastery of the Reading Strategy and Literary Analysis by having them answer the Review and Assess questions (SE/ATE p. 931)	10 min.
Use one or more of the print and media Assessment Resources (ATE p. 933) 🅰	up to 50 min.
EXTEND	
Apply Understanding	
Have students complete the Vocabulary Development Lesson and the Grammar Lesson (SE p. 932) 🅰	20 min.
Apply students' ability to use an objective tone using the Writing Lesson (SE p. 933) 🅰	45 min.
Apply students' understanding using one or more of the Extension Activities (SE p. 933)	20–90 min.

🅰 ACCELERATED INSTRUCTION:
Use the strategies and activities identified with an 🅰.

UNIVERSAL ACCESS
● = Below Level Students
▲ = On-Level Students
■ = Above Level Students

Time and Resource Manager

RESOURCES

PRINT 📝	TRANSPARENCIES	TECHNOLOGY 💿 🎧 📼
• **Beyond Literature,** Cultural Connection: Celtic Folklore, p. 55 ▲ ■		• **Interest Grabber Video,** Tape 5 ● ▲ ■
• **Selection Support Workbook:** ● ▲ ■ Literary Analysis, p. 220 Reading Strategy, p. 219 Build Vocabulary, p. 217	• **Literary Analysis and Reading Transparencies,** pp. 109 and 110 ● ▲ ■	
		• **Listening to Literature** ● ▲ ■ Audiocassettes, Side 32 Audio CDs, CD 19
• **Literatura en español** ● ▲ • **Literary Analysis for Enrichment** ■	• **Fine Art Transparencies, Volume 1,** Art Transparency 16 ● ▲ ■	
• **Formal Assessment:** Selection Test, pp. 195–197 ● ▲ ■ • **Open Book Test,** pp. 163–165 ● ▲ ■ • **Performance Assessment and Portfolio Management,** p. 19 ● ▲ ■ • PRENTICE HALL **ASSESSMENT** *SYSTEM* ● ▲ ■	• PRENTICE HALL **ASSESSMENT** *SYSTEM* ● ▲ ■ Skills Practice Answers and Explanations on Transparencies	• **Test Bank Software** ● ▲ ■ • **Got It! Assessment Videotapes,** Tape 5 ● ▲
• **Selection Support Workbook:** ● ▲ ■ Build Grammar Skills, p. 218 • **Writing and Grammar,** Platinum Level ● ▲ ■ • **Extension Activities,** p. 55 ● ▲ ■	• **Daily Language Practice Transparencies** ● ▲ • **Writing Models and Graphic Organizers on Transparencies,** pp. 79–81 ● ▲ ■	• **Writing and Grammar iText CD-ROM** ● ▲ ■ 💻 *Take It to the Net* www.phschool.com

BLOCK SCHEDULING: Use one 90-minute class period to preteach the selection and have students read it. Use a second 90-minute class period to assess students' mastery of skills and have them complete one of the Extension Activities.

Motivation

Tell students that this poem describes a choice between the reality of the human world and an escape to a magical world. On the chalkboard, create a pros-and-cons chart exploring the advantages and disadvantages of escaping reality. In the pros column, you might list "no responsibilities." In the cons column, you might list "losing friends and family." Have students brainstorm for other pros and cons. Leave the list on the chalkboard while students read the poem so that they can compare their ideas with those expressed in the poem.

▭ Interest Grabber Video

As an alternative, play "The Legacy of Harry Chapin" on Tape 5 to engage student interest.

❶ Background

Folklore

According to folklore, if you see a glow come from decaying wood, you have seen a fairy spark. In reality, this phenomenon is created from phosphorus (which glows) produced in decaying wood.

Prepare to Read

The Stolen Child

Untitled, Rob Wood, Illustration by Wood Ronsaville Harlin, Inc.

▭ *Take It to the Net*

Visit www.phschool.com for instruction and activities relating to "The Stolen Child," including
- background
- graphic organizers
- literary elements
- reading strategies

Preview

Connecting to the Literature

Almost every culture has tales of little people—fairies, elves, sprites, or pixies—who have supernatural powers to make a person rich, beautiful, or powerful. In these stories, there is usually a hidden price to pay. In "The Stolen Child," for example, fairies offer a child a world of delights—at a very high price.

❶ Background

In Irish, or Celtic, folklore, these little people are known as fairies. These creatures, which are said to be human in shape, come from folklore and legend. According to folklore, a circle of dark green grass or a circle of mushrooms may be a fairy ring—a place where fairies have danced.

TEACHING RESOURCES

The following resources can be used to enrich or extend the instruction for pp. 926-927.

Motivation

▭ **Interest Grabber Video**, Tape 5

Background

▭ **Beyond Literature**, p. 55 ▪

 Take It to the Net

Visit www.phschool.com for background and hotlinks for "The Stolen Child."

Literary Analysis

▭ **Selection Support:** Literary Analysis, p. 220 ▪

▭ **Literary Analysis and Reading Transparencies,** Atmosphere, p. 110

Reading

▭ **Literary Analysis and Reading Transparencies,** Responding, p. 109

▪ **BLOCK SCHEDULING:** Resources marked with this symbol provide varied instruction during 90-minute blocks.

Literary Analysis

Atmosphere

Atmosphere is the mood or the overall feeling that a story or poem conveys. A writer establishes atmosphere through details of the setting or action. Descriptive details, word choice, and rhyme and rhythm work together to produce atmosphere. The following lines from "The Stolen Child" create a mysterious, mystical atmosphere in which a meeting takes place between fairies and a human child.

> Where the wave of moonlight glosses / The dim grey sands with light, / Far off by furthest Rosses . . .

As you read the poem, notice the elements that the poet uses to create this atmosphere.

Connecting Literary Elements

In "The Stolen Child," the poet uses **alliteration**—the repetition of initial consonant sounds—to emphasize words and to create musical effects. Alliteration can occur within a single line or within a complete stanza. Notice the repetition of *w* sounds in the following lines:

> To the *waters* and the *wild*
> *With* a faery, hand in hand, . . .

As you read, notice how alliteration emphasizes words and images and adds to the atmosphere of the poem.

Reading Strategy

Responding

When you read a poem, you **respond** to it by thinking about your own reaction to the words. Consider these questions:

- What has the speaker said?
- How do the images in the poem affect you?
- What does the poem say to you?

To respond to "The Stolen Child," use a chart like the one here to record your thoughts.

Vocabulary Development

herons (her´ ənz) *n.* birds with long necks, legs, and bills, living along riverbanks and marshes (p. 929)

glosses (glôs´ əs) *v.* shines (p. 929)

slumbering (slum´ bər iŋ) *adj.* sleeping (p. 929)

---

❷ Literary Analysis

Atmosphere

- Tell students that they will focus on atmosphere—the mood or feeling of a piece—as they read "The Stolen Child."
- Read the instruction about atmosphere together as a class. Discuss with students the excerpt from the poem.
- Use the instruction for Connecting Literary Elements to demonstrate for students how alliteration affects the atmosphere of the poem.
- Encourage students to identify the words and lines that help create the poem's atmosphere as they read.

❸ Reading Strategy

Responding

- Remind students that whenever they read or watch something, they simultaneously respond to it.
- For example, ask students how they respond to television commercials: Do they believe the message? Do they want to buy the product? Do they laugh? Are they touched?
- Tell students that as they read the poem, they will be responding to the words, images, and message.
- Encourage students to use a chart like the one on p. 927 to record their responses to the poem.

Vocabulary Development

- Pronounce each vocabulary word for students, and read the definitions as a class. Have students identify any words with which they are already familiar.

CUSTOMIZE INSTRUCTION FOR UNIVERSAL ACCESS

For Less Proficient Readers	For English Learners	For Advanced Readers
Students may benefit from paraphrasing each stanza of the poem as they read. Encourage them to keep in mind the fairies' purpose—to tempt a human child away from human life. Also, have students point out words or phrases that add to the atmosphere of the poem.	Students may be confused by the inverted word order in the first and fourth stanzas. Help them to restate the lines, placing the words in standard order. Ask them how these lines might add to the atmosphere of the poem? Why do they think the poet wrote them this way?	Challenge students to identify and distinguish between the characteristics of the various literary elements used throughout the poem. Encourage them to explain how they think each element adds to the atmosphere the poet created.

 E-Teach

Visit E-Teach at www.phschool.com for teachers' essays on how to teach, with questions and answers.

**Step-by-Step Teaching Guide
for pp. 928–930**

CUSTOMIZE INSTRUCTION
For Musical/Rhythmic Learners

Encourage interested students to
set the poem to music. Suggest that
they use Irish music or any style that
they feel brings out the magic in the
poem. Some students may want to
create their own composition to
accompany the poem. Allow time
for students to present their poem
with musical accompaniment to the
class.

❶ About the Selection

In this poem, fairies tempt a child to
leave his life as a human, with all its
attendant suffering, and join them in
a fairyland where nature is friendly
and benign. In the last stanza, however, the fairies reveal that the child
will also leave the good things in
human life and go to the unknown—
the wild world of the fairies. Readers
are left to contemplate the price
that must be paid for escaping the
trials and responsibilities of the real
world.

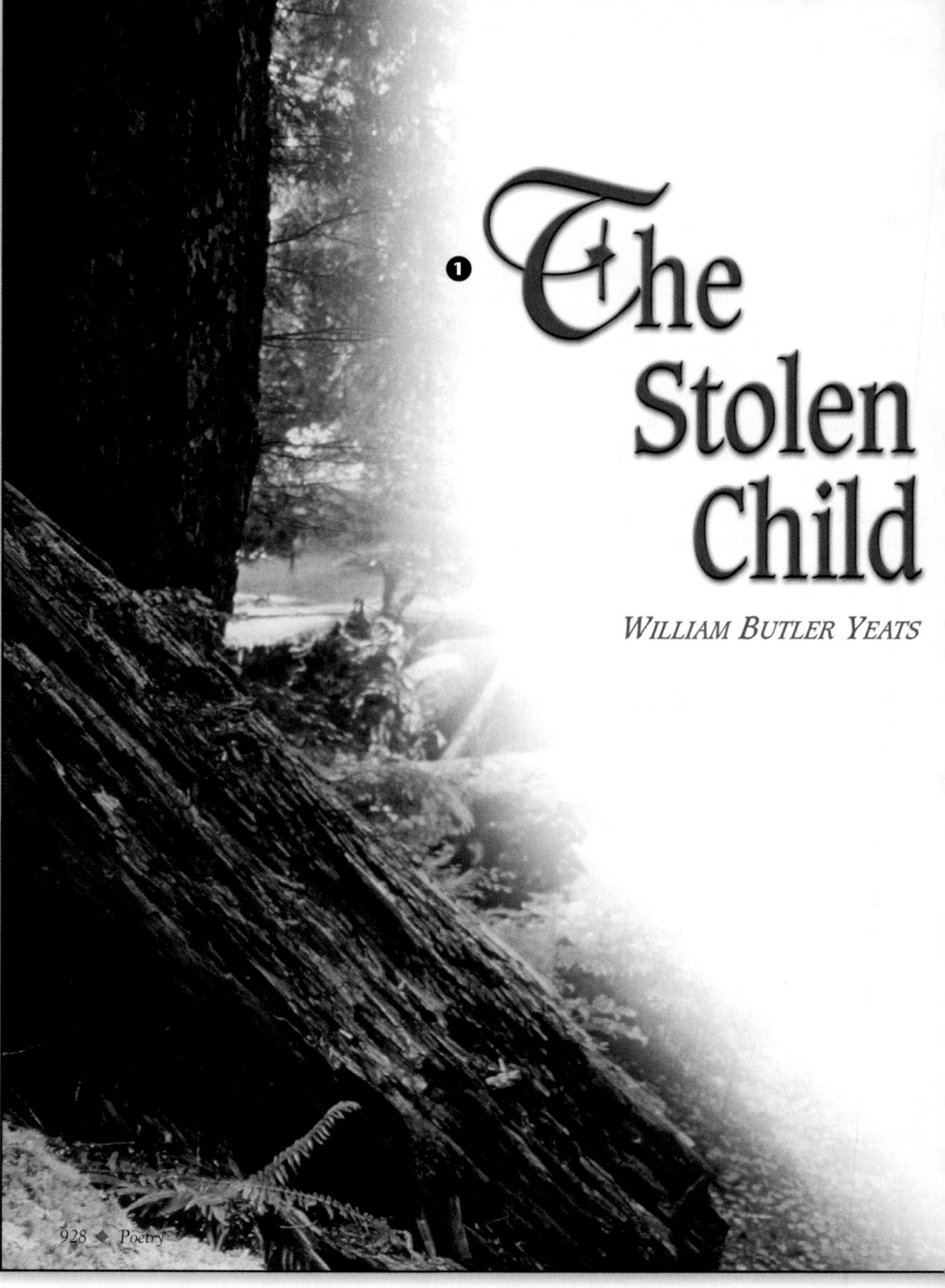

❶ The
Stolen
Child

WILLIAM BUTLER YEATS

928 ◆ Poetry

TEACHING RESOURCES

The following resources can be used to enrich or extend the instruction for pp. 928–930.

Literary Analysis

📄 **Writing Models and Graphic Organizers on
Transparencies,** p. 79–81

Reading

📖 **Selection Support:** Reading Strategy, p. 219;
Build Vocabulary, p. 217

🎧 **Listening to Literature Audiocassettes,** Side 32 ▪

💿 **Listening to Literature Audio CDs,** CD 19 ▪

Extension

📄 **Fine Art Transparencies, Volume 1,** Art
Transparency 16 (Call students' attention to what
the painting may suggest about the boundary
between fantasy and reality. Ask them why they
think the child in Yeats's poem chooses the world
of fantasy.) ▪

▪ **BLOCK SCHEDULING:** Resources marked with this symbol provide varied instruction during 90-minute blocks.

Where dips the rocky highland
Of Sleuth Wood in the lake,
There lies a leafy island
Where flapping <u>herons</u> wake
5   The drowsy water rats;
There we've hid our faery[1] vats,
Full of berries
And of reddest stolen cherries.
Come away, O human child!
10 *To the waters and the wild*
With a faery, hand in hand,
For the world's more full of weeping than you can understand.

Where the wave of moonlight <u>glosses</u>
The dim grey sands with light,
15 Far off by furthest Rosses[2]
We foot it all the night,
Weaving olden dances
Mingling hands and mingling glances
Till the moon has taken flight;
20 To and fro we leap
And chase the frothy bubbles,
While the world is full of troubles
And is anxious in its sleep.
Come away, O human child!
25 *To the waters and the wild*
With a faery, hand in hand,
For the world's more full of weeping than you can understand.

Where the wandering water gushes
From the hills above Glen-Car,
30 In pools among the rushes
That scarce could bathe a star,
We seek for <u>slumbering</u> trout
And whispering in their ears
Give them unquiet dreams;

---

1. faery a fairy.
2. Rosses marshes.

---

herons (her´ ənz) *n.* birds
with long necks, legs,
and bills, living along
riverbanks and marshes

glosses (glôs´ əs) *v.* shines

Literary Analysis
Atmosphere Describe the
mood that is set by this
stanza.

slumbering (slum´ bər iŋ)
adj. sleeping

◀ Critical Viewing In what way does this picture contribute to the dreamlike
atmosphere of "The Stolen Child"? **[Infer]**

④ ✔Reading Check
What do the fairies do all
night in the marshes?

The Stolen Child ◆ 929

❷ Reading Strategy
Responding
• Read aloud the bracketed passage. Ask students: Based on this description, does the fairyland sound like a nice place to go? Why?
Possible Response: Students may say that it sounds like a wonderful place to go—it's a beautiful, quiet, lazy place with lots of berries and cherries to eat.

• Instruct students to create a chart like the one shown on p. 927 to record their response to the details in this stanza. Students' charts should be similar to the one shown here.

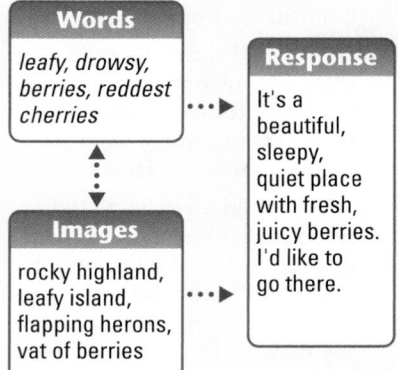

Words
leafy, drowsy, berries, reddest cherries

Images
rocky highland, leafy island, flapping herons, vat of berries

Response
It's a beautiful, sleepy, quiet place with fresh, juicy berries. I'd like to go there.

❸ Literary Analysis
Atmosphere
• Have students pay careful attention to details in the bracketed passage that help to establish a mood.

• Ask students the Literary Analysis question on p. 929: Describe the mood that is set by this stanza.
Answer: The mood is magical, light, happy, and carefree.

❹ ✔Reading Check
Answer: The fairies dance all night.

❺ ▶Critical Viewing
Answer: The misty, verdant forest in the photograph contributes to the magical, dream-like tone of Yeats's poem; it's easy to imagine the fairies leaping "to and fro" and chasing bubbles in this scene.

Review and Assess

1. Students' answers will depend upon their personal experiences, but they should support their opinions with evidence.

2. **(a)** The speakers like to eat berries and cherries; they like to dance and leap and talk to fish. **(b)** The speakers are fairies, and the words "we've" and "our" together with their descriptions reveal their identity.

3. **(a)** The vats are hidden on their leafy island. **(b)** Students will probably say the cherries have been stolen from humans.

4. **(a)** The fairies say the child should go with them because the world is full of sadness. **(b)** The fairies might want the child to become a fairy, too.

5. **(a)** The child gives up all the good parts of human life, such as hearing ". . . the lowing/Of the calves" and "the kettle on the hob . . ." **(b)** Students may say that the fairies think human beings suffer too much.

6. Students may think the fairies' promises are too ambiguous to take the risk.

---

35 Leaning softly out
From ferns that drop their tears
Over the young streams.
Come away, O human child!
To the waters and the wild
40 *With a faery, hand in hand,*
For the world's more full of weeping than you can understand.

Away with us he's going,
The solemn-eyed:
He'll hear no more the lowing[3]
45 Of the calves on the warm hillside
Or the kettle on the hob[4]
Sing peace into his breast,
Or see the brown mice bob
Round and round the oatmeal chest.

50 *For he comes, the human child,*
To the waters and the wild
With a faery, hand in hand,
From a world more full of weeping than he can understand.

---

3. **lowing** (lō´ iŋ) *n.* mooing.
4. **hob** (häb) *n.* ledge on a fireplace used for keeping a kettle or pan warm.

Review and Assess

Thinking About the Selection

1. **Respond:** Do you agree with the line repeated in "The Stolen Child" that "*the world's more full of weeping than you can understand*"? Why or why not?

2. **(a) Recall:** What activities do the speakers enjoy? **(b) Interpret:** What clues tell you the identity of the speakers?

3. **(a) Recall:** Where have the fairies hidden vats "Full of berries / And of reddest stolen cherries"? **(b) Infer:** From whom do you think the cherries have been stolen?

4. **(a) Recall:** Why do the fairies say the human child should go with them? **(b) Speculate:** Why do you think the fairies want the child?

5. **(a) Recall:** What does the child give up when he goes with the fairies? **(b) Make a Judgment:** What do you think is the fairies' attitude toward human beings? Explain.

6. **Assess:** The fairies list the features of the human world that the child must leave behind. Do you think the fairies promise enough to make such a sacrifice worthwhile? Explain.

William Butler Yeats

(1865–1939)

Yeats's poetry broke new ground. His writing was simple, natural, and more closely linked to the voice of the Irish people, their folklore, their traditions, and their national concerns than that of previous Irish poets. Yeats's interest in Irish politics and nationalism led him to help found the Irish Literary Theater in 1899.

For a time, Yeats moved to England because of political conflicts between people in Ireland of English and Irish ancestry. When he returned, he resided in Thoor Ballylee, a countryside tower that became an important symbol in his later poems. Yeats is considered one of the greatest twentieth-century poets who wrote in the English language.

ASSESSMENT PRACTICE: Critical Reading

Analyzing an Author's Meaning and Style   (For more practice, see Test Preparation Workbook, p. 55.)

Students preparing to take tests need to be reminded of the importance of determining what the author is implying when answering questions on a critical reading selection. For additional practice in using this skill, have students answer this question after reading "The Stolen Child":

Which of the choices best describes the author's opinions?

A Fairies will take good care of the child.

B The human child will sacrifice little by going with the fairies.

C The fairies' theft of the child will cause pain and sadness in the human world.

D The fairy world is superior.

Students should be able to determine that although the poem is told from the point of view of the fairies, the human child will be in a distant world and his loss will cause suffering. Therefore, answer *C* is best.

Review and Assess

Literary Analysis

Atmosphere

1. Using a diagram like the one here, describe the **atmosphere** of "The Stolen Child." What words or phrases, images, and techniques establish this atmosphere?

2. In what way does the atmosphere affect your expectations of how the poem will turn out?

Connecting Literary Elements

3. (a) Using a chart like the one here, list three passages in which the poet uses **alliteration,** and point out the initial consonant sounds he uses. (b) What images does the alliteration emphasize in each passage?

Passage	Sounds	Images

4. How does alliteration affect the mood or atmosphere of each passage?

Reading Strategy

Responding

5. What is your **response** to the fairies in this poem? Do you find them friendly, mysterious, threatening, or something else? Explain.
6. What are your feelings about the human child in this poem?
7. What overall feeling does the poem give you? Explain.

Extend Understanding

8. **Humanities Connection:** Which art form—film, theater, music, dance, painting, photography, or sculpture—do you think could best be used to interpret this poem? Explain.

Quick Review

Atmosphere is the mood or the overall feeling that a story or poem conveys.

Alliteration is the repetition of initial consonant sounds.

You **respond** to a poem by thinking about what the speaker has expressed, how the images in the poem affect you, and what the poem says to you.

 Take It to the Net

www.phschool.com
Take the interactive self-test online to check your understanding of the selection.

The Stolen Child ◆ 931

ENRICHMENT: Further Reading

Other Works by William Butler Yeats

"The Second Coming"
Collected Poems
Collected Plays

 Take It to the Net
Visit www.phschool.com for more information on William Butler Yeats.

Answers for p. 931

Review and Assess

1. Possible response:

Atmosphere

The poem has a magical, mysterious atmosphere.

Rhythm
The repeated chorus creates a hypnotic feel.

Words/Phrases
faery, frothy bubbles, slumbering trout, whispering in their ears

Rhyme
The changing rhyme scheme of each stanza creates a mysterious feeling.

Images
wave of moonlight, dim gray sands with light, bathe a star

2. Students might say the magical atmosphere of the poem suggests that the child might be taken by the fairies.

3. **(a)** Passages: "There lies a leafy island"; "Far off by furthest Rosses"; "Where the wandering water gushes." Sounds: l; f; w. **(b)** Images: A sleepy, quiet island; the faraway marshes; the winding water.

4. The alliteration emphasizes words and images and adds to the magical, mysterious atmosphere of the poem.

5. Possible response: The fairies seem friendly, but they also seem mysterious because they are tempting the child with vague descriptions.

6. Students might say they are worried about the child going with the fairies.

7. Some students will say the poem gives them an uneasy feeling, since the child has been lured away.

8. Some students may mention dance because the poem features an evocative moonlight dance.

931

❶ Vocabulary Development

Word Analysis

1. **(a)** *Lies* means "sits." **(b)** *Lies* means "statements that are not true."

2. **(a)** *Wave* means "beam (of light)." **(b)** *Wave* means "to motion with the hands."

3. **(a)** *Light* means "something that makes it possible to see." **(b)** *Light* means "not heavy."

Fluency: Elaboration

1. You'd expect to see a heron near water.

2. You might gloss a tabletop.

3. The most comfortable place for slumbering is a hammock.

Spelling Strategy

1. understanding

2. commandment

3. handed

❷ Grammar

1. There	4. There
2. their	5. They're
3. Their	

Writing Application

Sample summary: Fairies are trying to lure a child to their island. They're tempting the child with berries and descriptions of their carefree, mischievous activities. There they dance in the moonlight and whisper to trout. There are many beautiful places to go on their island. They're successful in getting the child to accompany them.

Integrate Language Skills

❶ Vocabulary Development Lesson

Concept Development: Words With Multiple Meanings

Many English words have more than one meaning. For example, the verb *gloss* means "to shine or make lustrous," and the noun *gloss* means "an explanatory note inserted in a text."

Identify the word in each sentence set that has multiple meanings. Explain the different meanings.

1. (a) There lies a leafy island where flapping herons wake the drowsy water rats. (b) The fairies lured the child with pleasant promises and lies.

2. (a) The wave of moonlight glosses the sands. (b) See the child wave as he fades into the forest.

3. (a) We saw the fairies dancing by the light of the moon. (b) Their steps were light on the sand.

❷ Grammar Lesson

Common Usage Problems: *their, there,* and *they're*

The words *their, there,* and *they're* can cause confusion if they are not used correctly. **Their** is a possessive pronoun and always modifies a noun. **There** can be used either as an expletive at the beginning of a sentence or as an adverb. **They're** is a contraction of *they are*.

Pronoun:	We seek for slumbering trout and whisper in *their* ears.
Expletive:	*There* are trout in the pond.
Adverb:	They lie in pools over *there* among the rushes.
Contraction:	*They're* calling softly to the child.

𝒲𝒢 *Prentice Hall Writing and Grammar Connection: Chapter 26, Section 2*

Fluency: Elaboration

Review the vocabulary list on page 927. Then, in your notebook, answer each question.

1. Where would you expect to see a *heron*?

2. What kind of item from your home would you *gloss*?

3. Where is the most comfortable place for *slumbering*?

Spelling Strategy

When you add a suffix to a word that ends in more than one consonant, do not double the final consonant. For example, *wound + -ed = wounded* and *gloss + -es = glosses.*

Combine each of the following to make a new word.

1. understand + *-ing*

2. command + *-ment*

3. hand + *-ed*

Practice Complete each of the sentences below with the correct word in parentheses.

1. (Their, There, They're) lies a leafy island where flapping herons nest.

2. The ferns drop (their, there, they're) tears over the young streams.

3. (Their, There, They're) chant lures children from their warm, loving homes.

4. (Their, There, They're) are the fairies.

5. (Their, There, They're) singing of a child.

Writing Application Write a summary of the plot of "The Stolen Child." Use *their, there,* and *they're* twice each.

TEACHING RESOURCES

The following resources can be used to enrich or extend the instruction for pp. 932–933.

Vocabulary

📝 **Selection Support**, Build Vocabulary, p. 217

📖 **Vocabulary and Spelling Practice Book** (Use this booklet for skills enrichment.) ▪

Grammar

📝 **Selection Support:** Build Grammar Skills, p. 218

𝒲𝒢 **Writing and Grammar**, Platinum Level, p. 620

💻 **Daily Language Practice Transparencies** ▪

Writing

𝒲𝒢 **Writing and Grammar**, Platinum Level, p. 109

💿 **Writing and Grammar iText CD-ROM** ▪

📄 **Writing Models and Graphic Organizers on Transparencies**, pp. 79–81

▪ **BLOCK SCHEDULING:** Resources marked with this symbol provide varied instruction during 90-minute blocks.

Writing Lesson

Crime Report

Imagine that you are a detective investigating the kidnapping of "The Stolen Child." Write a crime report describing what you found at the crime scene, including evidence, possible clues, and interviews with witnesses.

Prewriting   Review the poem to gather details about the fairies' habits and the setting. Draw a diagram of the scene, labeling each important object.

Drafting   Use precise nouns and vivid verbs to help readers picture the scene the way you encountered it. Keep your writing objective—if you include information from eyewitnesses, use direct quotations and name your sources. Refer to the diagram in your draft.

Model: Using an Objective Tone

The boy was last seen at about 8 P.M. His parents report putting him to bed in the bedroom marked on the diagram. As the diagram shows, the parents' bedroom is about ten feet down the hall from the boy's bedroom.

> Information is described in an orderly and objective way.

Revising   Review your draft and diagram to match the labeled objects in the sketch with the details in your report. This will help you identify any details that need to be added.

Prentice Hall Writing and Grammar Connection: Chapter 6, Section 4

Extension Activities

Listening and Speaking The pixies, sprites, and fairies of Irish folklore have equivalents in folklore from other cultures. Explore the folklore of another country, and select a story that reflects the theme of "The Stolen Child." In an **oral presentation,**

- Introduce the story
- Explain what culture it came from
- Explain the culture's view of these nonhuman creatures

After you present the story to classmates, compare it to "The Stolen Child," explaining the similarities and differences in the depiction of the fairies.

Research and Technology Working with a group, prepare a **timeline** that shows William Butler Yeats's place in the spectrum of Irish authors. Annotate the timeline to indicate any authors who influenced or were influenced by Yeats. Find out about Yeats's major literary works, and put them in the appropriate place on the timeline. [Group Activity]

 Take It to the Net www.phschool.com

Go online for an additional research activity using the Internet.

ASSESSMENT RESOURCES

The following resources can be used to assess students' knowledge and skills.

Selection Assessment

- **Formal Assessment,** pp. 195–197
- **Open Book Test,** pp. 163–165
- **Got It! Assessment Videotapes,** Tape 5
- **Test Bank Software**
- **Take It to the Net**
  Visit www.phschool.com for self-tests and additional questions on "The Stolen Child."

Writing Rubric

- **Performance Assess. and Portfolio Mgmt.,** p. 19

PRENTICE HALL ASSESSMENT SYSTEM

- **Workbook**
- **Skill Book**
- **Transparencies**
- **CD-ROM**

Lesson Support for p. 933

❸ Writing Lesson

- Have students use the Grid organizer in **Writing Models and Graphic Organizers on Transparencies,** pp.79–81, to help them in prewriting.

- Instruct them to write the six reporter's questions—who, what, where, when, how, why—along one axis and the names of relevant people along the other (i.e. child, parents, witnesses).

- They can use the Grid organizer as a guide when reviewing the poem and gathering details.

- When they finish, use the Description rubric, p. 19 in **Performance Assessment and Portfolio Management,** to assess students' work.

❹ Listening and Speaking

- Encourage students to choose a country that interests them or that they know very little about. You may want to use a globe or world map to aid students in their choices.

- Arrange with the librarian ahead of time to have a special section of folklore books set aside for the class. In addition, encourage students to search the Internet to find more information on the folklore of the country they have chosen.

- Have students share their presentation with the class when they finish.

CUSTOMIZE INSTRUCTION
for Universal Access

To address different learning styles, use the following activities suggested in the **Extension Activities** booklet. p. 55.

- For Musical/Rhythmic Learners, use Activity 5.

- For Visual/Spatial Learners, use Activity 6.

- For Interpersonal and Verbal/Linguistic Learners, use Activity 7.

Lesson Objectives

1. To make connections between William Butler Yeats' "The Stolen Child" and Harry and Sandy Chapin's "Cat's in the Cradle"

2. To understand how similar ideas can be communicated in different forms

3. To understand how a refrain or chorus can help communicate emotional meaning

Connections

In Yeats' "The Stolen Child," a child is lured away from the real world by the promise of a more imaginative life with the fairies. In Chapin's "Cat's in the Cradle," a father loses his son because the father is lured into a world apart from his home life.

The Poetic Talents of Harry Chapin

- Tell students that the lyrics of a song, as those on this page, are much like the lines of a poem.

- If possible, bring in examples of other folk songs to compare with Chapin's. Tom Paxton's "What Did You Learn in School Today?" is a good example.

- Point out to students that refrains, or repeated groups of lines, are much more common in songs than in straight poetry.

- Have students note that in Yeats's poem the point of view of the refrain does not vary from repetition to repetition, while the point of view in the song does vary. The first two "When you coming home . . . ? statements are sung by the son, while the last two are sung by the father.

- Ask students what is ironic about the photograph that accompanies the Chapin song on this page. **Answer:** The man in the song does not have time for his son, while the man and the boy in the photograph appear to be spending quality time together.

CONNECTIONS
Literature and Music

The Poetic Talents of Harry Chapin

Cat's in the Cradle
Harry Chapin and Sandy Chapin

"The Stolen Child" tells of a child lost through fairies' magical powers. "Cat's in the Cradle" tells of a father who stole the precious moments of his son's childhood from himself by being too busy and unavailable.

An artist in the American folk tradition of Woody Guthrie and Bob Dylan, Harry Chapin wrote songs that are essentially short stories set to music. A true humanitarian, over the course of his career he raised more than five million dollars for various causes. He died in 1981 in a car crash while on the way to perform at a benefit concert.

My child arrived just the other day,
He came to the world in the usual way.
But there were planes to catch and bills to pay,
He learned to walk while I was away.
And he was talking 'for I knew it, and as he grew
He said, "I'm gonna be like you, dad, you know I'm gonna be like you."

And the cat's in the cradle and the silver spoon,
Little boy blue and the man in the moon,
"When you comin' home dad?" "I don't know when,
But we'll get together then, You know we'll have a good time then."

My son turned ten just the other day.
He said, "Thanks for the ball, dad, come on let's play.
Can you teach me to throw?"
I said, "Not today, I got a lot to do." He said, "That's O.K."

934 ◆ Poetry

And he walked away but his smile never dimmed,
It said, I'm gonna be like him, yeah,
You know, I'm gonna be like him.

And the cat's in the cradle and the silver spoon,
Little boy blue and the man in the moon,
"When you comin' home dad?" "I don't know when,
But we'll get together then, You know we'll have a good
time then."

Well, he came from college just the other day.
So much like a man I just had to say
"Son I'm proud of you can you sit for a while?"
He shook his head and he said with a smile,
"What I'd really like dad is to borrow the car keys,
See you later. Can I have them please?"

And the cat's in the cradle and the silver spoon,
Little boy blue and the man in the moon,
"When you comin' home dad?" "I don't know when,
But we'll get together then, You know we'll have a good
time then."

I've long since retired, my son's moved away.
I called him up just the other day.
I said "I'd like to see you if you don't mind."
He said "I'd love to, dad, if I could find the time,
You see my new job's a hassle and the kids have the flu
But it's sure nice talkin' to you dad,
It's sure nice talkin' to you."

And as I hung up the phone it occurred to me,
He'd grown up just like me.
My boy was just like me.

And the cat's in the cradle and the silver spoon,
Little boy blue and the man in the moon,
"When you comin' home son?" "I don't know when,
But we'll get together then, Dad,
We're gonna have a good time then."

Connecting Literature and Music

1. What is the moral of "Cat's in the Cradle"?
2. In what way is the story told in "Cat's in the Cradle" a modern version of "The Stolen Child"?
3. Explain how the structure of "The Stolen Child" is similar to the structure of this song.

Harry Chapin

(1942–1981)
Singer/ songwriter Harry Chapin was a social activist as well as an artist. He committed time and money to the cause of ending world hunger, founding World Hunger Year in 1975.

Besides his life as a songwriter, Chapin was also a filmmaker (nominated for an Academy Award) and the composer of a musical play (nominated for two Tony Awards). Chapin died in a car accident on July 16, 1981, while on the way to perform at a benefit concert.

Connections: Cat's in the Cradle ◆ 935

Background
Music

Much of the non–Native American folk music of the United States developed from the British, Irish, and Scottish ballads brought by colonists and from African traditions brought by enslaved Africans. The ballads and blues of this heritage are storytelling forms. Traditional accompaniment includes guitar, violin, mandolin, banjo, and harmonica.

Beginning in the 1930s, the American singer and unionist Woody Guthrie revived traditional songs and also wrote his own songs in a similar style on social issues. He influenced the new generation of folk musicians, including Bob Dylan, that arose in the 1950s and 1960s. Chapin's songs of the 1970s extend this tradition of telling stories and commenting on life in musical form.

Answers
Connecting Literature and Music

1. The moral is do not ignore your children when they are growing up or they might ignore you when they are grown.
2. The modern situation in Chapin's song is one in which a child and a parent grow to be strangers because the parent is taken away from home by work. The fairy-tale situation in Yeats's poem is similar because, in it, a child and its parents are separated when the child is taken away to another world.
3. Both the poem and the song are divided into stanzas alternating with a repeated refrain. Both follow a regular rhyme scheme.

CUSTOMIZE INSTRUCTION FOR UNIVERSAL ACCESS

For Special Needs Students	For English Learners
Play a recording of "Cat's in the Cradle" for students and ask them to sing along. Have them pay attention to the structure of stanza and refrain to see how these elements contribute to the meaning of the song.	Ask students to do some research among their classmates and teachers to determine the meaning of some of the references in the song: "The cat's in the cradle," "silver spoon," "Little boy blue," and "man in the moon."

In Flanders Fields ✦ The Kraken ✦ Meeting at Night ✦ Reapers ✦ Prayer of First Dancers

Lesson Objectives

1. **To analyze and respond to literary elements**
   - Literary Analysis: Musical Devices
   - Comparing Literary Works

2. **To read, comprehend, analyze, and critique poems**
   - Reading Strategy: Listening
   - Reading Check questions
   - Review and Assess questions
   - Assessment Practice (ATE)

3. **To develop word analysis skills, fluency, and systematic vocabulary**
   - Vocabulary Development Lesson: Latin Prefix *mil-*

4. **To understand and apply written and oral language conventions**
   - Spelling Strategy
   - Grammar Lesson: *among* and *between*

5. **To understand and apply appropriate writing and research strategies**
   - Writing Lesson: Proposal for a Poetry Anthology
   - Extension Activity: Visual Presentation

6. **To understand and apply listening and speaking strategies**
   - Extension Activity: Poetry Reading

STEP-BY-STEP TEACHING GUIDE	PACING GUIDE
PRETEACH	
Motivate Students and Provide Background	
Use the Motivation activity (ATE p. 936)	5 min.
Read and discuss the Preview material and Background information (SE/ATE p. 936)	5 min.
Introduce the Concepts	
Introduce the Literary Analysis and Reading Strategy (SE/ATE p. 937)	15 min.
Pronounce the vocabulary words and read their definitions (SE p. 937)	5 min.
TEACH	
Monitor Comprehension	
Informally monitor comprehension by circulating while students read independently or in groups	10 min.
Monitor students' comprehension with the Reading Check notes (SE/ATE p. 943)	as students read
Develop vocabulary with Vocabulary notes (SE p. 939; ATE p. 939)	as students read
Develop Understanding	
Develop students' understanding of musical devices with the Literary Analysis annotations (SE p. 942; ATE pp. 939, 942)	10 min.
Develop students' understanding of listening with the Reading Strategy annotations (SE p. 943; ATE pp. 940, 943)	10 min.
ASSESS	
Assess Mastery	
Assess students' mastery of the Reading Strategy and Literary Analysis by having them answer the Review and Assess questions (SE/ATE p. 945)	20 min.
Use one or more of the print and media Assessment Resources (ATE p. 947)	up to 50 min.
EXTEND	
Apply Understanding	
Have students complete the Vocabulary Development Lesson and the Grammar Lesson (SE p. 946)	20 min.
Apply students' knowledge of using specific examples with the Writing Lesson (SE p. 947)	45 min.
Apply students' understanding using one or more of the Extension Activities (SE p. 947)	20–90 min.

A **ACCELERATED INSTRUCTION:**
Use the strategies and activities identified with an **A** .

UNIVERSAL ACCESS
- ● = Below Level Students
- ▲ = On-Level Students
- ■ = Above Level Students

Time and Resource Manager

Reading Level: Average/Challenging/Average/Easy/Easy
Average Number of Instructional Days: 4

RESOURCES		
PRINT 📖	**TRANSPARENCIES**	**TECHNOLOGY**
• **Beyond Literature,** Cross-Curricular Connection: Art, p. 56 ▲ ■		• **Interest Grabber Video,** Tape 5 ● ▲ ■
• **Selection Support Workbook:** ● ▲ ■ Literary Analysis, p. 224 Reading Strategy, p. 223 Build Vocabulary, p. 221	• **Literary Analysis and Reading Transparencies,** pp. 111 and 112 ● ▲ ■	
• **Authors In Depth,** Platinum Level ■		• **Listening to Literature** ● ▲ ■ Audiocassettes, Side 32 Audio CDs, CD 19
• **Literatura en español** ● ▲ • **Literary Analysis for Enrichment** ■		
• **Formal Assessment:** Selection Test, pp. 198–200 ● ▲ ■ • **Open Book Test,** pp. 166–168 ● ▲ ■ • **Performance Assessment and Portfolio Management,** p. 11 ● ▲ ■ • ASSESSMENT SYSTEM ● ▲ ■	• ASSESSMENT SYSTEM ● ▲ ■ Skills Practice Answers and Explanations on Transparencies	• **Test Bank Software** ● ▲ ■ • **Got It! Assessment Videotapes,** Tape 5 ● ▲
• **Selection Support Workbook:** ● ▲ ■ Build Grammar Skills, p. 222 • **Writing and Grammar,** Platinum Level ● ▲ ■ • **Extension Activities,** p. 56 ● ▲ ■	• **Daily Language Practice Transparencies** ● ▲	• **Writing and Grammar iText CD-ROM** ● ▲ ■ **Take It to the Net** www.phschool.com

BLOCK SCHEDULING: Use one 90-minute class period to preteach the selection and have students read it. Use a second 90-minute class period to assess students' mastery of skills and have them complete one of the Extension Activities.

Step-by-Step Teaching Guide
for pp. 936–937

Motivation

To capture students' interest in these musical poems, ask them to name their favorite songs, and write the five most popular on the chalkboard. Then, ask students to identify the mood of each song—for example, wistful, defiant, angry, or inspiring. Encourage students to think of situations in which songs are used to stir people's emotions. (Students may suggest religious ceremonies, celebrations, patriotic events, or movies.) Let them know that they will be reading five poems that also use "music"—the sounds and feelings of words—to create emotion.

▨ Interest Grabber Video

As an alternative, play "Public Monuments" on Tape 5 to engage student interest.

❶ Background

Social Studies

Flanders Field is also the name of an American military cemetery and memorial in Waregem, Belgium. The 368 American men who are buried there died in World War I, fighting to liberate Belgium from German occupation. In the middle of the cemetery is a chapel, on whose walls are inscribed the names of forty-three Americans missing in action—soldiers whose remains were either never identified or never recovered.

Prepare to Read

In Flanders Fields ◆ The Kraken ◆ Meeting at Night ◆ Reapers ◆ Prayer of First Dancers

▨ *Take It to the Net*

Visit www.phschool.com for instruction and activities relating to these selections, including
- background
- graphic organizers
- literary elements
- reading strategies

Preview

Connecting to the Literature

When you hear a poem, a story, a moving speech, or a dramatic proclamation read aloud, you may have the impression that you are hearing music. As you read these poems aloud, try to find the music of the words and hear them as songs.

❶ Background

World War I (1914–1918) is the backdrop for John McCrae's poem "In Flanders Fields." Territorial and economic rivalries between Russia, France, and Great Britain on one side and Germany and Austria-Hungary on the other had been brewing since the late nineteenth century. The battlefield of Flanders, a region in northern France and western Belgium, was littered with bomb craters, trenches—and bodies.

936 ◆ *Poetry*

TEACHING RESOURCES

The following resources can be used to enrich or extend the instruction for pp. 936–937.

Motivation
▨ **Interest Grabber Video**, Tape 5

Background
📖 **Beyond Literature**, p. 56 ▨

▨ *Take It to the Net*
Visit www.phschool.com for background and hotlinks for the selections.

Literary Analysis
▧ **Literary Analysis and Reading Transparencies,** Musical Devices, p. 112 ▨

Reading
📖 **Selection Support:** Reading Strategy, p. 223; Build Vocabulary, p. 221

▧ **Literary Analysis and Reading Transparencies,** Listening, p. 111

▨ **BLOCK SCHEDULING:** Resources marked with this symbol provide varied instruction during 90-minute blocks.

Literary Analysis

Musical Devices

Poets use a variety of **musical devices** to make their poetry sound a certain way:

- **Alliteration:** repetition of the first sound of several words, as in *silent swinging* or *roaring rise*
- **Onomatopoeia:** the use of words to imitate actual sounds, as in *bang, tap, swish*
- **Assonance:** repetition of similar vowel sounds, as in d*ee*p, b*e*n*ea*th, dr*ea*mless
- **Consonance:** repetition of similar consonant sounds at the ends of accented syllables, as in blue spur*t* of a ligh*t*ed ma*t*ch
- **Meter:** formal organization of rhythms; a pattern of alternating stressed and unstressed syllables
- **Repetition and rhyme:** repeated words and words that have the same sound

Comparing Literary Works

One of the things that distinguishes poetry from prose is the use of musical devices in poetry. Just as a composer of music must know harmony and melody in order to create the effects he or she desires, a poet must understand musical devices. As you read the poems in this grouping, compare the ways each poet uses these special tools to achieve an effect.

Reading Strategy

Listening

The sound of a poem gives you insight into the poet's intent. To appreciate the sound and musical qualities of a poem, **listen** to it as it is read aloud. Feel the rhythm of the lines, and pay attention to rhymes and other repeated sounds.

The rhythms and sounds of a poem often suggest a mood or reflect an idea. For example, "In Flanders Fields" has a regular, repetitive beat, suggesting the regularity of rows of grave markers. As you read, use a chart like the one shown to record the poems' sounds and what they suggest.

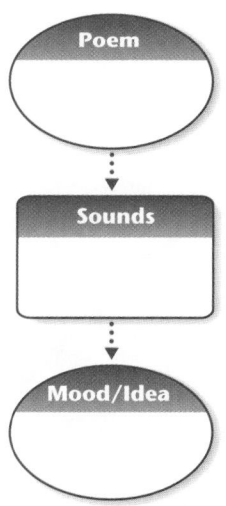

Vocabulary Development

abysmal (ə biz′ məl) *adj.* bottomless; too deep for measurement; profoundly deep (p. 939)

millennial (mi len′ ē əl) *adj.* lasting for one thousand years (p. 939)

In Flanders Fields / The Kraken / Meeting at Night / Reapers / Prayer of First Dancers ◆ 937

❷ Literary Analysis

Musical Devices

- Tell students that one of the things that sets poetry apart from most prose is the use of musical devices—the tools of language a poet uses to make a poem sound a certain way.
- Read the instruction for musical devices together as a class. Elicit from students other examples of some of the devices.
- Use the instruction for Comparing Literary Works to have students compare the use of musical devices among the selections.
- Use the Musical Devices transparency in **Literary Analysis and Reading Transparencies,** p. 112, to demonstrate for students the use of musical devices in the selections.

❸ Reading Strategy

Listening

- Tell students that listening is an important skill for appreciating poetry, which is created for the ear as well as for the eye.
- Encourage students to pay attention to poems that have a regular repetitive beat, as "In Flanders Fields" does, and to notice that when the regular rhythm is broken, their attention is drawn to the irregular lines.
- Encourage students to use a chart like the one shown on p. 937 to record the sounds of the poems as they read.

Vocabulary Development

- Pronounce each vocabulary word for students, and read the definitions as a class. Have students identify any words with which they are already familiar.

CUSTOMIZE INSTRUCTION FOR UNIVERSAL ACCESS

For Less Proficient Readers	For English Learners	For Advanced Readers
To help students understand the difficult vocabulary and complicated images expressed in the poems, invite them to read along as they listen to the recording of the poems on **Listening to Literature** Audiocassettes, Side 34, or Audio CDs, CD 17.	Pair up English learners with native speakers. Have the native speakers read aloud the poems once. Then, have students discuss unfamiliar vocabulary, looking up meanings in a dictionary if needed. Have students read aloud the poems again, each partner taking turns with the reading.	Engage students in a discussion about the effects of the musical devices. Ask students to read the poems, identifying the musical devices in each. Then, have them explain how each device adds to both the sound and the meaning of the poem.

 E-Teach

Visit E-Teach at www.phschool.com for teachers' essays on how to teach, with questions and answers.

**Step-by-Step Teaching Guide
for pp. 938–944**

CUSTOMIZE INSTRUCTION
For Verbal/Linguistic Learners

Because poets often use rich, descriptive words, students will find that reading poetry provides an excellent opportunity for them to expand their vocabulary. Suggest that students skim through the poems in the selection and make a list of the words they wish to use in their own writing and speaking.

❶ **About the Selection**

This poem, in its stark simplicity, calls on the living to acknowledge our bond with the dead—and our debt to those who gave their lives. The dead, the speakers of the poem, call upon us to take up the fight for a better world.

❷ **Critical Viewing**

Answer: The poet seems to like simple things, as evidenced by the poem's simple, straightforward language. He would probably like this simple marker.

---

❶ **IN FLANDERS FIELDS**

John McCrae

In Flanders fields the poppies blow
Between the crosses, row on row,
    That mark our place; and in the sky
    The larks, still bravely singing, fly
5 Scarce heard amid the guns below.

We are the Dead. Short days ago
We lived, felt dawn, saw sunset glow,
    Loved and were loved, and now we lie
        In Flanders fields.

10 Take up our quarrel with the foe:
To you from failing hands we throw
    The torch; be yours to hold it high.
    If ye break faith with us who die
We shall not sleep, though poppies grow
        In Flanders fields.

John McCrae

(1872–1918)
    A physician working as a medical officer in France during World War I, John McCrae saw firsthand the war about which he wrote. "In Flanders Fields" was published in Britain in 1915 and reprinted in the United States to boost the morale of soldiers and to encourage civilians to join the war effort.

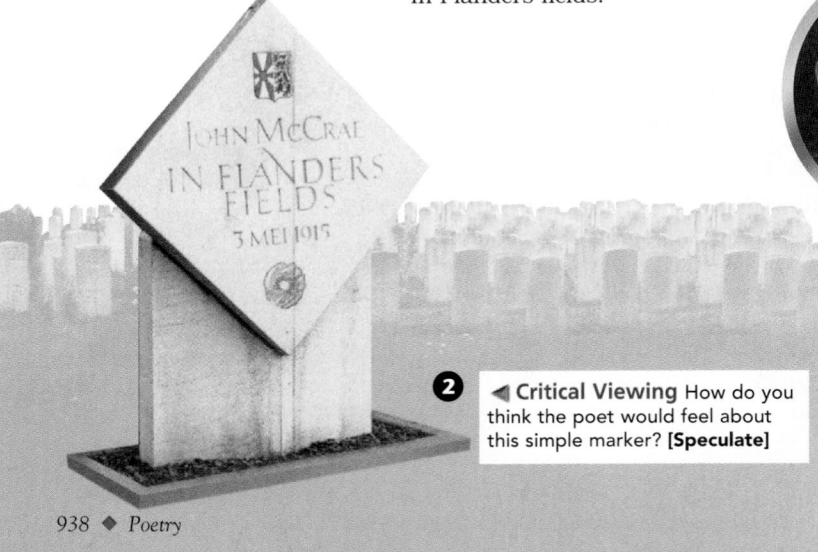

❷ ◀ **Critical Viewing** How do you think the poet would feel about this simple marker? **[Speculate]**

938 ◆ *Poetry*

TEACHING RESOURCES

The following resources can be used to enrich or extend the instruction for pp. 938–944.

Literary Analysis
📖 **Selection Support:** Literary Analysis, p. 224

Reading
🎧 **Listening to Literature Audiocassettes,** Side 32 ▪

💿 **Listening to Literature Audio CDs,** CD 19 ▪

Extension
📖 **Authors In Depth,** Platinum Level
(This collection includes seven additional selections by Alfred, Lord Tennyson for extended reading.) ▪

▪ **BLOCK SCHEDULING:** Resources marked with this symbol provide varied instruction during 90-minute blocks.

THE KRAKEN
Alfred, Lord Tennyson

❸ **About the Selection**
The poet's imagination is captured by the mythical sea monster that lives at the bottom of the ocean. An elemental force of nature, the Kraken dies only when the world ends. Like all creatures of the imagination, the Kraken thrives in an unexplored world, but loses its power when brought to light and examined.

❹ ▶**Critical Viewing**
Answer: Students may say that the many arms reflect the Kraken's "unnumbered polypi" and that the partially seen creature is mysterious like the Kraken.

❹ ◀ **Critical Viewing** How does this rendition of the Kraken compare and contrast with your impression of the Kraken in Tennyson's poem? **[Compare and Contrast]**

abysmal (ə biz´ məl) *adj.* bottomless; too deep for measurement; profoundly deep

millennial (mi len´ ē əl) *adj.* lasting for one thousand years

❺ **Literary Analysis**
Musical Devices
• Call on a volunteer to read aloud the bracketed passage. Then, ask students to identify the use of repetition and rhyme.
Answer: Students should see that *far* and forms of *sleep* are repeated; there are rhymes between *deep* and *sleep*, and *sea* and *flee*.
• Encourage students to identify other musical devices in this passage.
Answer: There is alliteration in the following places: *below* and *beneath* in lines 1–2; the repetition of *far* in line 2; *sea, sleep, sleepeth,* and *sunlights* in lines 2–4; and *faintest* and *flee* in line 4.

Below the thunders of the upper deep;
Far, far beneath in the <u>abysmal</u> sea,
His ancient, dreamless, uninvaded sleep
The Kraken[1] sleepeth: faintest sunlights flee
5 About his shadowy sides: above him swell
Huge sponges of <u>millennial</u> growth and height;
And far away into the sickly light,
From many a wondrous grot[2] and secret cell
Unnumbered and enormous polypi[3]
10 Winnow[4] with giant arms the slumbering green.
There hath he lain for ages and will lie
Battening[5] upon huge seaworms in his sleep,
Until the latter fire[6] shall heat the deep;
Then once by man and angels to be seen,
15 In roaring he shall rise and on the surface die.

---

1. **Kraken** (krä´ kən) *n.* sea monster resembling a giant squid; from Scandinavian folklore.
2. **grot** (grät) *n.* grotto; an underwater cave.
3. **polypi** (päl´ ip ē) *n.* corallike creatures with long, waving tentacles.
4. **Winnow** (win´ ō) *v.* to fan; to move wings or tentacles.
5. **Battening** (bat´ ən iŋ) *v.* feeding on; growing fat on.
6. **the latter fire** the apocalypse.

Alfred, Lord Tennyson

(1809–1892)

The most popular English poet of the nineteenth century and the first English writer ever to be made a baron, Alfred, Lord Tennyson lost favor with the public shortly after his death. Today, however, he is again known by many as the greatest Victorian poet and perhaps the most lyrical poet in the history of the English language.

The Kraken ◆ 939

❻ **Vocabulary Development**
The Latin Prefix *mil-*
• Call students' attention to the word *millennial* on p. 939. Tell students that the prefix *mil-* comes from the Latin *mille*, which means "one thousand."
• Challenge students to suggest other words containing this prefix.
Answer: Students might mention *millennium, millionaire,* and *millisecond.*
• Ask students how the word *millennial* contributes to the meaning of the stanza.
Possible response: The word *millennial* adds to the fantastic nature of the Kraken by alluding to its time in the grotto. The word also serves the poem musically through rhyme and consonance: *abysmal, swell, millennial, cell, will.*

CUSTOMIZE INSTRUCTION FOR UNIVERSAL ACCESS

For Advanced Readers

Suggest that students read additional works by Alfred, Lord Tennyson. Provide students with the title listed in the Enrichment box, ATE p. 945. You may also wish to use **Authors In Depth,** Platinum Level, which contains the following selections and others:

• "Tithonus" (poem, p. 161)
• "In Love, If Love Be Love" (poem, p. 163)
• "The Splendor Falls" (poem, p. 164)

After students have read these or other works by Tennyson, have them form discussion groups in which they compare and contrast the use of musical devices in each. Which devices does Tennyson seem to use most often, and what are their effects in each poem?

❼ About the Selection

Two lovers meet on a warm, moonlit night. The suspense and romance of this event is heightened by Browning's use of music, rhythm, and vivid imagery.

❽ Reading Strategy

Listening

- Ask students to listen to the sound of the poem as you read it aloud.
- Encourage students to notice the rhymes, repeated sounds, and rhythm of the lines.

▶ **Monitor Progress** Ask students: What is the mood of the poem?
Answer: The mood is quiet, romantic, and suspenseful.

❾ Background

Art

Atlantic Moon, by Jane Wilson American painter Jane Wilson was born in Iowa in 1924. Her work is exhibited in art galleries and museums around the country.

Use this question for discussion: Would you change this picture to make it more representative of the poem? Explain.
Answer: Some students might say that they would not change the picture because it represents the mood of the poem, if not its images. Other students might wish for a more detailed representation.

❿ ▶ Critical Viewing

Answer: Students should point out that, as in the poem, the picture portrays the sea meeting the shore, lit only by the moon.

❼ Meeting at Night
ROBERT BROWNING

1

The gray sea and the long black land;
And the yellow half-moon large and low;
And the startled little waves that leap
In fiery ringlets from their sleep,
5 As I gain the cove with pushing prow,
And quench its speed i' the slushy sand.

2

Then a mile of warm sea-scented beach;
Three fields to cross till a farm appears;
A tap at the pane, the quick sharp scratch
10 And blue spurt of a lighted match,
And a voice less loud, through its joys and fears,
Than the two hearts beating each to each!

Atlantic Moon, Jane Wilson, Fischbach Gallery, New York

❿ ▲ **Critical Viewing** Which elements of this picture reflect the setting and atmosphere of "Meeting at Night"? **[Support]**

Robert Browning

(1812–1889)

Browning worked for more than thirty years before his talent was acknowledged, devoting his time to the care of his more famous wife, Elizabeth Barrett Browning. Yet, it was his development of the dramatic monologue that had a greater influence on twentieth-century poetry. He is now considered a more significant poet than is his wife.

Reapers

JEAN TOOMER

Black reapers with the sound of steel on stones
Are sharpening scythes. I see them place the hones[1]
In their hip-pockets as a thing that's done,
And start their silent swinging, one by one.
5   Black horses drive a mower through the weeds,
And there, a field rat, startled, squealing bleeds,
His belly close to ground. I see the blade,
Blood-stained, continue cutting weeds and shade.

---

1. **hones** (hōnz) *n.* hard stones used to sharpen cutting tools.

Review and Assess

Thinking About the Selections

1. **Respond:** Which of these four poems seems most relevant to your life? Why?
2. **(a) Recall:** Who are the speakers of "In Flanders Fields"? **(b) Interpret:** What is their urgent message?
3. **(a) Recall:** In "The Kraken," what is the Kraken doing, and how do you know? **(b) Infer:** According to the poem, what is the only thing that would cause a change in the Kraken's activity? **(c) Analyze:** What would be the outcome of such an event?
4. **(a) Recall:** Describe the journey of the speaker in "Meeting at Night." **(b) Interpret:** At the end of "Meeting at Night," what is the reason for the "tap at the pane"?
5. **(a) Recall:** In "Reapers," what do the reapers do before they start swinging their scythes? **(b) Compare and Contrast:** Identify two items that the reapers cut, and explain the difference in the actions. **(c) Infer:** How does this contrast relate to the central message of the poem? Explain.
6. **Apply:** In what kinds of situations are poems or songs used to stir people's emotions?
7. **Relate:** Which of these poems do you think focuses the most on handing down something from the past? Explain.

Jean Toomer

(1894–1967)

French, Dutch, Welsh, German, Jewish, African, and Indian— Toomer was descended from all these ethnicities and races. "Because of these," he said, "my position in America has been a curious one." In 1923, Toomer earned early fame with the publication of his book *Cane*, which includes short stories, poems, and a short play.

Reapers ◆ 941

⓫ About the Selection

The reapers in this poem are too busy to notice the field rat injured by the blade of one of their mowers. Or, perhaps the impersonal, repetitive nature of their job has dulled their sense of pity for a small animal.

Answers for p. 941

Review and Assess

1. Students might cite "Meeting at Night," which features a romance.
2. **(a)** The speakers are the war dead. **(b)** Their urgent message is that their deaths will be in vain unless their successors, the audience of the poem, fight for the same principles they did.
3. **(a)** The Kraken is sleeping. Evidence includes "dreamless, uninvaded sleep," "The Kraken sleepeth," and "Battening upon huge seaworms in his sleep." **(b)** An apocalypse is the only thing that would change the Kraken's activity. **(c)** The outcome of this event would be the end of the world.
4. **(a)** The speaker travels over water, a mile of beach, and three fields to reach a farmhouse. **(b)** The tap at the pane announces to one lover the arrival of the other.
5. **(a)** They sharpen their scythes. **(b)** They cut weeds and shade— the weeds are cut by the scythes, and once the weeds have been cut, there is no shade in that spot and nowhere for small animals to hide. **(c)** The central message is that progress cannot be stopped, so this contrast relates to the negative effects of progress.
6. Students may suggest religious ceremonies, celebrations, patriotic events, or movies.
7. "In Flanders Fields" is about handing down a legacy—in this case, from the dead to the living.

⓬ PRAYER OF FIRST DANCERS

from *The Night Chant*

NAVAJO

Our Home and Native Land, 1983, Dannielle B. Hayes

⓮ ▲ Critical Viewing What technique used in this picture reflects a technique in "Prayer of First Dancers"? Explain. **[Connect]**

In Tse'gíhi,
In the house made of the dawn,
In the house made of the evening twilight,
In the house made of the dark cloud,
5   In the house made of the he-rain,
In the house made of the dark mist,
In the house made of the she-rain,
In the house made of pollen,
In the house made of grasshoppers,
10   Where the dark mist curtains the doorway,

Literary Analysis
Musical Devices What musical device is being employed in lines 2–9?

942 ◆ Poetry

The path to which is on the rainbow,
Where the zigzag lightning stands high on top,
Where the he-rain stands high on top,
Oh, male divinity!
15 With your moccasins of dark cloud, come to us.
With your leggings of dark cloud, come to us.
With your shirt of dark cloud, come to us.
With your head-dress of dark cloud, come to us.
With your mind enveloped in dark cloud, come to us.
20 With the dark thunder above you, come to us soaring.
With the shapen cloud at your feet, come to us soaring.
With the far darkness made of the dark cloud over your head,
    come to us soaring.
With the far darkness made of the he-rain over your head,
    come to us soaring.
With the far darkness made of the dark mist over your head,
    come to us soaring.
25 With the far darkness made of the she-rain over your head,
    come to us soaring.
With the zigzag lightning flung out on high over your head,
    come to us soaring.
With the rainbow hanging high over your head, come to us
    soaring.
With the far darkness made of the dark cloud on the ends
    of your wings, come to us soaring.
With the far darkness made of the he-rain on the ends
    of your wings, come to us soaring.
30 With the far darkness made of the dark mist on the ends
    of your wings, come to us soaring.
With the far darkness made of the she-rain on the ends
    of your wings, come to us soaring.
With the zigzag lightning flung out on high on the ends
    of your wings, come to us soaring.
With the rainbow hanging high on the ends of your wings,
    come to us soaring.
With the near darkness made of the dark cloud, of the he-
    rain, of the dark mist and of the she-rain, come to us.
35 With the darkness on the earth, come to us.
With these I wish the foam floating on the flowing water
    over the roots of the great corn.
I have made your sacrifice.
I have prepared a smoke for you.
My feet restore for me.
40 My limbs restore for me.

Reading Strategy

Listening This poem was originally intended as a chant and prayer. What do you hear when you read it aloud?

 Reading Check

What natural images are used in the poem?

---

❶❻ Reading Strategy

Listening

- Have students read the bracketed passage to themselves.
- Then ask students to close their eyes and listen as you read aloud the bracketed passage.
- Next, ask students the Reading Strategy question on p. 943: What do you hear when this passage is read aloud?
  Possible Response: Students will probably say that they hear the repetition most of all.
- Discuss with students the differences between reading the poem silently and hearing it read aloud.
  Possible Response: Students will probably say that hearing the poem makes its repetition more powerful and conveys its emotion more fully.

❶❼ ✓ Reading Check

Answer: Natural images used in the poem include rain, smoke, mist, clouds, thunder, lightning, rainbow, grasshoppers, pollen, dawn, twilight, wings, darkness, roots, and water.

CUSTOMIZE INSTRUCTION FOR UNIVERSAL ACCESS

For Less Proficient Readers	For Advanced Readers
The use of literary musical devices by poets is a difference between prose and poetry that students should be able to identify. Suggest that students make a chart of the devices listed on p. 937. Then, challenge them to find at least one example of each in this selection. You may wish to have students complete this exercise in pairs.	Challenge students to write a comparison of the different views of religion and nature suggested in "Prayer of First Dancers" and "The Kraken." Instruct students to use details from each poem to support their assertions. Have them include in their writings the connection between religion and nature evidenced in the poems, and the a comparison of different views of that connection.

943

Answers for p. 944

Review and Assess

1. Students might mention the repetition, which contributes to its lulling, chant-like quality.

2. **(a)** The speaker's request is for the divinity to restore his health. **(b)** Yes, the speaker is concerned with his community. The constant repetition of the pronoun *us* indicates this concern, and the refrain beginning *Happily* mentions all members of the community.

3. **(a)** "You" is the divinity. **(b)** The speaker's attitude toward "you" is one of reverence.

4. **(a)** Images include darkness, a rainbow, and lightning. **(b)** The Navajo hold nature in high esteem and feel humble before it.

5. Students should mention a song that describes nature's power.

My body restore for me.
My mind restore for me.
My voice restore for me.
Happily the old men will regard you.
45 Happily the old women will regard you.
Happily the young men will regard you.
Happily the young women will regard you.
Happily the boys will regard you.
Happily the girls will regard you.
50 Happily the children will regard you.
Happily the chiefs will regard you.
Happily, as they scatter in different directions,
they will regard you.
Happily, as they approach their homes, they will regard you.
Happily may their roads home be on the trail of pollen.
55 Happily may they all get back.
In beauty I walk.
With beauty before me, I walk.
With beauty behind me, I walk.
With beauty below me, I walk.
60 With beauty above me, I walk.
With beauty all around me, I walk.
It is finished again in beauty,
It is finished in beauty,
It is finished in beauty,
It is finished in beauty.

Review and Assess

Thinking About the Selection

1. **Respond:** Which elements of "Prayer of First Dancers" did you find most musical? Why?

2. **(a) Recall:** What is the speaker's request? **(b) Infer:** Even though the speaker's prayer is for himself, is he concerned about his community? How do you know?

3. **(a) Recall:** Who is the "you" addressed in the poem? **(b) Draw Conclusions:** What attitude does the speaker have toward the "you" being addressed?

4. **(a) Recall:** Identify three images from nature that are repeated throughout "Prayer of First Dancers." **(b) Generalize:** Basing your answer on these images, what does the poem reveal about the attitude of the Navajos toward nature?

5. **Relate:** Identify a contemporary song that contains images and ideas similar to those found in "Prayer of First Dancers."

Navajo

The Navajo nation is currently the largest Native American nation in the United States, with more than 100,000 members. Many live on the Navajo reservation, which covers 24,000 square miles of Arizona, Utah, and New Mexico.

Fierce warriors and hunters, the ancient Navajos settled in the Southwest about 1,000 years ago and eventually intermarried with the peaceful Pueblo people, who taught them to weave and raise crops.

Chants and sand paintings are part of the Navajos' complex system of ceremonials. "Prayer of First Dancers" from *The Night Chant* comes from that tradition of holy ceremonies.

ASSESSMENT PRACTICE: Critical Reading

Analyzing an Author's Meaning and Style   (For more practice, see Test Preparation Workbook, p. 56.)

Some tests require students to be prepared to paraphrase words and phrases in a poem in order to better interpret the writer's meaning. To help students with this skill, ask them to read the poem "In Flanders Fields" on p. 938 and then complete the following sentence.

The author's attitude toward war and death is most accurately described as—

A patriotism   **C** pride
B pain   **D** disrespect

Suggest that students paraphrase the poem and then eliminate choices that they recognize as incorrect, based on the poem's details. They should recognize that answer *B* is the best interpretation because the speaker mourns the lives of those who have died.

BLOCK SCHEDULING: Resources marked with this symbol provide varied instruction during 90-minute blocks.

Review and Assess

Literary Analysis

Musical Devices

1. How does the **meter** of "In Flanders Fields" relate to the purpose of the poem?

2. In the first five lines of "The Kraken," Tennyson combines both **assonance** and **consonance**. (a) Identify one example of each of these **musical devices.** (b) What is the effect of this combination?

3. Identify an example of each of the musical devices from the poems presented here.

Comparing Literary Works

4. In a chart like this one, choose adjectives to describe the effect or mood of each poem. Tell which musical devices contribute to this effect.

	"In Flanders Fields"	"The Kraken"	"Meeting at Night"	"Reapers"	"Prayer of First Dancers"
Effect					
Musical Device					

5. Which poet has used musical devices most successfully? Explain.

Reading Strategy

Listening

6. (a) Identify three pairs of rhyming words in "The Kraken." (b) What do the rhyme and rhythm of the poem add to its overall effect?

7. (a) What sound do you hear repeated in the first two lines of "Reapers"? (b) What action from the poem does this sound reflect?

8. (a) What sounds and rhythms do you hear in "Prayer of First Dancers"? (b) What effect do these sounds and rhythms produce?

Extend Understanding

9. **Cultural Connection:** Based on your reading of "Prayer of First Dancers," what important legacy do you think the Navajos have handed down to their children? Explain.

Quick Review

These **musical devices** are common in poetry:

alliteration—repetition of the first sound of several words

onomatopoeia—the use of words to imitate actual sounds

assonance—repetition of similar vowel sounds

consonance—repetition of similar consonant sounds at the ends of accented syllables

meter—formal organization of rhythms

repetition—repeated words

rhyme—words that have the same sound

You **listen** to the rhythms, rhymes, and repeated sounds in poetry to understand the mood or ideas reflected in the sounds.

 Take It to the Net

www.phschool.com

Take the interactive self-test online to check your understanding of these selections.

Answers for p. 945

Review and Assess

1. The meter of "In Flanders Fields" has the quality of a march, and the poem stresses the importance of marching on.

2. (a) Consonance: *thunders, upper, far, far.* Assonance: *thunders, upper.* (b) The combination creates a feeling of depth and mystery.

3. Alliteration: "Reapers" lines 1–2 *sound, steel, stone,* and *scythes.* Onomatopoeia: "Meeting at Night" lines 9–10 *tap, scratch,* and *spurt.* Assonance: "Meeting at Night" lines 7–8 *sea, beach,* and *Three.* Consonance: "The Kraken" lines 1–2 *thunders, upper, far, far.* Meter: "In Flanders Fields" most lines have four stressed syllables. Repetition: "Prayer of First Dancers" lines 2–9 *In the house made of.* Rhyme: "Reapers" lines 1–2 *stones* and *hones.*

4. "In Flanders Fields": Effect: structured, serious Musical Device: meter; "The Kraken": Effect: mysterious, scary Musical Device: assonance; "Reapers": Effect: impersonal, deadly; Musical Device: alliteration; "Meeting at Night": Effect: suspenseful, romantic, mysterious Musical Device: onomatopoeia; "Prayer of First Dancers": Effect: mesmerizing, lulling Musical Device: repetition

5. Some students may say that John McCrae used musical devices most effectively because the meter of "In Flanders Fields" is representative of marching soldiers.

6. (a) Rhyming words include *deep* and *sleep, sea* and *flee, height* and *light.* (b) The rhyme and rhythm create a sense of mystery and foreboding.

7. (a) The s sound is repeated in the first two lines. (b) The sound reflects the swishing motion and sound of the blades cutting through the grass.

8. (a) Repetition is the principal sound effect. (b) It creates the rhythm and builds the momentum of a chant.

9. Students are likely to mention a deep reverence for nature.

✳ **ENRICHMENT: Further Reading**

Other Works by the Authors

Works by John McCrae
In Flanders Fields, and Other Poems

Works by Alfred, Lord Tennyson
"Ulysses"

Works by Robert Browning
"My Last Duchess"

Works by Jean Toomer
Cane

 Take It to the Net
Visit www.phschool.com for more information on the authors.

❶ Vocabulary Development

Word Analysis

1. b   3. d
2. c   4. a

Fluency: Context

1. It would be very difficult because the pool would be too deep for measurement.
2. You would have to wait one thousand years.

Spelling Strategy

1. refusal   3. dismissal
2. proposal

❷ Grammar

1. between   4. between
2. between   5. between
3. among

Writing Application

Sample sentences: The crosses sit among the poppies in Flanders Fields. The poppies grow between two crosses.

Integrate Language Skills

❶ Vocabulary Development Lesson

Word Analysis: Latin Prefix *mil-*

In his poem "The Kraken," Tennyson uses the word *millennial* to describe the growth and height of the sponges. *Millennial*, which means "of or relating to a thousand-year period," contains the prefix *mil-* from the Latin *mille*, meaning "one thousand."

In your notebook, match each word beginning with *mil-* in the left column with its definition in the right column.

1. millennium   a. one thousand thousands
2. millipede   b. a period of one thousand years
3. millimeter   c. an insect with many legs
4. million   d. one one-thousandth of a meter

❷ Grammar Lesson

Common Usage Problems: *among* and *between*

Both *among* and *between* are prepositions. **Among** always implies a relationship of three or more items. **Between** is usually used only with two things.

> **Among:** Spent shells are scattered *among* the fallen bodies in Flanders fields. (many bodies)
>
> **Between:** The Kraken lies deep *between* the ocean surface and the ocean floor. (two items)

Fluency: Context

Answer the following questions, which are based on the vocabulary list on page 937.

1. If a pond were *abysmal*, how easy would it be for you to retrieve your sunglasses if you dropped them into it? Explain.
2. If you planted *millennial* roses, how long would you have to wait to see them bloom?

Spelling Strategy

The suffix *-al* is often used to turn nouns into related adjectives or verbs into related nouns. For example, the noun *abyss* becomes the adjective *abysmal*, which means "bottomless" or "profoundly deep." In your notebook, write the noun form of each of the following verbs.

1. refuse   2. propose   3. dismiss

Practice Complete these sentences with *among* or *between*.

1. The two sides could not settle the quarrel ___?___ them.
2. The Kraken lies ___?___ the seaweed and the giant sponges.
3. They moved ___?___ the sheaves of grain.
4. The meeting ___?___ the two friends was a joyful one.
5. He stands ___?___ the dark thunder above him and the cloud at his feet.

Writing Application Write two sentences about one of these poems. In one, correctly illustrate the use of *among*, and use *between* in the other.

𝒲𝒢 *Prentice Hall Writing and Grammar Connection: Chapter 26, Section 2*

TEACHING RESOURCES

The following resources can be used to enrich or extend the instruction for pp. 946–947.

Vocabulary

📓 **Selection Support:** Build Vocabulary, p. 221

📓 **Vocabulary and Spelling Practice Book** (Use this booklet for skills enrichment.) ▨

Grammar

📓 **Selection Support:** Build Grammar Skills, p. 222

𝒲𝒢 **Writing and Grammar,** Platinum Level, p. 613

🖥 **Daily Language Practice Transparencies** ▨

Writing

𝒲𝒢 **Writing and Grammar,** Platinum Level, p. 181

💿 **Writing and Grammar iText CD-ROM** ▨

▨ **BLOCK SCHEDULING:** Resources marked with this symbol provide varied instruction during 90-minute blocks.

Writing Lesson

Proposal for a Poetry Anthology

An anthology is a collection of works that have form or a theme in common. Using these poems, write a proposal for a poetry anthology that you would like to develop. Choose a controlling idea that links the poems, and explain it in your proposal.

Prewriting   Think of how you would like to arrange the poems, and gather details to support your idea. For example, if you were to propose an anthology based on musical devices, you might make a chart like the one shown.

Model: Gathering Specific Examples

Musical Device	Poem	Example
Alliteration	"Reapers"	Steel on stones
Onomatopoeia	"Meeting at Night"	A tap at the pane

Drafting   Begin by explaining the concept or organization of your anthology. Then, introduce specific examples to explain the points you make.

Revising   Review your proposal for clarity and supporting examples. Make sure that it is obvious why you have grouped the poems together. If your general idea is not clear, add information to explain your organization more effectively.

Prentice Hall Writing and Grammar Connection: Chapter 9, Section 3

Extension Activities

Listening and Speaking Choose one of the poems from this group, and give a **poetry reading** for the class. Practice reading the selection aloud in front of a mirror.

- Think about the poem's meaning to help determine which parts you should emphasize using voice, facial expressions, and gestures.
- Read according to punctuation, rather than stopping at the end of each line.

After practicing, present your reading to the class.

Research and Technology Work in a small group to produce a **visual presentation** showing mythological monsters, such as the Kraken, from various cultures. Divide the tasks of researching, writing, illustrating, and synthesizing the information among group members. Present your information on a poster, a scroll, or in a book. [Group Activity]

 Take It to the Net   www.phschool.com

Go online for an additional research activity using the Internet.

In Flanders Fields / The Kraken / Meeting at Night / Reapers / Prayer of First Dancers ◆ 947

ASSESSMENT RESOURCES

The following resources can be used to assess students' knowledge and skills.

Selection Assessment

- **Formal Assessment,** pp. 198–200
- **Open Book Test,** pp. 166–168
- **Got It! Assessment Videotapes,** Tape 5
- **Test Bank Software**
- *Take It to the Net*

   Visit www.phschool.com for self-tests and additional questions on the selections.

Writing Rubric

- **Performance Assessment and Portfolio Management,** p. 11

PRENTICE HALL ASSESSMENT *SYSTEM*

- **Workbook**
- **Skill Book**
- **Transparencies**
- **CD-ROM**

---

❸ **Writing Lesson**

- Tell students that they can choose a group of poems based on form, such as sonnets or haiku; on theme, such as love or hope; or on elements of language, such as musical devices.
- Remind students that once they have decided on the overall idea of the anthology, they should include in their proposals specific examples of poems that support their idea.
- Use the Writing Lesson to guide students in writing their proposals.
- Use the Persuasive Composition rubric in **Performance Assessment and Portfolio Management,** p. 11, to evaluate students' letters.

❹ **Research and Technology**

- Ask students to reread the poem on p. 939 and envision the Kraken based on the descriptive words Tennyson used.
- Have students find examples of monsters described by cultures from around the world, and decide which they wish to illustrate and how they plan to represent it.
- Tell students that they may draw the creatures themselves, or find artwork or photographs that illustrate them.
- Have students display their representations for the class. Assess them based on creativity and research.

CUSTOMIZE INSTRUCTION for Universal Access

To address different learning styles, use the following activities suggested in the **Extension Activities** booklet, p. 56.

- For Verbal/Linguistic Learners, use Activity 5.
- For Bodily/Kinesthetic Learners, use Activity 6.
- For Verbal/Linguistic Learners, use Activity 7.

The Wind—tapped like a tired Man ✦ A Pace Like That ✦ Metaphor ✦ Right Hand

Lesson Objectives

1. **To analyze and respond to literary elements**
   - Literary Analysis: Figurative Language
   - Comparing Literary Works

2. **To read, comprehend, analyze, and critique poems**
   - Reading Strategy: Paraphrasing
   - Review and Assess questions
   - Assessment Practice (ATE)

3. **To develop word analysis skills, fluency, and systematic vocabulary**
   - Vocabulary Development Lesson: Latin Word Root: -tac-

4. **To understand and apply written and oral language conventions**
   - Spelling Strategy
   - Grammar Lesson: Elliptical Clauses

5. **To understand and apply appropriate writing and research strategies**
   - Writing Lesson: Analysis of a Poem
   - Extension Activity: Biographical Report

6. **To understand and apply listening and speaking strategies**
   - Extension Activity: Interview

STEP-BY-STEP TEACHING GUIDE	PACING GUIDE
PRETEACH	
Motivate Students and Provide Background	
Use the Motivation activity (ATE p. 948)	5 min.
Read and discuss the Preview material and Background information (SE/ATE p. 948) **A**	5 min.
Introduce the Concepts	
Introduce the Literary Analysis and Reading Strategy (SE/ATE p. 949) **A**	15 min.
Pronounce the vocabulary words and read their definitions (SE p. 949)	5 min.
TEACH	
Monitor Comprehension	
Informally monitor comprehension by circulating while students read independently or in groups **A**	10 min.
Develop vocabulary with Vocabulary notes (SE pp. 950, 951, 954; ATE p. 954)	as students read
Develop Understanding	
Develop students' understanding of figurative language with the Literary Analysis annotation (ATE p. 952) **A**	10 min.
Develop students' understanding of paraphrasing with the Reading Strategy annotation (ATE p. 951)	10 min.
ASSESS	
Assess Mastery	
Assess students' mastery of the Reading Strategy and Literary Analysis by having them answer the Review and Assess questions (SE/ATE p. 955)	20 min.
Use one or more of the print and media Assessment Resources (ATE p. 957) **A**	up to 50 min.
EXTEND	
Apply Understanding	
Have students complete the Vocabulary Development Lesson and the Grammar Lesson (SE p. 956) **A**	20 min.
Apply students' ability to analyze a poem using the Writing Lesson (SE p. 957) **A**	45 min.
Apply students' understanding using one or more of the Extension Activities (SE p. 957)	20–90 min.

 ACCELERATED INSTRUCTION:
Use the strategies and activities identified with an **A**.

UNIVERSAL ACCESS
- ● = Below Level Students
- ▲ = On-Level Students
- ■ = Above Level Students

Time and Resource Manager

Reading Level: Average/Challenging/Easy/Average
Average Number of Instructional Days: 4

RESOURCES

PRINT 📖	TRANSPARENCIES 🗂	TECHNOLOGY 💿 🎧 📼
• **Beyond Literature,** Workplace Connection: Time Management Skills, p. 57 ▲ ■		• **Interest Grabber Video,** Tape 5 ● ▲ ■
• **Selection Support Workbook:** ● ▲ ■ Literary Analysis, p. 228 Reading Strategy, p. 227 Build Vocabulary, p. 225	• **Literary Analysis and Reading Transparencies,** pp. 113 and 114 ● ▲ ■	
		• **Listening to Literature** ● ▲ ■ Audiocassettes, Side 33 Audio CDs, CD 19
• **Literatura en español** ● ▲ • **Literary Analysis for Enrichment** ■	• **Fine Art Transparencies, Volume 1,** Art Transparency 11 ● ▲ ■	
• **Formal Assessment:** Selection Test, pp. 201–203 ● ▲ ■ • **Open Book Test,** pp. 169–171 ● ▲ ■ • **Performance Assessment and Portfolio Management,** p. 16 ● ▲ ■ • **PRENTICE HALL ASSESSMENT** *SYSTEM* ● ▲ ■	• **PRENTICE HALL ASSESSMENT** *SYSTEM* ● ▲ ■ Skills Practice Answers and Explanations on Transparencies	• **Test Bank Software** ● ▲ ■ • **Got It! Assessment Videotapes,** Tape 5 ● ▲
• **Selection Support Workbook:** ● ▲ ■ Build Grammar Skills, p. 226 • **Writing and Grammar,** Platinum Level ● ▲ ■ • **Extension Activities,** p. 57 ● ▲ ■	• **Daily Language Practice Transparencies** ● ▲ • **Writing Models and Graphic Organizers on Transparencies,** pp. 53–59 ● ▲ ■	• **Writing and Grammar iText CD-ROM** ● ▲ ■ 💻 *Take It to the Net* www.phschool.com

BLOCK SCHEDULING: Use one 90-minute class period to preteach the selection and have students read it. Use a second 90-minute class period to assess students' mastery of skills and have them complete one of the Extension Activities.

PRETEACH

Step-by-Step Teaching Guide for pp. 948–949

Motivation

Before students read, have them share the lyrics of favorite songs that they think express important messages about life. Help students to recognize any figurative language in the lyrics. If necessary, remind them that figurative expressions are imaginative comparisons used to describe a person, place, thing, or idea. Tell students that, like song lyrics, these poems use imaginative comparisons to make a point.

▭ Interest Grabber Video

As an alternative, play "Philip Fried on Poetry and Inspiration" on Tape 5 to engage student interest.

❶ Background

Social Studies

The Hebrew word *Torah* means "to teach" or "to show the way." The written Torah, to which the Background information on p. 948 refers, is handwritten on parchment scrolls and preserved in all Jewish synagogues. Readings from the Torah play a large role in many synagogue services.

Prepare to Read

The Wind—tapped like a tired Man ◆ A Pace Like That ◆ Metaphor ◆ Right Hand

▭ Take It to the Net

Visit www.phschool.com for instruction and activities relating to the selections, including
- background
- graphic organizers
- literary elements
- reading strategies

Preview

Connecting to the Literature

Some days just do not go the way we would like. Fortunately, every new day offers the chance to make a fresh start, right a wrong, or accomplish a goal. The speakers in these poems realize the importance of each day and the effect of the large and small choices they make.

❶ Background

In "A Pace Like That," the poet makes a comparison to a Torah scroll. A Torah scroll is a long, rolled parchment on which the first five books of the Bible are written in Hebrew. The Torah relates centuries of Jewish history. Specific readings from the Torah are assigned to each day, and the entire cycle of readings takes one year to complete.

TEACHING RESOURCES

The following resources can be used to enrich or extend the instruction for pp. 948–949.

Motivation

▭ **Interest Grabber Video**, Tape 5

Background

📖 **Beyond Literature**, p. 57 ▭

 Take It to the Net

Visit www.phschool.com for background and hotlinks for the selections.

Literary Analysis

📖 **Selection Support:** Literary Analysis, p. 228 ▭

📄 **Literary Analysis and Reading Transparencies,** Figurative Language, p. 114

Reading

📄 **Literary Analysis and Reading Transparencies,** Paraphrasing, p. 113

 BLOCK SCHEDULING: Resources marked with this symbol provide varied instruction during 90-minute blocks.

Literary Analysis

Figurative Language

Figurative language is writing or speech not meant to be interpreted literally. Here are some of the most often used figures of speech:

- A **simile** compares unlike things using the word *like* or *as*. In "Right Hand," the poet writes that a hand moves "back and forth *like* a Greek chorus."
- A **metaphor** also makes a comparison by writing or speaking about one thing as if it were another. In "Metaphor," the poet writes that "Morning *is* / a new sheet of paper."
- **Personification** describes an object, animal, or idea as if it had human characteristics. In "The Wind—tapped like a tired Man," the poet describes the wind as if it were a guest in a home.

Look for other examples of figurative language in these poems.

Comparing Literary Works

Writers and poets use figurative language to create vivid impressions and to help readers see things in new ways. Each figure of speech—simile, metaphor, and personification—produces a different result. As you read the poems that follow, compare the figurative language that is used and the effects that each produces.

Reading Strategy

Paraphrasing

Because poetry is so concise, it is helpful to **paraphrase,** or use your own words to restate the meaning of the lines. As you read, paraphrase complicated lines or stanzas. Keep a chart like the one here to paraphrase key passages in these poems.

Poet's Words

Paraphrase

Vocabulary Development

countenance (koun´ tə nəns) *n.* face (p. 950)

tremulous (trem´ yōō ləs) *adj.* quivering (p. 950)

flurriedly (flur´ əd lē) *adv.* in a flustered, agitated way (p. 950)

decipher (dē sī´ fər) *v.* make out the meaning (p. 951)

taciturn (tas´ ə turn´) *adj.* uncommunicative (p. 954)

eloquent (el´ ə kwənt) *adj.* vividly expressive (p. 954)

guttural (gut´ ər əl) *adj.* produced in the throat; harsh (p. 954)

diffused (di fyōōzd´) *v.* spread out (p. 954)

garrulity (gə rōō´ lə tē) *n.* talkativeness (p. 954)

The Wind—tapped like a tired Man / A Pace Like That / Metaphor / Right Hand ◆ 949

---

❷ Literary Analysis

Figurative Language

- Tell students that figurative language is used to create a feeling or special effect—it is not meant to be taken literally.
- Read the instruction about figurative language together as a class.
- Encourage students to think of other examples of similes, metaphors, and personification.
- Use the Figurative Language transparency in **Literary Analysis and Reading Transparencies,** p. 114, to demonstrate for students the different figures of speech they will see in the poems.

❸ Reading Strategy

Paraphrasing

- Remind students that when they read something and then restate it using their own words, they are paraphrasing.
- Tell students that, as an example, they might paraphrase the first four lines of "A Pace Like That" as "I realized when I was looking at the lemon tree I planted last year that I would like to slow down and take time to appreciate the things around me."
- Instruct students to complete a paraphrasing chart like the one on p. 949 as they read the poems.

Vocabulary Development

- Pronounce each vocabulary word for students, and read the definitions as a class. Have students identify any words with which they are already familiar.

CUSTOMIZE INSTRUCTION FOR UNIVERSAL ACCESS

For Less Proficient Readers	For English Learners	For Advanced Readers
Students may be able to better understand figurative language by discussing common expressions such as "This job is a piece of cake" (metaphor), "She was as fast as lightning" (simile), and "The wind is howling outside my window" (personification).	Invite students to share colloquial expressions and sayings about life from their native languages. If possible, have them write the sayings on the board, translate them into English, and point out any examples of similes, metaphors, and personification.	Suggest that students pick one of the poems to use as a model. First, have students identify the figurative language used in the poem and determine what effects it creates. Then, have them write a poem of their own using the same style and the same forms of figurative language.

 E-Teach

Visit E-Teach at www.phschool.com for teachers' essays on how to teach, with questions and answers.

**CUSTOMIZE INSTRUCTION
For Visual/Spatial Learners**

Encourage students to create or find a picture to accompany one of the poems. Students may want to draw the topic described in the poem or find a photograph or illustration that complements it. Suggest that students look through magazines or art books to find an image they feel is appropriate. Allow time for students to share their findings with the class.

❶ About the Selection

By personifying a gentle wind blowing through the speaker's room, Emily Dickinson conveys a sense of connection with nature and the importance of the everyday events of the natural world.

Answers for p. 950

Review and Assess

1. Students may say that just as the speaker enjoys the presence of the wind, so too have they enjoyed it, especially on warm days.

2. (a) The guest is the wind. **(b)** The wind sounds like hummingbirds and music, then taps again and is gone.

3. (a) Words or phrases include *tired Man, No Bone had He, tremulous, flitting,* and *timid Man.* **(b)** The speaker sees the wind as kind because she speaks of him as if he were a guest who keeps her company and plays music for her.

4. (a) The speaker invites the wind in and tries to offer him a chair. **(b)** The speaker seems kind, appreciative of nature, and lonely.

---

❶ The Wind — *tapped like a tired Man*

Emily Dickinson

The Wind—tapped like a tired Man—
And like a Host—"Come in"
I boldly answered—entered then
My Residence within

5 A Rapid—footless Guest—
To offer whom a Chair
Were as impossible as hand
A Sofa to the Air—

No Bone had He to bind Him—
10 His Speech was like the Push
Of numerous Humming Birds at once
From a superior Bush—

His <u>Countenance</u>—a Billow—
His Fingers, as He passed
15 Let go a music—as of tunes
Blown <u>tremulous</u> in Glass—

He visited—still flitting—
Then like a timid Man
Again, He tapped—'twas <u>flurriedly</u>—
And I became alone—

countenance (koun′ tə nəns) *n.* face

tremulous (trem′ yŏŏ ləs) *adj.* quivering

flurriedly (flur′ əd lē) *adv.* in a flustered, agitated way

Emily Dickinson

(1830–1886)
Emily Dickinson never married and spent almost her entire life in the home of her family. As she grew older, she rarely left the house. During the last ten years of her life, she dressed only in white and would not allow anyone to see her. When her health failed, she permitted her doctor to examine her only by observing her from a distance. In 1886, she died in the house in which she was born. (To learn more about Dickinson, see pages 159 and 284.)

Review and Assess

Thinking About the Selection

1. **Respond:** How does this poem relate to your experiences with the wind?

2. **(a) Recall:** In "The Wind—tapped like a tired Man," who is the "Guest" who enters the speaker's residence? **(b) Interpret:** What does the wind do when it blows through the house?

3. **(a) Interpret:** What words or phrases show the wind to be fleeting or fragile? **(b) Hypothesize:** Do you think the speaker sees the wind as menacing or kind? Explain.

4. **(a) Recall:** What two actions does the speaker try to complete? **(b) Interpret:** What impression of the speaker does the poem present?

TEACHING RESOURCES

The following resources can be used to enrich or extend the instruction for pp. 950–954.

Literary Analysis

📄 **Writing Models and Graphic Organizers on Transparencies,** pp. 53–59

Reading

📖 **Selection Support:** Reading Strategy, p. 227; Build Vocabulary, p. 225

🎧 **Listening to Literature Audiocassettes,** Side 33 ▦

💿 **Listening to Literature Audio CDs,** CD 19 ▦

Extension ·

📖 **Fine Art Transparencies, Volume 1,**
Art Transparency 11 (Invite students to compare the "magic" of the magician's right hand as he performs before a crowd with the influence of Grandfather's right hand in Philip Fried's poem, as he lives his heritage before his family.) ▦

▦ **BLOCK SCHEDULING:** Resources marked with this symbol provide varied instruction during 90-minute blocks.

❷ A Pace Like That

Yehuda Amichai

I'm looking at the lemon tree I planted.
A year ago. I'd need a different pace, a slower one,
to observe the growth of its branches, its leaves as they open.
I want a pace like that.
5 Not like reading a newspaper
but the way a child learns to read,
or the way you quietly <u>decipher</u> the inscription
on an ancient tombstone.

And what a Torah scroll takes an entire year to do
10 as it rolls its way from Genesis to the death of Moses,
I do each day in haste
or in sleepless nights, rolling over from side to side.

The longer you live, the more people there are
who comment on your actions. Like a worker
15 in a manhole: at the opening above him
people stand around giving free advice
and yelling instructions,
but he's all alone down there in his depths.

decipher (dē sīˊfər) v.
make out the meaning

Yehuda Amichai

(1924–2000)

Born in Germany, Yehuda Amichai immigrated with his family to Palestine, the region that became Israel, in 1948. He was a soldier in the Israeli defense forces and fought in several wars.

In addition to poetry, Amichai wrote short stories, a novel, and a play. He wrote in Hebrew, using this ancient language to write about timeless themes and contemporary topics. His Hebrew words have been translated into more than thirty languages.

A Pace Like That ◆ 951

Review and Assess

Thinking About the Selections

1. **Respond:** What kind of pace would you like to keep in your own life?

2. **(a) Recall:** According to the speaker in "A Pace Like That," what happens as you live longer? **(b) Infer:** Why might the speaker want to live at a slower pace?

3. **(a) Interpret:** Why does the poet compare the Torah scroll to his way of life? **(b) Draw Conclusions:** Why is the Torah scroll a good image for a slow pace?

4. **(a) Compare and Contrast:** In what ways do the images of nature in these poems reflect similar attitudes toward the natural world? **(b) Make a Judgment:** Do you think that most people live at a fast pace? Explain your answer.

Through an extended metaphor comparing each new morning to a blank sheet of paper, Eve Merriam conveys an optimistic view of life: that each new day is important because it brings an opportunity for a fresh start.

⑤ Literary Analysis

Figurative Language

• Call on a volunteer to read aloud the bracketed passage.

▶ **Monitor Progress** Then, ask students to identify the figurative expression in this stanza and explain what the poet means.
Answer: "Morning is/a new sheet of paper" is a metaphor—a new sheet of paper and a new day each offer a fresh start.

• Then, ask students what the used "sheet of paper" might represent, and where it might be filed away each day.
Answer: The used sheet of paper is the person's experience that day. The consequences of that experience are filed away in the person's memory, as a resource to be mined in the future.

952 ◆ *Poetry*

④ Metaphor

Eve Merriam

⑤ Morning is
a new sheet of paper
for you to write on.

Whatever you want to say,
5 all day,
until night
folds it up
and files it away.

The bright words and the dark words
10 are gone
until dawn
and a new day
to write on.

⑥ ◀ **Critical Viewing** How do you think the poet would evaluate the achievement shown in this photograph? **[Analyze]**

Review and Assess

Thinking About the Selection

1. **Respond:** To what would you compare the morning? Why?
2. **(a) Recall:** To what does the poet of "Metaphor" compare the morning? **(b) Interpret:** In what ways are these two alike?
3. **(a) Recall:** What happens when night falls? **(b) Infer:** What does "files it away" in line 8 suggest?
4. **(a) Recall:** What does dawn bring? **(b) Interpret:** What do you think the poet means by "The bright words and the dark words" in line 9?
5. **(a) Interpret:** What images, words, or actions help the poet carry the metaphor through the entire poem? **(b) Evaluate:** What makes this metaphor so effective? **(c) Take a Position:** Do you agree or disagree with the philosophy expressed in the poem? Explain.

Eve Merriam

(1916–1992)
Eve Merriam was born in Philadelphia, Pennsylvania. Because her family was always interested in books and reading, Merriam began her lifelong fascination with poetry at an early age. She has written books of poetry for children, including *There Is No Rhyme for Silver*, and for adults, including *Family Circle*. Merriam called poetry the most immediate and richest form of communication.

Metaphor ◆ 953

⑥ ▶ **Critical Viewing**
Answer: The poet might think the figure suggests the effort and accomplishment that are possible each new day.

Answers for p. 953

Review and Assess

1. Possible response: I would compare the morning to a child's first steps, because it is a time of day to be entered slowly.
2. **(a)** Morning is compared to a new sheet of paper. **(b)** Both offer the chance of a fresh start.
3. **(a)** Night folds up the day and files it away. **(b)** The phrase suggests storing it (the experience) for future use.
4. **(a)** Dawn brings a new day. **(b)** The poet is referring to good and bad feelings, moods, and experiences that people accumulate during the day.
5. **(a)** The image of night folding and filing the day away; the words *bright words, dark words,* and *a new day to write on* carry the metaphor through the entire poem. **(b)** It is an effective metaphor because it holds up to all of Merriam's examples: morning is like new paper because it gets used, stored away, and replaced by a new, fresh opportunity. **(c)** Some students will say they do not agree with the philosophy of the poem because your past becomes a part of you—you're never free to really start over each day.

CUSTOMIZE INSTRUCTION FOR UNIVERSAL ACCESS

For Gifted/Talented Students	For Advanced Readers
Suggest that students imagine that it is first thing in the morning and their journals are a "new sheet of paper." Have them write something that reflects a sense of freshness—it may be a poem, a scene from a story, or a description of an insight they had recently.	Suggest that students work in small groups to analyze and interpret the poems. You may want them to use a chart that includes the following questions: What is the theme? What is the tone? What is the speaker's attitude? How well does the poet convey her or his message? What types of figurative language does the poet employ? Is the poet's use of figurative language effective?

7 About the Selection

In this poem, the speaker honors his grandfather, a Jewish immigrant whose right hand—seamed, eloquent, and self-assured—reveals his character and the quality of his life. In this characterization, Fried celebrates the importance of an "ordinary" (yet extraordinary) man.

8 Vocabulary Development

The Latin Root –tac-

- Call students' attention to the word *taciturn* on p. 954. Tell students that the root -tac- comes from the Latin word *tacitus*, which means "silent."

- Ask students how the word *taciturn* contributes to the meaning of the stanza.
  Possible response: The word is used in a surprising way because it is applied to trousers. The uncommunicative nature of the trousers is contrasted with the "smiling," lively hand.

Answers for p. 954

Review and Assess

1. Some students might feel they would not be able to communicate with him, while his unique character would intrigue others.

2. **(a)** It "speaks" to the shirts. **(b)** The hand or grandfather might share stories about his boyhood, people he knew, or poems.

3. **(a)** These lines indicate that the grandfather's hand is a strong presence—meaning his true self is a strong presence. **(b)** The speaker comes from a Jewish immigrant family.

4. **(a)** The grandfather probably uses Yiddish most often because the last two lines state that he does not speak English very often. **(b)** He is self-conscious; he does not want his Yiddish self (the hand) to emerge.

5. The poem conveys respect and pride for Grandfather, based on words such as "eloquent" and "When it entered a room, even the corners/mumbled in Yiddish."

7 Right Hand

Philip Fried

Grandfather carried his voice in the seamed
palm of his right hand, the one
8 | that had ironed countless <u>taciturn</u> trousers.

What an <u>eloquent</u> hand, it broke into grins
5 and self-assured narration whenever
it opened—how could a hand carry nothing,
bear away nothing from its nation?
When it entered a room, even the corners
mumbled in Yiddish, the very dust
10 had sifted from consonants' <u>guttural</u> rubbing.

The poems this hand had proclaimed to shirts
as it moved back and forth like a Greek chorus
across the stage of the ironing board—
these poems had <u>diffused</u> in clouds of steam.

15 Grandpa himself had long been struck dumb
by the <u>garrulity</u> of this hand,
but sometimes he'd thrust it deep in his pocket
and, straightening up, display an uncanny
knack for spelling English words.

taciturn (tas′ ə tʉrn′) *adj.*
uncommunicative

eloquent (el′ ə kwənt) *adj.*
vividly expressive

guttural (gut′ ər əl) *adj.*
produced in the throat;
harsh

diffused (di fyoozd′) *v.*
spread out

garrulity (gə roo′ lə tē) *n.*
talkativeness

Philip Fried

(b. 1945)

Philip Fried, a poet and editor, is the founder of *The Manhattan Review*, an international poetry journal that features interviews with poets from around the world, as well as translations of their work. Fried is the author of two collections of poetry, *Mutual Trespasses* and *Quantum Genesis*. He has also collaborated with his wife, photographer Lynn Saville, on *Acquainted With the Night*, a collection of poems selected by him with photographs taken by her.

Review and Assess

Thinking About the Selection

1. **Respond:** Would you like to spend time with the man described in this poem? Why or why not?

2. **(a) Recall:** What does the grandfather's hand do as it irons shirts? **(b) Interpret:** What kinds of stories might the hand or the grandfather have to share?

3. **(a) Interpret:** Explain the meaning of lines 8–9. **(b) Infer:** What can you infer about the speaker's heritage based on this poem?

4. **(a) Infer:** What language do you think the grandfather uses most often? Explain. **(b) Speculate:** Why do you think he puts his hand in his pocket when he spells English words?

5. **Generalize:** What feeling toward Grandfather does this poem convey? Explain.

954 ◆ Poetry

✎ ASSESSMENT PRACTICE: Critical Reading

Analyzing an Author's Meaning and Style   (For more practice, see Test Preparation Workbook, p. 57.)

As students prepare to take tests, they may need further instruction in using critical reading as well as writing skills. Interpreting phrases by analyzing an author's meaning and style is a skill that students will find helpful when answering writing prompts. Use the following sample question.

Read the poem "The Wind—tapped like a tired Man" on p. 950 and respond to the following writing prompt:

What impression of the wind does Emily Dickinson create in her poem?

Responses should **(1)** include an appropriate thesis statement, developed with supporting details from Dickinson's poem; **(2)** be well organized; and **(3)** be written with appropriate sentence construction and punctuation.

Remind students to include details, examples, and impressions from the poem.

Review and Assess

Literary Analysis

Figurative Language

1. What qualities of the wind might lead Dickinson to **personify** it as "A Rapid—footless Guest"?
2. (a) What **simile** does Amichai use in "A Pace Like That" to describe the way people comment on his actions? (b) Explain how this comparison clarifies his meaning.
3. Explain the **metaphor** in "Metaphor."
4. Identify the simile Fried uses in "Right Hand" to describe the movement of his grandfather's hand while ironing shirts.

Comparing Literary Works

5. Using a chart like the one here, identify the type of figurative language used in each poem, give an example from the poem, and explain its effect on the overall tone of the poem.

Poem	Type of Figurative Language	Example	Effect

6. In your view, which poem presents the most effective figurative language? Explain.

Reading Strategy

Paraphrasing

7. **Paraphrase** the first and last stanzas of "The Wind—tapped . . ."
8. (a) Choose words that describe the speed of each activity in the first two stanzas of "A Pace Like That." (b) Use these words to paraphrase what Amichai says about the pace he wants to achieve.
9. (a) Identify two words Fried uses to describe his grandfather's hand, and give a synonym for each. (b) Paraphrase the description using the synonyms you have chosen.

Extend Understanding

10. **Cultural Connection:** In "Metaphor," the poet believes that each new day is like a blank piece of paper. What are some possible effects of a positive approach to each new day?

The Wind—tapped like a tired Man / A Pace Like That / Metaphor / Right Hand ◆ 955

Quick Review

Figurative language is writing or speech not meant to be interpreted literally.

Personification describes an object, animal, or idea as if it had human characteristics.

A **simile** compares unlike things using the word *like* or *as*.

A **metaphor** compares things by writing or speaking about one thing as if it were another.

When you **paraphrase**, you use your own words to restate what an author writes.

 Take It to the Net
www.phschool.com
Take the interactive self-test online to check your understanding of these selections.

Answers for p. 955

Review and Assess

1. The wind is stealthy and quick; it doesn't leave a trace.
2. **(a)** He says they're like people standing around a manhole yelling down advice. **(b)** The comparison conveys the speaker's sense of being observed.
3. A clean sheet of paper is a new start; so is a new day.
4. It moved back and forth like a Greek Chorus moves across a stage.
5. "The Wind": Personification, "A Rapid—footless Guest," The personification of the wind adds to the poem's breathless, lonely tone. "A Pace": Simile, "Like a worker in a manhole." The use of simile adds lightness to the poem. "Metaphor": Metaphor, "Morning is a new sheet of paper." The use of metaphor adds to the fresh, bright and hopeful tone of the poem. "Right Hand": Personification, "What an eloquent hand, it broke into grins and self-assured narration." The use of personification adds to the poem's tone of respect and pride.
6. Possible response: "The Wind" presents the most effective figurative language because it makes the wind seem like a quick, nervous person.
7. Sample response: The Wind came to my window, I invited him in, and he entered. He visited, but then nervously asked to leave and was gone, leaving me alone.
8. **(a)** Looking at the lemon tree—leisurely; sleeping and dreaming—hurriedly. **(b)** Sample response: He wants to observe things in a leisurely way.
9. **(a)** eloquent: expressive; garrulity: talkativeness **(b)** My grandfather's hand was expressive and talkative.
10. Possible response: A positive approach to each new day will lead people to accept new challenges and gather exciting or important new experiences.

❶ Vocabulary Development

Word Analysis

1. A taciturn judge doesn't talk much.
2. A reticent witness is reluctant to speak.
3. A tacit understanding is an unspoken understanding.

Spelling Strategy

1. writing   3. entirely
2. observed

Fluency: Word Choice

1. taciturn, eloquent, guttural, garrulity
2. tremulous, flurriedly
3. countenance
4. diffused
5. decipher

❷ Grammar

1. I do not understand the way (that) you decipher the inscription.
2. I hope (that) you can explain it.
3. I admire the way (that) he interprets the Torah.
4. Do you remember the morning (that) the sunrise was so brilliant?
5. He is the one (whom) I need to help me.

Writing Application

Sample sentences: My friend Lakeesha is a very talented artist. I admire the way she is able to draw pictures that look like photographs. Looking at the pictures she draws, I am constantly amazed by how detailed and accurate they are.

Integrate Language Skills

❶ Vocabulary Development Lesson

Word Analysis: Latin Root -tac-

Taciturn contains the Latin root *-tac-*, which along with its variation *-tic-*, means "silent." *Taciturn* means "silent" or "uncommunicative." In your notebook, describe the following:

1. A taciturn judge
2. A reticent witness
3. A tacit understanding

Spelling Strategy

For words ending in a silent *e*, drop the *e* before adding an ending beginning with a vowel. For example, *diffuse + -ed = diffused*. Match the suffixes with the words, and write the new word in your notebook.

1. write   a. *-ly*
2. observe   b. *-ing*
3. entire   c. *-ed*

Fluency: Word Choice

In your notebook, respond to each numbered item using words from the vocabulary list on page 949. Use each word only once.

1. List the four words that deal with speech or speaking.
2. Write one adjective and one adverb that could be used to describe the actions or attitude of a high-strung, excited, or nervous person.
3. Write a synonym for the word *face*.
4. Write the word that names what a shade or thin curtain does to light shining through it.
5. Identify the word you would most likely find in a story about solving the mystery of a secret code.

❷ Grammar Lesson

Elliptical Clauses

In an **elliptical clause,** one or more words are omitted because they are understood. Often, in adjective clauses, the relative pronoun *that* is not written or spoken.

> **Example:** I'm looking at the lemon tree [*that*] I planted.

The complete clause is "that I planted," but the word *that* is understood. Elliptical clauses in which the relative pronoun is not stated have an informal, conversational tone.

Practice Copy the following sentences in your notebook. Underline the elliptical clause in each, and then write the omitted word or words.

1. I do not understand the way you decipher the inscription.
2. I hope you can explain it.
3. I admire the way he interprets the Torah.
4. Do you remember the morning the sunrise was so brilliant?
5. He is the one I need to help me.

Writing Application Write a few sentences about someone whom you admire. Use two elliptical clauses in your writing.

𝒲𝒢 *Prentice Hall Writing and Grammar Connection: Chapter 20, Section 2*

TEACHING RESOURCES

The following resources can be used to enrich or extend the instruction for pp. 956–957.

Vocabulary

📖 **Selection Support:** Build Vocabulary, p. 225

📖 **Vocabulary and Spelling Practice Book** (Use this booklet for skills enrichment.) ▪

Grammar

📖 **Selection Support:** Build Grammar Skills, p. 224

𝒲𝒢 **Writing and Grammar,** Platinum Level, p. 472

▪ **Daily Language Practice Transparencies** ▪

Writing

𝒲𝒢 **Writing and Grammar,** Platinum Level, p. 285

💿 **Writing and Grammar iText CD-ROM** ▪

▪ **Writing Models and Graphic Organizers on Transparencies,** pp. 53–59

▪ **BLOCK SCHEDULING:** Resources marked with this symbol provide varied instruction during 90-minute blocks.

Writing Lesson

Analysis of a Poem

Each of the poems in this grouping conveys a broad meaning in a few words. Choose one of the poems that especially touches you, and analyze it more closely.

Prewriting   To begin your analysis, ask yourself general questions about the poem. Then, jot down ideas about how the poem looks, how it sounds, what images it presents, and how the poet uses figurative language.

> **Model: Analyzing a Poem**
>
> • What is the literal, or basic, meaning of this poem?
> • What is the central message, or greater meaning, of the poem?
> • How does each element contribute to that meaning?
> • What is my response to the poem?

Drafting   In the first paragraph, introduce the poem and identify the main idea you will address. Then, drawing on the ideas you have generated, explain how each of the poem's elements supports your interpretation. Conclude your analysis with a summary of your response to the poem.

Revising   Review your draft to make sure that each reference you make to the poem supports your interpretation. Delete or revise those ideas that do not fit your analysis.

W͞G Prentice Hall Writing and Grammar Connection: Chapter 13, Section 2

❹ Extension Activities

Listening and Speaking   With a partner, prepare an **interview** with the speaker of "The Wind—tapped like a tired Man." One of you should serve as the interviewer, and the other, as the poem's speaker.

- Prepare a list of questions about the wind's visit.
- Make notes of the kinds of responses the poem's speaker might make.
- Use language appropriate to the situation.

Perform your interview for the class. [Group Activity]

Research and Technology   Choose one of the poets in this grouping, and write a **biographical report** about him or her. Using resources in the library or on the Internet, discover some pertinent information about the poet's life. Write your report, and include a timeline showing when the poet published key works.

 Take It to the Net   www.phschool.com

Go online for an additional research activity using the Internet.

The Wind—tapped like a tired Man / A Pace Like That / Metaphor / Right Hand ◆ 957

❸ Writing Lesson

- Remind students that to support the main idea of a literary analysis, they must use specific details, including quotes from the poem.
- Tell students to be consistent in their purpose for writing—if their purpose is to explain the use of personification in "The Wind," then they should not discuss musical devices found in that poem.
- Remind students that they can also paraphrase specific passages to further describe images or explain details.
- As a model, show students the Interpreting a Work of Literature essay on pp. 53–59 of **Writing Models and Graphic Organizers on Transparencies.**
- Use the Response to Literature rubric in **Performance Assessment and Portfolio Management,** p. 16, to evaluate students' analyses.

❹ Research and Technology

- Discuss with students how to locate information in the library and on the Internet.
- Have students provide a bibliography that identifies where they found their resource materials.
- Remind students that they should include in the reports biographical information as well as examples of the poet's work.

CUSTOMIZE INSTRUCTION
for Universal Access

To address different learning styles, use the following activities suggested in the **Extension Activities** booklet, p. 57.

- For Interpersonal Learners, use Activity 5.
- For Verbal/Linguistic Learners, use Activity 6.
- For Visual/Spatial Learners, use Activity 7.

ASSESSMENT RESOURCES

The following resources can be used to assess students' knowledge and skills.

Selection Assessment

- 📖 **Formal Assessment,** pp. 201–203
- 📖 **Open Book Test,** pp. 169–171
- 📼 **Got It! Assessment Videotapes,** Tape 5
- 💿 **Test Bank Software**
- 💻 **Take It to the Net**
  Visit www.phschool.com for self-tests and additional questions on the selections.

Writing Rubric

- 📖 **Performance Assessment and Portfolio Management,** p. 16

PRENTICE HALL
ASSESSMENT *SYSTEM*

- 📖 **Workbook**
- 📄 **Transparencies**
- 📖 **Skill Book**
- 💿 **CD-ROM**

La Belle Dame sans Merci ✦ Danny Deever

Lesson Objectives

1. **To analyze and respond to literary elements**
   - Literary Analysis: Narrative and Dramatic Poetry
   - Comparing Literary Works
2. **To read, comprehend, analyze, and critique poems**
   - Reading Strategy: Identifying the Speaker
   - Reading Check questions
   - Review and Assess questions
   - Assessment Practice (ATE)
3. **To develop word analysis skills, fluency, and systematic vocabulary**
   - Vocabulary Development Lesson: Latin Root: -journ-
4. **To understand and apply written and oral language conventions**
   - Spelling Strategy
   - Grammar Lesson: Hyphens
5. **To understand and apply appropriate writing and research strategies**
   - Writing Lesson: News Bulletin
   - Extension Activity: Dialect Chart
6. **To understand and apply listening and speaking strategies**
   - Extension Activity: Reading

STEP-BY-STEP TEACHING GUIDE	PACING GUIDE
PRETEACH	
Motivate Students and Provide Background	
Use the Motivation activity (ATE p. 958)	5 min.
Read and discuss the Preview material and Background information (SE/ATE p. 958) **A**	5 min.
Introduce the Concepts	
Introduce the Literary Analysis and Reading Strategy (SE/ATE p. 959) **A**	10 min.
Pronounce the vocabulary words and read their definitions (SE p. 959)	5 min.
TEACH	
Monitor Comprehension	
Informally monitor comprehension by circulating while students read independently or in groups **A**	10 min.
Monitor students' comprehension with the Reading Check notes (SE/ATE pp. 961, 963)	as students read
Develop vocabulary with Vocabulary notes (SE pp. 961, 962, 964)	as students read
Develop Understanding	
Develop students' understanding of narrative and dramatic poetry with the Literary Analysis annotations (SE p. 961; ATE pp. 961, 962, 964) **A**	5 min.
Develop students' ability to identify the speaker with the Reading Strategy annotation (ATE p. 961)	5 min.
ASSESS	
Assess Mastery	
Assess students' mastery of the Reading Strategy and Literary Analysis by having them answer the Review and Assess questions (SE/ATE p. 965)	10 min.
Use one or more of the print and media Assessment Resources (ATE p. 967) **A**	up to 50 min.
EXTEND	
Apply Understanding	
Have students complete the Vocabulary Development Lesson and the Grammar Lesson (SE p. 966) **A**	10 min.
Apply students' knowledge of climax and resolution using the Writing Lesson (SE/ATE p. 967) **A**	45 min.
Apply students' understanding using one or more of the Extension Activities (SE p. 967)	20–90 min.

 ACCELERATED INSTRUCTION:
Use the strategies and activities identified with an **A**.

UNIVERSAL ACCESS
● = Below Level Students
▲ = On-Level Students
■ = Above Level Students

Time and Resource Manager

Reading Level: Average/Average
Average Number of Instructional Days: 3

PRINT 📖	TRANSPARENCIES 🗳	TECHNOLOGY 💿 🎧 📼
• **Beyond Literature,** Career Connection: The Military, p. 58 ▲ ■		• **Interest Grabber Video,** Tape 5 ● ▲ ■
• **Selection Support Workbook:** ● ▲ ■ Literary Analysis, p. 232 Reading Strategy, p. 231 Build Vocabulary, p. 229	• **Literary Analysis and Reading Transparencies,** pp. 115 and 116 ● ▲ ■	
• **Adapted Reader's Companion** ● • **Reader's Companion** ●		• **Listening to Literature** ● ▲ ■ Audiocassettes, Side 33 Audio CDs, CD 19
• **English Learner's Companion** ● ▲ • **Literatura en español** ● ▲ • **Literary Analysis for Enrichment** ■		
• **Formal Assessment:** Selection Test, pp. 204–206 ● ▲ ■ • **Open Book Test,** pp. 172–174 ● ▲ ■ • **Performance Assessment and Portfolio Management,** pp. 19, 28 ● ▲ ■ • 〔**ASSESSMENT** SYSTEM〕 ● ▲	• 〔**ASSESSMENT** SYSTEM〕 ● ▲ ■ Skills Practice Answers and Explanations on Transparencies	• **Test Bank Software** ● ▲ ■ • **Got It! Assessment Videotapes,** Tape 5 ● ▲
• **Selection Support Workbook:** ● ▲ ■ Build Grammar Skills, p. 230 • **Writing and Grammar,** Platinum Level ● ▲ ■ • **Extension Activities,** p. 58 ● ▲ ■	• **Daily Language Practice Transparencies** ● ▲	• **Writing and Grammar iText CD-ROM** ● ▲ ■ 💻 **Take It to the Net** www.phschool.com

BLOCK SCHEDULING: Use one 90-minute class period to preteach the selection and have students read it. Use a second 90-minute class period to assess students' mastery of skills and have them complete one of the Extension Activities.

Motivation

Write on the chalkboard the headings *choices* and *consequences*. Under *choices*, write "stayed up late watching an old movie." Under *consequences*, write "slept through next morning's soccer game." Encourage students to add some everyday choices and consequences to the list. Then, explain that many unwise choices are minor and their consequences short-lived. The poor choices the characters in these poems make, however, lead to more serious consequences.

▇ Interest Grabber Video

As an alternative, play "Danny Deever" on Tape 5 to engage student interest.

❶ Background

History

In the medieval power structure, knights were one step below the lords for whom they were dedicated to fight. A knight's training began by being sent away for seven years as a page to learn about religion, chivalry, and honor. When the page had proved himself, he became an assistant to a knight and was called a squire. The squire was really a knight's apprentice and learned to ride horses, fight in battles, and hunt. A squire became a knight when he swore to the knightly code of honor and chivalry.

Comparing Literary Works

Prepare to Read

La Belle Dame sans Merci ◆ Danny Deever

La Belle Dame sans Merci, Exh. 1902, oil on canvas, Sir Frank Dicksee, Bridgeman Art Library

▇ Take It to the Net

Visit www.phschool.com for interactive activities and instruction related to these selections, including

- background
- graphic organizers
- literary elements
- reading strategies

Preview

Connecting to the Literature

Our choices in life are based on what we want and need. Sometimes we want what we cannot have. In both of the poems in this grouping, the characters pay a heavy price for the choices they have made.

❶ Background

In "La Belle Dame sans Merci," a knight pines for a beautiful woman who is out of his reach. In the tradition of courtly love, a knight focuses his adoration on a beautiful, aristocratic woman whether or not she returns his love. This love is believed too noble and pure to be corrupted by physical affection. The knight performs great deeds to honor the lady, but he suffers terribly in the knowledge that his affection can never be returned.

958 ◆ *Poetry*

TEACHING RESOURCES

The following resources can be used to enrich or extend the instruction for pp. 958–959.

Motivation

▇ **Interest Grabber Video**, Tape 5 ▇

Background

▇ **Beyond Literature**, p. 58

 Take It to the Net

Visit www.phschool.com for background and hotlinks for the selections.

Literary Analysis

▇ **Literary Analysis and Reading Transparencies**, Narrative and Dramatic Poetry, p. 116 ▇

Reading

▇ **Selection Support:** Reading Strategy, p. 231; Build Vocabulary, p. 229

▇ **Literary Analysis and Reading Transparencies**, Identifying the Speaker, p. 115

▇ **BLOCK SCHEDULING:** Resources marked with this symbol provide varied instruction during 90-minute blocks.

Literary Analysis

Narrative and Dramatic Poetry

"La Belle Dame sans Merci" is a **narrative poem** that tells the tale of a knight enthralled by a woman. Like any story, a narrative poem has

- One or more characters—people who take part in the action
- Setting—time and place of the action
- Conflict—a struggle between opposing forces
- A series of events

"Danny Deever" is a **dramatic poem**—a poem that uses the techniques of drama. Dramatic poetry is verse that presents the speech of one or more characters.

Comparing Literary Works

Narrative and dramatic poetry combine the elements of a story with the structure of poetry. Perhaps the strongest story element is **plot,** the sequence of events that shows the action. As you read these poems, look for the stages of plot—from the exposition of characters, setting, and conflict through the climax, or high point, to the resolution of the story. Determine which writer presents the more complete plot, and compare the importance of the story with your understanding of the poetry.

Reading Strategy

Identifying the Speaker

Identifying the speaker, or the voice "telling" a poem, is an important first step in gaining insight into the poem. The speaker may be the poet or a fictitious character created by the poet. In "Danny Deever," the poet uses the characters as the speakers, and by doing so, he is able to delve into their minds. You can identify the speaker through direct statements or through hints and implications.

As you read, use a diagram like the one here to help you identify the speaker in these poems.

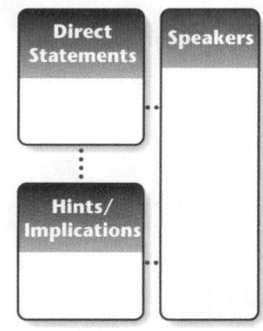

Vocabulary Development

sedge (sej) *n.* grassy plant that grows in wet areas (p. 961)

thrall (thrôl) *n.* complete control; slavery (p. 962)

sojourn (sō′ jʉrn) *v.* to stay temporarily (p. 962)

whimpers (hwim′ pərz) *v.* makes a low, whining sound (p. 964)

quickstep (kwik′ step′) *n.* pace used in normal military marching (p. 964)

La Belle Dame sans Merci / Danny Deever ◆ 959

---

❷ Literary Analysis

Narrative and Dramatic Poetry

- Reinforce the idea that a narrative poem tells a story and is usually longer than a dramatic poem. Dramatic poetry is poetry in which one or more characters speak. By using the words of one or more speakers, the poet creates the illusion of an actual dramatic event.

- Use the instructions for Comparing Literary Works to remind students of the elements of plot. Have them look for these elements as they read the selections.

- Use the Narrative and Dramatic Poetry transparency in **Literary Analysis and Reading Transparencies,** p. 116, to demonstrate for students how to identify these two types of poetry.

❸ Reading Strategy

Identifying the Speaker

- Explain that the speaker in a poem may be the poet or a character invented by the poet. Identifying the speaker helps the reader to comprehend the poem.

- Have students refer to the diagram on p. 959. Tell them to look for direct statements and hints that can help them identify the speaker in the poem.

- As they read, encourage students to use a diagram like the one shown to record hints or direct statements that may uncover the speaker's identity and give them insight into the poem.

Vocabulary Development

- Pronounce each vocabulary word for students, and read the definitions as a class. Have students identify any words with which they are already familiar.

 E-Teach

Visit E-Teach at www.phschool.com for teachers' essays on how to teach, with questions and answers.

CUSTOMIZE INSTRUCTION FOR UNIVERSAL ACCESS

For Special Needs Students	For Less Proficient Readers	For English Learners
Have students read the adapted version of these selections in the **Adapted Reader's Companion.** This version provides basic-level instruction in an interactive format with questions and write-on lines. Completing the adapted version will prepare students to read the selection in the Student Edition.	Have students read these selections in the **Reader's Companion.** This version provides basic-level instruction in an interactive format with questions and write-on lines. After students finish the selection in **Reader's Companion,** have them complete the questions and activities in the Student Edition.	Have students read the adapted version of these selections in the **English Learner's Companion.** This version provides basic-level instruction in an interactive format with questions and write-on lines. Completing the adapted version will prepare students to read the selection in the Student Edition.

Step-by-Step Teaching Guide
for pp. 960–964

CUSTOMIZE INSTRUCTION
For Musical/Rhythmic Learners

In "La Belle Dame sans Merci," as the knight pursues his idyllic romance with the beautiful lady, you can almost hear music on the hillsides. Have students find examples of music that would enhance the mood and atmosphere of this tale.

❶ About the Selection

"La Belle Dame sans Merci" (literally, "The Beautiful Woman Without Pity") is a character who appears in world literature under different names— Circe or Morgan le Fay, for example. In English, she is the *beldame*, a word for a woman who takes pleasure in destroying the unlucky men whom she enthralls. In this poem, a young man comes under her spell, only to find his life drained away after an enchanted night. Students might relate to the broader theme of this poem—things that seem attractive can sometimes disappoint or even endanger a person.

❷ Background

Art

La Belle Dame sans Merci, by John W. Waterhouse

English painter John William Waterhouse (1849–1917) was inspired by the poetry of Keats and Tennyson. His distinctive style— dreamy and romantic—perfectly captures the mood of Keats's poem.

Use this question for discussion:

How would you compare the lady in the painting to the one described in Keats's poem? Answer: Students might observe that the lady is similar because she has long hair, a mysterious air, and an intent expression.

❸ ▶Critical Viewing

Suggested response: She is pulling him toward her by wrapping her hair around his neck; she looks relaxed, and he is not resisting her.

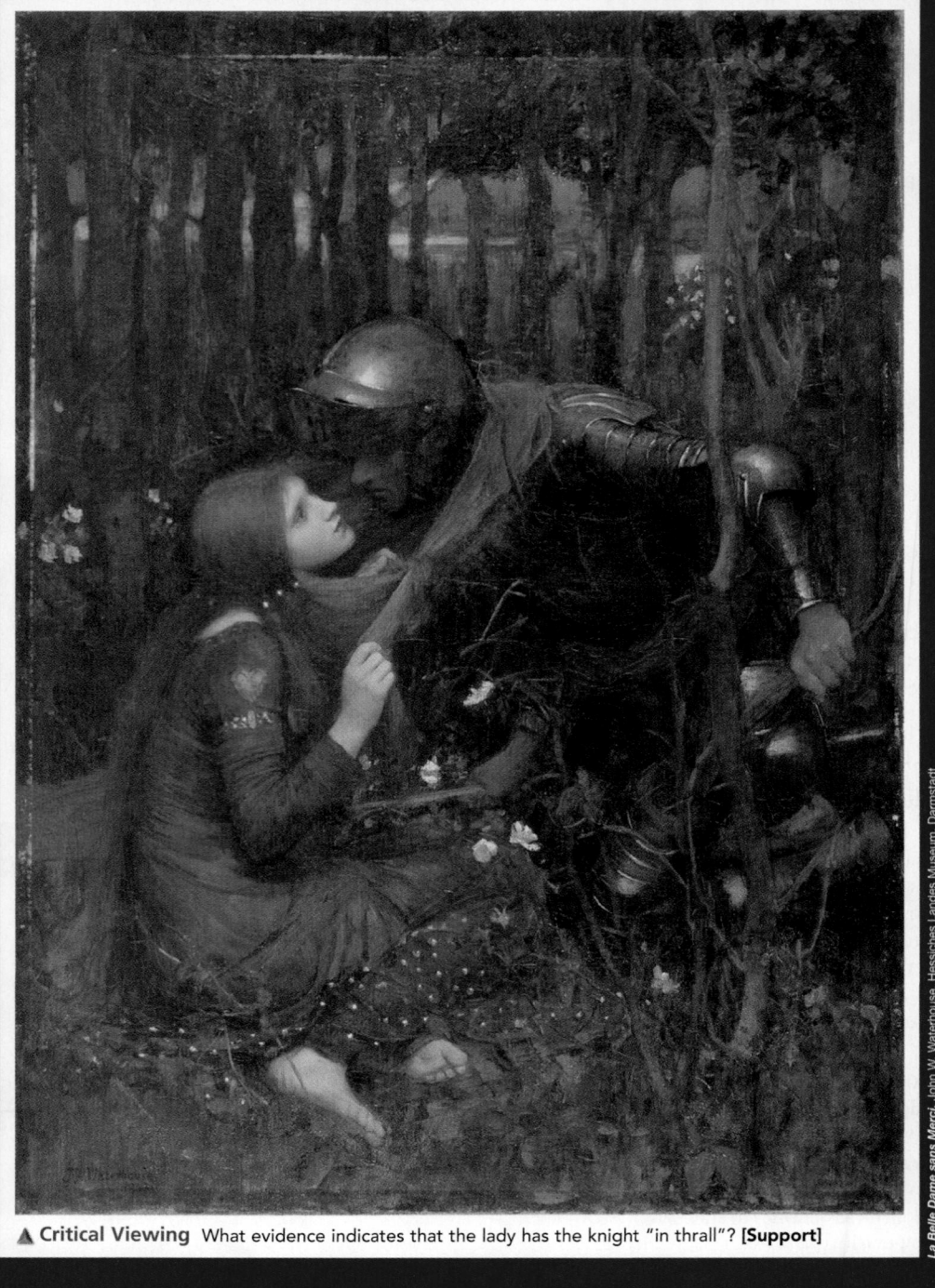

▲ **Critical Viewing** What evidence indicates that the lady has the knight "in thrall"? **[Support]**

La Belle Dame sans Merci, John W. Waterhouse, Hessisches Landes Museum, Darmstadt

960 ◆ *Poetry*

TEACHING RESOURCES

The following resources can be used to enrich or extend the instruction for pp. 960–964.

Literary Analysis

📖 **Selection Support:** Literary Analysis, p. 232

Reading

📖 **Reader's Companion**

📖 **English Learner's Companion**

🎧 **Listening to Literature Audiocassettes,** Side 33 ▪️

💿 **Listening to Literature Audio CDs,** CD 19 ▪️

▪️ **BLOCK SCHEDULING:** Resources marked with this symbol provide varied instruction during 90-minute blocks.

La Belle Dame sans Merci[1]

JOHN KEATS

O what can ail thee, knight-at-arms,
  Alone and palely loitering?
The sedge has withered from the lake,
  And no birds sing.

5   O what can ail thee, knight-at-arms,
  So haggard and so woe-begone?
The squirrel's granary is full,
  And the harvest's done.

I see a lily on thy brow,
10 With anguish moist and fever dew,
And on thy cheeks a fading rose
  Fast withereth too.

I met a lady in the meads,[2]
  Full beautiful—a faery's child,
15 Her hair was long, her foot was light,
  And her eyes were wild.

I made a garland for her head,
  And bracelets too, and fragrant zone;[3]
She looked at me as she did love,
20 And made sweet moan.

I set her on my pacing steed,
  And nothing else saw all day long,
For sidelong would she bend, and sing
  A faery's song.

25 She found me roots of relish sweet,
  And honey wild, and manna dew,[4]
And sure in language strange she said—
  'I love thee true.'

---

1. **La Belle Dame sans Merci** "The Beautiful Lady Without Pity" (French).
2. **meads** (mēdz) *n.* old-fashioned form of *meadow.*
3. **fragrant zone** sweet-smelling plant.
4. **manna** (man´ ə) **dew** (dōō) sweet substance obtained from the bark of certain ash trees.

sedge (sej) *n.* grassy plant that grows in wet areas

Literary Analysis
Narrative and Dramatic Poetry Describe the setting and the character introduced in the first two stanzas.

6 ✔**Reading Check**
What is the condition of the knight-at-arms?

---

❹ Literary Analysis
Narrative and Dramatic Poetry

- Read the bracketed passage aloud. Remind students that a narrative poem involves a setting, which is the time and place of the action, and also one or more characters who take part in the action.
- Ask students the Literary Analysis question on p. 961: Describe the setting and the character introduced in the first two stanzas.
  Answer: The setting is on the withered grass by a lake; the knight-at-arms is the character. He is alone and seems very distressed.

❺ Reading Strategy
Identifying the Speaker

- Remind students that the speaker in a poem may be the poet or a fictional character created by the poet. To identify the speaker, students should look for direct statements or hints in the text.
- Have a volunteer read aloud the bracketed passage on p. 961. Tell students that in these stanzas, a new speaker is established.
- Ask students to identify and describe both speakers.
  Answer: The first speaker is a minor character who finds the knight by the lake. The second speaker is the knight. Students should note that the knight is the main character; he tells his story.

❻ ✔Reading Check

Answer: The knight is "haggard" and "woe-begone." He is sitting alone by the lake, doing nothing.

CUSTOMIZE INSTRUCTION FOR UNIVERSAL ACCESS

For Special Needs Students	For Gifted/Talented Students	For Advanced Readers
Some students may have trouble with the vocabulary in "La Belle Dame sans Merci. " Remind them to use the text footnotes. Explain that when the Cockney dialect in "Danny Deever" is written, the letters "h" at the beginning of a word and "g" in "ing" words are often dropped, which makes the words look difficult to read.	Students may enjoy finding out more about the rules of courtly love. Encourage them to consider how the knight in "La Belle Dame sans Merci" follows or deviates from the rules.	Point out that both "La Belle Dame sans Merci" and "Danny Deever" use rhythm and rhyme to narrate stories. Have students identify and describe the rhythm and rhyme in each. Then, discuss how these literary devices add interest to the narratives.

Narrative and Dramatic Poetry

- Remind students that a narrative poem, like a story, will contain a conflict. Conflict is the struggle between opposing forces, in this case, the Knight and the Lady.

- Read the bracketed passage aloud. Have students explain the resolution of the conflict in this narrative poem.
  Answer: The knight is doomed to pine away for the lady until he dies.

Answers for p. 962

Review and Assess

1. Possible response: Some students may describe the knight as weak or lacking in valor because he allows himself to be taken in. Others may say that he is spellbound.

2. (a) The setting is the countryside by a lake in late autumn. (b) The late autumn setting reinforces the meaning and mood of the poem because in late autumn, nature is barren and depleted of vigor, similar to the way the lady has left the knight.

3. (a) The lady is beautiful, with long hair, a light step, and wild eyes. (b) The lady is a fairy who has held many men in thrall.

4. (a) The knight dreams of death-pale kings, princes, and warriors who warn him that La Belle Dame sans Merci has him in her thrall. (b) The people in the dream had all fallen victim to the beautiful lady in the past.

5. (a) The lady has left him for another victim. (b) The knight has now lost his vigor and sense of purpose.

6. This poem suggests that things that seem attractive on the surface are often disappointing or dangerous underneath.

She took me to her elfin grot,[5]
30   And there she wept, and sighed full sore,
And there I shut her wild wild eyes
      With kisses four.

And there she lullèd me asleep,
      And there I dreamed—Ah! woe betide!
35 The latest dream I ever dreamed
      On the cold hill's side.

I saw pale kings and princes too,
      Pale warriors, death-pale were they all;
They cried—'La Belle Dame sans Merci
40   Hath thee in thrall!'

I saw their starved lips in the gloam,
      With horrid warning gapèd wide,
And I awoke and found me here,
      On the cold hill's side.

45 And this is why I sojourn here,
      Alone and palely loitering,
Though the sedge has withered from the lake,
      And no birds sing.

5. **elfin** (elf´ in) **grot** cave belonging to a fairy.

thrall (thrôl) *n.* complete control; slavery

sojourn (sō´ jurn) *v.* to stay temporarily

John Keats

(1795–1821)

John Keats lived a short, often sad, life. His parents died while he was still a boy. Although he attended school in London and studied surgery, he decided to devote his life to poetry.

In 1816, Keats's sonnet "On First Looking into Chapman's Homer" was published. His editor introduced him to the poets Percy Bysshe Shelley and William Wordsworth. Like them, Keats emphasizes feeling and imagination over reason and logic in his poetry.

In 1818, Keats's brother died of tuberculosis. Keats had a premonition that he, too, would die of the disease. In a burst of creativity, he published his last and best volume of poetry in 1820. His premonition came true. He died of tuberculosis in 1821.

Review and Assess

Thinking About the Selection

1. **Respond:** What word or words would you use to describe the knight? Explain your answer.

2. (a) **Recall:** What is the setting of the poem? (b) **Connect:** In what way does the season of this setting reinforce the meaning and the mood of the poem?

3. (a) **Recall:** Describe the lady whom the knight meets. (b) **Infer:** What is unusual about her?

4. (a) **Recall:** Describe the knight's dream. (b) **Analyze:** Explain how the people in the knight's dream relate to his present condition.

5. (a) **Infer:** Where is the lady when the knight awakens from his dream? (b) **Draw Conclusions:** Why is the knight "Alone and palely loitering"?

6. **Generalize:** What does this poem suggest about things that seem attractive on the surface?

The Battle of Bunker Hill, Howard Pyle, Delaware Art Museum

DANNY DEEVER

Rudyard Kipling

"What are the bugles blowin' for?" said Files-on-Parade.[1]
"To turn you out, to turn you out," the Color-Sergeant[2] said.
"What makes you look so white, so white?" said Files-on-Parade.
"I'm dreadin' what I've got to watch," the Color-Sergeant said.
5   For they're hangin' Danny Deever, you can hear the Dead
       March play,
  The regiment's in 'ollow square[3] —they're hangin' him today;
  They've taken of his buttons off an' cut his stripes away,
  An' they're hangin' Danny Deever in the mornin'.

"What makes the rear-rank breathe so 'ard?" said Files-on-
     Parade.
10 "It's bitter cold, it's bitter cold," the Color-Sergeant said.
"What makes that front-rank man fall down?" says Files-on-
     Parade.

---

1. **Files-on-Parade** soldier who directs marching formation.
2. **Color-Sergeant** flag-bearer.
3. **'ollow square** for a hanging, soldiers' ranks form three sides of a square; the fourth side is the gallows.

⑩ ▲ Critical Viewing
Compare the method of fighting depicted in this painting with the way battles are fought today. **[Analyze]**

⑪ ✔Reading Check
What is going to happen to Danny Deever?

Danny Deever ◆ 963

⑫ Literary Analysis

Narrative and Dramatic Poetry

- Have a volunteer read aloud the bracketed passage. Encourage students to focus on the dramatic techniques the poet uses.

- Ask students how this passage helps readers feel they are actually witnessing the events being described.

  Answer: The conversation creates a sense of immediacy, as if the reader were standing near the two speakers and overhearing them.

Answers for p. 964

Review and Assess

1. Students are likely to respond that they would find it painful or uncomfortable to watch the hanging; some might also say they would identify with Danny Deever and feel afraid.

2. (a) The Color-Sergeant and Files-on-Parade relate the events. **(b)** The Color-Sergeant seems wiser, and perhaps more hardened, to the ways of the military; Files-on-Parade is more naïve and innocent.

3. (a) The Color-Sergeant has experience with military executions. **(b)** The conflicting explanations are not believable. **(c)** The Color-Sergeant is covering up the soldiers' horrified reaction at the brutal act they are witnessing—the hanging of Danny Deever.

4. (a) Danny Deever killed a comrade who was sleeping. **(b)** Many students will say that the lack of information makes them more sympathetic to Deever because Deever's side of the story is never heard, and he might have been unjustly accused.

"A touch o' sun, a touch o' sun," the Color-Sergeant said.
　They are hangin' Danny Deever, they are marchin' of 'im round,
　They 'ave 'alted Danny Deever by 'is coffin on the ground;
15　An' 'e'll swing in 'arf a minute for a sneakin' shootin' hound—
　O they're hangin' Danny Deever in the mornin'!

⑫ "'Is cot was right-'and cot to mine," said Files-on-Parade.
"'E's sleepin' out an' far tonight," the Color-Sergeant said.
"I've drunk 'is beer a score o' times," said Files-on-Parade.
20 "'E's drinkin' bitter beer alone," the Color-Sergeant said.
　They are hangin' Danny Deever, you must mark 'im to 'is place,
　For 'e shot a comrade sleepin'—you must look 'im in the face;
　Nine 'undred of 'is county an' the regiment's disgrace,
　While they're hangin' Danny Deever in the mornin'.

25 "What's that so black agin the sun?" said Files-on-Parade.
"It's Danny fightin' 'ard for life," the Color-Sergeant said.
"What's that that <u>whimpers</u> over'ead?" said Files-on-Parade.
"It's Danny's soul that's passin' now," the Color-Sergeant said.
　For they're done with Danny Deever, you can 'ear the
　　quick-step play,
30　The regiment's in column, an' they're marchin' us away;
　Ho! the young recruits are shakin', an' they'll want their beer
　　to-day,
　After hangin' Danny Deever in the mornin'.

whimpers (hwim´ pərz) *v.* makes a low, whining sound

quickstep (kwik´ step´) *n.* pace used in normal military marching

---

Review and Assess

Thinking About the Selection

1. **Respond:** If you were in the regiment, how would you feel about having to watch the hanging? Explain.

2. **(a) Recall:** Who are the two characters who relate the event through their dialogue? **(b) Compare and Contrast:** Compare and contrast the characters.

3. **(a) Recall:** Of the two speakers, which has some prior experience with military executions? **(b) Analyze:** The Color-Sergeant explains the rear-rank's hard breathing by saying it is "bitter cold." He explains a soldier's fainting as the result of a "touch o' sun." Are these conflicting explanations believable? **(c) Draw Conclusions:** What really accounts for the physical problems of the men?

4. **(a) Recall:** For what crime is Danny Deever being executed? **(b) Evaluate:** The poem provides few facts about Danny Deever or his crime. Explain whether this lack of information makes you more or less sympathetic to him.

Rudyard Kipling

(1865–1936)
Rudyard Kipling was born in India to English parents. He spoke both Hindustani and English until the age of six, when he was sent to England for a formal education. He returned to India at age sixteen and became a journalist, publishing many of his early works in newspapers. He is known mainly for his poetry and tales of India in the late 1800s, when Britain ruled India. In 1907, he became the first English author to be awarded the Nobel Prize for Literature.

✎ ASSESSMENT PRACTICE: Critical Reading

Author's Meaning and Style　　　　**(For more practice, see Test Preparation Workbook, p. 58.)**

Many tests require students to analyze an author's style and meaning. Use the following sample test item for students' preparation and practice:

Read the poem "La Belle Dame sans Merci" on pp. 961–962. What idea does the author suggest or imply in this poem?

A The knight is happy.
B The knight is lonely and sad.

C The autumn setting reflects the knight's good fortune.
D The beautiful lady was a good fairy.

To help students determine the author's main idea and implications, suggest that they paraphrase the poem. Lead students to notice that the author does not imply answers *A, C,* or *D.* Therefore, *B* is the best answer choice.

Review and Assess

Literary Analysis

Narrative and Dramatic Poetry

1. In "La Belle Dame sans Merci," which stanzas describe the setting and introduce the main character?
2. How does the last stanza of "La Belle Dame . . ." complete the story?
3. In "Danny Deever," what effect is created by having Files-on-Parade and the Color-Sergeant speak in dialect?

Comparing Literary Works

4. Use a **plot** diagram like the one here for each poem. (a) Describe the events that cause the conflict or the central problem of the story. (b) Identify the climax, or high point. (c) Name the events that resolve the problem.

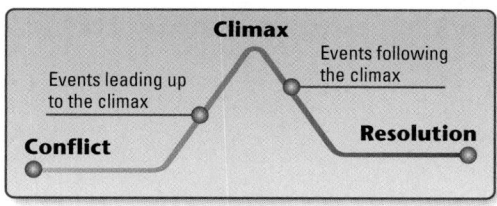

Climax

Events following the climax

Events leading up to the climax

Conflict

Resolution

5. (a) Which of the two poems has the strongest plot? (b) How does the presence or absence of a fully detailed plot influence your enjoyment of each poem? Explain.

Reading Strategy

Identifying the Speaker

6. The speaker of stanza 4 to the end of "La Belle Dame sans Merci" is different from the speaker of stanzas 1–3. What clues in the poem help you identify the change of speaker?
7. What does the second speaker in the poem reveal about the lady?
8. In the last half of each stanza of "Danny Deever," the poet employs a distinctive speech pattern but does not identify the speaker. Who do you think is speaking the words? Explain.

Extend Understanding

9. **Military Connection:** Why do you think that the men in Danny Deever's regiment had to be present at his hanging?

La Belle Dame sans Merci / Danny Deever ◆ 965

Quick Review

A **narrative poem** tells a story with one or more characters, a setting, a conflict, and a series of events that come to a conclusion.

In a **dramatic poem,** one or more characters speak, telling what is happening through dialogue.

Plot is the sequence of events in a narrative.

The **speaker** in a poem may be the poet or one or more fictitious characters created by the poet.

 Take It to the Net

www.phschool.com

Take the interactive self-test online to check your understanding of these selections.

---

❶ Vocabulary Development

Word Analysis

1. At the end of the day, the meeting was adjourned.
2. Each day I write my thoughts and impressions in my journal.
3. Television journalists report on the day's events.

Spelling Strategy

1. vice-president
2. sunburn
3. mother-in-law
4. Native American

Fluency

1. sedge
2. quickstep
3. sojourn
4. thrall
5. whimpers

❷ Grammar

The British army was based on <u>well-built</u> traditions and <u>rock-solid</u> rules that would not allow leniency for Danny Deever. <u>Files-on-Parade</u> had the cot on the <u>left-hand</u> side of Deever, and like the rest of the regiment, stood watching Deever's execution.

Writing Application

Sample sentences:

1. The merry-go-round was crowded with children.
2. The Color-Sergeant spoke loudly so that all could hear him.
3. The grayish-blue uniforms blended with the dark sky.
4. The well-prepared team took home many medals from the Olympics.

Integrate Language Skills

❶ Vocabulary Development Lesson

Word Analysis: Latin Root -journ-

Sojourn contains the root *-journ-*, which comes from the Latin *diurnalis*, meaning "day." It is easy to understand how the current meaning of *sojourn*, "temporary stay," could have evolved from "a day's stay." Write sentences using each word below in a way that defines it.

    1. adjourn   **2.** journal   **3.** journalist

Spelling Strategy

Some compound words, such as *quickstep*, are spelled as a single word. Others are spelled as separate words (*attorney general*) or are hyphenated (*great-grandson*). In your notebook, write each compound word below correctly.

  1. vice president   **3.** mother in law
  2. sun burn   **4.** Native American

Fluency: Sentence Completions

Review the vocabulary list on page 959. Then, copy the sentences, and fill in the blanks with the correct word from the list.

1. The ground near the pond was covered with ___?___.
2. The soldiers marched in ___?___ to the square.
3. After a brief ___?___, the knight continued his travels.
4. The beautiful woman held the knight in ___?___.
5. The knight heard the ___?___ of the young wolf cubs in the cave.

❷ Grammar Lesson

Hyphens

Hyphens are used to connect two or more words that function as a single word unless the dictionary gives a different spelling.

Compound nouns:	knight-at-arms Color-Sergeant

Use a hyphen to connect a compound modifier that comes before a noun.

Compound adjectives:	a *strong-willed* soldier front-rank an *up-to-date* report

Hyphens are not used in compound modifiers that include words ending in -ly (poorly trusted) or with compound proper adjectives (Chinese American customs).

Practice Copy the paragraph below into your notebook. Insert hyphens where necessary.

    The British Army was based on well built traditions and rock solid rules that would not allow leniency for Danny Deever. Files on Parade had the cot on the left hand side of Deever, and like the rest of the regiment, stood watching Deever's execution.

Writing Application Write two sentences using compound nouns and two using compound adjectives. Make sure that you hyphenate correctly.

W/G *Prentice Hall Writing and Grammar Connection: Chapter 28, Section 5*

966 ◆ *Poetry*

TEACHING RESOURCES

The following resources can be used to enrich or extend the instruction for pp. 966–967.

Vocabulary

📖 **Selection Support:** Build Vocabulary, p. 229

📖 **Vocabulary and Spelling Practice Book**
(Use this booklet for skills enrichment.)

Grammar

📖 **Selection Support:** Build Grammar Skills, p. 230

W/G **Writing and Grammar,** Platinum Level, p. 704 🔲

🔲 **Daily Language Practice Transparencies**

Writing

W/G **Writing and Grammar,** Platinum Level, p. 84

💿 **Writing and Grammar iText CD-ROM** 🔲

🔲 **BLOCK SCHEDULING:** Resources marked with this symbol provide varied instruction during 90-minute blocks.

Writing Lesson

News Bulletin

Imagine that you are a news reporter present at the hanging of Danny Deever. Write a news bulletin to inform your readers about the circumstances of the hanging and the mood of the soldiers. Include both the climax and the resolution.

Prewriting   Gather details from the poem about the mood of the soldiers. Use statements by the speakers as quotations in your report.

Drafting   Begin with a sensational lead-in to "hook" the readers. Then, start at the beginning and report the series of events that led to the climax you reported in your opening. Conclude with a description of the atmosphere following the event.

Model: Identifying the Climax

Just moments ago, an execution took place here at Kipling Army Base. . . . It was a somber ceremony. In the bitter cold early morning, bugles played sadly for the doomed man.

> The climax is mentioned right away to grab readers' attention. The resolution and details should follow in later paragraphs.

Revising   Review your report, and identify the exciting lead-in, the sequence of events leading to the climax, quotations from observers, and a wrap-up. If you cannot identify any one of these parts, revise your report to include it.

 Prentice Hall Writing and Grammar Connection: Chapter 5, Section 3

Extension Activities

Listening and Speaking   When poets present their work, they often begin with informal remarks that place their writing in context. With a group, prepare a **reading** of one of the poems. Introduce the poem, providing background information. The following tips may help:

- Assign different people to read the lines of the characters who speak in the poem.
- Vary your tone of voice to show emotion.

When you are prepared, give your reading to the class. **[Group Activity]**

Research and Technology   In addition to "Danny Deever," Rudyard Kipling wrote several other poems using this dialect. Use print, electronic, and Internet resources to find out more about this dialect. Present a **dialect chart** that would help readers of "Danny Deever" understand the Cockney language in the poem.

 Take It to the Net   www.phschool.com

Go online for an additional research activity using the Internet.

La Belle Dame sans Merci / Danny Deever ◆ 967

ASSESSMENT RESOURCES

The following resources can be used to assess students' knowledge and skills.

Selection Assessment

📖 **Formal Assessment**, pp. 204–206

📖 **Open Book Test**, pp. 172–174

📼 **Got It! Assessment Videotapes**, Tape 5

💿 **Test Bank Software**

🖥 *Take It to the Net*
Visit www.phschool.com for self-tests and additional questions on the selections.

Writing Rubric

📖 **Performance Assess. and Portfolio Mgmt.**, p. 19

Listening and Speaking Rubric

📖 **Performance Assess. and Portfolio Mgmt.**, p. 28

PRENTICE HALL
ASSESSMENT SYSTEM

📖 **Workbook**   🖥 **Transparencies**

📖 **Skill Book**   💿 **CD-ROM**

BLOCK SCHEDULING: Resources marked with this symbol provide varied instruction during 90-minute blocks.

Lesson Support for p. 967

❸ Writing Lesson

- Read the Writing Lesson instructions with the class, noting the importance of using details from the poem to construct an effective news bulletin.

- Give students six notecards each to implement the reporter's formula as they review the poem and gather details. They should be labeled *Who, What, Where, Why, When,* and *How.* Tell students that news bulletins require that they convey only the most important facts to the reader.

- Use the Writing Lesson to guide students in writing their bulletins.

- Use the Description rubric in **Performance Assessment and Portfolio Management,** p. 19, to assess students' bulletins.

❹ Listening and Speaking

- Suggest that students gather background information on the poems by doing research in the library or on the Internet.

- Have students rehearse the poems before presenting them to the class. Encourage them to look up all unfamiliar words so they can pronounce them without hesitation.

- To assess students' work, use the rubric for Narrative Presentation, p. 28 in **Performance Assessment and Portfolio Management.**

CUSTOMIZE INSTRUCTION
For Universal Access

To address different learning styles, use the activities suggested in the **Extension Activities** booklet, p. 58.

- For Musical/Rhythmic Learners, use Activity 5.

- For Logical/Mathematical Learners, use Activity 6.

- For Interpersonal and Verbal/Linguistic Learners, use Activity 7.

Jade Flower Palace ✦ The Moon at the Fortified Pass ✦ The Guitar ✦ What Are Friends For ✦ Making a Fist ✦ Some Like Poetry

Lesson Objectives

1. **To analyze and respond to literary elements**
   - Literary Analysis: Lyric Poetry
   - Comparing Literary Works
2. **To read, comprehend, analyze, and critique poems**
   - Reading Strategy: Reading in Sentences
   - Review and Assess questions
   - Assessment Practice (ATE)
3. **To develop word analysis skills, fluency, and systematic vocabulary**
   - Vocabulary Development Lesson: Greek Word Root: -path-
4. **To understand and apply written and oral language conventions**
   - Spelling Strategy
   - Grammar Lesson: Placement of only
5. **To understand and apply appropriate writing and research strategies**
   - Writing Lesson: Lyric Poem
   - Extension Activity: Brief Report
6. **To understand and apply listening and speaking strategies**
   - Extension Activity: Poetry Reading

STEP-BY-STEP TEACHING GUIDE	PACING GUIDE
PRETEACH	
Motivate Students and Provide Background	
Use the Motivation activity (ATE p. 968)	5 min.
Read and discuss the Preview material and Background information (SE/ATE p. 968) **A**	5 min.
Introduce the Concepts	
Introduce the Literary Analysis and Reading Strategy (SE/ATE p. 969) **A**	15 min.
Pronounce the vocabulary words and read their definitions (SE p. 969)	5 min.
TEACH	
Monitor Comprehension	
Informally monitor comprehension by circulating while students read independently or in groups **A**	15 min.
Develop vocabulary with Vocabulary notes (SE pp. 970, 971, 973; ATE p. 970)	as students read
Develop Understanding	
Develop students' understanding of lyric poetry with the Literary Analysis annotations (ATE pp. 969, 970, 971, 975) **A**	10 min.
Develop students' understanding of reading in sentences with the Reading Strategy annotation (ATE p. 969)	10 min.
ASSESS	
Assess Mastery	
Assess students' mastery of the Reading Strategy and Literary Analysis by having them answer the Review and Assess questions (SE/ATE p. 977)	20 min.
Use one or more of the print and media Assessment Resources (ATE p. 979) **A**	up to 50 min.
EXTEND	
Apply Understanding	
Have students complete the Vocabulary Development Lesson and the Grammar Lesson (SE p. 978) **A**	20 min.
Apply students' knowledge of creating a mood using the Writing Lesson (SE/ATE p. 979) **A**	45 min.
Apply students' understanding using one or more of the Extension Activities (SE p. 979)	20–90 min.

A **ACCELERATED INSTRUCTION:**
Use the strategies and activities identified with an **A**.

UNIVERSAL ACCESS
● = Below Level Students
▲ = On-Level Students
■ = Above Level Students

968a

Time and Resource Manager

Reading Level: Average/Average/Average/Easy/Easy/Easy
Average Number of Instructional Days: 4

RESOURCES

PRINT	TRANSPARENCIES	TECHNOLOGY
• **Beyond Literature,** Cross-Curricular Connection: Social Studies, p. 59 ▲ ■		• **Interest Grabber Video,** Tape 5 ● ▲ ■
• **Selection Support Workbook:** ● ▲ ■ Literary Analysis, p. 236 Reading Strategy, p. 235 Build Vocabulary, p. 233	• **Literary Analysis and Reading Transparencies,** pp. 117 and 118 ● ▲ ■	
• **Adapted Reader's Companion** ● • **Reader's Companion** ●		• **Listening to Literature** ● ▲ ■ Audiocassettes, Sides 33, 34 Audio CDs, CD 19
• **English Learner's Companion** ● ▲ • **Literatura en español** ● ▲ • **Literary Analysis for Enrichment** ■		
• **Formal Assessment:** Selection Test, pp. 207–209● ▲ ■ • **Open Book Test,** pp. 175–177 ● ▲ ■ • **Performance Assessment and Portfolio Management,** p. 29 ● ▲ ■ • PRENTICE HALL **ASSESSMENT** *SYSTEM* ● ▲	• PRENTICE HALL **ASSESSMENT** *SYSTEM* ● ▲ ■ Skills Practice Answers and Explanations on Transparencies	• **Test Bank Software** ● ▲ ■ • **Got It! Assessment Videotapes,** Tape 5 ● ▲
• **Selection Support Workbook:** ● ▲ ■ Build Grammar Skills, p. 234 • **Writing and Grammar,** Platinum Level ● ▲ ■ • **Extension Activities,** p. 59 ● ▲ ■	• **Daily Language Practice Transparencies** ● ▲	• **Writing and Grammar iText CD-ROM** ● ▲ ■ *Take It to the Net* www.phschool.com

BLOCK SCHEDULING: Use one 90-minute class period to preteach the selection and have students read it. Use a second 90-minute class period to assess students' mastery of skills and have them complete one of the Extension Activities.

Motivation

Write the word *poetry* in large block letters at the center of the chalkboard. Around it, write the words *Friendship, Beauty, Sadness, War,* and *Death.* Circle each word, and connect it to the word *poetry.* Let students know this is a cluster diagram showing some major themes of lyric poetry. Invite students to suggest words and phrases of their own, such as love, youth, age, growing up, and nature. Emphasize that a lyric poem can express anything a human being feels or observes. Tell students that they are going to read six lyric poems on six different themes and that each one is like a snapshot of the poet's feelings at a certain time. Urge students to "see" this snapshot as they read each poem.

Interest Grabber Video

As an alternative, play "What Are Friends For" on Tape 5 to engage student interest.

❶ Background

Theme

The poems in this group span the eighth through the twentieth centuries. Because the poets' thoughts are timeless, people of future generations can read the poems and reflect on them regardless of what poetic style they find appealing.

Comparing Literary Works

Prepare to Read

Jade Flower Palace ◆ The Moon at the Fortified Pass ◆ The Guitar
What Are Friends For ◆ Making a Fist ◆ Some Like Poetry

Take It to the Net

Visit www.phschool.com for interactive activities and instruction related to these selections, including
• background
• graphic organizers
• literary elements
• reading strategies

Preview

Connecting to the Literature

If you have ever reflected upon the meaning of friendship, beauty, war, or death, you already have something in common with the poets who wrote these poems. Considering such timeless themes is often where poetry begins.

❶ Background

Certain poems are classified as "lyric" poems because of their highly musical qualities. In ancient Greece, poems were recited or sung to the accompaniment of a lyre, a small stringed, harplike instrument. The word *lyric* is related to the word *lyre*. Even today, lyrics are associated with music: The words to songs are called lyrics.

968 ◆ *Poetry*

TEACHING RESOURCES

The following resources can be used to enrich or extend the instruction for pp. 968–969.

Motivation

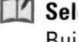 **Interest Grabber Video**, Tape 5

Background

 Beyond Literature, p. 59

Take It to the Net

Visit www.phschool.com for background and hotlinks for the selections.

Literary Analysis

Literary Analysis and Reading Transparencies, Lyric Poetry, p. 118

Reading

Selection Support: Reading Strategy, p. 235; Build Vocabulary, p. 233

Literary Analysis and Reading Transparencies, Reading in Sentences, p. 117

 BLOCK SCHEDULING: Resources marked with this symbol provide varied instruction during 90-minute blocks.

Literary Analysis

Lyric Poetry

Lyric poetry expresses the observations and feelings of a single speaker in highly musical verse. A lyric poem may follow a traditional form, such as a sonnet, or it may be written in *free verse*—verse not written in a formal rhythmical pattern. While reading, you will notice that a lyric poem, unlike a narrative poem, never tells a full story. Rather, it focuses on an experience or creates and explores a single effect. Use an organizer like the one here to explore how the details in each poem contribute to the main effect.

Comparing Literary Works

Like most lyric poetry, the poems presented here contain **imagery**—descriptive or figurative language that creates word pictures. These images are shaped by details of sight, sound, taste, touch, smell, or movement.

Notice the sounds of a swirling stream, a moaning wind, rats' claws scurrying and the sights of a stream, pines, gray rats, and broken tiles in this excerpt from "Jade Flower Palace."

> The stream swirls. The wind moans in
> The pines. Gray rats scurry over
> Broken tiles.

As you read these poems, notice the images each one contains. Consider the feeling or mood that each image conveys, and compare each poet's ability to use imagery to spark emotion.

Reading Strategy

Reading in Sentences

Poetry, like prose, achieves meaning through sentences. In poetry, a sentence may extend over several lines or it may even end in the middle of a line. To grasp the literal meaning of a poem, **read** it according to its **sentences,** not its lines. Do not stop at the end of a line unless there is a period, comma, colon, semicolon, or dash.

Vocabulary Development

pathos (pā´ thäs´) *n.* quality that arouses feelings of pity, sorrow, sympathy, or compassion (p. 970)

wistful (wist´ fəl) *adj.* expressing longing (p. 971)

monotonously (mə nät´ən əs lē) *adv.* going on and on without variation (p. 973)

Jade Flower Palace / The Moon at the Fortified Pass / The Guitar / What Are Friends For / Making a Fist / Some Like Poetry ◆ 969

---

❷ Literary Analysis

Lyric Poetry

- Tell students that as they read the selections, they will focus on lyric poetry, which expresses the feelings and observations of a single speaker.

- Read the instruction about lyric poetry together as a class. Tell students that the graphic organizer on p. 969 will help them explore how details contribute to the main effect of a lyric poem.

- Use the instruction for Comparing Literary Works to explore how the poets use sensory details to create images in lyric poems. Tell students that as they read the selections, they should note the images that are shaped by each poem.

- Use the Lyric Poetry transparency from **Literary Analysis and Reading Transparencies,** p. 118, to demonstrate for students how to identify details that contribute to the main effect.

❸ Reading Strategy

Reading in Sentences

- Remind students that reading poetry means stopping at the end of sentences. Reading poetry line by line makes its meaning difficult to understand.

- Tell students not to stop reading at the end of a line unless there is a period, comma, colon, semicolon, or dash.

Vocabulary Development

- Pronounce each vocabulary word for students, and read the definitions as a class. Have students identify any words with which they are already familiar.

📺 E-Teach

Visit E-Teach at www.phschool.com for teachers' essays on how to teach, with questions and answers.

CUSTOMIZE INSTRUCTION FOR UNIVERSAL ACCESS

For Special Needs Students	For Less Proficient Readers	For English Learners
Have students read the adapted version of "Making a Fist" in the **Adapted Reader's Companion.** This version provides basic-level instruction in an interactive format with questions and write-on lines. Completing the adapted version will prepare students to read the selection in the Student Edition.	Have students read "Making a Fist" in the **Reader's Companion.** This version provides basic-level instruction in an interactive format with questions and write-on lines. After students finish the selection in **Reader's Companion,** have them complete the questions and activities in the Student Edition.	Have students read the adapted version of "Making a Fist" in the **English Learner's Companion.** This version provides basic-level instruction in an interactive format with questions and write-on lines. Completing the adapted version will prepare students to read the selection in the Student Edition.

**CUSTOMIZE INSTRUCTION
For Verbal/Linguistic Learners**

As students read, have them make a list of the feelings that the speaker in each lyric poem expresses. Then, have them list the words and images that convey these feelings.

❶ About the Selections

"Jade Flower Palace" is a lyric poem that expresses the speaker's feeling about the impermanence of power and glory. The setting includes images of scurrying rats, ruins, and ghost fires that convey the message that power and glory are fleeting. In contrast, the setting of "The Moon at the Fortified Pass" is an active kingdom—its people alive and its armies on the move. Yet, it is in a lonely moment in the mountain setting that the speaker portrays the soldiers' homesickness and fear of death in order to emphasize the senselessness of war.

❷ Literary Analysis

Lyric Poetry

• Remind students that lyric poetry expresses the feelings and observations of the speaker.

• Ask students to suggest what feelings the speaker in this lyric poem expresses.
  Suggested responses: This speaker expresses the feelings of sadness, wistfulness, loneliness, and perhaps a sense of resignation.

❸ Vocabulary Development

The Greek Root -path-

• Tell students that the root of a word contains its basic meaning, and that *pathos* contains the Greek root -path-, which means "suffering, experience, and emotion."

• Have students suggest other words and phrases that contain this word root, and list them on the chalkboard.
  Possible responses: Students might mention *pathology, pathetic, sympathy,* and *empathy.*

❶ Jade Flower Palace

Tu Fu

*Translated by
Kenneth Rexroth*

The stream swirls. The wind moans in
The pines. Gray rats scurry over
Broken tiles. What prince, long ago,
Built this palace, standing in
5 Ruins beside the cliffs? There are
Green ghost fires in the black rooms.
The shattered pavements are all
Washed away. Ten thousand organ
Pipes whistle and roar. The storm
10 Scatters the red autumn leaves.
His dancing girls are yellow dust.
Their painted cheeks have crumbled
Away. His gold chariots
And courtiers are gone. Only

15 A stone horse is left of his
Glory. I sit on the grass and
Start a poem, but the <u>pathos</u> of
It overcomes me. The future
Slips imperceptibly away.
20 Who can say what the years will bring?

970 ◆ Poetry

pathos (pā′ thäs′) *n.* quality that arouses feelings of pity, sorrow, sympathy, or compassion

Tu Fu

(712–770)

Chinese poet Tu Fu was little known and unappreciated during his lifetime, but today he is regarded as a supreme craftsman. His poems are admired for their form as well as for their content. Tu Fu's poems celebrate nature, condemn the senselessness of war, and, as in "Jade Flower Palace," lament the passage of time.

TEACHING RESOURCES

The following resources can be used to enrich or extend the instruction for pp. 970–976.

Literary Analysis
📖 **Selection Support:** Literary Analysis, p. 236

Reading
📖 **Reader's Companion**
📖 **English Learner's Companion**
🎧 **Listening to Literature Audiocassettes,** Sides 33, 34 ▪
💿 **Listening to Literature Audio CDs,** CD 19 ▪

The Moon
at the Fortified Pass

Li Po

Translated by

Lin Yutang

The bright moon lifts from the Mountain of Heaven
In an infinite haze of cloud and sea,
And the wind, that has come a thousand miles,
Beats at the Jade Pass[1] battlements. . . .

❹
5 China marches its men down Po-teng Road
While Tartar[2] troops peer across blue waters of
     the bay. . . .
And since not one battle famous in history
Sent all its fighters back again,

❻
The soldiers turn round, looking toward the
     border,
10 And think of home, with wistful eyes,
And of those tonight in the upper chambers
Who toss and sigh and cannot rest.

---

1. **Jade Pass** gap in the Great Wall in northeastern China.
2. **Tartar** (tär´ tər) Tartars were nomadic tribes who originally lived in Mongolia, Manchuria, and Siberia. From A.D. 200 through 400, the Tartars were almost constantly at war with the Chinese. A thousand years later, under the leadership of Genghis Khan, the Tartars conquered China, as well as a number of other European and Asian countries.

❺ ▲ **Critical Viewing**
Imagine this picture as a setting for "The Moon at the Fortified Pass." What might make the soldiers "wistful"? **[Analyze]**

wistful (wist´ fəl) *adj.*
expressing longing

Li Po

(701–762)

A major Chinese classical poet of the Tang Dynasty, Li Po was a romantic who wrote about the joys of nature, love, friendship, and solitude. Although his writing was influenced by Taoist thought, he did not embrace the simple lifestyle that this philosophy encouraged.

The Moon at the Fortified Pass ◆ 971

---

❹ **Literary Analysis**
Lyric Poetry

• Point out that since this is a lyric poem, its historical situation is described in only two lines. In a narrative poem, the poet would have explained much more about the history of this conflict.

• Ask students to describe the setting for this event.
Answer: The place is the Jade Pass, a fortified gap in the Great Wall in northeastern China. The setting is moonlit, hazy, windy, and far from home.

❺ ▶**Critical Viewing**

Answer: These aspects of the setting would make the soldiers wistful: the darkness of night; the beauty of the moon; the loneliness of the mountains; the distance from home.

❻ **Critical Thinking**
Infer

• Have students read the bracketed passage. Ask them to describe how the soldiers feel.
Answer: The soldiers feel homesick.

• Then, have students identify the descriptive words in the passage that indicate the soldiers' feeling.
Answer: The phrases "looking toward the border" and "think of home" reflect the soldiers' homesickness.

CUSTOMIZE INSTRUCTION FOR UNIVERSAL ACCESS

For English Learners	For Advanced Readers	For Gifted/Talented Students
Ask students to skim the poems and write down easy as well as difficult words. Encourage students to explain the easy words; then, work with them to determine the meaning of the more difficult words using such aids as cognates and clues from the accompanying illustrations.	Invite students to describe the setting of each poem and analyze how it affects the poem's mood, or atmosphere.	Have students express the theme and spirit of one of these poems in a different form: for example, a journal entry, a brief musical interpretation, a painting, or a dance. Suggest that they begin by jotting down the theme and then deciding which art form would best express the feelings they associate with that theme.

❼ The Guitar

Federico García Lorca
Translated by Elizabeth du Gué Trapier

❽

❾ ▲ Critical Viewing What kind of song do you think the man in this painting is playing? Explain your answer. **[Infer]**

Now begins the cry
Of the guitar,
Breaking the vaults
Of dawn.
5   Now begins the cry
Of the guitar.
Useless
To still it.
Impossible
10   To still it.
It weeps <u>monotonously</u>
As weeps the water,
As weeps the wind
Over snow.
15   Impossible
To still it.
It weeps
For distant things,
Warm southern sands
20   Desiring white camellias.
It mourns the arrow without a target,
The evening without morning.
And the first bird dead
Upon a branch.
25   O guitar!
A wounded heart,
Wounded by five swords.

monotonously (mə nät′ən əs lē) *adv.* going on and on without variation

Review and Assess

Thinking About the Selections

1. **Respond:** To which of these poems do you relate? Explain.
2. **(a) Recall:** Where does the speaker of "Jade Flower Palace" sit, and what does he do? **(b) Interpret:** Why is the speaker overcome with pathos? **(c) Analyze:** How do the last six lines relate to the rest of the poem?
3. **(a) Recall:** Identify the event on which Li Po focuses in "The Moon at the Fortified Pass." **(b) Interpret:** In what way does the setting of the poem seem appropriate for a battle?
4. **(a) Recall:** To what does García Lorca compare the weeping of the guitar? **(b) Infer:** Which emotions does he attribute to it?
5. **Evaluate:** Which single image in these poems did you find the most striking? Explain.

Federico García Lorca

(1898–1936)

Federico García Lorca wrote many of his poems shortly after World War I, a culturally vibrant time in his homeland of rural Andalusia, outside Granada, Spain. Although García Lorca did not intend his work to be political, Nationalist forces found it offensive, and they assassinated him at the beginning of the Spanish Civil War.

The Guitar ◆ 973

973

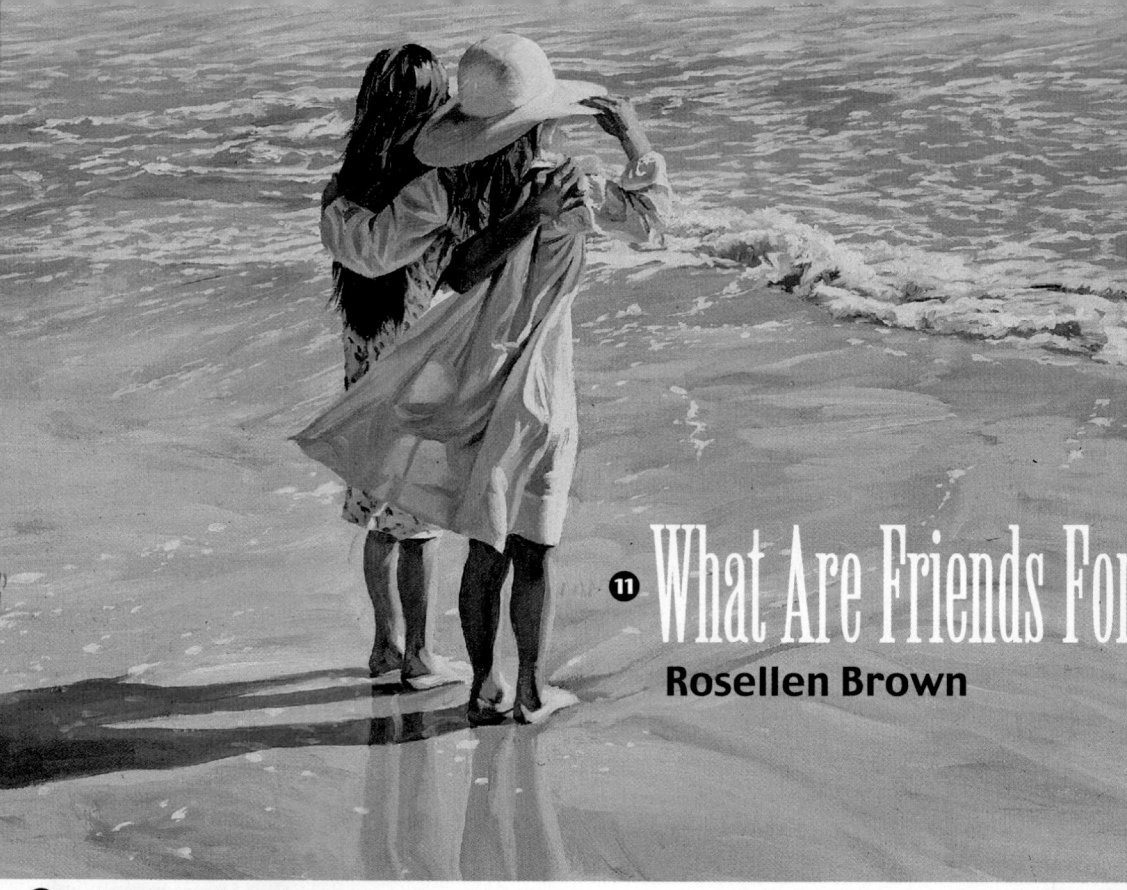

❶ What Are Friends For

Rosellen Brown

❹ ▲ Critical Viewing What qualities of friendship has the artist captured? [Analyze]

Best Friends, Craig Nelson/Bernstein & Andriulli, Inc.

What are friends for, my mother asks.
A duty undone, visit missed,
casserole unbaked for sick Jane.
Someone has just made her bitter.

5   Nothing. They are for nothing, friends,
I think. All they do in the end—
they touch you. They fill you like music.

Rosellen Brown

(b. 1939)

Besides being a poet, Rosellen Brown is an accomplished novelist and short-story writer. Her novel *Tender Mercies* was a national bestseller and became a major motion picture. Brown's latest book of poetry, *Cora Frye's Pillow Book,* was published in 1994.

974 ◆ Poetry

---

⑪ Making a Fist Naomi Shihab Nye

For the first time, on the road north of Tampico,[1]
I felt the life sliding out of me,
a drum in the desert, harder and harder to hear.
I was seven, I lay in the car
5 watching palm trees swirl a sickening pattern
   past the glass.
My stomach was a melon split wide inside my skin.

"How do you know if you are going to die?"
I begged my mother.
We had been traveling for days.
10 With strange confidence she answered,
"When you can no longer make a fist."

Years later I smile to think of that journey,
the borders we must cross separately,
stamped with our unanswerable woes.
15 I who did not die, who am still living,
⑮ still lying in the backseat behind all my questions,
clenching and opening one small hand.

---

1. **Tampico** (täm pē′ kō) seaport in eastern Mexico.

Review and Assess

Thinking About the Selections

1. **Respond:** Which poem do you like better? Why?
2. **(a) Recall:** What answer is given by the speaker to the title question, "What Are Friends For"? **(b) Contrast:** How do the speaker's feelings contrast with those of the mother?
3. **(a) Recall:** What does the speaker ask in "Making a Fist"? **(b) Recall:** What answer does the mother give? **(c) Infer:** How does the mother's answer affect the speaker throughout her life?
4. **(a) Analyze:** In "Making a Fist," what does the poet's childhood journey represent? **(b) Extend:** Explain one common method people use to deal with fear.
5. **(a) Evaluate:** What are some reasons for making a fist? **(b) Connect:** Based on your answers, how does the action suggest being alive?

Naomi Shihab Nye

(b. 1952)

Poet, songwriter, short-story writer, and children's book author, Naomi Shihab Nye lives in San Antonio, Texas. "Making a Fist" highlights her perception, imaginative sense of language, and ability to keep you close to an experience.

Making a Fist ◆ 975

⑮ Literary Analysis
Lyric Poetry
- Remind students that since this is a lyric poem, the observations and feelings of a single speaker are expressed.
- Read aloud the bracketed passage to the students. Ask students to summarize the speaker's feelings in these lines.
  Answer: As an adult, the speaker is still like a child with a painful curiosity about (and fear of) death.

Answers for p. 975

Review and Assess

1. Encourage students to support their choices with details from the text.
2. **(a)** Friends fill an emotional need. **(b)** The mother's feelings are cynical; the speaker's feelings are generous and optimistic.
3. **(a)** The speaker asks, "How do you know when you are going to die?" **(b)** The mother answers, "When you can no longer make a fist." **(c)** It makes the speaker think kindly of her mother for giving a simple answer to a very difficult question.
4. **(a)** The childhood journey in "Making a Fist" stands for the speaker maturing and learning to face her fears. **(b)** **Possible response:** People deal with fear by staying away from what they fear most.
5. **Possible response: (a)** One might make a fist to hold onto someone or something of value. **(b)** This motion suggests being alive because it shows a connection to other people or things.

CUSTOMIZE INSTRUCTION FOR UNIVERSAL ACCESS

For Less Proficient Readers	For Special Needs Students	For Advanced Readers
Have students discuss their answers to Review and Assess question 2 on p. 975. Students should refer to the poem and relate specific details to their own relationships with family members regarding friends. Encourage students to share their comparisons.	Have students work together to answer the Review and Assess questions on p. 975. Have students discuss their responses to question 5. How many reasons can they come up with for making a fist? How does the action suggest being alive?	Have students discuss the themes addressed in the selections. Allow time for them to look in the library for other poems that deal with these themes. Have students share poems they've found with the rest of the class.

16 About the Selection

In "Some Like Poetry," the speaker expresses her feelings about poetry. Each stanza of the poem examines one of the words in the title: *Some, Like,* and *Poetry.* In the end, the reader discovers that for the poet *like* is a vast understatement.

Answers for p. 976

Review and Assess

1. Students should offer reasons for their preferences.

2. **(a)** Possible answer: She compares it to a saving bannister. **(b)** Her point is that it is hard to evaluate who likes poetry and how much they like it, but the speaker herself places an ultimate, life-saving value on poetry.

3. Poetry is not to everyone's taste, but for those who value it, the message and imagery within poetry can be life-changing.

4. Possible answer: Poetry draws upon emotions, such as the fear of death and the love of friends, that people of all cultures experience.

16 Some Like Poetry

Wisława Szymborska
Translated by Joanna Trezciak

Some—
that means not all.
Not even the majority of all but the minority.
Not counting school, where one must,
5   and poets themselves,
there will be perhaps two in a thousand.

Like—
but one also likes chicken-noodle soup,
one likes compliments and the color blue,
10   one likes an old scarf,
one likes to prove one's point,
one likes to pet a dog.

Poetry—
but what sort of thing is poetry?
15   More than one shaky answer
has been given to this question.
But I do not know and do not know and
          clutch on to it,
as to a saving bannister.

Wisława Szymborska

(b. 1923)
The author of many collections of poetry, Wisława Szymborska of Poland has said, "No questions are of such significance as those that are naive." Her poetry asks direct questions about the meaning of life and death. Upon awarding her the 1996 Nobel Prize for Literature, the Swedish Academy called her the "Mozart of poetry."

Review and Assess

Thinking About the Selection

1. **Respond:** How do you feel about poetry? Explain.
2. **(a) Recall:** To what does the speaker compare poetry in the third stanza? **(b) Interpret:** What is the speaker's point in "Some Like Poetry"?
3. **Synthesize:** How can you apply the message of "Some Like Poetry" to the other poems in this group?
4. **Evaluate:** Why do you think that poetry exists in all cultures?

976 ◆ *Poetry*

✒ ASSESSMENT PRACTICE: Reading Comprehension

Author's Meaning and Style   (For more practice, see Test Preparation Workbook, p. 59.)

When completing test items that pertain to a critical reading passage, students need to be prepared to understand an author's implications. Have them read "What Are Friends For," p. 974, and answer the following sample test question:

Which of the following statements would the author most likely agree with?

    A Friends are worth nothing.
    B New friends are best.

    C Friendship is a lost art.
    D Friends are there when you need them.

    Choices *A, B,* and *C* are not supported by the poem's details. Because the author says "friends fill you like music," *D* is the best answer.

Review and Assess

Literary Analysis

Lyric Poetry

1. **(a)** What would you say is the central emotion or effect conveyed in "The Guitar"? **(b)** What words or details in the poem contribute to this effect?
2. **(a)** On what single subject does "Some Like Poetry" focus? **(b)** What is the speaker's personal feeling about the subject?
3. In your view, which of these **lyric poems** most effectively communicates the speaker's reaction to a single event? Explain.

Comparing Literary Works

4. Using a chart like the one here, compare the **imagery** in the poems.

Poem	Sight	Sound	Taste	Touch	Smell

5. **(a)** According to your chart, which poet makes the most use of the sense of sound? **(b)** Which poet makes use of the sense of touch?
6. What single image in these poems do you find most striking? Explain.

Reading Strategy

Reading in Sentences

7. Contrast the sentences in "Jade Flower Palace" and "The Moon at the Fortified Pass" based on the use of commas and periods.
8. The second sentence in "The Guitar" is a repetition of part of the first sentence. Explain how the punctuation leads you to read the two sentences differently.
9. "Some Like Poetry" interrupts one short sentence with elaboration about each word. What is the brief sentence "hidden" in Szymborska's poem?

Extend Understanding

10. **Music Connection:** "The Guitar" applies human qualities to a musical instrument. To what other instrument could you assign human qualities? Why?

Jade Flower Palace / The Moon at the Fortified Pass / The Guitar / What Are Friends For / Making a Fist / Some Like Poetry ◆ 977

Quick Review

Lyric poetry expresses the observations and feelings of a single speaker in highly musical verse.

Imagery is descriptive or figurative language that creates word pictures.

You get the literal meaning of a poem if you **read** it according to its **sentences**, not its lines.

 Take It to the Net
www.phschool.com
Take the interactive self-test online to check your understanding of these selections.

---

❶ Vocabulary Development

Word Analysis

1. **(b)** pathos   4. **(b)** sympathy
2. **(c)** pathology   5. **(c)** empathy
3. **(b)** antipathy

Fluency: Word Choice

1. pathos   3. monotonously
2. wistful

Spelling Strategy

1. mournful   3. playful
2. plentiful

❷ Grammar

1. Now begins the cry of the only guitar.
2. Only now begins the cry of the guitar.
3. Only China marches its men down the road.
4. China marches only its men down the road.
5. She likes only this brand of chicken-noodle soup.
6. Only she likes this brand of chicken-noodle soup.

Writing Application
Sample sentences:

1. Only I can read that poem aloud. (No one else can read the poem aloud.)
2. I can only read that poem aloud. (I cannot do anything else with the poem.)
3. I can read only that poem aloud. (I cannot read any other poems aloud.)
4. I can read that poem only aloud. (I cannot read it any other way.)

Integrate Language Skills

❶ Vocabulary Development Lesson

Word Analysis: Greek Root *-path-*

Pathos means "a quality that arouses feelings of pity or sorrow." The word contains the Greek root *-path-*, which means "feelings" or "suffering." Choose the word most closely associated with the person or thing in each numbered item.

1. very sad movie: (a) pathology, (b) pathos, (c) antipathy
2. medical researcher: (a) pathos, (b) sympathy, (c) pathology
3. enemy: (a) sympathy, (b) antipathy, (c) empathy
4. suffering animal: (a) antipathy, (b) sympathy, (c) pathology
5. very close friend: (a) pathos, (b) pathology, (c) empathy

❷ Grammar Lesson

Usage Problems: Placement of *only*

The placement of the word **only** can change—and sometimes confuse—the meaning of a sentence. Be sure to place *only* in front of the word you mean to modify.

> *Only* a stone horse is left of his glory. (All that was left was one stone horse.)
>
> A stone horse commemorates his *only* glory. (His single glory is commemorated by a stone horse.)

Practice In your notebook, write each sentence, adding the word *only* so that the sentence reflects the meaning in parentheses.

1. Now begins the cry of the guitar. (There is just one guitar.)

𝒲𝒢 *Prentice Hall Writing and Grammar Connection: Chapter 26, Section 2*

978 ◆ *Poetry*

Fluency: Word Choice

Identify the word from the vocabulary list on page 969 that is suggested by each book title.

1. *The Sick Little Girl*
2. *Love Lost Forever*
3. *Games to Play on Long Car Trips*

Spelling Strategy

The adjective suffix *-ful* means "full of." Remember that this suffix ends with just one *l*: *wist + -ful = wistful*. In your notebook, write the adjective ending in *-ful* that is associated with each phrase below.

1. full of sadness and *mourning*
2. something of which there is *plenty*
3. puppy that enjoys *playing*

2. Now begins the cry of the guitar. (At this moment, and no other, it cries.)
3. China marches its men down the road. (Just China and no other nation)
4. China marches its men down the road. (No women or children march.)
5. She likes this brand of chicken-noodle soup. (She will not eat anything else.)
6. She likes this brand of chicken-noodle soup. (No one else will eat it.)

Writing Application Place the word *only* in the following sentence in four different places, and then give the sense of each placement:

I can read that poem aloud.

Writing Lesson

Lyric Poem

Think about a moment that left a particularly strong impression on you—consider an ocean during a storm, a shared secret, or a shooting star. Write a lyric poem in which you let your readers experience that moment as you did.

Prewriting   Jot down notes about where your memorable moment took place, what the place looked like, and what feelings it gave you. Use descriptive language that appeals to the senses.

Drafting   Write your impressions and feelings using vivid, descriptive language to capture the mood of the setting. Although you may use partial sentences or break sentences over several lines, use punctuation to indicate pauses and stops.

Revising   Read your poem aloud as you revise. Listen for awkward rhythms or clumsy word choices. Add modifiers where more detail is needed to describe the setting or to create a mood.

> **Model: Revising to Create a Mood**
>
>   *strangely*   *as night approached,*
> The woods were ⋀ silent, ⋀
>   *in soft whispers,*
> And the snow fell ⋀
>
> The details *strangely, as night approached,* and *in soft whispers* help create a mystical mood.

 Prentice Hall Writing and Grammar Connection: Chapter 6, Connected Assignment

Extension Activities

Research and Technology   To learn more about the war that inspired "The Moon at the Fortified Pass," research the role of the Tartars in history and their conflict with the Chinese. Consider these sources:

- Electronic or online encyclopedia articles
- Other information from the Internet
- Magazine or journal articles and books

Write a **brief report** in which you present your findings, and explain how the information you learned adds to your understanding of the poem.

Listening and Speaking   Plan and present a **poetry reading** of "The Guitar." To set the mood, find and play a recording of classical Spanish guitar music. Play the recording softly the second time while you read "The Guitar." Explain how the music adds to the poetry.

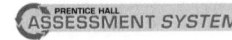 **Take It to the Net**   www.phschool.com

Go online for an additional research activity using the Internet.

Jade Flower Palace / The Moon at the Fortified Pass / The Guitar / What Are Friends For / Making a Fist / Some Like Poetry   ◆   979

ASSESSMENT RESOURCES

The following resources can be used to assess students' knowledge and skills.

Selection Assessment

- **Formal Assessment,** pp. 207–209
- **Open Book Test,** pp. 175–177
- **Got It! Assessment Videotapes,** Tape 5
- **Test Bank Software**

 Take It to the Net
Visit www.phschool.com self-tests and additional questions on the selections.

Listening and Speaking Rubric

- **Performance Assess. and Portfolio Mgmt.,** p. 29

PRENTICE HALL ASSESSMENT SYSTEM

- **Workbook**
- **Skill Book**
- **Transparencies**
- **CD-ROM**

Lesson Support for p. 979

❸ Writing Lesson

- A lyric poem's setting and its mood are often closely related. Remind students of "Jade Flower Palace": The setting of the decrepit palace creates a desolate mood. Have students focus on a setting that will create a distinct mood.

- Use the Writing Lesson to guide students in developing their poems. To help them move from prewriting to drafting, offer the following list of suggestions:
  - Make the first line interesting—start in the middle of things.
  - Use strong, vivid verbs.
  - Consider each and every word.
  - Don't use more words than you need.

❹ Listening and Speaking

- Since "The Guitar" is such a sorrowful lyric poem, students should consider finding a melancholy piece of music.

- Have students present their findings along with explanations of why they chose each particular accompaniment.

- Use the rubric for Delivering a Descriptive Presentation, p. 29 in **Performance Assessment and Portfolio Management,** to assess students' readings.

CUSTOMIZE INSTRUCTION
For Universal Access

To address different learning styles, use the following activities suggested in the **Extension Activities** booklet, p. 59.

- For Verbal/Linguistic and Interpersonal Learners, use Activity 5.
- For Logical/Mathematical and Intrapersonal Learners, use Activity 6.
- For Musical/Rhythmic and Bodily/Kinesthetic Learners, use Activity 7.

Lesson Objectives

1. To learn how to read historical essays for information
2. To learn how to analyze the basic patterns of organization of historical essays

About Historical Essays

- Have students read "About Historical Essays." Then, discuss examples of historical essays students have read.

  Possible response: Students may mention newspaper articles written about a person; articles on the history of a period, such as an encyclopedia entry on the Roman Empire; and articles on the history of a sport, which may be found in an encyclopedia, a non-fiction book, or a newspaper.

- Ask students why chronological order would be a logical pattern of organization to use in a historical essay.

  Answer: A historical essay generally considers events that occurred during a period of the past, so time order is a good pattern to use.

Reading Strategy

Analyzing Patterns of Organization

- Have students read the information about the Reading Strategy.

- Ask students which combination of patterns of organization would be the best for a historical essay on two different musicians and for an essay on the public views of war in history.

  Answer: An essay on two musicians would use chronological order and comparison and contrast. An essay on changing public views of war would use chronological order, comparison and contrast, and—since the subject is complex—order of importance.

Historical Essays

About Historical Essays

In a historical essay, the writer researches historical sources to find factual information about a particular person, event, or thing. Then, the writer records this information—usually in chronological order. In this essay, the writer presents information about the precursors to the guitar in Europe and Africa.

Reading Strategy

Analyzing Patterns of Organization

Writers may organize information in a variety of ways. Patterns of organization include chronological order, order of importance, comparison and contrast, and parts to whole.

In "The History of the Guitar," the author orders much of the information chronologically, starting with the earliest forerunners of the guitar and then moving to later instruments. He also compares instruments point by point.

The chart shown here explains the types of organization and provides examples to demonstrate an appropriate use of each type.

Types of Organization	Examples
Chronological Order	
• Presents events in the order in which they occurred • Ideal for reporting the history of a subject	Explaining the events leading up to the launch of the space shuttle
Order of Importance	
• Presents details in the order of increasing or decreasing importance • Ideal for writing persuasively or for building an argument	Defending or opposing an amendment to the Constitution
Comparison and Contrast	
• Presents similarities and differences • Ideal for addressing two or more subjects	Discussing the writing styles of two best-selling authors

As you read "The History of the Guitar," note which patterns of organization the writer uses.

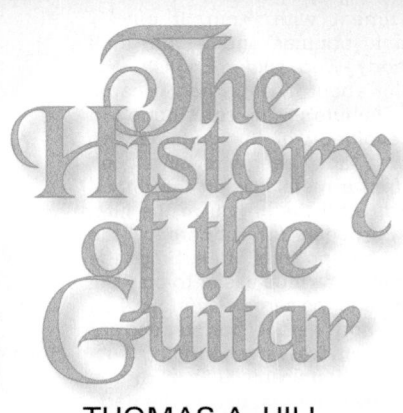

The History of the Guitar

THOMAS A. HILL

When we attempt to pinpoint the origins of deliberately produced, carefully designed instruments, we run into problems, because the very first instrument makers were not very concerned with posterity. They did not leave written records. One approach we might try, in an effort to find out where the guitar came from, would be an examination of languages. The ancient Assyrians,[1] four thousand years ago, had an instrument that they called a *chetarah*. We know little more about it other than that it was a stringed instrument with a sound-box, but the name is intriguing. The ancient Hebrews had their *kinnura*, the Chaldeans[2] their *qitra*, and the Greeks their *cithara* and *citharis*—which Greek writers of the day were careful to emphasize were *not* the same instrument. It is with the Greeks, in fact, that the first clear history of the evolution of an instrument begins; some of this history can again be traced with purely linguistic devices. The cithara and citharis were members of a family of musical instruments called *fides*—a word that is ancient Greek for "strings." From the *fides* family it is easy to draw lines to the medieval French *vielle*, the German *fiedel*, the English *fithele* or *fiddle*, and the *vihuela*, national instrument of medieval Spain. Significantly, much of the music for the vihuela (of which a great deal survives to the present day) can easily be transcribed[3] for the guitar.

> The writer begins his history with the earliest known facts.

> Hill uses the words for the instruments to trace their history.

---

1. **Assyrians** (ə sir´ ē ənz) founders of an ancient empire in the Middle East, flourishing in the seventh century B.C.
2. **Chaldeans** (kal dē´ ənz) a people that rose to power in Babylon, an ancient empire of the Middle East, during the sixth century B.C.
3. **transcribed** (tran skrībd´) v. adapted a piece of music for an instrument other than the one for which it was written.

The History of the Guitar

- Ask students to suggest where they might find an article like this one.

  Possible responses: Students may suggest a magazine sold to amateur and professional musicians, a non-fiction book on musical instruments, a Web site with the theme of either music or language, and so forth.

- Have students identify the basic organizational pattern Hill uses in the first part of his essay.

  Answer: He uses comparison and contrast to note various ancient cultures that had guitar-like instruments; he turns to chronological order when he traces the influence of the Greek word *fides* on other, later words in other languages.

- Have students determine what kind of early facts related to the guitar the author reports.

  Answer: He reports facts about words—the names of the instruments.

- What common, modern English word does Hill say has come from the Greek word *fides*, meaning "strings."

  Answer: The word *fiddle* derives from *fides*.

(continued on p. 982)

CUSTOMIZE INSTRUCTION FOR UNIVERSAL ACCESS

For Less Proficient Readers	For English Learners	For Advanced Readers
Have students discuss the characteristics of guitars. List the features they name. Divide students into groups and assign a different feature to each. Have members of each group determine what information on that feature appears in the article and report back to the class.	Ask students to use a dictionary to trace the origins of the names of a few instruments. Have them compare these words to the names of these instruments in their first language. Ask what these linguistic facts show about connections between cultures. Then, have them write a paragraph explaining what Hill learns from words.	Have students use this article and additional research to construct genealogical charts of the guitar. Charts should show related instruments, the features they share with or contributed to the guitar, the dates of their popularity, their culture of origin, and descriptions of the music they were used to play.

continued from p. 981

- Ask students why Hill shifts to a point-by-point comparison when he describes what the early instruments looked like.
  Answer: He wants the reader to understand the features of each instrument that make it similar to or different from others, including the modern guitar.

- Have students locate the point in the essay in which Hill moves back to a pattern of chronological order.
  Answer: He uses the word *Meanwhile* to shift back to time order, which he uses to discuss the introduction of the Moorish lute into Europe.

- Ask students to infer why the recent history of the guitar is more easily determined than the early history.
  Possible response: The early players of guitar-like instruments did not leave written records, and their instruments have perished.

In England, the influences of the cithara and citharis led to the evolution of such instruments as the *cither, zither, cittern,* and *gittern,* with which instrument the linguistic parallel we seek is fairly easy to draw. Gitterns dating back to 1330 can be seen in the British Museum. In Spain, there is music for the vihuela that dates back at least that far.

What did these instruments look like? Superficially, they bore a substantial resemblance to the guitar as we know it today, although the sides seldom curved in as far as do the sides of the modern guitar. They were usually strung with *pairs* of strings, or *courses,* much like a modern twelve-string guitar. The two strings of each course were tuned either in unison or an octave[4] apart. For a while, there seemed to be no standard for the number of courses an instrument should have; there are both vihuelas and gitterns with as few as four courses and as many as seven. By the fifteenth century, the vihuela seems to have settled on six as the standard number of courses. . . . In England, the gittern settled down to four courses. . . . Historians of this period do note the existence in Spain of an instrument called the *guitarra.* . . . But no music was being written for this instrument, and nobody seems to have been paying much attention to it.

Meanwhile, in Africa, the Arabs had been playing an instrument that they called *al-ud,* or "the wood," for centuries. When the Moors crossed the Straits of Gibraltar[5] in the twelfth century to conquer Spain, they brought this instrument with them. It quickly became popular, and by the time anybody who spoke English was talking about it, al-ud had become *lute.* The lute's main contribution to the evolution of the guitar as we know it today seems to have been the fret, a metal bar on the fingerboard. Until the arrival of the lute, the European forerunners of the guitar had no frets at all. Since the fret made it a little easier to play the same tune the same way more than once, and helped to standardize tunings, it was a resounding success. The first Arabic lutes in Europe had movable frets, tied to the neck, usually about eight in number. Consequently, the first vihuelas to which frets were added also had movable ones.

The lute—or rather the people who brought it to Europe—made another important contribution. The Moorish artistic influence, blowing the cobwebs away from stodgy Spanish art and society, created an artistic climate that encouraged music to flourish. And so the instruments on which the music was played flourished as well, and continued to evolve and improve. This is a contribution that cannot be overestimated.

If any general lines can be drawn, perhaps it can be said that descendants of the original al-ud, crossing the Straits of Gibraltar, collided in Spain with the descendants of the Greek cithara and citharis. Sprinkled with a little bit of gittern influence from England, the result led ultimately to what we know today as the guitar.

Hill uses point-by-point comparison to discuss the strings.

Transitions like *meanwhile* help the author move smoothly to his next point.

The writer concludes with a generalization.

---

4. **unison** (yo͞on´ ə sən) . . . **octave** (äk´ tiv) A unison consists of two tones of the same pitch. An octave consists of two tones that are eight notes apart in the scale. The pitches in an octave sound "the same" and are named by the same note.
5. **Moors** (mo͞orz) . . . **Gibraltar** (ji brôl´ tər) Groups of Moors, an Arab people of North Africa, invaded Spain at various times, starting in the eighth century A.D. The Straits of Gibraltar are waters dividing Spain from Africa.

Check Your Comprehension

1. What is the earliest stringed instrument described in the essay?
2. In what country can the early history of the guitar be most clearly traced?
3. What do these early instruments look like?
4. From which part of the world did the precursor of the lute come?
5. What is the contribution of the lute?

Apply the Reading Strategy

Analyzing Patterns of Organization

6. What pattern of organization does Hill use when he discusses the Assyrians before he discusses the Greek instruments? Explain.
7. What pattern of organization leads Hill to discuss the Arabian al-ud after describing the English gittern and Spanish vihuela? Explain.
8. What pattern of organization does Hill use in listing stringed instruments in the second paragraph? Explain.
9. What pattern best describes the general organization of this essay? Explain.

Activity

Studying a Variety of Formats

Find and read a newspaper article, a magazine article, and an online encyclopedia article. On a chart like the one shown at right, compare the main organizational plan used in each.

Comparing Informational Materials

Historical Essay and History Museum Exhibition

1. How would the information that you could obtain in a museum exhibit on the history of the guitar compare with the historical essay that you just read?
2. (a) From which informational materials might you gain more in-depth knowledge? (b) Which might you find more interesting? Explain your responses.

Analyzing Patterns

	Organizational Plan
Newspaper	
Magazine	
Online Encyclopedia	

Answers for p. 983

Check Your Comprehension

1. The earliest stringed instrument described is the *chetarah,* from Assyria.
2. The early history of the guitar can be most clearly traced in Greece.
3. They looked much like a modern guitar, with these differences: their sides did not curve in as far as those on a modern guitar; they were usually strung with pairs of strings, rather than single strings; the number of strings varied; and they had no frets.
4. The precursor of the lute came from Moorish countries in Africa.
5. The lute's main contribution was the fret, a metal bar on the fingerboard, which helped to standardize tunings.

Applying the Reading Strategy

6. He uses a chronological pattern, insofar as Assyrian culture predates classical culture; he uses order of importance, insofar as the Greeks are a clearer source of information and are a clearer influence on later cultures than are the Assyrians.
7. He uses a parts-to-whole organization, discussing the lute separately because it originated in another part of the world and because it contributed a distinctive part to the instrument—the frets.
8. He uses comparison and contrast, comparing each feature in turn.
9. The general organization of the essay is best described as chronological organization. Although the writer uses other types of organization throughout, he generally begins in the past and moves forward through time.

Activity

When students have completed their charts, ask for a show of hands to determine how many of each kind of organizational pattern, and what combinations of patterns, students found. In discussion, explore whether the patterns of organization have anything to do with the sources in which articles were found,

continued

Answers continued

or whether they are determined strictly by the subject matter.

Comparing Informational Materials

1. Students may say that the information obtained in a museum exhibit would probably not contain as much information as the historical essay and that the museum display would probably contain a great deal of graphic and color material, as well as examples of the instruments.
2. (a) Students may say that they would gain more in-depth knowledge from the essay.

(b) They may say they would find the museum display more interesting because of its visual interest and the actual presence of instruments.

The Waking ✦ Tanka ✦ Haiku ✦ Sonnet 18

Lesson Objectives

1. **To analyze and respond to literary elements**
   - Literary Analysis: Poetic Forms
   - Comparing Literary Works
2. **To read, comprehend, analyze, and critique poems**
   - Reading Strategy: Picturing the Imagery
   - Review and Assess questions
   - Assessment Practice (ATE)
3. **To develop word analysis skills, fluency, and systematic vocabulary**
   - Vocabulary Development Lesson: Forms of *temperate*
4. **To understand and apply written and oral language conventions**
   - Spelling Strategy
   - Grammar Lesson: *to, too, two*
5. **To understand and apply appropriate writing and research strategies**
   - Writing Lesson: Consumer Report of Poetic Forms
   - Extension Activity: Poster
6. **To understand and apply listening and speaking strategies**
   - Extension Activity: Oral Interpretation

STEP-BY-STEP TEACHING GUIDE	PACING GUIDE
PRETEACH	
Motivate Students and Provide Background	
Use the Motivation activity (ATE p. 984)	5 min.
Read and discuss the Preview material and Background information (SE/ATE p. 984)	5 min.
Introduce the Concepts	
Introduce the Literary Analysis and Reading Strategy (SE/ATE p. 985)	15 min.
Pronounce the vocabulary words and read their definitions (SE p. 985)	5 min.
TEACH	
Monitor Comprehension	
Informally monitor comprehension by circulating while students read independently or in groups	10 min.
Develop vocabulary with Vocabulary notes (SE pp. 989, 990)	as students read
Develop Understanding	
Develop students' understanding of poetic forms with the Literary Analysis annotation (ATE p. 987)	10 min.
Develop students' understanding of picturing imagery with the Reading Strategy annotations (ATE pp. 986, 989)	10 min.
ASSESS	
Assess Mastery	
Assess students' mastery of the Reading Strategy and Literary Analysis by having them answer the Review and Assess questions (SE/ATE p. 991)	20 min.
Use one or more of the print and media Assessment Resources (ATE p. 993)	up to 50 min.
EXTEND	
Apply Understanding	
Have students complete the Vocabulary Development Lesson and the Grammar Lesson (SE p. 992)	20 min.
Apply students' ability to compare and contrast using the Writing Lesson (SE/ATE p. 993)	45 min.
Apply students' understanding using one or more of the Extension Activities (SE p. 993)	20–90 min.

 ACCELERATED INSTRUCTION:
Use the strategies and activities identified with an .

UNIVERSAL ACCESS
● = Below Level Students
▲ = On-Level Students
■ = Above Level Students

Time and Resource Manager

RESOURCES

PRINT 📖	TRANSPARENCIES 🗒	TECHNOLOGY 💿 🎧 📼
• **Beyond Literature**, Cross-Curricular Connection: Science, p. 60 ▲ ■		• **Interest Grabber Video**, Tape 5 ● ▲ ■
• **Selection Support Workbook:** ● ▲ ■ Literary Analysis, p. 240 Reading Strategy, p. 239 Build Vocabulary, p. 237	• **Literary Analysis and Reading Transparencies,** pp. 119 and 120 ● ▲ ■	
		• **Listening to Literature** ● ▲ ■ Audiocassettes, Side 34 Audio CDs, CD 19
• **Literatura en español** ● ▲ • **Literary Analysis for Enrichment** ■		
• **Formal Assessment:** Selection Test, pp. 210–212 ● ▲ ■ • **Open Book Test,** pp. 178–180 ● ▲ ■ • **Performance Assessment and Portfolio Management,** p. 15 ● ▲ ■ • ⬡ PRENTICE HALL ASSESSMENT *SYSTEM* ● ▲	• ⬡ PRENTICE HALL ASSESSMENT *SYSTEM* ● ▲ ■ Skills Practice Answers and Explanations on Transparencies	• **Test Bank Software** ● ▲ ■ • **Got It! Assessment Videotapes,** Tape 5 ● ▲
• **Selection Support Workbook:** ● ▲ ■ Build Grammar Skills, p. 238 • **Writing and Grammar,** Platinum Level ● ▲ ■ • **Extension Activities,** p. 60 ● ▲ ■	• **Daily Language Practice Transparencies** ● ▲ • **Writing Models and Graphic Organizers on Transparencies,** p. 95 ● ▲ ■	• **Writing and Grammar iText CD-ROM** ● ▲ ■ 🖥 *Take It to the Net* www.phschool.com

BLOCK SCHEDULING: Use one 90-minute class period to preteach the selection and have students read it. Use a second 90-minute class period to assess students' mastery of skills and have them complete one of the Extension Activities.

Step-by-Step Teaching Guide for pp. 984–985

Motivation

To prepare students to envision the imagery of the poems, bring in posters or magazine photographs that depict different seasons and moods of nature. You might also play an audiotape of natural sounds such as wind, water, and bird songs. Have students discuss the feelings and memories they have when they see each photograph and hear each sound. Then, encourage them to make similar associations as they read the poetry.

▣ Interest Grabber Video

As an alternative, play "Sonnet 18: Reading and Student Response" on Tape 5 to engage student interest.

❶ Background

Literature

Sonnets developed from Italian songs in the Middle Ages. The word *sonnet* comes from the Italian word *sonetto,* which means "little sound or song." Villanelles originated in the "round" songs of medieval French farm workers. The repetition that derives from the round songs is a defining feature of villanelles.

Prepare to Read

The Waking ◆ Tanka ◆ Haiku ◆ Sonnet 18

 Take It to the Net

Visit www.phschool.com for interactive activities and instruction related to these selections, including
- background
- graphic organizers
- literary elements
- reading strategies

Preview

Connecting to the Literature

When you participate in a sport, you agree to follow certain rules. The rules exist, in part, to pose a challenge and to test the players' skills. In the same way, the rules governing certain forms of poetry challenge the poets' skills.

❶ Background

Poetry has many forms. For centuries, poetry in Japan was limited by a strict number of syllables. The tanka—only thirty-one syllables—was the only form used. The popularity of the tanka and, later, the seventeen-syllable haiku shows the Japanese preference for stark simplicity and suggestion over elaboration.

984 ◆ Poetry

TEACHING RESOURCES

The following resources can be used to enrich or extend the instruction for pp. 984–985.

Motivation

▣ **Interest Grabber Video,** Tape 5

Background

📖 **Beyond Literature,** p. 60

 Take It to the Net
Visit www.phschool.com for background and hotlinks for the selections.

Literary Analysis

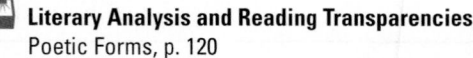 **Literary Analysis and Reading Transparencies,** Poetic Forms, p. 120

Reading

📖 **Selection Support:** Reading Strategy, p. 239; Build Vocabulary, p. 237

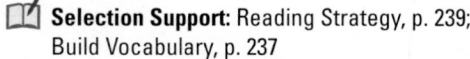 **Literary Analysis and Reading Transparencies,** Picturing the Imagery, p. 119

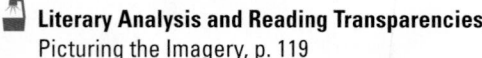 **BLOCK SCHEDULING:** Resources marked with this symbol provide varied instruction during 90-minute blocks.

Literary Analysis

Poetic Forms

Poets express their ideas in a variety of **poetic forms,** or structures. Following are a few examples:

- A **haiku** is an unrhymed lyric poem of three lines of five, seven, and five syllables. It usually includes an image from nature.
- A **tanka** consists of five unrhymed lines of five, seven, five, seven, and seven syllables. Like haiku, tanka also includes simple, straightforward images.
- A **sonnet** is a fourteen-line poem written in iambic pentameter (five unaccented syllables each followed by an accented one).
- A **villanelle** is a lyric poem written in three-line stanzas and ending in a four-line stanza. It has two refrains formed by repeating line 1 in lines 6, 12, and 18 and line 3 in lines 9, 15, and 19.

Comparing Literary Works

Poets choose the poetic form that will best allow them to express their ideas. For example, a sonnet is more suited to presenting a thoughtful explanation, and a haiku is best suited for conveying a striking, crisp image. Compare the rules for each structure, and consider how they affect the meaning of these poems.

Reading Strategy

Picturing the Imagery

When you **picture the imagery,** you use your memory and imagination to see, feel, hear, smell, and taste what the poets describe. In this excerpt from Ki no Tsurayuki's poem, feel the bitter wind blowing off the river and hear the birds' mournful cries:

> That winter night
> The river blew so cold
> That the plovers were crying.

In a chart like the one here, list associations and comparisons that help you picture the imagery.

Image	Association
"darling buds of May, . . ."	Warm sun Bright colors
Spring rain	Freshness Renewal

Vocabulary Development

camellia (kə mēl′ yə) *n.* flower of an Asiatic evergreen shrub (p. 989)

lapping (lap′ iŋ) *v.* dipping a liquid up with the tongue (p. 989)

temperate (tem′ pər it) *adj.* moderate in degree or quality (p. 990)

eternal (ē tʉr′ nəl) *adj.* everlasting; timeless (p. 990)

The Waking / Tanka / Haiku / Sonnet 18 ◆ 985

---

❷ Literary Analysis

Poetic Forms

- Reinforce the idea that poets can choose from a variety of poetic forms or structures to express their ideas.

- Read aloud the information on the four poetic structures that will be covered in this group of selections.

- Use the instruction for Comparing Literary Works to explain to students that poets choose the form of poetry that will best allow them to express their ideas. As they read the poems, students should consider how the form of each one helps to convey its meaning.

- Use the Poetic Forms transparency in **Literary Analysis and Reading Transparencies,** p. 120, to demonstrate for students how to identify the variety of poetic forms.

❸ Reading Strategy

Picturing the Imagery

- Remind students that imagery engages the senses and allows them to view mental pictures of what the poets describe.

- Then, tell students that when you use your memory and imagination to make associations with the sensory details, the imagery helps you see deeper into the poem.

- Instruct students to create imagery charts like the one on this page to record images from the poetry and associations that come from those images.

Vocabulary Development

- Pronounce each vocabulary word for students, and read the definitions as a class. Have students identify any words with which they are already familiar.

CUSTOMIZE INSTRUCTION FOR UNIVERSAL ACCESS

For Less Proficient Readers	For English Learners	For Advanced Readers
To help students picture the imagery in the poems, encourage them to draw sketches of the mental images that the sensory details bring to mind. When they finish, have students compare and contrast their sketches.	Model for students how to create an imagery chart by using the Picturing the Imagery transparency in **Literary Analysis and Reading Transparencies,** p. 119. Have students read the poems together. As they identify images and associations, have them record them in a chart like the one on the transparency.	Allow students to read the poems at their own pace, but encourage them to create imagery charts while they read. Have students compare and contrast the associations they make with each image.

 E-Teach

Visit E-Teach at www.phschool.com for teachers' essays on how to teach, with questions and answers.

**Step-by-Step Teaching Guide
for pp. 986–990**

CUSTOMIZE INSTRUCTION
For Verbal/Linguistic Learners

When reading poetry, it is likely that students will encounter unfamiliar words. Encourage them to use the dictionary to find precise meanings of words within the contexts of the poems.

❶ About the Selection

"The Waking" reflects upon our daily process of waking up—literally and figuratively—the process of becoming "awake" to the world of nature and the meaning of life.

❷ Reading Strategy

Picturing the Imagery

• Read aloud the bracketed passage to the students. Ask the students to envision the imagery in this stanza. Have them close their eyes and imagine morning sunlight shining on a tree that they know well.

• Ask them to write down as many details they envision as possible. Ask for volunteers to describe what they envision to the rest of the class. Have the students compare and contrast the various associations.

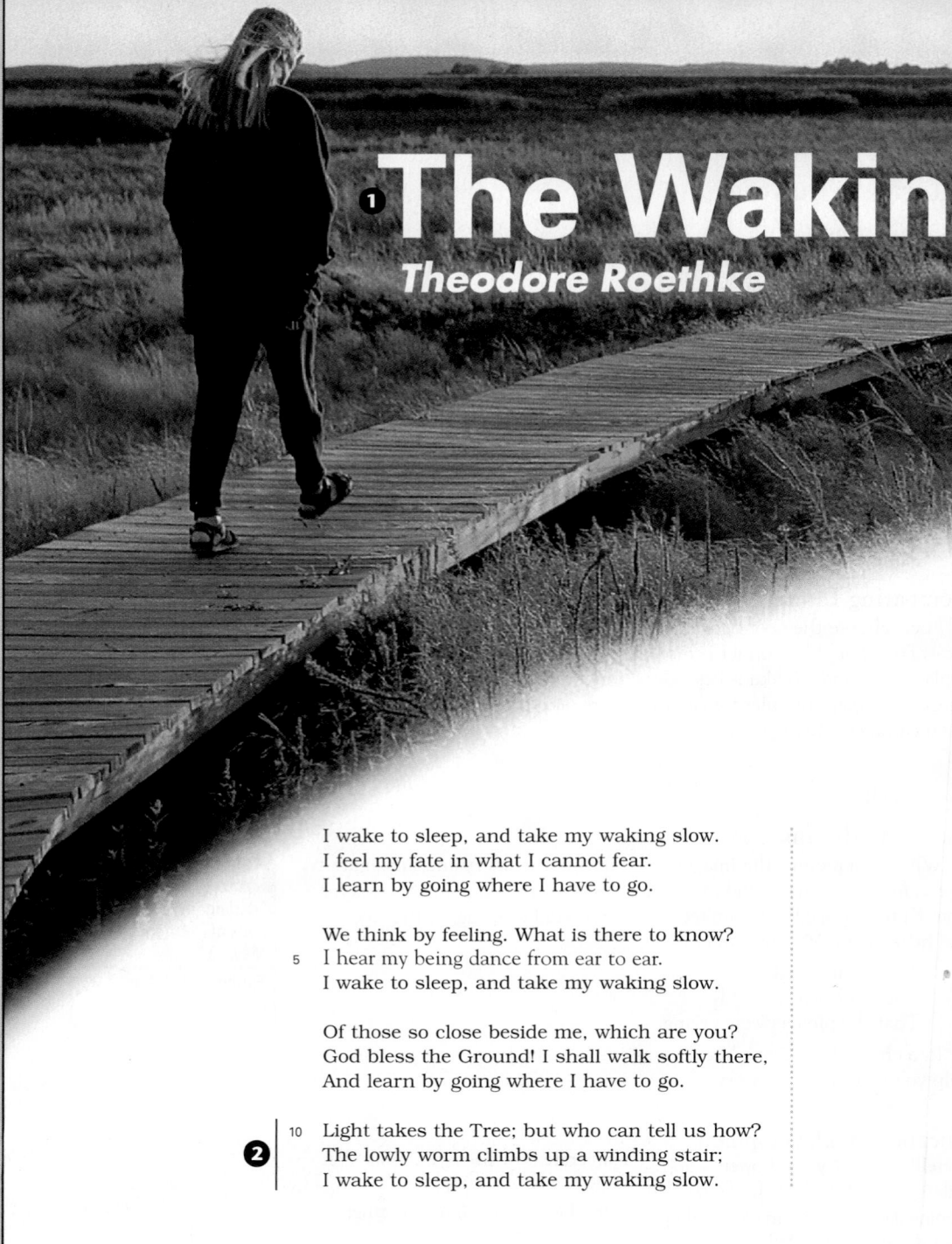

❶ # The Waking
Theodore Roethke

I wake to sleep, and take my waking slow.
I feel my fate in what I cannot fear.
I learn by going where I have to go.

We think by feeling. What is there to know?
5 I hear my being dance from ear to ear.
I wake to sleep, and take my waking slow.

Of those so close beside me, which are you?
God bless the Ground! I shall walk softly there,
And learn by going where I have to go.

❷ 10 Light takes the Tree; but who can tell us how?
The lowly worm climbs up a winding stair;
I wake to sleep, and take my waking slow.

986 ◆ *Poetry*

TEACHING RESOURCES

The following resources can be used to enrich or extend the instruction for pp. 986–990.

Literary Analysis

📖 **Writing Models and Graphic Organizers on Transparencies,** p. 95 ▪

📖 **Selection Support:** Literary Analysis, p. 240

Reading

🎧 **Listening to Literature Audiocassettes,** Side 34 ▪

💿 **Listening to Literature Audio CDs,** CD 19 ▪

▪ **BLOCK SCHEDULING:** Resources marked with this symbol provide varied instruction during 90-minute blocks.

Great Nature has another thing to do
To you and me; so take the lively air,
15 And, lovely, learn by going where to go.

This shaking keeps me steady. I should know.
What falls away is always. And is near.
I wake to sleep, and take my waking slow.
I learn by going where I have to go.

④

Review and Assess

Thinking About the Selection

1. **Respond:** After reading this poem, do you feel optimistic or pessimistic? Explain.

2. **(a) Recall:** According to the speaker, what dances "from ear to ear"? **(b) Interpret:** In what ways is the image contradictory? **(c) Interpret:** What is the emotion conveyed by this image?

3. **(a) Recall:** Identify two lines that address learning or thinking. **(b) Interpret:** What attitude toward knowledge do these lines convey? Explain.

4. **(a) Interpret:** What do you think the speaker means by the line "I wake to sleep, and take my waking slow"? **(b)** Why do you think so?

5. **(a) Analyze:** What advice about living can you find in this poem? **(b) Evaluate:** Do you think it is good advice? Why or why not?

Theodore Roethke

(1908–1963)

The American poet Theodore Roethke is known for his affectionate portrayals of children and the elderly. His works range from witty, realistic poems in strict form to free-form verse with exotic imagery. In 1954, Roethke received a Pulitzer Prize for his book, *The Waking, Poems: 1933–1953*.

The Waking ◆ 987

---

❻

The Monkey Bridge in Koshu Province,
1841, Hiroshige Hitsu, Christie's, New York

❺ Tanka

Translated by Geoffrey Bownas

Ki Tsurayuki

❼
When I went to visit
The girl I love so much,
That winter night
The river blew so cold
That the plovers[1] were crying.

---

1. **plovers** (pluv´ ərz) *n.* wading shore-birds with short tails; long, pointed wings; and short, stout beaks.

Priest Jakuren

One cannot ask loneliness
How or where it starts.
On the cypress-mountain,[1]
Autumn evening.

---

1. **cypress-mountain** Cypress trees are cone-bearing evergreen trees native to North America, Europe, and Asia.

❽ ▲ Critical Viewing Compare the mood of this painting with the mood or feelings evoked in these tankas. **[Compare and Contrast]**

❺ Haiku

Translated by Daniel C. Buchanan

Matsuo Bashō

Falling upon earth,
Pure water spills from the cup
Of the <u>camellia</u>.

落ちざまに
水こぼしけり
花椿

お
みづ
はな つばき

春雨や
鼠のなめる
隅田川

はる さめ
ねずみ
すみ だ がわ

Kobayashi Issa

A gentle spring rain.
Look, a rat is <u>lapping</u>
Sumida River.

camellia (kə mēl´ yə) *n.* flower of an Asiatic evergreen shrub

lapping (lap´ iŋ) *v.* dipping a liquid up with the tongue

Haiku

Matsuo Bashō (1644–1694)

Matsuo Bashō (mä tsoō´ bä shō) is generally regarded as the greatest Japanese haiku poet. He lived the life of a hermit, supporting himself by teaching and judging poetry contests. Bashō recorded his observations and insights in both poems and thoughtful travel diaries.

Kobayashi Issa (1763–1828)

Kobayashi Issa (kō bä yä´ shē ē´ sä) lived his life in urban poverty and struggled to overcome the loneliness and pain resulting from the deaths of loved ones. His difficult circumstances contributed to his appreciation of the fleeting lives of small creatures.

Haiku ◆ 989

Review and Assess

Thinking About the Selections

1. **Respond:** Which poem do you like best? Why?
2. **(a) Recall:** What does the word *it* refer to in the tanka by Priest Jakuren? **(b) Connect:** What is the connection between loneliness and the cypress-mountain?
3. **(a) Recall:** What does Bashō describe in his haiku? **(b) Recall:** What creature is the subject of Issa's haiku? **(c) Analyze:** To what senses do these haiku appeal?
4. **Speculate:** Why do you think nature plays such an important role in these poems?

10 About the Selection

Shakespeare's famous sonnet begins by praising the beauty and temperateness of his beloved as surpassing those of a summer day. It ends by testifying to the power of poetry to immortalize the person the poet loves.

11 ▶ Critical Viewing

Possible responses: Students should compare details of hairstyles, clothing, and jewelry and relate them to their own beliefs of what makes someone beautiful.

Answers for p. 990

Review and Assess

1. **Possible answers:** Students may feel flattered, overwhelmed, or embarrassed.

2. **(a)** The subject is compared to a summer's day. **(b)** The beloved fares better because unlike the summer day, she is not shaken by rough winds, the hot sun does not dim her complexion and, most of all, the beloved's beauty does not die as the season does.

3. **(a)** The sun is "the eye of heaven." **(b)** Sometimes the sun is too hot, and sometimes it does not shine brightly.

4. **(a)** "Thy eternal summer" (the subject's beauty) shall not fade. **(b)** The power of poetry immortalizes the beloved.

5. **(a)** Students may agree that literature has the power to make people and things immortal. **(b)** Students might mention books or poems that celebrate the lives of people who have died.

Frances Howard, Isaac Oliver, Victoria and Albert Museum

10 Sonnet 18

William Shakespeare

Shall I compare thee to a summer's day?
Thou art more lovely and more <u>temperate</u>:
Rough winds do shake the darling buds of May,
And summer's lease hath all too short a date:
5   Sometime too hot the eye of heaven shines,
And often is his gold complexion dimmed;
And every fair from fair sometime declines,
By chance or nature's changing course untrimmed;[1]
But thy <u>eternal</u> summer shall not fade,
10   Nor lose possession of that fair thou owest;[2]
Nor shall Death brag thou wander'st in his shade,
When in eternal lines to time thou grow'st:
     So long as men can breathe, or eyes can see,
     So long lives this, and this gives life to thee.

---

1. **untrimmed** (un trimd´) v. not made or kept neat; disordered.
2. **owest** (ō´ ist) v. own.

11 ▲ Critical Viewing
Compare the appearance of this woman with that of someone you consider beautiful. **[Compare and Contrast]**

temperate (tem´ pər it) adj. moderate in degree or quality

eternal (ē tur´ nəl) adj. everlasting; timeless

William Shakespeare

(1564–1616)

    Shakespeare's skill in writing English sonnets is one of the reasons his name has remained famous through the ages. Today, the English sonnet, which he perfected, is also known as the Shakespearean sonnet. He is even more famous as a playwright, having produced thirty-eight plays within about twenty years! For more about Shakespeare, see pages 818–819.

Review and Assess

Thinking About the Selection

1. **Respond:** How might you feel if you were the subject of a sonnet like this one? Explain.

2. **(a) Recall:** To what is the speaker comparing the subject of the poem? **(b) Draw Conclusions:** Does the subject fare better or worse than a summer's day? Explain.

3. **(a) Recall:** Who or what is "the eye of heaven"? **(b) Paraphrase:** In your own words, restate lines 5 and 6.

4. **(a) Recall:** What does the speaker say "shall not fade"? **(b) Draw Conclusions:** What makes the beloved immortal?

5. **(a) Evaluate:** Do you agree with the statement made in the last two lines? **(b) Apply:** What are some modern expressions of this sentiment?

✎ ASSESSMENT PRACTICE: Reading Comprehension

Analyzing an Author's Meaning and Style   **(For more practice, see Test Preparation Workbook, p. 60.)**

Help students practice analyzing an author's meaning and style to understand his or her message. Ask students to read "Sonnet 18," noting the details of the poem.

    According to the author, the speaker's love—

    A is like the wind
    B is ever changing like nature
    C will live as long as men breathe
    D is always changing

    Suggest that students analyze the answer choices and review the poem to determine which one best supports the author's meaning: he compares his love to many things, but believes it will live eternally—*C* is the best answer among the choices offered.

Review and Assess

Literary Analysis

Poetic Forms

1. (a) What are the two refrain lines in the villanelle "The Waking"? (b) What is the effect of their repetition in the poem?
2. Translations of Japanese poetry into English may not have the standard number of syllables. However, the poems retain other features of the form. Explain how the tanka and haiku presented here fit the form.
3. (a) A quatrain is a group of four lines. What is the message of the first two quatrains of Sonnet 18? (b) How does the third quatrain relate to the first two?

Comparing Literary Works

4. (a) How might the expression of the ideas in "The Waking" have to be changed to fit the tanka or haiku form? (b) How would one of the haiku have to change to fit the villanelle form?
5. Which of these forms do you think is most challenging for a poet to use? Explain.

Reading Strategy

Picturing the Imagery

6. Using a diagram like the one here, describe the feelings you experience when you picture the image of the "winding stair" in Roethke's "The Waking."

7. Identify one image from each tanka and haiku, and explain to which senses each image appeals.
8. In Sonnet 18, what sensory details do you associate with "Sometime too hot the eye of heaven shines, / And often is his gold complexion dimmed; . . ."?

Extend Understanding

9. **Cultural Connection:** (a) Which poems in this group—if any—are grounded in a specific culture? (b) What qualities of some poetry enable it to be timeless?

Quick Review

Poets express their ideas in a variety of **poetic forms,** or structures, which include the sonnet, villanelle, tanka, and haiku.

When you **picture the imagery,** you use your memory and imagination to see, feel, hear, smell, and taste what the poets describe.

 Take It to the Net
www.phschool.com
Take the interactive self-test online to check your understanding of these selections.

The Waking / Tanka / Haiku / Sonnet 18 ◆ 991

Answers for p. 991

Review and Assess

1. **(a)** "I wake to sleep and take my waking slow" and "I learn by going where I have to go." **(b)** Their repetition expresses the central meaning of the poem: that waking up to life and learning about life represent a gradual process that cannot be rushed or planned.

2. Both the tanka and the haiku include simple, straightforward images that relate to nature.

3. **(a)** The message is that the speaker's beloved is fairer than a summer's day. **(b)** The third quatrain contrasts the woman's fairness with summer by saying her fairness will not fade.

4. **(a)** "The Waking" would have to be simplified; perhaps the poet could focus on a single image of waking. **(b)** The haiku would have to be extended, and the poet might offer comments or insights about the central image.

5. Possible answer: Students might say the Shakespearean sonnet is the most challenging because its form and rhyme scheme create many restrictions.

6. Students may feel anticipation or curiosity.

7. Answers may include the following images: the plovers crying (hearing); the cypress mountain (sight); water spilling from a camellia (sight and touch); a rat lapping river water (taste and touch).

8. Students might associate these sensory details with hot summer days in which the temperature is very high and the sky is hazy rather than bright.

9. **(a)** The tanka and haiku reflect the stark, simple beauty often found in Japanese art. **(b)** Possible response: The simple yet profound form enables some poetry to be timeless.

❶ Vocabulary Development

Word Analysis

1. Priest Jaukuran lived a mild, temperate life.

2. A rash, intemperate act would have been unthinkable for him.

3. He practiced temperance in his activities by avoiding excess.

Spelling Strategy

1. coverage   **3.** watering

2. lyrical

Concept Development: Analogies

1. temperate   **3.** eternal

2. lapping   **4.** camellia

❷ Grammar

1. to   **4.** two

2. too   **5.** to; to

3. to

Writing Application

Sample sentences:

1. He wanted to join the group, too.

2. Too many people were involved in the situation.

3. We are going to the market.

4. She is going to give two nickels to you.

5. Two people jumped down from the tree.

6. The game requires two teams of five players each.

Integrate Language Skills

❶ Vocabulary Development Lesson

Word Analysis: Forms of *temperate*

The word *temperate* means "not extreme." Other forms of the word *temperate* also indicate moderation. Write a sentence for each of the following words, in which the idea of moderation is expressed:

    1. temperate   **2.** intemperate   **3.** temperance

Spelling Strategy

If a word of more than one syllable ends in a single consonant coming after a single vowel and the accent is not on the last syllable, do not double the final consonant before a suffix beginning with a vowel: *temper + -ate = temperate.*

Add a suffix—such as *-ing, -age,* or *-al*—to each word, forming a new word.

    1. cover   **2.** lyric   **3.** water

Concept Development: Analogies

Analogies present two word pairs. To complete analogies successfully, choose a word that forms a relationship in the second pair that matches the relationship of the first pair. The word relationships may be synonyms, antonyms, part to whole, or key characteristics.

Notice the relationship between the first pair of words in each item. Then, in your notebook, complete the second pair of words with a word from the vocabulary list on page 985.

    1. foolish : thoughtful :: excessive : ____?____

    2. tongue : ____?____ :: teeth : chewing

    3. mortal : ____?____ :: solar : lunar

    4. apple : tree :: ____?____ : shrub

❷ Grammar Lesson

Commonly Confused Words: *to, too, two*

Many people confuse the words *to, too,* and *two.* **To,** a preposition, begins a phrase or an infinitive. **Too,** an adverb, modifies adjectives and other adverbs. **Two** is a number.

Preposition:	Shall I compare thee *to* a summer's day?
Infinitive:	When I went *to* visit / The girl I love . . .
Adverb:	And summer's lease hath all *too* short a date: / . . .
Number:	The poet wrote *two* sonnets.

Practice Copy each sentence, inserting the correct word: *to, too,* or *two.*

    1. So long lives this, and this gives life ____?____ thee.

    2. Sometime ____?____ hot the eye of heaven shines, . . .

    3. I learn by going where I have ____?____ go.

    4. That winter night ____?____ lovers met.

    5. Great Nature has another thing ____?____ do / ____?____ you and me; . . .

Writing Application To illustrate the correct use of the words *to, too,* and *two,* write two sentences for each word.

*W*G *Prentice Hall Writing and Grammar Connection: Chapter 26, Section 2*

TEACHING RESOURCES

The following resources can be used to enrich or extend the instruction for pp. 992–993.

Vocabulary

📖 **Selection Support:** Build Vocabulary, p. 237

📖 **Vocabulary and Spelling Practice Book** (Use this booklet for skills enrichment.) 🔲

Grammar

📖 **Selection Support:** Build Grammar Skills, p. 238

*W*G **Writing and Grammar,** Platinum Level, p. 621 🔲

📖 **Daily Language Practice Transparencies**

Writing

*W*G **Writing and Grammar,** Platinum Level, p. 180

💿 **Writing and Grammar iText CD-ROM** 🔲

🔲 **BLOCK SCHEDULING:** Resources marked with this symbol provide varied instruction during 90-minute blocks.

Writing Lesson

Consumer Report of Poetic Forms

A consumer report outlines the strengths and weaknesses of a product or service. Write a consumer report of the poetic forms in this section, discussing the advantages and disadvantages of each and concluding with a recommendation to poets.

Prewriting   Classify the features of each form as advantages and disadvantages. Focus on the costs and benefits for a reader. For example, you might see the length of a haiku as a drawback because you do not get much poem for your money.

Drafting   Compare and contrast the specific advantages and disadvantages of each poetic form. Support your claims with examples from the poems in this section.

Model: Comparing and Contrasting

The haiku evokes a clear image in just a few words: "Pure water spills from the cup / Of the camellia." In contrast, the much longer sonnet might take up to four lines to fully develop the same image.

> The writer compares the number of words used to describe an image.

Revising   Review your draft for clarity and accuracy. Make sure that you have made valid comparisons. Finally, be sure your report makes a recommendation to readers.

WG   *Prentice Hall Writing and Grammar Connection: Chapter 9, Section 3*

Extension Activities

Listening and Speaking With a partner, prepare an **oral interpretation** of Sonnet 18 or "The Waking." Consider these tips:

- Modulate your voice to express meaning.
- Read according to punctuation.
- Experiment with alternating and combining your voices.

After you have practiced sufficiently, perform your reading for the class. Ask for feedback on your work. [Group Activity]

Research and Technology Design a **poster** to spark other students' interest in Japanese poetry. Use print, electronic, and Internet resources to research information about major ancient and modern Japanese poetic forms. Include poems or excerpts from poems, along with an explanation of the form and the history of each. Incorporate appropriate images, and display the poster in class.

Take It to the Net   www.phschool.com
Go on-line for additional research activity using the Internet.

The Waking / Tanka / Haiku / Sonnet 18 ◆ 993

---

❸ Writing Lesson

- Bring in some examples of consumer reports for students to review. Remind students that an informative consumer report provides information about a subject's strengths and weaknesses so that consumers can make informed choices.
- Encourage students to organize their prewriting notes on the Comparison-and-Contrast Organizer, p. 95 of **Writing Models and Graphic Organizers on Transparencies.**
- Use the Writing Lesson to guide students in developing their report. When they finish, use the rubric for Comparison-and-Contrast Compositions, p.15 in **Performance Assessment and Portfolio Management,** to assess students' work.

❹ Listening and Speaking

- Allow students to select partners. Have each pair decide on a selection to interpret orally.
- Encourage students to decipher words and lines they don't understand by rereading, using the dictionary, and having small-group discussions.
- Have students practice their interpretations before presenting them to the class.

CUSTOMIZE INSTRUCTION for Universal Access

To address different learning styles, use the following activities suggested in the **Extension Activities** booklet, p. 60.

- For Logical/Mathematical and Visual/Spatial Learners, use Activity 5.
- For Interpersonal Learners, use Activity 6.
- For Visual/Spatial Learners, use Activity 7.

Model From Literature

Many pieces of expository writing, such as Thomas A. Hill's "The History of the Guitar," can be viewed as if they were focused responses to a prompt. The imaginary prompt for Hill's essay might be, "Explain the history of the development of the guitar from its earliest known relatives."

Prewriting

- Have volunteers share their strategies for choosing a topic on which to write. Remind them to skim all the topics first, eliminating any about which they have little knowledge or in which they have no interest. A quick test is to list three or more details about the topic they are considering. Encourage students to reject any prompt for which this task is difficult and time consuming.

- Tell students to look carefully for key words that indicate the form their response should take. Students should relate the key word to the thesis statement they write to focus their answer on the question. The thesis stated will often repeat the key word in the question.

- Remind students that they will next need to gather details to support their thesis. Ask students to organize these details using lists, outlines, or cluster diagrams.

- Before students draft their essays, have them review the Rubric for Self-Assessment (p. 997) so they know what is expected.

Writing WORKSHOP

Writing for Assessment

When **writing for assessment,** you are writing to show how fully you have mastered a subject. In many cases, you are asked to write an essay within a specific amount of time without the aid of your notes or books. In this workshop, you will write a composition on a history topic to demonstrate how well you understand the topic.

Assignment Criteria Your assessment composition should have the following characteristics:

- Answers or responses match the questions asked
- Clearly stated main points supported with details
- A logical and effective organizational plan
- Correct grammar, spelling, and punctuation
- Standard American English

To preview the criteria on which your composition may be assessed, see the Rubric on page 997.

Prewriting

Choose a topic. In many cases, more than one essay question is provided, and you will be asked to choose one on which to write a composition. To choose, **skim the questions** first. Quickly eliminate any questions about which you have limited knowledge. To test your knowledge, you might immediately try to think of three details that you could use to answer a particular prompt. If you have to think for too long, move on and try another question.

Match key words to your thesis. Reread the question, and circle key words—such as *predict, trace, compare,* and *evaluate*—that indicate the form your response should take. Then, write a thesis statement that will focus your response on the answer to the question.

Gather details. When you have your thesis constructed, collect details to support it. You might try listing, outlining, or using a cluster diagram to help you brainstorm for the information you will use in your essay.

Analyzing a Test Question

In an essay, discuss the Constitution of the United States. (a) Explain how it came to be. (b) Analyze how a document written so long ago can still be of use today.

Discuss means to support a generalization with facts and examples. *Explain* means to clarify by probing reasons, causes, results, and effects. *Analyze* means to examine how various elements contribute to the whole.

---

994 ◆ *Poetry*

TEACHING RESOURCES

The following resources can be used to enrich or extend the instruction for pp. 994–997.

Writing and Grammar, Platinum Level, Chapter 14, pp. 304–315

Performance Assessment and Portfolio Management, p. 17

Writing Models and Graphic Organizers on Transparencies, pp. 103–106

 Writing and Grammar iText CD-ROM
Students can use the following tools as they complete their composition for assessment:

- Cluster Diagram
- Keyhole Organizer
- Unity and Coherence Checker

Student Model

Before you begin drafting, read this student model and review the characteristics of writing for assessment.

Aleksandra Wojtalewicz
Long Beach, California

In an essay, discuss the U.S. Constitution. (a) Explain how it came to be.
(b) Analyze how a document written so long ago can still be of use today.

In May 1787, in Philadelphia, the Constitutional Convention discussed what was happening to the government. Through debates and compromises, a draft defining the new government was finally completed. Each man signed the Constitution, which would mold and shape the government of the United States.

> The first two paragraphs provide an answer to part (a) of the question.

It took many skilled statesmen to contribute to this document. Without their knowledge, the Constitution would probably lack the power limits of the judicial, executive, and legislative branches and certain rights of the people. Without the Constitution, the country would not function smoothly because it would not have a plan to follow. The Constitution impacts the everyday problems that occur in the government. Who would have thought that this document would have such a great impact 211 years later?

> Here, the writer explains the key information in the Constitution.

> A transitional sentence indicates that the essay will move to address the second question.

In the presidential election of 2000, people waited impatiently until midnight to find out who would be the next president. The time came and went and the United States did not have a president-elect. The United States did not have a future president for about 38 days. During that time, candidates postured for the camera but also followed the rules set by the Constitution to try to reach a resolution. The case went from court to court, finally reaching the U.S. Supreme Court. In the end, the Supreme Court decided to stop recounting, and a president-elect was finally named.

Is the presidential election dilemma of 2000 the fault of the Constitution? The Constitution does not provide an obvious solution to problems such as an incorrect count of votes. There was a lot of talk in the media during the election of 2000 about changing the electoral-college system to allow the candidates to be elected by popular vote. This system was put into place with the signing of the Constitution. Under the original system, a board of electors represented the will of each state. Each elector cast two ballots.

How could a 211-year-old piece of paper have an influence on the wealthiest country in the world? If the Constitutional Convention had never met, then the United States would probably never have had this document. Even at the most difficult times, the Constitution provides a way for justice to be served.

> A conclusion presents the writer's insights into the issue.

Student Model

- Explain that the Student Model is a sample and that their essays may be longer or shorter.
- Ask students to explain how the first two paragraphs of the model relate to the prompt.
  Possible response: Part (a) of the prompt asks students to explain how the Constitution came to be. Aleksandra's first two paragraphs explain the events by which the document came to be and the contributions of its creators.
- Point out that the final sentence at the end of the second paragraph is a transitional sentence which introduces the impact of the Constitution on the lives of Americans in the twenty-first century.
- Ask students to explain how the essay responds to part (b) of the prompt.
  Answer: Aleksandra shows the Constitution's power today by describing a problem it caused—the dilemma of the presidential election of 2000. She indirectly suggests that the Constitution also provided a means of resolving the dilemma—an appeal to the Supreme Court.
- Finally, ask students what the writer has concluded about the question.
  Possible response: The writer has concluded that the Constitution serves justice even when the issues are difficult.

Real-World Connection

Although most people think of writing for assessment in testing situations, much of the writing that people do is assessed by others. In the business world, for instance, many of the same skills utilized in assessment writing are used to prepare memos for both peers and managers. These memos will, in effect, be assessed by their recipients in terms of organization, clarity, use of appropriate language, and effective expression. The skills students develop for writing for assessment may also apply in these real-world situations.

CUSTOMIZE INSTRUCTION FOR UNIVERSAL ACCESS

For Less Proficient Writers	For English Learners	For Advanced Writers
Present these prompts: "1. Evaluate the probability of achieving cold fusion. 2. Explain two causes of the American Revolution. 3. Compare the abilities of two athletes." Have students identify key terms and determine the topic about which they know most. Then, guide them in writing a thesis statement on the topic.	Present these prompts: "1. Evaluate the probability of achieving cold fusion. 2. Explain two causes of the American Revolution. 3. Compare the abilities of two athletes." Have students review the prompts for unfamiliar words they cannot decode using context. If these words are key terms, advise them to reject prompts containing them.	Present these prompts: "1. Evaluate the probability of achieving cold fusion. 2. Explain two causes of the American Revolution. 3. Compare the abilities of two athletes." Have them choose a prompt and write two or three different thesis statements for a possible answer. Ask them to determine which of their statements is strongest, and why.

Drafting

- Encourage students to organize their compositions using one of the listed organizational schemes. Suggest that they identify their approach as narrative, comparison and contrast, evaluation, or analysis. Have them pick the appropriate organization for each.

- Ask students to provide elaboration by listing details, examples, questions and personal observations or anecdotes based on their experience. Caution them to check that all are relevant to their topic.

Revising

- Supply students with colored pencils and have them follow the instructions in the text.

- Tell students that they should be able to explain how each paragraph links to their thesis statement. In each internal paragraph, they should be able to relate each detail to the topic sentence.

- Encourage students to check for and eliminate extraneous details that may relate to the topic but not to the thesis statement.

(continued on p. 977)

Writing WORKSHOP *continued*

Drafting

Organize your composition. Because you will have little time for revising, take time at the beginning to organize your thoughts and plan the structure of your composition. The following are three effective ways to organize it:

- **Comparison-and-contrast organization:** Use this method to show how two or more subjects are alike and different. You might discuss your topic point by point or subject by subject.
- **Chronological organization:** Write your composition to present events in the order in which they occurred.
- **Nestorian organization:** Use this plan if you are writing a composition to persuade, to evaluate, or to analyze a topic. Nestorian organization is shown at right.

Jot down a brief outline to help organize your material. Note the key details to include, but do not spend too much time creating a polished structure using roman numerals. Get the ideas down, and leave yourself time to develop a strong essay.

Elaborate with facts and examples. Make your writing convincing, and give it depth by providing supporting details. You might include examples, quotations, comparisons, or personal observations based on your experiences.

Revising

Revise to refine paragraph unity. In an essay written for a test, it is important to show what you know about a subject. However, you need to link every paragraph to your thesis and connect every detail in your body paragraphs to the topic sentence. To avoid turning in a paper with paragraphs that ramble, review your support of topic sentences.

Using a pencil, place a small check mark next to the topic sentence of each paragraph. Review each paragraph to see that you have concisely supported the point that the topic sentence presents. Insert revisions neatly, and cross out any deletions with a single line.

Revise your word choice. Review your draft, and locate "empty words" and "hedging words" (words that take away from the meaning). Replace or delete such words.

> **Example:** What I mean is that James Marshall got little out of his discovery.
> James Marshall got little out of his discovery.

Nestorian Organization

- Introduction
- Second-most persuasive point
- Third-most persuasive point
- Remaining points, decreasing in importance
- Most persuasive point
- Conclusion

USING TECHNOLOGY IN WRITING

If students are allowed to use computers for their test, they may want to make use of styling features such as boldface to introduce subheads that emphasize the organizational plan of the essay. They can also highlight their thesis statement and topic sentences to ensure that they have supplied them and placed them effectively. If test constraints allow, they can use a thesaurus, dictionary, and spell-checking functions to edit and revise their work. Students can also use the organizing tools and revision checkers available on the **Writing and Grammar Interactive CD-ROM**.

Compare the model and nonmodel. Why is the model more convincing and interesting?

Nonmodel	Model
How could a 211-year-old piece of parchment paper with rights, rules, and regulations of the American government written in ink with old english type writing have any influence at all on what is probably the wealthiest country in the world?	*How could a 211-year-old piece of paper have an influence on the wealthiest country in the world?*

Publishing and Presenting

Choose one of the following ways to share your writing with classmates or a wider audience.

Prepare for future exams. As you get ready to take midterms, finals, and state or national tests, form a discussion group and use your essay test responses to remind yourself of the topics and issues you have studied in class.

Publish your composition electronically. Post your composition on a Web site, or upload it onto a classroom computer.

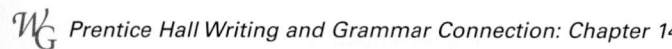 *Prentice Hall Writing and Grammar Connection: Chapter 14*

Rubric for Self-Assessment

Evaluate your writing using the following criteria and rating scale:

Criteria	Rating Scale				
	Not very				Very
Are the questions answered completely?	1	2	3	4	5
Are main points clearly stated?	1	2	3	4	5
Are there sufficient details to support each statement?	1	2	3	4	5
Is the organization logical and followed consistently throughout?	1	2	3	4	5
Have I used correct grammar, spelling, and punctuation?	1	2	3	4	5
Have I used Standard American English?	1	2	3	4	5

TEST-TAKING TIP

Encourage students to write a brief outline before they begin their compositions. Remind them that each main point must support their thesis statement. Tell them that the main points they choose to discuss can serve as topic sentences for the paragraphs that comprise the body of their essay.

Revising (continued)

- Have students explain why the Model is superior to the Nonmodel.

  Answer: The details and phrases in the Nonmodel that are deleted in the Model are either irrelevant—the use of Old English characters has nothing to do with the topic—or empty—"any influence at all" does not say anything more than "an influence." Including these phrases in the Nonmodel simply adds verbal clutter that blurs the writer's main point.

- Have students review their drafts for appropriate word choices. Have them identify "empty words" and "hedging words" and then delete or replace them. Often students add phrases like "What I mean" in an attempt to clarify. Encourage them to rethink what they want to say before writing rather than using such a phrase.

Publishing and Presenting

- Ask students to list what they have learned that will help them better prepare for essay questions on exams.

- Discuss the ways that students' essay questions are assessed on tests given in your classroom. You may want to share the weighting you give different aspects of the tests.

Assessment

- Review the assessment criteria in class.

- Before students proceed with self-assessment, have them score the Student Model in class, using one or more of the rubric categories, to help them see how to apply the criteria.

- The rubric on this page, and another rubric in an alternative format, can be found on pp. 17 and 66 of **Performance Assessment and Portfolio Management.**

Lesson Objectives

1. To use multimedia to make a presentation

2. To organize content and media for an effective presentation

3. To rehearse effective delivery and check equipment for a successful presentation

Prepare Your Content

- Remind students that outlines are as essential for a multimedia presentation as they are for a written composition. Outlines should allow students to plan the use of media effectively.

- Ask students to consider their choice of media. Sometimes their choice will depend upon what is available. Other times, the content can dictate the appropriate media choices. For example, in the explanation of a scientific topic, visuals in the form of diagrams may be most appropriate.

- Encourage students to use media evenly throughout a presentation.

- Have students test the intelligibility of their images before they give their presentation. You may want students to pair up and test each other's presentations for intelligibility.

Prepare Your Delivery

- Remind students to do a dry run of their presentation using the equipment they intend to use. They should know how all the necessary functions of the equipment work and try them out.

- If possible, encourage students to double-check their equipment just before their presentation to ensure that everything works. An extra extension cord is often a handy item.

- Have students design a backup plan. Key visuals can be copied for the audience. Even when the presentation is successful, such a backup is appreciated by audience members.

- After students complete their presentations, have them give out the Feedback Form. Have them consider classmates' responses and then give improved versions of their presentations.

Some kinds of information are most effectively presented with sounds and visuals. When preparing a **multimedia presentation,** consider using an overhead projector, a slide projector, a video or audio player, a computer, or other electronic devices. The following strategies will help you develop and deliver a multimedia presentation. The Feedback Form will help you prepare it.

Prepare Your Content

Although almost any kind of media can be used in a multimedia presentation, you should consider the topic, the audience, and the available equipment before you choose which media to use. Use the following suggestions to help you prepare:

- Outline your oral report, and decide which parts will be more effective if presented through visual or aural media.

- Choose media that will suit your topic. If your topic is American life during World War II, you might play popular music of that time as a background.

- Use media selections evenly throughout your presentation, not just at the beginning or end.

- Make sure that all visual images can be seen by the entire audience. Small images can be photocopied and enlarged before being shown on an overhead projector.

Prepare Your Delivery

A multimedia presentation will be more effective if it goes smoothly and the media do not detract from your topic. These tips may help you prepare:

- Rehearse your presentation with the multimedia equipment. Become familiar with making adjustments to the equipment.

- Before the presentation, double-check your equipment to make sure that everything is in working condition.

- Have a backup plan in case your equipment fails. You might have copies of illustrations or graphic organizers to give to the audience.

Activity: Presentation and Feedback — Choose an activity that especially interests you, and prepare a multimedia presentation in which you explain and demonstrate the activity. Practice your presentation. Make sure that you can use the equipment efficiently. Use the Feedback Form to evaluate your presentation.

Feedback Form for Multimedia Presentation
Rating System
+ = Excellent ✔ = Average –
Content
Media use effective _____
Media suits topic _____
Media spread throughout presentation _____
Media visible and audible _____
Delivery
Equipment functioning _____
Equipment enhances presentation _____

998 ◆ *Poetry*

CUSTOMIZE INSTRUCTION FOR UNIVERSAL ACCESS

For Less Proficient Readers	For Special Needs Students	For English Learners
This may be an opportunity for less proficient readers to shine. The use of multimedia will often enhance a presentation without the need for book research. Encourage these students to find multimedia examples around which to structure their presentations.	Some special needs students may have an affinity for multimedia equipment. Allow these students to help their less proficient classmates with equipment.	Encourage these students to use multimedia, including transparencies, music, and video, that will convey information to classmates irrespective of their language skills.

Assessment WORKSHOP

Analyzing an Author's Meaning

In the reading sections of some tests, you may be required to understand an author's ideas and to decide what the author suggests or implies.

- Identify the author's main idea and locate the details that support it.
- To make an inference, select an answer based on information in the passage and on your own knowledge.
- Eliminate answer choices that relate to something not suggested in the passage or that draw a conclusion that is too general.

Test-Taking Strategies

- To interpret phrases, try to restate them in your own words.
- Read test passages carefully. Details within sentences often give clues to the correct answer.

Sample Test Item

Directions: Read the passage, and answer the question that follows.

During the 1980s, marine scientists noticed that huge stretches of coral reefs, normally a variety of shades, had begun to turn white. Scientists eventually discovered the cause. The reefs had discharged the populations of microscopic organisms that gave the reefs their color. The bleaching has so far been linked to both natural environmental occurrences and interference from humans. Scientists continue to monitor the bleached reefs as they search for answers to this problem.

1 With which of the following statements might the author agree?

A The bleaching of coral reefs will probably be attributed to industrial pollutants.

B Further scientific study is needed to determine what role humans have played in bleaching the coral reefs.

C Scientists will probably discover in the near future the causes of the bleaching.

D The phenomenon has probably been occurring for some time.

Answer and Explanation

The correct answer is *B*. *A* is too far-reaching and is not supported by the text. *C* and *D* are not logical extensions of the information presented in the passage.

▶ Practice

Directions: Read the passage, and answer the question that follows.

The current trend toward reducing fat in our diets is an idea that requires careful examination. Fats are integral to proper body function. Besides serving to protect and support our organs, fat is a primary source of insulation. Our bodies also need fat as a source of energy and as a means of absorbing vitamins. A balanced diet includes the recommended proportions of carbohydrates, proteins, vitamins, minerals, and fats. This should be our goal.

1 The phrase "integral to proper body function" means that fat

A is a part of the body.

B helps the body work.

C is a key to the digestive system.

D is needed to help our bodies work.

Assessment Workshop ◆ 999

Lesson Objective

To analyze an author's meaning in a passage on a test

Applying Reading Strategies

- Explain to students that inferences from a passage must be directly linked to the writer's claims.
- Explain that inferences come in a few forms: a generalization based on a pattern of cases ("Most of these accidents involve carelessness, so carelessness is a cause of them"); a determination that a specific case fits a general rule ("Sidney is a chemist, and the writer states that chemists are well-paid, so the writer implies that Sidney is well-paid"); a restatement of part-whole relationships ("If the writer says scientists know some of the causes, then he implies they do not know all of them.")

Applying Test-Taking Strategies

- To answer test questions involving inferences, students should determine which answer choices are logically linked to claims in the passage. Explain that they should eliminate any choices that clearly go beyond scope of the passage.
- Have students read the Sample Test Item. Ask them to explain the ways in which answer choices A and C go beyond the scope of the passage. Answer: A refers to industrial pollutants; pollution is not discussed in the passage. C refers to the likelihood of finding an explanation; the passage does not indicate anything about this likelihood.
- Have students complete the Practice, using these strategies.

Answer

The correct answer is *D*. The passage discusses the importance of fat in the diet. From this fact, students can infer that *integral* means "necessary." *A* is incorrect because it suggests that the phrase refers to the composition of the body, when it refers to its function. *B* is incorrect because it does not explain the meaning of *integral*. *C* is incorrect because the passage does not discuss the digestive system.

TEACHING RESOURCES

The following resources can be used to enrich or extend the instruction for p. 999.

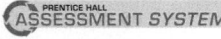
PRENTICE HALL
ASSESSMENT *SYSTEM*

📖 **Workbook**   📄 **Transparencies**

📖 **Skill Book**   💿 **CD-ROM**

999

Unit Objectives

1. To read epics and legends from around the world
2. To apply a variety of reading strategies appropriate for reading these selections
3. To analyze literary elements
4. To use a variety of strategies to build vocabulary
5. To learn elements of grammar, usage, and style
6. To use recursive writing processes to write in a variety of forms
7. To develop listening and speaking skills
8. To express and support responses to epics and legends
9. To prepare, organize, and present literary interpretations

Meeting the Objectives

With each selection, you will find instructional materials through which students can meet these objectives. Further, you will find additional practice pages for reading strategies, literary analysis, vocabulary, and grammar in the **Selection Support: Skills Development Workbook** in your Teaching Resources.

Background

Art

Knights About to Depart on the Quest for the Holy Grail, designed by Sir Edward Burne-Jones, tapestry woven by William Morris and Company

Two great Victorian artists, Edward Coley Burne-Jones (1833–1898) and William Morris (1834–1896) met at Oxford, where they were both divinity students. Burne-Jones was a painter and designer; Morris, a painter, also wrote poetry and designed furniture and wallpaper.

The subject of King Arthur and his knights exerted a strong hold over the imaginations of the Victorians, inspiring many beautiful works of art. Use this question for discussion:

Why do you think stories about legendary figures like King Arthur continue to interest readers?

Possible response: Such stories contain exciting adventures; the heroes they tell about embody qualities that are widely admired.

UNIT 10 **Epics and Legends**

Knights About to Depart on the Quest for the Holy Grail, Tapestry designed by Sir E. Burne-Jones, woven by William Morris & Co., Birmingham Museums and Art Gallery

1000 ◆ Epics and Legends

UNIT FEATURES

Connections	Reading Informational Materials
Every unit contains a feature that connects literature to a related topic, such as art, science, or history. In this unit, Eric P. Nash's essay, "*Star Wars:* An Epic for Today" (p. 1047), discusses the epic in modern popular films. Use the information and questions on the Connections page to enrich students' understanding of the selections presented within the unit.	These selections will help students learn to analyze and evaluate informational texts, such as workplace documents, technical directions, and consumer materials. They will expose students to the organization and features unique to nonnarrative texts. In this unit, students will learn to read and utilize information found in reference material.

Exploring the Genre

Great legends develop in every culture, reflecting the history and beliefs of the people who create them. These timeless stories serve two purposes: They explain important events in the history of a people, and they shape these events into a heroic and memorable form. The various tales of different cultures become identifying marks. People of other cultures can read these stories and sense how the culture was shaped and what figures and issues are central to its history.

Following are the types of folk literature you will encounter in this unit:

- An **epic** is a long narrative poem about the deeds of gods or heroes in war or travel.

- A **legend** is a widely told story about the past that may or may not have a foundation in fact. Most legends have some basis in history, but the details may have become lost or obscured through centuries of retelling and embellishment.

▲ **Critical Viewing** In this tapestry, a queen hands a shield to a knight. What does that gesture symbolize? **[Analyze]**

Exploring the Genre ◆ 1001

ASSESSMENT RESOURCES

- 📖 **Selection Support: Skills Development Workbook**
- 📖 **Formal Assessment**
- 📖 **Open Book Tests**
- 📖 **Performance Assessment and Portfolio Management**
- 📖 **Extension Activities**

1001

Why Read Literature?

The "Why Read Literature?" page in each unit presents a list of possible purposes for reading. Each purpose for reading is connected to one or more of the selections in the unit. Good readers set a purpose before reading in order to help them read actively and focus on meaningful details.

Unit 10 introduces three purposes for reading. "Read for the Love of Literature" encourages students to read about the adventures of Don Quixote and introduces students to the inspirational epic of the African hero Sogolon Djata. "Read to Appreciate the Author's Craft" helps students isolate the traditional elements of epic narration. When they "Read for Information," students learn to read for facts and details about an African republic.

How to Use This Page

- Tell students that before reading each selection in this unit, they should set a purpose for reading. This will help them read in an active and focused manner.

- Explain that reading epics from different cultures will help increase their love of literature.

- To appreciate an author's craft, a reader must see how the writer uses literary elements. In "Rama's Initiation," they will note the different elements that characterize epic composition.

- A third purpose for reading is to obtain information. Explain that when setting a purpose, students should specify the type of information they want to learn. For example, for reading the atlas entry on "Mali," they might set the purpose of learning about the land in which Sogolon Djata triumphed over adversity.

Why Read Literature?

When you read folk literature, you probably approach the text with a goal in mind—to appreciate, to learn, to be informed, or to be entertained. Your purpose will vary based on the context, style, or tone of the selection. Preview the three purposes you might set before reading the epics and legends in this unit.

Read for the Love of Literature

Don Quixote, in addition to entertaining readers, has inspired a musical—*Man of La Mancha*—and a new kind of literary hero. See what makes the story so timeless as you read the excerpt from **Don Quixote,** by Miguel de Cervantes, page 1006.

Sogolon Djata was not as advanced as the other children around him—he hardly spoke and still crawled when he should already have been walking. Despite his inabilities, this son of a king was destined for greatness. Find out why in the African epic **Sundiata,** by D. T. Niane, page 1064.

Read to Appreciate the Author's Craft

In epics and legends, the experiences and the characteristics of a hero or heroine often reveal the customs and values of the culture in which he or she lives. Note how R. K. Narayan effectively weaves these traditional aspects in the epic "Rama's Initiation," from the **Ramayana,** page 1052.

Read for Information

Sundiata is an epic of Mali, an African republic located in the heart of West Africa. To find out more about this culturally rich land, read the **"Mali"** entry, page 1076.

Take It to the Net

Visit the Web site for online instruction and activities related to each selection in this unit.
www.phschool.com

1002 ◆ *Epics and Legends*

How to Read Literature

Use Strategies for Reading Epics and Legends

Every culture has its epics and legends—stories of heroes who embody the values, strengths, and traditions of that culture. While the legends may differ from culture to culture, they all share a common feature: someone who achieves fame through great deeds. The following strategies will help you read epics and legends effectively:

1. Recognize author's attitude.

An author's attitude is the way he or she feels about a subject. It is reflected in the presentation of characters and events. To recognize an author's attitude, notice the details and events in the writing and think about the message that is being conveyed—either directly or indirectly—through this information.

2. Compare and contrast.

Take a close look at the selections in this unit by comparing and contrasting the characters and events in each one. Consider these points of comparison:

- Compare one character's behavior and actions with others in the story.
- Compare one epic or legend with another to determine which themes or ideas are universal and which are unique to a culture.

As you read the passage at right, compare Don Quixote's version of a knight with your image of a real knight.

3. Draw inferences about culture.

Use the details and descriptions in these selections to draw inferences about a culture's beliefs, values, and customs in a given period. In particular, the experiences of the hero or heroine will reveal the customs and values of the culture in which he or she lives.

4. Analyze a storyteller's purpose.

The information in most epics and legends was passed on through generations to preserve the history and values of a culture.

- In *Don Quixote,* the writer pokes fun at the values of his culture.
- In "Arthur Becomes King of Britain," the writer strives to bring some humanity and humor to a legendary hero.

To read the following epics and legends more effectively, use the notes in the side columns to help you apply these strategies.

Comparing and Contrasting

. . . for he contrived a kind of half-helmet of pasteboard which, fitted on to the morion, looked like a whole one. It is true that, in order to see if it was strong and fit to withstand a cut, he drew his sword and gave it a couple of slashes, the first of which undid in an instant what had taken him a week to do.—from *Don Quixote*

Comparison: He is like a knight because he has an element of armor—a helmet.

Contrast: His armor is not strong. The flimsy materials that protect him will not hold together for very long.

The "How to Read Literature" page in each unit presents a set of strategies to help readers understand authors' words and ideas. Each reading strategy is taught in conjunction with one or more of the selections within the unit. Good readers develop a bank of strategies from which they can draw as needed.

Unit 10 introduces four strategies for reading epics and legends. Students will learn to recognize the author's attitude, to compare and contrast characters and works, to draw inferences about the culture in which a work originates, and to analyze the storyteller's purpose.

How to Use This Page

Introduce the strategies for reading epics and legends, presenting each as a tool for developing understanding when reading the selections in this unit.

- As they read "from *Don Quixote*" (p. 1006), students will learn to compare and contrast characters.
- As they read "Morte d'Arthur" (p. 1020) and "Arthur Becomes King of Britain" (p. 1030), students will learn to use clues to recognize the author's attitude.
- As they read "Rama's Initiation" (p. 1052), students will use details and descriptions in the text to understand the cultural values and beliefs conveyed by the epic or legend.
- As they read "from *Sundiata:* An Epic of Old Mali" (p. 1064), students will use context clues to identify the author's purpose for retelling the legend or epic.

MODEL A READING STRATEGY: Recognize an Author's Attitude

Tell students that all writers have a particular attitude towards their subjects, and that by recognizing the author's attitude, they will gain more insight into the work. Tell students that noticing the way an author presents details and events in his or her works will help.

Show students how to recognize an author's attitude by modeling "Morte de Arthur." Have them follow along as you read lines 52–63 aloud.

Tell students:

Tennyson does not paint the battle with gore. Instead, he writes that "the noise of battle rolled / Among the mountains," as if the battle were a thunderstorm, and talks of "fallen" knights. His attitude towards the battle is dignified and serious. Describing the rescue of Arthur, Tennyson repeats the word *broken,* which chimes with *cross* and *barren*: "A broken chancel with a broken cross, / That stood on a dark strait of barren land." These words convey his attitude: Arthur's death is a hopeless, wasteful tragic ending.

from Don Quixote

Lesson Objectives

1. **To analyze and respond to literary elements**
   - Literary Analysis: Parody
   - Connecting Literary Elements: Epic Hero

2. **To read, comprehend, analyze, and critique an epic**
   - Reading Strategy: Comparing and Contrasting
   - Reading Check questions
   - Review and Assess questions

3. **To develop word analysis skills, fluency, and systematic vocabulary**
   - Vocabulary Development Lesson: Latin Word Root: -*son*-

4. **To understand and apply written and oral language conventions**
   - Spelling Strategy
   - Grammar Lesson: Capitalizing Proper Nouns and Adjectives
   - Assessment Practice (ATE)

5. **To understand and apply appropriate writing and research strategies**
   - Writing Lesson: Profile of a Modern Superhero
   - Extension Activity: Biographical Brochure

6. **To understand and apply listening and speaking strategies**
   - Extension Activity: Role Play

STEP-BY-STEP TEACHING GUIDE	PACING GUIDE
PRETEACH	
Motivate Students and Provide Background	
Use the Motivation activity (ATE p. 1004)	5 min.
Read and discuss the Preview material and Background information (SE/ATE p. 1004) [A]	5 min.
Introduce the Concepts	
Introduce the Literary Analysis and Reading Strategy (SE/ATE p. 1005) [A]	15 min.
Pronounce the vocabulary words and read their definitions (SE p. 1005)	5 min.
TEACH	
Monitor Comprehension	
Informally monitor comprehension by circulating while students read independently or in groups [A]	20 min.
Monitor students' comprehension with the Reading Check notes (SE/ATE pp. 1007, 1009, 1011)	as students read
Develop vocabulary with Vocabulary notes (SE pp. 1008, 1009, 1010, 1011; ATE p. 1010)	as students read
Develop Understanding	
Develop students' understanding of parody with Literary Analysis annotations (SE pp. 1007, 1008, 1011, 1012; ATE pp. 1007, 1008, 1009, 1012) [A]	10 min.
Develop students' ability to compare and contrast with the Reading Strategy annotations (SE pp. 1010, 1011; ATE pp. 1010, 1011)	10 min.
ASSESS	
Assess Mastery	
Assess students' mastery of the Reading Strategy and Literary Analysis by having them answer the Review and Assess questions (SE/ATE p. 1015)	20 min.
Use one or more of the print and media Assessment Resources (ATE p. 1017) [A]	up to 50 min.
EXTEND	
Apply Understanding	
Have students complete the Vocabulary Development Lesson and the Grammar Lesson (SE p. 1016) [A]	20 min.
Apply students' knowledge of gathering details using the Writing Lesson (SE/ATE p. 1017) [A]	45 min.
Apply students' understanding using one or more of the Extension Activities (SE p. 1017)	20–90 min.

[A] **ACCELERATED INSTRUCTION:**
Use the strategies and activities identified with an [A].

UNIVERSAL ACCESS
● = Below Level Students
▲ = On-Level Students
■ = Above Level Students

Time and Resource Manager

RESOURCES		
PRINT 📖	**TRANSPARENCIES**	**TECHNOLOGY** 💿 🎧 📼
• **Beyond Literature,** Cultural Connection: Spain's Golden Age, p. 61 ▲ ■		• **Interest Grabber Video,** Tape 5 ● ▲ ■
• **Selection Support Workbook:** ● ▲ ■ Literary Analysis, p. 244 Reading Strategy, p. 243 Build Vocabulary, p. 241	• **Literary Analysis and Reading Transparencies,** pp. 121 and 122 ● ▲ ■	
• **Adapted Reader's Companion** ● • **Reader's Companion** ● • **Authors In Depth,** Platinum Level ■		• **Listening to Literature** ● ▲ ■ Audiocassettes, Side 34 Audio CDs, CD 20
• **English Learner's Companion** ● ▲ • **Literatura en español** ● ▲ • **Literary Analysis for Enrichment** ■		
• **Formal Assessment:** Selection Test, pp. 217–219 ● ▲ ■ • **Open Book Test,** pp. 181–183 ● ▲ ■ • **Performance Assessment and Portfolio Management,** p. 28 ● ▲ ■ • **PRENTICE HALL ASSESSMENT SYSTEM** ● ▲ ■	• **PRENTICE HALL ASSESSMENT SYSTEM** ● ▲ ■ Skills Practice Answers and Explanations on Transparencies	• **Test Bank Software** ● ▲ ■ • **Got It! Assessment Videotapes,** Tape 5 ● ▲
• **Selection Support Workbook:** ● ▲ ■ Build Grammar Skills, p. 242 • **Writing and Grammar,** Platinum Level ● ▲ ■ • **Extension Activities,** p. 61 ● ▲ ■	• **Daily Language Practice Transparencies** ● ▲ • **Writing Models and Graphic Organizers on Transparencies,** pp. 13–16 ● ▲ ■	• **Writing and Grammar iText CD-ROM** ● ▲ ■ **Take It to the Net** www.phschool.com

BLOCK SCHEDULING: Use one 90-minute class period to preteach the selection and have students read it. Use a second 90-minute class period to assess students' mastery of skills and have them complete one of the Extension Activities.

Step-by-Step Teaching Guide
for pp. 1004–1005

Motivation

Ask students to describe some of the superheroes they've seen in films. Then, invite them to brainstorm for episodes in a film of their own invention that makes fun of superheroes. Encourage them to use exaggeration and distortion to heighten the humor of their scenes. Finally, point out that they are using techniques similar to those that Cervantes uses in his parody.

▣ Interest Grabber Video

As an alternative, play "Miguel de Cervantes" on Tape 5 to engage student interest.

❶ Background
Culture

Spain's fortunes were fast declining because of a series of disastrous wars, bad economic policies, and the stunning defeat of the Spanish Armada by the British Navy in 1588. This last event signaled the end of Spain's rule of the seas and the beginning of England's.

Prepare to Read

from Don Quixote

Don Quixote and the Windmill, c. 1900, Francisco J. Torrome

 Take It to the Net

Visit www.phschool.com for interactive activities and instruction related to this selection, including
- background
- graphic organizers
- literary elements
- reading strategies

Preview

Connecting to the Literature

You are reading a suspense novel that includes a devious villain. As the conflict intensifies, you silently shout at the pages, getting a little carried away. The main character in *Don Quixote* also gets carried away by the excitement of the stories he reads about knights and battles. As you will see, his imagination leads to some humorous scenes.

❶ Background

Miguel de Cervantes was born at a time when Spanish power and influence in the world was at its height. By the time Cervantes wrote *Don Quixote*, however, Spain's fortunes were fast declining. To some extent, Spain's transition from great confidence to deep despair is echoed in the novel, as Don Quixote takes refuge in chivalry to escape the realities of an unfriendly world.

1004 ◆ *Epics and Legends*

TEACHING RESOURCES

The following resources can be used to enrich or extend the instruction for pp. 1004–1005.

Motivation
▣ **Interest Grabber Video**, Tape 5 ▪

Background
📖 **Beyond Literature**, p. 61

 Take It to the Net
Visit www.phschool.com for background and hotlinks for *Don Quixote*.

Literary Analysis
▪ **Literary Analysis and Reading Transparencies**, Parody, p. 122

Reading
📖 **Selection Support:** Reading Strategy, p. 243; Build Vocabulary, p. 241
▪ **Literary Analysis and Reading Transparencies**, Comparing and Contrasting, p. 121 ▪

▪ **BLOCK SCHEDULING:** Resources marked with this symbol provide varied instruction during 90-minute blocks.

Literary Analysis

Parody

A **parody** is a comical piece of writing that mocks the characteristics of a specific literary form. By exaggerating or humorously imitating the ideas, language, tone, or action in a work of literature, a parody calls attention to the ridiculous qualities of its subject. In these lines from *Don Quixote*, you can see how Cervantes ridicules knights and the literature of chivalry by exaggerating the way his knight acts and speaks:

> Look there, friend Sancho Panza, where thirty or more monstrous
> giants rise up, all of whom I mean to engage in battle and slay, . . .

As you read, notice how Cervantes uses exaggerated tone, language, and description to add to the humor.

Connecting Literary Elements

An **epic** is a long narrative or narrative poem about the deeds of heroes. An **epic hero** is the brave and virtuous main character who proves his heroism on a long, dangerous journey. Despite his lifestyle, Don Quixote sees himself as an epic hero, and his "heroic" battles add to the parody.

Reading Strategy

Comparing and Contrasting

Much of the humor in *Don Quixote* comes from the sharp difference between the ideal knight and Don Quixote's version of a knight. **Comparing and contrasting** the two versions—looking for similarities and differences between them—will highlight the humor of Don Quixote, a mock "knight in shining armor."

Use a chart like the one shown to contrast Don Quixote's knightly attributes and possessions with those of an ideal knight.

Qualities or Things	Ideal Knight	Don Quixote
Armor		
Squire		
War horse		
Adventures		
Opponents		
Motivation		

Vocabulary Development

lucidity (lōō sid′ ə tē) *n.* clarity; ability to be understood (p. 1008)

adulation (a′ jōō lā′ shən) *n.* excessive praise or admiration (p. 1008)

interminable (in tʉr′ mi nə bəl) *adj.* lasting, or seeming to last, forever (p. 1008)

affable (af′ ə bəl) *adj.* pleasant (p. 1009)

sallying (sal′ ē iŋ) *v.* rushing forth suddenly (p. 1009)

requisite (rek′ wə zit) *adj.* required by circumstances (p. 1009)

sonorous (sän′ ər əs) *adj.* having a powerful, impressive sound (p. 1010)

veracious (və rā′ shəs) *adj.* truthful; accurate (p. 1010)

vanquish (van′ kwish) *v.* conquer; force into submission (p. 1010)

extolled (ek stōld′) *adj.* praised (p. 1011)

from *Don Quixote* ◆ 1005

---

❷ Literary Analysis

Parody

- Tell students that as they read these excerpts from *Don Quixote*, they will focus on parody, a comical piece of writing that mocks a specific literary form, in this case the literature of chivalry.

- Read the instruction about parody together as a class. Call students' attention to the example from the story.

- Use the instruction for Connecting Literary Elements to show how Don Quixote's view of himself as an epic hero adds to the parody.

- Use the Parody transparency in **Literary Analysis and Reading Transparencies**, p. 122, to show students how to analyze a parody.

❸ Reading Strategy

Comparing and Contrasting

- Remind students that comparing and contrasting means looking for similarities and differences.

- Then, tell students that comparing and contrasting the character of Don Quixote with that of an ideal knight will enhance the humor of the excerpts. To illustrate, review the chart on this page.

- As students read the excerpts from *Don Quixote*, have them complete a comparing-and-contrasting chart to help them appreciate the parodic elements of *Don Quixote*.

Vocabulary Development

- Pronounce each vocabulary word for students, and read the definitions as a class. Have students identify any words with which they are already familiar.

CUSTOMIZE INSTRUCTION FOR UNIVERSAL ACCESS

For Special Needs Students	For Less Proficient Readers	For English Learners
Have students read the adapted version of the excerpt from *Don Quixote* in the **Adapted Reader's Companion**. This version provides basic-level instruction in an interactive format with questions and write-on lines. Completing the adapted version will prepare students to read the selection in the Student Edition.	Have students read the excerpt from *Don Quixote* in the **Reader's Companion**. This version provides basic-level instruction in an interactive format with questions and write-on lines. After students finish the selection in **Reader's Companion**, have them complete the questions and activities in the Student Edition.	Have students read the adapted version of the excerpt from *Don Quixote* in the **English Learner's Companion**. This version provides basic-level instruction in an interactive format with questions and write-on lines. Completing the adapted version will prepare students to read the selection in the Student Edition.

 E-Teach

Visit E-Teach at www.phschool.com for teachers' essays on how to teach, with questions and answers.

**CUSTOMIZE INSTRUCTION
For Interpersonal and Verbal/Linguistic Learners**

Tell students to imagine that reports have reached the town council of a goofy old man pretending to be a knight who is attacking buses with a broken lance because he thinks they are monsters who go about the city kidnapping people. With a group of classmates, convene a meeting of the town council to discuss the situation. Is the man dangerous? Why or why not? What action should be taken?

❶ About the Selection

". . . enchantments, quarrels, battles, challenges, wounds, wooings, loves, agonies . . ." This list summarizes the "impossible nonsense" found in the stories of knights that Cervantes parodies. His main character is Don Quixote, an old gentleman who has gone crazy reading books of chivalry and now tries to emulate the knights of former times. He dons rusty armor, mounts a tired old horse, and calls a farm-girl his Lady. Later, he attacks a windmill he believes is a giant, ignoring the warnings of his "squire," Sancho Panza. Through Quixote, Cervantes humorously and touchingly contrasts romantic ideals with life's realities.

❷ Background

Art

Don Quixote and the Windmill, by Francisco J. Torrome

This artwork captures the comedy of the decisive moment in the "Terrible and Undreamed-of Adventure of the Windmills." Don Quixote loses his battle with the windmill and is dashed to the ground while a dismayed Sancho Panza clutches his head in the distance.

Use this question for discussion:

How does this illustration contrast Don Quixote and Sancho Panza?
Possible response: Don Quixote sees the windmills as monsters, while Sancho sees them for what they are. Quixote pays for his folly, while Sancho is dismayed but unharmed.

1006

from ❶ Don Quixote

Miguel de Cervantes
Translated by John Ormsby

Don Quixote and the Windmill, c. 1900, Francisco J. Torrome

1006 ◆ *Epics and Legends*

TEACHING RESOURCES

The following resources can be used to enrich or extend the instruction for pp. 1006–1014.

Literary Analysis

- **Writing Models and Graphic Organizers on Transparencies,** pp. 13–16
- **Selection Support:** Literary Analysis, p. 244

Reading

- **Adapted Reader's Companion**
- **Reader's Companion**

- **Listening to Literature Audiocassettes,** Side 34
- **Listening to Literature Audio CDs,** CD 20

Extension

- **Authors In Depth,** Platinum Level (The collection includes three additional selections by Miguel de Cervantes for extended reading.)

■ BLOCK SCHEDULING: Resources marked with this symbol provide varied instruction during 90-minute blocks.

CHAPTER I

Which Treats of the Character and Pursuits of the Famous Gentleman Don Quixote of La Mancha[1]

In a village of La Mancha, which I prefer to leave unnamed, there lived not long ago one of those gentlemen that keep a lance in the lance-rack, an old shield, a lean hack, and a greyhound for hunting. A stew of rather more beef than mutton, hash on most nights, bacon and eggs on Saturdays, lentils on Fridays, and a pigeon or so extra on Sundays consumed three quarters of his income. The rest went for a coat of fine cloth and velvet breeches and shoes to match for holidays, while on weekdays he cut a fine figure in his best homespun. He had in his house a housekeeper past forty, a niece under twenty, and a lad for the field and marketplace, who saddled the hack as well as handled the pruning knife. The age of this gentleman of ours was bordering on fifty. He was of a hardy constitution, spare, gaunt-featured, a very early riser, and fond of hunting. Some say that his surname was Quixada or Quesada (for there is no unanimity among those who write on the subject), although reasonable conjectures tend to show that he was called Quexana. But this scarcely affects our story; it will be enough not to stray a hair's breadth from the truth in telling it.

You must know that the above-named gentleman devoted his leisure (which was mostly all the year round) to reading books of chivalry—and with such ardor and avidity that he almost entirely abandoned the chase and even the management of his property. To such a pitch did his eagerness and infatuation go that he

1. **La Mancha** province in southcentral Spain.

5 ◀ **Critical Viewing** How does the artist of this painting feel about Don Quixote? **[Interpret]**

Literary Analysis
Parody What does the chapter title lead you to expect?

✓**Reading Check** **4**
What does the gentleman do in his spare time?

from *Don Quixote* ◆ 1007

---

3 Literary Analysis

Parody

- Remind students that one of the characteristics of a parody is that it mocks its subject matter.
- Read aloud the chapter title. Ask students how they would describe the style in which the title is written.
  Possible answers: The style is flowery, exaggerated, and mocking.
- Ask students what qualities they expect the "famous gentleman" of the title to have.
  Answer: Since a parody mocks its subject matter and the title seems mocking, the person in question is probably not really famous.
- Then, ask students the Literary Analysis question on p. 1007: What does the chapter title lead you to expect?
  Answer: The title leads the reader to expect a mocking treatment of a person who probably only considers himself to be a gentleman.

4 ✓**Reading Check**

Answer: In his spare time, the gentleman reads books of chivalry.

5 ▶ **Critical Viewing**

Answer: The artist feels that Don Quixote is ridiculous, bungling, and inept.

CUSTOMIZE INSTRUCTION FOR UNIVERSAL ACCESS

For Special Needs Students	For Less Proficient Readers	For Gifted/Talented Students
Because of Cervantes' florid and elaborate style, students may have trouble understanding the excerpts and appreciating their humor. Summarize passages for them, and play the **Listening to Literature** Audiocassette or CD while they follow along in the textbook.	Students may have difficulty at first with the elaborate style of the writing. Have them preview the picture on pp. 1006–1007 to be sure they know that Cervantes was making fun of flowery books about knights and their adventures.	Encourage students to distinguish the words and phrases that identify this selection as a parody. They can then rewrite a passage from *Don Quixote,* removing the parodic elements and discussing the effect on the humor of the passage.

Parody

- Have a volunteer read aloud the italicized text. What do students notice about the words in this passage?

Answer: Lead students to see that Cervantes repeats certain words to an absurd point.

- Then, ask students the Literary Analysis question on p. 1008: What qualities of writing does the italicized passage seem to mock?

Answer: Students should say that Cervantes is using exaggeration to ridicule the artificiality and convoluted language of the typical heroic novel.

---

sold many an acre of tillage land to buy books of chivalry to read, bringing home all he could find.

But there were none he liked so well as those written by the famous Feliciano de Silva, for their <u>lucidity</u> of style and complicated conceits[2] were as pearls in his sight, particularly when in his reading he came upon outpourings of <u>adulation</u> and courtly challenges. There ❻ he often found passages *like "the reason of the unreason with which my reason is afflicted so weakens my reason that with reason I complain of your beauty"*; or again, *"the high heavens, that of your divinity divinely fortify you with the stars, render you deserving of the desert your greatness deserves."*

Over this sort of folderol[3] the poor gentleman lost his wits, and he used to lie awake striving to understand it and worm out its meaning; though Aristotle[4] himself could have made out or extracted nothing, had he come back to life for that special purpose. He was rather uneasy about the wounds which Don Belianís gave and received, because it seemed to him that, however skilled the surgeons who had cured him, he must have had his face and body covered all over with seams and scars. He commended, however, the author's way of ending his book, with a promise to go on with that <u>interminable</u> adventure, and many a time he felt the urge to take up his pen and finish it just as its author had promised. He would no doubt have done so, and succeeded with it too, had he not been occupied with greater and more absorbing thoughts.

Many an argument did he have with the priest of his village (a learned man, and a graduate of Sigüenza[5]) as to which had been the better knight, Palmerín of England or Amadís of Gaul. Master Nicolás, the village barber, however, used to say that neither of them came up to the Knight of Phœbus, and that if there was any that could compare with *him* it was Don Galaor, the brother of Amadís of Gaul, because he had a spirit equal to every occasion, and was no wishy-washy knight or a crybaby like his brother, while in valor he was not a whit behind him.

In short, he became so absorbed in his books that he spent his nights from sunset to sunrise, and his days from dawn to dark, poring over them; and what with little sleep and much reading his brain shriveled up and he lost his wits. His imagination was stuffed with all he read in his books about enchantments, quarrels, battles, challenges, wounds, wooings, loves, agonies, and all sorts of impossible nonsense. It became so firmly planted in his mind that the whole fabric of invention and fancy he read about was true, that to him no history in the world was better substantiated. He used to say the Cid Ruy Díaz[6] was a very

---

2. **conceits** (kən sēts´) *n.* elaborate comparisons or metaphors.
3. **folderol** (fäl´ də räl´) *n.* mere nonsense.
4. **Aristotle** (ar´ is tät´əl) philosopher of ancient Greece.
5. **Sigüenza** (sē gwän´ sä) one of a group of "minor universities" granting degrees that were often laughed at by Spanish humorists.
6. **Cid Ruy Díaz** (sēd rōō´ē dē´ äs) famous Spanish soldier Ruy Diaz de Vivar: called "the Cid," a derivation of the Arabic word for *lord.*

lucidity (lōō sid´ ə tē) *n.* clarity; ability to be understood

adulation (a´ jōō lā´ shən) *n.* excessive praise or admiration

Literary Analysis
Parody Read the italicized passage aloud. What qualities of writing does it appear to mock?

interminable (in tur´ mi nə bəl) *adj.* lasting, or seeming to last, forever

---

✦ ENRICHMENT: History Connection

History of Armor

The first thing that Don Quixote does after deciding to become a knight-errant is to clean up some old and rusty armor that had belonged to his ancestors. The outfit that he restores would have dated from the period in which the manufacturing and use of armor reached its peak in Europe—the 1300s to the mid-1500s. After this time, gunpowder was increasingly used in battle and the production of armor, useful in hand-to-hand combat, declined.

Have students describe Don Quixote's armor and discuss how the description reinforces his identity as a hero who does not conform to his times. You might also have groups of students research and then report on the use and design of armor in various periods and cultures, ranging from ancient Greece to Spain of the 1500s. Encourage them to provide pictures of the various types of armor when they present their reports to the class.

good knight but that he was not to be compared with the Knight of the Burning Sword who with one backstroke cut in half two fierce and monstrous giants. He thought more of Bernardo del Carpio because at Roncesvalles he slew Roland in spite of enchantments, availing himself of Hercules' trick when he strangled Antæus the son of Terra in his arms. He approved highly of the giant Morgante, because, although of the giant breed which is always arrogant and ill-mannered, he alone was <u>affable</u> and well-bred. But above all he admired Reinaldos of Montalbán, especially when he saw him <u>sallying</u> forth from his castle and robbing everyone he met, and when beyond the seas he stole that image of Mohammed which, as his history says, was entirely of gold. To have a bout of kicking at that traitor of a Ganelon he would have given his housekeeper, and his niece into the bargain.

In a word, his wits being quite gone, he hit upon the strangest notion that ever madman in this world hit upon. He fancied it was right and <u>requisite</u>, no less for his own greater renown than in the service of his country, that he should make a knight-errant of himself, roaming the world over in full armor and on horseback in quest of adventures. He would put into practice all that he had read of as being the usual practices of knights-errant: righting every kind of wrong, and exposing himself to peril and danger from which he would emerge to reap eternal fame and glory. Already the poor man saw himself crowned by the might of his arm Emperor of Trebizond[7] at least. And so, carried away by the intense enjoyment he found in these pleasant fancies, he began at once to put his scheme into execution.

The first thing he did was to clean up some armor that had belonged to his ancestors and had for ages been lying forgotten in a corner, covered with rust and mildew. He scoured and polished it as best he could, but the one great defect he saw in it was that it had no closed helmet, nothing but a simple morion.[8] This deficiency, however, his ingenuity made good, for he contrived a kind of half-helmet of pasteboard which, fitted on to the morion, looked like a whole one. It is true that, in order to see if it was strong and fit to withstand a cut, he drew his sword and gave it a couple of slashes, the first of which undid in an instant what had taken him a week to do. The ease with which he had knocked it to pieces disconcerted him somewhat, and to guard against the danger he set to work again, fixing bars of iron on the inside until he was satisfied with its strength. Then, not caring to try any more experiments with it, he accepted and commissioned it as a helmet of the most perfect construction.

---

7. **Trebizond** (treb´ i zänd´) in medieval times, a Greek empire off the southeast coast of the Black Sea.
8. **morion** (mōr´ ē än´) *n.* old-fashioned soldier's helmet with a brim, covering the top part of the head.

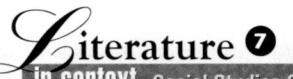

Literature ❼
in context Social Studies Connection

La Mancha

La Mancha, where Don Quixote lives, is a real region in central Spain located southeast of Madrid. Arabs who settled in the region called it al-Manshah, which means "dry land" or "wilderness." La Mancha is an area of flat, arid plains, characterized by high temperatures and strong winds. The landscape is dotted with windmills, such as those Don Quixote encounters. Several villages in the area are mentioned in the book and remain much as Cervantes described them more than four hundred years ago.

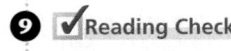

affable (af´ ə bəl) *adj.* pleasant

sallying (sal´ ē iŋ) *v.* rushing forth suddenly

requisite (rek´ wə zit) *adj.* required by circumstances

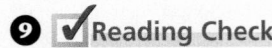

❾ ✓**Reading Check**

As a result of his reading, what does the gentleman decide to do?

from *Don Quixote* ◆ 1009

He next proceeded to inspect his nag, which, with its cracked hoofs and more blemishes than the steed of Gonela, that "*tantum pellis et ossa fruit,*"[9] surpassed in his eyes the Bucephalus of Alexander or the Babieca of the Cid.[10] Four days were spent in thinking what name to give him, because (as he said to himself) it was not right that a horse belonging to a knight so famous, and one with such merits of its own, should be without some distinctive name. He strove to find something that would indicate what it had been before belonging to a knight-errant, and what it had now become. It was only reasonable that it should be given a new name to match the new career adopted by its master, and that the name should be a distinguished and full-sounding one, befitting the new order and calling it was about to follow. And so, after having composed, struck out, rejected, added to, unmade, and remade a multitude of names out of his memory and fancy, he decided upon calling it Rocinante. To his thinking this was a lofty, sonorous name that nevertheless indicated what the hack's[11] status had been before it became what now it was, the first and foremost of all the hacks in the world.

Having got a name for his horse so much to his taste, he was anxious to get one for himself, and he spent eight days more pondering over this point. At last he made up his mind to call himself Don Quixote—which, as stated above, led the authors of this veracious history to infer that his name quite assuredly must have been Quixada, and not Quesada as others would have it. It occurred to him, however, that the valiant Amadís was not content to call himself Amadís and nothing more but added the name of his kingdom and country to make it famous and called himself Amadís of Gaul. So he, like a good knight, resolved to add on the name of his own region and style himself Don Quixote of La Mancha. He believed that this accurately described his origin and country, and that he did it honor by taking its name for his own.

So then, his armor being furbished, his morion turned into a helmet, his hack christened, and he himself confirmed, he came to the conclusion that nothing more was needed now but to look for a lady to be in love with, for a knight-errant without love was like a tree without leaves or fruit, or a body without a soul.

"If, for my sins, or by my good fortune," he said to himself, "I come across some giant hereabouts, a common occurrence with knights-errant, and knock him to the ground in one onslaught, or cleave him asunder at the waist, or, in short, vanquish and subdue him, will it not be well to have someone I may send him to as a present, that he may come in and fall on his knees before my sweet lady, and in a humble, submissive voice say, 'I am the giant Caraculiambro, lord of

9. **"*tantum pellis et ossa fruit*"** (tän′ tum pel′ is et äs′ ə frōō′ it) "It was nothing but skin and bones." (Latin)
10. **Bucephalus** (byōō sef′ ə ləs) **of Alexander or the Babieca** (bäb ē ä′ kä) **of the Cid** Bucephalus was Alexander the Great's war horse; Babieca was the Cid's war horse.
11. **hack's** horse's.

1010 ◆ *Epics and Legends*

the island of Malindrania, vanquished in single combat by the never sufficiently <u>extolled</u> knight Don Quixote of La Mancha, who has commanded me to present myself before your grace, that your highness may dispose of me at your pleasure'?"

Oh, how our good gentleman enjoyed the delivery of this speech, especially when he had thought of someone to call his lady! There was, so the story goes, in a village near his own a very good-looking farm-girl with whom he had been at one time in love, though, so far as is known, she never knew it nor gave a thought to the matter. Her name was Aldonza Lorenzo, and upon her he thought fit to confer the title of Lady of his Thoughts. Searching for a name not too remote from her own, yet which would aim at and bring to mind that of a princess and great lady, he decided upon calling her Dulcinea del Toboso, since she was a native of El Toboso. To his way of thinking, the name was musical, uncommon, and significant, like all those he had bestowed upon himself and his belongings.

CHAPTER VIII
Of the Good Fortune Which the Valiant Don Quixote Had in the Terrible and Undreamed-of Adventure of the Windmills, With Other Occurrences Worthy to Be Fitly Recorded

At this point they came in sight of thirty or forty windmills that are on that plain.

"Fortune," said Don Quixote to his squire, as soon as he had seen them, "is arranging matters for us better than we could have hoped. Look there, friend Sancho Panza,[12] where thirty or more monstrous giants rise up, all of whom I mean to engage in battle and slay, and with whose spoils we shall begin to make our fortunes. For this is righteous warfare, and it is God's good service to sweep so evil a breed from off the face of the earth."

"What giants?" said Sancho Panza.

"Those you see there," answered his master, "with the long arms, and some have them nearly two leagues[13] long."

"Look, your worship," said Sancho. "What we see there are not giants but windmills, and what seem to be their arms are the vanes that turned by the wind make the millstone go."

"It is easy to see," replied Don Quixote, "that you are not used to this business of adventures. Those are giants, and if you are afraid, away with you out of here and betake yourself to prayer, while I engage them in fierce and unequal combat."

So saying, he gave the spur to his steed Rocinante, heedless of the cries his squire Sancho sent after him, warning him that most certainly they were windmills and not giants he was going to attack. He,

---

12. **Sancho Panza** a simple countryman whom Don Quixote takes as his squire. In contrast to Don Quixote, Panza is practical and has common sense.

13. **leagues** a league is about three miles.

Literary Analysis
Parody How does Cervantes parody the style of tales of chivalry in Don Quixote's speech?

extolled (ek stōld') *adj.* praised

Reading Strategy
Comparing and Contrasting What is the difference in tone between the chapter title and the story?

14 ✔**Reading Check**
What leads the gentleman to call himself "Don Quixote"?

from Don Quixote ◆ 1011

---

12 **Reading Analysis**
Parody

- Ask a volunteer to read Don Quixote's speech. Then, ask students to describe the style of the speech. Is it written in plain language?
  Answer: The speech is not written in plain language. Instead, it is absurdly ornate and flowery.

- Then, ask the Literary Analysis question on p. 1011: How does Cervantes parody the style of tales of chivalry in Don Quixote's speech?
  Answer: Cervantes makes Don Quixote's speech as flowery as those found in tales of chivalry.

13 **Reading Strategy**
Comparing and Contrasting

- Have students read Chapter VIII in its entirety. Then, have students go back and read the chapter title.

- Ask students to identify the tone of the title and then the actual chapter.

- Then, ask students the Reading Strategy question on p. 1011: What is the difference in tone between the chapter title and the story?
  Answer: The tone of the chapter title is serious, while the tone of the story is parodic and mocking.

14 ✔**Reading Check**

Answer: The author believes the name is a variation of *Quixada*, perhaps the man's original name.

CUSTOMIZE INSTRUCTION FOR UNIVERSAL ACCESS

For Less Proficient Readers	For English Learners
Point out that the author provides a brief summary at this point in the tale. Invite students to expand upon this summary by making their own general statements about Don Quixote and his actions so far. **Possible summary:** Obsessed by romantic tales of chivalry, Don Quixote, a man who had led a quiet and ordinary life, prepares to embark upon new adventures as a knight-errant.	Don Quixote uses long, complex sentences with difficult and sometimes archaic vocabulary when he speaks. Help students break down and paraphrase his speeches. For example, introduce the sentence "Those are giants, and if you are afraid, away with you out of here and betake yourself to prayer, while I engage them in fierce and unequal combat." Guide students to see that this sentence could be broken down into three sentences: Those are giants. If you are afraid, go away and pray. I will fight them.

Parody

- Ask students what might happen in a battle between a traditional knight and his opponent.
  Answer: The knight would probably be victorious. Even if defeated, the knight would emerge from the battle with his dignity intact.

- Ask a volunteer to read aloud the bracketed passage. Then, ask the first Literary Analysis question on p. 1012: How does Don Quixote's battle with the windmills parody a traditional knight-giant battle?
  Answer: Don Quixote is defeated and humiliated in his battle with the windmill, whereas a traditional knight would come away proud and victorious from his battle with a giant.

❶❻ **Literary Analysis**

Parody and Epic Hero

- Discuss with students the attributes of an epic hero.
  Answer: An epic hero possesses bravery, great strength, and a desire to achieve immortality through heroic deeds.

- Have students read the bracketed passage to themselves. Then, ask the second Literary Analysis question on p. 1012: What qualities of an epic hero does Don Quixote display here?
  Answer: Don Quixote shows determination to do great deeds that will make him immortal.

1012

---

however, was so positive they were giants that he neither heard the cries of Sancho, nor perceived, near as he was, what they were.

"Fly not, cowards and vile beings," he shouted, "for a single knight attacks you."

A slight breeze at this moment sprang up, and the great vanes began to move.

"Though ye flourish more arms than the giant Briareus, ye have to reckon with me!" exclaimed Don Quixote, when he saw this.

❶❺ So saying, he commended himself with all his heart to his lady Dulcinea, imploring her to support him in such a peril. With lance braced and covered by his shield, he charged at Rocinante's fullest gallop and attacked the first mill that stood in front of him. But as he drove his lance-point into the sail, the wind whirled it around with such force that it shivered the lance to pieces. It swept away with it horse and rider, and they were sent rolling over the plain, in sad condition indeed.

Sancho hastened to his assistance as fast as the animal could go. When he came up he found Don Quixote unable to move, with such an impact had Rocinante fallen with him.

"God bless me!" said Sancho. "Did I not tell your worship to watch what you were doing, because they were only windmills? No one could have made any mistake about it unless he had something of the same kind in his head."

"Silence, friend Sancho," replied Don Quixote. "The fortunes of war more than any other are liable to frequent fluctuations. Moreover I think, and it is the truth, that that same sage Frestón who carried off my study and books, has turned these giants into mills in order to rob me of the glory of vanquishing them, such is the enmity he bears me. But in the end his wicked arts will avail but little against my good sword."

"God's will be done," said Sancho Panza, and helping him to rise got him up again on Rocinante, whose shoulder was half dislocated. Then, discussing the adventure, they followed the road to Puerto Lápice, for there, said Don Quixote, they could not fail to find adventures in abundance and variety, as it was a well-traveled thoroughfare. For all that, he was much grieved at the loss of his lance, and said so to his squire.

"I remember having read," he added, "how a Spanish knight, Diego Pérez de Vargas by name, having broken his sword in battle, tore from an oak a ponderous bough or branch. With it he did such things that day, and pounded so many Moors, that he got the surname of Machuca, and he and his descendants from that day forth were called Vargas y Machuca. I mention this because from the first oak I see I mean to tear such a branch, large and stout. I am determined ❶❻ and resolved to do such deeds with it that you may deem yourself very fortunate in being found worthy to see them and be an eyewitness of things that will scarcely be believed."

"Be that as God wills," said Sancho, "I believe it all as your worship says it. But straighten yourself a little, for you seem to be leaning to one side, maybe from the shaking you got when you fell."

1012 ◆ Epics and Legends

Literary Analysis
Parody How does Don Quixote's battle with the windmills parody a traditional knight-giant battle?

Literary Analysis
Parody and Epic Hero What qualities of an epic hero does Don Quixote display here?

✹ **ENRICHMENT: Cultural Connection**

Chivalry

Chivalry, a system of ethical ideals that developed under feudalism, reached its height in the twelfth and thirteenth centuries. It started out mainly in France and Spain but quickly spread to the rest of the European continent and to England. Chivalric ethics, which to this day are the basis of gentlemanly conduct, were a fusion of Christian and military ideas of morality. At the age of 7, boys from noble families became pages in the castles of noble families; when they were 14, they began their training as squires in the service of knights. After learn-

ing horsemanship and military skills, they were knighted as well, usually at the age of 21.

Chief among the chivalric virtues were piety, honor, valor, courtesy, chastity, and loyalty. The knight owed loyalty to his spiritual master, God; to his temporal master, the suzerain; and to the mistress of his heart, his lady love. Chivalric love was largely platonic. Usually, only a virgin or another man's wife could be chosen as the object of chivalric love.

Don Quixote, Honoré Daumier, Neue Pinakothek, Munich

17

▲ **Critical Viewing** What heroic qualities of Don Quixote are captured in this picture? What ridiculous qualities? **[Evaluate]**

18

from *Don Quixote* ◆ 1013

---

17 Background

Art

Don Quixote, **by Honoré Daumier**

The caricaturist, painter, and sculptor Honoré Daumier is best known for his cartoons satirizing the politics and society of nineteenth-century France. He found a wide audience for his cartoons attacking certain public figures and aspects of society. After 1850, Daumier produced a series of works based on *Don Quixote*. This image of Don Quixote on his horse is very loosely rendered and almost appears incomplete when compared with earlier, more detailed versions of the painting. Nevertheless, his lively use of line and texture captures the essence of the gentleman of La Mancha. Use these questions for discussion:

1. Why do you think Daumier painted Don Quixote as a faceless figure?
   Answer: In reality, Don Quixote was simply masquerading as a knight. By painting him as faceless, Daumier revealed the truth about him.

2. If you were painting a portrait of Don Quixote on his horse, how would your painting compare with this one?
   Answer: Students might exaggerate details to show Quixote's foolishness, or paint him as he saw himself—a regal and heroic figure.

18 ► Critical Viewing

Answer: Don Quixote's heroic qualities are shown through his upright posture—he is prepared to do heroic battle should the need arise. His emaciated horse and the fact that he is pictured without a face seem ridiculous.

Review and Assess

1. Students might find it most ridiculous when Don Quixote confuses the windmills for monsters that must be vanquished.

2. **(a)** Don Quixote cleaned up some old armor, gave himself and his horse "distinguished" names, and chose a farm-girl to call his lady. **(b)** This was not a sensible decision for him to make; it was based on pure fantasy.

3. **(a)** Sancho Panza was chosen by Don Quixote to be his squire. **(b)** Sancho is practical; Don Quixote is impractical. Sancho is a realist; Don Quixote is an idealist. Sancho is short and stocky; Don Quixote is tall and thin.

4. **(a)** Don Quixote mistakes the windmills for giants. **(b)** The battle between Don Quixote is humorous because it parodies a battle between a traditional knight and a giant or other foe.

5. Students should use details about Don Quixote's personality and behavior to support their answers.

6. The advantage of making the world fit one's illusions is that there may be some satisfaction in living in a world that exactly suits one's disposition. The disadvantage is that one bumps up against reality, sometimes forcefully.

"That is the truth," said Don Quixote, "and if I make no complaint of the pain it is because knights-errant are not permitted to complain of any wound, even though their bowels be coming out through it."

"If so," said Sancho, "I have nothing to say. But God knows I would rather your worship complained when anything ailed you. For my part, I confess I must complain however small the ache may be, unless this rule about not complaining applies to the squires of knights-errant also."

Don Quixote could not help laughing at his squire's simplicity, and assured him he might complain whenever and however he chose, just as he liked. So far he had never read of anything to the contrary in the order of knighthood.

Sancho reminded him it was dinner time, to which his master answered that he wanted nothing himself just then, but that Sancho might eat when he had a mind. With this permission Sancho settled himself as comfortably as he could on his beast, and taking out of the saddlebags what he had stowed away in them, he jogged along behind his master munching slowly. From time to time he took a pull at the wineskin with all the enjoyment that the thirstiest tavernkeeper in Málaga might have envied. And while he went on in this way, between gulps, he never gave a thought to any of the promises his master had made him, nor did he rate it as hardship but rather as recreation going in quest of adventures, however dangerous they might be.

Review and Assess

Thinking About the Selection

1. **Respond:** Which aspect of Don Quixote's appearance or behavior do you think is most ridiculous? Why?

2. **(a) Recall:** What actions does Don Quixote take in order to become a knight himself? **(b) Make a Judgment:** Do you think this was a sensible decision for him to make? Explain.

3. **(a) Recall:** Who is Sancho Panza? **(b) Compare and Contrast:** What are some differences between Sancho Panza and Don Quixote?

4. **(a) Recall:** Why does Don Quixote attack the windmills? **(b) Interpret:** What makes the battle between Don Quixote and the windmills humorous?

5. **Speculate:** What do you think will happen in the later adventures of Don Quixote and Sancho Panza? Why?

6. **Evaluate:** Don Quixote makes the world fit his illusions. What are the advantages and dangers of such an approach to life?

Miguel de Cervantes

(1547–1616)

Poet, playwright, and novelist Miguel de Cervantes is counted among the world's greatest writers. His masterpiece *Don Quixote* has been translated into more than sixty languages.

Cervantes was born in a small town outside Madrid, Spain. As a young soldier in Turkey, he was wounded and permanently lost the use of his left arm and hand. Sailing home, he was captured and enslaved by pirates for five years.

Once back in Spain, Cervantes married and became a purchasing agent for the navy. Problems with work and finances led to fines and imprisonment. His luck finally turned when he published the first part of *Don Quixote*. The book became a model for a new type of fiction in which the hero does not conform to his times.

✐ ASSESSMENT PRACTICE: Reading Comprehension

Writing Skills: Strategy	**(For more practice, see Test Preparation Workbook, p. 61.)**

Many tests ask students to demonstrate their knowledge of writing skills. Strategy questions may ask whether an addition to the passage is appropriate in the context of the writing. Give students this sample test item.

> Writing of Don Quixote, Cervantes says that he became so absorbed in his books and spent so much time reading stories of knights and their deeds that his brain was damaged and he lost his mind.

Suppose that Cervantes wanted to say more about the dangers of reading all the time. The most suitable addition is–

A Don Quixote lost touch with reality.
B Don Quixote sold off his land to buy books.
C Don Quixote used all his time for reading.
D Don Quixote read about one subject only.

The statements in *A, C,* and *D* are already implied or stated in the passage. *B* is the correct answer.

Review and Assess

Literary Analysis

Parody

1. In what ways is the incident with the windmills an example of a **parody**?
2. Which details in this selection poke fun at the way knights dressed?
3. What specific aspects of chivalry does Cervantes parody? Use a chart like the one shown to provide examples and explain how they are funny.

Chivalry	Parody
Impenetrable armor	Old, rusty, and breakable armor

Connecting Literary Elements

4. In what ways does the book *Don Quixote* resemble an **epic**?
5. What characteristics of an **epic hero** does Don Quixote himself embody?
6. In what ways is Don Quixote a parody of an epic hero?

Reading Strategy

Comparing and Contrasting

7. In what ways does Don Quixote, at least in his own mind, **compare** with the knights of old?
8. In what general ways does Don Quixote **contrast** with his idealized image of a knight?
9. What does the contrast between Don Quixote and the ideal knight tell us about Cervantes's view of chivalry?

Extend Understanding

10. **Career Connection:** Don Quixote reads romantic adventure stories to learn about being a knight. What sources would you use to find out about a career that interests you?

Quick Review

A **parody** is a comical piece of writing that mocks the characteristics of a specific literary form.

An **epic hero** is the brave and virtuous main character of an **epic**, a long narrative about the deeds of heroes.

To **compare**, look for similarities between characters or elements.

To **contrast**, look for differences between characters or elements.

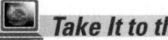 **Take It to the Net**
www.phschool.com
Take the interactive self-test online to check your understanding of the selection.

from Don Quixote ◆ 1015

---

❶ Vocabulary Development

Word Analysis

1. d
2. e
3. c
4. b
5. a

Concept Development: Synonyms

1. requisite
2. sallying
3. affable
4. sonorous
5. extolled
6. interminable
7. veracious
8. vanquish
9. lucidity
10. adulation

Spelling Strategy

1. rallying
2. babyish
3. essayist

❷ Grammar

1. Alexander the Great called his horse Bucephalus.
2. The brave knight who slew two giants was called Knight of the Burning Sword.
3. The innkeeper was a Málagan gentleman.
4. The farm girl he called Dulcinea was a native of Toboso.
5. The English translation of *Don Quixote* was written by John Ormsby.

Writing Application

Possible response: My friend Bob borrowed my book *Iberia,* by James Michener, to learn about the Iberian Peninsula.

1016

Integrate Language Skills

❶ Vocabulary Development Lesson

Word Analysis: Latin Root *-son-*

Don Quixote decides to name his horse Rocinante because he believes it is a "lofty, sonorous name." The Latin root *-son-*, which means "hearing" or "sound," appears in *sonorous*, a word meaning "having a powerful, rich sound." Using your knowledge of the root *-son-*, match each word below with its definition on the right.

1. sonic
2. consonance
3. dissonant
4. unison
5. sonogram

a. visual pattern of sound waves
b. unity of sound
c. not in harmony
d. having to do with sound
e. harmony of musical tones

Concept Development: Synonyms

Choose the word from the vocabulary list on page 1005 whose meaning is closest to that of each word below.

1. necessary
2. dashing forth
3. friendly
4. resonant
5. praised
6. unending
7. honest
8. conquer
9. clearness
10. excessive praise

Spelling Strategy

When you add a suffix beginning with *i* to a word ending in *y*, keep the *y* and simply add the ending: *sally + -ing = sallying.*

Add the suffix in parentheses to each word.

1. rally (*-ing*)   2. baby (*-ish*)   3. essay (*-ist*)

❷ Grammar Lesson

Capitalizing Proper Nouns and Adjectives

Proper nouns name specific people, places, or things. **Proper adjectives** are proper nouns used as modifiers or changed in form to become adjectives. For example, *Spain* is a proper noun, and *Spanish* is a proper adjective.

All proper nouns and proper adjectives begin with capital letters. In titles that contain proper nouns or adjectives, words of lesser importance—such as *of, by,* and *the*—are not capitalized. Proper nouns and proper adjectives are italicized in this example.

> I am the giant *Caraculiambro*, lord of the island of *Malindrania*. . . . The *Spanish* knight *Don Quixote of La Mancha* commanded me to present myself before your grace.

Practice Rewrite each sentence, capitalizing all proper nouns and proper adjectives.

1. Alexander the great called his horse bucephalus.
2. The brave knight who slew two giants was called knight of the burning sword.
3. The innkeeper was a málagan gentleman.
4. The farm girl he called dulcinea was a native of toboso.
5. The english translation of *don quixote* was written by john ormsby.

Writing Application Write a sentence that contains at least one proper noun, one proper adjective, and one book title.

𝒲𝒢 *Prentice Hall Writing and Grammar Connection: Chapter 27*

1016 ◆ Epics and Legends

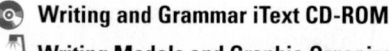

Writing Lesson

Profile of a Modern Superhero

Typically, the hero of an epic is serious. The challenge that the hero undertakes is life-threatening. Cervantes's comic hero Don Quixote, however, turned the heroic tale on its head. In the spirit of Cervantes, turn Don Quixote into a superhero.

Prewriting   Reread the selection, listing heroic qualities and knightly equipment that Don Quixote possesses. Then, update each item on your list. For example, you might turn his steed into a motor vehicle.

Model: Gathering Details

Don Quixote	My Superhero
brave	brave
crazy	fearless
delusional	imaginative
old	young

Drafting   Begin your profile with a catchy introduction that illustrates the quest to which your superhero has committed himself or herself. Then, develop the heroic qualities using your list, and update the knightly equipment with more modern superhero equipment.

Revising   Make sure that your superhero's qualities and equipment will help him or her achieve the quest. Delete unnecessary details.

 Prentice Hall Writing and Grammar Connection: Chapter 4, Section 2

Extension Activities

Listening and Speaking With a partner, perform a **role play** of the scene in which Sancho tries to talk Don Quixote out of attacking the windmills. For an effective reenactment, consider these tips:

- Develop distinctive ways of speaking and moving for each character.
- Incorporate funny body language and facial gestures into your acting.

Present your work for your classmates, and ask them to evaluate how well you captured the characters' personalities. **[Group Activity]**

Research and Technology Working with a group, conduct research for a **biographical brochure** of Miguel de Cervantes. Devise several questions to focus your work. Then, use books, biographical dictionaries, or Internet resources to find answers. Present your findings in an attractive final product. **[Group Activity]**

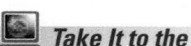 *Take It to the Net*   www.phschool.com

Go online for an additional research activity using the Internet.

from Don Quixote ◆ 1017

ASSESSMENT RESOURCES

The following resources can be used to assess students' knowledge and skills.

Selection Assessment

- **Formal Assessment,** pp. 217–219
- **Open Book Test,** pp. 181–183
- **Got It! Assessment Videotapes,** Tape 5
- **Test Bank Software**
- *Take It to the Net*

  Visit www.phschool.com for self-tests and additional questions on *Don Quixote*.

Listening and Speaking Rubric

- **Performance Assessment and Portfolio Management,** p. 28

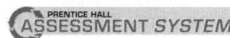 ASSESSMENT *SYSTEM*

- **Workbook**
- **Skill Book**
- **Transparencies**
- **CD-ROM**

---

❸ Writing Lesson

- Encourage students to discuss some of the ways in which Don Quixote parodies an epic hero, such as in his personality, his equipment, his battles.
- Have students use the discussion as a basis for doing the prewriting activity.
- As a model, show students the Biographical Profile transparencies, pp. 13–16 of **Writing Models and Graphic Organizers on Transparencies.**
- Then, use the rest of the writing lesson to guide students in developing their profiles.

❹ Listening and Speaking

- Point out that while Don Quixote and Sancho Panza go in quest of adventures together, they have very different views of the world, as indicated by the scene in which Sancho tries to talk Don Quixote out of attacking the windmills.
- Have students analyze the conversation that occurs before Don Quixote charges the windmills. They can identify the main points each character makes as well as the traits each shows.
- Have students work in pairs to prepare their role-plays. Suggest that partners create their own versions of the scene by elaborating on the points and traits they identified. Encourage them also to use both facial expressions and gestures to help communicate the personality traits of the characters.
- Have students use the rubric for Delivering a Narrative Presentation, p. 28 in **Performance Assessment and Portfolio Management.**

CUSTOMIZE INSTRUCTION
For Universal Access

To address different learning styles, use the activities suggested in the **Extension Activities** booklet, p. 61.

- For Visual/Spatial and Interpersonal Learners, use Activity 5.
- For Verbal/Linguistic Learners, use Activity 6.
- For Logical/Mathematical Learners, use Activity 7.

Morte d'Arthur ✦ Arthur Becomes King of Britain

Lesson Objectives

1. **To analyze and respond to literary elements**
   - Literary Analysis: Legend
   - Comparing Literary Works
2. **To read, comprehend, analyze, and critique a legend**
   - Reading Strategy: Recognizing Author's Attitude
   - Reading Check questions
   - Review and Assess questions
   - Assessment Practice (ATE)
3. **To develop word analysis skills, fluency, and systematic vocabulary**
   - Vocabulary Development Lesson: Latin Suffix: -ous
4. **To understand and apply written and oral language conventions**
   - Spelling Strategy
   - Grammar Lesson: Quotation Marks With Other Punctuation
5. **To understand and apply appropriate writing and research strategies**
   - Writing Lesson: Letter of Recommendation
   - Extension Activity: Chart
6. **To understand and apply listening and speaking strategies**
   - Extension Activity: Panel Discussion

STEP-BY-STEP TEACHING GUIDE	PACING GUIDE
PRETEACH	
Motivate Students and Provide Background	
Use the Motivation activity (ATE p. 1018)	5 min.
Read and discuss the Preview material and Background information (SE/ATE p. 1018) [A]	5 min.
Introduce the Concepts	
Introduce the Literary Analysis and Reading Strategy (SE/ATE p. 1019) [A]	15 min.
Pronounce the vocabulary words and read their definitions (SE p. 1019)	5 min.
TEACH	
Monitor Comprehension	
Informally monitor comprehension by circulating while students read independently or in groups [A]	45 min.
Monitor students' comprehension with the Reading Check notes (SE/ATE pp. 1021, 1023, 1025, 1027, 1031, 1033, 1035, 1037, 1039, 1041)	as students read
Develop vocabulary with Vocabulary notes (SE pp. 1027, 1028, 1031, 1036, 1038)	as students read
Develop Understanding	
Develop students' understanding of legends with the Literary Analysis annotations (SE/ATE pp. 1024, 1026, 1027, 1028, 1033, 1034, 1036, 1038, 1039) [A]	10 min.
Develop students' ability to recognize an author's attitude with the Reading Strategy annotations (SE/ATE pp. 1021, 1022, 1024, 1025, 1027, 1028, 1031, 1032, 1034, 1036, 1039, 1041)	10 min.
ASSESS	
Assess Mastery	
Assess students' mastery of the Reading Strategy and Literary Analysis by having them answer the Review and Assess questions (SE/ATE p. 1043)	20 min.
Use one or more of the print and media Assessment Resources (ATE p. 1045) [A]	up to 50 min.
EXTEND	
Apply Understanding	
Have students complete the Vocabulary Development Lesson and the Grammar Lesson (SE p. 1044) [A]	20 min.
Apply students' knowledge of revising for clarity using the Writing Lesson (SE/ATE p. 1045) [A]	45 min.
Apply students' understanding using one or more of the Extension Activities (SE p. 1045)	20–90 min.

 ACCELERATED INSTRUCTION:
Use the strategies and activities identified with an [A].

UNIVERSAL ACCESS
- ● = Below Level Students
- ▲ = On-Level Students
- ■ = Above Level Students

Time and Resource Manager

Reading Level: Challenging/Average
Average Number of Instructional Days: 4

PRINT 📑	TRANSPARENCIES 📄	TECHNOLOGY 💿 🎧 📼
• **Beyond Literature,** Humanities Connection: Courage, Honesty, and Compassion, p. 62 ▲ ■		• **Interest Grabber Video,** Tape 5 ● ▲ ■
• **Selection Support Workbook:** ● ▲ ■ Literary Analysis, p. 248 Reading Strategy, p. 247 Build Vocabulary, p. 245	• **Literary Analysis and Reading Transparencies,** pp. 123 and 124 ● ▲ ■	
• **Adapted Reader's Companion** ● • **Reader's Companion** ● • **Authors In Depth,** Platinum Level ■		• **Listening to Literature** ● ▲ ■ Audiocassettes, Side 35 Audio CDs, CD 20
• **English Learner's Companion** ● ▲ • **Literatura en español** ● ▲ • **Literary Analysis for Enrichment** ■		
• **Formal Assessment:** Selection Test, pp. 220–222 ● ▲ ■ • **Open Book Test,** pp. 184–186 ● ▲ ■ • **Performance Assessment and Portfolio Management,** p. 11 ● ▲ ■ • **PRENTICE HALL ASSESSMENT** *SYSTEM* ● ▲ ■	• **PRENTICE HALL ASSESSMENT** *SYSTEM* ● ▲ ■ Skills Practice Answers and Explanations on Transparencies	• **Test Bank Software** ● ▲ ■ • **Got It! Assessment Videotapes,** Tape 5 ● ▲
• **Selection Support Workbook:** ● ▲ ■ Build Grammar Skills, p. 246 • **Writing and Grammar,** Platinum Level ● ▲ ■ • **Extension Activities,** p. 62 ● ▲ ■	• **Daily Language Practice Transparencies** ● ▲	• **Writing and Grammar iText CD-ROM** ● ▲ ■ 💻 *Take It to the Net* www.phschool.com

BLOCK SCHEDULING: Use one 90-minute class period to preteach the selection and have students read it. Use a second 90-minute class period to assess students' mastery of skills and have them complete one of the Extension Activities.

Step-by-Step Teaching Guide
for pp. 1018–1019

Motivation

If possible, show a portion of *Monty Python and the Holy Grail* followed by a scene from *Camelot*. Ask students to compare and contrast the versions. Students will notice that plot details and language differ and that the writers have different attitudes toward the subject. Point out that this comically irreverent movie and romantic musical share the same source as Tennyson's formal and elegant "Morte d'Arthur" and T. H. White's "Arthur Becomes King of Britain."

Interest Grabber Video

As an alternative, play "Castles" on Tape 5 to engage student interest.

❶ Background

History

The task of unearthing information about King Arthur has not been easy. There are a few references to a great leader called Arthur in a handful of texts from the sixth to eighth centuries. However, these references usually mention his name in passing. Arthur, it seems, is claimed as the king of nearly every Briton kingdom known. The sixth century saw many men named Arthur born into the Celtic royal families of Britain but, despite attempts to identify the great man himself amongst them, there can be little doubt that most of these people were only named in his honor.

Prepare to Read

Morte d'Arthur ◆ Arthur Becomes King of Britain

The Crowning of Arthur, Royal MS, by permission of the British Library

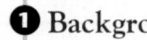 **Take It to the Net**

Visit www.phschool.com for interactive activities and instruction related to these selections, including

- background
- graphic organizers
- literary elements
- reading strategies

Preview

Connecting to the Literature

The heroes you admire reveal a great deal about what is important to you. In these selections, you will read about King Arthur, a legendary hero whose courage, honesty, and compassion have captivated people for hundreds of years.

❶ Background

The real King Arthur was most likely a British chieftain who defeated the Saxons in a decisive battle around A.D. 518. For years afterward, English bards sang about his exploits. In the 1100s, British writers revived legends about Arthur, and French troubadours added stories about Lady Guinevere and the Knights of the Round Table. The British writer Thomas Malory (1400–1471) reworked the expanded legends in *Le Morte d'Arthur* (French for "The Death of Arthur").

1018 ◆ *Epics and Legends*

TEACHING RESOURCES

The following resources can be used to enrich or extend the instruction for pp. 1018–1019.

Motivation

 Interest Grabber Video, Tape 5

Background

📖 **Beyond Literature**, p. 62

🖥 **Take It to the Net**

Visit www.phschool.com for background and hotlinks for "Morte d'Arthur" and "Arthur Becomes King of Britain."

Literary Analysis

📄 **Literary Analysis and Reading Transparencies,** Legend, p. 124

Reading

📖 **Selection Support:** Reading Strategy, p. 247
Build Vocabulary, p. 245

📄 **Literary Analysis and Reading Transparencies,** Recognizing Author's Attitude, p. 123

BLOCK SCHEDULING: Resources marked with this symbol provide varied instruction during 90-minute blocks.

Literary Analysis

Legend

A **legend** is a popular story handed down for generations. Most legends have some basis in historical fact, which may become obscured or lost through centuries of retelling and embellishment. Artists, poets, filmmakers, and novelists often turn to legends for inspiration, focusing on the following qualities:

- Exciting heroes and villains
- Adventures that blend historical fact with fiction
- Feelings of national pride generated by the heroes

Both novelist T. H. White and poet Alfred, Lord Tennyson based the works excerpted here on the Arthurian legends. As you read the selections, think about the ways in which the writing reflects the heroic qualities and oral traditions of legends.

Comparing Literary Works

In the Arthurian legends, Arthur is a **dynamic character**—one who changes and grows during the course of a literary work. Tennyson focuses on Arthur as he nears death after his years as king, whereas White presents Arthur as a young, innocent boy, unaware of the great things that are to come for him. As you read the selections, use a diagram like the one shown to contrast the ways Arthur's character changes from childhood to old age.

```
Young Arthur
  Innocent
  Playful

Old Arthur
  Tired
  Aristocratic
```

Reading Strategy

Recognizing Author's Attitude

All writers have a particular **attitude** that reflects their feelings toward their subjects. Recognizing the author's attitude will give you an insight into the work. As you read "Morte d'Arthur," look for clues that show the author's serious and respectful attitude toward his subject. Then, as you read "Arthur Becomes King of Britain," consider how the events and dialogue that White chooses convey a very different attitude.

Vocabulary Development

lamentation (lam′ ən tā′ shən) n. mourning (p. 1027)

swarthy (swôr′ thē) adj. having a dark complexion (p. 1028)

stickler (stik′ lər) n. person who insists uncompromisingly on the observance of something specified (p. 1031)

sumptuous (sump′ choo əs) adj. magnificent (p. 1036)

palfrey (pôl′ frē) n. saddle horse, especially one for a woman (p. 1038)

Morte d'Arthur / Arthur Becomes King of Britain ◆ 1019

Literary Analysis
Legend

- Tell students that as they read "Morte d'Arthur" and "Arthur Becomes King of Britain," they will focus on legends, popular stories handed down for generations.

- Read the instruction about legends together as a class. Call students' attention to the qualities of a legend.

- Use the instruction for Comparing Literary Works to acquaint students with the different depictions of the legendary Arthur that they will encounter in these two works.

- Have students create charts like the one shown on this page to compare and contrast the depictions of Arthur over the two selections.

Reading Strategy
Recognizing Author's Attitude

- Point out that all authors have certain feelings toward the characters they write about and that they reveal these feelings through their language and writing style.

- Then, tell students that the authors of "Morte d'Arthur" and "Arthur Becomes King of Britain" had quite different attitudes toward Arthur.

- As they read, remind students to look for clues that reveal these different attitudes.

Vocabulary Development

- Pronounce each vocabulary word for students, and read the definitions as a class. Have students identify any words with which they are already familiar.

CUSTOMIZE INSTRUCTION FOR UNIVERSAL ACCESS

For Special Needs Students	For Less Proficient Readers	For English Learners
Have students read the adapted version of "Morte d' Arthur" in the **Adapted Reader's Companion.** This version provides basic-level instruction in an interactive format with questions and write-on lines. Completing the adapted version will prepare students to read the selection in the Student Edition.	Have students read "Morte d' Arthur" in the **Reader's Companion.** This version provides basic-level instruction in an interactive format with questions and write-on lines. After students finish the selection in the **Reader's Companion,** have them complete the questions and activities in the Student Edition.	Have students read the adapted version of "Morte d' Arthur" in the **English Learner's Companion.** This version provides basic-level instruction in an interactive format with questions and write-on lines. Completing the adapted version will prepare students to read the selection in the Student Edition.

 E-Teach

Visit E-Teach at www.phschool.com for teachers' essays on how to teach, with questions and answers.

**Step-by-Step Teaching Guide
for pp. 1020–1042**

CUSTOMIZE INSTRUCTION
For Verbal/Linguistic Learners

Like Britain, Japan had a feudal era with warring *daimyo* (lords) and unifying *shoguns* (rulers). Have students research the subject of feudal Japan to find a leader like Arthur and prepare a brief oral report on his accomplishments.

❶ About the Selection

Several friends, while sitting around the fire on Christmas Eve, prevail upon the poet in the group to share his retelling of the Arthurian legend. The poet tells the story of Arthur's death, and Sir Bedivere's obedience to the dying king's last request. Like the men around the fire, Bedivere mourns the passing of an age, the death of all that seems noble and true. As the tale winds to a close, Arthur's funeral barge floats away and the friends are roused from their rapt involvement in the tale. Tennyson ends on an optimistic note, with bells singing out a return of Arthur and what he represented.

❷ Background

Art

How Sir Bedivere Cast the Sword Excalibur into the Water, by Aubrey Beardsley

Aubrey Beardsley (1872–1898) was a major figure in the 1890s Art Nouveau movement, which was marked by the use of an elegant style, featuring flowing curves and elaborate decorative elements. This illustration is one of 500 drawings by Beardsley for an edition of Sir Thomas Malory's fifteenth-century book, *Le Morte d'Arthur*, the source used by Tennyson for *The Idylls of the King.* Use this question for discussion:

How does this picture contrast with Tennyson's description of the event? Possible response: Students may say that Tennyson emphasizes action and movement while the illustration presents a stylized, motionless scene. Also, Tennyson's setting seems wilder, colder, and more barren than Beardsley's quiet lake.

❶ Morte d'Arthur

Alfred, Lord Tennyson

How Sir Bedivere Cast the Sword Excalibur Into the Water, Aubrey Beardsley, Houghton Library, Harvard University

❸ ▲ **Critical Viewing** This illustration depicts a significant moment in the Arthurian legend. What symbolic details does the illustrator include? Why are they important? **[Interpret]**

1020 ◆ *Epics and Legends*

TEACHING RESOURCES

The following resources can be used to enrich or extend the instruction for pp. 1020–1042.

Literary Analysis

📖 **Selection Support Workbook:** Literary Analysis, p. 248

Reading

🎧 **Listening to Literature Audiocassettes,** Side 35 ▦

💿 **Listening to Literature Audio CDs,** CD 20 ▦

Extension

📖 **Authors In Depth,** Platinum Level (The collection includes seven additional selections by Alfred, Lord Tennyson for extended reading.)

▦ **BLOCK SCHEDULING:** Resources marked with this symbol provide varied instruction during 90-minute blocks.

"Morte d'Arthur" is the most famous excerpt from Tennyson's epic Idylls of the King, *a set of twelve narrative poems based on the Arthurian legends.*

The Epic

At Francis Allen's on the Christmas eve—
The game of forfeits[1] done—the girls all kissed
Beneath the sacred bush and passed away—
The parson Holmes, the poet Everard Hall,
5   The host, and I sat round the wassail bowl,[2]
Then halfway ebbed; and there we held a talk,
How all the old honor had from Christmas gone,
Or gone or dwindled down to some odd games
In some odd nooks like this; till I, tired out
10 With cutting eights[3] that day upon the pond,
Where, three times slipping from the outer edge,
I bumped the ice into three several stars,
Fell in a doze; and half-awake I heard
The parson taking wide and wider sweeps,
15 Now harping on the church commissioners,
Now hawking at geology and schism;[4]
Until I woke, and found him settled down
Upon the general decay of faith
Right through the world: "at home was little left,
20 And none abroad; there was no anchor, none,
To hold by." Francis, laughing, clapped his hand
On Everard's shoulder, with "I hold by him."
"And I," quoth Everard, "by the wassail-bowl."
"Why yes," I said, "we knew your gift that way
25 At college; but another which you had—
I mean of verse (for so we held it then),
What came of that?" "You know," said Frank, "he burnt
His epic, his King Arthur, some twelve books"—
And then to me demanding why: "O, sir,
30 He thought that nothing new was said, or else
Something so said 'twas nothing—that a truth
Looks freshest in the fashion of the day;

---

1. **forfeits** (fôr´ fits) *n.* game in which something is taken away as a penalty for making a mistake.
2. **wassail bowl** (was´ əl bol) *n.* punch bowl.
3. **cutting eights** ice-skating so that skates cut figure eights in the ice.
4. **schism** (siz´ əm) *n.* division within an organization, especially a church, because of a difference of opinion.

Reading Strategy
Recognizing Author's Attitude Which words in the opening lines set the tone for this section of the poem?

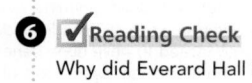

6 ✔**Reading Check**
Why did Everard Hall burn his epic?

Morte d'Arthur ◆ *1021*

❸ ▶ Critical Viewing
Possible responses: The illustration depicts the silk-clad arm taking the sword Excalibur into the lake. Sir Bedivere stands in a formal posture with his arm raised in a farewell salute. The darkness surrounding the scene suggests the serious and somber nature of this event.

❹ Background
Literature
The author frames the telling of "Morte d'Arthur" in his own era. The poem opens late on Christmas Eve after the festivities are done. A group of friends is sad that in modern times the serious aspects of Christmas are neglected in favor of games and lighter interests. The friends include the narrator (Tennyson), Holmes (a parson), and Everard Hall (the poet who will read his tale of King Arthur).

❺ Reading Strategy
Recognizing Author's Attitude
• Have students read the first nine lines of the poem. Ask them to record words and phrases, such as *passed away*, that they can use to help them determine the tone.
• Then, ask the Reading Strategy question on p. 1021: What words in the opening lines set the tone for this section of the poem? Answer: Such words as *done*, *passed away*, *ebbed*, *old*, *gone*, and *tired out* set the tone.

▶ **Monitor Progress** Ask students to describe the tone set in the opening lines.
Answer: The tone is nostalgic.

❻ ✔**Reading Check**
Answer: He thought that because the times had changed, the epic was old-fashioned and not worth saving.

CUSTOMIZE INSTRUCTION FOR UNIVERSAL ACCESS

For Less Proficient Readers	For Gifted/Talented Students	For Advanced Readers
Suggest to students that "Morte d'Arthur" needs special attention because of its stylized language. Direct them to keep a running summary of the poem and a list of puzzling words and phrases as they read (with the numbers of the lines where they appear) to review after they have finished the legend.	Have students follow Everard Hall's example and write a brief passage of unrhymed blank verse (iambic pentameter) describing some historical moment that other students will recognize. Challenge them to use *thou* and *thee* with the correct verb forms. Have them read their verses to the class.	Ask students to analyze lines 13–22 and suggest why a mid-nineteenth-century person might tie "geology" to a "decay of faith." They should recognize that geology represents science, which is often, but not necessarily, seen as being in opposition to religion and faith.

- Ask a volunteer to read aloud lines 57–63. Ask students to describe what feelings about Arthur the passage shows.

  Answer: The passage shows reverence and respect for Arthur.

- Then, ask the Reading Strategy question on p. 1022: What words and details in lines 57–63 reveal Tennyson's attitude toward King Arthur?

  Answer: Words such as *uplifted* and *bore* reveal Tennyson's reverence for Arthur; the details of the broken cross in the ruined chapel create the feeling that Arthur's defeat is also the defeat of goodness and virtue.

God knows; he has a mint of reasons; ask.
It pleased *me* well enough." "Nay, nay," said Hall,
35 "Why take the style of those heroic times?
For nature brings not back the mastodon,[5]
Nor we those times; and why should any man
Remodel models? these twelve books of mine
Were faint Homeric echoes,[6] nothing-worth,
40 Mere chaff and draff,[7] much better burnt." "But I,"
Said Francis, "picked the eleventh from this hearth,
And have it; keep a thing, its use will come.
I hoard it as a sugarplum for Holmes."
He laughed, and I, though sleepy, like a horse
45 That hears the corn-bin open, pricked my ears;
For I remembered Everard's college fame
When we were Freshmen. Then at my request
He brought it; and the poet, little urged,
But with some prelude of disparagement,
50 Read, mouthing out his hollow o's and a's,
Deep-chested music, and to this result.

Morte d'Arthur

So all day long the noise of battle rolled
Among the mountains by the winter sea,
Until King Arthur's table, man by man,
55 Had fallen in Lyonnesse[8] about their lord,
King Arthur; then, because his wound was deep,
The bold Sir Bedivere uplifted him,
Sir Bedivere, the last of all his knights,
And bore him to a chapel nigh the field,

60 A broken chancel[9] with a broken cross,
That stood on a dark strait of barren land.
On one side lay the ocean, and on one
Lay a great water, and the moon was full.
Then spake King Arthur to Sir Bedivere:
65 "The sequel of today unsolders[10] all
The goodliest fellowship of famous knights
Whereof this world holds record. Such a sleep
They sleep—the men I loved. I think that we
Shall never more, at any future time,
70 Delight our souls with talk of knightly deeds,
Walking about the gardens and the halls

---

5. **mastodon** (mas′ tə dän′) *n.* extinct animal resembling the elephant but larger.
6. **Homeric echoes** (hō mer′ ik ek′ ōz) imitations of the poems of the Greek poet Homer (of about the eighth century B.C.).
7. **chaff and draff** anything worthless; dregs.
8. **Lyonnesse** (lī′ ə nes′) legendary country off the southwestern coast of England, supposed to have sunk beneath the sea.
9. **chancel** (chan′ səl) *n.* part of a church around the altar.
10. **unsolders** (un säd′ ərs) *v.* separates.

Reading Strategy
Recognizing Author's Attitude What words and details in lines 57–63 reveal Tennyson's attitude toward King Arthur?

✸ ENRICHMENT: History Connection

Chivalry in Medieval Times

King Arthur and his retinue are thought of as advocates of chivalry—the code of behavior that was supposed to govern the actions of knights and nobles in the Middle Ages. The word comes from the French *chevalerie*, or mounted soldiers. The English word *cavalry* is derived from the same root.

The primary sources on the nature of chivalry are poems by eleventh- and twelfth-century minstrels in England and Europe. These epics celebrate the deeds and character of idealized heroes. These heroes were deeply devout and ever ready to defend their faith, even with their lives. They protected the weak and helpless and fought evil and injustice. Most were devoted to particular women, in whose names they performed their gallantries.

Of Camelot, as in the days that were.
I perish by this people which I made—
Though Merlin sware that I should come again
75 To rule once more—but let what will be be,
I am so deeply smitten through the helm
That without help I cannot last till morn.
Thou therefore take my brand Excalibur,
Which was my pride; for thou rememberest how
80 In those old days, one summer noon, an arm
Rose up from out the bosom of the lake,
Clothed in white samite,[11] mystic, wonderful,
Holding the sword—and how I rowed across
And took it, and have worn it, like a king;
85 And, wheresoever I am sung or told
In aftertime, this also shall be known.
But now delay not; take Excalibur,
And fling him far into the middle mere;[12]
Watch what thou seest, and lightly[13] bring me word."

90   To him replied the bold Sir Bedivere:
"It is not meet,[14] Sir King, to leave thee thus,
Aidless, alone, and smitten through the helm.
A little thing may harm a wounded man.
Yet I thy hest will all perform at full,[15]
95 Watch what I see, and lightly bring thee word."

So saying, from the ruined shrine he stepped
And in the moon athwart the place of tombs,
Where lay the mighty bones of ancient men,
Old knights, and over them the sea wind sang
100 Shrill, chill, with flakes of foam. He, stepping down
By zigzag paths and juts of pointed rock,
Came on the shining levels of the lake.

There drew he forth the brand Excalibur,
And o'er him, drawing it, the winter moon,
105 Brightening the skirts of a long cloud, ran forth
And sparkled keen with frost against the hilt;
For all the haft twinkled with diamond sparks,
Myriads of topaz lights, and jacinth work[16]
Of subtlest jewelry. He gazed so long
110 That both his eyes were dazzled, as he stood,
This way and that dividing the swift mind,
In act to throw; but at the last it seemed
Better to leave Excalibur concealed

---

1. **samite** (sam´ it) *n.* heavy silk fabric.
2. **mere** (mir) *n.* lake.
3. **lightly** *adv.* quickly.
4. **meet** *adj.* proper.
5. **I thy hest will all perform at full** I will carry out your order completely.
6. **topaz** (to´ paz) . . . **work** yellow and reddish-orange jewels.

Medieval Vocabulary
Tennyson's use of words of medieval origin to name parts of a knight's armor and weapons makes the legend seem more authentic. Look for these words as you read:

helm helmet
brand sword
haft handle or hilt of a sword
casque helmet
greaves armor for the legs below the knee
cuisses armor for the thigh

 Reading Check
Describe how Arthur first got the sword Excalibur.

Morte d'Arthur ◆ 1023

8 **Background**
Medieval Vocabulary
Many of these medieval words are derived from the Germanic language. *Brand* is an Old High German word for sword (and is also the source for the word *brandish*). Have students use a dictionary to find the derivations of the medieval words listed in the book. Encourage them to find modern words that are derived from these archaic terms.

9 ✔**Reading Check**
Answer: A silk-clad arm holding the sword arose from the lake. Arthur rowed to it and took it.

CUSTOMIZE INSTRUCTION FOR UNIVERSAL ACCESS

For Less Proficient Readers	For English Learners	For Gifted/Talented Students
Have students read lines 103–114 in pairs. Then, have them discuss what is going on at this point in the poem. Be sure they understand that Sir Bedivere has been commanded by Arthur to fling the sword Excalibur into the lake from which it came and that Bedivere is torn about whether to follow Arthur's wishes.	Encourage students to discuss Bedivere's dilemma and how they feel about it. What would they do if they were Bedivere? Why would they follow that course of action? What do they think Bedivere will eventually do? Will he hold out against his king or end up doing as Arthur wishes?	Encourage students who enjoy graphic arts to illustrate the scene of Bedivere at the lakeside, torn by his dilemma of whether to throw the sword into the lake or disobey his king's command. Before they begin, encourage students to think about which aspect of the scene they wish to highlight—Bedivere's indecision or the beauty of Excalibur.

Legend

- Review the qualities of a legend that are described on p. 1019. Remind students that a legend has exciting heroes and villains, the adventures it describes blend historical fact with fiction, and its heroes generate feelings of national pride.

- Ask students to identify the hero of this legend.
  Answer: Arthur is the hero.

- Then, ask the Literary Analysis question on p. 1024: What qualities of an oral legend does the story of Bedivere and the sword demonstrate?
  Answer: In this episode, Bedivere fulfills the role of villain in that he thwarts the will of and thereby betrays Arthur, the hero.

⓫ **Reading Strategy**

Recognizing Author's Attitude

- Have a volunteer read aloud lines 133–138. Ask students why Bedivere is pacing up and down beside the water.
  Answer: He can't decide what to do with Excalibur. Should he obey Arthur's order to throw it into the lake, or should he save it for posterity?

- Then, ask the Reading Strategy question on p. 1024: What attitude toward Bedivere do the words and details in lines 133–138 convey?
  Answer: Bedivere seems indecisive and weak-willed. He's letting the sword's glittering beauty distract him from his knightly obligation to Arthur.

There in the many-knotted water flags,[17]
115 That whistled still and dry about the marge.[18]
So strode he back slow to the wounded king.
      Then spake King Arthur to Sir Bedivere:
"Hast thou performed my mission which I gave?
What is it thou hast seen, or what hast heard?"
120 And answer made the bold Sir Bedivere:
"I heard the ripple washing in the reeds,
And the wild water lapping on the crag."
      To whom replied King Arthur, faint and pale:
"Thou hast betrayed thy nature and thy name,
125 Not rendering[19] true answer, as beseemed[20]
Thy fealty, nor like a noble knight;
For surer sign had followed, either hand,
Or voice, or else a motion of the mere.
This is a shameful thing for men to lie.
130 Yet now, I charge thee, quickly go again
As thou art lief and dear, and do the thing
I bade thee, watch, and lightly bring me word."
      Then went Sir Bedivere the second time
Across the ridge, and paced beside the mere,
135 Counting the dewy pebbles, fixed in thought;
But when he saw the wonder of the hilt,
How curiously and strangely chased,[21] he smote
His palms together, and he cried aloud:
      "And if indeed I cast the brand away;
140 Surely a precious thing, one worthy note,
Should thus be lost forever from the earth,
Which might have pleased the eyes of many men.
What good should follow this, if this were done?
What harm, undone? deep harm to disobey,
145 Seeing obedience is the bond of rule.
Were it well to obey then, if a king demand
An act unprofitable, against himself?
The king is sick, and knows not what he does.
What record, or what relic of my lord
150 Should be to aftertime, but empty breath
And rumors of a doubt? but were this kept,
Stored in some treasure-house of mighty kings,
Some one might show it at a joust of arms,
Saying, 'King Arthur's sword, Excalibur,
155 Wrought by the lonely maiden of the lake;
Nine years she wrought it, sitting in the deeps

---

17. **water flags** marsh plants.
18. **marge** (marj) *n.* margin; edge.
19. **rendering** (ren´ dər iŋ) *v.* giving.
20. **beseemed** (bē sēm´ əd) *v.* was suitable to.
21. **chased** *v.* decorated by engraving or embossing.

Reading Strategy
Recognizing Author's Attitude What attitude toward Sir Bedivere do the words and details in lines 133–138 convey?

ENRICHMENT: History Connection

The Round Table

The Round Table is a name used both as a designation for King Arthur's court and for a table where Arthur would sit with his knights. The earliest reference to this table is in a twelfth-century historical chronicle in verse, *Le Roman de Brut*, by Wace, a Norman poet. He wrote that the king wanted the table to be round to prevent fighting among the knights for the seats of highest honor. At a round table, all seats were equal in prestige.

A description of the Round Table by an English priest, Layamon, says that it could seat 1,600 men and could be folded up and carried on horseback. Another version says that the table sat twelve and that one seat, the *siege perilous* (*siege* is French for "seat") was left empty. It was reserved for a knight who was pure enough to find the Holy Grail, the cup used by Jesus at the Last Supper. Suddenly, this legend has it, the name of Sir Galahad appeared on this chair, and he occupied it from then on.

Upon the hidden bases of the hills.'
So might some old man speak in the aftertime
To all the people, winning reverence;
160 But now much honor and much fame were lost."
    So spake he, clouded with his own conceit,
And hid Excalibur the second time,
And so strode back slow to the wounded king.
    Then spoke King Arthur, breathing heavily:
165 "What is it thou hast seen, or what hast heard?"
    And answer made the bold Sir Bedivere:
"I heard the water lapping on the crag,
And the long ripple washing in the reeds."
    To whom replied King Arthur, much in wrath:
170 "Ah, miserable and unkind, untrue,
Unknightly, traitor-hearted! Woe is me!
Authority forgets a dying king,
Laid widowed of the power in his eye
That bowed the will. I see thee what thou art,
175 For thou, the latest-left of all my knights,
In whom should meet the offices[22] of all,
Thou wouldst betray me for the precious hilt;
Either from lust of gold, or like a girl
Valuing the giddy pleasure of the eyes.
180 Yet, for a man may fail in duty twice,
And the third time may prosper, get thee hence;
But, if thou spare to fling Excalibur,
I will arise and slay thee with my hands."
    Then quickly rose Sir Bedivere, and ran,
185 And, leaping down the ridges lightly, plunged
Among the bulrush beds,[23] and clutched the sword,
And strongly wheeled and threw it. The great brand
Made lightnings in the splendor of the moon,
And flashing round and round, and whirled in an arch,
190 Shot like a streamer of the northern morn,[24]
Seen where the moving isles of winter shock[25]
By night, with noises of the northern sea.
So flashed and fell the brand Excalibur;
But ere he dipped the surface, rose an arm
195 Clothed in white samite, mystic, wonderful,
And caught him by the hilt, and brandished him
Three times, and drew him under in the mere.
And lightly went the other to the king.
    Then spoke King Arthur, drawing thicker breath:
200 "Now see I by thine eyes that this is done.

---

22. **offices** *n.* duties.
23. **bulrush** (bool′ rush′) **beds** growth of marsh plants.
24. **a streamer of the northern morn** northern lights; the aurora borealis.
25. **the moving isles of winter shock** icebergs crash.

Reading Strategy
Recognizing Author's Attitude What is the author's attitude toward Arthur in lines 172–183?

Reading Check
Why does Sir Bedivere want to keep the sword?

Morte d'Arthur ◆ 1025

⑫ Reading Strategy
Recognizing Author's Attitude
- Ask a volunteer to read aloud lines 172–183. Ask students why Arthur is scolding Bedivere.
  Answer: He has seen into Bedivere's heart and knows that Bedivere has not followed his command to fling the sword into the lake.
- Ask whether the dying Arthur seems to think of himself as weak and helpless.
  Answer: No; Arthur threatens to kill Bedivere if the knight doesn't do as Arthur commands, and he seems convinced that he could accomplish this.
- Then, ask the Reading Strategy question on p. 1025: What is the author's attitude toward Arthur in lines 172–183?
  Answer: Tennyson feels that Arthur, even though he is close to death, is far from being a pathetic figure. He is as astute as ever, and he shows his nobility in his expectation of obedience from Bedivere. He is still capable of great strength of will and body.

▶ Monitor Progress Have students identify the details they used to recognize the author's attitude toward Arthur.

⑬ ✔Reading Check
Answer: Bedivere wants to preserve the sword for posterity.

CUSTOMIZE INSTRUCTION FOR UNIVERSAL ACCESS

For English Learners	For Gifted/Talented Students
On p. 1024, Arthur refers to Bedivere as "lief and dear." Have students check a dictionary to find the meaning of *lief* and other unusual words in the poem not defined in the notes. Encourage them to share their findings with the class.	The rigors of knighthood were intense. Besides the skill required for swordfighting and jousting, the knights spent a great deal of time on horseback and carried the weight of their armor. Have students research the type and amount of physical training required for a knight in medieval times and present their findings to the class.

⑭ Background

Art

The Dream of Arthur in Avalon, by Sir Edward Burne-Jones

It is not surprising that the British Pre-Raphaelite painter Sir Edward Coley Burne-Jones (1833–1898) chose this scene from Arthurian legend as a painting subject—he was known for his enthusiasm for the medieval. The subject of this painting is taken from Malory's *Morte d'Arthur.* Burne-Jones's dreamy, romantic "literary" style, executed in a flat technique, was effective not only in painting but in stained glass, tapestry, mosaic, and relief—all media that interested medieval artists as well. Use this question for discussion:

What seems to be happening to King Arthur in this picture? How do you know?

Answer: Arthur may be on his deathbed. The people around him seem to be mourning.

⑮ ▶ Critical Viewing

Answer: The painting depicts Arthur's death as a very formal occasion, whereas the description in the poem depicts a wild and natural scene. Also, in Tennyson's poem the scene showed in the painting takes place on a funeral barge on a lake.

⑯ Literary Analysis

Legend

• Ask students to summarize Sir Bedivere's actions regarding Excalibur.

Answer: Bedivere is commanded twice by Arthur to fling Excalibur into the lake, but twice he cannot bring himself to do it. After being threatened by Arthur, on the third time he manages to obey.

• Then, ask the Literary Analysis question on p. 1026: What aspects of Sir Bedivere's act are typical of a legend?

Possible response: Sir Bedivere twice fails to carry out Arthur's command before finally obeying. He gives the same reply, virtually word for word, when Arthur questions him after his first two failures to obey. This repetition of events heightens the suspense, stresses the magical qualities of Excalibur, and is typical of legend.

Speak out; what is it thou hast heard, or seen?"
    And answer made the bold Sir Bedivere:
"Sir King, I closed mine eyelids, lest the gems
Should blind my purpose, for I never saw,
205 Nor shall see, here or elsewhere, till I die,
Not though I live three lives of mortal men,
So great a miracle as yonder hilt.
Then with both hands I flung him, wheeling him;
But when I looked again, behold an arm,
210 Clothed in white samite, mystic, wonderful,
That caught him by the hilt, and brandished him
Three times, and drew him under in the mere."
    And answer made King Arthur, breathing hard:
"My end draws nigh; 'tis time that I were gone.
215 Make broad thy shoulders to receive my weight,
And bear me to the margin, yet I fear
My wound hath taken cold, and I shall die."
    So saying, from the pavement he half rose,
Slowly, with pain, reclining on his arm,
220 And looking wistfully with wide blue eyes
As in a picture. Him Sir Bedivere
Remorsefully regarded through his tears,
And would have spoken, but he found not words,
Then took with care, and kneeling on one knee,
225 O'er both his shoulders drew the languid hands,
And rising bore him through the place of tombs.
    But, as he walked, King Arthur panted hard,
Like one that feels a nightmare on his bed
When all the house is mute. So sighed the king,
230 Muttering and murmuring at his ear, "Quick, quick!
I fear it is too late, and I shall die."
But the other swiftly strode from ridge to ridge,
Clothed with his breath, and looking, as he walked,
Larger than human on the frozen hills.
235 He heard the deep behind him, and a cry
Before. His own thought drove him like a goad.[26]
Dry clashed his harness[27] in the icy caves
And barren chasms, and all to left and right
The bare black cliff clanged round him, as he based
240 His feet on juts of slippery crag that rang
Sharp-smitten with the dint of armèd heels—
And on a sudden, lo! the level lake,
And the long glories of the winter moon.
    Then saw they how there hove a dusky barge,
245 Dark as a funeral scarf from stem to stern,

---

26. **goad** (gōd) *n.* sharp pointed stick used to drive oxen.
27. **harness** (här′ nis) *n.* armor.

The Dream of Arthur in Avalon (detail), Sir Edward Burne-Jones, The Museo de Arte de Ponce, The Luis A. Ferré Foundation, Inc. Ponce, Puerto Rico

⑮ ▲ Critical Viewing How does this painting compare with Tennyson's description of Arthur's death? **[Compare and Contrast]**

Literary Analysis
Legend What aspects of Sir Bedivere's act are typical of a legend?

Beneath them; and descending they were ware
That all the decks were dense with stately forms
Black-stoled, black-hooded, like a dream—by these
Three queens with crowns of gold—and from them rose
250 A cry that shivered to the tingling stars,
And, as it were one voice, an agony
Of <u>lamentation</u>, like a wind that shrills
All night in a waste land, where no one comes,
Or hath come, since the making of the world.
255   Then murmured Arthur, "Place me in the barge,"
And to the barge they came. There those three queens
Put forth their hands, and took the king, and wept.
But she that rose the tallest of them all
And fairest laid his head upon her lap,
260 And loosed the shattered casque, and chafed his hands,
And called him by his name, complaining loud,
And dropping bitter tears against his brow
Striped with dark blood; for all his face was white
And colorless, and like the withered moon
265 Smote by the fresh beam of the springing east;
And all his greaves and cuisses dashed with drops
Of onset; and the light and lustrous curls—
That made his forehead like a rising sun
High from the dais-throne—were parched with dust;
270 Or, clotted into points and hanging loose,
Mixed with the knightly growth that fringed his lips.
So like a shattered column lay the king;
Not like that Arthur who, with lance in rest,
From spur to plume a star of tournament,
275 Shot through the lists at Camelot, and charged
Before the eyes of ladies and of kings.
    Then loudly cried the bold Sir Bedivere:
"Ah! my Lord Arthur, whither shall I go?
Where shall I hide my forehead and my eyes?
280 For now I see the true old times are dead,
When every morning brought a noble chance,
And every chance brought out a noble knight.
Such times have been not since the light that led
The holy Elders with the gift of myrrh.[28]
285 But now the whole ROUND TABLE is dissolved
Which was an image of the mighty world;
And I, the last, go forth companionless,
And the days darken round me, and the years,
Among new men, strange faces, other minds."
290   And slowly answered Arthur from the barge:

---

28. **the light . . . of myrrh** (mur) star that guided the three kings (the holy Elders) with their gift of incense (myrrh) to Bethlehem at the birth of Jesus.

lamentation (lam´ ən tā´ shən) *n.* mourning

Literary Analysis
Legend How do the details in lines 244–254 reflect Arthur's legendary status?

Reading Strategy
Recognizing Author's Attitude Which words in lines 265–266 reveal awe for Arthur?

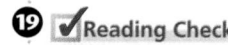 **Reading Check**
Where does Sir Bedivere take the dying Arthur?

Morte d'Arthur ◆ 1027

⓱ Literary Analysis
Legend
- Ask a volunteer to read aloud lines 244–254. Ask students to describe the mood of this scene.
  Answer: The mood is somber, eerie, and melancholy.
- Ask students to name some details that contribute to the mood of the scene.
  Answer: Details include a dusky barge, dark as a funeral scarf; black-stoled and black-hooded stately forms; three mysterious queens giving a shivering cry and an agony of lamentation.
- Then, ask the Literary Analysis question on p. 1027: How do the details in lines 244–254 reflect Arthur's legendary status?
  Possible response: The barge that appears in the lake from which Excalibur came creates a sense of mystery and wonder. The women on the barge must have some magical power to know of Arthur's death. His affiliation with these magical women makes Arthur seem larger than life.

⓲ Reading Strategy
Recognizing Author's Attitude
- Read aloud the bracketed lines. Ask students what attitude toward Arthur the lines show.
  Answer: The lines show an awe and reverence for Arthur.
- Then, ask the Reading Strategy question on p. 1027: Which words in these lines reveal awe for Arthur?
  Answer: The comparison between Arthur's face and the moon as it is illuminated by the beams of the rising sun reflects his legendary status.

⓳ ✔ Reading Check
Answer: Sir Bedivere takes Arthur to a funeral barge on a lake.

CUSTOMIZE INSTRUCTION FOR UNIVERSAL ACCESS

For Less Proficient Readers	For Gifted/Talented Students
Tell students that while in Tennyson's poem King Arthur acquires Excalibur when a mysterious arm lifts it from a lake, the next selection they will read describes Arthur getting the sword by a different means. Encourage students to discuss why the details of a legend may vary in different tellings. If necessary, remind students that legends were often passed on orally before they were written down.	The passage that describes King Arthur being placed in the barge with three queens to attend him uses many phrases, including "his brow / striped with dark blood, his face was white / And colorless, and like the withered moon" that appeal to the sense of sight. Have students create notes for a film version of this scene, describing camera angles, lighting, and other effects to heighten the visual effects of the scene.

- Read aloud the bracketed passage. Ask students to summarize the qualities that make Avilion a paradise.
  Answer: The weather is always fair and mild; flowers are always blooming.

- Then, ask the Literary Analysis question on p. 1028: How is Avilion similar to other legendary paradises?
  Answer: Like other legendary paradises, Avilion offers an escape from daily worries and pain; it is a place where all is fair and mild, a nurturing environment free of conflict.

❷⓵ Vocabulary Development

The Latin Suffix -ous

- Call students' attention to the word *grievous*. Tell them that the Latin suffix *-ous* means "like" or "pertaining to."

- Ask students what familiar word the first part of *grievous* reminds them of.
  Answer: *Griev-* is similar to *grief*.

- Then, ask students to define the word *grievous*.
  Answer: *Grievous* means "pertaining to grief."

- Ask students to look for words ending in *-ous* as they read the next selection.

"The old order changeth, yielding place to new,
And God fulfills himself in many ways,
Lest one good custom should corrupt the world.
Comfort thyself: what comfort is in me?
295 I have lived my life, and that which I have done
May He within himself make pure! but thou,
If thou shouldst never see my face again,
Pray for my soul. More things are wrought by prayer
Than this world dreams of. Wherefore, let thy voice
300 Rise like a fountain for me night and day.
For what are men better than sheep or goats
That nourish a blind life within the brain,
If, knowing God, they lift not hands of prayer
Both for themselves and those who call them friend?
305 For so the whole round earth is every way
Bound by gold chains about the feet of God.
But now farewell. I am going a long way
With these thou seest—if indeed I go—
For all my mind is clouded with a doubt—
310 To the island-valley of Avilion;²⁹
Where falls not hail, or rain, or any snow,
Nor ever wind blows loudly, but it lies
Deep-meadowed, happy, fair with orchard lawns
And bowery³⁰ hollows crowned with summer sea,
315 Where I will heal me of my grievous wound."
    So said he, and the barge with oar and sail
Moved from the brink, like some full-breasted swan
that, fluting a wild carol ere her death,
Ruffles her pure cold plume, takes the flood
320 With swarthy webs. Long stood Sir Bedivere
Revolving many memories, till the hull
Looked one black dot against the verge of dawn,
And on the mere the wailing died away.

    Here ended Hall, and our last light, that long
325 Had winked and threatened darkness, flared and fell;
At which the parson, sent to sleep with sound,
And waked with silence, grunted "Good!" but we
Sat rapt: it was the tone with which he read—
Perhaps some modern touches here and there
330 Redeemed it from the charge of nothingness—
Or else we loved the man, and prized his work;
I know not; but we sitting, as I said,
The cock crew loud, as at that time of year

---

29. island-valley of Avilion island paradise of Avalon where heroes were taken after death, according to Celtic mythology and medieval romances.
30. bowery (bou´ ər ē) *adj.* enclosed by overhanging boughs of trees or by vines.

Literary Analysis
Legend How is Avilion similar to other legendary paradises?

swarthy (swôr´ <i>thē</i>) *adj.* having a dark complexion

Reading Strategy
Recognizing Author's Attitude What does the speaker achieve by describing the group's "rapt" attention to the story?

☀ **ENRICHMENT: Art Connection**

Coats of Arms

In the eleventh century, around the time when the Arthurian legend is supposed to have taken place, knights and nobles began to display coats of arms on shields and flags. These were symbolic identifications of themselves and their families. The original purpose of these coats of arms was to allow the knights' followers to identify them in battle. Holding a shield in front of himself for protection, he would also display it prominently so a would-be attacker would quickly recognize a friend or foe.

Coats of arms often carried mottoes in addition to symbols and were handed down over generations, developing into an elaborate system. The study of coats of arms is called heraldry because it was the heralds, originally message bearers, who regulated and registered coats of arms in huge books called armorials. No two families could use the same design. Britain is the only country still to make use of these designs today, though a family's history often can be traced to a particular coat of arms.

³³⁵ The lusty bird takes every hour for dawn.
Then Francis, muttering, like a man ill-used,
"There now—that's nothing!" drew a little back,
And drove his heel into the smoldered log,
That sent a blast of sparkles up the flue.
And so to bed, where yet in sleep I seemed
³⁴⁰ To sail with Arthur under looming shores,
Point after point; till on to dawn, when dreams
Begin to feel the truth and stir of day,
To me, methought, who waited with the crowd,
There came a bark that, blowing forward, bore
³⁴⁵ King Arthur; like a modern gentleman
Of stateliest port;³¹ and all the people cried,
"Arthur is come again: he cannot die."
Then those that stood upon the hills behind
Repeated—"Come again, and thrice as fair";
³⁵⁰ And, further inland, voices echoed—"Come
With all good things, and war shall be no more."
At this a hundred bells began to peal,
That with the sound I woke, and heard indeed
The clear church bells ring in the Christmas morn.

---

31. Of stateliest port who carried himself in a most majestic or dignified manner.

Review and Assess

Thinking About the Selection

1. **Respond:** What is your opinion of Sir Bedivere's actions in response to Arthur's request? Explain.

2. **(a) Recall:** What occasion is celebrated at the start of the poem? **(b) Interpret:** Why might that connection be significant?

3. **(a) Recall:** In the poem within the poem, what has happened to Arthur? **(b) Analyze:** What are Arthur's feelings about what has happened?

4. **(a) Recall:** What does Arthur specifically request of Bedivere? **(b) Analyze:** Why does Bedivere hesitate to carry out Arthur's request?

5. **(a) Interpret:** Arthur says from the barge, "The old order changeth, yielding place to new." What does the old order represent to Arthur? **(b) Interpret:** What might the old order represent to Tennyson?

6. **Make a Judgment:** Why have writers, like Tennyson, continued to tell stories about Arthur's life and death?

Alfred, Lord Tennyson

(1809–1892)
Alfred, Lord Tennyson, the fourth son of twelve children, was born in Lincolnshire, England. He received his early schooling at his clergyman father's home and then attended Cambridge University for a few years. Financial problems forced him to withdraw before he received a degree. Living at home, he perfected his craft as a poet by experimenting with different poetic forms. His exquisite short lyrics and powerful longer works earned him great popularity and lasting fame.

Morte d'Arthur ◆ 1029

㉓ About the Selection

Legends are very adaptable. Where Tennyson sees Arthur as a heroic embodiment of ancient goodness and virtue, T. H. White views young Arthur in a more accessible way. Even figures of legend, he seems to say, are recognizably human. The characters in White's version of the Arthurian story are not stiff figures in an old-fashioned, still-life tableau. They live, breathe, and blunder. In fact, this excerpt from "The Once and Future King" tells how Arthur became king because Sir Kay forgot his sword.

㉔ Background

Art

The Crowning of Arthur (Royal MS)

This page of an illuminated manuscript shows Arthur being crowned. Although the drawing style is simple, even somewhat cartoonish, the illustration depicts a stately occasion. The most important figure, next to Arthur himself, is a bishop. The bishop is recognized by his pointed headdress, or miter, and his robes. Thus, one important aspect of the coronation is that it is approved by the Christian church. Arthur holds a scepter, which symbolizes his authority over wordly affairs. The other onlookers represent the acceptance of Arthur by his new subjects. Use these questions for discussion:

1. Does this illustration show you what you would expect to see at a coronation? Why or why not? Possible response: Students might say that they would expect to see more luxurious clothing and jewels at a coronation. However, the ritual of the bishop placing the crown upon the king, who is holding a scepter, and the expressions of the eager onlookers are probably what students would expect to see.

2. What impression of Arthur do you get from this painting? What gives you that impression? Possible response: With his benign expression and his subjects crowding around him, Arthur seems down-to-earth and accessible.

㉓ Arthur Becomes King of Britain

from THE ONCE AND FUTURE KING

T. H. WHITE

King Pellinore arrived for the important weekend in a high state of flurry.

"I say," he exclaimed, "do you know? Have you heard? Is it a secret, what?"

"Is what a secret, what?" they asked him.

"Why, the King," cried his majesty. "You know, about the King?"

"What's the matter with the King?" inquired Sir Ector. "You don't say he's comin' down to hunt with those darned hounds of his or anythin' like that?"

"He's dead," cried King Pellinore tragically. "He's dead, poor fellah, and can't hunt any more."

Sir Grummore stood up respectfully and took off his cap.

"The King is dead," he said. "Long live the King."

Everybody else felt they ought to stand up too, and the boys' nurse burst into tears.

"There, there," she sobbed. "His loyal highness dead and gone, and him such a respectful gentleman. Many's the illuminated picture I've cut out of him, from the Illustrated Missals, aye, and stuck up over the mantel. From the time when he was in swaddling bands,[1] right through them world towers till he was a-visiting the dispersed areas as the world's Prince Charming, there wasn't a picture of 'im but I had it out, aye, and give 'im a last thought o' nights."

"Compose yourself, Nannie," said Sir Ector.

"It is solemn, isn't it?" said King Pellinore, "what? Uther the Conqueror, 1066 to 1216."

"A solemn moment," said Sir Grummore. "The King is dead. Long live the King."

"We ought to pull down the curtains," said Kay, who was always a <u>stickler</u> for good form, "or half-mast[2] the banners."

"That's right," said Sir Ector. "Somebody go and tell the sergeant-at-arms."

It was obviously the Wart's duty to execute this command, for he was now the junior nobleman present, so he ran out cheerfully to find the sergeant. Soon those who were left in the solar[3] could hear a voice crying out, "Nah then, one-two, special mourning fer 'is lite majesty, lower awai on the command Two!" and then the flapping of all the standards, banners, pennons, pennoncells, banderolls, guidons, streamers and cognizances[4] which made gay the snowy turrets of the Forest Sauvage.

"How did you hear?" asked Sir Ector.

1. **swaddling bands** long, narrow bands of cloth wrapped around a newborn baby in former times.
2. **half-mast** (haf´ mast´) v. hang a flag at half-mast.
3. **solar** (sō´ lər) n. here, sun room. *Solar* is often used as an adjective.
4. **standards . . . cognizances** (käg´ nə zən´ sez) n. banners or flags.

◄ **Critical Viewing** Based on what you have read so far, how do you think T. H. White would feel about the formality and ceremony of this coronation scene? **[Draw Conclusions]**

Reading Strategy
Recognizing Author's Attitude What does the informal language in dialogue suggest about the author's feelings toward the characters?

stickler (stik´ lər) *n.* person who insists uncompromisingly on the observance of something specified

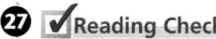 **Reading Check**
What command does the sergeant-at-arms give to show respect for the deceased King?

Arthur Becomes King of Britain ◆ 1031

㉙ "I was pricking through the purlieus[5] of the forest after that Beast, you know, when I met with a solemn friar of orders gray, and he told me. It's the very latest news."

"Poor old Pendragon," said Sir Ector.

"The King is dead," said Sir Grummore solemnly. "Long live the King."

"It is all very well for you to keep on mentioning that, my dear Grummore," exclaimed King Pellinore petulantly, "but who is this King, what, that is to live so long, what, accordin' to you?"

"Well, his heir," said Sir Grummore, rather taken aback.

"Our blessed monarch," said the Nurse tearfully, "never had no hair. Anybody that studied the loyal family knowed that."

"Good gracious!" exclaimed Sir Ector. "But he must have had a next-of-kin?"

㉚ "That's just it," cried King Pellinore in high excitement. "That's the excitin' part of it, what? No hair and no next of skin, and who's to succeed to the throne? That's what my friar was so excited about, what, and why he was asking who could succeed to what, what? What?"

㉛ "Do you mean to tell me," exclaimed Sir Grummore indignantly, "that there ain't no King of Gramarye?"

"Not a scrap of one," cried King Pellinore, feeling important. "And there have been signs and wonders of no mean might."

"I think it's a scandal," said Sir Grummore. "God knows what the dear old country is comin' to."

"What sort of signs and wonders?" asked Sir Ector.

"Well, there has appeared a sort of sword in a stone, what, in a sort of a church. Not in the church, if you see what I mean, and not in the stone, but that sort of thing, what, like you might say."

"I don't know what the Church is coming to," said Sir Grummore.

"It's in an anvil,"[6] explained the King.

"The Church?"

"No, the sword."

"But I thought you said the sword was in the stone?"

"No," said King Pellinore. "The stone is outside the Church."

"Look here, Pellinore," said Sir Ector. "You have a bit of a rest, old boy, and start again. Here, drink up this horn of mead[7] and take it easy."

"The sword," said King Pellinore, "is stuck through an anvil which stands on a stone. It goes right through the anvil and into the stone. The anvil is stuck to the stone. The stone stands outside a church. Give me some more mead."

"I don't think that's much of a wonder," remarked Sir Grummore. "What I wonder at is that they should allow such things to happen.

---

5. **purlieus** (pur′ lōoz) *n.* outlying part of a forest, exempted from forest laws.
6. **anvil** (an′ vəl) *n.* iron or steel block.
7. **mead** (mēd) *n.* drink made of fermented honey and water, often with spices or fruit added.

But you can't tell nowadays, what with all these Saxon agitators."[8]

"My dear fellah," cried Pellinore, getting excited again, "it's not where the stone is, what, that I'm trying to tell you, but what is written on it, what, where it is."

"What?"

"Why, on its pommel."[9]

"Come on, Pellinore," said Sir Ector. "You just sit quite still with your face to the wall for a minute, and then tell us what you are talkin' about. Take it easy, old boy. No need for hurryin'. You sit still and look at the wall, there's a good chap, and talk as slow as you can."

"There are words written on this sword in this stone outside this church," cried King Pellinore piteously, "and these words are as follows. Oh, do try to listen to me, you two, instead of interruptin' all the time about nothing for it makes a man's head go ever so."

"What are these words?" asked Kay.

"These words say this," said King Pellinore, "so far as I can understand from that old friar of orders gray."

"Go on, do," said Kay, for the King had come to a halt.

"Go on," said Sir Ector, "what do these words on this sword in this anvil in this stone outside this church, say?"

King Pellinore closed his eyes tight, extended his arms in both directions, and announced in capital letters, "Whoso Pulleth Out This Sword of this Stone and Anvil, is Rightwise King Born of All England."

"Who said that?" asked Sir Grummore.

"But the sword said it, like I tell you."

"Talkative weapon," remarked Sir Grummore skeptically.

"It was written on it," cried the King angrily. "Written on it in letters of gold."

"Why didn't you pull it out then?" asked Sir Grummore.

"But I tell you that I wasn't there. All this that I am telling you was told to me by that friar I was telling you of, like I tell you."

"Has this sword with this inscription been pulled out?" inquired Sir Ector.

"No," whispered King Pellinore dramatically. "That's where the whole excitement comes in. They can't pull this sword out at all, although they have all been tryin' like fun, and so they have had to proclaim a tournament all over England, for New Year's Day, so that the man who comes to the tournament and pulls out the sword can be King of all England forever, what, I say."

"Oh, father," cried Kay. "The man who pulls the sword out of the stone will be the King of England. Can't we go to the tournament, father, and have a shot?"

"Couldn't think of it," said Sir Ector.

"Long way to London," said Sir Grummore, shaking his head.

"My father went there once," said King Pellinore.

---

8. **Saxon** (saks′ sən) **agitators** Germanic people in ancient times who conquered parts of England.

9. **pommel** (pum′ əl) *n.* round knob on the end of the hilt of some swords.

Literary Analysis
Legend How do formal-sounding words, such as those written on the sword, contribute to the legend?

33 **Reading Check**
Where is the sword?

Arthur Becomes King of Britain ◆ 1033

32 Literary Analysis
Legend
- Ask a volunteer to read aloud the bracketed passage, keeping in mind that it should be read in "capital letters."
- Have students restate the passage in their own words.
  Answer: Whoever pulls this sword out of this stone and anvil was born to be King of England.
- Then, ask the Literary Analysis question on p. 1033: How do formal-sounding words, such as those written on the sword, contribute to the legend?
  Possible response: The formal, old-fashioned language points out the ancient origin of the legend and creates an amusing contrast to the everyday, comic world that most of the characters inhabit.

33 Reading Check
Answer: The sword is embedded in an anvil on a stone outside a church.

CUSTOMIZE INSTRUCTION FOR UNIVERSAL ACCESS

For Less Proficient Readers	For Advanced Readers
As with "Morte d'Arthur," tell students that this selection needs special attention because of its language and vocabulary. Have them read the vocabulary notes before reading a passage and keep a running list of puzzling words and phrases to review after they have finished the story.	Point out that the previous selection, "Morte d'Arthur," and "Arthur Becomes King of Britain" relate elements of the same legend from divergent viewpoints and attitudes. Have students discuss how White and Tennyson might have responded to each other's material. Which elements might have been useful to them in creating their own work, and which elements might they have responded to negatively?

Legend

- Read aloud the bracketed passage. Then, ask students whether T. H. White had any reason to know that this conversation about going to London ever took place between anyone associated with the historical King Arthur.
  Answer: No; White made up the conversation.

- Then, ask the Literary Analysis question on p. 1034: In what ways has the writer retold or revised the legend of King Arthur?
  Answer: White invented scenes and conversations and even characters for his retelling of the legend of King Arthur.

35 Reading Strategy

Recognizing Author's Attitude

- Ask students to describe the characters' feelings about going to London and why the characters feel that way.
  Answer: The characters have never been to such a large city and are awe-struck by the idea.

- Then, ask the Reading Strategy question on p. 1034: Why does the author make his characters seem so in awe of London?
  Possible response: Earlier the author ridiculed Pellinore, Ector, and Grummore for their lack of intelligence. Here he also wants to make it clear that they are unsophisticated local people, without any experience of the world beyond their immediate community.

Kay said, "Oh, surely we could go? When I am knighted I shall have to go to a tournament somewhere, and this one happens at just the right date. All the best people will be there, and we should see the famous knights and great kings. It does not matter about the sword, of course, but think of the tournament, probably the greatest there has ever been in Gramarye, and all the things we should see and do. Dear father, let me go to this tourney, if you love me, so that I may bear away the prize of all, in my maiden fight."

"But, Kay," said Sir Ector, "I have never been to London."

34 "All the more reason to go. I believe that anybody who does not go for a tournament like this will be proving that he has no noble blood in his veins. Think what people will say about us, if we do not go and have a shot at that sword. They will say that Sir Ector's family was too vulgar and knew it had no chance."

"We all know the family has no chance," said Sir Ector, "that is, for the sword."

"Lot of people in London," remarked Sir Grummore, with a wild surmise. "So they say."

He took a deep breath and goggled at his host with eyes like marbles.

35 "And shops," added King Pellinore suddenly, also beginning to breathe heavily.

"Dang it!" cried Sir Ector, bumping his horn mug on the table so that it spilled. "Let's all go to London, then, and see the new King!"

They rose up as one man.

"Why shouldn't I be as good a man as my father?" exclaimed King Pellinore.

"Dash it all," cried Sir Grummore. "After all, it is the capital!"

"Hurray!" shouted Kay.

"Lord have mercy," said the nurse.

At this moment the Wart came in with Merlyn, and everybody was too excited to notice that, if he had not been grown up now, he would have been on the verge of tears.

"Oh, Wart," cried Kay, forgetting for the moment that he was only addressing his squire, and slipping back into the familiarity of their boyhood. "What do you think? We are all going to London for a great tournament on New Year's Day!"

"Are we?"

"Yes, and you will carry my shield and spears for the jousts, and I shall win the palm[10] of everybody and be a great knight!"

"Well, I am glad we are going," said the Wart, "for Merlyn is leaving us too."

"Oh, we shan't need Merlyn."

"He is leaving us," repeated the Wart.

"Leavin' us?" asked Sir Ector. "I thought it was we that were leavin'?"

"He is going away from the Forest Sauvage."

---

10. **win the palm** be the winner. A palm leaf is a symbol of victory.

Literary Analysis
Legend In what ways has the writer retold or revised the legend of King Arthur?

Reading Strategy
Recognizing Author's Attitude Why does the author make his characters seem so in awe of London?

☀ ENRICHMENT: Literature Connection

The Legend of King Arthur

The first known reference to King Arthur appeared in *Gododdin*, a seventh-century Welsh poem. In the next few centuries, Arthur became a popular figure in Britain and Britanny in France. His stature grew in French Breton tales until he was seen as a great ruler and warlord. By the twelfth century, Britain had made him a national folk hero.

In Geoffrey of Monmouth's *Historia regnum Britanniae* (1137), Arthur is shown as the master of a great empire.

Tales of Arthur and his court spread all over Europe. A French poet, Chrétien de Troyes, wrote romances focusing on Sir Lancelot and Sir Perceval. German poets added more to Arthurian literature. Wolfram von Eschenbach wrote *Parzifal*, and Gottfried von Strassburg created the story of Tristan and Isolde.

In writing *Le Morte d'Arthur*, Sir Thomas Malory used these different stories to create the first comprehensive account of the legend in English.

37 ◀ **Critical Viewing** How can you tell that the young man in this picture is performing an amazing feat? **[Infer]**

Sir Ector said, "Come now, Merlyn, what's all this about? I don't understand all this a bit."

"I have come to say Goodbye, Sir Ector," said the old magician. "Tomorrow my pupil Kay will be knighted, and the next week my other pupil will go away as his squire. I have outlived my usefulness here, and it is time to go."

"Now, now, don't say that," said Sir Ector. "I think you're a jolly useful chap whatever happens. You just stay and teach me, or be the librarian or something. Don't you leave an old man alone, after the children have flown."

"We shall all meet again," said Merlyn. "There is no cause to be sad."

"Don't go," said Kay.

"I must go," replied their tutor. "We have had a good time while we were young, but it is in the nature of Time to fly. There are many things in other parts of the kingdom which I ought to be attending to just now, and it is a specially busy time for me. Come, Archimedes, say Goodbye to the company.'

"Goodbye," said Archimedes tenderly to the Wart.

38 ✔ **Reading Check**

Why is Merlyn leaving?

Arthur Becomes King of Britain ◆ 1035

---

36 ❻ Background

Art

Galahad's Sword in Stone (Royal MS)

This illuminated manuscript page shows the act of pulling a sword from a stone, one element of the legendary story of King Arthur. In the selection, Arthur becomes king after he removes the sword from the stone. Therefore, students may wonder why Galahad is portrayed here as removing the sword. In legend, Galahad (Lancelot's son) successfully repeated Arthur's feat. The drama of the moment is highlighted by an attentive audience, including a king and queen. Use these questions for discussion:

1. How are the circumstances of Arthur's feat different from the ones shown here?
   Answer: In Arthur's case, the sword was embedded in an anvil on a stone in front of a church; in Galahad's case, the stone was floating in a river, which is indicated by the fish. Also, in White's story, there were no witnesses to Arthur's feat.

2. The young man in this painting doesn't seem to be making much effort. How is he different from Arthur in the story you are reading?
   Answer: Arthur had to try very hard to remove the sword from the stone.

37 ▶ **Critical Viewing**

Possible response: The responses of the surrounding people, pointing and raising their hands in surprise, indicate that the young man is performing an amazing feat.

38 ✔ **Reading Check**

Answer: Merlyn is leaving because his students are going on—Sir Kay as a knight and Wart as his squire—and he feels he is no longer useful there.

CUSTOMIZE INSTRUCTION FOR UNIVERSAL ACCESS	
For English Learners	**For Advanced Readers**
Point out that the Wart barely looked up to say goodbye to Merlyn. Encourage students to write a journal entry from Wart's point of view expressing how he felt at saying good-bye to his beloved tutor.	Have students pay attention to White's mixture of modern idioms with medieval scenes that call for Tennyson's deliberately old-fashioned language. Kay asks his father if they can go to the tournament so that they can "have a shot" at it. When Pellinore decides to go to the tournament, he says, "Dang it!" Have students suggest more traditional responses to the situations in the story, such as "try our courage" and "Zounds!"

Legend

- Have students name some details used to describe the preparations for knighting.
  Possible response: Details include the old box of games and the worn-out straw dart board; the warm pants the nurse made; the sergeant's polishing of the armor until it was brittle.

- Ask students how they would characterize the details. Do they seem important or unimportant?
  Answer: They seem unimportant.

- Then, ask the Literary Analysis question on p. 1036: How does the inclusion of trivial information in this paragraph affect your reading of the legend?
  Possible response: The trivial details make the characters seem very human and make the legend seem very much like real life.

40 Vocabulary Development

The Latin Suffix -ous

- Call students' attention to the word *treacherous*. Ask what the suffix *-ous* means.
  Answer: It means "like" or "pertaining to."

- Ask what familiar word the beginning of *treacherous* resembles.
  Answer: It resembles *treachery*.

- Ask students to figure out what *treacherous* means.
  Answer: It means "pertaining to treachery," or "untrustworthy."

"Goodbye," said the Wart without looking up at all.

"But you can't go," cried Sir Ector, "not without a month's notice."

"Can't I?" replied Merlyn, taking up the position always used by philosophers who propose to dematerialize. He stood on his toes, while Archimedes held tight to his shoulder—began to spin on them slowly like a top—spun faster and faster till he was only a blur of grayish light— and in a few seconds there was no one there at all.

"Goodbye, Wart," cried two faint voices outside the solar window.

"Goodbye," said the Wart for the last time—and the poor fellow went quickly out of the room.

The knighting took place in a whirl of preparations. Kay's <u>sumptuous</u> bath had to be set up in the box room, between two towel-horses and an old box of selected games which contained a worn-out straw dart-board—it was called fléchette in those days—because all the other rooms were full of packing. The nurse spent the whole time constructing new warm pants for everybody, on the principle that the climate of any place outside the Forest Sauvage must be treacherous to the extreme, and, as for the sergeant, he polished all the armor till it was quite brittle and sharpened the swords till they were almost worn away.

At last it was time to set out.

Perhaps, if you happen not to have lived in the Old England of the twelfth century, or whenever it was, and in a remote castle on the borders of the Marshes at that, you will find it difficult to imagine the wonders of their journey.

The road, or track, ran most of the time along the high ridges of the hills or downs, and they could look down on either side of them upon the desolate marshes where the snowy reeds sighed, and the ice crackled, and the duck in the red sunsets quacked loud on the winter air. The whole country was like that. Perhaps there would be a moory marsh on one side of the ridge, and a forest of a hundred thousand acres on the other, with all the great branches weighted in white. They could sometimes see a wisp of smoke among the trees, or a huddle of buildings far out among the impassable reeds, and twice they came to quite respectable towns which had several inns to boast of, but on the whole it was an England without civilization. The better roads were cleared of cover for a bow-shot on either side of them, lest the traveler should be slain by hidden thieves.

They slept where they could, sometimes in the hut of some cottager who was prepared to welcome them, sometimes in the castle of a brother knight who invited them to refresh themselves, sometimes in the firelight and fleas of a dirty little hovel with a bush tied to a pole outside it—this was the signboard used at that time by inns—and once or twice on the open ground, all huddled together for warmth between their grazing chargers. Wherever they went and wherever they slept, the east wind whistled in the reeds, and the geese went over high in the starlight, honking at the stars.

sumptuous (sump´ choo əs) *adj.* magnificent

Literary Analysis
Legend How does the inclusion of the trivial information in this paragraph affect your reading of this legend?

Reading Strategy
Recognizing Author's Attitude What attitude is revealed by this description of the places where the travelers stayed?

✹ ENRICHMENT: History Connection

Castles

At the time the story of King Arthur takes place, kings lived in *castles*, fortified structures that housed the king and his advisers, stored food and arms, served as a prison, and protected the local population from attack.

A castle sat on high ground. If the land was flat, an artificial hill, or *motte*, was built. It was ringed by a *moat*, a water-filled ditch, crossed by a *drawbridge* that could be raised from inside the castle. The high stone walls were up to thirty feet thick, with platforms from which defenders could fight off attackers. Inside the wall was the courtyard, or *bailey*. Within the bailey stood a tall tower known as a *keep*, or *donjon*—the strongest point.

Attackers might attempt a siege and starve a castle's occupants into surrender. They could try to tunnel under the walls or knock the heavy wooden doors down with a battering ram. A stone castle was nearly invulnerable to attack, however, until the appearance of guns during the 1400s.

London was full to the brim. If Sir Ector had not been lucky enough to own a little land in Pie Street, on which there stood a respectable inn, they would have been hard put to it to find a lodging. But he did own it, and as a matter of fact drew most of his dividends from that source, so they were able to get three beds between the five of them. They thought themselves fortunate.

On the first day of the tournament, Sir Kay managed to get them on the way to the lists at least an hour before the jousts could possibly begin. He had lain awake all night, imagining how he was going to beat the best barons in England, and he had not been able to eat his breakfast. Now he rode at the front of the cavalcade, with pale cheeks, and Wart wished there was something he could do to calm him down.

For country people, who only knew the dismantled tilting ground[11] of Sir Ector's castle, the scene which met their eyes was ravishing. It was a huge green pit in the earth, about as big as the arena of a football match. It lay ten feet lower than the surrounding country, with sloping banks, and the snow had been swept off it. It had been kept warm with straw, which had been cleared off that morning, and now the closeworn grass sparkled green in the white landscape. Round the arena there was a world of color so dazzling and moving and twinkling as to make one blink one's eyes. The wooden grandstands were painted in scarlet and white. The silk pavilions of famous people, pitched on every side, were azure and green and saffron and checkered. The pennons and pennoncells which floated everywhere in the sharp wind were flapping with every color of the rainbow, as they strained and slapped at their flagpoles, and the barrier down the middle of the arena itself was done in chessboard squares of black and white. Most of the combatants and their friends had not yet arrived, but one could see from those few who had come how the very people would turn the scene into a bank of flowers, and how the armor would flash, and the scalloped sleeves of the heralds jig in the wind, as they raised their brazen trumpets to their lips to shake the fleecy clouds of winter with joyances[12] and fanfares.

"Good heavens!" cried Sir Kay. "I have left my sword at home."

"Can't joust without a sword," said Sir Grummore. "Quite irregular."

"Better go and fetch it," said Sir Ector. "You have time."

"My squire will do," said Sir Kay. "What an awful mistake to make! Here, squire, ride hard back to the inn and fetch my sword. You shall have a shilling[13] if you fetch it in time."

11. **tilting ground** ground on which a joust takes place.
12. **joyances** (joi′ əns iz) *n.* old word for *rejoicing*.
13. **shilling** (shil′ iŋ) *n.* British silver coin.

Literature in context — History Connection

Tournaments

The first tournaments were held in France in the 1100s. They were like war games, in which groups of knights would split up into two sides and fight each other. Unfortunately, many of the knights got hurt in these battles. In the 1200s, the real battles were replaced with mock ones call *jousts*. In a joust, two horsemen would charge at each other with blunt weapons and each would try to knock the other from his horse. Jousting tournaments were social gatherings attended by ladies and common people as well as by knights.

43 ✓ Reading Check

How does Kay feel on the morning of his first tournament?

Arthur Becomes King of Britain ◆ 1037

41 Reading Strategy

Recognizing Author's Attitude

- Read aloud the bracketed passage. Ask students whether they are surprised that the travelers had to stay in such primitive conditions.
  Answer: Students may say that they are surprised that royalty had to stay in places that were so primitive, unclean, and uncomfortable.

- Then, ask the Reading Strategy question on p. 1036: What attitude is revealed by this description of the places where the travelers stayed?
  Answer: An author may show her or his attitude toward a subject through contrast. Here, there is a huge contrast between images commonly associated with a group of nobles on a journey, such as luxurious housing and fine food, and the barren, scruffy, even squalid images the author presents. The contrast makes it clear that the author is making fun of the crude conditions that he sees as common in the provinces of Britain of that time.

42 Background

Tournaments

Tournaments were held in outlying areas of the kingdom, just as in London. In a poor and remote area such as King Pellinore's realm, however, there would not have been a permanent site for tournaments. An area would be cleared and the necessary facilities set up on a temporary basis.

43 ✓ Reading Check

Answer: Sir Kay feels nervous on the morning of the tournament.

CUSTOMIZE INSTRUCTION FOR UNIVERSAL ACCESS

For Less Proficient Readers	For Gifted/Talented Students	For Advanced Readers
Encourage students to empathize with Wart and the others in the group by comparing their own impressions on first seeing a very large city or a dazzling setting, such as a large amusement park, with those of the characters in the story. Have students write recollections of their impressions.	Have students create a mixed-media mural showing what the tournament grounds looked like. Encourage them to follow the description in the story while adding their own details. Encourage them to display their finished product in the classroom or hallway of the school.	Based on what they already know of the legend of King Arthur, have students begin at the point when Sir Kay sends Wart to fetch his sword and write their predictions of what will happen after Wart sets off to accomplish this errand.

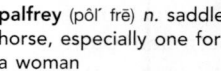

44 Literary Analysis

Legend and Dynamic Character

- Ask students to summarize the Wart's personality so far in the story.
  Possible response: The Wart is pleasant, eager to please, and obedient.

- Have a volunteer read aloud the bracketed passage. Ask students why the Wart is having to ponder ways to get a sword for Kay.
  Answer: The inn where Kay left his sword is closed tight.

- Then, ask the Literary Analysis question on p. 1038: What new aspects of the Wart's character are revealed as he attempts to find a sword for Sir Kay?
  Possible response: The Wart is showing a resourcefulness, determination, and spunk that he hasn't revealed before.

45 Background

Word Meaning

Pad in this context is a derogatory word for a horse that is old, infirm, or otherwise unimpressive.

46 Background

Culture

Much of the pleasure to be derived from earlier parts of *The Sword in the Stone* (1938) comes from the broad humor with which T. H. White satirizes twentieth-century English manners and mores by depicting the Middle Ages as a sort of bogus version of his own period. White was also reacting to the solemnity with which the Victorians regarded the Middle Ages.

The Wart went as pale as Sir Kay was, and looked as if he were going to strike him. Then he said, "It shall be done, master," and turned his ambling <u>palfrey</u> against the stream of newcomers. He began to push his way toward their hostelry[14] as best he might.

"To offer me money!" cried the Wart to himself. "To look down at this beastly little donkey-affair off his great charger and to call me Squire! Oh, Merlyn, give me patience with the brute, and stop me from throwing his filthy shilling in his face."

When he got to the inn it was closed. Everybody had thronged to see the famous tournament, and the entire household had followed after the mob. Those were lawless days and it was not safe to leave your house—or even to go to sleep in it—unless you were certain that it was impregnable.[15] The wooden shutters bolted over the downstairs windows were two inches thick, and the doors were double-barred.

"Now what do I do," asked the Wart, "to earn my shilling?"

He looked ruefully at the blind little inn, and began to laugh.

"Poor Kay," he said. "All that shilling stuff was only because he was scared and miserable, and now he has good cause to be. Well, he shall have a sword of some sort if I have to break into the Tower of London.

"How does one get hold of a sword?" he continued. "Where can I steal one? Could I waylay some knight even if I am mounted on an ambling pad, and take his weapons by force? There must be some swordsmith or armorer in a great town like this, whose shop would be still open."

He turned his mount and cantered off along the street. There was a quiet church-yard at the end of it, with a kind of square in front of the church door. In the middle of the square there was a heavy stone with an anvil on it, and a fine new sword was stuck through the anvil.

"Well," said the Wart, "I suppose it is some sort of war memorial, but it will have to do. I am sure nobody would grudge Kay a war memorial, if they knew his desperate straits"

He tied his reins round a post of the lych gate,[16] strode up the gravel path, and took hold of the sword.

"Come, sword," he said. "I must cry your mercy and take you for a better cause.

"This is extraordinary," said the Wart. "I feel strange when I have hold of this sword, and I notice everything much more clearly. Look at the beautiful gargoyles[17] of the church, and of the monastery which it belongs to. See how splendidly all the famous banners in the aisle are waving. How nobly that yew[18] holds up the red flakes of its timbers to worship God. How clean the snow is. I can smell something like sweet briar—and is it music that I hear?"

---

14. **hostelry** (häs′ təl rē) *n.* inn.
15. **impregnable** (im preg′ nə bəl) *adj.* not capable of being entered by force.
16. **lych** (lich) **gate** roofed gate at the entrance to a churchyard.
17. **gargoyles** (gar′ goilz) *n.* grotesquely carved animals or fantastic creatures on a building.
18. **yew** (yōō) *n.* type of evergreen tree with red cones.

palfrey (pôl′ frē) *n.* saddle horse, especially one for a woman

Literary Analysis

Legend and Dynamic Character What new aspects of the Wart's character are revealed as he attempts to find a sword for Sir Kay?

✹ ENRICHMENT: History Connection

Tournaments

A tournament such as the one to which Arthur and companions go in this story is quite different from the tournaments staged by knights in the 1100s. In these events a large number of knights would form two "armies" that would fight each other, often for several days and over large expanses of territory. Often, large sums of money were wagered on the outcome. Kings grew to dislike tournaments; when a number of armed knights gathered together, there was always a possibility of rebellion. Also, such mock battles usually resulted in the destruc- tion of property, and people might be injured or even killed.

By the 1200s, milder tournaments evolved, like the one in which Sir Kay hoped to compete. Knights would *joust*, or fight with blunted weapons. They also engaged in *tilting*. In this competition, two mounted knights with lances would charge each other in narrow lanes, or *lists*, on either side of a wooden barrier and attempt to knock each other from their horses.

It was music, whether of pan-pipes or of recorders, and the light in the churchyard was so clear, without being dazzling, that one could have picked a pin out twenty yards away.

"There is something in this place," said the Wart. "There are people. Oh, people, what do you want?"

Nobody answered him, but the music was loud and the light beautiful.

"People," cried the Wart, "I must take this sword. It is not for me, but for Kay. I will bring it back."

There was still no answer, and Wart turned back to the anvil. He saw the golden letters, which he did not read, and the jewels on the pommel, flashing in the lovely light.

"Come, sword," said the Wart.

He took hold of the handles with both hands, and strained against the stone. There was a melodious consort[19] on the recorders, but nothing moved.

The Wart let go of the handles, when they were beginning to bite into the palms of his hands, and stepped back, seeing stars.

"It is well fixed," he said.

He took hold of it again and pulled with all his might. The music played more strongly, and the light all about the churchyard glowed like amethysts; but the sword still stuck.

"Oh, Merlyn," cried the Wart, "help me to get this weapon."

There was a kind of rushing noise, and a long chord played along with it. All round the churchyard there were hundreds of old friends. They rose over the church wall all together, like the Punch-and-Judy[20] ghosts of remembered days, and there were badgers and nightingales and vulgar crows and hares and wild geese and falcons and fishes and dogs and dainty unicorns and solitary wasps and hedgehogs and griffins and the thousand other animals he had met. They loomed round the church wall, the lovers and helpers of the Wart, and they all spoke solemnly in turn. Some of them had come from the banners in the church, where they were painted in heraldry, some from the waters and the sky and the fields about—but all, down to the smallest shrew mouse, had come to help on account of love. Wart felt his power grow.

"Put your back into it," said a luce (or pike) off one of the heraldic banners, "as you once did when I was going to snap you up. Remember that power springs from the nape of the neck."

"What about those forearms," asked a badger gravely, "that are held together by a chest? Come along, my dear embryo,[21] and find your tool."

A merlin sitting at the top of the yew tree cried out, "Now then, Captain Wart, what is the first law of the foot? I thought I once heard something about never letting go."

---

19. **consort** (kän´ sôrt) *n.* harmony of sounds.
20. **Punch-and-Judy** puppets of the quarrelsome Punch and his wife, Judy, who constantly fight in a comical way.
21. **embryo** (em´ brē ō) *n.* anything in an early stage of development.

Reading Strategy
Recognizing Author's Attitude Do you think the writer treats this significant moment in the legend seriously? Explain.

Literary Analysis
Legend What does the inclusion of talking animals add to the Arthurian legend?

 Reading Check
What happens to the Wart when he takes hold of the sword?

Arthur Becomes King of Britain ◆ 1039

CUSTOMIZE INSTRUCTION FOR UNIVERSAL ACCESS

For Less Proficient Readers	For English Learners	For Advanced Readers
Ask students whether they would like to wake up some morning and discover that it is their destiny to be a leader and to change people's lives, or whether they would prefer to lead a quieter and more anonymous life. Have them record their thoughts in a journal entry.	Have students discuss how they feel about the Wart. Which of his qualities do they like and dislike? Do they find that their feelings about the Wart are changing as they get deeper into the story? Encourage students to write a paragraph describing their feelings.	Some scholars believe that Arthurian legend developed out of the stories of Celtic mythology. Have students research the history of the legend of King Arthur, including how it spread over the European continent. Encourage them to give examples of the Celtic tales that were absorbed into the legend.

---

47 Reading Strategy
Recognizing Author's Attitude

- Ask students to comment on the language of the passage. Is it simple or complicated?
  Answer: Except for the phrase "melodious consort," it is simple.

- Ask students what they think the author might have intended by saying that a "melodious consort" accompanied a failed attempt to get the sword from the stone.
  Possible response: The author was being humorous.

- Then, ask the Reading Strategy question on p. 1039: Do you think the author treats this significant moment in the legend seriously?
  Answer: The author does not treat this moment entirely seriously. Combining serious music with a failed attempt results in a comic effect.

48 Background
Literature

Students should know that in an earlier section of *The Once and Future King*, Merlyn used his powers to temporarily transform young Arthur into various animals, including a fish and a bird, so that he could learn their wisdom and communicate with them. These animals reappear here and repeat advice that they gave Arthur previously.

49 Literary Analysis
Legend

- Have students name some of the animals who have come to give the Wart advice on how to get the sword out of the stone.
  Answer: Among others, a luce, badgers, nightingales, crows, dogs, and fish have come to give Arthur advice.

- Ask the Literary Analysis question on p. 1039: What does the inclusion of talking animals add to the Arthurian legend?
  Possible response: The presence of the animals adds to the mystery and magic of the occasion and dramatizes Arthur's special powers.

50 Reading Check

Answer: The Wart feels strange and notices everything much more clearly.

This illustration shows the Round Table, twelve knights in various positions and rooms near the table, and the Holy Grail, the cup believed to have been used by Jesus at the Last Supper. Use these questions for discussion:

1. Would an illustration done in this style be appropriate for the story about King Arthur that you are now reading? Explain your answer.

   Possible response: The style of this illustration seems much too serious and formal for this story. "Arthur Becomes King of Britain" requires a more humorous and whimsical style.

2. Why do you think the attitudes of some of the people in the illustration are similar to those of people in the illustration on p. 1035?

   Possible response: Like the people witnessing Galahad's feat, the ones in this illustration are witnessing a marvel.

52 ▶Critical Viewing

Answer: By representing the Round Table and its knights and the Holy Grail in such detail, art such as this helps the viewer to create a mental image of important scenes from legends, thus preserving them in the viewer's mind.

The Round Table and the Holy Grail, Musée Condé, Chantilly, France

"Don't work like a stalling woodpecker," urged a tawny owl affectionately. "Keep up a steady effort, my duck, and you will have it yet."

A white-front said. "Now, Wart, if you were once able to fly the great North Sea, surely you can coordinate a few little wing-muscles here and there? Fold your powers together, with the spirit of your mind, and it will come out like butter. Come along, Homo sapiens,[22] for all we humble friends of yours are waiting here to cheer."

The Wart walked up to the great sword for the third time. He put out his right hand softly and drew it out as gently as from a scabbard.

There was a lot of cheering, a noise like a hurdy-gurdy[23] which went on and on. In the middle of this noise, after a long time, he saw Kay and gave him the sword. The people at the tournament were making a frightful row.

"But this is not my sword," said Sir Kay.

"It was the only one I could get," said the Wart. "The inn was locked."

"It is a nice-looking sword. Where did you get it?"

___

22. **Homo sapiens** (hō´ mō sā´ pē enz´) human being.
23. **hurdy-gurdy** (hur´ dē gur´ dē) *n.* musical instrument, like a barrel organ, played by turning a crank.

52 ▲ Critical Viewing
Explain how art, like the painting shown here, can preserve a legend visually. **[Infer]**

✳ ENRICHMENT: History Connection

Battle Protection

During the Middle Ages, types of armor changed as different kinds of warfare developed. In the twelfth century, the time of King Arthur, a knight's protection was chain mail, or tiny metal rings, linked together. A coat of chain mail deflected arrows, swords, and lances. Metal helmets protected the head and face.

Chain mail, however, was vulnerable to thirteenth-century weapons like longbows, maces, crossbows, and battle-axes. As a result, plate armor was introduced. It

was designed to cover the entire body and included armored *gauntlets*, or gloves, and *sollerets*, or shoes. Although full-plate armor was secure, it had disadvantages. It severely limited movement, and it was very expensive. It was also heavy; a knight in full armor had to be hoisted onto his horse by a machine.

The invention of guns made plate armor obsolete. By the sixteenth century, only breastplates and helmets were worn.

"I found it stuck in a stone, outside a church."

Sir Kay had been watching the tilting nervously, waiting for his turn. He had not paid much attention to his squire.

"That is a funny place to find one," he said.

"Yes, it was stuck through an anvil."

"What?" cried Sir Kay, suddenly rounding upon him. "Did you just say this sword was stuck in a stone?"

"It was," said the Wart. "It was a sort of war memorial."

Sir Kay stared at him for several seconds in amazement, opened his mouth, shut it again, licked his lips, then turned his back and plunged through the crowd. He was looking for Sir Ector, and the Wart followed after him.

"Father," cried Sir Kay, "come here a moment."

"Yes, my boy," said Sir Ector. "Splendid falls these professional chaps do manage. Why, what's the matter, Kay? You look as white as a sheet."

"Do you remember that sword which the King of England would pull out?"

"Yes."

"Well, here it is. I have it. It is in my hand. I pulled it out."

Sir Ector did not say anything silly. He looked at Kay and he looked at the Wart. Then he stared at Kay again, long and lovingly, and said, "We will go back to the church."

"Now then, Kay," he said, when they were at the church door. He looked at his firstborn kindly, but straight between the eyes. "Here is the stone, and you have the sword. It will make you the King of England. You are my son that I am proud of, and always will be, whatever you do. Will you promise me that you took it out by your own might?"

Kay looked at his father. He also looked at the Wart and at the sword.

Then he handed the sword to the Wart quite quietly.

He said, "I am a liar. Wart pulled it out."

As far as the Wart was concerned, there was a time after this in which Sir Ector kept telling him to put the sword back into the stone—which he did—and in which Sir Ector and Kay then vainly tried to take it out. The Wart took it out for them, and stuck it back again once or twice. After this, there was another time which was more painful.

He saw that his dear guardian was looking quite old and powerless, and that he was kneeling down with difficulty on a gouty[24] knee.

"Sir," said Sir Ector, without looking up, although he was speaking to his own boy.

"Please do not do this, father," said the Wart, kneeling down also. "Let me help you up, Sir Ector, because you are making me unhappy."

"Nay, nay, my lord," said Sir Ector, with some very feeble old tears.

---

24. **gouty** (gout′ ē) *adj.* having gout, a disease causing swelling and severe pain in the joints.

Reading Strategy
Recognizing Author's Attitude How do Sir Ector's comments to Sir Kay suit the tone of this selection?

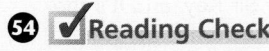 **Reading Check**
What does Sir Kay tell his father about the sword?

Arthur Becomes King of Britain ◆ 1041

53 Reading Strategy
Recognizing Author's Attitude

• Ask two volunteers to take the parts of Sir Kay and Sir Ector and read the bracketed passage aloud. Then, ask students why Sir Ector asks his son to promise him that Sir Kay removed the sword from the stone by his own might. Answer: He wants to be sure that it is Sir Kay who is destined to be King of England.

• Then, ask the Reading Strategy question on p. 1041: How do Sir Ector's comments to Sir Kay suit the tone of this selection? Possible response: The rectitude and honor with which Sir Ector approaches the issue suit the high moral tone of the selection. Also, the loving, patient, and kindly manner in which he resolves the matter with his son is in keeping with the loving tone of White's book.

54 ✔ Reading Check
Answer: Sir Kay tells his father that he found the sword stuck in a stone outside a church.

CUSTOMIZE INSTRUCTION FOR UNIVERSAL ACCESS

For Gifted/Talented Students	For Advanced Students
Have students work with several classmates to act out "Arthur Becomes King of Britain." Ask them to first adapt White's story for use as a script and then plan out how the action will take place. For example, how will they create a sense of motion on the journey to London? Then, have them rehearse and perform their play.	Ask students to prepare a report on the realities of life for common people in England in the eleventh or twelfth century. What kinds of houses did they live in? What did they eat and how did they acquire it? What kinds of occupations did they have? What kind of education was available? How were people affected by government? Ask students to present their findings to the class.

Review and Assess

1. Students might say young Arthur (or Wart) because he is sensible and honorable and, as revealed by the final scene, very human.

2. **(a)** He brings the news that the king is dead. **(b)** Sir Grummore reacts with great solemnity; the nurse bursts into tears; Sir Kay and Sir Ector see to it that the formality of half-masting the banners is observed.

3. **(a)** Whoever can pull the sword out of the anvil and stone will become king. **(b)** It adds to the mystery of the legend and ensures that the person who becomes king will be very special indeed.

4. **(a)** The Wart is trying to find a sword for Sir Kay, and it's the only one he comes across. **(b)** Magical forces of nature seem to unite to help Wart draw the sword from the stone; talking animals coax him to success.

5. **(a)** Wart is ambivalent about becoming king. He seems fearful and does not want to rise above his friends. **(b)** Wart is kind, loyal, sensible, and honorable.

6. **(a)** Possible answers: The dialogue is crude and unbecoming of knights; he uses malapropisms such as "next of skin"; he puts the knights in undignified situations, such as primitive lodgings in London. **(b)** Students may say that White's humor is successful because he has such obvious affection for his characters.

"I was never your father nor of your blood, but I wote[25] well ye are of an higher blood than I wend[26] ye were."

"Plenty of people have told me you are not my father," said the Wart, "but it does not matter a bit."

"Sir," said Sir Ector humbly, "will ye be my good and gracious lord when ye are King?"

"Don't!" said the Wart.

"Sir," said Sir Ector, "I will ask no more of you but that you will make my son, your foster-brother, Sir Kay, seneschal[27] of all your lands."

Kay was kneeling down too, and it was more than the Wart could bear.

"Oh, do stop," he cried. "Of course he can be seneschal, if I have got to be this King, and, oh, father, don't kneel down like that, because it breaks my heart. Please get up, Sir Ector, and don't make everything so horrible. Oh, dear, oh, dear, I wish I had never seen that filthy sword at all."

And the Wart also burst into tears.

---

25. **wote** (wōt) *v.* old word meaning "know."
26. **wend** (wend) *v.* here, old word meaning "thought."
27. **seneschal** (sen´ ə shəl) *n.* steward in the house of a medieval noble.

Review and Assess

Thinking About the Selection

1. **Respond:** Who is your favorite character in this retelling? Why?

2. **(a) Recall:** What significant news does King Pellinore bring? **(b) Compare and Contrast:** How do the different characters respond to the news?

3. **(a) Recall:** How is the new king of England to be chosen? **(b) Interpret:** What does this method of selecting the king add to the story?

4. **(a) Recall:** Why does the Wart attempt to pull the sword from the stone? **(b) Interpret:** In what ways is the Wart's accomplishment of drawing the sword from the stone a moment of magic and mystery?

5. **(a) Draw Conclusions:** How does the Wart feel about becoming king? Why? **(b) Evaluate:** What kingly qualities does the Wart reveal even as a boy?

6. **(a) Interpret:** What examples can you find to show that T. H. White pokes fun at the Arthurian legend? **(b) Evaluate:** Do you think his humor is successful? Explain.

T. H. White
(1906–1964)

At the age of thirty, Terence Hanbury White resigned his teaching position to devote himself to his many interests, which included flying, deep-sea diving, falconry, knitting, jumping horses, and, of course, writing. His most famous work, from which "Arthur Becomes King of Britain" is taken, is the four-part novel *The Once and Future King* (1958), a comic retelling of the Arthurian legends. White's version of the legends has inspired several movies as well as the musical *Camelot*.

ASSESSMENT PRACTICE: Writing Skills

| Style | (For more practice, see Test Preparation Workbook, p. 62.) |

Many tests ask students to demonstrate their knowledge of writing skills. Style questions focus on appropriate and effective use of language. Give students this sample test question.

> If you should never see my face again,
>
> Pray for my soul. More things are wrought by prayer
>
> Than this world dreams of. Wherefore, let thy voice
>
> Rise like a fountain for me night and day.

Tennyson's tone in this speech by Arthur to Bedivere is best described as—

A sentimental   **C** stern

B pessimistic   **D** exalted

Guide students to see that *D* is the correct answer. The dying Arthur is not speaking sternly, *C*, but with exaltation. Arthur does not face death with pessimism, *B*. There is nothing sentimental, *A*, about this particular expression of belief.

Review and Assess

Literary Analysis

Legend

1. (a) What historical facts does each writer include in his retelling of the Arthurian **legends**? (b) What parts are probably fictional?
2. What values or qualities in the Arthurian legends make it likely that they will continue to be enjoyed by successive generations?
3. Why do you think the details of a legend, such as how Arthur acquires Excalibur, may differ from version to version?

Comparing Literary Works

4. What aspects of Arthur's **dynamic character** does Tennyson stress in "Morte d'Arthur"?
5. What aspects of Arthur/Wart's character does White highlight in "Arthur Becomes King of Britain"?
6. Use a Venn diagram like the one here to identify the qualities that the two Arthurs have in common and those traits that are different.

Young Arthur   Old Arthur

Humble   Honorable   Regal

Reading Strategy

Recognizing Author's Attitude

7. Cite three passages in "Morte d'Arthur" that show Tennyson's **attitude** toward King Arthur.
8. Find three examples of words, phrases, and situations in the selection by T. H. White that show his light, humorous attitude toward the Arthurian legends.
9. Compare the ways in which the two writers use language and subject matter to reflect their attitudes.

Extend Understanding

10. **Cultural Connection:** To become king, Arthur has to carry out a task and demonstrate his kingly qualities. What task or test might we develop in our own culture to select a new leader?

Quick Review

A **legend** is a popular story handed down for generations. It blends historical facts with fiction.

A **dynamic character** changes or grows during the course of a literary work.

The **author's attitude** is the way he or she feels about the subject in the work.

 Take It to the Net
www.phschool.com
Take the interactive self-test online to check your understanding of these selections.

Morte d'Arthur / Arthur Becomes King of Britain ◆ 1043

Answers for p. 1043

Review and Assess

1. **(a)** Each writer bases his retelling on a historical King Arthur who drove the Saxons out of England. **(b)** The part of the tale about pulling the sword from the stone is fictional.

2. Qualities such as courage and honesty are paid tribute in the tales; future generations will also enjoy seeing these virtues triumph.

3. Legends are passed down through the generations along different channels. Each story-teller adds or changes something that he or she feels enhances the tale.

4. Tennyson stresses Arthur's acceptance that the old order changes and that he must make way for the new.

5. White highlights Wart's faithfulness, perseverance, and humility.

6. Young Arthur: innocent, playful; Old Arthur: tired, aristocratic; Common: determined, loyal

7. Tennyson's respectful attitude toward Arthur is shown in lines 50 and 51; his admiration for Bedivere shows in lines 56–59; his attitude of awe and reverence shows in lines 350–354.

8. Possible responses: Examples include "Compose yourself, Nanny"; all of Sir Grummore's dialogue; lines such as "Can't joust without a sword. Quite irregular."

9. Tennyson's language is formal, respectful, and serious; his subject, the death of King Arthur, is also serious. White's language is playful and humorous as well as affectionate; his subject, Arthur as a boy or young man, is full of vitality.

10. Possible responses: Tasks might include settling a difficult dispute, such as between fractious nations; or coming up with a good, workable idea for solving a domestic problem, such as poverty, crime, or pollution.

1043

❶ Vocabulary Development

Word Analysis

1. Feeling of envy or jealousy
2. Loving adventure or providing adventure
3. Full of lies

Spelling Strategy

1. valleys
2. allies
3. enemies

Fluency: Clarify Word Meaning

1. lamentation
2. sumptuous
3. palfrey
4. stickler
5. swarthy

❷ Grammar

1. "Watch out!" cried the little man. "Here comes the lance!"
2. A knight asked, "Where is the ring?"
3. "Go to the far side of that oak," said the little man, "and there you will see the target range."
4. "Thank you, sir," replied the knight.
5. "It was," said the Wart, "a sort of war memorial."

Writing Application

Possible Answer: "Now look, Kay," said Sir Pellinore, "don't you think you're stretching the truth a bit?"

"Oh, Father," sighed Kay. "How I wish it had been I instead of the Wart!"

Integrate Language Skills

❶ Vocabulary Development Lesson

Word Analysis: Latin Suffix -ous

The Latin suffix -ous means "having" or "full of." Because sumptu in Latin means "expense," sumptuous means "expensive" or "magnificent." Use your knowledge of the suffix -ous to define the following words:

    1. envious   2. adventurous   3. slanderous

Spelling Strategy

To pluralize a word that ends in y preceded by a vowel, add -s: palfrey becomes palfreys. To pluralize a word that ends in y preceded by a consonant, change the y to i and add -es: country becomes countries. Write the plural of each word below in your notebook.

    1. valley   2. ally   3. enemy

Fluency: Clarify Word Meanings

In your notebook, write the word from the vocabulary list on page 1019 that best fits each statement.

1. Sounds of this may be heard at funerals.
2. Things like this are usually expensive as well.
3. To avoid being thrown, you should hold on when you are riding one of these.
4. A fastidious person is probably one of these, too.
5. Spending a lot of time in the sun could make you look like this.

❷ Grammar Lesson

Quotation Marks With Other Punctuation

When you are writing dialogue, use **quotation marks** to set off the exact words of a speaker. Set off words that are not part of the quotation with commas or end marks.

Commas and periods always go inside the final quotation mark. However, question marks and exclamation marks go inside the final quotation mark only if the end mark is part of the quotation. Look at these examples:

> Sir Ector said, "Come now, Merlyn, what's all this about?"
>
> "Well, I am glad we are going," said the Wart, "for Merlyn is leaving us too."
>
> "We shall all meet again," said Merlyn.

Practice Rewrite the following sentences to correct any errors in punctuation.

1. "Watch out"! cried the little man. "Here comes the lance."
2. A knight asked Where is the ring?
3. "Go to the far side of that oak" said the little man "and there you will see the target range."
4. Thank you, sir replied the knight.
5. "It was said the Wart a sort of memorial".

Writing Application Write an exchange of dialogue between two characters in these selections using quotation marks correctly with other punctuation.

WG *Prentice Hall Writing and Grammar Connection: Chapter 28, Section 4*

TEACHING RESOURCES

The following resources can be used to enrich or extend the instruction for pp. 1044–1045.

Vocabulary

📖 **Selection Support:** Build Vocabulary, p. 245

📖 **Vocabulary and Spelling Practice Book**
(Use this booklet for skills enrichment.)

Grammar

📖 **Selection Support:** Build Grammar Skills, p. 246

WG **Writing and Grammar,** Platinum Level, p. 686

🖥 **Daily Language Practice Transparencies** ▪

Writing

WG **Writing and Grammar,** Platinum Level, p. 324 ▪

💿 **Writing and Grammar iText CD-ROM**

🖥 **BLOCK SCHEDULING:** Resources marked with this symbol provide varied instruction during 90-minute blocks.

Writing Lesson

Letter of Recommendation

In the grand land of Camelot, those worthy of honor were knighted and given the title "sir." Decide which author—Alfred, Lord Tennyson or T. H. White—deserves this honor. In a letter to Arthur, make your case for one of these men.

Prewriting   Review the selection of your choice as well as the author's biography to find evidence that the writer deserves knighthood. List several examples to support your position.

Drafting   Open with a clear statement of your purpose, identifying your recommendation for knighthood and your reasons. Then, present your details in your body paragraphs.

Revising   Reread your letter, making sure that every detail supports your purpose in a clear and consistent way. Revise your letter for clarity.

> **Where others may have given up, he demonstrated discipline.**

Model: Revising for Clarity

Alfred, Lord Tennyson studied at Cambridge University, but financial troubles forced him to leave the school. He eventually taught himself at home.

> The additional text identifies a quality—self-discipline—that concisely expresses the writer's main point.

 Prentice Hall Writing and Grammar Connection: Chapter 15, Section 1

Extension Activities

Listening and Speaking The musical *Camelot* is based on T. H. White's *The Once and Future King.* With several classmates, view the film or listen to the soundtrack of *Camelot.* Then, hold a **panel discussion.**

- Assign each panel member a different scene or song.
- Have each panelist explain how that scene or song depicts the Arthurian legend.

Follow up by presenting your findings to the class. **[Group Activity]**

Research and Technology The Arthurian legend is set in medieval England, where the rules of feudalism dictated a person's place in society. Feudalism was also practiced in other European countries and in Japan. Using library and Internet resources, make a list of information about feudalism in different countries. Then, prepare a **chart** comparing and contrasting how various countries practiced feudalism.

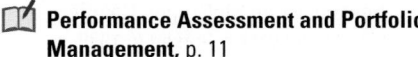 **Take It to the Net**   www.phschool.com

Go online for an additional research activity using the Internet.

Morte d'Arthur / Arthur Becomes King of Britain ◆ 1045

ASSESSMENT RESOURCES

The following resources can be used to assess students' knowledge and skills.

Selection Assessment

📖 **Formal Assessment,** pp. 220–222

📖 **Open Book Test,** pp. 184–186

📼 **Got It! Assessment Videotapes,** Tape 5

💿 **Test Bank Software**

 Take It to the Net

   Visit www.phschool.com for self-tests and additional questions on the selections.

Writing Rubric

📖 **Performance Assessment and Portfolio Management,** p. 11

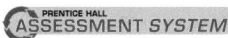 PRENTICE HALL **ASSESSMENT SYSTEM**

📖 **Workbook**   📖 **Transparencies**

📖 **Skill Book**   💿 **CD-ROM**

Lesson Objectives

1. To understand the connection between literary epics and the *Star Wars* trilogy

2. To understand how epic elements can be communicated in different forms

3. To understand how traditional values and beliefs are conveyed through contemporary mediums

Connections

Epics and legends tell of the struggle between good and evil. Like "Rama's Initiation," "from *Sundiata*: An Epic of Old Mali," and other epics, the films that comprise the *Star Wars* trilogy tell the story of a young hero battling to overcome obstacles and fighting evil. Have students review the selections, and ask them how Luke Skywalker and the Jedi knights compare to the heroes in these narratives.

Star Wars: An Epic for Today

• Remind students that *Star Wars* is a modern epic. Tell students that in this selection, the origins of the names of the characters in the *Star Wars* epic are explained.

• Then, have students explain some of the characteristic qualities of epic composition.
Answer: Some features are a hero who has many adventures and who faces great obstacles and terrible adversity; a hero who has special powers and gifts; and a reflection of the culture from which the epic comes.

• Ask students what the primary difference is between literary epics and film epics, and if this difference matters.
Possible response: Most students will point out that film consists of images and recorded sounds, recreating events with less assistance from the audience's imagination than a work of words. Students may say that the difference matters little as film and other forms of visual media function like literature as a form of entertainment and disseminator of cultural values and beliefs in our culture.

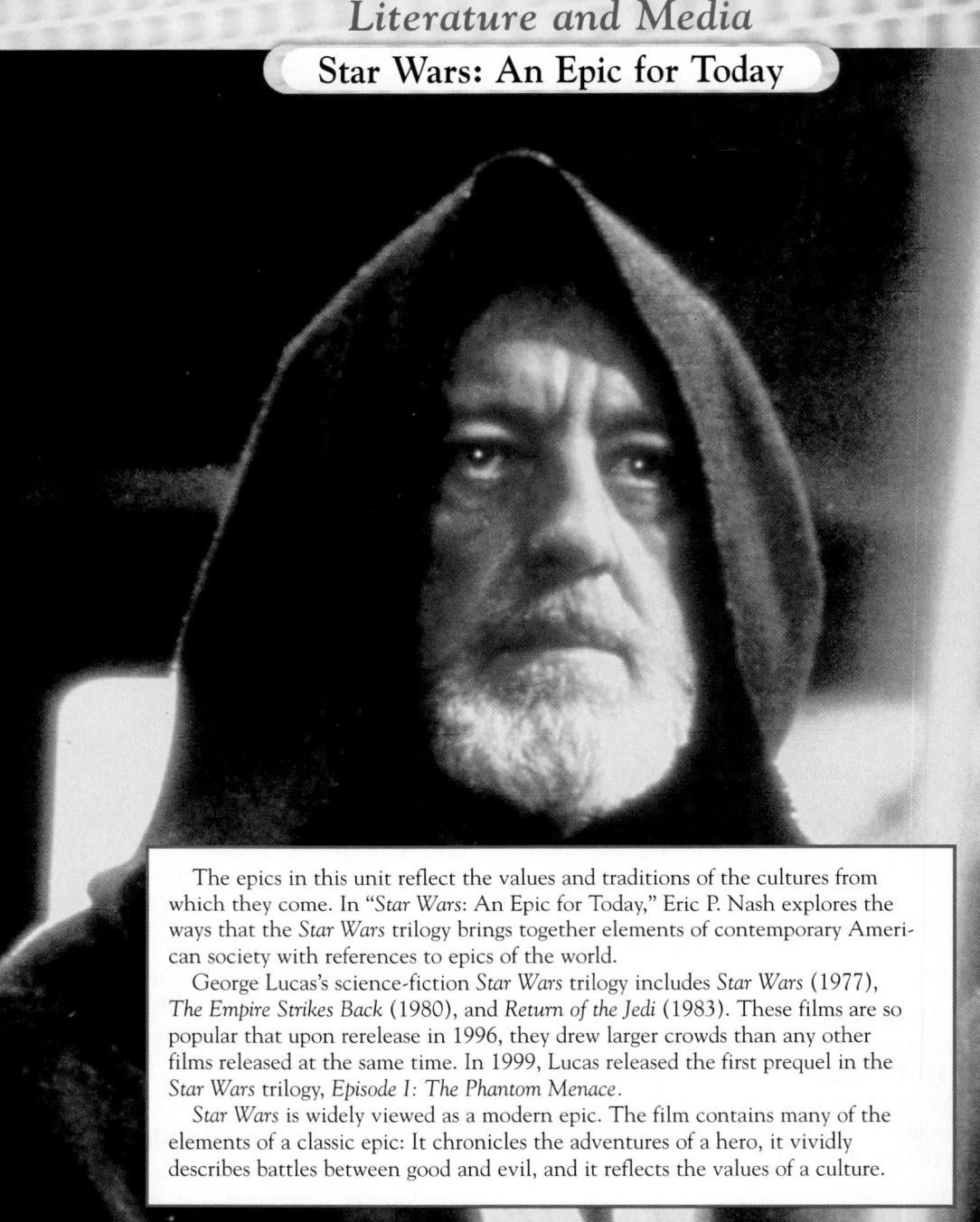

CONNECTIONS
Literature and Media
Star Wars: An Epic for Today

The epics in this unit reflect the values and traditions of the cultures from which they come. In "*Star Wars:* An Epic for Today," Eric P. Nash explores the ways that the *Star Wars* trilogy brings together elements of contemporary American society with references to epics of the world.

George Lucas's science-fiction *Star Wars* trilogy includes *Star Wars* (1977), *The Empire Strikes Back* (1980), and *Return of the Jedi* (1983). These films are so popular that upon rerelease in 1996, they drew larger crowds than any other films released at the same time. In 1999, Lucas released the first prequel in the *Star Wars* trilogy, *Episode I: The Phantom Menace*.

Star Wars is widely viewed as a modern epic. The film contains many of the elements of a classic epic: It chronicles the adventures of a hero, it vividly describes battles between good and evil, and it reflects the values of a culture.

1046 ◆ *Epics and Legends*

☼ ENRICHMENT: Film Connection

Star Wars Episode I: The Phantom Menace

George Lucas's *Star Wars: The Phantom Menace* (starring Liam Neeson, Ewan McGregor, Natalie Portman, and Jake Lloyd) was released in 1999, a much anticipated prequel to the *Star Wars* trilogy.

Set before the birth of Luke Skywalker, the episode tells the story of unrest that has engulfed the Galactic Republic. Characters include many who appear in the *Star Wars* trilogy, films that are set later in the story.

A young Obi-Wan Kenobi appears in the film. He and a fellow Jedi knight discover a young boy with unusual talent, Anakin Skywalker—a young and impressionable future Jedi warrior, who the viewer may realize, will later cross over to the "dark side" to become Darth Vader.

Thus the episode explains some of the history behind the *Star Wars* trilogy, continuing the epic scope of the story.

Star Wars: An Epic for Today

Eric P. Nash

Twenty years ago, the film maker George Lucas expanded everybody's notion of how fast a movie could really move with the first installment of his "Star Wars" trilogy. A new generation of movie-goers will be introduced to "Star Wars" on Friday, when the film returns to the big screen with a digitally remastered soundtrack, new scenes (including a meeting between Han Solo and the gelatinous Jabba the Hutt) and some visually enhanced effects. Part of what makes the "Star Wars" universe such fun is that the characters seem to emerge from their own complex cultures. Then there is the ear-tickling felicity of the names. It's hard to resist saying Boba Fett, Bounty Hunter, out loud just to try it on the lips. Just where did George Lucas come up with all these weird names?

"Basically, I developed the names for the characters phonetically," Mr. Lucas said. "I obviously wanted to telegraph a bit of the character in the name. The names needed to sound unusual but not spacey. I wanted to stay away from the kind of science fiction names like Zenon and Zorba. They had to sound indigenous and have consistency between their names and their culture."

Much has been made of the director's use of world myths from Joseph Campbell's "Hero With a Thousand Faces," but "Star Wars" is also a synthesis of the treasure trove of American pop culture—everything from comic strips, pulp fiction and films ranging from John Ford's "Searchers" to Victor Fleming's "Wizard of Oz" to Akira Kurosawa's "Hidden Fortress."

"Star Wars" in turn has spawned a galaxy of sub-industries—more than two dozen novels, trading cards, action figures, role-playing games, scores of websites and guides specializing in intergalactic arcana—many of which have been consulted in preparing this interstellar who's who.

Darth Vader: Mr. Lucas went back to the Dutch root for father to arrive at a name that approximates "Dark Father." Vader's original name is Anakin Skywalker. Anakin is a variation on a race of giants in Genesis, and Skywalker is an appellation for Loki, the Norse god of fire and mischief. The inspiration for Vader's face mask was in all likelihood the grille of a '56 Chevy.

◄ **Critical Viewing** What qualities of an epic hero do you see in the man in this picture? **[Analyze]**

---

gelatinous (jə lat′ ən əs) *adj.* resembling gelatin or jelly, especially in appearance and consistency

synthesis (sin′ thə sis) *n.* an integration or a combination of things

✔**Reading Check**

How did George Lucas come up with names for his characters?

CUSTOMIZE INSTRUCTION FOR UNIVERSAL ACCESS

For English Learners	For Gifted/Talented Students	For Advanced Readers
Have these students translate their impressions of the images presented with this piece on *Star Wars,* along with their knowledge of the movies, into verbal descriptions. You may wish to suggest words and phrases with which they can free-associate to come up with descriptions, such as: "glowing saber," and "legendary hero."	Have students review the selections in this unit and consult works on myth and legend to devise names for their own cast of epic characters. They should follow Lucas's example as described in the article, using combinations of names and suggesting references through sounds rather than simply picking up entire names verbatim.	Have these students find out more about some of the references used in this essay, such as J.R.R. Tolkien's *Lord of the Rings,* the John Carter of Mars tales by Edgar Rice Burroughs, and Frank Herbert's *Dune.* Students can present relevant information to the rest of the class to enhance their understanding of the essay.

▶**Critical Viewing**
Possible response: Students might cite the hooded cloak, the serious and thoughtful facial expression, the magical weapon, and the stature of the figure as qualities of an epic hero.

Star Wars: An Epic for Today

- Tell students that characters' names may reflect their personalities and may telegraph their roles in the story. Moreover, they may also reflect the author's or filmmaker's response to his or her cultural context. Have students consider some of the names in Lucas's trilogy.

- Ask students why they think the name Darth Vader is appropriate and what his role is in the epic.
  Possible response: The origin of the name Darth Vader—from the Dutch "Dark Father"—suits Darth Vader, who is a wicked person. He represents the forces of evil that Luke Skywalker must overcome.

- Then, have students explain how the origin of Luke Skywalker's name relates to his role in the epic.
  Possible response: Luke comes from the Greek "leukos," which means light. Skywalker is the name of Loki, the Norse god of fire. Thus Luke Skywalker will be the hero who uses the power of "the Force" (fire) to fight on the side of good (light) against the evil represented by Darth Vader.

- Finally, have a student volunteer read aloud the name explanations for Han Solo and R2-D2. Then, ask students how these two names reflect what George Lucas thinks about contemporary culture.
  Possible response: These names point out that George Lucas is aware of the role of contemporary mediums, such as television and movies, has played in shaping the American cultural psyche; that television and movies play an important role of in creating heroes of contemporary culture.

✔**Reading Check**

Answer: George Lucas chose symbolic names for his characters, some of which refer to characters in myth or scripture.

1047

Background

Film

Influenced by the heroes of epics and legends, George Lucas set a traditional hero tale in a futuristic setting. In the *Star Wars* saga, Lucas traces the adventures of Luke Skywalker. Pitting the young Skywalker against the experienced Darth Vader and a small rebel force against the powerful Empire, this epic space opera stages a grand battle between good and evil.

Like other epic heroes, Skywalker has his weaknesses as well as his strengths. He has to overcome the fears and disadvantages that come from being human as well as a hero. A hero's origin is often marked by unusual circumstances. Skywalker, like King Arthur, is raised by foster parents, ignorant of his true heritage.

Skywalker does not journey alone. In the tradition of other heroes, he has his trusty companions, including Han Solo, Princess Leia, Chewbacca, C-3PO, and R2-D2. Skywalker receives the gift of the Force from his spiritual guide, Obi-Wan Kenobi, whose role parallels that of Merlin in the Arthur legends.

In the trilogy, as often happens in epics, Skywalker is separated from his companions. Alone, he must seek out a spiritual teacher on a long quest. When he returns, he is prepared to confront the forces and temptations that would defeat an ordinary man, surviving a confrontation with Darth Vader, who is both enemy and father.

▶ **Critical Viewing**

Possible response: Students might cite trolls, werewolves, King Kong, or the yeti.

Luke Skywalker: The name of the character played by Mark Hamill derives from the Greek *leukos*, or light, an interesting contrast to Darth Vader. Luke of the Gospels was a gentile who converted to Christianity, an appropriate name for a boy who discovers the power of the Force.

Tatooine is the name of Luke's home planet, derived from the town of Tataouine in Tunisia, the country where the desert scenes in "Star Wars" were filmed. An early draft of the script was called "The Adventures of Luke Starkiller." It's easy to read Luke S. as a stand-in for Lucas.

Princess Leia Organa (Carrie Fisher) has braids that resemble dinner rolls, but her name evokes the lovely Dejah Thoris in the John Carter of Mars tales by Edgar Rice Burroughs, as well as Lady Galadriel of Lothlorien in J.R.R. Tolkien's "Lord of the Rings." The surname Organa reflects the conflict of nature and technology seen in the forest-dwelling heroes pitted against the machines of the Empire, according to Lucas's biographer, Dale Pollock.

The name **Han Solo** (Harrison Ford) capitalizes on the archaic sound of Han, a variation of John, to set us in a mythical world. The name Solo addresses his key character issue. Solo is a lone gun who must learn to trust others and identify with a greater cause. The swashbuckler's name also recalls one of the great pop culture adventurers, Napoleon Solo, "The Man from U.N.C.L.E." Napoleon Solo, by the way, first appeared as a minor hood in the James Bond novel "Goldfinger."

R2-D2 According to Mr. Lucas, the robot who resembles a whistling Hoover vacuum cleaner got his name from a sound editor's

▼ **Critical Viewing**
What other mythical creature does this Wookiee bring to mind? **[Relate]**

shorthand for "Reel Two, Dialogue Two" during the making of his earlier hit, "American Graffiti."

Chewbacca, the towering Wookiee, was a name inspired by Indiana, Mr. Lucas's rambunctious malamute. (The dog also lent his name to the hero of the film maker's Indiana Jones series.) Wookiee comes from an ad lib in "THX 1138," the film maker's first feature film: "I think I ran over a Wookiee back there."

Jedi, the name of the ancient knighthood, is a tip of the hat to Burroughs's Barsoom, where lords bear the title of Jed or Jeddak.

Obi-Wan Kenobi (Alec Guinness), also known as old Ben Kenobi, is revealed to us as a Jedi knight and introduces Luke to the power of the Force. Obi is the Japanese word for the sash used to tie a kimono; it may connote the Jedi knight's status as a martial arts master. Similarly, Wan sounds like the Japanese honorific suffix san. "OB" is also short for Old Ben, but there is chatter on the Internet that his name is really OB-1, a cryptic reference to Mr. Lucas's much anticipated history of the Clone Wars in future "Star Wars" installments.

Ewoks, those almost unbearably cute, highly marketable teddy-bear characters who saved the day in "The Return of the Jedi" inhabit the forest moon of Endor (the witch in the Book of Samuel hailed from a similarly named locale). Their name may sound like a variant of Wookiee, but it is taken from Miwok, the Indian tribe indigenous to San Rafael, California, the location of Mr. Lucas's Skywalker ranch.

Boba Fett, at least according to one fan on the World Wide Web, is a sly reference to another hotshot jockey, Bob Falfa, the drag racer played by none other than Mr. Ford in "American Graffiti."

Banthas, the shaggy, screw-horned mounts of the honking **Sand People,** are a variation on banth, a beast found on Barsoom. The Sand People bear similarities to nomadic tribes in the science fiction writer Frank Herbert's desert classic "Dune." The diminutive **Jawas,** who chatter like the cartoon chipmunks Chip 'n Dale, call to mind Indonesian Islam. Their name is perhaps echoic of Moroccan Gnawa trance music.

Connecting Literature and Media

1. Why do you think George Lucas looked to world myths, literature, and popular culture for the characters' names in *Star Wars*?
2. Name three sources Lucas used for names, and explain how the names and their sources are significant in terms of world cultures.
3. What does *Star Wars* reveal about contemporary American cultures?
4. In what ways is the *Star Wars* trilogy a modern-day epic?

Eric P. Nash

(b. 1956)
Eric P. Nash is the author of seven books on architecture and photography, including *Manhattan Skyscrapers.* He is a researcher for *The New York Times Magazine* and a frequent contributor to *The New York Times Book Review.* His articles have appeared in the *Wall Street Journal* and *Discover* magazine.

Nash says his interest in exotic cultures and languages comes partly from being "dragged around the world" by his anthropologist parents and from a "happily misspent youth reading comic books." Nash studied film at New York University.

Answers

Connecting Literature and Media

1. **Possible responses:** Lucas may have looked to world myths and literature to connect his tale to epic tradition. He may have included elements of popular culture because he knew that all epics reflect aspects of the culture from which they come. By combining these elements, he attempts to make a story that sums up other stories and so becomes weightier or grander.
2. **Possible responses:** Lucas uses names from Norse mythology, which connects his characters to world myths; he uses biblical references that tie to the religious beliefs of much of the Western world; he uses Moroccan Gnawan music, which ties his story to Eastern cultures.
3. The *Millennium Falcon*'s resemblance to a souped-up car reflects an admiration for an enterprising mind; the plot reflects an appreciation for pure adventure; and the unusual characters and names reflect diversity. All three are values in today's culture.
4. The epic features of *Star Wars* include a hero overcoming enormous odds, a hero with special abilities and powers, and a reflection of the culture from which it comes.

✴ ENRICHMENT: Film Connection

Film Criticism

The commercial success of *Star Wars,* the first in George Lucas's saga, surprised everyone, including its producers, who watched the advanced "rushes" with dismay. Most critics conceded that the film was fun but warned movie goers to "check your brains at the door." A typical reaction to the movie was that of film critic David Pirie:

Hollywood began as an amusement arcade, so it's appropriate that its most profitable film should

be as formally enchanting and psychologically sterile as a . . . pinball machine.

This reaction epitomizes many film critics' predicament. They are writing reviews of a form of mass entertainment. Yet, they may hold such mass entertainment to the standards set by high art. For this reason, film critics sometimes find themselves out of step with popular tastes, as was the case with *Star Wars.*

Rama's Initiation *from* the Ramayana

Lesson Objectives

1. **To analyze and respond to literary elements**
   - Literary Analysis: The Epic Hero
   - Connecting Literary Elements: Setting
2. **To read, comprehend, analyze, and critique an epic**
   - Reading Strategy: Drawing Inferences About Culture
   - Reading Check questions
   - Review and Assess questions
3. **To develop word analysis skills, fluency, and systematic vocabulary**
   - Vocabulary Development Lesson: Latin Word Root: *-min-*
4. **To understand and apply written and oral language conventions**
   - Spelling Strategy
   - Grammar Lesson: Commas With Introductory Phrases
   - Assessment Practice (ATE)
5. **To understand and apply appropriate writing and research strategies**
   - Writing Lesson: Script Proposal
   - Extension Activity: Annotated Poster
6. **To understand and apply listening and speaking strategies**
   - Extension Activity: Performance

STEP-BY-STEP TEACHING GUIDE	PACING GUIDE
PRETEACH	
Motivate Students and Provide Background	
Use the Motivation activity (ATE p. 1050)	5 min.
Read and discuss the Preview material and Background information (SE/ATE p. 1050) [A]	5 min.
Introduce the Concepts	
Introduce the Literary Analysis and Reading Strategy (SE/ATE p. 1051) [A]	15 min.
Pronounce the vocabulary words and read their definitions (SE p. 1051)	5 min.
TEACH	
Monitor Comprehension	
Informally monitor comprehension by circulating while students read independently or in groups [A]	15 min.
Monitor students' comprehension with the Reading Check notes (SE/ATE pp. 1053, 1055, 1057)	as students read
Develop vocabulary with Vocabulary notes (SE pp. 1053, 1054, 1055, 1057, 1058 ; ATE p. 1057)	as students read
Develop Understanding	
Develop students' understanding of the epic hero with the Literary Analysis annotations (SE p. 1057; ATE p. 1057) [A]	10 min.
Develop students' ability to draw inferences about culture with the Reading Strategy annotations (SE p. 1054; ATE pp. 1053, 1054, 1056)	10 min.
ASSESS	
Assess Mastery	
Assess students' mastery of the Reading Strategy and Literary Analysis by having them answer the Review and Assess questions (SE/ATE p. 1059)	20 min.
Use one or more of the print and media Assessment Resources (ATE p. 1061) [A]	up to 50 min.
EXTEND	
Apply Understanding	
Have students complete the Vocabulary Development Lesson and the Grammar Lesson (SE p. 1060) [A]	20 min.
Apply students' ability to use emotional language to convey their purpose using the Writing Lesson (SE/ATE p. 1061) [A]	45 min.
Apply students' understanding using one or more of the Extension Activities (SE p. 1061)	20–90 min.

[A] **ACCELERATED INSTRUCTION:**
Use the strategies and activities identified with an [A].

UNIVERSAL ACCESS
● = Below Level Students
▲ = On-Level Students
■ = Above Level Students

Time and Resource Manager

RESOURCES

PRINT 📖	TRANSPARENCIES 🖼	TECHNOLOGY 💿 🎧 📼
• **Beyond Literature,** Cultural Connection: Hinduism in India, p. 63 ▲ ■		• **Interest Grabber Video,** Tape 5 ● ▲ ■
• **Selection Support Workbook:** ● ▲ ■ Literary Analysis, p. 252 Reading Strategy, p. 251 Build Vocabulary, p. 249	• **Literary Analysis and Reading Transparencies,** pp. 125 and 126 ● ▲ ■	
		• **Listening to Literature** ● ▲ ■ Audiocassettes, Side 36 Audio CDs, CD 21
• **Literatura en español** ● ▲ • **Literary Analysis for Enrichment** ■	• **Fine Art Transparencies, Volume 1,** Art Transparency 14 ● ▲	
• **Formal Assessment:** Selection Test, pp. 223–225 ● ▲ ■ • **Open Book Test,** pp. 187–189 ● ▲ ■ • **Performance Assessment and Portfolio Management,** p. 28 ● ▲ ■ • **ASSESSMENT SYSTEM** ● ▲ ■	• **ASSESSMENT SYSTEM** ● ▲ ■ Skills Practice Answers and Explanations on Transparencies	• **Test Bank Software** ● ▲ ■ • **Got It! Assessment Videotapes** ● ▲
• **Selection Support Workbook:** ● ▲ ■ Build Grammar Skills, p. 250 • **Writing and Grammar,** Platinum Level ● ▲ ■ • **Extension Activities,** p. 63 ● ▲ ■	• **Daily Language Practice Transparencies** ● ▲	• **Writing and Grammar iText CD-ROM** ● ▲ ■ **Take It to the Net** www.phschool.com

BLOCK SCHEDULING: Use one 90-minute class period to preteach the selection and have students read it. Use a second 90-minute class period to assess students' mastery of skills and have them complete one of the Extension Activities.

Step-by-Step Teaching Guide for pp. 1050–1051

Motivation

Make the statement "Superheroes from all times and cultures possess certain traits in common." Then, have students generate a representative list of superheroes from ancient to present times—for example, Hercules, King Arthur, Robin Hood, and Xena, Warrior Princess. Discuss with students the characteristics that some of these heroes have in common, such as courage, loyalty, and integrity. Tell them that in reading this selection about a young Indian boy, they will get an opportunity to witness the making of a hero.

▣ Interest Grabber Video

As an alternative, you may wish to play "Celebrating Janamashtami" on Tape 5 to engage student interest.

❶ Background

Culture

Hinduism, one of the oldest living religions in the world, is the major religion of India. While there is no single book that outlines all its doctrines and beliefs, there are many sacred writings. These include the *Vedas*, which contain prayers, hymns, explanations, and philosophy; the *Puranas*, which tell the tales of Hindu gods and goddesses; the Hindu epics *Mahabharata* and the *Ramayana*; and the *Manu-Smitri*, a code of religious and social law. The *Ramayana* tells of Prince Rama, believed by many to be another incarnation of the Hindu god Krishna.

Prepare to Read

Rama's Initiation *from* the Ramayana

Take It to the Net

Visit www.phschool.com for interactive activities and instruction related to the *Ramayana,* including
- background
- graphic organizers
- literary elements
- reading strategies

Preview

Connecting to the Literature

What qualities do you think a hero possesses? As you read this episode from the *Ramayana*, you might be surprised to note that ancient heroes have much in common with contemporary superheroes. They combat evil and respect the land that nurtures all peoples.

❶ Background

Hinduism is the major religion of India. While there is no single book that outlines all its doctrines and beliefs, there are many sacred writings that contain prayers, describe the lives of the gods, or present codes of religious and social laws. The *Ramayana*, a great Hindu epic poem, tells of Prince Rama, believed by many to be another incarnation of the Hindu god Krishna.

1050 ◆ *Epics and Legends*

TEACHING RESOURCES

The following resources can be used to enrich or extend the instruction for pp. 1050–1051.

Motivation

▣ **Interest Grabber Video,** Tape 5 ▣

Background

📖 **Beyond Literature,** p. 63

Take It to the Net

Visit www.phschool.com for background and hotlinks for "Rama's Initiation."

Literary Analysis

Literary Analysis and Reading Transparencies, Epic Hero, p. 126

Reading

📖 **Selection Support:** Reading Strategy, p. 251; Build Vocabulary, p. 249

Literary Analysis and Reading Transparencies, Drawing Inferences About Culture, p. 125 ▣

▣ **BLOCK SCHEDULING:** Resources marked with this symbol provide varied instruction during 90-minute blocks.

Literary Analysis

The Epic Hero

The **epic hero** possesses certain qualities—bravery, great strength, and a desire to achieve immortality through heroic deeds. The hero is based on a legendary or historic person who travels on a long and challenging journey during which he proves his heroic qualities: He fights evil, falls in love, protects his honor, and rescues people in distress. In this passage, Rama protects his fellow travelers from a female demon's attack:

> Next she raised a hail of stones under which to crush her adversaries. Rama sent up his arrows, which shielded them from the attack.

As you read, look for Rama's heroic qualities and actions.

Connecting Literary Elements

The **setting**—the description of the time and place in which the action of a literary work takes place—is an important part of epic tales. On epic journeys, a hero, such as Rama, often encounters settings filled with natural and supernatural obstacles that must be overcome. These settings add mystery and wonder to the adventures of the epic hero.

Reading Strategy

Drawing Inferences About Culture

You probably do not know a great deal about life in India 2,000 years ago. However, if you combine the details you read in the adventures of Rama with your own experiences, you can **draw inferences** about the customs and values of Hindu culture. Use a chart like the one shown to record your inferences about Hindu culture.

Vocabulary Development

austerities (ô ster′ ə tēz) *n.* self-denials (p. 1053)

decrepitude (dē krep′ ə tōōd) *n.* state of being worn out by old age or illness (p. 1053)

sublime (sə blīm′) *adj.* noble; admirable (p. 1054)

august (ô gust′) *adj.* worthy of respect because of age and dignity (p. 1054)

secular (sek′ yə lər) *adj.* not sacred or religious (p. 1054)

obeisance (ō bā′ səns) *n.* gesture of respect (p. 1055)

exuberance (eg zōō′ bər əns) *n.* state of high spirits and good health (p. 1057)

diminutive (də min′ yōō tiv) *adj.* smaller than average (p. 1057)

esoteric (es′ ə ter′ ik) *adj.* beyond the understanding of most people (p. 1058)

Details

A sage teaches Rama about evil.

My Experience

The clergy relate religious stories to life.

Cultural Inferences

Hindu religious epics present messages about life.

Rama's Initiation ◆ 1051

---

❷ Literary Analysis

The Epic Hero

- Tell students that as they read "Rama's Initiation," they will focus on the epic hero, who goes on a long and challenging journey to prove his heroic qualities: bravery, strength, and the desire to achieve immortality.

- Read the instruction about the epic hero together as a class. Call students' attention to the example from the story.

- Use the instruction for Connecting Literary Elements to explain how the story's setting influences Rama's development as a hero.

- Use the Epic Hero transparency in **Literary Analysis and Reading Transparencies,** p. 126, to show students how to trace the development of the epic hero of the story.

❸ Reading Strategy

Drawing Inferences About Culture

- Point out to students that even if they do not know much about a culture, they can combine what they read with what they know from their own experience to make inferences about that culture. To illustrate, review the chart on this page.

- As students read "Rama's Initiation," have them complete an inference chart to help them draw inferences about Indian culture.

Vocabulary Development

- Pronounce each vocabulary word for students, and read the definitions as a class. Have students identify any words with which they are already familiar.

E-Teach

Visit E-Teach at www.phschool.com for teachers' essays on how to teach, with questions and answers.

Step-by-Step Teaching Guide for pp. 1052–1058

CUSTOMIZE INSTRUCTION
For Musical/Rhythmic Learners

Play a tape or CD of a classical Indian raga. Have students write a description of the music and the mood it evokes. Does it remind them of any type of Western music? What expectations about the story of Rama does the music inspire?

❶ About the Selection

In "Rama's Initiation," the young man Rama accepts his calling to help defend a sage and perform a sacrifice in a faraway sacred place. He proves himself by defeating a demon and thus begins his adventures as an epic hero. His adventures demonstrate the importance of bravery, strength, and respect for wisdom in Indian culture.

❷ Background

Art

Persian Translation of the Ramayana of Valmiki (detail)

This piece, by an unknown artist, illustrates a scene from the *Ramayana*. The picture plane is divided by the architectural elements of the columns, a device often used in Indian painting to suggest depth. Use this question for discussion:

> What might be the difference between the people sitting on the canopied platform and those in the foreground of the picture? Possible answer: Students might speculate that the people on the platform belong to a ruling or governing class. They might comment on the distance between the platform and the people surrounding it and observe that it might symbolize the distance between the two classes.

❸ ▶ Critical Viewing

Possible answer: The meeting might be about something that involves the whole community.

❷

Persian Translation of the Ramayana of Valmiki (detail), Mughal, school of Akbar, Freer Gallery of Art, Smithsonian Institution, Washington, D.C.

❸ ▲ **Critical Viewing** What do you think is the topic of this public meeting? **[Speculate]**

1052 ◆ *Epics and Legends*

TEACHING RESOURCES

The following resources can be used to enrich or extend the instruction for pp. 1052–1058.

Literary Analysis
📖 **Selection Support:** Literary Analysis, p. 252

Reading
🎧 **Listening to Literature Audiocassettes,** Side 38 ▪
💿 **Listening to Literature Audio CDs,** CD 19 ▪

Extension
📋 **Fine Art Transparencies, Volume 1,** Art Transparency 14 ▪ (Tell students that many Balinese dances are based on stories from the *Ramayana*. After students read the introductory information about the *Ramayana*, display the art transparency and have them discuss the connections between the painting and the Hindu epic.)

▪ **BLOCK SCHEDULING:** Resources marked with this symbol provide varied instruction during 90-minute blocks.

RAMA'S INITIATION
from the Ramayana • R. K. NARAYAN

The great Indian epic, the Ramayana, written by the poet Valmike, consists of 24,000 stanzas. Parts of the Ramayana *date from 500 B.C.*

The epic tells how Prince Rama wins his bride, Sita, by proving his strength. Just as he is about to inherit the throne, however, evil plots result in his banishment from the kingdom. For fourteen years, he wanders in exile with his wife, Sita, and his brother, Lakshmana. After Sita is kidnapped and Rama rescues her with the help of Hanuman, the monkey god, Rama is welcomed back to the kingdom.

The excerpt you are about to read tells of adventures from Rama's childhood that occur before his banishment. Even as boys, Rama and his brother Lakshmana show extraordinary strength and ability.

The new assembly hall, Dasaratha's [dä sä rä´ täz] latest pride, was crowded all day with visiting dignitaries, royal emissaries, and citizens coming in with representations or appeals for justice. The King was always accessible, and fulfilled his duties as the ruler of Kosala without grudging the hours spent in public service.

On a certain afternoon, messengers at the gate came running in to announce, "Sage Viswamithra" [vish wä´ mē trä].[1] When the message was relayed to the King, he got up and hurried forward to receive the visitor. Viswamithra, once a king, a conqueror, and a dreaded name until he renounced his kingly role and chose to become a sage (which he accomplished through severe <u>austerities</u>), combined in himself the sage's eminence and the king's authority and was quick tempered and positive. Dasaratha led him to a proper seat and said, "This is a day of glory for us; your gracious presence is most welcome. You must have come from afar. Would you first rest?"

"No need," the sage replied simply. He had complete mastery over his bodily needs through inner discipline and austerities, and was above the effects of heat, cold, hunger, fatigue, and even <u>decrepitude</u>. The King later asked politely, "Is there anything I can do?" Viswamithra looked steadily at the King and answered, "Yes. I am here to ask of you a favor. I wish to perform, before the next full moon, a yagna[2] at Sidhasrama [sēd häs rä´ mä]. Doubtless you know where it is?"

"I have passed that sacred ground beyond the Ganges[3] many times."

austerities (ô ster´ ə tēz) *n.* self-denials

decrepitude (dē krep´ ə tōōd) *n.* state of being worn out by old age or illness

⑤ ✓Reading Check

Why has the sage Viswamithra come to see the King?

---

1. **Viswamithra** (vish wä´ mē trä) teacher of Rama, the main character of the *Ramayana*.
2. **yagna** (yäg nä´) *n.* sacrifice.
3. **Ganges** (gan´ jēz) river in northern India.

---

❹ Reading Strategy
Drawing Inferences About Culture

• Read the bracketed passage aloud. Ask students to describe how Viswamithra suggests the evil creatures at Sidhasrama should be overcome.
Answer: He says that the creatures should be conquered in the same way men conquer "the five-fold evils within."

• Then, ask students what inference they can draw about the ancient Indians' view of evil.
Answer: Students might say that the ancient Indians saw evil as being both internal and external. The evils within a person are lust, anger, miserliness, egoism, and envy; evil in the world was believed to be caused by non-human creatures or powerful demons.

❺ ✓Reading Check
Answer: The sage wants Dasaratha to do him a favor so he can perform a sacrifice.

CUSTOMIZE INSTRUCTION FOR UNIVERSAL ACCESS

For Special Needs Students	For Less Proficient Readers	For Gifted/Talented Students
Use the phonetic spellings on pp. 1053, 1054, and 1056 to pronounce the names of the main characters for students, so that they will not spend too much time struggling with this on their own.	To avoid confusion, draw students' attention to p. 1056, "Thataka's Story." Explain that a story within a story is a common narrative technique in epics.	The *Ramayana,* like Homer's epic poems, was recited from memory for centuries before it was written down in verse. Suggest that students search for passages that they can render into verse by changing as few words as possible in this prose translation.

Drawing Inferences About Culture

- Have a volunteer read the bracketed passage aloud. Ask students what *unceremoniously* means in the second sentence.
  Answer: It means "informally" or "abruptly."

- Point out that the same sentence expresses that it was impolite not to show Viswamithra to the door. Then, ask the Reading Strategy question on p. 1054: What can you learn about Hindu culture and its concept of hospitality from this paragraph?
  Possible answer: Hindu culture places a strong emphasis on hospitality and on the rituals of politeness that must be observed when guests visit the home.

---

4 The sage interrupted. "But there are creatures hovering about waiting to disturb every holy undertaking there, who must be overcome in the same manner as one has to conquer the five-fold evils[4] within before one can realize holiness. Those evil creatures are endowed with immeasurable powers of destruction. But it is our duty to pursue our aims undeterred. The yagna I propose to perform will strengthen the beneficial forces of this world, and please the gods above."

"It is my duty to protect your <u>sublime</u> effort. Tell me when, and I will be there."

The sage said, "No need to disturb your <u>august</u> self. Send your son Rama with me, and he will help me. He can."

"Rama!" cried the King, surprised, "When I am here to serve you."

Viswamithra's temper was already stirring. "I know your greatness," he said, cutting the King short. "But I want Rama to go with me. If you are not willing, you may say so."

The air became suddenly tense. The assembly, the ministers and officials, watched in solemn silence. The King looked miserable. "Rama is still a child, still learning the arts and practicing the use of arms." His sentences never seemed to conclude, but trailed away as he tried to explain. "He is a boy, a child, he is too young and tender to contend with demons."

"But I know Rama," was all that Viswamithra said in reply.

"I can send you an army, or myself lead an army to guard your performance. What can a stripling[5] like Rama do against those terrible forces . . .? I will help you just as I helped Indra[6] once when he was harassed and deprived of his kingdom."

Viswamithra ignored his speech and rose to leave. "If you cannot send Rama, I need none else." He started to move down the passage.

6 The King was too stricken to move. When Viswamithra had gone half way, he realized that the visitor was leaving unceremoniously and was not even shown the courtesy of being escorted to the door. Vasishtha,[7] the King's priest and guide, whispered to Dasaratha, "Follow him and call him back," and hurried forward even before the King could grasp what he was saying. He almost ran as Viswamithra had reached the end of the hall and, blocking his way, said, "The King is coming; please don't go. He did not mean . . ."

A wry smile played on Viswamithra's face as he said without any trace of bitterness, "Why are you or anyone agitated? I came here for a purpose; it has failed: no reason to prolong my stay."

"Oh, eminent one, you were yourself a king once."

"What has that to do with us now?" asked Viswamithra, rather irked, since he hated all reference to his <u>secular</u> past and wanted always to be known as a Brahma Rishi.[8]

---

4. **five-fold evils** lust, anger, miserliness, egoism, and envy.
5. **stripling** (strip´ liŋ) *n.* young boy passing into manhood.
6. **Indra** (in´ drə) Hindu god associated with rain and thunderbolts.
7. **Vasishtha** (vä sē´ shtä) King's priest and guide.
8. **Brahma Rishi** (brä´ mä rī´ shē) enlightened sage.

sublime (sə blīm´) *adj.* noble; admirable

august (ô gust´) *adj.* worthy of respect because of age and dignity

Reading Strategy
Drawing Inferences About Culture What can you learn about Hindu culture and its concept of hospitality from this paragraph?

secular (sek´ yə lər) *adj.* not sacred or religious

✳ ENRICHMENT: Social Studies Connection

Hinduism

The major religion of India, Hinduism, is the oldest religion in the world. One of the important teachings of Hinduism is reincarnation. Hindus believe that when the body dies, the soul is reborn in a continuous process. The soul of someone who lives a good life will be reborn into a higher status, possibly one of wealth and high standing. The soul of a person who lives a bad life will be reborn into a lower condition, such as that of a pig or a cockroach.

Another major aspect of Hinduism in the past was the *caste system,* a strict system of hereditary social classes. Members of one caste could not mix with members of the other castes. In recent times, however, different castes do intermingle. There are four traditional castes: the *Brahmans,* or priests; the *Kshatriyas,* nobles and military leaders; the *Vaisyas,* business people and landowners; and the *Sudras,* farmers, workers, and servants. *Untouchables* were considered so low that they were outside the caste system. "Untouchability" was outlawed in 1949.

Vasishtha answered mildly, "Only to remind you of an ordinary man's feelings, especially a man like Dasaratha who had been childless and had to pray hard for an issue . . ."

"Well, it may be so, great one; I still say that I came on a mission and wish to leave, since it has failed."

"It has not failed," said Vasishtha, and just then the King came up to join them in the passage; the assembly was on its feet.

Dasaratha made a deep <u>obeisance</u> and said, "Come back to your seat, Your Holiness."

"For what purpose, Your Majesty?" Viswamithra asked.

"Easier to talk seated . . ."

"I don't believe in any talk," said Viswamithra; but Vasishtha pleaded with him until he returned to his seat.

When they were all seated again, Vasishtha addressed the King: "There must be a divine purpose working through this seer, who may know but will not explain. It is a privilege that Rama's help should be sought. Do not bar his way. Let him go with the sage."

"When, oh when?" the King asked anxiously.

"Now," said Viswamithra. The King looked woebegone and desperate, and the sage relented enough to utter a word of comfort. "You cannot count on the physical proximity of someone you love, all the time. A seed that sprouts at the foot of its parent tree remains stunted until it is transplanted. Rama will be in my care, and he will be quite well. But ultimately, he will leave me too. Every human being, when the time comes, has to depart and seek his fulfillment in his own way."

"Sidhasrama is far away . . .?" began the King.

"I'll ease his path for him, no need for a chariot to take us there," said Viswamithra reading his mind.

"Rama has never been separated from his brother Lakshmana. [läks mə´ nə] May he also go with him?" pleaded the King, and he looked relieved when he heard Viswamithra say, "Yes, I will look after both, though their mission will be to look after me. Let them get ready to follow me; let them select their favorite weapons and prepare to leave."

Dasaratha, with the look of one delivering hostages into the hand of an enemy, turned to his minister and said, "Fetch my sons."

Following the footsteps of their master like his shadows, Rama and Lakshmana went past the limits of the city and reached the Sarayu River, which bounded the capital on the north. When night fell, they rested at a wooded grove and at dawn crossed the river. When the sun came over the mountain peak, they reached a pleasant grove over which hung, like a canopy, fragrant smoke from numerous sacrificial fires. Viswamithra explained to Rama, "This is where God Shiva* meditated once upon a time and reduced to ashes the god of love when he attempted to spoil

Literature in context   Religion Connection

◆ *Hindu Gods*

Hindus worship thousands of gods. Each god is part of a single supreme force called Brahman, which only a few sages (such as Viswamithra) can truly understand. The three main gods of Hinduism are *Brahma*, the creator of the world; *Vishnu*, the preserver, who restores moral order; and *Shiva*, the destroyer, who regularly destroys the world in order to re-create it. *Indra*, the chief god mentioned in this selection, is associated with rain, lightning, and thunderbolts. Rama, the epic hero, is believed to be an incarnation of Vishnu who combines qualities of both a man and a god.

Shiva

obeisance (ō bā´ səns) *n.* gesture of respect

8 ✓ **Reading Check**

Who does Dasaratha suggest to go with Rama on his journey?

Rama's Initiation ◆ 1055

---

❼ Background

Hindu Religion

The Hindu religion has many gods and thus is called polytheistic. Three of the most important gods are Brahma (the Creator), Vishnu (the Preserver), and Shiva (the Destroyer).

On p. 1055, Vasishtha recognizes that a divine purpose is probably at work here. Vishnu, one of the Hindu gods, is known as the Preserver, or god of life. Hindus believe that Vishnu has appeared in nine forms, or avatars. One of these avatars is Rama. That Rama arrives at the place where Shiva meditated seems to set the stage for some kind of battle.

❽ ✓ **Reading Check**

Answer: Dasaratha suggests that Rama's brother, Lakshmana, go with Rama on his journey.

CUSTOMIZE INSTRUCTION FOR UNIVERSAL ACCESS

For Special Needs Students	For Gifted/Talented Students	For Advanced Readers
To keep students from getting mired in the long names in this text, encourage them to read to the accompaniment of the **Listening to Literature** Audiocassette or CD.	Allow groups of students to read the story aloud, with a different student taking each part and one student acting as narrator. After reading, students can discuss what their characters may have been thinking and feeling at various points.	Have students work together to think about their readings in literature and history with the purpose of identifying other literary works that reveal information about a culture as the *Ramayana* reveals information about India's. Encourage them to present their findings to the class.

Rama Chases a Demon Disguised as a Golden Deer

This visual interpretation of a scene from the *Ramayana* is in the collection of the Freer Gallery, a gift made to the United States by Charles Lang Freer (1854–1919), a financier and art collector with a particular interest in Asian art. Use these questions for discussion:

1. From what you have learned about Indian culture from this story, how might Rama know that the golden deer he is hunting is actually a demon?
   Possible answer: Because ancient Indians believed that the body could be transformed and forces of evil could assume other physical identities, Rama could conclude that a demonic force could disguise itself as an innocent creature.

2. Why might Rama want to kill the golden deer?
   Possible answer: If the deer is a demonic force, Rama would be ridding the empire of a source of evil.

❿ ▶ Critical Viewing

Possible answer: In this piece of art, Rama is admired for his prowess as a hunter.

⓫ Reading Strategy

Drawing Inferences About Culture

- Ask students what seemed to happen as a result of meditating and reciting incantations.
  Answer: The travelers no longer felt the arid heat but instead felt only coolness and freshness.

- Ask students whether they think the atmosphere really changed or whether the travelers only perceived it differently. If necessary, point out the phrase "felt as if" in the passage.
  Answer: The travelers perceived the air differently.

- Ask students what inferences they can make about the role of meditation and incantations in Indian culture and religion.
  Possible answer: The Indian people use meditation and incantation to help free the spirit to rise beyond the demands and discomforts of the body.

1056

his meditation. From time immemorial saints praying to Shiva come here to perform their sacrifices, and the pall of smoke you notice is from their sacrificial fires."

A group of hermits emerged from their seclusion, received Viswamithra, and invited him and his two disciples to stay with them for the night. Viswamithra resumed his journey at dawn and reached a desert region at midday. The mere expression "desert" hardly conveys the absolute aridity of this land. Under a relentless sun, all vegetation had dried and turned to dust, stone and rock crumbled into powdery sand, which lay in vast dunes, stretching away to the horizon. Here every inch was scorched and dry and hot beyond imagination. The ground was cracked and split, exposing enormous fissures everywhere. The distinction between dawn, noon, and evening did not exist here, as the sun seemed to stay overhead and burn the earth without moving. Bleached bones lay where animals had perished, including those of monstrous serpents with jaws open in deadly thirst; into these enormous jaws had rushed (says the poet) elephants desperately seeking shade, all dead and fossilized, the serpent and the elephant alike. Heat haze rose and singed the very heavens. While traversing this ground, Viswamithra noticed the bewilderment and distress on the faces of the young men, and transmitted to them mentally two *mantras*[9] (called "Bala" and "Adi-Bala"). When they meditated on and recited these

⓫ incantations, the arid atmosphere was transformed for the rest of their passage and they felt as if they were wading through a cool stream with a southern summer breeze blowing in their faces. Rama, ever curious to know the country he was passing through, asked, "Why is this land so terrible? Why does it seem accursed?"

"You will learn the answer if you listen to this story—of a woman fierce, ruthless, eating and digesting all living creatures, possessing the strength of a thousand mad elephants."

Thataka's Story

The woman I speak of was the daughter of Suketha [soo kā´ tä] a *yaksha*, a demigod of great valor, might, and purity. She was beautiful and full of wild energy. When she grew up she was married to a chieftain named Sunda. Two sons were born to them—Mareecha [mä´ rē chä] and Subahu [sä bä´ hoo]—who were endowed with enormous supernatural powers in addition to physical strength; and in their conceit and

❿ ▲ Critical Viewing
What details in this painting indicate Rama's strengths? **[Analyze]**

---

9. **mantras** (män´ trəz) sacred syllables.

✻ ENRICHMENT: Culture Connection

Language History

The Sanskrit language is considered part of the Indo-European family of languages, which includes English, German, Latin, and Farsi (spoken in ancient Persia and modern Iran). The beginnings of Sanskrit can be traced to approximately 1800 B.C., when the Aryans invaded India, bringing their language with them. This language evolved into Vedic Sanskrit, the language of the Indian upper classes. Gradually, Vedic Sanskrit fell out of use as a spoken language but became a standard form of written language, referred to now as classical Sanskrit. Sanskrit literature began orally and was passed down through many generations before the stories were written down. Two of the most important works of classical Sanskrit are the *Ramayana* and the *Mahabharata*.

exuberance they laid waste their surroundings. Their father, delighted at their pranks and infected by their mood, joined in their activities. He pulled out ancient trees by their roots and flung them about, and he slaughtered all creatures that came his way. This depredation came to the notice of the great savant Agasthya[10] (the diminutive saint who once, when certain demoniac beings hid themselves at the bottom of the sea and Indra appealed for his help to track them, had sipped off the waters of the ocean). Agasthya had his hermitage in this forest, and when he noticed the destruction around, he cursed the perpetrator of this deed and Sunda fell dead. When his wife learned of his death, she and her sons stormed in, roaring revenge on the saint. He met their challenge by cursing them. "Since you are destroyers of life, may you become *asuras* [ä soo´ räz] and dwell in the nether worlds." (Till now they had been demigods. Now they were degraded to demonhood.) The three at once underwent a transformation; their features and stature became forbidding, and their natures changed to match. The sons left to seek the company of superdemons. The mother was left alone and lives on here, breathing fire and wishing everything ill. Nothing flourishes here; only heat and sand remain. She is a scorcher. She carries a trident with spikes; a cobra entwined on her arm is her armlet. The name of this fearsome creature is Thataka. [tä tä´ kä] Just as the presence of a little loba (meanness) dries up and disfigures a whole human personality, so does the presence of this monster turn into desert a region which was once fertile. In her restlessness she constantly harasses the hermits at their prayers; she gobbles up anything that moves and sends it down her entrails.

Touching the bow slung on his shoulder, Rama asked, "Where is she to be found?"

Before Viswamithra could answer, she arrived, the ground rocking under her feet and a storm preceding her. She loomed over them with her eyes spitting fire, her fangs bared, her lips parted revealing a cavernous mouth; and her brows twitching in rage. She raised her trident and roared, "In this my kingdom, I have crushed out the minutest womb of life and you have been sent down so that I may not remain hungry."

Rama hesitated; for all her evil, she was still a woman. How could he kill her? Reading his thoughts, Viswamithra said, "You shall not consider her a woman at all. Such a monster must receive no consideration. Her strength, ruthlessness, appearance, rule her out of that category. Formerly God Vishnu [vēsh´ noo] himself killed Kyathi [kyä´ tē], the wife of Brigu [brē´goo], who harbored the asuras fleeing his wrath, when she refused to yield them. Mandorai, [mänd rä´ ē] a woman bent upon destroying all the worlds, was vanquished by Indra and he earned the gratitude of humanity. These are but two instances. A woman of demoniac tendencies loses all consideration to be treated as a woman. This Thataka is more dreadful than Yama, the god of death, who takes a life only when the time is ripe. But this monster, at the very scent of a living creature,

---

10. **savant** (sə vänt´) **Agasthya** (ä gus tē yä´) learned man named Agasthya.

Rama's Initiation ◆ 1057

exuberance (eg zoo´ bər əns) *n.* state of high spirits and good health

diminutive (də min´ yoo tiv) *adj.* smaller than average

Literary Analysis
Epic Hero and Setting In what ways is this setting the type of place an epic hero might be expected to encounter?

14 ✓ Reading Check
Why does nothing grow in the land where Thataka lives?

---

12 Literary Analysis
Epic Hero and Setting

- Have students read the bracketed passage. Ask them to describe the setting.
  Answer: The land is a desert where nothing grows; "only heat and sand remain."

- Then, ask the Literary Analysius question on p. 1057: In what ways is this setting they type of place an epic hero might be expected to encounter?
  Answer: The forbidding land itself is one of the challenges the epic hero encounters on his journey.

13 Vocabulary Development
The Latin Root -min-

- Call students' attention to the word *minutest*. Ask what familiar word they see in this word.
  Answer: Students will probably point out the word *minute*.

- Ask what part of an hour a minute is.
  Possible answers: A minute is one-sixtieth of an hour; a small part of an hour.

- Tell students that the Latin root -min- in *minutest* and *minute* means "small."

- Ask students the meaning of *minutest* in the text.
  Answer: *Minutest* means "smallest."

- Encourage students to look for other words with -min- as they read the story.

14 ✓ Reading Check

Answer: Nothing grows because as a result of a curse, Thataka's presence has turned a fertile land to dust.

CUSTOMIZE INSTRUCTION FOR UNIVERSAL ACCESS

For English Learners	For Gifted/Talented Students	For Advanced Readers
On p. 1055, Viswamithra uses the metaphor of a tree and its seedlings to explain why Rama must leave the home of his father. Now that Rama has defeated Thataka, challenge students to create a metaphor that describes his accomplishment.	After students have read about how Thataka created the desert that Viswamithra, Rama, and Lakshmana must cross, have them devise a mythic origin for a natural phenomenon, such as the Grand Canyon. Encourage them to write it as an episode in an epic and share it with the class.	Have students write an episode involving Viswamithra, Rama, and Lakshmana that might follow Rama's initiation. Ask them to focus the episode around another heroic quality Rama might develop, such as wisdom or resistance to temptation. Encourage them to share their writings with the class.

Review and Assess

1. Students might decide that he does the right thing because he teaches Rama not to accept things at face value.

2. **(a)** He wants Rama to help him perform a sacrifice at Sidhasrama. **(b)** Possible answer: In some mysterious way, the sage knows that Rama and no one else can help him.

3. **(a)** King Dasaratha says that his son is still a child and is not ready for such a mission. **(b)** Vasishtha senses that there is some divine purpose at work in the sage's choice of Rama.

4. **(a)** The region is parched and littered with bleached animal bones; there is no distinction between night and day. **(b)** The mantras help them overcome the discomforts and demands of the human body.

5. **(a)** Rama's arrow pierces Thataka's throat, killing her and initiating Rama into his mission of destroying evil. **(b)** With this battle, Rama initiates, or begins, his career of overcoming evil. **(c)** Possible answer: Rama will engage in his future battles against evil with great confidence.

6. Viswamithra is wise, worldly, and self-disciplined, and he can impart valuable lessons to Rama about the difference between how things appear and their true nature.

7. Possible answer: A child can be compared to a seed in any time period because the principle still applies: Like a seed growing into a tree, a child is small and needs nurturing to develop into a healthy adult.

---

craves to kill and eat. Do not picture her as a woman at all. You must rid this world of her. It is your duty."

Rama said, "I will carry out your wish."

Thataka threw her three-pronged spear at Rama. As it came flaming, Rama strung his bow and sent an arrow which broke it into fragments. Next she raised a hail of stones under which to crush her adversaries. Rama sent up his arrows, which shielded them from the attack. Finally Rama's arrow pierced her throat and ended her career; thereby also inaugurating Rama's life's mission of destroying evil and demonry in this world. The gods assembled in the sky and expressed their joy and relief and enjoined Viswamithra, "Oh, adept and master of weapons, impart without any reserve all your knowledge and powers to this lad. He is a savior." Viswamithra obeyed this injunction and taught Rama all the <u>esoteric</u> techniques in weaponry. Thereafter the presiding deities of various weapons, *asthras* [äs´ träz], appeared before Rama submissively and declared, "Now we are yours: command us night or day."

esoteric (es´ ə ter´ ik) *adj.* beyond the understanding of most people

---

Review and Assess

Thinking About the Selection

1. **Respond:** Do you think Viswamithra does the right thing by persuading Rama to overcome his hesitation about killing Thataka? Why or why not?

2. **(a) Recall:** Why does the sage Viswamithra want Rama to accompany him to Sidhasrama? **(b) Hypothesize:** Why does Viswamithra insist on taking Rama and not his father on this journey?

3. **(a) Recall:** Why is King Dasaratha at first reluctant to grant the sage's request? **(b) Infer:** Why does Vasishtha plead with the King to allow Rama to go on the journey?

4. **(a) Recall:** In what ways is the region through which Rama, Lakshmana, and Viswamithra pass inhospitable? **(b) Analyze:** How and why does the land seem different to Rama and Lakshmana when they use the mantras Viswamithra has given to them?

5. **(a) Recall:** What are the outcomes of Rama's first battle? **(b) Interpret:** Why do you think the battle is called "Rama's Initiation"? **(c) Hypothesize:** What impact do you think this battle will have on Rama's future behavior? Explain.

6. **Interpret:** Why is Viswamithra a worthy teacher for Rama in his quest to be a hero?

7. **Evaluate:** Does Viswamithra's comparison of a child to a seed apply today? Explain.

R. K. Narayan

(1906–2001)

For the Indian writer R. K. Narayan [nə rī´ ən], the *Ramayana* and *Mahabharata* (another Hindu epic) played a significant role in developing a love for literature, especially oral literature. Born into the priestly Hindu Brahman caste, Narayan spoke Tamil at home, used English at school, and was taught traditional Indian melodies and prayers in Sanskrit, India's ancient classical language. In addition to his contemporary versions of Indian epics, Narayan published dozens of novels and short-story collections.

ASSESSMENT PRACTICE: Writing Skills

Organization	(For more practice, see Test Preparation Workbook, p. 63.)

Some tests require that students choose the most logical sequence of ideas. To give students practice use the following test item.

(1) King Dasaratha watched apprehensively as his son Rama left the palace. (2) Viswamithra had made it clear that he wanted Rama to go with him. (3) Vasishtha suggested that it would be a good idea to send Rama along with Viswamithra. (4) Rama and his brother left the limits of the city.

(5) Viswamithra was the sort of man who knew what he wanted.

Choose the sequence of sentence numbers that will make the structure most logical.

A No change   **C** 1, 4, 2, 3, 5

B 2, 1, 3, 4, 5   **D** 5, 2, 3, 1, 4

The correct answer is *D*; the best organization for this information is chronological.

Review and Assess

Literary Analysis

Epic Hero

1. How does Rama begin the passage from childhood to adulthood?
2. How does Rama show his heroic powers?
3. What events during and after Rama's battle with Thataka indicate that Rama is an **epic hero**?

Connecting Literary Elements

4. (a) What is the **setting** at the beginning of the story? (b) Why is this setting appropriate for the childhood of an epic hero?
5. (a) Through what different settings does Rama pass on his first heroic journey? (b) What lessons does he learn in each? Use a chart like the one shown here to help with your analysis.

Place	Characteristics

 → **Lessons**

6. Why is the setting of Rama's battle with Thataka important in helping him understand evil in the world?

Reading Strategy

Drawing Inferences About Culture

7. Based on the role of the sage in this selection, what can you **infer** about the importance of the sage in Indian culture?
8. What does the *Ramayana* reveal about the relationship between kings and sages in ancient India?
9. Rama hesitates before killing Thataka because she is a woman. What inferences can you draw from this about Indian culture and society?

Extend Understanding

10. **Media Connection:** Compare and contrast Rama with a popular superhero in a short story, book, or film with which you are familiar.

Quick Review

An **epic hero**—the main character in an epic narrative—demonstrates bravery, great strength, and a desire to achieve immortality through heroic deeds while traveling on a long and dangerous journey.

The **setting** is the time and place in which the action of a literary work occurs.

You can use information revealed in literature to **draw inferences about a culture.**

 Take It to the Net

www.phschool.com

Take the interactive self-test online to check your understanding of the selection.

Rama's Initiation ◆ 1059

✳ ENRICHMENT: Further Reading

Other Works by R. K. Narayan

Under the Banyan Tree
Grandmother's Tale, Waiting for the Mahatma

 Take It to the Net
Visit www.phschool.com for more information on R. K. Narayan.

Answers continued

9. Readers can infer that ancient Indians honored and protected women.

10. Students might compare Rama with a superhero from a comic book, a science-fiction series, or a film in which the hero exhibits prowess to vanquish evil.

Answers for p. 1059

Review and Assess

1. Rama's journey with Viswamithra, on which he is introduced to the workings of evil, begins his passage from childhood to adulthood.

2. Rama shows his heroic powers by overcoming his reservations and killing Thataka, an evil force.

3. Rama fires an arrow that breaks Thataka's spear into fragments; next, he fires arrows that shield them from a hail of stones thrown by Thataka. After the battle, the people recognize Rama's heroism and ask Viswamithra to prepare him to lead them in all they do.

4. **(a)** The setting at the beginning of the story is the new assembly hall where the king, Rama's father, listens all day to citizens' appeals for justice and visits with dignitaries. **(b)** This is an appropriate place for Rama, a future epic hero, to spend his childhood, because there he can absorb principles of justice and learn about human nature.

5.

Place	Characteristics
pleasant grove	sacrifical smoke; hermits
arid desert	nothing grows; no distinction between day and night

Lessons

devotion to task

his role as destroyer of evil

6. The setting helps Rama realize the destructiveness of evil.

7. The selection shows that a sage is a prestigious and powerful position. The king will not risk offending him.

8. The Ramayana reveals that kings had great respect for sages in ancient India; they accepted the sages' counsel and followed their recommendations.

continued

Answers for p. 1060

❶ Vocabulary Development

Word Analysis

1. minimum: the least amount required
2. minority: a small number or part within a bigger group
3. minute: a very small amount
4. diminish: to become smaller or weaker

Spelling Strategy

1. allegiance
2. persistence
3. abundance
4. coincidence

Concept Development: Synonyms

1. b	**4.** b	**7.** a
2. a	**5.** a	**8.** b
3. c	**6.** c	**9.** a

❷ Grammar

1. Before Rama could strike, Thataka threw a spear at him.
2. To combat the evil woman, Rama gathered several weapons.
3. Thinking quickly, Rama sent up his arrows to shield them from the attack.
4. When the battle was over, the gods expressed joy and relief.
5. From that day on, Rama dedicated his life to fighting evil.

Writing Application
Sample sentences:
Traveling through the desert, Rama was confronted by the demon Thataka. He didn't know that by the end of the day, he would have fought the fiercest battle of his life against her.

Integrate Language Skills

❶ Vocabulary Development Lesson

Word Analysis: Latin Root -min-

The Latin root *-min-* means "small." The *diminutive* Agasthya is short in size. Use your knowledge of this root to help you define each of the following words.

1. minimum
2. minority
3. minute
4. diminish

Spelling Strategy

Because the word endings *-ance* (as in *exuberance*) and *-ence* (as in *confidence*) sound alike, you have to learn which ending is correct. If you can think of another form of the word, such as *exuberant* or *confident*, that spelling may help you. In your notebook, complete each word, supplying the correct ending.

1. allegi_____
2. persist_____
3. abund_____
4. coincid_____

Concept Development: Synonyms

Review the list of vocabulary words on page 1051. Then, choose the letter of the word below whose meaning is closest to that of the first wor

1. austerities: (a) savings, (b) deprivations, (c) blows
2. decrepitude: (a) weakness, (b) box, (c) fe
3. sublime: (a) pleasant, (b) tragic, (c) nobl
4. august: (a) warm, (b) dignified, (c) confus
5. secular: (a) nonreligious, (b) expansive, (c) serious
6. obeisance: (a) anger, (b) lie, (c) respect
7. exuberance: (a) excitement, (b) gloom, (c) conceit
8. diminutive: (a) sad, (b) little, (c) showy
9. esoteric: (a) secret, (b) accessible, (c) haughty

❷ Grammar Lesson

Commas With Introductory Phrases

Use a comma to separate an introductory phrase or clause from the main part of the sentence. Look at these examples from the text:

> **Introductory Phrase:** *On a certain afternoon,* messengers at the gate came running in to announce, "Sage Viswamithra."

> **Introductory Clause:** *When they were all seated again,* Vasishtha addressed the King: . . .

Practice Rewrite the following sentences, adding commas after any introductory expressions.

1. Before Rama could strike Thataka threw a spear at him.

2. To combat the evil woman Rama gathere several weapons.
3. Thinking quickly Rama sent up his arrow to shield them from the attack.
4. When the battle was over the gods expressed joy and relief.
5. From that day on Rama dedicated his life to fighting evil.

Writing Application Write two sentences abou Thataka, using an introductory phrase in one sentence and an introductory clause in the othe Review your writing to be sure that you have used commas properly.

WG Prentice Hall Writing and Grammar Connection: Chapter 28, Section 2

TEACHING RESOURCES

The following resources can be used to enrich or extend the instruction for pp. 1060–1061.

Vocabulary

📖 **Selection Support:** Build Vocabulary, p. 249
📖 **Vocabulary and Spelling Practice Book** (Use this booklet for skills enrichment.)

Grammar

📖 **Selection Support:** Build Grammar Skills, p. 250
WG **Writing and Grammar,** Platinum Level, p. 659
💻 **Daily Language Practice Transparencies** ▪

Writing

WG **Writing and Grammar,** Platinum Level, p. 282 ▪
💿 **Writing and Grammar iText CD-ROM**

▪ **BLOCK SCHEDULING:** Resources marked with this symbol provide varied instruction during 90-minute blocks.

Writing Lesson

Script Proposal

The *Ramayana* has all the ingredients for a summer blockbuster—exotic settings, a fearless superhero, an old sage with magical powers, and a scary villain. For a Hollywood producer, write a script proposal outlining how you plan to tell the story, cast the film, and use special effects and music to create a box-office success.

Prewriting	Before writing, picture the film in your mind. List ideas about plot, cast, special effects, and music that you think will keep the attention of a large audience. Choose one or two scenes to describe.
Drafting	As you draft, include vivid words and phrases to express the excitement and suspense of key scenes. Use emotional words, such as *stirring* and *sympathetic*.

Model: Using Emotional Language

In the *thrilling* climactic scene, Rama and Lakshmana let out a *rousing* cheer as they *charge* into a hail of stones flung by Thataka. As the music reaches a crescendo, Rama eyes his enemy.

> Vivid verbs, such as *charge,* and emotional modifiers, such as *thrilling* and *rousing,* add interest to the writing.

Revising	Reread your draft to evaluate whether the language is exciting and emotional. Then, revise any parts that need more detail or action.

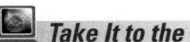 *Prentice Hall Writing and Grammar Connection: Chapter 13, Section 2*

Extension Activities

Research and Technology Rama is believed to be just one of the *avatars*, or incarnations, of the Hindu god Vishnu. Make an **annotated poster** using classical Hindu imagery that shows Vishnu in some of his other forms.

- Use Internet or library sources to research the incarnations of Vishnu.
- Include blocks of text on your poster that indicate what the different symbols represent.

Share your poster with the class, explaining the symbols you have included.

Listening and Speaking With a group, prepare a version of this episode of the *Ramayana* for an audience of young children. Pick out the main message of the story, and simplify the plot. Write dialogue that young children will understand. You may want to use puppets as your characters. Videotape your **performance** for young relatives or friends. [Group Activity]

Take It to the Net www.phschool.com

Go online for an additional research activity using the Internet.

Rama's Initiation ◆ 1061

Lesson Support for p. 1061

❸ Writing Lesson

- Remind students that every word of their script proposal has to count. Encourage them to use vivid words and phrases to express the excitement and suspense of key scenes as well as language that appeals to the emotions.

- Suggest that students use cubing as a prewriting technique. For an explanation of this method, see **Prentice Hall Writing and Grammar,** Platinum level, p. 202.

- Use the Writing Lesson to help students develop their script proposal.

❹ Listening and Speaking

- Encourage students to discuss the main message of the story—evil can be overcome through bravery, strength, and respect for wisdom.

- Before they begin to write, have students decide whether their script will require a narrator. If so, remind them to convey the qualities of their characters mainly through dialogue.

- When they have finished their script, have students create their puppets, assign roles, rehearse the script, and then videotape it before presenting it to the class and then to younger audiences.

- Use the rubric for Delivering a Narrative Presentation, p. 28 in **Performance Assessment and Portfolio Management,** to evaluate students' work.

CUSTOMIZE INSTRUCTION
For Universal Access

To address different learning styles, use the activities suggested in the **Extension Activities** booklet, p. 63.

- For Logical/Mathematical Learners, use Activity 5.

- For Musical/Rhythmic and Intrapersonal learners, use Activity 6.

- For Bodily/Kinesthetic and Interpersonal Learners, use Activity 7.

ASSESSMENT RESOURCES

The following resources can be used to assess students' knowledge and skills.

Selection Assessment

- **Formal Assessment,** pp. 223–225
- **Open Book Test,** pp. 187–189
- **Test Bank Software**
- **Got It! Assessment Videotapes,** Tape 5

 Take It to the Net
Visit www.phschool.com for self-tests and additional questions on the selection.

Listening and Speaking Rubric

- **Performance Assessment and Portfolio Management,** p. 28

PRENTICE HALL ASSESSMENT *SYSTEM*

- **Workbook**
- **Skill Book**
- **Transparencies**
- **CD-ROM**

from Sundiata: An Epic of Old Mali

Lesson Objectives

1. **To analyze and respond to literary elements**
   - Literary Analysis: Epic Conflict
   - Connecting Literary Elements: Relationships Between Characters

2. **To read, comprehend, analyze, and critique an epic**
   - Reading Strategy: Analyzing a Storyteller's Purpose
   - Reading Check questions
   - Review and Assess questions

3. **To develop word analysis skills, fluency, and systematic vocabulary**
   - Vocabulary Development Lesson: Latin Word Root: *-firm-*

4. **To understand and apply written and oral language conventions**
   - Spelling Strategy
   - Grammar Lesson: Semicolons
   - Assessment Practice

5. **To understand and apply appropriate writing and research strategies**
   - Writing Lesson: Storytelling Notes
   - Extension Activity: Research Report

6. **To understand and apply listening and speaking strategies**
   - Extension Activity: Story

STEP-BY-STEP TEACHING GUIDE	PACING GUIDE
PRETEACH	
Motivate Students and Provide Background	
Use the Motivation activity (ATE p. 1062)	5 min.
Read and discuss the Preview material and Background information (SE/ATE p. 1062) 🅰	5 min.
Introduce the Concepts	
Introduce the Literary Analysis and Reading Strategy (SE/ATE p. 1063) 🅰	15 min.
Pronounce the vocabulary words and read their definitions (SE p. 1063)	5 min.
TEACH	
Monitor Comprehension	
Informally monitor comprehension by circulating while students read independently or in groups 🅰	20 min.
Monitor students' comprehension with the Reading Check notes (SE/ATE pp. 1065, 1067, 1069, 1071)	as students rea
Develop vocabulary with Vocabulary notes (SE pp. 1065, 1066, 1067, 1070; ATE p. 1066)	as students rea
Develop Understanding	
Develop students' understanding of epic conflict with the Literary Analysis annotations (SE pp. 1067, 1070, 1071; ATE pp. 1067, 1070, 1071) 🅰	10 min.
Develop students' understanding of the storyteller's purpose with the Reading Strategy annotations (SE pp. 1069, 1071; ATE pp. 1065, 1069, 1071)	10 min.
ASSESS	
Assess Mastery	
Assess students' mastery of the Reading Strategy and Literary Analysis by having them answer the Review and Assess questions (SE/ATE p. 1073)	20 min.
Use one or more of the print and media Assessment Resources (ATE p. 1075) 🅰	up to 50 min.
EXTEND	
Apply Understanding	
Have students complete the Vocabulary Development Lesson and the Grammar Lesson (SE p. 1074) 🅰	20 min.
Apply students' ability to determine the audience's knowledge using the Writing Lesson (SE/ATE p. 1075) 🅰	45 min.
Apply students' understanding using one or more of the Extension Activities (SE p. 1075)	20–90 min.

 ACCELERATED INSTRUCTION:
Use the strategies and activities identified with an 🅰.

UNIVERSAL ACCESS
● = Below Level Student
▲ = On-Level Students
■ = Above Level Student

Time and Resource Manager

Reading Level: Average
Average Number of Instructional Days: 4

RESOURCES		
PRINT 📖	**TRANSPARENCIES** 🗂	**TECHNOLOGY** 💿 🎧 📼
• **Beyond Literature,** Cross-Curricular Connection: Geography, p. 64 ▲ ■		• **Interest Grabber Video,** Tape 5 ● ▲ ■
• **Selection Support Workbook:** ● ▲ ■ Literary Analysis, p. 256 Reading Strategy, p. 255 Build Vocabulary, p. 253	• **Literary Analysis and Reading Transparencies,** pp. 127 and 128 ● ▲ ■	
		• **Listening to Literature** ● ▲ ■ Audiocassettes, Side 36 Audio CDs, CD 21
• **Literatura en español** ● ▲ • **Literary Analysis for Enrichment** ■		
• **Formal Assessment:** Selection Test, pp. 226–228 ● ▲ ■ • **Open Book Test,** pp. 190–192 ● ▲ ■ • **Performance Assessment and Portfolio Management,** pp. 14, 28 ● ▲ ■ • **ASSESSMENT SYSTEM** ● ▲ ■	• **PRENTICE HALL ASSESSMENT SYSTEM** ● ▲ ■ Skills Practice Answers and Explanations on Transparencies	• **Test Bank Software** ● ▲ ■ • **Got It! Assessment Videotapes** ● ▲
• **Selection Support Workbook:** ● ▲ ■ Build Grammar Skills, p. 254 • **Writing and Grammar,** Platinum Level ● ▲ ■ • **Extension Activities,** p. 64 ● ▲ ■	• **Daily Language Practice Transparencies** ● ▲ • **Writing Models and Graphic Organizers on Transparencies,** p. 83 ● ▲ ■	• **Writing and Grammar iText CD-ROM** ● ▲ ■ 💻 *Take It to the Net* www.phschool.com

■ **BLOCK SCHEDULING:** Use one 90-minute class period to preteach the selection and have students read it. Use a second 90-minute class period to assess students' mastery of skills and have them complete one of the Extension Activities.

Motivation

Most good political leaders use brain, not brawn, to settle problems. Action heroes, however, often use more brawn than brain to fight evil. Ask students for examples of each—politicians who think out problems, and fictional superheroes who use extraordinary physical powers to make their impact on the world. Then, let students know that the storytellers, or griots, of Mali told of political leaders who were like action heroes. The excerpt from *Sundiata* describes a person who is both a great leader and the possessor of superhuman powers.

▦ Interest Grabber Video

As an alternative, you may wish to play "Ancient Mali" on Tape 5 to engage student interest.

❶ Background

History of the Mali Empire

The Mali Empire rose out of the decline of the Ghana Empire, which had flourished in earlier centuries.

Between the years of 1235 and 1240 A.D., Sundiata, the great warrior, conquered the lands of the Sosso, and then gained control of the trans-Saharan trade routes and the gold mines of Bouré (in present-day Guinea). With the revenues from the gold trade, Sundiata and subsequent kings—namely Mansa Musa, who ruled from 1307 to 1337—built alliances, conquered more peoples, and expanded the empire.

Under Mansa Musa, the empire reached its height. It comprised the lands of present-day Gambia, Senegal, Guinea, Mali, and parts of Burkina Faso, Niger, and Mauritania. It was then that Timbuktu (in present-day Mali) gained fame as a great city for learning, especially in law and the study of Islam.

Prepare to Read

from Sundiata: An Epic of Old Mali

Senegalese Glass Painting Used on Sundiata, Collection of Professor Donal Cruise-O'Brien, Courtesy of Longman International Education

▦ Take It to the Net

Visit www.phschool.com for interactive activities and instruction related to *Sundiata,* including

• background
• graphic organizers
• literary elements
• reading strategies

Preview

Connecting to the Literature

If you have ever been ridiculed—even over something as trivial as a bad haircut or a botched basketball shot—you know that the temptation to strike back can be strong. In this episode, the much belittled Mari Djata (Sundiata) finds a noble way not only to stop the ridicule, but also to become a hero.

❶ Background

Almost 1,000 years ago, western Africa was an unstable region. Rival kings fought for control of land and trade. Eventually, Sumanguru, from Ghana, gained control and cruelly oppressed the Mandinka people of Mali. Just when Mali needed a leader most, the hero Sogolon-Djata (Sundiata) united his people, defeated Sumanguru, and ushered in a period of peace and prosperity.

1062 ◆ *Epics and Legends*

TEACHING RESOURCES

The following resources can be used to enrich or extend the instruction for pp. 1062–1063.

Motivation

▦ **Interest Grabber Video,** Tape 5 ▦

Background

📖 **Beyond Literature,** p. 64

▦ **Take It to the Net**
Visit www.phschool.com for background and hotlinks for the excerpt from *Sundiata: An Epic of Old Mali.*

Literary Analysis

📄 **Literary Analysis and Reading Transparencies,** Epic Conflict, p. 128

Reading

📖 **Selection Support:** Reading Strategy, p. 255; Build Vocabulary, p. 253

📄 **Literary Analysis and Reading Transparencies,** Analyzing a Storyteller's Purpose, p. 127 ▦

 BLOCK SCHEDULING: Resources marked with this symbol provide varied instruction during 90-minute blocks.

Literary Analysis

Epic Conflict

At the heart of any epic is an **epic conflict**—a situation in which the hero struggles against an obstacle or enemy and emerges triumphant. Through these struggles, the hero passes from childhood to adulthood or gains some new understanding, while showing wisdom and bravery. In this passage, note how Sundiata, at age seven, struggles to walk for the first time:

> Djata was sweating and the sweat ran from his brow. In a great effort he straightened up and was on his feet at one go. . . .

As you read, note the obstacles that confront Mari Djata.

Connecting Literary Elements

In an epic, you can learn a lot about the hero by seeing how other characters relate to him or her. The **relationships between characters** are often part of the epic conflict, and they underscore the obstacles that the hero must overcome. In *Sundiata*, for example, the hero shows courage in response to insults heaped on his mother by another of the king's wives.

Reading Strategy

Analyzing a Storyteller's Purpose

African griots, or storytellers, had several **purposes,** or reasons for relating their stories. In retelling the story of Sundiata, the griots wanted to achieve these goals:

- To inform their people about important historic events
- To entertain them with exciting adventure stories
- To persuade the people to behave appropriately

To keep track of the storyteller's purposes, make a diagram like the one here. As you read, list events or passages that illustrate each purpose.

Vocabulary Development

fathom (fath´ əm) *v.* understand thoroughly (p. 1065)

taciturn (tas´ ə tʉrn´) *adj.* not liking to talk (p. 1065)

malicious (mə lish´ əs) *adj.* intentionally harmful (p. 1065)

infirmity (in fʉr´ mə tē) *n.* physical weakness (p. 1066)

innuendo (in´ yo̅o̅ en´ dō) *n.* indirect belittling remark (p. 1066)

diabolical (dī ə bäl´ ik əl) *adj.* wicked; cruel (p. 1066)

estranged (e strānjd´) *adv.* removed from; at a distance (p. 1067)

affront (ə frunt´) *n.* intentional insult (p. 1070)

---

❷ Literary Analysis
Epic Conflict

- Tell students that as they read the excerpt from *Sundiata: An Epic from Old Mali,* they will focus on epic conflict, a situation in which the hero struggles against an obstacle or enemy and emerges triumphant.
- Read the instruction about epic conflict together as a class. Call students' attention to the example from the story.
- Use the instruction for Connecting Literary Elements to connect the relationships between the story's characters to the obstacles the hero must overcome.
- Use the Epic Conflict transparency in **Literary Analysis and Reading Transparencies,** p. 128, to show students how to analyze the epic conflict of the story.

❸ Reading Strategy
Analyzing a Storyteller's Purpose

- Point out that every storyteller has a reason for telling a story—to entertain, to teach a lesson, to pass on some aspect of history. Use the chart on this page to explain African storytellers', or griots', reasons for telling *Sundiata.*
- As students read the excerpt from *Sundiata,* have them complete a similar chart to keep track of the griot's reasons for telling the story.

Vocabulary Development

- Pronounce each vocabulary word for students, and read the definitions as a class. Have students identify any words with which they are already familiar.

CUSTOMIZE INSTRUCTION FOR UNIVERSAL ACCESS

For Less Proficient Readers	For English Learners	For Advanced Readers
Ask students to think of and summarize a book or movie they have enjoyed. Included in their summary should be a statement of the writer's or filmmaker's purpose, whether to entertain, to convey some aspect of history, or to teach a lesson.	Ask students to describe their favorite kinds of books and movies. In general, are they ones that have been written to entertain, to teach, or to achieve some other purpose? Ask students why they like the kind of books and movies that they do.	Have students select a purpose for writing and then write a paragraph that fulfills that purpose. For example, if they select "to persuade" as their purpose, they could write a paragraph that tries to persuade fellow students to participate in a car wash whose proceeds would benefit a charity or go towards a class trip.

 E-Teach

Visit E-Teach at www.phschool.com for teachers' essays on how to teach, with questions and answers.

Step-by-Step Teaching Guide for pp. 1064–1072

**CUSTOMIZE INSTRUCTION
For Verbal/Linguistic Learners**

Tell students that the story they are about to read involves a conflict in which one of the parties is an underdog. The underdog as hero is a common theme in modern times. Have students discuss movies about underdogs who ultimately triumph over obstacles.

❶ About the Selection

In this translation of an African legend, future king Mari Djata (also known as Sogolon Djata and as Sundiata) seems a most unlikely hero, with his huge head and his inability to stand upright. How Mari Djata overcomes his infirmity and regains his honor is an exciting and instructive tale.

❷ Background

Art

Book Jacket, by David Wisniewski

David Wisniewski is both a storyteller and an illustrator. He attended Barnum & Bailey Clown College and spent three years as a circus clown before moving to the Washington, D.C. area and opening a puppet theater with his wife in 1980.

Wisniewski's first children's book was published in 1989. Since then, he has written and illustrated many award-winning books, including *Elfwyn's Saga, Rain Player,* and *Sundiata: Lion King of Mali.* His book *Golem* won the 1997 Caldecott Award. Use this question for discussion.

How do the bright colors affect the illustration's tone?
Answer: The bright yellows, reds, and blues convey a feeling of triumph and pride. Students might expect that the story will also tell of a bold triumph.

❸ ▶ Critical Viewing

Possible answer: Students might mention courage, strength, and determination.

❶ **SUNDIATA:**
AN EPIC OF OLD MAL

❷

D. T. NIANE

1064 ◆ Epics and Legends

TEACHING RESOURCES

The following resources can be used to enrich or extend the instruction for pp. 1064–1072.

Literary Analysis

📘 **Writing Models and Graphic Organizers on Transparencies,** p. 83

📙 **Selection Support:** Literary Analysis, p. 256

Reading

🎧 **Listening to Literature Audiocassettes,** Side 36 ▪

💿 **Listening to Literature Audio CDs,** CD 21 ▪

▪ **BLOCK SCHEDULING:** Resources marked with this symbol provide varied instruction during 90-minute blocks.

Characters in *Sundiata*:

Balla Fasséké (bä´ lä fä sä´ kä): Griot and counselor of Sundiata

Boukari (bōō kä´ rē): Son of the king and Namandjé, one of his wives; also called Manding (män´ diŋ) Boukari

Dankaran Touman (dän´ kä rän tōō´ män): Son of the king and his first wife, Sassouma, who is also called Sassouma Bérété

Djamarou (jä mä´ rōō): Daughter of Sogolon and the king; sister of Sundiata and Kolonkan

Farakourou (fä rä kōō´ rōō): Master of the forges

Gnankouman Doua (nän kōō´ män dōō´ ə): The king's griot; also called simply, Doua

Kolonkan (kō lōn´ kən): Sundiata's eldest sister

Namandjé (nä män´ jē): One of the king's wives

Naré Maghan (nä´ rä mäg´ hän): Sundiata's father

Nounfaïri (nōōn´ fä ē´ rē): Soothsayer and smith; father of Farakourou

Sassouma Bérété (sä sōō´ mä be´ re te): The king's first wife

Sogolon (sô gô lōn´): Sundiata's mother; also called Sogolon Kedjou (kä´ jōō)

Sundiata (sōōn dyä´ tä): Legendary king of Mali; referred to as Djata (dyä´ tä) and Sogolon Djata, which means "son of Sogolon." Sundiata is also called Mari (mä´ rē) Djata.

CHILDHOOD

God has his mysteries which none can <u>fathom</u>. You, perhaps, will be a king. You can do nothing about it. You, on the other hand, will be unlucky, but you can do nothing about that either. Each man finds his way already marked out for him and he can change nothing of it.

Sogolon's son had a slow and difficult childhood. At the age of three he still crawled along on all-fours while children of the same age were already walking. He had nothing of the great beauty of his father Naré Maghan. He had a head so big that he seemed unable to support it; he also had large eyes which would open wide whenever anyone entered his mother's house. He was <u>taciturn</u> and used to spend the whole day just sitting in the middle of the house. Whenever his mother went out he would crawl on allfours to rummage about in the calabashes[1] in search of food, for he was very greedy.

<u>Malicious</u> tongues began to blab. What three-year-old has not yet taken his first steps? What three-year-old is not the despair of his parents through his whims and shifts of mood? What three-year-old is not the joy of his circle through his backwardness in talking? Sogolon Djata (for it was thus that they called him, prefixing his mother's name

fathom (fath´ əm) v. understand thoroughly

taciturn (tas´ ə tʉrn´) adj. not liking to talk

malicious (mə lish´ əs) adj. intentionally harmful

---

1. **calabashes** (kal´ ə bash´ iz) n. dried, hollow shells of gourds, used as bowls.

◀ **Critical Viewing** Based on this illustration, what qualities would you expect Sundiata to have? **[Analyze]**

⑤ ✓ Reading Check
What distinguishing characteristics separate Sogolon Djata from others his age?

from Sundiata: An Epic of Old Mali ◆ 1065

---

to his), Sogolon Djata, then, was very different from others of his own age. He spoke little and his severe face never relaxed into a smile. You would have thought that he was already thinking, and what amused children of his age bored him. Often Sogolon would make some of them come to him to keep him company. These children were already walking and she hoped that Djata, seeing his companions walking, would be tempted to do likewise. But nothing came of it. Besides, Sogolon Djata would brain the poor little things with his already strong arms and none of them would come near him any more.

⑥ The king's first wife was the first to rejoice at Sogolon Djata's <u>infirmity</u>. Her own son, Dankaran Touman, was already eleven. He was a fine and lively boy, who spent the day running about the village with those of his own age. He had even begun his initiation in the bush.[2] The king had had a bow made for him and he used to go behind the town to practice archery with his companions. Sassouma was quite happy and snapped her fingers at Sogolon, whose child was still crawling on the ground. Whenever the latter happened to pass by her house, she would say, "Come, my son, walk, jump, leap about. The jinn[3] didn't promise you anything out of the ordinary, but I prefer a son who walks on his two legs to a lion that crawls on the ground." She spoke thus whenever Sogolon went by her door. The <u>innuendo</u> would go straight home and then she would burst into laughter, that <u>diabolical</u> laughter which a jealous woman knows how to use so well.

Her son's infirmity weighed heavily upon Sogolon Kedjou; she had resorted to all her talent as a sorceress to give strength to her son's legs, but the rarest herbs had been useless. The king himself lost hope.

infirmity (in fur′ mə tē) *n.* physical weakness

innuendo (in′ yōō en′ dō) *n.* indirect belittling remark
diabolical (dī ə bäl′ ik əl) *adj.* wicked; cruel

2. **initiation in the bush** education in tribal lore given to twelve-year-old West African boys so they can become full members of the tribe.
3. **jinn** (jin) *n.* supernatural beings that influence human affairs. Their promise was that the son of Sogolon would make Mali a great empire.

Literature ⑦
in context African Cultural Connection

♦ *Griot*

Naré Maghan gives Mari Djata important information about griots. The griot was an African storyteller and historian for his or her village. A griot would memorize all the births, deaths, marriages, hunts, seasons, and wars of a village. Sometimes speaking or singing for many hours or even days, the griot would repeat what his or her ancestors had memorized and passed on.

Because the griot's information was so important to the village leaders, the griot had a high place in African society and was also a counselor and spokesperson for the king.

How impatient man is! Naré Maghan became imperceptibly estranged but Gnankouman Doua never ceased reminding him of the hunter's words. Sogolon became pregnant again. The king hoped for a son, but it was a daughter called Kolonkan. She resembled her mother and had nothing of her father's beauty. The disheartened king debarred Sogolon from his house and she lived in semi-disgrace for a while. Naré Maghan married the daughter of one of his allies, the king of the Kamaras. She was called Namandjé and her beauty was legendary. A year later she brought a boy into the world. When the king consulted soothsayers[4] on the destiny of this son he received the reply that Namandjé's child would be the right hand of some mighty king. The king gave the newly-born the name of Boukari. He was to be called Manding Boukari or Manding Bory later on.

Naré Maghan was very perplexed. Could it be that the stiff-jointed son of Sogolon was the one the hunter soothsayer had foretold?

"The Almighty has his mysteries," Gnankouman Doua would say and, taking up the hunter's words, added, "The silk-cotton tree emerges from a tiny seed."

One day Naré Maghan came along to the house of Nounfaïri, the blacksmith seer of Niani. He was an old, blind man. He received the king in the anteroom which served as his workshop. To the king's question he replied, "When the seed germinates growth is not always easy; great trees grow slowly but they plunge their roots deep into the ground."

"But has the seed really germinated?" said the king.

"Of course," replied the blind seer. "Only the growth is not as quick as you would like it; how impatient man is."

This interview and Doua's confidence gave the king some assurance. To the great displeasure of Sassouma Bérété the king restored Sogolon to favor and soon another daughter was born to her. She was given the name of Djamarou.

However, all Niani talked of nothing else but the stiff-legged son of Sogolon. He was now seven and he still crawled to get about. In spite of all the king's affection, Sogolon was in despair. Naré Maghan aged and he felt his time coming to an end. Dankaran Touman, the son of Sassouma Bérété, was now a fine youth.

One day Naré Maghan made Mari Djata come to him and he spoke to the child as one speaks to an adult. "Mari Djata, I am growing old and soon I shall be no more among you, but before death takes me off I am going to give you the present each king gives his successor. In Mali every prince has his own griot.♦ Doua's father was my father's griot, Doua is mine and the son of Doua, Balla Fasséké here, will be your griot. Be inseparable friends from this day forward. From his mouth you will hear the history of your ancestors, you will learn the art of governing Mali according to the principles which our ancestors have bequeathed to us. I have served my term and done my duty too.

---

4. **soothsayers** (sō̍oth′ sā′ ərz) *n.* people who can foretell the future.

from *Sundiata: An Epic of Old Mali* ◆ 1067

---

estranged (e strānjd′) *adv.* removed from; at a distance

Literary Analysis
Epic Conflict What three things mentioned here appear to stand in the way of Mari Djata's success?

❾ ✓Reading Check
Who is the King's griot?

---

❽ Literary Analysis
Epic Conflict

- Remind students that in an epic conflict, the hero must overcome obstacles to reach his goal. Then, read the bracketed passage aloud.

- Have students answer the Literary Analysis question on p. 1067: What three things mentioned here appear to stand in the way of Mari Djata's success?
  Possible responses: The king has become disheartened over his son's infirmity; he barred Mari Djata's mother from his house; he remarried and had a son with his new wife.

❾ ✓Reading Check

Answer: The King's griot, or story-teller, is Gnankouman Doua.

CUSTOMIZE INSTRUCTION FOR UNIVERSAL ACCESS

For Less Proficient Readers	For Gifted/Talented Students	For Advanced Readers
Point out that people turn against Sogolon Djata because of his inability to walk. Have students write a journal entry about a time when they felt criticized for being different. Encourage them to reflect on why people sometimes ridicule or alienate others despite the pain it causes. Why do differences often invite ridicule?	Students might enjoy creating an epic that tells the (fictionalized) tale of an American leader. Have them pattern their epic after this one by providing a problem and its solution, supporting characters who create obstacles to the hero's success, and a hero who is able to overcome those obstacles.	Have students reread the first paragraph of the selection. Then, ask them to write a personal essay in which they state whether or not they agree with the narrator's statement that one's fate is fixed and cannot be altered. Encourage them to give reasons for their conclusions.

I have done everything which a king of Mali ought to do. I am handing an enlarged kingdom over to you and I leave you sure allies. May your destiny be accomplished, but never forget that Niani is your capital and Mali the cradle of your ancestors."

The child, as if he had understood the whole meaning of the king's words, beckoned Balla Fasséké to approach. He made room for him on the hide he was sitting on and then said, "Balla, you will be my griot."

"Yes, son of Sogolon, if it pleases God," replied Balla Fasséké.

The king and Doua exchanged glances that radiated confidence.

THE LION'S AWAKENING

A short while after this interview between Naré Maghan and his son the king died. Sogolon's son was no more than seven years old. The council of elders met in the king's palace. It was no use Doua's defending the king's will which reserved the throne for Mari Djata, for the council took no account of Naré Maghan's wish. With the help of Sassouma Bérété's intrigues, Dankaran Touman was proclaimed king and a regency council was formed in which the queen mother was all-powerful. A short time after, Doua died.

⑩ ▼ Critical Viewing
What skills might be needed to gather leaves from a baobab tree like this one? **[Infer]**

✸ ENRICHMENT: Social Studies Connection

Mali

The empire of Mali, which Sundiata formed in the thirteenth century, was in the region now known as the Republic of Mali. It is the largest country in West Africa.

This empire was a very rich state and one of the world's major producers of gold, but it has a history of instability. It was taken over in the fifteenth century by the Songhai empire, but that empire declined rapidly, and the region became a jumble of small states. In the

nineteenth century, Mali became part of the French empire. It broke from the French in 1960 under the leadership of Modibo Keita, a man from the same Keita tribe as Sundiata. Keita became the first president of the republic, but he was overthrown in 1968 by General Moussa Traoré, who in turn was overthrown in 1991.

Locate Mali on a map, and discuss with students how its location made it an important crossroads in Sundiata's time.

As men have short memories, Sogolon's son was spoken of with nothing but irony and scorn. People had seen one-eyed kings, one-armed kings, and lame kings, but a stiff-legged king had never been heard tell of. No matter how great the destiny promised for Mari Djata might be, the throne could not be given to someone who had no power in his legs; if the jinn loved him, let them begin by giving him the use of his legs. Such were the remarks that Sogolon heard every day. The queen mother, Sassouma Bérété, was the source of all this gossip.

Having become all-powerful, Sassouma Bérété persecuted Sogolon because the late Naré Maghan had preferred her. She banished Sogolon and her son to a back yard of the palace. Mari Djata's mother now occupied an old hut which had served as a lumber-room of Sassouma's.

The wicked queen mother allowed free passage to all those inquisitive people who wanted to see the child that still crawled at the age of seven. Nearly all the inhabitants of Niani filed into the palace and the poor Sogolon wept to see herself thus given over to public ridicule. Mari Djata took on a ferocious look in front of the crowd of sightseers. Sogolon found a little consolation only in the love of her eldest daughter, Kolonkan. She was four and she could walk. She seemed to understand all her mother's miseries and already she helped her with the housework. Sometimes, when Sogolon was attending to the chores, it was she who stayed beside her sister Djamarou, quite small as yet.

Sogolon Kedjou and her children lived on the queen mother's leftovers, but she kept a little garden in the open ground behind the village. It was there that she passed her brightest moments looking after her onions and gnougous.[5] One day she happened to be short of condiments and went to the queen mother to beg a little baobab leaf.[6]

"Look you," said the malicious Sassouma, "I have a calabash full. Help yourself, you poor woman. As for me, my son knew how to walk at seven and it was he who went and picked these baobab leaves. Take them then, since your son is unequal to mine." Then she laughed derisively with that fierce laughter which cuts through your

---

5. **gnougous** (noo′ gooz′) *n.* root vegetables.
6. **baobab** (bā′ ō bab′) **leaf** *n.* The baobab is a thick-trunked tree; its leaves are used to flavor foods.

Reading Strategy
Analyzing a Storyteller's Purpose What purpose might references to all types of kings serve?

 Reading Check
In what way is Sogolon publicly humiliated?

from *Sundiata: An Epic of Old Mali* ◆ 1069

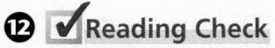

⓫ Reading Strategy
Analyzing a Storyteller's Purpose

- Read the bracketed passage aloud. Ask students to point out the different kinds of kings mentioned.
  Answer: One-eyed kings, one-armed kings, and lame kings are mentioned.

- Ask students what specific kind of king the storyteller says is not mentioned.
  Answer: Stiff-legged kings are not mentioned.

- Then, ask the Reading Strategy question on p. 1069: What purpose might references to all types of kings serve?
  Possible answer: It might serve to emphasize how unlikely it is that Mari Djata will amount to anything and how different he is from everyone else.

⓬ ✔ Reading Check
Answer: Sogolon is publicly humiliated when the queen mother invites everyone in to see Sogolon's child, who is still crawling at the age of seven.

CUSTOMIZE INSTRUCTION FOR UNIVERSAL ACCESS

For English Learners	For Gifted/Talented Students	For Advanced Readers
Encourage students to name some of the animals specifically mentioned in *Sundiata*. Then, have them research other animals native to specific areas of Mali. Students can then create a map of Mali that illustrates the variety of animals that live there.	As the story concludes, it will be clear that Sogolon Djata is a great hero. Encourage students to discuss other great heroes in fiction and in real life. Ask them to create a mural on paper that includes a drawing and a brief description of each hero.	Have students write an essay evaluating the central conflict in *Sundiata*. Encourage them to keep in mind the characteristics of an epic as they discuss whether the conflict is believable and engaging. Have them support their points with examples from the epic.

Relationships Between Characters

- Read the bracketed passage aloud. Ask students to describe how Sogolon feels.
  Answer: She feels humiliated, ashamed, angry, and possibly full of desire for revenge against Sassouma.

- Ask students how they as readers feel toward Sogolon, Mari Djata, and Sassouma.
  Possible answer: They probably side with Sogolon and Mari Djata, because they are the underdogs. They want to see Mari Djata vindicated.

- Have students answer the Literary Analysis question on p. 1070: How does the relationship between Sassouma and Sogolon serve to heighten the epic conflict?
  Possible answer: The relationship adds another obstacle to be overcome. Mari Djata must not only rise above his infirmity, he must do so in a way that allows his mother to rise above the person who has been so abusive to her.

---

flesh and penetrates right to the bone.

Sogolon Kedjou was dumbfounded. She had never imagined that hate could be so strong in a human being. With a lump in her throat she left Sassouma's. Outside her hut Mari Djata, sitting on his useless legs, was blandly eating out of a calabash. Unable to contain herself any longer, Sogolon burst into sobs and seizing a piece of wood, hit her son.

"Oh son of misfortune, will you never walk? Through your fault I have just suffered the greatest affront of my life! What have I done, God, for you to punish me in this way?"

Mari Djata seized the piece of wood and, looking at his mother, said, "Mother, what's the matter?"

"Shut up, nothing can ever wash me clean of this insult."

"But what then?"

"Sassouma has just humiliated me over a matter of a baobab leaf. At your age her own son could walk and used to bring his mother baobab leaves."

"Cheer up, Mother, cheer up."

"No. It's too much. I can't."

"Very well then, I am going to walk today," said Mari Djata. "Go and tell my father's smiths to make me the heaviest possible iron rod. Mother, do you want just the leaves of the baobab or would you rather I brought you the whole tree?"

"Ah, my son, to wipe out this insult I want the tree and its roots at my feet outside my hut."

Balla Fasséké, who was present, ran to the master smith, Farakourou, to order an iron rod.

Sogolon had sat down in front of her hut. She was weeping softly and holding her head between her two hands. Mari Djata went calmly back to his calabash of rice and began eating again as if nothing had happened. From time to time he looked up discreetly at his mother who was murmuring in a low voice, "I want the whole tree, in front of my hut, the whole tree."

All of a sudden a voice burst into laughter behind the hut. It was the wicked Sassouma telling one of her serving women about the scene of humiliation and she was laughing loudly so that Sogolon could hear. Sogolon fled into the hut and hid her face under the blankets so as not to have before her eyes this heedless boy, who was more preoccupied with eating than with anything else. With her head buried in the bed-clothes Sogolon wept and her body shook violently. Her daughter, Sogolon Djamarou, had come and sat down beside her and she said, "Mother, Mother, don't cry. Why are you crying?"

Mari Djata had finished eating and, dragging himself along on his legs, he came and sat under the wall of the hut for the sun was scorching. What was he thinking about? He alone knew.

The royal forges were situated outside the walls and over a hundred smiths worked there. The bows, spears, arrows and shields of Niani's warriors came from there. When Balla Fasséké came to order the iron

affront (ə frunt') n. intentional insult

Literary Analysis
Relationships Between Characters How does the relationship between Sassouma and Sogolon serve to heighten the epic conflict?

rod, Farakourou said to him, "The great day has arrived then?"

"Yes. Today is a day like any other, but it will see what no other day has seen."

The master of the forges, Farakourou, was the son of the old Nounfaïri, and he was a soothsayer like his father. In his workshops there was an enormous iron bar wrought by his father Nounfaïri. Everybody wondered what this bar was destined to be used for. Farakourou called six of his apprentices and told them to carry the iron bar to Sogolon's house.

When the smiths put the gigantic iron bar down in front of the hut the noise was so frightening that Sogolon, who was lying down, jumped up with a start. Then Balla Fasséké, son of Gnankouman Doua, spoke.

"Here is the great day, Mari Djata. I am speaking to you, Maghan, son of Sogolon. The waters of the Niger can efface the stain from the body, but they cannot wipe out an insult. Arise, young lion, roar, and may the bush know that from henceforth it has a master."

The apprentice smiths were still there, Sogolon had come out and everyone was watching Mari Djata. He crept on all-fours and came to the iron bar. Supporting himself on his knees and one hand, with the other hand he picked up the iron bar without any effort and stood it up vertically. Now he was resting on nothing but his knees and held the bar with both his hands. A deathly silence had gripped all those present. Sogolon Djata closed his eyes, held tight, the muscles in his arms tensed. With a violent jerk he threw his weight on to it and his knees left the ground. Sogolon Kedjou was all eyes and watched her son's legs which were trembling as though from an electric shock. Djata was sweating and the sweat ran from his brow. In a great effort he straightened up and was on his feet at one go—but the great bar of iron was twisted and had taken the form of a bow!

Then Balla Fasséké sang out the "Hymn to the Bow," striking up with his powerful voice:

"Take your bow, Simbon,
Take your bow and let us go.
Take your bow, Sogolon Djata."

When Sogolon saw her son standing she stood dumb for a moment, then suddenly she sang these words of thanks to God who had given her son the use of his legs:

"Oh day, what a beautiful day,
Oh day, day of joy;
Allah[7] Almighty, you never created a finer day.
So my son is going to walk!"

Standing in the position of a soldier at ease, Sogolon Djata, supported by his enormous rod, was sweating great beads of sweat.

---

7. **Allah** (al′ ə) Muslim name for God.

Literary Analysis
Epic Conflict How will the iron bar help Mari Djata with his epic conflict?

Reading Strategy
Analyzing a Storyteller's Purpose For what purpose might the griot have included songs in this story?

16 ☑ **Reading Check**
Why does Mari Djata decide to stand up?

---

14 **Literary Analysis**
Epic Conflict

- Read the bracketed passage aloud. Ask students what makes the iron bar mysterious.
  Possible answer: The iron bar was made a long time ago for some unspecified purpose. A soothsayer has associated it with something that will happen on a "great day."

- Ask students the Literary Analysis question on p. 1071: How will the iron bar help Mari Djata with his epic conflict?
  Possible answer: Mari Djata is going to use the iron bar to help him rise to his feet for the first time.

15 **Reading Strategy**
Analyzing a Storyteller's Purpose

- Ask students to describe the effect of the use of songs at this point in the story.
  Possible answer: Because it is the first time that songs have appeared in the story, it heightens the listener's/reader's awareness that something momentous is happening.

- Ask the Reading Strategy question on p. 1071: For what purpose might the griot have included songs in this story?
  Possible answer: One role of griots was to pass along their wisdom and knowledge in the form of song. Here, the griot sings songs of praise: They herald the phenomenal rise of King Sogolon Djata (Mari Djata), who has overthrown his enemies and overcome obstacles that would have daunted most people.

16 ☑ **Reading Check**
Answer: His mother has been humiliated and insulted, and Mari Djata decides to stand up so that he can accomplish a deed of strength that will erase her shame.

CUSTOMIZE INSTRUCTION FOR UNIVERSAL ACCESS

For English Learners	For Gifted/Talented Students	For Advanced Readers
In the first paragraph on p. 1070, Sogolon Kedjou is "dumbfounded." Prior knowledge and/or context will probably provide students with a sense of what the word means. However, they may be interested in discovering the precise meaning of this portmanteau word—a word that combines two other words in form and meaning—by using a dictionary.	Have students imagine that Sogolon and Sassouma Bérété meet each other right after Sundiata tears up the baobab tree. Have them role-play a conversation between the two.	Have students compare the epic conflict in this legend with that in the other legends in the unit. Does this story have the qualities of an epic? Have students categorize this story in a genre and defend their choices. Is it a tall tale or a legend, or does it rise to the level of an epic?

Answers for p. 1072

Review and Assess

1. Some students might have been surprised when Sogolon struck the son whom she loved and protected, but others will not be surprised that mounting pressures caused Sogolon to resort to this unjust act.

2. (a) The people of the kingdom spoke of Mari Djata with irony and scorn. (b) Some students may say that Mari Djata seems to be above insult; others will respond that he knows he will eventually prove his superiority over the crowds.

3. (a) They occupy an old hut on Sassouma's property. (b) The queen mother persecutes them because the late king, Mari Djata's father, preferred Mari Djata's mother over Sassouma.

4. (a) Mari Djata says, "I am going to walk today." (b) After his announcement, Mari Djata stops being passive and takes control over his life and what is happening to him and his mother.

5. (a) Mari Djata and his mother are scorned, tormented, and insulted because he cannot walk. (b) Through Mari Djata's triumph, the epic shows that cruel words and deeds must not be allowed free rein and that those with honor must protect those with little power; in a good world, honor will prevail.

6. A griot may hope that the story will show today's listeners that qualities of greatness can be found anywhere, even within people whom society deems weak or infirm.

7. Possible answer: (a) The qualities that make a hero are bravery, strength, and a desire to rectify evil in the world. (b) Some students may feel that the situation in this story required little bravery to rectify. Others may say that Mari Djata showed bravery by his patience and forbearance in the face of taunts and insults.

Balla Fasséké's song had alerted the whole palace and people came running from all over to see what had happened, and each stood bewildered before Sogolon's son. The queen mother had rushed there and when she saw Mari Djata standing up she trembled from head to foot. After recovering his breath Sogolon's son dropped the bar and the crowd stood to one side. His first steps were those of a giant. Balla Fasséké fell into step and pointing his finger at Djata, he cried:

"Room, room, make room!
The lion has walked;
Hide antelopes,
Get out of his way."

Behind Niani there was a young baobab tree and it was there that the children of the town came to pick leaves for their mothers. With all his might the son of Sogolon tore up the tree and put it on his shoulders and went back to his mother. He threw the tree in front of the hut and said, "Mother, here are some baobab leaves for you. From henceforth it will be outside your hut that the women of Niani will come to stock up."

Review and Assess

Thinking About the Selection

1. **Respond:** Were you surprised when Sogolon struck Mari Djata after she was insulted by Sassouma? Why or why not?

2. **(a) Recall:** What is the attitude of Sassouma Bérété and other people in the kingdom toward Mari Djata? **(b) Infer:** What prevents Mari Djata from responding to the crowds who torment and tease him?

3. **(a) Recall:** Where do Sogolon and her son go to live after the king dies? **(b) Infer:** Why are they mistreated in their new home?

4. **(a) Recall:** What surprising announcement does Mari Djata make after Sassouma Bérété insults his mother? **(b) Compare and Contrast:** What changes in Mari Djata's behavior and personality occur after his announcement?

5. **(a) Infer:** How do Mari Djata and his mother suffer dishonor in the story? **(b) Interpret:** In what specific ways does the epic illustrate the importance of honor?

6. **Make a Judgment:** What impact might the griot hope his story will have on listeners today? Explain.

7. **(a) Apply:** What specific qualities make a hero? **(b) Take a Position:** Do you think that Mari Djata possesses those qualities? Why or why not?

D. T. Niane

(b. 1932)

After listening to the stories told by Mamadou Kouyate (mä´ mä dōō kōō ya´ te), a griot of the Keita clan, Djibril Tamsir Niane (dye´ bril täm´ sēr nī´ yan) wrote *Sundiata: An Epic of Old Mali* in the Malinke language. Niane's work was translated into English and other languages, and now people all over the world can profit from the griot's wisdom.

Niane's own ancestors were griots. In addition to *Sundiata*, Niane has collected and retold many other ancient legends of Mali. His translations of the ancient oral histories are one way he affirms and preserves their value. Niane is also a respected scholar of African history.

ASSESSMENT PRACTICE: Writing Skills

Style   (For more practice, see Test Preparation Workbook, p. 64.)

Style questions focus on understanding the writer's point of view based on his or her use of language. The following question will help students assess their understanding of style.

Malicious tongues began to blab. What three-year-old has not yet taken his first steps? What three-year-old is not the despair of his parents through his whims and shifts of mood? What three-year-old is not the joy of his circle through his backwardness in talking?

Which of the following best replaces the word *malicious*?

A inappropriate   **C** friendly

B unkind   **D** deficient

The tone reflects the frustration of the child's mother. By process of elimination, students should determine that the attitude of others is *unkind,* answer *B*.

Review and Assess

Literary Analysis

Epic Conflict

1. (a) What obstacles does Mari Djata have to overcome in his **epic conflict**? (b) Use an organizer like the one shown to identify the heroic qualities he exhibits in his struggle.

Obstacles — Mari Djata — Heroic Qualities

2. How does Mari Djata respond to the way people react to his disability?

3. In what specific ways might Mari Djata's disability contribute to his effectiveness as a leader?

Connecting Literary Elements

4. Describe these **relationships between characters:** (a) Sundiata and his father, (b) Sundiata and the other children, (c) Sogolon and Sassouma.

5. What role does Mari Djata's relationship with his mother play in his epic conflict?

6. What important relationship exists between a griot and an epic hero such as Mari Djata?

Reading Strategy

Analyzing a Storyteller's Purpose

7. What do you think was the **storyteller's** main **purpose** for telling this epic?

8. Why do you think the storyteller includes a song praising Allah at the end of the epic?

Extend Understanding

9. **Social Studies Connection:** Think of a political leader you know about who had to overcome a physical disability. Explain how the leader's disability contributed to his or her effectiveness.

from Sundiata: An Epic of Old Mali ◆ 1073

Quick Review

An **epic conflict** is a situation in which the epic hero struggles against an obstacle or set of obstacles.

The **relationships between characters**—the way they act toward one another and toward the epic hero—add depth to the epic conflict.

Storytellers have **purposes,** or reasons for relating their stories: to inform, to entertain, or to persuade.

 Take It to the Net

www.phschool.com

Take the interactive self-test online to check your understanding of the selection.

Answers continued

9. **Possible answers:** Students may choose to write about Franklin D. Roosevelt, who coped with the effects of polio during his term as president of the United States, or contemporary senators wounded during the Vietnam War.

Answers for p. 1073

Review and Assess

1. **(a)** Mari Djata must overcome his physical disability, the taunts and ridicule of the community, the isolation imposed on him and his mother by his father and by the queen mother, and his mother's humiliation. **(b)** Obstacles include physical disabilities, taunts and ridicule, isolation from the community, and his mother's humiliation. Heroic qualities include patience, insight into human nature, knowledge that he must stand alone, and vindication through a show of greater strength.

2. Mari Djata seems unruffled by people's reaction to his disability. However, on one occasion he "brains" other children who walk near him.

3. Mari Djata's disability has enabled him to see people for what they truly are. He knows people are both loyal and cruel, and insight into people will make him an effective leader.

4. **(a)** Sundiata's father once had high expectations that he would do great things. His high hopes turned to disappointment, however. **(b)** Sundiata had no friends among the other children. They only taunted and insulted him, although he usually didn't seem to mind. **(c)** Sassouma took every opportunity to insult and humiliate Sogolon and Sundiata. Sogolon was furious at Sassouma and wanted to seek revenge through her son.

5. His mother's humiliation at the hands of Sassouma and her need to be avenged instigated Sundiata's first heroic act.

6. The griot's role is to inform the people about the adventures and exploits of a national hero.

7. The storyteller's main purpose was probably to prove that qualities of greatness could be found anywhere, including in those people society sees as infirm.

8. It is part of the Muslim culture to praise Allah, or God, who is regarded as responsible for shaping events.

continued

❶ Vocabulary Development

Word Analysis

1. confirm: to establish strongly
2. affirm: to state strongly that something is true
3. firmament: the vault or arch supporting the sky

Spelling Strategy

1. informing
2. insistence
3. expertly
4. depiction

Concept Development: Synonyms

1. b 3. b 5. b 7. a
2. c 4. b 6. a 8. c

❷ Grammar

1. Sassouma was a spiteful woman; she constantly pointed out Mari Djata's infirmities.
2. The boy's physical disability did not affect him emotionally; he was content.
3. Naré Maghan approached the blacksmith seer of Niani. He was an old, blind man.
4. Mari Djata's sister was helpful to her mother; she was a disappointment to the king.
5. The waters of the Niger can efface stains from the body; they cannot erase insults.

Writing Application

Sample paragraph:
Sogolon Kedjou was the best cook in the village; everyone praised her delicious gnougous. She always served these vegetables with a zesty peanut sauce. Her son was a great help in gathering the peanuts; it was his favorite chore.

Integrate Language Skills

❶ Vocabulary Development Lesson

Word Analysis: Latin Root -firm-

The Latin root -firm- means "to strengthen." Combined with the prefix in-, meaning "without," infirmity means "without strength," or "physical weakness." Incorporate the meaning of "strengthen" in the definitions of each of the following words:

1. confirm 2. affirm 3. firmament

Spelling Strategy

For words ending in two consonants, keep both consonants when you add a suffix starting with either a vowel or a consonant. For example, infirm + -ity = infirmity. Write the words formed by combining the base words and suffixes below.

1. inform + -ing
2. insist + -ence
3. expert + -ly
4. depict + -ion

❷ Grammar Lesson

Semicolons

Use a **semicolon** to form a compound sentence when the two ideas being joined are closely related and are not joined by a conjunction. If the clauses are not closely related, use a period to separate them into two sentences.

> **Closely Related:** He had a head so big that he seemed unable to support it; he also had large eyes which would open wide whenever . . .
>
> **Not Closely Related:** Mari Djata was born with a large head. He sat in the yard away from other children.

W̧G *Prentice Hall Writing and Grammar Connection: Chapter 28, Section 3*

1074 ◆ *Epics and Legends*

Concept Development: Synonyms

Review the vocabulary list on page 1063. Then, in your notebook, write the word in each item below whose meaning is closest to that of the first word.

1. fathom: (a) confuse, (b) understand, (c) remove
2. taciturn: (a) angry, (b) gracious, (c) quiet
3. malicious: (a) mournful, (b) harmful, (c) changeable
4. infirmity: (a) sadness, (b) illness, (c) fear
5. innuendo: (a) style, (b) hint, (c) allowance
6. diabolical: (a) evil, (b) passionate, (c) extreme
7. estranged: (a) removed, (b) indecent, (c) plentiful
8. affront: (a) coverup, (b) accident, (c) insult

Practice Revise each item below using either a semicolon or a period and capital letter.

1. Sassouma was a spiteful woman she constantly pointed out Mari Djata's infirmities.
2. The boy's physical disability did not affect him emotionally he was content.
3. Naré Maghan approached the blacksmith seer of Niani he was an old, blind man.
4. Mari Djata's sister was helpful to her mother she was a disappointment to the king.
5. The waters of the Niger can efface stains from the body they cannot erase insults.

Writing Application Write a paragraph about events in the story. Include two sentences in which clauses are connected by semicolons.

TEACHING RESOURCES

The following resources can be used to enrich or extend the instruction for pp. 1074–1075.

Vocabulary

📖 **Selection Support:** Build Vocabulary, p. 253
📖 **Vocabulary and Spelling Practice Book** (Use this booklet for skills enrichment.)

Grammar

📖 **Selection Support:** Build Grammar Skills, p. 254
W̧G **Writing and Grammar,** Platinum Level, p. 671
📄 **Daily Language Practice Transparencies** ▪

Writing

W̧G **Writing and Grammar,** Platinum Level, p. 256
💿 **Writing and Grammar iText CD-ROM**
📄 **Writing Models and Graphic Organizers on Transparencies,** p. 83

▪ **BLOCK SCHEDULING:** Resources marked with this symbol provide varied instruction during 90-minute blocks.

Writing Lesson

Storytelling Notes

Although the griots of ancient Mali presented epics from memory, a modern story-teller might want to work from a good set of notes. Combine the old and the new as you outline a retelling of the *Sundiata* epic.

Prewriting	Prepare note cards listing brief details about characters and events you will include. You do not need to write sentences, only notes.
Drafting	In your draft, elaborate on the details you listed on the note cards. Account for all the parts of a story: an introduction, a conflict, a climax, and a resolution. Also, be considerate of the knowledge level of your audience. Provide background information or definitions that listeners may need in order to follow your story.
Revising	Read through your notes to be sure that they will serve you well when you relate your story. Check to see whether you have included enough background information for your audience.

Model: Revising to Address Audience Knowledge

, a dish of root vegetables such as yams and carrots.

As any African cook knows, the leaves of the baobab tree are hard to gather but essential to seasoning gnougous. Mari Djata's mother begged Sassouma for baobab leaves, but the spiteful woman gave her the leaves with insults.

The audience can appreciate the use of authentic African terms as long as any unfamiliar words are defined.

W/G *Prentice Hall Writing and Grammar Connection: Chapter 12, Section 3*

Extension Activities

Listening and Speaking Many families keep their histories alive in the same way that Mali villagers do. Share a **story** that focuses on a key aspect of your family's background, such as

- Your earliest ancestor
- An important birth or death
- A special achievement

Present your story to the class using the story-telling style of a griot.

Research and Technology Sogolon used the rarest herbs to try to cure her son. Using library and Internet resources, prepare a written or an oral **research report** on the different ways that herbs have been used to heal people in ancient and modern times. Include photographs or drawings of herbs in your presentation.

 Take It to the Net www.phschool.com

Go online for an additional research activity using the Internet.

from Sundiata: An Epic of Old Mali ◆ 1075

❸ Writing Lesson

- Remind students to consider their audience's knowledge as they prepare their story. On their note cards, they should identify and define terms that might be unfamiliar, such as *baobab*, *soothsayer*, and *calabash*. They should also make a note to inform the audience where Mali is located.
- Encourage students to combine events and details of the *Sundiata* epic with the contemporary events and ideas they want to incorporate.
- Use the Writing Lesson to help students develop their retelling.
- Use the Narration: Short Story rubric in **Performance Assessment and Portfolio Management,** p. 14 to evaluate students' retellings.

❹ Listening and Speaking

- Brainstorm for other kinds of family oral tales: how a family came to live where they do, a family adventure, or how a family got into a business for which they are known.
- Point out that many oral tales provide details in chronological order. Students might use the Story Map transparency, p. 83 in **Writing Models and Graphic Organizers on Transparencies,** to help them organize their thoughts.
- Have students practice their tales by recording them, listening to them, and then revising them. Remind them to use a tone of voice that is appropriate to the action of their tale.
- Use the rubric for Delivering a Narrative Presentation, p. 28 in **Performance Assessment and Portfolio Management,** to assess students' work.

CUSTOMIZE INSTRUCTION FOR UNIVERSAL ACCESS

To address different learning styles, use the activities suggested in the **Extension Activities** booklet, p. 64.

For Verbal/Linguistic and Visual/Spatial Learners, use Activity 5.

For Verbal/Linguistic Learners, use Activity 6.

For Visual/Spatial and Logical/Mathematical Learners, use Activity 7.

About Reference Materials

- Have students read "About Reference Materials." Then, discuss the various reference tools that students have used or would like to learn to use. Ask students to list what they might use each reference tool for.

- Ask students what they have used maps for in their lives.
  Possible responses: going somewhere in a car, riding the buses or subways, locating a friend or relative in another state or country.

Reading Strategy
Skimming and Scanning

- Ask students what the main purpose of skimming is.
  Possible response: To get an idea of the organization and scope of a work.

- Ask students what the main purpose of scanning is.
  Possible response: To locate specific information quickly.

- Have students explain how they can use skimming and scanning together to get information from reference materials.
  Possible response: By skimming, a reader can find the section of text in which the desired information is likely to appear. By scanning the section for key words, the reader can then find the information.

- Discuss with students materials that might not be appropriate to skim and scan. For example, you probably should not skim and scan directions or ingredients for a medicine.

Reference Materials

About Reference Materials

Reference materials are sources of information such as encyclopedias, Internet resources, and atlases, all of which can be useful for a report or research project.

For example, the *Dorling Kindersley World Reference Atlas*, which is featured here, provides information on the West African country of Mali. It combines elements of two kinds of information in one visual display:

- Maps show physical features of the world, such as cities, mountains, rivers, and roads.
- Additional text provides information on climate, population, and political systems.

Reading Strategy

Skimming and Scanning

This atlas uses large-type headings and distinctive icons as a useful way of identifying and distinguishing one topic from another, as well as the information that falls under each topic.

- By **skimming** a text, you can get an idea of the organization and scope of a work before a careful reading of it. Read quickly, and take in groups of words. Stop for headings and other set-off text that is bold, italicized, or oversized, and draw a conclusion about the type of information presented.

- By **scanning,** you can locate specific information fast. Let your eyes move quickly over the page. Look for words related to the information you are seeking. Stop and read the sections. Scanning is useful for finding particular pieces of information, not for determining the kinds of information available.

Skim and scan this entry from an atlas. Use a graphic organizer such as the one shown here to record each kind of information you find.

Subjects Covered	Location of information	Answer
Countries bordering Mali	Map	
Language spoken in Mali	Icon of person with dialogue balloon	
Politics of Mali	Heading	

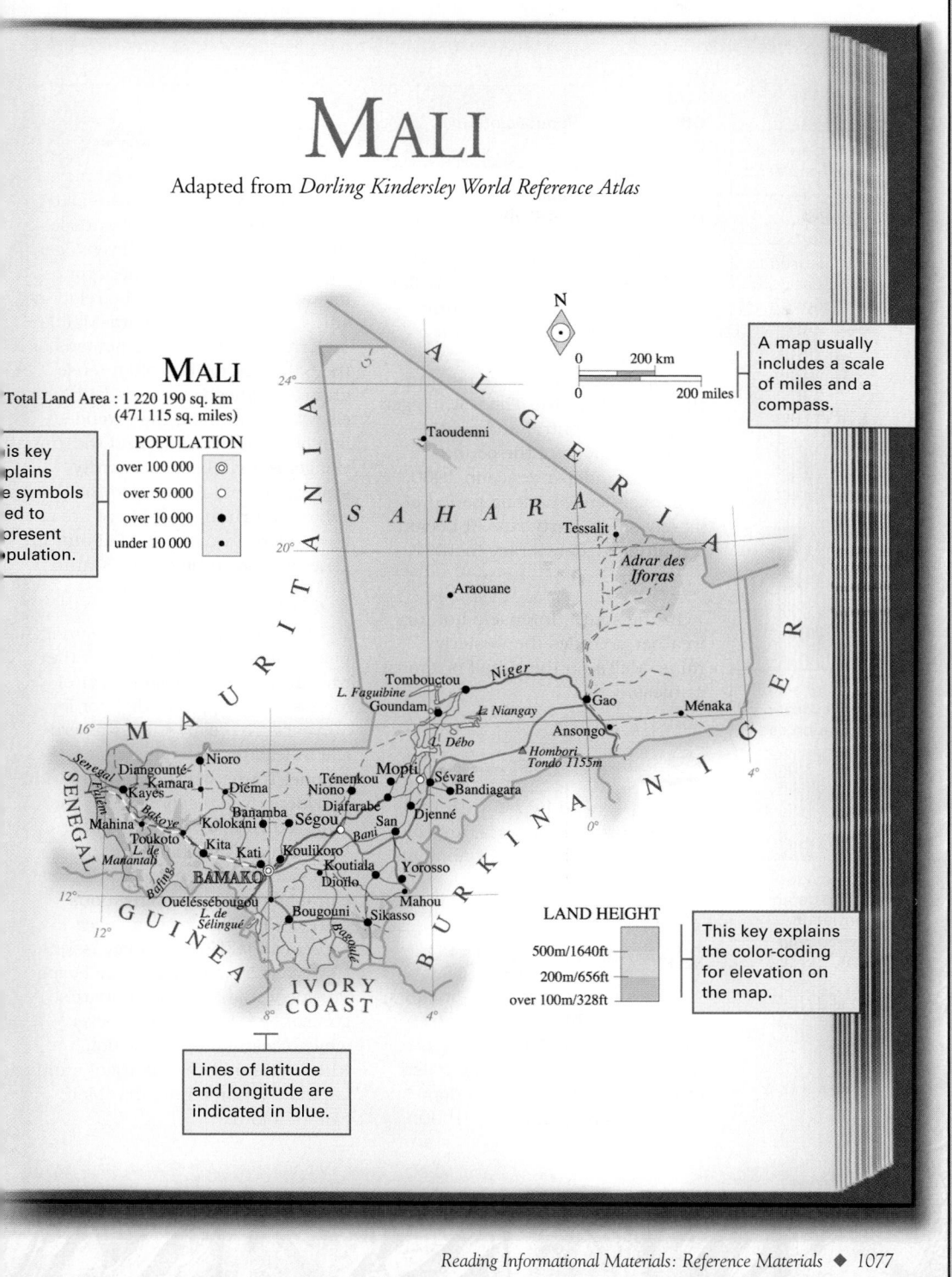

MALI

Adapted from *Dorling Kindersley World Reference Atlas*

MALI

Total Land Area : 1 220 190 sq. km
(471 115 sq. miles)

POPULATION

over 100 000	◎
over 50 000	○
over 10 000	●
under 10 000	·

is key
plains
e symbols
ed to
oresent
pulation.

N

0 _____ 200 km

0 _____ 200 miles

A map usually includes a scale of miles and a compass.

LAND HEIGHT

500m/1640ft	
200m/656ft	
over 100m/328ft	

This key explains the color-coding for elevation on the map.

Lines of latitude and longitude are indicated in blue.

ALGERIA

MAURITANIA

SAHARA

Taoudenni

Tessalit

Adrar des Iforas

Araouane

NIGER

Tombouctou

Niger

L. Faguibine

Goundam

Lac Niangay

Gao

Ménaka

L. Débo

Ansongo

▲ *Hombori Tondo 1155m*

Nioro

Diangounté-Kamara

Diéma

Ténenkou

Niono

Mopti

Sévaré

Bandiagara

SENEGAL

Kayes

Mahina

Banamba

Diafarabe

San

Djenné

Toukoto

Kolokani

Ségou

Kita

Koulikoro

Kati

Bani

BAMAKO

Koutiala

Djollo

Yorosso

Ouéléssebougou

L. de Sélingué

Bougouni

Mahou

Sikasso

BURKINA

GUINEA

IVORY COAST

Reading Informational Materials: Reference Materials ◆ 1077

Mali

- Point out the various features on the map. There are two keys. Lines of latitude and longitude are indicated in blue.
- Ask students what the key at the top indicates.
  Answer: It indicates populations in different cities or towns.
- Ask students what the key at the bottom indicates.
  Answer: The key indicates land height or elevation.

(continued on p. 1078)

CUSTOMIZE INSTRUCTION FOR UNIVERSAL ACCESS

For Special Needs Students	For Less Proficient Readers
Have students work in small groups. Each group can be responsible for finding information on Mali in one or two categories. Have each group share its information with other groups so that together the groups present a comprehensive picture of Mali.	Have these students start with an outline with heads like Climate, Transportation and so on. They should carefully scan each section and note important information. The resulting outline will be a quick picture of important information on Mali.

Mali (continued)

- Tell students that the key facts about Mali are summarized in the chart at the top. Ask students what categories of information they will find here.
  Answer: The categories include Official Name, Capital, Population, Currency, and Official Language.

- Have students list the main categories of information in the article.
  Answer: As given by the red heads, the categories include Climate, Transportation, Tourism, People, and Politics.

- Point out the various icons and have students identify each.
  Answer: The small plane indicates the airport at Bamako-Senou; the ship indicates a port; the suitcase indicates the number of visitors; the arrow indicates a statistical decline; the face with a speech ballon indicates major ethnicities or languages; the group of people indicates population density.

- Ask students explain how the system of boxed heads helps them read the article.
  Possible response: It makes locating information easy.

- Then, ask students under which head they would find information on roads in Mali.
  Answer: They would find information on roads under the head "Transportation."

1078

Key facts are summarized here.

Icons are used to call out basic information

Heads are set off to make locating information easy.

Text provides more in-depth information.

MALI

Official Name: *Republic of Mali*
Capital: *Bamako*
Population: *10.8 million*
Currency: *CFA franc*
Official Language: *French*

Mali is landlocked in the heart of West Africa. Its mostly flat terrain comprises virtually uninhabited Saharan plains in the north and more fertile savanna land in the south, where most of the population live. The River Niger irrigates the central and southwestern regions of the country. Following independence in 1960, Mali experienced a long period of largely single-party rule. It became a multiparty democracy in 1992.

CLIMATE

In the south, intensely hot, dry weather precedes the westerly rains. Mali's northern half is almost rainless.

TRANSPORTATION

 Bamako-Senou   Has no fleet

Mali is linked by rail with the port of Dakar in Senegal, and by good roads to the port of Abidjan in Ivory Coast.

TOURISM

 16,000 visitors   Down 33% in 1994

Tourism is largely safari-oriented, although the historic cities of Djénné, Gao and Mopti, lying on the banks of the River Niger, also attract visitors. A national domestic airline began operating in 1990.

PEOPLE

 Bambara, Fulani, Senufo, Soninke, French   24 people per sq. mile

Mali's most significant ethnic group, the Bambara, is also politically dominant. The Bambara speak the *lingua franca* of the River Niger, which is shared with other groups including the Malinke. The relationship between the Bambara–Malinke majority and the Tuareg nomads of the Saharan north is often tense and sometimes violent. As with elsewhere in Africa, the extended family, often based around the village, is a vital social security system and a link between the urban and rural poor. There are a few powerful women in Mali but, in general, women have little status.

POLITICS

The successful transition to multiparty politics in 1992 followed the overthrow in the previous year of Moussa Traoré, Mali's dictator for 23 years. The army's role was crucial in leading the coup, while Colonel Touré, who acted as interim president, was responsible for the swift return to civilian rule in less than a year. The change marks Mali's first experience of multiparty ism. Maintaining good relations with the Tuaregs, after a peace agreement in 1991, is a key issue. However, the main challenge facing President Alpha Oumar Konaré's government is to alleviate poverty while placating the opposition, which feels that the luxury of multipartyism is something that Mali cannot afford.

Check Your Comprehension

1. What is Mali's most significant ethnic group?
2. Which part of Mali almost always goes without rain?
3. When did Mali change from a dictatorship to a multiparty system?
4. What is Mali's official language?
5. For what tourist attraction is Mali most noted?

Applying the Reading Strategy

Skimming and Scanning

6. For items 1–5 above, explain whether you found the answer by skimming or by scanning.
7. Referring to the atlas entry, explain an important change to the political system of Mali in the 1990s. How did you find this information?
8. Scan the map to locate the capital of Mali. Explain how you found it.

Activity

Planning a Trip

Based on the information you can gather from this atlas entry, plan a trip to Mali. Decide the best time of year to go, what kind of clothing to take, and what you want to do while you are there. Generate a list of questions that you need answered in order to plan your trip more effectively.

Contrasting Informational Materials

Physical Maps and Road Maps

The map of Mali is a physical map, a type of map that shows the geographical features of an area. Another useful type of map is a road map. Get a road map, and answer these questions.

Physical Map		Road Map	
Keys	✓	✓	
Compass			
Scale of Miles			
Elevation			
Bodies of water			
Highways			

1. (a) What kinds of information can you find on a physical map that you cannot find on a road map? (b) What kinds of information can you find on a road map that you cannot find on a physical map?
2. Fill in a chart like the one shown at right to compare and contrast the features of a road map and a physical map.
3. In what situations would each of these maps be useful?

Answers continued

2.

Features	Road Map	Physical Map
Keys	Yes	Yes
Compass	Yes	Yes
Scale of Miles	Yes	Yes
Distances	Yes	No
Elevation	No	Yes
Bodies of Water	Yes	Yes
Other Natural Features	Some	Yes
Highways	Yes	Generally not
Towns/Cities	Yes	Generally fewer

3. Road maps would be useful when planning or taking a trip by car or bus. Physical maps would be useful to see relative locations of natural features at a glance.

Model From Literature

Letters to the editor share much in common with other persuasive forms, such as persuasive essays: They support a position with evidence, using appropriate, forceful language. Alexander Solzhenitsyn's Nobel Lecture is an example of such persuasive writing.

Prewriting

- Have volunteers share their ideas on controversial hot topics. Ask them to identify their source: television, newspapers, the Internet, or discussions with family and friends.

- Have students make a chart and identify the two sides of each topic. Then, have students decide which side they would like to present.

- Help students narrow their topics by looping: students write freely on their topic for five minutes, then circle their most important idea and write about that idea for five minutes. If students have trouble identifying their most important idea, have them work with partners and discuss which is the most important.

- Before students draft their letters, have them review the Rubric for Self-Assessment (p. 1083) so they know what is expected.

Writing WORKSHOP

Letter to the Editor

A **letter to the editor** is a type of business letter in which you present your opinion about a current event and support it with relevant facts, examples, or personal experiences. People write to the editors of magazines and newspapers to express their opinions on the content of the publication or on a public issue. In this workshop, you will write a letter to the editor of a publication.

Assignment Criteria Your letter to the editor should have the following characteristics:

- Standard business letter format, including heading, inside address, greeting, body, closing, and signature
- Formal language that states your opinion
- Relevant facts, examples, or personal experiences to support your opinion

To preview the criteria on which your letter to the editor may be assessed, see the Rubric on page 1083.

Prewriting

Choose a hot topic. Watch television, scan newspapers, or listen carefully to the issues your friends and family are discussing right now. In a chart like the one below, identify the two sides of several controversial topics, and then decide whether you feel strongly enough about any of the arguments to present it in a letter.

Narrow your topic. When you have chosen a topic, consider all the points you must make to convince your readers. Limiting your topic to one specific issue or problem enables you to cover your topic thoroughly. **Looping** is one strategy you can use.

Pro	Hot Topics	Con
Professional athletes have a responsibility to the public	Sports Heroes as Role Models	Excellent athletes necessarily models non-sports skills.
Restrictions can protect our youngest citizens.	Laws restricting the Internet	Freedom of speech nied by restrictions

1. First, write freely on your topic for about five minutes.

2. Read what you have written, and circle the most important idea.

3. Then, write for five minutes on that idea.

4. Continue this process until you come to a topic that is narrow enough to address in your letter to the editor.

5. If you keep writing, you may even be able to identify a thesis statement, or main idea, that you want your letter to communicate.

Student Model

Before you begin drafting, read this student model and review the characteristics of an effective letter to the editor.

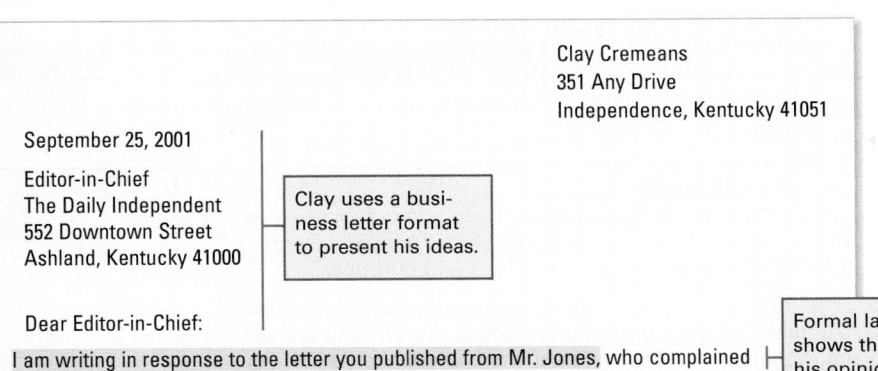

Clay Cremeans
351 Any Drive
Independence, Kentucky 41051

September 25, 2001

Editor-in-Chief
The Daily Independent
552 Downtown Street
Ashland, Kentucky 41000

> **Clay uses a business letter format to present his ideas.**

Dear Editor-in-Chief:

I am writing in response to the letter you published from Mr. Jones, who complained about our band's playing at the last football game.

> **Formal language shows that Clay takes his opinion—and his readers—seriously.**

The point of high-school band programs is to train students to play together to produce one stirring, harmonious sound. Because of a lack of instruction, education, and familiarity with music and instruments, this is difficult for some students. Band programs all over the country have inspired many students to go into the field of music, but many do not meet the requirements that they need to compete with those outside of high school. I personally know students who have been denied scholarships and have had scholarships revoked because they have not been properly trained. The Kenton County School District needs to devise a class that will alleviate these problems.

> **Clay supports his arguments with personal experiences.**

This new music class should have a staff composed of teachers who can play and teach all of the band instruments. Students need one-on-one, as well as group instruction. Of course, hiring a full staff of musicians for every school would cost a lot. Instead, full band directors could be hired for all the schools to share. This would allow students to gain a greater knowledge of music from a larger group of musicians. These teachers would offer more insight into the history and theory of music.

> **Clay points out a counterargument and suggests an alternative plan.**

With so many young people interested in fine arts, band directors cannot offer everyone the instruction that is needed. For the band to improve as a whole, everyone has to grow. Many of today's band directors try hard to develop better musicians, yet, because of a lack of time and staffing, feel disappointed and discouraged.

With adequate time and staffing, students will be able to make music together and demonstrate their talents. With an experienced music staff and better classes, I believe that Mr. Jones will be happier with our band's performance.

> **The conclusion reinforces Clay's ideas.**

Sincerely,

Clay Cremeans

Clay Cremeans

Student Model

- Explain that the letter to the editor is a sample. Students' letters may be longer or shorter depending upon their topics and what they wish to convey.
- Be sure students understand the importance of the correct return address, date, internal address and proper salutation.
- Point out that Clay clearly and succinctly states his reason for writing. In this way, he betters his chances of catching the editor's interest.
- Point out that the personal experiences Clay offers are an appropriate part of a letter to an editor.
- Discuss Clay's proposal. Ask students: How does he support his proposal?
  Answer: He provides evidence in the form of personal observations that the current band program is inadequate. He also notes that his proposal will be less costly than an alternative solution.
- Finally, ask students what the purpose of the final paragraph is.
  Possible response: Its purpose is to refer back to the reason for writing the letter and reinforce the proposal.

Real-World Connection

Tell students that they will often encounter situations about which they want to present an opinion. A letter to the editor is a good vehicle for that purpose. In class, discuss situations in which letters to editors might be warranted, such as local elections.

CUSTOMIZE INSTRUCTION FOR UNIVERSAL ACCESS

For Less Proficient Writers	For English Learners	For Advanced Writers
Have these students work with a partner with a similar opinion to decide on a topic and draft a letter.	Provide magazines or newspapers with examples of letters to editors that are good models. Have the students discuss why the models are good examples.	Find examples of letters to editors in newspapers or magazines. Have these students rewrite the letters to improve them.

Drafting

- Explain to students that using a block or modified block format means not indenting paragraphs. In block format, all elements, including addresses and the closing, are flush left. In modified block style, the return address, date, closing, and signature are indented to the center. Make sure their letters look professional and carry all the necessary information.

- Remind students that they should state the purpose of their letter up front and be sure that their details support their purpose. Conversely, remind them that extraneous information has no place in their letters and may dilute their purpose.

- Discuss appropriate tone and style with students. It will be most difficult to maintain a positive, polite tone in a letter of complaint. Encourage students to work at it, for a polite letter will obtain better results.

Revising

- Ask students to highlight topic sentences and underline their supporting statements. Then, have them assess support to see if their argument is strong enough.

- Encourage students to check for extraneous details that may relate to the topic but that detract from their overall message.

continued

Writing WORKSHOP *continued*

Drafting

Use a block or modified block format. A business letter is usually written in one of two general formats. See the chart at right for more information about these accepted styles.

Provide clear, purposeful information. Clearly explain your purpose in the opening lines of the letter. Then, support your position with details—such as examples, statistics, and facts—or with quotations from people who are familiar with the subject. Stay on track. Avoid adding information that does not directly support your main idea and purpose.

Use the appropriate vocabulary, tone, and style. Think about your audience. Use a tone that is positive and controlled. Even if you are voicing a complaint, remain polite. The style and vocabulary should suit your audience.

Provide supporting details. As you draft, make your writing convincing and give it depth by providing supporting details. The supporting details you choose should define, restate, explain, or illustrate your main points.

Revising

Revise to add support. Review your letter to evaluate whether you have included enough supporting details to make your argument successful. Highlight topic sentences, and underline supporting evidence. If a topic sentence has fewer than two supporting details, consider adding more evidence to support it or determine whether the point is worth including.

Block Format
• All elements of the letter begin flush left

Modified Block Format
• Heading, closing, and signature are indented to center of
• Everything else is flush

Model: Adding Supporting Details

Band programs all over the country have inspired many students to go into the field of music, but many do not meet the requirements that they need to compete with those outside of high school. The Kenton County School District needs to devise a class that will alleviate these problems.

I personally know students who have been denied scholarships and have had scholarships revoked because they have not been properly trained.

Clay has added personal knowledge to support his statement in this paragraph.

USING TECHNOLOGY IN WRITING

If students are using computers, they might want to boldface the type or use the highlight option to make their topic sentences stand out. This will make it easier for them to review their organization and to check for support. In addition, they can use the computer's thesaurus to help them find persuasive words. Emphasize the importance of checking a dictionary before using an unfamiliar word.

Students can also use the organizing tools and revision checkers available on the **Writing and Grammar iText CD-ROM**.

Revise to include appropriate language. Review your draft, giving special attention to your vocabulary, tone, and style. Use Standard American English, a polite tone, and a formal style.

Informal: The park's a mess cause you people are too lazy to pick up the trash.

Formal: The park is littered with trash because park employees have not done enough to remove it or to provide enough receptacles for it.

Compare the model and nonmodel. Why is the model more effective?

Nonmodel	Model
Look for words that can be revised to be more persuasive. This letter is an argument against that crabby Mr. Jones who insulted our band and how we played at the last football game.	*Look for words that are close in meaning but more powerful than those used in the nonmodel.* I am writing in response to the letter you published from Mr. Jones, who complained about our band's playing at the last football game.

Publishing and Presenting

Choose one of the following ways to share your writing with classmates or a wider audience.

Mail your letter. Write, type, or word-process your letter and mail it. When you get a response, share it with classmates.

Post your letter for classmates. Post your letter on a classroom bulletin board, or upload it onto a classroom computer so that other students can read it and discuss your ideas.

WG *Prentice Hall Writing and Grammar Connection: Chapters 7 and 15*

Rubric for Self-Assessment

Evaluate your letter to the editor using the following criteria and rating scale:

Criteria	Rating Scale				
	Not very				Very
Does your letter have each of the six main parts of a business letter: heading, inside address, salutation, body, closing, and signature?	1	2	3	4	5
Does the letter follow strict block or modified block format?	1	2	3	4	5
Are the vocabulary, tone, and style appropriate for your audience?	1	2	3	4	5
Is an opinion clearly stated?	1	2	3	4	5
Do all details support the central idea of your letter?	1	2	3	4	5

TEST-TAKING TIP

When taking a test that includes a letter-writing prompt, students should be careful to allow enough time for each step of the process. Though it is likely that a topic will be given, prewriting is still important, because this is the stage at which students gather support for their position. Suggest that students use a pro and con "T-chart" like the one on p. 1080 to jot down what they know about their topic. Remind them to use an appropriate format and include all the parts of a business letter.

continued from p. 1082

- Write on the board.

  Hey, you, get off that lousy cell phone.

  Would you please talk more softly on your cell phone.

  Ask students which request is more likely to get the results they want and why.
  Answer: The second statement is likelier to get results because it is polite and uses appropriate language.

- Have students compare the Model and the Nonmodel, noting the differences. Discuss what was changed and why the changes made the Model more effective.
  Answer: The Nonmodel uses insulting and confrontational language. The Model is more even-handed, and it introduces the subject of the letter with a more appropriate opening phrase.

- Ask students to go through their letters identifying examples of nonstandard American English, impolite tone, or informal style. Ask them to replace these items.

Publishing and Presenting

- Remind students of the proper way to address an envelope. Be sure that they include a return address and the correct postage.

- Encourage students to share positive comments about one another's letters. Discuss common areas of improvement.

Assessment

- Review the assessment criteria in class.

- Before students proceed with self-assessment, have them score the Student Model in class, using one or more of the rubric categories, to help them see how to apply the criteria.

Lesson Objectives

1. To learn about interviewing techniques
2. To learn how to prepare for an interview
3. To learn to take an active role in an interview

Preparation

- Remind students of the resources available to them to learn about a job or a company. Students can list these resources and then see what information they can get from each.

- Have students select a job, do research on a company, and then prepare questions to ask in the interview. Have them then work in pairs, each partner reviewing the other's questions. Then, have each partner suggest one way to present a positive attitude and professional appearance.

Participate in the Interview

- Emphasize the importance of appropriate language in the interview process. Ask students to give one example of an appropriate way to greet the interviewer and introduce themselves.

- Remind students to bring a notepad. Ask what kinds of notes they would take.
  Possible responses: They might take notes on job responsibilities, working conditions, pay rates, benefits, and education needed.

- Have students prepare for the Activity by listing questions they might be asked in an interview for the job they have selected. For each question, they should work out a response.

- After students complete the Activity on the student page, have them fill out the Feedback Form. When they finish the form, have them discuss their answers as a class or in small groups.

Listening and Speaking WORKSHOP

Interviewing Techniques

One of the most important skills you can learn, and one that you may use over and over in the years ahead, is that of **interviewing**. The following strategies will help you prepare for and participate in a job interview. Use the Feedback Form to help you improve your skills.

Preparation

A successful job interview requires more than showing up and answering questions. Above all, it requires preparation. Follow these planning steps:

Learn about the job and the company. Use the library and Internet, and ask friends and family about the company and the job you want.

Prepare to ask relevant questions. During an interview, you should share information about yourself and gather information about the company, the job, the benefits, and the working environment. Having thoughtful questions prepared in advance will help you make a good impression, so jot down a few to ask during the interview.

Participate in the Interview

Take an active role in an interview. In addition to good posture and a friendly attitude, keep these tips in mind:

- **Use language that conveys maturity, sensitivity, and respect.** Through your language, demonstrate that you will respond appropriately to the responsibilities of the job you are seeking.

- **Make notes of responses to questions.** Take a notepad with you, and jot down notes on what you learn, concerns you have, and issues you may want to think about or research later.

- **Respond correctly and effectively to questions.** Listen attentively, and respond precisely and fully to the questions asked. Listen to your interviewer's responses to help you determine what is important, and then use these cues to ask follow-up questions.

- **Demonstrate your knowledge of the subject or organization.** Draw on your research to volunteer information and to ask questions that reflect your knowledge of the company.

Activity:
Analyzing a Speech Working with a partner, review the help-wanted ads in a newspaper. Select a job, prepare for it, and role-play an interview. Use the Feedback Form to evaluate your interview.

1084 ◆ *Epics and Legends*

Feedback Form for an Interview

Rating System
+ = Excellent   ✔ = Average   – = Weak

Preparation
Knowledge of company _____
Knowledge of job requirements _____
List of specific questions _____

Interview
Appropriate language _____
Response to questions _____
Demonstration of knowledge _____

Answer the following questions:
What did I learn about the company during the interview?

What would I do differently in preparation for another interview?

CUSTOMIZE INSTRUCTION FOR UNIVERSAL ACCESS

Less Proficient Readers	Special Needs Students	English Learners
Have students print out or photocopy materials about the companies they have chosen. Then, have them highlight information that would affect them as employees. Have them devise questions and comments based on this information.	Have these students discuss as a group what they would expect from a job and what an employer would expect of them. Guide the discussion to lead students to formulate questions they might ask of an interviewer.	Students who are English learners may need special help with appropriate language. Before they begin the Activity, list out and define the following terms for them: *prior experience, benefits, hours, compensation, profit-sharing, initiative, self-starter, work ethic,* and *professionalism.*

Assessment WORKSHOP

Organization

In some tests, you may be required to demonstrate your knowledge of writing and revising skills in a multiple-choice format. The questions often test your ability to determine the correct order or sequence of sentences. To answer these kinds of questions, consider the following:

- Writers may organize material in a number of ways. They may explain events chronologically, build up ideas in order of importance, compare and contrast ideas or things, or show the effects of causes.

- Notice how the material is presented and developed in order to help you understand it.

Test-Taking Strategies

- Begin by locating the sentence that contains a main idea or concept.
- Eliminate any choice that begins the sequence with a sentence that would not logically begin a paragraph.

Sample Test Item

Directions: Read the passage, and answer the question that follows.

(1) Drivers are compelled to wear seat belts or be in violation of the law. (2) Because more people now wear seat belts, the number of automobile-related deaths has dropped. (3) Many states now have seat-belt laws. (4) More states should consider enacting seat-belt laws as a way to save lives. (5) Drivers who violate the law are given hefty fines.

1 Choose the sequence of sentence numbers that will make the structure of the paragraph most logical.

A NO CHANGE

B 5,4,3,1,2

C 3,1,5,2,4

D 1,4,2,3,5

Answer and Explanation

The correct answer is *C*. Any arrangement of sentences provides information, but the one in *C* makes the passage most logical because it introduces the concept of seat-belt laws, explains how they work, and presents a proposal based on the information.

▶ Practice

Directions: Read the passage, and answer the questions that follow.

(1) It is time for all citizens to realize that these laws make sense. (2) Several cities have enacted laws prohibiting bicycling on sidewalks. (3) When will people realize that bicycles should not be allowed on sidewalks? (4) Such laws have prevented injuries to pedestrians. (5) Many city sidewalks are clogged with cyclists competing for space with pedestrians.

1 Choose the sequence that will make the structure of the paragraph most logical:

A 3,5,2,4,1

B 1,2,3,5,4

C 5,3,1,2,4

D 4,2,1,3,5

2 Which of the following sentences would best support the ideas of this passage:

A Cyclists have rights, too.

B How many more pedestrians must be injured before we wake up?

C Bicycling can be fun.

D Dog walkers are a problem, too.

Applying Reading Strategies

Explain that the appropriate organization of a passage that presents an argument depends on the relation of sentences to a main topic. The sentence introducing the topic should appear at the beginning of the passage. Sentences giving further information about the topic should come next. Usually, sentences drawing conclusions about the topic should appear at the end.

Applying Test-Taking Strategies

- Have students read the sample test item and locate the sentence that contains the main idea.
  Answer: (3) Many states now have seat belt laws.

- Have students identify the sentences that give details about these laws. What is the best position for these sentences in the paragraph?
  Answer: Sentences (1), (2), and (5) each give details about the topic. Since these sentences tell more about the topic, they should follow the topic sentence.

- Have students identify the sentence that draws a conclusion from the other information in the passage. Why is the end of the paragraph the best position for this sentence?
  Answer: Sentence (4) draws a conclusion from other information in the passage. It belongs at the end because the reader needs to know the facts about seat-belt laws in sentence (2) before it will seem valid.

- Have students use these strategies to complete the Practice question.

Answers

1. The correct answer is *A*. Answers *B* and *C* are incorrect, because sentence (1) presents a conclusion about "these laws," so it must come after sentence (2), which introduces the laws. Answer *D* is incorrect because

sentence (4) tells more about the laws; it should follow (2).

2. The correct answer is *B*. Answers *A* and *C* are incorrect, because they speak positively of cycling and so contradict the main idea of the passage, which emphasizes a danger posed by cyclists. Answer *D* is incorrect because it merely distracts from this main idea.

TEACHING RESOURCES

The following resources can be used to enrich or extend the instruction on p. 1085.

 PRENTICE HALL
ASSESSMENT SYSTEM

 Workbook

 Transparencies

 Skill Book

💿 **CD-ROM**

RESOURCES

Suggestions for Sustained Reading R1

Glossary R7

Handbooks

Tips for Improving Reading Fluency R10

Literary Terms Handbook R12

Rubric Handbook R20

Writing Handbook R24
The Writing Process R24
The Modes of Writing R26

Formatting Business Letters R29

Spelling Handbook R30

Grammar and Mechanics Handbook R34
Summary of Grammar R34
Summary of Capitalization and Punctuation R35
Glossary of Common Usage R37

Internet Research Handbook R39

Writing Criticism and Citing Sources R41

Indexes

Index of Authors and Titles R44

Index of Skills R46

Index of Features R51

Acknowledgments (continued) R53

Credits R56

llowing are some suggestions for longer works
will give you the opportunity to experience the fun
stained reading. Each of the suggestions further
ores one of the themes in this book. All of the titles
ncluded in the **Prentice Hall Literature Library,** fea-
g the **Penguin Literature Library.**

u may want to consult your teacher before choos-
ne of these longer works.

it 1: On the Edge

Lord of the Flies
William Golding
Perigee Book, 1954

William Golding's exciting and
terrifying story has been a favorite
of high-school and college students
since it was published in 1954. A
plane crashes on a tropical island in
the Pacific, stranding a group of six-
velve-year-old boys from a private school. The boys
lly react to their plight by forming a cooperative
ety that enables everyone to share the bare essen-
necessary to survive. However, the boys' society
kly degenerates into a nightmarish power struggle
ght on by their darkest fears and impulses.

tes from Underground Selected Stories
lor Dostoyevsky, translated
ndrew R. MacAndrew
et Classic, 1961

m a sick man . . . a mean man."
opening lines of this book's title
take you deep into the mind of a
who sees the world as a dark,
rgiving place. This unlikely narrator lives life like a
jee from the outside world. He avoids communi-
g with co-workers and his interactions with old
ol friends are awkward and loaded with suspicion.
s from Underground is a record of the narrator's
sophy and thoughts as he lives his underground
By turns humorous, self-contradictory, arrogant,
pitying, and spiteful, the narrator provides a reveal-
ook at the inner psychology of a disturbed man.

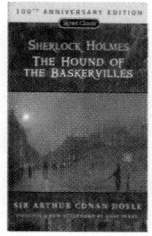

The Hound of the Baskervilles
Sir Arthur Conan Doyle
Signet Classic, 2001

A mysterious death on a dark, desolate moor prompts an urgent visit to
the famous detective Sherlock
Holmes. This fast-paced mystery novel
begins as the doctor of the deceased
man explains the suspicious circumstances of the
death to Holmes and his assistant Watson. An ancient
curse surrounds the dead man's family—the
Baskervilles. Centuries before, an ancestor had met a
violent death at the jaws of a large hellhound. Unlike
that grisly death, this time there were no apparent signs
of violent struggle surrounding the victim—just a frozen
look of horror on his face and the footprints of a gigantic hound. Holmes sends Watson to wander the marshy
grounds of the Baskerville estate and pore over the evidence. Will Watson and Holmes find the culprit before
the next Baskerville heir meets his own untimely death?

The Legend of Sleepy Hollow and Other Stories in The Sketch Book
Washington Irving
Signet Classic, 1961

Washington Irving, creator of such
well-known characters as Ichabod
Crane and Rip Van Winkle, put America
on the literary map. With his colorful
short stories, Irving invented a literary genre and introduced American customs and attitudes to Old World
readers. The title story of this collection tells the tale of
the high-strung Connecticut schoolteacher Ichabod
Crane. Crane settles in a quiet New York village and
starts teaching classes. He soon discovers the town is
not as sleepy as it seems. Late at night, a headless
horseman—a ghost from the Revolutionary War—is said
to haunt the dense, dark forests surrounding the village.
When Crane disappears without a trace one gloomy
night, the astonished villagers do not know whether to
blame a jealous rival—or the headless horseman.

To the Teacher:

Because great literature reflects
all of life's realities, both positive
and negative, classroom discussions of literature can raise sensitive and often controversial issues.
Before you recommend novels,
plays, and other literature to your
students, you may want to consider the values and sensitivities
of the community in which you
teach, as well as the age and
sophistication of your students.
It is also a good policy to preview
any literature that you are considering recommending to your
students. The notes below offer
some guidance on specific titles.

Unit 1

Lord of the Flies
by William Golding

Sensitive issues include the violence
and murder that occur when rifts
develop between the groups of boys.

***Notes from Underground
and Selected Stories***
by Fyodor Dostoyevsky

"Baklushkin's Story" contains murder, violence, and racial slurs.
"Akulka's Husband" contains gender
slurs, drunkenness, wife beating,
and murder. "In the Hospital" contains torture in prison. "Notes from
Underground" contains references
to sadism, prostitution, drinking,
and fighting. "The Dream of a
Ridiculous Man" mentions suicide.

The Hound of the Baskervilles
by Sir Arthur Conan Doyle

In addition to violent crimes, this
novel contains smoking; drinking;
instances of racial, gender, and class
prejudice; discussion of controversial
theories that relate skull shapes to
ethnic types; and references to the
supernatural.

***The Legend of Sleepy Hollow and
Other Stories in The Sketch Book***
by Washington Irving

Although Irving's treatment of
Native Americans may seem bigoted
by today's standards, his descriptions
were considered generous in his
day. Similarly, his depiction of
women may seem disparaging and
stereotypical, but it too is a product
of his times. The book contains
some instances of magic and the
supernatural.

Treasure Island
by Robert Louis Stevenson

Episodes of violence include Tom's knifing murder, the gun-and-cutlass battle in the fort in which several men are killed or injured, and the fight aboard the *Hispaniola* in which Hands is killed and Jim is pinned to the mast with a knife.

Unit 2

Silas Marner
by George Eliot

Students may be sensitive to the cruel aspects of the English class system and may disagree with Eliot's ideas about community-centered religion.

Jane Eyre
by Charlotte Brontë

In the course of this novel, there are instances of verbal, physical, and emotional abuse. Rochester's confession of bigamy at the wedding altar may disturb some students. Other sensitive issues include death, homelessness, and begging.

A Raisin in the Sun
by Lorraine Hansberry

Students may take issue with Walter's drinking and his desire to own a liquor store. Mama's emphasis on religion may offend some students. Ruth's dilemma over whether or not to have an abortion may be upsetting to certain students. The play contains profanity and racial slurs.

Treasure Island
Robert Louis Stevenson
Penguin Books, 1999

There is plenty of substance as well as style in Robert Louis Stevenson's thrilling adventure of pirates and treasure. The excitement begins when the narrator, the teenager Jim Hawkins, discovers a treasure map in the sea chest of an old pirate. He quickly sets sail with a group of friends to find the treasure. Unfortunately, others—led by the notorious pirate Long John Silver—have heard about the treasure as well. The pirates' lust for gold will drive them to great lengths, including treachery and murder, to be the first to uncover the treasure. Many familiar hallmarks of pirate stories can be found among the peg legs and mutinous crews of *Treasure Island*. Above all, however, the story is a gripping, masterly narrative beloved by readers and writers alike, from Mark Twain to Rudyard Kipling.

Unit 2: Striving for Success

Silas Marner
George Eliot
Signet Classic, 1999

George Eliot combines elements of social realism and fairy tale in this story of monetary loss and spiritual gain. The hero of Eliot's story is an extremely nearsighted linen weaver in nineteenth-century England. Silas Marner is unjustly accused of a theft that was actually committed by his best friend. Choosing exile over a life amongst his accusers, Marner remains a recluse in a small country village for fifteen years. There, he hoards the gold that he earns from his trade. When circumstances deprive him of that as well, Marner must end his long reclusiveness. Having lost everything he once held dear, he finds that all of his chances for redemption hinge on a little orphan girl with golden hair.

Jane Eyre
Charlotte Brontë
Signet Classic, 1997

When *Jane Eyre* was published 1844, the actions of the heroine shocked many critics, but the book was embraced by much of the English public. An orphan who refuses to bound by her low social class, Jane Eyre defies all who try to mistreat her. She fights back when the siblings in her adoptive family torment her continues to resist when she is banished to a dismal boarding school called Lowood. The arbitrary rules, tyrannical teachers, and harsh conditions of Lowood sap the spirit of most girls there, but not Jane's. Eventually, she leaves Lowood to become a governess in home of the mysterious Mr. Rochester. When the two develop an unexpected attraction and Rochester reveals a shocking secret, Jane must find the stren to demand mutual sacrifice before the two can unit

A Raisin in the Sun
Lorraine Hansberry
Vintage Books, 1988

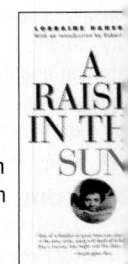

The riveting drama that brought Lorraine Hansberry national acclaim takes its inspiration from the Langston Hughes poem "A Dream Deferred." In *A Raisin in the Sun,* Hansberry answers Hughes's troubling question "What happens to a dream deferred?" by presenting the struggles of the Youngers. An African American family living in a Chicago housing projec the 1950s, the Youngers aspire to a different li As the family seeks to improve its lot, each charact wrestles with the questions that arise from their shared circumstances—questions of identity, justi assimilation, and survival. First performed in 1959, Hansberry's searing social drama was called "the that changed American theater forever" by *The Ne York Times*. Other critics have ranked it in importan with masterpieces like *Death of a Salesman* and *Th Glass Menagerie*.

Places Left Unfinished at the Time of Creation
John Phillip Santos
Penguin Books, 1999

John Phillip Santos's family memoir takes place amidst the rich hybrid of cultures along the border of Mexico and Texas. The Santos family was part of a wave of desperate immigrants that came to Texas to build a new life after the Mexican Revolution. Santos, a journalist and former Rhodes scholar, brings his family history to life with a magical, poetic style that effortlessly mixes the flavors of Spanish and English. Along the way, he creates a set of memorable characters that span generations. There is Madrina, a spiritual woman who has had the gift of prophecy since childhood, and Teofilo, a boy raised by the Kikapu Indians of northern Mexico. As he weaves the rich tapestry of his family's history, Santos conveys an important message about the preservation of memory across time and national borders.

Roughing It
Mark Twain
Signet Classic, 1962

Roughing It is a loosely autobiographical narrative of Mark Twain's efforts to strike it rich in the rough-and-tumble American West of the mid-nineteenth century. In the course of recounting his travels and tribulations, Twain does not feel the need to let the literal truth, or a neat story line, get in the way of a good yarn. As a result, Twain's memoirs of his time spent as a prospector, speculator, mill worker, and reporter are full of the colorful characters, rambling diversions, and humorous exaggerations that enliven his best fiction writing. Twain finds that he is not very good at silver prospecting or amassing millions, but he does uncover interesting characters like Slade the Terrible—whose wife could produce blazing guns from under her petticoats in the blink of an eye.

Unit 3: Clashing Forces

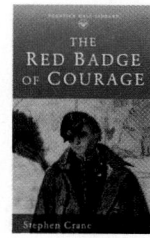

The Red Badge of Courage
Stephen Crane
Pearson Prentice Hall, 2000

Stephen Crane's classic novel about the American Civil War ushered in a new era of war stories. Instead of an epic about victory and defeat in battle, *The Red Badge of Courage* follows the personal reactions of one soldier, a young idealistic farm boy named Henry Fleming. He joins the Union Army out of a sense of patriotism, but also as a way of demonstrating his own maturity. When faced with real combat, though, Fleming struggles with feelings of doubt and fear. His crisis of nerve shames Fleming, and he steels himself to enter the fighting. Swept suddenly into the heat of battle, Henry must confront his fears and make a choice between cowardice and courage that may well cost him his life.

Animal Farm
George Orwell
Signet Classic, 1946, 1996

George Orwell wrote this simple tale with a powerful message about revolution to express his disillusionment with Soviet Russia. *Animal Farm* tells the allegorical story of the beasts of Manor Farm. Suffering from hunger and neglect at the hands of Mr. Jones, the animals rebel, driving the farmer and his wife from the land. The animals set up their own society in which "all animals are equal." Equality, however, means different things to different animals. To the dismay of some of the animals, they soon find that "some animals are more equal than others." Whether read as a scathing indictment of Joseph Stalin's totalitarian regime or as a fable about how easily ideals are corrupted by power, *Animal Farm* packs a tremendous punch.

Places Left Unfinished at the Time of Creation
by John Phillip Santos

This book deals with family secrets, including the apparent suicide of the author's grandfather. Some students may find the graphic description of killing a deer to be unsettling.

Roughing It
by Mark Twain

Students may react negatively to some of Twain's disparaging remarks about Native Americans, African Americans, and Asians.

Unit 3

The Red Badge of Courage
by Stephen Crane

This novel vividly depicts the horrors of war, including details of Henry's encounters with wounded, dying, and dead soldiers.

Animal Farm
by George Orwell

This book contains various depictions of cruelty to animals. For students whose families have lived in countries with repressive governments, this book may stir painful feelings.

Things Fall Apart
by Chinua Achebe

This book describes life in a rural Nigerian village where cultural practices include polygamy and both the social and the ritual drinking of alcohol (palm wine). Also present are instances of violence, including the ritual murder of a young man and the physical abuse of women and children. Some disturbing wartime practices, such as the taking of human heads, are described.

Les Misérables
by Victor Hugo

The various depictions of child abuse, from Cosette's beatings to Gavroche's neglect, may disturb some students. The issues surrounding prostitution and illegitimacy are a major focus of this book. There is also a great deal of violence, especially in the barricade scenes, where many die of gunshot wounds.

Four Major Plays, Volume 1
by Henrik Ibsen

All of the plays contain marital situations that some may find offensive. In *A Doll House,* the wife walks out on her husband, leaving her children behind. In *The Wild Duck,* a past affair, possibly adulterous, may have produced an illegitimate child. In *Hedda Gabler,* two of the characters seem to be carrying on an adulterous relationship. The main character in *The Master Builder,* who is married, seems to have an interest in two young women and may have had improper relations with one when she was underage. In addition, certain characters in *The Wild Duck* and *The Master Builder* drink excessively.

Unit 4

Of Mice and Men
by John Steinbeck

The shooting of Lenny, a mentally impaired man, may upset some readers. The novel also contains some profanity, drinking, and card games. Racial epithets are directed at Crooks, an African American, and sexist terms are directed at Curley's wife.

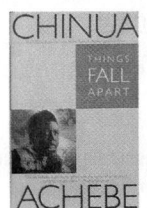

Things Fall Apart
Chinua Achebe
Anchor Books, 1959

One of the most dramatic developments in the second half of the twentieth century was the withdrawal of colonialist powers from Africa. Writers like Nigerian Chinua Achebe, who made a moral case for decolonization, had a significant impact on establishing support for African independence. *Things Fall Apart* tells the story of Okonkwo, a prosperous Ibo farmer and village elder. Life is complicated for Okonkwo even before the colonialists arrive. Once widely respected, he is banished for the accidental killing of a fellow Ibo. When he returns from exile, he finds that the traditional beliefs and cultural practices of his village have been undermined by the arrival of missionaries and colonial authorities. Through one man's story, told in a simple yet eloquent style, *Things Fall Apart* exposes the crippling effect that colonialism had on African societies.

Les Misérables
Victor Hugo, translated by Lee Fahnestock and Norman MacAfee
Signet Classic, 1987

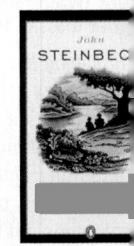

Victor Hugo's sweeping nineteenth-century epic centers around the French peasant Jean Valjean. Desperately poor, Valjean is driven to petty crime—stealing a loaf of bread—in an attempt to feed his starving family. Valjean is thrown into prison for nineteen years and emerges a bitter, unrepentant man. However, when a kind priest shows him mercy after catching Valjean trying to steal his household silver, Valjean vows to change his ways. He seeks to redeem himself by trying to help a poor, unfortunate young woman and her daughter. More than just an exciting story and interesting character study, *Les Misérables* is also a fascinating slice of early nineteenth-century French history. It chronicles a period when forces supporting royal authority and proponents of greater democracy tore apart and remolded French society.

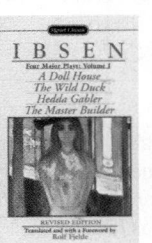

Four Major Plays, Volume
Henrik Ibsen, translated by Rolf Fje
Signet Classic, 1992

Great drama has the power to shock audiences and to shake them into a reexamination of themselves and society. When Henrik Ibsen's *A Doll House* first premiered in Decemb 1879, it had this type of galvanizing effect. Audiences watching the play witnessed the dramatic unraveling of a marriage under the pressur of rigid ideas about the duties of husbands and wive. The strong-willed attitude of the play's heroine, Nora Helmer, prompted outcry and debate about the expec tations of women in European society. Each of the other plays in this collection sparked a further questioning of social attitudes. Like *A Doll House,* they hav transcended their time and still have the power to su prise contemporary readers with their vivid characte and challenging ideas.

Unit 4: Turning Points

Of Mice and Men
John Steinbeck
Penguin Books, 1965

John Steinbeck's classic story relates the unforgettable friendship between two California migrant workers: Lenny, simple-minded but kindhearted, and George, headstrong, determined, and devoted to protecting Lenny. Clearly, the two have left some trouble behind them a have been forced to start over again and again. This time, however, the friends have a plan: They will make enough money to acquire a farm of their own and lea their life of dependence behind. Just when the plan seems within reach, however, a tragic turn of events brings an unexpected end to their dreams.

Selected Stories
Anton Chekhov, translated by Ann Dunnigan
Signet Classic, 1960

The general public knows Anton Chekhov mainly as a dramatist, but he was an accomplished short-story writer as well. In this collection of stories, Chekhov reveals the same brilliance in creating characters and depicting the lives of ordinary Russians that he exhibits in his plays. Choosing people from every walk of life—from landowner to peasant—he portrays their daily struggles without casting judgment.

The Mayor of Casterbridge
Thomas Hardy
Signet Classic, 1999

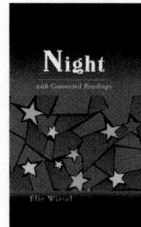

Few novels have such a dominant character, startling beginning, and tragic story line as *The Mayor of Casterbridge*. The figure of the deeply flawed title character, Michael Henchard, towers over the book like a figure in a Greek tragedy. In the shocking opening scene, Henchard publicly betrays his family in an unforgivable way. Much of the rest of his life is spent trying to atone for this act of betrayal, which he keeps to himself. Over the years, the secret gnaws at him and threatens to jeopardize his newfound respectability as the Mayor of Casterbridge.

A Separate Peace
John Knowles
Bantam Books, 1959

A Separate Peace examines the intense, often conflicting, feelings of a close friendship between two teenage boys. The story is told by one friend looking back from a perspective of fifteen years. The boys are roommates in an exclusive New England boarding school during the summer of 1942. Phineas and Gene, the two friends, could not be more dissimilar: Phineas is a fearless, athletic boy, and Gene is an intellectual who envies Phineas's easy self-assurance. Still, they form a bond that is part friendship, part rivalry.

Night with Connected Readings
Elie Wiesel
Pearson Prentice Hall, 2000

Elie Wiesel emerged from the Nazi death camps with an overwhelming desire to tell the world about the horrors he had experienced. Instead of writing an autobiographical account, he wrote a fictional story that closely mirrors his own struggle to survive. Like the fictional protagonist in *Night*, Wiesel was deported to a death camp as a teenager and endured the agony of the death of his entire family. *Night* describes in horrific detail the nightmarish world of the death camps, where survival is a combination of luck, resourcefulness, and sheer will. This shattering experience becomes a pivotal moment of his young life, when this devout boy asks the wrenching question, "How could this be allowed to happen?" As with most difficult questions, he finds no satisfying answers.

Unit 5: Expanding Horizons

The Song of the Lark
Willa Cather
Signet Classic, 1991

Music has the power to awaken people to important facets of themselves. When the young Thea Kronborg, the lead character in Willa Cather's *The Song of the Lark*, first hears Dvořák's New World Symphony, she immediately connects it to the flat, expansive, high-plains region where she was born. Cather traces Thea's development from a sheltered girl in Colorado to a successful opera singer. Along the way, people and places spark key moments of realization that inspire her to nurture her artistic voice. Singing onstage with a traveling musician, she suddenly notices the range and depth of her voice. Later, while visiting Arizona at a low point in her life, Thea experiences love and loss, and she draws from the desert landscape the strength she needs to continue as an artist.

Suggestions for Sustained Reading ◆ R5

Selected Stories
by Anton Chekhov

In some of these stories, students will encounter drunkenness and acts of physical violence against women and children. There may be some discomfort with certain sexual situations in the book as well.

The Mayor of Casterbridge
by Thomas Hardy

This novel opens with the drunken Michael Henchard selling his wife by auction at a county fair. Henchard's drinking, accompanied by fits of rage, is presented as a serious problem, which causes him to abstain from alcohol for the next two decades.

A Separate Peace
by John Knowles

The grimness of the war, Leper's insanity, Gene's psychological struggle, and Finny's death are potential sources of discomfort for students.

Night with Connected Readings
by Elie Wiesel

This book chronicles anti-Semitism and the enslavement, oppression, and genocide of European Jews during World War II. The main character experiences a loss of religious faith as a result of these events. Sexual abuse is mentioned, and language is used that may be considered offensive by some students.

Unit 5

The Song of the Lark
by Willa Cather

This story contains negative stereotypes of African Americans, Mexicans, Native Americans, and Jews; looting of sacred Native American burial grounds; alcoholism; and extramarital affairs.

Up From Slavery
by Booker T. Washington

Some students may be upset by this book's depiction of the brutal nature of slavery and the racist treatment that African Americans experienced during the post–Civil War period. Other students, particularly those unaware of the historical context, may find Washington's embrace of segregation difficult to understand.

Typical American
by Gish Jen

This novel alludes to sexual activity, including adultery and premarital sex. Some sensitive readers may find the overt and covert racism displayed by some of the characters discomforting.

Literature of the Expanding Frontier
Prentice Hall Anthology

In "Spirits of the Railways," issues of racism may disturb some students. In the excerpt from "The Life and Adventures of Nat Love," racial terms like *half-breed* and *colored* may prove controversial. In "Flight," name-calling leads to physical violence that some students may find disturbing.

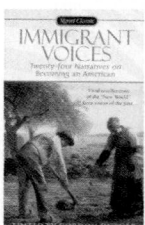

Immigrant Voices: Twenty-four Narratives on Becoming an American
Edited by Gordon Hutner
Signet Classic, 1999

The phrase "a nation of immigrants" is often used as shorthand for the constant change created in American society when new citizens reach its shores. However, this common phrase only captures immigration in its largest sense. In *Immigrant Voices,* Gordon Hutner lets immigrants tell their individual stories of struggle and sacrifice, broken dreams and unimagined successes. In this volume, immigrants from many nations of the world are represented. They describe the expanded opportunities that brought them to the United States and the diverse paths they took once they got here. A Pulitzer Prize winner, a rich industrialist, a social reformer, and a female pioneer are some of the various voices included in this informative book.

Up From Slavery
Booker T. Washington
Signet Classic, 2000

At the turn of the twentieth century, when the struggle for justice for African Americans was at a crossroads, the voices of two leaders were dominant. One of these leaders, Booker T. Washington, is the author of *Up From Slavery*. The book describes Washington's remarkable rise from slavery to become one of the leading advocates for African Americans. Through hard work, Washington sets out to disprove widespread stereotypes of African Americans. He founds the Tuskegee Institute as a place where former slaves can learn job skills. A powerful orator, he demands equality for all Americans. As a result, Washington finds himself both praised and criticized—praised for his message of self-empowerment, but criticized by the other eminent African American of his time, W.E.B. Du Bois, for accepting racist doctrines.

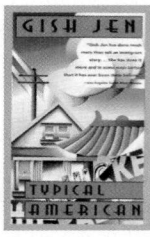

Typical American
Gish Jen
Plume, 1991

Some immigrants to the United States do not intend to stay long. They come to acquire a skill or go to school, then plan to return home. Sometimes, however, these events do not quite work out as planned. In Gish Jen's first novel, Yifeng leaves China to study engineering in the United States. When the Chinese Communists seize power in the late 1940s, he decides not to return to China. Yifeng easily becomes "Ralph Chang," but he finds it more difficult to leave his cultural values behind with his Chinese name. With his sister Theresa and his wife, Helen, Ralph tries to find compromise between the American dream of material success and the Chinese emphasis on family and education. The sometimes uneasy compromises the characters must make cast a revealing light on the immigrant experience.

Literature of the Expanding Frontier
Prentice Hall Anthology
Pearson Prentice Hall, 2000

To some extent, our contemporary view of frontier America is drawn from the media. Countless western television shows and movies contribute to this view, but they can also distort it. Taking a page from historians, it is interesting to go back to earlier sources to learn about the West from those with connections to the period. *Literature of the Expanding Frontier* achieves this aim by presenting works of literature from the earliest days of settlement to the closing of the frontier. The collection varies in focus and perspective, from Mark Twain's offbeat description of stagecoach travel to Rain-in-the-Face's description of life among Sioux warriors. In the course of the anthology, the West is constantly redefined as settlers push relentlessly toward the Pacific and northward to Alaska.

abashed (ə basht′) *adj.*: Embarrassed

adept (ə dept′) *adj.*: Expert; highly skilled

admonition (ad′ mə nish′ ən) *n.*: Warning; mild reprimand

adroit (ə droit′) *adj.*: Clever

aggrieved (ə grēvd′) *v.*: Wronged

alluvium (ə loo′ vē əm) *n.*: Material such as sand or gravel deposited by moving water

amenable (ə mē′ nə bəl) *adj.*: Responsive; open

amiably (ā′ mē ə blē) *adv.*: In a cheerful, friendly way

anarchists (an′ ər kists) *n.*: Those who disrespect laws or rules

annals (an′ əlz) *n.*: Historical records or chronicles; history

apotheosis (ə päth′ ē ō′ sis) *n.*: Glorification of a person or thing; raising of something to the status of a god

apprenticed (ə pren′ tist) *v.*: Assigned to work a specified length of time in a craft or trade in return for instruction

appurtenances (ə purt′ ən əns əz) *n.*: Accessories

arabesque (ar′ ə besk′) *adj.*: Elaborately designed

arable (ar′ ə bəl) *adj.*: Suitable for growing crops

ardent (är′ dənt) *adj.*: Warm or intense in feeling

arias (är′ ē əz) *n.*: Melodies in an opera, especially for solo voice with instrumental accompaniment

assailed (ə sāld′) *v.*: Attacked physically

assimilate (ə sim′ ə lāt′) *v.*: To absorb into a greater body

assuage (ə swāj′) *v.*: Calm; pacify

asunder (ə sun′ dər) *adv.*: Into pieces or parts

audaciously (ô dā′ shəs lē) *adv.*: In a bold way

august (ô gust′) *adj.*: Imposing and magnificent

austere (ô stir′) *adj.*: Severe; stern

avaricious (av′ ə rish′ əs) *adj.*: Greedy for riches

banal (bā′ nəl) *adj.*: Dull or stale because of overuse

belay (bi lā′) *n.*: Rope support

blasphemy (blas′ fə mē) *n.*: Disrespectful action or speech against a deity

bough (bou) *n.*: Tree branch

bouquet (boo kā′) *n.*: Fragrance

bowels (bou′ əlz) *n.*: Intestines

brittle (brit′ əl) *adj.*: Stiff and unbending; easily broken or shattered

centenarian (sen′ tə ner′ ē ən) *n.*: Person who is at least one hundred years old

cessation (se sā′ shən) *n.*: Stopping, either forever or for some time

chastisement (chas tīz′ mənt) *n.*: Punishment; severe criticism

choleric (cäl′ ər ik) *adj.*: Quick-tempered

chorister (kôr′ is tər) *n.*: Member of a chorus

clarity (klar′ ə tē) *n.*: The quality or condition of being clear

commiserate (kə miz′ ər āt′) *v.*: Sympathize; share suffering

communal (käm yoo′ nəl) *adj.*: Shared by the community

compelled (kəm peld′) *v.*: Forced to do something

condescension (kän′ di sen′ shən) *n.*: Looking down upon; regarding as below one's dignity

conferred (kən furd′) *v.*: Granted or bestowed

confounded (kən found′ id) *adj.*: Confused

consorted (kän sôr′ tid) *v.*: Joined; accompanied

conspicuous (kən spik′ yoo əs) *adj.*: Easy to see

constituents (kən stich′ oo ənts) *n.*: Components; parts

contagious (kən tā′ jəs) *adj.*: Spread by direct or indirect contact

contemplation (kän′ tem′ plə shən) *n.*: Thoughtful inspection; study

contemplatively (kən tem′ plə tiv lē) *adv.*: In a thoughtful or studious way

contention (kən ten′ shən) *n.*: Statement that one argues for

contrition (kən trish′ ən) *n.*: Feeling of remorse for having done something wrong

convalescents (kän′ və les′ ənts) *n.*: People who are recovering from illness

conviction (kən vik′ shən) *n.*: Strong belief

convoluted (kän′ və loot′ id) *adj.*: Intricate; twisted

convulsive (kən vul′ siv) *adj.*: Marked by an involuntary muscular contraction

cosmic (käz′ mik) *adj.*: Relating to the universe

countenance (koun′ tə nəns) *n.*: Expression on a person's face

counterfeiting (koun′ tər fit′ iŋ) *v.*: Making imitation money to pass off as real money

covert (kuv′ ərt) *adj.*: Hidden; secret

credulity (krə doo′ lə tē) *n.*: Tendency to believe too readily

crocheted (krō shād′) *v.*: Made with thread or yarn woven with hooked needles

cursory (kur′ sə rē) *adj.*: Superficial; done rapidly with little attention to detail

deference (def′ ər əns) *n.*: Yielding in thought

deftness (deft′ nis) *n.*: Skillfulness

demeanor (di mēn′ ər) *n.*: Behavior

deranged (də rānjd′) *adj.*: Unsettled

destitute (des′ tə toot′) *adj.*: Poverty stricken; in great need

destitute (des′ tə toot′) *n.*: Those living in poverty

detained (dē tānd′) *v.*: Kept in custody

dilapidated (də lap′ ə dāt′ id) *adj.*: Fallen into a shabby and neglected state

dire (dīr) *adj.*: Calling for quick action; urgent

disapprobation (dis ap′ rə bā′ shən) *n.*: Disapproval

discernible (di zurn′ i bəl) *adj.*: Recognizable; noticeable

disconsolate (dis kän′ sə lit) *adj.*: So unhappy that nothing will comfort

discourse (dis kôrs′) *v.*: Speak formally and at length

disparaged (di spar′ ijd) *v.*: Spoke slightly of; belittled

disparaging (di spar′ ij iŋ) *adj.*: Belittling; showing contempt for

disreputable (dis rep′ yoo tə bəl) *adj.*: Not respectable

divulge (də vulj′) *v.*: Reveal

doddering (däd′ ər iŋ) *adj.*: Shaky, tottering, or senile

doughty (dout′ ē) *adj.*: Brave; valiant

eclectic (ek lek′ tik) *adj.*: Composed of material from various sources

edifice (ed′ i fis) *n.*: Building

effete (e fēt′) *adj.*: Lacking vigor; overrefined

emanating (em′ ə nāt′ iŋ) *v.*: Coming forth

encroaching (en krōch′ iŋ) *v.*: Trespassing or intruding

engender (in jen′ dər) *v.*: Bring about; cause; produce

ensign (en′ sən) *n.*: Old word for a standard-bearer; one who carries a flag

enthralls (en thrôlz′) *v.*: Captivates; fascinates

envy (en′ vē) *n.*: Feeling of desire for another's possessions or qualities and jealousy at not having them

ephemeral (i fem′ ə rəl) *adj.*: Passing quickly

epitaph (ep′ ə taf) *n.*: Inscription on a tomb or gravestone

essence (es′ əns) *n.*: Crucial element or basis

euphemism (yoo′ fə miz′ əm) *n.*: Word or phrase substituted for a more offensive word or phrase

expedient (ek spē′ dē ənt) *adj.*: Convenient

expedition (eks′ pə dish′ ən) *n.*: Journey or voyage for a definite purpose

exploit (eks′ ploit) *n.*: Act or deed, especially a heroic achievement

expound (eks pound′) *v.*: Explain in detail

exquisite (eks′ kwi zit) *adj.*: Delicately beautiful

facetiousness (fə sē′ shəs nəs) *n.*: Act of making jokes at an inappropriate time

fallow (fal′ ō) *adj.*: Plowed but not planted

fastidious (fas tid′ ē əs) *adj.*: Not easy to please; discriminating

fervor (fur′ vər) *n.*: Passion; zeal

fettered (fet′ ərd) *adj.*: Restrained, as with a chain

flout (flout) *v.*: Show open contempt

fomentation (fō men tā′ shən) *n.*: Incitement; a stirring up

fomentations (fō′ mən tā′ shənz) *n.*: Applications of warm, moist substances in the treatment of an injury

forbore (fôr bôr′) *v.*: Refrained from

ford (fôrd) *n.*: Shallow place in a stream or river where people can cross

foreboding (fôr bōd′ iŋ) *n.*: Feeling that something bad will happen

forestalled (fôr stôld´) v.: Prevented by having done something ahead of time

forlorn (fər lôrn´) adj.: Abandoned; deserted

fortuitous (fôr tōō´ ə təs) adj.: Accidental and beneficial at the same time

frond (fränd) n.: Leaflike shoot of seaweed

furtively (fur´ tiv lē) adv.: Secretly; stealthily

fusillade (fyōō´ sə lād´) n.: Something that is like the rapid firing of many firearms

gibe (jīb) v.: Jeer; taunt

gout (gout) n.: Spurt; splash; glob

grimace (gri´ məs) n.: Twisted facial expression

grimacing (grim´ əs iŋ) v.: Making a twisted or distorted facial expression

guileless (gīl´ lis) adj.: Without slyness or cunning; frank

habiliments (hə bil´ ə mənts) n.: Clothing

hindrances (hin´ drəns əz) n.: People or things in the way; obstacles

hue (hū) n.: Color; tint

imminent (im´ ə nənt) adj.: About to happen

immutable (im myōōt´ ə bəl) adj.: Unchangeable

impediments (im pēd´ ə məntz) n.: Something standing in the way of something else

impending (im pen´ diŋ) adj.: About to happen

imperceptibly (im pər sep´ tə blē) adv.: In such a slight way as to be almost unnoticeable

imperious (im pir´ ē əs) adj.: Commanding; powerful

imperiously (im pir´ ē əs lē) adv.: Arrogantly

impertinence (im purt´ ən əns) n.: Inappropriate, rude action

impetuous (im pech´ ōō əs) adj.: Impulsive; passionate

implicit (im plis´ it) adj.: Essentially a part of; inherent

imploring (im plôr´ iŋ) v.: Asking or begging

importunity (im´ pôr tōōn´ i tē) n.: Persistence in requesting or demanding

impregnable (im preg´ nə bəl) adj.: Unconquerable; not able to be captured

incessantly (in ses´ ənt lē) adv.: Endlessly; constantly

incredulity (in´ krə dōō´ lə tē) n.: Unwillingness or inability to believe

indigence (in´ di jəns) n.: Poverty

indignant (in dig´ nənt) adj.: Feeling or expressing anger or scorn, especially at an injustice

indignantly (in dig´ nənt lē) adv.: Feeling anger as a reaction to ungratefulness

indomitable (in däm´ it ə bəl) adj.: Not easily defeated

induced (in dōōst´) v.: Caused

indulgence (in dul´ jəns) n.: Leniency; forgiveness

inert (i nurt´) adj.: Lacking the power to move; inactive

inestimable (in es´ tə mə bəl) adj.: Priceless; beyond measure

inexorably (in eks´ ə rə blē) adv.: Certainly

infested (in fest´ id) adj.: Overrun by

infirmity (in fur´ mə tē) n.: Illness; physical defect

influx (in´ fluks) n.: A coming in

ingratiating (in grā´ shē āt´ iŋ) adj.: Bringing into favor

inherent (in hir´ ənt) adj.: Inborn; existing naturally and inseparably

insatiable (in sā´ shə bəl) adj.: Cannot be satisfied; constantly wanting more

interminable (in tur´ mi nə bəl) adj.: Seemingly endless

irascible (i ras´ ə bəl) adj.: Easily angered; quick-tempered

itinerary (ī tin´ ər er´ ē) n.: Route

jangle (jaŋ´ gəl) n.: Discord; harsh sounds

jauntiness (jônt´ ē nis) n.: Carefree attitude

jovial (jō´ vē əl) adj.: Full of good humor

judicious (jōō dish´ əs) adj.: Showing good judgment; wise and careful

laborious (lə bôr´ ē əs) adj.: Involving or calling for much hard work; difficult

labyrinth (lab´ ə rinth) n.: Maze

laconic (lə kän´ ik) adj.: Terse; using few words

lacquered (lak´ ərd) adj.: Coated with varnish made from shellac or resin

lamentation (la mən tā´ shən) n.: Act of crying out in grief; wailing

legacies (leg´ ə sēz) n.: Money, property, or position left in a will to someone

lifeless (līf´ lis) adj.: Without life

limpid (lim´ pid) adj.: Perfectly clear; transparent

litany (lit´ ən ē) n.: Series of responsive religious readings

loomed (lōōmd) v.: Appeared in a large or threatening form

luminous (lōō´ mə nəs) adj.: Giving off light

malevolent (mə lev´ ə lənt´) adj.: Intended as evil or harmful

malice (mal´ is) n.: Desire to harm or see harm done to others

maligned (mə līnd´) adj.: Spoken ill of

manifestation (man´ ə fes tā´ shən) n.: Something that is made clear or plainly revealed

manifestations (man´ ə fes tā´ shənz) n.: Appearances or evidence

marginal (mär´ jən əl) adj.: Occupying the borderland of a stable area

mauled (môld) adj.: Roughly or clumsily handled

melancholy (mel´ ən käl´ ē) adj.: Sad and depressed

metamorphosis (met´ ə môr´ fə sis) n.: Change of form

misconstrued (mis kən strōōd´) v.: Misunderstood; misinterpreted

monosyllabic (mon´ ō si lab´ ik) adj.: Having only one syllable

moreover (môr ō´ vər) adv.: In addition to; further

mottled (mät´ əld) adj.: Marked with spots of different shades

mutable (myōōt´ ə bəl) adj.: Capable of change

mutiny (myōōt´ ən ē) n.: Open rebellion against authority

myriad (mir´ ē əd) adj.: Huge number; seemingly countless

nevertheless (nev´ ər thə les´) adv.: In spite of that; however

nonchalantly (nän´ shə länt´ lē) adv.: Casually; indifferently

obliterates (ə blit´ ə rāts´) v.: Destroys; erases without a trace

officious (ə fish´ əs) adj.: Overly ready to serve

opacity (ō pas´ ə tē) n.: Quality of not letting light pass through

oration (ô rā´ shən) n.: Formal speech, especially one given at a state occasion, ceremony, or funeral

oratory (ôr´ ə tôr´ ē) n.: Skill in public speaking

paddocks (pad´ əks) n.: Small enclosed fields

pallor (pal´ ər) n.: Lack of color; unnatural paleness

paranoia (par´ ə noi´ ə) n.: Mental disorder characterized by delusions of persecution

peons (pē´ änz) n.: Laborers

pervaded (pər vād´ id) v.: Spread throughout; filled

philosophy (fə läs´ ə fē) n.: System of principles or beliefs

piety (pi´ ə tē) n.: Holiness; respect for the divine

piously (pi´ əs lē) adv.: With actual or pretended religious devotion

piquancy (pē´ kən sē) n.: Pleasantly sharp quality

piqued (pēkt) v.: Offended

plausibility (plô´ zə bil´ ə tē) n.: Believability

poignant (poin´ yənt) adj.: Emotionally moving

portentous (pôr ten´ təs) adj.: Foreboding; full of unspecified meaning

portentously (pôr ten´ təs lē) adv.: Ominously; scarily

potency (pōt´ ən sē) n.: Power

precarious (prē ker´ ē əs) adj.: Dangerously lacking in security or stability

precipitous (prē sip´ ə təs) adj.: Steep

presage (prē sāj´) v.: Warn of a future event

prey (prā) n.: Animal hunted and killed for food

primeval (prī mē´ vəl) adj.: Ancient or primitive

procession (prō sesh´ ən) n.: Number of persons or things moving forward in an orderly or formal way

prodigious (prə dij´ əs) adj.: Enormous

proficiency (prō fish´ ən sē) n.: Expertise

profound (prō found´) adj.: Deep

promontories (präm´ ən tôr´ ēz) n.: High places extending out over a body of water

prosaic (prō zā´ ik) adj.: Commonplace; ordinary

protagonist (prō tag´ ə nist´) n.: Main character; person who plays a leading part

provender (präv´ ən dər) n.: Food

psychopathic (sī´ kō path´ ik) *adj.:* With a dangerous mental disorder

purified (pyoor´ ə fīd´) *v.:* Cleansed; made pure.

raked (rākt) *v.:* Scratched or scraped, as with a rake

rank (raŋk) *adj.:* Growing vigorously and coarsely

rapture (rap´chər) *n.:* State of being filled with joy

reap (rēp) *v.:* Gather

reciprocity (res´ ə präs´ ə tē) *n.:* Mutual action; dependence

refuse (ref´ yōōz) *n.:* Anything thrown away as useless

relish (rel´ ish) *n.:* Pleasure and enjoyment

repertoire (rep´ ə twär´) *n.:* Stock of songs that a singer knows and is ready to perform

replication (rep´ lə kā´ shən) *n.:* Echo or reverberation

repressed (ri prest´) *v.:* Held back or restrained

resolution (rez´ ə lōō´ shən) *n.:* Strong determination

reveling (rev´ əl iŋ) *v.:* Taking great pleasure

revere (ri vir´) *v.:* Regard with deep respect and love

rheumatic (rü ma´ tik) *adj.:* Suffering from a disease of the joints; able to move only with great pain

sagacity (sə gas´ ə tē) *n.:* Wisdom

sated (sāt´ əd) *v.:* Satisfied or pleased

satiated (sā´ shē ā tid) *v.:* Having had enough; full

saturated (sach´ ə rāt´ id) *v.:* Completely filled; thoroughly soaked

scrimmage (skrim´ ij) *n.:* Rough-and-tumble fight

scrutinized (skrōōt´ ən īzd´) *v.:* Looked at carefully; examined closely

sententiously (sen ten´ shəs lē) *adv.:* Pointed; expressing much in few words

sheaf (shēf) *n.:* Bundle of grain

shirked (shurkt) *v.:* Neglected or avoided

sidle (sī´ dəl) *v.:* Move sideways in a sneaky way

slanderous (slan´ dər əs) *adj.:* Damaging to a person's reputation

sordid (sôr´ did) *adj.:* Dirty; filthy

sovereigns (säv´ rənz) *n.:* British gold coins worth one pound each

spare (sper) *adj.:* Lean or thin

spurn (spurn) *v.:* Old word meaning "to kick disdainfully"

staidness (stād´ nəs) *n.:* State of being settled or resistant to change

stark (stärk) *adj.:* Bare; plain

staunch (stônch) *adj.:* Steadfast; loyal

stifle (stī´ fəl) *v.:* Hold back

stupefied (stōō´ pə fīd´) *adj.:* Dazed; stunned

stupor (stōō´ per) *n.:* Mental dullness, as if drugged

subjectively (səb jek´ tiv lē) *adv.:* Personally

sublimity (sə blim´ ə tē) *n.:* A noble or exalted state

sullen (sul´ ən) *adj.:* Gloomy; sad

sullenness (sul´ ən nəs) *n.:* Gloom; sadness

sultry (sul´ trē) *adj.:* Oppressively hot and moist; sweltering

supernal (sə purn´ əl) *adj.:* Celestial or divine

supplication (sup´ lə kā´ shən) *n.:* The act of asking humbly and earnestly

surly (sur´ lē) *adv.:* In a proud, commanding way

surpassed (sər past´) *v.:* Went beyond; excelled

syndrome (sin´ drōm) *n.:* Group of signs that occur together and may form a pattern

synthesis (sin´ thə sis) *n.:* Whole made up of separate elements put together

synthesized (sin´ thə sīzd´) *v.:* Made by bringing together different elements

synthetic (sin thet´ ik) *adj.:* Artificially made

taciturn (ta´ sə tərn) *adj.:* Preferring not to talk; uncommunicative; silent

taut (tôt) *adj.:* High-strung; tense

tempering (tem´ pə riŋ) *adj.:* Modifying or adjusting

tenuous (ten´ yōō əs) *adj.:* Slight; flimsy; not substantial or strong

terra firma (ter´ ə fur´ mə) *n.:* Latin for "solid earth."

thrall (thrôl) *n.:* Servant; slave

timorous (tim´ ər es) *adj.:* Full of fear; timid

titanic (tī tan´ ik) *adj.:* Huge and powerful

topography (tə päg´ rə fē) *n.:* Surface features of a place, such as rivers, lakes, mountains, and so on

transcends (tran sendz´) *v.:* Goes above or beyond limits; exceeds

transoms (tran´ səmz) *n.:* Small windows

tremulous (trem´ yōō ləs) *adj.:* Trembling; quivering

trod (träd) *v.:* Walked

trough (trôf) *n.:* Long, shallow V-shaped container from which farm animals drink water or eat feed

tumult (tōō´ mult) *n.:* Noisy commotion

ulterior (ul tir´ ē ər) *adj.:* Undisclosed; beyond what is openly stated

undulations (un´ dyōō lā´ shənz) *n.:* Waves

unwieldy (un wēl´ dē) *adj.:* Hard to manage because of shape or weight

usurped (yōō surpt´) *v.:* Taken power over; held by force

venerable (ven´ ər ə bəl) *adj.:* Worthy of respect by reason of age and dignity, character, or position

ventured (ven´ chərd) *v.:* Took a risk

veracity (və ras´ ə tē) *n.:* Truthfulness; honesty

vernal (vurn´ əl) *adj.:* Springlike

vertigo (vur´ ti gō) *n.:* Dizzy, confused state of mind

vestibule (ves´ tə byōōl´) *n.:* Small entrance hall or room

vigilance (vij´ ə ləns) *n.:* Watchfulness; alertness

vile (vīl) *adj.:* Extremely disgusting

vociferous (vō sif´ ər əs) *adj.:* Loud; noisy

volition (vō lish´ ən) *n.:* The act of using the will

wallowed (wäl´ ōd) *v.:* Enjoyed completely; took great pleasure

warrens (wôr´ ənz) *n.:* Mazelike passages

watershed (wô´ tər shed) *n.:* Moment or event after which nothing is the same

weir (wēr) *n.:* Low dam

zenith (zē´ nith) *n.:* Highest point

When you were younger, you learned to read. Then, you read to expand your experiences or for pure enjoyment. Now, you are expected to read to learn. As you progress in school, you are given more and more material to read. The tips on these pages will help you improve your reading fluency, or your ability to read easily, smoothly, and expressively.

Keeping Your Concentration

One common problem that readers face is the loss of concentration. When you are reading an assignment, you might find yourself rereading the same sentence several times without really understanding it. The first step in changing this behavior is to notice that you do it. Becoming an active, aware reader will help you get the most from your assignments. Practice using these strategies:

- Cover what you have already read with a note card as you go along. Then, you will not be able to reread without noticing that you are doing it.

- Set a purpose for reading beyond just completing the assignment. Then, read actively by pausing to ask yourself questions about the material as you read.

- Use the Reading Strategy instruction and notes that appear with each selection in this textbook.

- Stop reading after a specified period of time (for example, 5 minutes) and summarize what you have read. To help you with this strategy, use the Reading Check questions that appear with each selection in this textbook. Reread to find any answers you do not know.

✔ Reading Check

What common problem do many readers face?

Reading Phrases

Fluent readers read phrases rather than individual words. Reading this way will speed up your reading and improve your comprehension. Here are some useful ideas:

- Experts recommend rereading as a strategy to increase fluency. Choose a passage of text that is neither too hard nor too easy. Read the same passage aloud several times until you can read it smoothly. When you can read the passage fluently, pick another passage and keep practicing.

- Read aloud into a tape recorder. Then, listen to the recording, noting your accuracy, pacing, and expression. You can also read aloud and share feedback with a partner.

- Use the *Prentice Hall Listening to Literature* audiotapes or CDs to hear the selections read aloud. Read along silently in your textbook, noticing how the reader uses his or her voice and emphasizes certain words and phrases.

✔ Reading Check

In what ways will reading phrases rather than individual words affect your reading?

Understanding Key Vocabulary

If you do not understand some of the words in an assignment, you may miss out on important concepts. Therefore, it is helpful to keep a dictionary nearby when you are reading. Follow these steps:

- Before you begin reading, scan the text for unfamiliar words or terms. Find out what those words mean before you begin reading.
- Use context—the surrounding words, phrases, and sentences—to help you determine the meanings of unfamiliar words.
- If you are unable to understand the meaning through context, refer to the dictionary.

Paying Attention to Punctuation

When you read, pay attention to punctuation. Commas, periods, exclamation points, semicolons, and colons tell you when to pause or stop. They also indicate relationships between groups of words. When you recognize these relationships you will read with greater understanding and expression. Look at the chart below.

✔ **Reading Check**

Why should you look up words you do not know when reading an assignment?

Punctuation Mark	Meaning
comma	brief pause
period	pause at the end of a thought
exclamation point	pause that indicates emphasis
semicolon	pause between related but distinct thoughts
colon	pause before giving explanation or examples

Using the Reading Fluency Checklist

Use the checklist below each time you read a selection in this textbook. In your Language Arts journal or notebook, note which skills you need to work on and chart your progress each week.

Reading Fluency Checklist

- ❏ Preview the text to check for difficult or unfamiliar words.
- ❏ Practice reading aloud.
- ❏ Read according to punctuation.
- ❏ Break down long sentences into the subject and its meaning.
- ❏ Read groups of words for meaning rather than reading single words.
- ❏ Read with expression (change your tone of voice to add meaning to the word).

Reading is a skill that can be improved with practice. The key to improving your fluency is to read. The more you read, the better your reading will become.

ACT *See* Drama.

ALLEGORY An *allegory* is a story or tale with two or more levels of meaning—a literal level and one or more symbolic levels. The events, setting, and characters in an allegory are symbols for ideas or qualities.

ALLITERATION *Alliteration* is the repetition of initial consonant sounds. Writers use alliteration to give emphasis to words, to imitate sounds, and to create musical effects. Notice, in the following lines from Jean Toomer's "Reapers," how the *s* sounds suggest the sound of the blades sliding against stones to be sharpened:

> Black reapers with the sound of steel on stones
> Are sharpening scythes . . .

See also Assonance, Consonance, *and* Rhyme.

ALLUSION An *allusion* is a reference to a well-known person, place, event, literary work, or work of art. Writers often make allusions to famous works such as the Bible and William Shakespeare's plays. They also make allusions to mythology, politics, and current events. For example, the title of Stephen Vincent Benét's story "By the Waters of Babylon," p. 576, is an allusion to Psalm 137 in the Bible.

ANECDOTE An *anecdote* is a brief story about an interesting, amusing, or strange event. Anecdotes are told to entertain or to make a point.

See also Narrative.

ANTAGONIST The *antagonist* of a work is the character who opposes the protagonist (the character whom readers want to see succeed).

See also Character *and* Protagonist.

ANTICLIMAX Like a climax, an *anticlimax* is the turning point in a story. However, an anticlimax is always a letdown. It is the point at which you learn that the story will not turn out the way you had expected.

APHORISM An *aphorism* is a brief, memorable saying that expresses a basic truth. Many cultures pass on wisdom in the form of aphorisms, such as those from Confucius' *The Analects,* p. 220.

ASIDE An *aside* is a short speech delivered by an actor in a play, which expresses the character's thoughts. Traditionally, the aside is directed to the audience and is presumed to be inaudible to the other actors.

ASSONANCE *Assonance* is the repetition of vowel sounds followed by different consonants in two or more stressed syllables. In "The Kraken,"p. 939, Tennyson repeats the long *e* sound in the following lines:

> Below the thunders of the upper *deep*;
> Far, far *beneath* in the abysmal *sea*, . . .

See also Consonance.

ATMOSPHERE *Atmosphere*, or mood, is the feeling created in a reader by a literary work or passage. The following lines from "The Stolen Child," p. 928, create a mysterious, mystical atmosphere in which a meeting takes place between fairies and a human child:

> Where the wave of moonlight glosses
> The dim grey sands with light

AUTOBIOGRAPHY An *autobiography* is a form of nonfiction in which a person tells his or her own life story.

See also Biography *and* Nonfiction.

BIOGRAPHY A *biography* is a form of nonfiction in which a writer tells the life story of another person. "Marian Anderson: Famous Concert Singer," p. 702, is a brief biography by Langston Hughes.

See also Autobiography *and* Nonfiction.

BLANK VERSE *Blank verse* is poetry written in unrhymed iambic pentameter lines. This verse form was widely used by William Shakespeare. *The Tragedy of Julius Caesar,* p. 822, is written mostly in blank verse.

See also Meter.

CHARACTER A *character* is a person, an animal, or a thing that takes part in the action of a literary work. The *main character,* or *protagonist,* is the most important character in a story.

The *antagonist* opposes the main character. Round characters show many traits—faults as well as virtues. Flat characters demonstrate a single trait. Dynamic characters develop and grow during the course of the story. Static characters do not change.

See also Antagonist, Characterization, Motivation, *and* Protagonist.

CHARACTERIZATION *Characterization* is the act of creating and developing a character. In *direct characterization,* the author directly states a character's traits. A writer uses *indirect characterization* when showing a character's personality through his or her actions, thoughts, feelings, words, and appearance or through another character's observations and reactions.

See also Character.

CLIMAX The *climax* of a story, novel, or play is the high point of interest or suspense. The events that make up the rising action lead to the climax. The events that make up the falling action follow the climax.

See also Conflict, Plot, *and* Anticlimax.

CONFLICT A *conflict* is a struggle between opposing forces. Characters in conflict form the basis of stories, novels, and plays.

There are two kinds of conflict: external and internal. In an *external conflict,* the main character struggles against an outside force. An *internal conflict* involves a character in conflict with himself or herself. A story may have more than one conflict.

See also Plot.

CONNOTATION The *connotation* of a word is the set of ideas associated with it in addition to its explicit meaning. For example, the title "The Bean Eaters" refers literally to people who eat beans. The phrase connotes simplicity and poverty.

The connotation of a word can be personal, based on individual experiences, but more often, cultural connotations—those recognizable by most people in a group—determine a writer's word choices.

See also Denotation.

CONSONANCE *Consonance* is the repetition of similar consonant sounds at the ends of accented syllables. The repeated *t* and *ch* sounds in "the spurt of a lighted match" create consonance. Consonance is used to create musical effects and to emphasize particular words.

See also Assonance.

COUPLET A *couplet* is a pair of rhyming lines, usually of the same length and meter. A couplet generally expresses a single idea. Shakespeare's Sonnet 18, on p. 990, ends with the following couplet:

So long as men can breathe, or eyes can see
So long lives this, and this gives life to thee.

See also Stanza.

CRITICAL REVIEW A *critical review* offers one person's judgment of a movie, play, or other performance. In the review, the critic discusses the various elements of the performance and makes a recommendation.

See also Persuasion.

DENOTATION The *denotation* of a word is its dictionary meaning, independent of other associations that the word may have. The denotation of the word *lake,* for example, is an inland body of water.

See also Connotation.

DENOUEMENT *See* Plot.

DESCRIPTION A *description* is a portrait in words of a person, place, or object. Descriptive writing uses sensory details—those that appeal to the senses: sight, hearing, taste, smell, and touch.

DEVELOPMENT *See* Plot.

DIALECT *Dialect* is the form of language spoken by people in a particular region or group. Pronunciation, vocabulary, and sentence structure are affected by dialect. Writers use dialect to make their characters sound realistic and to create local color.

DIALOGUE A *dialogue* is a conversation between characters. Writers use dialogue to reveal character, to present events, and to add variety to a narrative.

DICTION *Diction* is word choice. To discuss a writer's diction is to consider the vocabulary used, the appropriateness of the words, and the vividness of the language. Diction can be formal, as in this excerpt from Edgar Allan Poe's "The Masque of the Red Death," which begins on p. 82:

It was a voluptuous scene, that masquerade. But first let me tell of the rooms in which it was held. There were seven—an imperial suite.

Diction can also be informal and conversational, as in these lines from "Flood" by Annie Dillard, on p. 712:

Women are bringing coffee in mugs to the road crew . . . Some kid starts doing tricks on a skateboard; I head home.

See also Connotation *and* Denotation.

DIRECT CHARACTERIZATION *See* Characterization.

DRAMA A *drama* is a story written to be performed by actors. The script of a drama is made up of dialogue—the words the actors say—and stage directions, which are comments on how and where action occurs.

Dramas are divided into large units called acts and into smaller units called scenes. A long play may include many sets that change with the scenes or a change of scene may be indicated with lighting.

See also Genre, Stage Directions, *and* Tragedy.

DRAMATIC IRONY *See* Irony.

DRAMATIC MONOLOGUE A *dramatic monologue* is a poem or speech in which a fictional character addresses a silent listener.

DRAMATIC POETRY *Dramatic poetry* is poetry that uses the techniques of drama. A dramatic poem is a verse that presents the speech of one or more characters. It usually involves many narrative elements, such as setting, conflict, and plot. Such elements may be found in Rudyard Kipling's "Danny Deever," on p. 963.

EPIC An *epic* is a long narrative or narrative poem about the deeds of gods or heroes. Ancient *folk epics* like the *Ramayana* and *Sundiata* were recited aloud as entertainment at feasts and were not written down until long after they were composed.

See also Narrative Poem.

ESSAY An *essay* is a short nonfiction work about a particular subject. In an *analytical essay,* the author breaks down a large idea into parts. By explaining how the parts of a concept or an object fit together, the essay helps readers understand the whole idea or thing.

A *descriptive essay* seeks to convey an impression about a person, place, or object. An *expository essay* gives information, discusses ideas, or explains a process. A *humorous essay* presents the author's thoughts on a subject in an amusing way. A *narrative essay* tells a true story. In a *reflective essay,* a writer shares his or her thoughts about and impressions of an idea or experience. A *persuasive essay* attempts to convince readers to adopt a particular opinion or course of action. A *visual essay* presents information or makes a point about a subject through photographs and other visual forms as well as through text.

This classification of essays is loose at best. Most essays contain passages that could be classified differently from the essay as a whole.

See also Description, Exposition, Genre, Narration, Nonfiction, *and* Persuasion.

EXPOSITION *Exposition* is writing or speech that explains a process or presents information. In the plot of a story or drama, the exposition is the part of the work that introduces the characters, setting, and situation.

EXTENDED METAPHOR In an *extended metaphor,* as in a regular metaphor, a subject is described as though it were something else. However, an extended metaphor differs from a regular metaphor in that several comparisons are made. Extended metaphors sustain the comparison for several lines or for an entire poem.

See also Figurative Language *and* Metaphor.

FALLING ACTION *See* Plot.

FANTASY A *fantasy* is highly imaginative writing that contains elements not found in real life. Examples of fantasy include stories that involve supernatural elements, stories that resemble fairy tales, and stories that deal with imaginary places and creatures.

See also Science Fiction.

FICTION *Fiction* is prose writing that tells about imaginary characters and events. The term is usually used for novels and short stories, but it also applies to dramas and narrative poetry. Some writers rely on their imaginations alone to create their works of fiction. Others base their fiction on actual events and people to which they add invented characters, dialogue, and plot situations.

See also Genre, Narrative, *and* Nonfiction.

FIGURATIVE LANGUAGE *Figurative language* is writing or speech not meant to be interpreted literally.

Figurative language is often used to create vivid impressions by setting up comparisons between dissimilar things. Look, for example, at this description from Emily Dickinson's "The Wind—tapped like a tired Man," on p. 950:

His Countenance—a Billow—
His Fingers, as He passed
Let go a music—as of tunes
Blown tremulous in Glass—

Some frequently used figures of speech are *metaphors, similes,* and *personification*.

See also Literal Language, Metaphor, Personification, *and* Simile.

FOIL A *foil* is a character who provides a contrast to another character. In *Julius Caesar,* on p. 822, the jealousy of Cassius serves as a foil to the good intentions of Brutus.

FOOT *See* Meter.

FORESHADOWING *Foreshadowing* is the use in a literary work of clues that suggest events that have yet to occur. This technique helps to create suspense, keeping readers wondering what will happen next.

See also Suspense.

FREE VERSE *Free verse* is poetry not written in a regular rhythmical pattern, or meter. Free verse seeks to capture the rhythms of speech. It is the dominant form of contemporary poetry. "Making a Fist" by Naomi Shihab Nye, p. 975, is written in free verse.

See also Meter.

GENRE A *genre* is a category or type of literature. Literature is commonly divided into three major genres: poetry, prose, and drama. Each major genre is in turn divided into smaller genres, as follows:

1. Poetry: Lyric Poetry, Concrete Poetry, Dramatic Poetry, Narrative Poetry, and Epic Poetry
2. Prose: Fiction (Novels and Short Stories) and Nonfiction (Biography, Autobiography, Letters, and Essays)
3. Drama: Serious Drama and Tragedy, Comic Drama, Melodrama, and Farce

See also Drama, Poetry, *and* Prose.

HAIKU The *haiku* is a three-line verse form. The first and third lines of a haiku each have five syllables. The second line has seven syllables. A haiku seeks to convey a single vivid emotion by means of images from nature.

HYPERBOLE *Hyperbole* is a deliberate exaggeration or overstatement. In Mark Twain's "The Notorious Jumping Frog of Calaveras County," the claim that Jim Smiley would follow a bug as far as Mexico to win a bet is hyperbole. Hyperboles are often used for comic effect.

IAMB *See* Meter.

IMAGE An *image* is a word or phrase that appeals to one or more of the five senses. Writers use images to re-create sensory experiences in words.

See also Description.

IMAGERY *Imagery* is the descriptive or figurative language used in literature to create word pictures for readers. These pictures, or images, are created by details of sight, sound, taste, touch, smell, and movement.

INDIRECT CHARACTERIZATION *See* Characterization.

IRONY *Irony* is the general term for literary techniques that portray differences between appearance and reality, expectation and result, or meaning and intention. In *verbal irony*, words are used to suggest the opposite of what is meant. In *dramatic irony,* there is a contradiction between what a character thinks and what the reader or audience knows to be true. In *irony of situation,* an event occurs that directly contradicts the expectations of the characters, the readers, or the audience.

During his monologue in William Shakespeare's *The Tragedy of Julius Caesar,* p. 822, Antony calls Brutus "an honorable man" when, in fact, he wants the people to think just the opposite. This is an example of verbal irony.

In the same play, dramatic irony occurs when the audience, knowing that Caesar will be assassinated, watches him set out on the ides of March.

In W. W. Jacobs's "The Monkey's Paw," p. 50, the Whites expect the paw to bring them happiness. Instead, the paw brings them nothing but grief. This is an example of irony of situation.

LEGEND A *legend* is a widely told story about the past that may or may not have a foundation in fact. A legend generally has more historical truth and less emphasis on the supernatural than does a myth.

See also Myth.

LITERAL LANGUAGE *Literal language* uses words in their ordinary senses. It is the opposite of *figurative language.* If you tell someone standing on a diving board to jump in, you are speaking literally. If you tell someone standing on a street corner to go jump in a lake, you are speaking figuratively.

See also Figurative Language.

LYRIC POEM A *lyric poem* is a musical verse that expresses the observations and feelings of a single speaker. Lyric poems have a musical quality achieved through rhythm and such other devices as alliteration and rhyme.

METAPHOR A *metaphor* is a figure of speech in which one thing is spoken of as though it were something else. Unlike a simile, which compares two things using *like* or *as,* a metaphor implies a comparison between them. In "Making a Fist," on p. 975, Naomi Shihab Nye uses this metaphor:

> My stomach was a melon
> split wide inside my skin.

See also Extended Metaphor *and* Figurative Language.

METER The *meter* of a poem is its rhythmical pattern. This pattern is determined by the number and types of stresses, or beats, in each line. To describe the meter of a poem, you must *scan* its lines, marking the syllables. Each strong stress is marked with a slanted accent mark (´), and each unstressed syllable is marked with a curved accent mark (˘). The stressed and unstressed syllables are then divided by vertical lines (|) into groups called *feet.* The following types of feet are common in English poetry:

1. *Iamb:* a foot with one unstressed syllable followed by a stressed syllable, as in the word *again*
2. *Trochee:* a foot with a stressed syllable followed by an unstressed syllable, as in the word *wonder*
3. *Anapest:* a foot with two unstressed syllables followed by one strong stress, as in the phrase *on the beach*
4. *Dactyl:* a foot with one strong stress followed by two unstressed syllables, as in the word *wonderful*
5. *Spondee:* a foot with two strong stresses, as in the word *spacewalk*

Depending on the type of foot that appears most often in them, lines of poetry are described as *iambic, trochaic, anapestic,* and so forth.

Lines are also described in terms of the number of feet that occur in them, as follows:

1. *Monometer:* one foot
   Ăll thíngs
   Aŕe ă
   Běcomíňg.
2. *Dimeter:*
   Ă búyĕr | fŏr thém
   Ă hándsŏme | yŏung mán
        —"The Bridegroom," p. 59
3. *Trimeter:*
   Sŭcceśs iš | cóuntĕd | sẃeetĕst
   Bў thóse| whŏ né'er | sŭcceéd.
        —"Success is counted sweetest," p. 158
4. *Tetrameter:* verse written in four-foot lines
5. *Pentameter:* verse written in five-foot lines
6. *Hexameter:* verse written in six-foot lines
7. *Heptameter:* verse written in seven-foot lines

Blank verse is poetry written in unrhymed iambic pentameter. Poetry that does not have a regular meter is called *free verse.*

MONOLOGUE A *monologue* is a speech by one character in a play, story, or poem. A monologue may be addressed to another character or to the audience, or it may be a *soliloquy*—a speech that presents the character's thoughts as though the character were overheard when alone.

See also Drama *and* Soliloquy.

MOOD *See* Atmosphere.

MORAL A *moral* is a lesson taught by a literary work. A fable usually ends with a moral that is directly stated.

MOTIVATION *Motivation* is a reason that explains or partially explains a character's thoughts or actions.

See also Character *and* Characterization.

MYTH A *myth* is a fictional tale that explains the actions of gods or the causes of natural phenomena. Unlike legends, myths have little historical truth and involve supernatural elements. Every culture has its collection of myths. Among the most familiar are the myths of the ancient Greeks and Romans.

See also Oral Tradition.

NARRATION *Narration* is writing that tells a story. The act of telling a story in speech is also called narration. Novels and short stories are fictional narratives. Nonfiction works such as news stories, biographies, and autobiographies are also narratives. A narrative poem tells a story in verse.

See also Anecdote, Essay, Narrative Poem, Nonfiction, Novel, *and* Short Story.

NARRATIVE A *narrative* is a story told in fiction, nonfiction, poetry, or drama.

See also Narration.

NARRATIVE POEM A *narrative poem* is one that tells a story. "La Belle Dame sans Merci," on p. 960, is an example of a narrative poem. It tells the story of a knight driven to despair because he loves a pitiless woman.

See also Dramatic Poetry, Epic, *and* Narration.

NARRATOR A *narrator* is a speaker or character who tells a story. The narrator may be either a character in the story or an outside observer. The writer's choice of narrator determines the story's *point of view,* which in turn determines the information the writer can reveal.

See also Speaker *and* Point of View.

NONFICTION *Nonfiction* is prose writing that presents and explains ideas or that tells about real people, places, objects, or events. To be classed as nonfiction, a work must be true. Among nonfiction forms are essays, newspaper and magazine articles, journals, travelogues, biographies, and autobiographies. Historical, scientific, technical, political, and philosophical writings are also nonfiction.

See also Autobiography, Biography, *and* Essay.

NOVEL A *novel* is a long work of fiction. Like a short story, a novel has a plot that explores characters in conflict. However, a novel is much longer than a short story and may have one or more subplots, or minor stories, and several themes.

OCTAVE *See* Stanza.

ONOMATOPOEIA *Onomatopoeia* is the use of words that imitate sounds. *Whirr, thud, sizzle,* and *hiss* are typical examples. Writers can deliberately choose words that contribute to a desired effect.

ORAL TRADITION The *oral tradition* is the passing of songs, stories, and poems from generation to generation by word of mouth. Many folk songs, ballads, fairy tales, legends, and myths originated in the oral tradition.

See also Myth.

PARABLE A *parable* is a simple, brief narrative that teaches a lesson by using characters and events to stand for abstract ideas. The parable "How Much Land Does a Man Need?" p. 138, teaches a lesson about greed.

PARODY A *parody* is a comical piece of writing that mocks the characteristics of a specific literary form. Through exaggeration of the types of ideas, language, tone, or action in a type of literature or a specific work, a parody calls attention to the ridiculous aspects of its subject. The excerpt from *Don Quixote,* p. 1006, is a parody of the sixteenth-century romantic literature.

PENTAMETER *See* Meter.

PERSONIFICATION *Personification* is a type of figurative language in which a nonhuman subject is given human characteristics. Emily Dickinson personifies the wind when she describes it as tapping like a tired man.

See also Figurative Language.

PERSUASION *Persuasion* is writing or speech that attempts to convince the reader to adopt a particular opinion or course of action. A newspaper editorial that says a city council decision was wrong is an example of persuasive writing attempting to mold opinion. Critical reviews, such as the reviews of the movie *Star Wars,* pp. 734 and 737, are a form of persuasive writing.

See also Critical Review *and* Essay.

PLOT *Plot* is the sequence of events in a literary work. In most novels, dramas, short stories, and narrative poems, the plot involves both characters and a central conflict. The plot usually begins with an exposition that introduces the setting, the characters, and the basic situation. This is followed by the inciting incident, which introduces the central conflict. The conflict then increases during the *development* until it reaches a high point of interest or suspense, the *climax.* All the events leading up to the climax make up the *rising action.* The climax is followed by the *falling action,* or *denouement.* The *resolution* is the end of the story, in which an insight or a change as a result of the conflict is shown.

POETRY *Poetry* is one of the three major types of literature; the others are prose and drama. Most poems make use of highly concise, musical, and emotionally charged language. Many also make use of imagery, figurative language, and special devices of sound such as rhyme. Poems are often divided into lines and stanzas and usually employ regular rhythmical patterns, or meters. However, some poems are written out just like prose, and some poems are written in free verse.

See also Free Verse, Genre, Meter, Rhyme, *and* Rhythm.

POINT OF VIEW The *point of view* is the perspective from which a story is told. If the narrator is part of the action, the story is told from the *first-person* point of view. We see and know only what the character telling the story sees and knows. In a story told by a *third person,* the narrator is someone outside the action. An *omniscient third-person* narrator is all-knowing; the narrator knows more about the characters and events than any one character can know. A *limited third-person* narrator tells only the thoughts and feelings of one character.

See also Narrator.

PROSE *Prose* is the ordinary form of written language. Most writing that is not poetry, drama, or song is considered prose. One of the major genres of literature, prose occurs in two forms: fiction and nonfiction.

See also Fiction, Genre, *and* Nonfiction.

PROTAGONIST The main character in a work of fiction— the character readers would like to see succeed—is the *protagonist.* Antigone is the protagonist in Sophocles' play *Antigone.*

See also Antagonist *and* Character.

REPETITION *Repetition* is the use of any element of language—a sound, word, phrase, clause, or sentence—more than once.

Poets use many kinds of repetition. Alliteration, assonance, rhyme, and rhythm are repetitions of certain sounds and sound patterns. A refrain is a repeated line or group of lines. In both prose and poetry, repetition is used for musical effects and for emphasis.

See also Alliteration, Assonance, Consonance, Rhyme, *and* Rhythm.

RESOLUTION *See* Plot.

RHYME *Rhyme* is the repetition of sounds at the ends of words. *End rhyme* occurs when the rhyming words come at the ends of lines, as in "The Kraken," by Alfred, Lord Tennyson, p. 939:

Below the thunders of the upper <u>deep</u>;
Far, far beneath in the abysmal *sea*,
His ancient, dreamless, uninvaded <u>sleep</u>
The Kraken sleepeth: faintest sunlights *flee*

Internal rhyme occurs when the rhyming words fall within a line.

See also Repetition *and* Rhyme Scheme.

RHYME SCHEME A *rhyme scheme* is a regular pattern of rhyming words in a poem. The rhyme scheme of a poem is indicated by using different letters of the alphabet for each new rhyme. In an *aabb* stanza, for example, line 1 rhymes with line 2 and line 3 rhymes with line 4.

See also Rhyme.

RHYTHM *Rhythm* is the pattern of beats, or stresses, in spoken or written language. Some poems have a very specific pattern, or meter, whereas prose and free verse use the natural rhythms of everyday speech.

See also Meter.

RISING ACTION *See* Plot.

SCENE *See* Drama.

SCIENCE FICTION *Science fiction* is writing that tells about imaginary events that involve science or technology. The setting can be on Earth, in space, on other planets, or in a totally imaginary place. Many science-fiction stories are set in the future.

See also Fantasy.

SENSORY LANGUAGE *Sensory language* is writing or speech that appeals to one or more of the senses.

See also Image.

SESTET *See* Stanza.

SETTING The *setting* of a literary work is the time and place of the action. Time can include not only the historical period—past, present, or future—but also a specific year, season, or time of day. Place may involve not only the geographical place—a country, state, or town—but also the social or cultural environment.

In some stories, setting serves merely as a backdrop for action, a context in which the characters move and speak. In others, however, setting is a crucial element.

Description of the setting often helps establish the mood of a story. For example, in Edgar Allan Poe's "The Masque of the Red Death," on p. 82, the setting contributes to the growing horror.

See also Mood.

SHORT STORY A *short story* is a brief work of fiction. The short story resembles the longer novel but generally has a simpler plot and setting. In addition, the short story tends to reveal character at a crucial moment rather than to develop it through many incidents.

See also Fiction, Genre, *and* Novel.

SIMILE A *simile* is a figure of speech in which *like* or *as* is used to make a comparison between two unlike ideas.

Poets often use similes. In "Right Hand," on p. 954, Fried compares a hand to a Greek chorus:

. . . as it moved back and forth like a Greek chorus across the stage of the ironing board

See also Figurative Language.

SOLILOQUY A *soliloquy* is a long speech expressing the thoughts of a character alone on stage. In William Shakespeare's *The Tragedy of Julius Caesar,* p. 822, Brutus begins a soliloquy while he is alone in his orchard. This soliloquy reveals Brutus' fears about how Caesar might change were he to be crowned king.

See also Monologue.

SONNET A *sonnet* is a fourteen-line lyric poem, usually written in rhymed iambic pentameter. The *English,* or *Shakespearean, sonnet* consists of three quatrains (four-line stanzas) and a couplet (two lines), usually rhyming *abab cdcd efef gg.*

The couplet usually comments on the ideas contained in the preceding twelve lines. The sonnet is generally not printed with the stanzas divided, but a reader can see distinct ideas in each. See Sonnet 18 by William Shakespeare on p. 866.

The *Italian,* or *Petrarchan, sonnet* consists of an octave (eight-line stanza) and a sestet (six-line stanza). Often the octave rhymes *abbaabba* and the sestet rhymes *cdecde.* The octave states a theme or asks a question. The sestet comments on or answers the question.

The Petrarchan sonnet took its name from Petrarch, a fourteenth-century Italian poet. Once the form was introduced in England, it underwent changes. The Shakespearean sonnet is, of course, named after William Shakespeare.

See also Lyric Poem, Meter, *and* Stanza.

SPEAKER The *speaker* is the imaginary voice assumed by the writer of a poem. In many poems, the speaker is not identified by name. The speaker within the poem may be a person, an animal, a thing, or an abstraction. The speaker in Gabriela Mistral's "Fear," on p. 95, is a woman who fears for her daughter's future.

STAGE DIRECTIONS *Stage directions* are notes included in a drama to describe how the work is to be performed or staged. These instructions are printed in italics and are not spoken aloud. They are used to describe sets, lighting, sound effects, and the appearance, personalities, and movements of characters.

See also Drama.

STANZA A *stanza* is a formal division of lines in a poem, considered as a unit. Often the stanzas in a poem are separated by spaces.

Stanzas are sometimes named according to the number of lines found in them. A *couplet,* for example, is a two-line stanza. A *tercet* is a stanza with three lines. Other types of stanzas include the following:

1. *Quatrain:* four-line stanza
2. *Cinquain:* five-line stanza
3. *Sestet:* six-line stanza
4. *Heptastich:* seven-line stanza
5. *Octave:* eight-line stanza

Sonnets, limericks, and haiku all have distinct stanza forms.

See also Haiku *and* Sonnet.

SURPRISE ENDING A *surprise ending* is a conclusion that violates the expectations of the reader but in a way that is both logical and believable. O. Henry's "Hearts and Hands," on p. 290, and Saki's "The Open Window," on p. 540, have surprise endings. Both authors were masters of this form.

SUSPENSE *Suspense* is the feeling of curiosity or uncertainty about the outcome of events in a literary work. Writers create suspense by raising questions in the minds of their readers.

SYMBOL A *symbol* is anything that stands for, or represents, something else. An object that serves as a symbol has its own meaning, but it also represents abstract ideas. Marks on paper can symbolize spoken words. A flag symbolizes a country. A flashy car may symbolize wealth. Writers sometimes use such conventional symbols in their work, but sometimes they also create symbols of their own through emphasis or repetition.

In Edgar Allan Poe's "The Masque of the Red Death," on p. 82, the masked figure symbolizes death and the clock symbolizes the passage of time.

TANKA A *tanka* consists of five unrhymed lines with a pattern of five, seven, five, seven, seven syllables. Tankas appear on p. 988.

TECHNICAL ARTICLE A *technical article* is a type of expository writing that explains a procedure, provides instructions, or represents specialized information. Often, specialized vocabulary is used. Sometimes, diagrams or charts illustrate complicated structures or steps. The technical article "Imitating Nature's Mineral Artistry," p. 748, explains how technology is used to create synthetic gems.

TETRAMETER *See* Meter.

THEME A *theme* is a central message or insight revealed through a literary work. It is a generalization about people or about life that is communicated through the literary work.

The theme of a literary work may be stated directly or implied. When the theme of a work is *implied,* readers think about what the work seems to say about the nature of people or about life. The story or poem can be viewed as a specific example of the generalization the writer is trying to communicate.

Note that there is usually no single correct statement of a work's theme, though there can be incorrect ones. Also, a long work, like a novel or a full-length play, may have several themes. Finally, not all literary works have themes. A work meant only to entertain may have no theme at all.

TONE The *tone* of a literary work is the writer's attitude toward his or her audience and subject. The tone can often be described by a single adjective, such as *formal* or *informal, serious* or *playful.* Rachel Carson uses a respectful tone in "The Marginal World," on p. 660, as she seeks the meaning behind the beauty of the natural world.

TRAGEDY A *tragedy* is a work of literature, especially a play, that results in a catastrophe for the main character. In ancient Greek drama, the main character was always a significant person, a king or a hero, and the cause of the tragedy was a tragic flaw, or weakness, in his or her character. The purpose of tragedy is not only to arouse fear and pity in the audience, but also, in some cases, to convey a sense of the grandeur and nobility of the human spirit.

In Shakespeare's *The Tragedy of Julius Caesar,* on p. 822, Brutus is a noble figure whose tragic flaw is assuming that honorable ends justify dishonorable means.

See also Drama.

TRIMETER *See* Meter.

UNIVERSAL THEME A *universal theme* is a message about life that can be understood by most cultures. Many folk tales and examples of classic literature address universal themes such as the importance of courage, the effects of honesty, or the dangers of greed.

VERBAL IRONY *See* Irony.

VILLANELLE A *villanelle* is a lyric poem written in three-line stanzas, ending with a four-line stanza. It has two refrain lines that appear initially in the first and third lines of the first stanza; then, they appear alternately as the third line of subsequent stanzas, and finally, as the last two lines of the poem. Theodore Roethke's "The Waking," on p. 986, is an example of a villanelle.

RUBRICS

What is a rubric?

A rubric is a tool, often in the form of a chart or a grid, that helps you assess your work. Rubrics are particularly helpful for writing and speaking assignments.

To help you or others assess, or evaluate, your work, a rubric offers several specific criteria to be applied to your work. Then the rubric helps you or an evaluator indicate your range of success or failure according to those specific criteria. Rubrics are often used to evaluate writing for standardized tests.

Using a rubric will save you time, focus your learning, and improve the work you do. When you know what the rubric will be before you begin writing a persuasive essay, for example, you will be aware as you write of specific criteria that are important in that kind of an essay. As you evaluate the essay before giving it to your teacher, you will focus on the specific areas that your teacher wants you to master— or on areas that you know present challenges for you. Instead of searching through your work randomly for any way to improve it or correct its errors, you will have a clear and helpful focus on specific criteria.

How are rubrics constructed?

Rubrics can be constructed in several different ways.
- Your teacher may assign a rubric for a specific assignment.
- Your teacher may direct you to a rubric in your textbook.
- Your teacher and your class may construct a rubric for a particular assignment together.
- You and your classmates may construct a rubric together.
- You may create your own rubric with criteria you want to evaluate in your work.

How will a rubric help me?

A rubric will help you assess your work on a scale. Scales vary from rubric to rubric but usually range from 6 to 1, 5 to 1, or 4 to 1, with 6, 5, or 4 being the highest score and 1 being the lowest. If someone else is using the rubric to assess your work, the rubric will give your evaluator a clear range within which to place your work. If you are using the rubric yourself, it will help you make improvements to your work.

What are the types of rubrics?

- A **holistic rubric** has general criteria that can apply to a variety of assignments. See p. R22 for an example of a holistic rubric.
- An **analytic rubric** is specific to a particular assignment. The criteria for evaluation address the specific issues important in that assignment. See p. R21 for examples of analytic rubrics.

SAMPLE ANALYTIC RUBRICS

Rubric With a 4-point Scale

The following analytic rubric is an example of a rubric to assess a persuasive essay.
It will help you evaluate audience and purpose, organization, elaboration, and use of language.

	Audience/Purpose	Organization	Elaboration	Use of Language
4	Demonstrates highly effective word choice; clearly focused on task.	Uses clear, consistent organizational strategy.	Provides convincing, well-elaborated reasons to support the position.	Incorporates transitions; includes very few mechanical errors.
3	Demonstrates good word choice; states focus on persuasive task.	Uses clear organizational strategy with occasional inconsistencies.	Provides two or more moderately elaborated reasons to support the position.	Incorporates some transitions; includes few mechanical errors.
2	Shows some good word choices; minimally states focus on persuasive task.	Uses inconsistent organizational strategy; presentation is not logical.	Provides several reasons but few are elaborated; only one elaborated reason.	Incorporates few transitions; includes many mechanical errors.
1	Shows lack of attention to persuasive task.	Demonstrates lack of organizational strategy.	Provides no specific reasons or does not elaborate.	Does not connect ideas; includes many mechanical errors.

Rubric With a 6-point Scale

The following analytic rubric is an example of a rubric to assess a persuasive essay.
It will help you evaluate presentation, position, evidence, and arguments.

	Presentation	Position	Evidence	Arguments
6	Essay clearly and effectively addresses an issue with more than one side.	Essay clearly states a supportable position on the issue.	All evidence is logically organized, well presented, and supports the position.	All reader concerns and counterarguments are presented effectively.
5	Most of essay addresses an issue that has more than one side.	Essay clearly states a position on the issue.	Most evidence is logically organized, well presented, and supports the position.	Most reader concerns and counterarguments are presented effectively.
4	Essay adequately addresses issue that has more than one side.	Essay adequately states a position on the issue.	Many parts of evidence support the position; some evidence is out of order.	Many reader concerns and counterarguments are presented adequately.
3	Essay addresses issue with two sides but does not present second side clearly.	Essay states a position on the issue, but the position is difficult to support.	Some evidence supports the position, but some evidence is out of order.	Some reader concerns and counterarguments are presented.
2	Essay addresses issue with two sides but does not present second side.	Essay states a position on the issue, but the position is not supportable.	Not much evidence supports the position, and what is included is out of order.	A few reader concerns and counterarguments are presented.
1	Essay does not address issue with more than one side.	Essay does not state a position on the issue.	No evidence supports the position.	No reader concerns or counterarguments are presented.

SAMPLE HOLISTIC RUBRIC

Holistic rubrics such as this one are sometimes used to assess writing assignments on standardized tests. Notice that the criteria for evaluation are focus, organization, support, and use of conventions.

Points	Criteria
6 Points	• The writing is strongly focused and shows fresh insight into the writing task. • The writing is marked by a sense of completeness and coherence and is organized with a logical progression of ideas. • A main idea is fully developed, and support is specific and substantial. • A mature command of the language is in evidence, and the writing may employ characteristic creative writing strategies. • Sentence structure is varied, and writing is free of all but purposefully used fragments. • Virtually no errors in writing conventions appear.
5 Points	• The writing is clearly focused on the task. • The writing is well organized and has a logical progression of ideas, though there may be occasional lapses. • A main idea is well developed and supported with relevant details. • Command of the language is mature. • Sentence structure is varied, and the writing is free of fragments, except when used purposefully. • Writing conventions are followed correctly.
4 Points	• The writing is clearly focused on the task, but extraneous material may intrude at times. • A clear organizational pattern is present, though lapses may occur. • A main idea is adequately supported, but development may be uneven. • Sentence structure is generally free of fragments but shows little variation. • Writing conventions are generally followed correctly.
3 Points	• Writing is generally focused on the task, but extraneous material may intrude at times. • An organizational pattern is evident, but writing may lack a logical progression of ideas. • Support for the main idea is generally present but is sometimes illogical. • Sentence structure is generally free of fragments, but there is almost no variation. • The work generally demonstrates a knowledge of writing conventions, with occasional misspellings.
2 Points	• The writing is related to the task but generally lacks focus. • There is little evidence of organizational pattern, and there is little sense of cohesion. • Support for the main idea is generally inadequate, illogical, or absent. • Sentence structure is unvaried, and serious errors may occur. • Errors in writing conventions and spelling are frequent.
1 Point	• The writing may have little connection to the task and is generally unfocused. • There has been little attempt at organization or development. • The paper seems fragmented, with no clear main idea. • Sentence structure is unvaried, and serious errors appear. • Poor word choice and poor command of the language obscure meaning. • Errors in writing conventions and spelling are frequent.
Unscorable	The paper is considered unscorable if: • The response is unrelated to the task or is simply a rewording of the prompt. • The response has been copied from a published work. • The student did not write a response. • The response is illegible. • The words in the response are arranged with no meaning. • There is an insufficient amount of writing to score.

STUDENT MODEL

Persuasive Writing

This persuasive letter, which would receive a top score according to a persuasive rubric, is a response to the following writing prompt, or assignment:

With the increased use of technology in the workplace, the skills that high-school graduates must possess have changed. Write a letter to your principal advocating new technology courses that could give high-school graduates a competitive edge.

Dear Principal:

I am writing to alert you to an urgent need in our school's curriculum. We need computer graphics courses!

> The letter begins with an engaging introduction that clearly states the persuasive focus.

Although you would have to find funds to buy the equipment, I've concluded that setting up this course would be well worth it. By adding this course, you would be adding many high-paying career options for students. Computer graphics is a type of art, and businesses all around us involve art in some form. You see computer graphics in commercials, movies, news broadcasts, weather broadcasts, architectural designs, and business presentations. Workers with computer graphics skills are well paid because they are in such high demand.

You may argue that the school already has computer science classes. Good point! I'm in a computer science class and it is mainly programming. Once we did have an assignment to design a graphic of a pumpkin. You wouldn't believe how much coding it takes to get a simple, animated drawing. In order to get a really creative image with definite lines, shading, lifelike colors, and texture, you need to use computer graphics software designed especially for that purpose. With software, you can make images that move and talk smoothly and environments with realistic colors and lighting. This is the same graphics software that businesses use for commercials, movies, and brochures. Students should be learning how to use this software.

> The author effectively counters an opposing argument to increase the persuasive power of her own argument.

Most importantly, computer graphics is a subject area that allows students to express their creativity. Adding a computer graphics course would have a positive effect on students. Course participants would enjoy doing their assignments, so they would earn good grades and turn in creative work. The energy and enthusiasm they would bring to their projects would catch the attention of the community at large. As a result, they would make the school and the principal look good.

> A positive argument that is well supported enhances the letter's persuasive appeal.

As you can see, adding a computer graphics course could be a very profitable idea for you, the students, and the community. You would be ensuring the success of students who desire an art or computer career. You would be opening hundreds of different career pathways. Wouldn't it be great to know you were the reason for these students' success? Thanks for your time and consideration.

Sincerely,

Dawn Witherspoon

The Writing Process

A polished piece of writing can seem to have been effortlessly created, but most good writing is the result of a process of writing, rethinking, and rewriting. The process can roughly be divided into stages: prewriting, drafting, revising, editing, proofreading, and publishing.

It is important to remember that the writing process is one that moves backward as well as forward. Even while you are moving forward in the creation of your composition, you may still return to a previous stage—to rethink or rewrite.

Following are stages of the writing process, with key points to address during each stage.

Prewriting

In this stage, you plan out the work to be done. You prepare to write by exploring ideas, gathering information, and working out an organization plan. Following are the key steps to take at this stage.

Step 1: Analyze the writing situation. Start by clarifying your assignment, so that you know exactly what you are supposed to do.

- *Focus your topic.* If necessary, narrow the topic—the subject you are writing about—so that you can write about it fully in the space you have.
- *Know your purpose.* What is your goal for this paper? What do you want to accomplish? Your purpose will determine what you include in the paper.
- *Know your audience.* Who will read your paper influences what you say and how you say it.

Step 2: Gather ideas and information. You can do this in a number of ways:

- *Brainstorm.* When you brainstorm, either alone or with others, you come up with possible ideas to use in your paper. Not all of your ideas will be useful or suitable. You will need to evaluate them later.
- *Consult other people about your subject.* Speaking informally with others may suggest an idea or an approach you did not see at first.
- *Make a list of questions about your topic.* When your list is complete, find the answers to your questions.
- *Do research.* Your topic may require information that you do not have, so you will need to go to other sources to find information. There are numerous ways to find information on a topic.

The ideas and information you gather will become the content of your paper. Not all of the information you gather will be needed. As you develop and revise your paper, you will make further decisions about what to include and what to leave out.

Drafting

When you draft, you put down your ideas on paper in rough form. Working from your prewriting notes and your outline or plan, you develop and present your ideas in sentences and paragraphs.

Organize. First, make a rough plan for the way you want to present your information. Sort your ideas and notes. Decide what goes with what and which points are the most important. You can make an outline to show the order of ideas, or you can use some other organizing plan that works for you.

There are many ways in which you can organize and develop your material. Use a method that works for your topic. Following are common methods of organizing information in the development of a paper:

- *Chronological Order* In this method, events are presented in the order in which they occurred. This organization works best for presenting narrative material or explaining in a "how-to" format.
- *Spatial Order* In spatial order, details are presented as seen in space; for example, from left to right, top to bottom, or from foreground to background. This order is good for descriptive writing.
- *Order of Importance* This order helps readers see the relative importance of ideas. You present ideas from the most to least important or from the least to most important.
- *Main Idea and Details* This logical organization works well to support an idea or opinion. Present each main idea, and back it up with appropriate support.

Once you have chosen an organization, begin writing your draft. Do not worry about getting everything perfect at the drafting stage. Concentrate on getting your ideas down.

Write your draft in a way that works for you. Some writers work best by writing a quick draft—putting down all their ideas without stopping to evaluate them. Other writers prefer to develop each paragraph carefully and thoughtfully, making sure that each main idea is supported by details.

As you are developing your draft, keep in mind your purpose and your audience. These determine what you say and how you say it.

Do not be afraid to change your original plans during drafting. Some of the best ideas are those that were not planned at the beginning. Write as many drafts as you like, until you are happy with the results.

Develop an Essay Most papers, regardless of the topic, are developed with an introduction, a body, and a conclusion. Here are tips for developing these parts:

Introduction In the introduction to a paper, you want to engage your readers' attention and let them know the purpose of your paper. You may use the following strategies in your introduction:

- Startle your readers.
- Use an anecdote.
- Take a stand.
- Quote someone.

Body of the Paper In the body of your paper, you present your information and make your points. Your organization is an important factor in leading readers through your ideas. Elaborating on your main ideas is also important. Elaboration is the development of ideas to make your written work precise and complete. You can use the following kinds of details to elaborate your main ideas:

- Facts and statistics
- Sensory details
- Explanations and definitions
- Anecdotes
- Examples
- Quotations

Conclusion The ending of your paper is the final impression you leave with your readers. Your conclusion should give readers the sense that you have pulled everything together. Following are some effective ways to end your paper:

- Summarize and restate.
- State an opinion.
- Call for action.
- Ask a question.
- Tell an anecdote.
- Provide an insight.

Revising

Once you have a draft, you can look at it critically or have others review it. This is the time to make changes—on many levels. Revising is the process of reworking what you have written to make it as good as it can be.

Revising Your Overall Structure Start by examining the soundness of your structure, or overall organization. Your ideas should flow logically from beginning to end. You may strengthen the structure by reordering paragraphs or by adding information to fill in gaps.

Revising Your Paragraphs Next, examine each paragraph in your writing. Consider the way each sentence contributes to the point of the paragraph. As you evaluate your draft, rewrite or eliminate any sentences that are not effective.

Revising Your Sentences When you study the sentences in your draft, check to see that they flow smoothly from one to the next. Look to see that you have avoided the pattern of beginning most of your sentences in the same way, and vary your sentence length.

Revising Your Word Choice The final step in the process of revising your work is to analyze your choice of words. Consider the connotations, or associations each word suggests, and make sure that each word conveys the exact meaning you intended. Also, look for the repetition of words, and make revisions to polish your writing.

Peer Review After you have finished revising your draft, work with one or more classmates to get a fresh perspective on your writing. First, have your reviewer look at one element of your writing, and ask your reviewer a specific question to get the most focused feedback possible. Weigh the responses you receive, and determine which suggestions you want to incorporate in your draft.

Editing

When you edit, you look more closely at the language you have used to ensure that the way you expressed your ideas is the most effective.

- Replace dull language with vivid, precise words.
- Cut or change unnecessary repetition.
- Cut empty words and phrases—those that do not add anything to the writing.
- Check passive voice. Usually, active voice is more effective.
- Replace wordy expressions with shorter, more precise ones.

Proofreading

After you finish your final draft, proofread it, either on your own or with the help of a partner.

It is useful to have both a dictionary and a usage handbook available to help you check that your work is correct. Here are the tasks in proofreading:

- Correct errors in grammar and usage.
- Correct errors in punctuation and capitalization.
- Correct errors in spelling.

Publishing

Now your paper is ready to be shared with others. Consider sharing your writing with classmates, family, or a wider audience.

The Modes of Writing

Writing is a process that begins with the exploration of ideas and ends with the presentation of a final draft. Often, the types of writing are grouped into modes according to form and purpose.

The modes addressed in this handbook are

- Narration
- Description
- Persuasion
- Exposition
- Research Writing
- Response to Literature
- Writing for Assessment
- Workplace Writing

NARRATION

Whenever writers tell any type of story, they are using **narration.** Although there are many kinds of narration, most narratives share certain elements, such as characters, a setting, a sequence of events, and, often, a theme. Following are some types of narration:

Autobiographical Writing Autobiographical writing tells a true story about an important period, experience, or relationship in the writer's life. An autobiographical narrative can be as simple as a description of a recent car trip or as complex as the entire story of a person's life. Effective autobiographical writing includes

- A series of events that involve the writer as the main character
- Details, thoughts, feelings, and insights from the writer's perspective
- A conflict or an event that affects the writer
- A logical organization that tells the story clearly
- Insights that the writer gained from the experience

A few types of autobiographical writing are autobiographical incidents, personal narratives, autobiographical narratives or sketches, reflective essays, eyewitness accounts, anecdotes, and memoirs.

Short Story A short story is a brief, creative narrative—a retelling of events arranged to hold a reader's attention. Most short stories include

- Details that establish the setting in time and place
- A main character who undergoes a change or learns something during the course of the story
- A conflict or a problem to be introduced, developed, and resolved

- A plot, the series of events that make up the action of the story
- A theme or generalization about life

A few types of short stories are realistic stories, fantasies, historical narratives, mysteries, thrillers, science-fiction stories, and adventure stories.

DESCRIPTION

Descriptive writing is writing that creates a vivid picture of a person, place, thing, or event. Descriptive writing can stand on its own or be part of a longer work, such as a short story. Most descriptive writing includes

- Sensory details—sights, sounds, smells, tastes, and physical sensations
- Vivid, precise language
- Figurative language or comparisons
- Adjectives and adverbs that paint a word picture
- An organization suited to the subject

Some examples of descriptive writing include description of ideas, observations, travel brochures, physical descriptions, functional descriptions, remembrances, and character sketches.

PERSUASION

Persuasion is writing or speaking that attempts to convince people to accept a position or take a desired action. When used effectively, persuasive writing has the power to change people's lives. As a reader and a writer, you will find yourself engaged in many forms of persuasion. Here are a few of them:

Persuasive Essay A persuasive essay presents your position on an issue, urges your readers to accept that position, and may encourage them to take an action. An effective persuasive essay

- Explores an issue of importance to the writer
- Addresses an issue that is arguable
- Uses facts, examples, statistics, or personal experiences to support a position
- Tries to influence the audience through appeals to the readers' knowledge, experiences, or emotions
- Uses clear organization to present a logical argument

Persuasion can take many forms. A few forms of persuasion include editorials, position papers, persuasive speeches, grant proposals, advertisements, and debates.

Advertisements An advertisement is a planned communication meant to be seen, heard, or read. It attempts to persuade an audience to buy a product or service, accept an idea, or support a cause. Advertisements may appear in printed form—in newspapers and magazines, on billboards, or as posters or flyers. They may appear on radio or television, as commercials or public-service announcements. An effective advertisement includes

- A memorable slogan to grab the audience's attention
- A call to action, which tries to rally the audience to do something
- Persuasive and/or informative text
- Striking visual or aural images
- Details that provide such information as price, location, date, and time

Several common types of advertisements are public-service announcements, billboards, merchandise ads, service ads, online ads, product packaging, and political campaign literature.

EXPOSITION

Exposition is writing that informs or explains. The information you include in expository writing is factual or based on fact. Effective expository writing reflects a well-thought-out organization—one that includes a clear introduction, body, and conclusion. The organization should be appropriate for the type of exposition you are writing. Here are some types of exposition:

Comparison-and-Contrast Essay A comparison-and-contrast essay analyzes the similarities and differences between two or more things. You may organize your essay either point by point or subject by subject. An effective comparison-and-contrast essay

- Identifies a purpose for comparison and contrast
- Identifies similarities and differences between two or more things, people, places, or ideas
- Gives factual details about the subjects being compared
- Uses an organizational plan suited to its topic and purpose

Types of comparison-and-contrast essays are product comparisons, essays on economic or historical developments, comparison and contrast of literary works, and plan evaluations.

Cause-and-Effect Essay A cause-and-effect essay examines the relationship between events, explaining how one event or situation causes another. A successful cause-and-effect essay includes

- A discussion of a cause, event, or condition that produces a specific result
- An explanation of an effect, outcome, or result

- Evidence and examples to support the relationship between cause and effect
- A logical organization that makes the explanation clear

Some appropriate subjects for cause-and-effect essays are science reports, current-events articles, health studies, historical accounts, and cause-and-effect investigations.

Problem-and-Solution Essay A problem-and-solution essay describes a problem and offers one or more solutions to it. It describes a clear set of steps to achieve a result. An effective problem-and-solution essay includes

- A clear statement of the problem, with its causes and effects summarized for the reader
- The most important aspects of the problem
- A proposal of at least one realistic solution
- Facts, statistics, data, or expert testimony to support the solution
- Language appropriate to the audience's knowledge and ability levels
- A clear organization that makes the relationship between problem and solution obvious

Some types of issues that might be addressed in a problem-and-solution essay include consumer issues, business issues, time-management issues, and local issues.

RESEARCH WRITING

Research writing is based on information gathered from outside sources, and it gives a writer the power to become an expert on any subject. A research paper—a focused study of a topic—helps writers explore and connect ideas, make discoveries, and share their findings with an audience. Effective research writing

- Focuses on a specific, narrow topic, which is usually summarized in a thesis statement
- Presents relevant information from a wide variety of sources
- Structures the information logically and effectively
- Identifies the sources from which the information was drawn

Besides the formal research report, there are many other specialized types of writing that depend on accurate and insightful research, including multimedia presentations, statistical reports, annotated bibliographies, and experiment journals.

Documented Essay A documented essay uses research gathered from outside sources to support an idea. What distinguishes this essay from other categories of research is the level and intensity of the research. In a documented essay, the writer consults a limited number of sources to elaborate an idea. In contrast, a formal research paper may include many more research sources. An effective documented essay includes

- A well-defined thesis that can be fully discussed in a brief essay
- Facts and details to support each main point
- Expert or informed ideas gathered from interviews and other sources
- A clear, coherent method of organization
- Full internal documentation to show sources of information

Subjects especially suited to the documented essay format include health issues, current events, and cultural trends.

Research Paper A research paper presents and interprets information gathered through an extensive study of a subject. An effective research paper has

- A clearly stated thesis statement
- Convincing factual support from a variety of outside sources, including direct quotations whose sources are credited
- A clear organization that includes an introduction, body, and conclusion
- A bibliography, or works-cited list, that provides a complete listing of research sources

Some research formats you may encounter include lab reports, annotated bibliographies, and multigenre research papers.

RESPONSE TO LITERATURE

When you write a **response-to-literature essay,** you give yourself the opportunity to discover *what, how*, and *why* a piece of writing communicated to you. An effective response

- Contains a reaction to a poem, story, essay, or other work of literature
- Analyzes the content of a literary work, its related ideas, or the work's effect on the reader
- Presents a thesis statement to identify the nature of the response
- Focuses on a single aspect of the work or gives a general overview
- Supports opinion with evidence from the work addressed

The following are just a few of the ways you might respond in writing to a literary work: reader's response journals, character analyses, literary letters, and literary analyses.

WRITING FOR ASSESSMENT

One of the most common types of school **assessment** is the written test. Most often, a written test is announced in advance, allowing you time to study and prepare. When a test includes an essay, you are expected to write a response that includes

- A clearly stated and well-supported thesis or main idea
- Specific information about the topic derived from your reading or from class discussion
- A clear organization

In your school career, you will probably encounter questions that ask you to address each of the following types of writing: explain a process; defend a position; compare, contrast, or categorize; and show cause and effect.

WORKPLACE WRITING

Workplace writing is probably the format you will use most after you finish school. It is used in offices, factories, and by workers on the road. Workplace writing includes a variety of formats that share common features. In general, workplace writing is fact-based writing that communicates specific information to readers in a structured format. Effective workplace writing

- Communicates information concisely to make the best use of both the writer's and the reader's time
- Includes a level of detail that provides necessary information and anticipates potential questions
- Reflects the writer's care if it is error-free and neatly presented

Some common types of workplace writing include business letters, memorandums, résumés, forms, and applications.

matting Business Letters

usiness letters follow one of several acceptable for-s. In **block format** each part of the letter begins at the margin. A double space is used between paragraphs. **odified block format,** some parts of the letter are nted to the center of the page. No matter which for-is used, all letters in business format have a heading, nside address, a salutation, or greeting, a body, a ing, and a signature. These parts are shown and annotated on the model business letter below, formatted in modified block style.

Model Business Letter

In this letter, Yolanda Dodson uses modified block format to request information.

The inside address indicates where the letter will be sent.

A salutation is punctuated by a colon. When the specific addressee is not known, use a general greeting such as "To whom it may concern:"

The body of the letter states the writer's purpose. In this case, the writer requests information.

The closing "Sincerely" is common, but "Yours truly" or "Respectfully yours" are also acceptable. To end the letter, the writer types her name and provides a **signature.**

Students for a Cleaner Planet
c/o Memorial High School
333 Veterans' Drive
Denver, Colorado 80211

January 25, 20--

Steven Wilson, Director
Resource Recovery Really Works
300 Oak Street
Denver, Colorado 80216

Dear Mr. Wilson:

Memorial High School would like to start a branch of your successful recycling program. We share your commitment to reclaiming as much reusable material as we can. Because your program has been successful in other neighborhoods, we're sure that it can work in our community. Our school includes grades 9–12 and has about 800 students.

Would you send us some information about your community recycling program? For example, we need to know what materials can be recycled and how we can implement the program.

At least fifty students have already expressed an interest in getting involved, so I know we'll have the people power to make the program work. Please help us get started.

Thank you in advance for your time and consideration.

Sincerely,

Yolanda Dodson

Yolanda Dodson

Applying Spelling Rules

Choosing Between *ie* and *ei*

When a word has a long *e* sound, use *ie*. When a word has a long *a* sound, use *ei*. When a word has a long *e* sound preceded by the letter *c*, use *ei*.

Long *e* Sound	Long *a* Sound	Long *e* Sound Preceded by *c*
believe	freight	deceive
grief	reign	receive

Exceptions: either, neither, seize, weird

Choosing the Ending *-cede*, *-ceed*, or *-sede*

There are ten words that end with this sound. You will need to memorize their spellings.

-cede Words	*-ceed* Words	*-sede* Words
accede	exceed	supersede
concede	proceed	
intercede	succeed	
precede		
recede		
secede		

Adding Prefixes

A *prefix* is one or more syllables added at the beginning of a word to form a new word. Adding a prefix to a word does not usually change the spelling of the original word.

re- + place = replace

un- + fair = unfair

mis- + spell = misspell

dis- + appear = disappear

il- + legal = illegal

Adding Suffixes

A *suffix* is one or more syllables added at the end of a word to form a new word. Adding a suffix often involves a spelling change in the original word.

Adding Suffixes That Begin With a Consonant

When adding a suffix that begins with a consonant—such as *-ly, -ness, -less, -ment,* and *-ful*—you usually do not change the spelling of the original word.

calm + *-ly* = calmly

open + *-ness* = openness

time + *-less* = timeless

employ + *-ment* = employment

help + *-ful* = helpful

Except for *truly, argument, judgment, daily*

Exceptions: If a word ends in *y* preceded by a consonant, change the *y* to *i* before adding these suffixes:

ready + *-ly* = readily

busy + *-ness* = business

Except for *shyness, slyly, spryness*

Adding Suffixes to Words That End in Silent *e*

If a word ends in a silent *e,* drop the *e* before adding a suffix that begins with a vowel.

love + *-able* = lovable

Except for *changeable, agreeable, useable*

Adding Suffixes That Begin With a Vowel to Words That End in *y*

When adding a suffix that begins with a vowel to a word that ends in *y* preceded by a consonant, change the *y* to *i* before adding the suffix.

greedy + *-er* = greedier

worry + *-ed* = worried

Exceptions: Do not change the *y* to *i* if the suffix begins with *i*—*carrying, babyish*

When adding a suffix that begins with a vowel to a word that ends in *y* preceded by a vowel, keep the *y* before adding the suffix.

portray + *-al* = portrayal

obey + *-ed* = obeyed

Exceptions: paid (not *payed*), said (not *sayed*), laid (not *layed*), gaiety (not *gayety*)

...bling the Final Consonant Before ...ding a Suffix If a one-syllable word ends in a ...e consonant preceded by a single vowel, double the ...consonant before adding a suffix that begins with a ...el.

...op + -*ed* = stopped

...m + -*ing* = dimming

...*ceptions:* Words that end in *x, y,* or *w* (*mixer, prayed, ...ng*)

...a word of more than one syllable ends in a single ...onant preceded by a single vowel and the accent is ...e final syllable, double the final consonant before ...ng a suffix that begins with a vowel.

...nit + -*ed* = omitted

...cur + -*ence* = occurrence

...*ceptions:* Words in which the accent shifts when the ...: is added (*prefer—preference*)

...> not double the final consonant if the accent is not ...e last syllable.

...avel + -*ing* = traveling

...danger + -*ed* = endangered

...ming the Plurals of Nouns

...ming Regular Plurals The rules below apply to ...nouns whose plurals are formed in regular ways.

n Ending	Rule	Examples
x, z, ..., ch	Add -*es*	circus, circuses
		lass, lasses
		fox, foxes
		waltz, waltzes
		buzz, buzzes
		bush, bushes
		church, churches
...ceded by ...sonant	Add -*es*	potato, potatoes
		hero, heroes
		Exceptions:
		Musical terms—
		solo, solos
		piano, pianos

Noun Ending	Rule	Examples
o preceded by a vowel	Add -*s*	radio, radios
		patio, patios
y preceded by a consonant	Change *y* to *i* and add -*es*	party, parties
		enemy, enemies
y preceded by a vowel	Add -*s*	key, keys
		convoy, convoys
ff	Add -*s*	staff, staffs
		sheriff, sheriffs
fe	Change *f* to *v* and add -*es*	life, lives
		knife, knives
f	Add -*s*	chief, chiefs
		roof, roofs
	OR	
	Change *f* to *v* and add -*es*	leaf, leaves
		shelf, shelves

Forming Irregular Plurals The plurals of some nouns are formed in irregular ways. You will need to memorize these:

goose, geese	foot, feet
man, men	woman, women
ox, oxen	child, children
tooth, teeth	mouse, mice
deer, deer	sheep, sheep

Forming Plurals of Compound Nouns Most one-word compound nouns have regular plural forms. If one part of a compound word is irregular, the plural form will also be irregular.

flashlight, flashlights (regular)

handful, handfuls (regular)

stepchild, stepchildren (irregular)

The plurals of most compound nouns written with hyphens or as separate words are formed by making the modified word—the word being described—plural.

mother-in-law, mothers-in-law

Web site, Web sites

Forming Plurals of Proper Nouns
To form the plurals of proper nouns, follow the same rules as with common nouns. In most cases, simply add -s to the proper noun. Add -es if the name ends in *s, ss, x, z, sh,* or *ch.*

> There are two Anns in our class.
>
> All of the Coxes arrived in one car.

For proper nouns ending in *y,* just add -s. Do not change the *y* to *i* and add -es.

> The Kennedys live in the house on the corner.
>
> There are two Kansas Citys; one in Missouri and one in Kansas.

Forming Plurals of Signs and Symbols
Use an apostrophe and an -s to write the plurals of numbers, symbols, letters, and words used to name themselves.

> Business names often include &'s.
>
> All of the 6's were written as 9's.
>
> She received only *A*'s and *B*'s.
>
> You used too many *and*'s in this sentence.

Writing Numbers

Spelling Out Numbers
If a number begins a sentence, spell it out.

> *Twenty-two* players are on the field during a football game.

Within a sentence, spell out numbers that can be written in one or two words.

> There are *fifty-two* weeks in a year.

Spell out numbers used to indicate place or order.

> Shelley came in *second* in the race.
>
> This is the *fifth* day in a row that it has rained.

Using Numerals
Use numerals for longer numbers that come within a sentence.

> Approximately *875* people attended the game.

If you include both small and large numbers in the same sentence, write them in the same way. It is best to use numerals.

> During a *12*-hour period, we counted *680* cars crossing the intersection.

Suggestions for Improving Your Spelling

Start a Personal Spelling List

Select the words that you have difficulty spelling, enter them in a special area in your notebook, and study them regularly. Add new words to your list, and cross out words you have mastered. You may find many of the words on your list among the Commonly Misspelled Words on the next page of this textbook.

Sound Out Difficult Words

Say the words aloud. Then, sound them out syllable by syllable as you study how to spell them.

Devise Memory Aids

Underline the part of a word that gives you the most trouble. Then, develop a memory device to help you remember the correct spelling.

Word	Memory Aid
dessert	My dessert is messy.
library	library branch
necessary	Only one c is necessary.

Look for Roots and Derivatives

Many words have common *roots.* Look for the root inside a word to help you focus on its spelling. Then, use the root to help you spell related words.

> benefit, beneficial, benefactor
>
> preferred, referred, inferred
>
> decide, incident, accident
>
> transmit, transmission, admit, admission

A *derivative* is a word that is formed from another word. Once you know how to spell a base word—the word from which the others are formed—you can more easily learn to spell its derivatives.

> decide, decision, decisive
>
> caution, cautious, precaution
>
> regular, regulation, regulate
>
> strong, strength, strengthen

Commonly Misspelled Words

The words on this page are ones that cause spelling problems for many people. As you review the list, check to see how many of the words give you trouble in your own writing. Then, try some of the suggestions for improving your spelling discussed on the previous page to help you conquer these "spelling demons."

abbreviate	bicycle	criticize	grammar	naturally	realize
absence	bookkeeper	cylinder	grievance	necessary	really
absolutely	boulevard	deceive	guarantee	negotiate	receipt
accelerate	brief	decision	guard	neighbor	recipe
accidentally	brilliant	defendant	guidance	neutral	recognize
accurate	bruise	definitely	handkerchief	nickel	recommend
ache	bulletin	delinquent	harass	niece	rehearse
achievement	buoy	dependent	height	ninety	relevant
acquaintance	bureau	descendant	humorous	noticeable	reminiscence
adequate	bury	description	hygiene	nuclear	renowned
advertisement	buses	desirable	immediately	nuisance	repetition
aerial	business	dessert	immigrant	obstacle	restaurant
aggravate	cafeteria	dining	independent	occasion	rhythm
agreeable	calendar	disappoint	individual	occurrence	ridiculous
aisle	campaign	disastrous	inflammable	omitted	sandwich
all right	canceled	discipline	interfere	opinion	satellite
aluminum	candidate	eighth	irritable	opportunity	schedule
amateur	captain	eligible	jewelry	optimistic	scissors
analysis	career	embarrass	judgment	outrageous	secretary
analyze	carriage	enthusiastic	knowledge	pamphlet	siege
ancient	cashier	entrepreneur	laboratory	parallel	sincerely
anecdote	category	envelope	lawyer	paralyze	solely
anniversary	ceiling	environment	legible	parentheses	sponsor
anonymous	cemetery	equipped	legislature	particularly	subtle
answer	census	equivalent	leisure	patience	superintendent
anxiety	certain	especially	liable	permanent	surveillance
apologize	characteristic	exaggerate	library	permissible	susceptible
appall	chauffeur	excel	license	perseverance	tariff
appearance	clothes	excellent	lieutenant	persistent	temperamental
appreciate	colonel	exercise	lightning	perspiration	theater
appropriate	column	existence	likable	persuade	threshold
architecture	commercial	extraordinary	liquefy	phenomenon	truly
argument	commitment	familiar	literature	physician	unmanageable
associate	committee	fascinating	maintenance	pneumonia	unwieldy
athletic	competitor	February	marriage	possession	usage
attendance	condemn	fiery	mathematics	prairie	usually
awkward	congratulate	financial	maximum	preferable	valuable
banquet	conscience	fluorescent	meanness	prejudice	various
bargain	conscious	foreign	mediocre	prerogative	vegetable
barrel	convenience	forfeit	mileage	privilege	voluntary
battery	cooperate	fourth	millionaire	probably	volunteer
beautiful	correspondence	fragile	minuscule	procedure	weight
beggar	counterfeit	gauge	miscellaneous	pronunciation	weird
beginning	courageous	genius	mischievous	psychology	whale
behavior	courteous	genuine	misspell	pursue	wield
benefit	criticism	government	mortgage	questionnaire	yield

Summary of Grammar

Nouns A noun is the name of a person, place, or thing. A common noun names any one of a class of people, places, or things. A proper noun names a specific person, place, or thing.

Common Noun	Proper Noun
city	Washington, D.C.

Pronouns A pronoun is a word that stands for a noun or for a word that takes the place of a noun.

A personal pronoun refers to (1) the person speaking, (2) the person spoken to, or (3) the person, place, or thing spoken about.

	Singular	Plural
First Person	I, me, my, mine	we, us, our, ours
Second Person	you, your, yours	you, your, yours
Third Person	he, him, his, she, her, hers it, its	they, them, their, theirs

A **reflexive pronoun** ends in -*self* or -*selves* and adds information to a sentence by pointing back to a noun or a pronoun earlier in the sentence.

I was saying to *myself,* "Ed, my boy, this is Everest—you've got to push it a bit harder!" — Edmund Hillary, p. 30

An **intensive pronoun** ends in -*self* or -*selves* and simply adds emphasis to a noun or a pronoun in the same sentence.

After a time, I myself was allowed to go into the dead houses and search for metal. — Stephen Vincent Benét, p. 576

A **demonstrative pronoun** directs attention to a specific person, place, or thing.

this   these   that   those

These are the juiciest pears I have ever tasted.

A **relative pronoun** begins a subordinate (relative) clause and connects it to another idea in the sentence.

The poet *who* wrote "Fear" is Gabriela Mistral.

An **indefinite pronoun** refers to a person, place, or thing, often without specifying which one.

And then, for a moment, *all* is still, . . . — Edgar Allan Poe, p. 82

Verbs A **verb** is a word that expresses time while showing an action, a condition, or the fact that something exists.

An **action verb** indicates the action of someone or something.

An action verb is **transitive** if it directs action toward someone or something named in the same sentence.

He *dusted* his hands, muttering. — Jack Finney, p. 6

An action verb is **intransitive** if it does not direct action toward something or someone named in the same sentence.

I *waved* and *shouted,* then as suddenly *stopped* as I realized my foolishness. — Edmund Hillary, p. 30

A **linking verb** is a verb that connects the subject of a sentence with a noun or a pronoun that renames or describes the subject. All linking verbs are intransitive.

Romance at short notice *was* her specialty. — Saki, p. 540

A **helping verb** is a verb that can be added to another verb to make a verb phrase.

Nor *did* I suspect that these experiences could be part of a novel's meaning.

Adjectives An **adjective** describes a noun or a pronoun or gives a noun or a pronoun a more specific meaning. Adjectives answer these questions:

What kind?	*blue* lamp, *large* tree
Which one?	*this* table, *those* books
How many?	*five* stars, *several* buses
How much?	*less* money, *enough* votes

The articles *the, a,* and *an* are adjectives. *An* is used before a word beginning with a vowel sound.

A noun may sometimes be used as an adjective.

diamond necklace   *summer* vacation

Adverbs An **adverb** modifies a verb, an adjective, or another adverb. Adverbs answer the questions *where, when, in what way,* or *to what extent.*

He could stand *there.* (modifies verb *stand*)

He was *blissfully* happy. (modifies adjective *happy*)

It ended *too* soon. (modifies adverb *soon*)

Prepositions A **preposition** relates a noun or a pronoun that appears with it to another word in the sentence.

before the end   near me   inside our fence

Conjunctions A **conjunction** connects other words or groups of words.

A **coordinating conjunction** connects similar kinds or groups of words.

mother *and* father   simple *yet* stylish

Correlative conjunctions are used in pairs to connect similar words or groups of words.

both Sue *and* Meg   *neither* he *nor* I

A **subordinating conjunction** connects two complete ideas by placing one idea below the other in rank or importance.

You would know him *if* you saw him.

Sentences A **sentence** is a group of words with a subject and a predicate. Together, these parts express a complete thought.

A **fragment** is a group of words that does not express a complete thought.

Subject and Verb Agreement To make a subject and verb agree, make sure that both are singular or both are plural.

Many *storms are* the cause of beach erosion.

Either the *cats* or the *dog is* hungry.

either *Angie* nor her *sisters were* present.

e *conductor,* as well as the soloists, *was applauded.*

se A **phrase** is a group of words, without a subject and a
 that functions in a sentence as one part of speech.

 prepositional phrase is a group of words that includes a
 sition and a noun or a pronoun that is the object of the
 sition.

 tside my window   below the counter

 adjective phrase is a prepositional phrase that modifies a
 or a pronoun by telling *what kind* or *which one.*

e wooden gates *of that lane* stood open.

 adverb phrase is a prepositional phrase that modifies a
 an adjective, or an adverb by pointing out *where, when, in
 way,* or *to what extent.*

 a sudden impulse, he got to his feet. — Jack Finney, p. 6

 appositive phrase is a noun or a pronoun with modifiers,
 d next to a noun or a pronoun to identify it or add informa-
 nd details.

 Morissot, watchmaker by trade but local militiaman for the
 e being, stopped short . . . — Guy de Maupassant, p. 102

 participial phrase is a participle with its modifiers or com-
 nts. The entire phrase acts as an adjective.

 oosing such a tide, I hoped for a glimpse of the pool.
 Rachel Carson, p. 660

 gerund phrase is a gerund with modifiers or a complement,
 ting together as a noun.

 , moving along the ledge was quite as easy as he thought
 vould be. — Jack Finney, p. 6

 infinitive phrase is an infinitive with modifiers, comple-
 , or a subject, all acting together as a single part of
 h.

 be alive to hear this song is a victory. . . . — Traditional,
 217

 ses A **clause** is a group of words with a subject and a

 independent clause has a subject and a verb and can
 by itself as a complete sentence.

 subordinate clause has a subject and a verb but cannot
 by itself as a complete sentence; it can only be part of a
 nce.

 adjective clause is a subordinate clause that modifies a
 or a pronoun by telling *what kind* or *which one.*

e people *who read the book* loved it.

 adverb clause modifies a verb, an adjective, an adverb, or
 al by telling *where, when, in what way, to what extent,
 what condition,* or *why.*

 ey read it *as soon as it was published.*

 noun clause is a subordinate clause that acts as a noun.

 hoever reads it is overcome with joy.

Summary of Capitalization and Punctuation

Capitalization

Capitalize the first word of a sentence and also the first word
in a quotation if the quotation is a complete sentence.

"Mummy," he said, "I can stay under water for two minutes— . . ." — Doris Lessing, p. 242

Capitalize all proper nouns and adjectives.

W. W. Jacobs   Flanders Fields   African writers

Capitalize a person's title when it is followed by the person's
name or when it is used in direct address.

Reverend Tallboys   Mrs. Prothero   Major Moberly

Capitalize titles showing family relationships when they refer
to a specific person unless they are preceded by a possessive
noun or pronoun.

Grandmother   his father

Capitalize the first word and all other key words in the titles
of books, periodicals, poems, stories, plays, paintings, and other
works of art.

Lord of the Flies   "Spring and All"

Punctuation

End Marks Use a **period** to end a declarative sentence,
an imperative sentence, an indirect question, and most
abbreviations.

The class will meet at noon.

Use a **question mark** to end a direct question, an incomplete
question, or a statement that is intended as a question.

Did you prepare your assignment?

Use an **exclamation mark** after a statement showing strong
emotion, an urgent imperative sentence, or an interjection
expressing strong emotion.

Wait until you hear the news!

Commas Use a **comma** before the coordinating conjunction
to separate two independent clauses in a compound sentence.

His arms had begun to tremble from the steady strain of
clinging to his narrow perch, and he did not know what to do
now. . . . — Jack Finney, p. 6

Use commas to separate three or more words, phrases, or
clauses in a series.

Animals took shape: yellow giraffes, blue lions, pink
antelopes, lilac panthers cavorting in crystal substance.
— Ray Bradbury, p. 614

Use commas to separate adjectives of equal rank. Do not use
commas to separate adjectives that must stay in a specific order.

Grammar and Mechanics Handbook ◆ *R35*

... I was immediately transported to the foot of mountains, with narrow defiles twisting in and out amongst their *towering, arid peaks.* — Rabindranath Tagore, p. 318

Use a comma after an introductory word, phrase, or clause.

When Marian Anderson again returned to America, she was a seasoned artist. — Langston Hughes, p. 702

Use commas to set off parenthetical and nonessential expressions.

All of these works, *of course,* had earlier left their marks. . . . — Vincent Canby, p. 734

Use commas with places, dates, and titles.

Poe was raised in Richmond, Virginia.

August 4, 2026

Alfred, Lord Tennyson

Use a comma to indicate words left out of an elliptical sentence, to set off a direct quotation, and to prevent a sentence from being misunderstood.

Vincent Canby writes for *The New York Times;* Roger Ebert, for the *Chicago Sun Times.*

Semicolons Use a **semicolon** to join independent clauses that are not already joined by a conjunction.

They could find no buffalo; *they had to hang an old hide from the sacred tree.* — N. Scott Momaday, p. 676

Use a semicolon to join independent clauses separated by either a conjunctive adverb or a transitional expression.

James Thurber wrote many books; moreover, he was a cartoonist and a journalist.

Use semicolons to avoid confusion when independent clauses or items in a series already contain commas.

There were the Useful Presents: engulfing mufflers of the old coach days, and mittens made for giant sloths; zebra scarfs of a substance like silky gum that could be tug-o'-warred down to the galoshes; . . . — Dylan Thomas, p. 694

Colons Use a **colon** in order to introduce a list of items following an independent clause.

The authors we are reading include a number of poets: Robert Frost, Octavio Paz, and Emily Dickinson.

Use a colon to introduce a formal quotation.

The next day Howard Taubman wrote enthusiastically in *The New York Times:* Marian Anderson has returned to her native land one of the great singers of our time. . . . — Langston Hughes, p. 702

Quotation Marks A **direct quotation** represents a person's exact speech or thoughts and is enclosed in quotation marks.

"Clara, my mind is made up."

An **indirect quotation** reports only the general meaning of what a person said or thought and does not require quotation marks.

She rattled on cheerfully about the shooting and the scarcity of birds, . . . — Saki, p. 540

Always place a comma or a period inside the final quotation mark.

"There are ceremonies going on," I said, "and I am busy." — Rabindranath Tagore, p. 318

Place a question mark or an exclamation mark inside the final quotation mark if the end mark is part of the quotation; if it is not part of the quotation, place it outside the final quotation mark.

"He asked, "Which poetry do you like best?"

Have you ever read the poem "Africa"?

Use single quotation marks for a quotation within a quotation.

Use quotation marks around the titles of short written works, episodes in a series, songs, and titles of works mentioned as parts of a collection.

"Making a Fist"   "These Are Days"

Underline or italicize titles of longer works, such as plays, movies, or novels.

Dashes Use **dashes** to indicate an abrupt change of thought, a dramatic interrupting idea, or a summary statement.

It made her so mad to see Muggs lying there, oblivious of the mice—they came running up to her—that she slapped him and he slashed at her, but he didn't make it. — James Thurber, p. 256

Parentheses Use **parentheses** to set off asides and explanations only when the material is not essential or when it consists of one or more sentences.

When I finished (What a lot of facts I found out!), I turned in my report.

Hyphens Use a **hyphen** with certain numbers, after certain prefixes, with two or more words used as one word, and with a compound modifier coming before a noun.

fifty-two   greenish-blue water

Apostrophes Add an **apostrophe** and *-s* to show the possessive case of most singular nouns.

Prospero's castle   the playwright's craft

Add an apostrophe to show the possessive case of plural nouns ending in *-s* and *-es.*

the sailors' ships   the babies' mothers

Add an apostrophe and *-s* to show the possessive case of plural nouns that do not end in *-s* or *-es.*

the children's games   the people's friend

Use an apostrophe in a contraction to indicate the position of the missing letter or letters.

I *didn't* love any one of you more than the other. — William Melvin Kelley, p. 182

Glossary of Common Usage

among, between *Among* is usually used with three or more items. *Between* is generally used with only two items.

Among the poems we read this year, Eve Merriam's "Metaphor" was my favorite.

"Like the Sun" tells of one man's conflict *between* telling the truth and telling white lies.

amount, number *Amount* refers to a mass or a unit, whereas *number* refers to individual items that can be counted. Therefore, *amount* generally appears with a singular noun, and *number* appears with a plural noun.

Being able to climb Mount Everest requires a huge *amount* of training.

In his story "The Masque of the Red Death," Poe uses a *number* of intriguing symbols.

any, all *Any* should not be used in place of *any other* or *all*.

Rajika liked Anne Tyler's "With All Flags Flying" better than *any other* short story.

Of *all* W. W. Jacobs's short stories, "The Monkey's Paw" is the most famous.

around In formal writing, *around* should not be used to mean *approximately* or *about*. These usages are allowable, however, in informal writing or in colloquial dialogue.

Romeo and Juliet had its first performance in *approximately* 1595.

Shakespeare was *about* thirty when he wrote it.

as, because, like, as to The word *as* has several meanings and can function as several parts of speech. To avoid confusion, use *because* rather than *as* when you want to indicate cause and effect.

Because Cyril was interested in African American poetry, he wrote his report on Langston Hughes.

Do not use the preposition *like* to introduce a clause that requires the conjunction *as*.

James Thurber conversed *as* he wrote—wittily.

The use of *as to* for *about* is awkward and should be avoided.

Rosa has a theory *about* Edgar Allan Poe's style.

bad, badly Use the predicate adjective *bad* after linking verbs such as *feel, look,* and *seem*. Use *badly* whenever an adverb is required.

Sara Teasdale's poem "There Will Come Soft Rains" shows clearly that the author felt *bad* about the destruction of the war.

In "Through the Tunnel," Jerry *badly* wants to be able to swim the length of the tunnel.

because of, due to Use *due to* if it can logically replace the phrase *caused by*. In introductory phrases, however, *because of* is better usage than *due to*.

The popularity of the mystery is largely *due to* the works of Edgar Allan Poe.

Because of lack of oxygen, Edmund Hillary and Tenzing Norgay moved more and more lethargically as they made their way up Everest.

being as, being that Avoid these expressions. Use *because* instead.

Because the protagonist of Anton Chekhov's "A Problem" is a static character, he changes little in the course of the story.

beside, besides *Beside* is a preposition meaning "at the side of" or "close to." Do not confuse *beside* with *besides,* which means "in addition to." *Besides* can be a preposition or an adverb.

As the men cross the lawn and approach the open window, a brown spaniel trots *beside* them.

There are many other Indian oral epics *besides* the *Ramayana*.

can, may The verb *can* generally refers to the ability to do something. The verb *may* generally refers to permission to do something.

Dylan Thomas describes his childhood Christmases so vividly that most readers *can* visualize the scene.

Creon's edict states that no one *may* bury Polyneices.

different from, different than The preferred usage is *different from*.

The structure and rhyme scheme of a Shakespearean sonnet are *different from* the organization of a Petrarchan sonnet.

farther, further Use *farther* when you refer to distance. Use *further* when you mean "to a greater degree" or "additional."

The *farther* the ants travel, the more ominous and destructive they seem.

The storm in Act I of *The Tragedy of Julius Caesar further* hints at the ominous deeds to come.

fewer, less Use *fewer* for things that can be counted. Use *less* for amounts or quantities that cannot be counted.

Poetry often uses *fewer* words than prose to convey ideas and images.

It takes *less* time to perform a Greek tragedy than to perform a Shakespearean play.

good, well Use the adjective *good* after linking verbs such as *feel, look, smell, taste,* and *seem*. Use *well* whenever you need an adverb or as an adjective describing health.

Caesar remarks that Cassius does not look *good;* on the contrary, his appearance is "lean."

Twain wrote especially *well* when he described eccentric characters.

hopefully Do not attach this adverb to a sentence loosely, as in "*Hopefully,* the rain will stop by noon." Rewrite the sentence so that *hopefully* modifies a specific verb. Other possible ways of revising such sentences include using the adjective *hopeful* or a phrase such as *everyone hopes that.*

> Dr. Martin Luther King, Jr., wrote and spoke *hopefully* about his dream of racial harmony.

> Mr. White was *hopeful* that the monkey's paw would bring him good fortune.

> *Everyone hopes that* the class production of *Antigone* will be a big success.

its, it's Do not confuse the possessive pronoun *its* with the contraction *it's,* used in place of "it is" or "it has."

> In *its* very first lines, "The Stolen Child" establishes an eerie mood.

> In "The Street of the Cañon," Pepe Gonzalez knows that *it's* dangerous to attend the party.

just, only When you use *just* as an adverb meaning "no more than," be sure you place it directly before the word it logically modifies. Likewise, be sure you place *only* before the word it logically modifies.

> *Just* one wish changed the Whites' lives forever.

> A short story can usually develop *only* a few characters, whereas a novel can include many.

kind of, sort of In formal writing, you should not use these colloquial expressions. Instead, use a word such as *rather* or *somewhat.*

> Poe portrays Prince Prospero as *rather* arrogant.

> The tone of the biography is *somewhat* long.

lay, lie Do not confuse these verbs. *Lay* is a transitive verb meaning "to set or put something down." Its principal parts are *lay, laying, laid, laid. Lie* is an intransitive verb meaning "to recline." Its principal parts are *lie, lying, lay, lain.*

> They laid the monkey's paw on the table for a while before anyone dared to pick it up.

> La belle dame sans merci enchants the knight as he *lies* in her "elfin grot."

leave, let Be careful not to confuse these verbs. *Leave* means "to go away" or "to allow to remain." *Let* means "to permit."

> Threatening Antigone not to disobey his orders, Creon angrily *leaves* the stage.

> Creon did not want to *let* Antigone bury her brother.

raise, rise *Raise* is a transitive verb that usually takes a direct object. *Rise* is an intransitive verb and never takes a direct object.

> In his speech, Antony unexpectedly *raises* the subject of Caesar's will.

> When the Cabuliwallah comes to call, Mini *rises* from her chair and runs to greet him.

set, sit Do not confuse these verbs. *Set* is a transitive verb meaning "to put (something) in a certain place." Its principal parts are *set, setting, set, set. Sit* is an intransitive verb meaning "to be seated." Its principal parts are *sit, sitting, sat, sat.*

> Antigone's conduct *sets* a high standard for us.

> Jerry's mother *sits* in her beach chair while Jerry swims in the ocean.

so, so that Be careful not to use the coordinating conjunction *so* when your context requires *so that. So* means "accordingly" or "therefore" and expresses a cause-and-effect relationship. *So that* expresses purpose.

> He wanted to do well on the test, *so* he read *The Tragedy of Julius Caesar* again.

> Antony uses eloquent rhetoric to stir up the people *so that* they will rebel.

than, then The conjunction *than* is used to connect the two parts of a comparison. Do not confuse *than* with the adverb *then,* which usually refers to time.

> I enjoyed "The Marginal World" more *than* "The Flood."

> Marian Anderson gave a triumphant singing recital in New York that evening, and she *then* embarked on a coast-to-coast American tour.

that, which, who Use the relative pronoun *that* to refer to things. Use *which* only for things and *who* only for people.

> The poem *that* Cheryl liked the most was "The street."

> Haiku, *which* consists of only seventeen syllables, is often built around one or two vivid images.

> The assassin *who* strikes Caesar first is Casca.

unique Because *unique* means "one of a kind," you should not use it carelessly to mean "interesting" or "unusual." Avoid such illogical expressions as "most unique," "very unique," and "extremely unique."

> Emily Dickinson's bold experiments with form make her *unique* in the history of nineteenth-century American poetry.

when, where Do not directly follow a linking verb with *when* or *where.* Be careful not to use *where* when your context requires *that.*

> **Faulty:** The exposition is *when* an author provides the reader with important background information.

> **Revised:** In the exposition, an author provides the reader with important background information.

> **Faulty:** Madras, India, is *where* R. K. Narayan was born.

> **Revised:** R. K. Narayan was born in Madras, India.

> **Faulty:** We read *where* the prizes were to be announced.

> **Revised:** We read *that* the prizes were to be announced.

Introduction to the Internet

The Internet is a series of networks that are interconnected all over the world. The Internet allows users to have almost unlimited access to information stored on the networks. Dr. Berners-Lee, a physicist, created the basis for the World Wide Web, the graphic-interface portion of the Internet, by writing a small computer program that allowed pages to be linked together using key words. The Internet was mostly text-based until 1992, when a computer program called the NCSA Mosaic (National Center for Supercomputing Applications) was created at the University of Illinois. This program was the first Web browser. The development of Web browsers greatly eased the ability of the user to navigate through all the pages stored on the Web. Very soon, the appearance of the Web was altered as well. More appealing visuals were added, and sound, too, was implemented. This change made the Web more user-friendly and more appealing to the general public.

Using the Internet for Research

Key Word Search

Before you begin a search, you should identify your specific topic. To make searching easier, narrow your subject to a key word or a group of key words. These are your search terms, and they should be as specific as possible. For example, if you are looking for the latest concert dates for your favorite musical group, you might use the band's name as a key word. However, if you were to enter the name of the group in the query box of the search engine, you might be presented with thousands of links to information about the group that is unrelated to what you want to know. You might locate such information as band member biographies, the group's history, fan reviews of concerts, and hundreds of sites with related names containing information that is irrelevant to your search. Because you used such a broad key word, you might need to navigate through all that information before you could find a link or subheading for concert dates. In contrast, if you were to type in "Duplex Arena and [band name]," you would have a better chance of locating pages that contain this information.

How to Narrow Your Search

If you have a large group of key words and still do not know which ones to use, write out a list of all the words you are considering. Once you have completed the list, scrutinize it. Then, delete the words that are least important to your search, and highlight those that are most important.

These **key search connectors** can help you fine-tune your search:

AND: Narrows a search by retrieving documents that include both terms. For example: *baseball* AND *playoffs*

OR: Broadens a search by retrieving documents including any of the terms. For example: *playoffs* OR *championships*

NOT: Narrows a search by excluding documents containing certain words. For example: *baseball* NOT *history of*

Tips for an Effective Search

1. Remember that search engines can be case-sensitive. If your first attempt at searching fails, check your search terms for misspellings and try again.

2. If you are entering a group of key words, present them in order from the most important to the least important key word.

3. Avoid opening the link to every single page in your results list. Search engines present pages in descending order of relevancy. The most useful pages will be located at the top of the list. However, read the description of each link before you open the page.

4. Some search engines provide helpful tips for specializing your search. Take the opportunity to learn more about effective searching.

Other Ways to Search

Using Online Reference Sites How you search should be tailored to what you are hoping to find. If you are looking for data and facts, use reference sites before you jump onto a simple search engine. For example, you can find reference sites to provide definitions of words, statistics about almost any subject, biographies, maps, and concise information on many topics. Here are some useful online reference sites:

Online libraries

Online periodicals

Almanacs

Encyclopedias

You can find these sources using subject searches.

Conducting Subject Searches As you prepare to go online, consider your subject and the best way to find information to suit your needs. If you are looking for general information on a topic and you want your search results to be extensive, consider the subject search indexes on most search engines. These indexes, in the form of category and subject lists, often appear on the first page of a search engine. When you click on a specific highlighted word, you will be presented with a new screen containing subcategories of the topic you chose.

Evaluating the Reliability of Internet Resources

Just as you would evaluate the quality, bias, and validity of any other research material you locate, check the source of information you find online. Compare these two sites containing information about the poet and writer Langston Hughes:

Site A is a personal Web site constructed by a college student. It contains no bibliographic information or links to sites that he used. Included on the site are several poems by Langston Hughes and a student essay about the poet's use of symbolism. It has not been updated in more than six months.

Site B is a Web site constructed and maintained by the English Department of a major university. Information on Hughes is presented in a scholarly format, with a bibliography and credits for the writer. The site includes links to other sites and indicates new features that are added weekly.

For your own research, consider the information you find on Site B to be more reliable and accurate than that on Site A. Because it is maintained by experts in their field who are held accountable for their work, the university site will be a better research tool than the student-generated one.

Tips for Evaluating Internet Sources

1. Consider who constructed and who now maintains the Web page. Determine whether this author is a reputable source. Often, the URL endings indicate a source.

   - Sites ending in *.edu* are maintained by educational institutions.
   - Sites ending in *.gov* are maintained by government agencies (federal, state, or local).

   - Sites ending in *.org* are normally maintained by non-profit organizations and agencies.
   - Sites ending in *.com* are commercially or personally maintained.

2. Skim the official and trademarked Web pages first. It is safe to assume that the information you draw from Web pages of reputable institutions, online encyclopedias, online versions of major daily newspapers, or government-owned sites produce information as reliable as the material you would find in print. In contrast, unbranded sites or those generated by individuals tend to borrow information from other sources without providing documentation. As information travels from one source to another, it could have been muddled, misinterpreted, edited, or revised.

3. You can still find valuable information in the less "official" sites. Check for the writer's credentials, and then consider these factors:

   - Do not be misled by official-looking graphics or presentations.
   - Make sure that the information is updated enough to suit your needs. Many Web pages will indicate how recently they have been updated.
   - If the information is borrowed, notice whether you can trace it back to its original source.

Respecting Copyrighted Material

Because the Internet is a relatively new and quickly growing medium, issues of copyright and ownership arise almost daily. As laws begin to govern the use and reuse of material posted online, they may change the way that people can access or reprint material.

Text, photographs, music, and fine art printed online may not be reproduced without acknowledged permission of the copyright owner.

Writing Criticism

Literary criticism involves studying, analyzing, interpreting, and evaluating works of literature. It can be as brief as an answer to a question or as lengthy as an essay or a book. Following are examples of three types of criticism.

Analysis

You are frequently asked to analyze, or break down into parts and examine, a passage or a work. Often you must support your analysis with specific references to the text. In this brief analysis, the writer uses words from the question to write a topic sentence and embeds quotations from the text as support.

Question In "Heat" by H.D., how does the speaker create the impression that heat is almost a solid substance?

Answer The speaker in "Heat" uses repetition and imagery to convey the impression that heat is almost a solid substance. By repeating the word *heat* in each of the three stanzas, the speaker emphasizes its physical presence. Further, the speaker uses images that appeal to the sense of touch in describing heat as if it were a substance. In the first stanza, the speaker asks the wind to "cut apart the heat," and in the third stanza, to "plow through it."

Biographical Criticism Critics who take a biographical approach use information about a writer's life to explain his or her work. In this passage of biographical criticism, Kenneth Silverman explains Edgar Allan Poe's preoccupation with death as Poe's response to the early death of his mother, Eliza.

"Much of his later writing, despite its variety of forms and styles, places and characters, is driven by the question of whether the dead remain dead. . . . The most persuasive and coherent explanation, . . . comes from the modern understanding of childhood bereavement. . . . [C]hildren who lose a parent at an early age, as Edgar lost Eliza Poe, . . . invest more feeling in and magnify the parent's image. . . . The young child . . . cannot comprehend the finality of death. . . . "

Historical Criticism Using this approach, a critic explains how an author's work responds to the events, circumstances, or ideas of the author's historical era. In the following passage of historical criticism, Jean H. Hagstrum shows how William Blake's character Urizen symbolizes the Enlightenment ideas of Newton, Locke, and Bacon that Blake detested.

"Urizen is also an active force. Dividing, partitioning, dropping the plummet line, applying Newton's compasses to the world, he creates abstract mathematical forms. Like Locke, he shrinks the senses, narrows the perceptions, binds man to natural fact. Like Bacon, he creates the laws of prudence and crucifies passion."

Using Ideas From Research

Below are three common methods of incorporating the ideas of other writers into your work. Choose the most appropriate style by analyzing your needs in each case. In all cases, you must credit your source.

- **Direct Quotation:** Use quotation marks to indicate the exact words.
- **Paraphrase:** To share ideas without a direct quotation, state the ideas in your own words.
- **Summary:** To provide information about a large body of work, identify the writer's main idea.

Avoiding Plagiarism

Whether you are presenting a formal research paper or an opinion paper on a current event, be careful to give credit for any ideas or opinions that are not your own. Presenting someone else's ideas, research, or opinion as your own—even if you have rephrased it in different words—is plagiarism, the equivalent of academic stealing, or fraud.

You can avoid plagiarism by synthesizing what you learn: Read from several sources, and let the ideas of experts help you draw your own conclusions and form your own opinions. When you choose to use someone else's ideas or work to support your view, credit the source of the material.

Preparing a Manuscript

The presentation of your written work is important. Your work should be neat, clean, and easy to read. Follow your teacher's directions for placing your name and class, along with the title and date of your work, on the paper.

Research Papers

Most formal research papers have these features:
- Title Page
- Table of Contents or Outline
- Works-Cited List or Bibliography

Citing Sources

In research writing, cite your sources. In the body of your paper, provide a footnote, an endnote, or a parenthetical citation, identifying the sources of facts, opinions, or quotations. At the end of your paper, provide a bibliography or a works-cited list, a list of all the sources you cite. Follow an established format, such as Modern Language Association (MLA) Style.

Works-Cited List (MLA Style)

A works-cited list must contain accurate information sufficient to enable a reader to locate each source you cite. The basic components of an entry are as follows:

- Name of the author, editor, translator, or group responsible for the work
- Title of the work
- Place and date of publication
- Publisher

For print materials, the information required for a citation generally appears on the copyright and title pages of a work. For the format of works-cited list entries, consult the examples at right and in the chart on page R43.

Parenthetical Citations (MLA Style)

A parenthetical citation briefly identifies the source from which you have taken a specific quotation, factual claim, or opinion. It refers the reader to one of the entries on your works-cited list. A parenthetical citation has the following features:

- It appears in parentheses.
- It identifies the source by the last name of the author, editor, or translator.
- It gives a page reference, identifying the page of the source on which the information cited can be found.

Punctuation A parenthetical citation generally falls outside a closing quotation mark but within the final punctuation of a clause or sentence. For a long quotation set off from the rest of your text, place the citation at the end of the excerpt without any punctuation following.

Special Cases

- If the author is an organization, use the organization's name, in a shortened version if necessary.
- If you cite more than one work by the same author, add the title or a shortened version of the title.

Sample Works-Cited Lists

Carwardine, Mark, Erich Hoyt, R. Ewan Fordyce, and Peter Gill. *The Nature Company Guides: Whales, Dolphins, and Porpoises.* New York: Time-Life Books, 1998.

Whales in Danger. "Discovering Whales." 18 Oct. 1999. <http://whales.magna.com.au/DISCOVER>

Neruda, Pablo. "Ode to Spring." *Odes to Opposites.* Trans. Ken Krabbenhoft. Ed. and illus. Ferris Cook. Boston: Little, Brown and Company, 1995.

The Saga of the Volsungs. Trans. Jesse L. Byock. London: Penguin Books, 1990.

An anonymous work is listed by title.

Both the title of the work and of the collection in which it is found are listed.

Sample Parenthetical Citations

It makes sense that baleen whales such as the blue whale, the bowhead whale, the humpback whale, and the sei whale (to name just a few) grow to immense sizes (Carwardine, Hoyt, and Fordyce 19–21). The blue whale has grooves running from under its chin to partway along the length of its underbelly. As in some other whales, these grooves expand and allow even more food and water to be taken in (Ellis 18–21).

Author's last name

Page numbers where information can be found

MLA Style for Listing Sources

Book with one author	Pyles, Thomas. *The Origins and Development of the English Language.* 2nd ed. New York: Harcourt Brace Jovanovich, Inc., 1971.
Book with two or three authors	McCrum, Robert, William Cran, and Robert MacNeil. *The Story of English.* New York: Penguin Books, 1987.
Book with an editor	Truth, Sojourner. *Narrative of Sojourner Truth.* Ed. Margaret Washington. New York: Vintage Books, 1993.
Book with more than three authors or editors	Donald, Robert B., et al. *Writing Clear Essays.* Upper Saddle River, NJ: Prentice-Hall, Inc., 1996.
Single work from an anthology	Hawthorne, Nathaniel. "Young Goodman Brown." *Literature: An Introduction to Reading and Writing.* Ed. Edgar V. Roberts and Henry E. Jacobs. Upper Saddle River, NJ: Prentice-Hall, Inc., 1998. 376–385. [Indicate pages for the entire selection.]
Introduction in a published edition	Washington, Margaret. Introduction. *Narrative of Sojourner Truth.* By Sojourner Truth. Ed. Washington. New York: Vintage Books, 1993. v–xi.
Signed article in a weekly magazine	Wallace, Charles. "A Vodacious Deal." *Time* 14 Feb. 2000: 63.
Signed article in a monthly magazine	Gustaitis, Joseph. "The Sticky History of Chewing Gum." *American History* Oct. 1998: 30–38.
Unsigned editorial or story	"Selective Silence." Editorial. *Wall Street Journal* 11 Feb. 2000: A14. [If the editorial or story is signed, begin with the author's name.]
Signed pamphlet	[Treat the pamphlet as though it were a book.]
Pamphlet with no author, publisher, or date	*Are You at Risk of Heart Attack?* n.p. n.d. [n.p. n.d. indicates that there is no known publisher or date]
Filmstrips, slide programs, videocassettes, DVDs, and other audiovisual media	*The Diary of Anne Frank.* Dir. George Stevens. Perf. Millie Perkins, Shelley Winters, Joseph Schildkraut, Lou Jacobi, and Richard Beymer. 1959. DVD. Twentieth Century Fox, 2004.
Radio or television program transcript	"Washington's Crossing of the Delaware." Host Liane Hansen. Guest David Hackett Fischer. *Weekend Edition Sunday.* Natl. Public Radio. WNYC, New York City. 23 Dec. 2003. Transcript.
Internet	"Fun Facts About Gum." NACGM site. National Association of Chewing Gum Manufacturers. 19 Dec. 1999. <http://www.nacgm.org/consumer/funfacts.html> [Indicate the date you accessed the information. Content and addresses at Web sites change frequently.]
Newspaper	Thurow, Roger. "South Africans Who Fought for Sanctions Now Scrap for Investors." *Wall Street Journal* 11 Feb. 2000: A1+ [For a multipage article that does not appear on consecutive pages, write only the first page number on which it appears, followed by a plus sign.]
Personal interview	Smith, Jane. Personal interview. 10 Feb. 2000.
CD (with multiple publishers)	Simms, James, ed. *Romeo and Juliet.* By William Shakespeare. CD-ROM. Oxford: Attica Cybernetics Ltd.; London: BBC Education; London: HarperCollins Publishers, 1995.
Signed article from an encyclopedia	Askeland, Donald R. "Welding." *World Book Encyclopedia.* 1991 ed.

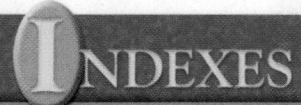

Index of Authors and Titles

Page numbers in *italics* refer to biographical information.

A

Achebe, Chinua, 444, *450*
Africa, 216
After Apple-Picking, 196
After 1,500 Years, Colosseum Reopens for Shows, 814
Akhmatova, Anna, *368*
All, 218
Also All, 219
Amichai, Yehuda, *951*
Analects, The, 220
Anaya, Rudolfo A., 128, *132*
Angela's Ashes, 475
Angelou, Maya, 199, *200*
Annie John, 70
Antigone, 772
Apple Tree, The, 206
Arthur Becomes King of Britain, 1030
Artzi-Pelossof, Noa Ben, 882
At Harvesttime, 200
Auto Wreck, 401

B

Bashō, Matsuo, *989*
Bean Eaters, The, 458
Before the Law, 404
Belle Dame sans Merci, La, 961
Benét, Stephen Vincent, 576, *586*
Bishop, Elizabeth, 293, *294*
Blackfeet, 492
Bradbury, Ray, 614, *620*
Brantley, Ben, 813, 814
Bridegroom, The, 59
Bridge, The, 366
Brontë, Emily, *367*
Brooks, Gwendolyn, *458*
Brown, Christy, 168, *174*, 178
Brown, Rosellen, *974*
Browning, Robert, *940*
Buck, Pearl S., 376, *392*
By the Waters of Babylon, 576

C

Cabuliwallah, The, 319
Calling Home, 414
Calvino, Italo, 621, *628*
Canby, Vincent, 734, *736*
Carson, Rachel, 660, *666*
Cassatt, Mary, 730
Cassian, Nina, *267*
Cat's in the Cradle, 934
Censors, The, 641
Cervantes, Miguel de, 1006, *1014*
Chapin, Harry, 934, *935*
Chapin, Sandy, 934
Chekhov, Anton, 596, *603*
Child's Christmas in Wales, A, 694
Civil Peace, 444
Columbus Dying, 162
Confucius, 220, *222*
Conscientious Objector, 266
Contents of the Dead Man's Pocket, 6

D

Damon and Pythias, 109
Danny Deever, 963
Dao, Bei, 218
Day-Lewis, Daniel, 178
Desai, Anita, 352, *360*
Dickinson, Emily, 158, 159, *284*, *464*, *950*
Dillard, Annie, 712, *718*
Diop, David, 216
Dog That Bit People, The, 256
Don Quixote, 1006
Douglas, Ann, 275
Dream Comes True, The, 39

E

Ebert, Roger, 737, *742*
Eco, Umberto, 456, *457*
Edwards, Julie Olsen, 724
Enzensberger, Hans, 633, *635*
Eulogy for a Fallen Leader, 882

F

Fear, 95
Feel the City's Pulse? It's Be-Bop, Man!, 275
Finney, Jack, 6, *20*
Fish, The, 293
Flood, 712
Ford, Gerald, 308
Fried, Philip, *954*
Frost, Robert, 196, *198*
Future of Luxury, The, 633

G

Games at Twilight, 352
García Lorca, Federico, 972, *973*
Garden of Stubborn Cats, The, 621
Globe Theater, The, 816
Going After Cacciato, 414
Good Deed, The, 376
Greek Theater, 768, 813
Guitar, The, 972
Guterson, David, 312, *315*

H

Haiku, 989
Hearts and Hands, 290
Henry, O., 290, *292*
Hill, Thomas A., 981
Hillary, Sir Edmund, 30, *36*
History of the Guitar, The, 981
How Much Land Does a Man Need?, 138
How to React to Familiar Faces, 456
Hughes, Langston, 268, *269*, 702, 706

I

I Am Not One of Those Who Left the Land, 368
Ibsen, Henrik, *513*
I dwell in Possibility—, 159

Imitating Nature's Mineral Artistry, 748
In Commemoration: One Million Volumes, 128
In Flanders Fields, 938
In the Orchard, 513
Into Thin Air, 37
Inzunza, Ernesto Ruelas, 753, *754*
Issa, Kobayashi, *989*

J

Jacobs, W. W., 50, *58*
Jade Flower Palace, 970
Jakuren, Priest, *988*
Jazz Fantasia, 270
Jussim, Estelle, 724, *726*

K

Kafka, Franz, 404, *406*
Keats, John, 961, *962*
Keep Memory Alive, 687
Kelley, William Melvin, 182, *190*
Kincaid, Jamaica, 70, 76
Kipling, Rudyard, 963, *964*
Krakauer, Jon, 37, *38*
Kraken, The, 939

L

La Belle Dame sans Merci, 960
Lagerkvist, Pär, 638, *640*
Lave, Charles, 411
Leiningen Versus the Ants, 550
Lessing, Doris, 242, *250*
Levertov, Denise, 514, *518*
Lightning and Thunder, 523
Like the Sun, 280
Li Po, *971*
Luck, 604

M

Making a Fist, 975
Man, A, 267
Mansfield, Katherine, 206, *210*
Marginal World, The, 660
Marian Anderson: Famous Concert Singer, 702
Masque of the Red Death, The, 82
Maupassant, Guy de, 102, *108*
McCourt, Frank, 475, *481*
McCrae, John, *938*
Meeting at Night, 940
Merriam, Eve, *952*
Metaphor, 952
Mexican Village, 498
Millay, Edna St. Vincent, *266*
Miller, Vassar, *162*
Mistral, Gabriela, 95
Momaday, N. Scott, 676, *682*
Monkey's Paw, The, 50
Moon at the Fortified Pass, The, 971
Mora, Pat, *160*
Morte d'Arthur, 1020

Mothers & Daughters, 724
Mowing, 198
Mühlberger, Richard, 466, 470
Munro, H. H., 540, 544
My Left Foot, 168

N

Nabokov, Vladimir, 342, 346
Narayan, R. K., 280, 283, 1052, 1058
Nash, Eric P., 1046, 1049
Native American Literature, 484, 492, 942
Navajo, 942, 944
New York Times, The, 813
Nguyen Thi Vinh, 398, 400
Niane, D. T., 1064, 1072
Niggli, Josephina, 498, 506
Night Chant, The, 942
Nobel Lecture, 683
Norgay, Tenzing, 39, 44
Nye, Naomi Shihab, 975

O

O'Brien, Tim, 414, 417
Oedipus, 769, 813
Old Song, 217
Old Stoic, The, 367
Olsen, Tillie, 724
Once and Future King, The, 1030
O'Neil, Paul, 748, 752
Open Window, The, 540
Orphan Boy and the Elk Dog, The, 484

P

Pace Like That, A, 951
Paz, Octavio, 96
Picture From the Past: Emily Dickinson, A, 464
Poe, Edgar Allan, 82, 88
Prayer of First Dancers, 942
Price, Reynolds, 464, 465
Pride, 402
Princess and All the Kingdom, The, 638
Private Horror Made Public, 813
Problem, A, 596
Pushkin, Alexander, 59, 64

R

Rama's Initiation, 1052
Ramayana, 1052
Ravikovitch, Dahlia, 402, 403
Reapers, 941
Right Hand, 954
Roethke, Theodore, 986, 987
Russell, William F., 109

S

Saki, 540, 544
Sandburg, Carl, 270
Shakespeare, William, 818, 822, 990
Shapiro, Karl, 401
65-MPH Speed Limit Is Saving Lives, 411
Snow Falling on Cedars, 312

Solzhenitsyn, Alexander, 512, 683, 686
Some Like Poetry, 976
Sonnet 18, 990
Sophocles, 769, 772, 808, 813
Speak, Memory, 342
Speech During the Invasion of Constantinople, 369
Speech on Japanese American Internment, 308
Spring and All, 94
Staff, Leopold, 366
Star Wars: An Epic for Today, 1046
Star Wars: Breakthrough Film Still Has the Force, 737
Star Wars—A Trip to a Far Galaxy That's Fun and Funny, 734
Stephenson, Carl, 550, 570
Stolen Child, The, 928
Storm in the Mountains, A, 512
Street, The, 96
Street of the Cañon, The, 498
Style, 199
Success is counted sweetest, 158
Sundiata: An Epic of Old Mali, 1064
Szymborska, Wisława, 976

T

Tagore, Rabindranath, 319, 326
Tanka, 988
Tell all the Truth but tell it slant—, 284
Tennyson, Alfred, Lord, 939, 1020, 1029
Theodora, Empress, 369, 370
There Will Come Soft Rains, 614
Thomas, Dylan, 694, 701
Thoughts of Hanoi, 398
Through the Tunnel, 242
Thurber, James, 256, 260
Tiger of the Snows, The, 39
Ting, Shu, 219
Tolstoy, Leo, 138, 152
Toomer, Jean, 941
Tragedy of Julius Caesar, The, 822
Tree Telling of Orpheus, A, 514
Tsurayuki, Ki, 988
Tu Fu, 970
Twain, Mark, 604, 608
Two Friends, 102

U

Uchida, Yoshiko, 300, 307
Ullman, James Ramsey, 39
Uncoiling, 160
Uprooting of a Japanese-American Family, The, 300

V

Valenzuela, Luisa, 641, 644
View From the Summit, 30
Visit to Grandmother, A, 182

W

Waking, The, 986
Walk to the Jetty, A, 70
Way to Rainy Mountain, The, 676

Weary Blues, The, 268
Welty, Eudora, 726
What Are Friends For, 974
What Makes a Degas a Degas?, 466
White, T. H., 1030, 1042
Widow and the Parrot, The, 430
Wiesel, Elie, 687, 688
Williams, William Carlos, 94
Wind—tapped like a tired Man, The, 950
Woolf, Virginia, 430, 438
Work That Counts, 753

Y

Yeats, William Butler, 928, 930

Index of Skills

LITERARY ANALYSIS

Act, R12
Allegory, R12
Alliteration, 927, 931, 937, 945, R12
Allusion, 205, 207, 211, 341, 345, 347, R12
Analytical essay, 463, 469, 471, R14
Anapest, R15
Anecdote, R12
Antagonist, 771, 773, 774, 778, 780, 782, 783, 784, 788, R12
Anticlimax, R12
Aphorisms, 215, 221, 223, R12
Aside, 860, 880, R12
Assonance, 937, 945, R12
Atmosphere, 927, 929, 931, R12
Author's
    attitude, 455, 459
    perspective, 29, 34, 43, 45
    purpose, 127, 130, 133, 463, 471
Autobiography, IN4, 167, 170, 172, 175, 655, 693, 696, 700, 707, R12
Biography, IN4, 655, 693, 696, 700, 707, R12
Blank verse, 840, 841, 843, 846, 848, 851, 853, 858, R12
Character rank, 840, 853, 856, 858
Characterization, 183, 184, 186, 187, 188, 189, R12
    direct, 181, 191, R12, R13
    indirect, 181, 191, R12, R15
Characters, IN2, 595, 600, 601, 606, 609, R12
    antagonist, 771, 773, 774, 778, 780, 782, 783, 784, 788, R12
    attitudes of, 443, 451
    decisions of, 771, 780, 788
    dynamic, 181, 187, 191, 317, 327, 375, 378, 379, 382, 386, 388, 390, 393, 1019, 1038, 1043
    flat, 137, 144, 148, 153
    protagonist, 771, 773, 774, 778, 780, 782, 783, 784, 788, R12, R17
    relationships between, 317, 324, 327, 375, 382, 385, 387, 391, 393, 1063, 1070, 1073
    round, 137, 148, 153
    static, 181, 187, 191, 317, 327, 375, 378, 379, 382, 386, 388, 390, 393, 595, 609
    tragic, 790, 792, 797, 800, 802, 806, 809
Cinquain, R19
Climax, 101, 106, 107, 112, 133, 241, 248, 251, 429, 439, 539, 545, 549, 568, 571, R12, R17
Comedy, IN6
Conflict, IN7, 429, 439, 497, 503, 507, 537, 549, 551, 557, 558, 561, 562, 563, 564, 565, 568, 569, 571, 883, 885, 887, 889, 891, 892, 894, 896, 898, R13
Connotation, 205, 211, R13
Consonance, 937, 945, R13
Couplet, R13, R19
Critical reviews, 655, 733, 740, 741, 743, R13
Dactyl, R15
Denotation, R13
Denouement, R13, R17

Description, 667, R13
Descriptive
    essay, IN5, 711, 713, 714, 715, 719, R14
    writing, 659, 663, 667
Development, R13
Dialect, R13
Dialogue, IN6, 351, 353, 361, 539, 545, 821, 831, 836, 838, R13
Diction, R13
Dimeter, R16
Direct characterization, 181, 191, R12, R13
Drama, IN6, R13, R15
Dramatic
    irony, R13, R15
    literature, IN1, IN6
    monologue, R14
    poem, IN8, 959, 961, 965, R14
    situation, 365, 371
    speeches, 860, 866, 868, 869, 872, 874, 877, 880, 890
Dynamic character, 181, 187, 191, 317, 327, 375, 378, 379, 382, 386, 388, 390, 595, 609, 1019, 1038, 1043, R12
Epic, IN11, 1005, 1015, R14
Epic conflict, 1063, 1067, 1071, 1073
Epic hero, 1005, 1015, 1051, 1057, 1059
Epiphany, 167, 170, 171, 172, 175
Essay, R14
    analytical, 463, 469, 471, 655, R14
    descriptive, IN5, 655, 711, 713, 714, 715, 719, R14
    expository, IN5, 655, 659, 662, 663, 667, R14
    humorous, 255, 257, 258, 261, R14
    narrative, R14
    persuasive, IN5, 675, 680, 682, 684, 689, R14
    reflective, IN5, 675, 680, 682, 684, 689, R14
    visual, IN5, 723, 727, R14
Exposition, 295, 429, 821, 828, 831, 832, 836, 837, 838, R14
Expository essay, IN5, 655, 659, 662, 663, 667, R14
Extended metaphor, R14
External conflict, 255, 258, 261, 549, 571, 883, 898, R13
Falling action, R14, R17
Fantasy, R14
Fate, 49, 65
Fiction, R14
Figurative language, IN9, 949, 955, R14
First-person point of view, 3, 69, 74, 77, 575, 587, R17
Flashback, 69, 74, 77
Flat characters, 137, 144, 153
Foil, R14
Folk literature, IN1, IN10
Folk tale, IN10
Foot, R14
Foreshadowing, 49, 52, 53, 56, 61, 63, 65, R14
Formats, 637
Free verse, R14
Genre, R15
Haiku, 985, R15
Heptameter, R16
Heptastich, R19

Hexameter, R16
Humorous essay, 255, 257, 258, 261, R14
Hyperbole, R15
Iambic, 840, R15, R16
Image, R15
Imagery, 93, 97, 195, 201, 969, 977, R15
Implied theme, 157, 163, R19
Inciting incident, 483, 493, 539
Indirect characterization, 181, 191, R12, R15
Informational texts, IN5
Internal conflict, 241, 242, 246, 247, 248, 251, 549, 571, 883, 898, R13
Irony, 279, 285, 613, 618, 629, R15
Legend, IN10, 1019, 1024, 1026, 1027, 1028, 1033, 1034, 1036, 1038, 1039, 1043, R15
Limerick, R19
Literal language, R15
Lyric poetry, IN8, 969, 977, R15
Metaphor, IN9, 949, 955, R14, R15
Meter, 937, 945, R15
Monologue, IN6, 860, 880, R16
Monometer, R16
Mood, R16
Moral, R16
Motivation, 351, 353, 356, 358, 361, 429, 431, 432, 439, R16
Musical devices, 265, 271, 937, 942, 945
Myth, IN10, 112, 483, 488, 490, 493, R16
Narration, R16
Narrative, R16
    essay, R14
    poem, IN8, 289, 959, 961, 965, R16
Narrator, 511, 519, R16
Nonfiction, xxvi, IN4, R16
Novel, R16
Octave, R16, R19
Omniscient point of view, 497, R17
Onomatopoeia, 937, 945, R16
Oral tradition, R16
Parable, 137, 139, 142, 145, 147, 148, 151, 153, R17
Parody, 1005, 1007, 1008, 1010, 1011, 1012, 1015, R17
Pentameter, 840, R16, R17
Personal narrative, 341, 345, 347
Personification, 397, 407, 949, 955, R14, R17
Persuasion, R17
Persuasive essay, IN5, 675, 680, 682, 684, 689, R14
Plays, IN6
Plot, IN2, IN7, 429, 439, 539, 541, 545, 959, 965, R17
Poems, IN1, IN8, R15, R17
    dramatic, IN8, 959, 961, 965, R14
    free verse, R14
    haiku, 985, R15, R19
    lyric, IN8, 969, 977, R15
    narrative, IN8, 289, 959, 961, 965, R16
    tanka, 985, R19
Poetic forms, IN8, 985, 991, R17
Point of view, IN3, 497, 499, 503, 507, 575, 577, 578, 581, 584, 587, R17
    author's, 29, 34, 43, 45
    first person, IN3, 69, 74, 77, 575, 587
    omniscient, 497, R17
    third person, IN3, 497, 575, 587, R17

Prose, R15, R17
Protagonist, 771, 773, 774, 778, 780, 782, 783, 784, 788, R12, R17
Quatrain, R19
Reflective essay, IN5, 675, 680, 682, 684, 689, R14
Repetition, 937, 945, R17
Resolution, 429, 439, 539, 545, 790, 806, 809, R17
Rhyme, IN9, 937, 945, R17
Rhyme scheme, R17
Rhythm, IN9, R18
Rising action, 5, 10, 12, 13, 21, R18
Round characters, 137, 153, R12
Scene, R18
Science fiction, R18
Sensory language, 93, 97, R18
Sestet, R18
Setting, IN3, 81, 89, 480, 575, 581, 584, 587, 613, 614, 616, 618, 622, 629, 1051, 1057, 1059, R18
Short story, xxvi, IN2, R18
Simile, IN9, 711, 719, 949, 955, R14, R18
Soliloquy, 860, 880, R18
Sonnet, 985, R18
Speaker, 365, 371, 511, 515, 519, R18
Spondee, R15
Stage directions, IN7, R18
Stanza, IN8, R18
Stated theme, 157, 163, R19
Static character, 181, 187, 191, 317, 327, 375, 378, 379, 382, 386, 388, 390, 393, 595, 609, R12
Surprise ending, 289, 295, R19
Suspense, 5, 8, 10, 12, 13, 14, 19, 20, 21, 883, 889, 894, 896, 898, R19
Symbols, 81, 85, 87, 89, R19
Tanka, 985, R19
Technical articles, 655, 747, 750, 754, 755, R19
Tetrameter, R16, R19
Theme, IN3, 157, 163, 279, 397, 399, 405, 407, 443, 447, 451, 637, 641, 643, 645, R19
    implied, 157, 163, R19
    stated, 157, 163, R19
    universal, 101, 113, 215, 223, R19
Third-person point of view, IN3, 497, 575, 587, R17
Tone, 127, 130, 133, 195, 201, 265, 271, 455, 459, 723, 727, R19
Tragedy, IN6, 900, 902, 910, 911, 912, 913, R19
Tragic character, 790, 792, 797, 800, 802, 806, 809
Tragic flaw, 900, 912, 913
Trimeter, R16, R19
Trochee, R15
Universal theme, 101, 113, 215, 223, R19
Verbal irony, R15, R19
Villanelle, 985, R19
Visual essay, IN5, 723, 727, R14
Writer's
    perspective, 733, 741, 743
    purpose, 299, 302, 304, 309

READING STRATEGIES

Author's
    attitude, 693, 695, 698, 703, 707, 1003, 1019, 1021, 1022, 1024, 1025, 1027, 1028, 1031, 1032, 1034, 1036, 1037, 1039, 1041, 1043
    perspective, 339, 365, 366, 371
    purpose, 125, 226, 229, 167, 169, 170, 172, 175, 339, 341, 347, 657, 675, 677, 680, 683, 685, 689, 1003, 1063, 1069, 1071, 1073
Background knowledge, 299, 301, 307, 309, 427
Cause and effect, 239, 279, 281, 285, 522, 659, 900, 901, 903, 905, 906, 908, 909, 910, 913
Challenging the message, 637, 645
Chronological patterns, 659
Clarifying, 125, 181, 185, 191, 537, 613, 615, 616, 621, 624, 625, 626, 627, 629
Comparing and contrasting, 659, 1003, 1005, 1010, 1011, 1015
    information from several sources, 812, 815
Constructing meaning, 537
Context clues, 3, 81, 84, 89, 121
Deduction, 410, 413
Diagrams, 747, 755
Drawing conclusions, 537, 575, 578, 579, 580, 583, 587
Drawing inferences, 69, 71, 73, 74, 75, 77, 157, 163, 339, 375, 377, 381, 383, 384, 389, 391, 393, 427, 429, 433, 436, 437, 439, 595, 597, 598, 601, 602, 609, 1003, 1051, 1054, 1059
Engaging the senses, 317, 320, 323, 427, 511, 517, 519
Evaluate
    a character's decision, 339, 351, 356, 358, 361
    credibility of information sources, 274, 277, 590, 593
    a writer's message, 397, 407
Forming mental images, 93, 96, 97, 239, 255, 258, 261, 985, 991
Identifying
    cause and effect, 279, 281, 285, 900, 901, 903, 905, 906, 908, 909, 910, 913
    with a character, 767, 790, 794, 795, 802, 805, 807, 809
    evidence, 657, 733, 740, 743
    relationships, 537, 539, 542, 545
    the speaker, 925, 959, 962, 965
Implied main idea, 335
Induction, 410, 413
Interactive reading, 239
Interpreting, 125, 195, 201, 483, 485, 486, 490, 493
    pictures, 657, 723, 727
Listening, 925, 937, 943, 945
Literal comprehension, 3
Main idea, 235, 335
Nonfiction, 657
Opinion and fact, 3, 29, 41, 45
Paraphrasing, 767, 860, 862, 865, 872, 874, 875, 876, 880, 949, 955
Patterns of organization, 659, 661, 667, 980, 983
Picturing the imagery, 255, 258, 261, 925, 985, 991
Predicting, 3, 239, 427, 497, 499, 504, 505, 507, 549, 552, 555, 556, 558, 559, 561, 562, 564, 566, 567, 571
    based on character traits, 137, 140, 144, 146, 149, 150, 153
    based on plot details, 537
outcomes, 3, 49, 50, 52, 54, 56, 59, 61, 65, 239, 289, 291, 295
Questioning, 125, 205, 209, 211, 239, 241, 242, 244, 246, 249, 251
    characters' motives, 771, 774, 776, 779, 782, 784, 785, 786, 788
Reading
    ahead, 3, 5, 7, 17, 21
    to appreciate author's craft, 2, 536, 766, 924, 1002
    between the lines, 767, 883, 887, 888, 890, 896, 898
    in blank verse, 840, 845, 847, 849, 850, 856, 858
    critically, 339
    to be entertained, 238, 426
    fiction, 427
    for information, 2, 124, 238, 338, 426, 536, 656, 766, 924, 1002
    to be inspired, 124, 338, 656
    for love of literature, 2, 124, 238, 338, 426, 536, 656, 766, 924, 1002
    in sentences, 925, 969, 977
    poetry, 925
Recall, 20, 36, 44, 58, 64, 76, 88, 96, 108, 112, 132, 152, 159, 162, 174, 190, 198, 200, 210, 217, 222, 250, 260, 267, 269, 270, 284, 292, 294, 308, 326, 346, 360, 367, 370, 392, 400, 403, 406, 438, 450, 457, 458, 470, 492, 506, 518, 544, 570, 586, 603, 608, 620, 628, 640, 644, 666, 682, 686, 688, 701, 706, 718, 726, 742, 752, 754, 787, 808, 837, 857, 879, 897, 912, 930, 941, 944, 950, 951, 953, 954, 962, 964, 973, 975, 976, 987, 989, 990, 1014, 1029, 1042, 1058, 1072
Recognizing facts and impressions, 657, 711, 712, 717, 719
Relating
    modes of persuasion, 410, 413
    text and pictures, 463, 471
    to what you know, 215, 223
Rereading, 3, 5, 7, 17, 21
Respond, 20, 36, 44, 58, 64, 76, 88, 96, 108, 112, 132, 152, 159, 162, 174, 190, 198, 200, 210, 217, 222, 250, 260, 267, 269, 270, 284, 292, 294, 308, 326, 346, 360, 367, 370, 392, 400, 403, 406, 438, 450, 457, 458, 470, 492, 506, 518, 544, 570, 586, 603, 608, 620, 628, 640, 644, 666, 682, 686, 688, 701, 706, 718, 726, 742, 752, 754, 787, 808, 837, 857, 879, 897, 912, 927, 930, 931, 941, 944, 950, 951, 953, 954, 962, 964, 973, 975, 976, 987, 989, 990, 1014, 1029, 1042, 1058, 1072
    to connotations, 455, 458, 459
    to images and ideas, 265, 271
Significant details, 101, 103, 104, 105, 106, 107, 113, 235
Skimming and scanning, 670, 673, 1076, 1079
Stated main idea, 335
Structure and format, 24, 27
Summarizing, 127, 128, 133
Text aids, 767, 821, 823, 825, 833, 835, 838
Using prior knowledge, 427, 443, 448, 451
Word meanings, 121

GRAMMAR, USAGE, AND MECHANICS

Active voice, 224
Adjective clauses, 372, 610, R35
Adjectives, 90, 98, 728, R34, R35
    capitalizing, 1016
    proper, 1016
Adverb clauses, 394, R35
Adverbs, 90, 202, 728, R34
Antecedents, 66, 899
Apostrophes, R36
Appositives, 440, 708, R35
Capitalization, 1016, R35
Clauses, 348, R35
Colons, R36
Commas, 1060, R35
Commonly confused words
    accept and *except*, 494
    among and *between*, 946, R37
    amount and *number*, R37
    any and *all*, R37
    around, R37
    as, because, like, as to, R37
    bad, badly, R37
    because of, due to, R37
    being as, being that, R37
    beside, besides, R37
    can, may, R37
    different from, different than, R37
    farther, further, R37
    fewer, less, R37
    good and *well*, 744, R37
    hopefully, R38
    its, it's, R38
    just, only, 546, R38
    kind of, sort of, R38
    lay and *lie*, 212, R38
    leave, let, R38
    raise, rise, R38
    set, sit, R38
    so, so that, R38
    than and *then*, 720, R38
    that, which, who, R38
    their, there, and *they're*, 932
    to, too, and *two*, 992
    unique, R38
    when, where, R38
    who, whom, who's and *whose*, 859
Comparative degree, 114, 690
Complete predicates, 262
Complete subjects, 252
Compound predicates, 296
Compound subjects, 310
Conjunctions, R34
Dashes, R36
Degrees of comparison, 668, 690
Demonstrative pronoun, R34
Direct address, 914
Direct object, 286
Elliptical clauses, 810, 956
End marks, R35
Exclamation mark, R35
Fragments, R34
Gerunds, 460, 520, R35
Hyphens, 966, R36
Imperative mood, 839
Indefinite pronoun, R34
Indicative mood, 839
Indirect object, 286
Infinitive phrases, 472, R35
Infinitives, 472, 508
Intensive pronoun, R34

Irregular comparative degrees, 690
Irregular verb forms, 154
Modifiers, 114, 756
Moods, 839
Nominative case, 78
Nonrestrictive appositives, 708
Noun clauses, 408, R35
Nouns, 22, 46, R34, R35
    capitalizing, 1016
    proper, 1016
Objective case, 78
Objective pronouns, 789
Parallel structure, 630
Parentheses, R36
Participial phrase, R35
Participles, 460
Passive voice, 224
Past perfect tense, 176
Past tense, 176
Period, R35
Phrase, R35
Placement of *only* and *just*, 546, 978, R38
Possessive case, 78
Predicate adjectives, 328
Predicate nominative, 328
Preposition, R34
Prepositional phrase, 508, R35
Present participial phrases, 452
Pronoun case, 78, 810
Pronouns, 66, 789, 881, 899, R34
Proper adjectives, 1016
Proper nouns, 1016
Punctuation, 966, 1044, 1060, 1074, R35
Question mark, R35
Quotation marks, 1044, R36
Reflexive pronoun, 881, R34
Regular verb forms, 154
Relative pronoun, R34
Restrictive appositives, 708
Semicolons, 1074, R36
Sentences, 588, R34
Subject and verb agreement, 164, 572, R34
Subjects, hard-to-find, 272
Subjunctive mood, 839
Subordination, 362, R35
Superlative degree, 114, 690
Tenses, 176, 192, 646
Usage problems, 859
    placement of *only*, 978
Verbs, 460, R34
    action, 134, R34
    forms of, 154
    helping, R34
    intransitive, R34
    irregular, 154
    lay and *lie*, 212
    linking, 134, R34
    regular, 154
    subject agreement, 164, R34
    tenses, 192, 646
    transitive, R34

VOCABULARY

Analogies, 98, 272, 372, 572, 756, 881, 992
Anglo-Saxon
  prefixes
    be-, 46
    mis-, 914
  suffixes
    -less, 98

-ly, 508
Antonyms, 114, 224, 328, 494, 668, 720, 744
Conjunctive adverbs, 588
Connotations, 690, 708, 744
Context, 154, 192, 588, 610, 946
Contrasting definitions, 394
Elaboration, 134, 932
Forms of
    portent, 839
    reciprocity, 690
    sagacity, 440
    temperate, 992
Greek
  prefixes
    epi-, 262
    syn-, 756
  roots
    -chol-, 272
    -chor-, 810
    -path-, 978
    -phil-, 899
Homographs, 494
Latin
  plural forms, 572
  prefixes
    counter-, 296
    im-, 164
    in-, 134
    mal-, 720
    mil-, 946
    pro-, 348
    super-, 362
    trans-, 789
  roots
    -ami-, 460
    -cent-, 472
    -cred-, 66
    -curs-, 310
    -dom-, 372
    -firm-, 1074
    -gratis-, 286
    -journ-, 966
    -jud-, 328
    -lum-, 252
    -min-, 1060
    -ora-, 881
    -pel-, 394
    -reput-, 452
    -sat-, 408
    -son-, 1016
    -spir-, 859
    -stup-, 78
    -tac-, 956
    -tain-, 114
    -term-, 22
    -ultra-, 646
    -ver-, 610
    -vol-, 176
  suffixes
    -able, 668
    -ment, 224
    -ous, 1044
    -tion, 90
  terms, 520
  word origins
    ventured, 192
Musical words, 708
Related words
    forms of *sagacity*, 440
Spelling vs. pronunciation, *-ough*, 202

Synonyms, 22, 66, 202, 212, 252, 494, 646, 668, 810, 839, 914, 1016, 1060, 1074
Words
choice of, 956, 978
about color, 728
in context, 408, 630
meanings, 78, 176, 262
multiple meanings, 932
from myths, 212, 630
from names, 546

CRITICAL THINKING AND VIEWING

Analyze, 20, 32, 34, 44, 58, 76, 86, 88, 108, 112, 123, 152, 158, 159, 162, 190, 196, 198, 200, 210, 237, 250, 260, 269, 270, 284, 292, 294, 300, 308, 326, 337, 346, 360, 367, 376, 404, 406, 425, 438, 446, 450, 456, 457, 468, 470, 492, 518, 535, 570, 586, 642, 644, 665, 678, 686, 701, 726, 738, 742, 752, 754, 765, 775, 781, 787, 798, 808, 816, 837, 857, 864, 879, 891, 902, 907, 911, 941, 953, 962, 963, 964, 971, 973, 974, 975, 987, 989, 1001, 1029, 1046, 1056, 1058, 1065
Analyze cause and effect, 152, 250, 308, 326, 392, 492, 502, 912
Apply, 20, 36, 88, 159, 162, 210, 222, 260, 269, 326, 346, 360, 467, 470, 682, 837, 941, 990
Assess, 162, 222, 686, 697, 768, 857, 930
Clarify, 187, 326
Compare, 75, 160, 326, 346, 540, 735, 742
Compare and contrast, 20, 58, 64, 76, 84, 88, 96, 102, 112, 152, 171, 182, 185, 190, 208, 210, 245, 248, 259, 260, 284, 292, 294, 326, 370, 403, 406, 450, 476, 478, 516, 543, 585, 617, 619, 620, 628, 640, 666, 701, 752, 857, 879, 897, 912, 939, 941, 951, 964, 988, 990, 1014, 1026, 1042, 1072
Connect, 18, 44, 88, 132, 159, 171, 188, 217, 220, 222, 292, 302, 319, 326, 343, 354, 358, 369, 386, 398, 406, 457, 470, 498, 513, 518, 544, 563, 570, 579, 597, 600, 608, 655, 663, 666, 687, 704, 706, 778, 804, 817, 854, 871, 873, 922, 942, 962, 975, 989, 990, 1042, 1072
Contrast, 144, 742, 751, 975
Deduce, 132, 198, 403, 458, 518, 586, 638, 688
Defend, 718
Distinguish, 608
Draw conclusions, 11, 16, 20, 30, 58, 64, 95, 96, 104, 174, 210, 250, 284, 292, 306, 346, 360, 392, 406, 458, 506, 544, 553, 604, 628, 644, 682, 684, 688, 694, 706, 725, 752, 754, 773, 857, 886, 897, 944, 951, 962, 964, 990, 1031, 1042
Evaluate, 20, 44, 64, 96, 108, 112, 132, 152, 159, 162, 174, 190, 200, 260, 269, 270, 284, 292, 346, 360, 370, 392, 450, 470, 492, 603, 620, 644, 666, 701, 712, 726, 808, 879, 897, 912, 953, 964, 973, 975, 976, 987, 990, 1013, 1014, 1042, 1058
Extend, 20, 44, 76, 96, 112, 132, 198, 210, 217, 250, 269, 308, 367, 392, 470, 975
Generalize, 36, 108, 198, 222, 270, 284, 360, 438, 518, 570, 944, 954, 962

Hypothesize, 58, 108, 138, 174, 190, 222, 260, 284, 370, 458, 950, 1058
Infer, 20, 36, 39, 42, 44, 50, 55, 62, 64, 76, 88, 96, 109, 112, 147, 152, 174, 198, 210, 217, 250, 267, 268, 294, 346, 360, 367, 370, 400, 406, 434, 438, 445, 450, 457, 464, 470, 474, 487, 492, 506, 570, 603, 620, 640, 666, 682, 686, 688, 706, 718, 726, 742, 791, 793, 823, 826, 830, 857, 897, 912, 929, 930, 941, 944, 951, 953, 954, 962, 972, 973, 975, 1035, 1040, 1058, 1068, 1072
Interpret, 6, 64, 76, 88, 96, 112, 132, 159, 162, 168, 174, 198, 200, 217, 222, 267, 284, 294, 367, 370, 392, 403, 406, 450, 458, 489, 492, 518, 544, 570, 628, 632, 666, 682, 686, 688, 701, 706, 724, 726, 777, 787, 808, 857, 879, 912, 930, 941, 950, 951, 953, 954, 973, 976, 987, 1007, 1014, 1020, 1029, 1042, 1058, 1072
Make a judgment, 36, 152, 217, 250, 270, 284, 308, 400, 403, 438, 450, 457, 506, 570, 620, 640, 644, 686, 688, 742, 754, 930, 951, 1014, 1029, 1072
Paraphrase, 269, 990
Predict, 256, 430, 484, 603, 608, 614, 676, 837, 879
Relate, 326, 603, 808, 857, 941, 944, 1048
Solve, 586
Speculate, 40, 58, 70, 141, 150, 174, 190, 206, 210, 267, 292, 308, 320, 326, 346, 368, 370, 400, 406, 450, 492, 506, 556, 586, 603, 608, 620, 640, 661, 682, 702, 706, 718, 737, 752, 787, 801, 846, 879, 897, 912, 930, 938, 954, 989, 990, 1014, 1052, 1065
State an opinion, 544
Summarize, 152, 200, 438, 620
Support, 266, 269, 270, 284, 603, 608, 742, 940, 960
Synthesize, 108, 216, 267, 754, 976
Take a position, 267, 360, 367, 406, 518, 544, 603, 608, 628, 640, 686, 706, 718, 752, 787, 879, 953, 1072

WRITING

Writing Applications

Advertisements, 631, R26
Advice column, 203
Analysis
of an image, 409
of a poem, 957
Analytical essay, 811
Assessment, 994, R28
Autobiographical narrative, 116, R26
Award speech, 395
Biographer's account, 709
Business letter, 1080, R28, R29
Cause-and-effect essay, R27
Character sketch, 116, 589
Citing sources, R42, R43
Cliffhanger scene, 23
Comparison-and-contrast essay, 47, 509, 758, R27
Consumer report, 993
Crime report, 933
Criticism, R41
Description of a Natural Setting, 99
Descriptive writing, 99, R26
Dialogue between children, 363
Documented essay, R27
Essays, 810, 811, R26, R27

Evaluation, 225
Exposition, R27
Extended definition of friendship, 115
Firsthand biography, 193
Interior monologue, 839
Internment camp research report, 311
Interview with the speaker, 273
Introduction
for an art exhibit, 729
for a collection, 547
Journal, 91, 135, 329
Last will and testament, 441
Letters, 691
business, 1080, R28, R29
to the editor, 297, 859, 1080
of introduction, 79
of recommendation, 1045
persuasive, 757
requesting information, 27
of submission, 165
Literary
comparison, 287
criticism, R41
Lyric poem, 979
Memo, 26
Monologue, 521, 839
Movie
review, 745
scene, 573
Museum placard, 473
Narration, R26
News
article, 263, 789
bulletin, 967
commentary, 373
interview, 453
Obituary, 881
Personal narrative, 177, 349
Persuasive
advertisements, 631, R26
argument, 461
composition, 330
essay, 332, 647, 915, R26
letter, 757
Problem-and-solution essay, R27
Profile, 899, 1017
Proposal
for nature documentary, 669
for poetry anthology, 947
for a script, 1061
Radio call-in transcript, 721
Reading journal, 135
Reflective essay, 418
Research writing, 526, R27, R28
Response to literature, 916, R28
Retelling
a myth, 495
a story, 213
Safety instructions, 67
Short story, 648, R26
Sketch of comic hero, 1017
Story ending, 611
Storytelling notes, 1075
Submission letter, 165
Technical manual, 230
Travel brochure, 253
Video script, 155
Workplace writing, R28

Writing Strategies

Adding a direct quotation, 287
Addressing
the critics, 647

a target audience, 631
Analyzing a poem, 957
Analyzing a character's behavior, 611
Anticipating questions, 473
Avoiding plagiarism, R41
Block format, 1082
Brainstorming, 91, 203, 418, 547, R24
Cause and effect, 67, 177
Character profile, 116
Chronological organization, 996, R24
Comparing and contrasting, 993, 996
Completing a timeline, 547
Conclusions, 918, R25
Consider
    the audience, 916
    the moment, 116
Details, 91, 115, 116, 118, 349, 420, 648,
    729, 758, 760, 916, 994, 1017, 1082,
    R24
Determining audience and purpose, 79
Dialogue, 118, 650
Directions, 155
Drafting, 118, 213, 232, 332, 420, 530,
    648, 760, 918, 996, 1082, R24
Editing, R25
Elaborating, 450, 760, 918, 996
    to give information, 165
    on a statement, 297
    with figurative language, 420
Evidence, 330
Facts and opinions, 263, 373, 757
Gathering specific examples, 526, 947, R26
Hexagonal writing, 758, 916
Identifying
    causes and effects, 67
    the climax, 967
    conflict, 116
    setting, 418
Interior monologue, 118
Introductions, 395, 918, R25
Investigative research, 526
Keeping a reading journal, 135
Listing, 758, 916
Logical order, 1017
Looping, 1080
Main idea, 418, R24
Modified block format, 1082
Narrowing a topic, 691
Nestorian organization, 996
Objective tone, 933
Order of importance, R24
Parallelism, 333
Paraphrasing, 915
Planning a sequence of events, 23
Plot diagram, 118, 650
Prewriting, 230, 330, 418, 526, 648, 758,
    916, 994, 1080, R24
Proofreading, R25
Quicklist, 1080
Recording the facts, 263
Revising, 232, 332, 420, 530, 648, 760,
    918, 996, R25
    to add sensory details, 349
    to add supporting details, 453, 1082
    to add transitions, 495
    to address audience knowledge,
        1075, 1083
    for appropriate language, 363
    to balance fact and opinion, 373
    to balance comparisons, 760
    for clarity, 919, 1045
    to create a mood, 979
    to create setting, 530

to elaborate, 224, 729
to evaluate coherence, 530
to evaluate structure, 509
to form parallel structures, 333
for logical order, 1017
for objectivity, 709
for organization, 1082
to provide examples, 193
to provide relevant support, 530
to replace forms of to be, 409
to replace vague words, 421
to strengthen analysis, 811
to strengthen support, 332
Scanning, 526
Sensory
    details, 99, 118, 408
    language, 721
Setting the scene, 573, 648
Spatial order, R24
Supporting
    generalizations, 589
    opinions with evidence, 745, 757
Thesis statement, 526, 758, 918
Topic, choosing, 116, 330, 418, 526, 758,
    916, 994, 1080
Transitions, 495, 669
Using
    appropriate language, 273
    emotional language, 1061
    first-person narration, 329
    objective tone, 33
    persuasive tone in a description, 253
    qualifiers for accuracy, 311
    sensory language, 721
    transitions to show comparisons, 669

LISTENING AND SPEAKING

Arguments, 530
Art exhibit, 473
Bibliography, 709
Book discussion, 349
Debate, 115, 165, 495, 509, 859
Demonstration, 757
Descriptive presentation, 234
Dialogue, 23, 253, 441, 453
Dramatic monologue, 67
Dramatic reading, 881
Effective listening, 652
Eulogy, 155
Games discussion, 363
Group discussion, 135, 729
Improvisational skit, 409
Informal debate, 165
Informal talk, 47
Interview, 225, 395, 957, 1084
Introduction, 461
Media coverage, 422
Media presentation, 762
Mock trial, 811
Monologue, 213, 611
Motivational speech, 573
Multimedia presentation, 349, 669, 920,
    998
Musical presentation, 967
Musical review, 709
Music analysis, 745
Narrative presentation, 120
Oral
    anecdote, 193
    argument, 287
    interpretation, 993
    reading, 273
    response, 762

Panel discussion, 1045
Perform a scene, 915
Persuasive
    argument, 311, 334, 631
    speech, 329
Poetry reading, 473, 947, 967, 979
Presentation, 933
Radio
    interview, 589
    script, 91
    show, 263
Research report, 979
Role play, 373, 1017
Royal speech, 647
Sound-effects tape, 297
Speech, 99, 177, 203, 573, 647
Speech analysis, 691
Storytelling, 547, 1075
Telephone interview, 79
Television interview, 521, 721
Visual symbol, 839

RESEARCH AND TECHNOLOGY

Annotated bibliography, 729
Annotated list, 647
Annotated map, 79, 155, 213, 453, 589
Art exhibit, 473
Bar graph, 495
Bibliography of reference materials, 709
Biographical
    brochure, 1017
    report, 957
    sketch, 263
Brochure, 165, 1017
Charts, 297, 1045
Collage, 373
Comparisons, 99, 745
Conflict-resolution workshop, 193
Conservation update, 757
Contrasting maps, 409
Copyright, R40
Dialect chart, 967
Flood report, 721
Floor plan, 631
Home pages, 441
Internet, R39, R40
Key word searches, R39
Library resources chart, 135
Manual, 253
Maps
    annotated, 79, 155, 213, 453, 589
    contrasting, 409
    floor plan, 631
Models, 915
Multimedia biography, 611
Multimedia presentation, 91, 177, 287,
    349, 395, 521, 811, 998
Musical review, 709
News article, 115, 225, 573
Oral history, 311
Photo essay, 509
Poster, 993, 1061
Presentation, 789
Reading list, 547
Reports, 363, 691, 721, 979
    research, 461, 1075
    scientific, 669
Slide-show presentation, 899
Survey, 67
Timelines, 23, 203, 273, 329, 933
Video game, 47
Visual presentation, 947

Index of Features

HOW TO READ LITERATURE

Analyze cause and effect, 239
Author's
    attitude, 1003
    perspective, 339
    purpose, 339, 657, 1003
Character's decision, 339
Clarify, 125, 537
Compare and contrast, 1003
Constructing meaning, 537
Context clues, 3
Cultural inferences, 1003
Drama, 767
Draw conclusions, 537
Engage senses, 427
Epics, 1003
Fact vs. opinion, 3, 657
Fiction, 427
Form mental images, 239
Identify
    author's purpose, 125
    with a character, 767
    evidence, 657
    relationships, 537
    speaker, 925
Inferences, 427
Interactive reading strategies, 125, 239
Interpret, 125, 657
Legends, 1003
Listening, 925
Literal comprehension, 3
Nonfiction, 657
Paraphrasing, 767
Picture the imagery, 925
Predict outcomes, 3, 239, 427, 537
Prior background knowledge, 427
Question, 125, 239
Read
    ahead, 3
    between the lines, 767
    critically, 339
    poetry, 925
    in sentences, 925
Reread, 3
Use text aids, 767

LITERATURE IN CONTEXT

African cultural connection, 1066
Agricultural vocabulary, 143
Animal behavior, 433
Ants, 566
Architectural features, 623
Black Death, 87
Cerebral palsy, 173
Children's games around the world, 357
Climbing essentials, 33
Crimean War, 607
Cultural connection, 60, 357, 380, 582
Design connection, 623
Dialect, 186
Dionysius the Elder, 110
Erebus, 843
Extended families, 380
From Kabul to Calcutta, 322
Geography connection, 72, 143, 322, 449
Griot, 1066
Health connection, 247
Hindu gods, 1055
History connection, 305, 322, 491, 599, 607, 1037
Horses, 491
How much is a million?, 131
Humanities connection, 560, 825, 843, 863, 904
Ides of March, 825
Indian clothing, 325
La Mancha, 1009
Landscape of Antigua, 72
Language connection, 186, 500, 1023
League, 869
Macbeth, 560
Market research, 9
Matchmaking, 60
Math connection, 9, 131
Media connection, 554
Medieval vocabulary, 1023
Mount Olympus, 863
Music connection, 282
Musical vocabulary, 705
Naked Jungle, The, 554
New York City, 582
Nigerian civil war, 449
Omens, 904
Physics, 15
Raga, 282
Religion, 1055
Science connection, 15, 87, 173, 344, 433, 566, 664
Sea birds, 664
Siberia, 599
Social studies connection, 110, 325, 696, 1009
Soomerki, 344
Spanish vocabulary, 500
Sports connection, 33
Tournaments, 1037
Vocabulary connection, 705, 848, 869
Wales, 696
Wartime heroes, 305
Water-safety rules, 247
Word forms, 848

READING INFORMATIONAL MATERIALS

Analyzing
    structure and format, 24, 27
    text structures, 522, 525
Arts-and-leisure articles, 812
Brochures, 670
Business documents, 24
Business letter, 25
Cause-and-effect articles, 522, 525
Compare information from several sources, 812, 815
Credibility of information sources, 274, 590, 593
Graphics, 276
Historical essay, 980
Home pages, 591
Instructions for use, 227
Memo, 26
Newspaper features, 274
Patterns of organization, 980, 983
Persuasive articles, 410
Reference materials, 1076
Skimming and scanning, 1076, 1079
Technical directions, 226
Visual representation, 276
Warranties, 226, 228
Web sites, 590
World atlas, 1076

CONNECTIONS

Art, 730

Geography, 37
History, 312, 414, 882
Humanities, 474
Media, 178, 1046
Music, 934
Technology, 632

WRITING WORKSHOPS

Autobiographical narrative, 116
Block format, 1082
Business letter, 1080
Chronological organization, 996
Compare-and-contrast essay, 758
Comparison-and-contrast
    organization, 996
Consider audience, 916, 1080
Drafting, 232, 332, 420, 530, 650,
    760, 996
Exposition, 230
Gather details, 420, 758, 916
How-to essay, 230
Investigative research, 526
Letter to the editor, 1080
Listing, 758, 916
Modified block format, 1082
Nestorian organization, 996
Parallelism, 333
Persuasive essay, 330
Publishing, 233, 333, 421, 531, 651,
    761, 919, 997, 1083
Reflective essay, 418
Research writing, 526
Response to literature, 916
Revising, 232, 332, 420, 530, 650,
    760, 918, 996, 1082
Scanning headlines, 526
Short story, 643
Thesis statement, 526
Topic selection, 116, 330, 418, 526,
    578, 916, 994, 1080
Writing for assessment, 994

LISTENING AND SPEAKING WORKSHOPS

Analyze a media presentation, 762
Analyzing types of arguments, 532
Comparing media coverage, 422
Delivering a persuasive argument,
    334

Descriptive presentations, 234
Effective listening, 652
Interviewing techniques, 1084
Multimedia presentation, 998
Narrative presentation, 120
Oral responses to literature, 920

ASSESSMENT WORKSHOPS

Author's meaning, 999
Cause and effect, 423
Characteristics of text, 921
Comparing and contrasting, 763
Context clues, 121
Details, 235
Facts, 235
Graphic Aids, 533
Main ideas, 335
Organization, 1085
Propaganda, 653
Word meanings, 121

Chana Bloch "Pride" by Dahlia Ravikovitch, translated by Chana Bloch and Ariel Bloch from *The Window,* Sheep Meadow Press, 1989. Reprinted by permission of Chana Bloch.

Brandt & Hochman Literary Agents, Inc. "By the Waters of Babylon" by Stephen Vincent Benet, from *The Selected Works of Stephen Vincent Benet,* Holt, Rinehart & Winston, Inc. Copyright © 1937 by Stephen Vincent Benet. Copyright renewed © 1965 by Thomas C. Benet, Stephanie Mahin and Rachel B. Lewis. Reprinted by permission of Brandt & Hochman Literary Agents, Inc.

Don Congdon Associates, Inc. "There Will Come Soft Rains" by Ray Bradbury, published in *Collier's Weekly,* 1950. Copyright © 1950 by Crowell-Collier Publishing, renewed 1977 by Ray Bradbury. "Contents of the Dead Man's Pocket" by Jack Finney, published in *Collier's,* 1950. Copyright © 1956 by Crowell Collier Publishing, renewed 1984 by Jack Finney. Reprinted and edited by permission of Don Congdon Associates, Inc.

Crown Publishers Inc., a division of Random House, Inc. "Damon and Pythias" from *Classic Myths to Read Aloud* by William Russell. Copyright © 1988 by William F. Russell. Used by permission of Crown Publishers, a division of Random House, Inc.

Darhansoff & Verrill Literary Agency "I am Not One of Those Who Left the Land" by Anna Akhmatova from *Poems of Akhmatova,* selected, translated and introduced by Stanley Kunitz and Max Hayward, copyright © 1973. Reprinted by permission of Darhansoff & Verrill Literary Agency.

Joan Daves Agency "Fear" by Gabriela Mistral from *Selected Poems of Gabriela Mistral,* translated by Doris Dana. Copyright © 1961, 1964, 1970, 1971 by Doris Dana. Reprinted by permission of The Joan Daves Agency on behalf of the estate of the author.

Dell Publishing, a division of Random House, Inc. "Calling Home" by Tim O'Brien, from *Going After Cacciato.* Copyright © 1976, 1977, 1978 by Tim O'Brien. Used by permission of Dell Publishing, a division of Random House, Inc.

Eric Dobby Publishing Ltd. "The Dream Comes True" by Tenzing Norgay and James Ramsey Ullman from *Tiger of the Snows.* Copyright © 1955 by Tenzing Norgay and James Ramsey Ullman. Used by permission.

Doubleday, a division of Random House, Inc. "The Waking" from *The Collected Poems of Theodore Roethke* by Theodore Roethke. Copyright © 1953 by Theodore Roethke. "Civil Peace" from *Girls at War* and *Other Stories* by Chinua Achebe. Copyright © 1972, 1973 by Chinua Achebe. Used by permission of Doubleday, a division of Random House, Inc.

Doubleday, A Division of Random House, Inc., and Harold Ober Associates, Inc. "Civil Peace" from *Girls at War and Other Stories* by Chinua Achebe. Copyright © 1972, 1973 by Chinua Achebe. Used by permission of Doubleday, a Division of Random House, Inc., and Harold Ober Associates, Inc.

Doubleday, a division of Random House, Inc., and The Wylie Agency, Inc. "The Bridge" by Leopold Staff from *Post War Polish Poetry,* selected and translated by Czeslaw Milosz. Translation copyright © 1965 by Czeslaw Milosz. Used by permission of Doubleday, a division of Random House, Inc. and The Wylie Agency, Inc.

Roger Ebert "Star Wars: Breakthrough Film Still Has the Force" by Roger Ebert. First published in January 1997, *Chicago Sun Times.* © 1997 The Ebert Co., Ltd. Reprinted by kind permission of the author.

Ann Elmo Agency, Inc. "Leiningen Versus the Ants" by Carl Stephenson, from *Leiningen Versus the Ants.* © 1938 by Carl Stephenson. Reprinted by permission of Ann Elmo Agency, Inc.

Farrar, Straus & Giroux, Inc. "What Are Friends For" by Rosellen Brown, from *Cora Fry's Pillow Book* by Rosellen Brown. Copyright © 1994. "A Walk to the Jetty" from *Annie John* by Jamaica Kincaid. Copyright © 1985 by Jamaica Kincaid. "The Fish" from *The Complete Poems 1927–1979* by Elizabeth Bishop. Copyright © 1979, 1983 by Alice Helen Methfessel. Excerpt from "Nobel Lecture, The One Great Heart" by Alexander Solzhenitsyn, from *Nobel Lecture.* Copyright © 1972 by the Nobel Foundation. Translation copyright © 1972 by Farrar, Straus & Giroux, Inc. "A Storm in the Mountains" from *Stories and Prose Poems* by Alexander Solzhenitsyn, translated by Michael Glenny. Translation copyright © 1971 by Michael Glenny.

Harcourt, Inc. "Antigone" from *Sophocles: The Oedipus Cycle,* An English Version by Dudley Fitts and Robert Fitzgerald. Copyright © 1939 by Harcourt, Inc. and renewed 1967 by Dudley Fitts and Robert Fitzgerald. CAUTION: All rights, including professional, amateur, motion picture, recitation, lecturing, performance, public reading, radio broadcasting, and television are strictly reserved. Inquiries on all rights should be addressed to Harcourt, Inc., Permissions Department, Orlando, FL 32887-6777. "Jazz Fantasia" from *Smoke and Steel* by Carl Sandburg, copyright 1920 by Harcourt, Inc., and renewed 1948 by Carl Sandburg. "How to React to Familiar Faces" from *How to Travel With a Salmon & Other Essays* by Umberto Eco, copyright © 1992 Gruppo Editoriale Fabbi, Bompiani, Sonzogno, Estas s.p.a., English translation by William Weaver, copyright © 1994 by Harcourt, Inc. Used by permission of the publisher. This material may not be reproduced in any form or by any means without the prior written permission of the publisher.

Harcourt, Inc., for The Executors of the Estate of Virginia Woolf, and The Hogarth Press, an imprint of Random House UK "The Widow and the Parrot" from *The Complete Shorter Fiction of Virginia Woolf,* copyright © 1985 Quentin Bell and Angelica Garnett. Used by permission of Harcourt, Inc., for The Executors of the Estate of Virginia Woolf, and The Hogarth Press, an imprint of Random House UK.

Harcourt, Inc., and The Wylie Agency "The Garden of Stubborn Cats" from *Marcovaldo or The Seasons in the City* by Italo Calvino, English translation copyright © 1983 by Harcourt, Brace, & Company and Martin Secker & Warburg, Ltd. Reprinted by permission of Harcourt, Inc.

HarperCollins Publishers, Inc. and Jonathan Clowes Ltd. "Through the Tunnel" from *The Habit of Loving* by Doris Lessing. Copyright © 1951 by Doris Lessing. Originally appeared in *The New Yorker.* Copyright renewed. Reprinted by kind permission of HarperCollins Publishers, Inc., and Jonathan Clowes Ltd., London, on behalf of Doris Lessing.

HarperCollins Publishers, Inc. "Flood" from *Pilgrim at Tinker Creek* by Annie Dillard. Copyright © 1974 by Annie Dillard. Used by permission of Harper Collins Publishers, Inc.

Harvard University Press and the Trustees of Amherst College "The Wind—tapped like a tired Man" (#436), "I dwell in Possibility— "(Poem #657), "Tell all the Truth but tell it slant (#1129), "Success is counted sweetest" (#67) by Emily Dickinson, from *The Poems of Emily Dickinson,* Thomas H. Johnson, ed., Cambridge, Mass.: The Belknap Press of Harvard University Press. Copyright © 1951, 1955, 1979 by the President and Fellows of Harvard College. Reprinted by permission of the publishers and the Trustees of Amherst College.

Hill and Wang, a division of Farrar, Straus, & Giroux, Inc. and Albert Bonniers Forlag AB "The Princess and All the Kingdom" from *The Marriage Feast* by Pär Lagerkvist, translated by Alan Blair. Translation copyright © 1954 by Random House, Inc.

Hispanic Society of America "The Guitar" by Federico García Lorca from *Translations from Hispanic Poets,* edited by Elizabeth du Gue Trapier. Reprinted by permission of the Hispanic Society of America.

National Council of Teachers of English (NCTE) "NCTE/IRA (National Council of Teachers of English/International Reading Association) Standards" is reproduced with kind permission of NCTE, 1111 W. Kenyon Road, Urbana, IL 61801. www.ncte.org

Henry Holt & Co. "Mowing" and "After Apple-Picking" from *The Poetry of Robert Frost,* edited by Edward Connery Lathem. Published by Holt, Rinehart, & Winston.

Houghton Mifflin Company and Frances Collin, Literary Agent "The Marginal World" from *The Edge of the Sea* by Rachel Carson. Copyright © 1955 by Rachel L. Carson, renewed 1983 by Roger Christie. Reprinted by permission of Houghton Mifflin Co. and Frances Collin, Literary Agent. All rights reserved.

International Creative Management, Inc., and Random House, Inc. "Homeless" from *Living Out Loud* by Anna Quindlen. Copyright © 1987 by Anna Quindlen. Reprinted by permission of International Creative Management, Inc. and Random House, Inc.

Japan Publications, Inc. "Falling upon earth" by Bashō and "A gentle spring rain" by Issa, reprinted from *One Hundred Famous Haiku,* translated by Daniel C. Buchanan, copyright © 1973. Used by permission.

John Johnson Ltd. "The Bridegroom" by Alexander Pushkin, from *The Bronze Horseman and Other Poems,* Penguin Books, 1982. Translation copyright © 1982 by D. M. Thomas. Used by permission.

Alfred A. Knopf, Inc., a Division of Random House, Inc. "The Weary Blues" from *The Collected Poems* by Langston Hughes. Copyright © 1994 by The Estate of Langston Hughes. From *Speak, Memory* by Vladimir Nabokov. Copyright © 1978 by The Estate of Vladimir Nabokov. Reprinted by permission of Alfred A. Knopf, a division of Random House, Inc.

Alfred A. Knopf, Inc., a division of Random House, Inc., and The Society of Authors as the Literary Representative of the Estate of Katherine Mansfield "The Apple Tree" from *The Scrapbook of Katherine Mansfield* by Katherine Mansfield, copyright © 1939 by Alfred A. Knopf, Inc. and renewed © 1967 by Mrs. Mary Middleton. Used by permission of Alfred A. Knopf, a division of Random House, Inc. and The Society of Authors as the Literary Representative of the Estate of Katherine Mansfield. "The Weary Blues" from *The Collected Poems by Langston Hughes.* Copyright © 1994 by The Estate of Langston Hughes. From *Speak, Memory* by Vladimir Nabokov. Copyright © 1978 by the Estate of Vladimir Nabokov. Reprinted by permission of Alfred A. Knopf, a division of Random House, Inc.

Library of America "Prayer of First Dancers," Navajo, from *The Night Chant,* by permission of The Library of America.

Liveright Publishing Company "Reapers" from *Cane* by Jean Toomer. Copyright 1923 by Boni & Liveright, renewed 1951 by Jean Toomer. Used by permission.

Long Beach Aquarium of the Pacific "Long Beach Aquarium of the Pacific" by Staff, from Aquarium of Pacific Educational Programs Brochure. Used by permission.

Martin Secker & Warburg, Ltd. Excerpt from *My Left Foot* by Christy Brown. Copyright © 1954 by Christy Brown.

Pat Mora "Uncoiling" from *Daughters of the Fifth Sun* by Pat Mora. Copyright © 1995 by Pat Mora. Published by Riverside Books.

William Morris Agency, Inc. "A Visit to Grandmother," copyright © 1964 by William Melvin Kelley, from *Dancers on the Shore* by William Melvin Kelley. Used by permission of William Morris Agency, Inc., on behalf of the author.

Natural History Magazine "Work That Counts" by Ernesto Ruelas Inzunza from *Natural History,* October 1996, Volume 105, Number 10. Copyright © the American Museum of Natural History, 1996. Used by permission of *Natural History* magazine.

New Directions Publishing Corp. "Jade Flower Palace" by Tu Fu, translated by David Hinston, from *The Selected Poems of Tu Fu.* Copyright © 1989 by David Hinton. "A Tree Telling of Orpheus" by Denise Levertov, from *Poems 1968–1972.* Copyright © 1970 by Denise Levertov. "Spring and All" by William Carlos Williams, from *Collected Poems: 1909–1939,* Volume 1. Copyright © 1938 by New Directions Publishing Corp. "The Street" by Octavio Paz, from *Selected Poems.* Copyright 1973 by Octavio Paz and Muriel Rukeyser. Reprinted by permission of New Directions Publishing Corp.

New Directions Publishing Corporation, and David Higham Associates Ltd. "A Child's Christmas in Wales" by Dylan Thomas. Copyright © 1952 by Dylan Thomas. Copyright © 1954 New Directions Publishing Corporation.

New Orleans Poetry Journal Press, Inc. "Columbus Dying" from *Adam's Footprint* by Vassar Miller, copyright © 1956 by Vassar Miller. Reprinted by permission of New Orleans Poetry Journal Press, Inc.

New Press "The Future of Luxury" by Hans Magnus Enzensberger, from *Zig Zag: The Politics of Culture and Vice Versa.* Copyright © 1998 by Hans Magnus Enzensberger. Reprinted by permission of The New Press.

New York Times Co. Excerpt from "Feel the City's Pulse? It's Bebop, Man!" by Ann Douglas from *Feel the City's Pulse? It's Bebop, Man! And sites of bop's triumphs & tragedies,* August 8, 1998. "Star Wars: An Epic for Today" (The Names Came From Earth) by Eric Nash, published in *The New York Times,* January 26, 1997. Copyright © 1997 by *The New York Times* Company. "Star Wars—A Trip to a Far Galaxy" by Vincent Canby, published in *The New York Times,* May 16, 1977. Copyright © 1977 by The New York Times Co. Reprinted by permission of The New York Times Company. "After 1,500 Years, Colosseum Reopens for Show" by Reuters News Service, from The New York Times Website, July 19, 2000. Copyright © 2000, The New York Times Co.

North Point Press, a division of Farrar, Straus & Giroux, Inc. "All" by Bei Dao, translated by Donald Finkel and Xueliang Chen, and "Also All" by Shu Ting, translated by Donald Finkel and Jinsheng Yi, from *A Splintered Mirror: Chinese Poetry from the Democracy Movement,* translated by Donald Finkel. Translation copyright © 1991 by Donald Finkel.

W. W. Norton & Company, Inc. From *Don Quixote, A Norton Critical Edition, The Ormsby Translation,* Revised by Miguel de Cervantes, edited by Joseph Jones & Kenneth Douglas. Copyright © 1981 by W. W. Norton & Company, Inc. Used by permission of W. W Norton & Company, Inc.

Norwegian Nobel Institute "Keep Memory Alive" by Elie Wiesel, from *Elie Wiesel's Nobel Prize Acceptance Speech.* Published by the Norwegian Nobel Institute.

Naomi Shihab Nye "Making a Fist" by Naomi Shihab Nye, from *Hugging the Jukebox, and Words Under the Words: Selected Poems.* Reprinted by permission of the author, Naomi Shihab Nye.

Harold Ober Associates Inc. "Marian Anderson: Famous Concert Singer" by Langston Hughes. Copyright © 1954 by Langston Hughes, renewed 1982 by George Houston Bass. "The Good Deed" by Pearl S. Buck. Copyright 1953 by Pearl S. Buck. Copyright renewed 1981. Used by permission of Harold Ober Associates Inc.

Tillie Olsen "Mothers and Daughters" from *Mothers and Daughters* by Tillie Olsen with Julie Olsen Edwards and Estelle Jussim. Copyright © 1987.

Pantheon Books, a division of Random House, Inc. "The Orphan Boy and the Elk Dog" from *American Indian Myths and Legends,* selected and edited by Richard Erdoes and Alfonso Ortiz. Copyright © 1984 by Richard Erdoes and Alfonso Ortiz. Used by permission of Pantheon Books, a division of Random House, Inc.

Penguin Books Ltd. "One cannot ask loneliness" by Priest Jakuren & "When I went to visit (Tanka)" by Ki Tsurayuki, from *The Penguin Book of Japanese Verse* edited and translated by Geoffrey Bownas and Anthony Thwaite (Penguin Books, 1964). Translation copyright © Geoffrey Bownas and Anthony Thwaite, 1964.

Peter Owen Ltd. "A Man" by Nina Cassian, translated by Roy MacGregor-Hastie.

Présence Africaine "Africa" from *Coups de Pilon* by David Diop, published by Présence Africaine, 1956. "Childhood" and "The Lion Awakening" from *Sundiata: An Epic of Old Mali* by D. T. Niane, translated by G. D. Picket. © Présence Africaine 1960 (original French version: Soundjata, ou L'épopée Mandingue). © Longman Group Ltd. (English Version) 1965. Reprinted by permission of Présence Africaine.

G. P. Putnam's Sons, a division of Penguin Putnam, Inc., and David Higham Associates "Arthur Becomes King" from *The Once and Future King* by T. H. White. Copyright © 1938, 1939, 1940 by T. H. White; renewed © 1958 by T. H. White. Used by permission of G. P. Putnam's Sons, a division of Penguin Putnam, Inc., and David Higham Associates.

Reynolds Price "What's in a Picture," retitled "A Picture from the Past" by Reynolds Price from the September/October 1996 issue of *Civilization Magazine,* copyright © 1996. Reprinted by permission of the author.

Random House, Inc. "At HarvestTime" and "Style" from *Wouldn't Take Nothing For My Journey Now* by Maya Angelou. Copyright © 1993 by Maya Angelou. "The Moon at the Fortified Pass" by Li Po, from *The Wisdom of China and India* edited by Lin Yutang. Copyright © 1942, and renewed 1970 by Random House, Inc. Used by permission of Random House, Inc.

Marian Reiner for Eve Merriam "Metaphor" from *It Doesn't Always Have to Rhyme* by Eve Merriam. Copyright © 1964 by Eve Merriam. Copyright renewed 1992 by Eve Merriam. Used by permission.

Rogers, Coleridge & White Ltd. "Games at Twilight" by Anita Desai. Copyright © 1978, Anita Desai. Reproduced by permission of the author c/o Rogers, Coleridge & White Ltd., 20 Powis Mews, London W11 1JN.

Rosemary Thurber and The Barbara Hogensen Agency "The Dog That Bit People," by James Thurber, from *My Life and Hard Times,* published by Harper & Row. Copyright © 1933, 1961 by James Thurber. Reprinted by arrangement with Rosemary Thurber and The Barbara Hogensen Agency. All rights reserved.

Schocken Books, Inc., a division of Random House, Inc. "Before the Law" from *Franz Kafka: The Complete Stories by Franz Kafka,* edited by Nahum N. Glatzer. Copyright © 1946, 1947, 1948, 1949, 1954, 1958, 1971 by Schocken Books. Used by permission of Schocken Books, a division of Random House, Inc.

Scribner "Angela's Ashes" by Frank McCourt, from *Angela's Ashes.* Copyright © 1996 by Frank McCourt. Reprinted with the permission of Scribner, a division of Simon & Schuster, Inc.

The Society of Authors as the literary representative of the Estate of W. W. Jacobs "The Monkey's Paw" from *The Lady of the Barge* by W. W. Jacobs.

Dr. Nigel Strudwick "Egyptology Resources" from Web site: www.newton.cam.ac.uk/egypt/index.html and www.newton.cam.ac.uk/egypt/museum.html. Copyright © Nigel Strudwick 1994–2001. Used by permission.

Time-Life Books "Imitating Nature's Mineral Artistry" from *Planet Earth: Gemstones* by Paul O'Neil and the Editors of Time-Life Books. Copyright © 1983 Time-Life Books, Inc.

Transworld Publishers, Ltd. Excerpt from "View from the Summit" by Sir Edmund Hillary. Copyright © 1999 by Sir Edmund Hillary. Used by permission.

Joanna Trzeciak "Some Like Poetry" by Wisława Szymborska, translated by Joanna Trzeciak, first appeared in *The New Yorker,* October 1996. © 1996 Wisława Szymborska. All rights reserved. Used by permission of the translator.

David Unger "The Censors" by Luisa Valenzuela. Copyright © 1976 by Luisa Valenzuela, renewed 1988. Translation copyright © 1982 by David Unger, first published in *Short Stories,* by David Godine Publishing.

University of California Press "A Pace Like That" translated by Chana Bloch, from *The Selected Poetry of Yehuda Amichai,* edited and translated by Chana Bloch and Stephen Mitchell. Copyright © 1996 The Regents of the University of California. Used by permission.

University of New Mexico Press "The Way to Rainy Mountain" by N. Scott Momaday. First published in *The Reporter,* January 26, 1967. © 1969 The University of New Mexico Press. Used by permission.

University of North Carolina Press "Street of the Cañon" from *Mexican Village,* by Josefina Niggli. Copyright © 1945 by the University of North Carolina Press, renewed 1972 by Josefina Niggli. Used by permission of the publisher.

Viking Penguin, Inc., a division of Penguin Putnam, Inc., and Metropolitan Museum of Art "What Makes a Degas a Degas?" from *What Makes a Degas a Degas?* by Richard Muhlberger, copyright © 1993 by The Metropolitan Museum of Art. Used by permission of Viking Penguin, a division of Penguin Putnam, Inc., and Metropolitan Museum of Art.

Viking Penguin, Inc., a division of Penguin Putnam, Inc., and Wallace Literary Agency for R. K. Narayan "Like the Sun," from *Under The Banyan Tree* by R. K. Narayan, copyright © 1985 by R. K. Narayan. Used by permission of Viking Penguin, a division of Penguin Putnam, Inc., and Wallace Literary Agency, Inc., for R. K. Narayan.

Villard Books, a division of Random House, Inc. from *Into Thin Air* by Jon Krakauer, copyright © 1997 by Jon Krakauer. Used by permission of Villard Books, a division of Random House, Inc.

Vintage Books, a division of Random House, Inc. Excerpt from "Snow Falling on Cedars," by David Guterson. Copyright © 1995 by David Guterson.

Visva-Bharati "Cabuliwallah" from *A Tagore Reader* by Rabindranath Tagore, copyright © 1945. Used by permission.

Estate of Arthur Waley From "The Analects of Confucius" by Confucius, translated by Arthur Waley. Copyright © 1938 by George Allen and Unwin Ltd.

Wallace Literary Agency for R. K. Narayan "Rama's Initiation" by R. K. Narayan from *The Ramayana* by R. K. Narayan. Published by Penguin Books. © 1972 by R. K. Narayan. Used by permission of the Wallace Literary Agency, Inc.

Warner/Chappell Music, Inc. "Cat's in the Cradle" by Sandy and Harry Chapin from *Verities & Balderdash.* Copyright ©1974 by Elektra.

A. P. Watt Ltd. Excerpt from "A Problem" by Anton Chekhov, translated from Russian by Constance Garnett.

Wieser and Wieser, Inc. "Auto Wreck" from *Collected Poems 1940–1978* by Karl Shapiro. Copyright ©1962 by Karl Shapiro. Used by permission of Wieser and Wieser, Inc.

Zohar Press Grateful acknowledgment to Zohar Press for permission to reprint "Right Hand" by Philip Fried from *Quantum Genesis and Other Poems.* Copyright © 1997 by Zohar Press.

Art Credits

Cover: Gustave Caillebotte (French, 1848–1894), *Rainy Day*, oil on canvas, 1876/77, 212.2 x 276.2 cm, Charles H. and Mary F. S. Worcester Collection, 1964.336/photograph © 1996, The Art Institute of Chicago, All Rights Reserved; **xxv:** Dennis MacDonald/PhotoEdit; **viii:** *Old Trees by Cold Waterfall*, 1470–1559, Wen Zhengming, The Los Angeles County Museum of Art, The Ernest Larsen Blancok Memorial Collection; **ix:** Gerard Lacz/Peter Arnold, Inc.; **x–xi:** Corel Professional Photos CD-ROM™; **xii:** Corel Professional Photos CD-ROM™; **xiii:** *Annie Old Crow*, James Bama, Courtesy of the artist; **xiv:** Time/Life Pictures; **xv:** Corel Professional Photos CD-ROM™; **ix:** Gerard Lacz /Peter Arnold, Inc.; **xvi–xvii:** Papilio/CORBIS; **1:** © Kazu Nitta/Stock Illustration Source, Inc.; **2:** The Granger Collection, New York; **4:** Ken Karp Photography; **6:** Joseph Nettis/Stock, Boston; **9:** Michael Newman/PhotoEdit; **11:** Ken Karp Photography; **15:** © Stone; **16:** Joseph Nettis/Stock, Boston; **18–19:** Joseph Nettis/Stock, Boston; **28, 30:** Fotopic/Omni-Photo Communications, Inc.; **33:** © Stone; **34–35:** Paul Keel/Photo Researchers, Inc.; **36:** Bettmann/CORBIS; **37:** Guido A. Rossi/The Image Bank; **38:** © 1997 Linda M. Morre/Villard Books; **39:** The Granger Collection, New York; **40–41:** Guido A. Rossi/The Image Bank; **42:** Fotopic/Omni-Photo Communications, Inc.; **44:** AP/Wide World Photos; **48:** *The Lights of Marriage* (detail), Marc Chagall, Kunsthaus, Zurich, © 1998 Artists Rights Society (ARS), New York/ADAGP, Paris; **58:** Bettman/CORBIS; **60:** Digital Imagery © Copyright 2001 PhotoDisc, Inc.; **62:** *The Lights of Marriage* (detail), Marc Chagall, Kunsthaus, Zurich, © 1998 Artists Rights Society (ARS), New York/ADAGP, Paris; **64:** Scala/Art Resource, NY; **68:** *Port de la Saline, Haiti*, n.d., Lois Mailou Jones, Courtesy of the artist; **70:** *San Antonio de Oriente* (detail), 1954, José Antonio Velásquez, Oil on canvas, Collection of the Art Museum of the Americas, Organization of American States; **75:** *Port de la Saline, Haiti*, n.d., Lois Mailou Jones, Courtesy of the artist; **76:** Photo by Sigrid Estrada; **80, 86:** *Les Masques et la Mort*, 1897, James Ensor, Giraudon/Art Resource, New York; **87:** Courtesy of the Library of Congress; **88:** Bettmann/CORBIS; **92:** © Kenneth Jarecke/Contact Press Images/PictureQuest; **94:** *William Carlos Williams* (detail), The National Portrait Gallery, Smithsonian Institution, Washington, D.C./Art Resource, NY; **95:** (t) *Woman with child*, Pablo Picasso, Museo Picasso, Barcelona, Spain, Scala/Art Resource, NY, © 1998 Estate of Pablo Picasso/Artists Rights Society (ARS), New York; **95** (b) Bettmann/CORBIS; **96:** AP/Wide World Photos; **100, 102:** *The Anglers*, Study for "La Grande Jatte," 1883, Georges Seurat, Oil on panel, 16 x 25 cm. Musée Nat. d'Art Moderne, Troyes, France, Giraudon/Art Resource, NY; **105:** *Les Maisons Cabassud à la Ville d'Avray*, Jean-Baptiste Camille Corot, The Louvre, Paris, Scala, Art Resource, New York; **108:** Bettmann/CORBIS; **109:** Culver Pictures, Inc.; **116:** PhotoEdit; **122–123:** *Steps to the Steps*, Brad Holland, Courtesy of the artist; **124** (l) *Orion*, 1984, Martin Wong, Acrylic on canvas, 36" diameter, Courtesy of Exit Art Gallery, New York; **124** (r) *Strong Steady Hands*, Alonzo Adams, Courtesy of the artist; **126:** *La Bibliothèque (The Library)*, 1949, Maria Elena Vieira da Silva, Musée National d'Art Moderne, Centre National d'Art et de Culture Georges Pompidou, Photo by Philippe Migeat © Centre G. Pompidou; **128–129:** Steve Dunwell/The Image Bank; **131:** © Jim Ballard/Stone; **132:** Prentice Hall; **136:** David Brookover/Photonica; **138–139:** Corel Professional Photos CD-ROM™; **141:** *Cornfield at Ewell* (detail), c.1846, William Holman Hunt, Oil on board, 20.2 x 31.8 cm. Tate Gallery, London, Great Britain/Art Resource, NY; **143:** CORBIS; **144:** *Rest During the Harvest*, Alexander Morosov, Tretyakov Gallery, Moscow, Russia, Scala/Art Resource, NY; **147:** *The Hay Harvest*, Boris Kustodiev, Scala/Art Resource, NY; **150–151:** Corel Professional Photos CD-ROM™; **152:** L. N. Tolstoi, I. E. Repin, Sovfoto/Eastfoto; **156, 158:** *The Terrace at Meric*, 1867, Frédéric Bazille, 21 3/4 x 36", Cincinnati Museum of Art, Oil on Canvas, Gift of Mark P. Herschede, 1976; **159:** The Granger Collection, New York; **160:** ARTE PÚBLICO PRESS; **161:** Steve Bronstein/The Image Bank; **162:** Photo by Maud Lipscomb; **166, 168, 171:** Photofest; **173:** © The Stock Market/Howard Sochurek; **174:** Rod Tuach/Globe Photos; **178:** (inset) Photofest; **178–179:** Joseph Sohm; ChromoSome Inc./CORBIS; **180:** *Spring Fever*, 1978, From the Profile Part I: The Twenties series (Mecklenburg County), Collage on board, 7 x 9 3/8" Private Collection, © Romare Bearden Foundation/Licensed by VAGA, New York, NY; **182:** *Strong Steady Hands*, Alonzo Adams, Courtesy of the artist; **185:** *Springtime Rain*, 1978, Ogden M. Pleissner, Ogden M. Pleissner Estate, Marion G. Pleissner Trust, Bankers Trust Company. Photo by Grace Davies/Omni-Photo Communications, Inc.; **188:** *Spring Fever*, 1978, From the Profile Part I: The Twenties series (Mecklenburg County), Collage on board, 7 x 9 3/8" Private Collection, © Romare Bearden Foundation/Licensed by

VAGA, New York, NY; **194:** Corel Professional Photos CD-ROM™; **198:** Dimitri Kessel/Life Magazine; **199:** *Wind on the Water*, bronze, 8 1/2 x 8 x 4 feet, Richard McDermott Miller; **200:** Henry McGee/Globe Photos; **204:** *Apple Plenty*, 1970, Herbert Shuptrine. Private Collection, Courtesy New York Graphic Society; **206:** Corel Professional Photos CD-ROM™; **208:** *Orchard with Flowering Fruit Trees, Springtime, Pontoise*, 1877, Camille Pissarro, Musée d'Orsay, Paris; **210:** CORBIS-Bettmann; **214:** Woodfin Camp & Associates; **216:** *Traditional Yam Harvest*, John Mainga, LAMU, The Gallery of Contemporary African Art, Photo by John Lei/Omni-Photo Communications, Inc.; **218:** Dorothy Alexander; **219:** *Old Trees by Cold Waterfall*, 1470–1559, Wen Zhengming, The Los Angeles County Museum of Art, The Ernest Larsen Blancok Memorial Collection; **220** (l) AP/Wide World Photos; **220** (r) Courtesy of Chi-Fong Lei; **222:** AP/Wide World Photos; **230:** Bob Daemmrich/The Image Works; **236–237:** *Two Figures in a Windy Landscape*, 1991, Clifford Goodenough; **238** (t) *Face in Sun*, Hal Lose, Stock Illustration Source, Inc.; **238** (b) © Frank Dirggs Collection/Archive Photos; **240:** *Coast Scene, Isles of Shoals*, 1901, Childe Hassam, The Metropolitan Museum of Art, Gift of George A. Hearn, 1909, Copyright © 1987 by The Metropolitan Museum of Art; **242–243:** Digital Imagery © Copyright 2001 PhotoDisc, Inc.; **245:** *The Beach Treat* (detail), Suzanne Nagler, Photograph © Stephen Tucker, Collection of Mr. and Mrs. X. Daniel Kafcas; **247:** David Perdew/Focus Group/PictureQuest; **248:** *The Diver*, Dennis Angel, oil on panel, 40" x 32"; **250:** Thomas Victor; **254, 256, 259:** *My Life and Hard Times* Copyright © 1933 by James Thurber. Copyright © renewed 1961 by James Thurber. Reprinted by arrangement with Rosemary A. Thurber and The Barbara Hogenson Agency; **260:** CORBIS-Bettmann; **264:** *Solo/Interval*, 1987. Romare Bearden, collage on board, 11x14", © Romare Bearden Foundation/Licensed by VAGA, New York, NY; **266** (b) *Edna St. Vincent Millay* (detail), Charles Ellis, The National Portrait Gallery, Smithsonian Institution, Washington, D.C./Art Resource, New York; **266** (t) Frank Siteman/PhotoEdit Communications, Inc.; **268:** © Frank Dirggs Collection/Archive Photos; **269:** *Langston Hughes* (detail), c.1925, Winold Reiss, The National Portrait Gallery, Smithsonian Institution, Washington, D.C./Art Resource, New York; **270** (b) *Carl Sandburg*, Miriam Svet, The National Portrait Gallery, Smithsonian Institution, Washington, D.C./Art Resource, New York; **270** (t) Digital Imagery © Copyright 2001 PhotoDisc, Inc.; **276:** Map.com; **278, 280:** *Face in Sun*, Hal Lose, Stock Illustration Source, Inc.; **282:** Dinodia/Omni-Photo Communications, Inc.; **283** (b) AP/Wide World Photos; **283** (t) Digital Imagery © Copyright 2001 PhotoDisc, Inc.; **284:** The Granger Collection, New York; **288:** *Hands of Helen Keller*, Jean Feuret/SuperStock; **290:** Fox Photos/Liaison Agency; **292:** CORBIS-Bettmann; **293:** Gerard Lacz /Peter Arnold, Inc.; **294** (t) Kenneth Redding/The Image Bank; **294** (b) Thomas Victor; **298:** Culver Pictures, Inc.; **300:** CORBIS-Bettmann; **303:** *Mess line: Noon at Manzanar*, Ansel Adams, Courtesy of the Library of Congress, Copywork by Grace Davies; **305:** The Mariners' Museum/CORBIS; **306:** Culver Pictures, Inc.; **308:** R. Dominguec/Globe Photos; **312:** Photofest/© 2000 Universal Studios Home Video. All Rights Reserved; **314:** Hulton Getty/Liaison Agency; **314–315:** Gary Braasch/CORBIS; **315:** Courtesy Jill Sabella; **315:** © IT STOCK INT'L/Index Stock Imagery/PictureQuest; **318–319:** P. & G. Bowater/The Image Bank; **320:** Corel Professional Photos CD-ROM™; **325:** Craig Lovell/CORBIS; **326:** The Granger Collection, New York; **330:** David Young-Wolff/PhotoEdit; **336–337:** *Summer Breeze*, 1995, Alice Dalton Brown, oil on canvas, 50" x 72", Courtesy Fischbach Gallery, NY, photo: Peter Jacobs; **338** (b) Art Zamur/Liaison International; **338** (t) © Dorling Kindersley; **340, 342:** Tina Merandon/Photonica; **344:** Chase Swift/CORBIS; **346:** Sovfoto/Eastfoto; **350:** Nancy Sheehan/PhotoEdit; **352:** Chase Swift/CORBIS; **354:** *Racing Game*, oil pastel/paper, Tony Wong, Courtesy of the Artist; **359:** *Hide and Seek*, oil pastel/paper, Tony Wong, Courtesy of the Artist; **364:** MacDuff Everton/The Image Bank; **367:** The Granger Collection, New York; **368** (b) Art Zamur/ Liaison International; **368** (t) The Granger Collection, New York; **369, 370:** © Archive Photos; **374:** © The Stock Market/Ned Gillette; **376:** *Mother and Daughter*. Leaf from a Manchu family album unidentified artist, ink and color on paper, H.13-1/8 in. x W.14-1/8in. The Metropolitan Museum of Art, anonymous gift, 1952. (52.209.3j) Copyright © 1980 by the Metropolitan Museum of Art; **379:** Courtesy of Chi-Fong Lei; **380:** © Keren Su/Stone; **383:** Courtesy of Chi-Fong Lei; **386:** Ken Karp Photography; **388:** © Dorling Kindersley; **390:** Courtesy of Chi-Fong Lei; **392:** *Pearl S. Buck* (detail), Vita Solomon, The National Portrait Gallery, Smithsonian Institution, Washington, D.C./Art Resource, New York; **396:** Digital Imagery © Copyright 2001 PhotoDisc, Inc.; **398:** *Peacefulness*

Tran Nguyen Dan, Indochina Arts Project; **401:** AP/Wide World Photos; **402:** G. R. Roberts/ Omni-Photo Communications, Inc.; **404:** *Enigma of the Hour,* 1912, Giorgio de Chirico, Coll. Mattioli, Milan, Italy, Scala/Art Resource, NY; © Foundation Georgio de Chirico/Licensed by VAGA, New York, NY, **406** (b) AP/Wide World Photos; **406** (t) Digital Imagery © Copyright 2001 Photo-Disc, Inc.; **414:** © Hulton Getty/Archive Photos; **416:** Digital Imagery © Copyright 2001 PhotoDisc, Inc.; **417:** AP/Wide World Photos; **418:** © Sven Martson/The Image Works; **424–425:** © Joy Gallowitz/Stock Illustration Source, Inc.; **426** (t) Corel Professional Photos CD-ROM™; **426** (b) © Jeanne White/Photo Researchers, Inc.; **428:** Digital Imagery © Copyright 2001 PhotoDisc, Inc.; **430, 432:** © Jeanne White/ Photo Researchers, Inc.; **434–435:** Corel Professional Photos CD-ROM™; **436:** Digital Imagery © Copyright 2001 PhotoDisc, Inc.; **438:** The Granger Collection, New York; **442:** United Nations; **444:** Betty Press/ Woodfin Camp & Associates; **446:** © The Stock Market/John Curtis; **450:** AP/Wide World Photos; **454:** *Audience B,* 1940, Diana Ong/SuperStock; **456:** Gifford/Liaison International; **457:** J. P. Gauthier/Globe Photos; **458** (t) Barrie Fanton/Omni-Photo Communications, Inc.; **458** (b) CORBIS-Bettmann; **462:** Corel Professional Photos CD-ROM™; **464:** The Granger Collection, New York; **465:** AP/Wide World Photos; **466:** *Dancers in Pink and Green,* Edgar Degas, oil on canvas, H. 32-3/8 in. W. 29-3/4 in. (82.2 x 75.6 cm) Signed (lower right): Degas. The Metropolitan Musem of Art, Bequest of Mrs. H. O. Havemeyer, 1929. The H. O. Havemeyer Collection. (29.100.42). Photograph Copyright © 1980 By The Metropolitan Museum of Art; **468:** *Carriage at the Races,* 1872, Edgar Degas, oil on canvas 14 3/8 x 22 in. (36.5 x55.9 cm) 1931 Purchase Fund, © 2000 Museum of Fine Arts, Boston. Courtesy, Museum of Fine Arts, Boston; **474–475:** Photofest; **477:** Liaison Agency; **478:** © Raymond Kleboe/Hulto/Archive Photos; **480** (b) Jacket design by John Fontana, Jacket photograph © Culver Pictures, Inc.; **481** (t) AP/Wide World Photos; **482:** *Following the Buffalo Run,* Charles M. Russell, Amon Carter Museum, Fort Worth; **484:** *The Color of Sun,* Howard Terpning, oil, 26 x 26, The Greenwich Workshop Inc.; **487:** *Crow Lodge of Twenty-five Buffalo Skins,* 1832–33, George Catlin, National Museum of American Art, Washington, D.C./Art Resource, NY; **489:** *Wild Horses at Play,* 1834–37, George Catlin, National Museum of American Art, Washington, D.C./Art Resource, NY; **491:** Dann Coffey/The Image Bank; **496:** *Fandango,* Gentilz, The Alamo, Daughters of the Republic of Texas; **498:** *The Alamo,* Daughters of the Republic of Texas; **500:** © David Hiser/Stone; **502:** Esbin/Anderson/ Omni-Photo Communications, Inc.; **504:** © Howard Kingsnorth/Stone; **510:** © John Deeks/Photo Researchers, Inc.; **512** (t) John Foster/Science Source/Photo Researchers, Inc.; **512** (b) Sovfoto/Eastfoto; **513** (t) Corel Professional Photos CD-ROM™; **513** (b) The Granger Collection, New York; **514, 516:** Corel Professional Photos CD-ROM™; **518:** Courtesy of New Directions Publishing Corporation; **523:** Digital Imagery © Copyright 2001 Photo-Disc, Inc.; **526:** Bob Daemmrich/Stock, Boston Inc./PictureQuest; **534–535:** *Final Departure,* oil on canvas, 42" x 70", Lisa Learner, Terry Putscher Artist Representative; **536** (t) *The Hunters,* Gari Melchers, Belmont, The Gari Melchers Estate & Memorial Gallery, Mary Washington College, Fredericksburg VA; **536** (b) Frank Siteman/Stock, Boston; **538:** *Summer Breeze,* 1995, Alice Dalton Brown, oil on canvas, 50" x 72", Courtesy Fischbach Gallery, NY, photo: Peter Jacobs; **540:** Superstock; **543:** *The Hunters,* Gari Melchers, Belmont, The Gari Melchers Estate & Memorial Gallery, Mary Washington College, Fredericksburg VA; **544:** The Granger Collection, New York; **548:** Photofest; **550:** © Kenneth H. Thomas/Photo Researchers, Inc.; **553, 554, 556:** Photofest; **560:** Corel Professional Photos CD-ROM™; **563:** Photofest; **566:** George D. Dodge/Bruce Coleman, Inc./PictureQuest; **574, 579:** *Red Hills and Bones,* 1941, Georgia O'Keeffe, Philadelphia Museum of Art, The Alfred Stieglitz Collection, © 1998 The Georgia O'Keeffe Foundation/Artists Rights Society (ARS), New York; **582:** Michael S. Yamasita/ CORBIS; **584:** *City Night,* 1926, Georgia O'Keeffe, Minneapolis Institute of Arts, Photo by Malcolm Varon, N.Y.C., © 1998 The Georgia O'Keeffe Foundation/Artists Rights Society (ARS), New York; **586:** AP/Wide World Photos; **594:** *The Charge of the Light Brigade,* Richard Caton Woodville, By permission of Cranston Fine Arts; **596:** Erich Lessing/Art Resource, NY, Private Collection, Switzerland; **600:** Corel Professional Photos CD-ROM™; **603:** CORBIS-Bettmann; **604:** *Scotland Forever,* Elizabeth Butler, Leeds City Art Galleries; **608:** *Samuel Langhorne Clemens (Mark Twain)* (detail), 1935, Frank Edwin Larson, The National Portrait Gallery, Smithsonian Institution, Washington, D.C./Art Resource, New York; **612:** © The Stock Market/Sanford/Agliolo; **614:** *Bikini,* 1987, Vernon Fisher, Collection of the Krannert Art Museum and Kinkead Pavilion, University of Illinois, Champaign-Urbana; **617:** *The Body of a House #1 of 8* © Robert Beckman 1993, oil on canvas, 69" x 96 1/2", photo by Tony Scodwell; **619:** *The Body of a House #6 of 8,* © 1993,

Robert Beckman, oil on canvas, 69" x 96 1/2", Photo by Tony Scodwell; **620:** Thomas Victor; **621:** Frank Siteman/Stock, Boston; **622:** Joan Slatkin/Omni-Photo Communications, Inc.; **623:** Pier Giorgio Sclarandis/ Black Star Publishing/PictureQuest; **625:** Catrina Genovese/Omni-Photo Communications, Inc.; **626:** Joan Slatkin/Omni-Photo Communications, Inc.; **628:** Sovfoto/Eastfoto; **632:** *L'Univers démasqué,* René Magritte, Art Resource, NY; **636:** Corel Professional Photos CD-ROM™; **638:** *Chronicles of St. Denis: Death of Clothar/View of the Ile de la Cité,* Jehan Fouquet, Bibliothèque Nationale, Paris/Bridgeman Art Library, London/Superstock, Inc.; **640:** The Granger Collection, New York; **642:** *Restricted Man,* 1961, © Jerry Uelsmann, Collection of the Center for Creative Photography; **648:** Myrleen Ferguson/PhotoEdit; **654–655:** *The Last Painter on Earth,* 1983, oil on canvas, 72" x 120" James Doolin, Courtesy of Koplin Gallery, Los Angeles, California; **656** (t) *The Aunts,* Fritz Eichenberg, © Estate of Fritz Eichenberg/Licensed by VAGA, New York, NY; **656** (m) UPI/CORBIS-Bettmann; **656** (b) © Carl Frank/Photo Researchers, Inc.; **658, 660:** Richard J. Green/Photo Researchers, Inc.; **661:** © Fred Winner/Jacana/ Photo Researchers, Inc.; **663:** Andrew J. Martinez/Photo Researchers, Inc.; **664:** Joe McDonald/CORBIS; **665:** Stephen J. Krasemann/DRK Photo; **666:** UPI/CORBIS-Bettmann; **674:** Robert Phillips/The Image Bank; **676:** *Old Ones Talking,* R. Brownell McGrew, Courtesy of the artist; **678:** *Annie Old Crow,* James Bama, Courtesy of the artist; **679:** Fan, Kiowa ca. 1900, eagle feathers, beads, cotton, leather H. 28-1/2 x W 7-1/2 inches. Gift of University of Tulsa, Bright Roddy Collection, Philbrook Art Center, Tulsa, Oklahoma, 1995.25.10; **681:** Pouch, ca. 1890–1910, KIOWA, hide, native pigment, glass and metal beads and silk binding. H. 6" W. 4 1/2" T328, Thaw Collection, Fenimore House Museum, New York State Historical Association, Cooperstown. Photo by John Bigelow Taylor, N.Y.C.; **682:** Thomas Victor; **686:** © Sergey Tetrin/Archive Photos; **687:** Photofest; **688:** AP/Wide World Photos; **692:** *Winter Scene,* Philip Gale Fine Art, Chepstow, Gwent, Wales, UK/Bridgeman Art Library, London/New York; **694:** *The Whistle,* Fritz Eichenberg © Estate of Fritz Eichenberg/Licensed by VAGA, New York, NY; **697:** *The Aunts,* Fritz Eichenberg, © Estate of Fritz Eichenberg/Licensed by VAGA, New York, NY; **698, 699:** *The Whistle* (detail), Fritz Eichenberg © Estate of Fritz Eichenberg/Licensed by VAGA, New York, NY; **701:** CORBIS-Bettmann; **702:** UPI/CORBIS-Bettmann; **704:** Digital Imagery © Copyright 2001 PhotoDisc, Inc.; **706:** *Langston Hughes* (detail), c.1925, Winold Reiss, The National Portrait Gallery, Smithsonian Institution, Washington, D.C./Art Resource, New York; **710, 712–713:** Steve Proehl/The Image Bank; **716:** Parvinder S. Sethi; **718:** Thomas Victor; **722:** Brookline, Massachusetts, 1986, Photograph by Sage Sohier © 1986; **724:** Danny Lyon/Magnum Photos, Inc.; **725:** Courtesy of the photographer; **726:** Nellie G. Morgan and Tammie Pruitt Morgan, Bicentennial Celebration, Philadelphia, Mississippi, 1976. Photo © 1997, Roland L. Freeman; **730:** Corel Professional Photos CD-ROM™; **731:** *Mother Combing Sara's Hair,* Mary Cassatt, Christie's Images, London, UK/Bridgeman Art Library, London/New York; **732, 734:** Photofest; **736:** © Frank Capri/Saga/Archive Photos; **737, 738–739:** Photofest; **742:** Lisa Rose/Globe Photos; **746:** © Alan Carey/Photo Researchers, Inc.; **748:** Andy Caulfield/The Image Bank; **751:** © Photo Researchers, Inc.; **752** (t) © Carl Frank/Photo Researchers, Inc.; **752** (b) Ralph Morse/Life Magazine © Time Inc.; **753, 754:** Photo by Scott Weidensaul; **758:** PhotoEdit; **764–765:** *Commedia dell'arte,* Andre Rouillard, Superstock, **766** (b) Etruscan Amphora, Black-figured, pontic Fighting soldiers, white dove on shield, National Museum, Warsaw, Poland, Erich Lessing/Art Resource, NY; **766** (t) New York Public Library Picture Collection; **768–769:** © Uniphoto, Inc.; **770, 772:** Fotopic/Omni-Photo Communications, Inc.; **775, 777, 778, 781:** TimePix; **791:** Fotopic/Omni-Photo Communications, Inc.; **793, 798, 801, 804:** TimePix; **806:** Etruscan Amphora, Black-figured, pontic Fighting soldiers, white dove on shield, National Museum, Warsaw, Poland, Erich Lessing/Art Resource, NY; **808:** Vatican Museum/Scala/Art Resource, NY; **816:** Robert Harding Picture Library; **817:** Illustration by Hugh Dixon from "Shakespeare in Performance" courtesy of Salamander Books, London; **818:** *William Shakespeare* (detail), Artist Unknown, by Courtesy of the National Portrait Gallery, London; **820:** Photofest; **823:** Culver Pictures, Inc.; **825:** Corel Professional Photos CD-ROM™; **826, 830:** Photofest; **843:** Hirmer Fotoarchive; **846–847:** Culver Pictures, Inc.; **863:** Gian Berto Vanni/CORBIS; **864, 871, 873:** Photofest; **877:** Extispicium relief (inspection of entrails) from the Forum of Trajan, Rome. Early Hadrianic. Louvre, Paris, France, Alinari/Art Resource, NY; **882:** Chuck Nacke/Woodfin Camp/PictureQuest; **886, 891:** Photofest; **902:** Relief of Domitius Ahenobarbus, scene of a census, Louvre, Paris, France, Erich Lessing/Art Resource, NY; **904:** © George Lepp/ Stone; **907:** Photofest; **911:** Barbarian fighting a Roman Legionary, Roman stone relief 2nd Cent.,

Art Credits ◆ R57

Staff Credits

The people who made up the **Prentice Hall Literature: Timeless Voices, Timeless Themes** team—representing design services, editorial, editorial services, market research, marketing services, media resources, online services & multimedia development, production services, project office, and publishing processes—are listed below. Bold type denotes the core team members.

Susan Andariese, Rosalyn Arcilla, Laura Jane Bird, Betsy Bostwick, **Anne M. Bray,** Evonne Burgess, **Louise B. Capuano, Pam Cardiff,** Megan Chill, Ed Cordero, Laura Dershewitz, Philip Fried, **Elaine Goldman,** Barbara Goodchild, Barbara Grant, **Rebecca Z. Graziano, Doreen Graizzaro,** Dennis Higbee, **Leanne Korszoloski,** Ellen Lees, David Liston, **Mary Luthi, George Lychock,** Gregory Lynch, Sue Lyons, **William McAllister,** Frances Medico, Gail Meyer, Jessica S. Paladini, Wendy Perri, Carolyn Carty Sapontzis, **Melissa Shustyk, Annette Simmons, Alicia Solis,** Robin Sullivan, Cynthia Sosland Summers, Lois Teesdale, **Elizabeth Torjussen, Doug Utigard,** Bernadette Walsh, Helen Young

The following persons provided invaluable assistance and support during the production of this program.

Gregory Abrom, Robert Aleman, Diane Alimena, Michele Angelucci, Gabriella Apolito, Penny Baker, Sharyn Banks, Anthony Barone, Barbara Blecher, Helen Byers, Rui Camarinha, Lorelee J. Campbell, John Carle, Cynthia Clampitt, Jaime L. Cohen, Martha Conway, Dina Curro, Nancy Dredge, Johanna Ehrmann, Josie K. Fixler, Steve Frankel, Kathy Gavilanes, Allen Gold, Michael E. Goodman, Diana Hahn, Kerry L. Harrigan, Jacki Hasko, Evan Holstrom, Beth Hyslip, Helen Issackedes, Cathy Johnson, Susan Karpin, Raegan Keida, Stephanie Kota, Mary Sue Langan, Elizabeth Letizia, Christine Mann, Vickie Menanteaux, Kathleen Mercandetti, Art Mkrtchyan, Karyl Murray, Kenneth Myett, Stefano Nese, Kim Ortell, Lissette Quinones, Erin Rehill-Seker, Patricia Rodriguez, Mildred Schulte, Adam Sherman, Mary Siener, Jan K. Singh, Diane Smith, Barbara Stufflebeem, Louis Suffredini, Lois Tatarian, Tom Thompkins, Lisa Valente, Ryan Vaarsi, Linda Westerhoff, Jeff Zoda

Prentice Hall gratefully acknowledges the following teachers who provided student models for consideration in the program.

Kate Anders, Suzanne Arkfeld, Elizabeth Bailey, Bill Brown, Diane Cappillo, Mary Chapman, Deedee Chumley, Terry Day, Cheryl Devoe, Dan Diercks, Ellen Eberly, Nancy Fahner, Terri Fields, Patty Foster, Joanne Giardino, Julie Gold, Christopher Guarraia, Dianne Hammond, Jo Higgins, Pauline Hodges, Gaye Ingram, Charlotte Jefferies, Bill Jones, Ken Kaiser, Linda Kramer, Karen Lopez, Catherine Lynn, Ashley MacDonald, Kathleen Marshall, LouAnn McCarty, Peggy Moore, Ann Okamura, Will Parker, Maureen Rippee, Tucky Roger, Terrie Saunders, Marilyn Shaw, Ken Spurlock, Mary Stevens, Sandra Sullivan, Wanda Thomas, Jennifer Watson, Amanda Wolf